abled. Plaintiffs primarily used the Rehabilitation Act of 1973 (29 U.S.C.A. § 701 et seq.), the earliest law of this type. But the Rehabilitation Act has a limited scope: it applies only to federally funded workplaces and institutions, and says nothing about those that do not receive government money.

With passage of the ADA in 1990, Congress gave broad protection to people with AIDS who work in the private sector. In general, the ADA is designed to increase access for disabled persons, and it also forbids discrimination in hiring or promotion in companies with fifteen or more employees. Specifically, employers may not discriminate if the person in question is otherwise qualified for the job. Moreover, they cannot use tests to screen out disabled persons, and they must provide reasonable accommodation for disabled workers. The ADA, which took effect in 1992, has quickly emerged as the primary means for bringing AIDS-related discrimination lawsuits.

AIDS and Health Care Closely related to work is the issue of health care. In some cases, the two overlap: health insurance, Social Security, and disability benefits for AIDS victims were often hard to obtain during the 1980s. Insurance was particularly difficult because employers feared rising costs and insurance companies did not want to pay claims. To avoid the costs of AIDS, insurance companies used two traditional industry techniques: they attempted to exclude AIDS coverage from general policies, and they placed caps (limits on benefits payments) on AIDS-related coverage.

In January 1995, the settlement in a lawsuit brought by a Philadelphia construction worker with AIDS illustrated that the ADA can be used to fight caps on coverage. In 1992, the joint union-management fund for the Laborers' District Council placed a $10,000 limit on AIDS benefits, in stark contrast to the $100,000 allowed for other catastrophic illnesses. At that time, the fund said the cap on AIDS benefits was designed to curb all health costs. In 1993, the EEOC ruled that it violated the ADA, and, backed by the AIDS Law Project of Philadelphia, the worker sued. Rather than fight an expensive lawsuit, the insurance fund settled.

AIDS and Education Issues in the field of education include the rights of HIV-positive students to attend class and of HIV-positive teachers to teach, the confidentiality of HIV records, and how best to teach young people about AIDS. A few areas have been settled in court: for instance, the right of students to attend classes was of greater concern in the early years of the epidemic, and no longer remains in dispute.

Certain students with AIDS may assert their right to public education under the Education for All Handicapped Children Act of 1975 (EAHCA), but the law is only relevant in cases involving special education programs. More commonly, students' rights are protected by the Rehabilitation Act.

Schools play a major role in the effort to educate the public on AIDS. Several states have mandated AIDS prevention instruction in their schools. But the subject is controversial: it evokes personal, political, and moral reactions to sexuality. During the 1980s, those who often criticized liberal approaches to sex education argued that AIDS materials should not be explicit, encourage sexuality, promote the use of contraceptives, or favorably portray gays and lesbians.

Civil Litigation TORT law has seen an explosion of AIDS-related suits. This area of law is used to discourage individuals from subjecting others to unreasonable risks, and to compensate those who have been injured by unreasonably risky behavior. The greatest number of AIDS-related LIABILITY lawsuits has involved the receipt of HIV-infected blood and blood products. A second group has concerned the sexual transmission of HIV. A third group involves AIDS-related psychic distress. In these cases, plaintiffs have successfully sued and recovered damages for their fear of having contracted HIV.

CROSS-REFERENCES

Disabled Persons; Discrimination; Food and Drug Administration; Gay and Lesbian Rights; Health Care; Patients' Rights; Physicians and Surgeons; Privacy.

Cross-references at end of article

BIOGRAPHY

Gloria Allred

ALLRED, GLORIA Gloria Allred, born July 3, 1941, in Philadelphia, is a flamboyant, widely recognized lawyer, feminist, activist, and radio talk show host. Though her critics dismiss her as a publicity monger and a dilettante, Allred has received praise from others who believe that she is a master at using the power of the news media to draw attention to the day-to-day struggles of ordinary people.

Born Gloria Rachel Bloom, Allred grew up in Philadelphia with her parents, Morris Bloom, a door-to-door salesman, and Stella Davidson Bloom, a homemaker. Her conventional middle-class childhood gave no hint of the outspoken activist to come. Allred graduated with honors from the University of Pennsylvania in 1963 with a bachelor's degree in English. She moved to New York to pursue a master's degree in teaching at New York University. Wh[...] interested in the CIVIL RIGHT[...] was beginning to gain mom[...] her master's degree in 19[...]

Biography of contributor to American law

GLORIA ALLRED 1941–

1968 Received master's in teaching from NYU; moved to Los Angeles to teach in Watts

1969 Watts riots in Los Angeles

Graduated from Univ. Pennsylvania, with honors

1941 Born, Philadelphia, Pa.

1955–68 Martin Luther King active in civil rights movement

1973 U.S. Supreme Court upheld Roe v. Wade, legalizing abortion

1974 Received J.D. from UCLA; Formed law partnership with Nathan Goldberg and Michael Maroko

1990 Sued L.A. County to stop shackling of pregnant inmates during labor and delivery; Lanzo v. Pitchess 1990

Wrote "Prostitution of Persecution" for L.A. Times, advocating legalization of prostitution

1990 Sued From Club L.A. for age discrimination

1925   1950   1975   2000

Timeline for subject of biography, including general historical events and life events

Philadelphia to teach at a high school with a predominantly black enrollment.

Allred says her interest in the struggle for equal rights arose from personal experiences. While she was in college, she married, gave birth to a daughter, and divorced. Unable to collect CHILD SUPPORT from her former husband, she was forced to return to her parents' home. She also recalls being paid less than a man for what she considered equal work. The reason given was that the man had a family to support, but at the time, Allred was the single mother of an infant.

After moving to California, Allred taught in the turbulent Watts section of Los Angeles and became the first full-time female staff member in United Teachers of Los Angeles, the union representing Los Angeles teachers. The experience stirred her interest in CIVIL RIGHTS and collective bargaining and prompted her to go to law school. She received her law degree, with honors, from Loyola Marymount University, Los Angeles, Law School in 1974. Soon after, she entered a law firm partnership with her classmates Nathan Goldberg and Michael Maroko.

Allred is probably the most flamboyant and well known member of her firm. She has achieved notoriety and name recognition through staged press conferences and demonstrations publicizing and dramatizing the cause she is championing at the time. She also accepts controversial cases that naturally attract media attention. During her years in practice, she has successfully sued Los Angeles County to stop the practice of shackling and chaining pregnant inmates during labor and delivery; put a halt on the city of El Segundo's quizzing job applicants about their sexual histories (*Thorne v. City of El Segundo*, 802 F.2d 1131 [9th Cir. 1986]); represented a client who was turned down for a job as a police officer after a six-hour lie detector exam that included questions about her sex life; and sued a dry cleaning establishment for discrimination because it charged more to launder women's shirts than men's.

Allred relishes confrontation, and her showy tactics have earned her both praise and criticism.

"THERE ARE ENOUGH HIGH HURDLES TO CLIMB, AS ONE TRAVELS THROUGH LIFE, WITHOUT HAVING TO SCALE ARTIFICIAL BARRIERS CREATED BY LAW OR SILLY REGULATIONS."

Defending what many have called self-promoting publicity stunts, Allred says she tries to use the few moments she is in the spotlight to make her point as forcefully as possible. Her detractors say that she wastes her time and energy on trivial issues that do not advance any worthwhile cause and deflect attention away from serious issues. Yet, she points out, she is often stopped on the street by people who recognize her and want to thank her for taking on the small fights that no one else wants.

Some critics say she is all show and no substance. But Allred has many supporters as well. Among them is Justice Joan Dempsey Klein, of the California Court of Appeal, who credits Allred with moving women's issues forward. Klein also points out that Allred saves her dramatics for outside the courtroom and always observes proper decorum when before the bench. According to Klein, Allred is always well-prepared and, for that reason, is quite successful.

Dressed in her trademark reds and electric blues, her striking black hair set off by deep red lipstick, Allred is a potent combination of scholarship and theatrics. Her keen intelligence and shrewd understanding of the power of the media have made her a contemporary success story in the world of law and politics.

ARBITER [*Latin, One who attends something to view it as a spectator or witness.*] Any person who is given an absolute power to judge and rule on a matter in a dispute.

Internal cross references

Quotation from subject of biography

Full cite for case

Definition enclosed in book logos with Latin translation provided

For Reference

Not to be taken from this room

WEST'S
ENCYCLOPEDIA
of
AMERICAN
LAW

WEST'S ENCYCLOPEDIA *of* AMERICAN LAW

Volume 11

WEST GROUP

This encyclopedia is the result of efforts by numerous individuals and entities from the Twin Cities and around the United States. West Group wishes to thank all who made this publication, its quality and content, a priority in their lives.

In addition to the individuals who worked on *West's Encyclopedia of American Law*, West Group recognizes Harold W. Chase (1922–1982) for his contributions to *The Guide to American Law: Everyone's Legal Encyclopedia*.

COPYRIGHT ©1998 By
   WEST GROUP
   610 Opperman Drive
   P.O. Box 64526
   St. Paul, MN 55164-0526
All rights reserved
Printed in the United States of America
05 04 03 02 01 00 99 98   8 7 6 5 4 3 2 1 0
Library of Congress Cataloging in
   Publication Data
ISBN: 0-314-20154-8 (Hard)

West's encyclopedia of American law.
      p.   cm.
      Includes bibliographical references and
      indexes.
      ISBN 0-314-20154-8 (hard :
      alk. paper)
      1. Law—United States—Encyclopedias.
      2. Law—United States—Popular works.
      I. West Publishing Company.
   KF154.W47   1997
   348.73'03 —dc20
   [347.30803]   96-34350
                                           CIP

PRODUCTION CREDITS

Cover, interior design, and page layout:
   David J. Farr, ImageSmythe
Composition: Carlisle Communications
Proofreading: Wiest International
Photo research: Elsa Peterson Ltd.
Art research: Nanette E. Bertaut
Editorial research: Pat Lewis
Artwork: Patricia Isaacs, Parrot Graphics
Indexing: Schroeder Indexing Services

This publication is designed to provide information on the subjects covered. It is sold with the understanding that the publisher is not engaged in rendering legal or other professional advice. If legal advice or other professional assistance is required, the services of a competent professional person should be sought.

WEST'S COMMITMENT TO THE ENVIRONMENT

In 1906, West Publishing Company began recycling materials left over from the production of books. This began a tradition of efficient and responsible use of resources. Today, 100 percent of our legal bound volumes are printed on acid-free, recycled paper consisting of 50 percent new paper pulp and 50 percent paper that has undergone a de-inking process. We also use vegetable-based inks to print all of our books. West recycles nearly 27,700,000 pounds of scrap paper annually—the equivalent of 229,300 trees. Since the 1960s, West has devised ways to capture and recycle waste inks, solvents, oils, and vapors created in the printing process. We also recycle plastics of all kinds, wood, glass, corrugated cardboard, and batteries, and have eliminated the use of polystyrene book packaging. We at West are proud of the longevity and the scope of our commitment to the environment.

West pocket parts and advance sheets are printed on recyclable paper and can be collected and recycled with newspapers. Staples do not have to be removed. Bound volumes can be recycled after removing the cover.

Production, printing, and binding by West Group.

CONTENTS

APPENDIX

ENGLISH LAW

The development of U.S. law is rooted in English political and legal history. The colonial settlers of North America were primarily from England, and until the 1760s they viewed themselves as English rather than "American." They brought with them the English common law and the English constitutional tradition.

Unlike the United States, England has never had a written constitution. Instead, the English constitutional tradition is based on the substance and procedures of the common law, along with key documents, such as Magna Charta and the English Bill of Rights. In the seventeenth and eighteenth centuries, political philosophers, especially John Locke, challenged the absolute authority of the monarchy and introduced the democratic idea that the people have a right to a government that meets their needs. These documents and ideas assumed great importance as the American colonists moved toward independence in the 1770s. In this sense English ideas paved the way for the American Revolution and the writing of the U.S. Constitution.

Magna Charta

The document that has come to be known as Magna Charta (spelled variously as "charta" or "carta"), or Great Charter, is recognized as a fundamental part of the English constitutional tradition. Although it is not a constitution, it contains provisions on criminal law that were incorporated into the Bill of Rights of the U.S. Constitution.

In 1215 King John of England (1199–1216) fought more than forty English barons and their followers in a civil war. The king had angered the barons by extracting revenues based on their feudal obligations in order to fight a war in France. After John lost the war, the barons rebelled against the king.

The rebels first demanded that the king confirm the Charter of Henry I, a coronation charter from 1100 in which King Henry I had promised to abolish all evil customs that oppressed the realm. Additional grievances were added to the charter, which King John was forced to accept at Runnymede in June 1215, after the rebels occupied London.

Magna Charta contains sixty-three chapters. Many of the chapters defined the king's feudal rights over his vassals, preventing the king from arbitrarily collecting revenue from the barons. Chapter 39 established the right to due process of law, and in chapter 40 the king promised that he would not sell, deny, or delay justice to anyone.

Magna Charta did not resolve the dispute between the barons and King John. Within months they were fighting again. In August 1215 the charter was annulled by Pope Innocent III, John's feudal overlord, on the grounds that it had been executed under duress. In 1216, however, after John's death the charter was reissued with some modifications. At the conclusion of the civil war in 1217, it was reissued again with minor revisions. This version of Magna Charta became part of the English constitutional tradition; confirmed by later kings and interpreted by Parliament, it is still revered as a symbol of English liberties.

English Bill of Rights

The English Bill of Rights grew out of the Glorious Revolution of 1688. During the revolution King James II abdicated and fled from England. He was succeeded by his daughter, Mary, and her husband, William of Orange, a Dutch prince. Parliament proposed a Declaration of Rights and presented it to William and Mary on February 13, 1689. Only after they accepted the declaration did Parliament proclaim them king and queen of England. Parliament then added several clauses to the declaration and formally enacted the amended bill as the Bill of Rights on December 16, 1689.

The Bill of Rights combined past grievances against the deposed king with a more general statement of basic liberties. The statute prohibited the monarch from suspending laws or levying taxes or customs duties without Parliament's consent and prohibited the raising and maintaining of a standing army during peacetime. More importantly, it proclaimed fundamental liberties, including freedom of elections, freedom of debate in Parliament, and freedom from excessive bail and from cruel and unusual punishments. To prevent a recurrence of the religious divisions that beset the Catholic James in ruling a largely Protestant England, the Bill of Rights also barred Roman Catholics from the throne.

The Bill of Rights became one of the cornerstones of the unwritten English constitution. The Bill of Rights has also had a significant impact on U.S. law, with many of its provisions becoming part of the U.S. Constitution and Bill of Rights.

Second Treatise on Government

The Englishman John Locke is regarded as one of the world's most important political philosophers, and his "Second Treatise on Government" has proved to be one of the seminal documents on the liberal political state. The U.S. system of government was built on Locke's ideas, including such core premises as the ultimate sovereignty of the people, the necessity of restraints on the exercise of arbitrary power by the executive or the legislature, and the revocability of the social contract by the people when power has been arbitrarily used against them. The Declaration of Independence and the U.S. Constitution are testaments to many of Locke's core ideas.

The "Second Treatise" (the second part of *Two Treatises on Government*) was written during the period preceding the abdication of King James II. Locke's work, which was published in 1690, became a justification for the Glorious Revolution of 1688, when government was reformed along the lines outlined by Locke in his *Two Treatises*. As a result of these reforms, England became a constitutional monarchy under Parliament's control. Greater measures of religious toleration and freedom of expression and thought were permitted, as set out in the English Bill of Rights.

In part, the *Two Treatises* were an attack upon political absolutism. The first treatise refuted the theory of the divine right of kings, which posited that monarchs derived their authority from God. The second treatise, however, has had the more lasting impact on the United States, for it sets out a theory of politics that found its way into U.S. law.

Locke maintained that people are naturally tolerant and reasonable, but that without a governing force, a certain amount of chaos and other inconveniences will occur. In his view all people are inherently equal and free to pursue "life, liberty, health, and property." To do this, they engage in a social contract in which they consent to give up a certain amount of power to a government dedicated to maintaining the well-being of the whole. At the same time, however, individuals' right to freedom of thought, speech, and worship must be preserved. In addition, the government must preserve citizens' private property.

Locke believed that the government is the trustee of the people's power and that it exercises power specifically for the purpose of serving the people. If the government abuses that trust, however, the people have a right to revoke the trust and assume the reins of government themselves or place them in new hands. This idea provided justification for the American Revolution in 1776.

Thomas Jefferson drew upon Locke's ideas of the law of nature, popular sovereignty, and the sanctity of the right of private property in writing the Declaration of Independence. The U.S. Constitution, with its separation of church and state and its guarantee of personal freedoms, reflects Locke's influence as well.

MAGNA CHARTA

John, by the grace of God, king of England, lord of Ireland, duke of Normandy and Aquitaine, count of Anjou, to all his archbishops, bishops, abbots, earls, barons, justiciars, foresters, sheriffs, stewards, servants, and all bailiffs and faithful men, health. Know that we by looking to God, and for the health of our soul, and of all our ancestors and heirs, to the honor of God, and the exaltation of his holy Church, and the rectifying of our realm by the counsel of our venerable fathers, Stephen, archbishop of Canterbury, primate of all England and cardinal of the holy Roman Church; Henry, archbishop of Dublin; William of London, Peter of Winchester, Joscelin of Bath and Glastonbury, Hugh of Lincoln, Walter of Worcester, William of Coventry and Benedict of Rochester, bishops; Master Pandulf, subdeacon of our lord pope and servant; brother Eymeric, master of the knights of the Temple in England; and of nobles, William Marshall, Earl of Pembroke; William, Earl of Salisbury; William, Earl Warrenne; William, Earl of Arundel; Alan of Galway, constable of Scotland; Warin, son of Gerold; Peter, son of Herbert; Hubert de Burg, seneschal of Poitou; Hugh de Neville; Matthew, son of Herbert; Thomas Basset; Alan Basset; Philip de Albini; Robert de Ropley; John Marshall; John, son of Hugh; and others our lieges.

Chapter 1

First, we grant to God, and by this our present charter we confirm, for us and our heirs forever, that the English church be free, and have its rights whole and its liberties unimpaired; *and so we will to be observed, which appears from the fact that we have of pure and free will, before difference arose between us and our barons, granted, and by our charter confirmed, freedom of elections, which is conceived greatest and most necessary for the English church, and have got it confirmed from our lord Pope Innocent III, which we will observe ourselves and will to be observed in good faith by our heirs forever.*[1] We have granted to all free men of our realm, for ourself and our heirs forever, all these underwritten liberties to have and to hold, for themselves and their heirs, from us and our heirs.

Chapter 2

If any of our earls or barons, or other tenant of us in chief by military service, die, and when he dies, his heir be of full age, and owe a relief, he shall have his inheritance by the old relief, to wit,

---

Source: William Stubbs, ed., *A Translation of Such Documents as Are Unpublished in Dr. Stubbs' Select Charters* (n.d.), pp. 187–197.

1. The full text of the Charter of 1215 has been included here. Sections that were omitted in later versions of the charter are printed in italic type on this and subsequent pages. Unless otherwise indicated, the omissions were made in 1216. Important alterations and additions have been indicated in the notes.

the heir, or heirs of an earl, for the whole barony of an earl by £100; the heir or heirs of a baron, the whole barony by £100; the heir or heirs of a knight for a whole military fee by 100*s.* at most, and he who owes less should pay less according to the ancient custom of fees.

Chapter 3

If the heir of any of these be below age, and be in wardship, when he comes to full age he shall have his inheritance without relief or fine.

Chapter 4

The guardians of the land of any heir, who is below age, shall not take from the land of the heir more than reasonable exits [revenues], and reasonable customs, and reasonable services, and this without destruction and waste of men or property; and if we commit the wardship of any such land to the sheriff or any one else, who is to answer to us for the exits, and he made destruction or waste of his wardship, we will take recompense of him, and the land shall be committed to two lawful and discreet men of that fee, who will answer to us of the exits, or to him to whom we have assigned them; and if we have given or sold to any one the wardship of any such land, and he does destruction or waste, he shall lose his wardship, and give it to two lawful and discreet men of that fee, who shall in like manner answer to us as is aforesaid.

Chapter 5

The guardian, as long as he have wardship of the land, shall keep up houses, parks, stews, pools, mills, and other things belonging to that land, from the exits of the same land, and restore to the heir, when he comes to full age, all that land stocked with teams, according to what the season of teams demands, and the exits of the land can reasonably sustain.[2]

Chapter 6

Heirs shall be married without disparagement, *so that before they contract matrimony it be communicated to the kinsmen in blood of the heir.*

Chapter 7

A widow after the death of her husband shall at once and without hindrance have her marriage and inheritance, nor give anything for her dower, or for her marriage, or for her inheritance, which inheritance she and her husband had on the day of her husband's death, and she shall remain in her husband's home for forty days after his death, within which her dower shall be assigned to her.[3]

Chapter 8

No widow shall be forced to marry as long as she wills to live without a husband, so that she give security that she will not marry without our assent, if she hold from us, or without the assent of the lord from whom she holds, if she holds from another.

Chapter 9

Neither we nor our bailiffs will seize any land or rent for any debt, as long as the chattels of the debtor suffice for paying the debt, nor shall the sureties of the debtor be distrained, as long as that debtor in chief suffices for the payment of the debt, and if the debtor in chief fail in paying the debt, not having whence to pay, the sureties shall answer for the debt, and if they will, shall have the land and rents of the debtor till they are satisfied of the debt which they paid for him, unless the debtor in chief show that he is quit thence against these sureties.

───────────

2. A clause added in 1216 stipulated that the chapter also applied to ecclesiastical properties except that those wardships should not be sold.

3. In 1217 a clause was added that guaranteed a widow one-third of her husband's lands unless a smaller dower had been assigned at the time of the marriage. In 1225 chapters 7 and 8 were combined into one.

Chapter 10

If anyone borrows anything from the Jews, more or less, and dies before the debt is paid, the debt shall not bear usury as long as the heir is under age, from whoever he holds it, and if that debt fall into our hands we will take only the chattel contained in the deed.

Chapter 11

And if anyone die and owes a debt to the Jews, his wife shall have her dower and pay nothing of that debt, and if the children of the dead man are under age, necessaries shall be provided for them according to the holding of the dead man, and the debt shall be paid from the residue, the service of the lords saved, and in the same way shall it be done with debts which are owed to other than Jews.

Chapter 12

No scutage or aid shall be laid on our realm except by the common counsel of our realm, unless for ransoming our person, and making our eldest son a knight, and marrying our eldest daughter once, and this must only be a reasonable aid, and so shall it be with the aids of the city of London.

Chapter 13

And the city of London shall have all its ancient liberties and its free customs, *both by land and by water*. Besides we will and grant that all other cities, and burghs [boroughs], and vills [towns], and ports shall have all their liberties and free customs.

Chapter 14

And to have a common counsel of our realm on assessing an aid other than in the three aforenamed cases, or assessing a scutage, we will cause to be summoned archbishops, bishops, abbots, earls, and greater barons, singly by our letters, and we will also cause to be summoned in general, by our sheriffs and bailiffs, all those who hold of us in chief, at a certain day, to wit, at least forty days after, and a certain place; and in all letters of summons we will express the cause of summons, and when summons is made the business assigned for the day shall proceed according to the council of those who are present, though not all who are summoned come.

Chapter 15

We will grant to no one in future that he take aid from his free men, except to ransom his person, to make his eldest son a knight, and to marry his eldest daughter once, and for this there shall only be a reasonable aid.

Chapter 16

No one shall be distrained to do a greater service for a knight's fee, or any other frank [free] tenement than is due from it.

Chapter 17

Common pleas shall not follow our court, but shall be held in some certain place.

Chapter 18

Recognizances of novel disseisin, mort d'ancestor, and darrein presentment shall not be taken except in their own counties and in this manner; we, or, if we be out of the realm, our chief justiciar, will send two justices to each county four times in the year, who, with four knights of each county, elected by the county, shall take in the county and day and place the aforenamed assises of the county.[4]

---

4. In 1217 the text was changed to say that justices (number unspecified) would be sent through each county once a year to hold assises with knights of the county (number unspecified). A separate chapter was created that stipulated that assises involving darrein presentment should always be held before the justices of the bench.

Chapter 19

And if the aforesaid assises of the county cannot be taken on that day, so many knights and free tenants shall remain of those who were at the county on that day, by whom judgments can be sufficiently effected, according as the business is great or small.

Chapter 20

A free man shall not be amerced for a small offense unless according to the measure of the offense, and for a great offense he shall be amerced according to the greatness of the offense, saving his tenement, and the merchant in the same manner, saving his merchandise, and the villein shall be amerced in the same manner, saving his tools of husbandry, if they fall into our mercy, and none of the aforenamed mercies shall be imposed except by the oath of reputable men of the vicinage.

Chapter 21

Earls and barons shall not be amerced but by their equals, and only according to the measure of the offense.

Chapter 22

No cleric shall be amerced *of his lay tenement*, except according to the measure of the other aforesaid, and not according to the size of his ecclesiastical benefice.[5]

Chapter 23

No vill or man shall be distrained to make bridges at rivers, unless he who of old, or by right, is bound to do so.

Chapter 24

No sheriff, constable, coroners, or others of our bailiffs shall hold pleas of our crown.

Chapter 25

All counties, hundreds, wapentakes, and ridings shall be at the old farms [rents] without any increase, saving the manors of our demesne.

Chapter 26

If anyone holding a lay fee [fief] of us dies, and the sheriff or our bailiff shows our letters patent of the summonses of a debt which the dead man owed us, it shall be lawful for our sheriff or bailiff to attach and enroll the chattels of the dead man found in this fee to the value of the debt by the view of lawful men, so that nothing be moved thence till our debt which is clear be paid us, and the residue shall be left to the executors to fulfill the testament of the deceased, and if nothing be owed us by the deceased, all his chattels shall go to the deceased, save the reasonable shares to his wife and children.

Chapter 27

If any free man die intestate, his chattels shall be distributed by his nearest relations and friends, by the view of the church, save the debts due to each which the deceased owed.

Chapter 28

No constable, or other bailiff of ours, shall take the corn or chattels of anyone, unless he forthwith pays money for them, or can have any respite by the good will of the seller.[6]

---

5. In 1225 chapters 20, 21, and 22 were combined in a single chapter.

6. In 1216 the chapter was modified to say that constables and their bailiffs should not take the goods of anyone who is not from the village where the castle is located unless they pay cash or make arrangements to pay later; persons from the village should be paid in three weeks. In 1217 the three weeks was changed to forty days.

Chapter 29

No constable shall distrain any knight to give money for the wardship of a castle [military service in the garrison of a castle], if he be willing to perform that wardship in his own person, or by some other reputable man, if he cannot do it himself for some reasonable cause, and if we have led or sent him to an army, he shall be quit of the wardship, according to the length of time that he is with us in the army.

Chapter 30

No sheriff or bailiff of ours, or any other, shall take horses and carts of any free man for carrying, except by the will of the free man.[7]

Chapter 31

Neither we nor our bailiffs will take any wood for our castles, or other our works, except by consent of the man whose wood it is.

Chapter 32

We will not hold the lands of those who are convict of felony, except for one year and one day, and then the lands shall be returned to the lords of the fees.

Chapter 33

All kidells [fish-weirs] shall for the future be wholly taken away from the Thames and the Medway, and through all England, except at the coast of the sea.

Chapter 34

The writ which is called *praecipe* for the future shall not issue to anyone about any tenement from which a free man may lose his court.

Chapter 35

There shall be one measure of wine throughout our whole realm, and one measure of beer, and one measure of corn, to wit, the London quarter, and one breadth of dyed cloth, and russet and haberget cloth, to wit, two ells within the lists, and of weights it shall be as of measures.

Chapter 36

Nothing shall be given or taken hereafter for the writ of inquisition on life or limb, but it shall be granted freely, and not denied.

Chapter 37

If anyone holds of us by fee-farm, either by socage or by burgage, or of any other land by military service, we shall not have the wardship of the heir or his land which belongs to another's fee, because of that fee-farm, or socage or burgage, nor shall we have wardship of that fee-farm, or socage or burgage, unless the fee-farm itself owes military service. We shall not either have wardship of heir or any land, which he holds of another by military service, by reason of some petty serjeanty which he holds of us, by the service of paying us knives, or arrows, or the like.

Chapter 38

No bailiff in future shall put anyone to law by his mere word, without trustworthy witnesses brought forward for it.

---

7. In 1216 the chapter was modified to say that the horses and carts should not be taken unless the owner received a specified amount of money. In 1217 a chapter was inserted that prohibited bailiffs from taking carts from the demesne of a cleric, a knight, or a lady. In 1225 chapters 30 and 31 from the Charter of 1215 and the new chapter were combined into a single chapter.

Chapter 39

No free man shall be seized, or imprisoned, or disseised, or outlawed, or exiled, or injured in any way, nor will we enter on him or send against him except by the lawful judgment of his peers, or by the law of the land.[8]

Chapter 40

We will sell to no one, or deny to no one, or put off right or justice.

Chapter 41

All merchants shall have safe conduct and security to go out of England or come into England, and to stay in, and go through England, both by land and water, for buying or selling, without any evil tolls, by old and right customs, except in time of war; and if they be of the land at war against us, and if such shall be found in our land, at the beginning of war, they shall be attached without loss of person or property, until it be known by us or our chief justiciar how the merchants of our land are treated who are found then in the land at war with us; and if ours be safe there, others shall be safe here.[9]

Chapter 42

It shall be lawful for anyone hereafter to go out of our realm, and return, safe and sound, by land or by water, saving fealty to us, except in time of war for some short time, for the common weal of the realm, except imprisoned men, and outlaws according to the law of the realm, and as natives of a land at war against us, and to the merchants of whom is done as is aforesaid.

Chapter 43

If any person holds of any escheat, as of the honor of Wallingford, Nottingham, Boulogne, Lancaster, or of other escheats which are in our hands, and they are baronies, and he dies, his heir shall not pay any other relief, or do us any other service but that which he would do for the baron, if the barony were in the hand of a baron, and we similarly will hold him in the same way that the baron held him.[10]

Chapter 44

Men who dwell without the forest shall not come hereafter before our justices of the forest, by common summonses, unless they are in plea, or sureties of one or more, who are attached for the forest.[11]

Chapter 45

We will not make justices, constables, sheriffs, or bailiffs except from those who know the law of the realm, and are willing to keep it.

Chapter 46

All barons who have founded abbeys, whence they have charters of the kings of England, or ancient tenure, shall have their custody while vacant, as they ought to have it.

---

8. In 1217 the words "of his freehold liberties or free customs" were inserted after "disseised." In 1225 the words "in the future" were inserted after "No free man shall," and the chapter and the one following it were joined together.

9. In 1216 the words "unless formerly they have been publicly prohibited" were inserted after "All merchants."

10. In 1217 a sentence added at the end of the chapter stipulated that the king would not have an escheat or wardship by reason of such an escheat or barony unless the person who held the property was a tenant-in-chief for other property.

11. Chapter 44 of the Charter of 1215 was retained in the Charter of 1216, but in 1217 it was transferred to the separate Charter of the Forest. In 1217 a new chapter was inserted at this point that stipulated that no free man should give or sell so much of his land that he would be prevented from doing the full service due from the fief.

Chapter 47

All forests which have been afforested in our time shall be forthwith deforested, and so with the rivers which have been forbidden by us in our time.[12]

Chapter 48

All ill customs of forests and warrens, and foresters and warreners, sheriffs and their servants, rivers and their keepers, shall be forthwith inquired into in each county by twelve sworn knights of the same county, who should be chosen by the reputable men of the same county; and, within forty days after the inquest is over, they shall be wholly done away by them, never to be recalled, so we know this first, or our justiciar, if we are not in England.

Chapter 49

We will forthwith return all hostages and charters which were delivered to us by the English as security of peace or faithful service.

Chapter 50

We will wholly remove from their bailiwicks the relations of Gerard de Athée so that hereafter they shall have no bailiwick in England, Engelard de Cigogné, Andrew, Peter, and Guy de Chanceux, Geoffrey de Martigny and his brothers, Philip Mark and his brothers, and Geoffrey his nephew, and all their following.

Chapter 51

And immediately after the restoration of peace, we will remove from the realm all foreign knights, bowmen, officers, and mercenaries who came with horses and arms to the harm of the realm.

Chapter 52

If anyone has been disseised or deprived by us without lawful judgment of his peers, from lands, castles, liberties, or his right, we will forthwith restore him; and if a dispute arise about this, judgment shall then be made by twenty-five barons, of whom mention is made below, for the security of peace, and of all those matters of which a man has been disseised or deprived without the lawful judgment of his peers, by King Henry our father, or by King Richard our brother, which lands we have in our hands, or which others have, which we ought to warrant, we will have respite up to the common term of the crusaders, those being excepted of which the plea was raised or inquisition was made by our order, before the taking of our cross, and when we return from our journey, or if we chance to remain from our journey, we will forthwith show full justice thence.

Chapter 53

We will have the same respite, and in the same way, about exhibiting justice of deforesting or maintaining the forests, which Henry our father, or Richard our brother afforested, and of the wardship of the lands which are of another's fee, of which thing we have hitherto had the wardship, by reason of the fee, because someone held of us by military service, and of the abbeys which were founded on the fee of another than our own, in which the lord of the fee says he has the right; and when we return, or if we stay from our journey, we will afford full justice to those who complain of these things.

Chapter 54

No one shall be seized or imprisoned for the appeal of a woman about the death of any other man but her husband.

Chapter 55

All fines which have been made unjustly and against the law of the land with us, and all amercements made unjustly and against the law of the land, shall be wholly excused, or it shall be done with them by the judgment of twenty-five barons, of whom mention will be made below on the security of the peace, or by the judgment of the greater part of them, along with the aforenamed Stephen, archbishop of Canterbury, if he can

---

12. In 1217 the first clause was transferred to the Charter of the Forest; the second clause became a separate chapter.

be present, and others whom he wills to summon to him, and if he be unable to be present, nevertheless the business shall go on without him, so that if one or more of the aforenamed twenty-five barons are in a like suit, they may be removed as far as this judgment is concerned, and others be appointed, elected, and sworn for this matter only, by the residue of the same twenty-five.

Chapter 56

If we have disseised or deprived the Welsh of their lands or liberties or other goods, without lawful judgment of their peers, in England or in Wales, let these things be forthwith restored, and if a dispute arise upon this, let it be thereafter settled in the march by the judgment of their peers; on tenements in England according to the law of England; on tenements in Wales according to the law of Wales; on tenements in the march according to the law of the march. The Welshmen shall do the same to us and ours.[13]

Chapter 57

In all these matters in which anyone of the Welsh was disseised or deprived without lawful judgment of his peers, by King Henry our father, or King Richard our brother, which we have in our hands, or which others hold, and which we ought to warrant, we will have respite to the common term of the crusaders, those excepted in which our plea has been raised, or inquisition has been made by our order, before we took the cross; but, when we return, or if by chance we wait from our journey, we will show full justice to them thence, according to the laws of Wales, and the aforesaid parties.

Chapter 58

We will restore the son of Llewellyn forthwith, and all the hostages of Wales, and the charters which have been delivered to us for the security of peace.

Chapter 59

We will do to Alexander, king of Scots, about his sisters, and restoring his hostages, and his liberties, and his right, according to the form in which we have dealt with our other barons of England, unless they are bound to other matters by the charters which we have of William his father, once king of the Scots, and this shall be by judgment of their peers in our court.

Chapter 60

All these aforesaid customs and liberties which we have granted to be held in our realm, as far as belongs to us, towards our own, all in our realm, both clergy and lay, shall observe, as far as belongs to them, towards their own.

Chapter 61

But since, for the sake of God and for the bettering of our realm, and for better quieting the discord which has arisen between us and our barons, we have ganted all the aforesaid, wishing to enjoy them in pure and firm security forever, we make and grant them the underwritten security: viz. that the barons choose twenty-five barons from the realm, whom they will, who should with all their power keep, hold, and cause to be kept, the peace and liberties which we grant them, and by this our present charter confirm, so that, if we, or our justiciar, or our bailiffs, or any of our servants, do wrong in any case to anyone, or we transgress any of the articles of peace and security, and the offense is shown to four out of the aforenamed twenty-five barons, those four barons shall come to us, or our justiciar, if we are out of the realm, to show the wrong; they shall seek that we cause that wrong to be rectified without delay. And if we do not rectify the wrong, or if we are without the realm, our justiciar does not rectify it within forty days from the time in which it was shown to us or our justiciar, if we are without the realm, the aforesaid four barons shall bring the case before the rest of the twenty-five barons, and those twenty-five barons, with the commonalty of the whole realm, shall distrain and distress us, in every way they can, to wit, by the capture of castles, lands, possessions, and other ways in which they can, till right is done according to their will, saving our person and that of our queen and our children; and, when right is done, they shall obey us as before. And whoever of the land wishes, may swear that he will obey the orders of the aforesaid twenty-five barons, in carrying out all the aforesaid, and that he will

---

13. Chapter 56 was retained in the Charter of 1216 but was omitted thereafter.

distress us as far as he can, with them, and we give publicly and freely license to all to swear who wills, and we will forbid no one to swear. But all those in the land who will not, by themselves and of their own accord, swear to the twenty-five barons about distraining and distressing us with them, we will cause them to swear by our orders, as is aforesaid. And if any one of the twenty-five barons dies, or quits the country, or in any way is hindered from being able to carry out the aforesaid, the remainder of the aforesaid twenty-five barons may choose another into his place, at their discretion, who shall be sworn in like manner with the rest. In all those matters which are committed to the barons to carry out, if these twenty-five happen to be present and differ on any one point, or others summoned by them will not or cannot be present, that must be had settled and fixed which the majority of those who are present provides or decides, just as if all the twenty-five agreed on it, and the aforesaid twenty-five shall swear that they will faithfully keep all the aforesaid, and cause them to be kept with all their power. And we will ask nothing from anyone, by ourselves or any other, by which any one of these grants and liberties shall be revoked or lessened; and if we do obtain any such thing, it shall be vain and void, and we will never use it by ourselves or by another.

Chapter 62

And all ill will, wrath, and rancor, which has arisen between us and our men, clerics and laymen, from the time of the discord, we fully have remitted and condoned to all. Besides, all the offenses done by reason of the same discord, from Easter in the sixteenth year of our reign to the renewal of peace, we wholly remit to all, clerics and laymen, and as far as we are concerned fully have condoned. And, moreover, we have caused letters patent to be made to them, in witness of this, of lord Stephen, archbishop of Canterbury, of lord Henry, archbishop of Dublin, and of the aforesaid bishops, and of Master Pandulf, as the aforenamed security and grants.

Chapter 63

Wherefore we will and firmly order that the English church should be free, and that the men of our realm should have and hold all the aforenamed liberties, rights, and grants, well and in peace, freely and quietly, fully and completely, for them and their heirs, from us and our heirs, in all things and places, forever, as is aforesaid. It is sworn both by us, and on the part of the barons, that all these aforesaid shall be kept in good faith and without ill meaning. Witnesses, the abovenamed and many others. Given by our hand, in the meadow which is called Runnymede, between Windsor and Staines, on the fifteenth day of June, in the seventeenth year of our reign.[14]

---

14. Several chapters were added in 1217 that regulated the sheriff's tourn (tour through the hundreds, or subdivisions, of a county to hold court) and view of frankpledge; made it illegal for anyone to give land to a religious house and receive it back to hold as a tenant; established that scutage should be taken as it had been during the reign of King Henry II (1154-1189); and decreed that all adulterine castles (castles built without the king's permission) that had been erected since the beginning of the war between John and the barons should be destroyed. All but the last chapter were retained in 1225.

ENGLISH BILL OF RIGHTS

AN ACT DECLARING THE RIGHTS AND LIBERTIES OF THE SUBJECT AND SETTLING THE SUCCESSION OF THE CROWN

Whereas the Lords Spiritual and Temporal and Commons assembled at Westminster, lawfully, fully, and freely representing all the states of people of this realm, did upon the thirteenth day of February in the year of our Lord one thousand six hundred eighty-eight present unto their Majesties, then called and known by the names and style of William and Mary, prince and princess of Orange, being present in their proper persons, a certain declaration in writing made by the said Lords and Commons in the words following, viz:[1]

Whereas the late King James the Second, by the assistance of divers evil councilors, judges, and ministers employed by him, did endeavor to subvert and extirpate the Protestant religion and the laws and liberties of the kingdom;

By assuming and exercising a power of dispensing with and suspending of laws and the execution of laws without consent of Parliament;

By committing and prosecuting divers worthy prelates for humbly petitioning to be excused from concurring to the said assumed power;

By issuing and causing to be executed a commission under the great seal for erecting a court called the Court of Commissioners for Ecclesiastical Causes;

By levying money for and to the use of the Crown by pretense of prerogative for other time and in other manner than the same was granted by Parliament;

By raising and keeping a standing army within this kingdom in time of peace without consent of Parliament and quartering soldiers contrary to law;

By causing several good subjects being Protestants to be disarmed at the same time when papists were both armed and employed contrary to law;

By violating the freedom of election of members to serve in Parliament;

By prosecutions in the Court of King's Bench for matters and causes cognizable only in Parliament and by divers other arbitrary and illegal courses;

And whereas of late years, partial, corrupt, and unqualified persons have been returned and served on juries in trials, and particularly divers jurors in trials for high treason which were not freeholders;

And excessive bail hath been required of persons committed in criminal cases to elude the benefit of the laws made for the liberty of the subjects;

And excessive fines have been imposed;

And illegal and cruel punishments inflicted;

Source: *Statutes of the Realm*, vol. 6 (1820), pp. 142–145.

1. Until 1752, the legal year in England began on March 25. Thus, in modern dating, February 13, 1688, would be February 13, 1689.

And several grants and promises made of fines and forfeitures before any conviction or judgment against the persons upon whom the same were to be levied;

All which are utterly and directly contrary to the known laws and statutes and freedom of this realm.

And whereas the said late King James the Second having abdicated the government, and the throne being thereby vacant, his Highness the prince of Orange (whom it hath pleased Almighty God to make the glorious instrument of delivering this kingdom from popery and arbitrary power) did, by the advice of the Lords Spiritual and Temporal and divers principal persons of the Commons, cause letters to be written to the Lords Spiritual and Temporal being Protestants and other letters to the several counties, cities, universities, boroughs, and cinque ports for the choosing of such persons to represent them as were of right to be sent to Parliament, to meet and sit at Westminster upon the two-and-twentieth day of January in this year one thousand six hundred eighty and eight, in order to such an establishment as that their religion, laws, and liberties might not again be in danger of being subverted; upon which letters, elections have been accordingly made.

And thereupon the said Lords Spiritual and Temporal and Commons, pursuant to their respective letters and elections being now assembled in a full and free representative of this nation, taking into their most serious consideration the best means for attaining the ends aforesaid, do in the first place (as their ancestors in like case have usually done) for the vindicating and asserting their ancient rights and liberties, declare

That the pretended power of suspending of laws or the execution of laws by regal authority without consent of Parliament is illegal;

That the pretended power of dispensing with laws or the execution of laws by regal authority, as it hath been assumed and exercised of late, is illegal;

That the commission for erecting the late Court of Commissioners for Ecclesiastical Causes, and all other commissions and courts of like nature, are illegal and pernicious;

That levying money for or to the use of the Crown by pretence of prerogative without grant of Parliament, for longer time or in other manner than the same is or shall be granted, is illegal;

That it is the right of the subjects to petition the king, and all commitments and prosecutions for such petitioning are illegal;

That the raising or keeping a standing army within the kingdom in time of peace, unless it be with consent of Parliament, is against law;

That the subjects which are Protestants may have arms for their defense suitable to their conditions and as allowed by law;

That election of members of Parliament ought to be free;

That the freedom of speech and debates or proceedings in Parliament ought not to be impeached or questioned in any court or place out of Parliament;

That excessive bail ought not to be required, nor excessive fines imposed, or cruel and unusual punishments inflicted;

That jurors ought to be duly impaneled and returned, and jurors which pass upon men in trials for high treason ought to be freeholders;

That all grants and promises of fines and forfeitures of particular persons before conviction are illegal and void;

And that, for redress of all grievances and for the amending, strengthening, and preserving of the laws, Parliaments ought to be held frequently.

And they do claim, demand, and insist upon all and singular the premises as their undoubted rights and liberties, and no declarations, judgments, doings, or proceedings to the prejudice of the people in any of the said premises ought in any wise to be drawn hereafter into consequence or example. To which demand of their rights, they are particularly encouraged by the declaration of his Highness the prince of Orange, as being the only means for obtaining a full redress and remedy therein. Having therefore an entire confidence that his said Highness the prince of Orange will perfect the deliverance so far advanced by him and will still preserve them from the violation of their rights which they have here asserted and from all other attempts upon their religion, rights, and liberties, the said Lords Spiritual and Temporal and Commons assembled at Westminster do resolve that William and Mary, prince and princess of Orange, be and be declared king and queen of England, France, and Ireland and the dominions thereunto belonging,[2] to hold the Crown and royal dignity of the said kingdom and dominions to them, the said prince and princess, during their lives and the life of the survivor of them; and that the sole and full exercise of the regal power be only in and executed by the said prince of Orange in the names of the said prince and princess during their joint lives, and after their deceases the said Crown and royal dignity of the said kingdoms and dominions to be to the heirs of the body of the said princess, and for default of such issue to the Princess Anne of Denmark and the heirs of her body, and for default of such issue to the heirs of the body of the said prince of Orange. And the Lords Spiritual and Temporal and Commons do pray the said prince and princess to accept the same accordingly; and that the oaths hereafter mentioned be taken by all persons of whom the oaths of allegiance and supremacy might be required by law, instead of them; and that the said oaths of allegiance and supremacy be abrogated:

I, A. B., do sincerely promise and swear that I will be faithful and bear true allegiance to their Majesties King William and Queen Mary. So help me God.

I, A. B., do swear that I do from my heart abhor, detest, and abjure as impious and heretical this damnable doctrine and position, that princes excommunicated or deprived by the pope or any authority of the see of Rome may be deposed or murdered by their subjects or any other whatsoever. And I do declare that no foreign prince, person, prelate, state, or potentate hath or ought to have any jurisdiction, power, superiority, preeminence, or authority, ecclesiastical or spiritual, within this realm. So help me God.

Upon which their said Majesties did accept the Crown and royal dignity of the kingdoms of England, France, and Ireland and the dominions thereunto belonging, according to the resolution and desire of the said Lords and Commons contained in the said declaration. And thereupon their Majesties were pleased that the said Lords Spiritual and Temporal and Commons, being the two Houses of Parliament, should continue to sit and, with their Majesties' royal concurrence, make effectual provision for the settlement of the religion, laws, and liberties of this kingdom, so that the same for the future might not be in danger again of being subverted. To which the said Lords Spiritual and Temporal and Commons did agree and proceed to act accordingly.

Now in pursuance of the premises, the said Lords Spiritual and Temporal and Commons in Parliament assembled, for the ratifying, confirming, and establishing the said declaration and the articles, clauses, matters, and things therein contained by the force of a law made in due form by authority of Parliament, do pray that it may be declared and enacted that all and singular the rights and liberties asserted and claimed in the said declaration are the true ancient and indubitable rights and liberties of the people of this kingdom and so shall be esteemed, allowed, adjudged, deemed, and taken to be; and that all and every the particulars aforesaid shall be firmly and strictly holden and observed as they are expressed in the said declaration; and all officers and ministers whatsoever shall serve their Majesties and their successors according to the same in all times to come. And the said Lords Spiritual and Temporal and Commons, seriously considering how it hath pleased Almighty God in his marvelous providence and merciful goodness to this nation to provide and preserve their said Majesties' royal persons most happily to reign over us upon the throne of their ancestors, for which they render unto him from the bottom of their hearts their humblest thanks and praises, do truly, firmly, assuredly, and in the sincerity of their hearts think, and do hereby recognize, acknowledge, and declare that King James the Second having abdicated the government and their Majesties having accepted the Crown and royal dignity as aforesaid, their said Majesties did become, were, are, and of right ought to be by the laws of this realm our sovereign liege lord and lady, king and queen of England, France, and Ireland and the dominions thereunto belonging; in and to whose princely persons, the royal state, Crown, and dignity of the said realms with all honors, styles, titles, regalities, prerogatives, powers, jurisdictions, and authorities to the same belonging and appertaining are most fully, rightfully, and entirely invested and incorporated, united and annexed.

---

2. English monarchs styled themselves king or queen of France between 1340 and 1801. The custom began when the English became embroiled in the Hundred Years War with France and King Edward III of England, whose mother was a French princess, claimed the French throne.

And for preventing all questions and divisions in this realm by reason of any pretended titles to the Crown, and for preserving a certainty in the succession thereof, in and upon which the unity, peace, tranquility, and safety of this nation doth under God wholly consist and depend, the said Lords Spiritual and Temporal and Commons do beseech their Majesties that it may be enacted, established, and declared that the Crown and regal government of the said kingdoms and dominions, with all and singular the premises thereunto belonging and appertaining, shall be and continue to their said Majesties and the survivor of them during their lives and the life of the survivor of them; and that the entire, perfect, and full exercise of the regal power and government be only in and executed by his Majesty in the names of both their Majesties during their joint lives; and after the deceases, the said Crown and premises shall be and remain to the heirs of the body of her Majesty and, for default of such issue, to her Royal Highness the Princess Anne of Denmark and the heirs of her body and, for default of such issue, to the heirs of the body of his said Majesty. And thereunto the said Lords Spiritual and Temporal and Commons do in the name of all the people aforesaid most humbly and faithfully submit themselves, their heirs, and posterities forever and do faithfully promise that they will stand to maintain and defend their said Majesties and also the limitation and succession of the Crown, herein specified and contained, to the utmost of their powers with their lives and estates against all persons whatsoever that shall attempt any thing to the contrary.

And whereas it hath been found by experience that it is inconsistent with the safety and welfare of this Protestant kingdom to be governed by a popish prince, or by any king or queen marrying a papist, the said Lords Spiritual and Temporal and Commons do further pray that it may be enacted that all and every person and persons that is, are, or shall be reconciled to, or shall hold communion with, the see or church of Rome, or shall profess the popish religion or shall marry a papist, shall be excluded and be forever incapable to inherit, possess, or enjoy the Crown and government of this realm and Ireland and the dominions thereunto belonging or any part of the same, or to have, use, or exercise any regal power, authority, or jurisdiction within the same. And in all and every such case or cases, the people of these realms shall be and are hereby absolved of their allegiance. And the said Crown and government shall from time to time descend to and be enjoyed by such person or persons being Protestants, as should have inherited and enjoyed the same in case the said person or persons so reconciled, holding communion, or professing or marrying as aforesaid were naturally dead. And that every king and queen of this realm, who at any time hereafter shall come to and succeed in the imperial Crown of this kingdom, shall on the first day of the meeting of the first Parliament next after his or her coming to the Crown, sitting in his or her throne in the House of Peers, in the presence of the Lords and Commons therein assembled, or at his or her coronation before such person or persons who shall administer the coronation oath to him or her at the time of his or her taking the said oath (which shall first happen), make, subscribe, and audibly repeat the declaration mentioned in the statute made in the thirtieth year of the reign of King Charles the Second entitled *An act for the more effectual preserving the king's person and government by disabling papists from sitting in either House of Parliament.* But if it shall happen that such a king or queen upon his or her succession to the Crown of this realm shall be under the age of twelve years, then every such king or queen shall make, subscribe, and audibly repeat the said declaration at his or her coronation, or the first day of the meeting of the first Parliament as aforesaid which shall first happen after such king or queen shall have attained the said age of twelve years. All which their Majesties are contented and pleased shall be declared, enacted, and established by authority of this present Parliament and shall stand, remain, and be the law of this realm forever. And the same are by their said Majesties, by and with the advice and consent of the Lords Spiritual and Temporal and Commons in Parliament assembled and by the authority of the same, declared, enacted, and established accordingly.

And be it further declared and enacted by the authority aforesaid that, from and after this present session of Parliament, no dispensation by *non obstante* of or to any statute, or any part thereof, shall be allowed but that the same shall be held void and of no effect, except a dispensation be allowed of in such statutes, and except in such cases as shall be specially provided for by one or more bill or bills to be passed during this present session of Parliament.

Provided that no charter or grant or pardon granted before the three-and-twentieth day of October in the year of our Lord one thousand six hundred eighty-nine shall be anyway impeached or invalidated by this act, but that the same shall be and remain of the same force and effect in law and no other than as if this act had never been made.

SECOND TREATISE ON GOVERNMENT

JOHN LOCKE, 1690

CHAPTER VII.
Of Political or Civil Society.

§ 77. God having made man such a creature, that in his own judgment it was not good for him to be alone, put him under strong obligations of necessity, convenience, and inclination, to drive him into society, as well as fitted him with understanding and language to continue and enjoy it. The first society was between man and wife, which gave beginning to that between parents and children; to which, in time, that between master and servant came to be added: and though all these might, and commonly did meet together, and make up but one family, wherein the master or mistress of it had some sort of rule proper to a family; each of these, or all together, came short of political society, as we shall see, if we consider the different ends, ties, and bounds of each of these.

* * *

§ 85. Master and servant are names as old as history, but given to those of far different condition; for a free-man makes himself a servant to another, by selling him, for a certain time, the service he undertakes to do, in exchange for wages he is to receive: and though this commonly puts him into the family of his master, and under the ordinary discipline thereof: yet it gives the master but a temporary power over him, and no greater than what is contained in the contract between them. But there is another sort of servants, which by a peculiar name we call slaves, who being captives taken in a just war, are by the right of nature subjected to the absolute dominion and arbitrary power of their masters. These men having, as I say, forfeited their lives, and with it their liberties, and lost their estates; and being in the state of slavery, not capable of any property; cannot in that state be considered as any part of civil society; the chief end whereof is the preservation of property.

§ 86. Let us therefore consider a master of a family with all these subordinate relations of wife, children, servants, and slaves, united under the domestic rule of a family; which, what resemblance soever it may have in its order, offices, and number too, with a little commonwealth, yet is very far from it, both in its constitution, power, and end: or if it must be thought a monarchy, and the pater-familias the absolute monarch in it, absolute monarchy will have but a very shattered and short power, when it is plain, by what has been said before, that the master of the family has a very distinct and differently limited power, both as to time and extent, over those several persons that are in it: for excepting the slave (and the family is as much a family, and his power as pater-familias as great, whether there be any slaves in his family or no), he has no legislative power of life and death over any of them, and none too but what a mistress of a family may have as well as he. And he certainly can

---

Source: Selections from *The Second Treatise on Government*, 5 J. Locke, WORKS (1823). The footnotes have been renumbered.

have no absolute power over the whole family, who has but a very limited one over every individual in it. But how a family, or any other society of men, differ from that which is properly political society, we shall best see by considering wherein political society itself consists.

§ 87. Man being born, as has been proved, with a title to perfect freedom, and uncontrolled enjoyment of all the rights and privileges of the law of nature, equally with any other man, or number of men in the world, hath by nature a power, not only to preserve his property, that is, his life, liberty, and estate, against the injuries and attempts of other men; but to judge of and punish the breaches of that law in others, as he is persuaded the offence deserves, even with death itself, in crimes where the heinousness of the fact, in his opinion, requires it. But because no political society can be, nor subsist, without having in itself the power to preserve the property, and, in order thereunto, punish the offences of all those of that society; there, and there only is political society, where every one of the members hath quitted this natural power, resigned it up into the hands of the community in all cases that exclude him not from appealing for protection to the law established by it. And thus all private judgment of every particular member being excluded, the community comes to be umpire, by settled standing rules, indifferent, and the same to all parties; and by men having authority from the community, for the execution of those rules, decides all the differences that may happen between any members of that society concerning any matter of right; and punishes those offences which any member hath committed against the society, with such penalties as the law has established: whereby it is easy to discern who are, and who are not, in political society together. Those who are united into one body, and have a common established law and judicature to appeal to, with authority to decide controversies between them, and punish offenders, are in civil society one with another: but those who have no such common appeal, I mean on earth, are still in the state of nature, each being, where there is no other, judge for himself, and executioner: which is, as I have before showed it, the perfect state of nature.

§ 88. And thus the commonwealth comes by a power to set down what punishment shall belong to the several transgressions which they think worthy of it, committed amongst the members of that society, (which is the power of making laws) as well as it has the power to punish any injury done unto any of its members, by any one that is not of it, (which is the power of war and peace:) and all this for the preservation of the property of all the members of that society, as far as is possible. But though every man who has entered into civil society, and is become a member of any commonwealth, has thereby quitted his power to punish offences against the law of nature, in prosecution of his own private judgment; yet with the judgment of offences, which he has given up to the legislative in all cases, where he can appeal to the magistrate, he has given a right to the commonwealth to employ his force, for the execution of the judgments of the commonwealth, whenever he shall be called to it; which indeed are his own judgments, they being made by himself, or his representative. And herein we have the original of the legislative and executive power of civil society, which is to judge by standing laws, how far offences are to be punished, when committed within the commonwealth; and also to determine, by occasional judgments founded on the present circumstances of the fact, how far injuries from without are to be vindicated; and in both these to employ all the force of all the members, when there shall be need.

§ 89. Whenever therefore any number of men are so united into one society, as to quit every one his executive power of the law of nature, and to resign it to the public, there and there only is a political or civil society. And this is done, wherever any number of men, in the state of nature, enter into society to make one people, one body politic, under one supreme government; or else when any one joins himself to, and incorporates with any government already made: for hereby he authorizes the society, or, which is all one, the legislative thereof, to make laws for him, as the public good of the society shall require; to the execution whereof, his own assistance (as to his own degrees) is due. And this puts men out of a state of nature into that of a commonwealth, by setting up a judge on earth, with authority to determine all the controversies, and redress the injuries that may happen to any member of the commonwealth; which judge is the legislative, or magistrate appointed by it. And wherever there are any number of men, however associated, that have no such decisive power to appeal to, there they are still in the state of nature.

§ 90. Hence it is evident, that absolute monarchy, which by some men is counted the only government in the world, is indeed inconsistent with civil society, and so can be no form of civil government at all: for the end of civil society being to avoid and remedy those inconveniences of the state of nature which necessarily follow from every man being judge in his own case, by setting up a known authority, to which every one of that society may appeal upon any injury received, or controversy that may arise, and which every one of the society ought to obey;[66] wherever any persons are, who have not such an authority to appeal to, for the decision of any difference between them, there those persons are still in the state of nature; and so is every absolute prince, in respect of those who are under his dominion.

§ 91. For he being supposed to have all, both legislative and executive power in himself alone, there is no judge to be found, no appeal lies open to any one, who may fairly, and indifferently, and with authority decide, and from whose decision relief and redress may be expected of any injury or inconveniency, that may be suffered from the prince, or by his order: so that such a man, however entitled, czar, or grand seignior, or how you please, is as much in the state of nature, with all under his dominion, as he is with the rest of mankind: for wherever any two men are, who have no standing rule, and common judge to appeal to on earth, for the determination of controversies of right betwixt them, there they are still in the state of nature[67], and under all the inconveniences of it, with only this woeful difference to the subject, or rather slave of an absolute prince: that whereas in the ordinary state of nature he has a liberty to judge of his right, and, according to the best of his power, to maintain it; now, whenever his property is invaded by the will and order of his monarch, he has not only no appeal, as those in society ought to have, but, as if he were degraded from the common state of rational creatures, is denied a liberty to judge of, or to defend his right: and so is exposed to all the misery and inconveniences, that a man can fear from one, who being in the unrestrained state of nature, is yet corrupted with flattery, and armed with power.

§ 92. For he that thinks absolute power purifies men's blood, and corrects the baseness of human nature, need read but the history of this, or any other age, to be convinced of the contrary. He that would have been insolent and injurious in the woods of America, would not probably be much better in a throne; where perhaps learning and religion shall be found out to justify all that he shall do to his subjects, and the sword presently silence all those that dare question it: for what the protection of absolute monarchy is, what kind of fathers of their countries it makes princes to be, and to what a degree of happiness and security it carries civil society, where this sort of government is grown to perfection; he that will look into the late relation of Ceylon may easily see.

§ 93. In absolute monarchies indeed, as well as other governments of the world, the subjects have an appeal to the law, and judges to decide any controversies, and restrain any violence that may happen betwixt the subjects themselves, one amongst another. This every one thinks necessary, and believes he deserves to be thought a declared enemy to society and mankind who should go about to take it away. But whether this be from a true love of mankind and society, and such a charity as we all owe one to another, there is reason to doubt: for this is no more than what every man, who loves his own power, profit, or greatness, may and naturally must do, keep those animals from hurting or destroying one another, who labour and drudge only for his pleasure and advantage; and so are taken care of, not out of any love the master has for them, but love of himself, and the profit they bring him: for if it be asked, what security, what fence is there, in such a state, against the violence and oppression of this absolute ruler? the very question can scarce be borne. They are ready to tell you, that it deserves death only to ask after safety. Betwixt subject and subject, they will grant, there must be measures, laws, and judges, for their mutual peace and security: but as for the ruler, he ought to be absolute, and is above all such circumstances; because he has power to do more hurt and wrong, it is right when he does it. To ask how you may be guarded from harm, or injury, on that side where the strongest hand is to do it, is presently the voice of faction and rebellion: as if when men quitting the state of nature entered into society, they agreed that all of them but one should be under the restraint of laws, but that he should still retain all the liberty of the state of nature, increased with

---

66. "The public power of all society is above every soul contained in the same society; and the principal use of that power is to give laws unto all that are under it which laws in such cases we must obey, unless there be reason showed which may, necessarily enforce that the law of reason, or of God, doth enjoin the contrary" (Hooker's *Eccl. Pol.* lib. i. sect. 16). [Ed. note] In the Keble edition of Hooker's Works, the appropriate citation for this passage would be Book I, chapter xvi, § 5.

67. [Ed. note] In a footnote, Locke here quotes a long passage from Hooker, LAWS OF ECCLESIASTICAL POLITY, Bk. I, c. x, § 4.

power, and made licentious by impunity. This is to think, that men are so foolish, that they take care to avoid what mischiefs may be done them by pole-cats, or foxes; but are content, nay think it safety, to be devoured by lions.

§ 94. But whatever flatterers may talk to amuse people's understandings, it hinders not men from feeling; and when they perceive that any man, in what station soever, is out of the bounds of the civil society which they are of, and that they have no appeal on earth against any harm they may receive from him, they are apt to think themselves in the state of nature in respect of him whom they find to be so; and to take care, as soon as they can, to have that safety and security in civil society for which it was instituted, and for which only they entered into it. And therefore, though perhaps at first (as shall be showed more at large hereafter in the following part of this discourse), some one good and excellent man having got a pre-eminency amongst the rest, had this deference paid to his goodness and virtue, as to a kind of natural authority, that the chief rule, with arbitration of their differences, by a tacit consent devolved into his hands, without any other caution but the assurance they had of his uprightness and wisdom; yet when time, giving authority, and (as some men would persuade us) sacredness to customs, which the negligent and unforeseeing innocence of the first ages began, had brought in successors of another stamp; the people finding their properties not secure under the government as then it was[68] (whereas government has no other end but the preservation of property), could never be safe nor at rest, nor think themselves in civil society, till the legislature was placed in collective bodies of men, call them senate, parliament, or what you please. By which means every single person became subject, equally with other the meanest men, to those laws which he himself, as part of the legislative, had established; nor could any one, by his own authority, avoid the force of the law when once made; nor by any pretence of superiority plead exemption, thereby to license his own, or the miscarriages of any of his dependents. "No man in civil society can be exempted from the laws of it:"[69] for if any man may do what he thinks fit, and there be no appeal on earth, for redress or security against any harm he shall do; I ask, whether he be not perfectly still in the state of nature, and so can be no part or member of that civil society; unless any one will say the state of nature and civil society are one and the same thing, which I have never yet found any one so great a patron of anarchy as to affirm.

CHAPTER VIII.
Of the Beginning of Political Societies.

§ 95. Men being, as has been said, by nature all free, equal, and independent, no one can be put out of this estate, and subjected to the political power of another, without his own consent. The only way whereby any one divests himself of his natural liberty, and puts on the bonds of civil society, is by agreeing with other men to join and unite into a community, for their comfortable, safe, and peaceable living one amongst another, in a secure enjoyment of their properties, and a greater security against any that are not of it. This any number of men may do, because it injures not the freedom of the rest; they are left as they were in the liberty of the state of nature. When any number of men have so consented to make one community or government, they are thereby presently incorporated, and make one body politic, wherein the majority have a right to act and conclude the rest.

§ 96. For when any number of men have, by the consent of every individual, made a community, they have thereby made that community one body, with a power to act as one body, which is only by the will and determination of the majority; for that which acts any community being only the consent of the individuals of it, and it being necessary to that which is one body to move one way; it is necessary the body should move that way whither the greater force carries it, which is the consent of the majority: or else it is impossible it should act or continue one body, one community, which the consent of every individual that united into it agreed that it should; and so every one is bound by that consent to be concluded by the majority. And therefore we see that in

---

68. [Ed. note] In a footnote, Locke here quotes from Hooker, LAWS OF ECCLESIASTICAL POLITY, Bk. I, c. x, § 5.

69. "Civil law, being the act of the whole body politic, doth therefore over-rule each several part of the same body" (Hooker, *Ibid.*). [Ed. note] Bk. I, c. x, § 13.

assemblies, empowered to act by positive laws, where no number is set by that positive law which empowers them, the act of the majority passes for the act of the whole, and of course determines; as having, by the law of nature and reason, the power of the whole.

§ 97. And thus every man, by consenting with others to make one body politic under one government, puts himself under an obligation to every one of that society to submit to the determination of the majority, and to be concluded by it; or else this original compact, whereby he with others incorporate into one society, would signify nothing, and be no compact, if he be left free, and under no other ties than he was in before in the state of nature. For what appearance would there be of any compact? what new engagement, if he were no farther tied by any decrees of the society than he himself thought fit, and did actually consent to? This would be still as great a liberty as he himself had before his compact, or any one else in the state of nature hath, who may submit himself and consent to any acts of it if he thinks fit.

§ 98. For if the consent of the majority shall not, in reason, be received as the act of the whole, and conclude every individual, nothing but the consent of every individual can make any thing to be the act of the whole: but such a consent is next to impossible ever to be had, if we consider the infirmities of health, and avocations of business, which in a number, though much less than that of a commonwealth, will necessarily keep many away from the public assembly. To which if we add the variety of opinions, and contrariety of interests which unavoidably happen in all collections of men, the coming into society upon such terms would be only like Cato's coming into the theatre, only to go out again.[70] Such a constitution as this would make the mighty leviathan of a shorter duration than the feeblest creatures, and not let it outlast the day it was born in: which cannot be supposed, till we can think that rational creatures should desire and constitute societies only to be dissolved: for where the majority cannot conclude the rest, there they cannot act as one body, and consequently will be immediately dissolved again.

§ 99. Whosoever therefore out of a state of nature unite into a community, must be understood to give up all the power necessary to the ends for which they unite into society, to the majority of the community, unless they expressly agreed in any number greater than the majority. And this is done by barely agreeing to unite into one political society, which is all the compact that is, or needs be, between the individuals that enter into, or make up a commonwealth. And thus that which begins and actually constitutes any political society, is nothing but the consent of any number of freemen capable of a majority, to unite and incorporate into such a society. And this is that, and that only, which did or could give beginning to any lawful government in the world.

§ 100. To this I find two objections made.

First, "That there are no instances to be found in story, of a company of men independent and equal one amongst another, that met together, and in this way began and set up a government."

Secondly, "It is impossible of right, that men should do so, because all men being born under government, they are to submit to that, and are not at liberty to begin a new one."

§ 101. To the first there is this to answer, that it is not at all to be wondered, that history gives us but a very little account of men that lived together in the state of nature. The inconveniences of that condition, and the love and want of society, no sooner brought any number of them together, but they presently united and incorporated, if they designed to continue together. And if we may not suppose men ever to have been in the state of nature, because we hear not much of them in such a state, we may as well suppose the armies of Salmanasser[71] or Xerxes were never children, because we

---

70. [Ed. note] The reference of course is to Cato the Elder (Marcus, 234–149 B.C.) who was called Cato the Censor because of his opposition to the introduction into Rome of Greek refinement and luxury. This is the same Cato who continually urged the destruction of Carthage, an event which finally occurred three years after his death.

71. [Ed. note] Undoubtedly a reference to Shalmaneser V (or IV), King of Assyria (727–22 B.C.) who defeated the Israelites (the inhabitants of the Northern Kingdom of Israel consisting of ten of the twelve tribes of Israel). He besieged the capital, Samaria, which fell to his successor Sargon II, who carried the inhabitants off to captivity in Assyria. These incidents are referred to in II Kings (in the Catholic Bible, IV Kings) 17. As "Salmanazar," he has achieved a certain measure of immortality by providing the name of an oversized bottle of wine holding 9.6 liters or the equivalent of 12 regular-size bottles of champagne (about ten U.S. quarts). Xerxes (d. 465 B.C.), who is mentioned next in the text is of course the "Great King" (of Persia) who led the second Persian invasion of Greece. He forced the pass at Thermopylae and burned

hear little of them till they were men, and embodied in armies. Government is every where antecedent to records, and letters seldom come in amongst a people till a long continuation of civil society has, by other more necessary arts, provided for their safety, ease, and plenty: and then they begin to look after the history of their founders, and search into their original, when they have outlived the memory of it: for it is with commonwealths as with particular persons, they are commonly ignorant of their own births and infancies: and if they know any thing of their original, they are beholden for it to the accidental records that others have kept of it. And those that we have of the beginning of any politics in the world, excepting that of the Jews, where God himself immediately interposed, and which favours not at all paternal dominion, are all either plain instances of such a beginning as I have mentioned, or at least have manifest footsteps of it.

§ 102. He must show a strange inclination to deny evident matter of fact, when it agrees not with his hypothesis, who will not allow, that the beginnings of Rome and Venice were by the uniting together of several men free and independent one of another, amongst whom there was no natural superiority or subjection. And if Josephus Acosta's[72] word may be taken, he tells us, that in many parts of America there was no government at all. "There are great and apparent conjectures," says he, "that these men, speaking of those of Peru, for a long time had neither kings nor commonwealths, but lived in troops, as they do this day in Florida, the Cheriquanas, those of Brasil, and many other nations, which have no certain kings, but as occasion is offered, in peace or war, they choose their captains as they please," l. i. c. *25*. If it be said that every man there was born subject to his father, or the head of his family; that the subjection due from a child to a father took not away his freedom of uniting into what political society he thought fit, has been already proved. But be that as it will, these men, it is evident, were actually free; and whatever superiority some politicians now would place in any of them, they themselves claimed it not, but by consent were all equal, till by the same consent they set rulers over themselves. So that their politic societies all began from a voluntary union, and the mutual agreement of men freely acting in the choice of their governors and forms of government.

§ 103. And I hope those who went away from Sparta with Palantus, mentioned by Justin,[73] l. iii. c. 4, will be allowed to have been freemen, independent one of another, and to have set up a government over themselves, by their own consent. Thus I have given several examples out of history, of people free and in the state of nature, that being met together incorporated and began a commonwealth. And if the want of such instances be an argument to prove that governments were not, nor could not be so begun, I suppose the contenders for paternal empire were better let it alone than urge it against natural liberty: for if they can give so many instances out of history, of governments begun upon paternal right, I think (though at best an argument from what has been, to what should of right be, has no great force) one might, without any great danger, yield them the cause. But if I might advise them in the case, they would do well not to search too much into the original of governments, as they have begun *de facto;* lest they should find, at the foundation of most of them, something very little favourable to the design they promote, and such a power as they contend for.

§ 104. But to conclude, reason being plain on our side, that men are naturally free, and the examples of history showing, that the governments of the world, that were begun in peace, had their beginning laid on that foundation, and were made by the consent of the people; there can be little room for doubt, either where the right is, or what has been the opinion or practice of mankind about the first erecting of governments.

§ 105. I will not deny that if we look back as far as history will direct us, towards the original of commonwealths, we shall generally find them under the government and administration of one

---

Athens, but was defeated in the famous sea battle of Salamis (480 B.C.); after he returned to Asia Minor, his Army was routed at the battle of Plataea in 479 B.C.

72. [Ed. note] José de Acosta, c.1539–1600, a Spanish Jesuit missionary who spent about fifteen years in the Spanish possessions in the new world, principally Peru, and who wrote *Historia Natural y Moral de las Indias* (*A Natural and Moral History of the Indians*), translated into English in 1604 and reprinted in 1880.

73. [Ed. note] The reference is to Marcus Junianus Justinus, a Roman historian of the third century A.D. (or possibly later) whose major work was a summary of an earlier history, now lost, of Gnaeus Pompeius Trogus, who flourished around the first century B.C. to the first century A.D. The event described in the text was the founding of Tarentum (modern Taranto) in Southern Italy by dissatisfied Spartans under Phalanthus at around 708 B.C. This was the only colony ever founded by Sparta.

man. And I am also apt to believe, that where a family was numerous enough to subsist by itself, and continued entire together, without mixing with others, as it often happens, where there is much land and few people, the government commonly began in the father: for the father having, by the law of nature, the same power with every man else to punish, as he thought fit, any offences against that law, might thereby punish his transgressing children, even when they were men, and out of their pupilage; and they were very likely to submit to his punishment, and all join with him against the offender in their turns, giving him thereby power to execute his sentence against any transgression, and so in effect make him the law-maker and governor over all that remained in conjunction with his family. He was fittest to be trusted; paternal affection secured their property and interest under his care; and the custom of obeying him in their childhood, made it easier to submit to him rather than to any other. If, therefore, they must have one to rule them, as government is hardly to be avoided amongst men that live together, who so likely to be the man as he that was their common father, unless negligence, cruelty, or any other defect of mind or body made him unfit for it? But when either the father died, and left his next heir, for want of age, wisdom, courage, or any other qualities, less fit for rule, or where several families met and consented to continue together, there, it is not to be doubted, but they used their natural freedom to set up him whom they judged the ablest, and most likely to rule well over them. Conformable hereunto, we find the people of America, who (living out of the reach of the conquering swords and spreading domination of the two great empires of Peru and Mexico) enjoyed their own natural freedom, though, *cæteris paribus*, they commonly prefer the heir of their deceased king; yet if they find him any way weak or incapable, they pass him by, and set up the stoutest and bravest man for their ruler.

§ 106. Thus, though looking back as far as records give us any account of peopling the world, and the history of nations, we commonly find the government to be in one hand; yet it destroys not that which I affirm, viz. that the beginning of politic society depends upon the consent of the individuals, to join into, and make one society; who, when they are thus incorporated, might set up what form of government they thought fit. But this having given occasion to men to mistake, and think that by nature government was monarchical, and belonged to the father; it may not be amiss here to consider, why people in the beginning generally pitched upon this form: which though perhaps the father's preeminency might, in the first institution of some commonwealth, give a rise to, and place in the beginning the power in one hand; yet it is plain that the reason that continued the form of government in a single person, was not any regard or respect to paternal authority; since all petty monarchies, that is, almost all monarchies, near their original, have been commonly, at least upon occasion, elective.

§ 107. First then, in the beginning of things, the father's government of the childhood of those sprung from him, having accustomed them to the rule of one man, and taught them that where it was exercised with care and skill, with affection and love to those under it, it was sufficient to procure and preserve to men all the political happiness they sought for in society; it was no wonder that they should pitch upon, and naturally run into that form of government, which from their infancy they had been all accustomed to; and which, by experience, they had found both easy and safe. To which, if we add, that monarchy being simple, and most obvious to men, whom neither experience had instructed in forms of government, nor the ambition or insolence of empire had taught to beware of the encroachments of prerogative, or the inconveniencies of absolute power, which monarchy in succession was apt to lay claim to, and bring upon them; it was not at all strange that they should not much trouble themselves to think of methods of restraining any exorbitancies of those to whom they had given the authority over them, and of balancing the power of government, by placing several parts of it in different hands. They had neither felt the oppression of tyrannical dominion, nor did the fashion of the age, nor their possessions, or way of living (which afforded little matter for covetousness or ambition), give them any reason to apprehend or provide against it; and therefore it is no wonder they put themselves into such a frame of government, as was not only, as I said, most obvious and simple, but also best suited to their present state and condition, which stood more in need of defence against foreign invasions and injuries, than of multiplicity of laws. The equality of a simple poor way of living, confining their desires within the narrow bounds of each man's small property, made few controversies, and so no need of many laws to decide them, or variety of officers to superintend the process, or look after the execution of justice, where there were but few trespasses, and few offenders. Since then those who liked one another so well as to join into society, cannot but be supposed to have some acquaintance and friendship together, and some trust one in another; they could not but have greater apprehensions of others than of one another: and therefore their first care and thought cannot but be supposed to be, how to secure themselves against foreign force. It was natural for them to put themselves under a frame of government which might best serve to that end, and choose the wisest and bravest man to conduct them in their wars, and lead them out against their enemies, and in this chiefly be their ruler.

§ 108. Thus we see that the kings of the Indians in America, which is still a pattern of the first ages in Asia and Europe, whilst the inhabitants were too few for the country, and want of people and money gave men no temptation to enlarge their possessions of land, or contest for wider extent of ground, are little more than generals of their armies; and though they command absolutely in war, yet at home and in time of peace they exercise very little dominion, and have but a very moderate sovereignty; the resolutions of peace and war being ordinarily either in the people, or in a council. Though the war itself, which admits not of plurality of governors, naturally devolves the command into the king's sole authority.

* * *

[Section 109 contains a discussion of illustrations taken from the history of Israel as contained in the Old Testament.]

§ 110. Thus, whether a family by degrees grew up into a commonwealth, and the fatherly authority being continued on to the elder son, every one in his turn growing up under it, tacitly submitted to it; and the easiness and equality of it not offending any one, every one acquiesced, till time seemed to have confirmed it, and settle a right of succession by prescription: or whether several families, or the descendants of several families, whom chance, neighbourhood, or business brought together, uniting into society: the need of a general, whose conduct might defend them against their enemies in war, and the great confidence the innocence and sincerity of that poor but virtuous age (such as are almost all those which begin governments, that ever come to last in the world) gave men of one another, made the first beginners of commonwealths generally put the rule into one man's hand, without any other express limitation or restraint, but what the nature of the thing and the end of government required: whichever of those it was that at first put the rule into the hands of a single person, certain it is that nobody was intrusted with it but for the public good and safety, and to those ends, in the infancies of commonwealths, those who had it, commonly used it. And unless they had done so, young societies could not have subsisted; without such nursing fathers, tender and careful of the public weal, all governments would have sunk under the weakness and infirmities of their infancy, and the prince and the people had soon perished together.

§ 111. But though the golden age (before vain ambition, and *amor sceleratus habendi*, evil concupiscence, had corrupted men's minds into a mistake of true power and honour) had more virtue, and consequently better governors, as well as less vicious subjects; and there was then no stretching prerogative on the one side, to oppress the people; nor consequently on the other, any dispute about privilege, to lessen or restrain the power of the magistrate; and so no contest betwixt rulers and people about governors or government: yet, when ambition and luxury in future ages[74] would retain and increase the power, without doing the business for which it was given; and, aided by flattery, taught princes to have distinct and separate interests from their people; men found it necessary to examine more carefully the original and rights of government, and to find out ways to restrain the exorbitancies, and prevent the abuses of that power, which they having intrusted in another's hands only for their own good, they found was made use of to hurt them.

§ 112. Thus we may see how probable it is, that people that were naturally free, and by their own consent either submitted to the government of their father, or united together out of different families to make a government, should generally put the rule into one man's hands, and choose to be under the conduct of a single person, without so much as by express conditions limiting or regulating his power, which they thought safe enough in his honesty and prudence: though they never dreamed of monarchy being *jure divino*, which we never heard of among mankind, till it was revealed to us by the divinity of this last age; nor ever allowed paternal power to have a right to dominion, or to be the foundation of all government. And thus much may suffice to show, that, as far as we have any light from history, we have reason to conclude, that all peaceful beginnings of

---

74. [Ed. note] In a footnote, Locke here quotes again (*see* note 67, *supra*) but at greater length from Hooker, LAWS OF ECCLESIASTICAL POLITY, Bk. I, c. x, § 5.

government have been laid in the consent of the people. I say peaceful, because I shall have occasion in another place to speak of conquest, which some esteem a way of beginning of governments.

The other objection I find urged against the beginning of politics, in the way I have mentioned, is this, viz.

§ 113. "That all men being born under government, some or other, it is impossible any of them should ever be free, and at liberty to unite together, and begin a new one, or ever be able to erect a lawful government."

If this argument be good, I ask, how came so many lawful monarchies into the world? for if any body, upon this supposition, can show me any one man in any age of the world free to begin a lawful monarchy, I will be bound to show him ten other free men at liberty at the same time to unite and begin a new government under a regal, or any other form; it being demonstration, that if any one, born under the dominion of another, may be so free as to have a right to command others in a new and distinct empire, every one that is born under the dominion of another may be so free too, and may become a ruler, or subject of a distinct separate government. And so by this their own principle, either all men, however born, are free, or else there is but one lawful prince, one lawful government in the world. And then they have nothing to do, but barely to show us which that is; which when they have done, I doubt not but all mankind will easily agree to pay obedience to him.

§ 114. Though it be a sufficient answer to their objection, to show that it involves them in the same difficulties that it doth those they use it against; yet I shall endeavour to discover the weakness of this argument a little farther.

"All men, 'say they,' are born under government, and therefore they cannot be at liberty to begin a new one. Every one is born a subject to his father, or his prince, and is therefore under the perpetual tie of subjection and allegiance." It is plain mankind never owned nor considered any such natural subjection that they were born in, to one or to the other, that tied them, without their own consents, to a subjection to them and their heirs.

§ 115. For there are no examples so frequent in history, both sacred and profane, as those of men withdrawing themselves, and their obedience, from the jurisdiction they were born under, and the family or community they were bred up in, and setting up new governments in other places; from whence sprang all that number of petty commonwealths in the beginning of ages, and which always multiplied as long as there was room enough, till the stronger, or more fortunate, swallowed the weaker; and those great ones again breaking to pieces, dissolved into lesser dominions. All which are so many testimonies against paternal sovereignty, and plainly prove that it was not the natural right of the father descending to his heirs, that made governments in the beginning, since it was impossible, upon that ground, there should have been so many little kingdoms; all must have been but only one universal monarchy, if men had not been at liberty to separate themselves from their families and the government, be it what it will, that was set up in it, and go and make distinct commonwealths and other governments, as they thought fit.

§ 116. This has been the practice of the world from its first beginning to this day; nor is it now any more hinderance to the freedom of mankind, that they are born under constituted and ancient polities, that have established laws and set forms of government, than if they were born in the woods, amongst the unconfined inhabitants that run loose in them: for those who would persuade us, that "by being born under any government, we are naturally subjects to it," and have no more any title or pretence to the freedom of the state of nature; have no other reason (bating that of paternal power, which we have already answered) to produce for it, but only because our fathers or progenitors passed away their natural liberty, and thereby bound up themselves and their posterity to a perpetual subjection to the government which they themselves submitted to. It is true, that whatever engagement or promises any one has made for himself, he is under the obligation of them, but cannot, by any compact whatsoever, bind his children or posterity: for his son, when a man, being altogether as free as the father, any "act of the father can no more give away the liberty of the son," than it can of any body else: he may indeed annex such conditions to the land he enjoyed as a subject of any commonwealth, as may oblige his son to be of that community, if he will enjoy those possessions which were his father's; because that estate being his father's property; he may dispose or settle it as he pleases.

§ 117. And this has generally given the occasion to mistake in this matter; because commonwealths not permitting any part of their dominions to be dismembered, nor to be enjoyed by any but those of their community, the son cannot ordinarily enjoy the possessions of his father, but under the same terms his father did, by becoming a member of the society; whereby he puts himself presently under the government he finds there established, as much as any other subject of that commonwealth. And thus "the consent of freemen, born under government, which only makes them members of it," being given separately in their turns, as each comes to be of age, and not in a multiude together; people take no notice of it, and thinking it not done at all, or not necessary, conclude they are naturally subjects as they are men.

§ 118. But it is plain governments themselves understand it otherwise; they claim "no power over the son, because of that they had over the father;" nor look on children as being their subjects, by their fathers being so. If a subject of England have a child by an English woman in France, whose subject is he? Not the king of England's; for he must have leave to be admitted to the privileges of it: nor the king of France's; for how then has his father a liberty to bring him away, and breed him as he pleases? and who ever was judged as a traitor or deserter, if he left or warred against a country, for being barely born in it of parents that were aliens there? It is plain then, by the practice of governments themselves, as well as by the law of right reason, that "a child is born a subject of no country or government."[75] He is under his father's tuition and authority till he comes to age of discretion; and then he is a freeman, at liberty what government he will put himself under, what body politic he will unite himself to: for if an Englishman's son, born in France, be at liberty, and may do so, it is evident there is no tie upon him by his father's being a subject of this kingdom; nor is he bound up by any compact of his ancestors. And why then hath not his son, by the same reason, the same liberty, though he be born any where else? Since the power that a father hath naturally over his children is the same, wherever they be born, and the ties of natural obligations are not bounded by the positive limits of kingdoms and commonwealths.

§ 119. Every man being, as has been showed, naturally free, and nothing being able to put him into subjection to any earthly power, but only his own consent; it is to be considered, what shall be understood to be a sufficient declaration of a man's consent, to make him subject to the laws of any government. There is a common distinction of an express and a tacit consent, which will concern our present case. Nobody doubts but an express consent of any man entering into any society, makes him a perfect member of that society, a subject of that government. The difficulty is, what ought to be looked upon as a tacit consent, and how far it binds, *i.e.* how far any one shall be looked on to have consented, and thereby submitted to any government, where he has made no expressions of it at all. And to this I say, that every man, that hath any possessions, or enjoyment of any part of the dominions of any government, doth thereby give his tacit consent, and is as far forth obliged to obedience to the laws of that government, during such enjoyment, as any one under it; whether this his possession be of land, to him and his heirs for ever, or a lodging only for a week; or whether it be barely travelling freely on the highway; and, in effect, it reaches as far as the very being of any one within the territories of that government.

§ 120. To understand this the better, it is fit to consider, that every man, when he at first incorporates himself into any commonwealth, he, by his uniting himself thereunto, annexes also, and submits to the community those possessions which he has, or shall acquire, that do not already

---

75. [Ed. note] In this connection it should be noted that Locke derives the power of sovereign nations to punish aliens who commit crimes within their borders from the right of every man in the state of nature to punish those who violate the laws of nature.

> . . . I desire them to resolve me by what right any prince or state can put to death or punish an alien for any crime he commits in their country. It is certain their laws, by virtue of any sanction they receive from the promulgated will of the legislative, reach not a stranger: they speak not to him, nor, if they did, is he bound to harken to them. The legislative authority, by which they are in force over the subjects of that commonwealth, hath no power over him. Those who have the supreme power of making laws in England, France, or Holland, are to an Indian but like the rest of the world, men without authority: and therefore, if by the law of nature every man hath not a power to punish offences against it, as he soberly judges the case to require, I see not how the magistrates of any community can punish an alien of another country; since, in reference to him, they can have no more power than what every man naturally may have over another.

J. Locke, THE SECOND TREATISE OF GOVERNMENT Para. 9 [5 J. Locke, WORKS 342 (1823 ed.) from which these readings were taken]. Locke seems driven to this *a priori* rejection of the *ius sanguinis* and *ius soli* as legitimate bases of jurisdiction by his insistence that governmental power can only originate from consent.

belong to any other government: for it would be a direct contradiction for any one to enter into society with others for the securing and regulating of property, and yet to suppose his land, whose property is to be regulated by the laws of the society, should be exempt from the jurisdiction of that government, to which he himself, the proprietor of the land, is a subject. By the same act therefore, whereby any one unites his person, which was before free, to any commonwealth, by the same he unites his possessions, which were before free, to it also: and they become, both of them, person and possession, subject to the government and dominion of that commonwealth, as long as it hath a being. Whoever, therefore, from thenceforth, by inheritance, purchase, permission, or otherways, enjoys any part of the land so annexed to, and under the government of that commonwealth, must take it with the condition it is under; that is, of submitting to the government of the commonwealth, under whose jurisdiction it is, as far forth as any subject of it.

§ 121. But since the government has a direct jurisdiction only over the land, and reaches the possessor of it (before he has actually incorporated himself in the society) only as he dwells upon, and enjoys that; the obligation any one is under, by virtue of such enjoyment, to "submit to the government, begins and ends with the enjoyment:" so that whenever the owner, who has given nothing but such a tacit consent to the government, will, by donation, sale, or otherwise, quit the said possession, he is at liberty to go and incorporate himself into any other commonwealth; or to agree with others to begin a new one, in *vacuis locis*, in any part of the world they can find free and unpossessed: whereas he that has once, by actual agreement, and any express declaration, given his consent to be of any commonwealth, is perpetually and indispensably obliged to be, and remain unalterably a subject to it, and can never be again in the liberty of the state of nature; unless, by any calamity, the government he was under comes to be dissolved, or else by some public act cuts him off from being any longer a member of it.

§ 122. But submitting to the laws of any country, living quietly, and enjoying privileges and protection under them, makes not a man a member of that society: this is only a local protection and homage due to and from all those, who, not being in a state of war, come within the territories belonging to any government, to all parts whereof the force of its laws extends. But this no more makes a man a member of that society, a perpetual subject of that commonwealth, than it would make a man a subject to another, in whose family he found it convenient to abide for some time; though, whilst he continued in it, he were obliged to comply with the laws, and submit to the government he found there. And thus we see, that foreigners, by living all their lives under another government, and enjoying the privileges and protection of it, though they are bound, even in conscience, to submit to its administration, as far forth as any denison; yet do not thereby come to be subjects or members of that commonwealth. Nothing can make any man so, but his actually entering into it by positive engagement, and express promise and compact. This is that which I think concerning the beginning of political societies, and that consent which makes any one a member of any commonwealth.

CHAPTER IX.
Of the Ends of Political Society and Government.

§ 123. If man in the state of nature be so free as has been said; if he be absolute lord of his own person and possessions, equal to the greatest, and subject to nobody, why will he part with his freedom, why will he give up this empire, and subject himself to the dominion and control of any other power? To which it is obvious to answer, that though in the state of nature he hath such a right, yet the enjoyment of it is very uncertain, and constantly exposed to the invasion of others; for all being kings as much as he, every man his equal, and the greater part no strict observers of equity and justice, the enjoyment of the property he has in this state is very unsafe, very unsecure. This makes him willing to quit a condition, which, however free, is full of fears and continual dangers: and it is not without reason that he seeks out, and is willing to join in society with others, who are already united, or have a mind to unite, for the mutual preservation of their lives, liberties and estates, which I call by the general name property.

§ 124. The great and chief end, therefore, of men's uniting into commonwealths, and putting themselves under government, is the preservation of their property. To which in the state of nature there are many things wanting.

First, There wants an established, settled, known law, received and allowed by common consent to be the standard of right and wrong, and the common measure to decide all controversies between them: for though the law of nature be plain and intelligible to all rational creatures: yet men being biassed by their interest, as well as ignorant for want of studying it, are not apt to allow of it as a law binding to them in the application of it to their particular cases.

§ 125. Secondly, In the state of nature there wants a known and indifferent judge, with authority to determine all differences according to the established law: for every one in that state being both judge and executioner of the law of nature, men being partial to themselves, passion and revenges very apt to carry them too far, and with too much heat, in their own cases; as well as negligence and unconcernedness, to make them too remiss in other men's.

§ 126. Thirdly, In the state of nature there often wants power to back and support the sentence when right, and to give it due execution. They who by any injustice offend, will seldom fail, where they are able, by force to make good their injustice; such resistance many times makes the punishment dangerous, and frequently destructive to those who attempt it.

§ 127. Thus mankind, notwithstanding all the privileges of the state of nature, being but in an ill condition, while they remain in it, are quickly driven into society. Hence it comes to pass, that we seldom find any number of men live any time together in this state. The inconveniencies that they are therein exposed to, by the irregular and uncertain exercise of the power every man has of punishing the transgressions of others, make them take sanctuary under the established laws of government, and therein seek the preservation of their property. It is this makes them so willingly give up every one his single power of punishing, to be exercised by such alone as shall be appointed to it amongst them; and by such rules as the community, or those authorized by them to that purpose, shall agree on. And in this we have the original right of both the legislative and executive power, as well as of the governments and societies themselves.

§ 128. For in the state of nature, to omit the liberty he has of innocent delights, a man has two powers.

The first is to do whatsoever he thinks fit for the preservation of himself and others within the permission of the law of nature: by which law, common to them all, he and all the rest of mankind are one community, make up one society, distinct from all other creatures. And, were it not for the corruption and viciousness of degenerate men, there would be no need of any other; no necessity that men should separate from this great and natural community, and by positive agreements combine into smaller and divided associations.

The other power a man has in the state of nature, is the power to punish the crimes committed against that law. Both these he gives up when he joins in a private, if I may so call it, or particular politic society, and incorporates into any commonwealth, separate from the rest of mankind.

§ 129. The first power, viz. "of doing whatsoever he thought fit for the preservation of himself" and the rest of mankind, he gives up to be regulated by laws made by the society, so far forth as the preservation of himself and the rest of that society shall require; which laws of the society in many things confine the liberty he had by the law of nature.

§ 130. Secondly, The power of punishing he wholly gives up, and engages his natural force (which he might before employ in the execution of the law of nature, by his own single authority, as he thought fit), to assist the executive power of the society, as the law thereof shall require: for being now in a new state, wherein he is to enjoy many conveniences, from the labour, assistance, and society of others in the same community, as well as protection from its whole strength; he is to part also with as much of his natural liberty, in providing for himself, as the good, prosperity, and safety of the society shall require; which is not only necessary, but just, since the other members of the society do the like.

§ 131. But though men, when they enter into society, give up the equality, liberty, and executive power they had in the state of nature, into the hands of the society, to be so far disposed of by the legislative as the good of the society shall require; yet it being only with an intention in every one the better to preserve himself, his liberty and property (for no rational creature can be supposed to change his condition with an intention to be worse); the power of the society, or legislative constituted by them, can never be supposed to extend farther than the common good; but is obliged to secure every one's property, by providing against those three defects above-mentioned, that made the state of nature so unsafe and uneasy. And so whoever has the legislative or supreme power of any commonwealth, is bound to govern by established standing laws, promulgated and known to the people, and not by extemporary decrees; by indifferent and upright judges, who are to decide controversies by those laws; and to employ the force of the community at home, only in the execution of such laws; or abroad to prevent or redress foreign injuries, and secure the community from inroads and invasion. And all this to be directed to no other end but the peace, safety, and public good of the people.

CHAPTER X.
Of the Forms of a Commonwealth.

§ 132. The majority having, as has been showed, upon men's first uniting into society, the whole power of the community naturally in them, may employ all that power in making laws for the community from time to time, and executing those laws by officers of their own appointing; and then the form of the government is a perfect democracy: or else may put the power of making laws into the hands of a few select men, and their heirs or successors; and then it is an oligarchy: or else into the hands of one man, and then it is a monarchy: if to him and his heirs, it is an hereditary monarchy: if to him only for life, but upon his death the power only of nominating a successor to return to them, an elective monarchy. And so accordingly of these the community may make compounded and mixed forms of government, as they think good. And if the legislative power be at first given by the majority to one or more persons only for their lives, or any limited time, and then the supreme power to revert to them again; when it is so reverted, the community may dispose of it again anew into what hands they please, and so constitute a new form of government: for the form of government depending upon the placing the supreme power, which is the legislative (it being impossible to conceive that an inferior power should prescribe to a superior, or any but the supreme make laws), according as the power of making laws is placed, such is the form of the commonwealth.

§ 133. By commonwealth, I must be understood all along to mean, not a democracy, or any form of government, but any independent community, which the Latines signified by the word *civitas;* to which the word which best answers in our language is commonwealth, and most properly expresses such a society of men, which community or city in English does not: for there may be subordinate communities in government; and city amongst us has a quite different notion from commonwealth: and therefore, to avoid ambiguity, I crave leave to use the word commonwealth in that sense, in which I find it used by king James the First; and I take it to be its genuine signification; which if any body dislike, I consent with him to change it for a better.

CHAPTER XI.
Of the Extent of the legislative Power.

§ 134. The great end of men's entering into society being the enjoyment of their properties in peace and safety, and the great instrument and means of that being the laws established in that society; the first and fundamental positive law of all commonwealths is the establishing of the legislative power; as the first and fundamental natural law, which is to govern even the legislative itself, is the preservation of the society, and (as far as will consist with the public good) of every person in it. This legislative is not only the supreme power of the commonwealth, but sacred and unalterable in the hands where the community have once placed it; nor can any edict of any body else, in what form soever conceived, or by what power soever backed, have the force and obligation of a law, which has not its sanction from that legislative which the public has chosen and appointed: for without this the law could not have that which is absolutely necessary to its being a law, the consent of the society; over whom nobody can have a power to make laws, but by their own consent, and by authority received from them.[76] And therefore all the obedience, which by the most solemn ties any one can be obliged to pay, ultimately terminates in this supreme power, and is directed by those laws which it enacts: nor can any oaths to any foreign power whatsoever, or any domestic subordinate power, discharge any member of the society from his obedience to the legislative, acting pursuant to their trust; nor oblige him to any obedience contrary to the laws so enacted, or farther than they do allow; it being ridiculous to imagine one can be tied ultimately to obey any power in the society which is not supreme.

§ 135. Though the legislative, whether placed in one or more, whether it be always in being, or only by intervals, though it be the supreme power in every commonwealth; yet,

---

76. [Ed. note] Locke, in a footnote here quotes several passages from Hooker, LAWS OF ECCLESIASTICAL POLITY, Bk. I, c. x, § 8. The quoted passages include the famous sentence "Laws they are not therefore which public approbation hath not made so."

First, It is not, nor can possibly be absolutely arbitrary over the lives and fortunes of the people: for it being but the joint power of every member of the society given up to that person or assembly which is legislator; it can be no more than those persons had in a state of nature before they entered into society, and gave up to the community: for nobody can transfer to another more power than he has in himself; and nobody has an absolute arbitrary power over himself, or over any other, to destroy his own life, or take away the life or property of another. A man, as has been proved, cannot subject himself to the arbitrary power of another; and having in the state of nature no arbitrary power over the life, liberty, or possession of another, but only so much as the law of nature gave him for the preservation of himself and the rest of mankind; this is all he doth, or can give up to the commonwealth, and by it to the legislative power, so that the legislative can have no more than this. Their power, in the utmost bounds of it, is limited to the public good of the society. It is a power that hath no other end but preservation, and therefore can never have a right to destroy, enslave, or designedly to impoverish the subjects.[77] The obligations of the law of nature cease not in society, but only in many cases are drawn closer, and have by human laws known penalties annexed to them, to enforce their observation. Thus the law of nature stands as an eternal rule to all men, legislators as well as others. The rules that they make for other men's actions must, as well as their own and other men's actions be conformable to the law of nature, *i.e.* to the will of God, of which that is a declaration; and the "fundamental law of nature being the preservation of mankind, no human sanction can be good or valid against it."

§ 136. Secondly, The legislative or supreme authority cannot assume to itself a power to rule by extemporary, arbitrary decrees; but is bound to dispense justice, and to decide the rights of the subject, by promulgated, standing laws, and known authorized judges.[78] For the law of nature being unwritten, and so nowhere to be found, but in the minds of men, they who, through passion, or interest, shall miscite, or misapply it, cannot so easily be convinced of their mistake, where there is no established judge: and so it serves not, as it ought, to determine the rights, and fence the properties of those that live under it; especially where every one is judge, interpreter, and executioner of it too, and that in his own case: and he that has right on his side, having ordinarily but his own single strength, hath not force enough to defend himself from injuries, or to punish delinquents. To avoid these inconveniences, which disorder men's properties in the state of nature, men unite into societies, that they may have the united strength of the whole society to secure and defend their properties, and may have standing rules to bound it, by which every one may know what is his. To this end it is that men give up all their natural power to the society which they enter into, and the community put the legislative power into such hands as they think fit; with this trust, that they shall be governed by declared laws, or else their peace, quiet, and property will still be at the same uncertainty as it was in the state of nature.

§ 137. Absolute arbitrary power, or governing without settled standing laws, can neither of them consist with the ends of society and government, which men would not quit the freedom of the state of nature for, and tie themselves up under, were it not to preserve their lives, liberties, and fortunes, and by stated rules of right and property to secure their peace and quiet. It cannot be supposed that they should intend, had they a power so to do, to give to any one, or more, an absolute arbitrary power over their persons and estates, and put a force into the magistrate's hand to execute his unlimited will arbitrarily upon them. This were to put themselves into a worse condition than the state of nature, wherein they had a liberty to defend their right against the injuries of others, and were upon equal terms of force to maintain it, whether invaded by a single man, or many in combination. Whereas by supposing they have given up themselves to the absolute arbitrary power

---

77. [Ed. note] Locke here, in a footnote, inserts a rather lengthy quote from Hooker, LAWS OF ECCLESIASTICAL POLITY, Bk. I, c. x, § 1.

78. "Human laws are measures in respect of men whose actions they must direct, howbeit such measures they are as have also their higher rules to be measured by, which rules are two, the law of God, and the law of nature; so that laws human must be made according to the general laws of nature, and without contradiction to any positive law of Scripture, otherwise they are ill-made" (Hooker's *Eccl. Pol.* lib. iii. sect. 9). [Bk. III, c. ix, § 2. In this passage, Hooker cites St. Thomas, SUMMA THEOLOGICA, Pt. II (1st Pt.), Q. 95, Art. 3, reprinted at p. 118, *supra*.] "To constrain men to anything inconvenient doth seem unreasonable" (*Ibid.* lib. i. sect. 10). [Bk. I, c. x, § 7].

and will of a legislator, they have disarmed themselves, and armed him, to make a prey of them when he pleases; he being in a much worse condition, who is exposed to the arbitrary power of one man, who has the command of 100,000, than he that is exposed to the arbitrary power of 100,000 single men; nobody being secure that his will, who has such a command, is better than that of other men, though his force be 100,000 times stronger. And therefore, whatever form the commonwealth is under, the ruling power ought to govern by declared and received laws, and not by extemporary dictates and undetermined resolutions; for then mankind will be in a far worse condition than in the state of nature, if they shall have armed one or a few men with the joint power of a multitude, to force them to obey at pleasure the exorbitant and unlimited degrees of their sudden thoughts, or unrestrained, and till that moment unknown wills, without having any measures set down which may guide and justify their actions: for all the power the government has being only for the good of the society, as it ought not to be arbitrary and at pleasure, so it ought to be exercised by established and promulgated laws; that both the people may know their duty, and be safe and secure within the limits of the law; and the rulers too kept within their bounds, and not be tempted, by the power they have in their hands, to employ it to such purposes, and by such measures, as they would not have known, and own not willingly.

§ 138. Thirdly, The supreme power cannot take from any man part of his property without his own consent: for the preservation of property being the end of government, and that for which men enter into society, it necessarily supposes and requires, that the people should have property, without which they must be supposed to lose that, by entering into society, which was the end for which they entered into it; too gross an absurdity for any man to own. Men therefore in society having property, they have such right to the goods, which by the law of the community are theirs, that nobody hath a right to take their substance or any part of it from them, without their own consent: without this they have no property at all; for I have truly no property in that, which another can by right take from me, when he pleases, against my consent. Hence it is a mistake to think, that the supreme or legislative power of any commonwealth can do what it will, and dispose of the estates of the subject arbitrarily, or take any part of them at pleasure. This is not much to be feared in governments where the legislative consists, wholly or in part, in assemblies which are variable, whose members, upon the dissolution of the assembly, are subjects under the common laws of their country, equally with the rest. But in governments where the legislative is in one lasting assembly always in being, or in one man, as in absolute monarchies, there is danger still that they will think themselves to have a distinct interest from the rest of the community; and so will be apt to increase their own riches and power, by taking what they think fit from the people: for a man's property is not at all secure, though there be good and equitable laws to set the bounds of it between him and his fellow-subjects, if he who commands those subjects have power to take from any private man what part he pleases of his property, and use and dispose of it as he thinks good.

§ 139. But government, into whatsoever hands it is put, being, as I have before showed, entrusted with this condition, and for this end, that men might have and secure their properties; the prince, or senate, however it may have power to make laws for the regulating of property between the subjects one amongst another, yet can never have a power to take to themselves the whole or any part of the subject's property without their own consent: for this would be in effect to leave them no property at all. And to let us see, that even absolute power, where it is necessary, is not arbitrary by being absolute, but is still limited by that reason, and confined to those ends, which required it in some cases to be absolute, we need look no farther than the common practice of martial discipline: for the preservation of the army, and in it of the whole commonwealth, requires an absolute obedience to the command of every superior officer, and it is justly death to disobey or dispute the most dangerous or unreasonable of them; but yet we see, that neither the serjeant, that could command a soldier to march up to the mouth of a cannon, or stand in a breach, where he is almost sure to perish, can command that soldier to give him one penny of his money; nor the general, that can condemn him to death for deserting his post, or for not obeying the most desperate orders, can yet, with all his absolute power of life and death, dispose of one farthing of that soldier's estate, or seize one jot of his goods; whom yet he can command any thing, and hang for the least disobedience; because such a blind obedience is necessary to that end for which the commander has his power, viz. the preservation of the rest; but the disposing of his goods has nothing to do with it.

§ 140. It is true, governments cannot be supported without great charge, and it is fit every one who enjoys his share of the protection, should pay out of his estate his proportion for the maintenance of it. But still it must be with his own consent, *i.e.* the consent of the majority, giving it either by themselves, or their representatives chosen by them: for if any one shall claim a power to lay and levy taxes on the people by his own authority, and without such consent of the people, he thereby invades the fundamental law of property, and subverts the end of government: for what property have I in that which another may by right take, when he pleases, to himself?

§ 141. Fourthly, The legislative cannot transfer the power of making laws to any other hands: for it being but a delegated power from the people, they who have it cannot pass it over to others. The people alone can appoint the form of the commonwealth, which is by constituting the legislative, and appointing in whose hands that shall be. And when the people have said, we will submit to rules, and be governed by laws made by such men, and in such forms, nobody else can say other men shall make laws for them; nor can the people be bound by any laws but such as are enacted by those whom they have chosen, and authorized to make laws for them. The power of the legislative being derived from the people by a positive voluntary grant and institution, can be no other than what that positive grant conveyed, which being only to make laws, and not to make legislators, the legislative can have no power to transfer their authority of making laws and place it in other hands.

§ 142. These are the bounds which the trust that is put in them by the society, and the law of God and nature, have set to the legislative power of every commonwealth, in all forms of government.

First, They are to govern by promulgated established laws, not to be varied in particular cases, but to have one rule for rich and poor, for the favourite at court, and the countryman at plough.

Secondly, These laws also ought to be designed for no other end ultimately, but the good of the people.

Thirdly, They must not raise taxes on the property of the people, without the consent of the people, given by themselves or their deputies. And this properly concerns only such governments where the legislative is always in being, or at least where the people have not reserved any part of the legislative to deputies, to be from time to time chosen by themselves.

Fourthly, The legislative neither must nor can transfer the power of making laws to any body else, or place it any where, but where the people have.

CHAPTER XII.
Of the legislative, executive, and federative Power of the Commonwealth.

§ 143. The legislative power is that, which has a right to direct how the force of the commonwealth shall be employed for preserving the community and the members of it. But because those laws which are constantly to be executed, and whose force is always to continue, may be made in a little time, therefore there is no need that the legislative should be always in being, not having always business to do. And because it may be too great a temptation to human frailty, apt to grasp at power, for the same persons who have the power of making laws, to have also in their hands the power to execute them; whereby they may exempt themselves from obedience to the laws they make, and suit the law, both in its making and execution, to their own private advantage, and thereby come to have a distinct interest from the rest of the community, contrary to the end of society and government: therefore in well ordered commonwealths, where the good of the whole is so considered, as it ought, the legislative power is put into the hands of divers persons, who, duly assembled, have by themselves or jointly with others, a power to make laws; which when they have done, being separated again, they are themselves subject to the laws they have made; which is a new and near tie upon them, to take care that they make them for the public good.

§ 144. But because the laws, that are at once, and in a short time made, have a constant and lasting force, and need a perpetual execution, or an attendance thereunto; therefore it is necessary there should be a power always in being, which should see to the execution of the laws that are made, and remain in force. And thus the legislative and executive power come often to be separated.

§ 145. There is another power in every commonwealth, which one may call natural, because it is that which answers to the power every man naturally had before he entered into society: for though in a commonwealth, the members of it are distinct persons still in reference to one another, and as such are governed by the laws of the society; yet in reference to the rest of mankind, they make one body, which is, as every member of it before was, still in the state of nature with the rest of mankind. Hence it is, that the controversies that happen between any man of the society with those that are out of it, are managed by the public; and an injury done to a member of their body engages the whole in the reparation of it. So that, under this consideration, the whole community is one body in the state of nature, in respect of all other states or persons out of its community.

§ 146. This therefore contains the power of war and peace, leagues and alliances, and all the transactions with all persons and communities without the commonwealth; and may be called federative, if any one pleases. So the thing be understood, I am indifferent as to the name.

§ 147. These two powers, executive and federative, though they be really distinct in themselves, yet one comprehending the execution of the municipal laws of the society within itself, upon all that are parts of it; the other the management of the security and interest of the public without, with all those that it may receive benefit or damage from; yet they are always almost united. And though this federative power in the well or ill management of it be of great moment to the commonwealth, yet it is much less capable to be directed by antecedent, standing, positive laws, than the executive; and so must necessarily be left to the prudence and wisdom of those whose hands it is in, to be managed for the public good: for the laws that concern subjects one amongst another, being to direct their actions, may well enough precede them. But what is to be done in reference to foreigners, depending much upon their actions, and the variation of designs, and interests, must be left in great part to the prudence of those who have this power committed to them, to be managed by the best of their skill, for the advantage of the commonwealth.

§ 148. Though, as I said, the executive and federative power of every community be really distinct in themselves, yet they are hardly to be separated, and placed at the same time in the hands of distinct persons: for both of them requiring the force of the society for their exercise, it is almost impracticable to place the force of the commonwealth in distinct, and not subordinate hands; or that the executive and federative power should be placed in persons that might act separately, whereby the force of the public would be under different commands; which would be apt some time or other to cause disorder and ruin.

CHAPTER XIII.
Of the Subordination of the Powers of the Commonwealth.

§ 149. Though in a constituted commonwealth, standing upon its own basis, and acting according to its own nature, that is, acting for the preservation of the community, there can be but one supreme power, which is the legislative, to which all the rest are and must be subordinate; yet the legislative being only a fiduciary power to act for certain ends, there remains still "in the people a supreme power to remove or alter the legislative," when they find the legislative act contrary to the trust reposed in them: for all power given with trust for the attaining an end, being limited by that end: whenever that end is manifestly neglected or opposed, the trust must necessarily be forfeited, and the power devolve into the hands of those that gave it, who may place it anew where they shall think best for their safety and security. And thus the community perpetually retains a supreme power of saving themselves from the attempts and designs of any body, even of their legislators, whenever they shall be so foolish, or so wicked, as to lay and carry on designs against the liberties and properties of the subject: for no man, or society of men, having a power to deliver up their preservation, or consequently the means of it, to the absolute will and arbitrary dominion of another; whenever any one shall go about to bring them into such a slavish condition, they will always have a right to preserve what they have not a power to part with; and to rid themselves of those who invade this fundamental, sacred, and unalterable law of self-preservation, for which they entered into society. And thus the community may be said in this respect to be always the supreme power, but not as considered under any form of government, because this power of the people can never take place till the government be dissolved.

§ 150. In all cases, whilst the government subsists, the legislative is the supreme power: for what can give laws to another, must needs be superior to him; and since the legislative is no otherwise legislative of the society, but by the right it has to make laws for all the parts, and for every member of the society, prescribing rules to their actions, and giving power of execution, where they are transgressed; the legislative must needs be the supreme, and all other powers, in any members or parts of the society, derived from and subordinate to it.

§ 151. In some commonwealths, where the legislative is not always in being, and the executive is vested in a single person, who has also a share in the legislative; there that single person in a very tolerable sense may also be called supreme; not that he has in himself all the supreme power, which is that of law-making; but because he has in him the supreme execution, from whom all inferior magistrates derive all their several subordinate powers, or at least the greatest part of them: having also no legislative superior to him, there being no law to be made without his consent, which cannot be expected should ever subject him to the other part of the legislative, he is properly enough in this sense supreme. But yet it is to be observed, that though oaths of allegiance and fealty are taken to him, it is not to him as supreme legislator, but as supreme executor of the law, made by a joint power of him with others: allegiance being nothing but an obedience according to law, which when he violates, he has no right to obedience, nor can claim it otherwise than as the public person invested with the power of the law; and so is to be considered as the image, phantom, or representative of the commonwealth, acted by the will of the society, declared in its laws; and thus he has no will, no power, but that of the law. But when he quits this representation, this public will, and acts by his own private will, he degrades himself, and is but a single private person without power, and without will, that has no right to obedience; the members owing no obedience but to the public will of the society.

§ 152. The executive power, placed any where but in a person that has also a share in the legislative, is visibly subordinate and accountable to it, and may be at pleasure changed and displaced; so that it is not the supreme executive power that is exempt from subordination: but the supreme executive power vested in one, who having a share in the legislative, has no distinct superior legislative to be subordinate and accountable to, farther than he himself shall join and consent; so that he is no more subordinate than he himself shall think fit, which one may certainly conclude will be but very little. Of other ministerial and subordinate powers in a commonwealth we need not speak, they being so multiplied with infinite variety, in the different customs and constitutions of distinct commonwealths, that it is impossible to give a particular account of them all. Only thus much, which is necessary to our present purpose, we may take notice of concerning them, that they have no manner of authority, any of them, beyond what is by positive grant and commission delegated to them, and are all of them accountable to some other power in the commonwealth.

§ 153. It is not necessary, no, nor so much as convenient, that the legislative should be always in being; but absolutely necessary that the executive power should; because there is not always need of new laws to be made, but always need of execution of the laws that are made. When the legislative hath put the execution of the laws they make into other hands, they have a power still to resume it out of those hands, when they find cause, and to punish for any male administration against the laws. The same holds also in regard of the federative power, that and the executive being both ministerial and subordinate to the legislative, which, as has been showed, in a constituted commonwealth is the supreme. The legislative also in this case being supposed to consist of several persons, (for if it be a single person, it cannot but be always in being, and so will, as supreme, naturally have the supreme executive power, together with the legislative) may assemble, and exercise their legislature, at the times that either their original constitution, or their own adjournment, appoints, or when they please; if neither of these hath appointed any time, or there be no other way prescribed to convoke them: for the supreme power being placed in them by the people, it is always in them, and they may exercise it when they please, unless by their original constitution they are limited to certain seasons, or by an act of their supreme power they have adjourned to a certain time; and when that time comes, they have a right to assemble and act again.

§ 154. If the legislative, or any part of it, be made up of representatives chosen for that time by the people, which afterwards return into the ordinary state of subjects, and have no share in the legislature but upon a new choice, this power of choosing must also be exercised by the people, either at certain appointed seasons, or else when they are summoned to it; and in this latter case the power of convoking the legislative is ordinarily placed in the executive, and has one of these two limitations in respect of time: that either the original constitution requires their assembling and acting at certain intervals, and then the executive power does nothing but ministerially issue directions for their electing and assembling according to due forms; or else it is left to his prudence to call them by new elections, when the occasions or exigencies of the public require the amendment of old, or making of new laws, or the redress or prevention of any inconveniences, that lie on, or threaten the people.

§ 155. It may be demanded here, What if the executive power, being possessed of the force of the commonwealth, shall make use of that force to hinder the meeting and acting of the legislative, when the original constitution or the public exigencies require it? I say, using force upon the people without authority, and contrary to the trust put in him that does so, is a state of war with the people, who have a right to reinstate their legislative in the exercise of their power: for having erected a legislative, with an intent they should exercise the power of making laws, either at certain set times, or when there is need of it; when they are hindered by any force from what is so necessary to the society, and wherein the safety and preservation of the people consists, the people have a right to remove it by force. In all states and conditions, the true remedy of force without authority is to oppose force to it. The use of force without authority always puts him that uses it into a state of war, as the aggressor, and renders him liable to be treated accordingly.

§ 156. The power of assembling and dismissing the legislative, placed in the executive, gives not the executive a superiority over it, but is a fiduciary trust placed in him for the safety of the people, in a case where the uncertainty and variableness of human affairs could not bear a steady fixed rule: for it not being possible that the first framers of the government should, by any foresight, be so much masters of future events as to be able to prefix so just periods of return and duration to the assemblies of the legislative, in all times to come, that might exactly answer all the exigencies of the commonwealth; the best remedy could be found for this defect was to trust this to the prudence of one who was always to be present, and whose business it was to watch over the public good. Constant frequent meetings of the legislative, and long continuations of their assemblies, without necessary occasion, could not but be burdensome to the people, and must necessarily in time produce more dangerous inconveniencies, and yet the quick turn of affairs might be sometimes such as to need their present help; any delay of their convening might endanger the public; and sometimes too their business might be so great, that the limited time of their sitting might be too short for their work, and rob the public of that benefit which could be had only from their mature deliberation. What then could be done in this case to prevent the community from being exposed some time or other to eminent hazard, on one side or the other, by fixed intervals and periods, set to the meeting and acting of the legislative; but to intrust it to the prudence of some, who being present, and acquainted with the state of public affairs, might make use of this prerogative for the public good? and where else could this be so well placed as in his hands, who was intrusted with the execution of the laws for the same end? Thus supposing the regulation of times for the assembling and sitting of the legislative not settled by the original constitution, it naturally fell into the hands of the executive, not as an arbitrary power depending on his good pleasure, but with this trust always to have it exercised only for the public weal, as the occurrences of times and change of affairs might require. Whether settled periods of their convening, or a liberty left to the prince for convoking the legislative, or perhaps a mixture of both, hath the least inconvenience attending it, it is not my business here to inquire; but only to show, that though the executive power may have the prerogative of convoking and dissolving such conventions of the legislative, yet it is not thereby superior to it.

§ 157. Things of this world are in so constant a flux, that nothing remains long in the same state. Thus people, riches, trade, power, change their stations, flourishing mighty cities come to ruin, and prove in time neglected desolate corners, whilst other unfrequented places grow into populous countries, filled with wealth and inhabitants. But things not always changing equally, and private interest often keeping up customs and privileges, when the reasons of them are ceased; it often comes to pass, that in governments, where part of the legislative consists of representatives chosen by the people, that in tract of time this representation becomes very unequal and disproportionate to the reasons it was at first established upon. To what gross absurdities the following of custom, when reason has left it, may lead, we may be satisfied, when we see the bare name of a town, of which there remains not so much as the ruins, where scarce so much housing as a sheepcote, or more inhabitants than a shepherd is to be found, sends as many representatives to the grand assembly of law-makers as a whole county, numerous in people, and powerful in riches. This strangers stand amazed at, and every one must confess needs a remedy; though most think it hard to find one; because the constitution of the legislative being the original and supreme act of the society, antecedent to all positive laws in it, and depending wholly on the people, no inferior power can alter it. And therefore the people, when the legislative is once constituted, having, in such a government as we have been speaking of, no power to act as long as the government stands; this inconvenience is thought incapable of a remedy.

§ 158. *Salus populi suprema lex*, is certainly so just and fundamental a rule, that he, who sincerely follows it, cannot dangerously err. If therefore the executive, who has the power of convoking the legislative, observing rather the true proportion than fashion of representation, regulates not by old custom, but true reason, the number of members in all places that have a right to be distinctly represented, which no part of the people, however incorporated, can pretend to, but in proportion to the assistance which it affords to the public; it cannot be judged to have set up a new legislative, but to have restored the old and true one, and to have rectified the disorders which succession of time had insensibly, as well as inevitably introduced; for it being the interest as well as intention of the people, to have a fair and equal representative; whoever brings it nearest to that, is an undoubted friend to, and establisher of the government, and cannot miss the consent and approbation of the community: prerogative being nothing but a power in the hands of the prince, to provide for the public good, in such cases, which depending upon unforeseen and uncertain occurrences, certain and unalterable laws could not safely direct; whatsoever shall be done manifestly for the good of the people, and the establishing the government upon its true foundations, is, and always will be, just prerogative. The power of erecting new corporations, and therewith new representatives, carries with it a supposition that in time the measures of representation might vary, and those places have a just right to be represented which before had none; and by the same reason, those cease to have a right, and be too inconsiderable for such a privilege, which before had it. It is not a change from the present state, which perhaps corruption or decay has introduced, that makes an inroad upon the government; but the tendency of it to injure or oppress the people, and to set up one part or party, with a distinction from and an unequal subjection of the rest. Whatsoever cannot but be acknowledged to be of advantage to the society, and people in general, upon just and lasting measures, will always, when done, justify itself; and whenever the people shall choose their representatives upon just and undeniably equal measures, suitable to the original frame of the government, it cannot be doubted to be the will and act of the society, whoever permitted or caused them so to do.

CHAPTER XIV.
Of Prerogative.

§ 159. Where the legislative and executive power are in distinct hands, (as they are in all moderated monarchies and well-framed governments) there the good of the society requires, that several things should be left to the discretion of him that has the executive power: for the legislators not being able to foresee, and provide by laws, for all that may be useful to the community, the executor of the laws having the power in his hands, has by the common law of nature a right to make use of it for the good of the society, in many cases, where the municipal law has given no direction, till the legislative can conveniently be assembled to provide for it. Many things there are, which the law can by no means provide for; and those must necessarily be left to the discretion of him that has the executive power in his hands, to be ordered by him as the public good and advantage shall require: nay, it is fit that the laws themselves should in some cases give way to the executive power, or rather to this fundamental law of nature and government, viz. That, as much as may be, all the members of the society are to be preserved: for since many accidents may happen, wherein a strict and rigid observation of the laws may do harm; (as not to pull down an innocent man's house to stop the fire, when the next to it is burning) and a man may come sometimes within the reach of the law, which makes no distinction of persons, by an action that may deserve reward and pardon; it is fit the ruler should have a power, in many cases, to mitigate the severity of the law, and pardon some offenders: for the end of government being the preservation of all, as much as may be, even the guilty are to be spared, where it can prove no prejudice to the innocent.

§ 160. This power to act according to discretion for the public good, without the prescription of the law, and sometimes even against it, is that which is called prerogative: for since in some governments the law-making power is not always in being, and is usually too numerous, and so too slow for the despatch requisite to execution; and because also it is impossible to foresee, and so by laws to provide for all accidents and necessities that may concern the public, or to make such laws as will do no harm, if they are executed with an inflexible rigour on all occasions, and upon all persons that may come in their way; therefore there is a latitude left to the executive power, to do many things of choice which the laws do not prescribe.

§ 161. This power, whilst employed for the benefit of the community, and suitably to the trust and ends of the government, is undoubted prerogative and never is questioned; for the people are very seldom or never scrupulous or nice in the point; they are far from examining prerogative, whilst it is in any tolerable degree employed for the use it was meant; that is, for the good of the people, and not manifestly against it: but if there comes to be a question between the executive power and the people, about a thing claimed as a prerogative, the tendency of the exercise of such prerogative to the good or hurt of the people will easily decide that question.

§ 162. It is easy to conceive, that in the infancy of governments, when commonwealths differed little from families in number of people, they differed from them too but little in number of laws: and the governors being as the fathers of them, watching over them for their good, the government was almost all prerogative. A few established laws served the turn, and the discretion and care of the ruler supplied the rest. But when mistake or flattery prevailed with weak princes to make use of this power for private ends of their own, and not for the public good, the people were fain by express laws to get prerogative determined in those points wherein they found disadvantage from it: and thus declared limitations of prerogative were by the people found necessary in cases which they and their ancestors had left, in the utmost latitude, to the wisdom of those princes who made no other but a right use of it; that is, for the good of their people.

§ 163. And therefore they have a very wrong notion of government, who say, that the people have encroached upon the prerogative, when they have got any part of it to be defined by positive laws: for in so doing they have not pulled from the prince any thing that of right belonged to him, but only declare, that that power which they indefinitely left in his or his ancestors' hands, to be exercised for their good, was not a thing which they intended him when he used it otherwise: for the end of government being the good of the community, whatsoever alterations are made in it, tending to that end, cannot be an encroachment upon any body, since nobody in government can have a right tending to any other end: and those only are encroachments which prejudice or hinder the public good. Those who say otherwise, speak as if the prince had a distinct and separate interest from the good of the community, and was not made for it; the root and source from which spring almost all those evils and disorders which happen in kingly governments. And indeed, if that be so, the people under his government are not a society of rational creatures, entered into a community for their mutual good; they are not such as have set rulers over themselves, to guard and promote that good; but are to be looked on as an herd of inferior creatures under the dominion of a master, who keeps them and works them for his own pleasure or profit. If men were so void of reason, and brutish, as to enter into society upon such terms, prerogative might indeed be, what some men would have it, an arbitrary power to do things hurtful to the people.

§ 164. But since a rational creature cannot be supposed, when free, to put himself into subjection to another, for his own harm; (though, where he finds a good and wise ruler, he may not perhaps think it either necessary or useful to set precise bounds to his power in all things) prerogative can be nothing but the people's permitting their rulers to do several things, of their own free choice, where the law was silent, and sometimes too against the direct letter of the law, for the public good; and their acquiescing in it when so done: for as a good prince, who is mindful of the trust put into his hands, and careful of the good of his people, cannot have too much prerogative, that is, power to do good; so a weak and ill prince, who would claim that power which his predecessors exercised without the direction of the law, as a prerogative belonging to him by right of his office, which he may exercise at his pleasure, to make or promote an interest distinct from that of the public; gives the people an occasion to claim their right, and limit that power, which, whilst it was exercised for their good, they were content should be tacitly allowed.

§ 165. And therefore he that will look into the history of England, will find, that prerogative was always largest in the hands of our wisest and best princes; because the people, observing the whole tendency of their actions to be the public good, contested not what was done without law to that end: or, if any human frailty or mistake (for princes are but men, made as others) appeared in some small declinations from that end; yet it was visible, the main of their conduct tended to nothing but the care of the public. The people, therefore, finding reason to be satisfied with these princes, whenever they acted without, or contrary to the letter of the law, acquiesced in what they did, and, without the least complaint, let them enlarge their prerogative as they pleased; judging rightly, that they did nothing herein to the prejudice of their laws, since they acted conformably to the foundation and end of all laws, the public good.

§ 166. Such God-like princes, indeed, had some title to arbitrary power by that argument, that would prove absolute monarchy the best government, as that which God himself governs the universe by; because such kings partook of his wisdom and goodness. Upon this is founded that saying, That the reigns of good princes have been always most dangerous to the liberties of their people: for when their successors, managing the government with different thoughts, would draw the actions of those good rulers into precedent, and make them the standard of their prerogative, as if what had been done only for the good of the people was a right in them to do for the harm of the people, if they so pleased; it has often occasioned contest, and sometimes public disorders, before the people could recover their original right, and get that to be declared not to be prerogative, which truly was never so: since it is impossible that any body in the society should ever have a right to do the people harm; though it be very possible and reasonable that the people should not go about to set any bounds to the prerogative of those kings or rulers, who themselves transgressed not the bounds of the public good; for "prerogative is nothing but the power of doing public good without a rule."

§ 167. The power of calling parliaments in England, as to precise time, place, and duration, is certainly a prerogative of the king, but still with this trust, that it shall be made use of for the good of the nation, as the exigencies of the times, and variety of occasions shall require: for it being impossible to foresee which should always be the fittest place for them to assemble in, and what the best season, the choice of these was left with the executive power, as might be most subservient to the public good, and best suit the ends of parliaments.

§ 168. The old question will be asked in this matter of prerogative, "But who shall be judge when this power is made a right use of?" I answer: between an executive power in being, with such a prerogative, and a legislative that depends upon his will for their convening, there can be no judge on earth; as there can be none between the legislative and the people, should either the executive or the legislative, when they have got the power in their hands, design or go about to enslave or destroy them. The people have no other remedy in this, as in all other cases where they have no judge on earth, but to appeal to heaven: for the rulers, in such attempts, exercising a power the people never put into their hands (who can never be supposed to consent that any body should rule over them for their harm), do that which they have not a right to do. And where the body of the people, or any single man, is deprived of their right, or under the exercise of a power without right, and have no appeal on earth, then they have a liberty to appeal to heaven, whenever they judge the cause of sufficient moment. And therefore, though the people cannot be judge, so as to have, by the constitution of that society, any superior power to determine and give effective sentence in the case; yet they have, by a law antecedent and paramount to all positive laws of men, reserved that ultimate determination to themselves which belongs to all mankind, where there lies no appeal on earth, viz. to judge whether they have just cause to make their appeal to heaven.—And this judgment they cannot part with, it being out of a man's power so to submit himself to another, as to give him a liberty to destroy him; God and nature never allowing a man so to abandon himself, as to neglect his own preservation: and since he cannot take away his own life, neither can he give another power to take it. Nor let any one think this lays a perpetual foundation for disorder; for this operates not till the inconveniency is so great that the majority feel it, and are weary of it, and find a necessity to have it amended. But this the executive power, or wise princes, never need come in the danger of: and it is the thing, of all others, they have most need to avoid, as of all others the most perilous.

*   *   *

CHAPTER XIX.
Of the Dissolution of Government.

§ 211. He that will with any clearness speak of the dissolution of government, ought in the first place to distinguish between the dissolution of the society and the dissolution of the government. That which makes the community, and brings men out of the loose state of nature into one politic society, is the agreement which every one has with the rest to incorporate, and act as one body, and so be one distinct commonwealth. The usual, and almost only way whereby this union is dissolved, is the inroad of foreign force making a conquest upon them: for in that case (not being able to maintain and support themselves as one entire and independent body), the union belonging to that body which consisted therein, must necessarily cease, and so every one return to the state he was in before, with a liberty to shift for himself, and provide for his own safety, as he thinks fit, in some other society. Whenever the society is dissolved, it is certain the government of that society cannot remain. Thus conquerors' swords often cut up governments by the roots, and mangle societies to pieces, separating the subdued or scattered multitude from the protection of, and dependence on, that society which ought to have preserved them from violence. The world is too well instructed in, and too forward to allow of, this way of dissolving of governments, to need any more to be said of it; and there wants not much argument to prove, that where the society is dissolved, the government cannot remain; that being as impossible, as for the frame of a house to subsist when the materials of it are scattered and dissipated by a whirlwind, or jumbled into a confused heap by an earthquake.

§ 212. Besides this overturning from without, governments are dissolved from within.

First, When the legislative is altered. Civil society being a state of peace, amongst those who are of it from whom the state of war is excluded by the umpirage, which they have provided in their legislative, for the ending all differences that may arise amongst any of them; it is in their legislative, that the members of a commonwealth are united, and combined together into one coherent living body. This is the soul that gives form, life, and unity to the commonwealth: from hence the several members have their mutual influence, sympathy, and connexion: and therefore, when the legislative is broken or dissolved, dissolution and death follows: for, the essence and union of the society consisting in having one will, the legislative, when once established by the majority, has the declaring, and as it were keeping of that will. The constitution of the legislative is the first and fundamental act of society, whereby provision is made for the continuation of their union, under the direction of persons, and bonds of laws, made by persons authorized thereunto, by the consent and appointment of the people; without which no one man, or number of men, amongst them, can have authority of making laws that shall be binding to the rest. When any one, or more, shall take upon them to make laws, whom the people have not appointed so to do, they make laws without authority, which the people are not therefore bound to obey; by which means they come again to be out of subjection, and may constitute to themselves a new legislative, as they think best, being in full liberty to resist the force of those, who without authority would impose any thing upon them. Every one is at the disposure of his own will, when those who had, by the delegation of the society, the declaring of the public will, are excluded from it, and others usurp the place, who have no such authority or delegation.

§ 213. This being usually brought about by such in the commonwealth who misuse the power they have, it is hard to consider it aright, and know at whose door to lay it, without knowing the form of government in which it happens. Let us suppose then the legislative placed in the concurrence of three distinct persons.

1. A single hereditary person, having the constant, supreme, executive power, and with it the power of convoking and dissolving the other two, within certain periods of time.

2. An assembly of hereditary nobility.

3. An assembly of representatives chosen, *pro tempore*, by the people. Such a form of government supposed, it is evident.

§ 214. First, That when such a single person, or prince, sets up his own arbitrary will in place of the laws, which are the will of the society, declared by the legislative, then the legislative is changed: for that being in effect the legislative, whose rules and laws are put in execution, and required to be obeyed; when other laws are set up, and other rules pretended, and enforced, than what the legislative, constituted by the society, have enacted, it is plain that the legislative is changed. Whoever introduces new laws, not being thereunto authorized by the fundamental appointment of the society, or subverts the old; disowns and overturns the power by which they were made, and so sets up a new legislative.

§ 215. Secondly, When the prince hinders the legislative from assembling in its due time, or from acting freely, pursuant to those ends for which it was constituted, the legislative is altered: for it is not a certain number of men, no, nor their meeting, unless they have also freedom of debating, and leisure of perfecting, what is for the good of the society, wherein the legislative consists: when these are taken away or altered, so as to deprive the society of the due exercise of their power, the legislative is truly altered: for it is not names that constitute governments, but the use and exercise of those powers that were intended to accompany them; so that he, who takes away the freedom, or hinders the acting of the legislative in its due seasons, in effect takes away the legislative, and puts an end to the government.

§ 216. Thirdly, When, by the arbitrary power of the prince, the electors, or ways of election, are altered, without the consent, and contrary to the common interest of the people, there also the legislative is altered: for if others than those whom the society hath authorized thereunto, do choose, or in another way than what the society hath prescribed, those chosen are not the legislative appointed by the people.

§ 217. Fourthly, The delivery also of the people into the subjection of a foreign power, either by the prince or by the legislative, is certainly a change of the legislative, and so a dissolution of the government: for the end why people entered into society being to be preserved one entire, free, independent society, to be governed by its own laws; this is lost, whenever they are given up into the power of another.

§ 218. Why, in such a constitution as this, the dissolution of the government in these cases is to be imputed to the prince, is evident; because he, having the force, treasure, and offices of the state to employ, and often persuading himself, or being flattered by others, that as supreme magistrate he is uncapable of control; he alone is in a condition to make great advances toward such changes, under pretence of lawful authority, and has it in his hands to terrify or suppress opposers, as factious, seditious, and enemies to the government: whereas no other part of the legislative, or people, is capable by themselves to attempt any alteration of the legislative, without open and visible rebellion, apt enough to be taken notice of; which, when it prevails, produces effects very little different from foreign conquest. Besides, the prince in such a form of government having the power of dissolving the other parts of the legislative, and thereby rendering them private persons, they can never in opposition to him, or without his concurrence, alter the legislative by a law, his consent being necessary to give any of their decrees that sanction. But yet, so far as the other parts of the legislative any way contribute to any attempt upon the government, and do either promote, or not (what lies in them) hinder such designs; they are guilty, and partake in this, which is certainly the greatest crime men can be guilty of one towards another.

§ 219. There is one way more whereby such a government may be dissolved, and that is, when he who has the supreme executive power, neglects and abandons that charge, so that the laws already made can no longer be put in execution. This is demonstratively to reduce all to anarchy, and so effectually to dissolve the government: for laws not being made for themselves, but to be, by their execution, the bonds of the society, to keep every part of the body politic in its due place and function; when that totally ceases, the government visibly ceases, and the people become a confused multitude, without order or connexion. Where there is no longer the administration of justice, for the securing of men's rights, nor any remaining power within the community to direct the force, or provide for the necessities of the public; there certainly is no government left. Where the laws cannot be executed, it is all one as if there were no laws; and a government without laws is, I suppose, a mystery in politics, inconceivable to human capacity, and inconsistent with human society.

§ 220. In these and the like cases, when the government is dissolved, the people are at liberty to provide for themselves, by erecting a new legislative, differing from the other, by the change of persons, or form, or both, as they shall find it most for their safety and good: for the society can never, by the fault of another, lose the native and original right it has to preserve itself; which can only be done by a settled legislative, and a fair and impartial execution of the laws made by it. But the state of mankind is not so miserable that they are not capable of using this remedy, till it be too late to look for any. To tell people they may provide for themselves, by erecting a new legislative, when by oppression, artifice, or being delivered over to a foreign power, their old one is gone, is only to tell them, they may expect relief when it is too late, and the evil is past cure. This is in effect no more than to bid them first be slaves, and then to take care of their liberty; and when their chains are on, tell them they may act like freemen. This, if barely so, is rather mockery than relief; and men can never be secure from tyranny, if there be no means to escape it till they are perfectly under it; and therefore it is, that they have not only a right to get out of it, but to prevent it.

§ 221. There is therefore, secondly, another way whereby governments are dissolved, and that is, when the legislative, or the prince, either of them act contrary to their trust.

First, the legislative acts against the trust reposed in them, when they endeavour to invade the property of the subject, and to make themselves, or any part of the community, masters, or arbitrary disposers of the lives, liberties, or fortunes of the people.

§ 222. The reason why men enter into society is the preservation of their property; and the end why they choose and authorize a legislative is, that there may be laws made, and rules set, as guards and fences to the properties of all the members of the society: to limit the power, and moderate the dominion, of every part and member of the society: for since it can never be supposed to be the will of the society that the legislative should have a power to destroy that which every one designs to secure by entering into society, and for which the people submitted themselves to legislators of their own making; whenever the legislators endeavour to take away and destroy the property of the people, or to reduce them to slavery under arbitrary power, they put themselves into a state of war with the people, who are thereupon absolved from any farther obedience, and are left to the common refuge, which God hath provided for all men, against force and violence. Whensoever therefore the legislative shall transgress this fundamental rule of society; and either by ambition, fear, folly, or corruption, endeavour to grasp themselves, or put into the hands of any other, an absolute power over the lives, liberties, and estates of the people; by this breach of trust they forfeit the power the people had put into their hands for quite contrary ends, and it devolves to the people, who have a right to resume their original liberty, and, by the establishment of a new legislative, (such as they shall think fit) provide for their own safety and security, which is the end for which they are in society. What I have said here, concerning the legislative in general, holds true also concerning the supreme executor, who having a double trust put in him, both to have a part in the legislative, and the supreme execution of the law, acts against both, when he goes about to set up his own arbitrary will as the law of the society. He acts also contrary to his trust, when he either employs the force, treasure, and offices of the society to corrupt the representatives, and gain them to his purposes; or openly pre-engages the electors, and prescribes to their choice, such, whom he has, by solicitations, threats, promises, or otherwise, won to his designs; and employs them to bring in such, who have promised beforehand what to vote, and what to enact. Thus to regulate candidates and electors, and new-model the ways of election, what is it but to cut up the government by the roots, and poison the very fountain of public security? for the people having reserved to themselves the choice of their representatives, as the fence to their properties, could do it for no other end, but that they might always be freely chosen, and so chosen, freely act, and advise, as the necessity of the commonwealth and the public good should, upon examination and mature debate, be judged to require. This, those who give their votes before they hear the debate, and have weighed the reasons on all sides, are not capable of doing. To prepare such an assembly as this, and endeavour to set up the declared abettors of his own will, for the true representatives of the people, and the law-makers of the society, is certainly as great a breach of trust, and as perfect a declaration of a design to subvert the government, as is possible to be met with. To which if one shall add rewards and punishments visibly employed to the same end, and all the arts of perverted law made use of, to take off and destroy all that stand in the way of such a design, and will not comply and consent to betray the liberties of their country, it will be past doubt what is doing. What power they ought to have in the society, who thus employ it contrary to the trust that went along with it in its first institution, is easy to determine; and one cannot but see, that he, who has once attempted any such thing as this, cannot any longer be trusted.

§ 223. To this perhaps it will be said, that the people being ignorant, and always discontented, to lay the foundation of government in the unsteady opinion and uncertain humour of the people, is to expose it to certain ruin; and no government will be able long to subsist, if the people may set up a new legislative, whenever they take offence at the old one. To this I answer, quite the contrary. People are not so easily got out of their old forms, as some are apt to suggest. They are hardly to be prevailed with to amend the acknowledged faults in the frame they have been accustomed to. And if there be any original defects, or adventitious ones introduced by time, or corruption; it is not an easy thing to get them changed, even when all the world sees there is an opportunity for it. This slowness and aversion in the people to quit their old constitutions, has in the many revolutions, which have been seen in this kingdom, in this and former ages, still kept us to, or, after some interval of fruitless attempts, still brought us back again to, our old legislative of king, lords, and commons: and whatever provocations have made the crown be taken from some of our princes' heads, they never carried the people so far as to place it in another line.

§ 224. But it will be said, this hypothesis lays a ferment for frequent rebellion. To which I answer,

First, No more than any other hypothesis: for when the people are made miserable, and find themselves exposed to the ill usage of arbitrary power, cry up their governors as much as you will, for sons of Jupiter; let them be sacred and divine, descended, or authorized from heaven; give them out for whom or what you please, the same will happen. The people generally ill-treated, and contrary to right, will be ready upon any occasion to ease themselves of a burden that sits heavy upon them. They will wish, and seek for the opportunity, which in the change, weakness, and accidents of human affairs, seldom delays long to offer itself. He must have lived but a little while in the world, who has not seen examples of this in his time; and he must have read very little, who cannot produce examples of it in all sorts of governments in the world.

§ 225. Secondly, I answer, such revolutions happen not upon every little mismanagement in public affairs. Great mistakes in the ruling part, many wrong and inconvenient laws, and all the slips of human frailty, will be borne by the people without mutiny or murmur. But if a long train of abuses, prevarications, and artifices, all tending the same way, make the design visible to the people, and they cannot but feel what they lie under, and see whither they are going; it is not to be wondered, that they should then rouse themselves, and endeavour to put the rule into such hands which may secure to them the ends for which government was at first erected; and without which, ancient names, and specious forms, are so far from being better, that they are much worse, than the state of nature, or pure anarchy; the inconveniencies, being all as great and as near, but the remedy farther off and more difficult.

§ 226. Thirdly, I answer, that this doctrine of a power in the people of providing for their safety anew, by a new legislative, when their legislators have acted contrary to their trust, by invading their property, is the best fence against rebellion, and the probablest means to hinder it: for rebellion being an opposition, not to persons, but authority, which is founded only in the constitutions and laws of the government; those, whoever they be, who by force break through, and by force justify their violation of them, are truly and properly rebels: for when men, by entering into society and civil government, have excluded force, and introduced laws for the preservation of property, peace, and unity amongst themselves; those who set up force again in opposition to the laws, do *rebellare*, that is, bring back again the state of war, and are properly rebels: which they who are in power, (by the pretence they have to authority, the temptation of force they have in their hands, and the flattery of those about them) being likeliest to do; the properest way to prevent the evil is to show them the danger and injustice of it, who are under the greatest temptation to run into it.

§ 227. In both the fore-mentioned cases, when either the legislative is changed, or the legislators act contrary to the end for which they were constituted, those who are guilty are guilty of rebellion: for if any one by force takes away the established legislative of any society, and the laws by them made pursuant to their trust, he thereby takes away the umpirage, which every one had consented to, for a peaceable decision of all their controversies, and a bar to the state of war amongst them. They, who remove, or change the legislative, take away this decisive power, which nobody can have but by the appointment and consent of the people; and so destroying the authority which the people did, and nobody else can set up, and introducing a power which the people hath not authorized, they actually introduce a state of war, which is that of force without authority; and thus, by removing the legislative established by the society (in whose decisions the people acquiesced and united, as to that of their own will) they untie the knot, and expose the people anew to the state of war. And if those, who by force take away the legislative, are rebels, the legislators themselves, as has been shown, can be no less esteemed so; when they, who were set up for the protection and preservation of the people, their liberties and properties, shall by force invade and endeavour to take them away; and so they putting themselves into a state of war with those who made them the protectors and guardians of their peace, are properly, and with the greatest aggravation, *rebellantes*, rebels.

§ 228. But if they, who say, "it lays a foundation for rebellion," mean that it may occasion civil wars, or intestine broils, to tell the people they are absolved from obedience when illegal attempts are made upon their liberties or properties, and may oppose the unlawful violence of those who were their magistrates, when they invade their properties contrary to the trust put in them; and that therefore this doctrine is not to be allowed, being so destructive to the peace of the world: they may as well say, upon the same ground, that honest men may not oppose robbers or pirates, because this may occasion disorder or bloodshed. If any mischief come in such cases, it is not to be charged upon him who defends his own right, but on him that invades his neighbour's. If the innocent honest man must quietly quit all he has, for peace sake, to him who will lay violent hands upon it, I desire it may be considered, what a kind of peace there will be in the world, which consists only in violence and rapine; and which is to be maintained only for the benefit of robbers and oppressors. Who would not think it an admirable peace betwixt the mighty and the mean, when the lamb, without resistance, yielded his throat to be torn by the imperious wolf? Polyphemus's den gives us a perfect pattern of such a peace, and such a government, wherein Ulysses and his companions had nothing to do, but quietly to suffer themselves to be devoured. And no doubt Ulysses, who was a prudent man, preached up passive obedience, and exhorted them to a quiet submission, by representing to them of what concernment peace was to mankind; and by showing the inconveniencies might happen, if they should offer to resist Polyphemus, who had now the power over them.

§ 229. The end of government is the good of mankind: and which is best for mankind that the people should be always exposed to the boundless will of tyranny; or that the rulers should be sometimes liable to be opposed, when they grow exorbitant in the use of their power, and employ it for the destruction, and not the preservation of the properties of their people?

§ 230. Nor let any one say, that mischief can arise from hence, as often as it shall please a busy head, or turbulent spirit, to desire the alteration of the government. It is true, such men may stir, whenever they please; but it will be only to their own just ruin and perdition: for till the mischief be grown general, and the ill designs of the rulers become visible, or their attempts sensible to the greater part, the people, who are more disposed to suffer than right themselves by resistance, are not apt to stir. The examples of particular injustice or oppression, of here and there an unfortunate man, moves them not. But if they universally have a persuasion, grounded upon manifest evidence, that designs are carrying on against their liberties, and the general course and tendency of things cannot but give them strong suspicions of the evil intention of their governors, who is to be blamed for it? Who can help it, if they, who might avoid it, bring themselves into this suspicion? Are the people to be blamed, if they have the sense of rational creatures, and can think of things no otherwise than as they find and feel them? And is it not rather their fault, who put things into such a posture, that they would not have them thought to be as they are? I grant, that the pride, ambition, and turbulency of private men have sometimes caused great disorders in commonwealths, and factions have been fatal to states and kingdoms. But whether the mischief hath oftener begun in the people's wantonness, and a desire to cast off the lawful authority of their rulers, or in the rulers' insolence, and endeavours to get and exercise an arbitrary power over their people; whether oppression, or disobedience, gave the first rise to the disorder; I leave it to impartial history to determine. This I am sure, whoever, either ruler or subject, by force goes about to invade the rights of either prince or people, and lays the foundation for overturning the constitution and frame of any just government, is highly guilty of the greatest crime, I think, a man is capable of; being to answer for all those mischiefs of blood, rapine, and desolation, which the breaking to pieces of governments bring on a country. And he who does it, is justly to be esteemed the common enemy and pest of mankind, and is to be treated accordingly.

§ 231. That subjects or foreigners, attempting by force on the properties of any people, may be resisted with force, is agreed on all hands. But that magistrates, doing the same thing, may be resisted, hath of late been denied: as if those who had the greatest privileges and advantages by the law, had thereby a power to break those laws, by which alone they were set in a better place than their brethren: whereas their offence is thereby the greater, both as being ungrateful for the greater share they have by the law, and breaking also that trust, which is put into their hands by their brethren.

§ 232. Whosoever uses force without right, as every one does in society, who does it without law, puts himself into a state of war with those against whom he so uses it; and in that state all former ties are cancelled, all other rights cease, and every one has a right to defend himself, and to resist the aggressor. This is so evident, that Barclay[79] himself, that great assertor of the power and sacredness of kings, is forced to confess, that it is lawful for the people, in some cases, to resist their king; and that too in a chapter, wherein he pretends to show, that the divine law shuts up the people from all manner of rebellion. Whereby it is evident, even by his own doctrine, that, since they may in some cases resist, all resisting of princes is not rebellion. . . .

*   *   *

---

79. [Ed. note] William Barclay, c. 1546–1608; Scottish jurist and political theorist who wrote in Latin. Even more than Filmer, it may be appropriate to say that Locke rescued him from (complete?) oblivion.

THE COLONIAL PERIOD

The development of the law in the thirteen American colonies between 1620 and 1776 was marked by the willingness of the colonists to apply elements of English common law and to devise new, and often simpler, ways of handling legal matters. Because many of the colonial settlements were geographically isolated, the law varied from place to place, and local traditions, customs, religious beliefs, and economic conditions often played major roles in shaping the law.

The Pilgrims who left England in 1620 to settle in Massachusetts were escaping from religious intolerance and persecution. Their religious beliefs, rooted in a strict version of Protestantism, led them to create a government that was dominated by the church leadership. By the beginning of the eighteenth century, however, Massachusetts had become a more heterogeneous and secular society with a growing commercial class that created a demand for trained lawyers and judges.

Other colonies were shaped by different traditions. In Pennsylvania the Quakers played a decisive role in the development of law and social arrangements. In the southern colonies, law became an instrument to support the institution of slavery. Laws in slaveholding colonies presumed that slaves were chattel (personal property) rather than human beings.

Mayflower Compact

In 1620 the ship *Mayflower* departed from England for the New World. Many of those on board were religious dissenters, known then as Separatists and later as Pilgrims or Puritans, who preferred to separate altogether from the Church of England rather than try to change the church as other dissenters attempted to do. The passengers also included emigrants who were not members of the Separatist congregation. The combined group of Separatists and "strangers," as they were called by the Separatists, had obtained a charter from the Virginia Company of London, giving them permission to settle within the boundaries of the colony of Virginia.

The *Mayflower*, however, did not reach Virginia. Instead, it arrived off the coast of what is now Cape Cod, Massachusetts, which was not within the boundaries of any established colonial government. The strangers asserted that they would not be bound by any laws, but William Bradford, the Separatists' leader, insisted that all male passengers sign an agreement to abide by the laws that the colonial leaders would establish at the colony they called Plymouth.

On November 21, 1620, forty-one adult male passengers signed the Mayflower Compact. The compact served as a device to preserve order and establish rules for self-government. The signers agreed to combine themselves into a "civil Body Politick" that would enact and obey "just and equal laws" that were made for the "general good of the colony." This commitment to justice and equality would be reiterated in many later documents, including the U.S. Constitution.

The Laws and Liberties of Massachusetts

The Laws and Liberties of Massachusetts, enacted in 1648, served as the basis for civil and criminal law in the colony until the eighteenth century. This code was a revision of a 1641 code known as *The Body of Liberties*, which was written by Nathaniel Ward, a Puritan minister and teacher. The Laws and Liberties reflect the Puritans' concern that members of the community should live a Christian life true to the principles of the sect. Laws were meant to guide the righteous and punish the wicked, but they were also to be administered fairly. Religious heresy was severely punished as were fornication, adultery, and other behavior that violated the moral teachings of the colonists. Nevertheless, the code mandated that individuals could not be punished or penalized without due process of law.

Frame of Government

In 1681 King Charles II of England granted William Penn a large tract of land on the west bank of the Delaware River, which Penn named Pennsylvania in honor of his father. Penn, a member and intellectual leader of the Quakers (Society of Friends), saw Pennsylvania as a refuge for Quakers and other persecuted peoples.

Penn believed in religious toleration on both pragmatic and moral grounds. He thought that a harmonious society, unhampered by intolerance, would be a prosperous society as well. In 1682, before he left England to become the first governor of Pennsylvania, Penn wrote the Frame of Government, which served as the colony's first constitution.

The Frame of Government was an expression of Penn's religious and political ideas. He sought to create a framework that would frustrate political mischief and prevent a ruler from assuming absolute power to the detriment of the community. To prevent absolutism, Penn employed the concept of balancing forces, a concept that the Framers of the U.S. Constitution later would use liberally. Freedom of worship was to be absolute, and all the traditional English rights were to be protected.

In practice, the government outlined in the Frame of Government proved in some respects to be unworkable. Penn, however, had included an amending clause, the first in any written constitution, so that the Frame of Government could be changed as circumstances required.

South Carolina Slave Code

The southern colonies relied on slave labor to cultivate the cash crops raised on large plantations. The first slave ships reached the colonies in the 1620s, and by the end of the century, the slave trade between West Africa and the southern colonies was thriving.

The social and legal relations between the English colonists and the African slaves were governed by racial beliefs and economics. Since the first meetings of West Africans and Europeans, Europeans had judged Africans to be their cultural inferiors. This belief shaped the slave codes that the colonies began to enact in the late seventeenth century. Africans were human chattel with no civil rights.

The South Carolina Slave Code of 1740 reflected concerns about controlling slaves. Section X authorized a white person to detain and examine any slave found outside a house or plantation who was not accompanied by a white person. Section XXXVI prohibited slaves from leaving their plantation, especially on Saturday nights, Sundays, and holidays. Slaves who violated the law could be subjected to a "moderate whipping." Section XLV prohibited white persons from teaching slaves to read and write.

Criminal behavior by slaves, especially actions directed against white persons, was severely punished under the code. Section IX provided that in the case of a capital crime, a slave must be brought to trial in a summary proceeding within three days of apprehension. Under section XVII, the killing of a white person by a slave was a capital crime, but section XXXVII treated a white person who killed a slave quite differently. Willfull murder of a slave was punished by a fine of 700 pounds. Killing a slave "on a sudden heat of passion" resulted in a fine of 350 pounds.

The code did recognize that slaves were entitled to a sufficient level of food, clothing, and shelter. Section XXXVIII permitted a complaint to be filed against a slave owner who was derelict in providing the necessities. A court could order the owner to provide relief to the slaves. Likewise, section XLIV authorized the fining of slave owners who worked their slaves more than fifteen hours a day during the hottest time of the year.

MAYFLOWER COMPACT

In the name of God, amen. We, whose names are underwritten, the loyal subjects of our dread sovereign lord King James, by the grace of God, of Great Britain, France, and Ireland, king, defender of the faith, &c. Having undertaken for the glory of God, and advancement of the Christian faith, and the honor of our king and country, a voyage to plant the first colony in the northern parts of Virginia, do by these presents, solemnly and mutually, in the presence of God and one another, covenant and combine ourselves together into a civil body politic, for our better ordering and preservation and furtherance of the ends aforesaid; and by virtue hereof do enact, constitute, and frame such just and equal laws, ordinances, acts, constitutions, and officers, from time to time, as shall be thought most meet and convenient for the general good of the colony; unto which we promise all due submission and obedience. In witness whereof we have hereunto subscribed our names at Cape Cod the eleventh of November, in the reign of our sovereign lord King James, of England, France, and Ireland, the eighteenth, and of Scotland, the fifty-fourth, anno Domini, 1620.[1]

Mr. John Carver	Mr. Samuel Fuller	Edward Tilly
Mr. William Bradford	Mr. Christopher Martin	John Tilly
Mr. Edward Winslow	Mr. William Mullins	Francis Cooke
Mr. William Brewster	Mr. William White	Thomas Rogers
Isaac Allerton	Mr. Richard Warren	Thomas Tinker
Miles Standish	John Howland	John Ridgdale
John Alden	Mr. Steven Hopkins	Edward Fuller
John Turner	Digery Priest	Richard Clark
Francis Eaton	Thomas Williams	Richard Gardiner
James Chilton	Gilbert Winslow	Mr. John Allerton
John Craxton	Edmund Margesson	Thomas English
John Billington	Peter Brown	Edward Doten
Joses Fletcher	Richard Bitteridge	Edward Liester
John Goodman	George Soule	

Source: Ben Perley Poore, ed., *The Federal and State Constitutions, Colonial Charters, and Other Organic Laws of the United States*, vol. 1 (1878), p. 931.

1. English monarchs styled themselves king or queen of France between 1340 and 1801. The custom began when the English became embroiled in the Hundred Years War with France and King Edward III of England, whose mother was a French princess, claimed the French throne.

THE LAWS AND LIBERTIES OF MASSACHUSETTS

To Our Beloved Brethren and Neighbours
the Inhabitants of the Massachusetts, the Governour, Assistants
and Deputies assembled in the Generall Court of that
Jurisdiction with grace and peace in our
Lord Jesus Christ

So soon as God had set up Politicall Government among his people Israel hee gave them a body of lawes for judgment both in civil and criminal causes. These were brief and fundamental principles, yet withall so full and comprehensive as out of them clear deductions were to be drawne to all particular cases in future times. For a Common-wealth without lawes is like a Ship without rigging and steeradge. Nor is it sufficient to have principles or fundamentalls, but these are to be drawn out into so many of their deductions as the time and conditions of that people may have use of. And it is very unsafe & injurious to the body of the people to put them to learn their duty and libertie from generall rules, nor is it enough to have lawes except they be also just. Therefore among other priviledges which the Lord bestowed upon his peculiar people, these he calls them specially to consider of, that God was neerer to them and their lawes were more righteous then other nations. God was sayd to be amongst them or neer to them because of his Ordinances established by himselfe, and their lawes righteous because himselfe was their Law-giver: yet in the comparison are implyed two things, first that other nations had something of Gods presence amongst them. Secondly that there was also somewhat of equitie in their lawes, for it pleased the Father (upon the Covenant of Redemption with his Son) to restore so much of his Image to lost man as whereby all nations are disposed to worship God, and to advance righteousness: ... They did by nature the things contained in the law of God. But the nations corrupting his Ordinances (both of Religion, and Justice) God withdrew his presence from them proportionably whereby they vvere given up to abominable lusts. .... Wheras if they had vvalked according to that light & lavv of nature they might have been preserved from such moral evils and might have injoyed common blessing in all their natural and civil Ordinances: now, if it might have been so with the nations who were so much strangers to the Covenant of Grace, what advantage have they who have interests in this Covenant, and may injoye the special presence of God in the puritie and native simplicitie of all his Ordinances by which he is so neer to his owne people. This hath been no small priviledge, and advantage to us New-England that our Churches, and civil State have been planted and growne up (like two vvines) together like that of Israel in the vvilderness by which we were put in minde (and had opportunity put into our hands) not only to gather our Churches, and set up the Ordinances of Christ Jesus in them according to the Apostolick patterne by such lights as the Lord graciously afforded us: but also withall to frame our civil Politie, and lawes according to the rules of his most holy word whereby each do help and strengthen other (the Churches the civil Authoritie, and the Civil Authoritie the Churches) and so both prosper the better without such emulation, and contention for priviledges or priority as have proved the misery (if not ruine) of both in other places.

*   *   *

These Lawes which were made successively in divers former years, we have reduced under several heads in an alphabeticall method, that so they might the more readilye be found . . . wherin (upon every occasion) you might readily see the rule which you ought to walke by.

*   *   *

You have called us from among the rest of our Bretheren and given us power to make the lawes: we must now call upon you to see them executed: remembring that old & true proverb, The execution of the law is the life of the law. If one sort of you viz: non-Freemen should object that you had no hand in calling us to this worke, and therfore think yourselvs not bound to obedience &c. Wee answer that a subsequent, or implicit consent is of like force in this case, as an express precedent power: for in puting your persons and estates into the protection and way of subsistance held forth and exercised within this Jursidiction, you doe tacitly submit to this Government and to all the wholesome lawes thereof[.]

*   *   *

If any of you meet with some law that seemes not to tend to your particular benefit, you must consider that lawes are made with respect to the whole people, and not to each particular person: and obedience to them must be yielded with respect to the common welfare, not to thy private advantage, and as thou yeildest obedience to the law for common good, but to thy disadvantage: so another must observe some other law for thy good, though to his own damage; thus must we be content to bear one anothers burden and so fullfill the Law of Christ.

That distinction which is put between the Lawes of God and the lawes of men, becomes a snare to many as it is mis-applied in the ordering of their obedience to civil Authoritie; for when the Authoritie is of God and that in way of an Ordinance . . . and when the administration of it is according to deductions, and rules gathered from the word of God, and the clear light of nature in civil nations, surely there is no humane law that tendeth to common good (according to those principles) but the same is mediately a law of God, and that in way of an Ordinance which all are to submit unto and that for conscience sake. . . .

THE
BOOK OF THE GENERAL LAVVES AND
LIBERTYES CONCERNING &C:

Forasmuch as the free fruition of such Liberties, Immunities, priviledges as humanitie, civilitie & christianity call for as due to everie man in his place, & proportion, without impeachment & infringement hath ever been, & ever will be the tranquility & stability of Churches & Comon-wealths; & the deniall or deprivall thereof the disturbance, if not ruine of both:

It is therefore ordered by this Court, & Authority thereof, That no mans life shall be taken away; no mans honour or good name shall be stayned; no mans person shall be arrested, restrained, bannished, dismembered nor any wayes punished; no man shall be deprived of his wife or children; no mans goods or estate shal be taken away from him; nor any wayes indamaged under colour of Law or countenance of Authoritie unless it be by the vertue or equity of some expresse law of the Country warranting the same established by a General Court & sufficiently published; or in case of the defect of a law in any particular case by the word of God. And in capital cases, or cases concerning dismembring or banishment according to that word to be judged by the General Court.

FRAME OF GOVERNMENT

WILLIAM PENN, 1682

Preface

I know what is said by the several admirers of monarchy, aristocracy and democracy, which are the rule of one, a few, and many, and are the three common ideas of government, when men discourse on the subject. But I chuse to solve the controversy with this small distinction, and it belongs to all three: Any government is free to the people under it (whatever be the frame) where the laws rule, and the people are a party to those laws, and more than this is tyranny, oligarchy, or confusion. . . .

*   *   *

Governments, like clocks, go from the motion men give them; and as governments are made and moved by men, so by them they are ruined too. Wherefore governments rather depend upon men, than men upon governments. Let men bee good, and the government cannot be bad; if it be ill, they will cure it. But, if men be bad, let the government be never so good, they will endeavor to warp and spoil it to their turn.

I know some say, let us have good laws, and no matter for the men that execute them: but let them consider, that though good laws do well, good men do better: for good laws may want good men, and be abolished or evaded by ill men: but good men will never want good laws, nor suffer ill ones. It is true, good laws have some awe upon ill ministers, but that is where they have not power to escape or abolish them, and the people are generally wise and good: but a loose and depraved people (which is the question) love laws and an administration like themselves. That, therefore, which makes a good constitution, must keep it, viz: men of wisdom and virtue, qualities, that because they descend not with worldly inheritances, must be carefully propagated by a virtuous education of youth; for which after ages will owe more to the care and prudence of founders, and the successive magistracy, than to their parents, for their private patrimonies. . . .

*   *   *

But, next to the power of necessity (which is a solicitor, that will take no denial) this induced me to a compliance, that we have (with reverence to God, and good conscience to men) to the best of our skill contrived and composed to the frame and laws of this government, to the great end of all government, viz: To support power in reverence with the people and to secure the people from the abuse of power; that they may be free by their just obedience, and the magistrates honourable, for their administration: for liberty without obedience is confusion, and obedience without liberty is slavery. To carry this evenness is partly owing to the constitution, and partly to the magistracy: where either of these fail, government will be subject to convulsions; but where both are wanting, it must be totally subverted; then where both meet, the government is like to endure. Which I humbly pray and hope God will please to make the lot of this Pensilvania. Amen.

SOUTH CAROLINA SLAVE CODE

**An Act for the better Ordering and Governing [of]
Negroes and other Slaves in this Province**

Whereas in his majesty's plantations in America, slavery has been introduced and allowed; and the people commonly called negroes, Indians, mulatos and mestizos have [been] deemed absolute slaves, and the subjects of property in the hands of particular persons the extent of whose power over slaves ought to be settled and limited by positive laws so that the slaves may be kept in due subjection and obedience, and the owners and other persons having the care and government of slaves, may be restrained from exercising too great rigour and cruelty over them; and that the public peace and order of this Province may be preserved:

Be it enacted, that all negroes, Indians (free Indians in amity with this government, and negroes, mulatos and mestizos who are now free excepted) mulatos or mestizos who now are or shall hereafter be in this Province, and all their issue and offspring born or to be born, shall be and they are hereby declared to be and remain for ever herafter absolute slaves, and shall follow the condition of the mother; and shall be deemed, . . . taken, reputed and adjudged in law to be chattels personal in the hands of their owners and possessors and their executors, administrators and assigns to all intents, constructions and purposes whatsoever, Provided that if any negro Indian mulato, or mestizo shall claim his or her freedom, it shall and may be lawful for such negro, Indian, mulato, or mestizo, or any person or persons whatsoever, on his or her behalf to apply to the justices of his Majesty's court of common pleas by petition or motion, either during the sitting of the said court, or before any of the justices of the same court at any time in the vacation. And the said court or any of the justices thereof, shall and they are hereby fully impowered to admit any person so applying, to be guardian for any negro, Indian, mulato or mestizo, claiming his, her or their freedom, and such guardians shall be enabled, intitled and capable in law to bring an action of trespass, in the nature of ravishment of ward against any person who shall claim property in, or who shall be in possession of any such negro, Indian, mulato or mestizo.

* * *

Provided that in any action or suit to be brought in pursuance of the direction of this act the burthen of the proof shall lay upon the plaintiff, and it shall be always presumed, that every negro, Indian, mulato, and mestizo, is a slave unless the contrary can be made appear (the Indians in amity with this government excepted) in which case the burden of the proof shall lie on the defendant.

* * *

III. And for the better keeping slaves in due order and subjection: be it further enacted that no person whatsoever, shall permit or suffer any slave under his or their care or management, and who lives, or is employed in Charlestown, or any other town in this Province to go out of the limits of the said town, or any such slave, who lives in the country to go out of the plantation to which such slave belongs, or in which plantation such slave is usually employed, without a letter subscribed and directed, or a ticket in the words following. . . .

* * *

V. If any slave who shall be out of the house or plantation where such slave shall live or shall be usually employed, or without some white person in company with such slave, shall refuse to submit or to undergo the examination of any white person, it shall be lawful for any such white Person to pursue, apprehend and moderately correct such slave; and if such slave shall assault and strike such white person, such slave may be lawfully killed.

* * *

IX. And whereas natural justice forbids, that any person of what condition soever should be condemned unheard, and the order of civil government requires that for the due and equal administration of justice, some convenient method and form of trial should be established, Be it therefore enacted, that all crimes and offences which shall be committed by slaves in this Province and for which capital punishment shall or lawfully may be inflicted, shall be heard, examined, tried, adjudged, and finally determined by any 2 justices assigned to keep the peace, and any number of freeholders not less than 3 or more than 5 in the county where the offence shall be committed and can be most conveniently assembled; either of which justices, on complaint made or information received of any such offence committed by a slave, shall commit the offender to the safe custody of the constable of the parish where such offence shall be committed, and shall without delay by warrant under his hand and seal, call to his assistance, and request any one of the nearest justices of the peace to associate with him; and shall by the same warrant summon such a number of the neighbouring freeholders as aforesaid, to assemble and meet together with the said justices, at a certain day and place not exceeding 3 days after the apprehending of such slave or slaves: and the justices and freeholders being so assembled, shall cause the slave accused or charged, to be brought before them, and shall hear the accusations which shall be brought against such slave, and his or her defence, and shall proceed to the examination of witnesses, and other evidence, and finally hear and determine the matter brought before them, in the most summary and expeditious manner; and in case the offender shall be convicted of any crime for which by law the offender ought to suffer death, the said justices shall give judgment, and award and cause execution of their sentence to be done, by inflicting such manner of death, and at such time as the said justices, by and with the consent of the freeholders shall direct, and which they shall judge will be most effectual to deter others from offending in the like manner.

* * *

[XVI.] Be it therefore enacted, that the several crimes and offences hereinafter particularly enumerated, are hereby declared to be felony without the benefit of the clergy, That is to say, If any slave, free negro, mulatto, Indian, or mestizo, shall willfully and maliciously burn or destroy any stack of rice, corn or other grain, of the product, growth or manufacture of this Province; or shall willfully and maliciously set fire to, burn or destroy any tar kiln, barrels of pitch, tar, turpentine or rosin, or any other of the goods or commodities of the growth, produce or manufacture of this Province; or shall feloniously steal, take or carry away any slave, being the property of another, with intent to carry such slave out of this Province; or shall willfully and maliciously poison, or administer any poison to any person, free man, woman, servant or slave; every such slave, free negro, mulatto, Indian (except as before excepted) and mestizo, shall suffer death as a felon.

XVII. Any slave who shall be guilty of homicide of any sort, upon any white person, except by misadventure or in defence of his master or other person under whose care and government such slave shall be, shall upon conviction thereof as aforesaid, suffer death. And every slave who shall raise or attempt to raise an insurrection in this Province, or shall endeavor to delude or entice any slave to run away and leave this Province; every such slave and slaves, and his and their accomplices, aiders and abettors, shall upon conviction as aforesaid suffer death. Provided always, That it shall and may be lawful to and for the justices who shall pronounce sentence against such slaves, and by and with the advice and consent of the freeholders as aforesaid, if several slaves shall receive sentence at one time, to mitigate and alter the sentence of any slave other than such as shall be convicted of the homicide of a white person, who they shall think may deserve mercy, and may inflict such corporal punishment (other than death) on any such slave, as they in their discretion shall think fit, any thing herein contained to the contrary thereof in any wise notwithstanding. Provided, That one or more of the said slaves who shall be convicted of the crimes or offences aforesaid, where several are concerned, shall be executed for example, to deter others from offending in the like kind.

* * *

XXXIII. And whereas several owners of slaves do suffer their slaves to go and work where they please, upon condition of paying to their owners certain sums of money agreed upon between the owner and slave; which practice occasioned such slaves to pilfer and steal to raise money for their owners, as well as to maintain themselves in drunkenness and evil courses; for prevention of which practices for the future, Be it enacted, that no owner, master or mistress of any slave, after the passing of this act, shall permit or suffer any of his, her or their slaves to go and work out of their respective houses or families, without a ticket in writing under pain of forfeiting the sum of current money, for every such offence.

* * *

XXXVI. And for that as it is absolutely necessary to the safety of this Province, that all due care be taken to restrain the wanderings and meetings of negroes and other slaves, at all times, and more especially on Saturday nights, Sundays and other holidays, and the using and carrying wooden swords, and other mischievous and dangerous weapons, or using and keeping of drums, horns, or other loud instruments, which may call together or give sign or notice to one another of their wicked designs and purposes; and that all masters, overseers and others may be enjoined diligently and carefully to prevent the same, Be it enacted, that it shall be lawfull for all masters, overseers and other persons whomsoever, to apprehend and take up any negro or other slave that shall be found out of the plantation of his or their master or owner, at any time, especially on Saturday nights, Sundays or other holidays, not being on lawful business, and with a letter from their master or a ticket, or not having a white person with them, and the said negro or other slave or slaves correct by a moderate whipping.

XXXVII. And whereas cruelty is not only highly unbecoming those who profess themselves Christians, but is odious in the eyes of all men who have any sense of virtue or humanity; therefore to restrain and prevent barbarity being exercised toward slaves, Be it enacted, That if any person or persons whosoever, shall willfully murder his own slave, or the slave of another person, every such person shall upon conviction thereof, forfeit and pay the sum of £700 current money, and shall be rendered, and is hereby declared altogether and forever incapable of holding, exercising, enjoying or receiving the profits of any office, place or employment civil or military within this Province: . . . And if any person shall on a sudden heat of passion, or by undue correction, kill his own slave or the slave of any person, he shall forfeit the sum of £350 current money, And in case any person or persons shall wilfully cut out the tongue, put out the eye, castrate or cruelly scald, burn, or deprive any slave of any limb or member, or shall inflict any other cruel punishment, other than by whipping or beating with a horsewhip, cow-skin, switch or small stick, or by putting irons on, or confining or imprisoning such slave; every such person shall for every such offence, forfeit the sum of £100 current money.

XXXVIII. That in case any person in this Province, who shall be owner, or who shall have the care government or charge of any slave, or slaves, shall deny, neglect or refuse to allow such slave or slaves under his or her charge, sufficient cloathing, covering or food, it shall and may be lawfull for any person or persons, on behalf of such slave or slaves, to make complaint to the next neighbouring justice in the parish where such slave or slaves live, or are usually employed; and if there shall be no justice in the parish, then to the next justice in nearest parish: and the said justice shall summon the party against whom such complaint shall be made, and shall enquire of, hear and determine the same: and if the said justice shall find the said complaint to be true, or that such person will not exculpate or clear himself from the charge, by his or her own oath, which such person shall be at liberty to do in all cases where positive proof is not given of the offence, such justice shall and may make such orders upon the same for the relief of such slave or slaves, as he in his discretion shall think fit, and shall and may let and impose a fine or penalty on any person who shall offend in the premises, in any sum not exceeding £20 current money, for each offence.

* * *

XLIV. And whereas many owners of slaves, and others who have the care, management and overseeing of slaves, do confine them so closely to hard labour; that they have not sufficient time for natural rest—Be it therefore enacted, That if any owner of slaves, or other person who shall have the care, management, or overseeing of any slaves, shall work or put any such slave or slaves to labour, more than 15 hours in 24 hours, from the 25th day of March to the 25th day of September, or more than 14 hours in 24 hours, from the 25th day of September to the 25th day of March; every such person shall forfeit any sum not exceeding or under £20, nor under £5 current money, for every time he, she or they shall offend herein, at the discretion of the justice before whom the complaint shall be made.

XLV. And whereas the having of slaves taught to write, or suffering them to be employed in writing, may be attended with great inconveniences; Be it enacted, that all and every person and persons whatsoever, who shall hereafter teach, or cause any slave or slaves to be taught to write, or shall use or employ any slave as a scribe in any manner of writing whatsoever, hereafter taught to write; every such person and persons shall, for every such offence, forfeit the sum of £100 current money.

CONFLICT AND REVOLUTION

By the 1750s the American colonies had grown in both population and economic strength. Increasingly, the colonists expressed dissatisfaction with Great Britain's control of their political and economic affairs. The colonies chafed under the rules of British mercantilism, the idea that colonies were to be exploited as a source of raw materials and a market for the mother country. The king and Parliament, however, viewed the colonies as part of the empire and sought to maintain the status quo.

The road to the American Revolution began with the French and Indian War (1756–1763), also known as the Seven Years' War. The war was fought to determine whether France or Great Britain would rule North America. Though Britain won the war, relations between Parliament and the colonies were strained. During the war the colonies had asserted their economic independence by trading with the enemy, flagrantly defying customs laws, and evading trade regulations. After the war the British government resolved to bring the colonies into proper subordination and to use them as a source of revenue for repaying the war debt.

Accordingly, Parliament passed a series of acts that required the colonies to pay taxes and import duties on a variety of goods and raw materials. The colonists, however, detested the Stamp Act and the Townshend Acts and refused to comply with them. Ultimately, these acts pushed the colonists to demand more autonomy in governing their affairs.

In 1774 armed conflict began in Massachusetts, and the colonies moved closer to declaring their independence. Nevertheless, many colonists still hoped to reach an accommodation with Britain. Public opinion shifted toward independence, however, when King George III issued orders to put down the colonial rebellion. The Continental Congress reacted by enacting the Declaration of the Causes and Necessity of Taking up Arms. In January 1776 Thomas Paine, the firebrand pamphleteer, published *Common Sense*, which was a direct attack on the king and a call for independence.

In July 1776 the Declaration of Independence cut the cord with the mother country by asserting the independence of the thirteen colonies. In writing the declaration, Thomas Jefferson borrowed phrases and ideas from the Virginia Declaration of Rights of 1776, which had been adopted a few weeks earlier. The War of Independence lasted from 1775 until 1783, when Britain renounced control of the colonies in the Treaty of Paris.

Stamp Act

In 1765 the British Parliament passed the Stamp Act, which imposed the first direct tax on the American colonies. The revenue measure was intended to help pay off the debt the British had incurred during the French and Indian War and to pay for the continuing defense of the colonies. To Parliament's great surprise, the Stamp Act ignited colonial opposition and outrage, leading to the first concerted effort by the colonists to resist Parliament and British authority.

The Stamp Act was designed to raise almost one-third of the revenue needed to support the military establishment permanently stationed in the colonies at the end of the French and Indian

War. The act placed a tax on newspapers, almanacs, pamphlets and broadsides, legal documents of all kinds, insurance policies, ship's papers, licenses, and even playing cards and dice. All these documents and objects had to carry a tax stamp.

In October 1765 nine of the thirteen colonies sent delegates to New York to attend the Stamp Act Congress. The Congress issued a "Declaration of Rights and Grievances" declaring that British subjects in the colonies had the same "rights and liberties" as the king's subjects in Britain. The Congress, noting that the colonies were not represented in Parliament, concluded that no taxes could be constitutionally imposed on them except by their own legislatures. Colonial merchants also organized an effective economic boycott that led to the bankruptcy of some London merchants.

The Stamp Act was repealed in 1766. Nevertheless, Parliament then passed the Declaratory Act, which asserted that Parliament had full authority to make laws that were legally binding on the colonies.

Townshend Acts

Parliament wasted little time in attempting to reassert its authority over the colonies. Between June 15 and July 2, 1767, it enacted four measures to raise revenue to pay the salaries of British governors and other officials in the colonies so that these officials would be independent of the colonial legislatures, which had been paying their salaries. The statutes came to be known as the Townshend Acts after Charles Townshend, the chancellor of the exchequer, who sponsored them.

The Townshend Acts accomplished four things. One act suspended the New York legislature until it complied with the Quartering Act of 1765, which required legislatures to house and provide supplies to British troops stationed in the colonies. Another act imposed import duties on tea, lead, paper, paint, and glass, while a third act allowed tea to be imported to the colonies free of the taxes that were levied in Great Britain. The fourth act restructured the customs service in the colonies, placing its headquarters in Boston.

As with the Stamp Act, the colonies met the new legislation with widespread opposition. The colonists saw the acts as a threat to their rights to govern themselves and levy taxes through colonial legislatures. Angry colonists threatened customs collectors and evaded the duties, while colonial merchants refused to import British goods. The situation in Boston escalated, culminating in the Boston Massacre

on March 5, 1770, in which five men were killed.

On the same day as the massacre, Parliament repealed all the import duties except that on tea, lifted the requirements of the Quartering Act, and ordered the removal of troops from Boston. Nevertheless, the Townshend Acts had had devastating effects on relations between the British government and the colonies. Colonists continued to argue that taxation without representation was not legitimate and began to discuss the necessity of political independence.

Declaration of the Causes and Necessity of Taking up Arms

Following the outbreak of hostilities in Concord and Lexington, Massachusetts, in April 1775, the Second Continental Congress met in Philadelphia. The Congress created the Continental Army, appointed George Washington commander, and, on July 8, adopted the Declaration of the Causes and Necessity of Taking up Arms.

John Dickinson, a delegate from Pennsylvania, was the principal author of the declaration. Although the declaration describes the actions by the British government that had angered the colonists and justifies the need to resist the British with arms, it does not proclaim a desire to break with the mother country. Instead the declaration expresses the need to conserve old liberties and the old order "in defence of the freedom that is our birth right and which we ever enjoyed until the late violation of it."

Common Sense

In January 1776 Thomas Paine published his fifty-page pamphlet *Common Sense*. It called for political independence and the establishment of a republican government. The pamphlet created a sensation, as much for its passionate rhetoric as for its political views. It sold more than 500,000 copies within a few months and is credited with creating the political momentum that led to the issuance of the Declaration of Independence on July 4, 1776.

In *Common Sense* Paine turned his vitriol on King George III and the institution of the monarchy, calling the king a "royal brute" and a "crowned ruffian." Insisting that people did not have to live under such a regime, he declared "that in America the law is king."

Virginia Declaration of Rights

The Virginia Declaration of Rights was adopted by the Virginia colonial constitutional convention on June 12, 1776. Its sixteen sections enumerated specific civil liberties that could not be legitimately taken away by government.

Most of the Declaration of Rights was written by George Mason, a plantation owner, real estate speculator, and neighbor of George Washington. A strong believer in human liberty and limited government, Mason crafted a document that guaranteed the citizens of Virginia, upon achieving independence from Great Britain, all the civil liberties they had lost under British rule.

The Declaration of Rights enumerates specific civil liberties, including freedom of the press, the free exercise of religion, and the injunction that "no man be deprived of his liberty, except by the law of the land or the judgement of his peers." Other provisions prohibited excessive bail or cruel and unusual punishments, required authorities to have evidence and good cause before obtaining a search warrant to enter a place, guaranteed the right to trial by jury, and said that a "well regulated militia" should be "under strict subordination" to the civilian government. Many of these provisions were later incorporated into the Bill of Rights.

Declaration of Independence

The Declaration of Independence, perhaps the most famous document in U.S. history, was adopted by the Second Continental Congress on July 4, 1776. The preparation of the declaration began on June 11, when Congress appointed a committee composed of Thomas Jefferson, John Adams, Benjamin Franklin, Robert R. Livingston, and Roger Sherman. Jefferson actually wrote the declaration, appropriating some of the language in the Virginia Declaration of Rights. Jefferson's famous phrase concerning "life, liberty, and the pursuit of happiness" is a slight reworking of the wording of the Virginia declaration.

After debate on Jefferson's draft, the Congress made several changes, yet the document remained an expression of the liberal political ideas articulated by John Locke and others. The second section, with its reference to "He," is an indictment of the actions of King George III. Like *Common Sense*, this section destroyed the aura surrounding the monarchy and helped move the colonists toward psychological as well as political independence from Great Britain.

For the members of the Continental Congress, the declaration served as a vehicle for publicizing their grievances and winning support for the revolutionary cause. It affirmed the natural rights of all people and the right of the colonists to "dissolve the political bands" with the British government. Later generations have laid more stress on the political ideals expressed in the declaration and, in particular, have found inspiration in the phrase "all men are created equal."

Treaty of Paris

The Treaty of Paris of 1783 ended the War of Independence and granted the thirteen colonies political freedom. A preliminary treaty between Great Britain and the United States had been signed in 1782, but the final agreement was not signed until September 3, 1783.

Peace negotiations began in Paris, France, in April 1782. The U.S. delegation included Benjamin Franklin, John Adams, John Jay, and Henry Laurens, while the British were represented by Richard Oswald and Henry Strachey. The negotiators concluded the preliminary treaty on November 30, 1782, but the agreement was not effective until Great Britain concluded treaties with France and Spain concerning foreign colonies.

In the final agreement, the British recognized the independence of the United States. The treaty established generous boundaries for the United States; U.S. territory now extended from the Atlantic Ocean to the Mississippi River in the west, and from the Great Lakes and Canada in the north to the 31st parallel in the south. The U.S. fishing fleet was guaranteed access to the fisheries off the coast of Newfoundland with their plentiful supply of cod.

Navigation of the Mississippi River was to be open to both the United States and Great Britain. Creditors of both countries were not to be impeded from collecting their debts, and Congress was to recommend to the states that loyalists to the British cause during the war should be treated fairly and their rights and confiscated property restored.

STAMP ACT

An Act for Granting and Applying Certain Stamp Duties, and Other Duties, in the British Colonies and Plantations in America, towards Further Defraying the Expenses of Defending, Protecting, and Securing the Same; and for Amending Such

Parts of the Several Acts of Parliament Relating to the Trade and Revenues of the Said Colonies and Plantations, as Direct the Manner of Determining and Recovering the Penalties and Forfeitures Therein Mentioned

Chapter 1

Whereas by an act made in the last session of Parliament, several duties were granted, continued, and appropriated towards defraying the expenses of defending, protecting, and securing the British colonies and plantations in America; and whereas it is just and necessary that provision be made for raising a further revenue within your Majesty's dominions in America, towards defraying the said expenses, we, your Majesty's most dutiful and loyal subjects, the Commons of Great Britain in Parliament assembled, have therefore resolved to give and grant unto your Majesty the several rates and duties hereinafter mentioned; and do most humbly beseech your Majesty that it may be enacted, and be it enacted by the king's most excellent Majesty, by and with the advice and consent of the Lords Spiritual and Temporal and Commons in this present Parliament assembled, and by the authority of the same, that from and after the first day of November, one thousand seven hundred and sixty-five, there shall be raised, levied, collected, and paid unto his Majesty, his heirs, and successors throughout the colonies and plantations in America which now are, or hereafter may be, under the dominion of his Majesty, his heirs, and successors,

For every skin or piece of vellum or parchment or sheet or piece of paper on which shall be engrossed, written, or printed any declaration, plea, replication, rejoinder, demurrer, or other pleading, or any copy thereof, in any court of law within the British colonies and plantations in America, a stamp duty of three pence.

For every skin or piece of vellum or parchment or sheet or piece of paper on which shall be engrossed, written, or printed any special bail and appearance upon such bail in any such court, a stamp duty of two shillings.

For every skin or piece of vellum or parchment or sheet or piece of paper on which shall be engrossed, written, or printed any petition, bill, answer, claim, plea, replication, rejoinder, demurrer, or other pleading in any court of chancery or equity within the said colonies and plantations, a stamp duty of one shilling and six pence.

Source: Danby Pickering, ed., *The Statutes at Large from Magna Carta to the End of the Eleventh Parliament of Great Britain, Anno 1761: Continued*, vol. 26 (1765), pp. 179-205.

For every skin or piece of vellum or parchment or sheet or piece of paper on which shall be engrossed, written, or printed any copy of any petition, bill, answer, claim, plea, replication, rejoinder, demurrer, or other pleading in any such court, a stamp duty of three pence.

For every skin or piece of vellum or parchment or sheet or piece of paper on which shall be engrossed, written, or printed any monition, libel, answer, allegation, inventory, or renunciation in ecclesiastical matters in any court of probate, court of the ordinary, or other court exercising ecclesiastical jurisdiction within the said colonies and plantations, a stamp duty of one shilling.

For every skin or piece of vellum or parchment or sheet or piece of paper on which shall be engrossed, written, or printed any copy of any will (other than the probate thereof), monition, libel, answer, allegation, inventory, or renunciation in ecclesiastical matters in any such court, a stamp duty of six pence.

For every skin or piece of vellum or parchment or sheet or piece of paper on which shall be engrossed, written, or printed any donation, presentation, collation, or institution of or to any benefice, or any writ or instrument for the like purpose, or any register, entry, testimonial, or certificate of any degree taken in any university, academy, college, or seminary of learning within the said colonies and plantations, a stamp duty of two pounds.

For every skin or piece of vellum or parchment or sheet or piece of paper, on which shall be engrossed, written, or printed any monition, libel, claim, answer, allegation, information, letter of request, execution, renunciation, inventory, or other pleading, in any admiralty court within the said colonies and plantations, a stamp duty of one shilling.

For every skin or piece of vellum or parchment or sheet or piece of paper on which any copy of any such monition, libel, claim, answer, allegation, information, letter of request, execution, renunciation, inventory, or other pleading shall be engrossed, written, or printed, a stamp duty of six pence.

For every skin or piece of vellum or parchment or sheet or piece of paper on which shall be engrossed, written, or printed, any appeal, writ of error, writ of dower, *ad quod damnum*, certiorari, statute merchant, statute staple, attestation, or certificate by any officer or exemplification of any record or proceeding in any court whatsoever within the said colonies and plantations (except appeals, writs of error, certiorari, attestations, certificates, and exemplifications, for or relating to the removal of any proceedings from before a single justice of the peace), a stamp duty of ten shillings.

For every skin or piece of vellum or parchment or sheet or piece of paper on which shall be engrossed, written, or printed any writ of covenant for levying of fines, writ of entry for suffering a common recovery, or attachment issuing out of, or returnable into, any court within the said colonies and plantations, a stamp duty of five shillings.

For every skin or piece of vellum or parchment or sheet or piece of paper on which shall be engrossed, written, or printed any judgment, decree, sentence, or dismission, or any record of *nisi prius* or *postea*, in any court within the said colonies and plantations, a stamp duty of four shillings.

For every skin or piece of vellum or parchment or sheet or piece of paper on which shall be engrossed, written, or printed any affidavit, common bail or appearance, interrogatory deposition, rule, order, or warrant of any court, or any *dedimus potestatem*, *capias*, *subpoena*, summons, compulsory citation, commission, recognizance, or any other writ, process, or mandate, issuing out of, or returnable into, any court or any office belonging thereto or any other proceeding therein whatsoever or any copy thereof or of any record not herein before charged within the said colonies and plantations (except warrants relating to criminal matters and proceedings thereon or relating thereto), a stamp duty of one shilling.

For every skin or piece of vellum or parchment or sheet or piece of paper on which shall be engrossed, written, or printed any license, appointment, or admission of any counselor, solicitor, attorney, advocate, or proctor to practice in any court, or of any notary within the said colonies and plantations, a stamp duty of ten pounds.

For every skin or piece of vellum or parchment or sheet or piece of paper on which shall be engrossed, written, or printed any note or bill of lading, which shall be signed for any kind of goods, wares, or merchandise to be exported from, or any cocket [a document sealed by the Custom House] or clearance granted within, the said colonies and plantations, a stamp duty of four pence.

For every skin or piece of vellum or parchment or sheet or piece of paper on which shall be engrossed, written, or printed letters of marque, or commission for private ships of war, within the said colonies and plantations, a stamp duty of twenty shillings.

For every skin or piece of vellum or parchment or sheet or piece of paper on which shall be engrossed, written, or printed any grant, appointment, or admission of or to any public beneficial office or employment for the space of one year, or any lesser time, of or above the value of twenty pounds per annum sterling money in salary, fees, and perquisites within the said colonies and plantations (except commissions and appointments of officers of the army, navy, ordnance, or militia, of judges, and of justices of the peace), a stamp duty of ten shillings.

For every skin or piece of vellum or parchment or sheet or piece of paper on which any grant of any liberty, privilege, or franchise under the seal of any of the said colonies or plantations, or under the seal or sign manual of any governor, proprietor, or public officer alone or in conjunction with any other person or persons, or with any council, or any council and assembly, or any exemplification of the same, shall be engrossed, written, or printed within the said colonies and plantations, a stamp duty of six pounds.

For every skin or piece of vellum or parchment or sheet or piece of paper on which shall be engrossed, written, or printed any license for retailing of spirituous liquors, to be granted to any person who shall take out the same within the said colonies and plantations, a stamp duty of twenty shillings.

For every skin or piece of vellum or parchment or sheet or piece of paper on which shall be engrossed, written, or printed any license for retailing of wine, to be granted to any person who shall not take out a license for retailing of spirituous liquors within the said colonies and plantations, a stamp duty of four pounds.

For every skin or piece of vellum or parchment or sheet or piece of paper on which shall be engrossed, written, or printed any license for retailing of wine, to be granted to any person who shall take out a license for retailing of spirituous liquors within the said colonies and plantations, a stamp duty of three pounds.

For every skin or piece of vellum or parchment or sheet or piece of paper on which shall be engrossed, written, or printed any probate of a will, letters of administration, or of guardianship for any estate above the value of twenty pounds sterling money; within the British colonies and plantations upon the continent of America, the islands belonging thereto, and the Bermuda and Bahama islands, a stamp duty of five shillings.

For every skin or piece of vellum or parchment or sheet or piece of paper on which shall be engrossed, written, or printed any such probate, letters of administration or of guardianship within all other parts of the British dominions in America, a stamp duty of ten shillings.

For every skin or piece of vellum or parchment or sheet or piece of paper on which shall be engrossed, written, or printed any bond for securing the payment of any sum of money, not exceeding the sum of ten pounds sterling money, within the British colonies and plantations upon the continent of America, the islands belonging thereto, and the Bermuda and Bahama islands, a stamp duty of six pence.

For every skin or piece of vellum or parchment or sheet or piece of paper on which shall be engrossed, written, or printed any bond for securing the payment of any sum of money above ten pounds, and not exceeding the sum of twenty pounds sterling money, within such colonies, plantations, and islands, a stamp duty of one shilling.

For every skin or piece of vellum or parchment or sheet or piece of paper on which shall be engrossed, written, or printed any bond for securing the payment of any sum of money above twenty pounds, and not exceeding forty pounds sterling money, within such colonies, plantations, and islands, a stamp duty of one shilling and six pence.

For every skin or piece of vellum or parchment or sheet or piece of paper on which shall be engrossed, written, or printed any order or warrant for surveying or setting out any quantity of land, not exceeding one hundred acres, issued by any governor, proprietor, or any public officer alone, or in conjunction with any other person or persons, or with any council or any council and assembly, within the British colonies and plantations in America, a stamp duty of six pence.

For every skin or piece of vellum or parchment or sheet or piece of paper on which shall be engrossed, written, or printed any such order or warrant for surveying or setting out any quantity of land above one hundred, and not exceeding two hundred acres, within the said colonies and plantations, a stamp duty of one shilling.

For every skin or piece of vellum or parchment or sheet or piece of paper on which shall be engrossed, written, or printed any such order or warrant for surveying or setting out any quantity of land above two hundred, and not exceeding three hundred and twenty acres, and in proportion for every such order or warrant for surveying or setting out every other three hundred and twenty acres within the said colonies and plantations, a stamp duty of one shilling and six pence.

For every skin or piece of vellum or parchment or sheet or piece of paper on which shall be engrossed, written, or printed any original grant or any deed, mesne conveyance, or other instrument whatsoever by which any quantity of land not exceeding one hundred acres shall be granted, conveyed, or assigned within the British colonies and plantations upon the continent of America, the islands belonging thereto, and the Bermuda and Bahama islands (except leases for any term not exceeding the term of twenty-one years), a stamp duty of one shilling and six pence.

For every skin or piece of vellum or parchment or sheet or piece of paper on which shall be engrossed, written, or printed any such original grant or any such deed, mesne conveyance, or other instrument whatsoever by which any quantity of land above one hundred, and not exceeding two hundred acres, shall be granted, conveyed, or assigned within such colonies, plantations, and islands, a stamp duty of two shillings.

For every skin or piece of vellum or parchment or sheet or piece of paper on which shall be engrossed, written, or printed any such original grant or any such deed, mesne conveyance, or other instrument whatsoever by which any quantity of land above two hundred, and not exceeding three hundred and twenty acres, shall be granted, conveyed, or assigned, and in proportion for every such grant, deed, mesne conveyance, or other instrument, granting, conveying, or assigning, every other three hundred and twenty acres within such colonies, plantations, and islands, a stamp duty of two shillings and six pence.

For every skin or piece of vellum or parchment or sheet or piece of paper on which shall be engrossed, written, or printed any such original grant or any such deed, mesne conveyance, or other instrument whatsoever by which any quantity of land not exceeding one hundred acres shall be granted, conveyed, or assigned within all other parts of the British dominions in America, a stamp duty of three shillings.

For every skin or piece of vellum or parchment or sheet or piece of paper on which shall be engrossed, written, or printed any such original grant or any such deed, mesne conveyance, or other instrument whatsoever by which any quantity of land above one hundred, and not exceeding two hundred acres, shall be granted, conveyed, or assigned within the same parts of the said dominions, a stamp duty of four shillings.

For every skin or piece of vellum or parchment or sheet or piece of paper on which shall be engrossed, written, or printed any such original grant or any such deed, mesne conveyance, or other instrument whatsoever whereby any quantity of land above two hundred, and not exceeding three hundred and twenty acres, shall be granted, conveyed, or assigned, and in proportion for every such grant, deed, mesne conveyance, or other instrument, granting, conveying, or assigning every other three hundred and twenty acres within the same parts of the said dominions, a stamp duty of five shillings.

For every skin or piece of vellum or parchment or sheet or piece of paper on which shall be engrossed, written, or printed any grant, appointment, or admission of or to any public beneficial office or employment, not herein before charged, above the value of twenty pounds per annum sterling money in salary, fees, and perquisites, or any exemplification of the same, within the British colonies and plantations upon the continent of America, the islands belonging thereto, and the Bermuda and Bahama islands (except commissions of officers of the army, navy, ordnance, or militia, and of justices of the peace), a stamp duty of four pounds.

For every skin or piece of vellum or parchment or sheet or piece of paper on which shall be engrossed, written, or printed any such grant, appointment, or admission, of or to any such public beneficial office or employment, or any exemplification of the same, within all other parts of the British dominions in America, a stamp duty of six pounds.

For every skin or piece of vellum or parchment or sheet or piece of paper on which shall be engrossed, written, or printed any indenture, lease, conveyance, contract, stipulation, bill of sale, charter party, protest, articles of apprenticeship, or covenant (except for the hire of servants not apprentices, and also except such other matters as are herein before charged) within the British colonies and plantations in America, a stamp duty of two shillings and six pence.

For every skin or piece of vellum or parchment or sheet or piece of paper on which any warrant or order for auditing any public accounts, beneficial warrant, order, grant, or certificate under any public seal, or under the seal or sign manual of any governor, proprietor, or public officer alone, or in conjunction with any other person or persons, or with any council or any council and assembly not herein before charged, or any passport or let-pass, surrender of office, or policy of assurance shall be engrossed, written, or printed within the said colonies and plantations (except warrants or orders for the service of the navy, army, ordnance, or militia, and grants of offices under twenty pounds per annum in salary, fees, and perquisites), a stamp duty of five shillings.

For every skin or piece of vellum or parchment or sheet or piece of paper on which shall be engrossed, written, or printed any notarial act, bond, deed, letter of attorney, procuration, mortgage, release, or other obligatory instrument not herein before charged within the said colonies and plantations, a stamp duty of two shillings and three pence.

For every skin or piece of vellum or parchment or sheet or piece of paper on which shall be engrossed, written, or printed any register, entry, or enrollment of any grant, deed, or other instrument whatsoever herein before charged within the said colonies and plantations, a stamp duty of three pence.

For every skin or piece of vellum or parchment or sheet or piece of paper on which shall be engrossed, written, or printed any register, entry, or enrollment of any grant, deed, or other instrument whatsoever not herein before charged within the said colonies and plantations, a stamp duty of two shillings.

And for and upon every pack of playing cards and all dice which shall be sold or used within the said colonies and plantations, the several stamp duties following (that is to say):

For every pack of such cards, the sum of one shilling.

And for every pair of such dice, the sum of ten shillings.

And for and upon every paper, commonly called a pamphlet, and upon every newspaper containing public news, intelligence, or occurrences, which shall be printed, dispersed, and made public, within any of the said colonies and plantations, and for and upon such advertisements as are hereinafter mentioned, the respective duties following (that is to say):

For every such pamphlet and paper contained in half a sheet, or any lesser piece of paper, which shall be so printed, a stamp duty of one halfpenny for every printed copy thereof.

For every such pamphlet and paper (being larger than half a sheet and not exceeding one whole sheet), which shall be so printed, a stamp duty of one penny for every printed copy thereof.

For every such pamphlet and paper being larger than one whole sheet and not exceeding six sheets in octavo, or in a lesser page, or not exceeding twelve sheets in quarto, or twenty sheets in folio, which shall be so printed, a duty after the rate of one shilling for every sheet of any kind of paper which shall be contained in one printed copy thereof.

For every advertisement to be contained in any gazette, newspaper, or other paper, or any pamphlet which shall be so printed, a duty of two shillings.

For every almanac or calendar for any one particular year, or for any time less than a year, which shall be written or printed on one side only of any one sheet, skin, or piece of paper, parchment, or vellum within the said colonies and plantations, a stamp duty of two pence.

For every other almanac or calendar for any one particular year, which shall be written or printed within the said colonies and plantations, a stamp duty of four pence.

And for every almanac or calendar written or printed within the said colonies and plantations to serve for several years, duties to the same amount respectively shall be paid for every such year.

For every skin or piece of vellum or parchment or sheet or piece of paper on which any instrument, proceeding, or other matter or thing aforesaid shall be engrossed, written, or printed within the said colonies and plantations in any other than the English language, a stamp duty of double the amount of the respective duties before charged thereon.

And there shall be also paid in the said colonies and plantations a duty of six pence for every twenty shillings, in any sum not exceeding fifty pounds sterling money, which shall be given, paid, contracted, or agreed for, with or in relation to any clerk or apprentice, which shall be put or placed to or with any master or mistress to learn any profession, trade, or employment.

* * *

Chapter 12

And be it further enacted by the authority aforesaid that the said several duties shall be under the management of the commissioners, for the time being, of the duties charged on stamped vellum, parchment, and paper in Great Britain: and the said commissioners are hereby empowered and required to employ such officers under them for that purpose as they shall think proper; and to use such stamps and marks to denote the stamp duties hereby charged as they shall think fit; and to repair, renew, or alter the same, from time to time, as there shall be occasion; and to do all other acts, matters, and things necessary to be done for putting this act in execution with relation to the duties hereby charged.

Chapter 13

And be it further enacted by the authority aforesaid that the commissioners for managing the said duties, for the time being, shall and may appoint a fit person or persons to attend in every court or public office within the said colonies and plantations to take notice of the vellum, parchment, or paper upon which any of the matters or things hereby charged with a duty shall be engrossed, written, or printed, and of the stamps or marks thereupon, and of all other matters and things tending to secure the said duties; and that the judges in the several courts and all other persons to whom it may appertain shall, at the request of any such officer, make such orders and do such other matters and things for the better securing of the said duties, as shall be lawfully or reasonably desired in that behalf: and every commissioner and other officer, before he proceeds to the execution of any part of this act, shall take an oath in the words, or to the effect following (that is to say):

I A.B. do swear that I will faithfully execute the trust reposed in me, pursuant to an act of Parliament made in the fifth year of the reign of his majesty King George the Third for granting certain stamp duties and other duties in the British colonies and plantations in America without fraud or concealment; and will from time to time true account make of my doing therein and deliver the same to such person or persons as his Majesty, his heirs, or successors shall appoint to receive such account; and will take no fee, reward, or profit for the execution or performance of the said trust or the business relating thereto from any person or persons other than such as shall be allowed by his Majesty, his heirs, and successors, or by some other person or persons under him or them to that purpose authorized.

Or if any such officer shall be of the people commonly called Quakers, he shall take a solemn affirmation to the effect of the said oath; which oath or affirmation shall and may be administered to any such commissioner or commissioners by any two or more of the same commissioners, whether they have or have not previously taken the same: and any of the said commissioners or any justice of the peace within the kingdom of Great Britain, or any governor, lieutenant governor, judge, or other magistrate within the said colonies or plantations, shall and may administer such oath or affirmation to any subordinate officer.

Chapter 14

And be it further enacted by the authority aforesaid that the said commissioners and all officers to be employed or entrusted by or under them as aforesaid shall, from time to time, in and for the better execution of their several places and trusts observe such rules, methods, and orders as they respectively shall, from time to time, receive from the high treasurer of Great Britain or the commissioners of the treasury or any three or more of such commissioners for the time being; and that the said commissioners for managing the stamp duties shall take especial care that the several parts of the said colonies and plantations shall, from time to time, be sufficiently furnished with vellum, parchment, and paper, stamped or marked with the said respective duties.

Chapter 15

And be it further enacted by the authority aforesaid that if any person or persons shall sign, engross, write, print, or sell, or expose to sale or cause to be signed, engrossed, written, printed, or sold or exposed to sale in any of the said colonies or plantations or in any other part of his Majesty's dominions any matter or thing for which the vellum, parchment, or paper is hereby charged to pay any duty before the same shall be marked or stamped with the marks or stamps to be provided as aforesaid, or upon which there shall not be some stamp or mark resembling the same; or shall sign, engross, write, print, or sell, or expose to sale or cause to be signed, engrossed, written, printed, or sold or exposed to sale any matter or thing upon any vellum, parchment, or paper that shall be marked or stamped for any lower duty than the duty by this act made payable in respect thereof; every such person so offending shall, for every such offense, forfeit the sum of ten pounds.

Chapter 16

And be it further enacted by the authority aforesaid that no matter or thing whatsoever by this act charged with the payment of a duty shall be pleaded or given in evidence or admitted in any court within the said colonies and plantations, to be good, useful, or available in law or equity, unless the same shall be marked or stamped in pursuance of this act with the respective duty hereby charged thereon, or with an higher duty.

Chapter 17

Provided nevertheless, and be it further enacted by the authority aforesaid that if any vellum, parchment, or paper containing any deed, instrument, or other matter or thing shall not be duly stamped in pursuance of this act at the time of the signing, sealing, or other execution or the entry or enrollment thereof, any person interested therein, or any person on his or her behalf, upon producing the same to any one of the chief distributors of stamped vellum, parchment, and paper, and paying to him the sum of ten pounds for every such deed, instrument, matter, or thing, and also double the amount of the duties payable in respect thereof, shall be entitled to receive from such distributor vellum, parchment, or paper stamped pursuant to this act to the amount of the money so paid; a certificate being first written upon every such piece of vellum, parchment, or paper, expressing the name and place of abode of the person by or on whose behalf such payment is made, the general purport of such deed, instrument, matter, or thing, the names of the parties therein and of the witnesses (if any) thereto, and the date thereof, which certificate shall be signed by the said distributor; and the vellum, parchment, or paper shall be then annexed to such deed, instrument, matter, or thing, by or in the presence of such distributor, who shall impress a seal upon wax to be affixed on the part where such annexation shall be made in the presence of a magistrate, who shall attest such signature and sealing; and the deed, instrument, or other matter or thing from thenceforth shall and may, with the vellum, parchment, or paper so annexed, be admitted and allowed in evidence in any court whatsoever and shall be as valid and effectual as if the proper stamps had been impressed thereon at the time of the signing, sealing, or other execution or entry or enrollment thereof: and the said distributor shall once in every six months, or oftener if required by the commissioners for managing the stamp duties, send to such commissioners true copies of all such certificates and an account of the number of pieces of vellum, parchment, and paper so annexed and of the respective duties impressed upon every such piece.

Chapter 18

And be it further enacted by the authority aforesaid that if any person shall forge, counterfeit, erase, or alter any such certificate, every such person so offending shall be guilty of felony and shall suffer death as in cases of felony without the benefit of clergy.

Chapter 19

And be it further enacted by the authority aforesaid that if any person or persons shall, in the said colonies or plantations or in any other part of his Majesty's dominions, counterfeit or forge any seal, stamp, mark, type, device, or label to resemble any seal, stamp, mark, type, device, or label which shall be provided or made in pursuance of this act; or shall counterfeit or resemble the impression of the same upon any vellum, parchment, paper, cards, dice, or other matter or thing thereby to evade the payment of any duty hereby granted; or shall make, sign, print, utter, vend, or sell any vellum, parchment, or paper or other matter or thing with such counterfeit mark or impression thereon, knowing such mark or impression to be counterfeited; then every person so offending shall be adjudged a felon and shall suffer death as in cases of felony without the benefit of clergy.

Chapter 20

And it is hereby declared that upon any prosecution or prosecutions for such felony, the dye, tool, or other instrument made use of in counterfeiting or forging any such seal, stamp, mark, type, device, or label, together with the vellum, parchment, paper, cards, dice, or other matter or thing having such counterfeit impression, shall, immediately after the trial or conviction of the party or parties accused, be broke, defaced, or destroyed in open court.

Chapter 21

And be it further enacted by the authority aforesaid that if any register, public officer, clerk, or other person in any court, registry, or office within any of the said colonies or plantations shall, at any time after the said first day of November, one thousand seven hundred and sixty-five, enter, register, or enroll any matter or thing hereby charged with a stamp duty, unless the same shall appear to be duly stamped; in every such case such register, public officer, clerk, or other person shall, for every such offense, forfeit the sum of twenty pounds.

* * *

Chapter 49

And be it further enacted by the authority aforesaid that the high treasurer of Great Britain, or the commissioners of his Majesty's treasury, or any three or more of such commissioners, for the time being shall once in every year at least set the prices at which all sorts of stamped vellum, parchment, and paper shall be sold by the said commissioners for managing the stamp duties and their officers; and that the said commissioners for the said duties shall cause such prices to be marked upon every such skin and piece of vellum and parchment and sheet and piece of paper: and if any officer or distributor to be appointed by virtue of this act shall sell, or cause to be sold, any vellum, parchment, or paper for a greater or higher price or sum than the price or sum so set or affixed thereon; every such officer or distributor shall, for every such offense, forfeit the sum of twenty pounds.

Chapter 50

And be it also enacted by the authority aforesaid that several officers who shall be respectively employed in the raising, receiving, collecting, or paying the several duties hereby charged within the said colonies and plantations shall every twelve months or oftener, if thereunto required by the said commissioners for managing the said duties, exhibit his and their respective account and accounts of the said several duties upon oath, or if a Quaker upon affirmation, in the presence of the governor, or commander in chief, or principal judge of the colony or plantation where such officers shall be respectively resident, in such manner as the high treasurer, or the commissioners of the treasury, or any three or more of such commissioners for the time being shall, from time to time, direct and appoint, in order that the same may be immediately afterwards transmitted by the said officer or officers to the commissioners for managing the said duties, to be comptrolled and audited according to the usual course and form of comptrolling and auditing the accounts of the stamp duties arising within this kingdom: and if any of the said officers shall neglect or refuse to exhibit any such account, or to verify the same upon oath or affirmation, or to transmit any such account so verified to the commissioners for managing the said duties in such manner, and within such time, as shall be so appointed or directed; or shall neglect or refuse to pay, or cause to be paid into the hands of the receiver general of the stamp duties in Great Britain, or to such other person or persons as the high treasurer, or commissioners of the treasury, or any three or more of such commissioners for the time being shall, from time to time, nominate or appoint, the monies respectively raised, levied, and received by such officers under the authority of this act, at such times, and in such manner as they shall be respectively required by the said high treasurer, or commissioners of the treasury; or if any such officers shall divert, detain, or misapply all or any part of the said monies so by them respectively raised, levied, and received, or shall knowingly return any person or persons *insuper* for any monies or other things duly answered, paid, or accounted for by such person or persons, whereby he or they shall sustain any damage or prejudice; in every such case, every such officer shall be liable to pay treble the value of all and every sum and sums of money so diverted or misapplied; and shall also be liable to pay treble damages to the party grieved, by returning him *insuper*.

Chapter 51

And be it further enacted by the authority aforesaid that the commissioners, receiver or receivers general, or other person or persons who shall be respectively employed in Great Britain in the directing, receiving, or paying the monies arising by the duties hereby granted shall, and are hereby required, between the tenth day of October and the fifth day of January following, and so from year to year, yearly, at those times, to exhibit their respective accounts thereof to his Majesty's auditors of the imprest in England for the time being, or one of them, to be declared before the high treasurer or commissioners of the treasury and chancellor of the exchequer for the time being, according to the course of the exchequer.

Chapter 52

And be it further enacted by the authority aforesaid that if the said commissioners for managing the said duties, or the said receiver or receivers general, shall neglect or refuse to pay into the exchequer all or any of the said monies in such manner as they are required by this act to pay the same, or shall divert or misapply any part thereof, then they, and every of them so offending, shall be liable to pay double the value of all and every sum and sums of money so diverted or misapplied.

Chapter 53

And be it further enacted by the authority aforesaid that the comptroller or comptrollers for the time being of the duties hereby imposed shall keep perfect and distinct accounts in books fairly written of all the monies arising by the said duties; and if any such comptroller or comptrollers shall neglect his or their duty therein, then he or they, for every such offense, shall forfeit the sum of one hundred pounds.

Chapter 54

And be it further enacted by the authority aforesaid that all the monies which shall arise by the several rates and duties hereby granted (except the necessary charges of raising, collecting, recovering, answering, paying, and accounting for the same, and the necessary charges from time to time incurred in relation to this act, and the execution thereof) shall be paid into the receipt of his Majesty's exchequer, and shall be entered separate and apart from all other monies, and shall be there reserved to be from time to time disposed of by Parliament towards further defraying the necessary expenses of defending, protecting, and securing the said colonies and plantations.

Chapter 55

And whereas it is proper that some provision should be made for payment of the necessary expenses which have been and shall be incurred in relation to this act and the execution thereof; and of the orders and rules to be established under the authority of the same before the said duties shall take effect, or the monies arising thereby shall be sufficient to discharge such expenses; be it therefore enacted by the authority aforesaid that his Majesty may, and he is hereby empowered by any warrant or warrants under his royal sign manual, at any time or times before the twentieth day of April, one thousand seven hundred and sixty-six, to cause to be issued and paid out of any of the surpluses, excesses, overplus monies, and other revenues composing the fund commonly called *The sinking fund* (except such monies of the said sinking fund as are appropriated to any particular use or uses, by any former act or acts of Parliament in that behalf) such sum and sums of money as shall be necessary to defray the said expenses; and the monies so issued shall be reimbursed by payment into the exchequer of the like sum or sums out of the first monies which shall arise by virtue of this act; which monies, upon the payment thereof into the exchequer, shall be carried to the account, and made part of the said fund.

Chapter 56

And it is hereby further enacted and declared that all the powers and authorities by this act granted to the commissioners for managing the duties upon stamped vellum, parchment, and paper shall and may be fully and effectually carried into execution by any three or more of the said commissioners, anything herein before contained to the contrary notwithstanding.

Chapter 57

And be it further enacted by the authority aforesaid that all forfeitures and penalties incurred after the twenty-ninth day of September, one thousand seven hundred and sixty-five, for offenses committed against an act passed in the fourth year of the reign of his present Majesty, entitled, *An act for granting certain duties in the British colonies and plantations in America*; for continuing, amending, and making perpetual an act passed in the sixth year of the reign of his late Majesty King George the Second, entitled, *An act for the better securing and encouraging the trade of his Majesty's sugar colonies in America*; for applying for produce of such duties, and of the duties to arise by virtue of the said act towards defraying the expenses of defending, protecting, and securing the said colonies and plantations; for explaining an act made in the twenty-fifth year of the reign of King Charles the Second, entitled, *An act for the encouragement of the Greenland and Eastland trades, and for the better securing the plantation trade*; and for altering and disallowing several drawbacks on exports from this kingdom, and more effectually preventing the clandestine conveyance of goods to and from the said colonies and plantations, and improving and securing the trade between the same and Great Britain, and for offenses committed against any other act or acts of Parliament relating to the trade or revenues of the said colonies of plantations; shall and may be prosecuted, sued for, and recovered in any court of record, or in any court of admiralty in the respective colony or plantation where the offense shall be committed, or in any court of vice admiralty appointed or to be appointed, and which shall have jurisdiction within such colony, plantation, or place (which courts of admiralty or vice admiralty are hereby respectively authorized and required to proceed, hear, and determine the same) at the election of the informer or prosecutor.

Chapter 58

And it is hereby further enacted and declared by the authority aforesaid that all sums of money granted and imposed by this act as rates or duties, and also all sums of money imposed as forfeitures or penalties, and all sums of money required to be paid, and all other monies herein mentioned shall be deemed and taken to be sterling money of Great Britain, and shall be collected, recovered, and paid to the amount of the value which such nominal sums bear in Great Britain; and that such monies shall and may be received and taken according to the proportion and value of five shillings and six pence the ounce in silver; and that all the forfeitures and penalties hereby inflicted, and which shall be incurred in the said colonies and plantations, shall and may be prosecuted, sued for, and recovered in any court of record, or in any court of admiralty in the respective colony or plantation where the offense shall be committed, or in any court of vice admiralty appointed or to be appointed, and which shall have jurisdiction within such colony, plantation, or place (which courts of admiralty or vice admiralty are hereby respectively authorized and required to proceed, hear, and determine the same) at the election of the informer or prosecutor; and that from and after the twenty-ninth day of September, one thousand seven hundred and sixty-five, in all cases where any suit or prosecution shall be commenced and determined for any penalty or forfeiture inflicted by this act, or by the said act made in the fourth year of his present Majesty's reign, or by any other act of Parliament relating to the trade or revenues of the said colonies or plantations in any court of admiralty in the respective colony or plantation where the offense shall be committed, either party, who shall think himself aggrieved by such determination, may appeal from such determination to any court of vice admiralty appointed or to be appointed, and which shall have jurisdiction within such colony, plantation, or place (which court of vice admiralty is hereby authorized and required to proceed, hear, and determine such appeal) any law, custom, or usage to the contrary notwithstanding; and the forfeitures and penalties hereby inflicted, which shall be incurred in any other part of his Majesty's dominions, shall and may be prosecuted, sued for, and recovered with full costs of suit in any court of record within the kingdom, territory, or place where the offense shall be committed, in such and the same manner as any debt or damage, to the amount of such forfeiture or penalty, can or may be sued for and recovered.

Chapter 59

And it is hereby further enacted that all the forfeitures and penalties hereby inflicted shall be divided, paid, and applied as follows; (that is to say) one-third part of all such forfeitures and penalties recovered in the said colonies and plantations shall be paid into the hands of one of the chief distributors of stamped vellum, parchment, and paper residing in the colony or plantation wherein the offender shall be convicted, for the use of his Majesty, his heirs, and successors; one-third part of the penalties and forfeitures so recovered, to the governor or commander in chief of such colony or plantation; and the other third part thereof to the person who shall inform or sue for the same; and that one moiety of all such penalties and forfeitures recovered in any other part of his Majesty's dominions shall be to the use of his Majesty, his heirs, and successors, and the other moiety thereof to the person who shall inform or sue for the same.

Chapter 60

And be it further enacted by the authority aforesaid that all the offenses which are by this act made felony and shall be committed within any part of his Majesty's dominions, shall and may be heard, tried, and determined before any court of law within the respective kingdom, territory, colony, or plantation where the offense shall be committed, in such and the same manner as all other felonies can or may be heard, tried, and determined in such court.

Chapter 61

And be it further enacted by the authority aforesaid that all the present governors or commanders in chief of any British colony or plantation shall, before the said first day of November, one thousand seven hundred and sixty-five, and all who hereafter shall be made governors or commanders in chief of the said colonies or plantations, or any of them, before their entrance into their government shall take a solemn oath to do their utmost that all and every the clauses contained in this present act be punctually and bona fide observed, according to the true intent and meaning thereof, so far as appertains unto the said governors or commanders in chief, respectively, under the like penalties, forfeitures, and disabilities, either for neglecting to take the said oath, or for wittingly neglecting to do their duty accordingly, as are mentioned and expressed in an act made in the seventh and eighth year of the reign of King William the Third, entitled, *An act for preventing frauds and regulating abuses in the plantation trade;* and the said oath hereby required to be taken shall be administered by such person or persons as hath or have been, or shall be appointed to administer the oath required to be taken by the said act made in the seventh and eighth year of the reign of King William the Third.

Chapter 62

And be it further enacted by the authority aforesaid that all records, writs, pleadings, and other proceedings in all courts whatsoever, and all deeds, instruments, and writings whatsoever, hereby charged, shall be engrossed and written in such manner as they have been usually accustomed to be engrossed and written, or are now engrossed and written within the said colonies and plantations.

Chapter 63

And it is hereby further enacted that if any person or persons shall be sued or prosecuted, either in Great Britain or America, for anything done in pursurance of this act, such person and persons shall and may plead the general issue, and give this act and the special matter in evidence; and if it shall appear so to have been done, the jury shall find for the defendant or defendants: and if the plaintiff or plaintiffs shall become nonsuited, or discontinue his or their action after the defendant or defendants shall have appeared, or if judgment shall be given upon any verdict or demurrer against the plaintiff or plaintiffs, the defendant or defendants shall recover treble costs and have the like remedy for the same, as defendants have in other cases by law.

TOWNSHEND ACTS

An Act for Restraining and Prohibiting the Governor, Council, and House of Representatives of the Province of New York, until Provision Shall Have Been Made for Furnishing the King's Troops with All the Necessaries Required by Law, from Passing or Assenting to Any Act of Assembly, Vote, or Resolution for Any Other Purpose

[Chapter 1]

Whereas an act of Parliament was made in the fifth year of his present Majesty's reign, entitled, *An act to amend and render more effectual, in his Majesty's dominions in America, an act passed in this present session of Parliament, entitled, An act for punishing mutiny and desertion and for the better payment of the army and their quarters;* wherein several directions were given, and rules and regulations established and appointed for the supplying his Majesty's troops in the British dominions in America with such necessaries as are in the said act mentioned during the continuance thereof, from the twenty-fourth day of March, one thousand seven hundred and sixty-five, until the twenty-fourth day of March, one thousand seven hundred and sixty-seven; and whereas the House of Representatives of his Majesty's province of New York in America have, in direct disobedience of the authority of the British legislature, refused to make provision for supplying the necessaries and in the manner required by the said act; and an act of assembly hath been passed within the said province for furnishing the barracks in the cities of New York and Albany with firewood and candles, and the other necessaries therein mentioned, for his Majesty's forces inconsistent with the provisions and in opposition to the directions of the said act of Parliament; and whereas by an act made in the last session, entitled, *An act to amend and render more effectual, in his Majesty's dominions in America, an act passed in this present session of Parliament entitled, An act for punishing mutiny and desertion, and for the better payment of the army and their quarters, the like directions, rules, and regulations were given and established for supplying with necessaries his Majesty's troops within the said dominions during the continuance of such act, from the twenty-fourth day of* March, *one thousand seven hundred and sixty-six, until the twenty-fourth day of* March, *one thousand seven hundred and sixty-eight;* which act was, by an act made in this present session of Parliament, entitled, *An act for further continuing an act of the last session of Parliament entitled, An act to amend and render more effectual, in his Majesty's dominions in America, an act passed in this present session of Parliament entitled, An act for punishing mutiny and desertion, and for the better payment of the army and their quarters, further continued until the twenty-fourth day of* March, *one thousand seven hundred and sixty-nine.* In order therefore to enforce within the said province of New York the supplying of his Majesty's troops with the necessaries and in the manner required by

Source: Danby Pickering, ed., *The Statutes at Large from Magna Carta to the End of the Eleventh Parliament of Great Britain, Anno 1761: Continued,* vol. 27 (1768), pp. 505–512.

the said acts of Parliament, may it please your Majesty that it may be enacted; and be it enacted by the King's most excellent Majesty, by and with the advice and consent of the Lords Spiritual and Temporal and Commons, in this present Parliament assembled, and by the authority of the same that from and after the first day of October, one thousand seven hundred and sixty-seven, until provision shall have been made by the said assembly of New York for furnishing his Majesty's troops within the said province with all such necessaries as are required by the said acts of Parliament, or any of them, to be furnished for such troops, it shall not be lawful for the governor, lieutenant governor, or person presiding or acting as governor or commander in chief, or for the council for the time being, within the colony, plantation, or province of New York in America, to pass, or give his or their assent to, or concurrence in, the making or passing of any act of assembly; or his or their assent to any order, resolution, or vote in concurrence with the House of Representatives for the time being within the said colony, plantation, or province; or for the said House of Representatives to pass or make any bill, order, resolution, or vote (orders, resolutions, or votes for adjourning such house only, excepted) of any kind, for any other purpose whatsoever; and that all acts of assembly, orders, resolutions, and votes whatsoever, which shall or may be passed, assented to, or made contrary to the tenor and meaning of this act after the said first day of October, one thousand seven hundred and sixty-seven, within the said colony, plantation, or province before and until provision shall have been made for supplying his Majesty's troops with necessaries as aforesaid, shall be and are hereby declared to be null and void, and of no force or effect whatsoever.

Chapter 2

Provided nevertheless, and it is hereby declared to be the true intent and meaning of this act that nothing herein before contained shall extend, or be construed to extend, to hinder, prevent, or invalidate the choice, election, or approbation of a speaker of the House of Representatives for the time being within the said colony, plantation, or province.

An Act for Granting Certain Duties in the British Colonies and Plantations in America; for Allowing a Drawback of the Duties of Customs upon the Exportation from This Kingdom of Coffee and Cocoa Nuts of the Produce of the Said Colonies or Plantations; for Discontinuing the Drawbacks Payable on China Earthenware Exported to America; and for More Effectually Preventing the Clandestine Running of Goods in the Said Colonies and Plantations

[Chapter 1]

Whereas it is expedient that a revenue should be raised in your Majesty's dominions in America for making a more certain and adequate provision for defraying the charge of the administration of justice and the support of civil government in such provinces where it shall be found necessary; and towards further defraying the expenses of defending, protecting, and securing the said dominions; we, your Majesty's most dutiful and loyal subjects, the Commons of Great Britain in Parliament assembled have therefore resolved to give and grant unto your Majesty the several rates and duties hereinafter mentioned; and do most humbly beseech your Majesty that it may be enacted, and be it enacted by the king's most excellent Majesty, by and with the advice and consent of the Lords Spiritual and Temporal and Commons in this present Parliament assembled, and by the authority of the same that from and after the twentieth day of November, one thousand seven hundred and sixty-seven, there shall be raised, levied, collected, and paid unto his Majesty, his heirs, and successors for and upon the respective goods herein after mentioned which shall be imported from Great Britain into any colony or plantation in America which now is, or hereafter may be, under the dominion of his Majesty, his heirs, or successors, the several rates and duties following; that is to say,

For every hundredweight avoirdupois of crown, plate, flint, and white glass, four shillings and eight pence.

For every hundredweight avoirdupois of green glass, one shilling and two pence.

For every hundredweight avoirdupois of red lead, two shillings.

For every hundredweight avoirdupois of white lead, two shillings.

For every hundredweight avoirdupois of painters colors, two shillings.

For every poundweight avoirdupois of tea, three pence.

For every ream of paper usually called or known by the name of Atlas Fine, twelve shillings.

For every ream of paper called Atlas Ordinary, six shillings.

For every ream of paper called Bastard, or Double Copy, one shilling and six pence.

For every single ream of blue paper for sugar bakers, ten pence half-penny.

For every ream of paper called Blue Royal, one shilling and six pence.

For every bundle of brown paper containing forty quires, not made in Great Britain, six pence.

Chapter 2

And it is hereby further enacted by the authority aforesaid that all other paper (not being particularly rated and charged in this act) shall pay the several and respective duties that are charged by this act upon such paper as is nearest above in size and goodness to such unrated paper.

Chapter 3

And be it declared and enacted by the authority aforesaid that a ream of paper chargeable by this act shall be understood to consist of twenty quires, and each quire of twenty such sheets.

Chapter 4

And it is hereby further enacted by the authority aforesaid that the said rates and duties charged by this act upon goods imported into any British American colony or plantation shall be deemed and are hereby declared to be sterling money of Great Britain; and shall be collected, recovered, and paid to the amount of the value which such nominal sums bear in Great Britain; and that such monies may be received and taken according to the proportion and value of five shillings and six pence the ounce in silver; and shall be raised, levied, collected, paid, and recovered in the same manner and form and by such rules, ways, and means and under such penalties and forfeitures as any other duties now payable to his Majesty upon goods imported into the said colonies or plantations, may be raised, levied, collected, paid, and recovered by any act or acts of Parliament now in force, as fully and effectually to all intents and purposes, as if the several clauses, powers, directions, penalties, and forfeitures relating thereto were particularly repeated and again enacted in the body of this present act: and that all the monies that shall arise by the said duties (except the necessary charges of raising, collecting, levying, recovering, answering, paying, and accounting for the same) shall be applied in the first place, in such manner as is hereinafter mentioned, in making a more certain and adequate provision for the charge of the administration of justice and the support of civil government in such of the said colonies and plantations where it shall be found necessary; and that the residue of such duties shall be paid into the receipt of his Majesty's exchequer, and shall be entered separate and apart from all other monies paid or payable to his Majesty, his heirs, or successors; and shall be there reserved, to be from time to time disposed of by Parliament towards defraying the necessary expenses of defending, protecting, and securing the British colonies and plantations in America.

Chapter 5

And be it further enacted by the authority aforesaid that his Majesty and his successors shall be, and are hereby empowered from time to time, by any warrant or warrants under his or their royal sign manual or sign manuals, countersigned by the high treasurer, or any three or more of the commissioners of the treasury for the time being, to cause such monies to be applied out of the produce of the duties granted by this act as his Majesty or his successors shall think proper or necessary for defraying the charges of the administration of justice and the support of the civil government within all or any of the said colonies or plantations.

Chapter 6

And whereas the allowing a drawback of all the duties of customs upon the exportation from this kingdom of coffee and cocoa nuts, the growth of the British dominions in America may be a means of encouraging the growth of coffee and cocoa in the said dominions, be it therefore enacted by the authority aforesaid that from and after the said twentieth day of November, one thousand seven hundred and sixty-seven, upon the exportation of any coffee or cocoa nuts, of the growth or produce of any British colony or plantation in America, from this kingdom as merchandise, the whole duties of customs payable upon the importation of such coffee or cocoa nuts shall be drawn back and repaid in such manner, and under such rules, regulations, penalties, and forfeitures as any drawback or allowance, payable out of the duties of customs upon the exportation of such coffee or cocoa nuts, was, could, or might be paid before the passing of this act; any law, custom, or usage to the contrary notwithstanding.

Chapter 7

And it is hereby further enacted by the authority aforesaid that no drawback shall be allowed for any china earthenware sold after the passing of this act as the sale of the united company of merchants of England trading to the East Indies, which shall be entered for exportation from Great Britain to any part of America; any law, custom, or usage to the contrary notwithstanding.

Chapter 8

And it is hereby further enacted by the authority aforesaid that if any china earthenware sold after the passing of this act at the sale of the said united company shall be entered for exportation to any part of America as china earthen ware that had been sold at the sale of the said company before that time, or, if any china earthenware shall be entered for exportation to any parts beyond the seas other than to some part of America in order to obtain any drawback thereon, and the said china earthenware shall nevertheless be carried to any part of America and landed there, contrary to the true intent and meaning of this act; that then, in each and every such case the drawback shall be forfeited; and the merchant or other person making such entry and the master or person taking the charge of the ship or vessel on board which the said goods shall be loaden for exportation shall forfeit double the amount of the drawback paid, or to be paid for the same, and also treble the value of the said goods; one moiety to and for the use of his Majesty, his heirs, and successors; and the other moiety to such officer of the customs as shall sue for the same; to be prosecuted, sued for, and recovered in such manner and form, and by the same rules and regulations, as other penalties inflicted for offenses against the laws relating to the customs may be prosecuted, sued for, and recovered by any act or acts of Parliament now in force.

Chapter 9

And for the more effectual preventing the clandestine running of goods in the British dominions in America, be it further enacted by the authority aforesaid that from and after the said twentieth day of November, one thousand seven hundred and sixty-seven, the master or other person having or taking the charge or command of every ship or vessel arriving in any British colony or plantation in America shall, before he proceeds with his vessel to the place of unlading, come directly to the customhouse for the port of district where he arrives and make a just and true entry, upon oath, before the collector and comptroller, or other principal officer of the customs there, of the burthen [burden], contents, and lading of such ship or vessel with the particular marks, numbers, qualities, and contents of every parcel of goods therein laden, to the best of his knowledge; also where and in what port she took in her lading; of what country built; how manned; who was master during the voyage, and who are owners thereof; and whether any and what goods during the course of such voyage had or had not been discharged out of such ship or vessel, and where: and the master or other person having or taking the charge or command of every ship or vessel going out from any British colony or plantation in America, before he shall take in or suffer to be taken into or laden on board any such ship or vessel any goods, wares, or merchandises to be exported shall in like manner enter and report outwards such ship or vessel, with her names and burden, of what country built, and how manned, with the names of the master and owners thereof, and to what port or place he intends to pass or sail. And before he shall depart with such ship or vessel out of any such colony or plantation, he shall also bring and deliver unto the collector and comptroller, or other principal officer of the customs at the port or place where he shall lade, a content in writing under his hand of the name of every merchant, or other person, who shall have laden or put on board any such ship or vessel any goods or merchandise, together with the marks and numbers of such goods or merchandise; and such master or person having or taking the charge or command of every such ship or vessel, either coming into or going out of any British colony or plantation as aforesaid, whether such ship or vessel shall be laden or in ballast, or otherwise, shall likewise publicly in the open customhouse, to the best of his knowledge, answer upon oath to such questions as shall be demanded of him by the collector and comptroller, or other principal officer of the customs for such port or place, concerning such ship or vessel and the destination of her voyage, or concerning any goods or merchandise that shall or may be laden on board her, upon forfeiture of one hundred pounds sterling money of Great Britain for each and every default or neglect; to be sued for, prosecuted, recovered, and divided in the same manner and form by the same rules and regulation in all respects as other pecuniary penalties for offenses against the laws relating to the customs or trade of his Majesty's colonies in America, may, by any act or acts of Parliament now in force, be prosecuted, sued for, recovered, and divided.

Chapter 10

And whereas by an act of Parliament made in the fourteenth year of the reign of King Charles the Second, entitled *An act for preventing frauds and regulating abuses in his Majesty's customs* and several other acts now in force, it is lawful for any officer of his Majesty's customs, authorized by writ of assistance under the seal of his Majesty's Court of Exchequer, to take a constable, headborough, or other public officer inhabiting near unto the place and in the daytime to enter and go into any house, shop, cellar, warehouse, or room or other place and, in case of resistance, to break open doors, chests, trunks, and other package there to seize, and from thence to bring, any kind of goods or merchandise whatsoever prohibited or uncustomed and to put and secure the same in his Majesty's storehouse next to the place where such seizure shall be made. And whereas by an act made in the seventh and eighth years of the reign of King William the Third, entitled, *An act for preventing frauds, and regulating abuses in the plantation trade*, it is, amongst other things, enacted that the officers for collecting and managing his Majesty's revenue and inspecting the plantation trade in America shall have the same powers and authorities to enter houses or warehouses to search and seize goods prohibited to be imported or exported into or out of any of the said plantations, or for which any duties are payable, or ought to have been paid; and that the like assistance shall be given to the said officers in the execution of their office, as, by the said recited act of the fourteenth year of King Charles the Second, is provided for the officers in England. But no authority being expressly given by the said act made in the seventh and eighth years of the reign of King William the Third to any particular court to grant such writs of assistance for the officers of the customs in the said plantations, it is doubted whether such officers can legally enter houses and other places on land to search for and seize goods in the manner directed by the said recited acts. To obviate such doubts for the future, and in order to carry the intention of the said recited acts into effectual execution, be it enacted, and it is hereby enacted by the authority aforesaid, that from and after the said twentieth day of November, one thousand seven hundred and sixty-seven, such writs of assistance to authorize and empower the officers of his Majesty's customs to enter and go into any house, warehouse, shop, cellar, or other place in the British colonies or plantations in America to search for and seize prohibited or uncustomed goods in the manner directed by the said recited acts shall and may be granted by the said superior or supreme court of justice having jurisdiction within such colony or plantation, respectively.

Chapter 11

And be it further enacted by the authority aforesaid that if any action or suit shall be commenced, either in Great Britain or America, against any person or persons for anything done in pursuance of this act, the defendant or defendants in such action or suit may plead the general issue and give this act and the special matter in evidence at any trial to be had thereupon; and that the same was done in pursuance and by the authority of this act. And if it shall appear so to have been done, the jury shall find for the defendant or defendants. And if the plaintiff shall be nonsuited, or discontinue his action after the defendant or defendants shall have appeared, or if judgment shall be given upon any verdict or demurrer against the plaintiff, the defendant or defendants shall recover treble costs and have the like remedy for the same as defendants have in other cases by law.

An Act to Enable His Majesty to Put the Customs, and Other Duties, in the British Dominions in America, and the Execution of the Laws Relating to Trade There, under the Management of Commissioners to be Appointed for that Purpose, and to be Resident in the Said Dominions

[Chapter 1]

Whereas in pursuance of an act of Parliament made in the twenty-fifth year of the reign of King Charles the Second, entitled, *An act for the encouragement of the Greenland and Eastland trades, and for the better securing the plantation trade*, the rates and duties imposed by that, and several subsequent acts of Parliament upon various goods imported into, or exported from the British colonies and plantations in America, have been put under the management of the commissioners of the customs in England for the time being, by and under the authority and directions of the high treasurer, or commissioners of the treasury for the time being; and whereas the officers appointed for the collection of the said rates and duties in America are obliged to apply to the said commissioners of the customs in England for their special instructions and directions, upon every particular doubt and difficulty which arises in relation to the payment of the said rates and duties, whereby all persons concerned in the commerce and trade of the said colonies and plantations are greatly obstructed and delayed in the carrying on and transacting of their business; and whereas the appointing of commissioners to be resident in some convenient part of his Majesty's dominions in America, and to be invested with such powers as are now exercised by the commissioners of the customs in England by virtue of the laws in being, would relieve the said merchants and traders from the said inconveniences, tend to the encouragement of commerce and to the better securing of the said rates and duties, by the more speedy and effectual collection thereof; be it therefore enacted by the King's most excellent Majesty, by and with the advice and consent of the Lords Spiritual and Temporal and Commons in this present Parliament assembled and by the authority of the same, that the customs and other duties imposed by any act or acts of Parliament upon any goods or merchandises brought or imported into, or exported or carried from any British colony or plantation in America, may from time to time be put under the management and direction of such commissioners to reside in the said plantations, as his Majesty, his heirs, and successors, by his or their commission or commissions under the great seal of Great Britain, shall judge to be most for the advantage of trade and security of the revenue of the said British colonies; any law, custom, or usage to the contrary notwithstanding.

Chapter 2

And it is hereby further enacted by the authority aforesaid that the said commissioners to be appointed, or any three or more of them, shall have the same powers and authorities for carrying into execution the several laws relating to the revenues and trade of the said British colonies in America, as were, before the passing of this act, exercised by the commissioners of the customs in England, by virtue of any act or acts of Parliament now in force, and it shall and may be lawful to and for his Majesty, his heirs, and successors, in such commission or commissions, to make provision for putting in execution the several laws relating to the customs and trade of the said British colonies; any law, custom, or usage to the contrary notwithstanding.

Chapter 3

Provided always, and it is hereby further enacted by the authority aforesaid, that all deputations and other authorities granted by the commissioners of the customs in England before the passing of this act, or which may be granted by them before any commission or commissions shall issue in pursuance of this act, to any officer or officers acting in the said colonies or plantations shall continue in force as fully, to all intents and purposes, as if this act had not been made, until the deputation, or other authorities so granted to such officer or officers, respectively, shall be revoked, annulled, or made void by the high treasurer of Great Britain, or commissioners of the treasury for the time being.

An Act for Taking Off the Inland Duty of One Shilling per Pound Weight upon All Black and Singlo Teas Consumed in Great Britain; and for Granting a Drawback upon the Exportation of Teas to Ireland and the British Dominions in America, for a Limited Time, upon Such Indemnification to Be Made in Respect Thereof by the East India Company, as Is Therein Mentioned; for Permitting the Exportation of Teas in Smaller Quantities Than One Lot to Ireland, or the Said Dominions in America; and for Preventing Teas Seized and Condemned from Being Consumed in Great Britain

[Chapter 1]

Whereas by an act of Parliament made in the eighteenth year of the reign of his late Majesty King George the Second, entitled, *An act for repealing the present inland duty of four shillings per poundweight upon all tea sold in Great Britain, and for granting to his Majesty certain other inland duties in lieu thereof; and for better securing the duty upon tea and other duties of excise; and for pursuing offenders out of one county into another;* an inland duty of one shilling per poundweight avoirdupois, and in that proportion for a greater or lesser quantity, was imposed and charged upon all tea to be sold in Great Britain; and also a further duty of twenty-five pounds for every one hundred pounds of the gross price at which such teas should be sold at the public sales of the united company of merchants of England trading to the East Indies, and proportionably for a greater or lesser sum; which duties were to commence from the twenty-fourth day of June, one thousand seven hundred and forty-five, over and above all customs, subsidies, and duties, payable to his Majesty for the same, upon importation thereof, to be paid in manner as in the said act is directed; and whereas by an act of Parliament made in the twenty-first year of his said late Majesty's reign, tea was allowed to be exported from this kingdom to Ireland and his Majesty's plantations in America without payment of the said inland duties; and whereas the taking off the said inland duty of one shilling per poundweight upon black and singlo teas, granted by the said act, and the allowing, upon the exportation of all teas which shall be exported to Ireland and his Majesty's plantations in America, the whole of the duty paid upon the importation thereof into this kingdom, appear to be the most probable and expedient means of extending the consumption of teas legally imported within this kingdom, and of increasing the exportation of teas to Ireland and to his Majesty's plantations in America, which are now chiefly furnished by foreigners in a course of illicit trade; and whereas the united company of merchants of England trading to the East Indies are willing and desirous to indemnify the public, in such manner as is hereinafter provided, with respect to any diminution of the revenue which shall or may happen from this experiment. We, your Majesty's most dutiful and loyal subjects, the Commons of Great Britain in Parliament assembled, do therefore most humbly beseech your Majesty, that it may be enacted; and be it enacted by the King's most excellent Majesty, by and with the advice and consent of the Lords Spiritual and Temporal and Commons in this present Parliament assembled and by the authority of the same, that for and during the space of five years, to be computed from the fifth day of July, one thousand seven hundred and sixty-seven, the said inland duty of one shilling per poundweight upon teas shall not be paid for or in respect of any bohea, congo, souchong, or pekoe teas, commonly called black teas, or any teas known by the denomination of singlo teas, which shall be cleared for consumption within Great Britain, out of the warehouses of the united company of merchants of England trading to the East Indies, or their successors; but that all such teas so to be cleared, whether the same have been already, or shall be hereafter, sold by the said company, or their successors, shall be and are hereby freed and discharged during the said term from the said inland duty.

Chapter 2

And it is hereby further enacted by the authority aforesaid, that for and during the like space of five years, to be computed from the fifth day of July, one thousand seven hundred and sixty-seven, there shall be drawn back and allowed for all teas exported from this kingdom as merchandise to Ireland, or any of the British colonies or plantations in America, the whole duties of customs payable upon the importation of such teas; which drawback or allowance, with respect to such teas as shall be exported to Ireland, shall be made to the exporter in such manner, and under such rules, regulations, securities, penalties, and forfeitures, as any drawback or allowance is now payable out of the duty of customs upon the exportation of foreign goods to Ireland; and with respect to such teas as shall be exported to the British colonies and plantations in America, the said drawback or allowance shall be made in such manner, and under such rules, regulations, penalties, and forfeitures, as any drawback or allowance payable out of the duty of customs upon foreign goods exported to foreign parts was, could, or might be made before the passing of this act (except in such cases as are otherwise provided for by this act).

Chapter 3

Provided always, and it is hereby enacted by the authority aforesaid, that the drawback allowed by this act shall not be paid or allowed for any teas which shall not be exported directly from the warehouse or warehouses wherein the same shall be lodged, pursuant to the directions of an act made in the tenth year of the reign of his late Majesty King George the First.

Chapter 4

And, for making good any diminution which may happen in the revenues of customs and excise by the discontinuance of the said duty and the allowance of the said drawback during the term aforesaid, be it enacted by the authority aforesaid, that on or before the first day of September, one thousand seven hundred and sixty-eight, and on or before the first day of September in each of the four succeeding years, a true and exact account shall be taken, slated, and made up by the proper officers of the customs and excise, respectively, of the net produce of all the duties of customs for and in respect of teas sold by the said company, or their successors, and also of the net produce of the duties of excise upon teas cleared out of the warehouses belonging to the said company, or their successors, within the year, ending the fifth day of July immediately preceding the taking, stating, and making up, such account; and that a sum, which shall be equal to the annual net produce of the duties of customs paid upon the importation of teas which were exported to Ireland and the British colonies and plantations in America, upon an average for five years preceding the fifth day of July, one thousand seven hundred and sixty-seven, shall be deducted from the total of the net produce, so stated, of the said duties of customs and excise in the said account, for the year ending the said fifth day of July, one thousand seven hundred and sixty-eight, and for each of the said four succeeding years, respectively; and if, after such deduction shall have been made, the remaining sum shall not amount to such a sum as shall be equal to the annual net produce of all the duties of customs for and in respect of teas sold by the said company; and also to the annual net produce of the duties of excise upon teas cleared out of the warehouses of the said company on an average for five years preceding the said fifth day of July, one thousand seven hundred and sixty-seven; then, and in every such case, from time to time, as often as such case shall so happen, the said company, or their successors, within forty days after a copy of such yearly account respectively shall have been delivered to their chairman, deputy chairman, secretary, cashier, or accomptant [accountant] general shall advance and pay, for every such year, respectively, into the receipt of his Majesty's exchequer, for his Majesty's use, such sum of money as shall, with the monies remaining in such respective annual account after the deduction aforesaid shall have been made, amount to such a sum as shall be equal to the annual net produce of all the said duties of customs and excise upon teas, on the said average of five years preceding the said fifth day of July, one thousand seven hundred and sixty-seven; so as the money to be paid by the said company, or their successors, in pursuance of this act, shall not, in any one of the said five years, exceed such a sum as shall be equal to the annual net amount of the said inland duty of one shilling per pound weight upon teas cleared from the warehouses of the said company for consumption within Great Britain; and also to the annual net amount of the duties of customs paid on the importation of teas which were exported to Ireland and the British colonies and plantations in America upon an average for five years preceding the said fifth day of July, one thousand seven hundred and sixty-seven.

Chapter 5

And be it further enacted by the authority aforesaid, that in case the said united company of merchants of England trading to the East Indies, or their successors, shall make failure in any of the payments hereby directed, required, or appointed to be made into the receipt of his Majesty's exchequer, in the manner, or on or before the respective times herein before limited or appointed for that purpose; that then, from time to time, as often as such case shall so happen, the money, whereof such failure in payment shall be made, shall and may be recovered to his Majesty's use, by action of debt, or upon the case, bill, suit, or information, in any of his Majesty's courts of record at Westminster; wherein no essoin, protection, privilege, or wager of law shall be allowed, or any more than one imparlance; in which action, bill, suit, or information, it shall be lawful to declare that the said united company of merchants of England trading to the East Indies, or their successors, are indebted to his Majesty the monies of which they shall have made default in payment, according to the form of this statute, and have not paid the same, which shall be sufficient; and in or upon such action, bill, suit, or information, there shall be further recovered to his Majesty's use, against the said united company of merchants of England trading to the East Indies, or their successors, damages, after the rate of twelve pounds per centum per annum, for the respective monies so unpaid, contrary to this act, together with full costs of suit; and the said united company, and their successors, and all their stock, funds, and all other their estate and property whatsoever and wheresoever shall be and are hereby made subject and liable to the payment of such monies, damages, and costs.

Chapter 6

And be it further enacted by the authority aforesaid, that all the monies which shall be paid into the receipt of his Majesty's exchequer in pursuance of this act shall be applied to such uses and purposes, and in such proportions, as the present duties on teas are now made applicable.

Chapter 7

And whereas by an act made in the twenty-first year of the reign of his late Majesty, entitled, *An act for permitting tea to be exported to Ireland, and his Majesty's plantations in America, without paying the inland duties charged thereupon by an act of the eighteenth year of his present Majesty's reign; and for enlarging the time for some of the payments to be made on the subscription of six millions three hundred thousand pounds, by virtue of an act of this session of Parliament*, it is enacted, that from and after the first day of June, one thousand seven hundred and forty-eight, no tea should be exported to the kingdom of Ireland, or to any of his Majesty's plantations in America, in any chest, cask, tub, or package whatsoever, other than that in which it was originally imported into Great Britain, nor in any less quantities than in the entire lot or lots in which the same was sold at the sale of the said united company, under the penalty of the forfeiture of such tea and the package containing the same; and whereas the prohibiting the exportation of tea in any less quantity than one entire lot has been very inconvenient to merchants and traders and tends to discourage the exportation of tea to Ireland, and the said colonies; be it therefore enacted by the authority aforesaid, that from and after the fifth day of July, one thousand seven hundred and sixty-seven, the said recited clause shall be, and is hereby, repealed.

Chapter 8

And be it further enacted by the authority aforesaid, that from and after the said fifth day of July, one thousand seven hundred and sixty-seven, no tea shall be exported to the kingdom of Ireland, or to any of his Majesty's plantations in America, in any chest, cask, tub, or package whatsoever other than that in which it was originally imported into Great Britain; nor in any less quantity than the whole and entire quantity contained in any chest, cask, tub, or package in which the same was sold at the public sale of the united company of merchants of England trading to the East Indies; under the penalty of the forfeiture of such tea, and the package containing the same, which shall and may be seized by any officer of the customs; and such forfeiture shall be recovered and applied in such and the same manner, as any of the penalties or forfeitures mentioned in the said act, made in the twenty-first year of the reign of his late Majesty, are thereby directed to be recovered and applied; and all tea exported under the authority of this act is hereby freed and discharged from the payment of the inland duties of excise, in such and the same manner, and shall be subject to the same rules and regulations, as are mentioned, appointed, and prescribed by the said act, in relation to tea exported by virtue thereof.

Chapter 9

And be it enacted by the authority aforesaid, that from and after the twenty-fourth day of July, one thousand seven hundred and sixty-seven, all teas which shall be seized and condemned for being illegally imported, or for any other cause, shall not be sold for consumption within this kingdom, but shall be exported to Ireland, or to the British colonies in America; and that no such teas, after the sale thereof, shall be delivered out of any warehouse belonging to his Majesty, otherwise than for exportation as aforesaid, or be exported in any package containing a less quantity than fifty pounds weight; which exportation shall be made in like manner, and under the same rules, regulations, penalties, and forfeitures, except in respect to the allowance of any drawback, as are by this act prescribed, appointed, and inflicted in relation to the exportation of teas sold by the said company; and upon the like bond and security as is required by the said act made in the twenty-first year of the reign of his late Majesty King George the Second, to be approved of by the commissioners of the customs or excise in England for the time being, or any three of them, respectively, or by such person or persons as they shall respectively appoint for that purpose.

Chapter 10

And be it further enacted by the authority aforesaid, that if any action or suit shall be commenced against any person or persons for anything by him or them done or executed in pursuance of this act, the defendant or defendants in such action or suit shall and may plead the general issue, and give this act, and the special matter, in evidence, at any trial to be had thereupon; and that the same was done in pursuance and by the authority of this act; and if afterwards a verdict shall pass for the defendant or defendants, or the plaintiff or plaintiffs shall become nonsuited, or discontinue his, her, or their action or prosecution, or judgment shall be given against him, her or them, upon demurrer, or otherwise, then such defendant or defendants shall have treble costs awarded to him or them against such plaintiff or plaintiffs.

DECLARATION OF THE CAUSES AND NECESSITY OF TAKING UP ARMS

A DECLARATION BY THE REPRESENTATIVES OF THE UNITED COLONIES OF NORTH AMERICA, NOW MET IN CONGRESS AT PHILADELPHIA, SETTING FORTH THE CAUSES AND NECESSITY OF THEIR TAKING UP ARMS

If it was possible for men, who exercise their reason to believe, that the divine Author of our existence intended a part of the human race to hold an absolute property in, and an unbounded power over others, marked out by his infinite goodness and wisdom, as the objects of a legal domination never rightfully resistible, however severe and oppressive, the inhabitants of these colonies might at least require from the parliament of Great-Britain some evidence, that this dreadful authority over them, has been granted to that body. But a reverence for our Creator, principles of humanity, and the dictates of common sense, must convince all those who reflect upon the subject, that government was instituted to promote the welfare of mankind, and ought to be administered for the attainment of that end. The legislature of Great-Britain, however, stimulated by an inordinate passion for a power not only unjustifiable, but which they know to be peculiarly reprobated by the very constitution of that kingdom, and desparate of success in any mode of contest, where regard should be had to truth, law, or right, have at length, deserting those, attempted to effect their cruel and impolitic purpose of enslaving these colonies by violence, and have thereby rendered it necessary for us to close with their last appeal from reason to arms. Yet, however blinded that assembly may be, by their intemperate rage for unlimited domination, so to sight justice and the opinion of mankind, we esteem ourselves bound by obligations of respect to the rest of the world, to make known the justice of our cause. Our forefathers, inhabitants of the island of Great-Britain, left their native land, to seek on these shores a residence for civil and religious freedom. At the expense of their blood, at the hazard of their fortunes, without the least charge to the country from which they removed, by unceasing labour, and an unconquerable spirit, they effected settlements in the distant and unhospitable wilds of America, then filled with numerous and warlike barbarians.—Societies or governments, vested with perfect legislatures, were formed under charters from the crown, and an harmonious intercourse was established between the colonies and the kingdom from which they derived their origin. The mutual benefits of this union became in a short time so extraordinary, as to excite astonishment. It is universally confessed, that the amazing increase of the wealth, strength, and navigation of the realm, arose from this source; and the minister, who so wisely and successfully directed the measures of Great-Britain in the late war, publicly declared, that these colonies enabled her to triumph over her enemies.—Towards the conclusion of that war, it pleased our sovereign to make a change in his counsels.—From that fatal movement, the affairs of the British empire began to fall into confusion, and gradually sliding from the summit of glorious prosperity, to which they had been advanced by the virtues and abilities of one man, are at length distracted by the convulsions, that now shake it to its deepest foundations.—The new ministry finding the brave foes of Britain, though frequently defeated, yet still contending, took up the unfortunate idea of granting them a hasty peace, and then subduing her faithful friends.

These colonies were judged to be in such a state, as to present victories without bloodshed, and all the easy emoluments of statuteable plunder.—The uninterrupted tenor of their peaceable and respectful behaviour from the beginning of colonization, their dutiful, zealous, and useful services during the war, though so recently and amply acknowledged in the most honourable manner by his majesty, by the late king, and by parliament, could not save them from the meditated innovations.—Parliament was influenced to adopt the pernicious project, and assuming a new power over them, have in the course of eleven years, given such decisive specimens of the spirit and consequences attending this power, as to leave no doubt concerning the effects of acquiescence under it. They have undertaken to give and grant our money without our consent, though we have ever exercised an exclusive right to dispose of our own property; statutes have been passed for extending the jurisdiction of courts of admiralty and vice-admiralty beyond their ancient limits; for depriving us of the accustomed and inestimable privilege of trial by jury, in cases affecting both life and property; for suspending the legislature of one of the colonies; for interdicting all commerce to the capital of another; and for altering fundamentally the form of government established by charter, and secured by acts of its own legislature solemnly confirmed by the crown; for exempting the *"murderers"* of colonists from legal trial, and in effect, from punishment; for erecting in a neighbouring province, acquired by the joint arms of Great-Britain and America, a despotism dangerous to our very existence; and for quartering soldiers upon the colonists in time of profound peace. It has also been resolved in parliament, that colonists charged with committing certain offences, shall be transported to England to be tried. But why should we enumerate our injuries in detail? By one statute it is declared, that parliament can *"of right make laws to bind us in all cases whatsoever."* What is to defend us against so enormous, so unlimited a power? Not a single man of those who assume it, is chosen by us; or is subject to our control or influence; but, on the contrary, they are all of them exempt from the operation of such laws, and an American revenue, if not diverted from the ostensible purposes for which it is raised, would actually lighten their own burdens in proportion, as they increase ours. We saw the misery to which such despotism would reduce us. We for ten years incessantly and ineffectually besieged the throne as supplicants; we reasoned, we remonstrated with parliament, in the most mild and decent language.

Administration sensible that we should regard these oppressive measures as freemen ought to do, sent over fleets and armies to enforce them. The indignation of the Americans was roused, it is true; but it was the indignation of a virtuous, loyal, and affectionate people. A Congress of delegates from the United Colonies was assembled at Philadelphia, on the fifth day of last September. We resolved again to offer an humble and dutiful petition to the King, and also addressed our fellow-subjects of Great-Britain. We have pursued every temperate, every respectful measure; we have even proceeded to break off our commercial intercourse with our fellow-subjects, as the last peaceable admonition, that our attachment to no nation upon earth should supplant our attachment to liberty.—This, we flattered ourselves, was the ultimate step of the controversy: but subsequent events have shewn, how vain was this hope of finding moderation in our enemies.

Several threatening expressions against the colonies were inserted in his majesty's speech; our petition, tho' we were told it was a decent one, and that his majesty had been pleased to receive it graciously, and to promise laying it before his parliament, was huddled into both houses among a bundle of American papers, and there neglected. The lords and commons in their address, in the month of February, said, that *"a rebellion at that time actually existed within the province of Massachusetts-Bay; and that those concerned with it, had been countenanced and encouraged by unlawful combinations and engagements, entered into by his majesty's subjects in several of the other colonies; and therefore they besought his majesty, that he would take the most effectual measures to inforce due obedience to the laws and authority of the supreme legislature."*—Soon after, the commercial intercourse of whole colonies, with foreign countries, and with each other, was cut off by an act of parliament; by another several of them were intirely prohibited from the fisheries in the seas near their coasts, on which they always depended for their sustenance; and large reinforcements of ships and troops were immediately sent over to general Gage.

Fruitless were all the entreaties, arguments, and eloquence of an illustrious band of the most distinguished peers, and commoners, who nobly and strenuously asserted the justice of our cause, to stay, or even to mitigate the heedless fury with which these accumulated and unexampled outrages were hurried on.—equally fruitless was the interference of the city of London, of Bristol, and many other respectable towns in our favor. Parliament adopted an insidious manoeuvre calculated to divide us, to establish a perpetual auction of taxations where colony should bid against colony, all of them uninformed what ransom would redeem their lives; and thus to extort from us, at the point of the bayonet, the unknown sums that should be sufficient to gratify, if possible to gratify, ministerial rapacity, with the miserable indulgence left to us of raising, in our own mode, the prescribed tribute. What terms more rigid and humiliating could have been dictated by remorseless victors to conquered enemies? in our circumstances to accept them, would be to deserve them.

Soon after the intelligence of these proceedings arrived on this continent, general Gage, who in the course of the last year had taken possession of the town of Boston, in the province of Massachusetts-Bay, and still occupied in it a garrison, on the 19th day of April, sent out from that place a large detachment of his army, who made an unprovoked assault on the inhabitants of the said province, at the town of Lexington, as appears by the affidavits of a great number of persons, some of whom were officers and soldiers of that detachment, murdered eight of the inhabitants, and wounded many others. From thence the troops proceeded in warlike array to the town of Concord, where they set upon another party of the inhabitants of the same province, killing several and wounding more, until compelled to retreat by the country people suddenly assembled to repel this cruel aggression. Hostilities, thus commenced by the British troops, have been since prosecuted by them without regard to faith or reputation.—The inhabitants of Boston being confined within that town by the general their governor, and having, in order to procure their dismission, entered into a treaty with him, it was stipulated that the said inhabitants having deposited their arms with their own magistrate, should have liberty to depart, taking with them their other effects. They accordingly delivered up their arms, but in open violation of honour, in defiance of the obligation of treaties, which even savage nations esteemed sacred, the governor ordered the arms deposited as aforesaid, that they might be preserved for their owners, to be seized by a body of soldiers; detained the greatest part of the inhabitants in the town, and compelled the few who were permitted to retire, to leave their most valuable effects behind.

By this perfidy wives are separated from their husbands, children from their parents, the aged and the sick from their relations and friends, who wish to attend and comfort them; and those who have been used to live in plenty and even elegance, are reduced to deplorable distress.

The general, further emulating his ministerial masters, by a proclamation bearing date on the 12th day of June, after venting the grossest falsehoods and calumnies against the good people of these colonies, proceeds to *"declare them all, either by name or description, to be rebels and traitors, to supercede the course of the common law, and instead thereof to publish and order the use and exercise of the law martial."*—His troops have butchered our countrymen, have wantonly burnt Charlestown, besides a considerable number of houses in other places; our ships and vessels are seized; the necessary supplies of provisions are intercepted, and he is exerting his utmost power to spread destruction and devastation around him.

We have received certain intelligence, that general Carleton, the governor of Canada, is instigating the people of that province and the Indians to fall upon us; and we have but too much reason to apprehend, that schemes have been formed to excite domestic enemies against us. In brief, a part of these colonies now feel, and all of them are sure of feeling, as far as the vengeance of administration can inflict them, the complicated calamities of fire, sword and famine. We are reduced to the alternative of chusing an unconditional submission to the tyranny of irritated ministers, or resistance by force.—The latter is our choice.—We have counted the cost of this contest, and find nothing so dreadful as voluntary slavery.—Honour, justice, and humanity, forbid us tamely to surrender that freedom which we received from our gallant ancestors, and which our innocent posterity have a right to receive from us. We cannot endure the infamy and guilt of resigning succeeding generations to that wretchedness which inevitably awaits them, if we basely entail hereditary bondage upon them.

Our cause is just. Our union is perfect. Our internal resources are great, and, if necessary, foreign assistance is undoubtedly attainable.—We gratefully acknowledge, as signal instances of the Divine favour towards us, that his Providence would not permit us to be called into this severe controversy, until we were grown up to our present strength, had been previously exercised in warlike operation, and possessed of the means of defending ourselves. With hearts fortified with these animating reflections, we most solemnly, before God and the world, declare, that, exerting the utmost energy of those powers, which our beneficent Creator hath graciously bestowed upon us, the arms we have been compelled by our enemies to assume, we will, in defiance of every hazard, with unabating firmness and perseverance, employ for the preservation of our liberties; being with one mind resolved to die freemen rather than to live slaves.

Lest this declaration should disquiet the minds of our friends and fellow-subjects in any part of the empire, we assure them that we mean not to dissolve that union which has so long and so happily subsisted between us, and which we sincerely wish to see restored.—Necessity has not yet driven us into that desperate measure, or induced us to excite any other nation to war against them.—We have not raised armies with ambitious designs of separating from Great-Britain, and establishing independent states. We fight not for glory or for conquest. We exhibit to mankind the remarkable spectacle of a people attacked by unprovoked enemies, without any imputation or even suspicion of offence. They boast of their privileges and civilization, and yet proffer no milder conditions than servitude or death.

In our own native land, in defence of the freedom that is our birthright, and which we ever enjoyed till the late violation of it—for the protection of our property, acquired solely by the honest industry of our fore-fathers and ourselves, against violence actually offered, we have taken up arms. We shall lay them down when hostilities shall cease on the part of the aggressors, and all danger of their being renewed shall be removed, and not before.

With an humble confidence in the mercies of the supreme and impartial Judge and Ruler of the Universe, we most devoutly implore his divine goodness to protect us happily through this great conflict, to dispose our adversaries to reconciliation on reasonable terms, and thereby to relieve the empire from the calamities of civil war.

COMMON SENSE

THOMAS PAINE, 1776

This is supposing the present race of kings in the world to have had an honorable origin; whereas it is more than probable, that, could we take off the dark covering of antiquity and trace them to their first rise, we should find the first of them nothing better than the principal ruffian of some restless gang; whose savage manners or preeminence in subtility obtained him the title of chief among plunderers: and who by increasing in power and extending his depredations, overawed the quiet and defenceless to purchase their safety by frequent contributions. . . .

* * *

England since the conquest hath known some few good monarchs, but groaned beneath a much larger number of bad ones; yet no man in his senses can say that their claim under William the Conqueror is a very honorable one. A French bastard landing with an armed banditti and establishing himself king of England against the consent of the natives is in plain terms a very paltry rascally original. It certainly hath no divinity in it. However it is needless to spend much time in exposing the folly of herditary rights: if there were any so weak as to believe it, let them promiscuously worship the ass and the lion, and welcome. I shall neither copy their humility, nor disturb their devotion. . . . The plain truth is, that the antiquity of English monarchy will not bear looking into.

* * *

In England a king hath little more to do than to make war and give away places; which, in plain terms, is to empoverish the nation and set it together by the ears. A pretty business indeed for a man to be allowed eight hundred thousand sterling a year for, and worshipped into the bargain! Of more worth is one honest man to society, and in the sight of God, than all the crowned ruffians that ever lived.

* * *

But where, say some, is the king of America? I'll tell you, he reigns above, and doth not make havoc of mankind like the royal brute of Great Britain. Yet that we may not appear to be defective even in earthly honors, let a day be solemnly set apart for proclaiming the charter; let it be brought forth placed on the divine law, the Word of God; let a crown be placed thereon, by which the world may know, that so far as we approve of monarchy, that in America the law is king. For as in absolute governments the king is law, so in free countries the law ought to be king; and there ought to be no other. But lest any ill use should afterwards arise, let the crown at the conclusion of the ceremony be demolished, and scattered among the people whose right it is.

Selections from *Common Sense* by Thomas Paine.

VIRGINIA DECLARATION OF RIGHTS

I

That all men are by nature equally free and independent, and have certain inherent rights, of which, when they enter into a state of society, they cannot, by any compact, deprive or divest their posterity; namely, the enjoyment of life and liberty, with the means of acquiring and possessing property, and pursuing and obtaining happiness and safety.

II

That all power is vested in, and consequently derived from, the people; that magistrates are their trustees and servants, and at all times amenable to them.

III

That government is, or ought to be, instituted for the common benefit, protection, and security of the people, nation, or community; of all the various modes and forms of government that is best, which is capable of producing the greatest degree of happiness and safety and is most effectually secured against the danger of maladministration; and that, whenever any government shall be found inadequate or contrary to these purposes, a majority of the community hath an indubitable, unalienable, and indefeasible right to reform, alter, or abolish it, in such manner as shall be judged most conducive to the public weal.

IV

That no man, or set of men, are entitled to exclusive or separate emoluments or privileges from the community, but in consideration of public services; which, not being descendible, neither ought the offices of magistrate, legislator, or judge to be hereditary.

V

That the legislative and executive powers of the state should be separate and distinct from the judicative; and, that the members of the two first may be restrained from oppression by feeling and participating the burthens of the people, they should, at fixed periods, be reduced to a private station, return into that body from which they were originally taken, and the vacancies be supplied by frequent, certain, and regular elections in which all, or any part of the former members, to be again eligible, or ineligible, as the laws shall direct.

Source: Ben Perley Poore, ed., *The Federal and State Constitutions, Colonial Charters, and Other Organic Laws of the United States*, vol. 2 (1878), pp. 1908–1909.

VI

That elections of members to serve as representatives of the people in assembly ought to be free; and that all men, having sufficient evidence of permanent common interest with, and attachment to, the community have the right of suffrage and cannot be taxed or deprived of their property for public uses without their own consent or that of their representatives so elected, nor bound by any law to which they have not, in like manner, assented, for the public good.

VII

That all power of suspending laws, or the execution of laws, by any authority without consent of the representatives of the people is injurious to their rights and ought not to be exercised.

VIII

That in all capital or criminal prosecutions a man hath a right to demand the cause and nature of his accusation to be confronted with the accusers and witnesses, to call for evidence in his favor, and to a speedy trial by an impartial jury of his vicinage, without whose unanimous consent he cannot be found guilty, nor can he be compelled to give evidence against himself; that no man be deprived of his liberty except by the law of the land or the judgment of his peers.

IX

That excessive bail ought not to be required, nor excessive fines imposed; nor cruel and unusual punishments inflicted.

X

That general warrants, whereby any officer or messenger may be commanded to search suspected places without evidence of a fact committed, or to seize any person or persons not named, or whose offense is not particularly described and supported by evidence, are grievous and oppressive and ought not be granted.

XI

That in controversies respecting property and in suits between man and man, the ancient trial by jury is preferable to any other and ought to be held sacred.

XII

That the freedom of the press is one of the greatest bulwarks of liberty and can never be restrained but by despotic governments.

XIII

That a well regulated militia, composed of the body of the people, trained to arms, is the proper, natural, and safe defense of a free state; that standing armies, in time of peace, should be avoided as dangerous to liberty; and that, in all cases, the military should be under strict subordination to, and governed by, the civil power.

XIV

That the people have a right to uniform government; and therefore, that no government separate from, or independent of, the government of Virginia, ought to be erected or established within the limits thereof.

XV

That no free government, or the blessings of liberty, can be preserved to any people but by a firm adherence to justice, moderation, temperance, frugality, and virtue and by frequent recurrence to fundamental principles.

XVI

That religion, or the duty which we owe to our Creator and the manner of discharging it, can be directed only by reason and conviction, not by force or violence; and therefore, all men are equally entitled to the free exercise of religion, according to the dictates of conscience; and that it is the mutual duty of all to practice Christian forbearance, love, and charity towards each other.

DECLARATION OF INDEPENDENCE

IN CONGRESS, JULY 4, 1776

THE UNANIMOUS DECLARATION
OF THE THIRTEEN UNITED
STATES OF AMERICA

When in the Course of human events, it becomes necessary for one people to dissolve the political bands which have connected them with another, and to assume among the powers of the earth, the separate and equal station to which the Laws of Nature and of Nature's God entitle them, a decent respect to the opinions of mankind requires that they should declare the causes which impel them to the separation.—We hold these truths to be self-evident, that all men are created equal, that they are endowed by their Creator with certain unalienable Rights, that among these are Life, Liberty and the pursuit of Happiness.—That to secure these rights, Governments are instituted among Men, deriving their just powers from the consent of the governed.—That whenever any Form of Government becomes destructive of these ends, it is the Right of the People to alter or to abolish it, and to institute new Government, laying its foundation on such principles and organizing its powers in such form, as to them shall seem most likely to effect their Safety and Happiness. Prudence, indeed, will dictate that Governments long established should not be changed for light and transient causes; and accordingly all experience hath shown, that mankind are more disposed to suffer, while evils are sufferable, than to right themselves by abolishing the forms to which they are accustomed. But when a long train of abuses and usurpations, pursuing invariably the same Object evinces a design to reduce them under absolute Despotism, it is their right, it is their duty, to throw off such Government, and to provide new Guards for their future security.—Such has been the patient sufferance of these Colonies; and such is now the necessity which constrains them to alter their former Systems of Government. The history of the present King of Great Britain is a history of repeated injuries and usurpations, all having in direct object the establishment of an absolute Tyranny over these States. To prove this, let Facts be submitted to a candid world.—He has refused his Assent to Laws, the most wholesome and necessary for the public good.—He has forbidden his Governors to pass Laws of immediate and pressing importance, unless suspended in their operation till his Assent should be obtained; and when so suspended, he has utterly neglected to attend to them.—He has refused to pass other Laws for the accommodation of large districts of people, unless those people would relinquish the right of Representation in the Legislature, a right inestimable to them and formidable to tyrants only.—He has called together legislative bodies at places unusual, uncomfortable, and distant from the depository or their public Records, for the sole purpose of fatiguing them into compliance with his measures.—He has dissolved Representative Houses repeatedly, for opposing with manly firmness his invasions on the rights of the people.—He has refused for a long time, after such dissolutions, to cause others to be elected; whereby the Legislative powers, incapable of Annihilation, have returned to the People at large for their

Source: *The United States Government Manual.*

exercise; the State remaining in the mean time exposed to all the dangers of invasion from without, and convulsions within.—He has endeavored to prevent the population of these States; for that purpose obstructing the Laws for Naturalization of Foreigners; refusing to pass others to encourage their migration hither, and raising the conditions of new Appropriations of Lands.—He has obstructed the Administration of Justice, by refusing his Assent to Laws for establishing Judiciary powers.—He has made Judges dependent on his Will alone, for the tenure of their offices, and the amount and payment of their salaries.—He has erected a multitude of New Offices, and sent hither swarms of Officers to harrass our people, and eat out their substance.—He has kept among us, in times of peace, Standing Armies, without the Consent of our legislatures.—He has affected to render the Military independent of and superior to the Civil power.—He has combined with others to subject us to a jurisdiction foreign to our constitution, and unacknowledged by our laws; giving his Assent to their Acts of pretended Legislation:—For quartering large bodies of armed troops among us:—For protecting them, by a mock Trial, from punishment for any Murders which they should commit on the Inhabitants of these States:—For cutting off our Trade with all parts of the world:—For imposing Taxes on us without our Consent:—For depriving us in many cases, of the benefits of Trial by Jury:—For transporting us beyond Seas to be tried for pretended offences:—For abolishing the free System of English Laws in a neighbouring Province, establishing therein an Arbitrary government, and enlarging its Boundaries so as to render it at once an example and fit instrument for introducing the same absolute rule into these Colonies:—For taking away our Charters, abolishing our most valuable Laws, and altering fundamentally the Forms of our Governments:—For suspending our own Legislatures, and declaring themselves invested with power to legislate for us in all cases whatsoever.—He has abdicated Government here, by declaring us out of his Protection and waging War against us.—He has plundered our seas, ravaged our Coasts, burnt our towns, and destroyed the lives of our people.—He is at this time transporting large Armies of foreign Mercenaries to compleat the works of death, desolation and tyranny, already begun with circumstances of Cruelty & perfidy scarcely paralleled in the most barbarous ages, and totally unworthy the Head of a civilized nation.—He has constrained our fellow Citizens taken Captive on the high Seas to bear Arms against their Country, to become the executioners of their friends and Brethren, or to fall themselves by their Hands.—He has excited domestic insurrections amongst us, and has endeavored to bring on the inhabitants of our frontiers, the merciless Indian Savages, whose known rule of warfare, is an undistinguished destruction of all ages, sexes and conditions. In every state of these Oppressions We have Petitioned for Redress in the most humble terms. Our repeated Petitions have been answered only by repeated injury. A Prince, whose character is thus marked by every act which may define a Tyrant, is unfit to be the ruler of a free people. Nor have We been wanting in attentions to our British brethren. We have warned them from time to time of attempts by their legislature to extend an unwarrantable jurisdiction over us. We have reminded them of the circumstances of our emigration and settlement here. We have appealed to their native justice and magnanimity, and we have conjured them by the ties of our common kindred to disavow these usurpations, which would inevitably interrupt our connections and correspondence. They too have been deaf to the voice of justice and consanguinity. We must, therefore, acquiesce in the necessity, which denounces our Separation, and hold them, as we hold the rest of mankind, Enemies in War, in Peace Friends.—

WE, THEREFORE, the REPRESENTATIVES of the UNITED STATES OF AMERICA, in General Congress, Assembled, appealing to the Supreme Judge of the world for the rectitude of our intentions, do, in the Name, and by Authority of the good People of these Colonies, solemnly publish and declare, That these United Colonies are, and of Right ought to be FREE AND INDEPENDENT STATES; that they are Absolved from all Allegiance to the British Crown, and that all political connection between them and the State of Great Britain, is and ought to be totally disolved; and that as Free and Independent States, they have full Power to levy War, conclude Peace, contract Alliances, establish Commerce, and to do all other Acts and Things which Independent States may of right do.—And for the support of this Declaration, with a firm reliance on the protection of Divine Providence, we mutually pledge to each other our Lives, our Fortunes and our sacred Honor.

John Hancock
Button Gwinnett
Lyman Hall
Geo. Walton
Wm. Hooper
Joseph Hewes
John Penn
Edward Rutledge
Thos. Heyward, Jr.
Thomas Lynch, Jr.
Arthur Middleton
Samuel Chase
Wm. Paca
Thos. Stone
Charles Carroll of
     Carrollton
George Wythe
Richard Henry Lee
Th. Jefferson

Benj. Harrison
Thos. Nelson, Jr.
Francis Lightfoot Lee
Carter Braxton
Robt. Morris
Benjamin Rush
Benj. Franklin
John Morton
Geo. Clymer
Jas. Smith
Geo. Taylor
James Wilson
Geo. Ross
Caesar Rodney
Geo. Read
Tho. M. Kean
Wm. Floyd
Phil. Livington
Frans. Lewis

Lewis Morris
Richd. Stockton
Jno. Witherspoon
Fras. Hopkinson
John Hart
Abra. Clark
Josiah Bartlett
Wm. Whipple
Saml. Adams
John Adams
Robt. Treat Paine
Elbridge Gerry
Step. Hopkins
William Ellery
Roger Sherman
Sam. Huntington
Wm. Williams
Oliver Wolcott
Matthew Thornton

TREATY OF PARIS

In the name of the most holy and undivided Trinity.

It having pleased the Divine Providence to dispose the hearts of the most serene and most potent Prince George the Third, by the grace of God, king of Great Britain, France, and Ireland, defender of the faith, duke of Brunswick and Lunebourg, arch-treasurer and prince elector of the Holy Roman Empire etc., and of the United States of America, to forget all past misunderstandings and differences that have unhappily interrupted the good correspondence and friendship which they mutually wish to restore, and to establish such a beneficial and satisfactory intercourse, between the two countries upon the ground of reciprocal advantages and mutual convenience as may promote and secure to both perpetual peace and harmony; and having for this desirable end already laid the foundation of peace and reconciliation by the Provisional Articles signed at Paris on the 30th of November 1782, by the commissioners empowered on each part, which articles were agreed to be inserted in and to constitute the Treaty of Peace proposed to be concluded between the Crown of Great Britain and the said United States, but which treaty was not to be concluded until terms of peace should be agreed upon between Great Britain and France and his Britannic Majesty should be ready to conclude such treaty accordingly; and the treaty between Great Britain and France having since been concluded, his Britannic Majesty and the United States of America, in order to carry into full effect the Provisional Articles above mentioned, according to the tenor thereof, have constituted and appointed, that is to say his Britannic Majesty on his part, David Hartley, Esqr., member of the Parliament of Great Britain, and the said United States on their part, John Adams, Esqr., late a commissioner of the United States of America at the court of Versailles, late delegate in Congress from the state of Massachusetts, and chief justice of the said state, and minister plenipotentiary of the said United States to their high mightinesses the States General of the United Netherlands; Benjamin Franklin, Esqr., late delegate in Congress from the state of Pennsylvania, president of the convention of the said state, and minister plenipotentiary from the United States of America at the court of Versailles; John Jay, Esqr., late president of Congress and chief justice of the state of New York, and minister plenipotentiary from the said United States at the court of Madrid; to be the plenipotentiaries for the concluding and signing the present definitive treaty; who after having reciprocally communicated their respective full powers have agreed upon and confirmed the following articles.

Source: United States. Department of State, *Treaties and Other International Agreements of the United States of America, 1776–1949* (compiled under the direction of Charles I. Bevans), vol. 12 (1974), pp. 8–12.

Article 1

His Britannic Majesty acknowledges the said United States, viz., New Hampshire, Massachusetts Bay, Rhode Island and Providence Plantations, Connecticut, New York, New Jersey, Pennsylvania, Delaware, Maryland, Virginia, North Carolina, South Carolina and Georgia, to be free sovereign and independent states, that he treats with them as such, and for himself, his heirs, and successors, relinquishes all claims to the government, propriety, and territorial rights of the same and every part thereof.

Article 2

And that all disputes which might arise in future on the subject of the boundaries of the said United States may be prevented, it is hereby agreed and declared, that the following are and shall be their boundaries, viz.: from the northwest angle of Nova Scotia, viz., that angle which is formed by a line drawn due north from the source of St. Croix River to the highlands; along the said highlands which divide those rivers that empty themselves into the river St. Lawrence, from those which fall into the Atlantic Ocean, to the northwesternmost head of Connecticut River; thence down along the middle of that river to the forty-fifth degree of north latitude; from thence by a line due west on said latitude until it strikes the river Iroquois or Cataraquy; thence along the middle of said river into Lake Ontario; through the middle of said lake until it strikes the communication by water between that lake and Lake Erie; thence along the middle of said communication into Lake Erie, through the middle of said lake until it arrives at the water communication between that lake and Lake Huron; thence along the middle of said water communication into the Lake Huron, thence through the middle of said lake to the water communication between that lake and Lake Superior; thence through Lake Superior northward of the Isles Royal and Phelipeaux to the Long Lake; thence through the middle of said Long Lake and the water communication between it and the Lake of the Woods, to the said Lake of the Woods; thence through the said lake to the most northwestern point thereof, and from thence on a due west course to the river Mississippi; thence by a line to be drawn along the middle of the said river Mississippi until it shall intersect the northernmost part of the thirty-first degree of north latitude. South, by a line to be drawn due east from the determination of the line last mentioned in the latitude of thirty-one degrees north of the equator, to the middle of the river Apalachicola or Catahouche; thence along the middle thereof to its junction with the Flint River, thence straight to the head of Saint Mary's River; and thence down along the middle of Saint Mary's River to the Atlantic Ocean; east, by a line to be drawn along the middle of the river Saint Croix, from its mouth in the Bay of Fundy to its source, and from its source directly north to the aforesaid highlands which divide the rivers that fall into the Atlantic Ocean from those which fall into the river Saint Lawrence; comprehending all islands within twenty leagues of any part of the shores of the United States, and lying between lines to be drawn due east from the points where the aforesaid boundaries between Nova Scotia on the one part and East Florida on the other shall, respectively, touch the Bay of Fundy and the Atlantic Ocean, excepting such islands as now are or heretofore have been within the limits of the said province of Nova Scotia.

Article 3

It is agreed that the people of the United States shall continue to enjoy unmolested the right to take fish of every kind on the Grand Bank and on all the other banks of Newfoundland, also in the Gulf of Saint Lawrence and at all other places in the sea, where the inhabitants of both countries used at any time heretofore to fish. And also that the inhabitants of the United States shall have liberty to take fish of every kind on such part of the coast of Newfoundland as British fishermen shall use, (but not to dry or cure the same on that island) and also on the coasts, bays, and creeks of all other of his Britannic Majesty's dominions in America; and that the American fishermen shall have liberty to dry and cure fish in any of the unsettled bays, harbors, and creeks of Nova Scotia, Magdalen Islands, and Labrador, so long as the same shall remain unsettled, but so soon as the same or either of them shall be settled, it shall not be lawful for the said fishermen to dry or cure fish at such settlement without a previous agreement for that purpose with the inhabitants, proprietors, or possessors of the ground.

Article 4

It is agreed that creditors on either side shall meet with no lawful impediment to the recovery of the full value in sterling money of all bona fide debts heretofore contracted.

Article 5

It is agreed that Congress shall earnestly recommend it to the legislatures of the respective states to provide for the restitution of all estates, rights, and properties, which have been confiscated belonging to real British subjects; and also of the estates, rights, and properties of persons resident in districts in the possession of his Majesty's arms and who have not borne arms against the said United States. And that persons of any other description shall have free liberty to go to any part or parts of any of the thirteen United States and therein to remain twelve months unmolested in their endeavors to obtain the restitution of such of their estates, rights, and properties as may have been confiscated; and that Congress shall also earnestly recommend to the several states a reconsideration and revision of all acts or laws regarding the premises, so as to render the said laws or acts perfectly consistent not only with justice and equity but with that spirit of conciliation which on the return of the blessings of peace should universally prevail. And that Congress shall also earnestly recommend to the several states that the estates, rights, and properties, of such last mentioned persons shall be restored to them, they refunding to any persons who may be now in possession the bona fide price (where any has been given) which such persons may have paid on purchasing any of the said lands, rights, or properties since the confiscation.

And it is agreed that all persons who have any interest in confiscated lands, either by debts, marriage settlements, or otherwise, shall meet with no lawful impediment in the prosecution of their just rights.

Article 6

That there shall be no future confiscations made nor any prosecutions commenced against any person or persons for, or by reason of, the part which he or they may have taken in the present war, and that no person shall on that account suffer any future loss or damage, either in his person, liberty, or property; and that those who may be in confinement on such charges at the time of the ratification of the treaty in America shall be immediately set at liberty, and the prosecutions so commenced be discontinued.

Article 7

There shall be a firm and perpetual peace between his Britannic Majesty and the said states, and between the subjects of the one and the citizens of the other, wherefore all hostilities both by sea and land shall from henceforth cease. All prisoners on both sides shall be set at liberty, and his Britannic Majesty shall with all convenient speed, and without causing any destruction, or carrying away any Negroes or other property of the American inhabitants, withdraw all his armies, garrisons, and fleets from the said United States, and from every post, place, and harbor within the same; leaving in all fortifications, the American artillery that may be therein; and shall also order and cause all archives, records, deeds, and papers belonging to any of the said states, or their citizens, which in the course of the war may have fallen into the hands of his officers, to be forthwith restored and delivered to the proper states and persons to whom they belong.

Article 8

The navigation of the river Mississippi, from its source to the ocean, shall forever remain free and open to the subjects of Great Britain and the citizens of the United States.

Article 9

In case it should so happen that any place or territory belonging to Great Britain or to the United States should have been conquered by the arms of either from the other before the arrival of the said Provisional Articles in America, it is agreed that the same shall be restored without difficulty and without requiring any compensation.

Article 10

The solemn ratifications of the present treaty expedited in good and due form shall be exchanged between the contracting parties in the space of six months or sooner, if possible, to be computed from the day of the signature of the present treaty. In witness whereof we the undersigned, their ministers plenipotentiary, have in their name and in virtue of our full powers, signed with our hands the present definitive treaty and caused the seals of our arms to be affixed thereto.

Done at Paris, this third day of September in the year of our Lord, one thousand seven hundred and eighty-three.

D. Hartley	[Seal]
John Adams	[Seal]
B. Franklin	[Seal]
John Jay	[Seal]

ORIGINS OF U.S. GOVERNMENT

After declaring their independence in 1776, the thirteen states had to determine both what type of central government they should form and how the individual states would be related to that central government. Their initial efforts to answer those questions resulted in the Articles of Confederation. The Articles were drafted in 1776 but were modified during the ratification process, which ended when the Articles went into effect on March 1, 1781.

The Articles of Confederation created a weak national government, which lacked both an executive and a judicial branch. The national government consisted only of a Congress, which prosecuted the end of the War of Independence and negotiated the Treaty of Paris. By the end of the war, however, the Congress of the Confederation of the States found itself receiving less cooperation from the individual states. The Congress did enact the Northwest Ordinance in 1787, which provided for the government of the Northwest Territory and established a procedure by which states could be carved out of the territory.

Dissatisfaction with the Articles of Confederation grew during the 1780s until Congress finally summoned a convention to amend and revise the Articles. All of the states except Rhode Island sent delegates to the convention, which convened in Philadelphia, Pennsylvania, in May 1787. A fundamental problem for the delegates was resolving a split between the states that favored a strong national government and those that preferred the strong state governments established by the Articles of Confederation.

As the convention debated the issues, it soon became apparent that a stronger national gov-

ernment was needed and that the Articles of Confederation would have to be replaced. A major conflict developed, however, between the large states, which favored a legislature apportioned by population, and the small states, which preferred a system under which each state would have an equal vote. The large states proposed the Virginia Plan, also known as the Randolph Plan, and the small states offered the New Jersey, or Paterson, Plan. At first, neither side would yield on the issue of representation. Finally, Roger Sherman, along with Oliver Ellsworth, proposed the Connecticut, or Great, Compromise, which called for a bicameral legislature with proportional representation in the lower house and equal representation in the upper house.

The U.S. Constitution was completed on September 17, 1787. It established three branches of government (legislative, executive, judicial) with an intricate set of checks and balances aimed at preventing one branch of government from gaining absolute control. The separation of powers is one of the hallmarks of the Constitution. The Framers did not, however, resolve the question of slavery. Southern states won the Three-fifths Compromise, which allowed them to count each slave as three-fifths of a white person in apportioning the House of Representatives and the electoral college.

Though opponents of the Constitution argued that it gave too much power to the national government, it was ratified by the requisite number of states by June 1788. George Mason, drafter of the Virginia Declaration of Rights, and other states' rights advocates opposed ratification because the Constitution included no guarantees of basic personal liberties. In response, the first Congress convened under the Constitution in 1789 enacted the first ten amendments to the Constitution, known as the Bill of Rights.

During the ratification battle of 1787 and 1788, Alexander Hamilton, James Madison, and John Jay wrote eighty-five short essays in support of the Constitution. The essays, known as the *Federalist Papers*, sought to convince the voters of New York to persuade their legislators to vote in favor of the proposed federal constitution. The writers so clearly articulated the reasoning and scope of many of the constitutional provisions that the *Federalist Papers* have taken on lasting historical and legal significance.

The early years of the Republic saw a clash between the Federalists, led by Hamilton, and the Republicans, led by Thomas Jefferson. Jefferson and other proponents of strong state governments accused Hamilton and other advocates of a strong national government of going beyond the constitutional restrictions on the power of the national government. This debate escalated after the federal Alien and Sedition Acts (1 Stat. 570, 596) were enacted in 1798. Jefferson and Madison prepared resolves, or resolutions, for the Virginia and Kentucky legislatures that proposed a "compact" theory of the U.S. Constitution. Under this theory state legislatures possessed all powers not specifically granted to the federal government, and states had the right to pass upon the constitutionality of federal legislation.

In the first years of the new nation, it was unclear whether the Supreme Court had the right to review an executive or legislative act and invalidate it if the act was contrary to constitutional principles. Article III of the Constitution was silent on the subject, but the Supreme Court settled the issue in 1803, when it ruled in *Marbury v. Madison*, 5 U.S. (1 Cranch) 137, 2 L. Ed. 60, that a particular act of Congress was unconstitutional.

The United States entered the field of international relations in 1823, when President James Monroe enunciated a statement on foreign policy that has come to be known as the Monroe Doctrine. The Monroe Doctrine asserted U.S. dominance over the Western Hemisphere and warned European nations not to interfere with the free nations of the region.

Articles of Confederation

The Articles of Confederation were the first constitution of the United States. During 1776–1777, a congressional committee led by John Dickinson of Pennsylvania (who had drafted the Declaration of the Causes and Necessity of Taking up Arms in 1775) wrote the Articles and submitted them to the states for ratification in 1777. Ratification was delayed by disputes between the states with extensive western lands and the "landless" states such as Maryland. On March 1, 1781, after the landed states agreed to cede their lands to Congress, the new government came into existence.

The Articles of Confederation reflected the new nation's fear of centralized power and authority. Under the Articles the states were more powerful than the central government, which consisted only of a Congress. Each state had one vote in Congress, with that vote determined by a delegation of from two to seven representatives. Though the Congress had the authority to regulate foreign affairs, wage war, and maintain the postal system, it had no power to levy and collect taxes or regulate interstate commerce.

Critics of the Articles multiplied until finally, in 1787, Congress summoned a convention to draft a revised constitution. On March 4, 1789, the new U.S. Constitution took effect, superseding the Articles of Confederation.

Northwest Ordinance

The Northwest Ordinance (officially the Ordinance of 1787) was enacted by the Congress of the Confederation of the States on July 13, 1787. This statute provided for the government of the Northwest Territory, an area bounded by the Ohio and Mississippi Rivers and the Great Lakes, and created a procedure by which states could be established within this territory and admitted to the Union. Congress was spurred to enact the ordinance when the Ohio Company of Associates, a group of land speculators, made plans to purchase more than one million acres in the territory.

The Northwest Ordinance set several important precedents. It established that unlike many nations, which left their new territories in a position inferior to the old, the United States would admit new states to the Union on an equal basis with the original states. The ordinance also set aside land in each township for schools, thus setting a precedent for federal support to education. In addition, the ordinance prohibited slavery in the territory and included the first full statement of U.S. Indian policy, which stressed that "utmost good faith shall always be observed toward the Indians."

The Virginia, or Randolph, Plan and the New Jersey, or Paterson, Plan

At the Constitutional Convention in 1787, a deep division emerged between the large, more populated states and the smaller states over the apportionment of the national legislature. The Virginia Plan, also known as the Randolph Plan, after its sponsor, Edmund Randolph, called for a two-house legislature with representation of each state based on its population or wealth. William Paterson, a delegate from New Jersey, proposed an apportionment plan on behalf of the small states that would allow each state to have one vote in a unicameral Congress.

Roger Sherman, along with Oliver Ellsworth, proposed the Connecticut, or Great, Compromise. This plan created a bicameral legislature with proportional representation in the lower house and equal representation in the upper house. All revenue measures would originate in the lower house. The compromise was accepted, and the Constitution was soon approved by the convention.

Constitution of the United States

The U.S. Constitution was drafted in 1787 in Philadelphia by delegates to the Constitutional Convention. The delegates decided soon after their arrival that the Articles of Confederation could not be saved through amendment and that an entirely new constitution should be written to replace it. The document that emerged from the convention was the product of a series of compromises.

Once the Constitution had been offered to the states for ratification, critics opposed it on several grounds. Most importantly, they argued that the Constitution created an overly powerful central government that could abuse the rights of citizens and criticized the Framers for failing to include a bill of rights. To win over the opposition, the supporters of the Constitution agreed that the enactment of a bill of rights should be among the business of the first Congress. By June 21, 1788, the requisite nine states had ratified the Constitution. Virginia and New York ratified it a few days later, while North Carolina did so in 1789 and Rhode Island agreed to the Constitution in 1790.

Since the Constitution went into effect in 1789, only twenty-seven amendments have been added to correct deficiencies in the original document or to adapt it to changing needs and principles.

Bill of Rights

The Bill of Rights, which consists of the first ten amendments to the U.S. Constitution, was drafted by the first Congress of the new government in 1789 and went into effect on December 15, 1791, when Virginia became the eleventh state to ratify the amendments.

The Bill of Rights followed a tradition in Anglo-American law of drawing up a list of basic rights to which all the people in the state were entitled. The English Bill of Rights, enacted in 1689, included the right to petition the government with grievances, the right to trial by jury, and the right not to be subjected to cruel and unusual punishments. In 1774 the First Continental Congress drew up a Declaration of Rights, which included such liberties as freedom of the press and a prohibition against standing armies in peacetime.

The Virginia Declaration of Rights, enacted in 1776, quickly became the model for other states. By 1781 eight states had enacted bills of rights, and four others had included statements guaranteeing individual rights either in the prefaces to their constitutions or in supplementary statutes. The Articles of Confederation did not include a bill of rights, however. The drafters of the Articles believed that the protection of individual rights was a state responsibility.

At the 1787 Constitutional Convention, Edmund Randolph and George Mason (the drafter of the Virginia Declaration of Rights) of Virginia and Elbridge Gerry of Massachusetts sought unsuccessfully to include a bill of rights in the new constitution. Most delegates took the view that the state bills of rights would continue to protect individual rights at the state level and that Congress would resist any attempts to infringe upon individual liberties at the federal level.

When the lack of a bill of rights became an issue in the ratification process, James Madison promised that the first Congress would enact a bill of rights as part of its business. As a member of the first House of Representatives, Madison reminded the members of this pledge. He drafted much of the final document, using Mason's Virginia Declaration of Rights as a model.

The Bill of Rights plays a central role in the protection of civil liberties and civil rights. When enacted, the ten amendments applied only to the actions of the federal government. In a long series of decisions, however, the U.S. Supreme Court has ruled that almost all the provisions in the Bill of Rights also apply to the states. Therefore, the Bill of Rights safeguards the basic rights of individuals from encroachment by all levels of government.

The Federalist Papers

The *Federalist Papers* were published by Alexander Hamilton, James Madison, and John Jay to help convince the citizens of New York that ratification of the U.S. Constitution was justified. The essays not only discuss many of the Constitution's provisions but also elaborate on the authors' own vision of the proper role of a national government.

Madison's first essay, *Federalist*, no. 10, is the most frequently quoted of the group. In it, Madison discussed the idea of political factions. At the time it was commonly agreed that democratic society needed to prevent factions because they would ultimately undermine the government and lead to violence. Madison agreed that factions can divide government but came to the opposite conclusion: the more factions, the better. In Madison's view more factions would make it less likely that any one party or coalition of parties would be able to gain control of government and invade the rights of other citizens. The system of checks and balances contained in the Constitution was part of Madison's plan for frustrating factions.

In *Federalist*, no. 78, Hamilton discussed the role of the judiciary. He defended the concept of judicial review, which was generally regarded as neither legitimate nor desirable by most political leaders. Hamilton defended the independence of the judiciary and the need for judicial discretion.

The Virginia and Kentucky Resolves

In 1798 James Madison wrote the Virginia Resolves, and Thomas Jefferson wrote the Kentucky Resolves. These legislative resolutions challenged the legitimacy of the federal Alien and Sedition Acts of 1798. Enacted as internal security laws, these acts restricted aliens and limited freedom of the press on the assumption that the United States might soon be at war with France.

Madison and Jefferson argued that Congress did not have the express constitutional authority to deport aliens nor to prosecute persons for seditious libel. They asserted in the resolves that state legislatures had the right to determine whether the federal government was complying with the mandate of the Constitution. In the second of the Kentucky Resolves, Jefferson contended that the "sovereign and independent states" had the right to "interpose" themselves between their citizens and improper national legislative actions and to "nullify" acts of Congress they deemed unconstitutional.

The resolves became an important component of Southern political resistance in the nineteenth century. These ideas ultimately became the legal justification for the secession of the Southern states from the Union in 1861.

Marbury v. Madison

Marbury v. Madison, 5 U.S. (1 Cranch) 137, 2 L. Ed. 60 (1803), is one of the most important cases in U.S. legal history. In *Marbury* the Supreme Court held that the Constitution gives it the right to determine the constitutionality of congressional legislation. Although Alexander Hamilton had defended the practice of judicial review in the *Federalist Papers*, the Supreme Court did not confront the issue until almost fifteen years later.

Chief Justice John Marshall reasoned that because a court's duty in a lawsuit is to declare the law and because the Constitution is the supreme law of the land, where a rule of statutory law conflicts with a rule of the Constitution, then the law of the Constitution must prevail. Marshall asserted that "i[t] is emphatically the province and duty of the judicial department, to say what the law is."

For a discussion of *Marbury v. Madison*, see volume 7, page 129.

Monroe Doctrine

On December 23, 1823, in his annual message to Congress, President James Monroe made a statement on foreign policy that came to be known as the Monroe Doctrine. At that time the United States feared that Russia intended to establish colonies in Alaska and, more importantly, that the continental European states would intervene in Central and South America to help Spain recover its former colonies, which had won their independence in a series of wars in the early nineteenth century.

President Monroe announced that North and South America were closed to colonization, that the United States would not become involved in European wars or colonial wars in the Americas, and, most importantly, that any intervention by a European power in the independent states of the Western Hemisphere would be viewed by the United States as an unfriendly act against the United States.

Later presidents reiterated the Monroe Doctrine. In the early twentieth century, it was extended to justify U.S. intervention in the states of Latin America.

ARTICLES OF CONFEDERATION

To all to whom these Presents shall come, we the undersigned Delegates of the States affixed to our Names send greeting

Whereas the Delegates of the United States of America in Congress assembled did on the fifteenth day of November in the Year of our Lord One Thousand Seven Hundred and Seventy-seven, and in the Second Year of the Independence of America agree to certain articles of Confederation and perpetual Union between the States of Newhampshire, Massachusetts-bay, Rhode-island, and Providence Plantations, Connecticut, New York, New Jersey, Pennsylvania, Delaware, Maryland, Virginia, North-Carolina, South-Carolina and Georgia in the Words following, viz.

Articles of Confederation and perpetual Union between the States of Newhampshire, Massachusetts-bay, Rhode-island and Providence Plantations, Connecticut, New-York, New-Jersey, Pennsylvania, Delaware, Maryland, Virginia, North-Carolina, South-Carolina and Georgia

Article I

The stile of this confederacy shall be "The United States of America."

Article II

Each State retains its sovereignty, freedom and independence, and every power, jurisdiction and right, which is not by this confederation expressly delegated to the United States, in Congress assembled.

Article III

The said States hereby severally enter into a firm league of friendship with each other, for their common defense, the security of their liberties, and their mutual and general welfare, binding themselves to assist each other, against all force offered to, or attacks made upon them, or any of them, on account of religion, sovereignty trade or any other pretence whatever.

Article IV

The better to secure and perpetuate mutual friendship and intercourse among the people of the different States in this Union, the free inhabitants of each of these States, paupers, vagabonds and fugitives from justice excepted, shall be entitled to all privileges and immunities of free citizens

---

Source: Ben Perley Poore, ed., *The Federal and State Constitutions, Colonial Charters, and Other Organic Laws of the United States*, vol. 1 (1878), pp. 7–12.

in the several States; and the people of each State shall have free ingress and regress to and from any other State, and shall enjoy therein all the privileges of trade and commerce, subject to the same duties, impositions and restrictions as the inhabitants thereof respectively, provided that such restrictions shall not exceed so far as to prevent the removal of property imported into any State, to any other State of which the owner is an inhabitant; provided also that no imposition, duties or restriction shall be laid by any State, on the property of the United States, or either of them.

If any person guilty of, or charged with treason, felony, or other high misdemeanor in any State, shall flee from justice, and be found in any of the United States, he shall upon demand of the Governor or Executive power, of the State from which he fled, be delivered up and removed to the State having jurisdiction of his offense.

Full faith and credit shall be given in each of these States to the records, acts and judicial proceedings to the courts and magistrates of every other State.

Article V

For the more convenient management of the general interests of the United States, delegates shall be annually appointed in such manner as the legislature of each State shall direct, to meet in Congress on the first Monday in November, in every year, with a power reserved to each State, to recall its delegates, or any of them, at any time within the year, and to send others in their stead, for the remainder of the year.

No State shall be represented in Congress by less than two, nor by more than seven members; and no person shall be capable of being a delegate for more than three years in any term of six years; nor shall any person, being a delegate, be capable of holding any office under the United States, for which he, or another for his benefit receives any salary, fees or emolument of any kind.

Each State shall maintain its own delegates in a meeting of the States, and while they act as members of the committee of the States.

In determining questions in the United States, in Congress assembled, each State shall have one vote.

Freedom of speech and debate in Congress shall not be impeached or questioned in any court, or place out of Congress, and the members of Congress shall be protected in their persons from arrests and imprisonments, during the time of their going to and from, and attendance on Congress, except for treason, felony, or breach of the peace.

Article VI

No State without the consent of the United States in Congress assembled, shall send any embassy to, or receive any embassy from, or enter into any conference, agreement, alliance or treaty with any king, prince or state; nor shall any person holding any office or profit or trust under the United States, or any of them, accept of any present, emolument, office or title of any kind whatever from any king, prince or foreign state; nor shall the United States in Congress assembled or any of them, grant any title of nobility.

No two or more States shall enter into any treaty, confederation or alliance whatever between them, without the consent of the United States in Congress assembled, specifying accurately the purposes for which the same is to be entered into, and how long it shall continue.

No State shall lay any imposts or duties, which may interfere with any stipulations in treaties, entered into by the United States in Congress assembled, with any king, prince or state, in pursuance of any treaties already proposed by Congress, to the courts of France and Spain.

No vessels of war shall be kept up in time of peace by any State, except such number only, as shall be deemed necessary by the United States in Congress assembled, for the defence of such State, or its trade; nor shall any body of forces be kept up by any State, in time of peace, except such number only, as in the judgment of the United States, in Congress assembled, shall be deemed requisite to garrison the forts necessary for the defence of such State; but every State shall always keep up a well regulated and disciplined militia, sufficiently armed and accoutered, and shall provide and constantly have ready for use, in public stores, a due number of field pieces and tents, and a proper quantity of arms, ammunition and camp equipage.

No State shall engage in any way without the consent of the United States in Congress assembled, unless such State be actually invaded by enemies, or shall have received certain advice of a resolution being formed by some nation of Indians to invade such State, and the danger is so imminent as not to admit of a delay, till the United States in Congress assembled can be consulted: nor shall any State grant commissions to any ships or vessels of war, nor letters of marque or reprisal, except it be after a declaration of war by the United States in Congress assembled, and then only against the kingdom or state and the subject thereof, against which war has been so declared and under such regulations as shall be established by the United States in Congress assembled, unless such State be infested by pirates, in which case vessels of war may be fitted out for that occasion, and kept so long as the danger shall continue, or until the United States in Congress assembled shall determine otherwise.

Article VII

When land-forces are raised by any State for the common defence, all officers of or under the rank of colonel, shall be appointed by the Legislature of each State respectively by whom such forces shall be raised, or in such manner as such State shall direct, and all vacancies shall be filled up by the State which first made the appointment.

Article VIII

All charges of war, and all other expenses that shall be incurred for the common defence or general welfare, and allowed by the United States in Congress assembled, shall be defrayed out of a common treasury, which shall be supplied by the several States, in proportion to the value of all land within each State, granted to or surveyed for any person, as such land and the buildings and improvements thereon shall be estimated according to such mode as the United States in Congress assembled, shall from time to time direct and appoint.

The taxes for paying that proportion shall be laid and levied by the authority and direction of the Legislatures of the several States within the time agreed upon by the United States in Congress Assembled.

Article IX

The United States in Congress assembled, shall have the sole and exclusive right and power of determining on peace and war, except in the cases mentioned in the sixth article—of sending and receiving ambassadors—entering into treaties and alliances, provided that no treaty of commerce shall be made whereby the legislative power of the respective States shall be restrained from imposing such imposts and duties on foreigners, as their own people are subjected to, or from prohibiting the exportation or importation of any species of goods or commodities whatsoever—of establishing rules for deciding in all cases, what captures on land or water shall be legal, and in what manner prizes taken by land or naval forces in the service of the United States shall be divided or appropriated—of granting letters of marque and reprisal in times of peace—appointing courts for trial of piracies and felonies committed on the high seas and establishing courts for receiving and determining finally appeals in all cases of captures, provided that no member of Congress shall be appointed a judge of any of the said courts.

The United States in Congress assembled shall also be the last resort on appeal in all disputes and differences now subsisting or that hereafter may arise between two or more States concerning boundary, jurisdiction or any other cause whatever; which authority shall always be exercised in the manner following. Whenever the legislative or executive authority or lawful agent of any State in controversy with another shall present a petition to Congress, stating the matter in question and praying for a hearing, notice thereof shall be given by order of Congress to the legislative or executive authority of the other State in controversy, and a day assigned for the appearance of the parties by their lawful agents, who shall then be directed to appoint by joint consent, commissioners or judges to constitute a court for hearing and determining the matter in question: but if they cannot agree, Congress shall name three persons out of each of the United States, and from the list of such persons each party shall alternately strike out one, the petitioners beginning, until the number shall be reduced to thirteen; and from that number not less than seven, nor more than nine names as Congress shall direct, shall, in the presence of Congress be drawn out by lot, and the persons whose names shall be so drawn or any five of them, shall be commissioners or judges, to hear and finally determine the controversy, so always as a major part of the judges who shall hear the cause shall agree in the determination: and if either party shall neglect to attend at the day appointed, without showing reasons, which Congress shall judge sufficient, or being present shall refuse to strike, the

Congress shall proceed to nominate three persons out of each State, and the Secretary of Congress shall strike in behalf of such party absent or refusing; and the judgment and sentence of the court to be appointed, in the manner before prescribed, shall be final and conclusive; and if any of the parties shall refuse to submit to the authority of such court, or to appear or defend their claim or cause, the court shall nevertheless proceed to pronounce sentence, or judgment, which shall in like manner be final and decisive, the judgment or sentence and other proceedings being in either case transmitted to Congress, and lodged among the acts of Congress for the security of the parties concerned: provided that every commissioner, before he sits in judgment, shall take an oath to be administered by one of the judges of the supreme court of the State where the cause shall be tried, "well and truly to hear and determine the matter in question, according to the best of his judgment, without favour, affection or hope of reward:" provided also that no State shall be deprived of territory for the benefit of the United States.

All controversies concerning the private right of soil claimed under different grants of two or more States, whose jurisdiction as they may respect such lands, and the States which passed such grants are adjusted, the said grants or either of them being at the same time claimed to have originated antecedent to such settlement of jurisdiction, shall on the petition of either party to the Congress of the United States, be finally determined as near as may be in the same manner as is before prescribed for deciding disputes respecting territorial jurisdiction between different States.

The United States in Congress assembled shall also have the sole and exclusive right and power of regulating the alloy and value of coin struck by their own authority, or by that of the respective States.—fixing the standard of weights and measures throughout the United States.—regulating the trade and managing all affairs with the Indians, not members of any of the States, provided that the legislative right of any State within its own limits be not infringed or violated—establishing and regulating post-offices from one State to another, throughout all the United States, and exacting such postage on the papers passing thro' the same as may be requisite to defray the expenses of the said office—appointing all officers of the land forces, in the service of the United States, excepting regimental officers—appointing all the officers of the naval forces, and commissioning all officers whatever in the service of the United States—making rules for the government and regulation of the said land and naval forces, and directing their operations.

The United States in Congress assembled shall have authority to appoint a committee, to sit in the recess of Congress, to be denominated "a Committee of the States," and to consist of one delegate from each State; and to appoint such other committees and civil officers as may be necessary for managing the general affairs of the United States under their direction—to appoint one of their number to preside, provided that no person be allowed to serve in the office of president more than one year in any term of three years; to ascertain the necessary sums of money to be raised for the service of the United States, and to appropriate and apply the same for defraying the public expenses—to borrow money or emit bills on the credit of the United States transmitting every half year to the respective States an account of the sums of money so borrowed or emitted,—to build and equip a navy—to agree upon the number of land forces, and to make requisitions from each State for its quota, in proportion to the number of white inhabitants in such State; which requisition shall be binding, and thereupon the Legislature of each State shall appoint the regimental officers, raise the men and cloath, arm and equip them in a soldier like manner, at the expense of the United States; and the officers and men so cloathed, armed and equipped shall march to the place appointed, and within the time agreed on by the United States in Congress assembled: but if the United States in Congress assembled shall, on consideration of circumstances judge proper that any State should not raise men, or should raise a smaller number than its quota, and that any other State should raise a greater number of men than the quota thereof, such extra number shall be raised, officered, cloathed, armed and equipped in the same manner as the quota of such State, unless the legislature of such State shall judge that such extra number cannot be safely spared out of the same, in which case they shall raise officer, cloath, arm and equip as many of such extra number as they judge can be safely spared. And the officers and men so cloathed, armed, and equipped, shall march to the place appointed, and within the time agreed on by the United States in Congress assembled.

The United States in Congress assembled shall never engage in a war, nor grant letters of marque and reprisal in time of peace, nor enter into any treaties or alliances, nor coin money, nor regulate the value thereof, nor ascertain the sums and expenses necessary for the defence and welfare of the United States, or any of them, nor emit bills, nor borrow money on the credit of the United States, nor appropriate money, nor agree upon the number of vessels of war, to be built or purchased, or the number of land or sea forces to be raised, nor appoint a commander in chief of the army or navy, unless nine States assent to the same: nor shall a question on any other point, except for adjourning from day to day be determined, unless by the votes of a majority of the United States in Congress assembled.

The Congress of the United States shall have power to adjourn to any time within the year, and to any place within the United States, so that no period of adjournment be for a longer duration than the space of six months, and shall publish the journal of their proceedings monthly, except such parts thereof relating to treaties, alliances or military operations, as in their judgment require secresy; and the yeas and nays of the delegates of each State on any question shall be entered on the journal, when it is desired by any delegate; and the delegates of a State, or any of them, at his or her request shall be furnished with a transcript of the said journal, except such parts as are above · excepted, to lay before the Legislatures of the several States.

Article X

The committee of the States, or any nine of them, shall be authorized to execute in the recess of Congress, such of the powers of Congress as the United States in Congress assembled, by the consent of nine States, shall from time to time think expedient to vest them with; provided that no power be delegated to the said committee, for the exercise of which, by the articles of confederation, the voice of nine States in the Congress of the United States assembled is requisite.

Article XI

Canada acceding to this confederation, and joining in the measures of the United States, shall be admitted into, and entitled to all the advantages of this Union: but no other colony shall be admitted into the same, unless such admission be agreed to by nine States.

Article XII

All bills of credit emitted, monies borrowed and debts contracted by, or under the authority of Congress, before the assembling of the United States, in pursuance of the present confederation, shall be deemed and considered as a charge against the United States, for payment and satisfaction whereof the said United States, and the public faith are hereby solemnly pledged.

Article XIII

Every State shall abide by the determinations of the United States in Congress assembled, on all questions which by this confederation are submitted to them. And the articles of this confederation shall be inviolably observed by every State, and the Union shall be perpetual; nor shall any alteration at any time hereafter be made in any of them; unless such alteration be agreed to in a Congress of the United States, and be afterwards confirmed by the Legislatures of every State.

And whereas it has pleased the Great Governor of the world to incline the hearts of the Legislatures we respectively represent in Congress, to approve of, and to authorize us to ratify the said articles of confederation and perpetual union. Know ye that we the undersigned delegates, by virtue of the power and authority to us given for that purpose, do by these presents, in the name and in behalf of our respective constituents, fully and entirely ratify and confirm each and every of the said articles of confederation and perpetual union, and all and singular the matters and things therein contained: and we do further solemnly plight and engage the faith of our respective constituents, that they shall abide by the determinations of the United States in Congress assembled, on all questions, which by the said confederation are submitted to them. And that the articles thereof shall be inviolably observed by the States we re[s]pectively represent, and that the Union shall be perpetual.

In witness whereof we have hereunto set our hands in Congress.

Done at Philadelphia in the State of Pennsylvania the ninth day of July in the year of our Lord one thousand seven hundred and seventy-eight, and in the third year of the independence of America.

On the part and behalf of the State of New Hampshire

JOSIAH BARTLETT,   JOHN WENTWORTH, Junr.,
                                                                        August 8th, 1778.

On the part and behalf of the State of Massachusetts Bay

JOHN HANCOCK,   FRANCIS DANA,
SAMUEL ADAMS,   JAMES LOVELL,
ELBRIDGE GERRY,   SAMUEL HOLTEN.

On the part and behalf of the State of Rhode Island and Providence Plantations

WILLIAM ELLERY,   JOHN COLLINS.
HENRY MARCHANT,

On the part and behalf of the State of Connecticut

ROGER SHERMAN,   TITUS HOSMER,
SAMUEL HUNTINGTON,   ANDREW ADAMS.
OLIVER WOLCOTT,

On the part and behalf of the State of New York

JAS. DUANE,   WM. DUER,
FRA. LEWIS,   GOUV. MORRIS.

On the part and in behalf of the State of New Jersey, Novr. 26, 1778

JNO. WITHERSPOON,   NATHL. SCUDDER.

On the part and behalf of the State of Pennsylvania

ROBT. MORRIS,   WILLIAM CLINGAN,
DANIEL ROBERDEAU,   JOSEPH REED,
JONA. BAYARD SMITH,   22d July, 1778.

On the part & behalf of the State of Delaware

THO. M'KEAN, Feby. 12, 1779.   NICHOLAS VAN DYKE.
JOHN DICKINSON, May 5th, 1779

On the part and behalf of the State of Maryland

JOHN HANSON,   DANIEL CARROLL,
       March 1, 1781.   Mar. 1, 1781.

On the part and behalf of the State of Virginia

RICHARD HENRY LEE,   JNO. HARVIE,
JOHN BANISTER,   FRANCIS LIGHTFOOT LEE.
THOMAS ADAMS,

On the part and behalf of the State of No. Carolina

JOHN PENN, July 21st, 1778.   JNO. WILLIAMS.
CORNS. HARNETT,

On the part & behalf of the State of South Carolina

HENRY LAURENS,   RICHD. HUTSON,
WILLIAM HENRY DRAYTON,   THOS. HEYWARD, Junr.
JNO. MATHEWS,

On the part & behalf of the State of Georgia

JNO. WALTON, 24th July, 1778.   EDWD. LANGWORTHY.
EDWD. TELFAIR,

Northwest Ordinance

An Ordinance for the Government of the Territory of the United States Northwest of the River Ohio

Be it ordained by the United States in Congress assembled that the said territory, for the purposes of temporary government, be one district, subject, however, to be divided into two districts, as future circumstances may, in the opinion of Congress, make it expedient.

Be it ordained by the authority aforesaid that the estates both of resident and nonresident proprietors in the said territory, dying intestate, shall descend to and be distributed among their children and the descendants of a deceased child in equal parts, the descendants of a deceased child or grandchild to take the share of their deceased parent in equal parts among them; and where there shall be no children or descendants, then in equal parts to the next of kin, in equal degree; and among collaterals, the children of a deceased brother or sister of the intestate shall have, in equal parts among them, their deceased parent's share; and there shall, in no case, be a distinction between kindred of the whole and half blood; saving in all cases to the widow of the intestate, her third part of the real estate for life, and one-third part of the personal estate; and this law relative to descents and dower shall remain in full force until altered by the legislature of the district. And until the governor and judges shall adopt laws as hereinafter mentioned, estates in the said territory may be devised or bequeathed by wills in writing, signed and sealed by him or her in whom the estate may be (being of full age) and attested by three witnesses;—and real estates may be conveyed by lease and release, or bargain and sale, signed, sealed, and delivered by the person, being of full age, in whom the estate may be, and attested by two witnesses, provided such wills be duly proved, and such conveyances be acknowledged, or the execution thereof duly proved, and be recorded within one year after proper magistrates, courts, and registers shall be appointed for that purpose; and personal property may be transferred by delivery, saving, however, to the French and Canadian inhabitants, and other settlers of the Kaskaskies, Saint Vincents, and the neighboring villages, who have heretofore professed themselves citizens of Virginia, their laws and customs now in force among them, relative to the descent and conveyance of property.

Be it ordained by the authority aforesaid that there shall be appointed from time to time, by Congress, a governor whose commission shall continue in force for the term of three years, unless sooner revoked by Congress; he shall reside in the district and have a freehold estate therein, in one thousand acres of land, while in the exercise of his office.

There shall be appointed from time to time, by Congress, a secretary whose commission shall continue in force for four years, unless sooner revoked; he shall reside in the district and have a

Source: Francis Newton Thorpe, ed., *The Federal and State Constitutions, Colonial Charters, and Other Organic Laws of the States, Territories, and Colonies Now or Heretofore Forming the United States of America*, vol. 2 (1909), pp. 957–962.

freehold estate therein, in five hundred acres of land, while in the exercise of his office. It shall be his duty to keep and preserve the acts and laws passed by the legislature, and the public records of the district, and the proceedings of the governor in his executive department, and transmit authentic copies of such acts and proceedings every six months to the secretary of Congress. There shall also be appointed a court, to consist of three judges, any two of whom to form a court, who shall have a common-law jurisdiction, and reside in the district and have each therein a freehold estate, in five hundred acres of land, while in the exercise of their offices; and their commissions shall continue in force during good behavior.

The governor and judges, or a majority of them, shall adopt and publish in the district such laws of the original states, criminal and civil, as may be necessary and best suited to the circumstances of the district, and report them to Congress from time to time, which laws shall be in force in the district until the organization of the general assembly therein, unless disapproved of by Congress; but afterwards the legislature shall have authority to alter them as they shall think fit.

The governor, for the time being, shall be commander in chief of the militia, appoint and commission all officers in the same below the rank of general officers; all general officers shall be appointed and commissioned by Congress.

Previous to the organization of the general assembly the governor shall appoint such magistrates and other civil officers in each county or township as he shall find necessary for the preservation of the peace and good order in the same. After the general assembly shall be organized, the powers and duties of magistrates and other civil officers shall be regulated and defined by the said assembly; but all magistrates and other civil officers, not herein otherwise directed shall, during the continuance of this temporary government, be appointed by the governor.

For the prevention of crimes and injuries, the laws to be adopted or made shall have force in all parts of the district, and for the execution of process, criminal and civil, the governor shall make proper divisions thereof; and he shall proceed from time to time, as circumstances may require, to lay out the parts of the district in which the Indian titles shall have been extinguished, into counties and townships, subject, however, to such alterations as may thereafter be made by the legislature.

So soon as there shall be five thousand free male inhabitants of full age in the district, upon giving proof thereof to the governor they shall receive authority, with time and place, to elect representatives from their counties or townships to represent them in the general assembly: provided that for every five hundred free male inhabitants there shall be one representative, and so on, progressively, with the number of free male inhabitants, shall the right of representation increase until the number of representatives shall amount to twenty-five; after which the number and proportion of representatives shall be regulated by the legislature: provided that no person be eligible or qualified to act as a representative unless he shall have been a citizen of one of the United States three years and be a resident in the district, or unless he shall have resided in the district three years; and in either case, shall likewise hold in his own right, in fee simple, two hundred acres of land within the same: provided also that a freehold in fifty acres of land in the district, having been a citizen of one of the states, and being resident in the district, or the like freehold and two years' residence in the district, shall be necessary to qualify a man as an elector of a representative.

The representatives thus elected shall serve for the term of two years; and in case of the death of a representative, or removal from office, the governor shall issue a writ to the county or township for which he was a member to elect another in his stead, to serve for the residue of the term.

The general assembly or legislature shall consist of the governor, legislative council, and a house of representatives. The legislative council shall consist of five members, to continue in office five years, unless sooner removed by Congress; any three of whom to be a quorum: and the members of the council shall be nominated and appointed in the following manner, to wit: As soon as representatives shall be elected the governor shall appoint a time and place for them to meet together, and when met they shall nominate ten persons, residents in the district, and each possessed of a freehold in five hundred acres of land, and return their names to Congress, five of whom Congress shall appoint and commission to serve as aforesaid; and whenever a vacancy shall happen in the council, by death or removal from office, the house of representatives shall nominate two persons, qualified as aforesaid, for each vacancy and return their names to Congress, one of whom Congress shall appoint and commission for the residue of the term; and every five years, four months at least before the expiration of the time of service of the members of the council, the said house shall nominate ten persons, qualified as aforesaid, and return their names to Congress, five of whom Congress shall appoint and commission to serve as members of the council five years, unless sooner removed. And the governor, legislative council, and house of representatives shall have authority to make laws in all cases for the good government of the district, not repugnant to the principles and articles in this ordinance established and declared. And all bills, having passed by a majority in the house and by a majority in the council, shall be referred to the governor for his assent; but no bill or legislative act whatever shall be of any force without his assent. The governor shall have power to convene, prorogue, and dissolve the general assembly when, in his opinion, it shall be expedient.

The governor, judges, legislative council, secretary, and such other officers as Congress shall appoint in the district shall take an oath or affirmation of fidelity and of office; the governor before the president of Congress, and all other officers before the governor. As soon as a legislature shall be formed in the district, the council and house, assembled in one room, shall have authority by joint ballot to elect a delegate to Congress who shall have a seat in Congress, with a right of debating, but not of voting, during this temporary government.

And for extending the fundamental principles of civil and religious liberty, which form the basis whereon these republics, their laws and constitutions, are erected; to fix and establish those principles as the basis of all laws, constitutions, and governments which forever hereafter shall be formed in the said territory; to provide also for the establishment of states, and permanent government therein, and for their admission to a share in the Federal councils on an equal footing with the original states, at as early periods as may be consistent with the general interest:

It is hereby ordained and declared by the authority aforesaid that the following articles shall be considered as articles of compact, between the original states and the people and states in the said territory, and forever remain unalterable, unless by common consent, to wit:

Article I
No person, demeaning himself in a peaceable and orderly manner, shall ever be molested on account of his mode of worship or religious sentiments in the said territory.

Article II
The inhabitants of the said territory shall always be entitled to the benefits of the writs of habeas corpus and of the trial by jury; of a proportionate representation of the people in the legislature and of judicial proceedings according to the course of the common law. All persons shall be bailable, unless for capital offenses, where the proof shall be evident or the presumption great. All fines shall be moderate; and no cruel or unusual punishments shall be inflicted. No man shall be deprived of his liberty or property, but by the judgment of his peers, or the law of the land, and should the public exigencies make it necessary for the common preservation to take any person's property, or to demand his particular services, full compensation shall be made for the same. And in the just preservation of rights and property, it is understood and declared that no law ought ever to be made or have force in the said territory that shall in any manner whatever interfere with or affect private contracts, or engagements, bona fide, and without fraud previously formed.

Article III
Religion, morality, and knowledge being necessary to good government and the happiness of mankind, schools and the means of education shall forever be encouraged. The utmost good faith shall always be observed towards the Indians; their lands and property shall never be taken from them without their consent; and in their property, rights, and liberty they never shall be invaded or disturbed, unless in just and lawful wars authorized by Congress; but laws founded in justice and humanity shall from time to time be made for preventing wrongs being done to them, and for preserving peace and friendship with them.

Article IV
The said territory, and the states which may be formed therein, shall forever remain a part of this confederacy of the United States of America, subject to the Articles of Confederation, and to such alterations therein as shall be constitutionally made; and to all the acts and ordinances of the United States in Congress assembled, conformable thereto. The inhabitants and settlers in the said territory shall be subject to pay a part of the Federal debts contracted or to be contracted, and a

proportional part of the expenses of government to be apportioned on them by Congress, according to the same common rule and measure by which apportionments thereof shall be made on the other states; and the taxes for paying their proportion shall be laid and levied by the authority and direction of the legislatures of the district, or districts, or new states, as in the original states, within the time agreed upon by the United States in Congress assembled. The legislatures of those districts, or new states, shall never interfere with the primary disposal of the soil by the United States in Congress assembled, nor with any regulations Congress may find necessary for securing the title in such soil to the bona fide purchasers. No tax shall be imposed on land the property of the United States; and in no case shall nonresident proprietors be taxed higher than residents. The navigable waters leading into the Mississippi and Saint Lawrence and the carrying places between the same shall be common highways and forever free, as well to the inhabitants of the said territory as to the citizens of the United States, and those of any other states that may be admitted into the confederacy, without any tax, impost, or duty therefore.

Article V

There shall be formed in the said territory not less than three nor more than five states; and the boundaries of the states, as soon as Virginia shall alter her act of cession and consent to the same, shall become fixed and established as follows, to wit: The western state in the said territory shall be bounded by the Mississippi, the Ohio, and the Wabash rivers; a direct line drawn from the Wabash and Post Vincents, due north to the territorial line between the United States and Canada; and by the said territorial line to the Lake of the Woods and Mississippi. The middle state shall be bounded by the said direct line, the Wabash from Post Vincents to the Ohio, by the Ohio, by a direct line drawn due north from the mouth of the Great Miami to the said territorial line, and by the said territorial line. The eastern state shall be bounded by the last-mentioned direct line, the Ohio, Pennsylvania, and the said territorial line: provided, however, and it is further understood and declared, that the boundaries of these three states shall be subject so far to be altered that, if Congress shall hereafter find it expedient, they shall have authority to form one or two states in that part of the said territory which lies north of an east and west line drawn through the southerly bend or extreme of Lake Michigan. And whenever any of the said states shall have sixty thousand free inhabitants therein, such state shall be admitted by its delegates into the Congress of the United States, on an equal footing with the original states in all respects whatever; and shall be at liberty to form a permanent constitution and state government: provided the constitution and government so to be formed shall be republican, and in conformity to the principles contained in these articles, and, so far as it can be consistent with the general interest of the confederacy, such admission shall be allowed at an earlier period, and when there may be a less number of free inhabitants in the state than sixty thousand.

Article VI

There shall be neither slavery nor involuntary servitude in the said territory, otherwise than in punishment of crimes, whereof the party shall have been duly convicted: provided always that any person escaping into the same, from whom labor or service is lawfully claimed in any one of the original states, such fugitive may be lawfully reclaimed and conveyed to the person claiming his or her labor or service as aforesaid.

Be it ordained by the authority aforesaid that the resolutions of the 23d of April, 1784, relative to the subject of this ordinance, be, and the same are hereby, repealed and declared null and void.

Done by the United States, in Congress assembled, the 13th day of July, in the year of our Lord one thousand seven hundred and eighty-seven, and of their sovereignty and independence the twelfth.

THE VIRGINIA, OR RANDOLPH, PLAN

[Virginia Governor Edmund Randolph] then commented on the difficulty of the crisis, and the necessity of preventing the fulfillment of the prophecies of the American downfall.

He observed that in revising the federal system we ought to inquire 1. into the properties, which such a government ought to possess, 2. the defects of the confederation, 3. the danger of our situation & 4. the remedy.

1. The Character of such a government ought to secure 1. against foreign invasion: 2. against dissensions between members of the Union, or seditions in particular states: 3. to procure to the several States various blessings, of which an isolated situation was incapable: 4. to be able to defend itself against incroachment: & 5. to be paramount to the state constitutions.

* * *

He then proceeded to enumerate the defects: 1. that the confederation produced no security against foreign invasion; congress not being permitted to prevent a war nor to support it by their own authority—Of this he cited many examples; most of which tended to shew, that they could not cause infractions of treaties or of the law of nations, to be punished: that particular states might by their conduct provoke war without controul; and that neither militia nor draughts being fit for defence on such occasions, inlistments only could be successful, and these could not be executed without money. 2. that the foederal government could not check the quarrels between states, nor a rebellion in any, not having constitutional power nor means to interpose according to the exigency:

3. that there were many advantages, which the U.S. might acquire, which were not attainable under the confederation—such as a productive impost—counteraction of the commercial regulations of other nations—pushing of commerce ad libitum—etc.etc.

4. that the foederal government could not defend itself against the incroachments from the states.

5. that it was not even paramount to the state constitutions, ratified, as it was in ma[n]y of the states.

3. He next reviewed the danger of our situation, appealed to the sense of the best friends of the U.S.—the prospect of anarchy from the laxity of government every where; and to other considerations.

4. He then proceeded to the remedy; the basis of which he said must be the republican principle.

He proposed as conformable to his ideas the following resolutions, which he explained one by one. . . .

1. Resolved that the Articles of Confederation ought to be so corrected & enlarged as to accomplish the objects proposed by their institution; namely, "common defence, security of liberty, and general welfare."

2. Resolved therefore that the rights of suffrage in the National Legislature ought to be proportioned to the Quotas of contribution, or to the number of free inhabitants, as the one or the other rule may seem best in different cases.

3. Resolved that the National Legislature ought to consist of two branches.

4. Resolved that the members of the first branch of the National Legislature ought to be elected by the people of the several States every   for the term of   [.]

* * *

5. Resolved that the members of the second branch of the National Legislature ought to be elected by those of the first, out of a proper number of persons nominated by the individual Legislatures[.]

* * *

6. Resolved that each branch ought to possess the right of originating Acts; that the National Legislature ought to be empowered to enjoy the Legislative Rights vested in Congress by the Confederation & moreover to legislate in all cases to which the separate States are incompetent, or in which the harmony of the United States may be interrupted by the exercise of individual Legislation; to negative all laws passed by the several States, contravening in the opinion of the National Legislature the articles of Union; and to call forth the force of the Union against any member of the Union failing to fulfill its duty under the articles thereof.

7. Resolved that a National Executive be instituted; to be chosen by the National Legislature for the term of   years, to receive punctually at stated times, a fixed compensation for the services rendered, in which no increase or diminution shall be made so as to affect the Magistracy, existing at the time of increase or diminution, and to be ineligible a second time; and that besides a general authority to execute the National laws, it ought to enjoy the Executive rights vested in Congress by the Confederation.

8. Resolved that the Executive and a convenient number of the National Judiciary, ought to compose a Council of revision with authority to examine every act of the National Legislature before it shall operate, & every act of a particular Legislature before a Negative thereon shall be final; and that the dissent of the said Council shall amount to a rejection, unless the Act of the National Legislature be again passed, or that of a particular Legislature be again negatived by   of the members of each branch.

9. Resolved that a National Judiciary be established to consist of one or more supreme tribunals, and of inferior tribunals to be chosen by the National Legislature, to hold their offices during good behaviour; and to receive punctually at stated times fixed compensation for their services, in which no increase or diminution shall be made so as to affect the persons actually in office at the time of such increase or diminution; that the jurisdiction of the inferior tribunals shall be to hear & determine in the first instance, and of the supreme tribunal to hear and determine in the dernier resort, all piracies & felonies on the high seas, captures from an enemy, cases in which foreigners or citizens of other States applying to such jurisdictions may be interested, or which respect the collection of the National revenue; impeachments of any National officers, and questions which may involve the national peace and harmony.

* * *

Mr. Wilson. He wished for vigor in the Government, but he wished that vigorous authority to flow immediately from the legitimate source of all authority. The Government ought to possess not only first the force, but secondly the mind or sense of the people at large. The Legislature ought to be the most exact transcript of the whole Society. Representation is made necessary only because it is impossible for the people to act collectively. The opposition was to be expected he said from the Governments, not from the Citizens of the States. The latter had parted as was observed (by Mr. King) with all the necessary powers; and it was immaterial to them, by whom they were exercised, if well exercised. The State officers were to be the losers of power. The people he supposed would be rather more attached to the national Government than to the State Governments as being more important in itself, and more flattering to their pride. There is no danger of improper elections if made by large districts. Bad elections proceed from the smallness of the districts which give an opportunity to bad men to intrigue themselves into office.

* * *

Colonel Mason. Under the existing Confederacy, Congress represent the States not the people of the States; their acts operate on the States, not on the individuals. The case will be changed in the new plan of Government. The people will be represented; they ought therefore to choose the Representatives. The requisites in actual representation are that the Representatives should sympathize with their constituents; should think as they think, & feel as they feel; and that for these purposes should even be residents among them. Much he said had been alleged against democratic elections. He admitted that much might be said; but it was to be considered that no Government was free from imperfections & evils; and that improper elections in many instances, were inseparable from Republican Governments. But compare these with the advantage of this Form in favor of the rights of the people, in favor of human nature. He was persuaded there was a better chance for proper elections by the people, if divided into large districts, than by the State Legislatures.

THE NEW JERSEY, OR PATERSON, PLAN

Mr. Paterson, said as he had on a former occasion given his sentiments on the plan proposed by Mr. Randolph he would now avoiding repetition as much as possible give his reasons in favor of that proposed by himself. He preferred it because it accorded 1. with the powers of the Convention, 2. with the sentiments of the people. If the confederacy was radically wrong, let us return to our States, and obtain larger powers, not assume them of ourselves.

* * *

. . . If the sovereignty of the States is to be maintained, the Representatives must be drawn immediately from the States, not from the people: and we have no power to vary the idea of equal sovereignty. The only expedient that will cure the difficulty, is that of throwing the States into Hotchpot.

* * *

Mr. Wilson entered into a contrast of the principal points of the two plans so far he said as there had been time to examine the one last proposed. These points were 1. in the Virginia plan there are two & in some degree three branches in the Legislature: in the plan from N.J. there is to be a single legislature only—2. Representation of the people at large is the basis of the one:—the State Legislatures, the pillars of the other—3. proportional representation prevails in one:—equality of suffrage in the other—4. A single Executive Magistrate is at the head of the one:—a plurality is held out in the other.—5. in the one the majority of the people of the U.S. must prevail:—in the other a minority may prevail. 6. the National Legislature is to make laws in all cases to which the separate States are incompetent &—:—in place of this Congress are to have additional power in a few cases only—7. A negative on the laws of the States:—in place of this coertion to be substituted—8. The Executive to be removable on impeachment & conviction;—in one plan: in the other to be removeable at the instance of majority of the Executives of the States—9. Revision of the laws provided for in one:—no such check in the other—10. inferior national tribunals in one:—none such in the other. 11. In the one jurisdiction of National tribunals to extend etc.—; an appellate jurisdiction only allowed in the other. 12. Here the jurisdiction is to extend to all cases affecting the National peace & harmony: there, a few cases only are marked out. 13. finally the ratification is in this way to be by the people themselves:—in that by the legislative authorities according to the thirteenth article of Confederation.

CONSTITUTION OF THE UNITED STATES

We the People of the United States, in Order to form a more perfect Union, establish Justice, insure domestic Tranquility, provide for the common defence, promote the general Welfare, and secure the Blessings of Liberty to ourselves and our Posterity, do ordain and establish this Constitution for the United States of America.

Article I

Section 1. All legislative Powers herein granted shall be vested in a Congress of the United States, which shall consist of a Senate and House of Representatives.

Section 2. The House of Representatives shall be composed of Members chosen every second Year by the People of the several States, and the Electors in each State shall have the Qualifications requisite for Electors of the most numerous Branch of the State Legislature.

No Person shall be a Representative who shall not have attained to the Age of twenty five Years, and been seven Years a Citizen of the United States, and who shall not, when elected, be an Inhabitant of that State in which he shall be chosen.

Representatives *and direct Taxes* shall be apportioned among the several States which may be included within this Union, according to their respective Numbers, *which shall be determined by adding to the whole Number of free Persons, including those bound to Service for a Term of Years, and excluding Indians not taxed, three fifths of all other Persons.*[1] The actual Enumeration shall be made within three Years after the first Meeting of the Congress of the United States, and within every subsequent Term of ten Years, in such Manner as they shall by Law direct. The Number of Representatives shall not exceed one for every thirty Thousand, but each State shall have at Least one Representative; *and until such enumerations shall be made, the State of New Hampshire shall be entitled to chuse three, Massachusetts eight, Rhode-Island and Providence Plantations one, Connecticut five, New-York six, New Jersey four, Pennsylvania eight, Delaware one, Maryland six, Virginia ten, North Carolina five, South Carolina five, and Georgia three.*

When vacancies happen in the Representation from any State, the Executive Authority thereof shall issue Writs of Election to fill such Vacancies.

Source: *The United States Government Manual.*

1. Provisions that have been changed by amendments or other legislation or have become obsolete have been printed in italic type. The Sixteenth Amendment overturned the provision on direct taxes. The provision on apportionment was overturned by the Thirteenth Amendment, which abolished slavery, and by the Fourteenth Amendment, which stipulated that all persons excluding Indians should be counted. Since 1940 Indians have also been counted.

The House of Representatives shall chuse their speaker and other Officers; and shall have the sole Power of Impeachment.

Section 3. The Senate of the United States shall be composed of two Senators from each State, *chosen by the Legislature thereof,*[2] for six Years; and each Senator shall have one Vote.

Immediately after they shall be assembled in Consequence of the first Election, they shall be divided as equally as may be into three Classes. The Seats of the Senators of the first Class shall be vacated at the Expiration of the second Year, of the second Class at the Expiration of the fourth Year, and of the third Class at the Expiration of the sixth Year, so that one third may be chosen every second Year; *and if Vacancies happen by Resignation, or otherwise, during the Recess of the Legislature of any State, the Executive thereof may make temporary Appointments until the next Meeting of the Legislature, which shall then fill such Vacancies.*[3]

No Person shall be a Senator who shall not have attained to the Age of thirty Years, and been nine Years a Citizen of the United States, and who shall not, when elected, be an Inhabitant of that State for which he shall be chosen.

The Vice President of the United States shall be President of the Senate, but shall have no Vote, unless they be equally divided.

The Senate shall chuse their other Officers, and also a President pro tempore, in the Absence of the Vice President, or when he shall exercise the Office of President of the United States.

The Senate shall have the sole Power to try all Impeachments. When sitting for that Purpose, they shall be on Oath or Affirmation. When the President of the United States is tried, the Chief Justice shall preside: And no Person shall be convicted without the concurrence of two thirds of the Members present. Judgment in Cases of Impeachment shall not extend further than to removal from Office, and disqualification to hold and enjoy any Office of honor, Trust or Profit under the United States: but the Party convicted shall nevertheless be liable and subject to Indictment, Trial, Judgment and Punishment, according to law.

Section 4. The Times, Places and Manner of holding Elections for Senators and Representatives, shall be prescribed in each State by the Legislature thereof; but the Congress may at any time by Law make or alter such Regulations, except as to the Places of chusing Senators.

The Congress shall assemble at least once in every Year, *and such Meeting shall be on the first Monday in December,*[4] unless they shall by Law appoint a different Day.

Section 5. Each House shall be the Judge of the Elections, Returns and Qualifications of its own Members, and a Majority of each shall constitute a Quorum to do business; but a smaller Number may adjourn from day to day, and may be authorized to compel the Attendance of absent Members, in such Manner, and under such Penalties as each House may provide.

Each House may determine the Rules of its Proceedings, punish its Members for disorderly Behaviour, and, with the Concurrence of two thirds, expel a Member.

Each House shall keep a journal of its Proceedings, and from time to time publish the same, excepting such Parts as may in their Judgment require Secrecy; and the yeas and Nays of the Members of either House on any question shall, at the Desire of one fifth of those Present, be entered on the Journal.

Neither House, during the Session of Congress, shall, without the Consent of the other, adjourn for more than three days, nor to any other place than that in which the two Houses shall be sitting.

Section 6. The Senators and Representatives shall receive a Compensation for their Services, to be ascertained by Law, and paid out of the Treasury of the United States. They shall in all Cases, except Treason, Felony and Breach of the Peace, be privileged from Arrest during their Attendance at the

---

2. Changed by the Seventeenth Amendment.
3. Modified by the Seventeenth Amendment.
4. Changed by the Twentieth Amendment, Section 2, to January 3.

Session of their respective Houses, and in going to and returning from the same; and for any Speech or Debate in either House, they shall not be questioned in any other Place.

No Senator or Representative shall, during the Time for which he was elected, be appointed to any civil Office under the Authority of the United States, which shall have been created, or the Emoluments whereof shall have been encreased during such time; and no Person holding any Office under the United States, shall be a Member of either House during his Continuance in Office.

Section 7. All Bills for raising Revenue shall originate in the House of Representatives; but the Senate may propose or concur with Amendments as on other Bills.

Every Bill which shall have passed the House of Representatives and the Senate, shall, before it become a Law, be presented to the President of the United States; If he approve he shall sign it, but if not he shall return it, with his Objections to that House in which it shall have originated, who shall enter the Objections at large on their Journal, and proceed to reconsider it. If after such Reconsideration two thirds of that House shall agree to pass the Bill, it shall be sent, together with the Objections, to the other House, by which it shall likewise be reconsidered, and if approved by two thirds of that House, it shall become a Law. But in all such Cases the Votes of both Houses shall be determined by yeas and Nays, and the Names of the Persons voting for and against the Bill shall be entered on the Journal of each House respectively. If any Bill shall not be returned by the President within ten Days (Sundays excepted) after it shall have been presented to him, the Same shall be a Law, in like Manner as if he had signed it, unless the Congress by their Adjournment prevent its Return, in which Case it shall not be a Law.

Every Order, Resolution, or Vote to which the Concurrence of the Senate and House of Representatives may be necessary (except on a question of Adjournment) shall be presented to the President of the United States; and before the Same shall take Effect, shall be approved by him, or being disapproved by him, shall be repassed by two thirds of the Senate and House of Representatives, according to the Rules and Limitations prescribed in the Case of a Bill.

Section 8. The Congress shall have Power To lay and collect Taxes, Duties, Imposts and Excises, to pay the Debts and provide for the common Defence and general Welfare of the United States; but all duties, Imposts and Excises shall be uniform throughout the United States;

To borrow Money on the Credit of the United States;

To regulate Commerce with foreign Nations, and among the several States, *and with the Indian Tribes;*[5]

To establish an uniform Rule of Naturalization, and uniform Laws on the subject of Bankruptcies throughout the United States;

To coin Money, regulate the Value thereof, and of foreign Coin, and fix the Standard of Weights and Measures;

To provide for the Punishment of counterfeiting the Securities and current Coin of the United States;

To establish Post Offices and post Roads;

To promote the Progress of Science and useful Arts, by securing for limited Times to Authors and Inventors exclusive Right to their respective Writings and Discoveries;

To constitute Tribunals inferior to the supreme Court;

To define and punish Piracies and Felonies committed on the high Seas, and Offences against the Law of Nations;

To declare War, *grant Letters of Marque and Reprisal,*[6] and make rules concerning Captures on Land and Water;

To raise and support Armies, but no Appropriation of Money to that Use shall be for a longer Term than two Years;

To provide and maintain a Navy;

To make rules for the Government and Regulation of the land and naval Forces;

---

5. Formal treaty arrangements with the Indians were abandoned after 1871.

6. The Declaration of Paris in 1856 and other treaties have outlawed letters of marque and reprisal.

To provide for calling forth the Militia to execute the Laws of the Union, suppress Insurrections and repel Invasions;

To provide for organizing, arming, and disciplining, the Militia, and for governing such Part of them as may be employed in the Service of the United States, reserving to the States respectively, the Appointment of the Officers, and the Authority of training the Militia according to the discipline prescribed by Congress;

To exercise exclusive Legislation in all Cases whatsoever, over such District (not exceeding ten Miles square), as may, by Cession of particular States, and the Acceptance of Congress, become the Seat of the Government of the United States,[7] and to exercise like Authority over all Places purchased by the Consent of the Legislature of the State in which the Same shall be for the Erection of Forts, Magazines, Arsenals, dock-Yards, and other needful Buildings;—And

To make all Laws which shall be necessary and proper for carrying into Execution the foregoing Powers, and all other Powers vested by this Constitution in the Government of the United States, or in any Department or Officer thereof.

Section 9. The Migration or Importation of such Persons as any of the States now existing shall think proper to admit, shall not be prohibited by the Congress prior to the Year one thousand eight hundred and eight, but a Tax or duty may be imposed on such Importation, not exceeding ten dollars for each Person.

The Privilege of the Writ of Habeas Corpus shall not be suspended, unless when in Cases of Rebellion or Invasion the public Safety may require it.

No Bill of Attainder or ex post facto Law shall be passed.

No Capitation, or other direct, Tax shall be laid, unless in Proportion to the Census or Enumeration herein before directed to be taken.[8]

No Tax or Duty shall be laid on Articles exported from any State.

No Preference shall be given by any Regulation of Commerce or Revenue to the Ports of one State over those of another: nor shall Vessels bound to, or from, one State, be obliged to enter, clear, or pay Duties in another.

No money shall be drawn from the Treasury, but in Consequence of Appropriations made by Law; and a regular Statement and Account of the Receipts and Expenditures of all public Money shall be published from time to time.

No Title of Nobility shall be granted by the United States: And no Person holding any Office of Profit or Trust under them, shall, without the Consent of the Congress, accept of any present, Emolument, Office, or Title, of any kind whatever, from any King, Prince, or foreign State.

Section 10. No State shall enter into any Treaty, Alliance, or Confederation; grant Letters of Marque and Reprisal; coin Money; emit Bills of Credit; make any Thing but gold and silver Coin a Tender in Payment of Debts; pass any Bill of Attainder, ex post facto Law, or Law impairing the Obligation of Contracts, or grant any Title of Nobility.

No State shall, without the Consent of the Congress, lay any Imposts or Duties on Imports or Exports, except what may be absolutely necessary for executing its inspection Laws: and the net Produce of all Duties and Imposts, laid by any State on Imports or Exports, shall be for the Use of the Treasury of the United States; and all such Laws shall be subject to the Revision and Controul of the Congress.

No State shall, without the Consent of Congress, lay any Duty of Tonnage, keep Troops, or Ships of War in time of Peace, enter into any Agreement or Compact with another State, or with a foreign Power, or engage in War, unless actually invaded, or in such imminent Danger as will not admit of delay.

Article II

Section 1. The executive Power shall be vested in a President of the United States of America. He shall hold his Office during the Term of four Years, and, together with the Vice President, chosen for the same term, be elected, as follows

---

7. Modified by the District of Columbia Home Rule Act of 1973.

8. Changed by the Sixteenth Amendment which permits a Federal income tax, and the Twenty-fourth Amendment, which prohibits Federal pollution.

Each State shall appoint, in such Manner as the Legislature thereof may direct, a Number of Electors, equal to the whole Number of Senators and Representatives to which the State may be entitled in the Congress: but no Senator or Representative, or Person holding an Office of Trust or Profit under the United States, shall be appointed an Elector.

The Electors shall meet in their respective States, and vote by Ballot for two Persons, of whom one at least shall not be an Inhabitant of the same State with themselves. And they shall make a List of all the Persons voted for, and of the Number of Votes for each; which List they shall sign and certify, and transmit sealed to the Seat of the Government of the United States, directed to the President of the Senate. The President of the Senate shall, in the Presence of the Senate and House of Representatives, open all the Certificates, and the Votes shall then be counted. The Person having the greatest Number of Votes shall be the President, if such Number be a Majority of the whole Number of Electors appointed; and if there be more than one who have such Majority, and have an equal Number of Votes, then the House of Representatives shall immediately chuse by Ballot one of them for President; and if no Person have a Majority, then from the five highest on the List the said House shall in like Manner chuse the President. But in chusing the President, the Votes shall be taken by States, the Representation from each State having one Vote; A quorum for this Purpose shall consist of a Member or Members from two thirds of the States, and a Majority of all the States shall be necessary to a Choice. In every Case, after the Choice of the President, the Person having the greatest Number of Votes of the Electors shall be the Vice President. But if there should remain two or more who have equal Votes, the Senate shall chuse from them by Ballot the Vice President.[9]

The Congress may determine the Time of chusing the Electors, and the Day on which they shall give their Votes; which Day shall be the same throughout the United States.

No Person except a natural born Citizen, *or a Citizen of the United States, at the time of the Adoption of this Constitution,* shall be eligible to the Office of President; neither shall any Person be eligible to that Office who shall not have attained to the Age of thirty five Years, and been fourteen Years a Resident within the United States.

In Case of the Removal of the President from Office, or of his Death, Resignation, or Inability to discharge the Powers and Duties of the said Office, the Same shall devolve on the Vice President, *and the Congress may by Law provide for the Case of Removal, Death, Resignation or Inability, both of the President and Vice President, declaring what Officer shall then act as President, and such Officer shall act accordingly, until the Disability be removed, or a President shall be elected.*[10]

The President shall, at stated Times, receive for his Services, a Compensation, which shall neither be encreased nor diminished during the Period for which he shall have been elected, and he shall not receive within that Period any other Emolument from the United States, or any of them.

Before he enter on the Execution of his Office, he shall take the following Oath or Affirmation:—"I do solemnly swear (or affirm) that I will faithfully execute the Office of President of the United States, and will to the best of my Ability, preserve, protect and defend the Constitution of the United States."

Section 2. The President shall be Commander in Chief of the Army and Navy of the United States, and of the Militia of the several States, when called into the actual Service of the United States; he may require the Opinion, in writing, of the principal Officer in each of the executive Departments, upon any Subject relating to the Duties of their respective Offices, and he shall have Power to grant Reprieves and Pardons for Offences against the United States, except in Cases of Impeachment.

He shall have Power, by and with the Advice and Consent of the Senate, to make Treaties, provided two thirds of the Senators present concur; and he shall nominate, and by and with the Advice and Consent of the Senate, shall appoint Ambassadors, other public Ministers and Consuls, Judges of the supreme Court, and all other Officers of the United States, whose Appointments are not herein otherwise provided for, and which shall be established by Law: but the Congress may by Law vest the Appointment of such inferior Officers, as they think proper, in the President alone, in the Courts of Law, or in the Heads of Departments.

The President shall have Power to fill up all Vacancies that may happen during the Recess of the Senate, by granting Commissions which shall expire at the End of their next Session.

---

9. Modified by the Twelfth and Twenty-third Amendments.

10. Clarified by the Presidential Succession Act of 1947 and by the Twenty-fifth Amendment.

Section 3. He shall from time to time give to the Congress Information of the State of the Union, and recommend to their Consideration such Measures as he shall judge necessary and expedient; he may, on extraordinary Occasions, convene both Houses, or either of them, and in Case of Disagreement between them, with Respect to the Time of Adjournment, he may adjourn them to such Time as he shall think proper; he shall receive Ambassadors and other public Ministers; he shall take Care that the Laws be faithfully executed, and shall Commission all the Officers of the United States.

Section 4. The President, Vice President and all civil Officers of the United States, shall be removed from Office on Impeachment for, and Conviction of, Treason, Bribery, or other High Crimes and Misdemeanors.

Article III

Section 1. The judicial Power of the United States, shall be vested in one supreme Court, and in such inferior Courts as the Congress may from time to time ordain and establish. The Judges, both of the supreme and inferior Courts, shall hold their Offices during good Behaviour, and shall, at stated Times, receive for their Services, a Compensation, which shall not be diminished during their Continuance in Office.

Section 2. The judicial Power shall extend to all Cases, in Law and Equity, arising under this Constitution, the Laws of the United States, and Treaties made, or which shall be made, under their Authority;—to all Cases affecting Ambassadors, other public Ministers and Consuls;—to all Cases of admiralty and maritime Jurisdiction;—to Controversies to which the United States shall be a Party;— to Controversies between two or more States; *between a State and Citizens of another State;*[11]— between Citizens of different States;—between Citizens of the same State claiming Lands under Grants of different States, and between a State, or the Citizens thereof, and foreign States, Citizens or Subjects.

In all Cases affecting Ambassadors, other public Ministers and Consuls, and those in which a State shall be Party, the supreme Court shall have original Jurisdiction. In all the other Cases before mentioned, the supreme Court shall have appellate Jurisdiction, both as to Law and Fact, with such Exceptions, and under such Regulations as the Congress shall make.

The Trial of all Crimes, except in Cases of Impeachment, shall be by Jury; and such Trial shall be held in the State where the said Crimes shall have been committed; but when not committed within any State, the Trial shall be at such Place or Places as the Congress may by Law have directed.

Section 3. Treason against the United States, shall consist only in levying War against them, or in adhering to their Enemies, giving them Aid and Comfort. No Person shall be convicted of Treason unless on the Testimony of two Witnesses to the same overt Act, or on Confession in open Court.

The Congress shall have Power to declare the Punishment of Treason, but no Attainder of Treason shall work Corruption of Blood, or Forfeiture except during the Life of the Person attainted.

Article IV

Section 1. Full Faith and Credit shall be given in each State to the public Acts, Records, and judicial Proceedings of every other State. And the Congress may by general Laws prescribe the Manner in which such Acts, Records, and Proceedings shall be proved, and the Effect thereof.

Section 2. The Citizens of each State shall be entitled to all Privileges and Immunities of Citizens in the several States.

A Person charged in any State with Treason, Felony, or other Crime, who shall flee from Justice, and be found in another State, shall on Demand of the executive Authority of the State from which he fled, be delivered up, to be removed to the State having Jurisdiction of the Crime.

---

11. Changed by the Eleventh Amendment.

No person held to Service or Labour in one State, under the Laws thereof, escaping into another, shall, in Consequence of any Law or Regulation therein, be discharged from such Service of Labour, but shall be delivered up on Claim of the Party to whom such Service or Labour may be due.[12]

Section 3. New States may be admitted by the Congress into this Union; but no new State shall be formed or erected within the Jurisdiction of any other State; nor any State be formed by the Junction of two or more States, or Parts of States, without the Consent of the Legislatures of the States concerned as well as of the Congress.

The Congress shall have Power to dispose of and make all needful Rules and Regulations respecting the Territory or other Property belonging to the United States; and nothing in this Constitution shall be so construed as to Prejudice any Claims of the United States, or of any particular State.

Section 4. The United States shall guarantee to every State in this Union a Republican Form of Government, and shall protect each of them against Invasion; and on Application of the Legislature, or of the Executive (when Legislature cannot be convened) against domestic Violence.

Article V

The Congress, whenever two thirds of both Houses shall deem it necessary, shall propose Amendments to this Constitution, or, on the Application of the Legislatures of two thirds of the several States, shall call a Convention for proposing Amendments, which, in either Case, shall be valid to all Intents and Purposes, as Part of this Constitution, when ratified by the Legislatures of three fourths of the several States, or by Conventions in three fourths thereof, as the one or the other Mode of Ratification may be proposed by the Congress; Provided *that no Amendment which may be made prior to the Year One thousand eight hundred and eight shall in any Manner affect the first and fourth Clauses in the Ninth Section of the first Article; and* that no State, without its Consent, shall be deprived of its equal Suffrage in the Senate.

Article VI

All Debts contracted and Engagements entered into, before the Adoption of this Constitution, shall be as valid against the United States under this Constitution, as under the Confederation.

This Constitution, and the Laws of the United States which shall be made in Pursuance thereof; and all Treaties made, or which shall be made, under the Authority of the United States, shall be the supreme Law of the Land; and the Judges in every State shall be bound thereby, any Thing in the Constitution or Laws of any State to the Contrary notwithstanding.

The Senators and Representatives before mentioned, and the Members of the several State Legislatures, and all executive and judicial Officers, both of the United States and of the several States, shall be bound by Oath or Affirmation, to support this Constitution; but no religious Test shall ever be required as a Qualification to any Office or public Trust under the United States.

Article VII

The Ratification of the Conventions of nine States, shall be sufficient for the Establishment of this Constitution between the States so ratifying the Same.

Done in Convention by the Unanimous Consent of the States present the Seventeenth Day of September in the Year of our Lord one thousand seven hundred and Eighty seven and of the Independence of the United States of America the Twelfth In witness whereof We have hereunto subscribed our Names,

G° Washington—Presid[t]
and deputy from Virginia

New Hampshire   John Langdon
                  Nicholas Gilman

———

12. Made obsolete by the Thirteenth Amendment.

Massachusetts	Nathaniel Gorham
	Rufus King
Connecticut	Wm Saml Johnson
	Roger Sherman
New York	Alexander Hamilton
New Jersey	Wil: Livingston
	David Brearley.
	Wm Paterson.
	Jona: Dayton
Pennsylvania	B Franklin
	Thomas Mifflin
	Robt Morris
	Geo. Clymer
	Thos. FitzSimons
	Jared Ingersoll
	James Wilson
	Gouv Morris
Delaware	Geo: Read
	Gunning Bedford jun
	John Dickinson
	Richard Bassett
	Jaco: Broom
Maryland	James McHenry
	Dan of St Thos. Jenifer
	Danl Carroll
Virginia	John Blair—
	James Madison Jr.
North Carolina	Wm Blount
	Richd Dobbs Spaight.
	Hu Williamson
South Carolina	J. Rutledge
	Charles Cotesworth Pinckney
	Charles Pinckney
	Pierce Butler.
Georgia	William Few
	Abr Baldwin

Amendments

(The first ten amendments were ratified December 15, 1791,
and form what is known as the "Bill of Rights.")

Amendment 1

Congress shall make no law respecting an establishment of religion, or prohibiting the free exercise thereof; or abridging the freedom of speech, or of the press; or the right of the people peaceably to assemble, and to petition the Government for a redress of grievances.

Amendment 2

A well regulated Militia, being necessary to the security of a free State, the right of the people to keep and bear Arms, shall not be infringed.

Amendment 3

No Soldier shall, in time of peace be quartered in any house, without the consent of the Owner, nor in time of war, but in a manner to be prescribed by law.

Amendment 4

The right of the people to be secure in their persons, houses, papers, and effects, against unreasonable searches and seizures, shall not be violated, and no Warrants shall issue, but upon probable cause, supported by Oath or affirmation, and particularly describing the place to be searched, and the persons or things to be seized.

Amendment 5

No person shall be held to answer for a capital, or otherwise infamous crime, unless on a presentment or indictment of a Grand Jury, except in cases arising in the land or naval forces, or in the Militia, when in actual service in time of War or public danger; nor shall any person be subject for the same offence to be twice put in jeopardy of life or limb; nor shall be compelled in any criminal case to be a witness against himself, nor be deprived of life, liberty, or property, without due process of law; nor shall private property be taken for public use, without just compensation.

Amendment 6

In all criminal prosecutions, the accused shall enjoy the right to a speedy and public trial, by an impartial jury of the State and district wherein the crime shall have been committed, which district shall have been previously ascertained by law, and to be informed of the nature and cause of the accusation; to be confronted with the witnesses against him; to have compulsory process for obtaining witnesses in his favor, and to have the Assistance of Counsel for his defence.

Amendment 7

In Suits at common law, where the value in controversy shall exceed twenty dollars, the right of trial by jury shall be preserved, and no fact tried by a jury, shall be otherwise re-examined in any Court of the United States, than according to the rules of the common law.

Amendment 8

Excessive bail shall not be required, nor excessive fines imposed, nor cruel and unusual punishments inflicted.

Amendment 9

The enumeration in the Constitution, of certain rights, shall not be construed to deny or disparage others retained by the people.

Amendment 10

The powers not delegated to the United States by the Constitution, nor prohibited by it to the States, are reserved to the States respectively, or to the people.

Amendment 11
(Ratified February 7, 1795)

The Judicial power of the United States shall not be construed to extend to any suit in law or equity, commenced or prosecuted against one of the United States by Citizens of another State, or by Citizens or Subjects of any Foreign State.

Amendment 12
(Ratified July 27, 1804)

The Electors shall meet in their respective states and vote by ballot for President and Vice-President, one of whom, at least, shall not be an inhabitant of the same state with themselves; they shall name in their ballots the person voted for as President, and in distinct ballots the person voted for as Vice-President, and they shall make distinct lists of all persons voted for as President, and of all persons voted for as Vice-President, and of the number of votes for each, which lists they shall sign and certify, and transmit sealed to the seat of the government of the United States, directed to the President of the Senate;—The President of the Senate shall, in the presence of the Senate and House of Representatives, open all the certificates and the votes shall then be counted;—The person having the greatest number of votes for President, shall be the President, if such number be a majority of the whole number of Electors appointed; and if no person have such majority, then from the persons having the highest numbers not exceeding three on the list of those voted for as President, the House of Representatives shall choose immediately, by ballot, the President. But in choosing the President, the votes shall be taken by states, the representation from each state having one vote; a quorum for this purpose shall consist of a member or members from two-thirds of the states, and a majority of all the states shall be necessary to a choice. And if the House of Representatives shall not choose a President whenever the right of choice shall devolve upon them, before the fourth day of March next following, then the Vice-President shall act as President, as in the case of the death or other constitutional disability of the President.—The person having the greatest number of votes as Vice-President, shall be the Vice-President, if such number be a majority of the whole number of Electors appointed, and if no person have a majority, then from the two highest numbers on the list, the Senate shall choose the Vice-President; a quorum for the purpose shall consist of two-thirds of the whole number of Senators, and a majority of the whole number shall be necessary to a choice. But no person constitutionally ineligible to the office of President shall be eligible to that of Vice-President of the United States.

Amendment 13
(Ratified December 6, 1865)

Section 1. Neither slavery nor involuntary servitude, except as a punishment for crime whereof the party shall have been duly convicted, shall exist within the United States, or any place subject to their jurisdiction.

Section 2. Congress shall have power to enforce this article by appropriate legislation.

Amendment 14
(Ratified July 9, 1868)

Section 1. All persons born or naturalized in the United States, and subject to the jurisdiction thereof, are citizens of the United States and of the State wherein they reside. No State shall make or enforce any law which shall abridge the privileges or immunities of citizens of the United States; nor shall any State deprive any person of life, liberty, or property, without due process of law; nor deny to any person within its jurisdiction the equal protection of the laws.

Section 2. Representatives shall be apportioned among the several States according to their respective numbers, counting the whole number of persons in each State, excluding Indians not taxed. But when the right to vote at any election for the choice of electors for President and Vice President of the United States, Representatives in Congress, the Executive and Judicial officers of a State, or the members of the Legislature thereof, is denied to any of the male inhabitants of such State, being twenty-one years of age, and citizens of the United States, or in any way abridged, except for participation in rebellion, or other crime, the basis of representation therein shall be reduced in the proportion which the number of such male citizens shall bear to the whole number of male citizens twenty-one years of age in such State.

Section 3. No person shall be a Senator or Representative in Congress, or elector of President and Vice President, or hold any office, civil or military, under the United States, or under any State, who, having previously taken an oath, as a member of Congress, or as an officer of the United States, or as a member of any State legislature, or as an executive or judicial officer of any State, to support the Constitution of the United States, shall have engaged in insurrection or rebellion against the same, or given aid or comfort to the enemies thereof. But Congress may by a vote of two-thirds of each House, remove such disability.

Section 4. The validity of the public debt of the United States, authorized by law, including debts incurred for payment of pensions and bounties for services in suppressing insurrection or rebellion, shall not be questioned. But neither the United States nor any State shall assume or pay any debt or obligation incurred in aid of insurrection or rebellion against the United States, or any claim for the loss or emancipation of any slave; but all such debts, obligations and claims shall be held illegal and void.

Section 5. The Congress shall have power to enforce, by appropriate legislation, the provisions of this article.

Amendment 15
(Ratified February 3, 1870)

Section 1. The right of citizens of the United States to vote shall not be denied or abridged by the United States or by any State on account of race, color, or previous condition of servitude.

Section 2. The Congress shall have power to enforce this article by appropriate legislation.

Amendment 16
(Ratified February 3, 1913)

The Congress shall have power to lay and collect taxes on incomes, from whatever source derived, without apportionment among the several States, and without regard to any census or enumeration.

Amendment 17
(Ratified April 8, 1913)

The Senate of the United States shall be composed of two Senators from each State, elected by the people thereof for six years; and each Senator shall have one vote. The electors in each State shall have the qualifications requisite for electors of the most numerous branch of the State legislatures.

When vacancies happen in the representation of any State in the Senate, the executive authority of such State shall issue writs of election to fill such vacancies: Provided, That the legislature of any State may empower the executive thereof to make temporary appointments until the people fill the vacancies by election as the legislature may direct.

This amendment shall not be so construed as to affect the election or term of any Senator chosen before it becomes valid as part of the Constitution.

Amendment 18
(Ratified January 16, 1919. Repealed December 5, 1933, by Amendment 21.)

Section 1. After one year from the ratification of this article the manufacture, sale, or transportation of intoxicating liquors within, the importation thereof into, or the exportation thereof from the United States and all territory subject to the jurisdiction thereof for beverage purposes is hereby prohibited.

Section 2. The Congress and the several States shall have concurrent power to enforce this article by appropriate legislation.

Section 3. This article shall be inoperative unless it shall have been ratified as an amendment to the Constitution by the legislatures of the several States as provided in the Constitution, within seven years from the date of the submission hereof to the States by the Congress.

Amendment 19
(Ratified August 18, 1920)

The right of citizens of the United States to vote shall not be denied or abridged by the United States or by any State on account of sex.

Congress shall have power to enforce this article by appropriate legislation.

Amendment 20
(Ratified January 23, 1933)

Section 1. The terms of the President and Vice President shall end at noon on the 20th day of January, and the terms of Senators and Representatives at noon on the 3d day of January, of the years in which such terms would have ended if this article had not been ratified; and the terms of their successors shall then begin.

Section 2. The Congress shall assemble at least once in every year, and such meeting shall begin at noon on the 3d day of January, unless they shall by law appoint a different day.

Section 3. If, at the time fixed for the beginning of the term of the President, the President elect shall have died, the Vice President elect shall become President. If a President shall not have been chosen before the time fixed for the beginning of his term, or if the President elect shall have failed to qualify, then the Vice President elect shall act as President until a President shall have qualified; and the Congress may by law provide for the case wherein neither a President elect nor a Vice President elect shall have qualified, declaring who shall then act as President, or the manner in which one who is to act shall be selected, and such person shall act accordingly until a President or Vice President shall have qualified.

Section 4. The Congress may by law provide for the case of the death of any of the persons from whom the House of Representatives may choose a President whenever the right of choice shall have devolved upon them, and for the case of the death of any of the persons from whom the Senate may choose a Vice President whenever the right of choice shall have devolved upon them.

Section 5. Sections 1 and 2 shall take effect on the 15th day of October following the ratification of this article.

Section 6. This article shall be inoperative unless it shall have been ratified as an amendment to the Constitution by the legislatures of three-fourths of the several States within seven years from the date of its submission.

Amendment 21
(Ratified December 5, 1933)

Section 1. The eighteenth article of amendment to the Constitution of the United States is hereby repealed.

Section 2. The transportation or importation into any State, Territory, or possession of the United States for delivery or use therein of intoxicating liquors, in violation of the laws thereof, is hereby prohibited.

Section 3. This article shall be inoperative unless it shall have been ratified as an amendment to the Constitution by conventions in the several States, as provided in the Constitution, within seven years from the date of the submission hereof to the States by the Congress.

Amendment 22
(Ratified February 27, 1951)

Section 1. No person shall be elected to the office of the President more than twice, and no person who has held the office of President, or acted as President, for more than two years of a term to which some other person was elected President shall be elected to the office of the President more than once. But this Article shall not apply to any person holding the office of President when this Article was proposed by the Congress, and shall not prevent any person who may be holding the office of President, or acting as President, during the term within which this Article becomes operative from holding the office of President or acting as President during the remainder of such term.

Section 2. This article shall be inoperative unless it shall have been ratified as an amendment to the Constitution by the legislatures of three-fourths of the several States within seven years from the date of its submission to the States by the Congress.

Amendment 23
(Ratified March 29, 1961)

Section 1. The District constituting the seat of Government of the United States shall appoint in such manner as the Congress may direct:

A number of electors of President and Vice President equal to the whole number of Senators and Representatives in Congress to which the District would be entitled if it were a State, but in no event more than the least populous State; they shall be in addition to those appointed by the States, but they shall be considered, for the purposes of the election of President and Vice President, to be electors appointed by a State; and they shall meet in the District and perform such duties as provided by the twelfth article of amendment.

Section 2. The Congress shall have power to enforce this article by appropriate legislation.

Amendment 24
(Ratified January 23, 1964)

Section 1. The right of citizens of the United States to vote in any primary or other election for President or Vice President, for electors for President or Vice President, or for Senator or Representative in Congress, shall not be denied or abridged by the United States or any State by reason of failure to pay any poll tax or other tax.

Section 2. The Congress shall have power to enforce this article by appropriate legislation.

Amendment 25
(Ratified February 10, 1967)

Section 1. In case of the removal of the President from office or of his death or resignation, the Vice President shall become President.

Section 2. Whenever there is a vacancy in the office of the Vice President, the President shall nominate a Vice President who shall take office upon confirmation by a majority vote of both Houses of Congress.

Section 3. Whenever the President transmits to the President pro tempore of the Senate and the Speaker of the House of Representatives his written declaration that he is unable to discharge the powers and duties of his office, and until he transmits to them a written declaration to the contrary, such powers and duties shall be discharged by the Vice President as Acting President.

Section 4. Whenever the Vice President and a majority of either the principal officers of the executive departments or of such other body as Congress may by law provide, transmit to the President pro tempore of the Senate and the Speaker of the House of Representatives their written declaration that the President is unable to discharge the powers and duties of his office, the Vice President shall immediately assume the powers and duties of the office as Acting President.

Thereafter, when the President transmits to the President pro tempore of the Senate and the Speaker of the House of Representatives his written declaration that no inability exists, he shall resume the powers and duties of his office unless the Vice President and a majority of either the principal officers of the executive department or of such other body as Congress may by law provide, transmit within four days to the President pro tempore of the Senate and the Speaker of the House of Representatives their written declaration that the President is unable to discharge the powers and duties of his office. Thereupon Congress shall decide the issue, assembling within forty-eight hours for that purpose if not in session. If the Congress, within twenty-one days after receipt of the latter written declaration, or, if Congress is not in session, within twenty-one days after Congress is required to assemble, determines by two-thirds vote of both Houses that the President is unable to discharge the powers and duties of his office, the Vice President shall continue to discharge the same as Acting President; otherwise, the President shall resume the powers and duties of his office.

Amendment 26
(Ratified July 1, 1971)

Section 1. The right of citizens of the United States, who are eighteen years of age or older, to vote shall not be denied or abridged by the United States or by any State on account of age.

Section 2. The Congress shall have the power to enforce this article by appropriate legislation.

Amendment 27

(Ratified May 7, 1992)

No law, varying the compensation for the services of the Senators and Representatives, shall take effect, until an election of Representatives shall have intervened.

BILL OF RIGHTS

Amendment 1

Congress shall make no law respecting an establishment of religion, or prohibiting the free exercise thereof; or abridging the freedom of speech, or of the press; or the right of the people peaceably to assemble, and to petition the Government for a redress of grievances.

Amendment 2

A well regulated Militia, being necessary to the security of a free State, the right of the people to keep and bear Arms, shall not be infringed.

Amendment 3

No Soldier shall, in time of peace be quartered in any house, without the consent of the Owner, nor in time of war, but in a manner to be prescribed by law.

Amendment 4

The right of the people to be secure in their persons, houses, papers, and effects, against unreasonable searches and seizures, shall not be violated, and no Warrants shall issue, but upon probable cause, supported by Oath or affirmation, and particularly describing the place to be searched, and the persons or things to be seized.

Amendment 5

No person shall be held to answer for a capital, or otherwise infamous crime, unless on a presentment or indictment of a Grand jury, except, in cases arising in the land or naval forces, or in the Militia, when in actual service in time of War or public danger; nor shall any person be subject for the same offence to be twice put in jeopardy of life or limb; nor shall be compelled in any criminal case to be a witness against himself, nor be deprived of life, liberty, or property, without due process of law; nor shall private property be taken for public use, without just compensation.

Amendment 6

In all criminal prosecutions, the accused shall enjoy the right to a speedy and public trial, by an impartial jury of the State and district wherein the crime shall have been committed, which district shall have been previously ascertained by law, and to be informed of the nature and cause of

---

Source: *The United States Government Manual.*

the accusation; to be confronted with the witnesses against him; to have compulsory process for obtaining Witnesses in his favor, and to have the Assistance of Counsel for his defence.

Amendment 7

In Suits at common law, where the value in controversy shall exceed twenty dollars, the right of trial by jury shall be preserved, and no fact tried by a jury, shall be otherwise reexamined in any Court of the United States, than according to the rules of the common law.

Amendment 8

Excessive bail shall not be required, nor excessive fines imposed, nor cruel and unusual punishments inflicted.

Amendment 9

The enumeration in the Constitution, of certain rights, shall not be construed to deny or disparage others retained by the people.

Amendment 10

The powers not delegated to the United States by the Constitution, nor prohibited by it to the States, are reserved to the States respectively, or to the people.

FEDERALIST, NUMBER 10

JAMES MADISON, 1787

Among the numerous advantages promised by a well constructed Union, none deserve to be more accurately developed than its tendency to break and control the violence of faction. The friend of popular governments, never finds himself so much alarmed for their character and fate, as when he contemplates their propensity to this dangerous vice. He will not fail therefore to set a due value on any plan which, without violating the principles to which he is attached, provides a proper cure to it. The instability, injustice and confusion introduced into the public councils, have in truth been the mortal diseases under which popular governments have every where perished; as they continue to be the favorite and fruitful topics from which the adversaries to liberty derive their most specious declamations. The valuable improvements made by the American Constitutions on the popular models, both ancient and modern, cannot certainly be too much admired; but it would be an unwarrantable partiality, to contend that they have as effectually obviated the danger on this side as was wished and expected. Complaints are every where heard from our most considerate and virtuous citizens, equally the friends of public and private faith, and of public and personal liberty; that our governments are too unstable; that the public good is disregarded in the conflicts of rival parties; and that measures are too often decided, not according to the rules of justice, and the rights of the minor party; but by the superior force of an interested and over-bearing majority. However anxiously we may wish that these complaints had no foundation, the evidence of known facts will not permit us to deny that they are in some degree true. It will be found indeed, on a candid review of our situation, that some of the distresses under which we labor, have been erroneously charged on the operation of our governments; but it will be found, at the same time, that other causes will not alone account for many of our heaviest misfortunes; and particularly, for the prevailing and increasing distrust of public engagements, and alarm for private rights, which are echoed from one end of the continent to the other. These must be chiefly, if not wholly, effects of the unsteadiness and injustice, with which a factious spirit has tainted our public administrations.

By a faction I understand a number of citizens, whether amounting to a majority or minority of the whole, who are united and actuated by some common impulse of passion, or of interest, adverse to the rights of other citizens, or to the permanent and aggregate interest of the community.

* * *

As long as the reason of man continues fallible, and he is at liberty to exercise it, different opinions will be formed. As long as the connection subsists between his reason and his self-love, his opinions and passions will have a reciprocal influence on each other; and the former will be objects to which the latter will attach themselves. The diversity in the faculties of men from which the rights of property originate, is not less an insuperable obstacle to a uniformity of interests. The protection of these faculties is the first object of Government. From the protection of different and unequal faculties of acquiring property, the possession of different degrees and kinds of property immediately results; and from the influence of these on the sentiments and views of the respective proprietors, ensues a division of the society into different interests and parties.

The latent causes of faction are thus sown in the nature of man; and we see them every where brought into different degrees of activity, according to the different circumstances of civil society. A zeal for different opinions concerning religion, concerning Government and many other points, as well of speculation as of practice; and attachment to different leaders ambitiously contending for pre-eminence and power; or to persons of other descriptions whose fortunes have been interesting to the human passions, have in turn divided mankind into parties, inflamed them with mutual animosity, and rendered them much more disposed to vex and oppress each other, than to co-operate for their common good. So strong is this propensity of mankind to fall into mutual animosities, that where no substantial occasion presents itself, the most frivolous and fanciful distinctions have been sufficient to kindle their unfriendly passions, and excite their most violent conflicts. But the most common and durable source of factions, has been the various and unequal distribution of property. Those who hold, and those who are without property, have ever formed distinct interests in society. Those who are creditors, and those who are debtors, fall under a like discrimination. A landed interest, a manufacturing interest, a mercantile interest, a monied interest, with many lesser interests, grow up of necessity in civilized nations, and divide them into different classes, actuated by different sentiments and views. The regulation of these various and interfering interests forms the principal task of modern Legislation, and involves the spirit of party and faction in the necessary and ordinary operations of Government.

* * *

The inference to which we are brought, is, that the causes of faction cannot be removed; and that relief is only to be sought in the means of controlling its effects.

If a faction consists of less than a majority, relief is supplied by the republican principle, which enables the majority to defeat its sinister views by regular vote: It may clog the administration, it may convulse the society; but it will be unable to execute and mask its violence under the forms of the Constitution. When a majority is included in a faction, the form of popular government on the other hand enables it to sacrifice to its ruling passion or interest, both the public good and the rights of other citizens. To secure the public good, and private rights, against the danger of such a faction, and at the same time to preserve the spirit and the form of popular government, is then the great object to which our enquiries are directed: Let me add that it is the great desideratum, by which alone this form of government can be rescued from the opprobrium under which it has so long labored, and be recommended to the esteem and adoption of mankind.

By what means is this object attainable? Evidently by one of two only. Either the existence of the same passion or interest in a majority at the same time, must be prevented; or the majority, having such co-existent passion or interest, must be rendered, by their number and local situation, unable to concert and carry into effect schemes of oppression. If the impulse and the opportunity be suffered to coincide, we well know that neither moral nor religious motives can be relied on as an adequate control. They are not found to be such on the injustice and violence of individuals, and lose their efficacy in proportion to the number combined together; that is, in proportion as their efficacy becomes needful.

From this view of the subject, it may be concluded, that a pure Democracy, by which I mean, a Society, consisting of a small number of citizens, who assemble and administer the Government in person, can admit of no cure for the mischiefs of faction. A common passion or interest will, in almost every case, be felt by a majority of the whole; a communication and concert results from the form of Government itself; and there is nothing to check the inducements to sacrifice the weaker party, or an obnoxious individual. Hence it is, that such Democracies have ever been spectacles of turbulence and contention; have ever been found incompatible with personal security, or the rights of property; and have in general been as short in their lives, as they have been violent in their deaths. Theoretic politicians, who have patronized this species of Government, have erroneously supposed, that by reducing mankind to a perfect equality in their political rights, they would, at the same time, be perfectly equalized and assimilated in their possessions, their opinions, and their passions.

A Republic, by which I mean a Government in which the scheme of representation takes place, opens a different prospect, and promises the cure for which we are seeking. Let us examine the points in which it varies from pure Democracy, and we shall comprehend both the nature of the cure, and the efficacy which it must derive from the Union.

The two great points of difference between a Democracy and a Republic are, first, the delegation of the Government, in the latter, to a small number of citizens elected by the rest: secondly, the greater number of citizens, and greater sphere of country, over which the latter may be extended.

The effect of the first difference is, on the one hand to refine and enlarge the public views, by passing them through the medium of a chosen body of citizens, whose wisdom may best discern the true interest of their country, and whose patriotism and love of justice, will be least likely to sacrifice it to temporary or partial considerations. Under such a regulation, it may well happen that the public voice pronounced by the representatives of the people, will be more consonant to the public good, than if pronounced by the people themselves convened for the purpose. On the other hand, the effect may be inverted. Men of factious tempers, of local prejudices, or of sinister designs, may by intrigue, by corruption or by other means, first obtain the suffrages, and then betray the interests of the people. The question resulting is, whether small or extensive Republics are most favorable to the election of proper guardians of the public weal: and it is clearly decided in favor of the latter by two obvious considerations.

In the first place it is to be remarked that however small the Republic may be, the Representatives must be raised to a certain number, in order to guard against the cabals of a few; and that however large it may be, they must be limited to a certain number, in order to guard against the confusion of a multitude. Hence the number of Representatives in the two cases, not being in proportion to that of the Constituents, and being proportionally greatest in the small Republic, it follows, that if the proportion of fit characters, be not less, in the large than in the small Republic, the former will present a greater option, and consequently a greater possibility of a fit choice.

In the next place, as each Representative will be chosen by a greater number of citizens in the large than in the small Republic, it will be more difficult for unworthy candidates to practise with success the vicious arts, by which elections are too often carried; and the suffrages of the people being more free, will be more likely to centre on men who possess the most attractive merit, and the most diffusive and established characters.

* * *

The other point of difference is, the greater number of citizens and extent of territory which may be brought within the compass of Republican, than of Democratic Government; and it is this circumstance principally which renders factious combinations less to be dreaded in the former, than in the latter. The smaller the society, the fewer probably will be the distinct parties and interests composing it; the fewer the distinct parties and interests, the more frequently will a majority be found of the same party; and the smaller the number of individuals composing a majority, and the smaller the compass within which they are placed, the more easily will they concert and execute their plans of oppression. Extend the sphere, and you take in a greater variety of parties and interests; you make it less probable that a majority of the whole will have a common motive to invade the rights of other citizens; or if such a common motive exists, it will be more difficult for all who feel it to discover their own strength, and to act in unison with each other.

FEDERALIST, NUMBER 78

ALEXANDER HAMILTON, 1788

According to the plan of the convention, all the judges who may be appointed by the United States are to hold their offices during good behaviour, which is conformable to the most approved of the state constitutions; and among the rest, to that of this state. Its propriety having been drawn into question by the adversaries of that plan, is no light symptom of the rage for objection which disorders their imaginations and judgments. The standard of good behaviour for the continuance in office of the judicial magistracy is certainly one of the most valuable of the modern improvements in the practice of government. In a monarchy it is an excellent barrier to the depotism of the prince: In a republic it is a no less excellent barrier to the encroachments and oppressions of the representative body. And it is the best expedient which can be devised in any government, to secure a steady, upright and impartial administration of the laws.

Whoever attentively considers the different departments of power must perceive, that in a government in which they are separated from each other, the judiciary, from the nature of its functions, will always be the least dangerous to the political rights of the constitution; because it will be least in a capacity to annoy or injure them. The executive not only dispenses the honors, but holds the sword of the community. The legislature not only commands the purse, but prescribes the rules by which the duties and rights of every citizen are to be regulated. The judiciary on the contrary has no influence over either the sword or the purse, no direction either of the strength or of the wealth of the society, and can take no active resolution whatever. It may truly be said to have neither Force nor Will, but merely judgment; and must ultimately depend upon the aid of the executive arm even for the efficacy of its judgments.

This simple view of the matter suggests several important consequences. It proves incontestibly that the judiciary is beyond comparison the weakest of the three departments of power; that it can never attack with success either of the other two; and that all possible care is requisite to enable it to defend itself against their attacks. It equally proves, that though individual oppression may now and then proceed from the courts of justice, the general liberty of the people can never be endangered from that quarter: I mean, so long as the judiciary remains truly distinct from both the legislative and executive. For I agree that "there is no liberty, if the power of judging be not separated from the legislative and executive powers." And it proves, in the last place, that as liberty can have nothing to fear from the judiciary alone, but would have everything to fear from its union with either of the other departments; that as all the effects of such an union must ensue from a dependence of the former on the latter, notwithstanding a nominal and apparent separation; that as from the natural feebleness of the judiciary, it is in continual jeopardy of being overpowered, awed or influenced by its coordinate branches; and that as nothing can contribute so much to its firmness and independence, as permanency in office, this quality may therefore be justly regarded as an indispensable ingredient in its constitution; and in a great measure as the citadel of the public justice and the public security.

The complete independence of the courts of justice is peculiarly essential in a limited constitution. By a limited constitution I understand one which contains certain specified exceptions to the legislative authority; such for instance as that it shall pass no bills of attainder, no ex post facto laws, and the like. Limitations of this kind can be preserved in practice no other way than through the medium of the courts of justice; whose duty it must be to declare all acts contrary to the manifest tenor of the constitution void. Without this, all the reservations of particular rights or privileges would amount to nothing.

Some perplexity respecting the right of the courts to pronounce legislative acts void, because contrary to the constitution, has arisen from an imagination that the doctrine would imply a superiority of the judiciary to the legislative power. It is urged that the authority which can declare the acts of another void, must necessarily be superior to the one whose acts may be declared void. As this doctrine is of great importance in all the American constitutions, a brief discussion of the grounds on which it rests cannot be unacceptable.

There is no position which depends on clearer principles, than that every act of a delegated authority, contrary to the tenor of the commission under which it is exercised, is void. No legislative act therefore contrary to the constitution can be valid. To deny this would be to affirm that the deputy is greater than his principal; that the servant is above his master; that the representatives of the people are superior to the people themselves; that men acting by virtue of powers may do not only what their powers do not authorise, but what they forbid.

If it be said that the legislative body are themselves the constitutional judges of their own powers, and that the construction they put upon them is conclusive upon the other departments, it may be answered, that this cannot be the natural presumption, where it is not to be collected from any particular provisions in the constitution. It is not otherwise to be supposed that the constitution could intend to enable the representatives of the people to substitute their will to that of their constituents. It is far more rational to suppose that the courts were designed to be an intermediate body between the people and the legislature, in order, among other things, to keep the latter within the limits assigned to their authority. The interpretation of the laws is the proper and peculiar province of the courts. A constitution is in fact, and must be, regarded by the judges as a fundamental law. It therefore belongs to them to ascertain its meaning as well as the meaning of any particular act proceeding from the legislative body. If there should happen to be an irreconcileable variance between the two, that which has the superior obligation and validity ought of course to be preferred; or in other words, the constitution ought to be preferred to the statute, the intention of the people to the intention of their agents.

Nor does this conclusion by any means suppose a superiority of the judicial to the legislative power. It only supposes that the power of the people is superior to both; and that where the will of the legislature declared in its statutes, stands in opposition to that of the people declared in the constitution, the judges ought to be governed by the latter, rather than the former. They ought to regulate their decisions by the fundamental laws, rather than by those which are not fundamental.

This exercise of judicial discretion in determining between two contradictory laws, is exemplified in a familiar instance. It not uncommonly happens, that there are two statutes existing at one time, clashing in whole or in part with each other, and neither of them containing any repealing clause or expression. In such a case, it is the province of the courts to liquidate and fix their meaning and operation; so far as they can by any fair construction be reconciled to each other; reason and law conspire to dictate that this should be done. Where this is impracticable, it becomes a matter of necessity to give effect to one, in exclusion of the other. The rule which has obtained in the courts for determining their relative validity is that the last in order of time shall be preferred to the first. But this is mere rule of construction, not derived from any positive law, but from the nature and reason of the thing. It is a rule not enjoined upon the courts by legislative provision, but adopted by themselves, as consonant to truth and propriety, for the direction of their conduct as interpreters of the law. They thought it reasonable, that between the interfering acts of an equal authority, that which was the last indication of its will, should have the preference.

But in regard to the interfering acts of a superior and subordinate authority, of an original and derivative power, the nature and reason of the thing indicate the converse of that rule as proper to be followed. They teach us that the prior act of a superior ought to be preferred to the subsequent act of an inferior and subordinate authority; and that, accordingly, whenever a particular statute contravenes the constitution, it will be the duty of the judicial tribunals to adhere to the latter, and disregard the former.

It can be of no weight to say, that the courts on the pretense of a repugnancy, may substitute their own pleasure to the constitutional intentions of the legislature. This might as well happen in the case of two contradictory statutes; or it might as well happen in every adjudication upon any single statute. The courts must declare the sense of the law; and if they should be disposed to exercise will instead of judgment, the consequence would equally be the substitution of their pleasure to that of the legislative body. The observation, if it proved anything, would prove that there ought to be no judges distinct from that body.

If then the courts of justice are to be considered as the bulwarks of a limited constitution against legislative encroachments, this consideration will afford a strong argument for the permanent tenure of judicial offices, since nothing will contribute so much as this to that independent spirit in the judges, which must be essential to the faithful performance of so arduous a duty.

This independence of the judges is equally requisite to guard the constitution and the rights of individuals from the effects of those ill humours which the arts of designing men, or the influence of particular conjunctures, sometimes disseminate among the people themselves, and which, though they speedily give place to better information and more deliberate reflection, have a tendency in the mean time to occasion dangerous innovations in the government, and serious oppressions of the minor party in the community. Though I trust the friends of the proposed constitution will never concur with its enemies in questioning that fundamental principle of republican government, which admits the right of people to alter or abolish the established constitution whenever they find it inconsistent with their happiness; yet it is not to be inferred from this principle, that the representatives of the people, whenever a momentary inclination happens to lay hold of a majority of their constituents incompatible with the provisions in the existing constitution, would on that account be justifiable in a violation of those provisions; or that the courts would be under a greater obligation to connive at infractions in this shape, than when they had proceeded wholly from the cabals of the representative body. Until the people have by some solemn and authoritative act annulled or changed the established form, it is binding upon themselves collectively, as well as individually; and no presumption, or even knowledge of their sentiments, can warrant their representatives in a departure from it, prior to such an act.

THE VIRGINIA AND KENTUCKY RESOLVES

Kentucky Resolve
November 10, 1798

1. Resolved, That the several states composing the United States of America are not united on the principle of unlimited submission to their general government; but that, by compact, under the style and title of a Constitution for the United States, and of amendments thereto, they constituted a general government for special purposes, delegated to that government certain definite powers, reserving, each state to itself, the residuary mass of right to their own self-government; and that whensoever the general government assumes undelegated powers, its acts are unauthoritative, void, and no force; that to this compact each state acceded as a state, and is an integral party; that this government, created by this compact, was not made the exclusive or final judge of the extent of the powers delegated to itself, since that would have made its discretion, and not the Constitution, the measure of its powers; but that, as in all other cases of compact among parties having no common judge, each party has an equal right to judge for itself, as well of infractions as the mode and measure of redress.

2. Resolved, That the Constitution of the United States having delegated to Congress a power to punish treason, counterfeiting the securities and current coin of the United States, piracies and felonies committed on the high seas, and offences against the laws of nations, and no other crimes whatever; and it being true, as a general principle, and one of the amendments to the Constitution having also declared "that the powers not delegated to the United States by the Constitution, nor prohibited by it to the states, are reserved to the states respectively, or to the people,"—therefore, also, the [Sedition Act] (and all other their acts which assume to create, define, or punish crimes other than those enumerated in the Constitution,) are altogether void, and of no force; and that the power to create, define, and punish, such other crimes is reserved, and of right appertains, solely and exclusively, to the respective states, each within its own territory.

3. Resolved, That it is true, as a general principle, and is also expressly declared by one of the amendments to the Constitution, that "the powers not delegated to the United States by the Constitution, nor prohibited by it to the states, are reserved to the states respectively, or to the people;" and that, no power over the freedom of religion, freedom of speech, or freedom of the press, being delegated to the United States by the Constitution, nor prohibited by it to the states, all lawful powers respecting the same did of right remain, and were reserved to the states, or to the people; . . . . That therefore the act of the Congress of the United States, passed on the 14th of July, 1798, entitled "An Act in Addition to the Act entitled 'An Act for the Punishment of certain Crimes against the United States,' " which does abridge the freedom of the press, is not law, but is altogether void, and of no force.

* * *

7. Resolved, That the construction applied by the general government [of the necessary-and-proper clause] goes to the destruction of all the limits prescribed to their power by the Constitution; that words meant by that instrument to be subsidiary only to the execution of the limited powers, ought not to be so construed as themselves to give unlimited powers, nor a part so to be taken as to destroy the whole residue of the instrument[.]

* * *

In questions of power, then, let no more be said of confidence in man, but bind him down from mischief by the chains of the Constitution. That this commonwealth does therefore call on its co-states for an expression of their sentiments on the acts concerning aliens, and for the punishment of certain crimes herein before specified, plainly declaring whether these acts are or are not authorized by the federal compact. And it doubts not that their sense will be so announced as to prove their attachment to limited government, whether general or particular, and that the rights and liberties of their co-states will be exposed to no dangers by remaining embarked on a common bottom with their own; but they will concur with this commonwealth in considering the said acts as so palpably against the Constitution as to amount to an undisguised declaration, that the compact is not meant to be the measure of the powers of the general government, but that it will proceed in the exercise over these states of all powers whatsoever. That they will view this as seizing the rights of the states, and consolidating them in the hands of the general government, with a power assumed to bind the states, not merely in cases made federal, but in all cases whatsoever, by laws made not with their consent, but by others against their consent; that this would be to surrender the form of government we have chosen, and live under one deriving its powers from its own will, and not from our authority; and that the co-states, recurring to their natural rights not made federal, will concur in declaring these void and of no force, and will each unite with this commonwealth in requesting their repeal at the next session of Congress.

Thomas Jefferson

Virginia Resolve
December 21, 1798

That this Assembly doth explicitly and peremptorily declare, that it views the powers of the federal government as resulting from the compact to which the states are parties, as limited by the plain sense and intention of the instrument constituting that compact, as no further valid than they are authorized by the grants enumerated in that compact; and that, in case of a deliberate, palpable, and dangerous exercise of other powers, not granted by the said compact, the states, who are parties thereto, have the right, and are in duty bound, to interpose, for arresting the progress of the evil, and for maintaining, within their respective limits, the authorities, rights and liberties, appertaining to them.

That the General Assembly doth also express its deep regret, that a spirit has, in sundry instances, been manifested by the federal government to enlarge it powers by forced constructions of the constitutional charter which defines them; and that indications have appeared of a design to expound certain general phrases (which, having been copied from the very limited grant of powers in the former Articles of Confederation, were the less liable to be misconstrued) so as to destroy the meaning and effect of the particular enumeration which necessarily explains and limits the general phrases, and so as to consolidate the states, by degrees, into one sovereignty, the obvious tendency and inevitable result of which would be, to transform the present republican system of the United States into an absolute, or, at best, a mixed monarchy.

James Madison

Kentucky Resolve
November 14, 1799

Resolved, That this commonwealth considers the federal Union, upon the terms and for the purposes specified in the late compact, conducive to the liberty and happiness of the several states: That it does now unequivocally declare its attachment to the Union, and to that compact, agreeably to its obvious and real intention, and will be among the last to seek its dissolution: That, if those who administer the general government be permitted to transgress the limits fixed by that compact, by a total disregard to the special delegations of power therein contained, an annihilation of the state governments, and the creation, upon their ruins, of a general consolidated government, will be the inevitable consequence: That the principle and construction, contended for by sundry of the state legislatures, that the general government is the exclusive judge of the extent of the powers delegated to it, stop not short of despotism—since the discretion of those who administer the government, and not the Constitution, would be the measure of their powers: That the several states who formed that instrument, being sovereign and independent, have the unquestionable right to judge of the infraction; and, That a nullification, by those sovereignties, of all unauthorized acts done under color of that instrument, is the rightful remedy: That this commonwealth does, under the most deliberate reconsideration declare, that the said Alien and Sedition Laws, are in their opinion, palpable violations of the said Constitution; and however cheerfully it may be disposed to surrender its opinion to a majority of its sister states, in matters of ordinary or doubtful policy, yet, in momentous regulations like the present, which so vitally wound the best rights of the citizen, it would consider a silent acquiescence as highly criminal: That, although this commonwealth, as a party to the federal compact, will bow to the laws of the Union, yet it does, at the same time, declare, that it will not now, or ever hereafter, cease to oppose, in a constitutional manner, every attempt, at what quarter soever offered, to violate that compact: And finally, in order that no pretext or arguments may be drawn from a supposed acquiescence, on the part of this commonwealth, in the constitutionality of those laws, and be thereby used as precedents for similar future violations of the federal compact, this commonwealth now enter against them in solemn Protest.

Thomas Jefferson

MONROE DOCTRINE

Fellow citizens of the Senate and House of Representatives:

Many important subjects will claim your attention during the present session, of which I shall endeavor to give, in aid of your deliberations, a just idea in this communication. I undertake this duty with diffidence, from the vast extent of the interests on which I have to treat and of their great importance to every portion of our Union. I enter on it with zeal from a thorough conviction that there never was a period since the establishment of our revolution when, regarding the condition of the civilized world and its bearing on us, there was greater necessity for devotion in the public servants to their respective duties, or for virtue, patriotism, and union in our constituents.

Meeting in you a new Congress, I deem it proper to present this view of public affairs in greater detail than might otherwise be necessary. I do it, however, with peculiar satisfaction, from a knowledge that in this respect I shall comply more fully with the sound principles of our government. The people being with us exclusively the sovereign, it is indispensable that full information be laid before them on all important subjects, to enable them to exercise that high power with complete effect. If kept in the dark, they must be incompetent to it. We are all liable to error, and those who are engaged in the management of public affairs are more subject to excitement and to be led astray by their particular interests and passions than the great body of our constituents, who, living at home in the pursuit of their ordinary avocations, are calm but deeply interested spectators of events and of the conduct of those who are parties to them. To the people every department of the government and every individual in each are responsible, and the more full their information the better they can judge of the wisdom of the policy pursued and of the conduct of each in regard to it. From their dispassionate judgment much aid may always be obtained, while their approbation will form the greatest incentive and most gratifying reward for virtuous actions and the dread of their censure the best security against the abuse of their confidence. Their interests in all vital questions are the same, and the bond, by sentiment as well as by interest, will be proportionably strengthened as they are better informed of the real state of public affairs, especially in difficult conjunctures. It is by such knowledge that local prejudices and jealousies are surmounted, and that a national policy, extending its fostering care and protection to all the great interests of our Union, is formed and steadily adhered to. . . .

At the proposal of the Russian imperial government, made through the minister of the emperor residing here, a full power and instructions have been transmitted to the minister of the United States at St. Petersburg to arrange by amicable negotiation the respective rights and interests

Source: James D. Richardson, ed., *A Compilation of the Messages and Papers of the Presidents*, vol. 2 (1897), pp. 207–219.

of the two nations on the northwest coast of this continent. A similar proposal had been made by his imperial Majesty to the government of Great Britain, which has likewise been acceded to. The government of the United States has been desirous by this friendly proceeding of manifesting the great value which they have invariably attached to the friendship of the emperor and their solicitude to cultivate the best understanding with his government. In the discussions to which this interest has given rise and in the arrangements by which they may terminate the occasion has been judged proper for asserting, as a principle in which the rights and interests of the United States are involved, that the American continents, by the free and independent condition which they have assumed and maintain, are henceforth not to be considered as subjects for future colonization by any European powers. . . .

It was stated at the commencement of the last session that a great effort was then making in Spain and Portugal to improve the condition of the people of those countries, and that it appeared to be conducted with extraordinary moderation. It need scarcely be remarked that the result has been so far very different from what was then anticipated. Of events in that quarter of the globe, with which we have so much intercourse and from which we derive our origin, we have always been anxious and interested spectators. The citizens of the United States cherish sentiments the most friendly in favor of the liberty and happiness of their fellow men on that side of the Atlantic. In the wars of the European powers in matters relating to themselves, we have never taken any part, nor does it comport with our policy so to do. It is only when our rights are invaded or seriously menaced that we resent injuries or make preparation for our defense. With the movements in this hemisphere we are of necessity more immediately connected, and by causes which must be obvious to all enlightened and impartial observers. The political system of the allied powers is essentially different in this respect from that of America. This difference proceeds from that which exists in their respective governments; and to the defense of our own, which has been achieved by the loss of so much blood and treasure, and matured by the wisdom of their most enlightened citizens, and under which we have enjoyed unexampled felicity, this whole nation is devoted. We owe it, therefore, to candor and to the amicable relations existing between the United States and those powers to declare that we should consider any attempt on their part to extend their system to any portion of this hemisphere as dangerous to our peace and safety. With the existing colonies or dependencies of any European power, we have not interfered and shall not interfere. But with the governments who have declared their independence and maintained it, and whose independence we have, on great consideration and on just principles, acknowledged, we could not view any interposition for the purpose of oppressing them, or controlling in any other manner their destiny, by any European power in any other light than as the manifestation of an unfriendly disposition toward the United States. In the war between those new governments and Spain, we declared our neutrality at the time of their recognition, and to this we have adhered, and shall continue to adhere, provided no change shall occur which, in the judgment of the competent authorities of this government, shall make a corresponding change on the part of the United States indispensable to their security.

The late events in Spain and Portugal show that Europe is still unsettled. Of this important fact no stronger proof can be adduced than that the allied powers should have thought it proper, on any principle satisfactory to themselves, to have interposed by force in the internal concerns of Spain. To what extent such interposition may be carried, on the same principle, is a question in which all independent powers whose governments differ from theirs are interested, even those most remote, and surely none more so than the United States. Our policy in regard to Europe, which was adopted at an early stage of the wars which have so long agitated that quarter of the globe, nevertheless remains the same, which is, not to interfere in the internal concerns of any of its powers; to consider the government *de facto* as the legitimate government for us; to cultivate friendly relations with it, and to preserve those relations by a frank, firm, and manly policy, meeting in all instances the just claims of every power, submitting to injuries from none. But in regard to those continents, circumstances are eminently and conspicuously different. It is impossible that the allied powers should extend their political system to any portion of either continent without endangering our peace and happiness; nor can anyone believe that our southern brethren, if left to themselves, would adopt it of their own accord. It is equally impossible, therefore, that we should behold such interposition in any form with indifference. If we look to the comparative strength and resources of Spain and those new governments, and their distance from each other, it must be obvious that she can never subdue them. It is still the true policy of the United States to leave the parties to themselves in the hope that other powers will pursue the same course.

SLAVERY

Slavery was introduced to the American colonies in the 1620s. By 1700 the slave population, located primarily in the southern colonies, had grown dramatically. After independence, the United States debated whether slavery should be allowed to continue. Though the Northwest Ordinance of 1787 banned slavery in the western territories, the Framers of the U.S. Constitution did not outlaw it. For the most part the Constitution ignored the issue, but the Three-fifths Compromise permitted southern states to count each slave as three-fifths of a white person for legislative apportionment.

The invention of the cotton gin by Eli Whitney, which revolutionized cotton processing and vastly increased the profitability of cotton growing, and the Louisiana Purchase of 1803 forced the United States to consider whether slavery should be confined to the Southern states or extended to the new states carved out of the territory west of the Mississippi River. Legislative compromises succeeded in holding the Union together until mid-century. However, the *Dred Scott* case (*Dred Scott v. Sandford*, 60 U.S. [19 How.] 393, 15 L. Ed. 691 [1857]) destroyed the legal basis for compromise by holding that Congress could not prohibit slavery in the territories.

Abolitionist opposition to slavery increased after *Dred Scott*. Abraham Lincoln's hostility to slavery, expressed in his "House Divided" speech, frightened the Southern states. His election as president in 1860 led to the secession of the Southern states and the U.S. Civil War. Though Lincoln saw the preservation of the Union as his main goal, he recognized that slavery had to be ended. The Emancipation Proclamation of January 1, 1863, decreed the freedom of slaves in Southern territories, but it took the Thirteenth Amendment, ratified in December 1865, to abolish slavery in the United States.

Missouri Compromise

The Missouri Compromise of 1820 was a congressional agreement that regulated the extension of slavery in the United States for thirty years. Under the agreement, the territory of Missouri was admitted as a slave state, the territory of Maine was admitted as a free state, and the boundaries of slavery were limited to the same latitude as the southern boundary of Missouri, 36°30′ north latitude.

By 1818 the rapid growth in population in the North had left the Southern states, for the first time, with less than 45 percent of the seats in the U.S. House of Representatives. The U.S. Senate was evenly balanced between eleven slave and eleven free states. Therefore, Missouri's 1818 application for statehood, if approved, would give the slave states a majority in the Senate and reduce the Northern majority in the House.

In 1819 the free territory of Maine applied for statehood. Speaker of the House Henry Clay of Kentucky saw this event as an opportunity to maintain the balance of free and slave states. He made it clear to Northern representatives that Maine would not be admitted without an agreement to admit Missouri. Clay persuaded opponents of slavery to drop efforts to ban it in the territories. In return, the Southern states agreed to limit slavery to the territory below 36°30′ north latitude. Under this provision the unsettled portions of the Louisiana Purchase north and west of Missouri would be free from slavery. The only area remaining for further expansion of slavery would be the territory that would become Arkansas and Oklahoma. To preserve the sectional equality in the Senate, Missouri and Maine were to be admitted to the Union simultaneously. Clay managed to pass the compromise in the House by a three-vote margin.

In 1821 Missouri complicated matters, however, by inserting a provision into its state constitution that prohibited free blacks and mulattoes from entering the state. Northern representatives objected to this language and refused to give final approval for statehood until it was removed. Clay then negotiated a second compromise that removed the offensive language from the Missouri constitution and substituted a provision that prohibited Missouri from discriminating against citizens from other states. Left unsettled was the question of who was a citizen. With this change Missouri and Maine were admitted to the Union.

Wilmot Proviso

The Wilmot Proviso was an unsuccessful congressional amendment, offered for the first time in 1846, that sought to ban slavery in the territories acquired from Mexico after the Mexican War. Named after its sponsor, Democratic Representative David Wilmot of Pennsylvania, the proviso never passed both houses of Congress, but it did ignite an intense national debate over slavery that led to the creation of the antislavery Republican party in 1854.

In August 1846 President James Polk asked Congress for $2 million to help him negotiate peace and settle the boundary with Mexico. Polk sought the acquisition of Texas and other Mexican territories. Wilmot quickly offered his amendment, which he attached to Polk's funding measure. The House approved the bill and sent it to the Senate for action. The Senate, however, adjourned before discussing the issue.

When the next Congress convened, a new appropriations bill for $3 million was presented, but the Wilmot Proviso was again attached to the measure. The House passed the bill, and the Senate was forced to consider the proposal. Under the leadership of Senator John C. Calhoun of South Carolina and other proslavery senators, the Senate refused to accept the Wilmot amendment and approved the funds for the negotiations without the proviso.

Though the amendment was never enacted, it became a rallying point for opponents of slavery. The creation of the Republican party in 1854 was based on an antislavery platform that endorsed the Wilmot Proviso.

Compromise of 1850

The Compromise of 1850 is the name given to a series of congressional statutes enacted in September 1850 in an attempt to resolve long-standing disputes over slavery. Southern slave owners had long demanded a more stringent fugitive slave law while Northern abolitionists insisted that slavery should be abolished in the District of Columbia. The unsuccessful Wilmot Proviso of 1846–1847 also revealed deep opposition to the expansion of slavery into the newly acquired Mexican territories. The debate over slavery intensified in 1849 when California applied for admission to the Union as a free state. Concern grew over the possibility that some Southern states might secede, leading to the dissolution of the Union.

Senator Henry Clay of Kentucky, aided by Senators Daniel Webster of Massachusetts and Stephen A. Douglas of Illinois, proposed a compromise that passed the Congress after much difficulty. The compromise consisted of five statutes. One statute created the New Mexico Territory, and a second created the Utah Territory. Both statutes left it up to the inhabitants to decide whether to enter the Union as a free state or a slave state. This approach, whose leading advocate was Douglas, became known as "popular sovereignty." A third statute admitted California to the Union as a free state, and a fourth statute prohibited bringing slaves into the District of Columbia for sale or transportation. The fifth statute was the most controversial, for it established a more rigorous fugitive slave law. The strengthening of federal enforcement of the Fugitive Slave Act (9 Stat. 462) angered many Northerners and led to growing sectional conflict.

Kansas-Nebraska Act

The Kansas-Nebraska Act of 1854 was the third and last of the series of compromises enacted before the Civil War in an attempt to resolve the question of whether slavery should be permitted in the western territories. Senator Stephen A. Douglas of Illinois, drafted the legislation that revoked the Missouri Compromise of 1820, which had banned slavery north of 36°30′ latitude. Douglas applied the doctrine of popular sovereignty to the Kansas and Nebraska Territories, as he had successfully urged Congress to do in the Compromise of 1850. The 1850 law left to New Mexico and Utah the decision of whether to enter the Union as free or slave states.

The Kansas-Nebraska Act failed to end the national conflict over slavery. Antislavery forces viewed the statute as a capitulation to the South, and many abandoned the Whig and Democratic parties to form the Republican party. Kansas soon became a battleground over slavery. On May 25, 1856, the militant abolitionist John Brown led a raid against proslavery supporters at Pottawatomie Creek, Kansas, killing five persons. The violence between the abolitionists and those who were proslavery soon gave the territory the name "Bleeding Kansas."

Dred Scott Case

The U.S. Supreme Court attempted to resolve the legal status of African Americans in *Dred Scott v. Sandford*. Chief Justice Roger Taney's belief that the Court could settle the issue proved mistaken, however. The decision heightened tensions and convinced abolitionists that the legal system was immoral.

Dred Scott was a slave owned by an army surgeon, John Emerson, who resided in Missouri. In 1836 Emerson took Scott to Fort Snelling, in what is now Minnesota, but then was a territory in which slavery had been expressly forbidden by the Missouri Compromise of 1820. In 1846 Scott sued for his freedom in Missouri state court, arguing that his residence in a free territory had released him from slavery. The Missouri Supreme Court rejected his argument, and Scott appealed to the U.S. Supreme Court.

The Court heard arguments on *Dred Scott* in 1855 and 1856. The Court could have disposed of the case on narrower grounds by holding that Scott had not become free through his temporary stay with Emerson in free territory. Instead, Taney decided that the Court needed to address the broader issue of the status of slavery in the territories. He wrote a tortuous opinion, arguing that because of the attitudes toward slavery and African Americans that prevailed in 1787–1789, when the Constitution was drafted and ratified, a slave was not and never could become a federal citizen. In addition, Taney ruled that the free descendants of slaves were not federal citizens and that property in slaves was entitled to such protection that Congress could not constitutionally forbid slavery in the territories.

The immediate effect of the *Dred Scott* decision was to convince abolitionists that the South and the Supreme Court planned to impose slavery throughout the Union. With the start of the Civil War in 1861, it became clear that Taney's decision had failed in its essential purpose.

"A House Divided" Speech

In 1856 Abraham Lincoln, an Illinois lawyer and politician, left the Whig party over the issue of slavery and joined the new antislavery Republican party. Lincoln was outraged at the Kansas-Nebraska Act of 1854 and the *Dred Scott* decision. He was particularly displeased with Illinois's Democratic Senator Stephen A. Douglas for championing the popular sovereignty doctrine, which allowed territories to decide whether to be free or slave states. The *Dred Scott* case suggested that there was no legal way to prevent slavery in the North as well.

The Republicans chose Lincoln as their candidate in the 1858 Illinois senatorial race against Douglas. The campaign was marked by a series of seven brilliant debates between the two contenders. Lincoln advocated loyalty to the Union, regarded slavery as unjust, and was opposed to any further expansion of slavery. He opened his campaign on June 16, 1858, with the declaration " 'A house divided against itself cannot stand.' I believe this government cannot endure permanently half *slave* and half *free*." His speech attacked the morality and legitimacy of popular sovereignty and warned that whether slavery could be permitted in the North was still an open question.

Lincoln lost the election due to an unfavorable apportionment of legislative seats in Illinois. At that time U.S. senators were elected by a vote of the state legislature. Though Lincoln garnered more popular votes, the legislators chose to reelect Douglas. Despite the loss, Lincoln's firm antislavery position had enhanced his national reputation and helped him win election as president in 1860.

Emancipation Proclamation

Lincoln supported the Civil War to preserve the Union, not to end slavery. Though he was personally opposed to slavery, he had been elected on a platform that pledged the continuation of slavery in states where it already existed. Wartime pressures, however, drove Lincoln toward emancipation of the slaves. Military leaders argued that an enslaved labor force in the South allowed the Confederate states to place more soldiers on the front lines. By the summer of 1862, Lincoln had prepared an Emancipation Proclamation, but he did not want to issue it until Union armies had had greater success on the battlefield. He feared that otherwise the proclamation might be seen as a sign of weakness.

The Union army's victory at the Battle of Antietam encouraged the president to issue a preliminary proclamation on September 22,

1862, that announced the abolition of slavery in areas occupied by the Confederacy effective January 1, 1863. The wording of the Emancipation Proclamation on that date made clear that slavery would still be tolerated in the border states and areas occupied by Union troops, so as not to jeopardize the war effort. Lincoln was uncertain that the Supreme Court would uphold the constitutionality of his action, so he lobbied Congress to adopt the Thirteenth Amendment, which totally abolished slavery.

MISSOURI COMPROMISE

An Act to Authorize the People of the Missouri Territory to Form a Constitution and State Government, and for the Admission of Such State into the Union on an Equal Footing with the Original States, and to Prohibit Slavery in Certain Territories

[Section 1]

Be it enacted by the Senate and House of Representatives of the United States of America, in Congress assembled, that the inhabitants of that portion of the Missouri territory included within the boundaries hereinafter designated, be, and they are hereby, authorized to form for themselves a constitution and state government and to assume such name as they shall deem proper; and the said state, when formed, shall be admitted into the Union, upon an equal footing with the original states, in all respects whatsoever.

Section 2

And be it further enacted, that the said state shall consist of all the territory included within the following boundaries, to wit: beginning in the middle of the Mississippi River, on the parallel of thirty-six degrees of north latitude; thence west, along that parallel of latitude, to the St. Francis River; thence up, and following the course of that river, in the middle of the main channel thereof, to the parallel of latitude of thirty-six degrees and thirty minutes; thence west, along the same, to a point where the said parallel is intersected by a meridian line passing through the middle of the mouth of the Kansas River, where the same empties into the Missouri River, thence, from the point aforesaid north, along the said meridian line, to the intersection of the parallel of latitude which passes through the rapids of the river Des Moines, making the said line to correspond with the Indian boundary line; thence east, from the point of intersection last aforesaid, along the said parallel of latitude, to the middle of the channel of the main fork of the said river Des Moines; thence down and along the middle of the main channel of the said river Des Moines, to the mouth of the same, where it empties into the Mississippi River; thence, due east, to the middle of the main channel of the Mississippi River; thence down, and following the course of the Mississippi River, in the middle of the main channel thereof, to the place of beginning: provided, the said state shall ratify the boundaries aforesaid. And provided also, that the said state shall have concurrent jurisdiction on the river Mississippi and every other river bordering on the said state, so far as the said rivers shall form a common boundary to the said state; and any other state or states, now or hereafter to be formed

---

Source: *Statutes at Large*, vol. 6 (1822), pp. 545–548, 645; Ben Perley Poore, ed., *The Federal and State Constitutions, Colonial Charters, and Other Organic Laws of the United States*, vol. 2 (1878), pp. 1107–1108.

and bounded by the same, such rivers to be common to both; and that the river Mississippi and the navigable rivers and waters leading into the same shall be common highways, and forever free, as well to the inhabitants of the said state as to other citizens of the United States, without any tax, duty, impost, or toll, therefore, imposed by the said state.

Section 3

And be it further enacted, that all free white male citizens of the United States, who shall have arrived at the age of twenty-one years, and have resided in said territory three months previous to the day of election, and all other persons qualified to vote for representatives to the general assembly of the said territory, shall be qualified to be elected, and they are hereby qualified and authorized to vote, and choose representatives to form a convention, who shall be apportioned amongst the several counties as follows:

From the county of Howard, five representatives. From the county of Cooper, three representatives. From the county of Montgomery, two representatives. From the county of Pike, one representative. From the county of Lincoln, one representative. From the county of St. Charles, three representatives. From the county of Franklin, one representative. From the county of St. Louis, eight representatives. From the county of Jefferson, one representative. From the county of Washington, three representatives. From the county of St. Genevieve, four representatives. From the county of Madison, one representative. From the county of Cape Girardeau, five representatives. From the county of New Madrid, two representatives. From the county of Wayne, and that portion of the county of Lawrence which falls within the boundaries herein designated, one representative.

And the election for the representatives aforesaid shall be holden on the first Monday and two succeeding days of May next, throughout the several counties aforesaid in the said territory, and shall be, in every respect, held and conducted in the same manner and under the same regulations as is prescribed by the laws of the said territory regulating elections therein for members of the general assembly, except that the returns of the election in that portion of Lawrence County included in the boundaries aforesaid shall be made to the county of Wayne, as is provided in other cases under the laws of said territory.

Section 4

And be it further enacted, that the members of the convention thus duly elected, shall be, and they are hereby authorized to meet at the seat of government of said territory on the second Monday of the month of June next; and the said convention, when so assembled, shall have power and authority to adjourn to any other place in the said territory, which to them shall seem best for the convenient transaction of their business; and which convention, when so met, shall first determine by a majority of the whole number elected, whether it be, or be not, expedient at that time to form a constitution and state government for the people within the said territory, as included within the boundaries above designated; and if it be deemed expedient, the convention shall be, and hereby is, authorized to form a constitution and state government; or, if it be deemed more expedient, the said convention shall provide by ordinance for electing representatives to form a constitution or frame of government; which said representatives shall be chosen in such manner, and in such proportion as they shall designate; and shall meet at such time and place as shall be prescribed by the said ordinance; and shall then form for the people of said territory, within the boundaries aforesaid, a constitution and state government: provided, that the same, whenever formed, shall be republican and not repugnant to the Constitution of the United States; and that the legislature of said state shall never interfere with the primary disposal of the soil by the United States, nor with any regulations Congress may find necessary for securing the title in such soil to the bona fide purchasers; and that no tax shall be imposed on lands the property of the United States; and in no case shall nonresident proprietors be taxed higher than residents.

Section 5

And be it further enacted, that until the next general census shall be taken, the said state shall be entitled to one representative in the House of Representatives of the United States.

Section 6

And be it further enacted, that the following propositions be, and the same are hereby, offered to the convention of the said territory of Missouri, when formed, for their free acceptance or rejection, which, if accepted by the convention, shall be obligatory upon the United States:

1. That section numbered sixteen in every township, and when such section has been sold or otherwise disposed of, other lands equivalent thereto and as contiguous as may be shall be granted to the state for the use of the inhabitants of such township for the use of schools.

2. That all salt springs, not exceeding twelve in number, with six sections of land adjoining to each, shall be granted to the said state for the use of said state, the same to be selected by the legislature of the said state, on or before the first day of January, in the year one thousand eight hundred and twenty-five; and the same, when so selected, to be used under such terms, conditions, and regulations as the legislature of said state shall direct. Provided, that no salt spring, the right whereof now is, or hereafter shall be, confirmed or adjudged to any individual or individuals, shall, by this section, be granted to the said state: and provided also, that the legislature shall never sell or lease the same, at any one time, for a longer period than ten years, without the consent of Congress.

3. That 5 percent of the net proceeds of the sale of lands lying within the said territory or state, and which shall be sold by Congress from and after the first day of January next, after deducting all expenses incident to the same, shall be reserved for making public roads and canals, of which three-fifths shall be applied to those objects within the state, under the direction of the legislature thereof; and the other two-fifths in defraying, under the direction of Congress, the expenses to be incurred in making of a road or roads, canal or canals, leading to the said state.

4. That four entire sections of land be, and the same are hereby, granted to the said state, for the purpose of fixing their seat of government thereon; which said sections shall, under the direction of the legislature of said state, be located, as near as may be, in one body, at any time, in such townships and ranges as the legislature aforesaid may select, on any of the public lands of the United States. Provided, that such locations shall be made prior to the public sale of the lands of the United States surrounding such location.

5. That thirty-six sections, or one entire township, which shall be designated by the president of the United States, together with the other lands heretofore reserved for that purpose, shall be reserved for the use of a seminary of learning, and vested in the legislature of said state, to be appropriated solely to the use of such seminary by the said legislature. Provided, that the five foregoing propositions herein offered, are on the condition that the convention of the said state shall provide by an ordinance, irrevocable without the consent of the United States, that every and each tract of land sold by the United States, from and after the first day of January next, shall remain exempt from any tax laid by order or under the authority of the state, whether for state, county, or township, or any other purpose whatever, for the term of five years from and after the day of sale; and further, that the bounty lands granted, or hereafter to be granted, for military services during the late war shall, while they continue to be held by the patentees or their heirs, remain exempt as aforesaid from taxation for the term of three years from and after the date of the patents, respectively.

Section 7

And be it further enacted, that in case a constitution and state government shall be formed for the people of the said territory of Missouri, the said convention or representatives, as soon thereafter as may be, shall cause a true and attested copy of such constitution, or frame of state government, as shall be formed or provided, to be transmitted to Congress.

Section 8

And be it further enacted, that in all that territory ceded by France to the United States under the name of Louisiana, which lies north of thirty-six degrees and thirty minutes north latitude, not included within the limits of the state contemplated by this act, slavery and involuntary servitude, otherwise than in the punishment of crimes whereof the parties shall have been duly convicted, shall be, and is hereby, forever prohibited. Provided always, that any person escaping into the same, from whom labor or service is lawfully claimed in any state or territory of the United States, such fugitive may be lawfully reclaimed and conveyed to the person claiming his or her labor or service as aforesaid.

Approved, March 6, 1820.

Sections of the Missouri Constitution of 1820 Dealing with Slavery
Section 26

The general assembly shall not have power to pass laws—

1. For the emancipation of slaves without the consent of their owners; or without paying them, before such emancipation, a full equivalent for such slaves so emancipated; and,

2. To prevent bona fide immigrants to this state, or actual settlers therein, from bringing from any of the United States, or from any of their territories, such persons as may there be deemed to be slaves, so long as any persons of the same description are allowed to be held as slaves by the laws of this state.

They shall have power to pass laws—

1. To prohibit the introduction into this state of any slaves who may have committed any high crime in any other state or territory;

2. To prohibit the introduction of any slave for the purpose of speculation, or as an article of trade or merchandise;

3. To prohibit the introduction of any slave, or the offspring of any slave, who heretofore may have been, or who hereafter may be, imported from any foreign country into the United States, or any territory thereof, in contravention of any existing statute of the United States; and,

4. To permit the owners of slaves to emancipate them, saving the right of creditors, where the person so emancipating will give security that the slave so emancipated shall not become a public charge.

It shall be their duty, as soon as may be, to pass such laws as may be necessary—

1. To prevent free Negroes and mulattoes from coming to and settling in this state, under any pretext whatsoever; and,

2. To oblige the owners of slaves to treat them with humanity and to abstain from all injuries to them extending to life or limb.

Section 27

In prosecutions for crimes, slaves shall not be deprived of an impartial trial by jury, and a slave convicted of a capital offense shall suffer the same degree of punishment, and no other, that would be inflicted on a white person for a like offense; and courts of justice, before whom slaves shall be tried, shall assign them counsel for their defense.

Section 28

Any person who shall maliciously deprive of life or dismember a slave shall suffer such punishment as would be inflicted for the like offense if it were committed on a free white person.

Resolution Providing for the Admission of the State of Missouri into the Union, on a Certain Condition

Resolved by the Senate and House of Representatives of the United States of America, in Congress assembled, that Missouri shall be admitted into this Union on an equal footing with the original states in all respects whatever upon the fundamental condition that the fourth clause of the twenty-sixth section of the third article of the constitution submitted on the part of said state to Congress shall never be construed to authorize the passage of any law, and that no law shall be passed in conformity thereto, by which any citizen, of either of the states in this Union, shall be excluded from the enjoyment of any of the privileges and immunities to which such citizen is entitled under the Constitution of the United States. Provided, that the legislature of the said state, by a solemn public act, shall declare the assent of the said state to the said fundamental condition and shall transmit to the president of the United States, on or before the fourth Monday in November next, an authentic copy of the said act; upon the receipt whereof, the president, by proclamation, shall announce the fact; whereupon, and without any further proceeding on the part of Congress, the admission of the said state into this Union shall be considered as complete.

Approved, March 2, 1821.

WILMOT PROVISO

Provided, that, as an express and fundamental condition to the acquisition of any territory from the Republic of Mexico by the United States, by virtue of any treaty which may be negotiated between them, and to the use by the executive of the moneys herein appropriated, neither slavery nor involuntary servitude shall ever exist in any part of said territory, except for crime, whereof the party shall first be duly convicted.

———

Source: *Congressional Globe*, 29th Congress, 1st session (August 12, 1846), p. 1217.

COMPROMISE OF 1850

An Act Proposing to the State of Texas the Establishment of Her Northern and Western Boundaries, the Relinquishment by the Said State of All Territory Claimed by Her Exterior to Said Boundaries, and of All Her Claims upon the United States, and to Establish a Territorial Government for New Mexico

[Section 1]

Be it enacted by the Senate and House of Representatives of the United States of America in Congress assembled, that the following propositions shall be, and the same hereby are, offered to the state of Texas, which, when agreed to by the said state, in an act passed by the general assembly, shall be binding and obligatory upon the United States, and upon the said state of Texas: provided, the said agreement by the said general assembly shall be given on or before the first day of December, eighteen hundred and fifty:

1. The state of Texas will agree that her boundary on the north shall commence at the point at which the meridian of one hundred degrees west from Greenwich is intersected by the parallel of thirty-six degrees thirty minutes north latitude, and shall run from said point due west to the meridian of one hundred and three degrees west from Greenwich; thence her boundary shall run due south to the thirty-second degree of north latitude; thence on the said parallel of thirty-two degrees of north latitude to the Rio Bravo del Norte, and thence with the channel of said river to the Gulf of Mexico.

2. The state of Texas cedes to the United States all her claim to territory exterior to the limits and boundaries which she agrees to establish by the first article of this agreement.

3. The state of Texas relinquishes all claim upon the United States for liability of the debts of Texas, and for compensation or indemnity for the surrender to the United States of her ships, forts, arsenals, custom houses, custom house revenue, arms and munitions of war, and public buildings with their sites, which became the property of the United States at the time of the annexation.

4. The United States, in consideration of said establishment of boundaries, cession of claim to territory, and relinquishment of claims, will pay to the state of Texas the sum of ten millions of dollars in a stock bearing 5 percent interest, and redeemable at the end of fourteen years, the interest payable half-yearly at the treasury of the United States.

5. Immediately after the president of the United States shall have been furnished with an authentic copy of the act of the general assembly of Texas accepting these propositions, he shall cause the stock to be issued in favor of the state of Texas, as provided for in the fourth article of this agreement: provided, also, that no more than five millions of said stock shall be issued until the

---

Source: *Statutes at Large*, vol. 9 (1851), pp. 446–458, 462–465, 467–468.

creditors of the state holding bonds and other certificates of stock of Texas for which duties on imports were specially pledged, shall first file at the treasury of the United States releases of all claim against the United States for or on account of said bonds or certificates in such form as shall be prescribed by the secretary of the treasury and approved by the president of the United States: provided, that nothing herein contained shall be construed to impair or qualify anything contained in the third article of the second section of the "joint resolution for annexing Texas to the United States," approved March first, eighteen hundred and forty-five, either as regards the number of states that may hereafter be formed out of the state of Texas, or otherwise.

Section 2

And be it further enacted, that all that portion of the territory of the United States bounded as follows: beginning at a point in the Colorado River where the boundary line with the republic of Mexico crosses the same; thence eastwardly with the said boundary line to the Rio Grande; thence following the main channel of said river to the parallel of the thirty-second degree of north latitude; thence east with said degree to its intersection with the one hundred and third degree of longitude west of Greenwich; thence north with said degree of longitude to the parallel of thirty-eighth degree of north latitude; thence west with said parallel to the summit of the Sierra Madre; thence south with the crest of said mountains to the thirty-seventh parallel of north latitude; thence west with said parallel to its intersection with the boundary line of the state of California; thence with said boundary line to the place of beginning—be, and the same is hereby, erected into a temporary government, by the name of the territory of New Mexico. Provided, that nothing in this act contained shall be construed to inhibit the government of the United States from dividing said territory into two or more territories, in such manner and at such times as Congress shall deem convenient and proper, or from attaching any portion thereof to any other territory or state. And provided, further, that, when admitted as a state, the said territory, or any portion of the same, shall be received into the Union, with or without slavery, as their constitution may prescribe at the time of their admission.

Section 3

And be it further enacted, that the executive power and authority in and over said territory of New Mexico shall be vested in a governor, who shall hold his office for four years, and until his successor shall be appointed and qualified, unless sooner removed by the president of the United States. The governor shall reside within said territory, shall be commander in chief of the militia thereof, shall perform the duties and receive the emoluments of superintendent of Indian affairs, and shall approve all laws passed by the legislative assembly before they shall take effect; he may grant pardons for offenses against the laws of said territory, and reprieves for offenses against the laws of the United States, until the decision of the president can be made known thereon; he shall commission all officers who shall be appointed to office under the laws of the said territory and shall take care that the laws be faithfully executed.

Section 4

And be it further enacted, that there shall be a secretary of said territory, who shall reside therein, and hold his office for four years, unless sooner removed by the president of the United States; he shall record and preserve all the laws and proceedings of the legislative assembly hereinafter constituted and all the acts and proceedings of the governor in his executive department; he shall transmit one copy of the laws and one copy of the executive proceedings, on or before the first day of December in each year, to the president of the United States, and, at the same time, two copies of the laws to the speaker of the House of Representatives and the president of the Senate, for the use of Congress. And, in case of the death, removal, resignation, or other necessary absence of the governor from the territory, the secretary shall have, and he is hereby authorized and required to execute and perform all the powers and duties of the governor during such vacancy or necessary absence, or until another governor shall be duly appointed to fill such vacancy.

Section 5

And be it further enacted, that the legislative power and authority of said territory shall be vested in the governor and a legislative assembly. The legislative assembly shall consist of a council and house of representatives. The council shall consist of thirteen members, having the qualifications of voters as hereinafter prescribed, whose term of service shall continue two years. The house of representatives shall consist of twenty-six members, possessing the same qualifications as prescribed for members of the council, and whose term of service shall continue one year. An apportionment shall be made, as nearly equal as practicable, among the several counties or districts, for the election of the council and house of representatives, giving to each section of the territory representation in the ratio of its population (Indians excepted), as nearly as may be. And the members of the council and of the house of representatives shall reside in, and be inhabitants of, the district for which they may be elected respectively. Previous to the first election, the governor shall cause a census or enumeration of the inhabitants of the several counties and districts of the territory to be taken, and the first election shall be held at such time and places and be conducted in such manner, as the governor shall appoint and direct; and he shall, at the same time, declare the number of the members of the council and house of representatives to which each of the counties or districts shall be entitled under this act. The number of persons authorized to be elected having the highest number of votes in each of said council districts, for members of the council, shall be declared by the governor to be duly elected to the council; and the person or persons authorized to be elected having the greatest number of votes for the house of representatives, equal to the number to which each county or district shall be entitled, shall be declared by the governor to be duly elected members of the house of representatives. Provided, that in case of a tie between two or more persons voted for, the governor shall order a new election to supply the vacancy made by such tie. And the persons thus elected to the legislative assembly shall meet at such place and on such day as the governor shall appoint; but thereafter, the time, place, and manner of holding and conducting all elections by the people, and the apportioning the representation in the several counties or districts to the council and house of representatives according to the population, shall be prescribed by law, as well as the day of the commencement of the regular sessions of the legislative assembly: provided, that no one session shall exceed the term of forty days.

Section 6

And be it further enacted, that every free white male inhabitant, above the age of twenty-one years, who shall have been a resident of said territory at the time of the passage of this act, shall be entitled to vote at the first election and shall be eligible to any office within the said territory; but the qualifications of voters and of holding office, at all subsequent elections, shall be such as shall be prescribed by the legislative assembly. Provided, that the right of suffrage, and of holding office, shall be exercised only by citizens of the United States, including those recognized as citizens by the treaty with the republic of Mexico, concluded February second, eighteen hundred and forty-eight.

Section 7

And be it further enacted, that the legislative power of the territory shall extend to all rightful subjects of legislation, consistent with the Constitution of the United States and the provisions of this act; but no law shall be passed interfering with the primary disposal of the soil; no tax shall be imposed upon the property of the United States; nor shall the lands or other property of nonresidents be taxed higher than the lands or other property of residents. All the laws passed by the legislative assembly and governor shall be submitted to the Congress of the United States, and, if disapproved, shall be null and of no effect.

Section 8

And be it further enacted, that all township, district, and county officers, not herein otherwise provided for, shall be appointed or elected, as the case may be, in such manner as shall be provided by the governor and legislative assembly of the territory of New Mexico. The governor shall nominate and, by and with the advice and consent of the legislative council, appoint all officers not herein otherwise provided for; and in the first instance the governor alone may appoint all said officers, who shall hold their offices until the end of the first session of the legislative assembly, and shall lay off the necessary districts for members of the council and house of representatives, and all other officers.

Section 9

And be it further enacted, that no member of the legislative assembly shall hold, or be appointed to, any office which shall have been created, or the salary or emoluments of which shall have been increased while he was a member, during the term for which he was elected, and for one year after the expiration of such term; and no person holding a commission or appointment under the United States, except postmasters, shall be a member of the legislative assembly, or shall hold any office under the government of said territory.

Section 10

And be it further enacted, that the judicial power of said territory shall be vested in a supreme court, district courts, probate courts, and in justices of the peace. The supreme court shall consist of a chief justice and two associate justices, any two of whom shall constitute a quorum, and who shall hold a term at the seat of government of said territory annually, and they shall hold their offices during the period of four years. The said territory shall be divided into three judicial districts, and a district court shall be held in each of said districts by one of the justices of the supreme court, at such time and place as may be prescribed by law; and the said judges shall, after their appointments, respectively, reside in the districts which shall be assigned them. The jurisdiction of the several courts herein provided for, both appellate and original, and that of the probate courts and of justices of the peace, shall be as limited by law. Provided, that justices of the peace shall not have jurisdiction of any matter in controversy when the title or boundaries of land may be in dispute, or where the debt or sum claimed shall exceed one hundred dollars; and the said supreme and district courts, respectively, shall possess chancery as well as common-law jurisdiction. Each district court, or the judge thereof, shall appoint its clerk, who shall also be the register in chancery and shall keep his office at the place where the court may be held. Writs of error, bills of exception, and appeals shall be allowed in all cases from the final decisions of said district courts to the supreme court, under such regulations as may be prescribed by law, but in no case removed to the supreme court shall trial by jury be allowed in said court. The supreme court, or the justices thereof, shall appoint its own clerk, and every clerk shall hold his office at the pleasure of the court for which he shall have been appointed. Writs of error and appeals from the final decisions of said supreme court shall be allowed, and may be taken to the Supreme Court of the United States, in the same manner and under the same regulations as from the circuit courts of the United States, where the value of the property or the amount in controversy, to be ascertained by the oath or affirmation of either party, or other competent witness, shall exceed one thousand dollars; except only that in all cases involving title to slaves, the said writs of error or appeals shall be allowed and decided by the said Supreme Court without regard to the value of the matter, property, or title in controversy; and except also that a writ of error or appeal shall also be allowed to the Supreme Court of the United States from the decision of the said supreme court created by this act, or of any judge thereof, or of the district courts created by this act, or of any judge thereof, upon any writ of habeas corpus involving the question of personal freedom; and each of the said district courts shall have and exercise the same jurisdiction in all cases arising under the Constitution and laws of the United States as is vested in the circuit and district courts of the United States; and the said supreme and district courts of the said territory, and the respective judges thereof, shall and may grant writs of habeas corpus in all cases in which the same are grantable by the judges of the United States in the District of Columbia; and the first six days of every term of said courts, or so much thereof as shall be necessary, shall be appropriated to the trial of causes arising under the said Constitution and laws; and writs of error and appeals in all such cases shall be made to the supreme court of said territory, the same as in other cases. The said clerk shall receive in all such cases the same fees which the clerks of the district courts of Oregon Territory now receive for similar services.

Section 11

And be it further enacted, that there shall be appointed an attorney for said territory, who shall continue in office for four years, unless sooner removed by the president, and who shall receive the same fees and salary as the attorney of the United States for the present territory of Oregon. There shall also be a marshal for the territory appointed, who shall hold his office for four years, unless sooner removed by the president, and who shall execute all processes issuing from the said courts when exercising their jurisdiction as circuit and district courts of the United States; he shall perform the duties, be subject to the same regulation and penalties, and be entitled to the same fees as the marshal of the district court of the United States for the present territory of Oregon, and shall, in addition, be paid two hundred (dollars) annually as a compensation for extra services.

Section 12

And be it further enacted, that the governor, secretary, chief justice and associate justices, attorney, and marshal shall be nominated and, by and with the advice and consent of the Senate, appointed by the president of the United States. The governor and secretary, to be appointed as aforesaid, shall, before they act as such, respectively take an oath or affirmation, before the district judge, or some justice of the peace in the limits of said territory, duly authorized to administer oaths and affirmations by the laws now in force therein, or before the chief justice or some associate justice of the Supreme Court of the United States, to support the Constitution of the United States, and faithfully to discharge the duties of their respective offices; which said oaths, when so taken, shall be certified by the person by whom the same shall have been taken, and such certificates shall be received and recorded by the said secretary among the executive proceedings; and the chief justice and associate justices, and all other civil officers in said territory, before they act as such, shall take a like oath or affirmation, before the said governor or secretary, or some judge or justice of the peace of the territory, who may be duly commissioned and qualified; which said oath or affirmation shall be certified and transmitted, by the person taking the same to the secretary, to be by him recorded as aforesaid; and afterwards, the like oath or affirmation shall be taken, certified, and recorded in such manner and form as may be prescribed by law. The governor shall receive an annual salary of fifteen hundred dollars as governor, and one thousand dollars as superintendent of Indian affairs. The chief justice and associate justices shall each receive an annual salary of eighteen hundred dollars. The secretary shall receive an annual salary of eighteen hundred dollars. The said salaries shall be paid quarter-yearly, at the treasury of the United States. The members of the legislative assembly shall be entitled to receive three dollars each per day during their attendance at the sessions thereof, and three dollars each for every twenty miles' travel in going to and returning from the said sessions, estimated according to the nearest usually traveled route. There shall be appropriated annually the sum of one thousand dollars, to be expended by the governor, to defray the contingent expenses of the territory; there shall also be appropriated annually a sufficient sum to be expended by the secretary of the territory, and upon an estimate to be made by the secretary of the treasury of the United States, to defray the expenses of the legislative assembly, the printing of the laws, and other incidental expenses; and the secretary of the territory shall annually account to the secretary of the treasury of the United States for the manner in which the aforesaid sum shall have been expended.

Section 13

And be it further enacted, that the legislative assembly of the territory of New Mexico shall hold its first session at such time and place in said territory as the governor thereof shall appoint and direct; and at said first session, or as soon thereafter as they shall deem expedient, the governor and legislative assembly shall proceed to locate and establish the seat of government for said territory at such place as they may deem eligible; which place, however, shall thereafter be subject to be changed by the said governor and legislative assembly.

Section 14

And be it further enacted, that a delegate to the House of Representatives of the United States, to serve during each Congress of the United States, may be elected by the voters qualified to elect members of the legislative assembly, who shall be entitled to the same rights and privileges as are exercised and enjoyed by the delegates from the several other territories of the United States to the said House of Representatives. The first election shall be held at such time and places, and be conducted in such manner, as the governor shall appoint and direct; and at all subsequent elections, the times, places, and manner of holding the elections shall be prescribed by law. The person having the greatest number of votes shall be declared by the governor to be duly elected, and a certificate thereof shall be given accordingly; provided, that such delegate shall receive no higher sum for mileage than is allowed by law to the delegate from Oregon.

Section 15

And be it further enacted, that when the lands in said territory shall be surveyed under the direction of the government of the United States, preparatory to bringing the same into market, sections numbered sixteen and thirty-six in each township in said territory shall be, and the same are hereby, reserved for the purpose of being applied to schools in said territory, and in the states and territories hereafter to be erected out of the same.

Section 16

And be it further enacted, that temporarily and until otherwise provided by law, the governor of said territory may define the judicial districts of said territory, and assign the judges who may be appointed for said territory to the several districts, and also appoint the times and places for holding courts in the several counties or subdivisions in each of said judicial districts, by proclamation to be issued by him; but the legislative assembly, at their first or any subsequent session, may organize, alter, or modify such judicial districts, and assign the judges, and alter the times and places of holding the courts, as to them shall seem proper and convenient.

Section 17

And be it further enacted, that the Constitution, and all laws of the United States which are not locally inapplicable, shall have the same force and effect within the said territory of New Mexico as elsewhere within the United States.

Section 18

And be it further enacted, that the provisions of this act be, and they are hereby, suspended until the boundary between the United States and the state of Texas shall be adjusted; and when such adjustment shall have been effected, the president of the United States shall issue his proclamation, declaring this act to be in full force and operation, and shall proceed to appoint the officers herein provided to be appointed in and for said territory.

Section 19

And be it further enacted, that no citizen of the United States shall be deprived of his life, liberty, or property, in said territory, except by the judgment of his peers and the laws of the land.

Approved, September 9, 1850.

An Act for the Admission of the State of California into the Union

Whereas the people of California have presented a constitution and asked admission into the Union, which constitution was submitted to Congress by the president of the United States, by message dated February thirteenth, eighteen hundred and fifty, and which, on due examination, is found to be republican in its form of government:

[Section 1]

Be it enacted by the Senate and House of Representatives of the United States of America in Congress assembled, that the state of California shall be one, and is hereby declared to be one, of the United States of America, and admitted into the Union on an equal footing with the original states in all respects whatever.

Section 2

And be it further enacted, that, until the representatives in Congress shall be apportioned according to an actual enumeration of the inhabitants of the United States, the state of California shall be entitled to two representatives in Congress.

Section 3

And be it further enacted, that the said state of California is admitted into the Union upon the express condition that the people of said state, through their legislature or otherwise, shall never interfere with the primary disposal of the public lands within its limits, and shall pass no law and do no act whereby the title of the United States to, and right to dispose of, the same shall be impaired or questioned; and that they shall never lay any tax or assessment of any description whatsoever upon the public domain of the United States, and in no case shall nonresident proprietors, who are citizens of the United States, be taxed higher than residents; and that all the navigable waters within the said state shall be common highways, and forever free, as well to the inhabitants of said state as to the citizens of the United States, without any tax, impost, or duty therefore: provided, that nothing herein contained shall be construed as recognizing or rejecting the propositions tendered by the people of California as articles of compact in the ordinance adopted by the convention which formed the constitution of that state.

Approved, September 9, 1850.

An Act to Establish a Territorial Government for Utah

Be it enacted by the Senate and House of Representatives of the United States of America in Congress assembled, that all that part of the territory of the United States included within the following limits, to wit: bounded on the west by the state of California, on the north by the territory of Oregon, and on the east by the summit of the Rocky Mountains, and on the south by the thirty-seventh parallel of north latitude, be, and the same is hereby, created into a temporary government, by the name of the territory of Utah; and, when admitted as a state, the said territory, or any portion of the same, shall be received into the Union, with or without slavery, as their constitution may prescribe at the time of their admission: provided, that nothing in this act contained shall be construed to inhibit the government of the United States from dividing said territory into two or more territories, in such manner and at such times as Congress shall deem convenient and proper, or from attaching any portion of said territory to any other state or territory of the United States.

* * *

Section 14

And be it further enacted, that the sum of five thousand dollars be, and the same is hereby, appropriated out of any moneys in the treasury not otherwise appropriated, to be expended by and under the direction of the said governor of the territory of Utah, in the purchase of a library, to be kept at the seat of government for the use of the governor, legislative assembly, judges of the supreme court, secretary, marshal, and attorney of said territory, and such other persons, and under such regulations, as shall be prescribed by law.

An Act to Amend, and Supplementary to, the Act Entitled "An Act Respecting Fugitives from Justice, and Persons Escaping from the Service of Their Masters," Approved February Twelfth, One Thousand Seven Hundred and Ninety-three

[Section 1]

Be it enacted by the Senate and House of Representatives of the United States of America in Congress assembled, that the persons who have been, or may hereafter be, appointed commissioners, in virtue of any act of Congress, by the circuit courts of the United States, and who, in consequence of such appointment, are authorized to exercise the powers that any justice of the peace, or other magistrate of any of the United States, may exercise in respect to offenders for any crime or offense against the United States, by arresting, imprisoning, or bailing the same under and by virtue of the thirty-third section of the act of the twenty-fourth of September, seventeen hundred and eighty-nine, entitled "An act to establish the judicial courts of the United States," shall be, and are hereby, authorized and required to exercise and discharge all the powers and duties conferred by this act.

Section 2

And be it further enacted, that the superior court of each organized territory of the United States shall have the same power to appoint commissioners to take acknowledgments of bail and affidavits, and to take depositions of witnesses in civil causes, which is now possessed by the circuit court of the United States; and all commissioners, who shall hereafter be appointed for such purposes by the superior court of any organized territory of the United States, shall possess all the powers, and exercise all the duties, conferred by law upon the commissioners appointed by the circuit courts of the United States for similar purposes and shall moreover exercise and discharge all the powers and duties conferred by this act.

Section 3

And be it further enacted, that the circuit courts of the United States and the superior courts of each organized territory of the United States shall from time to time enlarge the number of commissioners, with a view to afford reasonable facilities to reclaim fugitives from labor and to the prompt discharge of the duties imposed by this act.

Section 4

And be it further enacted, that the commissioners above named shall have concurrent jurisdiction with the judges of the circuit and district courts of the United States, in their respective circuits and districts within the several states, and the judges of the superior courts of the territories, severally and collectively, in termtime and vacation; and shall grant certificates to such claimants, upon satisfactory proof being made, with authority to take and remove such fugitives from service or labor, under the restrictions herein contained, to the state or territory from which such persons may have escaped or fled.

Section 5

And be it further enacted, that it shall be the duty of all marshals and deputy marshals to obey and execute all warrants and precepts issued under the provisions of this act, when to them directed; and should any marshal or deputy marshal refuse to receive such warrant, or other process, when tendered, or to use all proper means diligently to execute the same, he shall, on conviction thereof, be fined in the sum of one thousand dollars, to the use of such claimant, on the motion of such claimant, by the circuit or district court for the district of such marshal; and after arrest of such fugitive by such marshal or his deputy, or whilst at any time in his custody under the provisions of this act, should such fugitive escape, whether with or without the assent of such marshal or his deputy, such marshal shall be liable, on his official bond, to be prosecuted for the benefit of such claimant, for the full value of the service or labor of said fugitive in the state, territory, or district whence he escaped. And the better to enable the said commissioners, when thus appointed, to execute their duties faithfully and efficiently in conformity with the requirements of the Constitution of the United States and of this act, they are hereby authorized and empowered, within their counties respectively, to appoint, in writing under their hands, any one or more suitable persons, from time to time, to execute all such warrants and other process as may be issued by them in the lawful performance of their respective duties; with authority to such commissioners, or the persons to be appointed by them, to execute process as aforesaid, to summon and call to their aid the bystanders, or *posse comitatus* of the proper county, when necessary to ensure a faithful observance of the clause of the Constitution referred to, in conformity with the provisions of this act; and all good citizens are hereby commanded to aid and assist in the prompt and efficient execution of this law, whenever their services may be required, as aforesaid, for that purpose; and said warrants shall run, and be executed by said officers, anywhere in the state within which they are issued.

Section 6

And be it further enacted, that when a person held to service or labor in any state or territory of the United States has heretofore or shall hereafter escape into another state or territory of the United States, the person or persons to whom such service or labor may be due or his, her, or their agent or attorney, duly authorized by power of attorney in writing, acknowledged and certified under the seal of some legal officer or court of the state or territory in which the same may be executed, may pursue and reclaim such fugitive person, either by procuring a warrant from some one of the courts, judges, or commissioners aforesaid, of the proper circuit, district, or county, for the apprehension of such fugitive from service or labor or by seizing and arresting such fugitive, where the same can be done without process, and by taking, or causing such person to be taken, forthwith before such court, judge, or commissioner, whose duty it shall be to hear and determine the case of such claimant in a summary manner; and upon satisfactory proof being made, by deposition or affidavit in writing, to be taken and certified by such court, judge, or commissioner, or by other satisfactory testimony, duly taken and certified by some court, magistrate, justice of the peace, or other legal officer authorized to administer an oath and take depositions under the laws of the state or territory from which such person owing service or labor may have escaped, with a certificate of such magistracy or other authority, as aforesaid, with the seal of the proper court or officer thereto attached, which seal shall be sufficient to establish the competency of the proof, and with proof, also by affidavit, of the identity of the person whose service or labor is claimed to be due as aforesaid, that the person so arrested does in fact owe service or labor to the person or persons claiming him or her, in the state or territory from which such fugitive may have escaped as aforesaid, and that said person escaped, to make out and deliver to such claimant, his or her agent or attorney, a certificate setting forth the substantial facts as to the service or labor due from such fugitive to the claimant, and of his or her escape from the state or territory in which such service or labor was due, to the state or territory in which he or she was arrested, with authority to such claimant, or his or her agent or attorney, to use such reasonable force and restraint as may be necessary, under the circumstances of the case, to take and remove such fugitive person back to the state or territory whence he or she may have escaped as aforesaid. In no trial or hearing under this act shall the testimony of such alleged fugitive be admitted in evidence; and the certificates in this and the first (fourth) section mentioned, shall be conclusive of the right of the person or persons in whose favor granted, to remove such fugitive to the state or territory from which he escaped, and shall prevent all molestation of such person or persons by any process issued by any court, judge, magistrate, or other person whomsoever.

Section 7

And be it further enacted, that any person who shall knowingly and willingly obstruct, hinder, or prevent such claimant, his agent or attorney, or any person or persons lawfully assisting him, her, or them, from arresting such a fugitive from service or labor, either with or without process as aforesaid, or shall rescue, or attempt to rescue, such fugitive from service or labor, from the custody of such claimant, his or her agent or attorney, or other person or persons lawfully assisting as aforesaid, when so arrested, pursuant to the authority herein given and declared; or shall aid, abet, or assist such person so owing service or labor as aforesaid, directly or indirectly, to escape from such claimant, his agent or attorney, or other person or persons legally authorized as aforesaid; or shall harbor or conceal such fugitive, so as to prevent the discovery and arrest of such person, after notice or knowledge of the fact that such person was a fugitive from service or labor as aforesaid, shall, for either of said offenses, be subject to a fine not exceeding one thousand dollars and imprisonment not exceeding six months, by indictment and conviction before the district court of the United States for the district in which such offense may have been committed, or before the proper court of criminal jurisdiction, if committed within any one of the organized territories of the United States; and shall moreover forfeit and pay, by way of civil damages to the party injured by such illegal conduct, the sum of one thousand dollars, for each fugitive so lost as aforesaid, to be recovered by action of debt, in any of the district or territorial courts aforesaid, within whose jurisdiction the said offense may have been committed.

Section 8

And be it further enacted, that the marshals, their deputies, and the clerks of the said district and territorial courts, shall be paid, for their services, the like fees as may be allowed to them for similar services in other cases; and where such services are rendered exclusively in the arrest, custody, and delivery of the fugitive to the claimant, his or her agent or attorney, or where such supposed fugitive may be discharged out of custody for the want of sufficient proof as aforesaid, then such fees are to be paid in the whole by such claimant, his agent or attorney; and in all cases where the proceedings are before a commissioner, he shall be entitled to a fee of ten dollars in full for his services in each case, upon the delivery of the said certificate to the claimant, his or her agent or attorney; or a fee of five dollars in cases where the proof shall not, in the opinion of such commissioner, warrant such certificate and delivery, inclusive of all services incident to such arrest and examination, to be paid, in either case, by the claimant, his or her agent or attorney. The person or persons authorized to execute the process to be issued by such commissioners for the arrest and detention of fugitives from service or labor as aforesaid shall also be entitled to a fee of five dollars each for each person he or they may arrest and take before any such commissioner as aforesaid, at the instance and request of such claimant, with such other fees as may be deemed reasonable by such commissioner for such other additional services as may be necessarily performed by him or them: such as attending at the examination, keeping the fugitive in custody, and providing him with food and lodging during his detention, and until the final determination of such commissioner; and, in general, for performing such other duties as may be required by such claimant, his or her attorney or agent, or commissioner in the premises, such fees to be made up in conformity with the fees usually charged by the officers of the courts of justice within the proper district or county, as near as may be practicable, and paid by such claimants, their agents or attorneys, whether such supposed fugitives from service or labor be ordered to be delivered to such claimants by the final determination of such commissioners or not.

Section 9

And be it further enacted, that, upon affidavit made by the claimant of such fugitive, his agent or attorney, after such certificate has been issued, that he has reason to apprehend that such fugitive will be rescued by force from his or their possession before he can be taken beyond the limits of the state in which the arrest is made, it shall be the duty of the officer making the arrest to retain such fugitive in his custody and to remove him to the state whence he fled, and there to deliver him to said claimant, his agent, or attorney. And to this end, the officer aforesaid is hereby authorized and required to employ so many persons as he may deem necessary to overcome such force and to retain them in his service so long as circumstances may require. The said officer and his assistants, while so employed, to receive the same compensation, and to be allowed the same expenses, as are now allowed by law for transportation of criminals, to be certified by the judge of the district within which the arrest is made, and paid out of the treasury of the United States.

Section 10

And be it further enacted, that when any person held to service or labor in any state or territory, or in the District of Columbia, shall escape therefrom, the party to whom such service or labor shall be due, his, her, or their agent or attorney, may apply to any court of record therein, or judge thereof in vacation, and make satisfactory proof to such court, or judge in vacation, of the escape aforesaid, and that the person escaping owed service or labor to such party. Whereupon the court shall cause a record to be made of the matters so proved, and also a general description of the person so escaping, with such convenient certainty as may be; and a transcript of such record, authenticated by the attestation of the clerk and of the seal of the said court, being produced in any other state, territory, or district in which the person so escaping may be found, and being exhibited to any judge, commissioner, or other officer authorized by the law of the United States to cause persons escaping from service or labor to be delivered up, shall be held and taken to be full and conclusive evidence of the fact of escape, and that the service or labor of the person escaping is due to the party in such record mentioned. And upon the production by the said party of other and further evidence if necessary, either oral or by affidavit, in addition to what is contained in the said record of the identity of the person escaping, he or she shall be delivered up to the claimant. And the said court, commissioner, judge, or other person authorized by this act to grant certificates to claimants of fugitives, shall, upon the production of the record and other evidences aforesaid, grant to such claimant a certificate of his right to take any such person identified and proved to be owing service or labor as aforesaid, which certificate shall authorize such claimant to seize or arrest and transport such person to the state or territory from which he escaped: provided, that nothing herein contained shall be construed as requiring the production of a transcript of such record as evidence as aforesaid. But in its absence the claim shall be heard and determined upon other satisfactory proofs, competent in law.

Approved, September 18, 1850.

An Act to Suppress the Slave Trade in the District of Columbia
[Section 1]

Be it enacted by the Senate and House of Representatives of the United States of America in Congress assembled, that from and after the first day of January, eighteen hundred and fifty-one, it shall not be lawful to bring into the District of Columbia any slave whatever, for the purpose of being sold, or for the purpose of being placed in depot, to be subsequently transferred to any other state or place to be sold as merchandise. And if any slave shall be brought into the said district by its owner, or by the authority or consent of its owner, contrary to the provisions of this act, such slave shall thereupon become liberated and free.

Section 2

And be it further enacted, that it shall and may be lawful for each of the corporations of the cities of Washington and Georgetown, from time to time, and as often as may be necessary, to abate, break up, and abolish any depot or place of confinement of slaves brought into the said district as merchandise, contrary to the provisions of this act, by such appropriate means as may appear to either of the said corporations expedient and proper. And the same power is hereby vested in the Levy Court of Washington County, if any attempt shall be made, within its jurisdictional limits, to establish a depot or place of confinement for slaves brought into the said district as merchandise for sale contrary to this act.

Approved, September 20, 1850.

KANSAS-NEBRASKA ACT

AN ACT TO ORGANIZE THE TERRITORIES OF NEBRASKA AND KANSAS

[Section 1]

Be it enacted by the Senate and House of Representatives of the United States of America in Congress assembled, that all that part of the territory of the United States included within the following limits, except such portions thereof as are hereinafter expressly exempted from the operations of this act, to wit: beginning at a point in the Missouri River where the fortieth parallel of north latitude crosses the same; thence west on said parallel to the east boundary of the territory of Utah, on the summit of the Rocky Mountains; thence on said summit northward to the forty-ninth parallel of north latitude; thence east on said summit northward to the forty-ninth parallel of north latitude; thence east on said parallel to the western boundary of the territory of Minnesota; thence southward on said boundary to the Missouri River; thence down the main channel of said river to the place of beginning, be, and the same is hereby, created into a temporary government by the name of the territory of Nebraska; and when admitted as a state or states, the said territory, or any portion of the same, shall be received into the Union with or without slavery, as their constitution may prescribe at the time of their admission. Provided, that nothing in this act contained shall be construed to inhibit the government of the United States from dividing said territory into two or more territories, in such manner and at such times as Congress shall deem convenient and proper, or from attaching any portion of said territory to any other state or territory of the United States. Provided further, that nothing in this act contained shall be construed to impair the rights of person or property now pertaining to the Indians in said territory, so long as such rights shall remain unextinguished by treaty between the United States and such Indians, or to include any territory which, by treaty with any Indian tribe, is not, without the consent of said tribe, to be included within the territorial limits or jurisdiction of any state or territory; but all such territory shall be excepted out of the boundaries, and constitute no part of the territory of Nebraska, until said tribe shall signify their assent to the president of the United States to be included within the said territory of Nebraska, or to affect the authority of the government of the United States to make any regulations respecting such Indians, their lands, property, or other rights by treaty, law, or otherwise, which it would have been competent to the government to make if this act had never passed.

Section 2

And be it further enacted, that the executive power and authority in and over said territory of Nebraska shall be vested in a governor, who shall hold his office for four years, and until his successor shall be appointed and qualified, unless sooner removed by the president of the United

Source: *Statutes at Large*, vol. 10 (1855), pp. 277–290.

States. The governor shall reside within said territory and shall be commander in chief of the militia thereof. He may grant pardons and respites for offenses against the laws of said territory and reprieves for offenses against the laws of the United States, until the decision of the president can be made known thereon; he shall commission all officers who shall be appointed to office under the laws of the said territory and shall take care that the laws be faithfully executed.

Section 3

And be it further enacted, that there shall be a secretary of said territory, who shall reside therein and hold his office for five years, unless sooner removed by the president of the United States; he shall record and preserve all the laws and proceedings of the legislative assembly hereinafter constituted and all the acts and proceedings of the governor in his executive department; he shall transmit one copy of the laws and journals of the legislative assembly within thirty days after the end of each session and one copy of the executive proceedings and official correspondence semiannually, on the first days of January and July in each year, to the president of the United States and two copies of the laws to the president of the Senate and to the speaker of the House of Representatives, to be deposited in the libraries of Congress; and in case of the death, removal, resignation, or absence of the governor from the territory, the secretary shall be, and he is hereby, authorized and required to execute and perform all the powers and duties of the governor during such vacancy or absence, or until another governor shall be duly appointed and qualified to fill such vacancy.

Section 4

And be it further enacted, that the legislative power and authority of said territory shall be vested in the governor and a legislative assembly. The legislative assembly shall consist of a council and house of representatives. The council shall consist of thirteen members having the qualifications of voters, as hereinafter prescribed, whose term of service shall continue two years. The house of representatives shall, at its first session, consist of twenty-six members, possessing the same qualifications as prescribed for members of the council, and whose term of service shall continue one year. The number of representatives may be increased by the legislative assembly, from time to time, in proportion to the increase of qualified voters; provided, that the whole number shall never exceed thirty-nine. An apportionment shall be made, as nearly equal as practicable, among the several counties or districts, for the election of the council and representatives, giving to each section of the territory representation in the ratio of its qualified voters as nearly as may be. And the members of the council and of the house of representatives shall reside in, and be inhabitants of, the district or county or counties for which they may be elected, respectively. Previous to the first election, the governor shall cause a census, or enumeration of the inhabitants and qualified voters of the several counties and districts of the territory, to be taken by such persons and in such mode as the governor shall designate and appoint; and the persons so appointed shall receive a reasonable compensation therefore. And the first election shall be held at such time and places and be conducted in such manner, both as to the persons who shall superintend such election and the returns thereof, as the governor shall appoint and direct; and he shall at the same time declare the number of members of the council and house of representatives to which each of the counties or districts shall be entitled under this act. The persons having the highest number of legal votes in each of said council districts for members of the council shall be declared by the governor to be duly elected to the council; and the persons having the highest number of legal votes for the house of representatives shall be declared by the governor to be duly elected members of said house. Provided, that in case two or more persons voted for shall have an equal number of votes, and in case a vacancy shall otherwise occur in either branch of the legislative assembly, the governor shall order a new election; and the persons thus elected to the legislative assembly shall meet at such place and on such day as the governor shall appoint; but thereafter, the time, place, and manner of holding and conducting all elections by the people and the apportioning the representation in the several counties or districts to the council and house of representatives, according to the number of qualified voters, shall be prescribed by law, as well as the day of the commencement of the regular sessions of the legislative assembly; provided, that no session in any one year shall exceed the term of forty days, except the first session, which may continue sixty days.

Section 5

And be it further enacted, that every free white male inhabitant above the age of twenty-one years who shall be an actual resident of said territory and shall possess the qualifications hereinafter prescribed shall be entitled to vote at the first election and shall be eligible to any office within the said territory; but the qualifications of voters, and of holding office, at all subsequent elections, shall be such as shall be prescribed by the legislative assembly. Provided, that the right of suffrage and of holding office shall be exercised only by citizens of the United States and those who shall have declared on oath their intention to become such and shall have taken an oath to support the Constitution of the United States and the provisions of this act; and provided further, that no officer, soldier, seaman, or marine, or other person in the army or navy of the United States, or attached to troops in the service of the United States, shall be allowed to vote or hold office in said territory by reason of being on service therein.

Section 6

And be it further enacted, that the legislative power of the territory shall extend to all rightful subjects of legislation consistent with the Constitution of the United States and the provisions of this act; but no law shall be passed interfering with the primary disposal of the soil; no tax shall be imposed upon the property of the United States; nor shall the lands or other property of nonresidents be taxed higher than the lands or other property of residents. Every bill which shall have passed the council and house of representatives of the said territory shall, before it become a law, be presented to the governor of the territory; if he approve, he shall sign it; but if not, he shall return it with his objections to the house in which it originated, who shall enter the objections at large on their journal and proceed to reconsider it. If, after such reconsideration, two-thirds of that house shall agree to pass the bill, it shall be sent, together with the objections, to the other house, by which it shall likewise be reconsidered, and if approved by two-thirds of that house, it shall become a law. But in all such cases the votes of both houses shall be determined by yeas and nays, to be entered on the journal of each house respectively. If any bill shall not be returned by the governor within three days (Sundays excepted) after it shall have been presented to him, the same shall be a law in like manner as if he had signed it, unless the assembly, by adjournment, prevents its return, in which case it shall not be a law.

Section 7

And be it further enacted, that all township, district, and county officers, not herein otherwise provided for, shall be appointed or elected, as the case may be, in such manner as shall be provided by the governor and legislative assembly of the territory of Nebraska. The governor shall nominate and, by and with the advice and consent of the legislative council, appoint all officers not herein otherwise provided for; and in the first instance the governor alone may appoint all said officers, who shall hold their offices until the end of the first session of the legislative assembly, and shall lay off the necessary districts for members of the council and house of representatives and all other officers.

Section 8

And be it further enacted, that no member of the legislative assembly shall hold, or be appointed to, any office which shall have been created, or the salary or emoluments of which shall have been increased, while he was a member, during the term for which he was elected, and for one year after the expiration of such term; but this restriction shall not be applicable to members of the first legislative assembly; and no person holding a commission or appointment under the United States, except postmasters, shall be a member of the legislative assembly, or hold any office under the government of said territory.

Section 9

And be it further enacted, that the judicial power of said territory shall be vested in a supreme court, district courts, probate courts, and in justices of the peace. The supreme court shall consist of a chief justice and two associate justices, any two of whom shall constitute a quorum, and who shall hold a term at the seat of government of said territory annually, and they shall hold their offices during the period of four years, and until their successor shall be appointed and qualified. The said territory shall be divided into three judicial districts, and a district court shall be held in each of said districts by one of the justices of the supreme court at such times and places as may be prescribed by law; and the said judges shall, after their appointments, respectively, reside in the districts which shall be assigned them. The jurisdiction of the several courts herein provided for, both appellate and original, and that of the probate courts and of justices of the peace, shall be as limited by law: provided, that justices of the peace shall not have jurisdiction of any matter in controversy when the title or boundaries of land may be in dispute, or where the debt or sum claimed shall exceed one hundred dollars; and the said supreme and districts courts, respectively, shall possess chancery as well as commonlaw jurisdiction. Each district court, or the judge thereof, shall appoint its clerk, who shall also be the register in chancery, and shall keep his office at the place where the court may be held. Writs of error, bills of exception, and appeals shall be allowed in all cases from the final decisions of said district courts to the supreme court, under such regulations as may be prescribed by law; but in no case removed to the supreme court shall trial by jury be allowed in said court. The supreme court, or the justices thereof, shall appoint its own clerk, and every clerk shall hold his office at the pleasure of the court for which he shall have been appointed. Writs of error and appeals from the final decisions of said supreme court shall be allowed, and may be taken to the Supreme Court of the United States, in the same manner and under the same regulations as from the circuit courts of the United States, where the value of the property, or the amount in controversy, to be ascertained by the oath or affirmation of either party or other competent witness, shall exceed one thousand dollars; except only that in all cases involving title to slaves, the said writs of error or appeals shall be allowed and decided by the said supreme court, without regard to the value of the matter, property, or title in controversy; and except also that a writ of error or appeal shall also be allowed to the Supreme Court of the United States, from the decision of the said supreme court created by this act, or of any judge thereof, or of the district courts created by this act, or of any judge thereof, upon any writ of habeas corpus, involving the question of personal freedom. Provided, that nothing herein contained shall be construed to apply to or affect the provisions to the "Act respecting fugitives from justice, and persons escaping from the service of their masters," approved February twelfth, seventeen hundred and ninety-three, and the "Act to amend and supplementary to the aforesaid act," approved September eighteen, eighteen hundred and fifty; and each of the said district courts shall have and exercise the same jurisdiction in all cases arising under the Constitution and laws of the United States as is vested in the circuit and district courts of the United States; and the said supreme and district courts of the said territory, and the respective judges thereof, shall and may grant writs of habeas corpus in all cases in which the same are granted by the judges of the United States in the District of Columbia; and the first six days of every term of said courts, or so much thereof as shall be necessary, shall be appropriated to the trial of causes arising under the said constitution and laws and writs of error and appeal in all such cases shall be made to the supreme court of said territory, the same as in other cases. The said clerk shall receive in all such cases the same fees which the clerks of the district courts of Utah Territory now receive for similar services.

Section 10

And be it further enacted, that the provisions of an act entitled "An act respecting fugitives from justice, and persons escaping from the service of their masters," approved February twelve, seventeen hundred and ninety-three, and the provisions of the act entitled "An act to amend, and supplementary to, the aforesaid act," approved September eighteen, eighteen hundred and fifty, be, and the same are hereby, declared to extend to and be in full force within the limits of said territory of Nebraska.

Section 11

And be it further enacted, that there shall be appointed an attorney for said territory, who shall continue in office for four years, and until his successor shall be appointed and qualified, unless sooner removed by the president, and who shall receive the same fees and salary as the attorney of the United States for the present territory of Utah. There shall also be a marshal for the territory appointed, who shall hold his office for four years, and until his successor shall be appointed and qualified, unless sooner removed by the president, and who shall execute all processes issuing from the said courts when exercising their jurisdiction as circuit and district courts of the United States; he shall perform the duties, be subject to the same regulation and penalties, and be entitled to the same fees, as the marshal of the district court of the United States for the present territory of Utah, and shall, in addition, be paid two hundred dollars annually as a compensation for extra services.

Section 12

And be it further enacted, that the governor, secretary, chief justice and associate justices, attorney, and marshal shall be nominated and, by and with the advice and consent of the Senate, appointed by the president of the United States. The governor and secretary to be appointed as aforesaid shall, before they act as such, respectively take an oath or affirmation before the district judge or some justice of the peace in the limits of said territory, duly authorized to administer oaths and affirmations by the laws now in force therein, or before the chief justice, or some associate justice of the Supreme Court of the United States, to support the Constitution of the United States and faithfully to discharge the duties of their respective offices, which said oaths, when so taken, shall be certified by the person by whom the same shall have been taken; and such certificates shall be received and recorded by the said secretary among the executive proceedings; and the chief justice and associate justices, and all other civil officers in said territory, before they act as such, shall take a like oath or affirmation before the said governor or secretary, or some judge or justice of the peace of the territory, who may be duly commissioned and qualified, which said oath or affirmation shall be certified and transmitted by the person taking the same to the secretary, to be by him recorded as aforesaid; and afterwards, the like oath or affirmation shall be taken, certified, and recorded, in such manner and form as may be prescribed by law. The governor shall receive an annual salary of two thousand five hundred dollars. The chief justice and associate justices shall each receive an annual salary of two thousand dollars. The secretary shall receive an annual salary of two thousand dollars. The said salaries shall be paid quarter-yearly, from the dates of the respective appointments, at the treasury of the United States; but no such payment shall be made until said officers shall have entered upon the duties of their respective appointments. The members of the legislative assembly shall be entitled to receive three dollars each per day during their attendance at the sessions thereof and three dollars each for every twenty miles' travel in going to and returning from the said sessions, estimated according to the nearest usually travelled route; and an additional allowance of three dollars shall be paid to the presiding officer of each house for each day he shall so preside. And a chief clerk, one assistant clerk, a sergeant-at-arms, and doorkeeper may be chosen for each house; and the chief clerk shall receive four dollars per day, and the said other officers three dollars per day during the session of the legislative assembly; but no other officers shall be paid by the United States; provided, that there shall be but one session of the legislature annually, unless, on an extraordinary occasion, the governor shall think proper to call the legislature together. There shall be appropriated annually the usual sum, to be expended by the governor, to defray the contingent expenses of the territory, including the salary of a clerk of the executive department; and there shall also be appropriated annually a sufficient sum, to be expended by the secretary of the territory, and upon an estimate to be made by the secretary of the treasury of the United States, to defray the expenses of the legislative assembly, the printing of the laws, and other incidental expenses; and the governor and secretary of the territory shall, in the disbursement of all moneys entrusted to them, be governed solely by the instructions of the secretary of the treasury of the United States and shall, semiannually, account to the said secretary for the manner in which the aforesaid moneys shall have been expended; and no expenditure shall be made by said legislative assembly for objects not specially authorized by the acts of Congress, making the appropriations, nor beyond the sums thus appropriated for such objects.

Section 13

And be it further enacted, that the legislative assembly of the territory of Nebraska shall hold its first session at such time and place in said territory as the governor thereof shall appoint and direct; and at said first session, or as soon thereafter as they shall deem expedient, the governor and legislative assembly shall proceed to locate and establish the seat of government for said territory at such place as they may deem eligible; which place, however, shall thereafter be subject to be changed by the said governor and legislative assembly.

Section 14

And be it further enacted, that a delegate to the House of Representatives of the United States, to serve for the term of two years, who shall be a citizen of the United States, may be elected by the voters qualified to elect members of the legislative assembly, who shall be entitled to the same rights and privileges as are exercised and enjoyed by the delegates from the several other territories of the United States to the said House of Representatives, but the delegate first elected shall hold his seat only during the term of the Congress to which he shall be elected. The first election shall be held at such time and places and be conducted in such manner as the governor shall appoint and direct; and at all subsequent elections the times, places, and manner of holding the elections shall be prescribed by law. The person having the greatest number of votes shall be declared by the governor to be duly elected; and a certificate thereof shall be given accordingly. That the Constitution, and all laws of the United States which are not locally inapplicable, shall have the same force and effect within the said territory of Nebraska as elsewhere within the United States, except the eighth section of the act preparatory to the admission of Missouri into the Union, approved March sixth, eighteen hundred and twenty, which, being inconsistent with the principle of nonintervention by Congress with slavery in the states and territories, as recognized by the legislation of eighteen hundred and fifty, commonly called the Compromise Measures, is hereby declared inoperative and void; it being the true intent and meaning of this act not to legislate slavery into any territory or state, nor to exclude it therefrom, but to leave the people thereof perfectly free to form and regulate their domestic institutions in their own way, subject only to the Constitution of the United States: provided, that nothing herein contained shall be construed to revive or put in force any law or regulation which may have existed prior to the act of March sixth, eighteen hundred and twenty, either protecting, establishing, prohibiting, or abolishing slavery.

Section 15

And be it further enacted, that there shall hereafter be appropriated, as has been customary for the territorial governments, a sufficient amount, to be expended under the direction of the said governor of the territory of Nebraska, not exceeding the sums heretofore appropriated for similar objects, for the erection of suitable public buildings at the seat of government, and for the purchase of a library, to be kept at the seat of government for the use of the governor, legislative assembly, judges of the supreme court, secretary, marshal, and attorney of said territory, and such other persons, and under such regulations, as shall be prescribed by law.

Section 16

And be it further enacted, that when the lands in the said territory shall be surveyed under the direction of the government of the United States, preparatory to bringing the same into market, sections numbered sixteen and thirty-six in each township in said territory shall be, and the same are hereby, reserved for the purpose of being applied to schools in said territory and in the states and territories hereafter to be erected out of the same.

Section 17

And be it further enacted, that, until otherwise provided by law, the governor of said territory may define the judicial districts of said territory and assign the judges who may be appointed for said territory to the several districts; and also appoint the times and places for holding courts in the several counties or subdivisions in each of said judicial districts by proclamation, to be issued by him; but the legislative assembly, at their first or any subsequent session, may organize, alter, or modify such judicial districts and assign the judges and alter the times and places of holding the courts, as to them shall seem proper and convenient.

Section 18

And be it further enacted, that all officers to be appointed by the president, by and with the advice and consent of the Senate, for the territory of Nebraska, who, by virtue of the provisions of any law now existing, or which may be enacted during the present Congress, are required to give security for moneys that may be entrusted with them for disbursement, shall give such security at such time and place and in such manner as the secretary of the treasury may prescribe.

Section 19

And be it further enacted, that all that part of the territory of the United States included within the following limits, except such portions thereof as are hereinafter expressly exempted from the operations of this act, to wit, beginning at a point on the western boundary of the state of Missouri, where the thirty-seventh parallel of north latitude crosses the same; thence west on said parallel to the eastern boundary of New Mexico; thence north on said boundary to latitude thirty-eight; thence following said boundary westward to the east boundary of the territory of Utah, on the summit of the Rocky Mountains; thence northward on said summit to the fortieth parallel of latitude; thence east on said parallel to the western boundary of the state of Missouri; thence south with the western boundary of said state to the place of beginning, be, and the same is hereby, created into a temporary government by the name of the territory of Kansas; and when admitted as a state or states, the said territory, or any portion of the same, shall be received into the Union with or without slavery, as their constitution may prescribe at the time of their admission: provided, that nothing in this act contained shall be construed to inhibit the government of the United States from dividing said territory into two or more territories, in such manner and at such times as Congress shall deem convenient and proper, or from attaching any portion of said territory to any other state or territory of the United States. Provided further, that nothing in this act contained shall be construed to impair the rights of person or property now pertaining to the Indians in said territory, so long as such rights shall remain unextinguished by treaty between the United States and such Indians, or to include any territory which, by treaty with any Indian tribe, is not, without the consent of said tribe, to be included within the territorial limits or jurisdiction of any state or territory; but all such territory shall be excepted out of the boundaries and constitute no part of the territory of Kansas, until said tribe shall signify their assent to the president of the United States to be included within the said territory of Kansas, or to affect the authority of the government of the United States to make any regulation respecting such Indians, their lands, property, or other rights by treaty, law, or otherwise, which it would have been competent to the government to make if this act had never passed.

[Sections 20-30 and 32-36 are identical to the sections establishing a territorial government for Nebraska and have therefore been omitted.]

Section 31

And be it further enacted, that the seat of government of said territory is hereby located temporarily at Fort Leavenworth; and that such portions of the public buildings as may not be actually used and needed for military purposes may be occupied and used, under the direction of the governor and legislative assembly, for such public purposes as may be required under the provisions of this act.

Section 37

And be it further enacted, that all treaties, laws, and other engagements made by the government of the United States with the Indian tribes inhabiting the territories embraced within this act, shall be faithfully and rigidly observed, notwithstanding anything contained in this act; and that the existing agencies and superintendencies of said Indians be continued with the same powers and duties which are now prescribed by law, except that the president of the United States may, at his discretion, change the location of the office of superintendent.

Approved, May 30, 1854.

DRED SCOTT, Plff. in Er.,
v.
JOHN F. A. SANDFORD.
(See S. C. 19 How. 393–633.)

Plea in abatement, when may be reviewed—
the word "citizen" in the Constitution does
not embrace one of the negro race—negro
cannot become a citizen—slave not made free
by residence in a free state or territory—
Declaration of Independence does not include
slaves as part of the people—the rights and
privileges conferred by the Constitution upon
citizens do not apply to the negro race—Constitution should have the meaning intended
when it was adopted—court may examine
other errors besides plea in abatement—Constitution expressly affirms right of property
in slaves—Missouri compromise unconstitutional and void.

Where a plea in abatement, by defendant, to the
jurisdiction of the court below is overruled on demurrer, and the defendant thereupon pleads in bar,
upon which issues were joined and the trial and
verdict were in his favor, and the plaintiff thereupon brought the case into this court by writ of error, and the plea and demurrer and judgment of the
court below upon it are part of the record; held,
that this court has power to review the decision of
the court below upon the plea in abatement.

It is therefore the duty of the court to decide
whether the facts stated in the plea, are or are not
sufficient to show that the plaintiff is not entitled
to sue as a citizen in the court of the United States.

The provisions of the Constitution of the United
States in relation to the personal rights and privileges to which the citizen of a state should be entitled, do not embrace the negro African race, at
that time in this country, or who might afterwards
be imported, who had then been or should afterwards be made free in any state.

Such provisions of the Constitution do not put it
in the power of a single state to make out one of
the negro African race a citizen of the United
States, and to endue him with the full rights of
citizenship in every other state without their consent.

The Constitution of the United States does not
act upon one of the negro race whenever he shall
be made free under the laws of a state, and raise
him to the rank of a citizen, and immediately
clothe him with all the privileges of a citizen of
any other state, and in its own courts.

The plaintiff in error was a negro slave, and
brought into a free State (Illinois), and in the free
territory of the United States for about four years,
during which time he was married to another negro

691

slave who also was in said free territory. One of their children (Eliza) was born on the River Mississippi, north of the north line of Missouri, and another of their children was born in the State of Missouri, to which state he had returned.

Held, that the plaintiff in error could not be and was not a citizen of the State of Missouri, within the meaning of the Constitution of the United States, and consequently was not entitled to sue in its courts.

The legislation and histories of the times, and the language used in the Declaration of Independence, show that neither the class of persons who had been imported as slaves, nor their descendants, whether they had become free or not, were then acknowledged as part of the people, nor intended to be included in the general words used in that instrument.

The descendants of Africans who were imported into this country and sold as slaves, when they shall become emancipated, or who are born of parents who had become free before their birth, are not citizens of a state in the sense in which the word "citizen" is used in the Constitution of the United States.

The enslaved African race was not intended to be included in, and formed no part of, the people who framed and adopted the Declaration of Independence.

When the framers of the Constitution were conferring special rights and privileges upon the citizens of a state in every other part of the Union, it is impossible to believe that these rights and privileges were intended to be extended to the negro race.

The words of the Constitution should be given the meaning they were intended to bear, when that instrument was framed and adopted.

Where this court has decided against the jurisdiction of the Circuit Court on a plea of abatement, it has still the right to examine any question presented by exception or by the record, and may reverse the judgment for errors committed, and remand the case to the Circuit Court for it to dismiss the case for want of jurisdiction.

The right of property in a slave is distinctly and expressly affirmed in the Constitution.

The Act of Congress which prohibited a citizen from holding and owning property of this kind in the territory of the United States north of the line therein mentioned (thirty-six degrees thirty minutes north latitude), is not warranted by the Constitution, and is therefore void.

Neither Dred Scott himself, nor any of his family were made free by being carried into such territory; even if they had been carried there by their owner with the intention of becoming permanent residents.

Scott was not made free by being taken to Rock Island in the State of Illinois.

As Scott was a slave when taken into the State of Illinois by his owner, and was there held as such, and brought back into Missouri in that character, his status, as free or slave, depended on the laws of Missouri, and not of Illinois. He and his family were not free, but were, by the laws of Missouri, the property of defendant.

Argued Feb. 11, 12, 13 and 14, 1856. May 12, 1856, ordered to be re-argued at the next term. Re-argued Dec. 15, 16, 17 and 18, 1856. Decided March 6, 1857.

IN ERROR to the Circuit Court of the United States for the District of Missouri.

On November 2, 1853, Dred Scott, by his attorney, filed in the clerk's office of the Circuit Court of the United States for the District of Missouri, the following declaration against the defendant, John F. A. Sandford:

Dred Scott, of St. Louis, in the State of Missouri, and a citizen of the State of Missouri, complains of John F. A. Sandford, of the City of New York, and a citizen of the State of New York, in the plea of trespass for that the defendant heretofore, to wit: on the 1st day of January, A. D. 1853, at St. Louis, in the County of St. Louis and State of Missouri, with force and arms assaulted the plain-

tiff, and without law or right held him as a slave, and imprisoned him for the space of six hours and more, and then and there did threaten to beat the plaintiff and to hold him in prison, and restrained of his liberty, so that by means of such threats the plaintiff was put in fear and could not attend to his business, and thereby lost great gains and profits which he might have made and otherwise would have made in the prosecution of his business, to wit: $2,500, and other wrongs to the plaintiff then and there did, against the peace and to the damage of the plaintiff $3,000.

And also for that the defendant heretofore, on the 1st day of January, A. D. 1853, with force and arms at St. Louis aforesaid, an assault did make on Harriet Scott, then and still the wife of the plaintiff, and then and there did imprison said Harriet, and hold her as a slave, without law or right, for the space of six hours, and then and there did threaten to beat said Harriet and hold her as a slave, so that by means of the premises said Harriet was put in great fear and pain, and could not and did not attend to the plaintiff's business, and the plaintiff lost and was deprived of the society, comfort and assistance of his said wife, and thereby lost great gains and profits, of the value, to wit: of $2,500, and other wrongs to the plaintiff, the defendant then and there did, against the peace and to the plaintiff's damage, $3,000.

And also for that the defendant heretofore, to wit: on the 1st day of January, A. D. 1853, with force and arms at St. Louis aforesaid, made an assault on Eliza Scott and Lizzie Scott, then and still infant daughters and servants of the plaintiff, and then and there imprisoned and held as slaves said Eliza and Lizzie, for a long space of time, to wit: six hours, and then and there did threaten to beat said Eliza and Lizzie and hold them as slaves and restrained of their liberty, so that by means of the premises, said Eliza and Lizzie were put in great fear, and could not and did not attend to plaintiff's business as otherwise they might and would have done, and the plaintiff thereby lost the comfort, society, service and assistance of his said children and servants, of great value, to wit: $2,500, and other wrongs to the plaintiff, the defendant then and there did against the peace, and to the damage of plaintiff $3,000, and the plaintiff on account of the aforesaid several grievances, brings suit, etc., by his attorney,   R. M. Field.

The defendant, by his attorney, filed the following plea:

Plea to the jurisdiction of the court. April Term, 1854.

And the said John F. A. Sandford, in his own proper person, comes and says that this court ought not to have or take further cognizance of the action aforesaid, because he says that said cause of action, and each and every of them, if any such have accrued to the said Dred Scott, accrued to the said Dred Scott out of the jurisdiction of this court and exclusively within the jurisdiction of the courts of the State of Missouri; for that, to wit: the said plaintiff Dred Scott is not a citizen of the State of Missouri, as alleged in his declaration, because he is a negro of African descent, his ancestors were of pure African blood, and were brought into this country and sold as negro

1856.   DRED SCOTT V. SANDFORD.   393–633

slaves, and this the said Sandford is ready to verify; wherefore he prays judgment whether this court can or will take further cognizance of the action aforesaid.

The plea was verified.

The plaintiff filed the following demurrer to this plea:

And now comes the plaintiff and demurs in law to the plea of the defendant to the jurisdiction of the court, and says that the said plea and the matters therein contained are not sufficient in law to preclude the court of its jurisdiction of this case, and that the plaintiff is not bound by law to reply to said plea. Wherefore the plaintiff prays judgment of said plea, and that the defendant answer further to the plaintiff's said action, etc.

On April 24, 1854, the matters of law arising upon the demurrer were argued and submitted to the court. On April 25, the court rendered a decision that the law was for plaintiff on said demurrer, and that the said demurrer be, and the same is hereby sustained.

On May 4, 1854, in accordance with an agreement by the attorneys, the defendant filed pleas, Nos. 1, 2 and 3, to all of which pleas the plaintiff filed replications. Said attorneys also filed an agreement upon the statement of the facts in this case. The pleas are as follows:

1. And the said John F. A. Sandford, by H. A. Garland, his attorney, comes and defends the wrong and injury, when, etc., and says that he is not guilty of the said supposed trespass above laid to his charge, or any part thereof in manner and form as the said Dred Scott hath above thereof complained against him, and of this he, the said Sandford, putteth himself upon the country.

2. And for a further plea in this behalf, as to the making of said assault on said Dred Scott in the first count in said declaration mentioned, imprisoning him and keeping and detaining him in prison, etc., the said Sandford, by leave of the court obtained, says that the said Dred Scott ought not have or maintain his aforesaid action thereof against him, because he says that before, and at the time when, etc., in the said first count mentioned, the said Dred Scott was a negro slave, the lawful property of the defendant, and as such slave he gently laid his hands upon him, and only restrained him of such liberty as he had a right to do, and this the said Sandford is ready to verify, wherefore he prays judgment whether the said Scott ought to have or maintain his aforesaid action thereof against him.

3. And for a further plea in this behalf, as to making the said assault upon Harriet, the wife, and Eliza and Lizzie, the daughters of the said Dred Scott, in the second and third counts of the said declaration mentioned, and imprisoning them and keeping and detaining them in prison, etc., the said John F. A. Sandford, by leave of the court obtained, says that said Dred Scott out not to have or maintain his aforesaid action thereof against him, because he says that before and at the said time, etc., when etc., in the said second and third counts mentioned, the said Harriet, wife of said Scott, and Eliza and Lizzie, his daughters, were the lawful slaves of the said Sandford, and as such slaves he gently laid his hands upon them and restrained them of their liberty as he had a

15 L. ed.

right to do. And this he is ready to verify. Wherefore he prays judgment, etc.

           Garland, for defendant.

The replications are as follows:

The plaintiff, as to the plea of the defendant firstly above pleaded, and whereof he has put himself on the country, doth do like. Field.

And the plaintiff, as to the plea of the defendant secondly above pleaded as to said several trespasses in the introductory part of that plea mentioned and therein attempted to be justified, says that the plaintiff, by reason of anything in that plea alleged, ought not to be barred from having and maintaining his aforesaid action against the defendant, because he says that said defendant at said time, when, etc., of his own wrong, and without the cause by him in his said second plea alleged, committed the said several trespasses in the introductory part of that plea mentioned, in manner and form as the plaintiff has above in his declaration complained, and this the plaintiff prays may be inquired of by the country.

The replication to the third plea was similar to the second.

The agreed statement of facts was as follows:

In the year 1834 the plaintiff was a negro slave belonging to Doctor Emerson, who was a surgeon in the Army of the United States. In that year, 1834, said Doctor Emerson took the plaintiff from the State of Missouri to the military post at Rock Island in the State of Illinois, and held him there as a slave until the month of April or May, 1836. At the time last mentioned, said Doctor Emerson removed the plaintiff from said military post at Rock Island to the military post at Fort Snelling, situate on the west bank of the Mississippi River in the Territory known as Upper Louisiana, acquired by the United States of France, and situate north of the latitude of 36 degrees 30 minutes north, and north of the State of Missouri. Said Doctor Emerson held the plaintiff in slavery at said Fort Snelling, from said last-mentioned date until the year 1838.

In the year 1835, Harriet, who is named in the second count of the plaintiff's declaration, was the negro slave of Major Taliaferro, who belonged to the Army of the United States. In that year, 1835, said Major Taliaferro took said Harriet to said Fort Snelling, a military post situated as hereinbefore stated, and kept her there as a slave until the year 1836, and then sold and delivered her as a slave at said Fort Snelling unto the said Doctor Emerson hereinbefore named. Said Doctor Emerson held said Harriet in slavery at said Fort Snelling until the year 1838.

In the year 1836 the plaintiff and said Harriet, at said Fort Snelling, with the consent of said Doctor Emerson, who then claimed to be their master and owner, intermarried and took each other for husband and wife, Eliza and Lizzie named in the third count of the plaintiff's declaration, are the fruit of that marriage. Eliza is about fourteen years old, and was born on board of the steamboat Gipsey, north of the north line of the State of Missouri, and upon the River Mississippi. Lizzie is about seven years old, and was born in the State of Missouri, at the military post called Jefferson Barracks.

In the year 1838, said Doctor Emerson removed the plaintiff and said Harriet and their said daughter Eliza from said Fort Snelling to the State of Missouri, where they have ever since resided.

Before the commencement of this suit, said Doctor Emerson sold and conveyed the plaintiff, said Harriet, Eliza and Lizzie, to the defendant as slaves, and the defendant has ever since claimed to hold them, and each of them, as slaves.

At the times mentioned in the plaintiff's declaration, the defendant, claiming to be owner as aforesaid, laid his hands upon said plaintiff, Harriet, Eliza and Lizzie, and imprisoned them, doing in this respect, however, no more than what he might lawfully do, if they were of right his slaves at such time.

Further proof may be given on the trial for either party.

Mr. R. M. Field, for plaintiff.
Mr. H. A. Garland, for defendant.

The case was tried, at the Circuit Court held for the District of Missouri at St. Louis on May 15, 1854, before the court and a jury.

The jury found the following verdict, viz.:

"As to the first issue joined in this case, we of the jury find the defendant not guilty; and as to the issue secondly above joined, we of the jury find, that before and at the time when, etc., in the first count mentioned, the said Dred Scott was a negro slave, the lawful property of the defendant. And as to the issue thirdly above joined, we the jury find, that before and at the time when, etc., in the second and third counts mentioned, the said Harriet, wife of said Dred Scott, and Eliza and Lizzie the daughters of the said Dred Scott were negro slaves, the lawful property of the defendant." Whereupon it is now considered by the court, that the plaintiff take nothing by his writ in this case, and that the defendant John F. A. Sandford go hence without day and recover against said plaintiff, Dred Scott, the costs by him expended in the defense of this suit.

A motion for a new trial was made by the attorneys for the plaintiff, which the court overruled. Thereupon the said plaintiff filed a bill of exception, which is as follows:

Dred Scott
v.   } April Term, 1854.
John F. A. Sandford.

On the trial of this cause by the jury, the plaintiff, to maintain the issues on his part, read to the jury, the following agreed statement of facts.

"It is agreed that Dred Scott brought suit for his freedom, in the Circuit Court of St. Louis County; that there was a verdict and judgment in his favor; that on a writ of error to the Supreme Court, the judgment below was reversed, and the same remanded to the Circuit Court, where it has been continued to await the decision of this case.

Mr. Field, for plaintiff.
Mr. Garland, for defendant."

No further testimony was given to the jury by either party. Thereupon the plaintiff moved the court to give the jury, the following instructions:

Plaintiff's Instruction.

The jury are instructed, that upon the facts agreed to by the parties, they ought to find for the plaintiff.

The court refused to give such instruction to the jury, and the plaintiff to such refusal then and there duly excepted. The court then gave the following instruction to the jury, on motion of the defendant:

Defendant's Instruction.

The jury are instructed, that upon the facts in this case the law is with the defendant.

To the giving of such instruction the plaintiff then and there duly excepted.

The jury found the verdict as above. The plaintiff thereupon immediately filed in court the following motion for a new trial:

And now, after verdict, and before judgment, the plaintiff comes and moves the court to set aside the verdict and grant a new trial, because the court misdirected the jury in matter of law on said trial.   Field.

The court overruled the said motion and gave judgment on verdict for the defendant; and to such action of the court the plaintiff then and there duly excepted.

The plaintiff writes this bill of exceptions and prays that it may be allowed, and signed and sealed.   Field.

Allowed and signed and sealed, May 15, 1854.
R. W. Wells.   [seal.]

A writ of error was issued, and in the Supreme Court of the United States, December Term, 1854, the following was filed:

And now comes said plaintiff in error and says that in the record of the proceedings, and in the giving of judgment below, there is manifest error, because the court below, in the trial of the cause, misdirected the jury in matter of law, and because the court below gave judgment for the defendant below, when the judgment should have been for plaintiff below, wherefore for said errors and others the plaintiff prays judgment of reversal here, and that he may be restored to all he has lost.

By his attorney, Nathaniel Holmes.
Filed, Dec. 30, 1854.

Messrs. M. Blair and Curtis, for the plaintiff in error:

1. The first question is, whether this court will consider the question raised in the Circuit Court by the plea to the jurisdiction, no final judgment having been rendered on the demurrer to that plea, and the defendant having pleaded over after the demurrer was sustained, and the final judgment assigned for error having been rendered on the issue on the merits.

2. Whether, if the ruling of the Circuit Court on the demurrer to the plea in abatement is subject to be reviewed here, the judgment of the court, in holding the plaintiff to be "a citizen" in such sense as to enable him to maintain an action in that character in the courts of the United States, was erroneous.

3. Whether the facts stated in the agreed case entitle the plaintiff and his family to freedom, supposing the 8th section of the Act of 1820, known as the Missouri Compromise, to be constitutional.

4. Whether the said Act is constitutional.

Upon the first point the counsel cited, Sheppard v. Graves, 14 How. 519; U. S. v. Boyd, 5 How. 51; Smith v. Kernochen, 7 How. 216; Sims v. Hundley, 6 How. 1; Bailey v. Dozier, 6 How. 23; Conard v. Atlantic Ins. Co. 1 Pet. 386; De Wolf v. Rabaud, 1 Pet. 476; Evans v. Gee, 11 Pet. 89; 1 Wash. C. C. 70, 80; 2 Sumn. 251; 2 Dall. 341; 4 Dall. 330, and then said: In this case, as in those cited, the declaration gives jurisdiction, and the facts alleged in support of it can only be contested by making an issue as in other cases. If that issue be not made, or be waived in the conduct of the cause according to a well-settled practice of the court, there is no reason in this case more than in any other why the objection should be available at a later stage of the case. If the fact had been that plaintiff was not a resident of Missouri, and that was the reason why he was not a citizen, no advantage could be taken of the fact at any subsequent stage of the case. What difference does it make that another fact is relied on to show that he is not a citizen? It is the right to sue as "a citizen" of Missouri, which is questioned: and it is immaterial whether the right be questioned on account of residence, or on account of any other circumstance which deprives him of the character of a citizen of Missouri.

2. But if the court should be of opinion that the question raised by the plea in abatement, and the demurrer thereto, is not waived, and that the judgment of the Circuit Court therein must be maintained before it will consider the questions affecting his right to freedom, I submit the following considerations in support of the judgment on the demurrer:

The opinion of the court in Amy v. Smith, 1 Litt. 326, 4 Ga. 68, that free negroes are not citizens within the meaning of the 2d section of the 4th article of the Constitution, delivered in the spring of 1822, displays no research, logic or learning. On the other hand, the dissenting opinion of Judge Mills, p. 337, is sustained by the views of Judge Washington in Corfield v. Coryell, 4 Wash. C. C. 71.

21 Ala. 434; State v. Manuel, 4 Dev. & Bat. 24.

The other decisions relied on, Meigs, 339; 1 English, 509, are to the same effect as the decision in Amy v. Smith, and simply follow that.

The argument most relied on by those who deny the citizenship of free colored men is, that the Acts of Congress on the subject of naturalization provide for naturalizing white persons only. But even naturalization was not limited to the whites by the Constitution, and it has been extended repeatedly by treaty and Act of Congress to Indians and negroes.

Treaty with Choctaws, art. 14, 20th September, 1830; Treaty with the Cherokees, 12th art. Vol. V. U. S. Laws, 647; Treaties of 1803 for Louisiana, 1819 for Florida, 1847 for California; 21 Ala. 454; and as Judge Gaston says, 4 Dev. & Bat. 24, there is no connection between the subject of citizenship as acquired by birth and that acquired under the laws of Congress, and it would be a dangerous mistake to confound them. That citizenship is acquired by birth, is a well settled common law principle.

Vattel, ch. 19, secs. 212, 313, 314; Justinian, Lib. 1, Tit. 5, sec. 3; Constitution, sec. 5, art. 2.

The Constitution of the United States recognizes but two kinds of free persons, citizens and aliens. Nobody supposes that free negroes are aliens. They must therefore be citizens.

Opinions Atty.-Gen. Vol. IV. p. 417; 3d sec. Act March 6, 1820; 6th sec. Act of 1812, to form a territorial government in Missouri; Militia Act, May 17, 1792; Constitutions of Kentucky, Louisiana, Mississippi, Connecticut and Missouri.

All of the above define the qualifications of electors in terms, "free white male citizens;" and thus show that it is as a class of citizens that the negroes are excluded. These considerations would authorize the conclusion that the framers of the Constitution and the patriots of that era regarded this class of persons as citizens, and included them in that character in the provisions of the Constitution; and this is fully confirmed by reference to the laws and records of that day.

Act of Mass. 6th March, 1788; Proposal of South Carolina, Jan. 25, 1778, to amend the 4th article; Journals, Vol. II. p. 606; Journals, Vol. IV. p. 183; Organization of the Western Territory, Resolutions, April 23, 1784; Ordinance 1787, art. 4; 2 Kent's Com. p. 258, note b.

Missouri Rev. Laws of 1845, p. 755, and Code of 1835, allude to free negroes who were "citizens."

No reason can be imagined for permitting a suit between free white persons of different states, for wrongs which the local tribunals were deemed inadequate to redress, which will not apply with equal force to controversies to which a free negro may be a party. They have equal capacity with other citizens to hold property and carry on business, and therefore to create the mischief against which the national judiciary was provided. The words of a law are to be construed with reference to the object of the law.

16 Pet. 640; 12 Wheat. 441; 16 Pet. 104.

In 1 Paine, C. C. 394, the courts say that a person need not have acquired political rights; it is only necessary that he should have acquired a domicil, to enable him to sue as a citizen; and in 3 Wash. C. C. 546, that "citizenship means nothing but residence."

3. The next question to be considered is, whether Dred and his family, or either of them, was emancipated by being taken to Illinois, and to that part of Louisiana Territory lying north of 36 degrees 30 minutes, and being detained there in the manner described in the agreed case. The eldest child, Eliza, having been born north of the Missouri line, on the boat whilst descending the Mississippi, was free under the Constitution of Illinois, and well settled legal principles.

Constitution of Illinois, art. 6, secs. 1 and 2; 3 U. S. Stat. at L. p. 544; Spotts v. Gillaspie, 6 Rand. (Va.), 572; Commonwealth v. Holloway, 2 S. & R. 305.

The Circuit Court decided against the plaintiff on the strength of Scott v. Emerson, 15 Mo. 586.

But the question depends on general principles, and the courts of the United States, whilst they will respectfully consider the decisions of the State Court, decide such questions according to their own judgment of the law.

Swift v. Tyson, 16 Pet. 1; Carpenter v. Ins. Co. 16 Pet. 511; Lane v. Vick, 3 How. 476; Foxcroft v. Mallett, 4 How. 379.

During the time that Dr. Emerson kept Dred at his station at Rock Island, and Harriet at Fort Snelling, there is no evidence that he had or claimed a residence elsewhere, and this court, in Ennis v. Smith, 14 How. 423, "where a party lives, is taken prima facie to be his domicil."

See, also, Sylvia v. Kirby, 17 Mo. 434.

In the case of Scott v. Emerson, 15 Mo. 576, the court base their decision on two grounds:

1st. That by returning to Missouri to reside the master's right, which was suspended during the residence in Illinois, and in the Territory, is revived.

2d. The Constitution of Illinois, and the 8th sec. of the Act of 1820, are penal statutes which the courts of other States were not bound to enforce.

In support of the first position, Ex parte Grace, 2 Hagg. 90; Commonwealth v. Aves, 18 Pick. 193, and Mahoney v. Ashton, 4 H. & McH. 295, were cited.

These decisions are inapplicable to the case at bar, for in the present case the Constitution and Statute of Illinois expressly provide that emancipation shall be the effect of the violation of the provision. The laws under which the above decisions were made were different.

David v. Porter, 4 H. & McH. 418; Betty v. Horton, 1 Lee, 615.

The second ground relied upon by the court was equally untenable. See opinion of Judge Gambles, of the same case of Emerson v. Scott, "in this State it has been recognized from the beginning of the government as a correct position in law, that the master who takes his slave to reside in a state or territory where slavery is prohibited, emancipates his slave.

Also McMicken v. Amos, 4 Rand. 134; Bank v. Earle, 13 Pet. 590; Spencer v. Dennis, 8 Gill 321.

4. The freedom of Harriet and her daughter Lizzie depends on the validity of the 8th section of the Act of March 6, 1820, entitled "An Act to authorize the people of Missouri Territory to form a constitution and state government," etc.

The section is as follows:

That in all that territory ceded by France to the United States, which lies north of 36 degrees 30 minutes north latitude, not included within the limits of the State contemplated by this Act, slavery and involuntary servitude, otherwise than in the punishment of crimes whereof the party shall have been duly convicted, shall be, and the same is hereby forever prohibited.

Provided, always, that any person escaping into the same, from whom labor or service is lawfully claimed in any State or Territory of the United States, such fugitive may be lawfully reclaimed and conveyed to the person claiming his or her labor or service as aforesaid.

The validity of this section is denied, on the ground that Congress possessed no power to prohibit slavery in the Territories.

It is not the power to govern the Territories, but the extent of the power which is questioned. Even those who deny any constitutional power to govern the Territories, admit the power on the ground of necessity; but they say where the necessity stops, there the power ceases. But this concedes the whole question; for if it

be lawful to legislate at all, the quantum which may be necessary is purely a legislative question; and indeed, whether the Constitution confers directly the legislative power in question or not is immaterial, seeing that it owns the lands, and has power to pass what laws it may deem expedient to dispose of and make them available.

Undoubtedly, for temporary purposes, it is indispensable that provision be made to govern the people in order that the lands shall possess any value, or that what remains after part is sold, may not be seized and confiscated. What would be proper provisions to this end, is not within the scope of judicial inquiry. If it were, it is demonstrable that the provision in question is most judicious, as a mere regulation to facilitate the disposition of public lands.

But it is alleged that the particular provision prohibiting slavery is violative of some part of the Constitution, which establishes the equality of the States and the rights of slave holders to take that species of property into the Territories of the United States. I admit that whether the power of Congress to legislate be given expressly or by implication, it is given with the limitation that it shall be exercised in subordination to the Constitution, and that if it be exercised in violation of any provisions of the Constitution, the Act would be void. Subject to this limitation, Congress is at liberty to adopt any means to accomplish its object.

McCulloch v. Maryland, 4 Wheat. 316.

But where is it written in the Constitution that no law shall be passed prohibiting slavery in the territories? Not only was this measure adopted as one deemed advisable and proper to the well government of the territories under both the Confederation and the Constitution, but when the Mississippi Territory was ceded in 1798, it was deemed necessary to stipulate that slavery should not be prohibited, in order to limit the discretion of Congress. The limitation sought to be imposed is one dependent altogether upon state laws, and subjects Congress to the State Legislatures. The Act is now claimed as unconstitutional, because a species of property recognized in the laws of the States cannot be held in the Territories; but it would become constitutional if the States should cease to recognize such property; and again unconstitutional if the States should recognize it again. How the law in question affects the States as States, in any respect, is not perceived; it is not pretended that any State has legislative rights in the Territories.

Pollard v. Hagan, 3 How. 322.

On other subjects, there are difficulties in adjusting the rights of the general and state governments; but there can be no conflict on this. Over the Territories, the general government alone has any power; and in the exercise of that, as of all other powers, is a government of the people. "In form and substance (this court says), it emanates from them, its powers are granted by them, and are to be exercised on them and for their benefit."

On this branch of the subject, the counsel cited the following authorities: Story's Com. Const. Vol. III., pp. 193, 195; 1 Kent's Com. 360; Sergeant, Const. Law, 389; McCulloch v. Maryland, 4 Wheat. 422; Am. Ins. Co. v. Canter, 1 Pet. 543; Cherokee Nation v. Georgia, 5

Pet. 44; Menard v. Aspasia, 5 Pet. 505; Strader v. Graham, 10 How. 93; Cross v. Harrison, 16 How. 193; Hogg v. Zanesville Canal Co. 5 Ohio, 410; Phœbe v. Jay, Breese, 210; Spooner v. McConnell, 1 McL. 341; Merry v. Chexnaider, 8 Mart. (N. S.) 699; Harry v. Decker, Walker (Miss.) 36; Rachael v. Walker, 4 Mo. 350; 3 How. 223. And the following Acts of Congress; 1 Stat. at L., pp. 50, 551; 2 Stat. at L., pp. 58, 283, 309, 514; 3 Stat. at L., p. 546; 4 Stat. at L., p. 740; 5 Stat. at L., pp. 10, 235, 797; 9 Stat. at L., pp. 223, 447.

Messrs. H. S. Geyer and R. Johnson, for the defendant in error:

This cause was argued before this court at the December Term, 1855, when it was ordered to be re-argued by counsel for their respective parties, at a next term of court, and especially upon the following points:

1. Whether or not the facts being admitted by the demurrer to the plea to the jurisdiction, the judgment on the demurrer being that the defendant answer over, and the submission of the defendant to that judgment, by pleading over to the merits, the appellate court can take notice of these facts thus admitted upon the record, in determining the question of the jurisdiction to the court below, to hear and fully dispose of the case.

2. Whether or not, assuming that the appellate court is bound to take notice of the facts thus appearing upon the record, the plaintiff is a citizen of the State of Missouri within the meaning of the 11th section of the Judiciary Act of 1789.

1. The averment that the plaintiff is a citizen of the State of Missouri, is a necessary averment. If it had been omitted or defectively stated, it would have been error in the Circuit Court to entertain jurisdiction, even though the defendant had not traversed the averment, but pleaded to the merits.

3 Dall. 382; 2 Cranch, 1, 126; Sullivan v. Fulton Steamboat Co. 6 Wheat. 450; Turner v. Enrille, 4 Dall. 7; Capron v. Van Noorden, 2 Cranch, 126.

If the plea demurred to, is to be regarded as a traverse or averment of citizenship of the plaintiff, then the fact on which the plaintiff claims a right to sue in the Circuit Court does not appear by the record; on the contrary, it appears affirmatively that he had no right to sue in that court. The whole question, whether the court could entertain jurisdiction and allow the defendant to plead over, depends on the decision on the demurrer. If that was erroneous, it was error to proceed further, and the defendants pleading over could not give jurisdiction.

2. It appears by the record that the defendant is a negro, born a slave; and therefore, whether he is entitled to freedom or not, by his temporary residence at Rock Island or Fort Snelling, or both, he is not and cannot be a citizen of the State of Missouri, within the meaning of the Constitution, or sec. 11 of the Judiciary Act.

Citizens, within the meaning of art. 3, sec. 2, are citizens of the United States, who are citizens of the state in which they respectively reside.

Read v. Bertrand, 4 Wash. C. C. 516; Knox v. Greenleaf, 4 Dall. 360; 3 Story on Const. 565, secs. 1687, 1688; 6 Pet. 761.

15 L. ed.

Citizens are natives or naturalized. All persons born in the United States are not citizens.

Exceptions are:

First. Children of foreign ambassadors.

Second. Indians.

Third. In general, persons of color.

1 Bouv. Inst. pp. 16, 64; Amy v. Smith, 1 Lit. Ky. 334; 2 Kent's Com. p. 258, note b. Free blacks are not citizens within the provision of the Constitution, art. 4, sec. 2; so held by Dagget, Ch. J., in Connecticut. See note Kent's Com. supra.

See, also, State v. Claiborne, 1 Meigs, 331; Opinions Atty.-Gen. Vol. I. 382, ed. 41; Vol. I. p. 506, ed. 52. "An inquiry into the political grade of the free colored population, under the Constitution of the United States," by John P. Denny.

Persons who are not citizens of the United States by birth, can become such only by virtue of a treaty, or in pursuance of some law of the United States.

The power of naturalization is exclusively vested in Congress.

U. S. v. Villato, 2 Dall. 370; Chirac v. Chirac, 2 Wheat. 269; Houston v. Moore, 5 Wheat. 48.

A slave cannot become a citizen merely by a discharge from bondage.

3. Assuming that the Circuit Court had jurisdiction, the facts, as agreed by the parties, do not establish the right of the plaintiff, his wife and children, or either of them, to freedom.

Sec. 1 of art. 5 of the Constitution of Illinois, and sec. 8 of the Act of 6 March, 1820, do not declare the consequence of bringing a slave within the Territory, embraced. There is no exception or saving in respect to the rights of travelers. The effect of the provision is, in terms, the same, whether a slave is introduced to reside there or for some temporary purpose. Neither clause changes the condition of the slave brought into the Territory embraced by it. The slave is held to be free while he remains within such State or country, only because his owner has not the authority of law to restrain him of his liberty.

The owner's authority is restored if the slave is found within a State or country where slavery exists by law.

The Slave Grace, 2 Hagg. Adm. 94; Willard v. The People, 4 Scam. 461; Graham v. Strader, 5 B. Mon. 181; 7 B. Mon. 633; Collins v. America, 9 B. Mon. 565; Mercer v. Gilman, 11 B. Mon. 210; Maria v. Kirby, 12 B. Mon. 542; Lewis v. Fullerton, 1 Rand. 15.

It has been held that where an owner of a slave brings him into a State or country in which slavery does not exist, or is prohibited by law, with the intention to make it his domicil, it operates as an emancipation, and the master cannot resume domain, though the slave return to, or is found in a country where slavery exists by law.

Rankin v. Lydia, 2 A. K. Marsh. 467; Griffith v. Fanny, Gilm. (Va.) 143; Lunsford v. Coquillon, 2 Mart. N. S. 405; Josephine v. Poultney, 1 La. Ann. 329; Winney v. Whitesides, 1 Mo. 472; Milly v. Smith, 2 Mo. 172; Nat v. Ruddle, 8 Mo. 282; Rachel v. Walker, 4 Mo. 350; overruled in Scott v. Emerson, 15 Mo. 570; Sylvia v. Kirby, 17 Mo. 434.

These are cases of emancipation by the voluntary act of the master, binding upon him everywhere, as would be emancipation upon any other proof recognized by law. Slaves, however, attending their owners temporarily sojourning in, or traveling through a State wherein slavery does not exist by law, are not thereby emancipated.

2 A. K. Marsh. 467; Graham v. Strader, 5 B. Mon. 181; Mercer v. Gilman, 11 B. Mon. 210; Maria v. Kirby, 12 B. Mon. 542; Lewis v. Fullerton, 1 Rand. 15; Henry v. Ball, 1 Wheat. 1; Spragg v. Mary, 3 Harr. & J.; Pocock v. Hendricks, 8 Gill & J. 421; The Slave Grace, 2 Hagg. 94; Commonwealth v. Aves, 18 Pick. 193; Mahoney v. Ashton, 4 H. & McH. 295.

The present plaintiff in error was held not entitled to his freedom, on the same state of facts as is now in evidence, in Scott v. Emerson, 15 Mo. 576.

This decision was affirmed in Sylvia v. Kirby, 17 Mo. 434.

By the laws of Missouri, therefore, the claimants are slaves, and these laws must determine their condition in the courts of the United States.

Strader v. Graham, 10 How. 93.

4. No residence of a slave at Fort Snelling could change his condition or devest the title of his owner.

Slavery existed by law in all the territory ceded by France to the United States, and Congress has not the constitutional power to repeal that law, or abolish or prohibit slavery within any part of that Territory.

Sec. 8 of the Act of March 6, 1820, is the first, and almost the only instance of an assumption by Congress of the power to abolish slavery in the Territory. It has never been recognized by this court. It is understood to be claimed that authority of Congress to erect territorial governments is confirmed by art. 4, sec. 3, of the Constitution, which gives the "power to dispose of and make all needful rules and regulations respecting the territory or other property belonging to the United States," or to result from the power to acquire territory; and in either case, it comprehends a power of legislation exclusive, universal, absolute and unlimited.

3 Story, Const. secs. 1314, 1315, 1318, 1319, 1320, 1322; 1 Kent's Com. 423.

The clause of the Constitution, however, has been judicially interpreted to be a power to dispose of and make all needful rules and regulations respecting the lands and other property of the United States.

U. S. v. Gratiot, 14 Pet. 526, 537; Am. Ins. Co. v. Canter, 1 Pet. 342; see, also, Federalist, No. 43.

The subject of the power conferred by art. 4, sec. 3, is property, and the property only of the United States. This power is over unappropriated lands.

To organize a municipal government or corporation for the district or country, to prohibit slavery, or to interfere in any way with the law of property, is not to make needful rules and regulations respecting the territory or other property belonging within such district; therefore, the power to institute such a government, and more especially an unlimited power to legislate in all cases over the inhabitants in a territory and their property, cannot be deduced from the clause under consideration.

The power of Congress to institute temporary government over any territory, results necessarily from the fact that it is not within the jurisdiction of any particular State, and is within the power and jurisdiction of the United States. It is a power resulting from the necessity of the State, and is limited to the necessity from which it arises; to change the law of property, to emancipate slavery, to abolish slavery where, by the law it exists, to confiscate property, or devest vested rights, cannot be necessary or proper to the institution of a temporary government. The power of Congress over the territory belonging to the United States cannot authorize legislation which practically excludes from such territory the people of any portion of the Union, or prevents them from taking with them and holding in such territory any property recognized by the Constitution, and the local laws of the territory.

Mr. Chief Justice **Taney** delivered the opinion of the court:

This case has been twice argued. After the argument at the last term, differences of opinion were found to exist among the members of the court; and as the questions in controversy are of the highest importance, and the court was at that time much pressed by the ordinary business of the term, it was deemed advisable to continue the case, and direct a re-argument on some of the points, in order that we might have an opportunity of giving to the whole subject a more deliberate *consideration. [*400 It has accordingly been again argued by counsel, and considered by the court; and I now proceed to deliver its opinion.

There are two leading questions presented by the record:

1. Had the Circuit Court of the United States jurisdiction to hear and determine the case between these parties? And,

2. If it had jurisdiction, is the judgment it has given erroneous or not?

The plaintiff in error, who was also the plaintiff in the court below, was, with his wife and children, held as slaves by the defendant, in the State of Missouri, and he brought this action in the Circuit Court of the United States for that district, to assert the title of himself and his family to freedom.

The declaration is in the form usually adopted in that State to try questions of this description, and contains the averment necessary to give the court jurisdiction; that he and the defendant are citizens of different States; that is, he is a citizen of Missouri, and the defendant a citizen of New York.

The defendant pleaded in abatement to the jurisdiction of the court, that the plaintiff was not a citizen of the State of Missouri, as alleged in his declaration, being a negro of African descent, whose ancestors were of pure African blood, and who were brought into this country and sold as slaves.

To this plea the plaintiff demurred, and the defendant joined in demurrer. The court overruled the plea, and gave judgment that the defendant should answer over. And he thereupon put in sundry pleas in bar, upon which issues were joined, and at the trial the verdict and judgment were in his favor. Whereupon the plaintiff brought this writ of error.

Before we speak of the pleas in bar, it will be proper to dispose of the questions which have arisen on the plea in abatement.

That plea denies the right of the plaintiff to sue in a court of the United States, for the reasons therein stated.

If the question raised by it is legally before us, and the court should be of opinion that the facts stated in it disqualify the plaintiff from becoming a citizen, in the sense in which that word is used in the Constitution of the United States, then the judgment of the Circuit Court is erroneous, and must be reversed.

It is suggested, however, that this plea is not before us; and that as the judgment in the court below on this plea was in favor of the plaintiff, he does not seek to reverse it, or bring it before the court for revision by his writ of error; and also that the defendant waived this defense by pleading over, and thereby admitted the jurisdiction of the court. 401*] *But in making this objection, we think the peculiar and limited jurisdiction of courts of the United States has not been adverted to. This peculiar and limited jurisdiction has made it necessary, in these courts, to adopt different rules and principles of pleading, so far as jurisdiction is concerned, from those which regulate courts of common law in England and in the different States of the Union which have adopted the common law rules.

In these last mentioned courts, where their character and rank are analogous to that of a circuit court of the United States; in other words, where they are what the law terms courts of general jurisdiction, they are presumed to have jurisdiction unless the contrary appears. No averment in the pleadings of the plaintiff is necessary, in order to give jurisdiction. If the defendant objects to it, he must plead it specially, and unless the fact on which he relies is found to be true by a jury, or admitted to be true by the plaintiff, the jurisdiction cannot be disputed in an appellate court.

Now, it is not necessary to inquire whether in courts of that description a party who pleads over in bar, when a plea to the jurisdiction has been ruled against him, does or does not waive his plea; nor whether upon a judgment in his favor on the pleas in bar, and a writ of error brought by the plaintiff, the question upon the plea in abatement would be open for revision in the appellate court. Cases that may have been decided in such courts, or rules that may have been laid down by common law pleaders, can have no influence in the decision in this court. Because, under the Constitution and laws of the United States, the rules which govern the pleadings in its courts, in questions of jurisdiction, stand on different principles and are regulated by different laws.

This difference arises, as we have said, from the peculiar character of the government of the United States. For although it is sovereign and supreme in its appropriate sphere of action, yet it does not possess all the powers which usually belong to the sovereignty of a nation. Certain specified powers, enumerated in the Constitution, have been conferred upon it; and neither the Legislative, Executive nor Judicial Departments of the Government can lawfully

exercise any authority beyond the limits marked out by the Constitution. And in regulating the Judicial Department, the cases in which the courts of the United States shall have jurisdiction are particularly and specifically enumerated and defined; and they are not authorized to take cognizance of any case which does not come within the description therein specified. Hence, when a plaintiff sues in a court of the United States, it is necessary that he should *show, in his pleading, that [*402 the suit he brings is within the jurisdiction of the court, and that he is entitled to sue there. And if he omits to do this, and should, by an oversight of the Circuit Court, obtain a judgment in his favor, the judgment would be reversed in the appellate court for want of jurisdiction in the court below. The jurisdiction would not be presumed, as in the case of a common law, English, or state court, unless the contrary appeared. But the record, when it comes before the appellate court, must show, affirmatively, that the inferior court had authority, under the Constitution, to hear and determine the case. And if the plaintiff claims a right to sue in a circuit court of the United States, under that provision of the Constitution which gives jurisdiction in controversies between citizens of different states, he must distinctly aver in his pleading that they are citizens of different states; and he cannot maintain his suit without showing that fact in the pleading.

This point was decided in the case of Bingham v. Cabot, in 3 Dall. 382, and ever since adhered to by the court. And in Jackson v. Ashton, 8 Pet. 148, it was held that the objection to which it was open could not be waived by the opposite party, because consent of parties could not give jurisdiction.

It is needless to accumulate cases on this subject. Those already referred to, and the cases of Capron v. Van Noorden, in 2 Cranch, 126, and Montalet v. Murray, 4 Cranch, 46, are sufficient to show the rule of which we have spoken. The case of Capron v. Van Noorden strikingly illustrates the difference between a common law court and a court of the United States.

If, however, the fact of citizenship is averred in the declaration, and the defendant does not deny it, and put it in issue by plea in abatement, he cannot offer evidence at the trial to disprove it, and consequently cannot avail himself of the objection in the appellate court, unless the defect should be apparent in some other part of the record. For if there is no plea in abatement, and the want of jurisdiction does not appear in any other part of the transcript brought up by the writ of error, the undisputed averment of citizenship in the declaration must be taken in this court to be true. In this case, the citizenship is averred, but it is denied by the defendant in the manner required by the rules of pleading, and the fact upon which the denial is based is admitted by the demurrer. And if the plea and demurrer, and judgment of the court below upon it, are before us upon this record, the question to be decided is, whether the facts stated in the plea are sufficient to show that the plaintiff is not entitled to sue as a citizen in a court of the United States.

*We think they are before us. The [*403 plea in abatement and the judgment of the court upon it, are a part of the judicial proceedings in the Circuit Court, and are there recorded as such; and a writ of error always brings up to the superior court the whole record of the proceedings in the court below. And in the case of The Bank of the U. S. v. Smith, 11 Wheat. 172, this court said, that the case being brought up by writ of error, the whole record was under the consideration of this court. And this being the case in the present instance, the plea in abatement is necessarily under consideration; and it becomes, therefore, our duty to decide whether the facts stated in the plea are or are not sufficient to show that the plaintiff is not entitled to sue as a citizen in a court of the United States.

This is certainly a very serious question, and one that now for the first time has been brought for decision before this court. But it is brought here by those who have a right to bring it, and it is our duty to meet it and decide it.

The question is simply this: can a negro, whose ancestors were imported into this country and sold as slaves, become a member of the political community formed and brought into existence by the Constitution of the United States, and as such become entitled to all the rights, and privileges, and immunities, guarantied by that instrument to the citizen. One of these rights is the privilege of suing in a court of the United States in the cases specified in the Constitution.

It will be observed, that the plea applies to that class of persons only whose ancestors were negroes of the African race, and imported into this country, and sold and held as slaves. The only matter in issue before the court, therefore, is, whether the descendants of such slaves, when they shall be emancipated, or who are born of parents who had become free before their birth, are citizens of a state, in the sense in which the word "citizen" is used in the Constitution of the United States. And this being the only matter in dispute on the pleadings, the court must be understood as speaking in this opinion of that class only; that is, of those persons who are the descendants of Africans who were imported into this country and sold as slaves.

The situation of this population was altogether unlike that of the Indian race. The latter, it is true, formed no part of the colonial communities, and never amalgamated with them in social connections or in government. But although they were uncivilized, they were yet a free and independent people, associated together in nations or tribes, and governed by their own laws. Many of these political communities were situated in territories to which the white race claimed the ultimate **404*]** *right of dominion. But that claim was acknowledged to be subject to the right of the Indians to occupy it as long as they thought proper, and neither the English nor Colonial Governments claimed or exercised any dominion over the tribe or nation by whom it was occupied, nor claimed the right to the possession of the territory, until the tribe or nation consented to cede it. These Indian governments were regarded and treated as foreign governments, as much so as if an ocean had separated the red man from the white; and their freedom has constantly been acknowledged, from the time of the first emigration to the English

700

Colonies to the present day, by the different governments which succeeded each other. Treaties have been negotiated with them, and their alliance sought for in war; and the people who compose these Indian political communities have always been treated as foreigners not living under our government. It is true that the course of events has brought the Indian tribes within the limits of the United States under subjection to the white race; and it has been found necessary, for their sake as well as our own, to regard them as in a state of pupilage, and to legislate to a certain extent over them and the territory they occupy. But they may, without doubt, like the subjects of any other foreign government, be naturalized by the authority of Congress, and become citizens of a State, and of the United States; and if an individual should leave his nation or tribe, and take up his abode among the white population, he would be entitled to all the rights and privileges which would belong to an emigrant from any other foreign people.

We proceed to examine the case as presented by the pleadings.

The words "people of the United States" and "citizens" are synonymous terms, and mean the same thing. They both describe the political body, who, according to our republican institutions, form the sovereignty, and who hold the power and conduct the government through their representatives. They are what we familiarly call the "sovereign people," and every citizen is one of this people, and a constituent member of this sovereignty. The question before us is, whether the class of persons described in the plea in abatement compose a portion of this people, and are constituent members of this sovereignty. We think they are not, and that they are not included, and were not intended to be included, under the word "citizens" in the Constitution, and can, therefore, claim none of the rights and privileges which that instrument provides for and secures to citizens of the United States. On the contrary, they were at that time considered as a subordinate *and inferior class of [***405** beings, who had been subjugated by the dominant race, and whether emancipated or not, yet remained subject to their authority, and had no rights or privileges but such as those who held the power and the government might choose to grant them.

It is not the province of the court to decide upon the justice or injustice, the policy or impolicy of these laws. The decision of that question belonged to the political or law-making power; to those who formed the sovereignty and framed the Constitution. The duty of the court is to interpret the instrument they have framed, with the best lights we can obtain on the subject, and to administer it as we find it, according to its true intent and meaning when it was adopted.

In discussing this question, we must not confound the rights of citizenship which a state may confer within its own limits, and the rights of citizenship as a member of the Union. It does not by any means follow, because he has all the rights and privileges of a citizen of a State, that he must be a citizen of the United States. He may have all the rights and privileges of the citizen of a State, and yet not be entitled to the rights and privileges of a citizen in any other State. For, previous to the adoption of the Constitution of the United States, every State had the undoubted right to confer on whomsoever it pleased the character of a citizen, and to endow him with all its rights. But this character, of course, was confined to the boundaries of the State, and gave him no rights or privileges in other States beyond those secured to him by the laws of nations and the comity of States. Nor have the several States surrendered the power of conferring these rights and privileges by adopting the Constitution of the United States. Each State may still confer them upon an alien, or any one it thinks proper, or upon any class or description of persons; yet he would not be a citizen in the sense in which that word is used in the Constitution of the United States, nor entitled to sue as such in one of its courts, nor to the privileges and immunities of a citizen in the other States. The rights which he would acquire would be restricted to the State which gave them. The Constitution has conferred on Congress the right to establish an uniform rule of naturalization, and this right is evidently exclusive, and has always been held by this court to be so. Consequently, no State, since the adoption of the Constitution, can, by naturalizing an alien, invest him with the rights and privileges secured to a citizen of a State under the federal government, although, so far as the State alone was concerned, he would undoubtedly be entitled to the rights of a citizen, and clothed **406***] with all the *rights and immunities which the Constitution and laws of the State attached to that character.

It is very clear, therefore, that no State can, by any Act or law of its own, passed, since the adoption of the Constitution, introduce a new member into the political community created by the Constitution of the United States. It cannot make him a member of this community by making him a member of its own. And for the same reason it cannot introduce any person, or description of persons, who were not intended to be embraced in this new political family, which the Constitution brought into existence, but were intended to be excluded from it.

The question then arises, whether the provisions of the Constitution, in relation to the personal rights and privileges to which the citizen of a state should be entitled, embraced the negro African race, at that time in this country, or who might afterwards be imported, who had then or should afterwards be made free in any State; and to put it in the power of a single State to make him a citizen of the United States, and endue him with the full rights of citizenship in every other State without their consent. Does the Constitution of the United States act upon him whenever he shall be made free under the laws of a State, and raised there to the rank of a citizen, and immediately clothe him with all the privileges of a citizen in every other State, and in its own courts?

The court think the affirmative of these propositions cannot be maintained. And if it cannot, the plaintiff in error could not be a citizen of the State of Missouri, within the meaning of the Constitution of the United States, and, consequently, was not entitled to sue in its courts.

It is true, every person, and every class and **15 L. ed.**

description of persons, who were at the time of the adoption of the Constitution recognized as citizens in the several States, became also citizens of this new political body; but none other; it was formed by them, and for them and their posterity, but for no one else. And the personal rights and privileges guarantied to citizens of this new sovereignty were intended to embrace those only who were then members of the several state communities, or who should afterwards, by birthright or otherwise, become members, according to the provisions of the Constitution and the principles on which it was founded. It was the union of those who were at that time members of distinct and separate political communities into one political family, whose power, for certain specified purposes, was to extend over the whole territory of the United States. And it gave to each citizen rights and privileges outside of his State *which [**407** he did not before possess, and placed him in every other State upon a perfect equality with its own citizens as to rights of person and rights of property; it made him a citizen of the United States.

It becomes necessary, therefore, to determine who were citizens of the several States when the Constitution was adopted. And in order to do this, we must recur to the governments and institutions of the thirteen Colonies, when they separated from Great Britain and formed new sovereignties, and took their places in the family of independent nations. We must inquire who, at that time, were recognized as the people or citizens of a State, whose rights and liberties had been outraged by the English Government; and who declared their independence, and assumed the powers of government to defend their rights by force of arms.

In the opinion of the court, the legislation and histories of the times, and the language used in the Declaration of Independence, show, that neither the class of persons who had been imported as slaves, nor their descendants, whether they had become free or not, were then acknowledged as a part of the people, nor intended to be included in the general words used in that memorable instrument.

It is difficult at this day to realize the state of public opinion in relation to that unfortunate race, which prevailed in the civilized and enlightened portions of the world at the time of the Declaration of Independence, and when the Constitution of the United States was framed and adopted. But the public history of every European nation displays it, in a manner too plain to be mistaken.

They had for more than a century before been regarded as beings of an inferior order; and altogether unfit to associate with the white race, either in social or political relations; and so far inferior, that they had no rights which the white man was bound to respect; and that the negro might justly and lawfully be reduced to slavery for his benefit. He was bought and sold, and treated as an ordinary article of merchandise and traffic, whenever a profit could be made by it. This opinion was at that time fixed and universal in the civilized portion of the white race. It was regarded as an axiom in morals as well as in politics, which no one thought of disputing, or supposed to be open to dispute; and men in every grade and position in society daily and habitually acted upon it in their private pursuits, as well as in matters of public concern, without doubting for a moment the correctness of this opinion.

And in no nation was this opinion more firm-**408*]** ly fixed or more *uniformly acted upon than by the English government and English people. They not only seized them on the coast of Africa, and sold them or held them in slavery for their own use; but they took them as ordinary articles of merchandise to every country where they could make a profit on them, and were far more extensively engaged in this commerce than any other nation in the world.

The opinion thus entertained and acted upon in England was naturally impressed upon the colonies they founded on this side of the Atlantic. And, accordingly, a negro of the African race was regarded by them as an article of property, and held, and bought and sold as such, in every one of the thirteen Colonies which united in the Declaration of Independence, and afterwards formed the Constitution of the United States. The slaves were more or less numerous in the different Colonies, as slave labor was found more or less profitable. But no one seems to have doubted the correctness of the prevailing opinion of the time.

The legislation of the different Colonies furnishes positive and indisputable proof of this fact.

It would be tedious, **in this opinion**, to enumerate the various laws they passed upon this subject. It will be sufficient, **as a sample** of the legislation which then generally prevailed throughout the British Colonies, to give the laws of two of them; one being still a large slaveholding State, and the other the first State in which slavery ceased to exist.

The Province of Maryland, in 1717 (ch. 13, sec. 5), passed a law declaring "that if any **free negro or mulatto intermarry** with any white woman, or if any white man shall intermarry with any negro or mulatto woman, such negro or mulatto shall become a slave during life, excepting mulattoes born of white women, who, for such intermarriage, shall only become servants for seven years, to be disposed of as the Justices of the County Court, where such marriage so happens, shall think fit; to be applied by them towards the support of a public school within the said county. And any white man or white woman who shall intermarry as aforesaid, with any negro or mulatto, such white man or white woman shall become servants during the term of seven years, and shall be disposed of by the justices as aforesaid, and be applied to the uses aforesaid."

The other colonial law to which we refer was passed by Massachusetts in 1705 (chap. 6). It is entitled "An Act for the better preventing of a spurious and mixed issue," etc.; and it provides, that "if any negro or mulatto shall presume to smite or strike any person of the English or other Christian nation, such negro or mulatto shall be severely whipped, at **409*]** *the discretion of the justices before whom the offender shall be convicted."

And "that none of Her Majesty's English or Scottish subjects, nor of any other Christian nation, **within this province, shall contract**
702

matrimony with any negro or mulatto; **nor** shall any person, duly authorized to solemnize marriage, presume to join any such in marriage, on pain of forfeiting the sum of fifty pounds; one moiety thereof to Her Majesty, for and towards the support of the government within this province, and the other moiety to him or them that shall inform and sue for the same in any of Her Majesty's courts of record within the Province, by will, plaint, or information."

We give both of these laws in the words used by the respective legislative bodies, because the language in which they are framed, as well as the provisions contained in them, show, too plainly to be misunderstood, the degraded condition of this unhappy race. They were still in force when the Revolution began, and are a faithful index to the state of feeling towards the class of persons of whom they speak, and of the position they occupied throughout the thirteen colonies, in the eyes and thoughts of the men who framed the Declaration of Independence and established the State constitutions and governments. They show that a perpetual and impassable barrier was intended to be erected between the white race and the one which they had reduced to slavery, and governed as subjects with absolute and despotic power, and which they then looked upon as so far below them in the scale of created beings, that intermarriages between white persons and negroes or mulattoes were regarded as unnatural and immoral, and punished as crimes, not only in the parties, but in the person who joined them in marriage. And no distinction in this respect was made between the free negro or mulatto and the slave, but this stigma, of the deepest degradation, was fixed upon the whole race.

We refer to these historical facts for the purpose of showing the fixed opinions concerning that race, upon which the statesmen of that day spoke and acted. It is necessary to do this, in order to determine whether the general terms used in the Constitution of the United States, as to the rights of man and the rights of the people, was intended to include them, or to give to them or their posterity the benefit of any of its provisions.

The language of the Declaration of Independence is equally conclusive.

It begins by declaring that, "when in the course of human events it becomes necessary for one people to dissolve the political bands which have connected them with another, and to *assume among the powers of the [*410 earth the separate and equal station to which the laws of nature and nature's God entitle them, a decent respect for the opinions of mankind requires that they should declare the causes which impel them to the separation."

It then proceeds to say: "We hold these truths to be self-evident: that all men are created equal; that they are endowed by their Creator with certain inalienable rights; that among them is life, liberty, and pursuit of happiness; that to secure these rights, governments are instituted, deriving their just powers from the consent of the governed."

The general words above quoted would seem to embrace the whole human family, and if they were used in a similar instrument at this day, would be so understood. But it is too clear for dispute, that the enslaved African race were not intended to be included, and formed no part of the people who framed and adopted this Declaration; for if the language, as understood in that day, would embrace them, the conduct of the distinguished men who framed the Declaration of Independence would have been utterly and flagrantly inconsistent with the principles they asserted; and instead of the sympathy of mankind, to which they so confidently appealed, they would have deserved and received universal rebuke and reprobation.

Yet the men who framed this Declaration were great men—high in literary acquirements—high in their sense of honor, and incapable of asserting principles inconsistent with those on which they were acting. They perfectly understood the meaning of the language they used, and how it would be understood by others; and they knew that it would not, in any part of the civilized world, be supposed to embrace the negro race, which, by common consent, had been excluded from civilized governments and the family of nations, and doomed to slavery. They spoke and acted according to the then established doctrines and principles, and in the ordinary language of the day, and no one misunderstood them. The unhappy black race were separated from the white by indelible marks, and laws long before established, and were never thought of or spoken of except as property, and when the claims of the owner or the profit of the trader were supposed to need protection.

This state of public opinion had undergone no change when the Constitution was adopted, as is equally evident from its provisions and language.

The brief preamble sets forth by whom it was formed, for what purposes, and for whose **411***] benefit and protection. It declares *that it is formed by the people of the United States; that is to say, by those who were members of the different political communities in the several States; and its great object is declared to be to secure the blessings of liberty to themselves and their posterity. It speaks in general terms of the people of the United States, and of citizens of the several States, when it is providing for the exercise of the powers granted or the privileges secured to the citizen. It does not define what description of persons are intended to be included under these terms, or who shall be regarded as a citizen and one of the people. It uses them as terms so well understood that no further description or definition was necessary.

But there are two clauses in the Constitution which point directly and specifically to the negro race as a separate class of persons, and show clearly that they were not regarded as a portion of the people or citizens of the government then formed.

One of these clauses reserves to each of the thirteen States the right to import slaves until the year 1808, if it thinks proper. And the importation which it thus sanctions was unquestionably of persons of the race of which we are speaking, as the traffic in slaves in the United States had always been confined to them. And by the other provision the States pledge themselves to each other to maintain the right of property of the master, by delivering up to him any slave who may have escaped

from his service, and be found within their respective territories. By the first above-mentioned clause, therefore, the right to purchase and hold this property is directly sanctioned and authorized for twenty years by the people who framed the Constitution. And by the second, they pledge themselves to maintain and uphold the right of the master in the manner specified, as long as the government they then formed should endure. And these two provisions show, conclusively, that neither the description of persons therein referred to, nor their descendants, were embraced in any of the other provisions of the Constitution; for certainly these two clauses were not intended to confer on them or their posterity the blessings of liberty, or any of the personal rights so carefully provided for the citizen.

No one of that race had ever migrated to the United States voluntarily; all of them had been brought here as articles of merchandise. The number that had been emancipated at that time were but few in comparison with those held in slavery; and they were identified in the public mind with the race to which they belonged, and regarded as a part of the slave population rather than the free. It is obvious that they were not *even in the minds [***412** of the framers of the Constitution when they were conferring special rights and privileges upon the citizens of a State in every other part of the Union.

Indeed, when we look to the condition of this race in the several States at the time, it is impossible to believe that these rights and privileges were intended to be extended to them.

It is very true, that in that portion of the Union where the labor of the negro race was found to be unsuited to the climate, and unprofitable to the master, but few slaves were held at the time of the Declaration of Independence; and when the Constitution was adopted, it had entirely worn out in one of them, and measures had been taken for its gradual abolition in several others. But this change had not been produced by any change of opinion in relation to this race; but because it was discovered, from experience, that slave labor was unsuited to the climate and productions of these States: for some of the States, where it had ceased or nearly ceased to exist, were actively engaged in the slave trade, procuring cargoes on the coast of Africa, and transporting them for sale to those parts of the Union where their labor was found to be profitable, and suited to the climate and productions. And this traffic was openly carried on, and fortunes accumulated by it, without reproach from the people of the States where they resided. And it can hardly be supposed that, in the States where it was then countenanced in its worst form—that is, in the seizure and transportation—the people could have regarded those who were emancipated as entitled to equal rights with themselves.

And we may here again refer, in support of this proposition, to the plain and unequivocal language of the laws of the several States, some passed after the Declaration of Independence and before the Constitution was adopted, and some since the government went into operation.

We need not refer, on this point, particularly

to the laws of the present slaveholding States. Their statute books are full of provisions in relation to this class, in the same spirit with the Maryland law which we have before quoted. They have continued to treat them as an inferior class, and to subject them to strict police regulation, drawing a broad line of distinction between the citizen and the slave races, and legislating in relation to them upon the same principle which prevailed at the time of the Declaration of Independence. As relates to these States, it is too plain for argument, that they have never been regarded as a part of the people or citizens of the State, nor supposed to possess any political rights which the dominant race might not withhold or grant at their **413*]** pleasure. *And as long ago as 1822, the Court of Appeals of Kentucky decided that free negroes and mulattoes were not citizens within the meaning of the Constitution of the United States; and the correctness of this decision is recognized, and the same doctrine affirmed, in 1 Meigs' Tenn. 321.

And if we turn to the legislation of the States where slavery had worn out, or measures taken for its speedy abolition, we shall find the same opinions and principles equally fixed and equally acted upon.

Thus, Massachusetts, in 1786, passed a law similar to the colonial one of which we have spoken. The Law of 1786, like the Law of 1705, forbids the marriage of any white person with any negro, Indian or mulatto, and inflicts a penalty of £50 upon anyone who shall join them in marriage; and declares all such marriages absolutely null and void, and degrades thus the unhappy issue of the marriage by fixing upon it the stain of bastardy. And this mark of degradation was renewed, and again impressed upon the race, in the careful and deliberate preparation of their Revised Code published in 1836. This Code forbids any person from joining in marriage any white person with any Indian, negro or mulatto, and subjects the party who shall offend in this respect, to imprisonment, not exceeding six months, in the common jail, or to hard labor, and to a fine of not less than fifty nor more than two hundred dollars; and, like the Law of 1786, it declares the marriage to be absolutely null and void. It will be seen that the punishment is increased by the Code upon the person who shall marry them, by adding imprisonment to a pecuniary penalty.

So, too, in Connecticut. We refer more particularly to the legislation of this State, because it was not only among the first to put an end to slavery within its own territory, but was the first to fix a mark of reprobation upon the African slave trade. The law last mentioned was passed in October, 1788, about nine months after the State had ratified and adopted the present Constitution of the United States; and by that law it prohibited its own citizens, under severe penalties, from engaging in the trade, and declared all policies of insurance on the vessel or cargo made in the State to be null and void. But, up to the time of the adoption of the Constitution, there is nothing in the legislation of the State indicating any change of opinion as to the relative rights and position of the white and black races in this country, or indicating that it meant to place the latter, when free, upon a level with its

citizens. And certainly nothing which would have led the slaveholding States to suppose that Connecticut designed to claim for them, under *the new Constitution, the equal **[*414** rights and privileges and rank of citizens in every other state.

The first step taken by Connecticut upon this subject was as early as 1774, when it passed an Act forbidding the further importation of slaves into the State. But the section containing the prohibition is introduced by the following preamble:

"And whereas the increase of slaves in this State is injurious to the poor, and inconvenient."

This recital would appear to have been carefully introduced, in order to prevent any misunderstanding of the motive which induced the Legislature to pass the law, and places it distinctly upon the interest and convenience of the white population—excluding the inference that it might have been intended in any degree for the benefit of the other.

And in the Act of 1784, by which the issue of slaves, born after the time therein mentioned, were to be free at a certain age, the section is again introduced by a preamble assigning a similar motive for the Act. It is in these words:

"Whereas sound policy requires that the abolition of slavery should be effected as soon as may be consistent with the rights of individuals, and the public safety and welfare"—showing that the right of property in the master was to be protected, and that the measure was one of policy, and to prevent the injury and inconvenience, to the whites, of a slave population in the State.

And still further pursuing its legislation, we find that in the same Statute passed in 1774, which prohibited the further importation of slaves into the State, there is also a provision by which any negro, Indian or mulatto servant, who was found wandering out of the town or place to which he belonged, without a written pass such as is therein described, was made liable to be seized by anyone, and taken before the next authority to be examined and delivered up to his master—who was required to pay the charge which had accrued thereby. And a subsequent section of the same law provides, that if any free negro shall travel without such pass, and shall be stopped, seized or taken up, he shall pay all charges arising thereby. And this law was in full operation when the Constitution of the United States was adopted, and was not repealed till 1797. So that up to that time free negroes and mulattoes were associated with servants and slaves in the police regulations established by the laws of the State.

And again, in 1833, Connecticut passed another law, which made it penal to set up or establish any school in that State for the instruction of persons of the African race not inhabitants of the State, or to instruct or teach in any such school or *institution, or **[*415** board or harbor for that purpose, any such person, without the previous consent in writing of the civil authority of the town in which such school or institution might be.

And it appears by the case of Crandall v. The State, reported in 10 Conn. 340, that upon an information filed against Prudence Crandall for a violation of this law, one of the points raised in the defense was, that the law was a violation of the Constitution of the United States; and that the persons instructed, although of the African race, were citizens of other States, and therefore entitled to the rights and privileges of citizens in the State of Connecticut. But Chief Justice Daggett, before whom the case was tried, held, that persons of that description were not citizens of a State, within the meaning of the word "citizen" in the Constitution of the United States, and were not, therefore, entitled to the privileges and immunities of citizens in other States.

The case was carried up to the Supreme Court of Errors of the State, and the question fully argued there. But the case went off upon another point, and no opinion was expressed on this question.

We have made this particular examination into the legislative and judicial action of Connecticut, because, from the early hostility it displayed to the slave trade on the coast of Africa, we may expect to find the laws of that State as lenient and favorable to the subject race as those of any other State in the Union; and if we find that at the time the Constitution was adopted, they were not even there raised to the rank of citizens, but were still held and treated as property, and the laws relating to them passed with reference altogether to the interest and convenience of the white race, we shall hardly find them elevated to a higher rank anywhere else.

A brief notice of the laws of two other States, and we shall pass on to other considerations.

By the laws of New Hampshire, collected and finally passed in 1815, no one was permitted to be enrolled in the militia of the State but free white citizens; and the same provision is found in a subsequent collection of the laws made in 1855. Nothing could more strongly mark the entire repudiation of the African race. The alien is excluded, because, being born in a foreign country, he cannot be a member of the community until he is naturalized. But why are the African race, born in the State, not permitted to share in one of the highest duties of the citizen? The answer is obvious; he is not by the institutions and laws of the State numbered among its people. He forms no part of the sovereignty of the State, and is not, therefore, called on to uphold and defend it.

416*] *Again in 1822, Rhode Island in its Revised Code, passed a law forbidding persons who were authorize[l] to join persons in marriage from joining in marriage any white person with any negro, Indian or mulatto, under the penalty of $200, and declaring all such marriages absolutely null and void; and the same law was again re-enacted in its Revised Code of 1844. So that, down to the last mentioned period, the strongest mark of inferiority and degradation was fastened upon the African race in that State.

It would be impossible to enumerate and compress, in the space usually allotted to an opinion of a court, the various laws, marking the condition of this race, which were passed from time to time after the Revolution, and before and since the adoption of the Constitution of the United States. In addition to those

already referred to, it is sufficient to say that Chancellor Kent, whose accuracy and research no one will question, states in the sixth edition of his Commentaries, published in 1848, 2d vol. 258, note b, that in no part of the country, except Maine, did the African race, in point of fact, participate equally with the whites in the exercise of civil and political rights.

The legislation of the States therefore shows, in a manner not to be mistaken, the inferior and subject condition of that race at the time the Constitution was adopted, and long afterwards, throughout the thirteen States by which that instrument was framed; and it is hardly consistent with the respect due to these States, to suppose that they regarded at that time, as fellow citizens and members of the sovereignty, a class of beings whom they had thus stigmatized; whom, as we are bound, out of respect to the State sovereignties, to assume they had deemed it just and necessary thus to stigmatize, and upon whom they had impressed such deep and enduring marks of inferiority and degradation; or that when they met in convention to form the Constitution, they looked upon them as a portion of their constituents, or designed to include them in the provisions so carefully inserted for the security and protection of the liberties and rights of their citizens. It cannot be supposed that they intended to secure to them rights, and privileges, and rank, in the new political body throughout the Union, which every one of them denied within the limits of its own dominion. More especially, it cannot be believed that the large slaveholding States regarded them as included in the word "citizens," or would have consented to a constitution which might compel them to receive them in that character from another State. For if they were so received, and entitled to the privileges and immunities of citizens, it would exempt them from the operation of the special laws and from the police *regulations which they [*417 considered to be necessary for their own safety. It would give to persons of the negro race, who were recognized as citizens in any one State of the Union, the right to enter every other State whenever they pleased, singly or in companies, without pass or passport, and without obstruction, to sojourn there as long as they pleased, to go where they pleased at every hour of the day or night without molestation, unless they committed some violation of law for which a white man would be punished; and it would give them the full liberty of speech in public and in private upon all subjects upon which its own citizens might speak; to hold public meetings upon political affairs, and to keep and carry arms wherever they went. And all of this would be done in the face of the subject race of the same color, both free and slaves, inevitably producing discontent and insubordination among them, and endangering the peace and safety of the State.

It is impossible, it would seem, to believe that the great men of the slaveholding States, who took so large a share in framing the Constitution of the United States, and exercised so much influence in procuring its adoption, could have been so forgetful or regardless of their own safety and the safety of those who trusted and confided in them.

Besides, this want of foresight and care would have been utterly inconsistent with the caution displayed in providing for the admission of new members into this political family. For, when they gave to the citizens of each State the privileges and immunities of citizens in the several States, they at the same time took from the several States the power of naturalization, and confined that power exclusively to the Federal Government. No state was willing to permit another State to determine who should or should not be admitted as one of its citizens, and entitled to demand equal rights and privileges with their own people, within their own territories. The right of naturalization was therefore, with one accord, surrendered by the States, and confined to the Federal Government. And this power granted to Congress to establish an uniform rule of naturalization is, by the well-understood meaning of the word, confined to persons born in a foreign country, under a foreign government. It is not a power to raise to the rank of a citizen anyone born in the United States, who, from birth or parentage, by the laws of the country, belongs to an inferior and subordinate class. And when we find the States guarding themselves from the indiscreet or improper admission by other states of emigrants from other countries, by giving the power exclusively to Congress, we cannot fail to see that they could never have left with the States a much **418*]** *more important power—that is, the power of transforming into citizens a numerous class of persons, who in that character would be much more dangerous to the peace and safety of a large portion of the Union than the few foreigners one of the States might improperly naturalize. The Constitution, upon its adoption, obviously took from the States all power by any subsequent legislation to introduce as a citizen into the political family of the United States anyone, no matter where he was born, or what might be his character or condition; and it gave to Congress the power to confer this character upon those only who were born outside of the dominions of the United States. And no law of a State, therefore, passed since the Constitution was adopted, can give any right of citizenship outside of its own territory.

A clause, similar to the one in the Constitution, in relation to the rights and immunities of citizens of one State in the other States, was contained in the Articles of Confederation. But there is a difference of language, which is worthy of note. The provision in the Articles of Confederation was, "that the free inhabitants of each of the States, paupers, vagabonds, and fugitives from justice excepted, should be entitled to all the privileges and immunities of free citizens, in the several States."

It will be observed, that under this Confederation each State had the right to decide for itself, and in its own tribunals, whom it would acknowledge as a free inhabitant of another state. The term "free inhabitant," in the generality of its terms, would certainly include one of the African race who had been manumitted. But no example, we think, can be found of his admission to all the privileges of citizenship in any State of the Union after these Articles were formed, and while they continued in force. And notwithstanding the gen-

706

erality of the words "free inhabitants," it is very clear that, according to their accepted meaning in that day, they did not include the African race, whether free or not; for the 5th section of the 9th article provides that Congress should have the power "to agree upon the number of land forces to be raised, and to make requisitions from each State for its quota in proportion to the number of white inhabitants in such State, which requisition should be binding."

Words could hardly have been used which more strongly mark the line of distinction between the citizen and the subject—the free and the subjugated races. The latter were not even counted when the inhabitants of a State were to be embodied in proportion to its numbers for the general defense. And it cannot for a moment be supposed, that a class of *per- [*419 sons* thus separated and rejected from those who formed the sovereignty of the States, were yet intended to be included under the words "free inhabitants," in the preceding article, to whom privileges and immunities were so carefully secured in every State.

But although this clause of the Articles of Confederation is the same in principle with that inserted in the Constitution, yet the comprehensive word "inhabitant," which might be construed to include an emancipated slave, is omitted, and the privilege is confined to "citizens" of the State. And this alteration in words would hardly have been made unless a different meaning was intended to be conveyed, or a possible doubt removed. The just and fair inference is, that as this privilege was about to be placed under the protection of the general government, and the words expounded by its tribunals, and all power in relation to it taken from the State and its courts, it was deemed prudent to describe with precision and caution the persons to whom this high privilege was given—and the word "citizen" was on that account substituted for the words "free inhabitant." The word "citizen" excluded, and no doubt intended to exclude, foreigners who had not become citizens of some one of the States when the Constitution was adopted; and also every description of persons who were not fully recognized as citizens in the several States. This, upon any fair construction of the instruments to which we have referred, was evidently the object and purpose of this change of words.

To all this mass of proof we have still to add, that Congress has repeatedly legislated upon the same construction of the Constitution that we have given. Three laws, two of which were passed almost immediately after the government went into operation, will be abundantly sufficient to show this. The first two are particularly worthy of notice, because many of the men who assisted in framing the Constitution, and took an active part in procuring its adoption, were then in the halls of legislation, and certainly understood what they meant when they used the words "people of the United States" and "citizen" in that well considered instrument.

The first of these Acts is the Naturalization Law, which was passed at the second session of the first Congress, March 26, 1790, and confines the right of becoming citizens "to aliens being free white persons."

Now, the Constitution does not limit the power of Congress in this respect to white persons. And they may, if they think proper, authorize the naturalization of anyone, of any color, who was born under allegiance to another government. But the language of the law 420*] above quoted shows that citizenship *at that time was perfectly understood to be confined to the white race; and that they alone constituted the sovereignty in the government.

Congress might, as we before said, have authorized the naturalization of Indians, because they were aliens and foreigners. But, in their then untutored and savage state, no one would have though of admitting them as citizens in a civilized community. And, moreover, the atrocities they had but recently committed, when they were the allies of Great Britain in the Revolutionary War, were yet fresh in the recollection of the people of the United States, and they were even then guarding themselves against the threatened renewal of Indian hostilities. No one supposed then that any Indian would ask for, or was capable of enjoying, the privileges of an American citizen, and the word "white" was not used with any particular reference to them.

Neither was it used with any reference to the African race imported into or born in this country; because Congress had no power to naturalize them, and therefore there was no necessity for using particular words to exclude them.

It would seem to have been used merely because it followed out the line of division which the Constitution has drawn between the citizen race, who formed and held the government, and the African race, which they held in subjection and slavery, and governed at their own pleasure.

Another of the early laws of which we have spoken, is the first Militia Law, which was passed in 1792, at the first session of the second Congress. The language of this law is equally plain and significant with the one just mentioned. It directs that every "free able-bodied white male citizen" shall be enrolled in the militia. The word "white" is evidently used to exclude the African race, and the word "citizen" to exclude unnaturalized foreigners, the latter forming no part of the sovereignty; owing it no allegiance, and therefore under no obligation to defend it. The African race, however, born in the country, did owe allegiance to the government, whether they were slave or free; but it is repudiated, and rejected from the duties and obligations of citizenship in marked language.

The third Act to which we have alluded is even still more decisive; it was passed as late as 1813 (2 Stat. 809), and it provides: "That from and after the termination of the war in which the United States are now engaged with Great Britain, it shall not be lawful to employ, on board of any public or private vessels of the United States, any person or persons except citizens of the United States, or persons of color, natives of the United States.

421*] *Here the line of distinction is drawn in express words. Persons of color, in the judgment of Congress, were not included in the word "citizens," and they are described as another and different class of persons, and au-

15 L. ed.

thorized to be employed, if born in the United States.

And even as late as 1820 (chap. 104, sec. 8), in the charter to the City of Washington, the Corporation is authorized "to restrain and prohibit the nightly and other disorderly meetings of slaves, free negroes, and mulattoes," thus associating them together in its legislation; and after prescribing the punishment that may be inflicted on the slaves, proceeds in the following words: "And to punish such free negroes and mulattoes by penalties not exceeding twenty dollars for any one offense; and in case of the inability of any such free negro or mulatto to pay any such penalty and cost thereon, to cause him or her to be confined to labor for any time not exceeding six calendar months." And in a subsequent part of the same section, the Act authorizes the Corporation "to prescribe the terms and conditions upon which free negroes and mulattoes may reside in the city."

This law, like the laws of the States, shows that this class of persons were governed by special legislation directed expressly to them, and always connected with provisions for the government of slaves, and not with those for the government of free white citizens. And after such an uniform course of legislation as we have stated, by the Colonies, by the States, and by Congress, running through a period of more than a century, it would seem that to call persons thus marked and stigmatized, "citizens" of the United States, "fellow-citizens," a constituent part of the sovereignty, would be an abuse of terms, and not calculated to exalt the character of an American citizen in the eyes of other nations.

The conduct of the Executive Department of the government has been in perfect harmony upon this subject with this course of legislation. The question was brought officially before the late William Wirt, when he was the Attorney-General of the United States, in 1821, and he decided that the words "citizens of the United States" were used in the Acts of Congress in the same sense as in the Constitution; and that free persons of color were not citizens, within the meaning of the Constitution and laws; and this opinion has been confirmed by that of the late Attorney-General, Caleb Cushing, in a recent case, and acted upon by the Secretary of State, who refused to grant passports to them as "citizens of the United States."

But it is said that a person may be a citizen, and entitled to *that character, al- [*422 though he does not possess all the rights which may belong to other citizens; as, for example, the right to vote, or to hold particular offices; and that yet, when he goes into another State, he is entitled to be recognized there as a citizen, although the State may measure his rights by the rights which it allows to persons of a like character or class, resident in the State, and refuse to him the full rights of citizenship.

This argument overlooks the language of the provision in the Constitution of which we are speaking.

Undoubtedly, a person may be a citizen, that is, a member of the community who from the sovereignty, although he exercises no share of the political power, and is incapacitated from

707

holding particular offices. Women and minors, who form a part of the political family, cannot vote; and when a property qualification is required to vote or hold a particular office, those who have not the necessary qualification cannot vote or hold the office, yet they are citizens.

So, too, a person may be entitled to vote by the law of the State, who is not a citizen even of the State itself. And in some of the States of the Union foreigners not naturalized are allowed to vote. And the State may give the right to free negroes and mulattoes, but that does not make them citizens of the State, and still less of the United States. And the provision in the Constitution giving privileges and immunities in other States, does not apply to them.

Neither does it apply to a person who, being the citizen of a State, migrates to another State. For then he becomes subject to the laws of the State in which he lives, and he is no longer a citizen of the State from which he removed. And the State in which he resides may then, unquestionably, determine his status or condition, and place him among the class of persons who are not recognized as citizens, but belong to an inferior and subject race; and may deny him the privileges and immunities enjoyed by its citizens.

But so far as mere rights of person are concerned, the provision in question is confined to citizens of a State who are temporarily in another State without taking up their residence there. It gives them no political rights in the state as to voting or holding office, or in any other respect. For a citizen of one State has no right to participate in the government of another. But if he ranks as a citizen of the State to which he belongs, within the meaning of the Constitution of the United States, then, whenever he goes into another State, the Constitution clothes him, as to the rights of person, with all the privileges and immunities 423*] which belong to citizens of the *State. And if persons of the African race are citizens of a state, and of the United States, they would be entitled to all of these privileges and immunities in every State, and the State could not restrict them; for they would hold these privileges and immunities, under the paramount authority of the Federal Government, and its courts would be bound to maintain and enforce them, the Constitution and laws of the State to the contrary notwithstanding. And if the State could limit or restrict them, or place the party in an inferior grade, this clause of the Constitution would be unmeaning, and could have no operation; and would give no rights to the citizen when in another State. He would have none but what the State itself chose to allow him. This is evidently not the construction or meaning of the clause in question. It guarantees rights to the citizen, and the State cannot withhold them. And these rights are of a character and would lead to consequences which make it absolutely certain that the African race were not included under the name of citizens of a State, and were not in the contemplation of the framers of the Constitution when these privileges and immunities were provided for the protection of the citizen in other States.

The case of Legrand v. Darnall, 2 Pet. 664, has been referred to for the purpose of showing that this court has decided that the descendant of a slave may sue as a citizen in a court of the United States; but the case itself shows that the question did not arise and could not have arisen in the case.

It appears from the report that Darnall was born in Maryland, and was the son of a white man by one of his slaves, and his father executed certain instruments to manumit him, and devised to him some landed property in the State. This property Darnall afterwards sold to Legrand, the appellant, who gave his notes for the purchase money. But becoming afterwards apprehensive that the appellee had not been emancipated according to the laws of Maryland, he refused to pay the notes until he could be better satisfied as to Darnall's right to convey. Darnall, in the meantime, had taken up his residence in Pennsylvania, and brought suit on the notes and recovered judgment in the Circuit Court for the District of Maryland.

The whole proceeding, as appears by the report, was an amicable one; Legrand being perfectly willing to pay the money, if he could obtain a title, and Darnall not wishing him to pay unless he could make him a good one. In point of fact, the whole proceeding was under the direction of the counsel who argued the case for the appellee, who was the mutual friend of the parties, and confided in by both of them, and whose only *object was to [*424 have the rights of both parties established by judicial decision in the most speedy and least expensive manner.

Legrand, therefore, raised no objection to the jurisdiction of the court in the suit at law, because he was himself anxious to obtain the judgment of the court upon his title. Consequently, there was nothing in the record before the court to show that Darnall was of African descent, and the usual judgment and award of execution was entered. And Legrand thereupon filed his bill on the equity side of the Circuit Court, stating that Darnall was born a slave, and had not been legally emancipated, and could not, therefore, take the land devised to him, nor make Legrand a good title; and praying an injunction to restrain Darnall from proceeding to execution on the judgment, which was granted. Darnall answered, averring in his answer that he was a free man, and capable of conveying a good title. Testimony was taken on this point, and at the hearing the Circuit Court was of opinion that Darnall was a free man and his title good, and dissolved the injunction and dismissed the bill; and that decree was affirmed here, upon the appeal of Legrand.

Now, it is difficult to imagine how any question about the citizenship of Darnall, or his right to sue in that character, can be supposed to have arisen or been decided in that case. The fact that he was of African descent was first brought before the court upon the bill in equity. The suit at law had then passed into judgment and award of execution, and the Circuit Court, as a court of law, had no longer any authority over it. It was a valid and legal judgment, which the court that rendered it had not the power to reverse or set aside. And unless it had jurisdiction as a court of equity to restrain him from using its process as a court of law, Darnall, if he thought proper, would have been at liberty to proceed on his judgment, and compel the payment of the money, although the allegations in the bill were true, and he was incapable of making a title. No other court could have enjoined him, for certainly no State equity court could interfere in that way with the judgment of a circuit court of the United States.

But the Circuit Court as a court of equity certainly had equity jurisdiction over its own judgment as a court of law, without regard to the character of the parties; and had not only the right, but it was its duty—no matter who were the parties in the judgment—to prevent them from proceeding to enforce it by execution, if the court was satisfied that the money was not justly and equitably due. The ability of Darnall to convey did not depend upon his citizenship, but upon his title to freedom. And 425*] if he was free, he could hold and ·*convey property, by the laws of Maryland, although he was not a citizen. But if he was by law still a slave, he could not. It was, therefore, the duty of the court, sitting as a court of equity in the latter case, to prevent him from using its process, as a court of common law, to compel the payment of the purchase money, when it was evident that the purchaser must lose the land. But if he was free, and could make a title, it was equally the duty of the court not to suffer Legrand to keep the land, and refuse the payment of the money, upon the ground that Darnall was incapable of suing or being sued as a citizen in a court of the United States. The character or citizenship of the parties had no connection with the question of jurisdiction, and the matter in dispute had no relation to the citizenship of Darnall. Nor is such a question alluded to in the opinion of the court.

Besides, we are by no means prepared to say that there are not many cases, civil as well as criminal, in which a circuit court of the United States may exercise jurisdiction, although one of the African race is a party; that broad question is not before the court. The question with which we are now dealing is, whether a person of the African race can be a citizen of the United States, and become thereby entitled to a special privilege, by virtue to his title to that character, and which, under the Constitution, no one but a citizen can claim. It is manifest that the case of Legrand v. Darnall has no bearing on that question, and can have no application to the case now before the court.

This case, however, strikingly illustrates the consequences that would follow the construction of the Constitution which would give the power contended for, to a State. It would, in effect, give it also to an individual. For if the father of young Darnall had manumitted him in his lifetime, and sent him to reside in a State which recognized him as a citizen, he might have visited and sojourned in Maryland when he pleased, and as long as he pleased, as a citizen of the United States; and the state officers and tribunals would be compelled, by the paramount authority of the Constitution, to receive him and treat him as one of its citizens, exempt from the laws and police of the state in relation to a person of that description, and allow him to enjoy all the rights and privileges of citizenship, without respect to the laws of Maryland, although such laws were deemed by it absolutely essential to its own safety.

The only two provisions which point to them and include them, treat them as property, and make it the duty of the government to protect it; no other power, in relation to this race, is to be found in the Constitution; and as it is a government *of special, delegated pow- [*426 ers, no authority beyond these two provisions can be constitutionally exercised. The Government of the United States had no right to interfere for any other purpose but that of protecting the rights of the owner, leaving it altogether with the several States to deal with this race, whether emancipated or not, as each State may think justice, humanity, and the interests and safety of society, require. The States evidently intended to reserve this power exclusively to themselves.

No one, we presume, supposes that any change in public opinion or feeling in relation to this unfortunate race, in the civilized nations of Europe or in this country, should induce the court to give to the words of the Constitution a more liberal construction in their favor than they were intended to bear when the instrument was framed and adopted. Such an argument would be altogether inadmissible in any tribunal called on to interpret it. If any of its provisions are deemed unjust, there is a mode prescribed in the instrument itself by which it may be amended; but while it remains unaltered, it must be construed now as it was understood at the time of its adoption. It is not only the same in words, but the same in meaning, and delegates the same powers to the government, and reserves and secures the same rights and privileges to the citizen; and as long as it continues to exist in its present form, it speaks not only in the same words, but with the same meaning and intent with which it spoke when it came from the hands of its framers, and was voted on and adopted by the people of the United States. Any other rule of construction would abrogate the judicial character of this court, and make it the mere reflex of the popular opinion or passion of the day. This court was not created by the Constitution for such purposes. Higher and graver trusts have been confided to it, and it must not falter in the path of duty.

What the construction was at that time, we think can hardly admit of doubt. We have the language of the Declaration of Independence and of the Articles of Confederation, in addition to the plain words of the Constitution itself; we have the legislation of the different States, before, about the time, and since the Constitution was adopted; we have the legislation of Congress, from the time of its adoption to a recent period; and we have the constant and uniform action of the Executive Department, all concurring together, and leading to the same result. And if anything in relation to the construction of the Constitution can be regarded as settled, it is that which we now give to the word "citizen" and the word "people."

And upon a full and careful consideration of the subject, *the court is of opinion [*427 that, upon the facts stated in the plea in abatement, Dred Scott was not a citizen of Missouri within the meaning of the Constitution of the United States, and not entitled as such to sue in its courts; and, consequently, that the Circuit Court had no jurisdiction of the case, and that the judgment on the plea in abatement is erroneous.

We are aware that doubts are entertained by some of the members of the court, whether the plea in abatement is legally before the court upon this writ of error; but if that plea is regarded as waived, or out of the case upon any other ground, yet the question as to the jurisdiction of the Circuit Court is presented on the face of the bill of exception itself, taken by the plaintiff at the trial; for he admits that he and his wife were born slaves, but endeavors to make out his title to freedom and citizenship by showing that they were taken by their owner to certain places, hereinafter mentioned, where slavery could not by law exist, and that they thereby became free, and upon their return to Missouri became citizens of that State.

Now, if the removal of which he speaks did not give them their freedom, then by his own admission he is still a slave; and whatever opinions may be entertained in favor of the citizenship of a free person of the African race, no one supposes that a slave is a citizen of the State or of the United States. If, therefore, the acts done by his owner did not make them free persons, he is still a slave, and certainly incapable of suing in the character of a citizen.

The principle of law is too well settled to be disputed, that a court can give no judgment for either party, where it has no jurisdiction; and if, upon the showing of Scott himself, it appeared that he was still a slave, the case ought to have been dismissed, and the judgment against him and in favor of the defendant for costs, is, like that on the plea in abatement, erroneous, and the suit ought to have been dismissed by the Circuit Court for want of jurisdiction in that court.

But, before we proceed to examine this part of the case, it may be proper to notice an objection taken to the judicial authority of this court to decide it; and it has been said, that as this court has decided against the jurisdiction of the Circuit Court on the plea in abatement, it has no right to examine any question presented by the exception; and that anything it may say upon that part of the case will be extrajudicial, and mere obiter dicta.

This is a manifest mistake; there can be no doubt as to the jurisdiction of this court to revise the judgment of a circuit court, and to reverse it for any error apparent on the record, **428*]** *whether it be the error of giving judgment in a case over which it had no jurisdiction, or any other material error; and this, too, whether there is a plea in abatement or not.

The objection appears to have arisen from confounding writs of error to a state court, with writs of error to a circuit court of the United States. Undoubtedly, upon a writ of error to a state court, unless the record shows a case that gives jurisdiction, the case must be dismissed for want of jurisdiction in this court. And if it is dismissed on that ground, we have no right to examine and decide upon any question presented by the bill of exceptions, or any other part of the record. But writs of error to a state court, and to a circuit court of the

United States, are regulated by different laws, and stand upon entirely different principles. And in a writ of error to a circuit court of the United States, the whole record is before this court for examination and decision; and if the sum in controversy is large enough to give jurisdiction, it is not only the right, but it is the judicial duty of the court, to examine the whole case as presented by the record; and if it appears upon its face that any material error or errors have been committed by the court below, it is the duty of this court to reverse the judgment, and remand the case. And certainly an error in passing a judgment upon the merits in favor of either party, in a case which it was not authorized to try, and over which it had no jurisdiction, is as grave an error as a court can commit.

The plea in abatement is not a plea to the jurisdiction of this court, but to the jurisdiction of the Circuit Court. And it appears by the record before us, that the Circuit Court committed an error, in deciding that it had jurisdiction, upon the facts in the case, admitted by the pleadings. It is the duty of the appellate tribunal to correct this error; but that could not be done by dismissing the case for want of jurisdiction here—for that would leave the erroneous judgment in full force, and the injured party without remedy. And the appellate court, therefore, exercises the power for which alone appellate courts are constituted, by reversing the judgment of the court below for this error. It exercises its proper and appropriate jurisdiction over the judgment and proceedings of the Circuit Court as they appear upon the record brought up by the writ of error.

The correction of one error in the court below does not deprive the appellate court of the power of examining further into the record, and correcting any other material errors which may have been committed by the inferior court. There is certainly no rule of law—nor any practice—nor any decision of a *court—which even questions this **[*429** power in the appellate tribunal. On the contrary, it is the daily practice of this court, and of all appellate courts where they reverse the judgment of an inferior court for error, to correct by its opinions whatever errors may appear on the record material to the case; and they have always held it to be their duty to do so where the silence of the court might lead to misconstruction or future controversy, and the point has been relied on by either side, and argued before the court.

In the case before us, we have already decided that the Circuit Court erred in deciding that it had jurisdiction upon the facts admitted by the pleadings. And it appears that, in the further progress of the case, it acted upon the erroneous principle it had decided on the pleadings, and gave judgment for the defendant, where, upon the facts admitted in the exception, it had no jurisdiction.

We are at a loss to understand upon what principle of law, applicable to appellate jurisdiction, it can be supposed that this court has not judicial authority to correct the last mentioned error because they had before corrected the former; or by what process of reasoning it can be made out, that the error of an inferior court in actually pronouncing judgment for one of the parties, in a case in which it had no jurisdiction, cannot be looked into or corrected by this court, because we have decided a similar question presented in the pleadings. The last point is distinctly presented by the facts contained in the plaintiff's own bill of exceptions, which he himself brings here by this writ of error. It was the point which chiefly occupied the attention of the counsel on both sides in the argument—and the judgment which this court must render upon both errors is precisely the same. It must, in each of them, exercise jurisdiction over the judgment, and reverse it for the errors committed by the court below; and issue a mandate to the Circuit Court to conform its judgment to the opinion pronounced by this court, by dismissing the case for want of jurisdiction in the Circuit Court. This is the constant and invariable practice of this court where it reverses a judgment for want of jurisdiction in the Circuit Court.

It can scarcely be necessary to pursue such a question further. The want of jurisdiction in the court below may appear on the record without any plea in abatement. This is familiarly the case where a court of chancery has exercised jurisdiction in a case where the plaintiff had a plain and adequate remedy at law, and it so appears by the transcript when brought here by appeal. So, also, where it appears that a court of admiralty has exercised jurisdiction in a case belonging exclusively 430*] *to a court of common law. In these cases there is no plea in abatement. And for the same reason, and upon the same principles, where the defect of jurisdiction is patent on the record, this court is bound to reverse the judgment, although the defendant has not pleaded in abatement to the jurisdiction of the inferior court.

The cases of Jackson v. Ashton, 8 Pet. 148, and of Capron v. Van Noorden, 2 Cranch, 126, to which we have referred in a previous part of this opinion, are directly in point. In the last mentioned case, Capron brought an action against Van Noorden in a circuit court of the United States, without showing, by the usual averments of citizenship, that the court had jurisdiction. There was no plea in abatement put in, and the parties went to trial upon the merits. The court gave judgment in favor of the defendant with costs. The plaintiff thereupon brought his writ of error, and this court reversed the judgment given in favor of the defendant, and remanded the case with directions to dismiss it, because it did not appear by the transcript that the Circuit Court had jurisdiction.

The case before us still more strongly imposes upon this court the duty of examining whether the court below has not committed an error, in taking jurisdiction and giving a judgment for costs in favor of the defendant; for in Capron v. Van Noorden the judgment was reversed, because it did not appear that the parties were citizens of different States. They might or might not be. But in this case it does appear that the plaintiff was born a slave; and if the facts upon which he relies have not made him free, then it appears affirmatively on the record that he is not a citizen, and consequently his suit against Sandford was not a suit between citizens of different States, and the court had no authority to pass any judg-

ment between the parties. The suit ought, in this view of it, to have been dismissed by the Circuit Court, and its judgment in favor of Sandford is erroneous, and must be reversed.

It is true that the result either way, by dismissal or by a judgment for the defendant, makes very little, if any difference in a pecuniary or personal point of view to either party. But the fact that the result would be very nearly the same to the parties in either form of judgment, would not justify this court in sanctioning an error in the judgment which is patent on the record, and which, if sanctioned, might be drawn into precedent, and lead to serious mischief and injustice in some future suit.

We proceed, therefore, to inquire whether the facts relied on by the plaintiff entitled him to his freedom.

*The case, as he himself states it, [*431 on the record, brought here by his writ of error, is this:

The plaintiff was a negro slave, belonging to Dr. Emerson, who was a surgeon in the Army of the United States. In the year 1834, he took the plaintiff from the State of Missouri to the military post at Rock Island, in the State of Illinois, and held him there as a slave until the month of April or May, 1836. At the time last mentioned, said Dr. Emerson removed the plaintiff from said military post at Rock Island to the military post at Fort Snelling, situate on the west bank of the Mississippi River, in the Territory known as Upper Louisiana, acquired by the United States of France, and situate north of the latitude of thirty-six degrees thirty minutes north, and north of the State of Missouri. Said Dr. Emerson held the plaintiff in slavery at said Fort Snelling, from said last mentioned date until the year 1838.

In the year 1835, Harriet, who is named in the second count of the plaintiff's declaration, was a negro slave of Major Taliaferro, who belonged to the Army of the United States. In that year, 1835, said Major Taliaferro took said Harriet to said Fort Snelling, a military post, situated as hereinbefore stated, and kept her there as a slave until the year 1836, and then sold and delivered her as a slave, at said Fort Snelling, unto the said Dr. Emerson hereinbefore named. Said Dr. Emerson held said Harriet in slavery at said Fort Snelling, until the year 1838.

In the year 1836, the plaintiff and Harriet intermarried, at Fort Snelling, with the consent of Dr. Emerson, who then claimed to be their master and owner. Eliza and Lizzie, named in the third count of the plaintiff's declaration, are the fruit of that marriage. Eliza is about fourteen years old, and was born on board the steamboat Gipsey, north of the north line of the State of Missouri, and upon the River Mississippi. Lizzie is about seven years old, and was born in the State of Missouri, at the military post called Jefferson Barracks.

In the year 1838, said Dr. Emerson removed the plaintiff and said Harriet, and their said daughter Eliza, from said Fort Snelling, to the State of Missouri, where they have ever since resided.

Before the commencement of this suit, said Dr. Emerson sold and conveyed the plaintiff, and Harriet, Eliza, and Lizzie, to the defendant, as slaves, and the defendant has ever since claimed to hold them, and each of them, as slaves.

In considering this part of the controversy, two questions arise: 1st. Was he, together with his family, free in Missouri by reason of the stay in the territory of the United States 432*] hereinbefore *mentioned? And 2d. If they were not, is Scott himself free by reason of his removal to Rock Island, in the State of Illinois, as stated in the above admissions?

We proceed to examine the first question.

The Act of Congress, upon which the plaintiff relies, declares that slavery and involuntary servitude, except as a punishment for crime, shall be forever prohibited in all that part of that territory ceded by France, under the name of Louisiana, which lies north of thirty-six degrees thirty minutes north latitude, and not included within the limits of Missouri. And the difficulty which meets us at the threshold of this part of the inquiry is, whether Congress was authorized to pass this law under any of the powers granted to it by the Constitution; for if the authority is not given by that instrument, it is the duty of this court to declare it void and inoperative, and incapable of conferring freedom upon one who is held as a slave under the laws of any one of the States.

The counsel for the plaintiff has laid much stress upon that article in the Constitution which confers on Congress the power "to dispose of and make all needful rules and regulations respecting the territory or other property belonging to the United States;" but, in the judgment of the court, that provision has no bearing on the present controversy, and the power there given, whatever it may be, is confined, and was intended to be confined, to the territory which at that time belonged to, or was claimed by, the United States, and was within their boundaries as settled by the Treaty with Great Britain, and can have no influence upon a territory afterwards acquired from a foreign government. It was a special provision for a known and particular Territory, and to meet a present emergency, and nothing more.

A brief summary of the history of the times, as well as the careful and measured terms in which the article is framed, will show the correctness of this proposition.

It will be remembered that, from the commencement of the Revolutionary War, serious difficulties existed between the States, in relation to the disposition of large and unsettled territories which were included in the chartered limits of some of the States. And some of the other States, and more especially Maryland, which had no unsettled lands, insisted that as the unoccupied lands, if wrested from Great Britain, would owe their preservation to the common purse and the common sword, the money arising from them ought to be applied in just proportion among the several States to pay the expense of the war, and ought not to be appropriated to the use of State in whose chartered limits they might happen 433*] *to lie, to the exclusion of the other States by whose combined efforts and common expense the territory was defended and preserved against the claim of the British Government.

These difficulties caused much uneasiness

during the War, while the issue was in some degree doubtful, and the future boundaries of the United States yet to be defined by treaty, if we achieved our independence.

The majority of the Congress of the Confederation obviously concurred in opinion with the State of Maryland, and desired to obtain from the States which claimed it a cession of this territory, in order that Congress might raise money on this security to carry on the War. This appears by the resolution passed on the 6th of September, 1780, strongly urging the States to cede these lands to the United States, both for the sake of peace and union among themselves, and to maintain the public credit; and this was followed by the resolution of October 10th, 1780, by which Congress pledged itself, that if the lands were ceded, as recommended by the resolution above mentioned, they should be disposed of for the common benefit of the United States, and be settled and formed into distinct republican States, which should become members of the Federal Union, and have the same rights of sovereignty, and freedom, and independence as other States.

But these difficulties became much more serious after peace took place, and the boundaries of the United States were established. Every State, at that time, felt severely the pressure of its war debt; but in Virginia, and some other States there were large territories of unsettled lands, the sale of which would enable them to discharge their obligations without much inconvenience; while other States which had no such resource, saw before them many years of heavy and burdensome taxation, and the latter insisted, for the reasons before stated, that these unsettled lands should be treated as the common property of the States, and the proceeds applied to their common benefit.

The letters from the statesmen of that day will show how much this controversy occupied their thoughts, and the dangers that were apprehended from it. It was the disturbing element of the time, and fears were entertained that it might dissolve the Confederation by which the States were then united.

These fears and dangers were, however, at once removed, when the State of Virginia, in 1784, voluntarily ceded to the United States the immense tract of country lying northwest of the River Ohio, and which was within the acknowledged limits of the State. The only object of the State, in making *this ces- [*434 sion, was to put an end to the threatening and exciting controversy, and to enable the Congress of that time to dispose of the lands, and appropriate the proceeds as a common fund for the common benefit of the States. It was not ceded because it was inconvenient to the State to hold and govern it, nor from any expectation that it could be better or more conveniently governed by the United States.

The example of Virginia was soon afterwards followed by other States, and, at the time of the adoption of the Constitution, all of the States, similarly situated, had ceded their unappropriated lands, except North Carolina and Georgia. The main object for which these cessions were desired and made, was on account of their money value, and to put an end to a dangerous controversy, as to who was justly entitled to the proceeds when the lands should be sold. It is necessary to bring this part of the history of these cessions thus distinctly into view, because it will enable us the better to comprehend the phraseology of the Article of the Constitution so often referred to in the argument.

Undoubtedly the powers of sovereignty and the eminent domain were ceded with the land. This was essential, in order to make it effectual, and to accomplish its objects. But it must be remembered that, at that time, there was no Government of the United States in existence with enumerated and limited powers; what was then called the United States, were thirteen separate, sovereign, independent States, which had entered into a league or confederation for their mutual protection and advantage, and the Congress of the United States was composed of the representatives of these separate sovereignties, meeting together, as equals, to discuss and decide on certain measures which the States, by the Articles of Confederation, had agreed to submit to their decision. But this Confederation had none of the attributes of sovereignty in legislative, executive, or judicial power. It was little more than a congress of ambassadors, authorized to represent separate nations, in matters in which they had a common concern.

It was this Congress that accepted the cession from Virginia. They had no power to accept it under the Articles of Confederation. But they had an undoubted right, as independent sovereignties, to accept any cession of territory for their common benefit, which all of them assented to; and it is equally clear, that as their common property, and having no superior to control them, they had the right to exercise absolute dominion over it, subject only to the restrictions which Virginia had imposed in her Act of Cession. There was, as we have said, no Government of the United States **435*]** then in existence *with special enumerated and limited powers. The territory belonged to sovereignties, who, subject to the limitations above mentioned, had a right to establish any form of government they pleased, by compact or treaty among themselves, and to regulate rights of person and property in the territory as they might deem proper. It was by a Congress, representing the authority of these several and separate sovereignties, and acting under their authority and command (but not from any authority derived from the Articles of Confederation), that the instrument, usually called the Ordinance of 1787, was adopted; regulating in much detail the principles and the laws by which this Territory should be governed; and among other provisions, slavery is prohibited in it. We do not question the power of the States, by agreement among themselves, to pass this Ordinance, nor its obligatory force in the Territory, while the confederation or league of the States in their separate sovereign character continued to exist.

This was the state of things when the Constitution of the United States was formed. The territory ceded by Virginia belonged to the several confederated States as common property, and they had united in establishing in it a system of government and jurisprudence, in order to prepare it for admission as States, according to the terms of the cession. They were about to dissolve this federative

Union, and to surrender a portion of their independent sovereignty to a new government, which, for certain purposes, would make the people of the several States one people, and which was to be supreme and controlling within its sphere of action throughout the United States; but this government was to be carefully limited in its powers, and to exercise no authority beyond those expressly granted by the Constitution, or necessarily to be implied from the language of the instrument, and the objects it was intended to accomplish; and as this league of States would, upon the adoption of the new government, cease to have any power over the territory, and the Ordinance they had agreed upon be incapable of execution, and a mere nullity, it was obvious that some provision was necessary to give the new government sufficient power to enable it to carry into effect the objects for which it was ceded, and the compacts and agreements which the States had made each other in the exercise of their powers of sovereignty. It was necessary that the lands should be sold to pay the war debt; that a government and system of jurisprudence should be maintained in it, to protect the citizens of the United States, who should migrate to the Territory, in their rights of person and of property. It was also necessary that the new government, about to be *adopted, should be authorized to main- **[*436** tain the claim of the United States to the unappropriated lands in North Carolina and Georgia, which had not then been ceded, but the cession of which was confidently anticipated upon some terms that would be arranged between the general government and these two States. And, moreover, there were many articles of value besides this property in land, such as arms, military stores, munitions, and ships of war, which were the common property of the States, when acting in their independent characters as confederates, which neither the new government nor anyone else would have a right to take possession of, or control, without authority from them; and it was to place these things under the guardianship and protection of the new government, and to clothe it with the necessary powers, that the clause was inserted in the Constitution which gives Congress the power "to dispose of and make all needful rules and regulations respecting the territory or other property belonging to the United States." It was intended for a specific purpose, to provide for the things we have mentioned. It was to transfer to the new government the property then held in common by the States, and to give to that government power to apply it to the objects for which it had been destined by mutual agreement among the States before their league was dissolved. It applied only to the property which the States held in common at that time, and has no reference whatever to any territory or other property which the new sovereignty might afterwards itself acquire.

The language used in the clause, the arrangement and combination of the powers, and the somewhat unusual phraseology it uses, when it speaks of the political power to be exercised in the government of the territory, all indicate the design and meaning of the clause to be such as we have mentioned. It does not speak of any Territory, nor of Territories, but uses language which, according to its legitimate meaning, points to a particular thing. The power is given in relation only to the territory of the United States—that is, to a Territory then in existence, and then known or claimed as the territory of the United States. It begins its enumeration of powers by that of disposing, in other words, making sale of the lands, or raising money from them, which, as we have already said, was the main object of the cession, and which is accordingly the first thing provided for in the Article. It then gives the power which was necessarily associated with the disposition and sale of the lands—that is, the power of making needful rules and regulations respecting the Territory. And whatever construction may now be given to these 437*] words, everyone, we think, *must admit that they are not the words usually employed by statesmen in giving supreme power of legislation. They are certainly very unlike the words used in the power granted to legislate over territory which the new government might afterwards itself obtain by cession from a state, either for its seat of government, or for forts, magazines, arsenals, dockyards, and other needful buildings.

And the same power of making needful rules respecting the Territory is, in precisely the same language, applied to the other property belonging to the United States—associating the power over the Territory in this respect with the power over movable or personal property—that is, the ships, arms, and munitions of war, which then belonged in common to the State sovereignties. And it will hardly be said, that this power, in relation to the last mentioned objects, was deemed necessary to be thus specially given to the new government, in order to authorize it to make needful rules and regulations respecting the ships it might itself build, or arms and munitions of war it might itself manufacture or provide for the public service.

No one, it is believed, would think a moment of deriving the power of Congress to make needful rules and regulations in relation to property of this kind from this clause of the Constitution. Nor can it, upon any fair construction, be applied to any property but that which the new government was about to receive from the confederated States. And if this be true as to this property, it must be equally true and limited as to the territory, which is so carefully and precisely coupled with it—and like it referred to as property in the power granted. The concluding words of the clause appear to render this construction irresistible; for, after the provisions we have mentioned, it proceeds to say, "that nothing in the Constitution shall be so construed as to prejudice any claims of the United States, or of any particular State."

Now, as we have before said, all of the States, except North Carolina and Georgia, had made the cession before the Constitution was adopted, according to the resolution of Congress of October 10, 1780. The claims of other States, that the unappropriated lands in these two States should be applied to the common benefit, in like manner, was still insisted on, but refused by the States. And this member of the clause in question evidently applies to them, and can apply to nothing else. It was to exclude the conclusion that either party, by adopting the Constitution, would surrender what they deemed their rights. And when

the latter provision relates so obviously to the unappropriated lands not yet ceded by the States, and the first clause makes provision for those then actually ceded, it is *impos- [*438 sible, by any just rule of construction, to make the first provision general, and extend to all territories, which the Federal Government might in any way afterwards acquire, when the latter is plainly and unequivocally confined to a particular territory; which was a part of the same controversy, and involved in the same dispute, and depended upon the same principles. The union of the two provisions in the same clause shows that they were kindred subjects, and that the whole clause is local, and relates only to lands, within the limits of the United States, which had been or then were claimed by a State; and that no other Territory was in the mind of the framers of the Constitution, or intended to be embraced in it. Upon any other construction it would be impossible to account for the insertion of the last provision in the place where it is found, or to comprehend why, or for what object, it was associated with the previous provision.

This view of the subject is confirmed by the manner in which the present Government of the United States dealt with the subject as soon as it came into existence. It must be borne in mind that the same States that formed the Confederation also formed and adopted the new government, to which so large a portion of their former sovereign powers were surrendered. It must also be borne in mind that all of these same States which had then ratified the new Constitution were represented in the Congress which passed the first law for the government of this territory; and many of the members of that legislative body had been deputies from the States under the Confederation—had united in adopting the Ordinance of 1787, and assisted in forming the new government under which they were then acting, and whose powers they were then exercising. And it is obvious from the law they passed to carry into effect the principles and provisions of the Ordinance, that they regarded it as the Act of the States done in the exercise of their legitimate powers at the time. The new government took the territory as it found it, in the condition in which it was transferred, and did not attempt to undo anything that had been done. And among the earliest laws passed under the new government, is one reviving the Ordinance of 1787, which had become inoperative and a nullity upon the adoption of the Constitution. This law introduces no new form or principles for its government, but recites, in the preamble, that it is passed in order that this Ordinance may continue to have full effect, and proceeds to make only those rules and regulations which were needful to adapt it to the new government, into whose hands the power had fallen. It appears, therefore, that this Congress regarded the purposes *to which the land in [*439 this territory was to be applied, and the form of government and principles of jurisprudence which were to prevail there, while it remained in the territorial state, as already determined on by the States when they had full power and right to make the decision; and that the new government, having received it in this condition, ought to carry substantially into effect the plans and principles which had been previously adopted by the States, and which no doubt the

States anticipated when they surrendered their power to the new government. And if we regard this clause of the Constitution as pointing to this Territory, with a territorial government already established in it, which had been ceded to the States for the purposes hereinbefore mentioned—every word in it is perfectly appropriate and easily understood, and the provisions it contains are in perfect harmony with the objects for which it was ceded, and with the condition of its government as a Territory at the time. We can, then, easily account for the manner in which the first Congress legislated on the subject—and can also understand why this power over the Territory was associated in the same clause with the other property of the United States, and subjected to the like power of making needful rules and regulations. But if the clause is construed in the expanded sense contended for, so as to embrace any territory acquired from a foreign nation by the present government, and to give it in such territory a despotic and unlimited power over persons and property, such as the confederated States might exercise in their common property, it would be difficult to account for the phraseology used, when compared with other grants of power—and also for its association with the other provisions in the same clause.

The Constitution has always been remarkable for the felicity of its arrangement of different subjects, and the perspicuity and appropriateness of the language it uses. But if this clause is construed to extend to territory acquired by the present government from a foreign nation, outside of the limits of any charter from the British Government to a Colony, it would be difficult to say, why it was deemed necessary to give the government the power to sell any vacant lands belonging to the sovereignty which might be found within it; and if this was necessary, why the grant of this power should precede the power to legislate over it and establish a government there; and still more difficult to say, why it was deemed necessary so specially and particularly to grant the power to make needful rules and regulations in relation to any personal or movable property it might acquire there. For the words, "other property," necessarily, by every known rule of 440*] interpretation, must mean *property of a different description from territory or land. And the difficulty would perhaps be insurmountable in endeavoring to account for the last member of the sentence, which provides that "nothing in this Constitution shall be so construed as to prejudice any claims of the United States or any particular State," or to say how any particular State could have claims in or to a Territory ceded by a foreign government, or to account for associating this provision with the preceding provisions of the clause, with which it would appear to have no connection.

The words "needful rules and regulations" would seem, also, to have been cautiously used for some definite object. They are not the words usually employed by statesmen, when they mean to give the powers of sovereignty, or to establish a government, or to authorize its establishment. Thus, in the law to renew and keep alive the Ordinance of 1787, and to re-establish the government, the title of the law is: "An Act to provide for the government of the territory northwest of the River Ohio." And

in the Constitution, when granting the power to legislate over the territory that may be selected for the seat of government independently of a state, it does not say Congress shall have power "to make all needful rules and regulations respecting the territory;" but it declares that "Congress shall have power to exercise exclusive legislation in all cases whatsoever over such District (not exceeding ten miles square) as may, by cession of particular States and the acceptance of Congress, become the seat of the Government of the United States.

The words "rules and regulations" are usually employed in the Constitution in speaking of some particular specified power which it means to confer on the government, and not, as we have seen, when granting general powers of legislation. As, for example, in the particular power of Congress "to make rules for the government and regulation of the land and naval forces, or the particular and specific power to regulate commerce;" "to establish an uniform rule of naturalization;" "to coin money and regulate the value thereof." And to construe the words of which we are speaking as a general and unlimited grant of sovereignty over territories which the government might afterwards acquire, is to use them in a sense and for a purpose for which they were not used in any other part of the instrument. But if confined to a particular territory, in which a government and laws had already been established, but which would require some alterations to adapt it to the new government, the words are peculiarly applicable and appropriate for that purpose.

*The necessity of this special provi- [*441 sion in relation to property and the rights or property held in common by the confederated State, is illustrated by the 1st clause of the 6th article. This clause provides that "all debts, contracts and engagements entered into before the adoption of this Constitution, shall be as valid against the United States under this government as under the Confederation." This provision, like the one under consideration, was indispensable if the new Constitution was adopted. The new government was not a mere change in a dynasty, or in a form of government, leaving the nation or sovereignty the same, and clothed with all the rights, and bound by all the obligations of the preceding one. But, when the present United States came into existence under the new government, it was a new political body, a new nation, then for the first time taking its place in the family of nations. It took nothing by succession from the Confederation. It had no right, as its successor, to any property or rights of property which it had acquired, and was not liable for any of its obligations. It was evidently viewed in this light by the framers of the Constitution. And as the several States would cease to exist in their former confederated character upon the adoption of the Constitution, and could not, in that character, again assemble together, special provisions were indispensable to transfer to the new government the property and rights which at that time they held in common; and at the same time to authorize it to lay taxes and appropriate money to pay the common debt which they had contracted; and this power could only be given to it by special provisions in the Constitution.

The clause in relation to the territory and other property of the United States provided for the first, and the clause last quoted provided for the other. They have no connection with the general powers and rights of sovereignty delegated to the new government, and can neither enlarge nor diminish them. They were inserted to meet a present emergency, and not to regulate its powers as a government.

Indeed, a similar provision was deemed necessary, in relation to treaties made by the Confederation; and when in the clause next succeeding the one of which we have last spoken, it is declared that treaties shall be the supreme law of the land, care is taken to include, by express words, the Treaties made by the confederated States. The language is: "and all treaties made, or which shall be made, under the authority of the United States, shall be the supreme law of the land."

Whether, therefore, we take the particular clause in question, by itself, or in connection with the other provisions of the Constitution, we think it clear, that it applies only to the 442*] particular *territory of which we have spoken, and cannot, by any just rule of interpretation, be extended to a territory which the new government might afterwards obtain from a foreign nation. Consequently, the power which Congress may have lawfully exercised in this territory, while it remained under a territorial government, and which may have been sanctioned by judicial decision, can furnish no justification and no argument to support a similar exercise of power over territory afterwards acquired by the Federal Government. We put aside, therefore, any argument, drawn from precedents, showing the extent of the power which the general government exercised over slavery in this territory, as altogether inapplicable to the case before us.

But the case of The American and Ocean Insurance Companies v. Canter, 1 Pet. 511, has been quoted as establishing a different construction of this clause of the Constitution. There is, however, not the slightest conflict between the opinion now given and the one referred to; and it is only by taking a single sentence out of the latter and separating it from the context, that even an appearance of conflict can be shown. We need not comment on such a mode of expounding an opinion of the court. Indeed it most commonly misrepresents instead of expounding it. And this is fully exemplified in the case referred to, where, if one sentence is taken by itself, the opinion would appear to be in direct conflict with that now given; but the words which immediately follow that sentence show that the court did not mean to decide the point, but merely affirmed the power of Congress to establish a government in the Territory, leaving it an open question, whether that power was derived from this clause in the Constitution, or was to be necessarily inferred from a power to acquire territory by cession from a foreign government. The opinion on this part of the case is short, and we give the whole of it to show how well the selection of a single sentence is calculated to mislead.

The passage referred to is in page 542, in which the court, in speaking of the power of Congress to establish a territorial government

in Florida until it should become a State, uses the following language:

"In the meantime Florida continues to be a Territory of the United States, governed by that clause of the Constitution which empowers Congress to make all needful rules and regulations respecting the territory or other property of the United States. Perhaps the power of governing a territory belonging to the United States, which has not, by becoming a State, acquired the means of self-government, may result necessarily from the facts that it is not within the jurisdiction of any particular *State, and is within the power and ju- [*443 risdiction of the United States. The right to govern may be the inevitable consequence of the right to acquire territory. Whichever may be the source from which the power is derived, the possession of it is unquestionable."

It is thus clear, from the whole opinion on this point, that the court did not mean to decide whether the power was derived from the clause in the Constitution, or was the necessary consequence of the right to acquire. They do decide that the power in Congress is unquestionable, and in this we entirely concur, and nothing will be found in this opinion to the contrary. The power stands firmly on the latter alternative put by the court, that is, as "the inevitable consequence of the right to acquire territory."

And what still more clearly demonstrates that the court did not mean to decide the question, but leave it open for future consideration, is the fact that the case was decided in the Circuit Court by Mr. Justice Johnson, and his decision was affirmed by the Supreme Court. His opinion at the Circuit is given in full in a note to the case, and in that opinion he states, in explicit terms, that the clause of the Constitution applies only to the territory then within the limits of the United States, and not to Florida, which had been acquired by cession from Spain. This part of his opinion will be found in the note in page 517 of the report. But he does not dissent from the opinion of the Supreme Court; thereby showing that, in his judgment, as well as that of the court, the case before them did not call for a decision on that particular point, and the court abstained from deciding it. And in a part of its opinion subsequent to the passage we have quoted, where the court speak of the legislative power of Congress in Florida, they still speak with the same reserve. And in page 546, speaking of the power of Congress to authorize the Territorial Legislature to establish courts there, the court say: "They are legislative courts, created in virtue of the general right of sovereignty which exists in the government, or in virtue of that clause which enables Congress to make all needful rules and regulations respecting the territory belonging to the United States."

It has been said that the construction given to this clause is new, and now for the first time brought forward. The case of which we are speaking, and which has been so much discussed, shows that the fact is otherwise. It shows that precisely the same question came before Mr. Justice Johnson, at his circuit, thirty years ago—was fully considered by him, and the same construction given to the clause in the Constitution which is now given by this court. And that upon an appeal *from [*444 his decision the same question was brought before this court, but was not decided because a decision upon it was not required by the case before the court.

There is another sentence in the opinion which has been commented on, which even in a still more striking manner shows how one may mislead or be misled by taking out a single sentence from the opinion of a court, and leaving out of view what precedes and follows. It is in page 546, near the close of the opinion, in which the court say: "In legislating for them" (the Territories of the United States), "Congress exercises the combined powers of the general and of a state government." And it is said, that as a State may unquestionably prohibit slavery within its territory, this sentence decides in effect that Congress may do the same in a Territory of the United States, exercising there the powers of a State, as well as the power of the general government.

The examination of this passage in the case referred to, would be more appropriate when we come to consider in another part of this opinion what power Congress can constitutionally exercise in a Territory, over the rights of person or rights of property of a citizen. But, as it is in the same case with the passage we have before commented on, we dispose of it now, as it will save the court from the necessity of referring again to the case. And it will be seen upon reading the page in which this sentence is found, that it has no reference whatever to the power of Congress over rights of person or rights of property—but relates altogether to the power of establishing judicial tribunals to administer the laws constitutionally passed, and defining the jurisdiction they may exercise.

The law of Congress establishing a territorial government in Florida, provided that the Legislature of the Territory should have legislative powers over "all rightful objects of legislation; but no law should be valid which was inconsistent with the laws and Constitution of the United States."

Under the power thus conferred, the Legislature of Florida passed an Act, erecting a tribunal at Key West to decide cases of salvage. And in the case of which we are speaking, the question arose whether the Territorial Legislature could be authorized by Congress to establish such a tribunal, with such powers; and one of the parties, among other objections, insisted that Congress could not under the Constitution authorize the Legislature of the Territory to establish such a tribunal with such powers, but that it must be established by Congress itself; and that a sale of cargo made under its order, to pay salvors, was void, as made without legal authority, and passed no property to the purchaser.

445*] *It is in disposing of this objection that the sentence relied on occurs, and the court begin that part of the opinion by stating with great precision the point which they are about to decide.

They say: "It has been contended that by the Constitution of the United States, the judicial power of the United States extends to all cases of admiralty and maritime jurisdiction; and that the whole of the judicial power must be vested 'in one Supreme Court, and in

15 L. ed.

such inferior courts as Congress shall from time to time ordain and establish. Hence it has been argued that Congress cannot vest admiralty jurisdiction in courts created by the Territorial Legislature."

And after thus clearly stating the point before them, and which they were about to decide, they proceed to show that these territorial tribunals were not constitutional courts, but merely legislative, and that Congress might, therefore, delegate the power to the territorial government to establish the court in question; and they conclude that part of the opinion in the following words: "Although admiralty jurisdiction can be exercised in the states in those courts only which are established in pursuance of the 3d article of the Constitution, the same limitation does not extend to the Territories. In legislating for them, Congress exercises the combined powers of the general and state governments."

Thus it will be seen by these quotations from the opinion, that the court, after stating the question it was about to decide, in a manner too plain to be misunderstood, proceeded to decide it, and announced, as the opinion of the tribunal, that in organizing the Judicial Department of the government in a Territory of the United States, Congress does not act under, and is not restricted by, the 3d article in the Constitution, and is not bound, in a Territory, to ordain and establish courts in which the judges hold their offices during good behavior; but may exercise the discretionary power which a state exercises in establishing its judicial department, and regulating the jurisdiction of its courts, and may authorize the territorial government to establish, or may itself establish, courts in which the judges hold their offices for a term of years only, and may vest in them judicial power upon subjects confided to the judiciary of the United States. And in doing this, Congress undoubtedly exercises the combined power of the general and a state government. It exercises the discretionary power of a state government in authorizing the establishment of a court in which the judges hold their appointments for a term of years only, and not during good behavior; and it exercises the power of the general government in investing that *court with admiralty [*446 jurisdiction, over which the general government had exclusive jurisdiction in the Territory.

No one, we presume, will question the correctness of that opinion; nor is there anything in conflict with it in the opinion now given. The point decided in the case cited has no relation to the question now before the court. That depended on the construction of the 3d article of the Constitution, in relation to the judiciary of the United States, and the power which Congress might exercise in a territory in organizing the Judicial Department of the government. The case before us depends upon other and different provisions of the Constitution, altogether separate and apart from the one above mentioned. The question as to what courts Congress may ordain or establish in a territory to administer laws which the Constitution authorizes it to pass, and what laws it is or is not authorized by the Constitution to pass, are widely different—are regulated by different and separate articles of the Constitution, and stand

717

upon different principles. And we are satisfied that no one who reads attentively the page in Peters' Reports to which we have referred, can suppose that the attention of the court was drawn for a moment to the question now before this court, or that it meant in that case to say that Congress had a right to prohibit a citizen of the United States from taking any property which he lawfully held, into a Territory of the United States.

This brings us to examine by what provision of the Constitution the present Federal Government under its delegated and restricted powers, is authorized to acquire territory outside of the original limits of the United States, and what powers it may exercise therein over the person or property of a citizen of the United States, while it remains a territory, and until it shall be admitted as one of the States of the Union.

There is certainly no power given by the Constitution to the Federal Government to establish or maintain Colonies bordering on the United States or at a distance, to be ruled and governed at its own pleasure; nor to enlarge its territorial limits in any way, except by the admission of new States. That power is plainly given; and if a new State is admitted it needs no further legislation by Congress, because the Constitution itself defines the relative rights and powers and duties of the State, and the citizens of the State, and the Federal Government. But no power is given to acquire a Territory to be held and governed permanently in that character.

And indeed the power exercised by Congress to acquire territory and establish a government there, according to its own unlimited discretion, was viewed with great jealously by the 447*] *leading statesmen of the day. And in the Federalist, No. 38, written by Mr. Madison, he speaks of the acquisition of the Northwestern Territory by the confederated States, by the cession from Virginia and the establishment of a government there, as an exercise of power not warranted by the Articles of Confederation, and dangerous to the liberties of the people. And he urges the adoption of the Constitution as a security and safeguard against such an exercise of power.

We do not mean, however, to question the power of Congress in this respect. The power to expand the territory of the United States by the admission of new States is plainly given; and in the construction of this power by all the departments of the government, it has been held to authorize the acquisition of territory, not fit for admission at the time, but to be admitted as soon as its population and situation would entitle it to admission. It is acquired to become a State, and not to be held as a colony and governed by Congress with absolute authority; and as the propriety of admitting a new State is committed to the sound discretion of Congress, the power to acquire territory for that purpose, to be held by the United States until it is in a suitable condition to become a state upon an equal footing with the other States, must rest upon the same discretion. It is a question for the Political Department of the government, and not the judicial; and whatever the Political Department of the government shall recognize as within the limits of the United States, the Judicial Department is

718

also bound to recognize, and to administer in it the laws of the United States, so far as they apply, and to maintain in the territory the authority and rights of the government; and also the personal rights and rights of property of individual citizens, as secured by the Constitution. All we mean to say on this point is, that, as there is no express regulation in the Constitution defining the power which the general government may exercise over the person or property of a citizen in a territory thus acquired, the court must necessarily look to the provisions and principles of the Constitution, and its distribution of powers, for the rules and principles by which its decision must be governed.

Taking this rule to guide us, it may be safely assumed that citizens of the United States who migrate to a territory belonging to the people of the United States, cannot be ruled as mere colonists, dependent upon the will of the general government, and to be governed by any laws it may think proper to impose. The principle upon which our governments rest, and upon which alone they continue to exist, is the union of States, sovereign and independent within their own limits in *their inter- [*448 nal and domestic concerns, and bound together as one people by a general government, possessing certain enumerated and restricted powers, delegated to it by the people of the several States, and exercising supreme authority within the scope of the powers granted to it, throughout the dominion of the United States. A power, therefore, in the general government to obtain and hold Colonies and dependent Territories, over which they might legislate without restriction, would be inconsistent with its own existence in its present form. Whatever it acquires, it acquires for the benefit of the people of the several States who created it. It is their trustee acting for them, and charged with the duty of promoting the interests of the whole people of the Union in the exercise of the powers specifically granted.

At the time when the Territory in question was obtained by cession from France, it contained no population fit to be associated together and admitted as a State; and it therefore was absolutely necessary to hold possession of it as a Territory belonging to the United States until it was settled and inhabited by a civilized community capable of self-government, and in a condition to be admitted on equal terms with the other States as a member of the Union. But, as we have before said, it was acquired by the general government as the representative and trustee of the people of the United States, and it must, therefore, be held in that character for their common and equal benefit; for it was the people of the several States, acting through the agent and representative, the Federal Government, who in fact acquired the territory in question, and the government holds it for their common use until it shall be associated with the other States as a member of the Union.

But until that time arrives, it is undoubtedly necessary that some government should be established, in order to organize society, and to protect the inhabitants in their persons and property; and as the people of the United States could act in this matter only through the government which represented them, and through which they spoke and acted when the territory was obtained, it was not only within the scope of its powers, but it was its duty to pass such laws and establish such a government as would enable those by whose authority they acted to reap the advantages anticipated from its acquisition, and to gather there a population which would enable it to assume the position to which it was destined among the States of the Union. The power to acquire, necessarily carries with it the power to preserve and apply to the purposes for which it was acquired. The form of government to be established neces-**449***] sarily rested in the discretion *of Congress. It was their duty to establish the one that would be best suited for the protection and security of the citizens of the United States and other inhabitants who might be authorized to take up their abode there, and that must always depend upon the existing condition of the Territory, as to the number and character of its inhabitants, and the situation in the Territory. In some cases a government, consisting of persons appointed by the Federal Government, would best subserve the interests of the Territory, when the inhabitants were few and scattered, and new to one another. In other instances, it would be more advisable to commit the powers of self-government to the people who had settled in the territory, as being the most competent to determine what was best for their own interests. But some form of civil authority would be absolutely necessary to organize and preserve civilized society, and prepare it to become a state; and what is the best form must always depend on the condition of the territory at the time, and the choice of the mode must depend upon the exercise of a discretionary power by Congress acting within the scope of its constitutional authority, and not infringing upon the rights of person or rights of property of the citizen who might go there to reside or for any other lawful purpose. It was acquired by the exercise of this discretion and it must be held and governed in like manner, until it is fitted to be a state.

But the power of Congress over the person or property of a citizen can never be a mere discretionary power under our Constitution and form of government. The powers of the government and the rights and privileges of the citizen are regulated and plainly defined by the Constitution itself. And when the territory becomes a part of the United States, the Federal Government enters into possession in the character impressed upon it by those who created it. It enters upon it with its powers over the citizen strictly defined, and limited by the Constitution, from which it derives its own existence, and by virtue of which alone it continues to exist and act as a government and sovereignty. It has no power of any kind beyond it; and it cannot, when it enters a territory of the United States, put off its character, and assume discretionary or despotic powers which the Constitution has denied to it. It cannot create for itself a new character separated from the citizens of the United States, and the duties it owes them under the provisions of the Constitution. The territory being a part of the United States, the government and the citizen both enter it under the authority of the Constitution, with their respective rights defined and marked

out; and the Federal Government *can [*450 exercise no power over his person or property, beyond what that instrument confers, nor lawfully deny any right which it has reserved.

A reference to a few of the provisions of the Constitution will illustrate this proposition.

For example, no one, we presume, will contend that Congress can make any law in a territory respecting the establishment of religion or the free exercise thereof, or abridging the freedom of speech or of the press, or the right of the people of the territory peaceably to assemble and to petition the government for the redress of grievances.

Nor can Congress deny to the people the right to keep and bear arms, nor the right to trial by jury, nor compel anyone to be a witness against himself in a criminal proceeding.

These powers, and others in relation to rights of person, which it is not necessary here to enumerate, are, in express and positive terms, denied to the general government; and the rights of private property have been guarded with equal care. Thus the rights of property are united with the rights of person, and placed on the same ground by the fifth amendment to the Constitution, which provides that no person shall be deprived of life, liberty and property, without due process of law. And an Act of Congress which deprives a citizen of the United States of his liberty or property, merely because he came himself or brought his property into a particular Territory of the United States, and who had committed no offense against the laws, could hardly be dignified with the name of due process of law.

So, too, it will hardly be contended that Congress could by law quarter a soldier in a house in a territory without the consent of the owner, in time of peace; nor in time of war, but in a manner prescribed by law. Nor could they by law forfeit the property of a citizen in a territory who was convicted of treason, for a longer period than the life of the person convicted; nor take private property for public use without just compensation.

The powers over person and property of which we speak are not only not granted to Congress, but are in express terms denied, and they are forbidden to exercise them. And this prohibition is not confined to the States, but the words are general, and extend to the whole territory over which the Constitution gives it power to legislate, including those portions of it remaining under territorial government, as well as that covered by States. It is a total absence of power everywhere within the dominion of the United States, and places the citizens of a territory, so far as these rights are *concerned, on the same footing with [*451 citizens of the States, and guards them as firmly and plainly against any inroads which the general government might attempt, under the plea of implied or incidental powers. And if Congress itself cannot do this—if it is beyond the powers conferred on the Federal Government—it will be admitted, we presume, that it could not authorize a territorial government to exercise them. It could confer no power on any local government, established by its authority, to violate the provisions of the Constitution.

It seems, however, to be supposed, that there is a difference between property in a slave and other property, and that different rules may be applied to it in expounding the Constitution of the United States. And the laws and usages of nations, and the writings of eminent jurists upon the relation of master and slave and their mutual rights and duties, and the powers which governments may exercise over it, have been dwelt upon in the argument.

But in considering the question before us, it must be borne in mind that there is no law of nations standing between the people of the United States and their government and interfering with their relation to each other. The powers of the government, and the rights of the citizen under it, are positive and practical regulations plainly written down. The people of the United States have delegated to it certain enumerated powers, and forbidden it to exercise others. It has no power over the person or property of a citizen but what the citizens of the United States have granted. And no laws or usages of other nations, or reasoning of statesmen or jurists upon the relations of master and slave, can enlarge the powers of the government, or take from the citizens the rights they have reserved. And if the Constitution recognizes the right of property of the master in a slave, and makes no distinction between that description of property and other property owned by a citizen, no tribunal, acting under the authority of the United States, whether it be legislative, executive, or judicial, has a right to draw such a distinction, or deny to it the benefit of the provisions and guarantees which have been provided for the protection of private property against the encroachments of the governments.

Now, as we have already said in an earlier part of this opinion, upon a different point, the right of property in a slave is distinctly and expressly affirmed in the Constitution. The right to traffic in it, like an ordinary article of merchandise and property, was guaranteed to the citizens of the United States, in every State that might desire it, for twenty years. And the government in express terms is pledged to 452*] protect *it in all future time, if the slave escapes from his owner. This is done in plain words—too plain to be misunderstood. And no word can be found in the Constitution which gives Congress a greater power over slave property, or which entitles property of that kind to less protection than property of any other description. The only power conferred is the power coupled with the duty of guarding and protecting the owner in his rights.

Upon these considerations, it is the opinion of the court that the Act of Congress which prohibited a citizen from holding and owning property of this kind in the territory of the United States north of the line therein mentioned, is not warranted by the Constitution, and is therefore void; and that neither Dred Scott himself, nor any of his family, were made free by being carried into this territory; even if they had been carried there by the owner, with the intention of becoming a permanent resident.

We have so far examined the case, as it stands under the Constitution of the United States, and the powers thereby delegated to the Federal Government.

But there is another point in the case which

720

depends on state power and state law. And it is contended, on the part of the plaintiff, that he is made free by being taken to Rock Island, in the State of Illinois, independently of his residence in the territory of the United States; and being so made free he was not again reduced to a state of slavery by being brought back to Missouri.

Our notice of this part of the case will be very brief; for the principle on which it depends was decided in this court, upon much consideration, in the case of Strader et al. v. Graham, reported in 10th Howard, 82. In that case, the slaves had been taken from Kentucky to Ohio, with the consent of the owner, and afterwards brought back to Kentucky. And this court held that their status or condition, as free or slave, depended upon the laws of Kentucky, when they were brought back into that State, and not of Ohio; and that this court had no jurisdiction to revise the judgment of a state court upon its own laws. This was the point directly before the court, and the decision that this court had not jurisdiction, turned upon it, as will be seen by the report of the case.

So in this case: as Scott was a slave when taken into the State of Illinois by his owner, and was there held as such, and brought back in that character, his status, as free or slave, depended on the laws of Missouri, and not of Illinois.

It has, however, been urged in the argument, that by the laws of Missouri he was free on his return, and that this case, *therefore, cannot be governed by the [*453 case of Strader et al. v. Graham, where it appeared, by the laws of Kentucky, that the plaintiffs continued to be slaves on their return from Ohio. But whatever doubts or opinions may, at one time, have been entertained upon this subject, we are satisfied, upon a careful examination of all the cases decided in the State courts of Missouri referred to, that it is now firmly settled by the decisions of the highest court in the State, that Scott and his family upon their return were not free, but were, by the laws of Missouri, the property of the defendant; and that the Circuit Court of the United States had no jurisdiction, when, by the laws of the State, the plaintiff was a slave and not a citizen.

Moreover, the plaintiff, it appears, brought a similar action against the defendant in the State court of Missouri, claiming the freedom of himself and his family upon the same grounds and the same evidence upon which he relies in the case before the court. The case was carried before the Supreme Court of the State; was fully argued there; and that court decided that neither the plaintiff nor his family were entitled to freedom, and were still the slaves of the defendant; and reversed the judgment of the inferior State court, which had given a different decision. If the plaintiff supposed that this judgment of the Supreme Court of the State was erroneous, and that this court had jurisdiction to revise and reverse it, the only mode by which he could legally bring it before this court was by writ of error directed to the Supreme Court of the State, requiring it to transmit the record to this court. If this had been done, it is too plain for argument that the writ must have been dismissed for want of jurisdiction in this court. The case of Strader et al. v. Graham is directly in point; and, indeed, independent of any decision, the language of the 25th section of the Act of 1789 is too clear and precise to admit of controversy.

But the plaintiff did not pursue the mode prescribed by law for bringing the judgment of a state court before this court for revision, but suffered the case to be remanded to the inferior State court, where it is still continued, and is, by agreement of parties, to await the judgment of this court on the point. All of this appears on the record before us and by the printed report of the case.

And while the case is yet open and pending in the inferior State court, the plaintiff goes into the Circuit Court of the United States, upon the same case and the same evidence, and against the same party, and proceeds to judgment, and then brings here the same case from the Circuit Court, which the law would not have permitted him to bring directly from the 454*] *State court. And if this court takes jurisdiction in this form, the result, so far as the rights of the respective parties are concerned, is in every respect substantially the same as if it had, in open violation of law, entertained jurisdiction over the judgment of the State court upon a writ of error, and revised and reversed its judgment upon the ground that its opinion upon the question of law was erroneous. It would ill become this court to sanction such an attempt to evade the law, or to exercise an appellate power in this circuitous way, which it is forbidden to exercise in the direct and regular and invariable forms of judicial proceedings.

Upon the whole, therefore, it is the judgment of this court, that it appears by the record before us that the plaintiff in error is not a citizen of Missouri, in the sense in which that word is used in the Constitution; and that the Circuit Court of the United States, for that reason, had no jurisdiction in the case, and could give no judgment in it.

Its judgment for the defendant must, consequently, be reversed, and a mandate issued directing the suit to be dismissed for want of jurisdiction.

Mr. Justice Wayne:

Concurring as I do entirely in the opinion of the court, as it has been written and read by the Chief Justice—without any qualification of its reasoning or its conclusions—I shall neither read nor file an opinion of my own in this case which I prepared when I supposed it might be necessary and proper for me to do so.

The opinion of the court meets fully and decides every point which was made in the argument of the case by the counsel on either side of it. Nothing belonging to the case has been left undecided, nor has any point been discussed and decided which was not called for by the record, or which was not necessary for the judicial disposition of it, in the way that it has been done, by more than a majority of the court.

In doing this the court neither sought nor made the case. It was brought to us in the course of the administration of the laws which Congress has enacted, for the review of cases

from the circuit courts by the Supreme Court.

In our action upon it, we have only discharged our duty as a distinct and efficient department of the government, as the framers of the Constitution meant the judiciary to be, and as the States of the Union and the people of those States intended it should be, when they ratified the Constitution of the United States.

The case involves private rights of value, and constitutional principles of the highest importance, about which there had *be- [*455 come such a difference of opinion, that the peace and harmony of the country required the settlement of them by judicial decision.

It would certainly be a subject of regret, that the conclusions of the court have not been assented to by all of its members, if I did not know from its history and my own experience how rarely it has happened that the judges have been unanimous upon constitutional questions of moment, and if our decision in this case had not been made by as large a majority of them as has been usually had on constitutional questions of importance.

Two of the judges, Mr. Justices McLean and Curtis, dissent from the opinion of the court. A third, Mr. Justice Nelson, gives a separate opinion upon a single point in the case, with which I concur, assuming that the Circuit Court had jurisdiction; but he abstains altogether from expressing any opinion upon the 8th section of the Act of 1820, known commonly as the Missouri Compromise Law, and six of us declare that it was unconstitutional.

But it has been assumed, that this court has acted extrajudicially in giving an opinion upon the 8th section of the Act of 1820, because, as it has decided that the Circuit Court had no jurisdiction of the case, this court has no jurisdiction to examine the case upon its merits.

But the error of such an assertion has arisen in part from a misapprehension of what has been heretofore decided by the Supreme Court, in cases of a like kind with that before us; in part, from a misapplication to the circuit courts of the United States, of the rules of pleading concerning pleas to the jurisdiction which prevail in common law courts; and from its having been forgotten that this case was not brought to this court by appeal or writ of error from a state court, but by a writ of error to the Circuit Court of the United States.

The cases cited by the Chief Justice to show that this court has now only done what it has repeatedly done before in other cases, without any question of its correctness, speak for themselves. The differences between the rules concerning pleas to the jurisdiction in the courts of the United States and common law courts have been stated and sustained by reasoning and adjudged cases; and it has been shown that writs of error to a state court and to the circuit courts of the United States are to be determined by different laws and principles. In the first, it is our duty to ascertain if this court has jurisdiction, under the 25th section of the Judiciary Act, to review the case from the State court; and if it shall be found that it has not, the case is at end, so far as this court is concerned; for our power *to review the [*456 case upon its merits has been made, by the 25th section, to depend upon its having jurisdiction; when it has not, this court cannot criticise, controvert, or give any opinion upon the merits of a case from a state court.

But in a case brought to this court, by appeal or by writ of error from a circuit court of the United States, we begin a review of it, not by inquiring if this court has jurisdiction, but if that court has it. If the case has been decided by that court upon its merits, but the record shows it to be deficient in those averments which by the law of the United States must be made by the plaintiff in the action, to give the court jurisdiction of his case, we send it back to the court from which it was brought, with directions to be dismissed, though it has been decided there upon its merits.

So, in a case containing the averments by the plaintiff which are necessary to give the Circuit Court jurisdiction, if the defendant shall file his plea in abatement denying the truth of them, and the plaintiff shall demur to it, and the court should erroneously sustain the plaintiff's demurrer, or declare the plea to be insufficient, and doing so require the defendant to answer over by a plea to the merits, and shall decide the case upon such pleading, this court has the same authority to inquire into the jurisdiction of that court to do so, and to correct its error in that regard, that it had in the other case to correct its error, in trying a case in which the plaintiff had not made those averments which were necessary to give the court jurisdiction. In both cases the record is resorted to, to determine the point of jurisdiction, but, as the power of review of cases from a federal court, by this court, is not limited by the law to a part of the case, this court may correct an error upon the merits; and there is the same reason for correcting an erroneous judgment of the Circuit Court, where the want of jurisdiction appears from any part of the record, that there is for declaring a want of jurisdiction for a want of necessary averments. Any attempt to control the court from doing so by the technical common law rules of pleading in cases of jurisdiction, when a defendant has been denied his plea to it, would tend to enlarge the jurisdiction of the Circuit Court, by limiting this court's review of its judgments in that particular. But I will not argue a point already so fully discussed. I have every confidence in the opinion of the court upon the point of jurisdiction, and do not allow myself to doubt that the error of a contrary conclusion will be fully understood by all who shall read the argument of the Chief Justice.

I have already said that the opinion of the court has my unqualified assent.

457*]   *Mr. Justice Nelson:

I shall proceed to state the grounds upon which I have arrived at the conclusion that the judgment of the court below should be affirmed. The suit was brought in the court below by the plaintiff, for the purpose of asserting his freedom, and that of Harriet, his wife, and two children.

The defendant pleaded, in abatement to the suit, that the cause of action, if any, accrued to the plaintiff out of the jurisdiction of the court, and exclusively within the jurisdiction of the courts of the State of Missouri; for that the said plaintiff is not a citizen of the State of Missouri, as alleged in the declaration, because he is a negro of African descent; his ancestors were of pure African blood, and were brought into this country and sold as negro slaves.

To this plea the plaintiff demurred, and the defendant joined in demurrer. The court below sustained the demurrer, holding that the plea was insufficient in law to abate the suit.

The defendant then pleaded over in bar of the action.

1. The general issue. 2. That the plaintiff was a negro slave, the lawful property of the defendant. And 3. That Harriet, the wife of said plaintiff, and the two children, were the lawful slaves of the said defendant. Issue was taken upon these pleas, and the cause went down to trial before the court and jury, and an agreed state of facts was presented, upon which the trial proceeded, and resulted in a verdict for the defendant, under the instructions of the court.

The facts agreed upon were substantially as follows:

That in the year 1834, the plaintiff, Scott, was a negro slave of Dr. Emerson, who was a surgeon in the Army of the United States; and in that year he took the plaintiff from the State of Missouri to the military post at Rock Island, in the State of Illinois, and held him there as a slave until the month of April or May, 1836. At this date, Dr. Emerson removed, with the plaintiff, from the Rock Island post to the military post at Fort Snelling, situate on the west bank of the Mississippi River, in the Territory of Upper Louisiana, and north of the latitude thirty-six degrees thirty minutes, and north of the State of Missouri. That he held the plaintiff in slavery at Fort Snelling, from the last mentioned date until the year 1838.

That in the year 1835, Harriet, mentioned in the declaration, was a negro slave of Major Taliaferro, who belonged to the Army of the United States; and in that year he took her to Fort Snelling, already mentioned, and kept her there as a slave until the year 1836, and then sold and delivered her to Dr. Emerson, who held her in slavery, at Fort Snelling, until the year 1838. That in the year 1836 the plaintiff and Harriet *were married, at Fort   [*458 Snelling, with the consent of their master. The two children, Eliza and Lizzie, are the fruit of this marriage. The first is about fourteen years of age, and was born on board the steamboat Gipsey, north of the State of Missouri, and upon the Mississippi River; the other, about seven years of age, was born in the State of Missouri, at the military post called Jefferson Barracks.

In 1838 Dr. Emerson removed the plaintiff Harriet, and their daughter Eliza, from Fort Snelling to the State of Missouri, where they have ever since resided. And that before the commencement of this suit, they were sold by the Doctor to Sandford, the defendant, who has claimed and held them as slaves ever since.

The agreed case also states that the plaintiff brought a suit for his freedom, in the Circuit Court of the State of Missouri, on which a judgment was rendered in his favor; but that, on a writ of error from the Supreme Court of the State, the judgment of the court below was reversed, and the cause remanded to the circuit for a new trial.

722

On closing the testimony on the court below, the counsel for the plaintiff prayed the court to instruct the jury, upon the agreed state of facts, that they ought to find for the plaintiff; when the court refused, and instructed them that, upon the facts, the law was with the defendant.

With respect to the plea in abatement, which went to the citizenship of the plaintiff, and his competency to bring a suit in the federal courts, the common law rule of pleading is, that upon a judgment against the plea on demurrer, and that the defendant answer over, and the defendant submits to the judgment, and pleads over to the merits, the plea in abatement is deemed to be waived, and is not afterwards to be regarded as a part of the record in deciding upon the rights of the parties. There is some question, however, whether this rule of pleading applies to the peculiar system and jurisdiction of the federal courts. As, in these courts, if the facts appearing on the record show that the Circuit Court had no jurisdiction, its judgment will be reversed in the appellate court for that cause, and the case remanded with directions to be dismissed.

In the view we have taken of the case, it will not be necessary to pass upon this question, and we shall therefore proceed at once to an examination of the case upon its merits. The question upon the merits, in general terms, is whether or not the removal of the plaintiff, who was a slave, with his master, from the State of Missouri to the State of Illinois, with a view to a temporary residence, and after such 459*] residence and *return to the slave State, such residence in the free State works an emancipation.

As appears from an agreed statement of facts, this question has been before the highest court of the State of Missouri, and a judgment rendered that this residence in the free State has no such effect; but, on the contrary, that his original condition continued unchanged.

The court below, the Circuit Court of the United States for Missouri, in which this suit was afterwards brought, followed the decision of the State court, and rendered a like judgment against the plaintiff.

The argument against these decisions is, that the laws of Illinois, forbidding slavery within her territory, had the effect to set the slave free while residing in that State, and to impress upon him the condition and status of a freeman; and that, by force of these laws, this status and condition accompanied him on his return to the slave State, and of consequence he could not be there held as a slave.

This question has been examined in the courts of several of the slaveholding States, and different opinions expressed and conclusions arrived at. We shall hereafter refer to some of them, and to the principles upon which they are founded. Our opinion is, that the question is one which belongs to each State to decide for itself, either by its Legislature or courts of justice; and hence, in respect to the case before us, to the State of Missouri—a question exclusively of Missouri law, and which, when determined by that State, it is the duty of the federal courts to follow it. In other words, except in cases where the power is restrained by the Constitution of the United States, the law

of the State is supreme over the subject of slavery within its jurisdiction.

As a practical illustration of the principle, we may refer to the legislation of the free States in abolishing slavery, and prohibiting its introduction into their territories. Confessedly, except as restrained by the Federal Constitution, they exercised, and rightfully, complete and absolute power over the subject. Upon what principle, then, can it be denied to the State of Missouri? The power flows from the sovereign character of the States of this Union; sovereign, not merely as respects the federal government—except as they have consented to its limitation—but sovereign as respects each other. Whether, therefore, the State of Missouri will recognize or give effect to the laws of Illinois within her territories, on the subject of slavery, is a question for her to determine. Nor is there any constitutional power in this government that can rightfully control her.

*Every State or nation possesses an [*460 exclusive sovereignty and jurisdiction within her own territory; and her laws effect and bind all property and persons residing within it. It may regulate the manner and circumstances under which property is held, and the condition, capacity and state, of all persons therein; and, also, the remedy and modes of administering justice. And it is equally true, that no State or nation can affect or bind property out of its territory, or persons not residing within it. No State, therefore, can enact laws to operate beyond its own dominions, and, if it attempts to do so, it may be lawfully refused obedience. Such laws can have no inherent authority extraterritorially. This is the necessary result of the independence of distinct and separate sovereignties.

Now, it follows from these principles, that whatever force or effect the laws of one State or nation may have in the territories of another, must depend solely upon the laws and municipal regulations of the latter, upon its own jurisprudence and polity, and upon its own express or tacit consent.

Judge Story observes, in his Conflict of Laws, p. 24, "that a State may prohibit the operation of all foreign laws, and the rights growing out of them, within its territories." "And that when its code speaks positively on the subject, it must be obeyed by all persons who are within reach of its sovereignty; when its customary unwritten or common law speaks directly on the subject, it is equally to be obeyed."

Nations, from convenience and comity, and from mutual interest, and a sort of moral necessity to do justice, recognize and administer the laws of other countries. But, of the nature, extent and utility, of them, respecting property, or the state and conditions of persons within her territories, each nation judges for itself; and is never bound, even upon the ground of comity, to recognize them, if prejudicial to her own interests. The recognition is purely from comity, and not from any absolute or paramount obligation.

Judge Story again observes (398), "that the true foundation and extent of the obligation of the laws of one nation within another is the voluntary consent of the latter, and is inadmissible when they are contrary to its known interests." And he adds, "in the silence of any positive rule affirming or denying or restraining the operation of the foreign laws, courts of justice presume the tacit adoption of them by their own government, unless they are repugnant to its policy or prejudicial to its interests." See, also, 2 Kent's Com. p. 457; 13 Pet. 519, 589.

These principles fully establish that it be-**461***] longs to the sovereign *State of Missouri to determine by her laws the question of slavery within her jurisdiction, subject only to such limitations as may be found in the Federal Constitution; and, further, that the laws of other States of the Confederacy, whether enacted by their Legislatures or expounded by their courts, can have no operation within her territory, or affect rights growing out of her own laws on the subject. This is the necessary result of the independent and sovereign character of the State. The principle is not peculiar to the State of Missouri, but is equally applicable to each State belonging to the Confederacy. The laws of each have no extraterritorial operation within the jurisdiction of another, except such as may be voluntarily conceded by her laws or courts of justice. To the extent of such concession upon the rule of comity of nations, the foreign law may operate, as it then becomes a part of the municipal law of the State. When determined that the foreign law shall have effect, the municipal law of the State retires, and gives place to the foreign law.

In view of these principles, let us examine a little more closely the doctrine of those who maintain that the law of Missouri is not to govern the status and condition of the plaintiff. They insist that the removal and temporary residence with his master in Illinois, where slavery is inhibited, had the effect to set him free, and that the same effect is to be given to the law of Illinois, within the State of Missouri, after his return. Why was he set free in Illinois? Because the law of Missouri, under which he was held as a slave, had no operation by its own force extraterritorially; and the State of Illinois refused to recognize its effect within her limits, upon principles of comity, as a state of slavery was inconsistent with her laws, and contrary to her policy. But, how is the case different on the return of the plaintiff to the State of Missouri? Is she bound to recognize and enforce the law of Illinois? For, unless she is, the status and condition of the slave upon his return remains the same as originally existed. Has the law of Illinois any greater force within the jurisdiction of Missouri, than the laws of the latter within that of the former? Certainly not. They stand upon an equal footing. Neither has any force extraterritorially, except what may be voluntarily conceded to them.

It has been supposed, by the counsel for the plaintiff, that a rule laid down by Huberus had some bearing upon that question. Huberus observes that "personal qualities, impressed by the laws of any place, surround and accompany the person wherever he goes, with this effect: that in every place he enjoys and is subject to the same law which other persons of his **462***] *class elsewhere enjoy or are subject to." De Confl. Leg. lib. 1, tit. 3, sec. 12; 4 Dall. 375, n; 1 Story, Com. Laws, pp. 59, 60.

724

The application sought to be given to the rule was this; that as Dred Scott was free while residing in the State of Illinois, by the laws of that State, on his return to the State of Missouri he carried with him the personal qualities of freedom, and that the same effect must be given to his status there as in the former State. But the difficulty in the case is in the total misapplication of the rule.

These personal qualities, to which Huberus refers, are those impressed upon the individual by the law of the domicil; it is this that the author claims should be permitted to accompany the person into whatever country he might go, and should supersede the law of the place where he had taken up a temporary residence.

Now, as the domicil of Scott was in the State of Missouri, where he was a slave, and from whence he was taken by his master into Illinois for a temporary residence, according to the doctrine of Huberus, the law of his domicil would have accompanied him, and during his residence there he would remain in the same condition as in the State of Missouri. In order to have given effect to the rule, as claimed in the argument, it should have been first shown that a domicil had been acquired in the free State, which cannot be pretended upon the agreed facts in the case. But the true answer to the doctrine of Huberus is, that the rule, in any aspect in which it may be reviewed, has no bearing upon either side of the question before us, even if conceded to the extent laid down by the author; for he admits that foreign governments give effect to these laws of the domicil no further than they are consistent with their own laws, and not prejudicial to their own subjects; in other words, their force and effect depend upon the law of comity of the foreign government. We should add, also, that this general rule of Huberus, referred to, has not been admitted in the practice of nations, nor is it sanctioned by the most approved jurists of international law. Story, Com. secs. 91, 96, 103, 104; 2 Kent's Com. pp. 457, 458; 1 Burge, Con. Laws, pp. 12, 127.

We come now to the decision of this court in the case of Strader et al. v. Graham, 10 How. p. 82. The case came up from the Court of Appeals, in the State of Kentucky. The question in the case was, whether certain slaves of Graham, a resident of Kentucky, who had been employed temporarily at several places in the State of Ohio, with their master's consent, and had returned to Kentucky into his service, had thereby *become entitled to their free- [*463 dom. The Court of Appeals held that they had not. The case was brought to this court under the 25th section of the Judiciary Act. This court held that it had no jurisdiction, for the reason, the question was one that belonged exclusively to the State of Kentucky. The Chief Justice, in delivering the opinion of the court, observed that "every State has an undoubted right to determine the status or domestic and social condition of the persons domiciled within its territory, except in so far as the powers of the States in this respect are restrained, or duties and obligations imposed upon them by the Constitution of the United States. There is nothing in the Constitution of the United States, he observes, that can in any degree control the law of Kentucky upon this subject. And the condition of the negroes, therefore, as to freedom or slavery, after their return, depended altogether upon the laws of that State, and could not be influenced by the laws of Ohio. It was exclusively in the power of Kentucky to determine, for herself, whether their employment in another State should or should not make them free on their return."

It has been supposed, in the argument on the part of the plaintiff, that the 8th section of the Act of Congress passed March 6, 1820 (3 Stat. at L. p. 544), which prohibited slavery north of thirty-six degrees thirty minutes, within which the plaintiff and his wife temporarily resided at Fort Snelling, possessed some superior virtue and effect, extraterritorially and within the State of Missouri, beyond that of the laws of Illinois, or those of Ohio in the case of Strader et al. v. Graham. A similar ground was taken and urged upon the court in the case just mentioned, under the Ordinance of 1787, which was enacted during the time of the Confederation, and re-enacted by Congress after the adoption of the Constitution, with some amendments adapting it to the new government. 1 Stat. at L. p. 50.

In answer to this ground, the Chief Justice, in delivering the opinion of the court, observed: The argument assumes that the six articles which that Ordinance declares to be perpetual, are still in force in the States since formed within the territory, and admitted into the Union. If this proposition could be maintained, it would not alter the question; for the Regulations of Congress, under the old Confederation or the present Constitution, for the government of a particular territory, could have no force beyond its limits. It certainly could not restrict the power of the States, within their respective territories, nor in any manner interfere with their laws and institutions, nor give this court control over them.

464*] *"The Ordinance in question," he observes, "if still in force, could have no more operation than the laws of Ohio, in the State of Kentucky, and could not influence the decision upon the rights of the master or the slaves in that State."

This view, thus authoritatively declared, furnishes a conclusive answer to the distinction attempted to be set up between the extraterritorial effect of a state law and the Act of Congress in question.

It must be admitted that Congress possesses no power to regulate or abolish slavery within the States; and that if this Act had attempted any such legislation, it would have been a nullity. And yet the argument here, if there be any force in it, leads to the result, that effect may be given to such legislation; for it is only by giving the Act of Congress operation within the State of Missouri, that it can have any effect upon the question between the parties. Having no such effect directly, it will be difficult to maintain, upon any consistent reasoning, that it can be made to operate indirectly upon the subject.

The argument, we think, in any aspect in which it may be viewed, is utterly destitute of support upon any principles of constitutional law, as, according to that, Congress has no power whatever over the subject of slavery within the State; and is also subversive of the established doctrine of international jurisprudence, as, according to that, it is an axiom that

the laws of one government have no force within the limits of another, or extraterritorially, except from the consent of the latter.

It is perhaps not unfit to notice, in this connection, that many of the most eminent statesmen and jurists of the country entertain the opinion that this provision of the Act of Congress, even within the territory to which it relates, was not authorized by any power under the Constitution. The doctrine here contended for, not only upholds its validity in the territory, but claims for it effect beyond and within the limits of a sovereign state—an effect, as insisted, that displaces the laws of the State, and substitutes its own provisions in their place.

The consequences of any such construction are apparent. If Congress possesses the power, under the Constitution, to abolish slavery in a territory, it must necessarily possess the like power to establish it. It cannot be a one sided power, as may suit the convenience or particular views of the advocates. It is a power, if it exists at all, over the whole subject; and then, upon the process of reasoning which seeks to extend its influence beyond the territory, and within the limits of a state, if Congress should establish, instead of abolish, slavery, we do *not see but that, if a slave should be [*465 removed from the territory into a free State his status would accompany him, and continue, notwithstanding its laws against slavery. The laws of the free State, according to the argument, would be displaced, and the Act of Congress, in its effect, be substituted in their place. We do not see how this conclusion could be avoided, if the construction against which we are contending should prevail. We are satisfied, however, it is unsound, and that the true answer to it is, that even conceding, for the purposes of the argument, that this provision of the Act of Congress is valid within the territory for which it was enacted, it can have no operation or effect beyond its limits, or within the jurisdiction of a state. It can neither displace its laws nor change the status or condition of its inhabitants.

Our conclusion, therefore, is, upon this branch of the case, that the question involved is one depending solely upon the law of Missouri, and that the federal court sitting in the State, and trying the case before us, was bound to follow it.

The remaining question for consideration is: what is the law of the State of Missouri on this subject. And it would be a sufficient answer to refer to the judgment of the highest court of the State in the very case, were it not due to that tribunal to state somewhat at large the course of decision and the principles involved, on account of some diversity of opinion in the cases. As we have already stated, this case was originally brought in the Circuit Court of the State, which resulted in a judgment for the plaintiff. The case was carried up to the Supreme Court for revision. That court reversed the judgment below, and remanded the cause to the Circuit, for a new trial. In that state of the proceeding, a new suit was brought by the plaintiff in the Circuit Court of the United States, and tried upon the issues and agreed case before us, and a verdict and judgment for the defendant, that court following the decision of the Supreme Court of the State.

The judgment of the Supreme Court is reported in the 15 Mo. p. 576. The court placed the decision upon the temporary residence of the master with the slaves in the State and territory to which they removed, and their return to the slave State; and upon the principles of international law, that foreign laws have no extraterritorial force, except such as the State within which they are sought to be enforced may see fit to extend to them, upon the doctrine of comity of nations.

This is the substance of the grounds of the decision.

The same question has been twice before that court since, and the same judgment given. 15 Mo. 595; 17 Ib. 434. It must be admitted, therefore, as the settled law of the State, 466*] *and, according to the decision in the case of Strader et al. v. Graham, 10 How. 82, is conclusive of the case in this court.

It is said, however, that the previous cases and course of decision in the State of Missouri on this subject were different, and that the courts had held the slave to be free on his return from a temporary residence in the free State. We do not see, were this to be admitted, that the circumstance would show that the settled course of decision at the time this case was tried in the court below, was not to be considered the law of the State. Certainly, it must be, unless the first decision of a principle of law by a state court is to be permanent and irrevocable. The idea seems to be, that the courts of a state are not to change their opinions, or, if they do, the first decision is to be regarded by this court as the law of the State. It is certain, if this be so, in the case before us, it is an exception to the rule governing this court in all other cases. But what court has not changed its opinions? What judge has not changed his?

Waiving, however, this view, and turning to the decisions of the courts of Missouri, it will be found that there is no discrepancy between the earlier and the present cases upon this subject. There are some eight of them reported previous to the decision in the case before us, which was decided in 1852. The last of the earlier cases was decided in 1836. In each one of these, with two exceptions, the master or mistress removed into the free State with the slave, with a view to a permanent residence—in other words, to make that his or her domicil. And in several of the cases, this removal and permanent residence were relied on as the ground of the decision in favor of the plaintiff. All these cases, therefore, are not necessarily in conflict with the decision in the case before us, but consistent with it. In one of the two excepted cases, the master had hired the slave in the State of Illinois from 1817 to 1825. In the other, the master was an officer in the army, and removed with his slave to the military post of Fort Snelling, and at Prairie du Chien, in Michigan, temporarily, while acting under the orders of his government. It is conceded the decision in this case was departed from in the case before us, and in those that have followed it. But it is to be observed that these subsequent cases are in conformity with those in all the slave States bordering on the free—in Kentucky, 2 Marsh. 476; 5 B. Monroe, 176; 9 Ib. 565,—in Virginia, 1 Rand. 15; 1 Leigh, 172; 10 Grat. 495,—in Maryland, 4 Harr.

& McH. 295, 322, 325. In conformity, also, with the law of England on this subject, Ex parte Grace, 2 Hagg Adm. 94, and with the opinions of the *most eminent jurists of the [*467 country. Story's Confl. 396 a; 5 Kent's Com. 258 n; 18 Pick. 193, Chief Justice Shaw. See Corresp. between Lord Stowell and Judge Story, 1 vol. Life of Story, p. 552, 558.

Lord Stowell, in communicating his opinion in the case of The Slave Grace to Judge Story, states, in his letter, what the question was before him, namely: "Whether the emancipation of a slave brought to England insured a complete emancipation to him on his return to his own country, or whether it only operated as a suspension of slavery in England, and his original character devolved on him again upon his return." He observed, "the question had never been examined since an end was put to slavery fifty years ago," having reference to the decision of Lord Mansfield in the case of Somersett; but the practise, he observed, "has regularly been, that on his return to his own country, the slave resumed his original character as a slave." And so Lord Stowell held in the case.

Judge Story, in his letter in reply, observes: "I have read with great attention your judgment in the slave case, etc. Upon the fullest consideration which I have been able to give the subject, I entirely concur in your views. If I had been called upon to pronounce a judgment in a like case, I should have certainly arrived at the same result." Again he observes: "In my native State (Massachusetts), the state of slavery is not recognized as legal; and yet, if a slave should come hither, and afterwards return to his own home, we should certainly think that the local law attached upon him, and that his servile character would be reintegrated."

We may remark in this connection, that the case before the Maryland court, already referred to, and which was decided in 1799, presented the same question as that before Lord Stowell and received a similar decision. This was nearly thirty years before the decision in that case, which was in 1828. The Court of Appeals observed, in deciding the Maryland case, that "however the laws of Great Britain in such instances, operating upon such persons there, might interfere so as to prevent the exercise of certain acts by the masters, not permitted, as in the case of Somersett, yet, upon the bringing Ann Joice into this State (then the Province of Maryland), the relation of master and slave continued in its extent, as authorized by the laws of this State." And Luther Martin, one of the counsel in that case, stated, on the argument, that the question had been previously decided the same way in the case of slaves returning from a residence in Pennsylvania, where they had become free under her laws.

The State of Louisiana, whose courts had gone further in *holding the slave free [*468 on his return from a residence in a free State than the courts of her sister States, has settled the law, by an Act of her Legislature, in conformity with the law of the court of Missouri in the case before us. Sess. Law, 1846.

The case before Lord Stowell presented much stronger features for giving effect to the law of England in the case of The Slave Grace than exists in the cases that have arisen in this country, for in that case the slave returned to a colony of England over which the imperial government exercised supreme authority. Yet, on the return of the slave to the colony, from a temporary residence in England, he held that the original condition of the slave attached. The question presented in cases arising here, is as to the effect and operation to be given to the laws of a foreign State, on the return of the slave within an independent sovereignty.

Upon the whole, it must be admitted that the current of authority, both in England and in this country, is in accordance with the law as declared by the courts of Missouri in the case before us, and we think the court below was not only right, but bound to follow it.

Some question has been made as to the character of the residence in this case in the free State. But we regard the facts as set forth in the agreed case as decisive. The removal of Dr. Emerson from Missouri to the military posts was in the discharge of his duties as surgeon in the army, and under the orders of his government. He was liable at any moment to be recalled, as he was in 1838, and ordered to another post. The same is also true as it respects Major Taliaferro. In such a case, the officer goes to his post for a temporary purpose, to remain there for an uncertain time, and not for the purpose of fixing his permanent abode. The question we think too plain to require argument. The case of The Attorney General v. Napier, 6 Welsb. H. & G. Exch. 216, illustrates and applies the principle in the case of an officer of the English army.

A question has been alluded to, on the argument, namely: the right of the master with his slave of transit into or through a free State, on business or commercial pursuits, or in the exercise of a federal right, or the discharge of a federal duty, being a citizen of the United States, which is not before us. This question depends upon different considerations and principles from the one in hand, and turns upon the rights and privileges secured to a common citizen of the republic, under the Constitution of the United States. When that question arises, we shall be prepared to decide it.

469*] *Our conclusion is, that the judgment of the court below should be affirmed.

Mr. Justice Grier:

I concur in the opinion delivered by Mr. Justice Nelson on the questions discussed by him.

I also concur with the opinion of the court as delivered by the Chief Justice, that the Act of Congress of 6th March, 1820, is unconstitutional and void; and that, assuming the facts as stated in the opinion, the plaintiff cannot sue as a citizen of Missouri in the courts of the United States. But, that the record shows a prima facie case of jurisdiction, requiring the court to decide all the questions properly arising in it; and as the decision of the pleas in bar shows that the plaintiff is a slave, and therefore not entitled to sue in a court of the United States, the form of the judgment is of little importance; for whether the judgment be affirmed or dismissed for want of jurisdiction, it is justified by the decision of the court, and is the same in effect between the parties to the suit.

15 L. ed.

Mr. Justice Daniel:

It may with truth be affirmed, that since the establishment of the several communities now constituting the States of this Confederacy, there never has been submitted to any tribunal within its limits questions surpassing in importance those now claiming the consideration of this court. Indeed it is difficult to imagine, in connection with the systems of polity peculiar to the United States, a conjuncture of graver import than that must be, within which it is aimed to comprise, and to control, not only the faculties and practical operation appropriate to the American Confederacy as such, but also the rights and powers of its separate and independent members, with reference alike to their internal and domestic authority and interests, and the relations they sustain to their confederates.

To my mind it is evident that nothing less than the ambitious and far-reaching pretension to compass these objects of vital concern, is either directly essayed, or necessarily implied in the positions attempted in the argument for the plaintiff in error.

How far these positions have any foundation in the nature of the rights and relations of separate, equal and independent governments, or in the provisions of our own federal compact, or the laws enacted under and in pursuance of the authority of that compact, will be presently investigated.

In order correctly to comprehend the tendency and force of those positions, it is proper here succinctly to advert to the *facts [*470 upon which the questions of law propounded in the argument have arisen.

This was an action of trespass vi et armis, instituted in the Circuit Court of the United States for the District of Missouri, in the name of the plaintiff in error, a negro held as a slave, for the recovery of freedom for himself, his wife, and two children, also negroes.

To the declaration in this case the defendant below, who is also the defendant in error, pleaded in abatement that the court could not take cognizance of the cause because the plaintiff was not a citizen of the State of Missouri, as averred in the declaration, but was a negro of African descent, and that his ancestors were of pure African blood, and were brought into this country and sold as negro slaves; and hence it followed, from the 2d section of the 3d article of the Constitution, which creates the judicial power of the United States, with respect to controversies between citizens of different States, that the Circuit Court could not take cognizance of the action.

To this plea in abatement, a demurrer having been interposed on behalf of the plaintiff, it was sustained by the court. After the decision sustaining the demurrer, the defendant, in pursuance of a previous agreement between counsel, and with the leave of the court, pleaded in bar of the action: 1st, not guilty; 2d, that the plaintiff was a negro slave, the lawful property of the defendant, and as such the defendant gently laid his hands upon him, and thereby had only restrained him, as the defendant had a right to do; 3d, that with respect to the wife and daughters of the plaintiff, in the second and third counts of the declaration mentioned, the defendant had, as to them, only acted in the same manner, and in virtue of the same legal right.

Issues having been joined upon the above pleas in bar, the following statement, comprising all the evidence in the cause, was agreed upon and signed by the counsel of the respective parties, viz.:

"In the year 1834, the plaintiff was a negro slave belonging to Dr. Emerson, who was a surgeon in the Army of the United States. In that year, 1834, said Dr. Emerson took the plaintiff from the State of Missouri to the military post at Rock Island, in the State of Illinois, and held him there as a slave until the month of April or May, 1836. At the time last mentioned, said Dr. Emerson removed the plaintiff from said military post at Rock Island to the military post at Fort Snelling, situate on the west bank of the Mississippi River, in the Territory known as Upper Louisiana, acquired by the United States of France, and situate north **471***] of the latitude of thirty-six *degrees thirty minutes north, and north of the State of Missouri. Said Dr. Emerson held the plaintiff in slavery at said Fort Snelling, from said last mentioned date until the year 1838.

In the year 1835, Harriet, who is named in the second count of the plaintiff's declaration, was the negro slave of Major Taliaferro, who belonged to the Army of the United States. In that year, 1835, said Major Taliaferro took said Harriet to said Fort Snelling, a military post situated as hereinbefore stated, and kept her there as a slave until the year 1836, and then sold and delivered her as a slave at said Fort Snelling unto the said Dr. Emerson, hereinbefore named. Said Dr. Emerson held said Harriet in slavery at said Fort Snelling until the year 1838.

In the year 1836, the plaintiff and said Harriet, at said Fort Snelling, with the consent of said Dr. Emerson, who then claimed to be their master and owner, intermarried and took each other for husband and wife. Eliza and Lizzie, named in the third count of the plaintiff's declaration, are the fruit of that marriage. Eliza is about fourteen years old, and was born on board the steamboat Gipsey, north of the north line of the State of Missouri, and upon the River Mississippi. Lizzie is about seven years old, and was born in the State of Missouri, at a military post called Jefferson Barracks.

In the year 1838, said Dr. Emerson removed the plaintiff and said Harriet, and their said daughter Eliza, from said Fort Snelling to the State of Missouri, where they have ever since resided.

Before the commencement of this suit, said Dr. Emerson sold and conveyed the plaintiff, said Harriet, Eliza and Lizzie, to the defendant, as slaves, and the defendant has ever since claimed to hold them and each of them as slaves.

At the times mentioned in the plaintiff's declaration, the defendant, claiming to be owner as aforesaid, laid his hands upon said plaintiff, Harriet, Eliza and Lizzie, and imprisoned them, doing in this respect, however, no more than what he might lawfully do if they were of right his slaves at such times.

Further proof may be given on the trial for either party.

R. M. Field, for plaintiff,
H. A. Garland, for defendant."

728

"It is agreed that Dred Scott brought suit for his freedom in the Circuit Court of St. Louis County; that there was a verdict and judgment in his favor; that on a writ of error to the Supreme Court, the judgment below was reversed, and the *cause remanded to [*472 the Circuit Court, where it has been continued to await the decision of this case.

Field, for plaintiff,
Garland, for defendant."

Upon the aforegoing agreed facts, the plaintiff prayed the court to instruct the jury that they ought to find for the plaintiff, and upon the refusal of the instruction thus prayed for, the plaintiff excepted to the court's opinion. The court then, upon the prayer of the defendant, instructed the jury, that upon the facts of this case agreed as above, the law was with the defendant. To this opinion, also, the plaintiff's counsel excepted, as he did to the opinion of the court denying to the plaintiff a new trial after the verdict of the jury in favor of the defendant.

The question first in order presented by the record in this cause, is that which arises upon the plea in abatement, and the demurrer to that plea; and upon this question it is my opinion that the demurrer should have been overruled, and the plea sustained.

On behalf of the plaintiff it has been urged, that by the pleas interposed in bar of a recovery in the court below (which pleas both in fact and in law are essentially the same with the objections averred in abatement), the defense in abatement has been displaced or waived; that it could, therefore, no longer be relied on in the Circuit Court, and cannot claim the consideration of this court in reviewing this cause. This position is regarded as wholly untenable. On the contrary, it would seem to follow conclusively from the peculiar character of the courts of the United States, as organized under the Constitution and the statutes, and as defined by numerous and unvarying adjudications from this bench; and there is not one of those courts whose jurisdiction and powers can be deduced from mere custom or tradition; not one, whose jurisdiction and powers must not be traced palpably to, and invested exclusively by, the Constitution and statutes of the United States; not one that is not bound, therefore, at all times, and at all stages of its proceedings, to look and to regard the special and declared extent and bounds of its commission and authority. There is no such tribunal of the United States as a court of general jurisdiction, in the sense in which that phrase is applied to the superior courts under the common law; and even with respect to the courts existing under that system, it is a well settled principle, that consent can never give jurisdiction.

The principles above stated, and the consequences regularly deducible from them, have, as already remarked, been repeatedly *and unvaryingly propounded from this [*473 bench. Beginning with the earliest decisions of this court, we have the cases of Bingham v. Cabot et al. 3 Dall. 382; Turner v. Enrille, 4 Dall. 7; Abercrombie v. Dupuis et al. 1 Cranch, 343; Wood v. Wagnon, 2 Cranch, 9; The United States v. The Brig Union et al. 4 Cranch, 216; Sulivan v. The Fulton Steamboat Company,

19 How.

6 Wheat. 450; Mollan et al. v. Torrence, 9 Wheat. 537; Brown v. Keene, 8 Pet. 112, and Jackson v. Ashton, 8 Pet. 148; ruling, in uniform and unbroken current, the doctrine that it is essential to the jurisdiction of the courts of the United States, that the facts upon which it is founded should appear upon the record. Nay, to such an extent and so inflexibly has this requisite to the jurisdiction been enforced, that in the case of Capron v. Van Noorden, 2 Cranch, 126, it is declared, that the plaintiff in this court may assign for error his own omission in the pleadings in the court below, where they go to the jurisdiction. This doctrine has been, if possible, more strikingly illustrated in a latter decision, the case of The State of R. I. v. The State of Mass. 12 Pet. 657, 755.

In this case, on p. 718 of the volume, this court, with reference to a motion to dismiss the cause for want of jurisdiction, have said: "However late this objection has been made or may be made, in any cause in an inferior or appellate court of the United States, it must be considered and decided before any court can move one farther step in the cause, as any movement is necessarily to exercise the jurisdiction. Jurisdiction is the power to hear and determine the subject matter in controversy between the parties to a suit; to adjudicate or exercise any judicial power over them. The question is, whether on the case before the court their action is judicial or extrajudicial; with or without the authority of law to render a judgment or decree upon the rights of the litigant parties. A motion to dismiss a cause pending in the courts of the United States, is not analogous to a plea to the jurisdiction of a court of common law or equity in England; there, the superior courts have a general jurisdiction over all persons within the realm, and all causes of action between them. It depends on the subject matter, whether the jurisdiction shall be exercised by a court of law or equity; but that court to which it appropriately belongs can act judicially upon the party and the subject of the suit, unless it shall be made apparent to the court that the judicial determination of the case has been withdrawn from the court of general jurisdiction to an inferior and limited one. It is a necessary presumption that the court of general jurisdiction can act upon the given case; when nothing to the [474*] *contrary appears; hence has arisen the rule that the party claiming an exemption from its process must set out the reason by a special plea in abatement, and show that some inferior court of law or equity has the exclusive cognizance of the case; otherwise the superior court must proceed in virtue of its general jurisdiction. A motion to dismiss, therefore, cannot be entertained, as it does not disclose a case of exception; and if a plea in abatement is put in, it must not only make out the exception, but point to the particular court to which the case belongs. There are other classes of cases where the objection to the jurisdiction is of a different nature, as on a bill in chancery, that the subject matter is cognizable only by the King in Council, or that the parties defendant cannot be brought before any municipal court on account of their sovereign character or the nature of the controversy; or to the very common cases which present the question, whether the cause belong to a court of law or equity. To such cases, a plea in abatement would not be applicable, because the plaintiff could not sue in an inferior court. The objection goes to a denial of any jurisdiction of a municipal court in the one class of cases, and to the jurisdiction of any court of equity or of law in the other, on which last the court decides according to its discretion.

"An objection to jurisdiction on the ground of exemption from the process of the court in which the suit is brought, or the manner in which a defendant is brought into it, is waived by appearance and pleading to issue; but when the objection goes to the power of the court over the parties or the subject matter, the defendant need not, for he cannot, give the plaintiff a better writ. Where an inferior court can have no jurisdiction of a case of law or equity, the ground of objection is not taken by plea in abatement, as an exception of the given case from the otherwise general jurisdiction of the court; appearance does not cure the defect of judicial power, and it may be relied on by plea, answer, demurrer, or at the trial or hearing. As a denial of jurisdiction over the subject matter of a suit between parties within the realm, over which and whom the court has power to act, cannot be successful in an English court of general jurisdiction, a motion like the present could not be sustained consistently with the principles of its constitution. But as this court is one of limited and special original jurisdiction, its action must be confined to the particular cases, controversies, and parties over which the Constitution and laws have authorized it to act; any proceeding without the limits prescribed is coram non judice, and its action a nullity. And whether the want or excess of power is objected by a party, or is apparent *to the court, it must surcease [*475 its action or proceed extrajudicially."

In the constructing of pleadings either in abatement or in bar, every fact or position constituting a portion of the public law, or of known or general history, is necessarily implied. Such fact or position need not be specially averred and set forth; it is what the world at large and every individual are presumed to know—nay, are bound to know and to be governed by.

If, on the other hand, there exists facts or circumstances by which a particular case would be withdrawn or exempted from the influence of public law or necessary historical knowledge, such facts and circumstances form an exception to the general principle, and these must be specially set forth and established by those who would avail themselves of such exception.

Now, the following are truths which a knowledge of the history of the world, and particularly of that of our own country, compels us to know—that the African negro race never have been acknowledged as belonging to the family of nations; that as amongst them there never has been known or recognized by the inhabitants of other countries anything partaking of the character of nationality, or civil or political polity; that this race has been by all the nations of Europe regarded as subjects of capture or purchase; as subjects of commerce or traffic; and that the introduction of that race into every section of this country was not as members of civil or political society, but as slaves, as property in the strictest sense of the term.

In the plea in abatement, the character or capacity of citizen on the part of the plaintiff is denied; and the causes which show the absence of that character or capacity are set forth by averment. The verity of those causes, according to the settled rules of pleading, being admitted by the demurrer, it only remained for the Circuit Court to decide upon their legal sufficiency to abate the plaintiff's action. And it now becomes the province of this court to determine whether the plaintiff below (and in error here), admitted to be a negro of African descent, whose ancestors were of pure African blood, and were brought into this country and sold as negro slaves—such being his status, and such the circumstances surrounding his position—whether he can by correct legal induction from that status and those circumstances, be clothed with the character and capacities of a citizen of the State of Missouri.

It may be assumed as a postulate, that to a slave, as such, there appertains and can appertain no relation, civil or political, with the State or the government. He is himself strictly property, to be used in subserviency to the in- 476*] terests, the convenience *or the will, of his owner; and to suppose, with respect to the former, the existence of any privilege or discretion, or of any obligation to others incompatible with the magisterial rights just defined, would be by implication, if not directly, to deny the relation of master and slave, since none can possess and enjoy as his own, that which another has a paramount right and power to withhold. Hence it follows necessarily, that a slave, the peculium or property of a master, and possessing within himself no civil nor political rights or capacities, cannot be a citizen. For who, it may be asked, is a citizen? What do the character and status of citizen import? Without fear of contradiction, it does not import the condition of being private property, the subject of individual power and ownership. Upon a principle of etymology alone, the term "citizen," as derived from civitas, conveys the ideas of connection or identification with the State or government, and a participation of its functions. But beyond this, there is not, it is believed, to be found, in the theories of writers on government, or in any actual experiment heretofore tried, an exposition of the term "citizen," which has not been understood as conferring the actual possession and enjoyment, or the perfect right of acquisition and enjoyment, of an entire equality of privileges, civil and political.

Thus Vattel, in the preliminary chapter to his treatise on the Law of Nations, says: "Nations or States are bodies politic; societies of men united together for the purpose of promoting their mutual safety and advantage, by the joint efforts of their mutual strength. Such a society has her affairs and her interests; she deliberates and takes resolutions in common; thus becoming a moral person, who possesses an understanding and a will peculiar to herself." Again, in the first chapter of the first book of the treatise just quoted, the same writer, after repeating his definition of a State, proceeds to remark, that, "from the very de-
730

sign that induces a number of men to form a society, which has its common interests and which is to act in concert, it is necessary that there should be established a public authority, to order and direct what is to be done by each, in relation to the end of the association. This political authority is the sovereignty." Again this writer remarks: "The authority of all over each member essentially belongs to the body politic or the state."

By this same writer it is also said: "The citizens are the members of the civil society; bound to this society by certain duties, and subject to its authority; they equally participate in its advantages. The natives, or natural born citizens, are those born in the country, of parents who are citizens. As society *cannot perpetuate itself otherwise than [*477 by the children of the citizens, those children naturally follow the condition of their parents, and succeed to all their rights." Again: "I say, to be of the country, it is necessary to be born of a person who is a citizen; for if he be born there of a foreigner, it will be only the place of his birth, and not his country. The inhabitants, as distinguished from citizens, are foreigners who are permitted to settle and stay in the country." Vattel, Book 1, cap. 19, p. 101.

From the views here expressed, and they seem to be unexceptionable, it must follow, that with the slave, with one devoid of rights or capacities, civil or political, there could be no pact; that one thus situated could be no party to, or actor in the association of those possessing free will, power, discretion. He could form no part of the design, no constituent ingredient or portion of a society based upon common, that is, upon equal interests and powers. He could not at the same time be the sovereign and the slave.

But it has been insisted, in argument, that the emancipation of a slave, effected either by the direct act and assent of the master, or by causes operating in contravention of his will, produces a change in the status or capacities of the slave, such as will transform him from a mere subject of property, into a being possessing a social, civil, and political equality with a citizen; in other words, will make him a citizen of the State within which he was, previously to his emancipation, a slave.

It is difficult to perceive by what magic the mere surcease or renunciation of an interest in a subject of property, by an individual possessing that interest, can alter the essential character of that property with respect to persons or communities unconnected with such renunciation. Can it be pretended that an individual in any State, by his single act, though voluntarily or designedly performed, yet without the co-operation or warrant of the government, perhaps in opposition to its policy or its guaranties, can create a citizen of that State? Much more emphatically may it be asked, how such a result could be accomplished by means wholly extraneous, and entirely foreign to the government of the State. The argument thus urged must lead to these extraordinary conclusions. It is regarded at once as wholly untenable, and as unsustained by the direct authority or by the analogies of history.

The institution of slavery, as it exists and has existed from the period of its introduction
19 How.

into the United States, though more humane and mitigated in character than was the same institution, either under the republic or the empire of Rome, bears, both in its tenure and in 478*] the simplicity incident to the *mode of its exercise, a closer resemblance to Roman slavery than it does to the condition of villanage, as it formerly existed in England. Connected with the latter, there were peculiarities, from custom or positive regulation, which varied it materially from the slavery of the Romans, or from slavery at any period within the United States.

But with regard to slavery amongst the Romans, it is by no means true that emancipation, either during the republic or the empire, conferred, by the act itself, or implied, the status or the rights of citizenship.

The proud title of Roman citizen, with the immunities and rights incident thereto, and as contradistinguished alike from the condition of conquered subjects or of the lower grades of native domestic residents, was maintained throughout the duration of the Republic, and until a late period of the eastern empire and at last was in effect destroyed less by an elevation of the inferior classes than by the degradation of the free, and the previous possessors of rights and immunities civil and political, to the indiscriminate abasement incident to absolute and simple despotism.

By the learned and elegant historian of the decline and fall of the Roman Empire, we are told that "In the decline of the Roman Empire, the proud distinctions of the republic were gradually abolished; and the reason or instinct of Justinian completed the simple form of an absolute monarchy. The Emperor could not eradicate the popular reverence which always waits on the possession of hereditary wealth or the memory of famous ancestors. He delighted to honor with titles and emoluments his generals, magistrates and senators, and his precarious indulgence communicated some rays of their glory to their wives and children. But in the eye of the law all Roman citizens were equal, and all subjects of the empire were citizens of Rome. That inestimable character was degraded to an obsolete and empty name. The voice of a Roman could no longer enact his laws, or create the annual ministers of his powers; his constitutional rights might have checked the arbitrary will of a master; and the bold adventurer from Germany or Arabia was admitted with equal favor to the civil and military command which the citizen alone had been once entitled to assume over the conquests of his fathers. The first Cæsars had scrupulously guarded the distinction of ingenuous and servile birth, which was decided by the condition of the mother. The slaves who were liberated by a generous mater, immediately entered into the middle class of libertini or freedmen; but they could never be enfranchised from the duties of obedience and gratitude; whatever were the fruits 479*] of *their industry, their patron and his family inherited the third part, or even the whole of their fortune, if they died without children and without a testament. Justinian respected the rights of patrons, but his indulgence removed the badge of disgrace from the two inferior orders of freedmen; whoever ceased

15 L. ed.

to be a slave, obtained, without reserve or delay, the station of a citizen; and at length the dignity of an ingenuous birth was created or supposed by the omnipotence of the Emperor."[1]

The above account of slavery and its modifications will be found in strictest conformity with the institutes of Justinian. Thus, (book 1st, title 3d), it is said: "The first general division of persons in respect to their rights is into freemen and slaves." The same title, sec. 4th: "Slaves are born such, or become so. They are born such of bondwomen; they become so either by the law of nations, as by capture, or by the civil law." Section 5th: "In the condition of slaves there is no diversity; but among free persons there are many. Thus some are ingenui or freemen, others libertini or freedmen."

Tit. 4th De Ingenuis.—"A freeman is who is born free by being born in matrimony, of parents who both are free, or both freed; or of parents one free and the other freed. But one born of a free mother, although the father be a slave or unknown, is free."

Tit. 5th. De Libertinis.—"Freedmen are those who have been manumitted from just servitude."

Section 3d of the same title states that "freedmen were formerly distinguished by a threefold division." But the Emperor proceeds to say: "Our piety leading us to reduce all things into a better state, we have amended our laws, and re-established the ancient usage; for anciently liberty was simple and undivided— that is, was conferred upon the slave as his manumittor possessed it, admitting this single difference, that the person manumitted became only a freed man, although his manumittor was a free man." And he further declares: "We have made all freed men in general become citizens of Rome, regarding neither the age of the manumitted, nor the manumittor, nor the ancient forms of manumission. We have also introduced many new methods by which slaves may become Roman citizens."

By the references above given it is shown, from the nature and objects of civil and political associations, and upon the direct authority of history, that citizenship was not conferred *by the simple fact of emancipation, [*480 but that such a result was deduced therefrom in violation of the fundamental principles of free political association; by the exertion of despotic will to establish, under a false and misapplied denomination, one equal and universal slavery; and to effect this result required the exertions of absolute power—of a power both in theory and practice, being, in its most plenary acceptation, the sovereignty, the State itself—it could not be produced by a less or inferior authority, much less by the will or the act of one who, with reference to civil and political rights, was himself a slave. The master might abdicate or abandon his interest or ownership in his property; but his act would be a mere abandonment. It seems to involve an absurdity to impute to it the investiture of rights which the sovereignty alone had power to impart. There is not, per-

1.—Vide Gibbon's Decline and Fall of the Roman Empire. London edition of 1825, Vol. III., chap. 44, p. 183.

haps, a community in which slavery is recognized, in which the power of emancipation, and the modes of its exercise are not regulated by law—that is, by the sovereign authority; and none can fail to comprehend the necessity for such regulation, for the preservation of order, and even of political and social existence.

By the argument for the plaintiff in error. a power equally despotic is vested in every member of the association, and the most obscure or unworthy individual it comprises may arbitrarily invade and derange its most deliberate and solemn ordinances. At assumptions anomalous as these, so fraught with mischief and ruin, the mind at once is revolted, and goes directly to the conclusions, that to change or to abolish a fundamental principle of the society, must be the act of the society itself—of the sovereignty; and that none other can admit to a participation of that high attribute. It may further expose the character of the argument urged for the plaintiff, to point out some of the revolting consequences, which it would authorize. If that argument possesses any integrity, it asserts the power in any citizen, or quasi citizen, or a resident foreigner of any one of the States, from a motive either of corruption or caprice, not only to infract the inherent and necessary authority of such state, but also materially to interfere with the organization of the Federal Government, and with the authority of the separate and independent States. He may emancipate his negro slave, by which process he first transforms that slave into a citizen of his own State; he may next, under color of article 4th, section 2d, of the Constitution of the United States, obtrude him, and on terms of civil and political equality, upon any and every State in this Union, in defiance of all regulations of necessity or policy, ordained by those States for their internal happiness or safety. Nay, more: this manumitted **481*]** slave *may, by a proceeding springing from the will or act of his master alone, be mixed up with the institutions of the Federal Government, to which he is not a party, and in opposition to the laws of that government which, in authorizing the extension by naturalization of the rights and immunities of citizens of the United States to those not originally parties to the federal compact, have restricted that boon to free white aliens alone. If the rights and immunities connected with or practiced under the institutions of the United States can by any indirection be claimed or deduced from sources or modes other than the Constitution and laws of the United States, it follows that the power of naturalization vested in Congress is not exclusive—that it has in effect no existence, but is repealed or abrogated.

But it has been strangely contended that the jurisdiction of the Circuit Court might be maintained upon the ground that the plaintiff was a resident of Missouri, and that, for the purpose of vesting the court with jurisdiction over the parties, residence within the State was sufficient.

The first, and to my mind a conclusive reply to this singular argument, is presented in the fact that the language of the Constitution restricts the jurisdiction of the courts to cases in which the parties shall be citizens, and is entirely silent with respect to residence. A sec-

ond answer to this strange and latitudinous notion is, that it so far stultifies the sages by whom the Constitution was framed, as to impute to them ignorance of the material distinction existing between citizenship and mere residence or domicil, and of the well known facts, that a person confessedly an alien may be permitted to reside in a country in which he can possess no civil or political rights, or of which he is neither a citizen nor subject; and that for certain purposes a man may have a domicil in different countries, in no one of which he is an actual personal resident.

The correct conclusions upon the question here considered would seem to be these:

That in the establishment of the several communities now the States of this Union, and in the formation of the Federal Government, the African was not deemed politically a person. He was regarded and owned in every State in the Union as property merely, and as such was not and could not be a party or an actor, much less a peer in any compact or form of government established by the States or the United States. That if, since the adoption of the state governments, he has been or could have been elevated to the possession of political rights or powers, this result could have been effected by no authority less potent than that of the sovereignty—the State—exerted *to [***482** that end, either in the form of legislation, or in some other mode of operation. It could certainly never have been accomplished by the will of an individual operating independently of the sovereign power, and even contravening and controlling that power. That so far as rights and immunities appertaining to citizens have been defined and secured by the Constitution and laws of the United States, the African race is not and never was recognized either by the language or purposes of the former; and it has been expressly excluded by every Act of Congress providing for the creation of citizens by naturalization, these laws, as has already been remarked, being restricted to free white aliens exclusively.

But it is evident that, after the formation of the Federal Government by the adoption of the Constitution, the highest exertion of State power would be incompetent to bestow a character or status created by the Constitution, or conferred in virtue of its authority only. Upon those, therefore, who were not originally parties to the federal compact, or who are not admitted and adopted as parties thereto, in the mode prescribed by its paramount authority, no State could have power to bestow the character or the rights and privileges exclusively reserved by the States for the action of the Federal Government by that compact.

The States, in the exercise of their political power, might, with reference to their peculiar government and jurisdiction, guaranty the rights of person and property, and the enjoyment of civil and political privileges, to those whom they should be disposed to make the objects of their bounty; but they could not reclaim or exert the powers which they had vested exclusively in the government of the United States. They could not add to or change in any respect the class of persons to whom alone the character of citizen of the United States appertained, at the time of the adoption of the Federal Constitution. They could not create citizens of the United States by any direct or indirect proceeding.

According to the view taken of the law, as applicable to the demurrer to the plea in abatement in this cause, the questions subsequently raised upon the several pleas in bar might be passed by, as requiring neither a particular examination, nor an adjudication directly upon them. But as these questions are intrinsically of primary interest and magnitude, and have been elaborately discussed in argument, and as with respect to them the opinions of a majority of the court, including my own, are perfectly coincident, to me it seems proper that they should here be fully considered, and, so far as it is practicable for this court to accomplish such an end, finally put to rest.

483*]   *The questions, then, to be considered upon the several pleas in bar, and upon the agreed statement of facts between the counsel, are: 1st. Whether the admitted master and owner of the plaintiff, holding him as his slave in the State of Missouri, and in conformity with his rights guarantied to him by the laws of Missouri then and still in force, by carrying with him for his own benefit and accommodation, and as his own slave, the person of the plaintiff into the State of Illinois, within which State slavery had been prohibited by the Constitution thereof, and by retaining the plaintiff during the commorancy of the master within the State of Illinois, had, upon his return with his slave into the State of Missouri, forfeited his rights as master, by reason of any supposed operation of the prohibitory provision in the Constitution of Illinois, beyond the proper territorial jurisdiction of the latter State. 2d. Whether a similar removal of the plaintiff by his master from the State of Missouri, and his retention in service at a point included within no State, but situated north of thirty-six degrees thirty minutes of north latitude, worked a forfeiture of the right of property of the master, and the manumission of the plaintiff.

In considering the first of these questions, the acts or declarations of the master, as expressive of his purpose to emancipate, may be thrown out of view, since none will deny the right of the owner to relinquish his interest in any subject of property, at any time or in any place. The inquiry here bears no relation to acts or declarations of the owner as expressive of his intent or purpose to make such a relinquishment; it is simply a question whether, irrespective of such purpose, and in opposition thereto, that relinquishment can be enforced against the owner of property within his own country, in defiance of every guaranty promised by its laws; and this through the instrumentality of a claim to power entirely foreign and extraneous with reference to himself, to the origin and foundation of his title, and to the independent authority of his country. A conclusive negative answer to such an inquiry is at once supplied, by announcing a few familiar and settled principles and doctrines of public law.

Vattel, in his chapter on the general principles of the laws of nations, section 15th, tells us, that "nations being free and independent of each other in the same manner that men are naturally free and independent, the second

15 L. ed.

general law of their society is, that each nation should be left in the peaceable enjoyment of that liberty which she inherits from nature."

"The natural society of nations," says this writer, "cannot subsist unless the natural rights of each be respected." In *section [*484 16th he says, "as a consequence of that liberty and independence, it exclusively belongs to each nation to form her own judgment of what her conscience prescribes for her—of what it is proper or improper for her to do; and of course it rests solely with her to examine and determine whether she can perform any office for another nation without neglecting a duty she owes to herself. In all cases, therefore, in which a nation has the right of judging what her duty requires, no other nation can compel her to act in such or such a particular manner, for any attempt at such compulsion would be an infringement on the liberty of nations." Again, in section 18th of the same chapter, "nations composed of men, and considered as so many free persons living together in a state of nature, are naturally equal, and inherit from nature the same obligations and rights. Power or weakness does not produce any difference. A small republic is no less a sovereign state than the most powerful kingdom."

So, in section 20: "A nation, then, is mistress of her own actions, so long as they do not affect the proper and perfect rights of any other nation—so long as she is only internally bound, and does not lie under any external and perfect obligation. If she makes an ill use of her liberty, she is guilty of a breach of duty; but other nations are bound to acquiesce in her conduct, since they have no right to dictate to her. Since nations are free, independent, and equal, and since each possesses the right of judging, according to the dictates of her conscience, what conduct she is to pursue, in order to fulfill her duties, the effect of the whole is to produce, at least externally, in the eyes of mankind, perfect equality of rights between nations, in the administration of their affairs, and in the pursuit of their pretensions, without regard to the intrinsic justice of their conduct, of which others have no right to form a definitive judgment."

Chancellor Kent, in the 1st volume of his Commentaries, lecture 2d, after collating the opinions of Grotius, Heineccius, Vattel, and Rutherford, enunciates the following positions as sanctioned by these and other learned publicists, viz.: that "nations are equal in respect to each other, and entitled to claim equal consideration for their rights, whatever may be their relative dimensions and strength, or however greatly they may differ in government, religion, or manners. This perfect equality and entire independence of all distinct States is a fundamental principle of public law. It is a necessary consequence of this equality, that each nation has a right to govern itself as it may think proper, and no one nation is entitled to dictate a form of government or religion, or a course of internal *policy to an- [*485 other." This writer gives some instances of the violation of this great national immunity, and amongst them the constant interference by the ancient Romans, under the pretext of settling disputes between their neighbors, but with the real purpose of reducing those neighbors to bondage; the interference of Russia, Prussia, and Austria, for the dismemberment of Poland; the more recent invasion of Naples by Austria in 1821, and of Spain by the French Government in 1823, under the excuse of suppressing a dangerous spirit of internal revolution and reform.

With reference to this right of self-government in independent sovereign States, an opinion has been expressed, which, whilst it concedes this right as inseparable from, and as as a necessary attribute of sovereignty and independence, asserts, nevertheless, some implied and paramount authority of a supposed international law, to which this right of self-government must be regarded and exerted as subordinate; and from which independent and sovereign States can be exempted only by a protest, or by some public and formal rejection of that authority. With all respect for those by whom this opinion has been professed, I am constrained to regard it as utterly untenable, as palpably inconsistent, and as presenting in argument a complete felo de se.

Sovereignty, independence, and a perfect right of self-government, can signify nothing less than a superiority to and an exemption from all claims by any extraneous power, however expressly they may be asserted, and render all attempts to enforce such claims merely attempts at usurpation. Again; could such claims from extraneous sources be regarded as legitimate, the effort to resist or evade them, by protest or denial, would be as irregular and unmeaning as it would be futile. It could in nowise affect the question of superior right. For the position here combated, no respectable authority has been, and none, it is thought, can be adduced. It is certainly irreconcilable with the doctrines already cited from the writers upon public law.

Neither the case of James Somersett, 20 Howell's St. Tr. so often vaunted as the proud evidence of devotion to freedom under a government which has done as much perhaps to extend the reign of slavery as all the world besides; nor does any decision founded upon the authority of Somersett's case, when correctly expounded, assail or impair the principle of national equality, enunciated by each and all of the publicists already referred to. In the case of Somersett, although the applicant for the habeas corpus and the individual claiming property in that applicant were both subjects 486*] and residents *within the British Empire, yet the decision cannot be correctly understood as ruling absolutely and under all circumstances against the right of property in the claimant. That decision goes no farther than to determine, that within the realm of England there was no authority to justify the detention of an individual in private bondage. If the decision in Somersett's case had gone beyond that point, it would have presented the anomaly of a repeal by laws enacted for and limited in their operation to the realm alone, of other laws and institutions established for places and subjects without the limits of the realm of England; laws and institutions at that very time, and long subsequently, sanctioned and maintained under the authority of the British Government, and which the full and combined action of the King and Parliament was required to abrogate.

But could the decision in Somersett's case be correctly interpreted as ruling the doctrine which it has been attempted to deduce from it, still must be considered as having been overruled by the lucid and able opinion of Lord Stowell in the more recent case of The Slave Grace, reported in the second volume of Haggard, p. 94; in which opinion, whilst it is conceded by the learned judge that there existed no power to coerce the slave whilst in England, that yet, upon her return to the Island of Antigua, her status as a slave was revived, or, rather, that the title of the owner to the slave as property had never been extinguished, but had always existed in that Island. If the principle of this decision be applicable as between different portions of one and the same empire, with how much more force does it apply as between nations or governments entirely separate, and absolutely independent of each other? For in this precise attitude the States of this Union stand with reference to this subject, and with reference to the tenure of every description of property vested under their laws and held within their territorial jurisdiction.

A strong illustration of the principle ruled by Lord Stowell, and of the effect of that principle, even in a case of express contract, is seen in the case of Lewis v. Fullerton, decided by the Supreme Court of Virginia, and reported in the first volume of Randolph, p. 15. The case was this: a female slave, the property of a citizen of Virginia, whilst with her master in the State of Ohio, was taken from his possession under a writ of habeas corpus, and set at liberty. Soon, or immediately after, by agreement between this slave and her master, a deed was executed in Ohio by the latter, containing a stipulation that this slave should return to Virginia, and after a service of two years in that State, should there be free. The law of Virginia *regulating emancipa- [*487 tion required that deeds of emancipation should, within a given time from their date, be recorded in the court of the county in which the grantor resided, and declared that deeds with regard to which this requisite was not complied with should be void. Lewis, an infant son of this female, under the rules prescribed in such cases, brought an action, in forma pauperis, in one of the courts of Virginia, for the recovery of his freedom, claimed in virtue of the transactions above mentioned. Upon an appeal to the Supreme Court from a judgment against the plaintiff, Roane, Justice, in delivering the opinion of the court, after disposing of other questions discussed in that case, remarks:

"As to the deed of emancipation contained in the record, that deed, taken in connection with the evidence offered in support of it, shows that it had a reference to the State of Virginia; and the testimony shows that it formed a part of this contract, whereby the slave Milly was to be brought back (as she was brought back) into the State of Virginia. Her object was, therefore, to secure her freedom by the deed within the State of Virginia, after the time should have expired for which she had indented herself, and when she should be found abiding within the State of Virginia.

If, then, this contract had an eye to the State of Virginia for its operation and effect,

1856.   DRED SCOTT V. SANDFORD.   393-633

the lex loci ceases to operate. In that case it must, to have its effect, conform to the laws of Virginia. It is insufficient under those laws to effectuate an emancipation, for want of a due recording in the county court, as was decided in the case of Givens v. Mann, 6 Munf. 190, in this court. It is also ineffectual within the Commonwealth of Virginia for another reason. The lex loci is also to be taken subject to the exception, that it is not to be enforced in another country, when it violates some moral duty or the policy of that country, or is not consistent with a positive right secured to a third person or party by the laws of that country in which it is sought to be enforced. In such a case we are told, 'magis jus nostrum quam jus alienum servemus.' " Huberus, tom. 2, lib. 1, tit. 3; 2 Fonblanque, p. 444. "That third party, in this instance, is the Commonwealth of Virginia, and her policy and interests are also to be attended to. These turn the scale against the lex loci in the present instance."

The second or last mentioned position assumed for the plaintiff under the pleas in bar, as it rests mainly if not solely upon the provision of the Act of Congress of March 6, 1820, prohibiting slavery in Upper Louisiana north of thirty-six degrees thirty minutes north latitude, popularly called the Missouri Compromise, that assumption renews the question, for 488*] merly so *zealously debated, as to the validity of the provision in the Act of Congress, and upon the constitutional competency of Congress to establish it.

Before proceeding, however, to examine the validity of the prohibitory provision of the law, it may, so far as the rights involved in this cause are concerned, be remarked, that conceding to that provision the validity of a legitimate exercise of power, still this concession could by no rational interpretation imply the slightest authority for its operation beyond the territorial limits comprised within its terms; much less could there be inferred from it a power to destroy or in any degree to control rights, either of person or property, entirely within the bounds of a distinct and independent sovereignty—rights invested and fortified by the guaranty of that sovereignty. These surely would remain in all their integrity, whatever effect might be ascribed to the prohibition within the limits defined by its language.

But beyond and in defiance of this conclusion, inevitable and undeniable as it appears, upon every principle of justice or sound induction, it has been attempted to convert this prohibitory provision of the Act of 1820 not only into a weapon with which to assail the inherent —the necessarily inherent—powers of independent sovereign governments, but into a mean of forfeiting that equality of rights and immunities which are the birthright or the donative from the Constitution of every citizen of the United States within the length and breadth of the nation. In this attempt, there is asserted a power in Congress, whether from incentives of interest, ignorance, faction, partiality or prejudice, to bestow upon a portion of the citizens of this nation that which is the common property and privilege of all—the power, in fine, of confiscation, in retribution for no offense, or, if for an offense, for that of accidental locality only.

15 L. ed.

It may be that, with respect to future cases, like the one now before the court, there is felt an assurance of the impotence of such a pretension; still, the fullest conviction of that result can impart to it no claim to forbearance, nor dispense with the duty of antipathy and disgust at its sinister aspect, whenever it may be seen to scowl upon the justice, the order, the tranquillity, and fraternal feeling, which are the surest, nay, the only means, of promoting or preserving the happiness and prosperity of the nation, and which were the great and efficient incentives to the formation of this government.

The power of Congress to impose the prohibition in the 8th section of the Act of 1820 has been advocated upon an attempted construction of the 2d clause of the 3d section *of the 4th article of the Constitution, [*489 which declares that "Congress shall have power to dispose of and to make all needful rules and regulations respecting the territory and other property belonging to the United States."

In the discussions in both houses of Congress, at the time of adopting this 8th section of the Act of 1820, great weight was given to the peculiar language of this clause, viz.: territory and other property belonging to the United States, as going to show that the power of disposing of and regulating, thereby vested in Congress, was restricted to a proprietary interest in the territory or land comprised therein, and did not extend to the personal or political rights of citizens or settlers, inasmuch as this phrase in the Constitution, "territory or other property," identified territory with property, and inasmuch as citizens or persons could not be property, and especially were not property belonging to the United States. And upon every principle of reason or necessity, this power to dispose of and to regulate the territory of the nation could be designed to extend no farther than to its preservation and appropriation to the uses of those to whom it belonged, viz.: the nation. Scarcely anything more illogical or extravagant can be imagined than the attempt to deduce from this provision in the Constitution a power to destroy or in any wise to impair the civil and political rights of the citizens of the United States, and much more so the power to establish inequalities amongst those citizens by creating privileges in one class of those citizens, and by the disfranchisement of other portions or classes, by degrading them from the position they previously occupied.

There can exist no rational or natural connection or affinity between a pretension like this and the power vested by the Constitution in Congress with regard to the territories; on the contrary, there is an absolute incongruity between them.

But whatever the power vested in Congress, and whatever the precise subject to which that power extended, it is clear that the power related to a subject appertaining to the United States, and one to be disposed of and regulated for the benefit and under the authority of the United States. Congress was made simply the agent or trustee for the United States, and could not, without a breach of trust and a fraud, appropriate the subject of the trust to any other beneficiary or cestui que trust than the United States, or to the people of the Unit-

735

ed States, upon equal grounds, legal or equitable. Congress could not appropriate that subject to any one class or portion of the people, to the exclusion of others, politically and constitutionally equals; but every citizen would, if 490*] anyone *could claim it, have the like rights of purchase, settlement, occupation, or any other right, in the national territory.

Nothing can be more conclusive to show the equality of this with every other right in all the citizens of the United States, and the iniquity and absurdity of the pretension to exclude or to disfranchise a portion of them because they are the owners of slaves, than the fact that the same instrument, which imparts to Congress its very existence and its every function, guaranties to the slaveholder the title to his property, and gives him the right to its reclamation throughout the entire extent of the nation; and farther, that the only private property which the Constitution has specifically recognized, and has imposed it as a direct obligation both on the States and the Federal Government to protect and enforce, is the property of the master in his slave; no other right of property is placed by the Constitution upon the same high ground, nor shielded by a similar guaranty.

Can there be imputed to the sages and patriots by whom the Constitution was framed, or can there be detected in the text of that Constitution, or in any rational construction or implication deducible therefrom, a contradiction so palpable as would exist between a pledge to the slaveholder of an equality with his fellow-citizens, and of the formal and solemn assurance for the security and enjoyment of his property, and a warrant given, as it were, uno flatu, to another, to rob him of that property, or to subject him to proscription and disfranchisement for possessing or for endeavoring to retain it? The injustice and extravagance necessarily implied in a supposition like this, cannot be rationally imputed to the patriotic or the honest, or to those who were merely sane.

A conclusion in favor of the prohibitory power in Congress, as asserted in the 8th section of the Act of 1820, has been attempted, as deducible from the precedent of the Ordinance of the Convention of 1787, concerning the cession by Virginia of the territory northwest of the Ohio; the provision in which Ordinance, relative to slavery, it has been attempted to impose upon other and subsequently acquired territory.

The first circumstance which, in the consideration of this provision, impresses itself upon my mind, is its utter futility and want of authority. This court has, in repeated instances, ruled, that whatever may have been the force according to this Ordinance of 1787 at the period of its enactment, its authority and effect ceased, and yielded to the paramount authority of the Constitution, from the period of the adoption of the latter. Such is the principle ruled in the cases of Pollard's Lessee v. Hagan, 3 How. 212; Permoli v. New Orleans, 3 How. 491*] 589; *Strader v. Graham, 10 How. 82. But apart from the superior control of the Constitution, and anterior to the adoption of that instrument, it is obvious that the inhibition in question never had and never could have
736

any legitimate and binding force. We may seek in vain for any power in the convention, either to require or to accept a condition or restriction upon the cession like that insisted on; a condition inconsistent with, and destructive of, the object of the grant. The cession was, as recommended by the old Congress in 1780, made originally and completed in terms to the United States, and for the benefit of the United States, i. e., for the people, all the people, of the United States. The condition subsequently sought to be annexed in 1787 (declared, too, to be perpetual and immutable), being contradictory to the terms and destructive of the purposes of the cession, and after the cession was consummated, and the powers of the ceding party terminated, and the rights of the grantees, the people of the United States, vested, must necessarily, so far, have been ab initio void. With respect to the power of the convention to impose this inhibition, it seems to be pertinent in this place to recur to the opinion of one cotemporary with the establishment of the government, and whose distinguished services in the formation and adoption of our national charter, point him out as the artifex maximus of our federal system. James Madison, in the year 1819, speaking with reference to the prohibitory power claimed by Congress, then threatening the very existence of the Union, remarks of the language of the 2d clause of the 3d section of article 4th of the Constitution, "that it cannot be well extended beyond a power over the territory as property, and the power to make provisions really needful or necessary for the government of settlers, until ripe for admission into the Union."

Again he says, "with respect to what has taken place in the Northwest Territory, it may be observed that the Ordinance giving it its distinctive character on the subject of slaveholding proceeded from the old Congress, acting with the best intentions, but under a charter which contains no shadow of the authority exercised; and it remains to be decided how far the states formed within that Territory, and admitted into the Union, are on a different footing from its other member as to their legislative sovereignty. As to the power of admitting new States into the federal compact, the questions offering themselves are, whether Congress can attach conditions, or the new States concur in conditions, which after admission would abridge or enlarge the constitutional rights of legislation common to other States; whether Congress can, by a compact *with a new State, take power either to [*492 or from itself, or place the new member above or below the equal rank and rights possessed by the others; whether all such stipulations expressed or implied would not be nullities, and be so pronounced when brought to a practical test. It falls within the scope of your inquiry to state the fact, that there was a proposition in the convention to discriminate between the old and the new States by an article in the Constitution. The proposition, happily, was rejected. The effect of such a discrimination is sufficiently evident."[1]

In support of the Ordinance of 1787, there

1.—Letter from James Madison to Robert Walsh, November 27th, 1819, on the subject of the Missouri Compromise.

may be adduced the semblance at least of obligation deducible from compact, the form of assent or agreement between the grantor and grantee; but this form of similitude, as is justly remarked by Mr. Madison, is rendered null by the absence of power or authority in the contracting parties, and by the more intrinsic and essential defect of incompatibility with the rights and avowed purposes of those parties, and with their relative duties and obligations to others. If, then, with the attendant formalities of assent or compact, the restrictive power claimed was void as to the immediate subject of the Ordinance, how much more unfounded must be the pretension to such a power as derived from that source (viz.: the Ordinance of 1787), with respect to territory acquired by purchase or conquest under the supreme authority of the Constitution—territory not the subject of mere donation, but obtained in the name of all, by the combined efforts and resources of all, and with no condition annexed or pretended.

In conclusion, my opinion is, that the decision of the Circuit Court, upon the law arising upon the several pleas in bar, is correct, but that it is erroneous in having sustained the demurrer to the plea in abatement of the jurisdiction; that for this error the decision of the Circuit Court should be reversed, and the cause remanded to that court, with instructions to abate the action, for the reason set forth and pleaded in the plea in abatement.

In the foregoing examination of this cause, the circumstance that the questions involved therein had been previously adjudged between these parties by the court of the State of Missouri, has not been adverted to; for although it has been ruled by this court, that in instances of concurrent jurisdiction, the court first obtaining possession or cognizance of the controversy should retain and decide it, yet, as in this **493*]** case there had *been no plea, either of a former judgment or of autre action pendent, it was thought that the fact of a prior decision, however conclusive it might have been if regularly pleaded, could not be incidentally taken into view.

Mr. Justice Campbell:

I concur in the judgment pronounced by the Chief Justice, but the importance of the cause, the expectation and interest it has awakened, and the responsibility involved in its determination, induce me to file a separate opinion.

The case shows that the plaintiff, in the year 1834, was a negro slave in Missouri, the property of Dr. Emerson, a surgeon in the Army of the United States. In 1834, his master took him to the military station at Rock Island, on the border of Illinois, and in 1836 to Fort Snelling, in the present Minnesota, then Wisconsin Territory. While at Fort Snelling, the plaintiff married a slave who was there with her master, and two children have been born of this connection; one during the journey of the family in returning to Missouri, and the other after their return to that State.

Since 1838, the plaintiff and the members of his family have been in Missouri in the condition of slaves. The object of this suit is to establish their freedom. The defendant, who claims the plaintiff and his family, under the

15 L. ed.

title of Dr. Emerson, denied the jurisdiction of the Circuit Court, by the plea that the plaintiff was a negro of African blood, the descendant of Africans who had been imported and sold in this country as slaves, and thus he had no capacity as a citizen of Missouri to maintain a suit in the Circuit Court. The court sustained a demurrer to this plea; a trial was then had upon the general issue, and special pleas to the effect that the plaintiff and his family were slaves belonging to the defendant.

My opinion in this case is not affected by the plea to the jurisdiction, and I shall not discuss the questions it suggests. The claim of the plaintiff to freedom depends upon the effect to be given to his absence from Missouri, in company with his master, in Illinois and Minnesota, and this effect is to be ascertained by a reference to the laws of Missouri. For the trespass complained of was committed upon one claiming to be a freeman and a citizen, in that State, and who had been living for years under the dominion of its laws. And the rule is, that whatever is a justification where the thing is done, must be a justification in the forum where the case is tried.

20 How. St. Tri. 234; Cowp. S. C. 161.

The Constitution of Missouri recognizes slavery as a legal condition, extends guaranties to the masters of slaves, and invites *im- **[*494** migrants to introduce them, as property, by a promise of protection. The laws of the State charge the master with the custody of the slave, and provide for the maintenance and security of their relation.

The Federal Constitution and the Acts of Congress provide for the return of escaping slaves within the limits of the Union. No removal of the slave beyond the limits of the State, against the consent of the master, nor residence there in another condition, would be regarded as an effective manumission by the courts of Missouri, upon his return to the State. "Sicut liberis captis status restituitur sic servus domino." Nor can the master emancipate the slave within the State except through the agency of a public authority. The inquiry arises, whether the manumission of the slave is effected by his removal, with the consent of the master, to a community where the law of slavery does not exist, in a case where neither the master nor slave discloses a purpose to remain permanently, and where both parties have continued to maintain their existing relations. What is the law of Missouri in such a case? Similar inquiries have arisen in a great number of suits, and the discussions in the State courts have relieved the subject of much of its difficulty.

12 B. M. Ky. 545; Foster v. Foster, 10 Gratt. Va. 485; 4 Harr. & McH. Md. 295; Scott v. Emerson, 15 Mo. 576; 4 Rich. S. C. 186; 17 Mo. 434; 15 Mo. 596; 5 B. M. 173; 8 B. M. 540, 633; 9 B. M. 565; 5 Leigh, 614; 1 Rand. 15; 18 Pick. 193.

The result of these discussions is, that, in general, the status, or civil and political capacity of a person, is determined, in the first instance, by the law of the domicil where he is born; that the legal effect on persons, arising from the operation of the law of that domicil, is not indelible, but that a new capacity or status may be acquired by a change of domicil.

That questions of status are closely connected with considerations arising out of the social and political organization of the State where they originate, and each sovereign power must determine them within its own territories.

A large class of cases has been decided upon the second of the propositions above stated, in the Southern and Western courts—cases in which the law of the actual domicil was adjudged to have altered the native condition and status of the slave, although he had never actually possessed the status of freedom in that domicil.

Rankin v. Lydia, 2 A. K. Marsh. 467; Harny v. Decker, Walk. Miss. 36; 4 Mart. 385; 1 Mo. 472; Hunter v. Fulcher, 1 Leigh, 172.

I do not impugn the authority of these cases. No evidence is found in the record to establish **495*]** the existence of a domicil *acquired by the master and slave, either in Illinois or Minnesota. The master is described as an officer of the army, who was transferred from one station to another, along the Western frontier, in the line of his duty, and who, after performing the usual tours of service, returned to Missouri; these slaves returned to Missouri with him, and had been there for near fifteen years, in that condition, when this suit was instituted. But absence, in the performance of military duty, without more, is a fact of no importance in determining a question of a change of domicil. Questions of that kind depend upon acts and intentions, and are ascertained from motives, pursuits, the condition of the family, and fortune of the party, and no change will be inferred, unless evidence shows that one domicil was abandoned, and there was an intention to acquire another.

11 L. & Eq. 6; 6 Exch. 217; 6 M. & W. 511; 2 Curt. Ecc. 368.

The cases first cited deny the authority of a foreign law to dissolve relations which have been legally contracted in the State where the parties are, and have their actual domicil—relations which were never questioned during their absence from that State—relations which are consistent with the native capacity and condition of the respective parties, and with the policy of the State where they reside; but which relations were inconsistent with the policy or laws of the State or Territory within which they had been for a time, and from which they had returned, with these relations undisturbed. It is upon the assumption, that the law of Illinois or Minnesota was indelibly impressed upon the slave, and its consequences carried into Missouri, that the claim of the plaintiff depends. The importance of the case entitles the doctrine on which it rests to a careful examination.

It will be conceded, that in countries where no law or regulation prevails, opposed to the existence and consequences of slavery, persons who are born in that condition in a foreign State, would not be liberated by the accident of their introgression. The relation of domestic slavery is recognized in the law of nations, and the interference of the authorities of one State with the rights of a master belonging to another, without a valid cause is a violation of that law.

Wheat. Law of Na. 724; 5 Stats. at L. 601; Calh. Sp. 378; Reports of the Com. U. S. and G. B. 187, 238, 241.

738

The public law of Europe formerly permitted a master to reclaim his bondsman, within a limited period, wherever he could find him, and one of the capitularies of Charlemagne abolishes the rule of prescription. He directs, "that wheresoever, within the bounds of Italy, either the runaway slave of the King, or of *the church, or of any other man, shall [*496 be found by his master, he shall be restored without any bar or prescription of years; yet upon the provision that the master be a Frank or German, or of any other nation (foreign); but if he be a Lombard or a Roman, he shall acquire or receive his slaves by that law which has been established from ancient times among them." Without referring for precedents abroad, or to the colonial history, for similar instances, the history of the Confederation and Union affords evidence to attest the existence of this ancient law. In 1783, Congress directed General Washington to continue his remonstrances to the commander of the British forces respecting the permitting negroes belonging to the citizens of these States to leave New York, and to insist upon the discontinuance of that measure. In 1788, the resident minister of the United States at Madrid was instructed to obtain from the Spanish Crown orders to its governors in Louisiana and Florida, "to permit and facilitate the apprehension of fugitive slaves from the States, promising that the States would observe the like conduct respecting fugitives from Spanish subjects." The committee that made the report of this resolution consisted of Hamilton, Madison and Sedgwick (2 Hamilton's Works, 473); and the clause in the Federal Constitution providing for the restoration of fugitive slaves is a recognition of this ancient right, and of the principle that a change of place does not effect a change of condition. The diminution of the power of a master to reclaim his escaping bondsman in Europe commenced in the enactment of laws of prescription in favor of privileged communes. Bremen, Spire, Worms, Vienna, and Ratisbon, in Germany; Carcassonne, Béziers, Toulouse, and Paris, in France, acquired privileges on this subject at an early period. The Ordinance of William the Conqueror, that a residence of any of the servile population of England, for a year and a day, without being claimed, in any city, burgh, walled town, or castle of the King, should entitle them to perpetual liberty, is a specimen of these laws.

The earliest publicist who has discussed this subject is Bodin, a jurist of the sixteenth century, whose work was quoted in the early discussions of the courts in France and England on this subject. He says: "In France, although there be some remembrance of old servitude, yet it is not lawful here to make a slave or to buy any one of others, in so much as the slaves of strangers, as soon as they set their foot within France, become frank and free, as was determined by an old decree of the court of Paris against an ambassador of Spain, who had brought a slave with him into France." He states another case, which arose in the City of Toulouse, of a Genoese merchant, who had *carried a slave into that city on his [*497 voyage from Spain; and when the matter was brought before the magistrates, the "procureur of the city, out of the records, showed certain ancient privileges given unto them of Toulouse, wherein it was granted that slaves, so soon as they should come into Toulouse, should be free." These cases were cited with much approbation in the discussion of the claims of the West India slaves of Verdelin for freedom, in 1738, before the judges in admiralty (15 Causes Celébrés, p. 1; 2 Masse Droit Com. sec. 58), and were reproduced before Lord Mansfield, in the cause of Somersett, in 1772. Of the cases cited by Bodin, it is to be observed that Charles V. of France exempted all the inhabitants of Paris from serfdom, or other feudal incapacities, in 1371, and this was confirmed by several of his successors (3 Dulaire Hist. de Par. 546; Broud. Cout. de Par. 21), and the Ordinance of Toulouse is preserved as follows: "Civitas Tholosana fuit et erit sine fine libera, adeo ut servi et ancillæ sclavi et sclavæ, dominos habentes, cum rebus vel sine rebus suis, ad Tholosam vel infrà terminos extra urbem terminatos accedentes acquirant libertatem."

Hist. de Langue, tome 3, p. 69; Ibid. 6, p. 8; Loysel Inst. b. 1. sec. 6.

The decisions were made upon special ordinances, or charters, which contained positive prohibitions of slavery, and where liberty had been granted as a privilege; and the history of Paris furnishes but little support for the boast that she was a "sacro sancta civitas," where liberty always had an asylum, or for the "self-complacent rhapsodies" of the French advocates in the case of Verdelin, which amused the grave lawyers who argued the case of Somersett. The case of Verdelin was decided upon a special ordinance, which prescribed the conditions on which West India slaves might be introduced into France, and which had been disregarded by the master.

The case of Somersett was that of a Virginia slave carried to England by his master in 1770, and who remained there two years. For some cause, he was confined on a vessel destined to Jamaica, where he was to be sold. Lord Mansfield, upon a return to a habeas corpus, states the question involved. "Here, the person of the slave himself," he says, "is the immediate subject of inquiry. Can any dominion, authority or coercion be exercised in this country, according to the American laws?" He answers: "The difficulty of adopting the relation, without adopting it in all its consequences, is indeed extreme, and yet many of those consequences are absolutely contrary to the municipal law of England." Again, he says: "The return states that the slave departed, and refused to serve; whereupon, he was kept to be sold abroad." "So 498*] high *an act of dominion must be recognized by the law of the country where it is used. The power of the master over his slave has been extremely different in different countries." "The state of slavery is of such a nature, that it is incapable of being introduced on any reasons, moral or political, but only by positive law, which preserves its force long after the reasons, occasion, and time itself, from whence it was created, are erased from the memory. It is so odious, that nothing can be suffered to support it but positive law." That there is a difference in the systems of States, which recognize and which do not recognize the institution of slavery, cannot be disguised. Constitutional law, punitive law, police, domestic economy, industrial pursuits, and amuse-

ments, the modes of thinking and of belief of the population of the respective communities, all show the profound influence exerted upon society by this single arrangement. This influence was discovered in the Federal Convention, in the deliberations on the plan of the Constitution. Mr. Madison observed, "that the States were divided into different interests, not by their difference of size, but by other circumstances; the most material of which resulted partly from climate, but principally from the effects of their having or not having slaves. These two causes concur in forming the great division of interests in the United States."

The question to be raised with the opinion of Lord Mansfield, therefore, is not in respect to the incongruity of the two systems, but whether slavery was absolutely contrary to the law of England; for if it was so, clearly, the American laws could not operate there. Historical research ascertains that at the date of the Conquest the rural population of England were generally in a servile condition, and under various names, denoting slight variances in condition, they were sold with the land like cattle, and were a part of its living money. Traces of the existence of African slaves are to be found in the early chronicles. Parliament, in the time of Richard II., and also of Henry VIII., refused to adopt a general law of emancipation. Acts of emancipation by the last-named monarch and by Elizabeth are preserved.

The African slave trade had been carried on, under the unbounded protection of the Crown, for near two centuries, when the case of Somersett was heard, and no motion for its suppression had ever been submitted to Parliament, while it was forced upon and maintained in unwilling colonies by the Parliament and Crown of England at that moment. Fifteen thousand negro slaves were then living in that island, where they had been introduced under the counsel of the most illustrious jurists of the realm, and such slaves had been publicly *sold [*499 for near a century in the markets of London. In the northern part of the kingdom of Great Britain there existed a class of from 30,000 to 40,000 persons of whom the Parliament said, in 1775 (15 George III, chap. 28), "many colliers, coal heavers, and salters, are in a state of slavery or bondage, bound to the collieries and salt works, where they work for life, transferable with the collieries and salt works when their original masters have no use for them; and whereas the emancipating or setting free the colliers, coal heavers, and salters, in Scotland, who are now in a state of servitude, gradually and upon reasonable conditions, would be the means of increasing the number of colliers, coal heavers, and salters, to the great benefit of the public, without doing any injury to the present masters, and would remove the reproach of allowing such a state of servitude to exist in a free country," etc.; and again, in 1799, "they declare that many colliers and coal heavers still continue in a state of bondage." No statute, from the Conquest till the 15 George III., had been passed upon the subject of personal slavery. These facts have led the most eminent civilian of England to question the accuracy of this judgment, and to insinuate that in this judgment the offense of ampliare jurisdiction-em by private authority was committed by the eminent magistrate who pronounced it.

This sentence is distinguishable from those cited from the French courts in this: that there positive prohibitions existed against slavery, and the right to freedom was conferred on the immigrant slave by positive law; whereas here the consequences of slavery merely—that is, the public policy—were found to be contrary to the law of slavery. The case of The Slave Grace, 2 Hagg. 94, with four others, came before Lord Stowell in 1827, by appeals from the West India vice admiralty courts. They were cases of slaves who had returned to those islands, after a residence in Great Britain, and where the claim to freedom was first presented in the colonial forum. The learned judge in that case said: "This suit fails in its foundation. She (Grace) was not a free person; no injury is done her by her continuance in slavery, and she has no pretensions to any other station than that which was enjoyed by every slave of a family. If she depends upon such freedom conveyed by a mere residence in England, she complains of a violation of right which she possessed no longer than whilst she resided in England, but which totally expired when that residence ceased, and she was imported into Antigua."

The decision of Lord Mansfield was, "that so high an act of dominion" as the master exercises over his slave, in sending him abroad for sale, could not be exercised in England 500*] *under the American laws, and contrary to the spirit of their own.

The decision of Lord Stowell is, that the authority of the English laws terminated when the slave departed from England. That the laws of England were not imported into Antigua, with the slave, upon her return, and that the colonial forum had no warrant for applying a foreign code to dissolve relations which had existed between persons belonging to that island, and which were legal according to its own system. There is no distinguishable difference between the case before us and that determined in the admiralty of Great Britain.

The complaint here, in my opinion, amounts to this: that the judicial tribunals of Missouri have not denounced as odious the Constitution and laws under which they are organized, and have not superseded them on their own private authority, for the purpose of applying the laws of Illinois, or those passed by Congress for Minnesota, in their stead. The 8th section of the Act of Congress of the 6th of March, 1820 (3 Stat. at L. 545), entitled, "An Act to authorize the people of Missouri to form a State government," etc., etc., is referred to as affording the authority to this court to pronounce the sentence which the Supreme Court of Missouri felt themselves constrained to refuse. That section of the Act prohibits slavery in the district of country west of the Mississippi, north of thirty-six degrees thirty minutes north latitude, which belonged to the ancient Province of Louisiana, not included in Missouri.

It is a settled doctrine of this court, that the Federal Government can exercise no power over the subject of slavery within the States, nor control the intermigration of slaves, other than fugitives, among the States. Nor can that government affect the duration of slavery within the States, other than by a legislation over the

140

foreign slave trade. The power of Congress to adopt the section of the Act above cited must, therefore, depend upon some condition of the Territories which distinguishes them from States, and subjects them to a control more extended. The 3d section of the 4th article of the Constitution is referred to as the only and all-sufficient grant to support this claim. It is, that "new States may be admitted by the Congress to this Union; but no new State shall be formed or erected within the jurisdiction of any other State, nor any State be formed by the junction of two or more States, or parts of States, without the consent of the Legislatures of the States concerned, as well as of the Congress. The Congress shall have power to dispose of and make all needful rules and regulations respecting the territory, or other property *belonging to the United States; and [*501 nothing in this Constitution shall be so construed as to prejudice any claims of the United States, or of any particular State."

It is conceded, in the decisions of this court, that Congress may secure the rights of the United States in the public domain, provide for the sale or lease of any part of it, and establish the validity of the titles of the purchasers, and may organize territorial governments, with powers of legislation.

3 How. 212; 12 How. 1; 1 Pet. 511; 13 Pet. 436; 16 How. 164.

But the recognition of a plenary power in Congress to dispose of the public domain, or to organize a government over it, does not imply a corresponding authority to determine the internal polity, or to adjust the domestic relations, or the persons who may lawfully inhabit the territory in which it is situated. A supreme power to make needful rules respecting the public domain, and a similar power of framing laws to operate upon persons and things within the territorial limits where it lies, are distinguished by broad lines of demarcation in American history. This court has assisted us to define them. In Johnson v. McIntosh, 8 Wheat. 543–605, they say: "According to the theory of the British Constitution, all vacant lands are vested in the Crown; and the exclusive power to grant them is admitted to reside in the Crown, as a branch of the royal prerogative.

All the lands we hold were originally granted by the Crown, and the establishment of a royal government has never been considered as impairing its right to grant lands within the chartered limits of such colony."

And the British Parliament did claim a supremacy of legislation co-extensive with the absoluteness of the dominion of the sovereign over the crown lands. The American doctrine, to the contrary, is embodied in two brief resolutions of the people of Pennsylvania, in 1774: 1st. "That the inhabitants of these Colonies are entitled to the same rights and liberties, within the Colonies, that the subjects born in England are entitled to within the realm." 2d. "That the power assumed by Parliament to bind the people of these Colonies by statutes, in all cases whatever, is unconstitutional, and therefore the source of these unhappy difficulties." The Congress of 1774, in their statement of rights and grievances, affirm "a free and exclusive power of legislation" in their several provincial Legislatures, "in all cases of taxation and internal polity, subject only to the negative of their sovereign, in such manner as has been heretofore used and accustomed." 1 Jour. Cong. 32.

The unanimous consent of the people of the 502*] Colonies, then, *to the power of their sovereign, "to dispose of and make all needful rules and regulations respecting the territory" of the Crown, in 1774, was deemed by them as entirely consistent with opposition, remonstrance, the renunciation of allegiance, and proclamation of civil war, in preference to submission to his claim of supreme power in the Territories.

I pass now to the evidence afforded during the Revolution and Confederation. The American Revolution was not a social revolution. It did not alter the domestic condition or capacity of persons within the Colonies, nor was it designed to disturb the domestic relations existing among them. It was a political revolution, by which thirteen dependent Colonies became thirteen independent States. "The Declaration of Independence was not," says Justice Chase, "a declaration that the united Colonies jointly, in a collective capacity, were independent States, etc., etc., etc., but that each of them was a sovereign and independent State; that is, that each of them had a right to govern itself by its own authority and its own laws, without any control from any other power on earth."

3 Dall. 199; 4 Cranch, 212.

These sovereign and independent States, being united as a Confederation, by various public acts of cession, became jointly interested in territory, and concerned to dispose of and make all needful rules and regulations respecting it. It is a conclusion not open to discussion in this court, "that there was no territory within the (original) United States, that was claimed by them in any other right than that of some of the confederate States." Harcourt v. Gaillard, 12 Wheat. 523. "The question whether the vacant lands within the United States," says Chief Justice Marshall, "became joint property, or belonged to the separate States, was a momentous question, which threatened to shake the American Confederacy to its foundations. This important and dangerous question has been compromised, and the compromise is not now to be contested." 6 Cranch, 87.

The cessions of the States to the Confederation were made on the condition that the territory ceded should be laid out and formed into distinct republican States which would be admitted as members to the Federal Union, having the same rights of sovereignty, freedom and independence, as the other States. The first effort to fulfill this trust was made in 1785, by the offer of a charter or compact to the inhabitants who might come to occupy the land.

Those inhabitants were to form for themselves temporary state governments, founded on the constitutions of any of the States, but to be alterable at the will of their Legislature; and 503*] *permanent governments were to succeed these, whenever the population became sufficiently numerous to authorize the State to enter the Confederacy; and Congress assumed to obtain powers from the States to facilitate this object. Neither in the deeds of cession of the States, nor in this compact, was a sovereign power for Congress to govern the Territories asserted. Congress retained power, by this

Act, "to dispose of and to make rules and regulations respecting the public domain," but submitted to the people to organize a government harmonious with those of the confederate States.

The next stage in the progress of colonial government was the adoption of the Ordinance of 1787, by eight States, in which the plan of a territorial government, established by Act of Congress, is first seen. This was adopted while the Federal Convention to form the Constitution was sitting. The plan placed the government in the hands of a governor, secretary, and judges, appointed by Congress, and conferred power on them to select suitable laws from the codes of the States, until the population should equal 5,000. A legislative council, elected by the people, was then to be admitted to a share of the legislative authority, under the supervision of Congress; and States were to be formed whenever the number of the population should authorize the measure.

This Ordinance was addressed to the inhabitants as a fundamental compact, and six of its articles define the conditions to be observed in their Constitution and laws. These conditions were designed to fulfill the trust in the agreements of cession, that the States to be formed of the ceded Territories should be "distinct republican States." This Ordinance was submitted to Virginia in 1788, and the 5th article, embodying as it does a summary of the entire Act, was specifically ratified and confirmed by that State. This was an incorporation of the Ordinance into her Act of Cession. It was conceded, in the argument, that the authority of Congress was not adequate to the enactment of the ordinance, and that it cannot be supported upon the Articles of Confederation. To a part of the engagements, the assent of nine states was required, and for another portion no provision had been made in those Articles. Mr. Madison said, in a writing nearly contemporary but before the Confirmatory Act of Virginia, "Congress have proceeded to form new states, to erect temporary governments, to appoint officers for them, and to prescribe the conditions on which such States shall be admitted into the Confederacy; all this has been done, and done without the least color of constitutional authority." Federalist, No. 38. Richard Henry Lee, one of the committee who reported the Ordinance to Congress, *transmitted it to [*504 General Washington (15th July, 1787), saying: "It seemed necessary, for the security of property among uninformed and perhaps licentious people, as the greater part of those who go there are, that a strong-toned government should exist, and the rights of property be clearly defined." The consent of all the States represented in Congress, the consent of the Legislature of Virginia, the consent of the inhabitants of the territory, all concur to support the authority of this enactment. It is apparent, in the frame of the Constitution, that the Convention recognized its validity, and adjusted parts of their work with reference to it. The authority to admit new States into the Union, the omission to provide distinctly for territorial governments, and the clause limiting the foreign slave trade to States then existing, which might not prohibit it, show that they regarded this territory as provided with a government and organized permanently with a restriction on the subject of slavery. Justice Chase, in the opinion already cited, says of the government before, and it is in some measure true during the Confederation, "that the powers of Congress originated from necessity, and arose out of and were only limited by events, or, in other words, they were revolutionary in their very nature. Their extent depended upon the exigencies and necessities of public affairs;" and there is only one rule of construction, in regard to the acts done, which will fully support them, viz.: that the powers actually exercised were rightfully exercised, wherever they were supported by the implied sanction of the State Legislatures, and by the ratifications of the people.

The clauses in the 3d section of the 4th article of the Constitution, relative to the admission of new States, and the disposal and regulation of the territory of the United States, were adopted without debate in the Convention.

There was a warm discussion on the clauses that relate to the subdivision of the States, and the reservation of the claims of the United States and each of the States from any prejudice. The Maryland members revived the controversy in regard to the Crown lands of the Southwest. There was nothing to indicate any reference to a government of territories not included within the limits of the Union; and the whole discussion demonstrates that the Convention was consciously dealing with a Territory whose condition, as to government, had been arranged by a fundamental and unalterable compact.

An examination of this clause of the Constitution, by the light of the circumstances in which the Convention was placed, will aid us to determine its significance. The first clause is, "that new States may be admitted by the 505*] Congress into this *Union." The condition of Kentucky, Vermont, Rhode Island and the new States to be formed in the Northwest, suggested this, as a necessary addition to the powers of Congress. The next clause, providing for the subdivision of States, and the parties to consent to such an alteration, was required, by the plans on foot, for changes in Massachusetts, New York, Pennsylvania, North Carolina and Georgia. The clause which enables Congress to dispose of and make regulations respecting the public domain, was demanded by the exigencies of an exhausted treasury and a disordered finance, for relief by sales, and the preparation for sales, of the public lands; and the last clause, that nothing in the Constitution should prejudice the claims of the United States or a particular State, was to quiet the jealousy and irritation of those who had claimed for the United States all the unappropriated lands. I look in vain, among the discussions of the time, for the assertion of a supreme sovereignty for Congress over the territory then belonging to the United States, or that they might thereafter acquire. I seek in vain for an enunciation that a consolidated power had been inaugurated, whose subject comprehended an empire, and which had no restriction but the discretion of Congress. This disturbing element of the Union entirely escaped the apprehensive provisions of Samuel Adams, George Clinton, Luther Martin, and Patrick Henry; and, in respect to dangers from power vested in a central government over distant settlements, colonies, or provinces,

their instincts were always alive. Not a word escaped them, to warn their countrymen that here was a power to threaten the landmarks of this federative Union, and with them the safeguards of popular and constitutional liberty; or that under this Article there might be introduced, on our soil, a single government over a vast extent of country—a government foreign to the persons over whom it might be exercised, and capable of binding those not represented by statutes, in all cases whatever. I find nothing to authorize these enormous pretensions, nothing in the expositions of the friends of the Constitution, nothing in the expressions of alarm by its opponents—expressions which have since been developed as prophecies. Every portion of the United States was then provided with a municipal government, which this Constitution was not designed to supersede, but merely to modify as to its conditions.

The compacts of cession by North Carolina and Georgia, are subsequent to the Constitution. They adopt the Ordinance of 1787, except the clause respecting slavery. But the precautionary repudiation of that article forms an argument quite as satisfactory to the advocates for federal power, as its introduction *would have done. The refusal of a [*506 power to Congress to legislate in one place, seems to justify the seizure of the same power when another place for its exercise is found.

This proceeds from a radical error, which lies at the foundation of much of this discussion. It is, that the Federal Government may lawfully do whatever is not directly prohibited by the Constitution. This would have been a fundamental error, if no amendments to the Constitution had been made. But the final expression of the will of the people of the States, in the 10th Amendment, is, that the powers of the Federal Government are limited to the grants of the Constitution.

Before the cession of Georgia was made, Congress asserted rights, in respect to a part of her territory, which require a passing notice. In 1798 and 1800, Acts for the settlement of limits with Georgia, and to establish a government in the Mississippi Territory were adopted. A territorial government was organized, between the Chattahoochee and Mississippi Rivers. This was within the limits of Georgia. These Acts dismembered Georgia. They established a separate government on her soil, while they rather derisively professed, "that the establishment of that government shall in no respect impair the rights of the State of Georgia, either to the jurisdiction or soil of the territory." The Constitution provided that the importation of such persons as any of the existing States shall think proper to admit, shall not be prohibited by Congress before 1808. By these enactments, a prohibition was placed upon the importation of slaves into Georgia, although her Legislature had made none.

This court have repeatedly affirmed the paramount claim of Georgia to this territory. They have denied the existence of any title in the United States. 6 Cranch. 87; 12 Wheat. 523; 3 How. 212; 13 How. 381. Yet these Acts were cited in the argument as precedents to show the power of Congress in the Territories. These Statutes were the occasion of earnest expostulation and bitter remonstrance on the part of the authorities of the State, and the memory of their injustice and wrong remained long after the legal settlement of the controversy by the compact of 1802. A reference to these Acts terminates what I have to say upon the constitutions of the territory within the original limits of the United States. These constitutions were framed by the concurrence of the States making the cessions, and Congress, and were tendered to immigrants who might be attracted to the vacant territory. The legislative powers of the officers of this government were limited to the selection of laws from the States; and provision was made for the introduction of popular institutions, and their emancipation 507*] *from federal control, whenever a suitable opportunity occurred. The limited reservation of legislative power to the officers of the Federal Government was excused on the plea of necessity; and the probability is, that the clauses respecting slavery embody some compromise among the statesmen of that time; beyond these, the distinguishing features of the system which the patriots of the Revolution had claimed as their birthright, from Great Britain, predominated in them.

The acquisition of Louisiana, in 1803, introduced another system into the United States. This vast Province was ceded by Napoleon, and its population had always been accustomed to a viceroyal government, appointed by the Crowns of France or Spain. To establish a government constituted on similar principles, and with like conditions, was not an unnatural proceeding.

But there was a great difficulty in finding constitutional authority for the measure. The 3d section of the 4th article of the Constitution, was introduced into the Constitution on the motion of Mr. Gouverneur Morris. In 1803, he was appealed to for information in regard to its meaning. He answers: "I am very certain I had it not in contemplation to insert a decree de coercendo imperio in the Constitution of America. * * * I knew then, as well as I do now, that all North America must at length be annexed to us. Happy, indeed, if the lust of dominion stop here. It would, therefore, have been perfectly Utopian to oppose a paper restriction to the violence of popular sentiment, in a popular government." 3 Mor. Writ. 185. A few days later, he makes another reply to his correspondents. "I perceive," he says, "I mistook the drift of your inquiry, which substantially is, whether Congress can admit, as a new State, territory which did not belong to the United States when the Constitution was made. In my opinion, they cannot. I always thought, when we should acquire Canada and Louisiana, it would be proper to govern them as provinces, and allow them no voice in our councils. In wording the 3d section of the 4th article, I went as far as circumstances would permit, to establish the exclusion. Candor obliges me to add my belief,

that had it been more pointedly expressed, a strong opposition would have been made." 3 Mor. Writ. 192. The first territorial government of Louisiana was an Imperial one, founded upon a French or Spanish model. For a time, the Governor, judges, legislative council, marshal, secretary, and officers of the militia, were appointed by the President.[1]

*Besides these anomalous arrange- [*508 ments, the acquisition gave rise to jealous inquiries, as to the influence it would exert in determining the men and States that were to be "the arbiters and the rulers" of the destinies of the Union; and unconstitutional opinions, having for their aim to promote sectional divisions, were announced and developed. "Something," said an eminent statesman, "something has suggested to the members of Congress the policy of acquiring geographical majorities. This is a very direct step towards disunion, for it must foster the geographical enmities by which alone it can be effected. This something must be a contemplation of particular advantages to be derived from such majorities; and is it not notorious that they consist of nothing else but usurpations over persons and property, by which they can regulate the internal wealth and prosperity of States and individuals?"

The most dangerous of the efforts to employ geographical political power, to perpetuate a geographical preponderance in the Union, is to be found in the deliberations upon the Act of the 6th of March, 1820, before cited. The attempt consisted of a proposal to exclude Missouri from a place in the Union, unless her people would adopt a constitution containing a prohibition upon the subject of slavery, according to a prescription of Congress. The sentiment is now general, if not universal, that Congress had no constitutional power to impose the restriction. This was frankly admitted at the bar in the course of this argument. The principles which this court have pronounced condemn the pretension then made on behalf of the Legislative Department. In Groves v. Slaughter, 15 Pet., the Chief Justice said: "The power over this subject is exclusively with the several States, and each of them has a right to decide for itself whether it will or will not allow persons of this description to be brought within its limits." Justice McLean said: "The Constitution of the United States operates alike in all the States, and one State has the same power over the subject of slavery as every other State." In Pollard's Lessee v. Hagan, 3 How. 212, the court say: "The United States have no constitutional capacity to exercise municipal *jurisdiction, sovereignty, or em- [*509 inent domain, within the limits of a State or elsewhere, except in cases where it is delegated, and the court denies the faculty of the Federal Government to add to its powers by treaty or compact."

This is a necessary consequence, resulting from the nature of the Federal Constitution,

1.—Mr. Varnum said: "The bill provided such a government as had never been known in the United States." Mr. Eustis: "The government laid down in this bill is certainly a new thing in the United States." Mr. Lucas: "It has been remarked, that this bill establishes elementary principles never previously introduced in the government of any territory of the United States. Granting the truth of this observation," etc. etc. Mr. Macon: "My first objection to the principle contained in

this section is, that it establishes a species of government unknown to the United States." Mr. Boyle: "Were the President an angel instead of a man, I would not clothe him with this power." Mr. G. W. Campbell: "On examining the section, it will appear that it really establishes a complete despotism." Mr. Sloan: "Can anything be more repugnant to the principles of just government? Can anything be more despotic?—Annals of Congress, 1803–'4.

which is a federal compact among the States, establishing a limited government, with powers delegated by the people of distinct and independent communities, who reserved to their state governments, and to themselves, the powers they did not grant. This claim to impose a restriction upon the people of Missouri involved a denial of the constitutional relations between the people of the States and Congress, and affirmed a concurrent right for the latter, with their people to constitute the social and political system of the new States. A successful maintenance of this claim would have altered the basis of the Constitution. The new States would have become members of a Union defined in part by the Constitution and in part by Congress. They would not have been admitted to "this Union." Their sovereignty would have been restricted by Congress as well as the Constitution. The demand was unconstitutional and subversive, but was prosecuted with an energy, and aroused such animosities among the people, that patriots, whose confidence had not failed during the Revolution, began to despair for the Constitution.[1] Amid the utmost violence of this extraordinary contest, the expedient contained in the 8th section of this Act was proposed, to moderate it, and to avert the catastrophe it menaced. It was not seriously debated, nor were its constitutional aspects severely scrutinized by Congress. For the first time, in the history of the country, has its operation been embodied in a case at law, and been presented to this court for their judgment. The inquiry is, whether there are conditions in the constitutions of the Territories which subject the capacity and status of persons within their limits to the direct action of Congress. Can Congress determine the condition and status of persons who inhabit the Territories?

The Constitution permits Congress to dispose of and to make all needful rules and regulations respecting the territory of other property belonging to the United States. This power applies as well to territory belonging to the United States within the States, as beyond them. It comprehends all the public domain, wherever it may be. The argument is, that 510*] *the power to make "all needful rules and regulations" "is a power of legislation," "a full legislative power;" "that it includes all subjects of legislation in the territory," and is without any limitations, except the positive prohibitions which affect all the powers of Congress. Congress may then regulate or prohibit slavery upon the public domain within the new States, and such a prohibition would permanently affect the capacity of a slave, whose master might carry him to it. And why not? Because no power has been conferred on Congress. This is a conclusion universally admitted. But the power to "make rules and regulations respecting the territory" is not restrained by State lines, nor are there any constitutional prohibitions upon its exercise in the domain of the United States within the States; and whatever rules and regulations respecting

territory Congress may constitutionally make, are supreme and are not dependent on the situs of "the territory."

The author of the Farmer's Letters, so famous in the ante-revolutionary history, thus states the argument made by the American loyalists in favor of the claim of the British Parliament to legislate in all cases whatever over the Colonies: "It has been urged with great vehemence against us," he says, "and it seems to be thought their fort, by our adversaries, that a power of regulation is a power of legislation; and a power of legislation, if constitutional, must be universal and supreme, in the utmost sense of the word. It is, therefore, concluded that the Colonies, by acknowledging the power of regulation, acknowledged every other power."

This sophism imposed upon a portion of the patriots of that day. Chief Justice Marshall, in his Life of Washington, says "that many of the best informed men in Massachusetts had, perhaps, adopted the opinion of the parliamentary right of internal government over the Colonies;" "that the English statute book furnishes many instances of its exercise;" "that in no case recollected, was their authority openly controverted;" and "that the General Court of Massachusetts, on a late occasion, openly recognized the principle."

Marsh. Wash. Vol. II. pp. 75, 76.

But the more eminent men of Massachusetts rejected it; and another patriot of the time employs the instance to warn us of "the stealth with which oppression approaches," and "the enormities towards which precedents travel." And the people of the United States, as we have seen, appealed to the last argument, rather than acquiesce in their authority. Could it have been the purpose of Washington and his illustrious associates, by the use of ambiguous, equivocal, and expansive *words, [*511 such as "rules," "regulations," "territory," to re-establish in the Constitution of their country that fort which had been prostrated amid the toils and with the sufferings and sacrifices of seven years of war? Are these words to be understood as the Norths, the Grenvilles, Hillsboroughs, Hutchinsons, and Dunmores—in a word, as George III. would have understood them—or are we to look for their interpretation to Patrick Henry or Samuel Adams, to Jefferson, and Jay, and Dickinson; to the sage Franklin, or to Hamilton, who from his early manhood was engaged in combating British constructions of such words? We know that the resolution of Congress of 1780 contemplated that the new States to be formed under their recommendation were to have the same rights of sovereignty, freedom and independence, as the old. That every resolution, cession, compact and ordinance, of the States, observed the same liberal principle. That the Union of the Constitution is a Union formed of equal States; and that new States, when admitted, were to enter "this Union." Had another Union been proposed in "any pointed manner," it would have encountered not only "strong" but successful opposition. The disunion between Great Britain and her colonies originated in the antipathy of the latter to "rules and regulations" made by a remote power respecting their internal policy. In forming the

---

1.—Mr. Jefferson wrote: "The Missouri question is the most portentous one that ever threatened our Union. In the gloomiest moments of the Revolutionary War, I never had any apprehension equal to that I feel from this source."

Constitution, this fact was ever present in the minds of its authors. The people were assured by their most trusted statesmen "that the jurisdiction of the Federal Government is limited to certain enumerated objects, which concern all members of the republic," and "that the local or municipal authorities form distinct portions of supremacy, no more subject within their respective spheres to the general authority, than the general authority is subject to them within its own sphere." Still, this did not content them. Under the lead of Hancock and Samuel Adams, of Patrick Henry and George Mason, they demanded an explicit declaration that no more power was to be exercised than they had delegated. And the 9th and 10th amendments to the Constitution were designed to include the reserved rights of the States, and the people, within all the sanctions of that instrument, and to bind the authorities, state and federal, by the judicial oath it prescribes, to their recognition and observance. Is it probable, therefore, that the supreme and irresponsible power, which is now claimed for Congress over boundless territories, the use of which cannot fail to react upon the political system of the States, to its subversion, was ever within the contemplation of the statesmen who conducted the counsels of the people in the formation of this Constitution? 512*] When *the questions that came to the surface upon the acquisition of Louisiana were presented to the mind of Jefferson, he wrote: "I had rather ask an enlargement of power from the nation, where it is found necessary, than to assume it by a construction which would make our powers boundless. Our peculiar security is in the possession of a written Constitution. Let us not make it blank paper by construction. I say the same as to the opinion of those who consider the grant of the treaty-making power as boundless. If it is, then we have no Constitution. If it has bounds, they can be no others than the definitions of the powers which that instrument gives. It specifies and delineates the operations permitted to the Federal Government, and gives the powers necessary to carry them into execution." The publication of the journals of the Federal Convention in 1819, of the debates reported by Mr. Madison in 1840, and the mass of private correspondence of the early statesmen before and since, enable us to approach the discussion of the aims of those who made the Constitution, with some insight and confidence.

I have endeavored, with the assistance of these, to find a solution for the grave and difficult question involved in this inquiry. My opinion is, that the claim for Congress of supreme power in the Territories, under the grant to "dispose of and make all needful rules and regulations respecting territory," is not supported by the historical evidence drawn from the Revolution, the Confederation, or the deliberations which preceded the ratifications of the Federal Constitution. The Ordinance of 1787 depended upon the action of the Congress of the Confederation, the assent of the State of Virginia, and the acquiescence of the people who recognized the validity of that plea of necessity, which supported so many of the Acts of the governments of that time; and the Fed-

15 L. ed.

eral Government accepted the Ordinance as a recognized and valid engagement of the Confederation.

In referring to the precedents of 1798 and 1800, I find the Constitution was plainly violated by the invasion of the rights of a sovereign State, both of soil and jurisdiction; and in reference to that of 1804, the wisest statesmen protested against it, and the President more than doubted its policy and the power of the government.

Mr. John Quincy Adams, at a later period, says of the last Act, "that the President found Congress mounted to the pitch of passing those acts, without inquiring where they acquired the authority, and he conquered his own scruples as they had done theirs." But this court cannot undertake for themselves the same conquest. They acknowledge that our peculiar *security is in the possession of a writ- [*513 ten Constitution, and they cannot make it blank paper by construction.

They look to its delineation of the operations of the Federal Government, and they must not exceed the limits it marks out, in their administration. The court have said "that Congress cannot exercise municipal jurisdiction, sovereignty, or eminent domain, within the limits of a state or elsewhere, beyond what has been delegated." We are then to find the authority for supreme power in the Territories in the Constitution. What are the limits upon the operations of a government invested with legislative, executive and judiciary powers, and charged with the power to dispose of and to make all needful rules and regulations respecting a vast public domain? The feudal system would have recognized the claim made on behalf of the Federal Government for supreme power over persons and things in the Territories, as an incident to this title—that is, the title to dispose of and make rules and regulations respecting it.

The Norman lawyers of William the Conqueror would have yielded an implicit assent to the doctrine, that a supreme sovereignty is an inseparable incident to a grant, to dispose of and to make all needful rules and regulations respecting the public domain. But an American patriot, in contrasting the European and American systems, may affirm, "that European sovereigns give lands to their colonists, but reserve to themselves a power to control their property, liberty and privileges; but the American Government sells the lands belonging to the people of the several States (i. e., United States) to their citizens, who are already in the possession of personal and political rights, which the government did not give, and cannot take away." And the advocates for government sovereignty in the Territories have been compelled to abate a portion of the pretensions originally made in its behalf, and to admit that the constitutional prohibitions upon Congress operate in the Territories. But a constitutional prohibition is not requisite to ascertain a limitation upon the authority of the several departments of the Federal Government. Nor are the States or people restrained by any enumeration or definition of their rights or liberties.

To impair or diminish either, the Department must produce an authority from the peo-

745

ple themselves, in their Constitution; and as we have seen, a power to make rules and regulations respecting the public domain does not confer a municipal sovereignty over persons and things upon it. But as this is "thought their fort" by our adversaries, I propose a more definite examination of it. We have seen, Con- *514*]* gress does not *dispose of or make rules and regulations respecting domain belonging to themselves, but belonging to the United States.

These conferred on their mandatory, Congress, authority to dispose of the territory which belonged to them in common; and to accomplish that object beneficially and effectually, they gave an authority to make suitable rules and regulations respecting it. When the power of disposition is fulfilled, the authority to make rules and regulations terminates, for it attaches only upon territory "belonging to the United States."

Consequently, the power to make rules and regulations, from the nature of the subject, is restricted to such administrative and conservatory Acts as are needful for the preservation of the public domain, and its preparation for sale or disposition. The system of land surveys; the reservations for schools, internal improvements, military sites, and public buildings; the pre-emption claims of settlers; the establishment of land offices and boards of inquiry, to determine the validity of land titles; the modes of entry and sale, and of conferring titles; the protection of the lands from trespass and waste; the partition of the public domain into municipal subdivisions, having reference to the erection of territorial governments and States; and perhaps the selection, under their authority, of suitable laws for the protection of the settlers, until there may be a sufficient number of them to form a self-sustaining municipal government—these important rules and regulations will sufficiently illustrate the scope and operation of the 3d section of the 4th article of the Constitution. But this clause in the Constitution does not exhaust the powers of Congress within the territorial subdivisions, or over the persons who inhabit them. Congress may exercise there all the powers of government which belong to them as the Legislature of the United States, of which these Territories make a part. Loughborough v. Blake, 5 Wheat. 317. Thus the laws of taxation, for the regulation of foreign, federal and Indian commerce, and so for the abolition of the slave trade, for the protection of copyrights and inventions, for the establishment of postal communication and courts of justice, and for the punishment of crimes, are as operative there as within the States. I admit that to mark the bounds for the jurisdiction of the Government of the United States within the Territory, and of its power in respect to persons and things within the municipal subdivisions it has created, is a work of delicacy and difficulty, and, in a great measure is beyond the cognizance of the Judiciary Department of that government. How much municipal power may be exercised by the people of the Territory, before their admission to the Union, the courts of justice *515*]* cannot decide. This must depend, for *the most part, on political considerations, which cannot enter into the determination of a case of law or equity. I do not feel called upon to

define the jurisdiction of Congress. It is sufficient for the decision of this case to ascertain whether the residuary sovereignty of the States or people has been invaded by the 8th section of the Act of 6th March, 1820, I have cited, in so far as it concerns the capacity and status of persons in the condition and circumstances of the plaintiff and his family.

These States, at the adoption of the Federal Constitution, were organized communities, having distinct systems of municipal law, which, though derived from a common source, and recognizing in the main similar principles, yet in some respects had become unlike, and on a particular subject promised to be antagonistic.

Their systems provided protection for life, liberty and property, among their citizens, and for the determination of the condition and capacity of the persons domiciled within their limits. These institutions, for the most part, were placed beyond the control of the Federal Government. The Constitution allows Congress to coin money, and regulate its value; to regulate foreign and federal commerce; to secure, for a limited period, to authors and inventors, a property in their writings and discoveries; and to make rules concerning captures in war; and within the limits of these powers, it has exercised, rightly, to a greater or less extent, the power to determine what shall and what shall not be property.

But the great powers of war and negotiation, finance, postal communication and commerce, in general, when employed in respect to the property of a citizen, refer to, and depend upon, the municipal laws of the States, to ascertain and determine what is property, and the rights of the owner, and the tenure by which it is held.

Whatever these Constitutions and laws validly determine to be property, it is the duty of the Federal Government, through the domain of jurisdiction merely federal, to recognize to be property.

And this principle follows from the structure of the respective governments, state and federal, and their reciprocal relations. They are different agents and trustees of the people of the several States, appointed with different powers and with distinct purposes, but whose Acts, within the scope of their respective jurisdictions, are mutually obligatory. They are respectively the depositories of such powers of legislation as the people were willing to surrender, and their duty is to co-operate within their several jurisdictions to maintain the rights of the same citizens under both governments, unimpaired. *A proscription, [*516] therefore, of the constitution and laws of one or more States, determining property, on the part of the Federal Government, by which the stability of its social system may be endangered, is plainly repugnant to the conditions on which the Federal Constitution was adopted, or which that government was designed to accomplish. Each of the States surrendered its powers of war and negotiation, to raise armies and to support a navy, and all these powers are sometimes required to preserve a State from disaster and ruin. The Federal Government was constituted to exercise these powers for the preservation of the States, respectively, and to secure to all their citizens the enjoyment of the rights which were not surrendered to the Federal Government. The provident care of the statesmen who projected the Constitution was signalized by such a distribution of the powers of government as to exclude many of the motives and opportunities for promoting provocations and spreading discord among the States, and for guarding against those partial combinations, so destructive of the community of interest, sentiment and feeling, which are so essential to the support of the Union. The distinguishing features of their system consist in the exclusion of the Federal Government from the local and internal concerns of, and in the establishment of an independent internal government within, the States. And it is a significant fact in the history of the United States, that those controversies which have been productive of the greatest animosity, and have occasioned most peril to the peace of the Union, have had their origin in the well-sustained opinion of a minority among the people, that the Federal Government had overstepped its constitutional limits to grant some exclusive privilege, or to disturb the legitimate distribution of property or power among the States or individuals. Nor can a more signal instance of this be found than is furnished by the Act before us. No candid or rational man can hesitate to believe, that if the subject of the 8th section of the Act of March, 1820, had never been introduced into Congress and made the basis of legislation, no interest common to the Union would have been seriously affected. And certainly the creation, within this Union, of large confederacies of unfriendly and frowning States, which has been the tendency, and, to an alarming extent, the result, produced by the agitation arising from it, does not commend it to the patriot or statesman. This court have determined that intermigration of slaves was not committed to the jurisdiction or control of Congress. Wherever a master is entitled to go within the United States, his slave may accompany him, without any impediment from, or 517*] fear of, Congressional *legislation or interference. The question then arises, whether Congress, which can exercise no jurisdiction over the relations of master and slave within the limits of the Union, and is bound to recognize and respect the rights and relations that validity exist under the constitutions and laws of the States, can deny the exercise of those rights, and prohibit the continuance of those relations within the Territories.

And the citation of state statutes prohibiting the immigration of slaves, and of the decisions of state courts enforcing the forfeiture of the master's title in accordance with their rule, only darkens the discussion. For the question is, have Congress the municipal sovereignty in the territories which the State Legislatures have derived from the authority of the people, and exercise in the States.

And this depends upon the construction of the article in the Constitution before referred to.

And, in my opinion, that clause confers no power upon Congress to dissolve the relations of the master and slave on the domain of the United States, either within or without any of the States.

The 8th section of the Act of Congress of the 6th of March, 1820, did not, in my opinion, operate to determine the domestic condition and status of the plaintiff and his family during their sojourn in Minnesota Territory, or after their return to Missouri.

The question occurs as to the judgment to be given in this case. It appeared upon the trial that the plaintiff, in 1834, was in a state of slavery in Missouri, and he had been in Missouri for near fifteen years in that condition, when this suit was brought. Nor does it appear that he at any time possessed another state or condition, de facto. His claim to freedom depends upon his temporary elocation, from the domicil of his origin, in company with his master, to communities where the law of slavery did not prevail. My examination is confined to the case, as it was submitted upon uncontested evidence, upon appropriate issues to the jury, and upon the instructions given and refused by the court upon that evidence. My opinion is, that the opinion of the Circuit Court was correct upon all the claims involved in those issues, and that the verdict of the jury was justified by the evidence and instructions.

The jury have returned that the plaintiff and his family are slaves.

Upon this record, it is apparent that this is not a controversy between citizens of different States; and that the plaintiff, at no period of the life which has been submitted to the view of the court, has had capacity to maintain a suit in the courts *of the United States. [*518 And in so far as the argument of the Chief Justice upon the plea in abatement has a reference to the plaintiff or his family, in any of the conditions or circumstances of their lives as presented in the evidence, I concur in that portion of his opinion. I concur in the judgment which expresses the conclusion that the Circuit Court should not have rendered a general judgment.

The capacity of the plaintiff to sue is involved in the pleas in bar, and the verdict of the jury discloses an incapacity under the Constitution. Under the Constitution of the United States, his is an incapacity to sue in their courts, while, by the laws of Missouri, the operation of the verdict would be more extensive. I think it a safe conclusion to enforce the lesser disability imposed by the Constitution of the United States, and leave to the plaintiff all his rights in Missouri. I think the judgment should be affirmed on the ground that the Circuit Court had no jurisdiction, or that the case should be reversed and remanded that the suit may be dismissed.

Mr. Justice Catron:

The defendant pleaded to the jurisdiction of the Circuit Court, that the plaintiff was a negro of African blood; the descendant of Africans, who had been imported and sold in this country as slaves, and thus had no capacity as a citizen of Missouri to maintain a suit in the Circuit Court. The court sustained a demurrer to this plea, and a trial was had upon the pleas, of the general issue, and also that the plaintiff and his family were slaves, belonging to the defendant. In this trial a verdict was given for the defendant.

The judgment of the Circuit Court upon the plea in abatement is not open, in my opinion, to examination in this court upon the plaintiff's writ.

The judgment was given for him conformably to the prayer of his demurrer. He cannot assign an error in such a judgment.

Tidd's Pr. 1163; 2 Williams' Saund. 46a; 2 Iredell, N. C. 87; 2 W. & S. 391.

Nor does the fact that the judgment was given on a plea to the jurisdiction, avoid the application of this rule.

Capron v. Van Noorden, 2 Cranch, 126; 6 Wend. 465; 7 Met. 598; 5 Pike, 1005.

The declaration discloses a case within the jurisdiction of the court—a controversy between citizens of different States. The plea in abatement, impugning these jurisdictional averments, was waived when the defendant answered to the declaration by pleas to the merits. The proceedings on that plea remain a part of the technical record, to show the history of the case, but are not open to the review of this court by 519*] a writ *of error. The authorities are very conclusive on this point.

Shepherd v. Graves, 14 How. 505; Bailey v. Dozier, 6 How. 23; 1 Stewart (Ala.), 46; 10 Ben. Monroe (Ky.) 555; 2 Stew. (Ala.) 370, 443; 2 Scam. (Ill.) 78.

Nor can the court assume, as admitted facts, the averments of the plea from the confession of the demurrer. That confession was for a single object, and cannot be used for any other purpose than to test the validity of the plea.

Tompkins v. Ashby, 1 Moo. & Mal. 32; 33 Me. 96, 100.

There being nothing in controversy here but the merits, I will proceed to discuss them.

The plaintiff claims to have acquired property in himself, and became free, by being kept in Illinois during two years.

The Constitution, laws, and policy, of Illinois, are somewhat peculiar respecting slavery. Unless the master becomes an inhabitant of that State, the slaves he takes there do not acquire their freedom; and if they return with their master to the slave State of his domicil, they cannot assert their freedom after their return. For the reasons and authorities on this point, I refer to the opinion of my brother Nelson, with which I not only concur, but think his opinion is the most conclusive argument on the subject within my knowledge.

It is next insisted for the plaintiff, that his freedom (and that of his wife and eldest child) was obtained by force of the Act of Congress of 1820, usually known as the Missouri Compromise Act, which declares: "That in all that territory ceded by France to the United States, which lies north of thirty-six degrees thirty minutes north latitude, slavery and involuntary servitude shall be, and are hereby forever prohibited."

From this prohibition, the Territory now constituting the State of Missouri was excepted; which exception to the stipulation gave it the designation of a compromise.

The first question presented on this Act is, whether Congress has power to make such compromise. For, if power was wanting, then no freedom could be acquired by the defendant under the Act.

That Congress has no authority to pass laws and bind men's rights beyond the powers conferred by the Constitution, is not open to controversy. But it is insisted that, by the Constitution, Congress has power to legislate for and govern the Territories of the United States, and that, by force of the power to govern, laws could be enacted, prohibiting slavery in any portion of the Louisiana Territory; and, of course, to abolish slavery in all parts of it, whilst it was, or is, governed as a Territory.

My opinion is, that Congress is vested with power to govern *the Territories of the [*520 United States by force of the 3d section of the 4th article of the Constitution. And I will state my reasons for this opinion.

Almost every provision in that instrument has a history that must be understood, before the brief and sententious language employed can be comprehended in the relations its authors intended. We must bring before us the state of things presented to the Convention, and in regard to which it acted, when the compound provision was made, declaring: 1st. That "new States may be admitted by the Congress into this Union." 2d. "The Congress shall have power to dispose of and make all needful rules and regulations respecting the territory or other property belonging to the United States. And nothing in this Constitution shall be so construed as to prejudice any claims of the United States, or any particular State."

Having ascertained the historical facts giving rise to these provisions, the difficulty of arriving at the true meaning of the language employed will be greatly lessened.

The history of these facts is substantially as follows:

The King of Great Britain, by his proclamation of 1763, virtually claimed that the country west of the mountains had been conquered from France, and ceded to the Crown of Great Britain by the Treaty of Paris of that year, and he says: "We reserve it under our sovereignty, protection, and dominion, for the use of the Indians."

This country was conquered from the Crown of Great Britain, and surrendered to the United States by the Treaty of Peace of 1783. The colonial charters of Virginia, North Carolina and Georgia, included it. Other States set up pretentions of claim to some portions of the territory north of the Ohio, but they were of no value, as I suppose. 5 Wheat. 375.

As this vacant country had been won by the blood and treasure of all the States, those whose charters did not reach it, insisted that the country belonged to the States united, and that the lands should be disposed of for the benefit of the whole; and to which end, the Western Territory should be ceded to the States united. The contest was stringent and angry, long before the Convention convened, and deeply agitated that body. As a matter of justice, and to quiet the controversy, Virginia consented to cede the country north of the Ohio as early as 1783; and in 1784 the deed of cession was executed, by her delegates in the Congress of the Confederation, conveying to the United States, in Congress assembled, for the benefit of said States, "all right, title and claim, as well of soil as of jurisdiction, which this Commonwealth hath to the territory or tract of country within the limits of the Virginia *charter, situate, lying, and being to the [*521 northwest of the River Ohio." In 1787 (July 13), the Ordinance was passed by the old Congress to govern the Territory.

Massachusetts had ceded her pretension of claim to western territory in 1785, Connecticut hers in 1786, and New York had ceded hers. In August, 1787, South Carolina ceded to the Confederation her pretension of claim to territory west of that State. And North Carolina was expected to cede hers, which she did do, in April, 1790. And so Georgia was confidently expected to cede her large domain, now constituting the territory of the States of Alabama and Mississippi.

At the time the Constitution was under consideration, there had been ceded to the United States, or was shortly expected to be ceded, all the western country, from the British Canada line to Florida, and from the head of the Mississippi almost to its mouth, except that portion which now constitutes the State of Kentucky.

Although Virginia had conferred on the Congress of the Confederation power to govern the territory north of the Ohio, still, it cannot be denied, as I think, that power was wanting to admit a new State under the Articles of Confederation.

With these facts prominently before the Convention, they proposed to accomplish these ends:

1st. To give power to admit new States.

2d. To dispose of the public lands in the Territories, and such as might remain undisposed of in the new States after they were admitted.

And third, to give power to govern the different Territories as incipient States, not of the Union, and fit them for admission. No one in the Convention seems to have doubted that these powers were necessary. As early as the third day of its session (May 29th), Edmund Randolph brought forward a set of resolutions containing nearly all the germs of the Constitution, the 10th of which is as follows:

"Resolved, That provision ought to be made for the admission of States lawfully arising within the limits of the United States, whether from a voluntary junction of government and territory or otherwise, with the consent of a number of voices in the National Legislature less than the whole."

August 18th, Mr. Madison submitted, in order to be referred to the committee of detail, the following powers as proper to be added to those of the General Legislature:

"To dispose of the unappropriated lands of the United States." "To institute temporary governments for new States arising therein." 3 Madison Papers, 1353.

522*] *These, with the resolution, that a district for the location of the seat of government should be provided, and some others, were referred, without a dissent, to the committee of detail, to arrange and put them into satisfactory language.

Gouverneur Morris constructed the clauses, and combined the views of a majority on the two provisions, to admit new States; and second, to dispose of the public lands, and to govern the Territories, in the mean time, between the cessions of the States and the admission into the Union of new States arising in the ceded territory.

3 Madison Papers, 1456 to 1466.

It was hardly possible to separate the power "to make all needful rules and regulations" respecting the government of the territory and the disposition of the public lands.

15 L. ed.

North of the Ohio, Virginia conveyed the lands, and vested the jurisdiction in the thirteen original States, before the Constitution was formed. She had the sole title and sole sovereignty, and the same power to cede, on any terms she saw proper, that the King of England had to grant the Virginia Colonial Charter of 1609, or to grant the Charter of Pennsylvania to William Penn. The thirteen States, through their representatives and deputed ministers in the old Congress, had the same right to govern that Virginia had before the cession. Baldwin's Constitutional Views, 90. And the 6th article of the Constitution adopted all engagements entered into by the Congress of the Confederation, as valid against the United States; and that the laws, made in pursuance of the new Constitution, to carry out this engagement, should be the supreme law of the land, and the judges bound thereby. To give the compact, and the Ordinance, which was part of it, full effect under the new government, the Act of August 7th, 1789, was passed, which declares, "Whereas, in order that the Ordinance of the United States in Congress assembled, for the government of the territory northwest of the River Ohio, may have full effect, it is requisite that certain provisions should be made, so as to adapt the same to the present Constitution of the United States." It is then provided that the Governor and other officers should be appointed by the President, with the consent of the Senate; and be subject to removal, etc., in like manner that they were by the old Congress, whose functions had ceased.

By the powers to govern, given by the Constitution, those amendments to the Ordinance could be made, but Congress guardedly abstained from touching the compact of Virginia, further than to adapt it to the new Constitution.

It is due to myself to say, that it is asking much of a judge, *who has for nearly [*523 twenty years been exercising jurisdiction, from the western Missouri line to the Rocky Mountains, and, on this understanding of the Constitution, inflicting the extreme penalty of death for crimes committed where the direct legislation of Congress was the only rule, to agree that he had been all the while acting in mistake, and as an usurper.

More than sixty years have passed away since Congress has exercised power to govern the Territories, by its legislation directly, or by territorial charters, subject to repeal at all times, and it is now too late to call that power into question, if this court could disregard its own decisions; which it cannot do, as I think. It was held in the case of Cross v. Harrison, 16 How. 193, 194, that the sovereignty of California was in the United States, in virtue of the Constitution, by which power had been given to Congress to dispose of and make all needful rules and regulations respecting the territory or other property belonging to the United States, with the power to admit new States into the Union. That decision followed preceding ones, there cited. The question was then presented, how it was possible for the judicial mind to conceive that the United States Government, created solely by the Constitution, could, by a lawful treaty, acquire territory over which the acquiring power had no jurisdiction

749

to hold and govern it, by force of the instrument under whose authority the country was acquired; and the foregoing was the conclusion of this court on the proposition. What was there announced, was most deliberately done, and with a purpose. The only question here is, as I think, how far the power of Congress is limited.

As to the Northwest Territory, Virginia had the right to abolish slavery there; and she did so agree in 1787, with the other States in the Congress of the Confederation, by assenting to and adopting the Ordinance of 1787, for the government of the Northwest Territory. She did this also by an Act of her Legislature, passed afterwards, which was a treaty in fact.

Before the new Constitution was adopted, she had as much right to treat and agree as any European government had. And, having excluded slavery, the new government was bound by that engagement by Article six of the new Constitution. This only meant that slavery should not exist whilst the United States exercised the power of government, in the territorial form; for, when a State came in, it might do so, with or without slavery.

My opinion is, that Congress had no power, in face of the compact between Virginia and the twelve other States to force slavery into the Northwest Territory, because there, it was bound to that "engagement," and could not break it.

524*] *In 1790, North Carolina ceded her western territory, now the State of Tennessee, and stipulated that the inhabitants thereof should enjoy all the privileges and advantages of the Ordinance for governing the territory north of the Ohio River, and that Congress should assume the government, and accept the cession, under the express conditions contained in the Ordinance: Provided, "That no regulation made, or to be made, by Congress, shall tend to emancipate slaves."

In 1802, Georgia ceded her western territory to the United States, with the provision that the Ordinance of 1787 should in all its parts extend to the territory ceded, "that article only excepted which forbids slavery." Congress had no more power to legislate slavery out from the North Carolina and Georgia cessions, than it had power to legislate slavery in, north of the Ohio. No power existed in Congress to legislate at all, affecting slavery, in either case. The inhabitants, as respected this description of property, stood protected, whilst they were governed by Congress, in like manner that they were protected before the cession was made and when they were respectively, parts of North Carolina and Georgia.

And how does the power of Congress stand west of the Mississippi River? The country there was acquired from France, by Treaty, in 1803. It declares, that the First Consul, in the name of the French Republic, doth hereby cede to the United States, in full sovereignty, the Colony or Province of Louisiana, with all the rights and appurtenances of the said Territory. And, by article 3d, that "the inhabitants of the ceded territory shall be incorporated in the Union of the United States, and admitted as soon as possible, according to the principles of the Federal Constitution, to the enjoyment of all the rights, advantages and immunities,

of citizens of the United States; and, in the mean time, they shall be maintained and protected in the free enjoyment of their liberty, property, and the religion which they profess."

Louisiana was a Province where slavery was not only lawful, but where property in slaves was the most valuable of all personal property. The Province was ceded as a unit, with an equal right pertaining to its inhabitants, in every part thereof, to own slaves. It was, to a great extent, a vacant country, having in it few civilized inhabitants. No one portion of the Colony, of a proper size for a State of the Union, had a sufficient number of inhabitants to claim admission into the Union. To enable the United States to fulfill the Treaty, additional population was indispensable, and obviously desired with anxiety by both sides, so that the whole country should, as soon as possible, become States of the Union. And for this *contemplated future population, the [*525 Treaty as expressly provided as it did for the inhabitants residing in the Province when the Treaty was made. All these were to be protected "in the mean time;" that is to say, at all times, between the date of the Treaty and the time when the portion of the Territory where the inhabitants resided was admitted into the Union as a State.

At the date of the Treaty, each inhabitant had the right to the free enjoyment of his property, alike with his liberty and his religion, in every part of Louisiana; the Province then being one country, he might go everywhere in it, and carry his liberty, property, and religion, with him, and in which he was to be maintained and protected, until he became a citizen of a State of the Union of the United States. This cannot be denied to the original inhabitants and their descendants. And, if it be true that immigrants were equally protected, it must follow that they can also stand on the Treaty.

The settled doctrine in the State courts of Louisiana is, that a French subject coming to the Orleans Territory, after the Treaty of 1803 was made, and before Louisiana was admitted into the Union, and being an inhabitant at the time of the admission, became a citizen of the United States by that Act; that he was one of the inhabitants contemplated by the 3d article of the Treaty, which referred to all the inhabitants embraced within the new State on its admission.

That this is the true construction, I have no doubt.

If power existed to draw a line at thirty-six degrees thirty minutes north, so Congress had equal power to draw the line on the thirtieth degree—that is, due west from the City of New Orleans—and to declare that north of that line slavery should never exist. Suppose this had been done before 1812, when Louisiana came into the Union, and the question of infraction of the Treaty had then been presented on the present assumption of power to prohibit slavery, who doubts what the decision of this court would have been on such an Act of Congress; yet, the difference between the supposed line, and that on thirty-six degrees thirty minutes north, is only in the degree of grossness presented by the lower line.

The Missouri compromise line of 1820 was very aggressive; it declared that slavery was abolished forever throughout a country reaching from the Mississippi River to the Pacific Ocean, stretching over thirty-two degrees of longitude, and twelve and a half degrees of latitude on its eastern side, sweeping over four fifths, to say no more, of the original Province of Louisiana.

That the United States Government stipulat- **526***] ed in favor of *the inhabitants to the extent here contended for has not been seriously denied, as far as I know; but the argument is, that Congress had authority to repeal the 3d article of the Treaty of 1803, in so far as it secured the right to hold slave property, in a portion of the ceded territory, leaving the right to exist in other parts. In other words, that Congress could repeal the 3d article entirely, at its pleasure. This I deny.

The compacts with North Carolina and Georgia were Treaties also, and stood on the same footing of the Louisiana Treaty; on the assumption of power to repeal the one, it must have extended to all, and Congress could have excluded the slaveholder of North Carolina from the enjoyment of his lands in the Territory, now the State, of Tennessee, where the citizens of the mother State were the principal proprietors.

And so in the case of Georgia. Her citizens could have been refused the right to emigrate to the Mississippi or Alabama Territory, unless they left their most valuable and cherished property behind them.

The Constitution was framed in reference to facts then existing or likely to arise: the instrument looked to no theories of government. In the vigorous debates in the Convention, as reported by Mr. Madison and others, surrounding facts, and the condition and necessities of the country, gave rise to almost every provision; and among those facts, it was prominently true, that Congress dare not be intrusted with power to provide that, if North Carolina or Georgia ceded her western territory, the citizens of the State (in either case) could be prohibited, at the pleasure of Congress, from removing to their lands, then granted to a large extent, in the country likely to be ceded, unless they left their slaves behind. That such an attempt, in the face of a population fresh from the war of the Revolution, and then engaged in war with the great confederacy of Indians, extending from the mouth of the Ohio to the Gulf of Mexico, would end in open revolt, all intelligent men knew.

In view of these facts, let us inquire how the question stands by the terms of the Constitution, aside from the Treaty. How it stood in public opinion when the Georgia cession was made, in 1802, is apparent from the fact that no guaranty was required by Georgia of the United States for the protection of slave property. The Federal Constitution was relied on, to secure the rights of Georgia and her citizens during the territorial condition of the country. She relied on the indisputable truths, that the States were by the Constitution made equals in political rights, and equals in the right to participate in the common property of all the States **527***] united, and held in trust for *them. The Constitution having provided that "The citizens of each State shall be entitled to all privileges and immunities of citizens of the several

States," the right to enjoy the territory as equals was reserved to the States, and to the citizens of the States, respectively. The cited clause is not that citizens of the United States shall have equal privileges in the Territories, but the citizen of each State shall come there in right of his State, and enjoy the common property. He secures his equality through the equality of his State, by virtue of that great fundamental condition of the Union—the equality of the States.

Congress cannot do indirectly what the Constitution prohibits directly. If the slaveholder is prohibited from going to the Territory with his slaves, who are parts of his family in name and in fact, it will follow that men owning lawful property in their own States, carrying with them the equality of their State to enjoy the common property, may be told, you cannot come here with your slaves, and he will be held out at the border. By this subterfuge, owners of slave property, to the amount of thousands of millions, might be almost as effectually excluded from removing into the Territory of Louisiana north of thirty-six degrees thirty minutes, as if the law declared that owners of slaves, as a class, should be excluded, even if their slaves were left behind.

Just as well might Congress have said to those of the North, you shall not introduce into the territory south of said line your cattle or horses, as the country is already overstocked; nor can you introduce your tools of trade, or machines as the policy of Congress is to encourage the culture of sugar and cotton, south of the line, and so to provide that the Northern people shall manufacture for those of the South, and barter for the staple articles slave labor produces. And thus the Northern farmer and mechanic would be held out, as the slaveholder was for thirty years, by the Missouri restriction.

If Congress could prohibit one species of property, lawful throughout Louisiana when it was acquired, and lawful in the State from whence it was brought, so Congress might exclude any or all property.

The case before us will illustrate the construction contended for. Dr. Emerson was a citizen of Missouri; he had an equal right to go to the Territory with every citizen of other States. This is undeniable, as I suppose. Scott was Dr. Emerson's lawful property in Missouri; he carried his Missouri title with him; and the precise question here is, whether Congress had the power to annul that title. It is idle to say, that if Congress could not defeat the title directly, that it might be done *in- [***528** directly, by drawing a narrow circle around the slave population of Upper Louisiana, and declaring that if the slave went beyond it he should be free. Such assumption is mere evasion, and entitled to no consideration. And it is equally idle, to contend that because Congress has express power to regulate commerce among the Indian tribes, and to prohibit intercourse with the Indians, that therefore Dr. Emerson's title might be defeated within the country ceded by the Indians to the United States as early as 1805, and which embraces Fort Snelling. Am. State Papers, Vol. I. p. 734. We must meet the question whether Congress had the power to declare that a citizen of a State, carrying with him his equal rights, secured to him through his State, could be stripped of his goods and slaves, and be deprived of any participation in the common property. If this be the true meaning of the Constitution, equality of rights to enjoy a common country (equal to a thousand miles square) may be cut off by a geographical line, and a great portion of our citizens excluded from it.

Ingenious, indirect evasions of the Constitution have been attempted and defeated heretofore. In the Passenger Cases, 7 How. 283, the attempt was made to impose a tax on the masters, crews and passengers of vessels, the Constitution having prohibited a tax on the vessel itself; but this court held the attempt to be a mere evasion, and pronounced the tax illegal.

I admit that Virginia could, and lawfully did, prohibit slavery northwest of the Ohio, by her charter of cession, and that the Territory was taken by the United States with this condition imposed. I also admit that France could, by the Treaty of 1803, have prohibited slavery in any part of the ceded Territory, and imposed it on the United States as a fundamental condition of the cession, in the mean time, till new States were admitted into the Union.

I concur with Judge Baldwin, that federal power is exercised over all the territory within the United States, pursuant to the Constitution; and the conditions of the cession, whether it was a part of the original territory of a State of the Union, or of a foreign state, ceded by deed or treaty, the right of the United States in or over it depends on the contract of cession, which operates to incorporate as well the territory as its inhabitants into the Union. Baldwin's Constitutional Views, 84.

My opinion is, that the 3d article of the Treaty of 1803, ceding Louisiana to the United States, stands protected by the Constitution, and cannot be repealed by Congress.

And, secondly, that the Act of 1820, known **529*]** as the Missouri *Compromise, violates the most leading feature of the Constitution—a feature on which the Union depends, and which secures to the respective States and their citizens an entire equality of rights, privileges and immunities.

On these grounds, I hold the Compromise Act to have been void; and consequently, that the plaintiff, Scott, can claim no benefit under it.

For the reasons above stated, I concur with my brother judges that the plaintiff, Scott, is a slave, and was so when this suit was brought.

Mr. Justice McLean, dissenting:

This case is before us on a writ of error from the Circuit Court for the District of Missouri.

An action of trespass was brought, which charges the defendant with an assault and imprisonment of the plaintiff, and also of Harriet Scott, his wife, Eliza and Lizzie, his two children, on the ground that they were his slaves, which was without right on his part, and against law.

The defendant filed a plea in abatement, "that said causes of action, and each and every of them, if any such accrued to the said Dred

Scott accrued out of the jurisdiction of this court, and exclusively within the jurisdiction of the courts of the State of Missouri, for that, to wit: said plaintiff, Dred Scott, is not a citizen of the State of Missouri, as alleged in his declaration, because he is a negro of African descent, his ancestors were of pure African blood; and were brought into this country and sold as negro slaves; and this the said Sandford is ready to verify; wherefore he prays judgment whether the court can or will take further cognizance of the action aforesaid."

To this a demurrer was filed, which, on argument, was sustained by the court, the plea in abatement being held insufficient; the defendant was ruled to plead over. Under this rule he pleaded: 1. Not guilty; 2. That Dred Scott was a negro slave, the property of the defendant; and 3. That Harriet, the wife, and Eliza and Lizzie, the daughters of the plaintiff, were the lawful slaves of the defendant.

Issue was joined on the first plea, and replications of de injuria were filed to the other pleas.

The parties agreed to the following facts: in the year 1834, the plaintiff was a negro slave belonging to Dr. Emerson, who was a surgeon in the Army of the United States. In that year, Dr. Emerson took the plaintiff from the State of Missouri to *the post of Rock Island **[*530** in the State of Illinois, and held him there as a slave until the month of April or May, 1836. At the time last mentioned, Dr. Emerson removed the plaintiff from Rock Island to the military post at Fort Snelling, situate on the west bank of the Mississippi River, in the Territory known as Upper Louisiana, acquired by the United States of France, and situate north of latitude thirty-six degrees thirty minutes north, and north of the State of Missouri. Dr. Emerson held the plaintiff in slavery, at Fort Snelling, from the last-mentioned date until the year 1838.

In the year 1835, Harriet, who is named in the second count of the plaintiff's declaration, was the negro slave of Major Taliaferro, who belonged to the Army of the United States. In that year, Major Taliaferro took Harriet to Fort Snelling, a military post situated as hereinbefore stated, and kept her there as a slave until the year 1836, and then sold and delivered her as a slave, at Fort Snelling, unto Dr. Emerson, who held her in slavery, at that place, until the year 1838.

In the year 1836, the plaintiff and Harriet were married at Fort Snelling, with the consent of Dr. Emerson, who claimed to be their master and owner. Eliza and Lizzie, named in the third count of the plaintiff's declaration, are the fruit of that marriage. Eliza is about fourteen years old, and was born on board the steamboat Gipsey, north of the north line of the State of Missouri, and upon the River Mississippi. Lizzie is about seven years old, and was born in the State of Missouri, at the military post called Jefferson Barracks.

In the year 1838, Dr. Emerson removed the plaintiff and said Harriet and their daughter Eliza from Fort Snelling to the State of Missouri, where they have ever since resided.

Before the commencement of the suit, Dr. Emerson sold and conveyed the plaintiff, Harriet, Eliza and Lizzie, to the defendant, as slaves, and he has ever since claimed to hold them as slaves.

At the times mentioned in the plaintiff's declaration, the defendant, claiming to be the owner, laid his hands upon said plaintiff, Harriet, Eliza and Lizzie, and imprisoned them; doing in this respect, however, no more than he might lawfully do, if they were of right his slaves at such times.

In the first place, the plea to the jurisdiction is not before us, on this writ of error. A demurrer to the plea was sustained, which ruled the plea bad, and the defendant, on leave, pleaded over.

The decision on the demurrer was in favor of the plaintiff; and as the plaintiff prosecutes this writ of error, he does not complain of the decision on the demurrer. The defendant 531*] *might have complained of this decision, as against him, and have prosecuted a writ of error, to reverse it. But as the case, under the instruction of the court to the jury, was decided in his favor, of course he had no ground of complaint.

But it is said, if the court, on looking at the record, shall clearly perceive that the Circuit Court had no jurisdiction, it is a ground for the dismissal of the case. This may be characterized as rather a sharp practice, and one which seldom, if ever, occurs. No case was cited in the argument as authority, and not a single case precisely in point is recollected in our reports. The pleadings do not show a want of jurisdiction. This want of jurisdiction can only be ascertained by a judgment on the demurrer to the special plea. No such case, it is believed, can be cited. But if this rule of practice is to be applied in this case, and the plaintiff in error is required to answer and maintain as well the points ruled in his favor, as to show the error of those ruled against him, he has more than an ordinary duty to perform. Under such circumstances, the want of jurisdiction in the Circuit Court must be so clear as not to admit of doubt. Now, the plea which raises the question of jurisdiction, in my judgment, is radically defective. The gravamen of the plea is this: "That the plaintiff is a negro of African descent, his ancestors being of pure African blood, and were brought into this country, and sold as negro slaves."

There is no averment in this plea which shows or conduces to show an inability in the plaintiff to sue in the Circuit Court. It does not allege that the plaintiff had his domicil in any other State, nor that he is not a free man in Missouri. He is averred to have had a negro ancestry, but this does not show that he is not a citizen of Missouri, within the meaning of the Act of Congress authorizing him to sue in the Circuit Court. It has never been held necessary, to constitute a citizen within the Act, that he should have the qualifications of an elector. Females and minors may sue in the Federal courts, and so may any individual who has a permanent domicil in the State under whose laws his rights are protected, and to which he owes allegiance.

Being born under our Constitution and laws, no naturalization is required, as one of foreign birth, to make him a citizen. The most general and appropriate definition of the term "citizen" is "a freeman." Being a freeman, and

having his domicil in a State different from that of the defendant, he is a citizen within the Act of Congress, and the courts of the Union are open to him.

It has often been held, that the jurisdiction, as regards parties, can only be exercised between citizens of different States, *and that [*532 a mere residence is not sufficient; but this has been said to distinguish a temporary from a permanent residence.

To constitute a good plea to the jurisdiction, it must negative those qualities and rights which enable an individual to sue in the Federal courts. This has not been done; and on this ground the plea was defective, and the demurrer was properly sustained. No implication can aid a plea in abatement or in bar; it must be complete in itself; the facts stated, if true, must abate or bar the right of the plaintiff to sue. This is not the character of the above plea. The facts stated, if admitted, are not inconsistent with other facts, which may be presumed, and which bring the plaintiff within the Act of Congress.

The pleader has not the boldness to allege that the plaintiff is a slave, as that would assume against him the matter in controversy, and embrace the entire merits of the case in a plea to the jurisdiction. But beyond the facts set out in the plea, the court, to sustain it, must assume the plaintiff to be a slave, which is decisive on the merits. This is a short and an effectual mode of deciding the cause; but I am yet to learn that it is sanctioned by any known rule of pleading.

The defendant's counsel complain, that if the court take jurisdiction on the ground that the plaintiff is free, the assumption is against the right of the master. This argument is easily answered. In the first place, the plea does not show him to be a slave; it does not follow that a man is not free whose ancestors were slaves. The reports of the Supreme Court of Missouri show that this assumption has many exceptions; and there is no averment in the plea that the plaintiff is not within them.

By all the rules of pleading, this is a fatal defect in the plea. If there be doubt, what rule of construction has been established in the slave States? In Jacob v. Sharp, Meigs' Tenn. 114, the court held, when there was doubt as to the construction of a will which emancipated a slave, "it must be construed to be subordinate to the higher and more important right of freedom."

No injustice can result to the master, from an exercise of jurisdiction in this cause. Such a decision does not in any degree affect the merits of the case; it only enables the plaintiff to assert his claims to freedom before this tribunal. If the jurisdiction be ruled against him, on the ground that he is a slave, it is decisive of his fate.

It has been argued that, if a colored person be made a citizen of a State, he cannot sue in the Federal court. The Constitution declares that federal jurisdiction "may be exercised between citizens of different States," and the same is provided *in the Act of 1789. The [*533 above argument is properly met, by saying that the Constitution was intended to be a practical instrument; and where its language is too plain to be misunderstood, the argument ends."

In Chirac v. Chirac, 2 Wheat. 261, 15 U. S., this court says: "That the power of naturalization is exclusively in Congress does not seem to be, and certainly ought not to be, controverted." No person can legally be made a citizen of a State, and consequently a citizen of the United States, of foreign birth, unless he be naturalized under the Acts of Congress. Congress has power "to establish a uniform rule of naturalization."

It is a power which belongs exclusively to Congress, as intimately connected with our federal relations. A State may authorize foreigners to hold real estate within its jurisdiction, but it has no power to naturalize foreigners, and give them the rights of citizens. Such a right is opposed to the Acts of Congress on the subject of naturalization, and subversive of the federal powers. I regret that any countenance should be given from this bench to a practice like this in some of the States, which has no warrant in the Constitution.

In the argument, it was said that a colored citizen would not be an agreeable member of society. This is more a matter of taste than of law. Several of the States have admitted persons of color to the right of suffrage, and in this view have recognized them as citizens; and this has been done in the slave as well as the free States. On the question of citizenship, it must be admitted that we have not been very fastidious. Under the late Treaty with Mexico, we have made citizens of all grades, combinations, and colors. The same was done in the admission of Louisiana and Florida. No one ever doubted, and no court ever held, that the people of these Territories did not become citizens under the Treaty. They have exercised all the rights of citizens, without being naturalized under the Acts of Congress.

There are several important principles involved in this case, which have been argued, and which may be considered under the following heads:

1. The locality of slavery, as settled by this court and the courts of the States.

2. The relation which the Federal Government bears to slavery in the States.

3. The power of Congress to establish territorial governments, and to prohibit the introduction of slavery therein.

4. The effect of taking slaves into a new State or Territory, and so holding them, where slavery is prohibited.

5. Whether the return of a slave under the 534*] control of his *master, after being entitled to his freedom, reduces him to his former condition.

6. Are the decisions of the Supreme Court of Missouri, on the questions before us, binding on this court, within the rule adopted?

In the course of my judicial duties, I have had occasion to consider and decide several of the above points.

1. As to the locality of slavery. The civil law throughout the Continent of Europe, it is believed, without an exception, is, that slavery can exist only within the territory where it is established; and that, if a slave escapes, or is carried beyond such territory, his master cannot reclaim him, unless by virtue of some express stipulations.

Grotius, lib. 2, chap. 15, 5, 1; lib. 10. chap. 10, 2, 1; Wicqueposts Ambassador, lib. 1, p.

754

418; 4 Martin, 385; case of The Creole in the House of Lords, 1842; 1 Phillimore on International Law, 316, 335.

There is no nation in Europe which considers itself bound to return to his master a fugitive slave, under the civil law or the law of nations. On the contrary, the slave is held to be free where there is no treaty obligation, or compact in some other form, to return him to his master. The Roman law did not allow freedom to be sold. An ambassador or any other public functionary could not take a slave to France, Spain, or any other country of Europe, without emancipating him. A number of slaves escaped from a Florida plantation, and were received on board of ship by Admiral Cochrane. By the King's Bench, they were held to be free. 2 B. & C. 440.

In the great and leading case of Prigg v. The State of Pennsylvania, 16 Pet. 594, 41 U. S., this court say that, by the general law of nations, no nation is bound to recognize the state of slavery, as found within its territorial dominions, where it is in opposition to its own policy and institutions, in favor of the subjects of other nations where slavery is organized. If it does it, it is as a matter of comity, and not as a matter of international right. The state of slavery is deemed to be a mere municipal regulation, founded upon and limited to the range of the territorial laws. This was fully recognized in Somersett's case, Lafft's Rep. 1, 20 Howell's State Trials, 79, which was decided before the American Revolution.

There was some contrariety of opinion among the judges on certain points ruled in Prigg's case, but there was none in regard to the great principle, that slavery is limited to the range of the laws under which it is sanctioned.

No case in England appears to have been more thoroughly examined than that of Somersett. The judgment pronounced *by [*535 Lord Mansfield was the judgment of the Court of King's Bench. The cause was argued at great length, and with great ability, by Hargrave and others, who stood among the most eminent counsel in England. It was held under advisement from term to term, and a due sense of its importance was felt and expressed by the Bench.

In giving the opinion of the court, Lord Mansfield said:

"The state of slavery is of such a nature that it is incapable of being introduced on any reasons, moral or political, but only by positive law, which preserves its force long after the reasons, occasion, and time itself, from whence it was created, is erased from the memory; it is of a nature that nothing can be suffered to support it but positive law."

He referred to the contrary opinion of Lord Hardwicke, in October, 1749, as Chancellor: "That he and Lord Talbot, when Attorney and Solicitor-General, were of opinion that no such claim, as here presented, for freedom, was valid."

The weight of this decision is sought to be impaired, from the terms in which it was described by the exuberant imagination of Curran. The words of Lord Mansfield, in giving the opinion of the court, were such as were fit to be used by a great judge, in a most important case. It is a sufficient answer to all objections to that judgment, that it was pronounced before the Revolution, and that it was considered by this court as the highest authority. For near a century, the decision in Somersett's case has remained the law of England. The case of The Slave Grace, decided by Lord Stowell in 1827, does not, as has been supposed, overrule the judgment of Lord Mansfield. Lord Stowell held that, during the residence of the slave in England, "No dominion, authority, or coercion, can be exercised over him." Under another head, I shall have occasion to examine the opinion in the case of Grace.

To the position, that slavery can only exist except under the authority of law, it is objected, that in few if in any instances has it been established by statutory enactment. This is no answer to the doctrine laid down by the court. Almost all the principles of the common law had their foundation in usage. Slavery was introduced into the Colonies of this country by Great Britain at an early period of their history, and it was protected and cherished, until it became incorporated into the colonial policy. It is immaterial whether a system of slavery was introduced by express law, or otherwise, if it have the authority of law. There is no slave state where the institution is not recognized and protected by statutory enactments and judicial decisions. Slaves are made property by the laws of the slave States, and as such are liable to the claims of creditors; *they descend to heirs, are taxed, **536*] and in the South they are a subject of commerce.

In the case of Rankin v. Lydia, 2 A. K. Marsh, 467, Judge Mills, speaking for the Court of Appeals of Kentucky, says: "In deciding the question (of slavery), we disclaim the influence of the general principles of liberty, which we all admire, and conceive it ought to be decided by the law as it is, and not as it ought to be. Slavery is sanctioned by the laws of this State, and the right to hold slaves under our municipay regulations is unquestionable. But we view this as a right existing by positive law of a municipal character, without foundation in the law of nature, or the unwritten and common law."

I will now consider the relation which the Federal Government bears to slavery in the States:

Slavery is emphatically a state institution. In the 9th section of the 1st article of the Constitution, it is provided "that the migration or importation of such persons as any of the States now existing shall think proper to admit, shall not be prohibited by the Congress prior to the year 1808, but a tax or duty may be imposed on such importation, not exceeding ten dollars for each person."

In the Convention, it was proposed by a committee of eleven to limit the importation of slaves to the year 1800, when Mr. Pinckney moved to extend the time to the year 1808. This motion was carried—New Hampshire, Massachusetts, Connecticut, Maryland, North Carolina, South Carolina and Georgia voting in the affirmative; and New Jersey, Pennsylvania and Virginia, in the negative. In opposition to the motion, Mr. Madison said: "Twenty years will produce all the mischief that can be apprehended from the liberty to import slaves; so long a term will be more dishonorable to the

American character than to say nothing about it in the Constitution." Madison Papers.

The provision in regard to the slave trade shows clearly that Congress considered slavery a state institution, to be continued and regulated by its individual sovereignty; and to conciliate that interest, the slave trade was continued twenty years, not as a general measure, but for the "benefit of such States as shall think proper to encourage it."

In the case of Groves v. Slaughter, 15 Pet. 449, 40 U. S. Messrs. Clay and Webster contended that, under the commercial power, Congress had a right to regulate the slave trade among the several States, but the court held that Congress had no power to-interfere with slavery as it exists in the States, or to regulate what is called the slave trade among *them. If this trade were subject to [*537 the commercial power, it would follow that Congress could abolish or establish slavery in every State of the Union.

The only connection which the Federal Government holds with slaves in a State, arises from that provision of the Constitution which declares that "No person held to service in one State, under the laws thereof, escaping into another, shall, in consequence of any law or regulation therein, be discharged from such service or labor, but shall be delivered up, on claim of the party to whom such service or labor may be due."

This being a fundamental law of the Federal Government, it rests mainly for its execution, as has been held, on the judicial power of the Union; and so far as the rendition of fugitives from labor has become a subject of judicial action, the federal obligation has been faithfully discharged.

In the formation of the Federal Constitution, care was taken to confer no power on the Federal Government, to interfere with this institution in the States. In the provision respecting the slave trade, in fixing the ratio of representation, and providing for the reclamation of fugitives from labor, slaves were referred to as persons, and in no other respect are they considered in the Constitution.

We need not refer to the mercenary spirit which introduced the infamous traffic in slaves, to show the degradation of negro slavery in our country. This system was imposed upon our colonial settlements by the mother country, and it is due to truth to say that the commercial Colonies and States were chiefly engaged in the traffic. But we know as a historical fact, that James Madison, that great and good man, a leading member in the Federal Convention, was solicitous to guard the language of that instrument so as not to convey the idea that there could be property in man.

I prefer the lights of Madison, Hamilton, and Jay, as a means of construing the Constitution in all its bearings, rather than to look behind that period, into a traffic which is now declared to be piracy, and punished with death by Christian nations. I do not like to draw the sources of our domestic relations from so dark a ground. Our independence was a great epoch in the history of freedom; and while I admit the government was not made especially for the colored race, yet many of them were citizens of the New England States, and exercised the rights of suffrage when the Constitution was adopted, and it was not doubted by any intelligent person that its tendencies would greatly ameliorate their condition.

Many of the States, on the adoption of the 538*] Constitution, or *shortly afterward, took measures to abolish slavery within their respective jurisdictions; and it is a well-known fact that a belief was cherished by the leading men, South as well as North, that the institution of slavery would gradually decline, until it would become extinct. The increased value of slave labor, in the culture of cotton and sugar, prevented the realization of this expectation. Like all other communities and states, the South were influenced by what they considered to be their own interests.

But if we are to turn our attention to the dark ages of the world, why confine our view to colored slavery? On the same principles white men were made slaves. All slavery has its origin in power, and is against right.

The power of Congress to establish territorial governments, and to prohibit the introduction of slavery therein, is the next point to be considered.

After the cession of western territory by Virginia and other States, to the United States, the public attention was directed to the best mode of disposing of it for the general benefit.

While in attendance on the Federal Convention, Mr. Madison, in a letter to Edmund Randolph, dated the 22d April, 1787, says: "Congress are deliberating on the plan most eligible for disposing of the western territory not yet surveyed. Some alteration will probably be made in the ordinance on that subject." And in the same letter he says: "The inhabitants of the Illinois complain of the land jobbers, etc., who are purchasing titles among them. Those of St. Vincent's complain of the defective criminal and civil justice among them, as well as of military protection." And on the next day he writes to Mr. Jefferson: "The government of the settlements on the Illinois and Wabash is a subject very perplexing in itself, and rendered more so by our ignorance of the many circumstances on which a right judgment depends. The inhabitants at those places claim protection against the savages, and some provision for both civil and criminal justice."

In May, 1787, Mr. Edmund Randolph submitted to the Federal Convention certain propositions, as the basis of a Federal Government, among which was the following:

"Resolved, that provision ought to be made for the admission of States lawfully arising within the limits of the United States, whether from a voluntary junction of government and territory or otherwise, with the consent of a number of voices in the National Legislature less than the whole."

Afterward, Mr. Madison submitted to the Convention, in order to be referred to the committee of detail, the following powers, as proper to be added to those of general legislation: 539*] *"To dispose of the unappropriated lands of the United States. To institute temporary governments for new States arising therein. To regulate affairs with the Indians, as well within as without the limits of the United States."

756

Other propositions were made in reference to the same subjects, which it would be tedious to enumerate. Mr. Gouverneur Morris proposed the following:

"The Legislature shall have power to dispose of and make all needful rules and regulations respecting the territory or other property belonging to the United States; and nothing in this Constitution contained shall be so construed as to prejudice any claims either of the United States or of any particular State."

This was adopted as a part of the Constitution, with two verbal alterations—Congress was substituted for Legislature, and the word "either" was stricken out.

In the organization of the new government, but little revenue for a series of years was expected from commerce. The public lands were considered as the principal resource of the country for the payment of the Revolutionary debt. Direct taxation was the means relied on to pay the current expenses of the government. The short period that occurred between the cession of western lands to the Federal Government by Virginia and other States, and the adoption of the Constitution, was sufficient to show the necessity of a proper land system and a temporary government. This was clearly seen by propositions and remarks in the Federal Convention, some of which are above cited, by the passage of the Ordinance of 1787, and the adoption of that instrument by Congress, under the Constitution, which gave to it validity.

It will be recollected that the deed of cession of western territory was made to the United States by Virginia in 1784, and that it required the territory ceded to be laid out into States, that the land should be disposed of for the common benefit of the States, and that all right, title, and claim, as well of soil as of jurisdiction, were ceded; and this was the form of cession from other States.

On the 13th of July, the Ordinance of 1787 was passed, "for the government of the United States territory northwest of the River Ohio," with but one dissenting vote. This instrument provided there should be organized in the territory not less than three, nor more than five, States, designating their boundaries. It was passed while the Federal Convention was in session, about two months before the Constitution was adopted by the Convention. The members of the Convention must, therefore, have been well acquainted with the provisions of the *Ordinance. It provided for a [*540 temporary government, as initiatory to the formation of state governments. Slavery was prohibited in the territory.

Can anyone suppose that the eminent men of the Federal Convention could have overlooked or neglected a matter so vitally important to the country, in the organization of temporary governments for the vast territory northwest of the River Ohio? In the 3d section of the 4th article of the Constitution, they did make provision for the admission of new States, the sale of the public lands, and the temporary government of the territory. Without a temporary government, new States could not have been formed, nor could the public lands have been sold.

If the 3d section were before us now for consideration for the first time, under the facts stated, I could not hesitate to say there was adequate legislative power given in it. The power to make all needful rules and regulations is a power to legislate. This no one will controvert, as Congress cannot make "rules and regulations," except by legislation. But it is argued that the word "territory" is used as synonymous with the word "land"; and that the rules and regulations of Congress are limited to the disposition of lands and other property belonging to the United States. That this is not the true construction of the section, appears from the fact that in the first line of the section "the power to dispose of the public lands" is given expressly, and, in addition, to make all needful rules and regulations. The power to dispose of it is complete in itself, and requires nothing more. It authorizes Congress to use the proper means within its discretion, and any further provision for this purpose would be a useless verbiage. As a composition, the Constitution is remarkably free from such a charge.

In the discussion of the power of Congress to govern a territory, in the case of The Atlantic Insurance Company v. Canter, 1 Pet. 511; 7 Curt. 685, Chief Justice Marshall, speaking for the court, said, in regard to the people of Florida, "they do not, however, participate in political power; they do not share in the government till Florida shall become a state; in the mean time, Florida continues to be a territory of the United States, governed by virtue of that clause in the Constitution which empowers Congress 'to make all needful rules and regulations respecting the territory or other property belonging to the United States.'"

And he adds, "perhaps the power of governing a territory belonging to the United States, which has not, by becoming a state, acquired the means of self-government, may result 541*] *necessarily from the fact that it is not within the jurisdiction of any particular State, and is within the power and jurisdiction of the United States. The right to govern may be the inevitable consequence of the right to acquire territory; whichever may be the source whence the power is derived, the possession of it is unquestioned." And in the close of the opinion, the court say, "in legislating for them [the territories], Congress exercises the combined powers of the general and state governments."

Some consider the opinion to be loose and inconclusive; others that it is obiter dicta; and the last sentence is objected to as recognizing absolute power in Congress over Territories. The learned and eloquent Wirt, who, in the argument of a cause before the court, had occasion to cite a few sentences from an opinion of the Chief Justice, observed, "no one can mistake the style, the words so completely match the thought."

I can see no want of precision in the language of the Chief Justice; his meaning cannot be mistaken. He states, first, the 3d section as giving power to Congress to govern the territories, and two other grounds from which the power may also be implied. The objection seems to be, that the Chief Justice did not say which of the grounds stated he considered the source of the power. He did not specifically state this, but he did say, "whichever may be the source whence the power is derived, the

15 L. ed.

possession of it is unquestioned." No opinion of the court could have been expressed with a stronger emphasis; the power in Congress is unquestioned. But those who have undertaken to criticise the opinion, consider it without authority, because the Chief Justice did not designate specially the power. This is a singular objection. If the power be unquestioned, it can be a matter of no importance on which ground it is exercised.

The opinion clearly was not obiter dicta. The turning point in the case was, whether Congress had power to authorize the Territorial Legislature of Florida to pass the law under which the Territorial Court was established, whose decree was brought before this court for revision. The power of Congress, therefore, was the point in issue.

The word "territory," according to Worcester means "land, country, a district of country, under a temporary government." The words "territory or other property," as used, do imply, from the use of the pronoun other, that territory was used as descriptive of land; but does it follow that it was not used also as descriptive of a district of country? In both of these senses it belonged to the United States —as land, for the purpose of sale; as territory, for the purpose of government.

*But, if it be admitted that the word [*542 "territory" as used means land, and nothing but land, the power of Congress to organize a temporary government is clear. It has power to make all needful regulations respecting the public lands, and the extent of those "needful regulations" depends upon the direction of Congress, where the means are appropriate to the end, and do not conflict with any of the prohibitions of the Constitution. If a temporary government be deemed needful, necessary, requisite, or is wanted, Congress has power to establish it. This court says, in McCulloch v. The State of Maryland, 4 Wheat. 316, "If a certain means to carry into effect any of the powers expressly given by the Constitution to the government of the Union be an appropriate measure, not prohibited by the Constitution, the degree of its necessity is a question of legislative discretion, not of judicial cognizance."

The power to establish postoffices and postroads gives power to Congress to make contracts for the transportation of the mail, and to punish all who commit depredations upon it in its transit, or at its places of distribution. Congress has power to regulate commerce, and, in the exercise of its discretion, to lay an embargo, which suspends commerce; so under the same power, harbors, lighthouses, breakwaters, etc., are constructed.

Did Chief Justice Marshall, in saying that Congress governed a Territory, by exercising the combined powers of the federal and state governments, refer to unlimited discretion? A government which can make white men slaves? Surely, such a remark in the argument must have been inadvertently uttered. On the contrary, there is no power in the Constitution by which Congress can make either white or black men slaves. In organizing the government of a territory, Congress is limited to means appropriate to the attainment of the constitutional object. No powers can be exercised which are prohibited by the Constitution, or which are contrary to its spirit; so that, whether the object may be the protection of the persons and property of purchasers of the public lands, or of communities who have been annexed to the Union by conquest or purchase, they are initiatory to the establishment of state governments, and no more power can be claimed or exercised, than is necessary to the attainment of the end. This is the limitation of all the federal powers.

But Congress has no power to regulate the internal concerns of a State, as of a Territory; consequently, in providing for the government of a Territory, to some extent, the combined powers of the federal and state governments are necessarily exercised.

543*]   *If Congress should deem slaves or free colored persons injurious to the population of a free Territory, as conducing to lessen the value of the public lands, or on any other ground connected with the public interest, they have the power to prohibit them from becoming settlers in it. This can be sustained on the ground of a sound national policy, which is so clearly shown in our history by practical results, that it would seem no considerate individual can question it. And, as regards any unfairness of such a policy to our Southern brethren, as urged in the argument, it is only necessary to say that, with one fourth of the federal population of the Union, they have in the slave States a larger extent of fertile territory than is included in the free States; and it is submitted, if masters of slaves be restricted from bringing them into free territory, that the restriction on the free citizens of non-slaveholding States, by bringing slaves into free territory, is four times greater than that complained of by the South. But, not only so; some three or four hundred thousand holders of slaves, by bringing them into free territory, impose a restriction on twenty millions of the free States. The repugnancy to slavery would probably prevent fifty or a hundred freemen from settling in a slave Territory, where one slaveholder would be prevented from settling in a free Territory.

This remark is made in answer to the argument urged, that a prohibition of slavery in the free Territories is inconsistent with the continuance of the Union. Where a territorial government is established in a slave Territory, it has uniformly remained in that condition until the people form a State constitution; the same course where the Territory is free, both parties acting in good faith, would be attended with satisfactory results.

The sovereignty of the Federal Government extends to the entire limits of our territory. Should any foreign power invade our jurisdiction, it would be repelled. There is a law of Congress to punish our citizens for crimes committed in districts of country where there is no organized government. Criminals are brought to certain Territories or States, designated in the law, for punishment. Death has been inflicted in Arkansas and in Missouri, on individuals, for murders committed beyond the limit of any organized Territory or State; and no one doubts that such a jurisdiction was rightfully exercised. If there be a right to acquire territory, there necessarily must be an implied power to govern it. When the military force of the Union shall conquer a country, may not Congress provide for the government

of such country? This would be an implied power essential to the acquisition of new territory. *This power has been exercised, [*544 without doubt of its constitutionality on territory acquired by conquest and purchase.

And when there is a large district of country within the United States, and not within any state government, if it be necessary to establish a temporary government to carry out a power expressly vested in Congress—as the disposition of the public lands—may not such government be instituted by Congress? How do we read the Constitution? Is it not a practical instrument?

In such cases, no implication of a power can arise which is inhibited by the Constitution, or which may be against the theory of its construction. As my opinion rests on the 3d section, these remarks are made as an intimation that the power to establish a temporary government may arise, also, on the other two grounds stated in the opinion of the court in the insurance case, without weakening the 3d section.

I would here simply remark, that the Constitution was formed for our whole country. An expansion or contraction of our territory required no change in the fundamental law. When we consider the men who laid the foundation of our government and carried it into operation, the men who occupied the Bench, who filled the halls of legislation and the Chief Magistracy, it would seem, if any question could be settled clear of all doubt, it was the power of Congress to establish territorial governments. Slavery was prohibited in the entire Northwestern Territory, with the approbation of leading men, South and North; but this prohibition was not retained when this Ordinance was adopted for the government of southern Territories, where slavery existed. In a late republication of a letter of Mr. Madison, dated November 27, 1819, speaking of this power of Congress to prohibit slavery in a Territory, he infers there is no such power, from the fact that it has not been exercised. This is not a very satisfactory argument against any power, as there are but few, if any, subjects on which the constitutional powers of Congress are exhausted. It is true, as Mr. Madison states, that Congress, in the Act to establish a government in the Mississippi Territory, prohibited the importation of slaves into it from foreign parts; but it is equally true, that in the Act erecting Louisiana into two Territories, Congress declared, "it shall not be lawful for any person to bring into Orleans Territory, from any port or place within the limits of the United States, any slave which shall have been imported since 1798, or which may hereafter be imported, except by a citizen of the United States who settles in the Territory, under the penalty of the freedom of such slave." The inference of Mr. Madison, therefore, against the power of *Congress, is of no force, as it was [*545 founded on a fact supposed, which did not exist.

It is refreshing to turn to the early incidents of our history, and learn wisdom from the acts of the great men who have gone to their account. I refer to a report in the House of Representatives, by John Randolph, of Roanoke, as chairman of a committee, in March, 1803— fifty-four years ago. From the Convention held at Vincennes, in Indiana, by their president, and from the people of the Territory, a petition was presented to Congress, praying the suspension of the provision which prohibited slavery in that Territory. The report stated "that the rapid population of the State of Ohio sufficiently evinces, in the opinion of your committee, that the labor of slaves is not necessary to promote the growth and settlement of colonies in that region. That this labor, demonstrably the dearest of any, can only be employed to advantage in the cultivation of products more valuable than any known to that quarter of the United States; that the committee deem it highly dangerous and inexpedient to impair a provision wisely calculated to promote the happiness and prosperity of the Northwestern country, and to give strength and security to that extensive frontier. In the salutary operation of this sagacious and benevolent restraint, it is believed that the inhabitants will, at no very distant day, find ample remuneration for a temporary privation of labor and of emigration. 1 vol. State Papers, Public Lands, 160.

The judicial mind of this country, State and Federal, has agreed on no subject, within its legitimate action, with equal unanimity, as on the power of Congress to establish territorial governments. No court, State or Federal, no judge or statesman, is known to have had any doubts on this question for nearly sixty years after the power was exercised. Such governments have been established from the sources of the Ohio to the Gulf of Mexico, extending to the Lakes on the north and the Pacific Ocean on the west, and from the lines of Georgia to Texas.

Great interests have grown up under the territorial laws over a country more than five times greater in extent than the original thirteen States; and these interests, corporate or otherwise, have been cherished and consolidated by a benign policy, without anyone supposing the law-making power had united with the judiciary, under the universal sanction of the whole country, to usurp a jurisdiction which did not belong to them. Such a discovery at this late date is more extraordinary than anything which has occurred in the judicial history of this or any other country. Texas, under a previous or- 546*] ganization, *was admitted as a State; but no State can be admitted into the Union which has not been organized under some form of government. Without temporary governments, our public lands could not have been sold, nor our wilderness reduced to cultivation, and the population protected; nor could our flourishing States, west and south, have been formed.

What do the lessons of wisdom and experience teach, under such circumstances, if the new light, which has so suddenly and unexpectedly burst upon us, be true? Acquiescence; acquiescence under a settled construction of the Constitution for sixty years, though it may be erroneous; which has secured to the country an advancement and prosperity beyond the power of computation.

An act of James Madison, when President, forcibly illustrates this policy. He had made up his opinion that Congress had no power under the Constitution to establish a National Bank. In 1815, Congress passed a bill to estab-

15 L. ed.

lish a bank. He vetoed the bill, on objections other than constitutional. In his message, he speaks as a wise statesman and Chief Magistrate, as follows:

"Waiving the question of the constitutional authority of the Legislature to establish an incorporated bank, as being precluded, in my judgment, by the repeated recognitions under varied circumstances of the validity of such an institution, in acts of the Legislature, Executive, and Judicial branches of the Government, accompanied by indications, in different modes, of a concurrence of the general will of the nation."

Has this impressive lesson of practical wisdom become lost to the present generation?

If the great and fundamental principles of our Government are never to be settled, there can be no lasting prosperity. The Constitution will become a floating waif on the billows of popular excitement.

The prohibition of slavery north of thirty-six degrees thirty minutes, and of the State of Missouri, contained in the Act admitting that State into the Union, was passed by a vote of 134, in the House of Representatives, to 42. Before Mr. Monroe signed the Act, it was submitted by him to his Cabinet, and they held the restriction of slavery in a Territory to be within the constitutional powers of Congress. It would be singular, if in 1804 Congress had power to prohibit the introduction of slaves in Orleans Territory from any other part of the Union, under the penalty of freedom to the slave, if the same power embodied in the Missouri Compromise, could not be exercised in 1820.

But this law of Congress, which prohibits slavery north of *Missouri and of thirty- [*547 six degrees thirty minutes, is declared to have been null and void by my brethren. And this opinion is founded mainly, as I understand, on the distinction drawn between the Ordinance of 1787 and the Missouri compromise line. In what does the distinction consist? The Ordinance, it is said, was a compact entered into by the confederated States before the adoption of the Constitution; and that in the cession of territory, authority was given to establish a territorial government.

It is clear that the Ordinance did not go into operation by virtue of the authority of the Confederation, but by reason of its modification and adoption by Congress under the Constitution. It seems to be supposed, in the opinion of the court, that the articles of cession placed it on a different footing from Territories subsequently acquired. I am unable to perceive the force of this distinction. That the Ordinance was intended for the government of the Northwestern Territory, and was limited to such Territory, is admitted. It was extended to southern Territories, with modifications, by Acts of Congress, and to some northern Territories. But the Ordinance was made valid by the Act of Congress, and without such Act could have been of no force. It rested for its validity on the Act of Congress, the same, in my opinion, as the Missouri compromise line.

If Congress may establish a territorial government in the exercise of its discretion, it is a clear principle that a court cannot control that discretion. This being the case, I do not see on what ground the Act is held to be void.

It did not purport to forfeit property, or take it for public purposes. It only prohibited slavery; in doing which, it followed the Ordinance of 1787.

I will now consider the fourth head, which is: "The effect of taking slaves into a State or Territory, and so holding them, where slavery is prohibited.

If the principle laid down in the case of Prigg v. The State of Pennsylvania is to be maintained, and it is certainly to be maintained until overruled, as the law of this court, there can be no difficulty on this point. In that case, the court says: "The state of slavery is deemed to be a mere municipal regulation, founded upon and limited to the range of the territorial laws." If this be so, slavery can exist nowhere except under the authority of law, founded on usage having the force of law, or by statutory recognition. And the court further says: "It is manifest, from this consideration, that if the Constitution had not contained the clause requiring the rendition of fugitives from labor, every non-slaveholding State in the Union would have been at liberty to have 548*] declared free all runaway slaves *coming within its limits, and to have given them entire immunity and protection against the claims of their masters."

Now, if a slave abscond, he may be reclaimed, but if he accompany his master into a State or Territory where slavery is prohibited, such slave cannot be said to have left the service of his master where his services were legalized. And if slavery be limited to the range of the territorial laws, how can the slave be coerced to serve in a State or Territory, not only without the authority of law, but against its express provisions? What gives the master the right to control the will of his slave? The local law, which exists in some form. But where there is no such law, can the master control the will of the slave by force? Where no slavery exists, the presumption, without regard to color, is in favor of freedom. Under such a jurisdiction, may the colored man be levied on as the property of his master by a creditor? On the decease of the master, does the slave descend to his heirs as property? Can he sell him? Any one or all of these acts may be done to the slave, where he is legally held to service. But where the law does not confer this power, it cannot be exercised.

Lord Mansfield held that a slave brought into England was free. Lord Stowell agreed with Lord Mansfield in this respect, and that the slave could not be coerced in England; but on her voluntary return to Antigua, the place of her slave domicil, her former status attached. The law of England did not prohibit slavery, but did not authorize it. The jurisdiction which prohibits slavery is much stronger in behalf of the slave within it, than where it only does not authorize it.

By virtue of what law is it, that a master may take his slave into free territory, and exact from him the duties of a slave? The law of the territory does not sanction it. No authority can be claimed under the Constitution of the United States, or any law of Congress. Will it be said that the slave is taken as property, the same as other property which the master may own? To this I answer, that colored persons are made property by the law of

the State, and no such power has been given to Congress. Does the master carry with him the law of the State from which he removes into the Territory? And does that enable him to coerce his slave in the Territory? Let us test this theory. If this may be done by a master from one slave State, it may be done by a master from every other slave State. This right is supposed to be connected with the person of the master, by virtue of the local law. Is it transferable? May it be negotiated, as a promissory note or bill of exchange? If it be assigned to a man from a free State, may he coerce the slave by virtue of it? What shall this thing be *denominated? Is it per-   [*549 sonal or real property? Or is it an indefinable fragment of sovereignty, which every person carries with him from his late domicil? One thing is certain, that its origin has been very recent, and it is unknown to the laws of any civilized country.

A slave is brought to England from one of its islands, where slavery was introduced and maintained by the mother country. Although there is no law prohibiting slavery in England, yet there is no law authorizing it; and, for near a century, its courts have declared that the slave there is free from the coercion of the master. Lords Mansfield and Stowell agree upon this point, and there is no dissenting authority.

There is no other description of property which was not protected in England, brought from one of its slave islands. Does not this show that property in a human being does not arise from nature or from the common law, but, in the language of this court, "it is a mere municipal regulation, founded upon and limited to the range of the territorial laws?" This decision is not a mere argument, but it is the end of the law, in regard to the extent of slavery. Until it shall be overturned, it is not a point for argument; it is obligatory on myself and my brethren, and on all judicial tribunals over which this court exercises an appellate power.

It is said the Territories are common property of the States, and that every man has a right to go there with his property. This is not controverted. But the court say a slave is not property beyond the operation of the local law which makes him such. Never was a truth more authoritatively and justly uttered by man. Suppose a master of a slave in a British island owned a million of property in England; would that authorize him to take his slaves with him to England? The Constitution, in express terms, recognizes the status of slavery as founded on the municipal law. "No person held to service or labor in one State, under the laws thereof, escaping into another, shall," etc. Now, unless the fugitive escape from a place where, by the municipal law, he is held to labor, this provision affords no remedy to the master. What can be more conclusive than this? Suppose a slave escape from a Territory where slavery is not authorized by law, can he be reclaimed?

In this case, a majority of the court have said that a slave may be taken by his master into a Territory of the United States, the same as a horse, or any other kind of property. It is true, this was said by the court, as also many other things, which are of no authority. Nothing that has been said by them, which has not a direct bearing on the jurisdiction of the court, against which they decided, can be considered 550*] as *authority. I shall certainly not regard it as such. The question of jurisdiction, being before the court, was decided by them authoritatively, but nothing beyond that question. A slave is not a mere chattel. He bears the impress of his Maker, and is amenable to the laws of God and man; and he is destined to an endless existence.

Under this head I shall chiefly rely on the decisions of the Supreme Courts of the Southern States, and especially of the State of Missouri.

In the 1st and 2d sections of the 6th article of the Constitution of Illinois, it is declared that neither slavery nor involuntary servitude shall hereafter be introduced into this State, otherwise than for the punishment of crimes whereof the party shall have been duly convicted; and in the 2d section it is declared that any violation of this article shall effect the emancipation of such person from his obligation to service. In Illinois, a right of transit through the State is given the master with his slaves. This is a matter which, as I suppose, belongs exclusively to the State.

The Supreme Court of Illinois, in the case of Jarrot v. Jarrot, 2 Gilman, 7, said:

"After the conquest of this Territory by Virginia, she ceded it to the United States, and stipulated that the titles and possessions, rights and liberties of the French settlers, should be guarantied to them. This, it has been contended, secured them in the possession of those negroes as slaves which they held before that time, and that neither Congress nor the Convention had power to deprive them of it; or, in other words, that the Ordinance and Constitution should not be so interpreted and understood as applying to such slaves, when it is therein declared that there shall be neither slavery nor involuntary servitude in the Northwest Territory, nor in the State of Illionis, otherwise than in the punishment of crimes. But it was held that those rights could not be thus protected, but must yield to the Ordinance and Constitution.

The first slave case decided by the Supreme Court of Missouri, contained in the reports, was Winny v. Whitesides, 1 Mo. 473, at October Term, 1824. It appeared that, more than twenty-five years before, the defendant, with her husband, had removed from Carolina to Illinois, and brought with them the plaintiff; that they continued to reside in Illinois three or four years, retaining the plaintiff as a slave; after which, they removed to Missouri, taking her with them.

The court held, that if a slave be detained in Illinois until he be entitled to freedom, the right of the owner does not revive when he finds the negro in a slave State.
551*] *That when a slave is taken to Illinois by his owner, who takes up his residence there, the slave is entitled to freedom.

In the case of Lagrange v. Chouteau, 2 Mo. 20, at May Term, 1828, it was decided that the Ordinance of 1787 was intended as a fundamental law for those who may choose to live under it, rather than as a penal statute.

That any sort of residence contrived or permitted by the legal owner of the slave, upon the

faith of secret trusts or contracts, in order to defeat or evade the Ordinance, and thereby introduce slavery de facto, would entitle such slave to freedom.

In Julia v. McKinney, 3 Mo. 270, it was held, where a slave was settled in the State of Illinois, but with an intention on the part of the owner to be removed at some future day, that hiring said slave to a person to labor for one or two days, and receiving the pay for the hire, the slave is entitled to her freedom, under the 2d section of the 6th article of the Constitution of Illinois.

Rachel v. Walker, 4 Mo. 350, June Term, 1836, is a case involving, in every particular, the principles of the case before us. Rachel sued for her freedom; and it appeared that she had been bought as a slave in Missouri, by Stockton an officer of the army, taken to Fort Snelling, where he was stationed, and she was retained there as a slave a year; and then Stockton removed to Prairie du Chien, taking Rachel with him as a slave, where he continued to hold her three years, and then he took her to the State of Missouri, and sold her as a slave.

"Fort Snelling was admitted to be on the west side of the Mississippi River, and north of the State of Missouri, in the territory of the United States. That Prairie du Chien was in the Michigan Territory, on the east side of the Mississippi River. Walker, the defendant, held Rachel under Stockton."

The court said, in this case:

"The officer lived in Missouri Territory, at the time he bought the slave; he sent to a slaveholding country and procured her; this was his voluntary act, done without any other reason than that of his convenience; and he and those claiming under him must be holden to abide the consequences of introducing slavery both in Missouri Territory and Michigan, contrary to law; and on that ground Rachel was declared to be entitled to freedom."

In answer to the argument that, as an officer of the army, the master had a right to take his slave into free territory, the court said no authority of law or the government compelled him to keep the plaintiff there as a slave.

"Shall it be said, that because an officer of the army owns *slaves in Virginia, that [*552 when, as officer and soldier, he is required to take the command of a fort in the non-slaveholding States or Territories, he thereby has a right to take with him as many slaves as will suit his interests or convenience? It surely cannot be law. If this be true, the court say, then it is also true that the convenience or supposed convenience of the officer repeals, as to him and others who have the same character, the Ordinance and the Act of 1821, admitting Missouri into the Union, and also the prohibition of the several laws and constitutions of the nonslaveholding States.

In Wilson v. Melvin, 4 Mo. 592, it appeared the defendant left Tennessee with an intention of residing in Illinois, taking his negroes with him. After a month's stay in Illinois, he took his negroes to St. Louis, and hired them, then returned to Illinois. On these facts, the inferior court instructed the jury that the defendant was a sojourner in Illinois. This the Supreme Court held was error, and the judgment was reversed.

The case of Dred Scott v. Emerson, 15 Mo.

576, March Term, 1852, will now be stated. This case involved the identical question before us, Emerson having, since the hearing, sold the plaintiff to Sandford, the defendant.

Two of the judges ruled the case, the Chief Justice dissenting. It cannot be improper to state the grounds of the opinion of the court, and of the dissent.

The court says: "Cases of this kind are not strangers in our court. Persons have been frequently here adjudged to be entitled to their freedom, on the ground that their masters held them in slavery in Territories or States in which that institution is prohibited. From the first case decided in our court, it might be inferred that this result was brought about by a presumed assent of the master, from the fact of having voluntarily taken his slave to a place where the relation of master and slave did not exist. But subsequent cases base the right to 'exact the forfeiture of emancipation,' as they term it, on the ground, it would seem, that it was the duty of the courts of this State to carry into effect the constitution and laws of other States and Territories, regardless of the rights, the policy, or the institutions, of the people of this State."

And the court say that the States of the Union, in their municipal concerns, are regarded as foreign to each other; that the courts of one State do not take notice of the laws of other States, unless proved as facts, and that every State has the right to determine how far its comity to other States shall extend; and it is laid down, that when there is no act of manumission decreed to the free State, the courts of 553*] the slave States *cannot be called to give effect to the law of the free State. Comity, it alleges, between States, depends upon the discretion of both, which may be varied by circumstances. And it is declared by the court, "that times are not as they were when the former decisions on this subject were made." Since then, not only individuals but States have been possessed with a dark and fell spirit in relation to slavery, whose gratification is sought in the pursuit of measures whose inevitable consequence must be the overthrow and destruction of our government. Under such circumstances, it does not behoove the State of Missouri to show the least countenance to any measure which might gratify this spirit. She is willing to assume her full responsibility for the existence of slavery within her limits, nor does she seek to share or divide it with others.

Chief Justice Gamble dissented from the other two judges. He says:

"In every slaveholding State in the Union, the subject of emancipation is regulated by statute; and the forms are prescribed in which it shall be effected. Whenever the forms required by the laws of the State in which the master and slave are resident are complied with, the emancipation is complete, and the slave is free. If the right of the person thus emancipated is subsequently drawn in question in another State, it will be ascertained and determined by the law of the State in which the slave and his former master resided; and when it appears that such law has been complied with, the right to freedom will be fully sustained in the courts of all the slaveholding States, although the act of emancipation may

762

not be in the form required by law in which the court sits.

In all such cases, courts continually administer the law of the country where the right was acquired; and when that law becomes known to the court, it is just as much a matter of course to decide the rights of the parties according to its requirements, as it is to settle the title of real estate situated in our State by its own laws."

This appears to me a most satisfactory answer to the argument of the court. Chief Justice continues:

"The perfect equality of the different States lies at the foundation of the Union. As the institution of slavery in the States is one over which the Constitution of the United States gives no power to the general government, it is left to be adopted or rejected by the several States, as they think best; nor can any one State, or number of States, claim the right to interfere with any other State upon the question of admitting or excluding this institution.

"A citizen of Missouri, who removes with his slave to Illinois, *has no right to com- [*554 plain that the fundamental law of that State to which he removes, and in which he makes his residence, dissolves the relation between him and his slave. It is as much his own voluntary act, as if he had executed a deed of emancipation. No one can pretend ignorance of this constitutional provision, and," he says, "the decisions which have heretofore been made in this State, and in many other slaveholding States, give effect to this and other similar provisions, on the ground that the master, by making the free State the residence of his slave, has submitted his right to the operation of the law of such State; and this," he says, "is the same in law as a regular deed of emancipation."

He adds:

"I regard the question as conclusively settled by repeated adjudications of this court, and, if I doubted or denied the propriety of those decisions, I would not feel myself any more at liberty to overturn them, than I would any other series of decisions by which the law of any other question was settled. There is with me," he says, "nothing in the law relating to slavery which distinguishes it from the law on any other subject, or allows any more accommodation to the temporary public excitements which are gathered around it."

"In this State," he says, "it has been recognized from the beginning of the government as a correct position in law, that a master who takes his slave to reside in a State or Territory where slavery is prohibited, thereby emancipates his slave." These decisions, which come down to the year 1837, seemed to have so fully settled the question, that since that time there has been no case bringing it before the court for any reconsideration, until the present. In the case of Winny v. Whitesides, 1 Mo. 473, the question was made in the argument, "whether one nation would execute the penal laws of another," and the court replied in this language (Huberus, quoted in 4 Dallas), which says, "personal rights or disabilities obtained or communicated by the laws of any particular place are of a nature which accompany the person wherever he goes;" and the Chief Justice observed, in the case of Rachel v. Walker, 4 Mo. 350, the Act of Congress called the Missouri

Compromise was held as operative as the Ordinance of 1787.

When Dred Scott, his wife and children, were removed from Fort Snelling to Missouri, in 1838, they were free as the law was then settled, and continued for fourteen years afterwards, up to 1852, when the above decision was made. Prior to this, for nearly thirty years, as Chief Justice Gamble declares, the residence of a master with his slave in the State of Illinois, or the Territory north of Missouri, 555*] where slavery was prohibited *by the Act called the Missouri Compromise, would manumit the slave as effectually as if he had executed a deed of emancipation; and that an officer of the army who takes his slave into that State or Territory, and holds him there as a slave, liberates him the same as any other citizen—and down to the above time it was settled by numerous and uniform decisions; and that on the return of the slave to Missouri, his former condition of slavery did not attach. Such was the settled law of Missouri until the decision of Scott v. Emerson.

In the case of Sylvia v. Kirby, 17 Mo. 434, the court followed the above decision, observing that it was similar in all respects to the case of Scott v. Emerson.

This court follows the established construction of the statutes of a State by its Supreme Court. Such a construction is considered as a part of the Statute, and we follow it to avoid two rules of property in the same State. But we do not follow the decisions of the Supreme Court of a State beyond a statutory construction as a rule of decision for this court. State decisions are always viewed with respect and treated as authority; but we follow the settled construction of the statutes, not because it is of binding authority, but in pursuance of a rule of judicial policy.

But there is no pretense that the case of Dred Scott v. Emerson turned upon the construction of a Missouri Statute; nor was there any established rule of property which could have rightfully influenced in the decision. On the contrary, the decision overruled the settled law for nearly thirty years.

This is said by my brethren to be a Missouri question; but there is nothing which gives it this character, except that it involves the right to persons claimed as slaves who reside in Missouri, and the decision was made by the Supreme Court of that State. It involves a right claimed under an Act of Congress and the Constitution of Illinois, and which cannot be decided without the consideration and construction of those laws. But the Supreme Court of Missouri held, in this case, that it will not regard either of those laws, without which there was no case before it; and Dred Scott, having been a slave, remains a slave. In this respect it is admitted this is a Missouri question—a case which has but one side, if the Act of Congress and the Constitution of Illinois are not recognized.

And does such a case constitute a rule of decision for this court—a case to be followed by this court? The course of decision so long and so uniformly maintained established a comity or law between Missouri and the free States and Territories where slavery was prohibited, which must be somewhat regarded in this case. Rights sanctioned for twenty-eight

years *ought not and cannot be repudia- [*556 ated, with any semblance of justice, by one or two decisions, influenced, as declared, by a determination to counteract the excitement against slavery in the free States.

The courts of Louisiana having held, for a series of years, that where a master took his slave to France, or any free state, he was entitled to freedom, and that on bringing him back the status of slavery did not attach, the Legislature of Louisiana declared by an Act that the slave should not be made free under such circumstances. This regulated the rights of the master from the time the Act took effect. But the decision of the Missouri court, reversing a former decision, affects all previous decisions, technically, made on the same principles, unless such decisions are protected by the lapse of time or the Statute of Limitations. Dred Scott and his family, beyond all controversy, were free under the decisions made for twenty-eight years, before the case of Scott v. Emerson. This was the undoubted law of Missouri for fourteen years after Scott and his family were brought back to that State. And the grave question arises, whether this law may be so disregarded as to enslave free persons. I am strongly inclined to think that a rule of decision so well settled as not to be questioned, cannot be annulled by a single decision of the court. Such rights may be inoperatives under the decision in future; but I cannot well perceive how it can have the same effect in prior cases.

It is admitted, that when a former decision is reversed, the technical effect of the judgment is to make all previous adjudications on the same question erroneous. But the case before us was not that the law had been erroneously construed, but that, under the circumstances which then existed, that law would not be recognized; and the reason for this is declared to be the excitement against the institution of slavery in the free States. While I lament this excitement as much as anyone, I cannot assent that it shall be made a basis for judicial action.

In 1816, the common law, by statute, was made a part of the law of Missouri; and that includes the great principles of international law. These principles cannot be abrogated by judicial decisions. It will require the same exercise of power to abolish the common law, as to introduce it. International law is founded in the opinions generally received and acted on by civilized nations, and enforced by moral sanctions. It becomes a more authoritative system when it results from special compacts, founded on modified rules, adapted to the exigencies of human society; it is in fact an international morality, adapted to the best interests of nations. And in regard to the States *of this Union, on the subject [*557 of slavery, it is eminently fitted for a rule of action, subject to the Federal Constitution. "The laws of nations are but the natural rights of man applied to nations." Vattel.

If the common law have the force of a statutory enactment in Missouri, it is clear, as it seems to me, that a slave who, by a residence in Illinois in the service of his master, becomes entitled to his freedom, cannot again be reduced to slavery by returning to his former domicil in a slave State. It is unnecessary to say what legislative power might do by a general Act in such a case, but it would be singular if a freeman could be made a slave by the exercise of a judicial discretion. And it would be still more extraordinary if this could be done, not only in the absence of special legislation, but in a State where the common law is in force.

It is supposed by some that the 3d article in the Treaty of Cession of Louisiana to this country, by France, in 1803, may have some bearing on this question. The article referred to provides "that the inhabitants of the ceded Territory shall be incorporated into the Union, and enjoy all the advantages of citizens of the United States, and in the mean time they shall be maintained and protected in the free enjoyment of their liberty, property, and the religion they profess."

As slavery existed in Louisiana at the time of the cession, it is supposed this is a guaranty that there should be no change in its condition.

The answer to this is, in the first place, that such a subject does not belong to the treaty-making power; and any such arrangement would have been nugatory. And, in the second place, by no admissible construction can the guaranty be carried further than the protection of property in slaves at that time in the ceded Territory. And this has been complied with. The organization of the slave States of Louisiana, Missouri and Arkansas, embraced every slave in Louisiana at the time of the cession. This removes every ground of objection under the Treaty. There is, therefore, no pretense, growing out of the Treaty, that any part of the Territory of Louisiana, as ceded, beyond the organized States, is slave territory.

Under the fifth head, we were to consider whether the status of slavery attached to the plaintiff and wife on their return to Missouri.

This doctrine is not asserted in the late opinion of the Supreme Court of Missouri, and up to 1852 the contrary doctrine was uniformly maintained by that court.

In its late decision, the court say that it will not give effect in Missouri to the laws of Illi-558*] nois, or the law of Congress *called the Missouri Compromise. This was the effect of the decision, though its terms were, that the court would not take notice, judicially, of those laws.

In 1851, the Court of Appeals of South Carolina recognized the principle, that a slave, being taken to a free State, became free. Commonwealth v. Pleasant, 10 Leigh, 697. In Betty v. Horton, the Court of Appeals held that the freedom of the slave was acquired by the action of the laws of Massachusetts, by the said slave being taken there. 5 Leigh, 615.

The slave States have generally adopted the rule, that where the master, by a residence with his slave in a State or Territory where slavery is prohibited, the slave was entitled to his freedom everywhere. This was the settled doctrine of the Supreme Court of Missouri. It has been so held in Mississippi, in Virginia, in Louisiana, formerly in Kentucky, Maryland, and in other States.

The law, where a contract is made and is to be executed, governs it. This does not depend upon comity, but upon the law of the contract. And if, in the language of the Supreme Court

764

of Missouri, the master, by taking his slave to Illinois, and employing him there as a slave, emancipates him as effectually as by a deed of emancipation, is it possible that such an act is not matter for adjudication in any slave State where the master may take him? Does not the master assent to the law when he places himself under it in a free State?

The States of Missouri and Illinois are bounded by a common line. The one prohibits slavery, the other admits it. This has been done by the exercise of that sovereign power which appertains to each. We are bound to respect the institutions of each, as emanating from the voluntary action of the people. Have the people of either any right to disturb the relations of the other? Each State rests upon the basis of its own sovereignty, protected by the Constitution. Our Union has been the foundation of our prosperity and national glory. Shall we not cherish and maintain it? This can only be done by respecting the legal rights of each State.

If a citizen of a free State shall entice or enable a slave to escape from the service of his master, the law holds him responsible, not only for the loss of the slave, but he is liable to be indicted and fined for the misdemeanor. And I am bound here to say that I have never found a jury in the four States which constitute my circuit, which have not sustained this law, where the evidence required them to sustain it. And it is proper that I should also say that more cases have arisen in my circuit by reason of its extent and locality, than in all *other parts of the Union. This has [*559 been done to vindicate the sovereign rights of the Southern States, and protect the legal interests of our brethren of the South.

Let these facts be contrasted with the case now before the court. Illinois has declared in the most solemn and impressive form that there shall be neither slavery nor involuntary servitude in that State, and that any slave brought into it, with a view of becoming a resident, shall be emancipated. And effect has been given to this provision of the Constitution by the decision of the Supreme Court of that State. With a full knowledge of these facts, a slave is brought from Missouri to Rock Island, in the State of Illinois, and is retained there as a slave for two years, and then taken to Fort Snelling, where slavery is prohibited by the Missouri Compromise Act, and there he is detained two years longer in a state of slavery. Harriet, his wife, was also kept at the same place four years as a slave, having been purchased in Missouri. They were then removed to the State of Missouri, and sold as slaves, and in the action before us they are not only claimed as slaves, but a majority of my brethren have held that on their being returned to Missouri the status of slavery attached to them.

I am not able to reconcile this result with the respect due to the State of Illinois. Having the same rights of sovereignty as the State of Missouri in adopting a constitution, I can perceive no reason why the institutions of Illinois should not receive the same consideration as those of Missouri. Allowing to my brethren the same right of judgment that I exercise myself, I must be permitted to say that it seems to me the principle laid down will enable the people of a slave State to introduce slavery into a free State, for a longer or shorter time, as may suit their convenience; and by returning the slave to the State whence he was brought, by force or otherwise, the status of slavery attaches, and protects the rights of the master, and defies the sovereignty of the free State. There is no evidence before us that Dred Scott and his family returned to Missouri voluntarily. The contrary is inferable from the agreed case: "In the year 1838, Dr. Emerson removed the plaintiff and said Harriet, and their daughter Eliza, from Fort Snelling to the State of Missouri, where they have ever since resided." This is the agreed case; and can it be inferred from this that Scott and family returned to Missouri voluntarily? He was removed; which shows that he was passive, as a slave, having exercised no volition on the subject. He did not resist the master by absconding or force. But that was not sufficient to bring him within Lord Stowell's decision; he must have acted **560*]** voluntarily. It would be a *mockery of law and an outrage on his rights to coerce his return, and then claim that it was voluntary, and on that ground that his former status of slavery attached.

If the decision be placed on this ground, it is a fact for a jury to decide, whether the return was voluntary, or else the fact should be distinctly admitted. A presumption against the plaintiff in this respect, I say with confidence, is not authorized from the facts admitted.

In coming to the conclusion that a voluntary return by Grace to her former domicil, slavery attached, Lord Stowell took great pains to show that England forced slavery upon her Colonies, and that it was maintained by numerous Acts of Parliament and public policy, and, in short, that the system of slavery was not only established by Great Britain in her West Indian colonies, but that it was popular and profitable to many of the wealthy and influential people of England, who were engaged in trade, or owned and cultivated plantations in the Colonies. No one can read his elaborate views and not be struck with the great difference between England and her Colonies, and the free and slave States of this Union. While slavery in the Colonies of England is subject to the power of the mother country, our States, especially in regard to slavery, are independent, resting upon their own sovereignties, and subject only to international laws, which apply to independent States.

In the case of Williams, who was a slave in Granada, having run away, came to England, Lord Stowell said: "The four judges all concur in this—that he was a slave in Granada, though a free man in England, and he would have continued a free man in all other parts of the world except Granada."

Strader v. Graham, 10 How. 82, and 18 Curt. 305, has been cited as having a direct bearing in the case before us. In that case the court say: "It was exclusively in the power of Kentucky to determine, for itself, whether the employment of slaves in another State should or should not make them free on their return." No question was before the court in that case, except that of jurisdiction. And any opinion given on any other point is obiter dictum, and

15 L. ed.

of no authority. In the conclusion of his opinion, the Chief Justice said: "In every view of the subject, therefore, this court has no jurisdiction of the case, and the writ of error must on that ground be dismissed."

In the case of Spencer v. Negro Dennis, 8 Gill, 321, the court say: "Once free, and always free, is the maxim of Maryland law upon the subject. Freedom having once vested, by no compact between the master and the liberated slave, *nor by any condition subsequent, at- [***561** tached by the master to the gift of freedom, can a state of slavery be reproduced."

In Hunter v Fulcher, 1 Leigh, 172.

"By a Statute of Maryland of 1796, all slaves brought into that State to reside are declared free; a Virginian-born slave is carried by his master to Maryland; the master settled there, and keeps the slave there in bondage for twelve years, the statute in force all the time; then he brings him as a slave to Virginia, and sells him there. Adjudged, in an action brought by the man against the purchaser, that he is free."

Judge Kerr, in the case, says:

"Agreeing, as I do, with the general view taken in this case by my brother Green, I would not add a word, but to mark the exact extent to which I mean to go. The law of Maryland having enacted that slaves carried into that State for sale or to reside shall be free, and the owner of the slave here having carried him to Maryland, and voluntarily submitting himself and the slave to that law, it governs the case."

In every decision of a slave case prior to that of Dred Scott v. Emerson, the Supreme Court of Missouri considered it as turning upon the Constitution of Illinois, the Ordinance of 1787, or the Missouri Compromise Act of 1820. The court treated these Acts as in force, and held itself bound to execute them, by declaring the slave to be free who had acquired a domicil under them with the consent of his matser.

The late decision reversed this whole line of adjudication, and held that neither the Constitution and laws of the States, nor Acts of Congress in relation to Territories, could be judicially noticed by the Supreme Court of Missouri. This is believed to be in conflict with the decisions of all the courts in the Southern States, with some exceptions of recent cases.

In Marie Louise v. Marot et al. 9 La. 475, it was held, where a slave having been taken to the kingdom of France or other country by the owner, where slavery is not tolerated, operates on the condition of the slave, and produces immediate emancipation; and that, where a slave thus becomes free, the master cannot reduce him again to slavery.

Josephine v. Poultney, 1 La. Ann. 329, "where the owner removes with a slave into a State in which slavery is prohibited, with the intention of residing there, the slave will be thereby emancipated, and their subsequent return to the State of Louisiana cannot restore the relation of master and slave." To the same import are the cases of Smith v. Smith, 13 La. 441; Thomas v. Generis, 16 La. 483; Harry et al. v. Decker and Hopkins, Walk. (Miss.) 36. It was held that "slaves within the jurisdiction *of [***562** the Northwestern Territory became freemen by virtue of the Ordinance of 1787, and can assert their claim to freedom in the courts of Mississippi." Griffith v. Fanny, 1 Virginia, 143. It was decided that a negro held in servitude in Ohio, under a deed executed in Virginia is entitled to freedom by the Constitution of Ohio.

The case of Rhodes v. Bell, 2 How. 397, involved the main principle in the case before us. A person residing in Washington City purchased a slave in Alexandria, and brought him to Washington. Washington continued under the law of Maryland, Alexandria under the law of Virginia. The Act of Maryland of November, 1796, 2 Maxcy's Laws, 351, declared anyone who shall bring any negro, mulatto, or other slave, into Maryland, such slave should be free. The above slave, by reason of his being brought into Washington City, was declared by this court to be free. This, it appears to me, is a much stronger case against the slave than the facts in the case of Scott.

In Bush v. White, 3 Monroe, 104, the court say:

"That the Ordinance was paramount to the territorial laws, and restrained the legislative power there as effectually as a Constitution in an organized State. It was a public Act of the Legislature of the Union, and a part of the supreme law of the land; and, as such, this court is as much bound to take notice of it as it can be of any other law."

In the case of Rankin v. Lydia, 2 A. K. Marsh. 467, before cited, Judge Mills, speaking for the Court of Appeals of Kentucky, says:

"If, by the positive provision in our code, we can and must hold our slaves in the one case, and statutory provisions equally positive decide against that right in the other, and liberate the slave, he must, by an authority equally imperious, be declared free. Every argument which supports the right of the master on one side, based upon the force of written law, must be equally conclusive in favor of the slave, when he can point out in the statute the clause which secures his freedom."

And he further said:

"Free people of color in all the States are, it is believed, quasi citizens, or, at least, denizens. Although none of the States may allow them the privilege of office and suffrage, yet all other civil and conventional rights are secured to them; at least, such rights were evidently secured to them by the Ordinance in question for the government of Indiana. If these rights are vested in that or any other portion of the United States, can it be compatible with the spirit of our confederated government to deny their existence in any other part? Is there less comity existing between State and State, or 563*] State *and Territory, than exists between the despotic governments of Europe."

These are the words of a learned and great judge, born and educated in a slave State.

I now come to inquire, under the sixth and last head, "whether the decisions of the Supreme Court of Missouri, on the question before us, are binding on this court."

While we respect the learning and high intelligence of the state courts, and consider their decisions, with others, as authority, we follow them only where they give a construction to the state statutes. On this head, I consider myself fortunate in being able to turn to the decision of this court, given by Mr. Justice Grier, in Pease v. Peck, a case from the State

766

of Michigan, 18 How. 595, decided in December Term, 1855. Speaking for the court, Judge Grier said:

"We entertain the highest respect for that learned court (the Supreme Court of Michigan), and in any question affecting the construction of their own laws, where we entertain any doubt, would be glad to be relieved from doubt and responsibility by reposing on their decision. There are, it is true, many dicta to be found in our decisions, averring that the courts of the United States are bound to follow the decisions of the state courts on the construction of their own laws. But although this may be correct, yet a rather strong expression of a general rule, it cannot be received as the annunciation of a maxim of universal application. Accordingly, our reports furnish many cases of exceptions to it. In all cases where there is a settled construction of the laws of a State, by its highest judicature established by admitted precedent, it is the practice of the courts of the United States to receive and adopt it, without criticism or further inquiry. When the decisions of the State court are not consistent, we do not feel bound to follow the last, if it is contrary to our own convictions; and much more is this the case where, after a long course of consistent decisions, some new light suddenly springs up, or an excited public opinion has elicited new doctrines subversive of former safe precedent."

These words, it appears to me, have a stronger application to the case before us than they had to the cause in which they were spoken as the opinion of this court; and I regret that they do not seem to be as fresh in the recollection of some of my brethren as in my own. For twenty-eight years, the decisions of the Supreme Court of Missouri were consistent on all the points made in this case. But this consistent course was suddenly terminated, whether by some new light suddenly springing up, or an excited public opinion, or both, it is not *necessary to say. In the case of Scott [*564 v. Emerson, in 1852, they were overturned and repudiated.

This, then, is the very case in which seven of my brethren declared that they would not follow the last decision. On this authority I may well repose. I can desire no other or better basis.

But there is another ground which I deem conclusive, and which I will restate.

The Supreme Court of Missouri refused to notice the Act of Congress or the Constitution of Illinois, under which Dred Scott, his wife and children, claimed that they are entitled to freedom.

This being rejected by the Missouri court, there was no case before it, or at least it was a case with only one side. And this is the case which, in the opinion of this court, we are bound to follow. The Missouri court disregards the express provisions of an Act of Congress and the constitution of a sovereign State, both of which laws for twenty-eight years it had not only regarded, but carried into effect.

If a State court may do this, on a question involving the liberty of a human being, what protection do the laws afford? So far from this being a Missouri question, it is a question, as it would seem, within the 25th sec. of the Judiciary Act, where a right to freedom being

1856.   DRED SCOTT V. SANDFORD.   393–633

set up under the Act of Congress, and the decision being against such right, it may be brought for revision before this court, from the Supreme Court of Missouri.

I think the judgment of the court below should be reversed.

Mr. Justice Curtis, dissenting:

I dissent from the opinion pronounced by the Chief Justice, and from the judgment which the majority of the court think it proper to render in this case. The plaintiff alleged in his declaration, that he was a citizen of the State of Missouri, and that the defendant was a citizen of the State of New York. It is not doubted that it was necessary to make each of these allegations, to sustain the jurisdiction of the Circuit Court. The defendant denied, by a plea to the jurisdiction, either sufficient or insufficient, that the plaintiff was a citizen of the State of Missouri. The plaintiff demurred to that plea. The Circuit Court adjudged the plea insufficient, and the first question for our consideration is, whether the sufficiency of that plea is before this court for judgment, upon this writ of error. The part of the judicial power of the United States, conferred by Congress on the circuit courts, being limited to certain described cases and controversies, the 565*] question whether a particular *case is within the cognizance of a circuit court, may be raised by a plea to the jurisdiction of such court. When that question has been raised, the Circuit Court must, in the first instance, pass upon and determine it. Whether its determination be final, or subject to review by this appellate court, must depend upon the will of Congress; upon which body the Constitution has conferred the power, with certain restrictions, to establish inferior courts to determine their jurisdiction, and to regulate the appellate power of this court. The 22d section of the Judiciary Act of 1789, which allows a writ of error from final judgments of circuit courts, provides that there shall be no reversal in this court, on such writ of error, for error in ruling any plea in abatement, other than a plea to the jurisdiction of the court. Accordingly it has been held, from the origin of the court to the present day, that circuit courts have not been made by Congress the final judges of their own jurisdiction in civil cases. And that when a record comes here upon a writ of error or appeal, and, on its inspection, it appears to this court that the Circuit Court had not jurisdiction, its judgment must be reversed, and the cause remanded, to be dismissed for want of jurisdiction.

It is alleged by the defendant in error, in this case, that the plea to the jurisdiction was a sufficient plea; that it shows, on inspection of its allegations, confessed by the demurrer, that the plaintiff was not a citizen of the State of Missouri; that upon this record, it must appear to this court that the case was not within the judicial power of the United States, as defined and granted by the Constitution, because it was not a suit by a citizen of one State against a citizen of another State.

To this it is answered, first, that the defendant, by pleading over, after the plea to the jurisdiction was adjudged insufficient, finally waived all benefit of that plea.

15 L. ed.

When that plea was adjudged insufficient, the defendant was obliged to answer over. He held no alternative. He could not stop the further progress of the case in the Circuit Court by a writ of error, on which the sufficiency of his plea to the jurisdiction could be tried in this court, because the judgment on that plea was not final, and no writ of error would lie. He was forced to plead to the merits. It cannot be true, then, that he waived the benefit of his plea to the jurisdiction by answering over. Waiver includes consent. Here, there was no consent. And if the benefit of the plea was finally lost, it must be, not by any waiver, but because the laws of the United States have not provided any mode of reviewing the decision of the Circuit Court on such a plea, when that decision is against the defendant. This is not the *law. Whether [*566 the decision of the Circuit Court on a plea to the jurisdiction be against the plaintiff, or against the defendant, the losing party may have any alleged error in law, in ruling such a plea examined in this court on a writ of error, when the matter in controversy exceeds the sum or value of $2,000. If the decision be against the plaintiff, and his suit dismissed for want of jurisdiction, the judgment is technically final, and he may at once sue out his writ of error.

Mollan v. Torrance, 9 Wheat. 537.

If the decision be against the defendant, though he must answer over, and wait for a final judgment in the cause, he may then have have his writ of error, and upon it obtain the judment of this court on any question of law apparent on the record, touching the jurisdiction. The fact that he pleaded over to the merits, under compulsion, can have no effect on his right to object to the jurisdiction. If this were not so, the condition of the two parties would be grossly unequal. For if a plea to the jurisdiction were ruled against the plaintiff, he could at once take his writ of error and have the ruling reviewed here; while, if the same plea were ruled against the defendant, he must not only wait for a final judgment, but could in no event have the ruling of the Circuit Court upon the plea reviewed by this court. I know of no ground for saying that the laws of the United States have thus discriminated between the parties to a suit in its courts.

It is further objected, that as the judgment of the Circuit Court was in favor of the defendant, and the writ of error in this cause was sued out by the plaintiff, the defendant is not in a condition to assign any error in the record, and therefore this court is precluded from considering the question whether the Circuit Court had jurisdiction.

The practice of this court does not require a technical assignment of errors. See the rule. Upon a writ of error, the whole record is open for inspection; and if any error be found in it, the judgment is reversed.

Bank of U. S. v. Smith, 11 Wheat. 171.

It is true, as a general rule, that the court will not allow a party to rely on anything as cause for reversing a judgment, which was for his advantage. In this, we follow an ancient rule of the common law. But so careful was that law of the preservation of the course of its courts, that it made an exception out of that general rule, and allowed a party to assign for error that which was for his advantage, if it were a departure by the court itself from its settled course of procedure. The cases on this subject are collected in Bac. Abr. Error, H. 4. And this court followed this practice in Capron **567*]** v. Van Noorden, 2 *Cranch, 126, where the plaintiff below procured the reversal of a judgment for the defendant, on the ground that the plaintiff's allegations of citizenship had not shown jurisdiction.

But it is not necessary to determine whether the defendant can be allowed to assign want of jurisdiction as an error in a judgment in his own favor. The true question is, not what either of the parties may be allowed to do, but whether this court will affirm or reverse a judgment of the Circuit Court on the merits, when it appears on the record, by a plea to the jurisdiction, that it is a case to which the judicial power of the United States does not extend. The course of the court is, where no motion is made by either party, on its own motion, to reverse such a judgment for want of jurisdiction, not only in cases where it is shown, negatively, by a plea to the jurisdiction, that jurisdiction does not exist, but even where it does not appear, affirmatively, that it does exist. Piquignot v. The Pennsylvania R. R. Co. 16 How. 104. It acts upon the principle that the judicial power of the United States must not be exerted in a case to which it does not extend, even if both parties desire to have it exerted. Cutler v. Rae, 7 How. 729. I consider, therefore, that when there was a plea to the jurisdiction of the Circuit Court in a case brought here by a writ of error, the first duty of this court is, sua sponte, if not moved to it by either party, to examine the sufficiency of that plea; and thus to take care that neither the Circuit Court nor this court shall use the judicial power of the United States in a case to which the Constitution and laws of the United States have not extended that power.

I proceed, therefore, to examine the plea to the jurisdiction.

I do not perceive any sound reason why it is not to be judged by the rules of the common law applicable to such pleas. It is true, where the jurisdiction of the Circuit Court depends on the citizenship of the parties, it is incumbent on the plaintiff to allege on the record the necessary citizenship; but when he has done so, the defendant must interpose a plea in abatement, the allegations whereof show that the court has not jurisdiction; and it is incumbent on him to prove the truth of his plea.

In Sheppard v. Graves, 14 How. 505, the rules on this subject are thus stated in the opinion of the court: "That although, in the courts of the United States, it is necessary to set forth the grounds of their cognizance as courts of limited jurisdiction, yet wherever jurisdiction shall be averred in the pleadings, in conformity with the laws creating those courts, it must be taken prima facie, as existing; and **568*]** it is incumbent *on him who would impeach that jurisdiction for causes dehors the pleading, to allege and prove such causes; that the necessity for the allegation, and the burden of sustaining it by proof, both rest upon the party taking the exception." These positions are sustained by the authorities there cited, as well as by Wickliffe v. Owings, 17 How. 47.

When, therefore, as in this case, the necessary averments as to citizenship are made on the record, and jurisdiction is assumed to exist, and the defendant comes by a plea to the jurisdiction to displace that presumption, he occupies, in my judgment, precisely the position described in Bacon Abr. Abatement: "Abatement, on the general acceptation of the word, signifies a plea, put in by the defendant, in which he shows cause to the court why he should not be impleaded; or, if at all, not in the manner and form he now is."

This being, then, a plea in abatement, to the jurisdiction of the court, I must judge of its sufficiency by those rules of the common law applicable to such pleas.

The plea was as follows: "And the said John F. A. Sandford, in his own proper person, comes and says that this court ought not to have or take further cognizance of the action aforesaid, because he says that said cause of action, and each and every of them (if any such have accrued to the said Dred Scott), accrued to the said Dred Scott out of the jurisdiction of this court, and exclusively within the jurisdiction of the courts of the State of Missouri; for that, to wit: the said plaintiff, Dred Scott, is not a citizen of the State of Missouri, as alleged in his declaration, because he is a negro of African descent; his ancestors were of pure African blood, and were brought into this country and sold as negro slaves; and this the said Sandford is ready to verify. Wherefore, he prays judgment whether this court can or will take further cognizance of the action aforesaid."

The plaintiff demurred, and the judgment of the Circuit Court was, that the plea was insufficient.

I cannot treat this plea as a general traverse of the citizenship alleged by the plaintiff. Indeed, if it were so treated, the plea was clearly bad, for it concludes with a verification, and not to the country, as a general traverse should. And though this defect in a plea in bar must be pointed out by a special demurrer, it is never necessary to demur specially to a plea in abatement; all matters, though of form only, may be taken advantage of upon a general demurrer to such a plea. Chitty on Pl. 465.

The truth is, that though not drawn with the utmost technical accuracy, it is a special traverse of the plaintiff's allegation *of citi- **[*569** zenship, and was a suitable and proper mode of traverse under the circumstances. By reference to Mr. Stephen's description of the uses of such a traverse, contained in his excellent analysis of pleadings (Steph. on Pl. 176), it will be seen how precisely this plea meets one of his descriptions. No doubt the defendant might have traversed, by a common or general traverse, the plaintiff's allegation that he was a citizen of the State of Missouri, concluding to the country. The issue thus presented being joined, would have involved matter of law, on which the jury must have passed, under the direction of the court. But by traversing the plaintiff's citizenship specially—that is, averring those facts on which the defendant relied to show that in point of law the plaintiff was not a citizen, and basing the traverse on those facts as a deduction therefrom—opportunity was given to do what was done; that is, to present directly to the court, by a demurrer, the sufficiency of those facts to negative, in point of law, the plaintiff's allegation of citizenship. This, then, being a special, and not a general or common traverse, the rule is settled, that the facts thus set out in the plea, as the reason or ground of the traverse, must of themselves constitute, in point of law, a negative of the allegation thus traversed. Steph. on Pl. 183; Ch. on Pl. 620. And upon a demurrer to this plea, the question which arises is, whether the facts, that the plaintiff is a negro of African descent, whose ancestors were of pure African blood, and were brought into this country and sold as negro slaves, may all be true, and yet the plaintiff be a citizen of the State of Missouri, within the meaning of the Constitution and laws of the United States, which confer on citizens of one State the right to sue citizens of another State in the circuit courts. Undoubtedly, if these facts, taken together, amount to an allegation that, at the time of action brought, the plaintiff was himself a slave, the plea is sufficient. It has been suggested that the plea, in legal effect, does so aver, because, if his ancestors were sold as slaves, the presumption is they continued slaves; and if so, the presumption is, the plaintiff was born a slave; and if so, the presumption is, he continued to be a slave to the time of action brought.

I cannot think such presumptions can be resorted to, to help out defective averments in pleading; especially, in pleading in abatement, where the utmost certainty and precision are required. Chit. Pl. 457. That the plaintiff himself was a slave at the time of action brought, is a substantive fact, having no necessary connection with the fact that his parents were sold as slaves. For they might have been sold after he was born; or the plaintiff himself, if once a slave, might have *become a freeman before action was brought. To aver that his ancestors were sold as slaves, is not equivalent, in point of law to an averment that he was a slave. If it were, he could not even confess and avoid the averment of the slavery of his ancestors, which would be monstrous; and if it be not equivalent in point of law, it cannot be treated as amounting thereto when demurred to; for a demurrer confesses only those substantive facts which are well pleaded, and not other distinct substantive facts which might be inferred therefrom by a jury. To treat an averment that the plaintiff's ancestors were Africans, brought to this country and sold as slaves as amounting to an averment on the record that he was a slave, because it may lay some foundation for presuming so, is to hold that the facts actually alleged may be treated as intended as evidence of another distinct fact not alleged. But, it is a cardinal rule of pleading, laid down in Dowman's case, 9 Rep. b, and in even earlier authorities therein referred to, "that evidence shall never be pleaded, for it only tends to prove matter of fact; and therefore the matter of fact shall be pleaded." Or, as the rule is sometimes stated, pleadings must not be argumentative. Steph. Pl. 384, and authorities cited by him. In Com. Dig. Pleader, E. 3, and Bac. Abr. Pleas I. 5, and Steph. Pl., many decisions under this rule are collected. In trover, for an indenture whereby A granted a manor, it is no plea

[570*]**

15 L. ed.   49

that A did not grant the manor, for it does not answer the declaration except by argument. Yelv. 223.

So in trespass for taking and carrying away the plaintiff's goods, the defendant pleaded that the plaintiff never had any goods. The court said, "this is an infallible argument that the defendant is not guilty, but it is no plea." Dyer, a 43.

In ejectment, the defendant pleaded a surrender of a copyhold by the hand of Fosset, the steward. The plaintiff replied that Fosset was not steward. The court held this no issue, for it traversed the surrender only argumentatively. Cro. Eliz. 260.

In these cases, and many others reported in the books, the inferences from the facts stated were irresistible. But the court held they did not, when demurred to, amount to such inferable facts. In the case at bar, the inference that the defendant was a slave at the time of action brought, even if it can be made at all, from the fact that his parents were slaves, is certainly not a necessary inference. This case, therefore, is like that of Digby v. Alexander, 8 Bing. 416. In that case, the defendant pleaded many facts strongly tending to show that he was once Earl of Stirling; but as there was no positive allegation *that he was so at the time [*571 of action brought, and as every fact averred might be true, and yet the defendant not have been Earl of Stirling at the time of action brought, the plea was held to be insufficient.

A lawful seisin of land is presumed to continue. But if, in an action of trespass quare clausum, the defendant were to plead that he was lawfully seised of the locus in quo, one month before the time of the alleged trespass, I should have no doubt it would be a bad plea. See Mollan v. Torrance, 9 Wheat. 537. So if a plea to the jurisdiction, instead of alleging that the plaintiff was a citizen of the same State as the defendant, were to allege that the plaintiff's ancestors were citizens of that State, I think the plea could not be supported. My judgment would be, as it is in this case, that if the defendant meant to aver a particular substantive fact, as existing at the time of action brought, he must do it directly and explicitly, and not by way of inference from certain other averments, which are quite consistent with the contrary hypothesis. I cannot therefore, treat this plea as containing an averment that the plaintiff himself was a slave at the time of action brought; and the inquiry recurs, whether the facts, that he is of African descent, and that his parents were once slaves, are necessarily inconsistent with his own citizenship in the State of Missouri, within the meaning of the Constitution and laws of the United States.

In Gassies v. Ballon, 6 Pet. 761, the defendant was described on the record as a naturalized citizen of the United States, residing in Louisiana. The court held this equivalent to an averment that the defendant was a citizen of Louisiana; because a citizen of the United States, residing in any State of the Union, is, for purposes of jurisdiction, a citizen of that State. Now, the plea to the jurisdiction in this case does not controvert the fact that the plaintiff resided in Missouri at the date of the writ. If he did then reside there, and was also a citizen of the United States, no provisions

769

contained in the Constitution or laws of Missouri can deprive the plaintiff of his right to sue citizens of States other than Missouri, in the courts of the United States.

So that, under the allegations contained in this plea, and admitted by the demurrer, the question is, whether any person of African descent, whose ancestors were sold as slaves in the United States, can be a citizen of the United States. If any such person can be a citizen, this plaintiff has the right to the judgment of the court that he is so; for no cause is shown by the plea, why he is not so, except his descent and the slavery of his ancestors.

The 1st section of the 2d Article of the **572*]** Constitution *uses the language, "a citizen of the United States at the time of the adoption of the Constitution." One mode of approaching this question is, to inquire who were citizens of the United States at the time of the adoption of the Constitution.

Citizens of the United States at the time of the adoption of the Constitution can have been no other than the citizens of the United States under the Confederation. By the Articles of Confederation, a government was organized, the style whereof was, "The United States of America." This government was in existence when the Constitution was framed and proposed for adoption, and was to be superseded by the new Government of the United States of America, organized under the Constitution. When, therefore, the Constitution speaks of citizenship of the United States, existing at the time of the adoption of the Constitution, it must necessarily refer to citizenship under the government which existed prior to and at the time of such adoption.

Without going into any question concerning the powers of the Confederation to govern the territory of the United States out of the limits of the States, and consequently to sustain the relation of Government and citizen in respect to the inhabitants of such territory, it may safely be said that the citizens of the several States were citizens of the United States under the Confederation.

That government was simply a confederacy of the several States, possessing a few defined powers over subjects of general concern, each State retaining every power, jurisdiction, and right, not expressly delegated to the United States in Congress assembled. And no power was thus delegated to the government of the Confederation, to act on any question of citizenship, or to make any rules in respect thereto. The whole matter was left to stand upon the action of the several States, and to the natural consequence of such action, that the citizens of each State should be citizens of that Confederacy into which that State had entered, the style whereof was, "The United States of America."

To determine whether any free persons, descended from Africans held in slavery, were citizens of the United States under the Confederation, and consequently at the time of the adoption of the Constitution of the United States, it is only necessary to know whether any such persons were citizens of either of the States under the Confederation at the time of the adoption of the Constitution.

Of this there can be no doubt. At the time

of the ratification of the Articles of Confederation, all free native-born inhabitants of the States of New Hampshire, Massachusetts, New *York, New Jersey and North Carolina, **[*573** though descended from African slaves, were not only citizens of those States, but such of them as had the other necessary qualifications possessed the franchise of electors on equal terms with other citizens.

The Supreme Court of North Carolina, in the case of The State v. Manuel, 4 Dev. & Bat. 20, has declared the law of that State on this subject, in terms which I believe to be as sound law in the other States I have enumerated, as it was in North Carolina.

"According to the laws of this State," says Judge Gaston, in delivering the opinion of the court, "all human beings within it, who are not slaves, fall within one of two classes. Whatever distinctions may have existed in the Roman laws between citizens and free inhabitants, they are unknown to our institutions. Before our Revolution, all free persons born within the dominions of the King of Great Britain, whatever their color or complexion, were native-born British subjects—those born out of his allegiance were aliens. Slavery did not exist in England, but it did in the British Colonies. Slaves were not in legal parlance persons, but property. The moment the incapacity, the disqualification of slavery, was removed, they became persons, and were then either British subjects, or not British subjects, according as they were or were not born within the allegiance of the British King. Upon the Revolution, no other change took place in the laws of North Carolina than was consequent on the transition from a Colony dependent on a European King, to a free and sovereign State. Slaves remained slaves. British subjects in North Carolina became North Carolina freemen. Foreigners, until made members of the State, remained aliens. Slaves, manumitted here, became freemen, and therefore, if born within North Carolina, are citizens of North Carolina, and all free persons born within the State are born citizens of the State. The Constitution extended the elective franchise to every freeman who had arrived at the age of twenty-one, and paid a public tax; and it is a matter of universal notoriety, that, under it, free persons, without regard to color, claimed and exercised the franchise, until it was taken from free men of color a few years since by our amended Constitution."

In The State v. Newcomb, 5 Ired. 253, decided in 1844, the same court referred to this case of The State v. Manuel, and said: "That case underwent a very laborious investigation, both by the Bar and the Bench. The case was brought here by appeal, and was felt to be one of great importance in principle. It was considered with an anxiety and care worthy of the principle involved, and which give it a controlling *influence and authority on all **[*574** questions of a similar character."

An argument from speculative premises, however well chosen, that the then state of opinion in the Commonwealth of Massachusetts was not consistent with the natural rights of people of color who were born on that soil, and that they were not, by the Constitution of 1780 of that State, admitted to the condition of citizens, would be received with surprise by the people of that State, who know their own political history. It is true, beyond all controversy, that persons of color, descended from African slaves, were by that Constitution made citizens of the State; and such of them as have had the necessary qualifications, have held and exercised the elective franchise, as citizens, from that time to the present. See Com. v. Aves, 18 Pick. 210.

The Constitution of New Hampshire conferred the elective franchise upon "every inhabitant of the State having the necessary qualifications," of which color or descent was not one.

The Constitution of New York gave the right to vote to "every male inhabitant, who shall have resided," etc.; making no discrimination between the colored persons and others. See Con. of N. Y. Art. 2, Rev. Stats. of N. Y. Vol. I. p. 126.

That of New Jersey, to "all inhabitants of this Colony, of full age, who are worth £50 proclamation money, clear estate."

New York, by its Constitution of 1820, required colored persons to have some qualifications as prerequisites for voting, which white persons need not possess. And New Jersey, by its present Constitution, restricts the right to vote to white male citizens. But these changes can have no other effect upon the present inquiry, except to show, that before they were made, no such restrictions existed; and colored, in common with white persons, were not only citizens of those States, but entitled to the elective franchise on the same qualifications as white persons, as they now are in New Hampshire and Massachusetts. I shall not enter into an examination of the existing opinions of that period respecting the African race, nor into any discussion concerning the meaning of those who asserted, in the Declaration of Independence, that all men are created equal; that they are endowed by their Creator with certain inalienable rights; that among these are life, liberty, and the pursuit of happiness. My own opinion is, that a calm comparison of these assertions of universal abstract truths, and of their own individual opinions and acts, 575*] would not leave *these men under any reproach of inconsistency; that the great truths they asserted on that solemn occasion, they were ready and anxious to make effectual, wherever a necessary regard to circumstances, which no statesman can disregard without producing more evil than good, would allow; and that it would not be just to them, nor true in itself, to allege that they intended to say that the Creator of all men had endowed the white race, exclusively, with the great natural rights which the Declaration of Independence asserts. But this is not the place to vindicate their memory. As I conceive, we should deal here, not with such disputes, if there can be a dispute concerning this subject, but with those substantial facts evinced by the written constitutions of States, and by the notorious practice under them. And they show, in a manner which no argument can obscure, that in some of the original thirteen States, free colored persons, before and at the time of the formation of the Constitution, were citizens of those States.

15 L. ed.

The 4th of the fundamental articles of the Confederation was as follows: "The free inhabitants of each of these States, paupers, vagabonds and fugitives from justice excepted, shall be entitled to all the privileges and immunities of free citizens in the several States."

The fact that free persons of color were citizens of some of the several States, and the consequence, that this 4th Article of the Confederation would have the effect to confer on such persons the privileges and immunities of general citizenship, were not only known to those who framed and adopted those articles, but the evidence is decisive, that the 4th Article was intended to have that effect, and that more restricted language, which would have excluded such persons, was deliberately and purposely rejected.

On the 25th of June, 1778, the Articles of Confederation being under consideration by the Congress, the delegates from South Carolina moved to amend this 4th Article, by inserting after the word "free," and before the word "inhabitants," the word "white," so that the privileges and immunities of general citizenship would be secured only to white persons. Two States voted for the amendment, eight States against it, and the vote of one State was divided. The language of the article stood unchanged, and both its terms of inclusion, "free inhabitants," and the strong implication from its terms of exclusion, "paupers, vagabonds and fugitives from justice," who alone were excepted, it is clear, that under the Confederation, and at the time of the adoption of the Constitution, free colored persons of African descent might be, and, by reason of their citizenship in certain States, were, entitled to the *privileges and immunities of gen- [*576 eral citizenship of the United States.

Did the Constitution of the United States deprive them or their descendants of citizenship?

That Constitution was ordained and established by the people of the United States through the action, in each State, of those persons who were qualified by its laws to act thereon, in behalf of themselves and all other citizens of that State. In some of the States, as we have seen, colored persons were among those qualified by law to act on this subject. These colored persons were not only included in the body of "the people of the United States by whom the Constitution was ordained and established," but in at least five of the States they had the power to act, and doubtless did act, by their suffrages, upon the question of its adoption. It would be strange, if we were to find in that instrument anything which deprived of their citizenship any part of the people of the United States who were among those by whom it was established.

I can find nothing in the Constitution which, proprio vigore, deprives of their citizenship any class of persons who were citizens of the United States at the time of its adoption, or who should be native-born citizens of any State after its adoption; nor any power enabling Congress to disfranchise persons born on the soil of any State, and entitled to citizenship of such State by its constitution and laws. And my opinion is, that, under the Constitution of the United States, every free person born on the soil of a State, who is a citizen of that

State by force of its Constitution or laws, is also a citizen of the United States.

I will proceed to state the grounds of that opinion.

The 1st Section of the 2d Article of the Constitution uses the language, "a natural-born citizen." It thus assumes that citizenship may be acquired by birth. Undoubtedly, this language of the Constitution was used in reference to that principle of public law, well understood in this country at the time of the adoption of the Constitution, which referred citizenship to the place of birth. At the Declaration of Independence, and ever since, the received general doctrine has been, in conformity with the common law, that free persons born within either of the colonies were subjects of the King; that by the Declaration of Independence, and the consequent acquisition of sovereignty by the several States, all such persons ceased to be subjects, and became citizens of the several States, except so far as some of them were disfranchised by the legislative power of the States, or availed themselves, seasonably, of the right to adhere to the British Crown in the **577***] civil contest, *and thus to continue British subjects. McIlvaine v. Coxe's Lessee, 4 Cranch, 209; Inglis v. Sailors' Snug Harbor, 3 Pet. p. 99; Shanks v. Dupont, Ibid. p. 242.

The Constitution having recognized the rule that persons born within the several States are citizens of the United States, one of four things must be true:

First. That the Constitution itself has described what native-born persons shall or shall not be citizens of the United States; or,

Second. That it has empowered Congress to do so; or,

Third. That all free persons, born within the several States, are citizens of the United States; or,

Fourth. That it is left to each State to determine what free persons, born within its limits, shall be citizens of such State, and thereby be citizens of the United States.

If there be such a thing as citizenship of the United States acquired by birth within the States, which the Constitution expressly recognizes, and no one denies, then these four alternatives embrace the entire subject, and it only remains to select that one which is true.

That the Constitution itself has defined citizenship of the United States by declaring what persons, born within the several States, shall or shall not be citizens of the United States, will not be pretended. It contains no such declaration. We may dismiss the first alternative, as without doubt unfounded.

Has it empowered Congress to enact what free persons, born within the several States, shall or shall not be citizens of the United States?

Before examining the various provisions of the Constitution which may relate to this question, it is important to consider for a moment the substantial nature of this inquiry. It is, in effect, whether the Constitution has empowered Congress to create privileged classes within the States, who alone can be entitled to the franchises and powers of citizenship of the United States. If it be admitted that the Constitution has enabled Congress to declare what free persons, born within the several States,

772

shall be citizens of the United States, it must, at the same time, be admitted that it is an unlimited power. If this subject is within the control of Congress, it must depend wholly on its discretion. For, certainly, no limits of that discretion can be found in the Constitution, which is wholly silent concerning it; and the necessary consequence is, that the Federal Government may select classes of persons within the several States who alone can be entitled to the political privileges of citizenship of the United States. If this power exists, what persons born within the States may be President or Vice-President *of the United States, [***578** or members of either house of Congress, or hold any office or enjoy any privilege whereof citizenship of the United States is a necessary qualification, must depend solely on the will of Congress. By virtue of it, though Congress can grant no title of nobility, they may create an oligarchy, in whose hands would be concentrated the entire power of the Federal Government.

It is a substantive power, distinct in its nature from all others; capable of affecting not only the relations of the States to the General Government, but of controlling the political condition of the people of the United States. Certainly we ought to find this power granted by the Constitution, at least by some necessary inference, before we can say it does not remain to the States or the people. I proceed, therefore, to examine all the provisions of the Constitution which may have some bearing on this subject.

Among the powers expressly granted to Congress is "the power to establish a uniform rule of naturalization." It is not doubted that this is a power to prescribe a rule for the removal of the disabilities consequent on foreign birth. To hold that it extends further than this, would do violence to the meaning of the term naturalization, fixed in the common law (Co. Litt. 8 a, 129 a; 2 Ves. Sr. 286; 2 Bl. Com. 293), and in the minds of those who concurred in framing and adopting the Constitution. It was in this sense of conferring on an alien and his issue the rights and powers of a native-born citizen, that it was employed in the Declaration of Independence. It was in this sense it was expounded in the Federalist (No. 42), has been understood by Congress, by the Judiciary (2 Wheat. 259, 269; 3 Wash. 313, 322; 12 Wheat. 277), and by commentators on the Constitution. 3 Story's Com. on Const. 1–3; 1 Rawle on Const. 84–88; 1 Tucker's Bl. Com. App. 225–259.

It appears, then, that the only power expressly granted to Congress to legislate concerning citizenship, is confined to the removal of the disabilities of foreign birth.

Whether there be anything in the Constitution from which a broader power may be implied, will best be seen when we come to examine the two other alternatives, which are, whether all free persons, born on the soil of the several States, or only such of them as may be citizens of each State, respectively, are thereby citizens of the United States. The last of these alternatives, in my judgment, contains the truth.

Undoubtedly, as has already been said, it is a principle of public law, recognized by the Con-

situtation itself, that birth on the soil of a country both creates the duties and confers the rights of citizenship. But it must be remem-
579*] bered, that though *the Constitution was to form a government, and under it the United States of America were to be one united sovereign nation, to which loyalty and obedience on the one side, and from which protection and privileges on the other, would be due, yet the several sovereign States, whose people were then citizens, were not only to continue in existence, but with powers unimpaired, except so far as they were granted by the people to the National Government.

Among the powers unquestionably possessed by the several States, was that of determining what persons should and what persons should not be citizens. It was practicable to confer on the government of the Union this entire power. It embraced what may, well enough for the purpose now in view, be divided into three parts: First. The power to remove the disabilities of alienage, either by special acts in reference to each individual case, or by establishing a rule of naturalization to be administered and applied by the courts. Second. Determining what persons should enjoy the privileges of citizenship, in respect to the internal affairs of the several States. Third. What native born persons should be citizens of the United States.

The first named power, that of establishing a uniform rule of naturalization, was granted; and here the grant, according to its terms, stopped. Construing a constitution containing only limited and defined powers of government, the argument derived from this definite and restricted power to establish a rule of naturalization, must be admitted to be exceedingly strong. I do not say it is necessarily decisive. It might be controlled by other parts of the Constitution. But when this particular subject of citizenship was under consideration, and in the clause specially intended to define the extent of power concerning it, we find a particular part of this entire power separated from the residue, and conferred on the General Government, there arises a strong presumption that this is all which is granted, and that the residue is left to the States and to the people. And this presumption is, in my opinion, converted into a certainty by an examination of all such other clauses of the Constitution as touch this subject.

I will examine each which can have any possible bearing on this question.

The 1st clause of the 2d Section of the 3d Article of the Constitution is: "The judicial power shall extend to controversies between a State and citizens of another State; between citizens of different States; between citizens of the same State, claiming lands under grants of different States; and between States, or the citizens thereof, and foreign states,
580*] *citizens or subjects." I do not think this clause has any considerable bearing upon the particular inquiry now under consideration. Its purpose was, to extend the judicial power to those controversies into which local feelings or interests might so enter as to disturb the course of justice, or give rise to suspicions that they had done so, and thus possibly give occasion to jealousy or ill will between different States, or a particular State and a foreign na-

tion. At the same time, I would remark, in passing, that it has never been held—I do not know that it has ever been supposed—that any citizen of a State could bring himself under this clause and the 11th and 12th sections of the Judiciary Act of 1789, passed in pursuance of it, who was not a citizen of the United States. But I have referred to the clause, only because it is one of the places where citizenship is mentioned by the Constitution. Whether it is entitled to any weight in this inquiry or not, it refers only to citizenship of the several States; it recognizes that; but it does not recognize citizenship of the United States as something distinct therefrom.

As has been said, the purpose of this clause did not necessarily connect it with citizenship of the United States, even if that were something distinct from citizenship of the several States, in the contemplation of the Constitution. This cannot be said of other clauses of the Constitution, which I now proceed to refer to.

"The citizens of each State shall be entitled to all the privileges and immunities of citizens of the several States." Nowhere else in the Constitution is there anything concerning a general citizenship; but here, privileges and immunities to be enjoyed throughout the United States, under and by force of the national compact, are granted and secured. In selecting those who are to enjoy these national rights of citizenship—how are they described? As citizens of each State. It is to them these national rights are secured. The qualification for them is not to be looked for in any provision of the Constitution or laws of the United States. They are to be citizens of the several States, and, as such, the privileges and immunities of general citizenship, derived from and guarantied by the Constitution, are to be enjoyed by them. It would seem that if it had been intended to constitute a class of native born persons within the States, who should derive their citizenship of the United States from the action of the Federal Government, this was an occasion for referring to them. It cannot be supposed that it was the purpose of this article to confer the privileges and immunities of citizens in all the States upon persons not citizens of the United States.

*And if it was intended to secure these [*581 rights only to citizens of the United States, how has the Constitution here described such persons? Simply as citizens of each State.

But, further: though, as I shall presently more fully state, I do not think the enjoyment of the elective franchise essential to citizenship, there can be no doubt it is one of the chiefest attributes of citizenship under the American Constitutions; and the just and constitutional possession of this right is decisive evidence of citizenship. The provisions made by a constitution on this subject must therefore be looked to as bearing directly on the question what persons are citizens under that constitution; and as being decisive, to this extent, that all such persons as are allowed by the Constitution to exercise the elective franchise, and thus to participate in the Government of the United States, must be deemed citizens of the United States.

Here, again, the consideration presses itself upon us, that if there was designed to be a particular class of native-born persons within the States, deriving their citizenship from the Constitution and laws of the United States, they should at least have been referred to as those by whom the President and House of Representatives were to be elected, and to whom they should be responsible.

Instead of that, we again find this subject referred to the laws of the several States. The electors of President are to be appointed in such manner as the Legislature of each State may direct, and the qualifications of electors of members of the House of Representatives shall be the same as for electors of the most numerous branch of the State Legislature.

Laying aside, then, the case of aliens, concerning which the Constitution of the United States has provided, and confining our view to free persons born within the several States, we find that the Constitution has recognized the general principle of public law, that allegiance and citizenship depend on the place of birth; that it has not attempted practically to apply this principle by designating the particular classes of persons who should or should not come under it; that when we turn to the Constitution for an answer to the question, what free persons, born within the several States, are citizens of the United States, the only answer we can receive from any of its express provisions is, the citizens of the several States are to enjoy the privileges and immunities of citizens in every State, and their franchise as electors under the Constitution depends on their citizenship in the several States. Add to this, that the Constitution was ordained by the citizens of the several States; that they were "the people of the United States," for whom 582*] *and whose posterity the government was declared in the preamble of the Constitution to be made; that each of them was "a citizen of the United States at the time of the adoption of the Constitution," within the meaning of those words in that instrument; that by them the government was to be and was in fact organized; and that no power is conferred on the Government of the Union to discriminate between them, or to disfranchise any of them—the necessary conclusion is, that those persons born within the several States, who, by force of their respective constitutions and laws, are citizens of the State, are thereby citizens of the United States.

It may be proper here to notice some supposed objections to this view of the subject.

It has been often asserted that the Constitution was made exclusively by and for the white race. It has already been shown that in five of the thirteen original States, colored persons then possessed the elective franchise, and were among those by whom the Constitution was ordained and established. If so, it is not true, in point of fact, that the Constitution was made exclusively by the white race. And that it was made exclusively for the white race is, in my opinion, not only an assumption not warranted by anything in the Constitution, but contradicted by its opening declaration, that it was ordained and established by the people of the United States, for themselves and their posterity. And as free colored persons were then citizens of at least five States, and so in every sense part of the people of the United States, they were among those for whom and whose posterity the Constitution was ordained and established.

Again; it has been objected, that if the Constitution has left to the several States the rightful power to determine who of their inhabitants shall be citizens of the United States, the States may make aliens citizens.

The answer is obvious. The Constitution has left to the States the determination what persons, born within their respective limits, shall acquire by birth citizenship of the United States; it has not left to them any power to prescribe any rule for the removal of the disabilities of alienage. This power is exclusively in Congress.

It has been further objected, that if free colored persons, born within a particular State, and made citizens of that State by its constitution and laws, are thereby made citizens of the United States, then, under the 2d section of the 4th article of the Constitution, such persons would be entitled to all the privileges and immunities of citizens in the several States; and if so, then colored persons could vote, and be *eligible to not only federal offices, but [*583 offices even in those States whose Constitutions and laws disqualify colored persons from voting or being elected to office.

But this position rests upon an assumption which I deem untenable. Its basis is, that no one can be deemed a citizen of the United States who is not entitled to enjoy all the privileges and franchises which are conferred on any citizen. See 1 Lit. Ky. 326. That this is not true, under the Constitution of the United States, seems to me clear.

A naturalized citizen cannot be President of the United States, nor a Senator till after the lapse of nine years, nor a Representative till after the lapse of seven years, from his naturalization. Yet, as soon as naturalized, he is certainly a citizen of the United States. Nor is any inhabitant of the District of Columbia, or of either of the Territories, eligible to the office of Senator or Representative in Congress, though they may be citizens of the United States. So, in all the States, numerous persons, though citizens, cannot vote, or cannot hold office, either on account of their age or sex, or the want of the necessary legal qualifications. The truth is, that citizenship, under the Constitution of the United States, is not dependent on the possession of any particular political or even of all civil rights; and any attempt so to define it must lead to error. To what citizens the elective franchise shall be confided, is a question to be determined by each State, in accordance with its own views of the necessities or expediencies of its condition. What civil rights shall be enjoyed by its citizens, and whether all shall enjoy the same, or how they may be gained or lost, are to be determined in the same way.

One may confine the right of suffrage to white male citizens; another may extend it to colored persons and females; one may allow all persons above a prescribed age to convey property and transact business; another may exclude married women. But whether native-born women, or persons under age, or under guardianship because insane or spendthrifts, be excluded from voting or holding office, or allowed

774   19 How.

to do so, I apprehend no one will deny that they are citizens of the United States. Besides, this clause of the Constitution does not confer on the citizens of one State, in all other States, specific and enumerated privileges and immunities. They are entitled to such as belong to citizenship, but not such as belong to particular citizens attended by other qualifications. Privileges and immunities which belong to certain citizens of a State, by reason of the operation of causes other than mere citizenship, are not conferred. Thus, if the laws of a State require, 584*] in addition to *citizenship of the State, some qualification for office, or the exercise of the elective franchise, citizens of all other States, coming thither to reside, and not possessing those qualifications, cannot enjoy those privileges, not because they are not to be deemed entitled to the privileges of citizens of the State in which they reside, but because they, in common with the native-born citizens of that State, must have the qualifications prescribed by law for the enjoyment of such privileges under its constitution and laws. It rests with the States themselves so to frame their constitutions and laws as not to attach a particular privilege or immunity to mere naked citizenship. If one of the States will not deny to any of its own citizens a particular privilege or immunity, if it confer it on all of them by reason of mere naked citizenship, then it may be claimed by every citizen of each State by force of the Constitution; and it must be borne in mind, that the difficulties which attend the allowance of the claims of colored persons to be citizens of the United States are not avoided by saying that, though each State may make them its citizens, they are not thereby made citizens of the United States, because the privileges of general citizenship are secured to the citizens of each State. The language of the Constitution is: "The citizens of each State shall be entitled to all privileges and immunities of citizens in the several States." If each State may make such persons its citizens, they become, as such, entitled to the benefits of this article, if there be a native-born citizenship of the United States distinct from a native-born citizenship of the several States.

There is one view of this article entitled to consideration in this connection. It is manifestly copied from the 4th of the Articles of Confederation, with only slight changes of phraseology, which render its meaning more precise, and dropping the clause which excluded paupers, vagabonds and fugitives from justice, probably because these cases could be dealt with under the police powers of the States, and a special provision therefor was not necessary. It has been suggested, that in adopting it into the Constitution, the words "free inhabitants" were changed for the word "citizens." An examination of the forms of expression commonly used in the state papers of that day, and an attention to the substance of this article of the Confederation, will show that the words "free inhabitants," as then used, were synonymous with citizens. When the Articles of Confederation were adopted, we were in the midst of the War of the Revolution, and there were very few persons then embraced in the words "free inhabitants," who were not born on our soil. It was not a time

when many, save the *children of the [*585 soil, were willing to embark their fortunes in our cause; and though there might be an inaccuracy in the uses of words to call free inhabitants citizens, it was then a technical rather than a substantial difference. If we look into the constitutions and state papers of that period, we find the inhabitants or people of these Colonies or the inhabitants of this State, or Commonwealth, employed to designate those whom we should now denominate "citizens." The substance and purpose of the article prove it was in this sense it used these words: It secures to the free inhabitants of each State the privileges and immunities of free citizens in every State. It is not conceivable that the States should have agreed to extend the privileges of citizenship to persons not entitled to enjoy the privileges of citizens in the States where they dwelt; that under this article there was a class of persons in some of the States, not citizens, to whom were secured all the privileges and immunities of citizens when they went into other States; and the just conclusion is, that though the Constitution cured an inaccuracy of language, it left the substance of this article in the National Constitution the same as it was in the Articles of Confederation.

The history of this 4th article, respecting the attempt to exclude free persons of color from its operation, has been already stated. It is reasonable to conclude that this history was known to those who framed and adopted the Constitution. That under this 4th article of the Confederation, free persons of color might be entitled to the privileges of general citizenship, if otherwise entitled thereto, is clear. When this article was, in substance, placed in and made part of the Constitution of the United States, with no change in its language calculated to exclude free colored persons from the benefit of its provisions, the presumption is, to say the least, strong, that the practical effect which it was designed to have, and did have, under the former government, it was designed to have, and should have, under the new government.

It may be further objected, that if free colored persons may be citizens of the United States, it depends only on the will of a master whether he will emancipate his slave and thereby make him a citizen. Not so. The master is subject to the will of the State. Whether he shall be allowed to emancipate his slave at all; if so, on what conditions; and what is to be the political status of the freed man, depend, not on the will of the master, but on the will of the State, upon which the political status of all its native-born inhabitants depends. Under the Constitution of the United States, each State has retained this power of determining the political status of its native-born *inhabitants, and no exception thereto [*586 can be found in the Constitution. And if a master in a slaveholding State should carry his slave into a free State, and there emancipate him, he would not thereby make him a native-born citizen of that State, and consequently no privileges could be claimed by such emancipated slave as a citizen of the United States. For, whatever powers the States may exercise to confer privileges of citizenship on persons not born on their soil, the Constitution of the United States does not recognize such citizens. As has already been said, it recognizes the great principle of public law, that allegiance and citizenship spring from the place of birth. It leaves to the States the application of that principle to individual cases. It secured to the citizens of each State the privileges and immunities of citizens in every other State. But it does not allow to the States the power to make aliens citizens, or permit one State to take persons born on the soil of another State, and, contrary to the laws and policy of the States where they were born, make them its citizens, and so citizens of the United States. No such deviation from the great rule of public law was contemplated by the Constitution; and when any such attempt shall be actually made, it is to be met by applying to it those rules of law and those principles of good faith which will be sufficient to decide it, and not, in my judgment, by denying that all the free native-born inhabitants of a State, who are its citizens under its constitution and laws, are also citizens of the United States.

It has sometimes been urged that colored persons are shown not to be citizens of the United States, by the fact that the naturalization laws apply only to white persons. But whether a person born in the United States be or be not a citizen, cannot depend on laws which refer only to aliens, and do not affect the status of persons born in the United States. The utmost effect which can be attributed to them is, to show that Congress has not deemed it expedient generally to apply the rule to colored aliens. That they might do so, if thought fit, is clear. The Constitution has not excluded them. And since that has conferred the power on Congress to naturalize colored aliens, it certainly shows that color is not a necessary qualification for citizenship under the Constitution of the United States. It may be added, that the power to make colored persons citizens of the United States, under the Constitution, has been actually exercised in repeated and important instances. See the Treaties with the Choctaws, of Sept. 27, 1830, art. 14; with the Cherokees, of May 23, 1836, art. 12; Treaty of Guadaloupe Hidalgo, Feb. 2, 1848, art. 8.

I do not deem it necessary to review at length **587***] the legislation *of Congress having more or less bearing on the citizenship of colored persons. It does not seem to me to have any considerable tendency to prove that it has been considered by the Legislative Department of the government, that no such persons are citizens of the United States. Undoubtedly they have been debarred from the exercise of particular rights or privileges extended by white persons, but, I believe, always in terms which, by implication, admit they may be citizens. Thus the Act of May 17, 1792, for the organization of the militia, directs the enrollment of "every free, able-bodied, white male citizen." An assumption that none but white persons are citizens, would be as inconsistent with the just import of this language, as that all citizens are able-bodied, or males.

So the Act of February 28, 1803, 2 Stat. at L. 205, to prevent the importation of certain persons into States, when by the laws thereof their admission is prohibited, in its 1st section

forbids all masters of vessels to import or bring "any negro, mulatto, or other person of color, not being a native, a citizen, or registered seaman of the United States," etc.

The Acts of March 3, 1813, sec. 1, 2 Stat. at L. 809, and March 1, 1817, sec. 3, 3 Stat. at L. 351, concerning seamen, certainly imply there may be persons of color, natives of the United States, who are not citizens of the United States. This implication is undoubtedly in accordance with the fact. For not only slaves, but free persons of color, born in some of the States, are not citizens. But there is nothing in these laws inconsistent with the citizenship of persons of color in others of the States, nor with their being citizens of the United States.

Whether much or little weight should be attached to the particular phraseology of these and other laws, which were not passed with any direct reference to this subject, I consider their tendency to be, as already indicated, to show that, in the apprehension of their framers, color was not a necessary qualification of citizenship. It would be strange, if laws were found on our statute book to that effect, when by solemn treaties, large bodies of Mexican and North American Indians, as well as free colored inhabitants of Louisiana, have been admitted to citizenship of the United States.

In the legislative debates which preceded the admission of the State of Missouri into the Union, this question was agitated. Its result is found in the resolution of Congress, of March 5, 1821, for the admission of that State into the Union. The Constitution of Missouri, under which that State applied for admission into the Union, provided, that it should be the duty *of the Legislature "to pass laws to pre- [**588** vent free negroes and mulattoes from coming to and settling in the State, under any pretext whatever." One ground of objection to the admission of the State under this Constitution was, that it would require the Legislature to exclude free persons of color, who would be entitled, under the 2d section of the 4th article of the Constitution, not only to come within the State, but to enjoy there the privileges and immunities of citizens. The resolutions of Congress admitting the State was upon the fundamental condition, "that the Constitution of Missouri shall never be construed to authorize the passage of any law, and that no law shall be passed in conformity thereto, by which any citizen of either of the States of this Union shall be excluded from the enjoyment of any of the privileges and immunities to which such citizen is entitled under the Constitution of the United States." It is true, that neither this legislative declaration, nor anything in the Consitution or laws of Missouri, could confer or take away any privilege or immunity granted by the Constitution. But it is also true, that it expresses the then conviction of the legislative power of the United States, that free negroes, as citizens of some of the States, might be entitled to the privileges and immunities of citizens in all the States.

The conclusions at which I have arrived on this part of the case are:

First. That the free native-born citizens of each State are citizens of the United States.

Second. That as free colored persons born within some of the States are citizens of those

States, such persons are also citizens of the United States.

Third. That every such citizen, residing in any State, has the right to sue and is liable to be sued in the federal courts, as a citizen of that State in which he resides.

Fourth. That as the plea to the jurisdiction in this case shows no facts, except that the plaintiff was of African descent, and his ancestors were sold as slaves, and as these facts are not inconsistent with his citizenship of the United States, and his residence in the State of Missouri, the plea to the jurisdiction was bad, and the judgment of the Circuit Court overruling it, was correct.

I dissent, therefore, from that part of the opinion of the majority of the court, in which it is held that a person of African descent cannot be a citizen of the United States; and I regret I must go further, and dissent both from what I deem their assumption of authority to examine the constitutionality of the Act of Congress commonly called the Missouri Compromise *Act, and the grounds and con-589*] clusions announced in their opinion.

Having first decided that they were bound to consider the sufficiency of the plea to the jurisdiction of the Circuit Court, and having decided that this plea showed that the Circuit Court had not jurisdiction, and consequently that this is a case to which the judicial power of the United States does not extend, they have gone on to examine the merits of the case as they appeared on the trial before the court and jury, on the issues joined on the pleas in bar, and so have reached the question of the power of Congress to pass the Act of 1820. On so grave a subject as this, I feel obliged to say that, in my opinion, such an exertion of judicial power transcends the limits of the authority of the court, as described by its repeated decisions, and, as I understand, acknowledged in this opinion of the majority of the court.

In the course of that opinion, it became necessary to comment on the case of Legrand v. Darnall, reported in 2 Pet. 664. In that case, a bill was filed, by one alleged to be a citizen of Maryland, against one alleged to be a citizen of Pennsylvania. The bill stated that the defendant was the son of a white man by one of his slaves; and that the defendant's father devised to him certain lands, the title to which was put in controversy by the bill. These facts were admitted in the answer, and upon these and other facts the court made its decree, founded on the principle that a devise of land by a master to a slave was by implication also a bequest of his freedom. The facts that the defendant was of African descent, and was born a slave, were not only before the court, but entered into the entire substance of its inquiries. The opinion of the majority of my brethren in this case disposes of the case of Legrand v. Darnall, by saying, among other things, that as the fact that the defendant was born a slave only came before this court on the bill and answer, it was then too late to raise the question of the personal disability of the party, and therefore that decision is altogether inapplicable in this case.

In this I concur. Since the decision of this court in Livingston v. Story, 11 Pet. 351, the law has been settled, that when the declaration or bill contains the necessary averments of citizenship, this court cannot look at the record, to see whether those averments are true, except so far as they are put in issue by a plea to the jurisdiction. In that case, the defendant denied by his answer that Mr. Livingston was a citizen of New York, as he had alleged in the bill. Both parties went into proofs. The court refused to examine those proofs, with reference to the personal disability of the plaintiff. This is the *settled law of the court, af-[*590 firmed so lately as Sheppard v. Graves, 14 How. 505, and Wickliffe v. Owings, 17 How. 51; see, also, De Wolf v. Rabaud, 1 Pet. 476. But I do not understand this to be a rule which the court may depart from at its pleasure. If it be a rule, it is as binding on the court as on the suitors. If it removes from the latter the power to take any objection to the personal disability of a party alleged by the record to be competent, which is not shown by a plea to the jurisdiction, it is because the court are forbidden by law to consider and decide on objections so taken. I do not consider it to be within the scope of the judicial power of the majority of the court to pass upon any question respecting the plaintiff's citizenship in Missouri save that raised by the plea to the jurisdiction; and I do not hold any opinion of this court or any court, binding, when expressed on a question not legitimately before it. Carroll v. Carroll, 16 How. 275. The judgment of this court is, that the case is to be dismissed for want of jurisdiction, because the plaintiff was not a citizen of Missouri, as he alleged in his declaration. Into that judgment, according to the settled course of this court, nothing appearing after a plea to the merits can enter. A great question of constitutional law, deeply affecting the peace and welfare of the country, is not, in my opinion, a fit subject to be thus reached.

But as, in my opinion, the Circuit Court had jurisdiction, I am obliged to consider the question whether its judgment on the merits of the case should stand or be reversed.

The residence of the plaintiff in the State of Illinois, and the residence of himself and his wife in the Territory acquired from France lying north of latitude thirty-six degrees thirty minutes, and north of the State of Missouri, are each relied on by the plaintiff in error. As the residence in the Territory affects the plaintiff's wife and children as well as himself, I must inquire what was its effect.

The general question may be stated to be, whether the plaintiff's status, as a slave, was so changed by his residence within that Territory, that he was not a slave in the State of Missouri, at the time this action was brought.

In such cases, two inquiries arise, which may be confounded, but should be kept distinct.

The first is, what was the law of the Territory into which the master and slave went, respecting the relation between them?

The second is, whether the State of Missouri recognizes and allows the effect of that law of the Territory, on the status of the slave, on his return within its jurisdiction.

As to the first of these questions, the will of States and nations, *by whose municipal [*591 law slavery is not recognized, has been manifested in three different ways.

One is, absolutely to dissolve the relation, and terminate the rights of the master existing under the law of the country whence the parties came. This is said by Lord Stowell, in the case of The Slave Grace, 2 Hagg. Ad. 94, and by the Supreme Court of Louisiana in the case of Maria Louise v. Marot, 9 La. 473, to be the law of France; and it has been the law of several States of this Union, in respect to slaves introduced under certain conditions.

Wilson v. Isabel, 5 Call, 430; Hunter v. Fulcher, 1 Leigh, 172; Stewart v. Oakes, 5 Harr. & J. 107.

The second is, where the municipal law of a country not recognizing slavery, it is the will of the State to refuse the master all aid to exercise any control over his slave; and if he attempt to do so, in a manner justifiable only by that relation, to prevent the exercise of that control. But no law exists, designed to operate directly on the relation of master and slave, and put an end to that relation. This is said by Lord Stowell, in the case above mentioned, to be the law of England, and by Mr. Chief Justice Shaw, in the case of The Commonwealth v. Aves, 18 Pick. 193, to be the law of Massachusetts.

The third is, to make a distinction between the case of a master and his slave only temporarily in the country, animo non manendi, and those who are there to reside for permanent or indefinite purposes. This is said by Mr. Wheaton to be the law of Prussia, and was formerly the statute law of several States of our Union. It is necessary in this case to keep in view this distinction between those countries whose laws are designed to act directly on the status of a slave, and make him a freeman, and those where the master can obtain no aid from the laws to enforce his rights.

It is to the last case only that the authorities, out of Missouri, relied on by defendant, apply, when the residence in the non-slaveholding Territory was permanent. In The Commonwealth v. Aves, 18 Pick. 218, Mr. Chief Justice Shaw said: "From the principle above stated, on which a slave brought here becomes free, to wit: that he becomes entitled to the protection of our laws, it would seem to follow, as a necessary conclusion, that if the slave waives the protection of those laws, and returns to the State where he is held as a slave, his condition is not changed." It was upon this ground, as is apparent from his whole reasoning, that Sir William Scott rests his opinion in the case of The Slave Grace. To use one of his expressions, the effect of the law of England was to put the liberty of the slave into a parenthe-592*] sis. If there had been an *Act of Parliament declaring that a slave coming to England with his master should thereby be deemed no longer to be a slave, it is easy to see that the learned judge could not have arrived at the same conclusion. This distinction is very clearly stated and shown by President Tucker, in his opinion in the case of Betty v. Horton, 5 Leigh's Va. 615.

See, also, Hunter v. Fulcher, 1 Leigh's Va. 172; Maria Louise v. Marot, 9 La. 473; Smith v. Smith, 13 La. 441; Thomas v. Generis, 16 La. 483; Rankin v. Lydia, 2 A. K. Marsh. 467; Davis v. Tingle, 8 B. Mon. 539; Griffeth v. Fanny, Gilm. Va. 143; Lunsford v. Coquillon, 2 Mart. N. S. 405; Josephine v. Poultney, 1 La. Ann. 329.

But if the Acts of Congress on this subject

are valid, the law of the Territory of Wisconsin, within whose limits the residence of the plaintiff and his wife, and their marriage and the birth of one or both of their children, took place, falls under the first category, and is a law operating directly on the status of the slave. By the 8th section of the Act of March 6, 1820, 3 Stat. at L. 548, it was enacted that, within this Territory, "slavery and involuntary servitude, otherwise than in the punishment of crimes, whereof the parties shall have been duly convicted, shall be, and is hereby forever prohibited: Provided, always, that any person escaping into the same, from whom labor or service is lawfully claimed in any State or Territory of the United States, such fugitive may be lawfully reclaimed, and conveyed to the person claiming his or her labor or services, as aforesaid."

By the Act of April 20, 1836, 4 Stat. at L. 10, passed in the same month and year of the removal of the plaintiff to Fort Snelling, this part of the Territory ceded by France, where Fort Snelling is, together with so much of the territory of the United States east of the Mississippi as now constitutes the State of Wisconsin, was brought under a territorial government, under the name of the Territory of Wisconsin. By the 18th section of this Act, it was enacted, "That the inhabitants of this Territory shall be entitled to and enjoy all and singular the rights, privileges and advantages, granted and secured to the people of the Territory of the United States northwest of the River Ohio, by the articles of compact contained in the Ordinance for the government of said Territory, passed on the 13th day of July, 1787; and shall be subject to all the restrictions and prohibitions in said articles of compact imposed upon the people of the said Territory." The 6th article of that compact is, "there shall be neither slavery nor involuntary servitude in the said Territory, otherwise than in *the punishment of crimes, [*593 whereof the party shall have been duly convicted: Provided, always, that any person escaping into the same, from whom labor or service is lawfully claimed in any one of the original States, such fugitive may be lawfully reclaimed, and conveyed to the person claiming his or her labor or service, as aforesaid." By other provisions of this Act establishing the Territory of Wisconsin, the laws of the United States, and the then existing laws of the State of Michigan, are extended over the Territory; the latter being subject to alteration and repeal by the legislative power of the Territory created by the Act.

Fort Snelling was within the Territory of Wisconsin, and these laws were extended over it. The Indian title to that site for a military post had been acquired from the Sioux nation as early as September 23, 1805 (Am. State Papers, Indian Affairs, Vol. I. p. 744), and until the erection of the territorial government, the persons at that post were governed by the Rules and Articles of War, and such laws of the United States, including the 8th section of the Act of March 6, 1820, prohibiting slavery, as were applicable to their condition; but after the erection of the Territory, and the extension of the laws of the United States and the laws of Michigan over the whole of the Territory, including this military post, the persons residing there were under the dominion of those laws in all particulars to which the Rules and Articles of War did not apply.

It thus appears that, by these Acts of Congress, not only was a general system of municipal law borrowed from the State of Michigan, which did not tolerate slavery, but it was positively enacted that slavery and involuntary servitude, with only one exception, specifically described, should not exist there. It is not simply that slavery is not recognized and cannot be aided by the municipal law. It is recognized for the purpose of being absolutely prohibited, and declared incapable of existing within the Territory, save in the instance of a fugitive slave.

It would not be easy for the Legislature to employ more explicit language to signify its will that the status of slavery should not exist within the Territory, than the words found in the Act of 1820, and in the Ordinance of 1787; and if any doubt could exist concerning their application to cases of masters coming into the Territory with their slaves to reside, that doubt must yield to the inference required by the words of exception. That exception is, of cases of fugitive slaves. An exception from a prohibition marks the extent of the prohibition; for it would be absurd, as well as useless, to except from a prohibition 594*] *a case not contained within it. 9 Wheat. 200. I must conclude, therefore, that it was the will of Congress that the state of involuntary servitude of a slave, coming into the Territory with his master, should cease to exist. The Supreme Court of Missouri so held in Rachel v. Walker, 4 Mo. 350, which was the case of a military officer going into the Territory with two slaves.

But it is a distinct question, whether the law of Missouri recognized and allowed effect to the change wrought in the status of the plaintiff, by force of the laws of the Territory of Wisconsin.

I say the law of Missouri, because a judicial tribunal, in one State or nation, can recognize personal rights acquired by force of the law of any other State or nation, only so far as it is the law of the former State that those rights should be recognized. But, in the absence of positive law to the contrary, the will of every civilized State must be presumed to be to allow such effect to foreign laws as is in accordance with the settled rules of international law. And legal tribunals are bound to act on this presumption. It may be assumed that the motive of the State in allowing such operation to foreign laws is what has been termed comity. But, as has justly been said (per Chief Justice Taney, 13 Pet. 589), it is the comity of the State, not of the court. The judges have nothing to do with the motive of the State. Their duty is simply to ascertain and give effect to its will. And when it is found by them that its will to depart from a rule of international law has not been manifested by the State, they are bound to assume that its will is to give effect to it. Undoubtedly, every sovereign State may refuse to recognize a change, wrought by the law of a foreign State, on the status of a person, while within such foreign State, even in cases where the rules of international law require that recognition. Its will to refuse such recognition may be manifested by what we

term statute law, or by the customary law of the State. It is within the province of its judicial tribunals to inquire and adjudge whether it appears, from the statute or customary law of the State, to be the will of the State to refuse to recognize such changes of status by force of foreign law, as the rules of the law of nations require to be recognized. But, in my opinion, it is not within the province of any judicial tribunal to refuse such recognition from any political considerations, or any view it may take of the exterior political relations between the State and one or more foreign States, or any impressions it may have that a change of foreign opinion and action on the subject of slavery may afford a reason why the State should change its own action. To understand and give *just [*595 effect to such considerations, and to change the action of the State in consequence of them, are functions of diplomatists and legislators, not of judges.

The inquiry to be made on this part of the case is, therefore, whether the State of Missouri has, by its statute, or its customary law, manifested its will to displace any rule of international law, applicable to a change of the status of a slave, by foreign law.

I have not heard it suggested that there was any statute of the State of Missouri bearing on this question. The customary law of Missouri is the common law, introduced by statute in 1816. 1 Ter. Laws, 436. And the common law, as Blackstone says (4 Com. 67) adopts, in its full extent, the law of nations, and holds it to be a part of the law of the land.

I know of no sufficient warrant for declaring that any rule of international law, concerning the recognition, in that State, of a change of status, wrought by an extraterritorial law, has been displaced or varied by the will of the State of Missouri.

I proceed, then, to inquire what the rules of international law prescribe concerning the change of status of the plaintiff wrought by the law of the Territory of Wisconsin.

It is generally agreed by writers upon international law, and the rule has been judicially applied in a great number of cases, that wherever any question may arise concerning the status of a person, it must be determined according to that law which has next previously rightfully operated on and fixed that status. And further, that the laws of a country do not rightfully operate upon and fix the status of persons who are within its limits in itinere, or who are abiding there for definite temporary purposes, as for health, curiosity, or occasional business; that these laws, known to writers on public and private international law as personal statutes, operate only on the inhabitants of the country. Not that it is or can be denied that each independent nation may, if it thinks fit, apply them to all persons within their limits. But when this is done, not in conformity with the principles of international law, other States are not understood to be willing to recognize or allow effect to such applications of personal statutes.

It becomes necessary, therefore, to inquire whether the operation of the laws of the Territory of Wisconsin upon the status of the plaintiff was or was not such an operation as these principles of international law require other States to recognize and allow effect to.

And this renders it needful to attend to the particular facts and circumstances of this case. 596*] *It appears that this case came on for trial before the Circuit Court and a jury, upon an issue, in substance, whether the plaintiff, together with his wife and children, were the slaves of the defendant.

The court instructed the jury that, "upon the facts in this case, the law is with the defendant." This withdrew from the jury the consideration and decision of every matter of fact. The evidence in the case consisted of written admissions, signed by the counsel of the parties. If the case had been submitted to the judgment of the court, upon an agreed statement of facts, entered of record, in place of a special verdict, it would have been necessary for the court below, and for this court, to pronounce its judgment solely on those facts, thus agreed, without inferring any other facts therefrom. By the rules of the common law applicable to such a case, and by force of the 7th article of the Amendments of the Constitution, this court is precluded from finding any fact not agreed to by the parties on the record. No submission to the court on a statement of facts was made. It was a trial by jury, in which certain admissions, made by the parties, were the evidence. The jury were not only competent, but were bound to draw from that evidence every inference which, in their judgment, exercised according to the rules of law, it would warrant. The Circuit Court took from the jury the power to draw any inferences from the admissions made by the parties, and decided the case for the defendant. This course can be justified here, if at all, only by its appearing that upon the facts agreed, and all such inferences of fact favorable to the plaintiff's case, as the jury might have been warranted in drawing from those admissions, the law was with the defendant. Otherwise, the plaintiff would be deprived of the benefit of his trial by jury, by whom, for aught we can know, those inferences favorable to his case would have been drawn.

The material facts agreed, bearing on this part of the case, are, that Dr. Emerson, the plaintiff's master, resided about two years at the military post of Fort Snelling, being a surgeon in the Army of the United States, his domicil of origin being unknown; and what, if anything, he had done, to preserve or change his domicil prior to his residence at Rock Island, being also unknown.

Now, it is true, that under some circumstances the residence of a military officer at a particular place, in the discharge of his official duties does not amount to the acquisition of a technical domicil. But it cannot be affirmed, with correctness, that it never does. There being actual residence, and this being presumptive evidence of domicil, all the circumstances 597*] *of the case must be considered, before a legal conclusion can be reached, that his place of residence is not his domicil. If a military officer, stationed at a particular post, should entertain an exception that his residence there would be indefinitely protracted, and in consequence should remove his family to the place where his duties were to be discharged, form a permanent domestic establishment there, exer-

cise there the civil rights and discharge the civil duties of an inhabitant, while he did no act and manifested no intent to have a domicil elsewhere, I think no one would say that the mere fact that he was himself liable to be called away by the orders of the Government would prevent his acquisition of a technical domicil at the place of the residence of himself and his family. In other words, I do not think a military officer incapable of acquiring a domicil. Bruce v. Bruce, 2 Bos. & P. 230; Monroe v. Douglas, 5 Madd. Ch. 379. This being so, this case stands thus: there was evidence before the jury that Emerson resided about two years at Fort Snelling, in the Territory of Wisconsin. This may or may not have been with such intent as to make it his technical domicil. The presumption is that it was. It is so laid down by this court in Ennis v. Smith, 14 How. 400, and the authorities in support of the position are there referred to. His intent was a question of fact for the jury. Fitchburg v. Winchendon, 4 Cush. 190.

The case was taken from the jury. If they had power to find that the presumption of the necessary intent had not been rebutted, we cannot say, on this record, that Emerson had not his technical domicil at Fort Snelling. But, for reasons which I shall now proceed to give, I do not deem it necessary in this case to determine the question of the technical domicil of Dr. Emerson.

It must be admitted that the inquiry whether the law of a particular country has rightfully fixed the status of a person, so that in accordance with the principles of international law that status should be recognized in other jurisdictions, ordinarily depends on the question whether the person was domiciled in the country whose laws are asserted to have fixed his status. But, in the United States, questions of this kind may arise, where an attempt to decide solely with reference to technical domicil, tested by the rules which are applicable to changes of places of abode from one country to another, would not be consistent with sound principles. And in my judgment, this is one of those cases.

The residence of the plaintiff, who was taken by his master, Dr. Emerson, as a slave, from Missouri, to the State of Illinois, and thence to the Territory of Wisconsin, must be deemed to *have been for the time being, and until [*598 he asserted his own separate intention, the same as the residence of his master; and the inquiry, whether the personal statutes of the Territory were rightfully extended over the plaintiff, and ought, in accordance with the rules of international law, to be allowed to fix his status, must depend upon the circumstances under which Dr. Emerson went into that Territory, and remained there; and upon the further question, whether anything was there rightfully done by the plaintiff to cause those personal statutes to operate on him.

Dr. Emerson was an officer in the Army of the United States. He went into the Territory to discharge his duty to the United States. The place was out of the jurisdiction of any particular State, and within the exclusive jurisdiction of the United States. It does not appear where the domicil of origin of Dr. Emerson was, nor whether or not he had lost it, and gained another domicil, nor of what particular State, if any, he was a citizen.

On what ground can it be denied that all valid laws of the United States, Constitutionally enacted by Congress for the government of the Territory, rightfully extended over an officer of the United States and his servant who went into the Territory to remain there for an indefinite length of time, to take part in its civil or military affairs? They were not foreigners, coming from abroad. Dr. Emerson was a citizen of the country which had exclusive jurisdiction over the Territory; and not only a citizen, but he went there in a public capacity, in the service of the same sovereignty which made the laws. Whatever those laws might be, whether of the kind denominated personal statutes, or not, so far as they were intended by the legislative will, constitutionally expressed, to operate on him and his servant, and on the relations between them, they had a rightful operation, and no other State or country can refuse to allow that those laws might rightfully operate on the plaintiff and his servant, because such a refusal would be a denial that the United States could, by laws constitutionally enacted, govern their own servants, residing on their own territory, over which the United States had the exclusive control, and in respect to which they are an independent sovereign power. Whether the laws now in question were constitutionally enacted, I repeat once more, is a separate question. But, assuming that they were, and that they operated directly on the status of the plaintiff, I consider that no other State or country could question the rightful power of the United States so to legislate, or, consistently with the settled rules of international law, could refuse **599*]** to recognize the effects *of such legislation upon the status of their officers and servants, as valid everywhere.

This alone would, in my apprehension, be sufficient to decide this question.

But there are other facts stated on the record which should not be passed over. It is agreed that in the year 1836, the plaintiff, while residing in the Territory, was married, with the consent of Dr. Emerson, to Harriet, named in the declaration as his wife, and that Eliza and Lizzie were the children of that marriage, the first named having been born on the Mississippi River, north of the line of Missouri, and the other having been born after their return to Missouri. And the inquiry is, whether, after the marriage of the plaintiff in the Territory, with the consent of Dr. Emerson, any other State or country can, consistently with the settled rules of international law, refuse to recognize and treat him as a free man, when suing for the liberty of himself, his wife, and the children of that marriage. It is in reference to his status, as viewed in other States and countries, that the contract of marriage and the birth of children becomes strictly material. At the same time, it is proper to observe that the female to whom he was married having been taken to the same military post of Fort Snelling as a slave, and Dr. Emerson claiming also to be her master at the time of her marriage, her status, and that of the children of the marriage, are also affected by the same consideration.

If the laws of Congress governing the Territory of Wisconsin were constitutional and valid laws, there can be no doubt these parties were capable of contracting a lawful marriage, attended with all the usual civil rights and obligations of that condition. In that Territory they were absolutely free persons, having full capacity to enter into the civil contract of marriage.

It is a principle of international law, settled beyond controversy in England and America, that a marriage, valid by the law of the place where it was contracted, and not in fraud of the law of any other place, is valid everywhere: and that no technical domicil at the place of the contract is necessary to make it so. See Bishop on Mar. and Div. 125–129, where the cases are collected.

If, in Missouri, the plaintiff were held to be a slave, the validity and operation of his contract of marriage must be denied. He can have no legal rights; of course, not those of a husband and father. And the same is true of his wife and children. The denial of his rights is the denial of theirs. So that, though lawfully married in the Territory, when they came out of it, into the State of Missouri, they were no longer *husband and wife; and a [*600 child of that lawful marriage, though born under the same dominion where its parents contracted a lawful marriage, is not the fruit of that marriage, nor the child of its father, nor subject to the maxim, partus sequitur ventrem.

It must be borne in mind that in this case there is no ground for the inquiry, whether it be the will of the State of Missouri not to recognize the validity of the marriage of a fugitive slave, who escapes into a State or country where slavery is not allowed, and there contracts a marriage; or the validity of such a marriage, where the master, being a citizen of the State of Missouri, voluntarily goes with his slave in itinere, into a State or country which does not permit slavery to exist, and the slave there contracts marriage without the consent of his master; for in this case, it is agreed, Dr. Emerson did consent; and no further question can arise concerning his rights, so far as their assertion is inconsistent with the validity of the marriage. Nor do I know of any ground for the assertion that this marriage was in fraud of any law of Missouri. It has been held by this court, that a bequest of property by a master to his slave, by necessary implication entitles the slave to his freedom; because, only as a freeman could he take and hold the bequest. Legrand v. Darnall, 2 Pet. 664. It has also been held, that when a master goes with his slave to reside for an indefinite period in a State where slavery is not tolerated, this operates as an act of manumission; because it is sufficiently expressive of the consent of the master that the slave should be free. 2 Marsh. Ky. 470; 14 Mart. La. 401.

What, then, shall we say of the consent of the master, that the slave may contract a lawful marriage attended with all the civil rights and duties which belong to that relation; that he may enter into a relation which none but a free man can assume—a relation which involves not only the rights and duties of the slave, but those of the other party to the contract, and of their descendants to the remotest generation? In my judgment, there can be no more effectual abandonment of the legal rights of a master over his slave, than by the consent of the master that the slave should enter into a contract of marriage, in a free State, attended by all the civil rights and obligations which belong to that condition.

And any claim by Dr. Emerson, or anyone claiming under him, the effect of which is to deny the validity of this marriage, and the lawful paternity of the children born from it, wherever asserted, is, in my judgment, a claim inconsistent with good faith and sound reason, as well as with the rules of international law. And I go further: in my opinion, a law of the **601*]** State *of Missouri, which should thus annul a marriage, lawfully contracted by these parties while resident in Wisconsin, not in fraud of any law of Missouri, or of any right of Dr. Emerson, who consented thereto, would be a law impairing the obligation of a contract, and within the prohibition of the Constitution of the United States. See 4 Wheat. 629, 695, 696.

To avoid misapprehension on this important and difficult subject, I will state, distinctly, the conclusions at which I have arrived. They are:

First. The rules of international law respecting the emancipation of slaves, by the rightful operation of the laws of another State or country upon the status of the slave, while resident in such foreign State or country, are part of the common law of Missouri, and have not been abrogated by any statute law of that State.

Second. The laws of the United States, constitutionally enacted, which operated directly on and changed the status of a slave coming into the Territory of Wisconsin with his master, who went thither to reside for an indefinite length of time, in the performance of his duties as an officer of the United States, had a rightful operation on the status of the slave, and it is in conformity with the rules of international law that this change of status should be recognized everywhere.

Third. The laws of the United States, in operation in the Territory of Wisconsin at the time of the plaintiff's residence there, did act directly on the status of the plaintiff, and change his status to that of a free man.

Fourth. The plaintiff and his wife were capable of contracting, and, with the consent of Dr. Emerson, did contract a marriage in that Territory, valid under its laws; and the validity of this marriage cannot be questioned in Missouri, save by showing that it was in fraud of the laws of that State, or of some right derived from them; which cannot be shown in this case, because the master consented to it.

Fifth. That the consent of the master that his slave, residing in a country which does not tolerate slavery, may enter into a lawful contract of marriage, attended with the civil rights and duties which belong to that condition, is an effectual act of emancipation. And the law does not enable Dr. Emerson, or anyone claiming under him, to assert a title to the married persons as slaves, and thus destroy the obligation of the contract of marriage, and bastardize their issue, and reduce them to slavery.

But it is insisted that the Supreme Court of Missouri has settled this case by its decision in Scott v. Emerson, 15 Mo. 576; and that this de-**602*]** cision is in conformity *with the weight

782

of authority elsewhere, and with sound principles. If the Supreme Court of Missouri had placed its decision on the ground that it appeared Dr. Emerson never became domiciled in the Territory, and so its laws could not rightfully operate on him and his slave; and the facts that he went there to reside indefinitely, as an officer of the United States, and that the plaintiff was lawfully married there, with Dr. Emerson's consent, were left out of view, the decision would find support in other cases, and I might not be prepared to deny its correctness. But the decision is not rested on this ground. The domicil of Dr. Emerson in that Territory is not questioned in that decision: and it is placed on a broad denial, of the operation, in Missouri, of the law of any foreign State or country, upon the status of a slave, going with his master from Missouri into such foreign State or country, even though they went thither to become, and actually became, permanent inhabitants of such foreign State or country, the laws whereof acted directly on the status of the slave, and changed his status to that of a freeman.

To the correctness of such a decision I cannot assent. In my judgment, the opinion of the majority of the court in that case is in conflict with its previous decisions, with a great weight of judicial authority in other slaveholding States, and with fundamental principles of private international law. Mr. Chief Justice Gamble in his dissenting opinion in that case, said:

"I regard the question as conclusively settled by repeated adjudications of this court; and if I doubted or denied the propriety of those decisions, I would not feel myself any more at liberty to overturn them, than I would any other series of decisions by which the law upon any other question had been settled. There is with me nothing in the law of slavery which distinguishes it from the law on any other subject, or allows any more accommodation to the temporary excitements which have gathered around it. . . . But in the midst of all such excitement, it is proper that the judicial mind, calm and self-balanced, should adhere to principles established when there was no feeling to disturb the view of the legal questions upon which the rights of parties depend."

"In this State, it has been recognized from the beginning of the government as a correct position in law, that the master who takes his slave to reside in a State or Territory where slavery is prohibited, thereby emancipates his slave." Whinney v. Whitesides, 1 Mo. 473; Le Grange v. Chouteau, 2 Mo. 20; Milley v. Smith, 2 Mo. 36; Ralph v. Duncan, 3 Mo. 194; Julia v. McKinney, 3 Mo. 270; Nat v. Ruddle, 3 Mo. 400; Rachel v. Walker, 4 Mo. 350; Wilson v. Melvin, 4 Mo. 592.

*Chief Justice Gamble has also exam- **[*603** ined the decisions of the courts of other States in which slavery is established, and finds them in accordance with these preceding decisions of the Supreme Court of Missouri to which he refers.

It would be a useless parade of learning for me to go over the ground which he has so fully and ably occupied.

But it is further insisted we are bound to follow this decision. I do not think so. In

1856.   DRED SCOTT V. SANDFORD.   393-633

this case, it is to be determined what laws of the United States were in operation in the Territory of Wisconsin, and what was their effect on the status of the plaintiff. Could the plaintiff contract a lawful marriage there? Does any law of the State of Missouri impair the obligation of that contract of marriage, destroy his rights as a husband, bastardize the use of marriage, and reduce them to a state of slavery?

The questions which arise exclusively under the Constitution and laws of the United States, this court, under the Constitution and laws of the United States, has the rightful authority finally to decide. And if we look beyond these questions, we come to the consideration whether the rules of international law, which are part of the laws of Missouri until displaced by some statute not alleged to exist, do or do not require the status of the plaintiff, as fixed by the laws of the Territory of Wisconsin, to be recognized in Missouri. Upon such a question, not depending on any statute or local usage, but on principles of universal jurisprudence, this court has repeatedly asserted it could not hold itself bound by the decisions of State Courts, however great respect might be felt for their learning, ability, and impartiality. See Swift v. Tyson, 16 Pet. 1; Carpenter v. The Providence Ins. Co. 16 Pet. 495; Foxcroft v. Mallet, 4 How. 353; Rowan v. Runnels, 5 How. 134.

Some reliance has been placed on the fact that the decision in the Supreme Court of Missouri was between these parties, and the suit there was abandoned to obtain another trial in the courts of the United States.

In Homer v. Brown, 16 How. 354, this court made a decision upon the construction of a devise of lands, in direct opposition to the unanimous opinion of the Supreme Court of Massachusetts, between the same parties, respecting the same subject matter—the claimant having become nonsuit in the State Court, in order to bring his action in the Circuit Court of the United States. I did not sit in that case, having been of counsel for one of the parties while at the bar; but, on examining the report of the argument of the counsel for the plaintiff in error, I find they made the point, that this court ought to give effect to the construction put 604*] upon by the will by the State *Court, to the end that rights respecting lands may be governed by one law, and that the law of the place where the lands are situated; that they referred to the state decision of the case, reported in 3 Cushing, 390, and to many decisions of this court. But this court does not seem to have considered the point of sufficient importance to notice it in their opinions. In Millar v. Austin, 13 How. 218, an action was brought by the indorsee of a written promise. The question was, whether it was negotiable under a statute of Ohio. The Supreme Court of that State having decided it was not negotiable, the plaintiff became nonsuit, and brought his action in the Circuit Court of the United States. The decision of the Supreme Court of the State, reported in 4 Ves. L. J. 527, was relied on. This court unanimously held the paper to be negotiable.

When the decisions of the highest court of a State are directly in conflict with each other, it has been repeatedly held, here, that the last decision is not necessarily to be taken as the

rule. State Bank v. Knoop, 16 How. 369; Pease v. Peck, 18 How. 599.

To these considerations I desire to add, that it was not made known to the Supreme Court of Missouri, so far as appears, that the plaintiff was married in Wisconsin with the consent of Dr. Emerson, and it is not made known to us that Dr. Emerson was a citizen of Missouri, a fact to which that court seem to have attached much importance.

Sitting here to administer the law between these parties, I do not feel at liberty to surrender my own convictions of what the law requires, to the authority of the decision in 15 Missouri Reports.

I have thus far assumed, merely for the purpose of the argument, that the laws of the United States, respecting slavery in this Territory, were Constitutionally enacted by Congress. It remains to inquire whether they are constitutional and binding laws.

In the argument of this part of the case at bar, it was justly considered by all the counsel to be necessary to ascertain the source of the power of Congress over the Territory belonging to the United States. Until this is ascertained, it is not possible to determine the extent of that power. On the one side it was maintained that the Constitution contains no express grant of power to organize and govern what is known to the laws of the United States as a Territory. That whatever power of this kind exists, is derived by implication from the capacity of the United States to hold and acquire territory out of the limits of any State, and the necessity for its having some government.

*On the other side it was insisted that [*605 the Constitution has not failed to make an express provision for this end, and that it is found in the 3d Section of the 4th Article of the Constitution.

To determine which of these is the correct view, it is needful to advert to some facts respecting this subject, which existed when the Constitution was framed and adopted. It will be found that these facts not only shed much light on the question, whether the framers of the Constitution omitted to make a provision concerning the power of Congress to organize and govern Territories, but they will also aid in the construction of any provision which may have been made respecting this subject.

Under the Confederation, the unsettled territory within the limits of the United States had been a subject of deep interest. Some of the States insisted that these lands were within their chartered boundaries, and that they had succeeded to the title of the Crown to the soil. On the other hand, it was argued that the vacant lands had been acquired by the United States, by the war carried on by them under a common government and for the common interest.

This dispute was further complicated by unsettled questions of boundary among several States. It not only delayed the accession of Maryland to the Confederation, but at one time seriously threatened its existence. 5 Jour. of Cong. 208, 442. Under the pressure of these circumstances, Congress earnestly recommended to the several States a cession of their claims and rights to the United States. 5 Jour. of Cong. 442. And before the Constitution was framed, it had been begun. That by New

York had been made on the 1st day of March, 1781; that of Virginia on the 1st day of March, 1784; that of Massachusetts on the 19th day of April, 1785, that of Connecticut on the 14th day of September, 1786; that of South Carolina on the 8th day of August, 1787, while the convention for framing the Constitution was in session.

It is very material to observe, in this connection, that each of these Acts cedes, in terms, to the United States, as well the jurisdiction as the soil.

It is also equally important to note that, when the Constitution was framed and adopted, this plan of vesting in the United States, for the common good, the great tracts of ungranted lands claimed by the several States, in which so deep an interest was felt, was yet incomplete. It remained for North Carolina and Georgia to cede their extensive and valuable claims. These were made, by North Carolina on the 25th day of February, 1790, and by **606***] Georgia on the 24th day of April, *1802. The terms of these last mentioned cessions will hereafter be noticed in another connection; but I observe here that each of them distinctly shows, upon its face, that they were not only in execution of the general plan proposed by the Congress of the Confederation, but of a formed purpose of each of these States, existing when the assent of their respective people was given to the Constitution of the United States.

It appears, then, that when the Federal Constitution was framed, and, presented to the people of the several States for their consideration, the unsettled territory was viewed as justly applicable to the common benefit, so far as it then had or might attain thereafter a pecuniary value; and so far as it might become the seat of new States, to be admitted into the Union upon an equal footing with the original States. And also that the relations of the United States to that unsettled territory were of different kinds. The titles of the States of New York, Virginia, Massachusetts, Connecticut, and South Carolina, as well of soil as of jurisdiction, had been transferred to the United States. North Carolina and Georgia had not actually made transfers, but a confident expectation, founded on their appreciation of the justice of the general claim, and fully justified by the results, was entertained, that these cessions would be made. The Ordinance of 1787 had made provision for the temporary government of so much of the territory, actually ceded, as lay northwest of the River Ohio.

But it must have been apparent, both to the framers of the Constitution and the people of the several States who were to act upon it, that the government thus provided for could not continue, unless the Constitution should confer on the United States the necessary powers to continue it. That temporary government, under the Ordinance, was to consist of certain officers, to be appointed by and responsible to the Congress of the Confederation; their powers had been conferred and defined by the ordinance. So far as it provided for the temporary gov-

ernment of the Territory, it was an ordinary Act of legislation, deriving its force from the legislative power of Congress, and depending for its vitality upon the continuance of that legislative power. But the officers to be appointed for the Northwestern Territory, after the adoption of the Constitution, must necessarily be officers of the United States, and not of the Congress of the Confederation; appointed and commissioned by the President, and exercising powers derived from the United States under the Constitution.

Such was the relation between the United States and the Northwestern Territory, which all reflecting men must have foreseen would exist, when the government created by the *Constitution should supersede that of [*607 the Confederation. That if the new government should be without power to govern this Territory, it could not appoint and commission officers, to exercise their legislative, judicial and executive power; and that this Territory, which was even then foreseen to be so important, both politically and financially, to all the existing States, must be left not only without the control of the General Government, in respect to its future political relations to the rest of the States, but absolutely without any government, save what its inhabitants, acting in their primary capacity, might from time to time create for themselves.

But this Northwestern Territory was not the only Territory, the soil and jurisdiction whereof were understood to have been ceded to the United States. The cession by South Carolina, made in August, 1787, was of "all the territory included within the River Mississippi, and a line beginning at that part of the said river which is intersected by the southern boundary of North Carolina, and continuing along the said boundary line until it intersects the ridge or chain of mountains which divides the Eastern from the Western waters; then to be continued along the top of the said ridge of mountains, until it intersects a line to be drawn due west from the head of the southern branch of the Tugaloo River, to the said mountains; and thence to run a due west course to the River Mississippi."

It is true that by subsequent explorations it was ascertained that the source of the Tugaloo River, upon which the title of South Carolina depended, was so far to the northward, that the transfer conveyed only a narrow slip of land, about twelve miles wide, lying on the top of the ridge of mountains, and extending from the northern boundary of Georgia to the southern boundary of North Carolina. But this was a discovery made long after the cession, and there can be no doubt that the State of South Carolina, in making the cession, and the Congress in accepting it, viewed it as a transfer to the United States of the soil and jurisdiction of an extensive and important part of the unsettled territory ceded by the Crown of Great Britain by the Treaty of Peace, though its quantity or extent then remained to be ascertained.[1]

1.—Note by Mr. Justice Curtis. This statement that some territory did actually pass by this cession, is taken from the opinion of the court, delivered by Mr. Justice Wayne, in the case of Howard v. Ingersoll, reported in 13 How. 405. It is an obscure matter, and, on some examination of it, I have been led to doubt whether any territory actually passed by this cession. But as the fact is not important to the argument, I have not thought it necessary further to investigate it.

1856. DRED SCOTT V. SANDFORD. 393–633

It must be remembered also, as has been already stated, that not only was there a confident expectation entertained by the 608*] *other States, that North Carolina and Georgia would complete the plan already so far executed by New York, Virginia, Massachusetts, Connecticut, and South Carolina, but that the opinion was in no small degree prevalent, that the just title to this "back country," as it was termed, had vested in the United States by the Treaty of Peace, and could not rightfully be claimed by any individual State.

There is another consideration applicable to this part of the subject, and entitled, in my judgment, to great weight.

The Congress of the Confederation had assumed the power not only to dispose of the lands ceded, but to institute governments and make laws for their inhabitants. In other words, they had proceeded to act under the cession, which, as we have seen, was as well of the jurisdiction as of the soil. This Ordinance was passed on the 13th of July, 1787. The Convention for framing the Constitution was then in session at Philadelphia. The proof is direct and decisive, that it was known to the Convention.[1] It is equally clear that it was admitted and understood not to be within the legitimate powers of the Confederation to pass this Ordinance. Jefferson's Works, Vol. IX. pp. 251, 276; Federalist, Nos. 38, 43.

The importance of conferring on the new government regular powers commensurate with the objects to be attained, and thus avoiding the alternative of a failure to execute the trust assumed by the acceptance of the cessions made and expected, or its execution by usurpation, could scarcely fail to be perceived. That it was in fact perceived, is clearly shown by the Federalist (No. 38), where this very argument is made use of in commendation of the Constitution. Keeping these facts in view, it may confidently be asserted that there is very strong reason to believe, before we examine the Constitution itself, that the necessity for a competent grant of power to hold, dispose of, and govern territory, ceded and expected to be ceded, could not have escaped the attention of those who framed or adopted the Constitution; and that if it did not escape their attention, it could not fail to be adequately provided for.

Any other conclusion would involve the assumption that a subject of the gravest national concern, respecting which the small States felt so much jealousy that it had been almost an insurmountable obstacle to the formation of the Confederation, and as to which all the States had deep pecuniary and political interests, and which had been so recently and constantly 609*] agitated, *was nevertheless overlooked; or that such a subject was not overlooked, but designedly left unprovided for, though it was manifestly a subject of common concern, which belonged to the care of the General Government, and adequate provision for which could not fail to be deemed necessary and proper.

The admission of new States, to be framed out of the ceded territory, early attracted the attention of the Convention. Among the resolutions introduced by Mr. Randolph, on the 29th of May, was one on this subject (Res. No. 10, 5 Elliot, 128), which, having been affirmed in Committee of the Whole, on the 5th of June (5 Elliot, 156), and reported to the Convention on the 13th of June (5 Elliot, 190), was referred to the Committee of Detail, to prepare the Constitution, on the 26th of July (5 Elliot, 376). This committee reported an article for the admission of new States "lawfully constituted or established." Nothing was said concerning the power of Congress to prepare or form such States. This omission struck Mr. Madison, who, on the 18th of August (5 Elliot, 439), moved for the insertion of power to dispose of the unappropriated lands of the United States, and to institute temporary governments for new States arising therein.

On the 29th of August (5 Elliot, 492), the report of the committee was taken up, and after debate, which exhibited great diversity of views concerning the proper mode of providing for the subject, arising out of the supposed diversity of interests of the large and small States, and between those which had and those which had not unsettled territory, but no difference of opinion respecting the propriety and necessity of some adequate provision for the subject, Gouverneur Morris moved the clause as it stands in the Constitution. This met with general approbation, and was at once adopted. The whole section is as follows:

"New States may be admitted by the Congress into this Union; but no new States shall be formed or erected within the jurisdiction of any other State, nor any State be formed by the junction of two or more States, or parts of States, without the consent of the Legislatures of the States concerned, as well as of Congress.

The Congress shall have power to dispose of, and make all needful rules and regulations respecting the territory or other property belonging to the United States; and nothing in this Constitution shall be so construed as to prejudice any claims of the United States or any particular State."

That Congress has some power to institute temporary governments over the Territory, I believe all agree; and, if it be admitted that the necessity of some power to govern the Territory *of the United States could not [*610 and did not escape the attention of the Convention and the people, and the necessity is so great that, in the absence of any express grant, it is strong enough to raise an implication of the existence of that power, it would seem to follow that it is also strong enough to afford material aid in construing an express grant of power respecting that Territory; and that they who maintain the existence of the power, without finding any words at all in which it is conveyed, should be willing to receive a reasonable interpretation of language of the Constitution, manifestly intended to relate to the Territory, and to convey to Congress some authority concerning it.

It would seem, also, that when we find the subject matter of the growth and formation and admission of new States, and the disposal of the Territory for these ends, were under consideration, and that some provision therefor was expressly made, it is improbable that it would be, in its terms, a grossly inadequate provision; and that an indispensably necessary

---

1.—It was published in a newspaper at Philadelphia, in May, and a copy of it was sent by R. H. Lee to Gen. Washington, on the 15th of July. See p. 261, Cor. of Am. Rev. Vol. IV., and Writings of Washington, Vol. IX. p. 174.

power to institute temporary governments, and to legislate for the inhabitants of the Territory, was passed silently by, and left to be deduced from the necessity of the case.

In the argument at the bar, great attention has been paid to the meaning of the word "territory."

Ordinarily, when the territory of a sovereign power is spoken of, it refers to that tract of country which is under the political jurisdiction of that sovereign power. Thus Chief Justice Marshall, in United States v. Bevans, 3 Wheat. 386, says: "What, then, is the extent of jurisdiction which a State possesses? We answer, without hesitation, the jurisdiction of a State is co-extensive with its territory." Examples might easily be multiplied of this use of the word, but they are unnecessary, because it is familiar. But the word "territory" is not used in this broad and general sense in this clause of the Constitution.

At the time of the adoption of the Constitution, the United States held a great tract of country northwest of the Ohio; another tract, then of unknown extent, ceded by South Carolina; and a confident expectation was then entertained, and afterwards realized, that they then were or would become the owners of other great tracts, claimed by North Carolina and Georgia. These ceded tracts lay within the limits of the United States, and out of the limits of any particular State; and the cessions embraced the civil and political jurisdiction, and so much of the soil as had not previously been granted to individuals.

These words, "territory belonging to the 611*] United States," were *not used in the Constitution to describe an abstraction, but to identify and apply to these actual subjects, matter then existing and belonging to the United States, and other similar subjects which might afterwards be acquired; and this being so, all the essential qualities and incidents attending such actual subjects are embraced within the words "territory belonging to the United States," as fully as if each of those essential qualities and incidents had been specifically described.

I say, the essential qualities and incidents. But in determining what were the essential qualities and incidents of the subject with which they were dealing, we must take into consideration not only all the particular facts which were immediately before them, but the great consideration, ever present to the minds of those who framed and adopted the Constitution, that they were making a frame of government for the people of the United States and their posterity, under which they hoped the United States might be, what they have now become, a great and powerful nation, possessing the power to make war and to conclude treaties, and thus to acquire territory. See Sere v. Pitot, 6 Cranch, 336; Am. Ins. Co. v. Canter, 1 Pet. 542. With these in view, I turn to examine the clause of the article now in question.

It is said this provision has no application to any territory save that then belonging to the United States. I have already shown that, when the Constitution was framed, a confident expectation was entertained, which was speedily realized, that North Carolina and Georgia would cede their claims to that great Territory

which lay west of those States. No doubt has been suggested that the first clause of this same article, which enabled Congress to admit new States, refers to and includes new States to be formed out of this Territory, expected to be thereafter ceded by North Carolina and Georgia, as well as new States to be formed out of territory northwest of the Ohio, which then had been ceded by Virginia. It must have been seen, therefore, that the same necessity would exist for an authority to dispose of and make all needful regulations respecting this Territory, when ceded, as existed for a like authority respecting territory which had been ceded.

No reason has been suggested why any reluctance should have been felt, by the framers of the Constitution, to apply this provision to all the territory which might belong to the United States, or why any distinction should have been made, founded on the accidental circumstance of the dates of the cessions; a circumstance in no way material as respects the necessity for rules and regulations, or the propriety of conferring *on the Congress [*612 power to make them. And if we look at the course of the debates in the Convention on this article, we shall find that the then unceded lands, so far from having been left out of view in adopting this article, constituted, in the minds of members, a subject of even paramount importance.

Again; in what an extraordinary position would the limitation of this clause to territory then belonging to the United States, place the Territory which lay within the chartered limits of North Carolina and Georgia. The title to that Territory was then claimed by those States, and by the United States; their respective claims are purposely left unsettled by the express words of this clause; and when cessions were made by those States, they were merely of their claims to this Territory, the United States neither admitting nor denying the validity of those claims; so that it was impossible then, and has ever since remained impossible, to know whether this Territory did or did not then belong to the United States; and, consequently, to know whether it was within or without the authority conferred by this clause, to dispose of and make rules and regulations respecting the territory of the United States. This attributes to the eminent men who acted on this subject a want of ability and forecast, or a want of attention to the known facts upon which they were acting, in which I cannot concur.

There is not, in my judgment, anything in the language, the history, or the subject matter of this article, which restricts its operation to territory owned by the United States when the Constitution was adopted.

But it is also insisted that provisions of the Constitution respecting territory belonging to the United States do not apply to territory acquired by treaty from a foreign nation. This objection must rest upon the position that the Constitution did not authorize the Federal Government to acquire foreign territory, and consequently has made no provision for its government when acquired; or, that though the acquisition of foreign territory was contemplated by the Constitution, its provisions concerning the admission of new States, and the making of all needful rules and regulations respecting territory belonging to the United States, were not designed to be applicable to territory acquired from foreign nations.

It is undoubtedly true, that at the date of the Treaty of 1803, between the United States and France, for the cession of Louisiana, it was made a question, whether the Constitution had conferred on the Executive Department of the Government of the United States power to acquire foreign territory by a treaty. 613*] *There is evidence that very grave doubts were then entertained concerning the existence of this power. But that there was then a settled opinion in the executive and legislative branches of the government, that this power did not exist, cannot be admitted, without at the same time imputing to those who negotiated and ratified the Treaty, and passed the laws necessary to carry it into execution, a deliberate and known violation of their oaths to support the Constitution; and whatever doubts may then have existed, the question must now be taken to have been settled. Four distinct acquisitions of foreign territory have been made by as many different treaties, under as many· different administrations. Six States, formed on such territory, are now in the Union. Every branch of this government, during a period of more than fifty years, has participated in these transactions. To question their validity now, is vain. As was said by Mr. Chief Justice Marshall, in The American Insurance Company v. Canter, 1 Pet. 542, "the Constitution confers absolutely on the government of the Union the powers of making war and of making treaties; consequently, that government possesses the power of acquiring territory, either by conquest or treaty." See Sere v. Pitot, 6 Cranch, 336. And I add, it also possesses the power of governing it, when acquired, not by resorting to supposititious powers, nowhere found described in the Constitution, but expressly granted in the authority to make all needful rules and regulations, respecting the Territory of the United States.

There was to be established by the Constitution a frame of government, under which the people of the United States and their posterity were to continue indefinitely. To take one of its provisions, the language of which is broad enough to extend throughout the existence of the government, and embrace all territory belonging to the United States throughout all time, and the purposes and objects of which apply to all Territory of the United States, and narrow it down to territory belonging to the United States when the Constitution was framed, while at the same time it is admitted that the Constitution contemplated and authorized the acquisition, from time to time, of other and foreign territory, seems to me to be an interpretation as inconsistent with the nature and purposes of the instrument, as it is with its language, and I can have no hesitation in rejecting it.

I construe this clause, therefore, as if it had read, Congress shall have power to make all needful rules and regulations respecting those tracts of country, out of the limits of the several States, which the United States have acquired, or may hereafter acquire, by cessions, 614*] as well of the jurisdiction as of the *soil, so far as the soil may be the property of the

15 L. ed.

party making the cession, at the time of making it.

It has been urged that the words "rules and regulations" are not appropriate terms in which to convey authority to make laws for the government of the Territory.

But it must be remembered that this is a grant of power to the Congress—that it is, therefore, necessarily a grant of power to legislate—and certainly, rules and regulations respecting a particular subject, made by the legislative power of a country, can be nothing but laws. Nor do the particular terms employed, in my judgment, tend in any degree to restrict this legislative power. Power granted to a Legislature to make all needful rules and regulations respecting the Territory, is a power to pass all needful laws respecting it.

The word regulate, or regulation, is several times used in the Constitution. It is used in the 4th section of the 1st article to describe those laws of the States which prescribe the times, places, and manner, of choosing Senators and Representatives; in the 2d section of the 4th article, to designate the legislative action of a State on the subject of fugitives from service, having a very close relation to the matter of our present inquiry; in the 2d section of the 3d article, to empower Congress to fix the extent of the appellate jurisdiction of this court; and, finally, in the 8th section of the 1st article in the words, "Congress shall have power to regulate commerce."

It is unnecessary to describe the body of legislation which has been enacted under this grant of power; its variety and extent are well known. But it may be mentioned, in passing, that under this power to regulate commerce, Congress has enacted a great system of municipal laws, and extended it over the vessels and crews of the United States on the high seas and in foreign ports, and even over citizens of the United States resident in China; and has established judicatures, with power to inflict even capital punishment within that country.

If, then, this clause does contain a power to legislate respecting the Territory, what are the limits of that power?

To this I answer, that, in common with all the other legislative powers of Congress, it finds limits in the express prohibitions on Congress not to do certain things; that, in the exercise of the legislative power, Congress cannot pass an ex post facto law or bill of attainder; and so in respect to each of the other prohibitions contained in the Constitution.

Besides this, the rules and regulations must be needful. But undoubtedly the question whether a particular rule or regulation be needful, must be finally determined by Congress itself. Whether a law be needful, is a legislative or political, *not a judicial, ques- [*615 tion. Whatever Congress deems needful, is so, under the grant of power.

Nor am I aware that it has ever been questioned that laws providing for the temporary government of the settlers on the public lands are needful, not only to prepare them for admission to the Union as States, but even to enable the United States to dispose of the lands.

Without government and social order there can be no property; for without law, its ownership, its use and the power of disposing of it, cease to exist, in the sense in which those words are used and understood in all civilized States.

Since, then, this power was manifestly conferred to enable the United States to dispose of its public lands to settlers, and to admit them into the Union as States, when in the judgment of Congress they should be fitted therefor, since these were the needs provided for, since it is confessed that Government is indispensable to provide for those needs, and the power is, to make all needful rules and regulations respecting the Territory, I cannot doubt that this is a power to govern the inhabitants of the Territory, by such laws as Congress deems needful, until they obtain admission as States.

Whether they should be thus governed solely by laws enacted by Congress, or partly by laws enacted by legislative power conferred by Congress, is one of those questions which depend on the judgment of Congress—a question which of these is needful.

But it is insisted, that whatever other powers Congress may have respecting the Territory of the United States, the subject of negro slavery forms an exception.

The Constitution declares that Congress shall have power to make "all needful rules and regulations" respecting the Territory belonging to the United States.

The assertion is, though the Constitution says all, it does not mean all—though it says all, without qualification, it means all except such as allow or prohibit slavery. It cannot be doubted that it is incumbent on those who would thus introduce an exception not found in the language of the instrument, to exhibit some solid and satisfactory reason, drawn from the subject matter or the purposes and objects of the clause, the context, or from other provisions of the Constitution, showing that the words employed in this clause are not to be understood, according to their clear, plain, and natural signification.

The subject matter is the Territory of the United States out of the limits of every State, and consequently under the exclusive power of the people of the United States. Their **616*]** *will respecting it, manifested in the Constitution, can be subject to no restriction. The purposes and objects of the clause were the enactment of laws concerning the disposal of the public lands, and the temporary government of the settlers thereon, until new States should be formed. It will not be questioned that, when the Constitution of the United States was framed and adopted, the allowance and the prohibition of negro slavery were recognized subjects of municipal legislation; every State had in some measure acted thereon; and the only legislative Act concerning the Territory—the Ordinance of 1787, which had then so recently been passed— contained a prohibition of slavery. The purpose and object of the clause being to enable Congress to provide a body of municipal law for the government of the settlers, the allowance or the prohibition of slavery comes within the known and recognized scope of that purpose and object.

There is nothing in the context which qualifies the grant of power. The regulations must be "respecting the Territory." An enactment that slavery may or may not exist there, is a

788

regulation respecting the Territory. Regulations must be needful; but it is necessarily left to the legislative discretion to determine whether a law be needful. No other clause of the Constitution has been referred to at the bar, or has been seen by me, which imposes any restriction or makes any exception concerning the power of Congress to allow or prohibit slavery in the territory belonging to the United States.

A practical construction, nearly contemporaneous with the adoption of the Constitution, and continued by repeated instances through a long series of years, may always influence, and in doubtful cases should determine, the judicial mind, on a question of the interpretation of the Constitution. Stuart v. Laird, 1 Cranch, 299; Martin v. Hunter, 1 Wheat. 304; Cohens v. Virginia, 6 Wheat. 264; Prigg v. Pennsylvania, 16 Pet. 621; Cooley v. Port Wardens, 12 How. 315.

In this view, I proceed briefly to examine the practical construction placed on the clause now in question, so far as it respects the inclusion therein of power to permit or prohibit slavery in the Territories.

It has already been stated, that after the Government of the United States was organized under the Constitution, the temporary government of the Territory northwest of the River Ohio could no longer exist, save under the powers conferred on Congress by the Constitution. Whatever legislative, judicial, or executive authority should be exercised therein could be derived only from the people of the United States under the Constitution. And, accordingly, an Act was passed on the 7th *day[*617 of August, 1789, 1 Stat. at L. 50, which recites: "Whereas, in order that the Ordinance of the United States in Congress assembled, for the government of the Territory northwest of the River Ohio, may continue to have full effect, it is required that certain provisions should be made, so as to adapt the same to the present Constitution of the United States." It then provides for the appointment by the President of all officers, who, by force of the Ordinance, were to have been appointed by the Congress of the Confederation, and their commission in the manner required by the Constitution; and empowers the Secretary of the Territory to exercise the powers of the Governor in case of the death or necessary absence of the latter.

Here is an explicit declaration of the will of the first Congress, of which fourteen members, including Mr. Madison, had been members of the Convention which framed the Constitution, that the Ordinance, one article of which prohibited slavery, "should continue to have good effect." Gen. Washington, who signed this bill, as President, was the President of that Convention.

It does not appear to me to be important, in this connection, that that clause in the Ordinance which prohibited slavery was one of a series of articles of what is therein termed a compact. The Congress of the Confederation had no power to make such a compact, nor to act at all on the subject; and after what had been so recently said by Mr. Madison on this subject, in the thirty-eighth number of the Federalist, I cannot suppose that he, or any others who voted for this bill, attributed any intrinsic effect to what was denominated in the

Ordinance a compact between "the original States and the people and States in the new territory;" there being no new States then in existence in the Territory, with whom a compact could be made, and the few scattered inhabitants, unorganized into a political body, not being capable of becoming a party to a treaty, even if the Congress of the Confederation had had power to make one touching the government of that Territory.

I consider the passage of this law to have been an assertion by the first Congress of the power of the United States to prohibit slavery within this part of the Territory of the United States; for it clearly shows that slavery was there after to be prohibited there, and it could be prohibited only by an exertion of the power of the United States, under the Constitution; no other power being capable of operating within that Territory after the Constitution took effect.

On the 2d of April, 1790, 1 Stat. at L. 106, the first Congress passed an Act accepting a **618*]** deed of cession by North *Carolina of that Territory afterwards erected into the State of Tennessee. The fourth express condition contained in this deed of cession, after providing that the inhabitants of the Territory shall be temporarily governed in the same manner as those beyond the Ohio, is followed by these words: "Provided, always, that no regulations made or to be made by Congress shall tend to emancipate slaves."

This provision shows that it was then understood Congress might make a regulation prohibiting slavery, and that Congress might also allow it to continue to exist in the Territory; and accordingly, when a few days later, Congress passed the Act of May 20th, 1790, 1 Stat. at L. 123, for the government of the Territory south of the River Ohio, it provided, "and the government of the Territory south of the Ohio shall be similar to that now exercised in the Territory northwest of the Ohio, except so far as is otherwise provided in the conditions expressed in an Act of Congress of the present session, entitled 'An Act to accept a cession of the claims of the State of North Carolina to a certain district of western territory.'" Under the government thus established, slavery existed until the Territory became the State of Tennessee.

On the 7th of April, 1798, 1 Stat. at L. 649, an Act was passed to establish a government in the Mississippi Territory in all respects like that exercised in the Territory northwest of the Ohio, "excepting and excluding the last article of the Ordinance made for the government thereof by the late Congress on the 13th day of July, 1787." When the limits of this Territory had been amicably settled with Georgia, and the latter ceded all its claim thereto, it was one stipulation in the compact of cession, that the ordinance of July 13th, 1787, "shall in all its parts extend to the Territory contained in the present Act of Cession, that article only excepted which forbids slavery." The government of this Territory was subsequently established and organized under the Act of May 10th, 1800; but so much of the Ordinance as prohibited slavery was not put in operation there.

Without going minutely into the details of each case, I will now give reference to two

15 L. ed.

classes of Acts, in one of which Congress has extended the Ordinance of 1787, including the article prohibiting slavery, over different Territories, and thus exerted its power to prohibit it; in the other, Congress has erected governments over Territories acquired from France and Spain, in which slavery already existed, but refused to apply to them that part of the government under the Ordinance which excluded slavery.

Of the first class are the Act of May 7th, 1800, 2 Stat. at *L. 58, for the govern- **[*619** ment of the Indiana Territory; the Act of Jan. 11th, 1805, 2 Stat. at L. 309, for the government of Michigan Territory; the Act of May 3d, 1809, 2 Stat. at L. 514, for the government of the Illinois Territory; the Act of April 20, 1836, 5 Stat. at L. 10, for the government of the Territory of Wisconsin; the Act of June 12th, 1838, for the government of the Territory of Iowa; the Act of Aug. 14th, 1848, for the government of the Territory of Oregon. To these instances should be added the Act of March 6th, 1820, 3 Stat. at L. 548, prohibiting slavery in the Territory acquired from France, being northwest of Missouri, and north of thirty-six degrees thirty minutes north latitude.

Of the second class, in which Congress refused to interfere with slavery already existing under the municipal law of France or Spain, and established governments by which slavery was recognized and allowed, are: the Act of March 26th, 1804, 2 Stat. at L. 283, for the government of Louisiana; the Act of March 2d, 1805, 2 Stat. at L. 322, for the government of the Territory of Orleans; the Act of June 4th, 1812, 2 Stat. at L. 743, for the government of the Missouri Territory; the Act of March 30th, 1822, 3 Stat. at L. 654, for the government of the Territory of Florida. Here are eight distinct instances, beginning with the first Congress, and coming down to the year 1848, in which Congress has excluded slavery from the Territory of the United States; and six distinct instances in which Congress organized governments of Territories by which slavery was recognized and continued, beginning also with the first Congress, and coming down to the year 1822. These Acts were severally signed by seven Presidents of the United States, beginning with General Washington, and coming regularly down as far as Mr. John Quincy Adams, thus including all who were in public life when the Constitution was adopted.

If the practical construction of the Constitution contemporaneously with its going into effect, by men intimately acquainted with its history from their personal participation in framing and adopting it, and continued by them through a long series of Acts of the gravest importance, be entitled to weight in the judicial mind on a question of construction, it would seem to be difficult to resist the force of the Acts above adverted to.

It appears, however, from what has taken place at the bar, that notwithstanding the language of the Constitution, and the long line of legislative and executive precedents under it, three different and opposite views are taken of the power of Congress respecting slavery in the Territories.

*One is, that though Congress can **[*620** make a regulation prohibiting slavery in a Territory, they cannot make a regulation allowing

789

it; another is, that it can neither be established nor prohibited by Congress, but that the people of a Territory, when organized by Congress, can establish or prohibit slavery; while the third is, that the Constitution itself secures to every citizen who holds slaves, under the laws of any State, the indefeasible right to carry them into any Territory, and there hold them as property.

No particular clause of the Constitution has been referred to at the bar in support of either of these views. The first seems to be rested upon general considerations concerning the social and moral evils of slavery, its relations to republican governments, its inconsistency with the Declaration of Independence and with natural right.

The second is drawn from considerations equally general, concerning the right of self-government, and the nature of the political institutions which have been established by the people of the United States.

While the third is said to rest upon the equal right of all citizens to go with their property upon the public domain, and the inequality of a regulation which would admit the property of some and exclude the property of other citizens; and inasmuch as slaves are chiefly held by citizens of those particular States where slavery is established, it is insisted that a regulation excluding slavery from a Territory operates, practically, to make an unjust discrimination between citizens of different States, in respect to their use and enjoyment of the territory of the United States.

With the weight of either of these considerations, when presented to Congress to influence its action, this court has no concern. One or the other may be justly entitled to guide or control the legislative judgment upon what is a needful regulation. The question here is, whether they are sufficient to authorize this court to insert into this clause of the Constitution an exception of the exclusion or allowance of slavery, not found therein, nor in any other part of that instrument. To engraft on any instrument a substantive exception not found in it, must be admitted to be a matter attended with great difficulty. And the difficulty increases with the importance of the instrument, and the magnitude and complexity of the interests involved in its construction. To allow this to be done with the Constitution, upon reasons purely political, renders its judicial interpretation impossible—because judicial tribunals, as such, cannot decide upon political considerations. Political reasons have not the requisite certainty to afford rules of juridical 621*] *interpretation. They are different in different men. They are different in the same men at different times. And when a strict interpretation of the Constitution, according to the fixed rules which govern the interpretation of laws, is abandoned, and the theoretical opinions of individuals are allowed to control its meaning, we have no longer a Constitution; we are under the government of individual men, who for the time being have power to declare what the Constitution is, according to their own views of what it ought to mean. When such a method of interpretation of the Constitution obtains, in place of a republican government, with limited and defined powers, we have a government which is merely an exponent of the
790

will of Congress; or what, in my opinion, would not be preferable, an exponent of the individual political opinions of the members of this court.

If it can be shown by anything in the Constitution itself that when it confers on Congress the power to make all needful rules and regulations respecting the Territory belonging to the United States, the exclusion or the allowance of slavery was excepted; or if anything in the history of this provision tends to show that such an exception was intended by those who framed and adopted the Constitution to be introduced into it, I hold it to be my duty carefully to consider, and to allow just weight to such considerations in interpreting the positive text of the Constitution. But where the Constitution has said all needful rules and regulations, I must find something more than theoretical reasoning to induce me to say it did not mean all.

There have been eminent instances in this court closely analogous to this one, in which such an attempt to introduce an exception, not found in the Constitution itself, has failed of success.

By the 8th section of the 1st article, Congress has the power of exclusive legislation in all cases whatsoever within this district.

In the case of Loughborough v. Blake, 5 Wheat. 324, the question arose, whether Congress has power to impose direct taxes on persons and property in this district. It was insisted, that though the grant of power was in its terms broad enough to include direct taxation, it must be limited by the principle, that taxation and representation are inseparable. It would not be easy to fix on any political truth, better established or more fully admitted in our country, than that taxation and representation must exist together. We went into the War of the Revolution to assert it, and it is incorporated as fundamental into all American Governments. But however true and important *this maxim may be, it is not necessar- [*622 ily of universal application. It was for the people of the United States, who ordained the Constitution, to decide whether it should or should not be permitted to operate within this district. Their decision was embodied in the words of the Constitution; and as that maintained no such exception as would permit the maxim to operate in this district, this court interpreting that language, held that the exception did not exist.

Again; the Constitution confers on Congress power to regulate commerce with foreign nations. Under this, Congress passed an Act on the 22d of December, 1807, unlimited in duration, laying an embargo on all ships and vessels in the ports or within the limits and jurisdiction of the United States. No law of the United States ever pressed so severely upon particular States. Though the constitutionality of the law was contested with an earnestness and zeal proportioned to the ruinous effects which were felt from it, and though, as Mr. Chief Justice Marshall has said, 9 Wheat. 192, "a want of acuteness in discovering objections to a measure to which they felt the most deep-rooted hostility will not be imputed to those who were arrayed in opposition to this" I am not aware that the fact that its prohibited the use of a particular species of property, belonging almost exclusively to citizens of a few States, and this indefinitely, was ever supposed to show that it was unconstitutional. Something much more stringent, as a ground of legal judgment, was relied on—that the power to regulate commerce did not include the power to annihilate commerce.

But the decision was, that under the power to regulate commerce, the power of Congress over the subject was restricted only by those exceptions and limitations contained in the Constitution; and as neither the clause in question, which was a general grant of power to regulate commerce, nor any other clause of the Constitution, imposed any restrictions as to the duration of an embargo, an unlimited prohibition of the use of the shipping of the country was within the power of Congress. On this subject, Mr. Justice Daniel, speaking for the court in the case of U. S. v. Marigold, 9 How. 560, says: "Congress are, by the Constitution, vested with the power to regulate commerce with foreign nations; and however, at periods of high excitement, an application of the terms 'to regulate commerce,' such as would embrace absolute prohibition, may have been questioned, yet, since the passage of the Embargo and Non-Intercourse Laws, and the repeated judicial sanctions these statutes have received, it can scarcely, at this day, be open to doubt, that 623*] every subject falling legitimately *within the sphere of commercial regulation may be partially or wholly excluded, when either measure shall be demanded by the safety or the important interests of the entire nation. The power once conceded, it may operate on any and every subject of commerce to which the legislative discretion may apply it."

If power to regulate commerce extends to an indefinite prohibition of the use of all vessels belonging to citizens of the several States, and may operate, without exception, upon every subject of commerce to which the legislative discretion may apply it, upon what grounds can I say that power to make all needful rules and regulations respecting the territory of the United States is subject to an exception of the allowance or prohibition of slavery therein?

While the regulation is one "respecting the Territory," while it is, in the judgment of Congress, "a needful regulation," and is thus completely within the words of the grant, while no other clause of the Constitution can be shown, which requires the insertion of an exception respecting slavery, and while the practical construction for a period of upwards of fifty years forbids such an exception, it would, in my opinion, violate every sound rule of interpretation to force that exception into the Constitution upon the strength of abstract political reasoning, which we are bound to believe the people of the United States thought insufficient to induce them to limit the power of Congress, because what they have said contains no such limitation.

Before I proceed further to notice some other grounds of supposed objection to this power of Congress, I desire to say, that if it were not for my anxiety to insist upon what I deem a correct exposition of the Constitution; if I looked only to the purposes of the argument, the source of the power of Congress asserted in the opinion of the majority of the court would answer those purposes equally well. For they

admit that Congress has power to organize and govern the Territories until they arrive at a suitable condition for admission to the Union; they admit, also, that the kind of government which shall thus exist, should be regulated by the condition and wants of each Territory, and that it is necessarily committed to the discretion of Congress to enact such laws for that purpose as that discretion may dictate; and no limit to that discretion has been shown, or even suggested, save those positive prohibitions to legislate, which are found in the Constitution.

I confess myself unable to perceive any difference whatever between my own opinion of the general extent of the power of Congress and the opinion of the majority of the court, save *that I consider it derivable from [*624 the express language of the Constitution, while they hold it to be silently implied from the power to acquire territory. Looking at the power of Congress over the Territories as of the extent just described, what positive prohibition exists in the Constitution, which restrained Congress from enacting a law in 1820 to prohibit slavery north of thirty-six degrees thirty minutes north latitude?

The only one suggested is that clause in the 5th article of the Amendments of the Constitution which declares that no person shall be deprived of his life, liberty, or property, without due process of law. I will now proceed to examine the question, whether this clause is entitled to the effect thus contributed to it. It is necessary, first, to have a clear view of the nature and incidents of that particular species of property which is now in question.

Slavery being contrary to natural right, is created only by municipal law. This is not only plain in itself, and agreed by all writers on the subject, but is inferable from the Constitution, and has been explicitly declared by this court. The Constitution refers to slaves as "persons held to service in one State, under the laws thereof." Nothing can more clearly describe a status created by municipal law. In Prigg v. Pennsylvania, 16 Pet. 611, this court said: "The state of slavery is deemed to be a mere municipal regulation, founded on and limited to the range of territorial laws." In Rankin v. Lydia, 2 A. K. Marsh. 470, the Supreme Court of Appeals of Kentucky said: "Slavery is sanctioned by the laws of this State, and the right to hold them under our municipal regulations is unquestionable. But we view this as a right existing by positive law of a municipal character, without foundation in the law of nature or the unwritten common law." I am not acquainted with any case or writer questioning the correctness of this doctrine. See, also, 1 Burge, Col., and For. Laws, 738–741, where the authorities are collected.

The status of slavery is not necessarily always attended with the same powers on the part of the master. The master is subject to the supreme power of the State, whose will controls his action towards his slave, and this control must be defined and regulated by the municipal law. In one State, as at one period of the Roman law, it may put the life of the slave into the hand of the master; others, as those of the United States, which tolerate slavery, may treat the slave as a person when the master takes his life; while in others, the law may recognize a right of the slave to be protected from cruel treatment. In other words, the status of slavery embraces every condition, from that in which the slave is known to the law 625*] simply as a *chattel, with no civil rights, to that in which he is recognized as a person for all purposes, save the compulsory power of directing and receiving the fruits of his labor. Which of these conditions shall attend the status of slavery, must depend on the municipal law which creates and upholds it.

And not only must the status of slavery be created and measured by municipal law, but the rights, powers and obligations which grow out of that status, must be defined, protected and enforced by such laws. The liability of the master for the torts and crimes of his slave, and of third persons for assaulting or injuring or harboring or kidnapping him, the forms and modes of emancipation and sale, their subjection to the debts of the master, succession by the death of the master, suits for freedom, the capacity of the slave to be party to a suit, or to be a witness, with such police regulations as have existed in all civilized States where slavery has been tolerated, are among the subjects upon which municipal legislation becomes necessary when slavery is introduced.

Is it conceivable that the Constitution has conferred the right on every citizen to become a resident on the Territory of the United States with his slaves, and there to hold them as such, but has neither made nor provided for any municipal regulations which are essential to the existence of slavery?

Is it not more rational to conclude that they who framed and adopted the Constitution were aware that persons held to service under the laws of a State are property only to the extent and under the conditions fixed by those laws; that they must cease to be available as property, when their owners voluntarily place them permanently within another jurisdiction, where no municipal laws on the subject of slavery exist; and that, being aware of these principles, and having said nothing to interfere with or displace them, or compel Congress to legislate in any particular manner on the subject, and having empowered Congress to make all needful rules and regulations respecting the Territory of the United States, it was their intention to leave to the discretion of Congress what regulations, if any, should be made concerning slavery therein? Moreover, if the right exists, what are its limits, and what are its conditions? If citizens of the United States have the right to take their slaves to a Territory, and hold them there as slaves, without regard to the laws of the Territory, I suppose this right is not to be restricted to the citizens of slave-holding States. A citizen of a State which does not tolerate slavery can hardly be denied the power of doing the same thing. And what law of slavery does either take with him to the Territory? If it be said to be those laws 626*] respecting *slavery which existed in the particular State from which each slave last came, what an anomaly is this? Where else can we find, under the law of any civilized country, the power to introduce and permanently continue diverse systems of foreign municipal law, for holding persons in slavery? I say, not merely to introduce, but permanently to con-

tinue these anomalies. For the offspring of the female must be governed by the foreign municipal laws to which the mother was subject: and when any slave is sold or passes by succession on the death of the owner, there must pass with him, by a species of subrogation, and as a kind of unknown jus in re, the foreign municipal laws which constituted, regulated, and preserved, the status of the slave before his exportation. Whatever theoretical importance may be now supposed to belong to the maintenance of such a right, I feel a perfect conviction that it would, if ever tried, prove to be as impracticable in fact, as it is, in my judgment, monstrous in theory.

I consider the assumption which lies at the basis of this theory to be unsound; not in its just sense, and when properly understood, but in the sense which has been attached to it. That assumption is, that the Territory ceded by France was acquired for the equal benefit of all the citizens of the United States. I agree to the position. But it was acquired for their benefit in their collective, not their individual, capacities. It was acquired for their benefit, as an organized political society, subsisting as "the people of the United States," under the Constitution of the United States; to be administered justly and impartially, and as nearly as possible for the equal benefit of every individual citizen, according to the best judgment and discretion of the Congress; to whose power, as the Legislature of the nation which acquired it, the people of United States have committed its administration. Whatever individual claims may be founded on local circumstances, or sectional differences of condition, cannot, in my opinion, be recognized in this court, without arrogating to the judicial branch of the government powers not committed to it; and which, with all the unaffected respect I feel for it, when acting in its proper sphere, I do not think it fitted to wield.

Nor, in my judgment, will the position, that a prohibition to bring slaves into a Territory deprives any one of his property without due process of law, bear examination.

It must be remembered that this restriction on the legislative power is not peculiar to the Constitution of the United States; it was borrowed from Magna Charta; was brought to America by our ancestors, as part of their inherited liberties, and has existed in all the States, usually in the very words of *the [*627 Great Charter. It existed in every political community in America in 1787, when the Ordinance prohibiting slavery north and west of the Ohio was passed.

And if a prohibition of slavery in a Territory in 1820 violated this principle of Magna Charta, the Ordinance of 1787 also violated it; and what power had, I do not say the Congress of the Confederation alone, but the Legislature of Virginia, or the Legislature of any or all the States of the Confederacy, to consent to such a violation? The people of the States had conferred no such power. I think I may at least say, if the Congress did then violate Magna Charta by the Ordinance, no one discovered that violation. Besides, if the prohibition upon all persons, citizens as well as others, to bring slaves into a Territory, and a declaration that if brought they shall be free, deprives citizens of their property without due process of law, what shall we say of the legislation of many of the slaveholding States which have enacted the same prohibtion? As early as October, 1778, a law was passed in Virginia, that thereafter no slave should be imported into that Commonwealth by sea or by land, and that every slave who should be imported should become free. A citizen of Virginia purchased in Maryland a slave who belonged to another citizen of Virginia, and removed with the slave to Virginia. The slave sued for her freedom, and recovered it; as may be seen in Wilson v. Isbel, 5 Call. 425. See, also, Hunter v. Hulsher, 1 Leigh, 172; and a similar law has been recognized as valid in Maryland, in Stewart v. Oakes, 5 Harr. & Johns, 107. I am not aware that such laws, though they exist in many States, were ever supposed to be in conflict with the principle of Magna Charta incorporated into the state constitutions. It was certainly understood by the Convention which framed the Constitution, and has been so understood ever since, that, under the power to regulate commerce, Congress could prohibit the importation of slaves; and the exercise of the power was restrained till 1808. A citizen of the United States owns slaves in Cuba, and brings them to the United States, where they are set free by the legislation of Congress. Does this legislation deprive him of his property without due process of law? If so, what becomes of the laws prohibiting the slave trade? If not, how can a similar regulation respecting a Territory violate the 5th Amendment of the Constitution.

Some reliance was placed by the defendant's counsel upon the fact that the prohibition of slavery in this Territory was in the words, "that slavery, &c., shall be, and is hereby forever prohibited." But the insertion of the word "forever" can have no legal effect. Every enactment not expressly limited in its *duration continues in force until repealed or abrogated by some competent power, and the use of the word "forever" can give to the law no more durable operation. The argument is, that Congress cannot so legislate as to bind the future States formed out of the Territory, and that in this instance it has attempted to do so. Of the political reasons which may have induced the Congress to use these words, and which caused them to expect that subsequent Legislatures would conform their action to the then general opinion of the country that it ought to be permanent, this court can take no cognizance.

However fit such considerations are to control the action of Congress, and however reluctant a statesman may be disturb what has been settled, every law made by Congress may be repealed, and, saving private rights, and public rights gained by States, its repeal is subject to the absolute will of the same power which enacted it. If Congress had enacted that the crime of murder, committed in this Indian Territory, north of thirty-six degrees thirty minutes, by or on any white man, should forever be punishable with death, it would seem to me an insufficient objection to an indictment, found while it was a Territory, that at some future day States might exist there, and so the law was invalid, because, by its terms, it was to continue in force forever. Such an objection rests upon a misapprehension of the

province and power of courts respecting the constitutionality of laws enacted by the Legislature.

If the Constitution prescribe one rule, and the law another and different rule, it is the duty of courts to declare that the Constitution, and not the law, governs the case before them for judgment. If the law include no case save those for which the Constitution has furnished a different rule, or no case which the Legislature has the power to govern, then the law can have no operation. If it includes cases which the Legislature has power to govern, and concerning which the Constitution does not prescribe a different rule, the law governs those cases, though it may, in its terms, attempt to include others, on which it cannot operate. In other words, this court cannot declare void an Act of Congress which constitutionally embraces some cases, though other cases, within its terms, are beyond the control of Congress, or beyond the reach of that particular law. If, therefore, Congress had power to make a law excluding slavery from this Territory while under the exclusive power of the United States, the use of the word "forever" does not invalidate the law, so long as Congress has the exclusive legislative power in the Territory.

*But it is further insisted that the [*629 Treaty of 1803, between the United States and France, by which this Territory was acquired, has so restrained the constitutional powers of Congress, that it cannot, by law, prohibit the introduction of slavery into that part of this Territory north and west of Missouri, and north of thirty-six degrees thirty minutes north latitude.

By a treaty with a foreign nation, the United States may rightfully stipulate that the Congress will or will not exercise its legislative power in some particular manner, on some particular subject. Such promises, when made, should be voluntarily kept, with the most scrupulous good faith. But that a treaty with a foreign nation can deprive the Congress of any part of the legislative power conferred by the people, so that it no longer can legislate as it was empowered by the Constitution to do, I more than doubt.

The powers of the government do and must remain unimpaired. The responsibility of the government to a foreign nation, for the exercise of those powers, is quite another matter. That responsibility is to be met, and justified to the foreign nation, according to the requirements of the rules of public law; but never upon the assumption that the United States had parted with or restricted any power of acting according to its own free will, governed solely by its own appreciation of its duty.

The 2d section of the 4th article is: "This Constitution, and the laws of the United States which shall be made in pursuance thereof, and all treaties made or which shall be made under the authority of the United States, shall be the supreme law of the land." This has made treaties part of our municipal law; but it has not assigned to them any particular degree of authority, nor declared that laws so enacted shall be irrepealable. No supremacy is assigned to treaties over Acts of Congress. That they are not perpetual, and must be in some way repealable, all will agree.

15 L. ed.

793

If the President and the Senate alone possess the power to repeal or modify a law found in a treaty, inasmuch as they can change or abrogate one treaty only by making another inconsistent with the first, the Government of the United States could not act at all, to that effect, without the consent of some foreign government. I do not consider—I am not aware it has ever been considered—that the Constitution has placed our country in this helpless condition. The action of Congress in repealing the Treaties with France by the Act of July 7th, 1798, 1 Stat. at L. 578, was in conformity with these views. In the case of Taylor et al. 630]* v. Morton, 2 Curt. Cir. Ct. 454, *I had occasion to consider this subject, and I adhere to the views there expressed.

If, therefore, it were admitted that the Treaty between the United States and France did contain an express stipulation that the United States would not exclude slavery from so much of the ceded territory as is now in question, this court could not declare that an Act of Congress excluding it was void by force of the Treaty. Whether or no a case existed sufficient to justify a refusal to execute such a stipulation, would not be a judicial, but a political and legislative question, wholly beyond the authority of this court to try and determine. It would belong to diplomacy and legislation, and not to the administration of existing laws. Such a stipulation in a treaty, to legislate or not to legislate in a particular way, has been repeatedly held in this court to address itself to the political or the legislative power, by whose action thereon this court is bound, Foster v. Neilson, 2 Pet. 314; Garcia v. Lee, 12 Pet. 519.

But, in my judgment, this Treaty contains no stipulation in any manner affecting the action of the United States respecting the Territory in question. Before examining the language of the Treaty, it is material to bear in mind that the part of the ceded Territory lying north of thirty-six degrees thirty minutes, and west and north of the present State of Missouri, was then a wilderness, uninhabited save by savages, whose possessory title had not then been extinguished.

It is impossible for me to conceive on what ground France could have advanced a claim, or could have desired to advance a claim, to restrain the United States from making any rules and regulations respecting this Territory, which the United States might think fit to make; and still less can I conceive of any reason which would have induced the United States to yield to such a claim. It was to be expected that France would desire to make the change of sovereignty and jurisdiction as little burdensome as possible to the then inhabitants of Louisiana, and might well exhibit even an anxious solicitude to protect their property and persons, and to secure to them and their posterity their religious and political rights; and the United States, as a just government, might readily accede to all proper stipulations respecting those who were about to have their allegiance transferred. But what interest France could have in uninhabited Territory, which, in the language of the Treaty, was to be transferred "forever, and in full sovereignty," to the United States, or how the United

794

States could consent to allow a foreign nation to interfere in its purely internal affairs, in which that foreign nation had no concern *whatever, is difficult for me to conjec- [*631 ture. In my judgment, this Treaty contains nothing of the kind.

The 3d article is supposed to have a bearing on the question. It is as follows: "The inhabitants of the ceded Territory shall be incorporated in the Union of the United States, and admitted as soon as possible, according to the principles of the Federal Constitution, to the enjoyment of all the rights, advantages, and immunities, of citizens of the United States; and in the meantime they shall be maintained and protected in the enjoyment of their liberty, property, and the religion they profess."

There are two views of this Article, each of which, I think, decisively shows that it was not intended to restrain the Congress from excluding slavery from that part of the ceded Territory then uninhabited. The first is, that, manifestly, its sole object was to protect individual rights of the then inhabitants of the Territory. They are to be "maintained and protected in the free enjoyment of their liberty, property, and the religion they profess." But this Article does not secure to them the right to go upon the public domain ceded by the Treaty, either with or without their slaves. The right or power of doing this did not exist before or at the time the Treaty was made. The French and Spanish Governments, while they held the country, as well as the United States when they acquired it, always exercised the undoubted right of excluding inhabitants from the Indian country, and of determining when and on what conditions it should be opened to settlers. And a stipulation, that the then inhabitants of Louisiana should be protected in their property, can have no reference to their use of that property, where they had no right, under the Treaty, to go with it, save at the will of the United States. If one who was an inhabitant of Louisiana at the time of the Treaty had afterwards taken property then owned by him, consisting of fire-arms, ammunition, and spirits, and had gone into the Indian country north of thirty-six degrees thirty minutes, to sell them to the Indians, all must agree the 3d article of the Treaty would not have protected him from indictment under the Act of Congress of March 30, 1802, 2 Stat. at L. 139, adopted and extended to this Territory by the Act of March 26, 1804, 2 Stat. at L. 283.

Besides, whatever rights were secured were individual rights. If Congress should pass any law which violated such rights of any individual, and those rights were of such a character as not to be within the lawful control of Congress under the Constitution, that individual could complain, and the Act of Congress, as to such rights of his, would be inoperative; but it *would be valid and operative as to all [*632 other persons, whose individual rights did not come under the protection of the Treaty. And inasmuch as it does not appear that any inhabitant of Louisiana, whose rights were secured by Treaty, had been injured, it would be wholly inadmissible for this court to assume, first, that one or more such cases may have existed; and second, that if any did exist, the entire law was void—not only as to those cases, if any, in which it could not rightfully operate, but as to all others, wholly unconnected with the Treaty, in which such law could rightfully operate.

But it is quite unnecessary, in my opinion, to pursue this inquiry further, because it clearly appears from the language of the Article, and it has been decided by this court that the stipulation was temporary, and ceased to have any effect when the then inhabitants of the Territory of Louisiana, in whose behalf the stipulation was made, were incorporated into the Union.

In the case of New Orleans v. De Armas et al. 9 Pet. 224, the question was, whether a title to property, which existed at the date of the Treaty, continued to be protected by the Treaty after the State of Louisiana was admitted to the Union. The 3d article of the Treaty was relied on. Mr. Chief Justice Marshall said: "This article obviously contemplates two objects. One, that Louisiana shall be admitted into the Union as soon as possible, on an equal footing with the other States; and the other, that, till such admission, the inhabitants of the ceded Territory shall be protected in the free enjoyment of their liberty, property and religion. Had any one of these rights been violated while these stipulations continued in force, the individual supposing himself to be injured might have brought his case into this court under the 25th section of the Judicial Act. But this stipulation ceased to operate when Louisiana became a member of the Union, and its inhabitants were "admitted to the enjoyment of all the rights, advantages and immunities of citizens of the United States."

The cases of Choteau v. Marguerita, 12 Pet. 507, and Permoli v. New Orleans, 3 How. 589, are in conformity with this view of the Treaty.

15 L. ed.

To convert this temporary stipulation of the Treaty, in behalf of French subjects who then inhabited a small portion of Louisiana, into a permanent restriction upon the power of Congress to regulate territory then uninhabited, and to assert that it not only restrains Congress from affecting the rights of property of the then inhabitants, but enabled them and all other citizens of the United States to go into any part of the *ceded Territory [*633 with their slaves and hold them there, is a construction of this Treaty so opposed to its natural meaning, and so far beyond its subject matter and the evident design of the parties, that I cannot assent to it. In my opinion, this Treaty has no bearing on the present question.

For these reasons, I am of opinion that so much of the several Acts of Congress as prohibited slavery and involuntary servitude within that part of the Territory of Wisconsin lying north of thirty-six degrees thirty minutes north latitude, and west of the River Mississippi, were constitutional and valid laws.

I have expressed my opinion, and the reasons therefore, at far greater length than I could have wished, upon the different questions on which I have found it necessary to pass, to arrive at a judgment on the case at bar. These questions are numerous, and the grave importance of some of them required me to exhibit fully the grounds of my opinion. I have touched no question which, in the view I have taken, it was not absolutely necessary for me to pass upon, to ascertain whether the judgment of the Circuit Court should stand or be reversed. I have avoided no question on which the validity of that judgment depends. To have done either more or less, would have been inconsistent with my views of my duty.

In my opinion, the judgment of the Circuit Court should be reversed, and the cause remanded for a new trial.

795

End of Volume 60.

"HOUSE DIVIDED" SPEECH

ABRAHAM LINCOLN, JUNE 16, 1858

"A house divided against itself cannot stand."

I believe this government cannot endure, permanently half *slave* and half *free*.

I do not expect the Union to be *dissolved*—I do not expect the house to *fall*—but I *do* expect it will cease to be divided.

It will become *all* one thing, or *all* the other.

Either the *opponents* of slavery, will arrest the further spread of it, and place it where the public mind shall rest in the belief that it is in course of ultimate extinction; or its *advocates* will push it forward, till it shall become alike lawful in *all* the states, *old* as well as *new*—*North* as well as *South*.

Have we no *tendency* to the latter condition?

Let any one who doubts, carefully contemplate that now almost complete legal combination—piece of *machinery* so to speak—compounded of the Nebraska doctrine, and the Dred Scott decision. . . .

* * *

. . . [The Kansas-Nebraska Act] opened all the national territory to slavery. . . . This . . . had been provided for . . . in the notable argument of "*squatter sovereignty*," otherwise called "*sacred right of self government*," which latter phrase, though expressive of the only rightful basis of any government, was so perverted in this attempted use of it as to amount to just this: That if any *one* man, choose to enslave *another*, no *third* man shall be allowed to object.

* * *

While the Nebraska Bill was passing through Congress, a law case, involving the question of a negro's freedom . . . was passing through the U.S. Circuit Court for the District of Missouri; and both Nebraska Bill and law suit were brought to a decision in the same month of May, 1854. The Negro's name was "Dred Scott". . . .

* * *

[The points decided by the *Dred Scott* decision include] that whether the holding a negro in actual slavery in a free state, makes him free, as against the holder, the United States courts will not decide, but will leave to be decided by the courts of any slave state the negro may be forced into by the master.

This point is made, not to be pressed immediately . . . [that] the logical conclusion that what Dred Scott's master might lawfully do with Dred Scott, in the free state Illinois, every other master may lawfully do with any other *one*, or one *thousand* slaves, in Illinois, or in any other free state.

* * *

While the opinion of . . . Chief Justice Taney, in the Dred Scott case . . . expressly declare[s] that the Constitution of the United States neither permits congress nor a territorial legislature to exclude slavery from any United States territory, . . . [Taney] *omit*[s] to declare whether or not the same constitution permits a *state*, or the people of a state, to exclude it.

Possibly, this was a mere omission; but who can be quite sure. . . .

The nearest approach to the point of declaring the power of a state over slavery, is made by Judge Nelson. He approaches it more than once, using the precise idea, and *almost* the language too, of the Nebraska Act. On one occasion his exact language is, "except in cases where the power is restrained by the Constitution of the United States, the law of the State is supreme over the subject of slavery within its jurisdiction."

In what *cases* the power of the *states* is so restrained by the U.S. Constitution, is left an *open* question, precisely as the same question, as to the restraint on the power of the *territories* was left open in the Nebraska Act. Put *that* and *that* together, and we have another nice little niche, which we may, ere long, see filled with another Supreme Court decision, declaring that the Constitution of the United States does not permit a *state* to exclude slavery from its limits.

* * *

Such a decision is all that slavery now lacks of being alike lawful in all the states.

Welcome or unwelcome, such decision *is* probably coming, and will soon be upon us, unless the power of the present political dynasty shall be met and overthrown.

We shall *lie down* pleasantly dreaming that the people of Missouri are on the verge of making their state *free;* and we shall *awake* to the *reality*, instead, that the Supreme Court has made *Illinois* a *slave* state.

EMANCIPATION PROCLAMATION

BY THE PRESIDENT OF THE UNITED STATES OF AMERICA

A Proclamation

Whereas, on the twenty-second day of September, in the year of our Lord one thousand eight hundred and sixty-two, a proclamation was issued by the president of the United States, containing, among other things, the following, to wit:

"That on the first day of January, in the year of our Lord one thousand eight hundred and sixty-three, all persons held as slaves within any state or designated part of a state, the people whereof shall then be in rebellion against the United States, shall be then, thenceforward and forever, free; and the executive government of the United States, including the military and naval authority thereof, will recognize and maintain the freedom of such persons and will do no act or acts to repress such persons, or any of them, in any efforts they may make for their actual freedom.

"That the executive will, on the first day of January aforesaid, by proclamation, designate the states and parts of states, if any, in which the people thereof, respectively, shall then be in rebellion against the United States; and the fact that any state, or the people thereof, shall on that day be in good faith represented in the Congress of the United States, by members chosen thereto at elections wherein a majority of the qualified voters of such states shall have participated, shall, in the absence of strong countervailing testimony, be deemed conclusive evidence that such state, and the people thereof, are not then in rebellion against the United States."

Now, therefore, I, Abraham Lincoln, president of the United States, by virtue of the power in me vested as commander in chief of the army and navy of the United States, in time of actual armed rebellion against the authority and government of the United States, and as a fit and necessary war measure for suppressing said rebellion, do, on this first day of January, in the year of our Lord one thousand eight hundred and sixty-three, and in accordance with my purpose so to do, publicly proclaimed for the full period of one hundred days from the day first above mentioned, order and designate as the states and parts of states wherein the people thereof, respectively, are this day in rebellion against the United States, the following, to wit:

Arkansas, Texas, Louisiana (except the parishes of St. Bernard, Plaquemines, Jefferson, St. John, St. Charles, St. James, Ascension, Assumption, Terre Bonne, Lafourche, St. Mary, St. Martin, and Orleans, including the city of New Orleans), Mississippi, Alabama, Florida, Georgia, South Carolina, North Carolina, and Virginia (except the forty-eight counties designated as West Virginia, and also the counties of Berkeley, Accomac, Northampton, Elizabeth City, York, Princess Ann, and Norfolk, including the cities of Norfolk and Portsmouth), and which excepted parts are for the present left precisely as if this proclamation were not issued.

Source: *Statutes at Large*, vol. 12 (1864), pp. 1268–1269.

And by virtue of the power and for the purpose aforesaid, I do order and declare that all persons held as slaves within said designated states and parts of states are, and henceforward shall be, free; and that the executive government of the United States, including the military and naval authorities thereof, will recognize and maintain the freedom of said persons.

And I hereby enjoin upon the people so declared to be free to abstain from all violence, unless in necessary self-defense; and I recommend to them that, in all cases when allowed, they labor faithfully for reasonable wages.

And I further declare and make known that such persons, of suitable condition will be received into the armed service of the United States to garrison forts, positions, stations, and other places and to man vessels of all sorts in said service.

And upon this act, sincerely believed to be an act of justice, warranted by the Constitution upon military necessity, I invoke the considerate judgment of mankind and the gracious favor of Almighty God.

In witness whereof, I have hereunto set my hand and caused the seal of the United States to be affixed.

Done at the city of Washington this first day of January, in the year of our Lord one thousand eight hundred and sixty-three, and of the independence of the United States of America the eighty-seventh.

Abraham Lincoln

By the President:
William H. Seward, Secretary of State.

FROM SEGREGATION TO CIVIL RIGHTS

After the Civil War the Thirteenth, Fourteenth, and Fifteenth Amendments to the U.S. Constitution, along with many pieces of civil rights legislation, were enacted to protect the rights of the newly freed slaves. Nevertheless, African Americans were soon ensnared in a southern political and legal system that limited their political, economic, and social freedoms.

Initially after the war, during the Reconstruction era (1865–1876), the former Confederate states were placed under federal military control. During this time African Americans were able to register to vote and to be elected to state and local government posts. This period was also marked by white vigilantism, however, in the form of the Ku Klux Klan (KKK). The KKK used terror to discourage African Americans from voting or from asserting their other constitutional rights.

The presidential election of 1876 resulted in a deadlocked electoral college and allegations of election fraud. A congressional compromise was reached in which Republican Rutherford B. Hayes was elected president. In exchange, southern Democrats were rewarded with the withdrawal of federal troops and the end of Reconstruction.

During the 1870s the U.S. Supreme Court was called on to decide the scope of the Fourteenth Amendment. In the *Civil Rights* cases, 109 U.S. 3, 3 S. Ct. 18, 27 L. Ed. 835 (1883), the Court struck down the Civil Rights Act of 1875, which had been based on the Fourteenth Amendment. The Court held that the amendment prohibited only official, state-sponsored discrimination and did not reach discrimination by private parties. By the 1890s African Ameri-

cans had lost virtually all their civil rights as southern states, emboldened by the *Civil Rights* cases, passed laws that segregated all public facilities and public transportation on the basis of race. In *Plessy v. Ferguson*, 163 U.S. 537, 16 S. Ct. 1138, 41 L. Ed. 256 (1896), the Supreme Court endorsed "separate-but-equal" laws, holding that they did not violate the Constitution.

Beginning in the 1930s, the National Association for the Advancement of Colored People (NAACP) fought a series of court battles against various aspects of state-sponsored segregation. The NAACP's main focus, however, was the desegregation of public schools. A team of talented attorneys, which included future Supreme Court justice Thurgood Marshall, led the fight. Ultimately, they succeeded in having *Plessy* struck down. In *Brown v. Board of Education of Topeka, Kansas*, 347 U.S. 483, 74 S. Ct. 686, 98 L. Ed. 873 (1954), the Supreme Court ordered the end of state-sponsored segregated schools.

Despite these legal victories, most African Americans in the South were not able to vote or to exercise their civil rights. In response, Dr. Martin Luther King, Jr., started the modern civil rights movement in the 1950s. Instead of lawsuits, he used nonviolent public protests to attract the nation's attention to the conditions under which African Americans were forced to live. King and his followers were jailed for their demonstrations, but by the early 1960s it was clear that legal change must come.

President Lyndon B. Johnson pushed for the enactment of the landmark Civil Rights Act of 1964 (42 U.S.C.A. § 2000a et seq.), which prohibited racial and other types of discrimination in employment, education, and public accommodations. The act outlawed both state-sponsored and private segregation in hotels, restaurants, and public transportation. Johnson also introduced the Voting Rights Act of 1965 (42 U.S.C.A. § 1971 et seq.), which ensured protection against discriminatory voting practices. This act changed the South, as African Americans were allowed to register to vote for the first time since Reconstruction.

Civil Rights Cases

The *Civil Rights* cases involved five prosecutions and civil suits from California, Kansas, Missouri, New York, and Tennessee for denying African Americans access to public accommodations (hotels, theaters, and railroad cars) in violation of the Civil Rights Act of 1875. Justice Joseph P. Bradley, writing for the majority of the Supreme Court, held that the Fourteenth Amendment prohibited only official, state-sponsored discrimination and could not reach discrimination practiced by privately owned places of public accommodation.

Justice John M. Harlan, in a dissenting opinion, argued that segregation in public accommodations was a "badge of slavery" for the recently freed African Americans and that the act could be constitutionally justified by looking to the Thirteenth Amendment. This amendment gave Congress the authority to outlaw all "badges and incidents" of slavery. Not until the passage of title II of the Civil Rights Act of 1964 would the federal government achieve the desegregation of public accommodations.

Plessy v. Ferguson

At issue in *Plessy v. Ferguson* was an 1890 Louisiana law that required passenger trains operating within the state to provide "equal but separate" accommodations for "white and colored races." The Supreme Court upheld the law by a 7–1 vote, in the process putting a stamp of approval on all laws that mandated racial segregation. In his majority opinion, Justice Henry Billings Brown concluded that the Fourteenth Amendment "could not have intended to abolish distinctions based upon color, or to enforce social, as distinguished from political, equality, or a commingling of the two races upon terms unsatisfactory to either."

Justice John M. Harlan, the lone dissenter, responded that the "arbitrary separation of citizens on the basis of race" was equivalent to imposing a "badge of servitude" on African Americans. He contended that the real intent of the law was not to provide equal accommodations but to compel African Americans "to keep

to themselves." This was intolerable because "our Constitution is color-blind, and neither knows nor tolerates classes among citizens." Nevertheless, *Plessy* was the law of the land until 1954.

Brown v. Board of Education of Topeka, Kansas

The NAACP's legal strategy culminated in the Supreme Court's decision in *Brown v. Board of Education of Topeka, Kansas,* in 1954. The NAACP sought the overturning of *Plessy v. Ferguson*, which had protected state-mandated racial segregation in public schools. The Court had heard arguments in *Brown* during the 1953 term but was unable to reach a decision. The case was reargued in the 1954 term with the newly appointed chief justice, Earl Warren.

In May 1954 Warren issued the unanimous opinion of the Court, overruling *Plessy*. Writing that "separate educational facilities are inherently unequal," Warren held that racial segregation denied African Americans equal protection of the laws. *Brown* unleashed a torrent of controversy and protest in the South and immediately established Warren's image as a liberal. Billboards that read "Impeach Earl Warren" appeared throughout the South. Nevertheless, in 1955 the Court ordered states with segregated schools to move with "all deliberate speed" to dismantle their dual school systems (*Brown v. Board of Education [Brown II]*, 349 U.S. 294, 75 S. Ct. 753, 99 L. Ed. 1083 [1955]).

For a discussion of *Brown*, see volume 2, page 151. For the text of this case, see volume 2, page 349.

Letter from Birmingham City Jail

The civil rights protest marches and demonstrations led by Dr. Martin Luther King, Jr., met fierce resistance in Mississippi, Alabama, and Georgia. State and local authorities arrested King on various charges in hopes of driving him out of their states and stopping the civil rights movement. In contrast to the NAACP's methods, which centered on using the courts to strike down discriminatory laws, King and his followers used civil disobedience against white racism.

King's methods were criticized by white southerners who contended that the protests were illegal and that King was a lawbreaker. King was stung, however, by attacks on him by white clergy, who claimed that his methods were immoral. They counseled him to take lawful approaches and to avoid inciting public anger and bloodshed.

In 1963 King responded by writing "Letter from Birmingham City Jail." Imprisoned for failing to file an Alabama tax return, King defended the use of civil disobedience and argued that it was proper when citizens are confronted by unjust laws.

Civil Rights Act of 1964

After the assassination of President John F. Kennedy in 1963, President Lyndon B. Johnson announced his determination to pass a strong civil rights act that would end racial discrimination in employment, education, and other spheres of life. Deputy Attorney General Nicholas D. Katzenbach, Johnson's congressional liaison, worked with Senator Hubert H. Humphrey (D.-Minn.) and Senate minority leader Everett M. Dirksen (R.-Ill.) to achieve a compromise that would assure final passage. The result was the landmark Civil Rights Act of 1964.

Title I of the act guarantees equal voting rights by removing registration requirements and procedures biased against minorities and the underprivileged. Title II prohibits segregation or discrimination in places of public accommodation involved in interstate commerce. Title VII bans discrimination by trade unions, schools, and employers involved in interstate commerce or doing business with the federal government. This section also applies to discrimination on the basis of sex and established the Equal Employment Opportunity Commission to enforce these provisions. The act also calls for the desegregation of public schools (title IV), broadens the duties of the Civil Rights Commission (title V), and assures nondiscrimination in the distribution of funds under federally assisted programs (title VI).

Initially, the most controversial provision was title II. Because the 1883 *Civil Rights* cases held that the Fourteenth Amendment cannot reach private discrimination in public accommodations, Congress based title II on the Constitution's Commerce Clause, which gives Congress the authority to regulate interstate commerce. In *Heart of Atlanta Motel v. United States*, 379 U.S. 241, 85 S. Ct. 348, 13 L. Ed. 2d 258 (1964), the Supreme Court upheld title II as a constitutional application of the Commerce Clause.

Voting Rights Act of 1965

The Voting Rights Act of 1965 is a sweeping federal law that seeks to prevent voting discrimination based on race, color, or membership in a language minority group. The act was passed in the aftermath of one of the more violent episodes in the history of the civil rights movement. In 1965 Dr. Martin Luther King, Jr., led a group of civil rights supporters on a march to Selma, Alabama, to demand voting rights. They were met by police violence that resulted in the deaths of several marchers. The Selma violence galvanized voting rights supporters in Congress. President Lyndon B. Johnson responded by introducing the Voting Rights Act, the most sweeping piece of civil rights law in one hundred years. Congress enacted the measure five months later.

The passage of the Voting Rights Act was a watershed event in U.S. history. For the first time the federal government undertook voting reforms that had traditionally been left to the states. The act prohibits the states and their political subdivisions from imposing voting qualifications or prerequisites to voting or from imposing standards, practices, or procedures that deny or curtail the right of a U.S. citizen to vote because of race, color, or membership in a language minority group. The act was extended in 1970 and again in 1982, when its provisions were given an additional term of twenty-five years.

Southern states challenged the legislation as a dangerous attack on states' rights, but in *South Carolina v. Katzenbach*, 383 U.S. 301, 86 S. Ct. 803, 15 L. Ed. 2d 769 (1966), the U.S. Supreme Court upheld the constitutionality of the act, even though it was, in the words of Chief Justice Earl Warren, "inventive."

The initial act covered the seven states in the South that had used poll taxes, literacy tests, and other devices to obstruct registration by African Americans. Under the law a federal court can appoint federal examiners, who are authorized to place qualified persons on the list of eligible voters. The act waived accumulated poll taxes and abolished literacy tests and similar devices in the states to which it applied.

In addition, the act requires the seven states to obtain "preclearance" from the Justice Department or the U.S. District Court for the District of Columbia before changing the electoral system. The 1982 extension of the act expanded this provision to include all the states. Thus, a voter in any state may challenge a voting practice or procedure on the grounds that it is racially discriminatory either by intent or by effect.

The act has been used to create congressional districts that have a majority of minority voters so as to ensure minority representation. In *Shaw v. Hunt*, _U.S._, 116 S. Ct. 1894, 135 L. Ed. 2d 207 (1996), however, the Supreme Court ruled that the redrawing of a North Carolina congressional district into a "bizarre-looking" shape so as to include a majority of African Americans violated the Equal Protection Clause of the Fourteenth Amendment and therefore could not be justified by the Voting Rights Act.

3 S.Ct. 18
27 L.Ed. 835
(Cite as: 109 U.S. 3, 3 S.Ct. 18)

'THE CIVIL RIGHTS CASES.'
UNITED STATES
v.

STANLEY. [On a Certificate of Division in Opinion between the Judges of the Circuit Court of the United States for the District of Kansas.]
UNITED STATES
v.

RYAN. [In Error to the Circuit Court of the United States for the District of California.]
UNITED STATES
v.

NICHOLS. [On a Certificate of Division in Opinion between the Judges of the Circuit Court of the United States for the Western District of Missouri.]
UNITED STATES
v.

SINGLETON. [On a Certificate of Division in Opinion between the Judges of the Circuit Court of the United States for the Southern District of New York.]
ROBINSON and wife
v.

MEMPHIS & CHARLESTON R. CO. [In Error to the Circuit Court of the United States for the Western District of Tennessee.]

Supreme Court of the United States

October 15, 1883.

HARLAN, J., dissents.

CIVIL RIGHTS ☞ 103
78k103
Formerly 78k2.1
Congress has no power to legislate upon subjects which are within the domain of state legislation, but only to provide modes of redress against the operation of state laws and the action of state officers when these are subversive of the fundamental rights specified in the constitution; and therefore Act Cong. March 1, 1875, 18 Stat. 335, providing that all persons shall be entitled to full and equal enjoyment of the accommodations and advantages of inns, public conveyances, etc., and imposing penalties upon any person who shall violate said act, is unconstitutional.

STATES ☞ 4.16(2)
360k4.16(2)
Formerly 78k2.1
Congress has no power to legislate upon subjects which are within the domain of state legislation, but only to provide modes of redress against the operation of state laws and the action of state officers when these are subversive of the fundamental rights specified in the constitution; and therefore Act Cong. March 1, 1875, 18 Stat. 335, providing that all persons shall be entitled to full and equal enjoyment of the accommodations and advantages of inns, public conveyances, etc., and imposing penalties upon any person who shall violate said act, is unconstitutional.

CIVIL RIGHTS ☞ 103
78k103
Formerly 78k2.1
U.S.C.A.Const. Amend. 13, relates only to slavery and involuntary servitude; and, although it establishes universal freedom, it does not authorize congress to legislate upon subjects which are within the domain of state legislation; and therefore Act Cong. March 1, 1875, 18 Stat. 335, providing that any person who shall deny to any citizen the full enjoyment of any of the accommodations and advantages of inns, public conveyances, etc., shall be subject to a penalty, is unauthorized and void.

STATES ☞ 4.16(2)
360k4.16(2)
Formerly 78k2.1
U.S.C.A.Const. Amend. 13, relates only to slavery and involuntary servitude; and, although it establishes universal freedom, it does not authorize congress to legislate upon subjects which are within the domain of state legislation; and therefore Act Cong. March 1, 1875, 18 Stat. 335, providing that any person who shall deny to any citizen the full enjoyment of any of the accommodations and advantages of inns, public conveyances, etc., shall be subject to a penalty, is unauthorized

3 S.Ct. 18
(Cite as: 109 U.S. 3, 3 S.Ct. 18)

and void.

CIVIL RIGHTS ☜ 103
78k103
Formerly 78k2.1
The first and second sections of the civil rights act, passed March 1, 1875, 18 Stat. 335, in effect declaring that in all inns, public conveyances, and places of amusement colored citizens, whether slaves or not, and citizens of other races, shall have the same accommodations and privileges as are enjoyed by white citizens, and making it a penal offense in any person to deny to any citizen of any race or color, regardless of previous servitude, any of the said accommodations or privileges, are unconstitutional enactments as applied to the several states, not being authorized by either of thirteenth or fourteenth amendment to the constitution of the United States.

COMMERCE ☜ 3
83k3
Where Congress is clothed with direct and plenary powers over the whole subject, accompanied with an express or implied denial of such power to the states, as in the regulation of commerce with foreign nations and among the several states, Congress has power to pass laws for regulating such subjects in every detail, and the conduct and transactions of individuals in respect thereto.

CIVIL RIGHTS ☜ 103
78k103
Formerly 78k2.1
The fourteenth amendment, U.S.C.A. is not intended to protect individual rights against individual invasion, but to nullify and make void all state legislation and state action which impairs the privileges of citizens of the United States, etc.; and therefore congress has no authority to create a code of municipal law for the regulation of private rights.

CONSTITUTIONAL LAW ☜ 27
92k27
The fourteenth amendment, U.S.C.A. is not intended to protect individual rights against individual invasion, but to nullify and make void all state legislation and state action

which impairs the privileges of citizens of the United States, etc.; and therefore congress has no authority to create a code of municipal law for the regulation of private rights.

UNITED STATES ☜ 22
393k22
The fourteenth amendment, U.S.C.A. is not intended to protect individual rights against individual invasion, but to nullify and make void all state legislation and state action which impairs the privileges of citizens of the United States, etc.; and therefore congress has no authority to create a code of municipal law for the regulation of private rights.

CONSTITUTIONAL LAW ☜ 213(1)
92k213(1)
Formerly 92k209
Until some state law has been passed or some state action through its officers or agents has been taken adverse to the rights of citizens sought to be protected by the Fourteenth Amendment to the United States Constitution, U.S.C.A., no legislation of the United States under such amendment, nor any proceedings under such legislation, can be called into activity, for the prohibitions of the amendment are against state laws and acts done under state authority.

CONSTITUTIONAL LAW ☜ 213(1)
92k213(1)
Formerly 92k209
Positive rights and privileges are secured by the Fourteenth Amendment, U.S.C.A. by way of prohibition against state laws and state proceedings affecting such rights and privileges, and by power given to Congress to legislate for the purpose of carrying such prohibition into effect, and such legislation must necessarily be predicated upon such supposed state laws or state proceedings, and be directed to the correction of their operation and effect.

CONSTITUTIONAL LAW ☜ 213(4)
92k213(4)
Formerly 92k209
The provisions of the fourteenth amendment prohibiting state laws abridging the privileges of the citizen, or depriving any person of life,

3 S.Ct. 18
(Cite as: 109 U.S. 3, 3 S.Ct. 18)

liberty, or property without due process of law, or denying any person equal protection of the law, apply exclusively to state legislation, and have no reference to illegal acts of individuals. The power granted congress to enforce it, with appropriate legislation, applies to corrective legislation only, such as may be necessary to counteract and redress the effect of such forbidden state laws, and will not authorize direct legislation, such as Act Cong. March 1, 1875, 18 Stat. 335, known as the "Civil Rights Act."--

CONSTITUTIONAL LAW ☞ 206(1)
92k206(1)
The provisions of the fourteenth amendment prohibiting state laws abridging the privileges of the citizen, or depriving any person of life, liberty, or property without due process of law, or denying any person equal protection of the law, apply exclusively to state legislation, and have no reference to illegal acts of individuals. The power granted congress to enforce it, with appropriate legislation, applies to corrective legislation only, such as may be necessary to counteract and redress the effect of such forbidden state laws, and will not authorize direct legislation, such as Act Cong. March 1, 1875, 18 Stat. 335, known as the "Civil Rights Act."--

CONSTITUTIONAL LAW ☞ 213(4)
92k213(4)
Formerly 92k209
The legislation which Congress is authorized to adopt under the Fourteenth Amendment, U.S.C.A., is not general legislation upon the rights of the citizen, but corrective legislation such as may be necessary and proper for counteracting such laws as the States may adopt or enforce, and which, by the amendment, they are prohibited from making or enforcing, or such acts and proceedings as the states may commit or take, and which, by the amendment, they are prohibited from committing or taking.

CIVIL RIGHTS ☞ 101
78k101
Formerly 78k2
Civil rights, such as are guaranteed by the United States Constitution against state

aggression, cannot be impaired by the wrongful acts of individuals, unsupported by state authority in the shape of laws, customs, or judicial or executive proceedings, and the wrongful act of an individual, unsupported by any such authority, is simply a private wrong or a crime of the individual.

CONSTITUTIONAL LAW ☞ 215.1
92k215.1
Formerly 92k215
Civil rights, such as are guaranteed by the United States Constitution against state aggression, cannot be impaired by the wrongful acts of individuals, unsupported by state authority in the shape of laws, customs, or judicial or executive proceedings, and the wrongful act of an individual, unsupported by any such authority, is simply a private wrong or a crime of the individual.

CIVIL RIGHTS ☞ 103
78k103
Formerly 78k2.1
The thirteenth amendment relates only to slavery and involuntary servitude (which it abolishes); and although it establishes freedom to the United States, and Congress may probably pass laws directly enforcing its provisions, yet, such legislative power extends only to the subject of slavery and its incidents; and the denial of equal accommodations in inns, public conveyances, and places of public amusement, forbidden by Act Cong. March 1, 1875, 18 Stat. 335, imposes no badge of slavery or involuntary servitude upon the party, but, at most, infringes rights which are protected from state aggression by the fourteenth amendment, U.S.C.A.

CONSTITUTIONAL LAW ☞ 215.4
92k215.4
Formerly 92k211, 92k215
The thirteenth amendment relates only to slavery and involuntary servitude (which it abolishes); and although it establishes freedom to the United States, and Congress may probably pass laws directly enforcing its provisions, yet, such legislative power extends only to the subject of slavery and its incidents; and the denial of equal accommodations in inns, public conveyances, and places of public

3 S.Ct. 18
(Cite as: 109 U.S. 3, 3 S.Ct. 18)

amusement, forbidden by Act Cong. March 1, 1875, 18 Stat. 335, imposes no badge of slavery or involuntary servitude upon the party, but, at most, infringes rights which are protected from state aggression by the fourteenth amendment, U.S.C.A.

SLAVES ☞ 24
356k24

The thirteenth amendment relates only to slavery and involuntary servitude (which it abolishes); and although it establishes freedom to the United States, and Congress may probably pass laws directly enforcing its provisions, yet, such legislative power extends only to the subject of slavery and its incidents; and the denial of equal accommodations in inns, public conveyances, and places of public amusement, forbidden by Act Cong. March 1, 1875, 18 Stat. 335, imposes no badge of slavery or involuntary servitude upon the party, but, at most, infringes rights which are protected from state aggression by the fourteenth amendment, U.S.C.A.

CONSTITUTIONAL LAW ☞ 83(2)
92k83(2)

The thirteenth amendment relates only to slavery and involuntary servitude (which it abolishes); and although it establishes freedom to the United States, and Congress may probably pass laws directly enforcing its provisions, yet, such legislative power extends only to the subject of slavery and its incidents; and the denial of equal accommodations in inns, public conveyances, and places of public amusement, forbidden by Act Cong. March 1, 1875, 18 Stat. 335, imposes no badge of slavery or involuntary servitude upon the party, but, at most, infringes rights which are protected from state aggression by the fourteenth amendment, U.S.C.A.

CONSTITUTIONAL LAW ☞ 113
92k113

The provision in United States Constitution prohibiting states from passing any law impairing obligation of contract, does not give to Congress the power to provide laws for the general enforcement of contracts, nor power to invest the courts of the United States with jurisdiction over contracts, so as to enable

parties to sue upon them in such courts, but does give the power to provide remedies by which the impairment of contracts by state legislation can be counteracted and corrected.

FEDERAL COURTS ☞ 4
170Bk4
Formerly 106k258

The provision in United States Constitution prohibiting states from passing any law impairing obligation of contract, does not give to Congress the power to provide laws for the general enforcement of contracts, nor power to invest the courts of the United States with jurisdiction over contracts, so as to enable parties to sue upon them in such courts, but does give the power to provide remedies by which the impairment of contracts by state legislation can be counteracted and corrected.

SLAVES ☞ 24
356k24

Under the Thirteenth Amendment to the United States Constitution, Congress has a right to enact all necessary and proper laws for the obliteration and prevention of slavery with all its badges and incidents.

**19 *5 Sol. Gen. Phillips, for plaintiff, the United States.

No counsel for defendants, Stanley, Ryan, Nichols, and Singleton.

*7 Wm. M. Randolph, for plaintiffs in error, Robinson and wife.

*8 W. Y. C. Humes, for defendant in error, the Memphis & Charleston R. Co.

BRADLEY, J.

*4 These cases are all founded on the first and second sections of the act of congress known as the 'Civil Rights Act,' passed March 1, 1875, entitled 'An act to protect all citizens in their civil and legal rights.' 18 St. 335. Two of the cases, those against Stanley and Nichols, are indictments for denying to persons of color the accommodations and privileges of an inn or hotel; two of them, those against Ryan and Singleton, are, one an

3 S.Ct. 18
(Cite as: 109 U.S. 3, *4, 3 S.Ct. 18, **19)

information, the other an indictment, for denying to individuals the privileges and accommodations of a theater, the information against Ryan being for refusing a colored person a seat in the dress circle of Maguire's theater in San Francisco; and the indictment against Singleton being for denying to another person, whose color is not stated, the full enjoyment of the accommodations of the theater known as the Grand Opera House in New York, 'said denial not being made for any reasons by law applicable to citizens of every race and color, and regardless of any previous condition of servitude.' The case of Robinson and wife against the Memphis & Charleston Railroad Company was an action brought in the circuit court of the United States for the western district of Tennessee, to recover the penalty of $500 *5 given by the second section of the act; and the gravamen was the refusal by the conductor of the railroad company to allow the wife to ride in the ladies' car, for the reason, as stated in one of the counts, that she was a person of African descent. The jury rendered a verdict for the defendants in this case upon the merits under a charge of the court, to which a bill of exceptions was taken by the plaintiffs. The case was tried on the assumption by both parties of the validity of the act of congress; and the principal point made by the exceptions was that the judge allowed evidence to go to the jury tending to show that the conductor had reason to suspect that the plaintiff, the wife, was an improper person, because she was in company with a young man whom he supposed to be a white man, and on that account inferred that there was some improper connection between them; and the judge charged the jury, in substance, that if this was the conductor's bona fide reason for excluding the woman from the car, they might take it into consideration on the question of the liability of the company. The case is brought here by writ of error at the suit of the plaintiffs. The cases of Stanley, Nichols, and Singleton come up on certificates of division of opinion between the judges below as to the constitutionality of the first and second sections of the act referred to; and the case of Ryan, on a writ of error to the judgment of the circuit court for the district of California sustaining a demurrer to the information.

**20 *8 It is obvious that the primary and important question in all *9 the cases is the constitutionality of the law; for if the law is unconstitutional none of the prosecutions can stand.

The sections of the law referred to provide as follows:

'Section 1.   That all persons within the jurisdiction of the United States shall be entitled to the full and equal enjoyment of the accomodations, advantages, facilities, and privileges of inns, public conveyances on land or water, theaters, and other places of publie amusement; subject only to the conditions and limitations established by law, and applicable alike to citizens of every race and color, regardless of any previous condition of servitude.

'Sec. 2.   That any person who shall violate the foregoing section by denying to any citizen, except for reasons by law applicable to citizens of every race and color, and regardless of any previous condition of servitude, the full enjoyment of any of the accomodations, advantages, facilities, or privileges in said section enumerated, or by aiding or inciting such denial, shall, for every such offense, forfeit and pay the sum of $500 to the person aggrieved thereby, to be recovered in an action of debt, with full costs; and shall, also, for every such offense, be deemed guity of a misdemeanor, and upon conviction thereof shall be fined not less than $500 nor more than $1,000, or shall be imprisoned not less than 30 days nor more than one year: Provided, that all persons may elect to sue for the penalty aforesaid, or to proceed under their rights at common law and by state statutes; and having so elected to proceed in the one mode or the other, their right to proceed in the other jurisdiction shall be barred. But this provision shall not apply to criminal proceedings, either under this act or the criminal law of any state: And provided, further, that a judgment for the penalty in favor of the party aggrieved, or a judgment upon an indictment, shall be a bar to either prosecution respectively.'

3 S.Ct. 18
(Cite as: 109 U.S. 3, *9, 3 S.Ct. 18, **20)

Are these sections constitutional? The first section, which is the principal one, cannot be fairly understood without attending to the last clause, which qualifies the preceding part. The essence of the law is, not to declare broadly that all persons shall be entitled to the full and equal enjoyment of the accommodations, advantages, facilities, and privileges of inns, ***10** PUBLIC CONVEYANCES, AND THEATERS; BUT That such enjoyment shall not be subject to any conditions applicable only to citizens of a particular race or color, or who had been in a previous condition of servitude. In other words, it is the purpose of the law to declare that, in the enjoyment of the accommodations and privileges of inns, public conveyances, theaters, and other places of public amusement, no distinction shall be made between citizens of different race or color, or between those who have, and those who have not, been slaves. Its effect is to declare that in all inns, public conveyances, and places of amusement, colored citizens, whether formerly slaves or not, and citizens of other races, shall have the same accommodations and privileges in all inns, public conveyances, and places of amusement, as are enjoyed by white citizens; and vice versa. The second section makes it a penal offense in any person to deny to any citizen of any race or color, regardless of previous servitude, any of the accommodations or privileges mentioned in the first section.

Has congress constitutional power to make such a law? Of course, no one will contend that the power to pass it was contained in the ****21** constitution before the adoption of the last three amendments. The power is sought, first, in the fourteenth amendment, and the views and arguments of distinguished senators, advanced while the law was under consideration, claiming authority to pass it by virtue of that amendment, are the principal arguments adduced in favor of the power. We have carefully considered those arguments, as was due to the eminent ability of those who put them forward, and have felt, in all its force, the weight of authority which always invests a law that congress deems itself competent to pass. But the responsibility of an independent judgment is now thrown upon

this court; and we are bound to exercise it according to the best lights we have.

The first section of the fourteenth amendment,--which is the one relied on,--after declaring who shall be citizens of the United States, and of the several states, is prohibitory in its character, and prohibitory upon the states. It declares that ***11** *'no state shall make or enforce any law which shall abridge the privileges or immunities of citizens of the United States; nor shall any state deprive any person of life, liberty, or property without due process of law; nor deny to any person within its jurisdiction the equal protection of the laws.' It is state action of a particular character that is prohibited. Individual invasion of individual rights is not the subject-matter of the amendment. It has a deeper and broader scope. It nullifies and makes void all state legislation, and state action of every kind, which impairs the privileges and immunities of citizens of the United States, or which injures them in life, liberty, or property without due process of law, or which denies to any of them the equal protection of the laws. It not only does this, but, in order that the national will, thus declared, may not be a mere brutum fulmen, the last section of the amendment invests congress with power to enforce it by appropriate legislation. To enforce what? To enforce the prohibition. To adopt appropriate legislation for correcting the effects of such prohibited state law and state acts, and thus to render them effectually null, void, and innocuous. This is the legislative power conferred upon congress, and this is the whole of it. It does not invest congress with power to legislate upon subjects which are within the domain of state legislation; but to provide modes of relief against state legislation, or state action, of the kind referred to. It does not authorize congress to create a code of municipal law for the regulation of private rights; but to provide modes of redress against the operation of state laws, and the action of state officers, executive or judicial, when these are subversive of the fundamental rights specified in the amendment. Positive rights and privileges are undoubtedly secured by the fourteenth amendment; but they are secured by way of prohibition against state

3 S.Ct. 18
(Cite as: 109 U.S. 3, *11, 3 S.Ct. 18, **21)

laws and state proceedings affecting those rights and privileges, and by power given to congress to legislate for the purpose of carrying such prohibition into effect; and such legislation must necessarily be predicated upon such supposed state laws or state proceedings, **22 and be directed to the correction *12 of their operation and effect. A quite full discussion of this aspect of the amendment may be found in U. S. v. Cruikshank, 92 U. S. 542; Virginia v. Rives, 100 U. S. 313, and Ex parte Virginia, Id. 339.

An apt illustration of this distinction may be found in some of the provisions of the original constitution. Take the subject of contracts, for example. The constitution prohibited the states from passing any law impairing the obligation of contracts. This did not give to congress power to provide laws for the general enforcement of contracts; nor power to invest the courts of the United States with jurisdiction over contracts, so as to enable parties to sue upon them in those courts. It did, however, give the power to provide remedies by which the impairment of contracts by state legislation might be counteracted and corrected; and this power was exercised. The remedy which congress actually provided was that contained in the twenty-fifth section of the judiciary act of 1789, giving to the supreme court of the United States jurisdiction by writ of error to review the final decisions of state courts whenever they should sustain the validity of a state statute or authority, alleged to be repugnant to the constitution or laws of the United States. By this means, if a state law was passed impairing the obligation of a contract, and the state tribunals sustained the validity of the law, the mischief could be corrected in this court. The legislation of congress, and the proceedings provided for under it, were corrective in their character. No attempt was made to draw into the United States courts the litigation of contracts generally, and no such attempt would have been sustained. We do not say that the remedy provided was the only one that might have been provided in that case. Probably congress had power to pass a law giving to the courts of the United States direct jurisdiction

over contracts alleged to be impaired by a state law; and, under the broad provisions of the act of March 3, 1875, giving to the circuit courts jurisdiction of all cases arising under the constitution and laws of the United States, it is possible that such jurisdiction now exists. But under that or any other law, it must appear, as *13 well by allegation as proof at the trial, that the constitution had been violated by the action of the state legislature. Some obnoxious state law passed, or that might be passed, is necessary to be assumed in order to lay the foundation of any federal remedy in the case, and for the very sufficient reason that the constitutional prohibition is against state laws impairing the obligation of contracts.

And so in the present case, until some state law has been passed, or some state action through its officers or agents has been taken, adverse to the rights of citizens sought to be protected by the fourteenth amendment, no legislation of the United States under said amendment, nor any proceeding under such legislation, can be called into activity, for the prohibitions of the amendment are against state laws and acts done under state authority. Of course, legislation may **23 and should be provided in advance to meet the exigency when it arises, but it should be adapted to the mischief and wrong which the amendment was intended to provide against; and that is, state laws or state action of some kind adverse to the rights of the citizen secured by the amendment. Such legislation cannot properly cover the whole domain of rights appertaining to life, liberty, and property, defining them and providing for their vindication. That would be to establish a code of municipal law regulative of all private rights between man and man in society. It would be to make congress take the place of the state legislatures and to supersede them. It is absurd to affirm that, because the rights of life, liberty, and property (which include all civil rights that men have) are by the amendment sought to be protected against invasion on the part of the state without due process of law, congress may, therefore, provide due process of law for their vindication in every case; and that, because the denial by

3 S.Ct. 18
(Cite as: 109 U.S. 3, *13, 3 S.Ct. 18, **23)

a state to any persons of the equal protection of the laws is prohibited by the amendment, therefore congress may establish laws for their equal protection. In fine, the legislation which congress is authorized to adopt in this behalf is not general legislation upon the rights of the citizen, but corrective legislation; that is, such as may be necessary and proper for counteracting such laws as the states may *14 adopt or enforce, and which by the amendment they are prohibited from making or enforcing, or such acts and proceedings as the states may commit or take, and which by the amendment they are prohibited from committing or taking. It is not necessary for us to state, if we could, what legislation would be proper for congress to adopt. It is sufficient for us to examine whether the law in question is of that character.

An inspection of the law shows that it makes no reference whatever to any supposed or apprehended violation of the fourteenth amendment on the part of the states. It is not predicated on any such view. It proceeds ex directo to declare that certain acts committed by individuals shall be deemed offenses, and shall be prosecuted and punished by proceedings in the courts of the United States. It does not profess to be corrective of any constitutional wrong committed by the states; it does not make its operation to depend upon any such wrong committed. It applies equally to cases arising in states which have the justest laws respecting the personal rights of citizens, ans whose authorities are ever ready to enforce such laws as to those which arise in states that may have violated the prohibition of the amendment. In other words, it steps into the domain of local jurisprudence, and lays down rules for the conduct of individuals is society towards each other, and imposes sanctions for the enforcement of those rules, without referring in any manner to any supposed action of the state or its authorities.

If this legislation is appropriate for enforcing the prohibitions of the amendment, it is difficult to see where it is to stop. Why may **24 not congress, with equal show of authority, enact a code of laws for the enforcement and vindication of all rights of

life, liberty, and property? If it is supposable that the states may deprive persons of life, liberty, and property without due process of law, (and the amendment itself does suppose this,) why should not congress proceed at once to prescribe due process of law for the protection of every one of these fundamental rights, in every possible case, as well as to prescribe equal privileges in inns, public conveyances, and theaters. The truth is that the implication of a power to legislate in this manner is based *15 upon the assumption that if the states are forbidden to legislate or act in a particular way on a particular subject, and power is conferred upon congress to enforce the prohibition, this gives congress power to legislate generally upon that subject, and not merely power to provide modes of redress against such state legislation or action. The assumption is certainly unsound. It is repugnant to the tenth amendment of the constitution, which declares that powers not delegated to the United States by the constitution, nor prohibited by it to the states, are reserved to the states respectively or to the people.

We have not overlooked the fact that the fourth section of the act now under consideration has been held by this court to be constitutional. That section declares 'that no citizen, possessing all other qualifications which are or may be prescribed by law, shall be disqualified for service as grand or petit juror in any court of the United States, or of any state, on account of race, color, or previous condition of servitude; and any officer or other person charged with any duty in the selection or summoning of jurors who shall exclude or fail to summon any citizen for the cause aforesaid, shall, on conviction thereof, be deemed guilty of a misdemeanor, and be fined not more than five thousand dollars.' In Ex parte Virginia, 100 U. S. 339, it was held that an indictment against a state officer under this section for excluding persons of color from the jury list is sustainable. But a moment's attention to its terms will show that the section is entirely corrective in its character. Disqualifications for service on juries are only created by the law, and the first part of the section is aimed at certain disqualifying laws,

3 S.Ct. 18
(Cite as: 109 U.S. 3, *15, 3 S.Ct. 18, **24)

namely, those which make mere race or color a disqualification; and the second clause is directed against those who, assuming to use the authority of the state government, carry into effect such a rule of disqualification. In the Virginia case, the state, through its officer, enforced a rule of disqualification which the law was intended to abrogate and counteract. Whether the statute-book of the state actually laid down any such rule of disqualification or not, the state, through its officer, enforced such a rule; and it is against such state action, through its officers and agents, that the last clause of the section is directed. *16 This aspect of the law was deemed sufficient to divest it of any unconstitutional character, and makes it differ widely from the first and second sections of the same act which we are now considering.

**25 These sections, in the objectionable features before referred to, are different also from the law ordinarily called the 'Civil Rights Bill,' originally passed April 9, 1866, and re-enacted with some modifications in sections 16, 17, 18, of the enforcement act, passed May 31, 1870. That law, as re-enacted, after declaring that all persons within the jurisdiction of the United States shall have the same right in every state and territory to make and enforce contracts, to sue, be parties, give evidence, and to the full and equal benefit of all laws and proceedings for the security of persons and property as is enjoyed by white citizens, and shall be subject to like punishment, pains, penalties, taxes, licenses, and exactions of every kind, and none other, any law, statute, ordinance, regulation, or custom to the contrary notwithstanding, proceeds to enact that any person who, under color of any law, statute, ordinance, regulation, or custom, shall subject, or cause to be subjected, any inhabitant of any state or territory to the deprivation of any rights secured or protected by the preceding section, (above quoted,) or to different punishment, pains, or penalties, on account of such person being an alien, or by reason of his color or race, than is prescribed for the punishment of citizens, shall be deemed guilty of a misdememeanor, and subject to fine and imprisonment as specified in the act. This law

is clearly corrective in its character, intended to counteract and furnish redress against state laws and proceedings, and customs having the force of law, which sanction the wrongful acts specified. In the Revised Statutes, it is true, a very important clause, to-wit, the words 'any law, statute, ordinance, regulation, or custom to the contrary not-withstanding,' which gave the declaratory section its point and effect, are omitted; but the penal part, by which the declaration is enforced, and which is really the effective part of the law, retains the reference to state laws by making the penalty apply only to those who should subject *17 parties to a deprivation of their rights under color of any statute, ordinance, custom, etc., of any state or territory, thus preserving the corrective character of the legislation. Rev. St. §§ 1977, 1978, 1979, 5510. The civil rights bill here referred to is analogous in its character to what a law would have been under the original constitution, declaring that the validity of contracts should not be impaired, and that if any person bound by a contract should refuse to comply with it under color or pretense that it had been rendered void or invalid by a state law, he should be liable to an action upon it in the courts of the United States, with the addition of a penalty for setting up such an unjust and unconstitutional defense.

In this connection it is proper to state that civil rights, such as are guarantied by the constitution against state aggression, cannot be impaired by the wrongful acts of individuals, unsupported by state authority in the shape of laws, customs, or judicial or executive proceedings. The wrongful act of an individual, unsupported by any **26 such authority, is simply a private wrong, or a crime of that individual; an invasion of the rights of the injured party, it is true, whether they affect his person, his property, or his reputation; but if not sanctioned in some way by the state, or not done under state authority, his rights remain in full force, and may presumably be vindicated by resort to the laws of the state for redress. An individual cannot deprive a man of his right to vote, to hold property, to buy and to sell, to sue in the courts, or to be a witness or a juror; he may,

3 S.Ct. 18
(Cite as: 109 U.S. 3, *17, 3 S.Ct. 18, **26)

by force or fraud, interfere with the enjoyment of the right in a particular case; he may commit an assault against the person, or commit murder, or use ruffian violence at the polls, or slander the good name of a fellow-citizen; but unless protected in these wrongful acts by some shield of state law or state authority, he cannot destroy or injure the right; he will only render himself amenable to satisfaction or punishment; and amenable therefor to the laws of the state where the wrongful acts are committed. Hence, in all those cases where the constitution seeks to protect the rights of the citizen against discriminative and unjust laws of the state by prohibiting such laws, it is not individual offenses, but abrogation and *18 denial of rights, which it denounces, and for which it clothes the congress with power to provide a remedy. This abrogation and denial of rights, for which the states alone were or could be responsible, was the great seminal and fundamental wrong which was intended to be remedied. And the remedy to be provided must necessarily be predicated upon that wrong. It must assume that in the cases provided for, the evil or wrong actually committed rests upon some state law or state authority for its excuse and perpetration.

Of course, these remarks do not apply to those cases in which congress is clothed with direct and plenary powers of legislation over the whole subject, accompanied with an express or implied denial of such power to the states, as in the regulation of commerce with foreign nations, among the several states, and with the Indian tribes, the coining of money, the establishment of post-offices and post-roads, the declaring of war, etc. In these cases congress has power to pass laws for regulating the subjects specified, in every detail, and the conduct and transactions of individuals respect thereof. But where a subject is not submitted to the general legislative power of congress, but is only submitted thereto for the purpose of rendering effective some prohibition against particular state legislation or state action in reference to that subject, the power given is limited by its object, and any legislation by congress in the matter must necessarily be corrective in its character, adapted to counteract and redress the operation of such prohibited state laws or proceedings of state officers.

If the principles of interpretation which we have laid down are correct, as we deem them to be,--and they are in accord with the principles laid down in the cases before referred to, as well as in the recent case of U. S. v. Harris, decided at the last term of this court, **27 [1 SUP. CT. REP. 601,]--it is clear that the law in question cannot be sustained by any grant of legislative power made to congress by the fourteenth amendment. That amendment prohibits the states from denying to any person the equal protection of the laws, and declares that congress shall have power to enforce, by appropriate legislation, the provisions of the amendment. The law in question, without any reference to adverse state legislation on the subject, *19 declares that all persons shall be entitled to equal accommodation and privileges of inns, public conveyances, and places of public amusement, and imposes a penalty upon any individual who shall deny to any citizen such equal accommodations and privileges. This is not corrective legislation; it is primary and direct; it takes immediate and absolute possession of the subject of the right of admission to inns, public conveyances, and places of amusement. It supersedes and displaces state legislation on the same subject, or only allows it permissive force. It ignores such legislation, and assumes that the matter is one that belongs to the domain of national regulation. Whether it would not have been a more effective protection of the rights of citizens to have clothed congress with plenary power over the whole subject, is not now the question. What we have to decide is, whether such plenary power has been conferred upon congress by the fourteenth amendment, and, in our judgment, it has not.

We have discussed the question presented by the law on the assumption that a right to enjoy equal accommodations and privileges in all inns, public conveyances, and places of public amusement, is one of the essential rights of the citizen which no state can abridge or interfere with. Whether it is such a right or

3 S.Ct. 18
(Cite as: 109 U.S. 3, *19, 3 S.Ct. 18, **27)

not is a different question, which, in the view we have taken of the validity of the law on the ground already stated, it is not necessary to examine.

We have also discussed the validity of the law in reference to cases arising in the states only; and not in reference to cases arising in the territories or the District of Columbia, which are subject to the plenary legislation of congress in every branch of municipal regulation. Whether the law would be a valid one as applied to the territories and the district is not a question for consideration in the cases before us; they all being cases arising within the limits of states. And whether congress, in the exercise of its power to regulate commerce among the several states, might or might not pass a law regulating rights in public conveyances passing from one state to another, is also a question which is not now before us, as the sections in question are not conceived in any such view.

*20 But the power of congress to adopt direct and primary, as distinguished from corrective, legislation on the subject in hand, is sought, in the second place, from the thirteenth amendment, which abolishes slavery. This amendment declares 'that neither slavery, nor involuntary servitude, except as a punishment for crime, whereof the party shall have been duly convicted, shall exist within the United **28 States, or any place subject to their jurisdiction;' and it gives congress power to enforce the amendment by appropriate legislation.

This amendment, as well as the fourteenth, is undoubtedly self-executing without any ancillary legislation, so far as its terms are applicable to any existing state of circumstances. By its own unaided force and effect if abolished slavery, and established universal freedom. Still, legislation may be necessary and proper to meet all the various cases and circumstances to be affected by it, and to prescribe proper modes of redress for its violation in letter or spirit. And such legislation may be primary and direct in its character; for the amendment is not a mere

prohibition of state laws establishing or upholding slavery, but an absolute declaration that slavery or involuntary servitude shall not exist in any part of the United States.

It is true that slavery cannot exist without law any more than property in lands and goods can exist without law, and therefore the thirteenth amendment may be regarded as nullifying all state laws which establish or uphold slavery. But it has a reflex character also, establishing and decreeing universal civil and political freedom throughout the United States; and it is assumed that the power vested in congress to enforce the article by appropriate legislation, clothes congress with power to pass all laws necessary and proper for abolishing all badges and incidents of slavery in the United Stated; and upon this assumption it is claimed that this is sufficient authority for declaring by law that all persons shall have equal accommodations and privileges in all inns, public conveyances, and places of public amusement; the argument being that the denial of such equal accommodations and privileges is in itself a subjection to a species of servitude within the meaning of the amendment. Conceding the major proposition to be true, that that *21 congress has a right to enact all necessary and proper laws for the obliteration and prevention of slavery, with all its badges and incidents, is the minor proposition also true, that the denial to any person of admission to the accommodations and privileges of an inn, a public conveyance, or a theater, does subject that person to any form of servitude, or tend to fasten upon him any badge of slavery? If it does not, then power to pass the law is not found in the thirteenth amendment.

In a very able and learned presentation of the cognate question as to the extent of the rights, privileges, and immunities of citizens which cannot rightfully be abridged by state laws under the fourteenth amendment, made in a former case, a long list of burdens and disabilities of a servile character, incident to feudal vasslage in France, and which were abolished by the decrees of the national assembly, was presented for the purpose of showing that all inequalities and observances

3 S.Ct. 18
(Cite as: 109 U.S. 3, *21, 3 S.Ct. 18, **28)

exacted by one man from another, were servitudes or badges of slavery, which a great nation, in its effort to establish universal liberty, made haste to wipe out and destroy. But these were servitudes imposed by the old law, or by long custom which had **29 the force of law, and exacted by one man from another without the latter's consent. Should any such servitudes be imposed by a state law, there can be no doubt that the law would be repugnant to the fourteenth, no less than to the thirteenth, amendment; nor any greater doubt that congress has adequate power to forbid any such servitude from being exacted.

But is there any similarity between such servitudes and a denial by the owner of an inn, a public conveyance, or a theater, of its accommodations and privileges to an individual, even through the denial be founded on the race or color of that individual? Where does any slavery or servitude, or badge of either, arise from such an act of denial? Whether it might not be a denial of a right which, if sanctioned by the state law, would be obnoxious to the prohibitions of the fourteenth amendment, is another question. But what has it to do with the question of slavery? It may be that by the black code, (as it was called,) in the times when slavery prevailed, the proprietors of inns and public *22 conveyances were forbidden to receive persons of the African race, because it might assist slaves to escape from the control of their masters. This was merely a means of preventing such escapes, and was no part of the servitude itself. A law of that kind could not have any such object now, however justly it might be deemed an invasion of the party's legal right as a citizen, and amenable to the prohibitions of the fourteenth amendment.

The long existence of African slavery in this country gave us very distinct notions of what it was, and what were its necessary incidents. Compulsory service of the slave for the benefit of the master, restraint of his movements except by the master's will, disability to hold property, to make contracts, to have a standing in court, to be a witness against a white person, and such like burdens and incapacities were the inseparable incidents of the institution. Severer punishments for crimes were imposed on the slave than on free persons guilty of the same offenses. Congress, as we have seen, by the civil rights bill of 1866, passed in view of the thirteenth amendment, before the fourteenth was adopted, undertook to wipe out these burdens and disabilities, the necessary incidents of slavery, constituting its substance and visible from; and to secure to all citizens of every race and color, and without regard to previous servitude, those fundamental rights which are the essence of civil freedom, namely, the same right to make and enforce contracts, to sue, be parties, give evidence, and to inherit, purchase, lease, sell, and convey property, as is enjoyed by white citizens. Whether this legislation was fully authorized by the thirteenth amendment alone, without the support which it afterwards received from the fourteenth amendment, after the adoption of which it was re-enacted with some additions, it is not necessary to inquire. It is referred to for the purpose of showing that at that **30 time (in 1866) congress did not assume, under the authority given by the thirteenth amendment, to adjust what may be called the social rights of men and races in the community; but only to declare and vindicate those fundamental rights which appertain to the essence of citizenship, and the enjoyment or deprivation of which constitutes the essential distinction between freedom and slavery.

*23 We must not forget that the province and scope of the thirteenth and fourteenth amendments are different: the former simply abolished slavery: the latter prohibited the states from abridging the privileges or immunities of citizens of the United States, from depriving them of life, liberty, or property without due process of law, and from denying to any the equal protection of the laws. The amendments are different, and the powers of congress under them are different. What congress has power to do under one, it may not have power to do under the other. Under the thirteenth amendment, it has only to do with slavery and its incidents. Under the fourteenth amendment, it has power to counteract and render nugatory all state laws

3 S.Ct. 18
(Cite as: 109 U.S. 3, *23, 3 S.Ct. 18, **30)

and proceedings which have the effect to abridge any of the privileges or immunities which have the effect to abridge any deprive them of life, liberty, or property without due process of law, or to deny to any of them the equal protection of the laws. Under the thirteenth amendment the legislation, so far as necessary or proper to eradicate all forms and incidents of slavery and involuntary servitude, may be direct and primary, operating upon the acts of individuals, whether sanctioned by state legislation or not; under the fourteenth, as we have already shown, it must necessarily be, and can only be, corrective in its character, addressed to counteract and afford relief against state regulations or proceedings.

The only question under the present head, therefore, is, whether the refusal to any persons of the accommodations of an inn, or a public conveyance, or a place of public amusement, by an individual, and without any sanction or support from any state law or regulation, does inflict upon such persons any manner of servitude, or form of slavery, as those terms are understood in this country? Many wrongs may be obnoxious to the prohibitions of the fourteenth amendment which are not, in any just sense, incidents or elements of slavery. Such, for example, would be the taking of private property without due process of law; or allowing persons who have committed certain crimes (horse-stealing, for example) to be seized and hung by the posse comitatus without regular trial; or denying to any person, or class of persons, the right to pursue any peaceful *24 avocations allowed to others. What is called calss legislation would belong to this category, and would be obnoxious to the prhibitions of the fourteenth amendment, but would not to the prohibitions of the fourteenth when not involving the idea of any subjection of one man to another. The thirteenth amendment has respect, not to distinctions of race, or **31 class, or color, but to slavery. The fourteenth amendment extends its protection to races and classes, and prohibits any state legislation which has the effect of denying to any race or class, or to any individual, the equal protection of the laws.

Now, conceding, for the sake of the argument, that the admission to an inn, a public conveyance, or a place of public amusement, on equal terms with all other citizens, is the right of every man and all classes of men, is it any more than one of those rights which the states by the fourteenth amendment are forbidden to deny to any person? and is the consitution violated until the denial of the right has some state sanction or authority? Can the act of a mere individual, the owner of the inn, the public conveyance, or place of amusement, refusing the accommodation, be justly regarded as imposing any badge of slavery or servitude upon the applicant, or only as inflicting an ordinary civil injury, properly cognizable by the laws of the state, and presumably subject to redress by those laws until the contrary appears?

After giving to these questions all the consideration which their importance demands, we are forced to the conclusion that such an act of refusal has nothing to do with slavery or involuntary servitude, and that if it is violative of any right of the party, his redress is to be sought under the laws of the state; or, if those laws are adverse to his rights and do not protect him, his remedy will be found in the corrective legislation which congress has adopted, or may adopt, for counteracting the effect of state laws, or state action, prohibited by the fourteenth amendment. It would be running the slavery argument into the ground to make it apply to every act of discrimination which a person may see fit to make as to the guests he will entertain, or as to the people he will take into his coach or cab or car, or admit to his concert or theater, or deal with in *25 other matters of intercourse or business. Innkeepers and public carriers, by the laws of all the states, so far as we are aware, are bound, to the extent of their facilities, to furnish proper accommodation to all unobjectionable persons who in good faith apply for them. If the laws themselves make any unjust discrimination, amenable to the prohibitions of the fourteenth amendment, congress has full power to afford a remedy under that amendment and in accordance with it.

3 S.Ct. 18
(Cite as: 109 U.S. 3, *25, 3 S.Ct. 18, **31)

When a man has emerged from slavery, and by the aid of beneficent legislation has shaken off the inseparable concomitants of that state, there must be some stage in the progress of his elevation when he takes the rank of a mere citizen, and ceases to be the special favorite of the laws, and when his rights as a citizen, or a man, are to be protected in the ordinary modes by which other men's rights are protected. There were thousands of free colored people in this country before the abolition of slavery, enjoying all the essential rights of life, liberty, and property the same as white citizens; yet no one, at **32 that time, thought that it was any invasion of their personal status as freemen because they were not admitted to all the privileges enjoyed by white citizens, or because they were subjected to discriminations in the enjoyment of accommodations in inns, public conveyances, and places of amusement. Mere discriminations on account of race or color were not regarded as badges of slavery. If, since that time, the enjoyment of equal rights in all these respects has become established by constitutional enactment, it is not by force of the thirteenth amendment, (which merely abolishes slavery,) but by force of the fourteenth and fifteenth amendments.

On the whole, we are of opinion that no countenance of authority for the passage of the law in question can be found in either the thirteenth or fourteenth amendment of the constitution; and no other ground of authority for its passage being suggested, it must necessarily be declared void, at least so far as its operation in the several states is concerned.

This conclusion disposes of the cases now under consideration. In the cases of U. S. v. Ryan, and of Robinson v. Memphis & C. *26 R. Co., the judgments must be affirmed. In the other cases, the answer to be given will be, that the first and second sections of the act of congress of March 1, 1875, entitled 'An act to protect all citizens in their civil and legal rights,' are unconstitutional and void, and that judgment should be rendered upon the several indictments in those cases accordingly. And it is so ordered.

HARLAN, J., dissents.

**33 HARLAN, J., dissenting.

The opinion in these cases proceeds, as it seems to me, upon grounds entirely too narrow and artificial. The substance and spirit of the recent amendments of the constitution have been sacrificed by a subtle and ingenious verbal criticism. 'It is not the words of the law but the internal sense of it that makes the law. The letter of the law is the body; the sense and reason of the law is the soul.' Constitutional provisions, adopted in the interest of liberty, and for the purpose of securing, through national legislation, if need be, rights inhering in a state of freedom, and belonging to American citizenship, have been so construed as to defeat the ends the people desired to accomplish, which they attempted to accomplish, and which they supposed they had accomplished by changes in their fundamental law. By this I do not mean that the determination of these cases should have been materially controlled by considerations of mere expediency or policy. I mean only, in this form, to express an earnest conviction that the court has departed from the familiar rule requiring, in the interpretation of constitutional provisions, that full effect be given to the intent with which they were adopted.

The purpose of the first section of the act of congress of March 1, 1875, was to prevent race discrimination. It does not assume to define the general conditions and limitations under which inns, public conveyances, and places of public amusement may be conducted, but only declares that such conditions and limitations, whatever they may be, shall not be applied, by way of *27 discrimination, on account of race, color, or previous condition of servitude. The second section provides a penalty against any one denying, or aiding or inciting the denial, to any citizen that equality of right given by the first section, except for reasons by law applicable to citizens of every race or color, and regardless of any previous condition of servitude.

There seems to be no substantial difference between my brethren and myself as to what was the purpose of congress; for they say that

3 S.Ct. 18
(Cite as: 109 U.S. 3, *27, 3 S.Ct. 18, **33)

the essence of the law is, not to declare broadly that all persons shall be entitled to the full and equal enjoyment of the accommodations, advantages, facilities, and privileges of inns, public conveyances, and theaters, but that such enjoyment shall not be subject to any conditions applicable only to citizens of a particular race or color, or who had been in a previous condition of servitude. The effect of the statute, the court says, is that colored citizens, whether formerly slaves or not, and citizens of other races, shall have the same accommodations and privileges in all inns, public conveyances, and places of amusement as are enjoyed by white persons, and vice versa.

The court adjudges that congress is without power, under either the thirteenth or fourteenth amendment, to establish such regulations, and that the first and second sections of the statute are, in all their parts, unconstitutional and void.

**34 *28 *Before considering the particular language and scope of these amendments it will be proper to recall the relations which, prior to their adoption, subsisted between the national government and the institution of slavery, as indicated by the provisions of the constitution, the legislation of congress, and the decisions of this court. In this mode we may obtain keys with which to open the mind of the people, and discover the thought intended to be expressed.

In section 2 of article 4 of the constitution it was provided that 'no person held to service or labor in one state, under the laws thereof, escaping into another, shall, in consequence of any law or regulation therein, be discharged from such service or labor, but shall be delivered up on claim of the party to whom such service or labor may be due.' Under the authority of that clause congress passed the fugitive slave law of 1793, establishing the mode for the recovery of a fugitive slave, and prescribing a penalty against any person knowingly and willingly obstructing or hindering the master, his agent or attorney, in seizing, arresting, and recovering the fugitive, or who should rescue the fugitive from him, or who should harbor or conceal the slave after notice that he was a fugitive.

In Prigg v. Com. 16 Pet. 539, this court had occasion to define the powers and duties of congress in reference to fugitives from labor. Speaking by Mr. Justice STORY, the court laid down these propositions: That a clause of the constitution conferring a right should not be so construed as to make it shadowy, or unsubstantial, or leave the citizen without a remedial power adequate for its protection, when another mode, equally accordant with the words and the sense in which they were used, would enforce and protect the right so granted; that congress is not restricted to legislation for the exertion *29 of its powers expressly granted; but, for the protection of rights guaranteed by the constitution, it may employ, through legislation, such means, not prohibited, as are necessary and proper, or such as are appropriate, to attain the ends proposed; that the constitution recognized the master's right of property in his fugitive slave, and, as incidental thereto, the right of seizing and recovering him, regardless of any state law, or regulation, or local custom whatsoever; and that the right of the master to have his slave, so escaping, delivered up on claim, being guaranteed by the constitution, the fair implication was that the national government was clothed with appropriate authority and functions to enforce it.

The court said:
'The fundamental principle, applicable to all cases of this sort, would seem to be that when the end is required the means are given, and when the duty is enjoined the ability to perform it is contemplated to exist on the part of the functionary to whom it is intrusted.'

Again:
'It would be a strange anomaly and forced construction to suppose that the national government meant to rely for the due fulfillment of its own **35 proper duties, and the rights which it intended to secure, upon state legislation, and not upon that of the Union. A fortiori, it would be more objectionable to suppose that a power which

3 S.Ct. 18
(Cite as: 109 U.S. 3, *29, 3 S.Ct. 18, **35)

was to be the same throughout the Union should be confided to state sovereignty, which could not rightfully act beyond its own territorial limits.'

The act of 1793 was, upon these grounds, adjudged to be a constitutional exercise of the powers of congress.

It is to be observed, from the report of Prigg's Case, that Pennsylvania, by her attorney general, pressed the argument that the obligation to surrender fugitive slaves was on the states and for the states, subject to the restriction that they should not pass laws or establish regulations liberating such fugitives; that the constitution did not take from the states the right to determine the status of all persons within their respective jurisdictions; that it was for the state in which the alleged fugitive was found to determine, through her courts, or in such modes as she prescribed, whether the person arrested was, in fact, a freeman or a fugitive slave; that the sole power *30 of the general government in the premises was, by judicial instrumentality, to restrain and correct, not to forbid and prevent in the absence of hostile state action; and that, for the general government to assume primary authority to legislate on the subject of fugitive slaves, to the exclusion of the states, would be a dangerous encroachment on state sovereignty. But to such suggestions this court turned a deaf ear, and adjudged that primary legislation by congress to enforce the master's right was authorized by the constitution.

We next come to the fugitive slave act of 1850, the constitutionality of which rested, as did that of 1793, solely upon the implied power of congress to enforce the master's rights. The provisions of that act were far in advance of previous legislation. They placed at the disposal of the master seeking to recover his fugitive slave, substantially, the whole power of the nation. It invested commissioners, appointed under the act, with power to summon the posse comitatus for the enforcement of its provisions, and commanded 'all good citizens' to assist in its prompt and efficient execution whenever their services

were required as part of the posse comitatus. Without going into the details of that act, it is sufficient to say that congress omitted from it nothing which the utmost ingenuity could suggest as essential to the successful enforcement of the master's claim to recover his fugitive slave. And this court, in Ableman v. Booth, 21 How. 526, adjudged it to be, 'in all of its provisions, fully authorized by the constitution of the United States.'

The only other decision prior to the adoption of the recent amendments, to which reference will be made, is Dred Scott v. Sandford, 19 How. 393. That suit was instituted in a circuit court of the United States by Dred Scott, claiming to be a citizen of Missouri, the defendant being a citizen of another state. Its object was to assert the title of himself and family to freedom. The defendant pleaded in **36 abatement to the jurisdiction of the court that Scott--being of African descent, whose ancestors, of pure African blood, were brought into this country, and sold as slaves--was not a citizen. The only matter in issue, said the court, was whether the descendants of slaves so imported *31 and sold, when they should be emancipated, or who were born of parents who had become free before their birth, are citizens of a state in the sense in which the word 'citizen' is used in the constitution of the United States.

In determining that question the court instituted an inquiry as to who were citizens of the several states at the adoption of the constitution, and who, at that time, were recognized as the people whose rights and liberties had been violated by the British government. The result was a declaration by this court, speaking through Chief Justice TANEY, that the legislation and histories of the times, and the language used in the Declaration of Independence, showed 'that neither the class of persons who had been imported as slaves, nor their descendants, whether they had become free or not, were then acknowledged as a part of the people, nor intended to be included in the general words used in that instrument:' that 'they had for more than a century before been regarded as beings of an inferior race, and altogether unfit

3 S.Ct. 18
(Cite as: 109 U.S. 3, *31, 3 S.Ct. 18, **36)

to associate with the white race, either in social or political relations, and so far inferior that they had no rights which the white man was bound to respect, and that the negro might justly and lawfully be reduced to slavery for his benefit;' that he was 'bought and sold, and treated as an ordinary article of merchandise and traffic, whenever a profit could be made by it;' and that 'this opinion was at that time fixed and universal in the civilized portion of the white race. It was regarded as an axiom in morals as well as in politics, which no one thought of disputing, or supposed to be open to dispute; and men in every grade and position in society daily and habitually acted upon it in their private pursuits, as well as in matters of public concern, without for a moment doubting the correctness of this opinion.'

The judgment of the court was that the words 'people of the United States' and 'citizens' meant the same thing, both describing 'the political body who, according to our republican institutions, form the sovereignty and hold the power and conduct the government through their representatives;' that 'they are what we familiarly call the 'sovereign people,' and *32 every citizen is one of this people and a constituent member of this sovereignty;' but that the class of persons described in the plea in abatement did not compose a portion of this people, were not 'included, and were not intended to be included, under the word 'citizens' in the constitution;' that, therefore, they could 'claim none of the rights and privileges which that instrument provides for and secures to citizens of the United States;' that, 'on the contrary, they were at that time considered as a subordinate and inferior class of beings, who had been subjugated by the **37 dominant race, and, whether emancipated or not, yet remained subject to their authority, and had no rights or privileges but such as those who held the power and the government might choose to grant them.'

Such were the relations which, prior to the adoption of the thirteenth amendment, existed between the government, whether national or

state, and the descendants, whether free or in bondage, of those of African blood who had been imported into this country and sold as slaves.

The first section thereof provides that 'neither slavery nor involuntary servitude, except as a punishment for crime, whereof the party shall have been duly convicted, shall exist within the United States, or any place subject to their jurisdiction.' Its second section declares that 'congress shall have power to enforce this article by appropriate legislation.' This amendment was followed by the civil rights act of April 9, 1866, which, among other things, provided that 'all persons born in the United States, and not subject to any foreign power, excluding Indians not taxed, are hereby declared to be citizens of the United States.' 14 St. 27. The power of congress, in this mode, to elevate the race thus liberated to the plane of national citizenship, was maintained, by the supporters of the act of 1866, to be as full and complete as its power, by general statute, to make the children, being of full age, of persons naturalized in this country, citizens of the United States without going through the process of naturalization. The act of 1866, in this respect, was also likened to that of 1843, in which congress declared 'that the Stockbridge tribe of Indians, and each and every one of them, shall be deemed to be, and are hereby declared to be, citizens of the United States to *33 all intent and purposes, and shall be entitled to all the rights, privileges, and immunities of such citizens, and shall in all respects be subject to the laws of the United States.' If the act of 1866 was valid, as conferring national citizenship upon all embraced by its terms, then the colored race, liberated by the thirteenth amendment, became citizens of the United States prior to the adoption of the fourteenth amendment. But, in the view which I take of the present case, it is not necessary to examine this question.

The terms of the thirteenth amendment are absolute and universal. They embrace every race which then was, or might thereafter be, within the United States. No race, as such, can be excluded from the benefits or rights

3 S.Ct. 18
(Cite as: 109 U.S. 3, *33, 3 S.Ct. 18, **37)

thereby conferred. Yet it is historically true that that amendment was suggested by the condition, in this country, of that race which had been declared by this court to have had, according to the opinion entertained by the most civilized portion of the white race at the time of the adoption of the constitution, 'no rights which the white man was bound to respect,' none of the privileges or immunities secured by that instrument to citizens of the United States. It had reference, in a peculiar sense, to a people ****38** which (although the larger part of them were in slavery) had been invited by an act of congress to aid, by their strong right arms, in saving from overthrow a government which, theretofore, by all of its departments, had treated them as an inferior race, with no legal rights or privileges except such as the white race might choose to grant them.

These are the circumstances under which the thirteenth amendment was proposed for adoption. They are now recalled only that we may better understand what was in the minds of the people when that amendment was being considered, and what were the mischiefs to be remedied, and the grievances to be redressed.

We have seen that the power of congress, by legislation, to enforce the master's right to have his slave delivered up on claim was implied from the recognition and guaranty of that right in the national constitution. But the power conferred by the thirteenth amendment does not rest upon implication or ***34** inference. Those who framed it were not ignorant of the discussion, covering many years of the country's history, as to the constitutional power of congress to enact the fugitive slave laws of 1793 and 1850. When, therefore, it was determined, by a change in the fundamental law, to uproot the institution of slavery wherever it existed in this land, and to establish universal freedom, there was a fixed purpose to place the power of congress in the premises beyond the possibility of doubt. Therefore, ex industria, the power to enforce the thirteenth amendment, by appropriate legislation, was expressly granted. Legislation for that purpose, it is conceded, may be direct and primary. But to what

specific ends may it be directed? This court has uniformly held that the national government has the power, whether expressly given or not, to secure and protect rights conferred or guarantied by the constitution. U. S. v. Reese, 92 U. S. 214; Strauder v. West Virginia, 100 U. S. 303. That doctrine ought not now to be abandoned, when the inquiry is not as to an implied power to protect the master's rights, but what may congress do, under powers expressly granted, for the protection of freedom, and the rights necessarily inhering in a state of freedom.

The thirteenth amendment, my brethren concede, did something more than to prohibit slavery as an institution, resting upon distinctions of race, and upheld by positive law. They admit that it established and decreed universal civil freedom throughout the United States. But did the freedom thus established involve nothing more than exemption from actual slavery? Was nothing more intended than to forbid one man from owning another as property? Was it the purpose of the nation simply to destroy the institution, and then remit the race, theretofore held in bondage, to the several states for such protection, in their civil rights, necessarily growing out of freedom, as those states, in their discretion, choose to provide? Were the states, against whose solemn protest the institution was destroyed, ****39** to be left perfectly free, so far as national interference was concerned, to make or allow dircriminations against that race, as such, in the enjoyment of those fundamental rights that inhere in a state of freedom? ***35** Had the thirteenth amendment stopped with the sweeping declaration, in its first section, against the existence of slavery and involuntary servitude, except for crime, congress would have had the power, by implication, according to the doctrines of Prigg v. Com., repeated in Strauder v. West Virginia, to protect the freedom thus established, and consequently to secure the enjoyment of such civil rights as were fundamental in freedom. But that it can exert its authority to that extent is now made clear, and was intended to be made clear, by the express grant of power contained in the second

3 S.Ct. 18
(Cite as: 109 U.S. 3, *35, 3 S.Ct. 18, **39)

section of that amendment.

That there are burdens and disabilities which constitute badges of slavery and servitude, and that the express power delegated to congress to enforce, by appropriate legislation, the thirteenth amendment, may be exerted by legislation of a direct and primary character, for the eradication, not simply of the institution, but of its badges and incidents, are propositions which ought to be deemed indisputable. They lie at the very foundation of the civil rights act of 1866. Whether that act was fully authorized by the thirteenth amendment alone, without the support which it afterwards received from the fourteenth amendment, after the adoption of which it was re-enacted with some additions, the court, in its opinion, says it is unnecessary to inquire. But I submit, with all respect to my brethren, that its constitutionality is conclusively shown by other portions of their opinion. It is expressly conceded by them that the thirteenth amendment established freedom; that there are burdens and disabilities, the necessary incidents of slavery, which constitute its substance and visible form; that congress, by the act of 1866, passed in view of the thirteenth amendment, before the fourteenth was adopted, undertook to remove certain burdens and disabilities, the necessary incidents of slavery, and to secure to all citizens of every race and color, and without regard to previous servitude, those fundamental rights which are the essence of civil freedom, namely, the same right to make and enforce contracts, to sue, be parties, give evidence, and to inherit, purchase, lease, sell, and convey property as is enjoyed by white citizens; that under the thirteenth amendment congress has to do with slavery and *36 its incidents; and that legislation, so far as necessary or proper to eradicate all forms and incidents of slavery and involuntary servitude, may be direct and primary, operating upon the acts of individuals, whether sanctioned by state legislation or not. These propositions being conceded, it is impossible, as it seems to me, to question the constitutional validity of the civil rights act of 1866. I do not contend that the thirteenth amendment invests

congress with authority, by legislation, to regulate the entire body of the civil rights which citizens enjoy, or may enjoy, in the several states. But I do **40 hold that since slavery, as the court has repeatedly declared, was the moving or principal cause of the adoption of that amendment, and since that institution rested wholly upon the inferiority, as a race, of those held in bondage, their freedom necessarily involved immunity from, and protection against, all discrimination against them, because of their race, in respect of such civil rights as belong to freemen of other races. Congress, therefore, under its express power to enforce that amendment, by appropriate legislation, may enact laws to protect that people against the deprivation, on account of their race, of any civil rights enjoyed by other freemen in the same state; and such legislation may be of a direct and primary character, operating upon states, their officers and agents, and also upon, at least, such individuals and corporations as exercise public functions and wield power and authority under the state.

By way of testing the correctness of this position, let us suppose that, prior to the adoption of the fourteenth amendment, a state had passed a statute denying to freemen of African descent, resident within its limits, the same rights which were accorded to white persons, of making or enforcing contracts, or of inheriting, purchasing, leasing, selling, and conveying property; or a statute subjecting colored people to severer punishment for particular offenses than was prescribed for white persons, or excluding that race from the benefit of the laws exempting homesteads from execution. Recall the legislation of 1865-66 in some of the states, of which this court, in the Slaughter-*37 house Cases, said that it imposed upon the colored race onerous disabilities and burdens; curtailed their rights in the pursuit of life, liberty, and property to such an extent that their freedom was of little value; forbade them to appear in the towns in any other character than menial servants; required them to reside on and cultivate the soil, without the right to purchase or own it; excluded them from many occupations of gain; and denied them the privilege of giving

3 S.Ct. 18
(Cite as: 109 U.S. 3, *37, 3 S.Ct. 18, **40)

testimony in the courts where a white man was a party. 16 Wall. 57. Can there by any doubt that all such legislation might have been reached by direct legislation upon the part of congress under its express power to enforce the thirteenth amendment? Would any court have hesitated to declare that such legislation imposed badges of servitude in conflict with the civil freedom ordained by that amendment? That it would have been also in conflict with the fourteenth amendment, because inconsistent with the fundamental rights of American citizenship, does not prove that it would have been consistent with the thirteenth amendment.

What has been said is sufficient to show that the power of congress under the thirteenth amendment is not necessarily restricted to legislation against slavery as an institution upheld by positive law, but may be exerted to the extent at least of protecting the race, so liberated, against discrimination, in respect of legal rights belonging to freemen, where such discrimination is based upon race.

**41 It remains now to inquire what are the legal rights of colored persons in respect of the accommodations, privileges, and facilities of public conveyances, inns, and places of public amusement.

1. As to public conveyances on land and water. In New Jersey Steam Nav. Co. v. Merchants' Bank, 6 How. 382, this court, speaking by Mr. Justice NELSON, said that a common carrier is 'in the exercise of a sort of public office and has public duties to perform, from which he should not be permitted to exonerate himself without the assent of the parties concerned.' To the same effect is Munn v. Illinois, 94 U. S. 113. In Olcott v. Sup'rs, 16 Wall. 694, it was ruled that ***38** railroads are public highways, established, by authority of the state, for the public use; that they are none the less public highways because controlled and owned by private corporations; that it is a part of the function of government to make and maintain highways for the conveyance of the public; that no matter who is the agent, and what is the agency, the function performed is that of the

state; that although the owners may be private companies, they may be compelled to permit the public to use these works in the manner in which they can be used; that upon these grounds alone have the courts sustained the investiture of railroad corporations with the state's right of eminent domain, or the right of municipal corporations, under legislative authority, to assess, levy, and collect taxes to aid in the construction of railroads. So in Town of Queensbury v. Culver, 19 Wall. 91, it was said that a municipal subscription of railroad stock was in aid of the construction and maintenance of a public highway and for the promotion of a public use. Again, in Township of Pine Grove v. Talcott, 19 Wall. 676: 'Though the corporation [railroad] was private, its work was public; as much so as if it were to be constructed by the state.' To the like effect are numerous adjudications in this and the state courts with which the profession is familiar. The supreme judicial court of Massachusetts, in Inhabitants of Worcester v. Western R. Corp. 4 Metc. 566, said, in reference to a certain railroad:

'The establishment of that great thoroughfare is regarded as a public work, established by public authority, intended for the public use and benefit, the use of which is secured to the whole community, and constitutes, therefore, like a canal, turnpike, or highway, a public easement. * * * It is true that the real and personal property necessary to the establishment and management of the railroad is vested in the corporation; but it is in trust for the public.'

In Erie & N. E. R. Co. v. Casey, 26 Pa. St. 287, the court, referring to an act repealing the charter of a railroad, and under which the state took possession of the road, said, speaking by BLACK, J.:

'It is a public highway, solemnly devoted to public use. When the lands were taken it was for such use, or they could not have been taken at all. * * * Railroads established ***39** upon land taken by the right of eminent domain by authority of the commonwealth, created by her laws as thoroughfares for commerce, are her highways. No corporation has property in

3 S.Ct. 18
(Cite as: 109 U.S. 3, *39, 3 S.Ct. 18, **41)

them, though it may have franchises annexed to and exercisable within them.'

**42 In many courts it has been held that because of the public interest in such a corporation the land of a railroad company cannot be levied on and sold under execution by a creditor. The sum of the adjudged cases is that a railroad corporation is a governmental agency, created primarily for public purposes, and subject to be controlled for the public benefit. It is upon that ground that the state, when unfettered by contract, may regulate, in its discretion, the rates of fares of passengers and freight. And upon this ground, too, the state may regulate the entire management of railroads in all matters affecting the convenience and safety of the public; as, for example, by regulating speed, compelling stops of prescribed length at stations, and prohibiting discriminations and favoritism. If the corporation neglect or refuse to discharge its duties to the public, it may be coerced to do so by appropriate proceedings in the name or in behalf of the state.

Such being the relations these corporations hold to the public, it would seem that the right of a colored person to use an improved public highway, upon the terms accorded to freemen of other races, is as fundamental in the state of freedom, established in this country, as are any of the rights which my brethren concede to be so far fundamental as to be deemed the essence of civil freedom. 'Personal liberty consists,' says Blackstone, 'in the power of locomotion, of changing situation, or removing one's person to whatever place one's own inclination may direct, without restraint, unless by due course of law.' But of what value is this right of locomotion, if it may be clogged by such burdens as congress intended by the act of 1875 to remove? They are burdens which lay at the very foundation of the institution of slavery as it once existed. They are not to be sustained, except upon the assumption that there is still, in this land of universal liberty, a class which may yet be discrimated against, even in respect of rights of a character *40 so essential and so supreme, that, deprived of their enjoyment, in common with others, a freeman is not only branded as

one inferior and infected, but, in the competitions of life, is robbed of some of the most necessary means of existence; and all this solely because they belong to a particular race which the nation has liberated. The thirteenth amendment alone obliterated the race line, so far as all rights fundamental in a state of freedom are concerned.

2.   As to inns. The same general observations which have been made as to railroads are applicable to inns. The word 'inn' has a technical legal signification. It means, in the act of 1875, just what it meant at common law. A mere private boarding-house is not an inn, nor is its keeper subject to the responsibilities, or entitled to the privileges of a common innkeeper. 'To constitute one an innkeeper, within the legal force of that term, he must keep a house of entertainment or lodging for all travelers or wayfarers who might choose to accept the same, being of good character or conduct.' Redf. Carr. § 575. Says Judge STORY:

**43 'An innkeeper may be defined to be the keeper of a common inn for the lodging and entertainment of travelers and passengers, their horses and attendants. An innkeeper is bound to take in all travelers and wayfaring persons, and to entertain them, if he can accommodate them, for a reasonable compensation; and he must guard their goods with proper diligence. * * * If an innkeeper improperly refuses to receive or provide for a guest, he is liable to be indicted therefor. * * * They [carriers of passengers] are no more at liberty to refuse a passenger, if they have sufficient room and accommodations, than an innkeeper is to refuse suitable room and accommodations to a guest.' Story, Bailm. §§ 475, 476.

Said Mr. Justice COLERIDGE, in Rex v. Ivens, 7 Car. & P. 213, (32 E. C. L. 495:)
'An indictment lies against an innkeeper who refuses to receive a guest, he having at the time room in his house; and either the price of the guest's entertainment being tendered to him, or such circumstances occurring as will dispense with that *41 tender. This law is founded in good sense. The innkeeper is not to select his guests. He

3 S.Ct. 18
(Cite as: 109 U.S. 3, *41, 3 S.Ct. 18, **43)

has no right to say to one, you shall come to my inn, and to another you shall not, as every one coming and conducting himself in a proper manner has a right to be received; and for this purpose innkeepers are a sort of public servants, they having in return a kind of privilege of entertaining travelers and supplying them with that they want.'

These authorities are sufficient to show a keeper of an inn is in the exercise of a quasi public employment. The law gives him special privileges, and he is charged with certain duties and responsibilities to the public. The public nature of his employment forbids him from discriminating against any person asking admission as a guest on account of the race or color of that person.

3. As to places of public amusement. It may be argued that the managers of such places have no duties to perform with which the public are, in any legal sense, concerned, or with which the public have any right to interfere; and that the exclusion of a black man from a place of public amusement on account of his race, or the denial to him, on that ground, of equal accommodations at such places, violates no legal right for the vindication of which he may invoke the aid of the courts. My answer to that argument is that places of public amusement, within the meaning of the act of 1875, are such as are established and maintained under direct license of the law. The authority to establish and maintain them comes from the public. The colored race is a part of that public. The local government granting the license represents them as well as all other races within its jurisdiction. A license from the public to establish a place of public amusement, imports, in law, equality of right, at such places, among all the members of that public. This must be so, unless it be--which I deny--that the common municipal government of all the people may, in the exertion of its powers, conferred for the benefit of all, discriminate or authorize discrimination against a particular race, solely because of its former condition of servitude.

I also submit whether it can be said--in view

of the doctrines of this court as announced in Munn v. Illinois, *42 U. S. 123, and reaf **44 firmed in Peik v. Chicago & N. W. Ry. Co. 94 U. S. 178--that the management of places of public amusement is a purely private matter, with which government has no rightful concern. In the Munn Case the question was whether the state of Illinois could fix, by law, the maximum of charges for the storage of grain in certain warehouses in that state--the private property of individual citizens. After quoting a remark attributed to Lord Chief Justice HALE, to the effect that when private property is 'affected with a public interest it ceases to be juris privati only,' the court says:

'Property does become clothed with a public interest when used in a manner to make it of public consequence and affect the community at large. When, therefore, one devotes his property to a use in which the public has an interest, he in effect grants to the public an interest in that use, and must submit to be controlled by the public for the common good to the extent of the interest he has thus created. He may withdraw his grant by discontinuing the use, but, so long as he maintains the use, he must submit to the control.'

The doctrines of Munn v. Illinois have never been modified by this court, and I am justified, upon the authority of that case, in saying that places of public amusement, conducted under the authority of the law, are clothed with a public interest, because used in a manner to make them of public consequence and to affect the community at large. The law may therefore regulate, to some extent, the mode in which they shall be conducted, and consequently the public have rights in respect of such places which may be vindicated by the law. It is consequently not a matter purely of private concern.

Congress has not, in these matters, entered the domain of state control and supervision. It does not assume to prescribe the general conditions and limitations under which inns, public conveyances, and places of public amusement shall be conducted or managed. It simply declares in effect that since the nation has established universal freedom in this

3 S.Ct. 18
(Cite as: 109 U.S. 3, *42, 3 S.Ct. 18, **44)

country for all time, there shall be no discrimination, based merely upon race or color, in respect of the legal rights in the accommodations *43 and advantages of public conveyances, inns, and places of public amusement.

I am of opinion that such discrimination is a badge of servitude, the imposition of which congress may prevent under its power, through appropriate legislation, to enforce the thirteenth amendment; and consequently, without reference to its enlarged power under the fourteenth amendment, the act of March 1, 1875, is not, in my judgment, repugnant to the constitution.

It remains now to consider these cases with reference to the power congress has possessed since the adoption of the fourteenth amendment.

Before the adoption of the recent amendments it had become, as we have seen, the established doctrine of this court that negroes, whose ancestors had been imported and sold as slaves, could not become citizens of a state, or even of the United States, with the rights **45 and privileges guarantied to citizens by the national constitution; further, that one might have all the rights and privileges of a citizen of a state without being a citizen in the sense in which that word was used in the national constitution, and without being entitled to the privileges and immunities of citizens of the several states. Still further, between the adoption of the thirteenth amendment and the proposal by congress of the fourteenth amendment, on June 16, 1866, the statute-books of several of the states, as we have seen, had become loaded down with enactments which, under the guise of apprentice, vagrant, and contract regulations, sought to keep the colored race in a condition, practically, of servitude. It was openly announced that whatever rights persons of that race might have as freemen, under the guaranties of the national constitution, they could not become citizens of a state, with the rights belonging to citizens, except by the consent of such state; consequently, that their civil rights, as

citizens of the state, depended entirely upon state legislation. To meet this new peril to the black race, that the *44 purposes of the nation might not be doubted or defeated, and by way of further enlargement of the power of congress, the fourteenth amendment was proposed for adoption.

Remembering that this court, in the Slaughter-house Cases, declared that the one pervading purpose found in all the recent amendments, lying at the foundation of each, and without which none of them would have been suggested, was 'the freedom of the slave race, the security and firm establishment of that freedom, and the protection of the newly-made freeman and citizen from the oppression of those who had formerly exercised unlimited dominion over him;' that each amendment was addressed primarily to the grievances of that race,--let us proceed to consider the language of the fourteenth amendment. Its first and fifth sections are in these words:

'Section 1. All persons born or naturalized in the United States, and subject to the jurisdiction thereof, are citizens of the United States and of the state wherein they reside. No state shall make or enforce any law which shall abridge the privileges or immunities of citizens of the United States; nor shall any state deprive any person of life, liberty, or property without due process of law; nor deny to any person within its jurisdiction the equal protection of the laws.

* * *

'Sec. 5. That congress shall have power to enforce, by appropriate legislation, the provisions of this article.'

It was adjudged in Strauder v. West Virginia and Ex parte Virginia, 100 U. S. 307, 345, and my brethren concede, that positive rights and privileges were intended to be secured, and are in fact secured, by the fourteenth amendment.

But when, under what circumstances, and to what extent may congress, by means of legislation, exert its power to enforce the provisions of this amendment? The logic of

3 S.Ct. 18
(Cite as: 109 U.S. 3, *44, 3 S.Ct. 18, **45)

the opinion of the majority of the court--the foundation upon which its whole reasoning seems **46 to rest--is that the general government cannot, in advance of hostile state laws or hostile state *45 proceedings, actively interfere for the protection of any of the rights, privileges, and immunities secured by the fourteenth amendment. It is said that such rights, privileges, and immunities are secured by way of prohibition against state laws and state proceedings affecting such rights and privileges, and by power given to congress to legislate for the purpose of carrying such prohibition into effect; also, that congressional legislation must necessarily be predicated upon such supposed state laws or state proceedings, and be directed to the correction of their operation and effect.

In illustration of its position, the court refers to the clause of the constitution forbidding the passage by a state of any law impairing the obligation of contracts. The clause does not, I submit, furnish a proper illustration of the scope and effect of the fifth section of the fourteenth amendment. No express power is given congress to enforce, by primary direct legislation, the prohibition upon state laws impairing the obligation of contracts. Authority is, indeed, conferred to enact all necessary and proper laws for carrying into execution the enumerated powers of congress, and all other powers vested by the constitution in the government of the United States, or in any department or officer thereof. And, as heretofore shown, there is also, by necessary implication, power in congress, by legislation, to protect a right derived from the national constitution. But a prohibition upon a state is not a power in congress or in the national government. It is simply a denial of power to the state. And the only mode in which the inhibition upon state laws impairing the obligation of contracts can be enforced, is, indirectly, through the courts, in suits where the parties raise some question as to the constitutional validity of such laws. The judicial power of the United States extends to such suits, for the reason that they are suits arising under the constitution. The fourteenth amendment presents the first instance in our history of the investiture of congress with

affirmative power, by legislation, to enforce an express prohibition upon the states. It is not said that the judicial power of the nation may be exerted for the enforcement of that amendment. No enlargement of the judicial power was required, for it is clear *46 that had the fifth section of the fourteenth amendment been entirely omitted, the judiciary could have stricken down all state laws and nullified all state proceedings in hostility to rights and privileges secured or recognized by that amendment. The power given is, in terms, by congressional legislation, to enforce the provisions of the amendment.

The assumption that this amendment consists wholly of prohibitions upon state laws and state proceedings in hostility to its provisions, is unauthorized by its language. The first clause of the first section--'all persons born or naturalized in the United States, and subject to the jurisdiction thereof, are citizens of the United States, **47 and of the state wherein they reside'--is of a distinctly affirmative character. In its application to the colored race, previously liberated, it created and granted, as well citizenship of the United States, as citizenship of the state in which they respectively resided. It introduced all of that race, whose ancestors had been imported and sold as slaves, at once, into the political community known as the 'People of the United States.' They became, instantly, citizens of the United States, and of their respective states. Further, they were brought, by this supreme act of the nation, within the direct operation of that provision of the constitution which declares that 'the citizens of each state shall be entitled to all privileges and immunities of citizens in the several states.' Article 4, § 2.

The citizenship thus acquired by that race, in virtue of an affirmative grant by the nation, may be protected, not alone by the judicial branch of the government, but by congressional legislation of a primary direct character; this, because the power of congress is not restricted to the enforcement of prohibitions upon state laws or state action. It is, in terms distinct and positive, to enforce 'the provisions of this article' of amendment;

3 S.Ct. 18
(Cite as: 109 U.S. 3, *46, 3 S.Ct. 18, **47)

not simply those of a prohibitive character, but the provisions,--all of the provisions,--affirmative and prohibitive, of the amendment. It is, therefore, a grave misconception to suppose that the fifth section of the amendment has reference exclusively to express prohibitions upon state laws or state action. If any right was created by that amendment, the ***47** grant of power, through appropriate legislation, to enforce its provisions authorizes congress, by means of legislation operating throughout the entire Union, to guard, secure, and protect that right.

It is, therefore, an essential inquiry what, if any, right, privilege, or immunity was given by the nation to colored persons when they were made citizens of the state in which they reside? Did the national grant of state citizenship to that race, of its own force, invest them with any rights, privileges, and immunities whatever? That they became entitled, upon the adoption of the fourteenth amendment, 'to all privileges and immunities of citizens in the several states,' within the meaning of section 2 of article 4 of the constitution, no one, I suppose, will for a moment question. What are the privileges and immunities to which, by that clause of the constitution, they became entitled? To this it may be answered, generally, upon the authority of the adjudged cases, that they are those which are fundamental in citizenship in a free government, 'common to the citizens in the latter states under their constitutions and laws by virtue of their being citizens.' Of that provision it has been said, with the approval of this court, that no other one in the constitution has tended so strongly to constitute the citizens of the United States one people. Ward v. Maryland, 12 Wall. 430; Corfield v. Coryell, 4 Wash. C. C. 371; Paul v. Virginia, 8 Wall. 180; Slaughter-house Cases, 16 Wall. 77.

Although this court has wisely forborne any attempt, by a comprehensive ****48** definition, to indicate all the privileges and immunities to which the citizens of each state are entitled of right to enjoy in the several states, I hazard nothing, in view of former adjudications, in

saying that no state can sustain her denial to colored citizens of other states, while within her limits, of privileges or immunities, fundamental in republican citizenship, upon the ground that she accords such privileges and immunities only to her white citizens and withholds them from her colored citizens. The colored citizens of other states, within the jurisdiction of that state, could claim, under the constitution, every privilege and immunity ***48** which that state secures to her white citizens. Otherwise, it would be in the power of any state, by discriminating class legislation against its own citizens of a particular race or color, to withhold from citizens of other states, belonging to that proscribed race, when within her limits, privileges and immunities of the character regarded by all courts as fundamental in citizenship; and that, too, when the constitutional guaranty is that the citizens of each state shall be entitled to 'all privileges and immunities of citizens of the several states.' No state may, by discrimination against a portion of its own citizens of a particular race, in respect of privileges and immunities fundamental in citizenship, impair the constitutional right of citizens of other states, of whatever race, to enjoy in that state all such privileges and immunities as are there accorded to her most favored citizens. A colored citizen of Ohio or Indiana, being in the jurisdiction of Tennessee, is entitled to enjoy any privilege or immunity, fundamental in citizenship, which is given to citizens of the white race in the latter state. It is not to be supposed that any one will controvert this proposition.

But what was secured to colored citizens of the United States--as between them and their respective states--by the grant to them of state citizenship? With what rights, privileges, or immunities did this grant from the nation invest them? There is one, if there be no others--exemption from race discrimination in respect of any civil right belonging to citizens of the white race in the same state. That, surely, is their constitutional privilege when within the jurisdiction of other states. And such must be their constitutional right, in their own state, unless the recent amendments

3 S.Ct. 18
(Cite as: 109 U.S. 3, *48, 3 S.Ct. 18, **48)

be 'splendid baubles,' thrown out to delude those who deserved fair and generous treatment at the hands of the nation. Citizenship in this country necessarily imports equality of civil rights among citizens of every race in the same state. It is fundamental in American citizenship that, in respect of such rights, there shall be no discrimination by the state, or its officers, or by individuals, or corporations exercising public functions or authority, against any citizen because of his race or previous condition of servitude. In U. S. v. Cruikshank, 92 U. S. 555, it was said *49 that 'the equality of rights of citizens is a principle of republicanism.' And in Ex parte Virginia, 100 U. S. 344, the emphatic language of this court is that 'one great purpose of these amendments **49 was to raise the colored race from that condition of inferiority and servitude in which most of them had previously stood, into perfect equality of civil rights with all other persons within the jurisdiction of the states.' So, in Strauder v. West Virginia, Id. 306, the court, alluding to the fourteenth amendment, said: 'This is one of a series of constitutional provisions having a common purpose, namely, securing to a race recently emancipated, a race that through many generations had been held in slavery, all the civil rights that the superior race enjoy.' Again, in Neal v. Delaware, 103 U. S. 386, it was ruled that this amendment was designed, primarily, 'to secure to the colored race, thereby invested with the rights, privileges, and responsibilities of citizenship, the enjoyment of all the civil rights that, under the law, are enjoyed by white persons.'

Much light is thrown upon this part of the discussion by the language of this court in reference to the fifteenth amendment. In U. S. v. Cruikshank it was said:

'In U. S. v. Reese, 92 U. S. 214, we held that the fifteenth amendment has invested the citizens of the United States with a new constitutional right, which is exemption from discrimination in the exercise of the elective franchise on account of race, color, or previous condition of servitude. From this it appears that the right of suffrage is not a necessary attribute of national

citizenship, but that exemption from discrimination in the exercise of that right on account of race, etc., is. The right to vote in the states comes from the states; but the right of exemption from the prohibited discrimination comes from the United States. The first has not been granted or secured by the constitution of the United States, but the last has been.'

Here, in language at once clear and forcible, is stated the principle for which I contend. It can hardly be claimed that exemption from race discrimination, in respect of civil rights, against those to whom state citizenship was granted by the *50 nation, is any less for the colored race a new constitutional right, derived from and secured by the national constitution, than is exemption from such discrimination in the exercise of the elective franchise. It cannot be that the latter is an attribute of national citizenship, while the other is not essential in national citizenship, or fundamental in state citizenship.

If, then, exemption from discrimination in respect of civil rights is a new constitutional right, secured by the grant of state citizenship to colored citizens of the United States, why may not the nation, by means of its own legislation of a primary direct character, guard, protect, and enforce that right? It is a right and privilege which the nation conferred. It did not come from the states in which those colored citizens reside. It has been the established doctrine of this court during all its history, accepted as vital to the national supremacy, that congress, in the absence of a positive delegation of power to the state legislatures, may by legislation enforce and protect any right derived from or created by the national constitution. It was so declared in Prigg v. Com. It was reiterated in U. S. v. Reese, 92 U. S. **50 214, where the court said that 'rights and immunities created by and dependent upon the constitution of the United States can be protected by congress. The form and manner of the protection may be such as congress, in the legitimate exercise of its discretion, shall provide. These may be varied to meet the necessities of the particular right to protected.' It was distinctly

3 S.Ct. 18
(Cite as: 109 U.S. 3, *50, 3 S.Ct. 18, **50)

reaffirmed in Strauder v. West Virginia, 100 U. S. 310, where we said that 'a right or immunity created by the constitution or only guarantied by it, even without any express delegation of power, may be protected by congress.' Will any one claim, in view of the declarations of this court in former cases, or even without them, that exemption of colored citizens within their states from race discrimination, in respect of the civil rights of citizens, is not an immunity created or derived from the national constitution?

This court has always given a broad and liberal construction to the constitution, so as to enable congress, by legislation, to *51 enforce rights secured by that instrument. The legislation congress may enact, in execution of its power to enforce the provisions of this amendment, is that which is appropriate to protect the right granted. Under given circumstances, that which the court characterizes as corrective legislation might be sufficient. Under other circumstances primary direct legislation may be required. But it is for congress, not the judiciary, to say which is best adapted to the end to be attained. In U. S. v. Fisher, 2 Cranch, 358, this court said that 'congress must possess the choice of means, and must be empowered to use any means which are in fact conducive to the exercise of a power granted by the constitution.' 'The sound construction of the constitution,' said Chief Justice MARSHALL, 'must allow to the national legislature that discretion, with respect to the means by which the powers it confers are to be carried into execution, which will enable that body to perform the high duties assigned to it in the manner most beneficial to the people. Let the end be legitimate,--let it be within the scope of the constitution,--and all means which are appropriate, which are plainly adapted to that end, which are not prohibited, but consistent with the letter and spirit of the constitution, are constitutional.' McCulloch v. Maryland, 4 Wheat. 423.

Must these rules of construction be now abandoned? Are the powers of the national legislature to be restrained in proportion as the rights and privileges, derived from the nation, are more valuable? Are constitutional provisions, enacted to secure the dearest rights of freemen and citizens, to be subjected to that rule of construction, applicable to private instruments, *52 which requires that the words to be interpreted must be taken most strongly against those who employ them? Or shall it be remembered that 'a constitution of government, founded by the people for themselves and their posterity, and for objects of the most momentous nature,--for perpetual union, for the establishment of justice, for the general welfare, and for a **51 perpetuation of the blessings of liberty,--necessarily requires that every interpretation of its powers should have a constant reference to these objects? No interpretation of the words in which those powers are granted can be a sound one which narrows down their ordinary import so as to defeat those objects.' 1 Story, Const. § 422.

The opinion of the court, as I have said, proceeds upon the ground that the power of congress to legislate for the protection of the rights and privileges secured by the fourteenth amendment cannot be brought into activity except with the view, and as it may become necessary, to correct and annul state laws and state proceedings in hostility to such rights and privileges. In the absence of state laws or state action, adverse to such rights and privileges, the nation may not actively interfere for their protection and security. Such I understand to be the position of my brethren. If the grant to colored citizens of the United States of citizenship in their respective states imports exemption from race discrimination, in their states, in respect of the civil rights belonging to citizenship, then, to hold that the amendment remits that right to the states for their protection, primarily, and stays the hands of the nation, until it is assailed by state laws or state proceedings, is to adjudge that the amendment, so far from enlarging the powers of congress,--as we have heretofore said it did,--not only curtails them, but reverses the policy which the general government has pursued from its very organization. Such an interpretation of the amendment is a denial to congress of the power, by appropriate legislation, to enforce

3 S.Ct. 18
(Cite as: 109 U.S. 3, *52, 3 S.Ct. 18, **51)

one of its provisions. In view of the circumstances under which the recent amendments were incorporated into the constitution, and especially in view of the peculiar character of the new *53 rights they created and secured, it ought not to be presumed that the general government has abdicated its authority, by national legislation, direct and primary in its character, to guard and protect privileges and immunities secured by that instrument. Such an interpretation of the constitution ought not to be accepted if it be possible to avoid it. Its acceptance would lead to this anomalous result: that whereas, prior to the amendments, congress, with the sanction of this court, passed the most stringent laws-- operating directly and primarily upon states, and their officers and agents, as well as upon individuals--in vindication of slavery and the right of the master, it may not now, by legislation of a like primary and direct character, guard, protect, and secure the freedom established, and the most essential right of the citizenship granted, by the constitutional amendments. I venture, with all respect for the opinion of others, to insist that the national legislature may, without transcending the limits of the constitution, do for human liberty and the fundamental rights of American citizenship, what it did, with the sanction of this court, for the protection of slavery and the rights of the masters of fugitive slaves. If fugitive slave laws, providing modes and prescribing penalties whereby the master could seize and recover **52 his fugitive slave, were legitimate exertions of an implied power to protect and enforce a right recognized by the constitution, why shall the hands of congress be tied, so that--under an express power, by appropriate legislation, to enforce a constitutional provision, granting citizenship--it may not, by means of direct legislation, bring the whole power of this nation to bear upon states and their officers, and upon such individuals and corporations exercising public functions, as assume to abridge, impair, or deny rights confessedly secured by the supreme law of the land?

It does not seem to me that the fact that, by

the second clause of the first section of the fourteenth amendment, the states are expressly prohibited from making or enforcing laws abridging the privileges and immunities of citizens of the United States, furnishes any sufficient reason for holding or maintaining that the amendment was intended to deny congress the power, by general, primary, and direct legislation, of *54 protecting citizens of the United States, being also citizens of their respective states, against discrimination, in respect to their rights as citizens, founded on race, color, or previous condition of servitude. Such an interpretation of the amendment is plainly repugnant to its fifth section, conferring upon congress power, by appropriate legislation, to enforce, not merely the provisions containing prohibitions upon the states, but all of the provisions of the amendment, including the provisions, express and implied, of the grant of citizenship in the first clause of the first section of the article. This alone is sufficient for holding that congress is not restricted to the enactment of laws adapted to counteract and redress the operation of state legislation, or the action of state officers of the character prohibited by the amendment. It was perfectly well known that the great danger to the equal enjoyment by citizens of their rights, as citizens, was to be apprehended, not altogether from unfriendly state legislation, but from the hostile action of corporations and individuals in the states. And it is to be presumed that it was intended, by that section, to clothe congress with power and authority to meet that danger. If the rights intended to be secured by the act of 1875 are such as belong to the citizen, in common or equally with other citizens in the same state, then it is not to be denied that such legislation is appropriate to the end which congress is authorized to accomplish, viz., to protect the citizen, in respect of such rights, against discrimination on account of his race. As to the prohibition in the fourteenth amendment upon the making or enforcing of state laws abridging the privileges of citizens of the United States, it was impossible for any state to have enforced laws of that character. The judiciary could have annulled all such legislation under the provision that the constitution shall be the

3 S.Ct. 18
(Cite as: 109 U.S. 3, *54, 3 S.Ct. 18, **52)

supreme law of the land, anything in the constitution or laws of any state to the contrary notwithstanding. The states were **55 already under an implied prohibition not to abridge any privilege or immunity belonging to citizens of the United **53 States as such. Consequently, the prohibition upon state laws hostile to the rights belonging to citizens of the United States, was intended only as an express limitation on the powers of the states, and was not intended to diminish, in the slightest degree, the authority which ten nation has always exercised, of protecting, by means of its own direct legislation, rights created or secured by the constitution. The purpose not to diminish the national authority is distinctly negatived by the express grant of power, by legislation, to enforce every provision of the amendment, including that which, by the grant of citizenship in the state, secures exemption from race discrimination in respect of the civil rights of citizens.

It is said that any interpetation of the fourteenth amendment different from that adopted by the court, would authorize congress to enact a municipal code for all the states, covering every matter affecting the life, liberty, and property of the citizens of the several states. Not so. Prior to the adoption of that amendment the constitutions of the several states, without, perhaps, an exception, secured all persons against deprivation of life, liberty, or property, otherwise than by due process of law, and, in some form, recognized the right of all persons to the equal protection of the laws. These rights, therefore, existed before that amendment was proposed or adopted. If, by reason of that fact, it be assumed that protection in these rights of persons still rests, primarily, with the states, and that congress may not interfere except to enforce, by means of corrective legislation, the prohibitions upon state laws or state proceedings inconsistent with those rights, it does not at all follow that privileges which have been granted by the nation may not be protected by primary legislation upon the part of congress. The rights and immunities of persons recognized in the prohibitive clauses of the amendments were always *56 under the protection, primarily, of the states, while

rights created by or derived from the United States have always been, and, in the nature of things, should always be, primarily, under the protection of the general government. Exemption from race discrimination in respect of the civil rights which are fundamental in citizenship in a republican government, is, as we have seen, a new constitutional right, created by the nation, with express power in congress, by legislation, to enforce the constitutional provision from which it is derived. If, in some sense, such race discrimination is a denial of the equal protection of the laws, within the letter of the last clause of the first section, it cannot be possible that a mere prohibition upon state denial of such equal protection to persons within its jurisdiction, or a prohibition upon state laws abridging the privileges and immunities of citizens of the United States, takes from the nation the power which it has uniformly exercised of protecting, by primary direct legislation, those privileges and immunities which existed under the constitution before the adoption of the fourteenth amendment, or which have been created **54 by that amendment in behalf of those thereby made citizens of their respective states.

*57 It was said of Dred Scott v. Sandford that this court in that case overruled the action of two generations, virtually inserted a new clause in the constitution, changed its character, and made a new departure in the workings of the federal government. I may be permitted to say that if the recent amendments are so construed that congress may not, in its own discretion, and independently of the action or non-action of the states, provide, by legislation of a primary and direct character, for the security of rights created by the national constitution; if it be adjudged that the obligation to protect the fundamental privileges and immunities granted by the fourteenth amendment to citizens residing in the several states, rests, primarily, not on the nation, but on the states; if it be further adjudged that individuals and corporations exercising public functions may, without liability to direct primary legislation on the part of congress, make the race of

3 S.Ct. 18
(Cite as: 109 U.S. 3, *57, 3 S.Ct. 18, **54)

citizens the ground for denying them that equality of civil rights which the constitution ordains as a principle of republican citizenship,--then, not only the foundations upon which the national supremacy has always securely rested will be materially disturbed, but we shall enter upon an era of constitutional law when the rights of freedom and American citizenship cannot receive from the nation that efficient protection which heretofore was accorded to slavery and the rights of the master.

But if it were conceded that the power of congress could not be brought into activity until the rights specified in the act of 1875 had been abridged or denied by some state law or state action, I maintain that the decision of the court is erroneous. There has been adverse state action within the fourteenth amendment as heretofore interpreted by this court. I allude to Ex parte Virginia, supra. It appears, in that case, that one Cole, judge of a county court, was charged with the duty, by the laws of Virginia, of selecting grand and petit jurors. The law of the state did not authorize or permit him, in making such selections, to discriminate against colored citizens because of their race. But he was indicted in the federal court, under the act of 1875, for making such discriminations. *58 The attorney general of Virginia contended before us that the state had done its duty, and had not authorized or directed that county judge to do what he was charged with having done, and consequently that the state had not denied to the colored race the equal protection of the laws, and the act of Cole must therefore be deemed his individual act, in contravention of the will of the state. Plausible as this argument was, it failed to convince this court, and after saying that the fourteenth amendment had reference to the political body denominated a state, 'by whatever instruments or in whatever modes that action may be taken,' and that a state acts by its legislative, executive, and judicial authorities, and can act in no other way, we proceeded:

**55 'The constitutional provision, therefore, must mean that no agency of the state, or of the officers or agents by whom its powers are exerted, shall deny to any person within its jurisdiction the equal protection of the laws. Whoever, by virtue of public position under a state government, deprives another of property, life, or liberty without due process of law, or denies or takes away the equal protection of the laws, violates the constitutional inhibition; and, as he acts under the name and for the state, and is clothed with the state's power, his act is that of the state. This must be so, or the constitutional prohibition has no meaning. Then the state has clothed one of its agents with power to annul or evade it. But the constitutional amendment was ordained for a purpose. It was to secure equal rights to all persons, and, to insure to all persons the enjoyment of such rights, power was given to congress to enforce its provisions by appropriate legislation. Such legislation must act upon persons, not upon the abstract thing denominated a state, but upon the persons who are the agents of the state, in the denial of the rights which were intended to be secured.' 100 U.S. 346, 347.

In every material sense applicable to the practical enforcement of the fourteenth amendment, railroad corporations, keepers of inns, and managers of places of public amusement are agents of the state, because *59 amenable, in respect of their public duties and functions, to public regulation. It seems to me that, within the principle settled in Ex parte Virginia, a denial by these instrumentalities of the state to the citizen, because of his race, of that equality of civil rights secured to him by law, is a denial by the state within the meaning of the fourteenth amendment. If it be not, then that race is left, in respect of the civil rights under discussion, practically at the mercy of corporations and individuals wielding power under public authority.

But the court says that congress did not, in the act of 1866, assume, under the authority given by the thirteenth amendment, to adjust what may be called the social rights of men and races in the community. I agree that government has nothing to do with social, as distinguished from technically legal, rights of individuals. No government ever has brought,

3 S.Ct. 18
(Cite as: 109 U.S. 3, *59, 3 S.Ct. 18, **55)

or ever can bring, its people into social intercourse against their wishes. Whether one person will permit or maintain social relations with another is a matter with which government has no concern. I agree that if one citizen chooses not to hold social intercourse with another, he is not and cannot be made amenable to the law for his conduct in that regard; for no legal right of a citizen is violated by the refusal of others to maintain merely social relations with him, even upon grounds of race. What I affirm is that no state, nor the officers of any state, nor any corporation or individual wielding power under state authority for the public benefit or the public convenience, can, consistently either with the freedom established by the fundamental law, or with that equality of civil rights which now belongs to every citizen, discriminate against freemen or citizens, in their civil rights, because of their race, or because they once labored under disabilities imposed upon them as a race. The rights which congress, by the act of 1875, endeavored to secure and protect are legal, not social, rights. The right, for instance, of a **56 colored citizen to use the accommodations of a public highway upon the same terms as are permitted to white citizens is no more a social right than his right, under the law, to use the public streets of a city, or a town, or a turnpike road, or a public market, or a post-office, or his right to sit *60 in a public building with others, of whatever race, for the purpose of hearing the political questions ot the day discussed. Scarcely a day passes without our seeing in this court-room citizens of the white and black races sitting side by side watching the progress of our business. It would never occur to any one that the presence of a colored citizen in a court-house or court-room was an invasion of the social rights of white persons who may frequent such places. And yet such a suggestion would be quite as sound in law--1 say it with all respect--as is the suggestion that the claim of a colored citizen to use, upon the same terms as is permitted to white citizens, the accommodations of public highways, or public inns, or places of public amusement, established under the license of the law, is an invasion of the social rights of the white race.

The court, in its opinion, reserves the question whether congress, in the exercise of its power to regulate commerce among the several states, might or might not pass a law regulating rights in public conveyances passing from one state to anoher. I beg to suggest that that precise question was substantially presented here in the only one of these cases relating to railroads,--Robinson v. Memphis & C. R. Co. In that case it appears that Mrs. Robinson, a citizen of Mississippi, purchased a railroad ticket entitling her to be carried from Grand Junction, Tennessee, to Lynchburg, Virginia. Might not the act of 1875 be maintained in that case, as applicable at least to commerce between the states, notwithstanding it does not, upon its face, profess to have been passed in pursuance of the power given to congress to regulate commerce? Has it ever been held that the judiciary should overturn a statute because the legislative department did not accurately recite therein the particular provision of the constitution authorizing its enactment? We have often enforced municipal bonds in aid of railroad subscriptions where they failed to recite the statute authorizing their issue, but recited one which did not sustain their validity. The inquiry in such cases has been, was there in any statute authority for the execution of the bonds? Upon this branch of the case it may be remarked that the state of Louisiana, in 1869, passed a statute *61 giving to passengers, without regard to race or color, equality of right in the accommodations of railroad and street cars, steam-boats, or other water-crafts, stage-coaches, omnibuses, or other vehicles. But in Hall v. De Cuir, 95 U. S. 487, that act was pronounced unconstitutional so far as it related to commerce between the states, this court saying that 'if the public good requires such legislation it must come from congress and not from the states.' I suggest that it may become a pertinent inquiry whether congress may, in the exertion of its power to regulate commerce among the states, enforce **57 among passengers on public conveyances equality of right without regard to race, color, or previous condition of servitude, if it be true--which I do not admit--that such legislation would be an interference by government with the social

3 S.Ct. 18
(Cite as: 109 U.S. 3, *61, 3 S.Ct. 18, **57)

rights of the people.

My brethren say that when a man has emerged from slavery, and by the aid of beneficient legislation has shaken off the inseparable concomitants of that state, there must be some stage in the progress of his elevation when he takes the rank of a mere citizen, and ceases to be the special favorite of the laws, and when his rights as a citizen, or a man, are to be protected in the ordinary modes by which other men's rights are protected. It is, I submit, scarcely just to say that the colored race has been the special favorite of the laws. What the nation, through congress, has sought to accomplish in reference to that race is, what had already been done in every state in the Union for the white race, to secure and protect rights belonging to them as freemen and citizens; nothing more. The one underlying purpose of congressional legislation has been to enable the black race to take the rank of mere citizens. The difficulty has been to compel a recognition of their legal right to take that rank, and to secure the enjoyment of privileges belonging, under the law, to them as a component part of the people for whose welfare and happiness government is ordained. *62 At every step in this direction the nation has been confronted with class tyrany, which a contemporary English historian says is, of all tyrannies, the most intolerable, 'for it is ubiquitous in its operation, and weighs, perhaps, most heavily on those whose obscurity or distance would withdraw them from the notice of a single despot.' To-day it is the colored race which is denied, by corporations and individuals wielding public authority, rights fundamental in their freedom and citizenship. At some future time it may be some other race that will fall under the ban. If the constitutional amendments be enforced, according to the intent with which, as I conceive, they were adopted, there cannot be, in this republic, any class of human beings in practical subjection to another class, with power in the latter to dole out to the former just such privileges as they may choose to grant. The supreme law of the land has decreed that no authority shall be exercised in this country upon the basis of discrimination, in respect of civil rights, against freemen and citizens because of their race, color, or previous condition of servitude. To that decree--for the due enforcement of which, by appropriate legislation, congress has been invested with express power--every one must bow, whatever may have been, or whatever now are, his individual views as to the wisdom or policy, either of the recent changes in the fundamental law, or of the legislation which has been enacted to give them effect.

For the reasons stated I feel constrained to withhold my assent to the opinion of the court.

PLESSY v. FERGUSON.

(May 18, 1896.)

No. 210.

CIVIL RIGHTS — NEGROES — SEPARATE TRAVELING
ACCOMMODATIONS.

1. An act requiring white and colored persons to be furnished with separate accommodations on railway trains does not violate Const. Amend. 13, abolishing slavery and involuntary servitude. 11 South. 948, affirmed.

2. A state statute requiring railway companies to provide separate accommodations for white and colored persons, and making a passenger insisting on occupying a coach or compartment other than the one set apart for his race liable to fine or imprisonment, does not violate Const. Amend. 14, by abridging the privileges or immunities of United States citizens, or depriving persons of liberty or property without due process of law, or by denying them the equal protection of the laws. 11 South. 948, affirmed.

Mr. Justice Harlan dissenting.

In Error to the Supreme Court of the State of Louisiana.

This was a petition for writs of prohibition and certiorari originally filed in the supreme court of the state by Plessy, the plaintiff in error, against the Hon. John H. Ferguson, judge of the criminal district court for the parish of Orleans, and setting forth, in substance, the following facts:

That petitioner was a citizen of the United States and a resident of the state of Louisiana, of mixed descent, in the proportion of seven-eighths Caucasian and one-eighth African blood; that the mixture of colored blood was not discernible in him, and that he was entitled to every recognition, right, privilege, and immunity secured to the citizens of the United States of the white race by its constitution and laws; that on June 7, 1892, he engaged and paid for a first-class passage on the East Louisiana Railway, from New Orleans to Covington, in the same state, and thereupon entered a passenger train, and took possession of a vacant seat in a coach where passengers of the white race were accommodated; that such railroad company was incorporated by the laws of Louisiana as a common carrier, and was not authorized to distinguish between citizens according to their race, but, notwithstanding this, petitioner was required by the conductor, under penalty of ejection from said train and imprisonment, to vacate said coach, and occupy another seat, in a coach assigned by said company for persons not of the white race, and for no other reason than that petitioner was of the colored race; that, upon petitioner's refusal to comply with such order, he was, with the aid of a police officer, forcibly ejected from

PLESSY v. FERGUSON.   1139

said coach, and hurried off to, and imprisoned in, the parish jail of New Orleans, and
there held to answer a charge made by such
officer to the effect that he was guilty of
having criminally violated an act of the general assembly of the state, approved July 10,
1890, in such case made and provided.

The petitioner was subsequently brought
before the recorder of the city for preliminary
examination, and committed for trial to the
criminal district court for the parish of Orleans, where an information was filed against
him in the matter above set forth, for a violation of the above act, which act the petitioner affirmed to be null and void, because
in conflict with the constitution of the United States; that petitioner interposed a plea
to such information, based upon the unconstitutionality of the act of the general assembly,
to which the district attorney, on behalf of
the state, filed a demurrer; that, upon issue
being joined upon such demurrer and plea,
the court sustained the demurrer, overruled
the plea, and ordered petitioner to plead over
to the facts set forth in the information, and
that, unless the judge of the said court be enjoined by a writ of prohibition from further
proceeding in such case, the court will proceed
to fine and sentence petitioner to imprisonment, and thus deprive him of his constitutional rights set forth in his said plea, notwithstanding the unconstitutionality of the act under which he was being prosecuted; that no
appeal lay from such sentence, and petitioner
was without relief or remedy except by writs
of prohibition and certiorari. Copies of the
information and other proceedings in the criminal district court were annexed to the petition
as an exhibit.

Upon the filing of this petition, an order
was issued upon the respondent to show cause
why a writ of prohibition should not issue,
and be made perpetual, and a further order
that the record of the proceedings had in
the criminal cause be certified and transmitted to the supreme court.

To this order the respondent made answer,
transmitting a certified copy of the proceedings, asserting the constitutionality of the
law, and averring that, instead of pleading or
admitting that he belonged to the colored
race, the said Plessy declined and refused,
either by pleading or otherwise, to admit that
he was in any sense or in any proportion a
colored man.

The case coming on for hearing before the
supreme court, that court was of opinion that
the law under which the prosecution was had
was constitutional and denied the relief prayed for by the petitioner (Ex parte Plessy, 45
La. Ann. 80, 11 South. 948); whereupon petitioner prayed for a writ of error from this
court, which was allowed by the chief justice
of the supreme court of Louisiana.

A. W. Tourgee and S. F. Phillips, for plaintiff in error. Alex. Porter Morse, for defendant in error.

Mr. Justice BROWN, after stating the facts
in the foregoing language, delivered the opinion of the court.

This case turns upon the constitutionality
of an act of the general assembly of the state
of Louisiana, passed in 1890, providing for
separate railway carriages for the white and
colored races. Acts 1890, No. 111, p. 152.

The first section of the statute enacts "that
all railway companies carrying passengers in
their coaches in this state, shall provide equal
but separate accommodations for the white,
and colored races, by providing two or more
passenger coaches for each passenger train,
or by dividing the passenger coaches by a partition so as to secure separate accommodations: provided, that this section shall not be
construed to apply to street railroads. No
person or persons shall be permitted to occupy
seats in coaches, other than the ones assigned
to them, on account of the race they belong to."

By the second section it was enacted "that
the officers of such passenger trains shall have
power and are hereby required to assign each
passenger to the coach or compartment used
for the race to which such passenger belongs;
any passenger insisting on going into a coach
or compartment to which by race he does not
belong, shall be liable to a fine of twenty-five
dollars, or in lieu thereof to imprisonment for
a period of not more than twenty days in the
parish prison, and any officer of any railroad
insisting on assigning a passenger to a coach
or compartment other than the one set aside
for the race to which said passenger belongs,
shall be liable to a fine of twenty-five dollars,
or in lieu thereof to imprisonment for a period
of not more than twenty days in the parish
prison; and should any passenger refuse to
occupy the coach or compartment to which he
or she is assigned by the officer of such railway, said officer shall have power to refuse to
carry such passenger on his train, and for such
refusal neither he nor the railway company
which he represents shall be liable for damages in any of the courts of this state."

The third section provides penalties for the
refusal or neglect of the officers, directors,
conductors, and employés of railway companies to comply with the act, with a proviso
that "nothing in this act shall be construed as
applying to nurses attending children of the
other race." The fourth section is immaterial.

The information filed in the criminal district
court charged, in substance, that Plessy, being a passenger between two stations within
the state of Louisiana, was assigned by officers of the company to the coach used for the
race to which he belonged, but he insisted upon going into a coach used by the race to
which he did not belong. Neither in the information nor plea was his particular race or
color averred.

The petition for the writ of prohibition
averred that petitioner was seven-eighths Caucasian and one-eighth African blood; that the

mixture of colored blood was not discernible in him; and that he was entitled to every right, privilege, and immunity secured to citizens of the United States of the white race; and that, upon such theory, he took possession of a vacant seat in a coach where passengers of the white race were accommodated, and was ordered by the conductor to vacate said coach, and take a seat in another, assigned to persons of the colored race, and, having refused to comply with such demand, he was forcibly ejected, with the aid of a police officer, and imprisoned in the parish jail to answer a charge of having violated the above act.

The constitutionality of this act is attacked upon the ground that it conflicts both with the thirteenth amendment of the constitution, abolishing slavery, and the fourteenth amendment, which prohibits certain restrictive legislation on the part of the states.

1. That it does not conflict with the thirteenth amendment, which abolished slavery and involuntary servitude, except as a punishment for crime, is too clear for argument. Slavery implies involuntary servitude,—a state of bondage; the ownership of mankind as a chattel, or, at least, the control of the labor and services of one man for the benefit of another, and the absence of a legal right to the disposal of his own person, property, and services. This amendment was said in the Slaughter-House Cases, 16 Wall. 36, to have been intended primarily to abolish slavery, as it had been previously known in this country, and that it equally forbade Mexican peonage or the Chinese coolie trade, when they amounted to slavery or involuntary servitude, and that the use of the word "servitude" was intended to prohibit the use of all forms of involuntary slavery, of whatever class or name. It was intimated, however, in that case, that this amendment was regarded by the statesmen of that day as insufficient to protect the colored race from certain laws which had been enacted in the Southern states, imposing upon the colored race onerous disabilities and burdens, and curtailing their rights in the pursuit of life, liberty, and property to such an extent that their freedom was of little value; and that the fourteenth amendment was devised to meet this exigency.

So, too, in the Civil Rights Cases, 109 U. S. 3, 3 Sup. Ct. 18, it was said that the act of a mere individual, the owner of an inn, a public conveyance or place of amusement, refusing accommodations to colored people, cannot be justly regarded as imposing any badge of slavery or servitude upon the applicant, but only as involving an ordinary civil injury, properly cognizable by the laws of the state, and presumably subject to redress by those laws until the contrary appears. "It would be running the slavery question into the ground," said Mr. Justice Bradley, "to make it apply to every act of discrimination which a person may see fit to make as to the guests he will entertain, or as to the people

he will take into his coach or cab or car, or admit to his concert or theater, or deal with in other matters of intercourse or business."

A statute which implies merely a legal distinction between the white and colored races —a distinction which is founded in the color of the two races, and which must always exist so long as white men are distinguished from the other race by color—has no tendency to destroy the legal equality of the two races, or re-establish a state of involuntary servitude. Indeed, we do not understand that the thirteenth amendment is strenuously relied upon by the plaintiff in error in this connection.

2. By the fourteenth amendment, all persons born or naturalized in the United States, and subject to the jurisdiction thereof, are made citizens of the United States and of the state wherein they reside; and the states are forbidden from making or enforcing any law which shall abridge the privileges or immunities of citizens of the United States, or shall deprive any person of life, liberty, or property without due process of law, or deny to any person within their jurisdiction the equal protection of the laws.

The proper construction of this amendment was first called to the attention of this court in the Slaughter-House Cases, 16 Wall. 36, which involved, however, not a question of race, but one of exclusive privileges. The case did not call for any expression of opinion as to the exact rights it was intended to secure to the colored race, but it was said generally that its main purpose was to establish the citizenship of the negro, to give definitions of citizenship of the United States and of the states, and to protect from the hostile legislation of the states the privileges and immunities of citizens of the United States, as distinguished from those of citizens of the states.

The object of the amendment was undoubtedly to enforce the absolute equality of the two races before the law, but, in the nature of things, it could not have been intended to abolish distinctions based upon color, or to enforce social, as distinguished from political, equality, or a commingling of the two races upon terms unsatisfactory to either. Laws permitting, and even requiring, their separation, in places where they are liable to be brought into contact, do not necessarily imply the inferiority of either race to the other, and have been generally, if not universally, recognized as within the competency of the state legislatures in the exercise of their police power. The most common instance of this is connected with the establishment of separate schools for white and colored children, which have been held to be a valid exercise of the legislative power even by courts of states where the political rights of the colored race have been longest and most earnestly enforced.

One of the earliest of these cases is that of Roberts v. City of Boston, 5 Cush. 198, in

PLESSY *v.* FERGUSON.   1141

which the supreme judicial court of Massachusetts held that the general school committee of Boston had power to make provision for the instruction of colored children in separate schools established exclusively for them, and to prohibit their attendance upon the other schools. "The great principle," said Chief Justice Shaw, "advanced by the learned and eloquent advocate for the plaintiff [Mr. Charles Sumner], is that, by the constitution and laws of Massachusetts, all persons, without distinction of age or sex, birth or color, origin or condition, are equal before the law. * * * But, when this great principle comes to be applied to the actual and various conditions of persons in society, it will not warrant the assertion that men and women are legally clothed with the same civil and political powers, and that children and adults are legally to have the same functions and be subject to the same treatment; but only that the rights of all, as they are settled and regulated by law, are equally entitled to the paternal consideration and protection of the law for their maintenance and security." It was held that the powers of the committee extended to the establishment of separate schools for children of different ages, sexes and colors, and that they might also establish special schools for poor and neglected children, who have become too old to attend the primary school, and yet have not acquired the rudiments of learning, to enable them to enter the ordinary schools. Similar laws have been enacted by congress under its general power of legislation over the District of Columbia (sections 281–283, 310, 319, Rev. St. D. C.), as well as by the legislatures of many of the states, and have been generally, if not uniformly, sustained by the courts. State v. McCann, 21 Ohio St. 210; Lehew v. Brummell (Mo. Sup.) 15 S. W. 765; Ward v. Flood, 48 Cal. 36; Bertonneau v. Directors of City Schools, 3 Woods, 177, Fed. Cas. No. 1,361; People v. Gallagher, 93 N. Y. 438; Cory v. Carter, 48 Ind. 337; Dawson v. Lee, 83 Ky. 49.

Laws forbidding the intermarriage of the two races may be said in a technical sense to interfere with the freedom of contract, and yet have been universally recognized as within the police power of the state. State v. Gibson, 36 Ind. 389.

The distinction between laws interfering with the political equality of the negro and those requiring the separation of the two races in schools, theaters, and railway carriages has been frequently drawn by this court. Thus, in Strauder v. West Virginia, 100 U. S. 303, it was held that a law of West Virginia limiting to white male persons 21 years of age, and citizens of the state, the right to sit upon juries, was a discrimination which implied a legal inferiority in civil society, which lessened the security of the right of the colored race, and was a step towards reducing them to a condition of servility. Indeed, the right of a colored man

that, in the selection of jurors to pass upon his life, liberty, and property, there shall be no exclusion of his race, and no discrimination against them because of color, has been asserted in a number of cases. Virginia v. Rives, 100 U. S. 313; Neal v. Delaware, 103 U. S. 370; Bush v. Com., 107 U. S. 110, 1 Sup. Ct. 625; Gibson v. Mississippi, 162 U. S. 565, 16 Sup. Ct 904. So, where the laws of a particular locality or the charter of a particular railway corporation has provided that no person shall be excluded from the cars on account of color, we have held that this meant that persons of color should travel in the same car as white ones, and that the enactment was not satisfied by the company providing cars assigned exclusively to people of color, though they were as good as those which they assigned exclusively to white persons. Railroad Co. v. Brown, 17 Wall. 445.

Upon the other hand, where a statute of Louisiana required those engaged in the transportation of passengers among the states to give to all persons traveling within that state, upon vessels employed in that business, equal rights and privileges in all parts of the vessel, without distinction on account of race or color, and subjected to an action for damages the owner of such a vessel who excluded colored passengers on account of their color from the cabin set aside by him for the use of whites, it was held to be, so far as it applied to interstate commerce, unconstitutional and void. Hall v. De Cuir, 95 U. S. 485. The court in this case, however, expressly disclaimed that it had anything whatever to do with the statute as a regulation of internal commerce, or affecting anything else than commerce among the states.

In the Civil Rights Cases, 109 U. S. 3, 3 Sup. Ct. 18, it was held that an act of congress entitling all persons within the jurisdiction of the United States to the full and equal enjoyment of the accommodations, advantages, facilities, and privileges of inns, public conveyances, on land or water, theaters, and other places of public amusement, and made applicable to citizens of every race and color, regardless of any previous condition of servitude, was unconstitutional and void, upon the ground that the fourteenth amendment was prohibitory upon the states only, and the legislation authorized to be adopted by congress for enforcing it was not direct legislation on matters respecting which the states were prohibited from making or enforcing certain laws, or doing certain acts, but was corrective legislation, such as might be necessary or proper for counteracting and redressing the effect of such laws or acts. In delivering the opinion of the court, Mr. Justice Bradley observed that the fourteenth amendment "does not invest congress with power to legislate upon subjects that are within the domain of state legislation, but to provide modes of relief against state legislation or state action of the kind referred to. It does not authorize congress to create a code of municipal law for the regulation of private rights, but to provide modes of redress against the operation of state laws, and the action of state officers, executive or judicial, when these are subversive of the fundamental rights specified in the amendment. Positive rights and privileges are undoubtedly secured by the fourteenth amendment; but they are secured by way of prohibition against state laws and state proceedings affecting those rights and privileges, and by power given to congress to legislate for the purpose of carrying such prohibition into effect; and such legislation must necessarily be predicated upon such supposed state laws or state proceedings, and be directed to the correction of their operation and effect."

Much nearer, and, indeed, almost directly in point, is the case of the Louisville, N. O. & T. Ry. Co. v. State, 133 U. S. 587, 10 Sup. Ct. 348, wherein the railway company was indicted for a violation of a statute of Mississippi, enacting that all railroads carrying passengers should provide equal, but separate, accommodations for the white and colored races, by providing two or more passenger cars for each passenger train, or by dividing the passenger cars by a partition, so as to secure separate accommodations. The case was presented in a different aspect from the one under consideration, inasmuch as it was an indictment against the railway company for failing to provide the separate accommodations, but the question considered was the constitutionality of the law. In that case, the supreme court of Mississippi (66 Miss. 662, 6 South. 203) had held that the statute applied solely to commerce within the state, and, that being the construction of the state statute by its highest court, was accepted as conclusive. "If it be a matter," said the court (page 591, 133 U. S., and page 348, 10 Sup. Ct.), "respecting commerce wholly within a state, and not interfering with commerce between the states, then, obviously, there is no violation of the commerce clause of the federal constitution. * * * No question arises under this section as to the power of the state to separate in different compartments interstate passengers, or affect, in any manner, the privileges and rights of such passengers. All that we can consider is whether the state has the power to require that railroad trains within her limits shall have separate accommodations for the two races. That affecting only commerce within the state is no invasion of the power given to congress by the commerce clause."

A like course of reasoning applies to the case under consideration, since the supreme court of Louisiana, in the case of State v. Judge, 44 La. Ann. 770, 11 South. 74, held that the statute in question did not apply to interstate passengers, but was confined in its application to passengers traveling exclusively within the borders of the state. The case was decided largely upon the authority of Louisville, N. O. & T. Ry. Co. v. State, 66 Miss. 662, 6 South. 203, and affirmed by this court in 133 U. S. 587, 10 Sup. Ct. 348. In the present case no question of interference with interstate commerce can possibly arise, since the East Louisiana Railway appears to have been purely a local line, with both its termini within the state of Louisiana. Similar statutes for the separation of the two races upon public conveyances were held to be constitutional in Railroad v. Miles, 55 Pa. St. 209; Day v. Owen, 5 Mich. 520; Railway Co. v. Williams, 55 Ill. 185; Railroad Co. v. Wells, 85 Tenn. 613; 4 S. W. 5; Railroad Co. v. Benson, 85 Tenn. 627, 4 S. W. 5; The Sue, 22 Fed. 843; Logwood v. Railroad Co., 23 Fed. 318; McGuinn v. Forbes, 37 Fed. 639; People v. King (N. Y. App.) 18 N. E. 245; Houck v. Railway Co., 38 Fed. 226; Heard v. Railroad Co., 3 Inter St. Commerce Com. R. 111, 1 Inter St. Commerce Com. R. 428.

While we think the enforced separation of the races, as applied to the internal commerce of the state, neither abridges the privileges or immunities of the colored man, deprives him of his property without due process of law, nor denies him the equal protection of the laws, within the meaning of the fourteenth amendment, we are not prepared to say that the conductor, in assigning passengers to the coaches according to their race, does not act at his peril, or that the provision of the second section of the act that denies to the passenger compensation in damages for a refusal to receive him into the coach in which he properly belongs is a valid exercise of the legislative power. Indeed, we understand it to be conceded by the state's attorney that such part of the act as exempts from liability the railway company and its officers is unconstitutional. The power to assign to a particular coach obviously implies the power to determine to which race the passenger belongs, as well as the power to determine who, under the laws of the particular state, is to be deemed a white, and who a colored, person. This question, though indicated in the brief of the plaintiff in error, does not properly arise upon the record in this case, since the only issue made is as to the unconstitutionality of the act, so far as it requires the railway to provide separate accommodations, and the conductor to assign passengers according to their race.

It is claimed by the plaintiff in error that, in any mixed community, the reputation of belonging to the dominant race, in this instance the white race, is "property," in the same sense that a right of action or of inheritance is property. Conceding this to be so, for the purposes of this case, we are unable to see how this statute deprives him of, or in any way affects his right to, such property. If he be a white man, and assigned to a colored coach, he may have his

PLESSY *v.* FERGUSON.   1143

action for damages against the company for being deprived of his so-called "property." Upon the other hand, if he be a colored man, and be so assigned, he has been deprived of no property, since he is not lawfully entitled to the reputation of being a white man.

In this connection, it is also suggested by the learned counsel for the plaintiff in error that the same argument that will justify the state legislature in requiring railways to provide separate accommodations for the two races will also authorize them to require separate cars to be provided for people whose hair is of a certain color, or who are aliens, or who belong to certain nationalities, or to enact laws requiring colored people to walk upon one side of the street, and white people upon the other, or requiring white men's houses to be painted white, and colored men's black, or their vehicles or business signs to be of different colors, upon the theory that one side of the street is as good as the other, or that a house or vehicle of one color is as good as one of another color. The reply to all this is that every exercise of the police power must be reasonable, and extend only to such laws as are enacted in good faith for the promotion of the public good, and not for the annoyance or oppression of a particular class. Thus, in Yick Wo v. Hopkins, 118 U. S. 356, 6 Sup. Ct. 1064, it was held by this court that a municipal ordinance of the city of San Francisco to regulate the carrying on of public laundries within the limits of the municipality, violated the provisions of the constitution of the United States, if it conferred upon the municipal authorities arbitrary power, at their own will, and without regard to discretion, in the legal sense of the term, to give or withhold consent as to persons or places, without regard to the competency of the persons applying or the propriety of the places selected for the carrying on of the business. It was held to be a covert attempt on the part of the municipality to make an arbitrary and unjust discrimination against the Chinese race. While this was the case of a municipal ordinance, a like principle has been held to apply to acts of a state legislature passed in the exercise of the police power. Railroad Co. v. Husen, 95 U. S. 465; Louisville & N. R. Co. v. Kentucky, 161 U. S. 677, 16 Sup. Ct. 714, and cases cited on page 700, 161 U. S., and page 714, 16 Sup. Ct.; Daggett v. Hudson, 43 Ohio St. 548, 3 N. E. 538; Capen v. Foster, 12 Pick. 485; State v. Baker, 38 Wis. 71; Monroe v. Collins, 17 Ohio St. 665; Hulseman v. Rems, 41 Pa. St. 396; Osman v. Riley, 15 Cal. 48.

So far, then, as a conflict with the fourteenth amendment is concerned, the case reduces itself to the question whether the statute of Louisiana is a reasonable regulation, and with respect to this there must necessarily be a large discretion on the part of the legislature. In determining the question of reasonableness, it is at liberty to act with reference to the established usages, customs, and traditions of the people, and with a view to the promotion of their comfort, and the preservation of the public peace and good order. Gauged by this standard, we cannot say that a law which authorizes or even requires the separation of the two races in public conveyances is unreasonable, or more obnoxious to the fourteenth amendment than the acts of congress requiring separate schools for colored children in the District of Columbia, the constitutionality of which does not seem to have been questioned, or the corresponding acts of state legislatures.

We consider the underlying fallacy of the plaintiff's argument to consist in the assumption that the enforced separation of the two races stamps the colored race with a badge of inferiority. If this be so, it is not by reason of anything found in the act, but solely because the colored race chooses to put that construction upon it. The argument necessarily assumes that if, as has been more than once the case, and is not unlikely to be so again, the colored race should become the dominant power in the state legislature, and should enact a law in precisely similar terms, it would thereby relegate the white race to an inferior position. We imagine that the white race, at least, would not acquiesce in this assumption. The argument also assumes that social prejudices may be overcome by legislation, and that equal rights cannot be secured to the negro except by an enforced commingling of the two races. We cannot accept this proposition. If the two races are to meet upon terms of social equality, it must be the result of natural affinities, a mutual appreciation of each other's merits, and a voluntary consent of individuals. As was said by the court of appeals of New York in People v. Gallagher, 93 N. Y. 438, 448: "This end can neither be accomplished nor promoted by laws which conflict with the general sentiment of the community upon whom they are designed to operate. When the government, therefore, has secured to each of its citizens equal rights before the law, and equal opportunities for improvement and progress, it has accomplished the end for which it was organized, and performed all of the functions respecting social advantages with which it is endowed." Legislation is powerless to eradicate racial instincts, or to abolish distinctions based upon physical differences, and the attempt to do so can only result in accentuating the difficulties of the present situation. If the civil and political rights of both races be equal, one cannot be inferior to the other civilly or politically. If one race be inferior to the other socially, the constitution of the United States cannot put them upon the same plane.

It is true that the question of the proportion of colored blood necessary to constitute a colored person, as distinguished from a white person, is one upon which there is a difference of opinion in the different states; some holding that any visible admixture of black blood stamps the person as belonging to the colored race (State v. Chavers, 5 Jones [N. C.] 1); others, that it depends upon the preponderance of blood (Gray v. State, 4 Ohio, 354; Monroe v. Collins, 17 Ohio St. 665); and still others, that the predominance of white blood must only be in the proportion of three-fourths (People v. Dean, 14 Mich. 406; Jones v. Com., 80 Va. 544). But these are questions to be determined under the laws of each state, and are not properly put in issue in this case. Under the allegations of his petition, it may undoubtedly become a question of importance whether, under the laws of Louisiana, the petitioner belongs to the white or colored race.

The judgment of the court below is therefore affirmed.

Mr. Justice BREWER did not hear the argument or participate in the decision of this case.

Mr. Justice HARLAN dissenting.

By the Louisiana statute the validity of which is here involved, all railway companies (other than street-railroad companies) carrying passengers in that state are required to have separate but equal accommodations for white and colored persons, "by providing two or more passenger coaches for each passenger train, or by dividing the passenger coaches by a partition so as to secure separate accommodations." Under this statute, no colored person is permitted to occupy a seat in a coach assigned to white persons; nor any white person to occupy a seat in a coach assigned to colored persons. The managers of the railroad are not allowed to exercise any discretion in the premises, but are required to assign each passenger to some coach or compartment set apart for the exclusive use of his race. If a passenger insists upon going into a coach or compartment not set apart for persons of his race, he is subject to be fined, or to be imprisoned in the parish jail. Penalties are prescribed for the refusal or neglect of the officers, directors, conductors, and employés of railroad companies to comply with the provisions of the act.

Only "nurses attending children of the other race" are excepted from the operation of the statute. No exception is made of colored attendants traveling with adults. A white man is not permitted to have his colored servant with him in the same coach, even if his condition of health requires the constant personal assistance of such servant. If a colored maid insists upon riding in the same coach with a white woman whom she has been employed to serve, and who may need her personal attention while traveling, she is subject to be fined or imprisoned for such an exhibition of zeal in the discharge of duty.

While there may be in Louisiana persons of different races who are not citizens of the United States, the words in the act "white and colored races" necessarily include all citizens of the United States of both races residing in that state. So that we have before us a state enactment that compels, under penalties, the separation of the two races in railroad passenger coaches, and makes it a crime for a citizen of either race to enter a coach that has been assigned to citizens of the other race.

Thus, the state regulates the use of a public highway by citizens of the United States solely upon the basis of race.

However apparent the injustice of such legislation may be, we have only to consider whether it is consistent with the constitution of the United States.

That a railroad is a public highway, and that the corporation which owns or operates it is in the exercise of public functions, is not, at this day, to be disputed. Mr. Justice Nelson, speaking for this court in New Jersey Steam Nav. Co. v. Merchants' Bank, 6 How. 344, 382, said that a common carrier was in the exercise "of a sort of public office, and has public duties to perform, from which he should not be permitted to exonerate himself without the assent of the parties concerned." Mr. Justice Strong, delivering the judgment of this court in Olcott v. Supervisors, 16 Wall. 678, 694, said: "That railroads, though constructed by private corporations, and owned by them, are public highways, has been the doctrine of nearly all the courts ever since such conveniences for passage and transportation have had any existence. Very early the question arose whether a state's right of eminent domain could be exercised by a private corporation created for the purpose of constructing a railroad. Clearly, it could not, unless taking land for such a purpose by such an agency is taking land for public use. The right of eminent domain nowhere justifies taking property for a private use. Yet it is a doctrine universally accepted that a state legislature may authorize a private corporation to take land for the construction of such a road, making compensation to the owner. What else does this doctrine mean if not that building a railroad, though it be built by a private corporation, is an act done for a public use?" So, in Township of Pine Grove v. Talcott, 19 Wall. 666, 676: "Though the corporation [a railroad company] was private, its work was public, as much so as if it were to be constructed by the state." So, in Inhabitants of Worcester v. Western R. Corp., 4 Metc. (Mass.) 564: "The establishment of that great thoroughfare is regarded as a public work, established by public authority, intended for the public use and benefit, the use of which is secured to the whole community, and constitutes, therefore, like a canal, turnpike, or highway, a public easement." "It is true that the real and personal property, necessary to the establishment and management of the railroad, is vest-

PLESSY *v.* FERGUSON.   1145

ed in the corporation; but it is in trust for the public."

In respect of civil rights, common to all citizens, the constitution of the United States does not, I think, permit any public authority to know the race of those entitled to be protected in the enjoyment of such rights. Every true man has pride of race, and under appropriate circumstances, when the rights of others, his equals before the law, are not to be affected, it is his privilege to express such pride and to take such action based upon it as to him seems proper. But I deny that any legislative body or judicial tribunal may have regard to the race of citizens when the civil rights of those citizens are involved. Indeed, such legislation as that here in question is inconsistent not only with that equality of rights which pertains to citizenship, national and state, but with the personal liberty enjoyed by every one within the United States.

The thirteenth amendment does not permit the withholding or the deprivation of any right necessarily inhering in freedom. It not only struck down the institution of slavery as previously existing in the United States, but it prevents the imposition of any burdens or disabilities that constitute badges of slavery or servitude. It decreed universal civil freedom in this country. This court has so adjudged. But, that amendment having been found inadequate to the protection of the rights of those who had been in slavery, it was followed by the fourteenth amendment, which added greatly to the dignity and glory of American citizenship, and to the security of personal liberty, by declaring that "all persons born or naturalized in the United States, and subject to the jurisdiction thereof, are citizens of the United States and of the state wherein they reside," and that "no state shall make or enforce any law which shall abridge the privileges or immunities of citizens of the United States; nor shall any state deprive any person of life, liberty or property without due process of law, nor deny to any person within its jurisdiction the equal protection of the laws." These two amendments, if enforced according to their true intent and meaning, will protect all the civil rights that pertain to freedom and citizenship. Finally, and to the end that no citizen should be denied, on account of his race, the privilege of participating in the political control of his country, it was declared by the fifteenth amendment that "the right of citizens of the United States to vote shall not be denied or abridged by the United States or by any state on account of race, color or previous condition of servitude."

These notable additions to the fundamental law were welcomed by the friends of liberty throughout the world. They removed the race line from our governmental systems. They had, as this court has said, a common purpose, namely, to secure "to a race recently emancipated, a race that through many generations have been held in slavery, all the civil rights that the superior race enjoy." They declared, in legal effect, this court has further said, "that the law in the states shall be the same for the black as for the white; that all persons, whether colored or white, shall stand equal before the laws of the states; and in regard to the colored race, for whose protection the amendment was primarily designed, that no discrimination shall be made against them by law because of their color." We also said: "The words of the amendment, it is true, are prohibitory, but they contain a necessary implication of a positive immunity or right, most valuable to the colored race,—the right to exemption from unfriendly legislation against them distinctively as colored; exemption from legal discriminations, implying inferiority in civil society, lessening the security of their enjoyment of the rights which others enjoy; and discriminations which are steps towards reducing them to the condition of a subject race." It was, consequently, adjudged that a state law that excluded citizens of the colored race from juries, because of their race, however well qualified in other respects to discharge the duties of jurymen, was repugnant to the fourteenth amendment. Strauder v. West Virginia, 100 U. S. 303, 306, 307; Virginia v. Rives, Id. 313; Ex parte Virginia, Id. 339; Neal v. Delaware, 103 U. S. 370, 386; Bush v. Com., 107 U. S. 110, 116, 1 Sup. Ct. 625. At the present term, referring to the previous adjudications, this court declared that "underlying all of those decisions is the principle that the constitution of the United States, in its present form, forbids, so far as civil and political rights are concerned, discrimination by the general government or the states against any citizen because of his race. All citizens are equal before the law." Gibson v. State, 162 U. S. 565, 16 Sup. Ct. 904.

The decisions referred to show the scope of the recent amendments of the constitution. They also show that it is not within the power of a state to prohibit colored citizens, because of their race, from participating as jurors in the administration of justice.

It was said in argument that the statute of Louisiana does not discriminate against either race, but prescribes a rule applicable alike to white and colored citizens. But this argument does not meet the difficulty. Every one knows that the statute in question had its origin in the purpose, not so much to exclude white persons from railroad cars occupied by blacks, as to exclude colored people from coaches occupied by or assigned to white persons. Railroad corporations of Louisiana did not make discrimination among whites in the matter of accommodation for travelers. The thing to accomplish was, under the guise of giving equal accommodation for whites and blacks, to compel the latter to keep to themselves while traveling in railroad passenger coaches. No one would be so wanting in candor as to assert the contrary. The fundamental objection, therefore, to the statute, is that it interferes with the personal freedom of citizens. "Personal liberty," it has been well said, "consists in the power of locomotion, of changing situation, or removing one's person to whatsoever places one's own inclination may direct, without imprisonment or restraint, unless by due course of law." 1 Bl. Comm. *134. If a white man and a black man choose to occupy the same public conveyance on a public highway, it is their right to do so; and no government, proceeding alone on grounds of race, can prevent it without infringing the personal liberty of each.

It is one thing for railroad carriers to furnish, or to be required by law to furnish, equal accommodations for all whom they are under a legal duty to carry. It is quite another thing for government to forbid citizens of the white and black races from traveling in the same public conveyance, and to punish officers of railroad companies for permitting persons of the two races to occupy the same passenger coach. If a state can prescribe, as a rule of civil conduct, that whites and blacks shall not travel as passengers in the same railroad coach, why may it not so regulate the use of the streets of its cities and towns as to compel white citizens to keep on one side of a street, and black citizens to keep on the other? Why may it not, upon like grounds, punish whites and blacks who ride together in street cars or in open vehicles on a public road or street? Why may it not require sheriffs to assign whites to one side of a court room, and blacks to the other? And why may it not also prohibit the commingling of the two races in the galleries of legislative halls or in public assemblages convened for the consideration of the political questions of the day? Further, if this statute of Louisiana is consistent with the personal liberty of citizens, why may not the state require the separation in railroad coaches of native and naturalized citizens of the United States, or of Protestants and Roman Catholics?

The answer given at the argument to these questions was that regulations of the kind they suggest would be unreasonable, and could not, therefore, stand before the law. Is it meant that the determination of questions of legislative power depends upon the inquiry whether the statute whose validity is questioned is, in the judgment of the courts, a reasonable one, taking all the circumstances into consideration? A statute may be unreasonable merely because a sound public policy forbade its enactment. But I do not understand that the courts have anything to do with the policy or expediency of legislation. A statute may be valid, and yet, upon grounds of public policy, may well be characterized as unreasonable. Mr. Sedgwick correctly states the rule when he says that, the legislative intention being clearly ascertained, "the courts have no other duty to perform than to execute the legislative will,

without any regard to their views as to the wisdom or justice of the particular enactment." Sedg. St. & Const. Law, 324. There is a dangerous tendency in these latter days to enlarge the functions of the courts, by means of judicial interference with the will of the people as expressed by the legislature. Our institutions have the distinguishing characteristic that the three departments of government are co-ordinate and separate. Each must keep within the limits defined by the constitution. And the courts best discharge their duty by executing the will of the law-making power, constitutionally expressed, leaving the results of legislation to be dealt with by the people through their representatives. Statutes must always have a reasonable construction. Sometimes they are to be construed strictly, sometimes literally, in order to carry out the legislative will. But, however construed, the intent of the legislature is to be respected if the particular statute in question is valid, although the courts, looking at the public interests, may conceive the statute to be both unreasonable and impolitic. If the power exists to enact a statute, that ends the matter so far as the courts are concerned. The adjudged cases in which statutes have been held to be void, because unreasonable, are those in which the means employed by the legislature were not at all germane to the end to which the legislature was competent.

The white race deems itself to be the dominant race in this country. And so it is, in prestige, in achievements, in education, in wealth, and in power. So, I doubt not, it will continue to be for all time, if it remains true to its great heritage, and holds fast to the principles of constitutional liberty. But in view of the constitution, in the eye of the law, there is in this country no superior, dominant, ruling class of citizens. There is no caste here. Our constitution is color-blind, and neither knows nor tolerates classes among citizens. In respect of civil rights, all citizens are equal before the law. The humblest is the peer of the most powerful. The law regards man as man, and takes no account of his surroundings or of his color when his civil rights as guarantied by the supreme law of the land are involved. It is therefore to be regretted that this high tribunal, the final expositor of the fundamental law of the land, has reached the conclusion that it is competent for a state to regulate the enjoyment by citizens of their civil rights solely upon the basis of race.

In my opinion, the judgment this day rendered will, in time, prove to be quite as pernicious as the decision made by this tribunal in the Dred Scott Case.

It was adjudged in that case that the descendants of Africans who were imported into this country, and sold as slaves, were not included nor intended to be included under the word "citizens" in the constitution, and could not claim any of the rights and priv-

PLESSY *v.* FERGUSON.   1147

ileges which that instrument provided for and secured to citizens of the United States; that, at the time of the adoption of the constitution, they were "considered as a subordinate and inferior class of beings, who had been subjugated by the dominant race, and, whether emancipated or not, yet remained subject to their authority, and had no rights or privileges but such as those who held the power and the government might choose to grant them." 17 How. 393, 404. The recent amendments of the constitution, it was supposed, had eradicated these principles from our institutions. But it seems that we have yet, in some of the states, a dominant race,— a superior class of citizens,—which assumes to regulate the enjoyment of civil rights, common to all citizens, upon the basis of race. The present decision, it may well be apprehended, will not only stimulate aggressions, more or less brutal and irritating, upon the admitted rights of colored citizens, but will encourage the belief that it is possible, by means of state enactments, to defeat the beneficent purposes which the people of the United States had in view when they adopted the recent amendments of the constitution, by one of which the blacks of this country were made citizens of the United States and of the states in which they respectively reside, and whose privileges and immunities, as citizens, the states are forbidden to abridge. Sixty millions of whites are in no danger from the presence here of eight millions of blacks. The destinies of the two races, in this country, are indissolubly linked together, and the interests of both require that the common government of all shall not permit the seeds of race hate to be planted under the sanction of law. What can more certainly arouse race hate, what more certainly create and perpetuate a feeling of distrust between these races, than state enactments which, in fact, proceed on the ground that colored citizens are so inferior and degraded that they cannot be allowed to sit in public coaches occupied by white citizens? That, as all will admit, is the real meaning of such legislation as was enacted in Louisiana.

The sure guaranty of the peace and security of each race is the clear, distinct, unconditional recognition by our governments, national and state, of every right that inheres in civil freedom, and of the equality before the law of all citizens of the United States, without regard to race. State enactments regulating the enjoyment of civil rights upon the basis of race, and cunningly devised to defeat legitimate results of the war, under the pretense of recognizing equality of rights, can have no other result than to render permanent peace impossible, and to keep alive a conflict of races, the continuance of which must do harm to all concerned. This question is not met by the suggestion that social equality cannot exist between the white and black races in this country. That argument, if it

can be properly regarded as one, is scarcely worthy of consideration; for social equality no more exists between two races when traveling in a passenger coach or a public highway than when members of the same races sit by each other in a street car or in the jury box, or stand or sit with each other in a political assembly, or when they use in common the streets of a city or town, or when they are in the same room for the purpose of having their names placed on the registry of voters, or when they approach the ballot box in order to exercise the high privilege of voting.

There is a race so different from our own that we do not permit those belonging to it to become citizens of the United States. Persons belonging to it are, with few exceptions, absolutely excluded from our country. I allude to the Chinese race. But, by the statute in question, a Chinaman can ride in the same passenger coach with white citizens of the United States, while citizens of the black race in Louisiana, many of whom, perhaps, risked their lives for the preservation of the Union, who are entitled, by law, to participate in the political control of the state and nation, who are not excluded, by law or by reason of their race, from public stations of any kind, and who have all the legal rights that belong to white citizens, are yet declared to be criminals, liable to imprisonment, if they ride in a public coach occupied by citizens of the white race. It is scarcely just to say that a colored citizen should not object to occupying a public coach assigned to his own race. He does not object, nor, perhaps, would he object to separate coaches for his race if his rights under the law were recognized. But he does object, and he ought never to cease objecting, that citizens of the white and black races can be adjudged criminals because they sit, or claim the right to sit, in the same public coach on a public highway.

The arbitrary separation of citizens, on the basis of race, while they are on a public highway, is a badge of servitude wholly inconsistent with the civil freedom and the equality before the law established by the constitution. It cannot be justified upon any legal grounds.

If evils will result from the commingling of the two races upon public highways established for the benefit of all, they will be infinitely less than those that will surely come from state legislation regulating the enjoyment of civil rights upon the basis of race. We boast of the freedom enjoyed by our people above all other peoples. But it is difficult to reconcile that boast with a state of the law which, practically, puts the brand of servitude and degradation upon a large class of our fellow citizens,—our equals before the law. The thin disguise of "equal" accommodations for passengers in railroad coaches will not mislead any one, nor atone for the wrong this day done.

The result of the whole matter is that while this court has frequently adjudged, and at the present term has recognized the doctrine, that a state cannot, consistently with the constitution of the United States, prevent white and black citizens, having the required qualifications for jury service, from sitting in the same jury box, it is now solemnly held that a state may prohibit white and black citizens from sitting in the same passenger coach on a public highway, or may require that they be separated by a "partition" when in the same passenger coach. May it not now be reasonably expected that astute men of the dominant race, who affect to be disturbed at the possibility that the integrity of the white race may be corrupted, or that its supremacy will be imperiled, by contact on public highways with black people, will endeavor to procure statutes requiring white and black jurors to be separated in the jury box by a "partition," and that, upon retiring from the court room to consult as to their verdict, such partition, if it be a movable one, shall be taken to their consultation room, and set up in such way as to prevent black jurors from coming too close to their brother jurors of the white race. If the "partition" used in the court room happens to be stationary, provision could be made for screens with openings through which jurors of the two races could confer as to their verdict without coming into personal contact with each other. I cannot see but that, according to the principles this day announced, such state legislation, although conceived in hostility to, and enacted for the purpose of humiliating, citizens of the United States of a particular race, would be held to be consistent with the constitution.

I do not deem it necessary to review the decisions of state courts to which reference was made in argument. Some, and the most important, of them, are wholly inapplicable, because rendered prior to the adoption of the last amendments of the constitution, when colored people had very few rights which the dominant race felt obliged to respect. Others were made at a time when public opinion, in many localities, was dominated by the institution of slavery; when it would not have been safe to do justice to the black man; and when, so far as the rights of blacks were concerned, race prejudice was, practically, the supreme law of the land. Those decisions cannot be guides in the era introduced by the recent amendments of the supreme law, which established universal civil freedom, gave citizenship to all born or naturalized in the United States, and residing here, obliterated the race line from our systems of governments, national and state, and placed our free institutions upon the broad and sure foundation of the equality of all men before the law.

I am of opinion that the statute of Louisiana is inconsistent with the personal liberty of citizens, white and black, in that state, and hostile to both the spirit and letter of the constitution of the United States. If laws of like character should be enacted in the several states of the Union, the effect would be in the highest degree mischievous. Slavery, as an institution tolerated by law, would, it is true, have disappeared from our country; but there would remain a power in the states, by sinister legislation, to interfere with the full enjoyment of the blessings of freedom, to regulate civil rights, common to all citizens, upon the basis of race, and to place in a condition of legal inferiority a large body of American citizens, now constituting a part of the political community, called the "People of the United States," for whom, and by whom through representatives, our government is administered. Such a system is inconsistent with the guaranty given by the constitution to each state of a republican form of government, and may be stricken down by congressional action, or by the courts in the discharge of their solemn duty to maintain the supreme law of the land, anything in the constitution or laws of any state to the contrary notwithstanding.

For the reason stated, I am constrained to withhold my assent from the opinion and judgment of the majority.

LETTER FROM BIRMINGHAM CITY JAIL

MARTIN LUTHER KING, JR., APRIL 16, 1963

My Dear Fellow Clergymen:

While confined here in Birmingham city jail, I came across your recent statement calling my present activities "unwise and untimely." Seldom do I pause to answer criticism of my work and ideas. If I sought to answer all the criticisms that cross my desk, my secretaries would have little time for anything other than such correspondence in the course of the day, and I would have no time for constructive work. But since I feel that you are men of genuine good will and that your criticisms are sincerely set forth, I want to try to answer your statement in what I hope will be patient and reasonable terms.

I think I should indicate why I am here in Birmingham, since you have been influenced by the view which argues against "outsiders coming in." I have the honor of serving as president of the Southern Christian Leadership Conference, an organization operating in every southern state, with headquarters in Atlanta, Georgia. We have some eighty-five affiliated organizations across the South, and one of them is the Alabama Christian Movement for Human Rights. Frequently we share staff, educational and financial resources with our affiliates. Several months ago the affiliate here in Birmingham asked us to be on call to engage in a nonviolent direct-action program if such were deemed necessary. We readily consented, and when the hour came we lived up to our promise. So I, along with several members of my staff, am here because I was invited here. I am here because I have organizational ties here.

But more basically, I am in Birmingham because injustice is here. Just as the prophets of the eighth century B.C. left their villages and carried their "thus saith the Lord" far beyond the boundaries of their home towns, and just as the Apostle Paul left his village of Tarsus and carried the gospel of Jesus Christ to the far corners of the Greco-Roman world, so am I compelled to carry the gospel of freedom beyond my own home town. Like Paul, I must constantly respond to the Macedonian call for aid.

Moreover, I am cognizant of the interrelatedness of all communities and states. I cannot sit idly by in Atlanta and not be concerned about what happens to Birmingham. Injustice anywhere is a threat to justice everywhere. We are caught in an inescapable network of mutuality, tied in a single garment of destiny. Whatever affects one directly, affects all indirectly. Never again can we afford to live with the narrow, provincial "outside agitator" idea. Anyone who lives inside the United States can never be considered an outsider anywhere within its bounds.

You deplore the demonstrations taking place in Birmingham. But your statement, I am sorry to say, fails to express a similar concern for the conditions that brought about the demonstrations. I am sure that none of you would want to rest content with the superficial kind of social analysis that deals merely with effects and does not grapple with underlying causes. It is unfortunate that demonstrations are taking place in Birmingham, but it is even more unfortunate that the city's white power structure left the Negro community with no alternative.

In any nonviolent campaign there are four steps: collection of the facts to determine whether injustices exist; negotiation; self-purification; and direct action. We have gone through all these steps in Birmingham. There can be no gain saying the fact that racial injustice engulfs this community. Birmingham is probably the most thoroughly segregated city in the United States. Its ugly record of brutality is widely known. Negroes have experienced grossly unjust treatment in the courts. There have been more unsolved bombings of Negro homes and churches in Birmingham than in any other city in the nation. These are the hard brutal facts of the case. On the basis of these conditions, Negro leaders sought to negotiate with the city fathers. But the latter consistently refused to engage in good-faith negotiation.

Then, last September, came the opportunity to talk with leaders of Birmingham economic community. In the course of negotiations, certain promises were made by the merchants—for example, to remove the stores' humiliating racial signs. On the basis of these promises, the Reverend Fred Shuttlesworth and the leaders of the Alabama Christian Movement for Human Rights agreed to a moratorium on all demonstrations. As the weeks and months went by, we realized that we were the victims of a broken promise. A few signs, briefly removed, returned; the others remained.

As in so many past experiences, our hopes had been blasted, and the shadow of deep disappointment settled upon us. We had no alternative except to prepare for direct action, whereby we would present our very bodies as a means of laying our case before the conscience of the local and the national community. Mindful of the difficulties involved, we decided to undertake a process of self-purification. We began a series of workshops on nonviolence, and we repeatedly asked ourselves: "Are you able to accept blows without retaliating?" "Are you able to endure the ordeal of jail?" We decided to schedule our direct-action program for the Easter season, realizing that except for Christmas, this is the main shopping period of the year. Knowing that a strong economic-withdrawal program would be the by-product of direct action, we felt that this would be the best time to bring pressure to bear on the merchants for the needed change.

Then it occurred to us that Birmingham's mayoralty election was coming up in March, and we speedily decided to postpone action until after election day. When we discovered that the Commissioner of Public Safety, Eugene "Bull" Connor, had piled up enough votes to be in the run-off, we decided again to postpone action until the day after the run-off so that the demonstrations could not be used to cloud the issues. Like many others, we waited to see Mr. Connor defeated, and to this end we endured postponement after postponement. Having aided in this community need, we felt that our direct-action program could be delayed no longer.

You may well ask: "Why direct action? Why sit-ins, marches and so forth? Isn't negotiation a better path?" You are quite right in calling for negotiation. Indeed, this is the very purpose of direct action. Nonviolent direct action seeks to create such a crisis and foster such a tension that a community which has constantly refused to negotiate is forced to confront the issue. It seeks so to dramatize the issue that it can no longer be ignored. My citing the creation of tension as part of the work of the nonviolent-resister may sound rather shocking. But I must confess that I am not afraid of the word "tension." I have earnestly opposed violent tension, but there is a type of constructive nonviolent tension which is necessary for growth. Just as Socrates felt that it was necessary to create a tension in the mind so that individuals could rise from the bondage of myths and half-truths to the unfettered realm of creative analysis and objective appraisal, so must we see the need for nonviolent gadflies to create the kind of tension in society that will help men rise from the dark depths of prejudice and racism to the majestic heights of understanding and brotherhood.

The purpose of our direct-action program is to create a situation so crisis-packed that it will inevitably open the door to negotiation. I therefore concur with you in your call for negotiation. Too long has our beloved Southland been bogged down in a tragic effort to live in monologue rather than dialogue.

One of the basic points in your statement is that the action that I and my associates have taken in Birmingham is untimely. Some have asked: "Why didn't you give the new city administration time to act?" The only answer that I can give to this query is that the new Birmingham administration must be prodded about as much as the outgoing one, before it will act. We are sadly mistaken if we feel that the election of Albert Boutwell as mayor will bring the millennium to Birmingham. While Mr. Boutwell is a much more gentle person than Mr. Connor, they are both segregationists, dedicated to maintenance of the status quo. I have hope that Mr. Boutwell will be reasonable enough to see the futility of massive resistance to desegregation. But he will not see this without pressure from devotees of civil rights. My friends, I must say to you that we have not made a single gain in civil rights without determined legal and nonviolent pressure. Lamentably, it is an historical fact that privileged groups seldom give up their privileges voluntarily. Individuals may see the moral light and voluntarily give up their unjust posture; but, as Reinhold Niebuhr has reminded us, groups tend to be more immoral than individuals.

We know through painful experience that freedom is never voluntarily given by the oppressor; it must be demanded by the oppressed. Frankly, I have yet to engage in a direct-action campaign that was "well timed" in the view of those who have not suffered unduly from the disease of segregation. For years now I have heard the word "Wait!" It rings in the ear of every Negro with piercing familiarity. This "Wait" has almost always meant "Never." We must come to see, with one of our distinguished jurists, that "justice too long delayed is justice denied."

We have waited for more than 340 years for our constitutional and God-given rights. The nations of Asia and Africa are moving with jetlike speed toward gaining political independence, but we still creep at horse-and-buggy pace toward gaining a cup of coffee at a lunch counter. Perhaps it is easy for those who have never felt the stinging darts of segregation to say, "Wait." But when you have seen vicious mobs lynch your mothers and fathers at will and drown your sisters and brothers at whim; when you have seen hate-filled policemen curse, kick and even kill your black brothers and sisters; when you see the vast majority of your 20 million Negro brothers smothering in an airtight cage of poverty in the midst of an affluent society; when you suddenly find your tongue twisted and your speech stammering as you seek to explain to your 6-year-old daughter why she can't go to the public amusement park that has just been advertised on television, and see tears welling up in her eyes when she is told that Funtown is closed to colored children, and see ominous clouds of inferiority beginning to form in her little mental sky, and see her beginning to distort her personality by developing an unconscious bitterness toward white people; when you have to concoct an answer for a 5-year-old son who is asking: "Daddy, why do white people treat colored people so mean?"; when you take a cross-country drive and find it necessary to sleep night after night in the uncomfortable corners of your automobile because no motel will accept you; when you are humiliated day in and day out by nagging signs reading "white" and "colored"; when your first name becomes "nigger," your middle name becomes "boy" (however old you are) and your last name becomes "John," and your wife and mother are never given the respected title "Mrs."; when you are harried by day and haunted by night by the fact that you are a Negro, living constantly at tiptoe stance, never quite knowing what to expect next, and are plagued with inner fears and outer resentments; when you are forever fighting a degenerating sense of "nobodiness"—then you will understand why we find it difficult to wait. There comes a time when the cup of endurance runs over, and men are no longer willing to be plunged into the abyss of despair. I hope, sirs, you can understand our legitimate and unavoidable impatience.

You express a great deal of anxiety over our willingness to break laws. This is certainly a legitimate concern. Since we so diligently urge people to obey the Supreme Court's decision of 1954 outlawing segregation in the public schools, at first glance it may seem rather paradoxical for us consciously to break laws. One may well ask: "How can you advocate breaking some laws and obeying others?" The answer lies in the fact that there are two types of laws: just and unjust. I would be the first to advocate obeying just laws. One has not only a legal but a moral responsibility to obey just laws. Conversely, one has a moral responsibility to disobey unjust laws. I would agree with St. Augustine that "an unjust law is no law at all."

Now, what is the difference between the two? How does one determine whether a law is just or unjust? A just law is a man-made code that squares with the moral law or the law of God. An unjust law is a code that is out of harmony with the moral law. To put it in the terms of St. Thomas Aquinas: An unjust law is a human law that is not rooted in eternal law and natural law. Any law that uplifts human personality is just. Any law that degrades human personality is unjust. All segregation statues are unjust because segregation distorts the soul and damages the personality. It gives the segregator a false sense of superiority and the segregated a false sense of inferiority. Segregation, to use the terminology of the Jewish philosopher Martin Buber, substitutes an "I-it" relationship for an "I-thou" relationship and ends up relegating persons to the status of things. Hence segregation is not only politically, economically and sociologically unsound, it is morally wrong and sinful. Paul Tillich has said that sin is separation. Is not segregation an existential expression of man's tragic separation, his awful estrangement, his terrible sinfulness? Thus it is that I can urge men to obey the 1954 decision of the Supreme Court, for it is morally right; and I can urge them to disobey segregation ordinances, for they are morally wrong.

Let us consider a more concrete example of just and unjust laws. An unjust law is a code that a numerical or power majority group compels a minority group to obey but does not make binding on itself. This is *difference* made legal. By the same token, a just law is a code that a majority compels a minority to follow and that it is willing to follow itself. This is *sameness* made legal.

Let me give another explanation. A law is unjust if it is inflicted on a minority that, as a result of being denied the right to vote, had no part in enacting or devising the law. Who can say that the legislature of Alabama which set up that state's segregation laws was democratically elected? Throughout Alabama all sorts of devious methods are used to prevent Negroes from becoming registered voters, and there are some counties in which even though Negroes constitute a majority of the population, not a single Negro is registered. Can any law enacted under such circumstances be considered democratically structured?

Sometimes a law is just on its face and unjust in its application. For instance, I have been arrested on a charge of parading without a permit. Now, there is nothing wrong in having an ordinance which requires a permit for a parade. But such an ordinance becomes unjust when it is used to maintain segregation and to deny citizens the First-Amendment privilege of peaceful assembly and protest.

I hope you are able to see the distinction I am trying to point out. In no sense do I advocate evading or defying the law, as would the rabid segregationist. That would lead to anarchy. One who breaks an unjust law must do so openly, lovingly, and with a willingness to accept the penalty. I submit that an individual who breaks a law that conscience tells him is unjust, and who willingly accepts the penalty of imprisonment in order to arouse the conscience of the community over its injustice, is in reality expressing the highest respect for law.

Of course, there is nothing new about this kind of civil disobedience. It was evidenced sublimely in the refusal of Shadrach, Meshach and Abednego to obey the laws of Nebuchadnezzar, on the ground that a higher moral law was at stake. It was practiced superbly by the early Christians, who were willing to face hungry lions and the excruciating pain of chopping blocks rather than submit to certain unjust laws of the Roman Empire. To a degree, academic freedom is a reality today because Socrates practiced civil disobedience. In our own nation, the Boston Tea Party represented a massive act of civil disobedience.

We should never forget that everything Adolf Hitler did in Germany was "legal" and everything the Hungarian freedom fighters did in Hungary was "illegal." It was "illegal" to aid and comfort a Jew in Hitler's Germany. Even so, I am sure that, had I lived in Germany at the time, I would have aided and comforted my Jewish brothers. If today I lived in a Communist country where certain principles dear to the Christian faith are suppressed, I would openly advocate disobeying that country's anti-religious laws.

I must make two honest confessions to you, my Christian and Jewish brothers. First, I must confess that over the past few years I have been gravely disappointed with the white moderate. I have almost reached the regrettable conclusion that the Negro's great stumbling block in his stride toward freedom is not the White Citizen's Counciler or the Ku Klux Klanner, but the white moderate, who is more devoted to "order" than to justice; who prefers a negative peace which is the absence of tension to a positive peace which is the presence of justice; who constantly says: "I agree with you in the goal you seek, but I cannot agree with your methods of direct action"; who paternalistically believes he can set the timetable for another man's freedom; who lives by a mythical concept of time and who constantly advises the Negro to wait for a "more convenient season." Shallow understanding from people of good will is more frustrating than absolute misunderstanding from people of ill will. Lukewarm acceptance is much more bewildering than outright rejection.

I had hoped that the white moderate would understand that law and order exist for the purpose of establishing justice and that when they fail in this purpose they become the dangerously structured dams that block the flow of social progress. I had hoped that the white moderate would understand that the present tension in the South is a necessary phase of the transition from an obnoxious negative peace, in which the Negro passively accepted his unjust plight, to a substantive and positive peace, in which all men will respect the dignity and worth of human personality. Actually, we who engage in nonviolent direct action are not the creators of tension. We merely bring to the surface the hidden tension that is already alive. We bring it out in the open, where it can be seen and dealt with. Like a boil that can never be cured so long as it is covered up but must be opened with all its ugliness to the natural medicines of air and light, injustice must be exposed, with all the tension its exposure creates, to the light of human conscience and the air of national opinion before it can be cured.

In your statement you assert that our actions, even though peaceful, must be condemned because they precipitate violence. But is this a logical assertion? Isn't this like condemning a robbed man because his possession of money precipitated the evil act of robbery? Isn't this like condemning Jesus because his unique God-consciousness and never-ceasing devotion to God's will precipitated the evil act of crucifixion? We must come to see that, as the federal courts have consistently affirmed, it is wrong to urge an individual to cease his efforts to gain his basic constitutional rights because the quest may precipitate violence. Society must protect the robbed and punish the robber.

I had also hoped that the white moderate would reject the myth concerning time in relation to the struggle for freedom. I have just received a letter from a white brother in Texas. He writes: "All Christians know that the colored people will receive equal rights eventually, but it is possible that you are in too great a religious hurry. It has taken Christianity almost two thousand years to accomplish what it has. The teachings of Christ take time to come to earth." Such an attitude stems from a tragic misconception of time, from the strangely irrational notion that there is something in the very flow of time that will inevitably cure all ills. Actually, time itself is neutral; it can be used either destructively or constructively. More and more I feel that the people of ill will have used time much more effectively than have the people of good will. We will have to repent in this generation not merely for the hateful words and actions of the bad people but for the appalling silence of the good people. Human progress never rolls in on wheels of inevitability; it comes through the tireless efforts of men willing to be co-workers with God, and without this hard work, time itself becomes an ally of the forces of social stagnation. We must use time creatively, in the knowledge that the time is always ripe to do right. Now is the time to make real the promise of democracy and transform our pending national elegy into a creative psalm of brotherhood. Now is the time to lift our national policy from the quicksand of racial injustice to the solid rock of human dignity.

You speak of our activity in Birmingham as extreme. At first I was rather disappointed that fellow clergymen would see my nonviolent efforts as those of an extremist. I began thinking about the fact that I stand in the middle of two opposing forces in the Negro community. One is a force of complacency, made up in part of Negroes who, as a result of long years of oppression, are so drained of self-respect and a sense of "somebodiness" that they have adjusted to segregation; and in part of a few middle-class Negroes who, because of a degree of academic and economic security and because in some ways they profit by segregation, have become insensitive to the problems of the masses. The other force is one of bitterness and hatred, and it comes perilously close to advocating violence. It is expressed in the various black nationalist groups that are springing up across the nation, the largest and best-known being Elijah Muhammad's Muslim movement. Nourished by the Negro's frustration over the continued existence of racial discrimination, this movement is made up of people who have lost faith in America, who have absolutely repudiated Christianity, and who have concluded that the white man is an incorrigible "devil."

I have tried to stand between these two forces, saying that we need emulate neither the "do-nothingism" of the complacement nor the hatred and despair of the black nationalist. For there is the more excellent way of love and nonviolent protest. I am grateful to God that, through the influence of the Negro church, the way of nonviolence became an integral part of our struggle.

If this philosophy had not emerged, by now many streets of the South would, I am convinced, be flowing with blood. And I am further convinced that if our white brothers dismiss as "rabble-rousers" and "outside agitators" those of us who employ nonviolent direct action, and if they refuse to support our nonviolent efforts, millions of Negroes will, out of frustration and despair, seek solace and security in black-nationalist ideologies—a development that would inevitably lead to a frightening racial nightmare.

Oppressed people cannot remain oppressed forever. The yearning for freedom eventually manifests itself, and that is what has happened to the American Negro. Something within has reminded him that it can be gained. Consciously or unconsciously, he has been caught up by the *Zeitgeist,* and with his black brothers of Africa and his brown and yellow brothers of Asia, South America and the Caribbean, the United States Negro is moving with a sense of great urgency toward the promised land of racial justice. If one recognizes this vital urge that has engulfed the Negro community, one should readily understand why public demonstrations are taking place. The Negro has many pent-up resentments and latent frustrations, and he must release them. So let him march; let him make prayer pilgrimages to the city hall; let him go on freedom rides—and try to understand why he must do so. If his repressed emotions are not released in nonviolent ways, they will seek expression through violence; this is not a threat but a fact of history. So I have not said to my people: "Get rid of your discontent." Rather, I have tried to say that this normal and healthy discontent can be channeled into the creative outlet of nonviolent direct action. And now this approach is being termed extremist.

But though I was initially disappointed at being categorized as an extremist, as I continued to think about the matter I gradually gained a measure of satisfaction from the label. Was not Jesus an extremist for love: "Love your enemies, bless them that curse you, do good to them that hate you, and pray for them which despitefully use you, and persecute you." Was not Amos an extremist for justice: "Let justice roll down like waters and righteousness like an ever-flowing stream." Was not Paul an extremist for the Christian gospel: "I bear in my body the marks of the Lord Jesus." Was not Martin Luther an extremist: "Here I stand; I cannot do otherwise, so help me God." And John Bunyan: "I will stay in jail to the end of my days before I make a butchery of my conscience." And Abraham Lincoln: "This nation cannot survive half slave and half free." And Thomas Jefferson: "We hold these truths to be self-evident, that all men are created equal. . . ." So the question is not whether we will be extremists, but what kind of extremists we will be. Will we be extremists for hate or for love? Will we be extremists for the preservation of injustice or for the extension of justice? In that dramatic scene on Calvary's hill three men were crucified. We must never forget that all three were crucified for the same crime—the crime of extremism. Two were extremists for immorality, and thus fell below their environment. The other, Jesus Christ, was an extremist for love, truth and goodness, and thereby rose above his environment. Perhaps the South, the nation and the world are in dire need of creative extremists.

I had hoped that the white moderate would see this need. Perhaps I was too optimistic; perhaps I expected too much. I suppose I should have realized that few members of the oppressor race can understand the deep groans and passionate yearnings of the oppressed race, and still fewer have the vision to see that injustice must be rooted out by strong, persistent and determined action. I am thankful, however, that some of our white brothers in the South have grasped the meaning of this social revolution and committed themselves to it. They are still all too few in quantity, but they are big in quality. Some—such as Ralph McGill, Lillian Smith, Harry Golden, James McBride Dabbs, Ann Braden and Sarah Patton Boyle—have written about our struggle in eloquent and prophetic terms. Others have marched with us down nameless streets of the South. They have languished in filthy, roach-infested jails, suffering the abuse and brutality of policemen who view them as "dirty nigger-lovers." Unlike so many of their moderate brothers and sisters, they have recognized the urgency of the moment and sensed the need for powerful "action" antidotes to combat the disease of segregation.

Let me take note of my other major disappointment. I have been so greatly disappointed with the white church and its leadership. Of course, there are some notable exceptions. I am not unmindful of the fact that each of you has taken some significant stands on this issue. I commend you, Reverend Stallings, for your Christian stand on this past Sunday, in welcoming Negroes to your worship service on a nonsegregated basis. I commend the Catholic leaders of this state for integrating Spring Hill College several years ago.

But despite these notable exceptions, I must honestly reiterate that I have been disappointed with the church. I do not say this as one of those negative critics who can always find something wrong with the church. I say this as a minister of the gospel, who loves the church; who was nurtured in its bosom; who has been sustained by its spiritual blessings and who will remain true to it as long as the cord of life shall lengthen.

When I was suddenly catapulted into the leadership of the bus protest in Montgomery, Ala., a few years ago, I felt we would be supported by the white church. I felt that the white ministers, priests and rabbis of the South would be among our strongest allies. Instead, some have been outright opponents, refusing to understand the freedom movement and misrepresenting its leaders; all too many others have been more cautious than courageous and have remained silent behind the anesthetizing security of stained-glass windows.

In spite of my shattered dreams, I came to Birmingham with the hope that the white religious leadership of this community would see the justice of our cause and, with deep moral concern, would serve as the channel through which our just grievances could reach the power structure. I had hoped that each of you would understand. But again I have been disappointed.

I have heard numerous southern religious leaders admonish their worshipers to comply with a desegregation decision because it is the law, but I have longed to hear white ministers declare: "Follow this decree because integration is morally right and because the Negro is your brother." In the midst of blatant injustices inflicted upon the Negro, I have watched white churchmen stand on the sideline and mouth pious irrelevancies and sanctimonious trivialities. In the midst of a mighty struggle to rid our nation of racial and economic injustice, I have heard many ministers say: "Those are social issues, with which the gospel has no real concern." And I have watched many churches commit themselves to a completely other-worldly religion which makes a strange, un-Biblical distinction between body and soul, between the sacred and the secular.

I have traveled the length and breadth of Alabama, Mississippi and all the other southern states. On sweltering summer days and crisp autumn mornings I have looked at the South's beautiful churches with their lofty spires pointing heavenward. I have beheld the impressive outlines of her massive religious-education buildings. Over and over I have found myself asking: "What kind of people worship here? Who is their God? Where were their voices when the lips of Governor Barnett dripped with words of interposition and nullification? Where were they when Governor Wallace gave a clarion call for defiance and hatred? Where were their voices of support when bruised and weary Negro men and women decided to rise from the dark dungeons of complacency to the bright hills of creative protest?"

Yes, these questions are still in my mind. In deep disappointment I have wept over the laxity of the church. But be assured that my tears have been tears of love. There can be no deep disappointment where there is not deep love. Yes, I love the church. How could I do otherwise? I am in the rather unique position of being the son, the grandson and the great-grandson of preachers. Yes, I see the church as the body of Christ. But, oh! How we have blemished and scarred that body through social neglect and through fear of being nonconformists.

There was a time when the church was very powerful—in the time when the early Christians rejoiced at being deemed worthy to suffer for what they believed. In those days the church was not merely a thermometer that recorded the ideas and principles of popular opinion; it was a thermostat that transformed the mores of society. Whenever the early Christians entered a town, the people in power became disturbed and immediately sought to convict the Christians for being "disturbers of the peace" and "outside agitators." But the Christians pressed on, in the conviction that they were "a colony of heaven," called to obey God rather than man. Small in number, they were big in commitment. They were too God-intoxicated to be "astronomically intimidated." By their effort and example they brought an end to such ancient evils as infanticide and gladiatorial contests.

Things are different now. So often the contemporary church is a weak, ineffectual voice with an uncertain sound. So often it is an archdefender of the status quo. Far from being disturbed by the presence of the church, the power structure of the average community is consoled by the church's silent—and often even vocal—sanction of things as they are.

But the judgment of God is upon the church as never before. If today's church does not recapture the sacrificial spirit of the early church, it will lose its authenticity, forfeit the loyalty of millions, and be dismissed as an irrelevant social club with no meaning for the twentieth century. Every day I meet young people whose disappointment with the church has turned into outright disgust.

Perhaps I have once again been too optimistic. Is organized religion too inextricably bound to the status quo to save our nation and the world? Perhaps I must turn my faith to the inner spiritual church, the church within the church, as the true *ekklesia* and the hope of the world. But again I am thankful to God that some noble souls from the ranks of organized religion have broken loose from the paralyzing chains of conformity and joined us as active partners in the struggle for freedom. They have left their secure congregations and walked the streets of Albany, Ga. with us. They have gone down the highways of the South on tortuous rides for freedom. Yes, they have gone to jail with us. Some have been dismissed from their churches, have lost the support of their bishops and fellow ministers. But they have acted in the faith that right defeated is stronger than evil triumphant. Their witness has been the spiritual salt that has preserved the true meaning of the gospel in these troubled times. They have carved a tunnel of hope through the dark mountain of disappointment.

I hope the church as a whole will meet the challenge of this decisive hour. But even if the church does not come to the aid of justice, I have no despair about the future. I have no fear about the outcome of our struggle in Birmingham, even if our motives are at present misunderstood. We will reach the goal of freedom in Birmingham and all over the nation, because the goal of America is freedom. Abused and scorned though we may be, our destiny is tied up with America's destiny. Before the pilgrims landed at Plymouth, we were here. Before the pen of Jefferson etched the majestic words of the Declaration of Independence across the pages of history, we were here. For more than two centuries our forebears labored in this country without wages; they made cotton king; they built the homes of their masters while suffering gross injustice and shameful humiliation—and yet out of a bottomless vitality they continued to thrive and develop. If the inexpressible cruelties of slavery could not stop us, the opposition we now face will surely fail. We will win our freedom because the sacred heritage of our nation and the eternal will of God are embodied in our echoing demands.

Before closing I feel impelled to mention one other point in your statement that has troubled me profoundly. You warmly commended the Birmingham police force for keeping "order" and "preventing violence." I doubt that you would have so warmly commended the police force if you had seen its dogs sinking their teeth into unarmed, nonviolent Negroes. I doubt that you would so quickly commend the policemen if you were to observe their ugly and inhumane treatment of Negroes here in the city jail; if you were to watch them push and curse old Negro women and young Negro girls; if you were to see them slap and kick old Negro men and young boys; if you were to observe them as they did on two occasions, refuse to give us food because we wanted to sing our grace together. I cannot join you in your praise of the Birmingham police department.

It is true that the police have exercised a degree of discipline in handling the demonstrators. In this sense they have conducted themselves rather "nonviolently" in public. But for what purpose? To preserve the evil system of segregation. Over the past few years I have consistently preached that nonviolence demands that the means we use must be as pure as the ends we seek. I have tried to make clear that it is wrong to use immoral means to attain moral ends. But now I must affirm that it is just as wrong, or perhaps even more so, to use moral means to preserve immoral ends. Perhaps Mr. Connor and his policemen have been rather nonviolent in public, as was Chief Pritchett in Albany, Ga., but they have used the moral means of nonviolence to maintain the immoral end of racial injustice. As T. S. Eliot has said: "The last temptation is the greatest treason: To do the right deed for the wrong reason."

I wish you had commended the Negro sit-inners and demonstrators of Birmingham for their sublime courage, their willingness to suffer and their amazing discipline in the midst of great provocation. One day the South will recognize its real heroes. They will be the James Merediths, with the noble sense of purpose that enables them to face jeering and hostile mobs, and with the agonizing loneliness that characterizes the life of the pioneer. They will be old, oppressed, battered Negro women, symbolized in a 72-year-old woman in Montgomery, Ala., who rose up with a sense of dignity and with her people decided not to ride segregated buses, and who responded with ungrammatical profundity to one who inquired about her weariness: "My feet is tired, but my soul is at rest." They will be the young high school and college students, the young ministers of the gospel and a host of their elders, courageously and nonviolently sitting in at lunch counters and willingly going to jail for conscience sake. One day the South will know that when these disinherited children of God sat down at lunch counters, they were in reality standing up for what is best in the American dream and for the most sacred values in our Judaeo-Christian heritage, thereby bringing our nation back to those great wells of democracy which were dug deep by the founding fathers in their formulation of the Constitution and the Declaration of Independence.

Never before have I written so long a letter. I'm afraid it is much too long to take your precious time. I can assure you that it would have been much shorter if I had been writing from a comfortable desk, but what else can one do when he is alone in a narrow jail cell, other than write long letters, think long thoughts and pray long prayers?

If I have said anything in this letter that overstates the truth and indicates an unreasonable impatience, I beg you to forgive me. If I have said anything that understates the truth and indicates my having a patience that allows me to settle for anything less than brotherhood, I beg God to forgive me.

I hope this letter finds you strong in the faith. I also hope that circumstances will soon make it possible for me to meet each of you, not as an integrationist or a civil-rights leader but as a fellow clergyman and a Christian brother. Let us all hope that the dark clouds of racial prejudice will soon pass away and the deep fog of misunderstanding will be lifted from our fear-drenched communities, and in some not too distant tomorrow the radiant stars of love and brotherhood will shine over our great nation with all their scintillating beauty.

CIVIL RIGHTS ACT OF 1964

For Legislative History of Act, see p. 2355

PUBLIC LAW 88–352; 78 STAT. 241

[H. R. 7152]

An Act to enforce the constitutional right to vote, to confer jurisdiction upon the district courts of the United States to provide injunctive relief against discrimination in public accommodations, to authorize the Attorney General to institute suits to protect constitutional rights in public facilities and public education, to extend the Commission on Civil Rights, to prevent discrimination in federally assisted programs, to establish a Commission on Equal Employment Opportunity, and for other purposes.

Be it enacted by the Senate and House of Representatives of the United States of America in Congress assembled, That:

This Act may be cited as the "Civil Rights Act of 1964".

TITLE I—VOTING RIGHTS

Sec. 101. Section 2004 of the Revised Statutes (42 U.S.C. 1971), as amended by section 131 of the Civil Rights Act of 1957 (71 Stat. 637), and as further amended by section 601 of the Civil Rights Act of 1960 (74 Stat. 90),[55] is further amended as follows:

(a) Insert "1" after "(a)" in subsection (a) and add at the end of subsection (a) the following new paragraphs:

"(2) No person acting under color of law shall—

"(A) in determining whether any individual is qualified under State law or laws to vote in any Federal election, apply any

---

54. 5 U.S.C.A. § 133z—3.
55. 42 U.S.C.A. § 1971.

standard, practice, or procedure different from the standards, practices, or procedures applied under such law or laws to other individuals within the same county, parish, or similar political subdivision who have been found by State officials to be qualified to vote;

"(B) deny the right of any individual to vote in any Federal election because of an error or omission on any record or paper relating to any application, registration, or other act requisite to voting, if such error or omission is not material in determining whether such individual is qualified under State law to vote in such election; or

"(C) employ any literacy test as a qualification for voting in any Federal election unless (i) such test is administered to each individual and is conducted wholly in writing, and (ii) a certified copy of the test and of the answers given by the individual is furnished to him within twenty-five days of the submission of his request made within the period of time during which records and papers are required to be retained and preserved pursuant to title III of the Civil Rights Act of 1960 (42 U.S.C. 1974–74e; 74 Stat. 88): *Provided, however,* That the Attorney General may enter into agreements with appropriate State or local authorities that preparation, conduct, and maintenance of such tests in accordance with the provisions of applicable State or local law, including such special provisions as are necessary in the preparation, conduct, and maintenance of such tests for persons who are blind or otherwise physically handicapped, meet the purposes of this subparagraph and constitute compliance therewith.

"(3) For purposes of this subsection—

"(A) the term 'vote' shall have the same meaning as in subsection (e) of this section;

"(B) the phrase 'literacy test' includes any test of the ability to read, write, understand, or interpret any matter."

(b) Insert immediately following the period at the end of the first sentence of subsection (c) the following new sentence: "If in any such proceeding literacy is a relevant fact there shall be a rebuttable presumption that any person who has not been adjudged an incompetent and who has completed the sixth grade in a public school in, or a private school accredited by, any State or territory, the District of Columbia, or the Commonwealth of Puerto Rico where instruction is carried on predominantly in the English language, possesses sufficient literacy, comprehension, and intelligence to vote in any Federal election."

(c) Add the following subsection "(f)" and designate the present subsection "(f)" as subsection "(g)":

"(f) When used in subsection (a) or (c) of this section, the words 'Federal election' shall mean any general, special, or primary election held solely or in part for the purpose of electing or selecting any candidate for the office of President, Vice President, presidential elector, Member of the Senate, or Member of the House of Representatives."

(d) Add the following subsection "(h)":

"(h) In any proceeding instituted by the United States in any district court of the United States under this section in which the Attorney General requests a finding of a pattern or practice of discrimination pursuant to subsection (e) of this section the Attorney General, at the time he files the complaint, or any defendant in the proceeding, within twenty days after service upon him of the complaint, may file with the clerk of such court a request that a court of three judges be convened to hear and determine the entire case. A copy of the request for a three-judge court shall be immediately furnished by such clerk to the chief judge of the circuit (or in his absence, the presiding circuit judge of the circuit) in which the case is pending. Upon receipt of the copy of such request it shall be the duty of the chief judge of the circuit or the presiding circuit judge, as the case may be, to designate immediately three judges in such circuit, of whom at least one shall be a circuit judge and another of whom shall be a district judge of the court in which the proceeding was instituted, to hear and determine such case, and it shall be the duty of the judges so designated to assign the case for hearing at the earliest practicable date, to participate in the hearing and determination thereof, and to cause the case to be in every way expedited. An appeal from the final judgment of such court will lie to the Supreme Court.

"In any proceeding brought under subsection (c) of this section to enforce subsection (b) of this section, or in the event neither the Attorney General nor any defendant files a request for a three-judge court in any proceeding authorized by this subsection, it shall be the duty of the chief judge of the district (or in his absence, the acting chief judge) in which the case is pending immediately to designate a judge in such district to hear and determine the case. In the event that no judge in the district is available to hear and determine the case, the chief judge of the district, or the acting chief judge, as the case may be, shall certify this fact to the chief judge of the circuit (or, in his absence, the acting chief judge) who shall then designate a district or circuit judge of the circuit to hear and determine the case.

"It shall be the duty of the judge designated pursuant to this section to assign the case for hearing at the earliest practicable date and to cause the case to be in every way expedited."

TITLE II—INJUNCTIVE RELIEF AGAINST DISCRIMINATION IN PLACES OF PUBLIC ACCOMMODATION

Sec. 201. (a) All persons shall be entitled to the full and equal enjoyment of the goods, services, facilities, privileges, advantages, and accommodations of any place of public accommodation, as defined in this section, without discrimination or segregation on the ground of race, color, religion, or national origin.

(b) Each of the following establishments which serves the public is a place of public accommodation within the meaning of this title if its operations affect commerce, or if discrimination or segregation by it is supported by State action:

(1) any inn, hotel, motel, or other establishment which provides lodging to transient guests, other than an establishment located within a building which contains not more than five rooms for rent or hire and which is actually occupied by the proprietor of such establishment as his residence;

(2) any restaurant, cafeteria, lunchroom, lunch counter, soda fountain, or other facility principally engaged in selling food for consumption on the premises, including, but not limited to, any such facility located on the premises of any retail establishment; or any gasoline station;

(3) any motion picture house, theater, concert hall, sports arena, stadium or other place of exhibition or entertainment; and

(4) any establishment (A) (i) which is physically located within the premises of any establishment otherwise covered by this subsection, or (ii) within the premises of which is physically located any such covered establishment, and (B) which holds itself out as serving patrons of such covered establishment.

(c) The operations of an establishment affect commerce within the meaning of this title if (1) it is one of the establishments described in paragraph (1) of subsection (b); (2) in the case of an establishment described in paragraph (2) of subsection (b), it serves or offers to serve interstate travelers or a substantial portion of the food which it serves, or gasoline or other products which it sells, has moved in commerce; (3) in the case of an establishment described in paragraph (3) of subsection (b), it customarily presents films, performances, athletic teams, exhibitions, or other sources of entertainment which move in commerce; and (4) in the case of an establishment described in paragraph (4) of subsection (b), it is physically located within the premises of, or there is physically located within its premises, an establishment the operations of which affect commerce within the meaning of this subsection. For purposes of this section, "commerce" means travel, trade, traffic, commerce, transportation, or communication among the several States, or between the District of Columbia and any State, or between any foreign country or any territory or possession and any State or the District of Columbia, or between points in the same State but through any other State or the District of Columbia or a foreign country.

(d) Discrimination or segregation by an establishment is supported by State action within the meaning of this title if such discrimination or segregation (1) is carried on under color of any law, statute, ordinance, or regulation; or (2) is carried on under color of any custom or usage required or enforced by officials of the State or political subdivision thereof; or (3) is required by action of the State or political subdivision thereof.

(e) The provisions of this title shall not apply to a private club or other establishment not in fact open to the public, except to the extent that the facilities of such establishment are made available to the customers or patrons of an establishment within the scope of subsection (b).

Sec. 202. All persons shall be entitled to be free, at any establishment or place, from discrimination or segregation of any kind on the ground of race, color, religion, or national origin, if such discrimination or segregation is or purports to be required by any law, statute, ordinance, regulation, rule, or order of a State or any agency or political subdivision thereof.

Sec. 203. No person shall (a) withhold, deny, or attempt to withhold or deny, or deprive or attempt to deprive, any person of any right or privilege secured by section 201 or 202, or (b) intimidate, threaten, or coerce, or attempt to intimidate, threaten, or coerce any person with the purpose of interfering with any right or privilege secured by section 201 or 202, or (c) punish or attempt to punish any person for exercising or attempting to exercise any right or privilege secured by section 201 or 202.

Sec. 204. (a) Whenever any person has engaged or there are reasonable grounds to believe that any person is about to engage in any act or practice prohibited by section 203, a civil action for preventive relief, including an application for a permanent or temporary injunction, restraining order, or other order, may be instituted by the person aggrieved and, upon timely application, the court may, in its discretion, permit the Attorney General to intervene in such civil action if he certifies that the case is of general public importance. Upon application by the complainant and in such circumstances as the court may deem just, the court may appoint an attorney for such complainant and may authorize the commencement of the civil action without the payment of fees, costs, or security.

(b) In any action commenced pursuant to this title, the court, in its discretion, may allow the prevailing party, other than the United States, a reasonable attorney's fee as part of the costs, and the United States shall be liable for costs the same as a private person.

(c) In the case of an alleged act or practice prohibited by this title which occurs in a State, or political subdivision of a State, which has a State or local law prohibiting such act or practice and establishing or authorizing a State or local authority to grant or seek relief from such practice or to institute criminal proceedings with respect thereto upon receiving notice thereof, no civil action may be brought under subsection (a) before the expiration of thirty days after written notice of such alleged act or practice has been given to the appropriate State or local authority by registered mail or in person, provided that the court may stay proceedings in such civil action pending the termination of State or local enforcement proceedings.

(d) In the case of an alleged act or practice prohibited by this title which occurs in a State, or political subdivision of a State, which has no State or local law prohibiting such act or practice, a civil action may be brought under subsection (a): *Provided,* That the court may refer the matter to the Community Relations Service established by title X of this Act for as long as the court believes there is a reasonable possibility of obtaining voluntary compliance, but for not more than sixty days: *Provided further,* That upon expiration of such sixty-day period, the court may extend such period for an additional period, not to exceed a cumulative total of one hundred and twenty days, if it believes there then exists a reasonable possibility of securing voluntary compliance.

Sec. 205. The Service is authorized to make a full investigation of any complaint referred to it by the court under section 204(d) and may hold such hearings with respect thereto as may be necessary. The Service shall conduct any hearings with respect to any such complaint in executive session, and shall not release any testimony given therein except by agreement of all parties involved in the complaint with the permission of the court, and the Service shall endeavor to bring about a voluntary settlement between the parties.

Sec. 206. (a) Whenever the Attorney General has reasonable cause to believe that any person or group of persons is engaged in a pattern or practice of resistance to the full enjoyment of any of the rights secured by this title, and that the pattern or practice is of such a nature and is intended to deny the full exercise of the rights herein described, the Attorney General may bring a civil action in the appropriate district court of the United States by filing with it a complaint (1) signed by him (or in his absence the Acting Attorney General), (2) setting forth facts pertaining to such pattern or practice, and (3) requesting such preventive relief, including an application for a permanent or temporary injunction, restraining order or other order against the person or persons responsible for such pattern or practice, as he deems necessary to insure the full enjoyment of the rights herein described.

(b) In any such proceeding the Attorney General may file with the clerk of such court a request that a court of three judges be convened to hear and determine the case. Such request by the Attorney General shall be accompanied by a certificate that, in his opinion, the case is of general public importance. A copy of the certificate and request for a three-judge court shall be immediately furnished by such clerk to the chief judge of the circuit (or in his absence, the presiding circuit judge of the circuit) in which the case is pending. Upon receipt of the copy of such request it shall be the duty of the chief judge of the circuit or the presiding circuit judge, as the case may be, to designate immediately three judges in such circuit, of whom at least one shall be a circuit judge and another of whom shall be a district judge of the court in which the proceeding was instituted, to hear and determine such case, and it shall be the duty of the judges so designated to assign the case for hearing at the earliest practicable date, to participate in the hearing and determination thereof, and to cause the case to be in every way expedited. An appeal from the final judgment of such court will lie to the Supreme Court.

In the event the Attorney General fails to file such a request in any such proceeding, it shall be the duty of the chief judge of the district (or in his absence, the acting chief judge) in which the case is pending immediately to designate a judge in such district to hear and determine the case. In the event that no judge in the district is available to hear and determine the case, the chief judge of the district, or the acting chief judge, as the case may be, shall certify this fact to the chief judge of the circuit (or in his absence, the acting chief judge) who shall then designate a district or circuit judge of the circuit to hear and determine the case.

It shall be the duty of the judge designated pursuant to this section to assign the case for hearing at the earliest practicable date and to cause the case to be in every way expedited.

Sec. 207. (a) The district courts of the United States shall have jurisdiction of proceedings instituted pursuant to this title and shall exercise the same without regard to whether the aggrieved party shall have exhausted any administrative or other remedies that may be provided by law.

(b) The remedies provided in this title shall be the exclusive means of enforcing the rights based on this title, but nothing in this title shall preclude any individual or any State or local agency from asserting any right based on any other Federal or State law not inconsistent with this title, including any statute or ordinance requiring nondiscrimination in public establishments or accommodations, or from pursuing any remedy, civil or criminal, which may be available for the vindication or enforcement of such right.

TITLE III—DESEGREGATION OF PUBLIC FACILITIES

Sec. 301. (a) Whenever the Attorney General receives a complaint in writing signed by an individual to the effect that he is being deprived of or threatened with the loss of his right to the equal protection of the laws, on account of his race, color, religion, or national origin, by being denied equal utilization of any public facility which is owned, operated, or managed by or on behalf of any State or subdivision thereof, other than a public school or public college as defined in section 401 of title IV hereof, and the Attorney General believes the complaint is meritorious and certifies that the signer or signers of such complaint are unable, in his judgment, to initiate and maintain appropriate legal proceedings for relief and that the institution of an action will materially further the orderly progress of desegregation in public facilities, the Attorney General is authorized to institute for or in the name of the United States a civil action in any appropriate district court of the United States against such parties and for such relief as may be appropriate, and such court shall have and shall exercise jurisdiction of proceedings instituted pursuant to this section. The Attorney General may implead as defendants such additional parties as are or become necessary to the grant of effective relief hereunder.

(b) The Attorney General may deem a person or persons unable to initiate and maintain appropriate legal proceedings within the meaning of subsection (a) of this section when such person or persons are unable, either directly or through other interested persons or organizations, to bear the expense of the litigation or to obtain effective legal representation; or whenever he is satisfied that the institution of such litigation would jeopardize the personal safety, employment, or economic standing of such person or persons, their families, or their property.

Sec. 302. In any action or proceeding under this title the United States shall be liable for costs, including a reasonable attorney's fee, the same as a private person.

Sec. 303. Nothing in this title shall affect adversely the right of any person to sue for or obtain relief in any court against discrimination in any facility covered by this title.

Sec. 304. A complaint as used in this title is a writing or document within the meaning of section 1001, title 18, United States Code.

TITLE IV—DESEGREGATION OF PUBLIC EDUCATION

DEFINITIONS

Sec. 401. As used in this title—

(a) "Commissioner" means the Commissioner of Education.

(b) "Desegregation" means the assignment of students to public schools and within such schools without regard to their race, color, religion, or national origin, but "desegregation" shall not mean the assignment of students to public schools in order to overcome racial imbalance.

(c) "Public school" means any elementary or secondary educational institution, and "public college" means any institution of higher education or any technical or vocational school above the secondary school level, provided that such public school or public college is operated by a State, subdivision of a State, or governmental agency within a State, or operated wholly or predominantly from or through the use of governmental funds or property, or funds or property derived from a governmental source.

(d) "School board" means any agency or agencies which administer a system of one or more public schools and any other agency which is responsible for the assignment of students to or within such system.

SURVEY AND REPORT OF EDUCATIONAL OPPORTUNITIES

Sec. 402. The Commissioner shall conduct a survey and make a report to the President and the Congress, within two years of the enactment of this title, concerning the lack of availability of equal educational opportunities for individuals by reason of race, color, religion, or national origin in public educational institutions at all levels in the United States, its territories and possessions, and the District of Columbia.

TECHNICAL ASSISTANCE

Sec. 403. The Commissioner is authorized, upon the application of any school board, State, municipality, school district, or other governmental unit legally responsible for operating a public school or schools, to render technical assistance to such applicant in the preparation, adoption, and implementation of plans for the desegregation of public schools. Such technical assistance may, among other activities, include making available to such agencies information regarding effective methods of coping with special educational problems occasioned by desegregation, and making available to such agencies personnel of the Office of Education or other persons specially equipped to advise and assist them in coping with such problems.

TRAINING INSTITUTES

Sec. 404. The Commissioner is authorized to arrange, through grants or contracts, with institutions of higher education for the operation of short-term or regular session institutes for special training designed to improve the ability of teachers, supervisors, counselors, and other elementary or secondary school personnel to deal effectively with special educational problems occasioned by desegregation. Individuals who attend such an institute on a full-time basis may be paid stipends for the period of their attendance at such institute in amounts specified by the Commissioner in regulations, including allowances for travel to attend such institute.

GRANTS

Sec. 405. (a) The Commissioner is authorized, upon application of a school board, to make grants to such board to pay, in whole or in part, the cost of—

(1) giving to teachers and other school personnel inservice training in dealing with problems incident to desegregation, and

(2) employing specialists to advise in problems incident to desegregation.

(b) In determining whether to make a grant, and in fixing the amount thereof and the terms and conditions on which it will be made, the Commissioner shall take into consideration the amount available for grants under this section and the other applications which are pending before him; the financial condition of the applicant and the other resources available to it; the nature, extent, and gravity of its problems incident to desegregation; and such other factors as he finds relevant.

PAYMENTS

Sec. 406. Payments pursuant to a grant or contract under this title may be made (after necessary adjustments on account of previously made overpayments or underpayments) in advance or by way of reimbursement, and in such installments, as the Commissioner may determine.

SUITS BY THE ATTORNEY GENERAL

Sec. 407. (a) Whenever the Attorney General receives a complaint in writing—

(1) signed by a parent or group of parents to the effect that his or their minor children, as members of a class of persons similarly situated, are being deprived by a school board of the equal protection of the laws, or

(2) signed by an individual, or his parent, to the effect that he has been denied admission to or not permitted to continue in attendance at a public college by reason of race, color, religion, or national origin,

and the Attorney General believes the complaint is meritorious and certifies that the signer or signers of such complaint are unable, in his judgment, to initiate and maintain appropriate legal proceedings for relief and that the institution of an action will materially further the orderly achievement of desegregation in public education, the Attorney General is authorized, after giving notice of such complaint to the appropriate school board or college authority and after certifying that he is satisfied that such board or authority has had a reasonable time to adjust the conditions alleged in such complaint, to institute for or in the name of the United States a civil action in any appropriate district court of the United States against such parties and for such relief as may be appropriate, and such court shall have and shall exercise jurisdiction of proceedings instituted pursuant to this section, provided that nothing herein shall empower any official or court of the United States to issue any order seeking to achieve a racial balance in any school by requiring the transportation of pupils or students from one school to another or one school district to another in order to achieve such racial balance, or otherwise enlarge the existing power of the court to insure compliance with constitutional standards. The Attorney General may implead as defendants such additional parties as are or become necessary to the grant of effective relief hereunder.

(b) The Attorney General may deem a person or persons unable to initiate and maintain appropriate legal proceedings within the meaning of subsection (a) of this section when such person or persons are unable, either directly or through other interested persons or organizations, to bear the expense of the litigation or to obtain effective legal representation; or whenever he is satisfied that the institution of such litigation would jeopardize the personal safety, employment, or economic standing of such person or persons, their families, or their property.

(c) The term "parent" as used in this section includes any person standing in loco parentis. A "complaint" as used in this section is a writing or document within the meaning of section 1001, title 18, United States Code.

Sec. 408. In any action or proceeding under this title the United States shall be liable for costs the same as a private person.

Sec. 409. Nothing in this title shall affect adversely the right of any person to sue for or obtain relief in any court against discrimination in public education.

Sec. 410. Nothing in this title shall prohibit classification and assignment for reasons other than race, color, religion, or national origin.

TITLE V—COMMISSION ON CIVIL RIGHTS

Sec. 501. Section 102 of the Civil Rights Act of 1957 (42 U.S.C. 1975a; 71 Stat. 634) [56] is amended to read as follows:

"RULES OF PROCEDURE OF THE COMMISSION HEARINGS

"Sec. 102. (a) At least thirty days prior to the commencement of any hearing, the Commission shall cause to be published in the Fed-

---

56. 42 U.S.C.A. § 1975a.

eral Register notice of the date on which such hearing is to commence, the place at which it is to be held and the subject of the hearing. The Chairman, or one designated by him to act as Chairman at a hearing of the Commission, shall announce in an opening statement the subject of the hearing.

"(b) A copy of the Commission's rules shall be made available to any witness before the Commission, and a witness compelled to appear before the Commission or required to produce written or other matter shall be served with a copy of the Commission's rules at the time of service of the subpena.

"(c) Any person compelled to appear in person before the Commission shall be accorded the right to be accompanied and advised by counsel, who shall have the right to subject his client to reasonable examination, and to make objections on the record and to argue briefly the basis for such objections. The Commission shall proceed with reasonable dispatch to conclude any hearing in which it is engaged. Due regard shall be had for the convenience and necessity of witnesses.

"(d) The Chairman or Acting Chairman may punish breaches of order and decorum by censure and exclusion from the hearings.

"(e) If the Commission determines that evidence or testimony at any hearing may tend to defame, degrade, or incriminate any person, it shall receive such evidence or testimony or summary of such evidence or testimony in executive session. The Commission shall afford any person defamed, degraded, or incriminated by such evidence or testimony an opportunity to appear and be heard in executive session, with a reasonable number of additional witnesses requested by him, before deciding to use such evidence or testimony. In the event the Commission determines to release or use such evidence or testimony in such manner as to reveal publicly the identity of the person defamed, degraded, or incriminated, such evidence or testimony, prior to such public release or use, shall be given at a public session, and the Commission shall afford such person an opportunity to appear as a voluntary witness or to file a sworn statement in his behalf and to submit brief and pertinent sworn statements of others. The Commission shall receive and dispose of requests from such person to subpena additional witnesses.

"(f) Except as provided in sections 102 and 105(f) of this Act, the Chairman shall receive and the Commission shall dispose of requests to subpena additional witnesses.

"(g) No evidence or testimony or summary of evidence or testimony taken in executive session may be released or used in public sessions without the consent of the Commission. Whoever releases or uses in public without the consent of the Commission such evidence or testimony taken in executive session shall be fined not more than $1,000, or imprisoned for not more than one year.

"(h) In the discretion of the Commission, witnesses may submit brief and pertinent sworn statements in writing for inclusion in the record. The Commission shall determine the pertinency of testimony and evidence adduced at its hearings.

"(i) Every person who submits data or evidence shall be entitled to retain or, on payment of lawfully prescribed costs, procure a copy or transcript thereof, except that a witness in a hearing held in executive session may for good cause be limited to inspection of the official transcript of his testimony. Transcript copies of public sessions may be obtained by the public upon the payment of the cost thereof. An accurate transcript shall be made of the testimony of all witnesses at all hearings, either public or executive sessions, of the Commission or of any subcommittee thereof.

"(j) A witness attending any session of the Commission shall receive $6 for each day's attendance and for the time necessarily occupied in going to and returning from the same, and 10 cents per mile for going from and returning to his place of residence. Witnesses who attend at points so far removed from their respective residences as to prohibit return thereto from day to day shall be entitled to an additional allowance of $10 per day for expenses of subsistence, including the time necessarily occupied in going to and returning from the place of attendance. Mileage payments shall be tendered to the witness upon service of a subpena issued on behalf of the Commission or any subcommittee thereof.

"(k) The Commission shall not issue any subpena for the attendance and testimony of witnesses or for the production of written or other matter which would require the presence of the party subpenaed at a hearing to be held outside of the State wherein the witness is found or resides or is domiciled or transacts business, or has appointed an agent for receipt of service of process except that, in any event, the Commission may issue subpenas for the attendance and testimony of witnesses and the production of written or other matter at a hearing held within fifty miles of the place where the witness is found or resides or is domiciled or transacts business or has appointed an agent for receipt of service of process.

"(l) The Commission shall separately state and currently publish in the Federal Register (1) descriptions of its central and field organization including the established places at which, and methods whereby, the public may secure information or make requests; (2) statements of the general course and method by which its functions are channeled and determined, and (3) rules adopted as authorized by law. No person shall in any manner be subject to or required to resort to rules, organization, or procedure not so published."

Sec. 502. Section 103(a) of the Civil Rights Act of 1957 (42 U.S.C. 1975b(a); 71 Stat. 634) [57] is amended to read as follows:

"Sec. 103. (a) Each member of the Commission who is not otherwise in the service of the Government of the United States shall receive the sum of $75 per day for each day spent in the work of the Commission, shall be paid actual travel expenses, and per diem in lieu of subsistence expenses when away from his usual place of residence, in accordance with section 5 of the Administrative Expenses Act of 1946, as amended (5 U.S.C. 73b–2; 60 Stat. 808)."

---

57. 42 U.S.C.A. § 1975b(a).

Sec. 503.   Section 103(b) of the Civil Rights Act of 1957 (42 U.S.C. 1975b(b); 71 Stat. 634)[58] is amended to read as follows:

"(b) Each member of the Commission who is otherwise in the service of the Government of the United States shall serve without compensation in addition to that received for such other service, but while engaged in the work of the Commission shall be paid actual travel expenses, and per diem in lieu of subsistence expenses when away from his usual place of residence, in accordance with the provisions of the Travel Expenses Act of 1949, as amended (5 U.S.C. 835–42; 63 Stat. 166)."

Sec. 504.   (a) Section 104(a) of the Civil Rights Act of 1957 (42 U.S.C. 1975c(a); 71 Stat. 635), as amended,[59] is further amended to read as follows:

"DUTIES OF THE COMMISSION

"Sec. 104.   (a) The Commission shall—

"(1) investigate allegations in writing under oath or affirmation that certain citizens of the United States are being deprived of their right to vote and have that vote counted by reason of their color, race, religion, or national origin; which writing, under oath or affirmation, shall set forth the facts upon which such belief or beliefs are based;

"(2) study and collect information concerning legal developments constituting a denial of equal protection of the laws under the Constitution because of race, color, religion or national origin or in the administration of justice;

"(3) appraise the laws and policies of the Federal Government with respect to denials of equal protection of the laws under the Constitution because of race, color, religion or national origin or in the administration of justice;

"(4) serve as a national clearinghouse for information in respect to denials of equal protection of the laws because of race, color, religion or national origin, including but not limited to the fields of voting, education, housing, employment, the use of public facilities, and transportation, or in the administration of justice;

"(5) investigate allegations, made in writing and under oath or affirmation, that citizens of the United States are unlawfully being accorded or denied the right to vote, or to have their votes properly counted, in any election of presidential electors, Members of the United States Senate, or of the House of Representatives, as a result of any patterns or practice of fraud or discrimination in the conduct of such election; and

"(6) Nothing in this or any other Act shall be construed as authorizing the Commission, its Advisory Committees, or any person under its supervision or control to inquire into or investigate any membership practices or internal operations of any fraternal organization, any college or university fraternity or sorority, any private club or any religious organization."

58.   42 U.S.C.A. § 1975b(b).
59.   42 U.S.C.A. § 1975c(a).

(b) Section 104(b) of the Civil Rights Act of 1957 (42 U.S.C. 1975c(b); 71 Stat. 635), as amended,[60] is further amended by striking out the present subsection "(b)" and by substituting therefor:

"(b) The Commission shall submit interim reports to the President and to the Congress at such times as the Commission, the Congress or the President shall deem desirable, and shall submit to the President and to the Congress a final report of its activities, findings, and recommendations not later than January 31, 1968."

Sec. 505. Section 105(a) of the Civil Rights Act of 1957 (42 U.S.C. 1975d(a); 71 Stat. 636)[61] is amended by striking out in the last sentence thereof "$50 per diem" and inserting in lieu thereof "$75 per diem."

Sec. 506. Section 105(f) and section 105(g) of the Civil Rights Act of 1957 (42 U.S.C. 1975d(f) and (g); 71 Stat. 636)[62] are amended to read as follows:

"(f) The Commission, or on the authorization of the Commission any subcommittee of two or more members, at least one of whom shall be of each major political party, may, for the purpose of carrying out the provisions of this Act, hold such hearings and act at such times and places as the Commission or such authorized subcommittee may deem advisable. Subpenas for the attendance and testimony of witnesses or the production of written or other matter may be issued in accordance with the rules of the Commission as contained in section 102(j) and (k) of this Act, over the signature of the Chairman of the Commission or of such subcommittee, and may be served by any person designated by such Chairman. The holding of hearings by the Commission, or the appointment of a subcommittee to hold hearings pursuant to this subparagraph, must be approved by a majority of the Commission, or by a majority of the members present at a meeting at which at least a quorum of four members is present.

"(g) In case of contumacy or refusal to obey a subpena, any district court of the United States or the United States court of any territory or possession, or the District Court of the United States for the District of Columbia, within the jurisdiction of which the inquiry is carried on or within the jurisdiction of which said person guilty of contumacy or refusal to obey is found or resides or is domiciled or transacts business, or has appointed an agent for receipt of service of process, upon application by the Attorney General of the United States shall have jurisdiction to issue to such person an order requiring such person to appear before the Commission or a subcommittee thereof, there to produce pertinent, relevant and nonprivileged evidence if so ordered, or there to give testimony touching the matter under investigation; and any failure to obey such order of the court may be punished by said court as a contempt thereof."

Sec. 507. Section 105 of the Civil Rights Act of 1957 (42 U.S.C. 1975d; 71 Stat. 636), as amended by section 401 of the Civil Rights

60. 42 U.S.C.A. § 1975c(b).
61. 42 U.S.C.A. § 1975d(a).
62. 42 U.S.C.A. § 1975d(f), (g).

Act of 1960 (42 U.S.C. 1975d(h); 74 Stat. 89),[63] is further amended by adding a new subsection at the end to read as follows:

"(i) The Commission shall have the power to make such rules and regulations as are necessary to carry out the purposes of this Act."

TITLE VI—NONDISCRIMINATION IN FEDERALLY ASSISTED PROGRAMS

Sec. 601. No person in the United States shall, on the ground of race, color, or national origin, be excluded from participation in, be denied the benefits of, or be subjected to discrimination under any program or activity receiving Federal financial assistance.

Sec. 602. Each Federal department and agency which is empowered to extend Federal financial assistance to any program or activity, by way of grant, loan, or contract other than a contract of insurance or guaranty, is authorized and directed to effectuate the provisions of section 601 with respect to such program or activity by issuing rules, regulations, or orders of general applicability which shall be consistent with achievement of the objectives of the statute authorizing the financial assistance in connection with which the action is taken. No such rule, regulation, or order shall become effective unless and until approved by the President. Compliance with any requirement adopted pursuant to this section may be effected (1) by the termination of or refusal to grant or to continue assistance under such program or activity to any recipient as to whom there has been an express finding on the record, after opportunity for hearing, of a failure to comply with such requirement, but such termination or refusal shall be limited to the particular political entity, or part thereof, or other recipient as to whom such a finding has been made and, shall be limited in its effect to the particular program, or part thereof, in which such noncompliance has been so found, or (2) by any other means authorized by law: *Provided, however,* That no such action shall be taken until the department or agency concerned has advised the appropriate person or persons of the failure to comply with the requirement and has determined that compliance cannot be secured by voluntary means. In the case of any action terminating, or refusing to grant or continue, assistance because of failure to comply with a requirement imposed pursuant to this section, the head of the Federal department or agency shall file with the committees of the House and Senate having legislative jurisdiction over the program or activity involved a full written report of the circumstances and the grounds for such action. No such action shall become effective until thirty days have elapsed after the filing of such report.

Sec. 603. Any department or agency action taken pursuant to section 602 shall be subject to such judicial review as may otherwise be provided by law for similar action taken by such department or agency on other grounds. In the case of action, not otherwise subject to judicial review, terminating or refusing to grant or to continue financial assistance upon a finding of failure to comply with any requirement imposed pursuant to section 602, any person aggrieved

---

63. 42 U.S.C.A. § 1975d(h).

(including any State or political subdivision thereof and any agency of either) may obtain judicial review of such action in accordance with section 10 of the Administrative Procedure Act, and such action shall not be deemed committed to unreviewable agency discretion within the meaning of that section.

Sec. 604.   Nothing contained in this title shall be construed to authorize action under this title by any department or agency with respect to any employment practice of any employer, employment agency, or labor organization except where a primary objective of the Federal financial assistance is to provide employment.

Sec. 605.   Nothing in this title shall add to or detract from any existing authority with respect to any program or activity under which Federal financial assistance is extended by way of a contract of insurance or guaranty.

TITLE VII—EQUAL EMPLOYMENT OPPORTUNITY

DEFINITIONS

Sec. 701.   For the purposes of this title—

(a) The term "person" includes one or more individuals, labor unions, partnerships, associations, corporations, legal representatives, mutual companies, joint-stock companies, trusts, unincorporated organizations, trustees, trustees in bankruptcy, or receivers.

(b) The term "employer" means a person engaged in an industry affecting commerce who has twenty-five or more employees for each working day in each of twenty or more calendar weeks in the current or preceding calendar year, and any agent of such a person, but such term does not include (1) the United States, a corporation wholly owned by the Government of the United States, an Indian tribe, or a State or political subdivision thereof, (2) a bona fide private membership club (other than a labor organization) which is exempt from taxation under section 501(c) of the Internal Revenue Code of 1954: *Provided*, That during the first year after the effective date prescribed in subsection (a) of section 716, persons having fewer than one hundred employees (and their agents) shall not be considered employers, and, during the second year after such date, persons having fewer than seventy-five employees (and their agents) shall not be considered employers, and, during the third year after such date, persons having fewer than fifty employees (and their agents) shall not be considered employers: *Provided further*, That it shall be the policy of the United States to insure equal employment opportunities for Federal employees without discrimination because of race, color, religion, sex or national origin and the President shall utilize his existing authority to effectuate this policy.

(c) The term "employment agency" means any person regularly undertaking with or without compensation to procure employees for an employer or to procure for employees opportunities to work for an employer and includes an agent of such a person; but shall not include an agency of the United States, or an agency of a State or political subdivision of a State, except that such term shall include the United States Employment Service and the system of State and local employment services receiving Federal assistance.

(d) The term "labor organization" means a labor organization engaged in an industry affecting commerce, and any agent of such an organization, and includes any organization of any kind, any agency, or employee representation committee, group, association, or plan so engaged in which employees participate and which exists for the purpose, in whole or in part, of dealing with employers concerning grievances, labor disputes, wages, rates of pay, hours, or other terms or conditions of employment, and any conference, general committee, joint or system board, or joint council so engaged which is subordinate to a national or international labor organization.

(e) A labor organization shall be deemed to be engaged in an industry affecting commerce if (1) it maintains or operates a hiring hall or hiring office which procures employees for an employer or procures for employees opportunities to work for an employer, or (2) the number of its members (or, where it is a labor organization composed of other labor organizations or their representatives, if the aggregate number of the members of such other labor organization) is (A) one hundred or more during the first year after the effective date prescribed in subsection (a) of section 716, (B) seventy-five or more during the second year after such date or fifty or more during the third year, or (C) twenty-five or more thereafter, and such labor organization—

> (1) is the certified representative of employees under the provisions of the National Labor Relations Act, as amended, or the Railway Labor Act, as amended;
>
> (2) although not certified, is a national or international labor organization or a local labor organization recognized or acting as the representative of employees of an employer or employers engaged in an industry affecting commerce; or
>
> (3) has chartered a local labor organization or subsidiary body which is representing or actively seeking to represent employees of employers within the meaning of paragraph (1) or (2); or
>
> (4) has been chartered by a labor organization representing or actively seeking to represent employees within the meaning of paragraph (1) or (2) as the local or subordinate body through which such employees may enjoy membership or become affiliated with such labor organization; or
>
> (5) is a conference, general committee, joint or system board, or joint council subordinate to a national or international labor organization, which includes a labor organization engaged in an industry affecting commerce within the meaning of any of the preceding paragraphs of this subsection.

(f) The term "employee" means an individual employed by an employer.

(g) The term "commerce" means trade, traffic, commerce, transportation, transmission, or communication among the several States; or between a State and any place outside thereof; or within the District of Columbia, or a possession of the United States; or between points in the same State but through a point outside thereof.

(h) The term "industry affecting commerce" means any activity, business, or industry in commerce or in which a labor dispute would hinder or obstruct commerce or the free flow of commerce and includes any activity or industry "affecting commerce" within the meaning of the Labor-Management Reporting and Disclosure Act of 1959.

(i) The term "State" includes a State of the United States, the District of Columbia, Puerto Rico, the Virgin Islands, American Samoa, Guam, Wake Island, the Canal Zone, and Outer Continental Shelf lands defined in the Outer Continental Shelf Lands Act.

EXEMPTION

Sec. 702. This title shall not apply to an employer with respect to the employment of aliens outside any State, or to a religious corporation, association, or society with respect to the employment of individuals of a particular religion to perform work connected with the carrying on by such corporation, association, or society of its religious activities or to an educational institution with respect to the employment of individuals to perform work connected with the educational activities of such institution.

DISCRIMINATION BECAUSE OF RACE, COLOR, RELIGION, SEX, OR NATIONAL ORIGIN

Sec. 703. (a) It shall be an unlawful employment practice for an employer—

(1) to fail or refuse to hire or to discharge any individual, or otherwise to discriminate against any individual with respect to his compensation, terms, conditions, or privileges of employment, because of such individual's race, color, religion, sex, or national origin; or

(2) to limit, segregate, or classify his employees in any way which would deprive or tend to deprive any individual of employment opportunities or otherwise adversely affect his status as an employee, because of such individual's race, color, religion, sex, or national origin.

(b) It shall be an unlawful employment practice for an employment agency to fail or refuse to refer for employment, or otherwise to discriminate against, any individual because of his race, color, religion, sex, or national origin, or to classify or refer for employment any individual on the basis of his race, color, religion, sex, or national origin.

(c) It shall be an unlawful employment practice for a labor organization—

(1) to exclude or to expel from its membership, or otherwise to discriminate against, any individual because of his race, color, religion, sex, or national origin;

(2) to limit, segregate, or classify its membership, or to classify or fail to refuse to refer for employment any individual, in any way which would deprive or tend to deprive any individual of employment opportunities, or would limit such employment opportunities or otherwise adversely affect his status as an em-

ployee or as an applicant for employment, because of such individual's race, color, religion, sex, or national origin; or

(3) to cause or attempt to cause an employer to discriminate against an individual in violation of this section.

(d) It shall be an unlawful employment practice for any employer, labor organization, or joint labor-management committee controlling apprenticeship or other training or retraining, including on-the-job training programs to discriminate against any individual because of his race, color, religion, sex, or national origin in admission to, or employment in, any program established to provide apprenticeship or other training.

(e) Notwithstanding any other provision of this title, (1) it shall not be an unlawful employment practice for an employer to hire and employ employees, for an employment agency to classify, or refer for employment any individual, for a labor organization to classify its membership or to classify or refer for employment any individual, or for an employer, labor organization, or joint labor-management committee controlling apprenticeship or other training or retraining programs to admit or employ any individual in any such program, on the basis of his religion, sex, or national origin in those certain instances where religion, sex, or national origin is a bona fide occupational qualification reasonably necessary to the normal operation of that particular business or enterprise, and (2) it shall not be an unlawful employment practice for a school, college, university, or other educational institution or institution of learning to hire and employ employees of a particular religion if such school, college, university, or other educational institution or institution of learning is, in whole or in substantial part, owned, supported, controlled, or managed by a particular religion or by a particular religious corporation, association, or society, or if the curriculum of such school, college, university, or other educational institution or institution of learning is directed toward the propagation of a particular religion.

(f) As used in this title, the phrase "unlawful employment practice" shall not be deemed to include any action or measure taken by an employer, labor organization, joint labor-management committee, or employment agency with respect to an individual who is a member of the Communist Party of the United States or of any other organization required to register as a Communist-action or Communist-front organization by final order of the Subversive Activities Control Board pursuant to the Subversive Activities Control Act of 1950.

(g) Notwithstanding any other provision of this title, it shall not be an unlawful employment practice for an employer to fail or refuse to hire and employ any individual for any position, for an employer to discharge any individual from any position, or for an employment agency to fail or refuse to refer any individual for employment in any position, or for a labor organization to fail or refuse to refer any individual for employment in any position, if—

(1) the occupancy of such position, or access to the premises in or upon which any part of the duties of such position is performed or is to be performed, is subject to any requirement im-

posed in the interest of the national security of the United States under any security program in effect pursuant to or administered under any statute of the United States or any Executive order of the President; and

(2) such individual has not fulfilled or has ceased to fulfill that requirement.

(h) Notwithstanding any other provision of this title, it shall not be an unlawful employment practice for an employer to apply different standards of compensation, or different terms, conditions, or privileges of employment pursuant to a bona fide seniority or merit system, or a system which measures earnings by quantity or quality of production or to employees who work in different locations, provided that such differences are not the result of an intention to discriminate because of race, color, religion, sex, or national origin, nor shall it be an unlawful employment practice for an employer to give and to act upon the results of any professionally developed ability test provided that such test, its administration or action upon the results is not designed, intended or used to discriminate because of race, color, religion, sex or national origin. It shall not be an unlawful employment practice under this title for any employer to differentiate upon the basis of sex in determining the amount of the wages or compensation paid or to be paid to employees of such employer if such differentiation is authorized by the provisions of section 6(d) of the Fair Labor Standards Act of 1938, as amended (29 U.S.C. 206(d)).[64]

(i) Nothing contained in this title shall apply to any business or enterprise on or near an Indian reservation with respect to any publicly announced employment practice of such business or enterprise under which a preferential treatment is given to any individual because he is an Indian living on or near a reservation.

(j) Nothing contained in this title shall be interpreted to require any employer, employment agency, labor organization, or joint labor-management committee subject to this title to grant preferential treatment to any individual or to any group because of the race, color, religion, sex, or national origin of such individual or group on account of an imbalance which may exist with respect to the total number or percentage of persons of any race, color, religion, sex, or national origin employed by any employer, referred or classified for employment by any employment agency or labor organization, admitted to membership or classified by any labor organization, or admitted to, or employed in, any apprenticeship or other training program, in comparison with the total number or percentage of persons of such race, color, religion, sex, or national origin in any community, State, section, or other area, or in the available work force in any community, State, section, or other area.

OTHER UNLAWFUL EMPLOYMENT PRACTICES

Sec. 704. (a) It shall be an unlawful employment practice for an employer to discriminate against any of his employees or appli-

64. 29 U.S.C.A. § 206(d).

cants for employment, for an employment agency to discriminate against any individual, or for a labor organization to discriminate against any member thereof or applicant for membership, because he has opposed any practice made an unlawful employment practice by this title, or because he has made a charge, testified, assisted, or participated in any manner in an investigation, proceeding, or hearing under this title.

(b) It shall be an unlawful employment practice for an employer, labor organization, or employment agency to print or publish or cause to be printed or published any notice or advertisement relating to employment by such an employer or membership in or any classification or referral for employment by such a labor organization, or relating to any classification or referral for employment by such an employment agency, indicating any preference, limitation, specification, or discrimination, based on race, color, religion, sex, or national origin, except that such a notice or advertisement may indicate a preference, limitation, specification, or discrimination based on religion, sex, or national origin when religion, sex, or national origin is a bona fide occupational qualification for employment.

EQUAL EMPLOYMENT OPPORTUNITY COMMISSION

Sec. 705.   (a) There is hereby created a Commission to be known as the Equal Employment Opportunity Commission, which shall be composed of five members, not more than three of whom shall be members of the same political party, who shall be appointed by the President by and with the advice and consent of the Senate. One of the original members shall be appointed for a term of one year, one for a term of two years, one for a term of three years, one for a term of four years, and one for a term of five years, beginning from the date of enactment of this title, but their successors shall be appointed for terms of five years each, except that any individual chosen to fill a vacancy shall be appointed only for the unexpired term of the member whom he shall succeed. The President shall designate one member to serve as Chairman of the Commission, and one member to serve as Vice Chairman. The Chairman shall be responsible on behalf of the Commission for the administrative operations of the Commission, and shall appoint, in accordance with the civil service laws, such officers, agents, attorneys, and employees as it deems necessary to assist it in the performance of its functions and to fix their compensation in accordance with the Classification Act of 1949, as amended. The Vice Chairman shall act as Chairman in the absence or disability of the Chairman or in the event of a vacancy in that office.

(b) A vacancy in the Commission shall not impair the right of the remaining members to exercise all the powers of the Commission and three members thereof shall constitute a quorum.

(c) The Commission shall have an official seal which shall be judicially noticed.

(d) The Commission shall at the close of each fiscal year report to the Congress and to the President concerning the action it has taken; the names, salaries, and duties of all individuals in its employ and the moneys it has disbursed; and shall make such further reports on the cause of and means of eliminating discrimination and such recommendations for further legislation as may appear desirable.

(e) The Federal Executive Pay Act of 1956, as amended (5 U.S.C. 2201–2209),[65] is further amended—

(1) by adding to section 105 thereof (5 U.S.C. 2204) the following clause:

"(32) Chairman, Equal Employment Opportunity Commission"; and

(2) by adding to clause (45) of section 106(a) thereof (5 U.S.C. 2205(a)) the following: "Equal Employment Opportunity Commission (4)."

(f) The principal office of the Commission shall be in or near the District of Columbia, but it may meet or exercise any or all its powers at any other place. The Commission may establish such regional or State offices as it deems necessary to accomplish the purpose of this title.

(g) The Commission shall have power—

(1) to cooperate with and, with their consent, utilize regional State, local, and other agencies, both public and private, and individuals;

(2) to pay to witnesses whose depositions are taken or who are summoned before the Commission or any of its agents the same witness and mileage fees as are paid to witnesses in the courts of the United States;

(3) to furnish to persons subject to this title such technical assistance as they may request to further their compliance with this title or an order issued thereunder;

(4) upon the request of (i) any employer, whose employees or some of them, or (ii) any labor organization, whose members or some of them, refuse or threaten to refuse to cooperate in effectuating the provisions of this title, to assist in such effectuation by conciliation or such other remedial action as is provided by this title;

(5) to make such technical studies as are appropriate to effectuate the purposes and policies of this title and to make the results of such studies available to the public;

(6) to refer matters to the Attorney General with recommendations for intervention in a civil action brought by an aggrieved party under section 706, or for the institution of a civil action by the Attorney General under section 707, and to advise, consult, and assist the Attorney General on such matters.

(h) Attorneys appointed under this section may, at the direction of the Commission, appear for and represent the Commission in any case in court.

(i) The Commission shall, in any of its educational or promotional activities, cooperate with other departments and agencies in the performance of such educational and promotional activities.

65.   5 U.S.C.A. § 2201 et seq.

(j) All officers, agents, attorneys, and employees of the Commission shall be subject to the provisions of section 9 of the Act of August 2, 1939, as amended (the Hatch Act), notwithstanding any exemption contained in such section.

PREVENTION OF UNLAWFUL EMPLOYMENT PRACTICES

Sec. 706. (a) Whenever it is charged in writing under oath by a person claiming to be aggrieved, or a written charge has been filed by a member of the Commission where he has reasonable cause to believe a violation of this title has occurred (and such charge sets forth the facts upon which it is based) that an employer, employment agency, or labor organization has engaged in an unlawful employment practice, the Commission shall furnish such employer, employment agency, or labor organization (hereinafter referred to as the "respondent") with a copy of such charge and shall make an investigation of such charge, provided that such charge shall not be made public by the Commission. If the Commission shall determine, after such investigation, that there is reasonable cause to believe that the charge is true, the Commission shall endeavor to eliminate any such alleged unlawful employment practice by informal methods of conference, conciliation, and persuasion. Nothing said or done during and as a part of such endeavors may be made public by the Commission without the written consent of the parties, or used as evidence in a subsequent proceeding. Any officer or employee of the Commission, who shall make public in any manner whatever any information in violation of this subsection shall be deemed guilty of a misdemeanor and upon conviction thereof shall be fined not more than $1,000 or imprisoned not more than one year.

(b) In the case of an alleged unlawful employment practice occurring in a State, or political subdivision of a State, which has a State or local law prohibiting the unlawful employment practice alleged and establishing or authorizing a State or local authority to grant or seek relief from such practice or to institute criminal proceedings with respect thereto upon receiving notice thereof, no charge may be filed under subsection (a) by the person aggrieved before the expiration of sixty days after proceedings have been commenced under the State or local law, unless such proceedings have been earlier terminated, provided that such sixty-day period shall be extended to one hundred and twenty days during the first year after the effective date of such State or local law. If any requirement for the commencement of such proceedings is imposed by a State or local authority other than a requirement of the filing of a written and signed statement of the facts upon which the proceeding is based, the proceeding shall be deemed to have been commenced for the purposes of this subsection at the time such statement is sent by registered mail to the appropriate State or local authority.

(c) In the case of any charge filed by a member of the Commission alleging an unlawful employment practice occurring in a State or political subdivision of a State, which has a State or local law prohibiting the practice alleged and establishing or authorizing a State or local authority to grant or seek relief from such practice or to institute criminal proceedings with respect thereto upon receiving notice thereof, the Commission shall, before taking any action with respect to such charge, notify the appropriate State or local officials and, upon request, afford them a reasonable time, but not less than sixty days (provided that such sixty-day period shall be extended to one hundred and twenty days during the first year after the effective day of such State or local law), unless a shorter period is requested, to act under such State or local law to remedy the practice alleged.

(d) A charge under subsection (a) shall be filed within ninety days after the alleged unlawful employment practice occurred, except that in the case of an unlawful employment practice with respect to which the person aggrieved has followed the procedure set out in subsection (b), such charge shall be filed by the person aggrieved within two hundred and ten days after the alleged unlawful employment practice occurred, or within thirty days after receiving notice that the State or local agency has terminated the proceedings under the State or local law, whichever is earlier, and a copy of such charge shall be filed by the Commission with the State or local agency.

(e) If within thirty days after a charge is filed with the Commission or within thirty days after expiration of any period of reference under subsection (c) (except that in either case such period may be extended to not more than sixty days upon a determination by the Commission that further efforts to secure voluntary compliance are warranted), the Commission has been unable to obtain voluntary compliance with this title, the Commission shall so notify the person aggrieved and a civil action may, within thirty days thereafter, be brought against the respondent named in the charge (1) by the person claiming to be aggrieved, or (2) if such charge was filed by a member of the Commission, by any person whom the charge alleges was aggrieved by the alleged unlawful employment practice. Upon application by the complainant and in such circumstances as the court may deem just, the court may appoint an attorney for such complainant and may authorize the commencement of the action without the payment of fees, costs, or security. Upon timely application, the court may, in its discretion, permit the Attorney General to intervene in such civil action if he certifies that the case is of general public importance. Upon request, the court may, in its discretion, stay further proceedings for not more than sixty days pending the termination of State or local proceedings described in subsection (b) or the efforts of the Commission to obtain voluntary compliance.

(f) Each United States district court and each United States court of a place subject to the jurisdiction of the United States shall have jurisdiction of actions brought under this title. Such an action may be brought in any judicial district in the State in which the unlawful employment practice is alleged to have been committed, in the judicial district in which the employment records relevant to such practice are maintained and administered, or in the judicial district in which the plaintiff would have worked but for the alleged unlawful employment practice, but if the respondent is not found within any such district, such an action may be brought within the judicial district in which the respondent has his principal office. For purposes of sections 1404 and 1406 of title 28 of the United States Code, the judicial district in which the respondent has his principal office shall in all cases be considered a district in which the action might have been brought.

(g) If the court finds that the respondent has intentionally engaged in or is intentionally engaging in an unlawful employment practice charged in the complaint, the court may enjoin the respondent from engaging in such unlawful employment practice, and order such affirmative action as may be appropriate, which may include reinstatement or hiring of employees, with or without back pay (payable by the employer, employment agency, or labor organization, as the case may be, responsible for the unlawful employment practice). Interim earnings or amounts earnable with reasonable diligence by the person or persons discriminated against shall operate to reduce the back pay otherwise allowable. No order of the court shall require the admission or reinstatement of an individual as a member of a union or the hiring, reinstatement, or promotion of an individual as an employee, or the payment to him of any back pay, if such individual was refused admission, suspended, or expelled or was refused employment or advancement or was suspended or discharged for any reason other than discrimination on account of race, color, religion, sex or national origin or in violation of section 704(a).

(h) The provisions of the Act entitled "An Act to amend the Judicial Code and to define and limit the jurisdiction of courts sitting in equity, and for other purposes," approved March 23, 1932 (29 U.S.C. 101–115), shall not apply with respect to civil actions brought under this section.

(i) In any case in which an employer, employment agency, or labor organization fails to comply with an order of a court issued in a civil action brought under subsection (e), the Commission may commence proceedings to compel compliance with such order.

(j) Any civil action brought under subsection (e) and any proceedings brought under subsection (i) shall be subject to appeal as provided in sections 1291 and 1292, title 28, United States Code.

(k) In any action or proceeding under this title the court, in its discretion, may allow the prevailing party, other than the Commission or the United States, a reasonable attorney's fee as part of the costs, and the Commission and the United States shall be liable for costs the same as a private person.

Sec. 707. (a) Whenever the Attorney General has reasonable cause to believe that any person or group of persons is engaged in a pattern or practice of resistance to the full enjoyment of any of the rights secured by this title, and that the pattern or practice is of such a nature and is intended to deny the full exercise of the rights herein described, the Attorney General may bring a civil action in the appropriate district court of the United States by filing with it a complaint (1) signed by him (or in his absence the Acting Attorney General), (2) setting forth facts pertaining to such pattern or practice, and (3) requesting such relief, including an application for a permanent or temporary injunction, restraining order or other order against the person or persons responsible for such pattern or practice, as he deems necessary to insure the full enjoyment of the rights herein described.

(b) The district courts of the United States shall have and shall exercise jurisdiction of proceedings instituted pursuant to this section, and in any such proceeding the Attorney General may file with the clerk of such court a request that a court of three judges be convened to hear and determine the case. Such request by the Attorney General shall be accompanied by a certificate that, in his opinion, the case is of general public importance. A copy of the certificate and request for a three-judge court shall be immediately furnished by such clerk to the chief judge of the circuit (or in his absence, the presiding circuit judge of the circuit) in which the case is pending. Upon receipt of such request it shall be the duty of the chief judge of the circuit or the presiding circuit judge, as the case may be, to designate immediately three judges in such circuit, of whom at least one shall be a circuit judge and another of whom shall be a district judge of the court in which the proceeding was instituted, to hear and determine such case, and it shall be the duty of the judges so designated to assign the case for hearing at the earliest practicable date, to participate in the hearing and determination thereof, and to cause the case to be in every way expedited. An appeal from the final judgment of such court will lie to the Supreme Court.

In the event the Attorney General fails to file such a request in any such proceeding, it shall be the duty of the chief judge of the district (or in his absence, the acting chief judge) in which the case is pending immediately to designate a judge in such district to hear and determine the case. In the event that no judge in the district is available to hear and determine the case, the chief judge of the district, or the acting chief judge, as the case may be, shall certify this fact to the chief judge of the circuit (or in his absence, the acting chief judge) who shall then designate a district or circuit judge of the circuit to hear and determine the case.

It shall be the duty of the judge designated pursuant to this section to assign the case for hearing at the earliest practicable date and to cause the case to be in every way expedited.

EFFECT ON STATE LAWS

Sec. 708. Nothing in this title shall be deemed to exempt or relieve any person from any liability, duty, penalty, or punishment provided by any present or future law of any State or political subdivision of a State, other than any such law which purports to require or permit the doing of any act which would be an unlawful employment practice under this title.

INVESTIGATIONS, INSPECTIONS, RECORDS, STATE AGENCIES

Sec. 709. (a) In connection with any investigation of a charge filed under section 706, the Commission or its designated representative shall at all reasonable times have access to, for the purposes of examination, and the right to copy any evidence of any person being investigated or proceeded against that relates to unlawful employment practices covered by this title and is relevant to the charge under investigation.

(b) The Commission may cooperate with State and local agencies charged with the administration of State fair employment practices laws and, with the consent of such agencies, may for the purpose of carrying out its functions and duties under this title and within the limitation of funds appropriated specifically for such purpose, utilize the services of such agencies and their employees and, notwithstanding any other provision of law, may reimburse such agencies and their employees for services rendered to assist the Commission in carrying out this title. In furtherance of such cooperative efforts, the Commission may enter into written agreements with such State or local agencies and such agreements may include provisions under which the Commission shall refrain from processing a charge in any cases or class of cases specified in such agreements and under which no person may bring a civil action under section 706 in any cases or class of cases so specified, or under which the Commission shall relieve any person or class of persons in such State or locality from requirements imposed under this section. The Commission shall rescind any such agreement whenever it determines that the agreement no longer serves the interest of effective enforcement of this title.

(c) Except as provided in subsection (d), every employer, employment agency, and labor organization subject to this title shall (1) make and keep such records relevant to the determinations of whether unlawful employment practices have been or are being committed, (2) preserve such records for such periods, and (3) make such reports therefrom, as the Commission shall prescribe by regulation or order, after public hearing, as reasonable, necessary, or appropriate for the enforcement of this title or the regulations or orders thereunder. The Commission shall, by regulation, require each employer, labor organization, and joint labor-management committee subject to this title which controls an apprenticeship or other training program to maintain such records as are reasonably necessary to carry out the purpose of this title, including, but not limited to, a list of applicants who wish to participate in such program, including the chronological order in which such applications were received, and shall furnish to the Commission, upon request, a detailed description of the manner in which persons are selected to participate in the apprenticeship or other training program. Any employer, employment agency, labor organization, or joint labor-management committee which believes that the application to it of any regulation or order issued under this section would result in undue hardship may (1) apply to the Commission for an exemption from the application of such regulation or order, or (2) bring a civil action in the United States district court for the district where such records are kept. If the Commission or the court, as the case may be, finds that the application of the regulation or order to the employer, employment agency, or labor organization in question would impose an undue hardship, the

Commission or the court, as the case may be, may grant appropriate relief.

(d) The provisions of subsection (c) shall not apply to any employer, employment agency, labor organization, or joint labor-management committee with respect to matters occurring in any State or political subdivision thereof which has a fair employment practice law during any period in which such employer, employment agency, labor organization, or joint labor-management committee is subject to such law, except that the Commission may require such notations on records which such employer, employment agency, labor organization, or joint labor-management committee keeps or is required to keep as are necessary because of differences in coverage or methods of enforcement between the State or local law and the provisions of this title. Where an employer is required by Executive Order 10925, issued March 6, 1961, or by any other Executive order prescribing fair employment practices for Government contractors and subcontractors, or by rules or regulations issued thereunder, to file reports relating to his employment practices with any Federal agency or committee, and he is substantially in compliance with such requirements, the Commission shall not require him to file additional reports pursuant to subsection (c) of this section.

(e) It shall be unlawful for any officer or employee of the Commission to make public in any manner whatever any information obtained by the Commission pursuant to its authority under this section prior to the institution of any proceeding under this title involving such information. Any officer or employee of the Commission who shall make public in any manner whatever any information in violation of this subsection shall be guilty of a misdemeanor and upon conviction thereof, shall be fined not more than $1,000, or imprisoned not more than one year.

INVESTIGATORY POWERS

Sec. 710. (a) For the purposes of any investigation of a charge filed under the authority contained in section 706, the Commission shall have authority to examine witnesses under oath and to require the production of documentary evidence relevant or material to the charge under investigation.

(b) If the respondent named in a charge filed under section 706 fails or refuses to comply with a demand of the Commission for permission to examine or to copy evidence in conformity with the provisions of section 709(a), or if any person required to comply with the provisions of section 709(c) or (d) fails or refuses to do so, or if any person fails or refuses to comply with a demand by the Commission to give testimony under oath, the United States district court for the district in which such person is found, resides, or transacts business, shall, upon application of the Commission, have jurisdiction to issue to such person an order requiring him to comply with the provisions of section 709(c) or (d) or to comply with the demand of the Commission, but the attendance of a witness may not be required outside the State where he is found, resides, or transacts

314

business and the production of evidence may not be required outside the State where such evidence is kept.

(c) Within twenty days after the service upon any person charged under section 706 of a demand by the Commission for the production of documentary evidence or for permission to examine or to copy evidence in conformity with the provisions of section 709(a), such person may file in the district court of the United States for the judicial district in which he resides, is found, or transacts business, and serve upon the Commission a petition for an order of such court modifying or setting aside such demand. The time allowed for compliance with the demand in whole or in part as deemed proper and ordered by the court shall not run during the pendency of such petition in the court. Such petition shall specify each ground upon which the petitioner relies in seeking such relief, and may be based upon any failure of such demand to comply with the provisions of this title or with the limitations generally applicable to compulsory process or upon any constitutional or other legal right or privilege of such person. No objection which is not raised by such a petition may be urged in the defense to a proceeding initiated by the Commission under subsection (b) for enforcement of such a demand unless such proceeding is commenced by the Commission prior to the expiration of the twenty-day period, or unless the court determines that the defendant could not reasonably have been aware of the availability of such ground of objection.

(d) In any proceeding brought by the Commission under subsection (b), except as provided in subsection (c) of this section, the defendant may petition the court for an order modifying or setting aside the demand of the Commission.

NOTICES TO BE POSTED

Sec. 711. (a) Every employer, employment agency, and labor organization, as the case may be, shall post and keep posted in conspicuous places upon its premises where notices to employees, applicants for employment, and members are customarily posted a notice to be prepared or approved by the Commission setting forth excerpts from or, summaries of, the pertinent provisions of this title and information pertinent to the filing of a complaint.

(b) A willful violation of this section shall be punishable by a fine of not more than $100 for each separate offense.

VETERANS' PREFERENCE

Sec. 712. Nothing contained in this title shall be construed to repeal or modify any Federal, State, territorial, or local law creating special rights or preference for veterans.

RULES AND REGULATIONS

Sec. 713. (a) The Commission shall have authority from time to time to issue, amend, or rescind suitable procedural regulations to carry out the provisions of this title. Regulations issued under this section shall be in conformity with the standards and limitations of the Administrative Procedure Act.

(b) In any action or proceeding based on any alleged unlawful employment practice, no person shall be subject to any liability or punishment for or on account of (1) the commission by such person of an unlawful employment practice if he pleads and proves that the act or omission complained of was in good faith, in conformity with, and in reliance on any written interpretation or opinion of the Commission, or (2) the failure of such person to publish and file any information required by any provision of this title if he pleads and proves that he failed to publish and file such information in good faith, in conformity with the instructions of the Commission issued under this title regarding the filing of such information. Such a defense, if established, shall be a bar to the action or proceeding, notwithstanding that (A) after such act or omission, such interpretation or opinion is modified or rescinded or is determined by judicial authority to be invalid or of no legal effect, or (B) after publishing or filing the description and annual reports, such publication or filing is determined by judicial authority not to be in conformity with the requirements of this title.

FORCIBLY RESISTING THE COMMISSION OR ITS REPRESENTATIVES

Sec. 714. The provisions of section 111, title 18, United States Code, shall apply to officers, agents, and employees of the Commission in the performance of their official duties.

SPECIAL STUDY BY SECRETARY OF LABOR

Sec. 715. The Secretary of Labor shall make a full and complete study of the factors which might tend to result in discrimination in employment because of age and of the consequences of such discrimination on the economy and individuals affected. The Secretary of Labor shall make a report to the Congress not later than June 30, 1965, containing the results of such study and shall include in such report such recommendations for legislation to prevent arbitrary discrimination in employment because of age as he determines advisable.

EFFECTIVE DATE

Sec. 716. (a) This title shall become effective one year after the date of its enactment.

(b) Notwithstanding subsection (a), sections of this title other than sections 703, 704, 706, and 707 shall become effective immediately.

(c) The President shall, as soon as feasible after the enactment of this title, convene one or more conferences for the purpose of enabling the leaders of groups whose members will be affected by this title to become familiar with the rights afforded and obligations imposed by its provisions, and for the purpose of making plans which will result in the fair and effective administration of this title when all of its provisions become effective. The President shall invite the participation in such conference or conferences of (1) the members of the President's Committee on Equal Employment Opportunity, (2) the members of the Commission on Civil Rights, (3) representatives of

State and local agencies engaged in furthering equal employment opportunity, (4) representatives of private agencies engaged in furthering equal employment opportunity, and (5) representatives of employers, labor organizations, and employment agencies who will be subject to this title.

TITLE VIII—REGISTRATION AND VOTING STATISTICS

Sec. 801.   The Secretary of Commerce shall promptly conduct a survey to compile registration and voting statistics in such geographic areas as may be recommended by the Commission on Civil Rights. Such a survey and compilation shall, to the extent recommended by the Commission on Civil Rights, only include a count of persons of voting age by race, color, and national origin, and determination of the extent to which such persons are registered to vote, and have voted in any statewide primary or general election in which the Members of the United States House of Representatives are nominated or elected, since January 1, 1960.   Such information shall also be collected and compiled in connection with the Nineteenth Decennial Census, and at such other times as the Congress may prescribe.   The provisions of section 9 and chapter 7 of title 13, United States Code, shall apply to any survey, collection, or compilation of registration and voting statistics carried out under this title: *Provided, however,* That no person shall be compelled to disclose his race, color, national origin, or questioned about his political party affiliation, how he voted, or the reasons therefore, nor shall any penalty be imposed for his failure or refusal to make such disclosure.   Every person interrogated orally, by written survey or questionnaire or by any other means with respect to such information shall be fully advised with respect to his right to fail or refuse to furnish such information.

TITLE IX—INTERVENTION AND PROCEDURE AFTER REMOVAL IN CIVIL RIGHTS CASES

Sec. 901.   Title 28 of the United States Code, section 1447(d),[66] is amended to read as follows:

"An order remanding a case to the State court from which it was removed is not reviewable on appeal or otherwise, except that an order remanding a case to the State court from which it was removed pursuant to section 1443 of this title shall be reviewable by appeal or otherwise."

Sec. 902.   Whenever an action has been commenced in any court of the United States seeking relief from the denial of equal protection of the laws under the fourteenth amendment to the Constitution on account of race, color, religion, or national origin, the Attorney General for or in the name of the United States may intervene in such action upon timely application if the Attorney General certifies that the case is of general public importance.   In such action the United States shall be entitled to the same relief as if it had instituted the action.

---

66. 28 U.S.C.A. § 1447(d).

TITLE X—ESTABLISHMENT OF COMMUNITY RELATIONS SERVICE

Sec. 1001. (a) There is hereby established in and as a part of the Department of Commerce a Community Relations Service (hereinafter referred to as the "Service"), which shall be headed by a Director who shall be appointed by the President with the advice and consent of the Senate for a term of four years. The Director is authorized to appoint, subject to the civil service laws and regulations, such other personnel as may be necessary to enable the Service to carry out its functions and duties, and to fix their compensation in accordance with the Classification Act of 1949, as amended. The Director is further authorized to procure services as authorized by section 15 of the Act of August 2, 1946 (60 Stat. 810; 5 U.S.C. 55(a)), but at rates for individuals not in excess of $75 per diem.

(b) Section 106(a) of the Federal Executive Pay Act of 1956, as amended (5 U.S.C. 2205(a)),[67] is further amended by adding the following clause thereto:

"(52) Director, Community Relations Service."

Sec. 1002. It shall be the function of the Service to provide assistance to communities and persons therein in resolving disputes, disagreements, or difficulties relating to discriminatory practices based on race, color, or national origin which impair the rights of persons in such communities under the Constitution or laws of the United States or which affect or may affect interstate commerce. The Service may offer its services in cases of such disputes, disagreements, or difficulties whenever, in its judgment, peaceful relations among the citizens of the community involved are threatened thereby, and it may offer its services either upon its own motion or upon the request of an appropriate State or local official or other interested person.

Sec. 1003. (a) The Service shall, whenever possible, in performing its functions, seek and utilize the cooperation of appropriate State or local, public, or private agencies.

(b) The activities of all officers and employees of the Service in providing conciliation assistance shall be conducted in confidence and without publicity, and the Service shall hold confidential any information acquired in the regular performance of its duties upon the understanding that it would be so held. No officer or employee of the Service shall engage in the performance of investigative or prosecuting functions of any department or agency in any litigation arising out of a dispute in which he acted on behalf of the Service. Any officer or other employee of the Service, who shall make public in any manner whatever any information in violation of this subsection, shall be deemed guilty of a misdemeanor and, upon conviction thereof, shall be fined not more than $1,000 or imprisoned not more than one year.

Sec. 1004. Subject to the provisions of sections 205 and 1003(b), the Director shall, on or before January 31 of each year, submit to

---

67. 5 U.S.C.A. § 2205(a).

the Congress a report of the activities of the Service during the preceding fiscal year.

TITLE XI—MISCELLANEOUS

Sec. 1101. In any proceeding for criminal contempt arising under title II, III, IV, V, VI, or VII of this Act, the accused, upon demand therefor, shall be entitled to a trial by jury, which shall conform as near as may be to the practice in criminal cases. Upon conviction, the accused shall not be fined more than $1,000 or imprisoned for more than six months.

This section shall not apply to contempts committed in the presence of the court, or so near thereto as to obstruct the administration of justice, nor to the misbehavior, misconduct, or disobedience of any officer of the court in respect to writs, orders, or process of the court. No person shall be convicted of criminal contempt hereunder unless the act or omission constituting such contempt shall have been intentional, as required in other cases of criminal contempt.

Nor shall anything herein be construed to deprive courts of their power, by civil contempt proceedings, without a jury, to secure compliance with or to prevent obstruction of, as distinguished from punishment for violations of, any lawful writ, process, order, rule, decree, or command of the court in accordance with the prevailing usages of law and equity, including the power of detention.

Sec. 1102. No person should be put twice in jeopardy under the laws of the United States for the same act or omission. For this reason, an acquittal or conviction in a prosecution for a specific crime under the laws of the United States shall bar a proceeding for criminal contempt, which is based upon the same act or omission and which arises under the provisions of this Act; and an acquittal or conviction in a proceeding for criminal contempt, which arises under the provisions of this Act, shall bar a prosecution for a specific crime under the laws of the United States based upon the same act or omission.

Sec. 1103. Nothing in this Act shall be construed to deny, impair, or otherwise affect any right or authority of the Attorney General or of the United States or any agency or officer thereof under existing law to institute or intervene in any action or proceeding.

Sec. 1104. Nothing contained in any title of this Act shall be construed as indicating an intent on the part of Congress to occupy the field in which any such title operates to the exclusion of State laws on the same subject matter, nor shall any provision of this Act be construed as invalidating any provision of State law unless such provision is inconsistent with any of the purposes of this Act, or any provision thereof.

Sec. 1105. There are hereby authorized to be appropriated such sums as are necessary to carry out the provisions of this Act.

Sec. 1106. If any provision of this Act or the application thereof to any person or circumstances is held invalid, the remainder of the Act and the application of the provision to other persons not similarly situated or to other circumstances shall not be affected thereby.

Approved July 2, 1964.

VOTING RIGHTS ACT OF 1965

For Legislative History of Act, see p. 2437

PUBLIC LAW 89–110; 79 STAT. 437

[S. 1564]

An Act to enforce the fifteenth amendment to the Constitution of the
United States, and for other purposes.

*Be it enacted by the Senate and House of Representatives of the United
States of America in Congress assembled, That:*

This Act shall be known as the "Voting Rights Act of 1965".

Sec. 2. No voting qualification or prerequisite to voting, or standard, practice, or procedure shall be imposed or applied by any State

19. 42 U.S.C.A. § 242h.
20. 42 U.S.C.A. § 246(c).
21. 42 U.S.C.A. § 246(c).
22. 42 U.S.C.A. § 247a.

or political subdivision to deny or abridge the right of any citizen of the United States to vote on account of race or color.

Sec. 3.   (a) Whenever the Attorney General institutes a proceeding under any statute to enforce the guarantees of the fifteenth amendment in any State or political subdivision the court shall authorize the appointment of Federal examiners by the United States Civil Service Commission in accordance with section 6 to serve for such period of time and for such political subdivisions as the court shall determine is appropriate to enforce the guarantees of the fifteenth amendment (1) as part of any interlocutory order if the court determines that the appointment of such examiners is necessary to enforce such guarantees or (2) as part of any final judgment if the court finds that violations of the fifteenth amendment justifying equitable relief have occurred in such State or subdivision: *Provided,* That the court need not authorize the appointment of examiners if any incidents of denial or abridgement of the right to vote on account of race or color (1) have been few in number and have been promptly and effectively corrected by State or local action, (2) the continuing effect of such incidents has been eliminated, and (3) there is no reasonable probability of their recurrence in the future.

(b) If in a proceeding instituted by the Attorney General under any statute to enforce the guarantees of the fifteenth amendment in any State or political subdivision the court finds that a test or device has been used for the purpose or with the effect of denying or abridging the right of any citizen of the United States to vote on account of race or color, it shall suspend the use of tests and devices in such State or political subdivisions as the court shall determine is appropriate and for such period as it deems necessary.

(c) If in any proceeding instituted by the Attorney General under any statute to enforce the guarantees of the fifteenth amendment in any State or political subdivision the court finds that violations of the fifteenth amendment justifying equitable relief have occurred within the territory of such State or political subdivision, the court, in addition to such relief as it may grant, shall retain jurisdiction for such period as it may deem appropriate and during such period no voting qualification or prerequisite to voting, or standard, practice, or procedure with respect to voting different from that in force or effect at the time the proceeding was commenced shall be enforced unless and until the court finds that such qualification, prerequisite, standard, practice, or procedure does not have the purpose and will not have the effect of denying or abridging the right to vote on account of race or color: *Provided,* That such qualification, prerequisite, standard, practice, or procedure may be enforced if the qualification, prerequisite, standard, practice, or procedure has been submitted by the chief legal officer or other appropriate official of such State or subdivision to the Attorney General and the Attorney General has not interposed an objection within sixty days after such submission, except that neither the court's finding nor the Attorney General's failure to object shall bar a subsequent action to enjoin enforcement of such qualification, prerequisite, standard, practice, or procedure.

Sec. 4.   (a) To assure that the right of citizens of the United States to vote is not denied or abridged on account of race or color, no citizen shall be denied the right to vote in any Federal, State, or local election because of his failure to comply with any test or device in any State with respect to which the determinations have been made under subsection (b) or in any political subdivision with respect to which such determinations have been made as a separate unit, unless the United States District Court for the District of Columbia in an action for a declaratory judgment brought by such State or subdivision against the United States has determined that no such test or device has been used during the five years preceding the filing of the action for the purpose or with the effect of denying or abridging the right to vote on account of race or color: *Provided,* That no such declaratory judgment shall issue with respect to any plaintiff for a period of five years after the entry of a final judgment of any court of the United States, other than the denial of a declaratory judgment under this section, whether entered prior to or after the enactment of this Act, determining that denials or abridgments of the right to vote on account of race or color through the use of such tests or devices have occurred anywhere in the territory of such plaintiff.

An action pursuant to this subsection shall be heard and determined by a court of three judges in accordance with the provisions of section 2284 of title 28 of the United States Code and any appeal shall lie to the Supreme Court.   The court shall retain jurisdiction of any action pursuant to this subsection for five years after judgment and shall reopen the action upon motion of the Attorney General alleging that a test or device has been used for the purpose or with the effect of denying or abridging the right to vote on account of race or color.

If the Attorney General determines that he has no reason to believe that any such test or device has been used during the five years preceding the filing of the action for the purpose or with the effect of denying or abridging the right to vote on account of race or color, he shall consent to the entry of such judgment.

(b) The provisions of subsection (a) shall apply in any State or in any political subdivision of a state which (1) the Attorney General determines maintained on November 1, 1964, any test or device, and with respect to which (2) the Director of the Census determines that less than 50 per centum of the persons of voting age residing therein were registered on November 1, 1964, or that less than 50 per centum of such persons voted in the presidential election of November 1964.

A determination or certification of the Attorney General or of the Director of the Census under this section or under section 6 or section 13 shall not be reviewable in any court and shall be effective upon publication in the Federal Register.

(c) The phrase "test or device" shall mean any requirement that a person as a prerequisite for voting or registration for voting (1) demonstrate the ability to read, write, understand, or interpret any matter, (2) demonstrate any educational achievement or his knowledge of any particular subject, (3) possess good moral character, or

(4) prove his qualifications by the voucher of registered voters or members of any other class.

(d) For purposes of this section no State or political subdivision shall be determined to have engaged in the use of tests or devices for the purpose or with the effect of denying or abridging the right to vote on account of race or color if (1) incidents of such use have been few in number and have been promptly and effectively corrected by State or local action, (2) the continuing effect of such incidents has been eliminated, and (3) there is no reasonable probability of their recurrence in the future.

(e) (1) Congress hereby declares that to secure the rights under the fourteenth amendment of persons educated in American-flag schools in which the predominant classroom language was other than English, it is necessary to prohibit the States from conditioning the right to vote of such persons on ability to read, write, understand, or interpret any matter in the English language.

(2) No person who demonstrates that he has successfully completed the sixth primary grade in a public school in, or a private school accredited by, any State or territory, the District of Columbia, or the Commonwealth of Puerto Rico in which the predominant classroom language was other than English, shall be denied the right to vote in any Federal, State, or local election because of his inability to read, write, understand, or interpret any matter in the English language, except that in States in which State law provides that a different level of education is presumptive of literacy, he shall demonstrate that he has successfully completed an equivalent level of education in a public school in, or a private school accredited by, any State or territory, the District of Columbia, or the Commonwealth of Puerto Rico in which the predominant classroom language was other than English.

Sec. 5. Whenever a State or political subdivision with respect to which the prohibitions set forth in section 4(a) are in effect shall enact or seek to administer any voting qualification or prerequisite to voting, or standard, practice, or procedure with respect to voting different from that in force or effect on November 1, 1964, such State or subdivision may institute an action in the United States District Court for the District of Columbia for a declaratory judgment that such qualification, prerequisite, standard, practice, or procedure does not have the purpose and will not have the effect of denying or abridging the right to vote on account of race or color, and unless and until the court enters such judgment no person shall be denied the right to vote for failure to comply with such qualification, prerequisite, standard, practice, or procedure: *Provided*, That such qualification, prerequisite, standard, practice, or procedure may be enforced without such proceeding if the qualification, prerequisite, standard, practice, or procedure has been submitted by the chief legal officer or other appropriate official of such State or subdivision to the Attorney General and the Attorney General has not interposed an objection within sixty days after such submission, except that neither the Attorney General's failure to object nor a declaratory judgment entered under this section shall bar a subsequent action to enjoin enforcement of such qualification, prerequisite, standard, practice, or procedure. Any action under this section shall be heard and determined by a court of three judges in accordance with the provisions of section 2284 of title 28 of the United States Code and any appeal shall lie to the Supreme Court.

Sec. 6. Whenever (a) a court has authorized the appointment of examiners pursuant to the provisions of section 3(a), or (b) unless a declaratory judgment has been rendered under section 4(a), the Attorney General certifies with respect to any political subdivision named in, or included within the scope of, determinations made under section 4(b) that (1) he has received complaints in writing from twenty or more residents of such political subdivision alleging that they have been denied the right to vote under color of law on account of race or color, and that he believes such complaints to be meritorious, or (2) that in his judgment (considering, among other factors, whether the ratio of nonwhite persons to white persons registered to vote within such subdivision appears to him to be reasonably attributable to violations of the fifteenth amendment or whether substantial evidence exists that bona fide efforts are being made within such subdivision to comply with the fifteenth amendment), the appointment of examiners is otherwise necessary to enforce the guarantees of the fifteenth amendment, the Civil Service Commission shall appoint as many examiners for such subdivision as it may deem appropriate to prepare and maintain lists of persons eligible to vote in Federal, State, and local elections. Such examiners, hearing officers provided for in section 9(a), and other persons deemed necessary by the Commission to carry out the provisions and purposes of this Act shall be appointed, compensated, and separated without regard to the provisions of any statute administered by the Civil Service Commission, and service under this Act shall not be considered employment for the purposes of any statute administered by the Civil Service Commission, except the provisions of section 9 of the Act of August 2, 1939, as amended (5 U.S.C. 118i), prohibiting partisan political activity: *Provided*, That the Commission is authorized, after consulting the head of the appropriate department or agency, to designate suitable persons in the official service of the United States, with their consent, to serve in these positions. Examiners and hearing officers shall have the power to administer oaths.

Sec. 7. (a) The examiners for each political subdivision shall, at such places as the Civil Service Commission shall by regulation designate, examine applicants concerning their qualifications for voting. An application to an examiner shall be in such form as the Commission may require and shall contain allegations that the applicant is not otherwise registered to vote.

(b) Any person whom the examiner finds, in accordance with instructions received under section 9(b), to have the qualifications prescribed by State law not inconsistent with the Constitution and laws of the United States shall promptly be placed on a list of eligible voters. A challenge to such listing may be made in accordance with section 9(a) and shall not be the basis for a prosecution under section 12 of this Act. The examiner shall certify and transmit such list, and any supplements as appropriate, at least once a month, to the offices of the appropriate election officials, with copies to the Attorney General and the attorney general of the State, and any such lists and supplements thereto transmitted during the month shall be available for public inspection on the last business day of the month and in any event not later than the forty-fifth day prior to any election. The appropriate State or local election official shall place such names on the official voting list. Any person whose name appears on the examiner's list shall be entitled and allowed to vote in the election district of his residence unless and until the appropriate election officials shall have been notified that such person has been removed from such list in accordance with subsection (d): *Provided*, That no person shall be entitled to vote in any election by virtue of this Act unless his name shall have been certified and transmitted on such a list to the offices of the appropriate election officials at least forty-five days prior to such election.

(c) The examiner shall issue to each person whose name appears on such a list a certificate evidencing his eligibility to vote.

(d) A person whose name appears on such a list shall be removed therefrom by an examiner if (1) such person has been successfully challenged in accordance with the procedure prescribed in section 9, or (2) he has been determined by an examiner to have lost his eligibility to vote under State law not inconsistent with the Constitution and the laws of the United States.

Sec. 8. Whenever an examiner is serving under this Act in any political subdivision, the Civil Service Commission may assign, at the request of the Attorney General, one or more persons, who may be officers of the United States, (1) to enter and attend at any place for holding an election in such subdivision for the purpose of observing whether persons who are entitled to vote are being permitted to vote, and (2) to enter and attend at any place for tabulating the votes cast at any election held in such subdivision for the purpose of observing whether votes cast by persons entitled to vote are being properly tabulated. Such persons so assigned shall report to an examiner appointed for such political subdivision, to the Attorney General, and if the appointment of examiners has been authorized pursuant to section 3(a), to the court.

Sec. 9. (a) Any challenge to a listing on an eligibility list prepared by an examiner shall be heard and determined by a hearing officer appointed by and responsible to the Civil Service Commission and under such rules as the Commission shall by regulation prescribe. Such challenge shall be entertained only if filed at such office within the State as the Civil Service Commission shall by regulation designate, and within ten days after the listing of the challenged person is made available for public inspection, and if suported by (1) the affidavits of at least two persons having personal knowledge of the facts constituting grounds for the challenge, and (2) a certification that a copy of the challenge and affidavits have been served by mail or in person upon the person challenged at his place of residence set out in the application. Such challenge shall be determined within fifteen days after it has been filed. A petition for review of the decision of the hearing officer may be filed in the United States court of appeals for the circuit in which the person challenged resides within fifteen days after service of such decision by mail on the person petitioning for review but no decision of a hearing officer shall be reversed unless clearly erroneous. Any person listed shall be entitled and allowed to vote pending final determination by the hearing officer and by the court.

(b) The times, places, procedures, and form for application and listing pursuant to this Act and removals from the eligibility lists shall be prescribed by regulations promulgated by the Civil Service Commission and the Commission shall, after consultation with the Attorney General, instruct examiners concerning applicable State law not inconsistent with the Constitution and laws of the United States with respect to (1) the qualifications required for listing, and (2) loss of eligibility to vote.

(c) Upon the request of the applicant or the challenger or on its own motion the Civil Service Commission shall have the power to require by subpena the attendance and testimony of witnesses and the production of documentary evidence relating to any matter pending before it under the authority of this section. In case of contumacy or refusal to obey a subpena, any district court of the United States or the United States court of any territory or possession, or the District Court of the United States for the District of Columbia, within the jurisdiction of which said person guilty of contumacy or refusal to obey is found or resides or is domiciled or transacts business, or has appointed an agent for receipt of service of process, upon application by the Attorney General of the United States shall have jurisdiction to issue to such person an order requiring such person to appear before the Commission or a hearing officer, there to produce pertinent, relevant, and nonprivileged documentary evidence if so ordered, or there to give testimony touching the matter under investigation; and any failure to obey such order of the court may be punished by said court as a contempt thereof.

Sec. 10.   (a) The Congress finds that the requirement of the payment of a poll tax as a precondition to voting (i) precludes persons of limited means from voting or imposes unreasonable financial hardship upon such persons as a precondition to their exercise of the franchise, (ii) does not bear a reasonable relationship to any legitimate State interest in the conduct of elections, and (iii) in some areas has the purpose or effect of denying persons the right to vote because of race or color. Upon the basis of these findings, Congress declares that the constitutional right of citizens to vote is denied or abridged in some areas by the requirement of the payment of a poll tax as a precondition to voting.

(b) In the exercise of the powers of Congress under section 5 of the fourteenth amendment and section 2 of the fifteenth amendment, the Attorney General is authorized and directed to institute forthwith in the name of the United States such actions, including actions against States or political subdivisions, for declaratory judgment or injunctive relief against the enforcement of any requirement of the payment of a poll tax as a precondition to voting, or substitute therefor enacted after November 1, 1964, as will be necessary to implement the declaration of subsection (a) and the purposes of this section.

(c) The district courts of the United States shall have jurisdiction of such actions which shall be heard and determined by a court of three judges in accordance with the provisions of section 2284 of title 28 of the United States Code and any appeal shall lie to the Supreme Court. It shall be the duty of the judges designated to hear the case to assign the case for hearing at the earliest practicable date, to participate in the hearing and determination thereof, and to cause the case to be in every way expedited.

(d) During the pendency of such actions, and thereafter if the courts, notwithstanding this action by the Congress, should declare the requirement of the payment of a poll tax to be constitutional, no citizen of the United States who is a resident of a State or political subdivision with respect to which determinations have been made under subsection 4(b) and a declaratory judgment has not been entered under subsection 4(a), during the first year he becomes otherwise entitled to vote by reason of registration by State or local officials or listing by an examiner, shall be denied the right to vote for failure to pay a poll tax if he tenders payment of such tax for the current year to an examiner or to the appropriate State or local official at least forty-five days prior to election, whether or not such tender would be timely or adequate under State law. An examiner shall have authority to accept such payment from any person authorized by this Act to make an application for listing, and shall issue a receipt for such payment. The examiner shall transmit promptly any such poll tax payment to the office of the State or local official authorized to receive such payment under State law, together with the name and address of the applicant.

Sec. 11. (a) No person acting under color of law shall fail or refuse to permit any person to vote who is entitled to vote under any provision of this Act or is otherwise qualified to vote, or willfully fail or refuse to tabulate, count, and report such person's vote.

(b) No person, whether acting under color of law or otherwise, shall intimidate, threaten, or coerce, or attempt to intimidate, threaten, or coerce any person for voting or attempting to vote, or intimidate, threaten, or coerce, or attempt to intimidate, threaten, or coerce any person for urging or aiding any person to vote or attempt to vote, or intimidate, threaten, or coerce any person for exercising any powers or duties under section 3(a), 6, 8, 9, 10, or 12(e).

(c) Whoever knowingly or willfully gives false information as to his name, address, or period of residence in the voting district for the purpose of establishing his eligibility to register or vote, or conspires with another individual for the purpose of encouraging his false registration to vote or illegal voting, or pays or offers to pay or accepts payment either for registration to vote or for voting shall be fined not more than $10,000 or imprisoned not more than five years, or both: *Provided, however,* That this provision shall be applicable only to general, special, or primary elections held solely or in part for the purpose of selecting or electing any candidate for the office of President, Vice President, presidential elector, Member of the United

States Senate, Member of the United States House of Representatives, or Delegates or Commissioners from the territories or possessions, or Resident Commissioner of the Commonwealth of Puerto Rico.

(d) Whoever, in any matter within the jurisdiction of an examiner or hearing officer knowingly and willfully falsifies or conceals a material fact, or makes any false, fictitious, or fraudulent statements or representations, or makes or uses any false writing or document knowing the same to contain any false, fictitious, or fraudulent statement or entry, shall be fined not more than $10,000 or imprisoned not more than five years, or both.

Sec. 12. (a) Whoever shall deprive or attempt to deprive any person of any right secured by section 2, 3, 4, 5, 7, or 10 or shall violate section 11(a) or (b), shall be fined not more than $5,000, or imprisoned not more than five years, or both.

(b) Whoever, within a year following an election in a political subdivision in which an examiner has been appointed (1) destroys, defaces, mutilates, or otherwise alters the marking of a paper ballot which has been cast in such election, or (2) alters any official record of voting in such election tabulated from a voting machine or otherwise, shall be fined not more than $5,000, or imprisoned not more than five years, or both.

(c) Whoever conspires to violate the provisions of subsection (a) or (b) of this section, or interferes with any right secured by section 2, 3, 4, 5, 7, 10, or 11(a) or (b) shall be fined not more than $5,000, or imprisoned not more than five years, or both.

(d) Whenever any person has engaged or there are reasonable grounds to believe that any person is about to engage in any act or practice prohibited by section 2, 3, 4, 5, 7, 10, 11, or subsection (b) of this section, the Attorney General may institute for the United States, or in the name of the United States, an action for preventive relief, including an application for a temporary or permanent injunction, restraining order, or other order, and including an order directed to the State and State or local election officials to require them (1) to permit persons listed under this Act to vote and (2) to count such votes.

(e) Whenever in any political subdivision in which there are examiners appointed pursuant to this Act any persons allege to such an examiner within forty-eight hours after the closing of the polls that notwithstanding (1) their listing under this Act or registration by an appropriate election official and (2) their eligibility to vote, they have not been permitted to vote in such election, the examiner shall forthwith notify the Attorney General if such allegations in his opinion appear to be well founded. Upon receipt of such notification, the Attorney General may forthwith file with the district court an application for an order providing for the marking, casting, and counting of the ballots of such persons and requiring the inclusion of their votes in the total vote before the results of such election shall be deemed final and any force or effect given thereto. The district court shall hear and determine such matters immediately after the filing of such application. The remedy provided in this subsection shall not preclude any remedy available under State or Federal law.

(f) The district courts of the United States shall have jurisdiction of proceedings instituted pursuant to this section and shall exercise the same without regard to whether a person asserting rights under the provisions of this Act shall have exhausted any administrative or other remedies that may be provided by law.

Sec. 13. Listing procedures shall be terminated in any political subdivision of any State (a) with respect to examiners appointed pursuant to clause (b) of section 6 whenever the Attorney General notifies the Civil Service Commission, or whenever the District Court for the District of Columbia determines in an action for declaratory judgment brought by any political subdivision with respect to which the Director of the Census has determined that more than 50 per centum of the nonwhite persons of voting age residing therein are registered to vote, (1) that all persons listed by an examiner for such subdivision have been placed on the appropriate voting registration roll, and (2) that there is no longer reasonable cause to believe that persons will be deprived of or denied the right to vote on account of race or color in such subdivision, and (b), with respect to examiners appointed pursuant to section 3(a), upon order of the authorizing court. A political subdivision may petition the Attorney General for the termination of listing procedures under clause (a) of this section, and may petition the Attorney General to request the Director of the Census to take such survey or census as may be appropriate for the making of the determination provided for in this section. The District Court for the District of Columbia shall have jurisdiction to require such survey or census to be made by the Director of the Census and it shall require him to do so if it deems the Attorney General's refusal to request such survey or census to be arbitrary or unreasonable.

Sec. 14. (a) All cases of criminal contempt arising under the provisions of this Act shall be governed by section 151 of the Civil Rights Act of 1957 (42 U.S.C. 1995).

(b) No court other than the District Court for the District of Columbia or a court of appeals in any proceeding under section 9 shall have jurisdiction to issue any declaratory judgment pursuant to section 4 or section 5 or any restraining order or temporary or permanent injunction against the execution or enforcement of any provision of this Act or any action of any Federal officer or employee pursuant hereto.

(c) (1) The terms "vote" or "voting" shall include all action necessary to make a vote effective in any primary, special, or general election, including, but not limited to, registration, listing pursuant to this Act, or other action required by law prerequisite to voting, casting a ballot, and having such ballot counted properly and included in the appropriate totals of votes cast with respect to candidates for public or party office and propositions for which votes are received in an election.

(2) The term "political subdivision" shall mean any county or parish, except that where registration for voting is not conducted under the supervision of a county or parish, the term shall include

any other subdivision of a State which conducts registration for voting.

(d) In any action for a declaratory judgment brought pursuant to section 4 or section 5 of this Act, subpenas for witnesses who are required to attend the District Court for the District of Columbia may be served in any judicial district of the United States: *Provided*, That no writ of subpena shall issue for witnesses without the District of Columbia at a greater distance than one hundred miles from the place of holding court without the permission of the District Court for the District of Columbia being first had upon proper application and cause shown.

Sec. 15.   Section 2004 of the Revised Statutes (42 U.S.C. 1971),[23] as amended by section 131 of the Civil Rights Act of 1957 (71 Stat. 637), and amended by section 601 of the Civil Rights Act of 1960 (74 Stat. 90), and as further amended by section 101 of the Civil Rights Act of 1964 (78 Stat. 241), is further amended as follows:

(a) Delete the word "Federal" wherever it appears in subsections (a) and (c);

(b) Repeal subsection (f) and designate the present subsections (g) and (h) as (f) and (g), respectively.

Sec. 16.   The Attorney General and the Secretary of Defense, jointly, shall make a full and complete study to determine whether, under the laws or practices of any State or States, there are preconditions to voting, which might tend to result in discrimination against citizens serving in the Armed Forces of the United States seeking to vote.   Such officials shall, jointly, make a report to the Congress not later than June 30, 1966, containing the results of such study, together with a list of any States in which such preconditions exist, and shall include in such report such recommendations for legislation as they deem advisable to prevent discrimination in voting against citizens serving in the Armed Forces of the United States.

Sec. 17.   Nothing in this Act shall be construed to deny, impair, or otherwise adversely affect the right to vote of any person registered to vote under the law of any State or political subdivision.

Sec. 18.   There are hereby authorized to be appropriated such sums as are necessary to carry out the provisions of this Act.

Sec. 19.   If any provision of this Act or the application thereof to any person or circumstances is held invalid, the remainder of the Act and the application of the provision to other persons not similarly situated or to other circumstances shall not be affected thereby.

Approved August 6, 1965.

23. 42 U.S.C.A. § 1971.

WOMEN'S RIGHTS

The women's rights movement in the United States began in the nineteenth century when some women reformers demanded the right to vote and the same legal rights as men. The participation of women in the abolitionist movement played a crucial role in crystallizing their dissatisfaction with the lack of rights accorded to females. Some, like Lucy Stone, saw parallels between women and slaves: both were expected to be passive, cooperative, and obedient. In addition, the legal status of both slaves and women was unequal to that of white men. Sojourner Truth, an African American evangelist and reformer, also recognized this connection and soon was speaking before women's rights groups, advocating the right to vote.

After the Civil War ended in 1865, many of these women reformers devoted their energies to gaining women's suffrage. Susan B. Anthony, Elizabeth Cady Stanton, and Lucy Stone were the best-known suffrage leaders. Anthony and Stanton fought for a federal constitutional amendment granting women the right to vote, while Stone and her followers sought amendments in state constitutions. The Nineteenth Amendment to the U.S. Constitution, ratified in 1920, finally gave women the right to vote.

During the nineteenth century, women encountered rigid cultural and legal barriers when they sought to enter business and the professions. Women who married had traditionally suffered a loss of legal status, as the identity of the wife merged into that of the husband. He was a legal person but she was not. A married woman could not sign a contract without the signature of her husband. Upon marriage, he received all her personal property and managed all property that she owned. In return, the husband was obliged to support his wife and children. By the 1850s women's rights supporters had convinced many state legislatures to pass married women's separate property acts. These acts gave women the legal right to retain ownership and control of property they brought into the marriage.

Women also had difficulty entering the professions, because the cultural stereotypes of the period dictated that the proper role of an adult woman was to be a wife and mother. According to the prevailing viewpoint, the rough-and-tumble world of business and the professions was no place for women, who had more delicate natures than men. In addition, the male-dominated world believed women to be intellectually inferior and fundamentally incapable of handling the demands of white-collar jobs and the professions. This view was reinforced by the decision in *Bradwell v. Illinois*, 83 U.S. 130, 21 L. Ed. 442 (1872), when the U.S. Supreme Court ruled that it was not unconstitutional for Illinois to deny a woman a license to practice law solely on the basis of her gender.

The quest for women's rights reignited in the 1960s, fueled by the participation of women in the civil rights movement. Just as in the nineteenth century, women compared their legal, economic, and social status with that of persons of color and found similar problems. The National Organization for Women was established in 1966. It quickly became the nation's largest and most influential feminist organization, but in the process it stimulated opponents of modern feminism to organize as well.

Reproductive rights became a key issue for women in the 1960s. At that time the distribution of birth control devices and information was illegal in many states. In *Griswold v. Connecticut*, 381 U.S. 479, 85 S. Ct. 1678, 14 L. Ed. 2d 510 (1965), the Supreme Court struck down a Connecticut law that made the sale and possession of birth control devices a misdemeanor. More importantly, the Court declared that the Constitution contained a right to privacy. In *Eisenstadt v. Baird*, 405 U.S. 438, 92 S. Ct. 1029, 31 L. Ed. 2d 349 (1972), the Court established that the right of privacy is an individual right and is not limited to married couples.

The *Griswold* and *Eisenstadt* decisions paved the way for *Roe v. Wade*, 410 U.S. 113, 93 S. Ct. 705, 35 L. Ed. 2d 147 (1973), which struck down a Texas law that banned abortions. Justice Harry A. Blackmun concluded that the right to privacy "is broad enough to encompass a woman's decision whether or not to terminate her pregnancy." The *Roe* decision provided women with the right to continue or terminate a pregnancy, at least up to the point of viability. By the 1980s, however, a more conservative Supreme Court began upholding state laws that placed restrictions on this right.

Seneca Falls Declaration of Sentiments

The feminist political movement began in the nineteenth century with the call for female suffrage. At a convention in Seneca Falls, New York, in July 1848, a group of 240 people (200 women and 40 men) drafted and approved the Declaration of Sentiments. Among those present was Frederick Douglass, a former slave who was now an abolitionist leader. The convention was organized by Lucretia Mott and Elizabeth Cady Stanton, two Quakers whose concern for women's rights was aroused when Mott was denied a seat at an international antislavery meeting in London because she was a woman. The delegates adopted a statement of women's rights, deliberately modeled on the Declaration of Independence, as well as a series of resolutions calling for women's suffrage and the reform of marital and property laws that kept women in an inferior status.

Ain't I a Woman?

Sojourner Truth was a nineteenth-century African American evangelist who embraced abolitionism and women's rights. A charismatic speaker, she became one of the best-known abolitionists of her day. Born a slave and given the name Isabella Baumfree, she was freed in 1828 when a New York law abolished slavery within the state.

In 1843 she had a religious experience and came to believe that God had commanded her to travel beyond New York to spread the Christian gospel. She took the name Sojourner Truth and traveled throughout the eastern states as an evangelist. Truth soon became acquainted with the abolitionist movement and its leaders. She adopted their message, speaking out against slavery. Her speaking tours expanded as abolitionists realized her effectiveness as a lecturer. Though illiterate, she dictated her life story, *The Narrative of Sojourner Truth*, and sold the book at her lectures as a means of supporting herself.

In the early 1850s, she met leaders of the emerging women's rights movement, most notably Lucretia Mott. Truth recognized the connection between the inferior legal status of African Americans and women in general. Her most famous speech, "Ain't I a Woman?" first given in 1851, challenged cultural beliefs, including the natural inferiority of women, and biblical justifications for the second-class status of women.

Bradwell v. Illinois

Myra Bradwell's efforts to gain admission to the Illinois bar resulted in a Supreme Court decision. Bradwell had married a lawyer and read the law with her husband. In 1869 she passed the Illinois bar examination but was refused admission to the bar. She appealed to the Supreme Court, arguing that the Fourteenth Amendment's Equal Protection Clause prevented the state from imposing admission requirements based on gender.

In *Bradwell v. Illinois* in 1872, the Court rejected her constitutional argument. In a concurring opinion that revealed the cultural underpinnings of the period, Justice Joseph P. Bradley supported the Illinois Supreme Court's denial of Bradwell's application to practice law in the state. Bradley articulated the widely held view that the "natural and proper timidity and delicacy which belongs to the female sex evidently unfits it for many of the occupations of civil life." He further concluded that the "paramount destiny and mission of woman is to fulfill the noble and benign offices of wife and mother. This is the law of the Creator."

National Organization for Women Statement of Purpose

The establishment of the National Organization for Women (NOW) in 1966 signaled the growing strength of modern feminism. Initially,

NOW directed most of its resources toward the needs of working women. It attacked the exclusion of women from the professions, politics, and other areas of society because of outdated male views about women. It also denounced and attacked legal and economic discrimination, such as bank practices that denied married women credit in their own names.

NOW's Statement of Purpose defined the mainstream of the modern feminist movement. Though many women and men refused to be labeled "feminists," they agreed with NOW's basic demand that women in the workforce be treated equally with men, receive equal pay for equal work, and enjoy access to jobs and promotions to which their talents entitled them.

Griswold v. Connecticut

By 1960 almost every state had legalized birth control. Nevertheless, laws remained on the books that prevented the distribution of birth control information and contraceptives. One such law, passed in Connecticut in 1879, made the sale and possession of birth control devices a misdemeanor. The law also prohibited anyone from assisting, abetting, or counseling another in the use of birth control devices.

The U.S. Supreme Court reviewed the Connecticut law in *Griswold v. Connecticut* in 1965. Estelle Griswold, the director of Planned Parenthood in Connecticut, had been arrested for violating the birth control devices law three days after she opened a clinic in New Haven. She was convicted and fined $100. The Connecticut courts upheld her conviction, rejecting the contention that the state law was unconstitutional.

The Supreme Court struck down the Connecticut birth control law. In his majority opinion, Justice William O. Douglas announced that the law was unconstitutional because it violated a married couple's right to privacy. Douglas asserted that "specific guarantees in the Bill of Rights have penumbras, formed by emanations from those guarantees that help give them life and substance. Various guarantees create zones of privacy." Thus, these "penumbras" (things on the fringe of a major region) and "emanations" added up to a general, independent right of privacy. Connecticut could not be permitted "to search the sacred precincts of marital bedrooms for telltale signs of the use of contraceptives."

The *Griswold* decision invalidated the Connecticut law only insofar as it invaded marital privacy. Thus, the decision left open the question of whether states could prohibit the use of birth control devices by unmarried persons. In *Eisenstadt v. Baird*, in 1972, the Court reviewed a Massachusetts law that prohibited unmarried persons from obtaining and using contraceptives. The Court struck down the law, thereby establishing that the right of privacy is an individual right, not a right enjoyed only by married couples.

For a discussion of *Griswold v. Connecticut*, see volume 5, page 210.

Roe v. Wade

The establishment of an individual's right to privacy in *Eisenstadt* soon had dramatic implications for state laws that criminalized abortions. Until the 1960s every state prohibited abortion except when it was necessary to save the mother's life. The growth of the modern feminist movement in the 1960s led to calls for the legalization of abortion, and many state legislatures began to amend their laws to permit abortion when the pregnancy resulted from a rape or when the child was likely to suffer from a serious birth defect. In most cases, however, these laws required a committee of doctors, usually males, to approve the abortion.

These state restrictions on abortion were swept away by the Supreme Court's controversial decision in *Roe v. Wade* in 1973. The case began when a class action lawsuit challenged the state of Texas's abortion law. Sarah Weddington, the attorney for "Jane Roe," argued that the Constitution allows a woman to control her own body, including the decision to terminate an unwanted pregnancy.

The Supreme Court, by a 7–2 vote, struck down the Texas law. Justice Harry A. Blackmun, in his majority opinion, relied on the earlier right to privacy decisions to justify the Court's action. Blackmun concluded that the right to privacy "is broad enough to encompass a woman's decision whether or not to terminate her pregnancy." More important, he stated that the right of privacy is a fundamental right. This meant that the state of Texas had to meet the strict scrutiny test of constitutional review. Texas had showed a "compelling state interest" in protecting maternal health that justified reasonable state regulation of abortions performed after the first trimester (three months) of pregnancy. However, Texas also sought to proscribe all abortions and claimed a compelling state interest in protecting unborn human life. Though acknowledging that this was a legitimate interest, the Court held that it does not become compelling until that point in pregnancy when the fetus becomes "viable" (capable of "meaningful life outside the mother's womb"). Beyond the point of viability, said the Court, the state may prohibit abortion except in cases where it is necessary to preserve the life or health of the mother.

The *Roe* decision elicited a hostile reaction from those opposed to abortion. A "prolife" movement that sought the overturning of the *Roe* decision quickly emerged and became a new fixture in U.S. politics. Prolife forces sought a constitutional amendment to undo the decision, but the amendment fell one vote short in the U.S. Senate in 1983. Over time, as the composition of the Supreme Court has changed, the Court has modified its views without overturning *Roe*.

For the text of this case, see volume 1, page 313. For a discussion of *Roe v. Wade*, see volume 9, page 55.

SENECA FALLS
DECLARATION OF SENTIMENTS

When, in the course of human events, it becomes necessary for one portion of the family of man to assume among the people of the earth a position different from that which they have hitherto occupied, but one to which the laws of nature and of nature's God entitle them, a decent respect to the opinions of mankind requires that they should declare the causes that impel them to such a course.

We hold these truths to be self-evident: that all men and women are created equal; that they are endowed by their Creator with certain inalienable rights; that among these are life, liberty, and the pursuit of happiness; that to secure these rights governments are instituted, deriving their just powers from the consent of the governed. Whenever any form of government becomes destructive of these ends, it is the right of those who suffer from it to refuse allegiance to it, and to insist upon the institution of a new government, laying its foundation on such principles, and organizing its powers in such form, as to them shall seem most likely to effect their safety and happiness. Prudence, indeed, will dictate that governments long established should not be changed for light and transient causes; and accordingly all experience hath shown that mankind are more disposed to suffer, while evils are sufferable, than to right themselves by abolishing the forms to which they were accustomed. But when a long train of abuses and usurpations, pursuing invariably the same object evinces a design to reduce them under absolute despotism, it is their duty to throw off such government, and to provide new guards for their future security. Such has been the patient sufferance of the women under this government, and such is now the necessity which constrains them to demand the equal station to which they are entitled.

The history of mankind is a history of repeated injuries and usurpations on the part of man toward woman, having in direct object the establishment of an absolute tyranny over her. To prove this, let facts be submitted to a candid world.

He has never permitted her to exercise her inalienable right to the elective franchise.

He has compelled her to submit to laws, in the formation of which she had no voice.

He has withheld from her rights which are given to the most ignorant and degraded men—both natives and foreigners.

Having deprived her of this first right of a citizen, the elective franchise, thereby leaving her without representation in the halls of legislation, he has oppressed her on all sides.

He has made her, if married, in the eye of the law, civilly dead.

He has taken from her all right in property, even to the wages she earns.

He has made her, morally, an irresponsible being, as she can commit many crimes with impunity, provided they be done in the presence of her husband. In the covenant of marriage, she is compelled to promise obedience to her husband, he becoming, to all intents and purposes, her master—the law giving him power to deprive her of her liberty, and to administer chastisement.

He has so framed the laws of divorce, as to what shall be the proper causes, and in case of separation, to whom the guardianship of the children shall be given, as to be wholly regardless of the happiness of women—the law, in all cases, going upon a false supposition of the supremacy of man, and giving all power into his hands.

After depriving her of all rights as a married woman, if single, and the owner of property, he has taxed her to support a government which recognizes her only when her property can be made profitable to it.

He has monopolized nearly all the profitable employments, and from those she is permitted to follow, she receives but a scanty remuneration. He closes against her all the avenues to wealth and distinction which he considers most honorable to himself. As a teacher of theology, medicine, or law, she is not known.

He has denied her the facilities for obtaining a thorough education, all colleges being closed against her.

He allows her in Church, as well as State, but a subordinate position, claiming Apostolic authority for her exclusion from the ministry, and, with some exceptions, from any public participation in the affairs of the Church.

He has created a false public sentiment by giving to the world a different code of morals for men and women, by which moral delinquencies which exclude women from society, are not only tolerated, but deemed of little account in man.

He has usurped the prerogative of Jehovah himself, claiming it as his right to assign for her a sphere of action, when that belongs to her conscience and to her God.

He has endeavored, in every way that he could, to destroy her confidence in her own powers, to lessen her self-respect, and to make her willing to lead a dependent and abject life.

Now, in view of this entire disfranchisement of one-half the people of this country, their social and religious degradation—in view of the unjust laws above mentioned, and because women do feel themselves aggrieved, oppressed, and fraudulently deprived of their most sacred rights, we insist that they have immediate admission to all the rights and privileges which belong to them as citizens of the United States.

In entering upon the great work before us, we anticipate no small amount of misconception, misrepresentation, and ridicule; but we shall use every instrumentality within our power to effect our object. We shall employ agents, circulate tracts, petition the State and National legislatures, and endeavor to enlist the pulpit and the press in our behalf. We hope this Convention will be followed by a series of Conventions embracing every part of the country.

AIN'T I A WOMAN?

SOJOURNER TRUTH, 1851

Well, children, where there is so much racket there must be something out of kilter. I think that 'twixt the negroes of the South and the women at the North, all talking about rights, the white men will be in a fix pretty soon. But what's all this here talking about?

That man over there says that women need to be helped into carriages, and lifted over ditches, and to have the best place everywhere. Nobody ever helps me into carriages, or over mud-puddles, or gives me any best place! And ain't I a woman? Look at me! Look at my arm! I have ploughed and planted, and gathered into barns, and no man could head me! And ain't I a woman? I could work as much and eat as much as a man—when I could get it—and bear the lash as well! And ain't I a woman? I have borne thirteen children, and seen most all sold off to slavery, and when I cried out with my mother's grief, none but Jesus heard me! And ain't I a woman?

Then they talk about this thing in the head; what's this they call it? [member of audience whispers, "intellect"] That's it, honey. What's that got to do with women's rights or negroes' rights? If my cup won't hold but a pint, and yours holds a quart, wouldn't you be mean not to let me have my little half measure full?

Then that little man in black there, he says women can't have as much rights as men, 'cause Christ wasn't a woman! Where did your Christ come from? Where did your Christ come from? From God and a woman! Man had nothing to do with Him.

If the first woman God ever made was strong enough to turn the world upside down all alone, these women together ought to be able to turn it back, and get it right side up again! And now they is asking to do it, the men better let them.

Obliged to you for hearing me, and now old Sojourner ain't got nothing more to say.

MYRA BRADWELL, *Plff. in Err.,*
v.
STATE OF ILLINOIS.

(See S. C. 16 Wall. 130–142.)

*Constitutional law—female lawyer—privilege
to practice law—qualifications of attorneys.*

†1. The supreme court of Illinois having refused
to grant to plaintiff a license to practice law in
the courts of that state, on the ground that females are not eligible under the laws of that state,
such a decision violates no provision of the Federal Constitution.

2. The 2d section of the 4th article is inapplicable, because plaintiff is a citizen of the state of
whose action she complains, and that section only
guaranties privileges and immunities to citizens of
other states, in that state.

3. Nor is the right to practice law in the state
courts a privilege or immunity of a citizen of the
United States within the meaning of the 1st section of the 14th article of Amendment of the Constitution of the United States.

†Headnotes by Mr. Justice MILLER.

NOTE.—*The right of women to practice law*—
see note to In re Leach, 21 L. R. A. 701.

83 U. S.

4. The power of a state to prescribe the qualifications for admission to the bar of its own courts, is unaffected by the 14th Amendment, and this court cannot inquire into the reasonableness or propriety of the rules it may prescribe.

[No. 12.]

Argued Jan. 18, 1873.   Decided Apr. 15, 1873.

IN ERROR to the Supreme Court of the State of Illinois.

The petition in this case was filed in the court below, by the plaintiff in error, for license to practice law.   The said application having been denied, the petitioner sued out this writ of error.

The case is stated by the court.

Mr. **Matt. H. Carpenter,** for plaintiff in error:

The plaintiff in error is a married woman, of full age, a citizen of the United States, and of the state of Illinois; was ascertained and certified to be duly qualified in respect to character and attainments; but was denied admission to the bar for the sole reason that she was a married woman.   This is the error relied upon to reverse the proceedings below.

By the rules of this court, no person can be admitted to practice at the bar without service for a fixed term in the highest court of the state in which such person resides.   Consequently a denial of admission in the highest court of the state is an insurmountable obstacle to admission to the bar of this court.

This record, therefore, presents the broad question whether a married woman, being a citizen of the United States and of a state, and possessing the necessary qualifications, is entitled by the Constitution of the United States to be admitted to practice as an attorney and counselor at law in the courts of the state in which she resides.   This is a question, not of taste, propriety or politeness, but of civil right.

I have more faith in female suffrage, to reform the abuses of our election system in the large cities, than I have in the penal election laws to be enforced by soldiers and marines. Who believes that if ladies were admitted to seats in Congress, or upon the bench, or were participating in discussions at the bar, such proceedings would thereby be rendered less refined, or that less regard would be paid to the rights of all?

But whether women should be admitted to the right of suffrage is one thing and whether this end has already been accomplished is quite another.   The 14th Amendment forbids the states to make or enforce any law which shall abridge the privileges or immunities of a citizen.   But whether the right to vote is covered by the phrase "the privileges and immunities" was much discussed under the provisions of the old Constitution; and at least one of the earliest decisions drew a distinction between "privileges and immunities," and political rights.   On the other hand, Mr. Justice Washington, in a celebrated case, expressed the opinion that the right to vote and hold office was included in this phrase.   But in neither of the cases was this point directly involved, and both opinions are *obiter dicta* in relation to it.

But the 14th and 15th Amendments seem to settle this question against the right of female suffrage.   These Amendments seem to recognize the distinction at first pointed out between "privileges and immunities" and the right to vote.

The 14th Amendment declares "All persons born and naturalized in the United States, etc., are citizens of the United States, and of the state wherein they reside."   Of course women, as well as men, are included in this provision, and recognized as citizens.   This Amendment further declares: "No state shall make or enforce any law which shall abridge the privileges or immunities of citizens of the United States." If the privileges and immunities of a citizen cannot be abridged, then, of course, the privileges and immunities of all citizens must be the same.   The 2d section of this Amendment provides, that "representatives shall be apportioned among the several states according to their respective numbers, counting the whole number of persons in each state, excluding Indians, not taxed.   But when the right to vote at an election, etc., is denied to any of the male inhabitants, being twenty-one years of age, etc., the basis of representation therein shall be reduced in the proportion which the number of such male citizens shall bear to the whole number of male citizens twenty-one years of age in such state."

It cannot be denied that the right or power of a state to exclude a portion of its male citizens from the right to vote is recognized by this 2d section; from which it follows that the right to vote is not one of the privileges and immunities which the 1st section declared shall not be abridged by any state.

The 14th Amendment executes itself in every state of the Union.   Whatever are the privileges and immunities of a citizen in the state of New York, such citizen emigrating, carries them with him into any other state of the Union.   It utters the will of the United States in every state, and silences every state Constitution, usage or law which conflicts with it.   If to be admitted to the bar, on attaining the age and learning required by law, be one of the privileges of a white citizen in the state of New York, it is equally the privilege of a colored citizen in that state; and if in that state, then in any state.   If no state may make or enforce any law to abridge the privileges of a citizen, it must follow that the privileges of all citizens are the same.

The 14th and 15th Amendments distinguish between privileges and rights, and it must be confessed that it is paradoxical to say, as the 14th Amendment clearly does, that the privileges of a citizen shall not be abridged, while his right to vote may be.   But a judicial construction of the Constitution is wholly different from a mere exercise in philology.   The question is not whether certain words are aptly employed, but the context must be searched to ascertain the sense in which such words were used.

It is evident that there are certain privileges and immunities which belong to a citizen of the United States, as such; otherwise it would be nonsense for the 14th Amendment to prohibit a state from abridging them; and it is equally evident from the 14th Amendment that the right to vote is not one of those privileges.   And the question recurs, whether or not admission to the bar, the proper qualification being pos-

16 WALL.

sessed, is one of the privileges which a state may not deny.

In *Cummings* v. *Mo.* 4 Wall. 321, 18 L. ed. 362, this court says:

"In France, deprivation or suspension of civil rights or some of them—and among these the right of voting, of eligibility to office, of taking part in family councils, of being guardian or trustee, of bearing arms, and of teaching or being employed in a school or seminary of learning—are punishments prescribed by her Code.

The theory upon which our political institutions rest is, that all men have certain inalienable rights; that among these are life, liberty, and the pursuit of happiness; and that, in the pursuit of happiness, all avocations, all honors, all positions are alike open to every one, and that in the protection of these rights all are equal before the law. Any deprivation or extension of any of these rights for past conduct is punishment, and can be in no otherwise defined."

No broader or better enumeration of the privileges which pertain to American citizenship could be given. "Life, liberty, and the pursuit of happiness; and in the pursuit of happiness all avocations, all honors, all positions are alike open to every one; and in the protection of these rights all are equal before the law."

In *Ex parte Garland*, 4 Wall. 378, 18 L. ed. 370, this court says:

"The profession of an attorney and counselor is not, like an office, created by Congress, which depends for its continuance, its powers and its emoluments upon the will of its creator, and the possession of which may be burdened with any conditions not prohibited by the Constitution. Attorneys and counselors are not officers of the United States; they are not elected or appointed in the manner prescribed by the Constitution for the election and appointment of such officers. They are officers of the court, admitted as such by its order, upon evidence of their possessing sufficient legal learning and fair private character; . . . they hold their office during good behavior and can only be deprived of it for misconduct ascertained and declared by the judgment of the court, after opportunity to be heard has been offered."

Ex parte Heyfron, 7 How. (Miss.) 127; *Fletcher* v. *Daingerfield*, 20 Cal. 430.

"Their admission or their exclusion is not the exercise of a mere ministerial power. It is the exercise of judicial power, and has been so held in numerous cases."

It is now well settled that the courts in admitting attorneys to and in expelling them from the bar, act judicially, and that such proceedings are subject to review on writ of error or appeal, as the case may be.

In re Cooper, 22 N. Y. 67, *Strother* v. *Mo.* 1 Mo. 605; *Ex parte Secombe*, 19 How. 9, 15 L. ed. 565; *Ex parte Garland, supra*.

From these cases the conclusion is irresistible that the profession of the law, like the clerical profession and that of medicine, is an avocation open to every citizen of the United States. And while the legislature may prescribe qualifications for entering upon this pursuit, it cannot, under the guise of fixing qualifications, exclude a class of citizens from admission to the bar. The legislature may say at what age candidates

shall be admitted; may elevate or depress the standard of learning required. But a qualification to which a whole class of citizens can never attain is not a regulation of admission to the bar, but is, as to such citizens, a prohibition. For instance, a state legislature could not, in enumerating the qualifications, require the candidate to be a white citizen. I presume it will be admitted that such an act would be void. The only provision in the Constitution of the United States which secures to colored male citizens the privilege of admission to the bar, or the pursuit of the other ordinary avocations of life is the provision that "No state shall make or enforce any law which shall abridge the privileges or immunities of the citizens." If this provision protects the colored citizen, then it protects every citizen, black or white, male or female.

Why may a colored citizen buy, hold and sell land in any state of the Union? Because he is a citizen of the United States, and that is one of the privileges of a citizen. Why may a colored citizen be admitted to the bar? Because he is a citizen, and that is one of the avocations open to every citizen, and no state can abridge his right to pursue it. Certainly no other reason can be given.

Now, let us come to the case of Myra Bradwell. She is a citizen of the United States and of the state of Illinois, residing therein. She has been judicially ascertained to be of full age, and to possess the requisite character and learning. Indeed, the court below in its opinion found in the record says: "Of the ample qualifications of the applicant we have no doubt." Still, admission to the bar was denied the petitioner; not upon the ground that she was not a citizen; not for want of age or qualification; not because the profession of the law is not one of those avocations which are open to every American citizen as a matter of right, upon complying with the reasonable regulations prescribed by the legislature; but upon the sole ground that inconvenience would result from permitting her to enjoy her legal rights in this, to wit: that her clients might have difficulty in enforcing the contracts they might make with her as their attorney, because of her being a married woman.

Now, with entire respect to that court, it is submitted that this argument *ab inconvenienti*, which might have been urged with whatever force belongs to it against adopting the 14th Amendment in the full scope of its language, is utterly futile to resist its full and proper operation, now that it has been adopted.

I maintain that the 14th Amendment opens to every citizen of the United States, male or female, black or white, married or single, the honorable professions as well as the servile employments of life; and that no citizen can be excluded from any one of them. Intelligence, integrity and honor are the only qualifications that can be prescribed as conditions precedent to an entry upon any honorable pursuit or profitable avocation, and all the privileges and immunities which I vindicate to a colored citizen, I vindicate to our mothers, our sisters and our daughters.

Of a bar composed of men and women of equal integrity and learning, women might be more or less frequently retained as the taste or judgment of clients might dictate; but the broad shield of the Constitution is over all, and protects each in that measure of success which his or her individual merits may secure.

(No counsel appeared for the defendant in error.)

Mr. Justice **Miller** delivered the opinion of the court:

The plaintiff in error, residing in the state of Illinois, made application to the judges of the supreme court of that state for a license to practice law. She accompanied her petition with the usual certificate from an inferior court, of her good character, and that on due examination she had been found to possess the requisite qualifications. Pending this application, she also filed an affidavit to the effect "that she was born in the state of Vermont; that she was (had been) a citizen of that state; that she is now a citizen of the United States, and has been for many years past a resident of the city of Chicago in the state of Illinois." And with this affidavit she also filed a paper claiming that under the foregoing facts she was entitled to the license paid for, by virtue of the 2d section of the 4th article of the Constitution of the United States, and of the 14th article of Amendment of that instrument.

131*] *The statute of Illinois on this subject enacts that no person shall be permitted to practice as an attorney or counselor at law, or to commence, conduct, or defend any action, suit, or plaint, in which he is not a party concerned, in any court of record within this state, either by using or subscribing his own name or the name of any other person, without having previously obtained a license for that purpose from two justices of the supreme court, which license shall constitute the person receiving the same an attorney and counselor at law, and shall authorize him to appear in all the courts of record within this state and there to practice as an attorney and counselor at law according to the laws and customs thereof.

The supreme court denied the application apparently upon the ground that it was a woman who made it.

The record is not very perfect, but it may be fairly taken that the plaintiff asserted her right to a license on the grounds, among others, that she was a citizen of the United States, and that having been a citizen of Vermont at one time, she was, in the state of Illinois, entitled to any right granted to citizens of the latter state.

The court having overruled these claims of right founded on the clauses of the Federal Con-
138*] stitution before referred* to, those propositions may be considered as properly before this court.

As regards the provision of the Constitution that citizens of each state shall be entitled to all the privileges and immunities of citizens in the several states, the plaintiff in her affidavit has stated very clearly a case to which it is inapplicable.

The protection designed by that clause, as has been repeatedly held, has no application to a citizen of the state whose laws are complained of. If the plaintiff was a citizen of the state of Illinois, that provision of the Constitution gave her no protection against its courts or its legislation.

16 WALL.

The plaintiff seems to have seen this difficulty, and attempts to avoid it by stating that she was born in Vermont.

While she remained in Vermont that circumstance made her a citizen of that state. But she states, at the same time, that she is a citizen of the United States, and that she is now, and has been for many years past, a resident of Chicago, in the state of Illinois.

The 14th Amendment declares that citizens of the United States are citizens of the state within which they reside; therefore the plaintiff was, at the time of making her application, a citizen of the United States and a citizen of the state of Illinois.

We do not here mean to say that there may not be a temporary residence in one state, with intent to return to another, which will not create citizenship in the former. But plaintiff states nothing to take her case out of the definition of citizenship of a state as defined by the 1st section of the 14th Amendment.

In regard to that Amendment counsel for the plaintiff in this court truly says that there are certain privileges and immunities which belong to a citizen of the United States as such; otherwise it would be nonsense for the 14th Amendment to prohibit a state from abridging them, and he proceeds to argue that admission to the bar of a state, of a person who possesses the requisite learning and character, is one of those which a state may not deny.

*In this latter proposition we are not [*139 able to concur with counsel. We agree with him that there are privileges and immunities belonging to citizens of the United States, in that relation and character, and that it is these and these alone which a state is forbidden to abridge. But the right to admission to practice in the courts of a state is not one of them. This right in no sense depends on citizenship of the United States. It has not, as far as we know, ever been made in any state or in any case to depend on citizenship at all. Certainly many prominent and distinguished lawyers have been admitted to practice, both in the state and Federal courts, who were not citizens of the United States or of any state. But, on whatever basis this right may be placed, so far as it can have any relation to citizenship at all, it would seem that, as to the courts of a state, it would relate to citizenship of the state, and as to Federal courts, it would relate to citizenship of the United States.

The opinion just delivered in the *Slaughter-House Cases*, from Louisiana, *ante*, 394, renders elaborate argument in the present case unnecessary; for, unless we are wholly and radically mistaken in the principles on which those cases are decided, the right to control and regulate the granting of license to practice law in the courts of a state is one of those powers which are not transferred for its protection to the Federal government, and its exercise is in no manner governed or controlled by citizenship of the United States in the party seeking such license.

It is unnecessary to repeat the argument on which the judgment in those cases is founded. It is sufficient to say, they are conclusive of the present case.

The judgment of the State Court is, there-fore, affirmed.

Mr. Justice **Bradley:**

I concur in the judgment of the court in this case, by which the judgment of the supreme court of Illinois is affirmed, but not for the reasons specified in the opinion just read.

140*] *The claim of the plaintiff, who is a married woman, to be admitted to practice as an attorney and counselor at law, is based upon the supposed right of every person, man or woman, to engage in any lawful employment for a livelihood. The supreme court of Illinois denied the application on the ground that, by the common law, which is the basis of the laws of Illinois, only men were admitted to the bar, and the legislature had not made any change in this respect, but had simply provided that no person should be admitted to practice as attorney or counselor without having previously obtained a license for that purpose from two justices of the supreme court, and that no person should receive a license without first obtaining a certificate from the court of some county of his good moral character. In other respects it was left to the discretion of the court to establish the rules by which admission to the profession should be determined. The court, however, regarded itself as bound by at least two limitations. One was that it should establish such terms of admission as would promote the proper administration of justice, and the other that it should not admit any persons or class of persons not intended by the legislature to be admitted, even though not expressly excluded by statute. In view of this latter limitation the court felt compelled to deny the application of females to be admitted as members of the bar. Being contrary to the rules of the common law and the usages of Westminster Hall from time immemorial, it could not be supposed that the legislature had intended to adopt any different rule.

The claim that, under the 14th Amendment of the Constitution, which declares that no state shall make or enforce any law which shall abridge the privileges and immunities of citizens of the United States, and the statute law of Illinois, or the common law prevailing in that state, can no longer be set up as a barrier against the right of females to pursue any lawful employment for a livelihood (the practice of law included), assumes that it is one of the privileges and immunities of women as citizens to engage in any and every profession, occupation or employment in civil life.

141*] *It certainly cannot be affirmed, as a historical fact, that this has ever been established as one of the fundamental privileges and immunities of the sex. On the contrary, the civil law, as well as nature herself, has always recognized a wide difference in the respective spheres and destinies of man and woman. Man is, or should be, woman's protector and defender. The natural and proper timidity and delicacy which belongs to the female sex evidently unfits it for many of the occupations of civil life. The constitution of the family organization, which is founded in the divine ordinance, as well as in the nature of things, indicates the domestic sphere as that which properly belongs to the domain and functions of womanhood. The harmony, not to say identity, of interests and views which belong or should belong to the family institution, is repugnant to the idea of a woman adopting a distinct and independent career from that of her husband. So firmly fixed was this sentiment in the founders of the common law that it became a maxim of that system of jurisprudence that a woman had no legal existence separate from her husband, who was regarded as her head and representative in the social state; and, notwithstanding some recent modifications of this civil status, many of the special rules of law flowing from and dependent upon this cardinal principle still exist in full force in most states. One of these is, that a married woman is incapable, without her husband's consent, of making contracts which shall be binding on her or him. This very incapacity was one circumstance which the supreme court of Illinois deemed important in rendering a married woman incompetent fully to perform the duties and trusts that belong to the office of an attorney and counselor.

It is true that many women are unmarried and not affected by any of the duties, complications, and incapacities arising out of the married state, but these are exceptions to the general rule. The paramount destiny and mission of woman are to fulfill the noble and benign offices of wife and mother. This is the law of the Creator. And the rules of civil society *must be adapted to the general consti- [*142 tution of things, and cannot be based upon exceptional cases.

The humane movements of modern society, which have for their object the multiplication of avenues for woman's advancement, and of occupations adapted to her condition and sex, have my heartiest concurrence. But I am not prepared to say that it is one of her fundamental rights and privileges to be admitted into every office and position, including those which require highly special qualifications and demanding special responsibilities. In the nature of things it is not every citizen of every age, sex, and condition that is qualified for every calling and position. It is the prerogative of the legislator to prescribe regulations founded on nature, reason, and experience for the due admission of qualified persons to professions and callings demanding special skill and confidence. This fairly belongs to the police power of the state; and, in my opinion, in view of the peculiar characteristics, destiny, and mission of woman, it is within the province of the legislature to ordain what offices, positions, and callings shall be filled and discharged by men, and shall receive the benefit of those energies and responsibilities, and that decision and firmness which are presumed to predominate in the sterner sex.

For these reasons I think that the laws of Illinois now complained of are not obnoxious to the charge of abridging any of the privileges and immunities of citizens of the United States.

Mr. Justice **Field** and Mr. Justice **Swayne:** We concur in the opinion of Mr. Justice **Bradley.**

Dissenting, Mr. Chief Justice **Chase.**

NATIONAL ORGANIZATION FOR WOMEN STATEMENT OF PURPOSE

We, men and women who hereby constitute ourselves as the National Organization for Women, believe that the time has come for a new movement toward true equality for all women in America, and toward a fully equal partnership of the sexes, as part of the world-wide revolution of human rights now taking place within and beyond our national borders.

The purpose of NOW is to take action to bring women into full participation in the mainstream of American society now, exercising all the privileges and responsibilities thereof in truly equal partnership with men.

We believe the time has come to move beyond the abstract argument, discussion and symposia over the status and special nature of women which has raged in America in recent years; the time has come to confront, with concrete action, the conditions that now prevent women from enjoying the equality of opportunity and freedom of choice which is their right as individual Americans, and as human beings.

NOW is dedicated to the proposition that women first and foremost, are human beings, who, like all other people in our society, must have the chance to develop their fullest human potential. We believe that women can achieve such equality only by accepting to the full the challenges and responsibilities they share with all other people in our society, as part of the decision-making mainstream of American political, economic and social life.

We organize to initiate or support action, nationally or in any part of this nation, by individuals or organizations, to break through the silken curtain of prejudice and discrimination against women in government, industry, the professions, the churches, the political parties, the judiciary, the labor unions, in education, science, medicine, law, religion and every other field of importance in American society. . . .

There is no civil rights movement to speak for women, as there has been for Negroes and other victims of discrimination. The National Organization for Women must therefore begin to speak.

WE BELIEVE that the power of American law, and the protection guaranteed by the U.S. Constitution to the civil rights of all individuals, must be effectively applied and enforced to isolate and remove patterns of sex discrimination, to ensure equality of opportunity in employment and education, and equality of civil and political rights and responsibilities on behalf of women, as well as for Negroes and other deprived groups.

We realize that women's problems are linked to many broader questions of social justice; their solution will require concerted action by many groups. Therefore, convinced that human rights for all are indivisible, we expect to give active support to the common cause of equal rights for all those who suffer discrimination and deprivation, and we call upon other organizations committed to such goals to support our efforts toward equality for women.

WE DO NOT ACCEPT the token appointment of a few women to high-level positions in government and industry as a substitute for a serious continuing effort to recruit and advance women according to their individual abilities. To this end, we urge American government and industry to mobilize the same resources of ingenuity and command with which they have solved problems of far greater difficulty than those now impeding the progress of women.

WE BELIEVE that this nation has a capacity at least as great as other nations, to innovate new social institutions which will enable women to enjoy true equality of opportunity and responsibility in society, without conflict with their responsibilities as mothers and homemakers. In such innovations, America does not lead the Western world, but lags by decades behind many European countries. We do not accept the traditional assumption that a woman has to choose between marriage and motherhood, on the one hand, and serious participation in industry or the professions on the other. We question the present expectation that all normal women will retire from job or profession for ten or fifteen years, to devote their full time to raising children, only to reenter the job market at a relatively minor level. This, in itself, is a deterrent to the aspirations of women, to their acceptance into management or professional training courses, and to the very possibility of equality of opportunity or real choice, for all but a few women. Above all, we reject the assumption that these problems are the unique responsibility of each individual woman, rather than a basic social dilemma which society must solve. True equality of opportunity and freedom of choice for women requires such practical and possible innovations as a nationwide network of child-care centers, which will make it unnecessary for women to retire completely from society until their children are grown, and national programs to provide retraining for women who have chosen to care for their own children full time.

WE BELIEVE that it is as essential for every girl to be educated to her full potential of human ability as it is for every boy—with the knowledge that such education is the key to effective participation in today's economy and that, for a girl as for a boy, education can only be serious where there is expectation that it will be used in society. We believe that American educators are capable of devising means of imparting such expectations to girl students. Moreover, we consider the decline in the proportion of women receiving higher and professional education to be evidence of discrimination. This discrimination may take the form of quotas against the admission of women to colleges and professional schools; lack of encouragement by parents, counselors and educators; denial of loans or fellowships; or the traditional or arbitrary procedures in graduate and professional training geared in terms of men, which inadvertently discriminate against women. We believe that the same serious attention must be given to high school dropouts who are girls as to boys.

WE REJECT the current assumptions that a man must carry the sole burden of supporting himself, his wife, and family, and that a woman is automatically entitled to lifelong support by a man upon her marriage, or that marriage, home and family are primarily woman's world and responsibility—hers, to dominate, his to support. We believe that a true partnership between the sexes demands a different concept of marriage, an equitable sharing of the responsibilities of home and children and of the economic burdens of their support. We believe that proper recognition should be given to the economic and social value of homemaking and child care. To these ends, we will seek to open a reexamination of laws and mores governing marriage and divorce, for we believe that the current state of "half-equality" between the sexes discriminates against both men and women, and is the cause of much unnecessary hostility between the sexes.

WE BELIEVE that women must now exercise their political rights and responsibilities as American citizens. They must refuse to be segregated on the basis of sex into separate-and-not-equal ladies' auxiliaries in the political parties, and they must demand representation according to their numbers in the regularly constituted party committees—at local, state, and national levels—and in the informal power structure, participating fully in the selection of candidates and political decision-making, and running for office themselves.

IN THE INTERESTS OF THE HUMAN DIGNITY OF WOMEN, we will protest and endeavor to change the false image of women now prevalent in the mass media, and in the texts, ceremonies, laws, and practices of our major social institutions. Such images perpetuate contempt for women by society and by women for themselves. We are similarly opposed to all policies and practices—in church, state, college, factory, or office—which, in the guise of protectiveness, not only deny opportunities but also foster in women self-denigration, dependence, and evasion of responsibility, undermine their confidence in their own abilities and foster contempt for women.

NOW WILL HOLD ITSELF INDEPENDENT OF ANY POLITICAL PARTY in order to mobilize the political power of all women and men intent on our goals. We will strive to ensure that no party, candidate, president, senator, governor, congressman, or any public official who betrays or ignores the principle of full equality between the sexes is elected or appointed to office. If it is necessary to mobilize the votes of men and women who believe in our cause, in order to win for women the final right to be fully free and equal human beings, we so commit ourselves.

WE BELIEVE THAT women will do most to create a new image of women by acting now, and by speaking out in behalf of their own equality, freedom, and human dignity—not in pleas for special privilege, nor in enmity toward men, who are also victims of the current half-equality between the sexes—but in an active, self-respecting partnership with men. By so doing, women will develop confidence in their own ability to determine actively, in partnership with men, the conditions of their life, their choices, their future and their society.

NATIVE AMERICAN RIGHTS

When Europeans arrived in North America in the 1600s, they discovered that Native American tribes already occupied the land. Between the 1630s and the War of Independence, white settlers gradually pushed the Native Americans, whom they called "Indians," westward. The goals of the settlers, which included colonization, land exploitation, and religious conversion, led to cultural and social conflict that erupted in periodic "Indian wars."

After the formation of the United States, state and federal government leaders agreed that the nation needed to establish a national policy toward Native Americans. By the 1820s the government's policy was to remove Native Americans from their lands and resettle them in the "Great American Desert" to the west. In 1830 Congress passed the Indian Removal Act (4 Stat. 411) and appropriated $500,000 for this purpose. During the presidency of Andrew Jackson (1829–1837), ninety-four removal treaties were negotiated. By 1840 most of the Native Americans in the more settled states and territories had been sent west.

The U.S. Supreme Court confronted the issue of Native American rights in the *Cherokee* cases, the collective name for two cases of the 1830s: *Cherokee Nation v. Georgia*, 30 U.S. 1, 8 L. Ed. 25 (1831), and *Worcester v. Georgia*, 31 U.S. 515, 8 L. Ed. 483 (1832). In *Cherokee Nation*, Chief Justice John Marshall ruled that the Cherokee Indians were not a sovereign nation. The following year Marshall issued an opinion that, while not overruling *Cherokee Nation*, held that the Cherokees were a nation with the right to retain independent political communities. President Jackson refused to abide by

this ruling and supported the removal of the Cherokees to Oklahoma, which took place in 1838–1839.

Few tribes willingly moved westward, resulting in more Indian wars. The Black Hawk War of 1832, fought in Illinois, illustrates the situation Native Americans faced. The Sauk and Fox tribes, who had been forced from their lands by white settlers, faced the prospect of famine but were reluctant to move west where they would have to confront the hostile Sioux nation. Accordingly, Chief Black Hawk led the Sauk and Fox in an unsuccessful campaign to reoccupy their former lands.

Throughout the nineteenth century, treaties were made in which tribes ceded areas of land to the federal government in return for compensation in the form of livestock, merchandise, and annuities. These agreements were often accompanied by the establishment of reservations. All treaties that the United States entered into prior to 1871 were written in the formal language of international covenants. The parties would sign the draft treaty, and the document would be submitted to the U.S. Senate for ratification. After 1871 formal treaty arrangements were abandoned in favor of simple agreements between the government and Native American tribes. These agreements required the approval of both houses of Congress and had the same authority as the previous treaty forms, but they effectively abandoned the idea that Native American tribes were independent. For their part, the tribes came to distrust the federal government for not honoring the treaties, confining them to reservations, and ending a way of life that had endured for centuries. Not until the twentieth century, after the continent had been settled and the tribes restricted to reservations, did the federal government attempt to seek a different policy.

Worcester v. Georgia

The Cherokee nation, located in the state of Georgia, sought to remain on its territory and be viewed legally as an independent, sovereign nation. In *Cherokee Nation v. Georgia* (1831), the tribe fought the state of Georgia's attempts to assert jurisdiction over Cherokee lands. The Cherokees appealed to the U.S. Supreme Court, arguing that they were protected by treaties negotiated with the U.S. government. Chief Justice John Marshall, writing for the majority, ruled that the Court had no jurisdiction to hear the Cherokees' lawsuit. Marshall defined the Cherokees as a "domestic, dependent nation," rather than a sovereign nation. Therefore, under Article III of the Constitution, the Court had no basis for entertaining the lawsuit.

The following year, however, in *Worcester v. Georgia* (1832), the Court modified its holding. In *Worcester*, Georgia sought to prevent white persons from living in Cherokee country without first obtaining a license from the state. The Cherokees challenged this license requirement. The Supreme Court agreed with the Cherokees, ruling that the Georgia laws were unconstitutional because they violated treaties, the Contract and Commerce Clauses of the Constitution, and the sovereign authority of the Cherokee nation.

In his majority opinion, Chief Justice Marshall placed emphasis on the tribe's standing as a nation. He pointed out that the U.S. government had applied the words *treaty* and *nation* "to Indians as we have applied them to the other nations of the earth." In addition, he ruled that Indian nations were distinct peoples with the right to retain independent political communities.

Worcester's affirmation of the validity of the treaty the Cherokees had signed with the United States did not protect them. President Andrew Jackson refused to enforce the Court's ruling and encouraged the removal of the Cherokees. Nearly a quarter of the 15,000 Cherokees died during the relocation, which began in 1838. The Cherokee called the western trek to Oklahoma and Indian Territory the "Trail of Tears." Nevertheless, *Worcester* remains an important decision, for it endorsed the sovereignty of Native American nations and the need to respect the terms and conditions negotiated by treaty.

Surrender Speech

From April to August 1832, an armed band of Sauk and Fox Indians under Chief Black Hawk sought to reoccupy the lands they had held in the Illinois and Wisconsin Territory. The tribes, who faced famine and hostile Sioux to the west, wanted a place with decent land in which to plant their corn. The Illinois militia chased them into Wisconsin, killing women and children as the tribe attempted to escape across the Mississippi River.

Faced with annihilation, Black Hawk had no choice but to surrender. In his speech he recounted the history of lies and betrayal the white men had perpetuated on Native Americans. President Jackson then sent Black Hawk and his son Whirling Thunder on tour to be displayed as "trophies" of war. But the two prisoners showed such dignity in their ordeal that the public quickly began to sympathize with them.

Treaty with Sioux Nation

The Sioux were an important confederacy of the North American Indian tribes that inhabited the Great Plains. In the seventeenth century the Sioux had comprised small bands of Woodland Indians in the Mille Lacs region of present-day Minnesota. Conflict with the Ojibwa (also called Chippewa or Anishinabe) forced the Sioux to move to the buffalo ranges of the Great Plains. As they became adept buffalo hunters, the tribes grew and prospered. By 1750 the Sioux comprised some 30,000 persons firmly established in the heartland of the northern plains.

An 1825 treaty confirmed Sioux possession of an immense territory including much of present-day Minnesota, the Dakotas, Wisconsin, Iowa, Missouri, and Wyoming. As white settlers moved onto Sioux lands, violence erupted. Red Cloud's War (1866–1867) resulted in a treaty granting the Black Hills in perpetuity to the Sioux. The United States failed to honor the treaty, however, and allowed gold prospectors and miners to invade the territory in the 1870s. These events were the backdrop for the Battle of Little Bighorn on June 25, 1876, in which General George Armstrong Custer and three hundred troops were killed by Chief Sitting Bull and his Sioux warriors.

In 1877 Congress approved a treaty with certain bands of the Sioux (19 Stat. 254), which changed the terms of the treaty ratified in 1869. Because of pressure by white miners and settlers, the Great Sioux Reservation was reduced, three roads were to be constructed and maintained through the reservation, and the free navigation of the Missouri River was mandated.

In return, the Sioux nation continued to receive annuities negotiated in the 1869 treaty. More importantly, the Sioux were required to select land for a reservation "located in a country where they may eventually become self-supporting and acquire the arts of civilized life." The U.S. government promised the Sioux schools, instruction in "mechanical and agricultural arts," a ration of food, and a "comfortable house." The removal to the reservation meant the end of the Sioux people's traditional way of life. Sporadic resistance continued until the massacre at Wounded Knee, South Dakota, in December 1890, when U.S. troops slaughtered more than two hundred Sioux men, women, and children.

My Son, Stop Your Ears

On January 14, 1879, Chief Joseph, leader of the Nez Percé nation of the Northwest, addressed Congress to explain why his people had declared war on U.S. troops in 1877. Chief Joseph explained that he and his band had refused to leave their Oregon homes despite the yearly demands of U.S. Indian agents. In 1877, after local cowboys stole Nez Percé horses, the Native Americans struck back. For four months and over thirteen hundred miles, they conducted guerrilla warfare against U.S. troops as they sought to escape into Canada. Chief Joseph surrendered just before reaching the border. In this excerpt of his remarks, Chief Joseph discusses the treaties that the tribe had signed with the U.S. government and the subsequent efforts of the government to send his people to a reservation.

*SAMUEL A. WORCESTER, Plaintiff [*515
in Error,

v.

THE STATE OF GEORGIA.

Writ of error—practice—indictment for residing
in Cherokee territory contrary to laws of
Georgia—jurisdiction—rights of discoveries—
relations of Indians to European nations, to
the United States—legal status of the Cherokees—construction of treaties—act of Georgia
contrary to federal Constitution, acts of Congress and treaties.

A writ of error was issued to "the judges of the
Superior Court for the County of Gwinnett in the
State of Georgia," commanding them to send
to the Supreme Court of the United States, the
record and proceedings in the said Superior Court
of the County of Gwinnett, between the State
of Georgia, plaintiff, and Samuel A. Worcester,
defendant, on an indictment in that court. The
record of the court of Gwinnett was returned,
certified by the clerk, of the court, and was also
authenticated by the seal of the court. It was returned with, and annexed to, a writ of error issued
in regular form, the citation being signed by one
of the associate justices of the Supreme Court, and
served on the Governor and Attorney-General of
the State more than thirty days before the commencement of the term to which the writ of error
was returnable.

BY THE COURT: The judicial Act, so far as it
prescribes the mode of proceeding, appears to have
been literally pursued. In February, 1797, a rule
was made on this subject in the following words:
"It is ordered by the court that the clerk of the
court to which any writ of error shall be directed,
may make return of the same by transmitting a
true copy of the record, and of all proceedings in
the same, under his hand and the seal of the
court."

This has been done. But the signature of the
judge has not been added to that of the clerk. The
law does not require it. The rule does not require
it.

The plaintiff in error was indicted in the Superior
Court of the County of Gwinnett in the State of
Georgia, "for residing, on the 15th of July, 1831, in
that part of the Cherokee Nation attached by the
laws of the State of Georgia to that county, without a license or permit from the Governor of the
State, or from any one authorized to grant it, and
without having taken the oath to support and defend the constitution and laws of the State of
Georgia, and uprightly to demean himself as a citizen thereof, contrary to the laws of the said State."
To this indictment he pleaded that he was, on the

483

15th July, 1531, in the Cherokee Nation, out of the jurisdiction of the court of Gwinnett County; that he was a citizen of Vermont, and entered the Cherokee Nation as a missionary under the authority of the President of the United States, and has not been required by him to leave it, and that with the permission and approval of the Cherokee Nation he was engaged in preaching the gospel: that the State of Georgia ought not to maintain the prosecution, as several treaties had been entered into by the United States with the Cherokee Nation, by which that nation was acknowledged to be a sovereign nation, and by which the territory occupied by them was guaranteed to them by the United States, and that the laws of Georgia, under which the plaintiff in error was indicted, are repugnant to the treaties, and unconstitutional and void, and also that they are repugnant to the Act of Congress of March, 1802, entitled "An Act to regulate trade and intercourse with the Indian tribes." The Superior Court of Gwinnett overruled the plea, and the plaintiff in error was tried and convicted and sentenced "to hard labor in the penitentiary for four years." Held, that this was a case in which the Supreme Court of the United States **516***] had jurisdiction by writ of error, under *the twenty-fifth section of the "Act to establish the judicial court of the United States" passed in 1789.

The indictment and plea in this case draw in question the validity of the treaties made by the United States with the Cherokee Indians: if not so, their construction is certainly drawn in question; and the decision has been, if not against their validity, "against the right, privilege or exemption specially set up and claimed under them." They also draw into question the validity of a statute of the State of Georgia, "on the ground of its being repugnant to the Constitution, treaties and laws of the United States, and the decision is in favor of its validity."

It is too clear for controversy that the act of Congress by which this court is constituted has given it the power, and of course imposed on it the duty of exercising jurisdiction in this case. The record, according to the judiciary act and the rule and practice of the court, is regularly before the court.

The Act of the Legislature of Georgia, passed 22d December, 1830, entitled "An Act to prevent the exercise of assumed and arbitrary power by all persons, under pretext of authority from the Cherokee Indians," etc., enacts that "all white persons residing within the limits of the Cherokee Nation, on the first day of March next, or at any time thereafter, without a license or permit from his excellency the governor, or from such agent as his excellency the governor shall authorize to grant such permit or license, and who shall not have taken the oath hereinafter required, shall be guilty of a high misdemeanor, and upon conviction thereof shall be punished by confinement to the penitentiary at hard labor, for a term not less than four years." The eleventh section authorizes the governor, "should he deem it necessary for the protection of the mines or the enforcement of the laws in force within the Cherokee Nation, to raise and organize a guard," etc. The thirteenth section enacts, "that the said guard or any member of them shall be, and they are hereby authorized and empowered to arrest any person legally charged with or detected in a violation of the laws of this State, and to convey, as soon as practicable, the person so arrested before a justice of the peace, judge of the superior, justice of inferior court of this State, to be dealt with according to law." The extraterritorial power of every legislature being limited in its action to its own citizens or subjects, the very passage of this act is an assertion of jurisdiction over the Cherokee Nation, and of the rights and powers consequent thereto.

The principle, "that the discovery of parts of the continent of America gave title to the government by whose subjects, or by whose authority it was made, against all other European governments, which title might be consummated by possession," acknowledged by all Europeans, because it was the interest of all to acknowledge it; gave to the nation making the discovery, as its inevitable consequence, the sole right of acquiring the soil, and of making settlements on it. It was an exclusive principle, which shut out the right of competition among those who had agreed to it; not one which could annul the previous right of those who had not agreed to it. It regulated the right given by discovery among the European discoverers, but could not affect the rights of those already in possession, either as aboriginal occupants or as occupants by virtue of a discovery made before the memory of man. It gave the exclusive right to purchase, but did not found that right on a denial of the right of the possessor to sell.

The relations between the Europeans and the natives was determined in each case by the particular government which asserted and could maintain this pre-emptive *privilege in the particular [*517 place. The United States succeeded to all the claims of Great Britain, both territorial and political, but no attempt, so far as is known, has been made to enlarge them. So far as they existed merely in theory, or were in their nature only exclusive of the claims of other European nations, they still retain their original character, and remain dormant. So far as they have been practically exerted, they exist in fact, are understood by both parties, are asserted by the one, and admitted by the other.

Soon after Great Britain determined on planting colonies in America, the king granted charters to companies of his subjects, who associated for the purpose of carrying the views of the crown into effect, and of enriching themselves. The first of these charters was made before possession was taken of any part of the country. They purport generally to convey the soil, from the Atlantic to the South Sea. This soil was occupied by numerous and warlike nations, equally willing and able to defend their possessions. The extravagant and absurd idea that the feeble settlements made on the sea-coast, or the companies under whom they were made, acquired legitimate power by them to govern the people, or occupy the lands from sea to sea, did not enter the mind of any man. They were well understood to convey the title which, according to the common law of European sovereigns respecting America, they might rightfully convey, and no more. This was the exclusive right of purchasing such lands as the natives were willing to sell. The crown could not be understood to grant what the crown did not affect to claim, nor was it so understood.

NOTE.—Indians and Indian tribes; status; amenable to what laws; rights of; what courts have jurisdiction over; power of congress over. An Indian tribe or nation, occupying territory within the United States, cannot maintain an action in the United States courts. It is not a foreign state in the sense of the Constitution. Cherokee Nation v. Georgia, 5 Pet. 1.

Nor can such tribe be regarded as possessing such national character that they can claim immunity for homicide on the plea that it was committed in the course of legal war. Jim v. Washington Territory, 1 Wash. T. 76.

Cannot impose taxes on persons trading among them under the authority of the United States. 1 Op. Att. Gen. 645.

To be regarded for many purposes as a body politic within the Union, having the same general status as a territory. See Mackey v. Coxe, 18 How. 100.

Indians are not citizens of the United States but domestic subjects. The general statutes of naturalization do not apply to them. 7 Op. Att. Gen. 746. Not "enemies." 4 Op. Att. Gen. 81.

Responsible for debts, according to the laws of the State in which they live. Lowry v. Weaver, 4 McLean, 82.

Half-breed Indians are Indians so long as they remain in their tribe. 7 Op. Att. Gen. 746.

The child of a white woman, and Indian father, is a white person. United States v. Sanders, Hemp. 483.

A white man, adopted into an Indian tribe, does not thereby become an Indian, so as to cease to be amenable to the laws of the United States, or to lose the right of trial in their courts. United States v. Rogers, 4 How. 567; S. C. Hemp. 450; United States v. Rugsdale, Hemp. 497; 2 Op. Att. Gen. 402, 693; 4 Op. Att. Gen. 258; 7 Op. Att. Gen. 174.

Congress has power to pass laws punishing Indians for crimes and offenses against the United States. United States v. Cha-to-kah-na-pe-sha, Hemp. 27.

Jurisdiction of offenses in the Indian Territory by United States courts in Arkansas. United States v. Dawson, 15 How. 467; S. C. Hemp. 463; United States v. Ta-wan-ga-ca, Hemp. 304; United

1832   WORCESTER V. THE STATE OF GEORGIA.   517

Certain it is, that our history furnishes no example, from the first settlement of our country, of any attempt, on the part of the crown, to interfere with the internal affairs of the Indians farther than to keep out the agents of foreign powers, who, as traders or otherwise, might seduce them into foreign alliances. The king purchased their lands when they were willing to sell, at a price they were willing to take; but never coerced a surrender of them. He also purchased their alliance and dependence by subsidies, but never intruded into the interior of their affairs, or interfered with their self-government, so far as respected themselves only.

The third article of the Treaty of Hopewell acknowledges the Cherokees to be under the protection of the United States of America, and of no other power.

This stipulation is found in Indian treaties generally. It was introduced into their treaties with Great Britain; and may probably be found in those with other European powers. Its origin may be traced to the nature of their connection with those powers; and its true meaning is discerned in their relative situation.

The general law of European sovereigns respecting their claims in America, limited the intercourse of Indians, in a great degree, to the particular potentate whose ultimate right of domain was acknowledged by the others. This was the general state of things in time of peace. It was sometimes changed in war. The consequence was that their supplies were derived chiefly from that nation, and their trade confined to it. Goods, indispensable to their comfort, in the shape of presents, were received from the same hand. What was of still more importance, the strong hand of government was interposed to restrain the disorderly and licentious from intrusions into their country, from encroachments on their lands, and from those acts of violence which were often attended by reciprocal murder. The Indians perceived in this protection only what was beneficial to themselves—an engagement to punish aggressions on them. It involved practically no claim to their lands, no dominion **518*]** over their persons. *It merely bound the nation to the British crown, as a dependent ally claiming the protection of a powerful friend and neighbor, and receiving the advantages of that protection, without involving a surrender of their national character.

This is the true meaning of the stipulation, and is undoubtedly the sense in which it was made. Neither the British government nor the Cherokees ever understood it otherwise.

The same stipulation entered into with the United States is undoubtedly to be construed in the same manner. They receive the Cherokee Nation into their favor and protection. The Cherokees acknowledge themselves to be under the protection of the United States, and of no other power. Protection does not imply the destruction of the protected. The manner in which this stipulation was understood by the American government, is explained by the language and acts of our first president.

So with respect to the words "hunting-grounds." Hunting was at that time the principal occupation of the Indians, and their land was more used for that purpose than for any other. It could not, however, be supposed, that any intention existed of restricting the full use of the lands they reserved.

To the United States, it could be a matter of no concern whether their whole territory was devoted to hunting-grounds, or whether an occasional village, and an occasional corn field interrupted, and gave some variety to the scene.

These terms had been used in their treaties with Great Britain, and had never been misunderstood. They had never been supposed to imply a right in the British government to take their lands, or to interfere with their internal government.

The sixth and seventh articles stipulate for the punishment of the citizens of either country who may commit offenses on or against the citizens of the other. The only inference to be drawn from them is, that the United States considered the Cherokees as a nation.

The ninth article is in these words: "For the benefit and comfort of the Indians, and for the prevention of injuries or oppressions on the part of the citizens or Indians, the United States, in Congress assembled, shall have the sole and exclusive right of regulating the trade with the Indians, and managing all their affairs, as they think proper." To construe the expression "managing all their affairs," into a surrender of self-government would be a perversion of their necessary meaning, and a departure from the construction which has been uniformly put on them. The great subject of the article is the Indian trade. The influence it gave made it desirable that Congress should possess it. The commissioners brought forward the claim, with the profession that their motive was "the benefit and comfort of the Indians, and the prevention of injuries or oppressions." This may be true, as respects the regulation of their trade, and as respects the regulation of all affairs connected with their trade; but cannot be true, as respects the management of all their affairs. The most important of these is the cession of their lands and security against intruders on them. Is it credible that they could have considered themselves as surrendering to the United States the right to dictate their future cessions, and the terms on which they should be made; or to compel their submission to the violence of disorderly and licentious intruders? It is equally inconceivable that they could have supposed themselves, by a phrase thus slipped into an article, on another and more interesting subject, to have devested themselves of the right of self-government on subjects not connected with trade. Such a measure could not be *"for their benefit and comfort," or [*519 for "the prevention of injuries and oppression." Such a construction would be inconsistent with the spirit of this and of all subsequent treaties; especially of those articles which recognize the right of the Cherokees to declare hostilities and to make war. It would convert a treaty of peace covertly into an act annihilating the political existence of one of the parties. Had such a result been intended, it would have been openly avowed.

This treaty contains a few terms capable of being used in a sense which could not have been intended at the time, and which is inconsistent with the practical construction which has always been put on them; but its essential articles treat the Cherokees as a nation capable of maintaining the rela-

---

States v. Terrell, Hemp. 422; United States v. Starr, Hemp. 469; United States v. Sanders, Hemp. 483.

Indians have a right to the lands they occupy until that right is extinguished by voluntary cession to the government. Cherokee nation v. Georgia, 5 Pet. 1; Godfrey v. Beardsley, 2 McLean, 412.

But they are mere occupants; they do not hold a fee in the land of their original occupation, but only a usufruct, the fee being in the United States, or in some of the several States. United States v. Cook, 19 Wall. 591; Sparkman v. Porter, 1 Paine, 457; 8 Op. Att. Gen. 255; Marsh v. Brooks, 8 How. 223; Mann v. Wilson, 23 How. 457; Godfrey v. Beardsley, 2 McLean, 412; Minter v. Crommelin, 18 How. 87; Beecher v. Wetherby, 5 Otto, 517; Langford v. United States, 12 Ct. of Cl. 338.

Indians not capable of pre-empting public lands of the United States. 7 Op. Att. Gen. 746.

Indian residing in the United States is not a "foreign citizen or subject," within sec. 2. of art. 3 of the Constitution: and cannot maintain a suit in the Circuit Court of the United States. Karrahoo v. Adams, 1 Dill. 344.

8 L. ed.

Congress may exercise municipal legislation over the Indian country. United States v. Tobacco Factory, 1 Dill. 264; United States v. Flynn, 1 Dill. 451; Dwight's case, 13 Op. Att. Gen. 546.

Indians, though belonging to a tribe which maintains the tribal organization, occupying a reservation within a State, are amenable to State laws for murder or other offenses against such laws, committed by them off the reservation and within the limits of the State. United States v. Yellow Sun, 1 Dill. 271; S. C. sub nom.; United States v. Sacoo-da-cot, 1 Abb. U. S. 377.

The courts of the State alone have jurisdiction to try a white man for the murder of another, committed on the reservation of a tribe of Indians in that State. The national courts have no jurisdiction. United States v. Ward, 1 Woolw. 17; McCahon, 199; compare United States v. Stahl, McMahon, 206; 1 Woolw. 192.

Indian tribes, within territory of the United States, are independent political communities, and a child of one of such a tribe, is not born a citizen of the United States, although born within its territories. McKery v. Campbell, 5 Am. L. T. Rep. 407.

485

tions of peace and war, and ascertain the boundaries between them and the United States.

The treaty of Holston, negotiated with the Cherokees in July, 1791, explicitly recognizing the national character of the Cherokees, and their right of self-government, thus guarantying their lands; assuming the duty of protection, and of course pledging the faith of the United States for that protection, has been frequently renewed, and is now in full force.

To the general pledge of protection have been added several specific pledges, deemed valuable by the Indians. Some of these restrain the citizens of the United States from encroachments on the Cherokee country, and provide for the punishment of intruders.

The treaties and laws of the United States contemplate the Indian territory as completely separated from that of the States; and provide that all intercourse with them shall be carried on exclusively by the government of the Union.

The Indian nations had always been considered as distinct, independent political communities, retaining their original natural rights, as the undisputed possessors of the soil, from time immemorial; with the single exception of that imposed by irresistible power, which excluded them from intercourse with any other European potentate than the first discoverer of the coast of the particular region claimed: and this was a restriction which those European potentates imposed on themselves as well as on the Indians. The very term "nation," so generally applied to them, means "a people distinct from others." The Constitution, by declaring treaties already made, as well as those to be made, to be the supreme law of the land, has adopted and sanctioned the previous treaties with the Indian nations, and, consequently, admits their rank among those powers who are capable of making treaties. The words "treaty" and "nation" are words of our own language, selected in our diplomatic and legislative proceedings, by ourselves, having each a definite and well understood meaning. We have applied them to Indians, as we have applied them to the other nations of the earth. They are applied to all in the same sense.

Georgia, herself, has furnished conclusive evidence that her former opinions on this subject concurred with those entertained by her sister States, and by the government of the United States. Various acts of her Legislature have been cited in the argument, including the contract of cession made in the year 1802, all tending to prove her acquiescence in the universal conviction that the Indian nations possessed a full right to the lands they occupied, until that right should be extinguished by the United States with their consent; that their territory was separated from that of any State within whose chartered limits they might reside, by a boundary line, established by treaties; that, within their boundary, they possessed rights with which no State could interfere; and that the whole power of regulating the intercourse with them was vested in the United States.

520*] *In opposition to the original right possessed by the undisputed occupants of every country to this recognition of that right, which is evidenced by our history in every change through which we have passed, are placed the charters granted by the monarch of a distant and distinct region, parceling out a territory in possession of others, whom he could not remove, and did not attempt to remove, and the cession made of his claims, by the Treaty of Peace. The actual state of things at the time, and all history since, explain these charters; and the King of Great Britain, at the Treaty of Peace, could cede only what belonged to his crown. These newly asserted titles can derive no aid from the articles so often repeated in Indian treaties, extending to them, first, the protection of Great Britain, and afterwards that of the United States. These articles are associated with others, recognizing their title to self-government. The very fact of repeated treaties with them recognizes it; and the settled doctrine of the law of nations is, that a weaker power does not surrender its independence—its right to self-government, by associating with a stronger, and taking its protection. A weak state, in order to provide for its safety, may place itself under the protection of one more powerful, without stripping itself of the right of government, and ceasing to be a state. Examples of this kind are not wanting in Europe. "Tributary and feudatory states," says Vattel, "do not thereby cease to be sovereign and independent states, so long as self-government and sovereign and independent authority are left in the administration of the state." At the present day, more than one state may be considered as holding its right of self-government under the guarantee and protection of one or more allies.

The Cherokee Nation, then, is a distinct community, occupying its own territory, with boundaries accurately described, in which the laws of Georgia can have no force, and which the citizens of Georgia have no right to enter but with the assent of the Cherokees themselves, or in conformity with treaties, and with the acts of Congress. The whole intercourse between the United States and this nation is, by our Constitution and laws, vested in the government of the United States.

The act of the State of Georgia under which the plaintiff in error was prosecuted, is consequently void, and the judgment a nullity.

The acts of the Legislature of Georgia interfere forcibly with the relations established between the United States and the Cherokee Nation, the regulation of which, according to the settled principles of our Constitution, is committed exclusively to the government of the Union.

They are in direct hostility with treaties, repeated in a succession of years, which mark out the boundary that separates the Cherokee country from Georgia; guaranty to them all the land within their boundary; solemnly pledge the faith of the United States to restrain their citizens from trespassing on it; and recognize the pre-existing power of the nation to govern itself.

They are in equal hostility with the acts of Congress for regulating this intercourse and giving effect to the treaties.

The forcible seizure and abduction of the plaintiff in error, who was residing in the nation, with its permission, and by authority of the President of the United States, is also a violation of the acts which authorize the chief magistrate to exercise this authority.

Will these powerful considerations avail the plaintiff in error? We think they will. He was seized and forcibly carried away, while under guardianship of treaties guarantying the country in which he resided and taking it under the protection of the United States. He was seized while performing, under the *sanction of the chief [*521 magistrate of the Union, those duties which the humane policy adopted by Congress had recommended. He was apprehended, tried, and condemned, under color of a law which has been shown to be repugnant to the Constitution, laws, and treaties of the United States. Had a judgment, liable to the same objections, been rendered for property, none would question the jurisdiction of this court. It cannot be less clear when the judgment affects personal liberty, and inflicts disgrace-

---

Congress has power to regulate the sale and prohibit the unlicensed sale of spirituous liquors in the "Indian country." United States v. 43 gallons of whiskey, 3 Otto, 188; United States v. Shawmux, 2 Sawyer, 364; United States v. Winslow, 3 Sawyer, 337; Re Carr, 3 Sawyer, 116.

What constitutes the "Indian country." Bates v. Clark, 5 Otto, 204; United States v. Seveloff, 2 Sawyer, 311; Waters v. Campbell, 4 Sawyer, 121.

Indians cannot cut timber off of lands occupied by them, for the purposes of sale only, but may, for improving the land or better adapting it for occupation, and when cut off for the latter purposes, may sell the same. United States v. Cook, 19 Wall. 591.

Rights of Cherokee tribe in their lands, and of "actual settlers" thereon. Langdon v. Joy, 4 Dill. 391; United States v. Reese, 8 Cent. L. J. 453.

Indians maintaining tribal relations are not subject to the criminal jurisdiction of United States courts for acts done by them within Indian country. The district court cannot try one Indian for murder of another, done in Indian country. Ex-parte Reynolds, 18 Alb. L. J. 8.

Federal courts (not the courts of Kansas) have jurisdiction of larceny committed in Fort Leavenworth military reservation. Ex-parte Hebard, 4 Dill. 380.

Probate courts of a State cannot administer upon the property or effects of Indians, members of a tribe which maintains its tribal relations, without the assent of the general government. United States v. Payne, 4 Dill. 387; Stroud v. Missouri R. R. Co. 4 Dill. 396.

Jurisdiction to punish crimes committed by or against Indians. See note, 21 L. R. A. 169. Question relating to Indians as federal question,—see note, 62 L. R. A. 537.

ful punishment; if punishment could disgrace when inflicted on innocence. The plaintiff in error is not less interested in the operation of this unconstitutional law than if it affected his property. He is not less entitled to the protection of the Constitution, laws, and treaties of his country.

THIS was a writ of error to the Superior Court for the County of Gwinnett, in the State of Georgia.

On the 22d December, 1830, the Legislature of the State of Georgia passed the following act:

"An Act to prevent the exercise of assumed and arbitrary power by all persons, under pretext of authority from the Cherokee Indians and their laws, and to prevent white persons from residing within that part of the chartered limits of Georgia occupied by the Cherokee Indians, and to provide a guard for the protection of the gold mines, and to enforce the laws of the State within the aforesaid territory.

"Be it enacted by the Senate and House of Representatives of the State of Georgia in General Assembly met, and it is hereby enacted by the authority of the same that, after the 1st day of February, 1831, it shall not be lawful for any person or persons, under color or pretense of authority from said Cherokee tribe, or as headmen, chiefs or warriors of said tribe, to cause or procure by any means the assembling of any council or other pretended legislative body of the said Indians or others living among them, for the purpose of legislating (or for any other purpose whatever). And persons offending against the provisions of this section shall be guilty of a high misdemeanor, and subject to indictment therefor, and, on conviction, shall be punished by confinement at hard labor in the penitentiary for the space of four years.

"Sec. 2. And be it further enacted by the authority aforesaid that, after the time aforesaid, it shall not be lawful for any person or persons, under pretext of authority from the Cherokee tribe, or as representatives, chiefs, headmen or warriors of said tribe, to meet or 522*] assemble as a council, assembly, *convention, or in any other capacity, for the purpose of making laws, orders or regulations for said tribe. And all persons offending against the provisions of this section shall be guilty of a high misdemeanor, and subject to an indictment, and, on conviction thereof, shall undergo an imprisonment in the penitentiary at hard labor for the space of four years.

"Sec. 3. And be it further enacted by the authority aforesaid that, after the time aforesaid, it shall not be lawful for any person or persons, under color or by authority of the Cherokee tribe, or any of its laws or regulations, to hold any court or tribunal whatever, for the purpose of hearing and determining causes, either civil or criminal, or to give any judgment in such causes, or to issue, or cause to issue, any process against the person or property of any of said tribe. And all persons offending against the provisions of this section shall be guilty of a high misdemeanor, and subject to indictment, and, on conviction thereof, shall be imprisoned in the penitentiary at hard labor for the space of four years.

"Sec. 4. And be it further enacted by the authority aforesaid that, after the time aforesaid, it shall not be lawful for any person or persons, as a ministerial officer, or in any other capacity, to execute any precept, command or process issued by any court or tribunal in the Cherokee tribe, on the persons or property of any of said tribe. And all persons offending against the provisions of this section, shall be guilty of a trespass, and subject to indictment, and, on conviction thereof, shall be punished by fine and imprisonment in the jail or in the penitentiary, not longer than four years, at the discretion of the court.

"Sec. 5. And be it further enacted by the authority aforesaid that, after the time aforesaid, it shall not be lawful for any person or persons to confiscate, or attempt to confiscate, or otherwise to cause a forfeiture of the property or estate of any Indian of said tribe, in consequence of his enrolling himself and family for emigration, or offering to enroll for emigration, or any other act of said Indian, in furtherance of his intention to emigrate. And persons offending against the provisions of this section shall be guilty of high misdemeanor, and, on conviction, shall undergo an imprisonment in the penitentiary at hard labor for the space of four years.

*"Sec. 6. And be it further enacted [*523 by the authority aforesaid that none of the provisions of this act shall be so construed as to prevent said tribe, its headmen, chiefs or other representatives, from meeting any agent or commissioner, on the part of the State or the United States, for any purpose whatever.

"Sec. 7. And be it further enacted by the authority aforesaid that all white persons residing within the limits of the Cherokee Nation on the 1st day of March next, or at any time thereafter, without a license or permit from his excellency the governor, or from such agent as his excellency the governor shall authorize to grant such permit or license, and who shall not have taken the oath hereinafter required, shall be guilty of a high misdemeanor, and, upon conviction thereof, shall be punished by confinement to the penitentiary at hard labor for a term not less than four years; provided, that the provisions of this section shall not be so construed as to extend to any authorized agent or agents of the government of the United States or of this State, or to any person or persons who may rent any of those improvements which have been abandoned by Indians who have emigrated west of the Mississippi; provided, nothing contained in this section shall be so construed as to extend to white females, and all male children under twenty-one years of age.

"Sec. 8. And be it further enacted by the authority aforesaid that all white persons, citizens of the State of Georgia, who have procured a license in writing from his excellency the governor, or from such agent as his excellency the governor shall authorize to grant such permit or license, to reside within the limits of the Cherokee Nation, and who have taken the following oath, viz.: "I, A. B., do solemnly swear (or affirm, as the case may be) that I will support and defend the constitution and laws of the State of Georgia, and uprightly demean myself as a citizen thereof, so help me God," shall be, and the same are hereby declared, exempt and free from the operation of the seventh section of this act.

"Sec. 9. And be it further enacted that his

8 L. ed.

excellency the governor be, and he is hereby authorized to grant licenses to reside within the limits of the Cherokee Nation, according to the provisions of the eighth section of this act.

"Sec. 10. And be it further enacted by the **524***] authority aforesaid *that no person shall collect or claim any toll from any person for passing any turnpike gate or toll bridge, by authority of any act or law of the Cherokee tribe, or any chief or headman or men of the same.

"Sec. 11. And be it further enacted by the authority aforesaid that his excellency the governor be, and he is hereby empowered, should he deem it necessary, either for the protection of the mines, or for the enforcement of the laws of force within the Cherokee Nation, to raise and organize a guard, to be employed on foot, or mounted, as occasion may require, which shall not consist of more than sixty persons, which guard shall be under the command of the commissioner or agent appointed by the governor to protect the mines, with power to dismiss from the service any member of said guard (on paying the wages due for services rendered) for disorderly conduct, and make appointments to fill the vacancies occasioned by such dismissal.

"Sec. 12. And be it further enacted by the authority aforesaid that each person who may belong to said guard, shall receive for his compensation at the rate of fifteen dollars per month when on foot, and at the rate of twenty dollars per month when mounted, for every month that such person is engaged in actual service; and, in the event that the commissioner or agent herein referred to should die, resign, or fail to perform the duties herein required of him, his excellency the governor is hereby authorized and required to appoint, in his stead, some other fit and proper person to the command of said guard; and the commissioner or agent, having the command of the guard aforesaid, for the better discipline thereof, shall appoint three sergeants, who shall receive at the rate of twenty dollars per month while serving on foot, and twenty-five dollars per month when mounted, as compensation whilst in actual service.

"Sec. 13. And be it further enacted by the authority aforesaid that the said guard, or any member of them, shall be, and they are hereby authorized and empowered to arrest any person legally charged with, or detected in, a violation of the laws of this State, and to convey as soon as practicable the person so arrested before a justice of the peace, judge of the superior or justice of inferior court of this State, to be **525***] dealt *with according to law; and the pay and support of said guard be provided out of the fund already appropriated for the protection of the gold mines."

The Legislature of Georgia, on the 19th December, 1829, passed the following Act:

"An Act to add the territory lying within the chartered limits of Georgia, and now in the occupancy of the Cherokee Indians, to the counties of Carroll, DeKalb, Gwinnett, Hall, and Habersham, and to extend the laws of this State over the same, and to annul all laws and ordinances made by the Cherokee Nation of Indians, and to provide for the compensation
488

of officers serving legal process in said territory, and to regulate the testimony of Indians, and to repeal the ninth section of the Act of 1828 upon this subject.

"Sec. 1. Be it enacted by the Senate and House of Representatives of the State of Georgia in General Assembly met, and it is hereby enacted by the authority of the same, that from and after the passing of this act, all that part of the unlocated territory within the limits of this State, and which lies between the Alabama line and the old path leading from the Buzzard Roost on the Chattahoochee, to Sally Hughes's on the Hightower River; thence to Thomas Pelet's, on the old federal road; thence with said road to the Alabama line be, and the same is hereby added to, and shall become a part of, the County of Carroll.

"Sec. 2. And be it further enacted that all that part of said territory lying and being north of the last-mentioned line, and south of the road running from Charles Gait's ferry, on the Chattahoochee River, to Dick Roe's, to where it intersects with the path aforesaid, be, and the same is hereby added to, and shall become a part of, the County of DeKalb.

"Sec. 3. And be it further enacted that all that part of the said territory lying north of the last-mentioned line, and south of a line commencing at the mouth of Baldridge's Creek; thence up said creek to its source; from thence to where the federal road crosses the Hightower; thence with said road to the Tennessee line, be, and the same is hereby added to, and shall become part of, the County of Gwinnett.

"Sec. 4. And be it further enacted that all that part of the said territory lying north of said last-mentioned line, and south *of [*526 a line to commence on the Chestatee River, at the mouth of Yoholo Creek; thence up said creek to the top of the Blue Ridge; thence to the headwaters of Notley River; thence down said river to the boundary line of Georgia, be, and the same is hereby added to, and shall become a part of, the County of Hall.

"Sec. 5. And be it further enacted that all that part of said territory lying north of said last-mentioned line, within the limits of this State, be, and the same is hereby added to, and shall become a part of, the County of Habersham.

"Sec. 6. And be it further enacted that all the laws, both civil and criminal, of this State, be, and the same are hereby extended over said portions of territory, respectively; and all persons whatever residing within the same, shall, after the 1st day of June next, be subject and liable to the operation of said laws, in the same manner as other citizens of this State, or the citizens of said counties, respectively; and all writs and processes whatever, issued by the courts or officers of said courts, shall extend over, and operate on, the portions of territory hereby added to the same, respectively.

"Sec. 7. And be it further enacted that after the 1st day of June next, all laws, ordinances, orders and regulations, of any kind whatever, made, passed or enacted, by the Cherokee Indians, either in general council or in any other way whatever, or by any authority whatever of said tribe, be, and the same are hereby declared to be, null and void, and of no effect, as if the same had never existed; and in
Peters 6.

all cases of indictment or civil suits, it shall not be lawful for the defendant to justify under any of said laws, ordinances, orders or regulations; nor shall the courts of this State permit the same to be given in evidence on the trial of any suit whatever.

"Sec. 8. And be it further enacted that it shall not be lawful for any person or body of persons, by arbitrary power or by virtue of any pretended rule, ordinance, law or custom of said Cherokee Nation, to prevent by threats, menaces or other means, or endeavor to prevent, any Indian of said nation, residing within the chartered limits of this State, from enrolling as an emigrant, or actually emigrating or removing from said nation; nor shall it be lawful for any person or body of persons, by arbitrary power or by virtue of any pretended 527*] rule *ordinance, law or custom of said nation, to punish, in any manner, or to molest either the person or property, or to abridge the rights or privileges of any Indian, for enrolling his or her name as an emigrant, or for emigrating or intending to emigrate, from said nation.

"Sec. 9. And be it further enacted that any person or body of persons offending against the provisions of the foregoing section, shall be guilty of a high misdemeanor, subject to indictment, and on conviction shall be punished by confinement in the common jail of any county of this State, or by confinement at hard labor in the penitentiary, for a term not exceeding four years, at the discretion of the court.

"Sec. 10. And be it further enacted that it shall not be lawful for any person or body of persons, by arbitrary power, or under color of any pretended rule, ordinance, law or custom of said nation, to prevent or offer to prevent, or deter any Indian headman, chief or warrior of said nation, residing within the chartered limits of this State, from selling or ceding to the United States, for the use of Georgia, the whole or any part of said territory, or to prevent or offer to prevent, any Indian, headman, chief or warrior of said nation, residing as aforesaid, from meeting in council or treaty any commissioner or commissioners on the part of the United States, for any purpose whatever.

"Sec. 11. And be it further enacted that any person or body of persons offending against the provisions of the foregoing sections, shall be guilty of a high misdemeanor, subject to indictment, and on conviction shall be confined at hard labor in the penitentiary for not less than four nor longer than six years, at the discretion of the court.

"Sec. 12. And be it further enacted that it shall not be lawful for any person or body of persons, by arbitrary force, or under color of any pretended rules, ordinances, law or custom of said nation, to take the life of any Indian residing as aforesaid, for enlisting as an emigrant; attempting to emigrate, ceding, or attempting to cede, as aforesaid, the whole or any part of the said territory; or meeting or attempting to meet, in treaty or in council, as aforesaid, any commissioner or commissioners aforesaid; and any person or body of persons offending against the provisions of this section, shall be 528*] guilty of *murder, subject to indictment, and, on conviction, shall suffer death by hanging.

"Sec. 13. And be it further enacted that, should any of the foregoing offenses be committed under color of any pretended rules, ordinances, custom or law of said nation, all persons acting therein, either as individuals or as pretended executive, ministerial or judicial officers, shall be deemed and considered as principals, and subject to the pains and penalties hereinbefore described.

"Sec. 14. And be it further enacted that for all demands which may come within the jurisdiction of a magistrate's court, suit may be brought for the same in the nearest district of the county to which the territory is hereby annexed; and all officers serving any legal process on any person living on any portion of the territory herein named, shall be entitled to recover the sum of five cents for every mile he may ride to serve the same, after crossing the present limits of the said counties, in addition to the fees already allowed by law; and in case any of the said officers should be resisted in the execution of any legal process, issued by any court or magistrate, justice of the inferior court or judge of the Superior Court of any of said counties, he is hereby authorized to call out a sufficient number of the militia of said counties to aid and protect him in the execution of this duty.

"Sec. 15. And be it further enacted that no Indian or descendant of any Indian, residing within the Creek or Cherokee nations of Indians, shall be deemed a competent witness in any court of this State to which a white person may be a party, except such white person resides within the said nation."

In September, 1831, the grand jurors for the County of Gwinnett in the State of Georgia, presented to the Superior Court of the county the following indictment:

"Georgia, Gwinnett County: The Grand Jurors, sworn, chosen and selected for the County of Gwinnett, in the name and behalf of the citizens of Georgia, charge and accuse Elizur Butler, Samuel A. Worcester, James Trott, Samuel Mays, Surry Eaton, Austin Copeland, and Edward D. Losure, white persons of said county, with the offense of 'residing within the limits of the Cherokee Nation without a license:' For that the said Elizur Butler, Samuel A. Worcester, *James [*529 Trott, Samuel Mays, Surry Eaton, Austin Copeland, and Edward D. Losure, white persons, as aforesaid, on the 15th day of July, 1831, did reside in that part of the Cherokee Nation attached by the laws of said State to the said county, and in the county aforesaid, without a license or permit from his excellency the governor of said State, or from any agent authorized by his excellency the governor aforesaid to grant such permit or license, and without having taken the oath to support and defend the constitution and laws of the State of Georgia, and uprightly to demean themselves as citizens thereof, contrary to the laws of said State, the good order, peace and dignity thereof."

To this indictment the plaintiff in error pleaded specially as follows:

"And the said Samuel A. Worcester, in his own proper person, comes and says, that this court ought not to take further cognizance of the action and prosecution aforesaid, because

he says, that, on the 15th day of July, in the year 1831, he was, and still is, a resident in the Cherokee Nation; and that the said supposed crime or crimes, and each of them, were committed, if committed at all, at the town of New Echota, in the said Cherokee Nation, out of the jurisdiction of this court, and not in the County Gwinnett, or elsewhere within the jurisdiction of this court. And this defendant saith that he is a citizen of the State of Vermont, one of the United States of America, and that he entered the aforesaid Cherokee Nation in the capacity of a duly authorized missionary of the American Board of Commissioners for Foreign Missions, under the authority of the President of the United States, and has not since been required by him to leave it: that he was, at the time of his arrest, engaged in preaching the Gospel to the Cherokee Indians, and in translating the sacred Scriptures into their language, with the permission and approval of the said Cherokee Nation, and in accordance with the humane policy of the government of the United States for the civilization and improvement of the Indians; and that his residence there, for this purpose, is the residence charged in the aforesaid indictment: and this defendant further saith, that this prosecution the State of Georgia ought not to have or maintain, because, he saith, that several treaties have, from time to time, been entered **530*]** *into between the United States and the Cherokee Nation of Indians, to wit: at Hopewell, on the 28th day of November, 1785; at Holston, on the 2d day of July, 1791; at Philadelphia, on the 26th day of June, 1794; at Tellico, on the 2d day of October, 1798; at Tellico, on the 24th day of October, 1804; at Tellico, on the 25th day of October, 1805; at Tellico, on the 27th day of October, 1805; at Washington city on the 7th day of January, 1805; at Washington city, on the 22d day of March, 1816; at the Chickasaw Council House, on the 14th day of September, 1816; at the Cherokee Agency, on the 8th day of July, 1817, and at Washington city, on the 27th day of February, 1819; all which treaties have been duly ratified by the Senate of the United States of America, and by which treaties the United States of America acknowledge the said Cherokee Nation to be a sovereign nation, authorized to govern themselves, and all persons who have settled within their territory, free from any right of legislative interference by the several States composing the United States of America, in reference to acts done within their own territory; and by which treaties the whole of the territory now occupied by the Cherokee Nation, on the east of the Mississippi, has been solemnly guaranteed to hem; all of which treaties are existing treaties, at this day, and in full force. By these treaties, and particularly by the treaties of Hopewell and Holston, the aforesaid territory is acknowledged to lie without the jurisdiction of the several States composing the Union of the United States; and it is thereby especially stipulated that the citizens of the United States shall not enter the aforesaid territory, even on a visit, without a passport from the governor of a State, or from some one duly authorized thereto by the President of the United States; all of which will more fully and at large ap-
490

pear, by reference to the aforesaid treaties. And this defendant saith that the several acts charged in the bill of indictment were done, or omitted to be done, if at all, within the said territory so recognized as belonging to the said nation, and so, as aforesaid, held by them, under the guaranty of the United States: that for those acts the defendant is not amenable to the laws of Georgia, nor to the jurisdiction of the courts of the said State; and that the laws of the State of Georgia, which profess to add the said territory to the several adjacent counties of the said State, and to extend the laws of Georgia over the said territory *and per- **[*531** sons inhabiting the same; and, in particular, the act on which this indictment against this defendant is grounded, to wit: 'An Act entitled an Act to prevent the exercise of assumed and arbitrary power by all persons under pretext of authority from the Cherokee Indians and their laws, and to prevent white persons from residing within that part of the chartered limits of Georgia occupied by the Cherokee Indians, and to provide a guard for the protection of the gold mines, and to enforce the laws of the State within the aforesaid territory,' are repugnant to the aforesaid treaties; which, according to the Constitution of the United States, compose a part of the supreme law of the land; and that these laws of Georgia are, therefore, unconstitutional, void, and of no effect: that the said laws of Georgia are also unconstitutional and void, because they impair the obligation of the various contracts formed by and between the aforesaid Cherokee Nation and the said United States of America, as above recited: also, that the said laws of Georgia are unconstitutional and void, because they interfere with, and attempt to regulate and control the intercourse with the said Cherokee Nation, which, by the said Constitution, belongs exclusively to the Congress of the United States; and because the said laws are repugnant to the statute of the United States passed on the —— day of March, 1802, entitled 'An Act to regulate trade and intercourse with the Indian tribes, and to preserve peace on the frontiers:' and that, therefore, this court has no jurisdiction to cause this defendant to make further or other answer to the said bill of indictment, or further to try and punish this defendant for the said supposed offense or offenses aleged in the bill of indictment, or any of them; and, therefore, this defendant prays judgment whether he shall be held bound to answer further to said indictment."

This plea was overruled by the court, and the jurisdiction of the Superior Court of the County of Gwinnett was sustained by the judgment of the court.

The defendant was then arraigned, and pleaded "not guilty;" and the case came on for trial on the 15th day of September, 1831, when the jury found the defendants in the indictment guilty. On the same day the court pronounced sentence on the parties so convicted, as follows:

*"The State v. B. F. Thompson et al. **[*532** Indictment for residing in the Cherokee Nation without license. Verdict, Guilty."

"The State v. Elizur Butler, Samuel A. Worcester et al. Indictment for residing in the Cherokee Nation without license. Verdict, Guilty."

1832   WORCESTER V. THE STATE OF GEORGIA.   532

"The defendants in both of the above cases shall be kept in close custody by the sheriff of this county until they can be transported to the penitentiary of this State, and the keeper thereof is hereby directed to receive them, and each of them, into his custody, and keep them, and each of them, at hard labor in said penitentiary, for and during the term of four years."

A writ of error was issued on the application of the plaintiff in error, on the 27th of October, 1831, which, with the following proceedings thereon, was returned to this court:

"United States of America, ss.—The President of the United States to the honorable the judges of the Superior Court for the County of Gwinnett, in the State of Georgia, greeting:

"Because in the record and proceedings, as also in the rendition of the judgment of a plea which is in the said Superior Court for the County of Gwinnett, before you, or some of you, between the State of Georgia, plaintiff, and Samuel A. Worcester, defendant, on an indictment, being the highest court of law in said State in which a decision could be had in said suit, a manifest error hath happened, to the great damage of said Samuel A. Worcester, as by his complaint appears. We being willing that error, if any hath been, should be duly corrected, and full and speedy justice done to the parties aforesaid in this behalf, do command you, if judgment be therein given, that then under your seal distinctly and openly, you send the record and proceedings aforesaid, with all things concerning the same, to the Supreme Court of the United States, together with this writ, so that you have the same at Washington on the second Monday of January next, in the said Supreme Court, to be then and there held; that the record and proceedings aforesaid being inspected, the said Supreme Court may cause further to be done therein, to correct that error, what of right, and according to the laws and custom of the United States, should be done.

533*]   *"Witness, the Honorable John Marshall, Chief Justice of the said Supreme Court, the first Monday of August, in the year of our Lord one thousand eight hundred and thirty-one.   Wm. Thos. Carroll.

Clerk of the Supreme Court of the United States.

"Allowed by Henry Baldwin.

"United States of America to the State of Georgia, greeting:

"You are hereby cited and admonished to be and appear at a Supreme Court of the United States to be holden at Washington on the second Monday of January next, pursuant to a writ of error filed in the clerk's office of the Superior Court for the County of Gwinnett, in the State of Georgia, wherein Samuel A. Worcester is plaintiff in error, and the State of Georgia is defendant in error, to show cause, if any there be, why judgment rendered against the said Samuel A. Worcester, as in the said writ of error mentioned, should not be corrected, and why speedy justice should not be done to the parties in that behalf.

"Witness, the Honorable Henry Baldwin, one of the justices of the Supreme Court of the United States, this 27th day of October,

8 L. ed.

in the year of our Lord one thousand eight hundred and thirty-one.

Henry Baldwin.

"State of Georgia, County of Gwinnett, sct.— On this 26th day of November, in the year of our Lord eighteen hundred and thirty-one, William Potter personally appeared before the subscriber, John Mills, a justice of the peace in and for said county, and being duly sworn on the holy evangelists of Almighty God, deposeth and saith, that on the 24th day of November instant, he delivered a true copy of the within citation to His Excellency Wilson Lumpkin, Governor of the State of Georgia, and another true copy thereof he delivered, on the 22d day of November, instant, to Charles J. Jenkins, Esq., Attorney-General of the State aforesaid, showing to the said governor and attorney-general, respectively, at the times of delivery herein stated, the within situation.   Wm. Potter.

"Sworn to and subscribed before me, the day and year above written. John Mills, J. P."

This writ of error was returned to the Supreme Court with *copies of all the [*534 proceedings in the Superior Court of the county of Gwinnett, as stated, and accompanied with certificates of the clerk of that court in the following terms:

"Georgia, Gwinnett County. I, John G. Park, clerk of the Superior Court of the County of Gwinnett and State aforesaid, do certify that the annexed and foregoing is a full and complete exemplification of the proceedings and judgments had in said court against Samuel A. Worcester, one of the defendants in the case therein mentioned, as they remain, of record, in the said Superior Court.

"Given under my hand, and seal of the court, this 28th day of November, 1831.

John G. Park, Clerk.

"I also certify that the original bond, of which a copy is annexed (the bond was in the usual form), and also a copy of the annexed writ of error, were duly deposited and filed in the clerk's office of said court on the 10th day of November, in the year of our Lord eighteen hundred and thirty-one.

"Given under my hand and seal aforesaid, the day and date above written.

John G. Park, Clerk."

The case of Elizur Butler, plaintiff in error, v. The State of Georgia, was brought before the Supreme Court in the same manner.

The case was argued for the plaintiffs in error by Mr. Sergeant and Mr. Wirt, with whom also was Mr. Elisha W. Chester.

The following positions were laid down and supported by Mr. Sergeant and Mr. Wirt:

1. That the court had jurisdiction of the question brought before them by the writ of error; and the jurisdiction extended equally to criminal and to civil cases.

2. That the writ of error was duly issued, and duly returned, so as to bring the question regularly before the court, under the Constitution and laws of the United States, and oblige the court to take cognizance of it.

3. That the statute of Georgia under which the plaintiffs in error were indicted and convicted was unconstitutional and void; because:

491

535*] *1. By the Constitution of the United States, the establishment and regulation of intercourse with the Indians belonged exclusively to the government of the United States.

2. The power thus given, exclusively, to the government of the United States had been exercised by treaties and by acts of Congress, now in force, and applying directly to the case of the Cherokees; and that no State could interfere, without a manifest violation of such treaties and laws, which by the Constitution were the supreme law of the land.

3. The statute of Georgia assumed the power to change these regulations and laws: to prohibit that which they permitted; and to make that criminal which they declared innocent or meritorious; and to subject to condemnation and punishment, free citizens of the United States who had committed no offense.

4. That the indictment, conviction, and sentence being founded upon a statute of Georgia, which was unconstitutional and void; were themselves also void and of no effect, and ought to be reversed.

These several positions were supported, enforced and illustrated by argument and authority.

The following authorities were referred to: 2 Laws U. S. 65, sec. 25; Judiciary Act of 1789; Miller v. Nicholls, 4 Wheat. 311; Craig v. State of Missouri, 4 Peters, 400, 429; Fisher v. Cockerell, 5 Peters, 248; Ex-parte Kearney, 7 Wheat. 38; Cohens v. Virginia, 6 Wheat. 264; Martin v. Hunter, 1 Wheat. 304, 315, 361; 1 Laws U. S. 488, 470, 472, 482, 484, 486, 453; Blunt's Historical Sketch, 106, 107; Treaties with the Cherokees, 28th Nov. 1785; 2d July, 1791; 26th July, 1794; 2d Oct. 1798; 3 Laws U. S. 27, 125, 284, 303, 344, 460; 12 Journ. Congress, 82; Blunt's Hist. Sketch, 113, 110, 111, 114; Federalist, No. 42; 1 Laws U. S. 454; Holland v. Pack, Peck's Rep. 151; Johnson v. M'Intosh, 8 Wheat. 543; Cherokee Nation v. State of Georgia, 5 Peters, 1, 16, 27, 31, 48; Ware v. Hylton, 3 Dall. 199; Hughes v. Edwards, 9 Wheat. 489; Fisher v. Hamden, 1 Paine, 55; Hamilton v. Eaton, North Carolina Cases, 79; M'Culloch v. State of Maryland, 4 Wheat. 316; 2 Laws U. S. 121; 3 Laws U. S. 460; 3 Laws U. S. 750; Gibbons v. Odgen, 9 Wheat, 1.

536*] *Mr. Chief Justice Marshall delivered the opinion of the court:

This cause, in every point of view in which it can be placed, is of the deepest interest.

The defendant is a State, a member of the Union, which has exercised the powers of government over a people who deny its jurisdiction, and are under the protection of the United States.

The plaintiff is a citizen of the State of Vermont, condemned to hard labor for four years in the penitentiary of Georgia, under color of an act which he alleges to be repugnant to the Constitution, laws, and treaties of the United States.

The legislative power of the State, the controlling power of the Constitution and laws of the United States, the rights, if they have any, the political existence of a once numerous and powerful people, the personal liberty

492

of a citizen, are all involved in the subject now to be considered.

It behooves this court in every case, more especially in this, to examine into its jurisdiction with scrutinizing eyes, before it proceeds to the exercise of a power which is controverted.

The first step in the performance of this duty is the inquiry whether the record is properly before the court.

It is certified by the clerk of the court which pronounced the judgment of condemnation under which the plaintiff in error is imprisoned, and is also authenticated by the seal of the court. It is returned with, and annexed to, a writ of error issued in regular form, the citation being signed by one of the associate justices of the Supreme Court, and served on the Governor and Attorney-General of the State more than thirty days before the commencement of the term to which the writ of error was returnable.

The Judicial Act (sec. 22, 25, 2 Laws U. S. 64, 65), so far as it prescribes the mode of proceeding, appears to have been literally pursued.

In February, 1797, a rule (6 Wheat. Rules) was made on this subject in the following words: "It is ordered by the court that the clerk of the court to which any writ of error shall be directed, may make return of the same by transmitting a true *copy of [*537 the record, and of all proceedings in the same, under his hand and the seal of the court."

This has been done. But the signature of the judge has not been added to that of the clerk. The law does not require it. The rule does not require it.

In the case of Martin v. Hunter's Lessee, 1 Wheat. 304, 361, an exception was taken to the return of the refusal of the State court to enter a prior judgment of reversal by this court, because it was not made by the judge of the State court to which the writ was directed; but the exception was overruled, and the return was held sufficient. In Buel v. Van Ness, 8 Wheat, 312, also, a writ of error to a State court, the record was authenticated in the same manner. No exception was taken to it. These were civil cases. But it has been truly said at the bar that, in regard to this process, the law makes no distinction between a criminal and civil case. The same return is required in both. If the sanction of the court could be necessary for the establishment of this position, it has been silently given.

M'Culloch v. The State of Maryland, 4 Wheat. 316, was a qui tam action, brought to recover a penalty, and the record was authenticated by the seal of the court and the signature of the clerk, without that of a judge. Brown et al. v. The State of Maryland was an indictment for a fine and forfeiture. The record in this case, too, was authenticated by the seal of the court and the certificate of the clerk. The practice is both ways.

The record, then, according to the Judiciary Act, and the rule and the practice of the court, is regularly before us. The more important inquiry is, does it exhibit a case cognizable by this tribunal?

The indictment charges the plaintiff in error and others, being white persons, with the offense of "residing within the limits of the

Cherokee Nation without a license," and "without having taken the oath to support and defend the constitution and the laws of the State of Georgia."

The defendant in the State court appeared in proper person, and filed the following plea:

"And the said Samuel A. Worcester, in his own proper person, comes and says that this 538*] court ought not to take further *cognizance of the action and prosecution aforesaid, because, he says, that on the 15th day of July, in the year 1831, he was, and still is, a resident in the Cherokee Nation; and that the said supposed crime or crimes, and each of them, were committed, if committed at all, at the Town of New Echota, in the said Cherokee Nation, out of the jurisdiction of this court, and not in the county Gwinnett, or elsewhere, within the jurisdiction of this court; and this defendant saith that he is a citizen of the State of Vermont, one of the United States of America, and that he entered the aforesaid Cherokee Nation in the capacity of a duly authorized missionary of the American Board of Commissioners for Foreign Missions, under the authority of the President of the United States, and has not since been required by him to leave it; that he was, at the time of his arrest, engaged in preaching the Gospel to the Cherokee Indians, and in translating the sacred Scriptures into their language, with the permission and approval of the said Cherokee Nation, and in accordance with the humane policy of the government of the United States for the civilization and improvement of the Indians; and that his residence there, for this purpose, is the residence charged in the aforesaid indictment; and this defendant further saith that this prosecution the State of Georgia ought not to have or maintain, because, he saith, that several treaties have, from time to time, been entered into between the United States and the Cherokee Nation of Indians, to wit, at Hopewell, on the 28th day of November, 1785; at Holston, on the 2d day of July, 1791; at Philadelphia, on the 26th day of June, 1794; at Tellico, on the 2d day of October, 1798; at Tellico, on the 24th day of October, 1804; at Tellico, on the 25th day of October, 1805; at Tellico, on the 27th day of October, 1805; at Washington city, on the 7th day of January, 1805; at Washington city, on 22d day of March, 1816; at the Chickasaw Council House, on the 14th day of September, 1816; at the Cherokee Agency, on the 8th day of July, 1817; and at Washington city, on the 27th day of February, 1819: all which treaties have been duly ratified by the Senate of the United States of America, and by which treaties the United States of America acknowledge the said Cherokee Nation to be a sovereign nation, authorized to govern themselves, and all persons who have settled within their territory, free from any right of legislative interference by the several States composing the 539*] *United States of America, in reference to acts done within their own territory; and by which treaties the whole of the territory now occupied by the Cherokee Nation on the east of the Mississippi has been solemnly guaranteed to them; all of which treaties are existing treaties at this day, and in full force.

By these treaties, and particularly by the

treaties of Hopewell and Holston, the aforesaid territory is acknowledged to lie without the jurisdiction of the several States composing the Union of the United States; and it is thereby specially stipulated that the citizens of the United States shall not enter the aforesaid territory, even on a visit, without a passport from the governor of a State, or from some one duly authorized thereto by the President of the United States; all of which will more fully and at large appear by reference to the aforesaid treaties. And this defendant saith, that the several acts charged in the bill of indictment were done, or omitted to be done, if at all, within the said territory so recognized as belonging to the said nation, and so, as aforesaid, held by them, under the guarantee of the United States; that, for those acts, the defendant is not amenable to the laws of Georgia, nor to the jurisdiction of the courts of the said State; and that the laws of the State of Georgia, which profess to add the said territory to the several adjacent counties of the said State, and to extend the laws of Georgia over the said territory and persons inhabiting the same; and, in particular, the act on which this indictment against this defendant is grounded, to wit, 'An Act entitled an Act to prevent the exercise of assumed and arbitrary power by all persons under a pretext of authority from the Cherokee Indians, and their laws, and to prevent white persons from residing within that part of the chartered limits of Georgia occupied by the Cherokee Indians, and to provide a guard for the protection of the gold mines, and to enforce the laws of the State within the aforesaid territory,' are repugnant to the aforesaid treaties; which, according to the Constitution of the United States, compose a part of the supreme law of the land; and that these laws of Georgia are, therefore, unconstitutional, void, and of no effect; that the said laws of Georgia are also unconstitutional and void, because they impair the obligation of the various contracts formed by and between the aforesaid Cherokee Nation and the said United States of America, as above *recited; also, that the said laws of [*540 Georgia are unconstitutional and void, because they interfere with, and attempt to regulate and control the intercourse with the said Cherokee Nation, which, by the said Constitution, belongs exclusively to the Congress of the United States; and because the said laws are repugnant to the statute of the United States, passed on the —— day of March, 1802, entitled 'An Act to regulate trade and intercourse with the Indian tribes and to preserve peace on the frontier;' and that, therefore, this court has no jurisdiction to cause this defendant to make further or other answer to the said bill of indictment, or further to try and punish this defendant for the said supposed offense or offenses alleged in the bill of indictment, or any of them; and, therefore, this defendant prays judgment whether he shall be held bound to answer further to said indictment."

This plea was overruled by the court, and the prisoner, being arraigned pleaded not guilty. The jury found a verdict against him, and the court sentenced him to hard labor in the penitentiary for the term of four years.

By overruling this plea, the court decided that the matter it contained was not a bar to the action. The plea, therefore, must be examined for the purpose of determining whether it makes a case which brings the party within the provisions of the twenty-fifth section of the "Act to establish the judicial courts of the United States."

The plea avers that the residence charged in the indictment was under the authority of the President of the United States, and with the permission and approval of the Cherokee Nation. That the treaties subsisting between the United States and the Cherokees, acknowledge their right as a sovereign nation to govern themselves and all persons who have settled within their territory, free from any right of legislative interference by the several States composing the United States of America. That the act under which the prosecution was instituted is repugnant to the said treaties, and is, therefore, unconstitutional and void. That the said act is also unconstitutional, because it interferes with, and attempts to regulate and control the intercourse with the Cherokee Nation which belongs exclusively to Congress, and, because, also, it is repugnant to the statute of the United States, entitled "An Act to regu- **541***] late *trade and intercourse with the Indian tribes, and to preserve peace on the frontiers."

Let the averments of this plea be compared with the twenty-fifth section of the Judicial Act.

That section enumerates the cases in which the final judgment or decree of a State court may be revised in the Supreme Court of the United States. These are, "where is drawn in question the validity of a treaty, or statute of, or an authority exercised under the United States, and the decision is against their validity; or where is drawn in question the validity of a statute of, or an authority exercised under any State, on the ground of their being repugnant to the Constitution, treaties or laws of the United States, and the decision is in favor of such their validity; or where is drawn in question the construction of any clause of the Constitution, or of a treaty, or statute of, or commission held under the United States, and the decision is against the title, right, privilege or exemption, especially set up or claimed by either party under such clause of the said Constitution, treaty, statute or commission."

The indictment and plea in this case draw in question, we think, the validity of the treaties made by the United States with the Cherokee Indians; if not so, their construction is certainly drawn in question; and the decision has been, if not against their validity, "against the right, privilege or exemption, specially set up and claimed under them." They also draw into question the validity of a statute of the State of Georgia, "on the ground of its being repugnant to the Constitution, treaties and laws of the United States, and the decision is in favor of its validity."

It is, then, we think, too clear for controversy, that the act of Congress by which this court is constituted, has given it the power, and of course imposed on it the duty, of exercising jurisdiction in this case. This duty, however unpleasant, cannot be avoided. Those who fill the judicial department have no discretion in selecting the subjects to be brought

before them. We must examine the defense set up in this plea. We must inquire and decide whether the act of the Legislature of Georgia under which the plaintiff in error has been prosecuted and condemned, be consistent with, or repugnant to the Constitution, laws and treaties of the United States.

*It has been said at the bar that the [*542 acts of the Legislature of Georgia seize on the whole Cherokee country, parcel it out among the neighboring counties of the State, extend her code over the whole country, abolish its institutions and its laws, and annihilate its political existence.

If this be the general effect of the system, let us inquire into the effect of the particular statute and section on which the indictment is founded.

It enacts that "all white persons, residing within the limits of the Cherokee Nation on the 1st day of March next, or at any time thereafter, without a license or permit from his excellency the governor, or from such agent as his excellency the governor shall authorize to grant such permit or license, and who shall not have taken the oath hereinafter required, shall be guilty of a high misdemeanor, and, upon conviction thereof, shall be punished by confinement to the penitentiary, at hard labor for a term not less than four years."

The eleventh section authorizes the governor, should he deem it necessary for the protection of the mines, or the enforcement of the laws in force within the Cherokee Nation, to raise and organize a guard," etc.

The thirteenth section enacts, "that the said guard or any member of them, shall be, and they are hereby authorized and empowered to arrest any person legally charged with or detected in a violation of the laws of this State, and to convey, as soon as practicable, the person so arrested, before a justice of the peace, judge of the superior, or justice of inferior court of this State, to be dealt with according to law.

The extraterritorial power of every Legislature being limited in its action to its own citizens or subjects, the very passage of this act is an assertion of jurisdiction over the Cherokee Nation, and of the rights and powers consequent on jurisdiction.

The first step, then, in the inquiry which the Constitution and laws impose on this court, is an examination of the rightfulness of this claim.

America, separated from Europe by a wide ocean, was inhabited by a distinct people, divided into separate nations, independent of each other and of the rest of the world, having institutions of their own, and governing themselves by their *own laws. It is difficult [*543 to comprehend the proposition that the inhabitants of either quarter of the globe could have rightful original claims of dominion over the inhabitants of the other, or over the lands they occupied; or that the discovery of either by the other should give the discoverer rights in the country discovered which annulled the pre-existing rights of its ancient possessors.

After lying concealed for a series of ages, the enterprise of Europe, guided by nautical science, conducted some of her adventurous sons into this western world. They found it in possession of a people who had made small progress in agriculture or manufactures, and whose general employment was war, hunting, and fishing.

Did these adventurers, by sailing along the coast and occasionally landing on it, acquire for the several governments to whom they belonged, or by whom they were commissioned, a rightful property in the soil from the Atlantic to the Pacific; or rightful dominion over the numerous people who occupied it? Or has nature, or the great Creator of all things, conferred these rights over hunters and fishermen, on agriculturists and manufacturers?

But power, war, conquest, give rights, which, after possession, are conceded by the world; and which can never be controverted by those on whom they descend. We proceed, then, to the actual state of things, having glanced at their origin, because holding it in our recollection might shed some light on existing pretensions.

The great maritime powers of Europe discovered and visited different parts of this continent at nearly the same time. The object was too immense for any one of them to grasp the whole, and the claimants were too powerful to submit to the exclusive or unreasonable pretensions of any single potentate. To avoid bloody conflicts, which might terminate disastrously to all, it was necessary for the nations of Europe to establish some principle which all would acknowledge, and which should decide their respective rights as between themselves. This principle, suggested by the actual state of things, was, "that discovery gave title to the government by whose subjects or by whose authority it was made, against all other Euro-544*] pean *governments, which title might be consummated by possession." 8 Wheat. 573.

This principle, acknowledged by all Europeans, because it was the interest of all to acknowledge it, gave to the nation making the discovery, as its inevitable consequence, the sole right of acquiring the soil and of making settlements on it. It was an exclusive principle which shut out the right of competition among those who had agreed to it; not one which could annul the previous rights of those who had not agreed to it. It regulated the right given by discovery among the European discoverers, but could not affect the rights of those already in possession, either as aboriginal occupants, or as occupants by virtue of a discovery made before the memory of man. It gave the exclusive right to purchase, but did not found that right on a denial of the right of the possessor to sell.

The relation between the Europeans and the natives was determined in each case by the particular government which asserted and could maintain this pre-emptive privilege in the particular place. The United States succeeded to all the claims of Great Britain, both territorial and political; but no attempt, so far as is known, has been made to enlarge them. So far as they existed merely in theory, or were in their nature only exclusive of the claims of other European nations, they still retain their original character, and remain dormant. So far as they have been practically exerted, they exist in fact, are understood by both parties,

8 L. ed.

are asserted by the one, and admitted by the other.

Soon after Great Britain determined on planting colonies in America, the king granted charters to companies of his subjects, who associated for the purpose of carrying the views of the crown into effect, and of enriching themselves. The first of these charters was made before possession was taken of any part of the country. They purport, generally, to convey the soil, from the Atlantic to the South Sea. This soil was occupied by numerous and warlike nations, equally willing and able to defend their possessions. The extravagant and absurd idea that the feeble settlements made on the sea-coast, or the companies under whom they were made, acquired legitimate power by them to govern the people, or occupy the lands from *sea to sea, did not enter the mind of any [*545 man. They were well understood to convey the title which, according to the common law of European sovereigns respecting America, they might rightfully convey, and no more. This was the exclusive right of purchasing such lands as the natives were willing to sell. The crown could not be understood to grant what the crown did not affect to claim, nor was it so understood.

The power of making war is conferred by these charters on the colonies, but defensive war alone seems to have been contemplated. In the first charter to the first and second colonies, they are empowered, "for their several defenses, to encounter, expulse, repel, and resist, all persons who shall, without license," attempt to inhabit "within the said precincts and limits of the said several colonies, or that shall enterprise or attempt at any time hereafter the least detriment or annoyance of the said several colonies or plantations."

The charter to Connecticut concludes a general power to make defensive war with these terms: "and upon just causes to invade and destroy the natives or other enemies of the said colony."

The same power, in the same words, is conferred on the government of Rhode Island.

This power to repel invasion, and, upon just cause, to invade and destroy the natives, authorizes offensive as well as defensive war, but only "on just cause." The very terms imply the existence of a country to be invaded, and of an enemy who has given just cause of war.

The charter to William Penn contains the following recital: "and because, in so remote a country, near so many barbarous nations, the incursions, as well of the savages themselves, as of other enemies, pirates, and robbers, may probably be feared, therefore we have given," etc. The instrument then confers the power of war.

These barbarous nations, whose incursions were feared, and to repel whose incursions the power to make war was given, were surely not considered as the subjects of Penn, or occupying his lands during his pleasure.

The same clause is introduced into the charter to Lord Baltimore.

*The charter to Georgia professes to [*546 be granted for the charitable purpose of enabling poor subjects to gain a comfortable subsistence by cultivating lands in the American provinces, "at present waste and desolate." It

495

recites: "and whereas our provinces in North America have been frequently ravaged by Indian enemies, more especially that of South Carolina, which, in the late war by the neighboring savages, was laid waste by fire and sword, and great numbers of the English inhabitants miserably massacred; and our loving subjects, who now inhabit there, by reason of the smallness of their numbers, will, in case of any new war, be exposed to the like calamities, inasmuch as their whole southern frontier continueth unsettled, and lieth open to the said savages."

These motives for planting the new colony are incompatible with the lofty ideas of granting the soil and all its inhabitants from sea to sea. They demonstrate the truth that these grants asserted a title against Europeans only, and were considered as blank paper so far as the rights of the natives were concerned. The power of war is given only for defense, not for conquest.

The charters contain passages showing one of their objects to be the civilization of the Indians and their conversion to Christianity—objects to be accomplished by conciliatory conduct and good example; not by extermination.

The actual state of things, and the practice of European nations, on so much of the American continent as lies between the Mississippi and the Atlantic, explain their claims, and the charters they granted. Their pretensions unavoidably interfered with each other; though the discovery of one was admitted by all to exclude the claim of any other, the extent of that discovery was the subject of unceasing contest. Bloody conflicts arose between them, which gave importance and security to the neighboring nations. Fierce and warlike in their character, they might be formidable enemies or effective friends. Instead of rousing their resentments by asserting claims to their lands, or to dominion over their persons, their alliance was sought by flattering professions, and purchased by rich presents. The English, the French, and the Spaniards, were equally competitors for their friendship and their aid. Not well acquainted with the exact meaning 547*] of *words, nor supposing it to be material whether they were called the subjects, or the children of their father in Europe; lavish in professions of duty and affection, in return for the rich presents they received; so long as their actual independence was untouched, and their right to self-government acknowledged, they were willing to profess dependence on the power which furnished supplies of which they were in absolute need, and restrained dangerous intruders from entering their country; and this was probably the sense in which the term was understood by them.

Certain it is, that our history furnishes no example, from the first settlement of our country, of any attempt on the part of the crown to interfere with the internal affairs of the Indians, farther than to keep out the agents of foreign powers, who, as traders or otherwise, might seduce them into foreign alliances. The king purchased their lands when they were willing to sell, at a price they were willing to take; but never coerced a surrender of them. He also purchased their alliance and dependence by subsidies; but never intruded into the interior of their affairs, or interfered with their self-government, so far as respected themselves only.

The general views of Great Britain with regard to the Indians were detailed by Mr. Stuart, Superintendent of Indian Affairs, in a speech delivered at Mobile, in presence of several persons of distinction, soon after the peace of 1763. Towards the conclusion he says, "lastly, I inform you that it is the king's order to all his governors and subjects to treat Indians with justice and humanity, and to forbear all encroachments on the territories alloted to them; accordingly, all individuals are prohibited from purchasing any of your lands; but, as you know that, as your white brethren cannot feed you when you visit them unless you give them ground to plant, it is expected that you will cede lands to the king for that purpose. But, whenever you shall be pleased to surrender any of your territories to his majesty, it must be done, for the future, at a public meeting of your nation, when the governors of the provinces, or the superintendent shall be present, and obtain the consent of all your people. The boundaries of your hunting-grounds will be accurately fixed, and no settlement permitted to be made upon them. As you may be assured that all treaties *with your peo- [*548 ple will be faithfully kept, so it is expected that you, also, will be careful strictly to observe them."

The proclamation issued by the King of Great Britain in 1763, soon after the ratification of the articles of peace, forbids the governors of any of the colonies to grant warrants of survey, or pass patents upon any lands whatever, which, not having been ceded to, or purchased by, us (the King), as aforesaid, are reserved to the said Indians, or any of them.

The proclamation proceeds: "And we do further declare it to be our royal will and pleasure, for the present, as aforesaid, to reserve, under our sovereignty, protection, and dominion, for the use of the said Indians, all the lands and territories lying to the westward of the sources of the rivers which fall into the sea, from the west and north-west as aforesaid: and we do hereby strictly forbid, on pain of our displeasure, all our loving subjects from making any purchases or settlements whatever, or taking possession of any of the lands above reserved, without our special leave and license for that purpose first obtained.

"And we do further strictly enjoin and require all persons whatever, who have, either wilfully or inadvertently, seated themselves upon any lands within the countries above described, or upon any other lands which, not having been ceded to, or purchased by us, are still reserved to the said Indians, as aforesaid, forthwith to remove themselves from such settlements."

A proclamation issued by Governor Gage, in 1772, contains the following passage: "Whereas many persons, contrary to the positive orders of the king upon this subject, have undertaken to make settlements beyond the boundaries fixed by the treaties made with the Indian nations, which boundaries ought to serve as a barrier between the whites and the said nations, particularly on the Ouabache." The proclamation orders such persons to quit those countries without delay.

Such was the policy of Great Britain towards the Indian nations inhabiting the territory from which she excluded all other Europeans; such her claims, and such her practical exposition of the charters she had granted: she considered them as nations capable of maintaining the relations of peace and war; of governing themselves, under her protection; and 549*] she *made treaties with them, the obligation of which she acknowledged.

This was the settled state of things when the war of our Revolution commenced. The influence of our enemy was established; her resources enabled her to keep up that influence, and the colonists had much cause for the apprehension that the Indian nations would, as the allies of Great Britain, add their arms to hers. This, as was to be expected, became an object of great solicitude to Congress. Far from advancing a claim to their lands, or asserting any right of dominion over them, Congress resolved "that the securing and preserving the friendship of the Indian nations appears to be a subject of the utmost moment to these colonies."

The early journals of Congress exhibit the most anxious desire to conciliate the Indian nations. Three Indian departments were established, and commissioners appointed in each, "to treat with the Indians in their respective departments, in the name and on the behalf of the United Colonies, in order to preserve peace and friendship with the said Indians, and to prevent their taking any part in the present commotions."

The most strenuous exertions were made to procure those supplies on which Indian friendships were supposed to depend; and everything which might excite hostility was avoided.

The first treaty was made with the Delawares, in September, 1778.

The language of equality in which it is drawn evinces the temper with which the negotiation was undertaken, and the opinion which then prevailed in the United States.

"1. That all offenses or acts of hostilities, by one or either of the contracting parties against the other, be mutually forgiven, and buried in the depth of oblivion, never more to be had in remembrance.

"2. That a perpetual peace and friendship shall, from henceforth, take place and subsist between the contracting parties aforesaid, through all succeeding generations; and if either of the parties are engaged in a just and necessary war, with any other nation or nations, that then each shall assist the other, in due proportion to their abilities, till their enemies are brought to reasonable terms of accommodation," etc.

3. The third article stipulates, among other 550*] things, a free *passage for the American troops through the Delaware Nation; and engages that they shall be furnished with provisions and other necessaries at their value.

"4. For the better security of the peace and friendship now entered into by the contracting parties against all infractions of the same by the citizens of either party; to the prejudice of the other, neither party shall proceed to the infliction of punishments on the citizens of the

other, otherwise than by securing the offender or offenders, by imprisonment or any other competent means, till a fair and impartial trial can be had by judges or juries of both parties, as near as can be to the laws, customs and usages of the contracting parties, and natural justice," etc.

5. The fifth article regulates the trade between the contracting parties, in a manner entirely equal.

6. The sixth article is entitled to peculiar attention, as it contains a disclaimer of designs which were, at that time, ascribed to the United States by their enemies, and from the imputation of which Congress was then peculiarly anxious to free the government. It is in these words: "Whereas the enemies of the United States have endeavored, by every artifice in their power, to possess the Indians in general with an opinion that it is the design of the States aforesaid to extirpate the Indians and take possession of their country; to obviate such false suggestion the United States do engage to guaranty to the aforesaid nation of Delawares, and their heirs, all their territorial rights, in the fullest and most ample manner, as it hath been bounded by former treaties, as long as the said Delaware Nation shall abide by, and hold fast the chain of friendship now entered into."

The parties further agree that other tribes, friendly to the interest of the United States, may be invited to form a State, whereof the Delaware Nation shall be the heads, and have a representation in Congress.

This treaty, in its language and in its provisions, is formed as near as may be, on the model of treaties between the crowned heads of Europe.

The sixth article shows how Congress then treated the injurious calumny of cherishing designs unfriendly to the political and civil rights of the Indians.

*During the war of the Revolution, [*551 the Cherokees took part with the British. After its termination, the United States, though desirous of peace, did not feel its necessity so strongly as while the war continued. Their political situation being changed, they might very well think it advisable to assume a higher tone, and to impress on the Cherokees the same respect for Congress which was before felt for the King of Great Britain. This may account for the language of the Treaty of Hopewell. There is the more reason for supposing that the Cherokee chiefs were not very critical judges of the language, from the fact that every one makes his mark; no chief was capable of signing his name. It is probable the treaty was interpreted to them.

The treaty is introduced with the declaration that "the commissioners plenipotentiary of the United States give peace to all the Cherokees, and receive them into the favor and protection of the United States of America, on the following conditions."

When the United States gave peace, did they not also receive it? Were not both parties desirous of it? If we consult the history of the day, does it not inform us that the United States were at least as anxious to obtain it as the Cherokees? We may ask, further, did the Cherokees come to the seat of the American government to solicit peace; or, did the American

S L. ed.

commissioners go to them to obtain it? The treaty was made at Hopewell, not at New York. The word "give," then, has no real importance attached to it.

The first and second articles stipulate for the mutual restoration of prisoners, and are of course equal.

The third article acknowledges the Cherokees to be under the protection of the United States of America, and of no other power.

This stipulation is found in Indian treaties generally. It was introduced into their treaties with Great Britain; and may probably be found in those with other European powers. Its origin may be traced to the nature of their connection with those powers; and its true meaning is discerned in their relative situation.

The general law of European sovereigns, respecting their claims in America, limited the 552*] intercourse of Indians, in a *great degree, to the particular potentate whose ultimate right of domain was acknowledged by the others. This was the general state of things in time of peace. It was sometimes changed in war. The consequence was that their supplies were derived chiefly from that nation, and their trade confined to it. Goods, indispensable to their comfort, in the shape of presents, were received from the same hand. What was of still more importance, the strong hand of government was interposed to restrain the disorderly and licentious from intrusions into their country, from encroachments on their lands, and from those acts of violence which were often attended by reciprocal murder. The Indians perceived in this protection only what was beneficial to themselves—an engagement to punish aggressions on them. It involved, practically, no claim to their lands, no dominion over their persons. It merely bound the nation to the British crown as a dependent ally, claiming the protection of a powerful friend and neighbor, and receiving the advantages of that protection, without involving a surrender of their national character.

This is the true meaning of the stipulation, and is undoubtedly the sense in which it was made. Neither the British government nor the Cherokees ever understood it otherwise.

The same stipulation entered into with the United States, is undoubtedly to be construed in the same manner. They receive the Cherokee Nation into their favor and protection. The Cherokees acknowledge themselves to be under the protection of the United States, and of no other power. Protection does not imply the destruction of the protected. The manner in which this stipulation was understood by the American government is explained by the language and acts of our first President.

The fourth article draws the boundary between the Indians and the citizens of the United States. But, in describing this boundary, the term "allotted" and the term "hunting-ground" are used.

Is it reasonable to suppose that the Indians, who could not write, and most probably could not read, who certainly were not critical judges of our language, should distinguish the word "allotted" from the words "marked out." The actual subject of contract was the divid-553*] ing line between the two nations, *and their attention may very well be supposed to

498

have been confined to that subject. When, in fact they were ceding lands to the United States, and describing the extent of their cession, it may very well be supposed that they might not understand the term employed as indicating that instead of granting they were receiving lands. If the term would admit of no other signification, which is not conceded, its being misunderstood is so apparent, results so necessarily from the whole transaction, that it must, we think, be taken in the sense in which it was most obviously used.

So with respect to the words "hunting-grounds." Hunting was at that time the principal occupation of the Indians, and their land was more used for that purpose than for any other. It could not, however, be supposed that any intention existed of restricting the full use of the lands they reserved.

To the United States, it could be a matter of no concern whether their whole territory was devoted to hunting-grounds, or whether an occasional village, and an occasional corn field, interrupted and gave some variety to the scene.

These terms had been used in their treaties with Great Britain, and had never been misunderstood. They had never been supposed to imply a right in the British government to take their lands, or to interfere with their internal government.

The fifth article withdraws the protection of the United States from any citizen who has settled, or shall settle, on the lands allotted to the Indians, for their hunting-grounds; and stipulates that if he shall not remove within six months the Indians may punish him.

The sixth and seventh articles stipulate for the punishment of the citizens of either country, who may commit offenses on or against the citizens of the other. The only inference to be drawn from them is, that the United States considered the Cherokees as a nation.

The ninth article is in these words: "For the benefit and comfort of the Indians, and for the prevention of injuries or oppressions on the part of the citizens or Indians, the United States in Congress assembled, shall have the sole and exclusive right of regulating the trade with the Indians, and managing all their affairs, as they think proper."

To construe the expression "managing all their affairs," *into a surrender of self- [*554 government, would be, we think, a perversion of their necessary meaning, and a departure from the construction which has been uniformly put on them. The great subject of the article is the Indian trade. The influence it gave made it desirable that Congress should possess it. The commissioners brought forward the claim, with the profession that their motive was "the benefit and comfort of the Indians, and the prevention of injuries or oppressions." This may be true, as respects the regulation of their trade, and as respects the regulation of all affairs connected with their trade, but cannot be true as respects the management of all their affairs. The most important of these are the cession of their lands, and security against intruders on them. Is it credible that they should have considered themselves as surrendering to the United States the right to dictate their future cessions, and the terms on which they should be made? or to compel their submission

Peters 6.

to the violence of disorderly and licentious intruders? It is equally inconceivable that they could have supposed themselves, by a phrase thus slipped into an article on another and most interesting subject, to have devested themselves of the right of self-government on subjects not connected with trade. Such a measure could not be "for their benefit and comfort," or for "the prevention of injuries and oppression." Such a construction would be inconsistent with the spirit of this and of all subsequent treaties; especially of those articles which recognize the right of the Cherokees to declare hostilities and to make war. It would convert a treaty of peace covertly into an act annihilating the political existence of one of the parties. Had such a result been intended, it would have been openly avowed.

This treaty contains a few terms capable of being used in a sense which could not have been intended at the time, and which is inconsistent with the practical construction which has always been put on them; but its essential articles treat the Cherokees as a nation capable of maintaining the relations of peace and war, and ascertain the boundaries between them and the United States.

The Treaty of Hopewell seems not to have established a solid peace. To accommodate the differences still existing between the State of Georgia and the Cherokee Nation, the Treaty 555*] of *Holston was negotiated in July, 1791. The existing Constitution of the United States had been then adopted, and the government, having more intrinsic capacity to enforce its just claims, was perhaps less mindful of high sounding expressions denoting superiority. We hear no more of giving peace to the Cherokees. The mutual desire of establishing permanent peace and friendship, and of removing all causes of war, is honestly avowed, and, in pursuance of their desire, the first article declares that there shall be perpetual peace and friendship between all the citizens of the United States of America and all the individuals composing the Cherokee Nation.

The second article repeats the important acknowledgment that the Cherokee Nation is under the protection of the United States of America, and of no other sovereign whosoever.

The meaning of this has been already explained. The Indian nations were, from their situation, necessarily dependent on some foreign potentate for the supply of their essential wants, and for their protection from lawless and injurious intrusions into their country. That power was naturally termed their protector. They had been arranged under the protection of Great Britain; but the extinguishment of the British power in their neighborhood, and the establishment of that of the United States in its place, led naturally to the declaration, on the part of the Cherokees, that they were under the protection of the United States, and of no other power. They assumed the relation with the United States which had before subsisted with Great Britain.

This relation was that of a nation claiming and receiving the protection of one more powerful, not that of individuals abandoning their national character, and submitting as subjects to the laws of a master.

8 L. ed.

The third article contains a perfectly equal stipulation for the surrender of prisoners.

The fourth article declares that "the boundary between the United States and the Cherokee Nation shall be as follows: beginning," etc. We hear no more of "allotments" or of "hunting-grounds." A boundary is described, between nation and nation, by mutual consent. The national character of each; the ability of each to establish this boundary, is acknowledged by the other. To preclude forever all disputes, it is agreed *that it shall be [*556 plainly marked by commissioners, to be appointed by each party; and, in order to extinguish forever all claim of the Cherokees to the ceded lands, an additional consideration is to be paid by the United States. For this additional consideration the Cherokees release all right to the ceded land, forever.

By the fifth article, the Cherokees allow the United States a road through their country, and the navigation of the Tennessee River. The acceptance of these cessions is an acknowledgment of the right of the Cherokees to make or withhold them.

By the sixth article, it is agreed, on the part of the Cherokees, that the United States shall have the sole and exclusive right of regulating their trade. No claim is made to the management of all their affairs. This stipulation has already been explained. The observation may be repeated, that the stipulation is itself an admission of their right to make or refuse it.

By the seventh article, the United States solemnly guaranty to the Cherokee Nation all their lands not hereby ceded.

The eighth article relinquishes to the Cherokees any citizens of the United States who may settle on their lands; and the ninth forbids any citizen of the United States to hunt on their lands or to enter their country without a passport.

The remaining articles are equal, and contain stipulations which could be made only with a nation admitted to be capable of governing itself.

This treaty, thus explicitly recognizing the national character of the Cherokees, and their right of self-government, thus guarantying their lands; assuming the duty of protection, and of course, pledging the faith of the United States for that protection, has been frequently renewed and is now in full force.

To the general pledge of protection have been added several specific pledges, deemed valuable by the Indians. Some of these restrain the citizens of the United States from encroachments on the Cherokee country, and provide for the punishment of intruders.

From the commencement of our government Congress has passed acts to regulate trade and intercourse with the Indians; which treat them as nations, respect their rights, and manifest *a firm purpose to afford that protection [*557 which treaties stipulate. All these acts, and especially that of 1802, which is still in force, manifestly consider the several Indian nations as distinct political communities, having territorial boundaries, within which their authority is exclusive, and having a right to all the lands within those boundaries, which is not only acknowledged, but guaranteed by the United States.

In 1819, Congress passed an Act for promoting those humane designs of civilizing the neighboring Indians, which had long been cherished by the executive. It enacts, "that, for the purpose of providing against the further decline and final extinction of the Indian tribes adjoining to the frontier settlements of the United States, and for introducing among them the habits and arts of civilization, the President of the United States shall be, and he is hereby authorized, in every case where he shall judge improvement in the habits and condition of such Indians practicable, and that the means of instruction can be introduced with their own consent, to employ capable persons, of good moral character, to instruct them in the mode of agriculture suited to their situation; and for teaching their children in reading, writing and arithmetic; and for performing such other duties as may be enjoined, according to such instructions and rules as the President may give and prescribe for the regulation of their conduct in the discharge of their duties."

This act avowedly contemplates the preservation of the Indian nations as an object sought by the United States, and proposes to effect this object by civilizing and converting them from hunters into agriculturists. Though the Cherokees had already made considerable progress in this improvement, it cannot be doubted that the general words of the act comprehend them. Their advance in the "habits and arts of civilization," rather encouraged perseverance in the laudable exertions still farther to meliorate their condition. This act furnishes strong additional evidence of a settled purpose to fix the Indians in their country by giving them security at home.

The treaties and laws of the United States contemplate the Indian territory as completely separated from that of the States; and provide that all intercourse with them shall be carried on exclusively by the government of the Union. 558*] *Is this the rightful exercise of power, or is it usurpation?

While these States were colonies, this power, in its utmost extent, was admitted to reside in the crown. When our revolutionary struggle commenced, Congress was composed of an assemblage of deputies acting under specific powers granted by the legislatures, or conventions of the several colonies. It was a great popular movement, not perfectly organized; nor were the respective powers of those who were intrusted with the management of affairs accurately defined. The necessities of our situation produced a general conviction that those measures which concerned all, must be transacted by a body in which the representatives of all were assembled, and which could command the confidence of all: Congress, therefore, was considered as invested with all the powers of war and peace, and Congress dissolved our connection with the mother country, and declared these United Colonies to be independent States. Without any written definition of powers, they employed diplomatic agents to represent the United States at the several courts of Europe; offered to negotiate treaties with them, and did actually negotiate treaties with France. From the same necessity, and on the same principles, Congress assumed the management of Indian affairs; first in the name of these United Colonies, and afterwards in the name of the United States. Early attempts were made at negotiation, and to regulate trade with them. These not proving successful, war was carried on under the direction, and with the forces of the United States, and the efforts to make peace by treaty were earnest and incessant. The confederation found Congress in the exercise of the same powers of peace and war, in our relations with Indian nations, as with those of Europe.

Such was the state of things when the confederation was adopted. That instrument surrendered the powers of peace and war to Congress and prohibited them to the States, respectively, unless a State be actually invaded, "or shall have received certain advice of a resolution being formed by some nation of Indians to invade such State, and the danger is so imminent as not to admit of delay till the United States in Congress assembled can be consulted." This instrument also gave the United States in Congress assembled the sole and exclusive right of "regulating the trade and managing all the affairs with the Indians, not *members [*559 of any of the States: provided that the legislative power of any State within its own limits be not infringed or violated."

The ambiguous phrases which follow the grant of power to the United States were so construed by the States of North Carolina and Georgia as to annul the power itself. The discontent and confusion resulting from these conflicting claims produced representations to Congress, which were referred to a committee, who made their report in 1787. The report does not assent to the construction of the two States, but recommends an accommodation, by liberal cessions of territory, or by an admission on their part of the powers claimed by Congress. The correct exposition of this article is rendered unnecessary by the adoption of our existing Constitution. That instrument confers on Congress the powers of war and peace: of making treaties, and of regulating commerce with foreign nations, and among the several States, and with the Indian tribes. These powers comprehend all that is required for the regulation of our intercourse with the Indians. They are not limited by any restrictions on their free actions. The shackles imposed on this power, in the confederation, are discarded.

The Indian nations had always been considered as distinct, independent political communities, retaining their original natural rights, as the undisputed possessors of the soil from time immemorial, with the single exception of that imposed by irresistible power, which excluded them from intercourse with any other European potentate than the first discoverer of the coast of the particular region claimed: and this was a restriction which those European potentates imposed on themselves, as well as on the Indians. The very term "nation," so generally applied to them, means "a people distinct from others." The Constitution, by declaring treaties already made, as well as those to be made, to be the supreme law of the land, has adopted and sanctioned the previous treaties with the Indian nations, and consequently admits their rank among those powers who are capable of making treaties. The words "treaty" and "nation" are words of our own language, selected in our diplomatic and legislative proceedings, by ourselves, having each a definite 560*] and well understood meaning. We *have applied them to Indians, as we have applied them to the other nations of the earth. They are applied to all in the same sense.

Georgia herself has furnished conclusive evidence that her former opinions on this subject concurred with those entertained by her sister States, and by the government of the United States. Various acts of her Legislature have been cited in the argument, including the contract of cession made in the year 1802, all tending to prove her acquiescence in the universal conviction that the Indian nations possessed a full right to the lands they occupied, until that right should be extinguished by the United States, with their consent; that their territory was separated from that of any State within whose chartered limits they might reside, by a boundary line, established by treaties; that, within their boundary, they possessed rights with which no State could interfere, and that the whole power of regulating the intercourse with them was vested in the United States. A review of these acts, on the part of Georgia, would occupy too much time, and is the less necessary because they have been accurately detailed in the argument at the bar. Her new series of laws, manifesting her abandonment of these opinions, appears to have commenced in December, 1828.

In opposition to this original right, possessed by the undisputed occupants of every country; to this recognition of that right, which is evidenced by our history, in every change through which we have passed, is placed the charters granted by the monarch of a distant and distinct region, parceling out a territory in possession of others whom he could not remove and did not attempt to remove, and the cession made of his claims by the Treaty of Peace.

The actual state of things at the time, and all history since, explain these charters; and the King of Great Britain, at the Treaty of Peace, could cede only what belonged to his crown. These newly asserted titles can derive no aid from the articles so often repeated in Indian treaties; extending to them, first, the protection of Great Britain, and afterwards that of the United States. These articles are associated with others, recognizing their title to self-government. The very fact of repeated treaties with them recognizes it; and the settled doc-561*] trine *of the law of nations is that a weaker power does not surrender its independence—its right to self-government, by associating with a stronger and taking its protection. A weak State in order to provide for its safety, may place itself under the protection of one more powerful without stripping itself of the right of government, and ceasing to be a State. Examples of this kind are not wanting in Europe. "Tributary and feudatory states," says Vattel, "do not thereby cease to be sovereign and independent states so long as self-government and sovereign and independent authority are left in the administration of the state." At the present day, more than one State may be considered as holding its right of self-government under the guaranty and protection of one or more allies.

The Cherokee nation, then, is a distinct community, occupying its own territory, with

8 L. ed.

boundaries accurately described, in which the laws of Georgia can have no force, and which the citizens of Georgia have no right to enter but with the assent of the Cherokees themselves or in conformity with treaties and with the acts of Congress. The whole intercourse between the United States and this nation is, by our Constitution and laws, vested in the government of the United States.

The act of the State of Georgia under which the plaintiff in error was prosecuted is consequently void, and the judgment a nullity. Can this court revise and reverse it?

If the objection to the system of legislation lately adopted by the Legislature of Georgia in relation to the Cherokee Nation was confined to its extraterritorial operation, the objection, though complete, so far as respected mere right, would give this court no power over the subject. But it goes much further. If the review which has been taken be correct, and we think it is, the acts of Georgia are repugnant to the Constitution, laws, and treaties of the United States.

They interfere forcibly with the relations established between the United States and the Cherokee Nation, the regulation of which, according to the settled principles of our Constitution, are committed exclusively to the government of the Union.

They are in direct hostility with treaties, repeated in a succession of years, which mark out the boundary that separates *the [*562 Cherokee country from Georgia; guaranty to them all the land within their boundary; solemnly pledge the faith of the United States to restrain their citizens from trespassing on it; and recognize the pre-existing power of the nation to govern itself.

They are in equal hostility with the acts of Congress for regulating this intercourse, and giving effect to the treaties.

The forcible seizure and abduction of the plaintiff in error, who was residing in the nation with its permission, and by authority of the President of the United States, is also a violation of the acts which authorize the chief magistrate to exercise this authority.

Will these powerful considerations avail the plaintiff in error? We think they will. He was seized and forcibly carried away while under guardianship of treaties guarantying the country in which he resided, and taking it under the protection of the United States. He was seized while performing, under the sanction of the Chief magistrate of the Union those duties which the humane policy adopted by Congress had recommended. He was apprehended, tried, and condemned, under color of a law which has been shown to be repugnant to the Constitution, laws, and treaties of the United States. Had a judgment, liable to the same objections, been rendered for property, none would question the jurisdiction of this court. It cannot be less clear when the judgment affects personal liberty, and inflicts disgraceful punishment, if punishment could disgrace when inflicted on innocence. The plaintiff in error is not less interested in the operation of this unconstitutional law than if it affected his property. He is not less entitled to the protection of the Constitution, laws, and treaties of his country.

562   SUPREME COURT OF THE UNITED STATES.   1832

This point has been elaborately argued and, after deliberate consideration, decided, in the case of Cohens v. The Commonwealth of Virginia, 6 Wheat. 264.

It is the opinion of this court that the judgment of the Superior Court for the County of Gwinnett, in the State of Georgia, condemning Samuel A. Worcester to hard labor in the penitentiary of the State of Georgia for four years, was pronounced by that court under color of a law which is void, as being repugnant to the Constitution, treaties, and laws of the United 563*] *States, and ought, therefore, to be reversed and annulled.

Mr. Justice M'Lean.

As this case involves principles of the highest importance, and may lead to consequences which shall have an enduring influence on the institutions of this country; and as there are some points in the case on which I wish to state, distinctly, my opinion, I embrace the privilege of doing so.

With the decision just given, I concur.

The plaintiff in error was indicted under a law of Georgia "for residing in that part of the Cherokee Nation attached, by the laws of said State, to the County of Gwinnett, without a license or permit from his excellency the governor of the State, or from any agent authorized by his excellency the governor to grant such permit, or license and without having taken the oath to support and defend the constitution and laws of the State of Georgia, and uprightly to demean himself as a citizen thereof."

On this indictment the defendant was arrested, and, on being arraigned before the Superior Court for Gwinnett County, he filed, in substance, the following plea:

He admits that, on the 15th of July, 1831, he was, and still continued to be, a resident in the Cherokee Nation, and that the crime, if any were committed, was committed at the town of New Echota, in said nation, out of the jurisdiction of the court. That he is a citizen of Vermont, and that he entered the Indian country in the capacity of a duly authorized missionary of the American Board of Commissioners for Foreign Missions, under the authority of the President of the United States, and has not since been required by him to leave it. That he was, at the time of his arrest, engaged in preaching the Gospel to the Cherokee Indians, and in translating the sacred Scriptures into their language, with the permission and approval of the Cherokee Nation, and in accordance with the humane policy of the government of the United States for the improvement of the Indians.

He then states, as a bar to the prosecution, certain treaties made between the United States 564*] and the Cherokee Indians, by *which the possession of the territory they now inhabit was solemnly guaranteed to them; and also a certain Act of Congress, passed in March, 1802, entitled "An Act to regulate trade and intercourse with the Indian tribes." He also alleges that this subject, by the Constitution of the United States, is exclusively vested in Congress; and that the law of Georgia, being repugnant to the Constitution of the United States, to the treaties referred to, and to the
502

act of Congress specified, is void, and cannot be enforced against him.

This plea was overruled by the court, and the defendant pleaded not guilty.

The jury returned a verdict of guilty, and the defendant was sentenced by the court to be kept in close custody by the sheriff of the county until he could be transported to the penitentiary of the State, and the keeper thereof was directed to receive him into custody, and keep him at hard labor in the penitentiary, during the term of four years.

Another individual was included in the same indictment, and joined in the plea to the jurisdiction of the court, and was also included in the sentence; but his name is not adverted to, because the principles of the case are fully presented in the above statement.

To reverse this judgment, a writ of error was obtained, which, having been returned with the record of the proceedings, is now before this court.

The first question which it becomes necessary to examine is, whether the record has been duly certified, so as to bring the proceedings regularly before this tribunal.

A writ of error was allowed in this case by one of the justices of this court, and the requisite security taken. A citation was also issued, in the form prescribed, to the State of Georgia, a true copy of which, as appears by the oath of William Patten, was delivered to the governor on the 24th day of November last; and another true copy was delivered on the 22d day of the same month to the Attorney-General of the State.

The record was returned by the clerk, under the seal of the court, who certifies that it is a full and complete exemplification of the proceedings and judgment had in the case; and he *further certifies that the original [*565 bond, and a copy of the writ of error, were duly deposited and filed in the clerk's office of said court, on the 10th day of November last.

Is it necessary, in such a case, that the record should be certified by the judge who held the court?

In the case of Martin v. Hunter's Lessee, which was a writ of error to the Court of Appeals of Virginia, it was objected that the return to the writ of error was defective, because the record was not so certified; but the court in that case said, "the forms of process, and the modes of proceeding in the exercise of jurisdiction, are, with few exceptions, left by the Legislature to be regulated and changed, as this court may, in its discretion, deem expedient." By a rule of this court, "the return of a copy of a record, of the proper court, annexed to the writ of error, is declared to be a sufficient compliance with the mandate of the writ. The record in this case is duly certified by the clerk of the Court of Appeals, and annexed to the writ of error. The objection, therefore, which has been urged to the sufficiency of the return cannot prevail." 1 Wheat. 304.

In 9 Wheat. 526, in the case of Stewart v. Ingle et al., which was a writ of error to the Circuit Court for the District of Columbia, a certiorari was issued upon a suggestion of diminution in the record, which was returned by the clerk with another record; whereupon a
Peters 6.

motion was made for a new certiorari, on the ground that the return ought to have been made by the judge of the court below, and not by the clerk. The writ of certiorari, it is known, like the writ of error, is directed to the court.

Mr. Justice **Washington**, after consultation with the judges, stated that according to the rules and practice of the court, a return made by the clerk was a sufficient return.

To ascertain what has been the general course of practice on this subject, an examination has been made into the manner in which records have been certified from State courts to this court; and it appears that, in the year 1817, six causes were certified, in obedience to writs of error, by the clerk, under the seal of the court. In the year 1819, two were so certified, one of them being the case of M'Culloch v. The State of Maryland.

566*] *In the year 1821 three cases were so certified; and in the year 1823 there was one. In 1827 there were five, and in the ensuing year, seven.

In the year 1830 there were eight causes so certified, in five of which a State was a party on the record. There were three causes thus certified in the year 1831, and five in the present year.

During the above periods, there were only fifteen causes from State courts where the records were certified by the court or the presiding judge, and one of these was the case of Cohens v. The State of Virginia.

This court adopted the following rule on this subject in 1797:

"It is ordered by the court that the clerk of the court to which any writ of error shall be directed, may make the return of the same by transmitting a true copy of the record, and of all proceedings in the cause, under his hand, and the seal of the court."

The power of the court to adopt this rule cannot be questioned; and it seems to have regulated the practice ever since its adoption. In some cases, the certificate of the court, or the presiding judge has been affixed to the record; but this court has decided, where the question has been raised, that such certificate is unnecessary.

So far as the authentication of the record is concerned, it is impossible to make a distinction between a civil and a criminal case. What may be sufficient to authenticate the proceedings in a civil case, must be equally so in a criminal one. The verity of the record is of as much importance in the one case as in the other.

This is a question of practice; and it would seem that, if any one point in the practice of this court can be considered as settled, this one must be so considered.

In the progress of the investigation, the next inquiry which seems naturally to arise, is, whether this is a case in which a writ of error may be issued.

By the twenty-fifth section of the Judiciary Act of 1789, it is provided "that a final judgment or decree in any suit in the highest court of law or equity of a State, in which a decision in the suit could be had, where is drawn in **567***] question the validity *of a treaty, or statute of, or an authority exercised under, the

8 L. ed.

United States, and the decision is against their validity; or where is drawn in question the validity of a statute of, or an authority exercised under, any State, on the ground of their being repugnant to the Constitution, treaties, or laws of the United States, and the decision is in favor of such their validity; or where is drawn in question the construction of any clause of the Constitution, or of a treaty or statute of, or commission held under, the United States, and the decision is against the title, right, privilege, or exemption, specially set up or claimed by either party under such clause of the said constitution, treaty, statute, or commission, may be re-examined, and reversed or affirmed, in the Supreme Court of the United States."

Doubts have been expressed whether a writ of error to a State court is not limited to civil cases. These doubts could not have arisen from reading the above section. Is not a criminal case as much a suit as a civil case? What is a suit but a prosecution; and can any one suppose that it was the intention of Congress, in using the word "suit," to make a distinction between a civil prosecution and a criminal one?

It is more important that jurisdiction should be given to this court in criminal than in civil cases, under the twenty-fifth section of the Judiciary Act. Would it not be inconsistent both with the spirit and letter of this law, to revise the judgment of a State court, in a matter of controversy respecting damages, where the decision is against a right asserted under the Constitution or a law of the United States; but to deny the jurisdiction, in a case where the property, the character, the liberty and life of a citizen may be destroyed, though protected by the solemn guarantees of the Constitution?

But this is not an open question; it has long since been settled by the solemn adjudications of this court. The above construction, therefore, is sustained both on principle and authority. The provisions of the section apply as well to criminal as to civil cases, where the Constitution, treaties, or laws of the United States come in conflict with the laws of a State, and the latter is sustained by the decision of the court.

It has been said that this court can have no power to arrest *the proceedings of a [*568 State tribunal in the enforcement of the criminal laws of the State. This is undoubtedly true, so long as a State court, in the execution of its penal laws, shall not infringe upon the Constitution of the United States, or some treaty or law of the Union.

Suppose a State should make it penal for an officer of the United States to discharge his duties within its jurisdiction; as, for instance, a land officer, an officer of the customs, or a postmaster, and punish the offender by confinement in the penitentiary; could not the Supreme Court of the United States interpose their power, and arrest or reverse the State proceedings? Cases of this kind are so palpable, that they need only to be stated to gain the assent of every judicious mind. And would not this be an interference with the administration of the criminal laws of a State?

This court have repeatedly decided that they have no appellate jurisdiction in criminal cases

503

from the circuit courts of the United States; writs of error and appeals are given from those courts only in civil cases. But, even in those courts, where the judges are divided on any point in a criminal case, the point may be brought before this court, under a general provision in cases of division of opinion.

Jurisdiction is taken in the case under consideration exclusively by the provisions of the twenty-fifth section of the law which has been quoted. These provisions, as has been remarked, apply indiscriminately to criminal and civil cases, wherever a right is claimed under the Constitution, treaties, or laws of the United States, and the decision, by the State Court, is against such right. In the present case, the decision was against the right expressly set up by the defendant, and it was made by the highest judicial tribunal of Georgia.

To give jurisdiction in such a case, this court need look no further than to ascertain whether the right, thus asserted, was decided against by the State court. The case is clear of difficulty on this point.

The name of the State of Georgia is used in this case because such was the designation given to the cause in the State court. No one ever supposed that the State, in its sovereign capacity, in such a case, is a party to the cause. 569*] The form of *the prosecution here must. be the same as it was in the State court; but so far as the name of the State is used, it is a matter of form. Under a rule of this court, notice was given to the governor and Attorney-General of the State because it is a part of their duty to see that the laws of the State are executed.

In prosecutions for violations of the penal laws of the Union, the name of the United States is used in the same manner. Whether the prosecution be under a federal or State law, the defendant has a right to question the constitutionality of the law.

Can any doubt exist as to the power of Congress to pass the law under which jurisdiction is taken in this case? Since its passage, in 1789, it has been the law of the land; and has been sanctioned by an uninterrupted course of decisions in this court, and acquiesced in by the State tribunals, with perhaps a solitary exception; and whenever the attention of the national Legislature has been called to the subject, their sanction has been given to the law by so large a majority as to approach almost to unanimity.

Of the policy of this act there can be as little doubt as of the right of Congress to pass it.

The Constitution of the United States was formed, not, in my opinion, as some have contended, by the people of the United States, nor, as others, by the States; but by a combined power exercised by the people through their delegates, limited in their sanctions, to the respective States.

Had the Constitution emanated from the people, and the States had been referred to merely as convenient districts by which the public expression could be ascertained, the popular vote throughout the Union would have been the only rule for the adoption of the Constitution. This course was not pursued; and in this fact, it clearly appears that our fundamental law was not formed, exclusively, by the popular suffrage of the people.

504

The vote of the people was limited to the respective States in which they resided. So that it appears there was an expression of popular suffrage and State sanction, most happily united, in the adoption of the Constitution of the Union.

Whatever differences of opinion may exist as to the means *by which the Consti- [*570 tution was adopted, there would seem to be no ground for any difference as to certain powers conferred by it.

Three co-ordinate branches of the government were established—the executive, legislative and judicial. These branches are essential to the existence of any free government, and that they should possess powers, in their respective spheres, co-extensive with each other.

If the executive have not powers which will enable him to execute the functions of his office, the system is essentially defective; as those duties must, in such a case, be discharged by one of the other branches. This would destroy that balance which is admitted to be essential to the existence of free government, by the wisest and most enlightened statesmen of the present day.

It is not less important that the legislative power should be exercised by the appropriate branch of the government, than that the executive duties should devolve upon the proper functionary. And if the judicial power fall short of giving effect to the laws of the Union, the existence of the federal government is at an end.

It is in vain, and worse than in vain, that the national Legislature enact laws, if those laws are to remain upon the statute book as monuments of the imbecility of the national power. It is in vain that the executive is called to superintend the execution of the laws, if he have no power to aid in their enforcement.

Such weakness and folly are in no degree chargeable to the distinguished men through whose instrumentality the Constitution was formed. The powers given, it is true, are limited; and no powers, which are not expressly given, can be exercised by the federal government; but, where given, they are supreme. Within the sphere allotted to them, the co-ordinate branches of the general government revolve, unobstructed by any legitimate exercise of power by the State governments. The powers exclusively given to the federal government are limitations upon the State authorities. But, with the exception of these limitations, the States are supreme; and their sovereignty can be no more invaded by the action of the general government, than the action of the State governments can arrest or obstruct the course of the national power.

*It has been asserted that the federal [*571 government is foreign to the State governments, and that it must consequently be hostile to them. Such an opinion could not have resulted from a thorough investigation of the great principles which lie at the foundation of our system. The federal government is neither foreign to the State governments, nor is it hostile to them. It proceeds from the same people, and is as much under their control as the State governments.

Where, by the Constitution, the power of legislation is exclusively vested in Congress, they legislate for the people of the Union, and their acts are as binding as are the constitutional enactments of a State Legislature on the people of the State. If this were not so, the federal government would exist only in name. Instead of being the proudest monument of human wisdom and patriotism, it would be the frail memorial of the ignorance and mental imbecility of its framers.

In the discharge of his constitutional duties, the federal executive acts upon the people of the Union the same as a governor of a State, in the performance of his duties, acts upon the people of the State. And the judicial power of the United States acts in the same manner on the people. It rests upon the same basis as the other departments of the government. The powers of each are derived from the same source, and are conferred by the same instrument. They have the same limitations and extent.

The Supreme Court of a State, when required to give effect to a statute of the State, will examine its constitution, which they are sworn to maintain, to see if the legislative act be repugnant to it; and if the repugnancy exist, the statute must yield to the paramount law.

The same principle governs the supreme tribunal of the Union. No one can deny that the Constitution of the United States is the supreme law of the land; and, consequently, no act of any State Legislature or of Congress, which is repugnant to it, can be of any validity.

Now, if an act of a State Legislature be repugnant to the constitution of the State, the State court will declare it void; and if such act be repugnant to the Constitution of the Union, or a law made under that Constitution, which is declared to be the supreme law of the land, is it not equally void? And, under such 572*] *circumstances, if this court should shrink from a discharge of their duty in giving effect to the supreme law of the land, would they not violate their oaths, prove traitors to the Constitution, and forfeit all just claim to the public confidence?

It is sometimes objected, if the federal judiciary may declare an act of a State Legislature void, because it is repugnant to the Constitution of the United States, it places the legislation of a State within the power of this court. And might not the same argument be urged with equal force against the exercise of a similar power by the Supreme Court of a State. Such an argument must end in the destruction of all constitutions, and the will of the Legislature, like the acts of the Parliament of Great Britain, must be the supreme, and only law of the land.

It is impossible to guard an investiture of power so that it may not, in some form, be abused: an argument, therefore, against the exercise of power, because it is liable to abuse, would go to the destruction of all governments.

The powers of this court are expressly, not constructively, given by the Constitution; and within this delegation of power, this court are the Supreme Court of the people of the United States, and they are bound to discharge their duties, under the same responsibilities as the Supreme Court of a State; and are equally, within their powers, the Supreme Court of the people of each State.

When this court are required to enforce the laws of any State, they are governed by those laws. So closely do they adhere to this rule, that during the present term, a judgment of a Circuit Court of the United States, made in pursuance of decisions of this court, has been reversed and annulled because it did not conform to the decisions of the State Court, in giving a construction to a local law. But while this court conforms its decisions to those of the State courts on all questions arising under the statutes and constitutions of the respective States, they are bound to revise and correct those decisions, if they annul either the Constitution of the United States or the laws made under it.

It appears, then, that on all questions arising under the laws of a State, the decisions of the courts of such State form a rule for the decisions of this court, and that on all questions arising under the laws of the United States, the decisions of this court *form a rule [*573 for the decisions of the State courts. Is there anything unreasonable in this? Have not the federal, as well as the State courts, been constituted by the people? Why, then, should one tribunal more than the other be deemed hostile to the interests of the people?

In the second section of the third article of the Constitution, it is declared that "the judicial power shall extend to all cases in law and equity arising under the Constitution, the laws of the United States, and treaties made, or which shall be made, under their authority."

Having shown that a writ of error will lie in this case, and that the record has been duly certified, the next inquiry that arises is, what are the acts of the United States which relate to the Cherokee Indians and the acts of Georgia; and were these acts of the United States sanctioned by the federal Constitution?

Among the enumerated powers of Congress contained in the eighth section of the first article of the Constitution, it is declared that "Congress shall have power to regulate commerce with foreign nations, and among the Indian tribes." By the Articles of Confederation, which were adopted on the 9th day of July, 1778, it was provided that "the United States, in Congress assembled, shall also have the sole and exclusive right and power of regulating the alloy and value of coin struck, by their own authority, or by that of the respective States; fixing the standard of weights and measures throughout the United States; regulating the trade and management of all affairs with the Indians, not members of any of the States: Provided, that the legislative right of any State, within its own limits, be not infringed or violated."

As early as June, 1775, and before the adoption of the Articles of Confederation, Congress took into their consideration the subject of Indian affairs. The Indian country was divided into three departments, and the superintendence of each was committed to commissioners, who were authorized to hold treaties with the Indians, make disbursements of money for their use, and to discharge various duties designed to preserve peace and cultivate a friendly feeling with them towards the colonies. No person was permitted to trade with them without *a license from one or more of the com- [*574 missioners of the respective departments.

In April, 1776, it was "resolved, that the commissioners of Indian affairs in the middle department, or any one of them, be desired to employ, for reasonable salaries, a minister of the Gospel, to reside among the Delaware Indians, and instruct them in the Christian religion; a schoolmaster to teach their youth reading, writing, and arithmetic; also a blacksmith, to do the work of the Indians." The general intercourse with the Indians continued to be managed under the superintendence of the continental Congress.

On the 28th of November, 1785, the Treaty of Hopewell was formed, which was the first treaty made with the Cherokee Indians. The commissioners of the United States were required to give notice to the executives of Virginia, North Carolina, South Carolina, and Georgia, in order that each might appoint one or more persons to attend the treaty, but they seem to have had no power to act on the occasion.

In this treaty it is stipulated that "the commissioners plenipotentiary of the United States in Congress assembled, give peace to all the Cherokees, and receive them into the favor and protection of the United States of America, on the following conditions:"

1. The Cherokees to restore all prisoners and property taken during the war.

2. The United States to restore to the Cherokees all prisoners.

3. The Cherokees acknowledge themselves to be under the protection of the United States, and of no other sovereign whatsoever.

4. The boundary line between the Cherokees and the citizens of the United States was agreed to as designated.

5. If any person, not being an Indian, intrude upon the land "allotted" to the Indians, or, being settled on it, shall refuse to remove within six months after the ratification of the treaty, he forfeits the protection of the United States, and the Indians were at liberty to punish him as they might think proper.

6. The Indians are bound to deliver up to the United States any Indian who shall commit robbery, or other capital crime, on a white person living within their protection.
575*]   *7. If the same offense be committed on an Indian by a citizen of the United States, he is to be punished.

8. It is understood that the punishment of the innocent, under the idea of retaliation, is unjust, and shall not be practiced on either side, except where there is a manifest violation of this treaty; and then it shall be preceded, first, by a demand of justice; and, if refused, then by a declaration of hostilities.

"That the Indians may have full confidence in the justice of the United States respecting their interests, they shall have a right to send a deputy of their choice, whenever they think fit, to Congress."

The Treaty of Holston was entered into with the same people, on the 2d day of July, 1791.

This was a treaty of peace, in which the Cherokees again placed themselves under the protection of the United States, and engaged to hold no treaty with any foreign power, individual State, or with individuals of any State. Prisoners were agreed to be delivered up on

both sides; a new Indian boundary was fixed, and a cession of land made to the United States on the payment of a stipulated consideration.

A free, unmolested road, was agreed to be given through the Indian lands, and the free navigation of the Tennessee River. It was agreed that the United States should have the exclusive right of regulating their trade, and a solemn guarantee of their land, not ceded, was made. A similar provision was made as to the punishment of offenders, and as to all persons who might enter the Indian territory, as was contained in the Treaty of Hopewell. Also, that reprisal or retaliation shall not be committed until satisfaction shall have been demanded of the aggressor.

On the 7th day of August, 1786, an ordinance for the regulation of Indian affairs was adopted, which repealed the former system.

In 1794 another treaty was made with the Cherokees, the object of which was to carry into effect the Treaty of Holston. And on the plains of Tellico, on the 2d of October, 1798, the Cherokees, in another treaty, agreed to give a right of way, in a certain direction, over their lands. Other engagements were also entered into, which need not be referred to.

Various other treaties were made by the United States with *the Cherokee In- [*576 dians, by which, among other arrangements, cessions of territory were procured and boundaries agreed on.

In a treaty made in 1817, a distinct wish is expressed by the Cherokees to assume a more regular form of government, in which they are encouraged by the United States. By a treaty held at Washington on the 27th day of February, 1819, a reservation of land is made by the Cherokees for a school fund, which was to be surveyed and sold by the United States for that purpose. And it was agreed that all white persons, who had intruded on the Indian lands should be removed.

To give effect to various treaties with this people, the power of the executive has frequently been exercised; and at one time General Washington expressed a firm determination to resort to military force to remove intruders from the Indian territories.

On the 30th of March, 1802, Congress passed an Act to regulate trade and intercourse with the Indian tribes, and to preserve peace on the frontiers.

In this act it is provided that any citizen or resident of the United States, who shall enter into the Indian lands to hunt, or for any other purpose, without a license, shall be subject to a fine and imprisonment. And if any person shall attempt to survey, or actually survey, the Indian lands, he shall be liable to forfeit a sum not exceeding one thousand dollars, and be imprisoned not exceeding twelve months. No person is permitted to reside as a trader within the Indian boundaries, without a license or permit. All persons are prohibited, under a heavy penalty, from purchasing the Indian lands; and all such purchases are declared to be void. And it is made lawful for the military force of the United States to arrest offenders against the provisions of the act.

By the seventeenth section, it is provided that the act shall not be so construed as to "prevent any trade or intercourse with Indians living on lands surrounded by settlements of the citizens of the United States, and being within the ordinary jurisdiction of any of the individual States; or the unmolested use of a road, from Washington district to Mero district, or to prevent the citizens of Tennessee from keeping in repair said road." Nor was the act to be so construed as to prevent persons from traveling from 577*] Knoxville to Price's settlement, *provided they shall travel in the tract or path which is usually traveled, and the Indians do not object; but if they object, then all travel on this road to be prohibited, after proclamation by the President, under the penalties provided in the act.

Several acts, having the same object in view, were passed prior to this one; but as they were repealed either before, or by the Act of 1802, their provisions need not be specially noticed.

The acts of the State of Georgia, which the plaintiff in error complains of as being repugnant to the Constitution, treaties, and laws of the United States, are found in two statutes.

The first Act was passed the 12th of December, 1829, and is entitled "An Act to add the territory lying within the chartered limits of Georgia, and now in the occupancy of the Cherokee Indians, to the counties of Carroll, DeKalb, Gwinnett and Habersham; and to extend the laws of the State over the same, and to annul all laws made by the Cherokee Nation of Indians, and to provide for the compensation of officers serving legal process in said territory, and to regulate the testimony of Indians, and to repeal the ninth section of the Act of 1828 on this subject."

This act annexes the territory of the Indians within the limits of Georgia to the counties named in the title, and extends the jurisdiction of the State over it. It annuls the laws, ordinances, orders and regulations, of any kind, made by the Cherokees, either in council or in any other way, and they are not permitted to be given in evidence in the courts of the State. By this law, no Indian, or the descendant of an Indian, residing within the Creek or Cherokee Nation of Indians, shall be deemed a competent witness in any court of the State to which a white person may be a party, except such white person reside within the nation. Offenses under the act are to be punished by confinement in the penitentiary, in some cases not less than four nor more than six years, and others not exceeding four years.

The second Act was passed on the 22d day of December, 1830, and is entitled "An Act to prevent the exercise of assumed and arbitrary power, by all persons, on pretext of authority from the Cherokee Indians and their laws; and to prevent white persons from residing within 578*] that part of the *chartered limits of Georgia occupied by the Cherokee Indians; and to provide a guard for the protection of the gold mines, and to enforce the laws of the State without the aforesaid territory."

By the first section of this act, it is made a penitentiary offense, after the 1st day of February, 1831, for any person or persons, under color or pretense of authority from the said Cherokee tribe, or as headmen, chiefs or warriors of said tribe, to cause or procure, by any means, the assembling of any council or other pretended legislative body of the said Indians, for the purpose of legislating, etc.

They are prohibited from making laws, holding courts of justice, or executing process. And all white persons, after the 1st of March, 1831, who shall reside within the limits of the Cherokee Nation without a license or permit from his excellency the governor, or from such agent as his excellency the governor shall authorize to grant such permit or license, or who shall not have taken the oath hereinafter required, shall be guilty of a high misdemeanor; and, upon conviction thereof, shall be punished by confinement to the penitentiary at hard labor, for a term not less than four years. From this punishment, agents of the United States are excepted, white females, and male children under twenty-one years of age.

Persons who have obtained license, are required to take the following oath: "I, A B, do solemnly swear that I will support and defend the constitution and laws of the State of Georgia, and uprightly demean myself as a citizen thereof. So help me God."

The governor is authorized to organize a guard, which shall not consist of more than sixty persons, to protect the mines in the Indian territory, and the guard is authorized to arrest all offenders under the act.

It is apparent that these laws are repugnant to the treaties with the Cherokee Indians which have been referred to, and to the law of 1802. This repugnance is made so clear by an exhibition of the respective acts, that no force of demonstration can make it more palpable.

By the treaties and laws of the United States, rights are guaranteed to the Cherokees, both as it respects their territory and internal polity. By the laws of Georgia these rights are abolished; *and not only abolished, but an [*579 ignominious punishment is inflicted on the Indians and others, for the exercise of them. The important question then arises, which shall stand, the laws of the United States, or the laws of Georgia? No rule of construction, or subtlety of argument, can evade an answer to this question. The response must be, so far as the punishment of the plaintiff in error is concerned, in favor of the one or the other.

Not to feel the full weight of this momentous subject would evidence an ignorance of that high responsibility which is devolved upon this tribunal, and upon its humblest member, in giving a decision in this case.

Are the treaties and law which have been cited, in force? and what, if any obligations, do they impose on the federal government within the limits of Georgia?

A reference has been made to the policy of the United States on the subject of Indian affairs before the adoption of the Constitution, with a view to ascertaining in what light the Indians have been considered by the first official acts, in relation to them, by the United States. For this object, it might not be improper to notice how they were considered by the European inhabitants, who first formed settlements in this part of the continent of America.

The abstract right of every section of the human race to a reasonable portion of the soil, by which to acquire the means of subsistence, cannot be controverted. And it is equally clear that the range of nations or tribes, who exist in the hunter state, may be restricted within reasonable limits. They shall not be permitted to roam, in the pursuit of game, over an extensive and rich country, whilst in other parts, human beings are crowded so closely together, as to render the means of subsistence precarious. The law of nature, which is paramount to all other laws, gives the right to every nation to the enjoyment of a reasonable extent of country, so as to derive the means of subsistence from the soil.

In this view, perhaps, our ancestors, when they first migrated to this country, might have taken possession of a limited extent of the domain, had they been sufficiently powerful, without negotiation or purchase from the native Indians. But this course is believed to have been nowhere taken. A more conciliatory 580*] *mode was preferred, and one which was better calculated to impress the Indians, who were then powerful, with a sense of the justice of their white neighbors. The occupancy of their lands was never assumed, except upon the basis of contract, and on the payment of a valuable consideration.

This policy has obtained from the earliest white settlements in this country down to the present time. Some cessions of territory may have been made by the Indians, in compliance with the terms on which peace was offered by the whites, but the soil thus taken was taken by the laws of conquest, and always as an indemnity for the expenses of the war commenced by the Indians.

At no time has the sovereignty of the country been recognized as existing in the Indians, but they have been always admitted to possess many of the attributes of sovereignty. All the rights which belong to self-government have been recognized as vested in them. Their right of occupancy has never been questioned, but the fee in the soil has been considered in the government. This may be called the right to the ultimate domain, but the Indians have a present right of possession.

In some of the old States—Massachusetts, Connecticut, Rhode Island and others—where small remnants of tribes remain, surrounded by white population, and who, by their reduced numbers, had lost the power of self-government—the laws of the State have been extended over them, for the protection of their persons and property.

Before the adoption of the Constitution, the mode of treating with the Indians was various. After the formation of the confederacy, this subject was placed under the special superintendence of the United Colonies, though, subsequent to that time, treaties may have been occasionally entered into between a State and the Indians in its neighborhood. It is not considered to be at all important to go into a minute inquiry on this subject.

By the Constitution, the regulation of commerce among the Indian tribes is given to Congress. This power must be considered as exclusively vested in Congress, as the power to regulate commerce with foreign nations, to coin 581*] money, to *establish post-offices, and to declare war. It is enumerated in the same section, and belongs to the same class of powers. This investiture of power has been exercised

in the regulation of commerce with the Indians, sometimes by treaty, and, at other times, by enactments of Congress. In this respect they have been placed by the federal authority, with but few exceptions, on the same footing as foreign nations.

It is said that these treaties are nothing more than compacts, which cannot be considered as obligatory on the United States, from a want of power in the Indians to enter into them.

What is a treaty? The answer is, it is a compact formed between two nations or communities, having the right of self-government.

Is it essential that each party shall possess the same attributes of sovereignty to give force to the treaty? This will not be pretended; for, on this ground, very few valid treaties could be formed. The only requisite is, that each of the contracting parties shall possess the right of self-government, and the power to perform the stipulations of the treaty.

Under the Constitution, no State can enter into any treaty; and it is believed that, since its adoption, no State, under its own authority, has held a treaty with the Indians.

It must be admitted that the Indians sustain a peculiar relation to the United States. They do not constitute, as was decided at the last term, a foreign state, so as to claim the right to sue in the Supreme Court of the United States; and yet, having the right of self-government, they, in some sense, form a State. In the management of their internal concerns, they are dependent on no power. They punish offenses under their own laws, and, in doing so, they are responsible to no earthly tribunal. They make war and form treaties of peace. The exercise of these and other powers gives to them a distinct character as a people, and constitutes them, in some respects, a state, although they may not be admitted to possess the right of soil.

By various treaties, the Cherokees have placed themselves under the protection of the United States; they have agreed to trade with no other people, nor to invoke the protection of any other sovereignty. But such engagements do not devest *them of the right [*582 of self-government, nor destroy their capacity to enter into treaties or compacts.

Every State is more or less dependent on those which surround it; but, unless this dependence shall extend so far as to merge the political existence of the protected people into that of their protectors, they may still constitute a state. They may exercise the powers not relinquished, and bind themselves as a distinct and separate community.

The language used in treaties with the Indians should never be construed to their prejudice. If words be made use of which are susceptible of a more extended meaning than their plain import, as connected with the tenor of the treaty, they should be considered as used only in the latter sense. To contend that the word "allotted," in reference to the land guaranteed to the Indians in certain treaties, indicates a favor conferred rather than a right acknowledged, would, it would seem to me, do injustice to the understanding of the parties. How the words of the treaty were understood by this unlettered people, rather than their critical meaning, should form the rule of construction.

The question may be asked, is no distinction to be made between a civilized and savage people? Are our Indians to be placed upon a footing with the nations of Europe, with whom we have made treaties?

The inquiry is not what station shall now be given to the Indian tribes in our country? but, what relation have they sustained to us, since the commencement of our government?

We have made treaties with them; and are those treaties to be disregarded on our part because they were entered into with an uncivilized people? Does this lessen the obligation of such treaties? By entering into them, have we not admitted the power of this people to bind themselves, and to impose obligations on us?

The President of the Senate, except under the treaty-making power, cannot enter into compacts with the Indians, or with foreign nations. This power has been uniformly exercised in forming treaties with the Indians.

Nations differ from each other in condition, and that of the same nation may change by the 583*] revolutions of time, but the *principles of justice are the same. They rest upon a base which will remain beyond the endurance of time.

After a lapse of more than forty years since treaties with the Indians have been solemnly ratified by the general government, it is too late to deny their binding force. Have the numerous treaties which have been formed with them, and the ratifications by the President and Senate, been nothing more than an idle pageantry?

By numerous treaties with the Indian tribes we have acquired accessions of territory of incalculable value to the Union. Except by compact, we have not even claimed a right of way through the Indian lands. We have recognized in them the right to make war. No one has ever supposed that the Indians could commit treason against the United States. We have punished them for their violation of treaties; but we have inflicted the punishment on them as a nation and not on individual offenders among them as traitors.

In the executive, legislative and judicial branches of our government, we have admitted, by the most solemn sanctions, the existence of the Indians as a separate and distinct people, and as being vested with rights which constitute them a state, or separate community—not a foreign, but a domestic community—not as belonging to the confederacy, but as existing within it, and, of necessity, bearing to it a peculiar relation.

But, can the treaties which have been referred to, and the law of 1802, be considered in force within the limits of the State of Georgia?

In the act of cession made by Georgia to the United States in 1802, of all lands claimed by her west of the line designated, one of the conditions was, "that the United States should, at their own expense, extinguish, for the use of Georgia, as early as the same can be peaceably obtained, on reasonable terms, the Indian title to lands within the State of Georgia."

One of the counsel, in the argument, endeavored to show that no part of the country now inhabited by the Cherokee Indians. is within what is called the chartered limits of Georgia.

It appears that the charter of Georgia was surrendered *by the trustees, and that, [*584 like the State of South Carolina, she became a regal colony. The effect of this change was to authorize the crown to alter the boundaries, in the exercise of its discretion. Certain alterations, it seems, were subsequently made; but I do not conceive it can be of any importance to enter into a minute consideration of them. Under its charter, it may be observed that Georgia derived a right to the soil, subject to the Indian title, by occupancy. By the act of cession, Georgia designated a certain line as the limit of that cession, and this line, unless subsequently altered, with the assent of the parties interested, must be considered as the boundary of the State of Georgia. This line having been thus recognized, cannot be contested on any question which may incidentally arise for judicial decision.

It is important, on this part of the case to ascertain in what light Georgia has considered the Indian title to lands generally, and particularly within her own boundaries; and also, as to the right of the Indians to self-government.

In the first place, she was a party to all the treaties entered into between the United States and the Indians since the adoption of the Constitution. And prior to that period she was represented in making them, and was bound by their provisions, although it is alleged that she remonstrated against the Treaty of Hopewell. In the passage of the intercourse law of 1802, as one of the constituent parts of the Union, she was also a party.

The stipulation made in her act of cession, that the United States should extinguish the Indian title to lands within the State, was a distinct recognition of the right in the federal government to make the extinguishment; and also that, until it should be made, the right of occupancy should remain in the Indians.

In a law of the State of Georgia, "for opening the land-office, and for other purposes," passed in 1783, it is declared that surveys made on Indian lands were null and void; a fine was inflicted on the person making the survey, which, if not paid by the offender, he was punished by imprisonment. By a subsequent act, a line was fixed for the Indians, which was a boundary between them and the whites. A similar provision is found in other laws of Georgia, passed before the adoption *of [*585 the Constitution. By an act of 1787, severe corporeal punishment was inflicted on those who made or attempted to make surveys, "beyond the temporary line designating the Indian hunting-ground."

On the 19th of November, 1814, the following resolutions were adopted by the Georgia Legislature:

"Whereas, many of the citizens of this State, without regard to existing treaties between the friendly Indians and the United States, and contrary to the interest and good policy of this State, have gone, and are frequently going over, and settling and cultivating the lands allotted to the friendly Indians for their hunting-ground, by which means the State is not only deprived of their services in the army, but considerable feuds are engendered between us and our friendly neighboring Indians:

"Resolved, therefore, by the Senate and

House of Representatives of the State of Georgia in General Assembly met, that his excellency the governor, be, and is hereby requested to take the necessary means to have all intruders removed off the Indian lands, and that proper steps be taken to prevent future aggressions."

In 1817 the Legislature refused to take any steps to dispose of lands acquired by treaty with the Indians until the treaty had been ratified by the Senate; and, by a resolution, the governor was directed to have the line run between the State of Georgia and the Indians, according to the late treaty. The same thing was again done in the year 1819, under a recent treaty.

In a memorial to the President of the United States by the Legislature of Georgia in 1819, they say, "it has long been the desire of Georgia that her settlements should be extended to her ultimate limits." "That the soil within her boundaries should be subjected to her control, and that her police organization and government should be fixed and permanent." "That the State of Georgia claims a right to the jurisdiction and soil of the territory within her limits." "She admits, however, that the right is inchoate—remaining to be perfected by the United States, in the extinction of the Indian title; the United States pro hac vice as their agents.

The Indian title was also distinctly acknowl-**586***] edged by the Act *of 1796 repealing the Yazoo Act. It is there declared, in reference to certain lands, that "they are the sole property of the State, subject only to the right of the treaty of the United States, to enable the State to purchase, under its pre-emption right, the Indian title to the same;" and, also, that the land is vested in the "State, to whom the right of pre-emption to the same belongs, subject only to the controlling power of the United States, to authorize any treaties for, and to superintend the same." This language, it will be observed, was used long before the act of cession.

On the 25th of March, 1825, the Governor of Georgia issued the following proclamation:

"Whereas it is provided in said treaty that the United States shall protect the Indians against the encroachments, hostilities, and impositions of the whites, so that they suffer no imposition, molestation, or injury in their persons, goods, effects, their dwellings, or the lands they occupy, until their removal shall have been accomplished according to the terms of the treaty" which had been recently made with the Indians.

"I have therefore thought proper to issue this, my proclamation, warning all persons, citizens of Georgia or others, against trespassing or intruding upon lands occupied by the Indians, within the limits of Georgia, either for the purpose of settlement or otherwise, as every such act will be in direct violation of the provisions of the treaty aforesaid, and will expose the aggressors to the most certain and summary punishment by the authorities of the State and the United States." "All good citizens, therefore, pursuing the dictates of good faith, will unite in enforcing the obligations of the treaty, as the supreme law," etc.

Many other references might be made to the

public acts of the State of Georgia to show that she admitted the obligation of Indian treaties, but the above are believed to be sufficient. These acts do honor to the character of that highly respectable State.

Under the act of cession, the United States were bound, in good faith, to extinguish the Indian title to lands within the limits of Georgia, so soon as it could be done peaceably and on reasonable terms.

*The State of Georgia has repeatedly [*587 remonstrated to the President on this subject, and called upon the government to take the necessary steps to fulfill its engagement. She complained that, whilst the Indian title to immense tracts of country had been extinguished elsewhere, within the limits of Georgia but little progress had been made; and this was attributed either to a want of effort on the part of the federal government, or to the effect of its policy towards the Indians. In one or more of the treaties, titles in fee-simple were given to the Indians to certain reservations of land; and this was complained of by Georgia as a direct infraction of the condition of the cession. It has also been asserted that the policy of the government, in advancing the cause of civilization among the Cherokees, and inducing them to assume the forms of a regular government and of civilized life, was calculated to increase their attachment to the soil they inhabit, and to render the purchase of their title more difficult, if not impracticable.

A full investigation of this subject may not be considered as strictly within the scope of the judicial inquiry which belongs to the present case. But, to some extent, it has a direct bearing on the question before the court, as it tends to show how the rights and powers of Georgia were construed by her public functionaries.

By the first President of the United States, and by every succeeding one, a strong solicitude has been expressed for the civilization of the Indians. Through the agency of the government, they have been partially induced, in some parts of the Union, to change the hunter state for that of the agriculturist and herdsman.

In a letter addressed by Mr. Jefferson to the Cherokees, dated the 9th of January, 1809, he recommends them to adopt a regular government, that crimes might be punished and property protected. He points out the mode by which a council should be chosen, who should have power to enact laws; and he also recommended the appointment of judicial and executive agents, through whom the law might be enforced. The agent of the government, who resided among them, was recommended to be associated with their council, that he might give the necessary advice on all subjects relating to their government.

*In the Treaty of 1817, the Cherokees [*588 are encouraged to adopt a regular form of government.

Since that time, a law has been passed making an annual appropriation of the sum of ten thousand dollars, as a school fund for the education of Indian youths, which has been distributed among the different tribes where schools had been established. Missionary labors among the Indians have also been sanctioned by the government, by granting permits to those who were disposed to engage in such a work, to reside in the Indian country.

That the means adopted by the general government to reclaim the savage from his erratic life, and induce him to assume the forms of civilization, have had a tendency to increase the attachment of the Cherokees to the country they now inhabit is extremely probable; and that it increased the difficulty of purchasing their lands, as by act of cession the general government agreed to do, is equally probable.

Neither Georgia nor the United States, when the cession was made, contemplated that force should be used in the extinguishment of the Indian title, nor that it should be procured on terms that are not reasonable. But, may it not be said, with equal truth, that it was not contemplated by either party that any obstructions to the fulfillment of the compact should be allowed, much less sanctioned, by the United States?

The humane policy of the government towards these children of the wilderness must afford pleasure to every benevolent feeling; and if the efforts made have not proved as successful as was anticipated, still much has been done. Whether the advantages of this policy should not have been held out by the government to the Cherokees within the limits of Georgia, as an inducement for them to change their residence and fix it elsewhere, rather than by such means to increase their attachment to their present home, as has been insisted on, is a question which may be considered by another branch of the government. Such a course might, perhaps, have secured to the Cherokee Indians all the advantages they have realized from the paternal superintendence of the government; and have enabled it, on peaceable and reasonable terms, to comply with the act of cession.

Does the intercourse law of 1802 apply to the 589*] Indians who *live within the limits of Georgia? The nineteenth section of that act provides "that it shall not be construed to prevent any trade or intercourse with Indians living on lands surrounded by settlements of the citizens of the United States, and being within the ordinary jurisdiction of any of the individual States?" This provision, it has been supposed, excepts from the operation of the law the Indian lands which lie within any State. A moment's reflection will show that this construction is most clearly erroneous.

To constitute an exception to the provisions of this act, the Indian settlement, at the time of its passage, must have been surrounded by settlements of the citizens of the United States, and within the ordinary jurisdiction of a State; not only within the limits of a State, but within the common exercise of its jurisdiction.

No one will pretend that this was the situation of the Cherokees who lived within the State of Georgia in 1802; or, indeed, that such is their present situation. If then, they are not embraced by the exception, all the provisions of the Act of 1802 apply to them.

In the very section which contains the exception, it is provided that the use of the road from Washington district to Mero district should be enjoyed, and that the citizens of Tennessee, under the orders of the governor, might keep the road in repair. And in the same section, the navigation of the Tennessee River is reserved, and a right to travel from Knoxville to Price's settlement, provided the Indians should not object.

Now, all these provisions relate to the Cherokee country; and can it be supposed, by anyone, that such provisions would have been made in the act if Congress had not considered it as applying to the Cherokee country, whether in the State of Georgia or in the State of Tennessee?

The exception applied exclusively to those fragments of tribes which are found in several of the States, and which came literally within the description used.

Much has been said against the existence of an independent power within a sovereign State; and the conclusion has been drawn that the Indians, as a matter of right, cannot enforce their own laws, within the territorial limits of a State. The refutation of this argument is found in our past history.

*That fragments of tribes, having lost [*590 the power of self-government, and who lived within the ordinary jurisdiction of a State, have been taken under the protection of the laws, has already been admitted. But there has been no instance where the State laws have been generally extended over a numerous tribe of Indians living within the State and exercising the right of self-government, until recently.

Has Georgia ever, before her late laws, attempted to regulate the Indian communities within her limits? It is true, New York extended her criminal laws over the remains of the tribes within that State, more for their protection than for any other purpose. These tribes were few in number, and were surrounded by a white population. But, even the State of New York has never asserted the power, it is believed, to regulate their concerns beyond the suppression of crime.

Might not the same objection to this interior independent power by Georgia have been urged with as much force as at present, ever since the adoption of the Constitution? Her chartered limits, to the extent claimed, embraced a great number of different nations of Indians, all of whom were governed by their own laws, and were amenable only to them. Has not this been the condition of the Indians within Tennessee, Ohio, and other States?

The exercise of this independent power surely does not become more objectionable, as it assumes the basis of justice and the forms of civilization. Would it not be a singular argument to admit that, so long as the Indians govern by the rifle and the tomahawk, their government may be tolerated, but that it must be suppressed so soon as it shall be administered upon the enlightened principles of reason and justice?

Are not those nations of Indians who have made some advances in civilization better neighbors than those who are still in a savage state? And is not the principle, as to their self-government, within the jurisdiction of a State, the same?

When Georgia sanctioned the Constitution, and conferred on the national Legislature the exclusive right to regulate commerce or intercourse with the Indians, did she reserve the right to regulate intercourse with the Indians within her limits? This will not be pretended. If such had been the construction of her own

powers, would they not have been exercised?
591*] *Did her senators object to the numerous treaties which have been formed with the different tribes who lived within her acknowledged boundaries? Why did she apply to the executive of the Union, repeatedly, to have the Indian title extinguished; to establish a line between the Indians and the State, and to procure a right of way through the Indian lands?

The residence of Indians, governed by their own laws, within the limits of a State, has never been deemed incompatible with State sovereignty until recently. And yet, this has been the condition of many distinct tribes of Indians, since the foundation of the federal government.

How is the question varied by the residence of the Indians in a territory of the United States? Are not the United States sovereign within their territories? And has it ever been conceived by anyone that the Indian governments which exist in the territories are incompatible with the sovereignty of the Union?

A State claims the right of sovereignty commensurate with her territory, as the United States claim it, in their proper sphere, to the extent of the federal limits. This right or power, in some cases, may be exercised, but not in others. Should a hostile force invade the country, at its most remote boundary, it would become the duty of the general government to expel the invaders. But it would violate the solemn compacts with the Indians, without cause, to dispossess them of rights which they possess by nature, and have been uniformly acknowledged by the federal government.

Is it incompatible with State sovereignty to grant exclusive jurisdiction to the federal government over a number of acres of land for military purposes? Our forts and arsenals, though situated in the different States, are not within their jurisdiction.

Does not the constitution give to the United States as exclusive jurisdiction in regulating intercourse with the Indians as has been given to them over any other subjects? Is there any doubt as to this investiture of power? Has it not been exercised by the federal government ever since its formation, not only without objection, but under the express sanction of all the States?

The power to dispose of the public domain 592*] is an attribute *of sovereignty. Can the new States dispose of the lands within their limits which are owned by the federal government? The power to tax is also an attribute of sovereignty; but can the new States tax the lands of the United States? Have they not bound themselves, by compact, not to tax the public lands, nor until five years after they shall have been sold? May they violate this compact at discretion?

Why may not these powers be exercised by the respective States? The answer is, because they have parted with them, expressly for the general good. Why may not a State coin money, issue bills of credit, enter into a treaty of alliance or confederation, or regulate commerce with foreign nations? Because these powers have been expressly and exclusively given to the federal government.

Has not the power been as expressly con-

ferred on the federal government to regulate intercourse with the Indians, and is it not as exclusively given as any of the powers above enumerated? There being no exception to the exercise of this power, it must operate on all communities of Indians exercising the right of self-government; and, consequently, include those who reside within the limits of a State, as well as others. Such has been the uniform construction of this power by the federal government, and of every State government, until the question was raised by the State of Georgia.

Under this clause of the Constitution, no political jurisdiction over the Indians has been claimed or exercised. The restrictions imposed by the law of 1802 come strictly within the power to regulate trade; not as an incident, but as a part of the principal power. It is the same power, and is conferred in the same words, that has often been exercised in regulating trade with foreign countries. Embargoes have been imposed, laws of non-intercourse have been passed, and numerous acts restrictive of trade, under the power to regulate commerce with foreign nations.

In the regulation of commerce with the Indians, Congress have exercised a more limited power than has been exercised in reference to foreign countries. The law acts upon our own citizens, and not upon the Indians, the same as the laws referred to act upon our own citizens in their foreign commercial intercourse.

*It will scarcely be doubted by any- [*593 one that, so far as the Indians, as distinct communities, have formed a connection with the federal government by treaties; that such connection is political, and is equally binding on both parties. This cannot be questioned, except upon the ground that in making these treaties, the federal government has transcended the treaty-making power. Such an objection, it is true, has been stated, but it is one of modern invention, which arises out of local circumstances; and is not only opposed to the uniform practice of the government, but also to the letter and spirit of the Constitution.

But the inquiry may be made, is there no end to the exercise of this power over Indians within the limits of a State, by the general government? The answer is, that, in its nature, it must be limited by circumstances.

If a tribe of Indians shall become so degraded or reduced in numbers as to lose the power of self-government, the protection of the local law, of necessity, must be extended over them. The point at which this exercise of power by a State would be proper, need not now be considered; if, indeed, it be a judicial question. Such a question does not seem to arise in this case. So long as treaties and laws remain in full force, and apply to Indian nations exercising the right of self-government within the limits of a State, the judicial power can exercise no discretion in refusing to give effect to those laws, when questions arise under them, unless they shall be deemed unconstitutional.

The exercise of the power of self-government by the Indians within a State, is undoubtedly contemplated to be temporary. This is shown by the settled policy of the government in the extinguishment of their title, and especially by the compact with the State of Georgia. It is question, not of abstract right, but of public policy. I do not mean to say that the same moral rule which should regulate the affairs of private life should not be regarded by communities or nations. But, a sound national policy does require that the Indian tribes within our States should exchange their territories, upon equitable principles, or, eventually, consent to become amalgamated in our political communities.

At best they can enjoy a very limited inde- **594***] pendence within *the boundaries of a State, and such a residence must always subject them to encroachments from the settlements around them; and their existence within a State as a separate and independent community, may seriously embarrass or obstruct the operation of the State laws. If, therefore, it would be inconsistent with the political welfare of the States and the social advance of their citizens that an independent and permanent power should exist within their limits, this power must give way to the greater power which surrounds it, or seek its exercise beyond the sphere of State authority.

This state of things can only be produced by a co-operation of the State and federal governments. The latter has the exclusive regulation of intercourse with the Indians; and, so long as this power shall be exercised, it cannot be obstructed by the State. It is a power given by the Constitution and sanctioned by the most solemn acts of both the federal and State governments: consequently, it cannot be abrogated at the will of a State. It is one of the powers parted with by the States and vested in the federal government. But, if a contingency shall occur which shall render the Indians who reside in a State incapable of self-government, either by moral degradation or a reduction of their numbers, it would undoubtedly be in the power of a State government to extend to them the ægis of its laws. Under such circumstances, the agency of the general government, of necessity, must cease.

But, if it shall be the policy of the government to withdraw its protection from the Indians who reside within the limits of the respective States, and who not only claim the right of self-government but have uniformly exercised it; the laws and treaties which impose duties and obligations on the general government should be abrogated by the powers competent to do so. So long as those laws and treaties exist, having been formed within the sphere of the federal powers, they must be respected and enforced by the appropriate organs of the federal government.

The plaintiff, who prosecutes this writ of error, entered the Cherokee country, as it appears, with the express permission of the President, and under the protection of the treaties of the United States and the law of 1802. He entered, not to corrupt the morals of this people, nor to **595***] profit by their substance; but to *teach them, by precept and example, the Christian religion. If he be unworthy of this sacred office; if he had any other object than the one professed; if he sought, by his influence, to counteract the humane policy of the federal government towards the Indians, and to embarrass its efforts to comply with its solemn engagement with Georgia; though his sufferings **8 L. ed.**

be illegal, he is not a proper object of public sympathy.

It has been shown that the treaties and laws referred to come within the due exercise of the constitutional powers of the federal government; that they remain in full force, and consequently must be considered as the supreme laws of the land. These laws throw a shield over the Cherokee Indians. They guaranteed to them their rights of occupancy, of self-government, and the full enjoyment of those blessings which might be attained in their humble condition. But, by the enactments of the State of Georgia, this shield is broken in pieces—the infant institutions of the Cherokees are abolished, and their laws annulled. Infamous punishment is denounced against them for the exercise of those rights which have been most solemnly guaranteed to them by the national faith.

Of these enactments, however, the plaintiff in error has no right to complain, nor can he question their validity, except in so far as they affect his interests. In this view and in this view only, has it become necessary, in the present case, to consider the repugnancy of the laws of Georgia to those of the Union.

Of the justice or policy of these laws it is not my province to speak; such considerations belonging to the Legislature by whom they were passed. They have, no doubt, been enacted under a conviction of right, by a sovereign and independent State, and their policy may have been recommended by a sense of wrong under the compact. Thirty years have elapsed since the federal government engaged to extinguish the Indian title within the limits of Georgia. That she has strong ground of complaint arising from this delay must be admitted; but such considerations are not involved in the present case; they belong to another branch of the government. We can look only to the law, which defines our power, and marks out the path of out duty.

Under the administration of the laws of Georgia, a citizen of *the United States [**596** has been deprived of his liberty; and, claiming protection under the treaties and laws of the United States, he makes the question, as he has a right to make it, whether the laws of Georgia, under which he is now suffering an ignominious punishment, are not repugnant to the Constitution of the United States, and the treaties and laws made under it. This repugnancy has been shown; and it remains only to say, what has before been often said by this tribunal of the local laws of many of the States in this Union, that being repugnant to the Constitution of the United States, and to the laws made under it, they can have no force to devest the plaintiff in error of his property or liberty.

Mr. Justice **Baldwin** dissented, stating that in his opinion the record was not properly returned upon the writ of error, and ought to have been returned by the State court, and not by the clerk of that court. As to the merits, he said his opinion remained the same as was expressed by him in the case of The Cherokee Nation v. The State of Georgia, at the last term.

The opinion of Mr. Justice **Baldwin** was not delivered to the reporter.

This cause came on to be heard on the transcript of the record from the Superior Court for the County of Gwinnett, in the State of Georgia, and was argued by counsel; on consideration whereof, it is the opinion of this court that the act of the Legislature of the State of Georgia upon which the indictment in this case is founded, is contrary to the Constitution, treaties, and laws of the United States; and that the special plea in bar pleaded by the said Samuel A. Worcester, in manner aforesaid, and relying upon the Constitution, treaties, and laws of the United States aforesaid, is a good bar and defense to the said indictment, by the said Samuel A. Worcester; and as such ought to have been allowed and admitted by the said Superior Court for the County of Gwinnett, in the State of Georgia, before which the said indictment was pending and tried; and that there was error in the said Superior Court of the State of Georgia in overruling the plea so pleaded as aforesaid. It is therefore ordered and adjudged that the judgment rendered in the 597*] *premises by the said Superior Court of Georgia, upon the verdict upon the plea of "not guilty" afterwards pleaded by the said Samuel A. Worcester, whereby the said Samuel A. Worcester is sentenced to hard labor in the penitentiary of the State of Georgia, ought to be reversed and annulled. And this court proceeding to render such judgment as the said Superior Court of the State of Georgia should have rendered, it is further ordered and adjudged that the said judgment of the said Superior Court be, and hereby is reversed and annulled; and that judgment be, and hereby is, awarded, that the special plea in bar, so as aforesaid pleaded, is a good and sufficient plea in bar in law to the indictment aforesaid; and that all proceedings on the said indictment do forever surcease; and that the said Samuel A. Worcester be, and hereby is henceforth dismissed therefrom, and that he go thereof quit without day. And that a special mandate do go from this court to the said Superior Court, to carry this judgment into execution.

In the case of Butler, Plaintiff in Error, v. The State of Georgia, the same judgment was given by the court, and a special mandate was ordered from the court to the Superior Court of Gwinnett County, to carry the judgment into execution.

SURRENDER SPEECH

BLACK HAWK, 1832

Black-hawk is an Indian. He has done nothing for which an Indian ought to be ashamed. He has fought for his countrymen, the squaws and papooses, against white men, who came, year after year, to cheat them and take away their lands. You know the cause of our making war. It is known to all white men. They ought to be ashamed of it. The white men despise the Indians, and drive them from their homes. But the Indians are not deceitful. The white men speak bad of the Indian, and look at him spitefully. But the Indian does not tell lies; Indians do not steal.

An Indian, who is as bad as the white men, could not live in our nation; he would be put to death, and eat up by the wolves. The white men are bad schoolmasters; they carry false looks, and deal in false actions; they smile in the face of the poor Indian to cheat him; they shake them by the hand to gain their confidence, to make them drunk, to deceive them, and ruin our wives. We told them to let us alone, and keep away from us; but they followed on, and beset our paths, and they coiled themselves among us, like the snake. They poisoned us by their touch. We were not safe. We lived in danger. We were becoming like them, hypocrites and liars, adulterers, lazy drones, all talkers, and no workers.

We looked up to the Great Spirit. We went to our great father. We were encouraged. His great council gave us fair words and big promises; but we got no satisfaction. Things were growing worse. There were no deer in the forest. The opossum and beaver were fled; the springs were drying up, and our squaws and papooses without victuals to keep them from starving; we called a great council, and built a large fire. The spirit of our fathers arose and spoke to us to avenge our wrongs or die. We all spoke before the council fire. It was warm and pleasant. We set up the war-whoop, and dug up the tomahawk; our knives were ready, and the heart of Black-hawk swelled high in his bosom, when he led his warriors to battle. He is satisfied. He will go to the world of spirits contented. He has done his duty. His father will meet him there, and commend him.

––––––––

Source: Frank E. Stevens, *The Black Hawk War* (1903), 372-73.

TREATY WITH SIOUX NATION

1876

FORTIETH CONGRESS SECOND SESSION

CHAPTER 72, AN ACT TO RATIFY AN AGREEMENT WITH CERTAIN BANDS OF THE SIOUX NATION OF INDIANS AND ALSO WITH THE NORTHERN ARAPAHO AND CHEYENNE INDIANS.

BE IT ENACTED BY THE SENATE AND THE HOUSE OF REPRESENTATIVES OF THE UNITED STATES OF AMERICA IN CONGRESS ASSEMBLED,

that a certain agreement made by George W. Manypenny, Henry B. Whipple, Jared W. Daniels, Albert G. Boone, Henry C. Bulis, Newton Edumunds, and Augustine S. Gaylord, commissioners on the part of the United States, with the different bands of the Sioux Nation of Indians, and also the Northern Arapaho and Cheyenne Indians, be, and the same is hereby, ratified and confirmed:

PROVIDED, that nothing in this act shall be construed to authorize the removal of Sioux Indians to the Indian Territory and the President of the United States is hereby directed to prohibit the removal of any portion of the Sioux Indians to the Indian Territory until the same shall be authorized by an act of Congress hereafter enacted, except article four, except also the following portion of article six: "And if said Indians shall remove to said Indian Territory as hereinbefore provided, the Government shall erect for each of the principal chiefs a good and comfortable dwelling house" and said article not having been agreed to by the Sioux Nation: said agreement is in words and figures following: namely: "Articles of agreement made pursuant to the provisions of an act of Congress entitled "An act making appropriations for the current and contingent expenses of the Indian Department, and for fulfilling treaty stipulations with various Indian tribes, for the year ending June thirtieth, eighteen hundred and seventy-seven, and for other purposes," approved August 15, 1876, by and between George W. Manypenny, Henry B. Whipple, Jared W. Daniels, Albert G. Boone, Henry C. Bulis, Newton Edumunds, and Augustine S. Gaylord, commissioners on the part of the United States, with the different bands of the Sioux Nation of Indians, and also the Northern Arapaho and Cheyenne Indians, by their chiefs and headmen, whose names are hereto subscribed, they being duly authorized to act in the premises.

Article 1
[Reduction of the Great Sioux Reservation]

The said parties hereby agree that the northern and western boundaries of the reservation defined by article 2 of the treaty between the United States and different tribes of Sioux Indians, concluded April 29, 1868, and proclaimed February 24, 1869, shall be as follows: The western boundaries shall commence at the intersection of the one hundred and third meridian of longitude with the northern border of the State of Nebraska; thence north along said meridian to its intersection with the South Fork of the Cheyenne River; thence down said stream to its junction with the North Fork; thence up the North Fork of said Cheyenne River to the said one hundred and third meridian; thence north along said meridian to the South Branch of Cannon Ball River or Cedar Creek; and the northern boundary of the said reservation shall follow the said South Branch to its intersection with the main Cannon Ball River, and thence down the said main Cannon Ball River to the Missouri River; and the said Indians do hereby relinquish and cede to the United States all territory lying outside the said reservation, as herein, modified and described, including all privileges of hunting; and article 16 of said treaty is hereby abrogated.

Article 2
[Roads Through Reservation]

The said Indians also agree and consent that wagon and other roads, not exceeding three in number, may be constructed and maintained, from convenient and accessible points on the Missouri River, through said reservation, to the country lying immediately west thereof, upon such routes as shall be designated by the President of the United States; and they also consent and agree to the free navigation of the Missouri River.

Article 3
[Distribution Points for Annuities to Be Designated]

The said Indians also agree that they will hereafter receive all annuities provided by the said treaty of 1868, and all subsistence and supplies which may be provided for them under the present or any future act of Congress, at such points and places on the said reservation, and in the vicinity of the Missouri River.

Article 4
[Delegation to Select Home in Indian Territory]

The Government of the United States and the said Indians, being mutually desirous that the latter shall be located in a country where they may eventually become self-supporting and acquire the arts of civilized life, it is therefore agreed that the said Indians shall select a delegation of five or more chiefs and principal men from each band, who shall, without delay, visit the Indian Territory under the guidance and protection of suitable persons, to be appointed for that purpose by the Department of the Interior, with a view to selecting therein a permanent home for said Indians. If such delegation shall make a selection which shall be satisfactory to themselves, the people whom they represent, and to the United States, then the said Indians agree that they will remove to the country so selected within one year from this date. And the said Indians do further agree in all things to submit themselves to such beneficent plans as the Government may provide for them in the selection of a country suitable for a permanent home, where they may live like white men.

Article 5
[Assistance, Schools, Rations, Purchase of Surplus, Employment]

In consideration of the foregoing cession of territory and rights, and upon full compliance with each and every obligation assumed by the said Indians, the United States does agree to provide all necessary aid to assist the said Indians in the work of civilization; to furnish to them schools and instruction in mechanical and agricultural arts, as provided for by the treaty of 1868. Also to provide the said Indians with subsistence consisting of a ration for each individual of a pound and a half of beef, (or in lieu thereof, one half pound of bacon,) one-half pound of flour, and one-half pound of corn; and for every one hundred rations, four pounds of coffee, eight pounds of sugar, and three pounds of beans, or in lieu of said articles the equivalent thereof, in the discretion of the Commissioner of Indian Affairs. Such rations, or so much thereof as may be necessary, shall be continued until the Indians are able to support themselves. Rations shall, in all cases, be issued to the head of each separate family; and whenever schools shall have been provided by the Government for said Indians, no rations shall be issued for children between the ages of six and fourteen years (the sick and infirm excepted) unless such children shall regularly attend school. Whenever the said Indians shall be located upon lands which are suitable for cultivation, rations shall be issued only to the persons and families of those persons who labor, (the aged, sick, and infirm excepted;) and may provide that such persons be furnished in payment for their labor such other necessary articles as are requisite for civilized life. The Government will aid said Indians as far as possible in finding a market for their surplus productions, and in finding employment, and will purchase such surplus, as far as may be required, for supplying food to those Indians, parties to this agreement, who are unable to sustain themselves; and will also employ Indians, so far as practicable, in the performance of Government work upon their reservation.

Article 6
[Erection of Homes]

Whenever the head of a family shall, in good faith, select an allotment of land upon such reservation and engage in the cultivation thereof, the Government shall, with his aid, erect a comfortable house on such allotment; and if said Indians shall remove to said Indian Territory as hereinbefore provided, the Government shall erect for each of the principal chiefs a good and comfortable dwelling house.

Article 7
[Agency Employees to Be Married]

To improve the morals and industrious habits of said Indians, it is agreed that the agent, trader, farmer, carpenter, blacksmith, and other artisans employed or permitted to reside within the reservation belonging to the Indians, parties to this agreement, shall be lawfully married and living with their respective families on the reservation; and no person other than an Indian of full blood, whose fitness, morally or otherwise, is not, in the opinion of the Commissioner of Indian Affairs, conducive to the welfare of said Indians, shall receive any benefit from this agreement or former treaties, and may be expelled from the reservation.

Article 8
[Indians Subject to the Laws of the United States]

The provisions of the said treaty of 1868, except as herein modified, shall continue in full force, and, with the provisions of this agreement, shall apply to any country which may hereafter be occupied by the said Indians as a home; and Congress shall, by appropriate legislation, secure to them an orderly government; they shall be subject to the laws of the United States, and each individual shall be protected in his rights, property, person and life.

Article 9
[Indians Pledged to this Agreement]

The Indians, parties to this agreement, do hereby solemnly pledge themselves, individually and collectively, to observe each and all of the stipulations herein contained, to select allotments of land as soon as possible after their removal to their permanent home, and to use their best efforts to learn to cultivate the same. And they do solemnly pledge themselves that they will at all times maintain peace with the citizens and Government of the United States; that they will observe the laws thereof and loyally endeavor to fulfill all the obligations assumed by them under the treaty of 1868 and the present agreement, and to this end will, whenever called requested by the President of the United States, select so many suitable men from each band to co-operate with him in maintaining order and peace on the reservation as the President may deem necessary, who shall receive such compensation for their services as Congress may provide.

Article 10
[Annual Census]

In order that the Government may faithfully fulfill the stipulations contained in this agreement, it is mutually agreed that a census of all Indians affected hereby shall be taken in the month of December of each year, and the names of each head of family and adult person registered; said census to be taken in such manner as the Commissioner of Indian Affairs may provide.

Article 11
[Term "Reservation" Defined]

It is understood that the term reservation herein contained shall be held to apply to any country which shall be selected under the authority of the United States as the future home of said Indians.

This agreement shall not be binding upon either party until it shall have received the approval of the President and Congress of the United States.

Dated and signed at Red Cloud agency, Nebraska, September 26, 1876.

MY SON, STOP YOUR EARS

CHIEF JOSEPH, NEZ PERCÉ LEADER, 1879 ADDRESS TO CONGRESS

It has always been the pride of the Nez Percés that they were the friends of the white men. When my father was a young man there came to our country a white man [the Reverend Mr. Spaulding] who talked spirit law. He won the affections of our people because he spoke good things to them. At first he did not say anything about white men wanting to settle on our lands. Nothing was said about that until about twenty winters ago, when a number of white people came into our country and built houses and made farms. At first our people made no complaint. They thought there was room enough for all to live in peace, and they were learning many things from the white men that seemed to be good. But we soon found that the white men were growing rich very fast, and were greedy to possess everything the Indian had. My father was the first to see through the schemes of the white men, and he warned his tribe to be careful about trading with them. He had suspicion of men who seemed so anxious to make money. I was a boy then, but I remember well my father's caution. He had sharper eyes than the rest of our people.

Next there came a white officer [Governor Stevens], who invited all the Nez Percés to a treaty council. After the council was opened he made known his heart. He said there were a great many white people in the country, and many more would come; that he wanted the land marked out so that the Indians and white men could be separated. If they were to live in peace it was necessary, he said, that the Indians should have a country set apart for them, and in that country they must stay. My father, who represented his band, refused to have anything to do with the council, because he wished to be a free man. He claimed that no man owned any part of the earth, and a man could not sell what he did not own.

Mr. Spaulding took hold of my father's arm and said, "Come and sign the treaty." My father pushed him away, and said: "Why do you ask me to sign away my country? It is your business to talk to us about spirit matters, and not to talk to us about parting with our land." Governor Stevens urged my father to sign his treaty, but he refused. "I will not sign your paper," he said; "you go where you please, so do I; you are not a child. I am no child; I can think for myself. No man can think for me. I have no other home than this. I will not give it up to any man. My people would have no home. Take away your paper. I will not touch it with my hand."

My father left the council. Some of the chiefs of the other bands of the Nez Percés signed the treaty, and then Governor Stevens gave them presents of blankets. My father cautioned his people to take no presents, for "after a while," he said, "they will claim that you have accepted pay for your country." Since that time four bands of the Nez Percés have received annuities from the United States. My father was invited to many councils, and they tried hard to make him sign the treaty, but he was firm as the rock, and would not sign away his home. His refusal caused a difference among the Nez Percés.

Eight years later (1863) was the next treaty council. A chief called Lawyer, because he was a great talker, took the lead in this council, and sold nearly all the Nez Percés' country. My father was not there. He said to me: "When you go into council with the white man, always remember your country. Do not give it away. The white man will cheat you out of your home. I have taken no pay from the United States. I have never sold our land." In this treaty Lawyer acted without authority from our band. He had no right to sell the Wallowa [*winding water*] country. That had always belonged to my father's own people, and the other bands had never disputed our right to it. No other Indians ever claimed Wallowa.

In order to have all people understand how much land we owned, my father planted poles around it and said: "Inside is the home of my people—the white man may take the land outside. Inside this boundary all our people were born. It circles around the graves of our fathers, and we will never give up these graves to any man."

The United States claimed they had bought all the Nez Percés' country outside of Lapwai Reservation, from Lawyer and other chiefs, but we continued to live in this land in peace until eight years ago, when white men began to come inside the bounds my father had set. We warned them against this great wrong, but they would not leave our land, and some bad blood was raised. The white men represented that we were going upon the warpath. They reported many things that were false.

The United States Government again asked for a treaty council. My father had become blind and feeble. He could no longer speak for his people. It was then that I took my father's place as chief.

In this council I made my first speech to white men. I said to the agent who held the council: "I did not want to come to this council, but I came hoping that we could save blood. The white man has no right to come here and take our country. We have never accepted any presents from the Government. Neither Lawyer nor any other chief had authority to sell this land. It has always belonged to my people. It came unclouded to them from our fathers, and we will defend this land as long as a drop of Indian blood warms the hearts of our men."

The agent said he had orders, from the Great White Chief at Washington, for us to go upon the Lapwai Reservation, and that if we obeyed he would help us in many ways. "You *must* move to the agency," he said. I answered him: "I will not. I do not need your help; we have plenty and we are contented and happy if the white man will let us alone. The reservation is too small for so many people with all their stock. You can keep your presents; we can go to your towns and pay for all we need; we have plenty of horses and cattle to sell, and we won't have any help from you; we are free now; we can go where we please. Our fathers were born here. Here they lived, here they died, here are their graves. We will never leave them." The agent went away, and we had peace for a little while.

Soon after this my father sent for me. I saw he was dying. I took his hand in mine. He said: "My son, my body is returning to my mother earth, and my spirit is going very soon to see the Great Spirit Chief. When I am gone, think of your country. You are the chief of these people. They look to you to guide them. Always remember that your father never sold his country. You must stop your ears whenever you are asked to sign a treaty selling your home. A few years more, and white men will be all around you. They have their eyes on this land. My son, never forget my dying words. This country holds your father's body. Never sell the bones of your father and your mother." I pressed my father's hand and told him I would protect his grave with my life. My father smiled and passed away to the spirit-land.

I buried him in that beautiful valley of winding waters. I love that land more than all the rest of the world. A man who would not love his father's grave is worse than a wild animal.

For a short time we lived quietly. But this could not last. White men had found gold in the mountains around the land of winding water. They stole a great many horses from us, and we could not get them back because we were Indians. The white men told lies for each other. They drove off a great many of our cattle. Some white men branded our young cattle so they could claim them. We had no friend who would plead our cause before the law councils. It seemed to me that some of the white men in Wallowa were doing these things on purpose to get up a war. They knew that we were not strong enough to fight them. I labored hard to avoid trouble and bloodshed. We gave up some of our country to the white men, thinking that then we could have peace. We were mistaken. The white man would not let us alone. We could have avenged our wrongs many times, but we did not.

Whenever the Government has asked us to help them against other Indians, we have never refused. When the white men were few and we were strong, we could have killed them all off, but the Nez Percés wished to live at peace.

If we have not done so, we have not been to blame. I believe that the old treaty has never been correctly reported. If we ever owned the land we own it still, for we never sold it. In the treaty councils the commissioners have claimed that our country had been sold to the Government. Suppose a white man should come to me and say, "Joseph, I like your horses, and I want to buy them." I say to him, "No, my horses suit me, I will not sell them." Then he goes to my neighbor, and says to him: "Joseph has some good horses. I want to buy them, but he refuses to sell." My neighbor answers, "Pay me the money, and I will sell you Joseph's horses." The white man returns to me, and says, "Joseph, I have bought your horses, and you must let me have them." If we sold our lands to the Government, this is the way they were bought.

PRESIDENTIAL SPEECHES

Beginning with George Washington, U.S. presidents have addressed the nation concerning various issues of domestic and international policy. A small number of these speeches have become important documents in their own right. They contain ideas, symbols, and memorable statements that have captured the public's imagination and led to significant changes in U.S. law and government.

George Washington: Farewell Address

On September 17, 1796, leading newspapers published President George Washington's Farewell Address to the nation. Washington, who was nearing the end of his second four-year term, had rejected pleas by members of the Federalist party to seek a third term. The address, which was never delivered orally, is now remembered for its comments on foreign policy, but in 1796 Washington was also concerned with domestic politics.

Alexander Hamilton, who helped draft the Constitution and who wrote many of the essays contained in the *Federalist Papers*, prepared an initial version of the speech. Washington then revised and reshaped it into its final form. The president used the address both to end speculation that he would seek a third term and to help the chances of the Federalists in the forthcoming election.

Washington discussed the state of U.S. politics and lamented the bitter rivalry that had developed between the Federalists and the Republicans, who were led by Thomas Jefferson. A proponent of a strong national government, he warned against the dangers of sectionalism,

political revenge, and "the insidious wiles of foreign influence." The latter statement referred to the pro-French sentiments of Jefferson and the Republicans. Washington's policy during the wars between Great Britain and France in the early 1790s had been one of strict neutrality.

The most important section of the address dealt with U.S. foreign relations. Washington stated that the "true policy [of the United States] is to steer clear of permanent alliances with any parts of the foreign world." His views provided support and inspiration for U.S. isolationists who sought to prevent the United States from becoming involved with European governments. U.S. isolationism did not disappear as a viable political viewpoint until the nation's entry into World War II in 1941.

Abraham Lincoln: Gettysburg Address

On November 19, 1863, President Abraham Lincoln delivered an address at the dedication of the national cemetery in Gettysburg, Pennsylvania, that has become one of the most famous speeches of U.S. history. Lincoln's speech came less than six months after the conclusion of the Gettysburg campaign (June 27–July 4, 1863), one of the bloodiest battles of the U.S. Civil War. Confederate General Robert E. Lee and his forces were defeated by Union forces led by General George Meade. The losses for both sides were immense with more than 7,000 killed and 44,000 wounded or missing.

The principal orator at the dedication was Edward Everett, a senator, preacher, and scholar who spoke for more than two hours in the florid style of the time. Lincoln, who presided at the dedication, followed with a few brief remarks in a speech he had written in Washington and then revised slightly before the ceremony. Lincoln honored those who had died at Gettysburg and proclaimed that the cause for which they had died had given the nation a "new birth of freedom."

Lucid, terse, and precise, Lincoln's speech stood in stark contrast to Everett's. Though the crowd that day applauded Lincoln's address without enthusiasm, generations of schoolchildren have memorized and recited it, while Everett's speech was quickly forgotten.

Abraham Lincoln: Second Inaugural Address

Abraham Lincoln gave many memorable addresses during his political career, but his second inaugural address is ranked as perhaps his greatest speech. On March 4, 1865, as he began his second term as president, Lincoln delivered the address at the Capitol in Washington, D.C. With the Union forces close to victory—the Civil War would end the following month—Lincoln's address looked forward to the peace that would follow. Throughout the war Lincoln had expressed his desire to preserve the Union. In his address he reminded his listeners that the issue of slavery had been central to the Civil War and suggested that slavery had offended God and brought forth divine retribution in the form of the conflict. Now, with peace at hand, he urged a national reconciliation "with malice toward none, with charity for all." Lincoln did not have the opportunity to shape Reconstruction. He was shot on April 14, 1865, by John Wilkes Booth during the performance of a play at Ford's Theater in Washington, D.C. He died the next day.

Woodrow Wilson: Fourteen Points

By the end of the nineteenth century, U.S. presidents had begun to relax the traditional isolationism of U.S. foreign policy. Nevertheless, when World War I began in 1914, the United States remained aloof from the conflict. President Woodrow Wilson was reelected to a second term in 1916 on the slogan "He kept us out of war." Wilson and U.S. public opinion shifted, however, when Germany announced that it would engage in unrestricted submarine warfare beginning on February 1, 1917. On April 6, 1917, Wilson signed the congressional declaration of war against Germany.

Wilson, who had attempted to negotiate a peace among the belligerents in 1916, renewed his efforts by proposing a new framework for negotiations. On January 8, 1918, he delivered an address to Congress that named fourteen points to be used as the guide for a peace settlement. The speech became known as the Fourteen Points and served as a distillation of Wilson's vision of a postwar world. In the address Wilson said that the secret alliances that triggered the war must be replaced with "open covenants of peace, openly arrived at." He proclaimed the need to demilitarize the ocean and reduce military armaments. He also articulated the desire to end European colonialism and allow the various nationalities of the Austro-Hungarian and Ottoman Empires to create their own states. The most important point was the last, which called for a general association of nations that would guarantee political independence and territorial integrity for all countries.

Following the armistice that ended the war on November 9, 1918, President Wilson led the U.S. delegation to the Paris Peace Conference. Wilson was the only representative of the great powers (which also included Great Britain, France, and Italy) who truly wanted an international organization. His influence was instrumental in persuading the delegates to establish the League of Nations. At home, however, he was unable to secure Senate ratification of the peace treaty that included the league. He was opposed both by Republicans who did not want to commit the United States to supporting the league with financial resources and by isolationists from both major political parties who argued that the United States should not interfere in European affairs.

Franklin D. Roosevelt: First Inaugural Address

During the presidential campaign of 1932, with the United States mired in the Great Depression, Franklin D. Roosevelt called for action by the federal government to revive the economy and end the suffering of the thirteen million people who were unemployed. When he took office on March 4, 1933, the national mood was bleak. In his first inaugural address, Roosevelt reassured the nation that "the only thing we have to fear is fear itself." He proposed a New Deal for the people of the United States and promised he would use the power of the executive branch to address the economic crisis.

In his speech Roosevelt criticized the financial community for breeding a culture of greed during the 1920s that led to the economic depression. Declaring that "our greatest task is to put people to work," he proposed to use the government to reinvigorate the economy. He acknowledged that the need for "undelayed action" might require disturbing the "normal balance of executive and legislative authority."

Roosevelt's address helped rally the nation. His call for sweeping actions by the federal government produced a torrent of legislation from Congress in his first hundred days in office. Though the Supreme Court initially struck down many of these acts as unconstitutional, within a few years the Court changed its view. As a result, the federal government greatly expanded its power to regulate the economy. Through Roosevelt's bold initiatives, many U.S. citizens came to view the federal government in a new way—as the catalyst of progressive social change.

John F. Kennedy: Inaugural Address

John F. Kennedy was elected president in 1960 by a slim margin over Vice President Richard M. Nixon. During the campaign Kennedy had charged that the United States had fallen militarily behind the Soviet Union during the administration of President Dwight D. Eisenhower. Therefore, when Kennedy gave his inaugural address on January 20, 1961, he focused on U.S. foreign policy.

Kennedy's address revealed how far the United States had moved in international affairs. The isolationism of the 1930s had given way to a foreign policy based on fighting Communism anywhere in the world. He declared that "the torch has been passed to a new generation of Americans" committed to defending liberty.

The most quoted lines of the address—"ask not what your country can do for you, ask what you can do for your country"—became the patriotic rallying cry for Kennedy's New Frontier initiatives, which emphasized the space program, the Peace Corps, and increased defense spending.

Lyndon B. Johnson: Voting Rights Act Address

On March 15, 1965, President Lyndon B. Johnson addressed a joint session of Congress to urge the passage of new voting rights legislation. Although Johnson had successfully engineered the passage of the landmark Civil Rights Act of 1964 (42 U.S.C.A. § 2000a et seq.) the year before, problems remained. Dr. Martin Luther King, Jr., and other civil rights leaders demanded an end to racially discriminatory voting practices in the South. They organized public protests and voter registration drives that were met with intense resistance from local authorities.

When King and civil rights supporters marched to Selma, Alabama, in 1965 to demand voting rights, police met them with violence, and several marchers were murdered. The Selma violence, which was broadcast on television news programs, galvanized voting rights supporters in Congress. One week later, President Johnson responded by introducing the Voting Rights Act (42 U.S.C.A. § 1973 et seq.), which included the harshest penalties ever imposed for denials of civil rights. Congress enacted the measure five months later.

In his address Johnson confronted the problem of racism and racial discrimination. He declared that "every American citizen must have an equal right to vote. There is no reason which can excuse the denial of that right." Johnson reminded the nation that the Fifteenth Amendment, which was passed after the Civil War, gives all citizens the right to vote regardless of race or color, yet states had defied the Constitution and erected barriers based on those forbidden grounds. In Johnson's view no constitutional or moral issue was at stake. Congress simply needed to enforce the amendment with strict penalties.

Johnson, a native of Texas, surprised the nation near the close of his speech when he invoked the famous civil rights anthem and declared "we shall overcome." He was greeted by stunned silence, followed by thunderous applause and tears. It was reported that Dr. King, watching the speech on television from Selma, wept. Many historians view the speech as the watershed moment of the civil rights revolution of the 1960s.

Ronald W. Reagan: First Inaugural Address

Ronald Reagan was elected president in 1980, defeating the incumbent Jimmy Carter. Reagan, a Republican from California, had campaigned as much against the federal government as against his opponent. He charged that the federal government had become a bloated bureaucracy since its dramatic growth under Franklin D. Roosevelt in the 1930s and 1940s. He proposed to cut the size of the federal government and its budget and return power to the states.

In his first inaugural address, delivered on January 20, 1981, Reagan reaffirmed his campaign pledges. With the nation in an economic recession, he declared that "government is not the solution to our problem." Instead, he proposed to remove "the roadblocks that have slowed our economy and reduced productivity," reawaken "this industrial giant," get "government back within its means," and reduce "punitive tax burdens."

In addition, Reagan announced that he would restore the balance between the various levels of government. The federal government's growth would be reversed, and power would be returned to the states and the people. Though he denied any intention of doing away with government, Reagan made clear that "we are a nation that has a government—not the other way around."

Reagan's address signaled a turning point in modern U.S. history, as conservative political views became more popular with the electorate. Almost every facet of modern U.S. government became the subject of a conservative reevaluation that resulted in significant changes in the regulation of the economy and social welfare programs.

GEORGE WASHINGTON: FAREWELL ADDRESS

Friends and fellow citizens:

The period for a new election of a citizen to administer the executive government of the United States being not far distant, and the time actually arrived when your thoughts must be employed in designating the person who is to be clothed with that important trust, it appears to me proper, especially as it may conduce to a more distinct expression of the public voice, that I should now apprise you of the resolution I have formed to decline being considered among the number of those out of whom a choice is to be made.

I beg you at the same time to do me the justice to be assured that this resolution has not been taken without a strict regard to all the considerations appertaining to the relation which binds a dutiful citizen to his country; and that in withdrawing the tender of service, which silence in my situation might imply, I am influenced by no diminution of zeal for your future interest, no deficiency of grateful respect for your past kindness, but am supported by a full conviction that the step is compatible with both.

The acceptance of and continuance hitherto in the office to which your suffrages have twice called me have been a uniform sacrifice of inclination to the opinion of duty and to a deference for what appeared to be your desire. I constantly hoped that it would have been much earlier in my power, consistently with motives which I was not at liberty to disregard, to return to that retirement from which I had been reluctantly drawn. The strength of my inclination to do this previous to the last election had even led to the preparation of an address to declare it to you; but mature reflection on the then perplexed and critical posture of our affairs with foreign nations and the unanimous advice of persons entitled to my confidence impelled me to abandon the idea. I rejoice that the state of your concerns, external as well as internal, no longer tenders the pursuit of inclination incompatible with the sentiment of duty or propriety, and am persuaded, whatever partiality may be retained for my services, that in the present circumstances of our country you will not disapprove my determination to retire.

The impressions with which I first undertook the arduous trust were explained on the proper occasion. In the discharge of this trust I will only say that I have, with good intentions, contributed toward the organization and administration of the government the best exertions of which a very fallible judgment was capable. Not unconscious in the outset of the inferiority of my qualifications, experience in my own eyes, perhaps still more in the eyes of others, has strengthened the motives to diffidence of myself; and everyday the increasing weight of years admonishes me more and more that

---

Source: James D. Richardson, ed., *A Compilation of the Messages and Papers of the Presidents*, vol. 1 (1896), pp. 213–24.

the shade of retirement is as necessary to me as it will be welcome. Satisfied that if any circumstances have given peculiar value to my services they were temporary, I have the consolation to believe that, while choice and prudence invite me to quit the political scene, patriotism does not forbid it.

In looking forward to the moment which is intended to terminate the career of my political life, my feelings do not permit me to suspend the deep acknowledgment of that debt of gratitude which I owe to my beloved country for the many honors it has conferred upon me; still more for the steadfast confidence with which it has supported me, and for the opportunities I have thence enjoyed of manifesting my inviolable attachment by services faithful and persevering, though in usefulness unequal to my zeal. If benefits have resulted to our country from these services, let it always be remembered to your praise and as an instructive example in our annals that under circumstances in which the passions, agitated in every direction, were liable to mislead; amidst appearances sometimes dubious; vicissitudes of fortune often discouraging; in situations in which not unfrequently want of success has countenanced the spirit of criticism, the constancy of your support was the essential prop of the efforts and a guaranty of the plans by which they were effected. Profoundly penetrated with this idea, I shall carry it with me to my grave as a strong incitement to unceasing vows that Heaven may continue to you the choicest tokens of its beneficence; that your union and brotherly affection may be perpetual; that the free Constitution which is the work of your hands may be sacredly maintained; that its administration in every department may be stamped with wisdom and virtue; that, in time the happiness of the people of these states, under the auspices of liberty may be made complete by so careful a preservation and so prudent a use of this blessing as will acquire to them the glory of recommending it to the applause, the affection, and adoption of every nation which is yet a stranger to it.

Here, perhaps, I ought to stop. But a solicitude for your welfare which can not end but with my life, and the apprehension of danger natural to that solicitude, urge me on an occasion like the present to offer to your solemn contemplation and to recommend to your frequent review some sentiments which are the result of much reflection, of no inconsiderable observation, and which appear to me all important to the permanency of your felicity as a people. These will be offered to you with the more freedom as you can only see in them the disinterested warnings of a parting friend, who can possibly have no personal motive to bias his counsel. Nor can I forget as an encouragement to it your indulgent reception of my sentiments on a former and not dissimilar occasion.

Interwoven as is the love of liberty with every ligament of your hearts, no recommendation of mine is necessary to fortify or confirm the attachment.

The unity of government which constitutes you one people is also now dear to you. It is justly so, for it is a main pillar in the edifice of your real independence, the support of your tranquillity at home, your peace abroad, of your safety, of your prosperity, of that very liberty which you so highly prize. But as it is easy to foresee that from different causes and from different quarters much pains will be taken, many artifices employed, to weaken in your minds the conviction of this truth, as this is the point in your political fortress against which the batteries of internal and external enemies will be most constantly and actively (though often covertly and insidiously) directed, it is of infinite moment that you should properly estimate the immense value of your national union to your collective and individual happiness; that you should cherish a cordial, habitual, and immovable attachment to it; accustoming yourselves to think and speak of it as of the palladium of your political safety and prosperity; watching for its preservation with jealous anxiety; discountenancing whatever may suggest even a suspicion that it can in any event be abandoned, and indignantly frowning upon the first dawning of every attempt to alienate any portion of our country from the rest or to enfeeble the sacred ties which now link together the various parts.

For this you have every inducement of sympathy and interest. Citizens by birth or choice of a common country, that country has a right to concentrate your affections. The name of American, which belongs to you in your national capacity, must always exalt the just pride of patriotism more than any appellation derived from local discriminations. With slight shades of difference, you have the same religion, manners, habits, and political principles. You have in a common cause fought and triumphed together. The independence and liberty you possess are the work of joint councils and joint efforts, of common dangers, sufferings, and successes.

But these considerations, however powerfully they address themselves to your sensibility, are greatly outweighed by those which apply more immediately to your interest. Here every portion of our country finds the most commanding motives for carefully guarding and preserving the union of the whole.

The North, in an unrestrained intercourse with the South, protected by the equal laws of a common government, finds in the productions of the latter great additional resources of maritime and commercial enterprise and precious materials of manufacturing industry. The South, in the same intercourse, benefiting by the same agency of the North, sees its agriculture grow and its commerce expand. Turning partly into its own channels the seamen of the North, it finds its particular navigation invigorated; and while it contributes in different ways to nourish and increase the general mass of the national navigation, it looks forward to the protection of a maritime strength to which itself is unequally adapted. The East, in a like intercourse with the West, already finds, and in the progressive improvement of interior communications by land and water will more and more find, a valuable vent for the commodities which it brings from abroad or manufactures at home. The West derives from the East supplies requisite to its growth and comfort, and what is perhaps of still greater consequence, it must of necessity owe the secure enjoyment of indispensable outlets for its own productions to the weight, influence, and the future maritime strength of the Atlantic side of the Union, directed by an indissoluble community of interest as one nation. Any other tenure by which the West can hold this essential advantage, whether derived from its own separate strength or from an apostate and unnatural connection with any foreign power, must be intrinsically precarious.

While, then, every part of our country thus feels an immediate and particular interest in union, all the parts combined cannot fail to find in the united mass of means and efforts greater strength, greater resource, proportionably greater security from external danger, a less frequent interruption of their peace by foreign nations, and what is of inestimable value, they must derive from union an exemption from those broils and wars between themselves which so frequently afflict neighboring countries not tied together by the same governments, which their own rivalships alone would be sufficient to produce, but which opposite foreign alliances, attachments, and intrigues would stimulate and embitter. Hence, likewise, they will avoid the necessity of those overgrown military establishments which, under any form of government, are inauspicious to liberty, and which are to be regarded as particularly hostile to republican liberty. In this sense, it is that your union ought to be considered as a main prop of your liberty, and that the love of the one ought to endear to you the preservation of the other.

These considerations speak a persuasive language to every reflecting and virtuous mind, and exhibit the continuance of the union as a primary object of patriotic desire. Is there a doubt whether a common government can embrace so large a sphere? Let experience solve it. To listen to mere speculation in such a case were criminal. We are authorized to hope that a proper organization of the whole, with the auxiliary agency of governments for the respective subdivisions, will afford a happy issue to the experiment. It is well worth a fair and full experiment. With such powerful and obvious motives to union affecting all parts of our country, while experience shall not have demonstrated its impracticability, there will always be reason to distrust the patriotism of those who in any quarter may endeavor to weaken its bands.

In contemplating the causes which may disturb our union it occurs as matter of serious concern that any ground should have been furnished for characterizing parties by geographical discriminations—northern and southern, Atlantic and western—whence designing men may endeavor to excite a belief that there is a real difference of local interests and views. One of the expedients of party to acquire influence within particular districts is to misrepresent the opinions and aims of other districts. You cannot shield yourselves too much against the jealousies and heartburnings which spring from these misrepresentations; they tend to render alien to each other those who ought to be bound together by fraternal affection. The inhabitants of our western country have lately had a useful lesson on this head. They have seen in the negotiation by the executive and in the unanimous ratification by the Senate of the treaty with Spain, and in the universal satisfaction at that event throughout the United States, a decisive proof how unfounded were the suspicions propagated among them of a policy in the general government and in the Atlantic states unfriendly to their interests in regard to the Mississippi. They have been witnesses to the formation of two treaties—that with Great Britain and that with Spain—which secure to them everything they could desire in respect to our foreign relations toward confirming their prosperity. Will it not be their wisdom to rely for the preservation of these advantages on the union by which they were procured?

Will they not henceforth be deaf to those advisers, if such there are, who would sever them from their brethren and connect them with aliens?

To the efficacy and permanency of your union a government for the whole is indispensable. No alliances, however strict, between the parts can be an adequate substitute. They must inevitably experience the infractions and interruptions which all alliances in all times have experienced. Sensible of this momentous truth, you have improved upon your first essay by the adoption of a Constitution of government better calculated than your former for an intimate union and for the efficacious management of your common concerns. This government, the offspring of our own choice, uninfluenced and unawed, adopted upon full investigation and mature deliberation, completely free in its principles, in the distribution of its powers, uniting security with energy, and containing within itself a provision for its own amendment, has a just claim to your confidence and your support. Respect for its authority, compliance with its laws, acquiescence in its measures, are duties enjoined by the fundamental maxims of true liberty. The basis of our political systems is the right of the people to make and to alter their constitutions of government. But the constitution which at any time exists till changed by an explicit and authentic act of the whole people is sacredly obligatory upon all. The very idea of the power and the right of the people to establish government presupposes the duty of every individual to obey the established government.

All obstructions to the execution of the laws, all combinations and associations, under whatever plausible character, with the real design to direct, control, counteract, or awe the regular deliberation and action of the constituted authorities, are destructive of this fundamental principle and of fatal tendency. They serve to organize faction; to give it an artificial and extraordinary force; to put in the place of the delegated will of the nation the will of a party, often a small but artful and enterprising minority of the community, and, according to the alternate triumphs of different parties, to make the public administration the mirror of the illconcerted and incongruous projects of faction rather than the organ of consistent and wholesome plans, digested by common counsels and modified by mutual interests.

However combinations or associations of the above description may now and then answer popular ends, they are likely in the course of time and things to become potent engines by which cunning, ambitious, and unprincipled men will be enabled to subvert the power of the people, and to usurp for themselves the reins of government, destroying afterwards the very engines which have lifted them to unjust dominion.

Toward the preservation of your government and the permanency of your present happy state, it is requisite not only that you steadily discountenance irregular oppositions to its acknowledged authority, but also that you resist with care the spirit of innovation upon its principles, however specious the pretexts. One method of assault may be to effect in the forms of the Constitution alterations which will impair the energy of the system, and thus to undermine what can not be directly overthrown. In all the changes to which you may be invited remember that time and habit are at least as necessary to fix the true character of governments as of other human institutions; that experience is the surest standard by which to test the real tendency of the existing constitution of a country; that facility in changes upon the credit of mere hypothesis and opinion exposes to perpetual change, from the endless variety of hypothesis and opinion; and remember especially that for the efficient management of your common interests in a country so extensive as ours a government of as much vigor as is consistent with the perfect security of liberty is indispensable. Liberty itself will find in such a government, with powers properly distributed and adjusted, its surest guardian. It is, indeed, little else than a name where the government is too feeble to withstand the enterprises of faction, to confine each member of the society within the limits prescribed by the laws, and to maintain all in the secure and tranquil enjoyment of the rights of person and property.

I have already intimated to you the danger of parties in the state, with particular reference to the founding of them on geographical discriminations. Let me now take a more comprehensive view, and warn you in the most solemn manner against the baneful effects of the spirit of party generally.

This spirit, unfortunately, is inseparable from our nature, having its root in the strongest passions of the human mind. It exists under different shapes in all governments, more or less stifled, controlled, or repressed; but in those of the popular form it is seen in its greatest rankness and is truly their worst enemy.

The alternate domination of one faction over another, sharpened by the spirit of revenge natural to party dissension, which in different ages and countries has perpetrated the most horrid enormities, is itself a frightful despotism. But this leads at length to a more formal and permanent despotism. The disorders and miseries which result gradually incline the minds of men to seek security and repose in the absolute power of an individual, and sooner or later the chief of some prevailing faction, more able or more fortunate than his competitors, turns this disposition to the purposes of his own elevation on the ruins of public liberty.

Without looking forward to an extremity of this kind (which nevertheless ought not to be entirely out of sight), the common and continual mischiefs of the spirit of party are sufficient to make it the interest and duty of a wise people to discourage and restrain it.

It serves always to distract the public councils and enfeeble the public administration. It agitates the community with ill-founded jealousies and false alarms; kindles the animosity of one part against another; foments occasionally riot and insurrection. It opens the door to foreign influence and corruption, which find a facilitated access to the government itself through the channels of party passion. Thus the policy and the will of one country are subjected to the policy and will of another.

There is an opinion that parties in free countries are useful checks upon the administration of the government, and serve to keep alive the spirit of liberty. This within certain limits is probably true; and in governments of a monarchical cast patriotism may look with indulgence, if not with favor, upon the spirit of party. But in those of the popular character, in governments purely elective, it is a spirit not to be encouraged. From their natural tendency it is certain there will always be enough of that spirit for every salutary purpose; and there being constant danger of excess, the effort ought to be by force of public opinion to mitigate and assuage it. A fire not to be quenched, it demands a uniform vigilance to prevent its bursting into a flame, lest, instead of warming, it should consume.

It is important, likewise, that the habits of thinking in a free country should inspire caution in those entrusted with its administration to confine themselves within their respective constitutional spheres, avoiding in the exercise of the powers of one department to encroach upon another. The spirit of encroachment tends to consolidate the powers of all the departments in one, and thus to create, whatever the form of government, a real despotism. A just estimate of that love of power and proneness to abuse it which predominates in the human heart is sufficient to satisfy us of the truth of this position. The necessity of reciprocal checks in the exercise of political power, by dividing and distributing it into different depositories, and constituting each the guardian of the public weal against invasions by the others, has been evinced by experiments ancient and modern, some of them in our country and under our own eyes. To preserve them must be as necessary as to institute them. If in the opinion of the people the distribution or modification of the constitutional powers be in any particular wrong, let it be corrected by an amendment in the way which the Constitution designates. But let there be no change by usurpation; for though this in one instance may be the instrument of good, it is the customary weapon by which free governments are destroyed. The precedent must always greatly overbalance in permanent evil any partial or transient benefit which the use can at any time yield.

Of all the dispositions and habits which lead to political prosperity, religion and morality are indispensable supports. In vain would that man claim the tribute of patriotism who should labor to subvert these great pillars of human happiness—these firmest props of the duties of men and citizens. The mere politician, equally with the pious man, ought to respect and to cherish them. A volume could not trace all their connections with private and public felicity. Let it simply be asked, Where is the security for property, for reputation, for life, if the sense of religious obligations desert the oaths which are the instruments of investigation in courts of justice? And let us with caution indulge the supposition that morality can be maintained without religion. Whatever may be conceded to the influence of refined education on minds of peculiar structure, reason and experience both forbid us to expect that national morality can prevail in exclusion of religious principle.

It is substantially true that virtue or morality is a necessary spring of popular government. The rule indeed extends with more or less force to every species of free government. Who that is a sincere friend to it can look with indifference upon attempts to shake the foundation of the fabric? Promote, then, as an object of primary importance, institutions for the general diffusion of knowledge. In proportion as the structure of a government gives force to public opinion, it is essential that public opinion should be enlightened.

As a very important source of strength and security, cherish public credit. One method of preserving it is to use it as sparingly as possible, avoiding occasions of expense by cultivating peace, but remembering also that timely disbursements to prepare for danger frequently prevent much greater disbursements to repeal it; avoiding likewise the accumulation of debt, not only by shunning occasions of expense, but by vigorous exertions in time of peace to discharge the debts which unavoidable wars have occasioned, not ungenerously throwing upon posterity the burthen which we ourselves ought to bear. The execution of these maxims belongs to your representatives; but it is necessary that public opinion should cooperate. To facilitate to them the performance of their duty, it is essential that you should practically bear in mind that toward the payment of debts there must be revenue; that to have revenue there must be taxes; that no taxes can be devised which are not more or less inconvenient and unpleasant; that the intrinsic embarrassment inseparable from the selection of the proper objects (which is always a choice of difficulties), ought to be a decisive motive for a candid construction of the conduct of the government in making it, and for a spirit of acquiescence in the measures for obtaining revenue which the public exigencies may at any time dictate.

Observe good faith and justice toward all nations. Cultivate peace and harmony with all. Religion and morality enjoin this conduct. And can it be that good policy does not equally enjoin it? It will be worthy of a free, enlightened, and at no distant period a great nation to give to mankind the magnanimous and too novel example of a people always guided by an exalted justice and benevolence. Who can doubt that in the course of time and things the fruits of such a plan would richly repay any temporary advantages which might be lost by a steady adherence to it? Can it be that Providence has not connected the permanent felicity of a nation with its virtue? The experiment, at least, is recommended by every sentiment which ennobles human nature. Alas! is it rendered impossible by its vices?

In the execution of such a plan nothing is more essential than that permanent, inveterate antipathies against particular nations and passionate attachments for others should be excluded, and that in place of them just and amicable feelings toward all should be cultivated. The nation which indulges toward another in habitual hatred or an habitual fondness is in some degree a slave. It is a slave to its animosity or to its affection, either of which is sufficient to lead it astray from its duty and its interest. Antipathy in one nation against another disposes each more readily to offer insult and injury, to lay hold of slight causes of umbrage, and to be haughty and intractable when accidental or trifling occasions of dispute occur.

Hence frequent collisions, obstinate, envenomed, and bloody contests. The nation prompted by ill will and resentment sometimes impels to war the government contrary to the best calculations of policy. The government sometimes participates in the national propensity, and adopts through passion what reason would reject. At other times it makes the animosity of the nation subservient to projects of hostility, instigated by pride, ambition, and other sinister and pernicious motives. The peace often, sometimes perhaps the liberty, of nations has been the victim.

So, likewise, a passionate attachment of one nation for another produces a variety of evils. Sympathy for the favorite nation, facilitating the illusion of an imaginary common interest in cases where no real common interest exists, and infusing into one the enmities of the other, betrays the former into a participation in the quarrels and wars of the latter without adequate inducement or justification. It leads also to concessions to the favorite nation of privileges denied to others, which is apt doubly to injure the nation making the concessions by unnecessarily parting with what ought to have been retained, and by exciting jealousy, ill will, and a disposition to retaliate in the parties from whom equal privileges are withheld; and it gives to ambitious, corrupted, or deluded citizens (who devote themselves to the favorite nation) facility to betray or sacrifice the interests of their own country without odium, sometimes even with popularity, gilding with the appearances of a virtuous sense of obligation, a commendable deference for public opinion, or a laudable zeal for public good the base or foolish compliances of ambition, corruption, or infatuation.

As avenues to foreign influence in innumerable ways, such attachments are particularly alarming to the truly enlightened and independent patriot. How many opportunities do they afford to tamper with domestic factions, to practice the arts of seduction, to mislead public opinion, to influence or awe the public councils! Such an attachment of a small or weak toward a great and powerful nation dooms the former to be the satellite of the latter. Against the insidious wiles of foreign influence (I conjure you to believe me, fellow citizens), the jealousy of a free people ought to be constantly awake, since history and experience prove that foreign influence is one of the most baneful foes of republican government. But that jealousy, to be useful, must be impartial, else it becomes the instrument of the very influence to be avoided, instead of a defense against it. Excessive partiality for one foreign nation and excessive dislike of another cause those whom they actuate to see danger only on one side, and serve to veil and even second the arts of influence on the other. Real patriots who may resist the intrigues of the favorite are liable to become suspected and odious, while its tools and dupes usurp the applause and confidence of the people to surrender their interests.

The great rule of conduct for us in regard to foreign nations is, in extending our commercial relations to have with them as little political connection as possible. So far as we have already formed engagements let them be fulfilled with perfect good faith. Here let us stop.

Europe has a set of primary interests which to us have none or a very remote relation. Hence she must be engaged in frequent controversies, the causes of which are essentially foreign to our concerns. Hence, therefore, it must be unwise in us to implicate ourselves by artificial ties in the ordinary vicissitudes of her politics or the ordinary combinations and collisions of her friendships or enmities.

Our detached and distant situation invites and enables us to pursue a different course. If we remain one people, under an efficient government, the period is not far off when we may defy material injury from external annoyance; when we may take such an attitude as will cause the neutrality we may at any time resolve upon to be scrupulously respected; when belligerent nations, under the impossibility of making acquisitions upon us, will not lightly hazard the giving us provocation; when we may choose peace or war, as our interest, guided by justice, shall counsel.

Why forgo the advantages of so peculiar a situation? Why quit our own to stand upon foreign ground? Why, by interweaving our destiny with that of any part of Europe, entangle our peace and prosperity in the toils of European ambition, rivalship, interest, humor, or caprice?

It is our true policy to steer clear of permanent alliances with any portion of the foreign world, so far, I mean, as we are now at liberty to do it; for let me not be understood as capable of patronizing infidelity to existing engagements. I hold the maxim no less applicable to public than to private affairs that honesty is always the best policy. I repeat, therefore, let those engagements be observed in their genuine sense. But in my opinion it is unnecessary and would be unwise to extend them.

Taking care always to keep ourselves by suitable establishments on a respectable defensive posture, we may safely trust to temporary alliances for extraordinary emergencies.

Harmony, liberal intercourse with all nations are recommended by policy, humanity, and interest. But even our commercial policy should hold an equal and impartial hand, neither seeking nor granting exclusive favors or preferences; consulting the natural course of things; diffusing and diversifying by gentle means the streams of commerce, but forcing nothing; establishing with powers so disposed, in order to give trade a stable course, to define the rights of our merchants, and to enable the government to support them, conventional rules of intercourse, the best that present circumstances and mutual opinion will permit, but temporary and liable to be from time to time abandoned or varied as experience and circumstances shall dictate; constantly keeping in view that it is folly in one nation to look for disinterested favors from another; that it must pay with a portion of its independence for whatever it may accept under that character; that by such acceptance it may place itself in the condition of having given equivalents for nominal favors, and yet of being reproached with ingratitude for not giving more. There can be no greater error than to expect or calculate upon real favors from nation to nation. It is an illusion which experience must cure, which a just pride ought to discard.

In offering to you, my countrymen, these counsels of an old and affectionate friend I dare not hope they will make the strong and lasting impression I could wish—that they will control the usual current of the passions or prevent our nation from running the course which has hitherto marked the destiny of nations. But if I may even flatter myself that they may be productive of some partial benefit, some occasional good—that they may now and then recur to moderate the fury of party spirit, to warn against the mischiefs of foreign intrigue, to guard against the impostures of pretended patriotism—this hope will be a full recompense for the solicitude for your welfare by which they have been dictated.

How far in the discharge of my official duties I have been guided by the principles which have been delineated the public records and other evidences of my conduct must witness to you and to the world. To myself, the assurance of my own conscience is that I have at least believed myself to be guided by them.

In relation to the still subsisting war in Europe, my proclamation of the 22d of April 1793 is the index to my plan. Sanctioned by your approving voice and by that of your representatives in both houses of Congress, the spirit of that measure has continually governed me, uninfluenced by any attempts to deter or divert me from it.

After deliberate examination, with the aid of the best lights I could obtain, I was well satisfied that our country, under all the circumstances of the case, had a right to take, and was bound in duty and interest to take, a neutral position. Having taken it, I determined as far as should depend upon me to maintain it with moderation, perseverance, and firmness.

The considerations which respect the right to hold this conduct it is not necessary on this occasion to detail. I will only observe that, according to my understanding of the matter, that right, so far from being denied by any of the belligerent powers, has been virtually admitted by all.

The duty of holding a neutral conduct may be inferred, without anything more, from the obligation which justice and humanity impose on every nation, in cases in which it is free to act, to maintain inviolate the relations of peace and amity toward other nations.

The inducements of interest for observing that conduct will best be referred to your own reflections and experience. With me a predominant motive has been to endeavor to gain time to our country to settle and mature its yet recent institutions, and to progress without interruption to that degree of strength and consistency which is necessary to give it, humanly speaking, the command of its own fortunes.

Though in reviewing the incidents of my administration I am unconscious of intentional error, I am nevertheless too sensible of my defects not to think it probable that I may have committed many errors. Whatever they may be, I fervently beseech the Almighty to avert or mitigate the evils to which they may tend. I shall also carry with me the hope that my country will never cease to view them with indulgence, and that, after forty-five years of my life dedicated to its service with an upright zeal, the faults of incompetent abilities will be consigned to oblivion, as myself must soon be to the mansions of rest.

Relying on its kindness in this as in other things, and actuated by that fervent love toward it which is so natural to a man who views in it the native soil of himself and his progenitors for several generations, I anticipate with pleasing expectation that retreat in which I promise myself to realize without alloy the sweet enjoyment of partaking in the midst of my fellow citizens the benign influence of good laws under a free government—the ever-favorite object of my heart, and the happy reward, as I trust, of our mutual cares, labors, and dangers.

ABRAHAM LINCOLN: GETTYSBURG ADDRESS

Fourscore and seven years ago our fathers brought forth on this continent a new nation, conceived in liberty, and dedicated to the proposition that all men are created equal.

Now we are engaged in a great civil war, testing whether that nation, or any nation so conceived and so dedicated, can long endure. We are met on a great battlefield of that war. We have come to dedicate a portion of that field as a final resting-place for those who here gave their lives that that nation might live. It is altogether fitting and proper that we should do this.

But, in a larger sense, we cannot dedicate—we cannot consecrate—we cannot hallow—this ground. The brave men, living and dead, who struggled here, have consecrated it far above our poor power to add or detract. The world will little note nor long remember what we say here, but it can never forget what they did here. It is for us, the living, rather, to be dedicated here to the unfinished work which they who fought here have thus far so nobly advanced. It is rather for us to be here dedicated to the great task remaining before us—that from these honored dead we take increased devotion to that cause for which they gave the last full measure of devotion; that we here highly resolve that these dead shall not have died in vain; that this nation, under God, shall have a new birth of freedom; and that government of the people, by the people, for the people, shall not perish from the earth.

———

Source: *The Writings of Abraham Lincoln*, Constitutional ed., vol. 7 (G. P. Putnam's Sons, 1906), p. 20.

ABRAHAM LINCOLN: SECOND INAUGURAL ADDRESS

Fellow countrymen:

At this second appearing to take the oath of the presidential office, there is less occasion for an extended address than there was at the first. Then a statement somewhat in detail of a course to be pursued seemed fitting and proper. Now, at the expiration of four years, during which public declarations have been constantly called forth on every point and phase of the great contest which still absorbs the attention and engrosses the energies of the nation, little that is new could be presented. The progress of our arms, upon which all else chiefly depends, is as well known to the public as to myself, and it is, I trust, reasonably satisfactory and encouraging to all. With high hope for the future, no prediction in regard to it is ventured.

On the occasion corresponding to this four years ago, all thoughts were anxiously directed to an impending civil war. All dreaded it, all sought to avert it. While the inaugural address was being delivered from this place, devoted altogether to saving the Union without war, insurgent agents were in the city seeking to destroy it without war—seeking to disolve the Union and divide effects by negotiation. Both parties deprecated war, but one of them would make war rather than let the nation survive, and the other would accept war rather than let it perish, and the war came.

One-eighth of the whole population were colored slaves, not distributed generally over the Union, but localized in the southern part of it. These slaves constituted a peculiar and powerful interest. All knew that this interest was somehow the cause of the war. To strengthen, perpetuate, and extend this interest was the object for which the insurgents would rend the Union even by war, while the government claimed no right to do more than to restrict the territorial enlargement of it. Neither party expected for the war the magnitude or the duration which it has already attained. Neither anticipated that the cause of the conflict might cease with or even before the conflict itself should cease. Each looked for an easier triumph, and a result less fundamental and astounding. Both read the same Bible and pray to the same God, and each invokes His aid against the other. It may seem strange that any men should dare to ask a just God's assistance in wringing their bread from the sweat of other men's faces, but let us judge not, that we be not judged. The prayers of both could not be answered. That of neither has been answered fully. The Almighty has His own purposes. "Woe unto the world because of offenses; for it must needs be that offenses come, but woe to that man by whom the offense cometh." If we shall suppose that American slavery is one of those offenses which, in the providence of God, must needs come, but which, having continued through His appointed time, He now wills to remove, and that He gives to both North and South this terrible

---

Source: James D. Richardson, ed. *Messages and Papers of the Presidents: 1789–1897*, vol. 6 (1900), pp. 276–277.

war as the woe due to those by whom the offense came, shall we discern therein any departure from those divine attributes which the believers in a living God always ascribe to Him? Fondly do we hope, fervently do we pray, that this mighty scourge of war may speedily pass away. Yet, if God wills that it continue until all the wealth piled by the bondsman's two hundred and fifty years of unrequited toil shall be sunk, and until every drop of blood drawn with the lash shall be paid by another drawn with the sword, as was said three thousand years ago, so still it must be said, "the judgments of the Lord are true and righteous altogether."

With malice toward none, with charity for all, with firmness in the right as God gives us to see the right, let us strive on to finish the work we are in, to bind up the nation's wounds, to care for him who shall have borne the battle and for his widow and his orphan, to do all which may achieve and cherish a just and lasting peace among ourselves and with all nations.

WOODROW WILSON: FOURTEEN POINTS

It will be our wish and purpose that the processes of peace, when they are begun, shall be absolutely open and that they shall involve and permit henceforth no secret understandings of any kind. The day of conquest and aggrandizement is gone by; so is also the day of secret covenants entered into in the interest of particular governments and likely at some unlooked-for moment to upset the peace of the world. It is this happy fact, now clear to the view of every public man whose thoughts do not still linger in an age that is dead and gone, which makes it possible for every nation whose purposes are consistent with justice and the peace of the world to avow now or at any other time the objects it has in view.

We entered this war because violations of right had occurred which touched us to the quick and made the life of our own people impossible unless they were corrected and the world secure once for all against their recurrence. What we demand in this war, therefore, is nothing peculiar to ourselves. It is that the world be made fit and safe to live in; and particularly that it be made safe for every peace-loving nation which, like our own, wishes to live its own life, determine its own institutions, be assured of justice and fair dealing by the other peoples of the world as against force and selfish aggression. All the peoples of the world are in effect partners in this interest, and for our own part we see very clearly that unless justice be done to others it will not be done to us. The programme of the world's peace, therefore, is our programme; and that programme, the only possible programme, as we see it, is this:

I. Open covenants of peace, openly arrived at, after which there shall be no private international understandings of any kind but diplomacy shall proceed always frankly and in the public view.

II. Absolute freedom of navigation upon the seas, outside territorial waters, alike in peace and in war, except as the seas may be closed in whole or in part by international action for the enforcement of international covenants.

III. The removal, so far as possible, of all economic barriers and the establishment of an equality of trade conditions among all the nations consenting to the peace and associating themselves for its maintenance.

IV. Adequate guarantees given and taken that national armaments will be reduced to the lowest point consistent with domestic safety.

V. A free, open-minded, and absolutely impartial adjustment of all colonial claims, based upon a strict observance of the principle that in determining all such questions of sovereignty the interests of the populations concerned must have equal weight with the equitable claims of the government whose title is to be determined.

VI. The evacuation of all Russian territory and such a settlement of all questions affecting Russia as will secure the best and freest cooperation of the other nations of the world in obtaining for her an unhampered and unembarrassed opportunity for the independent determination of her own political development and national policy and assure her of a sincere welcome into the society of free nations under institutions of her own choosing; and, more than a welcome, assistance also of every kind that she may need and may herself desire. The treatment accorded Russia by her sister nations in the months to come will be the acid test of their good will, of their comprehension of her needs as distinguished from their own interests, and of their intelligent and unselfish sympathy.

VII. Belgium, the whole world will agree, must be evacuated and restored, without any attempt to limit the sovereignty which she enjoys in common with all other free nations. No other single act will serve as this will serve to restore confidence among the nations in the laws which they have themselves set and determined for the government of their relations with one another. Without this healing act the whole structure and validity of international law is forever impaired.

VIII. All French territory should be freed and the invaded portions restored, and the wrong done to France by Prussia in 1871 in the matter of Alsace-Lorraine, which has unsettled the peace of the world for nearly fifty years, should be righted, in order that peace may once more be made secure in the interest of all.

IX. A readjustment of the frontiers of Italy should be effected along clearly recognizable lines of nationality.

X. The peoples of Austria-Hungary, whose place among the nations we wish to see safeguarded and assured, should be accorded the freest opportunity to autonomous development.

XI. Rumania, Serbia, and Montenegro should be evacuated; occupied territories restored; Serbia accorded free and secure access to the sea; and the relations of the several Balkan states to one another determined by friendly counsel along historically established lines of allegiance and nationality; and international guarantees of the political and economic independence and territorial integrity of the several Balkan states should be entered into.

XII. The Turkish portion of the present Ottoman Empire should be assured a secure sovereignty, but the other nationalities which are now under Turkish rule should be assured an undoubted security of life and an absolutely unmolested opportunity of autonomous development, and the Dardanelles should be permanently opened as a free passage to the ships and commerce of all nations under international guarantees.

XIII. An independent Polish state should be erected which should include the territories inhabited by indisputably Polish populations, which should be assured a free and secure access to the sea, and whose political and economic independence and territorial integrity should be guaranteed by international covenant.

XIV. A general association of nations must be formed under specific covenants for the purpose of affording mutual guarantees of political independence and territorial integrity to great and small states alike.

In regard to these essential rectifications of wrong and assertions of right we feel ourselves to be intimate partners of all the governments and peoples associated together against the Imperialists. We cannot be separated in interest or divided in purpose. We stand together until the end.

For such arrangements and covenants we are willing to fight and to continue to fight until they are achieved; but only because we wish the right to prevail and desire a just and stable peace such as can be secured only by removing the chief provocations to war, which this programme does remove. We have no jealousy of German greatness, and there is nothing in this programme that impairs it. We grudge her no achievement or distinction of learning or of pacific enterprise such as have made her record very bright and very enviable. We do not wish to injure her or to block in any way her legitimate influence or power. We do not wish to fight her either with arms or with hostile arrangements of trade if she is willing to associate herself with us and the other peace-loving nations of the world in covenants of justice and law and fair dealing. We wish her only to accept a place of equality among the peoples of the world,—the new world in which we now live,—instead of a place of mastery.

FRANKLIN D. ROOSEVELT: FIRST INAUGURAL ADDRESS

I am certain that my fellow Americans expect that on my induction into the Presidency I will address them with a candor and a decision which the present situation of our Nation impels. This is preeminently the time to speak the truth, the whole truth, frankly and boldly. Nor need we shrink from honestly facing conditions in our country today. This great Nation will endure as it has endured, will revive and will prosper.

So, first of all, let me assert my firm belief that the only thing we have to fear is fear itself—nameless, unreasoning, unjustified terror which paralyzes needed efforts to convert retreat into advance. In every dark hour of our national life a leadership of frankness and vigor has met with that understanding and support of the people themselves which is essential to victory. I am convinced that you will again give that support to leadership in these critical days.

In such a spirit on my part and on yours we face our common difficulties. They concern, thank God, only material things. Values have shrunken to fantastic levels; taxes have risen; our ability to pay has fallen; government of all kinds is faced by serious curtailment of income; the means of exchange are frozen in the currents of trade; the withered leaves of industrial enterprise lie on every side; farmers find no markets for their produce; the savings of many years in thousands of families are gone.

More important, a host of unemployed citizens face the grim problem of existence, and an equally great number toil with little return. Only a foolish optimist can deny the dark realities of the moment.

Yet our distress comes from no failure of substance. We are stricken by no plague of locusts. Compared with the perils which our forefathers conquered because they believed and were not afraid, we have still much to be thankful for. Nature still offers her bounty and human efforts have multiplied it. Plenty is at our doorstep, but a generous use of it languishes in the very sight of the supply. Primarily this is because the rulers of the exchange of mankind's goods have failed, through their own stubbornness and their own incompetence, have admitted their failure, and abdicated. Practices of the unscrupulous money changers stand indicted in the court of public opinion, rejected by the hearts and minds of men.

True they have tried, but their efforts have been cast in the pattern of an outworn tradition. Faced by failure of credit they have proposed only the lending of more money. Stripped of the lure of profit by which to induce our people to follow their false leadership, they have resorted to exhortations, pleading tearfully for restored confidence. They know only the rules of a generation of self-seekers. They have no vision, and when there is no vision the people perish.

The money changers have fled from their high seats in the temple of our civilization. We may now restore that temple to the ancient truths. The measure of the restoration lies in the extent to which we apply social values more noble than mere monetary profit.

Happiness lies not in the mere possession of money; it lies in the joy of achievement, in the thrill of creative effort. The joy and moral stimulation of work no longer must be forgotten in the mad chase of evanescent profits. These dark days will be worth all they cost us if they teach us that our true destiny is not to be ministered unto but to minister to ourselves and to our fellow men.

Recognition of the falsity of material wealth as the standard of success goes hand in hand with the abandonment of the false belief that public office and high political position are to be valued only by the standards of pride of place and personal profit; and there must be an end to a conduct in banking and in business which too often has given to a sacred trust the likeness of callous and selfish wrongdoing. Small wonder that confidence languishes, for it thrives only on honesty, on honor, on the sacredness of obligations, on faithful protection, on unselfish performance; without them it cannot live.

Restoration calls, however, not for changes in ethics alone. This Nation asks for action, and action now.

Our greatest primary task is to put people to work. This is no unsolvable problem if we face it wisely and courageously. It can be accomplished in part by direct recruiting by the Government itself, treating the task as we would treat the emergency of a war, but at the same time, through this employment, accomplishing greatly needed projects to stimulate and reorganize the use of our natural resources.

Hand in hand with this we must frankly recognize the overbalance of population in our industrial centers and, by engaging on a national scale in a redistribution, endeavor to provide a better use of the land for those best fitted for the land. The task can be helped by definite efforts to raise the values of agricultural products and with this the power to purchase the output of our cities. It can be helped by preventing realistically the tragedy of the growing loss through foreclosure of our small homes and our farms. It can be helped by insistence that the Federal, State, and local governments act forthwith on the demand that their cost be drastically reduced. It can be helped by the unifying of relief activities which today are often scattered, uneconomical, and unequal. It can be helped by national planning for and supervision of all forms of transportation and of communications and other utilities which have a definitely public character. There are many ways in which it can be helped, but it can never be helped merely by talking about it. We must act and act quickly.

Finally, in our progress toward a resumption of work we require two safeguards against a return of the evils of the old order; there must be a strict supervision of all banking and credits and investments; there must be an end to speculation with other people's money, and there must be provision for an adequate but sound currency.

There are the lines of attack. I shall presently urge upon a new Congress in special session detailed measures for their fulfillment, and I shall seek the immediate assistance of the several States.

Through this program of action we address ourselves to putting our own national house in order and making income balance outgo. Our international trade relations, though vastly important, are in point of time and necessity secondary to the establishment of a sound national economy. I favor as a practical policy the putting of first things first. I shall spare no effort to restore world trade by international economic readjustment, but the emergency at home cannot wait on that accomplishment.

The basic thought that guides these specific means of national recovery is not narrowly nationalistic. It is the insistence, as a first consideration, upon the interdependence of the various elements in all parts of the United States—a recognition of the old and permanently important manifestation of the American spirit of the pioneer. It is the way to recovery. It is the immediate way. It is the strongest assurance that the recovery will endure.

In the field of world policy I would dedicate this Nation to the policy of the good neighbor—the neighbor who resolutely respects himself and, because he does so, respects the rights of others—the neighbor who respects his obligations and respects the sanctity of his agreements in and with a world of neighbors.

If I read the temper of our people correctly, we now realize as we have never realized before our interdependence on each other; that we can not merely take but we must give as well; that if we are to go forward, we must move as a trained and loyal army willing to sacrifice for the good of a common discipline, because without such discipline no progress is made, no leadership becomes effective. We are, I know, ready and willing to submit our lives and property to such discipline, because it makes possible a leadership which aims at a larger good. This I propose to offer, pledging that the larger purposes will bind upon us all as a sacred obligation with a unity of duty hitherto evoked only in time of armed strife.

With this pledge taken, I assume unhesitatingly the leadership of this great army of our people dedicated to a disciplined attack upon our common problems.

Action in this image and to this end is feasible under the form of government which we have inherited from our ancestors. Our Constitution is so simple and practical that it is possible always to meet extraordinary needs by changes in emphasis and arrangement without loss of essential form. That is why our constitutional system has proved itself the most superbly enduring political mechanism the modern world has produced. It has met every stress of vast expansion of territory, of foreign wars, of bitter internal strife, of world relations.

It is to be hoped that the normal balance of executive and legislative authority may be wholly adequate to meet the unprecedented task before us. But it may be that an unprecedented demand and need for undelayed action may call for temporary departure from that normal balance of public procedure.

I am prepared under my constitutional duty to recommend the measures that a stricken nation in the midst of a stricken world may require. These measures, or such other measures as the Congress may build out of its experience and wisdom, I shall seek, within my constitutional authority, to bring to speedy adoption.

But in the event that the Congress shall fail to take one of these two courses, and in the event that the national emergency is still critical, I shall not evade the clear course of duty that will then confront me. I shall ask the Congress for the one remaining instrument to meet the crisis—broad Executive power to wage a war against the emergency, as great as the power that would be given to me if we were in fact invaded by a foreign foe. For the trust reposed in me I will return the courage and the devotion that befit the time. I can do no less.

We face the arduous days that lie before us in the warm courage of the national unity; with the clear consciousness of seeking old and precious moral values; with the clean satisfaction that comes from the stem performance of duty by old and young alike. We aim at the assurance of a rounded and permanent national life.

We do not distrust the future of essential democracy. The people of the United States have not failed. In their need they have registered a mandate that they want direct, vigorous action. They have asked for discipline and direction under leadership. They have made me the present instrument of their wishes. In the spirit of the gift I take it.

In this dedication of a Nation we humbly ask the blessing of God. May He protect each and every one of us. May He guide me in the days to come.

JOHN F. KENNEDY: INAUGURAL ADDRESS

We observe today not a victory of party but a celebration of freedom—symbolizing an end as well as a beginning—signifying renewal as well as change. For I have sworn before you and Almighty God the same solemn oath our forebears prescribed nearly a century and three-quarters ago.

The world is very different now. For man holds in his mortal hands the power to abolish all forms of human poverty and all forms of human life. And yet the same revolutionary beliefs for which our forebears fought are still at issue around the globe—the belief that the rights of man come not from the generosity of the state but from the hand of God.

We dare not forget today that we are the heirs of that first revolution. Let the word go forth from this time and place, to friend and foe alike, that the torch has been passed to a new generation of Americans—born in this century, tempered by war, disciplined by a hard and bitter peace, proud of our ancient heritage—and unwilling to witness to or permit the slow undoing of those human rights to which this nation has always been committed, and to which we are committed today at home and around the world.

Let every nation know, whether it wishes us well or ill, that we shall pay any price, bear any burden, meet any hardship, support any friend, oppose any foe to assure the survival and the success of liberty.

This much we pledge—and more.

To those old allies whose cultural and spiritual origins we share, we pledge the loyalty of faithful friends. United, there is little we cannot do in a host of new cooperative ventures. Divided, there is little we can do—for we dare not meet a powerful challenge at odds and split asunder.

To those new states whom we welcome to the ranks of the free, we pledge our word that one form of colonial control shall not have passed away merely to be replaced by a far more iron tyranny. We shall not always expect to find them supporting our view. But we shall always hope to find them strongly supporting their own freedom—and to remember that, in the past, those who foolishly sought power by riding the back of the tiger ended up inside.

To those people in the huts and villages of half the globe struggling to break the bonds of mass misery, we pledge our best efforts to help them help themselves, for whatever period is required—not because the Communists may be doing it, not because we seek their votes, but because it is right. If a free society cannot help the many who are poor, it cannot save the few who are rich.

To our sister republics south of our border, we offer a special pledge—to convert our good words into good deeds—in a new alliance for progress—to assist free men and free governments in casting off the chains of poverty. But this peaceful revolution of hope cannot become the prey of hostile powers. Let all our neighbors know that we shall join with them to oppose aggression or subversion anywhere in the Americas. And let every other power know that this hemisphere intends to remain the master of its own house.

To that world assembly of sovereign states, the United Nations, our last best hope in an age where the instruments of war have far outpaced the instruments of peace, we renew our pledge of support—to prevent it from becoming merely a forum for invective—to strengthen its shield of the new and the weak—and to enlarge the area in which its writ may run.

Finally, to those nations who would make themselves our adversary, we offer not a pledge but a request: that both sides begin anew the quest for peace, before the dark powers of destruction unleashed by science engulf all humanity in planned or accidental self-destruction.

We dare not tempt them with weakness. For only when our arms are sufficient beyond doubt can we be certain beyond doubt that they will never be employed.

But neither can two great and powerful groups of nations take comfort from our present course—both sides overburdened by the cost of modern weapons, both rightly alarmed by the steady spread of the deadly atom, yet both racing to alter that uncertain balance of terror that stays the hand of mankind's final war.

So let us begin anew—remembering on both sides that civility is not a sign of weakness, and sincerity is always subject to proof. Let us never negotiate out of fear. But let us never fear to negotiate.

Let both sides explore what problems unite us instead of belaboring those problems which divide us.

Let both sides, for the first time, formulate serious and precise proposals for the inspection and control of arms—and bring the absolute power to destroy other nations under the absolute control of all nations.

Let both sides seek to invoke the wonders of science instead of its terrors. Together let us explore the stars, conquer the deserts, eradicate disease, tap the ocean depths and encourage the arts and commerce.

Let both sides unite to heed in all corners of the earth the command of Isaiah—to "undo the heavy burdens . . . [and] let the oppressed go free."

And if a beachhead of cooperation may push back the jungles of suspicion, let both sides join in creating a new endeavor—not a new balance of power, but a new world of law, where the strong are just and the weak secure and the peace preserved.

All this will not be finished in the first 100 days. Nor will it be finished in the first 1,000 days, nor in the life of this Administration, nor even perhaps in our lifetime on this planet. But let us begin.

In your hands, my fellow citizens, more than mine, will rest the final success or failure of our course. Since this country was founded, each generation of Americans has been summoned to give testimony to its national loyalty. The graves of young Americans who answered the call to service surround the globe.

Now the trumpet summons us again—not as a call to bear arms, though arms we need—not as a call to battle, though embattled we are—but a call to bear the burden of a long twilight struggle year in and year out, "rejoicing in hope, patient in tribulation"—a struggle against the common enemies of man: tyranny, poverty, disease and war itself.

Can we forge against these enemies a grand and global alliance, north and south, east and west, that can assure a more fruitful life for all mankind? Will you join in that historic effort?

In the long history of the world, only a few generations have been granted the role of defending freedom in its hour of maximum danger. I do not shrink from this responsibility—I welcome it. I do not believe that any of us would exchange places with any other people or any other generation. The energy, the faith, the devotion which we bring to this endeavor will light our country and all who serve it—and the glow from that fire can truly light the world.

And so, my fellow Americans: ask not what your country can do for you—ask what you can do for your country.

My fellow citizens of the world: ask not what America will do for you, but what together we can do for the freedom of man.

Finally, whether you are citizens of America or citizens of the world, ask of us here the same high standards of strength and sacrifice which we ask of you. With a good conscience our only sure reward, with history the final judge of our deeds, let us go forth to lead the land we love, asking His blessing and His help, but knowing that here on earth God's work must truly be our own.

LYNDON B. JOHNSON: VOTING RIGHTS ACT ADDRESS

I speak tonight for the dignity of man and the destiny of democracy.

I urge every member of both parties—Americans of all religions and of all colors—from every section of this country—to join me in that cause.

At times history and fate meet at a single time in a single place to shape a turning point in man's unending search for freedom. So it was at Lexington and Concord. So it was a century ago at Appomattox. So it was last week in Selma, Alabama.

There is no Negro problem. There is no southern problem. There is no northern problem. There is only an American problem.

And we are met here tonight as Americans—not as Democrats or Republicans—we are met here as Americans to solve that problem.

This was the first nation in the history of the world to be founded with a purpose. The great phrases of that purpose still sound in every American heart, north and south: "All men are created equal"—"Government by consent of the governed"—"Give me liberty or give me death.". . .

Those words are a promise to every citizen that he shall share in the dignity of man. This dignity cannot be found in man's possessions. It cannot be found in his power or in his position. It really rests on his right to be treated as a man equal in opportunity to all others. It says that he shall share in freedom, he shall choose his leaders, educate his children, provide for his family according to his ability and his merits as a human being. . . .

Many of the issues of civil rights are very complex and most difficult. But about this there can and should be no argument. Every American citizen must have an equal right to vote. There is no reason which can excuse the denial of that right. There is no duty which weighs more heavily on us than the duty we have to ensure that right.

Yet the harsh fact is that in many places in this country men and women are kept from voting simply because they are Negroes. . . .

Experience has clearly shown that the existing process of law cannot overcome systematic and ingenious discrimination. No law that we now have on the books—and I have helped to put three of them there—can ensure the right to vote when local officials are determined to deny it.

In such a case our duty must be clear to all of us. The Constitution says that no person shall be kept from voting because of his race or his color. We have all sworn an oath before God to support and to defend that Constitution.

We must now act in obedience to that oath.

Wednesday I will send to Congress a law designed to eliminate illegal barriers to the right to vote. . . .

To those who seek to avoid action by their National Government in their home communities—who want to and who seek to maintain purely local control over elections—the answer is simple. Open your polling places to all your people. Allow men and women to register and vote whatever the color of their skin. Extend the rights of citizenship to every citizen of this land. There is no constitutional issue here. The command of the Constitution is plain. There is no moral issue. It is wrong—deadly wrong—to deny any of your fellow Americans the right to vote in this country. There is no issue of States rights or National rights. There is only the struggle for human rights.

I have not the slightest doubt what will be your answer. . . .

But even if we pass this bill, the battle will not be over. What happened in Selma is part of a far larger movement which reaches into every section and State of America. It is the effort of American Negroes to secure for themselves the full blessings of American life.

Their cause must be our cause too, because it is not just Negroes but really it is all of us, who must overcome the crippling legacy of bigotry and injustice. And we shall overcome. . . .

This great, rich, restless country can offer opportunity and education and hope to all—all black and white, all North and South, sharecropper and city dweller. These are the enemies—poverty, ignorance, disease—they are our enemies, not our fellow man, not our neighbor. And these enemies too—poverty, disease, and ignorance—we shall overcome.

RONALD W. REAGAN: FIRST INAUGURAL ADDRESS

To a few of us here today, this is a solemn and most momentous occasion; and yet, in the history of our Nation, it is a commonplace occurrence. The orderly transfer of authority as called for in the Constitution routinely takes place as it has for almost two centuries and few of us stop to think how unique we really are. In the eyes of many in the world, this every-4-year ceremony we accept as normal is nothing less than a miracle.

Mr. President, I want our fellow citizens to know how much you did to carry on this tradition. By your gracious cooperation in the transition process, you have shown a watching world that we are a united people pledged to maintaining a political system which guarantees individual liberty to a greater degree than any other, and I thank you and your people for all your help in maintaining the continuity which is the bulwark of our Republic.

The business of our nation goes forward. These United States are confronted with an economic affliction of great proportions. We suffer from the longest and one of the worst sustained inflations in our national history. It distorts our economic decisions, penalizes thrift, and crushes the struggling young and the fixed-income elderly alike. It threatens to shatter the lives of millions of our people. Idle industries have cast workers into unemployment, causing human misery and personal indignity.

Those who do work are denied a fair return for their labor by a tax system which penalizes successful achievement and keeps us from maintaining full productivity. But great as our tax burden is, it has not kept pace with public spending. For decades, we have piled deficit upon deficit, mortgaging our future and our children's future for the temporary convenience of the present. To continue this long trend is to guarantee tremendous social, cultural, political, and economic upheavals. You and I, as individuals, can, by borrowing, live beyond our means, but for only a limited period of time.

Why, then, should we think that collectively, as a nation, we are not bound by that same limitation? We must act today in order to preserve tomorrow. And let there be no misunderstanding—we are going to begin to act, beginning today. The economic ills we suffer have come upon us over several decades. They will not go away in days, weeks, or months, but they will go away. They will go away because we, as Americans, have the capacity now, as we have had in the past, to do whatever needs to be done to preserve this last and greatest bastion of freedom.

In this present crisis, government is not the solution to our problem. From time to time, we have been tempted to believe that society has become too complex to be managed by self-rule, that government by an elite group is superior to government for, by, and of the people. But if no one among us is capable of governing himself, then who among us has the capacity to govern someone else? All of us together, in and out of government, must bear the burden. The solutions we seek must be equitable, with no one group singled out to pay a higher price.

We hear much of special interest groups. Our concern must be for a special interest group that has been too long neglected. It knows no sectional boundaries or ethnic and racial divisions, and it crosses political party lines. It is made up of men and women who raise our food, patrol our streets, man our mines and our factories, teach our children, keep our homes, and heal us when we are sick—professionals, industrialists, shopkeepers, clerks, cabbies, and truckdrivers. They are, in short, "We the people," this breed called Americans.

Well, this administration's objective will be a healthy, vigorous, growing economy that provides equal opportunity for all Americans, with no barriers born of bigotry or discrimination. Putting America back to work means putting all Americans back to work. Ending inflation means freeing all Americans from the terror of runaway living costs. All must share in the productive work of this "new beginning" and all must share in the bounty of a revived economy. With the idealism and fair play which are the core of our system and our strength, we can have a strong and prosperous America at peace with itself and the world. So, as we begin, let us take inventory.

We are a nation that has a government—not the other way around. And this makes us special among the nations of the Earth. Our Government has no power except that granted it by the people. It is time to check and reverse the growth of government which shows signs of having grown beyond the consent of the governed.

It is my intention to curb the size and influence of the Federal establishment and to demand recognition of the distinction between the powers granted to the Federal Government and those reserved to the States or to the people. All of us need to be reminded that the Federal Government did not create the States; the States created the Federal Government. Now, so there will be no misunderstanding, it is not my intention to do away with government. It is, rather, to make it work—work with us, not over us; to stand by our side, not ride on our back. Government can and must provide opportunity, not smother it; foster productivity, not stifle it.

If we look to the answer as to why, for so many years, we achieved so much, prospered as no other people on Earth, it was because here, in this land, we unleashed the energy and individual genius of man to a greater extent than has ever been done before. Freedom and the dignity of the individual have been more available and assured here than in any other place on Earth. The price for this freedom at times has been high, but we have never been unwilling to pay that price. It is no coincidence that our present troubles parallel and are proportionate to the intervention and intrusion in our lives that result from unnecessary and excessive growth of government.

It is time for us to realize that we are too great a nation to limit ourselves to small dreams. We are not, as some would have us believe, loomed to an inevitable decline. I do not believe in a fate that will fall on us no matter what we do. I do believe in a fate that will fall on us if we do nothing.

So, with all the creative energy at our command, let us begin an era of national renewal. Let us renew our determination, our courage, and our strength. And let us renew; our faith and our hope. We have every right to dream heroic dreams. Those who say that we are in a time when there are no heroes just don't know where to look. You can see heroes every day going in and out of factory gates. Others, a handful in number, produce enough food to feed all of us and then the world beyond. You meet heroes across a counter—and they are on both sides of that counter. There are entrepreneurs with faith in themselves and faith in an idea who create new jobs, new wealth and opportunity. They are individuals and families whose taxes support the Government and whose voluntary gifts support church, charity, culture, art, and education. Their patriotism is quiet but deep. Their values sustain our national life.

I have used the words "they" and "their" in speaking of these heroes. I could say "you" and "your" because I am addressing the heroes of whom I speak—you, the citizens of this blessed land. Your dreams, your hopes, your goals are going to be the dreams, the hopes, and the goals of this administration, so help me God. We shall reflect the compassion that is so much a part of your makeup. How can we love our country and not love our countrymen, and loving them, reach out a hand when they fall, heal them when they are sick, and provide opportunities to make them self-sufficient so they will be equal in fact and not just in theory? Can we solve the problems confronting us? Well, the answer is an unequivocal and emphatic "yes." To paraphrase Winston Churchill, I did not take the oath I have just taken with the intention of presiding over the dissolution of the world's strongest economy. In the days ahead I will propose removing the roadblocks that have slowed our economy and reduced productivity. Steps will be taken aimed at restoring the balance between the various levels of government. Progress may be slow—measured in inches and feet, not miles—but we will progress.

It is time to reawaken this industrial giant, to get government back within its means, and to lighten our punitive tax burden. And these will be our first priorities, and on these principles, there will be no compromise. On the eve of our struggle for independence a man who might have been one of the greatest among the Founding Fathers, Dr. Joseph Warren, President of the Massachusetts Congress, said to his fellow Americans, "Our country is in danger, but not to be despaired of. . . . On you depend the fortunes of America. You are to decide the important questions upon which rests the happiness and the liberty of millions yet unborn. Act worthy of yourselves."

Well, I believe we, the Americans of today, are ready to act worthy of ourselves, ready to do what must be done to ensure happiness and liberty for ourselves, our children and our children's children. And as we renew ourselves here in our own land, we will be seen as having greater strength throughout the world. We will again be the exemplar of freedom and a beacon of hope for those who do not now have freedom.

To those neighbors and allies who share our freedom, we will strengthen our historic ties and assure them of our support and firm commitment. We will match loyalty with loyalty. We will strive for mutually beneficial relations. We will not use our friendship to impose on their sovereignty, for our own sovereignty is not for sale.

As for the enemies of freedom, those who are potential adversaries, they will be reminded that peace is the highest aspiration of the American people. We will negotiate for it, sacrifice for it; we will not surrender for it—now or ever. Our forbearance should never be misunderstood. Our reluctance for conflict should not be misjudged as a failure of will. When action is required to preserve our national security, we will act. We will maintain sufficient strength to prevail if need be, knowing that if we do so we have the best chance of never having to use that strength.

Above all, we must realize that no arsenal, or no weapon in the arsenals of the world, is so formidable as the will and moral courage of free men and women. It is a weapon our adversaries in today's world do not have. It is a weapon that we as Americans do have. Let that be understood by those who practice terrorism and prey upon their neighbors. I am told that tens of thousands of prayer meetings are being held on this day, and for that I am deeply grateful. We are a nation under God, and I believe God intended for us to be free. It would be fitting and good, I think, if on each Inauguration Day in future years it should be declared a day of prayer.

This is the first time in history that this ceremony has been held, as you have been told, on this West Front of the Capitol. Standing here, one faces a magnificent vista, opening up on this city's special beauty and history. At the end of this open mall are those shrines to the giants on whose shoulders we stand. Directly in front of me, the monument to a monumental man: George Washington, Father of our country. A man of humility who came to greatness reluctantly. He led America out of revolutionary victory into infant nationhood. Off to one side, the stately memorial to Thomas Jefferson. The Declaration of Independence flames with his eloquence. And then beyond the Reflecting Pool the dignified columns of the Lincoln Memorial. Whoever would understand in his heart the meaning of America will find it in the life of Abraham Lincoln. Beyond those monuments to heroism is the Potomac River, and on the far shore the sloping hills of Arlington National Cemetery with its row on row of simple white markers bearing crosses or Stars of David. They add up to only a tiny fraction of the price that has been paid for our freedom. Each one of those markers is a monument to the kinds of heroes I spoke of earlier. Their lives ended in places called Belleau Wood. The Argonne, Omaha Beach, Salerno and halfway around the world on Guadalcanal, Tarawa, Pork Chop Hill, the Chosin Reservoir, and in a hundred rice paddies and jungles of a place called Vietnam.

Under one such marker lies a young man—Martin Treptow—who left his job in a small town barber shop in 1917 to go to France with the famed Rainbow Division. There, on the western front, he was killed trying to carry a message between battalions under heavy artillery fire. We are told that on his body was found a diary. On the flyleaf under the heading, "My Pledge," he had written these words: "America must win this war. Therefore, I will work, I will save, I will sacrifice, I will endure, I will fight cheerfully and do my utmost, as if the issue of the whole struggle depended on me alone."

The crisis we are facing today does not require of us the kind of sacrifice that Martin Treptow and so many thousands of others were called upon to make. It does require, however, our best effort, and our willingness to believe in ourselves and to believe in our capacity to perform great deeds; to believe that together, with God's help, we can and will resolve the problems which now confront us. And, after all, why shouldn't we believe that? We are Americans. God bless you, and thank you.

LEGAL SCHOLARSHIP

Since the nineteenth century, the role of lawyers and the nature of law in U.S. society have been the subject of ongoing debate and scrutiny. Legal scholars and practitioners have discussed whether the law is a self-contained body of rules, displaying logic and reason. Some have embraced this view and have aspired to make law a science. Since the early twentieth century, however, other important legal figures have expressed skepticism about the inner logic of the law, preferring to see legal rulings as responses to immediate social, political, and economic pressures. These skeptics eventually became known as legal realists, a school of thought that can be traced to the scholar and jurist Oliver Wendell Holmes, Jr.

The French writer Alexis de Tocqueville visited the United States in the 1830s and wrote about his travels in *Democracy in America* (1835), one of the classic works of social analysis. Tocqueville, a nobleman, was struck by the democratic character of U.S. society and devoted a section of his work to the role of lawyers and judges. He concluded that lawyers were vital to the preservation of civil order and democracy.

Lawyers have also been the target of popular criticism. In the late eighteenth and early nineteenth century, U.S. critics contended that lawyers and judges conspired to make the law a mysterious body of arcane language and procedures that needlessly complicated problems. Robert Rantoul, Jr., a Massachusetts attorney and member of Congress, was a prominent spokesman for the codification movement, which attacked the common law as unsuitable for a democratic republic. In a famous 1836 oration, Rantoul charged that "judge-made law is *ex post facto* law, and therefore unjust." People could not know the law because "no one knows what the law is before [the judge] lays it down." Moreover, a judge was able to rule differently from case to case.

For Rantoul and others, the only solution was to abandon the common-law system and codify all laws into one book that everyone could read and understand. The codification movement had limited success during the nineteenth century. Rantoul advocated a code but never tried to write one. David Dudley Field, a New York attorney, wrote what became known as the Field Code of civil procedure. His code was enacted in twenty-four states, most of them in the West.

The education and training of lawyers began to change in the nineteenth century. Traditionally, the most popular method of becoming a lawyer had been "reading the law" in a law office, learning legal rules and procedures under the tutelage of a practicing attorney. As the century progressed, however, more law schools were opened. The law school curriculum consisted of attending lectures, reading legal treatises, and memorizing legal rules and concepts. Christopher Columbus Langdell changed the course of U.S. legal education when he published his contracts casebook in 1871. Langdell, a professor and dean of Harvard Law School, introduced the case method, which required students to read judicial opinions and analyze the key points of each case. The Socratic method of logical inquiry was an integral part of the program: professors called on students in class, asked them to present their analysis, and challenged their presentation.

463

Langdell also embraced the nineteenth century's belief in progress and in the superiority of scientific inquiry. Langdell's conclusion that the law could be a science became a tenet of legal scholarship, but he was eventually challenged by Oliver Wendell Holmes, Jr. Holmes, a professor and scholar before serving on the Supreme Judicial Court of Massachusetts and the U.S. Supreme Court, rejected the assumption that law was a science or a logical system.

Holmes wrote a set of legal essays that was published in 1881 as *The Common Law*. In this volume, which is the most renowned work of legal philosophy in U.S. history, Holmes systematically analyzed, classified, and explained various aspects of U.S. common law, ranging from torts to contracts to crime and punishment. He concluded that:

> The life of the law has not been logic: it has been experience. The felt necessities of the time, the prevalent moral and political theories, intuitions of public policy, avowed or unconscious, even the prejudices which judges share with their fellow-men, have had a good deal more to do than the syllogism in determining the rules by which men should be governed.

By the beginning of the twentieth century, the United States had become an industrialized, urban nation. Some lawyers and legal scholars attempted to inject new ideas and information into the law in hopes of overturning stubbornly held doctrines and restoring public confidence in a legal system that appeared to be unprepared to face the realities of the new century. Famed lawyer and later Supreme Court justice Louis D. Brandeis revolutionized the law by submitting what has come to be known as the "Brandeis brief" in *Muller v. Oregon*, 208 U.S. 412, 28 S. Ct. 324, 52 L. Ed. 551 (1908). The brief contained sociological information on the health and well-being of women that Brandeis believed was relevant to deciding whether an Oregon law limiting work hours for women was constitutional. The U.S. Supreme Court upheld the law, lending credibility to Brandeis's use of nonlegal information.

Roscoe Pound, a scholar, teacher, reformer, and dean of Harvard Law School, worked to link law and society through his sociological jurisprudence and to improve the administration of the judicial system. His 1906 speech, "The Causes of Popular Dissatisfaction with the Administration of Justice," was a call to improve court administration and a preview of his theory of law. In 1908 he published "Mechanical Jurisprudence," attacking the notion that an unchanging and inflexible natural law formed the basis for the common law.

The twentieth century also saw the growth of law through legislation. As state legislatures and the U.S. Congress enacted more statutes containing complex and often unclear provisions, the courts were called upon to interpret these laws by using various rules of statutory construction to determine legislative purpose. In 1947, Harvard law professor and later Supreme Court justice Felix Frankfurter delivered a lecture entitled "Some Reflections on the Reading of Statutes," which expounds on the effect that legislative law has on the courts. Fifty years later, the torrent of legislation remains unabated.

Lawyers and Judges

Alexis de Tocqueville, a French political scientist, historian, and politician, is best known for *Democracy in America* (1835). A believer in democracy, he was concerned about the concentration of power in the hands of a centralized government. During his visit to the United States in 1831 and 1832, Tocqueville observed the deep social and political divisions produced by slavery. He was impressed, however, by the power of a free press and the importance that citizens placed upon the legal system.

In his observations on lawyers and judges, Tocqueville noted that U.S. courts of law possessed enormous political power. Judges had the power of judicial review, which allowed them to strike down laws as unconstitutional. He also observed that lawyers were active in politics, bringing to government and the political arena the knowledge, skills, and temperament peculiar to their profession. Tocqueville pointed out that lawyers are wedded to the public order and are often conservative. He concluded that "lawyers belong to the people by birth and interest, and to the aristocracy by habit and taste; they may be looked upon as the connecting link between the two great classes of society."

What Shall Be Done with the Practice of the Courts?

David Dudley Field was an attorney from a prominent New York family. His brother was Stephen J. Field, a U.S. Supreme Court justice. Field was a leading crusader for the codification movement. He attacked the rules of civil procedure of his time, which were based on English common-law pleading practices. Common-law pleading was an arcane practice filled with traps for the uninitiated that could result in the dismissal of the case on procedural grounds.

Field's essay of 1847, "What Shall Be Done with the Practice of the Courts," presented his case for what is now known as code pleading.

As a member of the New York pleading and practice commission, Field prepared a civil procedure code that the legislature adopted in 1848. The code simplified the filing and prosecution of lawsuits. It was a significant improvement over common-law systems of procedure, in that it required that the complaint contain "a plain and concise statement of the facts constituting plaintiff's cause of action." The code used the pleading as a way of narrowing and defining the dispute rather than as a general means of initiating a civil action.

The Field Code was later adopted by Missouri, California, and many other states. In time, however, code pleading became very technical, requiring the pleader to set forth the facts underlying and demonstrating the existence of the cause of action. Matters were simplified in 1938, when the Federal Rules of Civil Procedure were adopted. Rule 8(a) provides that the complaint shall contain "a short and plain statement of the claim showing that the pleader is entitled to relief." Likewise, the defendant "shall state in short and plain terms" the defenses to the plaintiff's complaint. There is no requirement that facts be alleged.

In the twentieth century, the desire for codification led to the drafting of various sets of uniform laws, including the Uniform Commercial Code and the Uniform Probate Code.

Contracts

The 1871 publication of *A Selection of Cases on the Law of Contracts* by Christopher Columbus Langdell revolutionized legal education. The book, which consisted of a collection of mostly English judicial opinions, was meant to assist the professor in developing within the student a scientific approach to the law. Langdell chose the cases for the fundamental principles they contained. Students were expected to dispense with the idea that they were attending a vocational school. Instead, they were to apply the principles they learned in the scientific search for truth. In his preface Langdell said that he sought to "select, classify, and arrange all cases which had contributed in any important degree to the growth, development, or establishment of any of its essential doctrines."

The Path of the Law

Oliver Wendell Holmes, Jr., is one of the most celebrated legal figures in U.S. history. His writings on jurisprudence have shaped discussions on the nature of law, and his court opinions have been studied as much for their style as their intellectual content.

Holmes rejected the idea that law could be studied as a science. He also emphatically dismissed Langdell's belief that legal systems obey rules of logic. While his book, *The Common Law* (1881), is a scholarly tour de force, his 1897 essay, "The Path of Law," has proved to be one of the most influential works in legal theory. In the essay Holmes builds on the themes of *The Common Law*, which included his disassociation of law from morality and his emphasis on policy over logic. He went on to define the law as a prediction of what the courts would do in a particular situation. He proposed a "bad man" theory of justice: a bad man will want to know only what the material consequences of his conduct will be; he will not be motivated by morality or conscience.

Holmes's jurisprudence led to the conclusion that judges make decisions first and then come up with reasons to explain them. His approach, which has been characterized as cynical, touched a nerve with succeeding generations of legal scholars.

Brief for the Defendant in Error, Muller v. Oregon

In *Muller v. Oregon* in 1908, the U.S. Supreme Court upheld an Oregon law that prohibited the employment of women for more than ten hours a day. The decision was based in large part on a brief submitted by Louis D. Brandeis in support of the law. The brief emphasized the differences between women and men and presented information showing that long work hours could have injurious effects on the health and welfare of women and their children, including their unborn children. The Court unanimously agreed, noting that "woman's physical structure and the performance of maternal functions place her at a disadvantage in the struggle for subsistence."

The Brandeis brief signaled a change in the type of evidence a court would consider in determining a case. With the growth of the social sciences, quantitative and qualitative studies conducted by researchers would increasingly find their way into U.S. courtrooms.

Mechanical Jurisprudence

Roscoe Pound followed in Holmes's footsteps. In "Mechanical Jurisprudence" (1908), Pound coined the term *mechanical jurisprudence* to refer to the common but odious practice whereby judges woodenly applied previous precedents to the facts of cases without regard to the consequences. For Pound, the logic of previous precedents alone would not solve jurisprudential problems. The essay decries the ossification of legal concepts into self-evident truths.

In opposition to mechanical jurisprudence, Pound offered his theory of sociological jurisprudence. He acknowledged that the common law contains some constant principles, particularly in regard to methods. He gave these principles the name "taught legal tradition." Pound believed that the implementation of this taught legal tradition by wise common-law judges resulted in substantive change, which reflected changes in society. As the interpreters of the common law, judges had a special duty to consider the practical effects of their decisions and to strive to ensure that they facilitated rather than hindered societal growth.

The Causes of Popular Dissatisfaction with the Administration of Justice

Roscoe Pound presented "The Causes of Popular Dissatisfaction with the Administration of Justice" at the annual convention of the American Bar Association in 1906. The lecture was a call to improve court administration and a preview of his theory of law. It has remained a classic statement on the need for efficient and equitable judicial administration.

Pound acknowledged that some people have always been dissatisfied with the law, but he contended that the courts did indeed need to be administered more effectively. He also noted that the adversary system often turned litigation into a game, irritating parties, jurors, and witnesses and giving the public the "false notion of the purpose and end of law." In addition, he attacked the overlapping jurisdiction of courts and argued that each state had too many courts.

In 1909 Pound organized the First National Conference on Criminal Law and Criminology, which gathered participants from many professions to discuss ways to reform the criminal law. The conference was one of the first of Pound's efforts to give practical application to sociological jurisprudence. Later, in 1929 President Herbert Hoover appointed Pound to the Wickersham Commission, the popular name for the National Commission on Law Observance and Enforcement. This commission conducted the first comprehensive national study of crime and law enforcement in U.S. history. The findings of the commission, which were published in fourteen volumes in 1931 and 1932, covered every aspect of the criminal justice system, including the causes of crime, police and prosecutorial procedures, and the importance of probation and parole.

Pound's lecture is a treasure trove of ideas concerning the management of courts. The area of court administration has grown since the 1960s, and court administrators now play an active role in monitoring and managing caseloads. Many states have also heeded Pound's advice and unified their trial courts, thereby eliminating several layers of courts.

Some Reflections on the Reading of Statutes

By 1947, when Felix Frankfurter delivered "Some Reflections on the Reading of Statutes" to New York City's bar association, he had been on the U.S. Supreme Court eight years. From 1914 until his appointment to the Court in 1939, Frankfurter had been a professor at Harvard Law School.

In his reflections Frankfurter noted that the work of the Supreme Court had changed over the years. In the nineteenth and early twentieth centuries, it heard a declining number of common-law cases. By the 1940s, not one case involved common law. This meant that the Supreme Court had become primarily an interpreter of statutes.

Frankfurter's essay discusses issues that have remained contentious. How does a judge divine legislative intent? What rules of construction should a judge apply to a statute? In the act of interpreting a statute, is the judge identifying legislative intent or acting as a surrogate legislator?

LAWYERS AND JUDGES

ALEXIS DE TOCQUEVILLE, 1835

Whenever a law that the judge holds to be unconstitutional is invoked in a tribunal of the United States, he may refuse to admit it as a rule; this power is the only one peculiar to the American magistrate, but it gives rise to immense political influence. In truth, few laws can escape the searching analysis of the judicial power for any length of time, for there are few that are not prejudicial to some private interest or other, and none that may not be brought before a court of justice by the choice of parties or by the necessity of the case. But as soon as a judge has refused to apply any given law in a case, that law immediately loses a portion of its moral force.

*   *   *

Within these limits the power vested in the American courts of justice of pronouncing a statute to be unconstitutional forms one of the most powerful barriers that have ever been devised against the tyranny of political assemblies.

*   *   *

When we have examined in detail the organization of the [United States] Supreme Court and the entire prerogatives which it exercises, we shall readily admit that a more imposing judicial power was never constituted by any people. The Supreme Court is placed higher than any other known tribunal, both by the nature of its rights and the class of justiciable parties which it controls.

*   *   *

The peace, the prosperity, and the very existence of the Union are vested in the hands of the seven Federal judges [of the United States Supreme Court]. Without them the Constitution would be a dead letter: the executive appeals to them for assistance against the encroachments of the legislative power; the legislature demands their protection against the assaults of the executive; they defend the Union from the disobedience of the states, the states from the exaggerated claims of the Union, the public interest against private interests, and the conservative spirit of stability against the fickleness of the democracy. Their power is enormous, but it is the power of public opinion. They are all-powerful as long as the people respect the law; but they would be impotent against popular neglect or contempt of the law. The force of public opinion is the most intractable of agents, because its exact limits cannot be defined; and it is not less dangerous to exceed than to remain below the boundary prescribed.

*   *   *

Democratic laws generally tend to promote the welfare of the greatest possible number; for they emanate from the majority of the citizens, who are subject to error, but who cannot have an interest opposed to their own advantage. The laws of an aristocracy tend, on the contrary, to

From *Democracy in America*.

concentrate wealth and power in the hands of the minority; because an aristocracy, by its very nature, constitutes a minority. It may therefore be asserted, as a general proposition, that the purpose of a democracy in its legislation is more useful to humanity than that of an aristocracy. This, however, is the sum total of its advantages.

* * *

No political form has hitherto been discovered that is equally favorable to the prosperity and the development of all the classes into which society is divided. These classes continue to form, as it were, so many distinct communities in the same nation; and experience has shown that it is no less dangerous to place the fate of these classes exclusively in the hands of any one of them than it is to make one people the arbiter of the destiny of another. When the rich alone govern, the interest of the poor is always endangered; and when the poor make the laws, that of the rich incurs very serious risks. The advantage of democracy does not consist, therefore, as has sometimes been asserted, in favoring the prosperity of all, but simply in contributing to the well-being of the greatest number.

The men who are entrusted with the direction of public affairs in the United States are frequently inferior, in both capacity and morality, to those whom an aristocracy would raise to power. But their interest is identified and mingled with that of the majority of their fellow citizens. They may frequently be faithless and frequently mistaken, but they will never systematically adopt a line of conduct hostile to the majority; and they cannot give a dangerous or exclusive tendency to the government.

* * *

It is not always feasible to consult the whole people, either directly or indirectly, in the formation of law; but it cannot be denied that, when this is possible, the authority of law is much augmented. This popular origin which impairs the excellence and the wisdom of legislation, contributes much to increase its power. There is an amazing strength in the expression of the will of a whole people; and when it declares itself, even the imagination of those who would wish to contest it is overawed. The truth of this fact is well known by parties, and they consequently strive to make out a majority whenever they can. If they have not the greater number of voters on their side, they assert that the true majority abstained from voting; and if they are foiled even there, they have recourse to those persons who had no right to vote.

In the United States, except slaves, servants, and paupers supported by the townships, there is no class of persons who do not exercise the elective franchise and who do not indirectly contribute to make the laws. Those who wish to attack the laws must consequently either change the opinion of the nation or trample upon its decision.

A second reason, which is still more direct and weighty, may be adduced: in the United States everyone is personally interested in enforcing the obedience of the whole community to the law; for as the minority may shortly rally the majority to its principles, it is interested in professing that respect for the decrees of the legislator which it may soon have occasion to claim for its own. However irksome an enactment may be, the citizen of the United States complies with it, not only because it is the work of the majority, but because it is his own, and he regards it as a contract to which he is himself a party.

In the United States, then, that numerous and turbulent multitude does not exist who, regarding the law as their natural enemy, look upon it with fear and distrust. It is impossible, on the contrary, not to perceive that all classes display the utmost reliance upon the legislation of their country and are attached to it by a kind of parental affection.

* * *

In visiting the Americans and studying their laws, we perceive that the authority they have entrusted to members of the legal profession, and the influence that these individuals exercise in the government, are the most powerful existing security against the excesses of democracy. This effect seems to me to result from a general cause, which it is useful to investigate, as it may be reproduced elsewhere. . . .

Men who have made a special study of the laws derive from [that] occupation certain habits of order, a taste for formalities, and a kind of instinctive regard for the regular connection of ideas, which naturally render them very hostile to the revolutionary spirit and the unreflecting passions of the multitude.

The special information that lawyers derive from their studies ensures them a separate rank in society, and they constitute a sort of privileged body in the scale of intellect. This notion of their superiority perpetually recurs to them in the practice of their profession: they are the masters of a science which is necessary, but not very generally known; they serve as arbiters between the citizens; and the habit of directing to their purpose the blind passions of parties in litigation inspires them with a certain contempt for the judgment of the multitude. Add to this that they naturally constitute a body; not by any previous understanding, or by an agreement that directs them to a common end; but the analogy of their studies and the uniformity of their methods connect their minds as a common interest might unite their endeavors.

Some of the tastes and the habits of the aristocracy may consequently be discovered in the characters of lawyers. They participate in the same instinctive love of order and formalities; and they entertain the same repugnance to the actions of the multitude, and the same secret contempt of the government of the people. I do not mean to say that the natural propensities of lawyers are sufficiently strong to sway them irresistibly; for they, like most other men, are governed by their private interests, and especially by the interests of the moment.

* * *

I do not, then, assert that all the members of the legal profession are at all times the friends of order and the opponents of innovation, but merely that most of them are usually so. In a community to which lawyers are allowed to occupy without opposition that high station which naturally belongs to them, their general spirit will be eminently conservative and anti-democratic. When an aristocracy excludes the leaders of that profession from its ranks, it excites enemies who are the more formidable as they are independent of the nobility by their labors and feel themselves to be their equals in intelligence though inferior in opulence and power.

* * *

Lawyers are attached to public order beyond every other consideration, and the best security of public order is authority. It must not be forgotten, also, that if they prize freedom much, they generally value legality still more; they are less afraid of tyranny than of arbitrary power; and, provided the legislature undertakes of itself to deprive men of their independence, they are not dissatisfied.

* * *

The government of democracy is favorable to the political power of lawyers; for when the wealthy, the noble, and the prince are excluded from the government, the lawyers take possession of it, in their own right, as it were, since they are the only men of information and sagacity, beyond the sphere of the people, who can be the object of the popular choice. If, then, they are led by their tastes towards the aristocracy and the prince, they are brought in contact with the people by their interests. They like the government of democracy without participating in its propensities and without imitating its weaknesses; whence they derive a two-fold authority from it and over it. The people in democratic states do not mistrust the members of the legal profession, because it is known that they are interested to serve the popular cause; and the people listen to them without irritation, because they do not attribute to them any sinister designs. The lawyers do not, indeed, wish to overthrow the institutions of democracy, but they constantly endeavor to turn it away from its real direction by means that are foreign to its nature. Lawyers belong to the people by birth and interest, and to the aristocracy by habit and taste; they may be looked upon as the connecting link between the two great classes of society.

The profession of the law is the only aristocratic element that can be amalgamated without violence with the natural elements of democracy and be advantageously and permanently combined with them. I am not ignorant of the defects inherent in the character of this body of men; but without this admixture of lawyer-like sobriety with the democratic principle, I question whether democratic institutions could long be maintained; and I cannot believe that a republic could hope to exist at the present time if the influence of lawyers in public business did not increase in proportion to the power of the people.

* * *

In America there are no nobles or literary men, and the people are apt to mistrust the wealthy; lawyers consequently form the highest political class and the most cultivated portion of society. They have therefore nothing to gain by innovation, which adds a conservative interest to their natural taste for public order. If I were asked where I place the American aristocracy, I should reply without hesitation that it is not among the rich, who are united by no common tie, but that it occupies the judicial bench and the bar.

The more we reflect upon all that occurs in the United States, the more we shall be persuaded that the lawyers, as a body, form the most powerful, if not the only, counterpoise to the democratic element. In that country we easily perceive how the legal profession is qualified by its attributes, and even by its faults, to neutralize the vices inherent in popular government. When the American people are intoxicated by passion or carried away by the impetuosity of their ideas, they are checked and stopped by the almost invisible influence of their legal counselors. These secretly oppose their aristocratic propensities to the nation's democratic instincts, their superstitious attachment to what is old to its love of novelty, their narrow views to its immense designs, and their habitual procrastination to its ardent impatience.

The courts of justice are the visible organs by which the legal profession is enabled to control the democracy. The judge is a lawyer who, independently of the taste for regularity and order that he has contracted in the study of law, derives an additional love of stability from the inalienability of his own functions. His legal attainments have already raised him to a distinguished rank among his fellows; his political power completes the distinction of his station and gives him the instincts of the privileged classes.

*   *   *

It must not be supposed, moreover, that the legal spirit is confined in the United States to the courts of justice; it extends far beyond them. As the lawyers form the only enlightened class whom the people do not mistrust, they are naturally called upon to occupy most of the public stations. They fill the legislative assemblies and are at the head of the administration; they consequently exercise a powerful influence upon the formation of the law and upon its execution. The lawyers are obliged, however, to yield to the current public opinion, which is too strong for them to resist; but it is easy to find indications of what they would do if they were free to act. The Americans, who have made so many innovations in their political laws, have introduced very sparing alterations in their civil laws, and that with great difficulty, although many of these laws are repugnant to their social condition. The reason for this is that in matters of civil law the majority are obliged to defer to the authority of the legal profession, and the American lawyers are disinclined to innovate when they are left to their own choice.

*   *   *

The influence of legal habits extends beyond the precise limits I have pointed out. Scarcely any political question arises in the United States that is not resolved, sooner or later, into a judicial question. Hence all parties are obliged to borrow, in their daily controversies, the ideas, and even the language, peculiar to judicial proceedings. As most public men are or have been legal practitioners, they introduce the customs and technicalities of their profession into the management of public affairs. The jury extends this habit to all classes. The language of the law thus becomes, in some measure, a vulgar tongue; the spirit of the law, which is produced in the schools and courts of justice, gradually penetrates beyond their walls into the bosom of society, where it descends to the lowest classes, so that at last the whole people contract the habits and the tastes of the judicial magistrate. The lawyers of the United States form a party which is but little feared and scarcely perceived, which has no badge peculiar to itself, which adapts itself with great flexibility to the exigencies of the time and accommodates itself without resistance to all the movements of the social body. But this party extends over the whole community and penetrates into all the classes which compose it; it acts upon the country imperceptibly, but finally fashions it to suit its own purposes.

WHAT SHALL BE DONE WITH THE PRACTICE OF THE COURTS?

DAVID DUDLEY FIELD, 1847

The Constitution of this State [New York, 1846], which goes into effect to-day, will render great changes necessary in our system of legal procedure. It remodels our Courts; unites the administration of law and equity in the same tribunal; directs testimony to be taken in like manner in both classes of cases; abolishes the offices of Master and Examiner in Chancery, hitherto important parts of our equity system; and, finally, directs that the next Legislature shall provide for the appointment of three commissioners, "whose duty it shall be to revise, reform, simplify, and abridge the rules of practice, pleadings, forms, and proceedings of the courts of record," and report thereon to the Legislature for its action.

Important modifications of the equity practice are thus made indispensable, in order to adapt it to the new mode of taking testimony. But I think that the Convention intended, and that the people expect, much greater changes than these. We know that radical reform in legal proceedings has long been demanded by no inconsiderable number of the people; that a more determined agitation of the subject has been postponed by its friends, till such time as there should be a reorganization of the judicial establishment, upon the idea that a new system of procedure and a new system of Courts ought to come in together; that it was a prominent topic in the Convention itself, where its friends were in an undoubted majority; and that the manifestations of public sentiment out of doors were no less clear than were the sentiments of that body. Indeed, if now, after all that has been done within the last five years, there should be made only such changes as the Constitution absolutely commands, there will be great and general disappointment.

* * *

Every consideration, as it seems to me, makes it expedient for us all now to enter heartily upon the work of amendment. Those of us who have long been laboring for a radical reformation of the law, and those who have felt less inclination for it, should find this an occasion to act together in the common pursuit of thorough and wise reforms. We feel the inconvenience of the present state of things. We know that the technicality and the drudgery of legal proceedings are discreditable to our profession. Justice is entangled in the net of forms.

* * *

Believing, therefore, that great changes are inevitable in any event, and that this is a period favorable to the adoption of all the reforms which are really required, I wish it were possible to engage every member of the legal profession in the promotion of a wise, safe, and radical reform. Radical reform will come sooner or later, with us or without us. Shall we cooperate to make it at the same time wise and safe?

Such a reform, I am persuaded, should have in view nothing less than a uniform course of proceeding, in all cases, legal and equitable.

* * *

What I propose, then, in respect to cases of legal cognizance, is this: that the present forms of action be abolished, and in their stead a complaint and answer required, each setting forth the real claim and defense of the parties. Such pleadings would be precisely similar to those proposed for equity cases, and we should thus have a uniform course of pleading for all cases, legal and equitable. The distinction between the two classes of cases is now merely a distinction in the forms of proceeding. The Court of Chancery has existed only in consequence of the narrow and fixed forms of the common law. If those forms had been abolished, and a natural procedure adopted, the course of the two Courts would long ago have been assimilated.

Let the plaintiff set forth his cause of action in his complaint briefly, in ordinary language, and without repetition; and let the defendant make his answer in the same way. Let each party verify his allegation by making oath that he believes it to be true. The complaint will then acquaint the defendant with the real charge, while the answer will inform the plaintiff of the real defense. The disputed facts will be sifted from the undisputed, and the parties will go to trial knowing what they have to answer. The plaintiff will state his case as he believes it, and as he expects to prove it. The defendant, on his part, will set forth what he believes and expects to establish, and he need set forth no more. He will not be likely to aver what he does not believe. His answer will disclose the whole of his defense, because he will not be allowed to prove anything which the answer does not contain. He will not be perplexed with questions of double pleading, nor shackled by ancient technical rules.

*   *   *

The legitimate end of every administration of law is to do justice, with the least possible delay and expense. Every system of pleading is useful only as it tends to this end. This it can do but one of two ways: either by enabling the parties the better to prepare for trial, or by assisting the jury and the Court in judging the causes.

*   *   *

If we adopt the plan of pleading which I propose, we shall save both time and expense. We shall avoid the risk of losing causes from mistaking the rules of pleading; and we take one step, and that a great one, toward introducing simplicity and directness into the machinery of the law.

*   *   *

And is, indeed, the learning of the profession bound up with the system of common-law pleading? Is the noble science of jurisprudence—the fruit of the experience of ages, at once the monument and the record of civilization—inseparable from such paltry learning as that, "after the declaration, the parties must at each stage demur, or plead by way of traverse, or by way of confession and avoidance," or that "upon a traverse issue must be tendered," or anything of that sort? Lawyers have enough to learn if their studies are confined to useful knowledge. To assert that the great body of the law, civil and criminal—the law which defines rights and punishes crimes; the law which regulates the proprietorship, the enjoyment, and the transmission of property in all its forms; which explains the nature and the obligations of contracts through all their changes; the law that prevails equally on the sea and the land; the law that is enforced in courts of chancery and courts of admiralty, as well as in the courts of common law—to assert that this vast body of law requires the aid of that small portion which regulates the written statement of the parties in the courts of common law, is to assert a monstrous paradox, fitter for ridicule than for argument.

CONTRACTS

CHRISTOPHER C. LANGDELL, 1871

Preface

I entered upon the duties of my present position, a year and a half ago, with a settled conviction that law could only be taught or learned effectively by means of cases in some form. I had entertained such an opinion ever since I knew anything of the nature of law or legal study; but it was chiefly through my experience as a learner that it was formed, as well as subsequently strengthened and confirmed. Of teaching indeed, as a business, I was entirely without experience; nor had I given much consideration to that subject, except so far as proper methods of teaching are involved in proper methods of study.

Now, however, I was called upon to consider directly the subject of teaching, not theoretically but practically, in connection with a large school with its more or less complicated organization, its daily routine, and daily duties. I was expected to take a large class of pupils, meet them regularly from day to day, and give them systematic instruction in such branches of law as had been assigned to me. To accomplish this successfully, it was necessary, first, that the efforts of the pupils should go hand in hand with mine, that is, that they should study with direct reference to my instruction; secondly, that the study thus required of them should be of the kind from which they might reap the greatest and most lasting benefit; thirdly, that the instruction should be of such a character that the pupils might at least derive a greater advantage from attending it than from devoting the same time to private study. How could this threefold object be accomplished? Only one mode occurred to me which seemed to hold out any reasonable prospect of success; and that was, to make a series of cases, carefully selected from the books of reports, the subject alike of study and instruction. But here I was met by what seemed at first to be an insuperable practical difficulty, namely, the want of books; for though it might be practicable, in case of private pupils having free access to a complete library, to refer them directly to the books of reports, such a course was quite out of the question with a large class, all of whom would want the same books at the same time. Nor would such a course be without great drawbacks and inconveniences, even in the case of a single pupil. As he would always have to go where the books were, and could only have access to them there during certain prescribed hours, it would be impossible for him to economize his time or work to the best advantage; and he would be liable to be constantly haunted by the apprehension that he was spending time, labor, and money in studying cases which would be inaccessible to him in after life.

It was with a view to removing these obstacles, that I was first led to inquire into the feasibility of preparing and publishing such a selection of cases as would be adapted to my purpose as a teacher. The most important element in that inquiry was the great and rapidly increasing number of reported cases in every department of law. In view of this fact, was there any satisfactory principle upon which such a selection could be made? It seemed to me that there was. Law, considered as a science, consists of certain principles or doctrines. To have such a mastery of these as to be able to apply them with constant facility and certainly to the ever-tangled skein of human affairs, is what constitutes a true lawyer; and hence to acquire that mastery should be the business of every earnest student of law. Each of these doctrines has arrived at its present state by slow degrees; in other words, it is a growth, extending in many cases through centuries. This growth is to be traced in the main through a series of cases; and much the shortest and best, if not the only way of mastering the doctrine effectually is by studying the cases in which it is embodied. But the cases which are useful and necessary for this purpose at the present day bear an exceedingly small proportion to all that have been reported. The vast majority are useless and worse than useless for any purpose of systematic study. Moreover, the number of fundamental legal doctrines is much less than is commonly supposed; the many different guises in which the same doctrine is constantly making its appearance, and the great extent to which legal treatises are a repetition of each other, being the cause of much misapprehension. If these doctrines could be so classified and arranged that each should be found in its proper place, and nowhere else, they would cease to be formidable from their number. It seemed to me, therefore, to be possible to take such a branch of the law as Contracts, for example, and, without exceeding comparatively moderate limits, to select, classify, and arrange all the cases which had contributed in any important degree to the growth, development, or establishment of any of its essential doctrines; and that such a work could not fail to be of material service to all who desire to study that branch of law systematically and in its original sources.

THE PATH OF THE LAW

OLIVER WENDELL HOLMES, JR., 1897

When we study law we are not studying a mystery but a well known profession. We are studying what we shall want in order to appear before judges, or to advise people in such a way as to keep them out of court. The reason why it is a profession, why people will pay lawyers to argue for them or to advise them, is that in societies like ours the command of the public force is intrusted to the judges in certain cases, and the whole power of the state will be put forth, if necessary, to carry out their judgments and decrees. People want to know under what circumstances and how far they will run the risk of coming against what is so much stronger than themselves, and hence it becomes a business to find out when this danger is to be feared. The object of our study, then, is prediction, the prediction of the incidence of the public force through the instrumentality of the courts.

The means of the study are a body of reports, of treatises, and of statutes, in this country and in England, extending back for six hundred years, and now increasing annually by hundreds. In these sibylline leaves are gathered the scattered prophesies of the past upon the cases in which the ax will fall. These are what properly have been called the oracles of the law. Far the most important and pretty nearly the whole meaning of every new effort of legal thought is to make these prophecies more precise, and to generalize them into a thoroughly connected system. The process is one, from a lawyer's statement of a case, eliminating as it does all the dramatic elements with which his client's story has clothed it, and retaining only the facts of legal import, up to the final analyses and abstract universals of theoretic jurisprudence. The reason why a lawyer does not mention that his client wore a white hat when he made a contract, while Mrs. Quickly would be sure to dwell upon it along with the parcel gilt goblet and the sea-coal fire, is that he foresees that the public force will act in the same way whatever his client had upon his head. It is to make the prophecies easier to be remembered and to be understood that the teachings of the decisions of the past are put into general propositions and gathered into textbooks, or that statutes are passed in a general form. The primary rights and duties with which jurisprudence busies itself again are nothing but prophecies. One of the many evil effects of the confusion between legal and moral ideas, about which I shall have something to say in a moment, is that theory is apt to get the cart before the horse, and to consider the right or the duty as something existing apart from and independent of the consequences of its breach, to which certain sanctions are added afterward. But, as I shall try to show, a legal duty so called is nothing but a prediction that if a man does or omits certain things he will be made to suffer in this or that way by judgment of the court;—and so of a legal right.

Source: Reprinted in its entirety from O. W. Holmes, Jr., *The Path of the Law*, 10 HARVARD LAW REVIEW 457 (1897). The footnotes have been renumbered.

The number of our predictions when generalized and reduced to a system is not unmanageably large. They present themselves as a finite body of dogma which may be mastered within a reasonable time. It is a great mistake to be frightened by the ever increasing number of reports. The reports of a given jurisdiction in the course of a generation take up pretty much the whole body of the law, and restate it from the present point of view. We could reconstruct the corpus from them if all that went before were burned. The use of the earlier reports is mainly historical, a use about which I shall have something to say before I have finished.

I wish, if I can, to lay down some first principles for the study of this body of dogma or systematized prediction which we call the law, for men who want to use it as the instrument of their business to enable them to prophesy in their turn, and, as bearing upon the study, I wish to point out an ideal which as yet our law has not attained.

The first thing for a business-like understanding of the matter is to understand its limits, and therefore I think it desirable at once to point out and dispel a confusion between morality and law, which sometimes rises to the height of conscious theory, and more often and indeed constantly is making trouble in detail without reaching the point of consciousness. You can see very plainly that a bad man has as much reason as a good one for wishing to avoid an encounter with the public force, and therefore you can see the practical importance of the distinction between morality and law. A man who cares nothing for an ethical rule which is believed and practised by his neighbors is likely nevertheless to care a good deal to avoid being made to pay money, and will want to keep out of jail if he can.

I take it for granted that no hearer of mine will misinterpret what I have to say as the language of cynicism. The law is the witness and external deposit of our moral life. Its history is the history of the moral development of the race. The practice of it, in spite of popular jests, tends to make good citizens and good men. When I emphasize the difference between law and morals I do so with reference to a single end, that of learning and understanding the law. For that purpose you must definitely master its specific marks, and it is for that that I ask you for the moment to imagine yourselves indifferent to other and greater things.

I do not say that there is not a wider point of view from which the distinction between law and morals becomes of secondary or no importance, as all mathematical distinctions vanish in presence of the infinite. But I do say that that distinction is of the first importance for the object which we are here to consider,—a right study and mastery of the law as a business with well understood limits, a body of dogma enclosed within definite lines. I have just shown the practical reason for saying so. If you want to know the law and nothing else, you must look at it as a bad man, who cares only for the material consequences which such knowledge enables him to predict, not as a good one, who finds his reasons for conduct, whether inside the law or outside of it, in the vaguer sanctions of conscience. The theoretical importance of the distinction is no less, if you would reason on your subject aright. The law is full of phraseology drawn from morals, and by the mere force of language continually invites us to pass from one domain to the other without perceiving it, as we are sure to do unless we have the boundary constantly before our minds. The law talks about rights, and duties, and malice, and intent, and negligence, and so forth, and nothing is easier, or, I may say, more common in legal reasoning, than to take these words in their moral sense, at some stage of the argument, and so to drop into fallacy. For instance, when we speak of the rights of man in a moral sense, we mean to mark the limits of interference with individual freedom which we think are prescribed by conscience, or by our ideal, however reached. Yet it is certain that many laws have been enforced in the past, and it is likely that some are enforced now, which are condemned by the most enlightened opinion of the time, or which at all events pass the limit of interference as many consciences would draw it. Manifestly, therefore, nothing but confusion of thought can result from assuming that the rights of man in a moral sense are equally rights in the sense of the Constitution and the law. No doubt simple and extreme cases can be put of imaginable laws which the statute-making power would not dare to enact, even in the absence of written constitutional prohibitions, because the community would rise in rebellion and fight; and this gives some plausibility to the proposition that the law, if not a part of morality, is limited by it. But this limit of power is not coextensive with any system of morals. For the most part it falls far within the lines of any such system, and in some cases may extend beyond them, for reasons drawn from the habits of a particular people at a particular time. I once heard the late

Professor Agassiz[29] say that a German population would rise if you added two cents to the price of a glass of beer. A statute in such a case would be empty words, not because it was wrong, but because it could not be enforced. No one will deny that wrong statutes can be and are enforced, and we should not all agree as to which were the wrong ones.

The confusion with which I am dealing besets confessedly legal conceptions. Take the fundamental question, What constitutes the law? You will find some text writers telling you that it is something different from what is decided by the courts of Massachusetts or England, that it is a system of reason, that it is a deduction from principles of ethics or admitted axioms or what not, which may or may not coincide with the decisions. But if we take the view of our friend the bad man we shall find that he does not care two straws for the axioms or deductions, but that he does want to know what the Massachusetts or English courts are likely to do in fact. I am much of his mind. The prophecies of what the courts will do in fact, and nothing more pretentious, are what I mean by the law.

Take again a notion which as popularly understood is the widest conception which the law contains;—the notion of legal duty, to which already I have referred. We fill the word with all the content which we draw from morals. But what does it mean to a bad man? Mainly, and in the first place, a prophecy that if he does certain things he will be subjected to disagreeable consequences by way of imprisonment or compulsory payment of money. But from his point of view, what is the difference between being fined and being taxed a certain sum for doing a certain thing? That his point of view is the test of legal principles is shown by the many discussions which have arisen in the courts on the very question whether a given statutory liability is a penalty or a tax. On the answer to this question depends the decision whether conduct is legally wrong or right, and also whether a man is under compulsion or free. Leaving the criminal law on one side, what is the difference between the liability under the mill acts or statutes authorizing a taking by eminent domain and the liability for what we call a wrongful conversion of property where restoration is out of the question? In both cases the party taking another man's property has to pay its fair value as assessed by a jury, and no more. What significance is there in calling one taking right and another wrong from the point of view of the law? It does not matter, so far as the given consequence, the compulsory payment, is concerned, whether the act to which it is attached is described in terms of praise or in terms of blame, or whether the law purports to prohibit it or to allow it. If it matters at all, still speaking from the bad man's point of view, it must be because in one case and not in the other some further disadvantages, or at least some further consequences, are attached to the act by the law. The only other disadvantages thus attached to it which I ever have been able to think of are to be found in two somewhat insignificant legal doctrines, both of which might be abolished without much disturbance. One is, that a contract to do a prohibited act is unlawful, and the other, that, if one of two or more joint wrongdoers has to pay all the damages, he cannot recover contribution from his fellows. And that I believe is all. You see how the vague circumference of the notion of duty shrinks and at the same time grows more precise when we wash it with cynical acid and expel everything except the object of our study, the operations of the law.

Nowhere is the confusion between legal and moral ideas more manifest than in the law of contract. Among other things, here again the so called primary rights and duties are invested with a mystic significance beyond what can be assigned and explained. The duty to keep a contract at common law means a prediction that you must pay damages if you do not keep it,—and nothing else. If you commit a tort, you are liable to pay a compensatory sum. If you commit a contract, you are liable to pay a compensatory sum unless the promised event comes to pass, and that is all the difference. But such a mode of looking at the matter stinks in the nostrils of those who think it advantageous to get as much ethics into the law as they can. It was good enough for Lord Coke, however, and here, as in many other cases, I am content to abide with him. In Bromage v.

---

29. [Ed. note] Jean Louis Rodolphe Agassiz (1807–73), a Swiss born naturalist and, *inter alia*, Professor of Natural History at Harvard. His second wife, Elizabeth Cabot (née Cary) (1822–1907) was one of the founders of Radcliffe College and its president from 1894 until 1902.

Genning,[30] a prohibition was sought in the King's Bench against a suit in the marches of Wales for the specific performance of a covenant to grant a lease, and Coke said that it would subvert the intention of the covenantor, since he intends it to be at his election either to lose the damages or to make the lease. Sergeant Harris for the plaintiff confessed that he moved the matter against his conscience, and a prohibition was granted. This goes further than we should go now, but it shows what I venture to say has been the common law point of view from the beginning, although Mr. Harriman, in his very able little book upon Contracts has been misled, as I humbly think, to a different conclusion.

I have spoken only of the common law, because there are some cases in which a logical justification can be found for speaking of civil liabilities as imposing duties in an intelligible sense. These are the relatively few in which equity will grant an injunction, and will enforce it by putting the defendant in prison or otherwise punishing him unless he complies with the order of the court. But I hardly think it advisable to shape general theory from the exception, and I think it would be better to cease troubling ourselves about primary rights and sanctions altogether, than to describe our prophecies concerning the liabilities commonly imposed by the law in those inappropriate terms.

I mentioned, as other examples of the use by the law of words drawn from morals, malice, intent, and negligence. It is enough to take malice as it is used in the law of civil liability for wrongs,—what we lawyers call the law of torts,—to show you that it means something different in law from what it means in morals, and also to show how the difference has been obscured by giving to principles which have little or nothing to do with each other the same name. Three hundred years ago a parson preached a sermon and told a story out of Fox's Book of Martyrs of a man who had assisted at the torture of one of the saints, and afterward died, suffering compensatory inward torment. It happened that Fox was wrong. The man was alive and chanced to hear the sermon, and thereupon he sued the parson. Chief Justice Wray instructed the jury that the defendant was not liable, because the story was told innocently, without malice. He took malice in the moral sense, as importing a malevolent motive. But nowadays no one doubts that a man may be liable, without any malevolent motive at all, for false statements manifestly calculated to inflict temporal damage. In stating the case in pleading, we still should call the defendant's conduct malicious; but, in my opinion at least, the word means nothing about motives, or even about the defendant's attitude toward the future, but only signifies that the tendency of his conduct under the known circumstances was very plainly to cause the plaintiff temporal harm.[31]

In the law of contract the use of moral phraseology has led to equal confusion, as I have shown in part already, but only in part. Morals deal with the actual internal state of the individual's mind, what he actually intends. From the time of the Romans down to now, this mode of dealing has affected the language of the law as to contract, and the language used has reacted upon the thought. We talk about a contract as a meeting of the minds of the parties, and thence it is inferred in various cases that there is no contract because their minds have not met; that is, because they have intended different things or because one party has not known of the assent of the other. Yet nothing is more certain than that parties may be bound by a contract to things which neither of them intended, and when one does not know of the other's assent. Suppose a contract is executed in due form and in writing to deliver a lecture, mentioning no time. One of the parties thinks that the promise will be construed to mean at once, within a week. The other thinks that it means when he is ready. The court says that it means within a reasonable time. The parties are bound by the contract as it is interpreted by the court, yet neither of them meant what the court declares that they have said. In my opinion no one will understand the true theory of contract or be able even to discuss some fundamental questions intelligently until he has understood that all contracts are formal, that the making of a contract depends not on the agreement of two minds in one intention, but on the agreement of two sets of external signs,—not on the parties' having *meant* the same thing but on their having *said* the same thing. Furthermore, as the signs may be addressed to one sense or another,—to sight or to hearing,—on the nature of the sign will depend the moment when the contract is made. If the sign is tangible, for instance, a letter, the contract is made when the letter of acceptance is delivered. If it is necessary that the minds of the parties meet, there will be no contract until the acceptance can be read,—none, for example, if the acceptance be snatched from the hand of the offerer by a third person.

---

30. 1 Roll[e] Rep. 368 [81 Eng.Rep. 540 (1616)].

31. See Hanson v. Globe Newspaper Co., 159 Mass. 293, 302 [34 N.E. 462, 465 (1893)].

This is not the time to work out a theory in detail, or to answer many obvious doubts and questions which are suggested by these general views. I know of none which are not easy to answer, but what I am trying to do now is only by a series of hints to throw some light on the narrow path of legal doctrine, and upon two pitfalls which, as it seems to me, lie perilously near to it. Of the first of these I have said enough. I hope that my illustrations have shown the danger, both to speculation and to practice, of confounding morality with law, and the trap which legal language lays for us on that side of our way. For my own part, I often doubt whether it would not be a gain if every word of moral significance could be banished from the law altogether, and other words adopted which should convey legal ideas uncolored by anything outside the law. We should lose the fossil records of a good deal of history and the majesty got from ethical associations, but by ridding ourselves of an unnecessary confusion we should gain very much in the clearness of our thought.

So much for the limits of the law. The next thing which I wish to consider is what are the forces which determine its content and its growth. You may assume, with Hobbes and Bentham and Austin, that all law emanates from the sovereign, even when the first human beings to enunciate it are the judges, or you may think that law is the voice of the Zeitgeist, or what you like. It is all one to my present purpose. Even if every decision required the sanction of an emperor with despotic power and a whimsical turn of mind, we should be interested none the less, still with a view to prediction, in discovering some order, some rational explanation, and some principle of growth for the rules which he laid down. In every system there are such explanations and principles to be found. It is with regard to them that a second fallacy comes in, which I think it important to expose.

The fallacy to which I refer is the notion that the only force at work in the development of the law is logic. In the broadest sense, indeed, that notion would be true. The postulate on which we think about the universe is that there is a fixed quantitative relation between every phenomenon and its antecedents and consequents. If there is such a thing as a phenomenon without these fixed quantitative relations, it is a miracle. It is outside the law of cause and effect, and as such transcends our power of thought, or at least is something to or from which we cannot reason. The condition of our thinking about the universe is that it is capable of being thought about rationally, or, in other words, that every part of it is effect and cause in the same sense in which those parts are with which we are most familiar. So in the broadest sense it is true that the law is a logical development, like everything else. The danger of which I speak is not the admission that the principles governing other phenomena also govern the law, but the notion that a given system, ours, for instance, can be worked out like mathematics from some general axioms of conduct. This is the natural error of the schools, but it is not confined to them. I once heard a very eminent judge say that he never let a decision go until he was absolutely sure that it was right. So judicial dissent often is blamed, as if it meant simply that one side or the other were not doing their sums right, and, if they would take more trouble, agreement inevitably would come.

This mode of thinking is entirely natural. The training of lawyers is a training in logic. The processes of analogy, discrimination, and deduction are those in which they are most at home. The language of judicial decision is mainly the language of logic. And the logical method and form flatter that longing for certainty and for repose which is in every human mind. But certainty generally is illusion, and repose is not the destiny of man. Behind the logical form lies a judgment as to the relative worth and importance of competing legislative grounds, often an inarticulate and unconscious judgment, it is true, and yet the very root and nerve of the whole proceeding.[32] You can give

----

32. [Ed. note] Cf. the famous opening lines from *The Common Law:*
The object of this book is to present a general view of the Common Law. To accomplish the task, other tools are needed besides logic. It is something to show that the consistency of a system requires a particular result, but it is not all. The life of the law has not been logic: it has been experience. The felt necessities of the time, the prevalent moral and political theories, intuitions of public policy, avowed or unconscious, even the prejudices which judges share with their fellow-men, have had a good deal more to do than the syllogism in determining the rules by which men should be governed. The law embodies the story of a nation's development through many centuries, and it cannot be dealt with as if it contained only the axioms and corollaries of a book of mathematics. In order to know what it is, we must know what it has been, and what it tends to become. We must alternately consult history and existing theories of legislation. But the most difficult labor will be to understand the combination of the two into new products at every stage. . . .
O. W. Holmes, Jr., THE COMMON LAW 1 (1881).

any conclusion a logical form. You always can imply a condition in a contract. But why do you imply it? It is because of some belief as to the practice of the community or of a class, or because of some opinion as to policy, or, in short, because of some attitude of yours upon a matter not capable of exact quantitative measurement, and therefore not capable of founding exact logical conclusions. Such matters really are battle grounds where the means do not exist for determinations that shall be good for all time, and where the decision can do no more than embody the preference of a given body in a given time and place. We do not realize how large a part of our law is open to reconsideration upon a slight change in the habit of the public mind. No concrete proposition is self-evident, no matter how ready we may be to accept it, not even Mr. Herbert Spencer's Every man has a right to do what he wills, provided he interferes not with a like right on the part of his neighbors.

Why is a false and injurious statement privileged, if it is made honestly in giving information about a servant? It is because it has been thought more important that information should be given freely, than that a man should be protected from what under other circumstances would be an actionable wrong. Why is a man at liberty to set up a business which he knows will ruin his neighbor? It is because the public good is supposed to be best subserved by free competition. Obviously such judgments of relative importance may vary in different times and places. Why does a judge instruct a jury that an employer is not liable to an employee for an injury received in the course of his employment unless he is negligent, and why do the jury generally find for the plaintiff if the case is allowed to go to them? It is because the traditional policy of our law is to confine liability to cases where a prudent man might have foreseen the injury, or at least the danger, while the inclination of a very large part of the community is to make certain classes of persons insure the safety of those with whom they deal. Since the last words were written, I have seen the requirement of such insurance put forth as part of the programme of one of the best known labor organizations. There is a concealed, half conscious battle on the question of legislative policy, and if any one thinks that it can be settled deductively, or once for all, I only can say that I think he is theoretically wrong, and that I am certain that his conclusion will not be accepted in practice *semper ubique et ab omnibus.*[33]

Indeed, I think that even now our theory upon this matter is open to reconsideration, although I am not prepared to say how I should decide if a reconsideration were proposed. Our law of torts comes from the old days of isolated, ungeneralized wrongs, assaults, slanders, and the like, where the damages might be taken to lie where they fell by legal judgment. But the torts with which our courts are kept busy to-day are mainly the incidents of certain well known businesses. They are injuries to person or property by railroads, factories, and the like. The liability for them is estimated, and sooner or later goes into the price paid by the public. The public really pays the damages, and the question of liability, if pressed far enough, is really the question how far it is desirable that the public should insure the safety of those whose work it uses. It might be said that in such cases the chance of a jury finding for the defendant is merely a chance, once in a while rather arbitrarily interrupting the regular course of recovery, most likely in the case of an unusually conscientious plaintiff, and therefore better done away with. On the other hand, the economic value even of a life to the community can be estimated, and no recovery, it may be said, ought to go beyond that amount. It is conceivable that some day in certain cases we may find ourselves imitating, on a higher plane, the tariff for life and limb which we see in the Leges Barbarorum.

I think that the judges themselves have failed adequately to recognize their duty of weighing considerations of social advantage. The duty is inevitable, and the result of the often proclaimed judicial aversion to deal with such considerations is simply to leave the very ground and foundation of judgments inarticulate, and often unconscious, as I have said. When socialism first began to be talked about, the comfortable classes of the community were a good deal frightened. I suspect that this fear has influenced judicial action both here and in England, yet it is certain that it is not a conscious factor in the decisions to which I refer. I think that something similar has led people who no longer hope to control the legislatures to look to the courts as expounders of the Constitutions, and that in some courts new principles have been discovered outside the bodies of those instruments, which may be generalized into acceptance of the economic doctrines which prevailed about fifty

---

33. [Ed. note] Literally "forever, everywhere and by everyone."

years ago, and a wholesale prohibition of what a tribunal of lawyers does not think about right. I cannot but believe that if the training of lawyers led them habitually to consider more definitely and explicitly the social advantage on which the rule they lay down must be justified, they sometimes would hesitate where now they are confident, and see that really they were taking sides upon debatable and often burning questions.

So much for the fallacy of logical form. Now let us consider the present condition of the law as a subject for study, and the ideal toward which it tends. We still are far from the point of view which I desire to see reached. No one has reached it or can reach it as yet. We are only at the beginning of a philosophical reaction, and of a reconsideration of the worth of doctrines which for the most part still are taken for granted without any deliberate, conscious, and systematic questioning of their grounds. The development of our law has gone on for nearly a thousand years, like the development of a plant, each generation taking the inevitable next step, mind, like matter, simply obeying a law of spontaneous growth. It is perfectly natural and right that it should have been so. Imitation is a necessity of human nature, as has been illustrated by a remarkable French writer, M. Tarde,[34] in an admirable book, "Les Lois de l'Imitation." Most of the things we do, we do for no better reason than that our fathers have done them or that our neighbors do them, and the same is true of a larger part than we suspect of what we think. The reason is a good one, because our short life gives us no time for a better, but it is not the best. It does not follow, because we all are compelled to take on faith at second hand most of the rules on which we base our action and our thought, that each of us may not try to set some corner of his world in the order of reason, or that all of us collectively should not aspire to carry reason as far as it will go throughout the whole domain. In regard to the law, it is true, no doubt, that an evolutionist will hesitate to affirm universal validity for his social ideals, or for the principles which he thinks should be embodied in legislation. He is content if he can prove them best for here and now. He may be ready to admit that he knows nothing about an absolute best in the cosmos, and even that he knows next to nothing about a permanent best for men. Still it is true that a body of law is more rational and more civilized when every rule it contains is referred articulately and definitely to an end which it subserves, and when the grounds for desiring that end are stated or are ready to be stated in words.

At present, in very many cases, if we want to know why a rule of law has taken its particular shape, and more or less if we want to know why it exists at all, we go to tradition. We follow it into the Year Books, and perhaps beyond them to the customs of the Salian Franks, and somewhere in the past, in the German forests, in the needs of Norman kings, in the assumptions of a dominant class, in the absence of generalized ideas, we find out the practical motive for what now best is justified by the mere fact of its acceptance and that men are accustomed to it. The rational study of law is still to a large extent the study of history. History must be a part of the study, because without it we cannot know the precise scope of rules which it is our business to know. It is a part of the rational study, because it is the first step toward an enlightened scepticism, that is, toward a deliberate reconsideration of the worth of those rules. When you get the dragon out of his cave on to the plain and in the daylight, you can count his teeth and claws, and see just what is his strength. But to get him out is only the first step. The next is either to kill him, or to tame him and make him a useful animal. For the rational study of the law the black-letter man may be the man of the present, but the man of the future is the man of statistics and the master of economics. It is revolting to have no better reason for a rule of law than that so it was laid down in the time of Henry IV. It is still more revolting if the grounds upon which it was laid down have vanished long since, and the rule simply persists from blind imitation of the past. I am thinking of the technical rule as to trespass *ab initio*, as it is called, which I attempted to explain in a recent Massachusetts case.[35]

Let me take an illustration, which can be stated in a few words, to show how the social end which is aimed at by a rule of law is obscured and only partially attained in consequence of the fact that the rule owes its form to a gradual historical development, instead of being reshaped as a whole,

---

34. [Ed. note] Gabriel Tarde (1843–1904). French sociologist and criminologist and from 1899 until his death Professor of Modern Philosophy, College de France. Tarde regarded man as an agent striving to realize ends suggested by the social environment and either sanctioned or rejected by that enactment. *Les Lois de l'Imitation* was published in 1890.

35. Commonwealth v. Rubin, 165 Mass. 453, [43 N.E. 200 (1896)].

with conscious articulate reference to the end in view. We think it desirable to prevent one man's property being misappropriated by another, and so we make larceny a crime. The evil is the same whether the misappropriation is made by a man into whose hands the owner has put the property, or by one who wrongfully takes it away. But primitive law in its weakness did not get much beyond an effort to prevent violence, and very naturally made a wrongful taking, a trespass, part of its definition of the crime. In modern times the judges enlarged the definition a little by holding that, if the wrongdoer gets possession by a trick or device, the crime is committed. This really was giving up the requirement of a trespass, and it would have been more logical, as well as truer to the present object of the law, to abandon the requirement altogether. That, however, would have seemed too bold, and was left to statute. Statutes were passed making embezzlement a crime. But the force of tradition caused the crime of embezzlement to be regarded as so far distinct from larceny that to this day, in some jurisdictions at least, a slip corner is kept open for thieves to contend, if indicted for larceny, that they should have been indicted for embezzlement, and if indicted for embezzlement, that they should have been indicted for larceny, and to escape on that ground.

Far more fundamental questions still await a better answer than that we do as our fathers have done. What have we better than a blind guess to show that the criminal law in its present form does more good than harm? I do not stop to refer to the effect which it has had in degrading prisoners and in plunging them further into crime, or to the question whether fine and imprisonment do not fall more heavily on a criminal's wife and children than on himself. I have in mind more far-reaching questions. Does punishment deter? Do we deal with criminals on proper principles? A modern school of Continental criminalists plumes itself on the formula, first suggested, it is said, by Gall,[36] that we must consider the criminal rather than the crime. The formula does not carry us very far, but the inquiries which have been started look toward an answer of my questions based on science for the first time. If the typical criminal is a degenerate, bound to swindle or to murder by as deep seated an organic necessity as that which makes the rattlesnake bite, it is idle to talk of deterring him by the classical method of imprisonment. He must be got rid of; he cannot be improved, or frightened out of his structural reaction. If, on the other hand, crime, like normal human conduct, is mainly a matter of imitation, punishment fairly may be expected to help to keep it out of fashion. The study of criminals has been thought by some well known men of science to sustain the former hypothesis. The statistics of the relative increase of crime in crowded places like large cities, where example has the greatest chance to work, and in less populated parts, where the contagion spreads more slowly, have been used with great force in favor of the latter view. But there is weighty authority for the belief that, however this may be, "not the nature of the crime, but the dangerousness of the criminal, constitutes the only reasonable legal criterion to guide the inevitable social reaction against the criminal."[37]

The impediments to rational generalization, which I illustrated from the law of larceny, are shown in the other branches of the law, as well as in that of crime. Take the law of tort or civil liability for damages apart from contract and the like. Is there any general theory of such liability, or are the cases in which it exists simply to be enumerated, and to be explained each on its special ground, as is easy to believe from the fact that the right of action for certain well known classes of wrongs like trespass or slander has its special history for each class? I think that there is a general theory to be discovered, although resting in tendency rather than established and accepted. I think that the law regards the infliction of temporal damage by a responsible person as actionable, if under the circumstances known to him the danger of his act is manifest according to common experience, or according to his own experience if it is more than common, except in cases where upon special grounds of policy the law refuses to protect the plaintiff or grants a privilege to the defendant.[38] I

---

36. [Ed. note] Probably Franz Joseph Gall (1758–1828), a German physician who eventually settled first in Vienna and later in Paris and was the founder of phrenology.

37. Havelock Ellis, "The Criminal," 41, citing Garofalo [Baron Raffaele, 1851–1934, Italian statesman, jurist, and criminologist].

38. An example of the law's refusing to protect the plaintiff is when he is interrupted by a stranger in the use of a valuable way, which he has traveled adversely for a week less than the period of prescription. A week later he will have gained a right, but now he is only a trespasser. Examples of privilege I have given already. One of the best is competition in business.

think that commonly malice, intent, and negligence mean only that the danger was manifest to a greater or less degree, under the circumstances known to the actor, although in some cases of privilege malice may mean an actual malevolent motive, and such a motive may take away a permission knowingly to inflict harm, which otherwise would be granted on this or that ground of dominant public good. But when I stated my view to a very eminent English judge the other day, he said: "You are discussing what the law ought to be; as the law is, you must show a right. A man is not liable for negligence unless he is subject to a duty." If our difference was more than a difference in words, or with regard to the proportion between the exceptions and the rule, then, in his opinion, liability for an act cannot be referred to the manifest tendency of the act to cause temporal damage in general as a sufficient explanation, but must be referred to the special nature of the damage, or must be derived from some special circumstances outside of the tendency of the act, for which no generalized explanation exists. I think that such a view is wrong, but it is familiar, and I dare say generally is accepted in England.

Everywhere the basis of principle is tradition, to such an extent that we even are in danger of making the rôle of history more important than it is. The other day Professor Ames wrote a learned article[39] to show, among other things, that the common law did not recognize the defence of fraud in actions upon specialties, and the moral might seem to be that the personal character of that defence is due to its equitable origin. But if, as I have said, all contracts are formal, the difference is not merely historical, but theoretic, between defects of form which prevent a contract from being made, and mistaken motives which manifestly could not be considered in any system that we should call rational except against one who was privy to those motives. It is not confined to specialties, but is of universal application. I ought to add that I do not suppose that Mr. Ames would disagree with what I suggest.

However, if we consider the law of contract, we find it full of history. The distinctions between debt, covenant, and assumpsit are merely historical. The classification of certain obligations to pay money, imposed by the law irrespective of any bargain as quasi contracts, is merely historical. The doctrine of consideration is merely historical. The effect given to a seal is to be explained by history alone.—Consideration is a mere form. Is it a useful form? If so, why should it not be required in all contracts? A seal is a mere form, and is vanishing in the scroll and in enactments that a consideration must be given, seal or no seal.—Why should any merely historical distinction be allowed to affect the rights and obligations of business men?

Since I wrote this discourse I have come on a very good example of the way in which tradition not only overrides rational policy, but overrides it after first having been misunderstood and having been given a new and broader scope than it had when it had a meaning. It is the settled law of England that a material alteration of a written contract by a party avoids it as against him. The doctrine is contrary to the general tendency of the law. We do not tell a jury that if a man ever has lied in one particular he is to be presumed to lie in all. Even if a man has tried to defraud, it seems no sufficient reason for preventing him from proving the truth. Objections of like nature in general go to the weight, not to the admissibility, of evidence. Moreover, this rule is irrespective of fraud, and is not confined to evidence. It is not merely that you cannot use the writing, but that the contract is at an end. What does this mean? The existence of a written contract depends on the fact that the offeror and offeree have interchanged their written expressions, not on the continued existence of those expressions. But in the case of a bond the primitive notion was different. The contract was inseparable from the parchment. If a stranger destroyed it, or tore off the seal, or altered it, the obligee could not recover, however free from fault, because the defendant's contract, that is, the actual tangible bond which he had sealed, could not be produced in the form in which it bound him. About a hundred years ago Lord Kenyon undertook to use his reason on this tradition, as he sometimes did to the detriment of the law, and, not understanding it, said he could see no reason why what was true of a bond should not be true of other contracts. His decision happened to be right, as it concerned a promissory note, where again the common law regarded the contract as inseparable from the paper on which it was written, but the reasoning was general, and soon was extended to other written contracts, and various absurd and unreal grounds of policy were invented to account for the enlarged rule.

_____

39. [Ed. note] Unquestionably, *Specialty Contracts and Equitable Defences*, 9 HARV. L.REV. 49 (1895).

I trust that no one will understand me to be speaking with disrespect of the law, because I criticise it so freely. I venerate the law, and especially our system of law, as one of the vastest products of the human mind. No one knows better than I do the countless number of great intellects that have spent themselves in making some addition or improvement, the greatest of which is trifling when compared with the mighty whole. It has the final title to respect that it exists, that it is not a Hegelian dream, but a part of the lives of men. But one may criticise even what one reveres. Law is the business to which my life is devoted, and I should show less than devotion if I did not do what in me lies to improve it, and, when I perceive what seems to me the ideal of its future, if I hesitated to point it out and to press toward it with all my heart.

Perhaps I have said enough to show the part which the study of history necessarily plays in the intelligent study of the law as it is to-day. In the teaching of this school and at Cambridge it is in no danger of being undervalued. Mr. Bigelow here and Mr. Ames and Mr. Thayer there have made important contributions which will not be forgotten, and in England the recent history of early English law by Sir Frederick Pollock and Mr. Maitland has lent the subject an almost deceptive charm. We must beware of the pitfall of antiquarianism, and must remember that for our purposes our only interest in the past is for the light it throws upon the present. I look forward to a time when the part played by history in the explanation of dogma shall be very small, and instead of ingenious research we shall spend our energy on a study of the ends sought to be attained and the reasons for desiring them. As a step toward that ideal it seems to me that every lawyer ought to seek an understanding of economics. The present divorce between the schools of political economy and law seems to me an evidence of how much progress in philosophical study still remains to be made. In the present state of political economy, indeed, we come again upon history on a larger scale, but there we are called on to consider and weigh the ends of legislation, the means of attaining them, and the cost. We learn that for everything we have to give up something else, and we are taught to set the advantage we gain against the other advantage we lose, and to know what we are doing when we elect.

There is another study which sometimes is undervalued by the practical minded, for which I wish to say a good word, although I think a good deal of pretty poor stuff goes under that name. I mean the study of what is called jurisprudence. Jurisprudence, as I look at it, is simply law in its most generalized part. Every effort to reduce a case to a rule is an effort of jurisprudence, although the name as used in English is confined to the broadest rules and most fundamental conceptions. One mark of a great lawyer is that he sees the application of the broadest rules. There is a story of a Vermont justice of the peace before whom a suit was brought by one farmer against another for breaking a churn. The justice took time to consider, and then said that he had looked through the statutes and could find nothing about churns, and gave judgment for the defendant. The same state of mind is shown in all our common digests and text-books. Applications of rudimentary rules of contract or tort are tucked away under the head of Railroads or Telegraphs or go to swell treatises on historical subdivisions, such as Shipping or Equity, or are gathered under an arbitrary title which is thought likely to appeal to the practical mind, such as Mercantile Law. If a man goes into law it pays to be a master of it, and to be a master of it means to look straight through all the dramatic incidents and to discern the true basis for prophecy. Therefore, it is well to have an accurate notion of what you mean by law, by a right, by a duty, by malice, intent, and negligence, by ownership, by possession, and so forth. I have in my mind cases in which the highest courts seem to me to have floundered because they had no clear ideas on some of these themes. I have illustrated their importance already. If a further illustration is wished, it may be found by reading the Appendix to Sir James Stephen's Criminal Law on the subject of possession, and then turning to Pollock and Wright's enlightened book.[40] Sir James Stephen is not the only writer whose attempts to analyze legal ideas have been confused by striving for a useless quintessence of all systems, instead of an accurate anatomy of one. The trouble with Austin was that he did not know enough English law. But still it is a practical advantage to master Austin, and his predecessors, Hobbes and Bentham, and his worthy successors, Holland and Pollock. Sir Frederick Pollock's recent little book is touched with the felicity which marks all his works, and is wholly free from the perverting influence of Roman models.

---

40. [Ed. note] AN ESSAY ON POSSESSION IN THE COMMON LAW (1888).

The advice of the elders to young men is very apt to be as unreal as a list of the hundred best books. At least in my day I had my share of such counsels, and high among the unrealities I place the recommendation to study the Roman law. I assume that such advice means more than collecting a few Latin maxims with which to ornament the discourse,—the purpose for which Lord Coke recommended Bracton. If that is all that is wanted, the title "De Regulis Juris Antiqui" can be read in an hour. I assume that, if it is well to study the Roman law, it is well to study it as a working system. That means mastering a set of technicalities more difficult and less understood than our own, and studying another course of history by which even more than our own the Roman law must be explained. If any one doubts me, let him read Keller's[41] "Der Römische Civil Process und die Actionen," a treatise on the prætor's edict, Muirhead's most interesting "Historical Introduction to the Private Law of Rome," and, to give him the best chance possible, Sohm's[42] admirable Institutes. No. The way to gain a liberal view of your subject is not to read something else, but to get to the bottom of the subject itself. The means of doing that are, in the first place, to follow the existing body of dogma into its highest generalizations by the help of jurisprudence; next, to discover from history how it has come to be what it is; and, finally, so far as you can, to consider the ends which the several rules seek to accomplish, the reasons why those ends are desired, what is given up to gain them, and whether they are worth the price.

We have too little theory in the law rather than too much, especially on this final branch of study. When I was speaking of history, I mentioned larceny as an example to show how the law suffered from not having embodied in a clear form a rule which will accomplish its manifest purpose. In that case the trouble was due to the survival of forms coming from a time when a more limited purpose was entertained. Let me now give an example to show the practical importance, for the decision of actual cases, of understanding the reasons of the law, by taking an example from rules which, so far as I know, never have been explained or theorized about in any adequate way. I refer to statutes of limitation and the law of prescription. The end of such rules is obvious, but what is the justification for depriving a man of his rights, a pure evil as far as it goes, in consequence of the lapse of time? Sometimes the loss of evidence is referred to, but that is a secondary matter. Sometimes the desirability of peace, but why is peace more desirable after twenty years than before? It is increasingly likely to come without the aid of legislation. Sometimes it is said that, if a man neglects to enforce his rights, he cannot complain if, after a while, the law follows his example. Now if this is all that can be said about it, you probably will decide a case I am going to put, for the plaintiff; if you take the view which I shall suggest, you possibly will decide it for the defendant. A man is sued for trespass upon land, and justifies under a right of way. He proves that he has used the way openly and adversely for twenty years, but it turns out that the plaintiff had granted a license to a person whom he reasonably supposed to be the defendant's agent, although not so in fact, and therefore had assumed that the use of the way was permissive, in which case no right would be gained. Has the defendant gained a right or not? If his gaining it stands on the fault and neglect of the landowner in the ordinary sense, as seems commonly to be supposed, there has been no such neglect, and the right of way has not been acquired. But if I were the defendant's counsel, I should suggest that the foundation of the acquisition of rights by lapse of time is to be looked for in the position of the person who gains them, not in that of the loser. Sir Henry Maine has made it fashionable to connect the archaic notion of property with prescription. But the connection is further back than the first recorded history. It is in the nature of man's mind. A thing which you have enjoyed and used as your own for a long time, whether property or an opinion, takes root in your being and cannot be torn away without your resenting the act and trying to defend yourself, however you came by it. The law can ask no better justification than the deepest instincts of man. It is only by way of reply to the suggestion that you are disappointing the former owner, that you refer to his neglect having allowed the gradual dissociation between himself and what he claims, and the gradual association of it with another. If he knows that another is doing acts which on their face show that he is on the way toward establishing such an association, I should argue that in justice to that other he was bound at his peril to find out whether the other was acting under his permission, to see that he was warned, and, if necessary, stopped.

---

41. [Ed. note] Friedrich Ludwig von Keller (1799–1860).
42. [Ed. note] Rudolph Sohm (1841–1917).

I have been speaking about the study of the law, and I have said next to nothing of what commonly is talked about in that connection,—text-books and the case system, and all the machinery with which a student comes most immediately in contact. Nor shall I say anything about them. Theory is my subject, not practical details. The modes of teaching have been improved since my time, no doubt, but ability and industry will master the raw material with any mode. Theory is the most important part of the dogma of the law, as the architect is the most important man who takes part in the building of a house. The most important improvements of the last twenty-five years are improvements in theory. It is not to be feared as unpractical, for, to the competent, it simply means going to the bottom of the subject. For the incompetent, it sometimes is true, as has been said, that an interest in general ideas means an absence of particular knowledge. I remember in army days reading of a youth who, being examined for the lowest grade and being asked a question about squadron drill, answered that he never had considered the evolutions of less than ten thousand men. But the weak and foolish must be left to their folly. The danger is that the able and practical minded should look with indifference or distrust upon ideas the connection of which with their business is remote. I heard a story, the other day, of a man who had a valet to whom he paid high wages, subject to deduction for faults. One of his deductions was, "For lack of imagination, five dollars." The lack is not confined to valets. The object of ambition, power, generally presents itself nowadays in the form of money alone. Money is the most immediate form, and is a proper object of desire. "The fortune," said Rachel, "is the measure of the intelligence." That is a good text to waken people out of a fool's paradise. But, as Hegel says,[43] "It is in the end not the appetite, but the opinion, which has to be satisfied." To an imagination of any scope the most far-reaching form of power is not money, it is the command of ideas. If you want great examples read Mr. Leslie Stephen's "History of English Thought in the Eighteenth Century," and see how a hundred years after his death the abstract speculations of Descartes had become a practical force controlling the conduct of men. Read the works of the great German jurists, and see how much more the world is governed to-day by Kant than by Bonaparte. We cannot all be Descartes or Kant, but we all want happiness. And happiness, I am sure from having known many successful men, cannot be won simply by being counsel for great corporations and having an income of fifty thousand dollars. An intellect great enough to win the prize needs other food beside success. The remoter and more general aspects of the law are those which give it universal interest. It is through them that you not only become a great master in your calling, but connect your subject with the universe and catch an echo of the infinite, a glimpse of its unfathomable process, a hint of the universal law.

––––––––––

43. Phil. des Rechts, § 190.

BRIEF FOR THE DEFENDANT IN ERROR, *MULLER V. OREGON*

LOUIS D. BRANDEIS, OCTOBER TERM, 1907

THE WORLD'S EXPERIENCE UPON WHICH THE LEGISLATION
LIMITING THE HOURS OF LABOR FOR WOMEN IS BASED

I. The Dangers of Long Hours
A. Causes
(1) Physical Differences Between Men and Women

The dangers of long hours for women arise from their special physical organization taken in connection with the strain incident to factory and similar work.

Long hours of labor are dangerous for women primarily because of their special physical organization. In structure and function women are differentiated from men. Besides these anatomical and physiological differences, physicians are agreed that women are fundamentally weaker than men in all that makes for endurance: in muscular strength, in nervous energy, in the powers of persistent attention and application. Overwork, therefore, which strains endurance to the utmost, is more disastrous to the health of women than of men, and entails upon them more lasting injury.

Report of Select Committee on Shops Early Closing Bill, British House of Commons, 1895.

Dr. Percy Kidd, physician in Brompton and London Hospitals:

The most common effect I have noticed of the long hours is general deterioration of health; very general symptoms which we medically attribute to over-action, and debility of the nervous system; that includes a great deal more than what is called nervous disease, such as indigestion, constipation, a general slackness, and a great many other indefinite symptoms.

Are those symptoms more marked in women than in men?

I think they are much more marked in women. I should say one sees a great many more women of this class than men; but I have seen precisely the same symptoms in men, I should not say in the same proportion, because one has not been able to make anything like a statistical inquiry. There are other symptoms, but I mention those as being the most common. Another symptom especially among women is anemia, bloodlessness or pallor, that I have no doubt is connected with long hours indoors.

Report of the Maine Bureau of Industrial and Labor Statistics, 1888.

Let me quote from Dr. Ely Van der Warker (1875):

Woman is badly constructed for the purposes of standing eight or ten hours upon her feet. I do not intend to bring into evidence the peculiar position and nature of the organs contained in the pelvis, but to call attention to the peculiar construction of the knee and the shallowness of the pelvis, and the delicate nature of the foot as part of a sustaining column. The knee joint of woman is a sexual characteristic. Viewed in front and extended, the joint in but a slight degree interrupts the gradual taper of the thigh into the leg. Viewed in a semi-flexed position, the joint forms a smooth ovate spheroid. The reason of this lies in the smallness of the patella in front, and the narrowness of the articular surfaces of the tibia and femur, and which in man form the lateral prominences, and thus is much more perfect as a sustaining column than that of a woman. The muscles which keep the body fixed upon the thighs in the erect position labor under the disadvantage of shortness of purchase, owing to the short distance, compared to that of man, between the crest of the ilium and the great trochanter of the femur, thus giving to man a much larger purchase in the leverage existing between the trunk and the extremities. Comparatively the foot is less able to sustain weight than that of man, owing to its shortness and the more delicate formation of the tarsus and metatarsus.

Report of the Massachusetts Bureau of Labor Statistics, 1875.

A "lady operator," many years in the business, informed us: "I have had hundreds of lady compositors in my employ, and they all exhibited, in a marked manner, both in the way they performed their work and in its results, the difference in physical ability between themselves and men. They cannot endure the prolonged close attention and confine-ment which is a great part of type-setting. I have few girls with me more than two or three years at a time; they must have vacations, and they break down in health rapidly. I know no reason why a girl could not set as much type as a man, if she were as strong to endure the demand on mind and body."

Report of the Nebraska Bureau of Labor and Industrial Statistics, 1901–1902.

They (women) are unable, by reason of their physical limitations, to endure the same hours of exhaustive labor as may be endured by men without injury to their health would wreck the constitution and destroy the health of women, and render them incapable of bearing their share of the burdens of the family and the home. The State must be accorded the right to guard and protect women as a class against such a condition, and the law in question to that extent conserves the public health and welfare.

In strength as well as in rapidity and precision of movement women are inferior to men. This is not a conclusion that has ever been contested. It is in harmony with all the practical experience of life. It is perhaps also in harmony with the results of those investigators . . . who have found that, as in the blood of women, so also in their muscles, there is more water than in those of men. To a very great extent it is a certainty, a matter of difference in exercise and environment. It is probably, also, partly a matter of organic constitution.

The motor superiority of men, and to some extent of males generally, is, it can scarcely be doubted, a deep-lying fact. It is related to what is most fundamental in men and in women, and to their whole psychic organization.

There appears to be a general agreement that women are more docile and amenable to discipline; that they can do light work equally well; that they are steadier in some respects; but that, on the other hand, they are often absent on account of slight indisposition, and they break down sooner under strain.

* * *

It has been estimated that out of every one hundred days women are in a semipathological state of health for from fourteen to sixteen days. The natural congestion of the pelvic organs during menstruation is augmented and favored by work on sewing machines and other industrial occupations necessitating the constant use of the lower part of the body. Work during these periods tends to induce chronic congestion of the uterus and appendages, and dysmenorrhea and flexion of the uterus are well known affections of working girls.

VII. Laundries

The specific prohibition in the Oregon Act of more than ten hours' work in laundries is not an arbitrary discrimination against that trade. Laundries would probably not be included under the general terms of "manufacturing" or "mechanical establishments"; and yet the special dangers of long hours in laundries, as the business is now conducted, present strong reasons for providing a legal limitation of the hours of work in that business.

Dangerous Trades. Thomas Oliver, Medical Expert on Dangerous Trades Committees of the Home Office. 1902.
Chapter XLVII. Laundry Workers.

It is perhaps difficult to realize that the radical change which has everywhere transformed industrial conditions has already affected this occupation (laundry work) also, and that for good or for evil the washerwoman is passing under the influences which have so profoundly modified the circumstances of her sister of the spinning-wheel and the sewing needle. When the first washing machine and ironing roller were applied to this occupation, alteration in the conditions became as much a foregone conclusion as it did in the case of the textile or the clothing manufactures, when the spinning frame, the power loom, or the sewing machine appeared.

Meanwhile, few industries afford at the present time a more interesting study. From a simple home occupation it is steadily being transformed by the application of power-driven machinery and by the division of labor into a highly organized factory industry, in which complicated labor-saving contrivances of all kinds play a prominent part. The tremendous impetus in the adoption of machinery, and the consequent modification of the system of employment so striking in the large laundries, is not greater than the less obvious but even more important development in the same direction among small laundries. Indeed the difference is rapidly becoming one of degree only. In the large laundries may be found perhaps more machinery and a greater number of the newest devices, but the fundamental change has affected all alike.

* * *

D. Bad Effect upon Morals

Report of British Chief Inspector of Factories and Workshops, 1900.

> One of the most unsatisfactory results of the present system of lack of working hours in laundries is the unfortunate moral effect on the women and girls. . . . Women who are employed at arduous work till far into the night are not likely to be early risers nor given to punctual attendance in the mornings, and workers who on one or two days in the week are dismissed to idleness or to other occupations, while on the remaining days they are expected to work for abnormally long hours, are not rendered methodical, industrious, or dependable workers by such an unsatisfactory training. The self-control and good habits engendered by a regular and definite period of moderate daily employment, which affords an excellent training for the young worker in all organized industries, is sadly lacking, and, instead, one finds periods of violent over-work alternating with hours of exhaustion. The result is the establishment of a kind of "vicious circle"; bad habits among workers make compliance by their employers with any regulation as to hours very difficult while a lack of loyal adherence to reasonable hours of employment by many laundry occupiers increases the difficulty for those who make the attempt in real earnestness.

MECHANICAL JURISPRUDENCE

ROSCOE POUND, 1908

"There is no way," says Sir Frederick Pollock, "by which modern law can escape from the scientific and artificial character imposed on it by the demand of modern societies for full, equal, and exact justice:" An Australian judge has stated the same proposition in these words: "The public is more interested than it knows in maintaining the highest scientific standard in the administration of justice." Every lawyer feels this, and every thoughtful student of institutions must admit it. But what do we mean by the word "scientific" in this connection? What is scientific law? What constitutes science in the administration of justice? Sir Frederick Pollock gives us the clue when he defines the reasons that compel law to take on this scientific character as three: the demand for full justice, that is for solutions that go to the root of controversies; the demand for equal justice, that is a like adjustment of like relations under like conditions; and the demand for exact justice, that is for a justice whose operations, within reasonable limits, may be predicted in advance of action. In other words, the marks of a scientific law are, conformity to reason, uniformity, and certainty. Scientific law is a reasoned body of principles for the administration of justice, and its antithesis is a system of enforcing magisterial caprice, however honest, and however much disguised under the name of justice or equity or natural law. But this scientific character of law is a means—a means toward the end of law, which is the administration of justice. Law is forced to take on this character in order to accomplish its end fully, equally, and exactly; and in so far as it fails to perform its function fully, equally, and exactly, it fails in the end for which it exists. Law is scientific in order to eliminate so far as may be the personal equation in judicial administration, to preclude corruption and to limit the dangerous possibilities of magisterial ignorance. Law is not scientific for the sake of science. Being scientific as a means toward an end, it must be judged by the results it achieves, not by the niceties of its internal structure; it must be valued by the extent to which it meets its end, not by the beauty of its logical processes or the strictness with which its rules proceed from the dogmas it takes for its foundation.

Two dangers have to be guarded against in a scientific legal system, one of them in the direction of the effect of its scientific and artificial character upon the public, the other in the direction of its effect upon the courts and the legal profession. With respect to the first danger, it is well to remember that law must not become too scientific for the people to appreciate its workings. Law has the practical function of adjusting everyday relations so as to meet current ideas of fair play. It must not become so completely artificial that the public is led to regard it as wholly arbitrary. No institution can stand upon such a basis today. Reverence for institutions of the past will not preserve, of itself, an institution that touches everyday life as profoundly as does the law. Legal theory can no

Source: Reprinted from 8 *Columbia Law Review* 605.

more stand as a sacred tradition in the modern world than can political theory. It has been one of the great merits of English law that its votaries have always borne this in mind. When Lord Esher said, "the law of England is not a science," he meant to protest against a pseudo-science of technical rules existing for their own sake and subserving supposed ends of science, while defeating justice. And it is the importance of the role of jurors in tempering the administration of justice with common-sense and preserving a due connection of the rules governing everyday relations with everyday needs of ordinary men that has atoned for the manifold and conspicuous defects of trial by jury and is keeping it alive. In Germany today one of the problems of law reform is how to achieve a similar tempering of the justice administered by highly trained specialists.

In the other direction, the effect of a scientific legal system upon the courts and upon the legal profession is more subtle and far-reaching. The effect of all systems is apt to be petrifaction of the subject systematized. Perfection of scientific system and exposition tends to cut off individual initiative in the future, to stifle independent consideration of new problems and of new phases of old problems, and to impose the ideas of one generation upon another. This is so in all departments of learning. One of the obstacles to advance in every science is the domination of the ghosts of departed masters. Their sound methods are forgotten, while their unsound conclusions are held for gospel. Legal science is not exempt from this tendency. Legal systems have their periods in which science degenerates, in which system decays into technicality, in which a scientific jurisprudence becomes a mechanical jurisprudence.

Roman law in its decadence furnishes a striking example. The Valentinian "law of citations" made a selection of jurisconsults of the past and allowed their writings only to be cited. It declared them, with the exception of Papinian, equal in authority. It confined the judge, when questions of law were in issue, to the purely mechanical task of counting and of determining the numerical preponderance of authority. Principles were no longer resorted to in order to make rules to fit cases. The rules were at hand in a fixed and final form, and cases were to be fitted to the rules. The classical jurisprudence of principles had developed, by the very weight of its authority, a jurisprudence of rules; and it is in the nature of rules to operate mechanically.

Undoubtedly one cause of the tendency of scientific law to become mechanical is to be found in the average man's admiration for the ingenious in any direction, his love of technicality as a manifestation of cleverness, his feeling that law, as a developed institution, ought to have a certain ballast of mysterious technicality. "Philosophy's queerest arguments," says James, "tickle agreeably our sense of subtlety and ingenuity." Every practitioner has encountered the lay obsession as to invalidity of a signing with a lead pencil. Every law teacher has had to combat the student obsession that notice, however cogent, may be disregarded unless it is "official." Lay hair-splitting over rules and regulations goes far beyond anything of which lawyers are capable. Experienced advocates have insisted that in argument to a jury, along with a just, common-sense theory of the merits, one ought to have a specious technicality for good measure. But apart from this general human tendency, there is the special tendency of the lawyer to regard artificiality in law as an end, to hold science something to be pursued for its own sake, to forget in this pursuit the purpose of law and hence of scientific law, and to judge rules and doctrines by their conformity to a supposed science and not by the results to which they lead. In periods of growth and expansion, this tendency is repressed. In periods of maturity and stability, when the opportunity for constructive work is largely eliminated, it becomes very marked.

> I have known judges, [said Chief Justice Erle] bred in the world of legal studies, who delighted in nothing so much as in a strong decision. Now a strong decision is a decision opposed to common-sense and to common convenience.... A great part of the law made by judges consists of strong decisions, and as one strong decision is a precedent for another a little stronger, the law at last, on some matters, becomes such a nuisance that equity intervenes, or an Act of Parliament must be passed to sweep the whole away.

The instance suggested in the conversation from which the foregoing extract is taken illustrates very well the development of a mechanical legal doctrine. Successive decisions upon the construction of wills had passed upon the meaning of particular words and phrases in particular wills. These decisions were used as guides in the construction of other wills. Presently rules grew up whereby it was settled that particular words and phrases had prescribed hard and fast meanings, and the construction of wills became so artificial, so scientific, that it defeated the very end of construction and compelled a series of sections in the Wills Act of 1836.

I have referred to mechanical jurisprudence as scientific because those who administer it believe it such. But in truth it is not science at all. We no longer hold anything scientific merely because it exhibits a rigid scheme of deductions from *a priori* conceptions. In the philosophy of today, theories are "instruments, not answers to enigmas, in which we can rest." The idea of science as a system of deductions has become obsolete, and the revolution which has taken place in other sciences in this regard must take place and is taking place in jurisprudence also. This revolution in science at large was achieved in the middle of the nineteenth century. In the first half of that century, scientific method in every department of learning was dominated by the classical German philosophy. Men conceived that by dialectics and deduction from controlling conceptions they could construe the whole content of knowledge. Even in the natural sciences this belief prevailed and had long dictated theories of nature and of natural phenomena. Linnaeus, for instance, lays down a proposition, *omne vivum ex ovo*, and from this fundamental conception deduces a theory of homologies between animal and vegetable organs. He deemed no study of the organisms and the organs themselves necessary to reach or to sustain these conclusions. Yet, today, study of the organisms themselves has overthrown his fundamental proposition. The substitution of efficient for final causes as explanations of natural phenomena has been paralleled by a revolution in political thought. We do not base institutions upon deduction from assumed principles of human nature; we require them to exhibit practical utility, and we rest them upon a foundation of policy and established adaptation to human needs. It has been asserted that to no small extent the old mode of procedure was borrowed from the law. We are told that it involved a "fundamentally juristic conception of the world in which all kinds of action and every sort of judgment was expressed in legal phraseology." We are told that "in the Middle Ages human welfare and even religion was conceived under the form of legality, and in the modern world this has given place to utility." We have, then, the same task in jurisprudence that has been achieved in philosophy, in the natural sciences and in politics. We have to rid ourselves of this sort of legality and to attain a pragmatic, a sociological legal science.

> What is needed nowadays, [it has been said] is that as against an abstract and unreal theory of State omnipotence on the one hand, and an atomistic and artificial view of individual independence on the other, the facts of the world with its innumerable bonds of association and the naturalness of social authority should be generally recognized, and become the basis of our laws, as it is of our life.

Herein is the task of the sociological jurist. Professor Small defines the sociological movement as "a frank endeavor to secure for the human factor in experience the central place which belongs to it in our whole scheme of thought and action." The sociological movement in jurisprudence is a movement for pragmatism as a philosophy of law; for the adjustment of principles and doctrines to the human conditions they are to govern rather than to assumed first principles; for putting the human factor in the central place and relegating logic to its true position as an instrument.

Jurisprudence is last in the march of the sciences away from the method of deduction from predetermined conceptions. On the continent of Europe, both the historical school of jurists and the philosophical school, which were dominant until at least the last quarter of the nineteenth century, proceeded in this way. The difference between them lay in the manner in which they arrived at their fundamental conceptions. The former derived them from the history of juristic speculation and the historical development of the Roman sources. The latter, through metaphysical inquiries, arrived at certain propositions as to human nature, and deduced a system from them. This was the philosophical theory behind the eighteenth-century movement for codification. Ihering was the pioneer in the work of superseding this jurisprudence of conceptions (*Begriffsjurisrudenz*) by a jurisprudence of results (*Wirklichkeitsjurisprudenz*). He insisted that we should begin at the other end; that the first question should be, how will a rule or a decision operate in practice? For instance, if a rule of commercial law were in question, the search should be for the rule that best accords with and gives effect to sound business practice. In the Civil Law, the doctrine as to mistake in the formation of a contract affords an example of the working of the two methods. Savigny treated the subject according to the jurisprudence of conceptions. He worked out historically and analytically the conception of a contract and deduced therefrom the rules to govern cases of mistake. It followed, from his conception, that if *A* telegraphed *B* to *buy* shares and the telegram as delivered to *B* read *sell*, there was no contract between *A* and *B*, and hence no liability of *A* to *B*; and for a time it was so held. But this and some of the other resulting rules were so far from just in their practical operation that, following the lead of Ihering, they have been abandoned and the ordinary understanding of businessmen has been given effect. And, in this same connection, the new German code has introduced, as a criterion of error in the content of an expression of the will, the question, what would be regarded as essential in the ordinary understanding of business. Even better examples of the workings of a jurisprudence of conceptions, for our purposes, may be found in the manner in which common-law courts have dealt with points of mercantile law. For instance, the law of partnership is made difficult and often unjust by the insistence of the courts upon deducing its rules from a conception of joint ownership and joint obligation, instead of ascertaining and giving effect to the actual situation as understood and practiced by merchants. The legal theory does not affect the actual course of business an iota. But it leads to unfortunate results when that course of business, for some reason, comes before the courts. Again, the refusal of Lord Holt to recognize the negotiability of promissory notes proceeded upon a deduction from the conception of a chose in action. A jurisprudence of ends would have avoided each of these errors.

In periods of legal development through juristic speculation and judicial decision, we have a jurisprudence of ends in fact, even if in form it is a jurisprudence of conceptions. The Roman *jus gentium* was worked out for concrete causes and the conceptions were later generalizations from its results. The *jus naturale* was a system of reaching reasonable ends by bringing philosophical theory into the scale against the hard and fast rules of antiquity. The development of equity in England was attained by a method of seeking results in concrete causes. The liberalizing of English law through the law merchant was brought about by substituting business practice for juridical conceptions. The development of the common law in America was a period of growth because the doctrine that the common law was received only so far as applicable led the courts, in adapting English case-law to American conditions, to study the conditions of application as well as the conceptions and their logical consequences. Whenever such a period has come to an end, when its work has been done and its legal theories have come to maturity, the jurisprudence of conceptions tends to decay. Conceptions are fixed. The premises are no longer to be examined. Everything is reduced to simple deduction from them. Principles cease to have importance. The law becomes a body of rules. This is the condition against which sociologists now protest, and protest rightly.

A period of legislative activity supervenes to supply, first new rules, then new premises, and finally a systematic body of principles as a fresh start for juristic development. But such periods hitherto have not been periods of growth. Usually legislative activity has not gone beyond the introduction of new rules or of new premises, and the chief result has been a summing up of the juristic accomplishment of the past in improved form. The further step, which is beginning to be taken in our present era of legal development through legislation, is in reality an awakening of juristic activity, as jurists perceive that they may effect results through the legislator as well as through the judge or the doctrinal writer. This step has yet to be taken outside of Germany. And in the first and second stages of a period of legislation the mechanical character of legal science is aggravated by the imperative theory, which is a concomitant of legislative activity. Austin's proposition that law is command so complete that even the unwritten law must be given this character, since whatever the sovereign permits he commands, was simply rediscovered during the legislative ferment of the reform movement in English law. In the flowering-time of Papal legislation the canon law had already asserted it. Moreover, a period of legislation and codification has brought German jurists to a like conclusion. At such times, when law is felt to be positive, to be the command of the law-maker, a tendency to enact rules as such becomes manifest. Roman law, in its period of legislation, can furnish more than one example of the sort of law-making of which we complain to-day.

Before the analytical school, which revived the imperative theory to meet the facts of an age of legislation, had become established, historical jurists led a revolt. But their jurisprudence is a jurisprudence of conceptions. Moreover, they have had little effect upon the actual course of Anglo-American law. The philosophical jurists have protested also and have appealed from purely legal considerations to considerations of reason and of natural law. But theirs, too, is a jurisprudence of conceptions, and their method, of itself, offers no relief. Their service has been in connection with the general sociological movement, in giving natural law a new and a modern aspect, and in promoting a general agreement among jurists on a sociological basis. In Europe, it is obvious that the different schools are coming together in a new sociological school that is to dominate juristic thought. Instead of seeking for an ideal universal law by metaphysical methods, the idea of all schools is to turn "the community of fact of mankind into a community of law in accord with the reasonable ordering of active life." Hence they hold that "the less arbitrary the character of a rule and the more clearly it conforms to the nature of things, the more nearly does it approach to the norm of a perfect law." The utilitarian theory of Bentham was a theory of legislation. The sociological theory of the present is a theory of legal science. Probably the chief merit of the new German code lies in its conformity in so large a degree to this theory. It lays down principles from which to deduce, not rules, but decisions; and decisions will indicate a rule only so long as the conditions to which they are applied cause them to express the principle. This, and not lax methods of equitable application, into which American courts are falling so generally, is the true way to make rules fit cases instead of making cases fit rules.

An efficient cause of the failure of much American legislation is that it is founded on an assumption that it is enough for the State to command. Legislation has not been the product of preliminary study of the conditions to which it was to apply. It has not expressed social standards accurately. It has not responded accurately to social needs. Hence a large proportion has been nugatory in practice. But the difficulty is not, as some have assumed, that matters of private law are not within the legitimate scope of legislation. It is rather that legislation has approached them upon a false theory. Judicial law-making also has acted upon an erroneous theory; and its results are often quite as much disregarded in practice as are statutes. Judicial law-making, however, cannot escape, except within very narrow limits, until it is given a new starting point from without. Legislative law-making, on the contrary, may do so and is beginning to do so.

That our case law at its maturity has acquired the sterility of a fully developed system, may be shown by abundant examples of its failure to respond to vital needs of present-day life. Its inadequacy to deal with employers' liability; the failure of the theory of "general jurisprudence" of the Supreme Court of the United States to give us a uniform commercial law; the failure of American courts, with centuries of discussion before them, to work out a reasonable or certain law of future interests in land; the breakdown of the common law in the matter of discrimination by public service companies because of inability to make procedure enforce its doctrines and rules; its breakdown in the attempt to adjust water rights in our newer states, where there was opportunity for free development; its inability to hold promoters to their duty and to protect the interests of those who invest in corporate enterprises against mismanagement and breach of trust; its failure to work out a scheme of responsibility that will hold legal entities, or those who hide behind their skirts, to their duty to the public—all these failures, and many more might be adduced, speak for themselves. But compare these failures with the great achievements of the youth of our case-law, with Lord Mansfield's development of a law of quasi-contracts from the fictions of the common counts, with Lord Mansfield's development of mercantile law by judicial decision, with Kent's working out of equity for America from a handful of English decisions, with Marshall's work in giving us a living constitution by judicial interpretation. Now and then, at present, we see vigorous life in remote corners of our case law, as, for instance, in the newer decisions as to surface and underground waters. But judicial revolt from mechanical methods to-day is more likely to take the form of "officious kindness" and flabby equitable application of law. Our judge-made law is losing its vitality, and it is a normal phenomenon that it should do so.

I have suggested some examples of the failure of our case law to rise to social and legal emergencies. Let me point to some phases of its active operation which lead to the same conclusion.

The manner in which the Fourteenth Amendment is applied affords a striking instance of the workings today of a jurisprudence of conceptions. Starting with the conception that it was intended to incorporate Spencer's Social Statics in the fundamental law of the United States, rules have been deduced that obstruct the way of social progress. The conception of liberty of contract, in particular, has given rise to rules and decisions which, tested by their practical operation, defeat liberty. As Mr. Olney says of the *Adair* Case, "it is archaic, it is a long step into the past, to conceive of and deal with the relations between the employer in such industries and the employee, as if the parties were individuals." The conception of freedom of contract is made the basis of a logical deduction. The court does not inquire what the effect of such a deduction will be, when applied to the actual situation. It does not observe that the result will be to produce a condition precisely the reverse of that which the conception originally contemplated. Again, the Commerce Clause of the Federal Constitution has been taken by one judge, at least, to be a constitutional enactment of a conception of free trade among the states. Deductions from this and like conceptions, assumed to express the meaning and the sole meaning of the clause, have given us rules which, when applied to the existing commercial and industrial situation, are wholly inadequate.

Procedure, with respect to which every thoughtful lawyer must feel that we are inexcusably behind the rest of the English-speaking world, suffers especially from mechanical jurisprudence. The conception of a theory of the case, developed by the common-law forms of action, has, in nearly half of our code jurisdictions, nullified the legislative intent and made the practice more rigid than at common law. But this conception is regarded by many as fundamental. In deductions from this conception they lose sight of the end of procedure, they make scientific procedure an end of itself, and thus, in the result, make adjective law an agency for defeating or delaying substantive law and justice instead of one for enforcing and speeding them. Aristotle discusses a project of a Greek reformer for enabling tribunals to render what he called a divided judgment. At that time, the judgment had to be absolute one way or the other. If a plaintiff claimed twenty *minæ* when but eighteen were proved to be due him, there was no course but to find for the defendant. The proposal to correct this and to allow a finding for the eighteen *minæ* due did not meet with Aristotle's approval. He said:

> A juror who votes acquittal decides, not that the defendant owes nothing, but that he does not owe the twenty *minæ* claimed.

We smile now at Aristotle's hard and fast deduction, in the face of a manifestly absurd result, from his conception of the trial of an issue. But at least half our jurisdictions do the same thing essentially in this matter of the theory of a plaintiff's case. That his pleadings and proofs disclose a case and a good case is not enough. The courts say they are not foreclosing that case; they are merely deciding upon the theory he has chosen to advance.

Again, in the practice as to parties, the common-law conception that there must be a joint interest or a joint liability, because there must be one controversy and joint parties are as one party, has seriously interfered with the liberal plan of the framers of the original Code of Civil Procedure. I can only cite some of the cases. But let me compare with our American cases a recent English decision. In that case two plaintiffs sued for an injunction against infringement of copyright and for an accounting of profits. Only one was owner of the copyright; the other was a mere licensee. But which one was owner was not clear. The court did not deem it necessary to take up this question and determine whether one only was owner and if so which, although a money recovery was to be had. So long as the plaintiffs were agreed among themselves and the defendant had wronged and owed money to one or the other of them, it affirmed a decree for an injunction and accounting. Although in strictness it might be that only *one* was entitled to judgment and so it would be necessary to determine *which* one, the court wasted no time on that question so long as nothing turned on it. Here the court was conscious that procedure was a mere means. It strove to vindicate the substantive law. It was not set upon adhering with scrupulous exactness to logical deductions from a conception of adjective law at the expense of the merits the latter exists to give effect to.

Trial procedure is full of mechanical jurisprudence born of deduction from conceptions. The decisions as to the effect of a view of the *locus* by a jury, in which judgments are reversed unless jurors are told, in the face of common-sense, not to use what they see as evidence, in order to vindicate a conception of the duty of a court of review; the wilderness of decisions as to the province of court and jury, in which, carrying a conception of distinction between law and fact to extreme logical results, the courts at one moment assume that jurors are perfect and will absolutely follow an abstract instruction to its logical consequences, in the face of common-sense and the evidence, and at the next assume that they are fools and will be misled by anything not relevant that drops from the court; and the practice of instructions, one way or the other, when doubtful points of law arise, a general verdict, and a new trial, if the court of review takes another view of the point, when the verdict could have been taken quite as well subject to the point of law reserved, and a new trial obviated, illustrate forcibly the extent to which procedural conceptions, pursued for their own sake, may defeat the end of procedure and defeat the substance of the law. For delay of justice is denial of justice. Every time a party goes out of court on a mere point of practice, substantive law suffers an injury. The life of the law is in its enforcement.

Evidence also has been a prolific field for the unchecked jurisprudence of conceptions. But one example must suffice. The decisions by which in a majority of jurisdictions jurors are not permitted to learn directly the views of standard texts upon scientific and technical subjects, but must pass upon the conflicting opinions of experts without the aid of the impartial sources of information to which any common-sense man would resort in practice, carry out a conception of the competency of evidence at the expense of the end of evidence. In one case, the question was whether death had taken place from strangulation. The trial was held in a rural community, and the medical experts accessible had had no actual experience of cases of strangulation of the sort involved. But standard medical works did relate cases precisely in point, and, after proof that they were standard authorities, a physician was allowed to testify with respect to the symptoms disclosed in the light of the recorded experience of mankind. For this, the judgment was reversed. To vindicate a juridical conception, the court shut out the best possible means of information, in the circumstances of the case in hand, and allowed an accused person to escape because of the inevitable limits of experience of a rural physician.

How far the mechanical jurisprudence, of which the example just given is an extreme case, forgets the end in the means, is made manifest by the stock objection to attempts at introducing a common-sense and business-like procedure. We are told that formal and technical procedure "makes better lawyers." One might ask whether the making of good lawyers is the end of law. But what is a good lawyer? Let Ulpian answer:

> *Ius est ars boni et æqui. Cuius merito quis nos sacerdotes appellet; iustitiam namque colimus et boni et æqui, notitiam profitemur, æquum ab iniquo separantes, licitum ab illicto discernentes, bonos non solum metu pœnarum, verum etiam præmiorum quoque exhortatione efficere cupientes veram, nisi fallor, philosophiam, non simulatam affectantes.*

The nadir of mechanical jurisprudence is reached when conceptions are used, not as premises from which to reason, but as ultimate solutions. So used, they cease to be conceptions and become empty words. James has called attention to a like vice in philosophical thought:

> Metaphysics has usually followed a very primitive kind of quest. You know how men have always hankered after unlawful magic, and you know what a great part in magic *words* have always played. If you have his name, or the formula of incantation that binds him, you can control the spirit, genie, afrite, or whatever the power may be. . . . So the universe has always appeared to the natural mind as a kind of enigma of which the key must be sought in the shape of some illuminating or power-bringing word or name. That word names the universe's *principle*, and to possess it is after a fashion to possess the universe itself. "God," "Matter," "Reason," "the Absolute," "Energy," are so many solving names. You can rest when you have them. You are at the end of your meta-physical quest.

Current decisions and discussions are full of such solving words: estoppel, malice, privity, implied, intention of the testator, vested and contingent—when we arrive at these we are assumed to be at the end of our juristic search. Like Habib in the Arabian Nights, we wave aloft our scimitar and pronounce the talismanic word.

With legislative law-making in the grip of the imperative theory and its arbitrary results, and judicial decision in the grip of a jurisprudence of conceptions and its equally arbitrary results, whither are we to turn? Judicial law-making cannot serve us. As things are, the cure would be worse than the disease. No court could hold such hearings as those had by legislative committees upon measures for the protection of operatives, described by Mrs. Kelley, or that recently had before the Interstate Commerce Commission as to uniform bills of lading. We must soon have a new starting-point that only legislation can afford. That we may put the sociological, the pragmatic theory behind legislation, is demonstrated every day. Legislative reference bureaus, the Comparative Law Bureau, the Conferences of Commissioners on Uniform State Laws, such hearings as the one before the Interstate Commerce Commission already referred to, hearings before legislative committees, such conferences as the one held recently with respect to the Sherman Anti-trust Law, bar-association discussions of reforms in procedure—all these are furnishing abundant material for legislation of the best type. No such resources are open to the courts. Hence common-law lawyers will some day abandon their traditional attitude toward legislation; will welcome legislation and will make it what it should be. The part played by jurists in the best days of Roman legislation, and the part they have taken in modern Continental legislation, should convince us, if need be, that juristic principles may be recognized and juristic speculation may be put into effect quite as well by legislation as by judicial decision.

Herein is a noble task for the legal scholars of America. To test the conceptions worked out in the common law by the requirements of the new juristic theory, to lay sure foundations for the ultimate legislative restatement of the law, from which judicial decision shall start afresh—this is as great an opportunity as has fallen to the jurists of any age. The end of a period of development by judicial decision is marked by the prevalence of two types of judges; those who think it a great display of learning and of judicial independence to render what Chief Justice Erle called "strong decisions," and those who fix their gaze upon the raw equities of a cause and forage in the books for cases to sustain the desired result. But the task of a judge is to make a principle living, not by deducing from it rules, to be, like the Freshman's hero, "immortal for a great many years," but by achieving thoroughly the less ambitious but more useful labor of giving a fresh illustration of the intelligent application of the principle to a concrete cause, producing a workable and a just result. The real genius of our common law is in this, not in an eternal case-law. Let the principles be formulated by whom or derived from whence you will. The Common Law will look to courts to develop and expound them, the Civil Law to doctrinal treatises. It is only a lip service to our common law that would condemn it to a perpetuity of mechanical jurisprudence through distrust of legislation.

THE CAUSES OF POPULAR DISSATISFACTION WITH THE ADMINISTRATION OF JUSTICE

ROSCO POUND, 1906

Dissatisfaction with the administration of justice is as old as law. Not to go outside of our own legal system, discontent has an ancient and unbroken pedigree. The Anglo-Saxon laws continually direct that justice is to be done equally to rich and to poor and the king exhorts that the peace be kept better than has been wont, and that "men of every order readily submit . . . each to that law which is appropriate to him." The author of the apocryphal *Mirror of Justices* gives a list of one hundred and fifty-five abuses in legal administration, and names it as one of the chief abuses of the degenerate times in which he lived that executions of judges for corrupt or illegal decisions had ceased. Wyclif complains that "lawyers make process by subtlety and cavilations of law civil, that is much heathen men's law, and do not accept the form of the gospel, as if the gospel were not so good as pagan's law." Starkey, in the reign of Henry VIII, says: "Everyone that can color reason maketh a stop to the best law that is beforetime devised." James I reminded his judges that "the law was founded upon reason, and that he and others had reason as well as the judges." In the eighteenth century, it was complained that the bench was occupied by "legal monks, utterly ignorant of human nature and of the affairs of men." In the nineteenth century the vehement criticism of the period of the reform movement needs only to be mentioned. In other words, as long as there have been laws and lawyers, conscientious and well-meaning men have believed that laws were mere arbitrary technicalities, and that the attempt to regulate the relations of mankind in accordance with them resulted largely in injustice. But we must not be deceived by this innocuous and inevitable discontent with all law into overlooking or underrating the real and serious dissatisfaction with courts and lack of respect for law which exists in the United States today.

In spite of the violent opposition which the doctrine of judicial power over unconstitutional legislation at first encountered, the tendency to give the fullest scope to the common law doctrine of supremacy of law and to tie down administration by common law liabilities and judicial review, was, until recently, very marked. Today, the contrary tendency is no less marked. Courts are distrusted, and executive boards and commissions with summary and plenary powers, freed, so far as constitutions will permit, from judicial review, have become the fashion. It will be assumed, then, that there is more than the normal amount of dissatisfaction with the present-day administration of justice in America. Assuming this, the first step must be diagnosis, and diagnosis will be the sole purpose of this paper. It will attempt only to discover and to point out the causes of current popular dissatisfaction. The inquiry will be limited, moreover, to civil justice. For while the criminal law attracts more notice, and punishment seems to have greater interest for the lay mind than the civil remedies of prevention and compensation, the true interest of the modern community is in the civil

---

Source: Reprinted from 29 *A.B.A. Rep.*, pt. I, 395–417, 1906.

administration of justice. Revenge and its modern outgrowth, punishment, belong to the past of legal history. The rules which define these invisible boundaries, within which each may act without conflict with the activities of his fellows in a busy and crowded world, upon which investor, promoter, buyer, seller, employer, and employee must rely consciously or subconsciously in their every-day transactions, are conditions precedent of modern social and industrial organization.

With the scope of inquiry so limited, the causes of dissatisfaction with the administration of justice may be grouped under four main heads: (1) Causes for dissatisfaction with *any* legal system, (2) causes lying in the peculiarities of our Anglo-American legal system, (3) causes lying in our American judicial organization and procedure, and (4) causes lying in the environment of our judicial administration.

It needs but a superficial acquaintance with literature to show that all legal systems among all peoples have given rise to the same complaints. Even the wonderful mechanism of modern German judicial administration is said to be distrusted by the people on the time-worn ground that there is one law for the rich and another for the poor. It is obvious, therefore, that there must be some cause or causes inherent in all law and in all legal systems in order to produce this universal and invariable effect. These causes of dissatisfaction with any system of law I believe to be the following: (1) The necessarily mechanical operation of rules, and hence of laws; (2) the inevitable difference in rate of progress between law and public opinion; (3) the general popular assumption that the administration of justice is an easy task, to which anyone is competent; and (4) popular impatience of restraint.

The most important and most constant cause of dissatisfaction with all law at all times is to be found in the necessarily mechanical operation of legal rules. This is one of the penalties of uniformity. Legal history shows an oscillation between wide judicial discretion on the one hand and strict confinement of the magistrate by minute and detailed rules upon the other hand. From time to time more or less reversion to justice without law becomes necessary in order to bring the public administration of justice into touch with changed moral, social, or political conditions. But such periods of reversion result only in new rules or changed rules. In time the modes of exercising discretion become fixed, the course of judicial action becomes stable and uniform, and the new element, whether custom or equity or natural law, becomes as rigid and mechanical as the old. This mechanical action of the law may be minimized, but it cannot be obviated. Laws are general rules; and the process of making them general involves elimination of the immaterial elements of particular controversies. If all controversies were alike or if the degree in which actual controversies approximate to the recognized types could be calculated with precision, this would not matter. The difficulty is that in practice they approximate to these types in infinite gradations. When we eliminate immaterial factors to reach a general rule, we can never entirely avoid eliminating factors which will be more or less material in some particular controversy. If to meet this inherent difficulty in administering justice according to law we introduce a judicial dispensing power, the result is uncertainty and an intolerable scope for the personal equation of the magistrate. If we turn to the other extreme and pile up exceptions and qualifications and provisos, the legal system becomes cumbrous and unworkable. Hence the law has always ended in a compromise, in a middle course between wide discretion and over-minute legislation. In reaching this middle ground, some sacrifice of flexibility of application to particular cases is inevitable. In consequence, the adjustment of the relations of man and man according to these rules will of necessity appear more or less arbitrary and more or less in conflict with the ethical notions of individuals.

In periods of absolute or generally received moral systems, the contrast between legal results and strict ethical requirements will appeal only to individuals. In periods of free individual thought in morals and ethics, and especially in an age of social and industrial transition, this contrast is greatly intensified and appeals to large classes of society. Justice, which is the end of law, is the ideal compromise between the activities of all in a crowded world. The law seeks to harmonize these activities and to adjust the relations of every man with his fellows so as to accord with the moral sense of the community. When the community is at one in its ideas of justice, this is possible. When the community is divided and diversified, and groups and classes and interests, understanding each other none too well, have conflicting ideas of justice, the task is extremely difficult. It is impossible that legal and ethical ideas should be in entire accord in such a society. The individual looks at cases one by one and measures them by his individual sense of right and wrong. The lawyer must look at cases in gross and must measure them largely by an artificial standard. He must apply the ethics of the community, not his own. If discretion is given him, his view will be that of the class from which he comes. If his hands are tied by law, he must apply the ethics of the past as formulated in common law and legislation. In either event, judicial and individual ethical standards will diverge. And this divergence between the ethical and the legal, as each individual sees it, makes him say with Luther, "Good jurist, bad Christian."

A closely related cause of dissatisfaction with the administration of justice according to law is to be found in the inevitable difference in rate of progress between law and public opinion. In order to preclude corruption, to exclude the personal prejudices of magistrates, and to minimize individual incompetency, law formulates the moral sentiments of the community in rules to which the judgments of tribunals must conform. These rules, being formulations of public opinion, cannot exist until public opinion has become fixed and settled, and cannot change until a change of public opinion has become complete. It follows that this difficulty in the judicial administration of justice, like the preceding, may be minimized, but not obviated. In a rude age the Teutonic moots in which every free man took a hand might be possible. But these tribunals broke under pressure of business and became ordinary courts with permanent judges. The Athenians conceived that the people themselves should decide each case. But the Athenian dikastery, in which controversies were submitted to blocks of several hundred citizens by way of reaching the will of the democracy, proved to register its caprice for the moment rather than its permanent will. Modern experience with juries, especially in commercial causes, does not warrant us in hoping much from any form of judicial referendum. Public opinion must affect the administration of justice through the rules by which justice is administered rather than through the direct administration. All interference with the uniform and automatic application of these rules, when actual controversies arise, introduces an anti-legal element which becomes intolerable. But, as public opinion affects tribunals through the rules by which they decide and these rules once made, stand till abrogated or altered, any system of law will be made up of successive strata of rules and doctrines representing successive and often widely divergent periods of public opinion. In this sense, law is often in very truth a government of the living by the dead. The unconscious changes of judicial law making and the direct alterations of legislation and codification operate to make this government by the dead reasonably tolerable. But here again we must pay a price for certainty and uniformity. The law does not respond quickly to new conditions. It does not change until ill effects are felt; often not until they are felt acutely. The moral or intellectual or economic change must come first. While it is coming, and until it is so complete as to affect the law and formulate itself therein, friction must ensue. In an age of rapid moral, intellectual, and economic changes, often crossing one another and producing numerous minor resultants, this friction cannot fail to be in excess.

A third perennial source of popular dissatisfaction with the administration of justice according to law may be found in the popular assumption that the administration of justice is an easy task to which anyone is competent. Laws may be compared to the formulas of engineers. They sum up the experience of many courts with many cases and enable the magistrate to apply that experience subconsciously. So, the formula enables the engineer to make use of the accumulated experience of past builders, even though he could not work out a step in its evolution by himself. A layman is no more competent to construct or to apply the one formula than the other. Each requires special knowledge and special preparation. Nonetheless, the notion that anyone is competent to adjudicate the intricate controversies of a modern community contributes to the unsatisfactory administration of justice in many parts of the United States. The older states have generally outgrown it. But it is felt in extravagant powers of juries, lay judges of probate and legislative or judicial law making against *stare decisis*, in most of the commonwealths of the South and West. The public seldom realizes how much it is interested in maintaining the highest scientific standard in the administration of justice. There is no more certain protection against corruption, prejudice, class feeling, or incompetence. Publicity will avail something. But the daily criticism of trained minds, the knowledge that nothing which does not conform to the principles and received doctrines of scientific jurisprudence will escape notice, does more than any other agency for the every-day purity and efficiency of courts of justice.

Another necessary source of dissatisfaction with judicial administration of justice is to be found in popular impatience of restraint. Law involves restraint and regulation, with the sheriff and his posse in the background to enforce it. But, however necessary and salutary this restraint, men have never been reconciled to it entirely. The very fact that it is a compromise between the individual and his fellows makes the individual, who must abate some part of his activities in the interest of his fellows, more or less restive. In an age of absolute theories, monarchical or democratic, this restiveness is acute. A conspicuous example is to be seen in the contest between the king and the common law courts in the seventeenth century. An equally conspicuous example is to be seen in the attitude of the frontiersman toward state-imposed justice. "The unthinking sons of the sage brush," says Owen Wister, "ill tolerate anything which stands for discipline, good order and obedience; and the man who lets another command him they despise. I can think of no threat more evil for our democracy, for it is a fine thing diseased and perverted, namely, the spirit of independence gone drunk." This is an extreme case. But in a lesser degree the feeling that each individual, as an organ of the sovereign democracy, is above the law he helps to make, fosters everywhere a disrespect for legal methods and institutions and a spirit of resistance to them. It is "the reason of this our artificial man the commonwealth," says Hobbes, "and his command that maketh law." This man, however, is abstract. The concrete man in the street or the concrete mob is much more obvious; and it is no wonder that individuals and even classes of individuals fail to draw the distinction.

A considerable portion of current dissatisfaction with the administration of justice must be attributed to the universal causes just considered. Conceding this, we have next to recognize that there are potent causes in operation of a character entirely different.

Under the second main head, causes lying in our peculiar legal system, I should enumerate five: (1) The individualist spirit of our common law, which agrees ill with a collectivist age; (2) the common law doctrine of contentious procedure, which turns litigation into a game; (3) political jealousy, due to the strain put upon our legal system by the doctrine of supremacy of law; (4) the lack of general ideas or legal philosophy, so characteristic of Anglo-American law, which gives us petty tinkering where comprehensive reform is needed; and (5) defects of form due to the circumstance that the bulk of our legal system is still case law.

The first of these, conflict between the individualist spirit of the common law and the collectivist spirit of the present age, has been treated of on another occasion. What was said then need not be repeated. Suffice it to point out two examples. From the beginning, the main reliance of our common law system has been individual initiative. The main security for the peace at common law is private prosecution of offenders. The chief security for the efficiency and honesty of public officers is mandamus or injunction by a taxpayer to prevent waste of the proceeds of taxation. The reliance for keeping public service companies to their duty in treating all alike at reasonable price is an action to recover damages. Moreover, the individual is supposed at common law to be able to look out for himself and to need no administrative protection. If he is injured through contributory negligence, no theory of comparative negligence comes to his relief; if he hires as an employee, he assumes the risk of the employment; if he buys goods, the rule is *caveat emptor*. In our modern industrial society, this whole scheme of individual initiative is breaking down. Private prosecution has become obsolete. Mandamus and injunction have failed to prevent rings and bosses from plundering public funds. Private suits against carriers for damages have proved no preventive of discrimination and extortionate rates. The doctrine of assumption of risk becomes brutal under modern conditions of employment. An action for damages is no comfort to us when we are sold diseased beef or poisonous canned goods. At all these points, and they are points of every-day contact with the most vital public interests, common law methods of relief have failed. The courts have not been able to do the work which the common law doctrine of supremacy of law imposed on them. A widespread feeling that the courts are inefficient has been a necessary result. But, along with this, another phase of the individualism of the common law has served to increase public irritation. At the very time the courts have appeared powerless themselves to give relief, they have seemed to obstruct public efforts to get relief by legislation. The chief concern of the common law is to secure and protect individual rights. "The public good," says Blackstone, "is in nothing more essentially interested than in the protection of every individual's private rights." Such, it goes without saying, is not the popular view today. Today we look to society for protection against individuals, natural or artificial, and we resent doctrines that protect these individuals against society for fear society will oppress us. But the common law guaranties of individual rights are established in our constitutions, state and federal. So that, while in England these common law dogmas have had to give way to modern legislation, in America they stand continually between the people, or large classes of the people, and legislation they desire. In consequence, the courts have been put in a false position of doing nothing and obstructing everything, which it is impossible for the layman to interpret aright.

A no less potent source of irritation lies in our American exaggerations of the common law contentious procedure. The sporting theory of justice, the "instinct of giving the game fair play," as Professor Wigmore has put it, is so rooted in the profession in America that most of us take it for a fundamental legal tenet. But it is probably only a survival of the days when a lawsuit was a fight between two clans in which change of venue had been taken to the forum. So far from being a fundamental fact of jurisprudence, it is peculiar to Anglo-American law; and it has been strongly curbed in modern English practice. With us, it is not merely in full acceptance, it has been developed and its collateral possibilities have been cultivated to the furthest extent. Hence in America we take it as a matter of course that a judge should be a mere umpire, to pass upon objections and hold counsel to the rules of the game, and that the parties should fight out their own game in their own way without judicial interference. We resent such interference as unfair, even when in the interests of justice. The idea that procedure must of necessity be wholly contentious disfigures our judicial administration at every point. It leads the most conscientious judge to feel that he is merely to decide the contest, as counsel present it, according to the rules of the game, not to search independently for truth and justice. It leads counsel to forget that they are officers of the court and to deal with the rules of law and procedure exactly as the professional football coach with the rules of the sport. It leads to exertion to "get error into the record" rather than to dispose of the controversy finally and upon its merits. It turns witnesses, and especially expert witnesses, into partisans pure and simple. It leads to sensational cross-examinations "to affect credit," which have made the witness stand "the slaughter house of reputations." It prevents the trial court from restraining the bullying of witnesses and creates a general dislike, if not fear, of the witness function which impairs the administration of justice. It keeps alive the unfortunate exchequer rule, dead in the country of its origin, according to which errors in the admission or rejection of evidence are presumed to be prejudicial and hence demand a new trial. It grants new trials because by inability to procure a bill of exceptions a party has lost the chance to play another inning in the game of justice. It creates vested rights in errors of procedure, of the benefit whereof parties are not to be deprived. The inquiry is not, What do substantive law and justice require? Instead, the inquiry is: Have the rules of the game been carried out strictly? If any material infraction is discovered, just as the football rules put back the offending team five or ten or fifteen yards, as the case may be, our sporting theory of justice awards new trials, or reverses judgments, or sustains demurrers in the interest of regular play.

The effect of our exaggerated contentious procedure is not only to irritate parties, witnesses and jurors in particular cases, but to give to the whole community a false notion of the purpose and end of law. Hence comes, in large measure, the modern American race to beat the law. If the law is a mere game, neither the players who take part in it nor the public who witness it can be expected to yield to its spirit when their interests are served by evading it. And this is doubly true in a time which requires all institutions to be economically efficient and socially useful. We need not wonder that one part of the community strain their oaths in the jury box and find verdicts against unpopular litigants in the teeth of law and evidence, while another part retain lawyers by the year to advise how to evade what to them are unintelligent and unreasonable restrictions upon necessary modes of doing business. Thus the courts, instituted to administer justice according to law, are made agents or abettors of lawlessness.

Another source of irritation at our American courts is political jealousy due to the strain put upon our legal system by the doctrine of the supremacy of law. By virtue of this doctrine, which has become fundamental in our polity, the law restrains, not individuals alone, but a whole people. The people so restrained would be likely in any event to be jealous of the visible agents of restraint. Even more is this true in that the subjects which our constitutional polity commits to the courts are largely matters of economics, politics, and sociology upon which a democracy is peculiarly sensitive. Not only are these matters made into legal questions, but they are tried as incidents of private litigation. This phase of the common law doctrine was felt as a grievance in the seventeenth century. "I tell you plainly," said Bacon, as attorney general, in arguing a question of prerogative to the judges, "I tell you plainly it is little better than a by-let or crooked creek to try whether the king hath power to erect this office in an assize between Brownlow and Michell." King Demos must feel much the same at seeing the constitutionality of the Missouri Compromise tried in an action of trespass, at seeing the validity of the legal tender laws tried on pleas of payment in private litigation, at seeing the power of the federal government to carry on the Civil War tried judicially in admiralty, at seeing the income tax overthrown in a stockholder's bill to enjoin waste of corporate assets and at seeing the important political questions in the Insular Cases disposed of in forfeiture proceedings against a few trifling imports. Nor is this the only phase of the common law doctrine of supremacy of law which produces political jealousy of the courts. Even more must the layman be struck with the spectacle of law paralyzing administration which our polity so frequently presents. The difficulties with writs of *habeas corpus* which the federal government encountered during the Civil War and the recent case of the income tax will occur to you at once. In my own state, in a few years we have seen a freight-rate law suspended by decree of a court and have seen the collection of taxes from railroad companies, needed for the every-day conduct of public business, tied up by an injunction. The strain put upon judicial institutions by such litigation is obviously very great.

Lack of general ideas and absence of any philosophy of law, which has been characteristic of our law from the beginning and has been a point of pride at least since the time of Coke, contributes its mite also toward the causes of dissatisfaction with courts. For one thing, it keeps us in the thrall of a fiction. There is a strong aversion to straightforward change of any important legal doctrine. The cry is *interpret it.* But such interpretation is spurious. It is legislation. And to interpret an obnoxious rule out of existence rather than to meet it fairly and squarely by legislation is a fruitful source of confusion. Yet the Bar are trained to it as an ancient common law doctrine, and it has a great hold upon the public. Hence if the law does not work well, says Bentham, with fine sarcasm, "it is never the law itself that is in the wrong; it is always some wicked interpreter of the law that has corrupted and abused it." Thus another unnecessary strain is imposed upon our judicial system and courts are held for what should be the work of the legislature.

The defects of form inherent in our system of case law have been the subject of discussion and controversy too often to require extended consideration. Suffice it to say that the want of certainty, confusion and incompleteness inherent in all case law, and the waste of labor entailed by the prodigious bulk to which ours has attained, appeal strongly to the layman. The compensating advantages of this system, as seen by the lawyer and by the scientific investigator, are not apparent to him. What he sees is another phase of the great game; a citation match between counsel, with a certainty that diligence can rake up a decision *somewhere* in support of any conceivable proposition.

Passing to the third head, causes lying in our judicial organization and procedure, we come upon the most efficient causes of dissatisfaction with the present administration of justice in America. For I venture to say that our system of courts is archaic and our procedure behind the times. Uncertainty, delay and expense, and above all the injustice of deciding cases upon points of practice, which are the mere etiquette of justice, direct results of the organization of our courts and the backwardness of our procedure, have created a deep-seated desire to keep out of court, right or wrong, on the part of every sensible business man in the community.

Our system of courts is archaic in three respects: (1) In its multiplicity of courts, (2) in preserving concurrent jurisdictions, (3) in the waste of judicial power which it involves. The judicial organizations of the several states exhibit many differences of detail. But they agree in these three respects. Multiplicity of courts is characteristic of archaic law. In Anglo-Saxon law, one might apply to the Hundred, the Shire, the Witan, or the king in person. Until Edward I broke up private jurisdictions, there were the king's superior courts of law, the itinerant justices, the county courts, the local or communal courts, and the private courts of lordships; besides which one might always apply to the king or to the Great Council for extraordinary relief. When later the royal courts had superseded all others, there were the concurrent jurisdictions of King's Bench, Common Pleas, and Exchequer, all doing the same work, while appellate jurisdiction was divided by King's Bench, Exchequer Chamber, and Parliament. In the Fourth Institute, Coke enumerates seventy-four courts. Of these, seventeen did the work that is now done by three, the County Courts, the Supreme Court of Judicature, and the House of Lords. At the time of the reorganization by the Judicature Act of 1873, five appellate courts and eight courts of first instance were consolidated into the one Supreme Court of Judicature. It was the intention of those who devised the plan of the Judicature Act to extend the principle of unity of jurisdiction by cutting off the appellate jurisdiction of the House of Lords and by incorporating the County Courts in the newly formed Supreme Court as branches thereof. The recommendation as to the County Courts was not adopted, and the appellate jurisdiction of the House of Lords was restored in 1875. In this way the unity and simplicity of the original design were impaired. But the plan, although adopted in part only, deserves the careful study of American lawyers as a model modern judicial organization. Its chief features were (1) to set up a single court, complete in itself, embracing all superior courts and jurisdictions; (2) to include in this one court, as a branch thereof, a single court of final appeal. In the one branch, the court of first instance, all original jurisdiction at law, in equity, in admiralty, in bankruptcy, in probate, and in divorce was to be consolidated; in the other branch, the court of appeal, the whole reviewing jurisdiction was to be established. This idea of unification, although not carried out completely, has proved most effective. Indeed, its advantages are self-evident. Where the appellate tribunal and the court of first instance are branches of one court, all expense of transfer of record, of transcripts, bills of exceptions, writs of error, and citations is wiped out. The records are the records of the court, of which each tribunal is but a branch. The court and each branch thereof knows its own records, and no duplication and certification is required. Again, all appellate practice, with its attendant pitfalls, and all waste of judicial time in ascertaining how or whether a case has been brought into the court of review is done away with. One may search the recent English reports in vain for a case where an appeal has miscarried on a point of practice. Cases on appellate procedure are wanting. In effect there is no such thing. The whole attention of the court and of counsel is concentrated upon the cause. On the other hand, our American reports bristle with fine points of appellate procedure. More than four per cent of the digest paragraphs of the last ten volumes of the *American Digest* have to do with Appeal and Error. In ten volumes of the *Federal Reporter*, namely volumes 129 to 139, covering decisions of the Circuit Courts of Appeals from 1903 till the present, there is an average of ten decisions upon points of appellate practice to the volume. Two cases to the volume, on the average, turn wholly upon appellate procedure. In the ten volumes there are six civil cases turning upon the question whether error or appeal was the proper mode of review, and in two civil cases the question was whether the Circuit Court of Appeals was the proper tribunal. I have referred to these reports because they represent courts in which only causes of importance may be brought. The state reports exhibit the same condition. In ten volumes of the Southwestern Reporter, the decisions of the Supreme Court and Courts of Appeals of Missouri show that nearly twenty per cent involve points of appellate procedure. In volume 87, of fifty-three decisions of the Supreme Court and ninety-seven of the Courts of Appeals, twenty-eight are taken up in whole or in part with the mere technics of obtaining a review. All of this is sheer waste, which a modern judicial organization would obviate.

Even more archaic is our system of concurrent jurisdiction of state and federal courts in causes involving diversity of citizenship; a system by virtue of which causes continually hang in the air between two courts, or, if they do stick in one court or the other, are liable to an ultimate overturning because they stuck in the wrong court. A few statistics on this point may be worth while. In the ten volumes of the Federal Reporter referred to, the decisions of the Circuit Courts of Appeals in civil cases average seventy-six to the volume. Of these, on the average, between four and five in a volume are decided on points of federal jurisdiction. In a little more than one to each volume, judgments of Circuit Courts are reversed on points of jurisdiction. The same volumes contain on the average seventy-three decisions of Circuit Courts in civil cases to each volume. Of these, six, on the average, are upon motions to remand to the state courts, and between eight and nine are upon other points of federal jurisdiction. Moreover, twelve cases in the ten volumes were remanded on the *form* of the petition for removal. In other words, in nineteen and three-tenths per cent of the reported decisions of the Circuit Courts the question was whether those courts had jurisdiction at all; and in seven per cent of these that question depended on the form of the pleadings. A system that permits this and reverses four judgments a year because the cause was brought in or removed to the wrong tribunal is out of place in a modern business community. All original jurisdiction should be concentrated. It ought to be impossible for a cause to fail because brought in the wrong place. A simple order of transfer from one docket to another in the same court ought to be enough. There should be no need of new papers, no transcripts, no bandying of cases from one court to another on orders of removal and of remand, no beginnings again with new process.

Judicial power may be wasted in three ways: (1) By rigid districts or courts or jurisdictions, so that business may be congested in one court while judges in another are idle; (2) by consuming the time of courts with points of pure practice, when they ought to be investigating substantial controversies; and (3) by nullifying the results of judicial action by unnecessary retrials. American judicial systems are defective in all three respects. The Federal Circuit Courts and Circuit Courts of Appeals are conspicuous exceptions in the first respect, affording a model of flexible judicial organization. But in nearly all of the states, rigid districts and hard and fast lines between courts operate to delay business in one court while judges in another have ample leisure. In the second respect, waste of judicial time upon points of practice, the intricacies of federal jurisdiction, and the survival of the obsolete Chinese Wall between law and equity in procedure make our federal courts no less conspicuous sinners. In the ten volumes of the *Federal Reporter* examined, of an average of seventy-six decisions of the Circuit Courts of Appeals in each volume, two turn upon the distinction between law and equity in procedure and not quite one judgment to each volume is reversed on this distinction. In an average of seventy-three decisions a volume by the Circuit Courts, more than three in each volume involve this same distinction, and not quite two in each volume turn upon it. But many states that are supposed to have reformed procedure scarcely make a better showing.

Each state has to a great extent its own procedure. But it is not too much to say that all of them are behind the times. We struck one great stroke in 1848 and have rested complacently or contented ourselves with patchwork amendment ever since. The leading ideas of the New York Code of Civil Procedure marked a long step forward. But the work was done too hurriedly and the plan of a rigid code, going into minute detail, was clearly wrong. A modern practice act lays down the general principles of practice and leaves details to rules of court. The New York Code Commission was appointed in 1847 and reported in 1848. If we except the Connecticut Practice Act of 1878, which shows English influence, American reform in procedure has stopped substantially where that commission left it. In England, beginning with 1826 and ending with 1874, *five* commissions have put forth *nine* reports upon this subject. As a consequence we have nothing in America to compare with the radical treatment of pleading in the English Judicature Act and the orders based thereon. We still try the *record*, not the *case*. We are still reversing judgments for nonjoinder and misjoinder. The English practice of joinder of parties against whom relief is claimed in the alternative, rendering judgment against any that the proof shows to be liable and dismissing the rest, makes an American lawyer rub his eyes. We are still reversing judgments for variances. We still reverse them because the recovery is in excess of the prayer, though sustained by the evidence.

But the worst feature of American procedure is the lavish granting of new trials. In the ten volumes of the *Federal Reporter* referred to, there are, on the average, twenty-five writs of error in civil cases to the volume. New trials are awarded on the average in eight cases a volume, or nearly twenty-nine per cent. In the state courts the proportion of new trials to causes reviewed, as ascertained from investigation of the last five volumes of each series of the National Reporter system, runs over forty per cent. In the last three volumes of the *New York Reports* (180–182), covering the period from December 6, 1904, to October 24, 1905, forty-five new trials are awarded. Nor is this all. In one case in my own state an action for personal injuries was tried six times, and one for breach of contract was tried three times and was four times in the Supreme Court. When with this we compare the statistics of the English Court of Appeal, which does not grant to exceed twelve new trials a year, or new trials in about three per cent of the cases reviewed, it is evident that our methods of trial and review are out of date.

A comparison of the volume of business disposed of by English and by American courts will illustrate the waste and delay caused by archaic judicial organization and obsolete procedure. In England there are twenty-three judges of the High Court who dispose on the average of fifty-six hundred *contested* cases, and have before them, in one form or another, some eighty thousand cases each year. In Nebraska there are twenty-eight district judges who have no original probate jurisdiction and no jurisdiction in bankruptcy or admiralty, and they had upon their dockets last year forty-three hundred and twenty cases, of which they disposed of about seventy per cent. England and Wales, with a population in 1900 of 32,000,000, employ for their whole civil litigation ninety-five judges, that is, thirty-seven in the Supreme Court and House of Lords and fifty-eight county judges. Nebraska, with a population in 1900 of 1,066,000, employs for the same purpose one hundred and twenty-nine. But these one hundred and twenty-nine are organized on an antiquated system and their time is frittered away on mere points of legal etiquette.

Finally, under the fourth and last head, causes lying in the environment of our judicial administration, we may distinguish six: (1) Popular lack of interest in justice, which makes jury service a bore and the vindication of right and law secondary to the trouble and expense involved; (2) the strain put upon law in that it has today to do the work of morals also; (3) the effect of transition to a period of legislation; (4) the putting of our courts into politics; (5) the making the legal profession into a trade, which has superseded the relation of attorney and client by that of employer and employee; and (6) public ignorance of the real workings of courts due to ignorant and sensational reports in the press. Each of these deserves consideration, but a few points only may be noticed. Law is the skeleton of social order. It must be "clothed upon by the flesh and blood of morality." The present is a time of transition in the very foundations of belief and of conduct. Absolute theories of morals and supernatural sanctions have lost their hold. Conscience and individual responsibility are relaxed. In other words, the law is strained to do double duty, and more is expected of it than in a time when morals as a regulating agency are more efficacious. Another strain upon our judicial system results from the crude and unorganized character of American legislation in a period when the growing point of law has shifted to legislation. When, in consequence, laws fail to produce the anticipated effects, judicial administration shares the blame. Worse than this is the effect of laws not intended to be enforced. These parodies, like the common law branding of felons, in which a piece of bacon used to be interposed between the branding iron and the criminal's skin, breed disrespect for law. Putting courts into politics and compelling judges to become politicians, in many jurisdictions has almost destroyed the traditional respect for the Bench. Finally, the ignorant and sensational reports of judicial proceedings, from which alone a great part of the public may judge of the daily work of the courts, completes the impression that the administration of justice is but a game. There are honorable exceptions, but the average press reports distract attention from the real proceeding to petty tilts of counsel, encounters with witnesses and sensational by-incidents. In Nebraska, not many years since, the federal court enjoined the execution of an act to regulate insurance companies. In press accounts of the proceeding, the conspiracy clause of the bill was copied *in extenso* under the headline "Conspiracy Charged," and it was made to appear that the ground of the injunction was a conspiracy between the state officers and some persons unknown. It cannot be expected that the public shall form any just estimate of our courts of justice from such data.

Reviewing the several causes for dissatisfaction with the administration of justice which have been touched upon, it will have been observed that some inhere in all law and are the penalty we pay for uniformity; that some inhere in our political institutions and are the penalty we pay for local self-government and independence from bureaucratic control; that some inhere in the circumstances of an age of transition and are the penalty we pay for individual freedom of thought and universal education. These will take care of themselves. But too much of the current dissatisfaction has a just origin in our judicial organization and procedure. The causes that lie here must be heeded. Our administration of justice is not decadent. It is simply behind the times. Political judges were known in England down to the last century. Lord Kenyon, as Master of the Rolls, sat in Parliament and took as active a part in political squabbles in the House of Commons as our state judges today in party conventions. Dodson and Fogg and Sergeant Buzzfuzz wrought in an atmosphere of contentious procedure. Bentham tells us that in 1797, out of five hundred and fifty pending writs of error, five hundred and forty-three were shams or vexatious contrivances for delay. Jarndyce and Jarndyce dragged out its weary course in chancery only half a century ago. We are simply stationary in that period of legal history. With law schools that are rivaling the achievements of Bologna and of Bourges to promote scientific study of the law; with active Bar Associations in every state to revive professional feeling and throw off the yoke of commercialism; with the passing of the doctrine that politics, too, is a mere game to be played for its own sake, we may look forward confidently to deliverance from the sporting theory of justice; we may look forward to a near future when our courts will be swift and certain agents of justice, whose decisions will be acquiesced in and respected by all.

SOME REFLECTIONS ON THE READING OF STATUTES

FELIX FRANKFURTER, 1947

A single volume of 320 octavo pages contains all the laws passed by Congress during its first five years, when measures were devised for getting the new government under way; 26 acts were passed in the 1789 session, 66 in 1790, 94 in 1791, 38 in 1792, 63 in 1793. For the single session of the 70th Congress, to take a predepression period, there are 993 enactments in a monstrous volume of 1014 pages—quarto not octavo—with a comparable range of subject matter. Do you wonder that one for whom the Statutes at Large constitute his staple reading should have sympathy, at least in his moments of baying at the moon, with the touching Congressman who not so long ago proposed a "Commission on Centralization" to report whether "the Government has departed from the concept of the founding fathers" and what steps should be taken "to restore the Government to its original purposes and sphere of activity"? Inevitably the work of the Supreme Court reflects the great shift in the center of gravity of lawmaking. Broadly speaking, the number of cases disposed of by opinions has not changed from term to term. But even as late as 1875 more than 40 per cent of the controversies before the Court were common-law litigation, fifty years later only five per cent, while today cases not resting on statutes are reduced almost to zero. It is therefore accurate to say that courts have ceased to be the primary makers of law in the sense in which they "legislated" the common law. It is certainly true of the Supreme Court, that almost every case has a statute at its heart or close to it.

This does not mean that every case before the Court involves questions of statutory construction. If only literary perversity or jaundiced partisanship can sponsor a particular rendering of a statute there is no problem. When we talk of statutory construction we have in mind cases in which there is a fair contest between two readings, neither of which comes without respectable title deeds. A problem in statutory construction can seriously bother courts only when there is a contest between probabilities of meaning.

Difficulties of Construction

Though it has its own preoccupations and its own mysteries, and above all its own jargon, judicial construction ought not to be torn from its wider, nonlegal context. Anything that is written may present a problem of meaning, and that is the essence of the business of judges in construing legislation. The problem derives from the very nature of words. They are symbols of meaning. But unlike mathematical symbols, the phrasing of a document, especially a complicated enactment, seldom attains more than approximate precision. If individual words are inexact symbols, with shifting variables, their configuration can hardly achieve invariant meaning or assured definiteness.

Source: Reprinted with permission from *The Record* of the Association of the Bar of the City of New York, © 1947. 2 *The Record* 213.

Apart from the ambiguity inherent in its symbols, a statute suffers from dubieties. It is not an equation or a formula representing a clearly marked process, nor is it an expression of individual thought to which is imparted the definiteness a single authorship can give. A statute is an instrument of government partaking of its practical purposes but also of its infirmities and limitations, of its awkward and groping efforts. With one of his flashes of insight, Mr. Justice Johnson called the science of government "the science of experiment." Anderson *v.* Dunn, 6 Wheat. 204, 226. The phrase, uttered a hundred and twenty-five years ago, has a very modern ring, for time has only served to emphasize its accuracy. To be sure, laws can measurably be improved with improvement in the mechanics of legislation, and the need for interpretation is usually in inverse ratio to the care and imagination of draftsmen. The area for judicial construction may be contracted. A large area is bound to remain.

The difficulties are inherent not only in the nature of words, of composition, and of legislation generally. They are often intensified by the subject matter of an enactment. The imagination which can draw an income tax statute to cover the myriad transactions of a society like ours, capable of producing the necessary revenue without producing a flood of litigation, has not yet revealed itself. (See 1 Report of Income Tax Codification Committee, Cmd. 5131, [1936] pp. 16 to 19.) Moreover, government sometimes solves problems by shelving them temporarily. The legislative process reflects that attitude. Statutes as well as constitutional provisions at times embody purposeful ambiguity or are expressed with a generality for future unfolding. "The prohibition contained in the Fifth Amendment refers to infamous crimes—a term obviously inviting interpretation in harmony with conditions and opinions prevailing from time to time." Mr. Justice Brandeis in United States *v.* Moreland, 258 U.S. 433, 451. And Mr. Justice Cardozo once remarked, "a great principle of constitutional law is not susceptible of comprehensive statement in an adjective." Carter *v.* Carter Coal Co., 298 U.S. 238, 327.

The intrinsic difficulties of language and the emergence after enactment of situations not anticipated by the most gifted legislative imagination, reveal doubts and ambiguities in statutes that compel judicial construction. The process of construction, therefore, is not an exercise in logic or dialectic. The aids of formal reasoning are not irrelevant; they may simply be inadequate. The purpose of construction being the ascertainment of meaning, every consideration brought to bear for the solution of that problem must be devoted to that end alone. To speak of it as a practical problem is not to indulge a fashion in words. It must be that, not something else. Not, for instance, an opportunity for a judge to use words as "empty vessels into which he can pour anything he will"—his caprices, fixed notions, even statesmanlike beliefs in a particular policy. Nor, on the other hand, is the process a ritual to be observed by unimaginative adherence to well-worn professional phrases. To be sure, it is inescapably a problem in the keeping of the legal profession and subject to all the limitations of our adversary system of adjudication. When the judge, selected by society to give meaning to what the legislature has done, examines the statute, he does so not in a laboratory or in a classroom. Damage has been done or exactions made, interests are divided, passions have been aroused, sides have been taken. But the judge, if he is worth his salt, must be above the battle. We must assume in him not only personal impartiality but intellectual disinterestedness. In matters of statutory construction also it makes a great deal of difference whether you start with an answer or with a problem.

The Judge's Task

Everyone has his own way of phrasing the task confronting judges when the meaning of a statute is in controversy. Judge Learned Hand speaks of the art of interpretation as "the proliferation of purpose." Who am I not to be satisfied with Learned Hand's felicities? And yet that phrase might mislead judges intellectually less disciplined than Judge Hand. It might justify interpretations by judicial libertines, not merely judicial libertarians. My own rephrasing of what we are driving at is probably no more helpful, and is much longer than Judge Hand's epigram. I should say that the troublesome phase of construction is the determination of the extent to which extraneous documentation and external circumstances may be allowed to infiltrate the text on the theory that they were part of it, written in ink discernible to the judicial eye.

Chief Justice White was happily endowed with the gift of finding the answer to problems by merely stating them. Often have I envied him this faculty but never more than in recent years. No matter how one states the problem of statutory construction, for me, at least, it does not carry its own answer. Though my business throughout most of my professional life has been with statutes, I come to you empty-handed. I bring no answers. I suspect the answers to the problems of an art are in its exercise. Not that one does not inherit, if one is capable of receiving it, the wisdom of the wise. But I confess unashamedly that I do not get much nourishment from books on statutory construction, and I say this after freshly reexamining them all, scores of them.

When one wants to understand or at least get the feeling of great painting, one does not go to books on the art of painting. One goes to the great masters. And so I have gone to great masters to get a sense of their practise of the art of interpretation. However, the art of painting and the art of interpretation are very different arts. Law, Holmes told us, becomes civilized to the extent that it is self-conscious of what it is doing. And so the avowals of great judges regarding their process of interpretation and the considerations that enter into it are of vital importance, though that ultimate something called the judgment upon the avowed factors escapes formulation and often, I suspect, even awareness. Nevertheless, an examination of some 2,000 cases, the bulk of which directly or indirectly involves matters of construction, ought to shed light on the encounter between the judicial and the legislative processes, whether that light be conveyed by hints, by explicit elucidation, or, to mix the metaphor, through the ancient test, by their fruits.

And so I have examined the opinions of Holmes, Brandeis, and Cardozo and sought to derive from their treatment of legislation what conclusions I could fairly draw, freed as much as I could be from impressions I had formed in the course of the years.

Holmes came to the Supreme Court before the great flood of recent legislation, while the other two, especially Cardozo, appeared at its full tide. The shift in the nature of the Court's business led to changes in its jurisdiction, resulting in a concentration of cases involving the legislative process. Proportionately to their length of service and the number of opinions, Brandeis and Cardozo had many more statutes to construe. And the statutes presented for their interpretation became increasingly complex, bringing in their train a quantitatively new role for administrative regulations. Nevertheless, the earliest opinions of Holmes on statutory construction, insofar as he reveals himself, cannot be distinguished from Cardozo's last opinion, though the latter's process is more explicit.

A judge of marked individuality stamps his individuality on what he writes, no matter what the subject. What is however striking about the opinions of the three Justices in this field is the essential similarity of their attitude and of their appraisal of the relevant. Their opinions do not disclose a private attitude for or against extension of governmental authority by legislation, or towards the policy of particular legislation, which consciously or imperceptibly affected their judicial function in construing laws. It would thus be a shallow judgment that found in Mr. Justice Holmes' dissent in the Northern Securities case (193 U.S. 197, 400) an expression of his disapproval of the policy behind the Sherman Law. His habit of mind—to be as accurate as one can—had a natural tendency to confine what seemed to him familiar language in a statute to its familiar scope. But the proof of the pudding is that his private feelings did not lead him to invoke the rule of indefiniteness to invalidate legislation of which he strongly disapproved (Compare Nash v. United States, 229 U.S. 373, and International Harvester Co. v. Kentucky, 234 U.S. 216), or to confine language in a constitution within the restrictions which he gave to the same language in a statute. (Compare Towne v. Eisner, 245 U.S. 418, and Eisner v. Macomber, 252 U.S. 189.)

The reservations I have just made indicate that such differences as emerge in the opinions of the three Justices on statutory construction, are differences that characterize all of their opinions, whether they are concerned with interpretation or constitutionality, with admiralty or patent law. They are differences of style. In the case of each, the style is the man.

If it be suggested that Mr. Justice Holmes is often swift, if not cavalier, in his treatment of statutes, there are those who level the same criticism against his opinions generally. It is merited in the sense that he wrote, as he said, for those learned in the art. I need hardly add that for him "learned" was not a formal term comprehending the whole legal fraternity. When dealing with problems of statutory construction also he illumined whole areas of doubt and darkness with insights enduringly expressed, however briefly. To say "We agree to all the generalities about not supplying criminal laws with what they omit, but there is no canon against using commonsense in construing laws as saying what they obviously mean," Rochen v. Ward, 279 U.S. 337, 339, is worth more than most of the dreary writing on how to construe penal legislation. Again when he said that "the meaning of a sentence is to be felt rather than to be proved," United States v. Johnson, 221, U.S.

448, 496, he expressed the wholesome truth that the final rendering of the meaning of a statute is an act of judgment. He would shudder at the thought that by such a statement he was giving comfort to the school of visceral jurisprudence. Judgment is not drawn out of the void but is based on the correlation of imponderables all of which need not, because they cannot, be made explicit. He was expressing the humility of the intellectual that he was, whose standards of exactitude distrusted pretensions of certainty, believing that legal controversies that are not frivolous almost always involve matters of degree, and often degree of the nicest sort. Statutory construction implied the exercise of choice, but precluded the notion of capricious choice as much as choice based on private notions of policy. One gets the impression that in interpreting statutes, Mr. Justice Holmes reached meaning easily, as was true of most of his results, with emphasis on the language in the totality of the enactment and the felt reasonableness of the chosen construction. He had a lively awareness that a statute was expressive of purpose and policy, but in his reading of it he tended to hug the shores of the statute itself, without much re-enforcement from without.

Mr. Justice Brandeis, on the other hand, in dealing with these problems as with others, would elucidate the judgment he was exercising by proof or detailed argument. In such instances, especially when in dissent, his opinions would draw on the whole arsenal of aids to construction. More often than either Holmes or Cardozo, Brandeis would invoke the additional weight of some "rule" of construction. But he never lost sight of the limited scope and function of such "rules." Occasionally, however, perhaps because of the nature of a particular statute, the minor importance of its incidence, the pressure of judicial business or even the temperament of his law clerk, whom he always treated as a co-worker, Brandeis disposed of a statute even more dogmatically, with less explicit elucidation, than did Holmes.

For Cardozo, statutory construction was an acquired taste. He preferred common law subtleties, having great skill in bending them to modern uses. But he came to realize that problems of statutory construction had their own exciting subtleties and gave ample employment to philosophic and literary talents. Cardozo's elucidation of how meaning is drawn out of a statute gives proof of the wisdom and balance which, combined with his learning, made him a great judge. While the austere style of Brandeis seldom mitigated the dry aspect of so many problems of statutory construction, Cardozo managed to endow even these with the glow and softness of his writing. The differences in the tone and color of their style as well as in the moral intensity of Brandeis and Cardozo made itself felt when they wrote full-dress opinions on problems of statutory construction. Brandeis almost compels by demonstration; Cardozo woos by persuasion.

Scope of the Judicial Function

From the hundreds of cases in which our three Justices construed statutes one thing clearly emerges. The area of free judicial movement is considerable. These three remembered that laws are not abstract propositions. They are expressions of policy arising out of specific situations and addressed to the attainment of particular ends. The difficulty is that the legislative ideas which laws embody are both explicit and immanent. And so the bottom problem is: What is below the surface of the words and yet fairly a part of them? Words in statutes are not unlike words in a foreign language in that they too have "associations, echoes, and overtones." (See Sir Ernest Barker's Introduction to his translation of Aristotle's Politics, p. lxiii.) Judges must retain the associations, hear the echoes, and capture the overtones. In one of his last opinions, dealing with legislation taxing the husband on the basis of the combined income of husband and wife, Holmes wrote: "The statutes are the outcome of a thousand years of history. . . . They form a system with echoes of different moments, none of which is entitled to prevail over the other." Hoeper v. Tax Commission, 284 U.S. 206, 219.

What exactions such a duty of construction places upon judges, and with what freedom it entrusts them! John Chipman Gray was fond of quoting from a sermon by Bishop Hoadley that "Whoever hath an *absolute authority* to *interpret* any written or spoken laws, it is he who is truly the law-giver to all intents and purposes, and not the person who first wrote or spoke them." Gray, *Nature and Sources of the Law* (2nd ed. 1921) 102, 125, 172. By admitting that there is some substance to the good Bishop's statement, one does not subscribe to the notion that they are lawgivers in any but a very qualified sense.

Even within their area of choice the courts are not at large. They are confined by the nature and scope of the judicial function in its particular exercise in the field of interpretation. They are under the constraints imposed by the judicial function in our democratic society. As a matter of verbal recognition certainly, no one will gainsay that the function in construing a statute is to ascertain the meaning of words used by the legislature. To go beyond it is to usurp a power which our democracy has lodged in its elected legislature. The great judges have constantly admonished their brethren of the need for discipline in observing the limitations. A judge must not rewrite a statute, neither to enlarge nor to contract it. Whatever temptations the statesmanship of policymaking might wisely suggest, construction must eschew interpolation and evisceration. He must not read in by way of creation. He must not read out except to avoid patent nonsense or internal contradiction. "If there is no meaning in it," said Alice's King, "that saves a world of trouble, you know, as we needn't try to find any." Legislative words presumably have meaning and so we must try to find it.

This duty of restraint, this humility of function as merely the translator of another's command, is a constant theme of our Justices. It is on the lips of all judges, but seldom, I venture to believe, has the restraint which it expresses, or the duty which it enjoins, been observed with so consistent a realization that its observance depends on self-conscious discipline. Cardozo put it this way: "We do not pause to consider whether a statute differently conceived and framed would yield results more consonant with fairness and reason. We take this statute as we find it." Anderson v. Wilson, 289 U.S. 20, 27. It was expressed more fully by Mr. Justice Brandeis when the temptation to give what might be called a more liberal interpretation could not have been wanting.

> The particularization and detail with which the scope of each provision, the amount of the tax thereby imposed, and the incidence of the tax, were specified, preclude an extension of any provision by implication to any other subject. . . . What the Government asks is not a construction of a statute, but, in effect, an enlargement of it by the court, so that what was omitted, presumably by inadvertence, may be included within its scope. (Iselin v. United States, 270 U.S. 245, 250-51.)

An omission, at the time of enactment, whether careless or calculated, cannot be judicially supplied however much later wisdom may recommend the inclusion.

The vital difference between initiating policy, often involving a decided break with the past, and merely carrying out a formulated policy, indicates the relatively narrow limits within which choice is fairly open to courts and the extent to which interpreting law is inescapably making law. To say that, because of this restricted field of interpretive declaration, courts make law just as do legislatures is to deny essential features in the history of our democracy. It denies that legislation and adjudication have had different lines of growth, serve vitally different purposes, function under different conditions, and bear different responsibilities. The judicial process of dealing with words is not at all Alice in Wonderland's way of dealing with them. Even in matters legal some words and phrases, though very few, approach mathematical symbols and mean substantially the same to all who have occasion to use them. Other law terms like "police power" are not symbols at all but labels for the results of the whole process of adjudication. In between lies a gamut of words with different denotations as well as connotations. There are varying shades of compulsion for judges behind different words, differences that are due to the words themselves, their setting in a text, their setting in history. In short, judges are not unfettered glossators. They are under a special duty not to overemphasize the episodic aspects of life and not to undervalue its organic processes—its continuities and relationships. For judges at least it is important to remember that continuity with the past is not only a necessity but even a duty.

There are not wanting those who deem naïve the notion that judges are expected to refrain from legislating in construing statutes. They may point to cases where even our three Justices apparently supplied an omission or engrafted a limitation. Such an accusation cannot be rebutted or judged in the abstract. In some ways, as Holmes once remarked, every statute is unique. Whether a judge does violence to language in its total context is not always free from doubt. Statutes come out of the past and aim at the future. They may carry implicit residues or mere hints of purpose. Perhaps the most delicate aspect of statutory construction is not to find more residues than are implicit nor purposes beyond the bound of hints. Even for a judge most sensitive to the traditional limitation of his function, this is a matter for judgment not always easy of answer. But a line does exist between omission and what Holmes called "misprision or abbreviation that does not conceal the purpose."

St. Louis–San Francisco Ry. *v.* Middlekamp, 256 U.S. 226, 232. Judges may differ as to the point at which the line should be drawn, but the only sure safeguard against crossing the line between adjudication and legislation is an alert recognition of the necessity not to cross it and instinctive, as well as trained, reluctance to do so.

In those realms where judges directly formulate law because the chosen lawmakers have not acted, judges have the duty of adaptation and adjustment of old principles to new conditions. But where policy is expressed by the primary lawmaking agency in a democracy, that is by the legislature, judges must respect such expressions by adding to or subtracting from the explicit terms which the lawmakers used no more than is called for by the shorthand nature of language. Admonitions, like that of Justice Brandeis in the Iselin case, that courts should leave even desirable enlargement to Congress will not by itself furnish the meaning appropriate for the next statute under scrutiny. But as is true of other important principles, the intensity with which it is believed may be decisive of the outcome.

The Process of Construction

Let me descend to some particulars.

The Text. Though we may not end with the words in construing a disputed statute, one certainly begins there. You have a right to think that a hoary platitude, but it is a platitude too often not observed at the bar. In any event, it may not take you to the end of the road. The Court no doubt must listen to the voice of Congress. But often Congress cannot be heard clearly because its speech is muffled. Even when it has spoken, it is as true of Congress as of others that what is said is what the listener hears. Like others, judges too listen with what psychologists used to call the apperception mass, which I take it means in plain English that one listens with what is already in one's head. One more caution is relevant when one is admonished to listen attentively to what a statute says. One must also listen attentively to what it does not say.

We must, no doubt, accord the words the sense in which Congress used them. That is only another way of stating the central problem of decoding the symbols. It will help to determine for whom they were meant. Statutes are not archaeological documents to be studied in a library. They are written to guide the actions of men. As Mr. Justice Holmes remarked upon some Indian legislation "The word was addressed to the Indian mind," Fleming *v.* McCurtain, 215 U.S. 56, 60. If a statute is written for ordinary folk, it would be arbitrary not to assume that Congress intended its words to be read with the minds of ordinary men. If they are addressed to specialists, they must be read by judges with the minds of the specialists.

And so we assume that Congress uses common words in their popular meaning, as used in the common speech of men. The cases speak of the "meaning of common understanding," "the normal and spontaneous meaning of language," "the common and appropriate use," "the natural straight-forward and literal sense," and similar variants. In McBoyle *v.* United States, 283 U.S. 25, 26, Mr. Justice Holmes had to decide whether an aeroplane is a "motor vehicle" within the meaning of the Motor Vehicle Theft Act. He thus disposed of it: "No doubt etymologically it is possible to use the word to signify a conveyance working on land, water or air, and sometimes legislation extends the use in that direction. . . . But in everyday speech 'vehicles' calls up a picture of a thing moving on land."

Sometimes Congress supplies its own dictionary. It did so in 1871 in a statute defining a limited number of words for use as to all future enactments. It may do so, as in recent legislation, by a section within the statute containing detailed definitions. Or there may be indications from the statute that words in it are the considered language of legislation. "If Congress has been accustomed to use a certain phrase with a more limited meaning than might be attributed to it by common practice, it would be arbitrary to refuse to consider that fact when we come to interpret a statute. But, as we have said, the usage of Congress simply shows that it has spoken with careful precision, that its words mark the exact spot at which it stops." Boston Sand Co. *v.* United States, 278 U.S. 41, 48. Or words may acquire scope and function from the history of events which they summarize or from the purpose which they serve.

However colloquial and uncertain the words had been in the beginning, they had won for themselves finally an acceptance and a definiteness that made them fit to play a part in the legislative process. They came into the statute . . . freighted with the meaning imparted to them by the mischief to be remedied and by contemporaneous discussion. . . . In such conditions history is a teacher that is not to be ignored. (*Cardozo,* Duparquet Co. *v.* Evans, 297 U.S. 216, 220-21.)

Words of art bring their art with them. They bear the meaning of their habitat whether it be a phrase or technical significance in the scientific or business world, or whether it be loaded with the recondite connotations of feudalism. Holmes made short shrift of a contention by remarking that statutes used "familiar legal expressions in their familiar legal sense." Henry v. United States, 251 U.S. 393, 395. The peculiar idiom of business or of administrative practice often modifies the meaning that ordinary speech assigns to language. And if a word is obviously transplanted from another legal source, whether the common law or other legislation, it brings the old soil with it.

The Context. Legislation is a form of literary composition. But construction is not an abstract process equally valid for every composition, not even for every composition whose meaning must be judicially ascertained. The nature of the composition demands awareness of certain presuppositions. For instance, the words in a constitution may carry different meanings from the same words in a statute precisely because "it is a constitution we are expounding." The reach of this consideration was indicated by Mr. Justice Holmes in language that remains fresh no matter how often repeated:

> "When we are dealing with words that also are a constituent act, like the Constitution of the United States, we must realize that they have called into life being the development of which could not have been foreseen completely by the most gifted of its begetters. It was enough for them to realize or to hope that they had created an organism; it has taken a century and has cost their successors much sweat and blood to prove that they created a nation. The case before us must be considered in the light of our whole experience and not merely in that of what was said a hundred years ago. (Missouri *v.* Holland, 252 U.S. 416, 433.)

And so, the significance of an enactment, its antecedents as well as its later history, its relation to other enactments, all may be relevant to the construction of words for one purpose and in one setting but not for another. Some words are confined to their history; some are starting points for history. Words are intellectual and moral currency. They come from the legislative mint with some intrinsic meaning. Sometimes it remains unchanged. Like currency, words sometimes appreciate or depreciate in value.

Frequently the sense of a word cannot be got except by fashioning a mosaic of significance out of the innuendoes of disjointed bits of statute. Cardozo phrased this familiar phenomenon by stating that "the meaning of a statute is to be looked for, not in any single section, but in all the parts together and in their relation to the end in view." Panama Refining Co. *v.* Ryan, 293 U.S. 388, 433, 439. And to quote Cardozo once more on this phase of our problem: "There is need to keep in view also the structure of the statute, and the relation, physical and logical, between its several parts." Duparquet Co. *v.* Evans, 297 U.S. 216, 218.

The generating consideration is that legislation is more than composition. It is an active instrument of government which, for purposes of interpretation, means that laws have ends to be achieved. It is in this connection that Holmes said "words are flexible." International Stevedoring Co. *v.* Haverty, 272 U.S. 50, 58. Again it was Holmes, the last judge to give quarter to loose thinking or vague yearning, who said that "the general purpose is a more important aid to the meaning than any rule which grammar or formal logic may lay down." United States *v.* Whitridge, 197 U.S. 135, 143. And it was Holmes who chided courts for being "apt to err by sticking too closely to the words of a law where those words import a policy that goes beyond them." Olmstead *v.* United States, 277 U.S. 438, 469. Note, however, that he found the policy in "those words"!

Proliferation of Purpose

You may have observed that I have not yet used the word "intention." All these years I have avoided speaking of the "legislative intent" and I shall continue to be on my guard against using it.

The objection to "intention" was indicated in a letter by Mr. Justice Holmes which the recipient kindly put at my disposal:

> Only a day or two ago—when counsel talked of the intention of a legislature, I was indiscreet enough to say I don't care what their intention was. I only want to know what the words mean. Of course the phrase often is used to express a conviction not exactly thought out—that you construe a particular clause or expression by considering the whole instrument and any dominant purposes that it may express. In fact intention is a residuary clause intended to gather up whatever other aids there may be to interpretation beside the particular words and the dictionary.

If that is what the term means, it is better to use a less beclouding characterization. Legislation has an aim; it seeks to obviate some mischief, to supply an inadequacy, to effect a change or policy, to formulate a plan of government. That aim, that policy is not drawn, like nitrogen, out of the air; it is evinced in the language of the statute, as read in the light of other external manifestations of purpose. That is what the judge must seek and effectuate, and he ought not be led off the trail by tests that have overtones of subjective design. We are not concerned with anything subjective. We do not delve into the mind of legislators or their draftsmen, or committee members. Against what he believed to be such an attempt Cardozo once protested:

> The judgment of the court, if I interpret the reasoning aright, does not rest upon a ruling that Congress would have gone beyond its power if the purpose that it professed was the purpose truly cherished. The judgment of the court rests upon the ruling that another purpose, not professed, may be read beneath the surface, and by the purpose so imputed the statute is destroyed. Thus the process of psychoanalysis has spread to unaccustomed fields. There is a wise and ancient doctrine that a court will not inquire into the motives of a legislative body. . . . (United States *v.* Constantine, 269 U.S. 287 at 298-99.)

The difficulty in many instances where a problem of meaning arises is that the enactment was not directed towards the troubling question. The problem might then be stated, as once it was by Mr. Justice Cardozo, "which choice is it the more likely that Congress would have made?" Burnet *v.* Guggenheim, 288 U.S. 280, 285. While in its context the significance and limitations of this question are clear, thus to frame the question too often tempts inquiry into the subjective and might seem to warrant the court in giving answers based on an unmanifested legislative state of mind. But the purpose which a court must effectuate is not that which Congress should have enacted, or would have. It is that which it did enact, however inaptly, because it may fairly be said to be imbedded in the statute, even if a specific manifestation was not thought of, as is often the very reason for casting a statute in very general terms.

Often the purpose or policy that controls is not directly displayed in the particular enactment. Statutes cannot be read intelligently if the eye is closed to considerations evidenced in affiliated statutes, or in the known temper of legislative opinion. Thus, for example, it is not lightly to be presumed that Congress sought to infringe on "very sacred rights." Milwaukee Publishing Co. *v.* Burleson, 255 U.S. 407, 438. This improbability will be a factor in determining whether language, though it should be so read if standing alone, was used to effect such a drastic change.

More frequently still, in the interpretation of recent regulatory statutes, it becomes important to remember that the judicial task in marking out the extent to which Congress has exercised its constitutional power over commerce, is not that of devising an abstract formula. The task is one of accommodation as between assertions of new federal authority and historic functions of the individual States. Federal legislation of this character cannot therefore be construed without regard to the implications of our dual system of government. In such cases, for example, it is not to be assumed as a matter of course that when Congress adopts a new scheme for federal industrial regulation, it deals with all situations falling within the general mischief which gave rise to the legislation. The underlying assumptions of our dual form of government, and the consequent presuppositions of legislative draftsmanship which are expressive of our history and habits, cut across what might otherwise be the implied range of legislation. The history of congressional legislation regulating not only interstate commerce as such but also activities intertwined with it, justify the generalization that, when the federal government takes over such local radiations in the vast network of our national economic enterprise and thereby radically readjusts the balance of State and national authority, those charged with the duty of legislating are reasonably explicit and do not entrust its attainment to that retrospective expansion of meaning which properly deserves the stigma of judicial legislation.

Search for Purpose

How then does the purpose which a statute expresses reveal itself, particularly when the path of purpose is not straight and narrow? The English courts say: look at the statute and look at nothing else. Lord Reading so advised the House of Lords when a bill was before it as to which the Attorney General had given an interpretative explanation during its passage in the House of Commons:

> Neither the words of the Attorney General nor the words of an ex-Lord Chancellor, spoken in this House, as to the meaning intended to be given to language used in a Bill, have the slightest effect or relevance when the matter comes to be considered by a Court of Law. The one thing which stands out beyond all question is that in a Court of Law you are not allowed to introduce observations made either by the Government or by anybody else, but the Court will only give consideration to the Statute itself. That is elementary, but I think it is necessary to bring it home to your Lordships because I think too much importance can be attached to language which fell from the Attorney-General. (94 Parl. Deb. 5th Series, Lords, col. 232, Nov. 8, 1934.)

How narrowly the English courts confine their search for understanding an English enactment is vividly illustrated by the pronouncements of Lord Haldane, surely one of the most broadminded of all modern judges.

> My Lords, (*Viscountess Rhondda's Claim*, [1922] 2 A. C. 339 at 383) the only other point made on the construction of the Act was that this Committee might be entitled to look at what passed while the Bill was still a Bill and in the Committee stage in the House. It was said that there amendments were moved and discussions took place which indicated that the general words of s. 1 were not regarded by your Lordships' House as covering the title to a seat in it. But even assuming that to be certain, I do not think, sitting as we do with the obligation to administer the principles of the law, that we have the least right to look at what happened while the Bill was being discussed in Committee and before the Act was passed. Decisions of the highest authority show that the interpretation of an Act of Parliament must be collected from the words in which the Sovereign has made into law the words agreed upon by both Houses. The history of previous changes made or discussed cannot be taken to have been known or to have been in view when the Royal assent was given. The contrary was suggested at the Bar, though I do not think the point was pressed, and I hope that it will not be thought that in its decision this Committee has given any countenance to it. To have done so would, I venture to say, have been to introduce confusion into well-settled law. In Millar v. Taylor the principle of construction was laid down in words, which have never, so far as I know, been seriously challenged, by Willes J. as long ago as in 1769: "The sense and meaning of an Act of Parliament must be collected from what it says when passed into a law; and not from the history of changes it underwent in the house where it took its rise. That history is not known to the other house or to the sovereign."

These current English rules of construction are simple. They are too simple. If the purpose of construction is the ascertainment of meaning, nothing that is logically relevant should be excluded. The rigidity of English courts in interpreting language merely by reading it disregards the fact that enactments are, as it were, organisms which exist in their environment. One wonders whether English judges are confined psychologically as they purport to be legally. The judges deem themselves limited to reading the words of a statute. But can they really escape placing the words in the context of their minds, which after all are not automata applying legal logic but repositories of all sorts of assumptions and impressions? Such a modest if not mechanical view of the task of construction disregards legal history. In earlier centuries the judges recognized that the exercise of their judicial function to understand and apply legislative policy is not to be hindered by artificial canons and limitations. The well-known resolutions in Heydon's Case, 3 Co. Rep. 7a, have the flavor of Elizabethan English but they express the substance of a current volume of U.S. Reports as to the considerations relevant to statutory interpretation. To be sure, early English legislation helped ascertainment of purpose by explicit recitals; at least to the extent of defining the mischief against which the enactment was directed. To take a random instance, an act in the reign of Edward VI reads: " 'Forasmuch as intolerable Hurts and Troubles to the Commonwealth of this Realm doth daily grow and increase through such Abuses and Disorders as are had and used in common Alehouses and other Houses called Tipling houses': (2) it is therefore enacted by the King our Sovereign Lord, etc." 6 Edward VI c. 25 (1552); 2 Stats. at Large 458. Judicial construction certainly became more artificial after the practice of elucidating recitals ceased. It is to be noted that Macaulay, a great legislative draftsman, did not think much of preambles. He believed that too often they are jejune because legislators may agree on what ought to be done, while disagreeing about the reasons for doing it. At the same time he deemed it most important that in some manner governments should give reasons for their legislative course. (See Lord Macaulay's Legislative Minutes (ed. by C. D. Dharker) pp. 145 *et seq.*) When not so long ago the Parliamentary mechanism was under scrutiny of the Lord Chancellor's Committee, dissatisfaction was expressed with the prevailing practice of English courts not to go outside the statutes. It was urged that the old practice of preambles be restored or that a memorandum of explanation go with proposed legislation. (See Professor Laski's Note to the Report of the Committee on Ministers' Powers, Cmd. 4060, Annex V, p. 135, 1932.)

At the beginning, the Supreme Court reflected the early English attitude. With characteristic hardheadedness Chief Justice Marshall struck at the core of the matter with the observation "Where the mind labours to discover the design of the legislature, it seizes everything from which aid can be derived." United States *v.* Fisher, 2 Cranch 358, 386. This commonsensical way of dealing with statutes fell into disuse, and more or less catchpenny canons of construction did service instead. To no small degree a more wooden treatment of legislation was due, I suspect, to the fact that the need for keeping vividly in mind the occasions for drawing on all aids in the process of distilling meaning from legislation was comparatively limited. As the area of regulation steadily widened, the impact of the legislative process upon the judicial brought into being, and compelled consideration of, all that convincingly illumines an enactment, instead of merely that which is called, with delusive simplicity, "the end result." Legislatures themselves provided illumination by general definitions, special definitions, explicit recitals of policy, and even directions of attitudes appropriate for judicial construction. Legislative reports were increasingly drawn upon, statements by those in charge of legislation, reports of investigating committees, recommendations of agencies entrusted with the enforcement of laws, etc., etc. When Mr. Justice Holmes came to the Court, the U.S. Reports were practically barren of references to legislative materials. These swarm in current volumes. And let me say in passing that the importance that such materials play in Supreme Court litigation carry far-reaching implications for bench and bar.

The change I have summarized was gradual. Undue limitations were applied even after Courts broke out of the mere language of a law. We find Mr. Justice Holmes saying, "It is a delicate business to base speculations about the purposes or construction of a statute upon the vicissitudes of its passage." Pine Hill Co. *v.* United States 259 U.S. 191, 196. And as late as 1925 he referred to earlier bills relating to a statute under review, with the reservation "If it be legitimate to look at them." Davis *v.* Pringle, 268 U.S. 315, 318.

Such hesitations and restraints are in limbo. Courts examine the forms rejected in favor of the words chosen. They look at later statutes "considered to throw a cross light" upon an earlier enactment. See United States *v.* Aluminum Co. Of America, 148 F. 2d. 416, 429. The consistent construction by an administrative agency charged with effectuating the policy of an enactment carries very considerable weight. While assertion of authority does not demonstrate its existence, long-continued, uncontested assertion is at least evidence that the legislature conveyed the authority. Similarly, while authority conferred does not atrophy by disuse, failure over an extended period to exercise it is some proof that it was not given. And since "a page of history is worth a volume of logic," N.Y. Trust Co. *v.* Eisner, 256 U.S. 345, 349, courts have looked into the background of statutes, the mischief to be checked and the good that was designed, looking sometimes far afield and taking notice also as judges of what is generally known by men.

Unhappily, there is no table of logarithms for statutory construction. No item of evidence has a fixed or even average weight. One or another may be decisive in one set of circumstances, while of little value elsewhere. A painstaking, detailed report by a Senate Committee bearing directly on the immediate question may settle the matter. A loose statement even by a chairman of a committee, made impromptu in the heat of debate, less informing in cold type than when heard on the floor, will hardly be accorded the weight of an encyclical.

Spurious use of legislative history must not swallow the legislation so as to give point to the quip that only when legislative history is doubtful do you go to the statute. While courts are no longer confined to the language, they are still confined by it. Violence must not be done to the words chosen by the legislature. Unless indeed no doubt can be left that the legislature has in fact used a private code, so that what appears to be violence to language is merely respect to special usage. In the end, language and external aids, each accorded the authority deserved in the circumstances, must be weighed in the balance of judicial judgment. Only if its premises are emptied of their human variables, can the process of statutory construction have the precision of a syllogism. We cannot avoid what Mr. Justice Cardozo deemed inherent in the problem of construction, making "a choice between uncertainties. We must be content to choose the lesser." Burnet *v.* Guggenheim, 288 U.S. 280, 288. But to the careful and disinterested eye, the scales will hardly escape appearing to tip slightly on the side of a more probable meaning.

Canons of Construction

Nor can canons of construction save us from the anguish of judgment. Such canons give an air of abstract intellectual compulsion to what is in fact a delicate judgment, concluding a complicated process of balancing subtle and elusive elements. All our three Justices have at one time or another leaned on the crutch of a canon. But they have done so only rarely, and with a recognition that these rules of construction are not in any true sense rules of law. So far as valid, they are what Mr. Justice Holmes called them, axioms of experience. See Boston Sand Co. *v.* United States, 278 U.S. 41, 48. In many instances, these canons originated as observations in specific cases from which they were abstracted, taken out of the context of actuality, and, as it were, codified in treatises. We owe the first known systematic discussion of statutory interpretation in England to the scholarship of Professor Samuel T. Thorne, Yale's Law Librarian. According to Professor Thorne, it was written probably prior to 1567. The latest American treatise on the subject was published in 1943. It is not unfair to say that in the four intervening centuries not much new wisdom has been garnered. But there has been an enormous quantitative difference in expounding the wisdom. "A Discourse upon the Exposicion & Understandinge of Statutes" is a charming essay of not more than thirty pages. Not even the freest use of words would describe as charming the latest edition of Sutherland's Statutory Construction, with its three volumes of more than 1500 pages.

Insofar as canons of construction are generalizations of experience, they all have worth. In the abstract, they rarely arouse controversy. Difficulties emerge when canons compete in soliciting judgment, because they conflict rather than converge. For the demands of judgment underlying the art of interpretation, there is no vade-mecum.

But even generalized restatements from time to time may not be wholly wasteful. Out of them may come a sharper rephrasing of the conscious factors of interpretation; new instances may make them more vivid but also disclose more clearly their limitations. Thereby we may avoid rigidities which, while they afford more precise formulas, do so at the price of cramping the life of law. To strip the task of judicial reading of statutes of rules that partake of the mysteries of a craft serves to reveal the true elements of our problem. It defines more accurately the nature of the intellectual responsibility of a judge and thereby subjects him to more relevant criteria of criticism. Rigorous analysis also sharpens the respective duties of legislature and courts in relation to the making of laws and to their enforcement.

Fair Construction and Fit Legislation

The quality of legislative organization and procedure is inevitably reflected in the quality of legislative draftsmanship. Representative Monroney told the House last July that "95 percent of all the legislation that becomes law passes the Congress in the shape that it came from our committees. Therefore if our committee work is sloppy, if it is bad, if it is inadequate, our legislation in 95 percent of the cases will be bad and inadequate as well." And Representative Lane added that "In the second session of the 78th Congress 953 bills and resolutions were passed, of which only 86 were subject to any real discussion." See 92 Cong. Rec. pp. 10040 and 10054, July 25, 1946. But what courts do with legislation may in turn deeply affect what Congress will do in the future. Emerson says somewhere that mankind is as lazy as it dares to be. Loose judicial reading makes for loose legislative writing. It encourages the practise illustrated in a recent cartoon in which a senator tells his colleagues "I admit this new bill is too complicated to understand. We'll just have to pass it to find out what it means." A modern Pascal might be tempted at times to say of legislation what Pascal said of students of theology when he charged them with "a looseness of thought and language that would pass nowhere else in making what are professedly very fine distinctions." And it is conceivable that he might go on and speak, as did Pascal, of the "insincerity with which terms are carefully chosen to cover opposite meanings." See Pater, *Miscellaneous Studies*, "Essay on Pascal," pp. 48, 51.

But there are more fundamental objections to loose judicial reading. In a democracy the legislative impulse and its expression should come from those popularly chosen to legislate, and equipped to devise policy, as courts are not. The pressure on legislatures to discharge their responsibility with care, understanding and imagination should be stiffened, not relaxed. Above all, they must not be encouraged in irresponsible or undisciplined use of language. In the keeping of legislatures perhaps more than of any other group is the well-being of their fellow-men. Their responsibility is discharged ultimately by words. They are under a special duty therefore to observe that "Exactness in the use of words is the basis of all serious thinking. You will get nowhere without it. Words are clumsy tools, and it is very easy to cut one's fingers with them, and they need the closest attention in handling; but they are the only tools we have, and imagination itself cannot work without them. You must master the use of them, or you will wander forever guessing at the mercy of mere impulse and unrecognized assumptions and arbitrary associations, carried away with every wind of doctrine." (See J. W. Allen's "Essay on Jeremy Bentham," in *The Social and Political Ideals of the Revolutionary Era* (ed. by Hearnshaw), pp. 181, 199.)

Perfection of draftsmanship is as unattainable as demonstrable correctness of judicial reading of legislation. Fit legislation and fair adjudication are attainable. The ultimate reliance of society for the proper fulfilment of both these august functions is to entrust them only to those who are equal to their demands.

Legal Miscellany

This section contains a diverse collection of legal, political, and historical information, most of which is organized in tabular form and in chronological order.

The tables provide readers with precise dates of the reigns of British monarchs and the terms of service of U.S. Supreme Court justices, presidents, vice presidents, and attorneys general. Readers may, for example, consult the succession of Supreme Court justices to determine which justices were on the Court when a major case was decided.

Using a chronological sequence, the congressional timeline links pertinent information about the House of Representatives and the Senate (size, political parties, procedural matters) with major court cases, laws, and investigations. Wars, presidential eras, and developments in science, technology, and communications are included as well.

The following tables are included:

- Presidents and Vice Presidents of the United States
- Presidential Nominations to the Supreme Court
- Time Chart of the Supreme Court
- Succession of Supreme Court Justices
- Attorneys General of the United States
- Congressional Timeline
- Regnal Years

PRESIDENTS AND VICE PRESIDENTS OF THE UNITED STATES

President	Service			Vice President	Congress
1 George Washington, F	April 30, 1789	to	March 3, 1797	1 John Adams	1, 2, 3, 4
2 John Adams, F	March 4, 1797		March 3, 1801	2 Thomas Jefferson	5, 6
3 Thomas Jefferson, D-R	March 4, 1801		March 3, 1805	3 Aaron Burr	7, 8
	March 4, 1805		March 3, 1809	4 George Clinton	9, 10
4 James Madison, D-R	March 4, 1809		March 3, 1813	"	11, 12
"	March 4, 1813		March 3, 1817	5 Elbridge Gerry	13, 14
5 James Monroe, D-R	March 4, 1817		March 3, 1825	6 Daniel D. Tompkins	15, 16, 17, 18
6 John Quincy Adams, D-R	March 4, 1825		March 3, 1829	7 John C. Calhoun	19, 20
7 Andrew Jackson, D	March 4, 1829		March 3, 1833	"	21, 22
"	March 4, 1833		March 3, 1837	8 Martin Van Buren	23, 24
8 Martin Van Buren, D	March 4, 1837		March 3, 1841	9 Richard M. Johnson	25, 26
9 William Henry Harrison[1], W	March 4, 1841		April 4, 1841	10 John Tyler	27
10 John Tyler, W	April 6, 1841		March 3, 1845		27, 28
11 James K. Polk, D	March, 4, 1845		March 3, 1849	11 George M. Dallas	29, 30
12 Zachary Taylor[1], W	March 5, 1849		July 9, 1850	12 Millard Fillmore	31
13 Millard Fillmore, W	July 10, 1850		March 3, 1853		31, 32
14 Franklin Pierce, D	March 4, 1853		March 3, 1857	13 William R. King	33, 34
15 James Buchanan, D	March 4, 1857		March 3, 1861	14 John C. Breckinridge	35, 36
16 Abraham Lincoln, R	March 4, 1861		March 3, 1865	15 Hannibal Hamlin	37, 38
"([1])	March 4, 1865		April 15, 1865	16 Andrew Johnson	39
17 Andrew Johnson, R	April 15, 1865		March 3, 1869		39, 40
18 Ulysses S. Grant, R	March 4, 1869		March 3, 1873	17 Schuyler Colfax	41, 42
	March 4, 1873		March 3, 1877	18 Henry Wilson	43, 44
19 Rutherford B. Hayes, R	March 4, 1877		March 3, 1881	19 William A. Wheeler	45, 46
20 James A. Garfield[1], R	March 4, 1881		September 19, 1881	20 Chester A. Arthur	47
21 Chester A. Arthur, R	September 20, 1881		March 3, 1885		47, 48
22 Grover Cleveland, D	March 4, 1885		March 3, 1889	21 Thomas A. Hendricks	49, 50
23 Benjamin Harrison, R	March 4, 1889		March 3, 1893	22 Levi P. Morton	51, 52
24 Grover Cleveland, D	March 4, 1893		March 3, 1897	23 Adlai E. Stevenson	53, 54
25 William McKinley, R	March 4, 1897		March 3, 1901	24 Garret A. Hobart	55, 56
"([1])	March 4, 1901		September 14, 1901	25 Theodore Roosevelt	57
26 Theodore Roosevelt, R	September 14, 1901		March 3, 1905		57, 58
"	March 4, 1905		March 3, 1909	26 Charles W. Fairbanks	59, 60
27 William H. Taft, R	March 4, 1909		March 3, 1913	27 James S. Sherman	61, 62
28 Woodrow Wilson, D	March 4, 1913		March 3, 1921	28 Thomas R. Marshall	63, 64, 65, 66
29 Warren G. Harding[1], R	March 4, 1921		August 2, 1923	29 Calvin Coolidge	67
30 Calvin Coolidge, R	August 3, 1923		March 3, 1925		68
"	March 4, 1925		March 3, 1929	30 Charles G. Dawes	69, 70
31 Herbert C. Hoover, R	March 4, 1929		March 3, 1933	31 Charles Curtis	71, 72
32 Franklin D. Roosevelt[2], D	March 4, 1933		January 20, 1941	32 John N. Garner	73, 74, 75, 76
"	January 20, 1941		January 20, 1945	33 Henry A. Wallace	77, 78
"([1])	January 20, 1945		April 12, 1945	34 Harry S. Truman	79
33 Harry S. Truman, D	April 12, 1945		January 20, 1949		79, 80
"	January 20, 1949		January 20, 1953	35 Alben W. Barkley	81, 82
34 Dwight D. Eisenhower, R	January 20, 1953		January 20, 1961	36 Richard M. Nixon	83, 84, 85, 86
35 John F. Kennedy[1], D	January 20, 1961		November 22, 1963	37 Lyndon B. Johnson	87, 88
36 Lyndon B. Johnson, D	November 22, 1963		January 20, 1965		88
"	January 20, 1965		January 20, 1969	38 Hubert H. Humphrey	89, 90
37 Richard M. Nixon, R	January 20, 1969		January 20, 1973	39 Spiro T. Agnew	91, 92, 93
"([3])	January 20, 1973		August 9, 1974	40 Gerald R. Ford[4]	93
38 Gerald R. Ford[5], R	August 9, 1974		January 20, 1977	41 Nelson A. Rockefeller	93, 94
39 Jimmy Carter, D	January 20, 1977		January 20, 1981	42 Walter F. Mondale	95, 96
40 Ronald Reagan, R	January 20, 1981		January 20, 1989	43 George Bush	97, 98, 99, 100
41 George Bush, R	January 20, 1989		January 20, 1993	44 Dan Quayle	101, 102
42 Bill Clinton, D	January 20, 1993			45 Al Gore	103, 104, 105[6]

[1]Died in office.
[2]First president to be inaugurated under 20th Amendment, Jan. 20, 1937.
[3]Resigned Aug. 9, 1974.
[4]First nonelected vice president, chosen under 25th Amendment procedure.
[5]First nonelected president.
[6]Through January 1999.
Party affiliation follows each president's name. F = Federalist, D-R = Democrat-Republican, D = Democrat, W = Whig, R = Republican.
Source: *The World Almanac 1997.*

PRESIDENTIAL NOMINATIONS TO THE SUPREME COURT

The following table shows the presidents who nominated the various Supreme Court justices and the states from which the justices were appointed. Chief justices appear in boldface type.

George Washington	**John Jay (N.Y.)**	1789
	John Rutledge (S.C.)	1789
	William Cushing (Mass.)	1789
	James Wilson (Pa.)	1789
	Robert H. Harrison (Md.)[1]	1789
	John Blair (Va.)	1789
	James Iredell (N.C.)	1790
	Thomas Johnson (Md.)	1791
	William Paterson (N.J.)	1793
	John Rutledge (S.C.)[2]	1795
	Samuel Chase (Md.)	1796
	Oliver Ellsworth (Conn.)	1796
John Adams	Bushrod Washington (Va.)	1798
	Alfred Moore (N.C.)	1799
	John Marshall (Va.)	1801
Thomas Jefferson	William Johnson (S.C.)	1804
	Henry Brockholst Livingston (N.Y.)	1806
	Thomas Todd (Ky.)	1807
James Madison	Joseph Story (Mass.)	1811
	Gabriel Duvall (Md.)	1812
James Monroe	Smith Thomson (N.Y.)	1823
John Quincy Adams	Robert Trimble (Ky.)	1826
Andrew Jackson	John McLean (Ohio)	1829
	Henry Baldwin (Pa.)	1830
	James M. Wayne (Ga.)	1835
	Roger B. Taney (Md.)	1836
	Philip B. Barbour (Va.)	1836
	John Catron (Tenn.)	1837

1. Declined appointment.
2. Accepted appointment but delayed taking his seat and later resigned.

Martin Van Buren	John McKinley (Ala.)	1837
	Peter V. Daniel (Va.)	1841
John Tyler	Samuel Nelson (N.Y.)	1845
James Polk	Levi Woodbury (N.H.)	1845
	Robert C. Grier (Pa.)	1846
Millard Fillmore	Benjamin R. Curtis (Mass.)	1851
Franklin Pierce	John A. Campbell (Ala.)	1853
James Buchanan	Nathan Clifford (Me.)	1858
Abraham Lincoln	Noah H. Swayne (Ohio)	1862
	Samuel F. Miller (Iowa)	1862
	David Davis (Ill.)	1862
	Stephen J. Field (Calif.)	1863
	Salmon P. Chase (Ohio)	1864
Ulysses S. Grant	William Strong (Pa.)	1870
	Joseph P. Bradley (N.J.)	1870
	Ward Hunt (N.Y.)	1873
	Morrison R. Waite (Ohio)	1874
Rutherford Hayes	John M. Harlan (Ky.)	1877
	William B. Woods (Ga.)	1881
James Garfield	Stanley Matthews (Ohio)	1881
Chester Arthur	Horace Gray (Mass.)	1882
	Samuel Blatchford (N.Y.)	1882
Grover Cleveland	Lucius Q. C. Lamar (Miss.)	1888
	Melville W. Fuller (Ill.)	1888
Benjamin Harrison	David J. Brewer (Kan.)	1889
	Henry B. Brown (Mich.)	1891
	George Shiras, Jr. (Pa.)	1892
	Howell E. Jackson (Tenn.)	1893
Grover Cleveland	Edward D. White (La.)	1894
	Rufus W. Peckham (N.Y.)	1895
William McKinley	Joseph McKenna (Calif.)	1898
Theodore Roosevelt	Oliver Wendell Holmes, Jr. (Mass.)	1902
	William R. Day (Ohio)	1903
	William H. Moody (Mass.)	1906
William Taft	Horace H. Lurton (Tenn.)	1910
	Edward D. White (La.)	1910
	Charles E. Hughes (N.Y.)	1910
	Willis Van Devanter (Wyo.)	1911
	Joseph R. Lamar (Ga.)	1911
	Mathlon Pitney (N.J.)	1912
Woodrow Wilson	James C. McReynolds (Tenn.)	1914
	Louis D. Brandeis (Mass.)	1916
	John H. Clarke (Ohio)	1916
Warren Harding	**William H. Taft (Conn.)**	1921
	George Sutherland (Utah)	1922
	Pierce Butler (Minn.)	1922
	Edward T. Sanford (Tenn.)	1923
Calvin Coolidge	Harlan F. Stone (N.Y.)	1925
Herbert Hoover	**Charles E. Hughes (N.Y.)**	1930
	Owen J. Roberts (Pa.)	1930
	Benjamin N. Cardozo (N.Y.)	1932
Franklin D. Roosevelt	Hugo L. Black (Ala.)	1937
	Stanley F. Reed (Ky.)	1938
	Felix Frankfurter (Mass.)	1939
	William O. Douglas (Conn.)	1939
	Frank Murphy (Mich.)	1940

	Harlan F. Stone (N.Y.) 1941
	James F. Byrnes (S.C.) 1941
	Robert H. Jackson (N.Y.) 1941
	Wiley B. Rutledge (Iowa)............................1943
Harry S. Truman ....Harold H. Burton (Ohio)....................1945
	Fred M. Vinson (Ky.) 1946
	Tom C. Clark (Tex.) 1946
	Sherman Minton (Ind.) 1949
Dwight D. Eisenhower..................**Earl Warren (Calif.)** 1953
	John M. Harlan (N.Y.)...............................1955
	William J. Brennan, Jr. (Ind.) 1956
	Charles E. Whittaker (Mo.) 1957
	Potter Stewart (Ohio)...............................1958
John F. Kennedy........................Bryon R. White (Colo.) 1962
	Arthur J. Goldberg (Ill.) 1962
Lyndon B. Johnson ....Abe Fortas (Tenn.)................................1965
	Thurgood Marshall (N.Y.)...........................1967
Richard M. Nixon......................**Warren Earl Burger (Minn.)** 1969
	Harry A. Blackmun (Minn.) 1970
	Lewis F. Powell (Va.) 1971
	William H. Rehnquist (Ariz.) 1971
Gerald Ford..........................John Paul Stevens (Ill.) 1976
Ronald Reagan ....Sandra Day O'Connor (Ariz.)....................1981
	William H. Rehnquist (Ariz.) 1986
	Antonin Scalia (Va.)...............................1986
	Anthony M. Kennedy (Calif.)........................1988
George Bush ....David H. Souter (N.H.) 1990
	Clarence Thomas (Va.) 1991
Bill Clinton ....Ruth Bader Ginsburg (D.C.)........................1993
	Stephen Breyer (Mass.) 1994

TIME CHART OF THE SUPREME COURT

Time Chart of the Supreme Court

This table is designed to aid the user in identifying the composition of the Supreme Court at any given time in U.S. history. Each listing is headed by the chief justice, whose name is italicized. Associate justices are listed following the chief justice in order of seniority. The name of each justice is followed by a symbol representing his or her party affiliation at the time of appointment.

1789	1790–91	1792	1793–94	1795	1796–97	1798–99
Jay (F)	*Jay* (F)	*Jay* (F)	*Jay* (F)	*J. Rutledge* (F)[1]	*Ellsworth* (F)	*Ellsworth* (F)
J. Rutledge (F)	J. Rutledge (F)	Cushing (F)	Cushing (F)	Cushing (F)	Cushing (F)	Cushing (F)
Cushing (F)	Cushing (F)	Wilson (F)	Wilson (F)	Wilson (F)	Wilson (F)	Iredell (F)
Wilson (F)	Wilson (F)	Blair (F)	Blair (F)	Blair (F)	Iredell (F)	Paterson (F)
Blair (F)	Blair (F)	Iredell (F)	Iredell (F)	Iredell (F)	Paterson (F)	S. Chase (F)
	Iredell (F)	T. Johnson (F)	Paterson (F)	Paterson (F)	S. Chase (F)	Washington (F)

1800	1801–03	1804–05	1806	1807–10	1811–22	1823–25
Ellsworth (F)	*J. Marshall* (F)	*J. Marshall* (F)	*J. Marshall* (F)	*J. Marshall* (F)	*J. Marshall* (F)	*J. Marshall* (F)
Cushing (F)	Cushing (F)	Cushing (F)	Cushing (F)	Cushing (F)	Washington (F)	Washington (F)
Paterson (F)	Paterson (F)	Paterson (F)	S. Chase (F)	S. Chase (F)	W. Johnson (DR)	W. Johnson (DR)
S. Chase (F)	S. Chase (F)	S. Chase (F)	Washington (F)	Washington (F)	Livingston (DR)	Todd (DR)
Washington (F)	Washington (F)	Washington (F)	W. Johnson (DR)	W. Johnson (DR)	Todd (DR)	Duval (DR)
Moore (F)	Moore (F)	W. Johnson (DR)	Livingston (DR)	Livingston (DR)	Duval (DR)	Story (DR)
				Todd (DR)	Story (DR)	Thompson (DR)

1826–28	1829	1830–34	1835	1836	1837–40	1841–43
J. Marshall (F)	*J. Marshall* (F)	*J. Marshall* (F)	*J. Marshall* (F)	*Taney* (D)	*Taney* (D)	*Taney* (D)
Washington (F)	Washington (F)	W. Johnson (DR)	Duval (DR)	Story (DR)	Story (DR)	Story (DR)
W. Johnson (DR)	W. Johnson (DR)	Duval (DR)	Story (DR)	Thompson (DR)	Thompson (DR)	Thompson (DR)
Duval (DR)	Duval (DR)	Story (DR)	Thompson (DR)	McLean (D)	McLean (D)	McLean (D)
Story (DR)	Story (DR)	Thompson (DR)	McLean (D)	Baldwin (D)	Baldwin (D)	Baldwin (D)
Thompson (DR)	Thompson (DR)	McLean (D)	Baldwin (D)	Wayne (D)	Wayne (D)	Wayne (D)
Trimble (DR)	McLean (D)	Baldwin (D)	Wayne (D)	Barbour (D)	Barbour (D)	Catron (D)
					Catron (D)	McKinley (D)
					McKinley (D)	Daniel (D)

1844	1845	1846–50	1851–52	1853–57	1858–60	1861
Taney (D)	*Taney* (D)	*Taney* (D)	*Taney* (D)	*Taney* (D)	*Taney* (D)	*Taney* (D)
Story (DR)	McLean (D)	McLean (D)	McLean (D)	McLean (D)	McLean (D)	McLean (D)
McLean (D)	Wayne (D)	Wayne (D)	Wayne (D)	Wayne (D)	Wayne (D)	Wayne (D)
Baldwin (D)	Catron (D)	Catron (D)	Catron (D)	Catron (D)	Catron (D)	Catron (D)
Wayne (D)	McKinley (D)	McKinley (D)	McKinley (D)	Daniel (D)	Daniel (D)	Nelson (D)
Catron (D)	Daniel (D)	Daniel (D)	Daniel (D)	Nelson (D)	Nelson (D)	Grier (D)
McKinley (D)	Nelson (D)	Nelson (D)	Nelson (D)	Grier (D)	Grier (D)	Campbell (D)
Daniel (D)	Woodbury (D)	Woodbury (D)	Grier (D)	Curtis (W)	Campbell (D)	Clifford (D)
		Grier (D)	Curtis (W)	Campbell (D)	Clifford (D)	

F = Federalist
DR = Democratic-Republican (Jeffersonian)
D = Democrat

W = Whig
R = Republican
I = Independent

(table continued on next page)

1. Rutledge was a recess appointment whose confirmation was rejected by the Senate after the 1795 term.

Time Chart of the Supreme Court—*continued*

1862	1863	1864–65	1866	1867–69	1870–71	1872–1873
Taney (D)	*Taney* (D)	*S. P. Chase* (R)	*S. P. Chase* (R)	*S. P. Chase* (R)	*S. P. Chase* (R)	*S. P. Chase* (R)
Wayne (D)	Wayne (D)	Wayne (D)	Wayne (D)[2]	Nelson (D)	Nelson (D)	Clifford (D)
Catron (D)	Cafron (D)	Catron (D)[2]	Nelson (D)	Grier (D)	Clifford (D)	Swayne (R)
Nelson (D)	Nelson (D)	Nelson (D)	Grier (D)	Clifford (D)	Swayne (R)	Miller (R)
Grier (D)	Grier (D)	Grier (D)	Clifford (D)	Swayne (R)	Miller (R)	Davis (R)
Clifford (D)	Clifford (D)	Clifford (D)	Swayne (R)	Miller (R)	Davis (R)	Field (D)
Swayne (R)	Swayne (R)	Swayne (R)	Miller (R)	Davis (R)	Field (D)	Strong (R)
Miller (R)	Miller (R)	Miller (R)	Davis (R)	Field (D)	Strong (R)	Bradley (R)
Davis (R)	Davis (R)	Davis (R)	Field (D)		Bradley (R)	Hunt (R)
	Field (D)	Field (D)				

1874–76	1877–79	1880	1881	1882–87	1888	1889
Waite (R)	*Waite* (R)	*Waite* (R)	*Waite* (R)	*Waite* (R)	*Fuller* (D)	*Fuller* (D)
Clifford (D)	Clifford (D)	Clifford (D)	Miller (R)	Miller (R)	Miller (R)	Miller (R)
Swayne (R)	Swayne (R)	Swayne (R)	Field (D)	Field (D)	Field (D)	Field (D)
Miller (R)	Miller (R)	Miller (R)	Bradley (R)	Bradley (R)	Bradley (R)	Bradley (R)
Davis (R)	Field (D)	Field (D)	Hunt (R)	Harlan (Ky.) (R)	Harlan (Ky.) (R)	Harlan (Ky.) (R)
Field (D)	Strong (R)	Bradley (R)	Harlan (Ky.) (R)	Woods (R)	Matthews (R)	Gray (R)
Strong (R)	Bradley (R)	Hunt (R)	Woods (R)	Matthews (R)	Gray (R)	Blatchford (R)
Bradley (R)	Hunt (R)	Harlan (Ky.) (R)	Matthews (R)	Gray (R)	Blatchford (R)	L. Lamar (D)
Hunt (R)	Harlan (Ky.) (R)	Woods (R)	Gray (R)	Blatchford (R)	L. Lamar (D)	Brewer (R)

1890–91	1892	1893	1894	1895–97	1898–1901	1902
Fuller (D)	*Fuller* (D)	*Fuller* (D)	*Fuller* (D)	*Fuller* (D)	*Fuller* (D)	*Fuller* (D)
Field (D)	Field (D)	Field (D)	Field (D)	Field (D)	Harlan (Ky.) (R)	Harlan (Ky.) (R)
Bradley (R)	Harlan (Ky.) (R)	Harlan (Ky.) (R)	Harlan (Ky.) (R)	Harlan (Ky.) (R)	Gray (R)	Brewer (R)
Harlan (Ky.) (R)	Gray (R)	Gray (R)	Gray (R)	Gray (R)	Brewer (R)	Brown (R)
Gray (R)	Blatchford (R)	Blatchford (R)	Brewer (R)	Brewer (R)	Brown (R)	Shiras (R)
Blatchford (R)	L. Lamar (D)	Brewer (R)	Brown (R)	Brown (R)	Shiras (R)	E. White (D)
L. Lamar (D)	Brewer (R)	Brown (R)	Shiras (R)	Shiras (R)	E. White (D)	Peckham (D)
Brewer (R)	Brown (R)	Shiras (R)	H. Jackson (D)	E. White (D)	Peckham (D)	McKenna (R)
Brown (R)	Shiras (R)	H. Jackson (D)	E. White (D)	Peckham (D)	McKenna (R)	Holmes (R)

1903–05	1906–08	1909	1910–11	1912–13	1914–15	1916–20
Fuller (D)	*Fuller* (D)	*Fuller* (D)	*E. White* (D)	*E. White* (D)	*E. White* (D)	*E. White* (D)
Harlan (Ky.) (R)	Harlan (Ky.) (R)	Harlan (Ky.) (R)	Harlan (Ky.) (R)	McKenna (R)	McKenna (R)	McKenna (R)
Brewer (R)	Brewer (R)	Brewer (R)	McKenna (R)	Holmes (R)	Holmes (R)	Holmes (R)
Brown (R)	E. White (D)	E. White (D)	Holmes (R)	Day (R)	Day (R)	Day (R)
E. White (D)	Peckham (D)	McKenna (R)	Day (R)	Lurton (D)	Hughes (R)	Van Devanter (R)
Peckham (D)	McKenna (R)	Holmes (R)	Lurton (D)	Hughes (R)	Van Devanter (R)	Pitney (R)
McKenna (R)	Holmes (R)	Day (R)	Hughes (R)	Van Devanter (R)	J. Lamar (D)	McReynolds (D)
Holmes (R)	Day (R)	Moody (R)	Van Devanter (R)	J. Lamar (D)	Pitney (R)	Brandeis (R)[3]
Day (R)	Moody (R)	Lurton (D)	J. Lamar (D)	Pitney (R)	McReynolds (D)	Clarke (D)

1921	1922	1923–24	1925–29	1930–31	1932–36	1937
Taft (R)	*Taft* (R)	*Taft* (R)	*Taft* (R)	*Hughes* (R)	*Hughes* (R)	*Hughes* (R)
McKenna (R)	McKenna (R)	McKenna (R)	Holmes (R)	Holmes (R)	Van Devanter (R)	McReynolds (D)
Holmes (R)	Holmes (R)	Holmes (R)	Van Devanter (R)	Van Devanter (R)	McReynolds (D)	Brandeis (R)
Day (R)	Van Devanter (R)	Van Devanter (R)	McReynolds (D)	McReynolds (D)	Brandeis (R)	Sutherland (R)
Van Devanter (R)	Pitney (R)	McReynolds (D)	Brandeis (R)	Brandeis (R)	Sutherland (R)	Butler (D)
Pitney (R)	McReynolds (D)	Brandeis (R)	Sutherland (R)	Sutherland (R)	Butler (D)	Stone (R)
McReynolds (D)	Brandeis (R)	Sutherland (R)	Butler (D)	Butler (D)	Stone (R)	Roberts (R)
Brandeis (R)	Sutherland (R)	Butler (D)	Sanford (R)	Sanford (R)	Roberts (R)	Cardozo (D)
Clarke (D)	Butler (D)	Sanford (R)	Stone (R)	Stone (R)	Cardozo (D)	Black (D)

1938	1939	1940	1941–42	1943–44	1945	1946–48
Hughes (R)	*Hughes* (R)	*Hughes* (R)	*Stone* (R)	*Stone* (R)	*Stone* (R)	*Vinson* (D)
McReynolds (D)	McReynolds (D)	McReynolds (D)	Roberts (R)	Roberts (R)	Black (D)	Black (D)
Brandeis (R)	Butler (D)	Stone (R)	Black (D)	Black (D)	Reed (D)	Reed (D)
Butler (D)	Stone (R)	Roberts (R)	Reed (D)	Reed (D)	Frankfurter (I)	Frankfurter (I)
Stone (R)	Roberts (R)	Black (D)	Frankfurter (I)	Frankfurter (I)	Douglas (D)	Douglas (D)
Roberts (R)	Black (D)	Reed (D)	Douglas (D)	Douglas (D)	Murphy (D)	Murphy (D)
Cardozo (D)	Reed (D)	Frankfurter (I)	Murphy (D)	Murphy (D)	R. Jackson (D)	R. Jackson (D)
Black (D)	Frankfurter (I)	Douglas (D)	Byrnes (D)	R. Jackson (D)	W. Rutledge (D)	W. Rutledge (D)
Reed (D)	Douglas (D)	Murphy (D)	R. Jackson (D)	W. Rutledge (D)	Burton (R)	Burton (R)

1949–52	1953–54	1955	1956	1957	1958–61	1962–65
Vinson (D)	*Warren* (R)	*Warren* (R)	*Warren* (R)	*Warren* (R)	*Warren* (R)	*Warren* (R)
Black (D)	Black (D)	Black (D)	Black (D)	Black (D)	Black (D)	Black (D)
Reed (D)	Reed (D)	Reed (D)	Reed (D)	Reed (D)	Frankfurter (I)	Douglas (D)
Frankfurter (I)	Frankfurter (I)	Frankfurter (I)	Frankfurter (I)	Frankfurter (I)	Douglas (D)	Clark (D)
Douglas (D)	Douglas (D)	Douglas (D)	Douglas (D)	Douglas (D)	Clark (D)	Harlan (N.Y.) (R)
R. Jackson (D)	R. Jackson (D)	Burton (R)	Burton (R)	Burton (R)	Harlan (N.Y.) (R)	Brennan (D)
Burton (R)	Burton (R)	Clark (D)	Clark (D)	Clark (D)	Brennan (D)	Stewart (R)
Clark (D)	Clark (D)	Minton (D)	Minton (D)	Harlan (N.Y.) (R)	Whittaker (R)	B. White (D)
Minton (D)	Minton (D)	Harlan (N.Y.) (R)	Brennan (D)	Brennan (D)	Stewart (R)	Goldberg (D)
				Whittaker (R)		

2. Upon the death of Catron in 1865 and Wayne in 1867, their positions were abolished according to a congressional act of 1866. The Court's membership was reduced to eight until a new position was created by Congress in 1869. The new seat has generally been regarded as a re-creation of Wayne's seat.

3. According to Professor Henry Abraham, "Many—and with some justice—consider Brandeis a Democrat; however, he was in fact a registered Republican when nominated" (Henry Abraham, *Freedom and the Court,* 3d ed. 455 [1977]).

Time Chart of the Supreme Court—*continued*

1965–67	1967–69	1969	1969–70	1970	1971	1972–75
Warren (R)	*Warren* (R)	*Burger* (R)	*Burger* (R)	*Burger* (R)	*Burger* (R)	*Burger* (R)
Black (D)	Black (D)	Black (D)	Black (D)	Black (D)	Douglas (D)	Douglas (D)
Douglas (D)	Douglas (D)	Douglas (D)	Douglas (D)	Douglas (D)	Brennan (D)	Brennan (D)
Clark (D)	Harlan (N.Y.) (R)	Harlan (N.Y.) (R)	Harlan (N.Y.) (R)	Harlan (N.Y.) (R)	Stewart (R)	Stewart (R)
Harlan (N.Y.) (R)	Brennan (D)	Brennan (D)	Brennan (D)	Brennan (D)	B. White (D)	B. White (D)
Brennan (D)	Stewart (R)	Stewart (R)	Stewart (R)	Stewart (R)	T. Marshall (D)	T. Marshall (D)
Stewart (R)	B. White (D)	B. White (D)	B. White (D)	B. White (D)	Blackmun (R)	Blackmun (R)
B. White (D)	Fortas (D)	Fortas (D)	T. Marshall (D)	T. Marshall (D)		Powell (D)
Fortas (D)	T. Marshall (D)	T. Marshall (D)		Blackmun (R)		Rehnquist (R)

1975–81	1981–85	1986–87	1988–89	1990	1991–92	1993
Burger (R)	*Burger* (R)	*Rehnquist* (R)	*Rehnquist* (R)	*Rehnquist* (R)	*Rehnquist* (R)	*Rehnquist* (R)
Brennan (D)	Brennan (D)	Brennan (D)	Brennan (D)	B. White (D)	B. White (D)	Blackmun (R)
Stewart (R)	B. White (D)	B. White (D)	B. White (D)	T. Marshall (D)	Blackmun (R)	Stevens (R)
B. White (D)	T. Marshall (D)	T. Marshall (D)	T. Marshall (D)	Blackmun (R)	Stevens (R)	O'Connor (R)
T. Marshall (D)	Blackmun (R)	Blackmun (R)	Blackmun (R)	Stevens (R)	O'Connor (R)	Scalia (R)
Blackmun (R)	Powell (D)	Powell (D)	Stevens (R)	O'Connor (R)	Scalia (R)	Kennedy (R)
Powell (D)	Rehnquist (R)	Stevens (R)	O'Connor (R)	Scalia (R)	Kennedy (R)	Souter (R)
Rehnquist (R)	Stevens (R)	O'Connor (R)	Scalia (R)	Kennedy (R)	Souter (R)	Thomas (R)
Stevens (R)	O'Connor (R)	Scalia (R)	Kennedy (R)	Souter (R)	Thomas (R)	Ginsburg (D)

1994–95
Rehnquist (R)
Stevens (R)
O'Connor (R)
Scalia (R)
Kennedy (R)
Souter (R)
Thomas (R)
Ginsburg (D)
Breyer (D)

SUCCESSION OF SUPREME COURT JUSTICES

Succession of Supreme Court Justices

This table is designed to aid the user in identifying the succession of justices on the Supreme Court. Read vertically, the table lists the succession of justices in each position of the Court and the years served by each.

The number of justices constituting the Supreme Court has varied. Initially, the Court comprised six justices, but Congress increased the number to seven in 1807, to nine in 1837, and to ten in 1863. In 1866, Congress reduced the number of justices to eight in an effort to prevent President Andrew Johnson from making any appointments to the Court. As a result, the positions of John Catron, who died in 1865, and James M. Wayne, who died in 1867, were abolished. In 1869, Congress raised the number of justices to nine, where it has remained. William Strong, the first justice appointed under the new statute, has generally been considered to have succeeded Wayne. Thus, Catron is the only person who has held the tenth seat on the Court.

Chief Justices   **Associate Justices**

Chief Justices	Associate Justices								
Jay 1789–1795	J. Rutledge 1789–1791	Cushing 1789–1810	Wilson 1789–1798	Harrison[6] 1789	Iredell 1790–1798	Todd 1807–1826	Field 1863–1897	McKinley 1837–1852	Catron 1837–1865
J. Rutledge[1] 1795	T. Johnson 1791–1793	Story 1811–1845	Washington 1798–1829	Blair 1789–1796	Moore 1799–1804	Trimble 1826–1828	McKenna 1898–1925	Campbell 1853–1861	
Ellsworth 1796–1799	Paterson 1793–1806	Woodbury 1845–1851	Baldwin 1830–1844	S. Chase 1796–1811	W. Johnson 1804–1834	McLean 1829–1861	Stone[8] 1925–1941	Davis 1862–1877	
J. Marshall 1801–1835	Livingston 1806–1823	Curtis 1851–1857	Grier 1846–1870	Duvall 1812–1835	Wayne 1835–1867	Swayne 1862–1881	R. Jackson 1941–1954	Harlan 1877–1911	
Taney 1836–1864	Thomson 1823–1843	Clifford 1858–1881	Bradley 1870–1892	Barbour 1836–1841	Strong 1870–1880	Matthews 1881–1889	Harlan 1955–1971	Pitney 1912–1922	
S. P. Chase 1864–1873	Nelson 1845–1872	Gray 1882–1902	Woods 1881–1887	Daniel 1841–1860	Shiras 1892–1903	Brewer 1889–1910	Rehnquist 1971–1986[9]	Sanford 1923–1930	
Waite 1874–1888	Hunt 1873–1882	Holmes 1902–1932	L. Lamar 1888–1893	Miller 1862–1890	Day 1903–1922	Hughes 1910–1916	Scalia 1986–	Roberts 1930–1945	
Fuller 1888–1910	Blatchford 1882–1893	Cardozo 1932–1938	H. Jackson 1893–1895	Brown 1891–1906	Butler 1922–1939	Clarke 1916–1922		Burton 1945–1958	
E. White[2] 1910–1921	E. White[4] 1894–1910	Frankfurter 1939–1962	Peckham 1895–1909	Moody 1906–1910	Murphy 1940–1949	Sutherland 1922–1938		Stewart 1958–1981	
Taft 1921–1930	Van Devanter 1911–1937	Goldberg 1962–1965	Lurton 1910–1914	J. Lamar 1911–1916	Clark 1949–1967	Reed 1938–1957		O'Connor 1981–	
Hughes 1930–1941	Black 1937–1971	Fortas[5] 1965–1969	McReynolds 1914–1941	Brandeis 1916–1939	T. Marshall 1967–1991	Whittaker 1957–1962			
Stone[3] 1941–1946	Powell 1971–1988	Blackmun 1970–1994	Byrnes 1941–1942	Douglas 1939–1975	Thomas 1991–	B. White 1962–1993			
Vinson 1946–1953	Kennedy 1988–	Breyer 1994–	W. Rutledge 1943–1949	Stevens 1976–		Ginsburg 1993–			
Warren 1953–1969			Minton 1949–1956						
Burger 1969–1986			Brennan 1956–1990						
Rehnquist[7] 1986–			Souter 1990–						

1. Appointment not confirmed.
2. Associate justice, 1894–1910.
3. Associate justice, 1925–1941.
4. Later chief justice, 1910–1921.
5. Appointment as chief justice not confirmed; resigned.
6. Declined appointment.
7. Associate justice, 1971–1986
8. Later chief justice, 1941–1946.
9. Later chief justice, 1986–.

ATTORNEYS GENERAL OF THE UNITED STATES

The following table lists the attorneys general of the United States, the appointing president, and the year appointed. The office of attorney general, who serves as the chief law officer of the Federal government and head of the Department of Justice, was organized by act of Congress on September 24, 1789. The Department of Justice was created on June 22, 1870.

George Washington	Edmund Randolph (Va.)	1789
	William Bradford (Va.)	1794
	Charles Lee (Va.)	1795
John Adams	Charles Lee (Va.)	1797
	Theophilus Parsons (Mass.)	1801
Thomas Jefferson	Levi Lincoln (Mass.)	1801
	Robert Smith (Md.)	1805
	John Breckenridge (Ky.)	1805
	Caesar A. Rodney (Del.)	1807
James Madison	Caesar A. Rodney (Del.)	1809
	William Pinkney (Md.)	1811
	Richard Rush (Pa.)	1814
James Monroe	Richard Rush (Pa.)	1817
	William Wirt (Va.)	1817
John Quincy Adams	William Wirt (Va.)	1817
Andrew Jackson	John McP. Berrien (Ga.)	1829
	Roger B. Taney (Md.)	1831
	Benjamin F. Butler (N.Y.)	1833
Martin Van Buren	Benjamin F. Butler (N.Y.)	1837
	Felix Grundy (Tenn.)	1838
	Henry D. Gilpin (Pa.)	1840
William H. Harrison	John J. Crittenden (Ky.)	1841
John Tyler	John J. Crittenden (Ky.)	1841
	Hugh S. Legaré (S.C.)	1841
	John Nelson (Md.)	1843
James Polk	John Y. Mason (Va.)	1845
	Nathan Clifford (Me.)	1846
	Issac Toncay (Conn.)	1848
Zachary Taylor	Reverdy Johnson (Md.)	1849
Millard Fillmore	John J. Crittenden (Ky.)	1850

Franklin Pierce . . . . .Caleb Cushing (Mass.) 1853

James Buchanan . . . . .Jeremiah S. Black (Pa.) 1857

Edwin M. Stanton (Ohio) 1860

Abraham Lincoln . . . . .Edward Bates (Mo.) 1861

Titian J. Coffey (Pa.) 1863

James Speed (Ky.) 1864

Andrew Johnson . . . . .James Speed (Ky.) 1865

Henry Stanbury (Ohio) 1866

William M. Evarts (N.Y.) 1868

Ulysses S. Grant . . . . .Ebenezer R. Hoar (Mass.) 1869

Amos T. Akerman (Ga.) 1870

George M. Williams (Ore.) 1870

Edwards Pierrepont (N.Y.) 1875

Alphonso Taft (Ohio) 1876

Rutherford Hayes . . . . .Charles Devens (Mass.) 1877

James Garfield . . . . .Wayne MacVeagh (Pa.) 1881

Chester Arthur . . . . .Benjamin H. Brewster (Pa.) 1881

Grover Cleveland . . . . .Augustus Garland (Ark.) 1885

Benjamin Harrison . . . . .William H. H. Miller (Ind.) 1889

Grover Cleveland . . . . .Richard Olney (Mass.) 1893

Judson Harmon (Ohio) 1895

William McKinley . . . . .Joseph McKenna (Cal.) 1897

John W. Griggs (N.J.) 1898

Philander C. Knox (Pa.) 1901

Theodore Roosevelt . . . . .Philander C. Knox (Pa.) 1901

William H. Moody (Mass.) 1904

Charles J. Bonaparte (Md.) 1906

William Taft . . . . .George W. Wickersham (N.Y.) 1909

Woodrow Wilson . . . . .James C. McReynolds (Tenn.) 1913

Thomas W. Gregory (Tex.) 1914

A. Mitchell Palmer (Pa.) 1919

Warren Harding . . . . .Harry M. Daugherty (Ohio) 1921

Calvin Coolidge . . . . .Harry M. Daugherty (Ohio) 1923

Harlan F. Stone (N.Y.) 1924

John S. Sargent (Vt.) 1925

Herbert Hoover . . . . .William D. Mitchell (Minn.) 1929

Franklin D. Roosevelt . . . . .Homer S. Cummings (Conn.) 1933

Frank Murphy (Mich.) 1939

Robert H. Jackson (N.Y.) 1940

Francis Biddle (Pa.) 1941

Harry S. Truman . . . . .Tom C. Clark (Tex.) 1945

J. Howard McGrath (R.I.) 1949

J. P. McGranery (Pa.) 1952

Dwight D. Eisenhower . . . . .Herbert Brownell, Jr. (N.Y.) 1953

William P. Rodgers (N.Y.) 1957

John F. Kennedy . . . . .Robert F. Kennedy (Va.) 1961

Lyndon B. Johnson . . . . .Robert F. Kennedy (Va.) 1963

Nicholas de B. Katzenbach (Pa.) 1964

Richard M. Nixon . . . . .John Mitchell (N.Y.) 1969

Richard G. Kleindienst (Ariz.) 1972

Elliot Richardson (Mass.) 1973

William S. Saxbe (Ohio) 1973

Gerald Ford . . . . .Edward H. Levi (Ill.) 1975

Jimmy Carter . . . . .Griffin Bell (Ga.) 1977

Benjamin R. Civiletti (Md.) 1979

Ronald Reagan	William French Smith (Calif.)	1981
	Edwin Meese III (Calif.)	1984
	Richard Thornburgh (Pa.)	1988
George Bush	Richard Thornburgh (Pa.)	1989
	William P. Barr (N.Y.)	1991
Bill Clinton	Janet Reno (Fla.)	1993

CONGRESSIONAL TIMELINE: NINETEENTH CENTURY

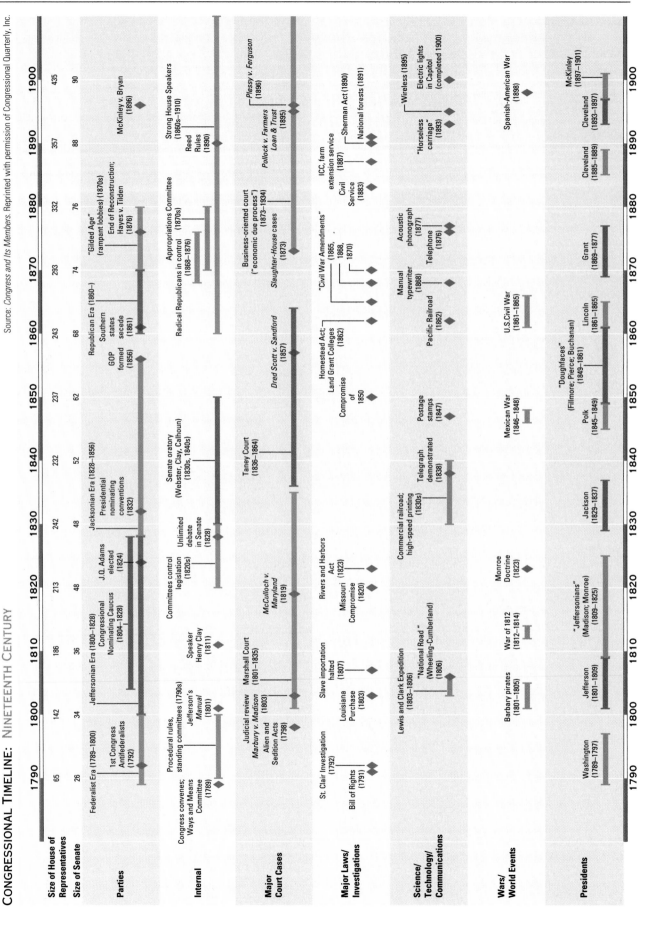

Source: *Congress and Its Members.* Reprinted with permission of Congressional Quarterly, Inc.

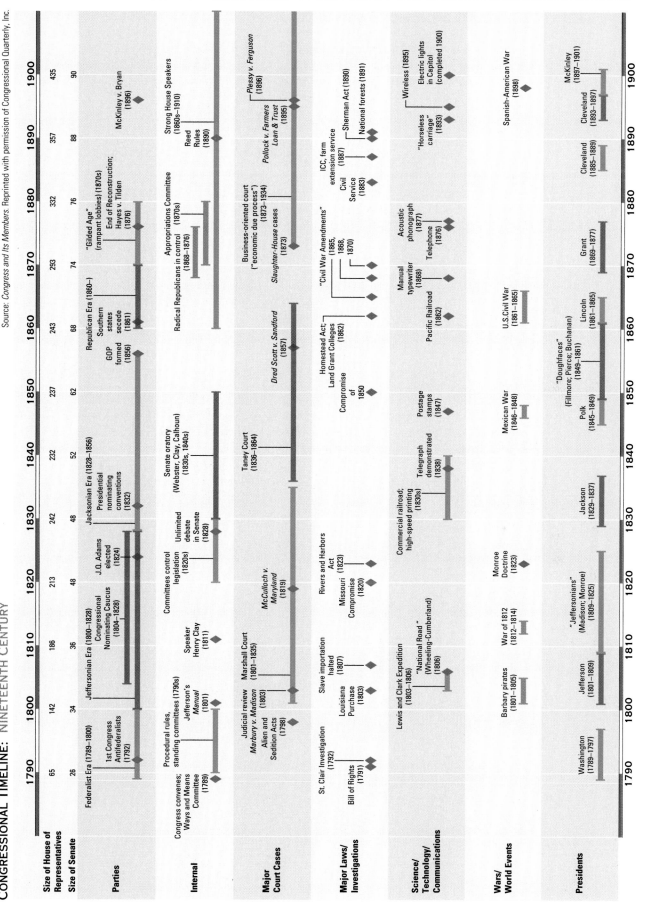

CONGRESSIONAL TIMELINE: NINETEENTH CENTURY

Source: *Congress and Its Members.* Reprinted with permission of Congressional Quarterly, Inc.

BRITISH REGNAL YEARS

Regnal years run from the date of a monarch's accession to the throne until the same date in the next calendar year. Thus an event occurring on March 24, 1626, would be in the first regnal year of King Charles I who acceded to the throne on March 27, 1625. British statutes are usually cited by regnal years.

Sovereign	Accession	Length of reign
William I	Oct. 14, 1066	21
William II	Sept. 26, 1087	13
Henry I	Aug. 5, 1100	36
Stephen	Dec. 26, 1135	19
Henry II	Dec. 19, 1154	35
Richard I	Sept. 23, 1189	10
John	May 27, 1199	18
Henry III	Oct. 28, 1216	57
Edward I	Nov. 20, 1272	35
Edward II	July 8, 1307	20
Edward III	Jan. 25, 1326	51
Richard II	June 22, 1377	23
Henry IV	Sept. 30, 1399	14
Henry V	March 21, 1413	10
Henry VI	Sept. 1, 1422	39
Edward IV	March 4, 1461	23
Edward V	April 9, 1483	—
Richard III	June 26, 1483	3
Henry VII	Aug. 22, 1485	24
Henry VIII	April 22, 1509	38
Edward VI	Jan. 28, 1547	7
Mary	July 6, 1553	6
Elizabeth	Nov. 17, 1558	45
James I	March 24, 1603	23
Charles I	March 27, 1625	24
The Commonwealth*	Jan. 30, 1649	11
Charles II	May 29, 1660	37
James II	Feb. 6, 1685	4
William III and Mary II	Feb. 13, 1689	14
Anne	March 8, 1702	13
George I	Aug. 1, 1714	13
George II	June 11, 1727	34
George III	Oct. 25, 1760	60
George IV	Jan. 29, 1820	11
William IV	June 26, 1830	7
Victoria	June 20, 1837	64
Edward VII	Jan. 22, 1901	9
George V	May 6, 1910	25
Edward VIII	Jan. 20, 1936	1
George VI	Dec. 11, 1936	15
Elizabeth II	Feb. 6, 1952	—

*The government established by Parliament after the abolition of the monarchy. The government of Oliver Cromwell and his son (1653-1658) is also known as the Protectorate.

represented by an FBI agent, Hollingsworth, and a former Soviet party official, McLeod, both living in a Brooklyn rooming house. Their protracted exchanges are reported by Mickey Lovett, a traumatized war veteran. Mailer was, apparently, trying to follow up on the keen-minded colloquies of Hearn and Cummings, but in the new novel he did not balance debate with sharply etched description as in *The Naked and the Dead*. Under the influence of Jean Malaquais, his French translator, Mailer had become fascinated with Marxist dialectics and the history of the Russian Revolution but was unable to find a way to dramatize this material. Consequently, the novel is claustrophobic, although its exploration of the nature and appeal of spies and spying is often trenchant. Mailer was conducting his continuing education in public, and the public was not appreciative, although the hallucinatory memories of some of the characters were a development of his art. *Barbary Shore* received the worst reviews of any Mailer book, and his confidence was weakened.

In his third novel, *The Deer Park* (1955), Mailer turned to Hollywood, where he had gathered impressions during a year (in 1949 and 1950) spent writing screenplays. The Cold War, and specifically the FBI and congressional witch hunts for communists and sympathizers of the early 1950s, form the background of the novel, but its chief concern is a portrait of the artist—director Charles Eitel—in search of lost artistic integrity. Blacklisted for his leftist activities, Eitel has retreated to a Southern California resort town to rebuild himself and write a new screenplay, one not based on meretricious commercial formulas. He has a new woman, Elena Esposito (modeled in part on Mailer's second wife, Adele Morales, whom he married in 1954), in his life, and the bounty of their affair rejuvenates him, at least initially. His old handlers want him to identify radicals before a congressional committee, but Eitel balks. Still, he misses his former stature and the emoluments of fame. The narrative follows Eitel's interactions with the town's pimps, drunks, actors, producers, and call girls—good and evil angels—each of whom makes him reflect on his quest for renewed confidence and energy, which he does with honesty and humor. It is narrated by twenty-three-year-old Sergius O'Shaugnessy, former air force pilot and another burned-out case, who drifts into an affair with Lulu Meyers, a young, beautiful, and wacky actress. Eitel (I-tell) eventually tells all, sells out, and breaks off with the passionate Elena, but only after an intense internal struggle.

Eitel's relations with Elena are brilliantly detailed by Mailer, although he has to drop Sergius as a narrator to present the interstices of their complex and near-tragic affair from an omniscient perspective. It is, perhaps, the most memorable portrait of a woman in Mailer's work. Eitel's final descent into the maw of Hollywood corruption is offset by Sergius's rise. Aided by the wisdom and negative example of Eitel, Sergius successfully resists the various baits offered by Herman Teppis, the head of Supreme Studios and one of Mailer's finest comic portraits. Because of a few explicit sexual scenes (which seem very tame today), Mailer had great difficulty in finding a publisher, although it is clear that the novel's intentions are the opposite of salacious. Indeed, as several critics have noted, *The Deer Park* is a modern morality play.

GREENWICH VILLAGE

Mailer's anger at the treatment of his third novel and his general dismay at the dull conformities of the 1950s made him seek a new identity for himself. He got interested in jazz, marijuana, and the nightlife of New York City's Greenwich Village and began writing for a variety of magazines—*Esquire*, *Dissent*, *Partisan Review*, and perhaps most important, the *Village Voice*, which he named and cofounded in 1955. His column, "Quickly," appeared there for several months in 1956. Attempts to write a new novel stalled, but his urban experiences and emerging belief in an embattled God led him in 1957 to write his most anthologized and controversial essay. "The White Negro" presented a philosophy based on the life of urban hipsters who emulated the existential experiences of African Americans living on the dangerous knife-edge of ecstasy and violence. If Mailer's first three novels dealt with larger social realities—war, warring ideologies, and Hollywood, respectively—"The White Negro" was all about the "rebellious imperatives of the self." In a world threatened by nuclear annihilation, the only recourse was to trust the body and religiously follow one's deepest instincts. American blacks, he argued, had been forced to do this, and their lives, while painful because of racism, were more authentic than those of white suburbanites.

The essay became the heart of Mailer's next book, *Advertisements for Myself* (1959), a sampler of previous work surrounded by extended and edgy commentary. Here Mailer created his characteristic narrative voice: direct, acerbic, self-referenced, digressive, and freewheeling, with a good deal of sardonic wit. This watershed volume led to two similar but less powerful collections, *The Presidential Papers* (1963) and *Cannibals and Christians* (1966), both derived from his magazine writing of the early 1960s. Intervening was an event that still resonates in his life, the penknife stabbing of his wife at a drunken party in November 1960 and his subsequent incarceration in a mental hospital. He later pleaded guilty to assault and received a suspended sentence, but the marriage to Adele was over. Mailer's varied forays of the late 1950s and early 1960s had only dampened his ability to get a new novel going. His frustration led him in late 1963 to up the ante by announcing that he would publish a novel, titled *An American Dream*, in monthly installments in *Esquire*; it ran from January to August 1964 and appeared in book form in 1965.

A NEW HERO

Until *An American Dream*, Mailer's major fictional characters were unsatisfactory in one way or another. None of them, not Hearn, Croft, Cummings, Lovett, McLeod, O'Shaugnessy, Eitel, or Elena Esposito, were invested with his deepest concerns: the desire to grow at all costs, a distrust of mechanistic reason, a willingness to take risks, a belief in the authority of the senses, faith in courage as the cardinal virtue, and fear and loathing for the rampant technology and the incipient totalitarianism he saw in American life. Stephen Richards Rojack, the protagonist of *An American Dream*, has these concerns, and he also shares Mailer's theological beliefs. Rojack is a war hero, former congressman, college professor, and a near alcoholic. Open to omens and portents and susceptible to every premonition, he hears voices, studies the moon, and waits for cancer to strike him. His wife Deborah taunts him with her infidelities, driving him to a physical attack that ends with her death and a plunge from her apartment window. Rojack claims that her fall was suicide, and the brunt of the story is devoted to his attempts to convince his friends, the police, and Deborah's father, Barney Oswald Kelly, the "solicitor for the devil," of his innocence. Narrated in a brisk, rococo style by Rojack, the novel shows Mailer at the height of his word power as he delineates the dread-filled inner life of his embattled protagonist. The air of the novel is haunted, filled with demonic and angelic presence, especially in the final scenes, when Rojack confronts Kelly in his penthouse apartment. *An American Dream* was an advance in several ways for Mailer. First, his existential cosmology of a warring universe is fully deployed; second, for the first time in Mailer's work the narrator and the chief protagonist are one; third, his energetic, lyrical style is now fully developed; and finally, all the spiritual dichotomies of the American urban landscape, Mailer's own New York City, are presented. Reviews of the novel were sharply divided, but the book was a best-seller and Mailer was lifted and empowered by its success.

From 1966 to 1975, Mailer was in constant motion. He was arrested for protesting the Vietnam War, covered prize fights and political conventions, staged a dramatic version of *The Deer Park*, appeared on countless television talk shows and college campuses, ran (and lost) for mayor of New York City, and made three experimental films. Married and divorced several times, he was by 1975 the father of seven children. He published nineteen books during this long spurt of productivity, only one of which, *Why Are We in Vietnam?* (1967), is a novel. Set in Alaska during the hunting trip of Texas corporate executives, it is narrated by D.J., the teenage son of the senior executive. D.J.'s jazzy, scatological style again demonstrated Mailer's comic abilities and linguistic inventiveness, but the descriptions of the hunters and the hunted in Alaska's majestic mountains are the novel's greatest achievement. It was nominated for the National Book Award, the first of five for Mailer.

CREATIVE NONFICTION

For the most part, however, Mailer was unwilling or unable to transform the fantastic cultural eruptions of the 1960s and 1970s into fiction. He needed a new way of seeing these events, and the optics of conventional journalism were too clumsy. Along with a number of other writers—Truman Capote, Joan Didion, Tom Wolfe, and Hunter Thompson are the most important—Mailer recognized that the well-refined techniques of modern fiction could be adapted to the task of capturing the unpredictable events of the postassassination years. He added a twist, however: he wrote about Norman Mailer's involvement in these events. He described himself in the third person, a rare usage, employed most notably by classical historians such as Xenophon and Julius Caesar. Sometimes he called himself "Mailer," but more often he came up with a new name such as "the Participant," "the Beast," or "Aquarius." From 1968 to 1975 he published seven full-length works of creative nonfiction dealing with the "double life" of Americans, which he described in *The Presidential Papers* as "the history of politics which is concrete, factual, practical and unbelievably dull" and "a subterranean river of untapped, ferocious, lonely and romantic desires, that concentration of ecstasy and violence which is the dream life of the nation." More specifically, three of these—*The Armies of the Night* (1968), *Miami and the Siege of Chicago* (1968), and *St. George and the Godfather* (1972)—examine the ways that the American political system dealt with, and did not deal with, the Vietnam War, as well as analyze the tumultuous presidential campaigns of 1968 and 1972.

The Armies of the Night is the most important of these because Mailer's third-person self-description lends itself perfectly to the account of his personal involvement in the antiwar March on the Pentagon in October 1967, including his arrest for crossing a police line at the Pentagon. This unique, best-selling narrative had a catalytic effect on subsequent antiwar activities and garnered Mailer the Pulitzer Prize, the George Polk Award, and the National Book Award. Part of the strength of the antiwar narratives comes from Mailer's ability to interleave personal testimony with analytic descriptions of complex social and political movements. His novelistic skill, reportorial acumen, and love of a good fight combined to make *The Armies of the Night* a classic of American nonfiction.

The other four nonfiction narratives deal with a variety of American events and issues and demonstrate Mailer's versatility: the 1969 flight to the moon (*Of a Fire on the Moon*, 1971), the rise of the women's movement and Mailer's contentious relations with it (*The Prisoner of Sex*, 1971), a biography of Marilyn Monroe (*Marilyn: A Biography*, 1973), and the 1974 heavyweight boxing match between Muhammad Ali and George Foreman (*The Fight*, 1975). Mailer complains openly in *The Fight* that he is tired of using himself as a narrative lens. He felt an urgency to break from the American scene and return to the novel, set in ancient Egypt, that he had begun in 1972. He worked on it intermittently through the early 1970s and then focused on it during the latter half of the decade, with only one major interruption to write *The Executioner's Song* (1979), an account of the life and death of Gary Gilmore, the Utah murderer who created a media sensation when he insisted that his death sentence by firing squad be carried out posthaste. To trace the tragic arc of Gilmore's life, Mailer saw that he must remove himself as an intrusive, self-referenced narrator. To highlight Gilmore, he banished Aquarius. Using a Hemingway-like style consonant with the open landscape of Utah and a point of view reminiscent of *The Naked and the Dead*, Mailer grounded his narrative in interviews with the principals of the story and an examination of thousands of pages of legal and psychological records. He was aided in this groundwork by Lawrence Schiller, a photographer, journalist, and film producer, with whom he has collaborated on a total of five books, including *Marilyn*. Mailer won his second Pulitzer for *The Executioner's Song*, which was later turned into a feature film using his Emmy-nominated screenplay. Some

readers feel that this "true life novel," as Mailer calls it, equals or surpasses *The Armies of the Night* in stature.

RETURN TO THE NOVEL

Reenergized by the success of *The Executioner's Song*, Mailer spent the next three years working almost exclusively on the Egyptian novel. He was now the father of nine children, all told, and since 1980 was married to his sixth wife, Barbara Norris Church Mailer. A painter, actress, novelist, and theatrical director, she "created a domestic climate that not only allows one to thrive at work but even to love the idea that there is work to do and it is worth doing," as he put it in the acknowledgments to his 1998 collection, *The Time of Our Time*. Unlike many of his earlier works, *Ancient Evenings* (1983) could not be written under deadline pressure. Mailer intended it to be his greatest work and did extensive rewriting and research on the customs, especially the military and funerary customs, of the Egypt of two millennia past. The remote temporal setting of the novel gave him freedom to explore matters such as magic, religion, telepathy, and reincarnation. His protagonist, Menenhetet I, lives four consecutive and very different lives in the course of this 709-page novel, having learned the secret of personal reincarnation from a Jewish slave. But the most powerful chapters of the novel deal with a well-known historical event: the Battle of Kadesh near the Orontes River in ancient Syria. Here Menenhetet's pharaoh, the great Ramses II, defeated the Hittites around the year 1300 B.C. The earlier sections of the novel dealing with the social customs and ruling ideas of the Egyptians, high and low, especially their violent and carnal religiosity, prepare the reader for Mailer's stunning depiction of the battle, which focuses on the chariot squadrons led personally by Ramses II. Other portions of the novel, however, are less compelling, especially the long description of Menenhetet's service as the pharaoh's harem master. Mailer's method of narration, which requires the entire novel to be told during one long evening many years after the chief events have taken place, had been criticized for its unnecessary detachment and convolution. But the novel's labyrinthine complexity has yet to be fully grasped by commentators; Mailer's most ambitious work may yet be seen as his masterwork.

In 1984, Mailer published *Tough Guys Don't Dance*, a gory and complicated murder mystery set in Provincetown, the town at the tip of Cape Cod in Massachusetts, where he began to spend the majority of his time from the mid-1980s on. In 1987 he took a break from his next major effort, a novel focused on the CIA, to direct a feature film based on *Tough Guys* that used his own screenplay. The CIA novel, *Harlot's Ghost*, appeared in 1991. The seven-year period between books is the longest such gap in Mailer's career to date. But *Harlot's Ghost*, at 1,300 pages, is also his longest work. It is also a crucial work for him in that it brings together two of his abiding interests: the power structures of the Cold War and the epistemology of identity. Forty years after *Barbary Shore*, Mailer returned to the world of false identities, dirty tricks, coded messages, intrigue, and covert operations. The novel follows the early life and CIA career of Harry Hubbard, son and godson of two CIA paladins who guide and test him as he advances through the ranks. He is stationed in Berlin and Uruguay and, in the novel's climax, takes part in the aborted CIA invasion of Cuba in 1961. Paralleling his agency work is his love affair with his godfather's young wife, Kittredge Montague (also a CIA operative), whom he later marries when she divorces Hugh Montague, the fabled "Harlot" of the title. The disappearance of Harlot in 1983, which sends shudders through intelligence organizations around the world, is the novel's culminating event. We learn of it early on, however, because the novel begins in the 1980s and after 100 pages turns back to follow Harry's early life and beginning years as an agent. This 1,200-page chronicle ends shortly after the 1963 assassination of President Kennedy with the words "To be continued." Presumably, we will learn of Harlot's fate if Mailer writes the sequel to what is his most ambitious work, excepting *Ancient Evenings*. Even if Mailer does not write the sequel (which has the working title "Harlot's Grave"), his even-handed anatomy of the CIA, his deft portraits of both fictional and historical figures (including Kennedy and CIA director Allen Dulles), and his powerful depiction of some of the most cataclysmic events of the mid-twentieth century assure the novel a prominent place among his works and in American fiction generally.

OSWALD, PICASSO, AND JESUS

It is not often noted that Mailer is an accomplished biographer, although not in the usual academic or historical modes. Mailer's biographies read like novels, which is, of course, his intention. He is not afraid of research or footnotes, and his biographies use both when necessary, but he relies more on his intuitions than on any archive. In addition to the fictive tone of his life studies, there is another commonality: they are all portraits of promethean figures, overreachers with divided souls. It might even be said that in their ambition, risk taking, and radical doubt

about their fundamental identities, they resemble Mailer. Each of his subjects from the 1970s—Marilyn Monroe, Muhammad Ali, Henry Miller, and Gary Gilmore—and those of his second biographical period—Lee Harvey Oswald, Pablo Picasso, and Jesus Christ—have artistic sensibilities, a thirst for fame, and a hidden life that is both an asset and a burden.

It is not much of an exaggeration to say that Mailer's magnificent seven all share Picasso's desire "to reach into mysteries of existence that no one else had even perceived," as Mailer put it in *Portrait of Picasso as a Young Man* (1995). The Picasso biography was completed in 1993, but because of various production problems it was not published until October 1995, four months after his study of Oswald appeared. *Oswald's Tale: An American Mystery* (1995) is arguably Mailer's finest biography, partly because of his obsession with the question of Oswald's role in President Kennedy's death, and partly because he and Lawrence Schiller were the first to gain access to KGB documents and agents who knew Oswald during his year in the Soviet Union. In *The Gospel According to the Son* (1997), Mailer retold the four Gospels from the point of view of the resurrected Jesus. Although it received mainly negative reviews, his depictions of several of the novel's characters—Judas, John the Baptist, and Satan—were praised, as was the authenticity of the voice of Jesus.

A CONTINUING CAREER

Mailer turned seventy-five in 1998 with no signs of diminished productivity. His birthday was marked by the publication of his largest collection, *The Time of Our Time*. This 1,286-page anthology includes selections from all of his important works arranged according to the dates of the events depicted rather than, as is customary, the dates of publication. Mailer thus defers to history rather than his own writing life. He followed this well-received volume with another collaboration with Lawrence Schiller. *Into the Mirror: The Life of Master Spy Robert P. Hanssen* was published in April 2002. Mailer had earlier written a television screenplay depicting the life of Hanssen; Schiller used it as the basis for *Into the Mirror*. Both the book and the four-hour television program (broadcast in November 2002) show that Mailer's skill with dialogue and his profound fascination with questions of identity continue with vigor. On 31 January 2003, his eightieth birthday, Random House published Mailer's forty-second book, *The Spooky Art: Some Thoughts on Writing*, a compilation of insights from over 150 different interviews, reviews, and essays of the past forty years, along with several new pieces. Mailer has surprised his readers countless times in the past and may do so again. He has challenged, beguiled, angered, and amazed three generations of readers worldwide. After more than fifty years, he still resides at the pinnacle of the American literary world, often castigated for his extra-literary activities but just as often praised for his ongoing construing of our national life and his relentless, brilliant narrative innovations.

[*See also* Hemingway, Ernest; Vietnam in Poetry and Prose; *and* War Literature.]

SELECTED WORKS

The Naked and the Dead (1948)
Barbary Shore (1951)
The Deer Park (1955)
Advertisements for Myself (1959)
The Presidential Papers (1963)
An American Dream (1965)
Cannibals and Christians (1966)
The Deer Park: A Play (1967)
Why Are We in Vietnam? (1967)
The Armies of the Night: History as a Novel, The Novel as History (1968)
Miami and the Siege of Chicago: An Informal History of the Republican and Democratic Conventions of 1968 (1968)
The Long Patrol: 25 Years of Writing from the Work of Norman Mailer (1971)
Of a Fire on the Moon (1971)
The Prisoner of Sex (1971)
Existential Errands (1972)
St. George and the Godfather (1972)
Marilyn: A Biography (1973)
The Fight (1975)
Genius and Lust: A Journey through the Major Writings of Henry Miller (1976)
The Executioner's Song (1979)
Pieces and Pontifications (1982)
Ancient Evenings (1983)
Tough Guys Don't Dance (1984)
Conversations with Norman Mailer (1988)
Harlot's Ghost (1991)
Oswald's Tale: An American Mystery (1995)
Portrait of Picasso as a Young Man: An Interpretive Biography (1995)
The Gospel According to the Son (1997)
The Time of Our Time (1998)
Into the Mirror: The Life of Master Spy Robert P. Hanssen (2002)
The Spooky Art: Some Thoughts on Writing (2003)

FURTHER READING

Adams, Laura. *Existential Battles: The Growth of Norman Mailer*. Athens, Ohio, 1976. Good discussion of themes and techniques, especially early narrators; includes discussion of extraliterary activities.

Adams, Laura. *Will the Real Norman Mailer Please Stand Up*. Port Washington, N.Y., 1974. Fourteen essays and reviews and one interview examining Mailer's protean activities, including two essays on his religious beliefs. Also contains extensive secondary bibliography.

Aldridge, John W. *Classics and Contemporaries*. Columbia, Mo., 1992. Contains important critiques of *The Long Patrol*, *Genius and Lust*, and *Harlot's Ghost*.

Begiebing, Robert J. *Acts of Regeneration: Allegory and Archetype in the Works of Norman Mailer*. Columbia, Mo., 1980. Close readings of major works from *Barbary Shore* to *The Executioner's Song*; contains a fine discussion of Mailer's "heroic consciousness."

Bloom, Harold, ed. *Norman Mailer: Modern Critical Views*. New York, 1986. Sixteen reviews and essays covering Mailer's major works and emphasizing Hemingway's influence.

Braudy, Leo, ed. *Norman Mailer: A Collection of Critical Essays*. Englewood Cliffs, N.J., 1972. Thirteen essays on Mailer's work through *Of a Fire on the Moon*; the editor's introduction has useful insights into *Miami and the Siege of Chicago*.

Bufithis, Philip M. *Norman Mailer*. New York, 1978. The most readable and reliable study of Mailer's early work through *Genius and Lust*.

Dearborn, Mary. *Mailer: A Biography*. New York, 1999. The most literary biography.

Dickstein, Morris. *Leopards at the Gate: The Transformation of American Fiction, 1945–1970*. Cambridge, Mass., 2002. The reshaping of American fiction by Mailer, Saul Bellow, James Jones, Philip Roth, James Baldwin, and Jack Kerouac.

Flaherty, Joe. *Managing Mailer*. New York, 1970. Account by his campaign manager of Mailer's 1969 campaign to be the Democratic nominee for mayor of New York City.

Glenday, Michael K. *Norman Mailer*. New York, 1995. Contains one of the finest discussions of *Why Are We in Vietnam?*

Kaufmann, Donald L. *Norman Mailer: The Countdown (The First Twenty Years)*. Carbondale, Ill., 1969. Pioneering discussion of the beast/seer conflict in the early work that overlooks Mailer's political ideas and activities.

Leeds, Barry H. *The Enduring Vision of Norman Mailer.* New York, 2002. Excellent discussion of boxing in Mailer's works and the film version of *Tough Guys Don't Dance.*

Leeds, Barry H. *The Structured Vision of Norman Mailer.* New York, 1969. First major study of Mailer's work; valuable for its analysis of *An American Dream* and *The Armies of the Night.*

Lennon, J. Michael. *Critical Essays on Norman Mailer.* Boston, 1986. Ten reviews and ten essays on Mailer's work through *Ancient Evenings.* Long introduction summarizes popular and critical response to his work.

Lennon, J. Michael, and Donna Pedro Lennon. *Norman Mailer: Works and Days.* Shavertown, Pa., 2000. Comprehensive, annotated, cross-referenced list of 1,100 Mailer items, including uncollected interviews, essays, letters to the editor, and ephemera. Also contains life chronology, 91 photographs, and the largest annotated secondary bibliography, with 387 items.

Lounsberry, Barbara. *The Art of Fact: Contemporary Artists of Nonfiction.* New York, 1990. Careful exploration of the parallels between *Advertisements for Myself* and Walt Whitman's *Leaves of Grass.*

Lucid, Robert F. *Norman Mailer: The Man and His Work.* Boston, 1971. Thirteen essays on Mailer's early work, four essays on his life, and an interview; contains the first major bibliography.

Manso, Peter. *Mailer: His Life and Times.* New York, 1985. Oral biography based on interviews with over 150 people; lacks synthesizing overview.

Merrill, Robert. *Norman Mailer Revisited.* Boston, 1992. Thoughtful examination of the formal structure of Mailer's narratives; contains perhaps the best analysis of *The Executioner's Song.*

Mills, Hilary. *Mailer: A Biography.* New York, 1982. Contains valuable interviews with Mailer's family and friends, including his first wife. First biography.

Poirier, Richard. *Norman Mailer.* New York, 1972. The most intelligent study of Mailer to date; excellent discussion of Mailer's dualisms and his relation to history.

Solotaroff, Robert. *Down Mailer's Way.* Urbana, Ill., 1974. Comprehensive discussion of Mailer's existentialism and "The White Negro."

Tabbi, Joseph. *Postmodern Sublime: Technology and American Writing from Mailer to Cyberpunk.* Ithaca, N.Y., 1995. Discusses Mailer's ambivalent attitude toward technology.

Whalen-Bridge, John. *Political Fiction and the American Self.* Urbana, Ill., 1998. Subtle examination of Mailer's relationship to American mythologies.

BERNARD MALAMUD

by Sanford Pinsker

In an 1 April 1968 interview with the *Jerusalem Post*, Bernard Malamud offered up the proposition that "every man is a Jew though he may not know it." The quip, slightly altered, enjoyed an oft-reprinted life as "all men are Jews." In some circles, the apocryphal version was taken as a comment on Malamud's universality; in others, it served as the flip side of Philip Roth's credo of edgy social realism: all Jews are men. During the heyday of the Jewish-American renaissance, the respective shorthands were used (and often misused) to distinguish Malamud's gentle soulfulness from Roth's biting satire.

Although suffering was a prominent feature of Malamud's most representative fiction, he did not sentimentalize life's troubles, much less embrace them. What he chronicled, with varying mixtures of realism and fantasy, was, as he put it, "simple people struggling to make their lives better in a world of bad luck." The best of Malamud's early stories make the heart crack, partly because they lay bare the soul of weariness and lament, and partly because they remind us that the same corrosive forces in life that bear down on one will sooner or later bear down on all.

Malamud's typical protagonists are immigrants scraping by on the city's meaner streets; their half-Yiddish, half-English speech rhythms suggest the historical baggage all carry on their bony shoulders. Malamud's style, a fusion of the magical and the mundane, fantasy and realistic fiction, reminds us that the heart, however troubled, can retain a vision of worlds more attractive.

LIFE AND MAJOR WORKS: A SUMMARY

Bernard Malamud was born in Brooklyn, New York, on 26 April 1914 to Max and Bertha Fidelman Malamud. His parents were Russian-Jewish immigrants who ran a small

Bernard Malamud. (*Courtesy of the Library of Congress*)

grocery store in Brooklyn, a mom-and-pop operation of the sort Malamud used as the setting for *The Assistant* (1957), his tale of suffering and spiritual redemption in Depression-era America.

From 1928 to 1932 Malamud was a student at Brooklyn's Erasmus Hall High School, where his earliest stories were published in the literary magazine, the *Erasmian*. In 1936 Malamud received his B.A. degree from the City College of New York, and in 1942 he earned an M.A. degree (with a thesis on Thomas Hardy's *The Dynasts*, 1903–1908) from Columbia University.

Initially, Malamud had planned on a career as a teacher of English in the New York City public schools, but a poor job market forced him to take a position in Washington, D.C., with the Bureau of Census. He soon returned to his native Brooklyn, however, where he wrote during the day and taught classes in English at Erasmus Hall High's night school division. On 6 November 1945 he married Ann De Chiara, an Italian American. Thus began a lifelong interest in Italian culture, as well as increasingly frequent trips to Italy itself. The result can be seen in those of Malamud's stories that feature Italian-American characters or Italian locales.

In 1949 Malamud accepted an instructorship in the English Department at Oregon State University in Corvalis. Eventually, he was promoted to associate professor and stayed at Oregon State until 1961. He continued write despite an onerous load of composition courses taught in a university more widely known for its commitment to agricultural and technical arts programs. His novel *A New Life* (1961) reflects Malamud's ambivalent feelings about the American West in general and Oregon State University in particular.

The year *A New Life* was published was also the year Malamud left Oregon to accept a position in the Division of Language and Literature at Bennington College in

Vermont. If Oregon State University was devoted to the pragmatic, Bennington had a deserved reputation as a school devoted to the arts. Malamud taught one creative writing course a year and divided his time between a residence in rural Vermont and an apartment in New York City. His novel *Dubin's Lives* (1979) reflects the lushness of Vermont's pastoral setting, although that work is also filled with the moral suffering and efforts at transcendence that always seem a part of Malamud's creative landscape.

Malamud died on 20 March 1986, at the age of seventy-one. His fiction was much honored during his lifetime. He received two National Book Awards, for *The Magic Barrel* (1958) and *The Fixer* (1966), in addition to a Pulitzer Prize for *The Fixer*. His reputation as one of the finest American writers of the second half of the twentieth century rests on a handful of extraordinarily crafted short stories, among them "The Magic Barrel," "Idiot's First," "The Angel Levine," and "The Last Mohican," as well as novels such as *The Natural* (1952), *The Assistant*, and *The Fixer*.

THE NATURAL

Malamud's first novel, *The Natural*, centers on baseball and a protagonist (Roy Hobbs) who yearns to be the best only to discover that ambition has cost him his humanity. The fablelike tale, filled as it is with elements of Arthurian legend and Jungian archetypes, is not as far from Malamud's portraits of the immigrant Jewish world as one might imagine. Hobbs is akin to the antiheroes and bumbling schlemiels who populate the bulk of Malamud's fiction. As do most of Malamud's protagonists, Hobbs struggles to make his life better in a world that has stacked the cards against him, regardless of how much the novel's mythic machinery suggests heroism and eventual triumph. *The Natural* continues to enjoy a deserved reputation as one of the finest American novels about baseball (the 1984 film version, starring Robert Redford as Roy Hobbs, served to enhance that estimate), and had Malamud continued to write such overtly American books, he would have been assured a successful career.

SHORT STORIES

Over his long career at the writing desk, Malamud produced four collections of short stories (*The Magic Barrel*; *Idiot's First*, 1963; *Pictures of Fidelman: An Exhibition*, 1969; and *Rembrandt's Hat*, 1973), along with an omnibus collection, *The Stories of Bernard Malamud* (1983); *Talking Horse: Bernard Malamud on Life and Work* (1996), a collection of interviews, talks, and notebook entries (many of them about his short fiction); and

The People, and Uncollected Stories (1989), a posthumous volume that contains his unfinished novel and a handful of uncollected stories.

The stories collected in *The Magic Barrel* were largely responsible for Malamud's growing reputation as a Jewish-American writer, a classification that he resisted all his life. "I have interests beyond that," Malamud insisted, stressing that he felt he wrote "for all men." Before one can write about—and for—"all men," however, one must learn how to write about a particular person anchored in a particular time, place, and situation. Malamud himself insisted as much in the foreword to his justly famous *The Stories of Bernard Malamud*: "Writing the short story is a good way to begin writing seriously." In Malamud's case, the beginning was a 1943 short story titled "The Grocery Store," which eventually grew into the novel we know as *The Assistant*. As a youngster Malamud had only to look beyond the end of his nose to see the near poverty and blasted dreams that came with the territory of his parents' grocery store. Teaching night school at Brooklyn's Erasmus High, Malamud wrote "The Grocery Store" as a way of giving shape and meaning to the place that defined, and delimited, his parents. Art was for Malamud what it was for Robert Frost—a "momentary stay against confusion."

When one gets beyond the conjunction of the empty shelves of "The Grocery Store" and its testy, quarrelsome characters, what makes one want to turn the pages is the high probability that Sam, the story's protagonist-grocer, has *genumen di gez*—committed suicide by sticking his head in an oven, as many other disappointed Jewish immigrants in fact did. Although Sam insists that he "made a mistake" and that he could not smell the escaping gas because of his cold, Ida—his wife—is not entirely convinced. This nagging doubt causes Ida radically to change her quarrelsome behavior and thus to push the tale toward something akin to a happy ending. As Malamud's final paragraph puts it, the next morning

> Ida reached over for the clock and shut off the alarm. It was nearly five. At six o'clock she would get up, dress, and go downstairs. She would pull in the milk box and the bread. Then she would sweep the store, and then the snow from the sidewalk. Let Sam sleep. Later, if he felt better, he could come downstairs.... The sleep would do him good.

In a Malamud short story or novel, the tale of immigrant Jewish poverty looks, sounds, and feels like nobody else's, largely because the rhythms of immigrant speech are so constricted that sorrow and joy, comic wonder and tragic recognition, fight for space in the same sparse paragraph. The story, "Take Pity," offers an example: "He was talking to me how bitter was his life, and he touched me on the sleeve to say something else, but the next minute his face got small and he fell down dead, the wife screaming, the little girls crying that it made in my heart pain. I am myself a sick man and when I saw him lying on the floor, I said to myself, 'Rosen, say goodbye, this guy is finished.' So I said it."

Partly moral fables, partly parables, Malamud's early stories pushed plot action into new configurations, ones that had been neither the concern nor the province of previous Jewish-American fiction. One thinks, for example, of Pinye Salzman in "The Magic Barrel," chanting the words of the Kaddish (the prayer for the dead) as his wayward daughter awaits the desperate, love-smitten rabbi rushing toward her; of the characters in "The Mourners," all sitting shivah (the seven-day period of Jewish mourning) for the others, and themselves; or of the white feather wafting gently downward from the heavens in "The Jewbird."

Quick brushstrokes set the typical Malamud story into motion, evoking a familiar landscape at the same time that they move us past it. His sense of motion is always in operation, as in the stories where Pinye Salzman flits about his business as a matchmaker with mercurial speed and a general disregard for the laws of physics.

In much of Malamud's early fiction, secret sharers slip out of their skins and become their antagonists. One thinks of Manishevitz and the Angel Levine ("The Angel Levine"), of Lieb the baker and Kobotsky ("The Loan"), and of George Stoyonovich and Mr. Cattanzara ("A Summer's Reading"). In Malamud's best stories the gritty surfaces of realistic detail give way to astonishing imaginative bursts, almost as if the essential features of the folktale had been filtered through quite another sensibility. The result makes for a daring experimentation that has not yet received its full due, for what is most thoroughly modern about Malamud's best writing—the conflation of landscape and psychological condition, the wrenching of expectation and outcome, the alternating currents of social realism and imaginative fancy—can be found less in the Yiddishized rhythms of his characters than in how he foregrounds the world in which they speak.

THE ASSISTANT

The Assistant is at once an extended example of cityscape as psychological condition (the back room of Bober's cramped and failing grocery store is an appropriate setting for sighs that seem to have had their genesis in the destruction of the Temple) and a moral fable about saintly transference. As in the social realism that Malamud renders in shorthand, Bober's patient suffering merely is, and it is the task of Frankie Alpine, his assistant, to learn what such suffering means and how it might overturned.

Bober suffers the slings and arrows of bad timing. In the prison of his grocery store there are no jailers, only prisoners. What Rosen, the protagonist of "Take Pity," says of his recently departed friend, Axel Kalish could—with a snip here, a tuck there—be said equally of Bober:

> He worked like a blind horse when he got to America, and saved maybe two-three thousand dollars that he bought with the money this pisher grocery in a dead neighborhood where he didn't have a chance. He called my company up for credit and they sent me I should see. . . . So right away I told him, without tricks, "Kiddo, this is a mistake. This place is a grave. Here they will bury you if you don't get out quick."

Only Frankie Alpine, ex-criminal and Jewish sufferer-in-training, keeps faith with Bober's complicated arithmetic of what it means to be fully human: "If you live, you suffer. Some people suffer more, but not because they want. But I think if a Jew don't suffer for the Law, he will suffer for nothing." But Frankie's stylized graduation from assistant to master is fraught with peril and riddled with ambivalence. His fate as Bober's psychological replacement reminds us of the fears Feld projects for his daughter in "The First Seven Years":

> Then he realized that what he had called ugly was not Sobel but Miriam's life if she married him. He felt for his daughter a strange and gripping sorrow, as if she were already Sobel's bride, the wife, after all, of a shoemaker, and had in her life no more than her mother had. And all his dreams for her—why he had slaved and destroyed his heart with anxiety and labor—all these dreams of a better life were dead.

In a similar, scary fashion, Frankie will replace Bober by becoming him: he will now slice a daily roll for the spiteful, vaguely anti-Semitic customer; he will share a morning cup of tea with Breitbart, the ironically named light bulb peddler, whose leitmotif is a long, soulful sigh; and most of all, he will surely marry Helen in a future Malamud leaves open to the reader's conjecture.

A NEW LIFE

A New Life may be a novel set in academia, but it is longer on artistic vision than most of the cardboard fictions set in Eyesore U. and known as academic novels. And while it is true that *A New Life* is often mentioned in the same breath as other classic novels of academic folly such as Mary McCarthy's *Groves of Academe* (1952) or Randall Jarrell's *Pictures from an Institution* (1954), it is, finally, about confronting the same inner torments that afflicted his earlier protagonists.

On its most immediate level, *A New Life* is about a young, idealistic English instructor from New York City, Seymour Levin, who finds himself out West and surrounded by philistines of the first water. One succeeds in Cascadia College's english department by not making waves and by doing one's best to introduce engineering students to the niceties of subject-verb agreement. As Professor Fairchild, department chairman and embodiment of its ethos, puts it: "Our main function, as I always tells everyone we employ here, is to satisfy the needs of the professional schools on the campus with respect to written communication."

The purpose of the English faculty is to be the consummate service department. In such a world, students get pretty much what they want—which is what they think they need—and the faculty is relieved of the pressures that come with the territory of english departments on the make: not only to publish but also to read and think about the inextricable relationship between a literate public and a healthy democracy. Rather than a collection of individuals (who can be problematic or worse), the department that chairman Fairchild imagines in his mind's eye is low speed, placid, and most of all, conforming: "There are two kinds of people I deplore in the teaching profession. One is the misfit who sneaks in to escape his inadequacy elsewhere and who ought to be booted out—and isn't very often; and the other is the aggressive pest whose one purpose is to upset other people's applecarts, and the more apples the better."

Not surprisingly, Levin turns out to be the applecart basher Fairchild talked about, because Malamud is interested in what happens to an essentially good man under extraordinary pressure. However, unlike Ernest Hemingway, who made exercises in grace under pressure his trademark, Malamud has little belief in the theatrics of defying death—whether the challenge comes from the battlefield, the bull ring, or the charge of an African rhino. Even more important, Malamud was not afraid (as Hemingway sometimes was) to add a sense of humor to the scenario.

THE FIXER

In *The Assistant*, visions of the future are inexorably linked to the past, to ghosts of the heart that cling to us stubbornly and without our full understanding. By contrast, Malamud grounded *The Fixer* in the nearly forgotten story of Mendel Beiliss and the spectacular blood libel trial of 1913 that swirled around him in the Russia of peasant superstition and czarist persecution. This, in short, was Jewish history of a decidedly different order than Morris Bober's makeshift Jewish theology. At the same time, however, Malamud so orchestrated the events of his retelling that they were simultaneously reinscribed on the sociopolitical landscape of his own time with the force of moral fable.

Yakov Bok, the novel's protagonist, is also the quintessential flop. Cuckolded and then deserted by his wife, he seems to have come from a long line of those who were the innocent victims of absurd accident: "His own father had been killed in an incident not more than a year after Yakov's birth—something less than a pogrom and less than useless: two drunken soldiers shot the first three Jews in their path, his father had been the second." Yet neither his father's death nor his own impoverished condition is enough to turn Yakov into a conventional handwringer. Rather, he brings to the poverty of the *shtetl* (an eastern European Jewish village) the same conflation of *kvetch* (complaint) and sigh that Morris Bober unpacked in his grocery store. About Morris we learn that "the world suffers. He felt every *schmerz*" (pain); about Yakov that he drank his tea unsweetened. ("It tasted bitter and he blamed existence.")

Opportunity turns out to be as dead in the *shtetl* as it proved to be in Morris Bober's mom-and-pop grocery store. But that said, Yakov, unlike Morris, tries to change his luck by setting off to Kiev. Perhaps things will go better there. Unfortunately (but hardly surprisingly) Yakov finds himself beleaguered by the accidents that befall him along the way—none of which (ironically enough) he is able to fix. Moreover, it is his penchant for doing good deeds that contributes to his misfortune and that ultimately seals his kinship with similar bunglers in Malamud's canon.

Yakov makes much of his insistence that he is not a political person, but the novel insists otherwise—first, by embroiling him in accusations of ritual murder and then forcing him to wait in jail for his trial. For those critics who have complained that Malamud was longer on vaguely spiritual metaphors than on dramatically convincing detail (for example, metaphorical Jews, metaphorical tenements, metaphorical suffering), the long, agonizing prison scenes in *The Fixer* must surely have given them pause, for his shackles were very real indeed.

Yakov also earns his rights as an Everyman. Caught in a web of bureaucratic absurdity, he suggests that "somebody has made a serious mistake," only to find that the case against him is growing stronger every day.

Yakov's learning comes slowly, interspersed by scenes in which momentary bits of self-deprecation are offset by his systematic torture. One by one former friends betray him—victims of bribery for the most part—until Yakov is left totally alone. Even his one Russian ally, Bibikov (a Russian version of Eugene Debs who spouts lines such as "if the law doesn't protect you, it will not, in the end, protect me"), either commits suicide or, more likely, is murdered. Yakov, by contrast, manages to survive. He has no compunctions about wearing a prayer shawl under his suit if it will keep him warm.

The novel ends with Yakov's realization that he "was the accidental choice for the sacrifice. He would be tried because the accusation had been made, there did not have to be any other reason. Being born a Jew meant being vulnerable to history, including its worst errors."

THE TENANTS

In *The Tenants* (1971), Malamud places Harry Lesser, his writerly Jew, in an apartment building that, like Lesser himself, has seen better days. Lesser's very name is a directional arrow of his writerly curve, one that threatens to go from lesser to least. His third book, now some ten years in the unmaking, may have started its life in the temple of Lesser's art, but now it quite literally stands for Lesser's life. Both are on the line and, as it were, in doubt.

For Levenspiel, the building's owner and the novel's one-man Greek chorus, the rickety steps and faulty plumbing, the erratic furnace and broken windows, represent an opportunity—that is, if only the fiercely stubborn Lesser would accept his generous offers to relocate and make it possible for a new, more profitable apartment building to rise, phoenixlike, from the ashes of the old. After all, Lesser is not the only man lugging his bundle of griefs through the world. He, Levenspiel, has *tsoris* (trouble) too: a crazy mother, a sick wife, and a knocked-up teenaged daughter. Not surprisingly, Lesser will not budge because the building, wretched though it may be, has become his triggering town, his sorrow-riddled doppelganger. As he puts it: "Home is where my book is."

Enter Willie Spearmint, an angry young black writer who stakes out a squatter's spot in Lesser's building. The Morris dance that results, as each writer becomes simultaneously the other—and the Other—is what Malamud's dark fable of deteriorating black-Jewish relations means to explore. Each needs the other because only with a merging

of Lesser's patient craft and Spearmint's passion can their art be an art that truly matters.

Malamud wrote about Jews and blacks earlier in his career (in, for example, "The Angel Levine" and "The Jewbird"), but now the ugly spectre of black anti-Semitism complicates the arithmetic. At the end of the novel Spearmint and Lesser are poised to kill each other, as the Yiddish word *rachmones* (compassion) repeats itself over and over on the final page.

DUBIN'S LIVES

The writers who struggle in *The Tenants* cannot match temperament and talent. By contrast, the William Dubin of *Dubin's Lives* is a disciplined, earnestly dogged biographer and a very productive one in the bargain. As the novel opens, he has a handful of successful biographies behind him and one—on D. H. Lawrence—in the works. Jogging, he meditates (or perhaps vice versa) about what it means to be William Dubin, "formerly of Newark, New Jersey," a fifty-six-year-old man who gives pattern and significance to dead men's lives. Rather than "lives of the saints," Dubin dryly chronicles the lives of passionate creatures such as Henry David Thoreau and Mark Twain.

Sensibility rather than suffering makes Dubin's character memorable. As Malamud's novel would have it, biographers become the lives they write about. Dubin is the condition writ large and comic. But that said, it should be added that some things about *Dubin's Lives* look very familiar indeed: a protracted winter follows Dubin's infatuation with the twenty-two-year-old Fanny Bick in much the same way that Shakespearean nights follow Shakespearean days. In such a world the heart swoons and the snowflakes fly; Dubin's book, "The Passion of D. H. Lawrence: A Life," is symmetrically balanced with Dubin's personal life in ways that smack of formalism's last hurrah, and yet again moral impulses lead, ironically, to botched results. By the usual measures, of course, Dubin, the biographer, has made it. He is by now a permanent, successful fixture of life in upstate New York's Center Campobello, a biographer rather than, say, an impoverished grocer or itinerant matchmaker. Which is to say, Dubin seems to be Malamud's effort to imagine a conflicted egghead of the sort who would be more at home in a Bellow novel. Indeed, Dubin even shares a penchant for writing cautionary notes to himself in ways that cannot help but remind us of Moses Herzog:

> He warned himself then as he often did, although it came to not much, that a good writer adventures beyond the uses of language, or what's there to put into words? Yet the truth

is some do not: of them Dubin is one. As though to make up for his limitations, from his pants pocket he dug out one of his impulsive notes to himself: "Everybody's life is mine unlived. One writes lives he can't live. To live forever is a human hunger."

Nonetheless, shadows of the Great Depression still fall across his orderly, reasonably comfortable existence. Dubin, in short, remains a Malamud character under the skin, however academic and scholarly his situation might be. It is hard for such men to feel entirely comfortable in the world. Malamud, of course, used to think of spiritual torment as a peculiarly Jewish condition. In *Dubin's Lives*, however, restlessness seems more a function of male menopause or middle-aged crisis or whatever fashionable term for low-level angst one prefers. Here, for example, is the cerebral Dubin alternately musing and panting about the nubile Fanny:

> It annoyed him a bit that he had felt her sexuality so keenly. It rose from her bare feet. She thus projects herself?—the feminine body, the beautifully formed hefty hips, full bosom, nipples visible—can one see less with two eyes? Or simply his personal view of her?—male chauvinism: reacting reductively? What also ran through his mind was whether he had responded to her as usual self, or as one presently steeped in Lawrence's sexual theories, odd as they were. He had thought much on the subject as he read the man's work.

Fortunately, *Dubin's Lives* is more complex, more interesting, and certainly more indebted to the comic spirit than most contemporary versions of the December-May syndrome tend to be. Part of the credit goes to Dubin's wife, Kitty. Her crime, as it were, is that after twenty-five years of marriage, raw sexuality no longer steams upwards from her bare toes. This fact about growing old will matter less to mature readers than it obviously does to the comically rendered Dubin. Moreover, those willing to pull Dubin up short, to hector him about the dangers of becoming an ersatz Lawrence, are hardly in short supply. Add Malamud's own flair for undercutting irony and the result takes the edge off Dubin's extensive, and allusion-filled, rationalizations. Malamud is far better on comic failure than he is on amorous success. Dubin's assignation with Fanny in romantic Venice is filled with comic interruptions and assorted pratfalls. Indeed, not since *A New Life*, where Seymour Levin gets lost in nature on the way to an assignation with one of his students, has Malamud been so funny about a would-be lover's parched forehead and cloying tongue. But contemporary novels demand more than a Dubin who trips over his feet while

chasing Fanny Bick. He must, eventually, slip her between the sheets or, in this case, tangle her among the Lawrentian flowers. Dubin may be Lawrence's biographer, but as these awkward scenes make clear, he is no Lawrence. Moreover, Malamud's efforts at this brand of sexuality were ill-considered and finally embarrassing. He was better, much better, at rendering passions of the PG sort.

GOD'S GRACE

God's Grace (1982), the last novel published during Malamud's lifetime, is at once a continuation of and a departure from his characteristic fiction. Because the novel often aspires to the condition of pure fable, *God's Grace* has a familiar look about it, but because the novel focuses on apocalyptic, end-of-history ruminations, it seems quite unlike Malamud's previous work.

The novel is a wild, often confusing description of the Second Great Flood and thus a way for Malamud to see the Holocaust through the lens of a new Holocaust. Calvin Cohn, a paleoanthropologist and son of a rabbi-cantor, was doing undersea research when the Djaniks and the Druzhkies (Yanks and Russians) launched an atomic Holocaust that destroyed every human being with the exception of himself. The novel traces Cohn's adventures and ruminations as he teams up with a chimpanzee named Buz and tries to make his way among other chimpanzees and albino apes. The stranded man in strange circumstances is a familiar enough literary ploy, but it seems far too mechanical, far too strained here. Moreover, Malamud adds a steady barrage of allusions from the Bible and Western literature: Adam and Eve, Abraham and Isaac, Parsifal and Prospero, and predictably enough, Robinson Crusoe.

The result is an ambitious, overly complex and confusing novel that is difficult to pin down and often hard to enjoy. Writing in the pages of the *Christian Science Monitor*, Victor Howes called *God's Grace* "somewhat east of science fi, somewhat west of allegory." The novel simply did not work on the level of engaging fiction. Unlike the case with most of Malamud protagonists, one did not especially care what happened, or did not happen, to Calvin Cohn. The novel had more bows to the Hebrew Bible and to the jeremiad of Puritan America than it did a convincing plot and engaging character ruminations. Nonetheless, *God's Grace* is surely Malamud's darkest novel and, in spots, one of his funniest.

THE PEOPLE

The People, and Uncollected Stories is a posthumous gathering that includes sixteen chapters of an uncompleted novel and fourteen previously uncollected short stories, five published now for the first time. The uncompleted novel *The People*—represents an effort to, in Malamud's words, "prime the pump" by seeking new material. As he put it, writing in the 1970s: "I may have done as much as I can with the sort of short story I have been writing so long—the somewhat mythological, biblically oriented tales.... What I see as possible is another variation of the comic-mythological—possibly working out the Chief Joseph of the Nez Percé idea—in other words, the Jewish Indian." The notion, long a favorite of the controversial literary critic Leslie Fiedler and the Mel Brooks of the parodic Western film *Blazing Saddles* (1974), seems merely insisted upon in the sketchy chapters we have. However, given what we know about Malamud's meticulous craftsmanship (he put every piece of his published writing through a long, agonizing series of drafts), there is every reason to believe that *The People* would have become a credible novel had Malamud lived long enough to complete it.

At the beginning of his career, the late Irving Howe, reviewing *The Magic Barrel* on the front page of *The New York Times Book Review*, not only proclaimed Malamud as "one of the very few American writers about whom it makes sense to say that his work has a distinctly 'Jewish' tone," but also argued that Malamud's work takes full possession of a distinctly Yiddish imagination: "Malamud can grind a character to the earth, but there is always a hard ironic pity, a wry affection better than wet gestures of love, which makes him seem a grandson of the Yiddish writers." Malamud's stature in American letters is secure for many reasons, but among them must surely be the way he added a dash of Yiddish flavoring to the rich, ever-changing stewpot of American fiction.

SELECTED WORKS

The Natural (1952)
The Assistant (1957)
The Magic Barrel (1958)
A New Life (1961)
Idiot's First (1963)
The Fixer (1966)
Pictures of Fidelman: An Exhibition (1969)
The Tenants (1971)
Rembrandt's Hat (1973)
Dubin's Lives (1979)
God's Grace (1982)
The Stories of Bernard Malamud (1983)
The People, and Uncollected Stories (1989)
Talking Horse: Bernard Malamud on Life and Work (1996)

FURTHER READING

Astro, Richard, and Jackson T. Benson, eds. *The Fiction of Bernard Malamud*. Corvalis, Ore., 1977. A solid collection of essays covering Malamud's fiction up to 1977.

Bloom, Harold. *Bernard Malamud*. New York, 1986. A collection of critical essays chosen by literary criticism's most eccentric genius.

Field, Leslie A., and Joyce W. Field, eds. *Bernard Malamud and the Critics*. New York, 1970. An anthology of critical essays that suggests the various ways that critics approach Malamud's work.

Field, Leslie A., and Joyce W. Field, eds. *Bernard Malamud: A Collection of Critical Essays*. Englewood Cliffs, N.J., 1975. An updated anthology pulling together the best critical thinking of its time.

Howe, Irving. "The Stories of Bernard Malamud." *Celebrations and Attacks*. New York, 1979. An early, important review by one of America's most influential critics.

Richman, Sidney. *Bernard Malamud*. New York, 1966. A pioneering work that retains its value.

Roth, Philip. *"Imagining Jews": Reading Myself and Others*. New York, 1975. May reveal more about Roth than it does about Malamud, but the essay is still an indispensable piece of criticism.

DAVID MAMET

by J. Chris Westgate

Three decades after David Mamet began writing for the stage, he is readily acknowledged to be among America's leading playwrights. His more than two dozen plays have enjoyed stage success and critical acclaim surpassing the work of most of his contemporaries. His awards, too numerous to list in their entirety, include the Obie Award, the Joseph Jefferson Award, the New York Drama Critics Circle Award, and the Pulitzer Prize. His highly provocative and continually evolving body of work has prompted a number of scholarly studies in the 1990s.

Yet Mamet remains decidedly circumspect about his considerable success. He is anything but comfortable with the resultant celebrity but welcomes the opportunity it affords him to realize his theatrical and cinematic projects. He usually downplays or deflects interviewers' presumptions that he speaks as an authority on American theater, but he is consistently outspoken about the stage. He cultivates a blue-collar persona more at home playing poker or frequenting pool halls than writing or directing plays, but he is perhaps most fulfilled, both intellectually and emotionally, by the theater. This penchant for equivocation (for which Mamet is infamous) is, in part, the means of securing the privacy that he highly values. But it equally reveals just how much his playful intellect delights in obfuscation. After all, he continually peoples his plays with equivocators. Nevertheless, Mamet does not equivocate when it comes to the theater. His conviction that the theater is much more than just a fashionable pastime, that it embodies and reaffirms defining cultural myths, that it has the potential to redeem a debauched and disillusioned society, is unwavering. And his love for the theater, for the wonder it evokes and the truth it reveals, is uncompromising.

David Mamet. (© *AFP/Corbis*)

THE MAKING OF A PLAYWRIGHT

Mamet's love of the theater almost certainly began as a love for words. He was born David Alan Mamet on 30 November 1947 and spent most of his childhood in Flossmoor, an Illinois suburb of Chicago. His mother, Lenore Silver Mamet, who was a schoolteacher, may have contributed to his fascination with language; but it was his father, Bernard Mamet, a labor lawyer and amateur semanticist, who truly cultivated Mamet's infatuation with words. While at the dinner table, his father would often encourage David and his sister Lyn to find the precise words to express themselves—almost certainly invaluable training for America's greatest language playwright. Writing of his childhood enthusiasm for words, Mamet underscores their incantatory power, their magical capacity to transform the everyday into the extraordinary, the banal into the transcendent. It was undoubtedly the magic of words that made Mamet initially gravitate toward the stage while attending Rich Central High. But it was not until he transferred to Francis Parker High in 1963, after going to live with his father (his parents divorced in 1958), that Mamet would become actively involved in the theater.

Much of Mamet's theatrical education derived from working at two Chicago theaters from 1963 to 1965, the first of which was Hull House. Working backstage for productions of Murray Schisgal's *The Typists* (1960) and *The Tiger* (1963) and acting in the chorus of Kurt Weill and Bertolt Brecht's *The Threepenny Opera* (1928), Mamet amassed invaluable practical experience under the tutelage of Bob Sichinger. Later, Mamet worked at Second City, Chicago's famed improvisational theater. Although his duties were generally limited to doing errands and busing tables, he maintains that his experience at Second

City exerts a profound influence upon his work. In 1965 Mamet enrolled at Goddard College in Vermont to study English literature, but he found the university such a poor substitute for the theater that he has written numerous essays urging writers, directors, and actors to hone their talents on the stage rather than in the classroom. While at Goddard, Mamet participated in the university's Junior Year Abroad program. That year, undoubtedly his most rewarding while in college, Mamet studied acting at the Neighborhood Playhouse in New York City under Sanford Meisner, a founding member of the Group Theatre in the 1930s. This experience was crucial to Mamet's growth as a playwright, as it was his first significant exposure to the work of Russian director Konstantinov Stanislavsky, whose writings have greatly influenced Mamet's dramaturgy. In 1969 Mamet wrote for his B.A. thesis an original Second City–style revue called *Camel*.

That first offering for the stage did far more than just earn Mamet his degree; it inaugurated the career of one of the most prolific and provocative playwrights in America. His plays range from absurdist parables like *Edmond* (1982) to children's plays such as *The Poet and the Rent* (1974) and *The Revenge of the Space Pandas* (1977) to the social satires like *American Buffalo* (1975) and *Glengarry Glen Ross* (1983) for which he is best known. This highly eclectic body of work is hardly surprising considering the many writers who have influenced Mamet, from novelists like Willa Cather, Ernest Hemingway, Sherwood Anderson, and Theodore Dreiser to nonfiction writers like economist Thorstein Veblen and psychologist D. W. Winnicott to dramatists such as Samuel Beckett, Eugene O'Neill, Arthur Miller, Bertolt Brecht, Anton Chekhov, and Harold Pinter. The last two playwrights have exerted the greatest influence upon Mamet's dramaturgy, as his plays combine Pinter's deceptively simple stories and ordinary characters with Chekhov's subtextual symbolism in a way that is distinctively Mamet's own. Consequently, Mamet's plays often depict the most commonplace incidents, such as arguments over a slice of toast in *American Buffalo* or the discussion of the mating habits of ducks in *The Duck Variations* (1972), that invariably suggest more universal themes such as betrayal, liminality, and estrangement. His plays are—often simultaneously—humorous and horrifying, simple and staggering, but always unsettling in the truth they bring to the stage.

NEGOTIATING A HARSH LAND

In *Writing in Restaurants* (1986) Mamet describes contemporary society as being inexorably, and almost mercifully,

in decline. Whether this apocalyptic theory accurately characterizes America or not, it certainly epitomizes the world that Mamet's characters inhabit. It is a world whose social myths have been corrupted beyond recognition or have collapsed altogether; a world where cultural artifacts have been reduced to commodities and where relationships, be they personal or professional, are nothing more than exploitable resources. Interestingly, Mamet's characters—who are, regardless of profession, all conmen, actors, and salesmen—are highly adapted to this world but continually at odds with it. They invariably express a profound sense of alienation and are constantly in search of what their world can never offer: a sense of belonging. Taken collectively, these characters are literary descendents of Yank from Eugene O'Neill's *The Hairy Ape* (1921); they are outcasts who not only do not belong but are tragically aware of their not belonging. They are beset by an emptiness they cannot name but equally cannot escape, an emptiness so overpowering that they do whatever they can, with little regard for moral or legal restraints, to fill it. They indulge their carnal desires in *Sexual Perversity in Chicago* (1974), *The Woods* (1977), and *Edmond*; they pursue, at any cost, business success in *American Buffalo*, *Speed-the-Plow* (1988), and *Glengarry Glen Ross*; or they continually re-create themselves through their own fictions in *Reunion* (1976), *Oleanna* (1992), and *A Life in the Theater* (1977). And Mamet's plays are dominated by the almost palpable sense that if his characters do not keep seducing, keep selling, or keep dissembling to themselves and to others, they will be overwhelmed by the emptiness.

Understanding Mamet's characters, though, is best accomplished through examining the words they exchange, as Mamet believes that language not only reveals character but also determines behavior. His characters are always talking, but they continually talk *at* each other, *over* each other, but almost never *to* each other—as is best exemplified by John and Carol from *Oleanna*, two characters who continually speak at right angles to each other. Words are rarely used to communicate the speaker's desires in Mamet's world; they are, instead, deployed to exploit the listener's desires. When Ricky Roma endeavors to sell James Lingk real estate in *Glengarry Glen Ross*, Roma discusses anything but property values. He speaks of gratifying hungers for food, sex, and security—what Abraham Maslow identified as the most fundamental of human needs—in an unbroken monologue that tacitly promises satisfaction of these desires. That Roma would draw upon something like Maslow's hierarchy, even if only intuitively, is hardly surprising. Roma is the quintessential Mametic antihero: part psychologist, part preacher, and part seducer. He is selling more than just real estate; he is selling understanding and approval. One of the most perilous things that anyone can do in Mamet's dramatic world, consequently, is listen. Like Roma's sales pitch, Mamet's dialogue is carefully crafted and highly poetic—not to exploit his audience but rather to reveal the existential condition of his dissemblers. The constant repetition of lines so common in Mamet's plays suggest the appalling reality that no one, not even God, is listening, that his characters are terribly alone. The frequent unanswered questions do not just reveal the characters' suspicious natures but also suggest that the universe those characters inhabit is both indifferent and indecipherable. The elliptical speech of his characters reflects their inchoate identities as they struggle to articulate themselves. Words, in effect, reify the characters' estrangement. Nevertheless, they keep talking, keep cajoling, and keep dissembling, perhaps because words are all they have.

THE EARLY PLAYS

In general, Mamet's body of work frustrates the most Herculean attempts at taxonomy, as he frequently reinterprets earlier themes or revisits earlier techniques in his later plays. Nevertheless, his first three plays, *Lakeboat* (1970), *The Duck Variations*, and *Sexual Perversity in Chicago* suggest that Mamet is working through his dramatic inheritance. All three plays exhibit similarities—such as the eschewal of Aristotelian plot for an episodic structure and the emphasis of narration over action—that evidence the influence of both Brecht's "epic" theater and drama critic Martin Esslin's *Theater of the Absurd* (1961), which includes playwrights such as Beckett and Pinter. Mamet's early plays appear to be little more than a series of disjunctive and overlapping conversations about incidents the audience rarely sees. In *Sexual Perversity in Chicago*, which was originally produced by the Organic Theatre Company, nearly all of the romance between Dan and Deb, which is the only real "action" within the play, takes place offstage, between the staccato scenes. The play's fragmentary structure, as many scholars have noted, highlights the characters' fragmented lives as they drift from one meaningless encounter to another, combating an almost palpable loneliness. Just as significantly, though, the episodic form suggests the helplessness of the characters to fulfill their needs or change their lives—as if those lives were entirely determined between the scenes. Mamet is clearly

fascinated with how dramatic structure influences the play's themes, as he returns to the episodic form in later plays like *A Life in the Theater* and *Edmond*. But even when Mamet writes more traditional plays of two or three acts, he routinely leaves much of the "action" between the scenes, so much so that it becomes a defining feature and a frequent criticism of his plays.

But in his early plays Mamet does more than pay homage to his dramatic forefathers by experimenting with theatrical conventions. In fact, *Sexual Perversity in Chicago*, which won Mamet his first Obie, is most noteworthy for the character type that it introduces. In Bernie Litko, Mamet creates more than just an obstacle to the romance between Dan and Deb; he establishes the blueprint for the Mametic antihero. The defining condition of this antihero is one of contradiction. He is highly charismatic but disdainful of others; he is gifted with language but rarely able to communicate; he is sensitive to the psychological and emotional needs of others but only so far as he can exploit them; and he is generally successful with women but almost invariably misogynist. This last characteristic is so prevalent throughout Mamet's plays that the playwright has often been implicated in the sins of his characters. In other words, many critics have accused Mamet, whose plays not only are dominated by men but also frequently portray women as victims, as being misogynist. Others argue that his characters' misogyny is just another theme that Mamet's plays explore and implicitly condemn, as does *Sexual Perversity in Chicago*. Even as Bernie's misogyny slowly poisons the romance between Dan and Deb, the play does anything but celebrate this accomplishment. In fact, the antihero's "triumph" over others—be it misogynist or capitalist—is usually at the expense of his own humanity, as it is with Bernie, who is, in effect, the precursor to such characters as Teach in *American Buffalo*, Charlie Fox in *Speed-the-Plow*, and Roma in *Glengarry Glen Ross*.

Although *Sexual Perversity in Chicago* garnered Mamet his earliest acclaim, it was *American Buffalo* that won him national renown. The play was originally produced in Chicago by the Goodman Theatre Stage Two in 1975; its Broadway production opened in 1977 at the Ethel Barrymore Theatre. While the play received mixed reviews during its initial run, largely because of its dearth of "action" and its enthusiasm for profanity, it also won numerous awards, including an Obie for 1976 and the New York Drama Critics Circle Award in 1977. What distinguishes this play among Mamet's early work is not just that it is his first traditionally structured, two-act play but also that it is the first of the social satires for which he has become best known. American capitalism is reduced to petty criminality within a play that dramatizes the absurd and appalling scheming of Don Dubrow, Bobby, and Teach—three would-be robber barons—who all endeavor to steal a buffalo-head nickel from a coin collector. It is not the potential profits the heist might yield that really motivate the characters, though. What fuels their willingness to deceive, betray, and exploit both the collector and each other is that in the world of free enterprise, at least the way it manifests itself within the play, social status is predicated upon business savvy. Like predatory animals within a pack structure, each character must constantly defend his status within the hierarchy by outsmarting or outmaneuvering the others. Weakness only invites usurpation. For Don, it hardly matters that he made a substantial profit from a coin that he previously thought worthless. What matters is the possibility that the collector got the better of him in a business deal. The heist, then, is really about reaffirming (for Don and Teach) or establishing (for Bobby) social dominance within this highly predatory society. In effect, the play satirizes not just the buying and selling of commodities but also the belief system endorsed by capitalism.

But Mamet does not write thesis plays; *American Buffalo* is much more than just a satire. When Mamet describes the play, in fact, he characterizes it as a tragedy. If it is a tragedy, then Don's tragic error is the fundamental mistake within Mamet's dramatic world: listening. From the opening scene it is clear that, despite the ethic of betrayal that pervades the play, Don enjoys a paternal relationship with Bobby, the young drug addict who works as his gofer. Don watches out for his protégé, both chastising him for his failures and involving him, despite the junkie's incompetence, in his business endeavors—including the proposed heist. But such sentimentality is a liability in the world of business, a world that requires the betrayal of others to get ahead, a world where the strong devour the weak. Unlike Don, Teach entertains no illusions about this world; in fact, he celebrates its ruthlessness. When he learns of the heist, he displaces Bobby by characterizing the burglary as a business transaction: it would only be good business to replace the inept junkie with the experienced thief. Don yields to Teach's argument, despite his genuine feelings for Bobby, and this is the first step of Teach's undermining all that Don believes so that Teach can make himself indispensable. Don becomes so suspicious of everyone that when Bobby arrives with the news of Fletcher's hospitalization, Don allows Teach to assault

Bobby when the junkie is evasive about the details of Fletcher's mugging. Only when Ruthie calls, confirming Bobby's story, does Don realize his mistake. But his efforts to make amends by promising to take Bobby to the hospital are futile. The damage, both to Bobby, who is bleeding from a head wound, and to Don's integrity, which is reduced to rubble like the wreckage of his shop, cannot be undone.

A STRING OF SUCCESS

The series of well-received plays that followed *American Buffalo* made 1977, the year that Mamet married the actress Lindsey Crouse, Mamet's most successful year on the stage. The St. Nicholas Theatre in Chicago premiered *The Water Engine* on May 11; on October 14 *Reunion* was presented in a double bill with *Dark Pony* at the Yale Repertory Theater; and *A Life in the Theater* opened at the Theatre de Lys in New York City on October 20. But perhaps the most interesting debut that year was a simple, Pinter-like play called *The Woods*. Most of Mamet's plays take place within a major city, but *The Woods*, which opened at the St. Nicholas Theatre, is set in a lakefront cabin during a weekend getaway for Nick and Ruth. These two lovers desperately need each other but for altogether different reasons. In Nick, Ruth sees someone to fulfill her adolescent fantasies, her own devoted lover like the one that her grandmother often described. Her giving the monogrammed bracelet to Nick reenacts the lover's gift of a necklace, which Ruth wore as a bracelet until she lost it, to her grandmother. But Nick fails to appreciate the significance of the gesture because he seeks, both in Ruth and presumably all women, comfort instead of passion. The tale he relates during their exchange of stories depicts two men who, like Nick, need to be rescued. His final declaration of love for Ruth is as a maternal figure, not as a lover. Like *Sexual Perversity in Chicago*, *The Woods* explores the inability of men and women to understand each other, much less fulfill each other's desires. They tell each other stories instead of talking to each other, and most of the stories highlight the same theme—decay. It is the same problem that haunts nearly all of the relationships between men and women in Mamet's plays, such as *Oleanna* and *The Cryptogram* (1994): the inability to communicate.

The years from 1978 to 1982 are a study in contrast for Mamet's continually evolving body of work. He produced three children's plays: *The Revenge of the Space Pandas*, *The Poet and the Rent*, and *The Frog Prince* (1984). But even as Mamet was staging these lighthearted plays, he brought

Edmond, perhaps his most cynical play, to the stage. This parable about humanity's quest for belonging, which of all Mamet's plays evinces the most immediate debt to O'Neill's *The Hairy Ape*, opened at the Goodman Theater in 1982, a year after Mamet's divorce from Crouse.

The play begins with Edmond's encounter with a fortune-teller who confirms what Edmond always suspected: that he, like O'Neill's brutish protagonist, does not belong. This "reading" of Edmond offers a startlingly accurate commentary upon his existential condition. He feels estranged from others, including the wife that he finds neither spiritually or sexually fulfilling; he feels abandoned by the social and religious myths that should afford him solace. Edmond leaves his wife and embarks upon an absurdly poignant quest for sexual gratification with a series of prostitutes. His would-be liaisons are stymied by various obstacles, but it seems unlikely that these encounters, even if successful, would have provided Edmond anything but the most transitory satisfaction, since sex is a metaphor for what he truly seeks. His quest is the most straightforward and yet simultaneously the most symbolic expression of what all Mamet's characters so desperately need: acceptance, approval, and belonging. What is tragic for Edmond is that even the most basic acknowledgement would suffice. He seemingly finds the belonging that he seeks with Glenna, the waitress he seduces, but when she rejects him after their encounter, he kills her in a fit of rage. Only after being imprisoned for the murder does Edmond truly find what he seeks through a homosexual union with another prisoner. It is an absurd solution to an absurd dilemma, perhaps the best that any of Mamet's characters can do.

HOLLYWOOD AND BACK

Although *Edmond* garnered its author another Obie, Mamet suffered several theatrical disappointments in 1978 and 1979. *The Water Engine*, though initially well received at Joseph Papp's Public Theatre in New York City, lasted only sixteen performances after moving uptown to the Plymouth Theatre. A new production of *The Woods* in 1979 was less than successful. And *Lone Canoe; or, the Explorer* failed so miserably in 1979 that it was parodied by Second City. Just how much these setbacks contributed to Mamet's overcoming his aversion to writing for Hollywood remains uncertain. Nevertheless, when director Bob Rafaelson approached him about writing the screenplay for an adaptation of James M. Cain's novel, *The Postman Always Rings Twice* (1934), with Jack Nicholson and Jessica Lange, Mamet jumped at the opportunity. This decision would do more than just afford the playwright a convenient distraction from his stage setbacks; it would effectively inaugurate Mamet's second career, as he has written predominantly for the big screen during the 1980s and 1990s, including several adaptations of his own plays. Writing for Hollywood was, despite his misgivings, something Mamet honestly enjoyed. It offered a new challenge for his restless intellect, as screenwriting was significantly different from the playwriting that he had known. But Mamet did anything but struggle with this new storytelling; in fact, he promptly mastered it. His second screenplay, *The Verdict* (1982), starring Paul Newman, earned Mamet an Academy Award nomination for Best Screenplay Adaptation. Hollywood turned out to be the perfect vehicle for Mamet's prolific output, as he followed these first two screenplays with *The Untouchables* (1987), *Things Change* (1988), *We're No Angels* (1989), and *Hoffa* (1992). With *House of Games* (1987) Mamet added Hollywood director to his résumé, and he went on to write and direct more movies, including *State and Main* (2000) and *Heist* (2001).

While writing for Hollywood, Mamet was doing more than just developing his talent for storytelling. He was, if *Speed-the-Plow* is any indication, amassing material for another satire. The play, which debuted in 1988 at the Royale Theater on Broadway, undoubtedly registers Mamet's dissatisfaction with Hollywood executives, as it caricatures the venality and cynicism of the movie industry through Charlie Fox and Bobby Gould, two producers who routinely sacrifice artistic merit for blockbuster profits. But Mamet does not merely use the stage to satirize Hollywood; the film industry also affords him the opportunity to explore several of his favorite themes. The play opens with Gould and Fox stumbling onto a career-making deal that is immediately complicated by the introduction of Karen, Gould's temporary secretary. Karen believes that films are about more than filling theater seats; they are chances to change the lives of the audience. To Fox, such naïveté is something to be exploited, and he bets Gould that he, Gould, cannot seduce her. Equally cynical, Gould eagerly accepts the wager and uses an overly sentimental novel as a ploy to win the bet. But when Karen arrives at his home, her idealism seduces him. Moved by Karen's apparent understanding of his loneliness, as well as by her sexual charms, Gould agrees to do the sentimental film that he believed laughable previously. This about-face may seem out of character for a Mametic character, but it is perfectly consistent. In Karen, Gould believes he has found what all Mamet's characters are seeking: understanding and belonging. This feeling, of course, is transitory. When Gould reveals that he intends to pass on the blockbuster deal that Fox brought him, Fox argues that Karen was only exploiting him. Karen's motives are ambiguous at best. But when she admits that she never would have slept with Gould if he had not given her film the green light, Gould dumps Karen, her film, and the values associated with it and once again endorses the blockbuster. Karen's idealism, along with Karen, is expelled from the studio; it has no place in the movie industry, and tragically (as Mamet's plays suggest), little place in today's capitalist world.

THE HIGHEST OF ACCOLADES

It was while writing predominantly for Hollywood that Mamet wrote his most highly acclaimed play. In 1983 *Glengarry Glen Ross* opened at the Cottlesloe Theater in London. The U.S. premiere came at the Goodman Theatre of the Art Institute of Chicago in 1984, the same year that it won the Pulitzer Prize. The play, which is dedicated to Harold Pinter, is a scathing critique of capitalism, much like *American Buffalo* eight years before. But whereas the earlier play depicted the amusing and appalling endeavors of three criminals masquerading as businessmen, *Glengarry Glen Ross* dramatizes the dealings of four real estate agents impersonating criminals. The driving force in the lives of Mamet's salesmen is, quite simply, selling. They work, and even live, under the unrelenting pressure to "always be closing," always be making the next sale. This pressure is best epitomized by the contest at the office, instituted by Mitch and Murray, the offstage business owners who are evoked almost mythically by the office manager and salesmen alike. The salesman with the highest sales wins a new Cadillac; second place wins a set of steak knives. The contest not only supplies Mamet's characters with ample motivation for their many indiscretions but also affords Mamet an ideal metaphor for capitalism. Success at selling commodities is rewarded with more commodities; anything other than first place is ridiculed. Just as significant is the absurdity associated with free enterprise that is underscored by the contest: only those with the premium leads can close deals, but only those who can close deals get the premium leads. It is Mamet's arresting interpretation of the old adage: the rich get richer while the poor get poorer. It is no wonder that the salesmen do whatever they can, regardless of the legality or ethicality of their actions, to get ahead: Levene feebly attempts to bribe Williamson for better leads; Roma willingly exploits both client and coworker; Moss

attempts to blackmail Aaronow and eventually recruits Levene to burglarize the office. Their actions, just short of the burglary, are not only accepted within the world of business; they are practically endorsed.

The most remarkable thing about the play that most critics regard as Mamet's masterpiece, though, is not its unflinching social commentary. It is, instead, how Mamet depicts these salesmen—despite their routine betrayals, dissembling, and criminality—sympathetically. They are not merely mouthpieces for the playwright's indignation; they are finely wrought portrayals of human beings thrust into a crucible. Shelley Levene was once the best of the real estate agents, but he has been eclipsed by his younger, more ambitious coworkers. His desperation to regain his former status, despite his inadequacy as a salesman in the highly predatory world that has surpassed him, is wonderfully human. Dave Moss, who orchestrates the office robbery, is driven by his outrage at the way in which Mitch and Murray—a metaphor for the corporate mentality that rationalizes firing longtime, hardworking employees through convenient euphemisms like downsizing—treat their workers. What he wants, above all else, is some small acknowledgement of his worth. Ricky Roma's confidence and charisma undoubtedly seduce as many spectators within the audience as they do clients in the restaurant where he does business. But Roma's bravado only thinly disguises his insecurity about staying on top of the leader board. He knows, even if only subconsciously, how easily he can be toppled. But it is George Aaronow who is the play's most sympathetic character. He is, by far, the most beleaguered of the salesmen—exploited by Moss, abused by the police and by Roma. He is the least effectual of the salesmen because he has too much empathy to exploit his clients; he cannot bring himself to do what is necessary to close deals. But it is this empathy that not only makes him the most human of Mamet's characters but also may provide the greatest critique of the business world. Through Aaronow, Mamet reveals that what is demanded by the religion of capitalism, what must be sacrificed at its altars for the salesmen to succeed, is their humanity.

A PLAYWRIGHT'S LEGACY

David Mamet may have become more widely recognized as a writer and director of films instead of plays, as he has worked predominantly and generally successfully in Hollywood since the early 1990s. Or his growing popularity may stem from his publication of nondramatic writing, including poetry, novels, and essay collections. Nevertheless, it is theater—where he began as an actor, realized his greatest gift as a writer, learned his craft as a director, and distinguished himself as a zealous advocate of the stage—that Mamet has left his most enduring mark. His contributions to the stage have been so significant that he won the Outer Circle Award for services to the American theater. But his greatest contribution is undoubtedly in his plays that explore and express distinctively American themes, most significantly the frontier ethic of the nineteenth century that conceptualized the continent as nothing more than an inexhaustible supply of exploitable resources—an ethic Mamet ascribes to American business today. Just as significantly, his dialogue, as actors have often noted, captures more than just a Chicago idiom; it is an unmistakably American idiom. Mamet's contributions to the stage have propelled American theater for more than thirty years, and Mamet still has much to offer. In June 1999 he debuted his play, *Boston Marriage*, at the Hasty Pudding Theater in Cambridge, Massachusetts; it starred Rebecca Pidgeon, whom Mamet married in 1991. This play is particularly noteworthy, as it has Mamet's first all-female cast and is his first historical play—suggesting that the playwright continues to explore and expand his own dramaturgy. If American theater was inaugurated by Eugene O'Neill in the 1920s, as it undoubtedly was, then that theater was cultivated in the final decades of the century, and perhaps will continue to be well into the next, by David Mamet.

[*See also* Anderson, Sherwood; Cather, Willa; Dreiser, Theodore; Hemingway, Ernest; Miller, Arthur; O'Neill, Eugene; *and* Theater in America.]

SELECTED WORKS

PLAYS (CHRONOLOGICALLY BY FIRST PRODUCTION)

Lakeboat (1970)
The Duck Variations (1972)
The Poet and the Rent (1974)
Sexual Perversity in Chicago (1974)
American Buffalo (1977)
Reunion (1976)
Dark Pony (1977)
A Life in the Theater (1977)
The Revenge of the Space Pandas (1977)
The Water Engine (1977)
The Woods (1977)
Lone Canoe; or, the Explorer (1979)
Edmond (1982)
Glengarry Glen Ross (1983)
The Frog Prince (1984)
The Shawl (1985)

Speed-the-Plow (1988)
Oleanna (1992)
The Cryptogram (1994)

PUBLISHED WORKS

Sexual Perversity in Chicago and *The Duck Variations* (1978)
The Water Engine and *Mr. Happiness* (1978)
Reunion and *Dark Pony* (1976)
Goldberg Street: Short Plays and Monologues (1985)
The Shawl and *Prairie du Chien* (1985)
Three Children's Plays (1986)
Writing in Restaurants (1986)
Three Jewish Plays (1987)
The Woods, Lakeboat, Edmond: Three Plays (1987)
Five Television Plays (1990)
On Directing Film (1991)
The Cabin: Reminiscence and Diversions (1992)
No One Will Be Immune and Other Plays and Pieces (1994)
Plays One (1994)
Plays Two (1994)
A Whore's Profession: Notes and Essays (1994)
Make-Believe Town: Essays and Remembrances (1996)
True and False: Heresy and Common Sense for the Actor (1997)
The Old Neighborhood: Three Plays (1998)
Three Uses of the Knife: On the Nature and Purpose of Drama (1998)
The Chinaman: Poems (1999)
Jafsie and John Henry: Essays (1999)
On Acting (1999)
Short Plays and Sketches (1999)
The Spanish Prisoner and *The Winslow Boy* (1999)
Wilson: A Consideration of the Sources (2000)

FURTHER READING

Bigsby, C. W. E. *David Mamet.* Edited by Malcolm Bradbury and Christopher Bigsby. London and New York, 1985. A revealing examination of the literary and thematic influences upon Mamet's major plays.

Brewer, Gay. *David Mamet and Film: Illusion/Disillusion in a Wounded Land.* Jefferson, N.C., and London, 1993. Interesting connections between the screenplays and the plays of the eighties, but often depends too heavily on biography.

Carroll, Dennis. *David Mamet.* Edited by Bruce King and Adele King. London, 1987. A good overview of Mamet's career up to 1987, including thematically organized chapters that examine the plays.

Dean, Anne. *David Mamet: Language as Dramatic Action.* London and Toronto, 1990. A thorough examination of Mamet's mastery of language throughout his body of

OPPORTUNITY KNOCKS

Teach, the play's most predatory character, has internalized this reality. While Teach's indignation over a trivial incident with Ruthie that morning initially suggests that he, too, believes that business and friendship must be kept separate, his actions quickly belie such an inference. As soon as he overhears Bobby saying that he saw the mark leaving with a suitcase, for example, Teach immediately exploits his friendship with Don for his own self-interest. He begins by complimenting Don on the way he runs his business. When flattery gets him only so far, he makes Don feel guilty for excluding him from his scheming until Don finally tells him about the customer who, a week earlier, bought a buffalo-head nickel that, it turns out, was a collector's item. Unlike Don, Teach champions the unscrupulousness encouraged by capitalism. Success justifies any tactic for Teach, who is not unlike the Renaissance Italian Niccolò Machiavelli, who argued that a ruler (substitute "businessman") is both justified and obligated to use whatever means necessary to maintain his reign (substitute "make a profit"). Consequently, Teach is all too willing to exploit friendship, double-cross Bobby, or do whatever is necessary to insinuate himself into the burglary of the coin collector's home. He finally convinces Don to include him by playing on Don's sense of himself as a businessman: Teach is the more experienced criminal than Bobby, and therefore the better man for the job. Anything else is bad business.

However, the proposed heist is less about making profit than it is about establishing or reestablishing the characters' reputations as businessmen. For Don, the real goal of the burglary is the recovery of the buffalo nickel, since he cannot get over his suspicion that the coin collector got the better of him in the business deal, even though Don sold the nickel that he previously considered worthless for ninety dollars. That Don may have been cheated is devastating to his self-identity because he ascribes so much importance to being a savvy businessman. Stealing the coin collection and selling it to another collector will, theoretically, assuage Don's ego as much as it will fill his wallet. Similarly, the robbery affords Teach the opportunity to compensate for his own feelings of inadequacy, though his ego is bruised by a fellow conman instead of a potential mark. It is not just Fletcher's repeated beating of Teach at poker that so discourages Teach. It is equally that Don champions Fletcher as the epitome of what a businessman should be, which frustrates Teach's need for Don's approval. That

is why Teach is so determined not only to participate in the heist but also to exclude Fletcher. Even Bobby's desire to be included is motivated largely by his need to impress Don. And when Bobby is cut out of the deal, he immediately devises his own business scheme: selling Don another buffalo nickel that he bought from a coin shop with Don's money. What is intriguing here is Bobby's motivation. He may be trying to make amends for missing the mark that morning, but he may equally be trying to advance himself at Don's expense by selling the coin for a profit. In other words, Bobby may have internalized the story of Fletcher, Ruthie, and the pig iron better than Don could have ever imagined.

UNWELCOME EPIPHANIES

Fletcher, though never seen, plays a pivotal role in not just Bobby's but also Don's initiation into the cutthroat world of business. After all, Don believes that Fletcher is the embodiment of the good businessman and that Fletcher's business savvy makes him a "standup guy." But when the second act opens, Fletcher is late for the rendezvous. This is not the "action" of a good businessman; this is the sort of ineptitude that requires apologies or excuses. More significantly, when Teach presses Don to go ahead with the robbery without Fletcher and Don refuses, Teach exposes—or fabricates—Fletcher's cheating at poker. Whether or not this cheating is a product of Teach's jealousy, Teach convinces Don by reminding him that Fletcher came up with a winning hand only after distracting everyone by spilling his drink. That Fletcher may cheat at cards undermines Don's admiration for him, since he had always believed that there was honor among thieves. But Teach's disclosure also reveals just how naïve is Don's belief that one can get ahead at business but still maintain one's friendships. Everything that Don believed at the play's opening is suddenly cast into doubt, and that is why when Bobby enters with the news that Fletcher is in the hospital after being mugged, Don remains skeptical. He no longer knows whom to trust or what to believe. And when Teach assaults Bobby, Don fails to defend him and callously tells him that he brought it on himself.

Teach too has his identity shaken, but it is done by Bobby, not Fletcher. When Bobby is already at the junk shop when Teach arrives that night, Teach is immediately suspicious. His first instinct is that Bobby has somehow regained Don's favor and displaced him in the robbery, just as Teach formerly did to Bobby. Such betrayals are the natural order of business for Teach. His suspicions are seemingly substantiated later when Bobby is evasive about the details of Fletcher's mugging. For Teach, it is obvious what is going on: Bobby and Fletcher have double-crossed Don and Teach. Teach may assault Bobby, then, as a way of reaffirming his self-image by reasserting his dominance over the junkie. It is for similar reasons that Teach erupts into his verbal and physical tirade after Bobby finally reveals that he never actually saw the mark that morning, with or without a suitcase. Teach and Don, it turns out, have been outsmarted by an incompetent junkie from the start. For Teach, this realization shatters his self-identity, and his lashing out in frustration derives from a moment of horrible self-knowledge. Teach finally sees himself as the petty, absurd criminal that he really is, and he can only cope with this brutal truth by inflicting as much damage onto the world as possible.

DIFFICULT DECISIONS AND HARSH REALITIES

While Mamet's play is extremely humorous in its reconfiguring of business executives as bumbling thieves who spend all their time planning a heist that never happens, its closing scene offers a compelling and caustic commentary on Social Darwinism masquerading as free enterprise. Don's junk shop, reduced to shambles by Teach's outburst, becomes an image of America ravaged by capitalism. The wreckage of Don's shop, the play suggests, is the inevitable outcome of encouraging success at any cost. This visual metaphor is thematically reinforced by the buffalo nickel at the heart of the play, which evokes the devastation wrought upon the natural resources, most notably the buffalo themselves, of nineteenth-century America by the frontier ethic of westward expansion. But the play's most poignant critique of the business world may be in Don's actions at the conclusion of the play, which ends with Bobby apologizing for another transgression, this one considerably more severe than the original. Instead of chastising Bobby for failing to act like a "standup guy," though, Don comforts and reassures him. The play concludes, in other words, with Don's implicit disavowal of the business ethic he advocated at the play's opening for his friendship with the junkie whose lie begat all the physical and psychological damage within the play. What this conclusion equally illustrates is that Mamet's play is not just a satire of corporate America. It is, just as significantly, an exploration of the undeniably human need for approval and belonging. To acknowledge only the satire is to overlook much of what has made *American Buffalo* a classic of modern American theater. Ultimately,

David Mamet's name remains one to remember almost three decades later, and *American Buffalo* is perhaps the Mamet play to remember, for if *Glengarry Glen Ross* is Mamet's masterpiece, then *American Buffalo* is his defining work.

[*See also* Theater in America.]

FURTHER READING

Barbera, Jack V. "Ethical Perversity in America: Some Observations on David Mamet's *American Buffalo*." *Modern Drama* 24 (1981): 270–275. A brief but interesting explication of the play's setting and subject matter in response to early criticisms of the play.

Bigsby, C. W. E. "*American Buffalo*." In *David Mamet*, edited by Malcolm Bradbury and Christopher Bigsby. London and New York, 1985. This article revealingly locates the play's themes within Mamet's overall body of work as well as discusses the literary and thematic influences upon *American Buffalo*.

Carroll, Dennis. "Business: *American Buffalo* (1975); *Glengarry Glen Ross* (1983)." In *David Mamet*, edited by Bruce King and Adele King. London, 1987. An examination of the consequences of capitalism for the personal relationships of Mamet's characters.

Dean, Anne. "*American Buffalo*." In Dean's *David Mamet: Language as Dramatic Action*. London and Toronto, 1990. A thorough and revealing discussion of the cultural and literary influences on the play.

Kane, Leslie. *Weasels and Wisemen: Ethics and Ethnicity in the Work of David Mamet*. New York, 1999. The chapter on *American Buffalo* intriguingly explicates the influence of Jewish history and literature on the play.

King, Thomas L. "Talk and Dramatic Action in *American Buffalo*." *Modern Drama* 34 (1991): 538–548. A fascinating argument that examines how language, not action, is the basis of conflict within the play.

Mamet, David. "Interview by Matthew C. Roudané." In *Speaking on Stage: Interviews with Contemporary American Playwrights*, edited by Philip C. Kolin and Colby H. Kullman. Tuscaloosa, Ala., and London, 1996. Mamet discusses *American Buffalo* and how its themes fit into the larger body of his work.

Schlueter, June, and Elizabeth Forsyth. "America as Junkshop: The Business Ethic in David Mamet's *American Buffalo*." *Modern Drama* 26 (1983): 492–500. This article offers a brief but revealing read of the corrupt and corrupting business ethic that characterizes the play.

Zeifman, Hersh. "Phallus in Wonderland: Machismo and Business in David Mamet's *American Buffalo* and *Glengarry Glen Ross*." In *David Mamet: A Casebook*, edited by Leslie Kane. New York and London, 1992. An engaging and highly readable examination of masculinity in Mamet's business plays.

See also the article on David Mamet, immediately preceding.

EDGAR LEE MASTERS

by Matthew J. Caballero

One of the most difficult accomplishments in the arts is to deliver a follow-up success. This dilemma is especially true in the case of the midwestern poet Edgar Lee Masters. In 1915, with the publication of what would become his greatest work, *Spoon River Anthology*, Masters gained immediate fame, and his voice was widely considered fresh and influential American poetry. His book received its share of criticism, both culturally and poetically, but contemporary writers such as Ezra Pound and Carl Sandburg lauded its expressionism and insight—comparing Masters's arrival to that of Walt Whitman's. Even today, this collection remains widely read and is considered a crucial text of early-twentieth-century poetry. The more than fifty works in Masters's canon (forty of which were published after *Spoon River*) did not bring the author the acclaim, both popularly and critically, that he enjoyed with the publication of *Spoon River*. Prolific though he was—writing plays, essays, and biographies, in addition to his verse, over the course of his forty-year career—his place in the American canon is still debated. As part of the "Chicago Renaissance," which included writers such as Vachel Lindsay, Carl Sandburg, and Theodore Dreiser, much of Masters's writing focused on America's people, their lives and dreams. This movement contributed significantly to the important shift of "artistic expectation" away from the cultural power centers of New York and the East. Midwest poetics were still in their infancy, as were many of their communities, and the Chicago Renaissance introduced new aesthetics into the American literary tradition, namely, the regional Midwest voice. There is a populism about his poetry, a descendant of Whitman's heritage, and Masters is deeply concerned with the themes of atrophy and cultivation he witnessed

Edgar Lee Masters, 1924.
(Photograph by Arnold Genthe. Courtesy of the Library of Congress)

in small-town America; his style reflects the ordinary rhythms of its language and life. For him, and for many of the characters whose wasted lives he depicts, the freedom of the romantic vision is critical to living life.

THE LIFE

Edgar Lee Masters was born in Garnett, Kansas, on 23 August 1868. He spent his childhood in the small western Illinois towns of Petersburg and Lewistown, whose nearby rivers, the Sangamon and Spoon, would provide the setting and inspiration for Masters throughout his life. Following in his father's legal footsteps, Masters did not attend college and instead, in 1891, began a distinguished law career that would last for nearly thirty years until his retirement in 1920. After moving to Chicago, he was a law partner of Clarence Darrow, the Chicago lawyer who would later gain notoriety for his defense against William Jennings Bryan in the Scopes Trial of 1925. The civic devotion at the foundation of his legal experience contributed significantly to the politics and populism that weave, sometimes overwhelmingly, through his artistic project. Following a financially and socially difficult divorce in the early 1920s (in which Darrow was retained by his wife), Masters left Chicago and remarried in New York. He spent the rest of his life publishing on an annual, if not semiannual basis, until the last decade of his life. He died on 5 March 1950 and was buried in his childhood home of Petersburg, Illinois.

Masters's early career (before the publication of *Spoon River* in 1915) is characterized by a heightened political consciousness and an uninspiring use of common poetic forms. *A Book of Verses* (1898) suffers from a romantic, immature vision of love that leads to uninteresting, straightforward observations about nature, myth, and other classical themes. "Ode to Autumn" and

"A Dream of Italy" display these poorly engaged ideas and imitative forms. His subsequent collection, *The Blood of the Prophets*, published under the pseudonym Dexter Wallace in 1905, was similarly received as undistinguished. Masters's inability to temper his strong political beliefs (which he had written about in a 1904 collection of essays titled *The New Star Chamber and Other Essays*) infused *The Blood of the Prophets* with a sanctimonious voice that critics found uncompelling, even though poetically he had developed a mature and exciting use of free verse. *Songs and Sonnets* (published in 1910, with a second series in 1912) seemed to detract from these advances as the poet wrote the familiar quatrains of love poetry that had characterized the previous decade's work. Along with these unsuccessful poetry collections, Masters also tried early in his career to be a successful playwright. He produced mostly Shakespearean, domestic dramas that romantically envisage unrequited love but poorly examine the personal and social relationships between a man and a woman. Beginning in 1907, he published *Althea*, *The Trifler* (1908), *The Leaves of the Tree* (1909), *Eileen* (1910), *The Locket* (1910), and *The Bread of Idleness* (1911), each of which received mixed and unenthusiastic support.

THE EARLY MASTERPIECE

It is Masters's 1915 publication, *Spoon River Anthology*, that is considered an American masterpiece. A collection of 214 epigraphs from various town members of a fictionalized community, *Spoon River* was based on the ancient text *Epigrams from a Greek Anthology*. His friend William Marion Reedy, editor of the St. Louis magazine *Reedy's Mirror*, gave this classical book to Masters; *Reedy's Mirror* began publishing Masters's epigraphs in 1914. The inspiration to write the anthology, as Masters relates in his autobiography, came from a visit by the author's mother during which the two discussed at length Masters's childhood homes. With these considerations fresh in his mind, Masters embarked on his portrait of the midwestern rural town by depicting, succinctly and with humble perspective, humankind in all its manifestations: enjoying life with family, enduring the pain of solitude, and exploring the meaning of life and its simple joys. Written in free verse, which was finally beginning to enjoy popular and critical welcome in American letters, the poems sincerely and with clear sadness relate each town member's experiences from which they have distilled one or two simple, yet profound, messages. This extensive narration is sustained by these individuals' perseverance, and it is precisely their simplicity and honesty that makes the reader able to believe in, and commiserate with, their personal stories.

"Theodore the Poet," epigraph number 39, talks about a young poet's fascination with nature and how that later develops into an interest in people's souls. Mirroring the author's own poetic dreams, this epigraph charges the poet to tell the heroic story of enduring a difficult, waning life. Number 85, "Petit, the Poet," confronts the passage of time and the self-doubt experienced by an artist who dares to explore it. His village is teeming with patterns of life, and yet the poet Petit fears that his iambics will be too small, too timid, and too poor to stand up to the symphonies of Homer and Whitman. "The Village Atheist," number 225, is a resounding affirmation of the prize of immortality for those who strive magnificently. Masters's accounts are also local and light-hearted. Two of the more popular characters from *Spoon River*, Knowlt Hoheimer (#25) and Lydia Puckett (#26), demonstrate the profound intimacy with which Masters wrote the collection. Knowlt, the first casualty of a military battle, laments the livestock theft that forced him to run to the army and an early grave. Lydia, however, explains right after his epigraph the real circumstances of his enlistment; it was not the pig stealing but her interest in another man that sends off the young soldier. Masters would add a prologue and epilogue to his collection for an expanded edition published in 1916. In the epilogue, Masters wrote almost four hundred lines of a conversation between devils and the cosmos, where his themes of life's universality and personal splendor are explored in a more theoretical, totalizing way. Masters's voice in this passage does not sink into pontification, however, as it approaches these potentially overwhelming ideas with the intent of exploration and understanding.

Most critics agree that Masters's work after *Spoon River* is characterized by two faults. First, his work has the careless feel of overproduction, and, second, his political ideologies took over much of his poetry's themes and left his verse exploring very limited aesthetic concerns. Of course, much of this artistic chaos had its roots in the personal difficulties engendered by Masters's literary success and his marital problems. However, in the decade following *Spoon River*, he was still able to publish eleven books. Of these, *Mitch Miller* (1920), his first novel, met with the most popular and critical success, even though audiences were split on whether Masters's voice really had achieved the meaningful sincerity of *Spoon River*. While a strong similarity to Mark Twain's *Tom Sawyer* undoubtedly exists—the rural setting dominated by a prominent river, two boys (Mitch and Skeeters

Kirby) and their exploratory coming of age, and the first-person narrative voice—the critical question remains as to how well Masters builds on this weighty foundation. Other notable titles from this period include *The Great Valley* (1916), *Toward the Gulf* (1918), and, especially, *Domesday Book* (1920), the last of which many believed poignantly recaptured and expanded the display of human universality that was the critical aspect of *Spoon River*'s success. *Mirage*, a novel published in 1924, was the third in a semiautobiographical trilogy that told of Masters's recent personal anguish from his troubled, intimate relationships.

A RETURN TO SPOON RIVER

Masters would return to Spoon River for what many would consider his last burst of quality poetic production. In 1924, he published *The New Spoon River*, which, while lacking in the convincing compassion and sadness of the original, is still one of his critical works. In this collection of epitaphs, most of the voices speak with distance from their defining event, and this dislocation makes it harder for them to appreciate the lessons learned. At times, when their principles are held up for judgment, the voice of Masters obtrudes into the picture, and the effective commonality of the poems gets lost. This is clearly seen in the relationships among the dead. In the original *Spoon River*, the connections between town members are rampant and explicit. This effect not only creates anticipation on the reader's part to understand this town's social web; it also displays a unique and fresh examination of the consciences that make up a village. In *The New Spoon River*, however, the town often has the feeling of simply being inhabited by different sides of the author, who, having experienced a good deal of personal and professional pain in the preceding decade, sometimes allows his self-pity to color the epitaphs. "Martin Venable" and "Ambrose Seyffert" are considered some of the stronger poems from this collection; they overcome the author's personal preoccupations to show some shred of the profound waste their common lives have been. These genuine and poignant examples are rarer in this collection, as a shift to a more melancholic and self-pitying tone pervades these epitaphs (leading many to question how effective a sequel this truly was). *Selected Poems* (1925) would be Masters's last successful book of poetry. This collection of 158 of his finest poems allowed the author to display some of his more effective writing in a smaller, more focused volume. The author's decisions were wise, and, for a while, the literary world again grew excited about the future productions from this talented voice.

THE QUASI-HISTORICAL LATER YEARS

The poetry that did follow, however, was not well received. *The Fate of the Jury: An Epilogue to Domesday Book* (1929) was not even given an appropriate ending. Without a doubt, Masters's later career is considered most successful because of the biographies he wrote. This historical focus was a natural continuation of the author's constant concern with understanding the constituent qualities of greatness; by examining the lives of some of the country's most important figures, Masters was able to ruminate on the causes of this common extraordinariness. While his intent in these works is to clarify many of the historical points he felt were interpreted poorly, his own opinion of the official record often overrides his historical concern. These problems are most evident in *Lincoln: The Man* (1931), where his Kentucky and western Illinois roots belie the attack contained inside the biography. Dedicated to the memory of Thomas Jefferson (a rural, populist Democrat who seems the opposite of the Republican president's use of federal power), the biography would fault Lincoln's gentle nature and confident decision making—as well as be faulted widely for its own shortcomings. He approached these books with less care for history and textual evidence than is usually the norm for historians or biographers; at his weakest moments, Masters displays his ignorance of previous scholarship and prefers to substitute his own account and explanation of facts and events. *Whitman* (1937) and *Mark Twain: A Portrait* (1938) both suffer from this problem. *Vachel Lindsay: A Poet in America* (1935), however, achieved greater success and is still one of the critical texts on this fellow Chicago Renaissance poet. Masters's exploration of Lindsay's development and search for success in an Eastern-based literary community were testaments to a struggle he knew well. He would also intimately and sincerely explain, with disarming candor, his own artistic development in *Across Spoon River: An Autobiography* (1936). The book displays Masters's strongly held political and poetic beliefs, and a reading of it explains much of the biographic specificity at which his poetry, especially *Spoon River Anthology*, only impressionistically hinted. Suffering from Masters's selective tendency, however, the autobiography ends in 1917 at the height of Masters's career, when *Spoon River* was widely popular and his law career successful. A projected follow-up was never written.

Contemporary reviewers fault much of Masters's work for being overly sentimental and lacking concern for the traditional, modern craft of poetic form. These criticisms have contributed to his declining popularity and significance during the late twentieth century. Yet even though his work suffered extensively from self-engendered problems, such as overpublication or his sometimes interruptive, preaching voice, there are still several instances of genius that assure his continued importance in American literature. His focus on the common person and the sadness to which many of these lives are destined presents an optimistic view on the power of art to address such threatening situations. His stark depictions of individuals' relationships to themselves, their communities, and their God played a part in encouraging American culture toward a more open exploration of the human condition—a journey that has not abated since. Masters's importance is both historical and poetic, and, in the end, his artistic message is one of optimism and the human community. As his tombstone reads, inscribed from the poem, "To-morrow Is My Birthday," which appeared in *Toward the Gulf*: "I am a dream out of a blessed sleep / Let's walk and hear the lark."

WORKS

A Book of Verses (1898)
Maximilian: A Play in Five Acts (1902)
The New Star Chamber and Other Essays (1904)
The Blood of the Prophets (as Dexter Wallace, 1905)
Althea: A Play in Four Acts (1907)
The Trifler: A Play (1908)
The Leaves of the Tree: A Play (1909)
Eileen: A Play in Three Acts (1910)
Songs and Sonnets (1910)
The Locket: A Play in Three Acts (1910)
The Bread of Idleness: A Play in Four Acts (1911)
Songs and Sonnets: Second Series (1912)
Spoon River Anthology (1915)
Songs and Satires (1916)
The Great Valley (1916)
Toward the Gulf (1918)
Starved Rock (1919)
Mitch Miller (1920)
Domesday Book (1920)
The Open Sea (1921)
Children of the Market Place (1922)
Skeeters Kirby (1923)
The Nuptial Flight (1923)
Mirage (1924)
The New Spoon River (1924)
Selected Poems (1925)
Lee: A Dramatic Poem (1926)
Kit O'Brien (1927)
Levy Mayer and the New Industrial Era (1927)

Jack Kelso: A Dramatic Poem (1928)
The Fate of the Jury: An Epilogue to Domesday Book (1929)
Gettysburg, Manila, Acoma (1930)
Lichee Nuts (1930)
Lincoln: The Man (1931)
Godbey: A Dramatic Poem (1931)
The Serpent in the Wilderness (1933)
The Tale of Chicago (1933)
Dramatic Duologues: Four Short Plays in Verse (1934)
Richmond: A Dramatic Poem (1934)
Invisible Landscapes (1935)
Vachel Lindsay: A Poet in America (1935)
Poems of People (1936)
The Golden Fleece of California (1936)
Across Spoon River: An Autobiography (1936)
Whitman (1937)
The Tide of Time (1937)
The New World (1937)
Hymn to the Unknown God (1937)
Mark Twain: A Portrait (1938)
More People (1939)
Ralph Waldo Emerson: The Living Thoughts of Emerson (1940)
Illinois Poems (1941)
The Sangamon (1942)
Along the Illinois (1942)
The Harmony of Deeper Music: Posthumous Poems of Edgar Lee Masters (1976)

FURTHER READING

Flanagan, John T. *Edgar Lee Masters: The Spoon River Poet and His Critics*. Metuchen, N.J., 1974. Early attempt to judge the appropriate place for Masters in the canon of American poetry.

Hallwas, John E., and Dennis J. Reader, eds. *The Vision of This Land: Studies of Vachel Lindsay, Edgar Lee Masters, and Carl Sandburg*. Macomb, Ill., 1976. An early work comparing the lives of three different poets whose long-term impacts varied, but whose comparison aids understanding.

Primeau, Ronald. *Beyond Spoon River: The Legacy of Edgar Lee Masters*. Austin, Tex., 1981. A positive look at the enduring influence the author has had throughout the twentieth century.

Russell, Herbert K. *Edgar Lee Masters: A Biography*. Urbana, Ill., 2001. A contemporary look at the life of Masters that shows the extensive relation between Masters's personal life and his poetry.

Wrenn, John H., and Margaret H. Wrenn. *Edgar Lee Masters*. Boston, 1983.

COTTON MATHER

by Adam Scott Miller

Cotton Mather, Puritan minister and historian, lived pen in hand. During the course of his life (1663–1728) he published more than four hundred works including histories, biographies, sermons, scientific treatises, discussions of demonology, and pamphlets dealing with health and medicine. Mather's life was itself no less zealous and eclectic. Bearing the weight of an impressive heritage, Mather wrote an invaluable history of New England, became involved in the Salem witchcraft trials, and was among the first to advocate smallpox inoculation.

Cotton Mather. (© *Bettmann/Corbis*)

FAMILY AND EDUCATION

Cotton Mather was born on 12 February 1663 in Boston, Massachusetts, an heir to Puritan prominence. Mather's life was profoundly shaped by this inheritance; even his name is a token of the weighty expectations he bore. Cotton Mather was named after his grandfathers, Richard Mather and John Cotton, two of Puritan New England's most prominent ministers. Mather's own father, Increase Mather, was also a powerful and influential figure. In addition to family expectations, Cotton Mather's Puritan world placed great emphasis on a son's need to meet the standard set by his father's model of behavior. This meant that meeting expectations mattered to his family *and* to God. Throughout his life, Mather was aware, to a fault, of his responsibility to bear his name properly and, by so doing, to honor his father, his grandfathers, and God.

Fortunately, Mather showed great promise from an early age. By his eleventh year, Mather had read extensively in Latin and Greek and had begun working on his Hebrew grammar. His drive to please his father, his hunger for learning, and his tremendous work ethic all combined to make possible his admission to Harvard before the age of twelve, making him the youngest student ever admitted. At Harvard, Mather excelled and he knew it. His success and

growing vanity were not appreciated by his fellow students, and it appears that he suffered significant abuse at their hands. During this time Mather also began to develop a serious problem with stuttering that, though eventually overcome, threatened both his pride and his plans to enter the clergy. Despite these difficulties, in 1678, at the age of fifteen, he received his bachelor's degree and became a member of his father's congregation, the Second Church of Boston. In 1680 Mather preached his first sermon and in 1681 he received his master's degree from Harvard and was elected a pastor of the Second Church. After his formal ordination in 1685, Mather turned his attention to a young minister's final matter of business, and on 4 May 1686 he married the first of his three wives, Abigail Phillips.

MINISTRY

In many ways, both as a man and a minister, Mather was a representative Puritan. As manifest in his diaries, his inner life was dominated by a Puritan bent toward self-awareness that resulted in a deep uneasiness about himself and his work. This constant sense of insecurity made him prone to sharp criticism of others. His periods of doubt prompted tireless and battering exercises of self-examination conducted in an attempt to determine that which Puritanism declared undeterminable: was he among the elect destined for salvation? On a weekly basis Mather would devote entire days to "secret prayer," examining and reviewing in detail the depth of his depravity. He frequently identified pride as his primary sin—an assessment shared by many of his contemporaries—and he worked constantly at finding ways to channel and harness that weakness.

As a result, Mather's religious convictions were also deeply practical. His convictions centered on a notion of "piety" that involved humility, patience, and a rejection of this world. His desire to excel in piety led him to be extremely generous with his money and deeply engaged in daily affairs. His concern for action and for the general welfare of the community found clear expression in 1710 in one of his major works, *Bonifacius* or *Essays to Do Good*. The work is shaped by Enlightenment ideals, is full of enthusiasm for comforting the downtrodden, and offers practical advice to ministers, doctors, and businessmen about how to be of greater use to others. Benjamin Franklin later remarked that reading it influenced his conduct for the rest of his life.

In addition to his concern for the general welfare of the community, Mather was particularly focused on the needs of his congregation. He approached his ministry with great care and thoughtful devotion, preparing nearly seventy formal sermons per year. He preached to a largely unconverted audience and took care to address the ordinary person. He recommended piety on the grounds that he felt common people valued most: piety, Mather taught, would produce a happy, prosperous, and well-oiled world. In conjunction with preparing and delivering sermons, Mather's ministerial work also involved keeping church records, visiting and comforting the sick and dying, baptizing and catechizing children, marrying couples, attending funerals, and promoting private religious societies.

In 1716, hoping to create a greater sense of shared Christian brotherhood among Protestant sects in America and England, Mather wrote *The Stone Cut out of the Mountain*, a work that attempted to reduce Christianity to fourteen universally shared maxims. Ultimately, Mather reduced these maxims to three: a belief in the Trinity, an utter reliance on Christ for salvation, and a love of neighbor out of respect for Christ. Mather also wrote a book-length manual for ministers, *Manuductio ad Ministerium* (1726), in which he urged ministers to be both thunderous preachers leading souls to God and humane, erudite gentlemen capable of concrete action.

CURIOSITIES, WITCHES, AND INOCULATIONS

Mather was something of an amateur scientist, and he was constantly engaged in the business of collecting scientific "curiosities" to present to the Royal Society, a British association dedicated to advancing science. Mather's letters to the Royal Society are eclectic and multidisciplinary. The letters deal with subjects as widely divergent as astronomy, botany, zoology, geology, and meteorology, and the posts eventually resulted in Mather's

election to the Royal Society in 1713, making him one of the first Americans to be so honored. In 1715 Mather completed a manuscript entitled *The Christian Philosopher*, the first general book on science to be written in America, and in 1721 it was published in a three-hundred-page volume. The title of the work shows that, for Mather, science (philosophy) and Christianity were deeply related endeavors. For Mather, a proper understanding of nature could only contribute to the good of man and the glory of God. This perspective is also evident in Mather's *The Angel of Bethesda* (1722), the only comprehensive American medical work written in the entire colonial period and his most important achievement in science. *The Angel of Bethesda* contains a mix of medical science, folk remedies, occult elements, and religious explanation. For Mather, the combination of clerical and medical functions was perfectly natural, and his concern for public health was fueled by his commitment to Christian benevolence in general.

It is important to note that Mather's scientific curiosity did not limit itself to the conventional. His controversial involvement in the Salem witchcraft trials, as well as his pioneering efforts to promote smallpox inoculation, both exemplify his willingness to believe in the exceptional. In 1688 Mather was introduced to a young woman named Martha Goodwin who appeared to be possessed by a demon. Mather brought her into his own home hoping to ease her pain, conduct a few experiments, and refute those skeptical of the Devil's, and God's, reality. While in his home, Martha suffered a number of demonic fits and seizures. When devotional exercises were performed on her behalf, her pain was provoked and magnified. These initial experiences with witchcraft convinced Mather of the existence of an "invisible world," and he resolved to have little patience for those who denied it. His time with Martha Goodwin prompted his first important book-length publication, *Memorable Providences, Relating to Witchcraft and Possessions* (1689). Although the book contained nothing not already popularly believed, it was widely read, and eighteen months after its appearance another group of girls fell victim to the kind of demonic convulsions described by Mather.

The first cases were reported around February 1692 in Salem Village, Massachusetts. The original claims of possession quickly multiplied as burgeoning confessions and accusations swiftly widened the circles of implication. It is estimated that at the height of the frenzy the number of those accused of witchcraft exceeded seven hundred. Mather believed in the reality of the "invisible war" being waged by the Devil in Salem, but he and others cautioned the judges against any simple reliance on "spectral evidence," evidence that consisted entirely of one person's testimony that another had appeared to them in spectral form and thereby afflicted them. Mather's cautions were not immediately heeded, and by the time the Salem witchcraft trials concluded, nineteen suspects had been hanged and another pressed to death. In October 1692, as the trials wound down, Mather began writing his *Wonders of the Invisible World* (1693), a work that defended and explored the events in Salem. The book is full of indecisive equivocations and was written to win the approval of those in powerful places. This book, more than anything else, has proved disastrous for Mather's reputation both then and now.

Mather would have recognized little difference between his belief in the "invisible world" and his confidence that smallpox inoculations could save lives. Experiments were experiments and science was science. In 1721 Boston was again ravaged by a smallpox epidemic. The epidemic lasted a full year and infected nearly half the city. Mather felt called to respond to the suffering. For a number of years he had devoted time and attention to the question of smallpox, and when it struck again he proposed to Boston physicians a new tactic: inoculation. Public reaction to this unorthodox treatment was predictable, and many feared that the practice of inoculation would simply cause the disease to spread more quickly. A year-long barrage of pamphlets and editorials ensued in which attacks and counterattacks concerning the question of inoculation became increasingly biting and personal. But Mather stood firm, confident of his position. Inoculations could save lives, and he was even willing to prove it by inoculating his own children. Mather and Dr. Zabdiel Boylston pressed forward, working with those willing to participate. Mather proceeded to publish his *Sentiments on the Small Pox Inoculated* (1721) and *An Account of Inoculating the Small Pox* (1722). In stark contrast to his involvement in the Salem witchcraft trials, history would, in this instance, vindicate Mather's convictions.

LITERATURE

Cotton Mather likely published more in his lifetime than all previous New England ministers combined. His output was staggering. He published more than four hundred works, the bulk of which were sermons. It is generally agreed that Mather had no gift for poetry; rhyming and meter were not among his literary strengths. However, Mather did succeed in fashioning a striking voice that was undeniably his own. The quality and tone of his prose are unmistakable. Once one is able to get past Mather's often cumbersome mannerisms, his prose demonstrates consistent grace and clarity. Mather's works are often noted for their control of language, their epigrammatic skill, their witty attachment to wordplay, and their tendency to make wide-ranging allusions.

Mather's best-known work is his *Magnalia Christi Americana* (1702), a kind of typological and documentary history of New England. The *Magnalia* is thoroughly American, and Mather meant it to be so. It is a major work of American historiography and an invaluable source of information about Puritan New England. Mather cast the *Magnalia* as a work meant to bring New England out of political and religious obscurity and into the light of world history, where he envisioned it playing a central role. Mather began working on the *Magnalia* in 1693, and shipped the manuscript for publication in June 1700. The first edition was published in 1702 and totaled 850 closely printed folio pages. The *Magnalia* is divided into seven sections: the first deals with the founding of New England; the next three sections contain the heart of the narrative and relate the lives of governors, ministers, and other noteworthy men of New England, emphasizing their experiences of conversion and their devotion to Puritanism; the fifth section is a collection of documents from Congregational Churches; the sixth relates remarkable providences; and the seventh deals with war.

The primary difficulty to be faced in reading the *Magnalia* is a nearly inevitable sense of incoherence. It is, at once, epic and prophetic, imaginative and archival. Mather draws on so many different sources and combines such various items of interest that it is easy to lose a sense of the essential unity that he saw so clearly at work: the histories, biographies, and documents collected all bear witness to the glorious work of God to be carried out in and through New England. In particular, the *Magnalia* demonstrates this unity in its attempt to illustrate the meaning of sainthood in New England. The biographies Mather presents of New England's political and religious leaders highlight their religious conversions, and each biography displays the same essential Puritan structure, almost to the point of utter predictability.

But for Mather, this duplication is precisely the point. Each life manifests a unique version of an essential type, a type that is at once a contemporary Puritan standard for conduct and an antitype to its predecessors in Biblical typology. Each biography roots its subject in both the redemptive past (the world of the Bible) and the redemptive present (Puritan New England). As a result, Mather intends the biographies to collectively form a lens through which New England's part in the redemptive future may be viewed. Each of the diverse pieces collected in the *Magnalia* is meant to work to that same salvific end. Whether Mather is always successful in creating this kind of compelling unity is a debatable question, but it is clear that the merit of the *Magnalia* is proportionate to the compelling persistence of its theme.

Mather's *Magnalia Christi Americana* is, in many respects, representative of his own life. Mather's life was filled and illuminated by the spirits of his predecessors, both Biblical and Puritanical. Its varied and often incongruent elements (his offensive vanity and his genuine generosity, his penchant for demonology and his commitment to modern science) leave us asking the same kinds of questions raised by the *Magnalia*: does Mather's life yield, as a whole, an additional example of the Puritan sainthood he worked so hard to portray in his history of New England? This is the very question that Mather himself perpetually asked and would continue asking until his death in 1728.

[*See also* Colonial Writing and Puritanism: The Sense of an Unending.]

SELECTED WORKS

The Declaration of the Gentlemen, Merchants, and Inhabitants of Boston (1689)
Memorable Providences, Relating to Witchcraft and Possessions (1689)
The Present State of New England (1690)
The Wonders of the Invisible World (1693)
The Life of His Excellency, Sir William Phips (1697)
A Family Well-Ordered (1699)

Reasonable Religion (1700)
Magnalia Christi Americana (1702)
The Negro Christianized (1706)
Bonifacius (1710)
The Stone Cut out of the Mountain (1716)
Psalterium Americanum (1718)
The Christian Philosopher (1721)
Sentiments on the Small Pox Inoculated (1721)
An Account of Inoculating the Small Pox (1722)
The Angel of Bethesda (1722)
Manuductio ad Ministerium (1726)

FURTHER READING

Beall, Otho T., Jr., and Richard H. Shryock. *Cotton Mather: First Significant Figure in American Medicine.* Baltimore, 1954. An assessment of Mather's contributions to the field of medicine.

Boas, Ralph, and Louise Boas. *Cotton Mather: Keeper of the Puritan Conscience.* New York, 1928. An early and sometimes superficial biography of Mather.

Levin, David. *Cotton Mather: The Young Life of the Lord's Remembrancer, 1663–1703.* Cambridge, Mass., 1978. A detailed biographical account of the first half of Mather's adult life.

Middlekauff, Robert. *The Mathers: Three Generations of Puritan Intellectuals, 1596–1728.* Berkeley, Calif., 1999. An examination of Cotton Mather; his father, Increase Mather; and his grandfather, Richard Mather, focused on their intellectual positions and contributions.

Silverman, Kenneth. *The Life and Times of Cotton Mather.* New York, 1984. An accurate, astute, and comprehensive treatment of Mather's life and work.

Wendell, Barrett. *Cotton Mather: The Puritan Priest.* New York, 1963. A balanced account of Mather's life and work.

WILLIAM MATTHEWS

by Matthew J. Caballero

William Matthews's poetry is characterized by a potent and eloquent voice that optimistically explores daily life. His work is often associated with the "Deep Image" movement of poets such as Robert Bly, W. S. Merwin, Mark Strand, and James Wright. With an impressionistic use of language, these poets sought to examine the location in the mind where life is lived and experienced. For Matthews as for these others, understanding the workings of the human psyche is always an emotionally difficult and psychologically complex adventure. Yet Matthews's verse is not accompanied by Bly's apocalyptic mysticism or Merwin's palling gloom. Matthews brings to his artistic project two important, uplifting considerations. First, he approaches the tribulations of self-understanding as the proof of life, which he considers an opportunity to be seized and lived. His poems focus on the pleasure of life's daily and domestic events, even if such pleasure is fleeting and complicated. Second, the poet also believes strongly in the power of verse to address, redress, and undress the mysterious workings of the psyche. Whether it was his fervent support of American poetry, the strong and powerful command of language thoroughly evinced in his poetry, or his energizing outlook on human experience, Matthews steadfastly believed in the importance of human language in unraveling the mysterious joys of existence.

LIFE AND EARLY SUCCESS

William Procter Matthews III was born in Cincinnati, Ohio, on 11 November 1942. After completing degrees at Yale and the University of North Carolina at Chapel Hill, Matthews went on to be a teacher and writer-in-residence at Cornell University; the universities of Colorado, Washington, and Iowa; and the City College of New York. He was the coeditor of the poetry journal *Lillabulero* from 1966 to 1974 and served on several other editorial boards during his lifetime. He received fellowships from the Guggenheim Foundation and the National Endowment for the Arts during his career, and his publication *Time & Money: New Poems* (1995) received the National Book

Critics Circle Award for poetry. He died on 12 November 1997, the day after his fifty-fifth birthday.

Matthews's first major publication was *Ruining the New Road: Poems* (1970), a collection of poems that was well received critically and demonstrated early Matthews's expressiveness and artistic project. In it, Matthews's style is quiet, direct, and assiduous. The poems do not lecture or harass; instead, the narrator entices the reader with sincere confessions about the joys and pain of daily life. The poems are often set in places of cloudy or suspended consciousness: states of sleep, night, dreams, and death become familiar settings in which Matthews works. He opens the collection with "The Search Party," a poem that cultivates a mutual sense of purpose in the poet's and the reader's exploration. Other poems, such as "Nothing But Bad News," "Newark under Martial Law," and "The Asian War," deal with the political and social situation of the United States in the early 1970s. However, Matthews does not integrate such social criticism on a sustained level. Here he does include poems dealing with basketball and jazz, two American creations he sees as predicated on the important balance of form and improvisation, and these settings and concerns occupied him throughout his career.

The Cloud and *The Moon* (both published in 1971) continue to work through these themes. But the most representative and powerful work of this early phase of Matthews's career was *Sleek for the Long Flight* (1972), a daring collection of forty-five poems that includes an array of free verse, prose poems, an ode, a letter, and two one-line poems. Here Matthews examines the mutability and limitless size of the outside world as a means to understanding the often more intense interior world. Beginning with the revisionary "Directions," the poet makes clear his intention to separate himself from the heavy-handedness of "Search Party" in a way that allows and encourages the reader to examine the interior dynamics of the human quest. In poems such as "Snow," "Sleep," "And So," and "The Cat," the transitional states of death, sleep, and unconsciousness blur into one another to reveal, with relief, our minds' universal responses to these cognitive transformations. These themes are complemented well by poems like "Praise," an ebullient look at a lover's constituent parts that simultaneously exalts the sum and its parts, and "La Tache, 1962," where the author's desire to taste the wine's "secrets" mirror his delight at self-discovery. In "Attention, Everyone," the poet triumphantly signals a new regime of love that dispels the gloom often engendered by that emotion.

RISING INTO FORM

Whereas Matthews's early work was characterized by free verse and a use of exploratory structures, in *Rising and Falling* (1979) he began to cultivate a tighter form of poetry that would continue through the rest of his career, marked by a shift to formal poetic elements coupled with the strong imagery for which he was known. In *Rising and Falling*, he works within this style to probe the outreaches of some of humankind's least structured experiences: childhood ("The Party" and "The Icehouse"), sleeping and dreams ("Waking at Dusk" and "Bedtime"), and death ("Living among the Dead"). Matthews uses these moments of suspended consciousness to demonstrate the importance of their residual images. Instead of fearing the opportunities presented by such unique states of mind, Matthews delves into their complications in a controlled way, both linguistically and poetically. In "A Walk," the narrator's early morning walk along Cape Cod is rife with memories and meanings that slowly disentangle themselves from the rocks and water and quickly disappear. Left are the joys and learning those experiences made possible.

A Happy Childhood (1984) focuses on these unique states of consciousness as Matthews makes explicit some of his implicit Freudian approaches to humankind's unique reception of the events and circumstances around us. By renewing the metaphors with which Freud discusses consciousness, Matthews embarks on a fresh examination of the complexities suggested by these ideas. This unpeeling of the psyche yields an understanding of the perpetually unraveling mystery of human existence. The conclusions of these poems display Matthews's reassuring belief in the individual's self-empowerment. These themes carry through to *Foreseeable Futures* (1987), where Matthews uses everyday human joys to foil the passage of time and death. In this collection of thirty-six poems, thirty of which are similarly structured in five tercets, Matthews confronts the potential emptiness of mortality. In "Days beyond Recall," Matthews admits to the overwhelming

circumstances of one person's existence. Yet the narrator will not succumb to this awe and decisively challenges all readers to choose between an empowered future or a defeated one. Examples of this sensibility are evinced in poems such as "Schoolboys with Dog, Winter"—where the narrator witnesses the triumphant sunrise on a landscape of children going to school on a wintry morning, delighting in the cloud of their frosty breath—and the poem "Blue Notes," where the cloudy state of waking up serves as a foundation for the "relentless joy" throughout our days.

EXPLORING THE BLUES IN POETRY

The blues sensibility is worked out with more complexity in Matthews' next book, *Blues If You Want* (1989). In this work, which borrows the titles of many jazz compositions, the poet expounds on the theme of sustainability and demonstrates the power such an awareness can have. He also begins to explore the relationships between language and music. His control of language is critical to the success of *Blues If You Want* as he develops rhythms that are as textually important as his words. With this deep, intricate understanding of the blues sensibility, Matthews is able to weather many of the temporary hardships that life presents—a journey of self-empowerment that he describes in *Time & Money*. Full of considerations about the transience of objects and experiences, the more than forty poems in this book display the optimism that is exemplary of, and expressed through, the poet's extraordinary linguistic gift.

After All, a collection published posthumously in 1998, continues the intensity, exploration, and optimism of Matthews's work. His fastidious effort to understand and explicate how and why our consciousness functions is always boldly undertaken through a self-critical analysis of his own interests and history. His work is an exceptional example of the relevance of poetry in the second half of the twentieth century, a goal he believed in and worked for throughout his life. Sincere and communicative, his poems explore humankind's greatest mystery, the self, and they inspire his readers with meaningful insights into that mystery.

WORKS

Broken Syllables (1969)
Ruining the New Road: Poems (1970)
The Cloud (1971)
The Moon (1971)
Sleek for the Long Flight (1972)
Without a Mouth (1972)

Sticks and Stones (1975)
Rising and Falling (1979)
Flood (1982)
A Happy Childhood (1984)
Foreseeable Futures (1987)
Blues If You Want (1989)
Curiosities (1989)
Selected Poems and Translations, 1969–1991 (1992)
Time & Money: New Poems (1995)
After All (posthumous, 1998)

FURTHER READING

Hanson, Danielle. "The Influence of Translation and Music on Poetry: An Interview with William Matthews." *Hayden's Ferry Review* 20 (Spring/Summer 1997), 75–85.

Ingersoll, Earl G., Judith Kitchen, and Stan Sanvel Rubin, eds. *The Post-confessionals: Conversations with American Poets of the Eighties.* London; Cranbury, N.J., 1989.

PETER MATTHIESSEN

by Patrick A. Smith

Peter Matthiessen, one of the most widely traveled and prolific American authors, has consistently produced fiction and nonfiction since the 1950s. He was born in New York City on 22 May 1927 to Erard and Elizabeth Matthiessen. His father, an architect by trade, was also a trustee of the National Audubon Society; the elder Matthiessen's interest in nature was influenced by Peter and his brother, George, who had a penchant for collecting wildlife and a native predilection for outdoor activities. The connection that Peter Matthiessen felt for his surroundings would manifest itself in all of his work.

Growing up in affluent surroundings that included both the solitude of nature and the vital chaos of New York City (the family kept an apartment overlooking Central Park, and the eight-year-old Matthiessen was to meet and become a lifelong friend of the author and New York literary fixture George Plimpton), the aspiring artist had ample opportunity to develop intellectually. By the time he was ten, Matthiessen was obsessed with birds; at sixteen, he knew that he would become a writer.

A RESTLESS SPIRIT

After graduating from the prestigious Hotchkiss School in Connecticut in 1945, Matthiessen enlisted in the U.S. Navy and was stationed at Pearl Harbor in Hawaii shortly after the end of World War II. In 1946, he enrolled at Yale, as his father had a generation before, and combined his studies in English with courses in natural history. A year of study abroad in Paris laid the foundation for an extended stay that began in 1951. In 1953, Matthiessen and Harold L. "Doc" Humes founded the *Paris Review*, a literary journal that focused on fiction and poetry from established and aspiring writers. The two enlisted the editorial talents of expatriate friends and fellow literati Plimpton and William Styron. Fifty years later, the *Paris Review* continued to be synonymous with excellence in cutting-edge literature.

By 1954, Matthiessen, his wife Patsy, and their young son, Lucas, had returned to New York, and Matthiessen's first novel, *Race Rock*, was published. Matthiessen and his wife grew apart; the restlessness that came to characterize both his lifestyle and his own eclectic work manifested itself when he wandered the United States for the better part of three years collecting material for his encyclopedic *Wildlife in America* (1959). What was to have been a three-part freelance job for *The New Yorker* instead placed Matthiessen squarely at the front of the conservation movement that Rachel Carson fueled three years later with *Silent Spring* (1962), her diatribe against the misuse of pesticides.

The moving opening pages of *Wildlife in America* are characteristic of Matthiessen's close—almost preternatural—association with the nature he observes, and they echo with the remarkable gravity and passion of his subsequent nonfiction. In those first passages, he describes what must have occurred to ensure the extinction of the great auk, as its last egg was smashed by hunters, and the bird and its mate were slaughtered for their skins. His conclusion is a mantra still repeated in today's conservation literature: "The finality of extinction is awesome, and not unrelated to the finality of eternity. Man, striving to imagine what might lie beyond the long light years of stars, beyond the universe, beyond the void, feels lost in space; confronted with the death of species, enacted on earth so many times before he came, and certain to

Peter Matthiessen. (© *Dan Lamont/Corbis*)

continue when his own breed is gone, he is forced to face another void, and feels alone in time." Human actions are inexorably connected with nature, Matthiessen writes, and the arbitrary political and economic boundaries that humans create only hinder that interaction.

In the space of a decade, Matthiessen developed a reputation as a hardworking and diversely talented writer. His connections to the publishing world—particularly his work for *The New Yorker*—allowed him sponsored travel on expeditions that would become legendary for their exoticism and the far-flung topics of the books that arose from those journeys: *The Cloud Forest* (1961), which explores the history, myth, and legend of South America, including the search for a fossil skull and a lost Inca city; *Under the Mountain Wall* (1962), an account of a Harvard University–Peabody Museum expedition to New Guinea, in which Matthiessen was given the rare opportunity to interact with the Kurelu tribe (the famous disappearance of Michael Rockefeller occurred on the trip); *The Shorebirds of North America* (1967), a lavishly illustrated book that describes the inhabitants of the ecosystems close to Matthiessen's home on Long Island; *Sal Si Puedes* (Escape if You Can) (1969), a social commentary on the plight of migrant farm workers and their relationship with big business that arose from the author's contact with Cesar Chavez; *Blue Meridian* (1971), an expedition with filmmaker Peter Gimbel in search of the great white shark; *The Tree Where Man Was Born* (1972), the author's exploration of human origins on the mysterious and awesome continent of Africa; *Sand Rivers* (1981), "the last safari into the last wilderness" of the Selous Game Reserve in Tanzania amid the political and economic strife of the Idi Amin regime in Uganda and an imminent oil crisis; and *The Birds of Heaven: Travels with Cranes* (2001), a chronicle of the author's search for the world's fifteen species of cranes on a journey that covers Siberia, Mongolia, India, Bhutan, China, Japan, Korea, Australia, Africa, Europe, and the United States.

THE ZEN YEARS

Matthiessen's experimentation with various drugs in order to examine and alter his perception of reality (a drug scene in *At Play in the Fields of the Lord* [1965] arose from that experimentation) became in the late 1960s a more sedate—and, judging from the extent to which the author has cultivated that study, a more enlightening—experience when his second wife, Deborah, introduced Matthiessen to Zen Buddhism. In 1973, after five years of Zen practice and a year after his wife's

death, Matthiessen journeyed to Nepal, a spiritual pilgrimage that resulted several years later in the publication of *The Snow Leopard* (1978). The effort garnered the National Book Award for Matthiessen and cemented a critical reputation that had grown steadily through more than two decades of attention to his craft.

Having fully dedicated himself to the study of Zen in the years following Deborah's death, Matthiessen, who was married in a Zen ceremony in 1980 to Tanzanian-born model Maria Eckhart, was ordained a Zen monk in 1981. That and other events related to both the author's practice of Zen and its history are recounted in *Nine-Headed Dragon River* (1986).

In the period following his ordination, Matthiessen turned his focus to socially important issues, as in the controversial *In the Spirit of Crazy Horse* (1983), a study of the case of Ojibwa-Sioux Leonard Peltier, who was convicted of killing two federal agents at Pine Ridge Reservation, South Dakota, on 26 June 1975 (more than twenty-five years later, Matthiessen and a group of writers and activists that included E. L. Doctorow, Kurt Vonnegut, and William Styron petitioned for Peltier's release from prison). In the book, Matthiessen proclaims the man's innocence of the charges against him. *In the Spirit of Crazy Horse* prompted one of the largest libel lawsuits in publishing history when Matthiessen and his publisher, Viking, were sued for forty-nine million dollars. After an eight-year court battle, author and publisher were vindicated, and the book, which had been removed from shelves in the interim, was once again available to the public.

Matthiessen followed that seething effort with *Indian Country* (1984), a documentary look at the plight of various Native American tribes around the United States, and *Men's Lives* (1986), an exploration of the fishermen who make their living from the waters off Long Island (as Matthiessen himself had for several seasons some years before).

FOCUSING ON FICTION

Despite his success with and obvious attention to nonfiction, Matthiessen has expressed disappointment that his fiction will likely always be overshadowed by the nonfiction's critical reception. As early as 1954, with the publication of *Race Rock*, Matthiessen balances a strong sense of style with a struggle for answers that are neither apparent nor easy. The novel traces the awakening of George McConville—like Matthiessen, the son of a well-to-do family—to the vagaries of class privilege.

The two novels that followed also contain obvious autobiographical references to Matthiessen's upbringing and examine the author's disquietude with his own position in society. *Partisans* (1955) introduces Barney Sand, the son of an American diplomat, who becomes interested in and ultimately entangled with the politics of Jacobi, a communist insurgent who has been exiled from the party. The resulting conflict between Sand's life of privilege and the disillusionment that he experiences when he discovers the truth behind Jacobi's exile (as it turns out, both systems are quite capable of treating people badly) forces Sand to rededicate himself to social change. In *Raditzer* (1961), Matthiessen refashions his experiences as a seaman after the culmination of World War II in his protagonist, Charlie Stark. Stark must come to terms with his own privileged life, while Raditzer, a character who evokes pathos in both his physical appearance and his questionable family background, sees Stark as his only friend. Stark, through Raditzer, comes to realize the dual nature of his own life, and he discovers the fine line between the life of privilege that he leads and the uglier, darker world that Raditzer inhabits.

Matthiessen followed up those novels with two tours de force that, as *The Snow Leopard* did for his nonfiction, would cement his reputation as a first-class stylist of fiction. In 1965, *At Play in the Fields of the Lord* drew on the author's travels to South America for its setting and played on his burgeoning interest in Zen for the themes that he would handle, specifically, religion, wealth, and the clash between civilization and nature. Ten years later, *Far Tortuga* (1975), an experimental novel that intersperses an objective narrator with the patois of the turtle hunters on board the *Lillias Eden*, uses the accretion of different voices and points of view for its effect. The novel, with its complex layering of narrative and dialogue, as well as brief but important narrative intrusions that move the story forward, is a poetic compilation of snapshot images that prefigures the comparison of Matthiessen to Faulkner upon the publication of the Watson trilogy.

Killing Mr. Watson (1990), the first of the three novels that detail the full, sordid life of Edgar J. Watson through the eyes of the people who interact with him, recalls the layering effect of the different voices in *Far Tortuga*. The first and subsequent novels in the trilogy, *Lost Man's River* (1997) and *Bone by Bone* (1999), are set in the Florida Everglades at the beginning of the twentieth century. Matthiessen became familiar with and interested in the area through his travels both as a child and an adult.

The story's plot came into focus for the author when he researched the legends he had heard about Watson, who was murdered, perhaps by a posse, in the early part of the century. The implications of Watson's story for the settling of the area and as a statement on the ecological implications of the American Dream were undoubtedly cultivated both by Matthiessen's later travels to the area and by his vast experience with other cultures and their relationships to the land. The trilogy has been acclaimed as the work of a mature author whose fiction and nonfiction both benefit from the strong ethical underpinnings of his vision.

Matthiessen is in the rare company of American writers to be nominated for the National Book Award in both fiction and nonfiction. He also has the distinction of having his work acclaimed by two groups whose opinions often diverge: literary critics, who extol Matthiessen for his contribution to the body of American literature in the last half of the twentieth century (particularly the later works, such as *At Play in the Fields of the Lord*, *Far Tortuga*, and the Watson trilogy), and scientists from the paleontologist Stephen Jay Gould to the anthropologist Hugh Brody, who understand the author's gift for elucidating and humanizing topics that were once considered the exclusive purview of jaunty adventurers such as Richard Halliburton or professionals in the hard sciences.

The sheer volume of Matthiessen's work—fiction and nonfiction, narrative, and polemic—the passion with which he documents a natural world that threatens to disappear before him (and, in large part, has disappeared), his keen sense of justice, and an intense and compassionate eye for his surroundings developed from a lifetime of close observation, all place Matthiessen in the first rank of American writers. The author compellingly articulates the contradictions inherent in American culture and the social and ecological implications of the decisions that arise from what Matthiessen implies is an increasingly shortsighted, impersonal, and venal society.

[*See also* Doctorow, E. L.; Nature Writing: Prose; Styron, William; *and* Vonnegut, Kurt.]

SELECTED WORKS

NOVELS

Race Rock (1954)
Partisans (1955)
Raditzer (1961)
At Play in the Fields of the Lord (1965)
Far Tortuga (1975)
Killing Mister Watson (1990)

Lost Man's River (1997)
Bone by Bone: A Novel (1999)

COLLECTIONS

On the River Styx and Other Stories (1989)

NONFICTION

Wildlife in America (1959)
The Cloud Forest: A Chronicle of the South American Wilderness (1961)
Under the Mountain Wall: A Chronicle of Two Seasons in the Stone Age (1962)
Oomingmak: The Expedition to the Musk Ox Island in the Bering Sea (1967)
The Shorebirds of North America (1967)
Sal Si Puedes: Cesar Chavez and the New American Revolution (1969)
Blue Meridian: The Search for the Great White Shark (1971)
Seal Pool (1972)
The Tree Where Man Was Born (1972)
The Wind Birds (1973)
The Snow Leopard (1978)
Sand Rivers (1981)
In the Spirit of Crazy Horse (1983)
Indian Country (1984)
Men's Lives: The Surfmen and the Baymen of the South Fork (1986)

Nine-Headed Dragon River: Zen Journals, 1969–1985 (1986)
African Silences (1991)
Baikal: Sacred Sea of Siberia (1992)
East of Lo Monthang: In the Land of Mustang (1995)
Tigers in the Snow (2000)
The Birds of Heaven: Travels with Cranes (2001)

FURTHER READING

Bonetti, Kay. "An Interview with Peter Matthiessen." *Missouri Review*, 12, no. 12 (1989): 109–124. Done with Bonetti's typical incisive questioning and sharp eye for detail, this interview examines Matthiessen's practice of Zen and his creative process.

Dowie, William. *Peter Matthiessen*. Boston, 1991. A biographical-critical work that details the author's career up to the publication of *Killing Mister Watson*.

Gatta, John. "Peter Matthiessen." In *American Writers: A Collection of Literary Biographies, Supplement V*. Edited by Jay Parini. New York, 2000. A biographical-critical overview of Matthiessen's long life and career, focusing a great deal of attention on the Watson trilogy and *The Snow Leopard*.

Roberson, William H. *Peter Matthiessen: An Annotated Bibliography*. Jefferson, N.C., 2001. A comprehensive listing of books and articles by and about Peter Matthiessen. An invaluable tool for discovering little-known primary or secondary works.

CORMAC McCARTHY

by Kimberly Lewis

Charles (Cormac) Joseph McCarthy Jr. was born on 20 July 1933 in Providence, Rhode Island. The family moved to Knoxville, Tennessee, in 1937, where Cormac grew up and attended Catholic school. He then studied at the University of Tennessee, first from 1951 to 1952 and then from 1957 to 1960, after four years in the U.S. Air Force. At Tennessee, he published his first two short stories, "Wake for Susan" (1959) and "A Drowning Incident" (1960), and left the university without a degree but with a grant—the first of many awards for his writing—from the Ingram-Merrill Foundation. In 1961, he married Lee Holleman, whom he divorced soon after the birth of his only son. Other than such skeletal details, the highly private writer has revealed little else about his early life, literary pursuits, or development.

His first novel, *The Orchard Keeper*, attracted the attention of William Faulkner's editor, Albert Erskine at Random House, and was published in 1965. Along with *Outer Dark* (1968), *Child of God* (1974), and the somewhat autobiographical *Suttree* (1979), it is set in the rural area near Knoxville, where the author lived with his second wife, Annie DeLisle, from 1966 to 1977. (In 1998, he married Jennifer Winkley.) These first novels were identified and praised by critics as "new" Southern literature and were grouped in with the work of other southern writers, including most notably William Faulkner, Robert Penn Warren, and Flannery O'Connor. McCarthy's characters, with regional dialects that recall certain Faulkner characters, are wanderers seeking an identity, alienated from the modernized and urban world, victims of and participants in the horrific violence of McCarthy's universe. These are all themes that reach their culmination in his fifth novel, *Blood Meridian* (1985).

His "southern" novels, along with a television screenplay, *The Gardener's Son* (1977), attracted little more than the attention of critics. Far from unimpressive, however, grants and awards, along with odd jobs, sufficed to support McCarthy's sparse lifestyle and his writing. They include the William Faulkner Foundation Award, a grant from the American Academy of Arts and Letters (with

which he traveled to Europe, where he met his second wife), a Rockefeller Foundation award, and a Guggenheim Fellowship. In 1981, four years after a life- and career-changing move to the Southwest, he was awarded a $236,000 "genius grant" from the MacArthur foundation. Nevertheless, both he and his writing remained surprisingly absent from the public scene, even after the publication of what is arguably his best novel, *Blood Meridian*.

TOWARD THE SOUTHWEST

With *Blood Meridian*, McCarthy became a southwestern writer. The tale is that of the kid, another searching and solitary orphan, whose capacity for violence earns him an invitation to join a band of Indian hunters on a murderous journey south and west, across the yet undefined and unbound wilderness of Mexico and the United States in the mid-nineteenth century. The novel is ruthlessly lyrical and violent, sweeping across a bloody and apocalyptic landscape; the Americans' only identity lies in their increasingly chaotic and undefined quest for massacre, dominance, and destruction. It is a vision of Manifest Destiny and western expansion in all its uncivilized and inglorious reality, laced with historical events and characters. It is also, however, a more universal vision of the brutality at the heart of human nature, of the insignificance of life in the hands of fate and endless repetition.

The dark antagonist of the nameless kid is Judge Holden, the most lucid, eloquent, and diabolical character of all of McCarthy's fiction. He appears out of nothing at the meridian of the day. He outlives all with unwavering confidence in his own godlike control over man and nature alike that, unlike the quest of Glanton and his band, never culminates in pure lust for riches or authority. He remains nothing more and nothing less than the calm and eternal catalyst of war and destruction, from his entrance into the kid's life to their final encounter, never reaching his own meridian:

The way of the world is to bloom and to flower and die but in the affairs of men there is no waning and the noon of his expression signals the onset of night. His spirit is exhausted at the peak of its achievement. His meridian is at once his darkening and the evening of his day. He loves games? Let him play for stakes. This you see here, these ruins wondered at by tribes of savages, do you not think that this will be again? Aye. And again. With other people, with other sons.

If the kid's turning away from violence upon reaching San Diego is a sign of his redemption, and if his initially innocent and later vehement opposition to Judge Holden indicates a possibility of triumph over evil and chaos, then the final scene of the dancing, fiddling judge whittles that possibility down to almost nothing.

Blood Meridian solidified McCarthy's place among the greatest living novelists—the book's depth, poetry, and intensity merit comparisons with not only his more obvious and continuing American influences, Herman Melville and Faulkner, but also with Shakespearean and Greek tragedy. Once again, despite critical acclaim, the novel only sold fifteen hundred copies. Popular recognition required the more traditional plot and protagonists of the first novel of the Border Trilogy, *All the Pretty Horses*.

THE BORDER TRILOGY

McCarthy's best-known book, *All the Pretty Horses*, appeared in 1992 and was soon adapted into a feature film by director Mike Nichols. Its release was accompanied by a rare interview in the 19 April 1992 *New York Times Magazine* that, however, did little to change the author's reputation as a recluse. At the time of the interview, he still resided in the Southwest, researching and writing (he writes only about places he knows), and occupied himself with various and numerous hobbies that he considers more interesting than talking about writing itself. He was inducted into the Southwest Writers Hall of Fame in El Paso in 1990, and in 1992 won the National Book Award for *All the Pretty Horses*. He published a play, *The Stonemason* (1994), and the other two highly successful pieces of the trilogy, *The Crossing* (1994) and *Cities of the Plain* (1998). Nevertheless, he continues to avoid photos and public appearances.

The Border Trilogy, set in the middle of the twentieth century, tells the tales of John Grady Cole and Billy Parham, two men of a dying breed of American cowboy. They have chosen to ignore the modernity of America, but they are capable neither of sinking into nor ignoring the past that, as in much Southern writing and here in McCarthy's postrevolutionary Mexico, is never really passed. As they live beside and cross over the border between America and Mexico, these characters attempt to exist in a narrow gap between a past and a future that is closing upon them.

The two men are as disoriented in modernity as the owl that crashes into Billy's truck at night in *Cities of the Plain*, and as doomed and determined as the wolf that Billy takes back to Mexico in *The Crossing*. Thus they turn south, with the practical and perhaps unconsciously metaphysical desire for new identity and expansion that is most often associated with the western frontier. As such, they are a glorification of the individual courage and values of that mythical American West. John Cole's devotion to Rawlins, Magdalena, and Alejandra, and Billy's attachment to the wolf, John, and Boyd, are rays of light cast upon McCarthy's otherwise still-sinister vision of human nature and destiny. Yet in their blind belief in the essential goodness and will of the individual, their ignorance of history, and their unconscious notions of moral and racial superiority, the protagonists also represent a harsh critique of the myth whose demise they witness and experience. They ultimately choose the only paths open to them, and they are those of the great tragic heroes of the Western tradition: death and exile.

The trilogy surpasses, however, this concrete tale of the American West. In a more spare and simple prose than that of *Blood Meridian*, McCarthy writes without the aid of such an articulate and conscious character as the judge. Instead, through the stories of secondary characters and of various prophets and sages met along the way, McCarthy provides glimpses into the region's and all of humanity's tragic past. His storytellers, themselves embattled and cast-out survivors of history and war, provide pieces of his obscure and eternally cyclical universe that, as the judge declares, did, does, and will exist long after even all traces of these tales have disappeared.

[*See also* Western Fiction.]

WORKS

The Orchard Keeper (1965)
Outer Dark (1968)
Child of God (1974)
Suttree (1979)
Blood Meridian; or, The Evening Redness in the West (1985)
All the Pretty Horses (1992)
The Crossing (1994)

The Stonemason (1994)
Cities of the Plain (1998)

FURTHER READING

Arnold, Edwin T., and Dianne C. Luce, eds. *Perspectives on Cormac McCarthy*. Jackson, Miss., 1993. Reprint of articles in Cormac McCarthy special issue of *Southern Quarterly* (Summer 1992).

Bell, Vereen M. *The Achievement of Cormac McCarthy*. Southern Literary Studies. Edited by Louis D. Rubin. Baton Rouge, La., 1988.

Bloom, Harold, ed. *Cormac McCarthy*. Philadelphia, 2002. A great collection of essays with partial emphasis on religion and violence.

Hall, Wade, and Rick Wallach, eds. *Sacred Violence: A Reader's Companion to Cormac McCarthy*. El Paso, Tex., 1995.

Jarrett, Robert L. *Cormac McCarthy*. New York, 1997. Good overview of McCarthy's work, especially with regard to postmodernism.

Lilley, James D., ed. *Cormac McCarthy: New Directions*. Albuquerque, N. Mex., 2002.

Sepich, John. *Notes on "Blood Meridian."* Louisville, Ky., 1993. Includes information on the historical facts contained in the fiction of *Blood Meridian*.

Woodward, Richard. "Cormac McCarthy's Venomous Fiction." *The New York Times Magazine* (19 April 1992). A rare and important interview with the author.

MARY McCARTHY

by Wendy Martin and Sharon Becker

Mary McCarthy's writing not only reflects a life lived across most of the twentieth century, but in its depth and breadth reveals a writer deeply engaged in the sociological, historical, and literary concerns of that tumultuous century. As America rapidly urbanized and commercialized and as its citizens embraced or rejected these developments, McCarthy's writing followed in step. McCarthy produced short stories, novels, and drama reviews as well as cultural and artistic critiques of modern America. Her fiction and nonfiction pieces are often deeply interrelated and share a profound concern with counterbalancing traditional approaches to race, class, and gender with more egalitarian cultural values. McCarthy's life defied conventional expectations for women living and working in the early decades of the twentieth century, and her writing mirrors her adventurous and forward-looking perspective. Though McCarthy openly wrote and lived against the grain, she was widely respected for her intellect, her sense of humor, and her wide-ranging literary contributions.

Mary McCarthy. (*Courtesy of the Library of Congress*)

CHILDHOOD AND YOUTH

McCarthy's ability to transcend the limitations of literary genres is a reflection of her own life, which was as turbulent as the century in which she lived. Born in Seattle, Washington, on 21 June 1912, Mary Therese McCarthy was orphaned along with her three younger brothers when her parents, Roy Winfield McCarthy and Therese (Tess) Preston McCarthy, died of influenza in the epidemic of 1918 while moving from Seattle to Minneapolis. This epidemic killed half a million people in the United States alone; more people died of influenza at this time than perished in World War I. Mary, then six, and her brothers—Kevin, four, Preston, three, and

Sheridan, one—were sent to live with their great-aunt Margaret Sheridan McCarthy and her husband, Myers Shriver.

As McCarthy's memoir, *Memories of a Catholic Girlhood* (1957), makes clear, the Shrivers provided little but the basics of human existence, if that. The children were exposed to abusive language; were expected to submit to severe punishment, including physical abuse; and were generally deprived of the nurturing environment they had previously known with their parents. Aunt Margaret cooked the children meals—consisting of cornmeal mush and cereal, prunes, rutabagas, and boiled potatoes—while she and her husband dined on, as McCarthy recalls in *Memories*, "pigs' feet and other delicacies." Aunt Margaret forced the children to play outside for six hours a day, no matter the weather, leaving them to their own devices to make up games to fill the time. As McCarthy remembers it, she and her brothers could often think of nothing else to do but "simply stand in the snow, crying."

Mary lived with the Shrivers for six years and then went to stay with her maternal grandparents, Harold and Augusta Preston, in Seattle, where her life was one of luxury and privilege. In Seattle, Mary attended the best Catholic schools in the area, easily learning Latin and discovering a love of writing. She was an outstanding student, winning prizes for essays and short stories. In 1929 McCarthy enrolled as an undergraduate at Vassar College, where she was immediately drawn to her courses in literature. In her second memoir, *How I Grew* (1987), McCarthy describes her blossoming love of reading the classics of English literature and the poetry and fiction of the American modernists; these replaced the popular romance and movie magazines she had favored in her high school years. Indeed, McCarthy's early writing reflects the

46

influence of her training in literature at Vassar in that this work unflinchingly creates a convergence of aesthetic and political concerns.

PERSONAL AND LITERARY DEVELOPMENT

In 1933, one week after graduation, Mary McCarthy, at age twenty-one, married an impoverished playwright named Harold Johnsrud. At the time McCarthy received financial support from her grandparents, which allowed her to take the risk of marrying Johnsrud, whom she thought to be her artistic and intellectual superior. Though McCarthy was attracting attention for a series of reviews written for *The Nation*, she still felt Johnsrud's writing career was more important than her own, an attitude reflecting the traditional assumption of masculine superiority in general. During these years, it was not easy to be a talented and ambitious woman when there was so much social resistance, and even hostility, toward powerful and accomplished women. In *How I Grew*, however, McCarthy admits that by her wedding night she was already regretting her marriage. She refers to this first marriage in her novel, *The Group* (1963), the story of a set of upper-middle- and upper-class girls who meet in college and grow to be very different kinds of women. In the novel Kay Strong, a smart and politically minded woman, marries a struggling playwright, Harald Petersen. Kay is caught between the choices of embracing traditional wifehood, which Harald seems to want, and maintaining the independent womanhood she gained in college.

After a series of extramarital affairs, McCarthy's marriage ended in divorce in 1936. She moved to an apartment in New York City's Greenwich Village and worked as an editorial assistant for the publisher Covici-Friede. The United States was in the midst of the Great Depression, and Greenwich Village was a center of great artistic and political ferment. Socially conscious writers such as John Dos Passos and Upton Sinclair, political activists, artists of all mediums, and those of simply a more bohemian bent were all drawn to the Village. McCarthy attended numerous Village parties, and her political values were honed while she listened to her friends argue over the finer points of communism. Aligning herself with Leon Trotsky, McCarthy embodies this political and social perspective in two of her short stories, "The Genial Host" and "Portrait of the Intellectual as a Yale Man," included in her singular collection of short stories, *The Company She Keeps* (1942). In both stories the female protagonist, Margaret Sargent, defends her political beliefs against men who align themselves with Joseph Stalin. In "The Genial

Host," Margaret attends a party and proudly defends Trotsky; she is pleased with herself for having an apparently persuasive effect on the party's guests until she realizes that she is giving the performance that the host, Pflaumen, expects. Thus, McCarthy deftly illuminates the position in which many women involved in political movements were placed: that of being an entertaining novelty whose intellect and opinions are not taken seriously.

In "Portrait of the Intellectual as a Yale Man," Margaret is placed again in the position of having to defend her beliefs against a man—in this instance, Jim Barnett, a shallow, clean-cut, all-American defender of Stalin who has been hired to work on a liberal and Stalinist-leaning magazine simply because he gives the magazine a wholesome and optimistic tone. By revealing her beliefs, Margaret risks losing her job and comes to learn that the stakes are high in the public workplace and that actions have palpable consequences. Margaret's integrity earns her the grudging respect of her peers and particularly of her political adversary: "You had to admire her courage," Jim thinks, "for undertaking something that cost her so much."

In the mid-1930s, McCarthy had an affair with Philip Rahv, a Ukrainian-born Marxist and the founder, with William Phillips, of *Partisan Review*. McCarthy and Rahv brought new life to the literary journal. Along with Dwight Macdonald, F. W. Dupee, and George L. W. Morris, Mary McCarthy served on the editorial board and was also drama critic for the journal. In 1938 McCarthy left Rahv and married Edmund Wilson, who was seventeen years older than she. A former managing editor of *Vanity Fair* and associate editor of *The New Republic*, Wilson was a well-respected and formidable literary critic as well as the author of an extremely influential book on literary modernism, *Axel's Castle* (1931). Though the match between this literary powerhouse and McCarthy, who was already capturing notice on the literary scene, would seem to be perfect, this was far from the truth.

Wilson and McCarthy's marriage, in fact, proved to be a destructive union that the McCarthy biographer Carol W. Gelderman has described as physically and emotionally abusive. Wilson's alcoholism-fueled behavior was destructive to McCarthy's self-esteem; at the same time, he was responsible for launching McCarthy's career in fiction. In the first year of their marriage, McCarthy said, Wilson insisted she stay in the study until she finished a short story. Submitting to Wilson's imperative, McCarthy wrote "Cruel and Barbarous Treatment," the story of her affair with John Porter, the man for whom she left her first husband. "Cruel and Barbarous Treatment" was published in the *Southern Review* in 1939. Following the success of this first story, McCarthy wrote several other related short stories that were eventually collected in *The Company She Keeps*. This collection drew the attention of *The New Yorker*, and McCarthy was asked to write for it.

McCarthy's literary career was taking off while her marriage to the man who, in some respects, helped make it possible was running aground. In 1945 McCarthy and the couple's six-year-old son, Reuel, moved into the Stanhope Hotel in New York City. At the deposition taken during the divorce proceedings, McCarthy cited "physical and mental humiliation" as her reason for securing a divorce. Just as McCarthy's marriage to Wilson served as a catalyst for her early writing, McCarthy's divorce from Wilson served as an impetus for an illustrious literary career.

A MATURE WRITER

In order to support herself and her son, McCarthy took a teaching position at Bard College for a year in 1945 and 1946. Though she decided not to return for a second year because she wanted to devote more time to her writing, McCarthy married her next husband, Bowden Broadwater, during her year at Bard. Eight years younger than McCarthy, Broadwater worked at *The New Yorker* and was impressed with her talent. Their fifteen years of marriage were some of the most productive of McCarthy's life. During that time she wrote *The Oasis* (1949), *Cast a Cold Eye* (1950), *The Groves of Academe* (1952), *A Charmed Life* (1955), *Sights and Spectacles* (1956), *Venice Observed* (1956), *The Stones of Florence* (1959), and *On the Contrary* (1961). McCarthy's writing during this time represents not only her maturation as a writer but also her increasing interest in engaging her readers in the larger political world.

Post–World War II New York City provided a very exciting and stimulating environment for artists and intellectuals as well as political activists. McCarthy was an organizer of and participant in the Europe-America groups of leftist artists and intellectuals, and her novel, *The Oasis*, was based on her own involvement in them. During this time McCarthy met Hannah Arendt, a philosopher whose works focus on the same issues of social injustice as McCarthy's. Their friendship lasted thirty years until Arendt's death in 1975. McCarthy, who was appointed Arendt's literary executor, took two years off from her own writing to edit and reorganize Arendt's *The Life of the Mind* (1978). The strong current of friendship between women surfaces as a theme in McCarthy's own work; for

example, the narrative intricacies of *The Group* tie together a group of college graduates who grow to womanhood within the nexus of their tightly bound friendships.

In December 1959, McCarthy, her son Reuel, and Broadwater left for a four-week tour of Poland where McCarthy was lecturing for the United States Information Agency. During the tour McCarthy fell in love with another man, James West, a public affairs officer for the American embassy. Though disappointed, Broadwater consented to a divorce, and McCarthy and West hoped to marry as soon as possible. However, West's children were young and his wife was unwilling to give him a divorce, so McCarthy continued to live and work in Europe while waiting for West to be free. The two were finally married in 1961.

McCarthy and West moved to Paris, where McCarthy finished *The Group*, which she had begun writing in the 1950s. The novel was published in 1963 to positive reviews and soon became a best-seller. While living in Paris, McCarthy embarked on the next phase of her writing career, in which she wrote books on a wide range of political issues. McCarthy's writing had always embodied political and cultural tensions and complexities in American culture. However, her more visible status as a writer of astute political insight stems in large part from the social changes brought about by the chaotic political and artistic experiments of the 1960s. During the 1960s and 1970s, McCarthy's books—*Vietnam* (1967), *Hanoi* (1968), *Medina* (1972), *The Seventeenth Degree* (1974), and *The Mask of State: Watergate Portraits* (1974)—were highly regarded as insightful commentary and critique of the political issues of those decades. In addition to writing about politics, McCarthy also wrote two more novels, *Birds of America* (1971) and *Cannibals and Missionaries* (1979); two books of literary criticism, *The Writing on the Wall and Other Literary Essays* (1970) and *Ideas and the Novel* (1980); and another autobiographical volume, *How I Grew*. At the time of her death at the age of seventy-seven of cancer in New York City on 25 October 1989, Mary McCarthy was widely recognized as one of the foremost American women writers and intellectuals.

CENTRAL THEMES

Throughout her long and successful career, McCarthy circled back to the same concerns. Whether she was writing short stories or penetrating criticisms of political issues, the politics of gender were repeatedly at the center of her writing. Like many other women of her generation, McCarthy resisted the label "feminist," but her work was clearly informed by a deeply held belief that traditional constructions of gender were ultimately destructive for both men and women. McCarthy understood that women needed to become economically independent from men in order to achieve psychological integrity; at the same time, it was almost impossible for her to create female characters that transcended the cultural limitations of their lives. Although the women in McCarthy's novels are liberated politically or sexually, they are often paradoxically hindered by their adherence to the traditional feminine code of passivity and dependence. McCarthy's women might give voice to striking out for a life of their own, but they are also waiting for a knight in shining armor to save them from the world and, by extension, themselves.

Margaret Sargent, the recurring character of the stories in *The Company She Keeps*, is a woman not unlike McCarthy herself. Sargent is a modern woman who struggles through marriage, divorce, and other intimate relationships; she is one of the rare women protagonists who actually has a job in the public sphere in American fiction. She is, then, a woman representative of the social and cultural concerns of the twentieth century. However, because she grew up in a culture that valued traditional femininity, her life is predicated on nurturing men who are morally, psychologically, or sexually weak. Her misplaced efforts to gain agency through the regeneration of these inappropriate men generally fail; ultimately, this narrative is an indictment of a restrictive, and even profoundly damaging, concept of redemptive womanhood.

Through the character of Margaret Sargent, McCarthy deconstructs the traditional trappings of courtship and love by demonstrating how these ideals damage relationships between women and men. As the romantic heroine, Margaret knowingly (and often begrudgingly) accepts the performative qualities of romance. For example, in "The Man in the Brooks Brothers Shirt," Margaret really does not want to be seduced by the man on the train, but she reflexively accepts this traditional scenario because no appealing alternative scripts seem available to her. However, her experience in the context of this seduction is one of self-abnegation; Margaret Sargent feels like a "slab of white lamb on an altar," but at the same time she feels "illuminated" by what she experiences as her self-sacrifice. McCarthy does not simply criticize the romantic performance as a patriarchal structure to create powerless and subjugated women; she also makes it clear that women are complicit in the creation of their own powerlessness and places pressure on women to examine their own false consciousness,

which eclipses their pursuit of self-knowledge. These concerns are repeated in McCarthy's later novel, *The Group*. However, here McCarthy creates the characters of the androgynous Helena and Lakey, a lesbian, who represent a protest against the submission to traditional gender roles that prove destructive to the other women in this group of friends.

In *The Company She Keeps*, Margaret Sargent is finally capable of attempting to reorder her own consciousness, but she still has to deal with the fact that the men in her life—and in the larger world in which she lives—are generally unaware of their egotistical masculinity. Trapped in infantile and self-indulgent behavior, as with the characters of Mr. Sheer in "Rogue's Gallery" and Pflaumen in "The Genial Host," or saddled with an inflated sense of self-importance, as with the Yale man, Jim Barnett, in "Portrait of the Intellectual as a Yale Man," the men in McCarthy's stories are ultimately ill equipped to embark on a rigorous examination of themselves and of their place in the world. This criticism of monolithic masculinity is echoed in later McCarthy works such as *The Mask of State: Watergate Portraits*. McCarthy crafts descriptions of the Watergate group that portray its politicians as self-indulgent, arrogant, and domineering, matching the fictional men in *The Company She Keeps* flaw for flaw.

Particularly interesting in McCarthy's career is the inclusion of her own life as a literary representation of a woman's struggle in the world. *In Memories of a Catholic Girlhood*, McCarthy steps outside of her childhood to focus on it from both historical and political perspectives. To better understand herself, McCarthy goes beyond the boundaries of her own life to examine the life of her grandmother, thereby connecting the life of one woman to the lives of all women. McCarthy's grandmother, Augusta Preston, a woman renowned for her beauty, represents the nineteenth-century ideal of decorative, static femininity that must be rendered powerless and anachronistic in order for McCarthy to control her own place in the world. Through heightened scrutiny of the importance that her grandmother placed on her status as a great beauty, McCarthy frees herself from the painful legacy of womanhood as a state of perpetual silence and ornamentality.

Conversely, McCarthy writes of her great aunt, Rosie Morgenstern Gottstein, as an illustration of a beauty that belies simple ornamentation. McCarthy looked to this aunt—bright, vibrant, and opinionated—as a model of twentieth-century womanhood. By contrast, McCarthy invokes the life her other great aunt, Eva, as one of mindlessness conventionality. Though McCarthy and her readers understand each of these women to be bound by the constrictions and limitations of traditional femininity at the time in which they live, by connecting them to the narrative of McCarthy's own life of a later period, she reanimates them as illustrations of an ongoing construction of limited feminine spheres. Discarding these traditional constructions as she moves through her narrative, McCarthy symbolically separates herself, and her readers, from the damaging effects of this gendered past. In her own life McCarthy stood in opposition to many of the powerless women she portrayed in her novels; in her work McCarthy aspired to the passionate and powerful ideals of contemporary womanhood.

Throughout her career, Mary McCarthy wrote about herself and her characters with the same unrelenting pursuit of truth. With each changing decade of the twentieth century, McCarthy reinvented her writing to reflect relevant social and political concerns as well as her personal priorities. From fiction and autobiography to literary and cultural criticism and political reportage and satire, McCarthy explores and exposes the underlying cultural assumptions of masculine privilege and the politics of gender, and she demands that her readers be as engaged as she was in the struggle to recognize that patriarchal values have repercussions far outside of the American home.

[See also Academic Novels and Wilson, Edmund.]

SELECTED WORKS

The Company She Keeps (1942)
The Oasis (1949)
Cast a Cold Eye (1950)
The Groves of Academe (1952)
A Charmed Life (1955)
Sights and Spectacles, 1937–1956 (1956)
Venice Observed (1956)
Memories of a Catholic Girlhood (1957)
The Stones of Florence (1959)
On the Contrary (1961)
The Group (1963)
Mary McCarthy's Theatre Chronicles, 1937–1962 (1963)
Vietnam (1967)
Hanoi (1968)
The Writing on the Wall and Other Literary Essays (1970)
Birds of America (1971)
Medina (1972)

The Mask of State: Watergate Portraits (1974)
The Seventeenth Degree (1974)
Cannibals and Missionaries (1979)
Ideas and the Novel (1980)
The Hounds of Summer and Other Stories (1981)
Occasional Prose (1985)
How I Grew (1987)
Intellectual Memoirs: New York, 1936–1938 (1992)

FURTHER READING

Brightman, Carol. *Writing Dangerously: Mary McCarthy and Her World*. New York, 1992. Brightman examines McCarthy from three perspectives: her personal life, her literary process, and her political interests.

Brightman, Carol, ed. *Between Friends: The Correspondence of Hannah Arendt and Mary McCarthy, 1949–1975*. New York, 1995. Traces the friendship between Arendt and McCarthy through their letters to each other. Of interest to scholars curious about the private thoughts of two public women.

Gelderman, Carol W. *Mary McCarthy: A Life*. New York, 1988. This biography should interest readers looking for a cohesive account of McCarthy's life and work.

Gelderman, Carol W., ed. *Conversations with Mary McCarthy*. Jackson, Miss., 1998.

Grumbach, Doris. *The Company She Kept*. New York, 1967.

Hardy, Willene Schaefer. *Mary McCarthy*. New York, 1981.

Kiernan, Francis. *Seeing Mary Plain*. New York, 2000. An examination of McCarthy's life and works through the words of her friends and literary contemporaries.

McKenzie, Barbara. *Mary McCarthy*. New York, 1966.

Stock, Irvin. *Mary McCarthy*. Minneapolis, Minn., 1968.

Stwertka, Eve, and Margo Viscusi, eds. *Twenty-four Ways of Looking at Mary McCarthy*. Westport, Conn., 1996. Divided into five sections, this book examines McCarthy's contribution to the intellectual culture of the United States, her relationship to Judaism, the influence of Edmund Wilson on her writing, her appearance as a fictional character in the writing of others, and McCarthy's use of her own life in her writing.

Taylor, Gordon O. "The Word for Mirror: Mary McCarthy." In his *Chapters of Experience: Studies in Twentieth Century American Autobiography*. New York, 1983.

J. D. McCLATCHY

by Heather Stephenson

Influential as a poet, critic, and editor at the turn of the twenty-first century, J. D. McClatchy is recognized for his erudition, verbal virtuosity, and interest in traditional poetic forms. He is also known for his friendship with the older poet James Merrill, whose literary executor he became after Merrill's death in 1995. Like his mentor, McClatchy writes with elegant lyricism and witty word-play. The elaborately polished surfaces of his early poems make it difficult to see more than their artful shimmer, but the technical mastery displayed in his later work allows his deeper moral concerns to shine through.

In addition to writing five books of poetry and two collections of essays, McClatchy has edited more than a dozen other volumes, including *The Vintage Book of Contemporary World Poetry* (1996) and *Love Speaks Its Name: Gay and Lesbian Love Poems* (2001). He has served as editor of *The Yale Review* since 1991 and as a chancellor of the Academy of American Poets since 1996 and has won fellowships from the Guggenheim Foundation and the National Endowment for the Arts. McClatchy's other awards include the Witter Bynner Award for poetry from the American Academy of Arts and Letters. He lives in Stonington, Connecticut, and New York City with his partner, the book designer and writer Chip Kidd.

Joseph Donald McClatchy Jr. was born in Bryn Mawr, Pennsylvania, on 12 August 1945. He attended a Jesuit high school, where he was introduced to the Latin and Greek classics that would later serve as models for his own writing. He earned a bachelor's degree summa cum laude from Georgetown University in 1967 and a doctorate in English from Yale University in 1974. The Vietnam War interrupted his graduate studies, but he avoided the draft by teaching English at two Philadelphia colleges and began reading contemporary poetry in his spare time, discovering a new focus for his studies. His doctoral thesis examined the traditions of American confessional poetry.

As a graduate student and young writer, McClatchy cultivated friendships with poets he admired. He met such greats as Elizabeth Bishop, W. H. Auden, Robert Lowell, and Anne Sexton, but in his quest for literary

forebears, James Merrill filled a primary role. An openly gay, apolitical man with cosmopolitan tastes and family money, Merrill wrote in traditional and invented forms with fastidious rigor, genially beating out his own musical path at a time when most poets were dancing to the irregular drum of free verse. McClatchy, still finding his own footing, met Merrill in 1972 after writing him a fan letter. As he tells it, Merrill impressed him as dauntingly sophisticated at first but soon became a friend to turn to for advice on everything from failed romance to poetic revision. McClatchy eventually moved to the seaside Connecticut town that had long been Merrill's home and still maintains a residence there. He and fellow American poet and scholar Stephen Yenser are Merrill's literary executors and have together edited his *Collected Poems* (2001). McClatchy is also the editor of *Recitative: Prose by James Merrill* (1986).

ALWAYS A STYLIST

McClatchy has always been a consummate stylist, working with traditional poetic forms even when they have been out of style. However, he does not class himself among the New Formalists. In *Twenty Questions* (1998), he criticizes the poets of that school for what he considers their narrow aims and "plodding, inaccurate lines." His own aim is to employ the traditional tools of the poetic craft—manipulating the shape and rhythm of a line, for example, or controlling its tone through the careful choice of a word—so skillfully that they help convey emotional and moral truths about the self.

McClatchy's early poems exhibit the strengths and flaws of his apprenticeship to masters such as Merrill, Auden, and Wallace Stevens. His first two books won ambivalent accolades for their virtuosity, which was perceived as either elegant style or rococo excess depending on the taste of the critic. But one section of his second collection, *Stars Principal* (1986), suggests that McClatchy was moving toward a more intimate and relaxed poetics. The long poem, titled "First Steps," offers a candid, often humorous narrative of McClatchy's struggle to come to terms with his homosexuality, from a childhood crush on a camp counselor called Red ("The namesake stubble, the sweatband, the upstart / Nipple" all seen during naptime) to the 1970s disco scene ("All that small talk / While a fantasy hurriedly undressed was getting / Nowhere"). As he writes about coming out as a gay man, McClatchy seems also to be coming out of the closet of his earlier, opaque style and into a more open, direct art.

While McClatchy writes from his perspective as a gay man, he does not expressly set out to compose "gay poems," and he eschews overt political agendas regarding sexuality or other issues of the day. Being gay, like being white, is part of his subjectivity, but it is not his subject. McClatchy edited a collection of lesbian and gay love poems, but he writes approvingly of Elizabeth Bishop's refusal to be included in any all-female anthology, seeing in it a fierce resistance to poetic isolation. He has also argued that the partial appeal of poetic subgroups undermines a poet's true function, which he says is to write a masterpiece.

McClatchy articulates his developing poetic aesthetic in the critical essays of the acclaimed 1989 volume *White Paper*. In its opening broadside, he decries the bland middlebrow poems that he says creative writing programs are churning out across the country. "Anything goes—as often as not in one ear and out the other," he quips, then calls for a poetry that fuses passion with artistic discipline, reinvigorating the formal conventions of the past. The remainder of the book is composed of close, sympathetic readings of poets he admires, particularly those whose work is often deemed difficult.

In the 1980s, McClatchy found a new outlet for his lyrical impulse in writing opera librettos. By 1996 he had written four: *A Question of Taste* (1989), *Mario and the Magician* (1994), *Orpheus Descending* (1994), and *Emmeline* (1996). He has also written the texts for several song cycles and translated the librettos of two operas, *The Magic Flute* (2000) and *Carmen* (2001). McClatchy says he has learned as much about writing poetry from listening to the music of composers such as Gustav Mahler and J. S. Bach as by reading. His command of sophisticated metrics and rhyme is evident in his own poems, and his admiration of such skill is clear in his criticism. He even extends his praise to American musical theater lyrics like those of the writer and composer Stephen Sondheim.

Yet it is in the literary and academic establishment that McClatchy continues to make his professional home. He taught at Yale through much of the 1970s and at Princeton University in the 1980s and early 1990s as well as at other universities. At *The Yale Review*, where he had served as poetry editor since 1980, he was promoted to editor in 1991.

His third volume of poems, *The Rest of the Way* (1990), was hailed as a poetic breakthrough. The book is a formal tour de force that climaxes in a series of linked sonnets titled "Kilim," in which McClatchy plays the instrument of language as skillfully as a coloratura sings. Throughout the volume, he seems at greater ease than before, his cadenzas no longer the labored efforts of an apprentice but the casual play of a man in command of his voice. Critics recognized the difference. A citation from the American Academy of Arts and Letters said that McClatchy might prove to be the most eloquent American poet of his generation.

McClatchy's newfound ease affected his prose as well. His second collection, *Twenty Questions*, includes highly readable autobiographical pieces along with its literary criticism. (One delightful essay links McClatchy's love of verbal disguise to being gay.) In the critical essays, he continues to praise those poets who extend the formal possibilities of their craft.

Twenty Questions was published at the same time as McClatchy's fourth volume of poetry, *Ten Commandments* (1998), a collection that confirmed his place among the nation's preeminent poets. In a tribute to the classical tradition that McClatchy admires, both books end with versions of poems by Horace. Rather than a literal translation from the original Latin, though, McClatchy offers up a lively transformation in "Late Night Ode," the widely anthologized poem that concludes *Ten Commandments*. The ode opens: "It's over, love. Look at me pushing fifty now, / Hair like grave-grass growing in both ears, / The piles and boggy prostate, the crooked penis." Like all McClatchy's best poems, this one combines the emotional candor of contemporary confessional poetry with the rhythmical precision of formal verse. As a mature poet, McClatchy moves beyond the mannered artifice of his early years and fulfills the injunction he translates from Horace's "Art of Poetry": "It's not enough that poems be exquisite. / Let empathy prevail and lead the listener's / Heart."

[*See also* Auden, W. H.; Bishop, Elizabeth; Lowell, Robert; Merrill, James; *and* Sexton, Anne.]

WORKS

Scenes from Another Life (1981)
Stars Principal (1986)
White Paper (1989)
The Rest of the Way (1990)

Twenty Questions (1998)
Ten Commandments (1998)
Hazmat (2002)

FURTHER READING

Logan, William. *Reputations of the Tongue: On Poets and Poetry*. Gainesville, Fla., 1999. Logan's discussion of McClatchy, found on pp. 171–174, covers the period through *The Rest of the Way*.

Link, Matt. "Pocketful of Poetry." *Los Angeles Advocate* (3 July 2001): 64. A short interview focusing on McClatchy as gay poet and editor.

McClatchy, J. D. "On 'My Mammogram.'" In *Introspections: American Poets on One of Their Own Poems*, edited by Robert Pack and Jay Parini. Hanover, N.H., 1997. Discussing how he wrote "My Mammogram," McClatchy illuminates broader issues about his approach to writing.

Stein, Lorin. "Confessions of a Poet: A Profile of J. D. McClatchy." *Poets & Writers Magazine* (January–February 1998): 30–43. A solid overview of McClatchy's life and work, including information gleaned from an interview with the poet as well as a brief commentary on his "Late Night Ode."

Trosky, Susan M., ed. *Contemporary Authors*. New Revision Series. Vol. 44, pp. 297–299. Washington, D.C., 1994. Detailed, though dated, entry on McClatchy includes bibliography.

CARSON McCULLERS

by Louis H. Palmer, III

To those who study her work, as well as to the public in general, Carson McCullers remains an enigma. Becoming a world-famous novelist by her middle twenties must have been quite a shock for a young woman from a small town. As she said to Rex Reed in her last interview, "I became an established literary figure overnight, and I was much too young to understand what happened to me or the responsibility it entailed. I was a bit of a holy terror. That, combined with all my illnesses, nearly destroyed me." Her literary career followed a stunningly productive decade, followed by twenty years in which she produced, comparatively, very little. This is generally attributed to the fact that she suffered from a series of debilitating physical conditions, including partial paralysis induced by stroke, breast cancer, and accidental injuries. These were further complicated by an array of psychological problems, including, according to some accounts, severe depression, suicidal tendencies, alcoholism, and a destructive, codependent relationship with the man she married twice, Reeves McCullers, who committed suicide in 1953.

McCullers seems to demonstrate, even embody, a series of contradictions. Was she a semieducated phenomenon from the provinces or a sophisticated literary figure from New York City's bohemian fringe? A devoted war wife, a closeted lesbian, or a bisexual adventuress? A minor writer with one theme or an important voice in the late modern period of American literature? A shy southern woman or a shameless self-promoter? A loyal and generous friend or a selfish egotist who used people as stepping stones? She has been described in all of these ways.

EARLY CAREER TO 1947

Born Lula Carson Smith on 19 February 1917, McCullers came from a respectable but not particularly affluent

Carson McCullers, 1959. (*Photograph by Carl Van Vechten. Courtesy of the Library of Congress*)

family in Columbus, Georgia, a medium-sized mill town on the western border with Alabama, situated near Fort Benning, a large military base. According to her biographer, Virginia Spencer Carr, Lula Carson's childhood was a normal one for the time and place. A dual interest in music and writing during her late teens is attested to by the fact that her father bought her first a piano and later a typewriter.

Carson (she dropped the "Lula" in her early teens) was an indifferent student who spent much of her out-of-school time practicing the piano. Much has been made of some fairly obvious connections between the young woman and her adolescent heroines, especially Mick Kelley in *The Heart Is a Lonely Hunter* (1940) and Frankie Adams in *The Member of the Wedding* (1946). Certainly, many of the settings, and presumably the characters and themes, found in her works correlate with her life, but it is difficult, and finally fruitless, to argue that any character is or is not an accurate version of the author's past.

At age seventeen Carson traveled to New York City, where she lived on and off for two years and enrolled in creative writing classes taught by Sylvia Chatfield Bates at New York University and Whit Burnett at Columbia University. In 1935, while back home, she met a young soldier, Reeves McCullers. In late 1936 she returned home with an illness, which was later believed to be rheumatic fever misdiagnosed as tuberculosis, and which probably did some of the physical damage responsible for her later strokes and heart disease. At this time she published her first story, "Wunderkind," in *Story*, a literary magazine. She and Reeves married in September 1937 and moved to Charlotte, North Carolina, where he worked for a credit company as an investigator. Later they moved to Fayetteville, another army post town located near Fort

Bragg, North Carolina. During these two years Carson completed two manuscripts, "The Mute" and "Army Post," which would become *The Heart Is a Lonely Hunter* and *Reflections in a Golden Eye* (1941). She submitted an outline of "The Mute" to Houghton Mifflin's contest for new fiction and received second prize, $500, and a contract to publish the finished manuscript. After she sent off this manuscript, she began to "amuse herself" by writing *Reflections in a Golden Eye*, a "fairy-tale" which she claimed to have written in two months. She also came up with the beginnings of a story of a three-way love affair, titled "The Bride and Her Brother," which would become *The Member of the Wedding*.

The Heart Is a Lonely Hunter was published in June 1940 to generally positive reviews. The title was an editorial choice, not McCullers's own. The novel revolves around a deaf-mute, John Singer, who attracts a series of small-town characters: Mick Kelley, an adolescent girl with musical aspirations; Jake Blount, a would-be Marxist reformer and an alcoholic; Benedict Copeland, an African-American doctor who wants racial reform; and Biff Brannon, a café owner who observes and comforts the others. Each character confesses to Singer, who is unable to communicate, and thus they form a cluster of isolated interests around a "center" who does not really understand their situations or what he means to them. Eventually he commits suicide, driven to despair by the death of his beloved, Antonopolis, another deaf-mute who was institutionalized and who had no idea of his importance to Singer. By the end of the novel, every character is further isolated and trapped, further away from his or her dreams. Mick Kelley is unable to escape to the greater world, as her creator did.

Carson and Reeves moved to Greenwich Village, where they participated in the lively literary gatherings of that time and place. In the summer of 1940, she attended the Breadloaf Writer's Conference in Vermont, where she met a variety of writers and critics, including John Ciardi, Louis Untermeyer, Katherine Anne Porter, and another young southerner, Eudora Welty. Returning to the city, she separated from Reeves and moved into a brownstone at 7 Middagh Street in Brooklyn Heights, just over the Brooklyn Bridge from Manhattan. This location, also known as February House, became legendary. Carson McCullers, W. H. Auden, and George Davis, the literary editor at *Harper's Bazaar*, ran a sort of bohemian boarding house there for artists and writers and their families. At one time or another in the next three years, guests and boarders included

Gypsy Rose Lee, the actress famous for having been a stripper; Richard Wright, the African-American novelist and author of *Native Son* (1940); Benjamin Britten, the avant-garde composer; Paul Bowles, the composer and the author of *The Sheltering Sky* (1949); Salvador Dali, the surrealist painter; Christopher Isherwood, the British playwright; the poet Louise MacNeice; and many others. This period is described by Carr as "a queer ménage" and presented as distracting and ruinous to Carson's health. By other accounts it was a time and place of creative ferment, where the young writer came into her own as a witty conversationalist and social manager. She alternated periods in Brooklyn with two long stretches at Yaddo, the writer's colony in Saratoga Springs, New York, and visits to Columbus to recover from bouts of illness.

From 1941 to 1943 McCullers published *Reflections in a Golden Eye*, continued work on *The Member of the Wedding*, and published a variety of short pieces. *Reflections in a Golden Eye* takes place on "an army post in peacetime." This short novel tells the story of an odd group of characters. Hypermasculine Major Langdon is having an affair with Captain Penderton's sensualist wife, Leonora. The analytic and compulsive Penderton harbors a secret desire for Private Elcee Williams. Langdon's neurotic wife Alison is cared for by an effeminate Filipino houseboy, Anacleto. She eventually mutilates herself by cutting off her nipples with garden shears and is placed in an institution, where she dies of a heart attack. Meanwhile, Private Williams, who cares for Leonora's horse, starts sneaking into her house to watch her as she sleeps. When Penderton discovers him, he shoots him. Again, no resolution that the novel provides benefits any of the characters, and here the most simple and brutal characters, Langdon and Leonora, seem to be the happiest.

During these three years in the early 1940s, McCullers—in addition to her invitations to stay at Yaddo—received a Guggenheim Fellowship and an American Academy of Arts and Letters grant. She initiated a divorce from Reeves when she discovered that he was forging checks in her name.

McCullers wrote *Ballad of the Sad Café* at Yaddo in 1941. It was published to little notice in *Harper's Bazaar* in August 1943. This novella follows a love triangle. Amelia Evans, a small-town general store owner, herb doctor, and moonshiner who looks and dresses like a man, falls in love with her cousin, Lymon Willis, a narcissistic hunchback dwarf. She changes her stingy ways and opens her store as a café, where he shows off. When her former husband, Marvin Macy, is released from prison and comes back to town, Lymon falls in love with him and follows him around. Eventually, Amelia and Marvin fight and Lymon intervenes to help Marvin win. The two men destroy the café and leave Ameila to waste slowly away. Compared with the earlier works, the story has a more intrusive narrator who functions as a not necessarily reliable commentator on the action, emphasizing the failure of love to be reciprocal.

The World War II years were ones of change for McCullers. Her father died from heart failure in August 1944 and her mother moved to Nyack, New York, where she eventually bought a house. Reeves, back in the army, led a battalion of Rangers, participating in the Normandy invasion. On his return, he and Carson remarried in 1945. *The Member of the Wedding* was published in March 1946. In this novel, Frances "Frankie" Adams, a twelve-year-old girl, spends a summer hanging around the kitchen talking to Berenice, an African-American cook, and John Henry, her six-year-old cousin. She develops an elaborate fantasy about becoming a "member of the wedding" of her brother and his bride. She decides that the three of them will become "the we of me" and go off on the honeymoon together. When she has to be physically restrained from joining the honeymooners, her dream comes to an abrupt end. By the end of the novel she seems to be reconciled to her new, more mature and more feminine role and has found a friend her own age. The novel abounds with imagery of people with "half" identities who fit into neither one nor the other of accepted categories, exemplified by the "morphodite" at the circus freak show.

THE FINAL TWENTY YEARS

Twenty years before her death, McCullers had completed her major work. While visiting Europe with Reeves, McCullers suffered two strokes in August and November of 1947. Her left side was paralyzed and would give her trouble for the rest of her life. In 1948 she separated from Reeves, was hospitalized for attempted suicide, and spent time on Nantucket. There, McCullers shared a house with Tennessee Williams and worked on a dramatization of *The Member of the Wedding*. The stage version opened on Broadway in January 1950 with Julie Harris as Frankie and Ethel Waters as Berenice. It won several awards and ran for 501 performances. It made enough money, along with the sale of its movie rights, to guarantee the author's financial well-being for the final sixteen years of her life.

During those years McCullers's physical problems increased and her literary productivity decreased. Reconciled once again to Reeves, she lived with him in a country house in France until his increasingly threatening and suicidal behavior drove her away. In November 1953 he killed himself in a hotel in Paris. In 1955 her mother died. *The Square Root of Wonderful* (1958) was a play about a woman with a charming, creative, but suicidal husband and an overbearing mother. It was produced on Broadway starring Anne Baxter (a well-known and critically respected film and stage actress) in late 1957. McCullers was bitterly disappointed when it received stinging reviews and closed after only forty-five performances. Her subsequent episode of depression was alleviated by treatment received from Dr. Mary Mercer, a psychoanalyst who became one of Carson's closest friends. McCullers underwent a series of surgeries to restore mobility in her left side and hands, but needed constant care. She became increasingly dependent on her nurse-housekeeper, Ida Reeder, a southern black woman whom she called Sister, and who was with her from 1954 until her death in 1967.

McCullers's final novel, *Clock without Hands*, on which she had been working since the early 1950s, was published in 1961 to mixed reviews. It was her most political novel since *The Heart Is a Lonely Hunter* and focused on issues of sexual identity and racial conflict in the segregated South. The plot centers around three characters: Judge Fox Clane, an aging segregationist going soft in the head; his grandson, Jester Clane, a high school senior with homosexual tendencies; and J. T. Malone, a pharmacist dying of leukemia. The action takes place in a small southern town during the year previous to the 1954 Supreme Court decision that abolished legal segregation. Jester has been raised by the judge, but finds himself attracted to Sherman Pew, a blue-eyed African-American orphan (found in a church, hence his surname). When Sherman moves into a white neighborhood, Malone and the judge meet as part of a vigilante group, but Malone refuses to go through with the bombing they plan. Jester warns Sherman, who brushes off the threat. After Pew is assassinated, Jester takes the man who did it up in his airplane to kill him, but chooses against revenge. The novel ends with the senile judge reciting the Gettysburg Address over the radio as a segregationist response to the Supreme Court decision. Malone dies peacefully. Despite lukewarm reviews, the book was on the best-seller lists for some months.

In 1962 McCullers was diagnosed with breast cancer and her right breast was removed. She collaborated with Edward Albee on a dramatic version of *The Ballad of the Sad Café*, which was moderately successful on Broadway in 1963–1964.

McCullers's final years saw more physical problems, including injuries from a fall. Films were made of three of her novels. *The Member of the Wedding* had been filmed with the Broadway cast and released in 1952. A film version of *The Heart Is a Lonely Hunter* was released in 1967 after her death. Her last major trip was a visit to Ireland to stay at film director John Huston's estate. He was in the editing phase after directing Elizabeth Taylor and Marlon Brando in *Reflections in a Golden Eye*. Carson suffered a major brain hemorrhage in August and died on 29 September 1967. She left several unfinished projects, including her autobiographical *Illumination and Night Glare*, which was published in 1999.

ART AND LIFE

Carson McCullers's life has been discussed here in some detail because, as already mentioned, there is a fair amount of correspondence between her experiences and the characters and settings about which she wrote. This is especially true in the minds of her readers, reviewers, and critics. With a few important exceptions, much of the work about McCullers focuses on "the world of Carson McCullers—a world of the lost, the injured, the eternal strangers at life's feast," to quote the Bantam paperback promotional blurb from 1971. Because she published her first novel at such an early age, because many of her characters are adolescent girls, and even because of her childlike physique (very large eyes in a round face and a thin, long-limbed body), she is often presented as a child genius or even a childlike simpleton. In a similar vein, because of her on-again, off-again relationship with Reeves and because she wrote stories where married people often had problems and the path of love did not follow the norms of gender expectations, she has been seen as a "queer" of various types, as well as a bad wife and partner. Because she became ill and was partially disabled from the time she was age thirty, her themes of bodily deformity and the grotesque have been emphasized.

As can be seen from these examples, the line between author and work has been seriously breached and has served to blind readers from seeing her as a conscious artist and careful craftsperson. Also, in the sixty-two years since the first novel was published, a variety of critical perspectives have been brought to bear on her work, each with its own set of blinders. The situation is further complicated by the fact that the writer herself was by necessity a critic and as such produced her own interpretive frameworks, which may have served her own needs and understandings but cannot be taken as ultimate truths.

CRITICAL REPUTATION

Judith Giblin James's *Wunderkind: The Reputation of Carson McCullers, 1940–1990* (1995) describes a development from "the protective enthusiasm of her earliest critics" through the New Critical formalism of the 1950s and 1960s, which tended to stress the themes of isolation, alienation, and adolescent angst set against a universal quest for Self or God. More specifically located interpretations were the psychoanalytic approaches of critics like David Madden that emerged in the 1970s and the feminist readings like those of Louise Westling in the 1980s, leading into a subsequent focus on gender identity and racial conflict, initiated by Gayatri Spivak's brilliant 1979 essay. James notes "the general and longstanding failure to explore the connection [McCullers] establishes between individualized and institutionalized cruelties" as a possibility for future work. Most of the important critical work can be found in one of the two essay collections, Harold Bloom's *Carson McCullers* (1986) and Beverly Lyon Clark and Melvin Friedman's *Critical Essays on Carson McCullers* (1996). Two articles are particularly noteworthy: Charles Hannon's cultural look at *Ballad of the Sad Café* in the light of women's labor issues of the 1940s and Rachael Adams's discussion of racial and gender blurring that moves away from either homosexual or heterosexual identity in the fiction toward a critique of the "normal" in both sexual-gender and racial terms. These two articles demonstrate the vitality of McCullers's scholarship as unitary readings give way to more culturally nuanced interpretations.

The question of the importance of Carson McCullers has yet to be resolved. Her themes and settings have caused her to be placed in the school of Southern Gothic or grotesque writers, formerly pejorative terms that subsequently have been treated as genres of interest. Her work has found a solid place in high school curricula, and she continues to be popular for a literary writer. What had been seen as modernist alienation has since been perceived as acute social analyses of difference and oppression within the contexts of gender, sexuality, race, region, and class. Critical opinion has tended to valorize the first four novels over *Clock without Hands* and to suggest that McCullers is a better novelist than she is a playwright, essayist, memoirist, or short-story writer. But more careful attention is being paid to her work as a whole and the establishment in 1997 of the Carson McCullers Society of the American Literature Association demonstrates the continuing scholarly interest in this provocative writer.

[*See also* Auden, W. H., *and* Wright, Richard.]

SELECTED WORKS

The Heart Is a Lonely Hunter (1940)
Reflections in a Golden Eye (1941)
The Ballad of the Sad Café (1943)
The Member of the Wedding (1946)
The Square Root of Wonderful (1958)
Clock without Hands (1961)
Collected Stories of Carson McCullers (1987)
Illumination and Night Glare (1999)
Complete Novels (2000)

FURTHER READING

Adams, Rachael. "A Mixture of Delicious and Freak: The Queer Fiction of Carson McCullers." *American Literature*. 71.3 (September 1999): 551–583. An excellent example of a new body of work on McCullers that examines her use of ideas of "in-betweenness" and indeterminacy to look at gender issues.

Bloom, Harold, ed. *Carson McCullers*. New York, 1986. The first collection of essays on McCullers.

Carr, Virginia Spencer. *The Lonely Hunter*. Garden City, N.Y., 1975. This biography set a new standard for literary biographies. It is an incredibly detailed work in a readable, almost conversational style. Carr is a southern academic, and this book reclaims McCullers for the South. Carr's Carson seems to want to be a good, respectable, middle-class southern woman and one gets the impression that she was subject to a series of bad influences, mainly emanating from a certain northern urban area. Nonetheless, this book is a great read and an indispensable source, based on interviews with McCullers's family, friends, neighbors, acquaintances, and enemies and on the extensive documentary archives at the Harry Ransom Humanities Research Center, University of Texas, Austin.

Carr, Virginia Spencer. *Understanding Carson McCullers*. Columbia, S.C., 1990. Relates biographical material to works.

Clark, Beverly Lyon, and Melvin Friedman, eds. *Critical Essays on Carson McCullers*. New York, 1996. Second collection of materials on McCullers. Includes reviews of all the major works, tributes by other authors, and a selection of critical essays.

Cook, Richard M. *Carson McCullers*. New York, 1975.

Edmonds, Dale. *Carson McCullers*. Austin, Tex., 1969.

Evans, Oliver. *Carson McCullers, Her Life and Work*. London, 1965. Reprinted as *The Ballad of Carson McCullers: An Intimate Biography* in 1966. The only biography published during McCullers's lifetime, it is based on extensive interviews with her as well as interviews with friends and family. Evans is an academic and his Carson comes off as a brilliant, if afflicted, intellectual.

Gaver, Lawrence. *Carson McCullers*. Minneapolis, Minn., 1969.

Hannon, Charles. "*The Ballad of the Sad Café* and Other Stories of Women's Wartime Labor." In *Bodies in Performance*, edited by Thomas Foster. New York, 1996. Looks at the novel in the context of its World War II–era publication in *Harper's Bazaar* and examines the magazine itself for clues to the gender-based ideology of the time.

James, Judith Giblin. *Wunderkind: The Reputation of Carson McCullers, 1940–1990*. Columbia, S.C., 1995. Indispensable analysis of everything written about McCullers through 1990.

McCullers, Carson. *The Mortgaged Heart*. Edited by Margarita G. Smith. Boston, 1971. The editor is also Carson's sister. This collection contains unpublished stories, magazine articles, poems, and other ancillary materials.

McDowell, Margaret. *Carson McCullers*. Boston, 1980. Probably the best of the short, critical introductions to McCullers.

Paulson, Suzanne Morrow. "Carson McCullers's *The Ballad of the Sad Café*: A Song Half-Sung, Misogyny, and Ganging Up." In *Critical Essays on Carson McCullers*, edited by Beverly Lyon Clark and Melvin J. Friedman. New York, 1996. An excellent recent feminist reading.

Savigneau, Josyane. *Carson McCullers: A Life*. Translated by Joan E. Howard. Boston, 2000. Savigneau, a French journalist and cultural editor from *Le Monde*, claims that McCullers needs defending, that "Virginia Spencer Carr's work creates a rather negative image of Carson McCullers," an image that Savigneau sets out to remedy. She had access to some new materials, especially to the "war letters" between Carson and Reeves, and was granted the only interview that psychoanalyst Mary Mercer has allowed. In all, her book presents a more positive image of Carson than does Carr as a dedicated artist and a more capable and worldly person. Moreover, Savigneau gives readers from the United States insight into the French audience, both scholarly and general, for McCullers's work and reminds us that more than one American author (Faulkner comes to mind) have gained reputations in France while being underappreciated in their native country.

Shapiro, Adrian M. et al. *Carson McCullers: A Descriptive Listing and Annotated Bibliography of Criticism.* New York, 1980.

Spivak, Gayatri. "Three Feminist Readings: McCullers, Drabble, Habermas." *Union Seminary Quarterly Review* 35.1 & 2 (Fall/Winter 1979–80): 15–34.

See also the article on *The Ballad of the Sad Café*, immediately following.

CARSON McCULLERS'S
THE BALLAD OF THE SAD CAFÉ

by Louis H. Palmer, III

The Ballad of the Sad Café was originally published in *Harper's Bazaar* in 1943. It was not published in book form until 1951, when it loaned its title to an omnibus collection of McCullers's works. This edition included her other three novels—*The Heart Is a Lonely Hunter* (1940), *Reflections in a Golden Eye* (1941), and *The Member of the Wedding* (1946)—and six short stories, so critics took this occasion for a reassessment of her work as a whole. Most chose either *The Ballad of the Sad Café* or *The Member of the Wedding* as her best work, a critical evaluation that continues to hold.

The Ballad of the Sad Café is unique among McCullers's longer fiction because it does not have an adolescent character. It is similar in length to *Reflections in a Golden Eye*. She referred to both as "fairy tales" on various occasions. Both novellas take place in closed, isolated communities—the former in "an army base in peacetime" and the latter in a small southern mill town described as "a place that is far-off and estranged from all other places in the world." Both involve a limited cast of strange, even grotesque, characters. But of the two, most readers see *The Ballad of the Sad Café* as the more successful and powerful narrative, comparing its world to that of myth and legend, whereas *Reflections in a Golden Eye* seems to garner comparison to a nightmare or a psychoanalytic case study. Certainly, the narrative voice in the former work, whether we take it to be the voice of the author or not, seems to be more confident, the tone more consistent. The characters seem more developed and plot more unified as well, perhaps because there are fewer characters in a simpler plot. McCullers may have realized her strengths as a storyteller in this story and in *The Member of the Wedding*, working with fewer characters in an intense and interactive plot where fewer actual "events" occur.

GENESIS OF THE STORY

According to McCullers's biographer Virginia Spencer Carr, *The Ballad of the Sad Café* was written during the summer of 1941 and finished at Yaddo, a writer's colony in Saratoga Springs, New York. At this time, McCullers was having romantic problems. She had developed a romantic attachment to a woman, Annemarie Clarac-Schwarzenbach, and was in the process of breaking up (for the first time; they would later remarry) with her husband Reeves, who was apparently involved in a same-sex relationship with the composer David Diamond, to whom she wrote that it was his book. In an article "Brooklyn Is My Neighborhood," published in March 1941 in *Vogue*, McCullers described a "hunchback, the pet of a nearby bar who was always wined and dined" as one of the odd and eccentric characters in her Brooklyn Heights neighborhood. This was obviously one source for Cousin Lymon, the story's birdlike hunchback dwarf.

THE STORY

The story revolves around Amelia Evans, the proprietor of the "sad café" of the title. She is the most prominent citizen of a dusty southern mill town. At age thirty she runs the local general store, distills moonshine, and serves as a folk doctor for the townspeople. She dresses like a man, is six foot two and muscular, and is fond of litigation, so most of the townspeople view her with fear and awe. As the story opens, a pitiful figure shows up and claims to be her cousin. Lymon Willis, a dwarf with a hunchback, breaks down in tears, literally on her doorstep. Uncharacteristically, she offers him liquor for free and invites him in. After three days the townspeople suspect that Amelia has done away with him, but a vigilante delegation sent to investigate finds him well taken care of; his clothes have been mended and he wears "a shawl of lime-green wool, the fringes of which almost touched the floor." Then Amelia appears and for the first time serves liquor in the store. This gesture demonstrates the transformation of Amelia, who has fallen in love with Lymon. She opens her store as a café at night, and the café, in turn, transforms the lonesome and isolated town into a lively community. Lymon holds forth in the café as "a great mischief-maker," instigating fights and interrupting conversations for attention. The strange love affair prompts the narrator to pontificate on the nature of love:

First of all, love is a joint experience between two persons—but the fact that it is a joint experience does not mean that it is a similar experience to the two persons involved. There are the lover and the beloved, but these come from two different countries. Often the beloved is only a stimulus for all the stored-up love which has lain quiet in the lover for a long time hitherto. And somehow every lover knows this. He feels in his soul that his love is a solitary thing.... Let it be added here that the lover about whom we are speaking need not necessarily be a young man saving for a wedding ring—this lover can be man, woman, or child, or indeed any human creature on this earth. Now the beloved can also be of any description. The most outlandish people can be the stimulus for love.... The beloved may be treacherous, greasy-headed and given to evil habits. Yes, and the lover may see this as clearly as anyone else—but that does not affect the evolution of his love one whit.... The value and quality of any love is determined solely by the lover himself. It is for this reason that most of us would rather love than be loved. Almost everyone wants to be the lover. And the curt truth is that, in a deep secret way, the state of being beloved is intolerable to many. The beloved fears and hates the lover, and with the best of reasons. For the lover is forever trying to strip bare his beloved. The lover craves any possible relation with the beloved, even if this experience can cause him only pain.

This digression has been quoted at length because it has been taken as the key to the novel by McCullers's early biographer, Oliver Evans, and others, and as a philosophical statement by the author on the nature of love. More recent treatments have tended to see the statement as ironic, or at least qualified by its context.

In any case, the quotation explains the basic mechanics of the plot. Six years after Lymon's arrival, Marvin Macy, a hardened criminal and Amelia's former husband (whom she kicked out after he tried to have sex with her) returns from a term in the penitentiary and comes back to town. Lymon falls in love with him: "Since first setting eyes on Marvin Macy, the hunchback was possessed by an unnatural spirit. Every minute he wanted to be following along behind this jailbird, and he was full of silly schemes to attract attention to himself. Still Marvin Macy either treated him hatefully or failed to notice him at all." Eventually, Macy finds a use for Lymon—to get revenge against Amelia. Macy even persuades her to allow him to move in with her and Lymon. The narrator observes that "it is better to take your mortal enemy in than to face the terror of living alone." At this point a fight between Amelia and Macy becomes inevitable. Amelia sets up a

punching bag and practices every day. Lymon mocks and humiliates her in the café. The townspeople take bets on Amelia's side. Once a series of omens have made it obvious—"a hawk with a bloody breast flew over the town and circled twice over the property of Miss Amelia"—and the townspeople have gathered, the contest begins. After a period of boxing, the opponents begin to wrestle. Finally, Amelia has the upper hand: "She had him down and straddled; her strong big hands were on his throat." At this point, with a cry, "the hunchback sprang forward and sailed through the air as if he had grown hawk wings. He landed on the broad strong back of Miss Amelia and clutched at her neck with his clawed little fingers." This final betrayal leads to Amelia's defeat, and after stealing her treasures and vandalizing the café and her liquor still, "they went off together, the two of them."

The story concludes with a description of the town as it was in the beginning: dull, isolated, and dead, with the café boarded up and Amelia's pale face occasionally visible in an upper window. The narrator's final words direct us to listen, out of boredom, to the song of the chain gang, described as "twelve mortal men," who sing together on the outskirts of town. It is a song that seems to "come from the earth itself, or the wide sky. It is music that causes the heart to broaden and the listener to grow cold with ecstasy and fright." The music diminishes and we are left with "just twelve mortal men who are together."

CRITICAL HISTORY

The Ballad of the Sad Café's reception really began with its publication in book form in 1951. At that time, V. S. Pritchett claimed in *The Nation* that the novel transcended "regional gossip" because "the compassion of the author gives [the characters] their Homeric moment as universal tragedy" (James, 1995, p. 41). Claims to universal truth of this sort dominate much early criticism, especially of the 1950s and 1960s. The early interpretations tend to have a philosophical perspective and to look for a unifying thematic structure, usually based on the love sermon. So in 1965 Oliver Evans sees the lack of reciprocal love as "a terrible law of nature that has sentenced man to a life of perpetual solitary confinement."

Two of McCullers's own pieces of literary criticism have been very influential in the critical history of her novel. In "The Flowering Dream: Notes on Writing," published in 1959 in *Esquire*, she describes an unconscious process by which characters and plots grow and "flower" by way of sudden illuminations. She defends the weirdness of some of her characters by quoting Terence, the Roman poet,

61

who states that "nothing human is alien to me." She also offers a reading of *The Ballad of the Sad Café* in terms of *eros* versus *agape*, two Greek terms for love: "Passionate, individual love—the old Tristan/Isolde love, the Eros love—is inferior to the love of God, to fellowship, to the love of Agapé—the Greek god of the feast, the God of brotherly love—and of man. This is what I tried to show in *The Ballad of the Sad Café* in the strange love of Miss Amelia for the hunchback, Cousin Lymon" (Carr, 1990, p. 63).

So we are to see the focused, compulsive loves in the story, such as Marvin Macy's (originally) for Amelia, Amelia's for Lymon, and Lymon's for Macy as *eros* and as inferior to the companionship of the town while the café is open, which represents *agape*. The flaw in such an interpretation is that in two cases, Macy's love for Amelia and Amelia's love for Lymon, *eros* results in *agape*: Macy reforms his evil ways and Amelia opens the café. It is only in the third instance, Lymon's love for Macy, that *eros* becomes a destructive force, and even then it forms a bond between the men. In McCullers's work, such abstract emotional states only seem to gain meaning when they interact with social conventions, especially with gender conventions like masculinity, femininity, and heterosexuality.

In her other piece, "The Russian Realists and Southern Literature," published in *Decisions* in 1941 and so written at about the same time as *The Ballad of the Sad Café*, McCullers takes on the Southern Gothic label, which had generally been used disparagingly since the novelist Ellen Glasgow introduced the term to criticize fellow southerners William Faulkner and Erskine Caldwell in 1936. In this essay McCullers claims that, instead of being opposed to a realist style, the Gothic or grotesque (she seems to use the terms interchangeably) as it is expressed in southern literature actually represents a type of realism. She claims, "the grotesque can serve the purposes of a more exact moral and psychological realism in art. By abjuring moral judgement and exaggerating rather than resolving contradictions in human experience, the writer could reveal the hidden abnormalities in 'normal' life." Such a technique is "prevalent in the best of recent Southern literature, especially in the fiction of William Faulkner" (James, 1995, p. 185). She compares southern literature to Russian literature in that they both exist in an environment where "human life is cheap." Rather than echo the grandiose claims of the Agrarians about the superiority of southern mores, she compared the southern poor to Russian peasants and noted the demoralizing

effects of racism on whites as well as blacks. The key way in which the Southern Gothic serves its writers and readers is, then, to hold up a mirror to show how wrong and sick the normal elements of life in a given culture—in McCullers's example, the segregated South—could be. This obviously points to the emphasis on class, racial, gender, and sexual identity issues that later critics have found interesting in McCullers's work.

By the late 1960s a growing interest in the narrator is evident, and the question arises whether the narrative voice is to be taken as omniscient—a difficult assumption given its folksy diction and strong statements of opinion—or as the voice of a limited perspective, and if so, what perspective? In an article in the *Mississippi Quarterly*, Dawson Gaillard (1972) sees the narrator as a community member, perhaps a mill worker. Joseph R. Millichap (1973) claims in an essay for the *Georgia Review* that the novel's success stems from its "unity of narrative voice" (p. 83), whereas Mary Ann Dazey (1985) discerns in the *Southern Literary Messenger* two distinct narrators, a "ballad maker" who tells the story and a "lamenter" who reflects on it.

Source studies also began to appear in the 1960s. These relate the story to either a specific source or a tradition. A 1964 article by Robert S. Phillips in *Short Fiction* is an example of the first type, which looks at the influence of a story by Danish writer Isak Dinesen. Broader criticism concerning influence tends to link the novel with either the ballad tradition or that of myth and folktale. This criticism includes Lawrence Graver's *Carson McCullers* (1969), which links the characters to Greek myths; Dale Edmonds's *Carson McCullers* (1969); and Robert Millichap's article, which look at character and narrative structure in terms of the traditional ballads. In *Carson McCullers, Her Life and Work* (1965), Evans compares the story to Sherwood Anderson's "*The Triumph of the Egg*" and Faulkner's "A Rose for Emily." Other influence studies include a 1989 article by Peter Messent that sees the work as a typical example of the post–Southern Renaissance novella tradition in the South. (The Southern Renaissance—or Renascence—refers to the flowering of modernist southern literature that began in the 1920s with authors such as Katherine Anne Porter, Robert Penn Warren, Thomas Wolfe, and William Faulkner.) An article by Mary A. Gervin in *Pembroke Magazine* (1988) analyzes three strands of influence: ancient myth, folk epic, and modern philosophy, especially Nietzsche. Willard Thorp (1960) in the *Mississippi Quarterly* and others have noted the story's indebtedness to the frontier or southwestern humor tradition, with its outlaw characters who engage in conflicts that break up the unity of the town.

Following the start of the women's movement, and especially since larger numbers of women have joined the ranks of scholars and critics, there have been a variety of studies from a feminist perspective. An article by Margaret Bolsterli (1978) in *Bucknell Review* suggests that the novel illustrates the double bind of a woman trapped in a patriarchal status quo. Amelia's downfall is her lack of a supportive community based on liberated values. Mary Roberts (1980) in *Studies in Literature* and Louise Westling (1996) both see Amelia as an androgyne who cannot fit into a gender-divided culture. Westling especially sees Amelia as a tomboy past her time who is punished by masculinist norms. In a *Pembroke Magazine* article, Ann Carlton (1988) sees Amelia as trapped by a male-based language and role system, a person to whom neither conventional masculinity nor femininity can provide an acceptable model. Suzanne Morrow Paulson points out that Amelia does not try to "strip bare" Lymon, as the love sermon suggests, but that her love gives him the confidence to reject her in favor of Marvin Macy. For Paulson, the conflict in the story is between patriarchal "gangs" of men, symbolized and reinforced by the framing device of the chain gang, and a woman who refuses to take a woman's role. She points out that the love Amelia feels for Lymon has the opposite effect from alienating and isolating the lover; instead, it makes her a catalyst for the town's brief foray into a community life that is not dominated by male "gangs."

Choosing to take a very different perspective, Charles Hannon's 1996 essay provides an engaging riposte to interpreters of the novel who insist on its mythic, folk, and timeless elements by placing it squarely in the context of its original publication in *Harper's Bazaar* in 1943. Looking at the actual issue of the magazine, he compares the messages in advertisements with those found in the story. He analyzes general ideological codes that include both the value of women's labor in the war effort and the contradictory insistence that such public labor be temporary for women and that women be prepared to return to the home and the unpaid norms of maintaining and reproducing the heterosexual family. *The Ballad of the Sad Café* can be seen in this context as a cautionary tale. Amelia becomes a model of the wartime laboring woman, punished by the community for her refusal to join the economy of the heterosexual family.

This survey provides us with an idea of the richness and variety of interpretations that this small novel has managed to stimulate. To summarize some of the most debated questions: How does the love sermon fit in? Is it McCullers's philosophy or the limited perspective of the narrator? Who or what is the narrator, or narrators? Which of the characters are sympathetic? What is the relationship of the townspeople to the characters? To the reader? What does the novel tell us about the South? About community? About conformity and unconventionality? About class, gender, sexuality? Finally, what does the ending signify? Is it an affirmation (because the men are together) of *agape*, of community, of hope? Or (because they are chained) of the impossibility of true *agape*, of community without oppression? We can look forward to many more debates from readers who are enchanted or disturbed by this "fairy tale."

FURTHER READING

Bloom, Harold, ed. *Carson McCullers*. New York, 1986. Collection of essays on all of McCullers's works.

Bolsterli, Margaret. " 'Bound' Characters in Porter, Welty, McCullers: A Pre-revolutionary Status of Women in American Fiction." *Bucknell Review* 24 (Spring 1978): 95–105. Important early "cultural feminist" interpretation.

Carlton, Ann. "Beyond Gothic and Grotesque: A Feminist View of Three Female Characters of Carson McCullers." *Pembroke Magazine* 20 (1988): 54–62. The three characters are Mick Kelly, Frankie Adams, and Amelia Evans. Looks at characters in terms of the Gothic-grotesque tradition.

Carr, Virginia Spencer. *The Lonely Hunter*. Garden City, N.Y., 1975. The most comprehensive biography of McCullers.

Carr, Virginia Spencer. *Understanding Carson McCullers*. Columbia, S.C., 1990. Short, biographically influenced study of McCullers.

Clark, Beverly Lyon, and Melvin Friedman, eds. *Critical Essays on Carson McCullers*. New York, 1996. The second collection of materials on McCullers, including reviews of all the major works, tributes by other authors, and a selection of critical essays.

Cook, Richard M. *Carson McCullers*. New York, 1975. A critical and biographical overview.

Dazey, Mary Ann. "Two Voices of the Single Narrator in *The Ballad of the Sad Café*." *Southern Literary Journal*

17 (Spring 1985): 33–40. A new look at the narrator question.

Edmonds, Dale. *Carson McCullers*. Austin, Tex., 1969. A critical and biographical overview.

Evans, Oliver. *Carson McCullers: Her Life and Work*. London, 1965. The first biography; it is more interpretive than Carr's.

Gaillard, Dawson F. "The Presence of the Narrator in Carson McCullers' *The Ballad of the Sad Cafe*." *Mississippi Quarterly* 25 (Fall 1972): 419–427.

Gervin, Mary A. "McCullers's Frames of Reference in *The Ballad of the Sad Café*." *Pembroke Magazine* 20 (1988): 37–42. Influence of myth, folk epic, Nietzsche.

Graver, Lawrence. *Carson McCullers*. Minneapolis, 1969. A critical-biographical overview.

Hannon, Charles. "*The Ballad of the Sad Cafe* and Other Stories of Women's Wartime Labor." In *Bodies in Performance*, edited by Thomas Foster et al. New York, 1996. Looks at the novel in the context of its World War II–era publication in *Harper's Bazaar* and examines the magazine itself for clues to the gender-based ideology of the time.

James, Judith Giblin. *Wunderkind: The Reputation of Carson McCullers, 1940–1990*. Columbia, S.C., 1995. Indispensable analysis of everything written about McCullers through 1990. Chapter 4 contains a detailed history of the novel's reception.

McCullers, Carson. *The Mortgaged Heart*. Edited by Margarita G. Smith. Boston, 1971. The editor is also Carson's sister. This collection contains unpublished stories, magazine articles, poems, and other ancillary materials.

McCullers, Carson. *Illumination and Night Glare: The Unfinished Autobiography of Carson McCullers*. Edited by Carlos Dews. Madison, Wis., 1999. Fragmentary autobiography that includes letters.

McDowell, Margaret. *Carson McCullers*. Boston, 1980. Probably the best of the short, critical introductions to McCullers.

McNally, John. "The Introspective Narrator in *The Ballad of the Sad Cafe*." *South Atlantic Bulletin* 38 (1973): 40–44.

Messent, Peter. "Continuity and Change in the Southern Novella." In *The Modern American Novella*, edited by A. Robert Lee. London, 1989. Looks at *The Ballad of the Sad Café* in terms of the regional novella.

Millichap, Joseph R. "Carson McCullers' Literary Ballad." *Georgia Review* 27 (Fall 1973): 329–339. Looks at the narrator and mythological influences.

Paulson, Suzanne Morrow. "Carson McCullers's *The Ballad of the Sad Cafe*: A Song Half-Sung, Misogyny, and Ganging Up." In *Critical Essays on Carson McCullers*, edited by Beverly Lyon Clark and Melvin J. Friedman. New York, 1996. An excellent feminist reading.

Phillips, Robert S. "Dinesen's 'Monkey' and McCullers' 'Ballad': A Study in Literary Affinity." *Studies in Short Fiction* 1 (1964): 184–190. A source study.

Roberts, Mary. "Imperfect Androgyny and Imperfect Love in the Works of Carson McCullers." *Studies in Literature* 12 (1980): 73–98.

Shapiro, Adrian M., et al. *Carson McCullers: A Descriptive Listing and Annotated Bibliography of Criticism*. New York, 1980. A bibliographical survey.

Thorp, Willard. "Suggs and Sut in Modern Dress: The Latest Chapter in Southern Humor." *Mississippi Quarterly* 13 (Fall 1960): 169–175. On the southwestern humor tradition in McCullers.

Westling, Louise. "Tomboys and Revolting Femininity." In *Critical Essays on Carson McCullers*, edited by Beverly Lyon Clark and Melvin J. Friedman. New York, 1996. Reads Amelia as a freak "stuck" in adolescence.

See also the article on Carson McCullers, immediately preceding.

TERRENCE McNALLY

by Karma Waltonen

Since his Broadway premier in 1964, Terrence McNally has matured into one of the most versatile yet consistently powerful voices in the theater. He has won, among other awards, numerous Tonys, an Emmy, a Pulitzer, two Guggenheim fellowships, and the Rockefeller Award. A member of the Dramatists Guild Council since 1970, he has been the vice president since 1981. He is also often labeled America's premier gay

Terrence McNally. (*Hulton Archive/Getty Images*)

playwright, yet he resists such a limiting classification. His most striking themes are alienation and our desire for connection. He is continually innovating theater with controversial ideas and experimental delivery. McNally's later plays, however varied, are always identifiable in their use of music, their delicately crafted dialogue, and their appeal to what is best in the human spirit.

McNally was born on 3 November 1939 in St. Petersburg, Florida, to Hubert and Dorothy McNally. He spent his childhood in Corpus Christi, Texas, where he was introduced to opera. His love for opera would influence his plays from the very beginning of his career. McNally obtained a degree in journalism from Columbia University. His *And Things Go Bump in the Night* was first produced in 1962. After revisions it was produced again and transferred to Broadway in 1964. The play, a surreal family drama about dysfunction, opened to harsh reviews and closed after two weeks. Notably, many critics writing about the play focused on gossip about McNally's sexuality and his past relationship with Edward Albee rather than the performance.

McNally took a short sabbatical from playwriting but soon returned with a series of shorter, satirical plays. Like many playwrights of the late 1960s and early 1970s his satires often involved a critique of the conflict in Vietnam. Among these early plays were *Next* (1967), *Botticelli* (1968), and *Bringing It All Back Home* (1969).

The Ritz (1975) was McNally's first big commercial success. The clever farce's action revolves around a straight man's calamities as he hides from the mob in a gay bathhouse. This play succeeded brilliantly, despite its perceived sexual subversiveness.

It's Only a Play (1985) marks a turning point in McNally's career. Up until this, he was best known for farcical comedies. As he says in his "A Few Words of Introduction": "It's one of the most serious plays I've ever written. It's my attempt to describe exactly what it was like to work in the Broadway theater in the 1980s. It is probably the closest thing I will ever write to a documentary." The action takes place at an opening-night party for a play, as all the characters wait for reviews. The desperation displayed by the characters is both funny and tragic. This tenor would continue through all his later plays.

However we might view *It's Only a Play*, its importance can never be underestimated if only because it is the play that forged McNally's relationship with Lynne Meadow and the Manhattan Theatre Club. McNally explains in his "A Few Words": "It was during one of the previews of *It's Only a Play* that Lynne Meadow said she would produce my next play sight unseen." The relationship between McNally and the MTC has endured.

The Lisbon Traviata (1985) was the most difficult play for McNally in all respects. Stephen, an opera fan, takes operatic vengeance on his lover, Michael, when Michael decides to end the relationship. In the first version of the play, Stephen stabs Michael with scissors to keep him from leaving. Critics denounced the operatic ending. When the play appeared again in 1989, Stephen brandished the scissors but Michael left unharmed. Whatever the ending, ultimately Stephen lives in an opera world and Michael doesn't belong there.

In his beautiful and touching *Frankie and Johnny in the Clair de Lune* (1987), McNally explores the difficulty working-class, middle-age people have in making a start. The play takes place in the hours before dawn after a first date as the characters struggle to connect. When the "wall of disparity" finally breaks down, the audience understands that this night has required great courage from them both.

McNally has said that *Lips Together, Teeth Apart* (1991) is his most operatic play and the one he considers his best. The play is indeed masterful. The action takes place on the Fourth of July at a beach house on Fire Island. Two couples come to the house Sally has inherited from her brother, who died of AIDS. The characters' frequent soliloquies not only illustrate inner thought but also demonstrate the characters' fundamental problem—they don't hear each other. Through the course of the drama, the couples must confront their various levels of homophobia as they struggle to maintain their relationships with each other.

A Perfect Ganesh (1993) was McNally's most expressionistic play to that point. We follow Margaret and Katharine as they travel in India. Katharine has two goals—to kiss a leper and to find the perfect Ganesh figurine. Both of these goals represent finding the part of herself that can love unconditionally. Their journey does not magically free either woman from the trappings of her prejudices, yet both become more aware of these feelings and of the consequences of failing to love others. Katharine is not able to kiss a leper, but she and Margaret are able find solace in the perfect Ganesh they receive from two AIDS-stricken men at the end.

Following closely on the heels of *A Perfect Ganesh* was the Tony-winning *Love! Valour! Compassion!* (1994). The action takes place at a country house over the three summer holiday weekends (one for each act). We watch as friends and lovers try to connect with each other through the hardships of death, disease, and all the other forces that pull people apart. Much of what we learn about the characters' histories is given to us through asides. The most striking direct audience addresses come very near the end of the play. The men are gathered together, arms intertwined, rehearsing "Dance of the Swans" for an AIDS benefit, complete with white tutus. One by one, the men step out to tell us how they will die. As the title indicates, love is the dominant theme in the play.

McNally's most controversial play to date is *Corpus Christi* (1998). The plan to produce the play resulted in numerous threats from various Christian and Muslim groups. It is, according to McNally's preface, "the life of Joshua, a young man from south Texas . . . told in the theatrical tradition of medieval morality plays." Joshua learns from God that He will teach the world a secret: "All men are divine." As he matures, the major moments of the Christ story are mirrored one by one. In this version of the passion play, Joshua ultimately is mocked as being "King of the Queers." The warning of this morality play is that we should not crucify our fellow humans for their difference, sexual difference in particular. The play's overriding message is that we are all divine and deserving of love.

McNally has written all the screenplays for the films based on his plays: *The Ritz* (1976), *Frankie and Johnny* (1991), and *Love! Valour! Compassion!* (1997). In 1984 McNally began experimenting with musicals. His first attempt was the book for *The Rink*. This was followed by the highly acclaimed book for *Kiss of the Spider Woman* in 1992. His book for *Ragtime* (1997) was also well received, and *Kiss* and *Ragtime* both won Tonys for best book. He is currently experimenting with librettos.

Many critics have noted that McNally's plays are highly dependent on music and dance. Music represents life and dance represents love and connection. These motifs are always played out in the shadow of death. AIDS lingers in the background of all the later works, just as the vision of Vietnam was present in his earlier plays. Yet AIDS is not the only agent of sickness or death in the plays. One recurring theme is the characters' acceptance of the failings of their own bodies and the bodies of others. McNally's obsession with the body on the road to death is ultimately about finding the beauty in life—something that is, of course, only possible through the fallible body.

When looking over his corpus, one is struck with the idea of inclusiveness. McNally wants us to learn that we are to love ourselves and each other. When Katharine from *A Perfect Ganesh* finally confronts a leper, she asks him, "Why are you diseased and hideous? What can I do to change that?" The leper replies simply, "Love me."

WORKS

There Is Something Out There (1962) (rewritten as *And Things Go Bump in the Night* and produced in 1964)

Next (1967)

Tour (1967)

Botticelli (1968)

Witness (1968)

Cuba Si! (1968)

Sweet Eros (1968)

Bringing It All Back Home (1969)

Whiskey (1973)

Bad Habits (1974)

The Ritz (1975)

It's Only a Play (1985)

The Lisbon Traviata (1985)

Frankie and Johnny in the Clair de Lune (1987)
Andre's Mother (1988)
Street Talk (1988)
Prelude & Liebestod (1989)
Lips Together, Teeth Apart (1991)
A Perfect Ganesh (1993)
The Wibbly, Wobbly, Wiggly Dance That Clepatterer Did (1993)
Love! Valour! Compassion! (1994)
Master Class (1996)
Corpus Christi (1998)

FURTHER READING

Bryer, Jackson R., ed. "Terrence McNally." In *The Playwright's Art: Conversations with Contemporary American Dramatists*. New Brunswick, N.J., 1995.

DiGaetani, John L. "Terrence McNally." In *A Search for a Postmodern Theater: Interviews with Contemporary Playwrights*, edited by John L. DiGaetani. New York, 1991.

Drukman, Steven. "Terrence McNally." In *Speaking on Stage: Interviews with Contemporary American Playwrights*, edited by Philip C. Kolin and Colby H. Kullman. Tuscaloosa, Ala., 1996.

Savran, David. *The Playwright's Voice*. New York, 1990.

Straub, Deborah. "Terrence McNally." In *Contemporary Authors*, New Revision Series. Vol. 2. Detroit, 1962–1981.

Zinman, Toby Silverman. *Terrence McNally: A Casebook*. New York, 1997.

JOHN McPHEE

by Jan Goggans

John McPhee, born on 8 March 1931 in Princeton, New Jersey, is universally praised for his intelligent, graceful prose. A writer's writer, a man whom other writers genuinely admire for his craft, he is the quintessential sponge, able to soak up a variety of information, assimilate and analyze it, and put it down into columns, essays, and book-length works that, grounded in traditional journalistic techniques but employing a number of literary strategies, read as smoothly and engrossingly as a Mark Twain novel. Indeed, Twain's two narrative reports, *Roughing It* and *Life on the Mississippi*, are among the works that precede McPhee's writing. Fact-based, sometimes taut and dramatic, sometimes spun with wit and charm, but always reading like a story, McPhee's prose compares to that in Twain's books, Stephen Crane's and E. B. White's reports from the war front, Truman Capote's exploration of a murder in *In Cold Blood*, and Joan Didion's social analysis, *Slouching towards Bethlehem*.

All illustrate the genre McPhee has mastered and has in many ways made his own: literary nonfiction or, in the class McPhee teaches at Princeton, "the literature of fact."

A SENSE OF WHERE HE WAS

McPhee was born to a former teacher, Mary Ziegler, and a general practitioner, Harry Roemer McPhee, whose practice included the U.S. Olympic teams and Princeton athletic squads for over a quarter of a century. His father's work may explain McPhee's lifelong interest in sports and athletes, an interest that began when he was very young. According to an interview he gave, he spent so much time playing sports that he could not say how he got any schoolwork done. In high school, while he remained active in sports—canoeing, tennis, basketball—he found a new passion, writing. This passion McPhee always attributes directly to his English teacher, Olive McKee. She required three compositions a week, all of which had to be clearly

John McPhee. (© *Bettmann/Corbis*)

outlined on a separate piece of paper. In a 1994 interview published in *Writing on the Edge*, McPhee explained the process, emphasizing that the teacher did not require a standard outline per se but something that clearly showed the "architecture" of the composition, something that demonstrated the writer's awareness of the start, end, and "in between" of the piece and the writer's "rationale" for it. All of that, McPhee says, "started us thinking about different ways to do things that make sense," a thought process he insists is still directly reflected in his work. In the interview, he compares that way of thinking to cooking, drawing a parallel between figuring out what to do with the information he has collected for a piece and the entire cycle of shopping at the market, returning home with what you have purchased, and figuring out what you can actually make: "You can't make a soufflé out of a red pepper," he points out; "You can, however, cook the red pepper in various ways."

With this background, it is not surprising that when McPhee entered Princeton University in 1949, he played for the basketball team and wrote for the college literary magazines. In addition, he was a regular contestant on a weekly radio and television show called "Twenty Questions," fashioned after the old game that begins with the question, "Is it animal, vegetable, or mineral?" and proceeds with only yes-or-no questions. Michael Pearson, who wrote a volume on McPhee for Twayne's United States Authors Series, argues that the show provided a solid groundwork for McPhee's nonfiction writing, showing him how to approach a subject by asking questions about it. At the same time, McPhee's submissions to the school publications the *Nassau Sovereign*, *Nassau Literary Magazine*, and *Princeton Tiger*, the last of which McPhee eventually edited, fostered in him his first clear literary goal—to be published in *The New Yorker*. He did not achieve that goal until 1963, ten years after he graduated from Princeton and nine years after the event the published article recounts: his experience playing basketball in England while engaged in postgraduate study at Cambridge University. McPhee submitted countless ideas and completed pieces to *The New Yorker*, even after securing a job at *Time* magazine's show business bureau. The piece *The New Yorker* finally accepted, "Basketball and Beefeaters," tells the story of McPhee's time on the Cambridge basketball team and their match against Her Majesty's Royal Fusiliers, which was scheduled to take place in the Tower of London. The game is moved at the last minute to a sports hall near the tower, but in any case McPhee's team wins—a modern "beheading," he claims.

Inspired by his publication, and perhaps following the time-honored writer's dictum to write what you know, McPhee proposed a piece on Bill Bradley, the former Princeton all-American basketball star. Receiving from the magazine only a promise to read the work, he sent in a 17,000-word profile on Bradley in December 1964. Accepted for publication in *The New Yorker*, it was published as a book, *A Sense of Where You Are*, in 1965. Just as important, it led to McPhee's being hired as a staff writer on *The New Yorker*, a position he has held ever since.

PIECES OF THE FRAMEWORK

In 1965, the year McPhee "extracted," to use William Howarth's term, an offer from *The New Yorker*'s editor to become a staff writer, the magazine was, along with *Harper's* and the *Atlantic Monthly*, literally rewriting the definition of journalism. Since the 1930s *The New Yorker* had been publishing pieces by E. B. White, A. J. Liebling, and Joseph Mitchell, all of whom wrote with a literary flair for character development and metaphor. Then, in August 1946, *The New Yorker* published John Hersey's article "Hiroshima," a 31,347-word piece that looked at six Japanese in the wake of the bombing, in the process focusing the reportorial notion of accurate accounts into the personal, even intimate details of actual people's lives. It was soon after published as a book, perhaps paving the way for the next wave of nonfiction literature in the 1960s. In 1966, the year after McPhee published *A Sense of Where You Are*, Truman Capote's *In Cold Blood* appeared, bringing with it a wave of controversy over what is fiction and what is reporting. Accused of factual inaccuracy in his reporting of a murder and its consequences, Capote replied that his book was a new art form, something that employed the reporter's research and the fiction writer's art. New Journalism soon appeared, the highly colorful, energetic, even frenetic form of writing Tom Wolfe perfected in novels like *The Right Stuff*. Characterized by Wolfe as accurate and literary, journalism that reads like a novel, the New Journalism introduced a type of profile never before seen, one that relied on scene-by-scene reconstruction of the subject's life, the use of third-person point of view, and the use of symbolic details to enhance the story. Most controversial, however, was Wolfe's insistence that the writer could come to know the subject of the profile so well that subject's entire dialogic process—including the monologue within his or her head—could be re-created.

Amid this near-carnival of new techniques for writers and new expectations from those who published them,

John McPhee set up literary shop in the offices of the magazine that had first drawn him in with its innovation and style. *The New Yorker* participated in this new configuration of journalism most notably in its profiles, pieces that gave readers interesting, sometimes intimate details about a person's life, combining personal interviews with secondary sources such as letters or interviews with family or friends, all within a highly readable prose style, lifting nonfiction to the realm of art. McPhee carried on with *The New Yorker* tradition, continuing the process of creating fresh new profiles of his subjects, but ultimately he reinvented the entire notion of a profile by extending the techniques—the massive compilation of details, the variety of sources, even the scene-by-scene reconstruction—to inanimate subjects such as oranges and abstract endeavors such as flood control or geology.

Even when McPhee writes about people who pick or grow or process oranges for a living, all of which he does in the 1967 book *Oranges*, he is really writing a profile of the orange itself, its history and future, its uses and, sometimes, abuses, how and where it grows and on what kind of trees, what kind of person picks it and how, and what happens to it after it is picked. McPhee's *Oranges* is more than natural history; it is a complete and absorbing cultural history, one in which he covers everything from the use of temple oranges in little-known sects of the Buddhist faith to the orange's role in literature (Shakespeare's *Much Ado about Nothing* and Boccaccio's *Decameron*), medicine (twenty-one cures, from acne to ulcers), art (Titian's *Last Supper*), and the sixteenth-century rage of building orangeries that provided some of the most beautiful European architecture to be found to date. All of this information McPhee conveys in a narrative structure that presents a variety of points of view without ever making overt judgments on the people or processes involved.

ASSEMBLING A CANON

McPhee's reportorial ability to convey others' judgments without making his own sets him apart from the heavily biased pieces of other New Journalists like Thomas Wolfe, who frequently includes himself in his pieces not simply as the interviewing character but as an essential part of the whole piece. McPhee, in contrast, is as quiet within his writing as he is in his life. In the handful of interviews he has granted, he talks mainly, and knowledgeably, about his own writing process, but he offers very few personal anecdotes. He has remained in Princeton his whole life, despite his many journeys to distant and exotic places.

Most tellingly, there seems to be only one photograph of McPhee; none of his many books carry dust-jacket photographs, and many people who read him avidly have no idea what he looks like. Similarly, readers do not get to know McPhee as a character in his essays and books. When he appears it is generally to set the scene, as in "A Forager," a profile of the naturalist Euell Gibbons, printed in *A Roomful of Hovings* (1968). After noting that Gibbons lives in Troxelville, Pennsylvania, McPhee opens a paragraph with "In November, I went to Troxelville, and on the morning of the fourth Gibbons and I started by car for the river." McPhee also "appears" in his work to ask questions, or even to think about things, but the result is the same: questions or thoughts always lead the reader not to McPhee but to the subject of the piece.

> I began to think of roast duck stuffed with oranges. Gibbons must have started to think about roast duck at that moment, too. "There's a difference between being hungry for foods that you're used to eating and being just plain hungry," he said, and he added, "I've been both." Then he went off foraging.

Noting this marked tendency, Michael Pearson argues that readers will find McPhee in his choice of characters and in the subjects he chooses to write about.

Characters and subject matter are indeed the "meat" on McPhee's literary table. While *A Sense of Where You Are* refers to Bill Bradley's extraordinary ability to play basketball, his innate sense of what is going on in the game at any given time, it also by extension refers to the general ability to know "where you are" in what you do. The Bradley piece was the first example of McPhee's ongoing pursuit of singular people who are good at what they do. While some, like Bradley, Arthur Ashe, Euell Gibbons, and David Brower, the lifelong Sierra Club activist, are famous, others are not, such as the canoe builder Henri Vaillancourt or the chef Alan Lieb (called Otto in *The New Yorker* essay "Brigade de Cuisine," reprinted in *Giving Good Weight*, 1979). What all share, Michael Pearson suggests, are those values celebrated in the works of Emerson and Thoreau, self-reliance and individualism.

McPhee's ability to immerse himself in those whose craft is the focus of his writing is remarkable. To write *Coming into the Country* (1977), his trilogy about people who live in the wilderness and urban landscapes of Alaska, McPhee spent months at a time over a two-year period in different parts of Alaska. To write the five geological books collected in 1998 as *Annals of the Former World*, awarded the Pulitzer Prize for nonfiction in 1999, McPhee turned what he had originally thought was a two-day project for a *New Yorker* piece into a series of geological expeditions that moved progressively west to California and then slightly back, ending at Pike's Peak, Colorado, spanning the years from 1979 to 1993. He was, as he describes it in *Writing on the Edge*, "at sea," scribbling down notes and typing them up without any idea of what they meant, feeling inadequate but knowing somehow that he could not and would not stop and that he had reached some place where, again in McPhee's words, "there's a kind of a vortex, and you're gone." The books McPhee wrote from that small idea provide for readers a complex and rich vision of the world as plate tectonics explains it. And while the subject matter is admittedly McPhee's most difficult, the geologists with whom he travels are vibrant and interesting: Princeton professor Ken Deffeyes and his then graduate student Karen Kleinspehn; U.S. Geological Survey workers Anita Harris and David Love; University of California professor Eldridge Moores, the man who theorized plate tectonics. For them and eventually for McPhee, the "former world" is instantiated in the current world, a newly active, living place. Through his immersion in the lives of these men and women and the fate they measure for this land, *Annals of a Former World* takes a backward dive into how this land came to have a fate at all. Thus, both the fate of humans and the fate of the land on which they live are elegantly and eloquently explored in McPhee's massive look at America's geological history.

McPhee turned early and seemingly easily to environmental issues and themes. Long before *Basin and Range* (1980), the first of his geological books, McPhee was looking at the fate of Americans in and on the American landscape. In his fourth book, *The Pine Barrens* (1968), McPhee focuses on a large tract of land in south-central New Jersey, a wilderness made legendary by its proximity to the populated coastal resorts and the industrial corridor of Interstate 95. For McPhee the Pine Barrens is a cultural crossroads, the place where North meets South in a far more complex interchange than traditional versus modern. The long tradition of free enterprise runs deep in this historical place, where conservatives believe in the right to develop and ecologists become intrusive outsiders even though they are fighting to save the historical land. Through dialogue, description, and explanation, McPhee treads deliberately through the tangle, never telling his readers how to think or feel but simply presenting the reality as he sees it.

It is of course the subjective quality of how McPhee sees it and its influence on what he chooses to present that has given McPhee his reputation as an environmental writer. Michael Pearson claims that, more than McPhee's frequent explorations into a specific sense of a place or even the journeys that take him to those places, McPhee's environmental reputation comes from the question he asks in *Coming into the Country*: "What will be the fate of this land?" That question, Pearson argues, could thematically work as the main point of all McPhee's work. McPhee himself says it is apparent from the topics he chooses that he cares about the outdoors, a concern he traces back to his childhood summers at a New Jersey camp, Keewaydin. Significantly, however, even in his overt explorations of human interaction with the environment, McPhee remains the observer. If, for example, *The Control of Nature* (1989) seems to suggest overall that the human attempt to reroute rivers and restrain the massive "debris flows" that mountains periodically and naturally spew is in vain, there is sympathy for the attempt. The opening description in "Los Angeles against the Mountain," the third piece in *The Control of Nature*, grips readers with its dramatically tense account of a family's near-burial in their own home, the parents bravely resigned to staying with their two teenage children, who were pinned between a bed and the house wall as the mud rose and rose and rose, stopping finally "near the children's chins."

LIFE IN THE ROUND

The Control of Nature is perhaps McPhee's signature book in that it combines all the elements of his craft: a carefully planned structure designed to express the theme of the book, interviews, research, a full immersion by whatever means possible in the subject matter, and finally, the many techniques of literature: narrative form, metaphor, allusion. All of his books, however, employ the techniques effectively, and choosing among his vast array of essays and books may simply come down to a reader's personal preference of subject matter.

For McPhee himself it is certainly a matter of personal preference; after a four-year hiatus, McPhee published in October 2002 a book about one of his fondest pursuits, shad fishing. From the craggy and complex geological history of the world and the equally complex minds and lives of those who are writing that history, McPhee turned, characteristically, to the next thing that interested him, the elusive and frustrating shad, a fish legendary for both its delicious taste and bones so pervasive its consumption frustrates all who approach it. In this book, as in the twenty-five that precede it, McPhee brings to light more than readers ever guessed existed on his subject matter. "Life in the round," he terms it, and it is his goal in all he writes. Studiously avoiding telling people how to feel or think, he instead prefers to give his readers the fullest view possible. To do so he avoids getting caught up in one issue and instead gets caught up in the whole of his subject, coming to that "vortex" he described at which he knows he is, somehow, "gone." Steadily, elegantly, prolifically, John McPhee has continued to produce pieces on a wealth of subjects, quietly mastering not simply those pursuits that form the topics for his books but the most difficult pursuit of all—that of great writing.

WORKS

A Sense of Where You Are (1965)
The Headmaster (1966)
Oranges (1967)
The Pine Barrens (1968)
A Roomful of Hovings (1968)
Levels of the Game (1969)
The Crofter and the Laird (1970)
Encounters with the Archdruid (1971)
The Deltoid Pumpkin Seed (1973)
The Curve of Binding Energy (1974)
Pieces of the Frame (1975)
The Survival of the Bark Canoe (1975)
Coming into the Country (1977)
Giving Good Weight (1979)
Basin and Range (1980)
In Suspect Terrain (1983)
La Place de la Concorde Suisse (1984)
Table of Contents (1985)
Rising from the Plains (1986)
The Control of Nature (1989)
Looking for a Ship (1990)
Assembling California (1993)
The Ransom of Russian Art (1994)
Irons in the Fire (1997)
Annals of the Former World (1998)
The Founding Fish (2002)

FURTHER READING

Drabble, Dennis. "Conversations with John McPhee." *Sierra* (October-December 1978): 61–63. A brief but entertaining interview that, like the Joan Hamilton profile/interview published in *Sierra* in 1990, reflects the concerns of the magazine and its readership.

Haynes, Jared. "The Size and Shape of the Canvas: An Interview with John McPhee." 2 parts. *Writing on the Edge* 5, no. 2 (Spring 1994) and 6, no. 1 (Fall 1994): 108–128. Haynes, a writing teacher at University of California, Davis, talks with McPhee at length about his writing and teaching processes. McPhee's answers are detailed, and the interview contributes substantively to an understanding of how McPhee perceives his craft.

Howarth, William, ed. *The John McPhee Reader.* New York, 1976. Howarth, an English professor at Princeton and noted scholar of American literature, provides what many consider to be the definitive account of McPhee's methods and motives. The biographical background on McPhee is well integrated into the various ideas and subjects in his canon. The description of McPhee's writing process is detailed and interesting.

Pearson, Michael. *John McPhee.* Twayne's United States Authors Series. Edited by Frank Day. New York, 1997. Pearson's is the only book-length work to date on McPhee. He covers the various literary movements that led up to the term "creative nonfiction" and provides a historical as well as artistic context for McPhee's work. Like *The John McPhee Reader, John McPhee* provides a good checklist of McPhee's books and articles as well as an annotated bibliography of published articles about McPhee. In addition, Pearson's book includes what may be the only photograph of John McPhee.

Pearson, Michael. "Twenty Questions: A Conversation with John McPhee." *Creative Nonfiction* (Fall 1993): 76–87.

Strachan, Patricia, ed. *The Second John McPhee Reader.* Introduction by David Remnick. New York, 1996.

HERMAN MELVILLE

by Benjamin Ivry

Herman Melville was born on 1 August 1819 on Pearl Street in downtown New York City. His father, Allan Melvill (as the family spelled its name at the time), was a trader whose own father, Thomas, had participated in the Boston Tea Party in 1773 as part of the American colonists' protest against high British tariffs. Herman Melville's mother, Maria Gansevoort, was from a distinguished family of Dutch origin. Maria's father, Peter Gansevoort, had been a revolutionary war officer known as the Hero of Fort Stanwix for his 1777 defense of an outpost in Rome, New York, against the British general John Burgoyne. Despite these distinguished ancestors, Allan Melvill could not turn a profit at his trade, importing dry goods from France to Boston. He dissipated the family fortune with ill-fated business ventures. In 1819, Allan Melvill wrote to his brother-in-law to announce Herman's birth: "The little stranger has good lungs, sleeps well and feeds kindly, he is in truth a chopping Boy," and to a business colleague in Paris, the proud father described the newborn as "un beau Garcon" (a handsome boy). He was named after his mother's brother, Herman Gansevoort, and baptized in the South Reformed Dutch Church. As part of the ceremony, the priest reminded his parents that according to the tenets of the church, children are "conceived and born in sin, and therefore are subject to all miseries, yea to condemnation itself." Before he was two years old, Herman had suffered a bout of measles, which his father described as including "very bad coughs, inflamed eyes, and virulent eruptions which characterize this troublesome disorder." This early illness may have been the origin of Melville's sensitive eyes, which he later described as "tender as young sparrows." Such passing ailments apart, the boy's health was generally good, as Allan explained in a family letter in 1821: "Little Herman

Herman Melville.
(Courtesy of the Library of Congress)

is in fine spirits and rugged as a Bear." When the Melvilles had another son in 1823, four-year-old Herman spoke his first recorded words: "Pa now got two ittle Boys." Three years later his father described him to an uncle as "an honest hearted double rooted Knicker-bocker of the true Albany stamp . . . he is very backward in speech and some-what slow in comprehension, but you will find him as far as he understands men and things both solid and pro-found." Herman's first ten years were spent in luxury, living in pleasant and spacious Manhattan homes. But in 1830 the family was forced to flee Manhattan for Albany to escape debts incurred by Allan Melvill in unsuccessful business ventures. Soon Allan went mad and died in January 1832 from stresses linked to his indebtedness. Herman witnessed his father's harrowing decline and death and his family's sufferings. These experiences would be echoed in the 1852 novel *Pierre*, in which a dying father "wander[s] so ambiguously in his mind."

As a result of his family's misfortune, Herman began work at age twelve as a bank clerk in Albany for $150 per year. Herman devoured books from his father's library, like Edmund Spenser's *The Faerie Queen* (1590), which he would later describe in *Pierre* as a "maze of all-bewildering beauty." Other books he read included Washington Irving's popular *Sketch Book* (1819–1820) and John Lloyd Stephens's *Incidents of Travel in Egypt, Arabian Petraea, and the Holy Land* (1837), both of which would influence his later writings. As a teenager he also joined a local debating group, the Philo Logos Society, where he revealed a feisty personality. When he was just under eighteen years old, Herman was ridiculed in an Albany newspaper as a "Ciceronian Baboon" and "moral Ethiopian whose conscience qualms not in view of the most atrocious guilt; whose brazen cheek never tingles with the blush of shame, whose moral principles, and sensibilities, have been destroyed by the corruption of his own black and bloodless heart." Herman's first recorded publication, in 1838, was a defense of his behavior in the debate group, in which he accused his foes of being "a train of bitter and caustic personalities." Thus, his first literary exercise was to defend himself from social ostracism. Having his speeches dismissed as "the raving of an unmasked hypocrite" must have hurt, with his father's madness still so vivid in his memory.

A widespread economic crisis began in 1837, and in 1839 the twenty-year-old Herman accepted an offer from his older brother Gansevoort to return to Manhattan in order to sign on as a hand aboard a whaler or merchant ship. His goal was to see the Pacific Ocean and escape the bank at Albany; his mother commented, "I think at heart he is rather agitated." As a boy on the ship *St. Lawrence*, he swabbed the decks and cleaned chicken coops and pigpens. Returning a few months later from his first sea voyage to Europe, Herman looked for work. He read Richard Henry Dana's best-seller, *Two Years Before the Mast* (1840), with what he later called a "Siamese link of affectionate sympathy." Young Dana wrote of wider adventures than Melville had yet experienced: rounding Cape Horn. With his brother Gansevoort's encouragement, Melville determined to sign up for a lengthy whaling voyage, the kind that sometimes lasted four years.

FURTHER VOYAGES AND *TYPEE*

Melville sailed on 3 January 1841 from Fairhaven, Massachusetts, on the *Acushnet*. He lived in close quarters with African Americans and Portuguese, which may have inspired his noteworthy racial tolerance later on. He left the ship for good without permission on 9 July, despite a sore leg. Melville made his way to Tahiti aboard another ship, gradually reaching Hawaii, where he again deserted ship. In 1843 he was working in a bowling alley in Honolulu as a pinsetter. The same year he signed up again with the U.S. Navy for a three-year stint and headed back for the Marquesas. There were other voyages, to Lima, Peru, and Rio de Janeiro, until his ship docked at Charleston in October 1844. Herman was twenty-five, his financial problems had not been solved, and he still lacked a profession. His family suggested that he publish an account of his adventures aboard ship, which he agreed to do, even though trying to earn a living as a writer was as difficult in Melville's time as it is today.

Typee (1846), the story of a young sailor, Toby, who escapes from a whaling boat in the South Seas, has clear parallels to the author's own experiences. Some of his memories were frankly erotic, deleted from the first edition of *Typee*, where Melville describes being bathed by naked local women "looking like so many mermaids sparkling in the billows that washed the sea weed covered sides of their lurking places.... [N]ever certainly was effeminate ottoman in the innermost shrine of his seraglio attended by lovelier houris with more excess of devotion than happened to me." *Typee* jests about sexuality aboard all-male ships, "regularly tacking twice in the twenty-four hours somewhere off Buggerry Island, or the Devil's-Tail Peak." Arriving at the Marquesas Islands, the protagonist explains, "Our ship was now wholly given up to every species of riot and debauchery. Not the feeblest barrier was interposed between the unholy passions of the crew and their unlimited gratification."

Washington Irving praised *Typee* as "exquisite" when Gansevoort Melville brought him the completed manuscript in London, where the book was accepted for publication by Putnam's. It appeared in 1846, and some British reviewers were shocked by its rough humor. Indeed, in the first chapter of *Typee* there was a racy reference about the queen of Hawaii showing off tattoos on her backside to French visitors who "fled the scene of so shocking a catastrophe." Worse, the book described missionaries in terms "of downright disrespect, of ridicule," as the *London Critic* charged, accusing Melville of not having "the real interests of Christianity very seriously at heart," an accurate, and damaging, accusation.

More enthused were the first reviewers of the American edition, published in March 1846, among them Nathaniel Hawthorne, who wrote in the *Salem Advertiser* about Melville's description of hearty cannibals: "Next, we catch a glimpse of a smoked human head, and the half-picked skeleton of what had been (in a culinary sense) a *well-dressed* man." Walt Whitman, as the editor of the *Brooklyn Eagle*, also praised *Typee*: "As a book to hold in one's hand and pore dreamily over of a summer day, it is unsurpassed." Herman's critical triumph was mixed with sadness over his brother Gansevoort's death in London in May 1846.

As expected, religious publications were outraged by the apparent immorality of *Typee*. The *Christian Parlor Magazine* wrote, "An apotheosis of barbarism! A panegyric on cannibal delights! An apostrophe to the spirit of savage felicity!" Apart from making Melville notorious as an author who lived among cannibals, *Typee* established his reputation as a writer of adventure stories in the tradition of Daniel Defoe and Tobias Smollett. During

Melville's lifetime *Typee* would often be rated as his finest work by those who could not or would not see him as anything but a writer of exotic tales.

OMOO

The publisher's accounts show that Melville earned only $86.26 from the first two thousand copies of *Typee* sold. At the time only two American writers, James Fenimore Cooper and Washington Irving, earned a satisfactory living by writing. Shortly after *Typee* appeared, Melville was hard at work on a sequel, *Omoo* (1847), an adventure tale set in Tahiti with as many criticisms of missionaries as his first book. In *Omoo* (the native word for beachcomber), Melville's style developed, juxtaposing images and metaphors: "In an instant, palm-trees and elms—canoes and skiffs—church spires and bamboos—all mingled in one vision of the present and past."

The literary influence of the Bible reached a new high point in Melville's work, with a tattooed sailor described as bearing a "sort of Urim and Thummim engraven upon his chest," an Old Testament reference to sacred tablets. *Omoo* includes details about whaling, a mutiny, beachcombing, and an enchanting maiden named Fayaway. British reviewers of *Omoo* applauded Melville's criticisms of missionaries and the French colonizers of Tahiti. *Blackwood's Magazine* admired the book and suspected that because the author's name was so euphonious, it must be a pen name: "Herman Melville sounds to us vastly like the harmonious and carefully selected appellation of an imaginary hero of romance." Reviewing the American edition of *Omoo*, Walt Whitman again was enthused, calling the book "thorough entertainment—not so light as to be tossed aside for its flippancy, nor so profound as to be tiresome."

MARDI

Once again, Melville set to work rapidly—he tended to spend what little he earned from publishers on books—and by the spring of 1847 had already begun his third book, *Mardi* (1849). The plot again involves a sailor deserting a whale ship to find adventure ashore in the South Seas. In August 1847, while working on the book, Herman became engaged to and married Elizabeth Shaw, the daughter of the eminent Massachusetts judge Lemuel Shaw. At this time, a number of American critics began to notice something immoral about *Typee*. The journalist Horace Greeley complained in the *New York Tribune*, "The tone is bad, and incidents of the most objectionable character are depicted with a racy lightness which would once have been admired but will now be justly condemned."

Greeley was particularly offended by "a penchant for bad liquors" and a "hankering after loose company not always of the masculine order." The *American Review* accused *Omoo* of trying to "excite unchaste desire." These charges came just weeks before Herman's wedding, along with a jesting reference in the *New York Daily Tribune* that "Mr. Herman Typee Omoo Melville" had just married a lady in Boston and could therefore expect a breach-of-promise lawsuit from "the fair forsaken Fayaway."

The attacks continued, and Melville was accused by the journalist William O. Bourne of being "the shameless herald of his own wantonness, and the pertinacious traducer of loftier and better men." Undaunted, in October 1847 Melville wrote to his British publisher to whet its appetite for his work in progress, a continuation of *Omoo* that would "possess more interest" than his previous works, "which treated of subjects comparatively trite." Yet privately, Melville was hurt by the criticism of his work and wrote to a relative that "hereafter I shall no more stab at a book (in print, I mean) than I would stab at a man."

The newlywed Melville set up house in Manhattan, where he took up a steady work routine, interrupted by walks through the city. His reading extended to Shakespeare, Montaigne, Rabelais, Dante, Defoe, Coleridge, Sir Thomas Browne, Robert Burton, Seneca, and Ossian. Melville's friends were aware of his bookworm tendencies, and one wrote: "By the way Melville reads old Books. He has borrowed Sir Thomas Browne of me and says finely of the speculations of the Religio Medici that Browne is a kind of 'crack'd Archangel.' Was ever anything of this sort said before by a sailor?" This intense reading was referred to in chapter 119 of *Omoo*: "In me, many worthies recline, and converse. I list to St. Paul who argues the doubts of Montaigne; Julian the Apostate cross-questions Augustine. . . . I am served like Bajazet: Bacchus my butler, Virgil my minstrel, Philip Sidney my page."

The rich resources of language had become a signal element of Melville's work. A poetic texture in his prose was inspired by a deep assimilation of strong precedents. *Mardi* begins as a lively narrative, but the story of a young sailor's adventures on a fictional Polynesian archipelago turns into a meditation on human experience on earth. Melville found room for political satire, discussions of morality, and metaphysical notions. Later, critics saw *Mardi* as a stepping stone to *Moby-Dick*, but at the time the author was concerned with the growing chorus of blame from critics, who doubted the accuracy of his first two autobiographical books.

In 1848 he wrote to his British publisher, John Murray, stating that since readers claimed that *Typee* and *Omoo* were invented rather than true, *Mardi* would be "a *real* romance of mine." By offering an undisguisedly novelistic work with elaborate concentration on language, he was ready to assert his artistic independence from the genre of travel memoir. The larger scope and ambitions of *Mardi* presented new difficulties, especially when Melville tried to incorporate elements of political satire, inspired by current events. As if in anticipation of how the book might be received, he included in it words about reviewers: "Critics?—Asses! Rather mules!—so emasculated, from vanity, they can not father a true thought. But at best, the greatest reviewers but prey on my leavings." This transition in Melville's writing clearly caused him stress. His wife Lizzie wrote to a family member about Herman: "His frequent exclamation is—'Oh Lizzy! The book!—the book!—what *will* become of the *Book*!'" Melville's first son Malcolm was born on 16 February 1849, just after Melville had completed work on *Mardi*. Before the baby arrived, Melville spent some time in what he considered to be his first truly intense reading of Shakespeare, during which he realized "the great Montaignism of Hamlet." His English publisher accepted *Mardi*, despite a reader's report declaring that the chapter "Dreams" seemed "to have been written by a madman," and the book's ending was "quite delirious."

By then, Melville was intimately aware of madness among his family and friends. When a friend went insane in 1849, he wrote to a mutual friend: "He who has never felt, momentarily, what madness is has but a mouthful of brains." At first, *Mardi* seemed to garner good reviews. Melville's friend Evert Duyckinck wrote about it in *The Literary World*, predicting that "the public will discover in him, at least, a capital essayist, in addition to the fascinating novelist and painter of sea life." Another early reviewer termed it "a regular Mardi-gras of a novel, to judge from the richness of its prose." But *The London Athenaeum* criticized the book for its "many madnesses," and the *Boston Post* claimed that the book recalled "the *talk* in Rabelais, divested of all its coarseness, and, it may be added, of all its wit and humor." The *New York Daily Tribune* stated, "If we had never heard of Mr. Melville before, we should soon have laid aside his book, as a monstrous compound of Carlyle, Jean-Paul, and Sterne, with now and then a touch of Ossian thrown in."

The *Boston Weekly Chronotype* claimed that the book "has greatly disappointed [Melville's] old admirers.... We cannot afford to let so vigorous and fascinating a writer in his own sphere become an imitator of Carlyle or of some fantastic German. Come back, O Herman, from thy cloudy, super-mundane flight, to the vessel's deck and the perfumed iles." Readers and reviewers longed for his return to the sea adventure tale, without meditations or metaphysics. With a family to support, Melville was ready to comply, for the time being.

REDBURN AND WHITE-JACKET

The relative failure of *Mardi* made Melville backtrack to a more straightforward genre of writing, a sea narrative in which the protagonist goes aboard ship, experiences Liverpool's sordid neighborhoods (as Melville himself had at age twenty), and returns home. Melville assured his publisher that *Redburn* (1849) would sell better than *Mardi* had, calling it "a plain, straightforward, amusing narrative of personal experience—the son of a gentleman on his first voyage to sea as a sailor—no metaphysics, no conic-sections, nothing but cakes and ale." He raced through the writing process, completing it in only about two months. He did not much value the result, writing to his father-in-law that the book was merely a job "done for money—being forced to it, as other men are to sawing wood." He would write even more harshly of *Redburn* to friends, calling it "a thing, which I, the author, know to be trash, and I wrote it to buy some tobacco with."

Melville soon understood that *Redburn*, however quickly finished, was not a solution to his financial problems. He decided to write another novel, *White-Jacket* (1850). Once again the narrative referred to sexual activity aboard ship: "What too many seamen are when ashore is very well known; but what some of them become when completely cut off from shore indulgences can hardly be imagined by landsmen. The sins for which the cities of the plain were overthrown still linger in some of these wooden-walled Gomorrahs of the deep."

Carefully based on research about shipboard medicine, the corporal punishment of sailors, and ports like Rio de Janeiro, Brazil, *White-Jacket* was greeted with positive reviews when it was published. Readers of the day were pleased by its good humor, as it presented a cozy amiability less iconoclastic than in his previous novels. Still, *White-Jacket* included some subtle allusions to homosexual activity aboard ship, describing an old sailor's "goggling glances" at a young sailor, who might be led "down into tarry perdition in his hideous store-rooms." More significantly, Melville used *White-Jacket* as a forum for discussing the evils of corporal punishment aboard ship, with chapters entitled "Some of the Evil Effects of Flogging," "Flogging Not Lawful," and "Flogging Not Necessary."

After his heavy schedule of writing, Melville planned a trip to England. His solo voyage was pleasant, once Melville managed to avoid on ship a "lisping youth of genteel capacity . . . quite disposed to be sociable," the son of a wealthy businessman whom Melville feared might be assigned as his cabin mate. Melville arrived in England in good spirits, stating in a letter that after ten years' absence, the British would surely describe him as the "author of 'Peedee' 'Hullabaloo' & 'Pog-Dog.' " The most impressive sight he saw during this 1849 journey was the Hôtel de Cluny in Paris (later the Musée de Cluny) and its ruins of Roman bath works, which he would evoke in his next novel, *Moby-Dick* (1851).

MOBY-DICK

Ten years earlier, as Melville was shipping out to England, the *Knickerbocker Magazine* in New York City had published an account of "Mocha Dick: or, The White Whale of the Pacific," about a white whale that had destroyed many boats. Melville probably meditated over this story for years, while intensely reading the Bible, which would dramatically influence *Moby-Dick; or, The Whale* in style and metaphor. An outsized book in every sense, breaking all boundaries and limits, *Moby-Dick* was also inspired by other summits of European literature: Shakespeare's plays, Goethe's *Faust* (1808–1832), Dante's *Divine Comedy* (ca. 1308–1321), Thomas Carlyle's essays, Laurence Sterne's *Tristram Shandy* (1760), and Robert Burton's *Anatomy of Melancholy* (1621), to name only a few. A massive wrestling with styles and subjects that the peaks of Western literature have struggled with, *Moby-Dick* is a rare book of infinite ambition that is at the height of its author's aims.

Typically jocular while writing it, Melville wrote to Richard Henry Dana in May 1850 that the book was half completed. "It will," he asserted, "be a strange sort of book, tho', I fear; blubber is blubber you know; tho' you may get oil out of it, the poetry runs as hard as sap from a frozen maple tree."

Melville moved to Massachusetts to be closer to a new friend, the novelist Nathaniel Hawthorne, with whom he was smitten. Indeed, in an essay-review of Hawthorne's book, *Mosses from an Old Manse* (1846), he wrote: "I felt that this Hawthorne has dropped germinous seeds into my soul. He expands and deepens down, the more I contemplate him; and further and further, shoots his strong New-England roots into the hot soil of my Southern soul." To a friend, Melville commented that compared with Hawthorne's soul, Washington Irving's was that of "a grasshopper." In turn, Hawthorne's wife Sophia wrote to her mother about Melville's "singularly quiet expression" that was "a strange, lazy glance, but with a power in it quite unique—It does not seem to penetrate through you, but to take you into himself." She added that Melville had described Hawthorne as "the first person whose physical being appeared to him wholly in harmony with the intellectual and spiritual. He said the sunny haze and the pensiveness, the symmetry of his face, the depth of eyes . . . were in exact response to the high calm intellect, the glowing, deep heart." With this attachment, it was no wonder that Melville decided suddenly to buy a farm, which he named Arrowhead, within walking distance of the Hawthorne home in Pittsfield, Massachusetts. The superhuman effort needed to write *Moby-Dick* in a few months required the extra inspiration brought by proximity to Hawthorne.

Working on his masterpiece, Melville seemed to concentrate more intensely on a reduced group of intimates, chief among whom was Hawthorne. When *Moby-Dick* was printed in 1851, he celebrated by inviting Hawthorne to a private dinner. According to one biographer, this was "the happiest day of Melville's life." The contentment would not last long, nor would the intense friendship. Hawthorne and his wife moved away from Pittsfield, but not before Melville modestly—and impractically—asked his friend not to write any review of *Moby-Dick*. Calling it a "wicked book" in its unconventional approach to moral questions, Melville was greeted by favorable reviews at first. *Harper's Magazine* observed,

> Beneath the whole story, the subtle, imaginative reader may perhaps find a pregnant allegory, intended to illustrate the mystery of human life. Certain it is that the rapid, pointed hints which are often thrown out, with the keenness and velocity of a harpoon, penetrate deep into the heart of things, showing that the genius of the author for moral analysis is scarcely surpassed by his wizard power of description.

However, the *Daily Palladium* of New Haven objected, "there is a little more irreverence and profane jesting than was needful to publish, however true to life the conversation may be." The *United States Magazine and Democratic Review* charged that Melville had "survived his reputation," and "in sober truth, Mr. Melville's vanity is immeasurable. . . . From this morbid self-esteem, coupled with a most unbounded love of notoriety, spring all Mr. Melville's efforts, all his rhetorical contortions, all his declamatory abuse of society, all his inflated sentiment, and all his insinuating licentiousness." The *Southern*

Quarterly Review opined that Captain Ahab's "ravings, and the ravings of some of the tributary characters, and the ravings of Mr. Melville himself, meant for eloquent declamation, are such as would justify a writ *de lunatico* [of madness] against all the parties." *Moby-Dick* sold fewer copies than Melville's previous two books, but he had more mouths than ever to feed after the birth of his son Stanwix in October 1851. Only posthumously would *Moby-Dick* be widely recognized as a masterpiece of world literature.

PIERRE AND "BARTLEBY THE SCRIVENER"

With financial pressures accumulating, Melville launched into another novel. *Pierre* (1852) describes erotically charged relationships between a mother and son and between the same young man and a young woman who might be his half sister. This incestuous subject matter was even more offensive to readers of the time than Melville's acceptance of a variety of religions instead of an exclusive Christian belief. Melville intended that *Pierre*, compared with *Moby-Dick*, would be "a rural bowl of milk," as he told Sophia Hawthorne, but it was an uncompromising work, in a style heavily influenced by Shakespeare: "In tremendous extremities human souls are like drowning men; well enough they know they are in peril; well enough they know the causes of that peril; nevertheless, the sea is the sea, and these drowning men do drown."

Given the poor sales of *Moby-Dick*, Melville was forced to accept a disadvantageous contract from Harper and Brothers in order to see *Pierre* into print. In *Pierre*, Melville may have drawn on recent memories of small-town life in Massachusetts. In addition to the novel's psychological investigations, the title character is a novelist who has conflicts with his publisher. Pierre's publishers write to him: "You are a swindler. Upon the pretense of writing a popular novel for us, you have been receiving cash advances from us, while passing through our press the sheets of a blasphemous rhapsody, filched from the vile Atheists, Lucian and Voltaire." This type of subversive humor was clearly informed by Melville's own adversarial relationships with his publishers. Harper was indeed unhappy with *Pierre*, and when Melville proposed to write a further book, they turned him down. His literary career had suffered a near-fatal blow.

When the British edition of *Moby-Dick* appeared in 1852, reviewers tended to point out literary influences, including Charles Lamb, Washington Irving, Thomas De Quincey, and Sir Thomas Browne. Critics also noted that Melville had arrived at a potentially dangerous new synthesis. *Bell's New Weekly Messenger*, based in London, stated that the book was ideal for readers who "love curry at its warmest point. Ginger cannot be too hot in the mouth for them. Such people, we should think, constitute the admirers of Herman Melville." The British reviews were better than those in America, but this did not help Melville's career or finances significantly. For the time being *Pierre* was not issued by any British publisher. American readers were informed by the *Boston Evening Gazette*, "Had Mr. Melville retired from the literary field after the production of 'Typee' and 'Omoo' he would have possessed an enviable reputation, but like many other authors he has spun the golden web so very fine in each succeeding work that it is almost valueless." At age thirty-two, Melville was a washed-up writer in the eyes of some influential critics.

Some charged him with even worse crimes. The *Boston Post* called *Pierre* "the craziest fiction extant," adding that to "save it from utter worthlessness, it must be called a prose poem, and even then, it might be supposed to emanate from a lunatic hospital rather than from the quiet retreats of Berkshire." Melville was accused of producing "more and sadder trash" than any writer of "undoubted ability." The theme of insanity was frequently repeated, as in the *Southern Quarterly Review*, which asserted, "The annals of Bedlam might be defied to produce such another collection of lunatics as the hero, his mother, his sister, and the heroine. Were there no mad doctors in that part of the country where they lived? Were the asylums all full?"

Some critics even claimed that Melville himself was insane, as a headline in the *New York Day Book* charged: "HERMAN MELVILLE CRAZY." The accompanying article stated that his last book was "composed of the ravings and reveries of a madman" and that "Melville was really supposed to be deranged." The *Southern Quarterly Review* similarly asserted that he had "gone 'clean daft' . . . [in] a very mad book." The British *New Monthly Magazine* joined the chorus with a review of *Moby-Dick* in 1853 that described the book's style as "maniacal—mad as a March hare—mowing, gibbering, screaming, like an incurable Bedlamite, reckless of keeper or strait-waistcoat."

Only rare readers and reviewers appreciated the complexities of Melville's psychological investigations in *Pierre*. The *Washington National Intelligencer* stated, "Melville has a strange power to reach the sinuousities of a thought, if we may so express ourselves." Into the genre of family novel Melville had introduced disturbing and unexpected elements (which continue to trouble some readers). *Putnam's Monthly* placed the blame on bad literary influences and asserted that Melville should have read prose by the lucid Joseph Addison instead of the complex, clotted works of Thomas Browne. By following this prescription, the well-intentioned critic hoped, Melville's writing would improve in "a year or two."

In understandable despair about his earnings and his literary career, Melville tried to obtain a consular appointment, a sinecure given to the political favorites of elected officials. Hawthorne was named consul to Liverpool, but Melville had no such luck. Meanwhile he worked on a new project for a novel, with the provisory title "The Isle of the Cross," which was never completed and is now lost.

Melville's family was losing any faith they might have previously had in his literary work. His mother wrote to her brother that Herman's ardent writing did not agree with him: "This constant working of the brain, and excitement of the imagination, is wearing Herman out." Her dream, to see her son appointed to a consular job and thus be saved from literary obsessions, would never be realized. Instead, after the "Isle of the Cross" project, he produced some short stories, including "Bartleby the Scrivener," one of his most permanently astonishing works. The tale of the office employee who would "prefer not to" has been seen as a precursor of modern writers from Franz Kafka to Samuel Beckett in its blend of gloomy comedy and outright despair. Its landscape of Lower Manhattan as a tragedy-laden shrine of commerce was as current 150 years later as when the story was written, making it perhaps one of the most perpetually relevant tales in American literature. Narrated by a perplexed employer, "Bartleby" opens unforgettably:

> I am a rather elderly man. The nature of my avocations for the last thirty years has brought me into more than ordinary contact with what would seem an interesting and somewhat singular set of men, of whom as yet nothing that I know of has ever been written:—I mean the law-copyists or scriveners. I have known very many of them, professionally and privately, and if I pleased, could relate divers histories, at which good-natured gentlemen might smile, and sentimental souls might weep. But I waive the biographies of all other scriveners for a few passages in the life of Bartleby, who was a scrivener the strangest I ever saw or heard of. While of other law-copyists I might write the complete life, of Bartleby nothing of that sort can be done. I believe that no materials exist for a full and satisfactory biography of this man. It is an irreparable loss to literature. Bartleby was one of those beings of whom nothing is ascertainable, except from the original sources, and in his

case those are very small. What my own astonished eyes saw of Bartleby, that is all I know of him, except, indeed, one vague report which will appear in the sequel.

"Bartleby" was greeted by an unusually comprehending review from the *Boston Daily Evening Traveler*. Its critic praised the story for "originality of invention and grotesqueness of humor . . . equal to anything from the pen of Dickens, whose writings it closely resembles, both as to the character of the sketch and the peculiarity of the style."

In 1853, when it seemed that Melville's fortunes in novel writing could not be lower, a fire broke out in the storerooms of Harper and Brothers and many of Melville's warehoused books were destroyed, thus removing any hope, already remote, of future royalties. Harper reacted by demanding that Melville pay in advance for any reprints of his books. Small wonder that he preferred to focus on publishing shorter works in magazines at this time, such as the humorous "I and My Chimney," with its fairly blatant phallic symbolism.

ISRAEL POTTER AND THE PIAZZA TALES

While working on short stories, Melville also prepared a new full-length work, a project he had contemplated for several years. It was inspired by *The Life and Remarkable Adventures of Israel R. Potter*, a true account that had first appeared in 1824. An eighteenth-century American farmer and adventurer, Potter fought in the Battle of Bunker Hill and later went to Europe as a courier of secret messages to Benjamin Franklin. Eventually, however, he became a beggar in London; perhaps Potter's troubled later life reminded Melville of his own career difficulties. The book was an occasion for Melville to research and recreate the lives of historical Americans such as Ethan Allen, Benjamin Franklin, and John Paul Jones. He described Franklin as "Jack of all trades, master of each and mastered by none—the type and genius of his land, Franklin was everything but a poet."

The presence of these real-life characters disarmed reviewers of Melville's *Israel Potter* (1855), such as the critic at the *New Bedford Mercury*, who called the book "veritable history, which is a mixture of fun, gravity, romance, and reality very taking from beginning to end." In his quintessential Americanness, Franklin's nonpoetic status must have struck Melville, who by now was surely aware that he himself was a strong poet. One of the most poetic of his prose pieces, later collected in *The Piazza Tales* (1856), was "Benito Cereno," based on a historical incident of shipboard mutiny described in an 1817 book by Captain Amasa Delano, *A Narrative of Voyages and Travels, in the Northern and Southern Hemispheres.*

Melville finished "Benito Cereno" in 1855, and reviews for *The Piazza Tales* were generally positive, led by William Ellery Channing's notice in the *New Bedford Daily Mercury*: "Hawthorne is more dry, prosaic and detailed, Irving more elegant, careful, and popular, but Melville is a kind of wizard; he writes strange and mysterious things that belong to other worlds beyond this tame and everyday place we live in."

In October 1856, desperately feeling the need of a change of scene, Melville sailed on a solitary trip to England, Italy, and the Near East. In Southport, England, in November he met Hawthorne once again, although the two old friends now felt uneasy in each other's company. Hawthorne later noted in his journal that he regretted his failure to find a consular appointment for Melville, who must have "suffered from too constant literary occupation, pursued without much success, latterly." According to Hawthorne, Melville's works "for a long while past, have indicated a morbid state of mind." The trip at times revealed stresses and tensions, as in Constantinople, where Melville noted in his journal, "Dread of the Arabs. Offering to lead me into a side-hole. . . . Horrible place for assassination." He described the ornate Church of the Holy Sepulcher in Jerusalem as "all is glitter and nothing is gold. A sickening cheat." He mocked commercialized tourism in the Holy Land of 1857 by recording a tour guide's typical spiel: "Yonder is the arch where Christ was shown to the people, and just by that open window is sold the best coffee in Jerusalem." He seemed relieved to return home to America.

THE CONFIDENCE-MAN, THE LECTURE CIRCUIT, AND POETRY

Melville's next novel, *The Confidence-Man* (1857), was based on a news item from 1849 in which a thief abused the trust of his victims in Manhattan. Melville transferred the story to a Mississippi riverboat, where deceivers from P. T. Barnum to Ralph Waldo Emerson are evoked. (Emerson was considered a fraud by Melville because he claimed that evil does not exist.) The satiric *Confidence-Man* expressed the writer's bitterness at what his life had become despite his accomplishments. Constant cheating and swindling fill the pages of this novel, one of Melville's most devastatingly dark works. Perhaps the bitterest irony for Melville was the American manner of optimistically claiming that everything is fine when manifestly it is not. His mood was doubtless not improved by a series of

health problems that he suffered while writing the novel, including rheumatism and sciatica.

The critic Newton Arvin has written of the "homogeneity" of Melville's writings at this time, expressing emotions drawn from life experiences: "ideas of failure, bankruptcy, anticlimax, the miscarriage of hopes, and a willful withdrawal from the life of men; . . . the closely related motive of exile, desertion, forlornness, or sterility; and . . . the motive of treachery, fraudulence, and falsity." Among the early reviews of *The Confidence-Man*, the one appearing in the *New York Journal* castigated Melville for the way "dogmatizing, theorizing, philosophising and amplifying upon every known subject are 'piled up' for forty-five chapters in the most eccentric and incomprehensible manner." The *Cincinnati Enquirer* expressed one of the common misunderstandings of the day about Melville's achievement: " 'Typee,' one of, if not the first of his works, is the best, and 'The Confidence-Man' the last, decidedly the worst. So Mr. M's authorship is toward the nadir rather than the climax." *The Critic* called *The Confidence-Man* "the hardest nut to crack" of the author's books and even doubted whether Melville's persona as adventurer-writer was genuine: "There are some parts of the story in which we feel half inclined to doubt whether this apostle of geniality is not, after all, an arch-imposter of the deepest dye."

As these reviews came in, Melville's finances reached a critical point, and he was obliged to sell his farm in piecemeal fashion. Meanwhile his family tried to persuade him to stop writing, given the disastrous results, both financially and on his mental health. In April 1857 his sister Augusta wrote to a relative that it was "of the utmost importance that something should be done to prevent the necessity of Herman's writing. . . . [To] return to the sedentary life which that of an author writing for his support necessitates, he would risk the loss of all the benefit to his health which he has gained by his tour, and possibly become a confirmed invalid. Of this his physicians have warned him."

Melville's brother-in-law, Lemuel Shaw, wrote to another relative that *The Confidence-Man* belonged to "that horribly uninteresting class of nonsensical books he is given to writing—where there are pages of crude theory and speculation to every line of narrative—and interspersed with strained and ineffectual attempts to be humorous. I wish he could or would do better, when he went away he was dispirited and ill." So that Melville would neither have to write nor labor at his farm, his family tried to find him a job at the U.S. Customs House in New York City, but without immediate success. In June

1857 Melville attended a dinner at which Oliver Wendell Holmes described a lecturer as "a literary strumpet subject for a greater than whore's fee to prostitute himself." Short of alternatives, Melville resolved nevertheless to try to make a living giving public lectures.

Melville offered to lecture on subjects like "Statues in Rome," about which he admitted he was no expert. As he was offered no bookings in Manhattan, his lectures—beginning in 1857—took place in smaller cities such as Albany, Syracuse, and Binghamton. These were a disaster. The *Lawrence Courier* complained that Melville's voice was so low that "a large part of the audience could not hear," while the *Bunker-Hill Aurora* and *Boston Mirror* stated that during the speech, some of his audience "left the hall; some read books and newspapers, some sought refuge in sleep, and some, to their praise be it spoken, seemed determined to use it as an appropriate occasion for self-discipline in the blessed virtue of patience."

Melville's habit of muttering was part of the problem, as the *Auburn American* claimed: "The lecture was completely, absolutely spoiled by his inexcusable blundering, sing song, monotonous delivery. It was the most complete case of infanticide we ever heard of; he literally strangled his own child. The words came through his moustache about as loud and with as much force as the creaking of a field mouse through a thick hedge." Still he pressed on, giving unsatisfactory speeches in Buffalo, Cincinnati, and other cities until February 1858. Shortly after finishing his tour, he had a physical collapse, after which, his wife later recalled, he "never regained his former vigor and strength."

As soon as he recovered somewhat, he went back to lecturing, going as far away as Wisconsin and Chicago since no organization ever invited him back for a second visit. This painful time was not entirely wasted. When not on the road, Melville still worked on his farm while deepening his passion for poetry, which would be his main literary outlet for the rest of his life.

From his early youth, Melville had learned many great poems by heart, and he now began to write verse of extraordinary quality. Like Walt Whitman, whose fascinating prose has been relatively neglected because of the fame of his poetry, Melville's poems may have been overlooked because of his renown as a novelist. Despite the praise of discerning writers like Robert Penn Warren, Melville's poetry at the turn of the twenty-first century had still not received the full attention it deserves. Turning his attention seriously to poetry, Melville read not only major and minor poets of America and England, but also

outstanding critical essayists. He researched the subject as thoroughly as he had the lore and history of whaling, and many other topics, when writing his novels.

Melville's first collection of poems, compiled in 1860, was unpublished, but he continued to write and plan future collections. In March 1861, still in search of a job, Melville went to Washington, D.C. There he attended a party at the White House given by the new president, Abraham Lincoln. Melville wrote to his wife, "Old Abe is much better looking than I expected and younger looking. He shook hands like a good fellow—working hard at it like a man sawing wood at so much per cord. Mrs. Lincoln is rather good-looking I thought." This somewhat exalted praise—few admired Mrs. Lincoln's looks—was not rewarded by any official appointment.

Melville returned to the Massachusetts countryside, where he felt, as before, permanently uneasy. In a book Melville owned, the British essayist William Hazlitt commented, "All country people hate each other. They have so little comfort that they envy their neighbors the smallest pleasure or advantage, and nearly grudge themselves the necessaries of life." Next to this, Melville jotted down, "That's a great truth." In November 1862 the disadvantages of rural life were reinforced by a road accident in which Melville was thrown from a wagon, breaking a shoulder and injuring his ribs. A friend recalled that after the accident, Melville avoided taking carriage rides and although eventually he seemed to recover from the shock, he probably never did so completely. In November 1863, when he finally sold his Pittsfield farm and moved back to Manhattan, it was with little nostalgia for rural life, even though Melville is still celebrated locally as a Berkshires writer.

BATTLE PIECES

From the beginning of the Civil War, Melville wrote poems inspired by some of the chief battles. In April 1863 he pulled strings with civil servant friends of his late father-in-law, Judge Shaw, to win permission to tour the Army of the Potomac's front lines. In 1864 he was "much shocked" to hear that Nathaniel Hawthorne had died, although the two friends had grown apart. The war had already inspired poems of anguished pity, as in Melville's most celebrated line, "All wars are boyish, and are fought by boys," from "The March into Virginia," inspired by the First Battle of Manassas in July 1861. His "Shiloh: A Requiem," following the Battle of Shiloh of April 1862, painted an uncanny scene of calm after the tragic events of war:

Skimming lightly, wheeling still,
The swallows fly low
Over the fields in clouded days,
The forest-field of Shiloh—
Over the field where April rain
Solaced the parched one stretched in pain
Through the pause of night
That followed the Sunday fight
Around the church of Shiloh—
The church so lone, the log-built one,
That echoed to many a parting groan
And natural prayer
Of dying foemen mingled there—
Foemen at morn, but friends at eve—
Fame or country least their care:
(What like a bullet can undeceive!)
But now they lie low,
While over them the swallows skim,
And all is hushed at Shiloh.

His elegy to the recently assassinated Abraham Lincoln, "The Martyr," rings truer than the more famous "O Captain, My Captain" by Walt Whitman, perhaps because genuine rage seeps through the prosody more than in Whitman's work. Melville subtitled his poem "Indicative of the Passion of the People on the 15th of April, 1865" and later added a note to indicate that he was not advocating revenge against the Southern rebels, although this is indeed the emotion behind his poem:

Good Friday was the day
    Of the prodigy and crime,
When they killed him in his pity,
    When they killed him in his prime
Of clemency and calm—
    When with yearning he was filled
    To redeem the evil-willed,
And, though conqueror, be kind;
    But they killed him in his kindness,
    In their madness and their blindness,
And they killed him from behind.

There is sobbing of the strong,
    And a pall upon the land;
But the People in their weeping
    Bare the iron hand:
Beware the People weeping
    When they bare the iron hand.

He lieth in his blood—
    The father in his face;
They have killed him, the Forgiver—
    The Avenger takes his place,

The Avenger wisely stern,
    Who in righteousness shall do
    What the heavens call him to,
And the parricides remand;
    For they killed him in his kindness,
    In their madness and their blindness,
And his blood is on their hand.

There is sobbing of the strong,
    And a pall upon the land;
But the People in their weeping
    Bare the iron hand:
Beware the People weeping
    When they bare the iron hand

Despite this powerful emotional aura, his collection, *Battle Pieces and Aspects of the War* (1866), was dismissed by most critics. The *American Literary Gazette and Publishers' Circular* called the rhymes "fearful" because one poem rhymed "law" with "Shenandoah." The *Cincinnati Enquirer* asserted that some of the poems "would be prose but for the typography," while the *Boston Post* somewhat ambiguously called them "pregnant, but not artistic." Melville was unfavorably compared with more conventional war poets like James Russell Lowell, and even the intelligent reader William Dean Howells complained in the *Atlantic Monthly*, "Mr. Melville's work possesses the negative virtues of originality in such degree that it not only reminds you of no poetry you have read, but of no life you have known."

Melville's new job as Deputy Inspector at the Customs House in New York City, from 1866 onward, permitted him much time outdoors, going from ship to ship to verify their cargoes. In 1867 domestic worries, fueled by continuing economic concerns, exploded when Melville's eighteen-year-old son Malcolm killed himself with a pistol at home. At first the coroner's verdict was suicide "under temporary insanity of mind," but the family appealed this judgment, which was revised to an accident. Whatever the truth was, Melville wrote to a friend about the funeral, "I wish you could have seen him as he lay in his last attitude, the ease of a gentle nature. Mackie never gave me a disrespectful word in his life, nor in any way ever failed in filialness."

The weight of this loss pursued Melville in his work days at the Customs House. In his off hours, he remained on the periphery of literary life, going to see a Manhattan reading by the touring novelist Charles Dickens in March 1868—a triumphant lecturer, in contrast to Melville—although not meeting him. Melville, who was still indebted to Harper's for advances that had not been earned by book sales, also studied the visual arts and collected engravings while continuing to concentrate on poetry. In 1869 he underlined an observation in Matthew Arnold's *Essays in Criticism* (1865): "Genius is mainly an affair of energy, and poetry is mainly an affair of genius." In the same book, Melville drew a box around a quotation from the French writer Maurice de Guérin: "The literary career seems to me unreal, both in its essence and in the rewards which one seeks from it, and therefore fatally marred by a secret absurdity." Melville added in the margin: "This is the finest verbal statement of a truth which every one who thinks in these days must have felt."

CLAREL

Having for a decade been mulling over his trip to the Middle East, Melville in 1870 began work on his book-length narrative poem, *Clarel* (1876). The title character is a divinity student who makes a pilgrimage to the Holy Land and meets two young men, Rolfe and Vine. Melville cast himself as the character Rolfe, while Vine is his late friend Hawthorne. Although *Clarel* remains one of Melville's least-read works, in its time the long narrative form was embraced by the poets Alfred Lord Tennyson, Elizabeth Barrett Browning, William Morris, and Robert Browning. There were also vivid older examples by such poets as Lord Byron and Walter Scott.

It took Melville five years to finish *Clarel*. The poem contains discourses on religious beliefs and politics, expressing Melville's personal philosophy, as when the character Rolfe states that Christianity

> made earth inhuman; yes, a den
> Worse for Christ's coming, since his love
> (Perverted) did but venom prove.

While laboring on *Clarel*, Melville had a rare experience of literary recognition when seven of his poems from *Battle Pieces* were included in an anthology, *Poets and Poetry of America* (1872), whose editor, Richard Henry Stoddard, would later call Melville "one of our great unrecognized poets." Later, Melville's uncle Peter Gansevoort paid for the publication of *Clarel*, perhaps hoping for a picturesque narrative.

Many critics of the day spoke of Melville as if he were already dead. The *Springfield Republican* wrote in 1876, "Mr. Melville lives in his novels—a sort of posthumous life, it is true, yet they are worth reading." The *Boston Daily Evening Transcript* found the massive work "rather apt to create a disgust for poetry if one is obliged to read them conscientiously and crucially." Although discovering in it

echoes of poets from William Blake to Hafez, the critic ultimately found the book confusing. Likewise, the *New York Independent* found Clarel "destitute of interest or metrical skill."

London's critics were more receptive. The *London Academy* stated, "in the subtle blending of old and new thought, in the unexpected turns of argument, and in the hidden connexion between things outward separate, Mr. Melville reminds us of A[rthur] H[ugh] Clough." However, *Clarel*'s reception made Melville even more obscure in the world of American letters. There were brief respites, as in 1882, when a newly founded Authors Club in New York City invited him to speak at one of their gatherings, but he refused, stating that "he had become too much of a hermit [whose] . . . nerves could no longer stand large gatherings." Melville's brother Thomas died in 1884, Herman himself suffered from rheumatic gout, and the rest of the family struggled with ill health as well. Melville kept on at the Customs House, where his wife stated, "the occupation is a great thing for him," declaring that working outdoors, going from boat to boat, suited him vastly better than a desk job that "required head work."

JOHN MARR AND OTHER SAILORS, TIMOLEON, AND BILLY BUDD

In his late sixties, Melville grew increasingly weary, but kept laboring on at his literary projects and day job. In 1888 he gathered poems into a new collection, *John Marr and Other Sailors*, portraits of sailors and adventurers he had known. He worked on another text, *Timoleon* (1891) and his last great prose work, *Billy Budd* (1924), which was unfinished when he died. The power of *Billy Budd* testifies to the fact that Melville still harbored a unique creative force despite his career reversals. Although Billy Budd's protagonist is a doomed, conventionally handsome sailor, the first example of physical beauty that Melville cites in the story is a black man in Liverpool, a common sailor,

> so intensely black that he must needs have been a native African of the unadulterate blood of Ham. A symmetric figure much above the average height. The two ends of a gay silk handkerchief thrown loose about the neck danced upon the displayed ebony of his chest; in his ears were big hoops of gold, and a Scotch Highland bonnet with a tartan band set off his shapely head. It was a hot noon in July; and his face, lustrous with perspiration, beamed with barbaric good humor. In jovial sallies right and left, his white teeth flashing into view, he rollicked along, the centre of a company of his shipmates.

As for *Timoleon*, the story of a Corinthian general of the fourth century B.C. was Melville's starting point for a poetry collection that explored his own family strife and career struggles. They included a poignant short meditation, "Monody," written after hearing of the death of Hawthorne in 1864:

> To have known him, to have loved him
>   After loneness long;
> And then to be estranged in life,
>   And neither in the wrong;
> And now for death to set his seal—
>   Ease me, a little ease, my song!
>
> By wintry hills his hermit-mound
>   The sheeted snow-drifts drape,
> And houseless there the snow-bird flits
>   Beneath the fir-trees' crape:
> Glazed now with ice the cloistral vine
>   That hid the shyest grape.

Despite the emotions expressed in such poignant late poems, a description of Melville in 1886 telling racy anecdotes in a barbershop suggests that he was still capable of joie de vivre. This joy may have had little to do with literature, however. One friend later recalled asking Melville at this time to borrow some of the books he had written, and Melville admitted he owned no copies of them.

In 1890, *New York Publishers' Weekly* explained, "There are more people today who believe Herman Melville dead than there are those who know he is living." He took strenuous walks around Manhattan, being ever restless, until finally he died on 28 September 1891 of an enlarged heart, aggravated by two years of erysipelas, a bacterial skin infection. Newspaper obituaries, like that of the *New York Press*, stated that Melville had "fallen into a literary decline," while the *New York Times* headlined the story: "THE LATE HIRAM MELVILLE," calling him "an absolutely forgotten man."

POSTHUMOUS RENOWN

At first, Melville's reputation fared little better after his death than when he was alive. In England, a Melville revival began, fueled by the admiration of writers like W. H. Hudson, who in the 1890s referred to *Moby-Dick* as a "great American book." This despite the novelist Joseph Conrad, who in 1907 wrote to a friend that he found *Moby-Dick* a "rather strained rhapsody with whaling for a subject and not a single sincere line in the 3 vols of it." In his *Studies in Classic American Literature* (1923), D. H. Lawrence, a more sensitive reader, applauded *Omoo* as "a fascinating book; picaresque, rascally, roving. Melville, as a bit of a beachcomber. . . . For once he is really reckless. For once he takes life as it comes. . . . That is good about

Melville: he never repents." Of *Moby-Dick*, Lawrence wrote that although Melville was "rather a sententious man," he created in that novel "a great book, a very great book, the greatest book of the sea ever written. It moves awe in the soul." Growing admiration of Melville was fueled by commemorations of his birthday centennial in 1919, followed by the generally unsatisfactory but significant first full-length biography, Raymond Weaver's *Herman Melville: Mariner and Mystic* (1921). Weaver presented Melville as a literary giant who "sinned blackly against the orthodoxy of his time." Appreciative books, like Lewis Mumford's *Herman Melville: A Study of His Life and Vision* (1929), appeared. F. O. Matthiessen's *American Renaissance* (1941), seeing Melville as a natural, ingenuous writer, was highly influential. After scolding Melville in schoolmasterish fashion for stylistic faults, Matthiessen states that Melville's "liberation in *Moby-Dick* through the agency of Shakespeare was almost an unconscious reflex." He added perceptively that in *Moby-Dick*, the character of Captain Ahab is "not so much a varied human being as a state of mind." Matthiessen underlined the tragic element in Melville's writings, calling *Pierre* "about the most desperate in our literature."

In the late twentieth century, critics have offered appreciative looks at even unpopular Melville works like *The Confidence-Man*, seeing it as a precursor of the Theatre of the Absurd, Albert Camus, Jorge Luis Borges, and Vladimir Nabokov. Others, like Warner Berthoff, have found his shorter writings like *The Piazza Tales* to be his most "instructive" achievement, that might "serve as a practical model" for today's writers. Melville's true value as a poet has still to be fully measured, worthy of a place alongside Emily Dickinson, Walt Whitman, and Ralph Waldo Emerson. As a novelist, he surely stands alone in nineteenth-century America.

[*See also* Short Story in America, The.]

SELECTED WORKS

Typee (1846)
Omoo (1847)
Mardi (1849)
Redburn (1849)
White-Jacket (1850)
Moby-Dick (1851)
Pierre (1852)
Israel Potter (1855)
Piazza Tales (1856)
The Confidence-Man (1857)
Battle Pieces and Aspects of the War (1866)
Clarel (1876)

John Marr and Other Sailors (1888)

Timoleon (1891)

Billy Budd (1924)

FURTHER READING

Allen, Gay Wilson. *Melville and His World*. New York, 1971.

Arvin, Newton. *Herman Melville*. New York, 1950. A combination of perceptiveness and hasty value judgments.

Auden, W. H. *The Enchafed Flood; or, The Romantic Iconography of the Sea*. New York, 1950. A major Anglo-American poet analyzes Melville's sea imagery.

Baird, James. *Ishmael*. Baltimore, 1956.

Bercaw, Mary K. *Melville's Sources*. Evanston, Ill., 1987.

Berthoff, Warner. *The Example of Melville*. Princeton, N.J., 1962.

Bloom, Harold. *Ahab*. New York, 1991.

Bloom, Harold. *Herman Melville: Modern Critical Views*. New York, 1986.

Bloom, Harold. *Herman Melville's* Moby-Dick: *Modern Critical Interpretations*. New York, 1986.

Bowen, James K., and Richard Vanderbeets. *A Critical Guide to Herman Melville: Abstracts of Forty Years of Criticism*. Glenview, Ill., 1971.

Branch, Watson G. *Melville: The Critical Heritage*. The Critical Heritage Series. London and Boston, 1974.

Braswell, William. *Melville's Religious Thought: An Essay in Interpretation*. New York, 1959.

Brodhead, Richard H. *Hawthorne, Melville, and the Novel*. Chicago, 1976.

Brodhead, Richard H. *New Essays on* Moby-Dick: *The American Novel*. Cambridge and New York, 1986.

Bryant, John. *A Companion to Melville Studies*. New York, 1986.

Bryant John. *Melville and Repose: The Rhetoric of Humor in the American Renaissance*. New York, 1993.

Bryant, John, and Robert Milder, eds. *Melville's Ever-moving Dawn: Centennial Essays*. Kent, Ohio, 1997.

Chase, Richard Volney. *Melville, A Collection of Critical Essays: Twentieth-Century Views*. Englewood Cliffs, N.J., 1962.

Cowen, Walker. *Melville's Marginalia*. New York, 1987. A study of Melville as engaged reader.

Davis, Clark. *After the Whale: Melville in the Wake of* Moby-Dick. Tuscaloosa, Ala., 1995.

Dillingham, William B. *Melville and His Circle: The Last Years*. Athens, Ga., 1996.

Eckardt, Sister Mary Ellen, and Harold Bloom, eds. *Herman Melville's* Billy Budd, *"Benito Cereno," "Bartleby the Scrivener," and Other Tales*. New York: Chelsea, 1987.

Eckardt, Sister Mary Ellen, and Robert Milder, eds. *Critical Essays on Melville's* Billy Budd, Sailor. Critical Essays on American Literature series. Boston, 1989.

Fiedler, Leslie. *Love and Death in the American Novel*. 1960. Reprint, New York, 1962. An early look at male bonding in *Moby-Dick* and other works by Melville.

Gale, Robert L. *A Herman Melville Encyclopedia*. Westport, Conn., 1995.

Garner, Stanton. *The Civil War World of Herman Melville*. Lawrence, Kans., 1993.

Gilman, William H. *Melville's Early Life and* Redburn. New York, 1951.

Haberstroh, Charles. *Melville and Male Identity*. Rutherford, N.J., 1980.

Hayes, Kevin, and Hershel Parker. *Checklist of Melville Reviews*. Evanston, Ill., 1991.

Hetherington, Hugh W. *Melville's Reviewers, British and American: 1846–1891*. Chapel Hill, N.C., 1961.

Higgins, Brian, and Hershel Parker. *Herman Melville: The Contemporary Reviews*. New York, 1995.

Hillway, Tyrus. *Herman Melville*. New York, 1963.

Hillway, Tyrus, ed. Moby-Dick *Centennial Essays*. Dallas, Tex., 1953.

Hoffman, Daniel. *Form and Fable in American Fiction*. New York, 1961.

Howard, Leon. *Herman Melville: A Biography*. Berkeley, Calif., 1951.

Jehlen, Myra. *Herman Melville: A Collection of Critical Essays*. Englewood Cliffs, N.J., 1994.

Knapp, Joseph G. *Tortured Synthesis: The Meaning of Melville's* Clarel. New York, 1972.

Lawrence, D. H. *Studies in Classic American Literature*. 1923. Reprint, London, 1971. Among the most readable of writings on Melville.

Levin, Harry. *The Power of Blackness: Hawthorne, Poe, Melville*. New York, 1958.

Levine, Robert S. *The Cambridge Companion to Herman Melville*. Cambridge Companions to Literature. Cambridge and New York, 1998.

Leyda, Jay. *The Melville Log: A Documentary Life of Herman Melville, 1819–1891*. 2 vols. New York, 1969. Massive and useful.

Lowell, Robert. *Benito Cereno in The Old Glory*. New York, 1965. An influential dramatization of Melville's story.

Martin, Robert K. *Hero, Captain, and Stranger: Male Friendship, Social Critique, and Literary Form in the*

Sea Novels of Herman Melville. Chapel Hill, N.C., 1986. A gender studies approach.

Matthiessen, F. O. *American Renaissance: Art and Expression in the Age of Emerson and Whitman.* London and New York, 1941. A lastingly influential study of Melville as a tragic, original American voice.

Mayoux, Jean-Jacques. *Melville.* Translated by John Ashbery. New York, 1960. A succinct appreciation from France, where Melville has long been appreciated.

Metcalf, Eleanor Melville. *Herman Melville: Cycle and Epicycle.* Cambridge, Mass., 1953.

Miller, Edwin Haviland. *Melville.* New York, 1975. Intelligent, sensitive overview.

Miller, James E., Jr. *A Reader's Guide to Herman Melville.* New York, 1962.

Miller, Perry. *The Raven and the Whale: Poe, Melville, and the New York Literary Scene.* New York, 1956. A look at the harsh literary controversies of the early nineteenth century in America.

Mumford, Lewis. *Herman Melville: A Study of His Life and Vision.* New York and London, 1929.

Mushabac, Jane. *Melville's Humor: A Critical Study.* Hamden, Conn., 1981.

Olsen, Charles. *Call Me Ishmael.* New York, 1947. A literary descendant of Melville's whale story.

Parker, Hershel. *Reading* Billy Budd. Evanston, Ill., 1990.

Parker, Hershel. *Herman Melville: A Biography.* 2 vols. Baltimore, 1996. Full of essential data and fervent interpretations.

Parker, Hershel, ed. *The Recognition of Herman Melville: Selected Criticism since 1846.* Ann Arbor, Mich., 1967.

Pavese, Cesare. "Herman Melville." In his *American Literature: Essays and Opinions.* Translated by Edwin Fussell. Berkeley, Calif., 1970. Pavese, Melville's Italian translator, had his own tragic aura.

Ricks, Beatrice, and Joseph D. Adams. *Herman Melville: A Reference Bibliography: 1900–1972, with Selected Nineteenth-Century Materials.* Boston, 1973.

Robertson-Lorant, Laurie. *Melville: A Biography.* Amherst, Mass, 1998.

Robillard, Douglas. *Melville and the Visual Arts: Ionian Form, Venetian Tint.* Kent, Ohio, 1997.

Rosenberry, Edward H. *Melville and the Comic Spirit.* Cambridge, Mass., 1955.

Sealts, Merton M. *The Early Lives of Melville: Nineteenth-Century Biographical Sketches and Their Authors.* Madison, Wis., 1974.

Sealts, Merton M., Jr. *Melville as Lecturer.* Cambridge, Mass., 1957.

Sealts, Merton M., Jr. *Melville's Reading.* Columbia, S.C., 1988.

Sedgwick, William Ellery. *Herman Melville: The Tragedy of Mind.* New York, 1962.

Sewall, Richard B. "Moby-Dick as Tragedy." In his *The Vision of Tragedy.* New Haven, Conn., 1959.

Shurr, William H. *The Mystery of Iniquity: Melville as Poet, 1857–1891.* Lexington, Ky., 1951.

Spark, Clare. *Hunting Captain Ahab.* Kent, Ohio, 2001.

Stein, William Bysshe. *The Poetry of Melville's Late Years: Time, History, Myth, and Religion.* Albany, N.Y., 1970.

Thompson, Lawrance Roger. *Melville's Quarrel with God.* Princeton, N.J., 1952.

Vincent, Howard P., ed. *Twentieth Century Interpretations of* Billy Budd. Englewood Cliffs, N.J., 1971.

Warren, Robert Penn. "Melville's Poems." *Southern Review* 3 (1967): 799–855. A respected American poet offers his views on Melville's work in verse.

Yannella, Donald, and Hershel Parker. *The Endless, Winding Way in Melville.* Glassboro, N.J., 1981.

See also the article on "Bartleby the Scrivener" and *Moby-Dick*, immediately following.

HERMAN MELVILLE'S "BARTLEBY THE SCRIVENER"

by Robert M. Dowling

Herman Melville anonymously published his first short story, "Bartleby, the Scrivener: A Story of Wall Street," in the November and December 1853 issues of *Putnam's Monthly Magazine*, and it was later included without the subtitle in Melville's *The Piazza Tales* (1856). "Bartleby" is a triumph of ambiguity, and the title character has been read as representing Henry David Thoreau, Jesus Christ, the Cherokee Indians, the Hindu ascetic Saniassi, and Melville himself, among dozens of others. Melville invites allegorical readings of this kind, as he implicitly likens Bartleby to Samuel Adams (a printer who was murdered with a hatchet by John C. Colt), Jesus Christ again, the forger Monroe Edwards, and Job. (One editor, M. Thomas Inge, even acknowledged the interpretive problem of "Bartleby" by titling his critical anthology, in contrite self-reflection, *Bartleby the Inscrutable*.) No matter which avatar is chosen, each one, if in singular ways, followed personal preferences rather than social assumptions.

"Bartleby" is set mainly in the offices of a Wall Street law firm, a profitable business that runs by the narrator's coda that "the easiest way of life is best." The narrator owns the firm, and like the protagonists of at least two of Melville's later stories, "Benito Cereno" (1855) and "The Paradise of Bachelors and the Tartarus of Maids" (1855), he is a well-meaning, liberal-minded, but ultimately ineffectual member of the professional class. At first he shares the "snug retreat" of his offices with only three employees, upon whom Melville confers the Dickensian nicknames Turkey, Nippers, and Ginger Nut. They are all fair workers, if in their own ways and on varying schedules. Nippers moonlights as a ward politician and small-time criminal lawyer; Turkey is an elderly eccentric who drinks heavily at noon. In the morning Turkey turns up penitent, ready to work, respectful, and most likely hung over, while Nippers arrives dyspeptic, aggressive from lack of sleep, and unfocused, but by the afternoon (following noontime potations), "their fits [relieve] each other like guards." This leaves the narrator, in effect, with only one employee rather than two, so he publishes an advertisement for extra help.

Bartleby appears at the office doorway with a genteel countenance that alarms the narrator as "pallidly neat, pitiably respectable, incurably forlorn!" The lawyer hires him, apparently out of pity as well as necessity. In his first few days, Bartleby proves an ideal copyist with an impeccable work ethic. "As if long famishing for something to copy," the lawyer says of Bartleby's productive beginnings, "he seemed to gorge himself on my documents." The lawyer is also gratified to have "a man of so singularly sedate an aspect" on his staff in order to temper the antipathetical company of Nippers and Turkey. After the third day, however, Bartleby begins to demur, fulfilling certain demands but replying to most with the same, sullen rejoinder: "I would prefer not to." This gentle, passive-aggressive word "prefer" enters the office vernacular, and Turkey, Nippers, and the lawyer begin speaking it as a matter of course. After a time, Bartleby refuses to leave, making the offices his home and abstaining from any labor at all, preferring instead to spend his time staring in "dead-wall reverie" at the sooty brick wall outside the office window.

THE LEAST OF MY BRETHREN

Once Bartleby makes the offices his home, while still preferring not to work, the lawyer grants him six days to leave "unconditionally." On the morning of the sixth day, the lawyer realizes that although being rid of Bartleby is a "beautiful thought," there was no guarantee the scrivener would agree to his terms: "After all, that assumption was simply my own, and none of Bartleby's. The great point was, not whether I had assumed that he would quit me, but whether he would prefer to do so. *He was more a man of preferences than assumptions*" (italics added). Bartleby does not leave, and the narrator sees that no common law of assumptions applies in the case of Bartleby.

Over time, the lawyer's worldview becomes unwound. He compares himself to Lot's wife, who was turned into a pillar of salt after disobeying God's command not to look back at the city of Sodom, and Bartleby becomes Godlike in his refusals. Irrationally, the lawyer considers himself to blame. His Christian compassion transcends common sense, and as Bartleby's obstinacy grows, so too does his employer's guilt. H. Bruce Franklin and Donald M. Fiene have identified two significant biblical passages, Matthew 25 and Mark 14, that further our understanding of "Bartleby" in its parabolic sense. The former closely resembles Melville's narrative arc, and its next-to-last line significantly says, "Inasmuch as ye have done unto one of the least of my brethren, ye have done to me." The passage refers to a good Christian's response to the sick, the hungry, the homeless, the imprisoned, and most important here, the alienated. In both Matthew and Mark, Christ is imprisoned, as Bartleby is in the final section of Melville's tale. And as Peter denies Christ's existence in Mark—"I know not this man of whom ye speak"—the lawyer insists to colleagues troubled by "the strange creature that I kept at my office" that Bartleby "is nothing to me" and that he knows "nothing about him," denying Bartleby, as Peter denied Christ, three times.

A SIGN OF OUR TIMES

In an 1851 letter to his close associate, Nathaniel Hawthorne, Melville famously pronounced that "There is the grand truth about Nathaniel Hawthorne. He says NO! in thunder; but the Devil himself cannot make him say *yes*. For all men who say *yes*, lie." The honesty Melville perceived in negation, the "grand truth" he admired in Hawthorne, prefigured twentieth-century existentialism (a link that Ronald Spector and Margaret Jennings have connected in different ways). Bartleby's mode of passive resistance dumbfounds those who live by the fixed doctrine of assumptions. The law itself contains no apparent recourse for the enigma Bartleby represents. The lawyer realizes that even if he wished to press charges against him for vagrancy, "it is because he will *not* be a vagrant . . . that you seek to count him *as* a vagrant. That is too absurd." In the final act of Bartleby's "ascendancy," the lawyer vacates the premises himself. Jorge Luis Borges writes of this conundrum, "It is as if Melville had written: 'It is enough that one man is irrational for others to be irrational and for the universe to be irrational.' "

Dan McCall (1989), John Seelye (1970), and Christopher W. Sten (1974) all contend that Ralph Waldo Emerson's "The Transcendentalist" is a text that must have informed the social and philosophical themes in "Bartleby." McCall pays closest attention to the passage that begins, "It is a sign of our times, conspicuous to the coarsest observer, that many intelligent and religious persons withdraw themselves from the common labors and competitions of the market and the caucus, and betake

themselves to a certain solitary and critical way of living, from which no solid fruit has yet appeared to justify their separation." Melville naturally read Emerson (few literate people of his day did not), and Sophia Hawthorne testified that for a full morning during a visit to the Hawthorne home in 1850, Melville "shut himself into the boudoir and read Mr. Emerson's essays." Both Bartleby and Melville removed themselves voluntarily from society's assumptions in the mode of Emerson's "many intelligent and religious persons." The ideals of American democracy seem to dictate that the individual's freedom of choice does not include choosing to be lonely and withdrawn, as it undermines the liberties of others. In the name of rational democracy, then, the radical democrat Bartleby must be hidden from the rest, locked away in New York City's most notorious prison, the Tombs, and left to die, which he does, in an embryonic coil at the base of its outer wall.

A STORY OF WALL STREET

Scriveners occupied a symbolic place in Wall Street life, as they were essentially human copy machines and existed to serve the market rather than profit from it. Cindy Weinstein likens Bartleby's preference not to continue labor-intensive copying with Melville himself figuratively going on strike, and the originality of this revolt "withholds from his employer the right to discipline and punish." Lionel Trilling adopts a similar view of Bartleby and his role in labor relations. Trilling draws from Karl Marx's theory that labor alienates man from himself, as labor is performed for society, not for the self. Later arguments along the same lines were made by Louise K. Barnett and John H. Randall. Trilling points out that Bartleby's "I would prefer not to" incantation only comes when asked to carry out laborious tasks. "What would have happened," Trilling puts to us, "if the narrator or one of Bartleby's fellow-copyists . . . had occasion to say 'Bartleby, I feel sick and faint. Would you help me to the couch and fetch me a glass of water?' "

Melville's subtitle, "A Story of Wall Street," invites the audience to regard "Bartleby" as another of the then-popular subgenre of Wall Street tales involving scriveners and other low-level office workers in Manhattan (although ironically the narrator boasts that "as yet nothing that I know of has ever been written" about the scrivener figure). Earlier in the same year that "Bartleby" appeared, for example, *The New York Times* and the *New York Tribune* simultaneously published on 18 February the first chapter of an anonymous novel titled *The Lawyer's*

Story; or, the Wrongs of the Orphans. By a Member of the Bar, and the *Sunday Dispatch* subsequently serialized it chapter by chapter. Johannes Dietrich Bergmann (1975) suggests that the first chapter may have provided the "narrative structure [Melville] could use for 'Bartleby.' " The narrator is also a kindhearted lawyer whose new clerk, Adolphus, is "shaded with constitutional or habitual melancholy" ("incurably forlorn!"), speaks the words "I would prefer" (if only once without emphasis), and mourns that "hope for the future is dead within me." This lawyer's story appeared ten months before Melville published his own, and as Dan McCall (1989) remarks of the finding, "I think anyone who has read 'Bartleby' carefully will tremble a little when reading the first sentence of the newspaper story." It begins like this: "In the summer of 1843, having an extraordinary amount of deeds to copy, I engaged, temporarily, an extra copying clerk, who interested me considerably, in consequence of his modest, quiet, gentlemanly demeanor, and in his intense application of his duties."

Bergmann later acknowledged that due to the sheer volume of these formulaic tales, this lawyer's story was "not necessarily a direct source" for Melville. David S. Reynolds (1988) connects the elements in "Bartleby" with those of the popular city mysteries of the 1840s and 1850s; Reynolds specifically cites the popular author George Foster's *New York in Slices* (1849), as it includes a whole chapter based, as Melville's tale is, on what Reynolds refers to as the "totally dehumanizing environment" of Wall Street, which produced "puppetlike people and universal misery cloaked by gentility." The story is undeniably a testimonial to life in the mechanized capital of American wealth, New York City, and its center of acquisition, Wall Street.

A MAN OF PREFERENCES

Critics often argue that the scrivener figure is an auto-biographical sketch of Melville himself, that "Bartleby" is a roman à clef borne of Melville's frustration with his own literary career. Raymond Weaver, Lewis Mumford, Richard Chase, David S. Reynolds, and most notably Alexander Eliot, Henry A. Murray, and Leo Marx have all made this argument in one form or another. More recent scholars like Johannes Bergmann (1975) have suggested that this point of view, as important as it is, is somewhat naïve, since among other things it reduces the multi-faceted tale to mere allegory, a mode Melville abhorred. The depth of the biographical correspondences between Bartleby and his author, however, cannot be entirely dismissed. Bartleby, of course, is a scrivener—someone who writes for a living. Melville worked as a low-level clerk for a time, his brothers Gansevoort and Allan were Wall Street lawyers, his father-in-law was a judge who supported Melville's career for years, and his literary career began as did Bartleby's, at first matching the assumptions, or expectations, of his audience. His first two novels, *Typee: A Peep at Polynesian Life* (1846) and *Omoo: A Narrative of Adventure in the South Seas* (1847), sold enormously well, as they recounted Melville's voyages in the South Pacific and allowed his landlocked audience to experience vicariously life among Polynesian cannibals and undomesticated seamen.

Like Bartleby, however, Melville initiated a series of negations, demurring from his audience's assumptions for a time with *Mardi* (1849) but then returning to work with *Redburn* (1849) and *White-Jacket; or, The World in a Man-of-War* (1850). After the relative failure of his masterpiece, *Moby-Dick* (1851), followed by the resounding failure of *Pierre; or, The Ambiguities* (1852), a novel that led critics to speculate as to Melville's sanity (one newspaper headline read, "HERMAN MELVILLE CRAZY"), it became clear that Melville no longer preferred to trade in the currency of the literary marketplace, and he paid, financially and psychologically, for his obstinacy. "Dollars damn me," he wrote Hawthorne while composing *Moby-Dick* in 1851, "My dear Sir, a presentiment is on me,—I shall at last be worn out and perish. . . . What I feel most moved to write, that is banned,—it will not pay. Yet, altogether, write the *other* way I cannot." But unlike Bartleby, Melville did continue writing, if inconsistently and with scant public recognition. The last novel Melville saw published was his masterpiece of false impressions, *The Confidence Man: His Masquerade* (1857), which went unappreciated in his own time.

In the short sequel that follows Bartleby's death, the narrator discovers one biographical fact about him: he worked for a time in Washington, D.C.'s Dead Letter Office, where letters with incorrect addresses were sorted and burned, their containments never revealed. The narrator's final ejaculation "Ah Bartleby! Ah humanity!" might be a hilarious satire of sentimental hyperbole; it might regard civilization and what leads to its discontents; it might be an expression of ecstasy through ambiguity. It is doubtful Melville himself would tell us. Instead, he might say, as Bartleby does, "Do you not see the reason for yourself."

[*See also* Emerson, Ralph Waldo; Hawthorne, Nathaniel; Short Story in America, The; Thoreau, Henry David; *and* Transcendentalism.]

FURTHER READING

Bergmann, Johannes Dietrich. " 'Bartleby' and *The Lawyer's Story*." *American Literature* 47 (1975): 432–436. A short piece in which Bergmann discusses a possible source for "Bartleby" from the *New York Times* and the *New York Tribune*, later published in a fuller, novel form by the popular novelist James A. Maitland.

Bergmann, Johannes Dietrich. "Melville's Tales." In *A Companion to Melville Studies*. Edited by John Bryant. New York, 1986. A helpful bibliographic essay on Melville's short fiction.

Franklin, H. Bruce. *The Wake of the Gods: Melville's Mythology*. Stanford, Calif., 1963. Franklin introduces possible sources for "Bartleby," most importantly Matthew 25.34–40, but also Sir Thomas Maurice's description of the Hindu ascetic Saniassi in *Indian Antiquities*. In the context of Matthew, Franklin argues, the narrator is a failed Christian.

Hardwick, Elizabeth. "Bartleby and Manhattan." *New York Review of Books*, 16 July 1981, 27–31. A lyrical explication of the tale's rhetorical devices, specifically regarding Melville's "reduction of language." In her words, "My own reading is largely concerned with the nature of Bartleby's short sentences."

Hayford, Harrison et al., eds. *The Piazza Tales and Other Prose Pieces, 1839–1860*. Chicago, 1987. A textual history of "Bartleby"—including the variants between the 1853 Putnam's original and the 1856 reprint in *The Piazza Tales*—and a short bibliographic essay. Contains a reproduction and transcription of the only known manuscript leaf (in the handwriting of Melville's sister Augusta) that has survived.

Inge, M. Thomas, ed. *Bartleby the Inscrutable: A Collection of Commentary on Herman Melville's Tale "Bartleby the Scrivener."* Hamden, Conn., 1979.

Maddox, Lucy. *Removals: Nineteenth-Century American Literature and the Politics of Indian Affairs*. New York, 1991. Compares Bartleby's experience with the Cherokee Indian removals to the Indian Territory (Oklahoma) in the 1830s. Maddox suggests a number of correspondences, including the false promise that if the Cherokee chose to civilize themselves, they could remain in Georgia.

Marx, Leo. "Melville's Parable of the Walls." In *Herman Melville's* Billy Budd, *"Benito Cereno," "Bartleby the Scrivener," and Other Tales*. Edited by Harold Bloom. New York, 1987. Marx argues that "Bartleby" is a parable of Melville's own life as a writer and metaphysical thinker who employed the symbolic walls that appear throughout the story (the walls outside the office windows, Wall Street, the outer walls of the Tombs, and so on) as "permanent, immovable parts of the structure of things, comparable to man's inability to surmount the limitations of his sense perceptions, or comparable to death itself."

McCall, Dan. *The Silence of Bartleby*. Ithaca, N.Y., 1989. A book-length synthesis of the mass of scholarly arguments that revolve around "Bartleby" through the 1980s, what McCall refers to as the "Bartleby industry." McCall compares the arguments and makes informed conclusions based on his experience "swimming through libraries" for commentary on "Bartleby."

Reynolds, David S. *Beneath the American Renaissance: The Subversive Imagination in the Age of Emerson and Melville*. Cambridge, Mass., 1988. Reynolds draws out the similarities between "Bartleby" and popular antebellum fiction, particularly the "city mysteries" novels of the 1840s and 1850s as represented by George Foster. Reynolds comprehensively demonstrates the correspondences between popular culture and the American Renaissance.

Seelye, John. "The Contemporary Bartleby." *American Transcendental Quarterly*, no. 7 (Summer 1970): 12–18. Finds sources for Melville's mysterious stranger, most notably in Washington Irving's "The Little Man in Black." Seelye argues that the narrator is a satirical prototype for Irving and the Whig Party and that Bartleby represents the New England transcendentalist figure we find in Emerson's "The Transcendentalist."

Smith, Herbert F. "Melville's Master in Chancery and His Recalcitrant Clerk." *American Quarterly* 17 (Winter 1965): 734–741. A discussion of the transition in jurisprudence from the law of equity, or chancery, and the law of propriety, or common law. Melville's narrator was master in chancery for a time before the changeover, and Smith aptly argues that this time in legal history illuminates our understanding of the tale.

Sten, Christopher W. "Bartleby the Transcendentalist: Melville's Dead Letter to Emerson." *Modern Language Quarterly* 35 (March 1974): 30–44.

Trilling, Lionel. *Prefaces to the Experience of Literature*. New York, 1981. Trilling applies Marx's theory of the alienation of labor as well as Freud's theory of suicide to tease out possible readings of "Bartleby." Since Marx, Trilling writes, argued that "the less you *are*, the more you *have*," the narrator, in the end, is a more alienated figure than Bartleby, as Bartleby refused to allow society to alienate him from himself.

Vincent, Howard P., ed. *Bartleby the Scrivener: A Symposium*. Kent, Ohio, 1966.

Weinstein, Cindy. "Melville, Labor, and the Discourses of Reception." *The Cambridge Companion to Melville*. Edited by Robert S. Levine. New York, 1998.

See also the article on Herman Melville that precedes this article, and the article on *Moby-Dick* that follows.

HERMAN MELVILLE'S
MOBY-DICK

by Joyce A. Rowe

As Ishmael, the narrator of Herman Melville's *Moby-Dick; or, The Whale* (1851), observes, the sea calls forth a "mystical vibration" that draws humans to seek the infinite in its depths. Melville's capacious novel tells of a whaling voyage that begins as a commercial venture but is soon overwhelmed by its captain's obsessive pursuit of the infinite in the form of a quasi-mythical sea monster (animal or god?), Moby Dick. For Captain Ahab, the white whale that sheared off his leg on a previous hunt has become the face of all that is inimical to humankind. His aim is to overcome and destroy this universal evil: "be the white whale agent, or be the white whale principal, [Ahab] will wreak his hate upon him."

The novel combines the reality and excitement of a mid-nineteenth-century hunt for whales that spans the globe (such ventures often lasted for more than three years) with elements of ribald humor and fantasy, gothic melodrama, political satire, and metaphysical speculation. The book is truly epic in its effort to comprehend both national and spiritual reality—humankind's political, psychological, and existential identity in an unknowable and incoherent universe. Once the maimed Captain Ahab (who combines qualities of the biblical Job with John Milton's Satan) subverts the voyage from its ostensible purpose, its ultimate catastrophe seems foredoomed. But the circular pattern of the narrative, as recounted by the venture's lone survivor, as well as the circular geography of the global voyage itself, suggests that the hubristic need that drives humans to pit themselves against the forces of nature and self is as infinite and eternal as the white whale seems to be. Yet like the "world-wandering whale ships" that Ishmael sees silently moored in port, human aspiration will never achieve its visionary goals: "one most perilous and long voyage ended, only begins a second; and a second ended only begins a third, and so on for ever and for aye. Such is the endlessness, yea, the intolerableness of all earthly effort." By the time Melville began *Moby-Dick* he knew something about the effort entailed in a writer's journey, having completed five books in less than five years. These, like his posthumously published final novella, *Billy Budd* (1924), were inspired by the few years he spent at sea, from 1839 to 1844. Although diverse in content and concerns, many of these books, like *Moby-Dick*, employ narrative rhythms and brief, contrapuntal chapters that suggest the tidal flux and reflux of the sea itself. But none prepares the reader for the astonishing leap in thought, language, and comprehensive artistry of the book Melville produced at the very moment the country was attempting to shore up, through the political Compromise of 1850, the high hopes of its problematic enterprise in nation building. Like Captain Ahab, America was struggling against looming catastrophe, brought on by the moral dismemberment of slavery that had crippled and perverted its founding ideals.

Although Melville sets the date of Ishmael's voyage on the *Pequod* near the time of the William Henry Harrison–Martin Van Buren contest for the presidency, which would place it early in 1841, the year he actually sailed on the whale ship *Acushnet*, the political concerns of the novel and the dark atmosphere in which it opens connect it directly to the time of Melville's writing. The narrator's apostrophe to the reader, "Call me Ishmael" (surely the most famous opening line in American literature), invites us to view this voyage as a richly symbolic, imaginative adventure as well as a dramatic one. Ishmael was a name often used in the early nineteenth century to signify the quintessential wanderer or outsider, a figure of romantic alienation and protest against the conventional social order. American readers in Melville's day, living in a Protestant culture that revered the Old Testament, would also be familiar with the story of the biblical Ishmael. The son of Hagar, Abraham's concubine and slave (bond servant), Ishmael was the outcast, illegitimate son contrasted with Isaac, the legitimate son through whose progeny God promises Abraham an everlasting covenant. It is through Isaac's line that the Israelites will claim their special status as God's chosen.

Like many of the biblical names that Melville scatters throughout *Moby-Dick*, the fate of the biblical Ishmael bears a slanted relation to that of Melville's character. In the King James Version of the Bible, it is predicted that Ishmael will be "a wild man; his hand will be against every man, and every man's hand against him" (Genesis 16:12); but the Lord also promises that Ishmael will be the progenitor of another mighty nation yet to be (Genesis 17:20). It is important to the modern reader's understanding of Melville's Ishmael to recall that the English Puritans (followers of John Calvin's Reformed theology) who settled New England in the seventeenth century traced their theological genealogy back to God's covenant with Abraham (which they believed to be reconceived in the Atonement). Their identification with the Old Testament Hebrews led them to interpret everyday experiences in the New World in terms of biblical precedents. Thus, God's promise to the ancient Israelites, if they kept true to their faith, would ultimately be fulfilled by the new Israelites, the Puritans, in America, the new Canaan, the City on the Hill, a beacon of hope to the whole world.

By the nineteenth century this theological belief had merged with a nationalistic messianism, a fervent belief in the exceptional qualities and destiny of the country, easily recognized in the political rhetoric of the day. But in assuming the mask of Ishmael, Melville, whose family still followed Calvin's Reformed theology and prided itself on its pre-Revolutionary American lineage, separates himself from this exclusive and excluding legacy—what he had already scouted as the vision of "a narrow tribe of men, with a bigoted Hebrew nationality—whose blood has been debased in the attempt to ennoble it." Ishmael provides him with an outsider's perspective, a critical stance on both the grandiose claims of national destiny and the moral pride of nineteenth-century individualism with which it was intertwined. The outcast Ishmael identifies himself with the lowliest slave ("who ain't a slave?"), with a crew of "meanest mariners, and renegades and castaways," pagan harpooners and New England Quakers, both practical and extraordinary. In other words, through the qualities of heart, mind, and imagination that characterize Ishmael, Melville proffers an exuberant alternative to what America has become. In this sense, *Moby-Dick* in its language and feeling draws energy from the nobility of an experiment gone tragically wrong. The *Pequod*'s voyage is a metaphor for a lost nation: it satirizes Manifest Destiny and speaks to the moral and spiritual horror of slavery, the hunger for gain that turns whales (all nature) into mere commodity, and the pusillanimity that makes challenge to the charismatic authority of a monomaniac leader unthinkable. Melville's story contains a prophetic and prescient warning to his countrymen—not just of

the war many already sensed lay ahead, but of the greater failure of humanity's own best hopes. Yet Ishmael's insight and final rescue suggest that Melville continued to cling to his own hope of an ideal democracy yet to be.

GOING TO SEA

In the first section of *Moby-Dick*, Melville encourages the reader's identification with Ishmael through a sequence of shifting moods that carries him from Manhattan to Nantucket, where he finds the whale ship *Pequod* and signs on as a common sailor. Ishmael tells us that going to sea is his regular antidote for the "hypos," a combination of personal rage and workaday boredom. But the sea offers a further lure. When, like Narcissus, we stare into its depths, we seek "the ungraspable phantom of life"—a mirror of the soul. With this seductive image of the sea in mind, Melville shifts the narrative to Ishmael's preparation for embarkation. Carrying only his carpet bag, Ishmael begins his foray into a new world of thought and feeling in stormy New Bedford, where he secures a bed at Peter Coffin's Spouter Inn. Here, as throughout the voyage, images of death and rebirth intertwine as the low, dark inn blossoms into an island of warmth and peace.

Ishmael is to bunk with an unknown man said to be peddling preserved heads on the streets of the town. This turns out to be a tattooed Polynesian "savage" from the cannibal South Pacific islands. But Queequeg, whom Ishmael later dubs "George Washington cannibalistically developed," is the least savage of human beings. An entirely noble fellow and island prince who worships a small idol that he carries around in a knapsack, Queequeg is a compendium of natural virtues—compassionate, wise, self-controlled, generous, and courageous. His humanity and friendship disarm Ishmael's prejudices and fears.

Melville has good fun dramatizing Ishmael's effort to adjust his stereotypical thinking as, gradually, he accepts the fact that the stranger in his bed is not a white man mutilated in a street brawl but a man with the body markings of another culture. Although Queequeg's skin is dramatically different from Ishmael's, Ishmael soon sees that what counts is the heart. Queequeg and Ishmael occupy the only available bed, one that the landlord announces was his own marriage bed. And the two, each initially frightened by the other's presence, soon find themselves embarking upon a friendship that is in effect a marriage of dark skinned and light. When they wake, Queequeg's arm is thrown over Ishmael "in the most loving and affectionate manner."

The elements of humor, sentiment, and erotic fantasy interwoven in Ishmael's respect for and fascination with Queequeg challenge conventional views of racial hierarchy and cultural difference. Ishmael's description of their signifying bond of bosom friendship—smoking a tomahawk pipe together, pressing their foreheads against one another, and Queequeg's immediate willingness to die for his friend—is capped off when Queequeg attempts to divide his money, "some thirty dollars in silver," with Ishmael, despite the latter's protests. This example of brotherhood in a culture where property is the hallmark of individual identity is a pointed attack on the hypocrisy of the Christian establishment that supports both slavery and the laissez-faire morality of the dollar. (It is the whites of New Bedford who are happy to buy Queequeg's embalmed New Zealand heads, which he had picked up as curios.) Ishmael notes that Queequeg's idolatry would horrify Ishmael's Presbyterian Church, yet it is Queequeg the Pagan who teaches Ishmael the Christian what love means and redeems him by taming his "splintered heart and maddened hand," no more to be "turned against the wolfish world." As they stroll out together they evoke stares, not because of Queequeg's outlandish tattooing (since New Bedford's whaling port draws a worldwide sailor population), but because of the easy companionship of a dark-skinned man with a white. Melville seems to raise the question, What might America have become if the European encounter with the wilderness had been directed by truly humane, universal values?

The two join a silent group of congregants and mourners at the Whaleman's Chapel (an actual site that Melville had visited, now a museum). Here, Melville's Father Mapple (modeled on a real-life favorite of the sailors) delivers an important sermon on the brief biblical Book of Jonah, whose story he recounts in the idiom of a seaman's experience. The chapel, with its wall of cenotaphs memorializing the dead buried at sea, and the sermon on Jonah's sin in attempting to escape a command of God by taking passage on a ship, only to find himself pitched into the boiling sea and buried in the body of a whale, remind us of the deadly power immanent in the creation. As Jonah discovers, there is no escaping God. He commands the sea as He does the whole fallen world. Thus, extending the Narcissus imagery, to go to sea is, symbolically, to plunge into the inescapable reality of life. In the heart of God's watery creation, in the belly of the whale, Jonah faces himself and finds the meaning of his existence. Jonah, a preacher who tried to escape his duty to preach "unwelcome truths" to the "wicked of Ninevah," might be

a model of a nation whose leaders refused "To preach the Truth to the face of Falsehood" in the year of the pernicious Fugitive Slave Law, which made protecting escaped slaves a federal crime. Certainly, Father Mapple seems to draw this conclusion from the story when he denounces "Senators and Judges" (such as those who supported the new slave law), and ends his peroration on his knees, covering his face with his hands—a gesture that suggests horror at what he sees ahead for the fallen nation, now like Jonah, buried in sin in the belly of the beast. Thus, the sermon prepares Ishmael and the reader for the events to come, and hints at Ishmael's Jonah-like purpose in telling his tale.

SHIP AND CREW

Like the history of the nation itself, the voyage that follows encompasses a promiscuous mix of reality and dream. For Ishmael, whose presence as narrator is often absorbed into the omniscient consciousness of Melville the writer, it is an expansive, mind-altering set of possibilities. For the mates and crew it is a commercial enterprise full of savage thrills. But for Captain Ahab it is the test of his potency—the power of his ego-driven soul.

Ishmael first hears of Ahab when he finds a ship whose strange appearance immediately attracts him. Surrounded by a necklace of the "long, sharp teeth of the sperm whale," her tiller "carved from the long narrow lower jaw of her hereditary foe," the *Pequod* seems part wild cannibal, part antique warrior. Her small, squarish shape and darkened, weather-stained hull suggest the complexion of a French grenadier "who has alike fought in Egypt and Siberia." Her masts come from the coast of Japan, her "ancient decks [are] worn and wrinkled, like the pilgrim-worshipped flag-stone in Canterbury Cathedral where [the Christian martyr] Becket bled." Her name, Ishmael recognizes, is that of a tribe of Massachusetts Indians, now extinct (having been slaughtered by seventeenth-century Puritan settlers). The ship, then, is not a simple new beginning but is freighted with the bloody world history to which America is heir. It is owned by the Bible-reading Quaker merchants Peleg and Bildad who, like their countrymen, are adept at finding religious sanction for commercial gain. Their chief principle is to buy cheap and sell dear, demonstrated in their good cop / bad cop tactics in contracting with Ishmael and Queequeg for each man's portion of the ship's profits.

Bildad's name recalls that of one of Job's false comforters, and his partner Peleg performs a version of this comfort when he assures Ishmael that Captain Ahab is a good man: "Oh, thou'lt like him well enough; no fear, no fear. He's a grand, ungodly, god-like man, Captain

Ahab... and Ahab of old, thou knowest, was a crowned king!" Ishmael responds that the biblical Ahab was a wicked king. But Peleg insists that the name is simply a misfortune, not a prediction of Ahab's character. Since Ahab, a man of sixty, leaves a new wife and a young child at home, how can there be "hopeless harm in Ahab?" asks Peleg. Stricken and blasted he may be but "Ahab has his humanities!" Peleg's words, however, suggest that something has happened to the captain's character since his leg was lost. Ishmael walks away, feeling both "sympathy and sorrow for him," and a strange awe.

Thus, like many epic heroes, or tragic ones, Ahab's mystery is felt first through rumor and portent before he actually appears, after the ship is under way. Ishmael's first sight of his captain produces a shock. Ahab stands on his quarterdeck, looking like a "man cut away from the stake, when the fire has overrunningly wasted all the limbs without consuming them.... His whole high, broad form, seem[s] made of bronze, like Cellini's cast Perseus." But threaded down from his grey hairs, along "one side of his tawny scorched face and neck, till it disappeared in his clothing, you saw a slender rod-like mark, lividly whitish." Ishmael compares this fire mark to that made by lightning on the "lofty trunk of a great tree." None of the crew knows its source. Later, we find that Ahab's mark has come to him as a sign of his worship of fire. For Ahab, though raised like many Nantucketers in the Quaker faith, has, like his biblical namesake, turned away from worship of the monotheistic God and sought power over nature in a fire-worshipping Eastern religion. The biblical Ahab, a king of Israel in Samaria, married Jezebel and adopted her religion, the worship of the fertility god Baal. Melville's Captain Ahab has at least as great aims as the Israelite king, who "did more to provoke the Lord God of Israel to anger than all the kings of Israel that were before him" (1 Kings 16:33). Ahab seeks what the Judeo-Christian tradition denies to man, absolute knowledge of God and dominion over His works. He is, in a sense, an anti-Jonah figure. Where Jonah ran from God, fearful of the burden God placed upon him, Ahab opposes himself to God.

When Melville completed his book he sent Hawthorne a letter saying, "I have written a wicked book and feel spotless as the lamb." Onto the figure of Captain Ahab, Melville projects all the blasphemous rage and despair of the romantic temperament that cannot accept human limitations. As Ishmael muses on Ahab, he sees a man of "superior natural force... who has... been led to think untraditionally and independently, [and learned] a bold and nervous lofty language—that man makes—a mighty

pageant creature, formed for noble tragedies." But it is also, perhaps, the fate of such a brooding man to succumb to a morbid monomania. Ahab embodies all the questions that religion, philosophy, and science cannot answer and a temperament that cannot rest in doubt or uncertainty, as Ishmael's can. Like many who have been traumatized by pain, Ahab rages against the universe, "his torn body and gashed soul bled into one another; and so interfusing, made him mad," speculates Ishmael. Unmanned by the white whale, he is most often seen on deck, rigid on his ivory leg and plotting his vengeance. As his monomania grows, he becomes, in effect, a self-created image of the power he believes has overwhelmed him. Ahab's suffering isolates him. The only other soul aboard the *Pequod* with the capacity to look deeply into the significance of things and so to understand Ahab's spiritual intensity—even to feeling a dangerous sympathy with him—is Ishmael.

The three mates who serve under Ahab—Starbuck, the chief mate, Stubb, the second mate, and Flask, the third mate—are, like their captain, native New Englanders. There their resemblance to him ends. Like Ahab, Starbuck is a native of Nantucket and a Quaker by descent, but his moral prudence and commercial instincts make him a thoroughly practical nineteenth-century rationalist, one unwilling to venture beyond what he knows as sane limits because he understands that nature is dangerous and awesome. Man's best recourse is intelligent care and self-restraint, Starbuck believes, even if at times he cannot help being carried away by the excitement of the whale hunt. Starbuck values a "useful courage." To him, "an utterly fearless man is a far more dangerous comrade than a coward." Having lost both father and brother to the whaling industry, he has no stomach for "fighting a fish that too much persisted in fighting him." But for all his good sense and physical prowess, Starbuck is not a man to challenge "the more spiritual terrors, which sometimes menace you from the concentrating brow of an enraged and mighty man." In this description of the only figure on the ship who might have the authority to avert its ultimate catastrophe, Melville suggests how difficult it is to oppose charismatic power, and why good men so often shrink from facing it down. Starbuck cannot seriously oppose Ahab, once he learns his plans, because he cannot face the psychological terrors within himself that a raging Ahab would provoke.

Stubb, the second mate, who operates on a moral and spiritual level a notch below Starbuck's, is a Cape Cod native, and a "happy-go-lucky" fellow who takes the world's perils as they come. He thinks little of death and nothing of the mortal questions that Starbuck respects and that torment Ahab. Stubb faces whales "coolly and off-handedly," humming as he works, keeping a pipe between his teeth. A comfort-seeking materialist, Stubb is a reliable, not unkindly figure. The third mate, Flask, a Martha's Vineyard native, is a "short, stout, ruddy fellow, who loves hunting whales, and manages to ignore their "majestic bulk and mystic ways" by reducing them in his mind to "a species of magnified mouse, or at least water-rat." Thus, each of these officers, like their captain, treats whales and the ocean itself in terms of his own capacity to apprehend (or imagine) the depths of existence. In descending order, they form an index to the moral and spiritual intelligence of mankind facing the unknown.

Each mate is supported by his harpooner, and each of these men, whose prowess is crucial to the whale hunt, is drawn as a great and powerful warrior: Daggoo, a native African; Tashtego, a Gayhead Indian; and Queequeg, a Polynesian. Taken together, they suggest the reach of American power, organized and directed by native-born whites but dependent upon the strength of dark-skinned races. Ishmael had mocked the distinction between savage and civilized in the privacy of his New Bedford marriage bed. But in the public sphere, which the ship represents, Melville finds racial categories built into the social and economic structure of the nation.

The rest of the crew are mostly foreign born, like the immigrants whose labor is creating America's expanding wealth. Ishmael calls the mariners "isolatoes." It is this crew, from Starbuck down to the lowliest castaway, that any captain must "[federate] along one keel" if the ship, like the country, is to prosper. Captain Ahab, however, has an extraordinary aim. He must mold these diverse individuals into a single will, infusing them with his own passion to hunt Moby Dick before they realize what the hunt will mean for their fate.

In chapter 36, "The Quarter-Deck," Melville shows us a demagogue in action. Ahab, blind to everything but his "intense bigotry of purpose," calls the ship's company together and initiates a series of chanted questions and responses intended to rouse the men's appetite for the hunt. Then he holds up a Spanish gold piece (worth sixteen dollars) and nails the doubloon to the mast, promising it to the first man who "raises me a white-headed whale with a wrinkled brow and a crooked jaw; . . . with three holes punctured in his starboard fluke." The pitch of his voice and the fixed gold piece (the sign, likened to a navel, attaches their ship to Moby Dick) carry the day for the ordinary crewmen. But Starbuck sees further and wonders,

"it was not Moby Dick that took off thy leg?" Taking his cue, Ahab unmasks his pain and horror and declares, "This is what ye have shipped for, men! To chase that white whale on both sides of land, and over all sides of earth till he spouts black blood and rolls fin out. What say ye, men, will ye splice hands on it, now?" Instinctively, the harpooners and seamen shout their "ayes" in support of their captain. But Starbuck holds back, telling Ahab, "I came here to hunt whales, not my commander's vengeance. How many barrels will thy vengeance yield thee even if thou gettest it, Captain Ahab? it will not fetch thee much in our Nantucket market." The chief mate's view of the whale, as simply a "dumb thing" that "smote thee from blindest instinct," would surely be that of most persons in Melville's day and ours. If Ahab is to keep his chief mate with him (along with the skeptical reader), Starbuck and we must better understand his cast of mind, which, however perverse, is that of an idealist. Ahab seeks meaning beyond the world of appearances, the material world that encloses our lives. To Starbuck he declaims: "All visible objects, man, are but as pasteboard masks. But in each event—in the living act, the undoubted deed—there some unknown but still reasoning thing puts forth the mouldings of its features from behind the unreasoning mask." Echoing Plato, Ahab insists that man is a prisoner in this world of appearances. But unlike the ancient philosopher, Ahab, a creature of the nineteenth-century, insists upon the Promethean power of the individual to overcome all obstacles to knowledge: "How can the prisoner reach outside except by thrusting through the wall?" he demands. "The white whale is that wall, shoved near to me." Sometimes, he admits, it seems there is nothing beyond. But to an Ahab this is intolerable. He would rather believe in a divinity, however inscrutably malicious, than in nothing at all. For what, then, would he be? "Talk not to me of blasphemy," he warns the orthodox Christian, Starbuck. "I'd strike the sun if it insulted me. For could the sun do that, then could I do the other; . . . Who's over me?" he cries in hyperbolic frenzy. "Truth has no confines."

At last, remembering the crew before him, Ahab gains control over himself and stages a final ritual to seal their bond. He passes a brimming pewter flagon among the men, giving a drink to each. Then he calls the harpooners to him and commands them to cross lances, turn the sockets up, and receive the "fiery waters" into them. The harpooners drink from their inverted lances, which Ahab names "murderous chalices," enjoining the pagans to swear, "Death to Moby Dick! God hunt us all, if we do not hunt Moby Dick to his death." Starbuck, recognizing the symbolism of an inverted (black) mass (and perhaps the grammatical punning in the hidden imperative, "let us hunt God" in Moby Dick), turns pale at this ritual bonding and what it portends.

THE WHALE

It is important to the multiple perspectives of the voyage that Ishmael, our silent witness, begins to brood upon just those symbolic possibilities in the whale that Ahab cannot but reject. Ahab takes his sense of the white whale as an agent of a malevolent creation from the myths of his ubiquity and supernatural malice that have long passed among the seamen. For Ishmael, though, what is most appalling about the whale is not its brutality but its color. While whiteness often signifies spotless purity and all that "is sweet, and honorable, and sublime," white also produces terror. Does not its all-color, no-color shadow "forth...the heartless voids and immensities of the universe...the thought of annihilation," which lies behind all the brilliant appearances we see? Indeed, in contemplating "the general rage and hate" that drive an Ahab, Ishmael wonders if humankind's greater terror does not lie in the possibility of "a dumb blankness, full of meaning, in a wide landscape of snows—a colorless, all-color of atheism from which we shrink." It is this "meaning" of no meaning, this sense of an intention that we only project onto a void we cannot know, that makes Ahab's "fiery hunt" so understandable. Without an organizing aim such as Ahab's vision provides, man is truly the orphan of the universe, alone with its mystery.

To further dramatize the significance of Ahab's condition, Melville provides his polar opposite in the black cabin boy Pip, the most vulnerable person on the voyage and the single soul for whom Ahab shows feeling. Pip, abandoned when he jumps in fright from a speeding whaleboat intent on the chase, is left utterly alone in the "heartless immensity" of the "shoreless ocean." The terror of this "intense concentration of self" drives him to idiocy. "By the merest chance" he is rescued. But though he speaks with an intuitive wisdom drawn from what he has seen in the "unwarped primal world," he can never speak coherently again.

Ahab, however, keeps his wits about him. He occupies his men with the normal activities of whaling to distract them from the full significance of what he intends. He has usurped the plain purpose of the voyage, and they could legally "refuse all further obedience to him, and even violently wrest from him the command." Thus, he encourages their hunt for ordinary sperm whales and all the factorylike labor which follows a kill: stripping the whale of its blubber; mincing and boiling and extracting the oil; pouring it into storage barrels in the hold of the ship; and squeezing the sweet-smelling sperm back into a fluid that will be sold for candles and other household goods. While Ishmael finds in these cooperative activities a source of bonding, of fraternal feeling among the men, and a stimulus to speculations about human relatedness, Ahab sees only a profit motive that he disdains. Muttering that "The permanent constitutional condition of the manufactured man...is sordidness," he likens the men to crusaders who pillaged and stole on their way to the Holy Land. For without these "pious perquisites," would they not have turned away "in disgust"? Imprisoned in the solitude of his own heart, Ahab is rarely stirred by sympathy for his people. As Starbuck observes, Ahab "would be a democrat to all above," but "lords it over all below."

Having circled a good portion of the globe, from Nantucket down to the eastern coast of South America, thence to the Cape of Good Hope and across the Indian Ocean to the South China Sea and the Japanese cruising ground, Ahab senses he is closing in on his prey. The several passing ships they meet along the way afford signs that the whale is near, though all flee him and at least one has already been thoroughly wrecked by him. But Ahab scorns all warnings and omens, refusing to let even the most pressing appeal for help from another vessel, the *Rachel*, whose captain is searching for his lost sons, turn him from his course. At the end even Starbuck, who pleads with him to forego his aim, is struck by his captain's strange courage in the face of the horrors that lie in wait.

The reader has seen throughout the story that Ahab and Moby Dick are described in similar terms—the whale's swollen, ridged, and wrinkled forehead is mirrored in Ahab's ribbed and dented brow. And just as Ahab carries a piece of sea life on his own body, his leg fashioned from a sperm whale's jawbone, so Moby Dick, stuck all over with harpoons that he cannot shake loose, is forever marked by the attempts of humans to ensnare and devour him. Ultimately, in this final portion, we are reminded of what Ahab is truly facing in Moby Dick, that Narcissus-like image of all that lies within a human's own soul: not its beauty alone, but the "horrors of the half known life" that we sense within and around us—the whale as something to which we half project and half respond.

Almost as if he can sniff his antagonist, Ahab calls all hands on deck and has himself hoisted to the main masthead. From this lookout, he himself is the first to sight the snow hill of a hump (or so he insists), crying,

"There she blows! . . . It is Moby Dick!" Claiming the doubloon for himself, Ahab insists on his special destiny: "Fate reserved the doubloon for me. . . . None of ye could have raised the White Whale first." The boats are lowered and he takes the lead. First seen, the swimming whale is indeed a godlike creature: "A gentle joyousness—a might mildness of repose in swiftness, invested the gliding whale. Not the white bull Jupiter swimming away with ravished Europa . . . did surpass the glorified White Whale as he so divinely swam."

But the godlike serenity of the whale has a darker side. As he breaches, rising from the water, "the hideousness" of his monstrous jaw is in full view. Then he disappears into the depths, only to emerge before Ahab's whaleboat, catch its bow in his mouth, shake it, and bite it in two. Ahab and his crew are thrown out. So begin three days of increasingly ferocious battle between the enraged captain and whale. Whether Moby Dick is maliciously aiming for Ahab or angered at being threatened by men who have already harmed him is deliberately unclear. Starbuck insists that Moby Dick is not seeking Ahab, but that Ahab madly, blasphemously, seeks him. Yet the whale often seems as satanically driven as Ahab. On the third day of the battle the whale, ignoring the boats bearing down on him, heads for the *Pequod* itself. He tears into its hull and turns it into a hearse for all the crew. Ahab, from his boat in the water aims his harpoon and cuts it deep into Moby Dick's flesh, only to have the harpoon line tangle like a boomerang and catch Ahab around the neck, shooting him out of the boat and carrying him down to the depths of the sea in a deathly embrace with Moby Dick. Meantime the ship has begun to sink. The *Pequod*, made of American wood (such wood was prophesied to be Ahab's second hearse), goes down with the American Indian, Tashtego, nailing Ahab's flag to the masthead and catching the wing of a sky hawk, "pecking at the flag," in its folds, as if taking a "living part of heaven" with her. The symbolic tableau blends American history and myth in a whirlpool of total destruction.

Yet, as the "great shroud of the sea" rolls on, one is saved to bear witness, having floated on the margin of the suction (the metaphoric position Ishmael has taken throughout the voyage). Fittingly, he is rescued by the *Rachel*—like its namesake, the mother of the exiled Hebrew people—still searching for its missing children, but finding only "another orphan."

FURTHER READING

Arvin, Newton. *Herman Melville*. Westport, Conn., 1950. Among earlier readings of Melville's work, this is one of the most astute and valuable by a major literary critic.

Brodhead, Richard. *Hawthorne, Melville, and the Novel*. Chicago, 1973. An elegant and concise analysis of the relation of the book's content to style and structure.

Brodtkorp, Paul, Jr. *Ishmael's White World: A Phenomenological Reading of "Moby-Dick."* New Haven, Conn., 1965. A study of Ishmael's consciousness.

Bryant, John, ed. *A Companion to Melville Studies*. Westport, Conn., 1986.

Gilmore, Michael T. "Introduction." In *Twentieth-Century Interpretations of "Moby-Dick": A Collection of Critical Essays*. Edited by Michael T. Gilmore. Englewood Cliffs, N.J., 1977.

Heimert, Alan. "*Moby-Dick* and American Political Symbolism." *American Quarterly* 15 (Winter, 1963): 498–534. The most thorough reading of the book as a political allegory. A valuable article, but the reader should be aware that the novel is richer than any simple allegorical scheme can render it.

Karcher, Carolyn. *Shadow over the Promised Land: Slavery, Race, and Violence in Melville's America*. Baton Rouge, La., 1980.

Kier, Kathleen, ed. *A Melville Encyclopedia: The Novels*. Troy, N.Y., 1990. A useful index to allusions in Melville's novels that a reader might puzzle over.

Parker, Hershel. *Herman Melville: A Biography*. Vol. 1, *1819–1851*. Baltimore, 1996. An extremely detailed, authoritative history by a scholar who has given many years of his own life to recovering the data of Melville's life and work. It has several chapters on the years leading up to and the time of the composition of *Moby-Dick*, but no critical analysis. However, for anyone who wants to know more about Melville's existence, particularly the early years that tell of his family, this work is invaluable.

Parker, Hershel, and Harrison Hayford. *"Moby-Dick" as Doubloon*. New York, 1970. A collection of critical responses to Melville's novel, from 1851 through 1970. An excellent resource.

Tuveson, Ernest Lee. *Redeemer Nation: The Idea of America's Millennial Role*. Chicago, 1968. A good introduction to the Puritan-messianic relationship.

See also the articles on Herman Melville and "Bartleby the Scrivener," immediately preceding.

H. L. MENCKEN

by Edward A. (Sandy) Martin

Henry Louis Mencken, better known as H. L. Mencken, was born on 12 September 1880 in Baltimore, Maryland. He became the most accomplished and widely known American journalist-author of the twentieth century. The skills and attitudes he acquired as a reporter carried over to his roles as book reviewer, editorial writer, columnist, and then editor for the *Smart Set* and the *American Mercury* magazines as well as for daily newspapers, especially the Baltimore *Sunpapers* and the *New York Evening Mail*. In his lifetime, thirty-one of his books were published, ten of them based on his own extensive research or experience, the rest in part revised and rewritten versions of his journalism. Mencken's career as a published author began in 1903 with a successful book of his poems and his last twentieth-century publication was the posthumous *A Second Mencken Chrestomathy* in 1995. With his ear for the rhythms and sounds of American English, Mencken moved his readers powerfully, some to anger at the outrageousness of his attitudes, others to gleeful celebration at the promise of liberation those attitudes represented. His blistering ridicule of nineteenth-century American moral and cultural values, and of the traditions that enshrined those values, was part of a resurgence in American life, a second renaissance, "America's Coming-of-Age" as the critic Van Wyck Brooks called it in 1915.

ANCESTRY, EDUCATION, AND INFLUENCES

Mencken was a third-generation German-American whose grandfather had immigrated to Baltimore in 1848. His family was more interested in assimilation into middle-class and mercantile American life than in its Germanic heritage. But as he became successful in his own career Mencken took great pride in his German ancestors and the traditional German culture of which they were a part. In 1898, when he was eighteen (as Fred Hobson tells the story [1994]), Mencken decided that his lifelong pursuits would be literature and writing. The sudden death of his father in 1899 released him from the expectation that he would continue in the family cigar-manufacturing business, where he had worked since his graduation two years earlier from the Baltimore Polytechnic Institute, a high school. His father had hoped that Henry would become an engineer. But the few courses available to him in the arts, English, and photography were what sustained him. He was largely self-educated in literature, with an extensive background in the classic English writers from Chaucer through the nineteenth century. He especially responded to eighteenth-century writers (such as Tobias Smollett, Laurence Sterne, Henry Fielding, James Boswell, Jonathan Swift, and Alexander Pope), but not to Samuel Johnson, to whom nevertheless he would later in his career be compared. His readings in romantic and Victorian prose and poetry were both broad and discriminating—he knew what he liked. William Makepeace Thackeray's novels were favorites, as were poems and fiction by Rudyard Kipling. Thomas Henry Huxley, a scientific rationalist and proponent of Darwin's evolutionary theory, became an inspiration and a model for him. He was fifteen when he began to read Huxley's essays, with admiration for his aggressive point of view and stylistic flare, as well as the clarity of his prose.

During this early self-education Mencken did not read very widely in the American classics. An exception was Mark Twain, whose *Huckleberry Finn* (1884) he had read for the first time when he was nine years old and which he celebrated again and again throughout his life. He was immediately taken with the relationship between Huck Finn as the narrator and the author Mark Twain, who "mainly . . . told the truth," along "with some stretchers." Using "stretchers" or exaggeration as vehicles for "the truth" became an element of style for Mencken, with a range from polemic to humor. As a teenager he also read Twain's *A Tramp Abroad* (1880), which helped broaden his interests to include Germany, its music and literature, and his own background. Not many other American writers at this point in his education evoked his respect; he sampled Emerson, Hawthorne, Melville, Whitman, and Thoreau but did not care for them. One notable exception was Ben Franklin, whose orderly, eighteenth-century pragmatism Mencken found to be exemplary.

Mencken and Aileen Pringle in Hollywood, 1926. (*Courtesy Enoch Pratt Free Library, Baltimore.*
Reprinted by permission)

In another aspect of his emerging aesthetic sensibility Mencken echoes the American romanticism of Thoreau, who in the conclusion to *Walden* (1854) wrote:

> I fear chiefly lest my expression may not be *extra-vagant* enough, may not wander far enough beyond the narrow limits of my daily experience, so as to be adequate to the truth of which I have been convinced. . . . I desire to speak somewhere *without* bounds; like a man in a waking moment, to men in their waking moments.

Like Thoreau, Mencken wrote with the conviction that joyous and committed language was the ultimate weapon in the warfare against the murderous, repressive aspects of modern life, and that irony was not the negation or inversion of joy but its most profound evoker. Thoreau had expressed an American version of the romantic evocation of reality through the power of language. Maturing as a writer, Mencken appreciated the ironic potential for extravagance, too. To speak without bounds the convincing truth would become for Mencken as much an ultimate joy as it had been for Thoreau.

There also was affinity to Walt Whitman. Edmund Wilson observed in *The New Republic* in 1921 that within Mencken's writings about American culture there is embedded a kind of "prose poem." Mencken's "poetry of America," Wilson wrote, was comparable to Whitman's "enumeration of another set of visions" in his cataloguelike accumulation of observations about American experience. As if from a version of Edgar Lee Masters's *Spoon River Anthology* (1915), an aggregation of Mencken's images from magazines, newspapers, and books sometimes ridicules small-town America but also recognizes the diversity, sadness, and sometimes pathos of the entire American provincial panorama. Beginning in 1924 some of the ridicule was gathered in the "Americana" section of the *American Mercury*. These recurring reports about the absurdities of American life were dispersed throughout the six books of collected essays and miscellany Mencken called his *Prejudices* (1919–1927). Other, more positive, images culled from his broad readings and travels, had previously appeared in the "Répétition Générale" section of the *Smart Set* and were called "Clinical Notes" in the *American Mercury*. Many were reprinted

100

in the volumes of *Prejudices*, as in the "People and Things" section of *Prejudices: Fourth Series* (1924). What Edmund Wilson called Mencken's Whitman-like "prose poem" about America forms a consistent pattern through many of Mencken's writings from 1910 and beyond.

JOURNALIST, BOOK REVIEWER, EDITOR, AUTHOR

Mencken's early career as a journalist, first for the *Baltimore Morning Herald*, then for the *Sunpapers* in Baltimore, soon led to assignments as Sunday edition editor for both. He wrote theater criticism for the *Herald*, and his interest in Shaw led to a book called *George Bernard Shaw: His Plays* (1905). In this first book about Shaw ever printed, Mencken presented the playwright primarily as an iconoclast and satirist. The book was an appreciation of the perspective toward which Mencken moved at this point—the intersection of lively prose with commentary about literature, culture, and philosophy. Mencken also had been writing poetry and fiction, with some success. A collection of his poems, *Ventures into Verse*, was published in 1903, and his efforts at short fiction were recognized in 1901 by Ellery Sedgwick, editor of *Frank Leslie's Popular Monthly* and later the *Atlantic Monthly*. Then, in 1908 Mencken's *The Philosophy of Friedrich Nietzsche* was published after nearly a year of intensive research and writing, which required the improvement of his rudimentary German so that he could read the works of Nietzsche as well as related works of German philosophy. His was the first book in English about Nietzsche; it went through five printings and, with the book on Shaw, marked the beginning of Mencken's national reputation. He presented Nietzsche both as a writer and as an iconoclast related to Shaw, Darwin, and Huxley.

By 1904, Mencken, a talented amateur pianist, was meeting regularly, as he would for the next fifty years, with friends on Saturday evenings to eat, drink, and make music, most of it from a classical eighteenth- and nineteenth-century repertoire, especially Bach, Beethoven, Schubert, Mozart, and Brahms. His ear for music complemented his love for what he praised as the "sough of words, the burble of phrases, the gaudy roll and hiss of sentences" in an essay about Upton Sinclair's style in the *New York Evening Mail* (21 June 1918). His aural sensitivity to the poetic dynamics of language would also be reflected in his selections for a canon of modernist writers, in his own writing, and in his books about the American language.

In 1910, Mencken was given the responsibilities of writing a column and at least two editorials each day for the newly created *Baltimore Evening Sun*. Then the next year the column was named "The Free Lance" because he had an almost unrestricted range of subjects. Politicians and reformers were fair game but not ministers, unless they attacked him first. The voice of an indignant historian spoke in startling metaphors and extravagant allusions to convey what he later called his "prejudices." He quickly became notorious as Baltimore's Bad Boy, much to his delight, and was also able to function effectively as a reformer in such areas as health services while attacking politicians and crusaders. There was a clear moral perspective underlying his skeptical satire of human motivation.

Mencken's assignments as a literary critic had expanded in 1908 when be became book reviewer for the *Smart Set* magazine. He met Theodore Dreiser at this time. Mencken, who had read and admired Dreiser's novel *Sister Carrie* (1900) in 1902, quickly became friends with him, beginning a close literary relationship. Mencken continued to write monthly columns of reviews and book notices for the *Smart Set* after he and the drama critic George Jean Nathan became co-editors of the magazine in August 1914. The cover of their first issue (in October) announced, "One civilized reader is worth a thousand boneheads." In the fifteen years before he left the magazine in 1923, Mencken wrote 182 review essays, and reviewed around 2,000 books. His book reviews and notices covered many subjects: politics, history, cultural and social studies, poetry, music, and fiction. In the *Smart Set*, fiction emerged as his main focus. Mark Twain and Joseph Conrad were his favorite writers, and he created opportunities to point out their influences. In a 1911 review, Mencken heralded the publication of Dreiser's *Jennie Gerhardt* (1911), in which he found the continuation of the power and success he had admired in *Sister Carrie*. Both Carrie and Jennie were characters rising out of ignorance and poverty into an "essential gentleness" and "innate, inward beauty." When he compared Dreiser and Conrad, he saw their heroes and heroines as "essentially tragic figures . . . [in whose tragedy] there is a deep and ghostly poetry."

His *Smart Set* reviews on works of Conrad and Dreiser were revised and expanded into essays that he included in his important volume, *A Book of Prefaces* (1917). One of these "Prefaces" was an essay called "Puritanism as a Literary Force," in which Mencken belligerently attacked the repressive influence of Puritan tradition on American culture. He echoed a thesis set forth by Van Wyck Brooks in *The Wine of the Puritans* (1909). Mencken focused on what he called the Puritans' "lack of aesthetic sense" and on the "prudishness and dirty-mindedness of Puritanism" that had victimized many American writers, including Mark Twain, Henry James, and William Dean Howells. A new generation of writers, whether they appreciated Mencken or not, was liberated by the power and energy of this formulation. Ernest Hemingway, F. Scott Fitzgerald, William Faulkner, Willa Cather, and many others, including poets and dramatists, found that an audience had been identified for them.

CULTURAL COMMENTATOR AND HISTORIAN OF LANGUAGE

Mencken recycled into his 1918 book, *In Defense of Women*, much of what he had been writing about women in the *Smart Set* since 1908. He appreciated the efforts women made to seek self-expression during the period that culminated with ratification in 1920 of the Nineteenth Amendment to the Constitution, which gave women the right to vote. He revised and amplified *In Defense of Women* (1918) in 1922. Attitudes limiting the rights of women were yet another manifestation of the influence of Puritanism on American life, Mencken felt. He recognized their ordeal, which he sensed was similar to the ordeal of artists, a path he had successfully navigated himself. In addition to celebrating Dreiser's heroines, Carrie and Jennie, he had written reviews highlighting depictions of women in novels by David Graham Phillips, Willa Cather, Sinclair Lewis, and the English writer H. G. Wells. For example, in Carol Kennicott, the Lewis heroine of *Main Street* (1920), Mencken recognized a character confined by the social and cultural conventions of small-town, midwestern life.

But Mencken's "defense" of women, in contrast to what he represented in some of his book reviews, to some readers seemed ironic: women were described as superior to men in intelligence and practicality, so why would they need a defense? Yet he ridiculed, rather than defended, women who were activists in political efforts for the expansion of women's rights. As in his other writings, it was as if he were addressing at least two different audiences. One read assertions about the intelligence and shrewdness of women as satire or ridicule, while another regarded the same text as a serious affirmation of women's capabilities. Some (perhaps Mencken's ideal audience) read it both ways and were delighted with the apparent paradox—or with the confusion.

In 1919, Mencken's *The American Language* was published. During the war years (1914–1918) he found that his negative views of American involvement in the war, along with his pro-German attitudes, were not acceptable perspectives for the critical essays and journalism about the ongoing American experience that he wanted to write. In 1915, Mencken's "Free Lance" column was withdrawn, with his consent, by the *Baltimore Evening Sun*. So he picked a neutral subject, the American language, and put much of his energy into research and writing about it. He had long been interested in the manifestations of American speech he had experienced as a reporter and had read in the works of Mark Twain.

However, there was an animus behind his efforts, for he saw himself as a spokesperson for the language of Americans, a defender of its expressiveness and integrity, including its slang and dialects, in the face of negative views of Americanisms and nonstandard British English. The volume represented an enormous scholarly undertaking, and to Mencken's happy surprise, it sold well; it would be followed by three revised editions in 1921, 1923, and 1936 and supplements one and two in 1945 and 1948. Each of these six publications stands by itself as a representation of Mencken's expanding theory and evidence about the importance of the American language. His efforts as an amateur philologist and linguist continued for the rest of his active life. Language had always fascinated him; his own skills as a writer drew on the diction, metaphors, rhythms, meters, and alliterations of traditional English, but especially the diverse energy of what he called General American, in all of its dialectical, regional, ethnic, and racial manifestations—a vast linguistic melting.

STYLE AND VOICE

Mencken's skill at creating and manipulating the responses of his readers had developed through a long apprenticeship and reached a high point in the 1920s. His trying out, or first drafting, ground had been his journalism for the Baltimore *Sunpapers*. In 1920 he began the "Monday Articles" for the *Evening Sun*, a column that he wrote until 1938. His subjects for satire were local and national politics, politicians, and characteristic American attitudes and beliefs. Believing as he did in freedom of expression, he ran letters from readers with dissenting views in the two columns adjacent to the "Monday Articles."

One stylistic extreme was his hoax-making delight at manipulating the responses of readers who perhaps believed him completely. For example, in an essay called

"A Neglected Anniversary," written for the *New York Evening Mail* in 1917, he described the invention of the bathtub in 1842, posing as an apparently reliable journalist-commentator, one of the everyday, myth-and-legend making voices of American culture. In this narrative, President Millard Fillmore, impressed by the supposed invention of the bathtub, installed one in the White House in 1851. To Mencken's delight, as well as disgust, the essay was cited as factual in various newspapers, encyclopedias, and dictionaries. He ridiculed those in his audience gullible enough to take his mock history seriously; those not taken in were amused by his parody.

Mencken's mature style and much of his best writing characteristically produced this range of responses from his readers. Here, as an example, are the opening sentences in his essay on William Jennings Bryan, called "In Memoriam: W.J.B.":

> Has it been duly marked by historians that William Jennings Bryan's last secular act on this globe of sin was to catch flies? A curious detail, and not without its sardonic overtones. He was the most sedulous flycatcher in American history, and in many ways the most successful. His quarry, of course, was not *Musca domestica* but *Homo neandertalensis*. For forty years he tracked it with coo and bellow, up and down the rustic backways of the Republic. Wherever the flambeaux of Chautauqua smoked and guttered, and the bilge of Idealism ran in the veins, and Baptist pastors dammed the brooks with the sanctified, and men gathered who were weary and heavy laden, and their wives who were full of Peruna and as fecund as the shad *(Aloso sapidissima)*—there the indefatigable Jennings set up his traps and spread his bait.

First published in the *Baltimore Evening Sun* in July 1925, this mock obituary was revised by Mencken for inclusion in *Prejudices: Fifth Series* (1926). The original context was Mencken's coverage of the Scopes trial, where Bryan testified for the prosecution in the case of John Thomas Scopes, a public school teacher in Dayton, Tennessee, accused of teaching evolution in violation of state law. Mencken was not interested in the free speech issue raised by the law. What he saw in the trial was an opportunity to show a national audience the foolish destructiveness and sheer irrationality of religious fundamentalism. Mencken had helped persuade the lawyer Clarence Darrow to take on the Scopes defense, and he wrote daily dispatches for the *Evening Sun*. The climax of the trial was Darrow's cross-examination of Bryan, in which he ridiculed Bryan's fundamentalism by exposing it to the rationalism of

Darwinian evolutionary theory. Bryan, elderly and in poor health, died shortly after this cross-examination.

Mencken's ridicule of Bryan amused and exhilarated many of his readers, but offended those who found this treatment of Bryan inappropriate upon the occasion of his death. Some were angered at the naming of Bryan as a hunter-scientist pursuing an insect-monster called man—Bryan, whose last notable action was to insist that man descended from the angels and was in no way related either to animals or to insects. These readers found the depiction of backwater, provincial Tennessee Christians both insulting and insensitive (as Mencken had intended). He used the exaggerated, authoritarian narrative voice we hear in much of his prose. His narrator asks, "Has it been duly marked by historians" and then goes on to mark, in imitation of an historian's rhetoric, what Bryan's last secular acts were. Mencken's extravagantly outrageous comparisons are calculated sources of amusement for sophisticated readers. His narrator interprets a broad spectrum of contemporary experiences and translates the circumstantial into the meaningful, fact into history, story into myth. Readers were either amused or angered by the inflated posturing of the voice and the outrageousness of the subject matter or of the metaphoric and imagistic vehicles for the subject matter. And there was also Mencken's own outrage behind the deft ridicule of Bryan's fundamentalism, with its puritanical, didactic dismissal of Darwin's theory of human evolution.

These extremes of response illustrate Mencken's capacity to delight as well as to offend and characterize, in broad contrasts, the readers he both addressed and satirized in much of his writing. His narrative strategies range from parody of the simple, matter-of-fact clarity of the reporter (as in "A Neglected Anniversary") to the high-in-oath voice of the historian-sociologist (as in "In Memoriam: W.J.B."), with many variations in between.

THE 1920s: FAME AND NOTORIETY

Walter Lippmann, also a journalist by background, wrote in the *Saturday Review* in 1926 that Mencken was a "force in America [with] an extraordinarily cleansing and vitalizing effect," "the most powerful personal influence on this whole generation of people." Through his "tremendous polemic" he succeeded in destroying, "by rendering...ridiculous and unfashionable," what was archaic in "the democratic tradition of the American pioneers." He identified and supported "a radical change of attitude...toward the whole conception of popular sovereignty and majority rule." Mencken's appeal,

Lippmann believed, was "sub-rational," in that his most influential writing, at its best, addressed "those vital preferences which lie deeper than coherent thinking."

Much of his journalism during these prolific years was revised and collected by Mencken into the six volumes of his *Prejudices*. He planned the series as a "slaughterhouse" where he would hang the victims of his wit. His main interests in *Prejudices: First Series* (1919) were literary. His topics included essays about several American critics, H. G. Wells, Thorstein Veblen, and Jack London. Two of the pieces were called the "New Poetry Movement" and "The American Magazine." He also ridiculed aspects of American provincialism and Puritanism, which became themes in the five subsequent volumes of the series.

In *Prejudices: Second Series* (1920) he fully deployed his voice as a sometimes astonished or bemused critic and commentator about the United States, a "Republic" he found both amusing and richly interesting. In "The National Letters" he noted the "respectable mediocrity" of American literary output and called for "a distinguished and singular excellence, a signal national quality, a ripe and stimulating flavor." Another essay was "The Sahara of the Bozart," revised and expanded from its November 1917 appearance in the *New York Evening Mail*. He called southern culture a desert landscape because of its mediocrity, stupidity, and absence of artistic and intellectual vitality. His coinage of "bozart" from the elegant French phrase "beaux arts" was only a beginning. "It is as if the Civil War stamped out all the bearers of the torch and left only a mob of peasants in the field. . . . You will not find a single Southern novelist whose work shows any originality or vitality," he wrote. Once again he evoked extremes of laughter and anger in his readers. One effect was support for a renaissance in southern literature, no doubt his hoped-for underlying purpose.

Prejudices: Third Series (1922) was organized around a theme established in its first essay, "On Being an American." Most immigrants before and after the Revolution, Mencken declared in his authoritative, historian's voice, were "botched and unfit." Mencken the mock historian took delight in a posture of disgust about what he called "this Eden of clowns." In the essay "Footnote on Criticism," he presented a credo about self-expression. "Criticism, at bottom, is indistinguishable from skepticism," he wrote in a context describing his ideal critic as one who values new ideas not "in proportion as they are likely to please," but "as they are amusing or beautiful." "The Novel," another significant essay in *Prejudices: Third Series*, begins by noticing "an unmistakable flavor

of effeminacy [that] hangs about the novel." Women, Mencken observed, were the main readers of novels. But contemporary women novelists were in the process of shedding their "lingering ladyism." Mencken described Willa Cather's extraordinary skill as a writer, in which he saw "first-hand representation" of what she as a woman had experienced and knew best. He called Cather's *My Ántonia* (1918) "a document in the history of American literature." He predicted that women novelists would depict the conduct of "[women as heroines] in the eternal struggle between . . . inspiration and . . . destiny."

And finally, as closure for this remarkable volume, were images taken from Mencken's readings in newspapers across America. They were arranged under the headings "Aspiration," "Virtue," and "Eminence" in a section called "Suite Americane." Edmund Wilson had read this section a year earlier, when it first appeared in the *Smart Set*, and quoted it to illustrate what he called Mencken's "poetry of America." For example:

> Aspiration: College professors in one-building universities on the prairie, still hoping, at the age of sixty, to get their whimsical essays into the *Atlantic Monthly*. . . . Car-conductors on lonely suburban lines, trying desperately to save up $500 and start a Ford garage. Virtue: Farmers plowing sterile fields behind sad meditative horses. . . . Women confined for the ninth or tenth time, wondering helplessly what it is all about. Methodist preachers retired after forty years of service in the trenches of God, upon pensions of $800 a year. . . . Decayed and hopeless men writing editorials at midnight for leading papers in Mississippi, Arkansas and Alabama.

Ridicule was modulated here (as in Sinclair Lewis's *Main Street*) by a vision of what was hopeless and sad about American provincial life.

In *Prejudices: Fourth Series* (1924) Mencken continued to revise and reprint writings that first appeared in the *American Mercury*, the *Baltimore Evening Sun*, and a weekly column for the *Chicago Tribune*. Although he seemed to be tiring of rewriting earlier journalism, the section called "People and Things" continued to gather images from American experience in his poetry of America: "Former plumbers, threshing-machine engineers and horse-doctors turned into United Brethren bishops. . . . The wilting flowers standing in ice-pitchers and spittoons in the hallways. . . . My first view of the tropics, the palm-trees suddenly bulging out of the darkness of dawn, the tremendous stillness, the sweetly acid smell."

Prejudices: Fifth Series (1926) and *Prejudices: Sixth Series* (1927) revisited many old subjects. Several essays illustrate how effectively and carefully Mencken reworked materials originally written to newspaper or magazine deadlines. Notable in the *Fifth Series* are "In Memoriam: W.J.B." and "The Hills of Zion," both from his reports for the *Evening Sun* on the Scopes trial. As Fred Hobson observes, Mencken thought of the *Sixth Series* as "a hack job, done to get some money," although it included poignant essays, one titled "On Suicide," and another about Rudolph Valentino, the film celebrity, written shortly after his fatal illness. Mencken responded to what he saw as a "fineness" in Valentino, a "man of relatively civilized feelings" caught up in "the whole grotesque futility of his life" as a Hollywood idol. Mencken coined a descriptive term for Hollywood, "Moronia," the land where "movie folks . . . have built their business upon a foundation of morons."

The Scopes trial in 1925 had been largely orchestrated by Mencken as one of the first of the staged media events that would become characteristic of twentieth-century American journalism. In the spring of 1926 along came another opportunity, this one a challenge to Mencken as the editor of the *American Mercury*. In the April issue the magazine had printed a story called "Hatrack," by Herbert Asbury, about a prostitute in a midwestern town. The New England Watch and Ward Society in Boston sought to censor the issue by having newsdealers return it to the *Mercury*. Mencken arranged to meet J. Franklin Chase, the society's secretary, on the Boston Common where, before a large audience, including many reporters, Mencken sold a copy of the April *Mercury* to Chase. Mencken was arrested and immediately released without trial on the grounds that no offense had been committed. In a more serious parallel action that could have had severe financial repercussions for the magazine, the April *Mercury* had been banned from the mails. But a counterinjunction blocked that order. So Mencken won in stylish fashion and upheld the freedom of the press, which to him was the central issue.

As the editor of the *American Mercury* during the ten-year period that began with its first issue in 1924, Mencken was able to solicit, select, and encourage submissions from authors of diverse backgrounds and persuasions. On the nonfiction side he identified controversial issues and published essays (some of them commissioned) on topics such as birth control and journalism; others were debunking profiles of politicians and literary notables, past and present. Among the authors were Max Eastman (Marxist literary critic), Emma Goldman (anarchist and editor of the magazine *Mother Earth*), Margaret Sanger

(birth control advocate and author), Clarence Darrow (labor and criminal lawyer), Upton Sinclair (socialist and muckraking novelist, author of *The Jungle*, 1906), Carl Van Vechten (music and drama critic, novelist, photographer), and Charles Beard (liberal historian). Although he published less fiction and poetry than nonfiction, authors included were Theodore Dreiser, Sherwood Anderson, F. Scott Fitzgerald, and Edgar Lee Masters. One of Mencken's notable omissions was Ernest Hemingway, who in 1924 sent him several stories. As always, Mencken knew what he liked, and neither Hemingway nor Gertrude Stein was published by him.

Mencken continued to write book review essays during his ten years as editor for the *American Mercury*. As reviewer and as editor he provided extensive support and advocacy for black American writers. Among them were W. E. B. Du Bois (author and editor of the NAACP's magazine, *The Crisis*); the poets Langston Hughes, Countee Cullen, and James Weldon Johnson; Walter F. White (later head of the NAACP); and George S. Schuyler (journalist). Mencken's own writing had a profound effect on black writers. A notable example was Richard Wright, who in his autobiography, *Black Boy* (1945), acknowledged Mencken's empowering influence. As both journalist and editor, Mencken was consistently concerned about abuses and denials of civil rights.

WOMEN, MARRIAGE, AND THE MIDLIFE CAREER

The years from 1925 to 1930 brought many changes to Mencken's life. His mother died in 1925. His *Notes on Democracy* (1926) was not well received, despite his more than ten years of research, planning, and intermittent bouts of writing. Also, he had a sense that he was losing the audience he had cultivated over a fifteen-year period. All of this combined to produce expressions of despair and depression. One such expression was the essay in *Prejudices: Sixth Series* titled "On Suicide."

During these unsettled years he was intimately involved with several women, with the possibility of marriage frequently at hand. The most intense and longest of these relationships was with Marion Bloom, whom he saw often between 1914 and 1923. Born in rural Maryland, she was, like Mencken, self-educated. An attractive person, she both fascinated and irritated him. They were lovers and talked of marriage, but finally, for Mencken, her lack of a genteel background stood in the way. Several other women were or thought they were significantly part of his life. Aileen Pringle, a film and stage star, met him whenever she could, and he made several trips to Hollywood to see her. She was a very willing candidate for marriage, as was Gretchen Hood, a handsome opera singer with whom Mencken carried on what was to him, but not to her, a mock courtship. There were others during these years, and the woman he finally decided to wed was Sara Haardt, whom he had met in 1923. She was eighteen years younger than he, a teacher at Goucher College when he met her, an aspiring writer whom he encouraged in her career. She came from a good southern family, thus satisfying Mencken's patrician expectations; she was poised, good-looking, and shared his ironic perspective. Her health, however, was fragile, and Mencken helped arrange several hospitalizations for her in Baltimore during the late 1920s. When, in 1929, he and Sara decided to marry, they kept their plans secret. His liaisons with the other women ended. Mencken was told by her doctors that Sara had perhaps no more than three years to live. They were married in 1930. Her periods of illness came more frequently, and she died in 1935. Mencken was very happy during their married years, although the tragedy of her illness was always present.

Mencken's comparative study of religions, *Treatise on the Gods*, was well received upon publication in 1930. It reflected his skepticism as well as wide reading over many years about comparative religions. However, around this time journalists as well as critics of Mencken were noting his loss of popularity and influence. He resigned from the *American Mercury* in December 1933 and continued to write "Monday Articles" for the *Baltimore Evening Sun* until 1938, when he became editor for the *Sun* papers. He also wrote for magazines, among them *The Nation*, *The New Yorker*, and *Harper's*. A major project during the years of his marriage was a book he called *Treatise on Right and Wrong* (1934). This *Treatise*, unlike *Treatise on the Gods*, did not do well with the reviewers and critics.

THE LATER CAREER

In 1935 he put his energy into the extensively revised and enlarged fourth edition of *The American Language* (1936). It was a great success, and a late, major phase in his career and reputation began.

Starting in 1936, when he wrote two short reminiscence essays for *The New Yorker*, Mencken planned an autobiographical book describing his earliest memories. *Happy Days, 1880–1892*, published in 1940, was the result. It was a mellow book; the voice was vintage Mencken, vivid but in nostalgic, often gentle, tones, richly textured with descriptive details and expressive scenes. He thought of

it as his *Tom Sawyer*, a sort of Mark Twain–like idyll, and he left out whatever would have darkened the sunny aspects of growing up in Baltimore, such as the dictatorial presence of his father, who appears mainly as a cheerful practical joker.

In 1939, Mencken, whose health had been in decline, had his first stroke. It was a minor one, and spurred by illness and a desire to shape his legacy, he began the project of organizing his many accumulated records, including correspondence, clippings, and scrapbooks. These efforts further stimulated his interest in memories of his early life in Baltimore. *The New Yorker*, a bastion of good writing in America, asked Mencken for new sketches, and these led him to a second volume in the autobiography, *Newspaper Days, 1890–1906* (1941). What he captured here was the diverse excitement of Baltimore at and after the turn of the century. There was a romantic, even heroic aspect to what he reported, and Mencken wrote in the full power of a skill honed through a lifetime.

In 1942, Mencken's *A New Dictionary of Quotations* appeared. It was a 1,300-page book and a task for which most writers would have needed at least several uninterrupted years. Next, at the urging of Harold Ross, editor of *The New Yorker*, he turned to *Heathen Days, 1890–1936*, published in 1943. This was a collection of autobiographical essays covering a thirty-year period that included stories about some of his travels. The audience Mencken had resurrected for himself at this late stage of his career was pleased to have him back in mellower form. The *Days* books were so popular that Alfred A. Knopf, Mencken's friend and publisher since 1917, put all three together in *The Days of H. L. Mencken* (1947). In spite of his outstanding successes as an author during these years, Mencken struck a melancholy tone in his author's note to *The Days*: "As the shadows close in . . . all I try to do here is to convey some of my joy to the nobility and gentry of this once great and happy Republic, now only a dismal burlesque of its former self." Each of the *Days* books had generated what Mencken called "Additions, Corrections, and Explanatory Notes." These remain at the Enoch Pratt Free Library in Baltimore as part of an enormous collection of manuscripts and letters that Mencken gathered as part of the record of his life.

This busy time was notable also for the two large supplements to *The American Language* in 1945 and 1948. For years he had corresponded with linguists and readers, who sent him clippings and anecdotes about Americanisms. The second and final *American Language* supplement came out to numerous laudatory reviews, including a letter from William Faulkner, who said, as Fred Hobson reports: "It's good reading, like Swift or Sterne." In the first edition of 1919, Mencken had described the "diverging streams" of American and British English. In the fourth edition of 1936 he had called the American stream the more powerful of the two. Then, in 1948, near the end of his active life as a writer, with these six substantial volumes completed, Mencken summarized his position in an essay, "The American Language," for the *Literary History of the United States*: "General American is much clearer and more logical than any of the other dialects, either English or American. It shows clear if somewhat metallic pronunciations, gives all necessary consonants their true values, keeps to simple and narrow speech tones, and is vigorous and masculine."

Mencken's interest in the organized record of his life continued with two posthumously published, book-length projects begun in 1941 and 1942: *Thirty-five Years of Newspaper Work* (1994) and *My Life as Author and Editor* (1993). Back in 1930, Mencken had begun a diary of personal reflections. Entries in the 1940s included many accounts of his failing health, along with nostalgic lamentations for the loss of what he had recently chronicled in the *Days* books. Nothing appeared in the diary about his female friends before or after his five years of marriage to Sara Haardt. He wrote two sad, affectionate entries about her. After her death many women were interested in him, and he in them. Mencken as always charmed them, and several were devoted to him. He enjoyed, perhaps thrived on, these relationships and responded with his usual courtliness while keeping his distance.

But the years from 1935 to 1948 were essentially dark ones for Mencken. His diary (which at his explicit direction was kept in a lockbox until twenty-five years after his death) had many despairing, melancholy entries, including some that were anti-Semitic, racist, and pro-Nazi. Sometimes when Mencken in his diary and letters referred to black Americans he used racist epithets common to his era (the late nineteenth and first half of the twentieth century), place (the border South), and class (white, privileged, comfortable). His writing about Jewish people occasionally used similar racist epithets, although many of his closest friends and colleagues, such as Alfred Knopf and George Jean Nathan, were Jews. These verbal insensitivities have been especially puzzling and vexing to late-twentieth- and early-twenty-first-century readers and students of Mencken.

In the diary and sometimes in correspondence, he wrote anecdotes about former friends and colleagues, chronicling their failures to control or manage their lives effectively (most notably, for example, Sinclair Lewis, F. Scott Fitzgerald, Theodore Dreiser, and Edgar Lee Masters). During World War II, as in World War I, Mencken felt a love of most things German, and he had a virulent distrust for President Franklin Roosevelt that was reminiscent of his earlier feelings about President Woodrow Wilson. There was not much he could write about the war effort that any of the mainstream media would have found publishable. So he kept quiet; exceptions were his extensive efforts in 1938 and 1939 to help Jewish friends whose families and other friends were trying to escape from Germany.

Although in 1945 his health continued to concern him, Mencken was still thinking about many new book-length projects. He was also sorting through files of correspondence, notes, clippings, photographs, and scrapbooks that he intended to give either to the New York Public Library or to the Enoch Pratt Free Library in Baltimore. In the late 1940s two biographers, Edgar Kemler and William Manchester, were working on books about him, and he cooperated generously—he wanted the record, while under his control, to be full and accurate.

Mencken continued to work on *My Life as Author and Editor* and went to the 1948 Democratic and Republican National Conventions in Philadelphia, a ritual of coverage that had begun in 1904. Then, in the late fall, he had a serious stroke that made it impossible for him to read or to write and affected his ability to talk. Mencken said about himself that 1948 was the year he died—the year his active career as an author, editor, journalist, and historian of the American language ended.

But there was still more to come. A *Mencken Chrestomathy*, which he had finished before his stroke, was published in 1949. A six-hundred-page selection of articles that had not yet been reprinted in book form, it sold well and was greeted as further evidence for Mencken's late-life success and popularity. Mencken had to cut the original typescript about in half to get it down to manageable form. He gave what he had edited out of the *Chrestomathy* to the Enoch Pratt Free Library.

Essentially Mencken now lived a kind of twilight life, seeing a few friends and continuing some correspondence through dictation. He showed some improvement in his speech. In 1955 he was cheered by the publication of *The Vintage Mencken*, a collection of writings selected and introduced by Alistair Cooke. And in 1955 he completed selections for *Minority Report: H. L. Mencken's Notebooks* (1956), short pieces that he hoped would be as controversial as some of his *Prejudices* in the 1920s. With the help of Alfred Knopf he edited or deleted the darker, pessimistic selections. On 29 January 1956, Mencken died at his home, 1524 Hollins Street in Baltimore, where he had lived for all except six years of his life.

THE AFTERLIFE CAREER

After his death, Mencken's career as an author continued to a major extent as he had planned. *Minority Report* resurrected the extravagant voice and attitudes of his prime years and made *The New York Times* best-seller list. But for the most part the initial postmortem image of Mencken rested on his acclaim for the six volumes about *The American Language* and for the popularity of the *Days* books. A selection called *A Choice of Days* came out in 1980.

Mencken had saved, selected, and organized his enormous lifelong correspondence as well as files of clippings and manuscripts. Repositories of the correspondence are at the New York Public Library, with copies at the Enoch Pratt Free Library and at the Dartmouth College Library. Notes, clippings, and manuscripts went to the Pratt Library. As Mencken had stipulated, some of this material was opened to the public fifteen years after his death, in 1971. Then, ten years later, as Mencken had further decreed, his diary was made available to students and researchers at the Pratt Library. It was published as *The Diary of H. L. Mencken* in 1989.

In 1991 the Pratt Library released the typescripts of two completed books: *My Life as Author and Editor* (published in 1993) and *Thirty-five Years of Newspaper Work* (published in 1994). Coming out in 1995 was the book-length typescript Mencken had left at his death, *A Second Mencken Chrestomathy*, with further selections from writings never reprinted in his lifetime.

Since his death in 1956, and following *Minority Report*, fourteen various selections from his work have been published in book form, made up primarily of material previously printed. Other of his writings not yet published, as well as some previously published, will no doubt be selected and edited as books in the future. Some may be correspondence, volumes to be added to the collections of letters already in book form.

A WAKING MOMENT

The 1920s were for Mencken what Thoreau in the 1850s had called a "waking moment." Mencken spoke without bounds to readers who welcomed the extravagance of his energetic prose and celebrated his skeptical deflation of what were perceived as outdated conventions of American life. The rolling thump of his writing, with its joyful flashes of metaphor and imagery, illuminated the attitudes of which he was convinced. His concerns focused on freedom of the individual from the repressions of government, social conventions, and fundamentalism in its many manifestations. Freedom of speech, freedom of the press, the emancipation of women, the rights of minorities (especially black Americans) were causes he supported in words and actions. As a book reviewer, editor, and by example as a writer, he advocated the liberation of the writer as artist. In this advocacy he was admirably successful. And his six encyclopedic volumes about the American language are enduring testimonials to his thesis that General American is not a dialect of British English but is, rather, a language with its own freedom, power, and energy to which British English has itself become a dialect. In his *Mencken: A Life*, Fred Hobson explains why Mencken's writing in the fourth, and final, edition of *The American Language* could interest and affect so powerfully both "popular and critical audiences": "Mencken was tying language to life, was writing social history, tracing patterns of migration and settlement, reflecting on questions of tradition and change, propriety and impropriety, dealing with the larger matters of culture." The same summation also describes the major works of the Mencken canon. And his own "Song of Myself," his lifelong accretions, revisions, and additions, echo Walt Whitman's in *Leaves of Grass*.

[*See also* Dreiser, Theodore; Thoreau, Henry David; Twain, Mark; Whitman, Walt; *and* Wilson, Edmund.]

SELECTED WORKS

Ventures into Verse (1903)
George Bernard Shaw: His Plays (1905)
The Philosophy of Friedrich Nietzsche (1908)
A Book of Prefaces (1917)
In Defense of Women (1918)
The American Language: A Preliminary Inquiry into the Development of English in the United States (1919)
Prejudices: First Series (1919)
Prejudices: Second Series (1920)
Prejudices: Third Series. (1922)
Prejudices: Fourth Series (1924)
Prejudices: Fifth Series (1926)
Notes on Democracy (1926)
Prejudices: Sixth Series (1927)
Treatise on the Gods (1930)

Treatise on Right and Wrong (1934)
Happy Days, 1880–1892 (1940)
Newspaper Days, 1890–1906 (1941)
Heathen Days, 1890–1936 (1943)
The American Language Supplement I (1945)
The American Language Supplement II (1948)
A Mencken Chrestomathy (1949)
The Vintage Mencken (1955)
H. L. Mencken: The American Scene, a Reader (1955)
Minority Report: H. L. Mencken's Notebooks (1956)
Prejudices, A Selection (1958)
The Diary of H. L. Mencken. (1989)
The Impossible H. L. Mencken: A Selection of His Best Newspaper Stories (1991)
My Life as Author and Editor (1993)
Thirty-five Years of Newspaper Work (1994)
A Second Mencken Chrestomathy (1995)
H. L. Mencken: A Documentary Volume (2000)
Menckeniana: A Quarterly Review (1962–)

FURTHER READING

Adler, Betty, comp. *H. L. M.: The Mencken Bibliography.* Baltimore, 1961.

Adler, Betty, comp. *H. L. M.: The Mencken Bibliography: A Ten-Year Supplement, 1962–1971.* Baltimore, 1971.

Bode, Carl. *Mencken.* Carbondale, Ill., 1969. An early study of the life in the context of the writing.

Bode, Carl, ed. *The New Mencken Letters.* New York, 1977.

Fecher, Charles A. *Mencken: A Study of His Thought.* New York, 1978. In addition to its topic, an especially useful study of the cultural impact of Mencken's writing.

Fitzpatrick, Vincent. "H. L. Mencken." In *Dictionary of Literary Biography.* Vol. 137. Detroit, Mich., 2000. A short introduction to the life and work, with bibliography.

Fitzpatrick, Vincent. *H. L. Mencken.* Macon, Ga., 2003. A reissue of the concise 1989 biography covering the life and the work, updated and expanded, with bibliography.

Fitzpatrick, Vincent, comp. *H. L. M.: The Mencken Bibliography, A Second Ten-Year Supplement, 1972–1981.* Baltimore, 1986.

Forgue, Guy Jean. *H. L. Mencken: L'homme, l'oeuvre, l'influence.* Paris, 1967.

Forgue, Guy Jean, ed. *Letters of H. L. Mencken.* Boston, 1981. Foreword by Daniel Aaron.

Hobson, Fred. *Mencken: A Life.* New York, 1994. A full-scale, well-documented and engagingly written study, including the context of the work, correspondence, and literary-historical background, with assessment of Mencken's place in American letters. Photographs.

Hobson, Fred. *Serpent in Eden: H. L. Mencken and the South.* Chapel Hill, N.C., 1974.

Lippmann, Walter. "H. L. Mencken," *Saturday Review* (11 December 1926), p. 413.

Martin, Edward A. *H. L. Mencken and the Debunkers.* Athens, Ga., 1984.

Martin, Edward A. *In Defense of Marion: The Love of Marion Bloom and H. L. Mencken.* Athens, Ga., and London, 1996. Letters and selected writings included.

Riggio, Thomas P., ed. *Dreiser-Mencken Letters: The Correspondence of Theodore Dreiser & H. L. Mencken, 1907–1945,* 2 vols. Philadelphia, 1986.

Rodgers, Marion Elizabeth, ed. *Mencken and Sara, a Life in Letters.* New York, 1987.

Schrader, Richard J., comp. *H. L. Mencken: A Descriptive Bibliography.* Pittsburgh, Pa., 1998.

Scruggs, Charles. *The Sage in Harlem: H. L. Mencken and the Black Writers of the 1920s.* Baltimore, 1984.

Singleton, M. K. *H. L. Mencken and the American Mercury Adventure.* Durham, N.C, 1962.

Teachout, Terry. *The Skeptic: A Life of H. L. Mencken.* New York, 2002. With a focus on Mencken as journalist, editor, and writer, a clear view of his relevance as critic and shaper of American cultural life is established.

Wilson, Edmund. "H. L. Mencken," *The New Republic* (1 June 1921), pp. 10–13.

JAMES MERRILL

by Willard Spiegelman

James Ingram Merrill was born on 3 March 1926 in New York City, the son of Charles Edward Merrill and Hellen Ingram Merrill, his second wife. Merrill had two older half-siblings. He was raised in a privileged household—his father founded the brokerage house that became Merrill Lynch—with residences in Manhattan, Long Island, and Palm Beach. When he was thirteen his beloved parents divorced; the breakdown of their marriage made national news. Although skeptical or overtly hostile readers criticized him throughout his life for writing "genteel" or pseudo-aristocratic poetry, he was also recognized before as well as after his death as one of the most important, innovative, and universally appealing poets of the second half of the twentieth century. He attended the Lawrenceville School and Amherst College, graduating summa cum laude in 1947. Between 1950 and 1952 he traveled in Europe (mostly in Italy) at a time when the first postwar tourists were returning to a continent that had been closed for more than a decade since the outbreak of World War II in 1939. His prose memoir, *A Different Person* (1993), tells the remarkable story of his coming of age, poetically, psychologically, and sexually, during this crucial period. In 1955, having come to accept his homosexuality, he settled down in Stonington, Connecticut with David Jackson, a talented painter, writer, and musician, whom he had met the previous year. For more than twenty years they divided their time between Connecticut and Athens, until the last decade of Merrill's life, when they replaced the Athens house with a small cottage in Key West, Florida.

Not obliged to labor at a job, even a university post, Merrill was one of the few poets of his generation who could afford to devote all of his efforts to literature. His collected work includes a massive epic, *The Changing Light*

James Merrill. (© *Bettmann/Corbis*)

at Sandover (1982), plus eleven single volumes of verse, his memoir, two novels, three plays, and collections of occasional prose pieces. At the beginning of his career, Merrill's poems seemed elegant, artful, indeed baroque and fanciful; objects and scenes of travels served as occasions or themes. Later on, he loosened his style and became freer and more varied in his choice of subjects. The poems came to sound both more personal and more expansive; critics and readers alike sat up and took notice. Many prizes followed, including two National Book Awards (in 1967 for *Nights and Days* and 1979 for *Mirabell: Books of Number*), a Pulitzer Prize in 1977 for *Divine Comedies*, a Bollingen Prize in 1972 (for *Braving the Elements*), the National Book Critics Circle Award in 1983 for *The Changing Light at Sandover*, and the Bobbitt National Prize for Poetry, given by the Library of Congress, in 1989 (for *The Inner Room*).

MERRILL AS A POET

Three gifts distinguish Merrill's poetry. First, from the very beginning he was a master of traditional verse forms and techniques. His ear, and his ability to vary the pacing, rhythm, and intonation of a poem, proved that he both listened to and re-created the patterns of human thought and speech while adding his own inflections to them. He was also a proficient user of puns and clichés, delighting in all the surprising possibilities of his native language.

Second, he recognized early on that "life was fiction in disguise" ("Days of 1935"), that a poet, like a novelist, can reimagine the real events of his life, use them in a poem, and add to them elements from his imagined or fictive life. Narrative, in other words, forms the basis of many of his shorter poems as well as his book-length epic. Merrill wrote his college undergraduate thesis on Marcel Proust.

110

He never lost the Proustian ability to record nuances of social life and to connect the inner life—whether his own or those of his "characters"—and the personal trials of love and loss with the greater society in which erotic and psychological dramas occur. Like Proust and Henry James he observed the surrounding social scene with a satirist's eye. And especially like Proust, Merrill developed as his great theme the recovery through time and memory of all of the losses and bequests of love. He is one of the great love poets of the twentieth century and, along with W. H. Auden, one of the greatest homosexual love poets.

Third, he followed a time-honored poetic path by building toward the writing of an epic, albeit a thoroughly unconventional one. Critics will debate for years to come whether *The Changing Light at Sandover* is Merrill's masterpiece or, in spite of brilliant glittering parts within, a misdirected effort and a betrayal of his own best talents. What he calls his "poems of science" flagrantly mingle chatty séances at a Ouija board with semi-serious investigations of molecular biology, genetic evolution, human history, and reincarnation. How soberly readers should take the mythic structures and cosmic revelations Merrill presents is a question that will continue to divide admirers from skeptics.

EARLY WORK

From the opening lines of the title poem of *The Black Swan and Other Poems* (1946), the reader can sniff the rarefied but intense bouquet of Merrill's rhythms and language: "Black on flat water past the jonquil lawns / Riding, the black swan draws / A private chaos warbling in its wake." *First Poems*, which contains and expands upon Merrill's earlier, shorter volume, likewise reins in feeling. Everything seems measured or seen from a distance. In "Portrait," Merrill joins the lushness of Keats's "The Eve of Saint Agnes" with the arch aestheticism of Wallace Stevens's "The Comedian as the Letter C":

> A lute, cold meats, a snifter somewhat full
> Like a crystal ball predicting what's unknown;
> Ingots of nougat, thumbsized cumquats sodden
> With juice not quite their own.

In accents "not quite [his] own," Merrill is also unintentionally preparing himself and his readers for the "crystal ball" predictions that will come later in his "prophetic" books.

Often lacking a human center, Merrill's early poems possess a cold perfection and a mannerly reticence. They are the exact opposite of poems written by the so-called confessional poets, although they obviously tell

us something about their maker. In an interview, the author once observed: "Manners are for me the touch of nature, an artifice in the very bloodstream." In the last poem of *First Poems*, Merrill alights upon a subject that will hold him throughout his career. "The House" explores human fragility via architecture. Whereas day is comfort, "Night is a cold house" whose "west walls take the sunset like a blow." Houses confer meaning, not just protection: the "listener" in the poem learns "soberly" at dusk that "a loss of deed and structure" is his plight. (Such loss will later inform more important poems like the sonnet sequence "The Broken Home" and "Clearing the Title," which concerns the "titles" of Merrill's epic poem and of his new house with David Jackson in Key West.) Things fall apart, ownership and actions fail, day is a flattering illusion, and "no key opens" the house of night. The speaker finally gains access to the house:

> I have entered, nevertheless,
> And seen the wet-faced sleepers the winds take
> To heart; have felt their dreadful profits break
> Beyond my seeing. At a glance they wake.

The open ending, whether revelation or submission, captures a moment full of possibilities.

Such possibilities expanded to include the ardors of seeing and traveling. In *The Country of a Thousand Years of Peace* (the title refers to Switzerland), Merrill dazzlingly demonstrates the limitations and attractions of the imagination and of his own aesthetic stances. For example, "The Octopus" alternates five- and four-stress lines, with rhymes on the first syllable of feminine endings and the second of masculine ones (for example, "translucence" / "unloose" and "fervor" / "observe"). Merrill compares "vision asleep in the eye's tight translucence" to a sleepy, caged octopus, only rarely coaxed out by the light into a waking dance; it uncurls its tentacles like the arms of a Hindu god toward the object of its attraction:

> He is willing to undergo the volition and fervor
> Of many fleshlike arms, observe
> These in their holiness of indirection
> Destroy, adore, evolve, reject—
> Till on glass rigid with his own seizure
> At length the sucking jewels freeze.

"Holiness" suggests the sacerdotal function of art, and "indirection" recalls T. S. Eliot's remarks on the need for artistic subtlety, opacity, and difficulty in our disjointed modern world. Like "The Doodler" (see below), "The Octopus" is an allegory of the artist's activity. Merrill's volume was published the same year as *Life Studies*, Robert

Lowell's "breakthrough" book. In his prose memoir "91 Revere Street," Lowell announces a theme that he shares with Merrill. In personal recollections, "the vast number of remembered *things* remains rocklike. Each is in its place, each has its function, its history, its drama. There, all is preserved by that motherly care that one either ignored or resented in his youth. The things and their owners come back with life and meaning—because finished, they are endurable and perfect." Memory, the family, residences: these became important issues for both Lowell and Merrill. And both men relied on external images to give weight and substance to inner conflicts.

Merrill recognized the limitations of his own imagination and work. In "The Book of Ephraim" (the first part of *The Changing Light*), he debates how to organize his weird material and confesses "My downfall was 'word-painting,'" but he opts for poetry over prose since "in verse the feet went bare." Throughout his career he veered between purely "descriptive" or "artful" poems and others that maintain a narrative or at least suggest the possibilities of storytelling. The poet-critic Richard Howard referred to the "patinated narcissism" of *First Poems*, which Merrill "literally roughed up" in *The Country of a Thousand Years of Peace*; "the resulting corrugation of surface corresponds . . . to a new agitation of the depth." Even early on, that is, Merrill was working with and through his strengths and limitations.

Merrill gives a name to these art poems: they are doodles. His signature piece "The Doodler" self-consciously warns against his limitations. Doodles are like children, "the long race that descends / From me." (Art as a substitute for children becomes a theme as well in *The Changing Light*, which defends homosexuality and its alternative ways of procreating.) These little icons grow on the page like lichens. Inflated and comic, the are both "art" and preparations for it, symbols of paintings yet to come. Looking at a page of random designs, the would-be artist confronts his past, from which the retrieval of meaning can be frustrating as well as fruitful: "Shapes never realized, were you dogs or chairs?" Like any person looking back on his life or work, the speaker seems to ask himself "What was I trying to do?" The question is a stand-in for that other question of self-examination that Merrill implicitly makes in all of his first-person poems: "What was I?" Or, "What was I like?" Like the voices he reads from the Ouija board later on, the doodles provide an antidote to the neat perfection of more polished poems: "nothing I do is at all fine / Save certain abstract forms. These come unbidden." The poet must look hopefully forward to future outbursts of energy that might turn into stories, designs, and characters ("I have learned / To do feet," he wryly announces).

WATER STREET AND NIGHTS AND DAYS

By the time of *Water Street* (1962), Merrill had moved to a new house in Stonington and discovered a symbol for his poetry as well as a subject for it. He greets guests in the final poem, "A Tenancy": "If I am host at last / It is of little more than my own past. / May others be at home in it." Many of these poems demonstrate a new ease in their reminiscence, especially "An Urban Convalescence" and "Scenes of Childhood." In both, themes of loss and compensation emerge as significant ways of accepting what he calls in the former poem "the dull need to make some kind of house / Out of the life lived, out of the love spent." What he came to label his "chronicles of love and loss" are already foreshadowed here. In the latter poem home movies reawaken consciousness and recapture the still-terrifying past. Repetition opens and also controls memory. The dead feed upon the living, but the living may control the dead (as Merrill demonstrates in *The Changing Light*) through machines like a movie "projector" (an appropriately Freudian word). The poet realizes he is "sun and air" and also "son and heir" by comparison to his dead father, whose presence casts a shadow on the movie screen. In the poem "For Proust," he announces that "The loved one always leaves," but throughout his work he proves that memory and imagination may often restore what life denies.

From the mid-1960s onward, Merrill's work began to enact such restoration. In *Nights and Days*, Merrill pays homage to the titles and subjects of poems by Constantin Cavafy (1863–1933), the Greek Alexandrian poet whose vignettes, characterizations, and multileveled diction Merrill took as models. Merrill began (as Lowell had in *Life Studies*) to make of his own history, and that of his family, the very stuff of myth. His work is at once personal and impersonal (manners, again, being an image of nature as well as of culture). He said in a 1972 interview: "You hardly ever need to *state* your feelings. The point is to feel and to keep your eyes open. Then what you feel is expressed, is mimed back at you by the scene. A room, a landscape. I'd go a step further. We don't *know* what we feel until we see it distanced by this kind of translation." Art and life sustain rather than rival one another. Watching a scene allows one to understand one's own feelings. "Translation" will reappear as the subject and title of one of his greatest long lyrics, "Lost in Translation" (1976).

With its own energies of masking and unmasking, love is the human experience that most allows us to witness illusion and reality working together and separately. In "Days of 1964," Merrill reanimates the gods of ancient Greece in modern Athenian guise. Aphrodite is reborn as Kyria Kleo, his cleaning woman, who masks her age and despair with a prostitute's cosmetics and tight clothing (the tools of her other employment), at the same time revealing the ravages of time she urgently wants to conceal. In love himself, the poet enthusiastically thinks his maid "*was* Love," both the ancient goddess and her modern reincarnation. He pays her generously because "Love [the deity and his current state of feeling] makes one generous," although ironically she is working at a different job in the hills, looking for erotic customers. Is love—the goddess or the feeling—a truth or an illusion? Kleo's makeup is "the erotic mask / Worn the world over by illusion / To weddings of itself and simple need." The poem unites all such oppositions at the end:

> If that was illusion, I wanted it to last long;
> To dwell, for its daily pittance, with us there,
> Cleaning and watering, sighing with love or pain.
> I hoped it would climb when it needed to the heights
> Even of degradation, as I for one
> Seemed, those days, to be always climbing
> Into a world of wide
> Flowers, feasting, tears—or was I falling, legs
> Buckling, heights, depths,
> Into a pool of each night's rain?
> But you were everywhere beside me, masked,
> As who was not, in laughter, pain, and love.

The Fire Screen (1969) begins to mark a middle-age retreat from the pains of love. Even grand opera (about which Merrill wrote beautiful poems throughout his career) seems too strenuous to confront after the age of forty. He acknowledges in the sonnet sequence "Matinées" that the real thing, whether art or life, is just "too silly or solemn": it is "Enough to know the score // From records or transcriptions / For our four hands." Sometimes, even, "it seems / Kinder to remember than to play." Merrill's prose footnote to "Mornings in a New House" shrugs cavalierly at the protection offered by a fancy fire screen (the French word for which is *contre-coeur*): "Oh well. Our white heats lead us no less than words do. Both have been devices in their day." One's "household opera" with its strong emotions develops through time and memory. Life comes to imitate art, as the young Merrill, recalling his first opera (a matinée performance of Wagner's *Rheingold*), acknowledges that

as he grew up he would have to arrange for his "own chills and fever, passions and betrayals, / Chiefly in order to make song of them."

Art and life come together again in "Days of 1935" (from *Braving the Elements*), a perfect ballad that treats one of Merrill's obsessive themes—the breakup of his parents' marriage and his identification with the Lindbergh baby—in the simplest of poetic forms. The poem reproduces a double fantasy: the adult's of childhood innocence and the child's of attention through victimization and heroics. The young boy dreams he is captured by a pair of Bonnie and Clyde look-alikes, movie stars right out of central casting. The characters, Floyd and Jean, are both coarse sexual creatures and parental surrogates. The kidnapped boy spins out tales for Jean all afternoon, realizing that he is like the Princess Scheherazade and she the real child in need of storytelling. After the criminals are captured, the boy returns to "real" life, and his mother puts him to sleep in a Proustian moment:

> She kisses him sweet dreams, but who—
> Floyd and Jean are gone—
>
> Who will he dream of? True to life
> He's played them false. A golden haze
> Past belief, past disbelief . . .
> Well. Those were the days.

"Life was fiction in disguise," he knew even as a child; now, the adult poet teaches that fiction is equally life transformed and feeling translated.

DIVINE COMEDIES

Divine Comedies (1976) begins Merrill's self-mythologizing epic. Traditionally a poet writes one great epic (such was the career of Virgil, who provided a model for subsequent poets like Dante, Spenser, Milton, and Wordsworth) for which his whole life is the preparation. The half-dozen smaller (but perfect) poems surrounding "The Book of Ephraim," like chapels around a grand cathedral, adumbrate the larger work's concerns. "Chimes for Yahya" and "Verse for Urania" echo Milton's "Nativity Ode"; "Chimes" also reworks Yeats's "The Second Coming" and repeats Merrill's themes of surrogate fathers, the Near East, the collision of cultures, and inheritance and bequests. The impressive "Lost in Translation" succinctly pinpoints issues of loss and possession. Recalling a childhood jigsaw puzzle with a missing piece, Merrill considers as well his vain attempts in the present to retrieve a translation by Rainer Maria Rilke of Paul Valéry's "Palme":

"So many later puzzles had missing pieces" that he finds compensation in cosmic housekeeping:

> But nothing's lost. Or else: all is translation
> And every bit of us is lost in it.

Robert Frost said that poetry is what is lost in translation; Merrill cleverly proves the adage wrong, since loss and retrieval—of poetry and of childhood memory—give rise to his poem (which, appropriately, contains his own translation of the Valéry poem as well as an epigraph from Rilke's German one).

"The Book of Ephraim" begins the three-part series that constitutes *The Changing Light*. Merrill and Jackson had been experimenting with a Ouija board since 1955, the second year of their tenancy in Stonington. The poem recounts both their daily life during a twenty-five year period and their communiqués from otherworldly spirits, starting with Ephraim, a Greek Jew (coincidentally from a broken home), who died in 36 C.E. He instructs "JM" and "DJ" (as the characters are called) through the twenty-six capital letters of the board. The poem's twenty-six sections begin with the letters of the alphabet, in sequence. (The second volume, *Mirabell: Books of Number*, is divided by the ten cardinal numbers; the third and longest, *Scripts for the Pageant*, has three sections entitled "Yes," "And," and "No." Along with letters and numbers, these words are the standard figures on a Ouija board. After a while, JM and DJ add pieces of punctuation to their homemade board in order to register subtler tones of voice as well as grammar.) Ephraim is a smiling, chatty schoolmaster, an epitome of worldly wit and wisdom who chides when necessary ("WILL / U NEVER LEARN LOOK LOOK LOOK LOOK YR FILL / BUT DO DO DO DO NOTHING") but more frequently adopts an affable, cooing tone ("U ARE SO QUICK MES CHERS I FEEL WE HAVE / SKIPPING THE DULL CLASSROOM DONE IT ALL / AT THE SALON LEVEL"). Ephraim gilds the philosophic pill, as Merrill does in his transcriptions that make up the poem: "huge tracts of information / Have gone into these capsules flavorless / And rhymed for easy swallowing." This is a good thing, too, since JM and DJ, as stand-ins for their audience, go in fear of abstractions. They have already slept through

> our last talk on Thomist
> Structures in Dante. Causes
> Were always lost—on us. We shared the traits
> Of both the dumbest
>
> Boy in school and that past master of clauses
> Whose finespun mind "no idea violates."

The allusion above to Henry James (in T. S. Eliot's characterization) appropriately sets the stage for a poem that contains Jamesian views of social life on this earth and beyond. The poem's "dramatis personae" (section D) include friends, family, strangers, and fictional characters among the living and the dead. Lacking a conventional plot line, the poem moves along parallel, sometimes intersecting, paths: discussions of reincarnation and of the structure of the universe and human history are interwoven with self-analysis and lyrical passages. Worldly wit and spiritual revelation go hand in hand: Ephraim tells DJ and JM, the hand and scribe, respectively (they use a teacup as a pointer to move from letter to letter, and JM writes down the various messages), that Mozart has been reborn as "A BLACK ROCK STAR / WHATEVER THAT IS."

MIRABELL AND SCRIPTS FOR THE PAGEANT

"The Book of Ephraim" is encyclopedic in its tonal calibrations as in its subject matter. Merrill admitted to having cared about music long before literature, and in a 1968 interview he essentially predicted his interest in the different "voices" he came to hear and record in his prophetic books: "'Voice' is the democratic word for 'tone.' 'Tone' always sounds snobbish, but without a sense of it, how one flounders." Merrill's epic poem plumbs the depths and scales the heights of the universe and also takes the measure of the human voice. In the same interview, Merrill asked: "How can you appreciate the delights of concision unless you abuse them?" Again, he has set the stage for the two subsequent chapters in the epic: the book-length *Mirabell* (1978) and *Scripts* (1980) are considerably longer and more complex than anything we might have imagined after "Ephraim." Mirabell, a semi-fallen angel from an earlier cosmos, takes over as a guiding spirit. He is joined by W. H. Auden and Merrill's Greek friend Maria Mitsotaki, spiritual guides and parent figures, both recently dead, "father of forms and matter-of-fact mother," whose common sense keeps JM and DJ from despair after their communication with the angels. All of these voices blend into a harmonious chorus, a new music corresponding to a focus away from the individual self. The twentieth century destroyed what D. H. Lawrence once called the old stable ego; otherness is both *Mirabell*'s theme and the condition of its world. One's former lives all run together (MM tells JM that "AS WITH THE OLD LOVES ONE FORGETS A FEW"). Heaven is "BOTH REALITY AND A FIGMENT OF THE IMAGINATION," a machine that WHA says "MAKES THE DEAD AVAILABLE TO LIFE." And although JM feels he is merely a "vehicle in this cosmic carpool," he is again reminded by Auden "WHAT A MINOR / PART THE SELF PLAYS IN A WORK OF ART." The whole universe is the intelligence that constitutes God.

"Ephraim" took twenty years to write; *Mirabell* was composed in Stonington during the summer of 1976. The former work seems a prologue to the main body, which was assembled under intense concentration. As a character, Ephraim befitted JM and DJ's novice status; Mirabell is more serious, appropriate to their new maturity and to the depth (or pretension, according to skeptical critics) of the newer revelations. Mirabell and his peers serve God Biology; they have fallen, having once trifled with creation (the result was black holes) but were forgiven. They must now "WARN MAN AGAINST THE CHAOS" that began with atomic fission in 1934 and threatens nature's 500-million-year-old greenhouse. God Biology himself, a distant kindly force, works eugenically with a few good souls whom he clones for the gradual improvement of the human race. JM's role as a scribe demands that he help speed an acceptance of God's (and his own) creative work. Mirabell, like God, needs JM because angels and deities lack two human gifts, language and feeling, for which they depend upon us. God has no words for his own power and grace: "Who, left alone, just falls back on flimflam / Tautologies like *I am that I am* / Or *The world is everything that is the case.*" The human scribes must translate angelic mathematical truths into their own "vocabulary of manners." Merrill has taken what readers have always identified as his salient gifts and put them at the service of cosmic or scientific principles.

JM wonders why God has chosen homosexuals (himself and DJ) for this work. The answer is a tongue-in-cheek, semipornographic self-defense:

Erection of theories, dissemination
Of thought—the intellectual's machismo.
We're more the docile takers-in of seed,
No matter what tall tale our friends emit,
Lately—you've noticed?—we just swallow it.

Mirabell assures them that God produced homosexuality to encourage poetry and music. (Many readers—gay as well as straight—have taken offense at such an easy proposal.) Merrill realizes that the quartet of JM and DJ in this world, and Auden and Maria in the other, are all childless. Likewise, type is traditionally set backward in order to appear correctly on a page. Reversion, like inversion, is correctness, just as a creation itself is "a reasoned indirection."

The third part of the trilogy, *Scripts for the Pageant* (1980), followed in the completed *Changing Light* by a coda entitled "The Higher Keys," is the epic's longest, most difficult part. Its primary new speakers are a pair of angels—Michael and Gabriel—who represent universal forces of creation and destruction, light and darkness, respectively. Because this book is organized around "Yes," "&" and "No," it is also—structurally—the simplest. Negation always counters affirmation. As the cast of characters expands it also reduces, because many people turn out to be a version of a single nature. Merrill's interest in masking and unmasking here receives its most dramatic and moving treatment. The epic at last has the heft of a pseudo-scientific treatise and the energy of a mystery novel, as readers proceed through a series of discoveries to learn the essential identities of the poem's characters. The poem strips away and expands at the same time. It also ends where it began. Having completed his life's work, JM now imagines the scene of its performance, before an audience of the living and the dead, the real and the imaginary, although he pledges his primary allegiance to the former: "For *their* ears I begin: 'Admittedly....'" The poem has come full circle, ending with the first word of "The Book of Ephraim."

AFTER *THE CHANGING LIGHT AT SANDOVER*

After completing what some readers think of as his masterpiece and others think of as a misdirection of his essential lyric talents, Merrill gathered three further volumes of short poems: *Late Settings* (1985), *The Inner Room* (1988), and *A Scattering of Salts*, published soon after his death on 6 February 1995. In these books, he returns to many of his earlier themes but with the maturity and simplicity that come from years of honing one's instrument. Merrill's syntax and diction careen between the ornate and baroque and the plain and simple. Merrill was gifted with an ear that registers all levels of language and tone, from the precise, the elevated, and the technical to the demotic, the colloquial, and the clichéd. In his last book especially he acknowledges mortality while never forgoing his characteristically lambent wit. His autobiographical memoir, *A Different Person*, continues the open self-examination begun in his epic. Merrill deepens and personalizes his defense of homosexuality, at least with regard to his own life, by recounting his years in Rome between 1950 and 1952, when he was asserting his independence from his family, seeing Europe and its culture for the first time, undergoing a successful psychoanalysis, and developing his artistic as well as his personal self. Like *The Changing Light*, the memoir tackles the whole issue of sameness and difference. Merrill was always of—at least—two minds about everything, as befits a poet whose primary tool is "metaphor," or the representation of one thing by the vehicle of another. The "different" person of the distant past is also, mutatis mutandis, the James Merrill writing in the present. One may recall a telling remark in one of John Keats's letters: "We are like the relict shirt of a Saint: the same and not the same: for the careful Monks patch it and patch it until there's not a thread of the original garment left, and still they show it for St. Anthony's shirt." Merrill's great theme turns out to have been, all along, that most basic of human questions: How does one become a person, both changing and making a self, and simultaneously staying true to one's given essence?

[*See also* McClatchy, J. D.]

WORKS

The Black Swan and Other Poems (1946)
First Poems (1951)
The Seraglio (1957)
The Country of a Thousand Years of Peace and Other Poems (1959)
Water Street (1962)
The (Diblos) Notebook (1965)
Nights and Days (1966)
The Fire Screen (1969)
Braving the Elements (1972)
Divine Comedies (1976)
Mirabell: Books of Number (1978)
Scripts for the Pageant (1980)
The Changing Light at Sandover (1982)
Late Settings (1985)

Recitative: Prose (1986)
The Inner Room (1988)
A Different Person: A Memoir (1993)
A Scattering of Salts (1995)
The Collected Poems (2001)
Collected Novels and Plays (2002)

FURTHER READING

Howard, Richard. *Alone with America: Essays on the Art of Poetry in the United States since 1950*. New York, 1971. The essay on Merrill is an interesting assessment of the pre-*Sandover* work.

Kalstone, David. *Five Temperaments*. New York, 1977. Another important early estimation in a volume that includes equally important coverage of John Ashbery, Elizabeth Bishop, Robert Lowell, and Adrienne Rich.

Labrie, Ross. *James Merrill*. Boston, 1982.

Lehman, David, and Berger, Charles, eds. *James Merrill: Essays in Criticism*. Ithaca, N.Y., 1983. Many excellent essays on various aspects of Merrill's poetry.

Moffett, Judith. *James Merrill: An Introduction to the Poetry*. New York, 1984. Good for beginners.

Polito, Robert. *A Reader's Guide to James Merrill's* The Changing Light at Sandover. Ann Arbor, Mich., 1994. Contains helpful guides to the entire trilogy.

Spiegelman, Willard. *The Didactic Muse: Scenes of Instruction in Contemporary American Poetry*. Princeton, N.J., 1989. Places Merrill and his poetry within the context of comparable contemporary poets.

Yenser, Stephen. *The Consuming Myth: The Work of James Merrill*. Cambridge, Mass., 1987. The best and most sophisticated guide to all of the poetry through the 1982 trilogy.

W. S. MERWIN

by Sean McDonnell

The son of a Presbyterian minister, William Stanley Merwin was born on 30 September 1927 in New York City and raised in Union City, New Jersey, and Scranton, Pennsylvania. One of the most prolific and successful postwar American poets, he has written more than fifteen books of poems and has won a range of prestigious prizes, including the Bollingen Prize, Tanning Prize, Ruth Lilly Poetry Prize, and Pulitzer Prize. After graduating from Princeton University in 1948 he left the United States to live in Europe, and over the course of his career he has lived in England, southern France, Mexico, and Hawaii, the landscapes and cultures of which all figure prominently in his poems. Although Merwin's poetic output is characterized by frequent and sometimes radical shifts in form and style, his work retains a high degree of unity by adhering to a consistent set of interrelated themes and concerns, which include the complexities of time, language, and memory; societal and existential alienation; myth; family; and the rhythms and patterns of the nonhuman world.

EARLY EXPLORATIONS

As a young poet, Merwin took to heart the advice given him by Ezra Pound to "read seeds, not twigs," and his early poems return to verse forms from the beginnings of European literature. *A Mask for Janus* (1952), chosen by W. H. Auden for the Yale Series of Younger Poets, and *The Dancing Bears* (1954) feature ballades, cantos, carols, roundels, and other early forms whose roots lie in the medieval and troubadour poetic traditions of the twelfth to fourteenth centuries. Merwin's typical speaker in these poems is a wanderer, often a sailor, who is cut off from the social forces that might otherwise help to flesh out his identity and who finds in the ocean's vast emptiness a corollary to his feeling of existential alienation. As many critics have noted, like his modernist predecessors Merwin has a keen interest in myth, though he often turns it on its head in order to suit his own purposes. In "Odysseus" (1960), for example, Merwin deflates the grandeur of the Homeric hero by suggesting that his journeys are defined not by bravery and superhuman feats but by repetition and

ennui. *Green with Beasts* (1956) contains a series of poems titled "Physiologus: Chapters for a Bestiary," which are some of Merwin's earliest ecological texts. Merwin values animals largely for the extent to which they resist the human attempt to control them, and in so doing point to a realm of knowledge and experience that lies outside of human language and understanding.

In 1956 Merwin returned to the United States after seven years in Europe, visiting the rural Pennsylvania of his childhood and staying for a time in Boston, where he spent time with Robert Lowell, Ted Hughes, and Sylvia Plath. The return home would inspire many of the poems in *The Drunk in the Furnace* (1960), a volume that stands in sharp contrast to his earlier work. In the book, Merwin loosens the formal trappings of his earlier verse, and like many of his contemporaries, he adopts a line that more closely resembles spoken language. He also relaxes the impersonality that marks his first three books and writes for the first time about his family. While many have compared the book to Lowell's *Life Studies*, published the previous year, Merwin's poems lack the intimate, revelatory nature of Lowell's confessional verse. Most often, Merwin's family poems underscore the distance he feels from his past and from his ancestors and rarely address his immediate family. The book frequently contrasts the restrictive religious code imposed by his grandmother with tales of his libertine grandfather, whose smoking, drinking, and swearing set him apart from her and who left the family before Merwin was born. The volume's title poem concerns a vagrant who sets up his home in an abandoned furnace at the town's edge. While the townspeople cringe at the riotous noise he makes in the furnace, their children are drawn to the music of his debased art. The drunk, like Merwin's grandfather, becomes a symbol of resistance to a kind of small-minded provincialism and religious dogmatism.

THE REVOLUTION OF THE 1960s

Few could predict the radical changes Merwin would introduce to his poetry in the 1960s, and the four books he wrote during that time—*The Moving Target* (1963), *The Lice* (1967), *The Carrier of Ladders* (1970), and *Writings to an Unfinished Accompaniment* (1973)—remain his most critically acclaimed works. In these books Merwin abandons the fixed forms of his previous work in favor of sparse, unpunctuated lyrics that capitalize on ambiguities in syntax and that often require multiple readings to decode. He uses jarring images and metaphors, influenced in part by the surrealist and French symbolist traditions, and often relies on a reduced, elemental vocabulary. The most distinguishing feature of these poems may well be their central voice, which extends the isolation of the speaker in Merwin's early work and which creates a distinctively harrowing mood at the same time that it seems to lack the substance of discrete personality. In this prophetic but apparently empty voice, many critics have heard the germs of a Zen-like spirituality.

As *The Drunk in the Furnace* reacts against the way the domestic space constrains individual identity, *The Moving Target* declares its independence from those larger social and cultural forces that seek to restrict and define the individual. In many of the poems, as the speaker realizes the way adherence to social codes has compromised him, he leaves society, casting himself into the desert in hopes of purifying himself and of finding a model of selfhood not tainted by the forces of social restriction. In "Lemuel's Blessing," the speaker prays to the independent wolf to help him overcome his own doglike nature, asking the wolf to save him from the need for the kinds of emotional dependencies that stem from socialization and to protect him as he seeks an independent source of being. The motif of stripping away the excesses of society in order to forge a pure self becomes one of the most powerful impulses of Merwin's work throughout this period, appearing again in poems like "Finally" and "I Live Up Here."

Merwin has always been an outspoken political activist, publishing reviews of obscure ecological texts in the 1950s, participating in the early stages of the anti-nuclear movement, and acting as a vocal critic of the Vietnam War. When he was awarded the Pulitzer Prize for *The Carrier of Ladders*, he requested that the prize money be divided between the draft resistance movement and a California painter who was blinded when police fired on Berkeley protesters. *The Lice* stands as one of the most sweeping critiques of the destructive human impulses that took the form of war and nuclear brinkmanship in the 1960s and as one of the most cohesive single volumes of verse published after World War II. Several poems in the book explicitly address political topics: Merwin elegizes the dead of the

Vietnam War in "The Asians Dying" and the victims of ecological catastrophe in "For a Coming Extinction" and "The Last One"; poems like "Bread at Midnight" and "Caesar" link political institutions to a kind of spiritual death. For Merwin these disasters are part of a larger impulse to dominate the world that indicts the entire human species, and in poems like "December Night" it is not clear that Merwin sees much hope that humanity can reverse the course of its destructiveness. Despite this bleak outlook, which borders at times on the apocalyptic, *The Lice* suggests that a source of value transcending human arrogance may be discovered in the patterns and order of the natural world. In "The Widow," he suggests that natural systems persevere in spite of human meddling, and in poems like "In One of the Retreats of Morning" and "Looking for Mushrooms at Sunrise," he proposes that by illustrating modes of being based on necessity, the natural world might provide an alternative model of being for humans as well.

LATER WORK

In the late 1970s, Merwin shifted his style again, tempering the difficulty of his 1960s work in favor of a more straightforward style marked by an increasing openness and intimacy. While still eschewing punctuation, Merwin began to write lucid, flowing narratives that utilized direct speech and vivid images in place of the jarring fragments that made up *The Lice*. During this time he continued to experiment with a wide range of forms: *Feathers from the Hill* (1978) draws on East Asian forms like the haiku; poems in *Opening the Hand* (1983) employ a mid-line break reminiscent of Middle English verse; and *The River Sound* (1999) and *The Pupil* (2001) feature a variety of fixed forms, many drawn from troubadour sources.

Nature and landscape, concerns of Merwin's throughout his career, take on a special importance in his later work. In the mid-1960s, Merwin purchased a house in rural southwest France, a landscape memorialized in *The Vixen* (1996) and in the prose works *The Lost Upland: Stories of Southwest France* (1992) and *The Mays of Ventadorn* (2002). In these books, landscape becomes, for Merwin, a means of connecting to vanishing ways of life attuned to natural rhythms, in the form of the rural, communal, agrarian lives of his neighbors, and to a vanishing language and literature, in the form of their native Provençal. Merwin has also written extensively on Hawaii, where he moved in 1976 to study with the Zen master Robert Aitken and where he maintains a grove of endangered palm trees. Much of *The Rain in the Trees* (1988) meditates on rich natural scenes and, in poems like "Hearing the Names of the Valleys," on the difficulty of capturing landscape and culture through language. *The Folding Cliffs* (1998), a book-length narrative poem set in nineteenth-century Hawaii, recounts the long-term damage wrought on the indigenous population and environment by American imperialism. Ultimately in these writings Merwin returns again to roots, and by exploring a personal connection with place he again affirms the need for a means of existence based in necessity and not domination.

As his career has progressed, Merwin's poetry has grown increasingly autobiographical, and he has found in family and in his childhood fertile ground for exploring his larger epistemological concerns. After the death of his father, he wrote about their troubled, distant relationship with a frankness unseen in his early work. The poems of *Opening the Hand* and the prose memoir *Unframed Originals* (1982) detail the way in which his father's restrictive injunctions—he frequently forbade Merwin from touching things, making noise, or moving outside of the confines of their front yard—dominated his childhood, revelations that help to shed light on the resistance to restrictive authority that is a hallmark of Merwin's career. "Testimony," a long poem in *The River Sound* written for Merwin's seventieth birthday, treats as a single fabric his entire life, beginning with fragments of childhood memories and family stories and moving through the events he witnessed and the literary friendships he held throughout his life. The poem connects particular, detailed moments with sweeping lyrical passages that ultimately seek to ground Merwin's memories not in the realm of the merely personal but in the larger context of history, nature, memory, and time.

Impressive as it is, Merwin's poetic output reflects only one part of his career. In the 1950s in England he worked as a playwright and wrote a number of successful plays, all of which remain unpublished. During this time he also worked as a translator for the BBC. He has translated poems from many periods and from many languages including French, Spanish, Italian, and Vietnamese and has published more than twenty-five volumes of translations, including authoritative versions of Pablo Neruda (1969), Jean Follain (1968), Dante's *Paradiso* (2000), *The Song of Roland* (1963), and *The Poem of the Cid* (1959). He has also published six books of prose, including several books about Southwest France.

SELECTED WORKS

A Mask for Janus (1952)
The Dancing Bears (1954)
Green with Beasts (1956)
The Drunk in the Furnace (1960)
The Moving Target (1963)
The Lice (1967)
The Carrier of Ladders (1970)
Writings to an Unfinished Accompaniment (1973)
The Compass Flower (1977)
Feathers from the Hill (1978)
Unframed Originals (1982)
Opening the Hand (1983)
The Rain in the Trees (1988)
The Lost Upland: Stories of Southwest France (1992)
Travels (1993)
The Vixen (1996)
The Folding Cliffs: A Narrative (1998)
The River Sound (1999)
The Pupil (2001)
The Mays of Ventadorn (2002)

FURTHER READING

Altieri, Charles. *Enlarging the Temple: New Directions in American Poetry during the 1960s.* Lewisburg, Pa., 1979. Altieri is Merwin's most articulate reader, and his treatment of Merwin's 1960s work remains the seminal critical text on the poet.

Davis, Cheri. *W. S. Merwin.* Boston, 1981. Davis takes on Merwin's entire career up to 1980. She provides many detailed readings, without an overarching theme.

Hix, H. L. *Understanding W. S. Merwin.* Columbia, S.C., 1997. A good general introduction to Merwin's work, arranged thematically.

Nelson, Cary, and Ed Folsom, eds. *W. S. Merwin: Essays on the Poetry.* Chicago, 1987. An edited anthology of essays written from a range of critical stances.

Scigaj, Leonard M. *Sustainable Poetry: Four American Ecopoets.* Lexington, Ky., 1999. Scigaj's polemical text examines Merwin's connection to the natural world, alongside the work of A. R. Ammons, Wendell Berry, and Gary Snyder.

METAFICTION

by Jerome Klinkowitz

Metafiction is a style of prose narrative in which attention is directed to the process of fictive composition. The most obvious example of a metafictive work is a novel about a novelist writing a novel, with the protagonist sharing the name of the creator and each book having the same title. Such an approach defies both the tradition of the novel itself, which for over two hundred years has insisted that the form be a representative account of doings in the world, and aesthetic theory, dominant since first expounded late in the eighteenth century by Samuel Taylor Coleridge, that the reader of such work will participate in a willing suspension of disbelief. The very term "novel" derives from the Italian word for "new," and after initial experiments by eighteenth-century English novelists involving formats such as letters (Samuel Richardson) and direct authorial comment (Laurence Sterne), a mainstream developed in which the role of writers both in Britain and in the United States was to make their novels reflect, in an illusionistic manner, the persons, places, and things of a recognizable time and place.

Although some American writers of the mid-nineteenth century (most notably Nathaniel Hawthorne in his preface to *The House of the Seven Gables*, published in 1851) argued that conditions in the young United States were more favorable to the romance (with its privileging of the imagination over the reason), the American novel developed with the same disposition toward realistic representation that had come to dominate the form. Even such a grandly romantic work as Herman Melville's *Moby-Dick* (1851) rested on a solid grounding of verifiable information about the people and materials involved in the whaling industry. And while succeeding eras would alternately stress and deemphasize such a factual bias—realism and naturalism in the later nineteenth century emulating an almost sociological and scientific accuracy, modernism in the twentieth century replacing it with a new mythological and psychological interest—novelists and readers shared a common expectation for the form. In the 1930s and 1940s, the social realism of John Steinbeck and Richard Wright offered works heavy on implied commentary, and from the 1950s on, stylists of morals (Flannery O'Connor, Saul Bellow) and manners (John Updike, John Cheever) would anchor their fiction in accounts drawn from an easily recognized, commonly inhabited world.

It was into this world, with its comfortably stable tradition for reality-affirming fiction, that the metafictive impulse asserted itself in the 1960s. Its motives run directly counter to the values that had defined the novel to date, placing a much greater emphasis on the act of making such a work of art and implying that representing news about the world was not a very important part of fiction's business at all. Literary theories, such as deconstruction and the death of the novel, contributed to this new style of writing, but its most important stimuli for innovation were the cultural changes evident at this time. The 1960s in America was a time of countercultural revolution, and a heady sense of revolt characterizes the work of emerging metafictionists. Political parties were changing, and so were allegiances to values and traditions that had been unquestioned for generations. The nation was at war (in Vietnam), and a sizable proportion of the population opposed that war. New attitudes toward sexuality and sexual behavior were expressed and took hold. Mainstream culture now seemed less dominant than a new multicultural mix. Men alone no longer served as the index to importance. Challenging old assumptions about fiction seemed just one more step in reformulating beliefs.

THE MOTIVE FOR METAFICTION

It is a high irony in the history of the novel that metafiction's strength may derive, at least in part, from the conventional novel's self-perceived weakness. The moment for this insight came in 1960, during the "death of the novel" controversy in which critics were complaining that the novel, an eighteenth-century form, might no longer be adequate to express the transformed nature of reality. The transformations in mind were scientific and philosophical, involving such ideas as relativity in physics, uncertainty in scientific method, and any number of philosophies that challenged the centrality of human intellect in the world's doings. Yet it was a novelist, Philip Roth, who in looking at the topical nature of his time's realities first expressed despair at representing them. As collected in his *Reading Myself and Others* (1974), Roth's complaints to a 1960 symposium on the novel's future capture the discomfort that realists of his era felt when faced with the nature of life as it had recently evolved.

What was Roth's problem with the just completed 1950s, in which he had struggled to locate his first two novels? "Simply this: that the American writer in the middle of the twentieth century has his hands full in trying to understand, describe, and then make *credible* much of American reality." To Roth, young and imaginatively vibrant as he was, the current scene was eclipsing conventional attempts at representation. "It stupifies, it sickens, it infuriates, and finally it is even a kind of embarrassment to one's meager imagination," he lamented. "The actuality is continually outdoing our talents, and the culture tosses up figures almost daily that are the envy of any novelist" (*Reading Myself*, p. 120). His immediate provocation was the way a local newspaper had reported a murder case, picturing the victims like comic strip characters and stationing a correspondent on the bereaved mother's front porch, generating human interest columns that sustained readership as loyally as had installments of a Charles Dickens novel one hundred years before. Press conferences were held to keep the material freshly spiced, and a popular song turned the event into a minstrel epic. Charitable contributions came in, enabling the mother to buy new kitchen appliances and a pair of matched parakeets, which she named after her murdered daughters.

From local interest to national issues (involving colorful characters and events from the last years of the Eisenhower administration), Roth regaled the symposium with material eclipsing any past, present, or future possibilities in fiction. Did this mean that the novel was indeed dead? If creating characters that test (but never exceed) credibility and spinning narratives that capture a quality of life as customarily lived are the necessary criteria, then its capacities may well have been exceeded by the enormities of current life. Roth's own response was to go ahead and include such apparently preposterous content anyway; from the excesses of President Richard Nixon's presidency in *Our Gang* (1971) to the uninhibited sexuality of *Portnoy's Complaint* (1969), he would emulate the black humor school of fiction (pioneered by such satirists as Terry Southern and Bruce Jay Friedman)

in order to let the shock value of his material distract from any concerns for literary form. Form itself would be left to the metafictionists, soon to appear among the ranks of even newer novelists who would in time expand fiction's boundaries sufficiently for even a mainstream novelist like Roth to introduce experiments with technique.

Literary theorists also began checking in around this time with their own objections. The early 1960s were the years when Americans first took heed of the critical practice known as deconstruction. Popularized in France with social and cultural essays written by Roland Barthes and literary analyses drawn by Jacques Derrida, deconstruction examines the unstated assumptions that stand behind conventional beliefs. The traditional novel would prove especially vulnerable to such a practice that could unmask its presumptions and undercut the viability of their basis. Deconstruction's favorite target is conventional fiction's totalizing effect, its assurance (to readers who have willingly suspended their disbelief) that the world it depicts is sufficiently manageable to be contained in a narrative under the author's absolute control. Such conditions are essential for the illusionistic novel to do its job, but these are the very assumptions most easily deconstructed. For Barthes in particular, classic fiction would prove especially illustrative of the novel's power to deceive; his analysis of Balzac's *Sarrasine* demonstrates just how such a work depends upon unquestioned assumptions. Not that writing novels is evil—just that the habits they encourage allow readers to be misled by similar uninterrogated manipulations in politics and social practice.

Deconstruction does more than disassemble statements in order to uncover hidden principles. It also provides a way of reading all human activities by interpreting them as signs. By looking back to the linguistic theories of Ferdinand de Saussure, theorists could see that just as language is generated by a grammar for the combination of linguistic signifiers, so all human activity could be understood in terms of the exchange of signs. The problem this caused for the traditional novel was that Saussure's method describes not identities but differences—*cat*, for instance, indicates not a certain animal but the way this term differs from other alphabetical constructions, such as *bat, hat, sat, dat*, and so forth through all possible permutations. Although the cat certainly exists, what matters for the system referring to it is how it differs from other linguistic constructions—how it is a different sign. Therefore, if one were to construct a system of representations, be it in language or in artistically conceived social practice, emphasis would need to be on the artifice of differences rather than on the thing in itself. Such a theory is anathema to the illusionistic business of conventional fiction, but is made to order for metafiction. It is no accident, then, that metafiction made its first major appearance in the 1960s, just as deconstruction arrived on American shores.

THE CHALLENGE FOR METAFICTION

"It seems a country-headed thing to say: that literature is language, that stories and the places and people in them are merely made of words as chairs are made of smoothed sticks and sometimes of cloth or metal tubes." So writes William H. Gass in 1970, his *Fiction and the Figures of Life* helping readers understand the challenges being faced in his own work and by any number of innovative novelists emerging in the middle to late 1960s. "Still, we cannot be too simple at the start," he allows, "since the obvious is often the unobserved." Yet to call such notions into question is alarming. "It seems incredible," he grants, "the ease with which we sink through books quite out of sight, pass clamorous pages into soundless dreams." Becoming aware of such practice can make for a rude awakening. "That novels should be made of words, and merely words, is shocking, really. It's as though you had discovered that your wife were made of rubber; the bliss of all those years, the fears . . . from sponge" (p. 27).

Metafiction—fiction that not only acknowledges the materials of its own composition but also makes that act of composition its own subject—broke onto the literary scene like so many other events of the American 1960s: brashly, even shockingly, but with an exuberance that conveyed a sense of joy rather than of malice. Yes, its practitioners would sweep away the conventions of traditional fiction, though for the most part it would happen with a great sense of humor. One of their points was that older novelists had taken the form too seriously, using it for ponderous moral statements or deadeningly meticulous descriptions. Fiction could do this, of course, but there was so much more that could be accomplished if writers would set aside the seriousness for a moment and have the fun that artistic creation provides.

Such playfulness typifies Richard Brautigan's novel *Trout Fishing in America* (1967), a work whose organization seems nothing more than the writer's fancy with language and the things it can do. Its many short chapters are given whimsical titles such as "Sea, Sea Rider," "The Shipping of Trout Fishing in America Shorty to Nelson Algren," and "The Cleveland Wrecking Yard," and most

are self-apparent regarding their ingenuity (the Shorty in question is such a stereotypical character of gritty social realism that Brautigan ends up putting him in a box and sending him to the author of *A Walk on the Wild Side* and *The Neon Wilderness*). The novel's final piece is called "The Mayonnaise Chapter." Why? Simply because the author has always wanted to write a book that ends with the word "mayonnaise." Because *Trout Fishing in America* is a work of metafiction, proudly proclaiming its own artifice, Brautigan is free to do so. Yet even here he makes it a trick, concluding with a banal letter of condolence replete with trite phrasing and meaningless sentiment, followed by the non sequitur of an apologetic P.S. that says "Sorry I forgot to give you the mayonaise" (p. 112; *sic*). The joke is doubled when readers see that thanks to the misspelling, Brautigan has yet to achieve his goal—and that, as Saussure and the later deconstructionists would argue, it's the word, and not the condiment, that's of substance here.

Playfulness on the page is a frequent feature of metafiction, serving as a friendly reminder that this new type of novel is less a representation of reality to be projected in the reader's mind than it is an event happening on the page. In *Willie Masters' Lonesome Wife* (1968) William H. Gass takes almost every step physically possible to emphasize the manufactured nature of his narrative: using different typefaces in different sizes, adding footnotes until they threaten to chase his story off the page, directing the publisher to use different colored paper for the book's successive sections, leaving the stained imprint of his coffee cup on the page, and, as a desperate attention-getter for the solid reality of his words, screening them across a woman's naked body. In the deliberately misspelled title of Steve Katz's novel *The Exagggerations of Peter Prince* (1968; *sic*) can be found another way typography draws attention to language's artificiality. Words do not happen naturally, but are made, Katz suggests; and sometimes they can be made incorrectly. The same goes for fictive narratives: they are made of words, and one narrative has no better claim to authority than another. Hence a second one soon appears in a rival second column, and then a third. Sometimes pages are crossed out but let allowed to stand, still easily legible, as a record of the author's process.

An important feature of the metafictive impulse is its delight in showing readers what can be done with the form. Robert Coover's 1968 novel *The Universal Baseball Association, Inc., J. Henry Waugh, Prop.* is a fine demonstration of metafiction's ability to instruct, starting as it does with a conventional narrative that by easy steps turns into a full-blown example of the new style.

J. Henry Waugh doesn't write a novel, but he does create a universe of representations: a card table baseball game that he plays with cards and dice. Such practice has long been a metaphor for God's operation of worldly existence, and at the beginning Coover has his fun with this notion. But soon Waugh becomes less of an omnipotent creator than a prisoner of the game he has devised. This happens because of his desire not just to throw the dice (of action) and turn the cards (for probabilities of occurrence) for the teams in his imaginary league, but also to keep records of each game and compile many years of league history (easily done, as an entire season can be played in a week or less, given the dice-thrower's time). Even more like a conventional novelist, he invents fully realized characters to go with the names on his roster. Again, this is a familiar enough property of real life, part of the baseball lore Coover absorbed as a child:

> You roll. Player A gets a hit or he doesn't, gets his man out or he doesn't. Sounds simple. But call Player A "Sycamore Flynn" or "Melbourne Trench" and something starts to happen. He shrinks or grows, stretches out or puts on muscle. Sprays singles to all fields or belts them over the wall. Throws mostly fastballs like Swanee Law or curves like Mickey Halifax. Choleric like Rag Rooney or slow and smooth like his old first-base rival Mose Stanford. Not easy to tell just how or why. (p. 47)

Henry Waugh seems in control of this, having both created the names and continuing to throw the dice. But he realizes that if he were to cease playing, a whole world would go out of existence, including his own role as creator of it. Once thrown, the dice dictate the action. In the meantime, Waugh develops his own favorites, including a rookie pitcher so talented (read: so lucky with Waugh's throws) that he's likely to break all records. But then a terrible probability comes up, a one-in-a-million chance that nevertheless rules the existence being played out in this game: the character is struck and killed by a line drive.

Here is the novel's crisis, not just in the fictively portrayed action but also in the narrative's own metafictional being. The pitcher's death will be a tragedy for both the game's participants and its maker, and so the maker intervenes, setting the card aside and choosing another. At this point a transition begins; slowly but steadily, the point of view shifts from Henry Waugh above the table to the action taking place on it—a literal version of the aesthetic behind the equivalent of metafiction in painting, the abstract expressionism of such midcentury artists as Jackson Pollock and Willem de Kooning, for whom the canvas was no longer a surface upon which to represent but an arena within which to act. To explain the pitcher's sudden salvation, the players devise a myth, one that comes to be acted out year after year in ritual fashion, as they struggle to participate in the sense of their own creation. From time to time they glance at the sky, especially at its shining source of illumination, a globe bearing a manufacturer's name and its wattage rating. And their life, inevitably, goes on, just as does the life of their creator, J. Henry Waugh, proprietor of the Universal Baseball Association, Inc.

Coover, born in 1932, is just a year older than Philip Roth, and is a graduate of the same University of Chicago master's program in English. However, service in the U.S. Navy delayed his schooling just long enough for him to graduate into a new generation of fiction writers, ones for whom Roth's fear about an increasingly preposterous style in American life was a provocation rather than an intimidation. Coover's teaching career had a significant start, at the University of Iowa Writers Workshop as a colleague of both Kurt Vonnegut, at the time writing early drafts of *Slaughterhouse-Five* (to be published in 1969), and Robert Scholes, whose critical study *The Fabulators* (1967) was the first to proclaim a new age of metafiction for the American novel. From these beginnings Coover continued as a quasi-metafictionist, using the style's principles and techniques as thematic material in his own narratives that draw equal strength from the materials of popular culture. As baseball helps locate Coover's metafictive doings within a commonly shared lore, so does politics (as another spectator sport) provide a familiar scene within which to enact a basically metafictive story. The author uses it several times, for both very long and relatively short (novella-length) works, creating what critic Linda Hutcheon has called *historiographic metafiction*, in which the historical record itself is shown to be quite an artificial construction.

The Public Burning (1977) is Coover's major work in this vein. It approaches the semiology that had paved the way for this new novelistic theory from another direction, using the textual nature of signs in a culture as elements in its essentially fictive nature. As if to answer Philip Roth's complaint about the absurdity of the American 1950s, Coover locates his narrative squarely within the sociopolitical doings of those years, including minor (yet colorful) scandals of the Eisenhower administration and the figments of popular imagination stirred by Cold War hysteria. Historically, the execution of atomic spies Julius and Ethel Rosenberg motivates the narrative, but more deeply characterizing it are the signs and symbols of Americana, from Uncle Sam (carrying on like a Yankee peddler in marketing his country's myths) to Richard Nixon, behaving in cartoonish form as an enfiguration of liberal anathemas. Anticommunist rages by such people as Senator Joseph McCarthy and FBI director J. Edgar Hoover are indeed challenges to the novelist's powers of creativity; Coover agrees with Roth that it would be hard for a fiction writer to imagine them, and even harder to be believed when presenting them as characters. But instead of using such materials for ludicrous satire, as Roth does in *Our Gang*, the author of *The Public Burning* addresses the issue of how they had been created. Americans themselves are the perpetrators of such spectacle, given their need to dramatize their concerns with melodramatic effects. In this novel Richard Nixon is less of a politician with his own agenda than a creation of the popular culture, expressing its fears and its hopes in a way so artificial as to broadcast his nature as a creature of image.

The Public Burning was a best-seller, as was E. L. Doctorow's novel *Ragtime* (1975), another work that uses history as just one more fictive construct among the many available to the writer. Richard Brautigan's *Trout Fishing in America* gained currency among the era's counterculture and became a staple of academic criticism as well, together with the fiction and commentary of William H. Gass that provided scholars with the philosophical background so helpful in justifying metafiction's role. Popular as this body of work is, it simply dallies with certain techniques of the new style, offering quotations of metafictive principles rather than wholeheartedly employing them as the artistic essence of its being. All are examples of metafiction emerging as a general trend in fiction during this cultural era of the late 1960s and early 1970s. More purely metafictive novels would remain within the province of the avant-garde, never attracting wide popular readership and limited in appeal to only a segment of critics, largely academic in nature, and even then having to fight off neoconservative arguments from scholars alarmed at the new form's presumed implications for morals and social manners. In time, a battle of the books would develop; and, after that, a purported resolution of the problem in the forms of satire and parody.

INNOVATION AS A CREDO
OF IMPROVEMENT

Because they have written important works of critical commentary that articulate the cause they expose in the reformation of fictive theory, Ronald Sukenick and Raymond Federman enjoy an influence as novelists disproportionate to the extent of their mass audience. While Thomas Pynchon may well be the greatest selling yet popularly unread author of his generation, Sukenick and Federman have exerted an innovative pressure on literary history well in excess of their books' marketing successes. As high-profile academics in an age when serious fiction was increasingly nurtured by the universities, the pair found themselves at the center of discussions and debates regarding the form's future. Not surprisingly, their work—both novels and supporting commentary—became the first choice for conservative critics eager to refute metafiction's disruption of tradition.

Each writer made his debut with a work of serious scholarship. Not surprisingly, because each had begun his career as an academic, these books are revised versions of their doctoral dissertations: for Federman, with his Ph.D. in French from the University of California, Los Angeles, a study titled *Journey to Chaos: Samuel Backett's Early Fiction*, published by the University of California Press in 1965; and Sukenick, who'd written a thesis on the great modernist poet for J. V. Cunningham and Irving Howe at Brandeis University, a scholarly book called *Wallace Stevens: Musing the Obscure*, issued in hardcover and paperback by the New York University Press in 1967. Beckett and Stevens are helpful in understanding metafiction's advance, thanks to problems they saw modernist writers facing, yet not completely solving. For Beckett, the challenge would forever be to produce a work that was not about something, but which was that something itself. Given that fiction was made of words, and that words by nature refer to things beyond themselves, the task would seem impossible. With Stevens, the issues are more philosophical, yet relate just as centrally to the writer's relationship with his work and with the world. Writing doctoral dissertations on these authors and then putting the problems they faced to the test in thoroughly new novels allowed both Sukenick and Federman to establish metafiction on a solid basis.

Sukenick's debut as a writer happened almost simultaneously on three fronts. His book on Wallace Stevens appeared only shortly before his first novel, *Up* (1968), and by the turn of the decade he was making frequent appearances on discussion panels and in the commentary sections of literary quarterlies. Many of these critical pieces are collected as *In Form: Digressions on the Act of Fiction* (1985), with the emphasis on "act," not "art," because whether in his fiction or in proposing a new theory for this form, Sukenick shifts emphasis from the literary nature of the product to the activity of its making, stressing the process of how a work is made and then functions in communication with the reader. Fiction is not about experience, he argues, but is more experience, on both ends of the artistic exchange. Rather than fiction presenting the news, it should present a response to the news. Lest this be considered idle impressionism, Sukenick called in Wallace Stevens to show how neither impressionism nor its more dignified cousin idealism is involved.

"Adequate adjustment to the present can only be achieved through ever fresh perception of it," Sukenick suggests, describing a credo for all genres of writing (and in fact for art in general). Looking at Stevens's project, he finds that "A fiction is not an ideological formulation of belief but a statement of a favorable rapport with reality" (p. 3), the challenge he describes at the start of *Wallace Stevens: Musing the Obscure*. The imagination is, for Stevens and Sukenick alike, one's most personal power for organizing the vast array of external reality into something freshly appealing. This is the quality of mind that does not project a reality and certainly does not impose ideas upon it, but instead works by "discovering significant relations within it" (p. 12). Here is the proper way for the world to take its part in the novel: not as a subject transcribed but as a circumstance made pertinent to the writer's concerns. The process is a rewarding one, for "When, through the imagination, the ego manages to reconcile reality with its own needs, the formerly insipid landscape is infused with the ego's emotion; and reality, since it now seems intensely relevant to the ego, suddenly seems more real" (pp. 14–15).

In *Up* a writer named Ronald Sukenick is writing two books: the one at hand and another for an academic requirement, presumably the Stevens book, though it is never cited. Why he is writing the novel at all can be explained by Stevens's own credo, because what passes for the reality of his life is indeed insipid. Part of metafiction's appeal to an academic audience is the way in which its concerns emerge from specific conditions of academic life, especially for those just entering the field. These include difficulties of employment, low pay, hard and often uninspiring work, substandard living conditions, and a pressure to publish or perish, certainly the only way writing in American society can be given such a possibly fatal edge. At the same time, these same conditions of life expose the author to the most exuberant forms of the counterculture taking hold in the 1960s. There are reenforcements between art and life, then, that allow the two to blend into one. Such is the method of *Up*, where not

just the author but even the reader may wonder whether an experience is being drawn from life or invented on the page. Occasionally the writer-protagonist will meet with characters from his novel. Are these people originals for his creations, or are they facets of characterization projected into reality? Because Sukenick's method is metafictive, the distinction doesn't matter, for the ultimate reality is the book itself. It doesn't matter if the characters are drawn from life or birthed into it; the point is that their activities are taking place on pages the writer is producing for the audience to read. The challenge is to live a life that allows the work to be produced, and the only measure of success is whether or not the novel is completed.

If there is a world described in Ronald Sukenick's *Up*, it is a life as it is being experienced by so many of its readers at the time: recent graduates from doctoral programs with theses on the great works of modernism and hopes to produce postmodern work of their own. In creating his novel, Sukenick lets his metafictive writer create within a full knowledge of the literary tradition. The book opens with a sense of prison narrative worthy of Solzhenitsyn, though within a page it becomes clear that the privations being suffered are not those imposed by a ruthlessly collective state but rather by a heat-stingy landlord. Other amorphous threats have their Kafkaesque nature, but are symptoms of teaching composition on a terminal contract. On the other hand, there are sexual delights (or at least fantasies of them) that run the gamut from D. H. Lawrence to Henry Miller. This literature is certainly real for the writer in *Up*, just as it is for the writer of *Up*, for each has been devoting his professional life to it through years of university training. Yet no example is allowed to exert its influence without being interrogated—a natural and expectable act, given the circumstances, and one in which the reader (by virtue of his or her knowledge of the canon) is invited to participate. The entire affair makes metafiction seem not an abstruse theory but rather the most likely way the person who is Ronald Sukenick and the people who are his readership can engage in the experience known as writing and reading a novel.

As Sukenick explains in *In Form*, "An essentialized narrative is still at the heart of fiction—it embodies the progression of the mind as it confronts and affects experience" (p. 14). This act is not a form of autobiography, nor is it a form of self-expression. Instead, such works as *Up* and Steve Katz's *The Exagggerations of Peter Prince* are examples of ways that those forms are, among others, "ways of incorporating our experience into fiction on the same level as any other data" (p. 24). Ultimately, the impulse to write fiction is the same as to take control of one's life. Creation of a future and not just recording of a past is what Sukenick sees as the higher calling of metafiction.

Raymond Federman's mentorship by Samuel Beckett creates an even stronger link with the problems of modernism awaiting solution in postmodern forms. As a postwar teenage immigrant to the United States and as a young man striving to write in an adopted language, Federman appealed to Beckett's own style of making a career in literature; and as the author of *Journey to Chaos* worked at becoming the author of a metafictive novel, *Double or Nothing* (1971), Beckett offered encouragement to the point of becoming a friend. In the older

Raymond Federman.
(*Photograph by Dama Ranga*)

writer's fiction, Federman finds an emphatic rejection of what the traditional novel tries to achieve. "Most works of fiction achieve coherence through a logical accumulation of facts about specific situations and more or less credible characters," he observes at the start of his study. "In the process of recording, or gradually revealing mental and physical experiences organized into aesthetic and ethical form, these works progress toward a definite goal: the discovery of knowledge" (*Journey to Chaos*, p. 4).

In Beckett's work, Federman finds, nothing of the sort happens. Here fiction cannot represent reality. Instead, novels such as *Watt* and *Molloy* exist as illusions that cannot reach the world, tempered only by moments in which the world itself seems too illusory to be captured in the hard materiality of fiction. At best, the author's characters, "like incurable poker players, are committed to their *mise en jeu*, and, win or lose, they cannot withdraw from the game until all the cards are played, all the while knowing that the deck of fictional cards can be dealt and redealt endlessly" (*Journey to Chaos*, p. 202). Federman's innovation is to address these conditions as a metafictionist, taking what are for the modernist writers problems in the human dilemma of existence and turning them into opportunities for creation. And not just for artistic play, because in his own case Raymond Federman faces a history that not even Samuel Beckett could have

devised. By hiding in a closet during the deportation of Jews from his native Paris, Federman as a youngster escaped the Holocaust. His father, mother, and two sisters did not, and their absence generates almost every narrative he has written since. His masterpiece, the novel *Double or Nothing*, has all the play of metafiction, as a young immigrant to America locks himself into a room with enough provisions to last a year, the time he has calculated it will take him to write his book. The calculations, of course, soon become their own subject, just as the typescript, reproduced photographically from the manually typed pages, reflects its own materiality. In that typescript are four X's, such as any typist might have used to indicate deletions, whose recurrent theme is the center of this novel: the loss of the writer's family members, the enormity of which defies articulation but whose absence remains the essence of his text, the meaninglessness that the other letters of the alphabet surround.

THE USES OF METAFICTION

Born as it was during the cultural turbulence of the 1960s, American metafiction proved useful to writers who wanted to vent their animosity against tradition and settle old scores. Yet after the dust of these confrontations settled, the metafictive impulse continued as talent for enriching even conventional narratives with an appreciation of language's creative power. In each case, readers are left with a better understanding of fiction's effect.

Gilbert Sorrentino's experience with metafiction characterizes how writers of other persuasions have been able to use this theory of the novel as a technique in works directed to other purposes. Primarily a poet following in the steps of William Carlos Williams and associated with the Black Mountain Group so heavily influenced by Charles Olson, Sorrentino began his novelist's career with *The Sky Changes* (1966), a conventionally modernist work that projects its narrator's psychological depression onto a bleak southwestern landscape that is experienced by means of a tedious auto journey. By the early

1970s, envying the success of younger metafictionists and disgusted with the commercial inhibitions of New York publishing (in which he had worked as an editor for Grove Press, publishing American editions of the Beckett novels that had inspired Raymond Federman), Sorrentino was adopting the fragmentation of this new style in his novel *Steelwork* (1970) and relishing his self-apparent presence as author in its companion, *Imaginative Qualities of Actual Things* (1971). This latter novel reads much like Sorrentino's vitriolic critical essays of the period (collected in 1984 as *Something Said*), where illusionistic fiction (especially as written by John O'Hara and lived in parodic fashion by some of Sorrentino's own hapless characters) is mocked for the way it lets fiction writers dodge their proper work (bringing their creative abilities to bear on the imaginative qualities of their material) while pandering to readers' comfortable familiarity with what they already know.

A user of metafiction can also become an abuser of it, which is how Sorrentino concluded his flirtation with the technique in *Mulligan Stew* (1979). Here he takes a deliberate look back at Irish writer Flann O'Brien's novel *At Swim-Two-Birds* (1939), a journalist's satire of self-reflective tendencies in modernist literature, and uses its slapstick narrative structure to make fun of the metafictional devices he had borrowed for his own work of the 1970s. As in the Irish classic, an author creates characters for unsavory purposes, abusing their own superior morals. In time they revolt, making the writer a prisoner in his own narrative. As in *Imaginative Qualities of Actual Things*, cultural pretensions of the art world are mercilessly satirized. The difference is that instead of driving the novel, metafictive practices are described secondhand and are made objects of ridicule.

Other writers less closely associated with the metafictive movement drew on its artistic philosophy more positively. In his 1969 novel *Slaughterhouse-Five*, Kurt Vonnegut solves his own problem in articulating the speechless horror of an undefended city's firebombing by making his struggle with form part of the novel's plot. Clarence Major, writing *Reflex and Bone Structure* in 1975, found a way to make the format of a detective novel come alive by making its focus of investigation the nature of language itself, especially the way language involves a person's deepest emotions, as in this passage where the narrator grieves for his dead wife and finds solace in the words for the experience:

> I am standing behind Cora. She is wearing a thin black nightgown. The backs of her legs are lovely. I love her.

The word standing allows me to watch like this. The word nightgown is what she is wearing. The nightgown itself is in her drawer with her panties. The word Cora is wearing the word nightgown. I watch the sentence: The backs of her legs are lovely. (p. 74)

In a similar manner, Grace Paley drew on a metafictive orientation to resolve issues in her story "The Long Distance Runner" from her 1974 collection *Enormous Changes at the Last Minute*. The narrative situation is somewhat unconventional, involving a mother's decision to take off on a long-distance run that keeps her away from her household for three full weeks. At first aimless, her run brings her across two New York boroughs to the neighborhood where she had lived as a child, now a nearly hopeless slum. Here she's sheltered by a woman living in what used to be the runner's family apartment; after three weeks of sharing experiences, the women part friends, the runner having solved what psychologists would call a midlife crisis of identity. But how to explain this? So that readers will understand her purpose, the narrator devises a metafictional encounter at the story's end, where she arrives home to find herself unmissed and her adventure of no real interest to her lover and teenage sons. She reports that she tells them the story—twice!—without any of them grasping its point. And so she becomes a metafictive author, for the reader's benefit retelling a twenty-page story in one short paragraph that concludes her tale:

> Because it usually isn't so simple. Have you known it to happen much nowadays? A woman inside the steamy energy of middle age runs and runs. She finds houses and streets where her childhood happened. She lives in them. She learns as though she was still a child what in the world is coming next. (p. 198)

In the years since it burst on the scene in the 1960s, American metafiction has become much like other innovations from that decade of radical change. No longer a surprise, its techniques have become less of a confrontational challenge to tradition than a helpful supplement to it. This is possible because in the course of literary history, metafiction has been accepted less as a destructive tendency that must overthrow mainstream fiction (or cease to exist itself) and more as a corrective to what had become a monological tendency among novelists to write fiction in only one way. By the turn of the twenty-first century, metafiction had become less of a strident policy than a reminder that novelists have a vast array of techniques at their disposal, and that readers can be trusted to appreciate approaches involving modes other than simple realism.

[*See also* Doctorow, E. L.; Paley, Grace; Roth, Philip; Stevens, Wallace; *and* Vonnegut, Kurt and his *Slaughterhouse-Five*.]

FURTHER READING

Brautigan, Richard. *Trout Fishing in America*. San Francisco, 1967.

Coover, Robert. *The Universal Baseball Association, Inc., J. Henry Waugh, Prop*. New York, 1968.

Coover, Robert. *The Public Burning*. New York, 1977.

Federman, Raymond. *Journey to Chaos: Samuel Beckett's Early Fiction*. Berkeley, Calif., 1965. Early evidence of Federman's fictive principles.

Federman, Raymond. *Double or Nothing*. Chicago, 1971.

Gass, William H. *Willie Masters' Lonesome Wife*. Evanston, Ill., 1968.

Gass, William H. *Fiction and the Figures of Life*. New York, 1970. Critical commentary on the aesthetics of metafiction.

Hutcheon, Linda. *A Poetics of Postmodernism*. London, 1988. Explains historiographic metafiction.

Katz, Steve. *The Exagggerations of Peter Prince*. New York, 1968.

Klinkowitz, Jerome. *Literary Disruptions: The Making of a Post-contemporary American Fiction*. Urbana, Ill., 1975. A literary history of metafiction's introduction into contemporary American fiction.

Klinkowitz, Jerome. *Structuring the Void: The Struggle for Subject in Contemporary American Fiction*. Durham, N.C., 1992. What fiction writers write about when subject matter is denied them.

Major, Clarence. *Reflex and Bone Structure*. New York, 1975.

Paley, Grace. *Enormous Changes at the Last Minute*. New York, 1974.

Roth, Philip. *Reading Myself and Others*. New York, 1974.

Scholes, Robert. *The Fabulators*. New York, 1967. Early look at key metafictive innovators in terms of their attention to the storytelling art.

Sorrentino, Gilbert. *The Sky Changes*. New York, 1966.

Sorrentino, Gilbert. *Steelwork*. New York, 1970.

Sorrentino, Gilbert. *Imaginative Qualities of Actual Things*. New York, 1971.

Sorrentino, Gilbert. *Mulligan Stew*. New York, 1979.

Sorrentino, Gilbert. *Something Said*. San Francisco, 1984. Critical essays on the need for metafiction.

Sukenick, Ronald. *Wallace Stevens: Musing the Obscure*. New York, 1967. Roots for Sukenick's interest in metafictive theory.

Sukenick, Ronald. *Up*. New York, 1968.

Sukenick, Ronald. *In Form: Digressions on the Act of Fiction*. Carbondale, Ill., 1985. Critical essays on the theory of metafiction.

Thiher, Allen. *Words in Reflection: Modern Language Theory and Postmodern Fiction*. Chicago, 1984.

EDNA ST. VINCENT MILLAY

by Gerry Cambridge

Edna St. Vincent Millay was one of the most famous American poets of her day, not least for her colorful love life, but her fame may well have made an objective evaluation of her art problematic. It is not much different today: even the titles of her most recent biographies, *Savage Beauty* (2001) and *What Lips My Lips Have Kissed* (2001), have a sensationalist aspect, and the nude photographs of her held by the Library of Congress and sealed until 2010 are unlikely to decrease the sensationalism. Millay made, and still makes, good copy. When the distinguished British poetry publisher Carcanet published her *Selected Poems* to mark the centenary of her birth in 1992, it could not resist prefacing the volume with an undated foreword by the American poet Richard Eberhart, which states that he had "worshipped" the poet because she possessed "immortality." "She was," he wrote, "too beautiful to live among mortals." Millay heard a lot of such mild compliments, and some critics have reacted against the like by dismissing the art as well as the artist.

Edna St. Vincent Millay.
(© *The Edna St. Vincent Millay Society.*
From the Library of Congress)

THE "RENASCENCE" CONTROVERSY

Even Millay's rise to prominence was controversial. As a penurious twenty-year-old, she entered, at her mother's encouragement, her poem "Renascence" in a competition for an anthology called *The Lyric Year*. It failed to win any of the first three monetary prizes. Yet, when the anthology was finally published, a sensation resulted. The literary consensus was that "Renascence" was the most outstanding contribution to the book. Millay received letters of congratulation and condolence from eminent contributors such as Witter Bynner and Arthur Davison Ficke, who wrote on Thanksgiving Day 1912 with thanks for the poem. Prominent reviewers such as Louis

Untermeyer, the poet and anthologist, singled out the poem for particular praise. The winner of the first prize, Orrick Johns, conceding that "Renascence" should have won, boycotted the award ceremony in embarrassment. No other poet can have so established herself with a poem that *didn't* win a prize.

Read today, the 214-line "Renascence" seems a literary curiosity. Its four-beat rhyming couplets are full of inversions and awkwardnesses, though it must have seemed an astonishing feat for a twenty-year-old woman in 1912. It charts a mystic rebirth that begins with a sort of Hitchcockian terror. The horizons crowd in on the narrator, space is compressed, and she undergoes a visionary experience after which she modestly claims knowledge of "the How and Why of all things, past, / And present, and forevermore." The experience leaves her with unbearable compassion for the suffering. She sinks six feet below the ground, rests there, undergoes a sort of cathartic death, wishes again for life above, and finally is gloriously resurrected. The poem is most interesting for its attempted fidelity to an experience difficult to convey. For all its faults, without it, Millay's life might have gone very differently.

EARLY LIFE AND EDUCATION

That life, at least in its early stages, reads like a stereotypical fairy tale. The story has poverty, beauty, brilliance, good fortune, and fame. Edna St. Vincent Millay was born at Rockland, Maine, on 22 February 1892, the eldest of three sisters. Her mother, Cora, was a nurse with an astonishing capacity for hard work. Expecting a boy, she had named her first child after St. Vincent's Hospital in New York, where, not long before, her brother's life had been saved. (Edna liked to be called "Vincent" at school, much to the annoyance of the school principal.) Cora divorced her feckless husband, Henry Tolman Millay, in 1900, and the family moved to Camden, Maine. Millay's early life was one of cooking, cleaning, and making do, although, like her sisters, she was also encouraged in the arts, and to be independent of spirit. She was precocious and gifted from an early age. As the eldest, however, she often had to take over the family duties while her formidable mother was away on a nursing case.

"Renascence" changed all that. When she read the poem—she was a superb reader of her own work—at the Whitehall Inn in Camden (she already had a reputation as a local poet of promise) in August 1912, a well-connected patron, Caroline Dow, stepped in. She offered to secure funds to give Millay an education. By 1913, after a term at Barnard College in New York, she went to Vassar. She proved a brilliant if at times dilatory student, studying every language offered, including Latin and Greek. She frequently flouted the college's rules, though without real fear of expulsion: she was more famous than the president, Henry MacCracken, who told her he did not want a "banished Shelley" on his doorstep. She conducted lesbian affairs in the all-woman climate of Vassar and generally stirred the place up as well as garnering the disapproval of her patroness. Miss Dow required a clean-living soul, taking the moral high ground. Instead she got Edna St. Vincent Millay, five feet, one inch tall, with heavy red hair down to her waist, green eyes, a milky complexion, and, having escaped the drudgery of Camden, a libido at least the match of any man's.

Despite her extracurricular shenanigans, Millay graduated with an A.B. in 1917 and was finally permitted to attend the commencement ceremony—she had been banned for unsuitable behavior—when the students got up a petition. That same year, she moved to New York, living a bohemian lifestyle and indulging in one of her passions, acting. She scraped a living by writing short stories under the pseudonym Nancy Boyd; she wrote poems; and, not least, she seduced men. Although named after a hospital, for some of her admittedly eager victims she proved no healing force. (One man's wife, in despair at the prospect of losing her husband, blinded herself by drinking bootleg liquor.) Though some have tried to make a case for her as a poet of wider themes, love—its thrills, agonies, and despairs—was, largely, her subject. And rhyming forms, especially the sonnet—"I will put chaos into fourteen lines," she proudly proclaimed in a late example—were, largely, her method.

THE FIRST BOOK

Millay's first book, *Renascence and Other Poems* (1917), published when she was twenty-five, showed a poet who, stylistically at least, apart from some relatively staid experiments in free verse, would hardly change thereafter. In content the poems are a subdued lot, with titles like "Sorrow" and "Kin to Sorrow." They have a wistful gentleness, and are most interesting for their emotional veracity. Apart from the now dated if significant "Renascence," the volume is most remarkable for a sequence of six love sonnets, several of which seem as fresh and readable today as when they were written.

The sonnet's fourteen lines and strict rhyme scheme, and its two main variations, the Petrarchan and the Shakespearean, in addition to its convention as an instrument for love poetry, stopped Millay from rambling and provided a ready-made vessel for the emotion—and its varieties—she was most interested in. All her published collections contain numerous examples of the form. The six sonnets in *Renascence* appear to have been addressed to Arthur Hooley, a New York editor and unattainable figure who was Millay's first real obsession. The first of the sonnets declares her intent to become "inured" to her beloved's beauty, and to beauty generally, little by little. Her sensitivity manifested itself early.

All six sonnets are interesting. One of the two outstanding pieces, "If I Should Learn, in Some Quite Casual Way"—titled by its first line, since Millay seldom titled any of her poems—imagines how she would respond if she discovered, in public, that her beloved had been killed. She wouldn't be hysterical, she concludes; her emotions, the narrator tells us, would be barely visible. She would only look up "and read with greater care / Where to store furs and how to treat the hair." It is an impressively subtle performance for a twenty-five-year-old, indicating her awareness that a failure to show emotion does not indicate its absence. She conjures perfectly the disconnected sense of someone receiving bad news. (Curiously, it was a semblance of cool restraint that, at times, she later found difficult to attain.) Technically, the sonnet unwinds in a single sentence through its fourteen lines, beginning with the conditional "If," which the final six lines resolve. The other outstanding sonnet, "Bluebeard," rewrites the myth of the husband who, planning to be absent from home, leaves the keys with his new wife, instructing her that she must never enter a particular room. She does, of course, and finds it full of the heads of her predecessors. In Millay's sonnet, the secret of Bluebeard's room is nothing: an empty, dusty room, it's symbolic only of his privacy. Encroached upon, he simply leaves, coldly disdainful of her breach of trust. She is left with the room's sterile emptiness. The sonnet may well have been inspired by her experiences with Arthur Hooley.

The next six years were full of astonishing productivity and moment for Millay. By 1923, she had not only published three more collections of poetry but had written a one-act play, *Aria da Capo*, about war, which is still in production today. Though she also wrote other verse dramas, this remains the best. In 1923, she had also become the first woman to win a Pulitzer Prize. Along the way, she solidly established her reputation as what one biographer, Daniel Mark Epstein, calls "the sex goddess of Greenwich Village."

POET AND "SEX GODDESS"

Sometimes a poet's "myth" is somewhat fabricated. The English poet Philip Larkin, for instance, wrote poems portraying himself as a sex-starved librarian, but after his death, his biographer revealed that he sometimes had concurrent affairs. With Millay, however, the myth was accurate. It was a significant part of her early external success. The famous opening quatrain and couplet—"First Fig" and "Second Fig"—of her second book, *A Few Figs from Thistles* (1920), which established her popular reputation, were, as it were, from the life. She was burning her candle at both ends. With dozens of willing supplicants to her charms—her ability to make both men and women fall in love with her was legendary—she was, subverting the biblical reference from Matthew about the fool who built his house upon the sand, building her "shining palace" there instead. She was one of those rare women who possess a curious ability to turn many men into doting puppies, and she made the most of it. She would be ruthless as a man, the poems in her second book suggested. On 31 May 1920, she informed the hapless John Peale Bishop, a poet and editor of *Harper's* who was infatuated with her, that she had just been in the arms of another man and was on her way to a third lover after she'd finished with Bishop. Edmund Wilson, later the eminent man of American letters, lost his virginity to her. (He would write that the experience of her, both intellectually and physically, was one of "the high points" of his life.) Her reputation was such that when she left for France in early 1921, partly to escape the complications of her private life, neither Bishop nor Wilson turned up to say goodbye. They were frightened of "the unknown others," as Wilson delicately put it, whom they might meet on the pier.

Sex sells, and, while it seems decidedly tame by contemporary standards, *A Few Figs from Thistles* was full of risqué implications. It showed Millay the libertine, cocking a snoot at societal conventions. It took conventions common enough in poetry by men—the brevity of being in love, for instance—and made them her own. In a literary sense, the book's subject matter was hardly unusual, but its provenance was. John Wilmot, second earl of Rochester and seventeenth-century English metaphysical poet, for instance, had specialized in such offhand dismissals as Millay adopts in "Thursday," when she chides a lover whom she loved the day before when he remonstrates with her for her inconstancy. "To the Not Impossible Him," with a lovely pun on "him," deftly conveys tones of religious import about her—as yet unfound—perfect lover. She pledges fidelity to a current love—but only until she travels. (Her poem's title is a reference to a line in the poem "Wishes. To His (Supposed) Mistresse" by the seventeenth-century English metaphysical poet Richard Crashaw. His forty-two-stanza piece details exhaustively the virtues of the perfect woman, "that not impossible shee," he has yet to meet.) In Millay's sonnet "Oh Think Not I Am Faithful to a Vow," she declares that she will be faithful only "to love's self alone," and that were the individual addressed in the poem "not lovely," she'd be off: "After the feet of beauty fly my own." In another sonnet, "I Do But Ask That You Be Always Fair," she warns the lover "not to lapse from beauty ever." That "fair" has nothing to do with "fair-minded." And in a sonnet to her first male lover, Floyd Dell, a New York playwright, to whom she lost her virginity, she informs him witheringly that she will forget him so quickly that he had better "make the most of this, [his] little day." Such abandon, haughtiness, and cynical sexiness from a woman poet in the 1920s were unusual enough to ensure that the book went through numerous printings.

Second April (1921), which appeared the following year, extended Millay's range a little; she returns to some of the country settings of her first book. She hears frogs at dusk in "Assault" and proclaims, "I am waylaid by beauty." She writes bleak little cris de coeur of lost love, such as "Ebb," and confesses her inability to resist taking any train, "No matter where it's going." Nonetheless, the volume contains little of the quality found in the previous two volumes. Some of its dozen sonnets are dated by Millay's use of overblown diction, a tendency that would grow as she aged. (At times she addresses the listener as if she were a queen on a throne.) The volume's sonnets are studded with poetical phrases and words: "Love's sacred grove," "irreligious brows," "fettered," "garlands." Often these hijack a poem, though occasionally in sonnets such as "When I Too Long Have Looked upon Your Face," in which the lover's face is compared to the dazzling sun, or "And you as well must die, beloved dust," written for Arthur Davison Ficke, the poem rises to a genuine dignity in an elevated style.

It would be two years before *The Harp-Weaver and Other Poems* (1923), Millay's next book, appeared. In the interim Millay had been living in France and Italy. She supported herself by writing for American magazines, but was not averse to relying on the generosity of lovers. Though she appears to have left America to escape love complications, she continued in Paris much the same pattern, beginning a relationship with George Slocombe, a married man who would later become an eminent journalist. She also became pregnant, perhaps by an Italian violinist. Her mother, who had joined her, performed an abortion, using local herbs, in Shillingstone, Dorset, England, where they were staying, in the autumn of 1922. Millay was beginning to think seriously about marriage, and even proposed to Witter Bynner, who eventually refused. (Bynner was gay.)

MARRIAGE AND FAME

Millay was not to know it, but when she returned with her mother to America in January 1923, an astonishing year awaited her. On 30 April she received notification from Columbia University that she'd won a Pulitzer Prize, with a check for $1,000. On 18 July she married Eugen Boissevain, a remarkable entrepreneur and general man of action, Dutch in origin, who made money as an importer. He was seriously rich—one of his gifts to her would be an emerald ring, worth over a quarter of a million dollars in today's currency—and a large enough personality to be wholly unfazed by Millay's celebrity. ("It is so obvious to anyone that Vincent is more important than I am," he said to one journalist.) Twelve years her senior, he would provide a buffer and source of strength for her until the end of his life. Caring for her, Boissevain began as he would continue, acting as her amanuensis, trying to make sure she was not "dulled by routine acts." This meant she had little to do but write poems and generally indulge herself, not necessarily the best way to produce lasting art.

When *The Harp-Weaver and Other Poems* was published on 19 November 1923, it was well received both in Britain and in America. One prominent English critic, Arthur Symons, compared her to Keats and Poe.

(The English poet Thomas Hardy would later be of the opinion that—along with skyscrapers—she was one of the two best things about America.) *The Harp-Weaver* was perhaps her most substantial collection to date. The book's title poem, "Ballad of the Harp-Weaver," is a mythical piece in thirty stanzas, loosely based on Millay's mother, Cora, and the family's straitened earlier years. The mother in the poem weaves clothes for "a king's son"—the poem's narrator. Some readers find the piece sentimental. At the end, as tragedy requires, the mother dies, but she leaves a pile of the king's son's clothes, "toppling to the skies." Elsewhere, in her poem "Feast," Millay praises thirst and want; she will "lie down lean," she tells us. Desire is better than satiety. Desire gives one something to aim for. "Departure" contrasts the grievous interior monologue of a suicidal girl with her mother's innocent question about her well-being: the narrator denies there's anything wrong and goes to make the tea. Despair is evoked in domestic surroundings. Millay's sassy, daredevil, sexually triumphal tone is largely absent from the book; instead, in "The Return from Town," perhaps an homage to her new husband, the poem's narrator recounts how she ignored temptation in the form of a boy and then a youth encountered on a journey home. She prefers returning "To such a man as any wife / Would pass a pretty lad for."

Again, the volume seems strongest for its sonnets, four of which are among Millay's most famous: "Pity Me Not Because the Light of Day," "I, Being Born a Woman and Distressed," "What Lips My Lips Have Kissed, and Where, and Why," and "Euclid Alone Has Looked on Beauty Bare." The seventeen-part sequence "Sonnets for an Ungrafted Tree," meanwhile, showed her experimenting intriguingly with new material.

The best of the love sonnets revisit familiar themes without simply recalling, as her weaker sonnets tend to, Shakespeare's famous sequence. In "Pity Me Not Because the Light of Day," after a catalog of things she should not be pitied for, she asks pity only because her heart is not as swift as her mind in grasping the truth about a relationship. Emotionality wins over intellect, a situation she resents in "I, Being Born a Woman and Distressed," where it represents "the poor treason" of her "stout blood" against her "staggering brain," with the ghost of a pun on the qualifier to "brain." "What Lips My Lips Have Kissed" is an elegy for her promiscuous youth. She has had so many lovers she can hardly remember them all, nor what she found attractive in them, though she regrets that young men will never again turn to her "at midnight with a cry." It is notable that the "cry" is theirs; the ability to produce it lies with her. She elegizes, it seems, the loss of that ability rather than the physical pleasure of having lovers. "Euclid Alone Has Looked on Beauty Bare" places beauty in the abstract—Euclid was the formulator of geometry—as superior to "dusty bondage." The poem praises abstract Beauty's "massive sandal set on stone." While in some of her worst examples, there is a disparity between her elevated diction and her subject matter, which leads to hyperbole, this sonnet has a memorable nobility: elevated diction and elevated perception combine convincingly.

By contrast, "Sonnets for an Ungrafted Tree," vaguely reminiscent of the Robert Frost of such poems as "The Hill Wife," is a loose narrative, spoken in the third person, about a woman who has returned to a house to look after her sick husband. The sequence is rich in domestic detail, full of solitude: when the grocer delivers food on the doorstep, the woman hides in the cellar until he goes away. Delineating the main character's emotional narrative, it is strongest for its local atmosphere and documentary detail. Millay studiously seems to avoid, here, the elevated diction that often flaws her love sonnets. At the sequence's close the man dies, and the woman resents the sudden change caused by funeral arrangements, having preferred the stasis of his illness. "Sonnets for an Ungrafted Tree" shows what Millay was capable of when opting for a quieter narrative style.

In the meantime, her life would prove anything but quiet. In 1924 she sailed around the world with her husband. In 1925, they bought "Steepletop," a 750-acre farm near Austerlitz, New York, which would remain their home until their deaths. It was named after the steeplebush flower Millay found growing there, and it provided a secluded base for what would become, in later years, her retirement into comparative isolation. In 1927, she was involved in the Sacco–Vanzetti case, involving two workers suspected of murdering a factory paymaster. The case was unproved, but Sacco and Vanzetti were known anarchists. The case split the country, with most artists taking their side. While Millay's involvement, despite her fame, failed to save them from execution, it increased her public profile. (In 1929, she was elected to the National Institute of Arts and Letters.)

THE FATAL INTERVIEW

In 1928, a key year for Millay, she published her fifth book, *The Buck in the Snow*, and mourned the first of three deaths that had a considerable effect on her—that of Elinor Wylie, a close poet friend. (It would be followed in 1931 and 1935, respectively, by the deaths of her mother and her father.) It was also the year in which she met George Dillon, a handsome and promising young poet who introduced her at a reading at the University of Chicago. The meeting would have ramifications for her work, herself, her tolerant husband, and Dillon himself for the next several years.

By now, of course, Millay was both famous and a publishing asset. Her books reliably sold in many thousands. During the second half of 1928 her royalty income from her publisher, Harper's, was the equivalent, at $15,000, of $200,000 today. That audience was partly built up, of course, of watchers of the Millay soap opera: she had partly made her life into art, always a dangerous procedure. *The Buck in the Snow*, however, reflecting her new surroundings, was a rather rural book. It was better received in an England finding pastoral relief after the horror of World War I, than in America. Notwithstanding, three months after publication it had sold forty thousand copies. Overall, it's a rather subdued performance. She begins to experiment unsuccessfully with a loose, end-rhymed free verse—she could seldom get far from rhyme—in poems like "The Bobolink," "There at Dusk I Found You," and "On First Having Heard the Skylark." "The Anguish" harks back nostalgically to a time of innocence before "the anguish of the world was on [her] tongue." As time went on, she would increasingly speak out on public issues. Perhaps the volume's outstanding poem is "Dirge Without Music," a piece proclaiming her lack of resignation to death. It has a hymnlike simplicity and a wide relevance. Of the seven sonnets included in the book, one of the most striking is a memorial to Inez Milholland, Eugen Boissevain's first wife (she had died in his arms) and a notable suffragette. "Take up the song," it exhorts, "forget the epitaph." Another fine sonnet is "To Jesus on His Birthday," an examination of the quotidian and banal end of great religious thought.

When Millay met George Dillon, therefore, on 2 November 1928, she was perfectly primed for a change. Dillon was twenty-one, tall, and of Greek-god good looks. Millay was thirty-six and famous. In a "fatal interview," the title she would give to the sequence of fifty-two sonnets she would write out of the ensuing relationship, the couple fell in love in Millay's dressing room and later at a modest reception after her reading. Ever accommodating, her husband, sensing this could prove a valuable experience for his wife, temporarily absented himself. So began a lengthy melodrama, in which the poet alternately harangued, commanded, and courted the at times infuriatingly dilatory

Dillon. In January 1929, she began writing the *Fatal Interview* sonnets. By May 1930 she could predict she would have a group of new love sonnets ready for publication in 1931. Whatever else she was, Millay was ever the conscious artist. When *Fatal Interview* was published on 15 April 1931, it received high praise from Edmund Wilson and the poet Robinson Jeffers, then at the height of his own fame.

Read today, *Fatal Interview* captures almost too successfully the absurd, overblown effect of full-out infatuation. The sequence's earlier sonnets are poems of solicitation. In VIII, she writes, with refreshing candor, "You shall be bowed and brought to bed with me...." By the following sonnet, the lover's eyes are compared, hyperbolically, to "two splendid planets"; Dillon, however, is still not in her bed. By sonnet XVI she's comparing him to a god (and, reassuringly for him, the relationship appears by then to have been consummated). Ten sonnets later, in XXVI, she claims that she is the only woman alive who suffers "love like a burning city" in her breast; we have to go back to an era when "heedless and wilful" queens "took their knights to bed," she tells us, to find her equal. When, by sonnet XXXIV, Dillon seems to have expressed doubt about the relationship, she commands him to thrust him—doubt, that is, personified—out, and arm the walls with spikes and shards of broken glass so that he will disembowel himself if he enters again. By sonnets XXXIX and XL the couple have argued, and plainly they have separated in the following six pieces. The remaining sonnets have a resigned distance and elegize the relationship.

As a sequence *Fatal Interview* is considerably flawed by its bombast and elevated terms. Some of it can be explained by the sequence's classical underpinning, which features the myth of Endymion, the beautiful young shepherd whom the goddess Selene falls in love with and makes immortal with her kiss—a myth of some relevance to Millay at this point. Notwithstanding, read now, some of its sonnets have a dated, antique feel, especially when Millay goes in for her characteristic hieratic gesturings and stock old-hat vocabulary—"sire," "physic," "liefer," "winged," "roseate," "sooth," "disesteem," "perfidious": these date the poems even when the perceptions seem fresh and original. The sequence is full of memorable lines, but Millay's penchant for the elevated phrase lessens many of the poems. She can describe without a blush beginning the morning like a sort of irritable queen "in a jeweled crown." All the poems are interesting, but perhaps the best of them is the superb sonnet XXXVI, "Hearing Your Words, and Not a Word among Them": the lover has

spoken words—whose content we must guess at—that the narrator doesn't want to hear. She imagines the island women of Matinicus, who wait for their men to come back from fishing. "The wind of their endurance," she writes, "Will flatten your words against your speaking mouth." It's noticeable that she doesn't say the wind of her own endurance will accomplish this, though the sonnet is usually read as presuming that that's what she means. Perhaps she knows herself all too well and is attempting to invoke the island women's constancy for herself. "Hearing Your Words" is beautifully constructed, unfolding in a single sentence through its fourteen lines. It also, incidentally, shows the resonance place names can have: "Matinicus" resounds wonderfully in the line in which it occurs.

THE LATER YEARS

Fatal Interview was to be the last great attempt at a theme that really captured Millay. She was still hugely popular—between 1934 and 1939 her annual income was the equivalent of over a quarter of a million dollars—but increasing age brought a retreat into reclusiveness, alcoholism, and drug dependency. Following the deaths of her parents, she was plagued by depression exacerbated by her extreme sensitivity. Whereas Eros, in Millay's heyday of the 1920s, had once been her ally, now it was turning against her. The last fifteen years of her life saw Millay publishing three more collections of poetry: the elegiac *Wine from These Grapes* (1934), *Huntsman, What Quarry?* (1939), and the propagandist *Make Bright the Arrows: 1940 Notebook* (1940). The later books were relatively undistinguished, though *Wine from These Grapes* included a sonnet sequence, "Epitaph for the Race of Man," that showed Millay using the sonnet for more than her traditional themes. Though ambitious, it reads at times like versified anthropology. *Huntsman, What Quarry?* includes the touching "To a Young Poet," and *Make Bright the Arrows*, an expression of support for Britain and the allies in World War II, was seen by critics as propaganda. In 1944 a nervous breakdown rendered Millay unable to write for two years. A visit by Edmund Wilson and his wife in 1948 left the critic shocked and surprised by how much she had changed physically since the glory days of the 1920s. She was, by then, frequently in and out of hospital in attempts to control her drug addiction. After Eugen Boissevain died of a stroke after having a cancerous lung removed, on 30 August 1949, she withdrew almost completely. She survived for just over a year, dying in what may well have been a drunken fall at Steepletop on 19 October 1950.

While a posthumously published volume, *Mine the Harvest* (1954), revealed nothing quite the equal of her most memorable poems, it showed an autumnal taking stock, as well as hints of a dry, late excellence she might have attained had she lived. The volume has a retrospective feel, but also shows her still willing to write out of unusual perceptions. "How Did I Bear It—How Could I Possibly as a Child" contrasts her quivering sensitivity as a child with her unwillingness as an adult to be so open and vulnerable to pure being and beauty. Among the better sonnets, "Those Hours When Happy Hours Were My Estate" is a celebration in her diminished present of a past she "lived with all [her] senses." The volume also contains the famous "I Will Put Chaos into Fourteen Lines," about the marriage of energy, personified as male, to the discipline of the sonnet's form.

MILLAY AND POSTERITY

Sometimes it seems the fate of poets popular in their lifetimes is a consignment to oblivion by posterity. Millay was certainly one of the most popular American poets of the twentieth century, yet a quarter of a century after her death she merited not even a single poem or mention in Richard Ellmann's *The New Oxford Book of American Verse* (1976). Certainly she is an uneven writer, and the orotund diction she at times favored has not worn well. While her "Shining palace on the sand" may not have survived, sufficient of its bright ruins have, in the form of many sonnets of considerable interest, as well as a dozen or so poems that seem, of their kind, the equal of anything else in twentieth-century American verse. Millay is more than a popular poet of her time. In their acute mapping of emotions, the best of her poems seem likely to remain "news," which Ezra Pound famously said was the hallmark of genuine literature.

WORKS

POETRY

Renascence and Other Poems (1917)
A Few Figs from Thistles (1920)
Second April (1921)
The Harp-Weaver and Other Poems (1923)
The Buck in the Snow (1928)
Poems Selected for Young People (1929)

Fatal Interview (1931)
Wine from These Grapes (1934)
The Flowers of Evil (1936)
Conversation at Midnight (1937)
Huntsman, What Quarry? (1939)
Make Bright the Arrows: 1940 Notebook (1940)
Mine the Harvest (1954)
Collected Poems (1956)
Edna St. Vincent Millay: Selected Poems: The Centenary Edition (1991)
The Selected Poetry of Edna St. Vincent Millay (2001)

PLAYS

Aria da Capo (1921)
The Lamp and the Bell (1921)
Two Slatterns and a King (1921)
The King's Henchman (1927)
The Princess Marries the Page (1932)
The Murder of Lidice (1942)

FURTHER READING

Brittin, Norman A. *Edna St. Vincent Millay*. New York, 1967; rev. ed., Boston, 1982. Useful for its criticism and biographical material, with an especially good annotated bibliography.

Epstein, Daniel Mark. *What Lips My Lips Have Kissed: The Loves and the Love Poems of Edna St. Vincent Millay*. New York, 2001. Biography with useful readings of the poetry, though Epstein is perhaps too adulatory toward the verse.

Freedman, Diane P., ed. *Millay at 100: A Critical Appraisal*. Carbondale, Ill., 1995. Thirteen essays, eleven of them by women, examining Millay's work from a markedly feminist perspective, broadly sympathetic to the poet.

Gould, Jean. *The Poet and Her Book*. New York, 1969. A stately and circumspect biography, with generous readings of the poetry.

Milford, Nancy. *Savage Beauty*. New York, 2001. The most detailed biography of Millay. Epstein's wins out on economy; this, on sheer weight of detail.

Thesing, William B., ed. *Critical Essays on Edna St. Vincent Millay*. New York, 1993. Articles and reviews covering a span of over seventy years that make up a sort of history of Millay's critical reputation, with an introduction overviewing that reputation.

ARTHUR MILLER

by Philip Parry

In 1990 Arnold Wesker, the British playwright, invited Arthur Miller in a seventy-fifth birthday tribute to "stop writing...and give us a break." Twelve years, four plays, and many essays and interviews later, this advice has plainly been ignored. Oddly, however, Miller's exceptionally productive later years have done little to extend his reputation. To the general public he remains, to his own considerable irritation and despite a great deal of converse evidence, a "naturalistic" or "realist" dramatist of the 1940s and 1950s. Although *All My Sons* (1947), *Death of a Salesman* (1949), *The Crucible* (1953), and *A View from the Bridge* (1956) are likely to remain the bedrock of his achievement, they are in an important respect unrepresentative of his work as a whole, for they leave out entirely Miller's identity as a Jew and the symbolic significance that he assigns to being Jewish. By contrast his only novel, *Focus* (1945), chronicles the rise of anti-Semitic movements in New York City, and most of his plays from *After the Fall* (1964) onward feature Jewish characters prominently. But although several Jewish actors have excelled as *Death of a Salesman*'s Willy Loman, the Kellers of *All My Sons* and the Lomans are not (explicitly at any rate) Jewish families; *The Crucible* is set in a New England Christian community; and the characters in *A View from the Bridge* are Italian Americans.

Arthur Miller. (*Hulton Archive / Getty Images*)

INFLUENCES AND EARLY PLAYS

Miller's origins are firmly embedded within the Jewish culture of New York City. Harlem, where he was born in 1915, was a gentler, more open, more ethnically diverse place than it subsequently became. When their clothing business, which at the height of its success employed eight hundred people, failed in the wake of the stock market collapse in 1929, his parents responded by moving their family to Brooklyn, another ethnically diverse area, where Jews and Italians and a small number of Irish families lived, for the most part, at peace with one another. It was only when Miller left this protected environment to raise money to support himself while in college that he began to encounter the pervasive anti-Semitism of mainstream New York City.

Integrity, both personal and social, is a persistent theme in Miller's plays. Despite the economic prosperity of the post–World War II decades, the most moving image of disintegration remains for him that moment, seventy years ago, when corporate America lost faith in itself. "Rose, the college men are jumping out of windows!" Quentin's father tells Quentin's mother in *After the Fall* (1964), when she cruelly upbraids him for losing all of his money. At exactly the same moment of revelation in *The Price* (1968), Victor tells Walter that their mother vomited over their father's hands: "Just kept on vomiting, like thirty-five years coming up. And he sat there. Stinking like a sewer. And a look came onto his face. I've never seen a man look like that." "Only the Civil War and the Great Depression touched nearly everyone wherever they lived and whatever their social class," Lee Baum, one of the narrators of *The American Clock* (and clearly a Miller self-portrait) tells his audience.

Miller wrote plays while at the University of Michigan and continued to write after graduating. None was included in *Collected Plays* (1957), though two were given retrospective recognition in the late 1980s; both of the plays investigate the risks and costs of passivity. In *The Golden Years* (written in 1940, but not performed until

136

1987), Montezuma, the leader of a fantastically wealthy, proud, and ancient civilization, cannot—because of a national belief in the imminent return to earth of a strong god—defend himself or his people from the brutal charms of an unprincipled invader. Despite this play's distant and exotic setting, the warning that Miller issues to contemporary Europe is clear. *The Man Who Had All the Luck*, which ran for under a week in 1944, is less ornate but covers similar moral territory. Subtitled *A Fable*, it is the story of David Beeves, a young man who prospers at whatever he does, but who feels that he does not truly own what he has not truly earned. Once again, paralleling *The Golden Years*, it is the superstitious vestige of an outmoded religion that weakens him. Anxious to see that life has meaning, David can keep his sanity only by believing that his advantages are either unmerited donations from a generous god or are both earned and deserved. Instead, by means of a mental aberration that builds the inevitability of failure into his vision of success, he convinces himself that his next venture must be a disaster that will reset the system and, once his debt to failure has been paid, allow him to resume his successful life. (Though only one Miller play is titled *The Price*, every Miller play has these words as its hidden subtitle.) Unable to explain or accept the good things that have happened to him, David superstitiously offers up the life and health of his unborn child to destruction. Traumatized by shame and paralyzed by dread, he is the passive victim of his own fears. What he must be taught to accept is that a positive response to circumstances, whether they are good or bad, is what indicates the truly active man. Once again the moral is clearly drawn: America must avoid the brutal, self-punishing urges that have allowed Europe to embrace fascism as its fate.

INTEGRITY AND IDENTITY

Concerns and issues adumbrated in these early plays are never left far behind; integrity's outward and inward assailants are Miller's persistent theme. "I want my name," Eddie calls out at the end of *A View from the Bridge*. "Marco's got my name—and . . . he's gonna give it back to me." Miller's own gloss is excellent: you need to be in control of your own conscience, he says in explaining *The Crucible*, because "with conscience goes the person, the soul immortal, and the *name*." His refusal to name names before the House Un-American Activities Committee in 1956, like Proctor's refusal at the deputy governor's court in Salem, links author and character; naming and not naming divides Mickey from Lou in *After the Fall*.

Personal and domestic principles and behavior cannot exist in isolation from the values and practices of a larger society. In "The Family in Modern Drama," published in the *Atlantic Monthly* in 1956, Miller argues that *Death of a Salesman* would be diminished in importance if Willy and Biff's struggle "were simply between father and son for recognition and forgiveness." Because it is a struggle that "extends itself out of the family circle and into society," it "broaches those questions of social status, social honor and recognition, which expand its vision and lift it out of the merely particular." Particular, but never merely particular, Miller's plays present us with representations of domestic and personal conflicts that are symbols of larger conflicts that in their turn reveal the moral structures of social life: both the HUAC hearings and the Salem trials are symbols of the real subject matter of *The Crucible*. John Proctor's opposition to the evil that engulfs him is corroded by his guilt over his adultery with Abigail. When he says that Hale is a cowardly minister who suspects the witchcraft allegations are spurious but cannot let go of them, Hale replies that there must be "some secret blasphemy that stinks to heaven" that has called down God's judgment upon Salem. Proctor ("reached by Hale's words") is paralyzed into inactivity. Weakened by a remorse that will not allow him to accept Elizabeth's forgiveness, he seeks a tainted compromise with dishonesty by dishonestly complying with the wishes of a corrupt court. He tries to justify doing so by taking the innocent and saintly Rebecca Nurse as a standard that only vanity could make him hope to match:

> I cannot mount the gibbet like a saint. It is a fraud. I am not that man. . . . My honesty is broke, Elizabeth; I am no good man. Nothing's spoiled by giving them this lie that were not rotten long before. . . . I'd have you see some honesty in it. Let them that never lied die now to keep their souls. It is pretense for me, a vanity that will not blind God nor keep my children out of the wind.

Proctor's desire to avoid death is entirely natural, but what ensures that he dies morally alive is his realization that a false confession has consequences, because it condemns as liars those who have truly maintained their innocence. His confrontation with Danforth is neither the story of two people who simply dislike each other nor an all-embracing conflict between good and evil. What the play exposes is the relationship between the values that a society proclaims and the integrity with which individual members of that society incorporate those values into their lives. Once integrity is lost topsy-turviness reigns:

the judge is corrupt, the guilty man is innocent. (When Danforth hears of Abigail's theft and flight, he knows that his court's proceedings are no longer sound, nor its decisions safe, but he chooses to continue his inquiry rather than admit to previous errors and injustices. Bound to uphold both law and justice, he sacrifices the latter to the former.)

"Nominal" integrity—which is certainly not nominal in the ordinary, diluted understanding of the term—pertains to groups and communities as well as to individuals: members of any self-respecting minority (Jews or homosexuals or liberals or vegetarians, or Protestants in a Catholic society, or Catholics in a Protestant society) must be willing to proclaim, without apology or the enforced or voluntary acceptance of demeaning stereotypes, that their integrity and honesty and distinctiveness are constituents of their being, not negotiable and excisable peripheral values. The clearest expression of this insight occurs in chapter 15 of *Focus* (1945), when Mr. Finkelstein, under threat from New York City's rapidly growing Christian Front, prepares to stand his ground:

> I am entirely innocent, he said to himself. I have nothing to hide and nothing to be ashamed of. If there are others who have something to be ashamed of, let them hide and wait for this thing that is happening, let them play the part they have been given and let them wait as though they are actually guilty of wrong. I have nothing to be ashamed of and I will not hide as though there were something stolen in my house.

Finkelstein, along with Gregory Solomon in *The Price*, are unusually Jewish Jews. More often Miller's Jews are (like Miller himself) secular and liberal and assimilated. What part should such Jews play—as Jews—in an overwhelmingly non-Jewish society? Questions about specifically Jewish identity lie deeply embedded in the plot of *The Ride Down Mount Morgan* (1991). Lyman Felt is a bigamist whose legal marriage is to a gentile; his wife is Theo, his daughter Bessie. His bigamous marriage, however, returns him to the fold; his wife is Leah, their nine-year-old son is Benjamin. The point that the contrasted names exist to make is stressed in an otherwise irrelevant scene where Lyman imagines that Theo and Leah are comparing their culinary achievements. "My gefulte fish," Leah says, "is feather-light." Lyman's imaging of Theo's response stresses how far he has departed from Jewish dietary observances: "He does love my glazed ham." The real Lyman, however, is both Theo's Lyman and Leah's Lyman: American Jews must be free to express themselves both within the smaller and the larger community.

"God, I always thought there'd be time to get to the bottom of myself!" the dying Phillip Gellburg cries out in *Broken Glass* (1994). He is yet one more Miller character who needs to establish a right relationship to his own identity by accepting its distinctiveness while at the same time understanding that it is not a unique affliction with a unique call upon the world's sympathy. ("*Everybody's* persecuted," his doctor, a self-accepting Jew, reminds him.) Gellburg's lack of integrity directs all of his actions. He is the only Jew working for a loan and mortgage company (a source of pride, a mark of distinction, and a badge of distinctiveness), but he is also a fall guy who, during years of repossession, acts out for the benefit of his employers a role for which they despise and condemn him. Similarly, he sends his son to West Point where the latter becomes the only Jewish captain, both an assertion of Jewishness and also a way of keeping Jerome away from the society of Jews. Symbolically, too, Gellburg suppresses his Jewishness: his powers of fatherhood are destroyed when he becomes impotent shortly after his son's birth. Many years later, his wife, deeply distressed by reports of Nazi mistreatment of elderly Jews, loses all feeling in her legs and takes permanently to her bed. Perhaps at the level at which this play is a psychological who-didn't-do-it-and-why, this is a symbolic protest at her husband's lack of sexual threat: bed is the one place where they never truly meet. But there is a larger and much clearer symbolism: Phillip and Sylvia are American Jews whose very desire to succeed as Americans leaves them paralyzed and impotent in the face of rising anti-Semitism. Right at the end of the play, just as he dies, Gellburg has his saving vision, and like Mr. Finkelstein, holds his ground: "Why we're different I will never understand but to live so afraid, I don't want that anymore. I tell you, if I live I have to try to change myself." Miller's irony is surely exquisite: Gellburg, a Jewish chameleon, must learn the virtues of visibility.

MOTIVATION

Since Miller is the author of a significant body of dramatic criticism and commentary, one way of constructing an account of his plays would be by asking questions about quite small-scale aspects of characterization and plotting, which one would then answer in Miller's own words. But these words themselves require interpretation. What can Miller have meant when he said, during an acting workshop, that Linda Loman "probably" knew of Willy's affair? To what examinable repository of pertinent information, lodged somewhere to the side of or behind the play, is Miller directing us? The clue is the occasion: "Assume Linda does know and see what you can make of her in the light of that assumption" is the task that Miller was setting his apprentice actresses. Nevertheless, one potent objection to this kind of approach, from within the bastions of orthodox literary criticism, is that it is insufficiently grounded in the play's text and requires an accompanying authorial (and authoritative because authorial) commentary. Miller provides rudimentary commentaries of this kind in all of his texts—very markedly in the stage directions to *The Price*—but his comments in his critical essays and interviews go far beyond what he is prepared to annotate within his texts. An extreme example is his utterly labyrinthine explanation of *Clara* (1987), a one-act piece in which a Jewish detective (one of a number of Freud-like Miller surrogates in the later plays) unpacks a witness's inhibitions and repressions. How can an art as properly superficial as theater probe such hidden depths?

The problem of knowing when, or whether, to halt interpretation of motive and conduct is one with which every Miller play confronts us. The title of *All My Sons* (1947), his first commercial success, contains the play's moral message. Joe Keller supplies defective aircraft parts, kills pilots, and escapes punishment. Eventually, he discovers that Larry (his elder son), who is also a pilot, has deliberately crashed his plane out of shame, in protest against his father's actions, and in order to bring an awareness of their consequences home to roost. "I think to him they were all my sons" is Joe's explanation and acceptance of Larry's point of view. As soon as Kate, Joe's wife, learns of her son's suicide, she—though hitherto she had been the most urgent and selfish believer in his survival—backs away from the implications of all that has happened and insists that he is dead, that the war is over, and that nothing will be gained by embracing guilt and the punishment that guilt merits. But their younger son, whose relationship with his father is the play's most intense aspect, reminds his mother that being sorry—while striving to live as though guilt had no consequences—is never enough. Instantly, we hear an off-stage shot that indicates that Joe has killed himself. Chris, aghast at this event, turns to his mother for absolution, and receives a version of what he seeks. ("Don't dear. Don't take it on yourself. Forget now. Live.")

As a morality play or fable, in which abstract propositions are given just enough flesh to hold the stage, *All My Sons* succeeds admirably and needs neither supplement nor complication. There are, however, important questions that scarcely get an airing until we fret away at its characters and their supposed motivations. Does Joe kill himself to embrace a more appropriate level of punishment than the legal code demands? Or is it shame that kills him? (He dies by his own hand to avoid having to admit his guilt to the wider community.) Does Chris Keller's refusal to let Joe rename the firm stem from an unacknowledged suspicion of his father's guilt? Or is he, like his mother, unwilling to put a line under his brother's death ("J. O. Keller and *Son*" rules out "J. O. Keller and Sons") even while—in his relations with his dead brother's fiancée—this line is precisely what he wishes to draw? At this point another explanation of Joe's suicide becomes possible: He dies to express kinship with his dead son and, at the same time, to yield ground to his living son by a supreme act of withdrawal. "Chris Keller and Sons" is his hope for the future. (A similar yielding of ground to Biff is arguably the "true" explanation of Willy Loman's suicide.) Why does Kate Keller refuse to accept Larry's death? Is this just the natural blindness of unresolved grieving? Or a possessive mother's attempt to bind her surviving son to herself by insisting that the girl whom he wishes to marry must remain bound to his elder brother? Or, sensing that Larry's death is part of a larger pattern, is she refusing to have Joe's guilt brought home to them (for if Larry is still alive his father's guilt is distanced and containable and deniable)? Or perhaps her primary motivation, Miller claimed in *Timebends: A Life* (1987), is "to take vengeance on her culpable husband by driving him psychically to his knees and ultimately to suicide." Are her last words ("Forget now. Live."), which are the play's final words, a plea for a sensible new beginning? Or evidence of her own continued desire for a compromise that blunts morality?

There are no easy answers to any of these questions, for there is no way of stopping the play to count its meanings. Originally, Miller tells us, Kate's conviction that Larry was still alive, backed up by Frank Lubey's astrological charts, made her role dominant. However, "as the play progressed the conflict between Joe and his son Chris pressed astrology to the wall until its mysticism gave way to psychology." But psychological explanation, once admitted, inaugurates a process that is not easily brought to heel. Thirty years after its first performance Miller saw a production of the play in Jerusalem in 1977. There, in a society engulfed in military conflict, the play renewed itself. Especially impressive was the performance of Hanna Marron, an actress whose leg had been blown off by a bomb in 1972: "her disfigurement as the result of war . . . seemed to add authenticity to Kate Keller's spiritual suffering," Miller wrote in *Timebends*. Eventually, as a result of seeing different emphases in different productions, Miller began to wonder whether he had not constructed a different play from the one he had originally intended.

The impossibility of halting interpretation—the need to clarify even clarification itself—is demonstrated by the interpretative history of *A View from the Bridge*. This play was written in order to clear up confusion in the theatergoing public's understanding of *The Crucible*; Alfieri's commentary was to relate the action of the play to its "generalized significance." Yet in this simple story of a man, his niece, and her lover, we never entirely learn (no more than does he) what fuels Eddie Carbone's intense dislike of Rodolpho. When, however, a reviewer of a 1997 London revival identified Catherine as Eddie's daughter, his mistake was not unique. Miller himself had for years, he admitted in an interview published in 1990, "unthinkingly thought" (a strange locution) "of Catherine as Eddie's daughter." What emerged into consciousness, long after the play was written, Miller wrote in *Timebends*, was "my father's adoration of my sister, and through this emotion, my own." Unsurprisingly, granted the unresolved matter out of which it grows, the play's ending settles for much less than half. "I confess," the play's lawyer and choric commentator says, "that something perversely pure calls to me from [Eddie's] memory—not purely good, but himself purely, for he allowed himself to be wholly known." But Miller's lawyer, perhaps echoing Miller himself in 1956, is retreating into a falsifying tidiness that clarifies nothing: what you really see from the bridge, if you are more interested in truth than poetry, is the dark and dirty waters below.

Miller is an acute observer of moral evasions, especially where disguised motives are in question. Often, indeed, he brings a Freud-like perceptiveness to his dissections of motivation and sometimes—as in *Incident at Vichy* (1964)—makes use of a Jewish doctor in order to do so. Essentially, the play is an evaluation of responsibility rather than guilt. Leduc (a Jewish psychiatrist) wants Von Berg, a patrician gentile, to recognize his human complicity with the Nazis in their extermination of the unassimilable other. Guilt, however, is not an adequate feeling unless it prompts action rather than paralysis. [Nor is innocence. Leduc's analysis of Monceau's actions reads like a brilliant exemplification of Freud's interpretative method in *The Psychopathology of Everyday Life* (1904). Monceau's passivity is merely another—intensely self-damaging—kind of complicity in the fate of the Jews.] Miller is not letting

anyone off here, but neither is he indulging in meaningless blaming. Von Berg's suicidal act of bravery is different from his earlier contemplated suicide back in Austria (which was simply despair and would leave the world as it was), for his self-sacrifice, which allows Leduc to escape and perhaps to survive, has now a real purpose.

THE PROBLEM OF CONSCIOUSNESS

Eventually, problems—of wholly knowing and of being wholly known—that *A View from the Bridge* raises but does not resolve were to have a grave impact on Miller's later plays. As early as 1957, however, he had identified the representation of consciousness, by which he meant a character's inward or mental life, as the major problem that faced the contemporary dramatist. Since in ordinary conversations, and leaving lying and other deliberate deceit to one side, we suppress as much as we express, how can an art form that relies on conventional dialogue penetrate beneath the emotional surface to the verbally unexpressed thoughts upon which conversation rides? Eugene O'Neill had identified the same problem, and in *Strange Interlude* (1928) had sought to resolve it by supplying massively expanded "asides" in which the characters' true feelings are directly presented to the audience. *Death of a Salesman*—subtitled *Certain Private Conversations in Two Acts and a Requiem* but originally to have been called *The Inside of His Head*—was an attempt to resolve this problem of consciousness by not entirely dissimilar means.

"I was never aware before," Miller told Tyrone Guthrie after seeing Guthrie's production of the play, that "this is a lyric; this is a long poem by Willy." But if this is so, the backer who withdrew funding from the 1949 production because he felt that nobody would know whether Willy was "imagining or really living through one or another scene" was making a substantial point. Sometimes, admittedly, the device is clear enough: when Linda, summoned up by memory, is seen darning stockings, this minor (but, in Willy's guilty eyes, demeaning) domestic chore summons up his next recollection, of the mistress to whom new stockings are a love token; and when Ben reassures Willy that he is a good father, it is Willy's attempts at self-reassurance that we witness.

What happens, however, in less clear-cut instances? When Miller angrily asserts in the interview that is the spine of *Arthur Miller and Company* (Bigsby, 1990) that playing Willy "like a real mad fellow" would be "bad acting and it would be a stupid way to do the show," how well does this square with his claim, given in the same interview, that "Willy is all the voices"? Is not the play seriously weakened—and above all weakened as a moral construction—if everything in it is simply still further evidence of what is happening inside Willy's head? In the very first "flashback," do we see Willy, feckless and dishonest from the start, lying to Linda about his commissions? Or is it the corruption of old age and failure that has led to this dishonest memory? At the beginning of the second act, do we see Linda discouraging Willy from striking out after Ben? Or is this Willy's manipulation of the past so as to put the blame onto her? (Is he not always shifting the blame? Are not his memories little self-flattering dramas in which—inside his head—he supplies all of the words?) *Death of a Salesman*, treated in this way, too easily becomes an exercise in persistent and interlocking ironies, the dramatic equivalent of a novel told to us by an unreliable narrator.

Willy is a salesman and Willy dies, but does he die the death of a salesman? His ideal (who is perhaps literally an ideal, since nobody else confirms even his existence) is Dave Singleman. "When he died—and by the way he died the death of a salesman... —hundreds of salesmen and buyers were at his funeral," Willy says. But in the infinitely plastic world of memories that have run riot, Singleman's name may do no more than symbolize Willy's resentful belief that marriage and family responsibilities have held him back. The bad joke is unavoidable: his own funeral brings him down to earth. Willy has never been, Biff tells Happy, much good at selling things. "Where are all the people he knew?" Linda asks. But if one thinks that *Death of a Salesman* is as much Biff's play as it is Willy's—if one recognizes that Biff, unlike Linda and Happy, is not just there to be manipulated (and remember that Willy cannot bear being in Biff's presence for long)—then the play ends not merely with a funeral but with a rebirth. Willy, finally recognizing that Biff's independence means that his is the only love that really matters, kills himself in order to yield to him the space that is the victory. "I know who I am, kid," Biff tells his hapless brother in words that mark his authentic existence outside his father's head.

No discussion of Miller's response to the problem of consciousness can avoid engagement with his most controversial play. *After the Fall* (1964) tries to explore and to embody dramatically "the surging, flitting, instantaneousness of a mind questing over its own surfaces and into its depths." Its action takes place "in the mind, thought, and memory"—a philosophically nightmarish trinity—of its central character, Quentin, who is Miller's by no means entirely flattering version of himself. Here truly is a play that takes place entirely inside its protagonist's head, but one which shows us (contrary to Miller's intention) what

a small and imprisoning space a human head can be. (Note: Quotations from *After the Fall* are taken from *Arthur Miller's Collected Plays*, Vol. II, London, 1981. This version differs from the text published in *The Portable Arthur Miller*, Christopher Bigsby, ed., New York, 1995.)

The play's basic problem is that, because of the way in which it is structured, Quentin is persistently self-presenting. Take, for example, that small but typical moment in the second act where Maggie begins the flirtation with Quentin that will lead to their disastrous marriage. She recalls for special praise an incident where, on their first chance meeting, Quentin told her that the hem of her dress was damaged and should be repaired. He did so, she tells him, because he valued her and wanted her to value herself; other men in the same situation would have laughed at her or would have tried "for a quick one." Instantly, Quentin turns to the listener to whom the entire play is addressed and reveals that he would have behaved no better than other men had he not feared rejection. Maggie's praise is, thus, misplaced and unmerited, and part of the program of self-discovery and self-cleansing that he has set himself requires him to reject it:

> (*to Listener*): Yes! It's all so clear: the honor! The first honor... was that I hadn't tried to go to bed with her! God, the hypocrisy!... Because, I was only afraid, and she took it for a tribute to her... "value"! No wonder I can't find myself here! (*He has gotten to his feet in agony.*)

But what justifies this agony? There is surely nothing culpable or superficial about a morality that encourages us to judge people (including ourselves) in terms of what they do rather than of what they think of doing. The quick calculations of right and wrong that Quentin spends the entire play making are not untrue to life; what is untrue, and very galling, is halting their rapid flow to hold them up for protracted inspection. The problem is a mechanical one: Miller's listener is a device designed to allow him to make Quentin's innermost thoughts available to us, a variant solution to the problem of getting us inside a character's head that is resolved differently in *Death of a Salesman*. But it is a severely flawed device, for it forces Quentin not merely into a perpetual act of self-justification but, worse still, into a perpetually public act of self-justification. That surely is why Quentin is intolerable. His constant attempt to cut himself down to size is ego-ridden and ego-driven.

After the Fall, as some of its earliest reviewers pointed out, is little more than a giant soliloquy with speeches given to others only as Quentin dictates. (Perhaps Willy has all the words; Quentin certainly does.) But what is the effect of having Quentin buttonhole us? "Were you able to give me two hours?" he says to his imagined listener. "It might not take that long [it takes nearly three], but I think it involves a great deal and I'd rather not rush. Fine." Of course, we are the listener, but unlike real listeners we cannot interrupt and "Fine" is issued as though in response to a response that we have no opportunity of registering. Such is the one-sided nature of theater. What in real life would you do if confronted with garrulous self-accusation and still more garrulous self-justification on this massive scale? Avoid the purveyor of it, of course, but also, surely, doubt the purveyor's claim to have achieved balance or poise or a sense of proportion. The very manner of the man discredits the claim. And that, surely, is the problem with *After the Fall*.

Or, rather, that is one of its problems. The other is sincerity, very much an Arthur Miller keyword but also something that theater is uniquely ill-equipped to illuminate. Take Quentin's telling us the saga of Felice's nose, which she wants to have altered by plastic surgery. There are a number of possible responses to this recital. Perhaps we simply think that surgical intervention is a sensible way of taking control of whatever aspect of our lives irritates or disappoints us, so that being strong means being strong enough to change your nose. Or perhaps we think that we should learn to accept what we are given, in which case being strong involves being strong enough not to change your nose. On this second, more overtly moralistic showing, not accepting your nose is akin to not accepting yourself, a kind of loss of (or lack of) integrity. And even of sincerity? "I mean," Felice says, "there's something sort of insincere about changing your nose." Her point is that you are deluding yourself if you think that all that is holding you back is your nose or that fixing your nose repairs all other faults. But she then tells Quentin that she fancied him and might therefore have had her nose fixed to snare him, but that her knowing that his wanting her had nothing to do with the shape of her nose left her free to change it in line with her own pure preference. She ends up doing what she had always wanted to do, but self-absolved from charges of insincerity; she is devious, but her nose is sincere. Quentin then tells his listener (but not Felice) that it is odd how something utterly peripheral in his life could be central to the life of another. But there is nothing odd here: the exact configuration of Felice's nose is bound to matter more to her than to anyone else. That what is important to her is less important to Quentin is merely the inevitable consequence of our leading lives

that are linked together in all sorts of ways. Perhaps what Quentin really wants to assert is that what is peripheral to him should be peripheral to others.

The special problem about sincerity in the theater stems from hypocrisy, defined as the art of the actor. Miller's stage directions in *After the Fall*, though they are generally brief, nevertheless annotate what is said in ways that can be considered illegitimate. Such directions do not merely tell actors and readers how things are to be said (as in "*loudly*," or "*softly*," or "*quickly*"), but also assign moral and emotional values, as in the following—again quite typical—exchange between Louise and Quentin:

QUENTIN: What do you think?
LOUISE, *in anguish*: It's not my decision, Quentin.
QUENTIN, *puzzled and surprised*: But aren't you involved?
LOUISE: Of course I'm involved.
QUENTIN, *genuinely foxed*: Is it that you're not sure of how you feel?

But where does that "genuinely" come from? What is the difference between sounding foxed and sounding genuinely foxed? What extra bit of art does an actor have to put in to get the "genuinely" across? And might not that extra bit of art be interpreted as evidence that the character is artfully simulating genuineness? Similarly Miller covers a crucial speech by Louise, who might herself seem merely manipulative, with this guidance: "*it is sincere, what she says, but she has had to learn the words, so there is the faintest air of a formula in her way of speaking*." This stage direction must mean that she is sincere despite sounding as though she is not. But how can this massive but hairline distinction be picked up in performance? Miller (like Quentin) may want sincerity to be the all-out issue in this play. We must, therefore, learn to penetrate disguise, but the very medium in which his art operates needs disguise as it foundational element. The truth is that real life—and that reading of social and personal signals of which so much real life consists—does not come with Miller's or Quentin's moral commentary attached; we make our choices, revoke and remake them, without benefit of an authorial guarantee. Once again, in this untidiest of plays, Miller is trying to tidy away life's characteristic untidiness.

The continued significance of this problem of consciousness is proved once we recognize that in a very late play—*Mr. Peters' Connections* (1998)—Miller returns us to *After the Fall* (1964) thirty-four years on. Both of these plays are attempts to give a voice to unvoiced desires and a physical form to unacted actions, and they exploit the same staging device in order to do so: *Mr. Peters' Connections* takes place "inside Mr. Peters' mind or at least on its threshold . . . the action of the play is the procession of Mr. Peters' moods, each of them summoning up the next." What has summoned up the later play, and has summoned up its title in particular, is that tiny moment in *After the Fall* when Quentin says that he has "lost the connection." Peters' sole task is to search for the goal that will give his life shape, meaning, and purpose, and will enable him to "connect up" his otherwise discrepant and unresolved experiences. He finds this unity and purpose (or "subject" as he calls it) at the very end of the play when his daughter says she loves him and asks him to love her in return: "I'm trying as hard as I can," he says: "I love you, darling, I wonder . . . could that be the subject!" The exclamation point, where a question mark might be expected, is telling us that Love is the answer; that Love is Peter's subject and Quentin's subject and everybody's subject; that Love makes the world go around.

Why is this ringing assertion of the centrality of love not convincing? *After the Fall* is a far from satisfactory play, and its least satisfactory part is its ending. By contrast, *Mr. Peters' Connections* is much neater and with beguiling simplicity smooths out the earlier work's irregularities. It does so at some cost, however. Not altogether surprisingly, the less well focused and less surely resolved play is the more demanding and the more commanding work. Nevertheless Miller's consistency of purpose over such a length of time is deeply impressive and entirely characteristic of him.

[*See also* Theater in America.]

SELECTED WORKS

The Man Who Had All The Luck (1944)
Focus (1945)
All My Sons (1947)
Death of a Salesman (1949)
An Enemy of the People (1950)
The Crucible (1953)
A Memory of Two Mondays (1955)
A View from the Bridge (one-act version, 1955)
A View from the Bridge (two-act version, 1956)
The Misfits (1961)
After the Fall (1964)
Incident at Vichy (1964)
The Price (1968)
In Russia (1969)
The Creation of the World and Other Business (1972)
The Archbishop's Ceiling (1977, 1984)

"Salesman" in Beijing (1984)
The American Clock (1980, 1984)
Two By A.M. (1982)
Playing for Time (1985)
Danger: Memory! (1987)
The Golden Years (1987)
Timebends: A Life (1987)
The Ride Down Mount Morgan (1991)
The Last Yankee (1993)
Broken Glass (1994)
The Theatre Essays of Arthur Miller (1994, 1996)
Mr. Peters' Connections (1998)
Echoes Down the Corridor: Collected Essays, 1944–2000 (2000)
The Misfits: Story of a Shoot (2000).

FURTHER READING

Bigsby, Christopher. *Confrontation and Commitment: A Study of Contemporary American Drama, 1959–66.* London, 1967. An early work by a leading British student of Miller's plays.

Bigsby, Christopher, ed. *Arthur Miller and Company: Arthur Miller Talks about His Work in the Company of Actors, Designers, Directors, and Writers.* London, 1990. The invaluable core of this book, giving unity to its disparate contents, is an interview with Arthur Miller (put together out of a series of interviews conducted over a ten-year period) in which Miller comments in detail on almost every aspect of his work. This book also contains the birthday tribute from Arnold Wesker cited in the text.

Bigsby, Christopher, ed. *The Cambridge Companion to Arthur Miller.* Cambridge and New York, 1997.

Cox, Brian. *Salem to Moscow: An Actor's Odyssey.* London, 1991. Cox's account of directing *The Crucible* at the Moscow Art Theatre School in 1988. Only indirectly a book about Miller but one that invites comparison with *"Salesman" in Beijing.*

Dukore, Bernard F. *"Death of a Salesman" and "The Crucible": Text and Performance.* London, 1989.

Foulkes, A. P. *Literature and Propaganda.* London and New York, 1983. This book's final chapter, "Demystifying the Witch Hunt," is a detailed discussion of early critical reaction to *The Crucible.*

Gussow, Mel. *Conversations with Miller.* London, 2002.

Martine, James J. *The Crucible: Politics, Property, and Pretense.* New York, 1993.

Murphy, Brenda. *Miller: Death of a Salesman.* Cambridge and New York, 1995. An indispensable discussion of the play's original Broadway production.

Savran, David. *Breaking the Rules: The Wooster Group*. New York, 1988. The third part of this book, titled "L.S.D. (...*Just the High Points*): History as Hallucination," chronicles the attempt by America's leading performance group to stage its own radical and controversial reworking of *The Crucible*.

Savran, David. *Communists, Cowboys, and Queers: The Politics of Masculinity in the Work of Arthur Miller and Tennessee Williams*. Minneapolis and London, 1992. A controversial reading in which Savran argues that Miller's liberalism masks an underlying misogyny.

See also the article on *Death of a Salesman*, immediately following.

ARTHUR MILLER'S
DEATH OF A SALESMAN

by Melissa Knox

Arthur Miller's play *Death of a Salesman* (1949) is an innovation in the genre of tragedy as well as a quintessentially American story by a master playwright. In some ways it conforms to the ancient Greek philosopher Aristotle's rules for tragedy, which have had a major influence on Western drama, affecting the plays of Shakespeare and other canonized writers. For instance, Aristotle stipulates that the action of the drama must take place within a single day, as it does in Miller's drama, which focuses on the last day in the life of Willy Loman. Tragedy is for Aristotle the "imitation of a good action," and Loman's efforts to keep himself going in the face of certain failure, to work and to provide for his family and to encourage his sons loosely conforms to Aristotle's notion of a good action. The tragic hero must be thoroughly human, that is, neither unrealistically angelic nor demonic, but a mixture of good and bad traits.

WILLY AS AN AMERICAN TRAGIC HERO

But Aristotle also writes that the tragic hero is also "famous or prosperous," adding that his fall must be caused not "by outright wickedness" but by some "serious flaw in . . . character." It is here that Miller's depiction of Willy Loman as a tragic hero departs significantly from Aristotle. Willy Loman has none of the traditional features of nobility required by Aristotle. He is not a king or a prince or a person of high estate; indeed, as more than one critic pointed out, to Miller's distaste, Loman sounds like "low man," as though Miller were trying to make a point of showing that an ordinary, average man can be a hero. Willy Loman is bracingly—one might even say spectacularly—average. In the opening scene he sits down and takes off his shoes, complaining, "These goddamn arch supports are killing me," something that the best-known tragic hero of ancient drama, Sophocles's Oedipus—whose name means "swollen foot," a fact that could not have escaped Miller—would never say.

Miller appears to have intended to contrast Willy Loman with Oedipus, who is famous for his failure to perceive that he has killed his father and conceived

children with his mother. This figurative blindness leads Oedipus to stab out his eyes in the final scenes. Not only do Willy's feet bother him but he cannot see very well, a trait his wife draws attention to in remarking that he never went to pick up his new glasses. Tragic heroes in classical and Shakespearean drama do not, in general, notice or bemoan the irritations and inconveniences of everyday life. Willy Loman is a salesman who has fallen on hard times because he has gotten too old and out of step with his customers' lifestyles to be able to sell much. Unable to earn a living wage, he spends much of his time dreaming and despairing, cadging money from a neighbor and seriously considering suicide.

Willy Loman is over sixty, and one of the first things he says is that he is "tired to death." Most of the heroes of classical and Shakespearean drama are young men filled with derring-do, whose larger-than-life, well-intentioned ambitions pave their particular roads to hell, inflaming the tragic flaw that undoes them. Willy Loman has no greater ambition than to stay alive and earn or borrow enough money to keep his family together. The poet T. S. Eliot's observation, "This is the way the world ends . . . not with a bang, but a whimper," perfectly describes the death of Willy Loman, which occurs offstage.

Unlike traditional tragic heroes—Oedipus, for instance, or Shakespeare's Macbeth—Willy Loman does not go out raging and fighting with operatic force but merely fades away. Technically, he drives away in his car, presumably crashing it, but none of this is seen on stage. His last onstage moments are quiet murmurings, an imagined conversation with a long-dead brother, Ben. While tragedies typically end with at least one corpse on stage, Miller's *Death of a Salesman* ends with the exposure of family relationships that have been exploited to foster illusions about the success of Willy and his sons. The strenuous attempts of Willy's son Biff to reach out and tell the truth force all members of the family to face—if just fleetingly—the lies that they have been living as well as their love for one another. Willy's grave is seen at the end.

The idea of the ordinary working man as a tragic hero is a particularly American concept, since one of the founding principles of American politics is Thomas Jefferson's notion of an aristocracy of virtue and talent as opposed to the European tradition of inherited status and privileges and an entire system and ranking of nobles akin to the hierarchy of angels in the Catholic Church. America's elected politicians are "noble" in the sense of having won the confidence of the electorate. The self-made, successful businessman—Willy Loman's identity in happier days, when, as he put it, "America is full of beautiful towns and fine, upstanding people. And they know me . . . they know me up and down New England. The finest people"—is the American version of nobility that Jefferson had in mind. By dint of his labors, Willy is a member of the elect of the "finest people," and there exists a long tradition of self-made, successful American citizens, "nobles" by virtue of their hard work and ingenuity—Donald Trump being a late-twentieth-century example. The prototypical American noble is the self-made entrepreneur, and Willy Loman exemplifies this tradition.

ACT ONE: HOPES AND DELUSIONS

Arthur Miller divides his drama into what he terms, in the play's subtitle, *Certain Private Conversations in Two Acts and a Requiem*. Although the two acts move forward in time, they are punctuated by many flashbacks and daydreams that define Miller's understanding of time as a concept. Miller remarked that in the play "nothing in life comes 'next,' but everything exists together and at the same time within us . . . there is no past to be 'brought forward' in a human being . . . he is his past at every moment . . . his present is merely that which his past is capable of noticing and smelling and reacting to."

The opening scene introduces an exhausted Willy, who is almost limping home after yet another of many unsuccessful days on the road trying to sell, and his wife, the long suffering and devoted Linda, who ministers to him and defends him to their sons, Biff and Happy. The names of the sons suggest an all-American casualness, an essential informality. Biff is as lightweight as his name suggests until the final scenes, when his ability to see and tell the truth transforms him. Happy is anything but—like the rest of the Loman family, he puts on a face to meet the faces that he meets, while inwardly feeling full of uncertainty and sorrow.

The sons' names also indicate their roles in the play. In American slang "biff" is a punch or a blow, an appropriate moniker for him, since he is a high school football hero,

at one point promising a play in which "when I take off my helmet, that means I'm breakin' out. Then watch me crash through that line!" In the end, it is Biff who gives an emotional one-two punch that knocks out Willy while also bringing him a certain peace of mind that appears to facilitate his urge to do himself in while still happy in the knowledge that Biff really loves him, despite all the difficulties they have had. Happy's role, as a salesman like his father, is to glad-hand people and sell merchandise. But he is dissatisfied with almost every aspect of his existence.

In the first scene, Willy and Linda have a conversation that reveals the depth of Willy's despair and mental instability. She calls to him, he reassures her that he has come back, and she wonders whether he smashed the car. This foreshadows his actual demise; the entire family fears this event so much throughout the drama that when it occurs offstage, there is a sense of almost transcendent relief. Linda tries to soothe Willy in this scene, encouraging him to talk to his boss about working closer to home in New York so he won't have an exhausting daily drive at his age and chatting with him about their sons, who went out double-dating together earlier that evening. Linda urges Willy not to lose his temper with Biff, who, it turns out, is thirty-four and without any real goals in life or any profession. He drifts from one menial job to another. But Willy is filled with illusions about this son: "He could be big in no time!" he insists, imagining all sorts of glory for Biff as a salesman. Almost in the same breath, Willy blows up at Linda for buying a new kind of cheese instead of the kind he always eats and asks whether they cannot open a window, "for God's sakes." Linda—who has the patience of Mother Teresa—mildly tells him that all the windows are open. Throughout the play, Willy's dreams of glory for himself and Biff alternate with his sense of being trapped.

The focus of the scene then shifts to Biff and Happy, who are lying in their beds listening to Willy and Linda and talking—about their father and the possibility he might wreck the car, about women in general ("About five hundred women would like to know what was said in this room," Happy quips), and about the girls with whom they spent the evening. Happy, the younger brother and outwardly the more successful because he earns a steady living, credits Biff with teaching him all he knows about women. This praise becomes the occasion for Happy to wonder why Biff has lost all the confidence he had in high school. The reason for Biff's aimlessness is one of the play's secrets, eventually answered in the second act, where it develops that Biff caught Willy with a woman at a particularly vulnerable point in Biff's life and never recovered from the shock and disappointment.

As Biff and Happy lie in their beds talking about Biff's future, Biff worries that he is "wasting my life" and is "mixed up very bad," but the only solution that immediately pops into his head is "maybe I oughta get married." He sees himself as being "like a boy," apparently imagining that marriage will make a man of him, a steady person able to make decisions, although this has obviously not happened with Willy, himself an overgrown boy given to flights of fancy and for whom his wife is more mother than partner. Happy comes up with the idea of getting Biff together with his former employer, one Bill Oliver, to try to make a fresh start, and from the way Happy talks—"he thought highly of you, Biff. I mean, they all do. You're well liked"—it becomes clearer that Happy, like Willy, thinks with delusional grandiosity about Biff's personality and its impact on others. In reality, Biff is utterly forgettable to most employers, an aimless if pleasant young man. To boot, he is a petty thief or kleptomaniac who takes things—without realizing why he does so—in an apparent blind urge to give himself some sense of control over his life. Biff listens to Happy complain about his job and about how the things he has wanted and now possesses—his own apartment and plenty of women—do not make him happy. Biff and Happy then indulge in a *folie à deux*, dreaming a typical American young man's dream of going out West, raising cattle, and working out in the open. They are not adolescents but grown men in their thirties, with little imagination about their own futures beyond this Western cliché.

The rest of act one moves between interludes of memory—one scene revives Willy's memories of Biff and Happy in high school, showing the three of them polishing the family car and dreaming of how great they will all be someday. In the course of the scene Biff's failing grades are mentioned, along with the danger that he will be flunked by his math teacher and not be able to use any of the three university football scholarships he has won. Bernard, son of the well-meaning neighbor, Charley (the man from whom Willy continually borrows large sums of money), is dismissed by Willy and Biff as a nobody, but as it turns out, Bernard is merely realistic. Another scene shows the ever-supportive Linda telling Willy he is the "handsomest man in the world," "idolized" by his children; the scene then fades into another, a memory of a tryst between a very lonely Willy and a woman he sleeps with on his unsuccessful trips as a traveling salesman. In other scenes Willy idealizes the life of his brother Ben, who lived in Africa; Linda chides Biff for making Willy unhappy; Linda reveals how little money Willy is now earning; and Happy and Biff fantasize about starting a million-dollar sporting goods business. The first act ends with Willy's jubilant plan for Biff to meet his former employer, Bill Oliver, to ask for help. Linda quietly wonders if Oliver will even remember Biff, momentarily infuriating Willy.

ACT TWO: TRUTH, LOVE, AND SUICIDE

In the second act Willy looks forward to a big dinner to which his sons will treat him at a New York City chop house on Forty-eighth Street near Sixth Avenue, an area filled with businessmen because it is in the neighborhood of Penn Station, a large commuter railroad station. The dinner is intended to be the culmination of a successful day in which Willy will ask his boss for a change of venue to New York from distant New England, along with a cash advance. Biff will meanwhile supposedly be having lunch with Bill Oliver, his employer of some years ago, asking him for money to start up a business with Happy. Willy goes off to work in high spirits, only moderately irritated by Linda's reminders of just how much money they need to pay off their refrigerator, their mortgage, and repairs on Willy's car. Just before leaving, Willy—inflated with the idea of his success—crows, "I'll never get behind a wheel the rest of my life!" But his ensuing actions complete his tailspin, ensuring that he will take one last fatal drive.

Willy goes to his employer, Howard, the son of the man for whom Willy originally worked. Unwisely, Willy reminds Howard, "I was with the firm when your father used to carry you here in his arms," which is perhaps what provokes Howard to call Willy "kid" for the rest of the conversation. In fact, Willy is a kid who can never stop dreaming and who has raised sons just like himself. Instead of giving him an easier commute and an advance, Howard effectually fires him. Willy staggers out of his office, goes to see his neighbor Charley, whose son Bernard is now a distinguished lawyer about to argue a case before the Supreme Court. Charley is ready with his weekly handout of fifty dollars, but also offers Willy a job. Willy turns it down, but wants even more money—one hundred ten dollars. Charley scoffingly indicates that he knows when he is being insulted, but pityingly gives the money to Willy.

While waiting for Charley, Willy has an upsetting conversation with Bernard. Suddenly emotional, Willy asks Bernard what his secret is, meaning why has Bernard achieved success and Biff not. Bernard at first parries Willy's question, cautiously observing that Biff never "trained himself for anything." But a desperate Willy persists, saying he has no one to talk to, and Bernard unwittingly reveals something that Willy has never been able to face merely by asking a few questions about Biff, who was Bernard's boyhood friend and even hero. Biff failed math in high school and lost the football scholarships, Bernard recounts, but Biff had then been quite ready to take a summer course and make up the math. Willy never knew that Biff was ready to do this, or more likely Willy had never admitted it to himself. Something must have happened, Bernard remarks, asking whether Biff went to see Willy and had a talk with him in New England. Willy immediately gets angry and defensive. The reason why becomes clear only a few scenes later, in a flashback of Biff coming unannounced to see him in Boston, ridiculing his math teacher's lisp to Willy's delight and then discovering that Willy has a woman in his room. Willy denies everything, alternating between apologizing and ordering Biff to forget all about it as Biff weeps, observing that his father has given the woman "Mama's stockings!" Meanwhile, in several previous scenes, the patient Linda has been mending her stockings. Biff can never understand or forgive his father's lonely escapade and becomes a drifter.

After leaving Charley's office, Willy goes to meet his sons. Before he gets there, the audience sees Happy chatting with a waiter in the restaurant and with Biff. Happy corrals some women to their table. It develops that Biff has never managed to see Bill Oliver, who did not remember him, and that in an agitated moment, Biff ran in and stole Oliver's fountain pen. Biff and Happy argue about what to tell their father. Happy, insisting "Dad is never so happy as when he's looking forward to something," urges Biff to tell Willy that he has a lunch date with Oliver the next day. Eventually, after a few days or weeks of saying Oliver is "thinking it over," Willy will forget the whole thing, Happy believes. Willy walks in and announces that he has been fired. Biff alternates between trying to tell Willy the truth and, egged on by Happy, telling him that he had lunch with Oliver. Willy drifts into a memory of the day Biff flunked math, and the scene becomes a dissonant meld of Willy's horrified memories of the day Biff appeared in Boston and Biff's attempts to tell him of the fiasco with Oliver.

Biff, Willy, and Happy have meanwhile been drinking, and the women at their table are aghast at their behavior. Happy at one point even tells them that Willy is not their father, just "a guy." The scene fades and then Willy is alone at the table, being told by the waiter that his sons left "with the chippies" and will see him at home. Disoriented, Willy asks if there is a seed store in the neighborhood, reiterating that he must get some seeds. Happy and Biff meanwhile arrive home after a good time with the women and try to give Linda long-stemmed roses. Enraged that they left Willy alone in the restaurant, she knocks them to Biff's feet and orders her sons out of the house.

Willy is then seen on his knees outdoors in the dark, trying to plant the seeds in the yard. He is talking to his dead brother, Ben. Biff goes to Willy and tries to speak with him. Biff finally finds the courage to tell Willy everything on his mind, how he is neither a "leader of men," or anything that Willy hoped for, nor full of spite, as Willy imagined. The effect is dramatic. Willy cries, understanding, as he says, that "Biff—he likes me!" Willy promises, at Linda's entreaties, to come up to bed, but he stays downstairs, immersed in an ominous conversation with Ben, who says, "We'll be late." Linda calls to Willy one more time and then the sound of a car is heard. It is clear that Willy has died, because Linda, Biff, and Happy are seen shortly thereafter kneeling at his grave.

The brief Requiem shows Charley, Linda, Biff, and Happy talking after the funeral. Charley explains that Willy had been out there as a salesman, "riding on a smile and a shoeshine," and that when the world started "not smiling back—that's an earthquake." Happy reverts to the dreamy world of the Loman family, promising that Willy has not died in vain, that he had "a good dream," that Happy will win the fight for him. In the final moments of the play, Linda sits by Willy's grave, trying to say goodbye, unable to weep, then sobbing that they were free, that the mortgage has finally been paid.

FURTHER READING

Brigsby, Christopher, ed. *The Cambridge Companion to Arthur Miller*. Cambridge, 1997. Useful collection of contemporary scholarly essays.

Miller, Arthur. *Death of a Salesman*. Edited by E. R. Wood. London, 1970.

Sophocles. *Oedipus Tyrannus*. Edited and translated by Luci Berkowitz and Theodore F. Brunner. New York, 1970. Classic ancient Greek tragedy; useful to compare to *Death of a Salesman*, which is partly modeled on it.

See also the article on Arthur Miller, immediately preceding.

HENRY MILLER

by David Ryan

Henry Miller's writing is perhaps best known for having set precedent, along with James Joyce's *Ulysses* and D. H. Lawrence's *Lady Chatterley's Lover*, in redefining legal and aesthetic distinctions between art and obscenity in the twentieth century. A truly enigmatic American writer, his first and most famous book, *Tropic of Cancer* (1934), originally published in France, was banned in the United States for some thirty years because of its frank sexual content. Several of Miller's subsequent books followed suit: *Black Spring* (1936), *Tropic of Capricorn* (1939), and part of the trilogy *The Rosy Crucifixion* could be obtained in the United States only illegally until the 1960s.

Henry Miller, 1940. (*Photograph by Carl Van Vechten. Courtesy of the Library of Congress*)

The self-trained Miller had a voracious reading appetite. Early influences on his writing include Fyodor Dostoyevsky, Walt Whitman, Louis-Ferdinand Céline, Marcel Proust, Knut Hamsun (whose novel *Hunger* helped shape *Tropic of Cancer*), and the European surrealists—in particular the film collaborations of Salvador Dali and Luis Buñuel.

Self-liberation constitutes a major theme of Miller's writing—liberation especially from what society deems countercultural or taboo. Miller was also known for taking an often self-aggrandizing liberty with the details of his life. Opting for a blurred marriage between fact and imagination, Miller's work celebrates a stratospheric zone of imaginative truth, in which biography is amended and used as it suits the fictional or heroic world of the narrative. If American literature of the nineteenth and early twentieth centuries had been dominated by a sense of verisimilitude, or the appearance of "how things really happened," Miller eschewed such a narrative stance. His claim was that literature was a truth unto itself, be it surreal, skewed, or inflated in its representation of fact.

EARLY YEARS

Henry Valentine Miller was born to German immigrants on 26 December 1891 at 450 East Eighty-fifth Street in the German section of New York City known as Yorkville. Shortly after his birth, his family moved to Brooklyn, where Miller spent his childhood and early adulthood. His father was a tailor, and for a time as a teenager Henry worked at his father's shop in Manhattan. After high school Miller attended City College of New York, but dropped out after two months and proceeded to take on a series of odd jobs. In 1917, now in his mid-twenties, Miller married Beatrice Sylvas Wickens and got a job in Manhattan as a manager at Western Union. Along with the job at his father's tailor shop, Miller's career at Western Union (the "Cosmodemonic-Cosmococcic Telegraph Company" of *Tropic of Cancer*) was one of the rare full-time day jobs Miller held in his life.

Miller used the failure of his first marriage as the subject of an early attempt at extended narrative; this work, *Crazy Cock*, was published posthumously in 1991. He returned to the subject of his first wife in his novel *Sexus* (1949).

While still married to his first wife, Miller met June Smith (aka June Mansfield) at a dance hall in 1923 and began an affair that proved as torturous to his personal life as it was elemental to his development as a writer. June was by most accounts eccentric, beautiful, and sexually liberated. In 1923 Miller and his first wife divorced, and a year later Miller married June. It was June who would later insist that Miller go to France.

THE AMERICAN IN PARIS

Although Miller would someday write much about his life in America, it was only after he moved to Paris in 1930 that he discovered his voice as a writer, gradually

149

abandoning straightforward formal narrative modes for the more liberated, open-ended, and anarchic writing associated with his first major success, *Tropic of Cancer*. Now in his late thirties Miller discovered the European art scene and avant-garde of the time, the works of the surrealists, including Buñuel and Dali's two films, *Un Chien andalou* and *L'Âge d'or*, which affected him greatly. The surrealists taught Miller to liberate himself from traditional linear, or chronological, ways of telling a story—to free himself from the conventions of the traditional novel as exemplified by Henry James.

While in France, Miller also befriended many whose lives he would fictionalize in his novels. He further developed his practice of letter writing—which was by his own account obsessive, and which to a great extent shaped his narrative voice. Many of these letters were preserved and later published.

In December 1931, Miller met the writer Anaïs Nin. Nin was wealthy, intelligent, and became a significant patron of Miller's. Late in 1932, Miller signed a three-book deal with the French publishing company Obelisk Press and in September 1934, *Tropic of Cancer* was published. Because Obelisk was at the time cash-strapped, Nin helped to bankroll the book's publication. It soon launched Miller as a raconteur of human nature celebrated at both its lowest and most noble states and as a stylist with the surrealist's emphasis on coherence of tone and unity of atmosphere. Often seemingly formless, and consistently defiant of convention, *Tropic of Cancer* compresses and inflates the fictionalized events of the author's life upon arriving in Paris. The book's antihero, "Henry Miller," plays fictional doppelgänger, a tendency the author would repeat in later work. Miller next published *Black Spring*, a collection of autobiographical sketches, in June 1936. *Tropic of Capricorn*, published in May 1939, returned to the anarchic spirit of *Tropic of Cancer*.

In June 1939, Miller traveled to Greece, staying predominately with a close friend, the writer Lawrence Durrell, and his wife. Miller chronicles his time there in *The Colossus of Maroussi* (1941). The imminence of World War II forced him to leave, reluctantly, at year's end for New York.

THE RETURN TO NEW YORK

In the United States, the publishing house New Directions had released a collection of Miller's essays and previously published extracts, titled *The Cosmological Eye*, in 1939. This became Miller's first American publication, his three prior books having been banned for importation by U.S. Customs. Upon arriving in New York, Miller embarked upon a solid period of writing output, completing *The Colossus of Maroussi, The World of Sex* (1940), a limited-edition exposition of the writer's views on sex, and *Quiet Days in Clichy* (1956), detailing the two years Miller spent in Clichy with his close friend and roommate, the Austrian writer Alfred Perlès, and their various sexual pursuits.

At the beginning of October 1940, Miller set out in a used Buick with the painter Abraham Rattner to chronicle his travels throughout the United States. The result was *The Air-Conditioned Nightmare* (1945), whose title the author had first penned in 1938. As suggested by the title, the author's depiction of his birth country was not intended to flatter. The sketches of Americans that the book includes unfold in Miller's characteristic fashion: Like a written-word version of the photography of Arthur Fellig (aka Weegee) or Diane Arbus, Miller's sympathetic portraits are of those too unglamorous or odd to be tallied into the country's usual mythmaking.

BIG SUR

In early 1942 Miller finished *Sexus*. Intended as a kind of Brooklyn-ized nod to Marcel Proust's *Remembrance of Things Past*, this first installment of what became the trilogy *The Rosy Crucifixion* detailed Miller's life with his first wife, and then with June, as well as his job at Western Union and early development as a writer. Published in France in 1949, it was not issued in the United States until 1965.

In the summer of 1942, Miller traveled to California and attempted to write films for Hollywood, but eventually gave this up. In 1944 he married a young philosophy student, Janina Martha Lepska. Miller's major output after World War II includes the aforementioned *The Air-Conditioned Nightmare* and *Remember to Remember* (1947). He also began to publish essays on the poet Arthur Rimbaud in the annual anthologies issued by New Directions. In 1948 Miller's novella *The Smile at the Foot of the Ladder* was written as an accompaniment text for drawings of the circus by the artist Fernan Léger, and brought on a shift in tone from the grittiness of his *Tropic of Cancer* and *Tropic of Capricorn*, to a more mature, lyrical style.

Miller found a permanent address in Big Sur, California, in 1947. He continued to work on the remaining two books of the *Rosy Crucifixion* trilogy, pausing to produce *The Books in My Life* in 1952 for New Directions. If Miller's love of literature is self-evident from a reading of his works, it is nowhere more exuberantly displayed than here. Miller details how he learned to write by marrying his prodigious reading with a keen interest in the details of living, to the extent that the two became inseparable.

Miller's second installment to *The Rosy Crucifixion*, *Plexus*, was published in Paris in 1953. It continues the story of Miller's writing apprenticeship after leaving Western Union, and his first two years of marriage to June.

In 1956 an English edition of Miller's collected essays on Rimbaud, *The Time of the Assassins*, was published. New Directions published Miller's *Big Sur and the Oranges of Hieronymous Bosch* in 1957, which located the writer in his home and transposed his figure from an expatriate American bohemian to a kind of proto-Beat Californian sage.

Miller finished the third installment of *The Rosy Crucifixion—Nexus—*in 1959. It was published in 1960 in Paris, like the prior two books in the series. Continuing where *Plexus* left off, *Nexus* furthers the saga of Miller's life with June, discussing the couple's live-in guest, Mara Andrews, whose intimate relationship with June is described by Miller with both fascination and disgust. Miller had allegedly intended on writing a fourth book for *The Rosy Crucifixion*, but the series ended with *Nexus*, the last book in which Miller would write about June Mansfield.

CENSORSHIP: MILLER AND THE 1960s

In June of 1961 the publishing house Grove Press—already locked into a First Amendment ruling over its publication of D. H. Lawrence's *Lady Chatterley's Lover* in 1959—published *Tropic of Cancer* in the United States. In both cases the courts debated the intricacies of what was deemed socially significant, and thereby entitled to constitutional protections. After a series of give-and-take rulings, *Tropic of Cancer* was legally cleared for distribution. The controversy over the book's release—and dozens of court battles (fifty-three were ongoing at one point) and arrests of booksellers in various states—ceased. Miller, now entering his seventies, found his first published work finally available in his home country. Because of the controversy over his work and the freedom its eventual acceptance allowed the arts in America, Miller became a symbol of the movement for free expression in the arts. The 1960s would remain the high point of his fame in the United States.

LATER YEARS

Miller's reputation took a downward turn in the 1970s, when feminist groups argued that the content of his books was sexist rather than sexual, and his sometimes controversial statements on race led to his works being removed from university curricula. Though his books were rigorously defended by many peers, including Norman Mailer and his old friend Durrell, Miller would never again achieve his former prominence.

Miller was awarded the French Legion of Honor in 1976. In 1978 he and several of his friends tried, unsuccessfully, to have him nominated for a Nobel Prize. His most notable book at this time, besides certain volumes of his letters (particularly his correspondence with Durrell and Nin), is the three-volume *Book of Friends* (published between 1976 and 1979).

Henry Miller died in his sleep on Saturday, 7 June 1980.

SELECTED WORKS

Tropic of Cancer (1934)
What Are You Going to Do about Alf? (1935)
Aller Retour New York (1935)
Black Spring (1936)
Scenario (A Film with Sound) (1937)
Money and How It Gets That Way (1938)
Max and the White Phagocytes (1938)
The Cosmological Eye (1939)
Tropic of Capricorn (1939)
The World of Sex (1940)
The Colossus of Maroussi (1941)
The Wisdom of the Heart (1941)
Sunday after the War (1944)
The Air-Conditioned Nightmare (1945)
Maurizius Forever (1946)
Remember to Remember (1947)
The Smile at the Foot of the Ladder (1948)
Sexus (1949)
The Books in My Life (1952)
Plexus (1953)
Nights of Love and Laughter (1955)
The Time of the Assassins: A Story of Rimbaud (1956)
Quiet Days in Clichy (1956)
A Devil in Paradise (1956)
Big Sur and the Oranges of Hieronymous Bosch (1957)
The Henry Miller Reader (1959)
The Intimate Henry Miller (1959)
Reunion in Barcelona (1959)
Nexus (1960)
To Paint Is to Love Again (1960)
Stand Still Like Hummingbird (1962)
Just Wild about Harry: A Melo Melo in Seven Scenes (1963)
Henry Miller on Writing (1964)
Insomnia; or, The Devil at Large (1971)
My Life and Times (1971)
On Turning Eighty: Journey to an Antique Land: Forward to the "Angel Is My Watermark" (1972)

Reflections on the Death of Mishima (1972)
First Impressions of Greece (1973)
Henry Miller's Book of Friends: A Tribute to Friends of Long Ago (1976)
Mother, China, and the World Beyond (1977)
Gliding into the Everglades (1977)
My Bike and Other Friends (1978)
Joey (1979)
The World of Lawrence: A Passionate Appreciation (1979)
The Paintings of Henry Miller: Paint As You Like and Die Happy (1982)
Opus Pistorum (1983)
Crazy Cock (1991)
Moloch; or, This Gentile World (1992)
Nothing but the Marvelous Wisdoms of Henry Miller (1999)

FURTHER READING

Brassaï. *Henry Miller: The Paris Years*. Translated by Timothy Bent. New York, 1995. Intimate, firsthand account of the writer in 1930s Paris by the famous photographer.

Dearborn, Mary V. *The Happiest Man Alive: A Biography of Henry Miller*. New York, 1991. See Ferguson, below.

Ferguson, Robert. *Henry Miller—A Life*. New York, 1991. Markedly more sympathetic and analytical than Dearborn's account, published the same year. The contradictions of the two books, taken together, add to the perception of Miller as enigmatic.

Jahshan, Paul. *Henry Miller and the Surrealist Discourse of Excess: A Post-structuralist Reading*. New York, 2001. Applies a poetics analysis to Miller's often discounted use of surrealist techniques, thereby forming an interesting discourse on an often ignored or disregarded—and ironically fundamental—aspect of Miller's writing.

Jong, Erica. *The Devil at Large: Erica Jong on Henry Miller*. New York, 1993. Jong's personal and biographical account, one of the best such studies of the writer.

Kersnowski, Frank L., and Alice Hughes. *Conversations with Henry Miller*. Jackson, Miss., 1995. A collection of interviews spanning 1956 to 1977, in which Miller discusses the subjects of art, the obscenity charges leveled against him, and life as an expatriate, among others.

Mailer, Norman, comp. *Genius and Lust: A Journey through the Major Writings of Henry Miller*. New York, 1976. Not a primary source, but the provocative and outspoken Mailer's analysis—and the backhanded dynamic of its praise and criticism of his subject—is interesting.

MARGARET MITCHELL'S
GONE WITH THE WIND

by Amanda Fields

When *Gone with the Wind* was published, it was an instant best-seller. The novel, which has never gone out of print, has succeeded in capturing a varied and devoted audience. When the book was first published by Macmillan in 1936, it sold a million copies within six months. In addition, its author, Margaret Mitchell, won the 1937 Pulitzer Prize, and the novel was made into one of the most popular films in American history.

The fascination of popular culture with *Gone with the Wind* lends authority to its appraisal as an epic. Numerous publications have attempted to imitate, parody, and add to the story in *Gone with the Wind*, including its film version. Mitchell did not like the film, but its popularity has made it nearly a hand-in-hand companion with the novel. In addition, sequels and parodies of the novel have been written, including Alice Randall's controversial novel, *The Wind Done Gone* (2002). In 1991 Alexandra Ripley's sequel, *Scarlett*, achieved best-seller status (and bad reviews), and eventually was made into a television miniseries. And the Atlanta Ballet included a version of *Gone with the Wind* in its 2002–2003 season. It is also worth noting that many Americans claim that the majority of their knowledge about the Civil War has come from this novel. Consequently, any critical attempt at this novel should be considered in relation to its popular appeal, the context from which it was written, and its controversial themes.

Margaret Mitchell, a journalist, began to write *Gone with the Wind* in 1926 and reluctantly gave it to a publisher in 1935. The manuscript was bought for $50,000 after a divisive discussion involving several editors—some thought it was overdone, sentimental, and didactic, while others considered the novel an epic. Perhaps the novel's enormous success and the effort put into creating it influenced Mitchell's decision not to publish another work; in fact, she demanded that all letters and evidence of other writing be destroyed upon her death.

Mitchell demonstrates a strong use of the elements of fiction in this novel. *Gone with the Wind* has a fast-moving and intriguing plot, despite its length. Although there are many characters, Mitchell is able to keep them separated and fresh in the minds of the reader. Perhaps this is in part because she succeeds in creating an entire world, one so full and compelling that the reader must recover back into reality after the final words of the lengthy book.

THE AMBIVALENT SCARLETT O'HARA

Gone with the Wind follows a young southern white girl, Scarlett O'Hara, through the Civil War. Scarlett undergoes several transformations through the plot, from a wealthy southern belle, to a widow, to a farmer, to a business owner, to the wife of the richest man in Atlanta. The story line centers on her personal life and struggles for independence; however, the theme of the dying culture and traditions of the South surrounds her every move.

Scarlett O'Hara's complex and often unappealing characteristics demonstrate the strength of Mitchell's anti-heroine. At the beginning of the novel, Scarlett plays the role of sweet southern belle with an agenda to be the most desirable of women. Men flock to her tiny waist and flirtatious manner, and many of the women hate her, for she can play the part better than all of them. What is significant to remember, however, is that Scarlett is playing a role that will help her receive what she believes she wants the most, and she succeeds in smoothly changing her role throughout the novel. In this sense, the book had a certain appeal for young white women who wanted to expand their choices in the 1930s. Yet Mitchell throws in a fresh complication, cleverly using the character of Melanie Wilkes as a foil to Scarlett. Melanie is sincere and kind, loving Scarlett no matter how many ways she offends the traditions she has grown up with. Melanie is also strong, enduring the awful ride from burning Atlanta with a newborn child and ready with a sword when Scarlett shoots a Yankee soldier. Yet Melanie seems perfectly content to be a gentle and wise "Southern lady," which is an interesting predicament for Mitchell's female readers, who may be faced with the desire to do anything they want but also desire to be fully accepted by others.

Within the boundaries of the white southern culture, Scarlett is impure, immoral, selfish, and fiercely concerned with always having what she needs, no matter what. In short, these complexities make Scarlett the intriguing and frustrating character who has enraptured millions of readers. It is possible that one could read the entire novel without cause for truly liking Scarlett O'Hara; however, another likely reaction is one of respect. The qualities mentioned above also translate to bravery, determination, and an admirable sense of independence and strength. And Scarlett's fallibility and humanity are shown by the mantra "I won't think about that now." This is a woman who has kept her family from starving, killed a man, and stolen her sister's beau for money. But she is also a woman who is able to adapt and continue to love her life and her family's land.

In the end, readers may not be sure who carries the torch of justice and who most certainly does not—who are the heroes and who are the enemies. While the main concern is Scarlett O'Hara, the vast world of characters and culture around her impinge upon the readers. *Gone with the Wind* allows readers to see the Civil War beyond black-and-white terms, literally and metaphorically. Mitchell's characterization of Scarlett O'Hara certainly aids this purpose.

Other readers, however, may argue that *Gone with the Wind* is at its core a love story. Although all kinds of love are presented in the novel—love for one's culture and values, love for a cause, love between people, love for money and class systems, love for an unchanging world—it is not a typical love story. Even though the film faces of Vivien Leigh (as Scarlett) and Clark Gable (as Rhett) are emblazoned into the myth of the novel as romantic, the text itself reveals Rhett Butler to be a supporting character. While he certainly is one of the strongest male characters in the novel, his purpose is to affect Scarlett rather than change or grow himself. He offers advice and reasoning; however, he is not very complex beyond this supporting purpose. Rhett also demonstrates traditionally feminine characteristics, such as an interest in verbally analyzing other people and a fastidious consciousness of dress and fashion. While a reader might be fascinated by Rhett's pursuit of Scarlett and her moments of submission with him, "love" does not ultimately seem like the appropriate word to describe their relationship. Granted, the question that pervades many readers' minds at the end of the novel is whether Scarlett and Rhett will get back together. However, Margaret Mitchell offered a telling response by refusing to write a sequel, claiming that the novel is complete as it stands. In addition, the concept of the dime store romance marks the lack of respect or serious criticism shown toward *Gone with the Wind* by intellectuals. However, if the novel is examined in light of the complex characterizations of the white women and the slaves, a rich trove of meaning becomes apparent.

RACE AND SEX: (DIS)EMPOWERMENT

One of the most controversial topics of Mitchell's novel is its offensive presentation of the black slaves. Readers might question the writer's beliefs about race relations when she uses an offensive portrayal, and Mitchell's awareness about her presentation is not clear. However, readers may also note the complexities of both southern white women and black male and female slaves, all victimized and enslaved by southern white men. Readers might interpret, also, the dynamics between the slaves and the white women, both in subjugated positions, both hurting each other as well. Mitchell shows that enslavement is always on the verge of being overthrown, that the white men of the Confederacy become impotent and ultimately are unable to solidify their power.

The white males in this book are by far the weakest characters. In an infamous scene, Confederate soldiers are moaning and dying in the dusty streets while doctors and citizens frantically rush around to help them. Readers bear witness not only to the tangible evidence of the death of a culture, but also to the helplessness of these men who have been complicit in building up an empire of oppression. It is to Mitchell's credit that Yankee men appear just as weak and simplistic, for it is not to be assumed by events in the book that anyone has truly been freed. Mitchell was able to imply both despair and hope from her 1926 vantage point. While a feminist interpretation must be careful to consider Mitchell's context in the 1930s, Mitchell seems aware of the subjugation of both slaves and women in the South.

Ironically, Mitchell pairs all the "weaker" traits of femininity with the males, a progressive emasculation that occurs throughout the book. For instance, Scarlett thinks of her first husband, Charles Hamilton, as a "pretty, flushed boy," one of the many who fawn upon her and whom she dominates from her submissive role. Frank Kennedy, her second husband, is seen as "an old maid in britches." While the men in the novel are weak and stereotypically feminine, Scarlett is both masculine and feminine, and she makes herself as free as possible to explore the strengths of both sets of traits.

Even as Scarlett recognizes the strengths of women like her mother, Ellen O'Hara, and, eventually, Melanie Wilkes, she is unable to acknowledge the strengths of the slaves. She is able to see beyond certain restrictions (such as those of women and terms of gentility) but not others (blacks and class). But readers do not need Scarlett's point of view to glean many of Mitchell's subtle characterizations. For example, Prissy, a slave who comes with Scarlett to Atlanta, is described as having a practiced smile of submission and a sly exterior of stupidity. Prissy's learned behavior and full awareness of it demonstrate her ability, just like Scarlett, to play a role and do her best to play it to her own advantage. Thus, an analysis of the novel's presentation of race relations would most certainly scrutinize the behaviors and coping mechanisms of the slaves and white women.

"TOMORROW IS ANOTHER DAY"

In the final sequence of *Gone with the Wind*, Scarlett O'Hara gazes at the house and the land (Tara) from which she draws a new strength and determination. Yet this scene also demonstrates her continued resistance to changing some of the basic principles of her life, despite her many transformations. She repeats a version of the phrase that has enabled her to avoid confronting many of the consequences of her decisions—"I'll think of it all tomorrow" (p. 1024). Yet her flaws uniquely enable her to thrive. In this final scene, Scarlett also links herself unswervingly to the culture whose boundaries she has consistently pushed through. While it seems certain that she will continue to survive, no matter what, Scarlett suddenly forms a solid connection between herself and the culture that has been destroyed. She yearns for Mammy, the house slave who has raised and worked with her, "Mammy, the last link with the old days" (p. 1024). In this sense, Scarlett has become a Confederate patriot, now that she sees what could be, and has been lost by the politics she once saw as so silly. Even those who opposed the war for various reasons (Scarlett because she did not have the opportunity to be educated about it, and Rhett because he was too educated about its complexities) eventually show a love for the culture and traditions that are being destroyed. Thus, this final scene depicts the very human ambiguities of Scarlett O'Hara's world, a world confronting the relevant complexities of class, culture, race, gender, and war.

FURTHER READING

Chadwick, Bruce. *The Reel Civil War: Myth-Making in American Film*. New York, 2001. A discussion of the abundance of films made about the Civil War and the perpetuation of Hollywood myths about American history. An intriguing read in relation to Mitchell's presentation of the Civil War era and the film's translation of Mitchell. Includes a bibliography and index.

Eskridge, Jane, ed. *Before Scarlett: Girlhood Writings of Margaret Mitchell*. Athens, Ga., 2000. A collection of Mitchell's writing: letters, fairy tales, short stories, plays, and journal entries.

Hanson, Elizabeth I. *Margaret Mitchell*. Boston, 1991. A brief biography that includes a selected bibliography and index.

Harwell, Richard, ed. *Margaret Mitchell's* Gone with the Wind *Letters: 1936–1949*. New York, 1976. For those interested in connecting a writer's personal life with his/her writings.

Mitchell, Margaret. *Lost Laysen*. Edited by Debra Freer. New York, 1996. A novella written when Mitchell was sixteen, discovered in the papers of Henry Love Angel, a close friend. Photos and a biography of their relationship are included.

Peacock, Jane Bonner, ed. *Margaret Mitchell: A Dynamo Going to Waste. Letters to Allen Edee, 1919–1921*. Atlanta, Ga., 1985. Of the relatively few surviving papers of Mitchell, these can be valuable when considering her writing, her personality, and her friendship with Edee.

Pyron, Darden Ashby, ed. *Recasting:* Gone with the Wind *in American Culture*. Gainesville, Fla., 1983. A collection of critical essays, ranging from the time of the novel's first publication to more current criticism.

Taylor, Helen. *Scarlett's Women:* Gone with the Wind *and Its Female Forms*. New Brunswick, N.J., 1989. Discusses the phenomenon of *Gone with the Wind*, with an emphasis on gender and race roles. Includes an intriguing discussion of several women's interpretations of the novel, as well as a bibliography and index.

Young, Elizabeth. *Disarming the Nation: Women's Writing and the American Civil War*. Chicago, 1999. Essays about women writers' presentations of the Civil War era (e.g., "The Rhett and the Black: Sex and Race in *Gone with the Wind*"). Includes a bibliography and index.

N. SCOTT MOMADAY

by Arnold E. Sabatelli

In 1969 a little known painter, poet, storyteller, and fiction writer of Kiowa descent won the Pulitzer Prize with his first novel, *House Made of Dawn* (1968). Since then N. Scott Momaday has been a prolific and steady presence in academic, literary, and Native American venues. His work has influenced and been largely responsible for what some have referred to as the Native American Renaissance, which includes such contemporary writers as Leslie Marmon Silko, Lousie Erdrich, and Sherman Alexie.

LIFE

Navarro Scott Mammedaty was born on 27 February 1934 in Lawton, Oklahoma, Kiowa country in southwestern Oklahoma. While well versed in oral narratives, histories, and Kiowa and other Native American literatures by a very young age, Momaday went on to study in a number of academic institutions. He spent a short time at the Virginia Military Academy but soon ended up studying at the University of New Mexico, where he received a B.A. degree in political science. He studied law at the University of Virginia but did not receive a degree. For a year he taught at the Apache reservation at Jicarilla before receiving a poetry fellowship to attend Stanford University. Here, under the guidance of the poet and critic Yvor Winters, he received M.A. and Ph.D. degrees in English. His dissertation was published by Oxford University Press as a critical edition of the poetry of Frederick Goddard Tuckerman (1965).

Momady gives frequent readings of his work and often combines them with discussions and speeches on various aspects of the Native American experience. He serves as a consultant for the National Endowment for the Humanities and the National Endowment for the Arts. His awards include a Guggenheim fellowship, the Academy of

N. Scott Momaday. (© *Corbis*)

American Poets Prize, the Pulitzer Prize, the Premio Letterario Internazionale Mondello, election into the Kiowa Gourd Clan, and honorary degrees from Yale and other American universities. He is a fellow of the American Academy of Arts and Sciences. Momaday has demonstrated his commitment to sustaining oral tradition and Indian culture, founding the Buffalo Trust, which places particular focus on teaching children about native histories, languages, and literature. For television, he was a commentator for the Ken Burns–Stephen Ives PBS series *The West* and also took part in the *This I Believe* series and the "Last Stand at Little Big Horn" episode of *The American Experience*. His voice is heard on many exhibits at the Museum of the American Indian at the Smithsonian Institution, and he has made numerous appearances on National Public Radio as a commentator on Indian affairs. His books have been translated into French, German, Italian, Russian, Japanese, and Spanish. He has taught at Berkeley and Stanford, and is currently Regents' Professor of the Humanities at the University of Arizona.

MULTICULTURALISM

Momaday has written several autobiographical works that deal directly with his Kiowa heritage and multicultural background, including *The Way to Rainy Mountain* (1969) and *The Names* (1976). His mother was of Cherokee and Euro-American descent, and during his childhood he was influenced by a range of cultural perspectives and languages—Navajo, San Carlos Apache, Anglo, Hispanic. In his work of both prose and poetry, *In the Presence of the Sun* (1992), Momaday explains that his early upbringing nurtured a love for Kiowa, Navajo, Jemez Pueblo, Spanish, and English words.

In Momaday's work, readers find themselves in a truly multicultural world. For the author, this is perfectly natural; there is no forced political agenda. It is simply the world he knows. In *House Made of Dawn*, in which a Jemez Pueblo veteran of World War II is imprisoned after murdering an albino whom he is convinced is a witch, the conflicts and interpenetrations of cultural paradigms and understandings become immediately apparent. In the long descriptive passages that open the novel, we view a young man running through a stark and powerful landscape, paying attention to everything. We concurrently view this same man many years later, hung over and disoriented, just returned to the landscape of his childhood and trying to sort through the forces that brought him there. Again and again in Momaday's work these fluid juxtapositions of different times bring to light his inherent assumptions about concepts of time and causality. For Momaday, Western constructs of linear time are at the very least problematic and quite possibly a reason for the deeper sickness that infects much of Western culture. Thus, in his fiction and poetry events from the past occur simultaneously with the present and even the future. These are not flashbacks in the traditional literary sense; rather, it is as if all times are occurring on the same plane.

Spanish and native and English words also coexist in Momady's work, for acknowledging the many languages people speak, the different ways of saying and seeing things, is an essential aspect of his worldview. His multicultural perspective is consistently fluid and natural, emphasizing in a nonjudgmental way that the world in which we live is far more vast and complex than any one cultural or linguistic perspective can account for.

FICTION

In 1968 Momaday's first novel, *House Made of Dawn*, took the literary world by storm as a wholly unique work of fiction. A young man schooled largely on reservations, an outsider to the literary scene of the times, had produced sparse, evocative passages reminiscent of Hemingway, complex shifts in time and place and point of view reminiscent of Faulkner, and cultural and narrative assumptions that were completely foreign to the mainstream. For the first time, the literary canon was opening its doors to the culmination of a long and extensive history of Native American literature that consisted of both oral and written narratives. In this work and throughout his career as a fiction writer, Momaday has consistently demonstrated the realities of Native American culture by blending together the many disparate forces at

work on the native consciousness. In *House Made of Dawn*, Abel, a World War II veteran and a tribal member, resides in several worlds at once. His downfall and his attempt to reemerge are emblematic of the struggles he has faced specifically because he straddles such often irresolvable forces. Abel struggles with alcoholism, sexual passion, and a litany of twentieth-century realities, the biggest perhaps being modern warfare. Momaday's portrait of Abel's plight explores the need for the traditions of his father as an antidote to the complexities of modernity. Never sentimental or overly romantic, *House Made of Dawn* casts a critical and poignant eye upon a world removed from its essence. This theme is continued in his next novel, *The Ancient Child* (1989), where we find a West Coast artist of Kiowa-Anglo descent trying to find stability at the midpoint of his life. Finally he is "healed" through a traditional ceremony that reconnects him with the bear spirit. His healer, a woman named Grey, is the ultimate multicultural entity, being of Navajo and Kiowa but also Mexican, French Canadian, Scotch, Irish, and English descent. In both of his major works of fiction, Momaday suggests that connection to the earth and healing are not relevant or available solely to Native Americans. His works reach outward to bring all humanity into their scope.

NONFICTION

For Momaday, the distinctions between fiction, poetry, and nonfiction are often self-consciously blurred. In his classic work *The Way to Rainy Mountain*, most commonly classified as a work of history, Momaday knits Kiowa tribal and private stories, history and descriptions of the land, and drawings into a text that does not fit neatly into any genre. The individual sentences are sparse and chantlike and rich in images. The drawings often occupy several pages in the midst of a story and move the text forward on their own. The narratives are extensive and frequently juxtaposed with italicized passages in the first person. While the work is accessible and very readable, it also invites further study into the rich background from which it springs. *The Journey of Tai-me* (1967) is an even more self-conscious experiment in creating a new genre that mixes poetry, fiction, and nonfiction elements. Amid private and public "narratives," Momaday also includes his own poetry and artwork. In *The Man Made of Words: Essays, Stories, Passages* (1997), he collects stories and essays written over thirty years that focus on language, the land, and the relationship between Native Americans and whites. Memorable portraits include one of Jay Silverheels (Tonto in the *Lone Ranger* television series) and a favorite dog, Cacique del Monte Chamiza (Momaday's black Labrador retriever).

POETRY

Over the years Momaday's poetry has garnered as much acclaim as his fiction and nonfiction. His most significant collections include *The Gourd Dancer* (1976), which includes the formerly published *Angle of Geese and Other Poems* (1974), *In the Presence of the Sun* (1992), and the poetry section of *In the Bear's House* (1999). His poems frequently focus on individual images or events, such as ceremonial shields, sacred landscapes, and individual moments in Kiowa or Navajo history, and they are frequently accompanied by his own provocative drawings. His poems more often than not work together toward a larger end, reflecting and emphasizing small parts of a broader theme that come to fruition when viewed within the context of the whole work. This very structure—of small, subtle moves toward a final meaning—demonstrates Momaday's fundamentally non-Western approach to literature. That said, Momaday's poems also integrate traditional poetic gestures such as rhyme and structure, so while the work strikes the reader as highly original and non-Western, it also demonstrates a synthesis of nonnative poetic values.

In the Bear's House, for instance, combines an intense focus on the image of the bear from a Kiowa perspective—where Bear represents all that is wild and untamed in the world—with Momaday's own personal connection with his bear spirit. His Indian name, Tsaoaitlee, he explains, means "Rock-tree boy," Rock-tree being the Devil's Tower in Wyoming where, in Kiowa legend, a young Kiowa boy was transformed into a bear and his sisters into the stars of the Big Dipper. In the book's "Bear-God Dialogues," poetry, prose, and Momaday's haunting, expressionistic paintings of bears are blended together. The old stories, legends, and myths are, for Momaday, quite real and relevant, with far-reaching importance for him and others. The bears of his poetry are holy and sacred creatures that speak to him and fill him with awe and deep mystery and a love for wilderness. The poems speak directly and concisely to this point and are at their strongest when read together with the art, drama, fiction, and nonfiction of this short work. The opening poem of the poetry section, "The Bear," also opens a number of his other collections, which suggests that not only do the integral sections of a book like *In the Bear's House* work in concert with each other but that the complete body of his work might well be seen as a single artistic expression. Momaday himself has said on numerous occasions that

he views his writing and painting as one continuous, lifelong work.

POWER OF THE IMAGE AND THE NATIVE AMERICAN VIEW

Grounded in a rich multicultural world, Momaday fuses together genre, voice, and structure in artistic works unlike any other contemporary artist. The inclusion of his own drawings and paintings is one of the more striking elements of Momaday's work. In his public appearances, the resonant, chantlike music of his own voice also makes a powerful contribution to the whole experience of his art. With these especially, the reader is forced momentarily to step outside the highly abstract realm of language and interact with pure image or sound. Further, Momaday's simple and understated language often puts abstraction aside and dwells instead on a fertile combination of images. That his poetry takes a range of forms, from traditional Kiowa chant to rhymed quatrains and free verse, is further testimony to his multicultural heritage. At the core of all his work is a passionate commitment to the hope that Native American ideals and views can heal and guide all of us through dark times.

[*See also* Native American Literature.]

WORKS

The Journey of Tai-me (1967)
House Made of Dawn (1968)
The Way to Rainy Mountain (1969)
Angle of Geese and Other Poems (1974)
The Gourd Dancer (1976)
The Names: A Memoir (1976)
The Ancient Child (1989)
In the Presence of the Sun: Stories and Poems, 1961–1991 (1992)
Circle of Wonder: A Native American Christmas Story (1994)
The Man Made of Words: Essays, Stories, Passages (1997)
In the Bear's House (1999)

FURTHER READING

Isernhagen, Hartwig, ed. *Momaday, Vizenor, Armstrong: Conversations on American Indian Writing.* Norman, Okla., 1998. An excellent resource for comparing viewpoints on Native American literature.

Frischkorn, Craig. "The Shadow of Tsoai: Autobiographical Bear Power in N. Scott Momaday's *The Ancient Child* (1989)." *Journal of Popular Culture* 3 (autumn 1999): 23. Frischkorn traces the connection between the image of the bear child in *The Ancient Child* and Momaday's own discovery of his ancestral bear nature.

Schubnell, Matthias, ed. *Conversations with N. Scott Momaday*. Jackson, Miss., 1997. Discussions with Momaday from 1970 through 1993 show the breadth and development of the author's thought. Some discussions move abruptly into heady abstraction.

Stevens, Jason W. "Bear, Outlaw, and Storyteller: American Frontier Mythology and the Ethnic Subjectivity of N. Scott Momaday." *American Literature* 73 (September 2001): 599. Stevens traces Momaday's focus on Indian identity as a negotiation between external and indigenous elements based in oral tradition.

Woodard, Charles L., ed. *Ancestral Voice: Conversations with N. Scott Momaday*. Lincoln, Neb., 1989. Each of the six conversations focuses on one aspect of the subject's life. Woodard includes pertinent examples of Momaday's writing as well as twenty-three illustrations of his pictorial art.

MARIANNE MOORE

by Brett C. Millier

For a long time the literary esta-blishment did not know quite what to make of the poems of Marianne Moore. Moore herself said that she thought of her work as poetry only because there did not seem to be any other category in which to place it, and in her best-known poem, "Poetry," she admitted of her subject, "I, too, dislike it." American popular culture embraced that apparent ambivalence, and Moore became famous late in her life—even a celebrity—without her best work being widely read. Feminist reclamations of neglected women writers, as well as reappraisals of the modernist movement in general, have revealed her unique contribution to modern poetry and to the English language, and she is

Marianne Moore. (*Photograph by George Platt Laynes. Courtesy of the Library of Congress*)

now considered an equal among the great modernist poets of her generation: Ezra Pound, T. S. Eliot, William Carlos Williams, Wallace Stevens.

Moore's idiosyncratic art is the result of a powerful tension in her nature. The child of a conservative and religious family, reserved in manner, fastidious in matters of propriety and decorum, she was at the same time a committed revolutionary in literary style, an early feminist, and an independent moral thinker. With Victorian personal modesty, she deployed a fierce intellect, extensive and eclectic reading, diligent work habits, and abiding self-confidence in the making of a literary career. Passionately interested in the world around her, she never married, and her poems show no abiding interest in sexuality. Personally and politically conservative, she was a social liberal and an early supporter of the civil rights movement. She tolerated in her friends lapses in judgment and values that she would not tolerate in herself: Ezra Pound's anti-Semitism appalled her, and she often worried about her young friend Elizabeth Bishop's liberal politics and alcohol abuse. She was fond

of W. H. Auden, despite the excesses of his personal life. Sincerity and authen-ticity, self-discipline, grace under pres-sure, and concentrated attentiveness were virtues that she celebrated in her poems—both in their composition and their content—and pursued in her life. Immune to the influence of literary fashion, she resolutely pursued her own goals of "humility, concentration and gusto" in the production of rigorously crafted poems that even today come off the page as sharp and fresh as crystal, and as uniquely her own.

A CLOSE-KNIT FAMILY

Marianne Craig Moore was born in Kirkwood, Missouri, outside St. Louis, on 15 November 1887. Her mother, Mary Warner Moore, had left John Milton Moore, Marianne's father, a few months before Marianne's birth, and had moved to the home of her widowed father, the Reverend John Riddle Warner. Marianne and her older brother, Warner, were young children in their grandfather's house, the parsonage of a Presbyterian church, where their mother served as hostess and housekeeper to the well-known minister until his death in 1893. Mrs. Moore next moved the family to an uncle's home in western Pennsylvania, and then to Carlisle, outside Philadelphia, in 1895. There Mrs. Moore raised her children alone, in the context of a supportive church community and sturdy Presbyterian values. The family was very close, and their later letters reveal a complex and playful social world, complete with nicknames and alternative identities. Mrs. Moore was the unchallenged authority in the family and remained a powerful influence on her daughter's moral thinking and poetic practice. She was ambitious about the education of her children, who attended the Metzger Institute in Carlisle, where she was employed as a teacher. The family's first separation came when Warner left for Yale in 1904. Although Warner never again lived at home, and in 1918 married a woman of whom his mother disapproved, the bond between the family members remained essentially unbroken until Mrs. Moore's death. Warner followed his grandfather's example and became a Presbyterian minister.

Marianne left home in 1905 to spend four years in college at Bryn Mawr. While there, Moore made use of a first-rate academic program—she majored in biology and histology—and a challenging social milieu to make herself into a writer and a woman of the world. She published poems and stories continuously in the college's literary magazine and visited New York City, catching a glimpse of that hub of American modernist art and thought. She left college in 1909 convinced that she would indeed be a poet. Without means, however, and with little inclination to leave her mother behind, Moore returned home to Carlisle after graduation, where she taught for a time at the Carlisle Indian School (and crossed paths with the Olympian Jim Thorpe, the school's most famous graduate) and took classes in typing and shorthand at the Carlisle Commercial College. In the summer of 1910 she worked at a camp school in Lake Placid, New York; in 1911 she and her mother traveled for the first time to England and cemented their lifelong Anglophilia. By 1912 she was beginning to publish poems in the most important journals of the day. In 1915 Moore became friends with the poet Hilda Doolittle, whom Ezra Pound would rechristen H.D. H.D. and her wealthy friend Bryher (Winifred Ellerman McPherson) would provide Moore with crucial moral and financial support for the rest of her life.

In the fall of 1915, Moore made an important trip alone to New York, during which she met many of the major writers and painters of the era, and visited museums and galleries where modernist art was being shown. In 1918, when her brother Warner became a U.S. Navy chaplain assigned to the Brooklyn Navy Yard, Moore and her mother took up residence in New York's Greenwich Village and Moore took a part-time job at the Hudson Park branch of the New York Public Library. Moore lived in New York and Brooklyn for the rest of her life, and her work is closely tied to the city.

THE DIAL AND OBSERVATIONS

Moore had a busy social life in her early years in New York, and became friends with the editors and publishers of the literary journal The Dial. Many of Moore's best early poems and most of her critical articles were published in this prestigious journal. She was its editor, and an important influence on how modernist work was received, from 1925 until the journal ceased publication in 1929.

Moore liked to say that she was surprised to receive in the mail in 1921 her own first book of poems, though there is evidence that she knew its publication was under way. H.D. and her then-husband, Richard Aldington, selected and printed the poems for the Egoist Press in London, under the title Poems. The book brought Moore's work to the attention of the critical establishment and was the occasion for important reviews by Eliot and Williams. While it gathers Moore's college poems and other work she would not reprint, the book also includes her earliest mature work, including "The Fish," "England," and the oft-revised "Poetry." In 1924 the Dial Press published Observations, which contained fifty-three poems (including most of those published in Poems) that Moore selected and arranged herself. Most critics consider this her first book.

Moore's poems are indeed rigorous, almost scientific, "observations" of the world in all its luminously significant detail. The word expresses her poetic practice in both its modes: rigorous seeing and selective description combined with deep (and often highly original) consideration of what is seen. Her eye, it is safe to say, is unique. Elizabeth Bishop called her the "World's Greatest Living Observer," and the title values the rigor of her looking and seeing while undervaluing the uniqueness of her perspective. Her friend Bryher remarked that Moore saw with her mind first, and the poet John Ashbery, perhaps her most direct inheritor in this regard, said that Moore's mind "moves in a straight line , . . . [but] does so over a terrain that is far from level." Her poems, composed always in complete and correct sentences, nonetheless proceed by association rather than open logic, and achieve much of their humor and effect by her deployment of antithesis, startling analogy, and surprising juxtaposition.

Moore's interpretations of the humans, animals, and landscapes around her are always moral. Like the aesthetic poets of a generation before, but with an utterly opposite result, Moore sought to embody the morality in her poetry in the aesthetic values of the poems themselves; like the younger modernist Ernest Hemingway, she expressed her ethical values—sincerity, authenticity, accuracy—in her style. Thus she is moral without being didactic; as her biographer, Charles Molesworth, noted, it is "more like the Augustan ideal of art conceived as an activity that seeks to instruct as well as delight, a subordinating of self-expression in order to tell people about the world and how to participate in it fully."

She considered most anything a potential subject for poetry, and most any piece of writing a potential source of inspiration or even quotation. The 1921 version of "Poetry" argues for " 'business documents and // schoolbooks' " as possible source material. Asked in 1924 to give an account of her influences, Moore began with canonical writers: Geoffrey Chaucer, Edmund Spenser, Samuel Johnson, Thomas Hardy, W. B. Yeats. But she went on to include books by contemporary sportswriters, a *National Geographic* guide to raising dogs, and the English journal *Punch*. The quoted sentence or phrase is perhaps the most characteristic aspect of Moore's work, and certain poems—"An Octopus" is the most successful example—are made up of extensive quoted material arranged not arbitrarily as in a cubist painting or a collage, but linked in an elaboration of meaning created by the almost prismatic juxtaposition of the remarks of different thinkers and writers on related ideas. High-culture and academic quotations stand alongside the words of popular and science writers. As the critic R. P. Blackmur wrote, quotations (and quotation marks) serve Moore as "boundaries for units of association which cannot be expressed by grammar or syntax." Her well-known poem "To a Snail" illustrates both her use of quotations and her drawing of moral analogy, in brief:

> If "compression is the first grace of style,"
> you have it. Contractility is a virtue
> as modesty is a virtue.
> It is not the acquisition of any one thing
> that is able to adorn,
> or the incidental quality that occurs
> as a concomitant of something well said,
> that we value in style,
> but the principle that is hid:
> in the absence of feet, "a method of conclusions";
> "a knowledge of principles,"
> in the curious phenomenon of your occipital horn.

Moore clearly sees in the unconscious "modesty" of the snail an analogy both to the realm of behavior—even deportment—and to the realm of writing. Notes in the back of the volume explain the sources of the quoted materials, and "the principle that is hid: / in the absence of feet" suggests the modernist values of compression and understatement in poetry and prose, values Moore embodied and used to great effect. The statement recalls (and predates) Ernest Hemingway's comment about his "iceberg" style, seven-eighths submerged.

Moore often disciplined her material in elaborate formal structures which are visible on the page but largely disappear when a poem is read aloud. She uses rhyme subtly, and her meter closely resembles the rhythm of elegant prose (several early reviewers questioned whether she was writing poetry at all); much of her verse is written in a form known as syllabics. Trusting her ear, she developed a pattern in which each line and each stanza contains a set number of syllables (exceedingly difficult to do, particularly in English), and the pattern is repeated throughout the poem. "The Fish" (the title of which begins the poem's first sentence) is an example:

> THE FISH
> wade
> through black jade.
>   Of the crow-blue mussel-shells, one keeps
>   adjusting the ash-heaps;
>   opening and shutting itself like
>
> an
> injured fan.
> The barnacles which encrust the side
> of the wave, cannot hide
>   there for the submerged shafts of the
>
> sun,
> split like spun
>   glass, move themselves with spotlight swiftness
>   into the crevices—
>   in and out, illuminating
>
> the
> turquoise sea
>   of bodies.

The poem continues in this pattern for five more stanzas, each with a rhyme in the first two lines (wade/jade; an/fan), a rhyme in the second pair of lines (side/hide) and a syllabic pattern of 1, 3, 9, 6, 8; twenty-seven syllables per stanza. Many of Moore's best poems employ some version of syllabics, including "The Steeple-Jack," "The Jerboa," and "Camellia Sabina," from *Observations*. Moore commented that her devotion to syllabics resulted from and expressed her "love of doing hard things," but the meticulous concentration that the form requires is also a value Moore often praises in her poems. Perhaps the most characteristic poem in the volume both embodies the form and expresses its value. "Critics and Connoisseurs" (in which the first line of each stanza has fourteen syllables, the second eight) begins with a statement: "There is a great amount of poetry in unconscious / fastidiousness." It ends with examples: first the studied movements of a swan in a stream at Oxford, then the labors of an ant.

I have seen this swan and
I have seen you; I have seen ambition without
understanding in a variety of forms. Happening to stand
   by an ant-hill, I have
      seen a fastidious ant carrying a stick north, south,
        east, west, till it turned on
      itself, struck out from the flower-bed into the lawn,
   and returned to the point
from which it had started. Then abandoning the stick as
   useless and overtaxing its
      jaws with a particle of whitewash—pill-like but
   heavy, it again went through the same course
     of procedure.
       What is
      there in being able
to say that one has dominated the stream in an attitude of
   self-defense;
   in proving that one has had the experience
      of carrying a stick?

The poem illustrates Moore's quirky and often self-deprecating sense of humor; surely the concentration required to make this statement in this form is analogous to the concentration of the swan and the mysterious determination of the ant, and thus is implicated in the rhetorical question that ends the poem. Calling it "ambition without understanding" acknowledges the point at which conscious effort gives way to unwilled inspiration in creating a work of art, or "a great amount of poetry."

"The Steeple-Jack," also a syllabic poem, is a painterly celebration of a peaceful town, and of the similar steady competence of the "man in scarlet" who "lets / down a rope as a spider spins a thread," and the steady attention of a college student named Ambrose, studying on the hillside above the town, "Liking an elegance of which / the source is not bravado, he knows by heart the antique / sugar-bowl shaped summer-house of / interlacing slats, and the pitch / of the church // spire." Moore concludes from their example:

   The hero, the student,
    the steeple-jack, each in his way,
  is at home.

It could not be dangerous to be living
   in a town like this, of simple people,
who have a steeple-jack placing danger-signs by the church
while he is gilding the solid-
   pointed star, which on a steeple
stands for hope.

Moore also saw examples of this "unconscious / fastidiousness" in the more exotic animals she admired, and learned about at the circus and zoo and museums,

and in the pages of the *National Geographic.* "The Jerboa" (which she tells us in the poem is "a small desert rat") expresses the principle in its very existence, finding sufficiency where human beings would die of hunger and thirst:

    It
honors the sand by assuming its color;
   closed upper paws seeming one with the fur
   in its flight from a danger.

By fifths and sevenths,
in leaps of two lengths,
   like the uneven notes
   of the Bedouin flute, it stops its gleaning
      on little wheel castors, and makes fern-seed
      foot-prints with kangaroo speed.

Its leaps should be set
to the flageolet;
   pillar body erect
   on a three-cornered smooth-working Chippendale
      claw—propped on hind legs, and tail as third toe,
      between leaps to its burrow.

Moore's animals are not allegorical representations of human attributes, but carefully observed and appreciated entities unto themselves, whose graceful adaptation to circumstances and environment provide a natural analogy to the human struggle to find a "home," and a dignified way of living, in the modern and postmodern world.

SELECTED POEMS AND WHAT ARE YEARS

In 1935 Moore published *Selected Poems*, which Eliot arranged and introduced. While the book added only nine poems to *Observations*, Eliot's influence ensured that this would be the book to cement Moore's reputation as a major American voice. Eliot's introduction to the volume provided much of the critical vocabulary about Moore's work for several decades, and she retained Eliot's arrangement of the poems, opening with "The Steeple-Jack," in subsequent collections. A year later, Bryher arranged for the publication of a slim fine-press volume of five poems, which Moore called *The Pangolin and Other Verse*. These poems were republished in 1941 with a few additions, in the volume titled *What Are Years*. *Selected Poems* and *What Are Years* contain most of the work upon which Moore's contemporary reputation rests.

Reading these poems, it is easy to be dazzled (or perhaps dismayed) by their odd apparent subjects, gleaming surfaces, and twisting logic, and to miss the depth and range of feeling the poems express. For all their formal reserve and intellectual intensity, the poems come to terms with places (Virginia, Mount Rainier, New York) and with emotions with unflinching honesty and at times with Moore's distinctive humor. In his introduction to the *Selected Poems*, Eliot remarked that "for a mind of such agility . . . the minor subject . . . may be the best release for the major emotions." The long poem misleadingly titled "An Octopus" (the subject is not a sea creature but an ice formation: the leg-like arrangement of eight glaciers on the slopes of Mount Rainier, which Moore visited when her brother was stationed in Seattle) is one of the great poetic contemplations of nature of the twentieth century. The poem quotes extensively from pamphlets produced by the National Park Service to discuss the Greek values of formal elegance, behavior both "noble" and "fair," finally recognizing the limitation of the Greek view in the face of overwhelming nature: "Neatness of finish! Neatness of Finish! / Relentless accuracy is the nature of this octopus / with its capacity for fact." Moore never sentimentalizes nature, as her great sea poem, "A Grave," attests. Written while her brother was at sea as a navy chaplain, the poem looks unflinchingly at humankind's vulnerability to nature, making gentle fun of the more common romantic view of the seaside vacationer:

> Man looking into the sea,
> taking the view from those who have as much right to it as
>   you have to it yourself,
> it is human nature to stand in the middle of a thing,
> but you cannot stand in the middle of this;
> the sea has nothing to give but a well excavated grave.

Moore manages emotion in her poems as part of her sense of decorum; like the subject of her poem "The Student" (from *What Are Years*), she is passionately detached in her pursuit of accuracy, "too reclusive for / some things to seem to touch / him; not because he / has no feeling but because he has so much." Moore's best poems do not grapple with politics or current events, but remain steadfastly focused on things of concern to human beings in any era or circumstances. "What Are Years?" addresses itself to a desperate human condition which may or may not be contemporary ("What is our innocence, / what is our guilt? All are / naked, none is safe") but the solution it offers is timeless. Happiness belongs to that creature which "accedes to mortality"; be like the caged bird, the poem advises, who "though he is captive, / his mighty singing / says, satisfaction is a lowly / thing, how pure a thing is joy. / This is mortality, / this is eternity."

Perhaps the oddest production of Moore's early and middle years is her long experimental poem called "Marriage." The poem is a meticulous and dispassionate examination of a sacrament and mode of existence in which Moore did not participate. Composed of fragments and quotations arranged so that their meanings clash and refract rather than resolve, the poem is at times humorous and at times darkly satirical. Her tone is both fascinated and ambivalent and her discussion of the "institution, / perhaps one should say enterprise," recalls the much briefer, but no less intense and ironic contemplations, of Emily Dickinson, in its reflections on "a thing one has believed in . . . / requiring all one's criminal ingenuity / to avoid!" The poem takes an institutional view of sexuality, and generally laments the human vulnerability to "beauty" in the opposite sex. "Unhelpful Hymen!" the poem exclaims, and it also laments the woman's apparently inevitable submission to the man: "experience attests / that men have power / and sometimes one is made to feel it." For all its apparent sociological analysis, the poem admits defeat in its attempt to understand, and finally sees marriage as a loss and individual vulnerability to it as weakness. Moore herself later retreated from this view and acknowledged that the state of marriage was "the proper thing for everybody but *me*."

Critics have long remarked on Moore's reticence and the lack of personal revelation in her poems, and on her apparent interest in the self-protective strategies of animals. Alicia Ostriker remarked cogently that woman poets of this era did well to adopt an impenetrable and dispassionate tone if they wished to be accepted by the masculine critical establishment, which was quick to dismiss work that was too "emotional" or that verged on sentimentality. Moore's poem "The Pangolin" seems to recognize this tendency in herself: "Another armored animal," the poem begins. But it goes on to celebrate both the superior design of the anteater's body ("scale / lapping scale with spruce-cone regularity until they / form the uninterrupted central / tail-row!") and the creature's graceful and harmonious existence on the land: "stepping in the moonlight, / on the moonlight peculiarly, that the outside / edges of his hands may bear the weight and save the claws / for digging." The details implicitly contrast the graceful existence of the pangolin with the desperate struggle of humankind to achieve grace, "man slaving / to make his life more sweet." Far from rejecting the model of the armored animal, Moore's poems find positive moral analogies in perhaps the least cuddly or potentially sentimental creatures.

In addition to poems, Moore wrote a considerable amount of prose during her career, even after the demise of the *Dial*, for which she had produced most of her critical writing. She attempted a novel, though it was rejected by several presses and never completed, and wrote several plays. Her prose is as quirky as her poetry, and proceeds along the lines of associative thought as well. But her many reviews and essays about contemporary poets and writers illustrate her enormous critical intelligence and her wide reading, and her reviews of Stevens and Auden, for example, helped to solidify their reputations among critics. Moore collected her essays and reviews in *Predilections* in 1955, and her *Complete Prose* appeared in 1986.

QUIET YEARS IN BROOKLYN

By the time the *Selected Poems* appeared in 1935, Moore had retreated from the hurly-burly of New York literary life. After *The Dial* folded in 1929, she and her mother left Greenwich Village and Manhattan for the Clinton Hill section of Brooklyn. The last years of the Depression and the World War II period were quiet for Moore, as much of her time and emotional energy were spent caring for her aging mother. The volume of poetry Moore published in 1944 has the evocative title *Nevertheless* and contained only six poems. The title poem asserts "What is there // like fortitude!" and "The Wood-Weasel" and "Elephants" celebrate the moral intelligence of animals that humankind has undervalued. The volume closes with her personal statement on the complex morality of war, "In Distrust of Merits," perhaps her most political poem. The poem acknowledges the reasons for war: "O / star of David, star of Bethlehem, / O black imperial lion / of the Lord—emblem / of a risen world—be joined at last, be / joined. There is hate's crown beneath which all is / death; there's love's without which none / is king"; and it sees the irony in the men "fighting fighting fighting that where / there was death there may / be life." But the poem ends with the poet addressing herself with a plea for Christian self-examination and confession of the "Iscariot-like crime" of inaction: "There never was a war that was / not inward."

Moore's mother died in July 1947 at the age of eighty-five. Devastated by the loss of her closest friend and companion and an important editor and critic, Moore took several months to find her bearings. When she did, she buried herself in a long work of translation. Inspired by a natural affinity for the ideal of illustrating human morality through animal behavior, Moore undertook to render a version of the fables of the seventeenth-century French poet Jean de La Fontaine in English verse; she spent the next several years on this painstaking work. The

book was rejected by several publishers and eventually appeared to mixed reviews in 1954.

BASEBALL AND CELEBRITY

In the midst of the translation project, in 1951, Moore published her *Collected Poems*, and at last achieved widespread recognition. The book won all of the poetry prizes for that year, including the National Book Award, the Pulitzer Prize, and the Bollingen Prize, and the distinctive face of the poet—tiny and pale, fading red hair coiled about her head, black tricorn hat inevitably on top—became familiar to millions of Americans. She resumed an active schedule of readings and lectures, and continued to receive awards and prizes, including a Gold Medal from the National Institute of Arts and Letters, the nation's highest cultural organization, in 1953. In the spirit of this newfound recognition, she agreed to a request from the Ford Motor Company that she help to name its new car model due to appear with much fanfare in 1958. Moore's suggestions say less about the car than about the richness of her imagination: they range from "Silver Sword" to "Regna Racer" and "Turcotingo" to "Mongoose Civique" and "Utopian Turtletop." The car, of course, was eventually called the Edsel, after Henry Ford's late son.

Moore's late poems were often literally written by request and have an "occasional" feel. Critics have dismissed this work (a few have even ridiculed it), but these are the poems by which she was known in the last years of her life. Moore's love of baseball became famous with the publication of her charming doggerel on the Brooklyn Dodgers, "Hometown Piece for Messrs. Alson and Reese" (in the 1959 collection *O to Be a Dragon*), and "Baseball and Writing" (in the 1966 volume *Tell Me, Tell Me*), inspired, she said, by postgame broadcasts. The poems are decidedly light verse, but Moore is not the first writer to find charm and even poetry in the bantering language of baseball. After the departure of the Dodgers and Giants for California after the 1957 season, Moore became a fan of both the Mets (and of the team's manager Casey Stengel in particular) and the Yankees. She attended a World Series game in 1963 with the writer George Plimpton and the poet Robert Lowell, an account of which Plimpton published the following year in *Harper's*. Her association with the game culminated in her being invited by Yankees owner Bill Burke to throw out the first pitch of the 1966 season at Yankee Stadium. In June of that year she was featured on the cover of *Esquire* magazine as one of eight "Unknockables"—a tiny, wizened figure dwarfed by the boxer Joe Louis and the singer Kate Smith, along with Jimmy Durante, Helen Hayes, and Norman Thomas, among others.

In 1965 the deterioration of her Brooklyn neighborhood forced Moore to move back to Manhattan, and she spent the last years of her life once again in Greenwich Village. In the care of a housekeeper and then a nurse, Moore continued to make personal appearances, including an interview with Joe Garagiola on NBC's *Today Show* in 1967, and to receive honors and awards, including eleven honorary degrees from Harvard, Princeton, and several other prestigious universities. She became a fellow of the Academy of American Poets in 1965, and a chevalier of the French Legion of Honor in 1968. Elaborate and well-publicized celebrations were held on her seventy-fifth, eightieth, and eighty-third birthdays, and Moore published articles, reviews, and poems in the popular press throughout the 1960s. Moore apparently enjoyed the trappings of celebrity, but the public's embrace of her as a quaint, eccentric, and comically dignified baseball enthusiast did much to obscure the value of her serious work and her contributions to American modernist poetry.

In 1967, to coincide with Moore's eightieth birthday, Macmillan and Viking published her *Complete Poems*. The book startled her faithful readers with its major revisions of long-published poems (most famously, "Poetry" was reduced from nearly thirty lines to three). Bedridden for most of the last two years of her life, Marianne Moore died on 5 February 1972, at the age of eighty-four. After her death, the figure of the celebrity faded from memory, and the works remained to speak of a fierce and revolutionary artist, whose poetry enables readers to participate in her singular imaginative vision.

[*See also* Writing as a Woman in the Twentieth Century.]

SELECTED WORKS

POETRY

Poems (1921)
Observations (1924)
Selected Poems (1935)
The Pangolin and Other Verse (1936)
What Are Years (1941)
Nevertheless (1944)
Collected Poems (1951)
The Fables of La Fontaine (1954)
Like a Bulwark (1956)
O to Be a Dragon (1959)
A Marianne Moore Reader (1961)
The Arctic Ox (1964)
Tell Me, Tell Me (1966)
The Complete Poems of Marianne Moore (1967)

PROSE

Predilections (1955)
The Complete Prose of Marianne Moore (1986)

FURTHER READING

Bishop, Elizabeth. "Efforts of Affection." In her *Complete Prose*. New York, 1984. A wonderful portrait of Moore in the middle years of her life.

Costello, Bonnie. *Marianne Moore: Imaginary Possessions*. Cambridge, Mass., 1981. Brilliant close analysis of Moore's poems.

Garrigue, Jean. *Marianne Moore*. Minneapolis, 1965. The best short introduction to Moore's imagination and craft.

Hadas, Pamela White. *Marianne Moore: Poet of Affection*. Syracuse, N.Y., 1977. Fine critical study of the poems, by a poet.

Merrin, Jeredith. *An Enabling Humility: Marianne Moore, Elizabeth Bishop and the Uses of Tradition*. Brunswick, N.J., 1990. Excellent study of Moore and her close friend Bishop, and their relationship to inherited poetic conventions.

Molesworth, Charles. *Marianne Moore: A Literary Life*. Boston, 1990. The excellent (and only) critical biography of Moore.

Nitchie, George W. *Marianne Moore: An Introduction to the Poetry*. New York, 1969. An early critical study of the poems.

Schulman, Grace. *Marianne Moore: The Poetry of Engagement*. Urbana, Ill., 1986. Monograph on Moore's work by a poet and friend of Moore's.

Tomlinson, Charles, ed. *Marianne Moore: A Collection of Critical Essays*. Englewood Cliffs, N.J., 1970.

TONI MORRISON

by Kristine Yohe

If Toni Morrison were to draw a map of her journeys of personal and creative exploration, the result would show many overlapping trajectories. Although Morrison has lived most of her life in the Northeast and Midwest, her parents' origins in the South, particularly Georgia and Alabama, have deeply influenced her cultural awareness. After growing up in Lorain, Ohio, Morrison attended college in Washington, D.C.; had an extended stay in the Caribbean (her former husband's home); did graduate work and editing in upstate New York; taught for a time in Houston, Texas; and even traveled to Stockholm, Sweden, to receive the Nobel Prize—yet she has lived in New York City or its vicinity for the bulk of her adult life. Likewise, her literary works span the country and even the

Toni Morrison. (*Photograph by Helen Marcus. Courtesy of the Library of Congress*)

hemisphere, the settings frequently drawn from her own experiences in the Midwest, the South, the Caribbean, Florida, New York City, and Oklahoma.

Morrison's real life landscapes permeate her fictional works, with characters exploring their geographic possibilities simultaneously with their personal and emotional treks. The characters often search for self through physical relocation when what they really need, Morrison demonstrates, is to take a serious look inside themselves, to take the essential journey within. This literary emphasis on the metaphysical quest seems also to apply to Morrison herself. An intensely private person, she only occasionally reveals any personal details about her life, such as when, in her published 1985 conversation with fellow African-American woman novelist Gloria Naylor, she stated that she has rarely felt a need for travel: "My interior life is so strong that I never associate anything important to any other place." Two years later, in an interview appearing in *Essence* magazine, Morrison said something similar in

the context of her intense focus on her work—which she found eminently satisfying—and her accompanying absence of need for an "elaborate social life." She stated simply, "I don't go anywhere to be happy." In other words, Morrison's emotional journeying has been extensive enough that she feels little need to search for her place externally. Apparently because she is comfortable inside herself, she is at home wherever she is.

Nevertheless—or perhaps consequently—homelessness is a major theme in her novels, ranging from the Breedlove family being put "out*doors*" in *The Bluest Eye* (1970), to the land-grabbing in *Song of Solomon* (1977) and *Jazz* (1992), to the denial of sanctuary suffered by the migrants in *Paradise* (1998). Throughout Morrison's works, a sense of place is profound, with search for home a frequent theme. This focus seems to spring simultaneously from her own deep roots in her Ohio hometown as well as her parents' acute awareness that they needed to leave the South for safer possibilities in the North. A southern sensibility pervades her work and accounts for her characters' sometimes bifurcated points of view about the South: it is home, but it is also the site of profound oppression.

Morrison's novels also include a deep awareness of history and culture, and their time frames range from the bleakest days of slavery and its aftermath, the mid-to late 1800s, as in *Beloved* (1987); to the era of her own childhood, the 1930s and 1940s, as in *The Bluest Eye*; to the late 1970s in *Tar Baby* (1981). Although not engaged in a decade-by-decade treatment of African-American history as August Wilson is for drama, Morrison still writes novels set in some of the most momentous eras of U.S. history. In addition to covering enslavement, she writes of World War I in *Sula* (1974); of the influence of the civil rights movement on Middle America, as in *Paradise*; and about Reconstruction and the Great Migration in *Paradise* and *Jazz*, respectively.

EARLY LIFE AND EDUCATION

Surrounded by family, Chloe Anthony Wofford grew up in Lorain, Ohio, a midwestern steel town on Lake Erie, west of Cleveland, where she was born at home on 18 February 1931. The second-oldest child, she shared her home with her parents, George Wofford and Ramah Willis Wofford; three siblings, Lois, George, and Raymond; and her maternal grandparents.

Her mother's parents, John Solomon Willis and Ardelia Willis, provided a vibrant southern link for Morrison, in part through their background as sharecroppers in Greenville, Alabama, where they lost their land around 1900. In approximately 1912 they joined other African Americans in the Great Migration, seeking greener pastures further north. Initially stopping over in Kentucky, where John Solomon Willis worked in a coal mine and Ardelia Willis washed clothes, the family later continued on to Lorain, mainly to find improved educational opportunities for their children.

As a young man, Morrison's father fled his home in Cartersville, Georgia, where he and his family had also been sharecroppers and where he had suffered terrible racial oppression that left him with an eternal antipathy for whites. Well into adulthood, he retained a negative impression of his Georgia roots, although he returned regularly to visit family members. Ironically, as Morrison described it in a 1998 interview with Carolyn Denard, his behavior was the opposite of her mother's, as Ramah Wofford spoke positively and nostalgically of her early years in the South but never returned, presumably out of fear.

As part of an apparently nurturing environment, Morrison's childhood was saturated with stories of and from the South, and she has said in several interviews that ghost stories, jokes, tales, music, and other elements of African-American folk culture were staples in her household. Additional influences came from Morrison's Roman Catholic upbringing, as well as from her grandmother's keeping a dream book in which she recorded and interpreted the symbols of dreams for "playing the numbers."

Also influential on Morrison's development was the fact that the community where she grew up was multicultural. Lorain was not large enough for a segregated educational system; her neighborhood and schools were integrated and included immigrants of many origins. And so at the beginning of her first-grade year, Morrison had the distinction of being not only the lone African American but the sole reader in the classroom. She has said that she did not personally experience racism in a disturbing way until she was older, when dating separated the races more clearly.

During this time, part of which covered the era of the Great Depression (from roughly 1929 to 1939), Morrison's hardworking parents sometimes struggled to make ends meet. One poignant example is that when one month they were unable to pay the rent on their house, the hostile landlord tried to burn it down with the family inside. All along, her father held a variety of jobs, often three at a time, including welding in a shipyard and a steel mill, working in building and road construction and even washing cars. Her mother—who was active in her church and sang in the choir—mostly worked in the home while her children were of school age. When Morrison was in college and graduate school, however, her mother often took menial jobs to help support her daughter financially. Her father died in 1975, her mother in 1994.

From childhood, Morrison was fascinated with books, even working as a student helper at the Lorain Public Library. She also earned money by doing jobs such as cleaning the houses of some of the white families in town, which, she has said, was not always a pleasant task for her. In addition, for a time she aspired to become a professional dancer. That did not happen, but she did manage to become the first person in her family to attend college.

After Morrison graduated with honors from Lorain High School in 1949, she moved to Washington, D.C., to attend Howard University, one of the most prestigious historically black universities. Intending to become a teacher, Morrison majored in English and minored in classics. In addition, while at Howard she adopted the name Toni from her middle name, Anthony. She has explained on several occasions that she dropped her given name, Chloe, because her classmates found it difficult to pronounce. While in college, Morrison also joined the Howard University Players, an acting troupe, and traveled throughout the South, getting a firsthand look at the region her parents and grandparents had told her about. She graduated with a B.A. degree from Howard in 1953.

Morrison then continued her education by pursuing her master's degree in English at Cornell University in Ithaca, New York, where she relocated shortly after graduating from Howard. She received her M.A. degree in 1955; her master's thesis was on the theme of suicide in the literature of William Faulkner and Virginia Woolf.

PERSONAL ADULTHOOD AND PROFESSIONAL CAREER

After leaving Cornell, Morrison moved to Houston to take a position teaching English at Texas Southern University. She stayed there two years, learning more, she has said, about southern African-American perspectives. In 1957 she returned to Washington, D.C., and Howard University, where she became an English instructor, a position she retained until 1964. During this time she met such future famous African Americans as Andrew Young (eventual mayor of Atlanta and ambassador to the United Nations) and Amiri Baraka (future poet). In addition, her students included the civil rights activist Stokely Carmichael and Claude Brown, who would later write *Manchild in the Promised Land* (1965). She also became involved with a writers' group while at Howard, which she has credited with starting her on the road to becoming a novelist.

Also at Howard, Toni Morrison met her future husband, Harold Morrison, whom she married in 1958. Originally from Jamaica, Harold Morrison had a career as an architect. The couple had two sons, Harold Ford, born in 1961, and Slade Kevin, born in 1964. During their marriage, they traveled to the Caribbean where, she has said, they had a long-term stay at one point. The marriage ended in divorce in 1964, while she was still pregnant with her second son, and Morrison generally declines to speak further of it. Around this same time, she took a trip to Europe.

After her divorce Morrison left Washington and returned with her sons to her parents' home in Lorain, Ohio, where they stayed for almost a year and a half before relocating to Syracuse, New York. There, Morrison began her editing work with Random House, first as a textbook editor and then as a senior editor at the New York City offices. She was an editor with Random House for almost the next twenty years, not leaving until 1983, and there she worked with such notable African-American writers as Henry Dumas, Angela Davis, Gayl Jones, Leon Forrest, June Jordan, Toni Cade Bambara, and Muhammad Ali. It was also during her early years in editing that Morrison became more serious about her own writing, which she has said came about in part because of her solitary existence as a single parent living away from her extended family. After many rejections, she finally managed to publish *The Bluest Eye*, her first novel, in 1970.

Morrison's work as a Random House editor included *The Black Book*, an anthology of African-American culture, almost a scrapbook, which was published in 1974. Although Morrison does not get formal editing credit—her name is not on the book, which was officially edited by Middleton Harris—she was greatly involved with its compilation. This experience exposed her to important and, for her, influential, relics of black history, including the story of Margaret Garner, which would inspire *Beloved* many years later.

While employed full time by Random House, Morrison also had several part-time teaching positions in English and creative writing. These ranged from a post at the State University of New York at Purchase in the early 1970s; to Yale University in the mid-1970s; and to Bard College, Rutgers University, and Stanford University thereafter. After her resignation from editing in 1983, she took a full-time teaching position as the Albert Schweitzer Professor of the Humanities at the State University of New York at Albany, where she stayed for the next five years. Since 1989, Morrison has been the Robert F. Goheen Professor in the Humanities at Princeton University, where she is affiliated with the programs in creative writing and African-American studies. She also directs the Princeton Atelier, a collaborative, interdisciplinary program focused on artistic creation that emphasizes connecting visiting artists with Princeton faculty and students.

Since 1970 Morrison has written and published seven novels—*The Bluest Eye, Sula, Song of Solomon, Tar Baby, Beloved, Jazz,* and *Paradise*—as well as a book of literary criticism, *Playing in the Dark: Whiteness and the Literary Imagination* (1992). Her 1993 *Nobel Prize acceptance speech* appeared in a single volume from Knopf in 1994. Upon her receipt in 1996 of the National Book Foundation Medal for Distinguished Contribution to American Letters, Morrison delivered a speech, "The Dancing Mind," also published in a slim separate volume by Knopf in 1996.

In addition, she edited a collection about Anita Hill—*Race-ing Justice, En-gendering Power: Essays on Anita Hill, Clarence Thomas, and the Construction of Social Reality* (1992)—and co-edited, with Claudia Brodsky Lacour, a work about O. J. Simpson, *Birth of a Nation'hood: Gaze, Script, and Spectacle in the O. J. Simpson Case* (1997). In 1998 she edited two volumes of James Baldwin's collected work for the Library of America. In 1996 and 1999 she edited a posthumous collection and a novel by Toni Cade Bambara.

Morrison also wrote a racially ambiguous short story, "Recitatif," published in 1983, as well as a play about the life of Emmett Till, *Dreaming Emmett*, performed in 1986 but never published. Morrison wrote the lyrics for two choral works, one in 1992 for Kathleen Battle, "Honey and Rue," composed by André Previn, and one in 1997 for Jessye Norman, "Sweet Talk," composed by Richard Danielpour. She also has written book chapters and magazine and journal articles for periodicals ranging from *The New York Times Magazine* to the *Michigan Quarterly Review*. In another direction, she co-wrote, with her son Slade Morrison, two children's books—*The Big Box* in 1999 and *The Book of Mean People* in 2002—with an agreement with Scribner to produce six more works for children, all inspired by Aesop's fables. The first of these, *Who's Got Game?: The Ant or the Grasshopper?*, appeared in 2003. Finally, in an on-line interview in May 2000 conducted by the *Oprah* show, Morrison stated that she had just begun to write a new novel, which is expected in the fall of 2003.

A prolific and flexible writer, Morrison is best known as a novelist. Her seven works of fiction cover a wide range of topics, emotions, characters, and settings. However, they share a number of thematic approaches, most notably a stress on the essential qualities of community connections, including family relationships, as well as on the importance of history. Each novel is also geographically oriented, as Morrison creates characters constantly on the go, exploring their physical worlds while also learning how crucial it is to venture into the internal landscape, into what she has called their "interior lives."

AWARDS AND RECOGNITIONS

After having some difficulty in finding a publisher for *The Bluest Eye*, her first novel, Morrison has found gradually increasing success as a writer, including strong critical acclaim and increasing attention from scholars. This first novel was itself well received, with overall positive reviews in *The New York Times*, *The New Yorker*, and elsewhere. *Sula* met with an even more encouraging response and greater sales when it was published in 1973. It was excerpted in *Redbook*, named as an alternate for the Book-of-the-Month Club, received the Ohioana Book Award in 1975, and was nominated for the National Book Award the same year.

In 1977, Morrison's stock rose further as *Song of Solomon* won the National Book Critics Circle Award and the American Academy and Institute of Arts and Letters Award. It also was named as a main selection by the Book-of-the-Month Club, making Morrison the

first African-American author to receive that honor since Richard Wright's *Native Son* in 1940. The following year, a PBS documentary appeared focusing entirely on Morrison. In 1980 she was appointed by President Jimmy Carter to the National Council on the Arts.

After *Tar Baby* was published in 1981 and appeared on *The New York Times* best-seller list, it sold well but was not reviewed as positively as expected, apparently in part because of its experimental and lush writing style. Nevertheless, it propelled Morrison to the cover of *Newsweek* magazine for 30 March 1981, which made her the first African-American woman to be so featured since Zora Neale Hurston in 1943. Also in 1981, Morrison was elected to the American Academy and Institute of Arts and Letters. In 1985 she received the New York State Governor's Arts Award.

The publication of her fifth novel, *Beloved*, in 1987, resulted in the greatest acclaim yet for Morrison. Although nominated for the National Book Award, it did not win, and nearly fifty African-American writers and critics signed a letter of protest, which was published in *The New York Times*. Yet *Beloved* did receive the Pulitzer Prize for fiction in 1988, as well as the Robert F. Kennedy Memorial Book Award, the Melcher Book Award, the Lyndhurst Foundation Award, and the Elmer Holmes Bobst Award.

Also in 1988, Morrison received the National Organization for Women's Elizabeth Cady Stanton Award, as well as the Before Columbus Foundation Award. The following year she won the Commonwealth Award in Literature from the Modern Language Association of America. In 1990 Morrison received the Chianti Ruffino Antico Fattore International Literary Prize. *Jazz*'s arrival in 1992 was warmly received, and it appeared on *The New York Times* best-seller list simultaneously with her nonfiction work, *Playing in the Dark: Whiteness and the Literary Imagination*. Some readers were less enthralled with *Jazz* than they had been with *Beloved*, although the critics were generally positive.

Then, in December 1993, Toni Morrison reached the capstone of her career, attaining the highest literary accolade possible: the Nobel Prize in literature. This distinction was made even sweeter by the fact that Morrison was the first African-American recipient and only the eighth woman in the world honored in this way. Morrison has said in interviews that she was especially pleased to have received this award while she was able to enjoy it with her mother, Ramah Wofford, who was still living—although she died a short time later, in February 1994. In a 1998 interview with Charlie Rose on the Public Broadcasting System, Morrison said of receiving the Nobel that she "felt weak, representative, patriotic," as well as seeing herself (in now familiar geographical-cultural terms) as powerfully emblematic of Ohio and African-American culture.

In 1996, Morrison received the National Book Foundation Medal for Distinguished Contribution to American Letters. Her seventh novel, *Paradise*, was published in January 1998. This work also received positive reviews and earned high sales, made even stronger by its participation in Oprah's Book Club shortly after its publication. In 2000 Morrison received the National Humanities Medal from President Bill Clinton.

THE BLUEST EYE

Morrison's first novel focuses on a forlorn young African-American girl, Pecola Breedlove, who believes that her devastating world will improve substantially if only she can wish and pray hard enough to make her eyes turn blue. The novel (whose germ came from someone she knew in childhood) originated from a short story Morrison had written during the early 1960s in a writing group, to which she has said she sought refuge from her troubled marriage. Told primarily from the points of view of two other young black girls, Claudia and Frieda MacTeer, *The Bluest Eye* is set in Lorain, Ohio, Morrison's hometown. Through the narration, which is primarily Claudia's, the novel creates startling contrasts between the sometimes bleak but always loving MacTeer household and that of the Breedlove family, which is quickly unraveling. Framed by the Dick and Jane story of an elementary primer, this novel examines the tensions between the ideal and the real in American culture.

Although the MacTeers have financial hardships of their own, their relatively stable environment becomes a brief haven for Pecola when her family loses its home. During Pecola's stay at the MacTeer home, she displays her fixation with blue eyes, in part through her fondness for drinking milk from a cup with a picture of Shirley Temple. While there, eleven-year-old Pecola begins menstruating, a circumstance that makes a great impact on Claudia and Frieda. Thereafter, Pecola returns home to her parents, Cholly and Pauline Breedlove, along with her older brother Sammy, who frequently runs away.

Pecola's family life is desolate and violent, and every member of the Breedlove family is utterly convinced of their own worthlessness and ugliness. Such despair causes Pecola to wish to disappear or die—or to have blue eyes, which, she believes, will prevent such terrible occurrences

as her parents' brutal fighting from taking place in front of her. In addition to worshipping Shirley Temple, Pecola loves blue-eyed Mary Jane candies, again clearly indicative of her sad internalization of a warped white value system.

When the Breedlove family deteriorates even further, Cholly, in a moment of tragic, twisted, drunken tenderness, rapes Pecola. This horrific act results in her pregnancy, although the baby dies after arriving prematurely. Astonishingly, the way that Morrison presents this unimaginable behavior provides a light into the remnants of Cholly's humanity. As Claudia says at the end of the novel: "He, at any rate, was the one who loved her enough to touch her, envelop her, give something of himself to her. But his touch was fatal, and the something he gave her filled the matrix of her agony with death."

In her complete withdrawal from the hell of her life, Pecola believes that, with the help of an odd man named Soaphead Church, she has achieved her goal of changing her eyes to the bluest ones of all. This utter break with reality leaves Pecola broken and unreachable, and she is thereafter seen wandering lost around town. Claudia realizes that her and others' willingness to go along with the widespread mistreatment of Pecola, as well as their endorsement of white values, makes the whole community complicit in the downward spiral of this sad young girl.

The Bluest Eye found a new, and perhaps wider, audience when Oprah Winfrey chose it in April 2000 as one of the Oprah's Book Club selections on her television show. In an interview from that time, Morrison explains that she still sees the novel as relevant, as contemporary girls and women are inundated with frequently negative messages about their appearances, with damaging repercussions for their self-images.

SULA

Most often hailed as one of the earliest works of fiction to focus on the friendship between African-American women, *Sula* the novel breaks rules much as Sula the character does. The friendship between Sula Peace and Nel Wright is the centerpiece of the work, with the two women representing varying perspectives on conventionality and values. At some points in their lives, the two balance each other perfectly; at other times, they clash. Likewise, the novel's narrative structure is sometimes linear and at other times more fragmented.

Also important in the novel are Sula's mother and grandmother, Hannah and Eva Peace. In her unorthodox house of disarray, Sula learns of the casual pleasures of sex from her mother Hannah's example and of how to be feisty, tough, and independent from Eva. Sula's father Rekus dies when she is three, yet Hannah still manages almost always to find "some touching every day." After Eva's husband BoyBoy, Sula's grandfather, leaves her with three children—Hannah, Pearl, and Plum—Eva disappears from town briefly and returns with one leg and a more stable financial status, a mystery never explained further. When Plum returns from World War I, he brings with him what appears to be a heroin addiction. Eva eventually decides that enough is enough and—in an act of brutal love that echoes similar events in Morrison's other novels (Cholly to Pecola in *The Bluest Eye*, Sethe to her daughter in *Beloved*, Joe to Dorcas in *Jazz*)—she kills him.

With a very different approach to life, Nel's mother, Helene Wright, holds sway over her daughter and husband, a cook on a Great Lakes ship. As she was born to a prostitute mother and raised by a staunchly religious grandmother in New Orleans, Helene is obsessed with order and propriety. She subdues Nel's imagination, just as she straightens her daughter's hair and puts a clothespin on her wide nose. Helene keeps her home spotless and tidy, and she does not tolerate any deviation from these norms in Nel.

Coming from these vastly differing influences, Sula and Nel learn to appreciate each other's lives and to learn about other possibilities for how to behave in the world. As Morrison writes of their shared perspectives: "Because each had discovered years before that they were neither white nor male, and that all freedom and triumph was forbidden to them, they had set about creating something else to be." Their unique friendship brings a welcome sense of completion to each other, as together they explore the depths of their previously lonely identities, particularly their growing interest in men.

As prominent as the characters in *Sula* is the Bottom, an African-American neighborhood of Medallion, Ohio. The novel is set in this outlying neighborhood, high up in the hills above the town, back when that land was considered undesirable. Morrison opens the novel with the genealogy of this place, delineating its unique history within a racist society. As we know from the opening, this community no longer exists, having been replaced with a golf course once the whites grew to appreciate the terrain. But *Sula* flashes back to when the Bottom was a lively place, long before ostensible progress has overrun it.

Presiding in a way over this town is another eccentric, Shadrack, a shell-shocked veteran of World War I who returns to Medallion mentally deranged and behaving inappropriately. Yet Shadrack fills a role in that society so that he is not a complete outcast, although he is laughed at. While he sells the townfolk the fish he catches, he also provides them with an other, someone they are not, as he exposes his genitals and invites them to march with him on National Suicide Day. Shadrack feels a kinship with Sula, as they both defy societal norms, something he recognizes in part through the stemmed-rose or tadpole-shaped birthmark above her eye.

Shadrack and Sula first interact while she is still an adolescent when he witnesses a scene of playfulness that results in tragedy. One summer day when they are twelve, Sula and Nel are cavorting near the river with a young boy named Chicken Little, when he flies from Sula's hands into the river and drowns. The girls are most concerned about whether or not they have been observed, implying that being caught matters more than trying to save Chicken Little or feeling regret over the loss of his life. In her concern that he has seen what happened, Sula visits Shadrack's cabin, where she says nothing but looks at him in wonder. His pleasant but inscrutable response, "Always," confounds Sula but seals a link between them.

As Sula and Nel grow up, they stay close for a while, although their opposing views on conventionality place pressure on their friendship. Nel marries young, to a man named Jude, and Sula goes away to college and to travel. After Sula's return, her place as the community's pariah becomes more pronounced. The breaking point between Sula and Nel occurs when, in the spirit of sharing everything with her close friend, Sula has sexual relations with Jude. When Nel discovers them together, Jude leaves forever, the women's friendship is broken, and Sula wonders what the problem is. Many years later, after self-righteous Nel visits the dying Sula, Nel realizes that what she has missed all of these years is not her wayward husband but her bosom friend, their lost closeness being the void at the center of her life.

In April 2002, *Sula* was the last selection in Oprah's Book Club, which was thereafter discontinued. At the time, Morrison said that she had been inspired to write the book by the incipient feminist movement of the early 1970s.

SONG OF SOLOMON

A coming-of-age story about a young man named Macon Milkman Dead, *Song of Solomon* was Morrison's longest and most fully developed novel when it was published. It covers multiple generations of the Dead family, whose name is an accident that came about when a drunk white man filling out freedom papers for those formerly enslaved wrote in the wrong blanks. The first Macon Dead, Milkman's grandfather, simply accepts this name and then passes it on to his son and grandson.

The novel centers on Milkman's aimless and materialistic life in an unnamed Michigan city on Lake Superior, during which he gradually acquires stronger values. While initial guidance comes from his capitalistic and heartless father, Milkman eventually embraces the more loving and spiritual teaching of his Aunt Pilate, his father's estranged sister. Yet before he gets to that point, Milkman must learn about his family history—including that of his mother, Ruth Foster—much of which takes him on a quest southward, first to Pennsylvania, and then farther south to Virginia. This journey, like the travels in all of Morrison's books, is both literal and figurative, as Milkman needs to scrutinize his own heart before he can begin to understand his family's secrets. The symbolism of these travels is echoed in Pilate's prized childhood possession: a geography book.

The first Macon Dead has a prosperous farm in Pennsylvania, Lincoln's Heaven, where he raises young Macon (Milkman's father) and Pilate after their mother dies in childbirth with Pilate, who is born, inexplicably, without a navel. Envious whites coveting his land kill him. Twelve-year-old Pilate and sixteen-year-old Macon flee, although they have sightings of his ghost thereafter. Pilate and Macon then have a falling out over some gold that they find, and they separate. Years later in Michigan they are reunited—albeit not amicably—just before Ruth conceives Milkman, which occurs with the help of herbal intervention by Pilate.

Years later Macon convinces his now-adult son Milkman to try to steal the gold that he believes Pilate kept after their disagreement in Pennsylvania years earlier. When it turns out not to be gold at all, Milkman heads to Pennsylvania and eventually Virginia in search of it. Having along the way alienated his former—and now a little crazy—friend Guitar, Milkman's life is in danger. However, an even more important development is that as Milkman heads further south and loses more and more of his material belongings, he gains respect for his family, for himself, and for other people. As he embraces less materialistic and more spiritual values, Milkman redeems himself. Most momentous to him is learning that ancestors of his were from the flying African tradition, in that they literally flew out of the fields of Virginia all the way back to Africa. Later, when Milkman returns to Virginia with Pilate, Guitar follows and a violent showdown results in her death. At the very end of the novel, Guitar and Milkman leap into thin air, perhaps dying or, as Morrison intimates, even flying.

This novel also was an Oprah selection, back in the earliest days of her book club in October 1996. That resulted in its return to the best-seller lists almost twenty years after it was first published, much to Morrison's initial surprise.

TAR BABY

Morrison's fourth novel is a departure from her earlier works, with its setting mostly on a mythical Caribbean island and its protagonists somewhat less sympathetic, which—although it sold well—may account for its relatively lower critical acclaim. This novel also places more emphasis on white characters than any of the earlier ones, with two of the six main characters a wealthy white couple. Yet *Tar Baby* reflects Morrison's trademark focus on the essential qualities of community and interpersonal relationships, history, journeying, and geography. Additionally, while *Song of Solomon* did include a ghost and people able to fly, this novel is thoroughly steeped in magic realism. Nature is sentient: rivers and trees resist real-estate development, and the ocean, a woman, steers a swimmer to a boat.

Set primarily in the vicinity of the whites' vacation home on the Isle des Chevaliers, the novel also takes place on a larger island nearby and in Eloe, Florida, and New York City. The story of three couples is told. Valerian and Margaret Street are the white owners of the Caribbean home, and Ondine and Sydney Childs are their African-American butler and cook. The final couple is Jadine Childs, Ondine and Sydney's Paris-based niece, and her short-term partner, Son Green, an African-American man who appears from nowhere.

Although *Tar Baby* has varying points of view, Jadine is its central consciousness. A famous and accomplished Paris fashion model, Jadine is not a typical Morrison protagonist. Along with being successful, Jadine is also arrogant, spoiled, and materialistic in some respects while remaining vulnerable and insecure. Although she is cared for by her aunt and uncle, Ondine and Sydney, Jadine's orphanhood rocks her moorings and results in a woman who has, as Morrison states, "forgotten her ancient properties." Disinclined to forge close ties with anyone, Jadine lacks the fundamental Morrisonian foundation: the essential reverence for and connection to one's ancestors.

Jadine's sometime romantic partner, Son Green, however, knows—to a fault, she would say—where he is from, namely, Eloe, Florida. Son's profound sense of his roots elicits resentment and contempt in Jadine, perhaps out of jealousy (although she has no envy of his lack of sophistication). Their fiery relationship seems to have potential at certain points, but their differences become too great, and by the end of the novel, she has flown back to Paris while he seems headed in the opposite direction. In a creative development that only Morrison seems capable of carrying off, *Tar Baby* ends with Son merging into the realm of myth through his apparent joining with a group of ancient blind horsemen.

The older couples, too, undergo changes. After a momentous secret is revealed about Margaret Street's abuse of her and Valerian's son, Michael, the tables turn, and the masters' control of the servants weakens. Too entrenched to go elsewhere, Sydney and Ondine will stay with the Streets, but the balance of power will never return to what it was before the revelation that Margaret, a beauty queen known in her youth as the Principal Beauty of Maine, took pleasure in sticking pins into her infant son's flesh. Now thirty years old, this son, Michael, is a powerful presence in his fraught absence. Supposed to join the family for the Christmas holidays, he never appears. Instead, the truth comes out, a demoralized Valerian yields control to Margaret, Ondine speaks her mind, and the formerly Edenic paradise has irrevocably fallen.

BELOVED

The Pulitzer Prize–winning *Beloved*, Morrison's fifth novel, has brought her the largest amount of praise. Ushering in a long string of even greater accolades for Morrison, this work goes back in time to the mid- and late 1800s, where Sethe and Paul D, now in Cincinnati, seek to reckon with their unmanageable pasts from the hell of slavery in Kentucky. Told in flashbacks—and, as Morrison has said, in the fragmented way that people remember—*Beloved* divulges its secrets piecemeal, although the linear story is eventually revealed.

Morrison's most supernatural novel thus far, *Beloved*, invites its readers to accept as its title character a ghostly woman who is the flesh-and-blood reincarnation of Sethe's murdered toddler girl. In having Sethe kill this daughter, Morrison was inspired by the bold decision of a historical enslaved woman, Margaret Garner, who chose death over reenslavement when she and her children were about to be captured in Cincinnati after escaping from Kentucky. As Morrison interprets this event fictionally, Sethe's rough actions actually spring from the intensity of her motherly love. Morrison has

described this circumstance several times, including a 1987 interview with Alan Benson: "For me, it was the ultimate gesture of the loving mother. It was also the outrageous claim of a slave. The last thing a slave woman owns is her children." Through this event, Morrison casts *Beloved* as the first portion of what she has visualized as a trilogy of works on excessive love, with this initial entry embodying overwhelming maternal love.

The novel also charts the entire life course of Denver, Sethe's surviving daughter. Within the province of the novel, she is born, grows up, remains isolated in the home, then breaks free and matures, finally finding a job and a community of her own. Baby Suggs, Denver's paternal grandmother, is a powerful, loving, spiritual leader-healer who later resigns herself to being a physically and emotionally spent, spirit broken old woman. Rounding out the list of main characters is Stamp Paid, the Underground Railroad–style conductor who transports Sethe and her infant Denver across the Ohio River and on to Baby Suggs's home, where they are reunited with Sethe's other children.

Echoing Milkman's travels southward in *Song of Solomon*, this novel features a remarkable journey in which, after sending her children north by wagon, Sethe—pregnant, recently whipped, and otherwise brutally assaulted—strikes out on foot. Because chaos now reigns at Sweet Home, the farm where she lives in Kentucky, Sethe cannot wait any longer, even though her husband Halle is missing. Yet she makes it to the Ohio River with the eventual serendipitous assistance of a poor white woman fleeing indentured servitude. Once successfully on the bank of that mighty river, Sethe goes into labor, and Denver is born.

Beloved's own journey, however, may be even more momentous, as she traverses the borders between the living and the dead. Emerging from limbo, the realm between life and death, Beloved wills herself into physical form based on her insatiable need to capture and hold Sethe's attention. When she dies she is but a toddler; in the current time of the novel, she is about twenty years old. As Morrison describes her emergence, Beloved materializes from a stream, which consists of that most basic of elements, water: "A fully dressed woman walked out of the water." And when Sethe first sees this woman, upon returning from a carnival with Denver and Paul D, she experiences a reenactment of her own water breaking in childbirth.

When Sethe eventually realizes that the woman is her lost daughter returned, she shuts out the rest of her life, including Paul D and even Denver and seeks to repay an insurmountable debt to Beloved. Beloved is never satisfied, however, and she will stop at nothing until Sethe has given up her own life. This downward spiral seems destined to end in Sethe's death until Denver becomes courageous enough to leave her house—124 Bluestone Road, itself carrying the import of a character—and seek help from the surrounding community. The citizens respond initially with food assistance and then aid of an even greater sort: they gather to exorcise Beloved's spirit from 124, and from Sethe. This purging succeeds, and by novel's end, Paul D has returned and Sethe and he begin healing in earnest.

JAZZ

The second installment in Morrison's trilogy on excessive love—here demonstrating the consequences of crushing romantic love—*Jazz* depicts a middle-aged married couple, Violet and Joe Trace, who have migrated from Virginia to "the City" (unnamed but clearly New York City). When Joe shockingly finds himself enthralled in the first adulterous affair of his life, with a much young woman named Dorcas, he panics and ends up shooting her. She refuses to name the shooter and dies shortly thereafter.

This murder—echoing the infanticide in *Beloved* and anticipating the killing of the Convent women in *Paradise*—opens the novel and imbues all of its plot developments with a special tone. Joe is so emotionally devastated that Dorcas's family does not seek a prosecution. Violet reacts initially by trying to maim the corpse at the funeral and then by trying to learn everything possible about Dorcas.

With an improvisational narrative structure, much like the musical genre of its name, *Jazz* also flashes back to Joe's and Violet's Virginia childhoods. Here, readers learn of Violet's bereft youth, during which her father disappears and her mother commits suicide, leaving Violet understandably scarred. Furthermore, Morrison explains that Joe's orphaned background in part leads him to become an apprentice to a local man, Henry Lestory, or Hunters Hunter, who teaches him to shoot. This woodsman's skill comes back to Joe many years later when he feels compelled to seek out Dorcas as prey—a circumstance that recollects for him his futile hunting for the mysterious woman Wild, whom he feared was his mother.

A distinct parallel to the eponymous character Beloved, Wild is a naked woman who exists in another realm, outside in the fields and in caves, as well as in the imaginations of local Vesper County, Virginia, residents. To a certain extent Morrison has confirmed this character linkage, as in a 1995 interview with Angels Carabi. Wild's initial appearance—naked and pregnant in a woody setting—closely resembles the way Beloved is last seen. Here, Morrison states, "Wild is a kind of Beloved" and then notes many parallels between them, but her final word on the matter is "I don't want to make all of these connections."

Wild's appearance also intersects with the other main story line, the journey of Golden Gray, a smug, white-appearing, young man who learns of his biracial parentage at age eighteen. As a consequence he leaves his mother, Vera Louise, in their Baltimore home and travels south to Virginia in search of his long-lost father. In an intricate plot development, Morrison reveals that this man is Hunters Hunter, the later father figure of Joe Trace. Furthermore, Golden Gray and Vera Louise have been coddled for many years by none other than Violet's grandmother, True Belle. And when Golden has almost arrived at Hunter's house, he comes across Wild, who has passed out. Therefore, Golden brings Wild to Hunter's house, and that is where she regains consciousness and subsequently gives birth—to Joe Trace. In these ways *Jazz*'s Golden Gray, Dorcas, and even Dorcas's friend Felice (in some ways like Beloved) serve as catalysts that greatly affect the dominant characters.

By the end of *Jazz*, Felice has provided the means by which Joe and Violet Trace can reunite. Violet's desolate childhood can finally be left behind, as can Joe's awkward family life, while for both of them, their virtual motherlessness can now be put to rest. The novel ends optimistically, implying that within a loving relationship—like that of Violet and Joe, just as with Sethe and Paul D of *Beloved*—healing, and even transcendence, are always possible.

PARADISE

In 1998 the final piece of Morrison's trilogy emerged with the novel *Paradise*, which espouses an extreme love for God, which becomes skewed into blind self-righteousness. Following a place-based trend begun as early as Morrison's second novel, *Sula*, this work features a town and a building not just as a characters, but as the main characters. Ruby, Oklahoma, a proud and self-satisfied domain, sees itself as the ultimate definer of morality and propriety. Its antagonist, the Convent, a school with much looser standards of behavior, is seventeen miles away. As Morrison's story unfolds, it is the tensions between these two places that form the heart of *Paradise*.

The modern-day town of Ruby is ruled by the officious offspring of migrants who had fled the South. Again emphasizing a monumental journey, Morrison writes that the townsfolk's grandparents and others had formed a group of itinerant African Americans who fled on foot from the violence of the racist South, especially Louisiana, in hopes that they would be able to create better lives out West. Heeding the call to "Come Prepared or Not at All!" these travelers hope to become homesteaders, new pioneers in a relatively open land. However, the 158 people or so discover that, primarily because of their particularly dark skin, they are turned away from the already-established all-black towns along the way. The travelers cope with this development, which becomes known as the Disallowing throughout the mythology of the novel, by redefining the intended insult so that they see their darkness as a source of pride.

With what appears to be supernatural intervention by means of the apparition of a walking man, the settlers follow the signs they are given and build their first town, Haven, Oklahoma, complete with a central cooking space, the Oven. When soldiers returning from World War II find open racial hostility, most of Haven's residents, taking the Oven with them, move further west, where they establish the town of Ruby. Within the time of the novel, 1973, the leaders of Ruby, particularly Deacon and Steward Morgan, exert their extreme control over the other residents, including their wives, Soane and Dovey.

Yet the Convent—not actually a convent but rather a school for Native American girls run by Roman Catholic nuns—allows for, and even welcomes, creativity, unconventionality, and even outsiders. The Convent women have all traveled circuitous and painful routes to get there, and they all retain devastating memories of the past. Through the evolving leadership of Consolata, by the novel's end the other women—Mavis, Gigi, Pallas, and Seneca—are able to begin the process of healing from their troubles and, therefore, to transcend their limitations.

As in other of Morrison's novels, supernatural occurrences come to bear in the wake of a defining murder. After the Ruby leaders decide that they need a scapegoat for the young people's embrace of the civil rights movement, they choose the Convent women as the offenders, as those who must have led astray the young citizens. Therefore, nine men travel the seventeen miles to the Convent before dawn one morning in July and shoot each of the women. "They shoot the white girl first" is how the novel opens, although which of the women this could be never becomes clear, as Morrison has intentionally stripped away racial markers from the Convent women.

The supernatural elements occur later, when Roger Best takes his hearse out to claim the deceased and finds that there are no bodies to collect, as they have all disappeared. Morrison explains this circumstance in a 1998 interview with Charlie Rose on the Public Broadcasting System just after the publication of *Paradise*. Although she says that she knew the first sentence when she began writing the novel, she did not know what would happen to the Convent women after the shooting. "Would they die or escape?" she wondered, then deciding, "Both—why can't they do both?" And that is precisely what happens—the women are killed, but they also are somehow resurrected, each visiting and making peace with the most hurtful elements of her past. When the Reverend Richard Misner and Anna Flood visit the Convent to investigate, another extraordinary experience occurs; they see an apparition of either a door or a window in the sky. Subsequently, some of the townspeople repent as they begin to recognize the errors of their ways and to see that they have become as exclusionary as those who rejected their ancestors in the Disallowing. As an outcast but spiritual character, Lone DuPres describes it: "God had given Ruby a second chance." In this way Morrison demonstrates the vastness of her vision, as the lines between the living and the dead are not distinct, and the potential for grace is limitless.

In each of her novels, Morrison creates a world where possibilities are wide open and people are able to heal and even transcend horrors. She builds a world where telepathy is commonplace, ghosts are real, and places exert energy. In each of her seven novels, Morrison quite simply gives us everything under the sun: "When I have been accused of making characters that are larger than life , . . . I realized that what I had in fact done was simply describe characters who were as large as life. Life is that large."

[*See also* Writing as a Woman in the Twentieth Century.]

SELECTED WORKS

The Bluest Eye (1970)
Sula (1974)
Song of Solomon (1977)
Tar Baby (1981)
Beloved (1987)
Jazz (1992)
Playing in the Dark: Whiteness and the Literary Imagination (1992)
The Nobel Prize Speech (1994)
The Dancing Mind (1996)
The Big Box (1999)
Paradise (1998)

The Book of Mean People (2002)
Who's Got Game?: The Ant or the Grasshopper? (2003)

FURTHER READING

Andrews, William L., and Nellie Y. McKay, eds. *Toni Morrison's* Beloved: *A Casebook*. New York, 1999. An exceptional resource that includes many essential primary materials, such as Frances Ellen Watkins Harper's poem about Margaret Garner, "The Slave Mother: A Tale of the Ohio."

Beaulieu, Elizabeth Ann. *The Toni Morrison Encyclopedia*. Westport, Conn., 2002. The most comprehensive Morrison resource available, including hundreds of entries on all seven novels.

Bouson, J. Brooks. *Quiet as It's Kept: Shame, Trauma, and Race in the Novels of Toni Morrison*. Albany, N.Y., 2000. A deeply analytical work, one of the few that is up-to-date enough to include *Paradise*.

Carabi, Angels. "Interview with Toni Morrison: Part Three." *Belles Lettres* (Spring 1995): 40–43.

Denard, Carolyn. "Toni Morrison." In *Modern American Women Writers*. Edited by Elaine Showalter et al. New York, 1991.

Gates, Henry Louis, Jr., and K. A. Appiah, eds. *Toni Morrison: Critical Perspectives Past and Present*. New York, 1993. A very thorough book on Morrison that includes insightful contemporary reviews of the first six novels by some of the most renowned Morrison scholars.

Harris, Trudier. *Fiction and Folklore: The Novels of Toni Morrison*. A very cogent and clear analysis of the influence of African-American folk traditions on Morrison's first five novels. Especially powerful insights on *Tar Baby* and *Beloved*.

Lubiano, Wahneema. "Toni Morrison." In *African-American Writers*. Edited by Valerie Smith. New York, 2001.

McKay, Nellie Y., and Kathryn Earle. *Approaches to Teaching the Novels of Toni Morrison*. New York, 1997. A perceptive book from the Modern Language Association series, it includes very useful background information on approaching the first six novels inside the classroom. Also useful for advanced students.

Morrison, Toni. *Profile of a Writer: Toni Morrison*. Directed by Alan Benson. 1987. One of the best and earliest interviews with Morrison about *Beloved*.

Morrison, Toni. Interview by Charlie Rose. *The Charlie Rose Show. Public Broadcasting System*, 20 January 1998. Focused primarily on her writing of *Paradise*, which had just been published, this conversation also emphasizes the other works in the trilogy, *Beloved* and *Jazz*, as well as Morrison's response to receiving the Nobel Prize.

Morrison, Toni. "Modernism and the American South: An Interview with Toni Morrison." *Studies in the Literary Imagination* 31, no. 2 (Fall 1998): 1–16. A deep and thorough interview by Carolyn Denard, with particularly valuable ideas about Morrison's views of the South.

Naylor, Gloria, and Toni Morrison. "A Conversation." In *Conversations with Toni Morrison*. Edited by Danille Taylor-Guthrie. Jackson, Miss., 1994. A 1985 discussion that provides a valuable peek into Morrison's private and creative lives, with interesting shared experiences between the two African-American women writers.

Page, Philip. *Dangerous Freedom: Fusion and Fragmentation in Toni Morrison's Novels*. Jackson, Miss., 1995. An excellent study of Morrison's first six works, with both thematic and theoretical approaches. Especially strong on *Beloved*.

Peach, Linden, ed. *Toni Morrison*. New York, 1998. As part of the New Casebooks Series, a valuable collection of scholarly essays, including all of the novels through *Jazz*.

Peterson, Nancy J., ed. *Toni Morrison: Critical and Theoretical Approaches*. Baltimore, 1997. A very useful collection, with essays covering the first six novels.

Reames, Kelly. *Toni Morrison's Paradise: A Reader's Guide*. New York, 2001. A helpful, though small, book entirely devoted to *Paradise*. It also includes the basic biographical material for Morrison.

Samuels, Wilfred D., and Clenora Hudson-Weems. *Toni Morrison*. Boston, 1990. A thematic study of the first five novels, this book is a good starting point for Morrison research.

Taylor-Guthrie, Danille, ed. *Conversations with Toni Morrison*. Jackson, Miss., 1994. A collection of over twenty interviews, spanning a wide range of years, this work is useful for finding out what Morrison has said about many topics, particularly her first six novels.

See also the article on *Beloved*, immediately following.

TONI MORRISON'S
BELOVED

by Kristine Yohe

A novel of fragments, flashbacks, and fractured narration, *Beloved* presents many of its readers with a challenging experience. Yet reading *Beloved*, which is Toni Morrison's fifth novel, also brings tremendous rewards through the sheer beauty of her writing—as well as the work's emphasis on spiritual renewal, personal transcendence, fierce love, and emotional healing. It is a novel that at once stretches the imagination and nurtures the soul.

Beloved was published in 1987 and immediately met with great critical and popular recognition, culminating in its receipt of the Pulitzer Prize for fiction in 1988. Hailed by many as Morrison's best work, this novel examines some of the most appalling atrocities of American slavery in uniquely compelling ways. As Morrison has said herself in several venues, in *Beloved* she avoids the wide, epic sweep of many other works about slavery and instead takes a very "narrow and deep" approach, seeking to convey what it felt like to be enslaved. Focusing primarily on the experiences of an African-American woman named Sethe, both within the grip of slavery and beyond, *Beloved* reveals some of the grisliest elements of what it means to try to be a mother—and indeed a human being—under a system of total oppression.

Beloved's place in Morrison's oeuvre is as the first installment of a trilogy of novels dealing with excessive forms of love. With its emphasis on the intensity of maternal love, *Beloved* sets into motion the sequence that next results in *Jazz* (1992), focusing on extreme romantic love, and then *Paradise* (1998), which treats overwhelming love for God. These three works share other thematic concerns, such as Morrison's attention to identity, motherhood, history, spirituality, geography, and migration. While the novels in this trilogy do not actually share characters, they do have some character types in common; for example, the eponymous Beloved is resurrected, to a degree, as the character Wild in *Jazz*.

Beloved also encompasses elements of the supernatural and of ghost stories, as the title character is the reincarnation of the "crawling-already? baby" daughter Sethe kills to save her from being returned to slavery. Because she invites us to accept this ghostly character Beloved as one of the central players in the text, Morrison requires any skeptics among her readers to suspend their disbelief. Combining concepts of African-American folklore with the influence of Vodun as well as with beliefs about shape shifting and communication between the living and the dead, *Beloved* creates a world where these various threads come together into an intricately woven whole. The novel also gained new attention when it was adapted into a movie released in 1998, starring Oprah Winfrey and directed by Jonathan Demme.

HISTORICAL AND CULTURAL BACKGROUND

Morrison has explained that she set out to write a work of fiction and not a documentary. Seminal aspects of *Beloved*'s plotline, however, were inspired by a unique historical account from American slavery, as well as by Morrison's deep awareness of a range of African-American cultural practices.

In January 1856 a woman named Margaret Garner fled enslavement near Richwood, Kentucky, traveling with her husband, children, and in-laws through northern Kentucky, over the frozen Ohio River, and into Cincinnati, Ohio. When they were followed and then confronted by the slave master, Archibald Gaines, and federal marshals, Garner decided that death was preferable to a return to slavery. She intended to kill all of her children and then kill herself, but succeeded only with one daughter. The surviving family members were taken into custody, and Garner ended up in court. One of the compelling issues at the time was whether she would be charged with murder or a property crime. In part because a murder charge would necessitate her late daughter being considered a human being, the overriding legal definitions of race and slavery prevailed. Subsequently, Margaret Garner was found guilty of the property crime, returned to slavery, and literally sold down the river, dying of typhoid fever two years later.

Much was made of this case, as abolitionists hailed Garner's actions as the ultimate evidence of slavery as hell if it would drive a mother to kill her child. However, the pro-slavery movement used these same facts to support their racist claims. The case was reported in newspapers throughout the country, and the African-American writer Frances Ellen Watkins Harper wrote an 1857 poem inspired by the case, "The Slave Mother: A Tale of the Ohio." Over 140 years later, Steven Weisenburger analyzed Margaret Garner's life and the resulting court case in his *Modern Medea: A Family Story of Slavery and Child-Murder from the Old South* (1998).

Toni Morrison learned of Margaret Garner's life in the process of editing the historical collection *The Black Book* (1974). Yet she has explained that she resisted learning anything more than the fact that an enslaved woman chose infanticide over returning her child to slavery. This fact became the kernel around which *Beloved* was created, with the rest being imagination, as she explained in a 1987 interview with Alan Benson. In addition, Morrison borrowed the Garner name, which is borne in the novel by the owners and some of the enslaved residents of Sweet Home, the Kentucky farm where Sethe meets Halle and the other main characters.

In the process of conducting her research for *Beloved*, Morrison incorporated into her novel some of the most brutal practices of slavery in the United States. She stated in the Benson interview that she was stunned to learn of the elaborate devices used within the slave system to enforce authority and punish those enslaved people who proved resistant. For example, Morrison represents Paul D as being forced to wear a spoked collar, which prevents him from lying down or finding any moment of comfort. Furthermore, in reference to the specious efforts of the era to justify slavery, Morrison's brutal character, schoolteacher, undergoes a pseudoscientific "investigation" to measure and then compare the supposedly human and animal features of the enslaved people.

Historically, *Beloved* also embraces many other features of the era in which it is set—primarily 1873 and 1874, with flashbacks to 1855, the time of Sethe's escape and Denver's birth, and to the earlier time at Sweet Home. For example, Stamp Paid—who serves as an informal Underground Railroad conductor—considers some contemporary atrocities, with references to Frederick Douglass's newspaper, the *North Star*, and to the rampant violence of Reconstruction: "Eighteen seventy-four and whitefolks still on the loose. Whole towns wiped clean of Negroes; eighty-seven lynchings in one year alone in Kentucky; four colored schools burned to the ground; grown men whipped like children; children whipped like

adults; black women raped by the crew; property taken, necks broken." In his rescue of Sethe and her newborn baby, Denver, across the Ohio River, Stamp Paid recalls historical Underground Railroad conductors such as John P. Parker, who was active in the Ripley, Ohio, area, east of Cincinnati. Beloved includes other Underground Railroad references, mainly through the plan to escape from Sweet Home, whereby Sethe, Halle, their children, and the others are to wait in a cornfield for a wagon to take them north. These characters are alerted to get ready by hearing an Underground Railroad song, one covert means of communication used by many enslaved people as they sought to escape. Moreover, Sethe and Denver await further transport once they have arrived in Ohio, and the next conductor, Ella, knows to pick them up because Stamp Paid leaves a sty open "when there's a crossing. Knots a white rag on the post if it's a child too." All of these historical markers contribute to *Beloved*'s aura of reality and accuracy, even amid its emphasis on imagination and spirituality.

SPIRITUAL CONTEXT

Morrison's conflation of history and the supernatural is one of the hallmarks of her overall fictional output and is most notable in *Beloved*. Its very premise—of accepting a ghost as a major character—stretches some readers' perspectives. Yet Morrison's worldview is eclectic and syncretic, and her novels embrace cultural elements of Christianity along with the more nature-based religions of African origin, such as Vodun. *Beloved* does so in part through not only espousing the presence of ghosts, but also through two main spiritual events: Baby Suggs's preaching and the virtual exorcism near the novel's end. In her calling of the Word, Baby Suggs exhorts her fellow African Americans to have the courage to value themselves within a world that regards them as inferior. Set in the Clearing, a sacred space in the woods behind their house outside Cincinnati, these spiritual gatherings involve Baby Suggs's heartfelt affirmations to her followers of the necessity of self-love.

The novel's exorcism occurs many years later, following Baby Suggs's death, long after she has abandoned her previously tremendous faith. When the community women finally decide that Beloved's haunting and overt mistreatment of Sethe have gone on long enough, they gather together to reclaim the rights of the living over the dead. Combining input from their various belief systems, these thirty women come together to pray and sing. Morrison implies that the women bring, in addition to traditional Christian beliefs and icons, more unconventional charms and fetishes, whatever they think will work. These symbols and aides are "stuffed in apron pockets, strung around their necks, lying in the space between their breasts. Others brought Christian faith—as shield and sword. Most brought a little of both." Echoing Baby Suggs's powerful call, this ceremony in effect brings community back to the isolated Sethe and achieves Beloved's final departure.

Finally, Morrison summons up the historical Middle Passage—the horrific slave ship passage from Africa to the Americas—through her descriptions of the "place" where Beloved exists before returning to life. In language recalling the unbearably cramped conditions of the overpacked ships, Morrison describes Beloved's situation as extremely "hot," with the dead and the living literally on top of one another, and barely enough room to crouch. From this realm, a sort of limbo between life and death, Beloved wills herself back to physical form, resulting in her arrival at 124 Bluestone Road—Baby Suggs's house in Ohio—after she emerges from the stream behind the house.

OVERVIEW

The plot of *Beloved* is complex and circuitous, as the narrative is shaped through flashbacks, memories, and its stream-of-consciousness structure. Its readers do not learn the story in a linear fashion; however, a sequential order does exist between its fragments.

The story begins on Sweet Home, a Kentucky farm run by Mr. and Mrs. Garner, who, ironically, practice a form of slavery in which the enslaved people are granted some degree of humanity and autonomy while nevertheless remaining fully enslaved. There, Baby Suggs and her young slave son Halle join four other young male slaves—Sixo, Paul D Garner, Paul F Garner, and Paul A Garner. After Halle is allowed to buy his mother's freedom through extra work, Mr. Garner takes Baby Suggs to Cincinnati, where he connects her with an abolitionist family, the Bodwins, who give her a house (at 124 Bluestone Road) and help her to find work. Feeling compelled to share the joy she discovers in freedom, Baby Suggs then begins to preach in her own free style.

Thereafter, Sethe, a young enslaved teenager, is brought to work at Sweet Home. Allowed to select her husband among the men, she chooses Halle. After they are informally married and begin having children, Mr. Garner dies mysteriously and Mrs. Garner is compelled to sell Paul F to pay debts. Thereafter, Mrs. Garner becomes ill and a relative of hers, schoolteacher, arrives to take control. Schoolteacher's enforcement of slavery is particularly brutal and dehumanizing, especially in comparison to

the Garners' style. Sethe, Halle, Sixo, and the two Pauls decide to escape and succeed in sending the three children to Baby Suggs in Cincinnati. But the other plans are discovered and thwarted by schoolteacher and his nephews. Consequently, Sixo and Paul A are killed for their rebellion, Sethe is beaten while pregnant, and the nephews steal her breast milk. Halle witnesses this and loses his mind and, apparently, his life. Paul D is then violently punished, sold away from Sweet Home, and taken to a prison camp in Alfred, Georgia, where he and the other inmates suffer excruciating torture, backbreaking work, and sexual abuse. Eventually escaping from Alfred, Paul D spends the next several years on the go.

Sethe, meanwhile, flees alone and on foot, somehow managing to make it almost to the Ohio River, where she collapses. She then confronts Amy Denver, a young "whitegirl" escaping indentured servitude and on her way to Boston. Amy ends up helping Sethe to survive and make it to the river, where Sethe gives birth to a baby girl she names Denver. Sethe and Denver are then discovered by Stamp Paid, allegedly out fishing but whose true purpose is to aid runaways. With the help of Ella, Stamp Paid gets the two to Baby Suggs's house, where Sethe's other children—Howard, Buglar, and the "crawling-already?" toddler girl (otherwise unnamed)—have already arrived.

Baby Suggs welcomes Sethe and the baby, and the reunited family, minus Halle, has "28 days" of relative happiness. Baby Suggs and Stamp Paid then arrange a large celebration to mark these limited successes. Yet the party givers somehow inadvertently go overboard in their generosity, and the community members become resentful. Therefore, when the white search party appears, the townsfolk refrain from warning Baby Suggs and Sethe.

Schoolteacher, his nephews, and the sheriff arrive at 124 Bluestone Road; Sethe sees them, gathers her children, and runs to a shed. Because she cannot bear the thought of their returning to Sweet Home, Sethe (like Margaret Garner) intends to kill her children and herself. She succeeds in killing the toddler girl and is in the process with Denver when Stamp Paid stops her. The sheriff takes Sethe and her baby, Denver, to jail, and through the intervention of the Bodwin family, they are eventually released and return to live with Baby Suggs at 124. Sethe then finds work cooking in a Cincinnati restaurant.

Soon, Sethe, Denver, and Baby Suggs realize that 124 Bluestone Road is haunted by the spirit of the deceased toddler girl. With various pranks—such as spilling food, cracking mirrors, moving furniture, and flooding a room with light or smells—the baby ghost makes her presence known. The two boys, Howard and Buglar, regard this haunting as hostile, and upon reaching adolescence they flee. The remaining women grow resigned to the ghost, in part because they feel obliged to pay it attention. Denver even regards the ghost as her only friend, particularly after she stops going to school when she is confronted by a classmate about her mother's harsh actions.

Subsequently, Baby Suggs, who dropped her preaching in the woods after the killing, takes to her bed and then gives up completely. After she dies, Sethe and Denver become even more isolated, though Sethe continues working. Then, several years later, Paul D Garner, "the last of the Sweet Home men," arrives looking for Baby Suggs. Immediately, the haunting accelerates, and Paul D fights back, seeming to win, at least temporarily.

Paul D and Sethe then begin a romantic relationship. Right after Paul D, Sethe, and Denver attend a carnival together—one of the few social events of Denver's whole life—they return home to discover a young woman sitting in the yard. This young woman, Beloved, embodies seemingly contradictory characteristics; though she appears about twenty years old, her behavior is that of a child.

Beloved simply stays on at 124, pleasing Denver, making Paul D uncomfortable, and bringing Sethe inexplicable satisfaction. Immediately, Denver realizes that this woman is her dead sister come back to life, and she protects her fiercely. Paul D, however, knows nothing of the killing, or of Beloved's origins. However, he finds himself "fixed," he thinks, by Beloved, who wants to intrude between Sethe and him. Eventually feeling compelled to sleep in an outbuilding, Paul D is stunned and guilt ridden when Beloved forces herself on him sexually. Yet when he tries to tell Sethe, he is unable to do so, though the conversation results in his return, for a time, to her bedroom.

Sethe does not fully realize that Beloved is her returned baby daughter until after Paul D leaves, which he does upon learning about the circumstances of the murder from Stamp Paid. Once he is out of the house, the three women, particularly Sethe and Beloved, focus completely inwardly, losing touch with the outside world and, gradually, with reality. After Beloved turns on Denver and becomes more violently obsessed with Sethe, Sethe stops going to work. Their food and money quickly diminish to almost nothing, and Denver is left with no choice; she must leave the house and seek help.

Significantly, this step outside, which so terrifies Denver, results in her and her mother's survival. By asking for help, Denver enlists the community members in acts of charity that save her and Sethe and enable Denver to break her social isolation. In the process of looking for work, Denver seeks out the Bodwins, the sympathetic people who had helped her mother and grandmother years earlier. On the day she is to begin working for them, Mr. Bodwin arrives to pick her up just as the thirty women have gathered to cast out the spirit that has returned to punish Sethe.

When Sethe sees Mr. Bodwin, she mistakes him for schoolteacher, who she thinks has returned to take her children. This time, her response is different; rather than killing her children as protection, Sethe instead tries to attack him. But the women stop her, the spell is broken, Beloved vanishes, and the haunting ends.

Denver's life continues to improve, though Sethe takes to her bed. At this point Paul D finds his way back to 124 and to Sethe. In the final scene, Paul D and Sethe are reunited, and she laments Beloved's departure, as her "best thing" is gone. Paul D, however, reflecting Baby Suggs's teaching, assures her that actually she is her own "best thing." Sethe's response—"Me? Me?"—marks her incipient development of self. Morrison shows that, in part because of the renewal of their loving, supportive relationship, both Sethe and Paul D can survive and begin to heal.

The final two pages, an epilogue, note that Beloved is sometimes remembered and sometimes avoided, though her spirit seems to linger in the vicinity, in the stream, in the weather itself. Noting repeatedly that "it was not a story to pass on," Morrison's narrator here assembles the various themes into an abstract yet beautiful acknowledgment of the ghost's effect on the others and on her intense loneliness. She is gone, but somehow not completely.

STYLE

The novel is written with a stream-of-consciousness approach, which is reminiscent in some respects of the writing manner embraced by such authors as William Faulkner, James Joyce, and Virginia Woolf, although Morrison's literary style is uniquely her own. Notably, Morrison's master's thesis at Cornell University was on Faulkner and Woolf.

Morrison has explained—in the Benson interview and elsewhere—that she wrote *Beloved* in fragments and flashbacks in order to reproduce the manner in which people remember. That is, rather than presenting a linear order, she depicts snippets much the way that the subconscious mind would recognize facets of any whole. The story comes together gradually through the memories—or "rememories," as Sethe calls them—of Sethe, Paul D, Denver, Baby Suggs, and Stamp Paid. This way, various versions and perspectives emerge for any given event, such as Sethe's escape, the killing of her daughter, or even the earlier history at Sweet Home. By the novel's end, this issue of memory and personal history has became more prominent, as Paul D, thinking of Sethe, "wants to put his story next to hers." Finally, in writing *Beloved*, Morrison was influenced by the slave narrative tradition, including those texts written by Frederick Douglass and Harriet Jacobs. Often referred to as a "neo-slave narrative"—as is Sherley Anne Williams's 1986 *Dessa Rose*—*Beloved* incorporates many of the essentials of this historical genre, including its emphasis on suffering under enslavement and the importance of escape.

[*See also* Autobiography in America: Slave Narratives *and* Writing as a Woman in the Twentieth Century.]

FURTHER READING

Andrews, William L., and Nellie Y. McKay, eds. *Toni Morrison's* Beloved: *A Casebook*. New York, 1999. An exceptional resource that includes many essential primary materials, such as Frances Ellen Watkins Harper's poem about Margaret Garner, "The Slave Mother: A Tale of the Ohio."

Beaulieu, Elizabeth Ann. *The Toni Morrison Encyclopedia*. Westport, Conn., 2003. The most comprehensive Morrison resource available, including hundreds of entries.

Bloom, Harold, ed. *Modern Critical Interpretations*: Beloved. Philadelphia, 1998. A helpful collection focused exclusively on *Beloved*.

Gates, Henry Louis, Jr., and K. A. Appiah, eds. *Toni Morrison: Critical Perspectives Past and Present*. New York, 1993. A very thorough book on Morrison that includes insightful reviews of *Beloved* by Ann Snitow and Margaret Atwood, as well as excellent scholarly essays on the novel by Trudier Harris, Valerie Smith, and Marilyn Sanders Mobley.

Morrison, Toni. *Profile of a Writer: Toni Morrison*. Produced and directed by Alan Benson. London, 1987. Videocassette. Interview by Alan Benson. One of the best, and earliest, interviews with Morrison about *Beloved*. It took place just before the novel was published.

Peach, Linden, ed. *Toni Morrison*. New York, 1998. Part of the New Casebooks series, a valuable collection of scholarly essays, several of which focus on *Beloved*.

Peterson, Nancy J., ed. *Toni Morrison: Critical and Theoretical Approaches*. Baltimore, 1997. A very useful collection with several essays dedicated to *Beloved*.

Weisenburger, Steven. *Modern Medea: A Family Story of Slavery and Child-Murder from the Old South*. New York, 1998. An essential work that tells a great deal about the life, and particularly the court case, of Margaret Garner.

See also the article on Toni Morrison immediately preceding.

VLADIMIR NABOKOV

by Ellen Pifer

On a summer's day in 1950, Vladimir Nabokov, fifty-one years old and riddled with doubts about the novel he was working on, headed for the garden incinerator to burn his drafts of *Lolita*'s first chapters. His wife, Véra, caught up with him, and at her urging Nabokov paused to reconsider. Slowly, and with many interruptions, Nabokov resumed work on the novel, which he completed in the spring of 1954. And the rest, as they say, is history—literary history. Not only did the publication of *Lolita* (1955) and its succès de scandale eventually make the novelist world famous, but they allowed him to give up his teaching post at Cornell University and devote himself

Vladimir Nabokov.
(*Courtesy of the Library of Congress*)

full-time to writing. *Lolita* marked a turning point in Nabokov's life and literary career in another crucial way. Because few Americans had read any of his Russian books, Nabokov could say in 1956 that their appraisal of his English ones was necessarily skewed. Lolita's arrival on the scene would soon change that situation. The economic and professional freedom granted Nabokov by *Lolita*'s success allowed him to embark on a systematic translation of his Russian work into English—a project that would, at last, begin to close the linguistic and cultural divide separating the two spheres of his literary production. By healing this rift at long last, Nabokov was able to realize in his own life—subject for decades to repeated upheaval, dislocation, and disruption—the elegant figure of the ampersand, or figure-eight, that recurs throughout his art and culminates in the pattern of a spiral whose overlapping arcs unlock the vicious circle of time.

RUSSIAN ROOTS

Born to wealth, privilege, and social prominence in St. Petersburg, Russia, on 23 April 1899, Vladimir Vladimirovich Nabokov was destined to lose, while still

a teenager, both his homeland and a vast estate inherited from his maternal uncle, Vasily Rukavishnikov, when the latter died in 1916. Although exile, loss, and longing are recurrent themes in his fiction, Nabokov remained remarkably serene throughout his life about the bouts of poverty and destitution that he and his family suffered, especially during the late 1930s, and the loss of what he jokingly called his "unreal estate." Infinitely more tragic was the loss of his beloved father, Vladimir Dmitrievich Nabokov, shot to death at a public meeting in Berlin on 28 March 1922, while trying to shield a colleague from the bullets of a Russian ultrarightist.

In *Speak, Memory: An Autobiography Revisited* (1966), the revised version of a memoir originally published as *Conclusive Evidence* (1951), Nabokov paints an idyllic picture of his early life as the eldest child of parents he adored. Initially educated at home by a series of English and French governesses and later by Russian tutors, Nabokov attended the liberal Tenishev School in St. Petersburg from 1911 to 1917. The family divided their time between an elegant town house in a fashionable district of St. Petersburg and their large country estate, Vyra, located fifty miles to the south. Nabokov's mother, born Elena Rukavishnikov, was a highly intelligent, cultivated woman who, like her husband, was a frequent traveler to Europe and fluent in several languages. Nabokov, who was trilingual, once said, "I don't think in any language, I think in images" (*Strong Opinions*, p. 14). His visual acuity and skills as a draftsman contributed to another lifelong pursuit, lepidopterology. As a researcher at Harvard's Museum of Comparative Zoology during the 1940s, he made painstaking drawings of butterflies based on his microscopic study of their anatomical features. The published results of his research, most notably his discoveries relating to a group of butterflies known as blues, are now recognized as pioneering contributions to the field.

In Nabokov's greatest Russian novel, *Dar* (1937–1938), later translated into English as *The Gift* (1963), the protagonist's father is a famous naturalist and explorer whose portrait is lovingly based on Nabokov's father. According to Nabokov's biographer, Brian Boyd, Nabokov's mother was astounded by the depth of her son's insight into the life and character of her husband. V. D. Nabokov, whose own father was state minister of justice under the czars Alexander II and III, trained as a jurist but dedicated himself, as a liberal politician and journalist, to the fight for constitutional democracy in Russia. An Anglophile and intellectual, Nabokov's father took a vital interest in literature, as his expressed admiration for Charles Dickens and his 5,000-volume library attest. It was in his father's paneled library that young Vladimir, between the ages of ten and fifteen, read more fiction and poetry than in any other five-year period of his life.

That the precocious youngster read these works in English, Russian, and French proved invaluable for his future: first as a student at Cambridge University; then as an émigré writer living in Berlin and Paris; and, most important, as a forty-year-old Russian novelist, midway through life and career, faced with the task of transforming himself into an American writer. "It had taken me some forty years to invent Russia and Western Europe," Nabokov said of his arrival in the United States, "and now I was faced by the task of inventing America" (*Lolita*, Afterword, p. 312). By the time Nabokov arrived in America, he had every reason to be personally and artistically exhausted. Yet through a monumental feat of imagination he managed, as the American writer John Updike wrote, "to bring an entirely new audacity and panache to American literature" (*Lectures on Literature*, pp. xxvi–xxvii).

EUROPEAN EXPATRIATION

Forced into exile by the Bolshevik coup of October 1917, Nabokov's family fled first to the Crimea and then to London; they ultimately settled in Berlin, where Nabokov's father became editor of the newly established Russian newspaper *Rul'* (The Rudder), which became a leading publication in émigré circles. Nabokov stayed on in England to continue his studies at Trinity College, Cambridge, where, while pursuing a B.A. degree in Russian and French literature, he devoted the majority of his time to becoming a Russian writer. At Cambridge he wrote

his first story, filled notebooks with verse, translated the poetry of Rupert Brooke into Russian, discovered the work of James Joyce, played soccer and tennis, and engaged in a number of romances. By the time Nabokov graduated from Cambridge in 1922, he had published widely in émigré periodicals and had two volumes of poetry in press. Taking up residence in Berlin, a major center for expatriate Russians, Nabokov launched the career of V. Sirin—a nom de plume he had adopted in 1921 to distinguish himself from his father, V. D. Nabokov, and would maintain throughout his career as an émigré Russian writer. To supplement his literary earnings, he gave tennis lessons, tutored pupils in English and French, and devised chess problems for the émigré dailies. In May 1923, he met and fell in love with Véra Slonim, a cultivated young woman born and raised in St. Petersburg and already an admirer of Sirin's work. They were married on 15 April 1925.

In the same year that Nabokov met Véra, he published a Russian version of Lewis Carroll's *Alice in Wonderland* (*Ania v strane chudes*, 1923), whose mirror world of absurd characters would be replayed, to nightmarish effect, in two of his later works of fiction reflecting the rise of totalitarianism in Germany and Russia: *Invitation to a Beheading* (*Priglashenie na kazn'*, 1938; trans. 1959) and his second novel in English, *Bend Sinister* (1947). For Nabokov, Carroll's Alice embodied all the qualities of wonder and imagination that the English Romantics celebrated in the child. He said in a lecture delivered in the mid-1950s, "In a sense we are all crashing to our death from the top story of our birth ... and wondering with an immortal Alice in Wonderland at the patterns of the passing wall. This capacity to wonder at trifles, these asides of the spirit, ... are the highest forms of consciousness" (*Lectures on Literature*, pp. 373–374). In Nabokov's view, consciousness, our "being aware of being aware of being," is what distinguishes humankind from the beast. "All the rest follows—the glory of thought, poetry, a vision of the universe" (*Strong Opinions*, p. 142). Consciousness not only shapes the world each of us inhabits, it calls "reality" into being—which is why the word "reality" must be enclosed in quotation marks (*Lolita*, Afterword, p. 312). In one sense, each of Nabokov's novels traces the way in which a central character constructs, out of myriad surrounding phenomena, the world he or she perceives as real. If he is a philosopher, like Adam Krug in *Bend Sinister*, he may come to the realization that consciousness "is the only real thing in the world and the greatest mystery of all" (p. 188). Few of Nabokov's protagonists achieve this overarching insight, however; gifted though they often are, they remain confined within the circle of their own solipsistic obsessions—whether in the guise of nymphets, chess patterns, an imagined "double," or a fantasized lost kingdom.

EARLY NOVELS

Nabokov's first novel, *Mary* (*Mashen'ka*, 1926; trans. 1970), offers a detailed picture of Berlin's émigré culture during the early 1920s. As Ganin, a young Russian exile, dreams of reuniting with a former sweetheart, her image becomes the focus of intense yearning for his lost homeland. After *Mary* was published, Nabokov was reportedly dissatisfied with its lack of aesthetic detachment. In his second novel, *King, Queen, Knave* (*Korol', dama, valet*, 1928), he achieved that detachment by calling attention to the fictional status of his universe—a construct of words taking life from the pen of the author. An arsenal of literary techniques—including wordplay, allusions, self-conscious references, and authorial intrusions—interrupts the reader's sympathetic participation in the characters' lives and world.

As the title *King, Queen, Knave* suggests, the main characters, like a "royal" triad of cards, play out the hand dealt them by their author as he plays with a favorite cliché of detective fiction: the adulterous love triangle. Franz, the myopic (in both senses) young knave of the novel, arrives in Berlin to work for his wealthy uncle, a prominent businessman named Dreyer. Martha, Dreyer's discontented wife, promptly seduces him, embroiling Franz in a scheme to murder her husband and get his money. The author's overt manipulations notwithstanding, each of the protagonists demonstrates the extent to which character—the psychology and moral consciousness of each character—is fate. Unable to resist Martha's despotic will, the cowardly Franz becomes not only her accomplice but also her puppet. She, on the other hand, is energized by her hatred for her husband, whose elusive inner life is a source of mysterious energy she cannot control and whose unpredictable actions inevitably thwart her plans. For each, "reality" proves to be a psychological construct, an incomplete but significant fusion of individual perception and the phenomenological world.

In *The Defense* (*Zashchita Luzhina*, 1930; trans. 1964), Nabokov, himself a composer of chess problems, deploys all the deceptive feints and false leads of the game to narrate the story of an inspired chess genius. Grand master Luzhin is a man rescued from the daunting confusion of life, its relentless sallies against his reclusive nature, by the elegant order of chess. The cold strategies of the chessboard have virtually eclipsed Luzhin's awareness of the world around him. The safety of his retreat is undermined, however, by an extraordinary woman who enters his life. When she and Luzhin's doctor convince him that he must, for the sake of his health and sanity, give up chess altogether, Luzhin tries, but fails, to ward off the deadly encroachments of the game. He ultimately seeks escape by leaping from a window. As he plummets to his death, the shadows in the courtyard declare his defeat as they "divide" before his eyes into the "dark and pale squares" of a chessboard.

The first of Nabokov's novels to receive wide recognition by Russian émigré critics, *The Defense* is paradigmatic of his later fiction. Sustaining dual, if not multiple, perspectives, it places unique demands on the reader. Luzhin, the hapless genius, is one of Nabokov's most touching protagonists, but his fate, while it provokes sympathy, is not to be "identified with" by the reader, who acquires a more detached perspective. From this vantage, the apparently three-dimensional world recedes into the artist's two-dimensional canvas, itself a kind of game board on which the reader and writer face off. *The Eye* (*Sogliadatai*, 1930; trans. 1965), Nabokov's fourth novel, plays with the relationship between life and art, imagination and reality, even more radically. It skillfully creates the illusion that the narrating "I" (and "eye") of the novel, a nameless Russian émigré living in Berlin, possesses a unique identity, distinct from that of a character named Smurov whom the narrator purports to be observing. In the end, Smurov turns out to be the narrator's projected self, or alter ego. Employing all the devices of a verbal illusionist, Nabokov constructs a hall of mirrors through which the delusional narrator leads his readers.

A LITERATURE OF EXILE

At the end of 1930, when *The Eye* was first published, Nabokov was already putting the finishing touches on his next novel, *Glory* (*Podvig*, 1932; trans. 1971). By 1931, fascist ideologues were taking to the streets of Berlin, and the offices of *Rul'* were attacked. Despite the threatening nature of these events, Nabokov continued to write at an astonishing rate, his imagination focused on the past rather than the present. The exile's longing to return to the land of his childhood constitutes *Glory*'s nostalgic theme. Martin Edelweiss, a romantic young Russian, dreams of returning to his beloved homeland, now in the grip of Soviet rule. Near the novel's end, as Martin entertains the possibility of his own death at the hands of executioners, he invokes the brave figure of the Russian

Acmeist poet Nikolai Gumilev, who was executed as a counterrevolutionary by the Bolsheviks in 1921. Although it received faint praise from émigré critics, *Glory* remained a favorite of its author, who counted Martin Edelweiss among his most "resplendent characters." Present-day readers may detect early soundings of some prominent Nabokovian themes. At one point in the novel, for example, Martin conjures an imaginary land called Zoorland, now bent under the weight of totalitarian rule—an image that would recur in many of Nabokov's later stories and novels, including *Invitation to a Beheading* and *Bend Sinister*, and would receive its apotheosis in the remarkable design of *Pale Fire*.

In contrast to *Glory*, the last of Nabokov's novels to be translated into English, *Laughter in the Dark* (*Kamera obskura*, 1932) received its first English translation as *Camera Obscura* in 1936. Dissatisfied with the translator's version, Nabokov retranslated it several years later as *Laughter in the Dark* (1938). Despite its flaws, the novel offers insight into some of the most important and least understood aspects of his fiction. The narrator's opening statement introduces the novel's detached perspective: "Once upon a time there lived in Berlin, Germany, a man called Albinus. He was rich, respectable, happy; one day he abandoned his wife for the sake of a youthful mistress; he loved; was not loved; and his life ended in disaster." True to this fablelike tone, the disaster in which Albinus's life ends is the result of his own moral failings. Psychologically blind from the story's outset, Albinus Kretschmar is, by the time he tries to murder his mistress, physically blind as well. The car crash that destroys his sight is brought on by his jealous rage at Margot's infidelity. His attempt at revenge similarly backfires: the gun goes off, but it is he who is fatally shot. These chilling ironies are greatly relished by the central villain of the tale, a sadistic artist named Axel Rex, who happens to be Margot's lover and delights in toying with the unwitting Albinus. A professional cartoonist, Rex proceeds to turn the rituals of daily life into clever vignettes evincing the same blend of cruelty and credulity that he creates in his newspaper sketches. His attempt to turn life into art for his own amusement represents a particularly vicious form of the misperception that befalls many a Nabokov character—from kindly Luzhin in *The Defense* to perverse Hermann in *Despair* and, most eloquently, to tormented Humbert in *Lolita*. Each fails to recognize the distinction between life and art and the laws governing the individual's prerogatives with respect to both.

Nabokov, by contrast, was rigorous about the distinction between life and art. Outside "that private world" in which the artist reigns as "perfect dictator," the rights and freedoms of the individual must obtain (*Strong Opinions*, p. 69). "Democracy is humanity at its best," he said, "because it is the natural condition of every man since the human mind became conscious not only of the world but of itself" (cited in Field, p. 375). To Nabokov, the artist's control over his fictional universe obviates his characters' autonomy—the right to life, liberty, and the pursuit of happiness on which democracy is founded. Because his highly wrought works of artifice underscore rather than hide this fact, he is often accused of the kind of aesthetic arrogance evinced by Axel Rex. The best argument against such a view is made by the novel itself. In one telling scene from *Laughter in the Dark*, Rex is engaging in his favorite pastime, taunting the blind Albinus, when Albinus's brother-in-law Paul arrives in search of his missing relative. Bursting into the room to find the naked Rex seated next to the blind man, tickling his face with a stem of grass, Paul delivers a blow to Rex's head, instantly reducing Albinus's tormentor to the naked wretch that he is.

The protagonist of Nabokov's sixth Russian novel, *Despair* (*Otchaianie*, 1936; trans. 1966), is another wretch with artistic pretensions. Hermann Karlovich, the first-person narrator, serves as a parody of the nineteenth-century Russian novelist Fyodor Dostoyevsky's confessional narrators. In the end, Hermann's plan to commit the "perfect" murder, which he repeatedly compares to the perfect work of art, proves to be a consummate bungle. Savaging Hermann's artistic pretensions, Nabokov subverts the assumptions of detective thrillers as he critiques Dostoyevsky's novel *Crime and Punishment* for its elevation of murder to the status of a philosophical paradigm. From Martha's thwarted attempt to murder her husband in *King, Queen, Knave* to Humbert's failure to redeem his crime against Lolita by murdering his rival, Clare Quilty, Nabokov's fiction demonstrates that the act of murder is never inspired, merely vicious and intrinsically banal.

TOTALITARIAN NIGHTMARES

It took Nabokov "one fortnight of wonderful excitement and sustained inspiration" to compose his next-to-last novel in Russian, *Invitation to a Beheading* (*Priglashenie na kazn'*, 1938; trans. 1959) (*Strong Opinions*, p. 68). The protagonist, Cincinnatus C., has been accused of an indefinite crime, "gnostical turpitude," apparently meaning that he is guilty of possessing a soul. Gradually,

Cincinnatus comes to see that the fortress in which he is imprisoned is only a stage set; the functionaries who run it, interchangeable dummies. The primary role of consciousness in Nabokov's world and vision here receives its most radical expression. As the sole prisoner in this macabre farce, Cincinnatus alone can grant it power. Whenever fear clouds his consciousness, Cincinnatus begins to conjure the farcical prison with dangerous intensity, inadvertently bestowing life on the dummies around him as he "inspire[s] the meaningless with meaning, and the lifeless with life" (p. 155). In the end, Cincinnatus holds on to his head in both senses. His delicate neck poised on the executioner's block, he suddenly rises and asks, "Why am I here?" With this simple challenge, the world of *Invitation* collapses: the fake scenery breaks up in a whirlwind of "dust, rags, chips of painted wood," the executioner's platform dissolves "in a cloud of reddish dust," and Cincinnatus makes his way toward "beings akin to him" (p. 223). Whether Cincinnatus finds liberation in death or in a world existing beyond the flimsy trappings of the prison is a question left for readers to ponder.

Depending on one's critical approach—political, metafictional, or metaphysical—Cincinnatus can be perceived as imprisoned in a fictionalized totalitarian regime, the author's plot, or the inferior world of matter. In each case, Nabokov's use of theatrical metaphors—the fortress's freshly painted walls, greasepainted characters, hastily improvised props—suggests the individual's entrapment in a sham world. If the fraudulent political trials staged by Stalin and his henchmen during the 1930s had some bearing on Nabokov's use of theatrical devices in *Invitation,* so did his own early activity as a playwright. *The Waltz Invention* (*Izobretenie val'sa,* 1938; trans. 1966), the only one of Nabokov's handful of Russian plays to be translated during his lifetime, is set in an invented country that offers some parallels with *Invitation.* Just as Cincinnatus's jailer, lawyer, and warden—Rodion, Roman, and Rodrig—turn out to be interchangeable dummies, so the government officials in *Waltz*—Grab, Grob, Gerb, Grib, and others—are similarly devoid of individual identity. Evincing characteristics of both Hitler's Germany and Stalin's Russia, *Waltz* anticipates the dropping of the atomic bomb seven years after its publication.

NABOKOV'S GIFT

Published serially in a Paris émigré journal during 1937–1938, *The Gift* (*Dar,* trans. 1963) is the crowning achievement of Nabokov's career as a Russian writer.

The complete text of the novel did not appear in book form until 1952, however, when it was brought out in Russian by a publisher based in New York. Displaying all of the stylistic and structural features that characterize Nabokov's most celebrated masterpieces—including *Lolita, Pale Fire,* and *Ada*—*The Gift* is set in émigré Berlin during 1926–1929. It centers on a young writer in exile named Fyodor Godunov-Cherdyntsev, his growth as an artist, the evolution of Russian literature, and the intensely debated issues defining Russian émigré culture of this period. For non-Russian readers there is much to appreciate as well. Interweaving themes and motifs from Nabokov's own personal history—Fyodor's loss of a cherished parent as well as of his native land and language—*The Gift* also depicts the profound literary and emotional rapport that develops between Fyodor and Zina, the young woman he meets and intends to marry. As he reviews the pattern of events that has led to his discovery of Zina, Fyodor gleans the operation of some benign force or fate at work in his life: "And not only was Zina cleverly and elegantly made to measure for him by a very painstaking fate, but both of them, forming a single shadow, were made to the measure of something not quite comprehensible, but wonderful and benevolent and continuously surrounding them" (p. 189).

From one vantage, the operation of a "painstaking fate" signals the author's controlling presence in the novel, guiding Fyodor toward his happy encounter with Zina. From another, it bespeaks Fyodor's apprehension of a realm existing beyond the world accessible to mortal sense. Although hints of a transcendent world, or "otherworld," tantalizingly recur throughout Nabokov's fiction, it was not until the 1970s—and, most particularly, not until his widow called explicit attention to this "principal theme" in her late husband's poetry and prose—that most critics began to explore this dimension of his work (Preface, p. 3). Whether or not individual readers wish to tease out this aspect of Nabokov's fiction, they can appreciate the value and meaning assigned to Fyodor's "gift" of creative vision. Inspired by love of art, of life, of Zina, he discovers in the dreary trappings of émigré life, with all of its poverty and dislocation, the sheer wonder of existence.

In *The Gift,* Fyodor's progress from talented young poet to mature prose writer echoes Nabokov's own literary career, launched by the private publication of his first book of poems at age seventeen and succeeded by what Nabokov would later dismiss as "a steady mass of verse" produced "with monstrous regularity" throughout the 1920s and 1930s (*Poems and Problems,* p. 13). Half a century later he would translate a small fraction of his Russian verse into English, publishing it alongside the fourteen poems he wrote in English in *Poems and Problems* (1970). Another aspect of Nabokov's personal history reflected in *The Gift* is Fyodor's abiding admiration for Aleksandr Pushkin (1799–1837), acknowledged by most Russians as the nation's greatest poet. The genius of Pushkin presides over *The Gift* as it does over Nabokov's monumental four-volume translation of and commentary to Pushkin's novel in verse, *Eugene Onegin* (*Evgenii Onegin*, 1833; trans. Nabokov, 1964). Nabokov's insistence on providing a literal translation of Pushkin's narrative poem, whose nuances he addresses in a thousand pages of scholarly commentary, sparked his public debate with the American critic Edmund Wilson. Their argument over the principles of translation and of Russian usage became so bitter that it ultimately ended the friendship. Chronicled in *Dear Bunny, Dear Volodya*, that friendship began with Wilson's early championship of Nabokov's work after Nabokov arrived in the United States.

Even before Nabokov set sail for America with his wife and six-year-old son, Dmitri (his father's future translator), he had made the decision—"one of the most difficult" in his life—to abandon his native tongue and henceforth write in English. By the time the threat of war was dismantling Europe's émigré communities, Nabokov had written nine novels, fifty-plus short stories, and a handful of plays, and was widely recognized as the leading Russian émigré writer of his generation. Launching his linguistic metamorphosis by translating two of his Russian novels into English (*Despair* in 1935, *Laughter in the Dark* in 1938), Nabokov began work in Paris, during the winter of 1938, on his first novel in English, *The Real Life of Sebastian Knight* (1941). Its narrator, identified only as V., is at work on a biography of his dead half brother, Sebastian Knight, a novelist whose personal history and idiosyncratic literary style bear marked affinities to Nabokov's. As V. attempts to bring the dead writer to life, his quest alludes to the process of artistic metamorphosis in which Nabokov himself was engaged. In his debut performance as an English writer, Nabokov sought to bring his own style and vision to life in another language. He was, moreover, about to do something still more extraordinary: to bring onto the stage of American letters a literary giant whose fame and influence even he could not have foretold.

JOURNEY TO AMERICA

During the winter and spring of 1940, while still engaged in the arduous process of obtaining visas for his family to flee Europe, Nabokov prepared for anticipated employment in America by writing a series of lectures on Russian literature. (Forty years later they were edited and published as *Lectures on Russian Literature*, a companion volume to his *Lectures on Literature*, devised for his classes on world literature at Wellesley and Cornell.) In May 1940, just before Hitler's armies marched into Paris, the Nabokovs set sail from St. Nazaire, Brittany. With the help of other Russian émigrés, they initially settled in New York and later in Massachusetts—first outside Boston and then in Cambridge. During his first five years in the United States, Nabokov worked on translations of Russian writers, conducted intensive research on Lepidoptera at the American Museum of Natural History in New York and Harvard's Museum of Comparative Zoology, and completed a commissioned study, *Nikolai Gogol* (1944), on one of his favorite Russian writers. In 1946, a year after Nabokov became a U.S. citizen, he completed his second novel in English, *Bend Sinister* (1947).

Bend Sinister and *Invitation to a Beheading* are, Nabokov said, "the two bookends of grotesque design between which my other volumes huddle" ("Anniversary Notes," p. 4). The metaphor aptly suggests the exposure to outside forces that the main characters of these novels suffer, imprisoned as they are in absurd but brutal regimes bent on the destruction of the individual. Both novels reflect in their "grotesque design" the repressive regimes that Nabokov was lucky enough to escape. (His younger brother Sergey, who died in a German concentration camp, was less fortunate.) In *Bend Sinister*, the totalitarian regime's hostility to individual identity and freedom is exercised by the Party of the Average Man, under the direction of a dictator named Paduk, in an invented country whose inhabitants speak a motley language comprised of Slavic and Germanic roots. Having recently suffered the death of his beloved wife, Olga, Adam Krug mourns her throughout—only to have his agony redoubled when the regime kidnaps his eight-year-old son, David, in an attempt to force Krug, a celebrated philosopher, to comply with the regime's ideological aims. In a manner grotesquely reminiscent of the Nazis' "scientific" experiments on concentration camp inmates, the child is mistakenly murdered. The novel's remarkable ending, which abruptly delivers readers back to the "comparative paradise" of the author's study, proved confusing to many of its early readers. Today those familiar with the self-referential, postrealist narrative strategies of younger American writers, from John Barth and John Hawkes to Don DeLillo (all keen admirers of Nabokov's fiction), are more intrigued than troubled by the prominent role played by Nabokov's authorial persona—in his words, "an anthropomorphic deity impersonated by me" (*Bend Sinister*, p. xviii).

Although the setting and theme of *Bend Sinister* appear to look back at Nabokov's Russian and European past rather than toward his American present, references to the life and landscape of the United States are scattered throughout the text. Allusions to Melville's *Moby-Dick*, the drawings of Saul Steinberg, and American immigration procedures are interwoven with a host of references to European literature from James Joyce and Stéphane Mallarmé to Shakespeare, whose *Hamlet* is discussed for the better part of a chapter. This density of cross-cultural and multilingual allusions has become a hallmark of Nabokov's American fiction. Otherwise, very little about *Bend Sinister* could have prepared readers for *Lolita*'s arrival on the scene.

LOLITA AND FAME

Considered too hot to handle by five American publishers, *Lolita* was finally published in Paris, in 1955, by the Olympia Press. One can only guess how long the novel would have remained hidden between pale green covers, muffled by the imprint of a press known for its "sexy" books, if Graham Greene, a prominent British novelist, had not rescued it from near-oblivion. Speaking to the *London Sunday Times* on Christmas Day (the timing could not have been lost on Nabokov), Greene named *Lolita* one of the three best books of the year. Once "discovered," it quickly became the focus of a legal and literary controversy. Despite its championship by writers and critics in the United States, *Lolita* did not receive an American edition until 1958—after which acclaim for its artistic merit quickly grew.

Since its publication, more than a few critics have proved unequal to the task of reading *Lolita* wisely or well. Ignoring the shifting tones and devious rhetorical strategies of the novel's first-person narrator—as well as the false leads provided by the author to trip up the inattentive—they have condemned the novelist's alleged identification with its scurrilous protagonist; some have even denounced Nabokov for his implicit promotion of the child's sexual exploitation. Yet all the puns, patterns, and wordplay spawned by Humbert's narration underscore the reader's need to stay alert, to maintain a critical distance from this most unreliable of narrators. As Humbert's voice shifts from rapturous evocation to mocking self-denigration, the narrative spins comedy out

of despair and tragedy out of farce. Set in prosperous postwar America, the novel paints an incongruous, often hilarious picture of a cosmopolitan European set adrift in a New World provincial backwater. Lolita's adolescent infatuation with handsome "Hum" quickly turns to contempt when, after the death of her mother (whom Humbert married to get at the daughter), he turns out to be a grotesque parody of the strict European papa, refusing to let her out of his clutches.

By all accounts, including Humbert's own, he is a pervert. What makes him so interesting, if untrustworthy, a character is the nature of his infernal passion, which derives not from some clinically definable disorder but from the depths of his fevered imagination. The nature of Humbert's quest is revealed early on by the "time terms" he substitutes for "spatial terms" when describing the "perilous" beauty of nymphets. Among young girls between the ages of nine and fourteen, he says, the bewitched nympholept discovers those rare few whose true nature "is not human but nymphic," or "demoniac" (p. 16). As readers soon discover, it is Humbert's own fantasizing imagination that works the demonic magic he ascribes to the nymphet. Only belatedly does he admit that, prey to his ardent imagination, he is the predator who captured Lolita and destroyed her childhood. If Humbert's confession of guilt at the end of the novel does not manage "to save his soul," as he hopes, it does afford him a modicum of saving grace (p. 308). The awakening that triggers his qualified redemption is both moral and aesthetic, because it depends both on the intensity of his remorse and on his vital perception of the child's autonomous identity. This link between ethics and aesthetics in Nabokov's fiction has generated increasing interest among scholars and critics, laying to rest his early reputation as an aesthete indifferent to the ethical concerns of human beings.

Once published in the United States, *Lolita* sold 100,000 copies in the first three weeks, catapulting it to the top of the best-seller list, where it remained for months. By this time Nabokov's next novel, *Pnin* (1957), had received its own share of acclaim. *Pnin*'s success, in contrast to *Lolita*'s, can largely be explained by the appeal of its main character, Timofey Pnin, a Russian émigré who teaches his native language at a New England college called Waindell. Awkward, absentminded, pedantic, Professor Pnin is, according to his author, not in the least a "clown"—although this assertion might surprise some of the nastier members of the Waindell faculty, whose lampoons of Pnin constitute a major pastime. The petty cruelty evinced by these and other characters is a reminder of the viciousness of which human beings are capable—a viciousness amply demonstrated by the recent history through which Pnin has lived. Less fortunate were many of Pnin's friends and acquaintances who, like his former sweetheart, Mira, perished in a Nazi concentration camp or were similarly "murdered" and "forgotten."

While *Lolita* declared Nabokov an American writer—its worldwide success making him an international celebrity—*Pnin* calls attention to the polarities of the novelist's cultural and linguistic identity. Timofey Pnin's hopeless grasp of English offers a comic counterpoint to Nabokov's mastery of his adopted language, just as Pnin's cultural dislocation and dismay contrast radically with Nabokov's expertise: the way he captures with perfect pitch the tones and rhythms of mid-century American life in *Lolita*. Indeed, so thoroughly had Nabokov steeped himself in his new language and country, so successful was he at transforming himself into an American writer that, when he turned his hand to translating *Lolita* into Russian, he was dismayed to find himself on the other side of the linguistic divide. Despite the admiration that Nabokov's translation of *Lolita* (1967) has won from leading Russian critics, Nabokov himself, as Alexander Dolonin points out, "expressed bitter disappointment with his own performance and complained that his old Russian strings had gotten rusty" (*The Garland Companion to Vladimir Nabokov*, pp. 323–324).

THE LAST ARC OF EXILE

In 1959, a year after *Lolita*'s arrival in America, Nabokov bid good-bye to academic life and to Cornell University, where he had taught for over a decade. After writing a screenplay of *Lolita* for Stanley Kubrick, which was later published (in 1974) but which the director largely ignored, Nabokov settled with Véra in Montreux, Switzerland, where he continued to reside until his death on 2 July 1977. Commenting on this ultimate phase of his life, Nabokov said, "I think I am trying to develop, in this rosy exile, the same fertile nostalgia in regard to America, my new country, as I evolved for Russia, my old one, in the first post-revolution years of West-European expatriation" (*Strong Opinions*, p. 49). Both phases of exile were recast in Nabokov's next novel, *Pale Fire* (1962), which juxtaposes a cozy American college town called New Wye, apparently located in upstate New York, with the remote kingdom of Northern Zembla, located in a fictional, Russified Scandinavia.

The novel opens with a brief foreword by Charles Kinbote, who introduces a 999-line narrative poem in rhyming couplets penned by a fictional American poet, John Shade. (It is worth noting that in Shade's poem Nabokov creates, for the first time in his career, a purely American voice—and does it within the strict parameters of rhyming couplets.) Recently deceased, Shade was for five months Kinbote's neighbor in New Wye, where he, like Kinbote, taught at Wordsmith College. Shade's poem in four cantos, "Pale Fire," occupies thirty-seven pages of the novel's text and is followed by Kinbote's lengthy commentary and index. By composing his huge commentary, Kinbote intends to reveal what he believes is the true subject of Shade's meditative poem: the story of Zembla's exiled king, Charles the Beloved, forced to flee after a revolution staged by the Extremist Party and pursued by an assassin sent to track him down in the United States. Kinbote's outrageous contention, that "without my notes Shade's text simply has no human reality at all," testifies to the delusion of a madman who believes himself to be the exiled king and reads Shade's poem through the distorting lens of his fantasy (p. 28). Conjuring a fairy-tale kingdom possessing its own unique history, politics, and people, Kinbote's riotous imagination and paranoid impulses trace a wild course over Shade's contemplative verse, which quietly explores the nature of art and the possible key to life's meaning. In his poem, Shade fashions a window through which to peer beyond the limits of the present; Kinbote gazes through it to discover a remote and mythical past.

Pale Fire's four distinct sections—Shade's poem and Kinbote's foreword, commentary, and index—constitute an intricately patterned, overarching design. As numerous critics have shown, many details of Kinbote's fantasized kingdom mirror elements of his academic life—from his anxieties about being exposed as a homosexual to the ridicule he suffers at the hands of certain colleagues. Threaded through Kinbote's commentary, moreover, are numerous skeins of interwoven images and motifs that resonate with and reflect elements of Shade's poem, beginning with its title. The opening lines of Shade's poem introduce the theme of reflection, a theme sustained and developed by the poem's recurrent images of windows, mirrors, and other shimmering surfaces: "I was the shadow of the waxwing slain / By the false azure of the windowpane" (p. 33). This image of "false azure," while bearing no literal relation to Kinbote's presumed identity as Charles the Beloved, resonantly comments on the illusory reality Kinbote has conjured to escape the confines of his unhappy existence. The kingdom of Zembla is a virtual world of mirrors—it has a palace of stained glass windows, a skyscraper of ultramarine glass, and a glass factory that serves as a focal point for the country's political crises. And just as Zembla reflects, as in a distortive mirror, Kinbote's life in New Wye, so the design of Shade's poem not only reflects details of Shade's domestic life but also at times appears, without the poet's knowing it, to foreshadow his untimely death. The agent responsible for these telling patterns of interlinking images is neither Kinbote nor Shade, as some critics have insisted, but Nabokov himself. At the end of the novel, John Shade dies senselessly, shot through the heart by a convict who mistakes him for someone else. But the "web of sense" he has sought to unravel by means of art's "combinational delight" emerges in the text's overarching design, in which Shade's poem and Kinbote's commentary play their assigned parts (pp. 63, 69).

ADA AND ANTITERRA

At the apex of his celebrity as an American writer, Nabokov published his longest and most difficult novel, *Ada; or Ardor: A Family Chronicle* (1969). The event was lavishly announced by *Time* magazine in its 23 May issue, which had the author's picture on the cover. How many of those who bought the book actually finished it poses an interesting question. What cannot be questioned is the complexity of its artistry. In *Ada* the artifice is more intricately contrived, the texture of allusions more densely interwoven, than in any previous or subsequent Nabokov novel—and that is saying a lot. By distorting and recombining the geographical, social, and historical facts of terrestrial life, Nabokov invents a world that leaves nothing to chance—and everything to art. The inhabitants of Antiterra are as extraordinary as their planet's topography; their experience, like Antiterran history and geography, is a dazzlingly distorted version of earthly existence. The characters pursue lives of remarkable excess: an excess both moral and material, from which the middle ground of human experience—the routine demands, constraints, and consolations—has been largely obliterated. Imbued with prodigious intelligence, energy, and appetite, Van and Ada Veen, siblings as well as lovers, are both monstrous and magnificent. Driven by a relentless capacity for "inhuman passion," they have little time and less inclination for the humbler forms of human affection (p. 252). From this perspective, Antiterra's alternative name, Demonia, suggests the demonic, or infernal, nature of the passion that rules not only their lives (the name of Van and Ada's father is Demon Veen) but the lives of virtually every other character in the novel.

As Van narrates, with Ada's help, the history of their lifelong love affair, the gardens of Ardis, where he and Ada first discovered the ecstasy of incest, exist in his memory as a perfect world of delight—one that parodies the myth of Eden and original innocence. The branches of the Zemski family tree, of which Van and Ada are the last surviving members, bear numerous forebears whose predilection for "old masters and young mistresses" offers suggestive variations on the siblings' own carnal and creative energies (p. 4). The interlinking relationships everywhere present in *Ada* are by no means confined to the familial, however. The text teems with linguistic references and intertextual allusions that investigate the interconnections between art and ardor, literature and painting, science and art, writing and acrobatics. On a global plane, myriad aspects of Antiterra tantalizingly evoke its possible relationship to a "sibling planet" that some Antiterran believers call Terra. In his novel, *Letters from Terra*, Van debunks the "strain of sweet happiness" pervading such visions of "Terra the Fair." The "purpose of the novel," he explains, "was to suggest that Terra cheated, that all was not paradise there, that perhaps in some ways human minds and human flesh underwent on that sibling planet worse torments than on our much maligned Demonia" (p. 341). True, Demonia's privileged and powerful practice every form of aesthetic and erotic indulgence at the expense of the lowly and weak. On the other hand, the scourges of war, revolution, and genocide are unknown to its inhabitants, who have enjoyed a "cloudless course of Demonian history in the twentieth century" (p. 580). In contrast to our Earth, Demonia appears to be, if not a "comparative paradise," a rather charming, old-fashioned version of hell.

NABOKOV'S SHADES

Following in the wake of *Ada*, *Transparent Things* (1972) marks a radical departure from Nabokov's previous novels in English. Brief in length and laconic in style, the novel centers on an inept protagonist whose name, like his character, lacks the dynamic features of a Humbert or a Kinbote, a Van or Ada Veen. Nor can Hugh Person claim any of these characters' prodigious talents. While he is affectionately regarded by the narrator, such fondness derives from sympathy rather than admiration. "Hugh, a sentimental simpleton, and somehow not a very *good* Person," says the narrator, "was merely a rather dear one" (p. 77). The novel, set in the 1950s and 1960s, follows Hugh Person from his days as a college student to his fortieth year. Events center on several European trips that he makes, the first with his widowed father and the last as a widower himself. An editor for a New York publisher, Hugh is assigned to work with Mr. R., a German-born novelist living in Switzerland, "who wrote English considerably better than he spoke it" and is known in his "adopted country" as a "master stylist" (p. 43). If these parodic references to the author's persona replay a familiar Nabokovian device, Mr. R. proves highly original in other ways. Not only is he an intrusive narrator, he is a posthumous one, having died by the time the novel opens.

Shortly after the publication of *Transparent Things*, Nabokov, taking note of the general incomprehension expressed by most reviewers, pointed to the novel's "behind-the-cypress inquiry into a tangle of random destinies" (*Strong Opinions*, pp. 194–196). Guided by this clue, critics returned to the novel to discover its ghostly theme and, subsequently, to trace that theme in other Nabokov novels. The information they have culled about these shades or ghosts suggests why notice of their presence came relatively late. Contrary to the conventions of folk or fairy tales, Nabokov's shades do not meddle directly in a person's life, dictating the course of the action or a character's fate. The influence they exert is both limited and oblique: by creating sudden shifts in the atmosphere, they encode phenomena with cryptic signs and messages. In *Transparent Things*, Mr. R. brings an otherworldly perspective to Hugh's story by revealing "things" that are "transparent" to a ghostly eye but opaque to those included among the novel's living. With the help of his fellow shades, the ghostly Mr. R. tries to assist Hugh as best he can; as the novel's narrator, he calls attention to patterns in Hugh's life that signal or foretell the design of his death. In the end, Hugh, like Cincinnatus and Krug before him, is liberated from the local landscape, gathered into a stylized eternity by the novel's invisible shades. "Easy . . . does it, son," says Mr. R., as he helps Hugh in the transition "from one state of being to another" (p. 158). The game of worlds in which this and other Nabokov novels playfully engage casts a speculative light on the nature of our own world and what may lie beyond its perceived confines.

Just as *Transparent Things* treats the theme of the otherworld more directly than any of Nabokov's previous fiction, so *Look at the Harlequins!* (1974) explicitly plays with and parodies the figure of the authorial persona—the shadowy V. in pursuit of Sebastian Knight's "real life," the N. who relates Pnin's history—that reappears throughout his fiction. LATH, as Nabokov referred to his last completed novel, is cast as the memoir of a successful Anglo-Russian writer, Vadim Vadimovich N., or VV,

whose life, like his name, is a distorted (and reductive) version of the author's. (Nabokov's own initials, V. V., stand for Vladimir Vladimirovich.) Born, like his near namesake, in 1899, VV has suffered a paralytic stroke that appears to have triggered or exacerbated his headaches and nervous disorders. He is haunted by the sense that he is only a pale reflection, or "parody," of a much greater writer, his life "an inferior variant" of "another man's life, somewhere on this or another earth" (p. 89). At the end of the novel, the tormented VV is able to break through the confines of his solipsistic perception and, in the form of the woman he loves, to embrace the larger world of "Reality." This theme has been sounded throughout Nabokov's novels and, it must be said, often to greater effect. Readers can trace its development from Ganin's awakening to the world around him, to Cincinnatus's epiphany concerning the flimsy trappings of the prison in which he is incarcerated, to Humbert's recognition that the real loss has been Lolita's, not his. In each case revelation, like a butterfly, breaks free of the cocoon spun by desire or obsession, fear or nostalgia—and makes contact, however briefly, with some higher truth or reality.

The dominant themes of Nabokov's career are also highlighted in the posthumously published collection *The Collected Stories of Vladimir Nabokov* (1995), which joins some fifty of the stories he wrote in Russian during the 1920s and 1930s with the ten he composed in English. The majority of these stories previously appeared in four definitive collections brought out in the aftermath of *Lolita*'s success—beginning with the English stories in *Nabokov's Dozen* (1958) and followed by three volumes of translations from the original Russian: *A Russian Beauty* (1973), *Tyrants Destroyed* (1975), and *Details of a Sunset* (1976). Unlike these volumes, however, the 1995 collection is organized chronologically and contains thirteen newly translated Russian stories to boot. It allows Nabokov's readers to trace the development, and intriguing metamorphoses, of themes and techniques he explored throughout his longer fiction. Those familiar with his novels will note the variations that both early and late stories ring on such dominant themes as the narrator's imaginative return to an idyllic first world; the presence of authorial agents or representatives within the text; the role of individual perception in creating or determining the nature of a character's "reality"; imagination's discovery of the extraordinary within the ordinary; the creative gestation of the work of art in the writer's consciousness; hints of an otherworld or metaphysical realm embedded in the fabric of existence, and the power of human thought, curiosity, and love to make fleeting contact with it.

NABOKOV'S GIFT TO AMERICAN LITERATURE

Rehearsing the dominant themes of Nabokov's fiction cannot begin to suggest, however, the impact and effects of his audacious language and style. The surprise of a Nabokov sentence, the charge of its linguistic layers and lapidary wit, defy description: you have to see (or read) it for yourself to believe it. Better to try capturing the arc of an airborne skater's triple axel or the leap of human thought as it soars like an acrobat into space. The self-conscious, self-referential nature of Nabokov's fiction celebrates the most daring feats of imagination, memory, thought, and art. The game of worlds in which Nabokov invites readers to participate is neither a superficial sport nor an escape from the exigencies of human experience. Rather, it serves as a model or reflection of the processes by which all of us, each in his or her own way, intimately register and record, shape and make known the world we inhabit. Nabokov liked to compare the artist to a conjurer and the tricks of his trade to the magician's sleights of hand. But the strategies of self-conscious artifice point to more than the prestidigitator's performance: like the magician whose deft fingers pluck a live bird from his hat, Nabokov summons the "real" in the very act of creating illusion.

Thirty years after Nabokov arrived in America, the journal *TriQuarterly* devoted its Winter 1970 issue to his achievement, celebrating the author's seventieth birthday and declaring him the greatest living American writer. Joining in the celebration was an impressive array of younger American writers, including John Updike, Herbert Gold, Richard Howard, and John Barth—each of whom paid his respects to the master. Speaking for a still younger generation of American writers, Edmund White, in a 1984 essay, said that Nabokov must ultimately be ranked alongside two other Russian artists of his generation who emigrated to America: the choreographer George Balanchine and the composer Igor Stravinsky. All three Russians, their genius "clarified" by French culture, embraced the "breezy short-order cook of American informality" (*Achievement*, pp. 25–26). White here alludes to the impact of New World culture on these formidable Russian innovators who, in their different media, would help fashion a new definition of American art and culture. When Nabokov arrived in America in 1940, many readers and writers were still caught in the spell of Ernest Hemingway's minimalist style, his code of understatement. But new voices—those of Jewish, African-American, and regional writers like Saul Bellow, Bernard Malamud, Ralph Ellison, Richard Wright, and Eudora Welty—were making themselves heard. To this vital infusion of new ethnic and racial perspectives, Nabokov added the charged rhythms of his language and the cross-cultural dimensions of his expatriate vision—helping to change forever what it means to write in the American grain.

WORKS

Laughter in the Dark (*Kamera obskura*, 1932) (1938)
The Real Life of Sebastian Knight (1941)
Nikolai Gogol (1944)
Bend Sinister (1947)
Lolita (1955)
Pnin (1957)
Nabokov's Dozen (1958)
Invitation to a Beheading (*Priglashenie na kazn'*, 1938) (1959)
Pale Fire (1962)
The Gift (*Dar*, 1952) (1963)
The Defense (*Zashchita Luzhina*, 1930) (1964)
Eugene Onegin: A Novel in Verse by Aleksandr Pushkin, trans. with commentary by Vladimir Nabokov, 4 vols. (1964; rev. ed. 1975)
The Eye (*Sogliadatai*, 1930) (1965)
Despair (*Otchaianie*, 1936) (1966)
The Waltz Invention (*Izobretenie val'sa*, 1938) (1966)
Speak, Memory: An Autobiography Revisited (1966)
King, Queen, Knave (*Korol', dama, valet*, 1928) (1968)
Ada; or Ardor: A Family Chronicle (1969)
Mary (*Mashen'ka*, 1926) (1970)
Poems and Problems (1970)
Glory (*Podvig*, 1932) (1971)
Transparent Things (1972)
A Russian Beauty and Other Stories (1973)
Strong Opinions (1973)
Lolita: A Screenplay (1974)
Look at the Harlequins! (1974)
Tyrants Destroyed and Other Stories (1975)
Details of a Sunset and Other Stories (1976)
Lectures on Don Quixote (1980)
Lectures on Literature (1980)
Lectures on Russian Literature (1981)
The Man from the USSR and Other Plays (1984)
The Enchanter (1986)
The Collected Stories of Vladimir Nabokov (1995)

FURTHER READING

Alexandrov, Vladimir E. *Nabokov's Otherworld*. Princeton, N.J., 1991. A detailed exploration of the metaphysical dimension of Nabokov's fiction and the relationship between ethics and metaphysics in his universe.

Alexandrov, Vladimir, ed. *The Garland Companion to Vladimir Nabokov*. New York, 1995. A comprehensive collection of authoritative analyses of Nabokov's works by many of the world's recognized experts.

Alter, Robert. *Partial Magic: The Novel as a Self-Conscious Genre*. Berkeley, Calif., 1975. Alter's seminal discussion of *Pale Fire*, in chapter 6, offers the most concise and illuminating introduction to the novel's structure and themes.

Appel, Alfred, Jr., ed. *The Annotated Lolita*. Rev. ed. New York, 1991. Appel's introduction to the novel offers valuable insights into Nabokov's major techniques and narrative devices.

Appel, Alfred, Jr., and Charles Newman, eds. *For Vladimir Nabokov on His Seventieth Birthday*. Supplement to *TriQuarterly*, no. 17 (Winter 1970).

Boyd, Brian. *Vladimir Nabokov: The Russian Years*. Princeton, N.J., 1990.

Boyd, Brian. *Vladimir Nabokov: The American Years*. Princeton, N.J., 1991. Boyd's definitive two-volume biography, covering the Russian and American phases of Nabokov's life, offers critical insights into virtually all of his Russian and English works.

Connolly, Julian W., ed. *Nabokov and His Fiction: New Perspectives*. Cambridge, Mass., 1999.

Field, Andrew. *Nabokov: His Life in Art*. Boston, 1967. An early critical biography that contains some insightful readings of Nabokov's fiction.

Grayson, Jane, Arnold McMillin, and Priscilla Meyer, eds. *Nabokov's World*. Vol. 1, *The Shape of Nabokov's World*. Vol. 2, *Reading Nabokov*. Houndmills, U.K., 2002.

Johnson, Kurt, and Steve Coates. *Nabokov's Blues: The Scientific Odyssey of a Literary Genius*. Cambridge, Mass., 1999. A fascinating account of Nabokov's pioneering contributions to the field of lepidoptery.

Karlinsky, Simon, ed. *Dear Bunny, Dear Volodya: The Nabokov-Wilson Letters, 1940–1971*. Rev. ed. Berkeley, Calif., 2001. The correspondence between Nabokov and the American writer and literary critic, Edmund Wilson, is helpfully annotated by the editor.

Nabokov, Dmitri, and Matthew J. Bruccoli, eds. *Vladimir Nabokov: Selected Letters, 1940–1977*. New York, 1989.

Page, Norman, ed. *Nabokov: The Critical Heritage*. London, 1982. A guide to the critical response to Nabokov from the 1930s through the 1970s, including samples of his early Russian and European reviews.

Pifer, Ellen. *Nabokov and the Novel*. Cambridge, Mass., 1980. A critical reassessment of Nabokov's highly wrought works of artifice, arguing for an ethical as well as aesthetic dimension in his art.

Pifer, Ellen, ed. *Vladimir Nabokov's Lolita: A Casebook*. New York, 2002. A representative collection of essays on Nabokov's most famous, and controversial, novel.

Rivers, J. E., and Charles Nicol, eds. *Nabokov's Fifth Arc: Nabokov and Others on His Life's Work*. Austin, Tex., 1982.

Rorty, Richard. *Contingency, Irony, and Solidarity*. New York, 1989. In chapter 7 of his study, this prominent American philosopher offers an interesting, if not always convincing, reading of Nabokov's treatment of human cruelty.

Schiff, Stacy. *Véra (Mrs. Vladimir Nabokov)*. New York, 1999. A portrait of the artist's wife that lends insight into their remarkable literary partnership.

Shapiro, Gavriel, ed. *Nabokov at Cornell*. Ithaca, N.Y., 2003. Selected essays by an international gathering of scholars who participated in the Nabokov centenary festival held at Cornell University in 1999.

Shrayer, Maxim D. *The World of Nabokov's Stories*. Austin, Tex., 1999. A comprehensive study of Nabokov's short stories that illuminates his Russian literary origins.

White, Edmund. "Nabokov: Beyond Parody." In *The Achievements of Vladimir Nabokov*, edited by George Gibian and Stephen Jan Parker. Ithaca, N.Y., 1984.

See also the article on *Lolita*, immediately following.

VLADIMIR NABOKOV'S
LOLITA

by Andrew Zawacki

*L*olita (1955) is Russian writer Vladimir Nabokov's novel about a fascinating, sometimes beautiful, often disquieting relationship between an older man, Humbert Humbert, and the twelve-year-old title character. Ostensibly Humbert's testimony recounted during his imprisonment for murder after the affair, the narrative is delivered not in Nabokov's native language but in English. The foreword by one John Ray Jr., Ph.D.—a further Nabokovian invention—argues that the case history to follow will become a classic in psychiatric circles and a moral touchstone, but Nabokov maintained a lifelong aversion to Freud's psychoanalytic apparatus, as well as to allegory, symbolism, didacticism, and literature promoting anything but aesthetic enjoyment. Born in Paris, Humbert is haunted by an unconsummated childhood romance with a thirteen-year-old girl named Annabel Leigh, an allusion to Edgar Allan Poe's poem, "Annabel Lee." A self-proclaimed "artist" and "madman" who vacillates between valorizing his good looks and European refinement and denigrating his shameful perversions, Humbert moves to New York after inheriting money. Following several bouts with insanity, when he is happily diagnosed as impotent and possibly homosexual, Humbert resides in New England at the home of widow Charlotte Haze and her daughter, Dolores. Twenty-four years after his formative frolics with the now-deceased Annabel, Humbert finds her reincarnated in the "dreamy childishness" and "eerie vulgarity" of young Dolores Haze, whose name suggests the mysterious pain she will cause her paramour. Humbert's ensuing obsession, documented in a diary, leads him to marry Charlotte, to consider murdering her in order to take sole possession of the girl he calls Lolita, and eventually to whisk the child away after her mother conveniently dies in an accident.

Lolita spends the summer at Camp Q, where Humbert fears she has been initiated into sex, so he henceforth struggles to keep her under close scrutiny. Humbert and Lolita commence a yearlong westward journey by car across the United States, during which they engage in sexual liaisons while staying in roadside motels. Humbert swears to the jury that he is not to blame for any immorality, since Lolita first seduced him into "strenuous intercourse." As Lo's modesty and willingness to disguise their rapport becomes increasingly lax, Humbert grows more guilty and paranoid, until he starts seeing—or imagines he sees—a convertible tailing them. The driver, Clare Quilty, is a famous dramatist, author of *The Little Nymph*, and Hum decides that he and Lo have likely been lovers ever since she acted in one of his plays. Humbert Humbert, whose divided, doubled name implies schizophrenia, believes he glimpses Lo speaking to the pursuer and preoccupies himself with outwitting the specter. Meanwhile, he has established a system of granting Lo money or freedoms in exchange for sexual favors, while bemoaning that what he considers their amorous solidarity has devolved, in her words, into "doing filthy things together and never behaving like ordinary people."

Lo contracts an infection, enters a hospital and, to her faux-father's despair, checks out with someone pretending to be her uncle. Humbert claims the subsequent part of his tale might be dubbed "Dolorès Disparue," hinting at a parallel with Marcel's jealousy toward Albertine in Proust's *À la recherche du temps perdu* (1913–1927) (*Remembrance of Things Past*, 1923–1930). Suspecting that Lo has run off with Quilty, H. H. undertakes a harried investigation of hotel directories, convinced Quilty has left cryptogrammic clues. After three fruitless years of searching, Humbert receives a letter from Lo, now Mrs. Richard F. Schiller, explaining that she and her husband need money. Hum visits her and finds that while her looks, at seventeen, have faded, he still loves her, while realizing that he has deprived her of a childhood. After Lo explains the part Quilty played in her exit, Humbert gives her four thousand dollars and departs to find the playwright. The homoerotic confrontation in Quilty's mansion further insinuates that the two men are perhaps only aspects of a split personality, and Humbert finally kills Quilty with a gun. The novel closes as the murderer, at once penitent and professing innocence, explains that he wishes his memoir to be published only after Lo has died. In a last nod toward the classical dictum that while life is short, art endures, Humbert tells Lolita that his story henceforth constitutes "the only immortality you and I may share."

PROVOCATIONS AND PRECURSORS

In a statement of 12 November 1956, appended to *Lolita*, Nabokov explains, somewhat evasively, that "the initial shiver of inspiration" for the novel was "prompted by a newspaper story about an ape in the Jardin des Plantes who, after months of coaxing by a scientist, produced the first drawing ever charcoaled by an animal: this sketch showed the bars of the poor creature's cage." Literary biographer Andrew Field argues that the motifs of imprisonment and of art as a mode of elegant caging are indeed present throughout Nabokov's work, even before *Lolita*. The protagonists Franz in *King, Queen, Knave* (1928) and Kretschmer in *Laughter in the Dark* (1932), like Humbert Humbert, are victims of their own or another's passion, while Hermann in *Despair* (1936) and Smurov in *The Eye* (1938) are also neurotic artists who, whether cleverly or compulsively, control the narratives they convey. Field further contends that the novel proposed by Zina's stepfather in *The Gift* (1952) prefigures the themes of *Lolita*: the elderly character imagines an "old dog" who marries a widow to seduce her daughter, a girl of the age "when nothing is formed yet but already she has a way of walking that drives you out of your mind." Alongside these mature books, a pair of Nabokov's early short stories, "A Fairytale" (1926) and "A Dashing Fellow" (1935–1937), addressed the dilemma of moral duty versus sexual desire.

The work considered to be *Lolita*'s most explicit forerunner is a short story that Nabokov, under his pseudonym, V. Sirin, composed in Russian in 1939, called "Volshebnik" ("The Enchanter"). Nabokov termed the tale—first published three decades after *Lolita*—"a kind of pre-*Lolita* novella," but critics have been quick to point out that the differences between the narratives are as pronounced as their rather superficial similarities. Nabokov himself cautioned that the unnamed protagonist of "Volshebnik" was, unlike H. H., central European, while the anonymous nymphet was French, the settings Paris and Provence. Like its better-known sister story, however, "The Enchanter" (1986) concerns a man seeking to justify his guilt after having married a dying widow in order to debauch her twelve-year-old daughter. The short story is perforated by themes of captivity, cunning, self-loathing, the elusiveness of beauty and purity, and the leitmotif of the wolf hungry to devour Little Red Riding

Hood. The forty-year-old's attempt to marry fatherhood with sexual love is frustrated at the tale's close when the girl, naked on a hotel bed as he waves "his magic wand" above her, wakes in horror at the moment of his ejaculation, forcing him to flee the authorities. Dmitri Nabokov, Vladimir's son, astutely observes that "the paternal shades rapidly into the infernal" here, as it does in *Lolita*, but the distinction between "protagonist and prey" is harder to ascertain in the more complex later work in which Lolita herself often incites seductions and emotional entrapment. By 1949, with Nabokov situated at Cornell University, what he called "the throbbing, which had never quite ceased" since "Volshebnik," started to "plague" him again, and he began devising a fresh rendition of his idea. Until his later claims that *Ada* (1969) caused him more trouble than his other novels, Nabokov was clear that *Lolita* had been "my most difficult book—the book that treated of a theme that was so distant, so remote, from my own emotional life." One source of difficulty was Nabokov's unfamiliarity with girls of Lolita's age. "I don't think I know a single little girl," he related. "I've met them socially now and then, but Lolita is a figment of my imagination." Another obstacle to the novel's creation, according to its author, was that "I did not know America; I had to invent America and Lolita." While writing his fiction—under the working title "The Kingdom by the Sea," about a girl who was named Juanita Dark until shortly before the novel's publication—Nabokov began taking the bus to observe the behavior of American teenage girls, paying special attention to their jargon.

AMERICA AND THE AMERICAN LANGUAGE

The result is a crass, bratty, often charming, semantically chameleonic preteen answering to the name Lo. No less enmeshed in Lolita's loquacity than Humbert, the reader becomes privy to an uncannily accurate American adolescent accent. "I think you stink," Lo tells her mother when directed to go to bed, "This is a free country." She badgers Humbert with a similar litany: "Swell chance. . . . I'd be a sap if I took your opinion seriously. . . . Stinker. . . . You can't boss me." Lolita's talk ranges from syllabic exaggerations like "Pulease, leave me alone" to deadpan exclamations such as "Wow! Looks swank" and "Gosh no." Occasionally she explains her vocabulary: "We washed zillions of dishes," she tells Humbert after camp, " 'Zillions' you know is schoolmarm's slang for many-many-many-many." And from time to time she deploys sarcastic French or Queen's English. "*Pardonnez*, Mother. I was not aiming at *you*," she tells Charlotte, later asking "fahther deah" if "*C'est entendu*?"

If, as Nabokov claims in his autobiography, *Lolita* was "a painful birth, a difficult baby," it is not just because he wrote it in English but because he attempted that peculiar brand of English that H. L. Mencken dubbed the American language. The first book that Nabokov wrote in English was *The Real Life of Sebastian Knight* (1941); that novel was followed by *Bend Sinister* (1947) and *Conclusive Evidence* (1951; revised as *Speak Memory*, 1966), before he finished *Lolita* in 1955. Nabokov was given to disparaging his ability to write in his adopted language, quipping that his "complete switch from Russian prose to English prose was exceedingly painful, like learning anew to handle things after losing seven or eight fingers in an explosion." Few would dispute his formidable command of English, however, and what he lamented as his "private tragedy" of having had to abandon "my untrammeled, rich, and infinitely docile Russian tongue for a second-rate brand of English" represents a windfall in American literature. Nabokov's earliest contact with English was through his governess in St. Petersburg, Russia, Miss Rachel Home; later he studied at Cambridge University. "I am an American writer, born in Russia and educated in England where I studied French literature, before spending fifteen years in Germany," he elaborated in a 1964 interview. "I came to America in 1940 and decided to become an American citizen, and make America my home." Repeatedly stating his admiration for the United States, especially its language and landscape, Nabokov vociferously defended *Lolita* against annoying charges that his novel ridiculed America. John Hollander, in *Partisan Review*, called *Lolita* a love affair with the Romantic novel. "The substitution 'English language' for 'romantic novel,'" Nabokov clarified, "would make this elegant formula more correct," and the novel indulges in grassroots American English. Humbert loves phrases like "it gave me the creeps" and "monkeying with the furniture," and as the story heats up he declares, "This, to use an American term, in which discovery, retribution, torture, death, eternity appear in the shape of a singularly repulsive nutshell, was *it*." He is equally adept at free indirect discourse, as when, in dialogue with Lolita's husband, he relates that Dick "guessed Bill and he would be going back to fix those wires. He guessed Mr. Haze and Dolly had loads of things to say to each other. He guessed he would be seeing me before I left. Why do these people guess so much and shave so little?" 258).

Written during Nabokov's butterfly-hunting excursions in Colorado, Wyoming, Arizona, and Oregon, the novel romances the natural and commercial American geography. The second half of *Lolita* roams 27,000 miles, from New England to Dixieland, across corn and cotton belts, the Rockies and western deserts, to the Pacific, then back through Reno, Death Valley, New Orleans, the Continental Divide, to Massachusetts. En route, Humbert and Lo luxuriate in shiny gasoline stations, soda fountains, roller-skating rinks, gaudy advertising billboards, and especially motels. Humbert admires functional motels and meticulously inventories their doors, beds, the ashes of a predecessor in the ashtray, the sound of a neighbor hanging his coat in the closet, the design of the hangers themselves. "I chose American motels instead of Swiss hotels or English inns," Nabokov explained, "only because I am trying to be an American writer and claim only the same rights that other American writers enjoy." A latter-day Alexis de Tocqueville of aesthetics, Humbert compares this American milieu with the setting of his infancy. The motels feature "yellow window shades pulled down to create a morning illusion of Venice and sunshine when actually it was Pennsylvania and rain," while the outdoors can deceive:

> I remember as a child in Europe gloating over a map of North America that had "Appalachian Mountains" boldly running from Alabama up to New Brunswick, so that the whole region . . . appeared to my imagination as a gigantic Switzerland or even Tibet, all mountain, glorious diamond peak upon peak, giant conifers, *le montagnard émigré* in his bear skin glory, and *Felis tigris goldsmithi*, and Red Indians under the catalpas. That it all boiled down to a measly suburban lawn and a smoking garbage incinerator, was appalling.

Nabokov exulted in this dissonance between philistine and formal, while simultaneously asserting that there was no intrinsic difference between a proletarian from Chicago and a bourgeois duke.

SEX, SCANDAL, THE BIG SCREEN

Nabokov's first published work was a translation of Lewis Carroll's *Alice's Adventures in Wonderland*, but the author of *Lolita* avoided, in his novel, any allusion to the perversion of the nineteenth-century English author and photographer of little girls. Nabokov did, however, while writing *Lolita*, note newspaper reports and court cases relevant to his theme and included several in the book. John Ray Jr. elucidates by noting that 12 percent of American males enjoy the "special experience" of Humbert Humbert, but Humbert's own theories on the appeal of young girls are more personal and metaphysical than statistics reveal. "Between the age limits of nine and fourteen," he declares, "there occur maidens who, to certain bewitched travelers, twice or many times older than they, reveal their true nature which is not human but nymphic (that is, demoniac); and these chosen creatures I propose to designate as 'nymphets.' " A self-declared "nympholept," Humbert is expert at discerning which girls possess the beatific, diabolical qualities to qualify. In Lolita's case it is a combination of her initially untainted, innocent beauty and a gum-chewing, bobby-soxing, impatient, obstinate vulgarity that gradually becomes self-aware and shameless. While clearly preoccupied by physical urges, Humbert insists that his quest transcends the merely tangible. "I am not concerned with so-called 'sex' at all," he declaims. "A greater endeavor lures me on: to fix once for all the perilous magic of nymphets." This aesthetic component, quite apart from being derivative of sexual desire, is constitutive of the special experience. "Sex is but the ancilla of art," Hum proposes, while Nabokov asserted that sex as an institution or problem bored him.

Through his protagonist's search to clarify his eccentric, sexual-artistic-mystical experience and to characterize the girls who provoke that half-blessed, half-damned impulse, Nabokov invented a phenomenon and a fury. The Pygmalion and Galatea myth woven into the novel has angered feminist critics, as has the phallocentrism and voyeurism that Humbert represents, while the implicit suggestion that art is a form of appropriation or murder has alarmed other commentators. The issue of pedophilia, of course, was taboo when the book appeared, and *Lolita* was deemed pornographic in various quarters. "That my novel does contain various allusions to the physiological urges of a pervert is quite true," Nabokov explained. "But after all we are not children, not illiterate juvenile delinquents, not English public school boys who after a night of homosexual romps have to endure the paradox of reading the Ancients in expurgated versions."

Under the advice of a friend who feared *Lolita* would be censored for its sexual content, Nabokov originally stipulated, when submitting the book to publishers, that it appear anonymously. Eventually, feeling such reticence would only add to the hype, he signed it, and after numerous publishing houses were shocked by what they read—or refused to read—Nabokov gave the book to the Olympia Press in Paris. Under the direction of Maurice Girodias, Olympia was infamous for disseminating pornographic texts. When *Lolita* appeared

in 1955, it sold poorly and received no reviews. It was not until Graham Greene named it one of the ten best books of the year in the Christmas 1955 issue of the *London Sunday Times* that the novel began attracting attention. It was censored in France, and more fuel was added to the fire when, in 1957, Girodias published *L'affaire Lolita* in an effort to fight the ban, taking up a crusade in which Nabokov was entirely disinterested and even deplored. *Lolita* entered its American phase that same year, when the U.S. Customs Service released its confiscated copies, hence permitting the book's American publication. *Lolita* appeared from Putnam on 18 August 1958 and sold 100,000 copies in three weeks, the fastest-selling American novel since *Gone with the Wind* (1936). The reviews it garnered ranged from self-righteous condemnation to vociferous praise. Nabokov sold the film rights to the novel to Harris-Kubrick Productions, and *Lolita* premiered in New York City in 1962. Director Stanley Kubrick used only portions of a screenplay that Nabokov had composed and which appeared in 1974 as *Lolita: A Screenplay*. Another film version by Adrian Lyne was released in 1997.

"*Lolita* is famous, not I," Nabokov once quipped. "I am an obscure, doubly obscure, novelist with an unpronounceable name."

FURTHER READING

Appel, Alfred, Jr. *The Annotated Lolita*. New York, 1970.

Field, Andrew. *Nabokov: His Life in Art*. Boston, 1967.

Maddox, Lucy. *Nabokov's Novels in English*. Athens, Ga., 1983.

Nabokov, Vladimir. *Strong Opinions*. New York, 1981. A collection of interviews with, letters to editors from, and articles by Nabokov.

Nabokov, Vladimir. *The Enchanter*. Translated from the Russian by Dmitri Nabokov. New York, 1986. Translated from Vladimir Nabokov's unpublished 1939 work, "Volshebnik."

Nabokov, Vladimir. *Speak, Memory*. New York, 1989. Nabokov's autobiography.

Nabokov, Vladimir. *Vladimir Nabokov: Novels 1955–1962* (Lolita, Pnin, Pale Fire, Lolita: A Screenplay). New York, 1996.

Page, Norman, ed. *Nabokov: The Critical Heritage*. Boston, 1982.

Proffer, Carl R. *Keys to Lolita*. Bloomington, Ind., 1968.

See also the article on Vladimir Nabokov immediately preceding.

NATIVE AMERICAN LITERATURE

by Margo Lukens

At the start of European voyages of exploration and empire building, the North American continent was populated by somewhere between 20 and 100 million people who spoke more than 300 different languages descending from 17 language families as different from one another as the Germanic from the Sino-Tibetan. Since their origins on the continent, each of the more than 300 distinct cultural groups had developed its own oral literature containing ritual drama, song, narrative, and oratory, all held in the vessel of human memory and transmitted through performance. These literatures—or "oratures" as some have called them—describe and express the abundant differences among culture groups, although there are some basic similarities among the worldviews of Native people in North America.

One salient similarity is a high value placed on community, the group within which one has one's identity and wherein lie the keys to safety and survival in a subsistence economy. North American Native peoples also share a belief in the close coexistence of physical and spiritual realities and the necessity for humans to maintain a harmonious connection with all parts of their world. In all cases, the Native peoples' oral traditions contain teachings and rituals for the specific purpose of keeping their relationships in balance with the universe. Finally, their cultural practices having evolved from making a living in a particular ecosystem (for example, coastal, woodland, desert, arid plains), Native peoples have identified strongly with traditional land and sometimes with particular features of familiar landscapes.

ORAL TRADITIONS: PRESERVATION IN WRITTEN TEXTS

Knowledge of the oral traditions of Native North Americans has been preserved in writing by Europeans and Euro-Americans since the early missionary incursions of the Spanish Franciscans and the French Jesuits. The first serious ethnographic collector in English was Henry Rowe Schoolcraft, an Indian agent who, with the assistance of his wife, Jane Johnston Schoolcraft (Ojibwa), published Ojibwa stories in *Algic Researches* (1839). What followed in the wake of his effort was a wide variation in collectors' approaches to the oral traditional material. Some nineteenth- and early-twentieth-century collectors, like Charles Godfrey Leland and Frank Cushing, polished their material with an Anglo-American audience in mind, using elevated literary language, reaching for parallels with Greco-Roman mythology, and eliding the sometimes prevalent and often humorous references to bodily functions. Others, like Abby Alger (who trained with Leland) and the Reverend Silas Rand (Micmac legends) managed to preserve the sensibility of the original in their translations and often credited the Native storytellers from whom they got their material.

The twentieth century saw the "salvage anthropology" of Franz Boas and his students, who worked in reaction to the military subjugation of tribes in the United States and the institution of the reservation system during the last decades of the nineteenth century. Anthropologists like J. D. Prince and James Mooney made the objective preservation of "vanishing" cultures and languages their project. This approach sometimes resulted in the publication of transliterated oral texts along with ungainly word-for-word translations; however, this work was initially intended for a specialized academic audience. It has been suggested that work in collaboration with Native informants by such scholars as Ruth M. Underhill, Frances Densmore, and Ruth Bunzel may also have stimulated some Native communities to value and remain attentive to continued practice of their oral traditions. As the importance of ethnography rose in the early twentieth century, many "as told to" life stories were collected by anthropologists seeking to understand tribal cultures. Notable among these are such narrators as Sam Blowsnake (Winnebago), Mountain Wolf Woman (Winnebago), Maria Chona (Papago), and Helen Sekaquaptewa (Hopi), all of whom collaborated with scholars or with friends to whom they entrusted their stories.

During the late nineteenth and early twentieth centuries, individual Native writers began to publish their own collected retellings of oral literature; one of the first was Joseph Nicolar (Penobscot), who published a version of the cycle of stories of Gluskap, the Wabanaki culture hero.

EUROPEAN COLONIAL AND MISSIONARY PERIOD

The Franciscan missionaries who accompanied Hernán Cortés in his conquest of the Aztec empire and tributaries set to work in the 1520s to convert Native people to Catholicism, hand in hand with a project to make them literate, first in Nahuatl and then in Spanish. Within the next one hundred years Aztec writers produced texts describing the conquest from the Native perspective, both in narrative and lyric form, which can be found in codices preserved in European ecclesiastical libraries.

Although the Mohegan preacher Samson Occom was the first Native writer to publish in English, it is clear that some Native people had been literate in English for a hundred years before his sermon on the death of Moses Paul (1772); letters of negotiation were written during King Philip's War (1675–1676) by Narragansett and Nipmuck men who had become literate as part of their conversion to Christianity. Occom himself was converted to Methodism and learned to read and write during his late teens, and although some Native people had been literate a century earlier, the experience of coming to literacy in late adolescence and in conjunction with religious conversion was recapitulated in the lives of numerous Native writers (and recounted in their texts) until the late nineteenth century. Occom's letters, sermon, and short autobiography reflect his frustration that even in his work as a missionary he encountered the racism of white ministers in the church hierarchy.

EARLY SELF-DETERMINATION AND SOVEREIGNTY

The late eighteenth and early nineteenth centuries produced conditions that required Native people to negotiate space and power with a new republic. A century and a half of occupation by Anglo-Americans had created mixed-blood and literate people for whom assimilation was a strategy for survival and for acquisition of power. In New England, the itinerant Methodist preacher William Apess (Pequot) published several texts including his autobiography *A Son of the Forest* (1829); his works range from religious conversion narratives to political protest and lectures on revisionist history, ending with *A Eulogy on King Philip* in 1836. Apess developed a concept of coalition among "people of color," a term he used; his most widely anthologized work, "An Indian's Looking-Glass for the White Man" (1833), analyzes racism and its expressions in the early republic.

In the southeast, meanwhile, the Cherokee linguist Sequoyah had invented a system for writing his Native language; his Cherokee syllabary made possible the publication, in Cherokee and English, of the first Native American newspaper, the *Cherokee Phoenix*. Elias Boudinot (Cherokee) was responsible for fundraising to launch the paper and gave his *Address to the Whites* in 1826 as part of the Cherokee effort to convince Anglo-Americans that the Cherokee people were equal in their attainments to whites and ought to be trusted to remain on their traditional lands and govern themselves. Boudinot became editor of the *Phoenix* in 1828 and continued to write persuasively about the Cherokees' civilization until his death in 1839 at the hands of his own people.

NINETEENTH-CENTURY AUTOBIOGRAPHERS AND NOVELISTS

Black Hawk, an Autobiography (1833) is the first example of an "as told to" life story, collected from Black Hawk (Sauk) by Antoine Le Claire and edited by John Patterson. Another early-nineteenth-century life story tells about the role of Governor Blacksnake (Seneca) in the revolutionary war; it did not reach publication until 1989 under the title *Chainbreaker*. The genre's most famous exemplar is *Black Elk Speaks* (1932), which appeared a full century after Black Hawk's life story.

John Rollin Ridge (Cherokee) grew up in the traditional Cherokee homeland of Georgia, but like Elias Boudinot, his father and grandfather were murdered in the internecine struggle between traditional and assimilationist Cherokee parties facing the forced removal of their people to Indian Territory (the Trail of Tears, 1838–1839). Ridge fled from the site of family horrors and migrated west. On the wave of gold fever, he worked as a journalist in California and there wrote the first Native American novel, *The Life and Adventures of Joaquín Murieta* (1854), under the nom de plume Yellow Bird. The legendary California bandit provided Ridge with a story on which he could displace his own consciousness of injustice at the hands of white people and wreak a heroic revenge.

His contemporary George Copway (Ojibwa) first published an autobiography, *The Life, History, and Travels of Kah-ge-gah-ga-bowh*, in 1847; he revised that work twice and republished it several times in the ensuing years. The autobiography contains several genres, including tribal ethnohistory, conversion narrative, and an account of his people's struggles with Anglo-American policy. Like William Apess, Copway devoted much of his life to working on behalf of Indian people in resistance to U.S. government plans for their relocation.

The first Native American woman to publish a volume on her own was Sarah Winnemucca Hopkins (Northern Paiute), who, like Copway, came to write after embarking on a career as a lecturer about her people. In her lectures she emphasized the parallels between Paiute and Christian morality and strove to demonstrate their potential for citizenship. Her cause to raise funds to establish a bilingual school for Native children in her community was taken up by the philanthropist Elizabeth Peabody, who introduced her to influential easterners (including Senator Henry Dawes, the sponsor of the General Allotment Act) and whose sister, Mary Peabody Mann, helped Winnemucca edit her manuscript for publication. *Life Among the Paiutes* (1883) resembles Copway's book in its inclusion of tribal ethnohistory, a memoir of the tribe's first contact with whites, and a detailed chronicle of the tribe's political relations with white settlers, Indian agents, and military personnel as well as Winnemucca's own role in these relationships. The text's purpose is social and political; it ends with a petition for readers (presumably sympathetic and enfranchised American citizens) to sign and circulate in support of the reunification of her people in a traditional homeland.

Sophia Alice Callahan (Muskogee Creek), the first Native American woman novelist, began *Wynema, A Child of the Forest* (1891) as a romance that celebrated both Creek traditional ways and the adaptability of Muskogee people to Anglo-American ways. The novel analyzes the prejudices of white people toward Indians and meditates on the issue of allotment of lands in severalty, a concern for Native reservation communities since the 1887 passage of the Dawes Act. However, before Callahan finished the manuscript, the December 1890 massacre of Sioux people at Wounded Knee, South Dakota, claimed her passionate attention, and her story swerves from its center at Muskogee, reaching out to incorporate Wounded Knee and in fact incorporating some of its survivors into

Sarah Winnemucca Hopkins (ca. 1844–1891). (*National Portrait Gallery, Smithsonian Institution/Art Resource*)

Muskogee's mixed-blood center. After a successful reception in the twenty years following its appearance, *Wynema* lay forgotten in a few libraries until late-twentieth-century scholarly attention by Annette Van Dyke and A. LaVonne Brown Ruoff brought it to the light of republication.

CULTURAL PRESERVATION AND INSTRUCTION BY NATIVE WRITERS

In the mid- to late nineteenth century, Native writers like Jane Johnston Schoolcraft (Ojibwa) and Joseph Laurent (Abenaki) perceived that preserving oral traditions in writing was one way to counteract cultural erosion; Schoolcraft published retellings in English of individual stories, while Laurent's 1884 *New Familiar Abenaki and English Dialogues* detailed the grammar of what Laurent called "the *uncultivated* Abenaki language," with the object of preserving it from "alterations." The Penobscot writer and tribal leader Joseph Nicolar wrote his 1893 *Life and Traditions of the Red Man*, an English-language version of traditional Penobscot stories, as an act of cultural preservation dedicated to the young people of his own nation. At the turn of the twentieth century Gertrude Simmons Bonnin, who wrote under the pen name Zitkala-Sa, published *Old Indian Legends* (1901), a collection of Dakota stories retold primarily for a juvenile non-Native audience; her writing career included journalism, fiction writing, autobiography, poetry, and political writing. The novelist Christine Quintasket (Okanogan/Colville), also known as Mourning Dove, collected stories from Okanogan elders for the 1933 volume *Coyote Stories*.

EARLY TWENTIETH CENTURY

Although literary scholars usually locate the Native American "renaissance" in the late 1960s and 1970s, the early twentieth century was a period of prolific activity by literate Native people in a wide range of genres and fields: autobiography, novel, short fiction, drama, poetry, ethnography, political writing, and publishing. The U.S. government's policies of assimilation had been aggressively advanced in the late nineteenth and early twentieth centuries by the General Allotment Act of 1887 and by a system of boarding schools for Indian children that removed them from the cultural influences of their home communities. In the process, however, children from numerous different tribes lived together at schools such as the Carlisle Indian Industrial School, where they used English as their common language, and published their exemplary work in school newspapers such as the Carlisle *Arrow*. This experience led to the rise of a pan-Indian consciousness, out of which grew both political organization and the creation of literary works in English.

One of the central figures at the turn of the twentieth century was Zitkala-Sa—"Red Bird" in Lakota, a name she gave herself. Educated at a Quaker missionary boarding school and at Earlham College, she was hired by Richard Henry Pratt to teach at Carlisle, the school he had founded on military principles to "kill the Indian and save the man." Her first major publication, three autobiographical articles in the *Atlantic Monthly* during the first three months of 1900, revealed her deep disagreement with her employer's policy, creating a rift that led to her departure from Carlisle. These articles were collected, along with her essay "Why I Am a Pagan" (1901) and some short fiction, in a 1921 Ginn and Company volume entitled *American Indian Stories*. In the meantime Bonnin had collaborated with the composer William Hanson on the libretto and music of an opera entitled *The Sun Dance* (1913) and became secretary of the pan-Indian Society of American Indians and editor of its journal *American Indian Magazine*, to which she contributed numerous poems, articles, and editorials. In 1924, the same year U.S. citizenship was finally granted to Native Americans, Bonnin coauthored *Oklahoma's Poor Rich Indians*, an exposé of the land grab that followed the discovery of oil on Indian land. She founded the National Council of American Indians in 1926, several years after the demise of the SAI, and served as its president until she died in 1938.

Contemporary with Bonnin were Charles Alexander Eastman (Santee Sioux) and Luther Standing Bear (Teton Sioux), both of whom wrote autobiographies, published retellings of traditional Sioux stories, and wrote some books intended for young audiences. Eastman was particularly known for his contributions to the early formation of the Boy Scouts and Campfire Girls in the early twentieth century. Eastman's *Indian Boyhood* (1902) is a memoir of his Santee childhood that ends with an optimistic view of his conversion to Christianity and entry into Anglo-American education; *From the Deep Woods to Civilization* (1916) problematizes Eastman's experiences and includes his view, as the first physician on the scene,

of the massacre of Big Foot's Oglala band at Wounded Knee. Standing Bear's autobiographical *My People, the Sioux* (1928) chronicles in positive terms his experiences among the first students admitted to Carlisle and as a performer in Buffalo Bill's Wild West Show; his *Land of the Spotted Eagle* (1933) reflects more on Sioux traditions and provides a critique of white people's treatment of Native Americans.

The early twentieth century also saw Native authors writing short fiction, poetry, and political satire, much of which appeared in ephemeral publications such as local and Native-run newspapers but sometimes in magazines of national circulation. The poet of first importance during this period was E. Pauline Johnson (Mohawk), from Grand River Reservation of the Six Nations in southern Ontario. Her mother was English and her father was Mohawk; consequently her upbringing gave her grounding in the English Romantic poets as well as great respect for Mohawk traditions. When her family fell on hard times after her father's death, Johnson began a twenty-five-year career of writing poetry and performing it live for general audiences in Canada, the United States, and Great Britain. Her first volume, *The White Wampum* (1895), is still one of the most published books of Canadian poetry; she also wrote numerous short stories, many of which deal with the issue of mixed blood. The last of these stories were collected in *The Moccasin Maker*, a volume published by friends after her death in 1913.

Contemporary scholarship has brought to light some poetry by Zitkala-Sa, who had likely been influenced by Johnson; her energies, however, were expressed more aptly in her prose fiction and in her overt political work and writings. Their contemporary Alexander Posey (Creek) used poetry as his primary vehicle, basing the style of his early works on the Anglo-European classics he had read in school or at Bacone Indian University in Muskogee, Oklahoma. Posey's unique contribution to Native American letters, however, is a style he developed as a mature writer based in the customs, values, and speech styles of Creek people. In 1902 Posey bought and took over the editorship of the *Indian Journal*, and for the next six years it was his vehicle for publishing the satirical Fus Fixico letters, which were often picked up by mainstream newspapers. Posey became known as an insightful humorist and biting satirist whose works express and incorporate the language, social values, and aesthetic sense of Native American people. After his death by drowning in 1908, his wife, Minnie Posey, published *The Poems of Alexander Lawrence Posey* (1910), the first collection of his works; the Fus Fixico letters were finally collected in one volume by Daniel Littlefield and Carol Hunter in 1993. In a similar instance, Henry "Red Eagle" Perley (Maliseet) made a sixty-year career of writing short fiction and nonfiction for national magazines and Maine sportsmen's magazines and newspapers between 1911 and 1972; decades after his death *Aboriginally Yours* (1997), a volume collecting a portion of his works, was published by Perley's niece and granddaughter.

The novelists of the early twentieth century are few but notable for their adaptation of genre to Native concerns. The young Christine Quintasket (Colville/Okanogan) spent four years in a convent school and two at a BIA (Bureau of Indian Affairs) school in Washington state; four years at the Fort Shaw Indian School near Great Falls, Montana; and two years at a business school in Calgary, Alberta, learning typing and correspondence skills. During her youth she had conceived a love for two narrative genres: the traditional tales of Okanogan culture and the romantic and melodramatic novels popular in Anglo-American culture. It was with these materials and styles that she set to work as Mourning Dove, or *Hum-is hu-ma*. Between 1912 and 1914, when she was in business school, Mourning Dove completed the first draft of her novel *Cogewea, the Half-Blood* (1927), but it would take more than a decade of struggle to publish it, even with the assistance of a white collaborator, Lucullus Virgil McWhorter, an amateur ethnographer and supporter of Indian causes. The published novel, although marred by McWhorter's editorial incursions, weaves together Okanogan traditional story lines and a western romance plot, in which the mixed-blood hero and heroine establish a safe and prosperous future for themselves and their white and Indian relatives. Although Mourning Dove's collection *Coyote Stories* had been published three years before her death in 1936, other editors brought out volumes of her renditions of traditional stories, *Tales of the Okanogans* (1976) and *Mourning Dove's Stories* (1991). Her memoirs were edited by Jay Miller in *Mourning Dove: A Salishan Autobiography* (1990).

John Milton Oskison (Cherokee), educated at Stanford and Harvard, was the son of an English father and a Cherokee mother; he used his family's experience farming and ranching in Indian Territory (present-day Oklahoma) as material and setting for numerous "western" short stories and novels of frontier life such as *Wild Harvest* (1925). The characters sometimes resemble Oskison or his family members, as in the dynastic novel *Brothers Three* (1935), and often his works meditate on negotiating mixed-blood identity amid the separations between Anglo and Native America. A world traveler who also possessed a degree in law, Oskison wrote numerous essays on topics as varied as scientific discovery, medicine, industry, international policy, and the political and economic issues affecting particular Native tribes.

MID-TWENTIETH CENTURY

The middle decades of the twentieth century were characterized by two policies enacted by the U.S. government. The first was the 1934 Wheeler-Howard Indian Reorganization Act; this act ended allotment of lands in severalty—which had resulted in the loss of 60 percent of previously reserved Indian land to non-Indians since 1887—and reestablished the authority of tribal governments. This act seemed a "New Deal" for Indian people. However, in 1953, when popular post–World War II sentiment pointed toward ending government involvement with Native communities, Congress passed House Concurrent Resolution 108, a policy known as "termination" of the government relationship of trusteeship with numerous tribes. Termination led to the loss of reservations and federal recognition for many tribes and to the forced migration of many Indian people to big cities in search of a non–land-based livelihood. Ironically these events brought many Native authors into the milieu of alienation that characterized the modern period for European and Anglo-American writers.

Some, like the Cherokee playwright Lynn Riggs, chose an urban lifestyle; Riggs spent most of his adult life alternating between Greenwich Village and Santa Fe, New Mexico. His plays and screenplays, however, partake of New Mexico and the Oklahoma of his childhood. Riggs's most famous play, *Green Grow the Lilacs* (1931), provided the libretto for Rodgers and Hammerstein's Pulitzer Prize–winning musical *Oklahoma!* (1943); Phyllis Cole Braunlich notes that Riggs used the taming and dividing of western land as "a metaphor for the spiritual change that was being forced on Native Americans, who believed that the land was a gift to all people from the Great Spirit." Some of Riggs's plays were more overt in their treatment of Indian themes and characters, most notably *The Cherokee Night* (1932), which deals with the situation of Native people in his day.

Two novelists who were most important and accomplished during this period were John Joseph Mathews (Osage) and D'Arcy McNickle (Salish). Mathews had experienced childhood in Indian Territory, military service in Europe during World War I, education at

Oxford University, and world travel before returning to Oklahoma to gather material for his first novel, *Wah'Kon-Tah* (1932). Mathews was elected to the tribal council the same year his second novel, *Sundown* (1934) was published. Both of his novels deal with the effects of allotment and assimilationist education on Native communities and individuals. Mathews published an autobiography entitled *Talking to the Moon* in 1945, after which his career turned toward biography and an epic history of the Osage people based on oral accounts, *The Osages: Children of the Middle Waters* (1961). At his death Mathews left behind the unpublished novel "Within Your Dream" and was still at work polishing his compendious autobiographical "Twenty Thousand Mornings." D'Arcy McNickle, the son of a Metis mother and a white father, was adopted into the Flathead tribe, and his family settled on allotted land. After being sent to the Indian boarding school in Chemawa, Oregon, McNickle went to public schools in Montana and Washington State, enrolling at the University of Montana in 1921. McNickle sold his allotment land to finance studies at Oxford, but when the money ran out in 1926 he settled in New York City, where he began work on his first novel, *The Surrounded* (1936). The novel went through numerous revisions before publication, corresponding with an evolution in McNickle's orientation toward his Indian and mixed-blood characters; he came to believe adherence to tribal ways and communities was better for Indian people than assimilation. The years John Collier served as commissioner of the Bureau of Indian Affairs (1933–1945) gave McNickle the promise of government employment as an Indian working on behalf of Indians. By 1936 he was living in Washington, D.C., working for the Bureau of Indian Affairs and beginning his path of publishing works of history. He published a juvenile novel *Runner in the Sun* in 1954, and his last novel, *Wind from an Enemy Sky*, was published posthumously in 1978. McNickle was honored during his lifetime by an honorary doctorate from the University of Colorado; in 1972 he became program director at the Newberry Library Center for the History of the American Indians, which was renamed for him after his death in 1977.

Unique among mid-twentieth-century Native American literature was *Black Elk Speaks*, a collaborative work narrated by Nicholas Black Elk (Oglala Lakota) and fashioned into prose by the German-born poet John Neihardt. The volume presents special problems to readers looking for Black Elk's voice, since he narrated his visions and experiences in his Native language; almost simultaneously,

Black Elk's son Ben translated his father's words into English, which Neihardt then rephrased for his daughter Enid to copy down in shorthand. She later typed them into longhand, from which Neihardt then composed the text. *Black Elk Speaks* is a work of hope perched at the edge of despair, the last-ditch effort of the Oglala holy man to provide spiritual teaching for his people and the world beyond; since the middle of the twentieth century *Black Elk Speaks* has provided a map for the spiritual seeking of many Native people outside the Oglala, as well as for non-Native people wishing to understand a Native American spiritual perspective.

LATE TWENTIETH CENTURY

The late twentieth century in Native American letters is marked by a widespread literary flowering across the genres, the "Native American Renaissance," heralded by the publication of Vine Deloria Jr.'s (Standing Rock Sioux) *Custer Died for Your Sins: An Indian Manifesto* (1969), the first of his numerous works of philosophy, religious studies, and political and legal critiques of American society. The same year, the mainstream literary establishment recognized the talent of N. Scott Momaday (Kiowa); his first novel, *House Made of Dawn* (1968), received the 1969 Pulitzer Prize in fiction. Momaday's poetry, fiction, and prose memoirs have influenced and inspired two generations of Native American and First Nations (Canadian-Native) writers. It is notable that many authors have published in multiple genres: for example, James Welch (Blackfeet) followed his first work of poetry with the influential novel *Winter in the Blood* (1974) and four more that have followed. Paula Gunn Allen (Laguna Pueblo) has produced a dozen volumes of poetry, fiction, and scholarship since 1973 and is probably most widely known for *The Sacred Hoop: Recovering the Feminine in American Indian Traditions* (1986). Louise Erdrich (Chippewa) began her literary career with poetry but, in collaboration with her husband Michael Dorris (Modoc), soon became a prolific writer of Faulkneresque novels including *Love Medicine* (1984) and *Tracks* (1988). Linda Hogan (Chickasaw) published numerous works of poetry before her work branched to produce the novels *Mean Spirit* (1990) and *Solar Storms* (1995). Diane Glancy (Cherokee) has published fifteen volumes including poetry (*Brown Wolf Leaves the Res*, 1984), short fiction (*Lone Dog's Winter Count*, 1991), and plays (*War Cries*, 1996). Foremost among these versatile writers is Leslie Marmon Silko (Laguna Pueblo), whose early work includes the volume of poetry entitled *Laguna*

Woman (1974) as well as the appearance of a number of her poems and short stories in anthologies of Native American writing published in the mid-1970s: *The Man to Send Rain Clouds* (1974), *Voices of the Rainbow* (1975), and *Carriers of the Dream Wheel* (1975). Silko's career blossomed with the publication of her novel *Ceremony* (1977), which weaves together mythic stories of Laguna spiritual tradition and a plot dealing with the experiences of a young mixed-blood Laguna man who serves in World War II; the novel blends the stylistic elements of oral tradition and postmodern narrative. Her later novels *Almanac of the Dead* (1991), a complex vision of self-interest and violence in the Americas, and *Gardens in the Dunes* (1999) explore the world beyond Laguna but with the sensibility and values she derives from Laguna. Silko also continues to range across genres, publishing poetry, fiction, and memoir in *Storyteller* (1981), letters between herself and the poet James Wright in a volume called *The Delicacy and Strength of Lace* (1986), and essays in *Yellow Woman and a Beauty of the Spirit* (1996).

Among those who work primarily in verse, Simon J. Ortiz (Acoma Pueblo) has been an influential poet since the early 1970s. The best-known of his fifteen volumes is *From Sand Creek* (1981). Ortiz's work is based in his strong Acoma identity, incorporating Keresan language and the spiritual traditions of his community. Joy Harjo (Muskogee Creek) went to college to learn painting but decided to become a writer after hearing Ortiz read. While she is primarily a poet (*She Had Some Horses*, 1983; *In Mad Love and War*, 1990), Harjo's works include a screenplay and recordings of musical performances with her band, Poetic Justice. The Hopi/Miwok poet Wendy Rose, trained academically as an anthropologist, has published eleven volumes since 1973. Primary among her philosophical concerns is the negotiating of identity, since having a non-Hopi mother situated her as an outsider to that community; *The Halfbreed Chronicles and Other Poems* (1985) is in many respects a complex response to and meditation on the conundrum of identity. *What Happened When the Hopi Hit New York* (1982) contemplates the specificity of different landscapes and connects her with Maurice Kenny (Mohawk), a prolific poet since the late 1950s, whose works have twice been nominated for Pulitzer Prizes; he received the American Book Award in 1984 for *The Mama Poems* (1984). Luci Tapahonso (Navajo) writes poetry from the perspective of Navajo as her first language, using both Navajo and English in her work. *Saani Dahataal: The Women Are Singing* (1993) is rooted in Tapahonso's

connection to her family and community and combines aspects of Navajo tradition and contemporary mainstream American life.

At work in his own direction before the 1969 flowering, Gerald Vizenor (Anishinaabe) began his prolific literary career in poetry after encountering haiku and other Asian literary forms while stationed in Japan with the U.S. Army. During the 1960s he published nine volumes of poetry, including some reworking of traditional Ojibwa (Anishinaabe) lyrics. During the mid-1960s he worked on behalf of urbanized Indians in the Minneapolis–St. Paul area and through this work began writing journalistic pieces; he wrote and edited for the *Minneapolis Tribune* from 1968 to 1976. In the 1970s Vizenor began publishing essays and fiction and made a transition from community service to college teaching and leadership in Native American studies. Vizenor's theoretical work on Indian identity as a construct ("terminal creeds are terminal diseases") and his stance on mixed blood as creative, similar to the energy of the "compassionate trickster," inform most of his work, including *Earthdivers: Tribal Narratives on Mixed Descent* (1981), *Griever: An American Monkey King in China* (1987), *Landfill Meditation* (1991), and *Chancers* (2000). N. Scott Momaday has called Vizenor "the supreme ironist among American Indian writers of the twentieth century," and for Louis Owens, Vizenor's work provides the most "outrageous challenge to all preconceived definitions."

Louis Owens (Cherokee/Choctaw) wrote novels and taught writing at the college level, becoming one of the most respected Native literary scholars of his generation. Owens published *American Indian Novelists: An Annotated Critical Bibliography* (1985) with his friend and colleague Tom Colonnese (Lakota), following that with *Other Destinies: Understanding the American Indian Novel* (1992) and *Mixedblood Messages: Literature, Film, Family, Place* (1998). His works of fiction partake of the popular genre of murder mystery but are always informed with tradition and sensibilities from his Choctaw heritage: *The Sharpest Sight* (1992), *Bone Game* (1994), *Wolfsong* (1995), and *Nightland* (1996) all rely on a Choctaw mixed-blood protagonist to unravel the mystery. In Owens's last novel, *Dark River* (1999), his protagonist Jake Nashoba dies of a gunshot wound in the process of discovering the answer to the puzzle, an intimation of Owens's untimely death in July 2002. Shorty Luke, "the surviving twin" of the story, gives him this epitaph: "It is said that Jacob Nashoba went home."

DIRECTIONS FOR THE
TWENTY-FIRST CENTURY

Most of the writers from the end of the twentieth century have survived into the twenty-first, and readers should expect an ever-increasing and changing body of work from Native American writers whose careers have lately begun. Sherman Alexie (Spokane/Coeur d'Alene) has kept up a pace of producing at least one book a year in his first ten years of writing, and two of his titles have been made into films: *The Business of Fancydancing* (1992) retained its title, and *The Lone Ranger and Tonto Fistfight in Heaven* (1993) became *Smoke Signals*. He has also worked on a screenplay based on his novel *Indian Killer* (1996). Greg Sarris (Pomo/Miwok) too has made the crossover into screenplay with his "novel in stories" *Grand Avenue* (1994), which is set in the tough Santa Rosa, California neighborhood where Sarris grew up. His biography of Pomo basketmaker Mabel McKay and his 1993 critical text *Keeping Slug Woman Alive* hold substantial promise for the future. Readers might also hope to see more from Betty Louise Bell (Cherokee), whose first novel, *Faces in the Moon*, a multigenerational story of women in one mixed-blood Cherokee family, appeared in 1994, and Susan Power (Dakota), author of *The Grass Dancer* (1994).

Another emerging direction in Native American literature is the proliferation of drama, a genre that flowered sooner in Canada than in the United States, with government support for the work of highly popular playwrights such as Tomson Highway (Cree), author of *The Rez Sisters* (1988) and *Dry Lips Oughta Move to Kapuskasing* (1989). In the United States, the Kiowa/Delaware playwright Hanay Geiogamah has been at work in theater since the early 1970s, publishing (*Body Indian*, 1972; *Foghorn*, 1973), directing, producing, and teaching Native American theater. For the past twenty years William Yellow Robe Jr. has acted, directed, taught, and written forty-two plays including *The Independence of Eddie Rose* (1986). The contemporary writers Gerald Vizenor (*Ishi and the Wood Ducks*, 1994), Diane Glancy (*The Truth Teller*, 1993), and LeAnne Howe (*Indian Radio Days*, 1993) have contributed to this growing field.

Increasingly it will be important for the field of Native American literary studies to be enriched and interrogated by the perspectives of Native American literary critics such as Paula Gunn Allen, Greg Sarris, Robert Allen Warrior (Osage), and Elizabeth Cook-Lynn (Dakota). Cook-Lynn has been an arbiter in Native American studies, having founded *Wicazo Sa Review* and operated it as an entirely Native-edited journal since 1985. She and fellow Native

critics, teachers, and publishers like Jeannette Armstrong and Joseph Bruchac will help foster the talent of new writers as well as the ongoing growth of the field.

[*See also* Erdrich, Louise; Momaday, N. Scott; *and* Silko, Leslie Marmon.]

FURTHER READING

Allen, Paula Gunn. *The Sacred Hoop: Recovering the Feminine in American Indian Traditions*. Boston, 1986; rev. 1992.

Bataille, Gretchen M., and Kathleen Mullen Sands. *American Indian Women: Telling Their Lives*. Lincoln, Neb., 1984.

Bruchac, Joseph, ed. *Survival This Way: Interviews with American Indian Poets*. Tucson, Ariz., 1987.

Brumble, H. David, 3d. *American Indian Autobiography*. Berkeley, Calif., 1988.

Colonnese, Tom, and Louis Owens, comps. *American Indian Novelists: An Annotated Critical Bibliography*. New York, 1985.

Harjo, Joy, and Gloria Bird, eds. *Reinventing the Enemy's Language: Contemporary Native Woman's Writings of North America*. New York, 1997.

Jaskoski, Helen, ed. *Early Native American Writing: New Critical Essays*. New York, 1996.

Krupat, Arnold. *The Voice in the Margin: Native American Literature and the Canon*. Berkeley, Calif., 1989.

Lincoln, Kenneth. *Native American Renaissance*. 2d revised edition. Los Angeles, 1985.

Littlefield, Daniel F., Jr., and James W. Parins, comps. *American Indian and Alaskan Native Newspapers and Periodicals, 1826–1924*. Westport, Conn., 1984.

Littlefield, Daniel F., Jr., and James W. Parins, comps. *A Biobibliography of Native American Writers, 1772–1924*. Metuchen, N.J., 1981.

Littlefield, Daniel F., Jr., and James W. Parins, comps. *A Biobibliography of Native American Writers, 1772–1924: A Supplement*. Metuchen, N.J., 1985.

Murray, David. *Forked Tongues: Speech, Writing, and Representation in North American Indian Texts*. Bloomington, Ind., 1991.

Nelson, Robert M. *Place and Vision: The Function of Landscape in Native American Fiction*. New York, 1993.

Owens, Louis. *Other Destinies: Understanding the American Indian Novel*. Norman, Okla., 1992.

Roemer, Kenneth M., ed. *Native American Writers of the United States. Dictionary of Literary Biography*, vol. 175. Detroit, 1997.

Ruoff, A. LaVonne Brown. *American Indian Literatures: An Introduction, Bibliographic Review, and Selected Bibliography*. New York, 1990.

Ruppert, James. *Mediation in Contemporary Native American Fiction*. Norman, Okla., 1995.

Sarris, Greg. *Keeping Slug Woman Alive: A Holistic Approach to American Indian Texts*. Berkeley, Calif., 1993.

Swann, Brian, and Arnold Krupat, eds. *Recovering the Word: Essays on Native American Literature*. Berkeley, Calif., 1987.

Trout, Lawana, ed. *Native American Literature: An Anthology*. Lincolnwood, Ill., 1999.

Vizenor, Gerald, ed. *Narrative Chance: Postmodern Discourse on Native American Indian Literatures*. Albuquerque, N.Mex., 1989.

Warrior, Robert Allen. *Tribal Secrets: Recovering American Indian Intellectual Traditions*. Minneapolis, 1995.

Wiget, Andrew O., ed. *Critical Essays on Native American Literature*. Boston, 1985.

Wiget, ed. *Handbook of Native American Literature*. Detroit, 1994.

Wyss, Hilary E. *Writing Indians: Literacy, Christianity, and Native Community in Early America*. Amherst, Mass., 2000.

NATURALISM AND REALISM

by Gary Scharnhorst

At the most elementary level, realism may be equated with verisimilitude or the approximation of truth. A mimetic artist, the literary realist claims to mirror or represent the world as it objectively appears. Naturalism may be given a trio of thumbnail definitions: pessimistic determinism, stark realism, and realism plus Darwin.

REALISM AS A LITERARY THEORY

William Dean Howells, the most prominent American advocate of realism in the arts, urged readers to apply this singular test to any work of the imagination: "Is it true?—true to the motives, the impulses, the principles that shape the life of actual men and women?" In *Criticism and Fiction* (1891), Howells proposed an evolutionary literary model, with realism superior to romance just as birds are a more sophisticated species than lizards. Although Howells admired the writings of Nathaniel Hawthorne, he nevertheless believed Hawthorne's fiction occupied a lower rung on the evolutionary scale of literature than realism, or "the truthful treatment of material." "Let fiction cease to lie about life," he declared. "Let it portray man and women as they are, actuated by the motives and the passions in the measure we all know; . . . let it not put on fine literary airs; let it speak the dialect, the language, that most Americans know—the language of unaffected people everywhere." Howells was also able to stretch his definition of realism to cover such wildly different works as Mark Twain's humorous sketches and his dystopian *A Connecticut Yankee in King Arthur's Court* (1889).

In all, according to Howells, realism insisted "that fidelity to experience and probability of motive are essential conditions of a great imaginative literature." Thus, it resisted or opposed allegory and romance, especially sentimental romance. Realistic fiction portrayed distinctive personalities and rounded or credible characters, developed linear plots, and depicted recognizable settings. (As the modern writer John Barth has noted, "God was not a bad novelist, except He was a realist.") Devaluing anecdote or story, it emphasized the importance of individual character. Sometimes claiming to portray a "slice of life" or "transcript of life," the realists often found their subjects amid the details and surfaces of middle-class, bourgeois experience. They shared with such pragmatists as William James a philosophical attitude, a method of "radical empiricism" that affirmed free will and equated motive and behavior.

Standard literary histories have long dated the start of the realistic period in American literature at the end of the Civil War. Ostensibly, the pioneering works of realism were such volumes as John W. De Forest's novel, *Miss Ravenel's Conversion from Secession to Loyalty* (1867), and Mark Twain's satirical travelogues, *The Innocents Abroad* (1869) and *Roughing It* (1872). With the critical recovery in the late twentieth century of women's writings from the mid-1800s, however, the beginning of the realistic period has been pushed back more than an entire generation to such texts as Caroline M. Kirkland's *A New Home, Who'll Follow? or, Glimpses of Western Life* (1839) and Rebecca Harding Davis's "Life in the Iron-Mills" (1861).

In the late twentieth century, too, proponents of poststructuralism assailed the notion of literary realism. How can any literary text replicate or imitate "reality" (whatever that may be?), they ask. Language creates the only reality we know. Any attempt to define the term absolutely is not only presumptuous but doomed. Roland Barthes, for example, has argued that so-called realistic texts are no more based on "reality" than other forms of writing and has indicted as simplistic the epistemological assumptions of those who purport to be realists. In effect, he suggested, the realists merely took reality for granted. Admittedly, it is easier to define what realism was not than what it actually was. (Mary E. Wilkins Freeman told an interviewer in 1890 that she "didn't even know" she was "a realist until [some reviewers] wrote and told me.") Such scholars as Donald Pizer, however, have attempted to recuperate or rehabilitate the terms "realism" and "naturalism." As Pizer writes in *The Cambridge Companion to American Realism and Naturalism* (1995), "Whatever the philosophical, moral, and social baggage that encumbers them, they will have to do." In a functional sense, the terms obviously meant something. What qualities in the writings of the self-described realists seemed innovative? Or, put another way, what was it about those writings that inspired such fierce opposition during the so-called Realism War of the 1880s and 1890s? Influenced by such European writers as Zola, Tolstoy, Guy de Maupassant, and Dostoyevsky, the realists certainly believed they were championing a new brand of fiction.

HOWELLS AND THE REALISM WAR

While he neither inspired nor founded a school or movement of realists, Howells was at the center of American literary culture for over fifty years. He was the most influential American novelist, editor, and critic of his generation. As editor of the *Atlantic Monthly* for over fifteen years and later as the contributor of the "Editor's Easy Chair" series to *Harper's Monthly*, he befriended and promoted such realists as Henry James, Mark Twain, Mary Freeman, John De Forest, Sarah Orne Jewett, Frank Norris, Charles Chesnutt, Paul Laurence Dunbar, Hamlin Garland, Edith Wharton, Charlotte Perkins Gilman, Abraham Cahan, and Stephen Crane. For Howells, realism was a democratic movement in the arts, a focus on the normal and ordinary, distinct from romanticism or "romanticistic" fiction with its emphasis on more ideal, bizarre, sentimental, fantastic, exotic, melodramatic, or aristocratic topics. "In life," he declared, the realist "finds nothing insignificant." In *The Rise of Silas Lapham* (1885), for example, Howells remarked on how "a great many novels" fail "as representations of life." The Reverend Mr. Sewell, a Howells spokesman, refers derisively to the "mischief" done by such popular fiction. "The novels might be the greatest possible good to us if they painted life as it is, and human feelings in their true proportion and relation, but for the most part they have been and are altogether noxious." The readers of such slop commit "psychical suicide." The novelist "who could interpret the common feelings of commonplace people," another character in the novel avers, "would have the answer to 'the riddle of the painful earth' on his tongue." In *The Minister's Charge* (1887), which again features the character of Sewell, Howells realistically rewrote the sentimental juvenile fiction of such authors as Alger and Oliver Optic. Similarly, Basil March, another Howells persona, opines in *A Hazard of New Fortunes* (1890) that

> I believe that this popular demand for the matrimony of others comes from our novel-reading. We get to thinking that there is no other happiness or good fortune in life except marriage, and it's offered in fiction as the highest premium for virtue, courage, beauty, learning, and saving human life. We all know it isn't. We know that in reality, marriage is dog-cheap.

Howells was profoundly influenced in the late 1880s by Tolstoy's ideas about nonviolence and economic equality. In 1887 he risked his reputation and livelihood by publicly repudiating the guilty verdicts brought against the Haymarket Square anarchists and what he called the "civic murder" of four of them. His novel *Annie Kilburn* (1889) glossed Tolstoy's *Anna Karenina* (1875–1877), as the identical initials of their respective heroines suggest. As a result, he became an easy target for some parochial critics. The so-called Realism War, waged in reviews and magazines throughout the 1880s and 1890s, pitted the realists, especially Howells, against editors and popular writers who espoused the sentimental or sensational brands of literary romance. For example, the genteel critic Hamilton Wright Mabie alleged in his review of Howells's *Silas Lapham* that realism was nothing more or less than "practical atheism applied to art." These skirmishes often smacked of politics; the controversy over realism began at the height of the debate over the fate of the Haymarket Square anarchists. Also, the war was fought largely along regional lines; the realists were largely easterners or transplanted westerners living in the East, whereas the most outspoken opponents of realism (including Maurice Thompson, author of *Hoosier Mosaics* [1875] and *Alice of Old Vincennes* [1901]; the poet James Whitcomb Riley; and Lew Wallace, author of the historical romances *The Fair God* [1873] and *Ben-Hur* [1880]) often resided in the Old South or the Old Northwest. The Association of Western Writers (later the Western Association of Writers), played a crucial role in the war by offering Thompson, its first president, a forum for his attacks. Over a period of some twenty years, beginning in 1887, Thompson repeatedly complained that Howells had foisted the "raw, nauseous realism of the Russians and the Zola school of France" onto a reading public hungry for "American books of a wholesome and patriotic kind." Realism was little more than decadent "worship of the vulgar, the commonplace and the insignificant." "Some years ago, before there had been so much said about realism in literature," Thompson declared in 1889, "I predicted that realism would in due time be found to mean materialism, socialism, and, at last, anarchy.... The progression will be: Realism, sensualism, materialism, socialism, communism, nihilism, absolute anarchy." Thompson and Howells's other opponents often compared realism to mere photography, or worse, cheap Kodak snapshots, lacking the artistry of the painter.

The war, in the end, took its toll on Howells's reputation. By the early twentieth century his brand of realism seemed dull and timid, a movement within the spurned genteel tradition in American letters. Ambrose Bierce defined realism in his *Devil's Dictionary* (1906) as "the art of depicting nature as it is seen by toads." In 1915 Howells wrote James that he had become "comparatively a dead cult with my statues cast down and the grass growing over them in the pale moonlight." Sinclair Lewis famously, or infamously, attacked him by name in his Nobel Prize acceptance speech in 1930: "Mr. Howells was one of the gentlest, sweetest, and most honest of men, but he had the code of a pious old maid whose greatest delight was to have tea at the vicarage."

In addition to Howells, many other novelists of the period defended the aesthetics of realism. In the preface to his novel *The Mammon of Unrighteousness* (1891), for example, H. H. Boyesen asserted that he had "disregarded all romantic traditions, and simply asked myself in every instance, not whether it was amusing, but whether it was to the logic of reality—true in color and tone to the American sky, the American soil, the American character." Henry James implicitly compared realistic fiction to painting in his essay, "The Art of Fiction" (1884). According to James, the novel should exude an "air of reality," which is its "supreme virtue," by "its immense and exquisite correspondence with life.... The only reason for the existence of a novel is that it does attempt to represent life. When it relinquishes this attempt, the same attempt that we see on the canvas of a painter, it will have arrived at a very strange pass." James's brand of realism was a form of literary portrai- ture, as may be inferred from several of his titles (including *Portraits of Places* [1883], *The Portrait of a Lady* [1881], *The American Scene* [1907], and *Par- tial Portraits* [1888]). And in his face- tious essay, "Fenimore Cooper's Liter- ary Offenses" (1895), Mark Twain listed "nineteen rules governing literary art." Among them: "when the personages of a tale deal in conversation, the talk shall sound like human talk, and be talk such as human beings would be likely to talk in the given circumstances," and "the personages of a tale shall confine them- selves to possibilities and let miracles

alone." Cooper's romance, *The Deerslayer* (1841), how- ever, was "simply a literary *delirium tremens*." Similarly, Stephen Crane reminisced that he had

> developed all alone a little creed of art which I thought was a good one. Later I discovered that my creed was identical with the one of Howells and Garland, and in this way I became involved in the beautiful war between those who say that ... we are the most successful in art when we approach the nearest to nature and truth, and those who ... don't say much.

REALISM AS LITERARY PRACTICE

The literary landscape in the late nineteenth century featured no organized or monolithic group of realists. As Elizabeth Ammons has suggested, "the most important characteristic of American realism was its racial, ethnic, sexual, and cultural range." There were, in effect, many "realities" or varieties of realism, including local color or regionalism (for example, the tales of Twain, Jewett, Freeman, Chopin, Bret Harte, James Lane Allen, Rose Terry Cooke, Joel Chandler Harris, Edward Eggleston, and Joseph Kirkland), psychological realism (James, Gilman, Sherwood Anderson), critical realism (Howells), and "veritism" (Garland's term for realism true to the perceptions of the writer, a protorealism or an overtly politicized form of realism). The various realists did not necessarily appreciate all contributions to the form; Mark Twain wrote Howells that he "would rather be damned to John Bunyan's heaven than read" James's *The Bostonians* (1886). Such Native-American storytellers as Zitkala-Sa and Sarah Winnemucca, the Jewish-American

Edward Eggleston. (© *Corbis*)

writer Anzia Yezierska, the Asian- American author Sui Sin Far, and such African Americans as W. E. B. Du Bois and Charles Chesnutt were also regarded as realists, though obviously their expe- riences were distinctly different from those of the canonical Anglo-American writers.

With their interest in local customs, mores, and dialects, local colorists were local historians in a sense. They iden- tified themselves with the communities they chronicled. Their tales often took the form of the anecdote or charac- ter sketch (Harte's "Tennessee's Part- ner" [1869], Freeman's "A New Eng- land Nun" [1891], and Harriet Beecher

Stowe's *Oldtown Folks* [1869], for example). Both Eggleston, the author of *The Hoosier Schoolmaster* (1871), and Kirkland, the author of *Zury: The Meanest Man in Spring County* (1887), turned formally late in their careers to writing local history. Eggleston was even elected president of the American Historical Association in 1900. The difference between literary romance and realism, at least of the local color variety, may be underscored by comparing two of Twain's novels, *The Adventures of Tom Sawyer* (1876) and *Adventures of Huckleberry Finn* (1884). As Leslie Fiedler has suggested in *Love and Death in the American Novel* (rev. ed., 1966), the two novels retell essentially the same story, the first nostalgically and sentimentally through a soft lens and the second more rigorously, honestly, and truthfully. The two novels are "alternative versions of the same themes" or "the same dream dreamed twice over, the second time as nightmare." "*Huckleberry Finn* is a true book," Fiedler adds, but "*Tom Sawyer* only 'mostly a true book' with 'some stretchers,' one of which is its ending." The contrast is perhaps most apparent in the respective depictions of Twain's hometown of Hannibal, Missouri. The bucolic St. Petersburg of *Tom Sawyer* and the opening chapters of *Huckleberry Finn* are an idealized representation of Hannibal, which is more realistically rendered in the latter work as Bricksville, the dirty little river town where hogs root in the muddy streets and the town drunk is killed in cold blood. Though his masterwork is rarely regarded as an exercise in local color, Twain also carefully recreated in *Huckleberry Finn* the several distinct dialects spoken by his characters. "The shadings have not been done in a hap-hazard fashion, or by guess-work," he insisted in an explanatory note, "but painstakingly, and with the trustworthy guidance and support of personal familiarity with those several forms of speech." In the Uncle Julius dialect tales collected in *The Conjure Woman* (1899), moreover, Chesnutt satirized Harris's popular Uncle Remus tales and the plantation tradition they evoked. Local colorists seemed drawn to compiling short story cycles. In addition to Chesnutt's *The Conjure Woman*, examples include Jewett's *The Country of the Pointed Firs* (1896), Garland's *Main-Travelled Roads* (1891), George Washington Cable's *Old Creole Days* (1879), and Kate Chopin's *Bayou Folk* (1894).

James's psychological realism was a more aestheticized form of fiction. By experimenting with refined narrators or "centers of consciousness," James presumed to recreate the play of their imaginations—in effect, to adapt his brother William's *Principles of Psychology* (1890) to the fictional page. Chapter 42 of *The Portrait of a Lady* (1881), in which Isabel Archer contemplates the state of her marriage to Gilbert Osmond, anticipated the modern stream of consciousness novels of Gertrude Stein, Virginia Woolf, James Joyce, and William Faulkner. In "The Turn of the Screw" (1898), Henry James recounted a ghost story from the point of view of a psychopathological narrator. Particularly in some of his later tales (including "The Beast in the Jungle" [1903]), he described almost no physical behavior, a technique that led to the joking complaint that James "chewed more than he bit off."

Very few American poets of the period between 1865 and 1915 presumed to be realists in their verse. The major poets—such as Longfellow, Riley, E. C. Stedman, Edwin Markham, Sidney Lanier, Ina Coolbrith, Thomas Wentworth Higginson, William Vaughan Moody, and Thomas Bailey Aldrich—were heirs of the sentimental tradition of British romanticism. Howells and other realists wrote poetry, to be sure, but most of it was utterly conventional and forgettable. Twain parodied sentimental verse in both *Tom Sawyer* and *Huckleberry Finn*, as in Emmeline Grangerford's funeral poetry, but his own poetry was unremarkable. The African-American poet Paul Laurence Dunbar published dialect verse, much as Chesnutt wrote dialect stories, but he was an exception to the rule. Both Crane and Edwin Arlington Robinson penned a brand of naturalistic poetry around the turn of the century. Crane's verse was enigmatic and bitterly ironic, and Robinson wrote such dramatic monologues as *Richard Cory* and *Miniver Cheevy* and the sonnets *Zola* and *Annandale*, the latter a defense of euthanasia.

The forte of the realists, however, was topical fiction. Even James's stories on the international theme (for example, *Daisy Miller* [1879], *The American* [1877], and *The Ambassadors* [1903]) exploited the growth in international travel during the last third of the nineteenth century. (With the development of the steamship, passenger departures from the United States for Europe increased from around 20,000 in 1860 to around 110,000 in 1900.) More to the point, realists often protested conditions, pilloried hypocrisy, or proposed social reforms. Few topics escaped their notice. It was, as Mark Twain and Charles Dudley Warner averred in their collaborative novel, a "gilded age," not a Golden Age. Among the topics that concerned them were political corruption (Twain and Warner's *The Gilded Age* [1873], Henry Adams's *Democracy* [1880], and Garland's *A Spoil of Office* [1892]); immigration and integration (Cahan's *The Rise of David Levinsky* [1917], Sui Sin Far's *Mrs. Spring Fragrance* [1912], and Yezierska's

Hungry Hearts [1920]); marriage and divorce (Howells's *A Modern Instance* [1882] and Wharton's *The Age of Innocence* [1920]); small-town parochialism or "the revolt from the village" (E. W. Howe's *The Story of a Country Town* [1883], Edgar Lee Masters's *Spoon River Anthology* [1915], Robinson's *The Children of the Night* [1897], Wharton's *Ethan Frome* [1911], Sinclair Lewis's *Main Street* [1920], and Sherwood Anderson's *Winesburg, Ohio* [1919]); military imperialism during the Spanish-American War (Howells's "Editha" [1905] and Twain's "The War Prayer" [1916]); lynchings (Twain's "The United States of Lyncherdom" [1923] and Walter V. T. Clark's *The Ox-Bow Incident* [1940]); urban squalor, prostitution, and the "fallen woman" or "the shame of the cities" (Crane's *Maggie: A Girl of the Streets* [1893]); economic injustice (James's *The Princess Casamassima* [1886], Howells's *A Hazard of New Fortunes* [1890], and Twain's *A Connecticut Yankee in King Arthur's Court*); alcoholism (Howells's *The Landlord at Lion's Head* [1897] and Norris's *McTeague* [1899]); and euthanasia (Wharton's *The Fruit of the Tree* [1907]). Such texts complemented some of the social essays of the period, including Henry Demarest Lloyd's *Wealth against Commonwealth* (1894), Thorstein Veblen's *The Theory of the Leisure Class* (1899), and Jacob Riis's *How the Other Half Lives* (1890). In "Under the Lion's Paw" (1889), Garland specifically endorsed the "single tax" on "unearned increment" advocated by Henry George in his book, *Progress and Poverty* (1879).

Other narratives were devoted to the "woman question" and the contemporary feminist movement, including Chopin's *The Awakening* (1899) and "The Story of an Hour" (1894), James's *The Bostonians*, Howells's *Dr. Breen's Practice* (1881), Freeman's "A New England Nun" (1891) and "The Revolt of 'Mother'" (1890), and Gilman's "The Yellow Wall-Paper" (1892). The latter tale specifically critiqued the rest cure for women suffering from hysteria or neurasthenia prescribed by S. Weir Mitchell, a Philadelphia nerve specialist and part-time novelist.

Realistic fiction published during the final decade of the nineteenth century was often a race-inflected fiction as well. The 1890s, punctuated by the Chinese Exclusionary Act (1892) and the *Plessy v. Ferguson* decision of the Supreme Court (1896) sanctioning "separate but equal" public facilities for blacks and whites, were the nadir of race relations in the United States. The public debate about it notwithstanding, Twain's *Adventures of Huckleberry Finn* was not a race novel, certainly not in the same sense as Howells's *An Imperative Duty* (1891) or Twain's *The Tragedy of Pudd'nhead Wilson* (1894). In the former, a young woman raised to believe she is white discovers that she has a black ancestor. In the latter, two baby boys are switched in their cradles, one of them freeborn and the other a slave but otherwise indistinguishable, with tragic results. In both novels the authors probed the meaning of racial identity. A cluster of other realistic race novels appeared in the early 1890s, among them Anna J. Cooper's *A Voice from the South* (1892) and Frances E. W. Harper's *Iola Leroy; or, Shadows Uplifted* (1892). Chesnutt also published a trio of realistic novels around the turn of the century that pondered the consequences of racial violence: *The House behind the Cedars* (1900); *The Marrow of Tradition* (1901), based on the race riot in Wilmington, North Carolina, in 1898; and *The Colonel's Dream* (1905), about the failure of the New South to secure racial justice.

Despite the early successes of the local colorists Bret Harte and Mark Twain, western American writers were slow to warm to realism. Western literature was epitomized by the sensational, blood-and-thunder of the dime novel westerns that celebrated westward expansion and conquest. As late as 1902, the same year Owen Wister's romanticized bestseller *The Virginian* appeared, Norris complained that rather than a school of western realists there were "the wretched 'Deadwood Dicks' and Buffalo Bills of the yellowbacks" and writers "who lied and tricked and strutted in Pathfinder and Leather-Stocking series." Still, a brand of western realism emerged in such neglected or unknown works as Mary Hallock Foote's novel *The Led-Horse Claim* (1883), Mary Austin's *Land of Little Rain* (1903), and Andy Adams's *The Log of a Cowboy* (1903), all of which deal with mining, ranching, or other forms of labor. Clarence Gohdes declared in 1951, in fact, that Foote was "more of a realist than either Harte or Clemens in portraying the life of the mining areas. . . . In the history of fiction dealing with the Far West she may claim attention as the first realist of the section."

American realists contributed to the national literary culture in another way; they belonged to the first generation of true literary professionals in America, as Howells suggested in his essay, "The Man of Letters As a Man of Business" (1893). The realists hired the first literary agents in the early 1880s, contributed to the first newspaper fiction syndicates in the mid-1880s, and lobbied for passage of legislation governing international copyright, finally adopted in 1891. They introduced marketing gimmicks such as subscription sales (Mark Twain was a director of the American Publishing Company of Hartford) and composite novels (such as *The Whole Family* [1908], to which Howells, James, Freeman, and nine other writers each contributed a chapter). Partly as a result of the invention of the Linotype machine, the number of magazines published in the nation increased from about two hundred in 1860 to some eighteen hundred in 1900, with a corresponding increase in the opportunities for literary careers. To be sure, most commercially successful novels were still pitched to middle-class women readers. Howells estimated that some 75 percent of all books sold in the United States were bought by women, and the novelist John W. De Forest similarly declared that women comprised four-fifths of the novel-reading public. The novel, even the realistic novel, usually contained a love interest (*Huckleberry Finn* was a rare and notable exception) if only to spur sales—but it was a love interest often disappointed. Many of the realists also scripted plays, often adaptations of their own stories and novels, because the market for new drama was more lucrative than for fiction. As Harte would write, plays were potentially "vastly more profitable" or lucrative than novels. A "good play" in production ought to pay its author about three thousand dollars per year, he thought. Similarly, James noted privately that he "simply *must* try, and try seriously, to produce half a dozen—a dozen, five dozen—plays for the sake of my pocket, my material future." In all, Twain, Howells, James, and Harte produced some sixty scripts, though many of them were never produced professionally.

NATURALISM AS A LITERARY THEORY

In his essay *Le roman expérimental* (The Experimental Novel) (1880), the French novelist Émile Zola developed an elaborate analogy between experimental or empirical fiction and the medical science of the French physician Claude Bernard. According to Zola, the experimental (that is, the naturalistic) novelist simply adopts "the scientific method, which has been in use for a long time." He "institutes the experiment, that is, sets the characters of a particular story in motion, in order to show that the series of events therein will be those demanded by the determinism of the phenomena under study." Richard Wright deployed a similar trope in his essay "How Bigger Was Born" (1940), often reprinted as an introduction to his *Native Son* (1940), one of the last American naturalistic novels: "Why should I not, like a scientist in a laboratory, use my imagination and invent test-tube situations, place Bigger in them, and...work out in fictional form a resolution of his fate?" The influence of Zola on American naturalists can hardly be understated. Norris, for example, sometimes signed his letters "the boy Zola," and Crane

wrote that his character Maggie Johnson "blossomed in a mud puddle," much as Zola's character Nana was "a plant nurtured on a dung heap."

In a word, the strategies of both realism and naturalism depend upon a quasi-scientific method of detailed observation, but in the case of naturalism the science is rooted in Darwin's theory of evolution. As Malcolm Cowley explained in " 'Not Men': A Natural History of American Naturalism" (*Kenyon Review*, Summer 1947), "The Naturalistic writers were all determinists in that they believed in the omnipotence of abstract forces. They were pessimists so far as they believed that men and women were absolutely incapable of shaping their own destinies." Similarly, Lars Åhnebrink, in *The Beginnings of Naturalism in American Fiction* (1950), allowed that the naturalist "portrays *life as it is in accordance with the philosophical theory of determinism*." Dreiser variously described Carrie Meeber, for example, as "a waif amid forces," "a wisp in the wind," a "wisp on the tide," and he referred in *Sister Carrie* (1900) and *An American Tragedy* in pseudoscientific terms to such body chemicals as "katastates" and "anastates" and to "chemisms" in an attempt to explain all thoughts and emotional responses as mere chemical reactions in the blood.

In all, naturalism was a literature of despair that repudiated the optimism and idealism of the Enlightenment. American naturalists tended to emphasize environmental factors in the formation of character, European naturalists heredity factors. Most American literary naturalists were also Social Darwinists who applied Darwin's biological theories of natural selection to models of social organization, arguing by analogy that just as the fittest of each species in nature struggles for existence by adapting to its environment, the fittest human competitors best adapt to social conditions and thrive and prosper. Crane made the point in a poem that is a virtual Social Darwinian parable:

The trees in the garden rained flowers.
Children ran there joyously.
They gathered the flowers
Each to himself.
Now there were some
Who gathered great heaps—
Having opportunity and skill—
Until, behold, only chance blossoms
Remained for the feeble.
Then a little spindling tutor
Ran importantly to the father, crying:
"Pray, come hither!
"See this unjust thing in your garden!"
But when the father had surveyed

213

He admonished the tutor:
"Not so, small sage!
"This thing is just.
"For, look you,
"Are not they who possess the flowers
"Stronger, bolder, shrewder
"Than they who have none?
"Why should the strong—
"The beautiful strong—
"Why should they not have the flowers?"
Upon reflection, the tutor bowed to the ground.
"My lord," he said,
"The stars are displaced
"By this towering wisdom."

Similarly, the opening chapter of Dreiser's *The Financier* (1912) portrayed a battle to the death between an octopus and a squid. Young Frank Cowperwood wonders how life is organized and observes the battle in a tank at a fish market near his home. Gradually, the lobster devours the squid and answers the riddle young Cowperwood had been pondering: "Lobsters lived on squids and other things," and men lived on "other men." Tennyson had mused on "Nature, red in tooth and claw" a half century before, but it remained for the naturalist writers to illustrate a ruthless struggle for existence. The theory of literary naturalism even informs such pulp novels as Edgar Rice Burroughs's *Tarzan of the Apes* (1914), which thematically suggests that a white child raised in the African jungle will inevitably grow up to be "king of the apes."

In truth, most naturalists came to Social Darwinism not through Darwin but through the social theories of Herbert Spencer. The poet Edwin Arlington Robinson lamented to a friend in 1890 that "Life was something before you came to Spencer." When Dreiser read Spencer's *First Principles* (1862) in 1894, he admitted, it "blew me, intellectually, to bits" and left him "numb." He realized that "Man was a mechanism, undevised and uncreated, and a badly and carelessly driven one at that.... When I read Spencer I could only sigh." He later told the novelist Frank Harris that Spencer "nearly killed me, took every shred of belief away from me; showed me that I was a chemical atom in a whirl of unknown forces; the realization clouded my mind." Similarly, Jack London recalled in his autobiographical novel, *Martin Eden* (1909), his own introduction to "the man Spencer.... There was no caprice, no chance. All was law." In brief, naturalism gleans from Darwin the metaphor of the jungle; from Spencer the metaphor of the "struggle for existence" in society; from Freud the inviolable determinism of the unconscious; from Marx a sense of economic determinism; from positivism in general and Auguste Comte in particular a doctrine of environmental determinism; and from Hippolyte Taine the notion of literature as the product of race or national character, moment, and social milieu.

While the canonical American naturalists are usually considered *sui generis*—some literary historians even assert that no American realist became a naturalist—both Howells and Twain commented on the doctrine of determinism in their late fiction. In *The Landlord at Lion's Head* and *The Son of Royal Langbrith* (1904), Howells considered the possibility of biological determinism along the lines of Zola. And *Huckleberry Finn* contains hints of Twain's belief in environmental determinism. ("I never thought no more about reforming. I shoved the whole thing out of my head; and said I would take up wickedness again, which was in my line, being brung up to it.") Both *A Connecticut Yankee in King Arthur's Court* and *The Tragedy of Pudd'nhead Wilson* were thematically devoted to illustrating how environment shapes character. "Training is everything"—this exact phrase appears in both chapter 18 of the former novel ("Training—training is everything; training is all there is to a person") and as an epigraph to chapter 5 of the latter. ("Training is everything. The peach was once a bitter almond; cauliflower is nothing but cabbage with a college education.") Twain expressed his ideas about environmental determinism most fully in his philosophical treatise *What Is Man?* (1906): "The human being is merely a machine, and nothing more.... A man is never anything but what his outside influences have made him."

Little wonder Cowley concluded that the net effect of naturalism was "to subtract from literature the whole notion of human responsibility." As Norris wrote of the brutish "second self" of his protagonist in *McTeague* (1899), "Below the fine fabric of all that was good in him ran the foul stream of hereditary evil, like a sewer. The vices and sins of his father and of his father's father, to the third and fourth and five hundredth generation, tainted him. The evil of an entire race flowed in his veins. Why should it be? He did not desire it. Was he to blame?" The author's answer is obvious: of course not. Or as Dreiser noted in chapter 7 of *Sister Carrie*, "On the tiger no responsibility rests." Crime in the naturalistic novel—such as McTeague's murder of Trina, Hurstwood's theft of money from his employers in *Sister Carrie*, or Clyde Griffith's murder of Roberta Alden in *An American Tragedy* (1925)—was the result of uncontrollable passions and forces, not personal volition. Similarly, Crane inscribed the flyleaf of a presentation copy of his novel *Maggie, A Girl of the Streets*:

It is inevitable that you will be greatly shocked by this book, but continue, please, with all courage to the end. For, it tries to show that environment is a tremendous thing in the world and frequently shapes lives regardless. If one proves that theory, one makes room in Heaven for all sorts of souls, notably an occasional street girl, who are not confidently expected to be there by many excellent people.

Yet Crane's comment also illustrates a dilemma faced by the naturalist. To the extent that he objectively portrayed the plight of the underclass and described the deterministic forces that shape character, he was faithful to the tenets of naturalism. To the extent he wrote a brief for the defense of the underclass or preached a message, however, he violated the principle of scientific objectivity and became an advocate for reform rather than an objective scientist. Form had been sacrificed to theme, as in *Maggie* or Upton Sinclair's *The Jungle* (1906), or even Steinbeck's *The Grapes of Wrath* (1939). Unlike realism, doctrinaire naturalistic texts rarely advocated social reform. Indeed, the naturalistic theory of mind went hand in glove with the Gospel of Wealth of such industrialists as Andrew Carnegie and John D. Rockefeller and Yale sociologist William Graham Sumner. Whereas naturalism shares with realism the ambition of depicting the experience of everyday men and women accurately, it also shares with modernism an epistemological skepticism, a belief in the nonteleological or purposeless nature of the universe. Though many of the naturalists were leftists (including Dreiser, London, Sinclair, and Steinbeck), their theoretically objective literary perspective warred with their politics. Or as Charles C. Walcutt explains in *American Literary Naturalism: A Divided Stream* (1956), "all 'naturalistic' novels exist in a tension between determinism and its antithesis. The reader is aware of the opposition between what the artist says about man's fate and what his saying it affirms about man's hope."

A naturalistic corollary to the doctrine of determinism was the indifference if not malevolence of nature. In Placer County, California, Norris writes in *McTeague*, nature "is a vast, unconquered brute of the Pliocene epoch, savage, sullen, and magnificently indifferent to man." Similarly, in *The Octopus* (1901) his narrator opines that "Nature is a gigantic engine, a vast cyclopean power, huge, terrible, a leviathan with a heart of steel, knowing no compunction, no forgiveness, no tolerance; crushing out the human atom standing in its way, with nirvanic calm." In "The Blue Hotel" (1898), Crane marvels on "the existence of man" suffering a blizzard and concedes "a glamour of wonder to these lice which were caused to cling to a whirling,

fire-smote, ice-locked, disease-stricken, space-lost bulb." Or, as Crane wrote in one of his poems,

A man said to the universe
"Sir, I exist!"
"However," replied the universe,
"The fact has not created in me
A sense of obligation."

NATURALISM AS LITERARY PRACTICE

Theoretically, the naturalistic tale might be a "success story," with the hero achieving ever greater triumphs. In practice, however, the naturalistic tale was almost always a "failure story" or "plot of decline," with an unfit protagonist like Eugene O'Neill's Brutus Jones slowly degenerating, falling ever lower on the evolutionary ladder. Norris's McTeague is depicted as an atavist fated eventually to die. Dreiser's *An American Tragedy* was among other things a parody of the Horatio Alger myth of success. Jack London's "To Build a Fire" (1908) features a foolish and unfit protagonist who deserves to die, and his "The Law of Life" (1901) depicts the necessary sacrifice of a tribal elder when he becomes a liability to the survival of the group. Such tales were often shocking to readers, and *Maggie*, *The Red Badge of Courage* (1895), and *Sister Carrie* were all published in expurgated versions at the insistence of publishers. Moreover, even though many naturalists (Dreiser, Crane, and Harold Frederic, for instance) began their careers as journalists, they employed a self-consciously crude style of writing. As Norris declared, "Give us stories now, give us men, strong, brutal men, with red-hot blood in 'em, with unleashed passions rampant in 'em, blood and bones and viscera in 'em, and women, too, that move and have their being, people that love and hate.... We don't want literature, we want life. We don't want fine writing, we want short stories."

However crude the naturalistic style, it did exhibit certain recurring hallmarks. Virtually all naturalistic novels were written from the third-person omniscient point of view. The naturalist was, after all, a type of scientist, his novel a type of laboratory report. (There were rare exceptions, such as Jack London's *The Sea-Wolf* [1904].) Whereas the realist aimed to draw "rounded" or credible individual characters, the naturalist portrayed representative and recurring types such as the brute (for example, Norris's *McTeague* and *Vandover and the Brute* [1914] and O'Neill's *The Hairy Ape* [1921]) and the spectator or observer (Presley in *The Octopus* or Ames in *Sister Carrie*, for instance). Unfortunately, the trend among naturalists to portray types also prompted them to reinforce racial and ethnic stereotypes and to assume the superiority of Anglo-Saxon civilization according to the standard science of the day. For example, Norris depicted a Jewish junk collector through anti-Semitic stereotyping in *McTeague*, Crane portrayed a comic Sambo in "The Monster" (1898), and London condescended to a number of racial types in his Klondike and South Seas fiction. Such belief in Anglo-Saxon superiority would point, in the end, to Gilman's endorsement of the early-twentieth-century eugenics movement in her novel, *Herland* (1915).

There were other formal characteristics of literary naturalism. Naturalists frequently employed organic, especially animal, metaphors. Obviously, such metaphors had been used prior to the publication of *On the Origin of Species* (1859), but after the publication of Darwin's theory of natural selection they would have an entirely new resonance. McTeague is a bull, Maggie's brother Jimmie is a fighting cock, and the Joad family in *The Grapes of Wrath* is implicitly compared to a land turtle. Naturalists also often invoked sports or gaming metaphors, as when Henry Fleming in *The Red Badge of Courage* compares a military battle to a football game. Plots were occasionally organized around such forms of cutthroat competition as labor strikes (for instance, *Sister Carrie*, Norris's *The Octopus*, Sinclair's *The Jungle*, Steinbeck's *In Dubious Battle* [1936] and *The Grapes of Wrath*) or, for obvious reasons, warfare (Crane's *The Red Badge of Courage*, Willa Cather's *One of Ours* [1922], Ernest Hemingway's *For Whom the Bells Tolls* [1940], Wharton's *A Son at the Front* [1923], Norman Mailer's *The Naked and the Dead* [1948], and James Jones's *From Here to Eternity* [1951] are examples). Naturalistic novels were often bloated with detailed descriptions of insulated settings, such as Rum Alley in *Maggie*, based on Hell's Kitchen on the West Side of Manhattan; the Polk Street neighborhood of San Francisco in *McTeague*; and first a ship and then an island in London's *The Sea-Wolf*. If a writer is an environmental determinist, after all, he or she labors under the obligation of depicting the environment in minute detail. Taking their cue from Zola's twenty-volume Rougon-Macquart cycle (1871–1893), moreover, several naturalists planned or completed trilogies of novels. Dreiser projected a "trilogy of Desire" and Norris anticipated a "trilogy of the Wheat." John Dos Passos's *U.S.A.* (1938) comprised three published novels, James T. Farrell wrote a "Studs Lonigan" and "Danny O'Neill" series, and Eugene O'Neill wrote *Mourning Becomes Electra* (1931) and later projected a cycle of plays on American history, of which the completed

A Touch of the Poet (1946) and *More Stately Mansions* (1964) were to be a part.

Above all, the naturalists tended to be critical of the "teacup tragedies" of Howellsian realism. "Realism is minute; it is the drama of a broken teacup, the tragedy of a walk down the block, the excitement of an afternoon call, the adventure of an invitation to dinner," Norris complained. Naturalism, in contrast, should explore "the unplumbed depths of the human heart, and the mystery of sex, and the problems of life, and the black, unsearched penetralia of the soul of man." In fine, "terrible things must happen to the characters in a naturalistic novel." Broadly speaking, too, there were generational differences between realists and naturalists. Realists like James and Howells matured as writers in the 1870s and 1880s, whereas naturalists like Crane and Norris matured in the 1890s. But these differences should not be exaggerated. After all, James and Howells remained essentially realistic and remarkably prolific writers until their deaths in 1916 and 1920, respectively, whereas Crane and Norris both were dead by 1902, Crane at the age of twenty-eight, Norris at thirty-two.

TWENTIETH-CENTURY DEVELOPMENTS

Some of Crane's later writings, such as *The Red Badge of Courage* and "The Blue Hotel," represent a variation on the naturalistic tradition and point in the direction of literary impressionism and modernism. Crane asserted in "War Memories" (1899) that he was trying to imitate in words what the French impressionists were doing with light and color: "I bring this to you merely as an effect—an effect of mental light and shade, if you like: something done in thought similar to that which the French Impressionists do in color; something meaningless and at the same time overwhelming, crushing, monstrous." *The Red Badge of Courage* essentially recounts through his impressions the fears and illusions of its ironic soldier-hero, Henry Fleming. All events are filtered through his vision, his sense perceptions. Not only is there no objectivity to his story, the very notion of reality is a shifting and unstable construction of Fleming's imagination. Put another way, by the end of his life Crane had begun to develop naturalistic themes in an impressionistic style. His later tales anticipate Hemingway's terse style, with frequent shifts in point of view, and in fact Hemingway later praised Crane's masterful method in such stories as "The Blue Hotel" and "The Open Boat" (1894).

The proletarian writers of the early twentieth century, such as Sinclair (*The Jungle*), Jack Conroy (*A World to Win*

[1935]), and Robert Cantwell (*The Land of Plenty* [1934]), attempted to graft their leftist politics onto naturalism, a project that met with decidedly mixed results. The hybrid betrayed the "divided stream" of American naturalism in unusual degree. *The Jungle* may have been the earliest American proletarian novel, and it is often credited with catalyzing support for the Pure Food and Drug Act (1906), but as a novel it is crudely constructed and basically breaks in half when the proletarian hero, Jurgis Rudkus, is thrown in jail and, upon his release, leaves Chicago. As Sinclair later conceded, he "aimed at the public's heart and by accident I hit it in the stomach." Naturalism, as Cowley explains in " 'Not Men,' " was fundamentally "unsuited" to the "essentially religious purpose" of the proletarian writers. Given the deterministic bias of naturalism, the proletarian writers were simply unable to explain the conversion of a character to socialism or other forms of radical politics.

The last major controversy over naturalism in literature occurred in the 1940s, and it centered on the possibility of "naturalistic tragedy." During the 1880s the Scandinavian playwrights Henrik Ibsen and August Strindberg had conceived of their plays *Ghosts* (1881) and *Miss Julie* (1888) as naturalistic tragedies. But tragedy, according to its Aristotelian definition, affirms the significance of human life: through the imitation of noble actions ending in catastrophe, a tragic hero falls from a high place and the audience experiences a catharsis of "pity and fear." Joseph Wood Krutch, in "The Tragic Fallacy," a chapter in *The Modern Temper* (1929), countered that the phrase "naturalistic tragedy" is an oxymoron. "We write no tragedies today," Krutch argued, because modern science has enfeebled the human spirit. "If the plays and novels of today deal with littler people and less mighty emotions," he added, "it is not because we have become interested in commonplace souls and their unglamorous adventures but because we have come, willy-nilly, to see the soul of man as commonplace and its emotions as mean." When writers turned "from the hero to the common man," they "inaugurated the era of realism." These arguments prompted Arthur Miller's dramatic experiment, *Death of a Salesman* (1948). In effect, Miller replied to Krutch in an essay explaining why he wrote the play: "In this age few tragedies are written," he declared. "It has often been held that the lack is due to a paucity of heroes among us, or else that modern man has had the blood drawn out of his organs of belief by the skepticism of science." The tragic mode may seem "archaic, fit only for the very highly placed, the kings or the kingly," but "I believe

that the common man is as apt a subject for tragedy in its highest sense as kings were." So Miller portrayed his hapless salesman Willy Loman (low man) as a tragic hero.

The tradition of realism and naturalism has left an indelible mark on American fiction. Even today, some elements of naturalism surface in the fiction of Saul Bellow and Norman Mailer, for example, and John Updike is a type of neo-realist with affinities to Howells. Whatever the posturings of the postmodernists, literary historians may claim for no other American literary tradition the achievements of the realists and naturalists.

[*See also* Anderson, Sherwood; Chesnutt, Charles W.; Chopin, Kate; Crane, Stephen, and his *The Red Badge of Courage*; Dreiser, Theodore; Dunbar, Paul Laurence; Garland, Hamlin; Harte, Bret; Howells, William Dean; James, Henry; Jewett, Sarah Orne; London, Jack; Masters, Edgar Lee; Miller, Arthur, and his *Death of a Salesman*; Norris, Frank; O'Neill, Eugene; Robinson, Edwin Arlington; Sinclair, Upton, and the Muckrakers; Steinbeck, John, and his *The Grapes of Wrath*; Twain, Mark; Wharton, Edith; *and* Wright, Richard.]

FURTHER READING

Åhnebrink, Lars. *The Beginnings of Naturalism in American Fiction.* Cambridge, Mass., 1950. A pioneering work on Zola's influence on Frank Norris.

Berthoff, Warner. *The Ferment of Realism: American Literature, 1884–1919.* New York, 1965. A useful survey of the period with particular reference to the major canonical texts.

Cady, Edwin H. *The Light of Common Day: Realism in American Fiction.* Bloomington, Ind., 1971. A traditional defense of the literary method, its unique sensibility, and its sources, with particular reference to James, Howells, and Twain.

Campbell, Donna M. *Resisting Regionalism: Gender and Naturalism in American Fiction, 1885–1915.* Athens, Ohio, 1997. Persuasively explains the emergence of naturalism as a response to the cultural mythology and feminine influence of the local colorists.

Condor, John J. *Naturalism in American Fiction: The Classic Phase.* Lexington, Ky., 1984. A jargon-free, traditional survey of the major naturalistic texts by Crane, Norris, Dreiser, Dos Passos, and Steinbeck.

Cowley, Malcolm. " 'Not Men': A Natural History of American Naturalism." *Kenyon Review* 9 (Summer 1947): 414–435. A succinct review of the form and many of the critical issues it raised.

Fiedler, Leslie. *Love and Death in the American Novel.* Rev. ed. New York, 1966. Though well-known for its thesis about the recurrence in American fiction of portrayals of interracial homosexual love, this study also dared to challenge other, privileged views of American literature.

Habegger, Alfred. *Gender, Fantasy, and Realism in American Literature*. New York, 1982. Examines how realist writers, social novelists by definition, defended masculinity and sought to correct the distortions in symbolic fiction by women.

Howard, June. *Form and History in American Literary Naturalism*. Chapel Hill, N.C., and London, 1985. A neo-Marxist approach to the topic of American naturalism.

Kaplan, Amy. *The Social Construction of American Realism*. Chicago, 1988. Reexamines the relation of realism to "social change," "the representation of class difference," and the emergence of a "mass culture."

Kolb, Harold H., Jr. *The Illusion of Life: American Realism as a Literary Form*. Charlottesville, Va., 1969. Revising traditional definitions of realism, this study suggests that realism was special not because it was an objective treatment of materials but because it offered the illusion of objectivity.

Martin, Jay. *Harvests of Change: American Literature, 1865–1914*. Englewood Cliffs, N.J., 1967. The study most sensitive to historical events during the period. A detailed literary history.

Martin, Ronald E. *American Literature and the Universe of Force*. Durham, N.C., 1981. A study of "the origins, transmission, and uses" of the concept of "force-universe," particularly in the writings of Henry Adams, Norris, London, and Dreiser.

Michaels, Walter Benn. *The Gold Standard and the Logic of Naturalism*. Berkeley, Calif., 1987. A New Historicist interpretation of American naturalism in which the writers work out conflicts between "material and representation, hard money and soft."

Mitchell, Lee Clark. *Determined Fictions: American Literary Naturalism*. New York, 1989. Considers "the narrative effects of determinism" on naturalistic texts, specifically London's "To Build a Fire," Dreiser's *An American Tragedy*, Norris's *Vandover and the Brute*, and Crane's *The Red Badge of Courage*.

Pizer, Donald. *Twentieth-Century American Literary Naturalism: An Interpretation*. Carbondale, Ill., 1982. A continuation of Pizer's work on nineteenth-century naturalism, with emphasis on the neglected naturalists of the 1930s and 1940s (including Dos Passos, Farrell, and Styron).

Pizer, Donald. *Realism and Naturalism in Nineteenth-Century American Literature*. Rev. ed. Carbondale, Ill., 1984. A formal approach to the study of realism and naturalism mediated through philosophy and aesthetics.

Pizer, Donald, ed. *The Cambridge Companion to American Realism and Naturalism: Howells to London*. Cambridge and New York, 1995. A collection of a dozen essays delineating the historical contexts, contemporary critical approaches, and "case studies" of works by Howells, Twain, James, Norris, Crane, Chopin, Wharton, London, Sinclair, and Du Bois.

Quirk, Tom, and Gary Scharnhorst, eds. *American Realism and the Canon*. Newark, Del., 1994. A collection of twelve essays from a variety of critical perspectives reassessing the accomplishments of both established and "new canonical" realists.

Sundquist, Eric J. *American Realism: New Essays*. Baltimore and London, 1982. A collection of fifteen revisionary essays on major texts by Howells, Twain, James, Crane, Norris, Wharton, Dreiser, and others.

Walcutt, Charles C. *American Literary Naturalism: A Divided Stream*. Minneapolis, Minn., 1956. Perhaps the most accessible studies of American naturalism, with chapters on Crane, London, Norris, Frederic, Garland, Dreiser, Anderson, and Farrell. Argues the now-familiar theme that naturalistic novels dramatize a tension between determinism and the exercise of free will.

Warren, Kenneth W. *Black and White Strangers: Race and American Literary Realism*. Chicago, 1993. Examines a variety of realistic texts on race written between Emancipation and the 1890s to argue for their "emancipatory" power.

NATURE WRITING: POETRY

by Aaron K. DiFranco

An interest in how the features of the real, physical universe give shape to human thought and experience remains a central preoccupation of American poetry. Whether as cells or solar systems, sensual or spiritual, wild or urban, animal or vegetable or mineral, the forms of nature have not only driven poets to expressions of awe and praise but also roused them to explore the implications of the world's processes and their own role within them. At stake is an understanding of the world close at hand but beyond the individual self, threatening and comforting, full of possibility and mystery, flourishing and decaying according to its own ways.

To just what extent poets are able to "write nature" has been a matter of much contention. Whereas prose lends itself to descriptive reporting and presumptions of a "factual" world, poetry usually arouses attention for its artistic, "fanciful" dimensions, and its ability to refer directly to the natural world has consequently been neglected. A dominant tradition in poetry criticism has focused primarily on how both language and the creative imagination can distort representations of the world. The excesses of emotion and whimsical imagery that often accompany popular romantic-era poetry, for example, only emphasize the way human beings can project meanings and values onto the world. As a result, analyses of poetic nature have tended to emphasize the human needs and interests motivating the verse. Although this practice has produced exceptional studies regarding nature within a humanist tradition, it has also helped perpetuate a way of thought that valorizes humanity and civilization over nature. Indeed, the category "nature poetry" not only has had to contend with the pejorative associations mentioned before but also claims that such poems merely present an escape from the "real" world of human affairs.

As environmental crises throughout the twentieth century fostered recognition of American society's continuing impact on nature on both local and global scales, renewed attention has been brought to the way poetry both reflects and constructs the culture's basic attitudes toward the nonhuman world. As history has shown, how people think about, talk about, and conceive of nature and their role in it can have great consequences for the surrounding world. Poetry is a place not only where language can be investigated and manipulated to push perceptions *of* the universe, but also where constructions of language can be tested to observe their effects *in* the world. Claims have been made that, in its broadest considerations, all poetry is inherently "nature poetry," in that poets, like all humans, are shaped by their basic existence as beings in the world and that the poem will thus show the influence of this "natural" condition. This line of thought—along with other generalizing lines that call poetry an imitation of nature, expressions of a natural condition, or a part of human nature—has encouraged nature-oriented critics at the turn of the twenty-first century to consider how all poetry responds materially, imaginatively, and ideologically to one's experience within the natural world.

Keeping in mind the real dangers to the environment—ranging from the extinction of species to soil erosion to toxic contamination—much of this criticism also takes on an advocacy role and often promotes the term "ecopoetry" to refer to those poems that try to place broader ecological concerns at the center of their work. But other modes of investigating how poetry engages nature are also prevalent. Bioregionalist approaches, for instance, emphasize an actual place as the subject of their investigations and look to the way poets use language to define and participate within their ecosystems. Stressing humanity as just one element in the totality of nature and its processes, bioregionalism considers how writers express the emotional, spiritual, and intellectual life of a culture and its interactions with the geology and biology—the organic and inorganic life—of a specific geographic region. Ecologically and anthropologically inclined, this method encourages exploration of all forms of imaginative writing for the way the natural history of the bioregion has influenced cultural practices and beliefs.

While this essay advocates a bioregional emphasis on the actual conditions of place evoked by poetry as well as on the intimate, personal expressions of local communities, such an undertaking is beyond its scope. Attention is brought rather to the poetic work that demonstrates a more conscious awareness of how language is simultaneously structured by and structuring of one's living experience within nature. An emphasis on how past attitudes have influenced contemporary considerations of poetic nature writing has led to this piece's construction as a cursory literary history. Although overlapping poetic careers are loosely arranged for the sake of convenience, this discussion is not intended as a linear narrative. Acknowledging the way such a history can participate in exclusionary canon formation as well as flatten out poets' individual differences in favor of the more general and conventional characteristics of a period, it intends to be extensive though not comprehensive. The variety of poetry dealt with here not only provides a spectrum of geographic, historic, scientific, and cultural influences that inform the current views of nature and poetry, but also represents vital, continuous perceptions that still yield both practical knowledge about the world and insight into nature's more ineffable qualities.

INDIGENOUS VOICES

To speak of the first poetries that engaged American nature is to speak of those who first tried to express the mind of the land. Indigenous peoples throughout North America, South America, and Mesoamerica developed cultures that bespoke a fundamental relationship to the ecology of their regions, whether they were seal hunting clans along the Arctic Circle, large agricultural communities in the Valley of Mexico or across the Andes, or hunting tribes of the Pampas in what is now Argentina. Indeed, different tribal groups are commonly associated within cultural areas determined by geography and prevailing natural resources. Even as tribes within these regions may have shared certain cultural practices and beliefs, each one also evolved traditions based on the specific circumstances of their location as well as on distinct social and linguistic modes. A tribe's oral tradition—songs, chants, prayers, stories, poems—maintains in expressive forms the heritage of the community, a heritage inscribed in and by the nature surrounding them. Estimates place the number of indigenous languages within the Americas before European contact at between two and three thousand, emphasizing not only the vast poetic legacy only beginning to be explored but also the diversity of cultural worldviews through which "American" nature could be perceived.

Although expansion and early assimilationist policies of the federal government have wrought considerable damage to the original tribal cultures, well over one hundred native languages are still spoken within the geopolitical borders of the United States, each of which maintains its own distinct oral tradition. While many songs are sacred to the tribe or to individual members and thus remain within the tribal community, still other forms—like publicly performed Powwow songs—are well known and continue to express allegiances to the seasons, the land, and its natural inhabitants. The advent of European contact brought with it the recording and translation into English of many tribal songs and stories. It is telling, however, that until the 1960s the best sources for translations into English were anthropologists and ethnologists like Frances Densmore, James Mooney, and others working for the federal government's Bureau of American Ethnology at the end of the nineteenth century and beginning of the twentieth. Both transcriptions and sound recordings are now located in the Library of Congress archives. Chippewa hunting songs from the Great Lakes, Inuit morning prayers, Navajo harvest chants, and countless other poetic declarations address the natural world from various perspectives and contain invaluable knowledge. Besides recording aspects of the natural history and local ecosystems, these songs demonstrate the spiritual, social, and philosophical dispositions that grew out of practices that were in turn integrated into the processes of the land and seasons. These practices also encouraged an ethical attitude that was ecologically minded, recognizing humans as just one component of the larger workings of nature, and imaginatively and respectfully considered the other members of the community, whether sun, wind, corn, deer, or bird.

From creation myths to the trickster tales of the Crow, Coyote, or Hare, these poetries express a conception of the natural world unimagined by conventional Western modes and reveal old and new ways of conceiving the human relationship to the continent. They also, as the sometimes tragic nineteenth-century songs of the Ghost Dance show, reflect how historical and cross-cultural pressures can affect tribal response to the natural world. Beginning in the 1960s, a renewed interest in these older forms has grown, directed in part by the emergence of new Native American literary voices such as N. Scott Momaday, Leslie Marmon Silko, and Gerald Vizenor. Also, anthologies by John Bierhorst, Natalie Burlin, and A. Grove Day were published through that decade, providing exceptional, modestly sized introductions to tribal literatures. Also, the growing field of ethnopoetics—exemplified by the journal *Alcheringa*, founded by Dennis Tedlock and Jerome Rothenberg in 1970 and active through the decade—began investigating the ways that poetry inflects a culture's behaviors in a given locale, as well as the way the field's own methods of investigation could maintain the values expressed there. Rothenberg also published several volumes with selections of indigenous poetry from North America and around the world, including *Technicians of the Sacred: A Range of Poetries from Africa, America, Asia, and Oceania* (1968). Although some of his work has been critiqued for its "imaginative" transformations of traditional native forms, it nevertheless highlights a sense of reverence toward the earth. The influence of these indigenous attitudes and poetic modes not only extends to his own poems but also manifests itself over and over throughout the tradition of poetry in American English.

POETS OF THE COLONIAL PERIOD AND EARLY REPUBLIC

Anne Bradstreet, the first writer of original poetry among the American colonists, is also often considered the first expression of a European sensibility marked by contact with the new continent. As expected, her poetry demonstrates characteristic attitudes toward nature that these colonists brought with them from Europe. Indeed, a biblical notion of the physical world as "fallen" from grace as well as a European bias toward civilization in part informed the colonial enterprise in the exoticized American wilderness. Bradstreet's poetry shows the conventions of seventeenth-century neoclassical poetry, and at times many of her "harts" and "hinds" more resemble tropes of the British commons than images of the hardwood forests of Massachusetts. Bradstreet perceived nature as part of a divinely created universe, though her Puritan background encouraged a moral resistance to its sensuality. More personal writings, such as "Correspondences," "Meditations," and the letter "To Her Children," demonstrate a complex spirituality responsive to contact with the continent's wonders, negotiating between Puritan doctrines and her experience of the new American landscape.

Although images of nature would regularly appear throughout the work of the dominant "American" poets into the middle of the eighteenth century, direct considerations of the country's nature were submerged by other artistic goals: pious and moral meditations, rustic satire, and revolutionary politics clothed in traditional verse forms, while slave spirituals and work songs provided

a different, more austere context for engaging the land through an expressive oral tradition. Occasional poems did appear that demonstrated greater degrees of felicity in their attentions to American environments, including some by Philip Freneau. These range from poems designed to promote the often feminized delights of various settlements, as in George Alsop's *A Character of the Providence of Maryland* (1666), to familiar pastoral or georgic meditations suited to the developing agrarian society. Almanac verse and descriptive, local color sketches like Timothy Dwight's *Greenfield Hill* (1794) also provided responses to the character of the territories.

By the beginning of the nineteenth century, poetry's ranging through nature began to transform, helped along by the Romantic movement sweeping through Europe and across the Atlantic. Responding to the growing remove of a Christian God from the earthly sphere and the emphasis on reason throughout the previous century, romanticism emphasized a sensitivity to wild nature and its alignment with the poetic imagination. For American poets, this meant a turn toward the distinct features of their own national landscape, particularly to moments of sublime encounter in the hinterlands of the country. Grounded in a more attentive consideration of the rustic American context and invested in a project of abstracting truths from the natural world, the poetic concern often sought emotional "recollections" for pastoral, moral, or aesthetic aims. The more popular poems of the era often traced a sentimental reconciliation between the individual and a domestically inflected natural world. Yet even the more popular Fireside Poets like John Greenleaf Whittier and Henry Wadsworth Longfellow drew on a pantheistic conception of nature as a source of spiritual value. Celebrations of wild nature also registered the growing damage from expansion, as in the work of Thomas Cole.

The earliest call in this era of nation building for an "American" poetry came from William Cullen Bryant, who in 1819 critiqued his contemporaries' traditional academic forms and lack of imagination. Although many of his own poems still embodied neoclassical impulses and provided readers pastoral consolation from the troubles of the developing agrarian society in occasionally predictable meditations, his work shows the growing influence of romantic ideas regarding poetic imagination and an immanent nature. His own naturalist inclinations as a student of botany also helped shape a homegrown aesthetic attentive to the details of the American continent. "The Prairies," in particular, has become emblematic for the way it turns from conceptions of nature as fallen to a more secular and attentive celebration of the Illinois landscape. Similarly, the work of William Gilmore Simms also began to explore the relationship between the poet and the physical world with great sensitivity.

TRANSCENDENTALISM

In the transcendental expression of its own romantic impulses, the United States developed its first distinctive literary tradition, and it was a tradition premised on how an individual engages with and eventually *knows* the world. Building from romanticism's sense of the poem as a form of knowledge counter to dogmatic rationality, as well as its turn toward experiences in nature to balance the alienations of civilization and increasing industrialization, transcendentalists were at the same time more grounded in the given world and more spiritually oriented. That their work tended toward visionary or philosophical sermons, however, leads to concerns over their idealist tendencies and the real place of nature within it. Although discussion of the era is dominated by a few major figures, a number of other poets also produced stirring and highly insightful representations of nature, including Caroline Sturgis Tappan and William Ellery Channing.

Significantly, two of the most noted figures in discussions of poetic nature writing are more well-known for their prose: Ralph Waldo Emerson and Henry David Thoreau. Many of Emerson's poems are still anthologized, but they are often overshadowed by the imaginative power of his essays, in which he traces out the demands for poetry. His essay *Nature* (1836) is generally considered a founding document of the dominant American tradition, not only for the way it sets out a philosophy of correspondences between the mind and the natural world, but also because of the way the prose evokes, in its own formal motions, how Emerson attempted to establish his own relationship to nature. Describing the world as "emblematic," he emphasized how the objects of nature were actually symbols for spiritual truths. Poetic language became a means by which these truths could be intuitively discovered by humans. His New England Unitarian background nurtured a continuing belief in nature as a divine creation, but Emerson's transcendental thought was less religiously doctrinal, encouraging direct encounters with the physical universe.

Where Emerson is seen as philosophical, Thoreau is upheld as a paragon for rendering a more common, direct experience of the natural world, an actual sense of contact like that he registered during a climb on the winter heights of Mount Katahdin. Like Emerson's verse, Thoreau's few poems express encounters with the transcendent particulars of the New England environment; though realistically depicted, they sometimes move toward a "poetic" sentiment that tends to obscure the real functioning of the environment. And, again like Emerson, it is Thoreau's imaginative prose, in *Walden* (1854) as well as his extensive *Journal*, that traces its influence into American nature poetry. If Emerson provided a method for engaging with nature, Thoreau not only carried it out in actual practice but provided a guiding ethic. His social criticism and championing of wilderness prompted a reconsideration of the fundamental relationship between civilization and the natural world, as well as of the functioning of the world beyond human enterprise. While his experiences in the wildernesses of New England have been variously characterized as pagan, escapist, or actually less "wild" than the texts present them to be, his writings have remained for many a source for articulate expression as well as for learning the manners of engagement with the natural world.

The persona of Walt Whitman in many ways finally blends the characteristics of Emerson's transcendental poet and Thoreau's rugged yet leisurely common man. *Leaves of Grass* (the first edition appearing in 1855) presented an attention to the rhythms of the land, the sense of everyday life in America *as* the poem, in an expansive free verse that did away with academic forms and expressions. Although frequently condemned for its sensuality by Victorian-minded society, Whitman's verse remains equally metaphysical, an investigation not only of his own place in the universe but also of his interrelation with all other things. Considered "democratic" for his inclusiveness, he attempts to comprehend everything in his poems and mark how it all makes up his own poetic identity. His scope also covers extensive catalogs of a nation diversely engaged in enterprises within nature—trapping, driving livestock, farming. Whitman evokes a mutual assimilation of the individual and land, though critics like Cecelia Tichi (1979) have pointed out how his poems reflect the period's concern with expansion and environmental reform.

Counter to Whitman's expansive, public persona is the recluse of Amherst, Emily Dickinson. Raised in a very strict Calvinist area of New England, as compared to Emerson's Unitarianism, she nonetheless broke with religious orthodoxy, finding in poetry an outlet for spiritual and metaphysical examinations. Her short lyrics pushed examinations of the natural world, relying less on intuitive feeling than on the circumlocutions of poetic logic. Dickinson's sharp attention traces the border between what can be known by human perception and the world beyond human cognition, and the natural world became a frontier where she continually confronted her own ability to conceive reality. Even more familiar tropes of nature, such as the sea in "I started early, took my dog," establish a personal, distinctive dimension for exploring the limits of self and world. Always mindful, her poems are conscious of the way the external world structures knowing.

TWENTIETH-CENTURY BORDER REGIONS

Despite Whitman's oracular bravado and Dickinson's poetic slant logic, a growing loss of faith in transcendent truths accompanied the increasing industrialization and social changes at the turn of the twentieth century. Nature remained potent both as a source of awe and as a forming limit of human consciousness, but the modernist poets demonstrated their own skepticism toward the meanings romantic poetry generated in its attempt to find significance in the emblems of nature. Most poets of the time turned toward Europe as a source for cosmopolitan civility and a refined intellectualism, borrowing from French symbolism and seventeenth-century British metaphysical poetry to represent psychological moods, fragmented consciousness, and well-wrought patterns of ambiguities. However, it should be kept in mind that even T. S. Eliot's *The Waste Land* (1922) concerns itself with a sense of civilization's distorted relation to nature: while using, for example, the image of a polluted Thames River to critique the decay of postwar society, the poem considers the tradition of seasonal fertility rituals in its efforts to find a right regard to the natural processes of existence.

The turn toward realism at the end of the nineteenth century had already provided for more careful descriptions of the conditions of existence, but this was later accompanied by concern over language's ability to accurately depict the "things" of the world without projecting human values and beliefs onto them. Despite this literary distrust of objective representation, many poets turned increasingly to the objects of nature—if not for "truth" then as a measure of their personal experiences. These poets followed Dickinson's example in using poetry to scrutinize the border between inventive mind and an opaque and textured nature, though without her occasional moments of faith and vision.

The most ready examples of modernist nature poetry are the era's two primary regionalists, Robert Frost and Robinson Jeffers. More enduringly popular, Frost made metaphors out of New England life. Caught perhaps in the aura of the transcendental tradition originating from the region, his poems differ both in their darker existentialist attitude and in their rural character. Although his poems certainly helped construct a belated national pastoral, they also established an American identity of belonging to the land as put forth by Whitman and a further attentiveness to how the forms of nature impress themselves into one's consideration. Using traditional forms, Frost's poems present themselves as spaces where the external world is met and constructed into an order to satisfy human emotional and spiritual needs, though these needs also seem to include repeated personal confrontations with the more daunting "orders" of nature, so that human meanings are kept in perspective.

Whereas Frost's poems often highlight the tension between humanity and nature, Robinson Jeffers has often been praised for the way he celebrates nature's distinct "inhuman" qualities. Jeffers also works through the modernist view of nature as ultimately unknowable, but his poems embrace the raw yet stunning world manifested by the rugged Pacific coast of California where he lived. Even as they reflect his anger over the continued despoiling of the American landscape, the poems perceive nature as having its own independent interest, as when imagining the land's indifferent response to suburban, human developments in "Carmel Point." Out of such attitudes Jeffers polemically encourages a turn away from human-centered concerns to consideration of the particulars of nature on their own terms. The resulting focus on how rock, hawk, ocean, or air construct in their relations the physical "ground" of experience has led to new critical evaluations of his ecological worldview.

MODERNIST THINGS AND A CULTURE'S IDEAS

More controversial, though no less salient, in discussions of modernist nature writing is Wallace Stevens, whose lyricism extended and exposed some limits to the romantic tradition's approach to nature. His visionary poetic practice emphasized how the imagination uses language to transform reality, and poems like "The Idea of Order at Key West" or "An Ordinary Evening in New Haven" enact these transformations with brilliance and sonorous clarity. As beautiful as they are, however, the poems highlight their inability to know the external world except through language. Such a practice has led some critics to emphasize the human needs that drive imagination and question his allegiance to real nature, but Stevens remained committed to the material world he saw as complementary to the imagination. Whereas nature provides a metaphysical direction for Frost's poems, Stevens's poetry continually points toward nature's phenomenological aspect, its existence outside of the poet's personal musings. Always skeptical of any transcendental or objective knowledge humanity may discover about the world, the poems do not deny an object world. Indeed, while Stevens may have paid little attention to natural history or natural processes, he nevertheless saw the role of the poet as directing attention back to the world of things, to the "thing itself."

Attention to phenomena in their particular form was also reflected by poetry's increasing break with traditional verse forms and the repeated aesthetic concentration on "things" over ideas. This project was perhaps carried out most extensively by the group of objectivists, who used their investigations of the structuring of poetry—that is, its use of sound, syntax, the placement of the printed word—to create a stronger correlation between the depicted world and the mind's apprehension of it through the poem. While this can be perceived in the wake of romantic and Emersonian correspondences between poet and nature, the break in form also signaled a turn from older contemplations of nature's transcendent meaning toward poetry's modes of revelation. Most familiar in this regard is William Carlos Williams. Even as his lyrics engaged the everyday life and common speech rhythms encountered around his small city home of Paterson, New Jersey, they were attentive to the vital elements of nature that quickened experience. Local flora—saxifrage, Queen Anne's lace, asphodel, willow—frequently provide subjects for imagistic structurings of experience.

Also interested in exploring poetry's ability to discover meanings was Marianne Moore. Her exuberant, syllabic forms often work associatively by bringing images of the world into collage. The title of her second book, *Observations* (1924), emphasizes her poetic manner. Not without her own moralizing, she took faith in the interrelatedness of things, how they expressed similarities and how by overlaying them in poems one could invent new impressions of nature's extent. Her oft-quoted description of poems as "imaginary gardens with real toads in them" highlights not only her artistic practice but also an ethical obligation toward the raw sources of her patternings. Her frequent use of zoological subjects—from katydids to mockingbirds to silkworms—is marked by an attentive precision of detail, as well as informed by her own readings of scientific literature. Direct and pragmatically

unsentimental, her poetry has often been compared to Dickinson's for the way it uses language to investigate nature and the way we render relationships with it.

Not usually considered under the rubric of "writing nature" is the group of southern Agrarian poets active through the 1920s and 1930s, including Allen Tate, John Crowe Ransom, and Robert Penn Warren. Only Warren's work takes a direct and distinctly mindful approach to nature, particularly in later works such as *Audubon: A Vision* (1969). Neoclassical in manner and voicing principles of stability and closeness to nature based on the South's agricultural and Christian heritage, the Agrarians generally took a humanist bent in their efforts to defend this heritage from the looming effects of industrialization after World War I. Despite—or even because of—criticisms that call them apologetic for the South's system of slaveholding or simply nostalgic, their work nevertheless deserves some attention for the way it expresses values grounded in the region's land-based practices. At the same time, focus on the body of work by black poets of the era, like Langston Hughes, Sterling Allen Brown, or Jean Toomer, demonstrates alternate ways the nature of the South has been "written" along with its antebellum history. Like the Agrarians, their poems were less interested in nature per se than in the way natural images symbolically articulate cultural heritage, but poems like Hughes's "The Negro Speaks of Rivers" or Brown's "Bitter Fruit of the Tree" show the way African-American experiences and social history have been inscribed diversely across the southern landscape.

MEDITATIONS OF THE MIDDLE GENERATION

Although modernist symbolism deepened the attention given over to nature, poets also started becoming more resistant to the overwhelming yet somewhat static conceptions of nature, especially as they usually reaffirmed past humanist doctrines in their quest for large, artistic truths. Poets of the next generation began to concern themselves with the implications of the poetic medium for coming to terms with the nature at hand. Theodore Roethke and Elizabeth Bishop turned toward more personal experiences in order to explore the surfaces of an immediate, palpable world. Although "demythified," the nature considered in their poetry still remains beyond the limits of total understanding. Yet, in directing attention toward common, everyday experiences, the poems suggest how a more literal, recognizable nature can be apprehended by the individual psyche. Bishop's travels throughout her life inform the terrain she travels in her poetry, terrain that is marked by the poet's own perceptual dislocations. Skeptical of transcendent orders like other modernist poets, her work is always conscious of the way it constructs its landscapes. Poems like those in *North and South* (1946) and *Geography III* (1976), though qualified, provide her a way to consider and revise her understanding of nature's meanings. Not explicitly "environmental," her work nevertheless questions the traditions and attitudes American poetry has relied upon to frame nature. More specifically placed, Roethke explored the nature he encountered in his family's greenhouses. Nature in his poems is often a dark mire, like the deep unconscious Roethke sounds out through his poems. Again, following a romantic tradition, the self intuits itself in its intuitions of nature. While it may seem that this suggests "deeper" levels of unconscious projection, the poems also demand a greater sensitivity to the hard, minute particulars of nature at work. His sonorous poetics depict a personal response to a sensuous world whose soil is devouring yet fecund. Though private, the persona is able to locate a real, intimately known nature outside of the self that, as a source and context for possibility, provides meaning.

Along with Williams, George Oppen and Lorine Niedecker are noted for their objectivist efforts to reveal an immanent nature. Oppen's poetry pays attention to the individual's cognitive responses to experience, yet it offers a careful balance between external and internal landscapes. Niedecker's work, in contrast, pays careful attention to place, specifically the isolate wilds of northern Wisconsin, blending personal knowledge of the region's history with precise observation. More radical in his formal departures is Charles Olson, whose conception of the poem as a "field" where the poet's experiences become enacted by the arrangement of language proved liberating for later poets as they constructed more "open" forms congruent with the mind's encounters with nature. Olson's stated goal was to turn away from the orders the ego provided and toward the particulars of a locale and how they structure awareness of one's always-present environment. His efforts in his *Maximus* poems to capture the spirit of his home in Gloucester, Massachusetts, reveal the real topography that shapes perception for his

Hildegarde Flanner. (*Courtesy of the Library of Congress*)

mythic persona. Furthermore, his awareness of the history and social construction of Gloucester places his perceptions in a context that no longer sees the external world in static opposition to the human mind, but rather as a place for vital interaction.

Personally motivated meditations on nature during this era also began to reimagine the sacred dimensions of nature. Stanley Kunitz turns to the forms of nature to demonstrate his commitment to its life-sustaining principles. His poems, crafted and passionate, sustain moments of transcendence out of attentive participation with the world. Blending Kunitz's celebratory attitude with Bishop's awareness of the limits of human perception, the work of Brewster Ghiselin consistently implicates the small actions of the individual within the larger, only vaguely understood motions of the natural world. Kenneth Rexroth and William Everson followed Jeffers's vital engagement with the Pacific coast along with his pantheistic leanings. Rexroth wrote about nature with an intuitive grace gained from translating Japanese and Chinese verse. At the same time, his poems possess an ecstatic—and at times erotic—embrace of the California coast as a source of spiritual vitality. Everson's sensual imagism and psychoanalytic background probed the region's symbolic resonances while upholding the divinity of the shorebird and cliff face. Less romantically inclined, but more outspoken regarding the threat of human impact on nature is the poetry of Hildegarde Flanner, Janet Lewis, and Lewis's husband, Yvor Winters. Flanner and Lewis in particular establish an environmentalist position, carrying subtle, elegiac tones as they question human accountability for their vividly rendered landscapes.

CONTEMPORARIES, PLACE, AND PROVISIONALITY

In the second half of the twentieth century, nature writing as a concept expanded with the growing awareness of the radical and, in some cases, permanent changes wrought on nature. Along with a new vocabulary and perspectives generated by the emerging field of ecology, poets also found new motivation in responding to the various modes of thought that had triggered the growing number of environmental crises in the United States. A consciousness of the limits of nature, emphasized by a growing global perspective that considered the biosphere as a whole, brought a new relevance to "nature poetry" as a form of social and political critique. The impact on nature as America transformed from an agrarian society to a dominant industrial nation after World War II revealed the delusion of considering it an inviolable, ahistorical other. Yet worldwide environmental concern has prompted a broader consideration of the innumerable ways the human and the nonhuman interact at every moment.

Perhaps the best known nature poet of the second half of the twentieth century is Gary Snyder, who consistently advocated from a public, counterculture position an ecological perception of the world, of how each particular of nature works interdependently not only with the poet but also with all other aspects. His life in the mountain regions of the West Coast prompted him, like Thoreau, to consider the workings of "wild" nature in ourselves and in the world. Although nourished by Asian and Native American aesthetics and philosophy, Snyder's conception of poetry as a tool to discover and know the "wildness" of nature, consciousness, and language also emphasizes his romantic and modernist heritage. Throughout his oeuvre, an "ecocentric" artistic goal focuses on how the mind forms relationships in a particular place and with the other members—whether river, mountain, or canyon wren—of that place. His efforts to express the interrelated ecological community of the Pacific Rim region were also taken up by close friends and colleagues such as Lew Welch and Phillip Whalen.

Nowhere is the sense of nature as a process more evident than in the poetry of A. R. Ammons. In works ranging from short, kinetic lyrics to expansive book-length poems like *Garbage* (1993) and *Sphere: The Form of a Motion* (1974), Ammons shows the movements of the world echoed in the movements of thought. His philosophical preoccupation with the tensions between the one and the many, the concrete and the abstract, finds its most ready images in the ever-changing manifestations of nature, particularly those he encountered on walks from his home, whether in upstate New York, coastal New Jersey, or rural North Carolina. A precise diction bolstered by his early scientific training gives his observations a solid, luminous clarity. Praise-filled yet unsentimental, his poetry of brooks, oaks, and bayberries demonstrates the continuous possibilities of perception and knowing.

A growing concern for the environment, especially after encountering Hawaii's sensitive tropical ecosystem, also directed the poetry of W. S. Merwin toward more explicit dealings with nature. Challenging American social attitudes that consistently overlook the natural world, Merwin's surreal, indirect style reconsiders the conventional relationships humans have developed with the earth. His later poems in particular confront the looming threat of extinction, not just of single species but of the entire planetary biosphere, that comes from an unwillingness to confront human implication in the natural world. A drive to reconceive and revitalize direct encounters with nature is inherently tied to his artistic goal of revitalizing language, resulting in almost propagandistic poems of intense perception and lyric force. This emphasis on perception as a means of discovering the world can also be found in the work of Denise Levertov, whose lines evoke a sensuality rarely encountered since Whitman. Spiritually inflected by Judeo-Christian mysticism, her poems command a continual apprehension of the world through all the senses. Her ecstatic, "organic" forms deftly unfold a reciprocal relation between an immanent nature and a corporeal self located firmly within the physical universe.

Whereas Snyder's philosophical and artistic emphasis on wilderness promotes a more idealistic counter to mainstream civilization, the work of Wendell Berry pushes a more socially aware bioregionalism grounded in the real conditions of the remnant agrarian culture of late twentieth-century America, giving a voice to the rural communities increasingly threatened by the overwhelming pressures of an urban-centered society. Having dedicated himself to the working of his Kentucky farm, his poems record the values and traditions of a human community committed to the land. From this position, he is able to share an intimate knowledge that comes not from "subduing" nature but rather from the acts of caretaking and husbandry. Like Snyder, he insists that a knowledge of the life of a place is necessary for ethical behavior, and poetry not only is shaped by these activities in the natural world but also provides the vehicle by which this knowledge can be passed from one generation to the next. Informed by the Western tradition's own strain of nature praise, Berry has become a respected and vocal champion of an individual and communal commitment to nature.

OBSERVANCES AND BEING

The continued attention to "being" in the world has led many contemporary poets to address those common, everyday encounters with the world that shape experience. For these poets the natural world plays an integral role, signifying not only the primary conditions for life but also how life extends in boundless varieties beyond the human. As with Berry, the work of Mary Oliver evokes a celebratory and religious embrace of the natural world. Expressive yet unsentimental, her intense awareness of a quotidian world of hawks, flowers, and hummingbirds demonstrates nature's capacity as a source of solace and renewal. Her sensual and exacting lines draw out a life lived deeply in the earth. Such metaphysical leanings can also be found in poetry by Richard Wilbur, whose detailed observations of the *Things of This World*, as his 1956 volume is called, delicately unfold moments of emotional and spiritual awareness. As apt to describe laundry as Queen Anne's lace, his poems hold faith in their ability to draw significance from a comprehensively envisioned universe. The verse of Maxine Kumin, on the other hand, finds its driving impulse in active participation with an environment both domestic and natural. Sensitive to the delicate yet vital motions of growth and decay, her direct tone subtly underscores a passion within her surroundings. Similarly, May Swenson's idiosyncratic forms enact the processes of perception inscribed by the kinetic processes of nature. Although Adrienne Rich is usually considered for her political engagement with women's issues, many of her poems are consistently discussed for their "ecofeminist" inclinations. Rich's evocations of the natural world challenge American conventions supported by a male-dominated tradition that typically conflates women and nature and draws stunning reconsiderations of the world around her.

A growing attentiveness to nature's cycles has also inspired a communal engagement socially, spiritually and politically minded. David Wagoner centers much of his poetry in the rugged landscape of the Pacific Northwest. Elegant and intuitive, his lyrics demonstrate how artistic insight participates with the motions of the local ecology, and his occasional use of the region's Native American tribal lore highlights his respect for nature's separate and distinctive workings. A gothic style indicative of his southern heritage infuses the nature poems of James Dickey. Although his poems admit the distinction of a human consciousness, they also emphasize humanity's primal subconscious as well as its bestial origin. For Dickey, this origin links humans with other animals, all of whom are part of the same species. While nature in poems like "In the Mountain Tent" is depicted as holy, his descriptions are more elemental than Edenic, conscious of the primal forces that drive it. A valuation of life and death also infuses the poetry of Galway Kinnell. Dedicated to recognizing the life-forms that humans share the planet with, his poems seek to overcome the limits of his own ego and reenter the active reality of porcupine, flower, or bear. With the poetry of John Haines, a naturalist's eye for detail imbues his direct, graceful evocations of the Alaskan wilderness. A similar calm celebration attends the precise descriptions of Donald Hall's nature poetry.

The growing interest in place and how aspects of one's region shape personal responses has been taken up by a number of poets of the second half of the twentieth century. Their work traces the edge of consciousness against an extreme sensitivity to the tangible and intangible details of their surroundings, and they have been criticized for the way their "scenic mode" can subsume the ineffability of the world to human responses, even in the more moralistic tones of William Stafford's nature poems. More specifically located, Richard Hugo and James Wright use images of their regions to probe the deeper workings of their own imaginations. Informed by penetrating lyric sensibilities, their poetry is less intent on depicting nature than on the emotional resonances that the natural world locates within their personal psychologies. Their work nevertheless explores the equivalencies between imagistic "inner" and "outer" landscapes: for Hugo, the towns and vistas of Montana and the Pacific Northwest create his poetic location; for Wright, it is Minnesota and his childhood home of Ohio. Edward Dorn mines the American West for his often satiric writings of the physical and social landscapes. More psychologically intense and more responsive to the actual realities of nature are the lyrics of Robert Bly. Like Merwin, his poems concern themselves with overcoming conventional, rational modes of apprehension, and they root themselves in landscapes—particularly those of his rural Minnesota home region—as a means to probe the "subconscious" drives of both self and nature. An active social critic who encourages a rediscovery of people's personal connections to nature, Bly seeks in his poetry the primal mechanisms of his own connections. James Merrill is also noted for the way his poems use landscapes to ground his poetic wanderings, as well as for his inclusion of scientific diction.

LATE TWENTIETH-CENTURY NATURES AND CULTURES

The success poetry has had in redirecting attention toward local ecosystems, environmental health, and the processes and needs of nature can be measured in part by the growing critical attention toward the genre. It can also be measured by the way this attention has been magnified and extended by another generation of poets exploring the implications of a renewed placement within nature. Within the last few decades, a growing number of exceptional poets writing about nature have been brought to wide public attention.

Prominent among the poets writing nature at the beginning of the twenty-first century are numerous Native American poets who continue to propagate tribal traditions and philosophies and bring increasing attention to the way nature renders the imagination. Leslie Marmon Silko became an influential early voice, not only for imaginative writings but also for the way she has presented aspects of the Pueblo cultural immersion in the life of the land. Simon J. Ortiz's crafted poems frequently sketch the tensions between cultural values as they meet in the Southwest, as in his moving "Vision Shadows." Just as often, however, his poems turn with ecstatic praise toward the open earth. Joy Harjo, implementing chants, legends, and stories from a variety of traditions, addresses the nonhuman, sacred world of eagle and moon, and her lyric style reminds us of the physical, vocal aspect of these ritual encounters. Luci Tapahonso weaves Navajo philosophy into her evocations of the Southwest landscape and the lives rooted there. Her graceful lines depict how an entire community, both other-than-human and human, participates in the movements of day and night. Significant for all these poets—including Ray A. Young Bear, Gretel Ehrlich, and Louise Erdrich—is not only the way they embrace a more expansive ecology in their poems but also how the various histories of tribal dislocations have inscribed themselves into the American landscape and into a collective social memory.

Visionary and sensitive, Linda Hogan almost resembles Marianne Moore at times for the way her images seek resonant patternings in nature. An air of deep necessity marks her evocations of stone and horse, acknowledging how they wake the life of the mind. Of mixed Chickasaw and European heritage, Hogan listens to nature with the same level of sensitivity as Emerson, finding both empirical and transcendent meaning in its changes. Her deeply considered approach to the environment and how we come to know the world through the information carried by wind, snow, and stone provides a clear grounding for her writings. Hogan's work is also sensitive to the history of social and environmental alteration, particularly with the introduction of industrial agriculture, that has literally shaped "Indian Territory" into "Oklahoma."

The kinds of ecological literacy advocated by Hogan's work can be found in the poems of Pattiann Rogers. Versed in physics as well as flora and fauna, her observations are marked by a clear knowledge of nature's processes, from the flight patterns of a hummingbird to the spin of the earth through space. With an emphasis on the sensuous and exhilarating expressiveness of language, her vibrant songs turn moments of attentiveness into moments of beauty. Her precision of word nevertheless enables a spiritual vision of nature both reverent and passionate. A similar virtuosity with science can be found in the work of Arthur Sze. His lyrical inquiries into nature also demonstrate how perception can be altered by being receptive to the actions of the world and the turns of language. While his translations of the eighth-century poets Tu Fu, Li Po, and other Chinese lyric masters have exposed him to the nature-influenced aesthetics and ethics of their poetry, his work also evolves out of his place in the American Southwest.

How culture works through language to adjust these impressions of nature is an issue at the center of much current poetry, as indicated by the variety and volume of Native American writings. A number of poets throughout the border regions of the West and Southwest are also investigating the intersections of Hispanic and Mesoamerican culture within the natural landscape. The fields and migrations of farm laborers serve as the basis of Gary Soto's alert renderings of California, bringing a social and historical perspective to its agricultural customs. Francisco X. Alarcón digs even deeper into the region's history, borrowing Aztec invocations in order to refashion attitudes of respect for nature's manifestations. Conscious of the way language carries feeling and inflects meaning, his verses mix Spanish and English in their efforts to find an alignment with nature compatible with his experience. The desert surrounding her home in El Paso provides a responsive setting for the work of Pat Mora, whose evocations of family and community celebrate the Hispanic heritage enmeshed in the region. How the natural features of one's region can become a means of articulating cultural identity can also be seen in work of several poets from Hawaii, including Garrett Hongo. Of Japanese-American descent, he uses the ecology and economics of the islands' plantation history for his confessional poems.

REGIONAL ECOLOGY AND WORLDVIEWS

Many poets have developed a naturalist's familiarity with their regions, and their poems often describe the contours of the terrain as clearly as any field guide. Not only do they provide an evocative knowledge of the scope of present, local nature, but their arrangements also seek to discover an individual stake in their surroundings. The observant lyrics of Alison Hawthorne Deming demonstrate how an intimacy with the natural world can provide a more intimate knowledge of one's self. Her poems turn to rain and butterflies to consider the folding and unfolding of life and form. Reg Saner's embrace of the American West has allowed him to orient his philosophical meditations along its mountains and plateaus. Calm descriptions of Chaco Canyon, home of the ancient Pueblo, or the mountains of Colorado slowly uncover the particulars of sun and cliff face to radiate in a penetrating stir of place and time. More rurally placed, Robert Pack's smooth, clear rhythms describe a domestic nature, familiar yet formed by its own cycles. A heft and vital holding that sustains lives can be found throughout his sensitive engagements with his New England landscapes, and a striking balance of discovery and restraint indicate the ethical dimensions of his meetings with nature. His sense of care for and desire to know the land can also be seen in the work of John Daniel, whose poems encounter a more rugged Pacific coast. Both of these poets remain always sensitive to nature's distinct being while evoking a sense of unity with it. Adamant about the importance of nature, their work avoids dogmatic "environmentalism" in favor of the complexities of direct contact and consideration.

The latest generation of poets has also begun exploring more thoroughly the emotional, social, and political dimensions of a life attentive to the motions of the nature around them. Robert Hass's poetry serves as a good example. His northern California home forms an evocative presence throughout his poems, supported by his own extensive knowledge of the region's ecology. Influenced by his translations of Japanese haiku masters, his poems attempt to align him with a whole and holistic sense of place. Although his poetry has been critiqued for the way it can foreground the human and avoid direct environmental advocacy, it nevertheless confronts the natural world through its deliberately conscious meditations and discovers emotional and cognitive possibilities for the poet. Aware of the instabilities and interdependencies of both nature and language, Hass's verse implicates his own personal doubts and desires in his considerations of nature.

Hass's poetry demonstrates how poets continue to rely on nature's forms to punctuate their experiences while remaining circumspect about the kinds of biases they bring to their worldviews. Nevertheless, their work tests itself and gauges how successfully their provisional responses not only express a life more deeply conscious of the natural world but also speak beyond the ken of an individual. The poems of Louise Glück discover in nature powerful symbols that help her elucidate her position in the universe. More directly placed in the texture of experience are the poems of Sandra McPherson. Precise exhibitions of the natural world lead inevitably to discovery through her work, not only making each thing and moment rich with felt presence but also readjusting our sensibility to nature's textures. This richness can also be found in the work of Jane Hirshfield, whose work generates sensitive meditations that celebrate the full existence of an everyday world of pebble and grass. More kinetic in her responses to nature is Jorie Graham. Her glimpses of swifts and cardinals are enough to send her poems on deep investigations of how these images can be imprinted and recalled by the mind. Through all these writers runs a sense of nature as a means of continuation and sustenance. This is perhaps most dramatically presented in the work of Sandra Alcosser, whose sensual images frequently recall nature's stages of rot and decomposition and emphasize the radical forms needed to keep nature and culture nourished.

The way these poets explore how symbols arise out of their descriptions of flowers, birds and jellyfish can also be seen in the way others approach conceptions of landscape and place. Deeply invested in their regions, their verse explores hollows, abandoned buildings, breakwaters, and canyons and the layers of life that accumulate there. The haunting verse of Dave Smith sinks into Virginia countryside, cottonmouths and a pulsing history rising out of its rich sedges. Luminous, almost surreal images fill the work of Charles Wright, whose memories of the South bring together present and past. His songs into the night dream him into a nature terrible and lovely. Place takes on mythic dimensions in works like Mark Doty's *Atlantis* (1995) and Brenda Hillman's *Cascadia* (2002). Stylistically and tonally unique, these volumes play out the relation between elemental nature and human being with wonderful shocks and wrenching aches.

To continue this discovery of the natural world was one aspect of the Watershed Environmental Poetry Festival, initiated in 1996 with the help of then-poet laureate Robert Hass. The campaign organized readings and events across the country, and it encouraged schools and communities to discover their local ecology through poetry, supporting the prospect that a more intimate knowledge of the bioregion would bring with it a greater sense of community and concern for all its inhabitants. Local and regional poetries still thrive throughout the country and still provide some of the best ways for learning not only about ecology of particular places on earth but also about the attitudes, practices, and vital life that attends that place.

[See also Ammons, A. R.; Berry, Wendell; Bishop, Elizabeth; Bradstreet, Anne; Dickey, James; Dickinson, Emily; Eliot, T. S.; Emerson, Ralph Waldo; Freneau, Philip; Frost, Robert; Glück, Louise; Hughes, Langston; Hugo, Richard; Jeffers, Robinson; Kinnell, Galway; Kunitz, Stanley; Levertov, Denise; Longfellow, Henry Wadsworth; Merrill, James; Merwin, W. S.; Momaday, N. Scott; Moore, Marianne; Nature Writing: Prose; Ransom, John Crowe; Rich, Adrienne; Roethke, Theodore; Silko, Leslie Marmon; Snyder, Gary; Soto, Gary; Stafford, William; Stevens, Wallace; Tate, Allen; Thoreau, Henry David; Warren, Robert Penn; Whitman, Walt; Wilbur, Richard; Williams, William Carlos; Wright, Charles; and Wright, James.]

FURTHER READING

Bryson, J. Scott, ed. *Ecopoetry: A Critical Introduction*. Salt Lake City, Utah, 2002. An extensive, lucid introduction to a variety of poets and critical approaches.

Buell, Lawrence. *The Environmental Imagination: Thoreau, Nature Writing, and the Formation of American Culture*. Cambridge, Mass., 1995. Seminal text of environmental criticism in the tradition of Thoreau. Extends Leo Marx's concept of the pastoral into the twentieth century.

Elder, John. *Imagining the Earth: Poetry and the Vision of Nature*. Urbana, Ill., and Chicago, 1985. A groundbreaking early study of twentieth-century poetry and its response to the natural world.

Elder, John, ed. *American Nature Writers*. 2 vols. New York, 1996. See especially "The Forms of American Nature Writing" by Christopher Merrill (vol. 2, pp. 1079–1098), which is an excellent, in-depth survey of canonical American nature poets; and David Robertson's "Bioregionalism in Nature Writing" (vol. 2, pp. 1013–1024), which establishes a methodology for bioregional investigations of literature.

Everson, William. *Archetype West: The Pacific Coast as a Literary Region*. Berkeley, Calif., 1976. A fascinating look at the cultural psychology revealed in the literature of the coastal region.

Gilbert, Roger. *Walks in the World: Representation and Experience in Modern American Poetry*. Princeton, N.J., 1991. A comprehensive examination of twentieth-century poets and their excursions into the physical world.

Harrington, Henry, and John Tallmadge, eds. *Reading under the Sign of Nature: New Essays in Ecocriticism*. Salt Lake City, Utah, 2000.

Kolodny, Annette. *The Lay of the Land: Metaphor as Experience and History in American Life and Letters*. Chapel Hill, N.C., 1975. A seminal text investigating conceptions of gender and femininity in descriptions of the early American landscape.

Marx, Leo. *The Machine in the Garden: Technology and the Pastoral Ideal in America*. New York, 1964. Seminal study regarding the roots of modern pastoral, its use as social critique, and its influence particularly on nineteenth-century literary texts.

Matthiessen, F. O. *American Renaissance: Art and Expression in the Age of Emerson and Whitman*. New York, 1949. Though dated in its approach, this text still provides a fundamental introduction to nineteenth-century literature.

Murphy, Patrick. *Farther Afield in the Study of Nature Oriented Literature*. Charlottesville, Va., 2000. Begins to develop cutting edge ecological and environmental considerations of recent poetry.

Paul, Sherman. *Hewing to Experience: Essays and Reviews on Recent American Poetry and Poetics, Nature and Culture*. Iowa City, 1989. Idiosyncratic yet illuminating readings of a variety of poets, including Emerson, Snyder, and Olson.

Quetchenbach, Bernard W. *Back from the Far Field: American Nature Poetry and the Late Twentieth Century*. Charlottesville, Va., 2000. Traces the way a number of nature poets in the second half of the century pursue a social advocacy role for nature through their poems.

Rotella, Guy. *Reading and Writing Nature: The Poetry of Robert Frost, Wallace Stevens, Marianne Moore, and Elizabeth Bishop*. Boston, 1991. Primary examination of modernist writers and their imaginative engagements with nature.

Scigaj, Leonard. *Sustainable Poetry: Four American Eco-poets*. Lexington, Ky., 1999. An academic study, it deals with many contemporary ideas regarding "ecopoetry." Though its jargon is difficult, it does provide some good close readings.

Silko, Leslie Marmon. "Landscape, History, and the Pueblo Imagination." In *On Nature: Nature, Landscape, and Natural History*, edited by Daniel Halpern. Berkeley, Calif., 1986. An important text for beginning considerations of Native American literature's relationship to the landscape.

Tichi, Cecelia. *New World, New Earth: Environmental Reform in American Literature from the Puritans through Whitman*. New Haven, Conn., 1979.

Vendler, Helen. *Part of Nature, Part of Us: Modern American Poets*. Cambridge, Mass., 1980. Comprehensive and lucid reviews of major twentieth-century figures from a humanist critical position.

NATURE WRITING: PROSE

by John Elder

The term "nature writing" conventionally refers to one particular category of nonfiction, rather than to the entire spectrum of literature about the natural world. Nature has, of course, like love, been a central topic for authors in every language and in nearly every form. Scholars who are interested in the broader range of genres thus sometimes prefer to use the term "environmental literature." That said, nature writing remains a remarkable, vivid, and continuous strand within the fabric of American literature. Such continuity comes from the fact that, above all, this genre has been a conversation. Authors within the lineage often address each other directly, as well as emulate each other's postures, personas, and excursions. Nature writing is a sort of ongoing experiment, an investigation of how imaginative literature and close observation of natural phenomena can be integrated.

To define this genre more precisely, it may be helpful to consider the example of Henry David Thoreau. His book *Walden; or, Life in the Woods* (1854) has proved to be an enduring inspiration for nature writers, with its story of a strategic retreat from society and its remarkably fresh and vigorous language. Another especially reverberant piece by Thoreau is the essay "Walking" (first published in *Excursions* in 1863), in which he makes the memorable statement, "In wildness is the preservation of the world." In the following passage, Thoreau reflects upon what wildness means for a writer:

> Where is the literature which gives expression to Nature? He would be a poet who could impress the winds and streams into his service, to speak for him; who nailed words to their primitive senses, as farmers drive down stakes in the spring, which the frost has heaved; who derived his words as often as he used them,—transplanted them to his page with earth adhering to their roots; whose words were so true and fresh and natural that they would appear to expand like the buds at the approach of spring, though they lay half-smothered between two musty leaves in a library,—ay, to bloom and bear fruit there, after their kind, annually, for the faithful reader, in sympathy with surrounding Nature.

(Emerson and Thoreau, 1991, p. 104)

Thoreau's distinction between merely using words and deriving them from their concrete, physical origins relates not only to his fascination with etymology but also to his desire to ground his ideas in nature. He believed that books "with earth adhering to their words" could blossom in the human spirit, revitalizing our lives and our musty institutions alike. Although Thoreau did not invent the genre of nature writing, the power of both his language and his convictions has made him central to the tradition in America. In light of the images above from his "Walking," this field of literature might be described as follows: a species of personal, and often narrative, nonfiction that is both knowledgeably appreciative of science and open to the spiritual potential of natural experience. The fact that such writing often includes elements of memoir is recognized by two of Thoreau's rhetorical questions in *Walden*: "Shall I not have intelligence with the earth? Am I not partly leaves and vegetable mould myself?" (Thoreau, 1983, p. 183).

There is a provisional quality to the term "nature writing"—as to any literary genre that tacks on the word "writing." In this it resembles the closely associated academic field of environmental studies. Such two-word titles contrast with familiar and assured categories like fiction and English. But such compound terminology may also reflect the emergence of nature writing along a dynamic edge—an edge both between conventional ways of classifying writing and between the arts and the sciences. Ecologists speak of "edge-effect" where two ecosystems meet. Examples of such an "ecotone" would be the brushy margin between woods and pasture or a rocky coastline. Ecotones in the physical world are characterized by their extraordinary richness, both in the numbers of species they harbor and in the biotic mass they produce. Similarly, where science and literature meet, with lyrical and figurative language becoming entangled with technical nomenclature, there is a special opportunity for an unpredictable and illuminating conversation. Nature writing not only typically offers a wider range of concrete information than is usually found in contemporary poetry and fiction but also displays an unusual array of formal and

232

stylistic innovations. A recent example of such originality would be Janisse Ray's book *Ecology of a Cracker Child-hood* (1999), in which chapters relating a memoir of the author's girlhood alternate with chapters on the natural history, ecology, and destruction of Georgia's native longleaf-pine forests.

ANTHOLOGIES AND CRITICAL STUDIES

Numerous anthologies of American nature writing have been published over the past century. Three works are particularly good resources for anyone wanting an overview of this genre. Thomas J. Lyon's *This Incomperable Lande: A Book of American Nature Writing* appeared in 1989. In addition to containing a sequence of substantial and well-chosen examples, from William Wood (*New Englands Prospect*, 1634) to John Hay (*The Immortal Wilderness*, 1987), Lyon's anthology contains an excellent introductory essay. The part of his introduction entitled "A Taxonomy of Nature Writing" proposes a spectrum running from "Field Guides and Professional Papers" through "Natural History Essays," "Rambles," "Solitude and Back-Country Living," "Travel and Adventure," and "Farm Life," to such philosophical essays as "Man's Role in Nature." Lyon's taxonomy brings out the diversity of the genre and suggests that the relative weight placed upon a given writer's personal experience is one good way to organize and unify the spectrum (Lyon, 1989, pp. 3–7). Robert Finch and John Elder's *The Norton Book of Nature Writing* (1990) begins with the scientist-parson Gilbert White, in order to emphasize the Linnaean origins of nature writing, and includes selections from other English-speaking countries as well as from America. A revised and expanded edition of *The Norton Book of Nature Writing* appeared in 2002, including many more contemporary selections and also representing a significantly wider range of racial and ethnic backgrounds of authors than in the first edition. *Sisters of the Earth: Women's Prose and Poetry about Nature*, edited by Lorraine Anderson, was published in 1991. This collection—which juxtaposes the work of woman nature writers with female authors in other genres and which organizes its table of contents thematically—has had an important role in stimulating scholarly research in the field.

Two other works are appropriate to mention as background for any thorough exploration of American nature writing. One is Lawrence Buell's 1995 study *The Environmental Imagination: Thoreau, Nature Writing, and the Formation of American Culture*, in which he relates the field of American nature writing to the larger framework of American literary history. It remains the authoritative critical work. *American Nature Writers* (1996), a two-volume collection of biographical and critical essays, surveys many of the important authors in this genre—including contemporary figures—and includes a bibliography for each of them.

This essay focuses on a particular sequence of writers who exemplify important developments in the field from the evolution of the genre in the revolutionary era to the early 1960s. Specifically, William Bartram, Susan Fenimore Cooper, Henry David Thoreau, John Muir, Mary Austin, Aldo Leopold, and Rachel Carson are the principal examples. The essay concludes with a look at the wealth of American nature writing at the beginning of the twenty-first century and a consideration of themes and voices emerging in the genre.

EARLY VOICES IN THE CONVERSATION

Many early voices in American literature placed a special emphasis upon the natural scene. From William Wood's *New Englands Prospect* (1634) to Thomas Jefferson's *Notes on the State of Virginia* (1784), the civic leaders of fledgling communities surveyed the geology, climate, flora, and fauna of their new homes in order to understand the available resources and the character of their landscapes. In such works, however, there was often a less individual voice than we have come to associate with the genre. The authors spoke for the larger educated community rather than focusing upon their own experience or feelings. The real impetus for the more personal accounts and reflections of what we now call nature writing came from the English clergyman and naturalist Gilbert White, who in 1789 published *The Natural History and Antiquities of Selborne*. White wrote in the generation after the Swedish scientist Carolus Linnaeus had published *Systema Naturae* (1735) and *Species Plantarum* (1753), the volumes that established and elaborated his binomial approach to identifying all organisms by genus and species. Linnaeus's system for keying out plants, birds, and animals inspired what the critic E. D. H. Johnson has called the "golden age of natural history." This flourishing of natural history as a pursuit of educated amateurs lasted for about a century, from the publication of *The Natural History and Antiquities of Selborne* through the lifetime of Charles Darwin. After Darwin's *Origin of Species* appeared in 1859, the life sciences became steadily more specialized and professionalized. Gilbert White, who served all his life as a curate of Selborne, the village in which he had also been born, typified the clerics, gentlemen and ladies of

John Muir, 1902. (*Courtesy of the Library of Congress*)

leisure, and poets who so enthusiastically ventured forth into the countryside armed with their Linnaean keys to the creation. Many readers were charmed by White's combination of acute observation with a humorous and charming personal narrative; his book had a place on those short shelves beside Darwin's bed aboard the ship *Beagle* and Thoreau's writing table in the cabin by Walden Pond. As the genre of nature writing flourished in America, explorations of the wilderness, speculations on evolution, and various forms of political advocacy took it in directions far from White's quiet village. Still, there has remained a family resemblance between these later, more boisterous books and the highly personal and reflective approach of the clergyman-scientist.

If White was the founder of a tradition of domestic natural history—in which scientific observation was part of a process of claiming one's home on earth—his younger American contemporary William Bartram took that combination of autobiographical narrative and Linnaean science on the road. A Quaker from Pennsylvania, and the son of John Bartram, one of Linnaeus's most important correspondents in the New World, he set off during the Revolution to explore the American Southeast. His *Travels through North & South Carolina, Georgia, East & West Florida, the Cherokee Country, the Extensive Territories of the Muscogulges, or Creek Confederacy, and the Country of the Chactaws* was widely read and praised on both sides of the Atlantic after its appearance in 1791. Bartram's reports on the natural history of this region were of the greatest interest to scientists of his time. But the main source of his appeal to a wider readership was the rapturous voice with which he expressed his observations. Watching mayflies drifting through the evening air before settling on the water and becoming food for trout, he writes, "Solemnly and slowly move onward, to the river's shore,

the rustling clouds of the Ephemera." Bartram describes with equal wonder a "subtle greedy" alligator rising out of the water to do battle with a competitor: "Behold him rushing forth from the flags and reeds. His enormous body swells. His plaited tail brandished high, floats upon the lake. The waters like a cataract descend from his opening jaws. Clouds of smoke issue from his dilated nostrils. The earth trembles with his thunder" (Bartram, 1988, pp. 88, 115). Studies by wildlife biologists in the twentieth century have confirmed the essential accuracy of Bartram's descriptions, even with all the exuberance of his language. White and Bartram, writing at the end of the eighteenth century, established two poles for American nature writing—the naturalist at home and the explorer reporting back the wonders of exotic landscapes. But in both instances scientific observations are interwoven with a personal quest for meaning and are inseparable from the observers' own engaging personality.

While Linnaean natural history, embodied in such observers as William Bartram, was one crucial influence in American nature writing, another was the transcendentalist vision and language of Ralph Waldo Emerson—in particular his 1836 volume *Nature*. Emerson's essays are often more abstract and speculative than the narrative form we associate with the term nature writing. But *Nature* has had a profound and abiding impact on writers in the tradition. Both Thoreau and John Muir, themselves so influential in the genre in their different ways, found a mentor in Emerson at the commencement of their careers—Thoreau through his conversations with the older man around Concord, Massachusetts, and through the example of Emerson's journal-keeping; Muir through reading Emerson's essays in college and carrying them with him as he commenced his travels. Thoreau and Muir, like so many others since, were impressed by Emerson's sense of nature as holy—a sanctuary where one might escape from humdrum routine and social restrictions. From passages like this one in *Nature*, they imbibed a religion of nature from passage in *Nature*. For example:

In the woods is perpetual youth. Within these plantations of God, a decorum and sanctity reign, a perennial festival is dressed, and the guest sees not how he should tire of them in a thousand years. In the woods, we return to reason and faith. There I feel that nothing can befall me in life,—no disgrace, no calamity (leaving me my eyes), which nature cannot repair. Standing on the bare ground,—my head bathed by the blithe air and uplifted into infinite space,—all mean egotism vanishes. I become a transparent eyeball; I am nothing; I see all; the currents of the Universal Being circulate through me; I am part or parcel of God.

(Emerson and Thoreau, 1991, p. 8)

While subsequent writers may sometimes go further than Emerson in regrounding their mystical revelations in the particulars of a landscape, experiences such as he describes here have continued to be essential to the genre's motivation, meaning, and appeal.

REPRESENTATIVE WOMAN WRITERS

Until about 1990, few women were included in collections of nature writing from the nineteenth and early twentieth centuries. One explanation that has been offered was the prominence of institutionally affiliated and subsidized explorers like Bartram, and his successors John Wesley Powell and Clarence King, in the early years of the genre. During that era, men were also dominant in the military, in government, and in the sciences. Celia Thaxter (1835–1894), who wrote about New Hampshire's Isles of Shoals (1873), and Mary Austin (1868–1934), who evoked the deserts of the Southwest beginning about 1903, were among the small number of women who were widely recognized before the middle of the twentieth century. However, one important result of the increasing prominence of nature writing, of related courses in environmental studies at the university level, and especially of anthologies like Lorraine Anderson's *Sisters of the Earth* has been a surge of scholarly interest in woman nature writers. This has led in turn to the rediscovery of a number of woman writers who were in fact well known during their lifetimes but whose books had largely gone out of print by World War II. Two such important writers who have been republished and are increasingly being taught and written about, are Mabel Osgood Wright (1859–1934) and Gene Stratton-Porter (1863–1924). Wright both anticipated today's renewed attention to gardens by such authors as Michael Pollan and Jamaica Kincaid and was an early advocate for the protection of wild birds. Stratton-Porter was best known as a novelist but also wrote knowledgeably and sympathetically about northeastern Indiana's Limberlost Swamp and became a distinguished photographer of its birds and moths.

The most significant recovery of an early woman nature writer, though, has been that of Susan Fenimore Cooper. Her book *Rural Hours by a Lady* went through several editions following its publication in 1850 and was read by Thoreau when he was writing *Walden*. Since Cooper was herself an appreciative reader of Gilbert White, her book thus forms an important bridge between the two main English and American influences on the genre. But between 1876 and 1998 there was no unabridged printing of *Rural Hours* available. Now that it is once more widely accessible, Cooper's work grows ever more interesting to scholars of the genre—in part because of its status as a sustained meditation on one small community. By including both human and nonhuman inhabitants in her reflections, and by speculating so thoughtfully about their interaction, Cooper anticipated today's bioregional movement at many points. She could read the histories of immigration, deforestation, and agriculture, as well as the underlying geological processes, from such signs as the prevailing flowers in a particular locale, the health of the crops, and the sandiness of the soils. An example of her ability to make these connections may be found the following passage from *Rural Hours*:

> A path made by the workmen and cattle crosses the field, and one treads at every step upon plantain, that regular path-weed of the Old World; following this track, we come to a little runnel, which is dry and grassy now, though doubtless at one time the bed of a considerable spring; the banks are several feet high, and it is filled with native plants; on one side stands a thorn-tree, whose morning shadow falls upon grasses and clovers brought from beyond the seas, while in the afternoon, it lies on gyromias and moose-flowers, sarsaparillas and cahoshes, which bloomed here for ages, when the eye of the red man alone beheld them. Even within the limits of the village spots may still be found on the bank of the river, which are yet unbroken by the plough, where the trailing arbutus, and squirrel-cups, and May-wings tell us so every spring; in older regions, these children of the forest would long since have vanished from all the meadows and villages, for the plough would have passed a thousand times over every rood of such ground.

(Cooper, 1998, p. 92)

Cooper tells the human history of her town through its natural history. As Thoreau also did, she bears in mind both the native flora and the native cultures that preceded her own family's founding of Cooperstown two generations before her birth. Another way in which rediscovering Cooper's work can orient us to Thoreau's is the recognition that he, despite his frequent celebrations of solitude, shares her central interest in neighbors as a part of the landscape of home. Not only in visiting a nearby railroad laborer's family and in conversing delightedly with a French-Canadian woodchopper, but also in his wry descriptions of "Brute Neighbors," Thoreau presents himself as a member of a community. Stepping out of the social mainstream offers him an opportunity to broaden his circle of acquaintance and to explore his affiliation with other living creatures, in what the contemporary writer David Abram has called "the more-than-human world."

THE WEST COAST AND THE DESERT

If Susan Fenimore Cooper represented a bridge between the intimate and domestic world of White and the more individualistic emphasis upon home in Thoreau, John Muir (1838–1914) accomplished a different kind of transition. He carried Emerson and Thoreau's sense of nature's holiness, and of its profound personal meaning, into the mountainous wilderness of the West. Born in Dunbar, Scotland, but raised from boyhood on a Wisconsin homestead, Muir grew up with remarkable physical energy and an insatiable hunger for wild beauty. Although he kept photographs of Emerson and Thoreau on the mantel of his Martinez, California, ranch in later years, Muir also scoffed at the idea that Concord could offer anything resembling the "wildness" that Thoreau called for in "Walking." His criterion for natural beauty, and his landscape of the heart from the day he first entered it, was the Yosemite Valley. His efforts to protect Yosemite (as well as his unsuccessful attempt to protect the nearby valley of Hetch Hetchy) led both to his 1892 founding of the Sierra Club and to a series of articles for the influential *Century* magazine. *The Mountains of California*, published in 1894, is a compilation of these articles. From the start, Muir's writing was motivated by an impulse of advocacy. Like Thoreau, he called for a less materialistic sense of "natural resources"—for an understanding of nature's meaning in our spiritual development. But in his political lobbying and his engagement in formulating legislation to protect wild spaces, Muir introduced a new, activist note in American nature writing.

Another characteristic of Muir's achievement was the sophisticated awareness of natural processes behind his response to individual phenomena. Bartram and Thoreau had both been highly skilled naturalists—fine botanists, in particular. But Muir's years at the University of Wisconsin (1860–1863) exposed him to both the glacial theories of Louis Agassiz and to Darwin's theory of biological evolution. It has often been noted that Muir's literary style tends to become florid and highly adjectival. Yet his scientific eye is so acute that he continually grounds his observations in highly persuasive analysis. He was the first writer to suggest, in contradiction to the theories of the California state geologist Josiah Whitney, that Yosemite Valley had been formed by glaciers. His explanation was

eventually proven to be right. A passage from *The Mountains of California* illustrates the integration of Muir's scientific authority with a rapturous voice recalling that of Bartram. He describes the formation of glaciers—in eras when snow annually accumulates in greater amounts than can melt in the following spring—and accounts for the shape of exposed rock through variations of mineral structure and hardness. But he also finds within such physical factors a providential power whose result is wild beauty.

> [O]ur admiration must be excited again and again as we toil and study and learn that this vast job of rockwork, so far-reaching in its influences, was done by agents so fragile and small are these flowers of the mountain clouds. Strong only by force of numbers, they carried away entire mountains, particle by particle, block by block, and cast them into the sea; sculptured, fashioned, modeled all the range and developed its predestined beauty.... Then, after their grand task was done, these bands of snow-flowers, these mighty glaciers, were melted and removed as if of no more importance than dew destined to last but an hour. Few, however, of Nature's agents have left monuments so noble and enduring as they. The great granite domes a mile high, the cañons as deep, the noble peaks, the Yosemite valleys, these, and indeed nearly all other features of the Sierra scenery, are glacier monuments.
>
> (Muir, 1985, p. 12)

Nature writing arrived at the West Coast on the heels of the Civil War—not only with John Muir but also with Clarence King, whose *Mountaineering in the Sierra Nevada* was published in 1872. Only after that did the tradition circle around to explore regions passed through too quickly in that wild migration. An important figure for filling in the map was Mary Austin. Like Muir, to whom she refers in her writing, Austin was raised in the Midwest (Illinois, in her case) but fell in love with the West. Her real love, though, was the deserts of southern California, Arizona, and, especially, New Mexico. A successful and prolific writer, known in her own day as a novelist and poet, as well as an essayist on feminism, language, native cultures, and natural history, Austin largely passed out of print following her death in 1934. Today, though, she has once more become celebrated as a key figure in the tradition of nature writing and an early, eloquent partisan of the desert's beauty. We have in American literature an impressive lineage of desert writers, who have reversed the conventional sense of these areas as "waste" lands and led to them being viewed more commonly as places of visionary beauty. Other writers in this line include John Van Dyke, Joseph Wood Krutch, Edward Abbey, and

Terry Tempest Williams. Although she was preceded by Van Dyke (whose book *The Desert* was published in 1901), Austin's tangy voice, and her passionate appreciation of the subtleties of the desert's ecology and its indigenous cultures alike, can really be said to have inaugurated this tradition. Here is the vivid opening of her best-known book, *The Land of Little Rain* (1903):

> East away from the Sierras, south from Panamint and Amargosa, east and south many an uncounted mile, is the Country of Lost Borders.
>
> Ute, Paiute, Mojave, and Shoshone inhabit its frontiers, and as far into the heart of it as a man dare go. Not the law, but the land sets the limit. Desert is the name it wears upon the maps, but the Indian's is the better word. Desert is a loose term to indicate land that supports no man; whether the land can be bitted and broken to that purpose is not proven. Void of life it never is, however dry the air and villainous the soil.
>
> This is the nature of that country. There are hills, rounded, blunt, burned, squeezed up out of chaos, chrome and vermilion painted, aspiring to the snow line. Between the hills lie high level-looking plains full of intolerable sun glare, or narrow valleys drowned in a blue haze. The hill surface is streaked with ash drift and black, unweathered lava flows.
>
> (Austin, 1988, p. 1)

Austin's opening passage is notable for its similarity to Georgia O'Keeffe's vision of the New Mexican landscape. A new palette entered into nature writing and painting alike through these artists' depictions of wind- and water-worked expanses of rock. In fact, a striking aspect of American nature writing is how frequently such a close connection is established between writers and painters in love with the same landscape, even though—as with Austin and O'Keeffe—they may not know each other or even be contemporaries. Similar pairings would include those between Emerson and the Hudson River and Luminist schools of painting and between John Muir and the Yosemite photography of Ansel Adams.

ENVIRONMENTAL ADVOCACY

Austin's celebration of the desert took a region that had been perceived as barren and celebrated it both as a place for communion with the stars and as a laboratory of evolution where the fundamental principles of ecological balance could be perceived. In both regards, she anticipated the achievement of Aldo Leopold (1888–1948) in *A Sand County Almanac, and Sketches Here and There* (1949). In effect, Leopold turns to the Wisconsin farmland from which John Muir had set off as a young man. He finds an abused and eroded farm not far from Madison, where he is teaching at the university, and sets out both to learn all he can about it and to restore it to health by his own efforts of practical stewardship. The actual location of Leopold's "shack" was Sauk County, Wisconsin. But his generic name Sand County encompasses all of those neglected or cut-over regions of America to which authors from Austin on have returned for a closer look, and with which they have developed an intimate sense relationship.

Leopold has another link with Muir, but one more significant than their shared connection with Wisconsin. Both of them contribute in crucial ways to the tradition of environmental advocacy within American nature writing. Muir was a prophet of conservation, who placed a special emphasis upon the sublime mountainous terrain of the West. Leopold looked at conservation not simply as a matter of protecting land but also as a marker of our cultural evolution. In one essay from *Sand County Almanac*, "Thinking Like a Mountain," he introduces this perspective through a story about killing wolves when he was a young man in New Mexico. Watching the fire die in the eyes of a wolf he had just shot gave Leopold a new realization about the importance of predators to a healthy ecosystem: "I was young then, and full of trigger-itch; I thought that because fewer wolves meant more deer, that no wolves would mean hunter's paradise. But after seeing the green fire die, I sensed that neither the wolf nor the mountain agreed with such a view" (Leopold, p. 130). Leopold went on to become a leading proponent of wilderness as the criterion of natural health and of predators as essential to that wild balance. In his central essay in *Sand County*, entitled "The Land Ethic," he called for an extension of human ethical standards to the entire community of life, writing that it was, "if I read the evidence correctly, an evolutionary possibility and an ecological necessity" (Leopold, 203).

Rachel Carson (1907–1964), like William Bartram, became famous for celebrating the wonders of a realm little imagined by most of her fellow citizens. In her case, this was not the alligator and orchid country of the southeastern swamps, but the evolutionary marvels of the sea. In *The Sea around Us* (1951) she portrayed the ocean as a single environment, while in *The Edge of the Sea* (1955) she explored the remarkable richness of shorelines, "the marginal world." Through these best-selling books, Carson became the first teacher about the science of ecology to a worldwide audience. She is especially remembered, however, for her book *Silent Spring* (1962), in which she traced the unintended consequences of widespread pesticide use, including substances like DDT that permeate the food chain—making it impossible for raptors to reproduce and contributing to cancer and other diseases in human beings. Just as she had earlier taught her readers about ecology, in *Silent Spring* she offered them a course in cellular biology. Her point throughout this book is that we need to intervene much more carefully in natural systems, out of an increased awareness of the web of life upon which we, too, directly depend. The upshot of Carson's careful exposition is an admonition to take a more modest and careful approach in our science and technology: "The 'control of nature' is a phrase conceived in arrogance, born of the Neanderthal age of biology and philosophy, when it was supposed that nature exists for the convenience of man" (Carson, 1994, p. 297).

NEW DIRECTIONS IN NATURE WRITING

If the century that followed Gilbert White's *Natural History and Antiquities of Selborne* can be called the "golden age of natural history," the decades since the publication of *Silent Spring* might well be characterized as the "golden age of American nature writing." This burgeoning of fine writing in the genre doubtless relates in part to an increased awareness of environmental problems. Just as Rachel Carson raised awareness of the unintended consequences of our large-scale agricultural practices, people have now become more conscious of the influence of burning fossil fuels on climate change, of the threat posed to biodiversity by human population growth and by the fragmentation of wild habitats, of the depletion of marine fisheries, and of the connection between first-world consumerism and third-world poverty. These are daunting issues, and a troubled tone pervades much contemporary nature writing. At the same time, by grappling with matters so essential to the human prospect—and by bringing to bear upon them a broad range of artistic, cultural, and scientific references—nature writing is increasingly impressive for its constructiveness and its moral dimension. Although many of them are quite sophisticated about current literary and academic conversations, today's nature writers tend to be less compliant to the coy, self-congratulatory aspects of deconstructive theories.

One can enumerate a group of accomplished nature writers whose energy, originality, and civic impact are difficult to equal with a comparably long tally of current novelists and poets. A highly incomplete list of authors who have achieved a major body of distinguished work

in this genre would include Peter Matthiessen, Rick Bass, Terry Tempest Williams, Edward Hoagland, Barry Lopez, Annie Dillard, Scott Russell Sanders, Robert Finch, Gretel Ehrlich, Wendell Berry, Gary Snyder, Ann Zwinger, Gary Paul Nabhan, and Richard K. Nelson. As environmental issues come more to the fore in our national conversation, a number of writers best known as poets or novelists have also begun to produce important pieces of nature writing. Among the authors in this category would be Maxine Hong Kingston, Alice Walker, Leslie Marmon Silko, Jim Harrison, Jamaica Kincaid, and Barbara Kingsolver. As a wider range of writers turn their hands to nature writing, even when it is not their principal field, one result has been greater diversity in the racial and ethnic backgrounds represented in the genre. In addition to several of the writers just mentioned, Ray Gonzalez, David Mas Masumoto, and Evelyn White have all produced striking pieces of nature writing that address the relation between their landscapes and their Chicano, Japanese-American, and African-American backgrounds, respectively.

Leslie Silko's 1986 essay "Landscape, History, and the Pueblo Imagination" (reprinted in *The Norton Book of Nature Writing*) deserves special comment. It has become widely recognized as a landmark for contemporary nature writing. While the figure of the Indian has long been prominent in America's literature of nature, before World War II there were relatively few Native American voices available in direct, untranslated form. Since the war, though, there have been an increasing number of distinguished works in this genre by Native American authors. Although Silko's reputation rests primarily on her novels, especially *Ceremony* (1977), her 1986 essay is a compelling statement of her Pueblo culture's reliance on stories to knit the people to their past and to their landscape. It offers a counterpoint to Western assumptions about a separation between wilderness and society. For Silko, stories may map the land, make a people at home in it, and enhance the human community's respect for all of the creatures in the ecosystem. Her point of view is congruent in these regards with powerful essays written by such other important Native American writers as N. Scott Momaday, Linda Hogan, and Louise Erdrich.

Just as a greater diversity of voices has entered into contemporary nature writing, certain themes have also gained prominence. One of these is the interest in gardens, both as natural landscapes and as cultural artifacts. Michael Pollan's book *Second Nature: A Gardener's Education* (1991) was a catalyst for this increasing attention to gardens. But the fiction writer Jamaica Kincaid has also written on this subject. Closely associated with gardens is the literature of farming. Wendell Berry has long and eloquently reflected upon the role of agriculture in America's landscape and culture alike. One representative piece by Berry would be "The Making of a Marginal Farm," in *Recollected Essays, 1965–1980* (1981). Other noteworthy works in this line include David Mas Masumoto's *Epitaph for a Peach: Four Seasons on My Family Farm* (1995) and Jane Brox's *Here and Nowhere Else: Late Seasons of a Farm and Its Family* (1995). As both of these titles suggest, there is often an elegiac cast to literature about the family farm; industrial agriculture and economic strictures can make this way of life feel like just one more gravely endangered habitat. At the same time, writers about the farm, like those about the garden, often bring a special perceptiveness to the wholeness of nature and culture. One of their contributions to nature writing—like that of the Native American writers—has been to discern continuity rather than separation between humanity and the natural world.

The twenty-first century has been described by the biologist E. O. Wilson as "the bottleneck" for biodiversity on this planet. Human population is projected to peak some time after 2050, along with the consumption of fossil fuels. In such an era, every major institution—religious, educational, scientific, and political—will be challenged to realign itself to new environmental realities. Nature writing, for so long a resource at the edge between literature and the earth, will certainly play an even more important role in illuminating these challenges and these efforts. While continuing to offer the fundamental literary values of wonder, delight, escape, and sympathy, it will become a crucial resource for readers—in America and around the world—who are striving for a more ecologically informed outlook on humanity and our natural home.

[*See also* Berry, Wendell; Dillard, Annie; Emerson, Ralph Waldo; Erdrich, Louise; Hoagland, Edward; Kincaid, Jamaica; Kingston, Maxine Hong; Lopez, Barry; Matthiessen, Peter; Momaday, N. Scott; Nature Writing: Poetry; Silko, Leslie Marmon; Snyder, Gary; Thoreau, Henry David, and his *Walden*; Walker, Alice; *and* Williams, Terry Tempest.]

FURTHER READING

Anderson, Lorraine, ed. *Sisters of the Earth: Women's Prose and Poetry about Nature.* New York, 1991. An influential anthology of women's writing about the natural world.

Austin, Mary. *The Land of Little Rain.* New York, 1988. An early celebration of the beauties of the desert, originally published in 1903.

Bartram, William. *Travels Through North & South Carolina, Georgia, East & West Florida, the Cherokee Country, the Extensive Territories of the Muscogulges, or Creek Confederacy, and the Country of the Chactaws.* New York, 1988. One of the first American travel books that integrated the nomenclature of Linnaean science. Originally published in 1791.

Buell, Lawrence. *The Environmental Imagination: Thoreau, Nature Writing, and the Formation of American Culture.* Cambridge, Mass., 1995. An authoritative and scholarly discussion of environmental literature, looking at nature writing as well as fiction and poetry.

Carson, Rachel. *Silent Spring.* Boston, 1994. The book that led to legislation restricting pesticide use in the United States and, eventually, allowed for the return of such endangered raptors as the peregrine falcon. Originally published in 1962.

Cooper, Susan Fenimore. *Rural Hours by a Lady.* Edited by Rochelle Johnson and Daniel Patterson. Athens, Georgia, 1998. The first publication of the full text of this important book since 1876.

Elder, John, ed. *American Nature Writers.* 2 vols. New York, 1996. Biographical and critical essays.

Emerson, Ralph Waldo, and Henry David Thoreau. *Nature and Walking.* Boston, 1991. A publication in one volume of two essays essential to the nature-writing tradition.

Finch, Robert, and John Elder, eds. *The Norton Book of Nature Writing.* New York, 1990. A collection of nature writing in English, starting with Gilbert White in 1789.

Finch, Robert, and John Elder, eds. *Nature Writing: The Tradition in English.* New York, 2002.

Lyon, Thomas J., ed. *This Incomperable Lande: A Book of American Nature Writing.* Boston, 1989. Includes a substantial and perceptive introduction surveying the genre in America.

Muir, John. *The Mountains of California.* New York, 1985. Originally published in 1894, this book did much to inspire the conservation in the mountainous West, by a man sometimes called the "father of the national parks."

Thoreau, Henry David. *Walden; or, Life in the Woods.* New York, 1983. The central work in the tradition of American nature writing originally published in 1854.

GLORIA NAYLOR

by Amanda Fields

Born on 25 January 1950 in New York City, Gloria Naylor is the eldest child of Alberta McAlpin Naylor and Roosevelt Naylor. The family lived in several places in New York as Naylor grew up, including the apartment building in Harlem owned by her grandmother Luecelia McAlpin. In addition to several physical transitions, a religious transition would soon have a strong impact on Gloria Naylor. Naylor's mother joined the Jehovah's Witnesses during the years 1963–1964, and Naylor was baptized a Jehovah's Witness and minister when she graduated from high school in 1968. This baptism eventually led her to North Carolina and Florida, where she preached full-time. In 1975, however, she left the Jehovah's Witnesses. After studying nursing at Medgar Evers College, she transferred to Brooklyn College to major in English.

Gloria Naylor. (*Courtesy of the New York Public Library*)

Toni Morrison's *The Bluest Eye* was the first book by a black woman that Naylor read. Like Morrison, Naylor often says of her writing that she had yet to see a book written about her. Once she began to pursue writing, Naylor's road to publication was fairly swift. In 1979 she received writing encouragement from Marcia Gillespie of *Essence*. She married in 1980 and divorced in 1981, the same year she received her B.A. degree in English and finished her first novel, *The Women of Brewster Place* (1982). After traveling to Spain and Tangiers, Naylor began graduate work in Afro-American Studies at Yale University. In 1983 she received her M.A. degree from Yale. Her master's thesis was her second novel, *Linden Hills* (1985). She received the American Book Award for best first novel, as well as the Distinguished Writer Award from the Mid-Atlantic Writers Association. In addition, she became a writer-in-residence at Cummington Community of the Arts and a visiting lecturer at George Washington University.

Naylor has received numerous awards since the publication of her first novel, including a National Endowment for the Arts fellowship (1985), the Candance Award of the National Coalition of One Hundred Black Women (1986), a Guggenheim fellowship (1988), and the Lillian Smith Award (1989). She has served as a visiting professor, lecturer, scholar-in-residence, and visiting writer at the University of Pennsylvania (1986), New York University (1986), Princeton (1986), Boston University (1987), Brandeis University (1988), Cornell University (1988), and the University of Kent in Great Britain (1992). In 1985 she traveled to India as a cultural exchange lecturer, and in 1993 she traveled, lectured, and did research in the Seregambian region of Africa as well as in Oslo. In 1990 Naylor established One Way Productions, a multi-ethnic production company. Her interest in theater was also fed by a stage reading of her fourth novel, *Bailey's Café* (1992), at Lincoln Center, followed by a stage production of *Bailey's Café* in 1994 by the Hartford Stage Company.

Naylor has published five novels, each with thematic and geographical connections to the others. In discussing these connections, many critics of Naylor tend to focus on the theological, cultural, and feminist implications of her work.

CHRISTIAN THEOLOGICAL INFLUENCE

Readers studying Naylor's work cannot ignore the influence of Christian theology on her characters and on the courses they choose to take. From symbolic names such as Eve and Esther to the circular pattern of Linden Hills downward to Luther Nedeed's house, Naylor's work is lush with biblical influence. Her stories often borrow from, parody, and reinvent the stories of the Christian Bible.

For instance, *Linden Hills* parodies Dante's *Inferno*. Luther Nedeed, the patriarch of Linden Hills, passes on his name and his land to each son. Each successive Luther watches from his vantage point at the bottom of the hill as the land he owns is populated by a neighborhood of people who yearn to be accepted. Luther promises a feeling of empowerment for these people, yet he, much like the Christian devil, truly holds the power he promises to give. In the *Inferno*, Judas, the betrayer of Jesus Christ, is trapped with Satan at the bottom of the circles of Hell. Willa, Luther's wife, may be seen as a symbol of Judas. In this version, however, Willa, who has "betrayed" her husband by not providing him with a child who has dark enough skin, finds redemption by uniquely finding herself. As a result, Willa becomes a savior.

There are other "saviors" in Naylor's work, including Eve from *Bailey's Café*. Eve literally rises up out of mud after being turned out by the minister who adopted her. After leaving the reach of the minister's belief system, Eve defines a sense of power and place for herself as the proprietor of a paradoxical whorehouse behind Bailey's Café. Eve takes in women she can heal in some way, women whose last sense of solace might come from her. Thus Eve sets off to establish her own ironic sense of redemption. In a pivotal scene, Eve slowly cuts open and scrapes out a plum with a sharp knife as the other women in the café silently watch. This act is a symbol of the pain felt by the character Mariam, who underwent genital mutilation, but it is also symbolic of a history that has been made invisible. As Eve cuts open the plum, readers of Naylor's work may be reminded of the significance of African-American women defining and establishing a history that has frequently been silenced.

AFRICAN-AMERICAN WOMEN AND HISTORY

The history of black women has been trivialized and misrepresented by a white (both male and female) perspective, and in most of her novels Naylor seems intent upon representing, re-visioning, and quite simply voicing the multiple perspectives of black women. One of these women, Mattie Michael, has a dream about the women of Brewster Place tearing down the wall where blood was spilled after a horrific rape. By removing each brick these women are shouting out their stories and moving beyond their silences. Similarly, in *Bailey's Café*, Eve's determination as the plum drips onto the café counter is symbolic of the attempt to expose and dig out a story, no matter how painful or messy, of womanhood.

Naylor uses different spaces to tell the stories of African-American women. Each novel is set in a specific place, and characters refer to other places in other novels (for example, Brewster Place is close to Linden Hills). This connection helps the reader establish a history, a community, and a functional sense of stability in a place where a story, however unconventional, can be told and believed. Indeed, several events occur in these books that the reader might be hard put to call believable in the conventional sense. Bailey's Café exists in no one place; it is as if the café is omniscient, knowing where and when it is most needed. The women in *Mama Day* (1988) live on a remote island called Willow Springs, where the healing powers of Miranda Day and her ancestors are fully accepted by the island's inhabitants. Willow Springs also provides a space where these women are quite distant from any white dominant culture.

By contrast, *Linden Hills* shows the effects of a place where human worth seems based on an intricate comparison to and insistent separation from the white middle class. But the rules of Linden Hills are made by a man. The women here do not have names; in fact, the most significant female character is only known as "Luther's wife" until nearly the end of the novel. Willa Prescott Nedeed, however, finds the strength to push through invisibility, own and proclaim her name, and break through the silencing of all of the Nedeed wives. Literary critics often point to Willa's actions at the end of the novel as a way of analyzing Naylor's feminist agenda. What is difficult to dispute, however, are the rich, complex, and individualized portraits of black women in Naylor's work.

SEAMS AND THREADS

Like the novels of Louise Erdrich and William Faulkner, Gloria Naylor's books work together to reveal multiple perspectives. Each book is a world unto itself while still connecting to and building upon the others. In *The Men of Brewster Place* (1998), Naylor tells the stories of the males who were on the periphery of the women in the first book. While some critics feel that this attempt was less than successful and that Naylor did not create complex male characters, the connections from her first to latest novel are clear. For instance, the people who live in Brewster Place are aware of Linden Hills; one of them, Kiswana Browne, grew up there. Willa Prescott Nedeed from *Linden Hills* is the niece of the indomitable Miranda Day (*Mama Day*). In *Mama Day*, George mentions Bailey's Café, and it is possible that he is the child named George who was born at the end of *Bailey's Café*. These connections, both literal and thematic, add to the fluidity of reading the novels in progression. Perhaps it is the reappearance of remnants of other stories and perspectives that lends Naylor's work an epic and lasting feel.

WORKS

The Women of Brewster Place (1982)
Linden Hills (1985)
Mama Day (1988)
Bailey's Café (1992)
Children of the Night: The Best Short Stories by Black Writers, 1967–Present (as editor) (1995)
The Men of Brewster Place (1998)

FURTHER READING

Felton, Sharon, and Michelle C. Loris, eds. *The Critical Response to Gloria Naylor*. Westport, Conn., 1997. A collection of critical essays that cover *The Women of Brewster Place* through *Bailey's Café*, including "Black Feminism and Media Criticism: *The Women of Brewster Place*" and "Gloria Naylor's *Mama Day* as Magic Realism."

Fowler, Virginia C. *Gloria Naylor: In Search of Sanctuary*. New York, 1996. In a critical discussion of spirituality and morality in relation to Naylor's first four novels, Fowler also attempts to draw connections between Naylor's time as a Jehovah's Witness and her writing.

Gates, Henry Louis, Jr., and K. A. Appiah, eds. *Gloria Naylor: Critical Perspectives Past and Present*. New York, 1993. Rita Mae Brown reviews *Mama Day*; Laura E. Tanner's "Reading Rape" and Larry R. Andrews's "Black Sisterhood in Naylor's Novels" are two critical essays.

Stave, Shirley A. *Gloria Naylor: Strategy and Technique, Magic and Myth*. Newark, Del., 2001. A collection of critical essays including such titles as "Hope from the Ashes: Naylor, Faulkner, and the Signifyin(g) Tradition" and "The Maternal Aesthetic of *Mama Day*."

Whitt, Margaret Earley. *Understanding Gloria Naylor*. Columbia, S.C., 1999. A brief biography of Naylor precedes a critical discussion of the novels from *The Women of Brewster Place* to *The Men of Brewster Place*.

Wilson, Charles E., Jr. *Gloria Naylor: A Critical Companion*. Westport, Conn., 2001. Includes a biography, a discussion of the African-American literary heritage in relation to Naylor, and critical responses to novels from *The Women of Brewster Place* to *The Men of Brewster Place*.

THE NEW CRITICS

by Philip Hobsbaum

The study of literature in the nineteenth century entailed such matters as philology and the editing of texts. Scholars had established a conception of methodological rigor that did duty until the early twentieth century as a condition of professional respectability. Value judgments were considered irrelevant to the study of literary history.

The rise of criticism in the university was a kind of reaction against this. It was closely bound up with the necessity of understanding modern poetry. Long before their work was identified as a school of debate, the New Critics—first named in 1941—were at work as a recognizable group, mostly inside the universities but holding temporary posts. Their characteristics included the close discussion of texts, the belief that texts should be looked at in isolation, and the assumption that a text was an independent entity capable of verbal analysis. It was assumed that the language of poetry carried an extra quality, variously defined but significantly different from prose. Along with this marched an emphasis upon evaluation. Frequently the techniques of the New Critics were used to privilege one work at the expense of another, proffered as a foil to the main work under discussion. One charge often leveled at them was that of formalism; the setting of style over content. That, if true, was not taken as a limiting judgment.

MAIN CHARACTERISTICS

The main characteristics of the New Critics are more positive than some of their expositors would allow. Their approach, in brief, discourages excursions into biography, social background, and the like. It favors quotation, backed up by analysis of the language deployed. Techniques such as these had been used before, but only as special effects, when a literary critic found himself in a particular kind of argumentative situation.

For example, Samuel Johnson in his *Life of Milton* questioned how Satan, transformed into a toad, was able to absorb his sword and shield into the batrachian body. Samuel Taylor Coleridge, seeking to indicate effects of metaphor in *Venus and Adonis*, resorted to an account of Shakespearean language. In "On Translating Homer," Matthew Arnold, up against the necessity of contrasting versions of the great Greek poet, was driven into comparison and analysis. And in a little-known essay, "A French Critic on Milton," Arnold took apart the rodomontade that he found in the early prose of Thomas Babington Macaulay. Similarly, Mark Twain anatomized the author of *Deerslayer* in his essay "Fenimore Cooper's Literary Offenses." These examples were, however, a departure from the norm and were often used in a negative capacity.

T. S. ELIOT

For T. S. Eliot (1888–1965), comparison and analysis was a key approach and accounts for the regard in which *The Sacred Wood* (1920) was held, if not by the public at large then certainly by his fellow littérateurs. This book of essays is one of the key texts in twentieth-century criticism. These essays form a program for contemporary poetry, and they are written with an edge that compels, rather than persuades, assent, as the following touchstones will show:

> Hamlet (the man) is dominated by an emotion which is inexpressible, because it is in excess of the facts as they appear.
>
> ("Hamlet and His Problems")

> If we look at the work of Jonson's great contemporaries, Shakespeare, and also Donne and Webster and Tourneur . . . their words have often a network of tentacular roots reaching down to the deepest terrors and desires. Jonson's most certainly have not.
>
> ("Ben Jonson")

> It is the poetry of a language which has undergone the discipline of prose.
>
> ("William Blake")

These essays, and several others that could be cited, are remarkable for the sheer wit with which they were written. In particular, they domesticated comparison and analysis among the critic's usual array of instruments.

In his essay "Philip Massinger," Eliot compares (greatly to the disadvantage of the former author) Massinger with Shakespeare:

> Massinger. Can I call back yesterday, with all their aids
> That bow unto my sceptre? or restore
> My mind to that tranquillity and peace
> It then enjoyed?
>
> Shakespeare. Not poppy, nor mandragora,
> Nor all the drowsy syrops of the world
> Shall ever medecine thee to that sweet sleep
> Which thou owedst yesterday.

Eliot comments:

> Massinger's is a general rhetorical question, the language just and pure, but colorless. Shakespeare's has particular significance; and the adjective "drowsy" and the verb "medecine" infuse a precise vigor. This is, on Massinger's part, an echo, rather than an imitation or a plagiarism—the basest, because least conscious form of borrowing. "Drowsy syrop" is a condensation of meaning frequent in Shakespeare, but rare in Massinger.

This is an early touchstone of the New Criticism. Its attention to verbal patterning and regard for evaluation mark it out from most precedent writing of a critical nature. Eliot is stern in "The Perfect Critic," another essay in *The Sacred Wood*, discounting biographical and background information and indeed anything that could distract the reader from the text.

Behind this is a specific view of literary history. Eliot believed that there had been a long deterioration from a period when, as he says in "Philip Massinger," "the intellect was immediately at the tips of the senses." He believed that, for example, blank verse was highly developed within Shakespeare's lifetime but that, with Massinger and "after the erection of the Chinese Wall of Milton, blank verse has suffered not only arrest but retrogression" ("Notes on the Blank Verse of Christopher Marlowe").

These essays, on Massinger, Marlowe, and the Perfect Critic, brought something new into criticism. Their influence in terms of approach and evaluation has been incalculable. As is the case with all good critical writing, the aperçus echo well beyond their immediate subjects.

F. R. LEAVIS

F. R. Leavis (1895–1978) records, "I bought *The Sacred Wood* just after it came out, in 1920. For the next few years I read it through several times a year, pencil in hand . . . if I had to characterize the nature of the debt briefly I should say that it was a matter of having had incisively demonstrated, for pattern and incitement, what the disinterested and effective application of intelligence to literature looks like" (*The Common Pursuit*, 1952). The proof of this is Leavis's early book, *Revaluation* (1936). Though it covers more ground, it is essentially an extension of Eliot's essays into a sustained history of poetry.

Revaluation begins with an account of the metaphysical poets, especially John Donne, and ends with discussions of Wordsworth, Shelley, and Keats. Leavis develops the comparison-and-analysis approach of Eliot very considerably. Here he compares Robert Herrick with Andrew Marvell:

> The Rose was sick and smiling died;
> And, being to be sanctified,
> About the bed there sighing stood
> The sweet and flowery sisterhood:
> Some hung the head, while some did bring,
> To wash her, water from the spring;
> Some laid her forth, while others wept.
> But all a solemn fast there kept:
> The holy sisters, some among,
> The sacred dirge and trental sung.
> But ah! what sweets smelt everywhere,
> As heaven had spent all perfumes there.
> At last, when prayers for the dead
> And rites were all accomplished,
> They, weeping, spread a lawny loom,
> And closed her up as in a tomb.

That is Herrick's "The Funeral Rites of the Rose," and this is a piece of Marvell:

> See how the flowers, as at parade,
> Under their colors stand display'd:
> Each regiment in order grows,
> That of the tulip, pink, and rose.
> But when the vigilant patrol
> Of stars walks round about the pole,
> Their leaves, that to the stalks are curl'd,
> Seem to their staves the ensigns furl'd.
> Then in some flower's beloved hut
> Each bee, as sentinel, is shut,
> And sleeps so too; but, if once stirred,
> She runs you through, nor asks the word.

That is from Marvell's poem "Upon Appleton House." Leavis comments:

> Now both of these may be fairly described as charmingly and gracefully playful. But it should be plain at once that

Marvell's in its playfulness has a strength that Herrick's has not—a seriousness that does not make it less playful and light. Herrick's game, Herrick's indulgence, in fact, is comparatively solemn; it does not refer us outside itself. "Let us," he virtually says, "be sweetly and deliciously sad," and we are to be absorbed in the game, the "solemn" rite. There is in Herrick's verse nothing of the crisp movement, nothing of the alert bearing, that, carrying as it does in its poise the element represented by "And sleeps so too," we recognize in Marvell's verse as the familiar urbane wit. What Marvell is doing is implicitly "placed"; not in the least solemn, he is much more serious. So he can, without any incongruity, any effect of an odd or uneasy transition, go on to a development such as is inconceivable in Herrick:

O thou, that dear and happy Isle,
The garden of the world erewhile,
Thou Paradise of the four seas
Which Heaven planted us to please,
But, to exclude the world, did guard
With wat'ry if not flaming sword;
What luckless apple did we taste
To make us mortal and thee waste.

It is clear that Leavis is building upon the foundations of Eliot. His privative comments upon Herrick are a way, by means of contrast, of establishing the superiority of Marvell. There are several presumptions here: that the text is available, that it is discussible, and that aesthetic values are inherent in the language thus discussed.

I. A. RICHARDS

Eliot's practice was theorized, four years after the event, by I. A. Richards (1893–1979), who himself taught Leavis at Cambridge, England, but spent his later years at Harvard. What he may be said to have done was stabilize critical terminology in his books *The Principles of Literary Criticism* (1924) and *Practical Criticism* (1929). The last-named demonstrated a technique of appraisal in proffering scripts without title or author to a class of students and eliciting their opinions.

Practical Criticism pioneered terms such as "sense," "feeling," "intention," and especially "tone." These were in use well before Richards, but Richards gave them a special application that lasted until well after his time:

the speaker has ordinarily an attitude to his listener. He chooses or arranges his words differently as his audience varies, in automatic or deliberate recognition of his relation to them. The tone of his utterance reflects his awareness of this relation, his sense of how he stands towards those he

is addressing. Again the exceptional case of dissimulation, or instances in which the speaker unwittingly reveals an attitude he is not consciously desirous of expressing, will come to mind.

This helps to lay a foundation of anti-intentionalism, on which much of the New Criticism stands. It also buttresses the basic account that Richards gives in his *Principles of Literary Criticism* of the way in which a text communicates with its reader. He uses the term "attitudes" to stand for much that previously was expressed in terms of the intention, philosophy, and even feeling in a work of literature. He believes that it is in terms of attitudes that the resolution, inter-inanimation and balancing of impulses—the most valuable effects of poetry—must be described. The value of the attitudes conveyed by a work of literature may be seen in terms of "the widening of the sphere of human sensibility." Communication takes place when one mind acts upon another, the implication being that an experience is induced in the reader similar to that which provoked the text he is reading. That communication is necessarily conveyed by words, and the words act upon one another to form a verbal entity. "What would be highly ambiguous by itself becomes definite in a suitable context."

Here, "ambiguity" seems to be a state to avoid. And indeed there are many examples in modern poetry where the meanings pull apart, as in "The sun above them is a bag of nails" or "The old man bearded with sickness," rendering the text difficult to understand. Yet in the most famous work of Richards's most famous pupil, ambiguity becomes a guarantee of poetic quality.

WILLIAM EMPSON

William Empson (1906–1984) writes, in *Seven Types of Ambiguity* (1930), "it will make poetry more beautiful" and claims that he has "almost always" discussed poems that he admires. He is recommending a use of language that he feels is distinct from that of the scientist, who is concerned to diminish ambiguity in language, using words to convey one single meaning. Empson, on the other hand, finds richness in the evocation of several meanings. This suggests that, by way of straight analysis as distinct from the comparative kind, it is possible to indicate layers of meaning, including atmosphere and implication, beyond the literal sense.

One piece of analysis, the first of many in *Seven Types of Ambiguity*, may be said especially to have influenced the American New Critics. Here Empson is writing of

Shakespeare's Sonnet 73 and concentrating upon the line "Bare ruined choirs, where late the sweet birds sang":

> ruined monastery choirs are places in which to sing, because they involve sitting in a row, because they are made of wood, are carved into knots and so forth, because they used to be surrounded by a sheltering building crystallized out of the likeness of a forest, and colored with stained glass and painting like flowers and leaves, because they are now abandoned by all but the grey walls colored like the skies of winter, because the cold and Narcissistic charm suggested by choir-boys suits well with Shakespeare's feeling for the object of the Sonnets, and for various sociological and historical reasons ("for oh, the hobby-horse is forgot," and the Puritans have cut down the Maypoles), which it would be hard now to trace out in their proportions; these reasons, and many more relating the simile to its place in the Sonnet, must all combine to give the line its beauty, and there is a sort of ambiguity in not knowing which of them to hold most clearly in mind. Clearly this is involved in all such richness and heightening of effect, and the machinations of ambiguity are among the very roots of poetry.

A good deal of the effect of such analysis is dependent upon the critic himself being able to write a suggestive prose, as Empson does.

JOHN CROWE RANSOM

Yet this very analysis was adversely criticized by John Crowe Ransom (1888–1974) in his book *The New Criticism* (1941), which gave this school its name. Ransom objects to what he sees as a failure on Empson's part to prioritize the more salient meanings in the complex of Sonnet 73. He uses a distinction that he found in Richards, where the "tenor" is the literal meaning of a phrase and the "vehicle" is the importation or foreign content. "I should wish to take exception to [Empson's] including those meanings that have to do with Shakespeare's narcissistic interest in the choir-boys, and the one about the Puritans' bad treatment of the songs and beauties of the churches; these are meanings within the vehicle that do not have any correspondents within the tenor, and are therefore ineligible on Empson's own terms."

Richard P. Blackmur.
(© *Bettmann/Corbis*)

For Ransom, the New Critics are Eliot, Richards, Empson, and Yvor Winters, and he finds fault with them all, mostly on the grounds of inconsistency and negativism. Yet his own approach to literature, behind a show of southern urbanity, is often negative and even hostile. In a famous essay, "Shakespeare at Sonnets" (1938), he commits the offense of which he has found others guilty, blaming the sonnets for divagations from conventional form. He himself deprecates Sonnet 73 for a failure to make the two images of the aging lover coexist; that is to say, the shaking boughs and the ruined choirs. One would certainly prefer the analysis of Empson, with its faults of overenthusiasm, to that of Ransom, with its lack of sympathy.

Sympathy indeed is not Ransom's strong point. His essay "A Poem Nearly Anonymous" (1933) concerns the highly individualistic "Lycidas" by John Milton. However, his is little more than an exercise in intentionalism—seeking to describe the mind of Milton when he produced the poem. With regard to the irregular stanzas and occasionally rhymeless lines, Ransom says "we imagine [Milton] thinking to himself, precisely like some modern poets we know, that he could no longer endure the look of perfect regimentation which sat upon the poor ideas objectified before him upon the page of poetry, as if that carried with it a reflection upon their sincerity." It is as though he wished to reduce both Shakespeare and Milton to some traditional norm. Thus, as a practical critic, Ransom fails to live up to criteria associated with the New Criticism. He further is less an advocate for the New Critics than perhaps the most discerning of their prosecuting witnesses.

Yet John Crowe Ransom was not only a distinguished poet but the most influential teacher of literature of his age. Among his pupils at Vanderbilt University and later, Kenyon College, were Allen Tate, Cleanth Brooks, Robert Penn Warren, Randall Jarrell, Robert Lowell, James Wright, and Anthony Hecht—most of them fine poets and several of them leading figures among the New Critics.

R. P. BLACKMUR

Although not dealt with as a central figure in Ransom's book on the New

Critics, R. P. Blackmur (1904–1965) is singled out in the introduction. Ransom cites Blackmur's discussion of a poem by Emily Dickinson, commenting that criticism of that nature "could not possibly have been written earlier than a few years ago." This is with reference to Blackmur's comment upon the following lines:

> Renunciation
> Is a piercing virtue,
> The letting go
> A presence for an expectation—
> Not now.

The comment by Blackmur in his essay "Emily Dickinson" (1937) runs:

> The words are all simple words, part of our stock vocabulary. Only one, "renunciation," belongs to a special department of experience or contains in itself the focus of a particular attitude, a department and an attitude we condition ourselves to keep mostly in abeyance. We know what renunciation is; we know it turns up as heroism or hypocrisy or sentimentality; and we do as little as possible about it. Only one word, "piercing," is directly physical; something that if it happens cannot be ignored but always shocks us into reaction. It is the shock of this word that transforms the phrase from a mere grammatical tautology into a metaphorical tautology which establishes as well as asserts identity. Some function of the word "pierce" precipitates a living intrinsic relation between renunciation and virtue; it is what makes the phrase incandesce.

Ransom remarks upon the "depth and precision" of this analysis. He is certainly persuasive in remarking that the attention to language manifest here would seem, like that of his contemporary practitioners, eclectic compared with the practice of their predecessors.

YVOR WINTERS

In Blackmur, as in Yvor Winters (1900–1968)—who seems more central to Ransom's argument—there may be noted a recognition of that local particularity of meaning peculiar to a poem. Winters defines this in his book *Primitivism and Decadence* (1937):

> [The poem] is composed of an almost fluid complex, if the adjective and the noun are not too nearly contradictory, of relationships between words (in the normal sense of the term), a relationship involving rational content, cadences, rhymes, juxtapositions, literary and other connotations, inversions, and so on, almost indefinitely. These relationships, it should be obvious, extend the poet's

vocabulary incalculably. They partake of the fluidity and unpredictability of experience and so provide a means of treating experience with precision and freedom.

In practice, this means characterizing what Ransom calls "the fringe of feeling" that differentiates poetry from prose. Winters, in his book *Maule's Curse* (1938), privileges the metrical patterning that one finds in Emily Dickinson; something that certainly cannot be replicated in prose. He quotes the poem "There's a certain slant of light." Its final stanza (the "it" referring to "the slant of light") runs:

> When it comes, the landscape listens,
> Shadows hold their breath;
> When it goes, 'tis like the distance
> On the look of death.

Winters comments:

> The first and third lines, like the second and fourth, are metrically identical; the first and third contain seven syllables each, with an additional extrametrical syllable at the end which takes the place of the missing syllable at the beginning of each subsequent short line, at the same time that the extrametrical syllable functions in the line in which it is written as part of a two-syllable rhyme. The elaborate structure of this poem results in the balanced hesitations and rapid resolutions which one hears in reading it.

"The balanced hesitations and rapid resolutions"—this is an acting out of the Richards concept of "tone."

ALLEN TATE

What in their apparently diverse ways Blackmur and Winters are pointing at is defined by Ransom's pupil, Allen Tate (1899–1979). His essay "Tension in Poetry" (1938) suggests "the meaning of poetry is its 'tension,' the full organized body of all the extension and intension that we can find in it. . . . [W]e may begin with the literal statement and by stages develop the complications of metaphor." It is what lies beyond the literal statement, one may infer, that constitutes "poetry." He quotes from John Donne's "Valediction: forbidding mourning":

> Our two soules therefore, which are one,
> Though I must goe, endure not yet
> A breach, but an expansion,
> Like gold to aiery thinnesse beate.

Tate comments:

> The interesting feature here is the logical contradiction of embodying the unitary, non-spatial soul in a spatial image:

247

the malleable gold is a plane whose surface can always be extended mathematically by one-half towards infinity; the souls are this infinity. The finite image of the gold, in extension, logically contradicts the intensive meaning (infinity) which it conveys; but it does not invalidate that meaning.

CLEANTH BROOKS

Another pupil of Ransom was Cleanth Brooks (1906–1994). What Tate terms "tension," Brooks regards as "irony." In *Modern Poetry and the Tradition* (1939), dedicated to Tate, Brooks writes, "the poet's attitude is a highly important element of what is communicated; and figurative language is continually used to indicate shadings of attitude. . . . Frequently, the more complex attitudes are expressed, and necessarily expressed, in varying degrees of irony: bitter, playful, whimsical, tragic, self-inclusive."

One example that Brooks cites is a stanza from "All Soul's Night" by W. B. Yeats. Here the poet invokes a dead friend, William Thomas Horton, who believed in God's will, yet who mourned the loss of his loved one:

Two thoughts were so mixed up I could not tell
Whether of her or God he thought the most,
But think that his mind's eye,
When upward turned, on one sole image fell;
And that a slight companionable ghost
Wild with divinity,
Had so lit up the whole
Immense miraculous house
The Bible promised us,
It seemed a gold-fish swimming in a bowl.

Brooks comments:

The final comparison comes as a shock in this particular context. It is hardly a decorative image. . . . The primary shock in the comparison rests in the clash between "Immense miraculous house / The Bible promised us" and the matter-of-fact domesticity of the goldfish bowl. But the comparison, shock and all, does justice to the various factors of the situation. If it is whimsical with a trace of irony, the whimsy grows legitimately out of what is, after all, only an accurate description of the friend's belief. The poet is aware of the element of magnificence in the belief, if at the same time aware of the fantastic element; and he has found means of letting the two elements work together in his picture of the crystal sphere of the heavens holding one golden and magnified image, "wild with divinity."

The direction of the critical comment here is to indicate a complexity more intricate than would be found in any straight statement of fact.

A kindred tendency may be found in Brooks's studies concerning the structure of poetry, collected as *The Well Wrought Urn* (1947). Here he is concerned to define a characteristic of poetry that he calls "paradox." Commenting upon William Wordsworth's sonnet "Composed upon Westminster Bridge," Brooks says:

Where, then, does the poem get its power? It gets it, it seems to me, from the paradoxical situation out of which the poem arises. The speaker is honestly surprised, and he manages to get some sense of awed surprise into the poem. It is odd to the poet that the city should be able to "wear the beauty of the morning" at all. Mount Snowden, Skiddaw, Mont Blanc—these wear it by natural right, but surely not grimy, feverish London. This is the point of the almost shocked exclamation:

Never did sun more beautifully steep
In his first splendor, valley, rock or hill . . .

The "smokeless air" reveals a city that the poet did not know existed: man-made London is a part of nature too, is lighted by the sun of nature, and lighted to as beautiful effect.

The point is that nothing in poetry is straight statement. There is always a complexity of effect that can be analyzed. Brooks quotes with approval T. S. Eliot's comment, in his Philip Massinger essay, on "that perpetual slight alteration of language, words perpetually juxtaposed in new and sudden combinations." This is in contrast, Brooks says, to science, where terms are frozen into strict denotations. What he is privileging and that which he here calls "paradox" he elsewhere terms "irony." This is substantially the same as the density of language Empson has called "ambiguity," Blackmur "incandescence," Winters "fluidity," and Tate "tension." A current term for this could be "multifacience," although some critics have preferred "plurisignation" or "polysemy."

UNDERSTANDING POETRY

Such a position as that of Tate and Brooks indicates how far Eliot is the true father of the New Criticism. This mode of discussion dominated literary discourse from 1920 for seventy years or more. It was helped by the university textbook that Brooks wrote in collaboration with his fellow student under Ransom, Robert Penn Warren (1905–1989), *Understanding Poetry* (1938). Here there is comment that is privative; for example, concerning the popular poem "Trees" by Joyce Kilmer. The authors quote:

A tree whose hungry mouth is pressed
Against the earth's sweet flowing breast.

They comment:

> Here the tree is metaphorically treated as a sucking babe and the earth, therefore, as the mother—a perfectly good comparison that has been made for centuries—the earth as "the great mother," the "giver of life," and so on. But the third stanza introduces a confusion:

> A tree that looks to God all day,
> And lifts her leafy arms to pray.

> Here the tree is no longer a sucking babe, but, without warning, is old enough to indulge in religious devotion.

However, most of the analyses found in *Understanding Poetry* are to do with poems that Brooks and Warren would recommend. For example, they quote "Ode to a Nightingale" by John Keats, and it is the fifth stanza that is here cited:

> I cannot see what flowers are at my feet,
> Nor what soft incense hangs upon the boughs,
> But, in embalmèd darkness guess each sweet
> Wherewith the seasonable month endows
> The grass, the thicket, and the fruit-tree wild;
> White hawthorn, and the pastoral eglantine;
> Fast-fading violets covered up in leaves;
> And mid-May's eldest child,
> The coming musk-rose, full of dewy wine,
> The murmurous haunt of flies on summer eves.

They comment:

> Having attained to the bird's dark covert, he "cannot see." Though the passage abounds in sensual detail and appeals so powerfully to all the senses, most of the images of sight are fancied by the speaker. He does not actually see the Queen-Moon or the stars. He "guess[es]" at what flowers are at his feet. He has found his way into a warm "embalmèd darkness." The last adjective means primarily "filled with incense," "sweet with balm," but it must also have suggested death—in Keats's day as in ours. In finding his way imaginatively into the dark covert, the speaker has approached death. He has wished to fade far away, "dissolve, and quite forget"; but the final dissolution and the ultimate forgetting is death. True, death here is apprehended in a quite different fashion from the death depicted in the third stanza. Here the balm is the natural perfume of growing flowers and the "gloom" is "verdurous," with suggestions of rich organic growth. . . . If his primary emphasis is on fertility and growth, he accepts the fact that death and change have their place here too: the violets, for instance, are thought of as "fast-fading."

Understanding Poetry held sway as the premier textbook for undergraduates studying English literature in American universities. Many of them went on to be teachers, not only in universities but in schools. Its influence was so paramount that it was almost forgotten that there were other ways of discussing literature.

CONCLUSION

The success of the New Critics was primarily with regard to short poems. The more dispersed effects of longer poems were not so susceptible to the School of Ambiguity, and novels demanded—to use Ransom's distinction—observation of structure at least as much as texture. Major literary figures such as C. S. Lewis and Edmund Wilson adopted quite different approaches. And it will be noticed that the New Critics emphasized here—Eliot, Leavis, Richards, Empson, Ransom, Tate, Brooks, and Warren—are all male. Of prominent women practitioners in this craft, Virginia Woolf may be termed an impressionist and Adrienne Rich an ideological critic. It is not so much that the New Criticism has disappeared as that it has been compelled to take its place among other modes of discourse. Ideologies such as feminism and cultural materialism encroached upon its ground, and other forms of thought, such as structuralism, poststructuralism, and the New Historicism, rose into apprehension.

Nevertheless, in order to be a New Critic, as Johnson said of the metaphysical poets, it was at least necessary to be able to write and to think. The approaches thus evinced proved useful in instituting pedagogical processes, especially the inculcation of intelligent reading. There has never been a satisfactory substitute for close attention to a text. Some critics, like those sheltering under the denomination of poststructuralism, have cast doubts upon the stability of the text, but this involves them in a degree of self-contradiction. For how, if a text cannot be properly ascertained, are we to understand their own statement, that a text cannot be properly ascertained? Would it not seem that their own statements are subject to the indeterminacy with which they characterize those of others? Further, after the researches of Michael Polànyi and Marjorie Grene, it would seem to be impossible to produce any comment, critical or otherwise, that did not suggest an extent of evaluation. Therefore it would seem that, whenever a teacher is required to substantiate a recommendation, some show of analysis is likely to be exacted. Further, in the competitive world of reviewing, some contact with the text is necessary, and some comment indicative of content and style is expected. To that extent, the lessons of the New Critics will continue to be taken to heart, even though they may not continue to enjoy the exemplary prestige that was theirs in the earlier to later twentieth century.

[*See also* Eliot, T. S.; Ransom, John Crowe; Tate, Allen; *and* Warren, Robert Penn.]

FURTHER READING

Blackmur, R. P. *Language as Gesture: Essays in Poetry*. London, 1954. Essays from 1937 onward, on Emily Dickinson, T. S. Eliot, Wallace Stevens, Hart Crane, and others.

Brooks, Cleanth. *Modern Poetry and the Tradition*. Chapel Hill, N.C., 1939. Influential (and approachable) book outlining irony as the basis of poetry.

Brooks, Cleanth. *The Well Wrought Urn*. Chapel Hill, N.C., 1947. A collection of analyses demonstrating paradox—which is seen as being akin to irony—to be the basis of poetry.

Brooks, Cleanth, and Robert Penn Warren. *Understanding Poetry*. New York, 1938. The dominant textbook for students of literature in American universities for several decades, demonstrating through many analyses the basic approaches of the New Criticism.

Eliot, T. S. *The Sacred Wood*. London, 1920. The key text and prototype of the New Criticism.

Eliot, T. S. *Selected Essays*. London, 1932. Enlarged version of above, adding essays on the metaphysical poets, Andrew Marvell, and John Dryden.

Empson, William. *Seven Types of Ambiguity*. London, 1930. Originated as essays written for his teacher, I. A. Richards, below, and demonstrating an approach to poetry as multifacient (plurisignant, polysemous) entity that has influenced literary criticism ever since.

Graff, Gerald. *Professing Literature: An Institutional History*. Chicago and London, 1987. Fascinating account of literary studies in American universities, providing historical framework for the New Critics.

Hobsbaum, Philip. *Theory of Criticism*. Bloomington, Ind., and London, 1970. Attempts to theorize certain aspects of New Critical practice.

Leavis, F. R. *Revaluation*. London, 1936. Account of English poetry developed from the practice of T. S. Eliot in *The Sacred Wood* and *Selected Essays*.

Leavis, F. R. *The Common Pursuit*. London, 1952. Essays dating from 1934 onward discussing Eliot, Lawrence, and other critics and poets, twentieth-century and otherwise.

Ransom, John Crowe. *The World's Body*. New York, 1938. Essays on Milton's "Lycidas," Shakespeare's sonnets, and aspects of theory designed to show that "the object of a proper society is to instruct its members how to transform instinctive experience into aesthetic experience."

Ransom, John Crowe. *The New Criticism*. New York, 1941. The book that first recognized the New Critics—Blackmur, Eliot, Richards, Empson, Winters—as an identifiable school of thought.

Richards, I. A. *The Principles of Literary Criticism*. London, 1924. One of the most sustained efforts ever to put forward a theory of literature.

Richards, I. A. *Practical Criticism*. London, 1929. A theoretical book kept down to earth by samples of Richards's teaching practice, especially the handouts returned by students with their comments on selected texts.

Scholes, Robert. *The Rise and Fall of English: Reconstructing English as a Discipline*. New Haven, Conn., and London, 1998. Gloomy account of and pessimistic prognostication for literary studies in the university.

Tate, Allen. *Essays of Four Decades*. Chicago, 1969; London, 1970. Essays from 1928 onwards, including "Tension in Poetry," "The Man of Letters in the Modern World," "A Note on Donne," "A Reading of Keats," and "Hart Crane."

Winters, Yvor. *In Defense of Reason*. Denver, Colo., 1947. Three books in one, dating from 1937, 1938, and 1943, dealing with aspects of poetry and theory in a manner at once combative and enlightening.

THE NEW FORMALISM

by Gerry Cambridge

The rise of New Formalism was probably the most significant development in American poetry in the last fifteen years of the twentieth century. It is a poetic movement that emphasizes writing in meter and rhyme, and to an extent narrative, against the institutionalized predominance of the free verse confessional lyric. Its proponents, however, have made exaggerated claims for it. At least equally exaggerated dismissals have been made by its detractors; such relatively innocent aesthetic choices as writing poetry in meter and rhyme or telling stories in one's poems have not only garnered accusations of political conservatism but have generated such vituperation on both sides that some commentators have somewhat hyperbolically referred to disputes over the movement as "the poetry wars." By the turn of the millennium, however, New Formalism was an established part of the American poetry scene. Major little magazines such as the *Hudson Review* and the *New Criterion* have proved sympathetic to the movement's professedly populist aims, while smaller concerns such as *The Formalist* print only work in meter and rhyme. The movement has even found supporters in Britain. The Scottish-American poetry journal, *The Dark Horse*, founded in 1995, retains a British skepticism towards many aspects of the movement but has printed many of its poets and given review space to numerous New Formalist publications. Additionally, the movement has its own poetry conference. Run each June in West Chester, Pennsylvania, the conference is the only one in the country to foreground poetic technique. Founded in June 1995, it is reputed to be one of the largest poetry conferences in America. New Formalism now routinely merits entries in literary encyclopedias. Whatever the value of the work it has produced, its place as a socio-poetic phenomenon seems secure.

HISTORY

New Formalism began in the late 1970s and early 1980s as an informal grouping of younger writers dissatisfied with the prevailing poetry orthodoxy in the academy. No doubt they felt limited and constrained by an aesthetic

there which focused on a subjective, confessional "I," usually in free verse, and as young poets of any curiosity at all are likely to, they began looking for other models. They found them particularly in the work of poets such as Robert Frost, Robinson Jeffers, and X. J. Kennedy, writers of wide import who had either kept faith with meter and rhyme or, in Jeffers's case, told stories. These young poets, who included Frederick Turner, Frederick Feirstein, Dana Gioia, Mark Jarman, and Robert McDowell also grew increasingly aware that poetry had lost its common audience. As Gioia, one of New Formalism's most prominent figures, would point out in his *Can Poetry Matter? Essays on Poetry and American Culture* (1992), an important polemic on contemporary American poetry and one linked to New Formalism, they became aware that poetry had become a subculture, cut off from the life of the mainstream culture and increasingly enervated. They saw the use of meter, rhyme, and narrative as perhaps a way of attempting to address this situation—to escape the ghettoization of contemporary free verse.

Free verse's dominance had been in part a reaction by poets such as Robert Bly, Adrienne Rich, Robert Lowell, John Berryman, and James Wright to the New Criticism favored in the universities in the 1940s and 1950s, which promulgated "difficult, labored" poems. After serving an apprenticeship in form, many such writers turned to free verse. In statements accompanying their poems in the influential anthology, *Naked Poetry: Recent American Poetry in Open Forms* (1969), younger poets such as Denise Levertov, Allen Ginsberg, Robert Bly, and Gary Snyder for the most part studiously avoided questions of technique, instead focusing on an aesthetic of sensibility. When, in their turn, they entered the academy as professors, as critic Keith Maillard has pointed out, they brought those predilections with them. The cultural upheavals of the Vietnam War era, with its suspicion of government and centralized power, were ripe for the growth of an aesthetic which favored free verse and a subjective "I" that rebelled against the New Critical orthodoxy still in vogue in the academy.

EARLY CONTROVERSIES

While not strictly New Formalist, the poet Brad Leithauser's essay, "Metrical Illiteracy," which appeared in the *New Criterion* in 1983, was an early indication of a backlash against free verse. It was a polemic castigating—by implication—the semiliterates claiming to be poets who had, nonetheless, never "worked seriously with form." He then accused many well-known poets in the United States of encouraging formlessness because they themselves would be seen as incompetent in form; their encouragement was therefore a kind of self-preservation. Leithauser's polemic foregrounded technical ability in form as the essential precursor of poetic achievement. "Metrical illiteracy," he asserted, was, for the poet, "functional illiteracy."

Two years later, in the *Associated Writing Programs Newsletter*, the main organ for the creative writing industry in America, a young free-verse advocate, Ariel Dawson, entered the fray. In "The Yuppie Poet" she first coined the phrase "new formalism"—as an insult. Dawson's polemic conflated the increasing prevalence of formalism with lifestyle, with "the glorification" of "competitiveness and the compulsion to acquire" possessed, she asserted, by "the yuppie poet." She also accused the New Formalism simply of being old formalism, as practiced by Anthony Hecht and Richard Wilbur, rehashed. Bizarrely, she opposed a concern with technique against "artistic integrity." Apparently, she judged them to be enemies of each other rather than complementary.

Dawson's polemic was soon followed by another, by poet-teacher Diane Wakoski of Michigan State University, which appeared in the *American Book Review* in 1986. "The New Conservatism in American Poetry" was a rambling and somewhat confused attack, most remarkable for Wakoski's hyperbolic assault on poet-academic John Hollander, an old formalist. In "denouncing the poetry which is the fulfillment of the American heritage," a Whitman-influenced free verse, Hollander was, in her opinion, a representative of Satan. Her attack linked rhyme and form with Reaganism.

This attack generated five responses, from Robert Mezey, Lewis Turco, David Radavich, Brian Richards, and Dana Gioia. Most of them denied any necessary link between aesthetics and politics, in particular between form and conservatism, citing Ezra Pound as an example of a fascist who wrote free verse. They also criticized as a kind of cultural fascism Wakoski's intolerance of literary pluralism, paradoxically in the guise of a democratic Whitmanism that declared form to be "un-American."

Gioia compared her tone and content to "the quest for pure Germanic culture led by the late Joseph Goebbels." He entertainingly suggested "the radical notion" that whatever poetry was written by Americans constituted American poetry.

Wakoski's polemic and these responses were the first real public controversy about the young movement. In autumn 1987 the *Hudson Review* published perhaps the first significant manifesto in the debate, Dan Gioia's "Notes on the New Formalism." The name given by Dawson as an insult had been capitalized, dusted down, and used as a moniker. Gioia's "Notes" identified the period as an exciting one for any young poet to be returning to writing in form, as the techniques had been largely neglected for twenty-five years—although, of course, numerous American poets had been writing in form without making an issue of the fact. Gioia's essay also linked the rise of work in rhyme and meter with dissatisfaction at poetry as a subculture. One of the so-called liberal New Formalists, Gioia cleverly avoided polarizing the debate around free and formal verse. Both techniques, he asserted, were valuable for different purposes. He discounted questions of political alliance, calling the decision to use meter not only politically neutral but purely aesthetic.

EARLY ANTHOLOGIES

Any literary movement is only as important as the quality of the poetry it produces. While Robert Richman's *The Direction of Poetry: An Anthology of Rhymed and Metered Verse Written in the English Language since 1975* (1988), in its provocative use of the definite article in the book's title, emphasized the increased profile for formal verse and contained a broader range of work than just that deemed to be New Formalist, including practitioners who had been writing formal verse for decades, most of the New Formalists were represented. Given its editor's pronouncements on lack of rigor in previous anthologies, it attracted criticism for Richman's apparent ignorance of what constituted meter. The poetry editor of the right-wing *New Criterion*, Richman was also criticized for his implicit linking of form to class. Commenting on the juxtaposition of form with working-class culture in the work of the British poet Tony Harrison, Richman had commented, bemusingly, "and what an unlikely coalition it is!" If nothing else, such a comment showed an astonishing ignorance of British, not to mention American, poetic tradition in which there is no necessary association between formal poetry and social status.

Richman's artificial juxtaposition of these may, however, have helped fuel the yoking together by the movement's detractors of aesthetics and politics.

Special issues of the American quarterly *Crosscurrents*, and of the British-American poetry journal *Verse*, followed in 1989 and 1990, respectively. They acted as more focused interim anthologies for the emerging movement. These issues showed, in general, New Formalism to be as yet more interesting in concept than in achievement. Nonetheless, in printing work by noted New Formalists such as R. S. Gwynn, Dana Gioia, Charles Martin, David Mason, and Rachel Hadas, they helped showcase some of the movement's most significant figures. The special issue of *Verse* also introduced New Formalism to an international audience. It enabled British readers to focus on an interesting new aspect of what was to them a bewildering American poetry scene. New Formalism, to use advertising parlance, had several unique selling points: it insisted on meter and rhyme; it was hospitable to narrative; it aimed at contemporary relevance and accessibility; and it assumed as an audience the "common reader." Such tenets were easy to remember.

In his introduction to the *Verse* special issue, Robert McPhillips reiterated ideas which had first appeared in his 1989 essay, "What's New about New Formalism?" He was careful to differentiate between old and new formalists, perhaps in part because the movement's detractors had frequently accused New Formalism of being a retrograde movement, harking back nostalgically to the academic formal poetry of the 1950s—an intriguing situation considering that these detractors were, themselves, mainly tenured in universities. A composite old formalist poem, McPhillips asserted, would be elegant, learned, ironic, often classically allusive. It would quite frequently focus on a cultural artifact, especially a European one. Its author would most likely be an English professor. By contrast, a New Formalist would be far less likely to be found in a university context: Dana Gioia was a businessman working for General Foods; Leithauser was a lawyer; Frederick Feirstein, one of the movement's founders, was a psychiatrist; and Tom Disch was a science-fiction writer. He or she would also be far less interested in displays of irony and erudition in verse (though many are notably erudite individuals). Growing up in the 1960s and 1970s surrounded by popular culture, the New Formalists prized colloquial diction, accessibility, and direct emotion. They attempted to use the old forms in a new way. They were, if anything, closer to Robert Frost than to poets in academe, formal or free.

EARLY POLEMICS BY NEW FORMALISTS

So, at least, went the theory. Meanwhile, in 1989 the first book of essays concerning New Formalism and its relation, New Narrative, appeared. (In practice, the two movements merge, and other commentators gather them under the New Formalism moniker.) *Expansive Poetry: Essays on the New Narrative and the New Formalism* collected thirteen pieces of unabashed advocacy by poet-critics. As promotion for a modest—at least in numbers—regiment engaged in a poetry war, the book's back cover copy did not inspire confidence. "DO YOU HATE READING POETRY?" it trumpeted in capitals. "THIS BOOK IS ABOUT POETRY YOU CAN READ!" It claimed that the new poetry possessed, among other things, "rhythms that ache to be felt."

Six of the book's essays deal exclusively with New Formalism. These opened with "Toward a Liberal Poetics," by Paul Lake, in which he combatively speculated whether tenured professors of creative writing would be embarrassed to be asked by their students about poetic forms about which they knew nothing. Lake also felt "sure" that meter, stress, and syllable count, as well as rhyme, were "rooted in our physiologies as well." This reasonable conviction—after all, such basic physiological actions as our heartbeats and lovemaking follow rhythmic patterns—received an attempt at scientific validation in the volume's closing essay, the extraordinary "The Neural Lyre." It was written by one of New Formalism's more visionary advocates, Frederick Turner, in association with Ernst Pöppel, an internationally distinguished psychophysicist working as head of the auditory research division of the Institute for Medical Psychology at the University of Munich. The essay is too complex to review in detail, but in brief it asserts that exposure to the regularity of metrical verse is an aid to the holistic use of our brains and that reading it can help develop "the positive emotions such as love and peacefulness." An education in such verse, the authors asserted, would help produce citizens "able to unite rational thought and calculation with values and commitment." Reading formal verse should therefore have a prime place in education. The implication is that metered verse is what the poet should write.

"The Neural Lyre" is astonishingly detailed in its particulars yet seems relatively simplistic in its conclusions. It contradicts the New Formalism's stated aim to write about poetry for a popular audience. It is specialist enough to be impervious to nonspecialized criticism. As one of New Formalism's more objective commentators, Keith Maillard, has pointed out, few readers would have sufficient scientific background to know whether it represents good science or not; we have to take it on trust. Nonetheless, one becomes vaguely uneasy at its authors' apparent desire to provide a scientific rationale for aesthetic practice, in particular when this is linked to social ends. For one thing, no poet ever wrote in meter because it would be good for society, except as a happy spin-off. As Robert Frost, one of New Formalism's mentors wrote, dreadfully but accurately, he did not mind the world being terrible provided he could capture it in art. A more worrying implication that could be taken from "The Neural Lyre," however, is of a kind of eugenics of the spirit quite as extreme as the stranglehold New Formalism claims free verse has held over American poetry.

Despite its amateur presentation and the lack still of a definitive anthology of New Formalist poetry, this book of essays established New Formalism as a force to be reckoned with. Interviews with American poets throughout the early 1990s routinely began including a question as to the interviewee's relationship to New Formalism; the "free or formal" controversy became a debating point in American poetry. The movement's increased profile also led to increased attacks, of which some attempted greater penetration than the earlier polemics of Dawson and Wakoski.

CRITIQUES OF NEW FORMALISM

One such attack was Ira Sadoff's "Neo-Formalism: A Dangerous Nostalgia," which appeared in the *American Poetry Review* in 1990. Unfortunately, the critique equated Robert Richman's *The Direction of Poetry* (1983) with the New Formalism. A rather more interesting critique was a 1992 article, "The Closing of the American Line: Expansive Poetry and Ideology," by Thomas B. Byers, in *Contemporary Literature*. Byers examines in some detail the ideology of New Formalism under the umbrella of Expansive Poetry. He concedes that there is no intrinsic connection between form and ideology in poetry and cites Ezra Pound as an illustration. He also wonders why New Formalism has not coopted the black poet Langston Hughes, who wrote often in meter and rhyme, to their cause in an attempt to defuse accusations that they are intrinsically feudal, right wing, and "un-American." But he proceeds to assert that there is a strong historical connection between received form and "the need to break with a colonial [that is, a British] past," at the same time pointing to "the persistent historical identification of poetic formalism with elite, genteel, and oppressive social class interests," among which he includes the

southern Agrarians. This conservative literary grouping included Allen Tate and John Crowe Ransom. Byers identifies "liberal formalists" such as Dana Gioia, Robert McPhillips, and Paul Lake as being apolitical. Their only politics is a politics of aesthetics to widen "the formal possibilities of poetry in our time." Byers argues that a right-wing formalist such as Frederick Turner, however, has as his view of the ideal society (in Byers's long-verse narrative, *The New World: An Epic Poem* [1985]) the "free countries,"(Turner describes them as "independent Jeffersonian aristocratic democracies, where art, sciences, and the graces of human life are cultivated to their highest") one hero of which is John Crowe Ransom. Byers quotes from Ransom's essay in *I'll Take My Stand: The South and the Agrarian Tradition* (1930), a prose broadside by the Fugitives arguing for the retention of feudal living in the South, in which one statement tacitly condones slavery—a moment which also troubled Anthony Hecht. Byers asserts that such implicit alliances, as well as the gender imbalance and lack of minorities in the New Formalism movement—there were no contributions by women at all in *Expansive Poetry*, for instance—proves its political conservatism. He denies that form can be dissociated from politics in the presence of such facts.

In a follow-up issue of *Contemporary Literature* (1993), there were several convincing refutations from New Formalists of the Byers essay. These pointed out his simplistic conflation of characters in poems with the author's own self and included an eloquent response from Frederick Turner accusing Byers of "selective quotation" and pointing out that, as a Caucasian married to a Chinese woman and father to a mixed race son, he made an unlikely fascist or racist. In later publications, however, New Formalists have opted where possible for a politically correct inclusiveness which indicates a desire to be seen as acceptable by the mainstream. Some commentators have indeed criticized them on these grounds. One, Joseph Salemi, a formal poet peripherally associated with the movement, sums up this attitude by asserting that New Formalism is not extreme enough. In trying to fulfill politically correct expectations, he believes, it displays a cap-doffing regard for the mainstream; its associated poets thereby place pursuit of power and status within the existing poetry culture before art.

ANTHOLOGIES

By 1994, when Aralia Press—a superb small press owned by Michael Peich (one of the co-founders of the West Chester formal poetry conference)—published *Formal*

Introductions, one of the first genuine New Formalist anthologies, the movement was already well established, so much so that the editor, Dana Gioia, commenting in his introduction on the anthology's delayed appearance, observed that it seemed "a relatively tame affair," not the radical item it would have been only five years earlier. He noted, however, that despite the publicity generated by the debate over New Formalism, there had been almost no real criticism of the movement's source texts.

Defined as "a modest guidebook," *Formal Introductions: An Investigative Anthology* was dedicated to X. J. Kennedy, "the godfather of this gang." (Kennedy, a superb, witty poet, had never stopped writing approachably in meter and rhyme.) The anthology comprised twenty-two poems by twenty-one poets, four of them women. The volume opens with a sonnet by Dick Allen that has an irregular rhyme scheme. Jack Butler's "Attack of the Zombie Poets" is a satire on writers of free verse, aimed at a coterie audience of other New Formalists. Frederick Feirstein writes two poems about his younger self that seem to contradict New Formalism's impatience with the autobiographical lyric (except that Feirstein writes one poem in blank verse and the other as a sonnet), while Brad Leithauser, in "Plexal," veers from the pleasingly concrete at times to the abstract register one might expect of a lawyer—

> where the modification, however slight
> of a single postulate must evert
> a balance somewhere.

It would be two years before a definitive trade anthology, the combatively titled *Rebel Angels: 25 Poets of the New Formalism* (1996), appeared from Story Line Press. Any movement is ultimately only as valuable as the poetry it gives rise to, is in fact at the mercy of the coal face of genuine creativity. It is one thing to theorize loftily. It is quite another to exemplify such pronouncements with remarkable poetry. This 259-page anthology, red as a fire truck or as William Carlos Williams's famous wheelbarrow, had as its cover illustration William Blake's *The Good and Evil Angels Struggling for Possession of a Child*. Its 126 poems came from poets born from 1940 to 1967. Ten of the volume's contributors are women; two contributors, Rafael Campo and Marilyn Nelson, are nonwhite; another, Marilyn Hacker, is an outspoken feminist. The anthology thus defuses possible criticisms that New Formalism represents merely an all-white, middle-class, predominantly male movement.

The book's poems are prefaced by a confident introduction by the editors, David Mason and Mark Jarman, both fine formal poets who, to their credit, omit their own work from the book. The anthology ends with a glossary of the forms that the poems employ, as well as a "key to the poems," which in chronological order notates each poem's form. These give the book an air of no-nonsense professionalism. The editors' opening statement, "Revolution is bred in the bone of the American character," prepares one for a dramatic reading experience.

Rebel Angels, predictably, received wide attention. In 1997 Robert McPhillips, an advocate for the movement, though one who at times seems keener on finding poems which demonstrate the tenets of New Formalism than anything else, praised the volume with reservations in *Sparrow*. He lamented the exclusion of Dana Gioia's "Cruising with the Beach Boys," perhaps not one of Gioia's best pieces, but seemingly exemplary of the movement's populist aims as it is written in impeccable meter and rhyme, dealing in unironic emotion and with a contemporary motif. The English critic John Lucas, meanwhile, writing in *The Dark Horse* in 1997, no doubt with the benefit of a British poetry scene equally at ease with free or formal verse, castigated the anthology for its "enervate dullness" as a whole. He pointed to antiquated language and the overpredominance of iambic meter, while praising some individual poets such as Gioia, Tom Disch, and Andrew Hudgins. Meanwhile, Eliot Weinburger, writing in the Australian Internet magazine *JACKET*, dismissed the anthology as dealing in outworn tropes and full of inept poems whose technical attributes often failed to live up to their editors' precise descriptions of them at the back of the book. For his taste, and despite the editors' assertion that "there is more variety in [the contributors'] approach to form . . . than in some work of the previous generations"—a vague statement which could be taken to imply a casualness in the approach to form—the New Formalists were not formal enough.

It has to be said that there is something to these criticisms. This, however, is hardly surprising. Despite hype and critical logrolling, it is unlikely that much of the poetry in any movement anthology will still be read in a hundred years time. Most of the work in *Rebel Angels* is iambic in meter; anapestic and dactylic substitutions, which can often inject rhythmic bounce into plodding lines, are predominantly absent. At times one remembers Randall Jarrell's stinging phrase, "Where poems have hearts, a metronome is beating here." The work tends not to be strong in image, in metaphor, or the visual;

the reverence one sees in Wilbur, Hecht, and Elizabeth Bishop, their loving, sometimes perceptually breathtaking delineation of the visual world, is largely absent. Some of the poems give the impression of dull competence and linguistic thinness. There are few remarkable imaginative leaps, little of the anarchy of sensibility of a William Carlos Williams or a John Crowe Ransom. Instead, the editors note in their introduction that making poems in meter "assumes a valued civility…but also a larger cultural vision that restores harmony and balance to the arts." It is a commendable but not very exciting assertion. The editors quote with approval Timothy Steele, one of the earliest and most technically adroit New Formalists, who in his *Missing Measures: Modern Poetry and the Revolt against Meter* (1990) credits the art of writing in meter with nourishing "in a way no other pursuit can" qualities such as "a love of nature," as well as "susceptibility to beauty and joy," among other attributes including humor and a sense of fairness generally contributory to the social good. It is difficult to see why any number of other "pursuits," even writing in free verse, should not be able to nourish those qualities equally well. Such an approved aesthetic generally produces the poems one would expect. There is little, for instance, of the sheer brazen heedlessness of an X. J. Kennedy, who can write a hilarious poem about sadomasochism in his "Flagellant's Song" or a heartbreaking lament spoken by an ageing floozy. Nor is there anything like the absurd yet agreeable hyperbole of a Whitman ("the scent of these armpits aroma finer than prayer") nor even, for all Anthony Hecht is an "old" formalist, typically associated therefore with refined civility and European artifacts, anything of the unflinched-from barbarities of "More Light! More Light!," a poem of what the Scottish critic Edwin Muir called "artistic heroism" in its facing up to horrific realities. Instead, decency and reasonableness rule in the main. They tend, however, as Philip Larkin believed happiness did, to "write white." They are social virtues, but not necessarily artistic ones without rather narrow limits.

Nonetheless, the anthology does have its high points. R. S. Gwynn and Tom Disch, both fine satirists, are represented by immaculately crafted stanzas (although even here one cavils at the rapist in Disch's "The Rapist's Villanelle" who can say, even making allowances for the irony of a rapist writing a villanelle, "My soul that bustling image would perfuse"!). Emily Grosholz's work has an attractive lyricism, while Frederick Feirstein's stylish and utterly contemporary couplets, spoken in the persona of a separated married man after an unsatisfactory one-night

stand in "Mark Stern Wakes Up," seem a fine fulfillment of some of the tenets of New Formalism. The crackling realism of Marilyn Hacker in "Cancer Winter," a sequence of fourteen autobiographical sonnets detailing her own experience with the disease and in "Elysian Fields," about the poor in New York—one of the few pieces that admit the existence of the poor—adds a strong note of streetwise reality. This is buttressed by narratives such as Sydney Lea's compelling "The Feud," about a country feud leading to tragedy, which delineates impressively the psychology of revenge, and Andrew Hudgins's "Saints and Strangers," spoken by a frank, loving daughter about her fervent Baptist father in the American South. Among others, Wyatt Prunty in his "A Note of Thanks" and Rachel Hadas in "The Red Hat" produce fine individual poems of wide import without sacrificing literary quality.

Also, all cavils about technique aside, some of the New Formalists are technical masters. Technical finesse and a delicacy of perception hallmarks some of Mary Jo Salter's work, while Charles Martin, another fine technician, writes a sharp dry sonnet about Guatemalan political murders in "Easter Sunday, 1985." Timothy Steele's work shows a fastidious elegance. Dana Gioia, one of the most prominent of the New Formalists, is well represented by several strong pieces, but most notably by the fine "Counting the Children," a narrative in blank verse tercets spoken by a Mr. Choi, a Chinese accountant. He is called in to audit the estate of a wealthy eccentric who, after her death, is found to have been a collector of dolls scavenged from anywhere. The poem begins with a scene that could be the opening of a film. The estate's executor shows Mr. Choi "hell": roomfuls of dismembered dolls. The narrative progresses to a moving meditation by an ordinary family man on time, fate, mortality, and children. It is at least as remarkable, its narrative power aside, for the power generated by a language register as plain as Frost's or William Wordsworth's at their barest.

Rebel Angels showcased these and other leading New Formalists such as Rachel Hadas and Brad Leithauser and began the process of establishing a formal canon for the movement. Many younger poets associated with New Formalism have since appeared on the scene. These include writers such as Diane Thiel, Kate Light, Wilmer Mills, Len Krisak, and A. E. Stallings, as well as fine formal poets yet to publish complete collections, such as the outstanding Leslie Monsour, Catherine Tufariello, and Chryss Yost. Many of these poets, some of whom are still in their thirties, have had first collections published by Story Line Press, owned by Robert McDowell, a narrative poet associated with the movement, or by the University of Evansville, which is associated with the partisan poetry journal *The Formalist*.

New Formalism has a secure place in the canon of contemporary American poetry. If the movement had done nothing more than emphasize that poets, like automobile mechanics, carpenters, or other tradespeople, should serve an apprenticeship in the art or craft they are working in, irrespective of whether they go off and write free verse or language poetry thereafter, it would have been immensely valuable. It has, of course, also attempted to resurrect the idea of poetry as a public and civic art, with a large potential audience not gathered from specialists but from among the "common reader." It seems doubtful, however, that the movement has effected the major shift in sensibility its supporters claim for it. A revolution in technique is more easily achieved than one in sensibility, a rather more fundamental thing.

NEW FORMALISM IN THE TWENTY-FIRST CENTURY

It is difficult to predict how New Formalism will evolve, though it has become more sophisticated in presenting its case. Books such as Kevin Walzer's broadly promotional overview of some of the movement's more significant figures, *Expansive Poetry and Postmodernism* (1998), have tended to emphasize its forward-looking nature. A reissued volume of essays, updating *Expansive Poetry* and called *New Expansive Poetry*, appeared in 1999, edited by the levelheaded R. S. Gwynn. It includes statements by women poets, in addition to men, on writing in form. Even the title of *After New Formalism: Poets on Form, Narrative, and Tradition* (1999), a volume of essays edited by Annie Finch, seems to attempt to move beyond New Formalism's tenets. The battles fought by the pioneers of the movement have cleared the ground for a younger generation that, presumably, will be able to take writing poetry in form as a given. The danger for younger poets within the existing hierarchy of New Formalism may well become one of, for the sake of acceptance, conforming to the movement's tenets at the expense of their own unrestrained development. It could well turn out, in fact, especially if New Formalism were to prove as influential as its advocates might wish, precisely as restrictive as the free verse orthodoxy rebelled against by the movement's earliest proponents. What is certain is that the future of American poetry hinges not upon narrow technical definitions of the art, but upon demonstrable excellence, whether in free or formal verse.

[*See also* Confessional Poetry; Fugitives, The, (and Southern Agrarianism); *and* Gioia, Dana.]

FURTHER READING

Berg, Stephen, and Robert Mezey, eds. *Naked Poetry: Recent American Poetry in Open Forms*. Indianapolis and New York, 1969. With contributions by Allen Ginsberg, W. S. Merwin, Denise Levertov, Gary Snyder, Robert Bly, and others. Offers a useful historical perspective of free verse and the attitude of its makers in the late 1960s.

Dacey, Philip, and David Jauss, eds. *Strong Measures: Contemporary American Poetry in Traditional Forms*. New York, 1986. A rather uneven volume, cramming 188 poets into just under 500 pages and somewhat lax in its definition of "formal"; nonetheless, a valuable overview of American formal poetry in the mid-1980s.

Feirstein, Frederick, ed. *Expansive Poetry: Essays on the New Narrative and the New Formalism*. Santa Cruz, Calif., 1989. Thirteen essays with a pronounced polemical tone, useful mainly as an overview of the movement near its beginnings.

Finch, Annie. *A Formal Feeling Comes: Poems in Form by Contemporary Women*. Ashland, Ore., 1994. Useful as an overview of work written by contemporary women poets, with prefatory statements to their selections (reprinted in Gwynn, below).

Finch, Annie, ed. *After New Formalism: Poets on Form, Narrative, and Tradition*. Ashland, Ore., 1999. Essays by nine women and fourteen men, from leading New Formalists as well as relative outsiders such as Adrienne Rich and Anne Stevenson. Especially valuable as an open debate ranging beyond the sometimes narrow early polemics of the movement.

Gioia, Dana. *Can Poetry Matter? Essays on Poetry and American Culture*. St. Paul, Minn., 1992. A volume of lucid essays by one of the most readable poet-critics writing. Includes several valuable and level-headed pieces about New Formalism.

Gwynn, R. S. ed. *New Expansive Poetry: Theory, Criticism, History*. Ashland, Ore., 1999. A more mature volume than Feirstein's *Expansive Poetry*, especially valuable for gathering seminal essays such as Leithauser's "Metrical Illiteracy" and for twelve statements by women poets (taken from Finch's *A Formal Feeling Comes*), in addition to an objective overview by outsider Keith Maillard.

Jarman, Mark, and David Mason, eds. *Rebel Angels: 25 Poets of the New Formalism*. Ashland, Ore., 1996. The closest thing yet to a canonical text for the movement.

Lindner, April. *New Formalist Poets of the American West*. Boise, Idaho, 2001. Trim little overview in a neat pamphlet format, especially valuable for its introduction to younger writers such as Chryss Yost and to those previously neglected, such as Leslie Monsour.

Mason, David. *The Poetry of Life and the Life of Poetry*. Ashland, Ore., 2000. Fine, readable essays by one of the foremost poets of the New Formalism. Useful as background.

Richman, Robert, ed. *The Direction of Poetry: An Anthology of Rhymed and Metered Verse Written in the English Language since 1975*. Boston, 1988. This book's seventy-six contributors are drawn from Britain, Ireland, and Australia as well as the United States, thus providing an international sampler of contemporary formal verse, though of uneven quality.

Steele, Timothy. *Missing Measures: Modern Poetry and the Revolt against Meter*. Fayetteville, Ark., 1990. Scholarly and impressively argued, tracing the decline of meter to distrust of its use by the early modernists.

Walzer, Kevin. *The Ghost of Tradition: Expansive Poetry and Post-modernism*. Ashland, Ore., 1998. Offers a useful perspective, in categories and with close readings, on fifteen of the most prominent New Formalist poets. Primarily advocative in tone.

THE NEW JOURNALISM

by Danielle Hinrichs

Amidst war protests, hippies, civil rights demonstrations, rock-and-roll festivals, assassinations, feminism, youth power, experimentation with drugs, and sexual revolution, many reporters and writers found that traditional literary categories could not capture the tumultuous changes of the 1960s. Concerned that fiction neglected the people and events of America at that time and that journalism ignored the complexity of the era, reporters and writers forged a new genre by applying the writing techniques and characteristics of the novel and short story to nonfiction, journalistic prose. Journalists like Tom Wolfe, Gay Talese, and Michael Herr joined fiction writers such as Truman Capote, Norman Mailer, and Joan Didion to create a nonfiction form characterized by its use of dialogue, scenic construction, point of view, and personal voice, all traditionally the terrain of fiction. The genre's many critics denied the originality of the form and worried about its threats to the objectivity and accuracy of traditional reportage. For New Journalists, the emerging genre was more responsive to cultural changes and more accurately, more thoroughly, and more interestingly conveyed the issues, events, and people of the 1960s and early 1970s. The New Journalism drew greater attention to nonfiction as a creative literary form and encouraged experimentation with genre and style.

TOM WOLFE

Tom Wolfe, the greatest advocate and one of the most prolific practitioners of the New Journalism, has been called the Big Bad Wolfe and Rebel-Doodle Dandy and is known for his fresh white suit and flawless style. His collection of essays, *The Kandy-Kolored Tangerine-Flake Streamline Baby* (1965), though not the first example of New Journalistic writing, was perhaps the most recognized and influential early example of the movement. The title essay emerged not from a calculated desire to try new techniques but out of frustration with the limitations of traditional practices for conveying the changing society and popular culture of the 1960s. Wolfe began writing an article for *Esquire* magazine about a hot rod and custom

car show in California run by teenagers with money and a dedication to style. Faced with a deadline, he resisted constructing the story in the usual way and finally resigned himself to leaving it unfinished. The editor asked Wolfe to send his notes so that someone else could write up the article. Wolfe sat down at his typewriter and began a letter to his editor, "Dear Byron." Rock-and-roll music blaring in the background, Wolfe wrote all night long, freely discussing his experiences in California of viewing cars as works of art and meeting people dedicated to a culture based on the freedom and sex appeal of the automobile. In the morning, he presented a forty-nine-page document to *Esquire*. The magazine struck the salutation and printed Wolfe's letter in its entirety.

This anecdote elucidates several important developments in the history and significance of New Journalism. The form grew out of attempts to write more freely about changes in the postmodern social world, and it often incorporated personal experience and an informal style. Like this early source, New Journalistic writing often reads as if it were a letter that includes the reporter's experiences and thoughts, conveying an intimacy with characters and revealing the context in which the story evolved. And, as Wolfe's groundbreaking letter did, the New Journalism developed amidst the noise of rock-and-roll and the sights, sounds, and turbulent emotions of the 1960s.

Journalism's movement toward a more fluid form and personal voice expanded the rules of journalistic writing to include more creative methods, wedding techniques of journalism and the novel and blurring the boundaries of fiction and nonfiction. In Wolfe's story about writing "Kandy-Kolored," he self-consciously reflects on the changes taking place in his own writing and in journalism as a whole. The New Journalism called attention to the creative potential of nonfiction writing, but the form was not entirely new. Many critics have shown that the New Journalism is just one development in a lengthy and diverse tradition of literary reportage that includes such important figures as William Hazlitt, Charles Dickens, Stephen Crane, Mark Twain, James Agee, Lillian Ross,

A. J. Liebling, and John Hersey. To varying degrees, all of these authors used narrative techniques in nonfiction writing. The New Journalism was new in the sense that it attracted a plethora of practitioners and critics in the 1960s and 1970s and declared itself a movement, explicitly challenging traditional practices and calling attention to its potential as an exciting and influential genre.

Tom Wolfe not only wrote some of the most influential New Journalistic works, but he also offered critical commentary and examples as the coeditor of an anthology called *The New Journalism* (1973). His interpretation greatly influenced the development and perception of the form. Wolfe described the fiction of the 1960s as "neo-fabulism" and listed its conventions as "No Background, No Place Name, No Dialogue, and the Inexplicable." In the midst of a literary revolution in which postmodern writers like Thomas Pynchon and John Barth began writing mythical and allegorical texts more tangentially related to historical reality, Wolfe and other New Journalists sought to recuperate the techniques of social realism as practiced by such writers as Honoré de Balzac and John Steinbeck in order to convey the rich and diverse social world of the late twentieth century. Wolfe defined the New Journalism according to realist writing strategies adapted by nonfiction writers: scene construction, dialogue, third person point of view, and the inclusion of status details like clothing and mannerisms.

Wolfe credited longtime journalist Gay Talese with introducing him to the possibilities of such techniques. Although Talese thoroughly researches his essays and interviews, they read as if they were short stories, including dialogue instead of direct quotations, exploring the interior thoughts of characters, and showing subjects interacting with their surroundings. For example, in an interview with Floyd Patterson, the boxer reveals intimate details of his life, telling Talese how it feels to be knocked out and why he avoids looking other fighters in the eye (otherwise he might not want to fight them). Rather than narrating the boxer's life, Talese shows him interacting with the places and people around him. The story depicts Patterson moving from one scene of action to another: running and throwing punches as he emerges from his training camp; speaking with a fan on the street; and relaxing in his apartment, with boxing trunks

Gay Talese.
(*Hulton Archive/Getty Images*)

drying in front of the fireplace. We begin to understand the complexity of character through the revelations of dialogue, scene, and point of view.

STYLE

Tom Wolfe's famously experimental vocabulary, alliteration, phrases from pop culture, long sentences, and unusual punctuation contribute to the feeling that we are in the mind of his characters and convey an immediacy and spontaneity of expression. Wolfe has remarked that he "found that things like exclamation points; italics; abrupt shifts (dashes) and syncopations (dots) helped give the illusion not only of a person talking but a person thinking." In *The Electric Kool-Aid Acid Test* (1968), Wolfe describes a crowd awaiting the Beatles from the point of view of various members of the audience. His unusual punctuation and use of onomatopoeia draw the readers into the crowd and convey the tremendous energy of participants. The following quotation is all one sentence, one gasp of pent-up anticipation and frantic release:

Each group of musicians that goes off the stage—the horde thinks *now* the Beatles, but the Beatles don't come, some other group appears, and the sea of girls gets more and more intense and impatient and the screaming gets higher, and the thought slips into Norman's flailing flash-frayed brain stem :::: the human lung cannot go beyond this :::: and yet when the voice says *And now—the Beatles*—what else could he say?—and out they come on stage—*them*—John and George and Ringo and uh the other one—it might as well have been four imported vinyl dolls for all it was going to matter—that sound he thinks cannot get higher, it doubles, his eardrums ring like stamped metal with it and suddenly *Ghhhhhhwooooooooowwwwww*, it is like the whole thing has snapped, and the whole front section of the arena becomes a writhing, seething mass of little girls waving their arms in the air, this mass of pink arms, it is all you can see, it is like a single colonial animal with a thousand waving pink tentacles—it *is* a single colonial animal with a thousand waving pink tentacles,—vibrating poison madness and filling the universe with the teeny agony torn out of them.

The punctuation marks demonstrate pauses in Norman's thinking and intensify the action throughout the passage, moving from three sequential colons to four, long dashes like holding one's breath while the Beatles emerge, and then the *Ghhhhhwoooooooooowwwwww* of release as the crowd goes wild. We move further and further into the observer's consciousness, hearing the ringing of his eardrums and seeing what he sees: the "seething mass of little girls waving their arms in the air." Through such undefined punctuation and visually audible words, Wolfe places the reader within a sensory world, one where we hear and see and feel as if we are in the audience.

THE MEDIA AND TRADITIONAL JOURNALISM

Although Wolfe defines the New Journalism by the techniques it uses and the forms it follows, it might be helpful to understand this new form in terms of what it does not do. To some extent, the New Journalism is less a creation of new methods and boundaries than a rejection of limiting, prescribed writing techniques. As Nicolaus Mills has suggested in *The New Journalism: A Historical Anthology* (1974), "A who, what, where, when, why style of reporting could not begin to capture the anger of a black power movement or the euphoria of a Woodstock." Many journalists felt that the detached, objective, and formulaic approach of traditional journalistic practices could not express the rebelliousness, confusion, and cultural questioning of Vietnam War protests, the civil rights movement, the women's movement, and the growing drug culture in the United States. While still claiming adherence to factual accuracy, New Journalists embraced subjectivity and resisted the inverted pyramid taught in journalism classes throughout the country. When Michael Herr published his personal account of time spent with soldiers at the war front in Vietnam, he remarked, "The press got all the facts (more or less); it got too many of them. But it never found a way to report meaningfully about death, which of course was really what it was all about." In *Dispatches* (1977), Herr does "report meaningfully," not by presenting statistics in decreasing order of importance but by recording his personal relationships with men in combat.

Similarly, works like Tom Wolfe's *The Electric Kool-Aid Acid Test* (1968) and Hunter S. Thompson's *Fear and Loathing in Las Vegas* (1971) sought to convey America's counterculture on its own terms, intimately exploring the drug culture from within. Thompson's work, in particular, shows how a more traditional journalistic approach makes 1960s America less comprehensible. Thompson and his drug-filled escapades become the central subject of *Fear and Loathing*. Trying to decide how to leave town quickly after accumulating thousands of dollars in room service

charges at a Las Vegas hotel, the reporter struggles to peruse the newspaper calmly. He reads:

TRIO RE-ARRESTED IN BEAUTY'S DEATH
An overdose of heroin was listed as the official cause of death for pretty Diane Hamby, 19, whose body was found stuffed in a refrigerator last week, according to the Clark County Coroner's office. Investigators of the sheriff's homicide team who went to arrest the suspects said that one, a 24-year-old woman, attempted to fling herself through the glass doors of her trailer before being stopped by deputies. Officers said she was apparently hysterical and shouted, "You'll never take me alive." But officers handcuffed the woman and she apparently was not injured.

This traditional news story, telling the who, what, when, and where in the first paragraph, leaves us with a resounding "Why?" There is no answer to this question and the attempt to fit this incredible story into the rigid form of traditional journalistic patterns remains unsatisfying and jarring. The objective phrases of formal newspaper language, such as "apparently hysterical" and "official cause of death," convey none of the shocking absurdity of the event. In contrast, Thompson's writing speaks to the confusion and tumultuousness of the political and social world with informal language, fluid form, and characters who continually travel across the country, looking for meaningful answers to life's questions.

The resounding rejection of traditional forms does not lead to a clearly categorized and easily defined set of New Journalistic practices. Rather, it brings journalists into an inventive period of fascinating experimentation and transgression of stylistic boundaries.

THE NONFICTION NOVEL

Well-known novelists joined reporters in creating and defining the New Journalism in its early stages. Truman Capote's *In Cold Blood: A True Account of a Multiple Murder and Its Consequences* appeared in serial form in *The New Yorker* in 1965, and then in book form in 1966. This immensely popular work revived Capote's career and elevated nonfiction writing in the view of the book-buying public. Capote remarked that he turned to nonfiction because he "wanted to produce a journalistic novel, something on a large scale that would have the credibility of fact, the immediacy of film, the depth and freedom of prose, and the precision of poetry." Nevertheless, he distanced himself from the New Journalism and declared *In Cold Blood* an entirely new form, the "nonfiction novel."

In order to re-create an accurate account of murder in novel form, Capote conducted extensive interviews and studied public documents to expose the minds of the criminals and the fears of the townspeople. He recreated the scene of the murder, conversations between participants, and the thoughts of the killers. Capote's obvious absence when the murder took place and his inclusion of dialogue and characters' thoughts initiated a far-reaching critical debate about the possibilities and problems of the New Journalism. How could his witnesses remember exactly what they thought or said? How could Capote trust his sources and record them accurately? Capote, however, both defended the accuracy of his account and questioned the possibility of complete objectivity. He spent six years becoming intimately involved with the lives of the criminals, reading about crime, interviewing murderers, training himself to memorize conversations, and relentlessly interviewing witnesses and participants.

Although Norman Mailer initially called Capote's work a "failure of imagination," demonstrating the literary world's preference for fiction, Mailer soon broke new ground with his own nonfiction writing when he won the Pulitzer Prize for *The Armies of the Night* (1968). Like Capote, he distanced himself from the New Journalism, subtitling his work, *History As a Novel/The Novel As History*, raising further questions about the relationship between fiction and nonfiction. In *The Armies of the Night*, Mailer describes an antiwar demonstration at the Pentagon. Unlike Capote, who maintains an objective distance from the events of his novel, Mailer includes himself as a primary character. He refers to himself in third-person, making Norman Mailer both a participant in and an explicit observer of a clash between protesters and police.

THE CRITICS

The New Journalism, its presence and its aspirations as a new literary genre, developed amidst tremendous controversy. Wolfe himself admitted doubts about the term "new" and outlined many important forerunners in his introduction to *The New Journalism*. Critics and naysayers like Dwight MacDonald asserted, "What is new is the pretension of our current parajournalists to be writing not hoaxes or publicity chit-chat but the real thing; and the willingness of the public to accept this pretense." The battle between New Journalists and their critics revolves around the question of newsworthiness and the power to define what is a significant part of history and worthy of public attention. Critics questioned both the importance and the accuracy of New Journalistic pieces, charging that reporters claimed the authority of factual journalism without complying with the rigor of traditional methods. According to MacDonald, "The parajournalist cozies up, merges into the subject so completely that the view point is wholly from inside, like family gossip. . . . There is no space between writer and topic, no 'distancing' to allow even the most rudimentary objective judgment, such as for factual accuracy." In response, New Journalists argued that the form does not distort the facts but, on the contrary, presents them in a more complete manner. Talese writes, "The New Journalism, though often reading like fiction, is not fiction. It is, or should be, as reliable as the most reliable reportage although it seeks a larger truth than is possible through the mere compilation of verifiable facts." Traditionalists, however, continued to equate fact and truth in opposition to the unreliability of fiction. In the end, this very criticism reveals the significance and power of the form. By transgressing boundaries between fact and fiction, New Journalists drew attention to literary techniques and claimed a revered space for nonfiction writing within American literature.

THE NEW JOURNALIST BEHIND THE SCENES

The New Journalism encompasses a wide variety of forms and modes, including sports writing, accounts of crimes, interviews, entertainment reports, analyses of social trends, and war correspondence. The writers of these very diverse New Journalistic works share the belief that the reporter must go beyond the surface, to become intimate with the subject of the piece, even participating if possible in events. Readers of the New Journalism often feel like they are being taken behind the scenes, observing the otherwise hidden motives and thoughts of public figures. Works by Joe McGinnis, George Plimpton, and John Sack demonstrate the diversity of New Journalistic topics—political candidates, sports teams, and combat—and the similarity of approaching these subjects with behind-the-scenes involvement. Rather than sitting down with Richard Nixon in a traditional interview or reporting on comments crafted for the press, McGinnis watched as the Nixon campaign taped several television commercials. This informal and time-consuming approach, what Gay Talese has called the "fine art of hanging out," revealed the process and development of Nixon's thoughts as well as the extent to which advisors shaped and censored his ideas. George Plimpton took this participatory involvement to a physical level, training for and playing in an exhibition game with the Detroit Lions for his book *Paper Lion* (1964). Plimpton becomes a central character in the book, and his inability to complete a single play in the exhibition game demonstrates the unique abilities and attitudes of professional football players. In *M* (1966), John Sack goes even further, risking his own life by joining (as a reporter) an infantry company in Vietnam. He gets to know the soldiers, intimately including their thoughts alongside accounts of their battles. After being harshly criticized for reporting people's thoughts, Sack sent the story to each soldier, gaining the entire troop's approval.

Gay Talese's "Flying to Dublin with Peter O'Toole" (1961) demonstrates that the expectations of intimacy require reporters to go beyond the techniques of traditional reporting. Sitting next to O'Toole on a flight to Ireland, Talese strikingly juxtaposes New Journalistic methods and traditional ones. On the airplane, the actor reveals "anger that can be sudden ('Why should I tell *you* the truth? Who are you, Bertrand Russell?') and . . . anger that quickly subsides ('Look, I'd tell you if I knew why, but I don't know, just don't know')." The exchange shows O'Toole's insecurity and doubts and allows readers to develop an understanding of the actor's evolving thoughts. But when O'Toole emerges from the plane to face "a crowd of photographers and reporters . . . flash bulbs fixed," we see an entirely different O'Toole: "He posed for pictures, gave a radio interview, bought everybody a drink; he laughed and backslapped, he was charming and suave, he was his public self, his airport self." The moral of Talese's story could be a motto for New Journalists: don't wait at the airport; get on the plane!

Perhaps the most remarkable quality of New Journalistic writing is the considerable flexibility of its styles and approaches. Certain magazines and newspapers allowed journalists the resources they needed for the form to flourish. Periodicals like *Esquire*, the *New York Herald Tribune*, the *Village Voice*, and *Rolling Stone* gave their reporters a great deal of freedom, encouraging them to dig deeply into each assignment. In 1972, Joe Eszterhas from *Rolling Stone* traveled to a small Missouri town where a hippie named Charlie Simpson had shot three people, two of them cops, and then himself. Long before the murder, the community had become divided; young "longhairs," speaking slang and listening to Jimi Hendrix, began meeting in the town square, encountering resistance from town officials who wanted to maintain the status quo. Eszterhas revealed the hostility of town traditionalists and the frustrations of young discontents by becoming a

part of both subcultures. Complete with tie, blazer, and cigar, he frequented bars and coffee shops, conversing with townspeople. When he felt that he understood their reaction to the crime, he donned blue jeans and a leather jacket and talked to Simpson's friends. Eszterhas's adaptability and awareness of his own role in the story contributes to a powerful portrayal of various points of view in Harrisonville, Missouri. He ends the story not with a simplistic statement about violence in the United States, but with a complex and confused questioning of the issues of the time, exposing a painful clash of values and ideals:

> It had been a long few days and I had scrutinized too many vivid details of four vicious killings and something in my mind flailed out now—Jesus Simpson, murderer, cold-blooded killer, compassionate, sensitive, sentimental. It could have been the fatigue or the Missouri weed or the beer mixed with wine, but I saw too many grotesqueries leaping about in that blazing bonfire.

The reporter's confusion is followed by the broken dialogue and unfinished thoughts of Simpson's friends. Like Eszterhas, many New Journalists leave their stories with questioning and uncertain endings, refusing to contain the confusion of wars, protests, drugs, and transformation in a neat and conclusive package. Instead, they urge the reader to confront the messiness, the disorder, and the pain of current events.

THE JOURNALIST AS CHARACTER

Although Wolfe saw New Journalism as a rejection of the practices of postmodern fiction, both respond to questions about objective experience through self-conscious allusions to the act of writing and the role of the author. Despite Capote's belief that "for the nonfiction-novel form to be entirely successful, the author should not appear in the work," the journalist's subjectivity enters the New Journalism in many ways, most significantly in works by Joan Didion and Hunter S. Thompson.

Joan Didion begins "John Wayne: A Love Song," published in *Slouching towards Bethlehem* (1968), with a story about going to the movies as a child. She then writes, "I tell you this neither in a spirit of self-revelation nor as an exercise in total recall, but simply to demonstrate that when John Wayne rode through my childhood, and perhaps through yours, he determined forever the shape of certain of our dreams." Didion calls attention to her own role in shaping the story and connects with the reader through references to her own thoughts, but she refuses to make herself too central in the story. Throughout the essay, she strives to illuminate the character and significance of John Wayne, and she feels the need to explain her own presence in the narrative.

Hunter S. Thompson, on the other hand, feels no need to explain himself. He takes the inclusion of the reporter to its furthest extreme, making himself the subject of his writings. Many critics have objected to Thompson's self-centered narratives, echoing Wayne Booth's comment that the thesis of Thompson's *Fear and Loathing in Las Vegas* is that "Hunter Thompson is interesting." Others, though, would happily agree, finding Thompson very interesting indeed. Nevertheless, *Fear and Loathing in Las Vegas* is not only about Thompson's travels but also about his attempts to research a story; his narratives become expositions on the process of writing a story, researching an event, and getting sidetracked time after time. In Thompson's own style of personal and participatory journalism, sometimes called "gonzo journalism," the rebel writer of the New Journalism rides with the Hell's Angels and takes psychedelic drugs, and the reader feels that writing is happening spontaneously as we watch.

LASTING INFLUENCE

Throughout the mid-1960s, Tom Wolfe offered grandiose claims for the New Journalism as a newly powerful genre that "would wipe out the novel as literature's main event." Although Wolfe's most dramatic expectations remain unfulfilled, the New Journalism has become an important and influential force in American literature. Decades after Wolfe's proclamation, writers and critics rarely use the term New Journalism to refer to contemporary writing, but its legacy continues in studies of literary journalism and creative nonfiction. Whereas Joan Didion is the only woman writer consistently included in studies of the New Journalism, broader consideration of the history of nonfiction writing has brought a greater diversity to literary discussions of the form. Most recently, the term "Way New Journalism," referring to journalism's encounter with the Internet, demonstrates the lasting

influence and significance of the New Journalism in American literature and life.

[*See also* Capote, Truman; Didion, Joan; *and* Mailer, Norman.]

FURTHER READING

Anderson, Chris. *Style as Argument: Contemporary American Nonfiction.* Carbondale, Ill., 1987. An in-depth analysis of works by Wolfe, Capote, Mailer, and Didion.

Hartsock, John C. *A History of American Literary Journalism.* Amherst, Mass., 2000. One of the best late-twentieth-century works that places the New Journalism in a historical tradition of literary journalism.

Hellmann, John. *Fables of Fact: The New Journalism as New Fiction.* Urbana, Ill., 1981. Helpful for comparing the New Journalism with fiction of the era. Hellmann offers insightful analyses of work by Mailer, Thompson, Wolfe, and Herr.

Johnson, Michael L. *The New Journalism: The Underground Press, the Artists of Nonfiction, and Changes in the Established Media.* Lawrence, Kans., 1971.

Mills, Nicolaus. *The New Journalism: A Historical Anthology.* New York, 1974. This collection contains works by many lesser-known authors, including several women writers. The anthology is organized thematically with useful introductions.

Talese, Gay, and Barbara Lounsberry, eds. *Writing Creative Nonfiction: The Literature of Reality.* New York, 1996. This collection includes classic New Journalism as well as more recent nonfiction writing. Talese's introduction is particularly engaging.

Weber, Ronald. *The Reporter as Artist: A Look at the New Journalism Controversy.* New York, 1974. An essential collection of writings about the New Journalism by New Journalists, critics, and literary analysts.

Wolfe, Tom, and E. W. Johnson, eds. *The New Journalism.* New York, 1973. An important anthology of New Journalistic works with an introduction and commentary by Wolfe.

NEW YORK SCHOOL OF POETS

by Catherine Daly

John Ashbery, Barbara Guest, Kenneth Koch, Frank O'Hara, and James Schuyler are among the leading New York School poets. Each wrote art criticism, plays, novels, and poetry in New York City during the late 1940s, 1950s, and early 1960s. Like the New York School of abstract expressionist painters for which the group of poets is named, the movement has proceeded in first, second, and third generations. The poets read and were influenced aesthetically by earlier art movement poetry such as dada and surrealist poetry. Their writing is abstract and informal. The poets have written in collaboration with each other and with visual artists. They have written long poems, encompassed art criticism in their poetry, and embraced pop culture as a subject. They have also been influential teachers of poetry.

Kenneth Koch.
(*Courtesy of the Library of Congress*)

HISTORY

The first generation of New York School painters, including Lee Krasner, Jackson Pollock, and Willem and Elaine de Kooning, began using the canvas as a field, employing aleatory techniques (those inviting chance, including paint dripping), and incorporating jazz-inspired improvisation in the late 1930s. Some of the painters were students of Hans Hoffman; others worked for Krasner as mural painters for the Works Progress Administration. The name "New York School" or "School of New York" is a reference to the nonacademic painters of the School of Paris, a group that included Chaim Soutine. The de Koonings went on to teach at Black Mountain College with Robert Creeley, a non-New York School poet who has collaborated with visual artists. The second generation of New York School painters includes Fairfield Porter, Philip Guston, Robert Rauschenberg, Jane Freilicher, Helen Frankenthaler, and Larry Rivers. In general, while these painters were affected by the gestural

abstraction of the earlier group, their work was more representational and the objects or scenes they represented were ambiguous, supporting more than one signification. They painted abstract portraits and landscapes and infused their paintings with found objects and references to pop culture before pop art.

The New York School of Poets is more of a coterie than a school, although many of the poets teach or have taught at, and most have attended, the same Ivy League institutions. The group incorporates overlapping clusters of friends and acquaintances. Like the West Coast School, the New York School is built around a coterie of homosexual men, and though women are associated with the New York School, the definition of the group according to all-male institutions and bars such as the San Remo and the Cedar has led many critics to ignore these female artists. While many academics have defined New York School poets as nonacademic, most of the writers in the second and third generation of New York School poets were students of other New York School poets in a college setting. Of course, many non-New York School poets, including John Yau, Ralph Angel, and the New York language poets Charles Bernstein and Bruce Andrews, were also students of New York School poets. John Tranter, an Australian poet who edits *JACKET*, an online journal, is in many ways a true New York School poet of the second generation, although he is outside the circles of acquaintance.

The first generation of New York School poets was drawn to minimalist form and sought to capture "life as it happens," including coincidences and random events. They incorporated references to and images from high and low culture in their work. The group was named by John Bernard Myers, director of the Tibor de Nagy Gallery and editor of the anthology *The Poets of the New York School* (1969).

Ashbery and O'Hara met through Ashbery's editorship of the *Harvard Advocate* after Koch graduated from Harvard and moved to New York City. Other writers attending Harvard immediately after World War II include Adrienne Rich, Robert Bly, and Alison Lurie. Barbara Guest met Ashbery and O'Hara through *Semi-Colon*, the magazine published by the Tibor de Nagy Gallery in New York City. James Schuyler was briefly a New York City roommate of O'Hara's.

Michael Brownstein, Sotere Torregian, and others in the second generation of New York School poets learned from the urban romanticism and informality of the first generation of poets. They deliberately set out to associate with the first-generation New York School poets. Like the preceding generation, they were interested in coterie poetry rather than official verse and collaborated with each other and with visual artists. The second generation helped found poetry institutions nationally and in New York City.

Tom Clark eventually served as poetry editor of *The Paris Review*. Ron Padgett and David Shapiro edited the 1970 anthology *An Anthology of New York Poets*, which was illustrated by Joe Brainard, and which infamously excluded all but one female New York School poet, Bernadette Mayer. Padgett has enjoyed a long career at Teachers & Writers, another New York poetry institution.

DEFINITION

John Myers's companion, Herbert Machiz, director of the Artists Theatre, matched painters creating stage sets with poets writing plays. In his introduction to his 1960 poetry anthology *The New American Poetry*, Donald Allen cited work with theater groups as a connection among the New York poets. O'Hara and Larry Rivers, Schuyler and Elaine de Kooning, Koch and Grace Hartigan, Ashbery and Nellie Blaine, Guest and Jane Freilicher, and James Merrill and Al Kress wrote and designed plays for Machiz at the Artists Theatre. While Merrill, whose use of form and meter was influenced by W. H. Auden, is a mainstream poet, Merrill and Auden both had relationships with the Tibor de Nagy Gallery and with the poets of the New York School. Merrill's long poem, *The Changing Light at Sandover*, partially written by chance and collaboration via Ouija board, is comparable to long poems written by the New York School poets. Schuyler was briefly Auden's secretary. Auden chose Ashbery's manuscript *Some Trees* (1956) for the Yale Series of Younger Poets over a manuscript by Frank O'Hara. Auden taught occasionally at Columbia University, while Koch enjoyed a long career there.

The first-generation poets collaborated with the second-generation painters to produce mixed media art. Guest, Schuyler, Ashbery, and O'Hara all wrote criticism of the first generation's works at *ARTNews*. Ted Berrigan, a poet of the second generation, wrote reviews for *ARTNews* before John Ashbery returned to the United States from France and became its executive editor. O'Hara and Schuyler both worked for the Museum of Modern Art (MoMA). Eventually, O'Hara became a MoMA curator. He collaborated closely with saxophonist-turned-painter Larry Rivers on projects that included *A City in Winter* (1952), O'Hara's first book and the first book published by the Tibor de Nagy Gallery. O'Hara wrote poems that were about paintings by Michael Goldberg and Norman Bluhm and that accompanied their print series. He also modeled for paintings by Rivers, Porter, Alice Neel, and Grace Hartigan, among others. In the latter part of his career, Rivers began writing and publishing. O'Hara collaborated with second-generation poet and painter Joe Brainard. Kenneth Koch collaborated with other poets and with painters; in fact, he was primarily interested in collaborations, not in working as an individual, in the 1950s. Schuyler lived with painter Fairfield Porter and his family for many years. Consequently, Porter painted many portraits of Schuyler.

Edwin Denby became famous for his dance criticism but also wrote New York School poetry and was one of the influences upon both Frank O'Hara and Ted Berrigan. Denby was slightly older than the first generation of poets and more closely acquainted with the first generation of painters than with the second. The Tibor de Nagy Gallery, which represents many abstract expressionist painters, still exhibits collaborations between the groups and publishes poetry.

In the late 1960s Ted Berrigan, a second-generation New York School poet, sold enrollments in the "school" for five dollars. Whether the New York School of poets is a school or coterie and whether the generations form a lineage or not is an active debate. Anthologies, relationships, and similarities in style, approach, and content define the group. The work has a relationship to visual art and criticism of visual art that goes beyond mere collaboration with visual artists. Critics do not always include essential writers of the New York School in the core group when listing New York School writers. Edward Field's poems, which share approach and content (such as monster movies) with other New York School poems, are in the New York section of Allen's *The New American Poetry*. This is the volume that first divided postmodern poets into the New York, San Francisco Renaissance, Black Mountain, and Beat groups. John Myers includes Kenward Elmslie in his anthology, although Elmslie, whose work engages sound and performance in a unique way, and who has written many librettos for theater works converted into operas, claims he is a friend, not a member, of the New York School. Harry Mathews met Ashbery in France and edited a journal with him. Furthermore, his work has appeared in several of the New York School anthologies. Still, he is better known as the American member of OuLiPo, the Organization of Potential Literature, an offshoot of 'pataphysics, than as a New York School poet.

OuLiPo, like the New York School poetic, has roots in surrealist game playing. Its member mathematicians and writers, including Italo Calvino and Georges Perec, are devoted to applying algorithms and other constraints to produce writing shaped by rule rather than chance. New York School poets have used collage or cut-ups, found poetry, and aleatory techniques in addition to directly collaborative processes. Kenneth Koch's "poem ideas" are closely related to conceptual poetry. Bernadette Mayer's influential poetry exercises are related both to Louis Zukofsky's phonetic translations of Catullus and to Koch's poem ideas. They carry Koch's concepts further into an investigation of language itself and a consideration of language as experience and poem content; her exercises were anthologized by the New York language poets.

LeRoi Jones, later Amiri Baraka, and Diane di Prima were associated with several postmodern poetry groups through editing and through the American Poet's Theatre. He is written into several New York School poems and published its writers early in their careers. Charles North, together with Schuyler, edited two anthologies of poetry by first- and second-generation New York School poets and sketches by New York School painters, including Red Coombs.

Some second-generation poets were associated directly with the older poets. Eileen Myles assisted Schuyler. David Lehman, Ron Padgett, and David Shapiro were Koch's students at Columbia University, then an all-male institution. Joseph Ceravolo, Bernadette Mayer, and Bill Berkson were Koch's students at The New School for Social Research. Others participated in the network of magazines, independent presses, anthologies, and gallery readings that gave life to New York School poetry. Sun Press published early poetry by Ron Padgett, Peter Schjeldahl, Jaimy Gordon, and Philip Lopate. Maureen Owen edited and published *Telephone* magazine and *Telephone Books*; the titles recall O'Hara's comparison

of a poem to a phone call. Lew Warsh and Anne Waldman edited the magazine *Angel Hair*, which became *United Artists* magazine and press, still publishing early in the twenty-first century. Anne Lauterbach's experimental poetry is New York School–inflected. Anne Waldman's work is performative and Beat-influenced in addition to being influenced by the New York School. Inclusion in anthologies and personal acquaintances link poets Clark Coolidge and Diane Ward with the New York School, although these poets are also closely associated with language poetry. Douglas Messerli, through his Los Angeles-based Sun and Moon Press and Green Integer Books, has published works by most of the New York School writers.

Second-generation poets Tom Clark, Bill Berkson, and Louis MacAdams relocated to the West Coast in the early 1970s and had both supportive or contentious relationships to the West Coast School poets. Anne Waldman, Lew Welch, and Ted Berrigan attended the 1965 Berkeley Poetry Conference, also attended by O'Hara. They associated with the poets and institutions supportive of the younger West Coast School writers and with the western language poets.

By the early 1970s, Clark Coolidge had moved to the Berkshires, and others closely associated with the group had moved from New York City. Ted Berrigan, through his teaching at Iowa and Yale in particular, would meet Barrett Watten, Robert Grenier, Kit Robinson, and Alice Notley. They would become interested in carrying the postmodernism of poem surfaces and language manipulation itself further through language-centered writing.

The third generation of New York School poets includes students or teachers at Columbia University, The New School for Social Research, the Teachers and Writers Collaborative, the Poetry Project at St. Marks's Church, Bard College, Brooklyn College of the City University of New York, and Naropa University in Boulder, Colorado. Many of these poets opted in by poetics or relationship. Anselm Berrigan and Edmund Berrigan, third-generation New York School poets, were sons of Ted Berrigan and Alice Notley. Lee Ann Brown and Lisa Jarnot studied with Mayer at the Poetry Project. Jordan Davis studied with Koch at Columbia.

O'Hara's death in 1966 ended the first period of New York School poetry. The second period stretched from the anthologies of 1969 and 1970, which published second-generation poets alongside first-generation poets, to Ted Berrigan's death in 1983. The third period ended with the publication of David Lehman's book, *The Last Avant-Garde*, in 1998. Both Koch and Rivers died in 2002. Ashbery and Guest were still writing as of then, collaborating with artists and reading, but their styles had been diverging from the styles of the New York School toward abstraction. The praxis and aesthetics of the New York School poetry now have a strong influence on many young poets.

CHARACTERISTICS

New York School poetics rejects many traditional forms and rejects mythology as content or model. While Guest has described all poetries as confessional, the confession and narration of the New York School poetry is not confrontational, as in the poetry of Robert Lowell, Sylvia Plath, or Anne Sexton. The poetry is dramatic but does not enact psychological drama. The abstract, intellectual poems written in plain American idiom place a value on pleasure and aesthetics. The poems are expressive: they clearly and carefully capture emotional states. The surface of the poems is elusive and allusive. The words delineate gestures and juxtapose ideas of different textures, evocative misunderstandings, and everyday events. O'Hara's poems about his urban environment, which he described as "I do this, I do that," form an autobiography. Ashbery's are allegorical in a mysterious way. Schuyler wrote intimate still lives.

Campy, ambiguous, and jazzed, this poetry is irreligious and not programmatically moral and political. During their New York period, Beats Jack Kerouac, Allen Ginsberg, and Gregory Corso were acquainted with the New York School poets, but New York School poets do not witness or espouse religious or political positions in poems, as do most Beat poets. While Kenneth Rexroth, Robert Lowell, and William Everson were conscientious objectors during World War II, Schuyler, O'Hara, and Koch were veterans of World War II who attended college on the GI Bill. Ted Berrigan was a veteran of the Korean War who also went to college on the GI Bill. O'Hara was homosexual both on the page and in person before the Stonewall Riot of 1969. The New York poets were liberal during the McCarthy era of the 1950s and were acquainted with the New York City intellectuals who founded the *New York Review of Books* in the early 1960s. Guest served as poetry editor for the leftist cultural publication *Partisan Review*.

Ashbery and Koch did academic work about and translated idiosyncratic presurrealist French writers Lautréamont (Isidore Ducasse), Raymond Roussel, and Pierre Reverdy. Ashbery and Mathews edited a journal they titled *Locus Solus* after one of Roussel's works. The poets found Russian poets Vladimir Mayakovsky and Boris Pasternak more congenial than poets and poetry receiving the approval of the New Critics in the postwar period. New York School poetry has the urbanity of Guillaume Appolinaire and the urban imagist landscape of Kay Boyle rather than the poetry of place or politics of the Fugitives. The poems are not written in order to adhere to a preceding standard or tradition. They are exploratory.

Each New York School poet and his poems display some but not all of the characteristics of New York School poets and poetry. Ashbery's work is polyvocal and allegorical. Guest's work is discontinuous and epitomizes the abstract lyric. Its lyrical beauty relates to the sense of the marvelous found in baroque poetry. She includes H.D. (Hilda Doolittle) in her influences and is more concerned with the self in history than the other poets. Schuyler did not complete a degree and began publishing poetry late in life. He writes about landscape, alternating a long-lined Whitmanian sweep and short-lined imagistic quality. Koch was a teacher and academic who, among other things, wrote parodies of academic verse, frequently using forms such as Byron's *ottava rima* or simplifications of Ariosto's baroque conceits. O'Hara had a career in art curation, specializing in abstract expressionism, and published monographs on Jackson Pollock, among others.

The poets do not typically rely on the forms and meanings of traditional verse. Instead, their poetry includes references to the theories, techniques, and thoughts used to write the poems, within the text. More poems than not are *ars poetica*, bildungsroman, process- or project-based (conceptual), or phenomenological in nature. The poets have contributed to contemporary long poetry, comic poetry, art criticism, unofficial verse culture, the teaching of poetry writing, and poetics.

Among the second generation, Ted Berrigan's first major work, *The Sonnets* (1964), was a collaged and cut-up sonnet sequence, where each line was discrete in an important way. Eileen Myles became better known for her fiction and autobiographical writing than for her poetry, as did Philip Lopate. Ron Padgett has published many translations from the French, including Reverdy's poetry, and he has edited many anthologies and books, including Edwin Denby's poems.

While John Ashbery is perhaps the New York School poet who has received the most accolades, Frank O'Hara was considered to be the center of the group during his lifetime. The group has always pointed out their friendship as well as the differences in their poetics.

THREE POETS: GUEST, SCHUYLER, AND BERRIGAN

While a member of the New York School of Poets, Barbara Guest has also written the biography *Herself Defined: The Poet H.D. and Her World* (1984), as well as fiction, plays, criticism and poetry. She traces her influence from imagism through H.D.'s later works, including *Trilogy* (1973). Like the other members of the New York School, she was influenced earlier in her career by Russian poets, although more by Anna Ahkmatova than by Boris Pasternak. She has not been as prolific a poet as O'Hara, Koch, or Ashbery, but her writing is at once more various and more condensed. She was associate editor of *ARTNews* from 1951 to 1954. Like the other first-generation New York School poets, she published poetry, and wrote and produced plays in the 1950s. Her first volume, however, was not published until the early 1960s. She left Manhattan for Long Island in New York State and then Berkeley, California.

Guest has continued to collaborate with young artists. Her work is more strikingly visual, while not imagistic, than the poetry of the other writers. She makes less use of pop cultural references and emotion than do the other writers.

James Schuyler's mental illness resulted in several psychotic episodes for which he was hospitalized. Despite this, he wrote two novels, in addition to the one in collaboration with John Ashbery, and plays, and he was published in New York School poetry anthologies and small journals for decades before his first full-length book was published in 1969. He did not give a public reading until 1988, three years before he died. He had especially close relationships with painters Darragh Park, his literary executor, and Fairfield Porter and Porter's family. Schuyler worked as a writer for *ARTNews* and worked briefly at MoMA.

His use of landscape and repetition recalls the imagists. Although they are not representative poets, some New York School poets are associated with imagist poets through a shared interest in the surface of the poem and in signs that reference more than one meaning, whether through allegory or pun.

Ted Berrigan was one of the leading second-generation New York School poets until his death in 1983. While at the University of Tulsa after his service in Korea, he met Ron Padgett, Joe Brainard, Dick Gallup, Tom Clark,

and Maureen Owen. In 1960, when Ron Padgett was admitted to Columbia University, Berrigan and eventually the remainder of the group followed. In New York City they met Anne Waldman, Lew Welch, Bernadette Mayer, Clark Coolidge, and other St. Mark's Place denizens. Padgett and Berrigan edited the influential mimeographed zine *C*. While his second wife, Alice Notley, attended Barnard, Berrigan did not meet Notley until he taught at the Iowa Writer's Workshop, where Notley earned a master of fine arts degree in fiction in 1969.

Berrigan's best-known work is his first book, *The Sonnets*, first published in 1964. Under the influence of Auden and like many of the first-generation poets who were also influenced by Auden in this regard, Berrigan used the names of friends to make his poems direct and intimate. His collaborators included the artists George Schneeman and Joe Brainard.

ART CRITICISM

Many of the poets, accustomed to interpreting art and familiar with the futurist manifesto and the various surrealist manifestos, have written poetics statements. Others, including Ashbery, have avoided making such statements about their own work although they write about other poetry, particularly about writings of the other New York School poets. Frank O'Hara wrote two notable poetics statements in 1959: "Personism: A Manifesto" and a statement published in *The New American Poetry* anthology. "Personism: A Manifesto" was reprinted in the introduction to *An Anthology of New York Poets* (1970) and elsewhere. In it, O'Hara claims that his poetics and opinions are in his poems, not in the manifesto, which was written as a self-assignment. It is the "opposite" of Charles Olson's "Projective Verse" essay. That is, O'Hara writes statements that directly contradict or pun on Olson's statements. Around the same time the West Coast poet Jack Spicer compared a poet to a radio that received and broadcast poems, meaning, that is, that the poet did not necessarily understand his poetry. O'Hara compared a poem to a telephone conversation between two people.

Schuyler mentions the influence on his work of the dominant art, painting, and of the anthology of dada poets and painters edited by painter Robert Motherwell (*The Dada Painters and Poets*, 1951) in his poetics statements. Koch's later poetry, including *Days and Nights* and *Circus II*, and his introductions to anthologies are poetics statements. Barbara Guest has written both film criticism and poetry criticism in poetry. Many critics consider John Ashbery's poetry to be primarily about the writing of poetry. Among the second generation of poets, Peter Schjeldahl, Marjorie Welish, Bill Berkson, David Shapiro, and John Perreault have written art criticism.

LONG POEMS

Most New York School poets have written long poems. Schuyler's *The Morning of the Poem* is possibly the most important New York School long poem because it typifies many of the characteristics of the school's poetry, including naturalness (not naturalism), discovered structure, and engagement with landscape and thought rather than place. Schuyler wrote two novels, *What's for Dinner?* (1978) and *Alfred and Guinivere* (2001). In collaboration with John Ashbery, he wrote *A Nest of Ninnies* (1969). Ashbery has written many long and book-length poems, including *Flow Chart* (1991), "A Wave," and *Girls on the Run* (1999). O'Hara's "Second Avenue" (1960) and "Ode to Michael Goldberg('s Birth and Other Births)" are long poems investigating the applicability of surreal imagery and liberation from the left margin. Koch's *Ko; or, A Season on Earth* (1960) is a book-length poem. *The Duplications* is his longest poem.

Alice Notley wrote the book-length poem *Descent of Alette* (1996) and the long series *Disobedience* (2001), which explore a female nonheroic epic. Bernadette Mayer's book-length poem, *Midwinter Day* (1982), was written on a single day. David Lehman has written two book-length sequences, *The Daily Mirror* (2000) and *The Evening Sun* (2002), which collect the daily poem he has written since 1996. Barbara Guest's *Seeking Air* (1978) is a novel as postcubist collage. Koch wrote a novel, *The Red Robins* (1975), which was later produced as a play, and the book *One Thousand Avant Garde Plays* (1988).

Koch's sound-based long poem, *When the Sun Tries to Go On*, was an exercise in lyric extension suggested by O'Hara. The imagery in O'Hara's *Second Avenue* is surreal and liberated from the left margin. *Europe*, Ashbery's first long poem, collaged text from a World War I book for teenage girls called *Beryl of the Biplane* (1917). Later, he titled a book *Girls on the Run* (1999) after a collage book written by the outsider artist Henry Darger. Repetition of details loosely inspired by canzone forms is what structures Schuyler's *The Morning of the Poem*. Other New York School long poems use diaries, telephone conversations, letters, and more recently e-mails and customer satisfaction survey cards as forms. Many of the poems' forms are discovered during the writing process. Joe Brainard's collection *I Remember* (2001) began with a self-imposed assignment

to write a number of lines that began with the title words. The assignment has since become a popular one in poetry workshops. The New York School long poem compares to the large canvas of the abstract expressionist painters.

HUMOR AND GENRES

There is a continuing debate about the extent to which comic poetry and occasional verse are light verse. Some of O'Hara's and Koch's poetry is light verse. More of it is truly funny or has a sublimely light sound, form, and tone. O'Hara's *Ode to Michael Goldberg('s Birth and Other Births)* is a birthday poem. His book *Lunch Poems* (1964), published in Lawrence Ferlinghetti's City Lights Press Pocket Poets Series, contains occasional poems written in midtown Manhattan. O'Hara's *The Day Lady Died*, written for Billie Holiday, is elegiac but not particularly solemn. It closes with a memory. The last phrase, mentioning "breath," converts the poem to a consideration of the death of the lyric, breath in poetry, and occasion or elegy itself. Ted Berrigan wrote a great deal of occasional verse for funerals, weddings, and birthdays. Koch's history of collaboration and postsurrealist game playing sharpens the satiric early poem *Fresh Air*. His later odes to intangibles surpass his self-imposed assignment to make a postmodern contribution to the ode. Even his serious poems are ironic in tone. Ashbery embraces culture high and low. In these ways, this postmodern poetry differs from anecdotal poetry and light verse. New York School poems refer to cartoon characters, children's books, friends, and celebrities but reject accepted modes of writing to expand the possibilities of urban verse, anticipating pop art and the era of post-Marxist cultural studies.

EDUCATION AND EXERCISES

While generally considered nonacademic or avant-garde poets, New York School poets were formally educated at competitive schools, and many of them have been teachers of writing. Kenneth Koch is widely recognized for his books teaching children, the elderly, and general readers how to read and write poetry. John Ashbery has been professor at Brooklyn College and then at Bard. Second-generation New York School poets formed the "nonacademic" academies that educated the third generation. For example, Anne Waldman was a director of The Jack Kerouac School of Disembodied Poetics at Naropa that Allen Ginsberg helped found. She was also an early codirector of the St. Mark's Poetry Project.

Koch's focus on exercises to teach writing and produce poetry has had a lasting effect in the academy across schools of poetry. The OuLiPo constraints used by Harry Mathews also influence classroom pedagogy. Ron Padgett has written books for teaching forms. Bernadette Mayer's experiments for poems are anthologized in *The* $L = A = N = G = U = A = G = E$ *Book*, edited by Bruce Andrews and Charles Bernstein, and her resulting poems have been included in Ron Silliman's anthology of experimental poetry, *In the American Tree* (1986). Conceptual poetry, poetry written according to constraints, and poetry exercises relate to the new forms used by experimental poets.

While mainstream anthologies through the 1970s ignored their work, anthologies have been key to the recognition of New York School poets. At the start of the twenty-first century, major presses such as Sun and Moon, New Directions, Farrar, Strauss and Giroux, Random House, and Penguin, along with publications including *Poetry*, *The New Yorker*, and *American Poetry Review*, publish New York School writing, as does the series of annual *Best American Poetry* anthologies edited by David Lehman. The poetry has become popular with readers who find its style, humor, and virtuoso free-verse technique a welcome relief from more stultifying verse. Experimental poets enjoy the difficult aspects of this poet's poetry. The poetry challenges critics, poets, and readers who seek engagement through a tradition or canon rather than an individual experience of the world.

[*See also* Ashbery, John; Gay Literature: Poetry and Prose; *and* Long Poem, The.]

FURTHER READING

Allen, Donald M., ed. *The New American Poetry*. New York, 1960. Groundbreaking anthology.

Lehman, David. *The Last Avant-Garde: The Making of the New York School of Poets*. New York, 1998.

Messerli, Douglas, ed. *From the Other Side of the Century: A New American Poetry, 1960–1990*. Los Angeles, 1994. Interesting successor to *The New American Poetry*.

Myers, John Bernard, ed. *The Poets of the New York School*. Philadelphia, 1969. Anthology by the director of the Tibor de Nagy gallery.

Padgett, Ron, and David Shapiro, eds. *An Anthology of New York Poets*. New York, 1970.

Perloff, Marjorie. *Frank O'Hara: Poet among Painters*. New York, 1977.

FRANK NORRIS

by Jan Goggans

Benjamin Franklin Norris Jr., the man who would become the writer Frank Norris, was born on 5 March 1870 in Chicago, Illinois, to Benjamin Norris and Gertrude Doggett. A scant thirty-two years later he died after fictively returning to Chicago, the setting for his final novel, *The Pit* (1903). During that span Norris wrote a collection of essays, verse, and novels that placed him for many years among the ranks of America's most famous and highly regarded writers. While Norris's reputation ultimately receded and he became less well-known than some of his contemporaries—such as Stephen Crane and the groundbreaking American writers who came a few decades after him—*The Pit, McTeague* (1899), and *The Octopus* (1901) are still widely read, taught, and discussed in the journals of literary scholarship.

Of those three novels, *The Octopus*, a study of the policies and politics behind California's great agricultural concerns, has been the most enduring, partly because of late-twentieth-century scholarship that focused on the role of literature in shaping our responses to the wilderness, and particularly the western landscape. Responses to Norris's writing at that time, however, looked not only at the content of his novels but at the philosophy that drives his plot and characterizations. In these analyses, the difficulties of limiting a writer to a certain genre became evident, for Norris was alternatively classified as a naturalist, a realist, a romantic, and a transcendentalist. Far from posing a problem, however, the discussion pointed to Norris's value as an American writer. It is because of the rich vein of philosophical thought found within his novels, and the wealth of historical detail they afford, that they remain as relevant

Frank Norris.
(*Courtesy of the Library of Congress*)

and important as they were in the early twentieth century.

FROM ARTIST TO WRITER

Norris's personal life has been studied as much, and with as diverse results, as his writing. On the surface he lived a relatively uneventful, if privileged, childhood. Born into a wealthy family, Norris—whose infant sisters died right before and after his birth—remained an only child until his brother Lester was born in 1878. A second brother, Charles, who would also become a writer, was born in 1881. The eight years Norris spent as a coddled only child led most to believe that he had received all the attention and pampering necessary to make a child happy, and for many years critics and readers agreed with his biographer, Franklin Walker, that Norris's wealthy upbringing, good looks, and free-ranging education had made him "naturally optimistic." Subsequent and deeper explorations into his psychological makeup and his family's difficulties have, however, led to a reassessment of Norris's inner life and its potential effect on his novels and stories. Beginning in 1969, William Dillingham, basing his work on research in Norris's archives, began to reconstruct the Norris family history in a way that made it seem less benign.

In 1884, when Norris was fourteen, the family moved west, first to Oakland and then San Francisco, where they purchased an expensive house on Sacramento Street. His mother, a former schoolteacher and stage actress, was sensitive, cultured, and artistic; she soon established herself among San Francisco's circle of art patrons, becoming a social success. His father, who had as a young man apprenticed himself to a Chicago jeweler and ultimately became the head of a large wholesale jewelry house, was quite literally a self-made man, someone who, without the benefit of any formal education, worked his way to financial success. He was not, however, a patron of the arts. The tension between two basically incompatible parents was a constant in their children's lives. As a teenager, Norris went to an exclusive college preparatory school at Belmont but dropped out after breaking his arm playing football. After a very brief attempt to study business at Boys' High School, he entered the San Francisco Art Association. Encouraged by a family friend, Norris pursued painting in London and Paris. Immersed in Parisian culture, he became infatuated with Jean Froissart's late medieval *Chronicles*. Reading the book was, his brother Charles wrote, "his daily recreation," a pursuit which led him to become "so imbued with the spirit of medievalism" that he was able to point out to his younger brother an anachronistic error in the armor worn by a character in Sir Walter Scott's *Ivanhoe* (1819).

It was during this time, according to Charles Norris, that his brother first began to write, a novel, "Robert d'Artois," that was the result of the many long hours the two boys spent playing with lead soldiers, the older brother spinning endless adventure tales about the toy soldiers. When Norris's parents took Charles back to San Francisco, leaving the older son in Paris, Charles received regular installments of a second never-published novel from his older brother, its pages "profusely illustrated with pencil sketches, mostly of myself as an esquire, a man-at-arms, an equerry, and finally as a knight. Plots and episodes from the works of Scott, Francis Bacon, Frank Stockton and others were lifted bodily, sometimes the actual wording was borrowed." Later, the older Norris would refer back to this attempt in the dedication he wrote for *The Pit*: "In memory of certain lamentable tales of the round (dining-room) table heroes; of the epic of the pewter platoon, and the romance-cycle of 'Gaston le Fox,' which we invented, maintained, and found marvelous at a time when we both were boys."

When his painting career did not materialize, Norris came back to California. His first paid published piece, "Clothes of Steel," appeared in the *San Francisco Chronicle* for 31 March 1889, and in 1890 he entered the University of California in Berkeley. It was while he was a college student that Norris's parents divorced after years of tension. During his sophomore year he published—with financial assistance from his mother—a three-canto poem, *Yvernelle: A Legend of Feudal France* (1892). The

publishers offered it during the Christmas season as a sort of coffee-table book, complete with lush illustrations and handsome binding. Norris was active in Phi Gamma Delta and constantly wrote for and published pieces in the campus newspaper. His course work was mainly in English and French. It was through these courses that Norris discovered the French writer, Émile Zola, considered for many years to have had the greatest influence on Norris. Most agree that Norris's novels all illustrate the technical influence of Zola, whose realistic descriptions have been characterized by some as microscopic in detail. There is greater debate over the degree to which Norris's writing reflects Zola's relentlessly deterministic philosophy. Some critics have pointed to course work Norris did with Professor Joseph Le Conte, a geologist and zoologist whose classes sought to reconcile the theory of evolution and traditional religious concepts of humankind, as having had a profound enough impact on Norris to permanently blunt Zola's pessimism. A discussion in Lawrence E. Hussman's *Harbingers of a Century: The Novels of Frank Norris* (1999), however, points to the difficulty in tracing the exact philosophical influences on Norris. Hussman looks at two early short stories—"Lauth," published in the *Overland Monthly* in 1893, and "The Puppets and the Puppy," published in *The Wave* in 1897—in order to locate the sources of Norris's later explorations of fate, free will, and the relationship between humankind and the forces of nature.

TOWARD A PHILOSOPHIC STANCE

According to Hussman, "Lauth" is Norris's most overtly optimistic work, one that in its exploration of the workings of the human soul suggests the Le Contian philosophy Norris studied at Berkeley. The title character discovers during a riot that he is capable of killing, and regresses to the savage condition of his Celtic ancestors. He is then killed, but soon after a doctor brings him back to "life." He never returns to humanity, however, for after reaching a condition close to his former existence, Lauth regresses through the ranks of the lower animals, ultimately sinking to the level "wherein the line between vegetable and animal cannot be drawn." The whole episode causes Lauth's friend, Anselm, to believe that Lauth's reanimation and subsequent descent into animalism proves that the soul differentiates human from beast and that "the most brutish man is still immeasurably higher than the most human brute." Such a philosophy, like Le Conte's work, attempts to construct a plausible bridge between the Darwinian chain of evolution and the Christian soul.

Hussman points out, however, that the stronger emphasis in Norris's novels—some of which retreat in various forms to what Norris in "Lauth" termed the "animal savagery latent in every human being"—is not on the soul but on humanity's subsurface animalism and its deterministic effect on people's lives.

Certainly in "The Puppets and the Puppy," the possibility that humans are brute animals, their destinies determined by a mechanistic force, drives the story. In this philosophical allegory, a lead soldier, a stuffed doll, a queen's bishop from a chess set, a toy rabbit, and a Noah's ark mannequin debate the question of what will happen when they are all "Thrown-away." The doll argues that there must be a "Boy" in whose image he is created and that the mechanism within him that cries when he is squeezed must be his immortal soul. The mannequin believes he will be temporarily discarded only to reemerge made of rosewood instead of pine. The lead soldier says he believes he will be remelted and recast "forever and ever," leading to the betterment of the race. The mechanical rabbit agrees with the doll that there is a "Boy" but that the "Boy" will not save the rabbit from "annihilation" when he is discarded. The queen's bishop believes that he has free will within the lines of the chessboard, but that a certain "Force" moves him about. For the bishop, the future holds "rot and decay" and final absorption into the elements. Moreover, within all of these points of view, each toy discusses various moral positions relating to their actions, and Hussman argues that this discussion of the individual's limited responsibility is a harbinger of Norris's ongoing attempt in his longer fiction to identify the proper moral stance in a world without religion.

The final section of the story introduces the puppy. In the midst of the toys' debate over their lack of choice in their own creation, Sobby, a fox terrier, enters the room. The dog chews up the mechanical rabbit, the doll, and the mannequin and knocks the lead soldier and the chess piece down the heat register, the bishop "mattering vaguely" about "vast, resistless forces of nature." Predictably, there is no single, agreed-upon reading of the story. It is clear, however, that it deals with the single question of free will in a determined universe. That same issue provides the constant tension in Norris's novels: Is the individual human fate determined by an impersonal force without moral authority, and if so, do humans have the obligation to define a moral position and act according to it? The differences in the critical responses to his novels consist in how the various critics and scholars interpret that force—whether, in their reading, it is a cold, imminently calculable, deterministic process or a vast, unknowable but ultimately impersonal force, or perhaps even a benign natural world that is simply beyond the grasp of an industrialized, overmechanized American society. Because of this diversity of opinions, contemporary readers can mine his fiction for a rich vein of philosophical debate.

THE NOVELS

Norris began writing novels perhaps as early as his Berkeley years. There is no doubt he was writing them during his year of postdoctoral study at Harvard, when he enrolled in writing classes and produced much of *McTeague* and a large section of what would become *Vandover and the Brute* (1914). Before Norris finished either, however, he sailed in 1895 for South Africa to write a series of articles for the *San Francisco Chronicle*. Upon arriving, he enlisted in the British army and joined in the Jameson Raid, one of the episodes that led to the Boer War. Norris caught South African fever and arrived back in San Francisco in the spring of 1896. After five weeks in bed, he took a position with the San Francisco paper *The Wave*. Sometime after that, either in October 1896 or the spring of 1897, Norris went to the Big Dipper Mine in Colfax, up in California's gold rush country. There, he finished *McTeague*, a novel that centers on a San Francisco dentist and the woman he marries—his best friend's cousin, Trina Sieppe. The deterministic bent of the novel comes early, when McTeague fights to resist "the foul stream of hereditary evil" running through his veins that urges him to molest Trina while she is under ether. Instead, he proposes and they marry. Soon after, Trina wins a lottery of five thousand dollars, and McTeague's best friend, Marcus, now convinced he, himself, wanted to marry his cousin, reports McTeague for practicing without a license. Unable to work, McTeague looks to Trina's lottery winnings, but she refuses to spend them. Enraged by her refusal to help him, a drunken McTeague breaks in on Trina in the kindergarten cloakroom where she is working, kills her, and steals her money. He flees to the gold country hills, pursued by Marcus, and on to Death Valley. In the novel's final scene, the slain Marcus is handcuffed to McTeague, who has run out of water and whose imminent death is chirped by a canary chittering feebly in the novel's last line.

McTeague's exploration of greed and the human desire to attain and possess at the price of all morality is paralleled by its analysis of the relationship between the sexes, an analysis Norris explored in two subplots of *McTeague* as well as in the next three novels he published: *Moran of the Lady Letty: A Story of Adventure Off the California Coast* (1898), *Blix* (1899), and *A Man's Woman* (1900). During that time he moved to New York City, arriving in February 1898 to accept a position reading submissions to *McClure's Magazine*. There he met William Dean Howells, who supported and encouraged Norris until the end of the latter's life. In May 1899, Norris, like fellow reporter Stephen Crane, was off to Cuba to write about the Spanish-American War. There, he contracted malaria and was sent back to San Francisco, where he married and began research for *The Octopus*. This novel, set in California, and its companion, *The Pit*, set in Chicago (the pit referring to the deep room in which stock trading occurs), look deeply and revealingly at the major philosophical issues raised in Norris's previous work: human greed; the possibility of a moral ethic in a world without moral authority; and the individual's responsibility to others, both in society and between the sexes.

Norris's biographer, Franklin Walker, writes that Norris spent a full year in writing *The Octopus*, for while other novels had often evolved on their own, he approached this one in a nearly scientific manner, carefully planning everything in advance to achieve what he called a "novel with a purpose." The novel is founded on an episode from California's history, the Mussel Slough affair, in which San Joaquin Valley farmers were dispossessed by the railroad and several farmers were killed in a subsequent riot.

Around that, Norris constructs the story of Presley, a poet spending the summer in the San Joaquin Valley in an attempt to find purpose and direction for his work, and his response to the conflict between ranchers like Magnus Derrick, an ex-governor who farms a large ranch, and the Pacific and Southwestern Railroad, which owns the titles to ranches like Derrick's. When the railroad attempts to raise its tenants' fees or evict them, an armed battle results: six men are killed, including Derrick's son and his neighbor, Annixter. Initially a rough, self-centered man who was "widely hated," Annixter—the second of three main characters in the novel—learns selflessness when he falls in love with Hilma Tree, a milkmaid, whom many critics see as a symbol of the natural world, a sort of earth goddess who is associated with the wheat itself. The third major character, Vanamee, is, according to Warren French, a "kind of latter-day Thoreau," well-read and intelligent, living the life of a recluse. He possesses a "sixth sense," as Norris calls it, which he uses to call forth the daughter of his dead lover, Angèle, who died in childbirth after being raped. This calling forth of something good, Angèle's daughter, from something evil, the rape, is articulated in Vanamee's statement at the end of novel that "through all shams, all wickednesses . . . all things surely, inevitably, resistlessly work together for good."

Although Vanamee's moral contribution to the novel has for many years caused controversy and even confusion among Norris scholars, he clearly shows the degree to which Norris indicts the California farmers, as well as the farming system. Vanamee's natural, innocent response to the land is in direct contrast to the exploitive practices that produce a false economy and ultimately wreak havoc on the land itself. At the novel's end, the false nature of the financial side of the wheat-growing industry is dramatized when S. Behrman, the railroad agent, suffocates in the hold of a wheat ship, suggesting the overriding power of the wheat itself and, for some critics, the futility of trying to harness that power.

The Pit, Norris's last novel, looks at the exploitive side of the wheat-growing industry as it is perpetuated on the Mercantile Exchange, the place in Chicago that sets the wheat prices. Even more than *The Octopus*, *The Pit* looks at the degree to which our lives are determined by brute forces beyond our control and the comparative freedom we have within that deterministic force to create moral relationships. The marriage of Laura Jadwin, an independent young woman, and Curtis Jadwin, a wealthy financial speculator, erodes increasingly as each pursues separate, selfish directions. Although she has married Jadwin for his money, Laura becomes increasingly obsessed with making him love her and, when she fails, begins to flirt with a former suitor. In the meantime, Jadwin devises a plan to corner the wheat market. Encouraged by rising wheat prices, farmers plant heavily, and unusually favorable growing conditions result in a bumper crop that Jadwin cannot corner. Warren French argues that the wheat triumphs once again over human greed but also that once again, as in *The Octopus*, some small kind of redemption exists. Jadwin's financial ruin comes on the night Laura has planned to run away with her lover, but when she sees her husband, "his eye sunken deep in his head, his face dead white, his hand shaking," and hears the newsboys outside crying the news of her husband's failure, she reaffirms her commitment to the marriage. They sell her property and go west together to start a new life.

Norris's planned trilogy of the wheat industry was never completed. He died on 25 October 1902 of a perforated appendix and peritonitis, his system undoubtedly weakened by the fevers he had contracted in South Africa and Cuba and his general neglect of his health. Probably helped by its author's death, *The Pit* sold nearly 100,000 copies in the original trade edition and in 1904 was made into a play that ran for seventy-seven performances. Norris's brother claimed that the third novel was not to be called "The Wolf," as had been announced, and that its

> pivotal episode was to deal with a famine-stricken county of Europe, and the timely appearance, from across the sea, of three huge American schooners—wheat ships—loaded to their capacity with the great crop that, in spite of the quarrels of farmers and railroads, and in spite of the manipulation of the bulls and bears on the stock market, was to fulfill its destiny as "the nourisher of nations."

Norris's great plan, never realized, was for a trilogy about the Civil War. It was to have centered on the Battle of Gettysburg.

[*See also* Naturalism and Realism.]

SELECTED WORKS

Yvernelle: A Legend of Feudal France (1892)
Moran of the Lady Letty: A Story of Adventure Off the California Coast (1898)
Blix (1899)
A Christmas in the Transvaal (1899)
McTeague (1899)
A Man's Woman (1900)
The Octopus; A Story of California (1901)
A Deal in Wheat, and Other Stories of the New and Old West (1903)
The Pit; A Story of Chicago (1903)
The Responsibilities of the Novelist, and Other Literary Essays (1903)
The Joyous Miracle (1906)
The Third Circle (1909)
Vandover and the Brute (1914)
Works (1928)
Letters (1956)
Literary Criticism of Frank Norris (1976)
Collected Letters of Frank Norris (1986)
Novels and Essays of Frank Norris (1986)
Perverted Tales: Frank Norris' 1897 Parodies of Rudyard Kipling, Stephen Crane, Bret Harte, Richard Harding Davis, Ambrose Bierce, Anthony Hope (1992)

The Apprenticeship Writings of Frank Norris, 1896–1898 (1996)
The Best Short Stories of Frank Norris (1998)

FURTHER READING

French, Warren. *Frank Norris*. New York, 1962. French looks at nearly all Norris wrote, including his criticism as well as his short stories and novels, along the way surveying most of the responses to Norris. He argues for his own reading of Norris as being far more a transcendentalist than a philosophical determinist.

Hussman, Lawrence E. *Harbingers of a Century: The Novels of Frank Norris*. Modern American Literature, vol. 21. New York, 1999. Hussman argues that Norris should be viewed as a lifelong philosophical materialist who developed an existential ethic of love for another and compassion for the other. The book covers both Norris's short stories and novels.

McElrath, Joseph R., Jr. and Katherine Knight. *Frank Norris: The Critical Reception*. New York, 1981. An interesting collection of newspaper, journal, and magazine publications responding to Norris's novels, the poem *Yvernelle*, and a handful of short stories and essays in criticism.

Walker, Franklin. *Frank Norris, A Biography*. Garden City, N.Y., 1932. Still considered to be the most comprehensive and best biography of Norris.

West, Lon. *Deconstructing Frank Norris's Fiction: The Male-Female Dialectic*. Modern American Literature, vol. 13. New York, 1998. This study expands on the more recent response to Norris's novels as more romantic than naturalistic by discussing the natural man and refined woman types in his works. West uses the archetypes of Carl Jung to establish a typology in Norris's work.

Zayani, Mohamed. *Reading the Symptom: Frank Norris, Theodore Dreiser, and the Dynamics of Capitalism*. Modern American Literature, vol. 15. New York, 1999. The book looks at the literary movement of naturalism in American fiction, tying it into capitalism as the "complex-structuring whole" from which naturalism cannot be separated. The book seeks to show how both are characterized by a dynamic property and are both, at their core, transgressive.

JOYCE CAROL OATES

by Maile Chapman

Joyce Carol Oates is a novelist, short-story writer, playwright, essayist, and poet of great intellectual complexity and stylistic range. Her body of work offers an interdisciplinary portrait of American culture that often depicts the darker aspects of human nature through psychological, physical, and sexual violence. Her prolific literary output is now legendary: she has published over one hundred books that include novels, short-story collections, novellas, books of poetry, books for children and young adults, and collections of literary criticism, reviews, and essays on topics ranging from tragedy to boxing. She

Joyce Carol Oates. (© *Bettmann/Corbis*)

has received awards and honors too numerous to catalog, including the National Book Award, the F. Scott Fitzgerald Award for Lifetime Achievement in American Literature, the PEN Malamud Award for Lifetime Achievement in the Short Story, a Bram Stoker Award for Superior Achievement in a Novel as well as for Life Achievement, a Heidemann Award for one-act plays, a Rosenthal Award from the National Institute of Arts and Letters, a Guggenheim Fellowship, the Mademoiselle College Fiction Award, and well over a dozen Pushcart Prizes. Her short fiction has appeared twenty-two times in the O. Henry Prize Stories anthologies, and she was the first recipient of an O. Henry special award for continuing achievement (1970). Her contribution to American letters extends beyond the enormous critical and popular response to her work: she has edited several anthologies of short fiction, was instrumental in establishing *The Ontario Review*, and since 1974 has managed a small press with her husband, Raymond Smith. She taught at the University of Detroit as an instructor (1961–1965) and assistant professor of English (1965–1967), and also at the University of Windsor (Ontario) as a member of the department of English (1967–1978). Since 1978 she has been writer-in-residence and currently is the

Roger S. Berlind Distinguished Professor of Humanities at Princeton University.

An academically precocious child, Oates was the first in her family to attend college, and the juxtaposition of her early education in a one-room schoolhouse with her later literary career is represented in several of her novels. Her childhood hometown of Lockport, in upstate New York (where she was born 16 June 1938), also appears often in her writing; it is sometimes described with nostalgia, but frequently poverty and violence appear as part of the social environment, and she has commented that despite the support and stability of her own family life, her memories of early violence in the economically depressed community have influenced and inspired her adult work. In 1956 she left Lockport with a scholarship to Syracuse University (from which she received the B.A. in 1960). While planning for a career in education, she continued to work steadily at her typewriter, producing several novels in a period of time that she has referred to as an "apprenticeship." Most of them remain unpublished, and many were subsequently destroyed. As an undergraduate she won the prestigious Mademoiselle College Fiction Award for her story "In the Old World," which would be included in her first published book, a collection of short stories titled *By the North Gate* (1963). Many reviews of the volume recognized her startling and original talent while singling out the violent content for debate. In fact these early stories deal with themes and preoccupations that appear throughout her later work, such as murder, suicide, rape, and violent assault, and the question of why her work contains such imagery has persisted. It was asked of her so many times that she responded in an essay titled "Why Is Your Work So Violent?," in which she exposed the essentially chauvinistic assumptions about suitable topics for "women's writing" behind the question.

Oates left Syracuse to earn her master's degree in English at the University of Wisconsin, where she met her husband, Raymond Smith. They married in 1960, and after completing their degrees the couple moved to Beaumont, Texas. She began a Ph.D. program in English at Rice University in Houston but decided to focus on writing rather than further graduate study when one of her stories was listed on the Honor Roll of Best American Short Stories. Soon after, she received notification that *By the North Gate* had been accepted for publication.

EARLY NOVELS

Oates's first published novel opened a phase of her writing that has been referred to as "psychological realism" and "American naturalism." *With Shuddering Fall* (1964) introduces Eden County, a fictionalized version of Oates's childhood landscape, which Karen Herz flees with Shar Rule, the race-car driver son of a neighbor. Their relationship is a struggle characterized by brutality and indifference, and one of their violent sexual encounters causes the pregnant Karen to miscarry. As she hemorrhages, Shar leaves for a racetrack, where he dies in a suicidal crash. The final section of the book describes Karen's subsequent breakdown and recovery in a mental institution and her eventual return to Eden County. Oates's next published novel, *A Garden of Earthly Delights* (1967), would become the first in a "triptych" of novels that examine American life from different social and economic viewpoints. Beginning with the itinerant and impoverished Walpole family traveling across the country in the 1920s and 1930s, the novel follows the life of Clara Walpole, who runs away from the poverty and uncertainty of her upbringing to seek a more secure existence. When her lover leaves her pregnant and stranded, she finds security as the mistress of a wealthy man. Violence once more complicates the relationships, and as an adult the child kills his foster father and himself, after which Clara goes insane and is committed to an institution.

Such instances of unwanted pregnancy, madness, and institutionalization in Oates's work question the limited horizons of women in difficult situations while documenting a distinctly female kind of madness, often with sexual elements. Instability, however, is not limited to female characters and also occurs in the second novel of the trilogy, which takes place among the privileged residents of a suburban community. *Expensive People* (1968) is the confession of Richard Everett, a gluttonous and repulsive young man who claims to have murdered his mother, Nada. He wants to be punished, but instead

he is diagnosed as delusional and his confession is not believed. The final novel of the triptych, *them* (1969), is the most critically acclaimed of Oates's early novels; it received the National Book Award in 1970. Based on the life of one of her students in Detroit, where Oates and her husband lived at the time of the race riots in 1967, *them* begins with Loretta, a sixteen-year-old girl living in the slums of Detroit, awakening to find her young lover dead. Realizing that her brother has murdered the boy, in her panic she is "saved" by Howard, a police officer who coerces her into having sex with him even before the body has been moved. Loretta, pregnant, marries Howard, who is later arrested for involvement in a prostitution ring, and the family is exiled. Loretta eventually takes the children back to Detroit, where she is almost immediately arrested for solicitation. And so the sordid cycle of poverty begins again and will lead her children, Maureen and Jules, into circumstances similar to those Loretta had earlier hoped to escape.

In 1967 Oates left the turmoil of Detroit for Windsor, Ontario, after accepting a teaching position at the University of Windsor. Her literary reputation now established, she continued to publish not only novels but also collections of short stories such as *The Wheel of Love* (1970) and *Marriages and Infidelities* (1972), as well as collections of essays such as *The Edge of Impossibility: Tragic Forms in Literature* (1972) and the poetry collections *Anonymous Sins* (1969) and *Love and Its Derangements* (1970). Though Oates's work was well received, some critics commented on the seeming lack of moral conclusions regarding the violence in her fiction. With *Wonderland* (1971), Oates began a shift toward addressing this issue in a novel that she has called an investigation into the "phantasmagoria" of personality. Also based on a true event, the novel follows Jesse Harte, who as a young boy survives the murderous and suicidal rage of his father that annihilates the other members of his family. As an adult, Jesse seeks replacement father figures and finds them in a series of physicians. *Wonderland* was published with two different endings, neither of which contains the kind of violent catharsis of her other novels, and one of which gives Jesse the chance to repudiate his father's act of destruction by finding and saving his runaway daughter.

THE GOTHIC NOVELS

A major stylistic change in Oates's writing is apparent in the best-selling *Bellefleur* (1980), a vivid tale that incorporates and critiques the genres of romance and historical fiction by blending historical facts with flamboyant and hallucinatory elements such as shape-shifting, clairvoyance, and vampirism. The novel was completed in Princeton, New Jersey, where Oates and her husband relocated in 1978 after she accepted a yearlong position as writer-in-residence at Princeton University that would eventually lead to the endowed chair that she holds today. Just as *Wonderland* marks the beginning of one shift in her writing, so *Bellefleur* marks another, and during her early years at Princeton, Oates wrote a series of Gothic novels that reveal her scholarly knowledge of literary convention alongside her ability to subvert the practices of different genres to describe life in America during historical periods. The first of these, *A Bloodsmoor Romance* (1982), capitalizes on the repressive narrative strategies of the romance form by telling the story of the Zinn sisters from the point of view of an elderly, thoroughly nineteenth-century female narrator who upsets everyone with an admission of unmarried motherhood. The next of these Gothic novels, "The Crosswicks Horror," takes place in Princeton during the early twentieth century; it remains, like a substantial quantity of Oates's work, unpublished. *Mysteries of Winterthurn* (1984) is a detective story in which the hero-sleuth must solve multiple outbreaks of violent murder. It is characteristic of Oates's productivity that while writing this series she also produced the realistic novel *Solstice* (1985), as well as numerous short stories unrelated to the Gothic project.

A RETURN TO REALISTIC NOVELS

Following the Gothic novels Oates published *Marya: A Life* (1986), *You Must Remember This* (1987), *Because It Is Bitter, and Because It Is My Heart* (1990), *Foxfire: Confessions of a Girl Gang* (1993), *We Were the Mulvaneys* (1996), and *Man Crazy* (1997), all of which critics have described as more visibly autobiographical than her earlier works. *Marya: A Life* is one example among many in these novels in which a female protagonist shares some of the background details of Oates's life, particularly the transition from a rural upbringing to a more intellectual or academic adulthood. Marya, raised by unsympathetic relatives in a small town, is sexually molested by an older cousin and later nearly raped by a group of male classmates during a going-away party on the night before she leaves to attend college as a scholarship student. As an adult, Marya becomes intellectually successful but unhappy in her emotional relationships, which prompts her to search for the mother who abandoned her. Intellectuals and academics also appear in *American Appetites* (1989),

which takes place in a fictionalized version of Princeton, and *Nemesis* (1990), which Oates, writing under her pseudonym of Rosamond Smith, based on a real sexual abuse scandal in the English department at Princeton.

In the 1990s Oates continued to write about disturbing and fascinating situations taken from contemporary American life. *Black Water* (1992) is a novella written from the point of view of a young woman who drowns in an accident reminiscent of the events at Chappaquiddick, in which a young woman died after an accident in a car driven by Senator Edward Kennedy. *Zombie* (1995) is based on the case of the gruesome serial killer Jeffrey Dahmer. *Man Crazy* (1997) is the story of a girl who willingly enters a cult where she is sexually used and abused by men, and *Blonde* (2000), nominated for a Pulitzer Prize, concerns the life of Norma Jean Baker, otherwise known as Marilyn Monroe. *Broke Heart Blues* (1999), like *Blonde*, examines the phenomena of celebrity and desire, in this case through the story of a teenage boy accused of murder in a small town. John Reddy Heart becomes a tragic idol, the object of intense public fascination and adoration, after he is tracked down by police in a manhunt following the shooting death of one of his mother's lovers. Another section of the book, from his perspective, gives a less romantic version of his flight, trial, and incarceration.

The tension between the external and interior lives of an individual is overtly clear in these works, and also exerts a subtle pressure in other recent novels, such as *We Were the Mulvaneys*, which has had enormous popular impact through its inclusion in Oprah Winfrey's Book Club. The Mulvaneys' initial happiness is based on solid values such as stability and love in the family home. The parents, Mike and Corinne, and the children—Mike Jr., the athlete; Patrick, the good student; Marianne, the cheerleader; and Judd, the baby of the family—have numerous affectionate nicknames for one another, and games and jokes illustrate their strong sense of themselves as a happy, lucky family envied by outsiders. But when Marianne is raped by a classmate, the family struggles, and fails, to help her and to heal itself in the face of antagonism from neighbors and former friends. As in the other novels, the characters' decline is told from behind the public façade. *Middle Age: A Romance* (2001) further examines loss and community obsession through the sudden death of Adam Berendt, a sculptor and relative newcomer to Salthill-on-Hudson, an affluent village outside New York City. His death affects the women of the village profoundly, forcing them to reexamine their life decisions. One, Marina Troy, finally accepts his gift of a secluded property where she returns to her own efforts at sculpture, a dream given up years before. Another woman vanishes, leaving her husband of many years in order to investigate the secrets of Adam Berendt's mysterious early life, and still another marries and begins a new family. The men of the community are also deeply affected, especially in their relationships to women. One of them, a jaded lawyer, finds happiness in an unexpected baby named for the deceased. Adam Berendt, sought after but reclusive in life, becomes in death an enigma with the power to change the lives of his friends, offering a positive outcome to a tragic death. This conclusion, like those of *We Were the Mulvaneys* and *Man Crazy*, has a redemptive quality that, even if tempered by tragedy, offers a more definite emotional resolution than those found in Oates's earlier novels.

SHORT STORIES

Oates is also a preeminent writer of short stories, many of which depict feelings of fear, impending violence, disintegration, loss of control, sexual unease, and anxiety. *The Wheel of Love* includes the widely anthologized "Where Are You Going, Where Have You Been?," in which Connie, a teenage girl alone in her parents' home, is visited by the stranger Arnold Friend. The two engage in a playful conversation that gradually, in classic Oatesian manner, darkens to reveal Friend's sinister, inexorable sexual intentions. The story is disturbing for its menace and psychological violence rather than for any overt act of force, and for Connie's complicity in her fate. The question of female passivity and complicity, often raised in Oates's fiction, is rarely resolved in comforting ways. The more formally experimental *Marriages and Infidelities* (1972) includes several of Oates's "re-imaginings" of masterworks of short fiction, such as "The Turn of the Screw," referring to the Henry James story of the same title. Other stories in this collection take inspiration from Franz Kafka, Henry David Thoreau, James Joyce, and Anton Chekhov, and are but a few examples of Oates's acknowledgment of her literary influences.

Other collections contain linked stories, such as *Crossing the Border* (1976), in which an American couple goes to Canada and the vicissitudes and infidelities of their relationship are subsequently examined. *The Assignation* (1988) includes "Tick," in which a woman newly separated from her husband discovers a tick embedded in her scalp. When, despite her persistent, frantic, bloody efforts, she cannot extricate it, her reactions vary from thoughts of suicide to resigning herself to a reconciliation with her husband, and the story is an example of Oates's dark, deadpan humor. Images of twins and doubles increasingly appear in Oates's work. *Heat and Other Stories* (1991) includes "Heat," in which identical twins are murdered by a slow-witted acquaintance, and "Desire," in which a middle-aged man unable to connect emotionally discovers the mummified remains of an undeveloped twin in his abdomen. The title story of *Haunted: Tales of the Grotesque* (1994) includes both doubling and the question of complicity in a story of two young girls trespassing on private property; one of them survives a terrifying, abusive encounter with sexual overtones but later sends her friend alone to the property, where she is murdered. *Faithless: Tales of Transgression* (2001) is her most recent collection, and while Oates's work always contains transgressive elements, these stories do so in new and aggressive ways, such as women meticulously planning acts of violence: one woman stalks her lover on the freeway, intending to kill them both in a crash ("Lover"), and another meditates on the weapons in her life ("Gunlove").

DEFYING CATEGORIZATION

Although some have been highlighted here for the purposes of examination, movements and phases in Joyce Carol Oates's literary work can be difficult to define. She frequently publishes realistic and fabular books within the same year, and often reexamines questions and tensions from past projects in new and innovative forms. An indication of her mastery of these multiple genres can be seen in the inclusion of her work in *The Best American Short Stories*, *The Best American Essays*, *The Best American Poetry*, *The Best American Short Plays*, and *The Best American Mystery Stories*. Regardless of the outdated complaints of some critics against her productivity and her ability to write in so many literary forms, the range and depth of her oeuvre have made her undeniably, and deservedly, one of the most distinguished and celebrated American authors.

[*See also* Short Story in America, The.]

WORKS

NOVELS

With Shuddering Fall (1964)
A Garden of Earthly Delights (1967)
Expensive People (1968)
them (1969)
Wonderland (1971)
Do with Me What You Will (1973)
The Assassins (1975)
Childwold (1976)

Son of the Morning (1978)
Cybele (1979)
Unholy Loves (1979)
Bellefleur (1980)
Angel of Light (1981)
A Bloodsmoor Romance (1982)
Mysteries of Winterthurn (1984)
Solstice (1985)
Marya: A Life (1986)
You Must Remember This (1987)
American Appetites (1989)
Because It Is Bitter, and Because It Is My Heart (1990)
Nemesis (1990)
Black Water (1992)
Foxfire: Confessions of a Girl Gang (1993)
What I Lived For (1994)
Zombie (1995)
We Were the Mulvaneys (1996)
Man Crazy (1997)
My Heart Laid Bare (1998)
Broke Heart Blues (1999)
Blonde (2000)
Middle Age: A Romance (2001)
Beasts (2002)

"ROSAMUND SMITH" NOVELS

Lives of the Twins (1987)
Soul/Mate (1989)
Nemesis (1990)
Snake Eyes (1992)
You Can't Catch Me (1995)
Double Delight (1997)
Starr Brigade Will Be with You Soon (1999)
The Barrens (2001)

SHORT-STORY COLLECTIONS

By the North Gate (1963)
Upon the Sweeping Flood and Other Stories (1966)
Cupid and Psyche (1970)
The Wheel of Love (1970)
Marriages and Infidelities (1972)
A Posthumous Sketch (1973)
The Girl (1974)
The Goddess and Other Women (1974)
Plagiarized Material (1974)
The Poisoned Kiss (1975)
The Poisoned Kiss and Other Stories from the Portuguese (1975)
The Seduction and Other Stories (1975)
The Blessing (1976)
Crossing the Border (1976)
Daisy (1977)

Night-Side (1977)
The Step-Father (1978)
All the Good People I've Left Behind (1979)
The Lamb of Abyssalia (1979)
A Middle-Class Education (1980)
A Sentimental Education (1980)
Funland (1983)
Last Days (1984)
Wild Saturday and Other Stories (1984)
Wild Nights (1985)
Raven's Wing (1986)
The Assignation (1988)
Heat and Other Stories (1991)
Where Is Here? (1992)
Where Are You Going, Where Have You Been? (1993)
Haunted: Tales of the Grotesque (1994)
Demon and Other Tales (1996)
"Will You Always Love Me?" and Other Stories (1996)
The Collector of Hearts: New Tales of the Grotesque (1998)
Faithless: Tales of Transgression (2001)

NOVELLAS

The Triumph of the Spider Monkey (1976)
I Lock My Door upon Myself (1990)
The Rise of Life on Earth (1991)
First Love: A Gothic Tale (1996)

POETRY

Women in Love and Other Poems (1968)
Anonymous Sins (1969)
Love and Its Derangements (1970)
Woman Is the Death of the Soul (1970)
In Case of Accidental Death (1972)
Wooded Forms (1972)
Angel Fire (1973)
Dreaming America and Other Poems (1973)
The Fabulous Beasts (1975)
Public Outcry (1976)
Abandoned Airfield 1977 (1977)
Season of Peril (1977)
Snowfall (1978)
Women Whose Lives Are Food, Men Whose Lives Are Money (1978)
Celestial Timepiece (1980)
The Stone Orchard (1980)
Nightless Nights: Nine Poems (1981)
Invisible Woman: New and Selected Poems, 1970–1982 (1982)
Luxury of Sin (1984)
The Time Traveler (1989)
Tenderness (1996)

ESSAYS

The Edge of Impossibility: Tragic Forms in Literature (1972)
The Hostile Sun: The Poetry of D. H. Lawrence (1973)
New Heaven, New Earth: The Visionary Experience in Literature (1974)
Contraries (1981)
The Profane Art: Essays and Reviews (1983)
On Boxing (1987)
(Woman) Writer: Occasions and Opportunities (1988)
George Bellows: American Artist (1995)
Where I've Been, and Where I'm Going: Essays, Reviews and Prose (1999)

SELECTED PLAYS

Miracle Play (1974)
Three Plays (1980)
I Stand before You Naked (1991)
In Darkest America (Tone Clusters and The Eclipse) (1991)
Twelve Plays (1991)
The Perfectionist and Other Plays (1995)
New Plays (1998)

CHILDREN'S AND YOUNG ADULT LITERATURE

Come Meet Muffin! (1998)
Big Mouth and Ugly Girl (2002)

FURTHER READING

Bender, Eileen Tepper. *Joyce Carol Oates: Artist in Residence*. Bloomington, Ind., 1987.

Bloom, Harold, ed. *Modern Critical Views: Joyce Carol Oates*. New York, 1981.

Friedman, Ellen G. *Joyce Carol Oates*. New York, 1980. Particularly helpful in locating Oates's early novels in American culture and literary tradition.

Johnson, Greg. *Invisible Writer: A Biography of Joyce Carol Oates*. New York, 1998. The definitive biography; a well-researched and insightful portrait of Oates's professional and personal life.

Milazzo, Lee, ed. *Conversations with Joyce Carol Oates*. Jackson, Miss., 1989. A compilation of interviews with Oates in which she discusses her life, her art, literature, and popular culture, this collection also gives the reader a sense of the often repeated questions regarding her productivity and the violent content in her writing.

Souther, Randy. *Celestial Timepiece: A Joyce Carol Oates Home Page*. <http://storm.usfca.edu/~southerr/jco.html>. This Web site offers the most up-to-date information about Oates's frequent publications and other aspects of her career; it includes links to reviews and other sites of interest.

OBJECTIVISM (REZNIKOFF, ZUKOFSKY, OPPEN)

by David Gunton

The objectivist poets—a loose association of American writers named by the poet Louis Zukofsky—distinguished themselves by a common objection to poetic excess and a trademark devotion to representing the world exactly as it is. The group was principally composed of Zukofsky, Charles Reznikoff, and George Oppen, the three of whom embarked on a series of publishing ventures together in the early 1930s, and also included Carl Rakosi and Lorine Niedecker, both of whom admired Zukofsky's aesthetic program and whose own careers were launched in part by his advocacy.

Zukofsky concocted the term "objectivist" at the request of the influential *Poetry* editor Harriet Monroe, and the objectivists would spend the rest of their careers questioning, qualifying, or openly rejecting the label. The zenith of the objectivist movement was a 1931 objectivist issue of *Poetry* guest-edited by Zukofsky at the request of his and Monroe's common acquaintance Ezra Pound. Monroe believed the issue would sell more copies if the writers whom Zukofsky assembled belonged to some kind of movement, and she implored him to brand them as such in his introduction. In coining "objectivism," Zukofsky may well have been thinking of Reznikoff's sparse lyrical fragments (his preface was adopted from an essay-in-progress on Reznikoff) or Oppen's equally minimalist urban images, but his declaration was nevertheless met with uniform surprise and disapproval. "His [Zukofsky's] aloof tone, the distant hauteur, the reasoning and language icily severe and rebuffing, I found that disturbing," Rakosi would later say of Zukofsky's manifesto (1983, p. 80).

The objectivists displayed an unusual and mostly unwitting knack for paradox. They were obsessed with writing clearly, yet produced some of the most notoriously difficult poetry of the twentieth century. Each was profoundly politically active but believed politics had no place in poetry and poetry no power to effect change in politics. While actively publishing together in the 1930s they attracted almost no critical or commercial attention whatsoever, yet each went on to produce master works in the 1960s and 1970s, thirty to forty years after

"objectivism" had fallen off the critical map. None were ever considered the preeminent poet of their day. But their accidental movement tells a compelling story of literary hijinks, personal integrity, and unique poetic accomplishment.

MYTHOLOGY

George Oppen and Louis Zukofsky met in New York City in 1928, when they were in their early twenties. Oppen and his wife, Mary, were concluding their elopement, having left their families in California; driven across country; married in Dallas, Texas; and settled in New York to pursue their literary ambitions on a modest annual income that Oppen inherited upon turning twenty-one. Zukofsky had recently received his master's degree in English from Columbia University and was looking for teaching work while writing admiring letters to his hero, Ezra Pound. Zukofsky and Oppen were enthusiastic disciples of America's modernists and desired to apply their predecessors' aesthetic principles to a suitable, clearly defined poetic form. The two would take long walks together on the Upper West Side, and with Mary would go to Coney Island to play in the ocean and ride the rides. Their mutual admiration for a poet several years their senior, Charles Reznikoff, soon brought them in contact with "Rezy," who by then had self-published several volumes of his own poetry and, as a graduate of New York University's law school, was working for *Corpus Juris*, an encyclopedia of law for lawyers. The three became fast friends.

As with all young poets, the thing to do was to set up a publishing operation and begin proselytizing, and in 1929 the Oppens moved to France and founded To Publishers on George's allowance. Shortly thereafter Zukofsky's persistent and appreciated correspondence with Pound led to Harriet Monroe's consent to an objectivist *Poetry* issue. The February 1931 volume included poems by Oppen and Reznikoff, the beginning sections of Zukofsky's lifelong poem "A," Zukofsky's controversial introduction, and two poems by a little-known Wisconsin poet,

Carl Rakosi. Other contributors included William Carlos Williams, Kenneth Rexroth, John Wheelwright, and Whittaker Chambers, some of who regarded Zukofsky's objectivism with enthusiasm and others with sarcastic disdain. In 1932 To Publishers published An "Objectivists" Anthology, a selection of poems from the Poetry issue coupled with new poems by the likes of T. S. Eliot, Basil Bunting, and Pound. Zukofsky prefaced the Anthology with a lengthy, spirited qualification of his Poetry preface. "The interest of the issue was in the few recent lines of poetry which could be found, and in the craft of poetry, NOT in a movement," Zukofsky wrote. "The contributors did not get up one morning all over the land and say 'objectivists' between tooth-brushes" (p. 12). He alluded to Vladimir Lenin's contention that it is better to have lived through a revolution than to write about one.

If the objectivist Poetry issue created but a small splash in the literary world, the Anthology produced barely a ripple. What reaction it did engender was condemnation from the critical powers that be. "Mr. Zukofsky's preface is so badly written that it is next to impossible to disentangle more than a few intelligible remarks," wrote Yvor Winters, whose New Criticism school would thoroughly outmaneuver the objectivists in the national aesthetic debate (Winters, 1973, p. 133). After publishing Williams's A Novelette and Other Prose (1932) and Pound's How to Read (1931) and The Spirit of Romance (1931), Oppen folded To Publishers, which he had entirely financed himself (and had even paid Zukofsky a nominal salary as editor), and returned with Mary to New York. But they, Williams, Reznikoff, and Zukofsky would soon reincorporate themselves as the Objectivist Press, a collective operation in which each author covered the costs of publishing his own book. The Press produced Williams's Collected Poems, 1921–1931 (1934), with a preface by Wallace Stevens; three books by Reznikoff; and Oppen's first book, Discrete Series (1934), which included a preface by Pound. Zukofsky, who would always have trouble finding publishers interested in his work, was not able to publish any of his poetry or criticism with the Objectivist Press because he did not have enough money to fund its publication.

The Objectivist Press published its last book in 1936. While the best work of each of the objectivists lay far into the future, in more than one case thirty or forty years later, any meaningful collaboration between them was already at an end. Oppen, Rakosi, Reznikoff, and Zukofsky each came from a Jewish, working-class family with a healthy appetite for socialist politics. The sincerity of their political convictions led Oppen and Rakosi to abandon poetry for over twenty years in the service of what they believed to be a higher, and incompatible, cause. The human emergencies of the Great Depression led Oppen and his wife, Mary, to join the Communist Party in 1935; they agitated for basic social services, organized workers, and conducted direct-action strikes. "Poetry . . . has nothing to do with helping people to survive and act," he later wrote (Seed, 1985, p. 17). Reznikoff self-published his work before the rise of the objectivists and continued to do so during their reign and afterward. As with the other objectivists, any meaningful recognition would come only at the end of his life. As the Objectivist Press folded, Zukofsky continued to search for teaching assignments, working briefly as an adjunct instructor at the University of Wisconsin in Madison and finally settling into a tenured literature post at Brooklyn Polytechnic Institute, where he referred to his students as "my plumbers." Carl Rakosi abandoned poetry in the 1930s for a career in social work, returning to writing only upon his retirement. Lorine Niedecker, who lived her entire life in rural Wisconsin, had read the objectivist Poetry issue with great interest, and embarked on a long, intense correspondence with Zukofsky. She ultimately produced poems that would rival any of the objectivists' in skill and accomplishment.

In 1969, Oppen won the Pulitzer Prize for his book Of Being Numerous (1968). The 1960s saw Zukofsky finally complete his book-length poem "A" and find a major publisher, W. W. Norton, to produce his collected short poems. Reznikoff received new attention for his landmark work Testimony (1965), a collection of "found" poems culled from turn-of-the-century legal accounts, and a publisher, Black Sparrow Press, dedicated to collecting and preserving his complete works. In a sense, however, any significant collaboration between the original objectivists was squelched upon Oppen's return in the early 1960s from a decade-long political exile in Mexico. When he returned to America, he also returned to poetry and found both enthusiastic publishers and readers, a phenomenon that the generally neglected Zukofsky found intolerable. Oppen claimed that Zukofsky did not dislike him any more than he disliked anyone whose work was published, though his wife, Mary, keenly recalled the precise moment of their break. Zukofsky asked Oppen if he preferred his own poetry to Zukofsky's. Zukofsky believed that Oppen had sacrificed the integrity of his work in order to sell books. Oppen replied that he did indeed prefer his own poetry. "You're tougher than I am, Louis," Mary remembered her husband saying, referring to his belief that Zukofsky used obscurity as a crutch (Hatlen and Mandel, 1981, p. 197). Zukofsky and Oppen, whose friendship was the genesis of their quixotic movement, would never speak to each other again.

THE INSTIGATOR: LOUIS ZUKOFSKY

In the course of his career, Louis Zukofsky produced an almost unbelievable volume of poetry, fiction, and criticism, the vast majority of which not only was not read by the general reading public but also was little read by the select literary public. Yet his admirers were passionately devoted to his work and convinced of his genius. "I never met anyone with such skill, such comprehending/steady eyes, and such an incisive continuum of scholarship, music, language and humor," his friend the writer Fielding Dawson remembered in a memoir of their relationship. "I often felt a fool beside him" (Terrell, 1980, p. 104).

Zukofsky spent much of his life bitter that he was not more widely published, even as he continued to produce obscure, arcane books—450-page volumes of Shakespeare criticism, transliterations of medieval Italian poetry—that could hardly be expected to attract a wide audience. This perpetual cycle of production and rejection was the engine that propelled Zukofsky throughout his life, even as it ultimately reduced him to a reclusive hypochondriac. For better or for worse, his hero Ezra Pound served him as a model until the end. As Pound was the high priest of early-twentieth-century modernism, so Zukofsky attempted to speak his own literary movement into life. And like Pound, increasing lack of interest in and rejection of his work led only to greater eccentricity. Yet Zukofsky's naming of objectivism undoubtedly stuck and raised the profile of a handful of poets who clearly deserved the attention.

Zukofsky was born on Manhattan's Lower East Side in 1904 to Pinchos and Chana Pruss Zukofsky, Orthodox Jews from the part of Russia that is now Lithuania. He early displayed his superhuman capacity for literary adsorption. By the age of eleven he had seen much of Ibsen, Strindberg, and Tolstoy performed, all in Yiddish; read Longfellow's *Hiawatha* and Aeschylus's *Prometheus Bound*, also in Yiddish; and read all of Shakespeare. His parents eschewed a free education at City College, scraping and saving to send their son to Columbia.

At Columbia, Zukofsky was a classmate of Lionel Trilling and studied under such luminaries as Mark Van Doren and John Dewey. Soon he was focusing on Ezra Pound as the only contemporary poet worthy of his emulation. In 1927 he began writing to Pound,

then in Italy, freely offering his opinions on contemporary literature, world affairs, Marxism, and Pound himself. Zukofsky's "Poem Beginning 'The' " particularly impressed Pound—it adhered to modernist experimental aesthetics in form while rejecting modernist pessimism in favor of his own optimism in content—and Pound included the poem in his short-lived magazine, *The Exile*:

1. The
2. Voice of Jesus I. Rush singing
3. in the wilderness
4. A boy's best friend is his mother,
5. It's your mother all the time.
6. Residue of Oedipus-faced wrecks
7. Creating out of the dead,—
8. From the candle flames of the souls of dead mothers
9. Vide the legend of thin Christ sending her out of the temple,—

Although one of his earliest, the poem is nevertheless a fine example of Zukofsky's trademark difficulty—the place, nature, and purpose of the action are unclear—and his linguistic playfulness—the pun on Oedipus "wrecks."

With the publication of the objectivist issue of *Poetry* and the *"Objectivists" Anthology*, Zukofsky planted his flag on the critical map, and while he would insist for the rest of his life that Harriet Monroe cajoled him into naming a movement, it is also clear that Zukofsky had thoroughly considered and passionately believed in the aesthetics he avowed. Zukofsky admired William Carlos Williams's imagist poetics but believed they required a more rigid form than Pound's brand of modernism could provide. He wanted a less romantic imagism that could represent things exactly as they are, a precise form that would accommodate sincerity and accuracy. "The interest of poets is after all in particulars," he wrote in his introduction to the *Anthology*. "Poems are only acts upon particulars outside of them. Only through such activity do they become particulars—i.e. poems" (p. 12). Objectivist poems, then, distill their focus to independent objects and, in eliminating subjective influence, become objects themselves. Zukofsky heeds Williams's famous command, "no ideas but in things," and then seeks to make the idea into a thing itself, an object. Carl Rakosi, however, doubted that Zukofsky ever applied his aesthetics to his own work. "I know from my talks with Zukofsky at the time," Rakosi wrote, "that Reznikoff was his model for an Objectivist, but if Reznikoff was an Objectivist, Zukofsky is not and never was one" (1983, p. 79). For Rakosi, there existed a "fundamental gulf" between Zukofsky's poetry and that of the other objectivists: "anything more un-Reznikoffian, un-Rakosian, un-Oppenesque . . . would be hard to imagine" (Rakosi, 1983, p. 80).

Zukofsky cut an undeniably dashing figure in his youth, impeccably dressed in three-piece suits in spite of his relative poverty, smoking imported cigarettes, wearing thick, dark eyeglasses underneath his imposing, arched eyebrows—the consummate academic. His *Poetry* issue brought him into lifelong correspondences and friendships with Rakosi and Niedecker, and in 1933 he met his future wife, Celia Thaew, a pianist, whom he married in 1939. In 1943 they had a son, Paul, who would become one of the most celebrated concert violinists of his day. From 1935 to 1942 Zukofsky, like many writers of his generation, was employed by the Works Progress Administration, working specifically on the *Index of American Design*, a scrupulous catalog of original American craftwork since colonial times. He later found work as a composition instructor at Brooklyn Polytechnic Institute, retiring as an associate professor in 1966. He remained a devoted correspondent of Pound's throughout his life, though the latter's steadily increasing anti-Semitic, fascist ravings would bitterly confound Zukofsky, forcing him into disagreement, admonishment, and ultimately simple disregard.

Zukofsky spent the majority of his adult life working on his most famous poem, the book-length *"A."* Written in twenty-four sections, its first seven "movements," collected in the *"Objectivists" Anthology*, are clearly indebted to Pound's *Cantos* in the authority of their declarations and their challenging free association of subjects.

> "They sang this way in deep Russia"
> He'd say and carry the notes
> Recalling the years
> Fly. Where stemmed
> The Jew among strangers?
> As the hummingbird
> Can fly backwards
> Also forwards—
> How else could it keep going?

In the early sections of the poem Zukofsky dealt with timeless, conventional themes such as death, resurrection, and immortality, but as the poem progressed and Zukofsky aged, later sections of the poem would become more experimental in nature, addressing topics such as the Kennedy assassination and the Vietnam War. The final section consists of a musical score composed by his wife, Celia. While Zukofsky placed sections of *"A"* in various periodicals as best he could, the poem would not be published as a whole until after his death.

While working on *"A,"* Zukofsky also wrote a long essay on Henry Adams, several short novels, a critical study of the French poet Guillaume Apollinaire, hundreds of short poems, an enormous two-volume study of Shakespeare, several collections of critical essays on poetry, a complete translation of the works of Catullus, a poetic catalog of his wife's garden (*80 Flowers*, 1978), and an autobiography, among other works. In his later years he began to receive some attention from his contemporaries and successors, though he could maddeningly, paradoxically foil their attempts to publish his work, particularly in conjunction with that of his former friend, George Oppen. He rarely ventured far beyond his Greenwich Village apartment on Seventh Avenue and constantly complained of aches, chills, and drafts. He never achieved the fame he felt he deserved, yet his prodigious output continues to astound.

THE NATURAL: CHARLES REZNIKOFF

"There is a learned article about my verse in *Poetry* for this month from which I learn that I am 'an objectivist,'" Charles Reznikoff wrote to his friend Albert Lewin upon the publication of the objectivist issue of *Poetry* in 1931 (1997, p. 84). His attitude is typical of that which he held toward all criticism or acclaim throughout his life. Reznikoff never endeavored to write objectivist or any kind of poetry but merely to represent the world as he found it, and yet it is precisely that sincere, unselfconscious aim that made him Zukofsky's ideal. "Rezy never talked about poetry," Oppen remembered (Hatlen and Mandel, 1981, p. 42). Methodically self-publishing collection after collection throughout his life, Reznikoff seemed to regard the poet's duties to be only to write and to publish, tacitly acknowledging circulation, readership, criticism, fame, and financial compensation as elusive quarries, probably the pure products of chance, and at the very least, best left to other people.

Reznikoff was born in 1894 in Brooklyn, New York, in the Jewish ghetto of Brownsville. His parents, Sarah Yetta (Wolwovsky) and Nathan Reznikoff, had immigrated to America from Russia in the 1880s, fleeing, like thousands of other Jews, the pogroms that followed the assassination of Tsar Alexander II. Though Reznikoff chronicled the prejudice and persecution his family experienced in his later works, and he included allusions and addresses to Jewish history, literature, and culture throughout the entire course of his career, as a young man he did not actively practice Judaism, and he moved away from his family as soon as he was able. After attending the University of Missouri School of Journalism in 1910, Reznikoff decided that this line of work was not for him (as he would do several times), and returned to New York to work in his father's business, selling hats. In 1912 he enrolled in the law school of New York University, graduated second in his class in 1915, and was admitted to New York State bar the following year. He did not, however, ever practice law. He attended graduate law classes at Columbia University for a while and ultimately found work as a writer for the legal encyclopedia *Corpus Juris*, along the way supporting himself as a freelance translator. His friend Lewin, a Hollywood film producer, sporadically employed Reznikoff as a researcher throughout the 1930s and 1940s, providing the poet what little income he received during the Great Depression. Earning money, and finding time for his writing after and among the countless hours devoted to wage-earning labor, were constant stresses throughout Reznikoff's life. He never tried, however, to sustain a peripheral career in literature as a professor or editor, as his friend Zukofsky did and as countless poets would do in subsequent generations. He sensed that his poetry demanded that he participate in the more general commerce of man, even when that work left him exhausted in the evenings. "Now my work has lost another day / I thought, but . . . ," Reznikoff wrote, "Surely the tide comes in twice a day" (Hindus, 1984, p. 16).

In 1930, Reznikoff married the writer and editor Marie Syrkin—his first marriage and her third. Syrkin had already established a sustainable career in literature, and Reznikoff's inconsistent income would strain their marriage throughout its duration. Depending on when he could find work in Hollywood and she in Boston, the two lived together only intermittently, sometimes being apart for long stretches. The considerable correspondence that survives testifies to Reznikoff's great affection and faithful devotion to his wife.

Reznikoff self-published his first collection, *Rhythms*, in 1919. He produced several more slim volumes before gaining admirers and friends in the persons of George Oppen and Louis Zukofsky in the late 1920s. Though Reznikoff actively participated in the nascent objectivists' various publishing schemes, he remained skeptical. He wrote to Lewin in 1933 that Zukofsky, "with whom I disagree as to both form and content of verse," was planning to publish one of his books, but "if nothing comes of his plans, as I expect," he would simply publish it himself (Reznikoff, 1997, p. 212). Following

the general dissolution of the objectivists in the late 1930s, Reznikoff did indeed resume privately publishing his work for approximately twenty years before finally winning a contract with New Directions in 1962. The firm published a collection of his selected poems, *By the Waters of Manhattan* (1962)—the title reprised from a modest edition Reznikoff printed in 1929—and three years later produced *Testimony: The United States, 1885–1890: Recitative*, a striking collection of "found poems" culled from documented court proceedings that Reznikoff encountered during his years working in law. Disappointing commercial and critical reception led New Directions to drop Reznikoff from its list, but the poet soon found his ultimate patron in the modest but plucky Black Sparrow Press, which would in the course of ten years publish his collected poems, sequels to *Testimony*, and *Holocaust* (1975), a similar "found" collection taken from transcripts of the Nuremberg and Eichmann trials.

While Reznikoff employed several poetic styles throughout his career, all of his work exhibits a marked concentration on images and facts with a bare minimum of editorializing or melodrama—an undeniably "objectivist" aesthetic. The poems that populate his early self-published collections typically consist of a few untitled lines that seek to capture a particular image:

Stubborn flies buzzing
In the morning when she wakes.

The flat roofs, higher, lower,
chimneys, water-tanks, cornices.

This, like many of his poems, identifies Reznikoff as a poet of the city. Although his search for work would occasionally take him elsewhere, he essentially lived in Manhattan his entire life, and his collections are largely populated by subways, streetcars, alleys, bridges, rivers, sidewalks, and distinctly urban characters. His favorite pastime, one he could always afford, was walking, and his short poems, without ever explicitly saying so, convey the sensibility of a lonely individual on a solitary, late night stroll:

Of course, we must die.
How else will the world be rid of
the old telephone numbers
we cannot forget?

The numbers
it would be foolish—
utterly useless—
to call.

"I like this secret walking / in the fog," he confides in another poem, "the solid path invisible / a rod away— /

and only the narrow present is alive." The speaker's attitude in the poem seems to mirror the poet's attitude to publishing success. In each case, the means become an end in themselves, the journey is itself the poet's only destination.

In addition to his short lyrics, the poems of Reznikoff's *Testimony* are a unique artistic accomplishment as well as an unwitting example of Zukofsky's aesthetic preference. Working on the law encyclopedia in the late 1920s, Reznikoff amused himself by reading dozens of casebooks containing the transcripts of every criminal trial from every state. On finding a case that particularly moved him, he would reduce the testimony to perhaps a couple of pages, perhaps half a dozen lines, scrupulously eliminating every unnecessary word while striving to isolate the case's emotional center. The poems of *Testimony* frequently chronicle seemingly minor disputes that turn horribly violent, accidental deaths caused by unsafe and unregulated machinery, and injustice brought on by social prejudice. The first poem of section V, "Boys and Girls," of "The South" describes a boy joy-riding on an excursion train after school:

> A crowd waiting
> to board the train.
> While it was moving toward the passengers,
> a man with a lantern
> in one hand and a stick in the other
> came through the cars,
> shouting at the boys
> to get off
> and striking at them with the stick.
>
> Trying to get off while the train was
>   moving,
> Joe fell between the cars.

The first poem of section IV, "Domestic Scenes" of "The West" describes the state of an impending divorce:

> When they told her husband
> that she had lovers
> all he said was:
> one of them
> might have a cigar
> and set the barn on fire.

In their sparsity, Reznikoff's *Testimony* poems achieve Zukofsky's goal of focusing on specific images, objects, and facts, and then creating a poem that is a kind of perfect object in itself, free of the poet's

subjective influences and imperfections. At the same time the poems are highly experimental, consisting ultimately of language entirely originating with other people—in a sense taking Zukofsky's objective mandate to an almost absurd extreme, yet foreshadowing the "found" poems of the Beat and New York School poets a generation in the future. This, like the rest of Reznikoff's work, stands as a kind of monument to pursuing absolute clarity in writing and to the craft of poem-writing itself. Reznikoff died in 1976 while correcting proofs for the first volume of Black Sparrow's *Complete Poems* (1976–1977).

THE SOLDIER: GEORGE OPPEN

The evidence of personal integrity in George Oppen's life is so overwhelming that were he a character encountered in fiction, he would likely be dismissed as too noble to be true. As a young man he devoted the lion's share of his time and money to his art. Moved by the plight of New York's unemployed, he then abandoned poetry, spending the next twenty-five years working to improve social services and fleeing his political enemies. "We knew we didn't know what the world was and we knew we had to find out, so it was a poetic exploration at the same time it was an action of conscience," he explained. "And I thought most of the poets [in the 1930s] didn't know about the world" (Hooker, 1985, p. 35). When he did return to poetry, he achieved a critical and commercial success unknown to his objectivist peers.

Oppen was born in New Rochelle, New York, to Elsie Rothfeld and George Oppenheimer, a diamond merchant, in 1908. When Oppen was four, his mother committed suicide. His father remarried in 1917, and the family moved to San Francisco.

George Oppen. (*Courtesy of the New York Public Library*)

As a senior at a military academy, Oppen was the driver in a one-car accident in which one of his passengers died. Soon after, he was expelled from the academy for drinking. He traveled through Europe for six months and ultimately gained admission to Oregon State University at Corvallis, where he met his future wife, Mary Colby. He was soon suspended, and she expelled, for violating curfew, so they left school, hitchhiked, were married, and settled in New York. They would be married for fifty-seven years.

The poetic culmination of Oppen's founding and financing of To Publishers and the Objectivist Press was his first book, *Discrete Series*, published in 1934. Although sparser and more cryptic than Oppen's volumes of the 1960s and 1970s, *Discrete Series* foreshadowed the economy of language that would garner Oppen, among other honors, the Pulitzer Prize. The book, only a couple of dozen pages, consisted primarily of untitled fragments of four to eight lines:

> This land:
> The hills, round under straw;
> A house
> With rigid trees
> And flaunts
> A family laundry,
> And the glass of windows

Although undeniably loyal to Zukofsky's objectivist demands of representing objects exactly as they are, Oppen drew mixed praise in a review of the book by William Carlos Williams and outright dismissal from the political radicals and intellectuals with whom he and Mary increasingly associated. That association was generally representative of the tentative, failed attempts by literary modernists and political leftists to find in each other an ally. Socialists, communists, and labor advocates required a literature that clearly advocated their cause and portrayed the worker in a flattering light, such as the state-mandated socialist realism of Stalin's Russia. Modernists such as Marianne Moore, T. S. Eliot, and James Joyce, touting the sanctity of the individual expression, could never meet the socialist realists' polemic demands, and in a way the two camps took out their frustration with each other on the objectivists. To the socialists, the objectivist poet was a passive bystander to economic injustice, merely cataloging objects, implicitly compliant with capitalist violence. Modernist critics doubted the objectivists' ability to truly see facts "just as they are," "objectively," and would ultimately acknowledge the poet as the supreme fact of the world in the person and poetics of Robert Lowell. By 1935, George Oppen lost interest in the debate and began to work to better the condition of New York's starving and homeless.

Oppen later characterized his Depression-era politics as liberal and antifascist—indeed, in 1942 he waived his draft exemption as a machinist, at the age of thirty-seven, to join the U.S. Army in the battle for Europe. In April 1945 his foxhole sustained direct artillery bombardment that seriously wounded Oppen and killed two of his comrades. He recovered, returned home, and was awarded the Purple Heart. In the late 1940s, though politically inactive and a decorated war hero, Oppen began to receive unwelcome attention from the FBI. The Oppens, now living in California, technically remained Communist Party members, and the FBI retained information on their activities and whereabouts, twice interviewing the couple in 1949. Fearing imprisonment and separation from their nine-year-old daughter, the Oppens moved to Mexico City, where they would live for almost ten years, only occasionally and briefly returning to the United States. Oppen was an accomplished carpenter and woodworker, and he used these skills to support his family during their exile.

In 1958, Oppen wrote his first poem in twenty-four years, "Blood from a Stone." Shortly thereafter, acknowledging their daughter's desire to attend college in America and sensing a change in the political climate, the Oppens returned to the United States. In 1962, Oppen published his collection *The Materials;* in 1965, *This in Which;* and in 1968, *Of Being Numerous,* for which he won the Pulitzer Prize. While Oppen insisted on a Chinese firewall between his poetry and politics, the sensibility accrued from his personal experience inevitably appeared in his work. *Of Being Numerous* in particular explores the phenomena of singularity, especially the singular person, in a world of mind-numbing multiplicity and moral duplicity. The poems reflect a sense of achieved coherence and accomplishment. "Solution" describes a completed jigsaw puzzle:

> The puzzle assembled
> At last in the box lid showing a green
> Hillside, a house,
> A barn and man
> And wife and children,
> All of it polychrome
> Lucid, backed by the blue
> Sky. The jigsaw of cracks
> Crazes the landscape but there is no gap, . . .

"There is no piece missing," the poem concludes, "The puzzle is complete / Now in its red and green and brown." The poem features the same concentration on objects as the poems of *Discrete Series,* yet here Oppen is able to offer a context that gives the poem a clear meaning. In affirming the singular in a world of multiplicity, he remains distinctly faithful to modernist principles, defending the sanctity of the individual while acknowledging the vast masses with equal claims to individuality. Likewise, Oppen's concentration on objects—"a green / Hillside, a house, / A barn and man / And wife and children"—as well his creating an object of the poem itself fulfills Zukofsky's prophecy of the objectivist poet.

In 1975, Oppen's *Collected Poems* was nominated for the National Book Award. He received significant critical attention throughout his final years, and while he remained estranged from Zukofsky, he maintained lively correspondences with both Charles Reznikoff and Carl Rakosi. He was diagnosed with Alzheimer's disease in 1982 and died in 1984.

CARL RAKOSI AND LORINE NIEDECKER

Carl Rakosi's expansive poetics distinguish him from his objectivist counterparts, but his intense dedication to the craft, his measured view of poetry's role in society, and his fruitful, lifelong correspondence with Zukofsky clearly define him as an integral player in the objectivist drama.

Like many of the objectivists, Rakosi grew up in an immigrant household. He was born in Hungary in 1903; his parents soon separated, and young Carl was left with his paternal grandmother while his father set out to establish himself in America. His father sent for Carl when he was four, and the two settled with Carl's new stepmother in Wisconsin, where Rakosi grew up and ultimately attended the state university at Madison. At the university Rakosi was part of a frenetic young poetry scene that included Kenneth Fearing and Margery Latimer (who would later marry Jean Toomer), both of whom Rakosi counted as close friends. They and his teachers encouraged Rakosi to aggressively peddle his poetry on a summer trip to New York City, and he soon found his poems in influential periodicals such as *The Little Review* and *The Nation*. Louis Zukofsky noticed and liked them, and he asked Rakosi to contribute to the objectivist issue of *Poetry*.

Rakosi later recalled that he found it "heady" to be branded as part of a movement, but, like Oppen and Reznikoff, he felt ill at ease with Zukofsky's manifesto. He appreciated Zukofsky's desire for that which is objectively perfect, but he doubted that this added up to a coherent aesthetic system: "There are Objectivists but no objectivism, in the sense of a type of poetry" (Rakosi, 1983, p. 85). Rakosi and Zukofsky became close friends while Rakosi lived in New York between 1935 and 1940, and they maintained a steady correspondence throughout their lives. But like Oppen, Rakosi would abandon poetry for over two decades. Aside from the time demands of starting a family, Rakosi attributed his long hiatus to "Marxian" doubts about poetry's social utility and to his earnest devotion to a career in social work, which he launched after earning a master's degree in clinical psychology from Wisconsin. He even changed his name to Callman Rawley, in the belief that his Hungarian name

would make it difficult for him to find work. A chance fan letter from a young scholar in 1965, two years prior to his retirement, encouraged Rakosi's return to poetry. His life's labor nearly completed, he believed he now had time to write.

While Zukofsky clearly believed that Rakosi's early poems adhered nicely to Zukofsky's aesthetic principles, much of Rakosi's work bears little resemblance to that of his objectivist colleagues. While Oppen and Reznikoff scrupulously reduced their poems to the bare essentials, and Zukofsky claimed to do so, Rakosi's poems incorporated a broad range of styles and subjects; some are written in strict form and others consist of pages of free verse, a few even going so far as to display a sense of humor. Indeed, many of Rakosi's poems are nothing if not gloriously *subjective*. "To a Collie Pup" is an affectionate address to the poet's dog:

> Lay off, you beggar,
> I just fed you
> and took you walking....
>
> how is it
> that you play
> with my shoelace
> and understand so well
> how to love me?
>
> For this you shall have
> the key to my bedroom
> and the degree
> of master of arts.

After returning to poetry, Rakosi became reacquainted with Reznikoff and close friends with Oppen, whom he had not met before. Rakosi compiled the dozens upon hundreds of his poems that appeared in small magazines and limited-edition volumes over the years into a *Collected Poems*, published by the National Poetry Foundation in 1986.

With the exception of a long, intense correspondence with Zukofsky, Lorine Niedecker had little contact with the objectivist poets, and her work remained largely unpublished and unknown during most of her life, obscure even by objectivist standards. Yet a recent reexamining of her poems has generated a great deal of critical attention, granting her a posthumous following that rivals any of her objectivist brethren.

Niedecker (1903–1970) was born in Wisconsin and spent her entire life there, much of it on tiny Black Hawk Island, on the Rock River near Fort Atkinson. She attended Beloit College for two years (1922–1924) and then returned home to care for her mother, who had lost her hearing. Her father's carp-fishing business provided them a comfortable middle-class life for some time, but when both of her parents died in the early 1950s, his deteriorating financial affairs forced Niedecker to sell almost all of the property they owned and return to the tiny farmhouse on the island where she was born. She had married and divorced a local man in the late 1930s. From 1957 to 1962 she supported herself by scrubbing floors at a local hospital, covering the five miles from her cabin to the hospital on foot every day. Her 1963 marriage, at the age of fifty-nine, to Albert Millen, a salesman, liberated her from this debilitating labor.

Passionately interested in poetry throughout her life, Niedecker read with great interest the 1931 objectivist issue of *Poetry* and soon struck up a correspondence with Zukofsky. In the 1930s she managed a couple of trips to New York, where she met him and the Oppens. "New York was overwhelming, and she was alone, a tiny, timid small-town girl," Mary Oppen remembered. "She escaped the city and returned to Wisconsin" (Penberthy, 1999, p. 4). Niedecker's first influence in poetry had been surrealism, the expansive, imaginative, and subjective nature of which Zukofsky disapproved and actively implored Niedecker to abandon. Their correspondence intensified, and one mid-1930s trip to visit him resulted in a pregnancy that Niedecker terminated at Zukofsky's insistence. Even after Zukofsky's marriage to Celia Thaew in 1939, however, they remained devoted correspondents for over twenty years.

Zukofsky always advised Niedecker to "condense" her poems in accordance with the minimalist objectivist standard, and Niedecker made constant, often ironic allusions to her "condensary" in her poems and letters throughout her life. "I went to school to Objectivism," she remarked late in her life, "but now I often say, 'There is something more' " (Penberthy, 1999, p. 4). On another occasion: "I'm going back to the Imagists, to the wordy ones and the strange rhythms, I have suppressed myself too long" (Penberthy, 1999, p. 4). After the birth of Zukofsky's son, Niedecker began a series of over fifty poems, divided into eight sections, titled "For Paul." Zukofsky probably objected to their broad, expansive style as much as he did to the increasingly sensitive autobiographical information that Niedecker included, and he scrupulously edited the sections that she sent him. As their correspondence waned, Niedecker increasingly returned to the surrealist influences of her youth, though much of what she published is in the sparse, objectivist vein. She

managed to publish a small book, *New Goose*, in 1946, and in the tradition of long objectivist hiatuses, not another original volume until the mid-1960s. A correspondence with the editor Cid Corman seems to have freed her to trust her instincts. *North Central* appeared in 1966, and she compiled two collected volumes, *T&G* for the Jargon Society in 1968 and *My Life by Water* for Fulcrum in 1970. She was obviously enjoying a new period of productivity when she died of a stroke that year.

"With her the external world, the object is primary," Rakosi commented, "it is most out front, and the subjective is most subsumed, so Objectivist is appropriate for her" (Penberthy, 1999, p. 1). It is hardly by chance that later critics have focused the bulk of their attention on Niedecker; her poems have an objectivist focus without sacrificing the agreeable sense of a human being, an artist, having penned the words. "Don't fall in love / with this face— / it no longer exists / in water / we cannot fish" concludes the first poem of *North Central*. A few short lines from an untitled poem in Niedecker's collected works present themselves as a tantalizing coda to the objectivist saga: "Far reach / of sand /A man // bends to inspect / a shell / Himself // part coral / and mud / clam."

WORKS

Niedecker, Lorine. *The Granite Pail: Selected Poems of Lorine Niedecker* (1985)

Niedecker, Lorine. *Lorine Niedecker: Collected Works* (2002)

Oppen, George. *The Collected Poems of George Oppen* (1975)

Rakosi, Carl. *The Collected Prose of Carl Rakosi* (1983)

Rakosi, Carl. *The Collected Poetry of Carl Rakosi* (1986)

Reznikoff, Charles. *Testimony: The United States, 1885–1910: Recitative* (1965)

Reznikoff, Charles. *Holocaust* (1975)

Reznikoff, Charles. *Poems 1918–1975: The Complete Poems of Charles Reznikoff* (1976–1977)

Zukofsky, Louis. *All: The Collected Short Poems, 1923–1964* (1965)

Zukofsky, Louis. *Prepositions: The Collected Critical Essays of Louis Zukofsky* (1967)

Zukofsky, Louis. *"A."* (1968)

Zukofsky, Louis, ed. *An "Objectivists" Anthology* (1932)

FURTHER READING

Auster, Paul. *The Art of Hunger and Other Essays.* London, 1982. Includes his essay on Reznikoff, "The Decisive Moment," an unusually perceptive close reading of the poetry.

Dawson, Fielding. "A Memoir: Louis Zukofsky." In *Louis Zukofsky: Man and Poet*, edited by Carroll Franklin Terrell. Orono, Maine., 1980.

Dembo, L. S. "Oppen on His Poems: A Discussion." In *George Oppen: Man and Poet*, edited by Burton Hatlen. Orono, Maine., 1981.

DuPlessis, Rachel Blau, and Peter Quartermain, eds. *The Objectivist Nexus: Essays in Cultural Poetics*. Tuscaloosa, Ala., 1999. The premier, most sophisticated collection of critical essays on the objectivist movement as a whole.

Hatlen, Burton, and Tom Mandel. "Poetry and Politics: A Conversation with George and Mary Oppen." In *George Oppen: Man and Poet*, edited by Burton Hatlen. Orono, Maine, 1981.

Heller, Michael. *Conviction's Net of Branches: Essays on the Objectivist Poets and Poetry*. Carbondale, Ill., 1985. Consisting of short essays on each major poet, this collection provides a good introduction to objectivist criticism.

Hindus, Milton. "Charles Reznikoff: A Biographical Essay." In his *Charles Reznikoff: Man and Poet*. Orono, Maine, 1984.

Hooker, Jeremy. "Seeing the World: The Poetry of George Oppen." In *Not Comforts, but Vision: Essays on the Poetry of George Oppen*. Budleigh Salterton, U.K., 1985.

Library of America. *American Poetry: The Twentieth Century*. Vol. 2. New York, 2000.

Penberthy, Jenny, ed. *Lorine Niedecker: Woman and Poet*. Orono, Maine, 1997. Interviews, criticism, and previously unpublished work, collected and presented by the preeminent Niedecker scholar.

Penberthy, Jenny. "A Little Too Little: Re-reading Lorine Niedecker." *How 2* 1, no. 1 (1999).

Rakosi, Carl. *The Collected Prose of Carl Rakosi*. Orono, Maine, 1983.

Reznikoff, Charles. *The Selected Letters of Charles Reznikoff*, edited by Milton Hindus. Santa Rosa, Calif., 1997.

Seed, John. "Living the Storm: George Oppen's 'Song of Experiences.' " In *Not Comforts, but Vision: Essays on the Poetry of George Oppen*. Budleigh Salterton, U.K., 1985.

Terrell, Carroll Franklin, ed. *Louis Zukofsky: Man and Poet*. Orono, Maine, 1980. A comprehensive critical anthology, including L. S. Dembo's famous interview with Zukofsky, memoirs, and obscure works by the poet.

Winters, Yvor. *Uncollected Essays and Reviews*, edited and introduced by Francis Murphy. Chicago, 1973.

Zukofsky, Louis, ed. *An "Objectivists" Anthology*. New York, 1932.

TIM O'BRIEN

by Judith Kitchen

For America, the Vietnam War is the war that does not end, and the name of Tim O'Brien has come to be synonymous with its continued examination. In 1967, when the war was at its height and 40,000 protesters were staging a rally at the Pentagon in Washington, D.C., Tim O'Brien was knocking on doors in Minnesota with petitions for presidential candidate Eugene McCarthy, who was running on an antiwar platform. In March 1968, when Lieutenant William Calley was leading a platoon that massacred between two hundred and five hundred civilians at My Lai in Quang Ngai Province, South Vietnam, O'Brien was about to graduate from Macalester College with a major in political science. In 1969, just as Richard M. Nixon was announcing the withdrawal of twenty-five thousand U.S. troops from Vietnam, O'Brien was an infantryman, fighting in Quang Ngai—Pinkville, as it was dubbed because of its color on army maps. In 1970, after four student demonstrators were killed at Kent State University and Lieutenant Calley had been court-martialed and sentenced to life imprisonment for murder, O'Brien returned from his stint in Vietnam with a purple heart. And in 1973, as the Paris Peace Accords were being signed, and two years before the fall of Saigon and the frenzy of the final helicopter flights from the roof of the U.S. embassy, O'Brien published a memoir entitled *If I Die in a Combat Zone, Box Me Up and Ship Me Home* (1973).

If I Die in a Combat Zone opens in the middle of a military mission in South Vietnam, then steps back to explore the issue of how O'Brien came to be a foot soldier in Third Platoon, Company A, Fifth Battalion, Forty-sixth Infantry Division, only a year after the My Lai massacre. The boredom, the fear, the never-ending confusion—none of these resembles what his education has taught him to expect:

Tim O'Brien.
(Photograph by Jerry Bauer)

"The men in war novels and stories and reportage seem to come off the typewriter as men resigned to bullets and brawn. Hemingway's soldiers especially. They are cynics. Not quite nihilists, of course, for that dooms them in the reader's eye." At this point, O'Brien asks himself the question—the still unanswered question of his generation—"But what about the people who are persuaded that their battle is not only futile but also dead wrong? What about *me*?"

Fascinatingly, in a newer edition of the memoir (1999), as though O'Brien had decided to raise more abstracted, philosophical stakes at the expense of the personal, that final question, with its self-conscious emphasis, was changed to "What about the conscripted Nazi?" The gesture suggests that O'Brien would like to distance himself from his preoccupation with self in order to consider political implications. Yet the book is effective precisely because it so carefully documents a particular sensibility wrestling with the questions that can only be answered by each individual.

The young narrator of *If I Die in a Combat Zone* represents himself as a kind of Everyman. Born 1 October 1946, the son of a veteran of the Pacific theater in World War II and a WAVE, O'Brien is the quintessential baby boomer. Growing up in Worthington, Minnesota (the Turkey Capital of the World), he learned to love baseball, the Fourth of July, maybe even apple pie. He knows that there is such a thing as conviction and has always been opposed to the war. As he writes in his memoir, after he received his draft notice, he found himself unable to flee to Canada (though he spent a summer contemplating doing so), and though he made elaborate plans to desert to Vancouver during basic training, in the end he found himself in Chu Lai and Landing Zone Gator. After that, it was a "hopelessly short ride" into the countryside, to the "clusters of hamlets, paddies, hedgerows, tunnel openings" where he came face-to-face with brutality. Thus, O'Brien comes off his own typewriter as unresigned—his legacy is not Ernest Hemingway's, but that of Stephen Crane: "It wasn't a matter of peace, as the pacifists argued, but rather a matter of when and when not to join others in making war."

The twenty-three short chapters of *If I Die in a Combat Zone* unfold in no particular order, disrupting the natural flow of narrative with polemics. Whenever the narrator comes too close to his own emotions, he shifts the kaleidoscope, looking for a new perspective. The point of view shifts from the intensity of the personal pronoun to the more general second person ("You try to second-guess the mine.... You try to trace the footprints of the man to your front"), then to the inclusive intimacy of "we" or the exclusive distance of "they." Some chapters act like stories, complete with dialogue and action, others are miniature treatises. Some are pure memory, others appear to be imagination. All are punctuated by the interwoven alter ego found in the long letters from his friend Erik: "Because there is no time, no cause or reason, for anything but truth, honesty has become fundamental to life itself. We must be honest or be silent." In short, the book argues with itself.

If I Die in a Combat Zone has often been called a novel. Not so. Its power is derived from its role as witness—and interpreter. O'Brien describes his own indecisiveness as "an intellectual and physical standoff," and the memoir perpetuates the standoff, asking questions that resist resolution. What would it have meant to refuse to join the others? O'Brien had failed his own test precisely because he wanted to retain a place to which, if he did die, they could "box me up and ship me home." Home, however, was elusive for the soldiers who returned to a country ashamed of its inability to win, disillusioned by its failed policies—a country willing to turn its back on the very men it had sent off to fight. The war in Vietnam was essentially a blue-collar war and yet, in telling his own story, O'Brien, who went on to do graduate work in government at Harvard University and then became a national affairs reporter for the *Washington Post*, seemed to be speaking for all the men who went in-country in Vietnam. In giving them such an early voice, O'Brien became the literary conscience of America.

THE MOVE TO FICTION

The limitations of memoir are the limits of the lived experience. For O'Brien, the realities of his imagination offered other ways to deal with an issue that would not go away. In 1975, he published his first novel, *Northern Lights*. The book explores the underlying tensions and ties between two brothers—one a wounded vet, one who had stayed home. The war figures only peripherally, though it colors the way each brother responds to the other. The novel is somewhat pedestrian, an apprenticeship for what was to come. What came was a surprise—*Going After Cacciato* (1978) appeared seemingly out of nowhere to win the National Book Award in 1979. O'Brien had transformed what might be only another war story into a visionary blend of stark reality and vivid fantasy. He had somehow found a structure that mimicked the very insanity he wanted to chronicle.

The novel's protagonist, Paul Berlin, spends a night of sentry duty on an observation post on the South China Sea. He has long hours to devote to memory—to get things straight: "Billy Boy Watkins, like the others, was among the dead.... It was a fact. It was the first fact, and leading from it were other facts. Now it was merely a matter of following the facts to where they ended." Even as Berlin recalls the recent days of sporadic combat in which the squad has lost several men (Billy Boy to fear, Pederson to sniper fire, others to tunnels or ambush or land mines), he spins for himself a tale in which one particular man, Cacciato, simply and definitively lays down his rifle and begins to walk the 6,800 miles to Paris, the city of dreams. The reverie proceeds, broken only by an occasional noise in the darkness or the intrusion of remembered details that give the dream its context.

The squad takes off on foot after Cacciato. They will keep him from going AWOL; they will show him how to handle his responsibilities; they will keep their shrinking ranks intact. For Berlin, however, the idea of the dream itself is life-sustaining: "It could be done. Wasn't that the critical point? It could truly be done." The powerlessness of the ordinary soldier is replaced by a sense of purpose—Berlin begins to identify with Cacciato, secretly hoping he will elude them. And he does. He fools them with every trick he has been taught: smoke grenades and tripflares and booby traps. He leaves traces—maps and empty candy wrappers—taunting them with his absence. Harold Murphy turns back, the lieutenant becomes ill, but most of them plod on. They become obsessed, going AWOL themselves in his pursuit. Along the way, they are joined by an adolescent girl with gold hoops in her ears and an uncanny knowledge of the terrain. In a sequence that mirrors Joseph Conrad in *Heart of Darkness*, she takes them into Vietcong territory, into the heart of the tunnels where darkness is deep, and an old general reminds them that they are the intruders, that "the land is your enemy." The days stretch into weeks, the weeks into months, and the trek takes them through Mandalay to Delhi to a prison cell in Iran. There is violence everywhere. Even the dream of freedom has been compromised by the war. At last, they arrive in "Gay Paree," and still Cacciato beckons to them—half real, half ghost. They stalk him, planning their assault; and in so doing, they become the furtive soldiers of the night.

The novel alternates its chapters, blurring the edges of memory and dream so that images mix and match, revealing source as well as consequence. Nothing is as it seems. O'Brien has reproduced a state of mind—a confusing nightmare where it is nearly impossible to tell friend from enemy, the real from the imagined. Berlin becomes obsessed with keeping track, making order out of chaos: "It was a matter of hard observation. Separating illusion from reality. What happened, and what might have happened." In a tone reminiscent of the memoir, Berlin reiterates O'Brien's question: "Why had Cacciato left the war? Was it courage or ignorance, or both?," and later answers it with "he believed that somewhere inside each man is a biological center for the exercise of courage...a fuse, that if ignited would release the full energy of what might be." Paul Berlin may echo the speaking voice of the memoir, but O'Brien also divides his arguments among a number of other fictional characters, as though to prove that "when a war is ended it is as if there have been a million wars, or as many wars as there were soldiers."

A million wars. The burden on the writer, then, is to capture as many versions as he can in order to approximate the larger truth. So O'Brien imagines Berlin, and Berlin imagines Cacciato, who becomes for him "an idea to develop, to tinker with and build and sustain, to draw out as an artist draws out his visions." *Going After Cacciato* has sometimes been referred to by critics as an example of magic realism. But the dream state does not occupy a realm of its own with an independent reality; rather, fact and illusion are deliberately fused into something that more closely resembles surrealism. The realism is the sheer, concentrated craziness of the war. The magic is the mind's ability to make an odd kind of sense of the senseless.

The book's final chapters both clarify and further obfuscate the ways this novel can be interpreted. Suddenly it is clear—or almost clear—that even the observation post exists only as the squad's ultimate destination.

Paul Berlin's long night is still in the future tense. And Cacciato? Missing in action. The lieutenant called it in to headquarters, spelling out his name—and the name, magically, transformed itself into hope. Maybe, just maybe, he can survive. Maybe, the novel suggests, the missing man will turn up again, in peacetime Paris, alive.

"War stories. That was what remained: a few stupid war stories, hackneyed and unprofound. Even the lessons were commonplace. It hurts to be shot. Dead men are heavy.... Stories that began and ended without transition. No developing drama or tension or direction. No order." Moving into fiction gave Tim O'Brien the space in which to invent the million stories of the million other wars. It allowed him to delve into the psyche of Paul Berlin. It gave him access to darker, more ambiguous thoughts—the shadowy, double-edged, double-faced thoughts we deny ourselves unless they catch us unaware, silently keeping watch some sleepless night.

FACT AND FICTION—"FACTION"

In 1985, O'Brien published a novel that did not directly have its roots in the Vietnam War. Set in 1995, ten years into the future, *The Nuclear Age* revives an image from O'Brien's first novel. In the book, William Cowling is digging a bomb shelter. "Balance of power, balance of mind," he says, and the book proceeds to throw everything out of balance. The novel captured some of the flavor of the absurd that haunted *Going After Cacciato*, but its sardonic humor and its fast-paced repartee did not contain the visionary sweep of the earlier book, nor did the subject have much currency in a time of lessening tensions between the superpowers.

Five years later, the publication of *The Things They Carried* (1990) had a different effect. This collection of linked stories (not quite a novel, although the stories are so interconnected that they reproduce the feel of a novel) met with instant success. America seemed ready to revisit the issues raised by Vietnam, and according to the critics, O'Brien had found just the right medium to convey the unreal qualities of the experience: "The line between fiction and fact is beautifully, permanently blurred" (Asa Baber, *Chicago Sun-Times*); "The integrity of a novel and the immediacy of an autobiography" (*The New Yorker*); "A dramatic redefinition of fiction itself" (*The Charlotte Observer*); "a kind of 'faction' presented as a collection of related stories that have the cumulative effect of a unified novel" (Martin Brady, *Booklist*). Dedicating the book to its own characters, fashioning a narrator who is at times called "Tim" and at others called "O'Brien," a character not quite himself even though the narrator, too, has written a novel called *Going After Cacciato*, the author has created a territory somewhere between fact and fiction, a distinction that O'Brien calls the difference between "happening truth" and "story truth."

The Things They Carried opens in the third person: "First Lieutenant Jimmy Cross carried letters from a girl named Martha." They all carried something—twenty-eight-pound mine detectors, P-38 can openers, pocketknives, C-rations, canteens, radios, malaria tablets, assault rifles, pencils, paper, dope, photographs, memories, dreams, their wounded buddies, a "kind of dignity." "They" are the platoon that populates these stories and "they carried all the emotional baggage of men who might die." Many of them did—graphically, dramatically, suddenly, surprisingly—and the reader is given the list of the dead long before their stories are told.

Many of the stories in *The Things They Carried* had been published in magazines before they were given new shape in the book, and it is important to remember that they were meant to stand on their own. That way, each character is granted his own subjective take on the collective experience. But story itself is at stake here—and, by extension, the nature of "truth." The stories take every imaginable form, and they come at the war from every possible angle. "The Sweetheart of Song Tra Bong," for example, is an example of embellishment, of the cumulative effect of hearsay and exaggeration and speculation, until the story has the ring of larger truth. On its surface, it could not have happened. No one was allowed to import a girlfriend to the front. And yet cute, blonde Mary Anne Bell arrives, wearing culottes and a sweet innocence, and she simply moves in. Later, she can be seen fraternizing with the Green Berets, the ones who have no time for the guys, in Alpha Company. Later still, she puts on her camouflage and heads out with them into the jungle. Eventually, she simply disappears, out there somewhere, indigenous now, one of them. Of course, the story cannot be true—the men take turns challenging it—and yet it fascinates them. Mary Anne represents something in all of them, something that intuitively understands that they hold a grudging empathy for the enemy—that, underneath, they are not very different from each other. Her initial innocence, her all-American innocence, is not so much corrupted as usurped.

So, asks the narrator's daughter, "Did you ever kill a man?" "Yes," he answers, in "The Man I Killed." "His jaw was in his throat, his upper lip and teeth were gone, his one eye was shut, his other eye was a star-shaped

hole." And then "no," he admits, in "Good Form." It is true that he is forty-three years old (Tim O'Brien's age at the time of writing the book), and it is true that he walked through Quang Ngai Province as a foot soldier, but "almost everything else is invented." Almost? What is the reader to make of it all? Suddenly he is saying that he was present when the man was killed, but "I did not kill him." And then, "even *that* story is made up."

Here is the happening truth: "I was once a soldier. There were many bodies, real bodies with real faces, but I was young then and I was afraid to look." Here is the story truth: "He was a slim, dead, almost dainty young man of about twenty. . . . His jaw was in his throat. His one eye was shut, the other eye was a star-shaped hole. I killed him." The truth is that all versions are true; there are a million wars, and these are some of them. Kathleen, like any good nine-year-old does not want to deal with the metaphysical. Come on, she pleads, tell me the real truth, before she drifts back to her fictional origins, conjured from the author's need for a questioner.

The real truth, the reader suspects, can be found at the end of "On the Rainy River," based on the summer before the speaker left for boot camp. "I was a coward. I went to the war." In two spare sentences, O'Brien indicts his protagonist (himself?) for choosing love and acceptance over principle and protest.

Perhaps the most poignant story is "Speaking of Courage." Norman Bowker is back from the war, at loose ends, driving around and around the lake. It is the Fourth of July, but Bowker has seen enough of fireworks in Nam; he would like to get on with a normal life, but how? Nothing seems to matter anymore. He is plagued with memories of Kiowa's death—his buddy, who drowned in a shit field; his buddy, who drowned because he, Norman, lost his hold on him. He tries out how he would tell the story to his father, tries on his words, and his father's responses, but nothing feels quite right.

This story is immediately followed by "Notes," in which an intrusive speaker (in the guise of O'Brien, as author) documents the letters he received from Bowker (containing his request that his story be written), and then he lets us know of Norman's subsequent suicide. The O'Brien character muses: "In ordinary conversation, I never spoke much about the war, certainly not in detail, and yet ever since my return I had been talking about it virtually nonstop through my writing." If writing is not therapy—and O'Brien does not consider it to be so—then what purpose does it serve? "By telling stories, you objectify your own experience. You separate it from yourself." O'Brien's narrative stance has provided the necessary distance (note how, even in talking about it, he has slipped into the second person). If he can pull back far enough, he might discover the angle from which the war makes any sense at all. Or, conversely, by drawing back, he may impose his own kind of sense on what might otherwise seem to be a haunted and overfertile imagination.

FACT VERSUS FICTION

In the story "Notes," O'Brien (or his interchangeable narrator) says, "*Going After Cacciato* was a war story; 'Speaking of Courage' was a postwar story. Two different time periods, two different sets of issues." So it becomes clear the war will never end; it will simply recede in time, offering up new perspectives. Certainly the Gulf War of 1990–1991, with its technological advances, its "clean kills" and "smart bombs," changed the nation's ideas of what a war could be like. The television news did not bring the nightly body count, and reporters were kept at a safe distance from the actual engagement. The commentators kept reminding us it was time to "regain" our image, or to "put Nam behind us." It was in this climate that *In the Lake of the Woods* made its appearance in 1994.

Postwar—and postmodern—the novel pulls up brutal images of My Lai like a repressed memory from the country's subconscious. The mystery of My Lai is the background to another, more current mystery. One night in 1986, a week after the protagonist John Wade, whose presence at My Lai was exposed, lost a primary vote for the U.S. Senate, his wife, Kathy, disappears from a remote cottage on Lake of the Woods in northern Minnesota where the two have retreated to decide what to do next. While the search for Kathy proceeds in the present, the search for the reasons for her disappearance moves in ever-widening circles, deeper and deeper into the past.

What happened that night? Did John Wade kill his wife? He was capable, wasn't he? Or did Kathy simply leave? Is she lost? Did the two of them plan to meet later, somewhere in Canada, somewhere where the past will not catch up with them? A fresh start? For all that O'Brien sets in motion, *In the Lake of the Woods* refuses to explain the unexplainable. "This book is about uncertainty," O'Brien asserted in an interview.

At the heart of the novel is a mystery so powerful even its author does not know its solution. Who was John Wade? What made him tick? The questions are framed in the past tense because the narrative present of the book is locked tightly in a set of footnotes in which a narrative presence makes itself felt. At the end of the sixth chapter, the author emerges in the guise of a journalist, saying, "biographer, historian, medium—call me what you want—but even after four years of hard labor I'm left with little but supposition and possibility." Later he reveals his motivations: "What drives me on, I realize, is a craving to force entry into another heart, to trick the tumblers of natural law, to perform miracles of knowing. It's human nature. We are fascinated, all of us, by the implacable otherness of others."

The novel becomes yet another set of "notes" that includes the known "facts" as they are uncovered, the "who, what, where, when, how" of the reporter's trade; a sequence of chapters, each entitled "Hypothesis," in which one plausible scenario after another is explored; a reconstructed history of John Wade, including his childhood, his obsessive relationship with first his father, then his wife; and a reconstructed history of John Wade's involvement at My Lai. The narrator (again in a ubiquitous, explanatory footnote) finds himself remembering his own time in Vietnam, and admits that he has his own "trapdoors." Looking for John Wade is like going after Cacciato: "All secrets lead to the dark, and beyond the dark there is only maybe."

Much of the story takes place in the "maybe" of the narrator's imagination, the places where he fills in the blanks. Who was John Wade? The love-starved child of an alcoholic father, the child devastated by his father's suicide, the child who was good at one thing—magic tricks? The young man who spied on his girlfriend and wondered if she could ever love him enough? The young lawyer-turned-politician who had come to crave the audience, the acceptance that translated into votes? The young politician whose liberal Democratic ideals were somehow lost in the process of getting elected? Memories of My Lai surface occasionally, brief moments of discomfort, as he stolidly puts it all behind him, makes it go away as if by magic.

Ironically, Wade had been almost a bystander at My Lai. Shocked and horrified by the atrocity, he stumbled around, viewing the carnage, and it was only late in the day, in a kind of reflex action, that he mistakenly shot an old man carrying a hoe, and then, not so mistakenly, shot one of the men from his platoon. And afterward, true to his nickname, "Sorcerer," he found a way to expunge all record of his having been there, transferred himself on paper to another company, and gave himself a fresh start. He gave himself the political career that exposure was now ending almost before it had begun.

If it was magic, it was magic on a grand scale. O'Brien positions his story in a public context, both literary and historical. There is yet another sequence of chapters, each entitled "Evidence." This is the reporter's actual "research" and, sprinkled throughout the comments from Wade's mother, Kathy's sister, Wade's political manager, an easygoing sheriff, and his skeptical assistant, are the "real-life" quotes from historians, writers, politicians, and newspaper articles—a prodigious compilation that reveals the annals of violence. From Sophocles to Hawthorne to Dostoyevsky to Pynchon, there is a running commentary on human nature, as in the quote from *Don Quixote*: "Love and War are the same thing, and stratagems and policy are as allowable in one as the other." This is further emphasized in quotes from Woodrow Wilson, Thomas Dewey, Richard Nixon. For carnage, O'Brien quotes Custer. For disappearance, Ambrose Bierce. For revenge, he cites letters from British soldiers, somewhere north of Lexington. And for explanation, he produces the flat voices of Paul Meadlo and William Calley in the actual court-martial transcripts.

If O'Brien the man is interested in political consequence, O'Brien's speaker is interested in mystery. "Why do we care about Lizzie Borden, or Judge Crater, or Lee Harvey Oswald, or the Little Big Horn? Mystery! Because of all that cannot be known. And what if we did know. . . . Nothing more would beckon, nothing would tantalize." True, but the book is more disturbing than its premise. It explodes the conventions of fiction, confronting fiction with fact. Lieutenant Calley was more than a "character," for all that he makes his appearance in this book. My Lai happened; hundreds of people died; Calley spent a total of forty months in jail. Just when you believe that some things are inviolable, O'Brien fictionalizes the actual trial, adding words in his footnotes—as though taken verbatim—that simply never were spoken. Anything to get a bead on the event.

Mystery may interest the reporter who is telling the story—but that is not the author's main concern. The author is interested in distance—a mirror reflecting a mirror reflecting a mirror—to give the book its odd angle of vision: the obsession buried in footnote, buried in the history of the history of violence.

IN THE DISTANCE

Distance: O'Brien's nemesis as well as his device. Fact to fend off fiction, but fact as deflection, a forced exit from the self. There are suggestions of complicity (if not collusion) in *In the Lake of the Woods*. Kathy knows that John spies on her. She suspects that he has secrets. And she has secrets of her own. In interviews, O'Brien talked at length about

America's complicity in the My Lai massacre—not so much a cover-up as a covering over. "There's a difference between explanation and exculpation," O'Brien stated in an online interview. The latter, he fears, has been America's response to a crime that he sees as having still gone unpunished. Recent disclosures about the past of real U.S. senators have underscored O'Brien's skeptical sense that, as a nation, we have refused to look at our darkest moments. In another interview, he said, "I think that we've healed the wounds too well, if anything. The country has obliterated the horror that was Vietnam. . . . My Lai is just a footnote in a history of a war that is also a kind of footnote."

In the 2 October 1994 edition of *The New York Times*, Tim O'Brien chronicled his return to Vietnam—to the jungles and paddies where he and his buddies fought off sniper fire, or were choppered out to field hospitals, or simply learned that the land was patient, that it would persist long after they were gone. In that article, "The Vietnam in Me," he also revealed his emotions over the ending of a relationship with Kate, his companion on the trip. Blending memory and reportage, he takes us there, in-country, talking to survivors, hearing the whisper of Paul Meadlo's flat "kill anything that breathes," watching Kate watch him. He is honest when he speaks of losing her: "This is a valance of horror that Vietnam never approximated. If war is hell, what do we call hopelessness?" O'Brien takes a risk when he juxtaposes the two experiences, but it is a risk we have come to expect from him. It is a risk he reiterates, in the article, when he repeats his old refrain, "I was a coward. I went to Vietnam."

Genre makes some important distinctions. Although fiction allowed O'Brien to explore the concepts of courage and cowardice, it was in nonfiction that O'Brien held himself accountable for his own choices. He does not quite forgive himself for needing love and acceptance. If he, and others, had been stronger, he implies, these stories might never have needed to be written.

In 1998, O'Brien tried once again to distance himself from the war. *Tomcat in Love* takes a comic look at obsessive love. It delighted some readers with its shenanigans, but failed to receive much critical attention. In 2002, O'Brien received several negative reviews of *July, July*, a book set on the campus of a fictitious Minnesota college where the class of 1969 is having its thirtieth reunion. Past relationships are explored and rekindled, while present ones seem about to break apart or begin. The result is a number of bizarre entanglements, while a lonely Vietnam vet serves as a ghostly reminder of their shared history. Love and war may very well be the same, but in O'Brien's hands, one turns a bit maudlin (however humorous) and the other achieves classical proportions. In "How to Tell a True War Story," O'Brien suggests that all his stories are really about love. And they are—love of friends, love of life, love of country. They demand the best of America by insisting of us that we face the past.

O'Brien has progressively distanced himself from his personal material in order to make it fresh again. Since 1973, he has shown us what Wilfred Owen called the "pity of war." In the future, he plans to return to nonfiction—a cultural study of what was happening at home during the time he was stationed in Vietnam. Thus he may be able to look through the eyes of those he left behind—patriots, resisters, students high on the power of protest, mothers, lovers, the politicians whose deliberate myopia he most despises. How will O'Brien's work be viewed? *Going After Cacciato* is perhaps a bit too self-consciously conceived and *In the Lake of the Woods* may play a few too many clever postmodern games for the general reader, but *The Things They Carried* is already considered a masterpiece and is destined to be read for generations to come—not as explanation, but as the eloquent, articulated voices of, and for, the men who carried the burden of the war. A million stories. There will be more stories, and, in O'Brien's own scrupulous words, "if they're told well, they will last."

[*See also* Vietnam in Poetry and Prose *and* War Literature.]

SELECTED WORKS

If I Die in a Combat Zone, Box Me Up and Ship Me Home (1973)
Northern Lights (1975)
Going After Cacciato (1978)
The Nuclear Age (1985)
The Things They Carried (1990)
In the Lake of the Woods (1994)
Tomcat in Love (1998)
July, July (2002)

FURTHER READING

Bruckner, D. J. R. "A Storyteller for the War That Won't End." *The New York Times* (3 April 1990). A running interview/commentary, especially good on the themes and devices of *The Things They Carried*.

Calloway, Catherine. " 'How to Tell a True War Story': Metafiction in *The Things They Carried*." In *Critique: Studies in Contemporary Fiction* 36, no. 4 (Summer 1995).

Franklin, H. Bruce. "Plausibility of Denial: Tim O'Brien, My Lai, and America," *The Progressive* (December 1994). Concentrates on My Lai as depicted in *In the Lake of the Woods*. Franklin gives a "definitive reading" of the book that O'Brien himself contradicts.

Herzog, Tobey C. *Tim O'Brien*, New York, 1997. Includes a bibliography.

Jones, Dale W. "The Vietnams of Michael Herr and Tim O'Brien: Tales of Disintegration and Integration." *Canadian Review of American Studies* 13, no. 3 (Winter 1982).

Kaplan, Steven. *Understanding Tim O'Brien*. Columbia, S.C., 1995. One in a well-known series on American letters, covering the life, the work, major themes, and issues.

Lee, Don. "Tim O'Brien Profile." *Ploughshares* (Winter 1995). Often cited as a comprehensive overview (available at *Ploughshares* Web site).

McCaffery, Larry. "An Interview with Tim O'Brien." In *Anything Can Happen: Interviews with Contemporary American Novelists*, edited by T. LeClair. Urbana, Ill., 1983.

O'Brien, Tim. "The Mystery of My Lai." In *Facing My Lai: Moving Beyond the Massacre*, edited by David L. Anderson, Lawrence, Kans., 1998. A discussion limited to My Lai and accountability.

Weber, Bruce. "Wrestling with War and Love; Raw Pain, Relived Tim O'Brien's Way." *The New York Times* (2 September 1998).

See also the article on *The Things They Carried*, immediately following.

TIM O'BRIEN'S
THE THINGS THEY CARRIED

by Pauls Toutonghi

"A true war story," Tim O'Brien writes in his collection of short fiction, *The Things They Carried* (1990) "is never moral. It does not instruct, nor encourage virtue, nor suggest models of proper human behavior, nor restrain men from doing the things men have always done. If a story seems moral, do not believe it." The story from which these lines are taken is the short piece, "How to Tell a True War Story," which first appeared in *Esquire* magazine. This sentence would be a fitting epigraph for much of O'Brien's work; he tells war stories and strives to refrain from any sense of instructional morality. His books entertain. They are predominantly filled with young, male military conscripts. O'Brien follows these men for short periods of time, displaying the junctures of conflict and pathos in their lives, capturing their voices, such as they are, stranded thousands of miles from home, submerged in a conflict over which they have little control.

Although it is sometimes unprofitable to trace the influence of an author's life on his or her work, *The Things They Carried* has a direct basis in O'Brien's own military service. He writes with the authority of experience; after graduating from Macalaster College in 1968, O'Brien was drafted into the army. He served a yearlong tour of duty in Vietnam. This time provided a fertile ground for his writing life, it seems; his reputation as a vivid and honest writer has been forged in the fires of war. Seldom do his characters avoid the brutality of the Vietnam War. Most of his books, if not overtly set in Vietnam during the late 1960s and early 1970s, consider veterans who are struggling to adapt to American society after the trauma of combat.

THE TEXT

The title story of the collection has been hailed as a stylistically innovative, entertaining, and moving work of fiction, and was included in the 1987 edition of *The Best American Short Stories*. It is part story, but also part index of items as it painstakingly details all of the things a foot soldier would carry in the field of deployment. The scene is the tropical rainforest of Vietnam, and mortality

is the constant background noise. At any moment, a sniper could shoot one of the soldiers; landmines are buried throughout the terrain. Yet instead of meditations on mortality, O'Brien chooses to move his authorial camera toward the details of physical weight. The prose painstakingly captures each element of the heaviness: "They carried USO stationery and pencils and pens. They carried Sterno, safety pins, trip flares, signal flares, spools of wire, razor blades, chewing tobacco, liberated joss sticks and statuettes of the smiling Buddha, candle, grease pencils." He considers the weapons that the soldiers bear; he lists each bullet by its weight, and each thirty-pound radio unit is described by its official military designation. Remarkably, as this list continues, it takes on a new significance. The weight—which is at first a physical and exterior weight—gradually becomes an interior weight, the weight of memory. O'Brien says this quite explicitly. It is clear that these items have become a set of signs, an intricate and variegated group of symbols: "Some things they carried in common. . . . They shared the weight of memory. They took up what others could no longer bear. Often, they carried each other, the wounded or weak." He is clearly staking out the psychological territory of the soldier; indeed, the book will trace this motion, from exterior detail to interior revelation.

The story "The Things They Carried" follows this pattern. Gradually, the plot focuses on the aborted relationship of First Lieutenant Jimmy Cross and the girl he has left behind in America—a young college student with whom he has had an innocent and unconsummated relationship. While carrying his heavy physical burdens through the field of combat, Cross must also be responsible for the safety of his men. He finds that his attention wanders; his weary body rebels at the daily dust, at the backbreaking pain of carrying these heavy items; he dreams of the girl, Martha, and loses touch with the dangerous environment that surrounds the soldiers. A sniper then kills one of his men; Cross is tormented by the thought that he could have saved the soldier, if only he had been paying more attention. "He would accept the blame for what had happened to Ted Lavender. He would be a man about it. . . . [H]is obligation was not to be loved but to lead. He would dispense with love." Here then, in microscopic clarity, is the process of closing off and distancing that any war can impose upon its soldiers.

BACK IN THE WORLD

This plot, in and of itself, would be sufficient for the needs of a short story. Yet O'Brien couples a lively attention to matters of plot and motivation with a robust sense of stylistic experimentation. He often eschews quotation marks and frequently breaks the narrative of a story into smaller sections, giving the reader bursts of powerfully moving text. Furthermore, the stories are intricately connected, constituting a latticework of common concerns and events told from a variety of perspectives. In the pages immediately after "The Things They Carried," O'Brien offers a story called "Love." Like many of the stories in the book, "Love" is barely three pages long—possibly eight hundred words at most.

Set in the United States several decades after the conflict, it occurs in what is ostensibly the house of O'Brien, or at least the fictionalization of the author who has written these stories. Cross has come to visit the man with whom he served his tour of duty; they talk a little bit about the war and Cross describes the way his relationship with Martha failed once he returned from Vietnam. They drink gin together—the writer character and Cross—and by the end of the night they are remembering the conflict. They recall its sadness and losses; they remember their violence-touched youth; they are amazed by snapshots of themselves "in country," when their faces were "incredibly soft and young." Memory becomes a tangible presence between the men, and their meeting displaces them from their present time and space.

But this is the essence of O'Brien's fiction. His characters are never fully comfortable with their lives, whether these lives occur in America or outside of the village of Tra Bong. O'Brien touches on all aspects of the war experience, enumerating the time during, before, and after the conflict. He details, of course, his experiences—or at least the experiences of a fictionalized young fiction writer—in combat. He details his encounters with friends and family after the war. And, perhaps most importantly, O'Brien's protagonist discusses the time before the war, when he is a newly graduated twenty-two year old and receives his draft card by surprise. This story, "On the Rainy River," is among the most powerful of the collection. It is not a violent story, and lacks the brutality and trauma of some of the other pieces. Yet its quiet composure and fictional reserve give it an energy that differentiates it from the other works in this suite of stories.

The young central character of this story leaves his Minnesota home upon receiving the draft notice and travels north to the Canadian border. While there, he checks into the Tip Top Lodge, a lonely, deserted motel run by its owner-proprietor, Elroy Berdahl. Tim, as the central character is called, vacillates between escape to Canada, where he will not have to worry about the draft and the war but will be separated from his family and friends, perhaps indefinitely. This, of course, was the quintessential dilemma facing many young, draft age men in 1968. Berdahl senses that the young man is in trouble; he gives away the room for free and does not charge for board. At one point, he proposes that he and Tim go fishing. They pilot the boat out into the Rainy River—the river that flows just behind the lodge. Berdahl steers the boat to within a few meters of Canadian soil, so that Tim can simply jump overboard and swim across. He realizes that the old man has decided to help him in this way, to offer him the opportunity for escape: What would you do? . . . Would you feel pity for yourself? Would you think about your family and your childhood and your dreams and all you're leaving behind? Would you cry, as I did?" Berdahl ignores the crying, fully aware of the drama playing itself out in the back of his boat; his silence is compassionate: "Elroy Berdahl remained quiet. He kept fishing. . . . And yet by his presence, his mute watchfulness, he made it real. He was the true audience. He was a witness, like God, or like the gods, who look on in absolute silence as we . . . make our choices or fail to make them." This passage begins to unearth the loneliness that animates many of the stories. It is a sad center—perhaps it is the isolation from the world that a soldier must have in order to survive—and one that is desperate for empathy and understanding. That is part of why these stories have such a shocking and immediate appeal; the writing needs to be heard.

THE NECESSITY OF EXPRESSION

Much in the way that a brief meditation on the nature of love by one of the soldiers in "The Things They Carried" leads to a subsequent story, "Love," many of the stories touch on interrelated themes. The reader can almost trace the pattern of the writer's mind as a casual word muttered by one of his characters prompts an entirely new direction within the book. The volume's style of writing is kinetic, and it gives the collection an identity and consistency beyond that which usually attaches itself to a group of short stories.

Another notable stylistic element is the rotation of characters; O'Brien moves people from one piece to the next, giving the collection a netlike cohesion. This cohesion disappears, however, once the setting shifts to the United States. The works set in Vietnam are peopled with a reliable cast of figures. For the most part, these are American soldiers—young and foolish and wide-ranging in political beliefs. The pieces set in America are much quieter and usually involve only a few reoccurring figures.

One of these is Norman Bowker, a soldier who served in Vietnam with the protagonist of the collection. In the fictional 1978 of *The Things They Carried*, Bowker kills himself, but only after writing Tim a rambling, seventeen-page letter in which he expresses—among other things—admiration for Tim's work as a fiction writer. Overall, the letter is disoriented and sadly confusing. It is filled with "the problem of finding a meaningful use for life after the war." The letter's arrival—and Bowker's subsequent suicide—is inspiration for one of the most haunting and least-known stories in the collection. Titled "Speaking of Courage," it was first published in the *Massachusetts Review* in 1976. Written from the point of view of an omniscient narrator who is familiar with Bowker's most intimate thoughts, the story follows Bowker through one of his solitary days. It shows his anguish over not having been able to save Kiowa—one of his fellow soldiers. The story catalogues the development of depression in Bowker's war-shocked mind. At the conclusion of the story, after driving around the lake twelve times, Bowker decides that he will wade into the water to watch a fireworks display that is scheduled for that evening: "After a time he got out, walked down to the beach, and waded into the lake without undressing. The water felt warm against his skin. He put his head under. He opened his lips, very slightly, for the taste, then . . . watched the fireworks. For a small town, he decided, it was a pretty good show."

The water rising over his head is a foretelling, of course, of his death, of the will-to-suicide that is expressing itself at the conclusion of this piece. Bowker's depression contrasts quite powerfully with the mindset of the book's narrator, who "took pride in sliding gracefully from Vietnam to graduate school, from Chu Lai to Harvard, from one world to another." This man, this mirrored O'Brien, has found his solace through writing, through written self-expression.

He, like Bowker, has had horrific experiences, and has come close to breakdown. In the story "The Man I Killed," the protagonist narrates his near breakdown upon shooting a man on a trail near the Song Tra Bong: "He was a slim, dead, almost dainty young man of about twenty. He lay with one leg bent beneath him, his jaw in his throat, his face neither expressive nor inexpressive. One eye was shut. The other was a star-shaped hole. 'Talk,' Kiowa said." Kiowa, whose death will be one of the saddest moments of the book, is urging the protagonist to speak. The protagonist cannot bring himself to move, to speak, to act in any way. He has shot this man in an encounter on the trail. It is the definitive war experience, and the protagonist's mental stability is almost destroyed.

In the context of this particular story, Kiowa is encouraging his friend to talk about anything so he will snap out of the shock that he has lapsed into after the shooting. But if this command is extended to the broader world of writing, Kiowa can be seen as a guiding force behind the entire collection. He encourages the writer O'Brien to find his voice so that the fictional Tim can again move through his fictional life and deal with his tragedies and traumas once more.

Yet what can be made of this Tim? Is this protagonist O'Brien himself? The most persuasive argument is that he is not, that this is a work of fiction, and that all of the characters—even the ones who are Vietnam veterans and writers living in New England at the time the book was written—are fictional. Yet O'Brien does write, after all: "I was a coward. I went to the war." Can this be interpreted as a direct salvo from the author, a dismayed assessment of his own life in a barely disguised fictional form? Speculation of this sort, in the end, is not profitable. Whether or not Tim O'Brien the writer is *Tim*, the protagonist of most of these stories, they remain powerful works of fiction, among the strongest to come out of the Vietnamese conflict. Ultimately, much of the work in *The Things They Carried* is revealed to be fictionalized. But this does not diminish its role or value in the turn-of-the-century literary culture of the English language.

In the story "Good Form," O'Brien confronts this issue directly. "It's time to be blunt," he writes. The word "blunt" is especially meaningful in this context. The things it connotes—blunt object, blunt force—are violent items or arrangements. Much of the danger of Vietnam came from sharp objects, such as projectile bullets and shrapnel. Now, through blunt words, through words that refer, associatively, to violence, O'Brien allows the reader to get toward the truth of the stories told in this collection:

"I'm forty-three years old, true, and I'm a writer now, and a long time ago I walked through Quang Ngai Province as a foot soldier. Almost everything else is invented. But it's not a game. It's a form." Then O'Brien narrates the death of the man whom he has previously admitted to killing. This time, when he tells the story, he says that he was not the one who fired the deadly shot; he was simply present when the man died. Yet this presence, he alleges, was enough. He is still guilty, guilty by association.

Then, however, O'Brien reveals more: "But listen. Even *that* story is made up." He then writes, "Here is the story-truth," and presents the exact description of the dead man reported in the previous piece, "The Man I Killed." Clearly, O'Brien is meditating on the shifting nature of truth in the written form, on the ways in which a writer can control the emotions of his or her readers. The story concludes: " 'Daddy, tell the truth,' Kathleen can say, 'did you ever kill anybody.' And I can say, honestly, 'Of course not.' Or I can say, honestly, 'Yes.' " That word "honestly," and all it entails, becomes the fulcrum of this passage. What importance does honesty have, O'Brien seems to be asking, when it comes to fiction? Indeed, the layering of irony upon irony—of point of view upon point of view—is truly a remarkable, disconcerting device. Truth and not truth exist simultaneously with each other, at the same location. They are not mutually exclusive; for O'Brien's fictional protagonist, the validity of all experiences can be brought into question.

REPRESENTATION AND FICTION

O'Brien, the writer—working in an American culture that is extremely desirous of truth and authentic representation—must struggle with the complexities of his fiction, which is penned in a traumatic and openly brutal vein of writing. The book constantly shifts back and forth between the Vietnam era and the United States in the mid-to-late 1980s. It deals with the issues of place and time and the difficulties of veterans as they continue trying to adjust to the wildly different lives that they led during the war. It is also a tremendously graphic and violent book. The works in *The Things They Carried* are indeed true war stories—honest, intricate, nightmarish, and highly accomplished.

[*See also* Vietnam in Poetry and Prose *and* War Literature.]

FURTHER READING

Bowie, Thomas J. "Reconciling Vietnam: Tim O'Brien's Narrative Journey." In *The United States and Vietnam from War to Peace*, edited by Richard M. Slabey. Jefferson, N.C., 1996. A concise and sharp article.

Heberle, Mark. *A Trauma Artist: Tim O'Brien and the Fiction of Vietnam*. Iowa City, Iowa, 2001. A significant trauma critic writes an important and far-reaching analysis.

McKay, Mary. "The Autobiography of Guilt: Tim O'Brien and Vietnam." In *Writing Lives: American Biography and Autobiography*, edited by Hans Bak and Hans Krabbendham. Amsterdam, 1998. A variety of scholarly articles, some quite useful.

Robinson, Daniel. "Getting It Right: The Short Fiction of Tim O'Brien." *Critique: Studies in Contemporary Fiction* 40, no. 3 (Spring 1999): 257–264. A coherent and carefully balanced article that focuses on *The Things They Carried*.

Tegmark, Mats. *In the Shoes of a Soldier: Communication in Tim O'Brien's Vietnam Narratives*. Uppsala, Sweden, 1998. A strong look at the role of speaking in several of O'Brien's books.

See also the article on Tim O'Brien, immediately preceding.

FLANNERY O'CONNOR

by Susan Balée

The southern writer Flannery O'Connor died before she was forty years old. Her father had died of lupus erythematosus when she was a teenager, and she endured its first attack on her system when she was in her mid-twenties. Lupus, a chronic and debilitating illness that causes the body's immune system to turn on itself, upended her plans to live the rest of her life in the Northeast. After the first onslaught of illness nearly killed her, O'Connor reluctantly moved back to the country where she had been born and bred—middle Georgia—to live with her mother on the family's dairy farm in Milledgeville.

Her location and her illness isolated her, but they hardly smothered her gifts. If anything, the forced return to her home place so early in her career fostered her ability to "write what she knew." What O'Connor knew was the South—its landscape, its people (black and white), its sense of humor, its manners, its food, its customs, and, perhaps most important, its religious obsessions.

Flannery O'Connor.
(*Photograph by Joe McTyre. Courtesy of the Library of Congress*)

A SOUTHERN WRITER

O'Connor, like William Faulkner before her, understood that the South's history had bestowed a mythic quality upon its landscape and its inhabitants. First, the fertile land, described as a new Garden of Eden by the first colonial settlers, needed only tilling to reap its bounty. (Even Thomas Jefferson, the founding father and famous espouser of "equality for all," had attempted to rationalize slavery by saying that the slaves performed a noble and necessary—and perhaps even divine—function for America as "the gardeners in the Garden.") Alas, that rich soil with its ample sunlight and nine-month growing season provided the impetus for the colonial importation

of enforced laborers. Africans, wrested from their native lands and cultures, became the involuntary tenders of the soil—generations of families in bondage sweated and suffered and died on fecund southern earth. However, slaves in the American South did more than endure—they also developed a new culture in the land of exile and passed it on to their children. A strong belief in the tenets of Christ's life and death remains a cornerstone of African-American culture in the South, and it is also, interestingly, a cornerstone of white southern culture.

Southern whites feel just as acutely the history of their landscape, even though only a small percentage of white southerners had ancestors who owned slaves. Despite this, and therefore paradoxically, a majority of white southerners felt their own liberty oppressed by the federal government before, during, and after the Civil War (1861–1865). Just as slaves had once poured their sweat into the greedy earth, white Confederate soldiers spilled their blood there during the Civil War. The death toll wiped out most of a generation of men and, as their black neighbors had learned before them, sometimes only a belief in Christ could make sense of the enormous loss.

Although to northerners race relations in the South appear especially acrimonious during the 1950s and early 1960s (the period of the civil rights movement), O'Connor understood that the majority of southerners, black and white, were bound together by a shared belief in the Christian Bible as well as the shared history of the land they had grown up on. For this reason, O'Connor referred to the South as "Christ-haunted." A devout Irish Catholic in the Baptist South, she had a deep awareness of the region's history of original sin and the fall. The original sin of the South was slavery, but with its evil came also the possibility of grace and redemption. O'Connor's black characters, like William Faulkner's, invariably possess dignity and grace far beyond that of the white characters with whom they are juxtaposed.

EARLY CREATIVITY

Born on 25 March 1925, Mary Flannery O'Connor (she later dropped the first name, saying it made her sound "like an Irish washerwoman") displayed a sharp wit and penetrating intelligence from her earliest days. By age five she was reading and writing and trying her hand at literary criticism in the margins of her books. In the flyleaf of Louisa May Alcott's *Little Men*, she scribbled, "first-rate. Splendid." But her opinion of a popular children's book of the period, Shirley Watkins's *Georgia Finds Herself*, received this harsh judgment: "This is the worst book I ever read next to 'Pinnocchio' [sic]."

She attended Catholic schools in Savannah, and later Milledgeville, where the family moved when she was twelve. Her mother, Regina Cline O'Connor, supervised her little wunderkind closely, but her father, Edward, spent most of his time in Atlanta, where he worked for the Federal Housing Administration. As O'Connor entered her teens her father's health worsened, and eventually he came home to Milledgeville to die. Lupus took his life when his daughter and only child was fifteen; ten years later she began to show the same symptoms.

After graduating from the local high school, O'Connor enrolled in Georgia College for Women (now Georgia College), walking a mere block from her house to the campus. Although she did not attend dances or parties and does not seem to have dated either in high school or college, she did expand her reputation as both a wit and a first-rate creative writer. In her senior year O'Connor became editor of *Corinthian*, the college's literary magazine, and immediately published an editorial laying out the magazine's new policy: "We will write as we feel, preserving a modicum of orthodox English and making a small effort at keeping our originality out of our spelling. Some of us will strive for Art, some of us for free publicity, and some, the wiser of us by far, will not strive. . . . If you like what we do, that's very nice. If you don't, please remember the paper drive when you dispose of your copy."

As her college career wound to its close, one of her professors urged her to apply to the University of Iowa's graduate writing program—then as now considered by many to be the best creative writing program in America. O'Connor took his advice, won a scholarship to the school, and moved to Iowa. She took a variety of classes, worked on her short stories with a vengeance, and wrote her mother every day. In 1946, when she was twenty-one years old, O'Connor sold her first story, "The Geranium," to *Accent* magazine.

"THE GERANIUM" AND "JUDGEMENT DAY": BOOKENDS OF A CAREER

O'Connor's stories, from the earliest ones to the last she wrote, are marked by their combination of laugh-out-loud humor and dorsal-hair-raising horror. This strange combination of terror and comedy is known variously as "Southern Gothic" (a term she hated) or "the grotesque." Perhaps it's not surprising that the first work O'Connor acknowledged as an influence on her own writing was Edgar Allan Poe's *Humorous Tales*. Although O'Connor's tales frequently end with violence, they are also hilarious.

"The Geranium" bears all the hallmarks of O'Connor's writing, both stylistically and thematically. In this first story she treated the themes that intrigued her throughout her career: displacement and homesickness, particularly of the southerner displaced to another region of America and of country people displaced to urban landscapes. Her other major theme, race relations between blacks and whites, also underpins this story.

"The Geranium" tells the story of Old Dudley, a Georgian from a county outside Atlanta who has moved to New York City to live with his daughter and son-in-law. Old Dudley is getting old and he knows that his daughter wants him to be near "family," but the old man's main reason for coming to New York derives from a misguided (but amusing to the reader) fantasy, a romanticized vision of the city he saw in the movie *Big Town Rhythm*.

He soon discovers how much he hates New York. He feels trapped in his daughter's small apartment and resents his dependence on her. Back in his boardinghouse in Coa County, he'd been "the man of the house" and the "master" of his black friend Rabie. He and Rabie had fished and hunted together, and Old Dudley had brought the catch home to the boardinghouse, where it provided meals for the elderly female tenants there. Those old women had looked up to him as their provider and protector, and Rabie looked up to him too. Old Dudley enjoyed his ability to explain complicated things to Rabie, such as the mechanical operation of guns.

Unfortunately, in New York City his daughter does not look up to him. Instead he exasperates her. For his part, the hallways of the apartment building look like "dog runs," the people are unfriendly, their living space is cramped. The women don't talk to him and the men he sees staring out windows snarl at him if he stares too long. But he does stare, particularly at an apartment window across the alley where a geranium pot is placed every morning. Like Old Dudley, the red flower is a displaced plant; it's in a city window when it should be in a yard. It subsists on the apartment's sill, but it cannot thrive.

The climactic scene of the story occurs when Old Dudley is running an errand for his daughter and begins to reminisce in the stairwell about his days hunting with Rabie. As he mimics the motions of firing a rifle, a black neighbor—a Yankee—comes up the stairs. "What are you hunting, old man?" the neighbor calls out. Old Dudley is stunned; blacks in the South would never address a white man in such a familiar tone. Old Dudley is so humiliated he sinks to his knees. The black neighbor, amiably enough, helps him up the stairs. Both mortified and enraged, the old man permits the neighbor to lead him to his daughter's door. Once inside, he rushes to the window and discovers that the geranium across the way has fallen off the sill. It lies broken in the alley, six floors below. Old Dudley begins to cry, and the geranium's owner laughs at him. One of the story's last images is of the dying geranium lying helplessly on the pavement, its roots exposed to the air.

What stands out in this story is Old Dudley's reaction to the friendly black neighbor whom he feels has made fun of him. Although Dudley is a sympathetic character, his attitude to the northern black man is that of a white supremacist—he feels humiliated when the black man speaks to him as an equal. Ironically, back in the South, the person with whom he feels the greatest sense of kinship (more than he feels for his own daughter) is also a black man, Rabie. The difference is that Rabie behaves in a subservient manner with Old Dudley; he listens politely to what the old man has to tell him and doesn't presume to be an equal.

In "The Geranium," O'Connor attempted to examine the racial issues that had suffused her home region since the days of slavery. Her exploration of these issues occupied her throughout her career, and racial conflict and communion appear in various forms in almost all of her fiction. In this first published short story she tried to sketch the dilemma of the Old South when confronted by the new. In a later interview she commented explicitly on the social situation in the South for blacks and whites, noting that "it requires considerable grace for two races to live together. . . . It can't be done without a code of manners based on mutual charity. . . . [The] old manners are obsolete, but the new ones will have to be based on what was best in the old ones." She went on to observe that "For the rest of the country, the race problem has been solved when the Negro has his rights, but for the Southerner, [white or black] that's only the beginning."

The breakdown of racial communication that animates "The Geranium" clearly stayed in Flannery O'Connor's mind for decades. In fact, she rewrote "The Geranium" in the 1960s and titled it "Judgement Day." That story, the closing piece in her second collection of short fiction, *Everything That Rises Must Converge* (1965), also centers on a climactic confrontation between an old white southerner and a young black northerner. However, nearly twenty years separated the two stories, and in that time the civil rights movement had radically changed the South.

In the revised version of the tale, the old white man displaced to his daughter's New York City apartment attempts to patronize the black man living next door, just as he has always patronized blacks in the South, but his overly familiar and superior manner is insulting to the northern neighbor. Tanner, the old man, greets the neighbor with the name of "Preacher," reasoning that "it had been his experience that if a Negro tended to be sullen, this title usually cleared up his expression."

The neighbor, however, is outraged by the salute, all the more so when the old man adds, "I reckon you wish you were back in South Alabama." The black neighbor retorts, "I'm not from South Alabama. . . . I'm from New York City. And I'm not no preacher. I'm an actor!" When Tanner persists in calling him "Preacher" and patronizing him, the neighbor grabs him by the shoulders and hisses, "I don't take no crap off no wool-hat red-neck son-of-a-bitch peckerwood old bastard like you." He then shoves Tanner against the wall and the old man, in shock, suffers a stroke.

What has changed here is the nature of O'Connor's critique. Southern racism is scathingly critiqued in the latter story, whereas the alienation of the displaced southerner in a northern city formed the sympathetic focus of the first tale. The civil rights movement had sunk into O'Connor's consciousness between her first and her last published story. Had she not died so young, who knows where her examination of racial reconciliation would ultimately have taken her fiction?

THE YADDO CONTROVERSY AND A SOJOURN IN NEW YORK

In 1947, O'Connor completed her thesis, *The Geranium: A Collection of Stories*, and began looking for college teaching jobs, which she did not find. Instead she stayed on as a postgraduate teaching assistant at Iowa until she received an invitation to spend the summer of 1948 at the Yaddo Foundation, the prestigious writers' colony near Saratoga Springs, New York. O'Connor's residency at Yaddo was extended several times, and while there she developed a close friendship with the Pulitzer Prize–winning poet Robert Lowell. Lowell, unfortunately, was at the beginning of one of the many nervous breakdowns that punctuated his life. In this instance, his mental malaise took a paranoid turn, and he became certain that the director of Yaddo was aiding and abetting communists. He urged O'Connor and the other writers in residence there to boycott the foundation, and most of them agreed to do so, not only because Lowell was eloquent and persuasive but because the postwar fear of Soviet communism that would later become full-blown during Senator Joseph McCarthy's era had already begun to influence American thinking.

To show her solidarity with Lowell, O'Connor moved temporarily to a friend's apartment in New York City in the spring of 1949. Lowell came for a visit and attended mass with O'Connor. After the mass, he felt his Catholicism suddenly being revived "with an incredible outpouring of grace." O'Connor, at first flattered that she had reintroduced him to the church, soon became alarmed—he kept insisting she was a saint. Meanwhile, the board at Yaddo dismissed Lowell's charges against the director, and O'Connor moved into a room at the YWCA that "smelled like an unopened Bible."

Lowell, after spending some time at a Trappist monastery, went on a "missionary tour" of the Midwest, where his delusions precipitated a complete psychotic break. After being jailed for disorderly conduct in Indiana, his family had him committed to a mental hospital outside Boston.

For her part, O'Connor had lost both the comforts of Yaddo and the company of the other writers there. The YWCA depressed her, and she hated New York City as much as any of the displaced southerners in her stories. In fact, she wrote to a friend that the only advantage to living in the city was that "although you see several people you wish you didn't know, you see thousands you're glad you don't know."

O'Connor continued to work on her first novel, *Wise Blood* (1952), but her money was running out.

Fortuitously her friendship with Robert Lowell had one excellent outcome: he had introduced her to Robert and Sally Fitzgerald, two people who would number among her best friends for the rest of her life.

SALLY AND ROBERT FITZGERALD

At the time O'Connor met them, Robert Fitzgerald was a poet and a celebrated translator of Greek classics. His wife, Sally, reviewed books and raised the couple's two children while waiting for the impending arrival of their third. They were devout Catholics, and Sally was from Texas; O'Connor felt an immediate kinship with them. For their part, the Fitzgeralds were immediately struck by the poise and intelligence of the twenty-four-year-old writer. Without realizing it at the time, the Fitzgeralds would ultimately write the best biographical sketches of their young friend and the most cogent introductions to her books. Of that first meeting, Robert remembered O'Connor sitting in a chair facing the windows of their New York apartment. The March light flickering off the East River illuminated her heart-shaped face; Robert observed that she looked "pale and glum, with fine eyes that could stop frowning and open brilliantly upon everything." She was shy but self-possessed, and the Fitzgeralds were much impressed by her sardonic wit and penetrating mind.

Thus, in July 1949, when they were preparing to move to Connecticut for the sake of their burgeoning family, they asked O'Connor if she would like to board with them. She agreed with alacrity. For a year and a half she lived with the Fitzgerald family in Ridgefield, and they seem to have had something of an idyllic domestic and literary life together. O'Connor had her own room and bathroom above the house's garage, and there she worked on her first novel, *Wise Blood*, every morning after attending Mass. The family ate dinner together, and after the kids were in bed the adults discussed books and writing and their lives. Robert later recalled, "Our talks then and at the dinner table were long and lighthearted, and they were our movies, our concerts, and our theatre."

This life might have gone on indefinitely except that by December 1950 O'Connor began to feel severe pain in her arms. A local doctor thought she might have arthritis but told her to check it at home when she returned to Milledgeville for Christmas. Unfortunately on the train home she became desperately ill. She spent most of the spring in the hospital, too sick even to write her friends.

WISE BLOOD

When O'Connor finally emerged from the hospital, it became clear to her that she would not be moving north again. Her illness had been temporarily arrested, but it could not be cured. Instead she moved with her mother into the house at Andalusia, the dairy farm that Regina O'Connor managed on the outskirts of Milledgeville. Mrs. O'Connor gave her daughter a bedroom on the ground floor because Flannery didn't have the strength to manage the stairs. Every day, Flannery had to give herself a shot of cortisone—which made her hair fall out and her face swell—and to maintain a rigorously salt-free diet. Slowly, however, her strength came back, and she began to write more letters to the Fitzgeralds and other friends; indeed, O'Connor was a marvelous letter writer, and much of what we know about her life and thoughts comes from her collected letters, *The Habit of Being* (1979), edited by Sally Fitzgerald.

On the farm, O'Connor raised a variety of birds. She owned flocks of geese, turkeys, mallard ducks, pheasants, quail, and a variety of chickens and roosters. After the May 1952 publication of her first novel, she added peacocks to the aviary. O'Connor delighted in her new and showy birds, and several of them appear in her fiction, where their regal spread tails, a green-bronze "galaxy of gazing, haloed suns," symbolize the presence of the divine.

Meanwhile, that first novel, *Wise Blood*, had made her something of a curiosity both nationally and in her hometown. In fact, although it was published to wide acclaim, many reviewers could not figure out what she was trying to do in the novel. O'Connor became annoyed by the apparent refusal of so many readers to take seriously the novel's preoccupation with religious matters. In a preface to a later edition of the book, she wrote: "That belief in Christ is to some a matter of life and death has been a stumbling block for readers who would prefer to think it a matter of no great consequence." Still, *Wise Blood* in no way resembles a conventional religious text. O'Connor explained that she wrote the novel with zest and wanted it to be read that way. "It is a novel about a Christian [in spite of himself], and as such, very serious, for all comic novels that are any good must be about matters of life and death."

The Christian-in-spite-of-himself protagonist of *Wise Blood* is Hazel Motes of Eastrod, Tennessee. Having completed his stint in the U.S. Army, Hazel returns to his hometown only to discover all the Moteses gone and Eastrod a ghost town. In shock, he travels to Taulkinham, a strange new city, where he meets a "blind" preacher, Asa

Hawks, and his daughter, Sabbath Lily. Hazel struggles to free himself from memories of his fundamentalist Christian upbringing and what he feels is his destiny to be a preacher. To fight against this fate, he founds "The Church Without Christ" and quickly acquires a not-very-bright disciple, Enoch Emery.

Enoch, in his zeal to serve Hazel, steals a mummy from a museum and offers it to Hazel as "a new Jesus." Enoch then nicks a gorilla suit, as a reward to himself, and feels that once he puts it on, everyone will want to shake his hand. There are many false preachers in the book, such as Asa, who serve as alter egos for Hazel. Hazel's sense of unredeemed guilt intensifies, and he runs over one of these alter egos with his car. Self-inflicted penance swiftly follows: Hazel blinds himself with quicklime, wraps his chest with barbed wire, and walks in shoes filled with broken glass and rocks. In the end, he is beaten to death by a policeman wielding a billy club.

One reviewer recognized *Wise Blood* as "an important addition to the grotesque literature of Southern decadence," but another wrote, "after an opening performance like this one, [where has she] left herself to go?" Some reviewers, however, were simply offended by the book's violence and its comically weird characters. O'Connor defended such characters, saying that she drew grotesque characters to show humankind's deformity in the modern world. She explained, "Whenever I'm asked why Southern writers particularly have a penchant for writing about freaks, I say it's because we are still able to recognize one."

In Milledgeville, though no one really understood her book, folks were proud of their young novelist. O'Connor amusingly wrote to the Fitzgeralds, "Around here if you publish the number of whiskers on the local pigs, everyone has to give you a tea."

A GOOD MAN IS HARD TO FIND

By 1953, O'Connor was working steadily on the collection of stories that would become *A Good Man Is Hard to Find* (1955). She had come to see there was one blessing in her illness: it had brought her home and forced her to write about the people and the region she knew best. Her thoughts on the notion of "displaced people" intensified as her hips disintegrated and her center of gravity was displaced. She described her condition to a friend: "I am not able to walk straight, but not crippled enough to walk with a cane so that I give the appearance of merely being a little drunk all the time." One of the earliest stories she wrote for this collection was "The Displaced Person," and it derives from her close observation of life on the farm. Her mother managed several sets of employees, including two black workers who lived on the farm, white hired help who ran the dairy, and finally a succession of Displaced Person's (D.P.'s) who came to live with her in the years after World War II. The miscommunications, clashes, and conflict occasioned by these people of different classes, races, and expectations living and working together animate several of O'Connor's stories, but especially "The Displaced Person."

In this story, Mrs. McIntyre, a farm owner, hires a displaced Polish family named Guizac. Mr. Guizac quickly upsets the balance of the farm workers by being far more industrious and thrifty than either the black laborers or white hired help. The more Mrs. McIntyre praises his efficiency and skill, the more the others hate him. Finally, however, even she comes to despise him when he tells her he wants to arrange a marriage between one of the black laborers and his niece, still incarcerated in a European refugee camp.

Mr. Guizac has touched a nerve; he has brought up the greatest sin of the South for white southerners: miscegenation (the intermarriage of blacks and whites). Mrs. McIntyre is horrified and decides to turn the Guizacs out, despite all of the Pole's hard work and despite the pleas of her parish priest. The priest tells her, "think of the thousands of them, think of the ovens and the boxcars and the camps and the sick children, and Christ Our Lord." But Mrs. McIntyre is resolute in shutting her mind to all of that, refusing to see that her lack of charity is precipitating a tragedy. In the end, the farm collapses due to an act of racism. O'Connor seems to hint that this is the fate that will befall the South if white southerners continue to treat black southerners as second-class citizens.

Another story in the collection, "The Artificial Nigger," also treats racism. The title refers to the sort of lawn statuary one used to see regularly in the South of black jockeys holding a horse's bridle ring. When an old white man and his grandson are lost in a black neighborhood of Atlanta (the old man is trying to prove to his grandson that the big city is an evil place), at odds with each other and afraid, the sight of one of these jockey figures reunites them. To a friend, O'Connor explained, "what I had in mind to suggest with the artificial nigger was the redemptive power of the Negro's suffering for us all."

The best-known story of this collection is probably the title one, about a thoughtless and rather selfish old lady, the Grandmother, who comes face-to-face with an escaped convict named the Misfit who has just killed every other member of her family. In later critical writing about

the story, O'Connor tried to explain that the central point of "A Good Man Is Hard to Find" is the central point of the life of every Christian: can God's grace be attained at the moment of death? She urged her readers, "In this story you should be on the lookout for such things as the action of grace in the Grandmother's soul, and not for the dead bodies." In fact, to be on the lookout for the action of grace in her characters is good advice for reading any of Flannery O'Connor's tales.

When *A Good Man Is Hard to Find* appeared in June 1955, it received excellent reviews, far better than those accorded *Wise Blood*. With trepidation O'Connor accepted an invitation to be interviewed on NBC-TV in New York City, telling a friend, "I have a mental picture of my glacial glare being sent out over the nation to millions of children who are impatiently waiting for The Batman to come on." Happily, the interview went well, as did a dramatization of a scene from one of the stories, "The Life You Save May Be Your Own," and it improved sales of the collection.

The success of that partial dramatization led to a contract from the producers of General Electric Playhouse, who wanted to make a television show of the entire story. O'Connor gladly sold them the rights and bought her mother a refrigerator. She told a friend, "While they make hash out of my story, she and me will make ice in the new refrigerator."

"The Life You Save May Be Your Own" is about a con man, Mr. Shiftlet, who appears on a poor southern farm seeking work. An old woman named Mrs. Crater and her retarded daughter, Lucynell, are the only two people living on the farm. Shiftlet is looking to get two things from Mrs. Crater: an old car she keeps in a garage and as much of her money as he can dig out of her. To achieve this end, he is forced to marry Lucynell. After the marriage, he drives them away for their "honeymoon," but when she falls asleep at a diner after the end of their first day on the road, he abandons her there. Mr. Shiftlet is a type of character that appears fairly frequently in O'Connor's stories—a "devil in disguise."

Of course, O'Connor was devilishly surprised herself when she found out who would play him in the television version of her story: the dancer Gene Kelly. "I am writing my agent to make haste and sell all my stories for musical comedies," she wrote. The TV show appeared in February 1957, and though O'Connor deemed it "slop of the third water," it made her even more famous in Milledgeville. "Dogs who live in houses with television have paused to sniff me," she joked. "One old lady said, 'That was a play that really made me think!' I didn't ask her what." As soon as her celebrity died down, O'Connor returned quietly to work on her second novel, *The Violent Bear It Away* (1960).

THE VIOLENT BEAR IT AWAY

O'Connor's second novel bears a good deal of resemblance to her first in that its main character, Francis Marion Tarwater, feels fated to be a preacher. Like Hazel Motes in *Wise Blood*, Tarwater fights against this sense of predestination; also like Motes before him, Tarwater is transformed and redeemed by violence. Tarwater does not want to become a preacher, but neither does he want to be an intellectual, like his Uncle Rayber, who believes only in nonreligious reason. Still, young Tarwater is drawn to Rayber's retarded son, Bishop, and he comes to believe that it is his duty to baptize the boy.

Eventually he does baptize Bishop, with tragic results. By the time the baptism occurs, Tarwater is tormented by the devil, first as a "Friend" that he hears talking in his head and later as an old-looking young man in a lavender car who takes him for a ride then rapes him in the woods. After these violent events, Tarwater gives in to the feeling that he is destined to be a prophet. The novel ends with his burning down the woods encircling his childhood home and anticipating the moment when he will see the final "revelation."

When she finished the book, O'Connor wrote to her friend A., "I expect this one to be pounced on and torn limb from limb." Although it wasn't exactly dismembered, the reviews for *The Violent Bear It Away* when it appeared in February 1960 were similar to the reviews that had attended the first publication of *Wise Blood*: mixed.

EVERYTHING THAT RISES MUST CONVERGE

In the mid-1950s, to add to her writing income, O'Connor had begun to give talks to writers' groups and college students around the nation. The talks helped financially, but they tired her. By 1954 she was walking with a cane, and by 1955 she had traded in the cane for crutches. Her hips were disintegrating because of the lupus, but the crutches humiliated her; she hated to be pitied or helped. Regarding Christ's words that into the kingdom of heaven "the lame shall enter first," she added, "This may be because the lame will be able to knock everybody else aside with their crutches."

In her last collection of stories, *Everything That Rises Must Converge* (1965), a tale called "The Lame Shall Enter First" features a juvenile delinquent with a clubfoot. No

doubt this story was connected to O'Connor's increasing lameness and its effect on her mentally.

O'Connor had also become very interested in the ideas of the French theologian Teilhard de Chardin (1881–1955). He believed that Christians must accept the fate that befalls them, whatever it is, for in the end, all of time will be seen to be moving toward an "omega point," an ultimate moment when all events merge. O'Connor took the title for her collection from this concept, and she also pondered hard his idea of accepting fate, which she called "passive diminishment."

O'Connor accepted her lupus in light of this idea. The lupus had consumed her life just as it had consumed her immune system, but it had been a gift for her writing. "I have never been anywhere but sick," she wrote to A. "In a sense sickness is a place more instructive than a long trip to Europe. . . . Sickness before death is a very appropriate thing and I think those who don't have it miss one of God's mercies."

The title story of *Everything That Rises Must Converge* treats the convergence of races, generations, and classes of people. Julian, an educated young man who dislikes his silly and old-fashioned mother, is pressured to escort her to her weight-reducing class at the YMCA. They travel by bus, in the South, where buses had only recently been integrated. Julian, miffed at his dependence on his mother, longs to humiliate her; he wants to break her spirit, her belief that she "was someone" from a good (white and upper-middle-class) southern family. To embarrass her, he attempts to chat with various black riders on the bus, and they ignore him.

Then a large black woman dragging her young son boards the bus. She wears a hat identical to the one on Julian's mother's head, and he attempts to get his mother's attention, to point out the "equality" in dress between her and the black mother, but Julian's mother is too busy playing with the black woman's son to notice him. Meanwhile, the black mother is enraged by Julian's mother's familiarity with her son. When they rise to get off at the same stop, Julian's mother tries to give the little boy a penny, and the boy's mother knocks her down with her purse. Julian gloats that his mother has finally received her comeuppance until he realizes that she is unconscious, perhaps even dead, and then his guilt and remorse begin and the story ends.

Flannery O'Connor died of complications from lupus on 3 August 1964, before the publication of her last collection of short stories. Despite her early death, her stories have continued to fascinate readers and critics alike. O'Connor worked to the end of her life, despite illness, and she never lost either her sense of humor or her courage.

Her deep religious faith allowed her to see her lupus as a blessing; it forced her to return to her home region and gave her the opportunity to explore the history and character of her region in writing. Not long before she died, O'Connor commented on her status as a southern writer: "To call yourself a Georgia writer is certainly to declare a limitation, but one which, like all limitations, is a gateway to reality. It is a great blessing, perhaps the greatest blessing a writer can have, to find at home what others have to go elsewhere seeking."

[*See also* Short Story in America, The.]

WORKS

Wise Blood (1952)
A Good Man Is Hard to Find (1955)
The Violent Bear It Away (1960)
Everything That Rises Must Converge (1965)
The Complete Stories of Flannery O'Connor (1971)

FURTHER READING

Asals, Frederick. *Flannery O'Connor: The Imagination of Extremity*. Athens, Ga., 1982. Asals makes sense of the violent endings of so many of O'Connor's stories by his analysis of her use of the grotesque (comedy combined with horror), the double motif (alter egos of main characters), and the intensity of her Catholic beliefs.

Bloom, Harold, ed. *Flannery O'Connor: Modern Critical Views*. New York, 1986. This collection remains the best smorgasbord of O'Connor criticism yet assembled. The major commentators are all here, from Asals on the double, to the theologian Ralph C. Woods on the violence of O'Connor's Catholicism. There are reprints of important biographical essays by Robert Fitzgerald and two excellent pieces of literary criticism by the novelists John Hawkes and Joyce Carol Oates.

Coles, Robert. *Flannery O'Connor's South*. Baton Rouge, La., 1980. The celebrated Harvard physician and writer reflects on his travels in the South during the civil rights movement, when O'Connor was writing her best and most important fiction. His is a brilliant portrait of the landscape—physically and culturally—that she lived in.

The Flannery O'Connor Bulletin. Milledgeville, Ga., 1972–. This periodical, edited by the O'Connor scholar Sarah Gordon, a professor at Georgia College, where the bulletin is based, serves as the primary organ of ongoing studies of the Georgia author. The newest work on O'Connor will be found here, as will many seminal critical articles on her life and work.

Gordon, Sarah. *Flannery O'Connor: The Obedient Imagination*. Athens, Ga., 2000. Another go-round on the biographical influences that shaped O'Connor's writing. Gordon's is a feminist approach and, far from perceiving O'Connor as an extremist (see Asals, above), she believes the author was hemmed in by a patriarchal, Catholic culture that limited the topics she could write about.

O'Connor, Flannery. *Mystery and Manners: Occasional Prose*. Edited by Sally and Robert Fitzgerald. New York, 1969.

O'Connor, Flannery. *The Habit of Being: Letters*. Edited by Sally Fitzgerald. New York, 1979.

O'Connor, Flannery. *The Presence of Grace and Other Book Reviews by Flannery O'Connor*. Compiled by Leo J. Zuber; edited by Carter W. Martin. Athens, Ga., 1983.

JOHN O'HARA

by James P. Austin

The short-story writer and novelist John O'Hara, whose popular fiction was known for its journalistic breeziness and its close attention to the details of contemporary American life in the mid-twentieth century, came to his success in roundabout yet dogged fashion. Born on 31 January 1905 in Pottsville, Pennsylvania, O'Hara was the first child of Dr. Patrick and Katherine Delaney O'Hara. The O'Haras represented, for some time, the combination of two powerful and staunchly Catholic families in the region, and John learned to assume early in life that his future place was among other influential young men and women in the Ivy League.

O'Hara's childhood was marked by a habitual mischievousness that would

John O'Hara.
(Courtesy of the Library of Congress)

assert itself often much later, in his adult life. This was perhaps due in part to ongoing tensions between O'Hara and his father, who wanted his son to go to medical school so badly that he offered his fourteen-year-old son $10,000 for the promise to go—an offer the younger O'Hara rejected. At a young age, O'Hara had settled on the prestige of Yale.

But his mischievous behavior often affected his studies; O'Hara spent several years in childhood bouncing from school to school as his father became increasingly incensed with his son's disappointing academic record. When O'Hara finally did graduate from a decent preparatory school, the Niagara University Prep School, his father doubted his dedication to Yale and decided that his son should work for a year, to develop a work ethic, before ultimately attending Yale. This decision had a tremendous impact on O'Hara's life, for two reasons. First, Dr. O'Hara arranged to have his son hired at the *Pottsville Journal*, at first for no salary and then only at modest salary. O'Hara loved the newspaper business, and this passion led him to New York, where he would eventually make his way as a writer.

The second reason for the significance of this decision is that Dr. O'Hara did not live through the end of the one-year deferral, dying in March 1925 of Bright's disease. This affected the O'Hara family in several ways, but it also ended John's intention to attend Yale. The death of Dr. O'Hara, and thus the end of his lucrative medical practice, reduced the family from one of considerable financial standing to near-poverty in only a matter of months. John O'Hara was twenty years old and working at the *Pottsville Journal* for a small salary.

MOVING ON TO NEW YORK

O'Hara's ambition to attend Yale faded after that—in part because the family could not afford it, in part because he was in love, and in part because he had latched on to newspaper work and enjoyed it. He left Pottsville for New York in 1928, and lived briefly in East Orange, New Jersey, while seeking newspaper work. In New York, O'Hara's writing career began taking shape, first as a newspaperman, then as a regular *New Yorker* contributor, and at last as a novelist and publisher of short-story collections.

O'Hara's first newspaper job in New York was with the *Herald-Tribune*, but it was certainly not his last. He worked at several newspapers during those early years, and became so desperate for living money as he toiled at literary writing that for a short time he lived in Pittsburgh and worked as managing editor for the *Bulletin-Index*. While in New York, he worked for *Time* magazine and the *Morning Telegraph*, among other newspapers and magazines. O'Hara typically lost these jobs because of frequent tardiness, being hung over, and often for being generally unpleasant.

It was also during these early years in New York that O'Hara began publishing for *The New Yorker*. His brief story "The Alumnae Bulletin" appeared in the 5 May 1928 issue of the magazine, and instigated a long relationship between O'Hara and the magazine. This relationship allowed O'Hara to make lifelong friends from *The New Yorker* staff, including Katharine Angell, E. B. White, and Wolcott Gibbs, and while beneficial to O'Hara—he would eventually place dozens of stories within *The New Yorker*'s pages—also resulted in over one hundred rejections, most of them for his stories.

In 1930, O'Hara met Helen Ritchie Petit, who he affectionately dubbed "Pet." Pet was a Wellesley College graduate who held a master's degree from Columbia University. By early 1931, O'Hara and Pet had married in an informal ceremony in New York, but their marriage was often uneven and stormy. O'Hara was still a frequent drinker, and he became moody, and perhaps violent, when he drank too much. Pet, too, drank more frequently as their marriage worsened. By 1933, it became apparent that they had made a mistake and separated. This failure caused O'Hara to spiral downward into a lengthy depression.

While O'Hara was establishing himself as a regular contributor to *The New Yorker*, he began publishing in other magazines, beginning with "Alone," which appeared in *Scribner's* in 1931. His story "Early Afternoon" was selected for the "Best Short Stories of 1932" issue. These successes developed a greater readership, and O'Hara's work began to be noticed.

FURTHER SUCCESSES

In 1933, O'Hara—still troubled by his failed marriage, inability to hold a steady job, and lingering insecurities with his own writing—began work on *Appointment in Samarra*, his first novel. He was granted an advance by Harcourt, Brace after the publisher read early work on the novel and approved it. This advance came just in time for O'Hara, who was out of work and residing in spartan quarters in New York.

Appointment in Samarra was published in 1934 and was widely reviewed. Many reviewers were favorable, while others were wary of the sexual nature of the book, considered racy for the times. But the novel sold well and was considered a success, and Harcourt, Brace requested that O'Hara collect some of his published short stories, which were published in 1935 under the title *The Doctor's Son and Other Stories*.

During this time, O'Hara began shuttling back and forth between New York and Los Angeles, where he began working in Hollywood, writing dialogue for scripts. His

stays in California were never permanent, and he often pined for the East while working in Hollywood. But he enjoyed the easy money, and returned to Hollywood fifteen times over twenty years. In 1936, O'Hara met and began dating Belle Wylie. Their courtship was intense and brief, and the couple eloped in December 1937—when O'Hara was thirty-two and his bride twenty-four. They would remain partners, and teammates of a sort, until her early death in 1954.

In the meantime, O'Hara was continuing to publish books, though they often did not generate much income for the author. His second novel, *Butterfield 8*, was published in 1935, followed in 1938 by *Hope of Heaven*, of which O'Hara was proud but which caused few ripples. That same year, however, O'Hara's short story "Pal Joey" appeared in *The New Yorker*. This one story had an enormous impact on O'Hara's future career and finances, since Harold Ross, editor of *The New Yorker* at that time, enjoyed the story and suggested that O'Hara expand the story into a series of stories following the exploits of the character Joey Evans. O'Hara took the suggestion and ran with it. O'Hara produced well over a dozen "Joeys," eventually collecting them together under the title *Pal Joey* in 1940, though some of the Joeys had appeared previously in O'Hara's 1939 collection *Files on Parade*. His collection *Pal Joey* became a steady seller, and O'Hara was even approached to sell the rights to his Joeys for production on Broadway as a musical. O'Hara agreed, and the musical *Pal Joey* premiered in New York and Philadelphia in late 1940. The musical was met with strong reviews—either for the better or the worse—and it was successful.

THE WAR

O'Hara was ardently patriotic, and when America entered World War II, he tried several times to enlist in the military, despite the fact that he was in his mid-thirties. His short-story production, which had been prolific for many years, fell off dramatically, plagued as he was by his inability to serve his country. O'Hara was turned away from military service for, among other things, bad teeth and an ulcer, and an abbreviated stint in the Office of Strategic Services revealed that O'Hara was physically unable to cope with the rigors of military service in any capacity.

Finally, in 1944, O'Hara began serving as a *Liberty* correspondent in the Pacific, and spent several weeks aboard the carrier *Intrepid* in this capacity. While on board, O'Hara was sober and healthy, and he missed his wife terribly. O'Hara returned from abroad in late

1944, and his daughter, Wylie O'Hara, was born on 14 June 1945.

After the war ended, O'Hara returned successfully to writing full-time. In 1945 he published a short-story collection, *Pipe Night*, and four years later the novel *A Rage to Live* was published. *A Rage to Live* was O'Hara's first novel to sell early and often, and was met with largely positive reviews. This was followed by a short novel, *The Farmers Hotel*, in 1951. This late success produced a renaissance of interest in O'Hara's earlier works, and several early works were reissued with new prefaces by O'Hara.

This run of success, however, was seriously tempered by two dramatic events in O'Hara's life. In August 1953, O'Hara suffered a stomach hemorrhage when it was punctured by an ulcer, and he would have died if Belle's sister had not found him in time, lying on the bathroom floor of his mother-in-law's apartment. The illness did not kill O'Hara, but it did make him realize that his days of heavy drinking were over. A few months later, in January 1954, Belle, who had been ill for months, went into the hospital for treatment, and shortly thereafter died, at age forty-one of acute auricular fibrillation. John O'Hara found himself alone, a single father to his daughter Wylie, and yet he did not drink. He did not drink again for the remainder of his life.

LATE CAREER

O'Hara was not alone for long. A few months after Belle's death, he began dating Katherine Barnes Bryan, known to her friends as Sister, and not long after that she was his exclusive partner. The following year they were married; the union was so successful that Sister eventually adopted Wylie.

This marriage and its success ushered in a productive period in O'Hara's writing career. Between 1955 and his death in 1970, O'Hara published eighteen books, including *Ten North Frederick*, which won the National Book Award in 1956; *From the Terrace* (1958); *Ourselves to Know* (1960); *The Big Laugh* (1962); *The Horse Knows the Way* (1964); *My Turn* (1966); and *And Other Stories* (1968). His books *Pal Joey, Ten North Frederick, Butterfield 8, From the Terrace,* and *A Rage to Live* were also adapted into screenplays and made into movies, although O'Hara himself had no direct involvement with these adaptations. His short stories also began to appear in *The New Yorker* again, ending a lengthy fallout with the magazine.

In 1957, O'Hara and Sister built a home outside of Princeton, New Jersey, that they named Linebrook.

O'Hara's study there would become the setting in which he produced the aforementioned prolific amounts of fiction in the final years of his life.

O'Hara's final book, *The Ewings*, was completed at Linebrook in February 1970, just two months before his death; the novel would not be published until 1972 because of estate problems. But on the last night of his life, John O'Hara was at work on a sequel to *The Ewings*, and stopped earlier than usual owing to pain in his chest and left arm. When Sister checked on him the following afternoon, she found her husband dead in his bed. John O'Hara was sixty-five years old.

WORKS

Appointment in Samarra (1934)
The Doctor's Son and Other Stories (1935)
Butterfield 8 (1935)
Hope of Heaven (1938)
Files on Parade (1939)
Pal Joey (1940)
Pipe Night (1945)
Hellbox (1947)
A Rage to Live (1949)
The Farmers Hotel (1951)
Sweet and Sour (1954)
Ten North Frederick (1955)
A Family Party (1956)
From the Terrace (1958)
Ourselves to Know (1960)
Sermons and Soda-Water (1960)
Assembly (1961)
The Big Laugh (1962)
The Cape Cod Lighter (1962)
Elizabeth Appleton (1963)
The Hat on the Bed (1963)
The Horse Knows the Way (1964)
The Lockwood Concern (1965)
My Turn (1966)
Waiting for Winter (1966)
The Instrument (1967)
And Other Stories (1968)
Lovey Childs: A Philadelphian's Story (1969)
The Ewings (1972)
The Time Element and Other Stories (1972)
A Cub Tells His Story (1974)
Good Samaritan and Other Stories (1974)

FURTHER READING

Bruccoli, Matthew J. *The O'Hara Concern: A Biography of John O'Hara.* New York, 1975. The first authorized biography of O'Hara's life.

Goldleaf, Steven. *John O'Hara: A Study of the Short Fiction*. New York, 1999. A study of many of O'Hara's most popular short stories and collections.

MacShane, Frank. *The Life of John O'Hara*. New York, 1980. Biography discussing the life and works of John O'Hara; includes bibliographical references and index.

Wolff, Geoffrey. *The Art of Burning Bridges: A Life of John O'Hara*. New York, 2003. A study of O'Hara's life and works.

SHARON OLDS

by Janet McCann

Sharon Olds has always been a controversial poet. The raw emotional power of her work and its sometimes intrusive physicality have many admirers and a few detractors. Accessible, highly personal (but not always autobiographical), these poems confront the reader with their frank female sensuality and their insistence that human experience is primarily of the body. Olds's poetry allows the body to speak. She articulates the physical at the extremes of human experience: birth, torture, sex, death. Her narratives come from observation, listening, reading of world events, experience. Her "body language" illuminates powerful truths.

Olds was born on 19 November 1942 in San Francisco and grew up in California. She received a B.A. degree from Stanford University in 1964 and a Ph.D. from Columbia in 1972. At Columbia she took part in student protests; she has described this participation in her poetry. She lives in Manhattan and teaches in the Creative Writing

Program at New York University, which she once directed; she was also New York Poet Laureate from 1998 to 2000. Through New York University, she founded a creative writing program for the severely physically disabled at Goldwater Hospital, another of the many ways she has found to give the body a voice. Because she has chosen to say little in public about the details of her personal life—she told an interviewer for *Salon* magazine that she had years ago taken a vow not to—the poems create an Olds mythology.

In childhood and young adulthood Olds read and wrote stories and poems; she says she has been influenced by Dickinson and Whitman as well as newer and older poets and also by other arts. She enumerates some of her sources: "Fats Domino, Charlie Parker, the Staples Singers, the Psalms . . . Beethoven, Puccini, MJQ, Mozart, 'Baby Owlet,' 'Desert Silv'ry Moon'—and then the whole idea of other languages and dance has had a big effect on my sense of shape, turn, line. I even want to say that human sobbing and coughing, say, influenced me" (personal communication). Her poems have an organic quality in all senses and reflect their multiple sources of inspiration.

SATAN SAYS

When Olds's first book appeared, she was thirty-seven years old, but her poems in noted journals had already drawn attention. *Satan Says* was published in 1980 by the University of Pittsburgh Press and received the San Francisco Poetry Center Award in 1981. This collection was perceived as "confessional" in the mode of Anne Sexton and Sylvia Plath, but it goes beyond its progenitors in its portrayal of violence, abuse, and the sexual. Moreover, it does not have the unbroken darkness of Plath and Sexton but finds energy and life even in destructive acts. What characterizes Olds's work from the beginning is its fleshiness, and indeed the words "matter" and "material" often appear in the work. While other poets seek translucence, Olds creates a glimmering opacity, a resistance of the body that highlights its materiality but

Sharon Olds. (*Margaretta K. Mitchell Photography*)

grants it a kind of sacredness. Pain and pleasure are very much mixed and melded in this poetry, and the poems reveal layers of love and hatred, delight and pain, rejection and acceptance of everything human. The poems describe violence, torment, and rebellion. They unveil a sensibility highly aware of and attuned to physical nature, the parts of the body, and the way these parts may be used and abused.

In *Satan Says*, Olds characteristically employs a flowing verse that piles detail on detail in a breathless narrative. Most of the poems are short; they usually tell stories about events in the speaker's life or in the lives of others. There is some wordplay and punning and a good deal of sound-echoing, but the power of the poem is really in the pileup of visual detail that pulls the sometimes unwilling reader into every scene. The run-on lines open out and pull in to heighten or release tension.

The voice in *Satan Says* is rebellious, direct, and confrontational, in the style of the 1980s. Marilyn Hacker called it "a daring and elegant first book," and the daring is not so much in what Olds says as in the attitude of the poems, which challenge the reader to accept the body and all its needs. While the scenes represented are sometimes shocking, the speaker remains irrepressible, energetic, open to delight. The speaker identifies herself as a follower of Whitman or Ginsberg who does not submit to life but rides it. In "The Language of the Brag" she applies the arrogant posture of the male poet to her female act of giving birth, "this glistening verb." Bearing and writing become one in this poem that celebrates female experience. Another poem with attitude is "The Sisters of Sexual Treasure," which describes two young girls trying to experience all the forbidden sexual acts possible to prove their "theory of the lost culture," which the speaker summarizes as: "if Mother said it wasn't there / it was there." Some of the poems focus on anatomical parts separately as the observer's gaze lingers on the body; some focus on the animality of human beings. But the energy in the poems and the acceptance of experience forbids any assessment of the speaker as a victim, no matter what experience is described.

SUBSEQUENT DIRECTIONS

Since her first book, Olds has published collections at fairly regular intervals, always to wide acclaim. She does not begin with the idea of a book but collects her best work from the previous three to five years and then proceeds to "refine, rewrite, shuffle, shape—work on the book as if it were a poem." *Satan Says* was followed by *The Dead and the Living* (1984), winner of the Lamont Award from the Academy of American Poets for a second book. It also won the National Book Critics Circle Award. This book handles some of the same materials as *Satan Says* but with a little more consciousness of craft and a wider range of subjects. While the first collection focused on the speaker's dysfunctional family, these poems include a powerful group (in the "Poems for the Dead" section) based on world events, such as "Portrait of a Child" (about a child dead of hunger in Yerevan) and "The Death of Marilyn Monroe." "Poems for the Living" return to her family and explore her sensual life and parenting experiences. As outspoken and graphic as those of *Satan Says*, the poems are sometimes more analytic. They demonstrate and expound the claim that love and hate are two sides of the coin of touch.

The Gold Cell (1987) follows the same themes, expressing compassion for public and private victims and exploring the bright and dark patches of the family quilt. Child abuse, political crimes, suffering, and neglect are on one side; joy in sensuous nature on the other. The poems addressing the speaker's own parenting are especially powerful as she focuses on the body and its vulnerabilities. In one poem, sleeping children are described through the details of their physical being; the physical details are the selves, the individuals. Olds concludes, "When love comes to me and says / What do you know, I say 'This girl, this boy.' " Another poem in which the daughter "is lost for an hour" finds the mother concentrating on her physical reality when she is found, "every gold cell of her body." The poems suggest that one must experience the worst to appreciate the best of physical life—that the dark and light strands are inextricably woven.

The concentration of Olds's work heightens its intensity, and no book is more concentrated or more intense than *The Father* (1992). In one painfully explicit poem after another, horrific experiences of the speaker's past are remembered as she notes the grisly details of her father's slow death. Yet even here the relationship is not all horrible; there is some love in it. Some reviewers found the book too concentrated, too disturbing. Others appreciated its probing honesty. The sequence describes the gritty details of the father's last conscious moments, and through his dying, the tortured relationship between the speaker and her father is reflected. Old violations are dissolved in compassion. The speaker describes the frantic rush to the hospital, the way the dying body looks, the last interactions between father and daughter, the death and cremation, and what happens afterward. Echoes of the earlier tormented relationship are reflected in the present.

"Nullipara" seems to sum up the book's theme, in the poem's richly ambiguous title and in the conclusion: "He knows he will live in me / after he is dead. I will carry him like a mother. / I do not know if I will ever deliver."

The Wellspring (1996) is intriguing in that it is a mostly positive collection that focuses on the body and on sexuality but in such a way as to redefine "family values" as centering on physical touch in all its manifestations. The speaker describes the expressed and suppressed violence that is at the core of family life, from couplings and births through small and large acts of rage involved in growing up to deaths that define the lives that led to them. Yet there is always a verve, an energy, so that even destructive acts are part of the lust for living that characterizes human and animal nature. The titles suggest the range: "Killing My Sister's Fish," "Dirty Memories," "Bathing the New Born," "My Son the Man," "High School Senior." Some of the poems suggest a lighter Olds—the parenting experiences are narrated with flickers of humor. The viscosity is still there but the more alarming fluids are less prominent—water and milk take an important place in poems of parenthood.

Blood, Tin, Straw (1999) again focuses on the physical, although many of the poems seem quieter, more distanced. This collection, winner of the 2000 Patterson Prize, revisits some of the scenes and people of earlier poems. The poems seem more metaphoric than some earlier ones in that the meanings of physical acts and even objects are explored—the poems do not stay with the acts and bodies themselves. For some readers accustomed to Olds's style this may seem a dilution, but for others the analytic element adds a new perspective. These poems also more often include the body's coverings as part of the body. Donna Seaman commented in her review, "If the body is the temple of the soul, then Olds is its priestess," and this collection seems to imply a little more formality, a little more distance, as though indeed the body were a temple, with its sacred objects and rituals. Inanimate objects also can speak for the body and for the soul. In "The Necklace," the speaker, who is feeling depressed, is wearing a pearl necklace inherited from her mother; as the necklace shifts on the speaker's throat she feels it as a message from her mother: "as if she slithered / along me to say, Come away from your gloom, / your father, that garden is a grave, come away." The pearls are hardened crumbs of her mother and show the connection as unbroken: they can "wobble along me, globe on her axis" to bring "morning." The poem plays with suggestions of roundness, pearls, circles, and Circe as it develops its extended comparison between the mother's voice and the pearls.

OLDS'S CONTRIBUTION

Olds's style has continued to change as her work has matured, although its subjects tend to remain constant and so does its emphasis on writing the body, the body writing. ("I like the physical feel of writing," she said in an interview with Esta Spalding in 2001, providing a glimpse of a poet who does not use a computer.) The poems have become longer and include more pauses. Rhythms that lurk beneath the surface are easier to spot; some of her poems approach hymn stanza, others blank verse. Her vocabulary has become more unusual, and words sometimes seem chosen for their heft and feel, as physical objects in a world of matter. Despite the changes, the poems remain accessible and achieve their power through detail.

Olds's work has remained popular over time despite changing tastes in poetry, during periods of postmodernist complexity as well as eras that favored outspoken personal poetry. Her focus on the father as a dark power invites comparison with Sylvia Plath, but Olds's assessment of the father's influence is more complex and her attitude toward the father figure is less passive. Olds's poems, however direct, do lend themselves to theorizing. For instance, Laura Tanner uses theories of the gaze, based on work by Michel Foucault, Laura Mulvey, and others, to discuss Olds's poems of terminal illness in *The Father*, and other critics focusing on the body as text have commented on Olds's reading of the physical. Olds's voice is immediately recognizable in any of her work: few contemporary poets can claim this distinction. The intensity of her poetry—its ability to seize even an unwilling reader—and its directness account for its success. The combination of the reticence of the poet with the outspokenness of the poems themselves increase its mystique. Olds's heady brew will not go out of style; its combination of image and wit will continue to compel readers.

WORKS

Satan Says (1980)
The Dead and the Living (1984)
The Gold Cell (1987)
The Matter of This World: New and Selected Poetry (1987)
The Sign of Saturn: Poems, 1980–1987 (1991)
The Father (1992)

The Wellspring: Poems (1996)
Blood, Tin, Straw (1999)
The Unswept Room (2002)

FURTHER READING

Argyros, Ellen. " 'Some Epic Use of My Excellent Body': Redefining Childbirth as Heroic in *Beloved* and 'The Language of the Brag.' " In *This Giving Birth: Pregnancy and Childbirth in American Women's Writing*, edited by Julie Tharp. Bowling Green, Ohio, 2000. Focuses on one poem but applies to many.

Dillon, Brian. " 'Never Having Had You, I Cannot Let You Go': Sharon Olds' Poems of a Father-Daughter Relationship." *Literary Review* 37, no. 1 (Fall 1994): 108–118.

McCallum-Whitcomb, Susan. "Claiming our Birth-Rite: The Poetry of American Mothers." In *This Giving Birth: Pregnancy and Childbirth in American Women's Writing*, edited by Julie Tharp. Bowling Green, Ohio, 2000. Centers on birth experiences.

Spalding, Esta. "The Earthly Matter: A Conversation with Sharon Olds." *Brick* 67 (Spring 2001): 85–92. Highly informative interview focused on Olds's techniques.

Tanner, Laura E. "Death Watch: Terminal Illness and the Gaze in Sharon Olds's *The Father*." *Mosaic* 29, no. 1 (March 1996): 104–121. Uses the film critic Laura Mulvey's ideas about the meaning of the gaze to analyze these poems, which closely observe the father's death.

Wright, Carolyne. "The Dead and the Living." *Iowa Review* 15, no. 1 (Winter 1985): 151–161. A review essay that gives a useful analysis of Olds's second book.

EUGENE O'NEILL

by Philip Parry

Eugene Gladstone O'Neill was born into a theatrical household on 16 October 1888 in a hotel room in New York City, and died in Boston, also in a hotel room, on 27 November 1953. Into the intervening sixty-five years, he managed to pack three marriages and a fair amount of marital infidelity, a lot of drinking, and an immense amount of writing. Excess is always dazzling, but it is O'Neill's writing that matters most.

He was the third and youngest son of James O'Neill (1845/6–1920)—an Irishman who, having emigrated to the United States in 1855, became one of nineteenth-century America's principal actors—and Mary Ellen Quinlan (1857–1922), known as Ella, also

Eugene O'Neill.
(*Courtesy of the Library of Congress*)

of an Irish family but born in New Haven, Connecticut. From these few facts, much of O'Neill's career as a dramatist, and many of the torments of his adolescent and adult life, can be derived. One incident in particular was traumatic. This third child had nonetheless only one elder brother, because in 1885 the O'Neill's seven-year-old eldest son, James O'Neill Jr. (1878–1923), infected their second son, Edmund Burke O'Neill, with measles. The death of the two-year-old, and the complex apportionment of guilt that resulted from it, naturally affected both parents but seems to have left Ella severely damaged emotionally. Perhaps her third son was conceived in a spirit of compensation: Eugene certainly grew to believe, probably prompted by his parents, that he was an inadequate replacement for his dead brother. (Sibling rivalry is scarcely unusual, but a dead rival is always the hardest to beat. In *Long Day's Journey into Night*, O'Neill is still in the thick of battle: by means of a highly significant reversal of names, Eugene becomes the dead second child, Edmund his guilt-ridden substitute. Freud could not have found clearer evidence of wish-fulfillment fantasy at work.) To add to the family's woes,

Ella had been prescribed morphine to numb the pains of Eugene's birth, became addicted, and remained under its distracting spell until 1914. Blighted by a death and a birth, her relationship with her sons was not ideal. Both Jamie and Eugene led deeply troubled adult lives.

At once dependent on female companionship and fiercely misogynistic, O'Neill was incapable of real emotional fidelity. Moreover, the Catholic faith into which he was born, far from being a consolation, set him moral standards that he lacked strength either to meet or to put aside. Instead, he sought a kind of querulous relief in drink and in the theater. What he never really found, and perhaps never truly wanted to find, was rest: the theater, in particular, was the venue where he fought his greatest rival, a living father rather than a dead brother. *Long Day's Journey into Night* was a reconciliation of sorts with a father who had died twenty years before it was written. Yet, had O'Neill's wishes been respected, this masterpiece of charity and compassion would never have seen its way through to performance. O'Neill's desire to impede the success of his best work (and he knew it was his best work) is fascinating evidence of just how complex and damaged were his relationships with both his family and his art.

One should not put too much emphasis, however, upon an image of O'Neill as a tormented artist, doomed forever to speak into a void, for perhaps surprisingly, he has never lacked public recognition. The only American dramatist to have received a Nobel Prize (awarded in 1936), he also won three Pulitzer prizes during his lifetime and a fourth posthumously in 1957. Remarkably, all save this last award predate the writing of *The Iceman Cometh* (1939–1940) and *Long Day's Journey into Night* (1940–1941) and long predate their first productions, in 1946 and 1956, respectively. Indeed, during the final twenty years of his life, plagued both by a neurological disorder that made writing physically arduous and by his commitment to several unduly ambitious theatrical projects, O'Neill largely fell away from public view. Yet to these difficult years, we now recognize, belong his finest achievements.

EXPERIMENTAL THEATER

O'Neill began his career as a dramatist by writing, between 1913 and 1918, nearly two dozen short plays, some of them not produced, others put on by the Provincetown Players, an amateur company, in the Wharf Theatre in Provincetown, Massachusetts, and various small theaters in New York City. *Beyond the Horizon* (1918), his first play to be given a professional Broadway production, was hailed as an authentic modern tragedy and won him a Pulitzer Prize. It reveals a persistent interest in antithetical characters and attitudes: two brothers—one by every instinct a farmer, the other a sailor—agree to reverse roles when the woman they both love decides that she would like to marry the wandering brother and settle down on the farm. The play traces the disappointment and defeat that both men experience when, for merely worldly and temporary benefits, they sacrifice their personal vision and aspiration.

Relatively straightforward in plotting and presentation, *Beyond the Horizon* brought the first phase of O'Neill's career to a close and ushered in fifteen years of radical experimentation. Granted that he was above all else a theatrical reformer, one way of coaxing clarity out of the resulting confusion is to see O'Neill's work of the 1920s and 1930s as a set of responses to deficiencies in the American theater, which he thought backward by European standards. Not all of his reforms worked or were needed, but all were seriously meant and he carried them through with quite fearsome sincerity. Some were generated not by defects in contemporary theater but by imperfections in his own vision of what theater could and should do. When in *Long Day's Journey into Night*, James Tyrone tells his son, Jamie, that he sneers at everyone except himself, Jamie replies ("wryly"): "That's not true, Papa. You can't hear me talking to myself, that's all." By 1940, when these lines were written, O'Neill was looking back on a long history of personal attempts to produce in the theater—by means of masks and asides and stage directions—a convincing record of interior monologue.

One persistent problem that every reader or producer of O'Neill's work faces is the result of his unrelenting attempt, fueled by enthusiasm for the work of Sigmund Freud, to give comprehensive expression to aspects of his characters' personalities that would remain hidden in ordinary life and circumstances. (One way of doing this without breaching naturalistic conventions is to write speeches for drunks and alcoholics. Both *The Iceman Cometh* and *Long Day's Journey into Night*, the fruits of O'Neill's triumphant return to naturalistic theater, rely heavily on such characters and on Mary Tyrone, a morphine addict.) Anxious that no scintilla of meaning should be lost, or be derived from anyone other than the playwright himself, O'Neill had always tried, he boasted, to *write out* his characters. The resulting subordination of performance to print is, or would be if it really succeeded, a denial of drama. (At the opposite end of the spectrum is Thornton Wilder's insistence that scripts are blank checks issued by playwrights to actors.)

O'Neill's principal weapon in this unnecessary fight against unlicensed interpretations of his plays is the stage direction. Other ways of expressing the unexpressed, most notably masks and asides, were adopted and pursued enthusiastically for a while, but were dropped when they proved unsatisfactory. To the explanatory and interpretive stage direction, by contrast, he remained permanently faithful. "Possibly my use of masks and asides is artifice and bombast," he conceded in 1934, eight years after *The Great God Brown* (his principal masked play) took to the stage, and six years after *Strange Interlude* (his most extended experiment in the employment of asides) (Bogard and Bryer, p. 440). Both masks and asides were failed solutions to the same problem. In 1932, in "Second Thoughts" on "Memoranda on Masks," he described *Strange Interlude* as a "new masked psychological drama . . . without masks" (Bogard, *Unknown O'Neill*, p. 409). Masked but without masks? This makes sense only because masks and asides were alternative revelations of the interior or mental life of his characters.

Like every theatrical invention, however, masks proved to be unruly beasts with a life of their own. In *The Great God Brown*, William Brown and Dion Anthony are, respectively, the Apollonian (rational) and Dionysian (passional) opposites of Nietzschean tragic theory. When Dion dies, Brown fakes his own disappearance, dons his rival's mask, and walks off with Dion's wife, Margaret, thus fulfilling a desire that he is otherwise too timid to realize. Clearly there is meaning here that in naturalistic drama would need lengthy exposition, but equally clearly O'Neill's masks are not just a convenient theatrical shorthand, mere symbols of our divided personalities, but are additionally, or instead, physical instruments of duplicity and error. Thus an explanatory device acquires a life of its own that requires further explanation. (Since, within the terms that the play sets, Margaret has every right to suppose that she is sleeping with her husband, what is the real-life equivalent of the situation in which Brown commits adultery with a woman who does not commit adultery with him?) There is a law of theater in operation here—the law of "endless semiosis"—which states that everything is interpretable, including interpretation itself. This argument, far from being a dismissal of *The Great God Brown*, suggests that not even O'Neill could have fully worked out the meaning of his play, not because he was stupid (he was not) or lacked industry (he did not), but because of the unalterable nature of theater (that it must always be interpreted) and of interpretation (that it is always incomplete).

Strange Interlude (1927), in some ways the oddest play in the O'Neill canon, is in other ways one of the least odd. There is massive reliance on asides, but once we accept that these are simply a means of making characters and their motivations comprehensively available to us, the very overexplicitness of the explanations and revelations that they contain renders the play unsurprising. Why did O'Neill rely so heavily on asides? That he was reviving a characteristic freedom of the Elizabethans is not convincing, for his asides are quite unlike most Elizabethan specimens and are much better described as interior monologue. What, apart from tens of thousands of words, would be lost if a modern director scraped away these monologues and presented the play without them?

There is, in any case, scattered about on the surface of the play enough for interpretation to work upon. Nina Leeds and Gordon Shaw are persuaded by Nina's father to postpone their marriage until after the war. Gordon is killed in a flying accident and, wracked by guilt and frustration at not having sexually yielded to him, Nina both nurses and seduces wounded soldiers. Two men who are interested in her (Charles Marsden, a novelist, and Edmund "Ned" Darrell, a doctor) are repelled by her behavior but try to repair her respectability by persuading her to marry Sam Evans, a not very bright young man who hero-worships Gordon Shaw. Nina does so, but when she becomes pregnant, Sam's mother tells her that she must abort her child because there is hereditary madness in the family. She should, instead, get pregnant by a healthy man and pass his child off as Sam's. Nina persuades Ned to father the replacement child, but they fall in love and are held back only by Nina's moral qualms from eloping and asking Sam for a divorce. Hurt by Nina's decision,

Ned leaves her. Eventually, when this son (Gordon Evans) is twenty-one and engaged to be married, Nina tries to tell Sam that Ned is Gordon's father but, held back by the difficulty of the situation, manages only to say that, spiritually, Gordon is the son of Gordon Shaw and has nothing of Sam in his spiritual being. The shock of this partial revelation kills Sam.

In the play's final scene, Gordon, suspecting his mother's wayward affections, strikes Ned. Nina tells him he has struck his father but, unable to comprehend her meaning, he assumes only that he has violated his father's express wishes by striking his friend. In remorse he suggests that his mother might now marry Ned. She and Ned agree to part, however, and Nina settles down with the faithful but sexless and mother-fixated Charles Marsden, who ends the play, appropriately enough, with an aside: "God bless dear old Charlie...who passed beyond desire, has all the luck at last!..." The play thus comes full circle. It is Professor Leeds's incestuous (though physically unexpressed) love for Nina that thwarts her happiness with Gordon. In the end she marries a man whom she has treated as a father substitute and father confessor throughout the play. Meanwhile, a new Gordon flies out of the play to marry, thus undoing the effect of the old Gordon's crash. The twenty-five years of the play's span are the strange interlude of its title.

Not entirely without controversy, for Nina clearly aborts her first child, *Strange Interlude* was nonetheless popular in its day. Now, however, partly because of its massive length, it is rarely performed. Most people who encounter it for the first time do so as readers, and many are taken aback by the clumsiness of O'Neill's writing, in his stage directions especially, but sometimes in dialogue as well. Two small examples must stand in for many more. First, in the play's opening direction there is the description of Charles Marsden: "*his face...too long for its width, his nose...high and narrow, his forehead broad, his mild blue eyes those of a dreamy self-analyst, his thin lips ironical and a bit sad.*" One might think this excessive, even redundant or unhelpful, but it is not, granted the date of its composition, especially odd. What, though, of how it continues? "*There is an indefinable feminine quality about him, but it is nothing apparent in either appearance or act.*" How can a thing be *apparent* if it does not *appear*? How, if we can neither see nor hear the evidence, are we to apprehend Marsden's feminine quality? What point is O'Neill struggling to make? He meant Marsden to be bisexual or homosexual, but why are we required to rummage about in elliptical stage directions and unpublished notes in order to find out something that, if it is relevant (and it is), ought to be made available to us through orthodox theatrical means, through words and actions, things we can hear and see? It is easy, and to an extent it is right, for a reader to interpret this direction as evidence of a move away from a genuinely dramatic mode of expression to one that is more purely literary, a move that compromises O'Neill's theatrical integrity.

The second example involves dialogue, but once again seems to call into question O'Neill's integrity as a dramatist working through properly dramatic channels. At the end of the play he puts into Nina's mouth a speech intended to allude to and to explain the play's title. "Strange interlude!" she exclaims (*"with a strange smile"*). "Yes, our lives are merely strange dark interludes in the electrical display of God the Father!" Is this not an authorial explanation masquerading, very unconvincingly indeed, as conversation? It is surely safe to say that in the whole history of humanity no one has ever uttered an even remotely similar sentence. Nevertheless, it makes some sense in O'Neill's vision of things: his next play is titled *Dynamo* (1929), is set in and around a hydroelectric power plant, features an insane hero named Reuben Light, and is a celebration of the beauty and destructiveness of life's feminine energies (whose "center must be the Great Mother of Eternal Life, Electricity, and Dynamo is her Divine Image on earth"). Moreover, the preposterousness of Nina's tag line is slightly reduced when we remember that throughout *Strange Interlude* she has been asserting female creativity by emphasizing the motherhood of God, but has been forced to recognize, from the example of her own son's development, that "sons are always their fathers. They pass through the mother to become their father again."

However, the complex situation that O'Neill has created is difficult to summarize neatly. Nina's son, the fruit of an illicit union, has been passed off as the legitimate offspring of her marriage. It is his "official father," rather than his biological one, whom he has grown to resemble, and Nina is lamenting the triumph of societal orthodoxy over mankind's passional life. This is a standard O'Neill theme. In a sense, though there are complicating ironies of an oedipal kind, *Dynamo* reverses the flow of the current of the earlier play and shows us the victory of passion over social convention. The Father God that Nina recognizes is a lawgiver, an inhibitor, and an upholder of appearances. In a deliberate act of submission, she brings her brief widowhood to an end by rejecting her lover in order to marry Marsden, who will neither trouble her sexually nor rouse her physically. But does any of this symbolic explanation (and it can be developed a great deal further) really justify the unconvincing way in which Nina Leeds is made to speak? What on earth can O'Neill's ear have been thinking about?

CONTROVERSIAL THEATER

O'Neill's theory of drama—and it is coherent enough to be called a theory—is genuinely interesting but will not of itself keep his plays alive. Despite his undoubted fame among historians and theorists of theater, many of his plays, overtaken by time and by shifts in fashion and politics and our sense of what is acceptable, have yet to be securely reestablished on the stage. A good example of a play that has now fallen from grace is *The Emperor Jones* (1920). It is a very brief work with an extraordinary structure. The first scene, which takes up one third of the play, is a typical piece of early and clumsy O'Neill that sets up what will follow. Brutus Jones, a double murderer, has fled prison in the United States and has washed up on an unidentified West Indian island, where he has established himself as emperor. News is brought of an impending insurrection, and Jones flees into the jungle in order to escape. In the seven scenes that comprise the rest of the play—scenes in which O'Neill makes a serious attempt to reinvent a drama of symbolic action rather than of naturalistic reportage—we witness, to the insistent accompaniment of the beating of a tom-tom, Jones's spiritual and social regression (he ends up as nearly naked as the theater of the time would allow) and eventual death. Here, in innovative staging that is deeply impressive, is the heart of the play. What makes *The Emperor Jones* all but unperformable now is O'Neill's well-meant but obtuse indulgence in racial stereotyping that is both physical and verbal. Lem, the leader of the insurrection (and, unlike Brutus Jones, a blacked-up white actor in the original production), is *"a heavy-set, ape-faced old savage of the extreme African type, dressed only in a loin cloth,"* and his language is still less subtly rendered: "He got um strong charm. I cook um money, make um silver bullet, make um strong charm too." Significantly, though the piece had been applauded by white theatergoers, when it was revived in a black theater in Harlem in 1927, a discerning but relatively benign audience laughed it off the stage, from embarrassment, surely, rather than outrage.

O'Neill's other famous "black piece"—*All God's Chillun Got Wings* (1923)—will strike most modern liberal readers as a well-intentioned but rather timid exploration of interracial marriage. In 1924, however, it provoked strong feelings. In a deliberate attempt to impede production, the mayor of New York withheld permission for children to appear on stage, which meant that the play's opening scene had to be read out to the audience. Worse still, when Mary Blair, a white actress who played a white character (Ella Downey), kissed the hand of Paul Robeson (Jim Harris)—in a deliberate act of submission and subordination ("*as a child might, tenderly and gratefully*")—Robeson, Blair, and O'Neill received racist death threats. Interestingly, as part of the complex of issues that have come to surround what is now termed color-blind casting, O'Neill was convinced that had a blacked-up white actor appeared as Harris, there would have been no controversy. When in 1927 he wanted Robeson to wear white makeup to play Lazarus in *Lazarus Laughed* (1926), he argued that since "white folks make up to play negroes . . . there's no reason why the reverse shouldn't be practiced" (Bogard and Bryer, 1988, p. 257). The logic is impeccable but, in the circumstances, perverse. Lazarus is the only character in the play who does not wear a mask: making a nonmasked Robeson paint himself would have been bound to generate an interpretative muddle.

The trouble that *All God's Chillun* ran into tells us more about American society in the 1920s than it does about the play itself. More interesting from a strictly dramatic perspective is the way in which O'Neill planned for it to be staged. The first three scenes of act 1 represent "*a corner in lower New York, at the edge of a colored district*" (1) "*Years ago,*" (2) "*Nine years later,*" and (3) "*Five years later.*" They are brief scenes that sketch—diagrammatically (almost in Brechtian style) rather than naturalistically—the passage of time. The stage set, too, is like a pattern or diagram that gives visible expression to the play's theme. The street to the right is filled with blacks; the street to the left is filled with whites; only at the corner, where the streets meet, is there racial mingling. In the "*street of the whites*" a high-pitched, nasal tenor sings a song to an audience that laughs "*constrainedly, awkward in natural emotion.*" In "*the street of the blacks*" there is a different song and different, less inhibited laughter—"*distinctive in quality*" that "*expresses the difference in race.*"

Such expressive, indeed expressionist, staging is characteristic of O'Neill's approach to theater and provides powerful evidence with which to challenge the claim (itself very powerfully supported by the disposition of his plays on the page) that he was basically a novelist in the way his imagination worked. He is, one must admit, an intensely verbal dramatist who is often a merely verbose one. Paradoxically, though, his verbosity sometimes annotates an absence of words. In *The Emperor Jones*, for example, as Brutus Jones regresses into primitivism, both his clothes and his language disappear. (The two disappearances are linked because language is the dress of thought.) Scene 6 contains fewer than one hundred spoken words, but there are four times as many in the descriptive and prescriptive stage directions that surround this short speech. These directions clearly show the symbolic way in which O'Neill was making use of setting:

> *The interlocked ropes of creepers reaching upward to entwine the tree trunks give an arched appearance to the sides. The space thus enclosed is like the dark, noisome hold of some ancient vessel.*

They also provide what, elsewhere in the play, O'Neill terms "narrative in pantomime." Negroes appear; they are shackled and naked, swaying backward and forward as though answering the rhythms of the sea; their voices swell; they wail in despair; they fall back into silence. On stage, in front of us, we see speechless (but not voiceless) performers act out for us Brutus Jones's terrified vision of his own racial history. How long is scene 6 of *The Emperor Jones*? Fewer than one hundred words (the number of words that are spoken and heard)? Or four hundred words (the number of words that we read)? Both answers are wrong because both assume that a play is text rather than performance. The true answer is that scene 6 is as long as it takes to perform it adequately. We should not allow the appearance of the play on the page to deceive us into believing that it is a merely typographical artifact.

Equally expressive, though by different means, is the way in which, in act 2 (scenes 2 and 3) of *All God's Chillun Got Wings*, the room in which Jim Harris lives grows smaller as his hopes shrink and despair imprisons him: "*The walls of the room appear shrunken in, the ceiling lowered, so that the furniture, the portrait, the mask, look unnaturally large and domineering. . . . The walls appear shrunken in still more, the ceiling now seems barely to clear the people's heads, the furniture and the characters appear enormously magnified.*" Despite his fondness for words on a page, O'Neill is a physical as well as a verbal playwright.

Desire under the Elms (1924) was O'Neill's other controversial play of the 1920s. Some reviewers (the degree of whose sensitiveness one can scarcely imagine) thought it a tale of almost unrelieved sordidness, in which sin and appalling freedom of speech were frankly illustrated. Once again, because of its sensationalist subject matter (and, it must be admitted, some rather clumsy dialogue), the play's considerable and specifically theatrical virtues were overlooked. In particular, O'Neill worked hard to suggest throughout the play "the flow of life from room to room," and succeeded brilliantly. Here the device that O'Neill explored is physical simultaneity. In part 3, scene 1, we are shown Ephraim Cabot's farmhouse sliced through as though it were a doll's house. Downstairs is a rowdy party thrown to celebrate the birth of Ephraim's son by Abbie, his young and frisky third wife. Upstairs in one bedroom a cradle stands by a double bed, the perfect image of a fruitful marriage; in the adjacent bedroom Eben Cabot, Ephraim's son and the true father of the child, sits on the side of the bed and "*scowls at the floor.*" The partygoers, sensing the child's true paternity, enjoy themselves at Ephraim's expense; he, dimly aware of their derision, reasserts his authority by vigorous dancing and heavy drinking. Eben moves from his bedroom and stands beside the cradle. "*At the same moment that he reaches the cradle, Abbie seems to sense something. She gets up weakly and goes to Cabot.*" That simple action speaks volumes silently, and for once O'Neill resists the temptation to decorate it with too many words, but even had he yielded to temptation, the fact remains that this is a brilliant piece of true theater.

PAGE AND STAGE

The O'Neill paradox is easily summed up: America's foremost dramatist is scarcely a dramatist at all. Too many of his plays, so the argument goes, are either grandiose ideas in the mind, unrealizable on any material stage, or they are arrangements of printed words upon the pages of a book that are fully apprehensible only by a reader, and they are designed to encourage and reward the kind of inspection that good readers habitually bestow upon significant texts. "A Play for an Imaginative Theatre," O'Neill's subtitle for *Lazarus Laughed*, concedes that what we read will only—and perhaps can only—find its proper fulfillment in the mind.

Evidence to support the claim that O'Neill was essentially a writer of books rests, inevitably, upon the printed page and is, initially at least, compelling. Anyone who bought a copy of *Strange Interlude* in 1928 would have made a substantial purchase. It is a volume of 348 pages (twice or three times the length of a normal play) filled with words that are variously presented upon the page: one font size for dialogue; a smaller size for interior "unvoiced" speech; two sizes of italics for stage directions, depending upon whether dialogue or interior speech is being

annotated. This arrangement sounds confusing but, in fact, is not, because it more sharply differentiates O'Neill's two kinds of speech than does the standard Library of America edition, which relies entirely on indentation to mark the difference. But what every reader is very much aware of, regardless of which edition is consulted, is the huge verbosity of *Strange Interlude* and the way in which its peripheries seem to have swollen out of all proportion. The first thousand or so words that begin scene 4 comprise only one word of public utterance ("Hell!"), two speech headings (EVANS, NINA), 467 words of stage direction, and 584 words of interior monologue. It is tempting to see in these figures evidence of the abdication of a dramatist's traditional responsibilities and a decisive move into the territory of the novel. Even if one discounts interior monologue from one's argument, on the grounds that it is meant to be spoken, it is still the case that more than forty percent of the words on the page are directed at the reader rather than the playgoer.

What can have prompted such a huge diversion of energy? The answer can only be a very considerable disquiet about the nature of performance itself. Drama is the most objective of all of the arts, in the simple sense (which follows from Aristotle's formal division of poetry into lyric, epic, and dramatic) that it has traditionally (though not always in fact) made no provision for an authorial or narratorial or personally privileged voice. Thus, at any rate until Brecht claimed the epic as a theatrical form, everything that was heard "on stage" was mediated to an audience through a character who, however special an author might wish to make him or her, remained a character and not merely a spokesperson. O'Neill's stage directions—many of them not genuine directions at all—are best understood as a way of negating theater's defining objectivity. A single example from *A Touch of the Poet* (1935–1936; first performed 1957) makes the case compellingly. When Cornelius "Con" Melody, the play's dissolute principal character, enters, initially O'Neill supplies him with an extended description of a traditional kind ("*forty-five, tall, broad-shouldered, deep-chested, and powerful, with long muscular arms, big feet, and large hairy hands*") that rapidly develops into a piece of character assessment ("*There is a look of wrecked distinction . . . of brooding, humiliated pride. His bloodshot gray eyes have an insulting gray stare which anticipates insult*") and is then extended on the assumption that the reader's judgment matches O'Neill's own ("*His manner is that of a polished gentleman. Too much so. He overdoes it and one soon feels that he is overplaying a role which has become more real than his real self to him*").

"*More real than his real self*" is the kind of observation that a few years earlier had encouraged O'Neill to use masks and asides and that, in *Days without End* (1932–1933), led him to divide the morally divided John Loving between two actors (the second visible only to the audience): "*John nervously writes a few words on a pad—then stops abruptly, and stares before him. Loving watches him.*" Moreover, the notion that every man is an actor would eventually reconcile O'Neill to his father's memory and his father's chosen art form long enough for him to mine the insight exhaustively in *Long Day's Journey into Night*. More relevant at present is the way in which O'Neill simply folds the reader's judgment into his own. "One soon feels." But who soon feels this? The writer and reader, obviously. But what if the spectator, who does not have access to these words in performance, does not feel this? Who is then at fault?

O'Neill does not simply doubt what he can do through the medium of drama but also doubts, much more fundamentally, what drama itself can do. Lying behind both his restless experimentalism and his heavy reliance on stage directions is a desire to extend the expressive range of drama. What perturbed him is that a playwright who relies on dialogue and action alone can never be sure—because too many things intervene, especially the vagaries of performance—that he has enabled playgoers to get to the bottom of a character's motivation. The novel, because it incorporates authorial comment in order to reveal a character's thoughts as well as speeches, seemed to him capable of a greater degree of realism than was available to the dramatist. (Was he right? Is novelistic realism really real? Since in life the only sources of information about others are what they say and what they do, perhaps dramatists—more realistically and more honestly than novelists—acknowledge and accept ineradicable restrictions upon our knowledge of others.)

But was O'Neill—a practicing dramatist of vast experience who had lived out his formative years in the very shadow of the theater—really as naïve as the foregoing arguments seem to assume? There are counterarguments, and in any case appearances can be deceptive. An instructive example occurs in act 3 of "The Haunted," which is the third part of *Mourning Becomes Electra* (1929–1931). Orin, driven mad by guilty lust (an incestuous love for his mother that has been renewed as an incestuous affection for his sister), kills himself while cleaning his service revolver. Lavinia hears the shot and, being now the last

of the Mannons, seeks to proclaim her independence of them by asserting her kinship with her mother, who was merely a Mannon through marriage. But she does so in a room dominated by their portraits: a visual reminder of the power of the past. "I'll live in spite of you," she asserts, but then marches stiffly out of the room, her gait a physical expression of her kinship with her father and a visible contradiction of what she is saying. What is going on here is quite subtle and genuinely dramatic, and it works upon an audience by legitimate theatrical means. But then, characteristically, O'Neill adds to his perfectly orthodox stage direction thirty-seven words that spell out its meaning for readers: "*She squares her shoulders, with a return of the abrupt military movement copied from her father which she had of old—as if by the very act of disowning the Mannons she had returned to the fold.*" Nonetheless, one's irritation at being told why Lavinia marches out of the room should not take too much away from what is an overannotated but nonetheless genuinely theatrical moment.

Perhaps we are wrong and O'Neill's directions are designed for those readers who are actors, rather than for readers generally. "Are the Actors to Blame?" was the startling title of a brief paper that he wrote in 1925. Were actors to blame for the current poor state of the theater? He answered that they were, but made significant concessions. First he grants the centrality of acting. "In the acting lies the acted play," he says, and adds that "the immediate future of the theatre is in the actor." The problem that actors face, and why O'Neill wants to moderate his blaming of them, is that they are too often the victims of the theater that they serve ("actors are conceived by and born of the parts they have been permitted to play"). O'Neill's conclusion—contained in his opening sentence—is austere:

> I believe that there is no possibility of real progress in the creative interpretation of plays of arresting imagination and insight until we develop a new quality of depth of feeling and comprehensive scope of technique in actors and actresses. For only when a play is self-expressed through sensitive, truthful, trickless acting is "the play the thing."
>
> (Bogard, *Unknown O'Neill*, pp. 390–391)

These comments help us to see that the two aspects of O'Neill's work which dominate modern critical discussion are linked: a strong personal or biographical element in all that he writes, and a radical mistrust of actors and the stage that is at odds with an equally strong commitment to theater. His relationships with his parents—James O'Neill (1846–1920) and Ella Quinlan

O'Neill (1857–1922)—explain both aspects. James was a famous actor who blunted his talents in pursuit of financial security by repeatedly performing in *The Count of Monte Cristo*; Ella, addicted to morphine, was alternately possessive and indifferent. The conflicting emotions toward his parents that O'Neill never fully managed to control are reflected in incidents that occur in a variety of disguises throughout his plays and that rise to the surface explicitly in *Long Day's Journey into Night*.

O'Neill's dramatic experimentation—the creative equivalent of an obsession with ceaseless traveling that characterized his early years especially—is evidence that his relationship with the theater was a vexed and contentious one that reflects his equally difficult relationship with a father who, for obvious reasons, represented Theater itself. O'Neill links the two in a letter to an associate in 1921. "My main trouble in theatre-going," he noted, was that "I can't help seeing with the relentless eyes of heredity, upbringing and personal experience every little trick they pull as actors. Thus the actor is ever present to me and the character is lost" (Bogard and Bryer, 1988, pp. 150–151). This closely parallels "Are the Actors to Blame?" (proper performance requires "sensitive, truthful, trickless acting") and anticipates criticism put into the mouth of Jamie Tyrone in *Long Day's Journey into Night*, when he compares his father's deadening repetitions in an overrehearsed, too-often performed role to the perfection of a seal that, through long hours of deadening training, learns to balance a ball on its nose: "I shall give the art of acting," he says, "back to the performing seals, which are its most perfect expression." Jamie's worst moment of self-abasement comes when, in *A Moon for the Misbegotten* (1941–1943), he remembers his own ham acting (but in real life rather than on stage) when, drunkenly accompanying his mother's coffin back for burial, he is forced to act out his grief:

> There were several people around and I knew they expected me to show something. Once a ham, always a ham! So I put on an act. I flopped on my knees and hid my face in my hands and faked some sobs and cried, "Mama! Mama! My dear mother!" But all the time I kept saying to myself, "You lousy ham! You God-damned lousy ham!"

The grief was genuine; the performance false, and the resulting self-consciousness (of oneself as a critical inspector of one's own inadequate acting) is emotionally self-destructive. That acting is a dangerous activity is a point made more than once in *A Moon for the Misbegotten*,

which is really a coda to *Long Day's Journey into Night* and is set eleven years after the earlier play. In it Jamie (known as Jim Tyrone)—middle-aged, dissolute, and desperately lonely—loses his last hope of a saving emotional attachment when, through an excess of self-loathing, he fails to commit himself to Josie Hogan. Instead, fearful of the emotional cost of contact with another human being, he spends the night in childlike submission to her, leaning on her breast in a state of regressive dependency. He awakens to glimpse a beautiful dawn but, unable to accept it at face value, immediately insists that Josie should not spoil it for him by reminding him of the many squalid dawns that he has greeted in the arms of a whore:

> Don't spoil this dawn! (*A pause. She watches him tensely. He turns slowly to face the east, where the sky is now glowing with all the colors of an exceptionally beautiful sunrise. He stares, drawing a deep breath. He is profoundly moved. . . .*)

Dramatists frequently frame their stage directions in either a "technical" manner that emphasizes the mechanics of performance or a "fictive" manner that ignores performance entirely. "Exit stage left" is a good example of the former kind, and tells us what an *actor* does. "He dies" is an equally good example of the latter kind, and tells us what a *character* does. O'Neill's phrasing is undoubtedly fictive, here and elsewhere generally, but this stage direction is nonetheless genuine and not a novelistic obtrusion into the play. What O'Neill expects an audience to see is a performance in which the actor who plays Jim Tyrone responds to lighting effects that represent sunrise:

> (*. . .He stares, drawing a deep breath. He is profoundly moved but immediately becomes self-conscious and tries to sneer it off—cynically*) God seems to be putting on quite a display. I like Belasco better. Rise of curtain, Act-Four stuff.

When reading the play, it is tempting to interpret this as a very simple contrast. Jim Tyrone, rotted both by theatrical artifice and by alcohol, cannot get beyond a view of reality corroded by the self-consciousness of an artist. Even a natural event to his diseased eye seems stagier than a set from a production by David Belasco (1845–1921). But in performance this contrast is blunted. Since the natural display that Tyrone accuses of artificiality is necessarily an artificial display, we are compelled by the simple physical fact of performance to share his viewpoint. The theater in which Jim's image of a theater-infested world is presented to us becomes itself an image of the truth of that image. Here is theater turned against itself.

This, indeed, is one of O'Neill's principal images. There is a hatred of theater in every theatrical piece he ever created, a powerful sense of the crushing constraints imposed by theatrical representation and a correspondingly intense desire to break down and break through these constraints. That is why O'Neill is in so many ways a tester of theater's limits. Once one has a sense of this, one begins to spot it everywhere and sees in it an image of life's entrapment by art. In *The Great God Brown,* for example—one of his more outrageous experiments—there is a conventional fourth-wall-removed set of its period, complete with painted wings and a backdrop, that seems not at all innovative. But, most peculiarly, the backdrop "*on which the rear wall [of Mrs. Anthony's sitting room] is painted*" is described as being "*painted with the intolerable lifeless realistic detail of the stereotyped paintings which usually adorn the sitting rooms of such houses.*" This is not just a dull sitting room decorated with pictures of equally dull sitting rooms, though that is part of O'Neill's point. It is, rather, the very epitome of such sitting rooms: its entire back wall not a back wall at all but the painted representation of a back wall. The entire play, we are to understand, is set not in a sitting room but in the theatrical representation of a sitting room. Why this advanced degree of introversion?

The constant devaluing of the play and the playwright at the expense of performance thoroughly depressed O'Neill, and in a letter written in 1926, he voiced his disgust eloquently: "I am certainly getting God damn tired of...eternally putting up with inexcusable...*approximations* to what I've written.... What's the use of my trying to get ahead with new stuff until some theatre can give that stuff the care and opportunity it must have in order to register its new significance outside of the written page in a theatre?" (Bogard and Bryer, 1988, pp. 213–214). Here O'Neill's impatience with existing (or, his standard terms of abuse, unoriginal or conventional) theater is clearly evident, though he accepts that plays must exist in performance ("outside of the written page"). Nonetheless, his objection to performance proved unappeasable. When in a letter written in 1942 he stated that "the play as written and the play as produced, no matter how excellently or successfully, can never be the same," he did so without accepting an inevitable but far from malignant consequence: the fact that no play belongs, wholly and exclusively, to whomever writes its words (Bogard and Bryer, 1988, p. 531). Nine years later, in a remarkable act of self-injury, he consigned his greatest play to the permanent limbo of nonperformance by reminding his publisher that *Long Day's Journey*

into Night was not to be printed until twenty-five years after his death and must "never [be] produced as a play" (Bogard and Bryer, 1988, p. 589). This restriction goes far beyond any need to protect family and friends: the ban on performing the play, unlike the ban on publishing it, was to be absolute (but unenforceable; it was breached by his widow within three years of his death). Since he was convinced that *Long Day's Journey* was his masterpiece, the only plausible explanation is that he feared that, of its very nature, performance would degrade and sully it: just as perhaps our living out our lives in the flesh betrays the (surely sentimental) idealism of our conception.

LATE PLAYS

The Iceman Cometh and *Long Day's Journey into Night* are perhaps the two greatest plays in the American repertoire. It would be foolish to subordinate them entirely to the argument developed in this essay, but equally foolish to suppose that they have nothing in common with his other plays. What is a pipe dream if it is not a mask? Or, to borrow O'Neill's own conceit, a mask without a mask? Each man in *The Iceman Cometh* is two men, one drunk and the other sober. Unusually, in Harry Hope's hopeless home of lost hopes it is the drunken man who is the norm; his sober self is the scary exception. They are each of them performers and frauds, but the greatest performer and fraud of them all is Hickey. As soon as he enters, late in the first act, he "*immediately puts on an entrance act.*" The lie that he tells is that he tells no lies. He killed his wife, he says, because he loved her and wanted to spare her the constant disappointments that loving him would bring her. That is very nearly the truth but absolutely not true. He killed her because he hated her, and he hated her because she loved him more than he loved himself, and by doing so set him standards that he would always fail to meet: "I remember I heard myself speaking to her, as if it was something I'd always wanted to say: 'Well, you know what you can do with your pipe dream now, you damned bitch!'"

The "deep pity and understanding and forgiveness for *all* the four haunted Tyrones" that enabled O'Neill to write *Long Day's Journey into Night* extended also to the theatrical art to which his father, his brother (fitfully), and he himself (most devotedly of all) had dedicated their lives. The play's great last act, which O'Neill was sure was the best thing that he had ever written, is inexplicable unless we see it as a set of performances, of poems and other party pieces, that are read aloud for pleasure and applause. Because there are many of them and the play is very long, there is a great temptation to cut them, but they are essential, should be retained, and must be done well. The two greatest of them are Edmund's description of his life at sea (which is not a recitation at all but an original utterance) and Mary's extraordinary descent of the staircase, trailing her wedding dress and speaking of the past to which, in her drug-charged imagination, she is compelled to return. This last, in particular, is physically set up to resemble a theatrical performance: in its own very distinctive manner it is as self-conscious a piece of theatrical conceit-making as Shakespeare's interlude of Pyramus and Thisbe or, perhaps a more likely influence, the dramatic vignette with which Henrik Ibsen ends *Hedda Gabler* (1890).

There is a final paradox. For a period of fifteen years Eugene O'Neill did more to shake the pillars of the naturalistic stage than did any of his contemporaries. At the last, however, he returned to it, dropped his masks and the asides (though he never managed to drop, nor even to prune, his stage directions), and produced his very best work, in which at long last he seemed at peace in a medium that he had frequently reviled but had never deserted.

[*See also* Theater in America.]

WORKS

(Note: Dates are presumed years of composition rather than of first performance.)

Recklessness (1913)
Thirst (1913)
Warnings (1913)
The Web (1913)
A Wife for a Life (1913)
Bread and Butter (1913–1914)
Abortion (1914)
Fog (1914)
The Movie Man (1914)
Servitude (1914)
Bound East for Cardiff (1914–1915)
The Personal Equation (1915)
The Sniper (1915)
Before Breakfast (1916)
Now I Ask You (1916–1917)
'Ile (1917)
In the Zone (1917)
The Long Voyage Home (1917)
The Moon of the Caribbees (1917)
Beyond the Horizon (1918)
The Rope (1918)
Shell Shock (1918)
Where the Cross Is Made (1918)
The Dreamy Kid (1918–1919)
The Straw (1918–1919)

Anna Christie (1920)
Diff'rent (1920)
The Emperor Jones (1920)
Gold (1920; 1921)
The First Man (1921)
The Hairy Ape (1921)
The Fountain (1921–1922)
Welded (1922–1923)
All God's Chillun Got Wings (1923)
Desire under the Elms (1924)
The Great God Brown (1924–1925)
Marco Millions (1924–1925)
Lazarus Laughed (1926)
Strange Interlude (1927)
Dynamo (1928–1929)
Mourning Becomes Electra (1929–1931)
Ah, Wilderness! (1932–1933)
Days without End (1932–1933)
A Touch of the Poet (1935–1936)
More Stately Mansions (1936–1940)
The Iceman Cometh (1939–1940)
Long Day's Journey into Night (1941)
Hughie (1941–1942)
A Moon for the Misbegotten (1941–1943)

FURTHER READING

Barlow, Judith E. *Final Acts: The Creation of Three Late O'Neill Plays.* Athens, Ga., 1985. A book that makes pioneering use of O'Neill's manuscripts and typescripts.

Black, Stephen A. *Eugene O'Neill: Beyond Tragedy and Mourning.* New Haven, Conn., 1999. A long book, though the shortest of three major biographies; its heavy commitment to psychoanalytic investigation is a questionable feature.

Bogard, Travis, ed. *The Complete Plays of Eugene O'Neill.* New York, 1988.

Bogard, Travis, ed. *The Unknown O'Neill: Unpublished or Unfamiliar Writings of Eugene O'Neill.* New Haven, Conn., 1988.

Bogard, Travis, and Jackson R. Bryer, eds. *Selected Letters of Eugene O'Neill.* New Haven, Conn., 1988.

Brietzke, Zander. *The Aesthetics of Failure: Dynamic Structure in the Plays of Eugene O'Neill.* Jefferson, N.C., 2001. Includes many interesting production photographs.

Chothia, Jean. *Forging a Language: A Study of the Plays of Eugene O'Neill.* Cambridge and New York, 1979.

Floyd, Virginia. *The Plays of Eugene O'Neill: A New Assessment.* New York, 1985. A helpful volume with brief but detailed discussions of every play in chronological order of composition.

Floyd, Virginia, ed. *Eugene O'Neill: The Unfinished Plays.* New York, 1988. Describes three late plays (begun between 1940 and 1943) that were left unfinished.

Gallup, Donald C. *Eugene O'Neill and His Eleven-Play Cycle: "A Tale of Possessors Self-Dispossessed."* New Haven, Conn., 1998. Describes O'Neill's uncompleted magnum opus, parts of which have been published as *More Stately Mansions* and *A Touch of the Poet.*

Halfmann, Ulrich, ed. *Eugene O'Neill: Comments on the Drama and the Theater.* Tübingen, 1987.

Manheim, Michael, ed. *The Cambridge Companion to Eugene O'Neill.* Cambridge and New York, 1998. One of the best volumes in a generally distinguished series; especially good on theatrical background and performance history.

Moorton, Richard F., ed. *Eugene O'Neill's Century: Centennial Views of America's Foremost Tragic Dramatist.* New York, 1991.

Ranald, Margaret Loftus, ed. *The Eugene O'Neill Companion.* Westport, Conn., 1984. An encyclopedia in all but name and an indispensable reference work.

Vena, Gary. *O'Neill's "The Iceman Cometh": Reconstructing the Premiere.* Ann Arbor, Mich., 1988. An immensely detailed reconstruction of the initial performance of the play on 9 November 1946 at the Martin Beck Theatre in New York City. The cast photographs (in costume) are particularly interesting. It was performed with three intervals: of seventy-five minutes after act 1, and of ten minutes each after acts 2 and 3.

Voglino, Barbara. *"Perverse Mind": Eugene O'Neill's Struggle with Closure.* Madison, N.J., 1999.

See also the article on *Long Day's Journey into Night*, immediately following.

EUGENE O'NEILL'S
LONG DAY'S JOURNEY INTO NIGHT

by Josef Raab

The writing of *Long Day's Journey into Night* was completed in 1941, after Eugene O'Neill had already secured his position as the most successful American playwright of his time by winning the Nobel Prize in literature in 1936. This play, however, remained unpublished until 1955 and unproduced until 1956, three years after the author's death. O'Neill had actually stipulated that it not be performed until twenty-five years after his death. The reason for this stipulation as well as for the play's strong emotional appeal is its painful personal background. This is by far the most autobiographical play by Eugene O'Neill, and it dramatizes difficult family issues that the author did not want to make public during his lifetime. Writing about them without any intent of staging or publishing the play in his lifetime can therefore be seen as a therapeutic attempt on O'Neill's part to come to terms with his painful memories of his parents and to reconcile himself with his earlier experiences. As he pointed out in his dedication to his wife Carlotta, he wrote the piece "in tears and blood" but also "with deep pity and understanding and forgiveness for all the four haunted Tyrones." When it finally was performed, critics and audiences were overwhelmed: the play earned Eugene O'Neill a fourth Pulitzer Prize in drama, awarded posthumously.

In *Long Day's Journey into Night*, O'Neill preserves the unities of time, place, and action ascribed to classical tragedy. The staged events take place in less than twenty-four hours (from the morning of one beautiful day in August 1912 until midnight); they are all set in and around the summer home of the Tyrone family in New London, Connecticut; and there are no significant subplots that divert the audience's attention from the main course of events, the gradual breakup of the Tyrone family. The cast of characters is small: James Tyrone, an aging Irish-American actor; his wife Mary, a nervous woman who tries to cope with the disappointments she has experienced and with the sacrifices she has made; their older son Jamie, a hard-drinking rake who still relies financially on his parents and who is not keen to help his father with repairs

and yard work; his sickly brother Edmund, a poet suffering from tuberculosis; and their maid Cathleen, who serves as a confidante for Mary Tyrone and as a comic relief figure for the play. From the start of the drama there is tension—especially between the father and his elder son—but more important there is a feeling that the three male family members are self-conscious in their ways of dealing with Mary, carefully avoiding anything that might upset her. However, in the course of the play we move from the facade of normalcy (metaphorically represented by the title word "day") to the painful truths of Mary's morphine addiction and the seriousness of Edmund's disease (the title's "night"). This journey is completed with little action, but instead through dialogue and small but significant gestures. It is psychological realism more than anything else that this drama of revelation is after.

LITERARY AND
BIOGRAPHICAL BACKGROUND

In the history of American drama, Eugene O'Neill is commonly credited with having moved the theater away from the melodrama that characterized it all through the second half of the nineteenth century. The work of playwrights like Dion Boucicault, Augustin Daly, and David Belasco used a rather superficial brand of realist depiction and relied on sentimentality as a means of drawing audiences. Psychological explorations, if they existed at all in melodrama, remained very much on the surface. The Little Theatre Movement of the early twentieth century, by contrast, sought to reinvigorate drama as an art form. One of the companies to constitute this movement was the Provincetown Players, whose main direction and outlook came from Susan Glaspell and Eugene O'Neill. The troupe's performance of O'Neill's one-act play *Bound East for Cardiff* in 1916 proved an immense success. After World War I the Theatre Guild, perhaps the most successful manifestation of the art theater movement, was looking to perform the best contemporary playwrights writing in English, namely, the Irishman George Bernard Shaw and the American Eugene

O'Neill. By the 1920s at the latest, with the Little Theatre Movement and Eugene O'Neill, American drama had abandoned escapism, sensationalism, and action-driven plays and was ready to transfer to the stage Sigmund Freud's recent discoveries concerning the human psyche.

Despite his own disclaimers, O'Neill was profoundly influenced by both Freud and Carl Gustav Jung. He underwent psychoanalysis in 1927 and was convinced of the important function of illusions and delusions. Yet it seems that O'Neill is not so much interested in individual psychology as in what he called "the forces behind—Fate, God, man's biological past creating his present. Instead of God, modern man has the subconscious, the mother of all Gods."

In the playwright's opinion, moments of self-revelation, of realizing a certain truth, are moments of compassion, which allow us to see people as victims of life's ironies. In Aristotelian terms, the result of such insights is both terror and pity; indeed, O'Neill believes that only pity can make life endurable, for pity implies understanding. It is through pity (i.e., compassion, or caring) that we can overcome selfish narcissism. This is the essence of O'Neill's tragic view of life. To make life endurable, the playwright is convinced, we need human solidarity, understanding, and forgiveness—love in the sense of *agape*, *caritas*, and *sympatheia*. But faced with cynicism and with our own vulnerability, we put on masks, life-sustaining illusions. O'Neill is preoccupied with the problem that our only choice seems to be between the masks assigned to us and the masks we invent for ourselves: "One's outer life passes in a solitude haunted by the masks of others, one's inner life passes in a solitude hounded by the masks of oneself." Rather than unmasking such illusions or life lies in the manner of Ibsen, however, O'Neill believes them to be necessary for survival.

His tragic view of mankind influences both his plots and his dialogue—in *Long Day's Journey into Night* and throughout his work. Human relationships often appear as battles for dominance (similar to the drama of August Strindberg or Harold Pinter). These battles are fought primarily with language as a weapon, which is why numerous of O'Neill's characters (especially Mary in *Long Day's Journey*) try to withdraw from communication and from the social arena. As a result, physical gestures, visual devices, musical elements, and a symbolic setting often complement the dialogue of O'Neill's plays.

While Eugene O'Neill's early phase (which culminated in *Desire under the Elms*, produced in 1925) was characterized primarily by one-act plays that explore fate, determinism, the life at sea, and the role of illusions or masks, his middle period is less realistic and more expressionist, relying on Greek models, as exemplified in a play like *Mourning Becomes Electra* (produced in 1931). In his late phase, with plays like *The Iceman Cometh* (produced in 1946) and *Long Day's Journey into Night*, he returns to realism, leaving behind his earlier emphasis on mythic dimensions. What we tend to get in this mature period are realistic American tragedies.

Among these, *Long Day's Journey* is the one that comes most strongly out of O'Neill's autobiographical experiences. The author's father, James O'Neill, of Irish descent, played the leading role in *The Count of Monte Cristo* for a long time. This assured him financial success but ruined his artistic talent. James O'Neill drank heavily, and he is said to have been tightfisted and domineering. All of these qualities can be found in the play's James Tyrone character. Eugene O'Neill's mother, Ella, usually accompanied her husband on his acting tours. Instead of a home, she had to content herself with hotel rooms. When she had complications after giving birth, a careless doctor prescribed morphine, to which she then got addicted. It took her many years to conquer that addiction. The alcoholism of Eugene O'Neill's brother is likewise suggested in *Long Day's Journey*. And the author himself is the model for the play's Edmund Tyrone. By 1912, the year when the play is set, O'Neill had contracted malaria in Honduras, had attempted suicide, had suffered a nervous breakdown, and was infected with tuberculosis, which required a stay at a sanatorium. The relatively structured life there seems to have had a positive effect on the young man, who had by that time started writing poetry.

During the late 1930s and early 1940s, when he wrote *Long Day's Journey*, Eugene O'Neill also worked on a colossal cycle of plays, which was to be titled "A Tale of Possessors Self-Dispossessed." This was to be the saga of an American family from colonial times to the present day. But only two plays of this prospective cycle were eventually finished: *A Touch of the Poet* and *More Stately Mansions*, both produced posthumously, in 1958 and 1967, respectively. Nonetheless, the project suggests that the themes of family and disintegration were strongly on the author's mind at the time, as he was also struggling with alcoholism, Parkinson's disease, and the frustration of not being able to execute all his artistic ambitions.

THE PLAY

When the play begins, the audience sees the living room—with one door opening onto a front parlor (where we can hear a piano) and the other leading to a back parlor, which is shunned by all as if it reminded them of something in their past lives that they would rather forget. This duality indirectly announces the family's journey to be depicted by the play, moving from a hopeful belief that the present problems can be overcome to the painful recognition that things are likely not to improve and that the sins of the past will continue to haunt this family.

As always in O'Neill's plays, there are precise, elaborate stage directions. The various characters in *Long Day's Journey into Night* are described in much detail. Mary, the mother, is a nervous woman, lonely, constantly touching her hair and—symbolically—always looking for her glasses. She had wanted to become a concert pianist, but now is painfully aware of her crippled hands; she had planned to enter a nunnery but instead she married an actor. These failures to go through with her intentions suggest from the start of the play that her fight against her drug addiction is bound to fail. She had become addicted to morphine when her husband did not want to spend the money for a good doctor and the cheap quack he consulted prescribed morphine. The result of this so-called treatment is that in the time of the play she can only function if she has had a fix. Edmund, who resembles his mother most, is a hypersensitive young man, a poetic nature who finds unity only in the dissolving contours of the fog. With a flourish of bourgeois respectability, Tyrone, the father, comes across throughout the play as the actor he is; he is always playing a role, yet at the end he, too, emerges as what he truly is, namely, a sad and bewildered old man. Edmund's brother Jamie is a downright cynic whose philosophy is summarized in one phrase: "forget it." His love of cheap women and cheap whiskey does not bode well. Nonetheless, Jamie is the character who is most aware of his loneliness and of his dead-end position. "We are all in the bag. . . . [W]e can't beat the game," he acknowledges. One character is absent from the play and yet motivates the whole action: a third son named Eugene, who died as a baby and for whose death Mary blames herself and Jamie.

The summer house in which the Tyrone family is staying is an almost exact replica of the playwright's New England family home. Its isolation is emphasized by the fog that swirls in from the ocean and in which, as Edmund says, "life can hide from itself." But the sound of the foghorn serves as a danger signal, namely, the danger of Mary's relapse into her morphine habit. It dispels any illusions and, as Mary observes, it is "calling you back."

Apart from the set, choreography is also an important factor. The introductory scene opens with Mary and Tyrone on stage. Tyrone's arm is around his wife's waist—for the one and only time in this play, underlining the hope that characterizes the morning and which gradually fades as the day progresses. The careful grouping of the four main characters continues throughout the play; as new alliances are formed and old ones are abandoned, O'Neill uses all possible constellations. At the end of the play, the four figures are once again assembled, although each of them is feeling isolated and depressed now. It is a scene full of pathos and pain: Mary—addressing the Virgin Mary—has brought down her wedding gown as if to suggest that life had been full of promise until she got married.

Dialogue in *Long Day's Journey* is used most often to hide the truth, and it is usually against the will of the *dramatis personae* that the painful past is uncovered. In fact, one of the principle functions of dialogue as it is used in the play is that of refusing to accept any guilt. Defensive and offensive strategies alternate. One last, desperate move is the total refusal of communication, either by accusing the other person of lying or by leaving, looking out the window, or avoiding eye contact. O'Neill's interest in the workings of the human psyche becomes very clear here.

In the play's opening scene, there is still joking and playfulness: Jamie and Edmund laugh together in the dining room, while Mary, supposedly cured after a stay in a sanatorium, teases her husband about his real-estate deals. But very soon the topic of conversation turns to Mary's worries about Edmund's health, while all characters shy away from talking about Mary and from looking at her too carefully. Later, Tyrone and Jamie discuss Edmund's diagnosis, and Jamie accuses his father of being too cheap to pay for good medical care for his son. Jamie's fear that Mary has relapsed into her drug habit is confirmed by midday. The effect that this discovery has on the men is resignation on Tyrone's part, cynicism on Jamie's, and a sickly disposition on Edmund's. All the while Mary denies her drug use and keeps insisting that Edmund only has a cold. In the afternoon, once the men have gone to town, Mary reminisces about her past dreams and the housekeeper Cathleen enjoys Tyrone's whiskey. After the men's return Edmund tries again to get through to his mother, but she only accuses him of being "gloomy and morbid" and retires to the upper floor. In the evening Edmund and Tyrone sit together, wavering between mutual affection and accusations. They get drunk in order to forget their worries. Once Jamie comes home and openly refers to their mother as a "hophead," there is a fight and immediate remorse. In the play's painful closing scene, then, the foghorn is sounding outside and Mary comes down the stairs in a completely drugged state, dragging her wedding dress and mumbling about something she has lost and can no longer remember. The men stare at her speechlessly.

While there was a constant masking and unmasking of the various characters throughout the play, all illusions are gone by the end. The painful issues that were veiled at the beginning—Mary's drug addiction, Edmund's tuberculosis, Jamie's frustrations, and Tyrone's refusal to accept any blame—are obvious to all by the end. O'Neill puts his conviction of the tragic inevitability of life into Mary's statement: "The past is the present, it's the future too, we all try to lie [our way] out of that but life won't let us." And later: "none of us can help the things life has done to us: They are done before you realize it, and once they are done they make you do other things, until at last everything comes between you and what you'd like to be, and you have lost your true self for ever." The ways of coping with this pain and dilemma that the play mentions—denial, alcohol, drugs, and sex—are all revealed to be inadequate. O'Neill implies that the best way of dealing with life's suffering is the approach of Edmund, the poet, who tries to experience life consciously, to be ecstatic about life, and to relish its beauty.

SIGNIFICANCE

Long Day's Journey into Night conveys a sense of determinism or fate, with which the characters find it hard to cope. Attempts at forgetting, escape, and illusion are therefore frequent, since facing reality would lead to despair. Apart from using the play as a means of reconciling himself with his family history, Eugene O'Neill also takes up modernist concerns like the interest in the workings of the human mind, the breakdown of communication, the self's dissolution into role-playing, or the general feeling of pessimism. The resulting impression is that of a life-in-death existence. Moreover, there is an echo of the country's situation in 1941; like the play's foghorn, the attack on Pearl Harbor dispelled the illusion that the United States could stay out of World War II.

Throughout his career, Eugene O'Neill was fascinated by the element of ambivalence in human behavior. The most revealing quality of O'Neill's characters, therefore, is their tendency to waver continuously between opposite moods: love and hatred, aggression and compassion, reproach and apology, self-contempt and self-pride,

hope and despair. Indeed, most characters in O'Neill's works—including the four principal figures in *Long Day's Journey*—are split characters.

O'Neill's pronouncement that "the tragic alone has that significant beauty which is truth" underlines his decidedly tragic view of life. Once he declared that he was concerned not with man's relation to other people but with man's relation to God. He tended to consider man a lost creature who is trying to escape despair. The very fact, however, that man is capable of despairing is at the same time his unique chance for redemption. Out of this paradox comes O'Neill's expression "hopeless hope," which is all that he believes is left of nineteenth-century American optimism after the carnage of World War I. And this is what he seeks to represent in *Long Day's Journey* and elsewhere: "the theatre to me is life... [and] life is struggle.... [There is] something in us which prevents us from accomplishing what we dream and desire." The cause as well as the effect of striving to make one's illusions come true is suffering. Therefore, the playwright contends that in tragedy "we are brought face to face with great suffering... [which shows] the vanity of all human effort." Nonetheless, for Eugene O'Neill, man's nobility consists in the act of resistance to his inevitable fate. Human life, though, is tragic and ironic, a fact that can be neutralized for a while by the struggle of individual characters, by their stoic acceptance or active resistance, but that cannot be overcome.

[*See also* Theater in America.]

FURTHER READING

Black, Stephen A. *Eugene O'Neill: Beyond Mourning and Tragedy*. New Haven, Conn., 1999. A psychobiography of the author that considers his playwriting a form of self-psychoanalysis.

Bloom, Harold, ed. *Eugene O'Neill's* Long Day's Journey into Night. New York, 1987. A collection of ten essays by eminent scholars and an introduction that examine a variety of aspects of the play, ranging from its form and language and its use of monologue, symbolism, and setting to autobiographical issues, revolt, and remembering.

Hinden, Michael. Long Day's Journey into Night: *Native Eloquence*. Boston, 1990. A very useful introduction to the play, containing character analyses, background information, the play's history, and an extensive bibliography.

O'Neill, Eugene. *Long Day's Journey into Night*. New Haven, Conn., 2001. The authoritative Yale University Press edition of the play, which was originally published in 1955.

Porter, Laurin. *The Banished Prince: Time, Memory, and Ritual in the Late Plays of Eugene O'Neill*. Ann Arbor, Mich., 1988. Explores O'Neill's uses of the past in his mature phase.

See also the article on Eugene O'Neill, immediately preceding.

ALICIA OSTRIKER

by Rachel Barenblat

Alicia Ostriker is a poet, literary critic, and midrashist who gained recognition during the latter part of the twentieth century (and into the twenty-first). Born in 1937, Ostriker holds a B.A. degree from Brandeis University (1959), and an M.A. degree (1961) and Ph.D. (1964) from the University of Wisconsin. She began her teaching career at Rutgers University in 1965 and has served as a professor of English there since 1972.

Her doctoral dissertation, on the work of William Blake, became her first book, *Vision and Verse in William Blake* (1965). That early engagement with Blake continues to color Ostriker's perspectives; although she now takes issue with his misogyny, she admires his utopian vision, his commitment to social justice, and the daring transgressiveness of his subject matter and form.

Much of what Ostriker praises in Blake can be found in her own work. At present she is the author of ten collections of poems, among them *The Imaginary Lover* (1986), which won the William Carlos Williams Award of the Poetry Society of America; *The Crack in Everything* (1996), a National Book Award finalist that won the Paterson Poetry Award and the San Francisco State Poetry Center Award; and *The Little Space: Poems Selected and New, 1968–1998* (1998), a finalist for the 1999 Lenore Marshall Poetry Prize. Her most recent collection is *The Volcano Sequence* (2002).

POETRY BOTH PERSONAL AND POLITICAL

Ostriker's poetry is characterized by both passion and clarity. She is not afraid to tackle dangerous subjects, such as war, childbirth, and breast cancer. She brings grand topics—gender construction, the nature of justice, the implications of theology—down to earth; she elevates small topics—turning fifty, eating a pear, men watching other men in locker rooms—beyond their ordinariness. As her critical exploration of women's poetry interrogates the assumed "otherness" of women within the literary canon, her poems speak in the voices of women as diverse as Hagar, Miriam, Sheba, the "crazy lady" on a subway train, and herself.

The feminist credo "the personal is political" is exemplified in many of Ostriker's poems, among them the prose poem "Cambodia" (*The Mother/Child Papers*, 1980). In "Cambodia," Ostriker addresses the Vietnam War, the 1970 demonstrations at Kent State College that resulted in four student deaths, and the uncomprehending obstetrician who refused to believe that labor could be pleasurable and insisted on numbing Ostriker against the birth of her son in 1970. It is left to the reader to draw connections between childbirth and war (that every son is a potential soldier?), between a president invading a country and an obstetrician invading a woman's body (technology as superior power over the helpless?), and between filial love and love of country (even, or especially, when both parenting and patriotism are fraught with difficulties).

Another representative poem, "A Meditation in Seven Days" (*Green Age*, 1989), explores the roles of women and images of femaleness within Jewish tradition, from Sarah to the Sabbath Queen, all of which are "never enough." The poem interrogates the tradition: Why is Jewishness matrilineal when most Jewish interpretations of God have been masculine? How can Jewish women celebrate both their Jewishness and their womanhood? Can there be a balance in the tradition's divine tension between judgment and compassion? In the poem's final segment, Ostriker concludes that there is no one with whom to wrestle (an allusion to the biblical story of Jacob wrestling with the angel) but herself, that although "the father" is old and asleep and impotent, his three children—Judaism, Christianity, Islam—still love him, because he is the only God we have. The poem ends at the threshold of revelation: "Fearful, I see my hand is on the latch / I am the woman, and about to enter."

Ostriker's continuing engagement with justice and power, with politics, the nature of womanhood, the Jewish tradition, and the question of God's presence in a damaged world evokes the early rabbinic injunction that while it is not incumbent upon us to finish the task of healing the world, neither are we free from the responsibility of beginning it.

Alicia Ostriker, from *The Volcano Sequence*, 2002. (*Photograph by J. P. Ostriker. Reprinted by permission of the University of Pittsburgh Press*)

Although her central themes are relatively constant, her relationship to them changes over time. For instance, her early collections contain poems of childbirth; in the mid-1980s she chronicled the separation of a daughter departing for college; in *The Volcano Sequence* she approaches her mother's aging and infirmity, the terrible desire to rail at a parent whose frailty unmakes anger. Ostriker's other themes include history and politics, marriage and family, and painters and painting.

WRITING "LIKE A WOMAN"

Although the fields of poetry, criticism, and midrash are separable, Ostriker's work in each of these genres informs and affects her work in the other two. As Ostriker's poetry seeks to explore female experience through themes including motherhood, speech and silence, and desire and sexuality, so her criticism engages with female experience by examining women's writing and women's exegesis of sacred texts.

Writing Like a Woman (1983) was Ostriker's first major work of literary criticism focusing on women's writing. Here she delves into the work of H.D., Sylvia Plath, Anne Sexton, May Swenson, and Adrienne Rich; non-poet-specific essays examine the relationship between motherhood and poetry and explore what it means to write "like a woman." Ostriker resists the urge to either glorify or essentialize womanhood. Writing like a woman, she says, just means writing as one is, from one's entire self, and though we may now believe that women are more inclined than men to approach certain themes (the body, relationships) or write in a certain style (intimately), the truth of the matter is that "woman poet" is no more precise a term than "American poet" or "man poet." The labels describe but do not prescribe.

Stealing the Language: The Emergence of Women's Poetry in America (1986) continues the work begun in *Writing Like a Woman* with a major survey of American women's poetry, beginning with colonial-era poet Anne Bradstreet and continuing through the twentieth century. With copious quotations, Ostriker illustrates the themes and driving forces she finds in American women's poetry, among them the quest for identity and voice, the use of the body as a metaphor for (and locus of) female experience, and the making of revisionist mythology that enables women poets to create breathing room for themselves within traditionally masculine religious and mythological traditions.

WRESTLING WITH THE ANGEL

Religious tradition, also a primary theme in Ostriker's poetry, is the subject of *Feminist Revision and the Bible* (1993) and *The Nakedness of the Fathers: Biblical Visions and Revisions* (1994). The former collects Ostriker's Bucknell Lectures on such subjects as "The Buried Woman in

Biblical Narrative" and "A Word Made Flesh: The Bible and Women's Poetry." The latter book is a more ambitious project, combining feminist exegesis of Torah, midrashim (texts—in this case both prose and poems—that reinterpret Torah from within its own narrative framework), and fragments of memoir relating to Ostriker's own wrestle with the proverbial angel of Judaism.

Ostriker's exegesis is characterized by the trifold approach she identifies as characteristic of feminist exegesis of biblical texts: a hermeneutics of suspicion, a hermeneutics of desire, and a hermeneutics of indeterminacy. *The Nakedness of the Fathers* blurs genre boundaries; Ostriker does not limit herself to critical analysis but also dives into her own personal relationship with the texts and their interpretations. "To the rest of the world the Jew is marginal. But to Judaism I am marginal. Am woman, unclean," she writes. "What right have I to comment? None, none, none. What calls me to do it? I have no answer but the drops of my blood, that say try" (*The Nakedness of the Fathers*, p. 6).

Ostriker's life-work to date can be summed up as a process of creating and exploring sacred texts. Her explorations of Torah and new midrash are sacred work, and because she believes literary criticism should be born out of love and not purely out of intellectualism, it is arguable that her essays on poetry are in their own way exegesis of sacred text, the sacred text of how women poets (primarily in the twentieth century) have inscribed their lives.

WORKS

Vision and Verse in William Blake (1965)
Songs (1969)
Once More out of Darkness (1974)
William Blake: The Complete Poems (1977)
A Dream of Springtime (1979)
The Mother/Child Papers (1980)
A Woman under the Surface: Poems and Prose Poems (1982)
Writing Like a Woman (1983)

Stealing the Language: The Emergence of Women's Poetry in America (1986)
The Imaginary Lover (1986)
Green Age (1989)
Feminist Revision and the Bible (1993)
The Nakedness of the Fathers: Biblical Visions and Revisions (1994)
The Crack in Everything (1996)
The Little Space: Poems Selected and New, 1968–1998 (1998)
Dancing at the Devil's Party: Essays on Poetry, Politics, and the Erotic (2000)
The Five Scrolls (2000)
The Volcano Sequence (2002)

FURTHER READING

Bryan, Sharon, ed. *Where We Stand: Women Poets on Literary Tradition*. New York, 1993. Includes "The Road of Excess: My William Blake," an essay by Ostriker that serves as a brief history of her "romance" with her "most significant literary Other."

Cook, Pamela. "Secrets and Manifestos: Alicia Ostriker's Poetry and Politics." *Borderlands: Texas Poetry Review* 2 (Spring 1993). A look at how Ostriker's poetry expresses her worldview.

George, Diana Hume. "Forcing an Entry into Eternity: Alicia Ostriker's Poetry and Criticism." *Spoon River Poetry Review* 25, no. 2 (Summer/Fall 2000). An overview of Ostriker's work, both poetry and prose.

Heller, Janet Ruth. "Exploring the Depths of Relationships in Alicia Ostriker's Poetry." *Literature and Psychology* 38, 1–2 (1992). An analysis of the central role relationships, especially familial ones, play in Ostriker's poetry.

Mullaney, Janet Palmer, ed. *Truthtellers of the Times: Interviews with Contemporary Women Poets*. Ann Arbor, Mich., 1998. Includes an interview with Ostriker, focusing on how motherhood has affected Ostriker's poetry and her writing life.

CYNTHIA OZICK

by Elaine M. Kauvar

In *Fame & Folly: Essays* (1996), her fourth collection of essays, Cynthia Ozick chronicles other writers' disappointments, their early success, and in some cases, the mistakes that have cost them their fame. She is interested in what divides a major writer from a minor one, in why one writer's work fades into oblivion and another's thrives. It is a small wonder that she titled the volume as she did. Writing about *Fame & Folly* in 1996, James Wood described it this way: "Her essays invent language, for one thing, and this language—busy, rhapsodic, willful—is congruous with the language of her fiction" (p. 92). Such a description of Ozick's work is not difficult to

Cynthia Ozick. (*Photograph by Julius Ozick; courtesy of Knopf*)

understand, for the breadth of Ozick's subjects become as universal as they are inclusive; she does not confine herself to the special, the parochial, or the limited—all characteristics, as her searching essays suggest, of minor writers. The radiance of her language and the universality of the subjects that obsess her have ushered Cynthia Ozick into the forefront of American letters, where the numerous prizes and awards she has won testify to her status as a major American writer.

OZICK'S EARLY YEARS

Born in New York City on 17 April 1928, Cynthia Ozick is the youngest child of Celia and William Ozick, Russian immigrants who ran a drugstore in the Pelham Bay region of the Bronx. "A Drugstore in Winter," the last essay in Ozick's first collection of essays *Art & Ardor* (1983), tells of life in the Park View Pharmacy and its importance to the writer's early reading, her "old school hurts," her enduring and perdurable "craving ... for nothing but an old scarred pen" to record "the poetry side of life"—the realm of the imagination.

Painful school memories haunt Ozick's work. They began in the *cheder* (the room or school in which Hebrew is taught), where she learned Hebrew and the principles of Judaism. Here, the rabbi told her grandmother to take the child home because "a girl doesn't have to study." She suffered unforgettable hurt at P.S. 71 in the Bronx where she was regarded as stupid and where it was "brutally difficult to be a Jew." About those experiences she has observed: "It was very strange to me to have two lives like this; on the school side, where I was almost always the only Jew, and in *cheder* where I was almost always the only girl." When she entered Hunter College High School in Manhattan, her crowning intellect was finally acknowledged. Later she graduated from New York University, and in 1950 she received a master's degree in English literature from Ohio State University. Her thesis "Parable in Henry James" transformed a twenty-two-year-old woman who "lived like the elderly bald-headed Henry James" into a "worshiper of literature." Of James's impact on her, she resolutely announced, "Influence is perdition."

When Ozick was twenty-five, she read Leo Baeck's "Romantic Religion," an essay, she told an interviewer, that "in some way broke open the conceptual egg of [her] life" (Kauvar, 1985, p. 385). Like Enoch Vand, a main character in her first published novel, *Trust* (1966), she devoted herself to studying Judaic texts, reinforcing her apprehension that Jews are "quite the opposite of the parochial." But the label "Jewish writer" is something else entirely: "As a writer of fiction, I know today that I essentially don't want to be responsible for Jewish culture, responsible, that is, within the fiction itself, in the sense of being a spokesperson or assuming the task of carrier of a tradition" (Kauvar, 1985, p. 385). For Ozick the writer's loyalties lie elsewhere. However much she celebrates the particulars of her culture, Ozick insists that a writer's "method and [her] goal must be freedom, freedom, and more freedom," that a Jew must be differentiated from a writer. In the act of writing, "a writer is a writer."

To the prolonged period in which she labored on *Trust*, Ozick attributes an ardent but mistaken attempt to be a "ripened artist" rather than to accept the "faltering, imperfect, dreaming youth" she was (Kauvar, "Interview," 1993, p. 361). She attributes the sacrifice of her youth to the thirteen years of her earlier travail, writing a novel she ultimately abandoned. But the resplendent sentences her struggle for exactitude produces capture and enthrall her readers. Rather than consign her work to narrow categories and rigid ideologies like gender and ethnicity, her readers should celebrate the capaciousness of her mind. There issues clash and reverberate; there ambiguity triumphs over certainty and resolution. Hers is a consciousness that views the universe through its own prism.

BRIEF BEGINNINGS IN POETRY

Having written and translated poetry and having once said she was "obsessed and possessed" by it, Cynthia Ozick no longer writes it, nor does she consider herself a poet. To a suggestion that she collect her poems in a single volume she replied, "I'm not a poet and shouldn't masquerade as one" (Lowin, 1988, p. 12). Yet the subjects of her poems—the last of which she wrote two years before the publication of *Trust*—have the range of her tales and are wedded to them. The titles of such poems as "Greeks, "The Fish in the Net," "Caryatid," "The Seventeen Questions of Rabbi Zusya," and "When That with Tragic Rapture Moses Stood" reflect her core dispute between Hebraism and Hellenism. A glance at a scene in a Harlem apartment from a passing train in "Commuter's Train through Harlem" sparks the Keatsian formula of truth and beauty. Still another poem, "Urn-Burial," muses on Sir Thomas Browne. The variousness of their forms, the splendor of their language, their remarkable revelations—these attributes radiate Cynthia Ozick's "meticulous language-love."

FOCUS ON PROSE FICTION

Described by the artist herself as "In certain ways . . . simply an immensely long poem," the first novel Ozick published is a portrait of the artist as a young woman, at once ingenious and moving. Vast in scope, morally engaged, and arguably the most important book she has written, *Trust* constitutes the thematic matrix of Cynthia

Ozick's oeuvre. A dialectic pulses through that oeuvre; its terms concern two of the three cultural forces Ozick investigates in her novel as she establishes the signal importance of memory and history to humankind.

Their disclosures are imperative for the unnamed narrator of *Trust*, who lacks awareness of her father's identity. On the occasion of her graduation, the threshold of her future, she is rootless and belongs nowhere. The two figures to which the narrator is drawn, her unknown father Gustave Nicholas Tilbeck and her mother's husband Enoch Vand, represent the divided pathways confronting her and embody the debate central to Ozick's work on which Enoch Vand writes an essay titled "Pan Versus Moses." Neither is the victor at the end of the novel, for the narrator remains caught between two worlds. Gravitating toward Enoch Vand, drawn to Gustave Nicholas Tilbeck, she is unable to declare one superior to the other. They stand like heralds beckoning her in opposite directions. And those poles of attraction have provoked what Cynthia Ozick calls the "central quarrel of the West," which is the provenance of her "unholy conflict," the competition between moral seriousness and aestheticism. However instructively divergent for the narrator of *Trust* and however responsible for its topography, the two cultural forces are nonetheless transcended by the power of the novel, journeying as it does into the interior of human experience.

Ozick continues to explore the two cultural forces in *The Pagan Rabbi, and Other Stories* (1971), her first collection of stories. Its title story contains a tree on which the main character sees fit to end his life and which revivifies the Hebraism and Hellenism controversy in two ruined paradises: Arcadia and the Garden of Eden. Unlike the narrator of *Trust*, the protagonist of "The Pagan Rabbi," Isaac Kornfeld, crosses the boundaries of Judaism into paganism. But the narrator of *Trust* and the narrator of the short story both face an uncertain future. Another story in *The Pagan Rabbi*, "Envy; or, Yiddish in America," concerns the cultural conflict with which the Jewish artist must contend. It is a maze leading to sorrow, as Hershel Edelshtein discovers when he finds in himself the two irreconcilable desires that destroy Isaac Kornfeld, a belief in Jewish history together with the seductions of pagan culture. The issue of art and tradition at their crux, the stories in *The Pagan Rabbi* embody the dichotomy between religious belief and the religion of art. And that dichotomy encompasses inherited tradition, which in *The Pagan Rabbi* is subsumed in the embattled convictions of the generations.

If the characters in Ozick's first collection of fiction wrestled with their tradition, those in *Bloodshed and Three Novellas* (1976) have repudiated it. The betrayal of that tradition, indeed any tradition, leads to cultural rootlessness, a divided identity—worse, marginality. To fabricate an identity is to appropriate a life unlike one's own and then to await liberation. The truth is otherwise, as the characters in *Bloodshed* who spurn their tradition or remain on its margins make plain. In "A Mercenary," for example, Ozick sets forth not only the reasons for impersonation but also the consequences of dissemblance. Believing they will be "made free by unbelonging," the impersonators in this tale end instead by annihilating their selves. Marginality offers no better sustenance, as the title story shows in its character's choice of secularism over Judaism. Bearing thematic resemblances to the first two stories in the collection but without their darkness, "An Education" and "Usurpation" impart divided views and diverse perspectives and culminate in the injunction against idolatry—the defining idea of Jewish identity.

That resolution, however, generates the conflicts informing *Levitation: Five Fictions* (1982). Her conclusions "less logically decisive" than those of other writers, the narrator of "Usurpation" wittily foreshadows the emphasis Cynthia Ozick places on the artistic imagination—its inventiveness, its moral truths, and its perils. Indeed, the five fictions in the collection are all portraits of artists. Not devoted to the imagination but addicted to power, the Feingolds, the main characters of the story "Levitation," delight in transforming harrowing stories into aesthetic experiences. The photographer-narrator of "Shots" ends by choosing art over life. And the attorney whose biography Ozick recounts lives alone like the photographer-narrator "among other people's decaying old parents." Puttermesser's "personal history" highlights the discord between the law and the imagination and yields another portrait of the artist. ("Puttermesser" means "butter knife" in Yiddish.) In creating the golem Xanthippe (the name of Socrates' wife), Ruth Puttermesser hopes for the golem's help carrying out her "*PLAN* for the Resuscitation, Reinvigoration & Redemption of the City of New York"; instead, Puttermesser ends with the sorrowful recognition that her Utopia is a forbidden idol and her construction of it is rivalry with the Creator.

The contest between Hebraism and Hellenism abides in Ozick's second novel, written nearly twenty years after *Trust*. In *The Cannibal Galaxy* (1983), a fifty-eight-year-old schoolmaster attempts to resolve that debate by establishing a "dual curriculum" at the Edmund Fleg Primary School. Akin to Ruth Puttermesser's golem and conjured up for equally noble reasons, the dual curriculum nonetheless founders because of Joseph Brill's conviction that it can predict failure or success from "earliness." What the second novel has in common with Puttermesser and Xanthippe is the schoolmaster's competition with the Supreme Being, the forbidden transgression of the Second Commandment. Their concern with the artist's enterprise and moral substance yoke *The Cannibal Galaxy* to *Levitation*.

If a metaphoric hell of his own invention houses Joseph Brill at the end of *The Cannibal Galaxy*, two authentic hells confront Rosa Lublin in *The Shawl* (1989), a short story and a novella that Ozick, over six years later, would make into a play. Her tragic experience in the Nazi death camps has forced Rosa into the situation in which she finds herself. After helplessly watching her child Magda in "The Shawl" thrown against an electrified fence in a death camp, Rosa suffers from unrelenting and agonizing memories of the Nazis' butchery. Of undeniable significance to Holocaust literature, the novella hearkens back to *Trust* in its concern with the father, its struggle over Hellenism, and its preoccupation with imaginative writing. The play, an affecting attack on Holocaust denial, exposes the lies certain German historians promoted to erase historical actuality—the horror of the Nazi machinery of destruction whose aftermath continues to torment Rosa Lublin.

Another link to *Trust* is forged in *The Messiah of Stockholm* (1987), Cynthia Ozick's third novel. The search for a father resides at the heart of the first novel Ozick published; it continues in another form in *The Shawl*, and in *The Messiah of Stockholm* the idea is inverted. Lars Andemening, the novel's main character, fancies himself the son of Bruno Schulz, the Polish writer gunned down in Drohobycz by the SS. Lars becomes his imagined father's double, patterning his life after his until Lars finally relinquishes the fantasized but nevertheless idolized father. The significance of the father inheres in the three fathers that the novel includes, one of whom is Lars Andemening himself. Although she explores the father's relationship to tradition as well as art's relationship to reality and illusion, Cynthia Ozick, as is her practice, holds out not a simple solution but a multiple choice, deepening rather than resolving the perplexities of Hebraism and Hellenism in her third novel.

In 1997 Ruth Puttermesser reappeared, this time with her life story completed in the novel *The Puttermesser*

Papers. One of Cynthia Ozick's most memorable characters, Puttermesser, in addition to the two tales published in *Levitation,* is accorded three more chapters before the reader learns her final fate. We see Puttermesser at "the unsatisfying age of fifty-plus" still single but now willing to listen to "her mother's refrain"—that she must marry. Together she and Rupert Rabeeno read George Eliot and copy her life with similar and painful results. After her experience with her Muscovite cousin in the novel's fourth chapter, Ruth Puttermesser at last resides in the Paradise she first longed for in "Puttermesser: Her Work History, Her Ancestry, Her Afterlife." Of that idyllic place she concludes, "The secret meaning of Paradise is that it too is hell."

A cultural patrimony—Cynthia Ozick once called it the "hinge of generation"—accounts for the presence of fathers throughout her fiction. Continuity, the idea of transmission, the capacity to inherit a culture, the nurturings of a heritage—these are critical to her work and irradiate her tales, which are never monolithic. Ozick's work is nothing if not dialectical: warring motives reside in all the characters she creates; each fiction ends by upholding a value that the next fiction tears down. Absolutes and certainties are alien to her vision, which is to say "the central quarrel of the West" remains alive and the question of art's relation to illusion and reality abides. But one thing is sure: in her next novel, a part of which appeared in the *Princeton Library Journal* in 2002, positions will compete and perspectives shift.

OTHER PROSE

Here is the way Ozick begins her preface to *Metaphor & Memory: Essays* (1989), her second collection of essays: "While stories and novels under the eye of a good reader are permitted to bask in the light of the free imagination, essays are held to a sterner standard. No good reader of fiction will suppose that a character's ideas and emotions are consistently, necessarily, inevitably, the writer's ideas and emotions; but most good readers of essays unfailingly trust the veracity of non-narrative prose." For Cynthia Ozick, an essay, as well as a story, can "be a bewitched contraption in the way of a story." There is a reason why she is at pains to make that distinction. Readers have always expected her to be single-minded and decisive in her essays—everything her fiction is not.

Instead, the essays often impart contrary convictions, complicating rather than clarifying the contrivance furnished by the tale. If the dual curriculum collapses at the end of *The Cannibal Galaxy,* for instance, Ozick

continues to reflect on it in "Bialik's Hint," an essay she published in 1983 after the novel appeared. Rather than render the conclusion she reaches at the end of *The Cannibal Galaxy* resolute, "Bialik's Hint" posits the means to fuse the free imagination and "the Sinaitic challenge of distinctive restraint and responsibility." But no idea of Cynthia Ozick's is univocal. Consider the title of her essay: its equivocal conclusion lies in its title—a hint, not a surety.

Metaphor & Memory contains Cynthia Ozick's musings on various writers—writers as diverse as Cyril Connolly, William Gaddis, Italo Calvino, J. M. Coetzee, Primo Levi, Saul Bellow, Henry James, and Theodore Dreiser—in addition to meditations on her own writing, a memory of her first day at New York University, translation, the postmodern condition, the relation between metaphor and memory, and much more. *Art & Ardor,* her first collection of essays, demonstrates an equally broad range of subjects. In that volume are essays on other writers as dissimilar as Edith Wharton and I. B. Singer. The literature of the Holocaust, literary convictions, feminist issues, cultural beliefs—to name just a few of the volume's subjects—suffuse *Art & Ardor* with intellectual splendor.

That splendor crowds Ozick's other collections of essays, including *Fame & Folly* and *Quarrel & Quandary: Essays* (2000). The first volume centers on writers and their work; the cleavage between art and life. "T. S. Eliot at 101: 'The Man Who Suffers and the Mind Which Creates'" exemplifies her approach. To argue that biography is not a fallacious method with which to elucidate a writer's poems is to refuse to divide the author from the text. From the perspective of some forty years, she offers a divided judgment of T. S. Eliot. Granting him the author of that invaluable thought that "history underlies poetry" and the equally momentous belief that "poetry can be redemptive," Ozick ends with a somber moral truth: "It is now our unsparing obligation to disclaim the reactionary Eliot." Her acute psychological insights illuminate the workings of Henry James's psyche in "What Henry James Knew" (also the title of a collection of her essays published in 1993 in England), and insights of various kinds clarify the reasons for the exclusion of Anthony Trollope's works, oppose Salman Rushdie's, and recover the once-revered Alfred Chester.

An astute critic of contemporary culture, the sleuth who detects other writers' motivations, Ozick also reflects on translation, history, the imagination, and formative experiences, as well as the Holocaust in *Quarrel & Quandary.* The essays in that collection proclaim her altercations with other writers, set forth her disputes with postmodern issues, and register her deep engagement with imaginative writing, her own and others'. "Who Owns Anne Frank?" quarrels with the way contemporary culture regards Anne Frank and the metamorphosis of her diary for the stage: it is "an unholy speculation; it tampers with history, with reality, with deadly truth." Contrary to many others who have mulled over Anne Frank, Ozick allows herself to imagine Anne's diary burned. Why imagine such a thing? To save it from a world that has woefully mistaken it and utterly misjudged the diarist.

Cynthia Ozick recalls her own vanished youth in "A Drug Store Eden," a companion to "A Drugstore in Winter." We meet the people who come to the Park View Pharmacy and we observe the events as they unfolded there in both essays, but "A Drug Store Eden" yields up the hidden garden "nested in a wilderness of empty lots all around," secluded and invisible. Long destroyed but still alive as the "secret Eden behind [her] eyes," the garden serves as a powerful metonymy for the ravages of time, and the loss of youth.

Never as faltering or imperfect as she once imagined, she has found her way "in the bliss of American prose," and found her way supremely, too, into its pantheon. Out of her work whirl up multiple revelations not only about the uses of imaginative writing, the nature of literary culture, and the discoveries of history, but about deeds and their consequences—the nature of human life itself. To purloin E. M. Forster's phrase, her writing educates the heart.

SELECTED WORKS

Trust (1966)
The Pagan Rabbi, and Other Stories (1971)
Bloodshed and Three Novellas (1976)
Levitation: Five Fictions (1982)
Art & Ardor: Essays (1983)
The Cannibal Galaxy (1983)
Rosa (1983)
Seymour: An American Muse (1985)
The Messiah of Stockholm (1987)
Metaphor & Memory: Essays (1989)
The Shawl (1989)
What Henry James Knew: And Other Essays on Writers (1993)
Fame & Folly: Essays (1996)
Selections (1996)
The Puttermesser Papers (1997)
Quarrel & Quandary: Essays (2000)

FURTHER READING

Bloom, Harold, ed. *Cynthia Ozick*. New York, 1986. This collection includes a valuable introduction by Harold Bloom and many helpful essays on Cynthia Ozick's work.

Cohen, Sarah Blacher. *Cynthia Ozick's Comic Art: From Levity to Liturgy*. Bloomington, Ind., 1994. Blacher Cohen attempts to show the relationship between the comic and the sacred in Ozick's work, in contrast to other critics who foreground the writer's intellect and seriousness.

Kauvar, Elaine M. *Cynthia Ozick's Fiction: Tradition and Invention*. Bloomington, Ind., 1993. This book is arranged chronologically and provides readings of Ozick's fiction from *Trust* through *The Messiah of Stockholm*. Contrary to Joseph Lowin and other critics, Kauvar not only places Ozick's work in the context of American literature but shows her use of her tradition in her fiction as well.

Kauvar, Elaine M. "An Interview with Cynthia Ozick." *Contemporary Literature* 26 (Winter 1985).

Kauvar, Elaine M. "An Interview with Cynthia Ozick." *Contemporary Literature* 34 (Fall 1993).

Lowin, Joseph. *Cynthia Ozick*. Boston, 1988. The first critic to discuss all of the genres in which Ozick has written, Lowin sees Ozick primarily in the Jewish and Yiddish traditions. His book contains generous portions of his correspondence with the artist.

Pinsker, Sanford. *The Uncompromising Fictions of Cynthia Ozick*. Columbia, Mo., 1987. An early book on Ozick's work written in an off-handed manner and containing a number of errors that have been subsequently corrected by other critics.

Rainwater, Catherine, and William J. Scheick, eds. *Contemporary American Women Writers: Narrative Strategies*. Lexington, Ky., 1985. The volume contains a chapter "Invention and Orthodoxy" by Ellen Pifer on Ozick and a valuable, but not updated, bibliography of her work.

Strandberg, Victor. *Greek Mind/Jewish Soul: The Conflicted Art of Cynthia Ozick*. Madison, Wis., 1994. Examines the influences of the Western literary tradition and the artist's social circumstance. Both the American and the Jewish characteristics of her work are considered with illuminating results.

Wood, James. "Cynthia Ozick's *Fame and Folly*." *The New Yorker* (13 May 1996): 88–93.

GRACE PALEY

by Ellen McGrath Smith

"There is a long time in me between knowing and telling," Grace Paley writes in her short story "Debts." For nearly a half-century, Paley's short fiction, essays, and poetry have borne witness to that slow, engaged process of knowing and telling. Since 1959, she has published some forty-five short stories that have made their stylistic and thematic marks on the American short fiction genre. Widely anthologized and recognized as a "writer's writer," Paley is most celebrated for her fiction, although she has written and published nonfiction and poetry as well.

Paley's literary output draws on her multiple identities as an American woman of the World War II generation, a political activist, a parent and grandparent, a lifelong New Yorker, and a Jew born to immigrant parents who fled the Russian pogroms at the turn of the twentieth century. Paley incorporates these identities into her literary endeavors, perhaps because of her stated belief that meaningful writing is not only well crafted in the literary sense but also close to the lives and speech of ordinary people. She has written that great storytellers must also be great listeners and that literature is more a "work of truth" than a "work of art."

The "truth" that Paley's work most consistently illuminates has to do with the lives of women as they strive to act within and against established social roles. Though frequently sidelined from the public sphere because of their gender and their responsibilities as wage earners and mothers, most of Paley's female characters are concerned about the issues of their day—from the Vietnam War to nuclear arms buildup to women's rights; in their own ways, such characters become aware of how their personal lives and the public sphere intersect. In this sense, much of Paley's fiction is autobiographical, written in the hope

Grace Paley.
(© *Christopher Felver/Corbis*)

that, by telling the stories of people often eclipsed in conventional literature, it might be possible to "save a few lives."

While truthfulness and simplicity have been Paley's stated goals, her narrative style and attention to individual speech patterns have drawn the praise of critics and readers. Some have seen her work as avant-garde in its unconventional sentence structures, shifts in time, and fusion of inner thought and spoken dialogue. Many attribute such innovative features to her upbringing in a multicultural, multilingual community and extended family, surrounded by the sounds of Russian, Yiddish, and the dialects and languages of the modern New York "melting pot." Though she did not finish college, she studied in her late teens with the poet W. H. Auden, who encouraged her to eschew stilted language in favor of a language closer to her own milieu and experience. Auden's advice was not lost on her, for the most striking aspect of her short fiction is the fineness of her ear, her knack for revealing the quirky poetry found in the streets of New York. Paley's more directly literary influences include the Russian authors Anton Chekhov and Isaac Babel; she shares a literary affinity and friendship with the working-class feminist author Tillie Olsen.

Paley did not publish her first book, *The Little Disturbances of Man: Stories of Women and Men at Love* (1959), until she was thirty-seven years old. Although she had been writing for some time, her energies went to caring for the two children she had with her first husband, Jess Paley, whom she married in 1942. She was also working at miscellaneous jobs and volunteering in her community. Today, in her eighties, she spends part of the year in the Vermont countryside, where her second husband, Bob Nichols, has roots, but she continues to keep an apartment in the Greenwich Village neighborhood where she spent most of her adult life.

Born on 11 December 1922, Paley was the youngest child of Manya and Isaac Goodside (anglicized from the Russian name Gutseit). Isaac Goodside, a Jewish socialist, had been imprisoned and exiled by the tsar; one of his brothers was killed during a workers' demonstration. The Goodsides immigrated to the United States in 1905 and were later joined by Isaac's mother and two sisters. Isaac initially worked as a photographer but went on to attend medical school, and by the time his daughter Grace was born, he was established in the Bronx as a family physician. Paley was a precocious child, but as an adolescent she neglected school and, like many young women of her generation, sought marriage and family. After briefly attending college and secretarial school, she married Jess Paley. Under the cloud of World War II, she spent much of the early 1940s on U.S. Army bases, since her husband was enlisted in the Signal Corps. When they were finally able to settle again in New York, Jess Paley worked as a filmmaker. The couple struggled financially, piecing jobs together to pay bills and care for their young children.

A NEW VOICE WITH NEW ACCENTS

Paley wrote in the nooks and crannies of available time. Her 1959 publication of *The Little Disturbances of Man*, despite its modest reception, established her reputation as a fiction writer. That reputation grew when the collection was reissued in 1968 and 1973.

This debut collection begins with "Goodbye and Good Luck," in which an older aunt, speaking to her niece, looks back on her unconventional life choices, particularly her involvement with a married man regarded as a star in the heyday of New York Yiddish theater. Highlighting the aunt's inflections and self-preserving philosophies, the story documents a period in Jewish immigrant culture that, even as Paley came of age, was passing away. A more controversial story, "A Woman, Young and Old," tells of a fourteen-year-old girl's seduction of her aunt's boyfriend, a military man. " 'I know exactly what I want,' " Josephine, the Lolita-like narrator and protagonist, announces to the older man she aims to seduce and marry. This story was published in the men's magazine *Nugget*, which suggests that some of Paley's early readers were attracted to her work's sexual directness; others have alternatively seen "A Woman" as exposing the ways in which women have been raised to focus solely on the sexual-romantic aspects of life. A male point of view frames "The Contest." Built around two young adults' collaboration to win a trivia contest sponsored by a Yiddish newspaper, the story also dramatizes the tension between the sexes. After helping his girlfriend, Dotty Wasserman, identify "Jews in the News" and win the newspaper's grand prize, the first-person narrator finds himself in a marriage trap that he ultimately escapes. Like many of the stories in this debut collection, "The Contest" underscores the sense that being in love can be akin to being at war.

One of the most memorable stories in *The Little Disturbances*, "In Time Which Made a Monkey of Us All," rivals Faulkner's fiction in its mixture of local color, tragedy, and humor. "Two Sad Stories from a Long and Happy Life" introduces many of the characters who reappear in Paley's later work, including the single mother Faith (Darwin) Asbury, modeled on Paley herself; Faith's quixotic and mostly absent former husband, Ricardo; and Faith's sons, Richard and Tonto. Some of the people in Faith's diverse and struggling neighborhood are introduced as well, including Dolly Raftery, an Irish-American tenement version of Chaucer's Wife of Bath. These characters receive fuller elaboration in Paley's second and third collections, establishing her not only as a writer of short fiction but as the author of a story cycle in which separate works overlap, expand, or even work in counterpoint to one another.

Paley's second book of stories, *Enormous Changes at the Last Minute* (1974), is a fuller exploration of the lives of characters like Faith Asbury and her urban neighbors. Moreover, it reflects the author's growing political activism. As the 1960s advanced, her involvement in nonviolent protest against U.S. military action in Vietnam deepened; in 1969, she was one of the American antiwar delegates sent to Hanoi to negotiate with the North Vietnamese for the release of U.S. prisoners of war. Also during the late 1960s, Paley's first marriage ended. She had become more overtly feminist in her outlook, believing that sexism, military imperialism, and the destruction of the environment were related issues. The reformist spirit of this period permeates this second book, whose title story brings together the liberalism of Alexandra, a social worker in her thirties; the utopianism of Dennis, a young cab driver/songwriter; and the world-weariness of Alexandra's elderly father, a Russian-Jewish immigrant who had "read Dickens, gone to medical school, and shot like a surface-to-air missile right into the middle class." Each character offers a distinct generational view of the advantages and ills of American life, creating a field of possibility for interaction, growth, and even, as the story's title indicates, "enormous changes."

In 1965 Paley began teaching writing at Sarah Lawrence College, a position she held until 1988. This work, coupled with her own experiences as a mother, attuned her to the interests, hopes, and anxieties of younger people. The story "Faith in a Tree" enacts the main character's "evolution" from a discontented divorced mother in search of a man to an active woman who thinks "more and more and every day about the world." The evolutionary aspect of the story is symbolized by Faith's positioning, in the beginning, in a tree in Washington Square Park, where mothers are gathered as their children play. Hidden in the tree, Faith chimes in with the other women's gripes and gossip, and joins them in assessing and flirting with men who pass by. Suddenly, a group protesting U.S. policy in Vietnam appears and is stopped by police. When the skirmish passes, Faith's son indicts the adults for not standing up to the police. It is then that Faith comes down from the tree, plants her feet in the ground, and takes her son's idealism and disappointment to heart.

GOING THE DISTANCE: MID-CAREER AND BEYOND

In the story "The Long-Distance Runner," which closes *Enormous Changes*, Faith, her children nearly grown, one day simply begins to run through New York (evoking the jogging-craze of the 1970s), visiting landmarks from her past and reaching the "old neighborhood" of her childhood, now predominately black. The premise of a forty-two-year-old woman spontaneously becoming a distance runner corresponds with the unlikeliness of what follows: she stays for three weeks in the apartment where she grew up, with the current residents, a black woman and her four children. During her stay, Faith learns the limits of her understanding of racial issues as well as the bonds she and Mrs. Luddy share as women. The allegory, with its interface of past and future, is encapsulated in the closing lines: "A woman inside the steamy energy of middle age runs and runs. She finds the houses and streets where her childhood happened. She lives in them. She learns as though she were still a child what in the world is coming next."

The most directly autobiographical story in *Enormous Changes* is "Conversations with My Father," which in many ways elucidates Paley's approach to fiction, centering on the disparity between an aging father's idea of what a good story is and his daughter's reluctance to follow traditional plot, "the absolute line between two points which I've always despised . . . because it takes all hope away. Everyone, real or invented, deserves the open destiny of life." Indeed, Paley's work is more invested in dialogue, point of view, and subjective efforts to make sense of events than in the events themselves.

In Paley's third collection, *Later the Same Day* (1985), the division between fiction and autobiography is further blurred, and the sociopolitical concerns of the previous book are firm parts of the landscape. Faith and her friends are now middle-aged and the children they shepherded at the playground grown, but the bond between them holds, as is seen in "Friends," in which the group of women visits a friend dying of cancer. "Dreamer in a Dead Language," which picks up where "Faith in the Afternoon" left off in the previous book, is set in a retirement home, where Faith's mother is happy but her father is restless. When he opens up to her, she reciprocates, only to be chastised for her failed marriage and numerous romantic partners. The story captures the painful love of a daughter for her parents, a mother for her sons, and the isolating moments when those closest to Faith seem the least able to understand her.

Later the Same Day opens with the story "Love." In it, Faith shares with her lover a poem she has written that recalls how being attentive to younger people led her to "descend into remembering love," echoing that moment in "Faith in a Tree" when she resolves to climb down from the tree of selfhood and involve herself in the world. Poetry, Paley has often said, is her first love. Her first book of poems, *Leaning Forward*, was published in 1985. Paley's poems are usually free-verse lyrics in which the use of space and the line as a breath/thought unit takes the place of punctuation. They often deal with the subjects that concern her in her fiction but in a more telescopic fashion and with a more minimalist tone. The poem "Responsibility" is a catalog of Paley's beliefs in the writer's duties as a social witness and critic. While this poem is direct and prosaic, another, "A Poem about Storytelling," is more convoluted in its articulation of the symbiotic relationship between the storyteller and the listener, the living and the dead. Paley's poems tend to be closer than the fiction to the author's inner experiences and feelings; this is particularly true of her later poetry, which bears evidence of the urban fiction writer's discoveries of nature and rural community in her later years. In *Begin Again: Collected Poems* (2000), she interweaves poems about aging and pastoral contemplation with a sense of history—the history of the past as well as the making of history in the present. In her lyrics, Paley documents mothers' losses of children in El Salvador, the slow and often hidden ravages of AIDS, and the paradoxical love of the abusive parent, connecting these instances of suffering and inhumanity to the Holocaust and Vietnam—the history that, the poet insists, we cannot afford to forget. The importance of poetry as an act of remembering is made clear in the poem "The Immigrant Story," in which Paley recalls "enter[ing] the English language" as a child, the sense of accomplishment she felt at assimilating, and the more mature recognition that assimilation is not without loss: "is there a literature that chants the disappearance / of tongues," she wonders at the end of the poem.

Paley has written numerous essays and talks on the art of writing and the writer's role in local and global events. These works, along with her poetry and fiction, underscore her belief that writers can and should be both active and contemplative.

WORKS

The Little Disturbances of Man: Stories of Women and Men at Love (1959)
Enormous Changes at the Last Minute (1974)
Later the Same Day (1985)
Leaning Forward: Poems (1985)
Long Walks and Intimate Talks (1991)
The Collected Stories (1994)
New and Collected Poems (1992)
Just As I Thought (1998)
Begin Again: Collected Poems (2000)

FURTHER READING

Arcana, Judith. *Grace Paley's Life Stories: A Literary Biography*. Urbana, Ill., 1993. A complete biographical account of Paley's development as a writer and activist, with detailed attention to the short fiction.

Bach, Gerhard, and Blaine H. Hall, eds. *Conversations with Grace Paley*. Jackson, Miss., 1997. Reprints twenty-one interviews with Paley, on topics ranging from feminism to the short fiction genre.

Isaacs, Neil D. *Grace Paley: A Study of the Short Fiction*. Boston, 1990. Thorough readings of the individual short stories and the major collections, along with a section on the author's craft and biography, reviews of critical reception, a chronology, and a bibliography.

Taylor, Jacqueline. *Grace Paley: Illuminating the Dark Lives*. Austin, Tex., 1990. Study of Paley's fiction with an emphasis on giving voice to traditionally marginalized groups.

DOROTHY PARKER

by Joy Arbor

Dorothy Parker is often remembered as a wit of the 1920s and 1930s, the author of such quips as "You can lead a horticulture, but you can't make her think" and "Boys seldom make passes / At girls who wear glasses." She is associated with the Algonquin Round Table and the early *New Yorker*. Infamous for her biting remarks, outrageous behavior, and heavy drinking, she has been the subject of numerous novels, plays, and screenplays, most recently Alan Rudolph's 1994 film, *Mrs. Parker and the Vicious Circle*, with Jennifer Jason Leigh in the title role. In the public imagination, Parker's celebrity and caustic personality often overshadow her significant literary achievements as a short-story writer, poet, critic, screenwriter, and playwright, as well as her political commitments. Yet Dorothy Parker's work ought not to be overlooked. Parker is important to literary and cultural history as a writer, a sharp-eyed critic, and a champion of political freedom. During her life, Parker was also a wildly popular writer; her books of poetry and short stories were best-sellers. *The Portable Dorothy Parker*, arranged by Parker in 1943 and released by Viking in 1944 specifically for servicemen overseas, is one of only three in the series (they now number more than seventy-five) that has sold steadily and never gone out of print. The other two are *The Portable Shakespeare* and *The Portable World Bible*.

Dorothy Parker.
(*Courtesy of the Library of Congress*)

DOROTHY ROTHSCHILD: EARLY YEARS

Dorothy Parker was born Dorothy Rothschild on 22 August 1893 in West End, New Jersey. She was born two months premature, a fact that was important to her—later, she would say that it was the last time she was early for anything. Her mother, Eliza A. Marston, was Scottish. Her father, J. Henry Rothschild, a prosperous garment manufacturer, was said by Wyatt Cooper in a 1968 *Esquire* article to be a "distinguished Talmudic scholar." Dorothy was not, however, raised as a Jew. Born to a Jewish father and a gentile mother, she claimed later in life that if she wrote her autobiography, she would title it "Mongrel".

After her mother died when she was five, her father soon remarried a pious Catholic spinster. Young Dorothy did not get along with her stepmother and was terrified of her father. Her stepmother told her that (contrary to Talmudic law, which determines a child's religion based on the mother) she was Jewish because of her father and set her on a course of moral indoctrination to save her soul. She sent Dorothy to a nearby school run by nuns of the Blessed Sacrament Convent. Dorothy's stepmother died of a brain hemorrhage in 1903.

It is unknown exactly when young Dorothy realized that the wealth that surrounded her came from New York City sweatshops that exploited poor immigrant workers, forced to labor in hot temperatures for long hours. We do know that the sharp disparity between the rich and the poor and unemployed haunted her as a child. The youngest of four children many years older than she—Helen, twelve; Harold, nine; and Bertram, six—she often found herself left to her own devices. She spent most of her time reading.

In the fall of 1907, the adolescent Dorothy was sent away to Miss Dana's, an exclusive private boarding school in Morristown, New Jersey. Her fellow students included wealthy heiresses, southern belles, and northern debutantes. Miss Dana's had a classical curriculum, as advanced as those of most junior colleges today. Parker would later draw on Latin poetry and her knowledge of French. Once a week, the entire school met to discuss political and social issues, which perhaps fueled Dorothy's later political concerns. In this atmosphere, she started writing poems. Her biographers disagree on when she left Miss Dana's.

What is known is that Dorothy's father died in 1912 and the young woman who had not been brought up to work suddenly had no money. She contacted Frank Crowninshield, who had bought an early poem. He got her a job at *Vogue* for ten dollars a week. Her first caption there expressed both her wit and her dissatisfaction with the world of fashion: "Brevity is the Soul of Lingerie, as the Petticoat said to the Chemise." In 1915, Dorothy was transferred from *Vogue* to *Vanity Fair*, under Crowninshield's editorship.

BECOMING DOROTHY PARKER

In 1917, Dorothy met and fell in love with Edwin Parker II, a handsome Wall Street broker of distinguished ancestry. He was also a heavy regular drinker. In May, he volunteered for military service, and in June, he and Dorothy were married. During the weekdays, Dorothy Parker worked at *Vanity Fair*, and on the weekends she joined "Eddie" wherever he was stationed, until he was shipped to France. After the war, he did not come home immediately; he was stationed in the Rhineland. Later, she would draw on her experience as a wife waiting for her soldier husband to return in her important short story, "The Lovely Leave."

In April 1918, while Eddie was still away, Parker was appointed drama critic of *Vanity Fair*, succeeding P. G. Wodehouse. In May 1919, Crowninshield hired two Harvard graduates, Robert Benchley and Robert E. Sherwood, to *Vanity Fair*'s editing staff; both Mr. Benchley and Mr. Sherwood, as she called them, would become very important to Mrs. Parker, as they called her. The three of them carried on witty conversations, dining regularly at the nearby Algonquin Hotel, which was then a meeting place for theater people. At the Algonquin, the three *Vanity Fair* wits met Alexander Woolcott; Franklin P. Adams (F.P.A.), who wrote the important column "The Conning Tower" in *The New York Tribune*; and Harold Ross, who would later found *The New Yorker*. The six soon became the center of the group of literary and theater people who spent much of their time making wisecracks and puns; the group was later called the Algonquin Round Table because the hotel manager gave them a large round table when their numbers could not fit at an ordinary table. F.P.A.'s column began to record the group's quips, making Parker an oft-quoted celebrity.

Parker's career as a play reviewer became strained. Instead of merely summarizing performances, she used sardonic quips to poke fun at the shallowness she saw on the stage. She compared Florenz Ziegfeld's wife, Billie Burke, who overacted badly in a play, to the burlesque star Eva Tanguay. She also attacked two other productions. Ziegfeld and the other two producers were important advertisers in *Vanity Fair*, and in January 1920, Crowninshield removed Parker as drama critic. Both she and Benchley resigned in protest.

Parker took a monthly drama column at *Ainslee's* and freelanced, getting her poems published. She was also contributing poetry and prose almost weekly to *Life*, which helped build her popularity and public persona. By April 1921, her witty poems were introducing issues of *Life*. At *Ainslee's* and *Life*, there were no taboos; she honed her irreverent style, using sophisticated wit and puns. Characteristic of her work is when she notes that Avery Hopwood's play goes "from bed to worse." Further, she learned to marry the critical incisiveness that bespoke her dedication to serious art with a sarcastic tone.

She worked with the best wits on *Life*, including many members of the burgeoning Algonquin Round Table. She also began writing character sketches (which served what became her most important work—her fiction) and essays for *Saturday Evening Post*, *Ladies' Home Journal*, and *Everybody's*. Her productivity ensured that Dorothy Parker was becoming a household name.

When Eddie returned from military service in 1919, their relationship became rocky. He did not fit easily into the Round Table. Parker's association with the Algonquin wits included late-night parties at a variety of apartments and speakeasies around New York. To keep Eddie company, she had begun to drink. As her relationship with Eddie got worse and worse, she began to drink more frequently. When Eddie finally asked her to help him dry out at his family's home in Hartford, Connecticut, she refused, claiming that his family disliked her because her father had been a Jew. When he left, depression set in, and she found it more and more difficult to write. A perfectionist who always wrote slowly—"I can't write five words but change seven"—she reputedly put a towel over her typewriter so visitors would not see what, if anything, she was working on. Much later in her life, she would become famous for missing deadlines.

She took her discouragement and self-disgust out on others. Her caustic remarks to the editor of the *Saturday Evening Post* prevented her work from appearing there again. Her tearful admissions that she wished for a family and a house in the country were dismissed by her friends as a parody of drunken sentimentalizing. Nor was her self-pitying poem "News Item" about men not making passes at girls who wear glasses taken seriously.

A painful affair with the reporter and budding playwright Charles MacArthur left her pregnant. She had an abortion and became more depressed. She drank more and tried to commit suicide. Her poetry, which had once been merely witty, now deepened to reflect her despair:

> There's little in taking or giving,
> There's little in water or wine;
> This living, this living, this living,
> Was never a project of mine.
>
> ("Coda")

Later, Parker would become famous for this suicidal streak in her poems as she began to write the poems that she would publish in collections. Parker used the bad times as material for her writing during the good times, a pattern that would last the rest of her life, with mixed success. During this time, she also wrote the story, "Such a Pretty Picture," an interior monologue that conveys the pain of a suburban husband trapped in a bad marriage. Parker's first published story, based on her observations of Benchley's marriage, appeared in *Smart Set* in 1922.

Parker collaborated with her Algonquin cohorts on a number of mediocre musicals, plays, articles, and even a book. She also collaborated with Elmer L. Rice on a play, *Close Harmony* (1929), but it closed in four weeks despite some good reviews. Having reviewed other dramatists for years, the failure of the play must have been a great disappointment. She also wrote a short film with George S. Kaufman called *Business Is Business* for Paramount Studios; she would later write more scripts for Hollywood.

BEST-SELLING PARKER

Parker continued to publish poems and short stories. In December 1926, her first collection of poems, *Enough Rope*, was published. The collection was a best-seller and went through eleven editions. Reviewing the collection, Genevieve Taggard stated, "Dorothy Parker runs her little show as if it were a circus," not recognizing that Parker's witty voice was just a pose in poems like "Resume":

> Razors pain you;
> Rivers are damp;
> Acids stain you;
> And drugs cause cramp.
> Guns aren't lawful;
> Nooses give;
> Gas smells awful;
> You might as well live.

In 1928, Parker published her second book of poems, *Sunset Gun*, to excellent reviews. Her final collection of poems, *Death and Taxes*, was published in 1931 to fine reviews, except in *Poetry*.

Harold Ross and Jane Grant had started *The New Yorker* in 1925, winning financial support by listing Parker among an impressive list of "advisory editors"; yet Parker contributed little to the magazine's first year. Off and on from 1927 to 1931, Parker reviewed books for *The New Yorker*. Though she signed the reviews "Constant Reader," it was well known that she authored the reviews. She praised writers she liked, but the acerbity of her commentary on those she did not is entertaining and insightful. She praised Ernest Hemingway and Ring Lardner but said of Margot Asquith's autobiography, "The affair between Margot Asquith and Margot Asquith will live as one of the prettiest love stories in all literature." Of A. E. Milne, she wrote, "Tonstant weader fwowed up."

In 1929, Parker's most daring story was published. "Big Blonde" is the story of Hazel Morse. When her marriage that was supposed to save her from being a "good sport" falls apart, Hazel begins drinking and becomes a party girl. The men in her life support her yet do not stay long. Hazel lives in a haze of alcohol that does not prevent her from being depressed. Finally, she decides to kill herself but does not succeed. For the story, in which Parker clearly drew upon her own life experiences, she won the O. Henry Prize for the best short story appearing in an American magazine for that year. In 1930, it was collected with other stories, including "Mr. Durant," about a man's insensitive handling of his mistress's abortion, to form *Laments for the Living*. Published in 1933, *After Such Pleasures*, her second collection of stories, exposed the shallowness of society and featured portraits of aging women.

HOLLYWOOD

In 1933, Benchley introduced Parker to Alan Campbell, a young Broadway actor eleven years her junior. They were married in 1934 and began to work on scripts for Paramount Studios. Though Parker did not like living in Los Angeles, she and Campbell collaborated on a number of films, earning high salaries. Between their salaries and the royalties of her collected poems, *Not So Deep as a Well* (1936), they had enough money to buy and renovate a 111-acre farm in Bucks County, Pennsylvania, in 1937, while much of the country was plunged in the Depression.

Of the many scripts that Campbell and Parker collaborated on, their most famous was the 1937 *A Star Is Born*; the film starred Frederic March and Janet Gaynor. *A Star Is Born* is the story of a relationship between an aging, once-successful but alcoholic actor and an up-and-coming actress. When the actress becomes increasingly successful, the relationship is torn apart. Finally, the aging actor kills himself. Since Parker drank heavily and was almost considered a has-been at that point, it is easy to see that she and her young attractive husband may have had some insight into that story. Their screenplay was nominated for an Academy Award; the film was remade with the same screenplay in 1954 starring Judy Garland and James Mason. The 1976 version, starring Barbra Streisand and Kris Kristofferson, used a new script written by Joan Didion and John Gregory Dunne.

In Los Angeles, Parker met the playwright and writer Lillian Hellman, who would be a close friend in later years and would become executor of Parker's estate. With Hellman and Hellman's lover, writer Dashiell Hammett, Parker became an organizer of the Screen Writers Guild. Later, she became more politically active; she organized events for the Anti-Nazi League and went to Spain to report on the war there.

When World War II began, Parker again became a waiting wife, as Campbell had, at forty, enlisted in the army. At the end of the war, her husband did not immediately return; Parker and Campbell divorced in 1947 and remarried in 1950. In 1949, Parker was blacklisted by the California State Senate Committee on Un-American Activities. In 1951, the screenwriter Martin Berkeley named her and Campbell in his list of communists in Hollywood, making it impossible for them to find work there.

Parker left for New York and collaborated with Arnaud D'Usseau on the play *The Ladies of the Corridor* (1954), which was named the best play of the year by George Jean Nathan. In 1956, she returned to Hollywood with Campbell. Though she was commissioned by *Esquire* to write book reviews, writing had become hard for her, and she often missed deadlines. In 1963, Campbell took an overdose of sleeping pills and died in bed next to her.

Parker moved back to New York, where she died in 1967, leaving over twenty thousand dollars to Martin Luther King Jr., a man she admired but had never met.

Today, feminist critics are reassessing Parker's work, finding in her fiction portraits of women and relationships well ahead of their time.

[*See also* Algonquin Round Table *and* Writing as a Woman in the Twentieth Century.]

WORKS

Enough Rope (1926)
Sunset Gun (1928)
Close Harmony (1929)
Laments for the Living (1930)
Death and Taxes (1931)
After Such Pleasures (1933)
Not So Deep as a Well (1936)
Here Lies (1939)
Collected Stories of Dorothy Parker (1942)
Collected Poetry of Dorothy Parker (1944)
The Viking Portable Dorothy Parker (1944)
The Best of Dorothy Parker (1952)
The Ladies of the Corridor (1954)
Short Story: A Thematic Anthology (1965)
Constant Reader (1970)
The Portable Dorothy Parker (1973)
The Penguin Dorothy Parker (1977)
The Coast of Illyria (1990)
Complete Stories (1995)
Not Much Fun: The Lost Poems of Dorothy Parker (1996)

FURTHER READING

Keats, John. *You Might as Well Live: The Life and Times of Dorothy Parker*. New York, 1970. The first biography of Parker. Highly readable.

Kinney, Arthur F. *Dorothy Parker, Revised*. New York, 1998. A solid introduction to Parker's work. One of the few here that includes Parker's politics.

Meade, Marion. *Dorothy Parker: What Fresh Hell Is This?* New York, 1988. Considered the most authoritative biography to date.

Melzer, Sondra. *The Rhetoric of Rage: Women in Dorothy Parker*. New York, 1997. Analysis of women in selected short stories.

Pettit, Rhonda S. *A Gendered Collision: Sentimentalism and Modernism in Dorothy Parker's Poetry and Fiction*. Madison, Wisc., 2000. Analyzes Parker in the tradition of female sentimentalism.

ROBERT PINSKY

by James Longenbach

Robert Pinsky.
(Margaretta K. Mitchell Photography)

"My mother's dreadful fall," runs a line by Robert Pinsky in "Biography," a poem from his *Jersey Rain* (2000); "Her mother's dread / Of all things: death, life, birth." One thing leads to another: "My brother's birth / Just before the fall, his birth again in Jesus." And another: "Wobble and blur of my soul, born only once, / That cleaves to circles." What may seem like a pattern of events in "Biography" is more precisely a pattern of words—a swirl of language that seems at once fateful and arbitrary. The mother's "dreadful" fall leads to the grandmother's "dread." Her dread of "birth" invokes her grandson's "birth again in Jesus." His second birth allows his brother, who was "born only once," into the poem. This man, the author of the poem, is a soul who "cleaves to circles." He is a poet who recognizes that his being is determined by ever-widening circles of experience, history, and chance—the "unseen multitudes" (as he puts it in "An Alphabet of My Dead," also from *Jersey Rain*) who have determined the shape of his body, his house, the world through which he walks.

Pinsky was born in Long Branch, New Jersey, in 1940. After attending Rutgers and Stanford University, he published his first collection of poems, *Sadness and Happiness*, in 1975. Five more books of poetry and two books of criticism have followed. So has *Mindwheel* (1986), an electronic novel, and a much-acclaimed translation of Dante's *Inferno* (1994). In 1997, Pinsky was named Poet Laureate of the United States, a position he held for an unprecedented three years. "Circle of causes or chaos or turns of chance," he intones in "Biography": How *does* one thing lead to another?

Part of what has made Pinsky such a successful laureate is that he has never stopped feeling like an interloper—a saxophone-blasting kid from a lower-middle-class Jewish family in Long Branch. He wants both to revere and to ruffle the tradition; more profoundly, he suggests that we cannot possibly revere the tradition—continue it, make it live—without ruffling it. "The poet's first social responsibility, to continue the art," says Pinsky in *Poetry and the World* (1988), "can be filled only through the second, opposed responsibility to change the terms of the art as given—and it is given socially, which is to say politically."

How does a poet—who spends most of his time alone, pushing words around—actually fulfill these momentous responsibilities? In *The Sounds of Poetry* (1998) Pinsky notes that both Allen Ginsberg's poem "Howl" and W. E. B. Du Bois's essay "On the Training of Black Men" end with what can be heard as lines of iambic pentameter: "Door of my cottage in the Western night"; "I sit with Shakespeare and he winces not." But Pinsky neither upbraids the radicals with the tradition nor beats the tradition with the radicals. To him, there is nothing ironic about Ginsberg's or Du Bois's use of the great English line; since the tradition is an ongoing process rather than a static body of achievement, the tradition is available to everyone. And since English is a mongrel tongue, the tradition itself is fruitfully compromised: as Pinsky puts it, the sound of Thomas Jefferson's phrase "life, liberty, and the pursuit of happiness" combines the Anglo-Saxon bluntness of "life" and "hap" with the "Roman, legalistic force of Latin 'liberty' " and the "courtly, equestrian connotations of Norman French 'pursuit.' " This is a reticent way of saying that a kid from Long Branch and the Declaration of Independence are cut from the same ragged cloth.

As the poem "Biography" suggests by its very design, the events of Pinsky's life do not tell us very much. What interests Pinsky is the movement between those events, the way in which the sound of one word generates another. Consequently, to discover the "biography" of this poet one has merely to listen to anything he has ever written—to hear that his poems feel simultaneously anarchic and well made, reckless and traditional. In "Shirt," from *The Want Bone* (1990), Pinsky thinks about the innumerable historical forces that have produced the very clothes on his back (the "shirt" serves as a kind of emblem for "identity"). The poem's pentameter lines swirl from sweatshops in Korea to Scottish mills, from the seventeenth-century Anglican poet George Herbert to an almost anonymous African-American woman in South Carolina.

> The kilt, devised for workers
> To wear among the dusty clattering looms.
> Weavers, carders, spinners. The loader,
>
> The docker, the navvy. The planter, the picker, the sorter
> Sweating at her machine in a litter of cotton
> As slaves in calico headrags sweated in fields:
>
> George Herbert, your descendant is a Black
> Lady in South Carolina, her name is Irma
> And she inspected my shirt. Its color and fit
>
> And feel and its clean smell have satisfied
> Both her and me. We have culled its cost and quality
> Down to the buttons of simulated bone,
>
> The buttonholes, the sizing, the facing, the characters
> Printed in black on neckband and tail. The shape,
> The label, the labor, the color, the shade. The shirt.

As these lines suggest, Pinsky is deeply interested in the racial and ethnic components of identity, and though all the ingredients for an identity politics are contained in his poems, such a politics never emerges. Far more interesting is the way in which one thing leads unpredictably to another: the rhythm of the phrase "The loader, / The docker, the navvy" generates the phrase "The planter, the picker, the sorter" in the same way that Irma leads us back to George Herbert. Things are themselves because they are made of other things, and the links between them feel simultaneously inexplicable and incontrovertible. Pinsky's poems are not often about Long Branch, New Jersey, but their linguistic texture feels like Long Branch, which is to say that they feel like Robert Pinsky: courtly yet provincial, elegant yet homemade, preserved out of time yet as relentlessly in motion as the waves on the shore. From Pinsky's point of view, his poems could not be otherwise. "Our very sentences," he says in his second book of poems, *An Explanation of America* (1979), "are like a cloth / Cut shimmering from conventions of the dead."

In his second critical book, *The Situation of Poetry* (1977), Pinsky helped create the taste by which he would be judged, offering the word "discursive" to describe a poetry that might be organized by the unfolding of abstract statement rather than the eruption of primal images. But the discursiveness of *An Explanation of America* was never destined to become Pinsky's signature. The poems in his next books, *History of My Heart* (1984) and *The Want Bone*, continue to address Pinsky's signature theme (the dialectical relationship of the self and the social structure), but they don't explain anything; instead, they allow us to experience the movement of this dialectical process through unpredictable turns of syntax, diction, and metaphor. In "The Uncreation" various ideas of singing hold the poem's disparate materials together. In "At Pleasure Bay" some version of the phrase "never the same" recurs. And, as we've already seen, the repeated motif in "Shirt" is neither a theme nor a phrase but simply a rhythm: "The back, the yoke, the yardage" or "The planter, the picker, the sorter."

But "if gorgeous, impressive language and profound, crucial ideas were all that poetry offered to engage us," asks Pinsky in *Poetry and the World*, "would it seem—as it does to many of us—as necessary as food?" What engages us in poetry is not the product (the achieved word or thought) but the process of moving through those thoughts and words: "This movement—physical in the sounds of a poem, moral in its relation to the society implied by language, and the person who utters the poem—is near the heart of poetry's mysterious appeal, for me." Pinsky's fully mature poems not only describe this appeal but also enact it.

In this regard, "Ode to Meaning" is the major poem of *Jersey Rain* and possibly the major poem of Pinsky's career:

> Gesturer, when is your spur, your cloud?
> You in the airport rituals of greeting and parting.
> Indicter, who is your claimant?
> Bell at the gate. Spiderweb iron bridge.
> Cloak, video, aroma rue, what is your
> Elected silence, where was your seed?

The "you" Pinsky addresses in these lines is meaning itself. Where do you come from, he asks, what provokes you, what receives you? Meaning is everywhere in the poem—everywhere in the world—yet its very abundance is overwhelming; it continually escapes our best efforts to pin it down. We crave meaning, yet once clearly defined, meaning threatens to determine us. "Dire one and desired one," begins "Ode to Meaning," "Savior, sentencer." In the same way that the sounds of the phrases "dire one" and "desired one" threaten to become identical (while their meanings are opposed), meaning is a force that we cannot help spurning even as we crave it.

"You are the wound," ends "Ode to Meaning," "You / Be the medicine." However much this poetry courts the sound of madness, Pinsky craves sanity. "Let those scorn you who never / Starved in your dearth," he says of meaning, and his poem—turning swiftly from literary history to biography—points to the origins of his hunger.

> Untrusting, I court you. Wavering
> I seek your face, I read
> That Crusoe's knife
> Reeked of you, that to defile you
> The soldier makes the rabbi spit on the torah.
> "I'll drown my book," says Shakespeare.

> Drowned walker, revenant.
> After my mother fell on her head, she became
> More than ever your sworn enemy. She spoke
> Sometimes like a poet or critic of forty years later.
> Or she spoke of the world as Thersites spoke of the heroes,
> "I think they have swallowed one another. I
> Would laugh at that miracle."

The phrase "fell on her head" appears several times throughout the poems of *Jersey Rain*; it names the central event in the biography Pinsky constructs for himself throughout this book: "My mother's dreadful fall," as he puts it in "Biography." Throughout "Ode to Meaning" Pinsky presents the "fall" into a swirling world of language as a fortunate fall. Everyone grapples with the sounds of language, and we could not be comforted if we were not confused—and confused again. Meaning, Pinsky insists in the "Ode," is to be found "not in the words, not even / Between the words, but a torsion, / A cleaving, a stirring."

Which is to say that meaning exists in movement, in the ever-shifting way in which one thing leads to another, making us who we are, unmaking us so that we might be made again.

SELECTED WORKS

Landor's Poetry (1968)
Sadness and Happiness (1975)
The Situation of Poetry (1977)
An Explanation of America (1979)
History of My Heart (1984)
Mindwheel (1986)
Poetry and the World (1988)
The Want Bone (1990)
The Inferno of Dante (translator) (1994)
The Figured Wheel (1996)
The Sounds of Poetry (1998)
Jersey Rain (2000)
Democracy, Culture and the Voice of Poetry (2002)

FURTHER READING

Glück, Louise. "Story Tellers." *American Poetry Review* 26 (July-August 1997): 9–12. A major poet's reading of lyric and narrative elements in Pinsky's later poems.

Longenbach, James. *Modern Poetry after Modernism*. New York, 1997. The most complete account available of Pinsky's career.

McClatchy, J. D. "Shapes of Desire." *New Republic* (24 September 1990): 46–48. A perceptive survey of Pinsky's career up to *History of My Heart*.

Parini, Jay. "Explaining America: The Poetry of Robert Pinsky." *Chicago Review* 33 (1981): 16–26. An account of the discursive elements of Pinsky's earlier poems.

SYLVIA PLATH

by Caitriona O'Reilly

On the morning of 11 February 1963, Sylvia Plath committed suicide in London. At the time of her death, she was known as the author of a first, moderately well received book of poems, *The Colossus* (1960). In addition, she had recently published a novel, *The Bell Jar* (1963), under the pseudonym Victoria Lucas. She had published a number of prose stories and sketches in various magazines and journals. Plath also left behind a manuscript of newer work, titled *Ariel*, which consisted of poems written for the most part in the last five months of her life. The eventual publication of this book, somewhat altered in form from Plath's original intention, occurred in 1965. Plath's considerable renown as a writer dates from the publication of *Ariel*, which was quickly recognized as a poetic work of the highest order. As the facts about her life, and particularly the manner of her death, became widely known, she developed a cult status. Many critical commentators found themselves taking sides in a startlingly polarized debate about the merit of Plath's late work. Much of the critical controversy centered around poems such as "Daddy" and "Lady Lazarus," in which Plath conflates details from the recent past of Europe (in particular references to the concentration camps and the Nazi persecution of the Jews) with images depicting the trauma of her personal history.

Rather than clarifying the "identity" of Sylvia Plath and the root cause of her madness or genius, the publication of *Letters Home: Correspondence, 1950–1963* in 1975, and of her journals in America in 1982, seemed only to fuel the fires of controversy. Unfortunately, in a highly public and grotesque exaggeration of the blame-apportioning that can follow a death of such tragic nature, Sylvia Plath's family and friends were caught in the crossfire of a critical debate often dominated and made rancorous by

Sylvia Plath.
(© *Bettmann/Corbis*)

the gender politics of the 1970s. The personal fallout from this almost unprecedented collision between a writer's work and her biography is incalculable. What can be asserted, however, is that Plath's notoriety has obscured to a great extent the true value of her best work, tending to foreground the more sensational of her poems at the expense of other, quieter, and perhaps more important aspects of her writing. Decades after her death, when several of the main protagonists of Plath's biographical drama are no longer living, it has become somewhat easier to view her work in the balanced critical light it deserves.

BACKGROUND AND EARLY LIFE

Sylvia Plath was born in Boston, Massachusetts, on 27 October 1932, the first child of Otto Plath and his second wife, Aurelia Schober Plath. Otto Plath was forty-seven at the time of his daughter's birth, twenty-one years older than his wife, and a dominant patriarchal presence in the household. He had emigrated to the United States from Grabow, a town in the then "Polish Corridor" (later called by Plath a "manic-depressive hamlet in the black heart of Prussia") in 1901. Estranged from his devoutly Lutheran family because of his conversion to Darwinism, Otto Plath independently pursued advanced studies in languages, biology, zoology, and entomology, eventually receiving a doctorate from Harvard in 1928 for research into the life cycle of the bumblebee. Aurelia Schober had been born in the United States to Austrian parents, and had worked as a high-school teacher of languages before her marriage at the age of twenty-two. From both parents, Plath seems to have inherited her strong idealism and drive toward self-improvement, and perhaps also an immigrant's sense of the precariousness of worldly success, a sense of its having to be continually renewed and bolstered. Otto Plath died following an operation to amputate a gangrenous leg in 1940, when Sylvia was eight and her brother, Warren, five. He had stubbornly refused to seek medical advice for his declining health, and was much weakened by the time a diagnosis of diabetes was made. There is some evidence to suggest that Plath considered her father's carelessness about his health as tantamount to suicide and therefore as blameworthy. Written in 1962, "Daddy" is an angry tirade against the father who has deserted her, a Freudian drama of repetition-compulsion in which the speaker resurrects her vampiric father only to kill him again in a contradictory attempt to efface the original source of her psychological pain. In Plath's poetry and prose, Otto Plath was to become a potent symbol of absence, signifying the impossibility of lasting love, of God, or of any real meaning in life. The death of her father was a shock from which Plath never properly recovered.

COLLEGE LIFE AND ATTEMPTED SUICIDE

Following Otto Plath's death, the family moved inland from Winthrop to Wellesley, Massachusetts. At this early stage in her life, Sylvia Plath was already embarked on a brilliant academic career, aspiring with immense discipline and hard work to become the ideal all-around student. She won a scholarship to study at Smith College, where she maintained her high grade average while enjoying an active social life, serving as an editor of the *Smith Review*, and publishing stories in *Seventeen*, the *Christian Science Monitor*, and *Mademoiselle*. Plath was later to find the transition from her initial success as a precocious student, publishing in the "slicks," as she called them, to becoming a more mature and considered writer a difficult one. As a teenager she had mastered the art of tailoring her writing to meet the perceived requirements of the magazines in which she wanted to publish, and finding her own independent voice was to be a gradual and often painful process.

In June 1953, at the end of her second year at Smith, Plath embarked on a guest editorship for *Mademoiselle* in New York City, together with nineteen other young high achievers from colleges all over the country. She later satirized this period in her strongly autobiographical novel *The Bell Jar*, and from her descriptions of the overwhelming summer heat of the city, the exhausting routine of hard work and socializing, and the competitive cattiness of the young women with whom she was thrown, it is clear that Plath did not enjoy her stint on *Mademoiselle* as much as she felt she ought to have, but was left drained by the experience. On returning home

to Wellesley, she was dismayed to discover that she had not been accepted for Frank O'Connor's summer writing class at Harvard. At loose ends in Wellesley, suffering badly from insomnia, and panicking at her inability to impose a disciplined routine on herself, Plath began to slip into depression. The family doctor prescribed sleeping pills and referred her to a psychiatrist, who recommended electroconvulsive therapy (ECT) after a brief consultation. The ECT was ineptly administered, and the resulting pain and terror that Plath suffered apparently propelled her toward suicide.

On 24 August she hid herself in the family basement and took a massive overdose of sleeping pills. Having vomited up a large quantity of the pills, she lay undiscovered in a comatose state for two days, while police searched the surrounding area for her. She was eventually discovered and brought to the psychiatric wing of Massachusetts General Hospital. Her physical health was recovered, but the severity of her mental condition became clear, and she was transferred to McLean Hospital in Belmont, Massachusetts, at the expense of her Smith benefactress, Olive Higgins Prouty. Plath remained at McLean (whose other illustrious literary patients had included Robert Lowell and Anne Sexton) until February 1954, when she was judged fit to return to Smith. The Freudian analysis she underwent as part of her treatment at McLean was to have a profound influence on her writing. In 1958, while living in Boston with her husband, Ted Hughes, Plath voluntarily reentered analysis with her McLean psychiatrist, Dr. Ruth Beuscher, and further refined her own interpretation of the Freudian "family romance." Plath's artistic debt to her analysis, and the rather programmatic narrative version of the traumatic events of her life with which it seemed to furnish her, remains one of the more controversial aspects of her biography.

GRADUATION AND MARRIAGE

Plath returned to Smith in February 1954 and resumed her challenging work and social schedule, graduating summa cum laude in 1955. In the autumn of that year, she embarked on a master's degree course at Newnham College, Cambridge. At a party in Cambridge in February 1956, she met the young English poet Ted Hughes. The couple married within four months of their first meeting, in a ceremony that took place in London on 16 June 1956. They spent their honeymoon in Benidorm, Spain, and then returned to Cambridge, where Plath completed her studies, graduating with a master's degree in 1957. The couple moved back to the United States in the summer of that year, Plath to take up a teaching job at Smith College, and Hughes to teach and write. Her journals testify to Plath's difficulties with teaching and her frustration with the lack of time it afforded her to concentrate on her poetry and prose. During the difficult year of 1957–1958 Plath and Hughes resolved to try to live by their writing. They spent the following year in Boston, where they met many writers, including Robert Frost, Robert Lowell, Marianne Moore, and Adrienne Rich. Plath participated (with Anne Sexton) in Robert Lowell's writing workshop at Boston University for a time, and in December 1958 reentered psychotherapy with Dr. Ruth Beuscher.

Plath and her husband spent the summer of 1959 traveling across the United States by car, returning home in late August. The autumn of 1959 saw them at Yaddo, the artists' colony in Saratoga Springs, New York. Her stay there was to be a productive time for Plath. She was by this time pregnant with her first child, and many of the poems she wrote at Yaddo, including the breakthrough sequence "Poem for a Birthday," show her musing on her condition. "Poem for a Birthday" posits a connection between pregnancy and her personal reemergence after the nightmare of psychological disintegration and "electrocution" by ECT. As well as this important poem, Plath also wrote several successful lyrics at Yaddo, including "Mushrooms" and "The Colossus," which was to become the title poem of her first collection.

RETURN TO ENGLAND, MOTHERHOOD, AND THE GENESIS OF *ARIEL*

Late in 1959, Plath and Hughes left the United States for England, where they intended to settle and raise a family. Until August 1961 they lived in London (their daughter Frieda Rebecca was born in April 1961); thereafter they moved to Court Green, a former rectory in the village of North Tawton in Devon. A second child, Nicholas Farrar, was born there in January 1962. Heinemann had published *The Colossus* in London in 1960, and in 1962 Knopf published it in New York. While in Devon, Plath began work on the poems that would eventually be gathered into the *Ariel* volume. In the early autumn of 1962, Plath and Hughes separated acrimoniously after Plath's discovery that Hughes had begun an affair with Assia Wevill, wife of the young Canadian poet David Wevill. Alone with her children in Devon, Plath entered upon the most productive phase of her creative life. Between September and December 1962, she produced as many as forty lyric poems of immense

power, often writing two in a day. For a writer as self-conscious and painstaking as Plath had been, it was a true watershed.

In December, tired of her enforced isolation in Devon but exultant at her creative breakthrough, Plath moved back to London with her children. She continued to write poems, but with less ferocity than the initial outburst of the autumn. It seems she was also working on a second novel, which dealt with the subject of her marriage. The manuscript of this work, if it still exists, has never been released by Plath's estate. *The Bell Jar* (a work Plath dismissed to friends as "a potboiler," probably because of the extremely unfavorable biographical portraits it contained) was published pseudonymously by Heinemann in January 1963. However, difficulties with her new flat and with finding a nanny for her children, as well as ill health and the harshest winter England had seen for many years, combined to make her seriously depressed. Despite the ministrations of concerned friends and of her doctor, Plath was clearly unable to cope, and she gassed herself in the kitchen of her flat in the early hours of 11 February, having first taken steps to ensure the safety of her two children, who were asleep in an upstairs bedroom. She was thirty years of age.

THE LEGACY

Sylvia Plath died intestate, and her husband, Ted Hughes, together with his sister Olwyn, took over the administration of Plath's literary estate after 1963. The publication of *Ariel* in 1965 was followed by two further volumes of poetry in 1971, *Crossing the Water* (which contains poems written between *The Colossus* and *Ariel*) and *Winter Trees* (containing eighteen previously uncollected poems and a verse play for radio titled *Three Women*). Aurelia Schober Plath published a volume of Plath's correspondence in 1975, and a children's book titled *The Bed Book*, written by Plath in the late 1950s, appeared the following year. In 1977 Hughes published *Johnny Panic and the Bible of Dreams*, a collection of Plath's short stories and miscellaneous prose pieces, and in 1981 Plath's *Collected Poems* was published, a volume that also included a substantial amount of juvenilia. It was awarded the Pulitzer Prize.

A heavily edited edition of *The Journals of Sylvia Plath* appeared in the United States only in 1982, and it was not until after Hughes's death that a more comprehensive edition of the journals appeared in Britain and the United States in 2000, edited by Karen V. Kukil. In addition, it is thought that a substantial amount of Sylvia Plath's writing either did not survive or has been withheld by her estate. This includes two volumes of her journals covering the years 1960–1963 and a novel that she is believed to have finished, or at least brought close to completion, by the time of her death. Of the journals, Ted Hughes wrote: "Two more notebooks survived for a while, maroon-backed ledgers like the 1957–1959 volume, and continued the record from late 1959 to within three days of her death. The last of these contained entries for several months, and I destroyed it because I did not want her children to have to read it.... The other disappeared."

SHORTER PROSE WORKS AND *THE BELL JAR*

Even despite such absences, however, the totality of Plath's published work indicates what a remarkably precocious and multifaceted talent she possessed. Many of the early stories contained in *Johnny Panic and the Bible of Dreams* are somewhat stilted and amply illustrate what Plath wrote about so eloquently in the journals, her struggle to imbue her material with convincing life and psychological insight. An early success was "Superman and Paula Brown's New Snowsuit," written when Plath was twenty-three. This semiautobiographical story is set in Plath's childhood during World War II and deals subtly with the theme of discrimination against German-Americans in this period. However, such success in prose before 1960 was the exception for Plath. It is in the later, more directly autobiographical pieces, such as "America! America!" (an amusing satire on American patriotism written for *Punch*) or "Ocean 1212-W," that a freer, more confident prose voice can be seen emerging. The latter piece, written for the BBC series "Writers on Themselves," is a tremendously skillful evocation of Plath's early childhood in Winthrop, Massachusetts. Ostensibly it is about a young child's jealousy at the birth of her baby brother, an event that brings her own isolation home to her: "Hugging my grudge, ugly and prickly, a sad sea urchin, I trudged off on my own, in the opposite direction toward the forbidding prison. As from a star I saw, coldly and soberly, the separateness of everything. I felt the wall of my skin: I am I. That stone is a stone. My beautiful fusion with the things of this world was over." On a deeper level, however, the piece can be said to revisit the site of Plath's obsession with the death of her father, since it deals with a period of happiness she now regards as forever out of reach. The abruptness of the story's ending underlines the shock of loss: "My father died, we moved inland. Whereon those nine first years of my life sealed themselves off like a ship

in a bottle—beautiful, inaccessible, obsolete, a fine, white flying myth."

The Bell Jar deals with the theme of isolation and unhappiness in greater detail. The book is really a roman à clef detailing the traumatic summer of Plath's breakdown in 1953, and contains thinly disguised portraits of her family and friends. It is generally supposed that Plath published the novel under an assumed name and discouraged her mother from reading it because of the acidity with which some of these portraits are drawn. Mrs. Greenwood, the mother of the book's protagonist, comes off particularly badly. In another recasting of her versatile Freudian-inflected myth of self, Plath makes clear that it is her heroine's enforced proximity to her well-meaning but hopelessly naïve mother that leads to suicidal depression. During one climactic scene an insomniac and desperate Esther Greenwood fantasizes about killing her sleeping mother: "My mother turned from a foggy log into a slumbering, middle-aged woman, her mouth slightly open and a snore raveling from her throat. The piggish noise irritated me, and for a while it seemed to me that the only way to stop it would be to take the column of skin and sinew from which it rose and twist it to silence between my hands." The extreme detachment of this description borders on the pathological, and is symptomatic of Esther's feeling of general disconnectedness from reality. This is the "bell jar" state that Plath describes being trapped in, as though a glass wall were separating her from her life. Its similarity to the sealed-off ship-in-a-bottle quality of her childhood described above underlines the profound continuity of imagery throughout Plath's work. A version of the bell jar would return in her late poem "Medusa," a counterpart to "Daddy" in which the speaker violently rejects her smothering, controlling mother, whom she also envisages as an airless receptacle: "Bottle in which I live, / Ghastly Vatican."

The Bell Jar is written with considerable verve and displays Plath's gifts for gallows humor, forceful imagery, and skillful inflection of voice, characteristics that she later raised to virtuosic level in the poems of *Ariel*. However, the novel is less convincing as a bildungsroman or psychological self-portrait. The critic Stan Smith (1989) has written of Plath's "irony of artifice," suggesting that Plath uses her heroine's paranoia to "penetrate the bland benevolent surfaces of other people's motives to discover their inner and unconscious significance." However, other critics of the novel, such as Pat MacPherson and Elisabeth Bronfen, have noted that the novel's almost nonchalant resolution, given the apparent severity of Esther's psychological collapse, is unconvincing. The growth in self-knowledge and insight one expects from a novel of crisis has failed to materialize, but this aesthetic weakness is perhaps indicative of another, more disturbing meaning. In *The Bell Jar*, "cure" is viewed not as a form of internal healing but instead as a test one must pass in order to rejoin the competitive society beyond the asylum walls. The novel depicts an encompassing dystopia to which there seems no viable alternative, and at its core is a nihilism that is avoided only by denial, a willed redirection of the gaze. Esther's suicide can in fact be seen as a last-ditch attempt of the will to avoid coming face-to-face with this more profound, unspoken reality, not an outcome of having already confronted it. *The Bell Jar*, despite its jaunty, slangy narrative style, is a work that studiously avoids admitting its own deepest implications.

THE *ARIEL* POEMS

If *The Bell Jar* provides unsatisfying glimpses of a darker truth, then it is in Plath's poetry, with the resources of myth at her disposal, that Plath gives full voice to her particular tragic vision, and it is upon these late poems that her reputation as a writer ultimately rests. "The Fearful" provides an arresting image of selves being devoured by their attributes:

> This man makes a pseudonym
> And crawls behind it like a worm.
>
> This woman on the telephone
> Says she is a man, not a woman.
> The mask increases, eats the worm,
> Stripes for mouth and eyes and nose,
>
> The voice of the woman hollows—
> More and more like a dead one . . .

The image is that of a fiction taking on an autonomous life, hollowing out or abstracting the living matter of which it was initially composed, in cannibalistic fashion. Throughout Plath's work, the figure of a self subsumed or reduced to its various, separable appurtenances has a counterpart in images of wholeness and intuitions of an essential core of self. The latter trope has been emphasized by those who regard *Ariel* as a triumphant culmination; indeed, it may be regarded as the most commonly accepted interpretation of Plath's achievement, although it involves a strong teleological bias, with either *Ariel* or the poet's suicide as the inevitable end point of the process. According to this interpretation of Plath's life and works, the *Ariel* poems

represent a triumphant, and permanent, release from years of seemingly fruitless toil, psychological difficulties, and paralyzing writer's block. Plath's husband and executor, Ted Hughes, possibly the most important critic of her work, has argued that Plath's poems represent stages in her healing and rediscovery of self. In a number of influential essays about Plath's writing, Hughes portrays her as a uniquely self-referential writer: "Sylvia Plath's poetry, like a species on its own, exists in little else but the revelation of that birth and purpose. Although her whole considerable ambition was fixed on becoming the normal flowering and fruiting kind of writer, her work was roots only" (Hughes 1995, p. 178). But perhaps to regard Plath as quite such a unique writer is to begin to pathologize her. Hughes, far from demystifying Plath, has added greatly to her posthumous mythology by emphasizing her helpless passivity before a ferocious muse: "It [i.e., her development] gave the impression of being a secret crucible, or rather a womb, an almost biological process—and just as much beyond her manipulative interference" (Hughes, 1995, p. 180).

The image of the woman artist which emerges from this portrait is that of a sibyl in the grip of a powerful, biologically determined process which it is beyond her power to actively control. Hughes diagnoses Plath as a unique case in the history of poetry: "The difficulty is the extreme peculiarity in kind of her poetic gift. And the difficulty is not lessened by the fact that she left behind two completely different kinds of poetry" (Hughes, 1995, p. 178). The first kind of poetry, in Hughes's analysis, was everything before the true "*Ariel* voice" emerged in "Elm," which was written on 19 April 1962. Hughes's assertion that the end point of this process was a new, triumphant self and that "all her poems are in a sense by-products" (Hughes, 1995, p. 189) indicates that his interpretation of Plath has, ironically, much in common with feminist readings of her work, as the critic Jacqueline Rose (1991) has observed: "Let's . . . note how close, aesthetically, that notion of the emergent real self is to the feminist reading of Plath in terms of an isolate selfhood that Hughes has also been seen as suppressing." Rose argues convincingly that Plath's work is indicative of a less triumphant vision of self and reality: "I think we should be very cautious about attempting to read Plath's writing in terms of a positive emergence of selfhood, of turning what may be better thought of in terms of the unbearable coexistence of opposites into a narrative progression from suffering into self-discovery or flight."

A careful chronological reading of the poems indicates that Plath's themes are in fact remarkably consistent. While the *Ariel* poems may seem to represent a self that has emerged from the inimical reality in which it has been forced to exist, Plath's best poems illustrate, conversely, a troubling philosophical acquiescence to such realities. Thus, in an early poem such as "The Thin People," Plath establishes the vampire metaphor she would later use to greater dramatic effect in "Daddy." The "thin people" of the poem are never named, although it is clear that she is thinking of the starved inmates of the Nazi concentration camps as they appeared in 1940s newsreels during the speaker's childhood. Although she argues that the passage of time should logically make them disappear, they seem paradoxically to grow in power by virtue of their tenacity in memory. Vampirelike, they return from the scene of their repression in "the contracted country of the head" and begin to drain reality of its richness, as if in revenge: "They persist in the sunlit room: the wallpaper / Frieze of cabbage-roses and cornflowers pales / Under their thin-lipped smiles, / Their withering kingship."

Similarly, in the 1957 poems "All the Dead Dears" and "The Disquieting Muses," Plath introduces the theme of maternal blame she would later fine-tune in "Medusa." Although Plath's early lyrics are rather stilted and self-conscious, demonstrating how heavily, at first, she relied on the formal poetic resources of rhyme and meter, her development as a poet was rapid. By the time of her return to England in 1959, following the decisive breakthrough of "Poem for a Birthday," she was writing lyrics full of disturbingly powerful and suggestive imagery. In "Crossing the Water," for example, she imagines herself and her husband as "two black, cut-paper people" whose fragile identities are threatened by the immensity of the ocean. Such themes—the terrible insecurity of the self, the reality of indifference and lovelessness, and the inevitability of death and loss—preoccupied Plath from the beginning of her writing life to the end. It is in the poems of *Ariel* that they are most powerfully reiterated, however. Apart from the controversial poems such as "Daddy" and "Lady Lazarus," in which Plath dubiously inflates her personal trauma to rival that of the Jewish victims of the Nazis (an aesthetic lapse for which she has attracted a great deal of critical opprobrium), it is in other, better poems that the poignancy of her tragic vision comes through most clearly.

Plath's most beautiful poems present images of absolute self-loss. One of these, "The Night Dances," describes, according to Ted Hughes, "a revolving dance which her baby son performed at night in his crib" (Plath, 1981, note, p. 294). The smile that falls surrealistically into the grass at the beginning of this poem is "irretrievable," and the speaker compares this to the dancing gestures of her baby, which seem so significant to her that she finds it hard to believe they are merely ephemeral: "Surely they travel / The world forever, I shall not entirely / Sit emptied of beauties, the gift / Of your small breath, the drenched grass / Smell of your sleeps, lilies, lilies." The image of the lilies is then considered in its uniqueness—it is as if Plath is deconstructing the poem as she writes it—"their flesh bears no relation. Cold folds of the ego, the calla, / And the tiger, embellishing itself— / Spots, and a spread of hot petals." This is the alienation of extreme self-involvement: a lily is not just a lily but is classified according to species; the calla lily is wrapped up in its own cold beauty (there is a submerged pun here on "callous") while the tiger lily embellishes itself alone. This introduces the theme of indifference, or, as this poem expresses it, amnesia: "The comets / Have such a space to cross, / Such coldness, forgetfulness." She considers the movement of the comets to be a more appropriate metaphor for her son's gestures: "so your gestures flake off— / Warm and human, then their pink light / Bleeding and peeling / Through the black amnesias of heaven." By this time the speaker seems to have given up her belief that the self and its gestures can retain their identity, and the image is a disturbing one, a vision of dismemberment.

In "The Night Dances" the self is a disintegrating structure, its gestures inevitably swallowed up in inhospitable and unconscious space. The fatalistic tone of the poem is reflected in Plath's avoidance of the question mark, a technique she uses here twice: "And how will your night dances lose themselves." And again at the end, when she compares her son's dances to falling snow: "Why am I given / these lamps, these planets / Falling like blessings, like flakes / Six-sided, white / On my eyes, my lips, my hair / Touching and melting. / Nowhere." The speaker of "The Night Dances" entertains no hope of an answer to her questions. This poem provides an image of self not as emergent but as fragmented, dissipated, obsolescent.

The consciousness of *Ariel* has many different masks and positions; part of the excitement of the volume comes from the restless dynamism of a voice that repeatedly insists on escaping from deadening enclosures. Such a movement always entails loss, however; the speaker of "Ariel" imagines sloughing off "dead hands, dead stringencies"; the ascending consciousness of "Fever 103" experiences orgiastic self-loss, "my selves dissolving, old whore petticoats"; and the symbolically liberated queen bee of "Stings" is horribly injured, a metonymic "red scar" already murdered by the "wax house" that has engulfed her. In other, remarkable poems such as "Totem," Plath restates her disabused and fatalistic recognition that "there is no terminus, only suitcases / Out of which the same self unfolds like a suit / Bald and shiny, with pockets of wishes, / Notions and tickets, short circuits and folding mirrors." "Words," written the week before her death, posits an absolute division between the autonomy of "words dry and riderless" and the "fixed stars" that "govern a life." This poem stands as a salutary reminder to those who would simplistically conflate Plath's biography with the personae of her writings. At its extreme, this critical approach has tended to view Plath's entire oeuvre as an extended suicide note, or (in Hughes's analysis) as the "by-product[s]" of her quest for self-realization. But the connections between a writer's life and her work are numerous, indirect, and mysterious. Plath's poems stand as a poignant testament to the tragic loss of a remarkable talent, but they are also undeniably powerful and achieved works of art in their own right.

[*See also* Writing as a Woman in the Twentieth Century.]

WORKS

The Colossus (1960)
The Bell Jar (1963)
Ariel (1965)
Crossing the Water (1971)
Winter Trees (1971)
Letters Home: Correspondence, 1950–1963 (1975)
The Bed Book (1976)
Johnny Panic and the Bible of Dreams (1977)
Collected Poems (1981)
The Journals of Sylvia Plath (1982)
The Unabridged Journals of Sylvia Plath (2000)

FURTHER READING

Alvarez, A. "Prologue: Sylvia Plath." In his *The Savage God: A Study of Suicide*. London, 1971. A controversial early contribution to the Plath mythography, Alvarez's account was objected to by her estate. This article examines Plath's work in the light of her suicide.

Axelrod, Steven Gould. *Sylvia Plath: The Wound and the Cure of Words*. Baltimore, 1990. A Freudian reading of Plath's career and work.

Bloom, Harold, ed. *Sylvia Plath*. New York, 1989. Aside from the dismissive introduction by the editor, this is a useful collection of essays.

Brain, Tracy. *The Other Sylvia Plath*. Harlow, U.K., 2001. An interesting examination of the social and environmental concerns of Plath's writing.

Brennan, Claire, ed. *The Poetry of Sylvia Plath: A Reader's Guide to Essential Criticism*. Duxford, U.K., 2000. A very useful sourcebook of the main Plath criticism.

Britzolakis, Christina. *Sylvia Plath and the Theatre of Mourning*. Oxford, 1999. A complex study of the function of mourning in Plath's writings.

Bronfen, Elisabeth. *Sylvia Plath*. London, 1998. A comprehensive and readable introductory study of Sylvia Plath.

Gilbert, Sandra M. "In Yeats's House: The Death and Resurrection of Sylvia Plath." In *Sylvia Plath: The Critical Heritage*, edited by Linda Wagner-Martin. London, 1988. This and the 1989 essay are insightful works by an important feminist critic.

Gilbert, Sandra M. "'A Fine, White Flying Myth': Confessions of a Plath Addict." In *Sylvia Plath*, edited by Harold Bloom. New York, 1989.

Heaney, Seamus. "The Indefatigable Hoof-Taps." In his *The Government of the Tongue*. London, 1988. A review-essay of Plath's *Collected Poems*.

Hughes, Ted. *Winter Pollen: Occasional Prose*. Edited by William Scammell. London, 1995.

Hughes, Ted. *Birthday Letters*. London, 1998. These two Hughes items are indispensable reference works for the study of Sylvia Plath.

Kendall, Tim. *Sylvia Plath: A Critical Study*. London, 2001. A good introductory study.

Lane, Gary, ed. *Sylvia Plath: New Views on the Poetry*. Baltimore, 1979. An illuminating collection of essays.

MacPherson, Pat. *Reflecting on* The Bell Jar. London, 1991. An excellent reference work, containing sharp criticism and social commentary.

Malcolm, Janet. *The Silent Woman: Sylvia Plath and Ted Hughes*. London, 1994. Examines the controversy surrounding Plath's literary estate and the difficulties encountered by her biographers.

Rose, Jacqueline. *The Haunting of Sylvia Plath*. London, 1991. Examines the function of fantasy both in Plath's work and in the controversy that surrounds her legacy.

Smith, Stan. *Inviolable Voice: History and Twentieth-Century Poetry*. Dublin, 1981.

Smith, Stan. "Attitudes Counterfeiting Life: The Irony of Artifice in Sylvia Plath's *The Bell Jar*." In *Sylvia Plath*, edited by Harold Bloom. New York, 1989.

Stevenson, Anne. *Bitter Fame: A Life of Sylvia Plath*. Harmondsworth, U.K., 1990. Well written but very controversial, this is the only biography fully authorized by the Plath estate.

Wagner-Martin, Linda. *Sylvia Plath: A Biography.* London, 1988.

Wagner-Martin, Linda. *Sylvia Plath: A Literary Life.* London, 1999. Wagner-Martin's biographical studies of

Plath provide an interesting contrast to Stevenson's *Bitter Fame.*

Wagner-Martin, Linda, ed. *Critical Essays on Sylvia Plath.* Boston, 1984.

Wagner-Martin, Linda, ed. *Sylvia Plath: The Critical Heritage.* London, 1988.

See also the article on *The Bell Jar*, immediately following

SYLVIA PLATH'S
THE BELL JAR

by Arielle Greenberg

Sylvia Plath's only novel, *The Bell Jar* (1963), begins with a memorable sentence that sets the tone for a searing, vivid story about modern angst, a sense of dislocation and paranoia that are at once internal and part of the culture. Perhaps only *The Catcher in the Rye* (1951) has mined adolescent ambivalence in the moment between Cold War complacency and the countercultural revolution as effectively and engagingly. But although taken less seriously and given less credit, Plath's work is ultimately more indicting: while both novels document the rise of a middle-class depression that would plague Americans in the latter half of the twentieth century, only *The Bell Jar* bears witness to the ways in which traditional gender roles contribute to the seemingly pandemic condition.

First published a month before its author's death, *The Bell Jar* is the story of an intelligent young woman's despair, her attempted suicide, and her shaky journey back to mental health, as she questions the limited choices she faces on the edge of adulthood. The novel is replete with the literary device of the double, or doppelganger: the narrator, whose senior thesis is supposed to be about twins in Joyce's epic *Finnegan's Wake*, encounters people and images in her own life that represent opposing visions of what it means to be a successful and contented woman. Throughout the book, the struggle to resolve the two halves of her identity—her ambitious, intellectual need for self-determination with the societal pressure to fulfill her feminine role as a wife and mother—are depicted as the crux of her emotional meltdown.

When the reader first meets Esther Greenwood, a straight-A scholarship student at a prestigious women's college, she has recently arrived in New York City, having won a temporary editorial position on the college issue of a fashion magazine. She knows she is supposed to be thrilled but instead feels out of place, whisked from photography shoot to editorial meeting, graceless and incompetent among the fashionable and worldly. Esther has spent her whole life winning merit awards, and as she leaves her childhood behind, she suspects that her academic success will end with her fraudulent intellect

revealed and nothing to show for all her prizes. The women she meets are either successful writers or happy homemakers, wholesome virgins or femmes fatales, but nothing in between—Esther senses that choosing one path will mean eliminating the other. (Her boyfriend, Buddy Willard, has assured her that after they are married, she will no longer want to write poems, and proposes to her by offering to turn her into "Mrs. Buddy Willard.") Stifled by these dual, and dueling, identities, Esther rejects them all, in a series of lively and disturbing vignettes: she turns down the proposal, fights off a date who tries to rape her, falls asleep midway through a seduction, throws away the outfits and makeup given to her by the magazine, and then returns to her mother's house in the Boston suburbs for the remainder of the summer.

Once home, Esther's options narrow further: rejected by a summer writing course at Harvard, her future as an author is in doubt, and she is surrounded by such women as the well-liked young housewife up the street who has subverted her ambitions for her family. Esther's mother, also bright and talented, gave up her career to raise her children; Esther sees her devoted mother as representative of all she stands to lose, and resents her for it. The future Esther had imagined for herself, as a glamorous and talented poet and editor or academic who also has a handsome husband and darling kids, does not seem possible. At nineteen, Esther is exhausted—a female overachiever, patronized by mentors and men, often valued for her beauty rather than her intellect, and torn between other people's incompatible visions for her adult self. Esther seeks to be "purified" and made whole and considers whether such purity can be reached only through death. Plagued by insomnia, she is referred to a psychiatrist, but the psychiatrist is another man who does not take Esther seriously, and the electroshock treatment he prescribes is administered incorrectly. Esther begins to contemplate suicide in earnest but finds that her will to live outweighs her attempts at drowning and hanging, each of which she describes with wry black humor. Only after a distraught visit to her father's grave does she make a serious attempt on her life, hiding in a crawl space in her basement and overdosing on sleeping pills.

Miraculously, Esther is found and revived, and for the remainder of the book she describes being "patched" together, first in state hospitals and then in a private asylum, where once again she is a scholarship student, her recovery paid for by a wealthy woman author. There she is treated by a sympathetic female psychiatrist, Dr. Nolan, who helps Esther face her anger toward her mother and treats her with insulin and shock therapy until Esther feels that the "bell jar," the distorting sense of dissociation and detachment that depression lowers over its victims, has been lifted. Dr. Nolan also helps Esther obtain an illegal diaphragm as a means to her independence, although her first sexual experience results in a massive hemorrhaging. Another of Esther's doubles, a fellow psychiatric patient named Joan whom Esther knew from her former, normal life, helps Esther through this ordeal, only to regress in her own recovery and kill herself on the grounds of the hospital. At the novel's end, Esther is preparing to exit the asylum, return to college, and heed the "brag" of her heartbeat, but although she recognizes her triumph in relation to Joan's failure, the bell jar hovers above her head, ready to descend again at any moment.

Acclaimed primarily for her poetry, Plath in fact wrote a great deal of fiction in her short life and had published several short stories before her first collection of poems appeared in 1960. *The Bell Jar* was her primary fiction project and absorbed much of her time and energy in her final years. Many essays about *The Bell Jar* remark on the prevalent baby imagery—one of the most memorable scenes depicts Buddy, a medical student, bringing Esther to witness a woman giving birth—but the way Plath uses infants shifts throughout the book. Sometimes babies represent death or the grotesque, such as the fetus in a jar Esther sees; at other times they signify the displacement of self when a woman becomes a mother. Elsewhere, babies are described as innocent and blank, a state Esther desires to reenter when she climbs into the womblike space in the basement to die. Plath began thinking about *The Bell Jar* in the mid-1950s, a couple of years after the events that inspired it, but most of it was composed in the early 1960s, when in three years Plath had three pregnancies: two children and a miscarriage. Her final poems, and the novel, attest to both the joy and the paralyzing fatigue and anxiety motherhood caused her.

Decades after its publication, *The Bell Jar* still sells steadily, owing as much of its popularity to the cult of Sylvia Plath and the book's thinly veiled autobiographical

detail as to its sharp, vibrant writing and accurate depiction of depression. A brilliant and driven poet, Plath had already established a reputation by the time she died at thirty, but it grew exponentially after her death. Plath thought of her first novel as a way to make money (writing was her sole source of income) and as a way to reexamine her most harrowing ordeal; like her best poems, her fiction came from personal experience, and she had planned to write a second novel dealing with infidelity, based on the breakup of her marriage to the British poet Ted Hughes. When *The Bell Jar* was first published, only in England and under the pseudonym Victoria Lucas (Plath did not want to hurt the actual Americans—many of them friends and relatives—on whom the characters were based), it received favorable reviews but did not have a large impact. But by 1971, the posthumous publication of her final poems, *Ariel*, was a sensation: coinciding with the rise of feminism, full of searing, ferocious verse, and written by a tragic young suicide, *Ariel* sold extremely well, and *The Bell Jar* was reissued in America under Plath's own name, becoming a best-seller.

The publication inflicted great pain on Plath's mother, who fought its release, and it was the impetus for at least one lawsuit, by a woman who claimed that the character Joan was based on herself. Indeed, the majority of the novel's particulars are Plath's own: like Esther's father, Plath's father died when she was young; like Esther, Plath had won a prestigious college board prize the summer of her first suicide attempt, which happened almost exactly as she describes in *The Bell Jar*. It is no surprise, therefore, that *The Bell Jar* became a kind of public diary for the legions of women in the early 1970s for whom Plath transcribed, beautifully and brutally, the disheartening choices those women faced.

In the wake of the autobiographical furor, it can be difficult to read *The Bell Jar* as a work of literature. The fact of Plath's own suicide erases the hopefulness she tried to convey in *The Bell Jar*: although Esther is unsure of herself at the novel's end, the book is narrated from the future, in which she has a child happily playing in the background. Plath's real-life tragedy overshadows the book's comedy, as much of it is in fact a wickedly funny, if dark, commentary on 1950s life. Structurally, the first half of the novel concentrates on the colorful details of the magazine internship, crammed full of wisecracks about that rarified world, and then moves on to lambast suburbia. Although *The Bell Jar* is often cited as a book about mental hospitals, Esther is hospitalized only in the last quarter of the novel, and even this section is marked by an acerbic wit.

Also missing in all the commotion over *The Bell Jar* is acknowledgment of what a groundbreaking work it was. Plath had *The Catcher in the Rye* in mind while writing, and was obviously influenced by the glib, vernacular tone made popular by Salinger and other *New Yorker* writers of that era, but Plath's heroine, unlike Holden Caulfield, is able to pinpoint the part of her culture that has caused her malaise—sexual inequality. It is easy to think of *The Bell Jar* as a novel of the women's movement, but in fact it was written a decade earlier, from experiences and notes dating from a full decade before that. Plath had identified the most pressing concerns of the movement—Why must a woman give up her own identity to her romantic partner? Why are there so many double standards that put women at a powerful cultural disadvantage? How can a woman balance motherhood with a career? Why does society not allow for healthy sexual desire in women?—long before such questions became part of the accepted rhetoric of feminism.

It is also a stylistically daring book. Though less accomplished than her poems, *The Bell Jar* could not have remained so popular were it not a satisfying read, narrated by an engaging, accessible heroine, and replete with the kind of visceral imagery Plath is known for in her verse. Many contemporary novelists employ morbid humor, vivid descriptions of sex and violence, and an ironic, dry tone, but in the early 1960s Plath was a young woman depicting rape, suicide, depression, and psychotherapy with humor and candor, long before any of these topics were openly discussed. Without *The Bell Jar*, one could theorize, the hundreds of novels about bright young career girls steeling themselves for dates, diapers, and disillusionment might not exist, nor would the outpouring of literary memoirs chronicling mental illness and recovery. What is perhaps most tragic about *The Bell Jar* is how relevant these issues have remained.

FURTHER READING

Alexander, Paul, ed. *Ariel Ascending: Writings about Sylvia Plath*. New York, 1985. Accessible collection of critical essays that seeks to provide literary analysis of the work in place of biographical, psychoanalytical analysis of the writer. Includes pieces by Hardwick, Moss, and Brown that deal specifically with *The Bell Jar*.

Macpherson, Pat. *Reflecting on The Bell Jar*. London, 1991. Part of Routledge's "Heroines?" series of feminist critiques of literary heroines, this is one of the few serious book-length analyses of Plath's novel, placing it in the useful context of McCarthyism and the Freudian culture of the 1950s.

Rose, Jacqueline. *The Haunting of Sylvia Plath*. Cambridge, Mass., 1992. Original theories on Plath's writing, including work on *The Bell Jar* as part of the *New Yorker* aesthetic, mixing high and low culture.

See also the article on Sylvia Plath, immediately preceding.

EDGAR ALLAN POE

by Thomas Wright

At the beginning of the twenty-first century, Edgar Allan Poe was more popular than ever. "The Raven" and a number of his Gothic and detective tales were among the most famous writings in the English language, and they were often some of the first works of literature that young adults read. They had also entered the popular imagination—football teams and beers were named after them, and they had inspired episodes of the animated television show *The Simpsons* and a number of rock songs.

Poe also continued to exercise a profound influence over writers and artists. Two of the most popular authors of the

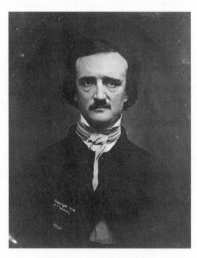

Edgar Allan Poe.
(Courtesy of the Library of Congress)

second half of the twentieth century, Stephen King and Isaac Asimov, acknowledged Poe as an important precursor. Countless novels published at the end of the twentieth century, such as Peter Ackroyd's *The Plato Papers: A Prophesy* (1999) and Mark Z. Danielewski's *House of Leaves* (2000), also bear definite traces of his influence. The Argentinean author Jorge Luis Borges, whose own works are greatly indebted to Poe, once called him the unacknowledged father of twentieth-century literature, and Poe's influence shows no signs of diminishing. Despite his enormous popularity and influence, Poe's canonical status is still challenged by certain commentators. Harold Bloom, for instance, regards Poe's writings as vulgar and stylistically flawed. Bloom follows in a long line of Poe detractors, many of whom have been amazed by the fact that what T. S. Eliot called his "puerile" and "haphazard" productions could have influenced "great" writers such as the French poets Charles Baudelaire and Stéphane Mallarmé.

Poe criticism was, however, far more favorable (and far more plentiful) over the last half of the twentieth century than previously. Poe is indeed something of a boom industry in academia. New Critics, New Historicists,

psychoanalysts, and poststructuralists all find his works suggestive. Few of these critics are interested in making aesthetic judgements, however, and those who concern themselves with such things continue to express doubts about Poe's achievement.

As a result, Poe remains something of an enigma. To many he is a formative influence, a genius, and an inspiration; to others he is a shoddy stylist and a charlatan. It would be more reasonable, perhaps, to regard Poe as all of these things and to accept James Russell Lowell's famous judgment that he was "Three fifths . . . genius, and two fifths sheer fudge." Few of Poe's readers are reasonable, however, as he is one of those writers who is either loved or hated.

POE'S PERSONA

One of the reasons Poe has been far more popular and influential than writers who, according to some, have produced works of greater literary value is that he created, with a little help from others, a fascinating literary persona. That persona was of an author at once bohemian and extremely intellectual. The bohemian aspect was largely the creation of his "friend" Rufus Wilmot Griswold, who in his obituary of Poe described him as a depraved and demonic writer. Poe himself was responsible for the intellectual element: he presented himself to the public in his writings as an erudite and bookish scholar.

Poe's persona captured the imagination of the world; like Byron before him, he became a kind of mythical or archetypal figure. Nineteenth-century poets such as Ernest Dowson and Baudelaire (who prayed to Poe and dressed up as him) regarded Poe as the original bohemian *poète maudit* (a tradition in which the poet explores extremes of experience and emotional depth) and as the first self-conscious literary artist. As such, he seemed to be a prefiguring type of themselves. This legendary persona may be at odds with Poe's real personality and the actual facts of his biography, but that is beside the point. What matters is that it fascinated and continues to fascinate people.

Poe's legendary personality and life have also provided people with a context in which his writings can be read (and it is worth noting here that an account of Poe's life has traditionally appeared as a preface to anthologies of his works). As is the case with the Irish writer Oscar Wilde, we tend to read Poe's works as expressions of his (real or mythical) character and as dramatizations of his personality. This confers a degree of homogeneity on his writings; although he experimented in a variety of forms and wrote on numberless topics, we think of all of his productions as "Poe performances."

EARLY POETRY

Edgar Allan Poe was born in Boston on 19 January 1809, the son of the itinerant actors David Poe Jr. and Elizabeth Arnold, both of whom died when he was still an infant. He was brought up by the Richmond tobacco merchant John Allan, with whom he had a difficult relationship. Educated in London and then, for a brief period, at the University of Virginia, Poe entered the U.S. Army in 1827. It was always Poe's ambition to be recognized as a great poet, and in 1827 he published his first volume of verse, *Tamerlane and Other Poems*, under the name "a Bostonian."

The title poem of the slim collection is a monologue by Tamerlane, the Renaissance Turkish warrior. The other poems are conventional romantic meditations on death, solitude, nature, dreams, and vanished youth in which Poe comes before us, as it were, in the theatrical garb of the romantic poet. The poems display Poe's considerable gift for imitation (which he later used to great effect in his prose parodies) and his habit of half quoting from his favorite authors. They contain countless echoes from romantic poets (especially Lord Byron). It is not, however, so much a question of plagiarism as it is of Poe serving a literary apprenticeship and placing himself within a poetic tradition.

In 1829 Poe published, under his own name, his second verse collection, *Al Aaraaf, Tamerlane, and Minor Poems*. It contained revised versions of some of the poems that had been published in *Tamerlane* (Poe was a zealous reviser) and seven new poems. "Sonnet—To Science," Poe's famous poem on the antagonistic relationship between science and poetry, opens the book. It is followed by the title poem, "Al Aaraaf," which has been variously interpreted

as a lament for the demise of the creative imagination in a materialistic world and as an allegorical representation of Poe's aesthetic theories. The poem is characterized by its variety of meter, its heavy baroque effects, and its extreme obscurity. The volume has its lighter moments, however. "Fairyland," with its "Dim vales," "Huge moons," and yellow albatrosses is one of Poe's first exercises in burlesque and self-parody. It was typical of Poe to include, within the same volume, serious poems and comic pieces that seem to parody those compositions.

In 1831, wishing to leave the army, Poe got himself expelled from the West Point military academy. In that year he also brought out a third volume of poetry, *Poems by Edgar A. Poe*. This collection represents a considerable advance on his earlier efforts and contains famous poems such as "To Helen" and "The Doomed City" (later called "The City in the Sea"). The former, which is perhaps the most beautiful of all Poe's lyrics, is a stately hymn to Helen of Troy, which in its later, revised form, contained the celebrated lines:

> Thy Naiad airs have brought me home
> To the Glory that was Greece,
> And the grandeur that was Rome.

"The Doomed City" is a wonderful evocation of a silent city beneath the sea.

Both poems create a haunting atmosphere through the use of alliteration, assonance, measured rhythms, and gentle rhymes; they also contain words with long open vowel sounds such as "loom," "gloom," "yore," and "bore" that were to become a Poe trademark. Because of Poe's fondness for such techniques, it is hardly surprising that his poems have been compared to music. Poe believed that music was the art that most effectively excited, elevated, and intoxicated the soul and thus gave human beings access to the ethereal realm of supernal beauty, a realm in which Poe passionately believed and for which he seems to have pined throughout his life. As Poe aimed to create similar effects with his verse, he attempted to marry poetry and music. This is why the rhythm of his verse is perfectly measured and often incantatory; it is also why he frequently chose words for their sounds rather than for their sense. In "To Helen," for example, he writes of "those *Nicéan* barks of yore," a rather confused classical allusion but a word that produces wonderfully musical vibrations.

Poe offers us what he called "a suggestive indefiniteness of meaning with a view of bringing about vague and therefore spiritual *effects*." Decadent and symbolist poets of the nineteenth century, including Baudelaire and Paul Verlaine, were heavily influenced by Poe's method, and they consciously imitated his "word-music." They also regarded Poe as their most important precursor because of his theoretical statements about poetry. Indeed, Poe was (and perhaps remains) as famous a critic and theoretician of verse as he was a poet. He is particularly remembered for his powerful denunciation of didactic poetry and for his emphasis on the self-consciousness and deliberateness of the poet's art.

Most of Poe's important theoretical pronouncements were made in the essays and lectures he wrote toward the end of his life. In *Poems* he wrote a prefatory "Letter to Mr —, " which represents his first theoretical statement about verse. Here he defined poetry as a pleasurable idea set to music. He also argued, with more than a slight nod to the English poet Samuel Taylor Coleridge, that poetry "is opposed to a work of science by having, for its *immediate* object, pleasure, not truth; to romance, by having for its object an *indefinite* instead of a *definite* pleasure." At its best, Poe's poetry embodies such ideas by creating vague yet powerful atmospheric effects and by giving the reader intense aesthetic pleasure.

Poe's early poetry received mixed reviews and failed to establish him as either a popular or a critically acclaimed author. Later commentators, such as T. S. Eliot and Walt Whitman, criticized its limited range and extent; they also bemoaned its lack of intellectual and moral content. Others dismissed Poe as a mere verse technician; Emerson famously referred to him as "the jingle man." Poe's verse was, however, revered by later nineteenth-century poets such as Mallarmé and Dowson, and considering his influence on such Decadent and symbolist writers, he can perhaps be regarded as the most influential American poet of that century after Whitman.

TALES OF THE GROTESQUE AND ARABESQUE

Numerous connections exist between Poe's early verse and the short stories he started to write for magazines and newspapers around 1830. (Poe's decision to turn his hand to prose was partly because of the lack of commercial and critical success achieved by his poetry.) In some of his stories Poe included poems; he also returned to forms, such as the dramatic monologue and the dialogue between disembodied spirits, that he had used in poems such as "Tamerlane" and "Al Aaraaf." And yet Poe's tales are clearly distinguished from his early verse, most obviously by their variety of mood, content, and theme. Poe seems to have been liberated as a writer when he turned from romantic verse to the more flexible, capacious, and traditionally heterogeneous genre of the short story. He now had at his disposal a multitude of tones and devices, and in the twenty-five stories that he wrote in the 1830s and that were collected in the anthology *Tales of the Grotesque and Arabesque* (2 vols., 1840), he exploited these to great effect.

In fact, such is the diversity of the style and mood of Poe's early stories that the division of the contents of *Tales* into the two categories of grotesque and arabesque seems simplistic and inadequate. Poe's grotesques are comic and burlesque stories that usually involve exaggeration and caricature. In this group we can include the tales "Lionizing" and "The Scythe of Time" (earlier called "A Predicament"), which are satires of the contemporary literary scene. Another characteristic of Poe's grotesque stories is the introduction of elements of the ludicrous and the absurd. In the tale "Loss of Breath," the protagonist literally loses his breath and goes out in search of it. It is a shame that Poe's early grotesques are generally neglected, because not only do they testify to his range and resourcefulness as a writer, but some of them are compelling and funny. The neglect results partly from the fact that, in order to be appreciated, they require extensive knowledge of the literary and political state of antebellum America and partly because they have been overshadowed by his arabesque tales.

Poe's arabesque tales are intricately and elaborately constructed prose poems. The word "arabesque" can also be applied to those stories in which Poe employed Gothic techniques. Gothic literature, which typically aimed to produce effects of mystery and horror, was established in the latter half of the eighteenth century by writers such as the English novelist Anne Radcliffe and the German story writer E. T. A. Hoffmann. By the beginning of the nineteenth century, the Gothic short story had become one of the most popular forms of magazine literature in England and America.

It is generally agreed that Poe's particular contribution to Gothic literature was his use of the genre to explore and describe the psychology of humans under extreme and abnormal conditions. Typically, his characters are at the mercy of powers over which they have no control and which their reason cannot fully comprehend. These powers may take the form of sudden, irrational impulses ("the imp of the perverse" that inspires the protagonist of "Berenice" to extract the teeth of his buried wife, for example), or as is the case with the eponymous hero of "William Wilson," a hereditary disease. *Tales of the Grotesque and Arabesque* contains some of Poe's most famous Gothic productions, including "Morella," "Ligeia," and "Berenice" (the stories of the so-called "marriage group," which concern the deaths of beautiful young women), along with perhaps the most popular of all his tales, "The Fall of the House of Usher."

"Usher" is a characteristic arabesque production. It exhibits many of the trappings of Gothic fiction: a decaying mansion located in a gloomy setting, a protagonist (Roderick Usher) who suffers from madness and a peculiar sensitivity of temperament inherited from his ancient family, and a woman (his sister) who is prematurely buried and who rises from her tomb. Yet from Gothic clichés such as these, Poe produced a tale of extraordinary power. Indeed, perhaps only Stephen King in *The Shining* (1977) has succeeded in investing a building with such horror and in conveying the impression that it is alive.

Apart from the grotesque and arabesque stories, *Tales of the Grotesque and Arabesque* includes other varieties of writing. "Hans Phaall" has been classed as science fiction, and "King Pest" is a surreal historical adventure. Several stories contain elements of all of these genres; "Metzengerstein," for example, is at once a work of historical fiction, a powerful Gothic tale, and a witty and grotesque parody of the latter genre. The diversity of the contents of the tales, and the variety of theme and style within individual stories, must be seen in the context of the original form in which they appeared. All of the tales were first published in popular newspapers and magazines from 1832 to 1839. The audience for such publications was extremely heterogeneous, and Poe was clearly trying to appeal to as large a cross-section as possible. We should also remember that, unlike subscribers to weightier publications, the magazine- and newspaper-reading public had a very limited attention span. Readers craved novelty, sensation, and diversity.

Poe was profoundly influenced by the tastes of this public. In a letter to Thomas Willis White, a newspaper editor, he remarked that the public loves "the ludicrous heightened into the grotesque: the fearful colored into the horrible: the witty exaggerated into the burlesque: the singular wrought out into the strange and mystical." In *Tales of the Grotesque and Arabesque* this is precisely what he gave them. The most obvious characteristic of his stories is their sensationalism: they include accounts of balloon journeys to the moon, premature burials, encounters with the devil, and a number of gruesome deaths.

From the early 1830s Poe planned to gather together his short stories and publish them in book form. In the mid-1830s he unsuccessfully offered for publication a collection of stories under the title "Tales of the Folio Club." Poe devised an elaborate plan for the "Folio Club" volume. The tales were to be read out, over the course of a single evening, by various members of a literary club, and each story was to be followed by the critical remarks of the rest of the company. The book was evidently intended as a satire of popular contemporary modes of fiction and criticism; as such it can be compared to the work of Poe's English contemporary, Thomas Love Peacock. The satirical intent is clearly indicated by the names and descriptions of the various club members, which include "Mr Snap, the President, who is a very lank man with a hawk nose." Many of the figures were based on real people.

When considering *Tales of the Grotesque and Arabesque*, it is important to remember the dramatic nature of its forerunner. Our knowledge of the Folio Club gathering encourages us to read Poe's stories as the compositions of various personae and to regard Poe as author of the authors of the tales. W. H. Auden described Poe's writing as operatic, and *Tales of the Grotesque and Arabesque* does indeed resemble an opera in which Poe's narrators walk on and off the stage. Thus, the narrator of "Morella" mutters, melodramatically, "Years—years, may pass away, but the memory of that epoch—never!" as he leaves the stage to make way for the narrator of "Lionizing." "I am," the latter remarks to the reader-audience by way of introduction, "that is to say, I *was*—a great man."

Poe's gift for impersonating his narrators is remarkable, and like a great dramatist, he seemed to contain multitudes of characters. The comparison with the playwright is appropriate because the world of Poe's writing is a thoroughly theatrical one. In it the laws of "real life" (of psychological accuracy and consistency, for instance) do not apply, and in this context we can recall Poe's famous distinction between "Hamlet the dramatis persona" and "Hamlet the man." In the Poe universe, bizarre and absurd incidents occur on a regular basis, the dialogue and the settings are distinctly stagy, and everything is hyperbolic. As the above quotations from "Morella" and "Lionizing" suggest, it is also a world in which tragedy can be quickly followed by comedy.

And here we might recall that Poe was the son of two itinerant actors. It is particularly interesting to note that Poe's beloved mother, Eliza, was renowned for her ability to play an enormous range of tragic and comic roles, often in the same theatrical season. Her son seems to have inherited this gift as, in his writings, he effortlessly swaps a suit of sables for motley attire. At times, as in

"The Visionary" (later called "The Assignation"), which contains elements of tragedy, parody, and self-parody, Poe wore both costumes at the same time. And this in turn may help us understand the appeal of Gothic literature for Poe, because it is a form of writing in which comedy intensifies the horror by setting it in relief. Those who have adapted Poe's tales for the cinema have appreciated the humorous elements of the Gothic, as their films are at once terrifying and hilarious.

Drama and theatricality are in fact everywhere in Poe's writing. As a young poet, he effortlessly mimicked the styles of writers such as Byron; as a reviewer he convincingly adopted the tone of the authoritative critic. Throughout his works he seems to entertain and juggle ideas rather than to offer them as articles of faith, and the idea of literary performance is central to his authorship. Poe is a writer-performer whose productions can be compared to virtuoso literary displays. As readers we are like members of a theater audience who are by turns enthralled, horrified, and dazzled, and when the performance is over we applaud Poe's artistry.

An appreciation of the theatrical nature of Poe's work has important consequences for criticism. If we view Poe's writing as fundamentally dramatic, it becomes impossible to discover Poe's individual voice in the universe of voices that is his work or to analyze it from the point of view of his authorial intentions. It also becomes essential to judge the work's style and content in terms of its dramatic appropriateness: when Poe's writing is weak and verbose, for example, this may be the appropriate style for a particular narrator.

THE NARRATIVE OF ARTHUR GORDON PYM OF NANTUCKET

The only full-length novel that Poe would write, *The Narrative of Arthur Gordon Pym of Nantucket* (1838), was begun on the suggestion of a publisher to whom he had unsuccessfully offered "Tales of the Folio Club." Its first two installments appeared in the *Southern Literary Messenger*, and it came out in book form in 1838. In choosing to write a sensational sea adventure—the plot includes, among other things, a mutiny, a shipwreck, a famine, and a massacre—Poe once again selected an extremely popular subject and form.

As a realistic chronicle of an utterly fantastic journey, the novel is similar to some of the stories Poe had written in the 1830s, such as "MS. Found in a Bottle." Cast in the form of a first-person account of a real sea voyage and including journal entries, "factual" information,

and scholarly footnotes, *Pym* is written with a sharp attention to significant detail that recalls the novels of the eighteenth-century author Daniel Defoe. This attention to detail, which can be found throughout Poe's fiction, confers a degree of verisimilitude on narrations that lack psychological realism. Poe's fictional works are not, in other words, realistic, but they have a reality of their own. *Pym* is also similar to a Defoe novel in that it is digressive and loosely structured. In contrast to Poe's short stories, it lacks a definite architecture and fails to create a unified impression or effect. Curiously enough, this is precisely what makes it such a hypnotic book. *Pym*'s journey, like that of Karl Rossman in Franz Kafka's *Amerika* (1927), is imbued with a vague sense of horror.

Pym also contains a preface, reminiscent of Defoe, in which the narrator claims that the book is a real account of a voyage although its first installments in the *Southern Literary Messenger* had appeared under the name of the short-story writer, "Mr Poe." Few reviewers were taken in by this typical Poe hoax, and the novel was generally reviewed with varying degrees of enthusiasm, as a work of fiction. Until around the 1960s, critics tended to agree with Poe's own dismissive estimation of his "very silly" novel. Since then, however, it has received much better press and has inspired a variety of readings that range from the autobiographical to the allegorical. Like many of Poe's works, it is *Pym*'s ambiguity and indefiniteness that make it so suggestive. These qualities are perfectly embodied in the novel's famous last line. As the eponymous hero's boat heads toward a cataract, a shrouded human figure suddenly appears, "And the hue of the figure was of the perfect whiteness of the snow." At about the same time Poe also wrote two other works, both unfinished, that can be briefly mentioned here. "The Journal of Julius Rodman," a *Pym*-like account of an expedition across the Rocky Mountains, appeared in *Gentleman's Magazine* in 1840. Five years previously the *Southern Literary Messenger* had published scenes from *Politian*, a blank verse tragedy set in Renaissance Italy that would later be included in *The Raven and Other Poems* (1845).

POE'S CRITICISM

Throughout his life Poe wrote a great deal of literary journalism and worked in an editorial capacity for a variety of newspapers. It was also one of his great ambitions to edit his own magazine. As a critic he was outspoken, vitriolic, and fearless. He highlighted the technical limitations of the books he reviewed, accused several authors (most famously Henry Wadsworth Longfellow) of plagiarism, and took great delight in attacking the New England literary establishment.

Poe was not simply motivated by a disinterested concern for the health of letters; he was also desperately trying to carve his way to literary fame. That is why his criticism tended to be as sensational as his short-story writing: controversy was the equivalent of the Gothic and grotesque effects of his fiction. Without money or regular employment, Poe had to achieve celebrity status in order to survive in the literary marketplace, and if he could not be famous then he would be notorious. He did everything he could to keep his name before the public, even going to the extent of anonymously reviewing his own works.

Poe also used the pages of the popular press to fashion and present an image of himself as a man of immense erudition. In his articles, as in his short stories, he included countless quotations and phrases from various languages; he also made a great exhibition of his learning. Poe's "Marginalia," published in newspapers during the 1840s, consists of comments and meditations that he claimed to have scribbled in the margins of the books in his library. "I sought relief," he commented, like a latter-day Renaissance connoisseur of fine literature, "from *ennui* in dipping here and there at random among the volumes of my library." The reality was quite different, however. Poe wrote the pieces as fillers for newspapers when they were short of copy, and the sad fact of the matter was that he could never afford to assemble an extensive library of his own.

Poe's most important contributions to literary criticism were his theories concerning the short story and poetry. It has been suggested that his comments on the short story, which were scattered throughout reviews of books such as Nathaniel Hawthorne's *Twice-Told Tales* (1837), helped establish the genre in its modern form. Poe's theory can be briefly summarized. He was concerned above all with the effect of his tale on the reader. This effect should, he thought, be single and unified. When readers finished the story they ought be left with a totality of impression, and every element of the story—character, style, tone, plot, and so on—should contribute to that impression. Stories too long to be read at a single sitting could not, in Poe's view, achieve such powerful and unified effects—hence the brevity of his own productions. Poe also advocated the Aristotelian unities of place, time, and action and put special emphasis on the opening and conclusion of his tales. In addition, he encouraged authors to concentrate exclusively on powerful emotional

and aesthetic effects—the aim of fiction, he suggested, was not a didactic one. Finally, instead of providing the reader with a transparent upper current of meaning, he thought that the meaning of a tale should be indefinite and ambiguous.

Obviously, such ideas help us understand Poe's own short stories. "The Tell-Tale Heart" and "The Masque of the Red Death," for example, exhibit most of the above-mentioned characteristics. The theories of poetry that Poe adumbrated in book reviews and in lectures such as "The Poetic Principle" (1849) also help us understand his verse. In Poe's criticism there is a sense in which he was justifying his own practice as a creative writer and also attempting to create the kind of critical atmosphere in which his work would be favorably judged. Other writers, such as T. S. Eliot and Ezra Pound, have also found this to be an effective strategy for achieving literary success. More broadly, it can be suggested that writing such as Poe's that lacks a definite content and an unambiguous message requires a theory in order to, as it were, support it and make it intelligible to the reader.

Poe's statements about poetry are similar to his pronouncements on the short story. Thus, in a review of Longfellow's *Hyperion, A Romance* (1839), he criticized its lack of a definite design and unified effect. Later, when commenting on the same author's *Ballads and Other Poems* (1841), he complained of Longfellow's didacticism and his failure to appreciate that the aim of poetry was not to instruct readers but to give them access to the world of supernal beauty. These ideas were expressed in a more theoretical form in "The Poetic Principle," in which Poe criticized what he referred to as "the heresy of the didactic" and famously defined poetry as "the Rhythmical Creation of Beauty." These ideas proved to be extremely influential and were later adapted by "art-for-art's-sake" aesthetes such as Oscar Wilde and by symbolists such as Paul Valéry. It has also been suggested that Poe's emphasis on the words on the page, rather than on external considerations such as the writer's biography, make him an important precursor of the New Critics.

THE RAVEN AND OTHER POEMS

Poe's most influential theoretical essay was probably "The Philosophy of Composition," published in *Graham's Magazine* in 1846. Before we turn to it, however, it is necessary to consider "The Raven," the inception and writing of which the essay describes. "The Raven," first published in the *New York Evening Mirror* in January 1845, was an instant hit with the reading public. This allusion to pop music is apt because the immediate and enormous success of the poem has been accurately compared to that of a present-day song. On its publication, Poe became an overnight sensation, and thereafter he would always be associated with the poem. In a sense this association is unfortunate, because it obscures the fact that the poem, like many of Poe's short stories, is a dramatic production. The narrator, a young man mourning the death of his love Lenore, sits in his study musing "over many a quaint and curious volume of forgotten lore"—a character and a setting typical of Poe. As well as being a dramatic poem, it is also an intensely theatrical one: the gloomy weather, the speaking bird, and props such as the purple curtain and the bust of Pallas could have been filched from the set of a Gothic drama. The young man's language, too, is distinctly stagy; at one point he remarks to the Raven: "'Sir . . . or Madam, truly your forgiveness I implore.'" The effect of such distinctly camp lines is complicated; you are not sure whether to laugh or scream. In the theater, and in the theatrical world of the poem, it is of course possible to do both.

Given the theatricality of the poem, it is fitting that Poe performed it, just as Dickens performed his novels, in public and private readings. During his recitations Poe once again proved that the theater was in his blood: he would dress in black, turn the lamps down low, and chant the poem in a melodious voice. The content of the poem is of course unrealistic; like a great drama, however, it creates its own vivid and convincing reality through its solemn rhymes and its stately rhythm.

Poe's raven has become as famous as those other birds of romanticism, Keats's nightingale, Shelley's skylark, and Coleridge's albatross. This is ironic because, in "The Philosophy of Composition," he insisted that the poem was not a romantic one. The essay was written to demonstrate that, far from being a work of inspiration, the composition of "The Raven" proceeded with what he called "the precision and rigid consequence of a mathematical problem." Along with metaphors drawn from mathematics, Poe typically (and revealingly) used images of acting to convey his detachment and self-consciousness during the writing of the poem.

Desiring to create a powerful effect of melancholy beauty that would appeal to both "the popular and the critical taste," Poe tells us that he hit upon the saddest of all subjects: the death of a beautiful woman. This had, of course, been the subject of several of his earlier writings, such as the "marriage group" of stories in *Tales of the Grotesque and Arabesque*. In order to make the effect of the poem intense and unified, he decided that it should be limited to around one hundred lines and that it would include a refrain composed of the single, sonorous word, "Nevermore." In the remainder of the essay Poe, who might be compared here to a magician who enjoys explaining away his tricks, goes on to make numerous comments of a similar nature.

It has been suggested that "The Philosophy of Composition" was a typical Poe hoax, and it is highly unlikely that it is a veracious account of the actual writing of "The Raven." This, however, is largely irrelevant since the essay's importance lies in the fact that it offered a novel theory of composition and a new conception of the poet. Poe was attempting to replace the idea of the inspired poet that had been established by the ancients and by contemporaries such as Coleridge with his notion of the cold and calculating author. Once again, Poe's idea proved to be extremely influential in the history of literature. It informs Valéry's conception of the poet as an extremely self-conscious artist and T. S. Eliot's idea of the impersonal author.

It is doubtful that Poe's theories would have exercised such a powerful influence had he not also embodied and dramatized them in his writings. Perhaps even more important, he also offered himself as an archetype of the kind of author he was describing. Poe presented himself, in other words, as the exemplar of the self-conscious poet, an original that poets such as Baudelaire copied.

"The Raven" was republished in Poe's most substantial and famous collection of verse, *The Raven and Other Poems*, in 1845. The book, which was prefaced by a statement that typically succeeded in being at once self-effacing and arrogant, contained revised versions of earlier compositions such as *Israfel* and poems that had never previously appeared in book form. Also included in the collection were several poems that had appeared, or would later appear, in Poe's short stories. (This is a striking demonstration of the homogeneous nature of Poe's oeuvre.) The most famous of these poems are "The Haunted Palace," a powerful atmospheric poem improvised by Roderick Usher, and "The Conqueror Worm," written by the eponymous hero of "Ligeia." In the latter, angels are in a theater watching humankind play out its meaningless "motley drama" in which there is "much of Madness and more of Sin / And horror the soul of the plot." Suddenly, "a blood-red thing" comes onto the stage. The lights go out, the curtain comes down, and death (for it is he) holds illimitable dominion over all. In its Gothic style, its dark vision of the world, and its theatricality, the poem is characteristic of its author and indeed reads like a microcosm of his oeuvre. One obvious point that can be made in connection with the poems that appeared in Poe's short stories is that they are dramatic works (a comparison here might be made with Robert Browning's monologues). Yet again, Poe displays his great gifts as a mimic or actor, and once more we are alerted to the difficulties of reading his work in an autobiographical light.

Many of Poe's finest poems were written after the publication of "The Raven" and were collected in volume form posthumously. These include the onomatopoeic "The Bells," the beautiful ballad "Annabel Lee," and the musical masterpiece "Ulalume." This last poem is perhaps the most perfect example of Poe's ability to create a mysterious and unearthly atmosphere through repetition, assonance, and the use of languorous, usually trisyllabic, words. While discussing the poem, Poe is reported to have remarked that he deliberately wrote verse that would be unintelligible to the many. "Ulalume" is certainly hard to understand, but like the rest of Poe's verse, its ambiguity heightens rather than diminishes its power.

POE, THE DETECTIVE STORY, AND SCIENCE FICTION

Between the publication of *Tales of the Grotesque and Arabesque* in 1840 and his death in 1849, Poe wrote numerous short stories. Among them are some of the most famous of all his writings, such as "The Black Cat," "The Tell-Tale Heart," "The Cask of Amontillado," "The Pit and the Pendulum," "Hop-Frog," and "The Masque of the Red Death." These stories have achieved the status of myths in the Western world; even those who have not read them know their plots. Because of the exigencies of space, and also because some of Poe's arabesque and grotesque productions have already been discussed, the focus here is on the stories that appeared in *Tales* (1845) and, in particular, on Poe's detective tales and science fiction. Although reviewers of *Tales* were, as usual, divided between those who described Poe as a great original and those who dismissed him as a showy and stylistically incompetent writer, the volume sold better than any of Poe's other publications.

Four detective stories (or "Tales of ratiocination," as Poe called them) appeared in *Tales*: the prize-winning "The Gold-Bug" and three tales that featured the detective C. Auguste Dupin: "The Purloined Letter," "The Mystery of Marie Roget," and "The Murders in the Rue Morgue." Although writers such as Voltaire, William Godwin, and

Tobias Smollet had produced examples of what might be loosely termed crime fiction in the eighteenth century, it was these tales that established the modern short detective story as a definite and distinct form.

In "The Murders in the Rue Morgue," the most famous and entertaining of Poe's detective stories, we immediately recognize the structure of the modern detective tale. A hideous and inexplicable crime is committed (the brutal murder of two women in a locked room in Paris), and all the evidence is placed before us. The police, who rely on cunning and instinct rather than rational method and imagination, are utterly baffled. Fortunately for them, an amateur genius, Dupin, is on hand to unravel the mystery. The tale (which in terms of its action is written backward) thus includes two stories: that of the crime and that of its solution and explanation by Dupin.

In creating Dupin, Poe invented the archetype of the modern detective. Among Dupin's descendents are Agatha Christie's Hercule Poirot, G. K. Chesterton's Father Brown, and of course Sir Arthur Conan Doyle's Sherlock Holmes, who in one of Conan Doyle's stories actually discusses Dupin's merits. An eccentric and reclusive genius, Dupin is both a poetic visionary and a detached man of reason; he combines the attributes of the poet with those of the mathematician. In "The Purloined Letter," where he unravels a mystery by identifying with the criminal, Dupin also displays an actor's power of empathy. He is, in other words, a glorified and aristocratic version of Poe. Poe also created the original of the detective's companion: a friend of average intelligence who narrates the tale and who acts, as it were, as the reader's representative within it. In "The Murders in the Rue Morgue," the character is nameless; in later works by other authors he will be called Doctor Watson and Captain Hastings.

Poe is thus in large part responsible for one of the most popular and dominant forms of modern literature. After reading Poe, the French writers the Goncourt brothers believed that they had discovered "the literature of the twentieth century—love giving place to deductions... the interest of the story moved from the heart to the head... from the drama to the solution." This prediction proved correct. Twentieth-century writers such as Jorge Luis Borges (who believed that Poe's ghost dictated detective stories to him) consciously imitated Poe, and the popularity and influence of the detective story has been, and still is, enormous. The broader point made by the Goncourt brothers concerning a literature of "the head" is also interesting. The detective story is essentially an intellectual exercise or game, and much of Poe's writing can be described in these terms. Perhaps it is this quality in his work that made it so popular and influential in the twentieth century.

The invention, or at the very least the foundation, of the modern detective story is surely Poe's greatest contribution to world literature. He has also been hailed as the father of modern science fiction. The extent to which Poe established the genre is, however, a matter of controversy. Those who have argued for his formative influence point to the futuristic, technological, and rationalistic elements of his work. It is perhaps better to approach the question through a consideration of Poe's influence, which was enormous. Poe's science fiction stories profoundly influenced later masters of the genre such as Jules Verne, H. G. Wells, and Isaac Asimov (who conflated the science fiction tale and the detective story). Among the Poe stories that have been classed as science fiction are "Hans Phaall," the eponymous hero's account of his nineteen-day balloon journey to the moon, and the futuristic "Mellonta Tauta." Two stories in *Tales*, "The Colloquy of Monos and Una" and "The Conversation of Eiros and Charmion," have also been classified as science fiction tales.

Both are dialogues between disembodied spirits set sometime in the distant future. The dialogue form, which derives from ancients such as Lucian and Plato, was very popular in Poe's time among satirical writers such as Thomas Love Peacock, Giacomo Leopardi, and William Blake. Poe also used it for satirical purposes; in these dialogues he criticizes his age for, among other things, its exclusive belief in science. Poe's argument with science was in some respects a typically romantic one. Science and industrialization, it is suggested in "The Colloquy," have given humans the false idea that they have dominion over nature and have devalued the poetic intellect.

Yet Poe went further than this conventional romantic position and challenged science's claims to objectivity and its emphasis on empiricism. So far as objectivity is concerned, reading hoax stories such as "Hans Phaall" leaves the impression that scientific explanations of the world are not unlike stories and that science itself may be a kind of fiction. Regarding the limitations of empiricism, Poe believed that the discovery of facts was not enough and that it is what is done with them that is important. It requires, Poe suggests, a visionary rather than a scientist to sort, connect, and shape them into theories. This visionary figure, who is both poet and mathematician, appears throughout Poe's writings. Sometimes he is Dupin, the great detective; at other times he is Poe, the theorist of poetic composition and the author of the scientific prose poem *Eureka*.

EUREKA

Poe evidently believed that *Eureka*, published in 1848, was his greatest achievement: "I have no desire to live since I have done 'Eureka,'" he wrote to his mother-in-law. "I could accomplish nothing more." Indeed, he appears to have regarded it as nothing less than the solution to the secret of the universe. It is most unfortunate for humanity, therefore, that *Eureka* makes extremely dull reading and is very difficult to understand. One of the best attempts at a summary is contained in Kenneth Silverman's (1991) excellent biography of Poe. Suffice it to say here that *Eureka*, subtitled as "Essay on the material and the spiritual universe" predicted, among other things, the annihilation and the rebirth of the universe.

Although *Eureka* has traditionally been regarded as a distinct work within the Poe canon, there are many connections between it and the rest of his oeuvre. Passages in short stories such as "Mellonta Tauta" prefigure some of its contents. In his preface to the book Poe described it as a poem rather than a "scientific" work. "I offer this Book of Truths," he wrote, adapting Keats's famous line, "not in the character of a Truth-Teller, but for the Beauty that abounds in its Truth; constituting it True."

The rather confused critical reception that *Eureka* received also made it a typical Poe production. Some reviewers read it as an elaborate hoax in the manner of "Hans Phaall"; others considered it to be a prolix and labored satire of scientific discourse. Certain critics regarded it as a brilliant and sincere work of genius, yet it was also dismissed as arrant fudge. Such diverse and extreme reactions to Poe's work have already been noted; they testify to the fact that, whatever else his writing is, it is impossible to ignore.

POE'S INFLUENCE

When Poe died in Baltimore on 7 October 1849 from causes that are still the subject of debate, some commentators predicted that his works would be forgotten. They could not have been more wrong, as his books are currently read throughout the world and his influence on world literature has been extraordinary. With their consummate artistry, their self-consciousness, and their heavy atmosphere of decay, Poe's poems and tales (along with his literary persona and his theories) inspired Decadent and symbolist writers of the nineteenth century. Baudelaire, among whose earliest works were translations of Poe's stories, famously died with a copy of Poe's tales beside his bed. Mallarmé, Verlaine, Dowson, and Wilde also worshipped at the Poe shrine.

At the end of the nineteenth century, science fiction writers such as Verne and Wells and authors of detective stories such as Conan Doyle acknowledged their profound debt to Poe. It was Conan Doyle who remarked that Poe's tales "have been so pregnant with suggestion . . . that each is a root from which a whole literature has developed." In the twentieth century Poe's influence was no less profound. His short stories were of immense importance to authors as diverse as Kafka, H. P. Lovecraft (who referred to his tales of horror as "Poe stories"), Vladimir Nabokov, and Stephen King. He has also had a powerful effect on every other branch of the arts. Painters such as René Magritte and Edmund Dulac were fascinated by him, and film directors such as Roger Corman and Alfred Hitchcock also took inspiration from his writings.

Poe continues to inspire and enchant people today. In the future he will no doubt attract as much hostile criticism as he has in the past, but he will survive because he will continue to be read. And despite all of the faults and all of the fudge in his writings, it is hard, in conclusion, to think of another American writer who has so drastically altered the landscape of the popular imagination or who has had such a powerful effect on his fellow artists.

[*See also* Detective Fiction; Popular Fiction; Romanticism in America: The Emersonian Tradition; Science Fiction; *and* Short Story in America, The.]

SELECTED WORKS

Tamerlane and Other Poems (1827)
Al Aaraaf, Tamerlane, and Minor Poems (1829)
Poems by Edgar A. Poe (1831)

The Narrative of Arthur Gordon Pym of Nantucket (1838)
Tales of the Grotesque and Arabesque (1840)
The Raven and Other Poems (1845)
Tales (1845)
Eureka (1848)
Collected Works of Edgar Allan Poe (1969–1978)
The Science Fiction of Edgar Allan Poe (1976)
The Fall of the House of Usher and Other Writings (1986)
Poetry, Tales, and Selected Essays (1996)

FURTHER READING

Carlson, Eric W., ed. *The Recognition of Edgar Allan Poe: Selected Criticism since 1829.* Ann Arbor, Mich., 1966. Collection of all of the famous essays on Poe, including those by T. S. Eliot, W. H. Auden, and Walt Whitman.

Carlson, Eric W., ed. *A Companion to Poe Studies.* Westport, Conn., 1996. A comprehensive collection of modern appraisals of every aspect of Poe's life and work.

Hayes, Kevin J. *The Cambridge Companion to Edgar Allan Poe.* Cambridge, 2002. Excellent and wide-ranging collection of late-twentieth-century Poe scholarship.

Hyneman, Esther F. *Edgar Allan Poe: An Annotated Bibliography of Books and Articles in English, 1827–1973.* Boston, 1974.

Silverman, Kenneth. *Edgar A. Poe: Mournful and Never-ending Remembrance.* New York, 1991. Its psycho-analytic explanations are sometimes unconvincing, but it is easily the best biography available.

Walker, I. M., ed. *Edgar Allan Poe: The Critical Heritage.* New York, 1986. Anthology of contemporary reviews of Poe's work.

THE POETESS IN AMERICAN LITERATURE

by Annie Finch

In the nineteenth century, the term "poetess" was typically a conventional compliment to, or acknowledgement of, any female poet's femininity. During the twentieth century it became more often a label of contempt and condescension. In the twenty-first century, the word "poetess" has taken on an objective literary meaning for the first time. It has been revived to delineate a specific poetic tradition in which many women poets, and some men, have taken part. This poetic tradition involves particular techniques and strategies that are markedly different from those of the romantic and postromantic poetic traditions. In this essay, the term "sentimentism" refers to the poetic techniques and conventions developed by the poetesses, in order to clearly distinguish their methods and aims from those of poetic romanticism.

The lineage of the "poetess" in America includes such poets as Lydia Sigourney, Frances Osgood, Elinor Wylie, Alice Dunbar-Nelson, Sara Teasdale, Edna St. Vincent Millay, Anna Hampstead Branch, Louise Imogen Guiney, Frances Harper, Babette Deutsch, Louise Bogan, Emma Lazarus, Leonie Adams, and many others. The poetess tradition has also affected or influenced the work of such poets as Phillis Wheatley, Emily Dickinson, Edgar Allan Poe, Henry Wadsworth Longfellow, Elizabeth Bishop, and Marianne Moore. More recently, poets as different as Carolyn Kizer, Louise Glück, Lucille Clifton, and Jorie Graham have been influenced by this tradition. Because the romantic and postromantic poetic traditions have dominated American poetry since the early nineteenth century, to consider poetess poetry in its own terms is both a challenge and a source of great potential rewards. Although the techniques of repetition and conscious artificiality in sentimentist poetry can strike contemporary readers as unnaturally simple, if the poems are read as they were meant to be read—slowly, with an open heart—and listened to with the body as well as the mind, it is possible for even highly educated contemporary readers to experience the appeal that has kept the poems of such writers as Teasdale and Millay alive and well-loved for decades after the works of more sophisticated poets have been abandoned.

Unfortunately, many of the most important works by the poetesses, such as Lydia Sigourney's *Selected Poems* (1800) and Frances Osgood's *Poems* (1850) were out of print during the entire twentieth century. The best primary sources for poetess poetry are two recent anthologies: Cheryl Walker's *American Women Poets of the Nineteenth Century* and Joan Sherman's *African-American Poetry of the Nineteenth Century*.

POETIC SELF IN THE POETESS TRADITION

One of the most important ways that poetess poetry differs from romantic poetry is in the poet's treatment and positioning of the poetic speaker, or "self." Romantic poems enable the reader to identify with a strong central poetic speaker who appropriates nature and the world as a vehicle for accessing the poet's own emotions. In John Keats's "Ode to a Nightingale," for example, the speaker's self provides the sole locus of subjectivity in the poem. Similarly, in William Cullen Bryant's "Thanatopsis," where a feminized Nature solaces the speaker with her "voice of gladness," her "smile," and her "healing sympathy," the existence of nature is refracted through the lens of the poet's individual self. Poetess poems, on the other hand, allow nature and the world a more independent existence. Over the centuries, poetesses developed several methods to achieve a balance among subjectivities within their poems. Innovative (from a romantic point of view) approaches to metaphor played a key role in this central achievement of sentimentism.

Lydia Sigourney is typical of the sentimentist poetesses in that she rarely personifies or even relates a metaphor to natural objects in order to make statements about her own feelings. Her poems are not organized around a central poetic subject or ego, but instead they attribute an independent subjectivity, often conventionalized, to nature: "Then the sea answer'd—spoils are mine / From many an argosy, / And pearl-drops sleep in my bosom deep, / But naught have I there for thee." They lend to natural objects voices and identities separate from that of the speaker, who may even address them directly: "Yes, we have need of thee; / thanks, tree of sympathy." Perhaps because the poetess, usually a woman, was used to being objectified herself, the speakers in poetess poems do not take on the role of objectifying central bard. Significantly, the very few poems in which Sigourney does use nature as a device to describe a central human state are poems celebrating public institutions or involving male speakers, such as the patriotic poem "Connecticut River," with its theme of "devotion" for the "fatherland," or "The Dying Philosopher," in which she adopts a male persona.

In the work of early poetesses such as Sigourney, Christianity can play a key role in the sentimentist approach to nature. In such poems, God takes on the role of the romantic subjectivity, and the speaker, along with all the poem's human and natural characters, are equally objectified in relation to God—called by Sigourney the "One Dread Name." A later, less religious poetess such as Helen Hunt Jackson might use other strategies to allow nature its freedom. One technique is for the poetess to assert the power to describe nature, while in the same poem undercutting or contradicting her own power. In Jackson's "The Wall-Flower of the Ruins of Rome," for example, the speaker attributes human qualities to the flower, but the poem ends with a qualification: "the whole of thy deep spell / I cannot fathom, and thou wilt not tell." Because of such strategies, a reader of these sentimentist poems takes away not so much a sense of the power of the poet's self as a sense of that which Dickinson might call "circumference": a world of endless and equal entities in which the poetic "I" is not necessarily more privileged than any other self.

An even more complex strategy of self-presentation occurs in the work of some early twentieth-century poetesses. Although the lyric self and its emotions are an increasing concern of poetesses of this period, the speaker of such poems does not express her emotions by making metaphors about nature. Instead, she objectifies herself. The projected reader or listener taking on the role of the lover, and the speaker of such poems prevents the addressee from "metaphorizing" her, instead making herself into a wave, a river, a storm, a candle, or a tree, as in the following lyric by Sara Teasdale:

My heart is heavy with many a song
Like ripe fruit bearing down the tree,
But I can never give you one—
My songs do not belong to me.

Yet in the evening, in the dusk
When moths go to and fro,
In the gray hour if the fruit has fallen,

Take it, no one will know.
("My Heart is Heavy," 1918)

Through the techniques of entering in dialogue with nature, the qualification of lyric insights, and self-metaphor, the speaker of a sentimentist lyric refuses to act the part of the central bardic romantic poet-speaker. Instead, the sentimentist lyric enacts, through the structure of its own voices, a communal and compassionate multiplicity of subjectivities.

FORM AND THE POETESS

Poetess poetry often makes use of poetic forms that were easily imitated by people without access to much formal education, a group that included most women of the eighteenth and nineteenth centuries. Laura Mandell (2003) has pointed out the influence of class and gender considerations on such stylistic choices. Ballad stanzas and iambic tetrameters and trimeters were akin to the popular ballad forms familiar to people of the working classes. Many poetesses did not have access to the money and time necessary to thoroughly learn the most prestigious poetic meter, iambic pentameter, whose mastery involved reading and studying books by canonical male poets. This fact alone helped until recently to bar poetesses from the canon of respected writers, a view that John Crowe Ransom made explicit by claiming, in his essay on Dickinson, that she never achieved true greatness as a poet because she did not use iambic pentameter.

Although many poetesses, notably Maria Brooks, Lydia Sigourney, and Phoebe Cary, did write some poems in iambic pentameter, most favored other meters, including ballad stanzas, anapests, and trochees. These meters have had a much longer life in oral poetic tradition than in written poetry, and they were frequently used in children's and popular poetry through the mid-twentieth century. Because of their association with oral tradition, such meters often have not been varied as subtly as iambic pentameter, a fact that added to the feeling that poetess poetry was not as metrically complex as romantic poetry.

Aside from its insistent meters, one of the key formal aspects of sentimentist poetry is its free use of repetition. Repetition is an oral-based poetic technique, undermining the primacy of written over spoken language and reminding the eye of the ear's primacy. It pulls the reader down from the vicarious bardic literary perch and into the preliterate, childlike, even nonhuman body. The very same qualities that make obvious verbal repetition anathema to the post-romantic contemporary reader are the qualities that make it such an integral part of the successful sentimentist lyric. Repetition's qualities of unself-consciousness, physical pleasure in form, orality, and slowness of texture are all qualities intrinsic to poetess poetry generally. They connect a sentimentist lyric to its roots in folk and oral-based poetry.

Repetition can function at its most effective to render language unfamiliar and to lend words a totemic power that is not based on their representational powers. Sara Teasdale's "Let It Be Forgotten," for example, uses a subtle texture of repetition to enact the process of forgetting, giving the very word "forgotten" a reified presence through insistent repetition and finally covering up the word itself, like the forgotten thing, in snow:

> Let it be forgotten, as a flower is forgotten,
> Forgotten as a fire that once was singing gold,
> Let it be forgotten forever and ever,
> Time is a kind friend, he will make us old.
>
> If anyone asks, say it was forgotten
> Long and long ago,
> As a flower, as a fire, as a hushed footfall
> In a long forgotten snow.

The word "forgotten" occurs four times in the first stanza, along with one "forever" and one "fire." The second stanza has only one "forgotten" and one "fire." One "flower" and one "footfall" take the place of two of the forgotten "forgottens"; one "forgotten" is buried in snow in the final line; and the final "forgotten" from the first stanza has, indeed, disappeared without a trace. Teasdale's poem shows an achievement on a literal level of linguistic tangibility, of "opacity," to use experimentalist Charles Bernstein's term.

Repetition in sentimentist poems appeals to the reader's sense of space, being, and unindividuated consciousness. In Teasdale's "Night Song at Amalfi," for instance, the device of repetition links the speaker viscerally with the sky and the sea, echoing through the heart of the poem like a vacuum. At the same time it allows a new mood to enter the poem, as the tone of the concluding question changes from plaintive to defiant in the echoing silence following the repetitions. But it does all this without words, because repetition is, paradoxically, a wordless technique.

> I asked the heaven of stars
> What I should give my love—
> It answered me with silence,
> Silence above.
>
> I asked the darkened sea
> Down where the fishers go—

> It answered me with silence,
> Silence below.
>
> Oh, I could give him weeping,
> Or I could give him song—
> But how can I give silence
> My whole life long?

CONVENTIONALITY AND THE POETESS

Another key way in which sentimentist poetics differs from the poetics of romantic tradition is in the poetess's attitude toward the stylistic choices of conventionality and artificiality. Mandell remarks that, while for a poet such as Wordsworth it was a point of honor to defamiliarize ordinary language, the poetess did not have the benefit of Wordsworth's education. For the poetess, as for writers of lower social class, highly conventional and even clichéd poetic diction could function as a value, a sign of education and culture. Thus, poetess poetry not only is open to simple meters and conventional diction but also evinces a conscious comfort with artificiality in general.

Often, artificiality can be seen in the use of metaphor and conceit. For example, none of Lydia Sigourney's nature poems transform natural objects in the service of the poetess's own concerns, unless they make it clear that is what they are doing. Such clarity is often attained through the use of those exaggerated figures that have given poetess poetry the epithet "artificial." The consciousness of artificiality is developed to great complexity near the end of Sigourney's "Autumn," where several of the poem's symbols explicitly explain their own significance to the poetess. Sigourney places the words spoken by the symbols in quotation marks:

> "We are symbols, ye say, of the hasting doom
> Of youth, and of health, and of beauty's bloom,
> When Disease, with a hectic flush doth glow,
> And Time steal on with his tress of snow."

Not only do the symbols describe their own meaning to the poetess, but the phrase "ye say," which Sigourney has them address to her, indicates an additional level of self-consciousness. The words emphasize that the symbolism occurs in the poetess's mind alone and that the symbols do not seem to represent a truth outside the text of the poem. In other words, the poetess herself is aware that the meanings she sees in nature are constructed ones. This fact is not hidden in any way but is one of the most apparent aspects of the poem. As a result, this poem cannot be deconstructed in the same terms as a romantic lyric. The reader in a sense has nothing at all to lose by seeing through the arbitrariness of the poem's imaginary meanings, since the arbitrariness is built into the poem's most accessible surface. This point is reinforced by the poet in the line, "Yet ye still have a voice to the musing heart, / Tree, Stream and Rose." When the symbols proceed to give a moral at the end of the poem, it is clear that this metaphorical moral,

> "The soul that admits in an evil hour
> The breath of vice to its sacred bower
> Will find its peace with its glory die,
> Like the fading hues of an autumn sky."

is not any extratextual truth but only a further continuation of the poetess's very self-conscious musing. But, by putting the poem's meanings and morals into the voices of the natural objects rather than into her own voice, Sigourney has managed simultaneously to make it clear that all the meanings in the poem are obviously her own fictions and to avoid the subjective self that would be created if she were to draw these conclusions in a central human voice.

Like the lack of a central subject-speaker, the choices of conventional diction, simple meters, and artificial conceits doomed the poetesses during the twentieth century to the invisibility of the supposed "sentimental." Conventionality is, after all, the most instantly recognizable aspect of sentimentality and, in our age of aggressive individualism and the pursuit of novelty, the easiest to despise. Sentimental conventionality involves transparent language, familiar figures, and an underlying conviction of artificiality that not only renders a lyric familiar and accessible but also marks it as part of the larger literary and social community. It is hard to recall now, in the age that has been so dominated by postromanticism, that originality was not always a key value in poetry. In many eras, including the ancient world, the Renaissance, and the Enlightenment, it was more important for a poet to capture a conventional idea with skill than to break new ground. In order to read the work of the poetesses in its own terms, it is similarly necessary to set aside postromantic and post–New Critical assumptions that originality and innovation in language and concept are axiomatic poetic values.

SENTIMENTALITY AND THE POETESS

If the romantic lyric aims to emphasize the integrity and emotional authenticity of the poet's individual, passionate self, the sentimentist lyric aims to position both poet and reader within a web of larger relationships, a world, a community. Faith in the aesthetic value of a commonly shared, accessible understanding of the world forms the crucial distinction between the poetesses and what we think of as the postmodern sensibility—and, along with sexism, it is probably the true basis of their denigration throughout most of the twentieth century. The poetesses wrote of close relationships and communally shared feelings, blending their lives with those of the people around them in an intimacy that easily crossed the boundaries of individual selves. That they wrote this way in the nineteenth and early twentieth centuries, when the lyric poetic self was by definition male, and when the level of self-assertion required of a lyric poet was almost impossible for most women even to envision, is a measure of their alienation from the most powerful hierarchies of poetic value.

The poetesses embodied the sentimental worldview—based on diffuse lyric subjectivity, communal values, and a self-consciously artificial aesthetic—with great consistency. Their poems often attempted purposefully to reflect common values, as in the following passage from "The Aged" by Marguerite St. Leon Loud.

> Lovely the aged! when like shocks of corn,
> Full ripe and ready for the reaper's hand,
> Which garners for the resurrection morn
> The bodies of the just—in hope they stand.
> And dead must be the heart, the bosom cold,
> Which warms not with affection for the old.

Many of the poetess poems center on relationships between women: close friends, young nieces and daughters, babies, and mothers are frequent addressees. Frances Sargent Osgood's 1850 volume *Poems*, for example, includes numerous poems addressed directly to intimate female friends, including "To Sarah," "To Mrs. O," "To Mary," "To a Slandered Poetess," "I Dearly Love a Changing Cheek," "To Amelia Welby," and many others. Numerous other poems are meant to provide information and advice from one woman to another, including "Venus and the Modern Belle," "To a Maiden in Doubt," and "Golden Rules in Rhyme from a Matron to a Maiden." Others are addressed to or concern young girls: "Fanny's First Smile," "Ellen Learning to Walk," "Marion's Song in the Schoolroom," "Little May Vincent," and more. This is the female-centered and domestic literary culture in which Emily Dickinson was participating when she included so many of her own poems in letters to friends and family members.

The "sentimentality" in the work of the poetesses had its origin in the eighteenth-century culture of "sensibility," the desire to return to feelings as the ground of truth, in reaction to the overreliance on reason during the

Enlightenment. The poetry of Phillis Wheatley is a link between eighteenth-century sensibility and nineteenth-century sentimentality. When Wheatley writes, in her poem "To the University of Cambridge, in New England," "Ye blooming plants of human race divine, / an Ethiop tells you [sin is] your greatest foe," she sentimentalizes herself as an object, from the public position of an outsider like the reader. An African-American woman brought to America as a slave when she was a child, Wheatley allegorizes herself and her race in such poems. Wheatley's numerous poems on the deaths of acquaintances and children also draw on conventional images of death in order to allegorize domestic scenes, in the same way that the nineteenth-century poetesses would later write poems explicitly in their capacity as mothers. Such a poetic focus on external images rather than on a centralized subjectivity is one of the key characteristics that distinguishes sentimental poetry from the poetry of sensibility.

Sentimental writing presupposes a public community of readers who will feel what the writer has intended them to feel. This presumption that the reader will react as planned is probably a major reason that contemporary readers, reared on the romantic ethos of individuality, generally dislike sentimental art. Although evoking certain kinds of emotion is sentimentality's central aim, sentimentality accomplishes this aim not by ignoring persuasive, publicly comprehensible rhetorical logic but by manipulating it. The fear of being violated, of being known so intimately by a writer that one can be too obviously manipulated (not in the subtle way of high art, but in a way that is embarrassingly evident to any other person), connects with fears of intimacy and dependence. Nonetheless, the most salient aspects of sentimental poetry are well-suited to achieving the aim of establishing poet and reader within a shared communal world.

The most stereotypically sentimental subject of the poetess in America is the death of an infant. Mark Twain's parody of poetess Emmeline Grangerford in *Adventures of Huckleberry Finn* (1884) focuses on this aspect of the poetess. In fact, the death of infants was an extremely common experience of nineteenth-century domestic life, and the poetess elegies served a necessary social function as well as an aesthetic one. Sigourney infuses her elegies with Christianity in order to give them the quality of a spiritual lesson. Frances Osgood's "Ashes of Roses" is more personal in its emotion:

> I know her little heart is glad; some gentle angel guides
> My loved one on her joyous way, where'er in heaven
>   she glides,

> Some angel far more wisely kind than I could ever be,
> With all my blind, wild, mother-love,—my Fanny, tends
>   on thee!
> And every sweet want of thy heart her care benign fulfils,
> And every whisper'd wish for me, with lulling love she stills.

Of course, it is not so much certain subjects as the way they are treated that causes contemporary readers the most difficulty appreciating the sentimentist aesthetic. Conventional language and the evocation of shared emotion can embarrass some readers by making a blatant appeal to a shared and common humanity. Diffuse subjectivity embarrasses some readers by giving us the poet naked of the dignity conferred by lyric authority, and evident formal devices and stylized repetition further distance the speaker from the appearance of authentic subjectivity. Yet we are used to ignoring conventionalized religious sentiments and other artifacts in the work of poets from previous centuries. When read with an open mind, poems using sentimentist strategies can create a strong emotional pull, a physical pleasure in words, and a sense of common humanity.

THE POETESS TRADITION

Independent of romanticism and modernism, the poetesses developed and explored their own poetic traditions and techniques to embody their view of a shared, accessible world, open to tradition and convention, and an often diffused, uncentered self that did not have a privileged subjectivity. The poetesses built very successful careers writing formal, accessible poems about spiritual and political as well as domestic and emotional themes. Lydia Sigourney was paid the then-huge sum of $500 annually by *Godey's Lady's Book* just to list her name on their masthead. Edna St. Vincent Millay enjoyed celebrity status unheard of for a poet today, as well as gigantic book sales. And, as the decades went on and women won more power in society, early-twentieth-century poetesses such as Teasdale, Millay, Wylie, and Adams adapted many of their predecessors' sentimentist techniques to a wider range of attitudes and themes.

But despite these poetesses' successful careers, the poetess tradition was studied during the late twentieth century mostly through the work of Emily Dickinson. Dickinson was herself an admirer of many of the poetesses, and the traits she shares with them include her use of ballad stanza instead of iambic pentameter, her unashamed whimsicality, her commitment to making poetry part of daily life, the writing of poems for friends and relatives, and most of all her ability to locate her own subjectivity outside of the central lyric persona. One of the specific techniques that Dickinson must have learned from the poetesses is the stated or implied question, emphasizing the speaker's inability to understand nature fully: "The tidy Breezes, with their Brooms / Sweep vale—and hill—and tree! / Prithee, My pretty Housewives! / Who may expected be?" writes Dickinson. Sigourney asks the stream, "Stream! why is thy rushing step delayed?" "O helpless body of hickory tree, / What do I burn, in burning thee?" asks Helen Hunt Jackson. And Dickinson: "What tenements of clover / are fitting for the bee." Dickinson uses several such techniques to diffuse the impact of her own lyric subjectivity; in fact, some of the very qualities that have made Dickinson seem so utterly alone and anomalous among "poets" are the qualities she shares with the invisible tradition of the poetesses.

But Emily Dickinson, as a female poet, was a very lonely figure in the American poetic landscape during most of the twentieth century. In the five decades following New Criticism, the once-thriving classic tradition of women's poetry had been torn apart. As Sandra Gilbert and Susan Gubar explain in their essay "Forward into the Past" (1983), the price of poetic success for any woman after mid-century has been to despise virtually all pre-twentieth-century poetry by women, ignoring the similarities between Dickinson, not to mention H.D. and Gertrude Stein, and the poetesses. Feminist poets who came of age in the 1960s and 1970s distanced themselves from the poetesses because of subject matter as well as form. In the postmodern climate of the 1980s and 1990s, the hermetic tradition of Stein and H.D. pushed the poetesses even further distant on the basis of accessibility, while the intimate connections between Dickinson and the poetesses continued to be ignored.

But even in the late twentieth century, the poetess tradition continued to live on in unlikely places. Marianne Moore's quirky approach to description and Elizabeth Bishop's discomfort with using simile and metaphor both have their roots in poetess poetics. More recently, Carolyn Kizer has made her link with poetess poetics a conscious, if an ambivalent, one. In her long poem "Pro Femina," Kizer writes:

I will speak about women of letters, for I'm in the racket . . .
Our biggest successes to date? Old maids to a woman.

Carolyn Kizer.
(© *Christopher Felver/Corbis*)

And our saddest conspicuous failures?
    The married spinsters
On loan to the husbands they treated
    like surrogate fathers.
Think of that crew of self-pitiers, not
    very distant,
Who carried the torch for themselves
    and got first-degree burns.
Or the sad sonneteers,
    toast-and-teasdales we loved
    at thirteen;
Middle-aged virgins seducing the
    puerile anthologists
Through lust-of-the-mind;
    barbituate-drenched Camilles
With continuous periods, murmuring
    softly on sofas
When poetry wasn't a craft but a
    sickly effluvium,
The air thick with incense, musk, and
    emotional blackmail.

Kizer's description here leads to an attack on poetesses like Teasdale and Millay, both childless, married to older businessman husbands, and eventually suicidal. Yet the number of lines that Kizer devotes to these "conspicuous failures" shows how impossible it is for her to ignore them completely, and her tirade incorporates a note of compassion for the early-twentieth-century poetesses' attempt to combine heterosexual love with artistic freedom.

While Kizer's connection with the poetess tradition is made ironically clear in "Pro Femina," numerous other contemporary poets, both well-known and unknown, also write in ways that are influenced less self-consciously by sentimentism. Jorie Graham's use of natural objects such as butterflies and flowers as starting points for meditations on subjectivity, Lucille Clifton's use of direct emotional statement and repetition, and Louise Glück's use of dialogue with nature in her book *The Wild Iris* are just a few examples. At the same time, male writers who participated directly in the poetess tradition, such as Henry Wadsworth Longfellow, with his careful craft and conscious artificiality, and Edgar Allan Poe (friend and reviewer of many poetesses), with his intense, palpable verbal repetition, are beginning to be reevaluated as well.

It may be no coincidence that the work of the poetesses is starting to enjoy a revival in an age dominated by postmodernist ideas about the contingency and fluidity of the self, because in many respects the work of the poetesses is oddly consistent with the tenets of late-twentieth-century experimental poetry. The poetesses do not write

381

with the same kind of "I" that romantic poets do; instead, they imbue their lyrics with multiple interacting voices and perspectives, both human and natural. The poetess does not objectify the natural world with the proprietary ease of the romantic poet. Instead, she approaches nature with multiple points of view and continual questioning. She is just as likely to objectify herself as to objectify the natural world. But the product of the poetess's diffuse subjectivity is not the fragmented presentation of self and nature that characterizes so much postmodern writing. For the poetesses, a fluid self is not linked to outer chaos; in fact, self-diffusion may only be possible insofar as the outer world is perceived as a stable place linked by natural cycles and the ties of community.

The sentimentist women poets have been relegated to silence because their poetry threatens the most basic tenets of romanticism. Their poems call into question the importance and solidity of the individual self, the possibility of objectifying nature, and the fundamental alienation of self from the world. Insofar as the poetess poetic tradition involves particular techniques and strategies that are markedly different from those of the romantic and postromantic poetic traditions, a poet such as Sara Teasdale is a poetess; Elizabeth Barrett Browning, who adopted many of the strategies of romanticism, is not; and Dickinson falls somewhere in between. From Lydia Sigourney through Leonie Adams, the poetesses have been united not so much by an interest in common subject matter as by a consistent alternative approach to the lyric poem that relies on "antiromantic" or "sentimentist" assumptions that run counter to current standards of literary value.

For exactly these reasons, the "poetesses" offer a valuable strategy of renewal for poets in the twenty-first century, particularly for women poets who need a new way to connect with pre-twentieth-century poetic traditions.

In a cycle of self-fulfilling prophecies, poetess poetry has been so routinely dismissed as trivial and inferior over the last 150 years that it is difficult to gain the critical distance to even begin to read it on its own terms, apart from the criteria established by romantic dominance. Yet it is important to attempt do so, for three reasons: the fresh perspective the poetess tradition offers from which to view romanticism, the light that understanding of poetess aesthetics can shed on the practices of a range of canonical and contemporary poets, and the potential vitality of poetess poetics in its own right.

[*See also* Bishop, Elizabeth; Dickinson, Emily; Glück, Louise; Lazarus, Emma; Millay, Edna St. Vincent; Moore, Marianne; *and* Sentimental Literature.]

FURTHER READING

Gray, Janet, ed. *She Wields a Pen: American Women Poets of the Nineteenth Century.* Iowa City, Iowa, 1997.

Mandell, Laura. "The Poetess Tradition." *Romanticism on the Net* 29–30 (February–May 2003) <www.sul.stanford.edu/mirrors/romnet>.

Sherman, Joan R. *African-American Poetry of the Nineteenth Century: An Anthology.* Urbana, Ill., 1992.

Walker, Cheryl, ed. *American Women Poets of the Nineteenth Century: An Anthology.* New Brunswick, N.J., 1992.

MARIE PONSOT

by Marilyn Hacker

In her poetry, Marie Ponsot negotiates an edgy territory of loss and discovers that it shares a border with the breathtaking landscape of intellectual freedom. The skill of her prosody is such that one need not remark upon it. A careful reader notices that her words mean what they have always said: every inflection and connotation rippling through the common usage from a point of origin has been accounted for. She teaches us thought's verbal

Marie Ponsot.
(*Photograph by Eleanor M. Hamilton*)

anatomies the way a mother (she would permit the simile) teaches what she knows, not from a syllabus but in the context of conversation, storytelling, even admonition: loving discourse. Ponsot's poetry is always demanding, but it is never "difficult" in the contemporary critical sense. Rigorous and generous with readers, it is unsparing in what it indicates as it shares what it loves.

One of the delicious paradoxes of Marie Ponsot's work is its examination of the double consciousness of a writer who is bilingual (English and French, with a strong background in Latin) in culture as well as in usage, but in whose writing that profoundly international culture is annealed to a very specific sense of place. Though Paris and other French, North African, and varied North American landscapes are significant in her work, Ponsot is primarily one of the most eloquent poets of New York City, one who can be placed alongside Hart Crane, Muriel Rukeyser, and Frank O'Hara in her realization of an urban poetics, in the way in which her work inhabits and is inhabited by this city in particular. For Ponsot, New York is not only Manhattan but that "other" New York of "the outer boroughs," in her case Queens, where she grew up, and where she spent decades teaching at Queens College and raising, mostly single-handedly, her seven children.

SOURCES AND RESOURCES

The poet was born Marie Birmingham in New York City on 21 April 1921; her parents, William and Marie

(Candee) Birmingham, were a wine and spirits importer and a schoolteacher, of families long established in the city. She has one brother. At first educated in the New York public school system, she received her B.A. degree from St. Joseph's College for Women in Brooklyn, New York, in 1940 (at age nineteen) and an M.A. degree from Columbia University in seventeenth-century English literature in 1941. She lived and worked on her own in Manhattan during the war years—from bookselling at Brentano's to being a production manager of juvenile books at Thomas Crowell and Company—writing and reading in the ferment of new voices, the emergence of the first literally postmodernist generation. Possibly the figures in the "classic" modernist movement to have the greatest presence in her development were H.D. and Djuna Barnes, both marginalized by their gender and life choices and the emerging epic ambitions of their work, and both of whose books the young poet purchased, read, and reflected upon (and both of whom appear themselves as tutelary figures in her mature work). The young poet read H.D.'s *Trilogy* (1946) as its volumes were published, and this confrontation of a woman poet with quotidian life and spiritual quest in wartime may have helped Ponsot form her own lifetime concern, in her work, with the connections between public events, private life, and the broader and less predictable life of the mind. The presence of Joyce's ludic and radical derangement of language in Ponsot's work is also indubitable and warmly acknowledged. An early poem, "Private and Profane," names some of the other figures in her intellectual hagiography: Mary Wortley Montague, John Skelton, Mathias Grünewald, Mozart, Couperin, St. Thomas Aquinas, John Donne, Jane Austen (perhaps also Montaigne and William Blake). But the war years were also the time when her pacifist convictions were both tested and examined and in which she found the resource of engagement with the pacifist *Catholic Worker* newspaper, cofounded by Dorothy Day.

In 1948 she went to Paris, where she pursued postgraduate studies at the Sorbonne and worked as an archivist for UNESCO. It was on the boat to France that she made the acquaintance of another young poet, Lawrence Ferlinghetti, who would, eight years later, publish her first book. In Paris she met the painter Claude Ponsot, whom she married in December 1948; their first child, Monique, was born there in September of the following year. The family then moved to New York, living first in Little Italy and then in Jamaica, Queens. Six more children, all boys, were born between 1951 and 1962.

Ponsot had been writing poems since her childhood, and as *Springing* (2002), her volume of new, selected, and uncollected poems shows, her mature style, with its modulations, its prosodic fine-tuning, its concentric ripples of context, was more than implicit in poems she wrote in her twenties. But she was (and still is) reticent about publication. It was the good taste of her fellow former expatriate Lawrence Ferlinghetti—who had founded San Francisco's City Lights Bookshop and its accompanying publishing venture—that brought her work into print. *True Minds*, solicited by Ferlinghetti, was published in 1956 in his Pocket Poets series, best known for (in the same year) the publication of Allen Ginsberg's *Howl* (1956) but also of books by Denise Levertov and Frank O'Hara.

The serendipitous incongruity of Marie Ponsot's work first appearing in the context of the Beat explosion leads a reader to think of her in the context of her astounding generation of American poets, those born in the 1920s. Ginsberg, O'Hara, Levertov, Hayden Carruth, James Wright, Carolyn Kizer, Anthony Hecht, James Merrill, W. S. Merwin, Jane Cooper, and John Ashbery are only some of them: the range of approaches, contexts, connections, ruptures, and evolutions in style seems infinite, as does their breadth of development and response and reaction to what had become the modernist canon. While most of these poets were and are involved in schools, movements, circles of literary criticism and influence, Ponsot has made her own, initially fairly isolated, way, though her prodigious and continual reading has connected her with all the possibilities—the choices of her contemporaries, the parallel development of pre- and postwar French writing and of Irish writing, but also, perennially, English, French, and Latin poetry of the preceding centuries. The "argument" (particularly in the sense of "dialogue") and reconciliation of past and present are constant undercurrents in her poetry, whatever the primary theme.

AN EXIGENT CAREER

In the years following the publication of *True Minds*, Marie Ponsot wrote much, published little of her own, and began a parallel career as a translator of works ranging from classic fairy tales (her fascination with tales and fables transfigured what would have been mere bread-and-butter work for another writer) to verse drama by Paul Claudel for radio broadcast. There was a sequence of poems in *Poetry* duly acknowledged by a prize. There was a divorce. In 1965 Ponsot published her verse translations of a significant selection of La Fontaine's *Fables* with Signet Books (reissued in 2002 by Welcome Rain Press). The project of a verse translation of the *Lais* of Marie de France did not survive the loss of the manuscript-in-progress.

In 1966, as a single mother of seven, Marie Ponsot began what was to become a passionately committed teaching career, in the SEEK program at Queens College. She remained at Queens College for thirty years (eventually as a tenured full professor) and continues to teach in the graduate writing programs at New York University and Columbia University as well as at the 92nd Street Y. Her teaching commitment began and has always been rooted in the teaching of composition (which in her mind is in no way different in kind from the teaching of "creative writing"). It led her to coauthor, with her colleague the scholar and writer Rosemary Deen, two invaluable and practical texts on the teaching of composition (useful for any writer, at any time): *Beat Not the Poor Desk* and *The Common Sense*, published by the Boynton Press in 1981 and 1985, respectively. In 1986 she spent a semester teaching in mainland China.

In 1981, Alfred A. Knopf published *Admit Impediment*—whose title wryly indicated its connection with and disjunction from the earlier volume. But while the first collection had been chapbook-brief, the new book, the work of a woman in the prime of life, was polyvalent and generous in its scope as well as in its length, in its formal, intellectual, and affective claims for the possibilities of poetry. *The Green Dark* was published in 1988 and *The Bird Catcher* in 1998; the latter received the National Book Critics Circle Award, and an article by Dinitia Smith about the poet in *The New York Times* signaled the beginning of an overdue critical acclaim. *Springing*, published in the spring of 2002, includes—as well as work completed since *The Bird Catcher*—previously unpublished or uncollected poems, many written between the publication of *True Minds* and the poems gathered in *Admit*

Impediment; these are the work of a mature poet in her late thirties and forties, firm in her art but at that time apparently reticent about publication.

Ponsot is, despite the spacing of her book publications, a prolific poet, but she is a near-unbelievably exigent one, who will keep drafts of a significant work in progress for years, if necessary, until she is satisfied with it; who will even withdraw poems that have been published in journals from a book manuscript in progress for reworking she deems necessary. Apart from the demands of her life as a young and then a single mother, it was this, and not any sparseness of the work itself, that resulted in the wide spacing of her first four published books.

KNOWLEDGE AS A SOURCE OF JOY

Although Ponsot's work has not yet been extensively discussed in the context of second-wave American feminism, even by feminist critics, or made part of the feminist literary "canon," its assumptions, and even more the questions it poses, place it in that line (though never to the exclusion of other investigations). The poet considers the role of women in history, including the recovery of lost or insufficiently studied figures like Jacqueline Pascal (the poet and sister of Blaise, silenced in the Jansenist convent of Port-Royal) or Elena Cornaro (a seventeenth-century Italian, the first woman doctor of philosophy), but also the meaning of all women's exclusion from traditions of exploration and exchange. From her first book on, she observes and verbally constructs childbirth and mothering as essential human endeavors, not apart from but essential to the ongoing examined life and examined mind. A variety of ordinary women are given speech in her poems, often only discreetly indicated as dramatic monologues by the presence of quotation marks framing the text. Neither men nor women (nor children) are reified in her work: sexuality is appreciated but divested of what she aptly names "the usual criminal metaphors."

Ponsot is a gardener and a birdwatcher, both of which are endeavors that imply a concentration of attention, a fine-tuning of observation, that are essential to her work as a poet. Poems such as "Gliding" (hang-gliders in the Alpes-Maritimes), "Pourriture Noble" (the creation of Sauternes), or "In Abeyance" (the migration of hawks above upstate New York) amaze the reader with the acuity of the poet's knowledge of how and why something happens, so that these events are never reduced to the facility of metaphor or simile, whatever other or larger human instance they may also imply. And it is because of (not despite) the poet's polymath range of knowledge,

because of the way she, teacher and mother, makes clear what she knows, that her work, while often complex and seldom predictable, remains not merely accessible but a source of joy and discovery to a wide range of readers.

While numerous reviewers have called attention to Ponsot's virtuoso performances in renewing received forms such as terza rima, the sonnet (and crown of sonnets), villanelle and sestina, *rimas dissolutas*, and the Gaelic rann, not enough attention has been paid to her genius as a creator of nonce forms, in complex, sometimes long poems that visually resemble "free verse" but in which the reader aurally perceives patterns of meter, rhyme, and sonority that structure a complex progression of mental discovery. Even in elegies, her genius and penchant for wordplay are irrepressible—as if the human penchant for structuring words and syntax were, as it may well be, the mind's only bastion against death's annihilation. Death itself is disarmed in her poems by turns of phrase: "A decade, a week a second, then / time shrugs and shudders out of touch / into a perfect fit / and that's it" ("I've Been Around, It Gets Me Nowhere").

Marie Ponsot is at once a poet eminently of her time, whose work bridges the assimilation of and resistance to modernism in contemporary anglophone poetry, and one whose work is comprehensible as part of the ongoing enterprise of poetry as she understands it, not limited to national borders or even to the English language but an irreplaceable part of what defines the human mind and the human community.

WORKS

True Minds (1956)
Admit Impediment (1981)
Beat Not the Poor Desk (with Rosemary Deen) (1981)
The Common Sense (with Rosemary Deen) (1985)
The Green Dark (1988)
The Bird Catcher (1998)
Springing (2002)

FURTHER READING

Boland, Eavan. Review of *The Green Dark. Commonweal* (4 November 1988).

Dillingham, Thomas F. Review of *Admit Impediment. Open Places* (Fall 1982).

Gilbert, Sandra. Review of *The Bird Catcher. Women's Review of Books* (October 1998).

Howard, Richard. "Poetry Unyoked." *The Nation* (20 March 1982). Review of *Admit Impediment.*

Ivry, Benjamin. Review of *The Bird Catcher. PIF* magazine (online) and *Time Out: New York.*

Jacobsen, Josephine. "Flexible Flyer." *The Nation* (28 May 1988). Review of *The Green Dark*.

Jacobsen, Josephine. Review of *Admit Impediment. Commonweal* (6 November 1981).

Jalon, Allan. "A Poet's Progress." *Los Angeles Times* (April 2002). Review of *Springing*.

Margaronis, Maria. Review of *The Green Dark. Voice Literary Supplement* (1988).

Orr, David. "What's Not a Poem Has Been Discarded." *New York Times Book Review* (21 April 2002). Review of *Springing*.

Ostriker, Alicia. Review of *Admit Impediment. 13th Moon* (1982).

Smith, Dinitia. "Recognition at Last for Poet of Elegant Complexity." *New York Times* (13 April 1999).

POPULAR FICTION

by John Sutherland

Insofar as the distinction holds, literary fiction roots itself inextricably in popular fiction: materially, aesthetically, culturally, and economically. The energies of fiction surge up; they rarely trickle down. The novel, a late-arriving literary form, required a massive and literate readership, sophisticated productive and distributive apparatus, large investments of venture capital on one side, and considerable amounts of disposable income on the other. Fiction is, as Ian Watt argued half a century ago, the child born of capitalism and the natural partner of commercialism.

Popular fiction is, essentially, a fast-selling, high-volume product that, typically, leaves little or no residue (who now reads the book "everyone" was reading in 1933, *Anthony Adverse*?). Rate-of-sale and replaceability (this year's best-sellers are rarely last year's) are two key criteria. For these reasons, best-sellers, as the term is conventionally applied, might better be called fast-sellers.

America was peculiarly suited for the development of a popular-fiction industry and its most dynamic manifestation, best- (or fast-) sellerism. As a country, America came into being at the same time as the rise of the novel. With their revolutionary declarations, the new state's founders enshrined freedom of expression. There was (unlike in Europe) no tradition of state control over literature. Commercial control via privilege or monopoly is similarly absent from American literary culture, historically considered. America has never imposed (apart from a brief attempt in 1915) any system of retail price maintenance such as Great Britain's Net Book Agreement, devised to discourage entrepreneurial "underselling"—in other words, competition.

America has enjoyed (and, typically, invented) the world's advanced printing, transport, and communication technologies. Most important, in its formative nineteenth-century phase, and until the early 1890s, the American book trade was unfettered by any adherence to protocols of international copyright. It was in the happy position of being able to plunder mature European—principally British—literary cultures at will. Frank Luther Mott's "Over-all Best Sellers in the United States" uses for its survey the calculus of "a total sale equal to one percent of the population of the continental United States for the decade in which it was published." Mott lists, by this finicky reckoning, 124 best-selling "American" novels, in the period from 1776 to 1900. Of those, 74 are British, 15 mainland European (mainly French), and a mere 55 are native products. Volume sales are impossible to calculate: but the biggest-selling titles were, by trade anecdotal evidence, overseas authors—Sir Walter Scott, Charles Dickens, Eugene Sue, Grace Aguilar, Edward Bulwer-Lytton, Daphne DuMaurier, Robert Louis Stevenson, H. Rider Haggard, Sir Hall Caine, and Marie Corelli.

The rampant expansion of the American book trade in that crucial century arose from being able to concentrate on selling rather than originating its products. For the American bookman, the main task was not the cultivation of authors but the capture of customers. Typically, this was done by speedy delivery, gimmickry, high-powered advertising, and—most important—by lowering retail costs to dirt-cheap level. A novel such as *The Last Days of Pompeii* (1834) cost a deterring guinea and a half in England. In America, Bulwer-Lytton's (pirated) novel would, typically, be available as a new novel in various imprints at well under a dollar.

During the Civil War, the most popular reading matter among combatants on both sides of the conflict were pirated copies of *Les Misérables*. It is probably the most bloodstained novel in the history of literature. Scant remuneration returned from the American battlefield to the Victor Hugo estate. Mrs. Humphry Ward's *Robert Elsmere* (1888) was the best-selling novel of the century in its home territory. Her British royalties, from tens of thousands of British sales, made the author rich. The revenues from millions of sales in America (where, as a final indignity, her masterpiece ended up being given away free with bars of soap) were, by contrast, a few hundred dollars—a pittance that she grandly, if impotently, spurned. With Congress voting to observe international copyright regulation in April 1891, Ward's next novel, *The History of David Grieve* (1892), earned her a record-breaking seven-thousand-pound advance—on the strength of its surefire American popularity.

Three nineteenth-century events stand out as landmarks in American popular fiction. The first is the Walter Scott mania from 1814 to 1832. The Wizard of the North's spell extended across the Atlantic. Scott was, in the first half of the century, *the* American best-seller. That mania was succeeded, seamlessly, by the Dickens mania. Dickens, like other English writers, was not charmed to be popular but unremunerated; he repaid his loyal transatlantic readers with the venomous *American Notes*. These sales bonanzas forged and organized a market for popular fiction—a vacuum sucking in quantities of overseas material and gradually encouraging the growth of domestic talent.

As important as the pirate haul is what is called the "great revolution" in American bookselling, namely the distribution in the 1840s of novels as twenty-five-cent (or less) "extras"—off-printed supplements sold with newspapers. The innovation is credited to two New York journalists, Park Benjamin and Rufus Wilmot Griswold. The extras consolidated a mass-market readership for good, new fiction at a throwaway price.

Logically, it was in America that the first best-seller list originated—a wonderful instrument both for recording popularity and stimulating it. The chart of "Books in Order of Demand" (preeminently novels) was the brainchild of Harry Thurston Peck, in the *Bookman*, in 1895. Old habits died hard—seven out of the top ten novels listed in the first year were of British origin. The term "best-seller" is first recorded as coming into use in 1902. The most reliable, and long-lived, of the best-seller lists was launched in *Publisher's Weekly* in 1912.

Other innovations were pioneered in America in the twentieth century. "Pulp fiction" originated with Frank A. Munsey's *All-Story Magazine*, which had achieved a circulation of half a million by 1907 and helped launch the careers of Zane Grey, Edgar Rice Burroughs, and Max Brand. It was in America that mail-order bookselling perfected itself with the establishment of the Book of the Month Club (BOMC) and the Literary Guild, in 1926 and 1927. In 1933 the first "blockbuster," *Anthony Adverse*, topped the best-seller list for two years (boosted by a tie-in movie, massive advertising, and BOMC adoption).

The mass-market paperback was pioneered in America with Robert de Graff's Pocket Books in 1939. Like the book club, the twenty-five-cent paperback—which could be retailed in drug stores or on newsstands—circumvented the traditional bookshop. The "quality" or "glossy" paperback in the 1960s added new impetus to de Graff's

innovation, as did the sophisticated, "synergistically" tied-in novels and "novelizations" of the later twentieth century (was *Star Wars* a movie, a novelization, a comic-book line, or a multiproduct franchise?). Finally, under American commercial auspices, came the internet bookstore in the late 1990s.

There is no advance in the merchandising of books—preeminently popular fiction—which America has not either pioneered or perfected. This is the background against which the following chronological survey should be set.

PREHISTORY: 1790–1900

The long history of the American novel starts with the republication of Susanna Haswell Rowson's tale of female trial, *Charlotte Temple* (1794; first published in London in 1791). With its New York setting, and two hundred identified editions over the next century, this novel can be seen as the first American popular novel.

The market for fiction, from the Revolution to the mid-nineteenth century, was largely supplied by London. Nonetheless, some distinctly national flavors can be detected. Riding the wave of the Waverley novels' extraordinary popularity, James Fenimore Cooper cannily "Americanized" Scott's romance formula. *The Last of the Mohicans* (1826) is seminal in many ways. As Scott had elegized the passing of the Celtic clan, Cooper elegized the passing of the indigenous American tribe. And in the character of its buckskin-clad frontiersman (a clear derivative of Scott's Rob Roy) Cooper patented the most durable heroic type in American popular fiction.

Arguably the first popular American novel to break away from the Scott mold is Daniel P. Thompson's *The Green Mountain Boys* (1839). This tale of land-grabbing and a bloody feud in Revolution-period Vermont was published through fifty editions in twenty years and spawned imitations. But by most definitions the first "true" American best-seller is Harriet Beecher Stowe's *Uncle Tom's Cabin* (1852). The novel sold amazingly—the demand for ten thousand copies a week wore out the publishers' presses. Stowe can also be seen as creating what would be a vital and enduring link between the American best-seller and the American social conscience. "What an accursed thing slavery is!" her novel asserts. The other best-selling work of the nineteenth century that can be said to have had a visibly social effect is Edward Bellamy's *Looking Backward* (1888)—a work which, like William Morris's concurrent *A Dream of John Ball* (1888) and *News from Nowhere* (1890), domesticated utopian socialism for a mass market.

Popular fiction, as does literary fiction, oscillates restlessly between poles of engagement and escapism, realism and romance. Women novelists, less polemical and socially engaged than Stowe, "feminized" the early 1850s with popular works such as Susan Warner's *The Wide, Wide World* (1850), Caroline Lee Hentz's *The Planter's Northern Bride* (1854; a romantic retort to Stowe), Maria S. Cummins's *The Lamplighter* (1854), Mary Jane Holmes's *Tempest and Sunshine* (1854), and Augusta J. Evans's *Beulah* (1859). These works were overpoweringly sentimental and aimed principally at the American woman reader (often in her leisurely, premarital teens). They derive, clearly enough, from the governess plot of Charlotte Brontë's *Jane Eyre* (itself a derivative of Richardson). Byronic heroes and masterful guardians (ultimately destined to be husbands) are as recurrent as orphan girls (destined, of course, to be maiden brides).

Few items from the "Feminized Fifties" survive. More durable, culturally, were the "dime novels," pioneered by the enterprising publisher Beadle and Adams in the early 1860s. Cheapness and portability were the principal attractions of these modern chapbooks that, like their ancestors, required no bookshop to reach their readers. They were also the soil from which two of the twentieth-century mass-market genres sprang. The "Western" was the dime novel's staple subject. The first of them was, surprisingly, the composition of a woman, Mrs. Ann S. Stephens, with *Malaeska, the Indian Wife of the White Hunter* (1860). Among other best-selling (and much imitated) dime novels were Edward S. Ellis's *Seth Jones* (1860) and the Deadwood and Buffalo Bill Cody series (by many hands) of the 1870s.

As the titles indicate, these were proto-Westerns. Dime novels were also, two decades later, the literary vehicle for proto-detective fiction with the Nick Carter series. The young crime buster survived, in pulps, radio serials, comic books, and films into the 1960s—still young at the age of one hundred twenty. He was also the creation of many hands—most notably Frederic Van Rensselaer Dey, author of more than two hundred Nick Carter stories (typically portraying him in combat with the similarly indestructible series villain, Doc Quartz). A conventional starting point for the American detective novel proper is Anna Katharine Green's *The Leavenworth Case* (1878), a whodunit that introduced the immensely successful series hero, Ebenezer Gryce.

By the 1870s, American popular fiction had cultivated a remarkable speed of response to current events—as witnessed by E. P. Roe's best-seller set against the great Chicago fire of 1871, *Barriers Burned Away* (1872). Newspaper headlines would regularly supply material for opportunistic writers over the next century. But there were constituencies other than newspaper readers to cater to. Ever since its foundation, America had been a Bible-reading population. Lew Wallace's *Ben-Hur: A Tale of the Christ* (1880), one of the biggest sellers of the late nineteenth century, was that useful thing: a novel that could be read on Sunday. The other religious superseller of the period, Charles Monroe Sheldon's *In His Steps* (1897), was estimated to have racked up cumulative sales of over six million dollars by 1945.

On the fringe of the religious market for fiction were such essentially improving works for children as Louisa May Alcott's *Little Women* (1868) and, more spectacularly, the rags-to-riches fables of Horatio Alger. A Unitarian minister, Alger infused evangelical fervor into such Social Darwinistic tracts as *Ragged Dick; or, Street Life in New York with the Boot-blacks* (1868) and *Mark the Match Boy* (1869) or—most challengingly to the aspirant youth of America—*Abraham Lincoln, the Backwoods Boy; or, How a Young Rail-splitter Became President* (1883).

Famously, Ernest Hemingway declared that all genuinely American fiction can be tracked back to Twain's *Adventures of Huckleberry Finn* (1884). Its primacy lay in its having forged a distinctly vernacular idiom for subsequent novelists. One can, however, point to earlier popular works, appealing through their comic use of regional dialects, such as the Hoosier tales of Edward Eggleston. These antipastorals, with their authentically registered Indiana speech, enjoyed huge success—most of all *The Hoosier School-Master* (1871).

Émile Zola had an easier ride into American popular culture than into England (where his luckless publisher was imprisoned). Works such as *Nana* (1880) were bestsellers, and American Zolaism took off with Stephen Crane's *Maggie: A Girl of the Streets* (1893). It would reach its apogee with Upton Sinclair's *j'accuse!* about the Chicago stockyards, *The Jungle* (1906). He had, Sinclair ruefully observed, aimed for the conscience of America and succeeded only in kicking it in the stomach. Patrons would, over the next century, regularly pay good money for similar kickings.

THE EARLY TWENTIETH CENTURY

The twentieth century opened with what was plausibly claimed to be the fastest-selling novel of all time, Irving Bacheller's *Eben Holden* (1900). It was, appropriately for the period, a romance of immigration. Bacheller's novel was propelled by dynamic advertising. Hype, as it would later be called, also helped make Maurice Thompson's *Alice of Old Vincennes*—a historical romance set in Revolutionary times—the number one novel in overall sales for the first year of the new century.

The twentieth century's accelerated tempo was reflected in a market appetite for short, quickly consumed literature. This appetite for short stories made possible the huge success of O. Henry, the "Yankee Maupassant." William Sydney Porter, the man behind the nom de plume, had begun writing his fiction while a prisoner, on charges of embezzlement, in 1901—something on which even Alger could scarcely have improved.

Arguably, the most momentous event for popular fiction in the twentieth century happened outside the booktrade. The "motion picture" became a marketable commodity with *The Great Train Robbery* (a dime novel narrative) in 1903. The "movies" would transform the popular entertainment industry. The "King of the Adventure Writers," Rex Beach (the "poor man's Jack London"), regularly crested the *Bookman* best-seller lists in the early years of the century with his Alaskan Adventures, tales of the Yukon gold strikes, which began with *Pardners* (1905). Shrewdly, Beach set up his own film company to exploit his property. The modern tie-in was born.

As John G. Cawelti (1976) has argued, "melodrama" is a thick strand in twentieth-century American popular fiction. The large, sweeping "melodrama" was exploited, with spectacular success in the early years of the century, by Winston Churchill, whose string of big (in every sense) best-sellers began with *The Crisis* (1901). Churchill's popularity peaked with *A Far Country* (1915), the bildungsroman of an American prodigal son, Hugh Paret, from error-strewn boyhood to manly maturity. Churchill's formula can be traced down to such later exponents of the high melodramatic style as James T. Farrell, John O'Hara, and Herman Wouk.

Less ambitiously than Churchill, Booth Tarkington popularized the trials of adolescence in wry comic studies such as *Penrod* (1914) and *Seventeen* (1916). The young reader had always been more of a force in the United States than in Europe. And with eighteen-year-olds dying by the hundred thousand in France between 1914 and 1918, Tarkington's idylls had an added escapist charm.

World War I provoked a surge of Anglophilia in the American best-selling lists. The years 1924 and 1925 saw American lists dominated by Percival Christopher Wren's *Beau Geste* (1925; prototype of innumerable, preposterous Foreign Legion romances), P. G. Wodehouse's ultra-English butler-comedy *Jeeves* (1923), E. M. Hull's triumphant sequel, *The Sons of the Sheik* (1925; *The Sheik* had been filmed in 1921, starring Rudolph Valentino), Michael Arlen's cosmopolitan comedy *The Green Hat* (1924), Margaret Kennedy's *The Constant Nymph* (1924; a work which distantly inspired Vladimir Nabokov's 1958 superseller, *Lolita*), and Warwick Deeping's "returned hero" saga, *Sorrell and Son* (1925). Not since 1891 had British popular fiction so coincided with American taste. The English strain continued, if less predominantly, through the following decades with best-selling works such as James Hilton's *The Lost Horizon* (1933) and *Good-Bye Mr. Chips* (1934).

Nationalist themes were also prominent in the aftermath of the war. Edna Ferber inaugurated what would become a string of American epics with *So Big*, the number one novel of 1925. Ferber's consistently popular (and massive) novels included *Show Boat* (1926; adapted into an even more popular musical, by Jerome Kern and Oscar Hammerstein), and concluded almost three decades later with *Giant* (1952), the dynastic saga of two generations of Texans. This last work was filmed in 1956, starring James Dean, Rock Hudson and Elizabeth Taylor. Ferber's twelve novels and nine plays were made into twenty films.

The 1920s witnessed a qualitative high point of bestsellerism: a rare convergence of literary and popular. Representative of this temporary trend is the number one title of 1927, Thornton Wilder's *The Bridge of San Luis Rey*. The narrative begins with a (historical) bridge collapse in Peru, on 20 July 1714, and goes on to reconstruct the (fictional) lives of the five travelers killed in the disaster. Wilder's novel was a runaway success, with sixteen editions called for in six months. Wilder headed the American best-seller lists again almost ten years later with *Heaven's My Destination*, a Voltairean satire on Sinclair Lewis's blast against "the religion business" (predatory evangelism), *Elmer Gantry* (1927). Lewis's un-Voltairean novel was itself a number one title, selling 200,000 copies in its first week of publication.

One of the interesting subgenres of popular fiction in the 1920s was the so-called "sex novel"—a light confection combining raciness, urban sophistication, and Jazz Age flapperdom. The best of these works, and another novel of quality, was Anita Loos's *Gentlemen Prefer Blondes* (1925). Adapted from a *Harper's Bazaar* serial (written in deliciously comic semiliterate style), it pioneered a gallery of enduring sexual stereotypes. The story was filmed (starring, inevitably, Marilyn Monroe) in 1953. Loos's novel topped the 1926 lists with the equally deft comic fantasia *The Private Life of Helen of Troy* by John Erskine. Other sex novels of the period—less noteworthy—are Vina Delmar's *Bad Girl* (1928; the bad girl of the title is Dot Haley, a telephone operator of loose morals) and Donald Henderson Clarke's *Impatient Virgin* (1931). These novels widened the aperture of permissibility—something spectacularly exploited in Erskine Caldwell's steamy sex-and-southern-squalor tales, *God's Little Acre* (1933) and *Tobacco Road* (1932).

There are, largely, five main categories of genre fiction (romance, Westerns, detective, science fiction, and male action). The most venerable is romance, following a direct line from *Charlotte Temple* to Danielle Steel, catering mainly to the woman reader. The primal male action genre—rooted in the dime novel—is the Western, or cowboy romance (with its many variations of setting). Owen Wister, author of *The Virginian*, declared the West to be "the great playground of young men." It would be the favorite location for male readers of all ages. Wister supplied the blueprint for Zane Grey (a Munsey stalwart), who went on to produce such best-sellers as *Riders of the Purple Sage* (1912) and *The Lone Star Ranger* (1915). For a decade Grey could claim to be the most popular novelist in the English-speaking world. Lifetime sales of his novels (boosted by reciprocating pulp and celluloid versions) are estimated at two-hundred fifty million. His roughly sixty novels produced over one hundred twenty film adaptations.

Trailing behind Grey in the early decades of the twentieth century were creators of series heroes such as Clarence E. Mulford's *Bar 20* cowpoke, Hopalong Cassidy (introduced in 1910 and played by William Boyd on the screen for twenty years). Street and Smith's *Western Story Magazine*, begun in 1919 and costing a talismanic dime, launched the career of Max Brand. With two hundred full-length novels to his credit (aided by his "red-hot typewriter"), Brand was one of the contenders in the 1920s and 1930s for the "King of the Pulps" title. Brand's successor as a mass producer of fictional "oaters" was Louis L'Amour, with one hundred four titles to his credit by the time of his death in 1988. Other distinguished performances in the genre include Ernest Haycox, whose *Stage to Lordsburg* (1937) was adapted into the classic John Ford film, *Stagecoach* (1939), with John Wayne as the Ringo Kid.

The third of the long-established genres is the detective story. The early decades of the twentieth century are seen as the golden age of this genre. S. S. Van Dine's patrician Philo Vance ("Lord Wimsey's American cousin") is one of myriad popular sleuth-heroes. It was Van Dine who introduced the famous "twenty rules" for golden-age detective fiction. The Anglophile taint was removed mainly through *Black Mask* magazine and the arrival of its new editor, Captain Joseph T. Shaw, in 1926. This magazine pioneered the hardboiled detectives and the private-eye thrillers of Dashiell Hammett (whose *Maltese Falcon* introduced the archetypal Sam Spade in 1930), James M. Cain (whose noir masterpiece, *The Postman Always Rings Twice* came out in 1934), and Raymond Chandler (whose Philip Marlowe was introduced in 1939 with *The Big Sleep*). The "softer-boiled" line continued with Rex Stout's Nero Wolfe and his "Dr. Watson," Archie Goodwin.

As with Westerns, the productivity of the leaders in this genre was legendary. H. Bedford-Jones was, in the 1930s, selling a million a year under some ten pseudonyms. He graciously ceded his title "King of the Woodpulps" to Erle Stanley Gardner in March 1933, on receiving a complimentary copy of the first Perry Mason adventure, *The Case of the Velvet Claws*. Gardner, under his battery of pen names, would go on to sell over three hundred million copies of his crime and mystery novels over the next four decades. His detective defense lawyer Perry Mason (always his lead commodity) was given an even wider audience by the television series, starring Raymond Burr, from 1957 to 1966.

Science fiction (with its subgenres fantasy, horror, and Gothic) is the fourth of the great genre families. The patriarchal figure is Edgar Rice Burroughs. Burroughs as a young man had steeped himself in Darwin and manuals of self-help. These can be tracked in his most famous conception, *Tarzan of the Apes*, first published in *All-Story Magazine* in 1912. In 1912, Burroughs had brought out *John Carter of Mars*. His hollow-earth Pellucidar series was launched in 1914. With these best-selling products in his stable, the author incorporated himself in 1923 as Edgar Rice Burroughs Inc. He was, at this date, earning the then-fabulous sum of $100,000. Burroughs would go on to publish some seventy-five novels (many of which are still in print).

A purer form of science fiction was concocted in Hugo Gernsback's *Amazing Stories* (founded in 1926) and its great rival *Astounding Science Fiction* (founded in 1930). After being taken over by John W. Campbell in 1937, *Astounding Science Fiction* became the vehicle for the brightest talents in the genre, with the work of writers such as Isaac Asimov, Robert Heinlein, and Theodore Sturgeon.

A full anatomy of interwar genre would need to take into account such offshoots as war novels, thrillers, spy novels, and pornography. Although genre products rarely make it into the period's best-seller lists (Zane Grey and Edgar Rice Burroughs excepted), their effects can be traced easily enough. Gertrude Atherton's *Black Oxen*, the number one title of 1923, is an elixir of youth romance in which (fantastically) the antique heroine is restored to flapper youth by having her ovaries bombarded by "Dr. Steinach's new X-ray technique." The gimmick is patently borrowed from science fiction. Sometimes the borrowings were entirely cynical. William Faulkner (later a Nobel Prize–winner) composed *Sanctuary* (1931) by asking himself what would sell ten thousand copies in 1931, and then "invented the most horrific tale I could imagine and wrote it in about three weeks." The tale of sadistic rape and violence duly sold its expected quantity.

As genre diversified its energies of popular fiction elsewhere they went into the formation of what the booktrade would call "the blockbuster." One can conveniently mark its arrival with Hervey Allen's *Anthony Adverse* (1933). At twelve hundred pages, and costing three dollars, the publishers, Farrar and Rinehart, advertised the novel as "three books for the price of one." Boosted as a BOMC title and by the 1936 film, *Anthony Adverse* headed the American best-seller lists for two years. It sold an estimated six hundred thousand copies, in hardback, in four years.

The main line of top-selling titles through the 1930s remained the melodrama. Pearl S. Buck's saga of the self-improving Chinese peasant Wang Lung, *The Good Earth* (1931), earned her a Nobel Prize in 1938. An offshoot of melodrama, the doctor's tale, had emerged in 1935 with Lloyd C. Douglas's *The Green Light*, a "surgeon's dilemma" tale. This line of fiction was developed into an inexhaustibly popular genre in 1940 with the versatile Max Brand's *Calling Dr. Kildare*—the first of a series of narratives chronicling the trials of a young Irish-American physician, his wise old mentor, Dr. Leonard Gillespie, and the love of his life, nurse Mary Lamont. Kildare was adapted into the emergent television medium and was the procreator of such subsequent hits (on small screen and in novelization) as *Marcus Welby, M.D.*; *M*A*S*H*; and *ER*.

Not all doctors in popular fiction were saintly. Ambivalence about the profession was given memorable expression in Henry Bellamann's best-selling title of 1940, *Kings Row*, in which the villainous Dr. Gordon amputates (unnecessarily) the legs of a young man he considers ineligible as a suitor for his daughter. The novel was filmed in 1942, with Ronald Reagan as the luckless, limbless Drake McHugh, delivering his most famous line: "Where's the rest of me?" The depiction of the unrelenting malignity of small-town life in *Kings Row* anticipates Grace Metalious's 1956 superseller, *Peyton Place*.

Rarely have the poles of realism and romance been more divided than in the best-sellers of the late 1930s. Margaret Mitchell's *Gone with the Wind* (1936) was, like *Anthony Adverse* before it, the biggest blockbuster ever. Its canvas, taking in the Civil War, was panoramic. It was also, famously, "The Greatest Love Story of all Time" and the reticent Atlanta author's only published work. At one thousand seventy-three pages, it was vast and at three dollars costly. Mitchell's novel had achieved worldwide sales of nearly thirty million by the mid-1990s, boosted by the equally blockbusting 1939 film, starring Vivien Leigh and Clark Gable.

Alongside Mitchell's historical melodrama, John Steinbeck's social protest tract, *The Grapes of Wrath*, headed the 1939 best-seller list. The story of the Joad family's doomed odyssey from their parched Oklahoma farm to the false paradise of southern California promoted, with propagandistic urgency, the idealisms of Franklin Roosevelt's New Deal (crossed with the author's own idiosyncratic neo-Darwinism). Steinbeck's novel was filmed, with a disconcertingly upbeat ending, by John Ford in 1940.

The Second World War, as had its predecessor, propelled British authors such as A. J. Cronin and Richard Llewellyn to the top of the American best-seller list. The line of social seriousness introduced by Steinbeck was continued with such enraged number-one best-sellers as Lillian Smith's antilynching tract *Strange Fruit* (1944; dramatized in 1945 and subsequently immortalized by Billie Holiday's jazz vocal version) and Betty Smith's *A Tree Grows in Brooklyn* (1943). Also continued was the line of blockbusting escapist romance—most successfully with Kathleen Winsor's English civil war romp, *Forever Amber* (1944). The heroine, Amber St. Clare, sleeps with everyone—including the Merry Monarch. Her uncompromising motto is: "Adultery's no crime—it's an amusement." Millions of readers agreed.

POST–WORLD WAR II TO TODAY

In 1946, Robert Penn Warren produced what was, probably, the biggest seller of the immediate postwar period (by literary critical criteria) with his roman à clef based on the demagogue Huey Long, *All the King's Men*. World War II had, it seemed, made America thoughtful about the ideals its citizens were fighting for. National conscience was wrenched by Laura Z. Hobson's exposure of the discreet mechanisms of anti-Semitism in *Gentleman's Agreement*. The novel was filmed in 1947 by Elia Kazan, starring Gregory Peck as the journalist Philip Green, who pretends to be Jewish. The solemn film won three Oscars. There was, oddly, no serious best-seller about World War II from the serving soldier's point of view until Norman Mailer's *The Naked and the Dead* in 1948—a novel which broached new ground in explicitness (specifically with its "three-letter word"—"fug"). In 1951, James Jones's *From Here to Eternity* was the year's number one best-seller and Herman Wouk's *The Caine Mutiny* was number two. These novels aimed, as Jones put it, "to blow the lid of the war."

A more ponderous approach to "great issues" was evident in the saga of the Apostle Peter, *The Big Fisherman* by Lloyd C. Douglas, which topped best-seller lists in 1948. Douglas was a Lutheran minister before becoming a popular novelist. His 1942 best-seller, about the most sacred relic of the Crucifixion, *The Robe*, was filmed—in the grand Cecil B. DeMille Technicolor style—in 1953.

Crime fiction was, in the mid-1940s, even "harder boiled" than it had been in the trendsetting *Black Mask* era of the mid-1930s. W. R. Burnett's *The Asphalt Jungle* (1949) opened with an apt quotation from William James: "Man is the most formidable of all beasts of prey, and indeed the only one that preys systematically on his own species." The most predatory invention in crime fiction of the period was Mickey Spillane's series hero, Mike Hammer, introduced in *I the Jury* (1947). The vigilante private eye played executioner as well as jury on the last page by shooting a (guilty) woman in the stomach. "It was easy," he observes, laconically. For several years Spillane's sales outstripped all rivals in the United States.

There was, in the Dwight Eisenhower era, a preference for large, meaty, quasi-realistic novels. Henry Morton Robinson made it to the top of the 1950 best-seller list with his life-and-trials story of an American prince of the Catholic Church, *The Cardinal*. Four years later, Morton Thompson wrote the best-seller of 1954, *Not as a Stranger*. This multistrand story of young men undergoing medical training would be much imitated—not least in television soap operas (soap and white coats made natural partners). Thompson's novel was regarded as "daring" for its time and was made into a big-budget film in 1955. The rapid sequence by which the film hit the screen at the same time as the mass-market paperback hit the stands was, by the mid-1950s, well established. James Gould Cozzens's wildly overpraised (at the time) *By Love Possessed*, the best-seller of 1957, was filmed in 1961. More interesting, with hindsight, are Allen Drury's John Gunther–style "Inside Washington" political romans à clef, of which the most popular was *Advise and Consent* (1959).

As had Edward Bellamy's *Looking Backward* in the 1880s, Ayn Rand's paean to capitalism, *Atlas Shrugged*, a best-seller of 1957, popularized the author's philosophy (in her case, frankly summed up as the "doctrine of the dollar"). A slow starter (it only made number ten on the 1957 list, eight places behind *Peyton Place*), Rand's massive tract had sold five million copies (and reaped many dollars) by 1984 and had influenced many of America's most influential decision makers.

Rand was one of three "Russians" to figure in the best-seller lists of the late 1960s. Vladimir Nabokov's fantasia on pedophilia, *Lolita*, was after some years' nervous suppression, released in the United States in 1958. It shot to the top of the best-seller lists, to be challenged, over succeeding months by Boris Pasternak's *Doctor Zhivago*—a work that could only be read in its *samizdat* version in the author's native Soviet Union. Nabokov became rich, and Pasternak was offered a consolatory Nobel Prize (which he could not accept).

The early 1960s best-seller lists were dominated by Irving Stone's massive "bio-fictions"—such as *The Agony and the Ecstasy* (1961). Michelangelo's story required, the author recorded, six years of research. It was made into a suitably reverent film starring Charlton Heston in 1965. Stone's biographical massiveness of biofictional design was rivaled by the geofictions of James A. Michener, whose first epic, *Hawaii*, topped the American lists in 1959, coinciding with the region's accession to statehood.

From a literary-historical point of view, the most significant work of popular fiction over the year from 1959 to 1960 was a thirty-year-old romance of illicit love in the woods, D. H. Lawrence's *Lady Chatterley's Lover*. This novel, with its "four-letter words" was cleared in successive court hearings and—not being protected under American copyright law—duly pirated in millions of copies. The "stampede" of editions of Lawrence's novel is plausibly credited with triggering the 1960s "paperback revolution." The new parameters of expression which it defined made possible not only literary efforts, like Philip Roth's *Portnoy's Complaint* (1969), but a new fictional brutalism—most emetically displayed in Harold

Robbins's series of supersellers, beginning with *The Carpetbaggers* (1961).

For the consumer of less salacious wares, Arthur Hailey began his series of heavily researched novels, dealing with the institutions of modern life, with *Hotel* in 1965. He would go on to cover airports, banks, auto factories, and hospitals. Hailey claimed that it took him four years to produce a novel: three years' research, one year writing. He had a golden touch throughout the late 1960s and 1970s.

Genre fiction had, since World War II, progressed well beyond its pulpy origins and aspired—at its top level—to literary respectability. Much of the credit belongs to the self-adjudicating nature of these lines of "category" fiction, through their institutional awards: "Edgars," "Nebulas," "Hugos," and "Silver Daggers." In addition to the staple product represented by such writers as "Ellery Queen" (i.e., Frederic Dannay and Manfred B. Lee), the genres diversified in unconventional ways. Chester Himes, with the first of his Coffin Ed and Grave Digger cop stories, *A Rage in Harlem* (1965), successfully mixed noir and African-American genres. Tony Hillerman introduced an even more unusual line of *romans policiers* with his Navajo cops, Joe Leaphorn and Jim Chee, in *The Blessing Way* (1970). The most respected writer in the crime-adventure genre, Elmore Leonard, gave up writing film scripts and embarked on a new and fabulously successful career with his first published novel, *The Big Bounce*, in 1969.

Science fiction was similarly raising itself (to the distress of its harder-line fans). Ray Bradbury, with novels such as *Fahrenheit 451* (1953), broke out of the science-fiction ghetto into popular readership and high critical respect. He was, cynics said, the favorite science-fiction writer among readers who did not like science fiction. Works such as Frank Herbert's *Dune* (1965)—which had originated with research into the preservation of Oregon's coastline—became cult classics, as did Isaac Asimov's *Foundation Trilogy* (1961). They were even studied on American campuses—that deadliest of accolades.

Women's romance entered new, uninhibited, territory with Jacqueline Susann's *The Valley of the Dolls* in 1966. The intertwined story of three young women in New York—sexual and chemical adventurers ("dolls" are pills)—blazed

John Grisham. (*John Grisham Papers, Special Collections Department, Mitchell Memorial Library, Mississippi State University*)

a trail for what later became known as "bodice rippers." The mood of the late 1960s, even in "straight" melodrama, was notably dissident. Everything was ripping. Elia Kazan's number one title of 1967, *The Arrangement*, is the story of what in the 1950s would have been called (after Sloan Wilson's 1955 best-seller) a man in a gray flannel suit, a cigarette advertising executive, who methodically destroys the successful life he has laboriously constructed for himself. Pro-Vietnam war novels, such as Robin Moore's *The Green Berets* (1965, filmed by John Wayne, starring John Wayne, in 1968) attracted obloquy in equal measure to their success.

There remained some things on which Americans could agree. Michael Crichton's technothriller, *The Andromeda Strain* (1969), was the first "true" science fiction to make it to the upper reaches of the best-seller lists. A celebration of American (specifically NASA's) science, it did so on popular excitement about the Apollo moon landings. So too did Arthur C. Clarke's 1968 "novelization" of Stanley Kubrick's film, *2001: A Space Odyssey* (itself based on one of Clarke's short stories).

The late 1960s and 1970s are most notable for marking new scales of sale. The origin of Mario Puzo's *The Godfather* (1969) is legendary. The author, as he later declared, decided that "I was forty-five years old, I owed $20,000 to relatives, finance companies, banks and assorted bookmakers and loan sharks. It was really time to grow up and sell out." The subsequent novel, which did for the Mafia what Hailey had done for airports, went on to sell some ten million copies over the following decade. The same threshold was passed, in the same short period, by Richard Bach's *Jonathan Livingston Seagull* (1970), William Peter Blatty's *The Exorcist* (1971), Peter Benchley's *Jaws* (1974), Erich Segal's *Love Story* (1970), and Erica Jong's *Fear of Flying* (1974; a feminist "Portnoy's Complaint"). Works such as Harper Lee's *To Kill a Mockingbird* (1960) and *Peyton Place* (1956) had, cumulatively, cleared almost as many copies, but not so rapidly.

There emerged in the late 1970s and 1980s a nucleus of novelists who could, for the first time in American book-trade history, clear a million copies in hardback in a year, at full retail price.

They were headed by Stephen King (who came on the scene, inauspiciously, with *Carrie* in 1974). King's reliably prodigious output over the next quarter of a century would establish him as the twentieth century's Edgar Allan Poe and an unmatched money machine. Others in the top division of authors who could sell as many in hardback as best-selling authors of the 1960s in paperback were: James A. Michener (maker of grandiose epics), Jean M. Auel (creator of an unusual string of prehistoric sagas, beginning with *The Clan of the Cave Bear* in 1980), Robert Ludlum (master of the "paranoid" thriller), and Danielle Steel. In 1984, Tom Clancy came to the fore with his Cold War technothriller, *The Hunt for Red October*. He would, thereafter, top the best-seller lists with everything he wrote.

Thomas Harris laid the way, with *The Silence of the Lambs* (1988), for what would be the most successful thriller-movie tie-in ever (Hannibal Lecter became as mythically famous in the popular mind as Dracula or Frankenstein). More fluently than Harris—a notoriously slow producer—John Grisham patented with *The Firm* (1991) a line of legal thrillers that in turn generated an unbroken string of hugely successful film adaptations. Michael Crichton pulled off the same trick with his heavily researched high-tech thrillers—most successfully *Jurassic Park* (1990; filmed by Steven Spielberg in 1993).

Feminism had made its mark on the detective novel with Sara Paretsky's V. I. Warshawski, introduced with *Indemnity Only* (1982), and Sue Grafton's Kinsey Millhone, introduced in *"A" is for Alibi* (1982). It was Patricia Cornwell, with her chief medical examiner heroine Kay Scarpetta (introduced with *Postmortem* in 1990) who would sell the most copies and earn the highest advances ever paid to a woman writer in American book trade history.

New markets emerged in the late twentieth century. Young readers had more disposable income than at any time in American history. V. C. Andrews's strangely combined amalgam of horror and domesticity, which began with *Flowers in the Attic* in 1979, successfully targeted a teenaged, mainly female, constituency. By the late 1990s, Andrews's novels (some of them produced after her death in 1986, but under her franchised brand-name) had sold one hundred million copies worldwide. An even younger readership (or viewership) made William Kotzwinkle's novelization *E. T.: The Extra-Terrestrial Storybook* the number one title of 1982, and *The Return of the Jedi Storybook* the number one title a year later.

What literary historians would regard as "canonical" works were pulled up by the updraft. E. L. Doctorow's jaundiced antibicentennial *Ragtime* (a novel that itself should surely last for two hundred years) was the best-seller of 1975. Nobel Prize–winner Saul Bellow's *Humboldt's Gift* also figured in that year's top ten. The "quality" superseller was a regular feature of the popular market—with titles such as William Styron's *Sophie's Choice* (1979), Margaret Atwood's *The Handmaid's Tale* (1985), Tom Wolfe's *Bonfire of the Vanities* (1987), and Salman Rushdie's *The Satanic Verses* (1988). Whatever else, the American literary sensibility had not been prostituted by the ever-expanding popularity of popular fiction.

FURTHER READING

Bailey, Dale. *American Nightmares: The Haunted House Formula in American Popular Fiction*. Bowling Green, Ohio, 1999. Bailey's book is model of the "topos"—or recurrent figure—in popular fiction.

Baym, Nina. *Woman's Fiction: A Guide to Novels by and about Women in America, 1820–1870*. Ithaca, N.Y., 1978. This work has been influential and instrumental in throwing new critical light on a previously neglected subgenre—"feminized fiction."

Bleiler, Richard, ed. *Science Fiction Writers: Critical Studies of the Major Authors from the Early Nineteenth Century to the Present Day*. New York, 1998. Bleiler draws on a massive database of the science fiction genre.

Bloom, Clive. *Bestsellers: Popular Fiction Since 1900*. New York, 2002. An up-to-date survey, drawing on recent statistical information and similarly recent critical theory.

Bode, Carl. *Anatomy of American Popular Culture, 1840–1861*. Westport, Conn., 1983. Bode sensibly incorporates popular fiction into the whole ensemble of American cultural practice—something routinely overlooked by tunnel-visioned literary critics.

Cawelti, John G. *Adventure, Mystery, and Romance: Formula Stories as Art and Popular Culture*. Chicago, 1976. A landmark work in theorizing the subject. His distinction between formulaic "popular" and non-formulaic "canonical" fiction still holds up usefully.

Cawelti, John G. *Six-Gun Mystique Sequel*. Bowling Green, Ohio, 1999. Limits itself to the Western.

Davidson, Cathy. *Reading in America: Literature and Social History*. Baltimore, 1989. A sophisticatedly symptomatic approach—posing the question: "What does popular fiction say about its host society?"

Hackett, Alice Payne. *80 Years of Best Sellers, 1895–1975*. New York, 1977.

Hart, James D. *The Popular Book: A History of America's Literary Taste.* Westport, Conn., 1976. An early, synoptic, monograph: an entertaining catalog raisonée.

Hinckley, Karen, and Barbara Hinckley. *American Best Sellers: A Reader's Guide to Popular Fiction.* Bloomington, Ind., 1989. This is even more of a catalogue.

Mott, Frank Luther. *Golden Multitudes: The Story of Best Sellers in the United States.* New York, 1947. This was the first critical work to methodically attempt to anatomize the American popular novel. It remains a much-cited source book.

Nye, Russel. *The Unembarrassed Muse: The Popular Arts in America.* New York, 1970. A readable discussion of the nation's reading matter and connected cultural products.

Radway, Janice A. *A Feeling for Books: The Book-of-the-Month Club, Literary Taste, and Middle-Class Desire.* Chapel Hill, N.C., 1997. A much (and rightly) applauded case study of a subsection of the popular fiction industry.

Radway, Janice A. *Reading the Romance: Women, Patriarchy, and Popular Literature.* Chapel Hill, N.C., 1991. This work is more dogmatic, but equally well grounded in primary research.

Sullivan, Larry E., and Lydia Cushman Schurman, eds. *Pioneers, Passionate Ladies, and Private Eyes: Dime Novels, Series Books, and Paperbacks.* New York, 1996. Skims entertainingly over an array of pulp and genre.

Sutherland, John. *Bestsellers.* Boston, 1981. Does the same for the 1970s blockbuster.

KATHERINE ANNE PORTER

by Denise Larrabee

Against her wishes, Katherine Anne Porter's literary reputation rests on her expertise as a stylist. "I've been called a stylist until I really could tear my hair out," she said in a 1963 interview. "I simply don't believe in style. The style is you." Porter is considered one of the finest American short story writers of the twentieth century primarily because of her precise and highly visual stories that reveal unsettling truths about human nature. A woman devoted to her career and artistic excellence, Porter helped shape modern American literature with fiction drawn from ordinary life but exploring profound human issues.

Born Callie Russell Porter on 15 May 1890 in the rural community of Indian Creek, Texas, she was the third child of Harrison Boone Porter and Mary Alice Jones. Porter began calling herself Katherine Anne by the age of fifteen, making the name change legal years later. She took the name from her paternal grandmother, Catherine Anne Porter, who helped raise her and her three siblings after their mother died in 1892. Her father, despondent and unsuccessful, had moved his young family to Kyle, Texas, where his mother, a devout Methodist and respected member of her community, provided stability, security, and an education for his children, despite her meager circumstances.

Porter found the disparity between the family's social standing in the community and their financial means painful. Throughout her life, she claimed an aristocratic southern heritage that belied the truth of her family's economic situation. She later drew on this experience for her fiction in such short stories as "The Grave." In this story, the children feel displaced and uneasy among the sharecroppers who have recently acquired their family's land. It is important to note that "The Grave" features Miranda, Porter's alter ego, along with Paul, a fictional

Katherine Anne Porter. (*Permission granted by Barbara Thompson Davis, Literary Trustee for the Estate of Katherine Anne Porter*)

representation of her brother. Several of Porter's southern stories feature fictional representations of her family, including "Old Mortality," "Pale Horse, Pale Rider," and "The Fig Tree."

After her grandmother died when Porter was eleven, the family lived with various relatives throughout Texas. In San Antonio, Porter received the last of her formal education at the Thomas School, a nonsectarian school with a strong Methodist influence. Here she studied drama, singing, and music. In 1906, at the age of sixteen, she married John Henry Koontz, a member of a wealthy Catholic ranching family. The marriage lasted nine years, during which Porter, whose family were conservative Protestants, converted to Catholicism. Throughout her life she vacillated between devoutness and skepticism, sometimes mocking organized religion and always deploring its authoritarianism. Her most eloquent criticism of organized religion appears in her essay "On a Criticism of Thomas Hardy" (1940).

EARLY CAREER

After performing songs and reciting poems on the lyceum circuit for a time, Porter began writing for the *Fort Worth Critic* in 1917. She worked there a year before moving to Denver to write for the *Rocky Mountain News*. She never again lived in Texas, although she returned to her southern origins repeatedly for inspiration. Porter believed the atmosphere too repressive for a creative and independent woman writer. Although she rejected the label of "feminist," Porter lived the life of one, and her essays and fiction are full of strong women who seek knowledge, express their opinions, defy authority, and enjoy sex—women much like herself.

While living in Denver, Porter nearly died during the influenza epidemic of 1919. This profound experience helped her develop a stronger self-identity and make a commitment to her art, although she continued to accept writing assignments for screenplays, newspaper articles, book reviews, and essays for the much-needed income.

Porter met a number of successful and stimulating artists, musicians, and writers in Denver who inspired her to move to New York near the end of 1919. In fact, Porter knew many of the influential artistic and political figures of the twentieth century. Many friends and associates, such as the writer and historian Josephine Herbst, belonged to the Communist Party, and Porter became an active communist supporter. Communist sympathizers were not uncommon among artists and writers of the time, and Porter was attracted to Marxist ideology through her empathy with the poor and intolerance for social injustice.

LIFE IN MEXICO

Communist ideology's influence on her writing is evident in the work Porter produced during frequent trips to Mexico throughout the 1920s. She published articles, reviews, and essays on Mexican art, music, religion, and politics, promoting the creations of indigenous people, relating the history of Mexican folk songs and printed ballads, criticizing the Catholic Church for its neglect of the poor, and supporting the communist revolution in Mexico.

Mexico's influence on Porter's fictional writing cannot be overstated. She began viewing herself as a working artist, developing a theory of artistic integrity from which she never deviated. Through her association with politically radical Mexican artists, such as Diego Rivera, she developed an unaffected but vivid style. Like the Mexican artists who drew on their heritage with pride, Porter would later look to her own past for creative inspiration. Her experiences in Mexico inspired a number of Porter's best short stories, including "Maria Concepción" and "Hacienda," both of which explore two recurring themes in her fiction—exploitation of the poor and class struggle.

"Maria Concepción," her first published short story, appeared in the prestigious periodical *Century* in 1922. The story is highly regarded, despite some dated stereotypical portrayals of indigenous Mexicans. Porter, believing the Mexican revolution failed to help the poorest Mexicans, presents the themes of exploitation and class struggle with remarkable subtlety in a story of a powerful, independent, and vengeful woman who gets away with murder. The villagers in the story, desperate for money, work for an archaeologist, ironically unearthing their own history only to give it away.

"Hacienda" also reflects Porter's disillusionment with Mexican politics and the revolution. It appeared in the *Virginia Quarterly Review* in 1932 and as a small book in 1934. The story is based on Porter's observations during a visit to the Hacienda Tetlapayac during the filming of *Qué Viva Mexico!* by the director Sergei Eisenstein. In "Hacienda," Porter emphasizes the misery of indigenous Mexicans, the injustice and arrogance of landed aristocracy, and the ignorance of foreigners exploiting the beauty and drama of the landscape and its people.

By 1929 Porter was living in New York again, working as a part-time editor for Macauley and as a freelance writer. She had married and divorced twice more; the name of her second husband is unknown; the third was Ernest Stock, an aspiring artist. She traveled to Bermuda with financial help from friends to work in solitude on a biography of Cotton Mather, a project she never finished. Porter often relied on friends for financial assistance until she became financially secure later in life.

In 1930 she returned to Mexico for the last time, after publishing her first collection of stories, *Flowering Judas*. This collection featured six stories, all of which had been published in American periodicals such as *Hound & Horn*, *New Masses*, and *Transition*.

Flowering Judas attracted critical attention and established a place for Porter among American literary writers. Reviewers focused on her style and praised her craftsmanship and unaffected voice. The themes of class struggle and exploitation of the poor appear in this collection as well, but this time they play out in the American South in the stories "He" and "Magic." Porter's disillusion with the Mexican revolution again appears in "Flowering Judas," but a preoccupation with death predominates in this story. Life appears meaningless to the title character, trapped between a fear of living and a fear of dying. Porter too was preoccupied with death, probably resulting from her mother's death and her own near-death experience in 1919.

Darlene Unrue (1985) reveals a unifying theme of truth in Porter's fiction, evident in five of the six stories in this collection. "He," "Maria Concepción," and "Flowering Judas" focus on the confrontation with our primitive selves that is essential for self-revelation. "The Jilting of Granny Weatherall" and "Magic" question the usefulness of organized religion, and faith in general, as a pathway to truth.

TRAVELS TO EUROPE

In 1931 Porter received a Guggenheim Fellowship, which she used to finance a trip to Europe. With her companion

Eugene Pressly, whom she would marry in 1933, Porter sailed to Germany on the *Werra*. This ocean voyage would inspire her best-selling novel, *Ship of Fools* (1962). Porter and Pressly traveled to Berlin, Paris, Madrid, and Switzerland. From 1932 to 1936 they lived in Paris.

During this time, Porter published "Hacienda" as a small book, *Flowering Judas and Other Stories* (an expanded edition of the 1930 publication), and *Katherine Anne Porter's French Song-Book,* which contained English translations of French songs. Porter accepted this project, conceived by her friend the publisher Barbara Harrison, because of her early interest in music.

After Porter and Pressly returned to the United States in 1936, Porter settled in Pennsylvania to write while Pressly lived in Washington, D.C. She moved many times throughout her life, and biographers theorize that she yearned for a home but felt like an outsider wherever she lived. This nomadic tendency often interfered with Porter's work, contributing to her financial difficulties.

In 1937 Porter traveled to Texas, visiting family for the first time in eighteen years. While she is not regarded as a poet, Porter occasionally wrote verse and attempted to publish it. Generally considered an average poet, during this trip to Texas, Porter composed what many consider her two best poems: "After a Long Journey" and "Anniversary in a Country Cemetery," which she left at her mother's grave.

PALE HORSE, PALE RIDER

After divorcing Pressly in 1938, Porter married for the last time. Her fifth husband was Albert Erksine, a graduate student twenty-one years younger than she who worked as business manager for the *Southern Review*. They would divorce in 1942. In 1939 she published *Pale Horse, Pale Rider*, which contains three novellas (a term Porter disliked): "Old Mortality," "Noon Wine," and the title story.

Overwhelmingly considered superior examples of short fiction, these three novellas are tragedies that explore the power of the past in our lives, a recurring theme in Porter's fiction. The characters change and grow as their relationship with the past changes and grows. But Porter's genius is most evident in the moments of enlightenment her characters experience in lieu of pat resolutions.

In "Old Mortality," Miranda and her sister grow up learning a romantic version of their Aunt Amy's life and death. When Miranda returns home for her Uncle Gabriel's funeral, she learns another version of the tale. Miranda's future is left unresolved as she realizes she will never know the truth and decides to break with the past altogether. "Noon Wine" tells the tragic story of Mr. Thompson, a dairy farmer acquitted of murder. He travels the countryside trying to absolve himself in the eyes of his neighbors. Unable to obtain the deeper resolution he seeks, he kills himself. The title story, "Pale Horse, Pale Rider," revisits Miranda, who contracts influenza during the flu epidemic that occurred during World War I. Her lover, Adam, tries to nurse her back to health, but he becomes infected and dies. Miranda emerges from the hospital at the end of the war deeply scarred, facing a bleak future alone.

While "Pale Horse, Pale Rider" draws heavily on Porter's life experience, "Old Mortality" and "Noon Wine" draw on Porter's southern past, a past she often magnified and biographers still debate, although her stories are repeatedly anthologized in collections of southern fiction. Clearly she saw herself as a southern writer, and her fiction, with some characteristic southern elements—tragic story lines, an acute awareness of history, the overriding power of family—supports the claim.

Porter's southern heritage led to her affiliation with the Agrarians, a group of southern writers including Robert Penn Warren, Allen Tate, and Caroline Gordon, who believed capitalism had failed America and the nation needed to reinstitute traditional values with an agricultural rather than industrial economy. Their radically conservative approach promoted clear class and racial distinctions, which they attempted to balance with paternalism. By the late 1930s Porter was becoming less and less leftist in her politics; by World War II she had adopted a centrist position. Her affinity with the Agrarians developed largely because in some ways their ideology overlapped with the communist values Porter still held dear, such as anti-industrialism, while allowing her to connect with her southern roots.

Most of the stories in *The Leaning Tower and Other Stories* (1944) draw on Porter's southern past, including, "The Source," "The Last Leaf," and "The Witness." Most of these were previously published in the *Southern Review*. However, the major work in this collection is the title story. Based on her trip to Berlin in 1931, "The Leaning Tower" revisits one of the themes found in her stories of Mexico—disillusion with communism. In addition to elegantly weaving the personal and political lives of the Germans, Porter's use of symbolism makes "The Leaning Tower" one of her more important works. The cold winter setting symbolizes Germany between the world wars, during the rise of Nazism. When Charles Upton, the main character, picks up a replica of the leaning tower of Pisa and it crumbles in his hand, it is clear that the Germans, with their inordinate pride, will fail.

Porter's first collection of essays, *The Days Before*, came out in 1952, followed in 1955 by a collection of her southern short stories, *The Old Order*. Both of these volumes compiled works that Porter had published previously, many as far back as the 1920s. Throughout the 1950s, most of Porter's publications were excerpts from her novel-in-progress, *Ship of Fools*. One exception, "Holiday" (1960), won the O. Henry Memorial Award.

SHIP OF FOOLS

In order to supplement her income from publications, Porter taught at a number of universities, including the University of Liège in Belgium as a Fulbright fellow. In 1959, she received a grant from the Ford Foundation. An engaging speaker, Porter also gave readings and lectures and appeared on radio and television. When she finally published *Ship of Fools* in 1962, she was recognizable and popular with the general public.

Porter worked on *Ship of Fools* intermittently for over twenty-five years, beginning in 1936 with the story "Promised Land." Throughout her career Porter fluctuated among periods of quiet enterprise, social diversion, emotional upheaval, domestic activity, and depression. Consequently it was difficult for her to maintain the discipline needed to construct a novel. For seven years, beginning in 1955, Seymour Lawrence of Atlantic–Little Brown provided Porter with encouragement, financial support, and seclusion so that she could complete the novel.

Ship of Fools chronicles the journey of nearly forty passengers onboard the *Vera*, a German ship sailing from Vera Cruz to Bremerhaven in 1931. The *Vera*, which means "truth," represents the world and humankind—its passengers—on a journey through life. This allegorical novel captures the state of the Western world as it blindly tolerated the totalitarian ideologies and political tensions that culminated in World War II. The passengers, representing various nationalities and backgrounds, interact with each other; complications arise and tensions escalate. For example, a number of Germans make anti-Semitic remarks, and an American woman is mistaken for a prostitute. By the time they disembark in Bremerhaven, the passengers have learned a considerable amount about each other and have experienced intense confrontations. Even so, they are little changed and content to continue their lives as before.

Ship of Fools was a spectacular commercial success: it was a best-seller, later made into a film, and made Porter financially secure in her own right. The critical response to the novel remains mixed. As expected, the author excels with her stylistic prose and clarity of expression. But the novel is often criticized for its countless stagnant, unredeemable characters and blatant anti-Semitism. A few of the passengers are more attractive, such as Dr. Schumann, a religious man with a heart condition who often shows compassion toward his fellow passengers. However, the book exhibits a hopeless representation of human nature, the origins of which may be Porter's own prejudices against Jews, African Americans, and Germans, to name a few.

The structure of the novel is also problematic, for it is episodic and lacks a conventional plot. Some critics maintain it is unfair to judge *Ship of Fools* against a conventional novel structure, as it was never Porter's intention to write a conventional novel. Others believe Porter was simply out of her element—a master short story writer pressured into writing a novel in order to win the respect of the literary establishment.

Although *Ship of Fools* was not the literary success Porter had hoped for, the novel succeeds at capturing the disillusionment of a particular historical moment and fully develops the recurring theme of self-delusion in Porter's work—the idea that all humans share responsibility for the ills of the world, whether or not we realize it.

LATER YEARS

Within three years, Porter would gain the recognition she had longed for throughout her career. The publication of *The Collected Stories of Katherine Anne Porter* in 1965 received both the National Book Award and the Pulitzer Prize. She followed this success with the publication of *The Collected Essays and Occasional Writings of Katherine Anne Porter* in 1970. Throughout her career, Porter wrote countless book reviews, thirteen of which are included in this collection, along with eight poems and numerous essays.

Porter's essays are praised almost as much as her short stories. Again, it is her style that draws attention. She is direct, opinionated, and confident, which may be attributed to the fact that many of her essays grew out of her voluminous correspondence with friends, family, and colleagues. In fact, her personal writing is almost as well regarded as her professional writing.

Porter's essays and book reviews illuminate the high literary standards to which she held herself and other writers. She insisted on form and structure, serious or worthwhile subject matter (she disliked popular fiction), and authentic voice. In her nonfiction she discusses the artistic theory behind her fiction writing as well as the artists and writers who influenced her, such as Ernest Hemingway, Henry James, and Virginia Woolf. She believed that the artist must be free to express his or her "truth," remaining independent and accountable to no one. Indeed, it was this tenet that ultimately led Porter to end her support of the Communist Party, which expected party loyalty in all facets of life from its members.

Porter produced very little new work after the publication of her *Collected Stories*. She liked her celebrity status and accepted several honorary degrees. Her last full-length work was *The Never-Ending Wrong* (1977), a memoir of her experience protesting the Sacco and Vanzetti case in 1927.

In 1977, several strokes left Porter unable to care for herself. She required full-time nursing care until she died on 18 September 1980.

SELECTED WORKS

Flowering Judas (1930)
Flowering Judas and Other Stories (1935)
Pale Horse, Pale Rider: Three Short Novels (1939)
Anniversary in a Country Cemetery (1942)
The Leaning Tower and Other Stories (1944)
Selected Short Stories (1945)
The Days Before (1952)
A Defense of Circe (1955)
The Old Order: Stories of the South from Flowering Judas; Pale Horse, Pale Rider; and The Leaning Tower (1955)
Ship of Fools (1962)
The Collected Stories of Katherine Anne Porter (1965)
The Collected Essays and Occasional Writings of Katherine Anne Porter (1970)
The Never-Ending Wrong (1977)

FURTHER READING

Alvarez, Ruth M., and Thomas F. Walsh. *Uncollected Early Prose of Katherine Anne Porter*. Austin, Tex., 1993.

Bayley, Isabel, ed. *Letters of Katherine Anne Porter*. New York, 1990.

Brinkmeyer, Robert H., Jr. *Katherine Anne Porter's Artistic Development: Primitivism, Traditionalism, and Totalitarianism*. Baton Rouge, La., and London, 1993.

Busby, Mark, and Dick Heaberlin. *From Texas to the World and Back: Essays on the Journeys of Katherine Anne Porter*. Fort Worth, Tex., 2001.

Chandra, Lakshmi. *Katherine Anne Porter: Fiction as History*. New Delhi, India, 1992.

Givner, Joan. *Katherine Anne Porter: A Life*. Rev. ed. Athens, Ga., 1991. Biography exploring key events in Porter's life and their effect on her work.

Givner, Joan, ed. *Katherine Anne Porter: Conversations*. Jackson, Miss., and London, 1987.

Hilt, Kathryn, and Ruth M. Alvarez. *Katherine Anne Porter: An Annotated Bibliography*. New York, 1990. Most complete bibliography to date.

Machann, Clinton, and William Bedford Clark, eds. *Katherine Anne Porter and Texas: An Uneasy Relationship*. College Station, Tex., 1990.

Stout, Janis P. *Katherine Anne Porter: A Sense of the Times*. Charlottesville, Va., 1995. Most recent biography; more analytical than Givner's biography.

Tanner, James F. *The Texas Legacy of Katherine Anne Porter*. Denton, Tex., 1990.

Unrue, Darlene Harbour. *Truth and Vision in Katherine Anne Porter's Fiction*. 1985. A study of unifying themes in Porter's work. Lists critical sources.

Unrue, Darlene Harbour. *Understanding Katherine Anne Porter*. Columbia, S.C., 1988. Biographical information and analysis of her fiction and nonfiction for students and general readers. Good annotated bibliography.

Unrue, Darlene Harbour, ed. *"This Strange, Old World" and Other Book Reviews by Katherine Anne Porter*. Athens, Ga., 1991.

Unrue, Darlene Harbour, ed. *Katherine Anne Porter's Poetry*. Columbia, S.C., 1996. Contains previously unpublished poems as well as poems published during her lifetime and the text of *Katherine Anne Porter's French Song-Book*.

Unrue, Darlene Harbour, ed. *Critical Essays on Katherine Anne Porter*. New York, 1997.

Vanashree. *Feminine Consciousness in Katherine Anne Porter's Fiction*. New Delhi, India, 1991.

Walsh, Thomas F. *Katherine Anne Porter and Mexico: The Illusion of Eden*. Austin, Tex., 1992.

EZRA POUND

by Michael Coyle

On the morning of 2 May 1945, Ezra Pound walked down the hill of Sant'Ambrogio into the seaside town of Rapallo, Italy, intending (as biographer Humphrey Carpenter tells it) "to go and identify himself" to "the American forces who were setting up military headquarters in one of the waterfront hotels." He told the soldiers that he wanted "to give information to the State Department." Before he made that walk he must have wondered whether he would come to harm (he was, after all, under indictment for treason), or whether indeed his attempt to cooperate—to help his country—might be appreciated; perhaps, rather than forcible custody, he might actually meet gratitude. What happened to him that morning was, however, something he likely did not anticipate—something that might well stand as emblematic of his lifelong relation with the public. There was no one on the scene who had any idea who he was. No one there had the slightest clue as to why the U.S. government should be interested in him. Eventually, Pound returned to the home that wartime constraints had compelled him to share with both his mistress, Olga Rudge, and his wife, Dorothy. It was only on the next day, when two antifascist partisans pounded on his door with the butt of a tommy gun and marched him back down to the American headquarters, that Pound's painful, thirteen-year incarceration was to begin in earnest.

No poet in the history of the language has had a more complex relation with his readers than Pound. He could be haughtily dismissive of the "iggurant masses," and yet throughout his career was passionately albeit paradoxically committed to the ideals of popularization—which he once pronounced "the ultimate goal of scholarship." Pound's deepest poetic aspirations were ineluctably tied to his hopes to revitalize Western culture in general and American culture in particular. To do this he became

Ezra Pound, 1943.
(Courtesy of the Library of Congress)

convinced that the art of poetry must itself be revivified—made once more to matter in the way that poetry had mattered in Homer's day. This revivification would come not from any pandering to popular tastes, however, but from an insistence on the most exacting of aesthetic standards. Pound was in this singular way the most Whitmanian of poets—containing multitudes, embracing apparently irreconcilable contradictions. Sometimes the contradictions were in fact irreconcilable. The *Cantos* (1917–1968) are perhaps impossibly ambitious. But in all things Pound risked greatly; sometimes he erred greatly, but greatness was always his goal. What errors he made came never from selfish or egoistic impulses. In fact, Pound was hugely generous to young talent wherever he found it, regarding his work to get others published as but part of his struggle to make poetry matter—to change the sociocultural role of the poet.

EARLY LIFE

"Nothing so boring as trype re/infancy," Pound wrote to one of his early biographers, and that conviction deserves respect. He was born in a modest clapboard house in Hailey, Idaho, on 30 October 1885 to Homer and Isabel Weston Pound. Ultimately, the family settled in Wyncote, Pennsylvania, a northern suburb of Philadelphia. Much doted on as an only child, Pound entered the University of Pennsylvania at the age of fifteen, but transferred to Hamilton College at the end of his sophomore year. He took his M.A. degree back at Penn, and then in the summer of 1907 found a job at Wabash University, a job that forever ended not only his interest in an academic career but also in continued life in the United States. In February 1908 he accepted an offer of financial compensation (never fully paid) for the college's termination of his contract.

The European travels he began thereafter took him first to Gibraltar and then to Venice, where Pound published his first book of poems. Called *A Lume Spento* ("With Tapers Quenched"—the phrase is from Dante; 1908), it was, though passionate, in most respects derivative. It proved nevertheless enormously important. Pound had the book brought out—"published" is hardly the word for an edition of 150 copies paid for by the author—to establish his credentials as a serious poet. After *A Lume Spento*, Pound never looked back, never again seriously doubted that he had found his calling.

THE POET

Pound arrived in London on 14 August 1908. The city was then still very much an imperial city—seat of the largest empire the world had ever known. But for Pound its attraction was its comparative smallness; the London literary world was close-knit, and Pound rightly concluded it would be easier to make his name there than in the diffuse and sprawling republic of letters back home. Over the next couple of years he would make many acquaintances, connecting with younger writers while showing a talent for attracting the attention of mentors. This latter group included publishers as well as numerous writers and poets.

But there were two figures to whom he was especially drawn. First, William Butler Yeats, arguably even then the greatest living poet in the language—though his best work yet lay ahead—and whose work as a dramatist (ten plays already completed by 1908) was rapidly drawing him away from the pale symbolist work of the 1890s. Moreover, as an Irishman, Yeats also knew something about making it in London as an outsider. Pound and Yeats became close, perhaps because of rather than in spite of all the differences between them in manners and personality: where Yeats was dignified and refined, Pound delighted in appearing brash and so impatient of fastidiousness as to verge on the vulgar. By 1915–1916 they had come to rely on one another to the extent that they spent winters together in a Sussex cottage, with Pound serving as something of Yeats's rather imperious secretary.

The second figure was Ford Madox Ford. The young English poet Richard Aldington described Ford as "a sort of literary Falstaff," but Ford held several attractions for Pound. A prolific novelist, he was an established figure in the London world and, as Wyndham Lewis remarked, became Pound's go-between with the London literary establishment. It was to Ford that Pound ascribed his next major lesson. Pound's third volume of poems, *Canzoni* (1911), essentially endeavored to show that the forms

of the twelfth-century troubadours were still viable in English. On its publication, Pound went to see Ford to present him with a copy. Sitting in his chair, Ford began to read but, Pound recalled, he "felt the errors of [Pound's lack of] contemporary style to the point of rolling (physically, and if you look at it as a mere superficial snob, ridiculously) on the floor.... And that roll saved me at least two years, perhaps more. It sent me back to my own proper effort, namely toward using the living tongue."

Sure enough, *Canzoni* proved the last such book that Pound would ever write, although his predilection for archaic speech would reappear from time to time in individual cantos, such as in the much-discussed "Usura" canto (XLV), where he writes, "With Usura hath no man a house of good stone," and so on. The several volumes that Pound had published in London prior to *Canzoni* were all similarly caught in the romance of history, in Pound's fascination with the poets of Provence, the troubadours, and with language that seemed outside the world of Victorian getting and spending. The very titles of these collections suffice to make the point: *A Quinzaine for this Yule* (privately printed, 1908), *Personae* (1909), *Exultations* (1909), and *Provença* (1910). The strongest poems from these early volumes speak through personae—dramatis personae—typically medieval in identity. They serve Pound in much the same way that the form of dramatic monologue served Victorian poets like Tennyson or Browning, giving the poet space to explore subject matter he could not claim from his individual experience along with sentiments that it might be socially inconvenient to espouse in unmediated lyrical voice. Pound's interest in masks or personae is as old as his interest in poetry, and in "Mask," from *A Lume Spento*, he asks:

> These tales of old disguisings, are they not
> Strange myths of souls that found themselves among
> Unwonted folk that spake an hostile tongue,
> Some soul from all the rest who'd not forgot
> The star-span acres of a former lot

In other words, Pound took the deployment of a poetic mask—"old disguisings"—as a connection with an older world where poetry mattered and where poets lived more freely among ordinary folk.

Ripostes (1912) was Pound's first concerted attempt "toward using the living tongue." Poems like "Portrait d'une femme" occasioned a new directness in his writing. In this volume, too, however there remain sustained exercises in archaic speech—but Pound's translation of "The Seafarer," which a year or so earlier might well have occasioned any number of "forsooths," "thines," and "thous," proves to be of much tougher material. There are a few archaisms like "nathless" and inversions of word order, but their presence is tempered by a new directness of language. What is most striking about the translation is the degree to which Pound strives to reproduce the effect of the original by recreating the alliterative formulae of the original Anglo-Saxon. The most striking poem of all from this collection, however, is "The Return," a poem that Hugh Kenner has observed could only have been composed at a typewriter:

> See, they return, one, and by one,
> With fear, as half-awakened;
> As if the snow should hesitate
> And murmur in the wind,
>   And half turn back;
> These were the "Wing'd-with-Awe,"
>   Inviolable.

There is a new kind of self-consciousness here—not the kind evident in the young man who thought that to sound like a poet he needed to speak in flowery archaisms, but of a poet keenly alert to the signifying power of language. The second of the two similes in this stanza builds on and amplifies the first, and "Wing'd-with-Awe" is less about the qualities of the ancient gods (it is they whose return the poet imagines) than about the way in which they were perceived by humankind. "Wing'd-with-Awe" is less an adjective than it is a radiant detail from a vanished world. This attempt to supercharge his language anticipated the next great development in Pound's work—and career.

IMAGISM

The story of imagism, or *Imagisme*, as Pound called it, has been much retold and much debated—in large part because the subsequent accounts of the principals involved are often sectarian and contradictory. In general, however, it can be said that imagism had a longish prehistory, that it was Pound who thrust it before the attention of the world, and that quickly thereafter Pound lost control of it.

Again, one of the things that made London an attractive destination for the young Pound was the comparative smallness of its literary scene—the extent to which that scene was concentrated in a few circles, alliances, or groups. One such group into which Pound gained admission centered around philosopher-controversialist T. E. Hulme. It was here that Pound came to know the work of French aestheticians like Henri Bergson and Rémy de Gourmont, and his exposure to their work helped him rethink "his own proper effort." Between December 1911 and March 1912 he read Gourmont, and the results of this reading are evident in his first important series of critical essays, "I Gather the Limbs of Osiris," published in A. R. Orage's journal, *The New Age*. The essay, whose title alludes to the scattering of the limbs of the slain god (material right out of James Frazer's *The Golden Bough*, 1907–1915, which would ten years later prove one of the underpinnings of T. S. Eliot's *The Waste Land*, 1922), is where Pound first developed his notion of "the luminous detail." This notion would take several different forms over the next ten years, but its most influential form would appear in the manifesto of Pound's *Des Imagistes* (1914).

In launching his first coordinated salvo against the niceties of contemporary English verse, Pound made use of his official role as overseas editor for Harriet Monroe's *Poetry*. The salvo was opened by F. S. Flint's short report, "Imagisme." (It mattered greatly that the label assumed French form—that in itself signaled a departure from polite English convention toward potentially dangerous predecessors like Charles Baudelaire or Paul Verlaine.) Flint announced that he had "sought out an *imagiste* with intent to discover whether the group itself knew anything about the movement." There was not actually a group already in place; Pound was reporting on the revolution even before he had fomented it. In any case, Pound's own contribution immediately followed Flint's. Pound opened with a definition: "an 'image' is that which presents an intellectual and emotional complex in an instant of time."

In February 1914 all the theorizing produced its first collected work—although Pound had in fact sent the manuscript to America the previous summer. It was an anthology that Pound called "Des imagistes," and was first published as a special issue of the *Glebe* in New York City. The several reprintings of the work in book form soon after tell much about its reception. In March 1914, the New York City publishers Albert and Charles Boni brought out the anthology in book form; the following month it was reprinted in London by the Poetry Bookshop. In 1917 the New York City publisher Frank Shay brought out a new edition, and he did so again in 1920. The influence of this little volume of mostly forgettable poems was enormous, and it produced a groundswell of interest, in the United States especially, that almost immediately escaped Pound's control. Pound's loss of control indicates that other poets, and readers, saw in imagism something very different from what he saw. What imagism became is not pertinent here, but Pound's initial vision most certainly is. The idea for imagism, or *Imagisme*, came together in Pound's mind while talking poetry with H.D. and Richard Aldington. In particular, it was a certain compression that Pound saw in H.D.'s poetry that seems first to have brought together his previously inchoate impulses and yearnings. The compression of H.D.'s short poem "Oread" (the Greek word for a mountain nymph), exemplifies the potential power that led Pound to believe he had encountered the future of modern poetry:

> Whirl up, sea—
> whirl your pointed pines,
> splash your great pines
> on our rocks,
> hurl your green over us,
> cover us with your pools of fir.

What the poem does is confuse the conventional distinction between the two parts of any metaphor, "tenor" and "vehicle"; when we say "love is rose," "rose" is the vehicle that the poet hopes will help us understand something new about love (here, the tenor). But in "Oread" it is unclear whether the crashing of sea upon rocks is deployed to explain the sensation of being in a forest during a storm, or whether the forest is deployed to illuminate the experience of standing before the titanic energy of the sea—or whether both, in fact, work simultaneously to figure the experience of being surrounded and perhaps transported by enormous natural forces. There is Pound's "intellectual and emotional complex in a moment of time."

But most of the hundreds of poets who thought they recognized in *Des Imagistes* their own ideals were not after the same kind of compression and discipline that Pound held ideal. The popular readership for the volume saw instead the possibilities of loose, almost haikulike structure, unfettered by rhyme or regular meter. In particular, the American poet Amy Lowell, a woman of established family name and fortune, decided that she, too, was an imagiste, and journeyed to London with a letter of introduction from Harriet Monroe. Pound—sensing that Lowell had her own ideas and the resources to make them happen, took an immediate dislike to her. The feeling was mutual. By August, insisting that all future imagist anthologies be assembled on a democratic basis, Lowell had rallied most of Pound's former contributors around her. In May 1915 she saw through publication the first of three volumes entitled *Some Imagist Poets*. The Frenchified "e" had disappeared, and so too had Pound. But by that time he had long since moved on to further projects.

MARRIAGE AND CHILDREN

In April 1914, Pound married Dorothy Shakespear, daughter of Henry Hope Shakespear, a successful solicitor, and his wife Olivia—who twenty years before had a secret affair with Yeats. Intelligent and committed to the arts, Dorothy herself was a talented amateur painter. (Most of her surviving work is now at Hamilton College.) The marriage seems not to have been a passionate one—Pound later told Daniel Cory that, lovely as Dorothy was when he first had met her, "I fell in love with a beautiful picture that never came to life." But Dorothy spent the rest of her life doing what she could to be involved in Pound's career. She did illustrations for the *Cantos* that were never published, and also for the magazine *Blast*. She shouldered—especially in later years—a good part of Pound's correspondence. The annuity that her father set up for her on her marriage was not enough ever to allow her and Pound to live grandly, but it was enough to save them from poverty. And in 1926 (when she was age thirty-nine) she gave birth to a son, Omar, conceived shortly after Dorothy learned that Pound's mistress, Olga Rudge, was herself expecting a child.

Pound met Olga, a concert violinist, after hearing her play in London late in 1920; immediately afterward, he encountered her at Natalie Barney's salon. Ten years younger than Ezra, Olga was energetic and cosmopolitan. After Pound introduced her to George Antheil, the self-professed "bad boy of music," the three of them began organizing performances together, with Pound pounding out rhythm on tambourines or bass drums. In the summer and early autumn of 1924, when Dorothy was in England visiting with her mother, the friendship of Pound and Olga, both living in northern Italy, deepened. Late that fall they conceived a child, Mary, who was born in July 1925. Shortly afterwards, Olga and Pound took the child to be reared by foster parents in the Italian Tirol, where Pound thought the mountain air would be especially healthy for her. Like Omar, who was raised by his grandparents in London, Mary was to spend her childhood in more or less distant relation to her parents. Pound, Dorothy, and Olga all regarded their responsibilities as artists as coming before their responsibility as parents.

VORTICISM

Marriage seems only to have consolidated other choices that Pound had made rather than itself occasioning new departures. New departures were, however, in the offing, and were, as was often his case, instigated by interaction with other dynamic minds. In 1914 two such figures

405

played an especially important role in his life. The first was the young English painter, poet, and novelist Wyndham Lewis; Pound and Lewis had actually met as early as 1909, but their relationship entered a new phase in March 1914, when Lewis and Kate Lechmere opened the Rebel Art Centre. Lewis proposed to Pound that the center hold an "Imagist Meeting"; that event never came off, but it put the two of them in a new kind of collaborative posture. Lewis was perhaps even more combative by nature than Pound, and his anti-romantic tendencies were considerably more pronounced. When he decided to amplify the rebel tendencies of his center by publishing a new magazine dedicated to similar principles, he invited Pound's collaboration. Thus was born both *Blast*—which was to survive only two issues before the outbreak of World War I rendered trivial its militant agitations—and also the vorticist program which it aimed to launch.

Vorticism might be understood as an English reaction to futurism, which was an essentially Italian movement launched in 1909 by Filippo Tommaso Marinetti. Marinetti's futurism turned its back on the museums that then and now dominate the art world and celebrated action and movement above all things. "Let us murder the moonshine," he proclaimed, meaning by "moonshine" poetic tradition, romanticism, and its glorification of nature. Marinetti's boredom with tradition led to a fetishizing of machinery—which is why Lewis retorted that futurism could only have been conceived in so backward a country as Italy: "We've had machines in England for a donkey's years. They're no novelty to *us*." But for all that Pound and Lewis would learn from Marinetti's entrepreneurialism, his great talent for self-promotion, they developed a very different sense of what was needful for further progress in the arts. Where Marinetti celebrated energy as speed and movement, Pound and Lewis celebrated the concentrated energy of pattern. Pound defined a "vortex" as "the point of maximum energy" and as he went on returned to the language of the luminous detail that had marked his critical work for several years now. Tying his new movement to his last, Pound wrote: "The image is not a idea. It is a radiant node or cluster; it is what I can, and must perforce, call a VORTEX, from which, and through which, and into which, ideas are constantly rushing." It is not movement, then, but a still point like the eye of a hurricane. With Pound's vorticist manifestos, his critical sensibility reached full maturity; his poetics would still need another five years or so to catch up, and even

at that depended heavily on interaction with another new contact.

T. S. ELIOT AND *MAUBERLEY*

In late September 1914, Pound was called on by another aspiring poet, a young American fresh out of Harvard University named T. S. Eliot. In showing Pound the manuscript of "The Love Song of J. Alfred Prufrock," Eliot scattered any lingering bitterness Pound might have had over the imagist business (and a business is precisely what it had quickly become), demonstrating that imagism was not sufficient anodyne for the lifelessness of the poetry of the time. When Pound forwarded Eliot's manuscript to Harriet Monroe, he called it "the most interesting contribution I've had from an American," adding that "he is the only American I know of who has made what I can call adequate preparation for writing. He has actually trained himself *and* modernized himself *on his own*." A transformed dramatic monolog where the implied interlocutor is not another person but rather the speaker's own unconscious, "Prufrock" represented a way of parleying with tradition, of using tradition to establish modernity. Pound immediately incorporated Eliot into his vorticist activities and included Eliot's "Preludes" and "Rhapsody on a Windy Night" in the second number of *Blast*—an inclusion that would become almost inconceivable ten years later, given Eliot's increasingly conservative turn. In November, Pound published a second anthology—which included nothing imagist and no one published in *Des Imagistes* except William Carlos Williams, but featured five poems by Eliot. Then, in 1917, Pound and Eliot embarked on a joint venture. Reacting against what seemed to them the dilution of imagist principles by Amy Lowell and her clique, they agreed to assume a particular formal discipline: they would each write a twentieth-century update of the satirical quatrains of Théophile Gautier, a French poet from the middle of the previous century. What resulted was Eliot's second volume of poems, *Poems* (1920), and Pound's *Hugh Selwyn Mauberley (Life and Contacts)* (1920).

Mauberley was the last important poem that Pound would publish that was not a part of the *Cantos*. As such, it is particularly important that the poem comprises a complex, ambivalent farewell to the aestheticism of his early career. The poem in some sense might be Pound's greatest tribute to Ford, in that it treats a character in almost novelistic fashion, though written in Gautier-like quatrains. Developing Gustave Flaubert's technique of free-indirect discourse (we are told in "Mauberley

1920" that "His true Penelope / Was Flaubert"), the poem destabilizes perspective, so that sometimes we seem to be following Mauberley's career from the perspective of his contacts, and at other times, as in the celebrated "Envoi" (1919), it seems to be Mauberley's own voice that speaks. The poem divides into two sections, one dated 1919, and one 1920, and the relation between them remains a matter of critical controversy: does the second part further develop the first, or does it reject, even cancel the first? Whatever else might be uncertain, there can be no doubt that this instability is built into the poem and is part of its design. As a farewell to his own, early aestheticism, "Mauberley" was both an admission of error and an implicit affirmation of vision. Mauberley is both Pound, himself, and he is not Pound. The poem opens:

> For three years, out of key with his time,
> He strove to resuscitate the dead art
> Of poetry; to maintain "the sublime"
> In the old sense. Wrong from the start—
>
> No, hardly, but . . .

It is possible to read those "three years" as the period of Pound's concentrated agitation for imagism and then for vorticism. But what to make of the immediately canceled affirmation of line four, "wrong from the start," in his attempt to "maintain 'the sublime' / In the old sense."? The poem takes this canceled admission of error as a point of departure, not closure. The "but" clause begun in line five is never completed (which is why we break off the quotation in mid-line). Is the project of resuscitating poetry, of reaching again for "the sublime" as opposed to the conventional pretty, necessarily wrong? The poem gives us reasons to think why it might be, but Pound's own answer comes only implicitly, in his virtually tireless activities over the next forty-some-odd years, activities stilled neither by public indifference, political error and isolation, nor even by long incarceration in St. Elizabeths Hospital.

FIRST ATTEMPTS AT CANTOS

There were several false starts at what was to become his life's work. Published in the June 1917 number of *Poetry*, still some three years before even *Mauberley*, "Three Cantos" appeared to inaugurate Pound's long-considered attempt to write a modern epic. The sequence opened with an address to Robert Browning, whose long narrative poem *Sordello* represented the last previous effort of consequence:

> Hang it all, there can be but one *Sordello*!
> But say I want to, say I take your whole bag of tricks

> Let in your quirks and tweeks, and say the thing's an
>   art-form,
> Your *Sordello*, and that the modern world
> Needs such a rag-bag to stuff all its thought in . . .

For all the apparent brashness of the opening grumble, this was a tentative beginning—a poem about the poet's inability to compose poetry. The poem is not even positive that "the modern" world needs such a thing as epic. Later in the same canto, Pound questions the value of poetic personae:

> Is't worth the evasion, what were the use
> of setting figures up and breathing life upon them
> Were't not *our* life . . .

Still struggling for the right form wherein to relate modernity to history, "Three Cantos" was an inconclusive affair and, like *Mauberley*, notable primarily as a kind of exorcism. Pound would republish the sequence twice over the next eight months. Thereafter, nothing further of the *Cantos* appeared in print until the first version of "The Fourth Canto" appeared in the June 1920 number of *The Dial*. Between 1919 and 1925, Canto IV went through numerous revisions, but was at last the first canto to reach final form. After that, and after the publication of *A Draft of XVI Cantos* in late January 1925, Pound never again looked back.

Of course, the idea of final form in the *Cantos* is itself a vexed question. The very title of the poem—*Cantos*—suggests a provisional quality. The word in its most literal sense is simply Italian for "song." This provisional quality is amplified by the titles of the various parts of the work. *A Draft of XVI Cantos* was followed five years later by *A Draft of XXX Cantos* (1930). The other sections of the poem published before World War II perpetuate this pattern of inconclusive or themeless titles. More than any poem in history before it, the *Cantos* is open in form. It is a poem that values the play of mind and imagination more than it does mere finish, and that makes extraordinary demands on its readers in an attempt to engage them in that play. But then, as Pound put it in his singular *Guide to Kulchur* (1938): "Man reading shd. be man intensely alive. The book shd. be a ball of light in one's hand."

THE "POEM INCLUDING HISTORY" AS *NEKUIA*

Pound's real progress on the *Cantos* seems to have been launched by his work with Eliot on the manuscripts and typescripts of *The Waste Land* (1922), which Eliot in near despair had given him to read in November 1921. The "caesarian operation" (Pound's phrase) that he performed to bring the poem into the world has been justly celebrated, by Eliot himself first and foremost. But Pound evidently got as good as he gave: Eliot's use of the blind seer, Tiresias, whom Odysseus seeks out in the underworld in order to learn the way back home, suggested to Pound in a way that it did not to Eliot a new way of engaging the past.

Canto I begins *in medias res*, or mid-sentence: "And then went down to the ship." What precedes this sentence is the Homeric material of Book XI of the *Odyssey*, where the witch goddess, Circe, sends Odysseus to the underworld to learn how to evade the wrath of Poseidon and make his way home. What is notable about Pound's presentation, however, is that he does not simply translate from Homer, but rather translates from the sixteenth-century Latin translation of Andreas Divus. More than this, Pound translates in language that recalls the Anglo-Saxon of the eleventh-century manuscript (the poem itself probably dating from the ninth century) *The Seafarer*. This move, this leaving visible of the various tissues of mediation, heralds one of the enduring features of the work.

Nekuia (pronounced ne-KWEE-a) is the name that scholars have long given to Book XI of the *Odyssey*; the word denotes a magical rite in which ghosts are called up and questioned about the future, and some form of this rite figures in virtually all ancient epics. For Pound there was something especially primal about this scene; he knew that the Homeric poems comprise a gathering of various elements from oral tradition, and of these the *nekuia* is regarded to be among the most ancient. To open his poem with a *nekuia* would thus be to begin by communing with the potential entirety of human cultural history. Moreover, Canto I breaks off as it began, *in medias res* (the last words of the canto are "so that:"), and the poem never actually takes us out of the underworld. One way of understanding the structural importance of this is to conceive of the rest of the poem as a continual conversing with the dead and an attempt to find order in the throng and clamor in which the poet finds himself.

Nekuia suggests a principle of organization whereby the *Cantos* can be understood as a sustained communion with ghosts—a calling forth of voices from the past in order to question them about the future. This would in any case comprise one way of attempting "a poem including history"—which is the way in which Pound defined "epic" in his *ABC of Reading* (1934). Indeed, this emphasis on history grew increasingly pronounced over the next decade. By the time he was writing *Guide to Kulchur* (1938), his major effort to expound the historiographical method pursued in the *Cantos*, Pound was insisting that "the 'new' historic sense in our time demands . . . whole slabs of the records." By "whole slabs" he meant unmediated blocks of text from older materials. He wanted a historical method that included "concrete" pieces of historical evidence, rather like the way that, in collage, found objects are affixed to one surface. He wanted a method that could include that evidence "whole," and because the force of his claims for universal truth rested on a primary demonstration of a multifariousness of evidence, he wanted a means of presenting his evidence in all its "strangeness" from the familiarities of modern life; this strangeness would charge his demonstration of parallels through time with that much extra force.

Most of these later developments were apparent even in Canto I. There was the large block of concrete evidence, in the form of the translation from Homer. There was the "strangeness" that necessarily arises from contact with ghosts, or with the dead, but that ultimately connected with familiar modern speech; for instance, just as Odysseus beat back the approach of his own mother to ensure that the prophet Tiresias would have an opportunity to speak, so too does Pound turn on his medieval source, commanding, "Lie Quiet, Divus," as though telling him to stand back so that Homer himself might come forward. (But that very command paradoxically calls attention to the presence of a mediating voice.) Indeed, Odysseus's struggle to ensure that it is Tiresias who gets the opportunity to speak prefigures Pound's later struggles to condense masses of primary material into the few, intensely luminous details that he believed his purpose required. By the time he was working on *Eleven New Cantos* (1934), his primary materials had become much more historical-political in nature than literary, with his principal subjects being certain American presidents like Thomas Jefferson and, sadly, the Italian dictator Benito Mussolini. (Pound also proposed these parallels more directly in his polemic, *Jefferson and/or Mussolini: L'idea statale, Fascism As I Have Seen It*, 1935). As the *Cantos* developed, the didactic features of Pound's work became increasingly unmistakable, but this aspect, too, represents an amplification of previous tendencies more than something new.

DIDACTIC POETRY AND LYRICIZED ECONOMICS

In July 1922, Pound wrote to one of his former professors at the University of Pennsylvania that "it's all rubbish to pretend that art isn't didactic. A Revelation is always didactic." But, he added, "art can't offer a patent medicine. A failure to distinguish that from a profounder didacticism has led to the errors of 'aesthete's critique'"—the latter phrase referring to the poets of the 1890s who insisted on "art for art's sake." This phrase, "a profounder didacticism," suggests much about the nature of the *Cantos*. The poem was not going to speechify and tell people what to do; it was not to talk about experience at all but aimed rather itself to be a unique experience that might move readers from their accustomed ways of thinking toward a vision of patterns that unite diverse civilizations. Ultimately, Pound's goal was to aestheticize the sociopolitical and to politicize the aesthetic in order to release poetry from the stifling, perfumed rooms into which he believed it had been forced during the nineteenth century, and in order to release his readers from the compartmentalized lives that made it possible for the avaricious and soulless continually to exploit and manipulate them.

Sometimes, despite these aims, Pound's didactic impulses found quite thematically direct expression. Canto XLV, for instance, the celebrated "Usura" canto, inveighs passionately against the age-old practice of usury—lending money for interest:

With Usura hath no man a house of good stone
each block cut smooth and well fitting
that design might cover their face
with usura
hath no man a painted paradise on his church wall

From *The Fifth Decad* [sic] *of Cantos* (1937), the "Usura" canto is particularly striking in that it joins Pound at his most pedantic with Pound at his most archaic; the quasi-Renaissance language of the canto has a kind of distancing effect on its didactic message, implicitly suggesting that the poem itself has no connection with that usury-dependent economic system even as it reminds readers that it was not Pound, but the ancients, who first conceived this prohibition.

The next published section of the poem, *Cantos LII-LXXI* (1940), completed just before the outbreak of World War II, further developed this synthesis of didactic aims on the present with lyrical distancing devices. In this case, baffling many of his first readers, Pound turned to China. This decad of cantos not only charts a course through Chinese history, it also—drawing heavily on Ernest Fenollosa's theory of the ideogram—includes large Chinese ideograms on the page (as had Canto LI, the last canto of the previous sequence). Pound laid out

the purpose of this volume in *Guide to Kulchur*: "The LESSON of Chinese history? As I can have no pretence to 'potting' it here, might nevertheless be of two kinds. By implication, we might more despise and suspect the kind of education which we (my generation) received, and we might acquire some balance in NOT mistaking recurrence for innovation." The cantos have a lesson, and they aim to reveal pattern ("recurrence") in the manifold details of history, bringing out that pattern by isolating luminous details from narrative detailing.

THE PISAN CANTOS AND A PRIZE FIGHT

In 1934, Pound published a volume of essays that he called *Make It New*, and the volume began with an essay called "Date Line" that carried the subheading, "Rapallo Jan. 28th Anno XII." The essay itself is an important restatement of the connections among poetry, history, and economics, but when T. S. Eliot included it in his collection *Literary Essays of Ezra Pound* (1954), he omitted the subheading (even though its content is repeated toward the end of the essay). The reason for the omission is that "Anno XII" indicates the twelfth year of the fascist era—Mussolini had been in power since the so-called March on Rome of 1922. Pound had followed Mussolini's career since 1927. By 1934 he had become an outspoken supporter of all for which he understood Mussolini to stand. The reasons for Pound's enormous political failings remain subject to debate. Some scholars have purported to identify Pound's fascism as implicit in even his earliest work, while others would identify a falling into error at some point in the mid-1930s. Nevertheless, there is no mistaking that Pound thought of himself as part of the fascist experiment in Italy. That said, Mussolini's fascism should not indiscriminately be associated with Hitler's National Socialism. Pound's enthusiasm for Mussolini most likely owed first to his comparative isolation in Rapallo, a small town on the Italian Riviera where Pound and Dorothy had moved in 1924, and second to his increasingly pronounced dissatisfaction with liberal democracy—which he had come to dismiss as "a mess of mush." Less certain, however, is the extent that Pound's political commitments require any particular political reading. As the poet and critic Robert Perelman has suggested, there are roads in the *Cantos* that lead to fascism, but readers do not have to take them. There are fascist elements in the poem, but to read the poem so as to insist on them is unnecessarily to adhere to a course that the structural dynamics of the poem do not warrant.

As an open-form work that turns on repeated leitmotifs or, as Pound calls them, "subject rhymes," the *Cantos* characteristically works by overdetermining the meaning of particular details, any one of which usually connects with not one but several other details in a given canto, and with other motifs from other cantos both backwards and forwards in the poem. That is, the *Cantos* functions by juxtaposing voices and materials from widely heterogeneous sources into dynamic—ideogrammic—relation. Pound's poem represents the world as he knew it; Italian fascism was part—a large part—of his world, but he understood it in terms of its relations to older, even ancient values. Pound was interested in how fascism fit into a larger scheme of values, not into remaking the world to fit a fascist schema.

Nevertheless, his support for Mussolini eventually attracted the attention of Washington. He had already begun making radio broadcasts for Minculpop, the Italian Ministry of Popular Culture, in support of the Italian cause. (The first was on 11 January 1935, and the broadcasts had become regular in early 1941.) When the United States entered the World War II and U.S. citizens were ordered repatriated, Pound appeared before George Wadsworth, the U.S. chargé d'affaires in Rome, only to have his passport confiscated on the spot—apparently because of his radio broadcasts. In mid-July 1942 the government offered Pound a conditional passport allowing his return to the United States on condition that he remain there for the duration of the war. Returning to the United States was already a difficult prospect. Pound's parents were by that point also living in Rapallo, and his father had just suffered a broken hip and was too frail to travel. Furthermore, the American chargé made difficulties over Pound's English wife and then told him that his daughter, who was not a U.S. citizen, could not join him. Indignant, Pound resolved to wait out the war in Rapallo. That decision would have serious consequences.

The FBI began its investigation of Pound in December 1942, and a Washington, D.C., grand jury indicted him in absentia for treason in July 1943. During the war years, Pound's progress on the *Cantos* slowed from the astonishing pace of the late 1930s to next to nothing. Between the confiscation of his passport and his capture by Italian partisans, he completed only two cantos. Both overtly treat the war, and the first summons the spirit of Marinetti; both were quietly suppressed in all postwar printings of the *Cantos* until the tenth printing of the poem in 1986. But the most celebrated part of his work was yet to come.

After being taken into custody by American troops, Pound was shortly transferred to a military detention camp outside of Pisa. Once there, Pound was put into what he later called "the gorilla cage," a six by six-and-a-half feet cage hastily constructed—just for Pound—of jagged airstrip metal. Exposed to the elements and under intense floodlights at night, the sixty-five-year-old Pound suffered inflammation of the eyes, claustrophobia, and mental confusion. In short, convinced that he was soon to be executed, he collapsed physically, and with a temporary loss of memory. As a consequence of this collapse, a pup tent was set up in his cage, and he was allowed to use the typewriter in the camp medical center.

It was here, under these grave circumstances, that he wrote much of the volume that came to be known as *Pisan Cantos* (1948). This volume would win the 1949 Bollingen Prize for poetry and spark the greatest and most bitter debate of American literary history—the only national debate over poetry that the United States has ever known. Much of the volume is marked by the poet's struggle to discern what is left of his dreams, now that all his material hopes have apparently come to ruin. Here again Pound's language becomes self-consciously archaic, as though taking in the wreck of Europe from a Tieresian perspective:

> What thou lovest well remains,
> $\qquad$ The rest is dross
> What thou lov'st well shall not be reft from thee
> What thou lov'st well is thy true heritage
> Whose world, or mine or theirs
> $\qquad$ Or is it of none?

Pound was returned to Washington by military transport in November 1945. On 13 February in a sanity hearing, he was declared to be of "unsound mind" and thus unfit for trial. He was remanded to St. Elizabeths Hospital in Washington, D.C., until his condition improved sufficiently for that trial to take place. His day in court never came; it does not look good for a democratic government to execute poets for political crimes, and no one representing the government pressed hard for anything more than simply getting Pound out of the way and out of the limelight. As for the limelight, their move backfired.

At the end of 1948, a committee of the most eminent poets in the country, including W. H. Auden, Louise Bogan, T. S. Eliot, Robert Lowell, Allen Tate, and Robert Penn Warren, selected *Pisan Cantos* for the first annual Bollingen Prize—the first and last time the federal government ever sponsored a prize for poetry. Whipped up by conservative voices like poet Robert Hillyer, or by

Norman Cousins and Harrison Smith of the *Saturday Review*, a public outcry erupted that lasted for over two years. Even mass circulation organs like *Time* magazine covered the story. The Bollingen controversy, as most parties to it recognized, marked the exasperated backlash of middle-class culture to the academic culture that now proposed more to lead it than to serve it. In the end Pound got to keep his prize, but the Library of Congress terminated its association with the Bollingen award, and while Pound's defenders succeeded in making their case for the separation of the poet from the poetry, they did so at the cost of further removing poetry from ordinary discourse. The realm of poetry was made safe from politics, but it was a much reduced realm—a terrible irony, given that Pound's lifelong aim had been to expand the concerns of modern poetry and make it once more matter to cultural life in the broadest sense. Given that Pound had endeavored his entire career to capture the attention of the public, whether in the publication of his numerous popularizing primers, his radio broadcasts, or his periodical columns and essays, there was an especially pointed irony in that with the Bollingen controversy, Pound finally received genuinely broad public attention—but attention that was for the most part hostile. Strangely, perhaps, Pound himself stayed quiet throughout this long, national donnybrook, but he would not keep his own counsel for long.

In fact, the Bollingen controversy was just the beginning of Pound's creating embarrassment for his captors. While incarcerated at St. Elizabeths, Pound worked more actively than ever, maintaining (with Dorothy's help) a furious level of correspondence; writing cantos; doing translations of Sophocles, Confucian odes, and Egyptian love songs; writing critical essays; and continuing to stump for the economic reform that had preoccupied him since meeting C. H. Douglas, founder of the Social Credit movement, back in 1919. (Douglas's basic A+B Theorem is that the cost of raw materials and the cost of labor added together are never enough to pay for all the goods produced—which means a constant need for export, and eventually war to open up new markets.) Pound became, in additional to all this, something approaching a site of pilgrimage for the next generation of poets, poets who, had he remained in Italy, might never have been able to meet him—poets like Charles Olsen, Hayden Carruth, and Allen Ginsberg.

Pound's being in Washington also facilitated his regular contact with James Laughlin, an aspiring poet who under Pound's encouragement founded New Directions Press, which retains the copyright on most of Pound's North American publications. During the 1950s, Laughlin brought out—in a series of paperback books that look rather like a uniform edition—new titles, such as T. S. Eliot's *Literary Essays of Ezra Pound*, William Cookson's *Selected Prose of Ezra Pound*, Confucius (1951), *Translations* (1953; with an introduction by Hugh Kenner, who became the don of Pound studies with his magisterial 1972 study, *The Pound Era*); and *Pavannes and Divagations* (1958); and reprints in the 1950s and afterward of older titles like *Guide to Kulchur*, *ABC of Reading* (1934), and *The Spirit of Romance* (1910), as well as expanded editions of *Personae* (1990; the selected, pre-*Cantos* poetry) and of the *Cantos*.

THE FINAL VOLUMES

The second volume of cantos to be published during Pound's incarceration carried the defiant title of *Section: Rock-Drill: LXXXV–XCV* (1955)—a title that announced his enduring determination to make his case, to get his ideas through to an indifferent or even resistant public. The title recalled something Pound had published in the pages of *Poetry* forty years before, where he averred that "I am boring my little hole in the adamantine stupidity of England, America, New Zealand and a few places elsewhere. I even enjoy the job." Neither his sense of mission, nor his zeal, had changed much in the course of his lifetime.

The final volume of cantos that Pound completed is called *Thrones de los Cantares: XCVI–CIX* (1959). These cantos contain some of the most lyrical passages in the entire work, but they are also the most challenging. Pound's pressing sense that he still had not gotten through to the public led him not to ease up on his principles of ideogrammic inclusion or his engaging in the "new historical method," but rather to press the principles harder.

While Pound focused on *Thrones*, friends and allies were renewing their efforts to win him freedom. Led by the poets Robert Frost and Archibald MacLeish, they at last prevailed. The court ruled on 18 April 1958 that there could be no benefit to the United States in maintaining Pound in indefinite custody, since that custody could not contribute to his recovery, and it ordered him to be released into his wife's custody (technically, into the custody of "the committee for Ezra Pound"). Pound was released on 7 May. After another month visiting with friends, he set sail on 30 June for Italy. The liner reached Italy on 9 July, and Pound—notoriously unrepentant and in a way that embarrassed most of those who had agitated for his release—greeted the awaiting press by raising his arm in the fascist salute. Later that month, he and his small entourage reached Schloss Brunnenberg, an old castle in the Italian Tirol that daughter Mary was working to transform into a center for the Ezuversity—a material embodiment of Pound's vision. As winter set in, however, the altitude and cold proved too much for the aging poet, and in March 1959 he and Dorothy moved back to Rapallo.

THE POUND LEGACY

In 1960, Pound told the poet Donald Hall (who had come to interview him) that what remained for him in the *Cantos* was the finding of "a verbal formula to combat the rise of brutality." But something was happening to Pound, something that ushered in the final phase of his life. Pound sank into a deep depression that left him increasingly challenged for words. He began to tell visitors that he had made a "botch" of his life's work and that the *Cantos* were a failure. At the time, and for many years afterward, commentators assumed that Pound's silence in these years was a self-imposed penance. Pound himself claimed otherwise, telling one reporter, "I did not enter silence; silence captured me." There were increasingly fewer days of productive writing, and there were to be no further completed volumes of *Cantos*.

The *Cantos* could not have been finished, however, even if Pound had another twenty years to work on them, because his sense of closure depended at last not on the organic unity of his poem—perfect coherence among the individual parts—but on the organic integrity of culture. Among Pound's oldest and deepest convictions was the sense that human relations constitute a totality or wholeness wherein all forms of activity are profoundly connected; the structure of the *Cantos* aimed to represent this totality—the ways in which poetry and economics and politics and ethics are profoundly interrelated. Thus, the perfectly realized poem would leave its trace on a more perfectly realized society, and poetic closure could come only with the revitalization of culture to which the poem was dedicated. So much might be seen in the relentless determination of *Rock-Drill* and *Thrones*. For as long as he physically was able, Pound struggled under this impossibly demanding sense of mission. When in his last years he confessed his sense of failure, he limited that failure to his actual work. He never renounced the vision of ideal wholeness and rejuvenation.

Pound left behind a complex legacy that is still unfolding. Since he undertook the *Cantos*, any number of other poets have followed his lead and struggled to craft a modern epic: William Carlos Williams (*Paterson*), H.D. (*Trilogy* and *Helen in Egypt*), Basil Bunting (*Briggflatts*), Charles Olson (*Maximus*), Louis Zukofsky (*A*), Robert Lowell (*History* and *Notebooks*), and Melvin Tolson (*Harlem Gallery*). For thirty years there have been three literary journals (two in the United States, *Paideuma* and *Sagetrieb*, and one in the United Kingdom, *Agenda*) dedicated to promoting the writing and study of poetry in the Poundian tradition. Pound's example continues to inform the dynamics of poetic translation, with poet-translators like Robert Fitzgerald insisting that the translation should be a real poem in its own right and one that parleys the original into a modern idiom. And finally, and perhaps most problematically, Pound has probably forever changed the relation of literary study to the broader reading public, and even the relation of that public to poetry itself; as Donald Davie remarked in 1964, "Pound has made it impossible any longer to regard the poet as seer." And so, as the significance of the *Cantos* continues to be as fiercely debated as its meaning, Pound's work remains as open to the future as it was to the past.

[*See also* Confessional Poetry; Eliot, T. S.; H.D.; Imagism and American Poets; *and* Long Poem, The.]

SELECTED WORKS

A Lume Spento (1908)
The Spirit of Romance (1910)
Patria mia (1912)
Des Imagistes (1914)
Cathay (1915)
Catholic Anthology (1915)
The Classic Noh Theatre of Japan (1916)
A Memoir of Gaudier-Brzeska (1916)
Dialogues of Fontenelle (1917)
The Chinese Written Character as a Medium for Poetry (1919)
Hugh Selwyn Mauberley (1920)
Instigations (1920)
Fancy Goods and Open All Night (1922)
The Natural Philosophy of Love (1922)
The Call of the Road (1923)
Indiscretions; or, Une revue de deux mondes (1923)
How to Read (1931)
Profile (1932)
ABC of Economics (1933)
Active Anthology (1933)
ABC of Reading (1934)
Make It New (1934)

*Jefferson and/or Mussolini: L' idea statale, Fascism As I Have
    Seen It* (1935)
Polite Essays (1937)
Guide to Kulchur (1938)
Elektra (1949)
Translations (1953)
Shih Ching: The Classic Anthology Defined by Confucius
    (1954) *Moscardino* (1956)
Selected Poems (1957)
Women of Trachis (1957)
Pavannes and Divagations (1958)
*Impact: Essays on Ignorance and the Decline of American
    Civilization* (1960)
Love Songs of Ancient Egypt (1961)
Confucius to Cummings (1964)
*Confucius: The Unwobbling Pivot, The Great Digest, The
    Analects* (1969)
Selected Cantos (1970)
Selected Prose (1973)
Collected Early Poems of Ezra Pound (1976)
Ezra Pound and Music: The Complete Criticism (1977)
Ezra Pound Speaking: Radio Speeches of World War II (1978)
Ezra Pound and the Visual Arts (1980)
Ezra Pound and Japan: Letters and Essays (1987)
Personae (1990)
*Ezra Pound's Poetry and Prose: Contributions to
    Periodicals* (1991)
Cantos (1995)
Selected Letters, 1907–1941

FURTHER READING

Alexander, Michael. *The Poetic Achievement of Ezra Pound.* Berkeley, Calif., 1979. A general overview that essentially ignores Pound's extra-literary activities.

Bell, Ian F. A. *The Critic as Scientist: The Modernist Poetics of Ezra Pound.* London and New York, 1981.

Bischoff, Volker. *Ezra Pound Criticism, 1905–1985: A Chronological Listing of Publications in English.* An authoritative bibliography of critical books and essays about Ezra Pound.

Bush, Ronald. *The Genesis of Ezra Pound's Cantos.* Princeton, N.J., 1976. The best account of how Pound moved from the *Three Cantos* of 1917 to the real beginning of the poem.

Carpenter, Humphrey. *A Serious Character: The Life of Ezra Pound.* There still is no biography of Pound that demonstrates a sensitivity to both the poet and his work, but Carpenter, though generally hostile and even dismissive of Pound, offers the most thorough attempt yet.

Coyle, Michael. *Ezra Pound, Popular Genres, and the Discourse of Culture.* University Park, Pa., 1995. A study of how Pound's combinations of poetry with other kinds of writing relate to nineteenth-century notions of culture.

Coyle, Michael, ed. *Ezra Pound and African American Modernism.* Orono, Me., 2001.

Dasenbrock, Reed. *The Literary Vorticism of Ezra Pound and Wyndham Lewis.* Baltimore, 1985. A tough-minded account of vorticism.

Davie, Donald. *Ezra Pound: The Poet as Sculptor.* New York, 1964. Possibly the first nonpartisan examination of Pound's work, by one of his most influential critics.

Davie, Donald. *Ezra Pound.* London, 1975.

Espey, John. *Ezra Pound's Mauberley: A Study in Composition.* Los Angeles, 1955. Still the definitive study of *Hugh Selwyn Mauberley.*

Froula, Christine. *A Guide to Ezra Pound's Selected Poems.* New York, 1973.

Froula, Christine. *To Write Paradise: Style and Error in Pound's Cantos.* New Haven, Conn., 1984. A rigorous account of Canto IV and a richly suggestive study of how error functions as a constituent feature of the *Cantos.*

Gallup, Donald. *A Bibliography of Ezra Pound.* London, 1983. Indispensable for any thorough navigation through Pound's voluminous publications.

Kenner, Hugh. *The Poetry of Ezra Pound.* New York, 1951. An influential contribution to the ending of the Bollingen controversy and the beginning of modern Pound studies.

Kenner, Hugh. *The Pound Era.* Berkeley, Calif., 1971. A hugely influential book, written in an allusive and paratactic style that recalls Pound's own, which attempts to represent the whole of modernism in Pound's image.

Lindberg, Kathryne. *Reading Pound Reading: Modernism after Nietzsche.* New York, 1987. A compelling study that examines Pound through a Nietzschean lens.

Longenbach, James. *Stone Cottage: Pound, Yeats, and Modernism.* New York, 1988. Focuses on Pound's relationship with Yeats, and suggests how Yeats encouraged Pound to conceive of the task of the modern poet in elite, even hermetic terms.

MacDonald, Gail. *Learning to Be Modern: Pound, Eliot, and the American University.* New York, 1993. Examines how Pound and Eliot shaped the nature and structure of modern education, also discusses the analytical tools we now use to understand them.

Marsh, Alec. *Money and Modernity: Pound, Williams, and the Spirit of Jefferson*. Tuscaloosa, Ala, 1998. The most important study of Pound and economics.

Nicholls, Peter. *Ezra Pound: Politics, Economics, and Writing*. London, 1984. A groundbreaking study—the first to explore the connections between the literary and political dimensions of Pound's writing.

Norman, Charles. *The Case of Ezra Pound*. New York, 1968. A sourcebook for the salvos and fusillades of the Bollingen controversy.

Rainey, Lawrence S. *Institutions of Modernism: Literary Elites and Public Culture*. New Haven, Conn., 1998. A cultural studies approach to Pound that attends to how Pound attempted to excite public interest in his work.

Redman, Tim. *Ezra Pound and Italian Fascism*. New York, 1987. A thorough examination of the writings of Pound's Italian period, in both English and Italian.

Ruthven, K. K. *A Guide to Ezra Pound's Personae*. Berkeley, Calif., 1969. An annotated gloss and guide through the poems Pound collected in *Personae*.

Sherry, Vincent. *Ezra Pound, Wyndham Lewis, and Radical Modernism*. New York, 1993. Revisionist approach to vorticism that relates its emphasis on the eye to a radical politics.

Sieburth, Richard. *Instigations: Ezra Pound and Rémy de Gourmont*. Cambridge, Mass., 1978.

Sullivan, J. P. *Ezra Pound and Sextus Propertius: A Study in Creative Translation*. The definitive account of Pound's most accomplished poem prior to the *Cantos*.

Surette, Leon. *The Birth of Modernism: Ezra Pound, T. S. Eliot, W. B. Yeats, and the Occult*. Montreal, 1993. Situates Pound's work in the context of late nineteenth- and early-twentieth-century spiritualism and fascination with the occult.

Terrell, Carroll F., ed. *A Companion to the Cantos of Ezra Pound*. 2 vols. Berkeley, Calif., 1980. A canto-by-canto gloss of allusions, quotations, and foreign phrases.

Yao, Steven G. *Translation and the Languages of Modernism: Gender, Politics, Language*. New York, 2002. An innovative account of Pound's work as translator, and the relation of that work to modernism as a broader field.

See also the article on *The Pisan Cantos*, immediately following.

EZRA POUND'S
THE PISAN CANTOS

by Ronald Bush

The Pisan Cantos (1948) depart from Ezra Pound's usual historical focus in the *Cantos* (1917–1968) to depict the explosive personal crisis that swallowed Pound up at the end of World War II. Like Winston Churchill and the editors of the *New Republic*, Pound had been an early admirer of Mussolini, and in 1924 he took up residence in the Ligurian seaside resort of Rapallo. However, unlike most of Mussolini's other admirers, Pound remained stalwart even after Mussolini invaded Abyssinia in 1935 and enacted a series of anti-Semitic laws in 1938. Early in World War II, Pound accepted an invitation to broadcast on Rome radio and used it to condemn hostilities between America and Italy, which he was convinced were the work of bankers, arms dealers, and Jews. When the United States declared war on the Axis, Pound made the fateful decision to continue these broadcasts (which grew ever more anti-Semitic) and was placed under indictment in absentia for treason in July 1943. As 1944 wore on, Pound could not help but see that the inevitable fall of Mussolini would mean the end of his own dream of a fascist utopia and the destruction of much that he held dear, including the cultural treasures around him. Nor was it clear that he would be allowed to survive the peace.

By the end of May 1944, Pound and his wife Dorothy were forced to flee their flat in Rapallo and moved in with Pound's lifelong companion, Olga Rudge, in an excruciating ménage à trois. Their house was situated on cliffs above Rapallo in the village of Sant'Ambrogio. It was here that Pound read the news that many of Italy's artistic treasures had been blasted by Allied air forces. Pound turned to anger and lamentation, and the extremity of his condition realized itself in visionary encounters on the hillside.

Pound channeled his defiance into Cantos 72 and 73, written in an Italian that combined the philosophical idiom of Dante and Guido Cavalcanti with colloquial rage. These fascist apologies were left out of collected editions of the *Cantos* from 1948 until 1991, with no explanation of why the poet skipped from Canto 71 to Canto 74. His visionary moments were incorporated into sequels that

he drafted in Italian from December 1944 to February 1945, poems that absorbed the extended preparations for an epic Paradise which he had contemplated since the beginning of the war. Pound's winter poetry entertains "ancient voices" and affirms a paradisal bedrock in human experience that cannot be destroyed.

Before Pound could polish these Italian verses, though, he found himself a prisoner of the American army. The government vacillated about what to do with him, but finally ordered him incarcerated, aged nearly sixty, at the U.S. Army Disciplinary Training Center (DTC), a GI prison camp located near the Viareggio road just north of Pisa. From 24 May to 15 June 1945, he stayed in a concrete-floored, wire isolation cage in the open air of a fierce sun and slept under constant illumination. He suffered acute symptoms of confusion, anxiety, and fatigue, and ultimately broke down. He was transferred to an officer's tent in the medical compound, and he remained there until 16 November, when he was taken without warning to a Washington-bound plane.

A MULTILAYERED CONFESSIONAL POEM

In the period between June and November, 1945, Pound composed a powerful and multilayered confessional poem that refashioned his own despair, humility, contrition, and rage into a modernist psychodrama in which he cast himself as the last voice of the languages and cultures of Europe—"a lone ant from a broken ant-hill / from the wreckage of Europe, ego scriptor" (Canto 76). The difficulties of this work have to do not only with the reaches of its cultural reference but from the way it presents with great immediacy (but without explanation) the movements of Pound's mind. Take, for example, this passage from Canto 74, the long first poem of *The Pisan Cantos*:

> Butterflies, mint and Lesbia's sparrows,
>   the voiceless with bumm drum and banners,
>   and the ideogram of the guard roosts
>   el triste pensier si volge
>   ad Ussel. A Ventadour
>   va il consire, el tempo rivolge

and at Limoges the young salesman
bowed with such french politeness "No that is impossible."
I have forgotten which city
But the caverns are less enchanting to the unskilled explorer
   than the Urochs as shown on the postals,
we will see those old roads again, question,
       possibly
but nothing appears much less likely,
      Mme Pujol,
and there was a smell of mint under the tent flaps
especially after the rain

Here the sight of butterflies and the smell of mint after a rain quicken Pound's imagination, causing him to associate the sparrows in front of him with Catullus's poem about "Lesbia's sparrows," and by implication, with Venus herself. Pound's intimations, though, are set against the stark reality of the camp, where prison voices are drowned out by drumming. What began in joy turns to sorrow, and Pound (shifting now to his adopted Italian) remembers a rainy trip in better times to the medieval towns of Ussel and Ventadour in southern France. The bleakness of the present moment suffuses Pound's fading recall of a gracious French salesman who answered some request with a phrase that now seems emblematically sad: "No that is impossible."

But Pound cannot remember the name of the Frenchman, though he has not forgotten the disappointment he felt visiting cave paintings nearby. Nor is this disappointment likely to be remedied, as his indefinite confinement will prevent him from revisiting "those old roads" again. Then, inexplicably, he remembers the name of another benign figure from that time, the innkeeper "Mme Pujol," and the power of that recovery (fixed in the ambiguities of a syntax that seems to call out her name) miraculously restores his spirit ("smell of mint under the tent flaps / especially after the rain").

THE DTC, MEMORY, AND THE NATURAL WORLD

In innumerable small moments like this, *The Pisan Cantos* reknit a shattered psyche. Always, though, they are grounded in the here and now. As Pound explained in a contemporary "Note to [the] Base Censor" in which he tried to persuade the military authorities that his typescripts were not encoded sedition, the poems are also alive with the sounds of the camp. In Pound's words, "the form of the poem and main progress is conditioned by its own inner shape, but the life of the DTC passing OUTSIDE the scheme cannot but impinge, or break into the main flow." So the cantos faithfully register the noise

of roll call and drill and the birds on the barbed wire and most importantly the conversation of his fellow prisoners. ("The proper names given," he explains to the censor, "are mostly those of men on sick call seen passing my tent.")

Amid these extraordinary circumstances, Pound draws on memories, the natural world, and ghostly presences to sustain his will to survive. Memory provides his primary resource. Terrified that he might have lost his life's thread when he broke down, he strains to recall the times when he was a boy in Philadelphia and New York City, a young man on his first grand tour of Europe, a fledgling poet in the salons of the great in Venice and London and Paris, a backpacker on the roads of Provence, a husband and lover in Rapallo and Venice, an aging man on the winding paths of Sant'Ambrogio.

Beyond these reminiscences, instances of close natural observation extend the poetry's intense concentration, never more so than in a critical moment near its conclusion, where Pound tenderly records the fall of an infant wasp from its mother's nest and suddenly reflects that "When the mind swings by a grass-blade / an ant's forefoot shall save you" (Canto 83). Like Henry David Thoreau, however, Pound in his naturalism is intent on higher laws. And so he goes on to link the descent and initiation of the infant wasp with the cycles of the sun and seasons, the figures of Persephone and Christ, and the power of the human imagination to transcend mortality. The more Pound loads the immediate with significance, though, the more the quotidian asserts itself. From such tensions, exaggerated by the poem's fragmented technique (which makes us work to follow the reverie's gathering significance), comes a sense of extraordinary authenticity.

"SUAVE EYES, QUIET, NOT SCORNFUL"

Meanwhile, as *The Pisan Cantos*' "winds veer" (Canto 74), we start to notice larger structures. The most obvious concerns a quest like that in Dante's *Purgatorio* for reunion with a beloved whose countenance promises peace. This pattern is much clearer if we consider the sequence in the form that Pound first intended it. His first complete draft began with these lines (later lines eleven and following of Canto 74):

The suave eyes, quiet, not scornful,
   rain also is of the process
What you depart from is not the way

Lines two and three are taken from the writings of Confucius that Pound was translating when he was taken prisoner, and suggest not only the disorder of his current travail but (in terms like "the process" and "the way") also hope and permanence. The line that precedes them brings that hope to life. It presents the shock of an encounter with a pair of eyes that Pound had expected to be "scornful" but which he now discovers to be "suave" and "quiet" instead.

As *The Pisan Cantos* progresses, this haunting vision repeats itself with increasing portentousness and reaches a first climax in Canto 81. Near despair, Pound there senses his beloved's half-seen but radiant presence enter his tent, overpowering "the other lights" around him:

> there came new subtlety of eyes into my tent,
> whether of spirit or hypostasis,
> but what the blindfold hides
> or at carneval
> nor any pair showed anger
> Saw but the eyes and stance between the eyes,
> colour, diastasis,
> careless or unaware it had not the
> Whole tent's room
> nor was place for the full Ειδως ["seeing" or "knowing"]
> interpass, penetrate
> casting but shade beyond the other lights
> sky's clear
> night's sea
> green of the mountain pool
> shone from the unmasked eyes in half-mask's space.
> What thou lovest well remains

The next two cantos reenact this cycle of despair and elevation, until in Canto 83 the beloved's eyes join with his own, and his anguish disappears in a true and compassionate vision of the world around him:

> The eyes, this time my world,
> But pass and look *from* mine
> between my lids.

SOCIETY AND RAGE

This moment of transformation concludes the poem's quest, but not the canto or the sequence, both of which in Pound's first plan end a page later with a tender memory of his mother attending sessions of the U.S. Senate. Personal redemption, Pound implies, cannot in itself redeem society, which has been reduced during the course of his own life to "a dam'd supercilious era." In fact, the sequence's concerns had always been more than personal, and Pound had paid more attention to the world around him than his note to the base censor acknowledged. A considerable part of the sequence's attraction, for example, has to do with the cadences and the generosity of Pound's mostly black fellow prisoners (and with Pound's own

generosity as he opened his poem up to them). So in Canto 74 we overhear one of them warning Pound, "doan you tell no one / I made you that table."

The importance of the quotidian, though, impelled Pound to fashion a structure looser than Dante's epic narrative. In fashioning a nervous and flexible poetic diary, Pound anticipates Robert Lowell's *Day by Day* (1977). His own model seems to have been the lyric and episodic *Testament* (1461) of François Villon, and he took his cue especially from Villon's questions in stanza 29:

> Where are those laughing comrades
> that I was with in former days
> who sang so well, talked so well
> and so excelled in word and deed?
> Some are dead and stiff—
> nothing now remains of them:
> may they find peace in Paradise,
> and may God save the rest.

The very first lines Pound wrote at Pisa memorialize the hanging, on 2 July 1945, of a prisoner named Louis Till, and from then on the *Testament*'s gallows setting helped Pound organize the loose progress of his recovery.

Emphasizing the theme of prison life, though, also stoked Pound's rage against his captors and modern society. So in Canto 74, Pound invokes the *Odyssey* to suggest that the criminals in the camp have been turned into swine by the poison of financial corruption, which Pound observes "in all the veins of the commonweal." Against this horror, *The Pisan Cantos* fulminate in cadences drawn from the prophets. Again like Thoreau, Pound claims as poet a special affinity with nature and decries America's destiny to remain Nature's Nation. The most famous of these passages immediately follows the beloved's epiphany in Canto 81 and addresses the "half black half white" American army:

> The ant's a centaur in his dragon world.
> Pull down thy vanity, it is not man
> Made courage, or made order, or made grace,
> Pull down thy vanity, I say pull down.
> Learn of the green world what can be thy place
> In scaled invention or true artistry
> . . .
> Pull down thy vanity
> Thou art a beaten dog beneath the hail,
> A swollen magpie in a fitful sun,
> Half black half white
> Nor knowst'ou wing from tail

Ultimately this prophetic rage took over the work. Pound thought he had finished the sequence when on

2 October 1945 he wrote his wife Dorothy that "I have done a Decad 74/83 . . . which dont seem any worse than the first 70." On its way to him, though, was a letter of Dorothy's which informed him that J. P. Angold, a promising poet, had died, and that several fascist collaborators were facing death. The news stirred Pound into further composition, and he immediately began a coda to the sequence he thought he had completed. The new canto (84) begins with a cry of grief and includes a bitter farewell to "il Capo [Mussolini], / Pierre [Laval], [and] Vidkun [Quisling]." This unforeseen conclusion changed the sequence irrevocably, and Pound completed the job by moving ten other angry lines to the start of the sequence. Pound's elegy to Mussolini send *The Pisan Cantos* on their way bristling with self-protective hostility and hurtling toward Canto 84.

Without *The Pisan Cantos*, Pound would probably have become known as a fellow traveler of the T. S. Eliot of *The Waste Land* (1922), who self-destructed like so many others on the ideological reefs of the 1930s. It was his ability to portray moments when "the mind swings by a grass blade" that made a new generation regard him as a poet who lived long enough to doubt his strongest convictions and make haunting poetry of the remaining disarray.

FURTHER READING

Bacigalupo, Massimo. *The Forméd Trace: The Later Poetry of Ezra Pound*. New York, 1980. A full thematic and political analysis of *The Pisan Cantos* by a fine Italian critic who is also the son of Pound's friend and physician.

Bush, Ronald. " 'Quiet, Not Scornful': The Composition of the *Pisan Cantos*." In *A Poem Containing History: Textual Studies in the* Cantos, edited by Lawrence Rainey. Ann Arbor, Mich., 1997. A rereading of the *Pisan Cantos* based on archival materials and including an account of Pound's early Italian drafts.

Carne-Ross, D. S. *Instaurations*. Boston, 1979. Includes a fine, close reading of Canto 81.

Kenner, Hugh. *The Pound Era*. Berkeley, Calif., 1971. The best single book on Pound, including an important chapter on *The Pisan Cantos*.

Nicholls, Peter. *Ezra Pound: Politics, Economics, and Writing*. Atlantic Highlands, N.J., 1984. Revisionary criticism that is also deeply historical.

Pound, Omar, and Robert Spoo, eds. *Ezra and Dorothy Pound, Letters in Captivity: 1945–1946*. New York, 1999. Pound's letters to his wife during confinement. Essential material annotated with great care and thoroughness.

Read, Forrest. "The Pattern of the *Pisan Cantos*." *Sewanee Review* 65.3 (1957): 400–419. The earliest and still essential reading of the shape of *The Pisan Cantos*.

Woodward, Anthony. *Ezra Pound and* The Pisan Cantos. London, 1980. A book-length treatment of *The Pisan Cantos* that addresses the poetry's philosophical implications with admirable subtlety.

See also the article on Ezra Pound, immediately preceding.

PROLETARIAN LITERATURE

by Robert Niemi

The heyday for proletarian literature was the 1930s, when the Great Depression pitched capitalism into a severe and protracted crisis and spawned a burgeoning Marxist literary culture bitterly hostile to capitalist values and institutions and committed to revolt. In concert with the virulent backlash against communism in the 1940s and 1950s, the American literary community turned on Depression-era proletarian literature with a vengeance, denouncing it as nothing more than aesthetically worthless propaganda for a disgraced political doctrine. That reductive judgment largely prevailed until the 1960s, when some literary scholars and historians argued for a more nuanced and fair-minded reassessment. After the end of the Cold War, another and much more sweeping and rigorously researched wave of revisionist scholarship has emerged that continues to dispel the old stereotypes about the crudities of proletarian literature. What emerges from the new scholarship is a complex and variegated literature quite unlike the caricature advanced by its detractors.

NINETEENTH-CENTURY PRECURSORS

More than any other major American writer of his day, Herman Melville limned the plight of the industrial proletariat. Born into an affluent New York City mercantile family, Melville lived a charmed youth until his father's bankruptcy and death plunged the family into poverty and eventually forced young Melville to go to sea. Melville's years as a sailor on whalers and warships opened his eyes to the spiritually numbing world of physical labor. Though his relationship to the proletariat was a mixture of helpless pity and aversion, he came to understand the ironclad imperatives of the American class system as few of his contemporaries ever would. After making his literary reputation with South Seas adventure yarns, Melville used his fiction to probe the gap between America's official ideology and its social realities. His fourth book, the quasi-autobiographical *Redburn* (1849), tells the story of a downwardly mobile bourgeois with artistic aspirations forced to adapt to the brutal proletarian life of a sailor. In the process, Melville's alter ego, Redburn, learns that manual labor and mental labor are mutually exclusive, as are the social classes they constitute—an unpopular insight that was central to Melville's tortured artistic vision. His next book, *White-Jacket* (1850), was an exposé of flogging aboard American men-of-war. Even Melville's allegorical masterpiece, *Moby-Dick* (1851) was proletarian fiction inasmuch as it featured mostly working-class characters and a detailed representation of the grisly work of whaling. Some of Melville's short stories, most notably "The Tartarus of Maids" (1855) and "Bartleby the Scrivener" (1856), counted the cost of an ascendant industrial capitalism that reduced its workers to dehumanized cogs in a machine.

Just as the Civil War was breaking out in April 1861, the *Atlantic Monthly* published Rebecca Harding Davis's fine novella *Life in the Iron Mills*, perhaps the first detailed account of factory life in American fiction and an early example of literary realism. The novel's tragic protagonist, Hugh Wolfe, is a gifted sculptor condemned by poverty to work in an iron mill. Convicted of a theft that was actually committed by his cousin Deborah, Wolfe commits suicide in jail, the hapless victim of powerful social forces beyond his control.

Inspired by *Life in the Iron Mills*, Elizabeth Stuart Phelps interviewed survivors of the 1860 Pemberton Mill disaster in Lawrence, Massachusetts, in which eighty-eight factory girls died in a fire after the building they were working in collapsed. Phelps's meticulously researched account of the tragedy, "The Tenth of January," appeared in the *Atlantic Monthly* in March 1868 and was well received. In 1871 Phelps brought out *The Silent Partner*, a novel that focuses on the relationship between Sip, a mill worker, and Miss Kelso, the eponymous "silent partner" in the mill after her father's death. Though on opposite sides of the class divide, both women find solidarity in their rejection of marriage in favor of personal autonomy. Amanda Douglas's *Hope Mills* (1880), Beverly Warner's *Troubled Waters* (1885), and Henry Francis Keenan's *The Money-Makers* (1885) also dealt with labor and class issues.

Attempting to duplicate the success of Edward Bellamy's popular utopian novel, *Looking Backward* (1889), Ignatius Donnelly's strange, anti-Semitic romance, *Caesar's Column* (1890), envisioned a technocratic future America run by a ruthless plutocracy of very rich Jews that keep the working masses in penurious misery. The Brotherhood of Destruction, a revolutionary proletarian group, revolts against and destroys the plutocrats but brings down civilized society in the process. A populist reformer (and failed politician), Donnelly feared the unchecked power of America's Gilded Age ruling elites but was even more horror-stricken at the prospect of all-out class warfare.

Edward Bellamy, ca. 1890.
(*Courtesy of the Library of Congress*)

PROLETARIAN FICTION OF THE LATER PROGRESSIVE ERA

The period from the turn of the century to World War I saw a tremendous increase in working-class consciousness and labor agitation in America. Manifestations of growing radicalism include the 1901 formation of the Socialist Party and the extreme left-wing Industrial Workers of the World (IWW or "Wobblies") in 1905. These and a host of other leftist organizations and unions enjoyed burgeoning membership and influence over the next decade.

A true proletarian literature reflecting the changing political climate begins with Isaac Kahn Friedman, a socialist from an affluent background whose settlement-house work in Chicago in the 1890s brought him firsthand knowledge of working-class life. Friedman's novel *By Bread Alone* (1901), is a fictionalized version of the infamous Homestead Strike that ran from July to November 1892 in Pittsburgh. Locked out of the Homestead Works by its ruthless manager, Henry Clay Frick, after a wage dispute, members of the Amalgamated Association of Iron and Steel Workers defeated Pinkerton Detective Agency strikebreakers in a bloody battle on 6 July and took charge of the works. Six days later, however, Pennsylvania governor Robert Pattison sent 8,000 militiamen to reoccupy Homestead and get production going again. When Emma Goldman's companion, Alexander Berkman, tried to assassinate Frick in his office on 23 July he only managed to turn public sentiment against the striking workers. The eventual defeat of the strike six months later was a terrible setback for the nascent labor movement. Friedman's fictionalized version of the Homestead

events accurately depicts the workers' plight: long hours and low pay, wage cuts, dangerous working conditions, and overcrowded company housing. He also supplies a convincing portrayal of the famous battle between the strikers and the Pinkertons and the subsequent attempt on Frick's life. Though clearly on the side of the workers, Friedman was more reformist than radical; in the end he condemns anarchism and violent class struggle and affirms the virtues of peaceful change.

Of vastly greater impact than Friedman's book was Upton Sinclair's *The Jungle* (1906), a searing exposé of the filthy, dangerous working conditions within the Chicago meatpacking industry that brought the plight of the industrial working class to a huge readership and prompted passage of the Meat Inspection and Pure Food and Drug Acts (1906 and 1907, respectively). *The Jungle* focuses on Jurgis Rudkus, a Lithuanian immigrant who comes to Chicago with his fiancée, Ona Lukoszaite, and extended family in hopes of forging a better life. Jurgis secures a job in a meatpacking plant and marries Ona, but their prospects soon dim. Injured at work, Jurgis loses his job and is forced to take even more degrading employment at a fertilizer plant. When Jurgis discovers that Ona has to provide sexual favors to her boss, Connor, in order to keep her job, he assaults Connor and is sentenced to thirty days in jail. Upon release Jurgis finds his family evicted from their home. Tragically, Ona dies in childbirth. Jurgis, broken in body and spirit, descends ever lower into the social pit—until he hears an illuminating socialist speech, converts to socialism as his last, best hope, and commits all his efforts to the 1904 elections in which the Socialist Party made dramatic gains at the polls. Critics of the novel pointed out flaws: Sinclair tended to overemphasize workers' victimization and slighted their efforts at organized resistance; his characters were one dimensional; and his depiction of the workers' hell was far more memorable than Jurgis's political conversion, which was, after all, the point of the book. Nonetheless, *The Jungle* remains historically crucial as the first great proletarian novel that brought the harsh realities of working-class life into mainstream American literature.

Sinclair's friend, mentor, and fellow socialist Jack London, though best known for his adventure stories, was an authentic and powerful voice for proletarian literature in his day. In his radical speeches and essays, collected in *War of the Classes* (1905) and *Revolution* (1910), London eloquently espoused his anticapitalist politics. His *People of the Abyss* (1903), an exposé of slum conditions in London's East End, was a pioneering work of investigative journalism and progressive advocacy. While a number of London's short stories and portions of his longer works—for example, *Martin Eden* (1908), "South of the Slot" (1909), "The Human Drift" (1910), *John Barleycorn* (1913), and *The Valley of the Moon* (1913)—can be classified as "proletarian" in sympathy and subject matter, his most important work in this vein was *The Iron Heel* (1907). Set in the halcyon days of a twenty-seventh-century socialist world utopia, *The Iron Heel* purports to look back on America circa 1912, when the capitalist-turned-fascist oligarchy takes over the country by military force and crushes all progressive opposition. Though wrong (or at least premature) about America's becoming a police state in response to capitalist crisis and revolutionary ferment, London was certainly prescient in regards to modernity as a whole, and *The Iron Heel* remains a fascinating if underappreciated classic of revolutionary literature.

WORLD WAR I TO THE CRASH OF 1929

American radicalism reached its high-water mark around 1912. That year the IWW won the "Bread and Roses" strike in Lawrence, Massachusetts, and Socialist Party presidential candidate Eugene V. Debs polled nearly a million votes, or 6 percent of the total—the largest vote for a socialist in American history. America's subsequent involvement in World War I had a devastating effect on the Socialist Party. Government repression against socialist war resisters and bitter conflict among the membership over nationalist loyalties destabilized the party and pushed its leadership to the right. As a result, Socialist Party membership and power declined precipitously. In 1919 the party effectively destroyed itself when it expelled two-thirds of its membership for being too radical. During and after the war, government repression of leftist radicals accelerated into a full-blown "red scare." Wilson's attorney general, A. Mitchell Palmer, a zealous anticommunist crusader, staged a series of raids that targeted socialist, communist, and labor organizations; offices were smashed, thousands were arrested, and hundreds of "reds" were subsequently deported back to Europe and Russia.

Despite the increasingly hostile political climate, proletarian fiction continued to appear, albeit at a much slackened pace. A noteworthy prewar example is Arthur Bullard's *Comrade Yetta* (1913), which charts the radicalization of Yetta Rayefsky, a feisty New York City garment worker who leads a wildcat strike, is jailed, goes on to help form a union, joins the staff of a socialist journal, and even marries the editor. Briefly attracted to the IWW's doctrine of revolutionary violence, Yetta ultimately opts for peaceful change: a position consistent with Bullard's own socialist ideology.

While Bullard's novel featured a working-class protagonist converted to leftist politics, other proletarian novels of the period had a tendency to focus their conversion plots on bourgeois protagonists. For example, Billy, the hero of Ernest Poole's best-selling novel *The Harbor* (1915), is a middle-class, college-educated journalist initially smitten with the plutocracy. Persuaded by a college friend to do a story on a radical labor leader, Bill covers a violent strike, is jailed, and finds his sympathies are with the downtrodden dockworkers. He dedicates his life as a writer to their cause.

Upton Sinclair was guilty of the same sort of implicit class condescension with his novel *King Coal* (1917), a fictionalized account of the Colorado coal wars of 1913–1914. The bitter labor struggles in Colorado led up to the infamous Ludlow Massacre (20 April 1914) in which nine men and eleven women and children were shot or burned to death in their tents by National Guardsmen and coal company thugs—an atrocity not depicted in Sinclair's novel. *King Coal* does, however, expose the coal companies' routine abuses: endangering miners by flouting mining laws, cheating miners of their wages by underweighing coal yields, using intimidation and violence to thwart union organizing. Writing to a middle-class audience, Sinclair casts the novel from the point of view of Hal Warner, son of a coal company mogul, who goes undercover to investigate conditions in the mines and in the miners' communities. The novel centers on Warner's labor education, his conversion to a pro-union stance, and his activities in behalf of the miners: an elitist, individualist point of view palatable to a bourgeois readership but one that keeps the workers in the background.

If proletarian literature languished in the oppressive political climate of the 1920s, theorizing about it began in earnest. In the February 1921 issue of the Marxist journal the *Liberator*, Irwin Granich (later known as Michael Gold) published "Towards Proletarian Art," a landmark essay that called for American artists to eschew individualist aloofness, cast their lot with the working masses, and dedicate themselves to chronicling social revolution. In

Gold's view, proletarian literature was broadly equivalent to radical literature—in other words, the emphasis was placed on the author's ideology rather than on working-class pedigree or choice of subject matter. Leon Trotsky voiced a similar position in his essay "Communist Policy toward Art" (1923), in which he wrote, "It is untrue that revolutionary art can be created only by workers." Trotsky went on to warn against a too-precipitous rejection of bourgeois art but also assured his readers that a socialist society need not lead to "a decline of individuality or an impoverishment of art." Unlike Gold, Trotsky considered proletarian art a temporary and transitional phenomenon that would evaporate with the coming dissolution of class society through socialist revolution.

PROLETARIAN LITERATURE OF THE DEPRESSION ERA

While the Great Depression began on "Black Thursday," 29 October 1929, when the stock market crashed, the era's proletarian literature actually had its conceptual genesis in 1928. In that year the *New Masses*, a progressive literary magazine descended from Max Eastman's radical journal, *Masses* (1911–1917) came under the editorial control of the avowed communists Michael Gold and Joseph Freeman. Founded in 1926 by an amalgam of bohemians, liberals, and radicals and open to writers of all political persuasions, the *New Masses* under Gold and Freeman took a sharp turn to the left and initially became a "proletcult" magazine specializing in publishing work by, in Gold's words, "as yet, semiarticulate voices hidden in the mines, textile mills, farms, sawmills, and lumber camps." In October 1929, in an effort to broaden the scope of its content and make the magazine more commercially viable, *New Masses* inaugurated the first John Reed Club (JRC), a Marxist writers' group whose central tenet—"art is a class weapon"—pointedly repudiated the art for art's sake cult of modernism in favor of a quasi-propagandistic, anti-idealist aesthetic in line with the American Communist Party and Soviet cultural dictates. Over the next five years a dozen other John Reed Clubs would spring up in major U.S. cities and serve as vital gestation grounds for a 1930s proletarian literature that was ideologically quite consistent but by no means uniform in style or content.

In his pioneering and still indispensable study *The Radical Novel in the United States, 1900–1954* (1956), Walter Rideout makes a case for the considerable diversity of 1930s proletarian fiction by identifying four main groupings in terms of subject matter and content: (1) "those centered about a strike; (2) those concerned with the development of an individual's class consciousness and his conversion to Communism; (3) those dealing with the 'bottom dogs,' the lowest layers of society; and (4) those describing the decay of the middle class." In many instances these categories overlap, and Rideout's taxonomy also applies to proletarian literature that precedes the Depression. For example, Upton Sinclair's *The Jungle* would be classified as mainly a "conversion" novel but also contains elements of the strike and "bottom dogs" genres.

THE STRIKE NOVEL

On 1 April 1929, Fred Erwin Beal, organizer for the communist-led National Textile Workers Union (NTWU), called for a strike at the Loray Mill in Gastonia, North Carolina. Embittered by paltry wages, long hours, poor housing and working conditions, bad food, and "stretch-outs" (work load increases without increased compensation), 1,800 of 2,200 workers, most of whom were poor whites, went out on strike the next day. The mill owners enlisted local law enforcement to guard the 400 nonstrikers as they entered and left the mill. On 3 April, as unrest mounted, Governor O. Max Gardner (himself a textile mill owner) sent in the National Guard. The *Gastonia Gazette* also abetted the efforts of the strikebreakers by taking every opportunity to demonize the Communist Party, proclaiming, for example, that it "has no religion, it has no color line, it believes in free love." In the ensuing weeks the mill owners sent masked vigilantes to ransack NTWU headquarters and later evicted sixty-two families from company housing. On 7 June a strikebreakers' raid on the evicted workers' tent camp resulted in the shooting death of Gastonia police chief O. F. Adderholt, an event that sealed the defeat of the strike. Fourteen strike leaders were indicted for Adderholt's killing and the seven eventually convicted sought political asylum in the Soviet Union. A final tragedy: Ella May Wiggins, a prominent strike organizer, was shot and killed by deputized thugs on 14 September 1929. Though the strike collapsed under intense journalistic, legal, and paramilitary pressures, it did at least broach possibilities for radical change normally repressed in the South. The strike also exposed class exploitation, sexism, racism, an antilabor press, and the role of religion in maintaining the capitalist status quo.

The symbolic centrality of the Gastonia strike for the radical left was made manifest by the appearance of no less than six novels based on it: Mary Heaton Vorse's *Strike!* (1930); Sherwood Anderson's *Beyond Desire* (1932); Fielding Burke's [Olive Tilford Dargan],

Call Home the Heart (1932); Grace Lumpkin's *To Make My Bread* (1932); Myra Page's [Dorothy Gary Markey] *Gathering Storm: A Story of the Blackbelt* (1932); and William Rollins's *The Shadow Before* (1934). With varying degrees of thoroughness and detail, all six novels presented a more or less accurate depiction of conditions at the Loray Mill, the course of the strike, and the political ramifications. What really distinguishes the books is their respective handling of gender and sexual issues, race, religion, and the culture of the South.

An experienced labor reporter assigned to cover the strike, Mary Heaton Vorse had the advantage of being an eyewitness to Gastonia. She wrote *Strike!* as the actual events unfolded, a vantage point that enabled her to document the lives of mill families and poor southern white women in considerable detail. Nonetheless, Vorse, a northerner, tended to slight racial issues and to accept and reproduce stereotypes regarding the backwardness of southern culture.

Famous for his groundbreaking collection *Winesburg, Ohio* (1919), Sherwood Anderson was the most prominent of the Gastonia chroniclers. He was also the most modernist in style and sensibility—and therefore the least proletarian. Only the final section of *Beyond Desire* deals with the Gastonia strike. The rest of the book is taken up with Anderson's stock-in-trade: an impressionistic, poetically expressed examination of individual subjectivity and sexuality that cannot begin to address the systemic issues of gender, class, and race that were vital determinants at Gastonia.

More successful as proletarian fiction is Fielding Burke's *Call Home the Heart* and Grace Lumpkin's *To Make My Bread*. Both novels embed the story of the strike in a much larger historical narrative tracing the transformation of the South from a rural, agricultural society into a more modern, industrial culture. Like many a strike novel, Burke's book is basically a conversion novel that plots the political radicalization of its protagonist, in this case a white Appalachian woman named Ishma, who is forced by poverty to come down from the mountains to work in the mill. Ishma is inevitably drawn into the strike and has an epiphany about her lot when she hears a communist organizer speak. Ultimately, though, the novel's pivotal scene depicts Ishma's discovery of her own deep-seated racism: a sobering realization that sends her back to the hills and her traditional way of life. Though the novel's resolution blunts its ideological force, it still manages to treat issues of gender, race, and radicalism with fairness and clarity.

Somewhat broader and more collectivist in perspective, Lumpkin's novel spans thirty years as it follows the story of the three generations of McClures, a poor Appalachian clan that is forced by family misfortune and changing economic conditions to move from the backwoods to the textile mill. The last section of the novel presents a faithful rendition of the worsening working conditions that led up to the Gastonia strike, the company's brutal tactics, the violence that ensued, and the strike's eventual defeat. Among the Gastonia chroniclers, Lumpkin is best at emphasizing the critical role that white women workers played in waging the strike and seeking out common cause with black workers, a historic development in southern race relations. Furthermore, despite the actual outcome, Lumpkin refuses to end her book on a defeatist note. John Stevens, her fictional counterpart to NTWU organizer Fred Beal, advises John, the youngest McClure, that the strike, though lost, is just a beginning. Lessons learned can and will be applied to future labor actions.

Among the Gastonia novels, Myra Page's *Gathering Storm* is, in historical terms, the most thorough and didactically Marxist treatment of the events. A Ph.D. in sociology (University of Minnesota, 1928) and a devout communist, Page published *Southern Cotton Mills and Labor* (1929), a critique of failed union organizing in the South, before she tried her hand at a fictionalized version of the same subject matter. To underscore the crucial role of race in class oppression, Page structured her narrative around two poor working families, one white (the Crenshaws) and the other black (the Morgans). After young Martha Morgan is raped and murdered by white men, her fiancé, Jim, kills one of the ringleaders, and a white mob retaliates by killing the entire Morgan family—except for Fred Morgan, who is working in the North. The rest of the novel focuses not only on the strike but on the friendship and radicalization of Tom Crenshaw and Fred Morgan: a motif that symbolizes the coming together of the black and white proletariat against a common class foe. Starting in the 1870s and dealing with World War I, the Russian Revolution, and the Soviet socialist experiment, Page's novel has contextual amplitude far surpassing the efforts of her contemporaries—a virtue undercut by the author's tendency to too often interrupt her story with redundant political preachments.

The last of the Gastonia strike novels, William Rollins's *The Shadow Before*, contrasts sharply with Page's *Gathering Storm* both in terms of aesthetic technique and faithfulness of historical adaptation. As regards form, Rollins eschewed realism for the kinds of experimental narrative techniques introduced by John Dos Passos in his *U.S.A.* trilogy, especially the use of stream-of-consciousness narration. In terms of setting, Rollins shifted the strike from the South to New England, a move that robs his version of the vital element of race and tends to distort the underlying history. More problematically Rollins advances the notion that the abstract dynamic of historical change, abetted by the decadence of the capitalist class, will bring about socialist revolution: a position that minimizes the historical agency of the working class.

Besides the Gastonia novels, Walter Rideout identifies ten other strike novels published in the 1930s: Louis Colman's *Lumber* (1931), Mike Pell's *S. S. Utah* (1932), Arnold B. Armstrong's *Parched Earth* (1934), Robert Cantwell's *The Land of Plenty* (1934), Fielding Burke's sequel to *Call Home the Heart*, *A Stone Came Rolling* (1935), Clara Weatherwax's *Marching! Marching!* (1935), Leane Zugsmith's *A Time to Remember* (1936), Clifton Cuthbert's *Another Such Victory* (1937), Josephine Johnson's *Jordanstown* (1937), and Edwin Moultrie Lanham's *The Stricklands* (1939). Of this number, only three have enduring literary merit: Cantwell's *The Land of Plenty*, Weatherwax's *Marching! Marching!*, and Zugsmith's *A Time to Remember*.

PROLETARIAN "CONVERSION" NOVELS

Rideout's second category, the proletarian bildungsroman (novel of self-development) almost inevitably culminates in the protagonist's conversion to leftist radicalism. A key example is Agnes Smedley's *Daughter of Earth* (1929), a quasi-autobiographical novel that charts a young woman's personal, sexual, and political coming-of-age in the years leading up to World War I. Smedley's alter ego, Marie Rogers, is born into a desperately poor farm family in Missouri, grows up in the midst of the Colorado coal wars after the family moves west, fends off sexual harassment while working a variety of low-wage jobs, and struggles to obtain an education. Along the way she becomes a militant socialist, marries and divorces twice, gets involved with a group of revolutionary nationalists who seek India's independence from the British Empire, and is jailed for her antiwar activism. The novel ends on a somewhat problematic note, politically, when Marie decides to leave America for Europe. However ambiguous its conclusion might be, *Daughter of Earth* remains a remarkable and historically significant novel. With great passion and eloquence Smedley is able to relate personal issues (for example, gender inequality) to larger public issues (class

inequality and imperialism) in a thoroughgoing critique of the capitalist system.

A tireless advocate for proletarian literature, *New Masses* editor Michael Gold also practiced what he preached. In 1930 he published *Jews Without Money*, like Smedley's novel a quasi-autobiographical bildungsroman, but in this case the setting throughout is New York City's Lower East Side, a Jewish ghetto also populated by immigrants of many other nationalities. Gold mounts his critique of American capitalism in two ways: by frankly evoking the hardships, corruption, and random violence caused by extreme poverty; and through the pathetic figure of Herman Gold, the protagonist's father, who clings to a naive faith in the American Dream despite overwhelming experiential evidence to the contrary. Like Smedley's Marie Rogers, "Mikey Gold" finds a way out of the social pit by converting to revolutionary activism.

Another key conversion novel is Jack Conroy's *The Disinherited* (1934). A true worker-writer from Moberly, Missouri, Conroy drew heavily on his own experience in presenting the picaresque saga of Larry Donovan, son of a coal miner from Monkey Nest Camp, Missouri, who loses his two brothers and his father to mining accidents. Forced to go to work in a railroad repair shop at the age of thirteen, Donovan drifts through a series of industrial jobs in the Detroit automobile industry until the Depression deprives him of steady work. Along the way he meets and befriends Ed, a cynical coworker, and Hans, a German Army deserter turned communist labor organizer who helps to imbue Donovan with class consciousness. Accompanied by Ed, Donovan returns to Monkey Nest Camp, where they reunite with Hans. The novel ends on an optimistic note, with all three men setting off to organize the local farmers.

Other conversion novels include Maxwell Bodenheim's *Run, Sheep, Run* (1932) and *Slow Vision* (1934); George Marlen's [George Spiro] *The Road: A Romance of the Proletarian Revolution* (1932); Meyer Levin's *The New Bridge* (1933); Dale Curran's *A House on the Street* (1934); Waldo Frank's *The Death and Birth of David Markand* (1934); Albert Halper's *The Foundry* (1934); Edward Newhouse's *You Can't Sleep Here* (1934); Thomas Boyd's *In Time of Peace* (1935); Jack Conroy's sequel to *The Disinherited*, *A World to Win* (1935); Isidor Schneider's *From the Kingdom of Necessity* (1935); James Steele's [Robert Cruden] *Conveyor* (1935); Thomas Bell's *All Brides Are Beautiful* (1936); James T. Farrell's *A World I Never Made* (1936) and *No Star Is Lost* (1938); and John Hyde Preston's *The Liberals: A Novel* (1938).

BOTTOM DOGS

Edward Dahlberg's *Bottom Dogs* (1929) inaugurated a new genre of proletarian fiction that dealt exclusively with what Karl Marx referred to, in *The Communist Manifesto*, as the "'dangerous class,' the social scum, that passively rotting mass thrown off by the lowest layers of the old society." Marx considered society's dregs as more likely fodder for "reactionary intrigue" than proletarian revolution—a sentiment borne out by Dahlberg's work and other "bottom dogs" novels that invariably featured deracinated, nihilistic drifters prone to all manner of violence, criminality, and degradation. The point of these gruesome, apocalyptic narratives was to show that capitalism in its dotage was spawning monsters that threatened civilization itself. Other examples of the "bottom dogs" genre include Charles Yale Harrison's *A Child Is Born* (1931); Edward Dahlberg's *From Flushing to Calvary* (1932); Henry Roth's *Call It Sleep* (1934); Nelson Algren's *Somebody in Boots* (1935); Tom Kromer's *Waiting for Nothing* (1935); Edward Anderson's *Hungry Men* (1935); Martin Delaney's *Journal of a Young Man* (1936); and Joseph Vogel's *Man's Courage* (1938).

EXPOSÉS OF MIDDLE-CLASS DECAY

Counterpoised against novels of working-class struggle, political conversion, and lumpen despair was a fourth genre of proletarian fiction that depicted the gradual disintegration of the bourgeoisie—stories of decay usually mitigated by the conversion to radicalism of one or two characters. Foremost among these books were two trilogies: James T. Farrell's Studs Lonigan trilogy (*Young Lonigan: A Boyhood in Chicago Streets*, 1932; *The Young Manhood of Studs Lonigan*, 1934; and *A World I Never Made*, 1936) and Josephine Herbst's trilogy (*Pity is Not Enough*, 1933; *The Executioner Waits*, 1934; and *Rope of Gold*, 1939). Other examples include Edwin Seaver's *The Company* (1930) and *Between the Hammer and the Anvil* (1937); Albert Halper's *The Chute* (1937); Joseph Vogel's *At Madame Bonnard's* (1935); and Leane Zugsmith's *The Summer Soldier* (1938).

WPA FEDERAL WRITERS' PROJECT

To a far greater extent than the John Reed Clubs or the Communist Party, the U.S. government nurtured radical writers and proletarian voices through the Federal Writers' Project (FWP), a branch of Roosevelt's massive Works Progress Administration (WPA). Established in 1935 as an employer of last resort for out-of-work writers, the Federal Writers' Project provided temporary jobs for thousands of writers in all forty-eight states and, over its seven-year life span, managed to publish some 1,200 books and pamphlets, including the famous American Guide series. FWP workers also conducted extensive oral history interviews throughout the country and created a priceless archive of workers' stories, slave narratives, and folklore that otherwise would have been lost. Equally important, the FWP supported and helped launch the careers of Ralph Ellison, Richard Wright, Studs Terkel, John Cheever, Saul Bellow, Margaret Walker, Arna Bontemps, and Zora Neale Hurston, to name just a few. Anticommunist fervor whipped up by the Dies House Un-American Activities Committee brought an end to the FWP in 1943.

[*See also* Algren, Nelson; Anderson, Sherwood; London, Jack; Melville, Herman, and his *Moby-Dick*; Naturalism and Realism; Roth, Henry; *and* Sinclair, Upton, and the Muckrakers.]

FURTHER READING

Aaron, Daniel. *Writers on the Left: Odysseys in American Literary Communism*. New York, 1964. A sweeping and erudite social chronicle of leftist writers from 1912 to the early 1940s that examines the complex politics of the period.

Blake, Fay M. *The Strike in the American Novel*. Metuchen, N.J., 1972. A comprehensive and fascinating reference book that provides detailed summaries of every known strike novel from the 1870s through the Depression era.

Bogardus, Ralph, and Fred Honson, eds. *Literature at the Barricades: The American Writer in the 1930s*. University, Ala., 1982. Presents thirteen essays on major 1930s writers, for example, Edmund Wilson, John Dos Passos, James T. Farrell, John Steinbeck, Richard Wright, James Agee, and Harriet Arnow.

Booker, M. Keith. *The Modern American Novel of the Left: A Research Guide*. Westport, Conn., 1999. Offers detailed synopses and critiques of dozens of twentieth-century radical novels.

Brommel, Nicholas K. *By the Sweat of the Brow: Literature and Labor in Antebellum America*. Chicago, 1993. In chapters on Thoreau, Melville, Hawthorne, Rebecca Harding Davis, Susan Warner, Harriet Beecher Stowe, and Fredrick Douglass, Brommel examines the affinities between physical and mental labor in nineteenth-century American culture.

Coiner, Constance. *Better Red: The Writing and Resistance of Tillie Olsen and Meridel LeSuer*. New York, 1995. The first book-length study to explore these feminist writers' ties to the American Communist Party, it contributes to a reenvisioning of 1930s U.S. communism as well as to efforts to promote working-class writing as a legitimate category of literary analysis.

Cook, Sylvia Jenkins. *From Tobacco Road to Route 66: The Southern Poor White in Fiction.* Chapel Hill, N.C., 1976.

Foley, Barbara. *Radical Representations: Politics and Form in U.S. Proletarian Fiction, 1929–1941.* Durham, N.C., 1993. A magisterial study of Depression-era proletarian fiction that seeks to recover the true political climate of the 1930s. Theoretically sophisticated but always lucid, this is a key critical work in its field.

Hapke, Laura. *Labor's Text: The Worker in American Fiction.* New Brunswick, N.J., 2001. An extremely ambitious and exhaustively researched survey of writing by and about the U.S. working class that covers the entire twentieth century. An invaluable addition to working-class literature studies.

Herreshoff, David Sprague. *Labor into Art: The Theme of Work in Nineteenth-Century American Literature.* Detroit, 1991. Explores the representation of work in Thoreau's *Walden*, Melville's *Moby-Dick*, Dickinson's poetry, Douglass's *Slave Narrative*, and the poetry of Whitman.

Homberger, Eric. *American Writers and Radical Politics: Equivocal Commitments.* New York, 1986. Examines the evolving political stances of Jack London, Upton Sinclair, John Reed, Edmund Wilson, and 1930s proletarian writers.

Madden, David, ed. *Proletarian Writers of the Thirties.* Carbondale, Ill., 1968. Compilation of articles about key proletarian writers—for example, John Dos Passos, Richard Wright, Edward Dahlberg, Robert Cantwell, Jack Conroy, Daniel Fuchs, Dalton Trumbo, B. Traven. Almost exclusive focus on white male writers makes this otherwise excellent collection dated.

Mangione, Jerre. *The Dream and the Deal: The Federal Writers Project, 1935–1943.* Philadelphia, 1983. An excellent history of the FWP from a former national coordinating editor.

Murphy, James F. *The Proletarian Moment: The Controversy over Leftism in Literature.* Chicago, Ill., 1991. This original and thoroughly researched work summarizes the intense international debates of the 1930s about leftism and proletarian literature. Until 1937 the *Partisan Review* was a leading theoretical organ of the American proletarian literature movement.

Nekola, Charlotte, and Paula Rabinowitz, eds. *Writing Red: An Anthology of American Women Writers, 1930–40.* New York, 1987. The first anthology of poetry and prose from the 1930s by women writers on the Left who were both class-conscious and feminist.

Nelson, Cary. *Repression and Recovery: Modern American Poetry and the Politics of Cultural Memory, 1910–1945.* Madison, Wis., 1992. Resurrects the work of dozens of forgotten poets—especially women, blacks, and writers on the Left—whose work has been repressed by the postwar backlash against communism.

Olsen, Tillie. *Silences.* New York, 1978. Discusses how adverse circumstances, especially those related to class, race, sex, and the sociopolitical climate, combine to militate against the creation of literature.

Pells, Richard H. *Radical Visions and American Dreams.* New York, 1973.

Rabinowitz, Paula. *Labor and Desire: Women's Revolutionary Fiction in Depression America.* Chapel Hill, N.C., 1991. Arguing that "the histories of literature, women, and radicalism must be told as interlocking narratives," Rabinowitz describes and critiques several works of women's revolutionary fiction.

Rideout, Walter B. *The Radical Novel in the United States, 1900–1954: Some Interrelations of Literature and Society.* Cambridge, Mass., 1956. The first major study of its kind, Rideout's book remains indispensable.

Shulman, Robert. *The Power of Political Art: The 1930s Literary Left Reconsidered.* Durham, N.C., 2000.

Swados, Harvey, ed. *The American Writer and the Great Depression.* Indianapolis, 1966. Anthology of proletarian prose and poetry by thirty Depression-era writers.

Wald, Alan. *The New York Intellectuals: The Rise and Decline of the Anti-Stalinist Left from the 1930's to the 1980's.* Chapel Hill, N.C., 1987.

Wixon, Douglas. *The Worker-Writer in America: Jack Conroy and the Tradition of Midwestern Literary Radicalism, 1898–1990.* Urbana, Ill., 1994. This amply documented study focuses on the author as a worker-writer and views his career in terms of the changing fortunes of midwestern literary radicalism.

Zandy, Janet, ed. *Calling Home: Working-Class Women's Writings: An Anthology.* New Brunswick, N.J., 1990.

FRANCINE PROSE

by Lani Wolf

A sharp observer of the contemporary world, Francine Prose is known for her gifts of irony and wit. Often characterized as a "cultural satirist," Prose addresses such charged subjects as political correctness, sexual harassment, feminism, and New Ageism. Though critics have described her work as "scathing," "withering," and "mocking"—"dark comedy" at its height—she remains a defender of humanity, addressing such topics as love and marriage, the difficulty of middle age and personal failure, and the search for spirituality, albeit misguided. Rendering her characters endearingly, she allows us to see ourselves, our own weaknesses, eccentricities, and foibles, within them; in her own words, "I do not find them guilty of anything that I am not guilty of myself." Thus, her work may be perhaps more accurately described as "irony with heart."

BIOGRAPHY

The author of over twenty books to date, among them novels, short-story collections, novellas, and children's books, Prose is the recipient of numerous grants and awards, including a Guggenheim and a Fulbright. She has taught at several prestigious writing programs, including Iowa, Sewanee, and Breadloaf, and at Sarah Lawrence, Harvard, and Johns Hopkins Universities. Her work has appeared in *The New Yorker*, *Atlantic Monthly*, *GQ*, and *Paris Review*. A journalist as well as a fiction writer, Prose has written regularly on art for *The Wall Street Journal*, served as an editor at *Double Take*, and has been a contributing editor at *Harper's*. Her June 1998 article in *Harper's* on women's writing, "The Scent of a Woman's Ink," for example, has garnered a variety of impassioned responses to her view that the majority of "women's culture," whether it be literary or media-driven, is grossly substandard to that geared for men.

Her careers as writing teacher, editor, and journalist have greatly influenced the themes and story lines of her fiction. Her love of travel, especially, emerges in her fiction as a transformative force. As Prose explains: "So many things are crystallized when you are in a strange country. Questions about your life, or the world, suddenly become very clear. The answers don't necessarily become clear, but the questions become clear." Prose has traveled extensively, to Prague, Paris, and Poland, for example, and has lived in such faraway places as Bombay. She currently resides in New York City with her husband and two sons.

MAJOR WORKS

Prose began writing shortly after her graduation from Radcliffe College in 1968, in her own words, "unqualified to do anything else." Her early collection of short stories, *Household Saints* (1981), takes as its subject a young woman's religious upbringing in a Catholic household like her own. Her second story collection, *Women and Children First* (1988), with such characters as Janet, an antique buyer who explores mother-son ESP, and Ceci, a kindergarten teacher who turns toward Tibetan Buddhism, reveals the kernel of the extraordinary within seemingly ordinary lives. Set in eighteenth-century Poland, her first novel, *Judah the Pious* (1973), is a tale, a story within a story about the salvation of Jews from a pogrom. Though this fantasy has little in common with her later works, set in the very real modern world and addressing contemporary issues, *Judah* points toward the artistic control and technical skill for which she is known.

Stylistically, Prose is a master, her sentences fluid, varied, and architecturally balanced. "It's the only thing I care about," she said in a 2000 interview. "Perfecting the rhythms, the cadences, the momentum. Everything else in putting a novel or story together is a vehicle for getting to the sentences." Elsewhere she adds: "I'll rewrite something a zillion times until it shows improvement." She believes in the hard work, the day-to-day routine, that fiction writing requires: "As Flaubert said, it's a life that requires bourgeois habits."

If a common thematic strand can be found in her fiction, it is the despair, self-doubt, and self-consciousness of her characters. Not initially endearing or likable, certainly not admirable, they represent imperfect humanity, common humanity, full of missteps and vanities, uncertainties and delusions. Weak-willed, hungry-hearted sinners, they are the authors of their own downfalls. Yet Prose is so able to situate the reader inside her protagonists' consciousnesses that we cannot help but sympathize with them and perhaps even admit to seeing a bit of ourselves in them. Professor Swenson of *Blue Angel* (2000) serves as a case in point. Despairing over his own failure as a writer, he has an affair with a talented, antiestablishment creative writing student, Angela Argo. A witch hunt for "faculty Romeos" ensues, and Swenson is brought before the university's judiciary board. The situation worsens with intimations that he had molested his teenage daughter when she was a child. What rescues Swenson, aside from the ambiguity surrounding Angela's own role in beginning the affair, is the very real humanity, and even pathos, underlying his actions—the pain of lost youth and approaching middle age, the allure of fame and literary success, the urge to somehow rediscover his own talent through another's. In short, envy, vanity, and narcissism—powerful, albeit unattractive, emotions common to us all.

Like Professor Swenson, the playwright Landau of *Guided Tours of Hell* (1997) is an overly cerebral solipsist suffering from the spiritual turmoil of failure in his career and personal life. He travels to a Kafka conference in Prague to promote his poorly acclaimed epistolary drama *To Kafka from Felice*, only to end up in an absurd debate over concentration camp conditions with the star of the conference, the poet and camp survivor Jiri Krakauer. Krakauer seems to upstage Landau in just about everything: in his artistic talent, with his authentic, I-was-there poetry; in his masculinity, with his strong, manly build and sexual magnetism; and in his personality, with his expressive demeanor and notion that his is the heart of a Primo Levi. Krakauer's successes, illusory as they may be, bring into relief Landau's "failures"—failures that, as we see but he cannot, add up to nothing more than being who he is: a self-centered, petty, peevish, not very talented, very human guy. On the way to the concentration camp, "tiny nips of transcendence nibble at his line, but given even the gentlest tug, they slip back into the water, the oily shoals of boredom, ego and resentment, and let's be honest, fury at Jiri Krakauer, that terrible poet and memoirist whose only claim to fame is that he survived two years in the camp, where he somehow conducted a love affair with Kafka's sister Ottla." Like so many of Prose's protagonists, Landau, reveling in despair but too paralyzed with doubt to do anything about it, is not capable of achieving complete epiphany and change.

"Three Pigs in Five Days," the second and longer novella in *Guided Tours of Hell*, offers a greater sense of redemption for the protagonist. Nina, a travel writer sent to Paris by her lover-boss, Leo, to write a story about a former brothel that is now a popular hotel, struggles obsessively over whether Leo really loves her, and if not, what does anything matter? Unlike Landau, however, her emotional turmoil leads to some critical realizations that affirm that all life within her is not lost. During a personal tour at the Rodin Museum, for example, the curator shows her a collection of Rodin's erotic drawings, explaining that when the artist made love to models, he hung out a sign: "Absent. Visiting cathedrals"—and this despite Camille Claudel's consuming love for him. Sex, it occurs to Nina, likewise rapt with obsessive love, is just a form of tourism, a visitation of surfaces, not necessarily with underlying depth or meaning. By the end of the story, she realizes Leo's transparency yet continues to believe in the existence of passionate love, even if only as figured through historical models, such as the French Revolution, and mythology, such as Orpheus and Eurydice. More able than Landau to listen to voices other than her own and to see the reality of her situation, she emerges with a greater sense of self, which, we hope, will save her.

Prose's early novel *Bigfoot Dreams* (1986) likewise addresses the debilitating sense of self-doubt that personal failure can bring. After a series of career mishaps, Vera Perl is fired from her job as a reporter for a Brooklyn tabloid, but instead of losing hope she journeys west to search for Bigfoot. In *Hunters and Gatherers* (1995) Prose ties this sense of self-doubt to failed love. After the most recent in a long series of breakups, Martha, a thirty-year-old fact checker at a Manhattan fashion magazine, seeks solace with a group of priestesses she meets by chance on a Fire Island beach. On one level she feels flattered by their easy acceptance of her and affirmed by their overt feminism; on another she sees "her association with the Goddess group for the walking nervous breakdown it was." Eventually the group travels to Arizona to study with a Native American shaman, experiencing a medicine walk, a fast, ritual drumming, and a vision quest in a sweat lodge. Though they do not achieve true self-realization through these rituals, exposing themselves as being just as flawed as men, they reach toward transcendence in the sheer fact and process of the search. As Prose explains, "I've been made uneasy by the goofy intensity of these rituals—and at the same time been deeply moved by these women's need for a religion in which they can feel included."

Although Prose is certainly a "lampooner of lifestyles," armed with a biting wit, she remains true to her characters, striving to create particular and unique individuals instead of archetypes or straw men in service of a point, targeting instead contemporary moods and mores. A supreme novelist of manners, she offers us fiction that is consistently humorous, satirical, and thought-provoking and characters who can perhaps teach us to laugh at ourselves.

WORKS

Judah the Pious (1973)
The Glorious Ones (1974)
Stories from Our Living Past (1974)
Marie Laveau (1977)
Animal Magnetism (1978)
Household Saints (1981)
Hungry Hearts (1983)
Bigfoot Dreams (1986)
Women and Children First: Stories (1988)
Primitive People (1992)
The Peaceable Kingdom: Stories (1993)
Hunters and Gatherers (1995)
Dybbuk: A Story Made in Heaven (1996)
Guided Tours of Hell: Novellas (1997)
The Angel's Mistake: Stories of Chelm (1997)
You Never Know: A Legend of the Lamed-Vavniks (1998)
Janis (screenplay, with Nancy Savoca) (1999)
Blue Angel (2000)
The Demon's Mistake: A Story from Chelm (2000)

FURTHER READING

Aarons, Victoria. "Responding to an Old Story: Susan Fromberg, Leslea Newman, and Francine Prose." In *Daughters of Valor: Contemporary Jewish-American Women Writers*, edited by Jay L. Halio and Ben Siegel. Newark, Del., 1997.

Atlantic Unbound: Interviews. "A Conversation with Francine Prose." http://www.theatlantic.com/unbound/factfict/ff9803.html. Comprehensive interview covering Prose's personal and writing life, literary influences, and major works.

Baker, John F. "Francine Prose." *Publishers Weekly* (13 April 1992), pp. 38–39.

Bookreporter.com. "*Francine Prose. Interview: July 28, 2000.*" http://www.bookreporter.com/authors/auprosefrancine.asp. Interview addressing themes of *Blue Angel* and *Guided Tours of Hell*.

Eisenberg, Deborah. "Francine Prose." *Bomb* 45 (Fall 1993).

Kessler, Rod. "Behind the Buzz." *Radcliffe Quarterly* (Summer 2000). http://www.radcliffe.edu/quarterly/200003/read-7.html. Excellent essay addressing Prose's major works, particularly regarding style and philosophy of writing.

New York State Writers' Institute, State University of New York. "*Francine Prose.*" http://www.albany.edu/writers-inst/prosefrancine.html. Brief but informative biography including critical praise.

Pearlman, Mickey. "Francine Prose." In *Inter/View: Talks with America's Writing Women*, edited by Mickey Pearlman and Katherine Usher Henderson. Lexington, Ky., 1990.

Potak, Rena. "Francine Prose." In *Jewish-American Women Writers: A Bio-Bibliographical and Critical Sourcebook*, edited by Sara R. Horowitz. Westport, Conn., 1994.

Thibodeaux, Troy L. "Francine Prose." In *Dictionary of Literary Biography*. Vol. 234: *American Short-Story Writers since World War II*. Third Series. Edited by Patrick Meanor and Richard E. Lee. Detroit, 2001.

ANNIE PROULX

by Robert Dowling

Annie Proulx.
(*Photograph by Jim McHugh*)

Annie Proulx is a vital force in contemporary American literature. She has produced six books of fiction to date: *Heart Songs and Other Stories* (1988), *Postcards* (1992), *The Shipping News* (1993), *Accordion Crimes* (1996), *Close Range: Wyoming Stories* (1999), and *That Old Ace in the Hole* (2003). Between 1991 and 1994 she was awarded a National Endowment for the Arts grant, a Guggenheim Fellowship, a PEN/Faulkner Award for *Postcards*, and a *Chicago Tribune* Heartland Prize, an *Irish Times* International Fiction Prize, a National Book Award, and a Pulitzer Prize for *The Shipping News*. Though Proulx currently enjoys minor celebrity status (a significant achievement for a prose writer in the twenty-first century), responses from the general reading public have been mixed—her themes are as confounding as they are enlightening, depressing as they are uplifting, violent as they are compassionate, exotic as they are commonplace, and erotic as they are a turnoff. Proulx has infused a bitter tonic into the tradition of American storytelling that will, for better or worse, affect the way American writers approach their nation's physical and social landscapes for years to come.

Proulx was born Edna Annie Proulx (sounds like "true") on 22 August 1935 in Norwich, Connecticut, a historic mill town that the maternal side of her family, the Gills, helped found in the early seventeenth century. Her father, George Napolean Proulx, was a textile manufacturer and her mother, Lois "Nelly" Gill Proulx, was a painter and amateur naturalist. Her family relocated frequently, roaming from Connecticut to Vermont, down to North Carolina, and back up to Maine and Rhode Island. The eldest of five girls, Proulx often imagined having a brother, which partly explains the pervasiveness of "the other side of the [gender] equation" in her fiction

(Bolick interview). She received her undergraduate degree from the University of Vermont in 1969 (though she attended some classes at Colby College in the 1950s), graduating *cum laude*, and earned a masters degree in history from Sir George Williams University (now Concordia) in 1973. She has since received honorary doctorates from Concordia and the Universities of Maine and Toronto. At Sir George Williams, Proulx was trained in the methods of the French Annales school of history, an approach that in her words, "pioneered minute examination of the lives of ordinary people through account books, wills, marriage and death records, farming and crafts techniques, the development of technologies" (Rood, 2001, p. 2). Any reader with a cursory knowledge of Proulx's work can grasp the correlation between the methods of the Annales school and her fiction, which is rife with quotidian details. These details are designed, like literary naturalism a century before, to illuminate the psychological effects of overbearing social conventions and the determining role of history and environment on ordinary lives.

Proulx has married and divorced three times, with at least one child from each marriage (her only daughter, Sylvia "Muffy" Marion, from the first; Jonathan Edward and Gillis Crowell from the second; and Morgan Hamilton from the third). Although she is very close to her children (*Close Range* is dedicated to them), nearly all of her characters experience dysfunctional family relations. Quoyle, the protagonist of *The Shipping News*, marries the unloving Petal Bear, who bears him two daughters, both of whom she sells off to a child pornographer just before dying in an automobile accident. The musician Joey Przybysz from *Accordion Crimes* molests his daughter and forces his wife to drink liniment in order to enhance her singing voice, thus aggravating the throat cancer that kills her. Rancher Croom imagines leaping off a cliff in "55 Miles to the Gas Pump" (*Close Range*), and his wife dreams of prying open her locked attic to discover a stack of her husband's former "paramours," all of whom are dead, some "desiccated as jerky," each "used hard," and all recognizable from missing persons ads. The discourse of domestic relations in Proulx goes beyond the ordinary, suburban breakdown of the family. In her hunt for the extreme, she finds the gothic aspect of marital and parental collapse where we might least expect it—in the small-town American countryside. According to Proulx, however, one does not find the provenance of these thoughts and actions in the countryside itself, but from the grotesqueries of the urban media. In the case of "55 Miles to the Gas Pump," for instance, "what their imaginations conjure up . . . is certainly adult material, fed by the sensational journalism and television that is their source of knowledge of the outside world. How far a leap is it to demons and witches?" (Dowling interview).

GOOD COUNTRY PEOPLE

Proulx passed her Ph.D. orals examination at Sir George Williams in 1975 before resolving to skirt a glutted teaching market and pursue a career in freelance journalism. As a nonfiction writer, she gravitated toward subjects that on the surface appear mundane—"weather, apples, canoeing, mountain lions, mice, cuisine, libraries, African beadwork, cider and lettuces" (*Contemporary Authors* 145)—but which provided a foundation of material knowledge that she later employed, along with her mother's artistic influence and her theoretical graduate school training, to tease out the extraordinary aspects of everyday life in rural America.

Proulx wrote numerous articles through the 1960s, 1970s, and 1980s in a range of journals including *Gourmet, Horticulture, Blair and Ketchums, Outdoor Life, National Wildlife, Organic Gardening,* and *Country Journal.* She was also developing, thanks in part to the material and practice these assignments afforded her, as a fiction writer. Her first short story, "All the Pretty Little Horses," appeared in *Seventeen* in June 1964, and *Gray's Sporting Journal* also published her early fiction, importantly introducing her to a small, motivated cadre of New England nature writers who encouraged her to press on with her writing (Rood, p. 4). In the 1980s, she produced a number of how-to books on practical, homespun subjects with titles like *Plan and Make Your Own Fences and Gates, Walkways, Walls, and Drives* (1983), and *The Fine Art of Salad Gardening* (1985).

She also founded a community newsletter in Vermont called *The Vershire Behind the Times,* which she ran from 1984 to 1986. On this proclivity for rural life, and hostility toward most things urban, she says,

> Rural subjects are of interest to me because the people who live in the country are adept at managing, able to do things, familiar with physical work, cognizant of climate, weather and storm, aware of the natural world in ways urban and suburban dwellers are not. By a cruel twist of economic fate their lives and livelihoods are controlled by distant urban power structures. I don't so much make a distinction between rural and urban subjects as write about events and people in rural places, even urbanites who come to the country to live but rarely accept the place on its own terms. I have great respect for rural people and the complicated lines of cooperation that emerge in country places. I find cities rather boring once you get past the restaurants and bijoux shops. I can't bear the bloody noise of traffic and the clack of high heels. I feel crowded and acutely uncomfortable in cities. The west still has silence and relatively clear air, long sight-lines. That's for me, thanks.

> (Dowling interview)

Proulx's first short story for a nationwide adult audience, "The Wer-Trout," appeared in the June 1982 issue of *Esquire*—it was the first of a string of successes in short fiction, now considered some of the finest stories ever written by an American. Tom Jenks, the *Esquire* editor who originally accepted "The Wer-Trout," was hired at the prominent publishing house Charles Scribners Sons, and soon after persuaded Proulx to submit a full volume of short fiction. Proulx's response was *Heart Songs and Other Stories* (1988). Based in the hardscrabble terrain of working-class New England, *Heart Songs* contains nine stories in the 1988 edition (two more were added in the 1995 edition) that together revise the more sentimental representations of nineteenth-century New England local colorists like Harriet Beecher Stowe and Sarah Orne Jewett, and even the later rhapsodies of Robert Frost and Wallace Stegner. Her view of the countryside is consistent with older portraits of the land and its beauty, but only up to a point; rather than presenting self-reliant agrarians sustaining themselves in idyllic solitude, her characters are typically observers of a systemic corporate reality that they are powerless to check. Rural people in Proulx's stories futilely, if nobly, protect what little there is left of their ancestral past. Though *Heart Songs* received typically scant reviews for a debut collection, critics welcomed her as a promising and enigmatic new voice in American letters.

COMING OF AGE

Unlike so many top writers who achieve notoriety at unreasonably early ages, one might say Annie Proulx, a middle-aged woman from the New England sticks, has willed her reputation into existence. Proulx published her first novel, *Postcards*, in 1992 at the age of fifty-seven. The fact that *Postcards* was her first novel stunned reviewers, considering the novel's ambitious narrative scope and stylistic precision. *Postcards* is the story of a rural New Englander, Loyal Blood, who rapes his fiancée and unintentionally takes her life in the process. Though his secret remains with him, he deserts his family farm in Vermont and peregrinates through Western states over a period of forty years, from the end of the Second World War to the late 1980s. Loyal is a fugitive from his own demons. He takes jobs and seeks out opportunities in various states: Illinois, Colorado, the Dakotas, New Mexico, Minnesota—wherever chance delivers him. The farm back home cannot survive without him, and it slowly perishes in his absence. Loyal's aimless wanderings and the consequences of his flight, as Proulx herself professes, represent "an ironic version of American expansion westward" (Rood, 2001, p. 59). Manifest destiny is reduced in Proulx's invented world to a fugitive murderer and rapist wandering aimlessly about inhospitable terrain.

Her second novel, the highly acclaimed *The Shipping News*, opens in upstate New York with Quoyle, a lonely, barely employable simpleton whose name refers to a one-dimensional knot that "may be walked on if necessary." Quoyle becomes emotionally unwound by the death of his pernicious wife Petal Bear in a grisly car accident, and he and their two daughters move with his aunt to Killick-Claw, Newfoundland, the seat of their brutish ancestral clan. Toward the end of the narrative, however, Quoyle becomes the subject of his own actions; he becomes whole, a man with agency, no longer victimized by forces beyond his control. Eventually overcoming his inexorable stream of bad luck, Quoyle finds employment as the managing editor of a local newspaper, settles down with his family, and ultimately redeems his forefather's besmirched history on the Newfoundland peninsula. This redemptive aspect of her novel has in many ways opened it to a broader audience than her more fatalistic tales, but the irony of Quoyle's so-called happiness escaped many of her readers:

> The "redemptive aspect" of *Shipping News* is something of an illusion. I had so many comments from readers and editors who read *Postcards* to the effect that "I love the writing but it's so DARK!" that I somewhat spitefully determined to write

something with an illusory happy ending. *Shipping News* was my second novel and the tradition is that the second novel is a bomb, so I figured that it would be the right book to get this faux happy ending out of my system. In fact, Quoyle's "happiness" at the end is nothing more than the absence of pain. Almost no one picked up on this. . . . Of course later I thought maybe that's all happiness is anyway.

(Dowling interview)

Her next novel, *Accordion Crimes*, perhaps her most ambitious book to date, trails a handmade accordion through a battery of owners. In it we find an admixture of Proulx's dark humor, violent imagery, and sensitivity to historical currents that looks back to older traditions of the realistic novel, most notably, as Karen L. Rood indicates, John Dos Passos's *U.S.A.* trilogy. Like *U.S.A.*, both Proulx's *Postcards* and *Accordion Crimes* cover long periods in American history: *Postcards* extends across the second half of the twentieth century and *Accordion Crimes* takes up the first half as well, charting the course of the accordion from the 1890s to the 1990s. There are eight sections in all, each dealing with the historical trends and events that characterize the time and place of each section—anti-immigration, World War I, the Great Depression, World War II, the civil rights movement, and the corporatization of American culture. As the narrative progresses, regional, ethnic, and personal individuality become subsumed by the tide of commercialization and mass media. In *Heart Songs*, her small New England farmers are in too close a proximity to the urban centers to effectively maintain their cultural isolation. In *Postcards*, Loyal's Vermont home is destroyed by his self-imposed exile into the American West. In *The Shipping News*, Quoyle's life improves because he revitalizes his ancestral past in Newfoundland and escapes the influences of acculturation to the south, while in *Accordion Crimes*, little remains to save or not save, return to or flee from—white ethnic groups are now simply white, not Scandinavian, Italian, Irish, or Polish. Whatever was worth saving from those group identities exists only residually by the late twentieth century. Proulx's ironic ending this time is that groups who suffer from prejudice, almost exclusively racial now, will be America's cultural survivors, since they are systematically ghettoized and therefore left alone.

"THE FAR SIDE OF THE FENCE"

The title of her next work, *Close Range: Wyoming Stories*, accentuates the distinction between it and the rest of her fiction. This collection of short stories is written from a "close" observational platform, since Proulx now resides in Wyoming. Proulx thus digs deeper into the consciousnesses of her case studies, thickly describing what aspects of the Wyoming culture are salvageable during the commercial and corporate onslaught of the late twentieth century. Wyoming's physical isolation can prolong its identity, Proulx implies, but outside influences are still dangerously viable. Again, "the sensational journalism and television" intrudes upon their lives, invidiously acting as their "source of knowledge of the outside world."

Although the stories reveal an intimacy with the Wyoming cultural landscape, she rejects the suggestion that she has achieved insider status in that state, and argues that regional writing should not be restricted to insiders:

> I am an outsider in Wyoming and everywhere I have lived. That is the natural condition of most writers. When you develop a writerly eye that watches others and how they behave and interact, you are necessarily on the far side of the fence. It is much harder—at least for me—to write from my personal life, inner knowledge or long familiarity with a place or set of people.

(Dowling interview)

The Wyoming stereotype typically involves pickup trucks, rodeos, spousal abuse, rural machismo, alcoholism, loneliness, and regret, all of which Proulx embraces in *Close Range*. In a *New Yorker* essay, "Blue Skies and Empty Places" (25 December 2000 and 1 January 2001), she paradoxically applauds the often violent masculinity of Wyoming's countryside and its inhabitants, adding that "the characters in a story, like people in life, behave as their landscape makes them behave." She refines this treatment of behavior and landscape further in her latest novel, *That Old Ace in the Hole*, which is set on the Texas panhandle. When asked how she reconciles her fondness for the Western landscape and how it "makes [her characters] behave," she replies in unapologetic terms:

> There *is* lingering violence in the contemporary west, people do drink, men are often alternately rough with women and sentimental about them. That I see the landscape and the people who live in it as connected is hardly unusual. That I like both may seem a contradiction . . . but one of the traits in humans that I find deeply interesting is contradiction. Human beings are endlessly complex, our lives ricocheting between yin/yang behavior. Apparently sweet and kind people are capable of atrocities; foul and cruel louts exhibit streaks of tenderness. Societies also exhibit contradictory behaviors. I find exploring these contradictions the stuff of fiction.

(Dowling interview)

[*See also* Popular Fiction.]

SELECTED WORKS

Heart Songs and Other Stories (1988)
Postcards (1992)
The Shipping News (1993)
Accordion Crimes (1996)
Close Range: Wyoming Stories (1999)
That Old Ace in the Hole: A Novel (2003)

FURTHER READING

Bolick, Katie. *Atlantic Unbound*. 12 November 1997. www.theatlantic.com/unbound/factfict/eapint.htm. An insightful interview, which challenges Proulx to comment on her celebrity status and the complications of achieving this status as an older writer.

Dowling, Robert. Unpublished email interview, 17 August 2002, exclusively for this volume.

Flaven, Louise. "Quoyle's Quest: Knots and Fragments as Tools of Narration in *The Shipping News*." *Critique* (1999): 239–247. A close reading of *The Shipping News* and its unorthodox syntactical sentence and narrative structure. Flaven points out that the more anxious and lost Quoyle becomes, the more clipped and jolting the structure of the sentences; and, she elaborates, "because they are often participial fragments, phrases that lack subjects of actions, we sense a lack of subjective character in Quoyle" (p. 241).

Myers, B. R. "A Reader's Manifesto: An Attack on the Growing Pretentiousness of American Literary Prose." *Atlantic Monthly* (July/August 2001): 104–122. An attack on Proulx and other contemporary authors, such as Cormac McCarthy, Don DeLillo, Paul Aster, and Toni Morrison, in which he condemns Proulx's fragmented style as an attempt to "exploit the license of poetry while claiming exemption from poetry's rigorous standards" (p. 105).

"Proulx, E(dna) Annie." *Contemporary Authors*, 1995. Includes an exclusive autobiographical essay by Proulx.

Rood, Karen L. *Understanding Annie Proulx*. Columbia, S.C., 2001. Rood provides a concise biographical and critical introduction to Proulx and her writing, and dedicates a chapter to each of Proulx's books.

Steiner, Wendy. *Postmodern Fictions, 1960–1990*. New York, 1999. Steiner argues that Proulx's fiction surpasses postmodernist fiction as "the strategies of coping are not hyperrationality, paradox, and the absurd, but a kind of nurturing steadfastness" (p. 538).

PURITANISM: THE SENSE OF AN UNENDING

by John McWilliams

On the rare occasion when a contemporary American recalls "the Puritans," the image likely to come to mind is of a killjoy, sure of his own spiritual rectitude, anxious to enforce it upon others, and possessed by the nagging fear that someone, somewhere, might be happy. "The Puritans," we believe, could have had no appreciation of earthly beauty, let alone of sensual pleasure, because they saw this world darkly through the lens of their corrosive sense of universal sin and therefore lived only to pursue the radiance of the afterlife. This perspective, to modern readers, may seem mere simpleminded unreason and angry rant. Above all, we associate the historical Puritan with ministers and governors whose minds were blinded with patriarchal certitude of the most repellent sort. We imagine the Puritan to be smugly reflecting, in darkest night: "Because I know that God has elected me for an eternity of heavenly bliss, I am entitled to rule over all unworthy sinners, over all you women, children, and common laborers, and to force you to follow in my virtuous path. I have God's assurance that I am more pure than thou."

To the extent that we are conscious of the source of this image of Puritanism, we are likely to recall a compulsory high school reading of Hawthorne's *The Scarlet Letter*, a local performance of Arthur Miller's *The Crucible*, or the sensationalized films recently and loosely made from both of them. The Puritan is the unsmiling domineering man dressed in a black suit, wearing a steeple crowned hat, grasping (as Hawthorne pictured his first ancestor) a Bible in one hand and a sword in the other. Or, as Hawthorne also imagined him, the Puritan is the weak-willed minister, immobilized by his secret sin, treasuring up the sexual secret he does not have the courage to reveal. From our memories of *The Scarlet Letter*, *The Crucible*, and the films made from them, we associate Puritan women either with defiantly sensual victims of male suppression (Hawthorne's Hester Prynne) or with adolescent slatterns who gleefully spread the deadly hysteria of the Salem witch hunt (Miller's Abigail Williams). Wherever we turn in popular culture, what remains associated in our minds with "Puritanism" is a curious mix of prudery, lust, and religious pretense, all of it safely historicized into a remote, dark, and superstitious past that, we are assured, can no longer have anything to do with our enlightened selves.

Such half-readings and half-filmings turn the complexities of Hawthorne's novel and Miller's play into starkest caricature. Our readiness to oversimplify shows our need to continue a pattern of cultural accusation now almost two centuries old. Because Hawthorne is the chief source of our national image of Puritanism, it is important to remember that Hawthorne's compelling fictions themselves encourage historical distortion. Hawthorne exaggerated the loveless and sadistic qualities of Puritan forefathers even as he granted them the strengths of the founders. Recently we have found powerful new reasons to disparage the Puritans. Since the rise of the Red Power and counterculture movements of the late 1960s, centuries of violent dispossession of the Indian can now be traced back to Puritan origin. Never mind that the Spanish oppression of native peoples in the New World makes the Puritan record look tolerant or that many a present-day accuser of Puritan racial wrong owns a piece of suburban land and brings his book royalties to a bank where his land title deed rests in a safety deposit box. Similarly, ever since Earth Day, our awareness of environmental degradation has made us more than ready to charge the Puritans with having transformed the near-wilderness of New England's 1620 coastal and interior lands into something other than pastoral plenty. And again, never mind that the very real ecological sins of the Puritans were as nothing compared with the damage wrought upon New England by nineteenth-century railroads, textile mills, and shoe factories—economic forces that the Puritans could not possibly have foreseen.

The crucial moment in forming our present kind of scorn for the Puritan heritage occurred not in Hawthorne's time but during the 1920s. Under the modernist pressure to "make it new" and the modernist demand to free individual creativity from communal moral restraint, the Puritans became the bête noire of our national origin, the blocking force that needed, once and for all, to be denounced and removed from the pedestal of influence. H. L. Mencken, editor of the *Smart Set* and the darling pundit of the era's intelligentsia, charged that the Puritans had eagerly enforced a "theology of the most grotesque and insane sort ever cherished by man" ("Last New Englander"). To Mencken, "the whole Puritan theological and political apparatus" could be summarized as "the pervasiveness of sin, the importance of moral problems, the need of harsh and inquisitorial laws" ("Notes"). What resulted, Mencken declared, was even worse than the Puritans' "almost total lack of aesthetic aspiration." The Puritans left a double inheritance of repressive behavior among men of Anglo-Saxon stock: on the one hand, the "intolerable prudishness and dirty-mindedness of Puritanism"; on the other, "that timorousness and reticence which are the distinguishing marks of the Puritan" (shades of Arthur Dimmesdale). Puritan prudishness and dirty-mindedness were, in Mencken's view, still surviving in "the old heat" of biblical fundamentalism that underlies the opinions of the half-educated American ("Last New Englander"). Conversely, the "timorousness and reticence" of the Puritan survived in the evasive high-sounding words and professorial Protestantism of Woodrow Wilson, whom Mencken never tired of dubbing "the archangel Woodrow."

In the formation of the American literary canon, no book has been more important than D. H. Lawrence's *Studies in Classic American Literature* (1923). Convinced that the spirit of place was essential to good literature, and anxious to deflate the cliché that the Pilgrims came to America to practice freedom of worship, Lawrence portrayed newfound America as a wilderness that could release the potential of the deepest self only if one brought the deepest self to it. The underside of American origins, Lawrence charged, was that the Puritans brought to America not freedom of conscience but "a black spirit" based upon both revulsion from oneself and "a black revulsion from Europe." In the era of Puritan founding Lawrence saw a self-defeating flight from Renaissance humanism rather the dawning of Protestant liberty. As early as 1630 America became a culture of "escaped slaves" controlled by a dark fear of their own emptiness. Two hundred pages later, when Lawrence considers *The Scarlet Letter*, he ascribes the prudery of Adam's fig leaf to Hawthorne's Puritans, and notes that, in Dimmesdale's self-flagellation, we see "the myth of New England," "a form of masturbation" in which one hugs one's own sins in secret but gloats over others' sins in public.

William Carlos Williams's stature as a modernist poet was eventually to make *In the American Grain* (1925), little read upon its first publication, almost as influential as Lawrence's *Studies*. *In the American Grain* casts a wider historical and cultural net, from Eric the Red to Abraham Lincoln, but its fastening upon the evils of Puritanism is no less intense. Again and again, the metaphor of the Puritans as hard little seeds, "little pips," incapable of growth because of their inner emptiness, is repeated to show the hollowness of American materialist values. Inner emptiness leads Puritans and their Yankee descendants to fierce opposition to all outsiders, all non-Protestants. The Puritans' "jargon of God . . . was their dialect by which they kept themselves surrounded as with a palisade." Unwilling to acknowledge the "intensity of their emptiness," the Puritans went on, generation after generation, "praising zero in themselves," trusting that the material symbols of technological expertise and industrial might would compensate for their spiritual failings and sensual self-deprivation. As a consequence, Puritanism in its later incarnations has remained the "malfeasant ghost that dominates us all." Into a remembered conversation with Valéry Larbaud in Paris, Williams inserts a judgment releasing his detestation of everything he associates with the word "Puritanism": "There is a 'puritanism'—of which you hear, of course, but you have never felt it stinking all about you—that has survived to us from the past. It is an atrocious thing, a kind of mermaid with a corpse for tail. Or it remains, a bad breath in the room. This THING, strange, inhuman, powerful, is like a relic of some died out tribe whose practices were revolting."

The stridency of the 1920s attack on Puritanism depends on the authors' belief that Puritanism was not a past regional oddity but a living national spirit that continues to infect us all. In Williams's terms, the "relic" has remained as "powerful" as a "bad breath in the room." No one today, no matter how contemptible "Puritanism" is thought to be, could write such an intensely repellent denunciation; neither the Puritans nor Puritanism now seem important enough to merit it. Nonetheless, stripped of hyperbole, the substance of the charges leveled against the Puritan by Mencken, Lawrence, and Williams remains alive and well; the words "Puritan" and "Puritanism" retain many of those same connotations today. It is the purpose of this essay to expose the historical falsity of these connotations, at least insofar as they are verifiable in Puritan literature, if not in Puritan culture. In particular, by looking at the endings and resolutions of the most widely known and highly regarded of Puritan writings,

I seek to counter the continuing assumption that the Puritans were a people of absolute certitude, sure of their own election, proud of their righteousness, and anxious to reveal it in order to disparage others.

The assumptions about endings and resolutions as well as the title of this essay derive from Frank Kermode's lively, probing book of lectures *The Sense of an Ending* (1966). Rephrasing Aristotle, Kermode argues that "Men die because they cannot join the beginning and the end." If we were present at the beginning or the end, we would be immortal. In fact, however, everyone in historical memory has been born in the middle of time, unable to see the beginning or the end, longing to find coherence in the passing of time and to find meaning in the happenings of life, yet sensing that, unless beginnings and ends can be truly seen, coherence and meaning are impossible. We wish to live through identifiable crises, Kermode argues, because crises are spots in time that force us to define our ends and our beginnings. For Kermode, this human predicament is an essential element of the appeal of the written word. Much of the world's enduring literature has a beginning, a middle, a crisis, and an end. For Christians, the Bible has its beginning (Genesis), its crisis (the Crucifixion), and its end (Revelations). However, just as the end of time has, since the Middle Ages, come to seem immanent but no longer not imminent, so in literature "Beginnings are always troublesome and conclusions are the weak point of most authors."

Without ever mentioning the American Puritans, Kermode's argument is especially applicable to them. For greatly varied purposes (individual salvation, a City on a Hill, restoration of the first-century church community, prosperity as the sign of enduring virtue), the Puritans left behind British origins they had come to perceive as constrictions. As in Kermode's model, the American Puritan wished to see each day as a potential crisis because to do so might satisfy the yearning for an ultimate revelation, "our deep need for intelligible Ends." But if the Ends proved neither imminent nor clearly discernible, what then would become of the certitude, the assurance, the sense of righteousness, that is so essential to our stereotype of the Puritan? Instead of exhibiting Mencken's "old heat" of biblical fundamentalism, the Puritan might be left in precisely the troubling position Kermode postulated for any honest post-Renaissance thinker: "We project ourselves—a small humble elect, perhaps—past the End, so as to see the structure whole, a thing we *cannot do* from our spot of time in the middle"

(italics added). In sum, the Puritan might well acquire, to his own vexation, a bewildering sense of unending.

THE ENDS OF ARRIVAL

Among the diverse genres (diaries, letters, poems, promotional tracts, histories) recording the motives for the first Puritan settlements, two writings by the two founding governors have been rightly singled out for decades of anthologizing: William Bradford's *Of Plymouth Plantation* (1630–1654) and John Winthrop's "A Model of Christian Charity" (1630). Our ways of anthologizing them have, however, distorted the intentions and arguments of both authors. By identifying them as "Puritan" writings, we affix a label that Bradford and Winthrop not only never used but sought to avoid. Among British Anglicans, "Puritan" had been a term of contempt since the 1570s (The *Oxford English Dictionary* quotes Thomas Nashe: "they take themselves to be pure, when they are filthy in God's sight."). To Bradford, his group of British separatists who settled Plymouth from Amsterdam in 1620 should best be called simply "pilgrims." To Winthrop, who repeatedly denied that he had separated from the Anglican church, the settlers of the "great migration" he led to Boston in 1630 should best think of themselves as "a company professing ourselves fellow members of Christ." When we repeatedly select for our anthologies Bradford's uplifting accounts of the arrivals at Cape Cod and Plymouth and the forming of the Mayflower Compact, we falsify the historical overview of Bradford's text. Similarly, scholars and politicians who reduce Winthrop's model of Christian charity to the sure prediction that America will be a City on a Hill violate the essence of his argument.

When Bradford set out in 1630 to record the history of Plymouth plantation, he confidently expected to pen, "in a plain style, with singular regard unto the simple truth in all things," the Pilgrims' part in Satan's continuing war against the saints. Although Satan proves to be little more than a metaphor for evils that men enact rather than an intervening agent, the first book of Bradford's history, ending with the Pilgrims' arrival in Plymouth Bay and the building of their first houses, sustains the progressive, even heroic tone with which colonial and republican Americans would long memorialize their past. After eighty pages, however, Bradford without explanation stopped writing his history. When he resumed work on it at least a decade later, he changed its form, deciding to recount the events to be described in Book 2 (from 1620 to 1646) in the form of annals rather than a sustained narrative, presumably "for brevity's sake." Throughout the first book, Bradford controls Plymouth's past, selecting events and then interpreting them under the assumption that history is controlled by God's providence. In the second book, even though Bradford insists upon God's overruling providence again and again, it is evident that, as a writer, Bradford is now controlled by Plymouth's past. The demanding sequence of yearly events threatens to become not a coherent narrative with a known end but beads upon a string. Should we credit Bradford's claim that he changed his form "for brevity's sake"? If so, why do the annals of Plymouth plantation require over three hundred pages, whereas the entire narrative of exile, migration, and arrival required but eighty?

The answer may be sought in the subject matter of the annals themselves. During the first years recounted in the annals, there had been dire issues of survival: Would the Pilgrims starve, would the Indians destroy them, would the adventurers withdraw all support, would the Pilgrims ever secure an uncontested deed to their land, could they pay off their debt, could their fish, fur, and lumber trades survive French and Dutch competition? In later years, however, Plymouth's history declines into a dispiriting mix of subversions from within, attacks from without, and slow lessening of the founders' strength. Sometimes in anger, sometimes in melancholy, Bradford recounts the following debacles: the commercial sabotage of Thomas Weston; the teary deceit of Reverend John Lyford, their first resident minister; the deaths of John Robinson, Robert Cushman, and William Brewster; the rivalry of the nearby "atheist" settlement at Merrymount, whose leader Thomas Morton was arming the Indians; the divisive virtues of Roger Williams, who seemed to value purity to the disregard of communal order; sodomy and buggery; the imprisonment and emigration of Edward Winslow; and finally and most decisively, a prosperity that induced settlers to disperse from Plymouth to remote farmlands and new communities.

When Bradford began writing his history, aware both of Plymouth's problems and the coming of Winthrop's larger group to Massachusetts Bay, Bradford had sought to justify the Pilgrims' settlement in Plymouth "as stepping-stones unto others" in the great work of "advancing the gospel of the kingdom of Christ in those remote parts of the world." At some point during his last years of writing the annals, however, Bradford added a footnote lamenting that the "sacred bond" and "sweet communion" of the first settlement had decayed unto dissolution, thus accounting for "my misery in old age," a fact he is now acknowledging "for others' warning and admonition,

and my own humiliation." *Of Plymouth Plantation* ends not in any summary of achievement or failure but in Bradford's listing the bare dates "1647–1648" without placing any entries underneath them. His inability to bring his history to resolution was not due to sickness, death, or disinterest. By 1654 Bradford had abandoned *Of Plymouth Plantation* and had turned to writing angry, despairing poems attacking Boston's new love of "gold and silk" and warning "Oh, New England, thou canst not boast; / Thy former glory thou hast lost." Trying to make the discouraging annals of Plymouth fit the progressive assumptions of providential history had evidently become, at the last, unmanageable.

Unlike Bradford, Winthrop needed to speak to only one moment of historical crisis, but his message was no more assured. Seeking to unify and strengthen the spirits of his fellow emigrants, Winthrop paused near the end of "A Model of Christian Charity" to define, in four consecutive, numbered paragraphs, the identity, work, purpose, and means of their passage to a new world. All "persons" in the fleet were to think of themselves collectively as a "company professing ourselves fellow members of Christ" both in the financial sense of the term (they were the Massachusetts Bay Trading Company) and in their church polity (a congregational community, self-formed under willing covenant with their God). Their "work," a similarly collective endeavor, did not require the union of church and state (as Mencken charged) but a compromise that would keep political and religious powers separate under one government: "to seek out a place of cohabitation and consortship under a due form of government both civil and ecclesiastical." With evident care for priority among the settlers' purposes, Winthrop defined their "end" as a sequence rising from improving their earthly lives, to doing service to God, to thereby preserving themselves from "the common corruptions of this evil world" and ultimately to "work out our Salvation under the power and purity of His holy Ordinances." As for the "means" of achieving these ends, Winthrop could only insist that in America the settlers would have the opportunity to practice what in England was only professed—namely the New Testament "Law of Grace" commanding men to do good unto others, to love their enemy. "We must bear one another's burdens," Winthrop concludes at the end of his discussion of "means." His central concern is whether his community will be able to extend and sustain the needed spirit of Christian charity toward each other rather than displaying their special election. Nothing in John Winthrop's formulations is exclusively Puritan; everything derives from the broad reach of Pauline Christianity.

Read in their original context, the famous phrases "We shall be as a City upon a Hill, the eyes of all people are upon us" are offered only as the possible end of attaining a spiritual wholeness not yet achieved: "We shall find the God of Israel is among us, when ten of us shall be able to resist a thousand of our enemies." In the preceding sentences, Winthrop warns his audience that if we "fall to seeking great things for ourselves and our posterity, the Lord will surely break out in wrath against us." In the following sentences, Winthrop voices his fear that if we deal falsely with our God we shall not only become "a story and a by-word throughout the world" but "be consumed out of the good land where we are going." The closing words of "A Model of Christian Charity" say nothing about a City on a Hill but warn that if we worship "other Gods, our pleasures and profits . . . we shall surely perish out of the good land." Which settler aboard the *Arbella*, upon hearing John Winthrop's words, could possibly have felt assured of his own salvation or have been confident of the community's glorious future? As in this sentence, so in "A Model of Christian Charity" as a whole, the future is nothing more than a conditional "if" fraught with anxiety.

THE ENDS OF MEDITATION

When John Bunyan published *The Pilgrim's Progress* (1678–1684), a novel that would be, for more than a century, the second best-selling book in the English language, Bunyan's fellow Protestants in America read it eagerly, even though they wrote no fiction themselves, insisting publicly that to reinvent the world with words was to risk assuming the role of God. Nonetheless, the closet appeal of *The Pilgrim's Progress* for many an American Protestant reader surely lay in the opportunity to discover how Christian's and Christiana's travails through a world full of constant reversal and recurrent despair could finally earn them, apparently without regard to church membership, the reward of arriving at the Celestial City. Christian's joyful arrival in heaven was what the American Puritan longed for but could not quite credit; *The Pilgrim's Progress* had to remain, therefore, suspect as fiction. Writing poetry, however, was quite another matter. Not only had there been in the recent past great British religious poets of both Puritan and Anglican persuasion (Edmund Spenser, John Donne, George Herbert, Andrew Marvell); the rhythms and rhymes of poetry could convey, to some slight degree, the heavenly music of the spheres, the

harmonies of God's laws. Eulogies, elegies, translations of the Psalms, versified theology, incidental poems on personal and community experiences flowed continually from New England pens. The best of these poems, by Bunyan's near contemporaries Anne Bradstreet and Edward Taylor, partake of the tradition Louis Martz has identified as the poetry of meditation: to pause from this world's busy-ness and to consider, in a sustained way, the weight of the world's and the self's evil, the possibilities of release from them, and ways in which the music of words might somehow lift the "Affections" (emotions) beyond life's daily ruck toward the ecstasy of salvation. Could our dismissal of the Puritan tradition be partly accountable to our refusal to engage in a meditative process so utterly foreign to the ever-accelerating daily focus of our lives?

The short, personal poems Anne Bradstreet wrote in her later years would, according to Mencken's or Lawrence's definition, have to be described as almost anti-Puritan. Writing from and about her own emotional experience rather than theology, Bradstreet sought to understand life's reversals and mysteries in a world presumed to be ordered by a just and merciful God. Her subject range is necessarily limited: her intense love, physical and spiritual, for her often absent husband; the pains and promise of childbirth; bodily sickness; sudden household disaster; the untimely death of too many of her children and grandchildren; the beauty of October in New England. Her emotional range, however, is not limited. As a mature poet she found the strength to abandon pretentious diction and pretentious subjects for simple words that do not immediately grasp for the easy or customary answer. In her inner conflict of Flesh and Spirit, sometimes expressed in dialogue form, Spirit should prevail, but does not always do so. Her questioning was as real as her piety. Moreover, Bradstreet knew that a mocking self-deferential irony was the effective tone for subverting, without directly attacking, the presumption of male superiority she experienced all her life. Although she knew that Queen Elizabeth had been no friend to outspoken Puritans, Bradstreet praised Elizabeth unreservedly as the woman who "hath wiped off th'aspersion of her sex" and trusts that Elizabeth will somehow prove to be, at least in spirit, the "Phoenix Queen."

Two meditative poems suggest how little assurance this presumably "Puritan" woman ever found. "As Weary Pilgrim," written in her fifty-seventh year, begins with an eighteen-line description of the welcome rest the weary pilgrim earns in late life surcease from the world's vexations. Such welcome rest, we suddenly and unexpectedly learn, is not for her:

A pilgrim I, on earth perplexed
With sins, with cares and sorrows vext,
By age and pains brought to decay,
And my clay house mold'ring away.

Bradstreet ends her poem longing that the Lord might come as "dear Bridegroom" to take her away from a world of pain and confusion and to finally unite her body with her soul. Longing is, however, her only recourse. Without complaint, she expresses no confidence in arriving at the Celestial City, no end to her earthly weariness, no pride in her familial and poetic achievements, no evidence that her pilgrimage has been progress.

"Contemplations," Bradstreet's most sustained meditation, assumes from first line to last that any verifiable meaning in life must arise from one's own contemplative thinking, not from sermon, liturgy, or even the Word itself. On a solitary late afternoon walk in the autumn of her life, the glory of fall foliage leave her senses so "rapt" that she remarks "I wist not what to wish." Four stanzas of ecstatic sun worship follow, stanzas in which the sun is *not* an allegorical stand-in for Christ. Musings upon the biblical account of Creation lead Bradstreet to renewed notice of the created life around her and to presume from evidence of this world the existence of the Deity. (Here is a forerunner of the eighteenth-century "argument from design.") Nonetheless, in Bradstreet's experience of earthly life, mankind "never finds cessation, /But day or night, within, without, vexation." The wonder is that, despite all the wrack and sorrow, in the face of all our declared faith in the heavenly afterlife, we still fear to die, still will not "deeply groan for that divine translation." In the poem's five concluding stanzas, time remains the inexorable destroyer. The expected consolation arrives only in the final couplet, which leaves us wondering, for reasons beyond the gender of pronouns, whether Bradstreet believes herself included in her reference to how "he whose named is graved in the white stone / Shall last and shine when all of these are gone."

Bradstreet used the title "Meditations" for a series of short prose reflections that resemble epigrams. Some of them recall Ecclesiastes and some Benjamin Franklin, but very few would be suitable to a catechism. Quoting two of them should suffice to show how little Anne Bradstreet resembles the stereotypical Puritan: "Wisdom with an inheritance is good, but wisdom without an inheritance is better than an inheritance without wisdom"; "How

unsearchable are His ways and His footsteps past finding out." The grieving strength of Anne Bradstreet's spirit fully emerges in her autobiographical prose letter "To My Dear Children," in which the conventional Puritan act of a written testimony of faith is undertaken more for her children's sake than for her own. Bradstreet unashamedly admits to her own questionings of God's existence, her resentment at the barrenness of the New World, her wonder whether Protestant anti-Catholicism was merest prejudice. Amidst sickness and love, Bradstreet's letter serves to assure her children that atheism, relativism, sickness, death, and joy are all natural and all transient. There is, for her, and presumably for her children, no recourse but to have faith. She has come to believe that heaven and hell are in fact not places but states of mind: "it is the absence or presence of God that makes heaven and hell." If Anne Bradstreet is labeled a "Puritan" woman, she is certainly no fit example of William Carlos Williams's notion of the Puritan "blind seed" who projects inner emptiness onto a feared world. No "little pip" was she.

If one were to select the single major achievement of American Puritan poetry, there is no choice other than the *Preparatory Meditations* of Edward Taylor (1642–1729). Born in England, educated first at Cambridge and then, after emigration to America, at Harvard, Taylor accepted a call to be the minister for the struggling frontier town of Westfield, Massachusetts, a position he would retain for over fifty years. As his community's factotum as well as spiritual leader, Taylor willingly served as sometime schoolmaster, physician, and town policy adviser, even as he strove to continue granting church membership only to apparently sincere believers at a time when open church membership was being increasingly demanded. Such probity, endurance, and strength of commitment earned him the admiration of Massachusetts leaders and, as the decades went on, the deep respect, tinged with resentment, of his own congregation. Few of Taylor's contemporaries knew, however, that his commitment to writing poetry was equally strong and equally sustained; it seems characteristic of Taylor that he made no effort to publish his poetry during his lifetime.

Taylor's title, "Preparatory Meditations," suggests that the personal and clerical purposes of writing verse were for him quite inseparable. To prepare himself to be worthy to express God's Word in a sermon, and more particularly to be worthy to offer communion in the body and blood of Christian fellowship, Taylor would compose a meditation in verse. The sermon prepared the verse meditation and vice versa. To try to purify his language in verse and prose was to try to purify his soul, not merely for his sake but for the community he served. Taylor did not have our rather convenient ability to distance religious concerns into safely intellectual or even academic categories. What we would call theology was to him emotional belief; what we would call psychology was a search for readiness of spirit. Consequently, in the world of Taylor's *Preparatory Meditations*, only the representative self and God exist; other relationships certainly matter but are wholly dependent upon the need of the self to prepare to receive God's grace, to feel that moment of holiness within that might become a moment of holiness without.

The writing of a preparatory meditation thus becomes an often desperate search for metaphors that might accurately express some small part of the infinitely varied relationship of God and Man. Man is the crumb and God the baker; man is the coin and God the mint-maker; man is the lute and God the composer; man is the seed and God the gardener; man is the iron and God the blacksmith; man is the stopped pipe whose halting voice God must unclog; man hopes to be the bidden guest at the sumptuous feast God prepares; man is the twig who would be grafted onto God's tree. Within almost every preparatory meditation (five to ten stanzas of six iambic pentameter lines, with an *ababcc* rhyme scheme) Taylor shifts abruptly from one metaphor, to another, searching to find, if not the precisely accurate metaphor, at least a better one, even as he despairs of the blotted, botched, constricted lines through which he is trying to convey God's glory. What remains constant within this ever-widening field of metaphor is the imbalance of agency. Taylor may, through the prayer of his poem, try to prepare himself to be worthy to receive God's grace, but God always remains the prime mover, the only true agent, the source of all power.

Taylor's emotions toward his God range from ecstasy to despair; his hope ranges from eternal salvation to sensing just one instant of God's flaming flake of love; his tone ranges from exclamatory joy to self-conscious obscurantism. Almost all of the preparatory meditations end, however, in one of two ways. The first is a direct plea to God for grace: "Lord, blow the Coal: Thy Love Enflame in Me"; "Pass o'er my Faults; shine forth, bright sun, arise / Enthrone Thy Rosy-self within mine Eyes"; "Let me thy Angel be, be Thou my Lord." The second is a conditional bargain in which Taylor promises to make recompense for God's mercy: "If Thou wilt plead my Case before the King: / I'll wagon loads of love and glory bring"; "If in this stream Thou cleanse and cherish me / My heart Thy Hallelujah's Pipe shall be"; "If with Thy

precious robes will't dress me here / My present tunes shall sing Thy praise when there." Never, however, can Taylor himself be the initiator, the one who determines, or even the one who chooses. Whether Taylor thinks of himself as a botch of leprosy or God's golden angel, he has received no sign of his abiding condition and no assurance that God's grace might be present in him either on this coming Sabbath day or at any time hereafter.

What emerges from such lifelong uncertainty? The inner compulsion, based upon spiritual need, to write 217 preparatory meditations over a period of forty-three years. And what spiritual state does one reach? The last completely legible preparatory meditation, dated Westfield 1722 and written probably in Taylor's eighty-first year, describes his condition as follows:

> My Love alas is but a shrimpy thing
> > A sorry Crickling a blasted bud
> A little drachm, too light a gift to bring.
> > It's but a grain weight and scarce ever good,
> > And shall I then presume thee to obtain
> > If I should rob thee of so small a grain?

The metaphors, the exclamations, the mockery of his own presumption cannot be distinguished from the preparatory meditations he had written forty years earlier. The individual meditations, even sometimes the stanzas among them, prove interchangeable for the most plausible of reasons. For Edward Taylor there was no end to the search for grace, no end to the doubt of his own condition, no resolution save a plea or a question. Preparatory meditation must continue, unresolved, until death.

One of Taylor's lyrics, poems deriving from a particular incident or occasion, nicely summarizes his sense of the condition of life. Called to guest minister at another church, Taylor hesitates whether or not to set off into a threatening rainstorm. The first two stanzas of the poem, titled "When Let by Rain," are characteristically full of self-mocking questions:

> Ye Flippering Soul,
> > Why dost between the Nippers dwell?
> Not stay, nor go. Not yea, nor yet Control,
> > Doth this do well?
> > > Rise journy'ng when the skies fall weeping Showers.
> > > Not o're nor under th'Clouds and Cloudy Powers?
> Not yea, nor no:
> > On tiptoes thus? Why sit on thorns?
> Resolve the matter; Stay thyself or go,
> > Be'nt both ways born.
> > > Wager thyself against thy surplice, see,
> > > And win thy Coat; or let thy Coat win thee.

As the poem continues, Taylor debates whether it would be better to remain behind like a pent-up cask, like a bottle of ale ready to burst, or to go and strike a spark in God's temple that could enlighten the distant listeners—and perhaps burn up God's building. This homely incident surely had some kind of resolution in Taylor's personal experience (he must have decided either to go or to stay), but in the poem, no resolution whatsoever is provided. Taylor was moved to write "When Let by Rain" because it afforded him an opportunity to convey the stark condition of the flippering soul caught, apparently forever, between life's nippers. A pilgrimage apparently to nowhere.

THE ENDS OF AUTOBIOGRAPHY

For the Puritan, writing about oneself, whether in a diary, a letter, or autobiography, was indirectly connected to the need to provide testimony of one's faith in order to qualify for church membership. The Puritans' admirable and democratic quest for widespread literacy and compulsory public schooling in the Commonwealth of Massachusetts reflected the double hope that, from an early age, adults could read Scriptures for themselves and could preserve in writing the providential spiritual experiences of their daily lives. Self-examination through writing was, therefore, one form of spiritual and civic preparation, enabling an individual to ready himself or herself for receiving the gift of grace and/or church membership. But the autobiographical impulse was also fraught with peril. Too much self-examination was a sure sign of the root sin of pride, of placing oneself before others or even before one's God. Puritans were acutely aware that such pride was most likely to manifest itself as hypocrisy. In its milder form, hypocrisy was the pretense of virtue and spirituality displayed for public purpose; its more insidious form was honest self-deception, the need to believe in a strength of personal faith that was not real. As Daniel Shea has shown, the consequence was that Puritan autobiographical writing was, from the outset, a guarded, oddly communal act in which the self was offered as exemplary for others precisely because it was *not* especially pure. Conversion was not a blinding single experience that marked one out forever as of the elect. It was a lifelong process in which one's momentary emotional crisis, however compelling, becomes suspect over the length of time. In Shea's words, "As long as the Puritan magistracy held sway, enthusiastic autobiography was for the closet only." To seek to display what Mencken would call "the old heat" would have been to expose oneself to being duped by the Satan within.

These self-suspecting qualities are apparent in the surviving autobiographical testimonies of fifty-one ordinary men and women who founded Thomas Shepard's Cambridge congregation in the mid-1630s (see Caldwell, Shepard). More important for literary purposes, we find them in acute form in the two best known and most admired of Puritan autobiographies, written by Thomas Shepard and by Jonathan Edwards near the beginning and end of the American Puritan movement respectively. The stereotypical view of "the Puritan" would hold that clergymen like Shepard and Edwards, because they were prominent members of the ministerial elite, would be sure of their own election and therefore certain of their own authority. The evidence of their autobiographies suggests that the opposite is true. Neither of these autobiographies reaches a conclusion or even a clear ending; both seem to have been left unfinished, with no sign of the author intending publication. Having thought long and deeply about what we might call the psychology of attaining spiritual certainty, Shepard and Edwards were acutely aware of a debilitating paradox. Because there is no assurance of salvation for anyone, ministers included, to remain fearful that one is the worst of sinners may be a sign of greater assurance. Conversely, to be confident of one's holiness suggests that one should be less confident of receiving grace. Here is the Puritan catch-22, discernible to people of the acuity, ministerial experience, and literary skill of Shepard or Edwards but not likely to be understood by those who would judge "the Puritan" from without. The conundrum is best phrased as an alternative: Which is the more insidious form of human pride: to be sure of one's purity, or to be sure of one's sin?

Like Anne Bradstreet and Benjamin Franklin after him, Thomas Shepard (1603–1649) at an advancing age dedicated his autobiographical reflections to the benefit of children, in this case Shepard's son and namesake. All of the temptations to which Shepard succumbed would be later experienced by either Bradstreet or Franklin: "loose and lewd company, lust and pride and gaming and bowling and drinking"; love of besting fellow students in intellectual dispute; "a depth of atheism and unbelief in the main matters of salvation and whether the Scriptures were God's word"; recurrent doubt whether Catholicism or Protestantism was true Christianity; a "deceitfulness of the heart" in which one pretends to repent for sin; and, lastly, an inability to be truly convinced of the inner cancer of sin even as one totals up one's sinful acts. Three times Shepard sets himself a course of "daily meditation" and then falls away from it, acknowledging at one point, well after his supposed conversion, that "Christ was not so sweet as my lust." To take pride in denouncing his own sin, Shepard knows, is a temptation so perverse that he calls it, in a passage anticipating both Cotton Mather and Hawthorne, "the impardonable sin."

The stereotypical Puritan is supposed to have been a resolute "come-outer," certain that emigration to the New World would preserve him from the corruption of the Old World. Nearly half of Shepard's autobiography is concerned with the five years of indecision (1630–1635) during which, as a banned preacher, he remained a semi-fugitive in England primarily because he could not resolve to leave. The external difficulties of emigration, Shepard shows, were considerable, but the true problem was that "others began to pursue me and to threaten me, as thinking I was a Nonconformable man (when for the most of that time I was not resolved either way, but was dark in those things)." The eight reasons Shepard lists for finally deciding to emigrate are overwhelmingly practical, sometimes even a bit cowardly, beginning with "1) I saw no call to any other place in old England nor way of subsistence in peace and comfort to me and my family" and proceeding to "8) Though my ends were mixed, and I looked much to my own quiet, yet the Lord let me see the glory of those liberties in New England." For Shepard there clearly had been no moment of forthright decision, no conviction that purity lay in separation.

Thomas Shepard's autobiography ends not with a summary of his own spiritual condition but with a paragraph describing the death of his beloved second wife, Joanna. There can be no more moving account of the dignity of human loss than this closing passage, regrettably too long to quote. As Shepard nears the end of his own life, Joanna dies in childbirth, causing him, for the second time, to feel the "heartbreaking affliction . . . that I should provoke the Lord to strike at my innocent children for my sake." Joanna's virtues far transcended her constant, quiet ability to "order my family affairs"; she possessed, Shepard insists, "an excellency to reprove for sin and discerned the evils of men"—his own in particular. As Joanna dies in a protracted fever, crying out "Lord, though I am unworthy, Lord, one word, one word," Shepard can conclude only that her last moments, like her last sacrament, "*seemed* to be full of Christ and thereby fitted for heaven" (italics added). Shepard does not try to hide his human protest at the severity of this final affliction, acknowledging that "He [the Lord] did teach me to prize a little grace gained by a cross as a sufficient recompense for all outward losses. But this loss

was very great." The only conclusion Shepard is able to reach about Joanna's death is: "Thus God hath visited and scourged me for my sins and sought to wean me from this world, but I have ever found it a difficult thing to profit even but a little by the sorest and sharpest afflictions." With these muted, honest, and self-depreciating words the autobiography ends. Although Shepard would live for three more years, he wrote no further in it. Surely Shepard must have known that he could not, at the last, get beyond the cloud of life's difficulties to find spiritual benefit in the extremity of suffering God had granted him. Amidst such doubt and uncertainty, there could be only silence.

The name Jonathan Edwards, a decade ago associated with a pop singer, has once again returned to its century-old association with the infamous revival sermon "Sinners in the Hands of an Angry God" (1741). To continue to judge Jonathan Edwards, let alone American Puritanism, by this one sermon is rather like judging the entirety of the Bible by the Book of Job or all of American culture by the Jerry Springer TV show. Because "Sinners in the Hands of an Angry God" was meant to shock a congregation of backsliders by summoning up all the accusatory power of apocalyptic metaphor, it can be readily cited by those who wish to confirm Menckenite notions of the American Puritan as a nasty ranter luxuriating in the old heat of someone else's sin. This particular sermon was, however, written to be delivered for a one-time, one-place occasion. It is not representative of Edwards's complex thought, balanced temperament, and lifelong insistence on a quiet search for the sweetness of God's grace. The essence of "True Virtue," Edwards wrote repeatedly, did not reside in any scriptural text, and certainly not in condemnatory hate, but rather in "love to Being"—that is, love to the universal principle of Being—a love which was more readily glimpsed alone in a field than together in church and which showed itself as "a Divine and Supernatural Light," not as the flames of hellfire.

Edwards's "Personal Narrative" (1739?) is his private record of the quest for love of Being during the years of his early maturity. Without mentioning his astonishing academic and ministerial accomplishments, Edwards unfolds his life as a sequence of separate experiences in which he momentarily felt the sweetness of God's grace and was momentarily taken out of himself to be both annihilated and filled by divine love, becoming at once nothing and all. As in Taylor's *Preparatory Meditations* and Shepard's autobiography, there proves to be no end and no resolution to the process. Although Edwards uses the term "conversion," he cannot trace it to one experience but rather insists "I have had a vastly greater sense of my own wickedness, and the badness of my own heart, since my conversion, than ever I had before." At some point in early adulthood the Calvinistic doctrine of God's absolute sovereignty in choosing whom to save and whom to damn stopped seeming "a horrible doctrine," but Edwards makes no attempt to explain logically how the change occurred. Logic cannot explain it. As Edwards recalls his life, such moments of ecstatic union keep on recurring, but so do the long, low periods in between. The "Personal Narrative" ends, quietly but fittingly, with an anticlimactic diarylike entry: "Another Saturday night (January, 1739), had such a sense, how sweet and blessed a thing it was." Because the original manuscript of the "Personal Narrative" is lost, we cannot know whether Edwards intended to continue it further, but the question is of little importance because there could have been no finality to the searching it recounts. Life's most important question—Will God grant me the sweet holiness of Christ's love?—can never be answered beyond one's present moment in the middle of earthly time. The quest for certainty can bring only uncertainty.

Because of Edwards's interest in epistemology, he was especially aware that the Puritan quest for assurance was beset by problems of human language. On the one hand, the Protestant legacy granted great importance to the written word, human as well as divine. On the other hand, Edwards well knew that, as T. S. Eliot was to insist in "Burnt Norton," our words "Slip, slide, perish, / Decay with imprecision, will not stay in place." Consequently the exasperated phrase "I know not how to express" arises repeatedly in Edwards's writing, never more so than in those passages of the "Personal Narrative" in which Edwards tries to apprehend the Deity:

> I walked abroad alone, in a solitary place in my father's pasture, for contemplation. And as I was walking there, and looked up on the sky and clouds; there came into my mind so sweet a sense of the glorious majesty and grace of God, that I know not how to express. I seemed to see them both in sweet conjunction; majesty and meekness joined together; it was a sweet and gentle, and holy majesty; and also a majestic meekness; an awful sweetness; a high, and great, and holy gentleness.

The triune God is by definition both absolute majesty (Jehovah) and its opposite, absolute meekness (Christ), but how can human language possibly convey both qualities in one term? In this passage, Edwards struggles to find the word for this "sweet conjunction" five separate times, but all he can create are various combinations of multiple terms, none of them adequate. Human language, which is necessarily flawed, cannot accurately apprehend the Divine, which is by definition perfect.

By life's end, Edwards had written hundreds of thousands of words trying to apprehend the Deity by a means he had long known to be futile. It is no wonder that Edwards was so often drawn toward asserting the power of a purely *sensual* apprehension of God. Edwards knew, however, that he could not avoid using words as the means of expressing this antiverbal hope. The depth of this problem, embedded in the very act of writing, would surface later in unexpected, decidedly un-Puritan, places in American literature. Edgar Allan Poe, for example, insisted that although great poetry must always be a quest for "Supernal Beauty," the writing of poetry was like the quest of the moth for the star, more effectively realized through music than through the flawed medium of words.

Paradoxically, Edwards's "Personal Narrative" arrives at a clear, detailed definition of what it means to be, not a true Puritan, but a true Christian:

> The soul of a true Christian, as I then wrote my meditations, appeared like such a little white flower as we see in the spring of the year; low and humble on the ground, opening its bosom to receive the pleasant beams of the sun's glory; rejoicing as it were, in a calm rapture; diffusing around a sweet fragrancy; standing peacefully and lovingly, in the midst of other flowers round about; all in like manner opening their bosoms, to drink in the light of the sun.

Because Edwards remains the measure of the American Puritan writer, we should recognize that the virtues that emerge in this well known passage—humility, joy, quietude, silence, unity with nature—are the opposite of those commonly associated with "American Puritanism." The wonder is that, for an author so self-conscious about the inevitably flawed nature of language, the passage flows so smoothly toward the "light" of the sun/Son. Perhaps Edwards's easy fluency is due to the comparatively modest task of developing only one natural metaphor; he can quietly but intently observe a spring jonquil rising out of a New England winter and infer its equivalencies of spirit. If God is thus approached metaphorically, through words that apply to the observable nature of our world, the Deity may be apprehended with a clarity that any enumeration of His abstract qualities ("majestic meekness") can never approach.

Benjamin Franklin's *Autobiography* (1771, 1784, 1818) signals the end of the Puritan era, though certainly not the end of the Puritans' concerns. It too is unfinished, though for quite different reasons. Franklin worked on it at various stages of adulthood but died before he could complete it. To Benjamin Franklin, few issues are likely to remain irresolvable if we will patiently apply reason to them. Had he lived to finish the *Autobiography*, he surely would have provided concluding observations, reaffirming his introductory paragraphs, about a man's likely rise to affluence, reputation, and felicity through diligence, reason, and self-control—with a reference to the blessings of God added in parenthetically and perhaps a last ironic joke at his own expense. Because man was to live for this world, without searching after any absolute, a greater degree of certitude was, for Franklin, both possible and welcome. His writings also contain an occasional note of complacency, a complacency quite foreign to Cotton Mather and the Puritans who had controlled the Boston of Franklin's youth and against whom he had rebelled. As a measure of the change within the continuity, one need look no farther than the two questions Franklin urged himself and others to meditate upon every morning and every evening: "What good shall I do this Day?" and "What Good have I done to day?" Live for today's good, Franklin urges, in order to benefit others as well as oneself. Edward Taylor would surely have wondered what so time-bound and presentist a "meditation" could possibly be "preparatory" to. The day-to-day nature of Franklin's activist virtues, which many Americans have pursued since his time, has surely made our earthly world, in the main, a better world. Perhaps, however, amidst our pursuit of secular virtues, we had better hope that our denial of any world hereafter will prove to be valid.

One closing prediction. As long as we continue to apply the misnomer of "Puritan," it will be futile to protest against its overwhelmingly negative associations. As the catchall term of historical reference, "Puritan" is unlikely ever to lose its accusatory weight. Beyond this surmise, however, silence seems best. An essay like this one, asserting that the American Puritan could see no end to the crucial civic and spiritual problems of life, should surely be wary of arriving at a resolute ending. Absolute conclusions are perhaps best left to self-declared non-Puritans who are assured of certain certainties—to opinion leaders like, say, H. L. Mencken.

[*See also* Bradstreet, Anne; Colonial Writing in America; Edwards, Jonathan; Franklin, Benjamin; Hawthorne, Nathaniel, and his *The Scarlet Letter*; Mencken, H. L.; Miller, Arthur; Taylor, Edward; *and* Williams, William Carlos.]

FURTHER READING

Bercovitch, Sacvan. *The American Jeremiad*. Madison, Wis., 1978. Influential study of changing rhetoric within the Puritan tradition of prophesying God's punishment of New England's decline.

Bradford, William. *The Collected Verse*. Edited by Michael G. Runyan. St. Paul, Minn., 1974.

Bradford, William. *Of Plymouth Plantation 1620–1647*. Edited by Francis Murphy. New York, 1981.

Bradstreet, Anne. *The Works of Anne Bradstreet*. Edited by Jeannine Hensley. Cambridge, Mass., 1967.

Bremer, Francis J. *The Puritan Experiment*. Rev. ed. Hanover, N.H., 1995. The best single-volume introductory survey of American Puritanism.

Bunyan, John. *The Pilgrim's Progress*. New York, 1964.

Caldwell, Patricia. *The Puritan Conversion Narrative*. Cambridge, Mass., 1983. An informative study of the Puritan testimonies of faith required for church membership.

Delbanco, Andrew. *The Puritan Ordeal*. Cambridge, Mass., 1989. Insightful study of the psychology of Puritan emigration/immigration as well as other Puritan ordeals.

Edwards, Jonathan. *A Jonathan Edwards Reader*. Edited by John E. Smith, Harry S. Stout, and Kenneth P. Minkema. New Haven, Conn., 1995.

Eliot, T. S. "Burnt Norton." In *Four Quartets*. London, 1971.

Foster, Stephen. *The Long Argument*. Chapel Hill, N.C., 1991. A much-needed and informative study of American Puritanism in its British contexts.

Franklin, Benjamin. *Autobiography and Other Writings*. Edited by Ormond Seavey. Oxford and New York, 1993.

Grabo, Norman. *Edward Taylor*. Rev. ed. Boston, 1988. The best single-volume study of Taylor's life, thought, and poetry.

Gura, Philip. *A Glimpse of Sion's Glory*. Middletown, Conn., 1983. Effectively compares the millennial impulses among differing groups of American Puritans.

Kermode, Frank. *The Sense of an Ending: Studies in the Theory of Fiction*. New York, 1966. Lectures reflecting on life's beginnings and endings and their bearing on literature from Aristotle to modernism.

Knight, Janice. *Orthodoxies in Massachusetts*. Cambridge, Mass. 1995. Challenges Perry Miller's assumption that there was one dominant orthodoxy in seventeenth-century Massachusetts.

Lawrence, D. H. *Studies in Classic American Literature.* New York, 1923; rev. ed. 1981.

Martz, Lewis. *The Poetry of Meditation.* New Haven, 1962. Authoritative study of the seventeenth-century British tradition of religious poetry from which American Puritan poetry derived.

Mencken, H. L. "The Last New Englander." In *A Mencken Chrestomathy.* New York, 1949.

Mencken, H. L. "More Notes for a Work upon the Origin and Nature of Puritanism." In *The Impossible H. L. Mencken,* edited by Marion Elizabeth Rodgers. New York, 1991.

Miller, Perry. *Errand into the Wilderness.* Cambridge, Mass., 1956. Contains Miller's "From Edwards to Emerson" and "The Marrow of Puritan Divinity," the two most influential essays on American Puritanism to date. These essays are the best possible introduction to a reading of Miller's monumental multivolume study *The New England Mind.*

Morgan, Edmund S. *Visible Saints.* Ithaca, N.Y., 1963. A clear, lively study of the Puritan problem of assurance and its connection to church membership. Now challenged but not superseded.

Pettit, Norman. *The Heart Prepared.* New Haven, 1966. A study of ways by which the Puritans hoped to prepare the heart for grace despite predestination.

Poe, Edgar Allan. "The Poetic Principle." In *Great Short Works of Edgar Allan Poe,* edited by G. R. Thompson. New York, 1970.

Scheick, William J. *The Writings of Jonathan Edwards.* College Station, Tex., 1975. The most accessible single-volume introduction to the writings of Jonathan Edwards.

Shea, Daniel B. *Spiritual Autobiography in Early America.* Rev. ed. Madison, Wis., 1988. Influential study of how, in Puritan autobiographies, the remembered life is shaped to accord with spiritual needs.

Shepard, Thomas. *God's Plot: Puritan Spirituality in Thomas Shepard's Cambridge.* Edited by Michael McGiffert. Amherst, Mass., 1994. McGiffert's introductory essay is especially insightful.

Staloff, Darren. *The Making of an American Thinking Class.* Oxford and New York, 1998. Neo-Marxist study of class and power relationships among governors and ministers in seventeenth-century Massachusetts.

Stannard, David E. *The Puritan Way of Death.* Oxford and New York, 1977. Puritan attitudes and practices regarding the death of infants, children, and adults.

Stout, Harry S. *The New England Soul.* Oxford and New York, 1986. Authoritative study of American Puritan preaching and the sermon form from their origins in England to the American Revolution.

Taylor, Edward. *The Poems of Edward Taylor.* Edited by Donald E. Stanford. Chapel Hill, N.C., 1989.

Williams, William Carlos. *In The American Grain.* New York, 1925; rev. ed. 1956.

Winthrop, John. *The Journal of John Winthrop 1630–1649.* Edited by Richard S. Dunn and Laetitia Yeandle. Cambridge, Mass., 1996.

THOMAS PYNCHON

by David Ryan

Thomas Pynchon is regarded among the leading figures of postwar American literature, in particular the postmodern school, which includes writers such as William Gaddis, John Barth, Robert Coover, William Gass, and Donald Barthelme. He was born Thomas Ruggles Pynchon, in Glen Cove, New York, on 8 May 1937. His earliest published writing appeared in his high school newspaper, the Oyster Bay *Purple and Gold*, under various pen names: Boscoe Stein, Roscoe Stein, and Bosc. Pynchon graduated from high school in 1953 and attended Cornell University, majoring in engineering physics. He left school temporarily to serve a two-year tour of duty in the navy as a signal corpsman. Afterward, he returned to Cornell and changed majors, earning a B.A. in English in 1959 and working on the university literary magazine.

Two of Pynchon's short stories were published while he was studying at Cornell—"Mortality and Mercy in Vienna" (*Epoch*, 1959) and "The Small Rain" (*Cornell Writer*, 1959). He published two other stories—"Entropy" (*Kenyon Review*, 1960) and "Low-lands" (*New World Writing*, 1960)—shortly after he graduated. Pynchon's early stories, most collected in *Slow Learner* (1984), establish certain characteristic aesthetic principles he would develop in his novels.

"Entropy" is particularly instructive regarding the development of Pynchon's literary aesthetic because it is the first extended exploration of a theme that follows through much of his writing. The term *entropy* refers to a thermodynamic measure of energy available for work in a closed system or the tendency for energy in a closed system to deteriorate to an inert uniformity. This property has also been applied to communication theory: the more information is added to a system, the more the appearance of disorder tends to increase. Pynchon's novels would be driven one way or another by the concept of entropic decline or distortion. The term's metaphoric meaning and utility have evolved over the course of Pynchon's literary output, from its early use in the story "Entropy," where it provides a social and physical environment—a split view of two rooms, one filling with partygoers,

the other holding its two tenants' delicately maintained ecosystem, a "heat death" implicit in the unchanging temperature of the thermometer—to the more intimate, personal meaning Pynchon describes in *Slow Learner* in 1984: "When I think about the property nowadays, it is more and more in connection with time, that human one-way time we're all stuck with locally here, and which terminates, it is said, in death. Certain processes, not only thermodynamic ones but also those of a medical nature, can often not be reversed. Sooner or later we all find this out, from the inside" (pp. 14–15).

After graduating from Cornell, Pynchon worked as a technical writer at Boeing Aircraft in Seattle, Washington. An essay written by him on missile safety, titled "Togetherness," was published in *Aerospace Safety* in December 1960. The combination of events in Pynchon's life up to this point seems to have established the bedrock of his writing to come: from the study of engineering and physics during his early undergraduate years, to his two-year tenure in the navy and subsequent switch, back at Cornell, to a major in English; and finally his brief career at Boeing. Add to this the influence of the Beat writers of the time, such as Jack Kerouac, and one sees the origins of Pynchon's writing as remarkably autobiographical.

V.

Two previously published short stories—"Low-lands" (*Cornell Writer*, 1959) and "Under the Rose" (*The Noble Savage*, 1961)—were absorbed into Pynchon's first novel, *V.*, which was completed after he left Boeing. Published in 1963 and subsequently awarded the William Faulkner Award for the best first novel of the year, the novel's multiple antirealistic narratives, characters, settings, and formal challenges demonstrated Pynchon's ambition and range early on.

After the novel's publication, Pynchon, then twenty-six, effectively disappeared from public life. From this point forward, piecing together fragments of his biography becomes extremely difficult, beyond the facts surrounding publication of the literary work he produced. He would become notorious for his ability to keep his personal life clear of public scrutiny.

V.'s story alternates between "historical" chapters and those recounting events of one anchor year, 1956. The historical passages travel around the world in time—Mallorca, 1946; France, 1913 and 1918; Florence, 1899; South West Africa, 1922 and 1904; Malta, 1939–1943; and Valletta, 1919—the multiple stories revolving around, to greater or lesser degree, Herbert Stencil's father, and then Herbert himself, as they search for the impossibly elusive "V." of the title—a woman or a place or perhaps simply an idea.

The lives of the novel's large cast of characters are complicated by paranoia, a sometimes compelling, at other times inexplicable fear that a complex network of shadow powers larger than themselves controls the world around them. Pynchon typically sets paranoia at the level of masked identity in *V.*: governments and individuals alike are seldom what they appear to be. This provokes an often hallucinatory quality in the novel, as one character's identity and affiliations become clear only after the reader has registered a prior identity against which to compare them. Characters, like the namesake of the title *V.*, become fleshed out in relation to shifting sets of relationships between themselves and those around them.

The passages, set in 1956, take place predominantly in New York, and feature Benny Profane as he wanders, seemingly without purpose, drifting from job to job, and carouses with a crowd known collectively as The Whole Sick Crew. Profane exists in life with as little effort as possible, even as the events around him oscillate from the banal to the ridiculous: a self-described schlemiel, he appears to be as comfortable riding the subway endlessly up and down its line (yo-yoing) as he is hunting abandoned pet alligators in the New York City sewer system. His stasis in the midst of the meaningless though often turbulent surroundings is typical of his crowd, The Whole Sick Crew—as is the absurdity of his name. In *V.*, as in later novels, Pynchon intentionally reduces the plausibility of his characters as living, breathing beings, at the level of their naming: Clayton ("Blood") Chiclitz, Pig Bodine, Herbert Stencil, Roony Winsome, Fergus Mixolydian, Mafia Winsome, Yoyodyne (one of the nation's biggest defense contractors, suggesting Boeing Aircraft), among others. As if to ensure that his characters remain objects rather than believably human building blocks whose names suggest consumerism and popular culture, Pynchon moves his characters around the maze of his story, rendering them as self-consciously mechanized, animated media.

The sense of literary self-consciousness—in naming conventions, manipulation of historical references, the mixture of "high" and "low" forms of comedy, and the infusion of pop culture into the text—is a hallmark of postmodern fiction, and Pynchon is often credited as the archetype of the postmodern writer. Postmodern literature reflects the culture of its time: the barrage of information and stimuli the electronic age has embedded into daily life so that media and existence become impossible to dissociate from one another. Two police officers, appearing at one of The Whole Sick Crew's many parties in *V.*, can only impersonate the mannered acting of the police officers in the popular *Dragnet* television series of the time. A consistently antinatural setting of name and event pervades the 1956 passages, portraying postwar contemporary life—its hyperevolved structures and humanity looted by consumerism and the mass media—as having reached an absurdly accelerated distortion and lassitude, recalling Pynchon's interest in the properties of entropy.

The historical passages in *V.* are markedly different in style and tone, the story line often Byzantine in complexity, its prose liquid. The chaotic structure and setting lean toward the surreal, countering the Beat styling of the 1956 sections with the more baroque, often clownish, paranoia of Herbert Stencil, whose obsessive quest seeks meaning from the letter V.

Colonialism, fascism, genocide, and subterranean sexual exploitation (though often willing) mark the historical world in *V.*: its participants are objectified, most often literally, as targets, sexual objects, machines, corpses, or tourists.

V.'s thematic linkages subordinate the linear chronology of events as the novel's historical sections jump backward and forward in time, woven into the episodes of Profane and The Whole Sick Crew in 1956. The seeming absence of linear time forces the reader's attention on theme: love, death, paradoxical representations of humanity and mechanization as desire and apathy, "fill up the novel" until its borders can sustain no more. And so the novel ends. The questions the reader is left with deny a simple reduction. Pynchon would develop this complex, open-ended novel's form in work to come.

THE CRYING OF LOT 49

Pynchon's next novel, *The Crying of Lot 49* (1966), won the Richard and Hilda Rosenthal Foundation Award of the National Institute of Arts and Letters. The action of the novel revolves around the small epic quest of its 1960s housewife protagonist, Oedipa Maas. At the outset, Oedipa is given the task of executing the estate of the recently deceased tycoon Pierce Inverarity, a former lover. But she is distracted by an increasingly hallucinatory trail of discovery, the strands of which may or may not identify the presence of a conspiracy spanning centuries, rooted in an old and still extant private mail delivery system known as the Tristero.

Because of its shorter length and somewhat less dense, comic treatment of its subject, *The Crying of Lot 49* has been considered by many critics a kind of Pynchon in schematic. Pynchon himself, in *Slow Learner*, refers to it as a "story" rather than a novel, "in which I seem to have forgotten most of what I thought I'd learned up till then" (p. 22).

On her quest, Oedipa encounters a number of men (Metzger, Genghis Cohen, Randolph Driblette, John Nefastis, Stanley Koteks, Mike Fallopian, among others), who appear to direct her toward evidence of an underground conspiracy, apparently centered around the Tristero system. If Oedipa's clues can be trusted, there exists a complex and long-standing conflict between competing mail-delivery systems (carriers of information), originating in northern Europe during the Renaissance and continuing in some form throughout the present tense of the novel.

As Oedipa encounters the men who will lead, or mislead, her along her search for meaning, she also discovers a number of physical "clues": among them, a flawed postage stamp; an ideogram scrawled on the bathroom wall in the shape of a trumpet, or muted "post" horn, the acronym W.A.S.T.E. written beneath; and different "pure" and "corrupt" text editions of a Renaissance drama (whose Jacobean text references have certain parallels to the novel's events). The signs add up, but not to anything conclusive. The goal of this novel is not the traditional build-up and resolution of central and subordinate conflicts, so much as puzzling through a gathering web of insinuations that develop and then multiply from the chase itself: Will Oedipa uncover a secret society capable of resolving the suspicions she herself cannot shape into coherence? Or will the questions simply continue to grow and disperse into a state of maximum information around her? Will she ultimately comprehend or simply unravel, giving in to the tangled logic she is compelled to unknot from the waking nightmare of the quest's narrative?

In the end it doesn't seem to matter. Meaning, in this case, is found in its increasing self-distortion. Pynchon places more emphasis on the strands framing the search, and the pollution of evidence found in the spaces between, than on any traditional sense of outcome, leaving the reader to sort the "fast and slow molecules" of the narrative.

At one point in the novel, Oedipa's quest leads her to the scientist John Nefastis, who has created a machine that Oedipa suspects may provide insight into the growing evidence of conspiracy around her. Much critical discussion of *The Crying of Lot 49* has focused on this "Nefastis Machine" and the demon kept inside it. The science upon which it is based is related once again to entropy. Though complicated and resistant to cursory discussion, the way it integrates this novel, and Pynchon's fiction at large, warrants some explanation here.

Pynchon's source for the Nefastis Machine, and the demon inside, is James Clerk Maxwell's *Theory of Heat*, published in 1871. In it, Maxwell proposed an imaginary creature, or demon, able to sort hot (fast) molecules from cold (slow) molecules inside a box without expending energy, thereby violating the second law of thermodynamics, which states that entropy tends to increase in a closed system.

What makes this rather abstruse theory germane to a study of Pynchon's writing is simply how Oedipa's story, which begins in relatively placid middle-class comfort, fills up with bits of information (as molecules fill the Nefastis Machine). As this information continues to bombard Oedipa's, and the reader's, sensibilities, she gravitates not toward any manageable way of sorting or deriving meaning from the information, but rather toward a state of madness. At the most rudimentary level, Pynchon has wrapped his novel around metaphors of energy and its kinship with information theory.

Ultimately, even the Nefastis Machine only produces another layer of false meaning in the novel. Because the fictional inventor, John Nefastis, reveals himself as a lunatic, what Oedipa gains by the end is only her personal relation to "meaning" as she increasingly finds herself alone and closer to madness. Pynchon might imply that pursuing meaning in a fictional universe is dependent on the interpretive sensitivity of the reader; that ultimately the trip is the *event* itself, not some succinct "point" or tidy concluding statement. By the conclusion, the action of the novel proves to be circular, any traditional notion of resolution dispersed and open-ended. Indeed, the circularity of Oedipa's quest is built into the very last line of the book: "waiting for the crying of Lot 49" simply restates the title, and in a sense reestablishes a beginning rather than putting an end to the matter.

GRAVITY'S RAINBOW

Gravity's Rainbow (originally titled *Mindless Pleasures*) was published in 1973. It won the National Book Award in 1974 (shared with Isaac Bashevis Singer's *A Crown of Feathers and Other Stories*); the prize was accepted on Pynchon's behalf by the comedian "Professor" Irwin Cory. *Gravity's Rainbow* was also nominated for the Pulitzer Prize, though the nomination was later withdrawn by the Pulitzer advisory board. The controversy resulted in *no* prize for fiction given that year (1974). In 1975 Pynchon declined a William Dean Howells Medal from the American Academy of Arts and Letters.

Encyclopedic, shifting radically from the darkly comic to mythic, to simply pitch black in tone, *Gravity's Rainbow* is a staggering accomplishment of form, erudition, and historical observation. It has been compared widely and favorably with masterpieces such as Melville's *Moby-Dick*, and Joyce's *Ulysses*, and is considered one of the great American novels of the twentieth century.

Pynchon's third novel is a minefield of societal, psychological, linguistic, dialectical, and historical references set within the labyrinth of a deceptively loose matrix. There are literally hundreds of characters, and their fictional world comes perhaps as close as any novel of the twentieth century to the real-world endlessness of possibilities in story and transmutation within a grid of logically contradicting (and contrary) arguments, themes, and character representations. Though traces of linear story line prevail, many events within the novel travel laterally to one another along metaphor and lines of language: regional, popular, professional dialects; Hebrew cabalistic mysticism; esoterica; Teutonic myth; the poetry of Rainer Maria Rilke; the language of the Kazakhs; and the parlance of Soviet bureaucracy, among others. Its historical network includes that of the preliterate African Herero tribe and its clash with German colonialists (and eventual genocide in the nineteenth and twentieth centuries), rocket science (literally), Calvinism as forerunner of fascism (suggestive of controversies involving Pynchon's own American colonial antecedent, William Pynchon), Pavlov's *Lectures*, and myriad others.

Much of the novel's primary action occurs in the years 1944 and 1945, though the time frame of the overall narrative is difficult to measure because it deals not only with a tangible past—roughly nine months beginning in December 1944—but also with a protohistory,

descending into the preconscious minds of its characters. Mimicking the elasticity of time as perceived through memory, the text's seamless jumps into stream of consciousness dominate by the end of the novel.

Tyrone Slothrop is ostensibly the closest the reader gets to a hero in *Gravity's Rainbow*. He has the uncanny tendency to become sexually excited at the precise location at which German V-2 rockets will land. Because the V-2's supersonic speed allows it to hit its target before the delayed scream of its trail is heard, Slothrop's ability to "locate" ground zero in advance of the explosion becomes the subject of much interest and analysis. His form of telepathy is a negotiable source of power to various factions within a network of elite, most notably warmongering, commercial interests, a seemingly invisible *They*. This sends Slothrop further and further into the underground, shape-shifting as necessary (at one point disguised as a pig) to escape the various forces against him. As with Pynchon's prior two novels, the idea of an unattainable concept (Stencil's elusive V., Oedepa's Tristero, and here, the origins of Slothrop's erection) simultaneously stimulates the desire for illumination as well as the potential for danger if ever actually discovered.

A major thematic concern in *Gravity's Rainbow*, as in much of Pynchon's work, develops relationships between a "preterite," or underclass, and elite religious, political, or technological forces that coerce the former into subservience by means of their seemingly omnipotent, omnipresent tentacles. These elite forces (*They*) see themselves as preordained to exploit their victims (*Us*).

On a more architectonic level, this sense of polar opposites identifies one of Pynchon's techniques for generating the structure of his stories: introducing opposing (binary) concepts and then circulating various metaphors inside their center. For example, ideas generated from the concept of white versus black appear throughout *Gravity's Rainbow*: white as a race is codified in Von Trotha's Germans as they colonize the African Herero population (black), eventually committing genocide against them. White appears as death or bleaching of life, as a blinding light or obliteration (as from the detonation of the V-2, and later of the A-bomb), as Christianity, to name only a few. Black is manifested with equal weight and resistance to moral implication: as race, death, decomposition; as pre-Christian; as subterranean, organic, fecal, preconscious, and inherently spiritual. By the end of the discourse, the universe between white and black has become too complicated to reduce back to its simple originating terms. The conceptual opposition between the two poles exists only to serve a greater purpose. *Gravity's Rainbow* creates a remarkably dense structure, only to have it chipped away at by the proliferation of its interior components.

Pynchon achieves this "filling up" by a strategic arrangement of metaphor. Within the novel's many structural poles, metaphors often operate in parallel: for instance, the *advent* of Christ (and Christianity) runs as a parallel image to the *advent* of the A-bomb. Both, in some regard, might be classified within the white spectrum of the matrix. Indeed, the very organization of the novel is set, among other key elements, in relative accordance with the Christian liturgical calendar of 1944–1945. As the imminent threat of various technologies of destruction looms, holidays such as Christmas and Easter mark key events, and form a linear time line concurrent with various pagan festivals.

The resulting metaphors generated by this method bridge the vast space between the poles, showing the shades of gray that exist, for example, between white and black, while complicating the very meaning such a bridge attempts to suggest. Rarely can anything be reduced to a simple essence. White and black become, among other things, the domination of one culture over another, shown in a variety of forms ranging from a protofascist Calvinist theocracy, to German colonization and genocide, to twentieth-century Nazism, to the corporate and technological forces (Shell Oil, I. G. Farben, etc.) benefiting from the perpetuation of war. With such contexts embedded in the structure, white and black are no longer so simple or so plain.

SLOW LEARNER

Throughout the last half of the 1970s and the greater part of the 1980s, Pynchon's literary output was extremely limited. In 1984 *Slow Learner* collected most of his early shorter fiction, and includes an insightful and forthright introduction by the author. Given the relative dearth of self-commentary written by Pynchon, and considering the difficulty and diverse interpretability of his work, *Slow Learner*'s introduction is an extremely useful source. Pynchon seems particularly incisive and blunt about the supposed failings of the stories collected here.

The collection includes the published stories of the late 1950s and early 1960s, the aforementioned "The Small Rain," "Low-lands," "Under the Rose," and "Entropy," as well as "The Secret Integration," published in 1964 in *The Saturday Evening Post*.

VINELAND

In 1988 Pynchon received a MacArthur Foundation Award. At the end of 1989, sixteen years after the publication of *Gravity's Rainbow*, Pynchon's next novel, *Vineland*, was published. The primary story is set in a northern California logging town during the 1980s. Its characters—feds, hippies, and other throwbacks to the 1960s—locate the poles of Pynchon's opposing worlds, his elite and preterite classes. *Vineland*'s ultimate subject regards the dead, phosphorus still-water reflection of the hopes and fears of the 1960s. As such, most of the players in the novel emerge as anachronistic, devoured by the times, in light of the changed world and conservative atmosphere of the Reagan era.

The story starts from a conspiracy against ex-hippie Zoyd Wheeler (reminiscent of the ambitionless primary "heroes" of Pynchon's earlier fictions), whose annual play of jumping through windows for government medical benefits on the grounds of insanity has earned him the role of local eccentric. Many of Pynchon's earlier themes remain: the attainment of humanity against the inevitable odds of death and ironclad systems of control, for instance. Conspiracy again resides just out of reach of complete grasp, though its presence is felt as overarching, all encompassing. There is much to be mistrusted, and personal lives cannot escape the palpable evidence of a hierarchy of control, even if such a hierarchy cannot be seen. Plots and political factions interweave, remaining simultaneously elusive and evident in characters' lives. *Vineland* retains the shape of a quest as one of its primary drives. Leading the quest is Wheeler's daughter Prairie, who—like Stencil in *V.*, Oedipa Maas in *The Crying of Lot 49*, and nominally Slothrop in *Gravity's Rainbow*—searches for details of something both unavoidable and unattainable. In *Vineland*, Prairie's quest is for information about her estranged mother, Zoyd's ex-wife, Frenesi Gates, a sixties film student turned FBI informant. What follows, among the many narrative strands of the novel, is the history of three generations rebelling against the existing powers of their age. As such, the notion of family as a political unit emerges as integral to Pynchon's novel.

The marriage of low and high forms in past novels—idiom and slang injected in equal parts with a lyricism—exists in *Vineland*, though the novel's emphasis is American and middle-class, and its language resides generally within the slang and television nomenclature of the 1980s. An attention to the surfaces of history emerges—historical event with its context heightened or removed for the purpose of the fiction—as in prior novels, though the scope is far more contained. As much as certain operating principles of paranoia, control, and an enforced determinism prevail in *Vineland*, and as much as the novel operates as its own individual statement, perhaps what is more interesting is how it differs from Pynchon's earlier work.

Vineland's historical frame remains located predominantly in the period spanning from the 1960s to the mid-1980s, rather than reaching back hundreds of years, as had each of his prior novels. Its history does extend further than "the summer of love"—for example, in the stories of three generations of liberal activism opposing a palpably destructive right-wing political agenda—but compared to novels such as *V.* and *Gravity's Rainbow*, Pynchon's fourth novel seems uniquely current in scope.

Moreover, the influence of television and popular culture removes much of the pretense of "literary" enterprise. Where this was evident in the earlier novels—especially *The Crying of Lot 49* with its rock bands, television reruns, and pop psychology—it is predominant in *Vineland*. Focusing its scope on contemporary popular modes—cataloging brand names, television programs, "lowbrow" films and music, mocking almost anything that might appear to intrude as highbrow—what unfolds from the reading is a remarkably *American* narrative. The countercultural politics and dreams of the 1960s have metastasized into the tumors of the Reagan/Bush years. Whether Pynchon's fascination with brand names and consumerist culture is genuine, cynical, or an amalgam of both, one general impression of the novel is that it clearly emphasizes the conspiracy of commerce and how it "brands" the American consciousness with its vapidity. As such, the enthusiasm or depression of such a reading is left entirely up to the reader.

MASON & DIXON

Mason & Dixon was released in late 1997 to much anticipation. Pynchon's telling of the lives of Charles Mason (1728–1786), assistant to the Astronomer Royal, and Jeremiah Dixon (1733–1779), a Quaker surveyor, fabricates a unique *fableau* from the recorded history of the two men. As with prior novels—*Gravity's Rainbow* and *V.* in particular—Pynchon creates his own fictional universe by refracting its historical surfaces from the tangle of their actual context. In other words, even when events and minutiae match up with historically supportable "truths," their inclusion in Pynchon's narratives serves a higher purpose: fictional truth, the gathering of data with linguistic and mnemonic "triggers" to form visceral, *human* meaning. As such, *Mason & Dixon*'s encyclopedia doesn't recount history, but rather reinvents it altogether, complete with its own entries, divisions, and nomenclature.

History, like fiction, is not solely the cataloging of so-called facts into some chain-link causality. Rather, it is a "great disorderly Tangle of Lines, long and short, weak and strong, vanishing into the Mnemonick Deep, with only their Destination in common" (p. 349). Fiction gathers its power by appealing to the alchemy of a reader's experience, memory, and perception of chronology and "fact." In *Mason & Dixon*, Pynchon convincingly argues for the power of art to convey history with a greater humanity and verisimilitude than those traditionally in charge of recording it: political, industrial, and religious bureaucracies, by now a familiar *Them*.

Mason & Dixon is narrated in an unusually linear, first-person point of view by the Reverend Wicks Cherrycoke (who claims to have accompanied the famous surveyors on certain trips). Its most immediately noticeable difference from Pynchon's earlier work is in its use of a particular dialect with such singular emphasis. If past novels often draw from a number of high and low idioms (which in themselves form an encyclopedia or lexicon of references within the novel), *Mason & Dixon* is written using only one: eighteenth-century English.

The choice of this linguistic yoke for the narrative does far more than lend it a ring of authenticity. On a very immediate level, the barrier to the contemporary reader of *Mason & Dixon*'s eighteenth-century language, grammar, and jargon—the archaic, constant use of Title Case, and the strange poetry of its clause construction, for example—serves to continually draw out the difference between the narrative's *Then* and the current reader's *Now*. The language not only invokes the fictional dream of two adventurers from another time, but also reminds the reader that the period unfolding from each strange linguistic construction is impossibly anachronistic to our own present tense, language being the most immediate surface we experience in a novel, the lens we must look through to find a book's meaning.

Language emerges as a metaphor in itself, a metaphor for the past potential of America (and the world) set against its eventual failure to realize its promise. Any difficulty in reading *Mason & Dixon* effectively draws out just how much things have changed. The reader is constantly reminded that the potential which America's Old World discoverers found when they arrived has long since been lost: thwarted by slavery, civil war, overdevelopment, pollution, and the genocide of the land's native population.

Certain similarities of formal construction and theme in *Mason & Dixon* recall Pynchon's previous work. The novel uses a number of binary poles—Heavens (celestial) and Earth (terrestrial), God and Science, Old World and New World, America's North and South, Mason's melancholic nature and Dixon's sanguinity, among others—to establish the various structures through which the story circulates. Political and religious conspiracies abound, as in Mason's thwarted induction into the British Royal Society through the intrigues and opportunism of Nevil Maskelyne. A fraternity of sinister nuns and Jesuits emerges among a tapestry of odd religious and secret societies, reminding us of Pynchon's elite controlling classes. Mason and Dixon themselves evolve as subordinated by the French, English, and Dutch bureaucracies that to a great extent control the pair's destiny.

Manifest in the human need to chart the earth and skies, we discover one of *Mason & Dixon*'s central quests: the unending desire to understand cosmic design in light of our mortality on earth. Two expeditions to witness the transit of Venus, in 1761 and in 1769, frame the beginning and the end of the novel. The placement of these events reinforces the presence of incomprehensible forces controlling the heavens, while below on earth we can only watch, record, demarcate, battle, and plunder.

Pynchon again seems to suggest that humankind can only complicate, rather than satisfy, this desire to *know*. In a desire to understand cosmic and celestial phenomena—metaphors for the meaning of life itself—all one on earth can do is feebly map one's tangible, material surroundings. Meanwhile, time passes, we grow old, and eventually we die. It is this helplessness in the face of desire set against our mortality that gives the novel its emotional center and, perhaps most forcefully of any of Pynchon's previous work, communicates an emotional weight in its investigation of desire, misdirected fulfillment, loss, and decay.

SELECTED WORKS

V. (1963)
The Crying of Lot 49 (1966)
Gravity's Rainbow (1973)
Slow Learner (1984)
Vineland (1989)
Mason & Dixon (1997)

FURTHER READING

Green, Geoffrey, Donald J. Greiner, and Larry McCaffery, eds. *The* Vineland *Papers: Critical Takes on Pynchon's Novel*. Normal, Ill., 1994. Essays by various writers on *Vineland*.

Hite, Molly. *Ideas of Order in the Novels of Thomas Pynchon*. Columbus, Ohio, 1993. An excellent treatment of Pynchon's formal methods, most important, ideas of duplicity and opposition used in his first three novels.

Levine, George, and David Leverenz, eds. *Mindful Pleasures: Essays on Thomas Pynchon*. Boston, 1976. Seminal source on Pynchon's writing, up to and including *Gravity's Rainbow*.

O'Donnell, Patrick, ed. *New Essays on* The Crying of Lot 49. New York, 1991. Essays offering diverse postmodern, modern, feminist, and European interpretations on Pynchon's second "minor" novel that are applicable to much of his work before and after.

Seed, David. *The Fictional Labyrinths of Thomas Pynchon*. Iowa City, 1988. Essays on Pynchon's fiction, including his short stories, up to *Gravity's Rainbow*.

Weisenburger, Steven. *A* Gravity's Rainbow *Companion: Sources and Contexts for Pynchon's Novel*. Athens, Ga., 1988. A remarkably detailed annotated companion to Pynchon's most dense and difficult novel.

JOHN CROWE RANSOM

by Gerry Cambridge

John Crowe Ransom's life was in one sense extraordinary—though in his lifetime well known as a critic, an acute theorist on poetry, and an influential teacher under whom studied eminent twentieth-century poets including Robert Lowell, Anthony Hecht, James Wright, and Robert Penn Warren, at the center of his achievement are a few dozen poems, unique in tone, written over the space of four or five years in the early to mid-1920s. This small body of work forms the vital nucleus of everything else, in a literary sense, that he did.

EARLY LIFE

Ransom was born on 30 April 1888 at Pulaski, Tennessee. He was the son of a Methodist minister, and owing to the itinerant nature of his father's profession was largely taught within the family until the age of ten. He excelled academically, graduating from Vanderbilt University at the top of his class in 1909. Apart from three years as a Rhodes Scholar at Christ Church College, Oxford (1910–1913), from which he took a degree in classics, and two years in France (1917–1919) as an artillery officer, he spent most of his earlier life in the American South, as an academic and teacher at Vanderbilt. In 1937 he moved to Kenyon College in Ohio, at the age of forty-nine. A scrupulous and, to all accounts, most mannerly academic, he was married to Robb Reavill for over fifty years. The couple had three children and remained married until Ransom's death in 1974.

Ransom himself observed that most of his poems were about familiar and often familial situations. He complained, perhaps tongue in cheek, about what a "bourgeois" poet they had turned him into. This is true only in the most shallow sense. The best poems deal with existential fundamentals.

John Crowe Ransom.
(© Bettmann/Corbis)

He was a poet whom the muse visited only briefly: almost his entire published output of just under 160 poems was written between 1915 and 1927, that is, between the ages of twenty-eight and thirty-nine, and most of the best, during the early and mid-1920s, when the poet was in his thirties. Thereafter, he concentrated mainly on criticism, teaching, editing, and, unfortunately, rewriting some of the poems, often to their detriment.

EARLY POETRY

Ransom's poetic career started intriguingly. His first volume, *Poems about God* (1919) by "John Crowe Ransom, 1st Lieutenant," was published when he was on active duty in France. The volume's poems had been written between 1915 and 1918, and were recommended to Henry Holt and Company by Robert Frost. Though it is usually dismissed, and Ransom suppressed it, never reprinting any of its poems, the volume offers a fascinating insight into the young poet. An introduction by the author, who refers to the writer of the poems in the third person, as if to indicate how far he has developed from him, explains the volume's raison d'être: taking the term "God" as emblematic of the big experiences of life, the poet attempts to delineate as many situations as possible in which God would be invoked sincerely and unaffectedly. The poems are seldom uncomplicatedly devotional, though the method led to moments of sometimes comic bathos. In "Noon Day Grace," for instance, the narrator is a food-obsessed fundamentalist who praises God, and his mother and father in equal measure, for the Earth's abundance. Among the qualities and objects covered by his relentless eulogy is his father's ability to cure country ham, not forgetting necessary homage to the Creator, because, as he says, "God was behind it, it seems to me." It is difficult to discern how seriously Ransom meant this to be taken. The poem reads now as a lampoon of its narrator.

Many of the other poems' characters are in dispute with God. "Sunset," perhaps Ransom's only venture into free verse, and the first poem he wrote, is spoken by a man whose intended is overly enamored of God. He cannot get her to pay him the attention he feels he merits. God is the only rival he fears. Out watching a sunset with her, he waits patiently with her dog, Rover, until his beloved "And her strange eyes / come home from God." Apart from the mention of "Rover," which introduces an unsettling bathos, the poem has a genuine gravitas. Other pieces, however, break through any possible ambiguities. "Grace" is a powerful narrative poem that becomes a diatribe by the narrator against God for "His" killing of a hired field hand. The poem strikes a much less ironic attitude than that in the later poems. It has a raw energy. The impression conveyed by this initial volume is that of a strong and distinct intellect observing the world from unpredictable angles. The poems' oddness of diction and ringing metric also prefigure aspects of Ransom's mature style.

POETIC MATURITY

A number of events which may have contributed to the development of that style happened between the publication of *Poems about God* and Ransom's mature collections, *Chills and Fever* (1924) and *Grace after Meat* (published in the same year by Leonard and Virginia Woolf's Hogarth Press in London) and his final collection, barring volumes of *Selected Poems*, *Two Gentlemen in Bonds* (1927). One was that Ransom had been offered secure employment after his return from France in 1919 as a lecturer at Vanderbilt University, where he would be promoted in 1927 to professor. Another was that he had married, after a brief courtship, in December 1920, and become the father of a girl, Helen, in January 1922, and a son, Reavill, in September 1923. And the third was that in 1919 he had begun attending the unofficial group "The Fugitives," which, while originally interested in philosophical debate, was soon meeting to discuss its members' poetry. The pugnacious and widely read Allen Tate was in attendance by 1921, initially as a student, followed, in 1923, by Robert Penn Warren. Much of the poetry produced by group members was published in nineteen issues of a little magazine, *The Fugitive*, which ran from April 1922 to December 1925. Many of Ransom's major poems appeared in its pages.

THE WORK'S QUALITIES AND THEMES

Evident in all the poems is Ransom's unique voice. He is an original: the poetry is immediately identifiable as his by a line or two. Encountering a Ransom poem is as memorable as meeting an old, utterly distinctive crofter at a gathering of business executives. Technically, strange locutions, latinisms, and unusual words such as "pernoctated"—to stay up all night debating, a verb he learned as a Rhodes Scholar—are mixed with Anglo-Saxon monosyllables and an almost knockabout rhythm. Stylistically, the poems have an idiosyncrasy reminiscent of Thomas Hardy's. While quite distinct, they share something of the crusty unfoolableness of Hardy's tone. The voice in them is, generally, cool, distanced, and ironic, lit with a rhythmical energy that makes the effect, at times, one of comic vigor. Ransom often achieves this by inversions of syntax, overblown verbs, and unexpected nouns: "Strong was the heart that clanged within her bosom," he writes of the female character in "Spectral Lovers." The sentence construction is typical.

The poems' main themes are death, energies subdued by routine—very often sexual energy or love thwarted by the deadweight of respectability and social convention—and the sometimes absurd mismatchings of desire. The narrator in the poems is fully aware of what Ransom himself called "that entire vitality which Providence meant for [a man]." The poems bear witness to such primal energies as well as to their restraint. If there is no God in the world of the mature poems, and therefore neither afterlife nor possibility of spiritual "reward," or if His presence is decidedly ambiguous, this absence or ambiguity foregrounds instinctual energies and grants them a new tension and power. For example, a couple physically attracted in the sonnet "Good Ships" are, though vessels "fit for storm and sport," unable to break through social mores into that new existence. They have been "converted" into "miserly merchant hulks." Pragmatic realities of earning a living, of the world where money is essential, take precedence. Beauty here is associated with impulse acted upon, ugliness with suppression of energies. Idealism versus reality, sexual energy versus convention, are held in thrumming counterpoise in Ransom's best verse. But while reality and convention are often the victors, the reader senses that the poems' narrators are invariably on the side of the stifled impulse. The narrator of "Old Man Playing among Grandchildren," who depicts an inscrutable old man, has him dismiss with amusing peremptoriness the whole paraphernalia of conventional adult life. Exclaimed about by one of his adult offspring, he indicates to readers that he prefers the wild vivacity of his grandchildren and has now escaped to join them, dancing round a backyard fire, "having performed ignominies unreckoned," as an adult, to satisfy the exactions of the adult world.

The wild old man helps to strike a typical note in Ransom's work: it is peopled with eccentrics and outsiders—"Miriam Tazewell," "Captain Carpenter," "Robert Crocodile." The poems often mingle comedy with gravity. "Crocodile" is a wonderful cartoonish fable about the ultimate inability of the poem's central character to thwart instinct and predilection. "Old Robert Crocodile," of Florida, an unlikely cultural emissary, journeys to Europe, but finds himself gauchely uncomfortable in the cultural glories of that continent—in a series of stanzas that proceed with filmic abruptness as he visits Paris and Oxford, but longs for the bayous of home. Suddenly, unable to take any more, he flees from the genteel culturedness of society ladies writing to him on lavender paper, and returns to Florida—a wiser, if not a sadder, reptile. Such a poem draws its power from Ransom's sense of being, despite his background in classics, something of a cultural outsider in the face of European history and tradition.

Ransom is also a fine elegist, though his elegies sound no bass notes. They are threnodies in a minor key. Their lack of overstatement increases the force of such poems, which include "Bells for John Whiteside's Daughter," "Dead Boy," and "Here Lies a Lady." While the first of these has been widely discussed and elucidated, its five rhyming quatrains remain remarkably self-sufficient. The first stanza records how the little girl's attitude in death "astonishes" the observers. The middle three stanzas recount her vivacity in life. The closing stanza changes the observers' attitudes: no longer are they astonished, but "vexed" at the dead little girl, "lying so primly propped." The trim efficiency of the poem's stanzas and tone contrast ironically with the tragedy of the situation.

In "Dead Boy," in some ways a companion piece, the child's demise is "by foul subtraction"—the arithmetical term helps increase the coldness of the boy's death—and the narrator informs us at the close of the first stanza that none of the boy's family like the "transaction" between them and death; nor do "*some* of the world of outer dark," such as the poem's narrator (italics added). The saturnine note sounded by him seems to imply that, unlike others who occupy that world and presumably observe the proceedings with schadenfreude, pleasure at others' ills, the narrator does so unwillingly. Yet either his judgment, his inability to lie to himself about reality,

or some unknown quality of his temperament condemns him to that world. The obscurely unhappy note struck by this poem's narrator echoes elsewhere in Ransom's mature verse.

It has been observed that the relative treatments of the characters in these two elegies bear out the inherent sexism in Ransom's work: the little girl's death causes vexation; the little boy's, however, has dynastic consequences. Here, though, the poet surely is merely recording the sexual conservatism of the American South in the 1920s. Within limits, poets are more fairly judged on the perfection of their art than on the perfection or otherwise of their moral vision, and Ransom's poems are, usually, impeccably constructed; with some notable exceptions, it is true, nonetheless, that his poems' narrators' view of the sexes tends to the stereotypical. His *Selected Poems'* first two sections are titled, not wholly ironically, "The Innocent Doves" and "The Manliness of Men." The poems are full of timid ladies, "blue girls," a virgin called "this richest of cities" ready to be sacked by the warrior male. Female sexuality is threatening: in "Her Eyes," the narrator upbraids an unnamed woman for the beauty of her eyes. They are too beautiful to be true. The narrator can only state that she will "get some blame / On her good name." In "April Treason," the woman character is a mere cipher, simply a beautiful body "which he honored as he must."

Other poems, such as "The Equilibrists" or "Piazza Piece," set up situations of irreconcilable sexual irony. The latter is a variation on the Petrarchan sonnet, a more difficult form in English than in its rhyme-rich Italian original on account of English's paucity of rhymes. Ransom uses the conventional division of the poem's fourteen-line form into octet and sestet, eight- and six-line stanzas, to astonishing effect. An ironic rewriting of the balcony scene in Romeo and Juliet, the poem is structured as two terse dramatic monologues. In the first, an old man attempts, futilely, to make a young woman waiting for her "truelove" hear him. He occupies the first eight lines of the poem, the young woman, the sonnet's six concluding lines. The old gentleman, emblematic of death, is trapped in his desire for her, yet confident of his inevitable triumph. She hears him finally, but rebuffs him: she waits for the young men to romance her. The first and concluding lines of each stanza are identical: in the octet, they depict the old man "in a dustcoat trying," in the sestet, the young woman "in beauty waiting." While the verbs at the end of the opening line of each stanza—"trying," "waiting"—are resolved like an exhaled breath in their succeeding lines, when they recur at the end of each stanza,

455

they can't be resolved: they become intransitive. An initial possibility becomes a final futility. This is increased by the meaning of the verbs themselves. They lock the poem's two characters, forever interlinked yet separate, into their barren, perpetual present. "Piazza Piece" is a minor masterpiece of irony with a wonderful aesthetic logic.

THE OLDER MAN OF LETTERS

Ransom's poetic career, in a real sense of writing original poems, had practically finished by the late 1920s. He followed this period of his greatest work by consolidation: the theorist, essayist, and teacher took over from the poet. By 1926 the Fugitives had moved from discussions of poetry to wider themes. In *I'll Take My Stand: The South and the Agrarian Tradition* (1930), to which Ransom contributed a foreword and an essay, he argued for the value of agricultural society as a response against industrialism, though this argument contained a hint of tacit agreement with slavery, as Anthony Hecht has pointed out. (Ransom would later change his mind about the value of the Agrarian tradition.) Ransom also began to elucidate his own poetic ideals in a series of complex theoretical essays, somewhat influenced by the New Criticism of the English critic I. A. Richards, with its emphasis on the actual texts of poems at the expense of their biographical or sociological contexts.

In 1937 Ransom moved to Kenyon College, Ohio, which had offered financial benefits Vanderbilt refused to match, despite many protests by luminaries including Allen Tate: Ransom was by now a hugely respected figure. Randall Jarrell and Robert Lowell followed him from Vanderbilt to Kenyon in order to continue studying under him. There, as well as teaching, he edited the influential little magazine *The Kenyon Review* from 1939 to 1959.

THE CLOSING PHASE

Yet, finally, Ransom's entire career is built around the achievement of the poems. Numerous "Selected" volumes were published between 1945 and 1969. He received many awards in his later years, including a Bollingen Award for poetry in 1950 and a National Book Award in 1964 for his *Selected Poems* of the previous year. Unable to produce new poems, Ransom spent almost half a century rewriting some of the old ones, gathering the new versions along with their precursors in "Sixteen Poems in Eight Pairings" in his final "Selected" volume, along with commentary on his "improvements." Although he had observed in his critical writing that poetry escaped "the strictures and reductions" of logic (*Selected Poems*, p. 153), he seemed

to do his best to ignore this in these rewritings. Enlarging ambiguities in the originals are tediously clarified; the poems usually increase considerably in length; the surer poetic instinct of the younger man becomes encrusted with the overelaborations of the old scholar (Ransom was eighty by the time he finished these rewritings). Despite the poet's intentions, however, some readers have preferred the original versions, in "Tom, Tom, the Piper's Son," for example, enjoying the wonderfully ambiguous description of the character as "Privy to great dreams," which disappears entirely in the final version, or finding the stark description of the old lady on her deathbed as "a thin stalk white and blown" plainly superior to the poetically conventional "wan like a rose overblown" that replaced it in the final version of "Here Lies a Lady."

Many of his best poems, however, Ransom left largely untouched. Among others, pieces such as "Prelude to an Evening," "Dog," "Judith of Bethulia," "Philomela," "Old Mansion," "Vision by Sweetwater," and "Necrological," in addition to a number of those previously mentioned, form a small body of minor masterpieces that seem as fresh and relevant and surprising as when they were written. When Ransom died in his sleep at Gambier, Ohio, on 3 July 1974, it was as a much laureled and fêted old poet who had not been able to write a poem of significance for over forty years, an irony a character in one of his best poems may well have wryly relished.

[*See also* Fugitives, The, (and Southern Agrarianism); Tate, Allen; *and* Warren, Robert Penn.]

WORKS

Poems about God (1919)
Chills and Fever (1924)
Grace after Meat (1924)
Two Gentlemen in Bonds (1927)
God without Thunder: An Unorthodox Defense of Orthodoxy (1930)
The World's Body (1938)
The New Criticism (1941)
Poetics (1942)
A College Primer of Writing (1943)
Selected Poems (1945, 1963, 1969)
Poems & Essays (1955)
Beating the Bushes: Selected Essays, 1941–1970 (1972)
Selected Letters of John Crowe Ransom (1985)

FURTHER READING

Buffington, Robert. *The Equilibrist: A Study of John Crowe Ransom's Poems, 1916–1963*. Nashville, Tenn., 1967.

Knight, Karl F. *The Poetry of John Crowe Ransom: A Study of Diction, Metaphor and Symbol.* London, 1964.

Parsons, Thornton H. *John Crowe Ransom.* New York, 1969.

Williams, Miller. *The Poetry of John Crowe Ransom.* New Brunswick, N.J., 1972. Useful overview of the life, written by an accomplished poet, with interesting glosses on significant poems, and the evolution of "Tom, Tom, the Piper's Son" traced through its eight drafts.

Young, Thomas Daniel. *Gentleman in a Dustcoat: A Biography of John Crowe Ransom.* Baton Rouge, La., 1976. The standard biography, extremely detailed at 475 pages.

Young, Thomas Daniel, ed. *John Crowe Ransom: Critical Essays and a Bibliography.* Baton Rouge, La., 1968. Seminal essays on various aspects of Ransom, primarily as a poet but also as critic and editor, by writers including Robert Penn Warren, Delmore Schwartz, Cleanth Brooks, and Randall Jarrell.

ISHMAEL REED

by Lynn Orilla Scott

Among contemporary African-American writers, Ishmael Reed is one of the most innovative, prolific, and controversial. To date he has published nine novels, five collections of poems, four collections of essays, and four plays. He has also authored three television productions, an opera, and a "gospera." Some of his poetry has been set to music and produced on record. A sampling of his fiction, poetry, and essays has been collected in *The Reed Reader* (2000). As a teacher, a cultural activist, and especially an editor and publisher, Reed has been an advocate of multiculturalism in American literature since the early 1970s. His experimental work, which draws from myth, history, popular culture, and African-American oral culture, can be classified as "populist postmodernist." The most characteristic attribute of his work is its aggressive, provocative, and sometimes outrageous humor.

EARLY YEARS

Born on 22 February 1938 in Chattanooga, Tennessee, to Thelma V. Coleman and Henry Lenoir, Ishmael Reed moved to Buffalo, New York, in 1942 with his mother and her new husband, Bennie Stephen Reed. Reed says that he started writing in his late teens and was first influenced by Nathanael West and H. L. Mencken. He graduated from high school in 1956 and enrolled in Millard Fillmore College in Buffalo, where he wrote his first story, "Something Pure," a satire about the second coming of Christ. His English teacher was so impressed that he brought the story to the attention of other faculty, and Reed was offered a four-year scholarship to the University of Buffalo. However, Reed never received the scholarship because his stepfather, afraid of being deceived, refused to fill out forms that asked him to reveal his assets. Reed's stepfather, an assembly-line worker who had taught himself to read, knew that many blacks had had their property stolen in the South for signing documents they didn't understand. Without the scholarship, Reed had a difficult time paying for college; he also did not like conforming to other people's reading lists. After leaving college he wrote for *The Empire Star Weekly*, a militant

Ishmael Reed.
(*Margaretta K. Mitchell Photography*)

black paper founded by A. J. Smitherman, an antilynching newspaper editor who had fled Oklahoma after being indicted for inciting the 1921 Tulsa "riot." Writing about local politics, police brutality, and segregated schools, Reed and editor Joe Walker "shook up the town." In 1961 Reed first met Malcolm X, whom he interviewed for a Buffalo radio station. Conversations with Malcolm X and Reed's interest in jazz would soon take him to New York. In 1962 Reed married Priscilla Rose Thompson, and their daughter, Timothy Bret Reed, was born.

After moving to New York City, Reed started attending meetings of the Umbra Society, a group of African-American writers who became associated with the Black Aesthetic movement, including David Henderson, Calvin Hernton, Lorenzo Thomas, and Tom Dent. During the five years that Reed lived in New York, he met a number of literary celebrities and civil rights figures including

James Baldwin, Ralph Ellison, Norman Mailer, Langston Hughes, Amiri Baraka, and James Meredith. Hughes would publish an early poem of Reed's, "The Feral Pioneers," in the 1970 edition of *The Poetry of the Negro*. While living in New York, Reed helped establish the *East Village Other*, one of the first "underground" newspapers, and he served as an editor for a Newark, New Jersey, weekly. Reed also published his first novel, *The Free-Lance Pallbearers* (1967), a surrealistic work influenced by Voltaire's *Candide* that parodies Ellison's *Invisible Man* and, among other things, satirizes the complicity of the Catholic Church, some black political leaders, and the university in the Vietnam War. Shortly after the publication of *Pallbearers*, Reed moved to California and began teaching at the University of California at Berkeley. Separated from his first wife since 1963, Reed married the dancer and choreographer Carla Blank in 1970, and in 1977 his second daughter, Tennessee Reed, was born. Reed and his family have lived in Berkeley and Oakland since the late sixties. Although he was denied tenure in the English Department in 1977, he has continued to teach at Berkeley. He has also taught at the University of Washington in Seattle, at Yale, SUNY-Buffalo, Dartmouth, Columbia, Harvard, and the University of California at Santa Barbara. In 1995 he received an honorary doctorate from the State University of New York at Buffalo.

MAJOR WORKS

Reed's eclectic style is challenging for the first-time reader. His narratives incorporate parallel stories and texts and often conflate past and present. Reed draws from various forms of popular culture including music, TV, film, and painting as well as myth, history, and African-American religion. His comic language includes satire, exaggeration, parody, invective, and bawdy humor. "Gumbo is like a metaphor for my writing style," Reed told an interviewer in the early 1970s. "I think that is what I try to deal in, exquisite and delicious combinations." "Neo-hoodoo," another metaphor for his aesthetic, like gumbo, signifies Reed's indebtedness to African-American culture. Hoodoo is the African-American version of Vodoun, the Haitian religion developed from West African religious practices, and the term "gumbo," meaning a savory soup, is derived from the Bantu word *ngombo*. Both neo-hoodoo and gumbo effectively suggest Reed's opposition to a monolithic Western aesthetic and his value of the syncretic style of indigenous religious and cultural traditions. Several poems in *Conjure* (1972) are direct expressions of neo-hoodooism, especially the "Neo-HooDoo Manifesto." His two most celebrated novels, *Mumbo Jumbo* (1972) and *Flight to Canada* (1976), are brilliant realizations of his aesthetic.

Mumbo Jumbo, an elaborate pastiche that incorporates drawings, photos, quotes, and a "partial bibliography," is a double parody directed against both the derogatory Western description of black language and religion as "mumbo jumbo" and against the essentialism of the Black Aesthetic movement, which romanticized a transcendent black subject. A detective story that takes place during the Harlem Renaissance, *Mumbo Jumbo* develops a conflict between Western civilization and "Jes Grew," an "anti-plague" sweeping the country and manifesting itself in jazz music and dance. The plot revolves around Jes Grew "seeking its words. Its text. For what good is a liturgy without a text?" The central conflict is over who will get possession of Jes Grew's sacred text: the hoodoo detective, PaPa LaBas, head of the Mumbo Jumbo Kathedral, who wants to preserve the text; or the atonists represented by The Wallflower Order, who want to destroy it. Working for the Wallflower Order is Hinckle Von Vampton (a satirical allusion to the white patron and writer of the Harlem Renaissance, Carl Van Vechten), who is, in fact, hundreds of years old and a member of the medieval order of the Knights Templar. PaPa LaBas provides a "historical" exposition near the end of the novel that traces the origins of the conflict to the mythical Prince Osiris and his brother, Set, the original enemy of the spirit of Jes Grew. The text, the Book of Thoth, is a choreography of Osiris's dance movements. Those who have misread and suppressed the sacred text extend in a line from Set to Moses, to Christ, to the Apostles, to the Knights Templar, to the Wallflower Order. In addition to the race for the sacred text, one of the novel's parallel stories involves the *Mu'tafikah*, a group stealing indigenous artifacts from museums (or Art Detention Centers) and returning them to the places from which they were plundered. Although the sacred text is destroyed, unexpectedly, by a Black Muslim, the irrepressible Jes Grew survives the destruction of its text. In the *Signifying Monkey*, Henry Louis Gates has described *Mumbo Jumbo* as an "allegory of the nature of writing itself," a novel that celebrates the indeterminacy of interpretation and "addresses the play of the black literary tradition."

Flight to Canada continues Reed's playful reflections on the black literary tradition and its relationship to Western literary forms. A parody of the nineteenth-century antebellum slave narrative, *Flight to Canada* is

459

a wildly comic novel that reverses a number of the genre's formulas, in particular the association of freedom with the movement from south to north. Reed's narrator, Raven Quickskill, is an escaped slave who has returned south to tell the story of Uncle Robin, a loyal house slave.

Flight to Canada is also a commentary on the ways in which the slave's story was appropriated by whites. Early in the narrative Quickskill identifies Uncle Robin with Harriet Beecher Stowe's Uncle Tom and states his intention to reappropriate the slave's story from the white author. Determined to give Uncle Robin "the protection" that Uncle Tom didn't have, Quickskill will tell Robin's story "using a process the old curers used, [so that] to lay hands on the story would be lethal to the thief." Reed liberates the slave narrative from its didactic and melodramatic roots by overlaying the present on the past and reinventing character types. Quickskill makes his escape to Canada on a jumbo jet, the country hears the Emancipation Proclamation on the radio, and the Lincoln assassination is replayed on television. Various twentieth-century figures like Barbara Walters and Yul Brynner make appearances, as does Abraham Lincoln, who dances to "Hello Dolly" with the house slave, Mammy Barracuda. Quickskill's naive idealism is the source of much of Reed's satire. Booed on the antislavery circuit and disillusioned by the unheroic and self-serving behavior of his companions, Quickskill concludes that Canada is no different from the United States and returns south. Yet the South he returns to is very different from the one he left. Massa Swille is dead, because his sister's ghost pushed him into the fireplace in the heat of an incestuous embrace. Clever Robin manipulated Massa Swille's will, inherited the plantation, and has turned it into a home for black artists and craftsmen. Reed's romp with the slave narrative is a metaphor of the black artist's struggle to gain narrative control over his story.

CONTROVERSY AND LATER WORK

Throughout his career Reed has seen himself in combat with powerful literary interests that would circumscribe black male expression. As a result, his work has engendered considerable controversy for its satirical portrayal of black nationalism but even more for its portrayal of women and of feminism. *Reckless Eyeballing* (1986), Reed's attack on what he calls "the hypocrisies and contradictions of the feminist movement," is an outrageously funny novel about a black playwright, Ian Ball, who has been sex-listed (equivalent to the 1950s blacklists of suspected communists). As the novel opens, Ball has written a new

play, also called "Reckless Eyeballing," that he hopes will appease powerful New York white feminists and their black women supporters. The play is about exhuming the body of a lynch victim, Ham Hill (Emmett Till), so he can be prosecuted on behalf of the white woman whom he recklessly eyeballed. Although Ian Ball's play is successful (after the ending is rewritten by the leading feminist and Ham Hill is convicted), Reed's novel was not. Often viewed as an attack on Alice Walker's *The Color Purple*, *Reckless Eyeballing* alienated many readers and critics and damaged Reed's reputation. Yet the novel, which satirizes several groups and positions, is complex, involving a larger cultural critique than just antifeminism and bears more than a dismissive or cursory reading.

The 1980s began what Reed has called his "writin' is fightin'" period. After moving from the suburbs to inner-city Oakland in 1979, Reed's work became increasingly concerned with the effect of Ronald Reagan's policies on African Americans, the abandonment of the poor, and the introduction of crack cocaine into black communities, issues addressed in his play *Hubba City* and his novel *The Terrible Twos* (1982). Reed has consistently exposed the media's negative portrayals of black men, its double standard of reporting "pathologies" in the black community but not in white ethnic communities, and the double standard by which the label of misogyny is applied to white and black men by feminists. His essay "Airing Dirty Laundry" describes his media activism and takes a stand against the "unscientific blame-the-victim explanation of America's racial crisis." By the end of the 1980s Reed embarked on yet another new direction, studying Japanese and Yoruba. *Japanese by Spring* (1993), which reflects his interest in both languages, satirizes neoconservatives and the racial and gender politics in a fictional California college.

As coeditor and publisher of *Y'Bird*, *Quilt*, and of a number of anthologies including *MultiAmerica: Essays on Cultural Wars and Cultural Peace* (1997), Reed has promoted writers with divergent views, working from a variety of ethnic traditions. He has received deserved recognition for his contributions to American literature including nominations for a Pulitzer Prize and for two National Book awards in 1973, the National Institute for Arts and Letters Award for the best noncommercial novel of 1974, the Poetry in Public Places Award in 1976, and the Lewis Michaux and American Civil Liberties awards in 1978. In 1998 he received the Lila Acheson Wallace–Reader's Digest Writers' Award and the MacArthur "genius" award.

WORKS

The Free-Lance Pallbearers (1967)

Yellow Back Radio Broke-Down (1969)

Catechism of d Neoamerican Hoodoo Church (1970)

Mumbo Jumbo (1972)

Conjure (1972)

Chattanooga (1973)

The Last Days of Louisiana Red (1974)

Flight to Canada (1976)

Shrovetide in Old New Orleans (1978)

A Secretary to the Spirits (1978)

The Terrible Twos (1982)

God Made Alaska for the Indians: Selected Essays (1982)

Reckless Eyeballing (1986)

New and Collected Poems (1988)

Writin' Is Fightin': Thirty-Seven Years of Boxing on Paper (1988)

The Terrible Threes (1989)

Japanese by Spring (1993)

Airing Dirty Laundry (1993)

Hubba City, The Preacher and the Rapper, and Savage Wilds (1997) plays

Gethsemane Park (1998)

Writing Is Fighting: Forty-three Years of Boxing on Paper (1998)

C Above High C (1999)

The Reed Reader (2000)

FURTHER READING

Dick, Bruce, and Pavel Zemliansky, eds. *The Critical Response to Ishmael Reed*. Westport, Conn., 1999.

Dick, Bruce, and Amritjit Singh, eds. *Conversations with Ishmael Reed*. Jackson, Miss., 1995.

Fox, Robert Elliot. *Conscientious Sorcerers: The Black Postmodernist Fiction of Leroi Jones/Amiri Baraka, Ishmael Reed, and Samuel R. Delany*. New York, 1987.

Gates, Henry Louis. "On 'The Blackness of Blackness': Ishmael Reed and a Critique of the Sign." In *The Signifying Monkey: A Theory of African-American Literary Criticism*, pp. 217–238. New York, 1988.

McGee, Patrick. *Ishmael Reed and the Ends of Race*. New York, 1997.

Martin, Reginald. *Ishmael Reed and the New Black Aesthetic Critics*. Basingstoke, U.K., 1988.

Settle, Elizabeth A., and Thomas A. Settle, eds. *Ishmael Reed: A Primary and Secondary Bibliography*. Boston, 1982.

ADRIENNE RICH

by Claire Keyes

Adrienne Rich.
(© *Christopher Felver/Corbis*)

Adrienne Rich has earned a place in American literature as the leading feminist poet of the twentieth century. Most critics agree that she has accomplished what no woman writer has done before: to speak—in poetry—with a public voice. Although some aspects of her verse might be considered in the confessional mode, she demands that her poetry be more than a personal expression. As a result of her prose as well as her verse, she has developed a wide, international readership. A feminist trailblazer at a time when one was needed, Rich moves beyond feminism to speak her poetic truth and unabashedly allies that truth with politics. In forging her identity as poet, public intellectual, nurturer of other women, and advocate for causes, she challenges women to seek a larger, more equitable world for themselves and others.

THE YOUNG POET

Her early life, family background, and education helped shape the poet Rich was to become. She was born in Baltimore, Maryland, on 16 May 1929. Her father was a doctor; her mother was a talented pianist who gave up a potential career to devote herself to being wife and mother, home-schooling Adrienne and her younger sister for several years. Rich's father treated her as a son, expected her to achieve, and gave her access to his library. As a young girl, she was familiar with great literature, from Shakespeare and Keats to the Norwegian playwright Henrik Ibsen. Encouraged to read and write and to memorize poetry, she excelled in school and earned her bachelor's degree from Radcliffe College in 1951. It is no surprise, then, that she had the confidence in herself to enter the competition for the Yale Younger Poets Award while she was an undergraduate, and that she won

and had her first book of poems published the year she graduated—1951.

Her early poems reflect her life and yet at the same time point to her later achievement as a radical feminist poet. The poems in Rich's first book, *A Change of World* (1951), were praised by the contest judge, W. H. Auden, for their "modesty" and "respect [for] their elders." Indeed, Rich's poems use conventional forms, solid metrical patterns, and end rhyme. She imitates male poets she had studied and admired all her young life: Auden himself, William Butler Yeats, Wallace Stevens, Robert Frost, and Edwin Arlington Robinson. She resembles them in her tone, her subject matter, even her persona, taking on, in some cases, a male voice and experience. At times, however, when her subject comes closer to female experience, a strong female voice emerges that acts to subvert the conventions. The often-anthologized "Aunt Jennifer's Tigers" is a prime example of this subversion. The theme is art versus life as experienced by a married woman who practices needlework and fashions a tapestry of tigers who "prance across a screen, / bright topaz denizens of a world of green." In contrast to the dashing tigers and their lack of fear, Aunt Jennifer is portrayed as weak and nervous, her "fingers fluttering through her wool"; her hands "find even the ivory needle hard to pull." In Rich's second stanza, she suggests that the reason for Jennifer's weakness lies in "the massive weight of Uncle's wedding band." Paradoxically, this fearful, oppressed woman produces a work of art that will outlive her. Even more compelling is the sheer power contained in the tigers, the product of Jennifer's female imagination. Rich's poem, formally serene and conventional in its meters and its end rhyme, expresses a profoundly unconventional concept: the terrible sacrifice of womanly power and imagination in a traditional marriage.

EMERGING FEMINIST POET

As Rich matured as a poet, her subversion of conventionality became more overt and more exciting for her and for her readers. The decade (1951–1961) following Rich's graduation from college saw her both embracing conventional roles of wife and mother and experiencing her choices as increasingly problematic. She married Alfred H. Conrad, a divorced, Jewish graduate student, and gave birth to three sons. In this same period, she traveled to Europe, wrote many new poems, and published a second book of poetry (*The Diamond Cutters and Other Poems*, 1955). While she was being recognized and praised for work that she herself found too conventional and imitative, Rich was having increasing difficulty reconciling the role of artist with the traditional female roles.

Because Rich illuminates her writing process in essays, reviews, and nonfiction books, the reader can gain insight into the dilemmas she faced during these years by reading her essay "When We Dead Awaken: Writing as Re-Vision (1971) and *Of Woman Born: Motherhood as Experience and Institution* (1976). She describes what it feels like to be both a nurturer of children and an artist who must allow the imagination to exert its power. The artistic imagination must have free rein, she says; the artist must not be afraid to see day as night, to see that "nothing can be too sacred for the imagination to turn into its opposite." Being a mother, Rich says in "When We Dead Awaken," "requires a holding back, a putting-aside of that imaginative activity" (Gelpi and Gelpi, 1993, p. 174). Because so few women artists—be they poets or visual artists, musicians or dancers—have also been mothers, Rich's explanation of the conflicts she experiences are extremely valuable and illuminating. Marriage and motherhood put demands on women that their lovers or husbands need not necessarily confront. In her prose, Rich addresses such issues and opens up numerous other issues concerning the patriarchal structure of society. These same issues inform her poetry.

Early volumes such as *The Diamond Cutters, Snapshots of a Daughter-in-Law* (1963), *Necessities of Life* (1966), *Leaflets* (1969), and *The Will to Change* (1971) might usefully be seen as precursors to the full-blown feminism of Rich's award-winning volume, *Diving into the Wreck* (1973). When she was young, Rich's artistic consciousness was dominated by her perception that literature was written by men, with a few exceptions like Emily Dickinson, the Bronte sisters, or Virginia Woolf. This perception translated, at times, to her writing like a man. While Rich was too gifted to write truly "bad" poetry

in these early volumes, she sometimes went through contortions to bring her creativity into line with the male poets she admired. She writes, for instance, like the Irish poet William Butler Yeats, in "The Loser" (1958), to describe a situation in which her male persona expresses longing for a woman who has spurned his love and married another man. He feels "envy" for her husband, but decides merely to "turn my head and wish him well / who chafed your beauty into use." She writes Frost imitations in a rhyming dramatic monologue such as "The Perennial Answer" and succeeds in expressing a Frostian tone of bleak New England realism: "He knew I'd have the blackest word told straight," even if it were "my child that couldn't live."

Rich is honing her craft in poems like these, learning how to develop the voice of a persona and how to write a strong iambic line. In a dramatic monologue like "Antinous: the Diaries" (1959), the choice of subject matter leads her to articulate themes that she probably had not anticipated. A notoriously beautiful young man during the reign of the Roman emperor Hadrian, Antinous was admired for his beauty and treated by the emperor and others as a love object. Yet like anyone else he had an inner life of importance to him—if to no one else. He ends up committing suicide, "helpless, disgraced, alone." In writing about this historical figure, Rich is also touching upon issues that were becoming increasingly important to her and many other women: women's second-class status, the primacy of the male in a patriarchal social structure, the denial of woman's freedom to express her own self and her own needs, the "lies, secrets and silences" that being a woman—or a homosexual—entailed.

INFLUENCE OF WOMEN AUTHORS

During the 1960s and early 1970s, Rich was writing increasingly unconventional poems and the essays, lectures, reviews, and introductions that would compose her second volume of prose, *On Lies, Secrets, and Silences: Selected Prose, 1966–1978* (1979). These prose pieces are extremely helpful in understanding the tone, themes, and imagery of her poetry, and most of her critics, including myself, use the essays as a guide to understanding her poetic intent. While helpful, Rich's attempts to guide critical response should not be allowed to limit the reader's interpretation. Her essays in *On Lies* explore the novels and poetry of such writers as Charlotte Bronte and Emily Dickinson. Studying literature by women can be regarded as Rich's attempt to validate herself as a woman. Whereas her early works can be regarded as male-identified, the poetry of the 1960s and early 1970s became increasingly woman-identified. To understand how this development in Rich's psyche expresses itself poetically, the reader can turn to "I am in Danger, Sir—" (1964), Rich's poem about Emily Dickinson.

Just looking at this poem on the page, the reader can see that Rich has abandoned any sort of rigid stanza form as well as rhyme schemes. Her style is less conventional, more in the free verse mode of the second half of the twentieth century. It is not formless, however, but sharp and precise. She quotes from the letters written by Emily Dickinson and her correspondent Thomas Higginson. Dickinson sought validation from an editor she admired; Higginson was baffled by the eccentricities of the Amherst poet. There was no true meeting of minds until Dickinson gave it up and had it out at last, as Rich writes, "on her own premises." There is a wonderful play of words in the last line of the poem, where Rich is both referring to Dickinson's hermit-like retreat to her own house and also to Dickinson's courageous stand—because so isolated and unsupported—on the aesthetic principles she deemed central to her art. She would not conform to what editors expected of a "poetess" in the nineteenth century; nor would Adrienne Rich any more seek the validation of powerful male figures. By turning to a study of Dickinson and other women authors, Rich grew more firm in her own identity.

POETRY AND THE CULTURAL REVOLUTION

Rich's development as a poet coincided with that period in American history when there was a dramatic and revolutionary movement for civil rights and women's rights, and against America's involvement in the Vietnam War. Rich and her husband were politically involved. They lived and taught in New York City, where Rich worked at the City College of New York, among other places. In the swirl of cultural revolution, Rich was on the leading edge. Her poetry and prose helped to ignite the flame of consciousness-raising in many women, both in America and abroad.

Rich put herself and her poetry at the heart of a great political movement: the liberation of women. Her poem "Planetarium" (1968) helps illuminate Rich's role as she lived it. "Planetarium" celebrates the life and achievements of Caroline Herschel (1750–1848), an astronomer who discovered eight comets in her ninety-eight years of life. Few of us have heard of her. Rich has dedicated herself to uncovering the lives of women

like Herschel and celebrating them in poetry. This is her way of "re-visioning" history and women's place in it. She places Herschel and her discoveries in the context of other women's lives, specifically women accused of being witches. Like Herschel, they "rode the night sky" on their proverbial broomsticks. Rich regards the witch-burning craze of the fifteenth, sixteenth, and seventeenth centuries as an obscene misperception: "A woman in the shape of a monster / a monster in the shape of a woman"—even someone as accomplished as Caroline Herschel. Society regards any kind of female aberration as deviant and punishable—or to be ignored, like Herschel's achievements.

Placing Herschel in the context of the history of women, Rich enlarges the scope of her subject and then moves her poem back to herself as a woman and a poet. She sees herself as "an instrument in the shape / of a woman." She has been standing, she says, "in the direct path of a battery of signals"—as if she were a transformer—"trying to translate pulsations / into images." She does the poet's work not for herself alone, but "for the relief of the body / and the reconstruction of the mind." Thus Rich takes upon herself the role of poet as seer, transforming the "impulses" she gets from the universe via the language of her poetry for the purposes of the general good. This image of the poet as seer goes back at least as far as Homer. Rich assumes the poetic mantle as a woman and places it upon herself. Does she have the right to make such a statement? The poems of Rich's middle period and the great works of *Diving into the Wreck* and *The Dream of a Common Language* (1978) give us a clearer sense of her poetic power, its range, and its limitations.

RADICAL FEMINIST POET

Although her poems grew increasingly radical in the 1970s, Adrienne Rich garnered more awards and public recognition. In her personal life she experienced problems in her marriage, her husband's suicide, and her coming out as a lesbian. A woman for whom principles mean more than prizes, she accepted the National Book Award in 1974 (shared with Allen Ginsberg) for *Diving into the Wreck* along with two other nominees, Audre Lorde and Alice Walker. They received the award in the name of all women who had been silenced and lacked recognition. Rich's expansiveness is an acknowledgment that the power of her poetry comes from a groundswell of feminist energy. As a spokesperson for that energy, she both absorbs and reflects it.

Rich's title poem, "Diving into the Wreck," is perhaps her most well-known. The poem is mythic in its scope, dramatic in its rendering. Rich creates a protagonist who is capable of performing physical feats that the poet, afflicted with rheumatoid arthritis since the early 1950s, would be unable to do. The poem engages us with an adventurous speaker who prepares for, and then descends into, the ocean, to explore a wreck. The scuba diver is not identified as female or male. In fact, one of the major discoveries of the poem is that the diver could be either. "I am she: I am he . . . ," the diver says, circling the wreck. The diver is also a reader, and his or her first step in preparing for the dive is to check out "the book of myths." Rich's diver discovers that the sea is "not a question of power," but another element entirely, and that "the words [of the myths] are purposes. / The words are maps." That is, language helps the diver figure out where to go. Once there, the diver wants to study the wreck and see "what treasures prevail." The poem never reveals what the wreck stands for, teasing us with its possible significance. The ship is a man-made thing whose purpose was never fully achieved. Given Rich's interests, the wreck most likely refers to human civilization, perhaps the ideals of the Enlightenment that were supposed to lead us to greater equality, fraternity, unity. What went wrong? Is there an old ideal we can bring back to the surface? The poem concludes by suggesting we all must make the journey the diver has made—but singly. Each of us must become "the one who find our way / back to this scene."

From the psychic adventure of "Diving into the Wreck," the reader turns to "The Phenomenology of Anger" and encounters Rich as the angry, man-hating feminist—though she detests that label. Suffice it to say that even a quick reading of the multipart poem gives a thrilling (if you are a woman and taught not to express anger) embodiment in striking poetic images of pure, cleansing anger against the perverted forms of "manliness" that lead to the subjugation of woman and the rape of the earth. She imagines training "white acetylene . . . / on the true enemy," not to kill him but to "[leave] him in a new / world; a changed / man."

The angry feminist Rich can also be gentle and lyrical, as in her poem "Song," which brings us back to her own story and the tragic suicide of her husband, although he is not mentioned directly. In fact, Rich refused for a long time to treat her husband's death as a subject for poetry, her way of showing him respect. Even so, this poem provides the reader with a sense of how she handled the period following his death. "You're wondering," she writes, "if I'm lonely." The answer is yes, but not the way we might think a widow to be lonely. Rich gives us a striking image of herself as an airplane that "rides lonely and level" toward its destination. Her images of loneliness show her not forlorn, but simply someone "waking first, of breathing dawn's first cold breath." These images convey a clear sense of a new beginning and of a woman with hope.

Rich is not lonely for long—if *The Dream of a Common Language* is any indication. Included as a centerpiece in this collection are "Twenty-one Love Poems." These poems address her love for another woman. While there are romantic moments ("You kissed my hair to wake me."), and moments where the loved one is praised (in her lover's small hands, she "could trust the world"), these poems are striking for their honesty and their realism. These are mainly city poems, and Rich emphasizes the dirt and danger as well as the lover's dreams: "our animal passion rooted in the city."

The most striking poem, for me, is not the erotic "Floating Poem, Unnumbered," but one that comes at the end of the sequence and that Rich sets in a place like Stonehenge, where there is a great round of ancient monoliths arranged to capture the light at the solstice. She concludes her poem by emphasizing her choice "to be a figure in that light," in effect becoming one of the monoliths, "yet more than stone / a woman." Clearly, Rich's being is centered in her womanhood. Being a woman is the source of her strength ("more than stone") and at the core of her aesthetic sensibility. This "female core" leads to her choice of subject matter (for example, Marie Curie in her opening poem, "Power") and to her taking on the voice of Elvira Shatayev in a poem about a team of Russian women mountain climbers ("Phantasia for Elvira Shatayev"). Rich's poetry is, indubitably, the poetry of a woman: her themes, her tone, her strategies, the voices she assumes, and the aesthetic she espouses are female to the core.

"Transcendental Etude," the last poem in *The Dream of a Common Language*, makes this abundantly clear. The title might remind us of a romantic era musical composition, something, say, by Franz Liszt. While there are musical references in the poem, it is more a study (etude) that moves from the particular and local (driving on a Vermont country road, seeing a deer) to a vision which is thrilling because it signifies "a whole new poetry beginning here." That vision is the articulation of Rich's female aesthetic. She creates a scenario in which the speaker leaves a crowded room filled with argument and jargon and goes to a female space—a kitchen. On the margin, as it were, the female outsider quietly begins to assemble a "construction" out of various natural artifacts ("the shed silver whisker of a cat"). There is no vaulting ambition in her efforts, just the desire to connect her materials into a meaningful whole. She creates her composition with a feeling of "care for the many-lived, unending / forms in which she finds herself." Among these forms are a "sherd of broken glass," capable of inflicting a deep cut (like the pure acetylene torch of "Phenomenology of Anger"?); a "plentiful soft leaf," capable of soothing a "wound"; and finally "the stone foundation, rockshelf further / forming underneath everything that grows." This "rockshelf" on which the poem and the volume end recalls the twenty-first love poem in its imagery and its import. More important, Rich conveys her continuing belief in the potential for growth and change—a constant motif in her work for over fifty years.

THE MULTIFACETED MATURE POET

The decade of the 1980s was significant for Rich in many ways. She moved from New England with her partner, Michelle Cliff, to Santa Cruz, California; underwent two operations for arthritis; won numerous honors and awards, including the National Poetry Association Award for Distinguished Service to the Art of Poetry; received honorary doctorates; and was granted prestigious professorships, including professor of English at Stanford University. At the same time, she published five books, including three new collections of poetry. This is a prodigious output for any writer and a strong indicator of establishment status—but not for Rich. She has never been comfortable with any kind of establishment, particularly if it means the exclusion of others because they are too poor, the wrong color, or the wrong sex. She remained strong in her identity as a radical feminist and a lesbian, as is demonstrated in her essay "Compulsory Heterosexuality and Lesbian Existence." In her fifties, however, she was increasingly aware of aging, of the ailments that led to her two operations, and of her own roots as a Jewish woman. Whatever her status, she was cognizant of change. As a poet, she recorded that change and illuminated it.

In "Transit," from *A Wild Patience Has Taken Me This Far* (1981), Rich imagines a scenario in which she encounters another woman, a skier who might have been herself if she were physically healthy and less attuned to the workings of her own soul. The speaker feels envy when she sees "how strong [the skier's] knees carry her." At the same time, she notices "how unaware she is, how simple" it is for her to move in her body. The poem ends in a question about whether or not the two women will

"decide / to recognize" the other and perhaps opposite self. It may be quite difficult for someone strong and physically competent to recognize another side of the self that is less able. The opposite is equally true: the "crippled" self resists recognizing areas of strength and competence. As in "Transcendental Etude," Rich continues to develop her theme of a multifaceted self. In her poem "Integrity," she writes that she had "nothing but my self to go by," and then revises this perception to "nothing but my selves." Rich becomes convinced that the self is not a fixed entity, but fluid and dynamic.

Early in the 1980s, she revisited a memory from her young womanhood in a poem titled "For Ethel Rosenberg," who, as Rich's headnote tells us, was "convicted, with her husband, of 'conspiring to commit espionage' "; executed in the electric chair, 19 June 1953, at the same time Rich was getting married. Rich explores a significant woman from the past, asking questions about that woman's life and the choices she made, her strengths, her weaknesses, where her life intersects with Rich's, where it splits. One theme that emerges strongly in "For Ethel Rosenberg" is the concept of woman as monster (see "Planetarium") and Rosenberg as "that daughter of a family like so many / needing its female monster." Why was she a "monster"? Because she was a "bad daughter" and wanted "to distinguish herself"? Because she wanted "revolution"? If Rosenberg was a monster, then how many other women, including Rich, could be labeled the same? And executed? It's pretty scary.

POETRY AND POLITICS

Rich's poem "For Ethel Rosenberg" is more ruminative than lyrical, more "political" than most of us expect or even want from poetry. More and more, Rich would write this type of discursive poem with a strong political element. It has neither the drama nor the flash of "Diving into the Wreck," but "Diving into the Wreck" enabled this poem. It is part of a continuing exploration of the "wreck" and part, indeed, of the complex of ideas that Rich expands upon more fully in her selected prose of this period: *Blood, Bread, and Poetry* (1986).

Rich speaks of alienation in her title essay—of being cut off from the sources of one's strength, whether that be gender, race, history, ethnicity—and the need to overcome that alienation. In her poem "Sources," from *Your Native Land, Your Life* (1986), she explores her own roots as a Jewish woman. The poem begins with a specific place—northern New England, most likely Vermont—where she and her family had a vacation home.

466

She hasn't returned, she says, in "sixteen years." She recalls on this same trip a fox she saw, a vixen ("dead now") who represented the art of survival. She had written about this vixen before ("5:30 A.M.," 1967) and would title her 2001 volume of poetry *Fox*. The fox is Rich's "power animal." Gutsy and female, it is instinctual and protective of its offspring. This recurring image in Rich's poetry leads naturally to her question in this poem: "From where does your strength come, you Southern Jew?" And further, "With whom do you believe your lot is cast?" These two questions, she writes, are behind almost everything she has written.

"Sources," a long poem with many parts, addresses her deceased father in section VII. It is written in prose paragraphs (as is section XXII, about her husband), as if prose would be closer to the way she might actually speak to him. She used to see him as the embodiment of the "Kingdom of the Fathers" but feminist ideology made it appropriate, it seems, to dismiss him. She regrets not seeing beneath her father's "power and arrogance," what she calls "the suffering of the Jew," and "it is only now, under a powerful, womanly lens, that I can decipher your suffering and deny no part of my own." Rich softens her stance toward her father under the influence of her sense of herself as a woman. She has empathy for him and "the alien stamp [he] bore, because [he] had deliberately arranged that it should be invisible to [her]." She recognizes in him the gap between the man and the Jew, just as in her own case there was a gap between the woman and the poet, the woman and the Jew. Bringing her identity as a Jew into the construction of her many "selves," Rich is empowered to turn in this poem and speak to her husband.

Like her father, her husband cut himself off from his Jewish identity—except for the food, which Rich describes in lush detail. She speaks to him now, she says, because "no person, trying to take responsibility for her or his identity, should have to be so alone." She sees herself allied with him in a common cause: "an end to suffering," and a desire "to change the laws of history." In this emotional appeal to her husband, Rich is reconnecting to her personal past and seeing her efforts as part of a larger, historical goal.

THE AGING SURVIVOR

Rich continued to develop this emphasis on history—both personal and political—in her next volume, *Time's Power* (1989). She looks back upon her relationship with her mother in "Solfegietto," or "little study," a term used by keyboard composers. Since Rich's mother was a pianist, this is a fitting title. Unlike Rich's coming to understand her father in "Sources," "Solfeggieto" ends in questions to her mother that remain unresolved: "What did you want from me?" and "What did I want from you?" Rich is more likely in her later poems to leave such questions unanswered.

"Time's power," as the poem "Living Memory" tells us, "is the only just power" because it treats everyone equally and does not make judgments. As Rich grows older and realizes she is in "the last age of her life" ("Dreamwood," 1987), she comes to a deeper understanding of herself and her avowed intention to "change the laws of history." Her long poem "The Desert as Garden of Paradise" ruminates in its eleven sections on a typical North American environment, the desert. As a resident of California, Rich is closer to the desert than she was in the Northeast. Its reality has become a part of her lived experience, and she meditates on it. Section four speaks metaphorically about desert plants. In simple, albeit beautiful, language Rich describes plants that must live in drought conditions, but she is pointing to a human truth which she has come to acknowledge: change does happen, but incrementally. We are more likely to understand and accept this if we consider that some desert plants must "persist, not by species betrayal," but through minute changes. To survive, such plants must make "a steady bargain with the way things are"—as must most people. This is not a revolutionary stance; it lacks the passionate fire. It is a mature stance and the statement of a survivor, more realist than romantic.

CONTINUED ACCOMPLISHMENT

In the period from 1991 to 2001, Rich published four new collections of poetry and her *Collected Early Poems, 1950–1970* (1993), plus two books of prose. Age and a fragile body have not slowed her down. Her work also regularly appears in important anthologies and textbooks. Adrienne Rich is a significant literary figure, not only for her poetry but also for the prose that illuminates it. Central to her poetics is "the drive to connect, the dream of a common language." This desire on Rich's part is admirable. On the simplest level she appears to be saying that she wants to be a poet who truly communicates and who is understood by everyone. Often, however, when we read her poetry—especially the later work—we find it difficult to understand. Rich anticipates this difficulty by attaching "Notes" to her poetry volumes explaining the writers she is referring to or the particular historical event (for example, Operation Desert Storm) that informs her poems. Reading Adrienne Rich is not easy; she challenges us to know as much as she does and to love the writers she finds important, the poet Muriel Rukeyser, for instance.

Rich writes long discursive poems such as her title poem "An Atlas of the Difficult World" (1991). She ranges all over the United States and admonishes us to "Catch if you can your country's moment" (section V). She writes this poem as a citizen of a country whose purposes she can no longer fathom. She asks twice in the poem, "Where are we moored? What / are the bindings? What behooves us?" Rich in many places in this poem sounds Whitmanesque. For example, in section IV's long, loose lines she finds something "that binds / the map of this country together: the girasol /, orange gold-petalled with her black eye." She finds this flower no matter where she goes in the United States. From this plant "so generous" she starts considering "nature's waste" and then simply the waste of human lives "in this segregate republic." Many critics have noted the similarities between Rich's verse and Walt Whitman's. The chief difference, it seems to me, is Rich's lack of unbridled optimism. As in the "girasol" image, she finds something that connects us all, but then moves to a gloomy insight about lives wasted in prison or poverty. Like Walt Whitman, Rich cajoles and admonishes us from her position as a public voice.

Her poems in *Dark Fields of the Republic* (1995) are in a similar vein. She takes her title from F. Scott Fitzgerald's *The Great Gatsby*, an image suggesting the collapse of the great American Dream—or at least its corruption. "Calle Vision" (literally "vision street") takes us on a journey on the dark side of America, not the open spaces where we might find the girasol but, in section 6, to a slaughterhouse where workers on an assembly line cut up millions of chickens. Rich deals with an event she read about in the news, a fire in one of these slaughterhouses where the doors were locked from the outside and the workers were trapped: "some fleeing to the freezer / some found 'stuck in poses of escape'—." Rich imaginatively enters the experience of those workers—"how dead birds [come] at you along the line /—how you smell them in your sleep. . . . " Her approach is not detached or abstract; she inhabits the workers' lives through the power of imagination and the poetic skill of her words. While she recognizes the tragedy and cruelty of "the dark fields of the republic," she is aware of beauty and how "it will leap / from all directions." In our own history, for example, "once we were dissimilar / yet unseparate that's beauty." Rich can see both the tragedy of this country and its beautiful idealism.

In *Midnight Salvage* (1999), Rich's long title poem works toward and then away from an image in section 6 that mentions "a yard called Midnight Salvage," which is "past the curve where the old craftsman was run down." "Salvage" refers to something saved from destruction or waste and reminds me, once again, of the powerful imagery of "Diving into the Wreck," where the diver explores the wreck to see the damage, but also what "treasures" might prevail. Rich focuses on the young driver who killed the craftsman and how unfamiliar he was with the road. He did not know "that you could speed yet hold the curve / watching for those who walked there." He is not evil, simply "unpracticed" in necessary life skills. Rich's language in this poem is simple and direct. We need no footnotes to understand her.

The second stanza operates as a contrast to the first and brings in a speaker who is an autobiographical "I." She recounts the many times over the years she has driven the same road, under all sorts of conditions, yet she has "killed nobody left no trace / practiced in life as I am." Rich does not judge the young driver except to say he is "unpracticed." She is no better than he is, just "lucky" and "practiced in life." This is the poem of an older woman, no longer on the rampage against men or anyone else, but, as she says in section 7 of "Midnight Salvage," coming to grips with the "horrible patience" it takes to "wait for language for meaning for the last sign."

The poems of the 1990s see the old revolutionary accepting the fact that change takes time, comes in tiny increments, and requires the luck and the wisdom of an old hand like herself. This does not mean she is complacent. Rich in this period began a serious study of Karl Marx and his *Communist Manifesto*. As with any author she takes seriously, Marx enters her poetry. Her poem "A Long Conversation" (1997–1998) incorporates passages from the *Manifesto*. This poem is in unnumbered sections, although the pagination breaks it up into units. Rich had been taught when she was young that Marx's ideas were "evil." She decides to find out for herself. In addition to quoting Marx, she brings in others, including President Richard Nixon, who mangled the language and said, "the Arts, you know—they're Jews, they're left-wing, in other words, stay away." Rich juxtaposes prosy sections with rhyming sections, and at times it is difficult to perceive any kind of coherence or order. Is this the common language? Always the poet, she comes back to what remains valuable for her: "charred, crumpled, ever-changing human language." Rich involves us with her process of discovery, and like her we must develop a "horrible patience" simply to stay there with her: she who has come so far.

It is difficult to stay the course with Adrienne Rich in *Fox* unless you have traveled with her through many other books of poetry and prose. She expects you—as reader—to know her and her concerns. Even the experienced reader of Rich needs her "Notes" to decipher such a poem as "Twilight." How else would we know it concerns the "Old Stone House" of Brownington, Vermont, built in 1836 by an African-American architect? It also takes an experienced reader to appreciate the reappearance of the fox in Rich's title poem. Rich states boldly, "I needed the fox," describing it fully and carefully, saying she "needed recognition" from it. For Rich, the fox represents the art of survival: "the truth of briars she had to have run through," and also a kind of brute courage: "a vixen's courage in vixen terms." She pursues her image and what it signifies for her: "it means tearing and torn endless / and sudden." More strikingly, it brings forth a powerful, womanly image: "the birth-yell of the yet-to-be human child / pushed out of a female the yet-to-be woman." She needs this fox in a visceral way. What she seeks—mature and "experienced" though she may be—is a rebirth or at least a renewal of her courage to survive the trials she must face.

POET FOR ALL OR NONE

It is striking that *Fox*, a book of poems by a woman in her "last age," should contain poems that graphically address the continued quest for rebirth. For Adrienne Rich, poetry has always been a vehicle for such rebirth. The poem "For This" addresses Rich's enduring relationship with her art. This poem is more structured and lyrical than her longer, more ruminative poems. It contains four stanzas and the speaker addresses a "you" who must be poetry. The first two stanzas begin with conditional phrases: "If I've reached for your lines" and "If I've touched your finger." In both stanzas she depicts in vivid terms how essential poetry is for her survival. She frames this relationship in an image of a transfusion: "a pack of blood fresh-drawn / hanging dark red from a hook."

In the subsequent two stanzas, she configures poetry as her energy source: "A pilot light lies low / while the gas jets sleep." With her energy ignited, she knows that "language uncommon and agile as truth / melts down the most intractable silence." In other words, she still believes in the power of language—as well she must, having remained faithful to it for over fifty years. Of course, what is interesting about her statement is that she uses the

word "uncommon" to modify "language." It seems she has given up her dream of a "common language." The last stanza of the poem, however, corrects this impression. She imagines the poet's ethics as "A light keeper's ethics: / you tend for all or none." The lighthouse is a compelling image. Poetry is not for a restricted few; if it is, it is no longer poetry: "as if the lamp could be shut off at will / rescue denied for some." Erected on dangerous coasts, the lighthouse deflects mariners away from destructive rocks or ledges, helping to save lives. Poetry is also that essential and nondiscriminatory. Most of the time, Rich comes close to achieving that goal. When she gets too exotic in her references, too loosely didactic and preachy, she risks losing us. Nonetheless, she is a woman who has given her mature being to poetry. What she has found there has sustained her in a long, productive, and accomplished life. Reading Adrienne Rich can enlarge our perceptions of poetry and sustain us in the challenges we face in this twenty-first century.

[*See also* Writing as a Woman in the Twentieth Century.]

WORKS

POETRY

A Change of World (1951)
The Diamond Cutters and Other Poems (1955)
Snapshots of a Daughter-in-Law (1963)
Necessities of Life (1966)
Selected Poems (1967)
Leaflets (1969)
The Will to Change (1971)
Diving into the Wreck (1973)
Poems: Selected and New, 1950–1974 (1975)
Twenty-one Love Poems (1976)
The Dream of a Common Language (1978)
A Wild Patience Has Taken Me This Far (1981)
Sources (1983)
*The Fact of a Doorframe: Poems Selected and New,
    1950–1984* (1984)
Your Native Land, Your Life (1986)
Time's Power: Poems, 1985–1988 (1989)
An Atlas of the Difficult World: Poems, 1988–1991 (1991)
Collected Early Poems, 1950–1970 (1993)
Dark Fields of the Republic: Poems, 1991–1995 (1995)
Midnight Salvage: Poems, 1995–1998 (1999)
Fox: Poems, 1998–2000 (2001)

NONFICTION

*Of Woman Born: Motherhood as Experience and
    Institution* (1976)
*On Lies, Secrets, and Silences: Selected Prose,
    1966–1978* (1979)

Blood, Bread, and Poetry: Selected Prose, 1979–1985 (1986)
What Is Found There: Notebooks on Poetry and Politics (1993)
Arts of the Possible: Essays and Conversations (2001)

FURTHER READING

Cooper, Jane Roberta, ed. *Reading Adrienne Rich: Reviews and Re-Visions, 1951–1981*. Ann Arbor, Mich., 1984. This is an edited collection of reviews and articles on Rich, some of which cannot be found anywhere else. Cooper also includes a complete list of reviews of Rich's work from 1951 to 1981.

Diaz-Diocaretz, Myriam. *Translating Poetic Discourse: Questions on Feminist Strategies in Adrienne Rich*. Amsterdam and Philadelphia, 1985. This text deals with specific feminist issues confronted by translators of Rich's work into foreign languages, with Spanish providing the leading instance. Although it is chiefly for specialists, the author's insights into Rich's relationship with language are brilliant.

Gelpi, Barbara Charlesworth, and Albert Gelpi, eds. *Adrienne Rich's Poetry and Prose*. A Norton Critical Edition. New York, 1993. An earlier edition of this book was published in 1975. Both editions contain samples of Rich's poetry and prose and include reviews of her work and some critical essays. The newer edition attempts to stay current with Rich's prodigious output and contemporary criticism of her work. The Gelpis are Rich's long-term friends, and two of Albert Gelpi's valuable essays on her work are in the 1993 volume.

Keyes, Claire. *The Aesthetics of Power: The Poetry of Adrienne Rich*. Athens, Ga., 1986. This study covers the development of Rich's poetry up to *A Wild Patience* by pursuing the theme of power in her work. Keyes attempts to establish that Rich developed a female aesthetic. Individual chapters are devoted to each book Rich published, starting with *A Change of World*.

Templeton, Alice. *The Dream and the Dialogue: Adrienne Rich's Feminist Poetics*. Knoxville, Tenn., 1994. This book is for scholars interested in how Rich's feminism informs her poetry and vice versa. An early chapter gives an overview of Rich's debt to and departure from the romantic tradition in poetry. Later chapters provide in-depth readings of individual books of poems from *Diving into the Wreck* up to *An Atlas of the Difficult World*.

Werner, Craig Hansen. *Adrienne Rich: The Poet and Her Critics*. Chicago and London, 1988. Werner analyzes the varied responses of literary critics to Rich's work. He points out which critics have been helpful and which ones have missed the point of what Rich is doing. He clarifies her major themes with special emphasis on Rich's poetry as an evolving process. His helpful index leads readers to discussions of significant individual poems and the critical responses they have received.

EDWIN ARLINGTON ROBINSON

by Scott Donaldson

Edwin Arlington Robinson (1869–1935) was the first great modernist American poet. He grew up during a period of prettified poetry and rejected its archaisms and artificialities out of hand. For a long time, the diction of his verse was thought to be too much in the common grain, too plainspoken, to be deserving of publication alongside the work of such once-eminent practitioners as Thomas Bailey Aldrich and Richard Watson Gilder. Robinson was revolutionary too in his concentration on ordinary people as subjects for poetry. He was forced to pay for publication of his first book, *The Torrent and the Night Before* (1896). "There is very little tinkling water, and there is not a red-bellied robin in the whole collection," he wrote a friend. Instead there were incisive short glimpses, some in restrictive sonnet form, of the people he observed around him—among them the elderly clerks at a dry goods store.

Edwin Arlington Robinson.
(*Painting by Lilla Cabot Perry.*
Colby Library)

> I did not think that I should find them there
> When I came back again . . .

it began in wonderful monosyllables. He sent it off to the *New York Sun*, and it came back with a one-word rejection notice: "Unavailable." This would change.

E. A. (as he liked to be called) was born on 22 December 1869 in Head Tide, Maine, a hamlet where his canny father, Edward, kept a general store. Edward Robinson was past fifty years of age at the time. He and his wife, Mary, already had two sons—twelve-year-old Dean and four-year-old Herman—and neither particularly welcomed their third (and last) child. Baby boy Robinson was not provided with a name until, six months after he was born, his mother went on vacation to South Harpswell, where a number of ladies dropped slips of paper into a hat and the slip with "Edwin" on it was drawn. The woman who

proposed the name was a summer visitor from Arlington, Massachusetts, hence Edwin Arlington Robinson.

Later that same year the family moved to the well-situated town of Gardiner, where ice was harvested from the Kennebec river and a dozen lumber and paper mills operated on the fast-flowing Cobbossee stream. The Robinsons prospered financially, and young Win—painfully shy and unathletic—spent his childhood admiring his older brother Dean, who became a doctor, and in unequal competition with Herman, who, with his handsome outgoing ways, was very nearly his opposite. Then the family suffered a series of reverses. Dean became addicted to morphine and died young, probably by taking an overdose. Herman married Emma Shepherd, the girl both he and E. A. loved. Herman started out well in business but suffered losses in the panic of 1893 and descended into alcoholism. E. A. assumed the role of dutiful son, doing chores around the Robinson house, looking after his father during his last days and wondering what he should do with himself. He resolved early on to be a poet, even if he should starve into the bargain, and was constantly warding off the inquiries of well-meaning neighbors who thought he should forget such foolishness and get a regular job. "Dear friends," he answered them in a poem, "reproach me not for what I do,

> The shame I win for singing is all mine,
> The gold I miss for dreaming is all yours.

In 1891 E. A. undertook a two-year term as a special student at Harvard. There he made friends with a number of young men who shared or sympathized with his ambitions and was exposed to the worlds of music and theater. After returning home, Robinson tried writing short stories for a time, but poetry had him in thrall.

In 1896 the blue-backed pamphlets of his first book reached him a few days after the death of his mother from black diphtheria. Robinson remained in Gardiner only one more year before departing for New York, the "town down the river," but during that year he published *The Children of the Night*, a second book of poems, and formed an important friendship with Laura Richards, the daughter of Julia Ward Howe (who wrote "The Battle Hymn of the Republic") and herself a successful author. Recognizing Robinson's talent at once, she more or less adopted him as a supplementary member of her own patrician family and introduced him to Harvard professor John Hays Gardiner, the scion of the family that gave the town of Gardiner its name.

THE LIFE OF POETRY

Robinson has been called the nation's first professional poet—that is, the first to earn his living from poetry and not from more conventional occupations like teaching and journalism. It took him more than twenty years to reach that goal. The wonder is that he stuck to "the life of poetry," as Louis O. Coxe called it in his fine book on Robinson, through the lean years of disappointment. At the end of 1897 Robinson arrived in New York possessed by the conviction that he had been put on the earth for one thing alone—to write poetry—and confident that in due course he would find an audience. He brought with him a tiny income, and he labored at his poems in a series of boardinghouses and cheap hotel rooms. A meticulous craftsman, he was willing to invest weeks in a single sonnet. He traveled light and required only minimal funds to survive, but when his poems did not sell and the family fortune ran dry, he was forced to take on a number of jobs. Hays Gardiner wangled a post for him as a clerk in the office of Harvard president Charles Norton Eliot. Robinson liked Boston, where he befriended the composer Daniel Gregory Mason and the poet Josephine Preston Peabody, but hated the work. After six months he was through and returned to New York. He moved in with George Burnham, a lifelong friend he had met when both were special students at Harvard, subsisted on two meals a day with an apple for lunch, and reveled in his companions from the city's bohemian subculture.

The most striking of these was Alfred H. Louis, a diminutive and bearded English Jew who looked and smelled like a tramp but who spoke familiarly of Gladstone and Ruskin, the archbishop of Canterbury and the Rossettis, George Meredith and George Eliot. Despite such apparent pretensions, Louis played Chopin and recited his own verse beautifully. In the eyes of the world Louis was certainly a failure, but Robinson was fascinated by him: Weren't the failures invariably more interesting than the successful? So he undertook the long serio-comic poem about Louis that finally appeared as *Captain Craig* in 1902, following a number of rejections.

Captain Craig contained in addition to the title poem several of Robinson's best poems of short and medium length, but the critics were not impressed. They missed the humor in "Isaac and Archibald" and the poignancy of "Aunt Imogen," a portrait-in-disguise of Robinson himself as "Uncle Win" to the three nieces who had been born to Herman and Emma. Robinson insisted that he was not to be found in his poetry, but admitted to certain exceptions—among them "Aunt Imogen" and the slyly self-deprecating figure of "Miniver Cheevy":

> Miniver scorned the gold he sought,
> But sore annoyed was he without it;
> Miniver thought and thought and thought,
> And thought about it.
>
> Miniver Cheevy, born too late,
> Scratched his head and kept on thinking;
> Miniver coughed, and called it fate,
> And kept on drinking.

Robinson himself came to rely on the bottle to get him through the days of poverty and discouragement. To scratch out a meager existence, he worked as a time checker during construction of the New York subway. Ten hours a day in the fetid underground air, with the roar of the machinery torturing his ears, drove him close to madness. A friend from Harvard, William Butler, rescued him into an advertising post for a Boston department store, another position for which he was almost entirely unsuited. Then came an unexpected reprieve in the form of a letter from the White House. President Theodore Roosevelt's son Kermit was studying at Groton, where his English master, Henry (Dick) Richards, son of Laura Richards, introduced the lad to such Robinson portraits in brief—drawn, mostly, from his Gardiner origins—as the miserly "Aaron Stark," with "eyes like little dollars in the dark," and the butcher "Reuben Bright," so grief-stricken when his wife died that he "tore down the slaughter house." Kermit Roosevelt was taken by Robinson and interested his father in the little-recognized poet from Maine. T. R. characteristically decided to do something to help him. Would Robinson be interested in a consular post in Canada or Mexico? Robinson would not, but if something could be found in New York....

472

So it was that Robinson went to a desk at the U.S. Customs Office in New York more or less regularly from 1905 to 1909, when Roosevelt's term as president and the government's largesse ended. It was understood that Robinson had no real duties at the customhouse. He showed up during lunch hour, read his newspaper, and left it behind as a signal to the regular employees that he had been there. The regimen should have been conducive to the writing of poetry, but it did not work out that way. Discouraged by the failure of *Captain Craig* and his inability to sell his work to the magazines, Robinson had begun to doubt himself as a poet. For a time he tried writing plays in prose, but these were not produced. Evenings, he made the rounds of the saloons.

Robinson consumed prodigious amounts of whiskey—two and three drinks to each one drunk by his companions. His capacity seemed boundless, and he showed hardly any effects—except that gradually the alcohol liberated his silent tongue, and he could talk freely and well about any number of topics, including the writers he admired, such as Dickens, Kipling, and Hardy. A collateral benefit was that the saloons were required by law to provide some kind of food in order to secure a liquor license. Robinson maintained that he could draw a map showing the location of every free lunch counter in New York City.

In the short term, the drinking served to ward off shyness and melancholy. Over a period of time, liquor only deepened his depression. "For seven years," he told a friend late in life, "I had *ab-so-lute-ly* nothing but the bottle" (Smith, 1965, p. 33). He swore off his demon (as he called it) in 1912, not for the last time. For the remainder of his life Robinson vacillated between periods of heavy drinking and periods on the wagon.

POEMS OF HEARTACHE

In the summer of 1911, Robinson first went to the MacDowell Colony in Peterborough, New Hampshire. He was wary of the idea of an artists' colony and prepared an avenue of escape in advance: a telegram was to arrive, calling him away. When the time came, he ignored the telegram, for MacDowell turned out to be his salvation. Like the other colonists, E. A. walked to his private studio in the woods each morning (lunch arrived surreptitiously outside the door) and returned each evening to the fellowship of a shared dinner. For the rest of his life, he followed a regular migratory pattern: Boston for a month or two in the spring and fall, winters in New York, and June through September at MacDowell. Almost all of his writing was done during those summer months. Eventually, as his reputation developed, he became the colony's most distinguished resident and, despite his notorious reticence, a much-sought-after dinner companion. But he always felt that he owed the place, and the widow of the composer Edward MacDowell who ran it, a considerable debt. In "Hillcrest" (the name of Mrs. MacDowell's home on the grounds) Robinson celebrates the healing qualities of his surroundings.

> He [the creative artist] may, if he but listen well,
> Through twilight and the silence here,
> Be told what there are none may tell
> To vanity's impatient ear;
>
> And he may never dare again
> Say what awaits him, or be sure
> What sunlit labyrinth of pain
> He may not enter and endure.

By the summer of 1911 Robinson had somewhat unwillingly settled into permanent status as a bachelor. In February 1909 his disgraced brother Herman died in the public ward of Boston City Hospital. In September of that year E. A. went to Gardiner and proposed to his sister-in-law Emma. Had she accepted and Robinson become her husband and stepfather to the three nieces he adored, his career would surely have followed a different path. But Emma refused him, and that was that. The brother-wife predicament naturally found expression in his verse. As Chard Powers Smith points out in *Where the Light Falls*, many Robinson poems explore triangular love relationships.

"Eros Turannos," one of Robinson's greatest poems, addresses the situation of a woman attached to an unworthy husband. Soon after they are married, the woman recognizes her error. She chooses to suffer the consequences alone, rather than submit to the gossiping of her neighbors.

> The falling leaf inaugurates
> The reign of her confusion;
> The pounding wave reverberates
> The dirge of her illusion;
> And home, where passion lived and died,
> Becomes a place where she can hide,
> While all the town and harbor side
> Vibrate with her seclusion.

In a masterful inversion of regularly iambic meter, the accent falls hard on the first syllable of "Vi-brate." It is as if the town were ahum with rumors.

"Meanwhile we do no harm," a subsequent stanza begins, but the very baldness of the statement suggests the irony underneath. Here as elsewhere in Robinson's poetry the choral "we" includes the speaker among the Tilbury townspeople (collectively fashioned on the model of Gardiner's citizens) who persistently misunderstand the plight of their fellows. Thus the solitary Pamela, of "The Tree in Pamela's Garden," can make all Tilbury Town believe she does not care about love. And in the final lines of the much-anthologized "Richard Cory," the envy-driven ignorance of the townspeople prevents them from recognizing the distress of the rich man among them.

> So on we worked, and waited for the light,
> And went without the meat, and cursed the bread;
> And Richard Cory, one calm summer night,
> Went home and put a bullet through his head.

Many remember the final two lines for their shock value. Not enough recall the two that precede them, where the chorus's incapacity for sympathy for someone of a different social stratum is aligned with the sacrilege of cursing the bread.

Robinson is often at his best in his portraits of the bereft and sometimes suicidal. He wrote, as Robert Frost said, about griefs and not about grievances. These poems can be exquisitely painful, for they are about real people and what really happened to them. Old people, some of them, like "The Poor Relation" languishing alone above the rumbling of the city, or poor Eben Flood, with no one but himself to take a drink with on the journey to his upland hermitage.

> There was not much that was ahead of him,
> And there was nothing in the town below—
> Where strangers would have shut the many doors
> That many friends had opened long ago.

Robinson teeters on the brink of sentimentality but avoids the plunge by the simplicity of the diction and by the humor that pervades the rest of "Mr. Flood's Party." As the poet himself repeatedly commented, no one who missed his humor—and his irony—could properly value what he wrote.

An implicit question underlying many of these poems of heartache is Why? Robinson's "secret," as James Dickey phrased it, "is that there *is* no secret, no answer. One cannot, finally, judge; one can only present." In his lifetime Robinson came to be regarded as something of a sage, but he disavowed the role. If he was wise, it was in realizing what he could not know and in repudiating the easy solutions offered by church and state. In "The Man against the Sky" (1916), he tried—and failed—to come

to a religious accommodation with twentieth-century materialism. He repudiated the Eighteenth Amendment, which attempted to legislate alcohol out of existence, by promptly falling off the wagon. Robinson did not consider himself a philosopher, yet in his own way adopted the pragmatic position that dominated the climate of opinion of his time. Like the pragmatists, he repudiated abstractions. Beliefs changed, and beliefs held too strongly could lead to violent suppression of contrary views.

THE QUESTION OF SUCCESS

Most of Robinson's most lasting poems were written by 1921. These are works of short to medium length concentrated closely on a single human being or on a small group of people. Invariably they suggest far more than they say. In their extraordinary condensation some of them read like entire novels drastically cut, and the better for it. Robinson resisted being called a psychologist or philosopher, but he plumbed the depths of his characters nonetheless. A few of them are presented through dramatic monologues that reach into the past, for example, "Ben Jonson Entertains a Man from Stratford" and "Rembrandt to Rembrandt."

His continuing production earned Robinson enough critical recognition so that in 1921 Macmillan brought out his *Collected Poems*, he won his first Pulitzer, and Yale gave him the first of his honorary degrees. But these honors did not secure him a living. Until well past the age of fifty he was dependent on the support of well-wishers. A principal benefactor was Lewis Isaacs, a New York lawyer and composer E. A. met at the MacDowell Colony. In 1916 Isaacs assembled a consortium of Robinson's friends to contribute to his support, and a dozen of them gave $100 each annually. The $1,200 enabled Robinson to get along reasonably well and occasionally to buy a ticket to listen to Wagner or to Gilbert and Sullivan, two of his eclectic musical favorites.

During the decade from 1917 to 1927 Robinson wrote three long narrative poems based on the Arthurian legend: *Merlin* (1917), *Lancelot* (1920), and *Tristram* (1927). The first two are regarded as superior to the third. The third made his fortune. The newly founded Literary Guild took *Tristram*, enlisted Mark Van Doren to write a laudatory introduction, and gave the 4,400-line blank-verse poem a theatrical sendoff by having a famous actress read passages at New York's Little Theatre. Robinson, who would not make public appearances promoting his work, did not attend the reading but turned up afterward to accept congratulations. He was alarmed to hear that the Guild had ordered 12,000 copies from Macmillan; ordinarily, his books sold only a thousand or two. But the well-advertised *Tristram*, which had a love story to tell, appealed to a much wider audience than his previous work. Sales ran to nearly 60,000 copies in the first year. The royalties amounted to $14,535, "which," he remarked to Isaacs, "isn't so bad for blank verse."

Success did not change his migratory habits or his work routine. From 1929 to 1935 he turned out long narrative poems at the rate of one a year. The short poems had stopped coming, and the longer ones did not reach their standard. He had often been accused of obscurity, but where Robinson's work up to 1921 is concerned, the fault usually lay in the inability of his readers to detect irony. In the case of the long poems, the charge of obscurity has more merit. Robinson's sense that there were no final answers led him into convoluted passages of qualification that resemble the late novels of Henry James. In addition, the plot lines of the final seven books, from *Cavender's House* (1929) to *King Jasper* (1935), often delve into criminal behavior. In some of them, as in some of the detective stories he was reading, Robinson was guilty of withholding essential information for unconscionable stretches of time.

Early in January 1935 doctors detected the well-advanced cancer that would take Robinson's life. Many friends came to see him during the hospitalization that followed. Making light of his illness, E. A. seemed more concerned with the plight of others. The window of his room at New York Hospital offered a fine view of the East River, the poet Ridgely Torrence commented. He hated to look out, E. A. replied, for he could catch a glimpse of Welfare Island and couldn't help thinking of the old men down there, their crowded dingy quarters, their loneliness. "I mustn't tire you," the poet Winfield Townley Scott said at the end of his visit. "It's not so much a matter of your tiring me as it is of my tiring you," Robinson said. The consummate professional to the end, he finished reading proofs for *King Jasper* days before his death on 5 April 1935.

At the time Edwin Arlington Robinson was generally regarded as the greatest American poet, and he maintained a prominent position in the canon of American literature into the latter decades of the century. Then his reputation waned, only to begin an upward climb in the 1990s, when three editions of his selected poems were published and a number of practicing poets called for a restoration. Among the most eloquent was Donald Hall in *The Essential Robinson*. "We must restore Robinson to the American

pantheon," he wrote. "The generation of great poets, after the magnificent solitaries Dickinson and Whitman, begins with Robinson and Frost before it moves to Pound, Stevens, Moore, and Eliot." Robinson was masterful, Hall pointed out, in his handling "of verse and poetry, of metric and diction, syntax and tone, rhyme and understanding, ethics, metaphor, and the exposure of greed." He was better in his early work than in his later work, but this is true of almost all the major American writers of the twentieth century. What matters is that he looked around him and gave us wonderfully moving pictures of what he saw.

WORKS

The Torrent and the Night Before (1896)
The Children of the Night (1897)
Captain Craig (1902)
The Town Down the River (1910)
Van Zorn (1914)
Captain Craig (rev. ed.) (1915)
The Porcupine (1915)
The Man against the Sky (1916)
Merlin (1917)
The Three Taverns (1920)
Lancelot (1920)
Avon's Harvest (1921)
Collected Poems (1921)
Roman Bartholow (1923)
The Man Who Died Twice (1924)
Dionysius in Doubt (1925)
Tristram (1927)
Sonnets 1889–1927 (1928)
Cavender's House (1929)
Collected Poems (1929)
The Glory of the Nightingales (1930)
Matthias at the Door (1931)
Nicodemus (1932)
Talifer (1933)
Amaranth (1934)
King Jasper (1935)
Collected Poems (1936)

FURTHER READING

Anderson, Wallace L. *Edwin Arlington Robinson: A Critical Introduction*. Boston, 1967. Offers a fine introduction to Robinson and his work, with close analysis of some twenty poems.

Barnard, Ellsworth. *Edwin Arlington Robinson: A Critical Study*. New York, 1952. Pioneering critical volume that emphasizes the early work.

Cary, Richard, ed. *Edwin Arlington Robinson's Letters to Edith Brower*. Cambridge, Mass., 1968.

Coxe, Louis O. *Edwin Arlington Robinson: The Life of Poetry*. New York, 1969. Extremely well-written and interesting study, with a splendid concluding chapter on "The Poet as Modernist."

Dickey, James. "The Poet of Secret Lives and Misspent Opportunities." *New York Times Book Review* (18 May 1969): 1, 10. Review of Coxe's study.

Faggen, Robert, ed. *Selected Poems*. (By E. A. Robinson.) New York, 1997.

Hagedorn, Hermann. *Edwin Arlington Robinson: A Biography*. New York, 1938. The first biography, published three years after Robinson's death: often lively but handicapped by lack of access to sources.

Hall, Donald. *The Essential Robinson*. Hopewell, N.J., 1994.

Joyner, Nancy Clark. *Edwin Arlington Robinson: A Reference Guide*. Boston, 1978. Invaluable reference work, with brief comments on all the available Robinson scholarship through 1976.

Neff, Emery. *Edwin Arlington Robinson*. New York, 1948. This critical biography in the American Men of Letters series places primary emphasis on the work rather than the life.

The Poetry of E. A. Robinson. Edited and introduced by Robert Mezey. New York, 1999.

Richards, Laura E. *E. A. R.* Cambridge, Mass., 1936. A reminiscence of Robinson in the environment of his hometown.

Scott, Winfield Townley. *Exiles and Fabrications*. Garden City, N.Y., 1961. "To See Robinson" (pp. 154–169) provides an excellent word portrait of Robinson in his later years.

Smith, Chard Powers. *Where the Light Falls: A Portrait of Edwin Arlington Robinson*. New York, 1965. Smith's biography establishes the triangular love relationship in Robinson's life and finds it reflected in many poems.

Sutcliffe, Denham. *Untriangulated Stars: Letters of Edwin Arlington Robinson to Harry de Forest Smith, 1890–1905*. Cambridge, Mass., 1947.

Selected Letters of Edwin Arlington Robinson. Edited and introduced by Ridgely Torrence. New York, 1940.

Winters, Yvor. *Edwin Arlington Robinson*. New York, 1947. The idiosyncratic and boldly authoritative Winters evaluates Robinson's accomplishment by close attention to a number of poems.

Zabel, Morton Dauwen. *Selected Poems of Edwin Arlington Robinson*. Introduction by James Dickey. New York, 1965.

THEODORE ROETHKE

by Gerry Cambridge

Not long before his premature death in 1963 at the age of fifty-five, Theodore Roethke (pronounced "Rett-key") gave a reading in Seattle, which was reported in the local press anonymously under the title "Voice of Balder Through Mouth of Groucho." It described the overweight poet "straining out of his tux like a precocious panda," and compared him to a juggler: the poet as a sort of vaudeville act who, at intervals, smuggled in readings from his greatest poems.

Theodore Roethke was—at least on the surface—a paradox: a bulky six-foot-two, fleshy, ungainly in size twelve feet (he was often compared to a bear)

Theodore Roethke. (*Courtesy of the New York Public Library*)

who wrote delicately of the natural world and the journeys of the soul; an obsessive and grimly competitive tennis player who even coached the sport yet who wrote poems in praise of meditation; the roaring bard who in his more manic moments claimed to have been close friends with gangsters, yet was easily disturbed by the sight of blood. (Once, having accidentally killed a mouse that had given him a fright, he went to his wife and burst into tears.) Roethke himself was aware of his paradoxes. Being interviewed for a job at Bennington College, in 1943, he introduced himself by announcing, "I may look like a beer salesman, but I'm a poet."

OVERVIEW OF THE POETRY

Sometimes it seemed as if he were two poets—writing, at least technically, two different types of poems. Even a glance through his *Collected Poems* (1966) shows that, among the often genteel vases of the rhymed and metered lyrics, which at times bore a heavy influence of the Irish poet W. B. Yeats, the tendril of the more expansive pieces in free verse—long-lined, more casual, and more energetic—seem to show the real Roethke, despite a manner that he learned from admired poets such as Gerard

Manley Hopkins, Walt Whitman, and D. H. Lawrence. Yet throughout his work, irrespective of influence, the reader hears Roethke's distinctive note, a note at once questing and vulnerable: "Have I come to always? Not yet." If Robert Lowell, considered one of Roethke's most eminent contemporaries, said of himself that he wanted his work to be "heartbreaking," Roethke at least aspires to optimism, despite the darkness present in parts of his output. The poems are at times lit with an achieved gaiety, reverence for the small, and a humane empathy that, at times, veers close to sentimentality. His writing has some of the irrepressible life energy of that nature which serves it as backdrop and, sometimes, main subject. He is the great poet of the psychic quest; of nature emblematic of the psyche, in which natural growth mirrors spiritual development. Roethke's is a creaturely and flowery kingdom, one in which at its best, as a late villanelle notes, "the right thing happens to the happy man," in which happiness seems to denote a trust in the rightness of the universe, almost beyond self-interest. Although his writing could have all the duality of his personality, down to the beery exuberance of "Gob Music" (a late song-poem left out of his last book as inappropriate, in which "the slop pail is the place to think" of the dangers of heavy drinking), it is in the poems of inner life, rooted in his own childhood, that much of the essential Roethke is found.

EARLY LIFE

Theodore Huebner Roethke—usually known as "Ted"—was born on 25 May 1908 on Gratiot Avenue in Saginaw, Michigan, the eldest child of a Prussian father and a German mother. It was a childhood and adolescence dominated by two things: his father's greenhouse business, which was shared with a brother, Charles, and which had been inherited from their own father, Wilhelm; and the death of Otto, Roethke's father, when the boy was fifteen. Both had a profound effect on the developing poet. Roethke Greenhouses took up some twenty-five acres or, as Roethke later estimated, a quarter of a million feet under glass. The business specialized in roses and orchids, but with carnations and other flowers too. In a letter to the critic Kenneth Burke in 1949, the poet described its atmosphere as "feudal"; it often kept people employed for sentimental reasons; its bookkeeping was, Roethke wrote, "chaotic." Nevertheless, one visitor from Holland, a bulb specialist, pronounced it "the finest greenhouse in America." Often, as a concession to creativity, its flowers were planted in complementary color schemes. It was a massed botanical world that would later provide a major source of inspiration for the maturing poet.

At age fourteen, in 1922, Roethke saw the greenhouses sold following a dispute between his father and his uncle Charles, who owned 54 percent. In January 1923, his uncle committed suicide; three months later, Otto Roethke, the poet's powerful, patriarchal father, died a slow and painful death of bowel cancer. Roethke took his place at the head of the family. He seemed to adapt well enough to his father's death at the time, but the shadow the event left occurs frequently in the poetry he wrote later.

Without friends with whom to discuss his interests, Roethke was the first member of his family to attend college. In the fall of 1925 he entered the University of Michigan at Ann Arbor, focusing on language and literature. When he graduated in 1929, familial pressure coerced him into entering law school, again at Michigan. He lasted only a short time, withdrew in February 1930, and entered the graduate school, in the fall of that year going on to Harvard Graduate School—mainly, as he wrote in a letter, to work under the English literary critic I. A. Richards, whose practice of close reading texts would lead to the so-called "New Criticism."

Meanwhile, Roethke had begun writing seriously, aiming for publication. (Not that this was new to him: as a freshman, his speech written for the junior branch of the Red Cross was translated into twenty-six languages, a greater coverage than he would ever achieve as a poet.) He published three modest little poems in the *Harp*, a tiny magazine, for May–June 1930. The poems were strictly conventional, metered, and rhymed. "Sweep up the broken dreams of youth!" the twenty-two-year-old exhorted in one epigram. What one had to use to do so was, apparently, the broom of "utter truth." Roethke was, not surprisingly, ambitious to do better. One night at Harvard, when he bumped into the poet Robert Hillyer, he spontaneously asked him to read some of his work.

Hillyer agreed to do so the following day, and reputedly burst out at the time, "Any editor who wouldn't buy these is a fool!"—considerable encouragement to the youth from unliterary Saginaw.

EARLY TEACHING CAREER

Roethke was on his way, not just as a poet, but also as a teacher, though he did not realize it. The Depression forced him to withdraw from Harvard and look for a job. Fortunately, he was taken on at Lafayette College, teaching English, in the fall of 1931, on a salary of $1,200 a year—a comfortable amount in the depressed economic climate. He proved to be an inspiring teacher, some of whose students clearly remembered him thirty years later. His popularity was understandable: he was, after all, only twenty-three, and socialized—basically, drank—with his students. His teaching, too, was passionately engaged and unusual. On one occasion in his teaching career he instructed his students to describe his actions—and climbed out of a classroom window, navigated around the entire classroom on the outside ledge, making faces every now and then through the windows at the class, before climbing back in on the opposite side of the building. He remained at Lafayette until 1935, employed twice as long as the customary two-year term because of his exceptional teaching abilities. While there, he not only published early poems—thirteen in 1934 alone—but fell in love with Mary Kunkel, an aspiring artist (they got as far as contemplating marriage) and met poets including Stanley Kunitz and Louise Bogan. Roethke's relationship with Kunkel helped bolster his ego against the invariable setbacks of any writing life; Bogan's and Kunitz's friendship and advice helped consolidate his growing sense of himself as a poet.

It was at Michigan State College (now University) in the fall of 1935 that Roethke had his first breakdown, which set a pattern of future episodes—manic activity, followed by hospitalization. Many observers, including Roethke's biographer, Allan Seager, believe he brought these on deliberately, to "improve" his poetry. Roethke was highly ambitious—as late as 25 September 1961, in a letter to the English man of letters Stephen Spender, he was writing: "I can write rings around some of those punks on [Eliot's] list." (The "list" was Faber and Faber's, Britain's foremost poetry publisher, then edited by T. S. Eliot.) Roethke was also an exploratory poet of inner vision. Being able to accomplish this appears to have involved episodes of psychological rebirth occasioned by his breakdowns.

The first lasted from November 1935 to mid-January 1936. He lost his job at Michigan State, and that spring spent several dreary months at the family home in Saginaw—a regular retreat during his recuperations, especially in the early days. By the fall of 1936 he had again begun teaching, to his considerable relief—he had feared his hospitalization might make him unemployable—at Pennsylvania State University. There, as everywhere else, he established a reputation as a gifted and idiosyncratic teacher, indulged by the college principal because "he stirred the place up." It was here that he had his second serious relationship, with Kitty Stokes, a college librarian who typed out many of the poems that appeared in his first book. *Open House*—its title something of a misnomer—was published in 1941. Its contents had been arranged by Stanley Kunitz. Roethke was launched.

OPEN HOUSE

First books by poets are usually one of two kinds. Sometimes they include some of the best work the poet will ever produce. More often, they have all the imperfections of immaturity, of false starts, and of influences not quite worked through. They are works of promise, not achievement. *Open House*'s five sections and forty-seven poems were well received by critics as eminent and scrupulous as W. H. Auden, Louise Bogan, and Yvor Winters, and reviewed in leading periodicals such as the *Atlantic Monthly*, *The New Republic*, and *The New Yorker*. Over sixty years later, the book seems a rather mannered performance. All its poems were quite strictly metered and rhymed, and sometimes windily abstract in tone. They deal at times in the manner of Allen Tate, in portentous statement such as "The winds of hatred blow," or in earnest concern—"Corruption reaps the young"—and their generalizations are presented in lines of often metronomic regularity. The verse has a plodding seriousness that at least seemed genuine but, often, has a voice borrowed from other poets: "No Bird" and "Death Piece" are reminiscent in tone and form of Emily Dickinson and her hymn measures; "The Signals" reads like a close imitation of Robert Frost's "A Passing Glimpse." When the poet is able, however, to get down off his plinth and keep the verse rooted in particulars as in "Mid Country Blow" or "On the Road to Woodlawn," one hears the true Roethkean note, soon to be used to wonderful effect: "I remember the crossing-tender's geranium border / that blossomed in soot," as his poem "The Reminder," seemingly a memory of his father, begins. Unimpressive in itself, this opening line-and-a-half is remarkable for several reasons: the energy of its

rhythm points forward to much of the later Roethke; there is the reference to "blossoming," quickly undercut by "soot"; and lastly, the poet is looking back, announced in that ungainsayable "I remember. . . ."

When he focused on the particulars of his own experience it granted the writing an incontrovertible authority that the windy rhetoric lacked elsewhere. Interestingly, the other poem that pointed ahead—by being retrospective—also used "I remember" in its opening line. "The Premonition," refers to the boy's memory of seeing his father's face, reflected, being "lost in a maze of water," when he stood up, as presaging his early death. Yet its subject matter is also premonitory of the poet's second and perhaps most famous book, *The Lost Son and Other Poems* (1948). For Roethke, as for William Wordsworth, going forward as an artist would mean a return to origins.

THE BREAKTHROUGH

A poet's artistic advances are often mysterious. We know that as early as 1942, Roethke had written "The Minimal," which would appear in his second book; it is a brief free-verse paean of kinship with the smaller creatures of the earth, "cleaning and caressing, / creeping and healing." (He had sent it to Stanley Kunitz, who had responded affirmingly: "You're a great fellow with bugs and bogs.") In 1943, Roethke moved to teach at Bennington College in Vermont, and the change may have stimulated his childhood memories. A further factor may have been Roethke's hospitalization for another manic phase in late 1945.

When *The Lost Son and Other Poems* appeared in 1948, from its vigorous first line—"Sticks in a drowse droop over sugary loam"—readers of Roethke's first book found themselves in a radically different imaginative world. The second volume's four sections opened with a group of fourteen pieces, the so-called "Greenhouse Poems": memories of Roethke's childhood. The poems are lush, fecund, full of tendrils and blossoms, roots and mildew, with steam and greenhouse warmth expressed in a springy free verse a world away from the somewhat marmoreal tone of much of *Open House*. Roethke called the world of the greenhouse his "symbol for the whole of life, a womb, a heaven-on-earth." It can also be seen as a symbol of his own work: the cultivated environment under glass representing his control over his material, and the floral growth and steamy blossomings the world of the unconscious that provides the vigor of genuine art. The poems are vignettes of the child's memories of flower dumps, weirdly sprouting cellars, "perverse life"; of a world where the very soil itself is "breathing a small breath." Anyone who has ever been astonished at the bizarre sprouting of potatoes left in a dark cupboard will recognize Roethke's remembered universe.

The poems represent one of the most approachable parts of his oeuvre: they are vivid in their particulars, sharply descriptive, tautly made, and operate on at least two levels. When the English poet Philip Larkin, reviewing the *Collected Poems* of Sylvia Plath (who was influenced by Roethke in her early work) referred to Roethke's air of "something nasty in the greenhouse," he was doubtless responding to the creepy unkillable urge toward life manifested in Roethke's vegetable kingdom. It is a world without grief or sorrow in which the highest moral value—if morality can be said to exist at all—is survival, as in "Flower Dump," in which a surviving tulip sways triumphantly "Over the dying, the newly dead." Vegetable growth becomes a symbol for psychic growth, yet the sequence also captures all the vigor of Roethke's boyhood experience: in one poem a greenhouse full of roses in a gale is a ship, sailing "until the calm morning"; it survives unscathed. Thirteen lines of this thirty-three-line poem begin with an active verb, among them "Flinging," "Flailing," "Creaking," and "Cracking," which reinforce the poem's sense of action—a device the poet uses throughout the sequence. The poems have a winning clarity, which perhaps reaches its peak in "Child on Top of a Greenhouse," a seven-line vignette and memory by the poet that is as vivid as a photograph, though, again, the active verbs—"billowing," "flashing," "crackling," "tossing"—give it a pleasing vivacity. Lacking a main verb to resolve it, the poem is curiously suspended in time.

The sequence closes with the famous "Frau Bauman, Frau Schmidt and Frau Schwartz," the poet's recollection of three old greenhouse ladies, "nurses of nobody else" except, the poem's syntax suggests, the greenhouse flowers; interestingly, the latter seem personified by the poet as personalities. The three accompany the adult poet in memory like a trio of ambiguous fairy godmothers. They "plotted for more than themselves," he tells us, and the verb is used in both strategic and horticultural senses. "They trellised the sun" he puns again, referring to himself, the lost son of the book's title: within the compassed and yet universal world of the greenhouse, where vegetal and psychic growth correspond, the implication is that they are also custodians of the poet's psychic development. Rather eerily, they still bend over him as he drifts to sleep.

Memorable pieces from the brief middle sections of the book included "My Papa's Waltz" (an uneasy reminiscence of being swung as a child by his drunken father), "The Minimal," and "Night Crow," but it was the book's closing section that contained the title sequence and instituted a style and voice that would be uniquely Roethke's. The poems take the form of an interior monologue, at times bizarre, and full of gnomic statements and rhetorical questions; they are a sort of psychic shorthand, like nothing else in literature. (Roethke himself said that his influences were the Bible, Mother Goose, and the seventeenth-century British poet and mystic Thomas Traherne.) While some critics have attempted to annotate and explicate them, they remain relatively resistant to convincing detailed analysis, although Roethke, in a letter to the critic Babette Deutsch on 22 January 1948, indicated that the five-part narrative structure of "The Lost Son" made it perhaps the easiest of these poems to follow. The sequence charts a psychic rebirth, beginning with the death of the poet's father, passing through a submergence into the subhuman world, despair, the obsessiveness of mania, and reemergence through a childhood memory of Otto Roethke in the greenhouse. It culminates in section five, "It was beginning winter," with the frail promise of a "lively understandable spirit," and instructs the poem's narrator simply to "wait."

While convincing critical exegesis of the poems following is almost impossible, that is not the point: one might as well ask what a stone means, or a river's sound. These poems present their peculiar otherworld in an entirely distinctive language, a queer literary infant talk; they float in and out of comprehensibility. What they mean is, largely, what they say, and that is not paraphrasable. The poems should be read aloud. They are finally small hymns to spiritual renewal, invocations to spiritual growth, and affirmations of the poet's connection to, and kinship with, the small creeping and blossoming things of the earth.

Praise to the End!—the title taken from Wordsworth's *Prelude*, that poem full of childhood memories—appeared in 1951, and continued this new style. There are distinct flashes of autobiography, with sad and wistful references to the poet's dead father and uncle, and memorable invocations to the vegetable kingdom for reassurance: the poet asks a begonia to whisper to him that "There's no alas / Where I live." He seeks confirmation that, even if not for him, a world without "alas" exists.

The Lost Son volume and *Praise to the End!*—in particular the former—established Roethke as a poet to reckon with. *The Lost Son* earned rave reviews by figures like Louise Bogan, Babette Deutsch, and Robert Fitzgerald. The poems gave contemporary criticism plenty to explicate; read today, they retain some of their power, though *Praise to the End!* can be wearing to read in bulk. Its air of inspired child talk eventually seems repetitive, and one longs for the clearer harsher note of Roethke's more lucid writing.

MID-CAREER

That more lucid writing was to be largely on display in the three volumes Roethke had yet to publish, beginning with *The Waking*, a selection of poems that added several new pieces and appeared on 8 September 1953. In the interim, several significant life changes had taken place for Roethke. In 1947, he was appointed to the University of Washington at Seattle (where he remained as a teacher to the end of his life). In 1950, he had another bout of illness. These usually meant not just unpaid absence from his teaching duties, but substantial medical bills. Luckily, from June 1952 to September 1953 a Ford Foundation grant let the poet concentrate on his own work. The most significant event, however, was that he got married. He was forty-four, and had reencountered, by accident in New York, a former student from Bennington, Beatrice O'Connell. Although she was seventeen years his junior, and beautiful, like many another of his students she had had a crush on him at Bennington. They were married just a month after meeting again. W. H. Auden was Roethke's best man at the wedding, on 3 January 1953. Louise Bogan was the maid of honor. Not surprisingly, his marriage seems to have prompted Roethke's development as a love poet in his later books.

The poems added to *The Waking* seemed to show that Roethke had largely moved beyond the style that had made his reputation. His poem "Elegy for Jane," ostensibly about one of his students, Jane Bannick, who died after being thrown by a horse, has something of the lucidity of the Greenhouse Poems, while being unconnected to Roethke's childhood. (Roethke usually seems an especially self-concerned poet.) Written in a lucid free verse, by the poet "neither father nor lover," it compares the dead girl to "a wren," "a sparrow," and a "skittery pigeon," affectionate comparisons in his natural lexicon. Death becomes "this sleep" in Roethke's holistic universe: though the girl is dead it is implied that what makes up her body shall have other lives. The poem marked a style he would revisit in significant later poems—free-verse vignettes of people, such as "Elegy," for an indomitable

aunt of the poet's, or of animals, such as "Slug," which honor the external world. The book also included the Yeatsian sequence "Four for Sir John Davies," and the title villanelle, remarkable in that Roethke was able to retain something of his own tone in what can be a tedious repetitive form.

The Waking was awarded the Pulitzer Prize for poetry in 1954. It marked the beginning of the close of his career, in a shower of awards and prizes. When *Words for the Wind*, a collection of poems adding forty-three new poems in five different sections, followed in the fall of 1958, it won six awards; Richard Eberhart praised it in *The New York Times* as "a major achievement in the Romantic tradition of American Poetry." It would be the last volume of poetry Roethke would publish in his lifetime. Such praise for Roethke's achievement to that date was understandable. In his second and third books, Roethke had spoken in a voice unmistakably his own. The new poems added to *Words for the Wind* included the collection's title poem, the theme of which is the completion of the self through love of another, as well as classics such as "I Knew a Woman." Though a commentator such as the English critic Ian Hamilton has called its sentiments "cloying"—"I swear she cast a shadow white as stone," its narrator proclaims in the final stanza—for others this overdone sentiment may be part of its charm. Hyperbolic in tone, and at times bawdy, punning, and romantic, it is an unabashed love poem, and love is, by definition, an unhinged experience. But it was the volume's five "Meditations of an Old Woman," collected at the end of the volume, that seemed the real breakthrough. The woman character bears comparison to the speaker in the Irish Gaelic poem "The Old Woman of Beare," because Roethke was always deeply interested in Irish literature. However, while the Old Woman of Beare, at the end of a rich life, laments her lost loves and the ugliness of age, the old lady in the "Meditations" recounts her spiritual autobiography. These "meditations" are written in a fast-moving free verse using Roethke's characteristic technique of rhetorical questions and epigrammatic answers; they are full of closely observed details and concrete particulars. Near death, she recounts the sensual awakening of her adolescence, and equates the soul's journey to physical travel. She has become peculiar, she confides, "whiskery / With a cheek soft as a hound's ear." She needs "an old crone's knowing." It is noticeable, however, that she does not speak in a voice radically different from Roethke's own; the most frequent pronoun is "I." On the edge of life one might expect her to regret, to reminisce, and to recount details and memories of others, but not so. She is an extraordinarily self-concerned speaker, obsessed by her soul's condition, trapped in the self. Nonetheless, the situation posited by the poem—an old lady, musing on life—provides a solid background to the sequence's content, which helps ground her spiritual preoccupations.

EARLY DEATH AND *THE FAR FIELD*

It was a style that Roethke would continue, ostensibly autobiographically, in his last book. Although *The Far Field* was only published in 1964, the year after Roethke's death, it has the air of a "last poems" and was largely completed in manuscript by the time he died. Fittingly, it gathers together some of the finest poems he ever wrote. In it is found Roethke the spiritual voyager, in the "North American Sequence"; Roethke the elegist, writing of his father in the poem "Otto"; and Roethke the observer of and empathizer with the small in nature in "The Lizard," "The Meadow Mouse," and "The Geranium."

The volume opened with the magnificent five-part "North American Sequence"—long rangy pieces in Whitmanesque free verse. They are poems full of desire for transformation, to be out of the human, to be a part of instinctive nature; finally, they are freighted with desire for death. Where Roethke's return to fundamentals in his Greenhouse Poems was a desire for spiritual development, these are largely poems of stasis. The narrator is locked in his personality and invokes—through vivid descriptions of seacoast, water, and coastal creatures—a transformation; a place where, as he writes at the close of the second poem in the sequence, "Meditation at Oyster River," in the early moonlight "All's a scattering, / A shining." The book's title poem, "The Far Field"—referring to a field at the back of the greenhouse in Roethke's childhood—is full of presentiment of death. It begins, "I dream of journeys repeatedly," imagining the narrator as a driver stalling in a snowdrift until the car's headlights are extinguished. The poet skillfully mixes tones to make the more elevated phrases convincing: in section two, five lines of concrete description of the field's end lead him to the observation that there "One learned of the eternal"; in section four, "All finite things reveal infinitude," is demonstrated by five lines of vivid visual description. The poems of a man preparing for death, the sequence—insofar as it is one, for it hardly develops—finishes with "The Rose": both a wild rose in a sea-wind on the coast, and the roses of memory and the child's father. "What need for heaven, then, / With that man and those roses?" he writes, touchingly. The whole sequence has an elegiac tone, a sense of the

significance of the temporal; it strikes a plangent note not present in Roethke's earlier work.

The volume's love poems, sometimes spoken in the voice of a woman, are less successful. Sometimes, as in "Her Reticence," they are embarrassingly Yeatsian, but substandard Yeats; Roethke's "Wish for a Young Wife," undoubtedly addressed to his own wife, Beatrice, is touching but somewhat mawkish. He calls her "my lizard"—considerable praise in a Roethke poem, and concludes with a wish for her continued happiness after his death. It is a sentimentality also present in "The Meadow Mouse," which, despite that, is one of the three most striking of the volume's "nature" poems. Roethke's baby mouse found in a meadow is straight out of Walt Disney. The sentimentality almost, but not quite, sinks the poem, which compares at its closure the escaped rodent to "All things innocent, hapless, forsaken." "The Lizard," however, the volume's neighboring poem, set in Italy, has a dry-eyed accuracy and clarity of description that skirts the possibility of sentimentality; it acknowledges the lizard's position, along with the cockroach, as a more senior citizen of the planet than the human observer. "The Geranium" comically depicts a beery, womanizing, cigar-smoking narrator's neglectful "relationship" with a potted geranium. The poem revisits, in part, the strange world of the greenhouse. The flower becomes a personality, unsettling the narrator. When the "snuffling cretin of a maid" throws it out, he says nothing, but fires her the following week. The poem wittily portrays the almost erotic intimacy between flower and narrator, though the maid is badly treated: plainly, in this narrator's plant-centered universe, a geranium is valued over the dignity of a servant.

Roethke's formal verse often foundered in its abstractions and narcotic Yeatsian rhythms. His last volume closed with "Once More, The Round," a rather orotund hymn of kinship with all things. It is a world away from the difficult and troubled affirmations of the "North American Sequence," giving a somewhat programmatic air to the end of Roethke's poetic quest; perhaps more genuinely, his poem "Otto," a memory of his father, showed what the poet could achieve in formal stanzas when he had a real subject to work with. The poem is a touching, unsentimental recollection of his Prussian father "who learned early to be rude / To fools and frauds." More touching still is Roethke's heartfelt invocation at the poem's close: "O world so far away! O my lost world!" The line could function as his epigraph.

Theodore Roethke died suddenly and relatively young at the age of fifty-five. On 1 August 1963, at the home of friends on Bainbridge Island, Washington, he mixed some juleps, put them in the refrigerator, and in the afternoon heat at 5 o'clock went swimming in their pool. He was found floating face down having suffered a coronary occlusion. He was a poet of the spirit, always seemingly uncomfortable in the large body he had occupied, who made of his discomfort, and a life plagued by psychological problems doubtless exacerbated by the artistic ambition common in numerous American poets of the 1950s, an art unique in the country's literature. He would never "cadenza again of flowers," as an elegy by John Berryman shortly after his untimely death put it. "The Garden Master," as Berryman christened him, had finally been translated into nature—an action that the later poems invoked and seemed to desire.

WORKS

Open House (1941)
The Lost Son and Other Poems (1948)
Praise to the End! (1951)
The Waking: Poems, 1933–1953 (1953)
Words for the Wind (1958)
I Am! Says the Lamb (1961)
Party at the Zoo (1963)
The Far Field (1964)
On the Poet and His Craft: Selected Prose (1965)
Collected Poems (1966)
Selected Letters (1968)
Selected Poems (1969)
Straw for the Fire: From the Notebooks of Theodore Roethke, 1943–1963 (1972)
Dirty Dinky and Other Creatures: Poems for Children (1973)

FURTHER READING

Blessing, Richard Allen. *Theodore Roethke's Dynamic Vision*. Bloomington, Ind., 1974. A useful close reading of the poems.

Bogen, Don. *Theodore Roethke and the Writing Process*. Athens, Ohio, 1991. A study that makes extensive use of unpublished papers in the Roethke Collection at the Suzallo Library of the University of Washington to trace the evolution of significant Roethke poems.

Bowers, Neal. *Theodore Roethke: The Journey from I to Otherwise*. Columbia, Mo., 1982. A study that interprets Roethke's oeuvre in the light of mysticism.

Malkoff, Karl. *Theodore Roethke: An Introduction to the Poetry*. New York, 1966. Valuable close readings of Roethke poems, including "I Knew a Woman," and "The Flight."

Parini, Jay. *Theodore Roethke: An American Romantic*. Amherst, Mass., 1979. A study of the whole career in the context of Emersonian romanticism, with a good deal of new material drawn from Roethke's unpublished notebooks.

Seager, Allan. *The Glass House: The Life of Theodore Roethke*. Ann Arbor, Mich., 1991. The standard biography, detailed and affectionate, written by a close friend and long time associate of the poet.

Stein, Arnold, ed. *Theodore Roethke: Essays on the Poetry*. Seattle, 1965. Nine disparate essays by poets and critics including W. D. Snodgrass, Stephen Spender, and William Meredith. Useful as an overview.

Sullivan, Rosemary. *Theodore Roethke: The Garden Master*. Seattle, 1975. A look at Roethke's vision of nature.

ROMANTICISM IN AMERICA: THE EMERSONIAN TRADITION

by Donald Pease

Literary historians have divided American romanticism into historical periods that are distinguished by the different revolutionary events out of which each was organized. The historical relationship between the phases of American romanticism can be formulated in terms of contraries. Romanticism emerged in the United States during the revolutionary era, when writers and painters invented a tradition that endowed the American Revolution with a history. Writers in the second generation of American romanticism attempted to meet the challenge Ralph Waldo Emerson posed in the 1836 essay *Nature,* when he asked, "Why should not we have a poetry and philosophy of insight and not of tradition, and a religion of revelation to us and not the history of theirs?" The first generation of American romantics wanted to displace revolutionary violence with the Enlightenment ideals they shared with European romanticism. Emerson then transformed the American revolution into an event that took place within the individual's consciousness. The first generation generated a dynamic interaction between European models and the American artists who desired a comparable culture; after Emerson, American romantics aspired to be liberated from every form of institutional determination.

Although literary historians have characteristically divided American romantic literature into works that came before and those that came after Emerson, his writing in fact sits uneasily within the genre of romantic discourse. Although literary historians have described discourse of American romanticism as the source of the conceptual framework that explained, qualified, refined, and specified what Emerson meant to say, Emerson did not align his project with any preexisting literary movement or political institution, and he refused to conform to any principle of association other than the singularity of the private individual. Emerson's way of thinking differed from romanticism in that it was not governed by the rule of progress, and insofar as it replaced the romantics' need to transform the social order with trust in the limitless creative potential of the solitary individual.

When Emerson asked "Why cannot we also enjoy an original relation to the universe? Why should not we have a poetry and philosophy of insight and not of tradition, and a religion of revelation to us and not the history of theirs?" he did not represent literary originality as a new state of literary affairs. The interrogatives in which the opening paragraph of *Nature* is organized are not propositions. In posing these questions, Emerson did not presume the success of his generation's responses. Indeed, the paragraph presupposes a discord between the questions Emerson has addressed to them and any answers the second generation of American romantics might supply. The sole common denominator of these questions is that the answers to them cannot be made to conform to any existing structure of belief.

Although Emerson's essays disrupted the discourse of American romanticism within which they often have been placed, American romanticism owed its present standing as a period concept to Emerson's placement within it. But the Emerson who legitimated the historical standing of American romanticism was the Emerson whose work twentieth-century literary historians described as the fulfillment of the Enlightenment dream of the liberation of humankind from its subjection to historical necessity. In the wake of this description, Emerson no longer simply designated the transition from an earlier to a later phase of American romanticism. His work was instead interpreted as gratifying the historian's desire that temporality should make sense and that American literary history should be significant.

Emerson wrote neither novels nor histories, and little poetry. His writings nevertheless created the taste by which American romanticism was valued. His work became the romantic epitome, embracing all its individual cases, as well as the exemplar of the originality American romantics pursued. The self-reflexivity and the dense linguistic structure of Emerson's essays were interpreted by modern literary critics as signs of romantic literature's autonomy as an independent domain with laws and obligations belonging to it alone. But while an example is usually said to elucidate a general trend, Emerson is impossible to fit within either the first or the second generation of American romantics. In "Self-Reliance," he proposed that his relation to historical events be interpreted after the example of his essays, which did not culminate in imaginative syntheses but characteristically turned on moments in which their governing conceptual themes foundered upon the discovery of new anomalies.

Perhaps it was their aversion to the discontinuity effected by Emerson's essays that led literary historians to represent them as part of an American romantic tradition. In assessing the difficulties Emerson poses to this categorization, Harold Bloom describes him as a standard of uniqueness that other romantics unsuccessfully aspired to attain. Bloom's magisterial *The Anxiety of Influence* considers the anxious response of Emerson's literary descendants to Emerson's originality within a theory of literary history, wherein the absence of any standardized line through which his project could be continued, became the medium through which the Emersonian tradition was interpreted and transmitted.

When Norman Foerster's 1929 volume *The Reinterpretation of American Literature* enshrined American literature as an academic discipline, Emerson and American romanticism supplied the organizing schema reflected in its institutionalization. American romanticism—along with Puritanism, the Frontier, realism, and modernism—took up its historical position as one of the core period concepts that were thought to represent particular stages in the development of the "American Mind." Subsequently, literary anthologists have consecrated Emerson as the founder of a national literary heritage that extended back to Jonathan Edwards of the Puritan period and projected forward to include the literary modernist Wallace Stevens. Emerson's literary predecessors were interpreted as prefigurations, and his descendants as involved in a relation of anxious dependency on this central figure. To be seen as integral, American literature required this heuristic epitomizing.

The tradition of American romantic literature into which Foerster, Bloom, and subsequent literary historians assimilated Emerson's prose was crucial to the emergence of a public culture and the bourgeois class, both of which were foundational to the modern nation-state. After they were augmented with the doctrine of manifest destiny and the belief in American uniqueness, Emerson and American romanticism shaped the contours of American history and endowed it with a narrative in which the liberal individual became the hero of a quest romance set against the backdrop of a modern Eden.

Despite the growing body of commentary dedicated to the historic role Emerson played in the articulation of its tradition, however, he holds a highly contradictory relation with the period concept of American romanticism. According to modern literary historians, "Emerson" is the name of an author whose work is included within the historical period in which American romanticism predominated, but "Emerson" also names a literary project that is not altogether reducible to this period. As the representative of the consolidated value of the discourse of American romanticism, Emerson stood in the whole tradition of which he was a part. After his elevation as the standard against which other American romantics were evaluated, he also constituted an exception to the discourse he regulated. Emerson at once represented what other American romantics lacked and what completed them.

Over the past century, scholars of American literature have vacillated in their representation of Emerson's relationship to the romantic tradition. Whereas Foerster characterized Emerson as a literary model for his descendants and a regulatory ideal for the tradition, Bloom described Emerson's achievement as an obstacle to the American romantics who labored in his wake. As a consequence of these contradictory placements, "Emerson" remains the name of a literary project for which literary historians continue to seek adequate descriptions.

Not all representations of Emerson's relationship to American romanticism are reducible to either Foerster's description or Bloom's. Americanist scholars have more recently described Emerson and romanticism as engaged in a defensive reaction against the unfinished work of the American Revolution—the social emancipation of blacks, the political enfranchisement of women, and the extension of social justice to the working poor—with which romanticism is historically linked. A new generation of American scholars has raised fresh questions that are concerned less with discerning the relationship between Emerson and American romanticism than with examining the deleterious effect of the categorization on American culture. In addition to accounts of American romanticism before and after Emerson, this article briefly considers Emerson's paradoxical relationship with that period, as well as recent critiques of the genre.

AMERICAN ROMANTICISM
BEFORE EMERSON

The first generation of American romanticism included the poets William Cullen Bryant and Edgar Allan Poe, the novelist James Fenimore Cooper, the folklorist Washington Irving, the historian George Bancroft, and the Hudson River painters Thomas Cole and Asher Durand. Literary historians have assumed that the writers and artists who composed this generation were the target of the critique with which Emerson began his 1836 manifesto *Nature*:

> Our age is retrospective. It builds the sepulchres of the fathers. It writes biographies, histories and criticism. The foregoing generations beheld God and nature face to face; we through their eyes. Why cannot we also enjoy an original relation to the universe? Why should not we have a poetry and philosophy of insight and not of tradition, and a religion of revelation to us and not the history of theirs? Enbosomed for a season in nature, whose floods of life stream around and through us, and invite us by the powers they supply, to action proportioned to nature, why should we grope among the dead bones of the past and put the living generation into masquerade out of its faded wardrobe? The sun shines today also. There is more wool and flax in the fields. There are new lands, new men, new thoughts. Let us demand our own works and laws and worship.

Before Emerson's complaint that this generation of American writers was insufficiently nationalist in orientation, there existed no shared criteria under which to organize their disparate cultural achievements. After Emerson's negative evaluation of their work as subservient to European models, however, the members of this otherwise unrelated group of writers and painters were subsequently brought into coherence as the exponents of the first phase of American romanticism. Individually and as group, they valued the tradition that Emerson criticized. Rather than engendering stylistic innovations or exporting revolutionary ideals, they willingly took up apprenticeship to their European masters.

Bryant's *Thanatopsis and Other Poems* and Poe's 1831 edition of *Poems* presented American themes within an idiom forged by William Wordsworth, Percy Bysshe Shelley, and the English Lakes School of poetry. Irving's "Rip Van Winkle" and "The Legend of Sleepy Hollow" adapted German fairy tales to legends transmitted orally in the Dutch sections of New York state. In *The Leatherstocking Tales*, the novelist James Fenimore Cooper accommodated the themes and techniques of Sir Walter Scott's historical romances to frontier culture. Thomas Cole and Asher Durand considered their landscape projects as part of a transatlantic exchange of symbolic geographies through which they gave expression to their solidarity with a shared Enlightenment project. The recognition of their work in European capitals was understood to confer on these artists, and by extension on the American national culture, the prestige required for recognition of America's place among older nations.

Whereas Emerson declared America's cultural independence from preexisting models, these artists fashioned a national tradition out of European examples. The romantics, establishing a kind of secular scripture, endowed the nation's foundational political compacts, the Declaration of Independence and the Constitution, with what Eric Hobsbawm has called "an invented historical tradition." Hobsbawm has observed of such romantic inventions that a national tradition refers to a set of practices that are normally governed by overtly or tacitly accepted rules, and that are of a ritual or symbolic nature. Through the invention of a national tradition for the rights and liberties promoted in the nation's foundational texts, the first wave of American romantics sought retroactively to characterize them as values and norms of behavior comparable with the nationalist movements then emerging across Europe.

The historical discontinuity generated by the American Revolution stimulated the artists' efforts to render its values part of Euro-American history and tradition. Bryant and the so-called Fireside School of American poetry reconceptualized the revolution as a mythological representation that regulated the understanding of past actions and the hope for future ones. In explaining the significance of this myth, Longfellow's *The Song of Hiawatha* and Whittier's "Snowbound" assimilated themes associated with the European Enlightenment to indigenous materials. Washington Irving's tales related the grand events of the American Revolution to the local needs of the Dutch settlers of New York state so that these Dutch-Americans could discover in his tales an imaginative sense in which they too belonged to the new nation. James Fenimore Cooper's *The Last of the Mohicans* described the disappearance of the last survivors of a noble tribe in a sublime historical romance designed to arouse noble romantic sentiments. The historians Francis Parkman and George Bancroft in their romantic historiographies constructed exemplars of the revolutionary virtues of patriotism and love of liberty; their historical tableaux rivaled Cooper's in their subordination of historical facts to the themes of manifest destiny and American Indian savagery. Their mastery of the techniques of historical romance and romantic history discloses the profound allegiance of these disparate artists to the common task of inventing America.

In purging the inhabitants of the new nation of their attachments to the Old World, these American romantics also inscribed the American landscape with images and figures of speech drawn from the Bible. They cast the prototypical American hero as an Adamic figure chosen by divine providence for a mission in the American wilderness, and they represented the United States as a redeemer nation with the manifest destiny to propagate the principles and the ideals of democratic culture. Individually and as a group, these writers ratified the belief that United States was propagating an empire of liberty after the European model.

EMERSON'S PLACE

The early romantics who solicited comparison with the work of European romantics were motivated by the desire to overcome the traumatic discontinuity generated by the American Revolution. But after Emerson endowed American romanticism with the quality of national uniqueness, he disrupted that continuum. Before the publication of *Nature*, American romanticism lacked criteria by which to differentiate Euro-American and American romanticism. The stirring questions in the essay's opening paragraph have provided subsequent generations of literary historians with criteria—originality of viewpoint, singularity of style, and uniqueness of execution—to distinguish the earlier and later phases of American romanticism. Each of these literary values—originality, uniqueness, insight—was thereafter employed to account for the Americanness of Emerson's romanticism.

Although *American* romanticism cannot be understood to have existed without Emerson, Emerson would not have positioned himself within the tradition, nor would he have recognized his project within this interpretive framework. The categorization of his work as an example of American romanticism betrayed Emerson's grounding conviction in his writing's singularity. At the same time that Emerson's essays were construed as the inspiring foundation of an authentically American romanticism, they also constituted glaring exceptions to the assumptions of the genre upon which understanding them paradoxically still depends. When he struggled to liberate it from every preexisting historical context, Emerson set his literary project in opposition to the notion of continuity that makes literary history possible. By institutionalizing Emerson's essays as the origin of a new phase of American romanticism, American literary historians removed Emerson from the position of the unmediated referent of the "we" in the question "Why cannot we also enjoy an original relation to the universe?" and reinstalled him as the founder of the school of American romanticism founded on the desire to be original.

But after American romanticism authorized itself through twentieth-century interpreters of the romantic tradition who retroactively designated Emerson as its founding figure, it also institutionalized the figure who defied inclusion within this category. The fact that Emerson could not be unambiguously included within the discourse that originated with his intervention did not impede this historical project but facilitated its accomplishment. Emerson established the relation of internal exclusion as foundational to his work when he transmuted the drama surrounding his resignation from his post as minister into the scene within which he composed his essays, addresses, and poetry.

When Emerson resigned from the Second Church of Boston on 9 September 1831, he preached a sermon entitled "The Lord's Supper," in which he offered as his reason the conviction that Jesus had not intended to institute a permanent ritual of commemoration when he celebrated Passover with his disciples. Emerson's decision to discontinue this rite derived from his insight that the authority of the Christian tradition was dependent on the perpetuation of conventions that were inimical to the creative self.

Rather than participating in the continuation of the tradition commemorating Jesus' transformation into Christ the Messiah, Emerson focused his attention on the internal event—the liberation of the creative self—that the ceremony of the Lord's Supper commemorated. After Emerson distinguished the minister who commemorates the transformation of Jesus from the creative self who lays bare its significance, he transferred his belief to the latter figure. In trusting in the self who was the recipient of the revelation rather than the outward signs of this interior event, Emerson affirmed his belief in the self's powers of creative reception.

When he dislodged himself from his identity as a Unitarian minister, Emerson opened up a new space outside the prescribed order of places. As an event that the church was required to exclude in order to sustain the coherence of the Christian tradition, Emerson's resignation took place at the limit of the representable, but Emerson nevertheless transformed this literally incongruous space into the scene within which he composed his essays.

Emerson followed his resignation with a series of manifestos: *Nature* in 1836; "The American Scholar," an address delivered to the Harvard Phi Beta Kappa Society in

1837; and the "Divinity School Address," given to the Harvard Divinity School in 1838. In them, he announced his liberation from determinations, respectively, by nature, by school, and by religious creed. Because each of these manifestos reenacted the disidentification from a mandated identity that Emerson had first accomplished when he resigned from the church, they retroactively endowed that drama with the qualities of a foundational event.

AMERICAN ROMANTICISM AFTER EMERSON

After he resigned from the ministry, Emerson replaced the Christian tradition with the creative self as the secular authority under whose tutelage he addressed his readers. He intended his essays as sites wherein his individual readers might be restored to the infinitude of the creative self. Rather than encouraging his readers to accommodate to existing social models, Emerson's essays were designed to turn them away from their assigned social positions and toward their powers of creative reception. In "Self-Reliance," Emerson represented the gap between individuality and social identity as the passage through which his readers would obtain access to their own creative resources.

The point of departure for Emerson's essays entailed the generalized rejection of existing social positions and the assumptions, canons, and institutions that supported them. Although Emerson never identified with any existing social role, however, two of the figures over which he ruminated in his essays—"The American Scholar" and "The Poet"—acquired social significance after Henry David Thoreau and Walt Whitman designated these representations in Emerson's essays as the models on which they fashioned their literary identities.

Thoreau transformed Emerson's proposition that the true American Scholar would emerge only when the individual is unafraid to "plant himself indomitably on his own instincts" into a personal challenge, which Thoreau set about meeting in two linked ventures. The first was his year-long residency in a shack next to Walden Pond. The second entailed the publication of the journal he composed during this ordeal as material evidence of his having attained the standing of an American Scholar.

Although Emerson idealized the poet as a liberating god in his essays, he never developed a poetic form into which he could fully release his thinking. In the 1855 preface to *Leaves of Grass*, however, Walt Whitman announced himself as the incarnation of the Poet prophesied by Emerson. Whitman, unlike Bryant and Poe, invented a flexible style of free verse whose open poetic form and lack of finish depended for its imaginative completion on the contributions of his democratic readers.

Thoreau and Whitman wanted to reconcile their literary ambitions to existing social determinations; Emerson, by contrast, created his essays within a space withdrawn from the social order. In his essays and addresses, he opened up fields of possibility in which thought and action were brought into crises that could not be resolved. The immense social respect that his contemporaries conferred on the "Sage of Concord" derived in part from the influence over the conduct of their lives that Thoreau and Whitman (along with prominent members of the Boston Brahmin class) attributed to Emerson. After Thoreau and Whitman credited Emerson's essays as the source of the social roles with which they identified, they endowed Emerson with the powers of symbolic investiture that Harold Bloom has associated with the founding of an American religion: "The mind of Emerson is the mind of America, for worse and for glory, and the central concern of that mind was the American religion, which most memorably was named 'self-reliance' " (Bloom, 1982, p. 145).

That supposed American religion, however, was not continuous with Emerson's lifelong project that rejected every form of organized religion. The religion that has been made out of Emerson's essays was in fact the invention of the critic F. O. Matthiessen, whose 1941 masterwork, *American Renaissance: Art and Expression in the Age of Emerson and Whitman,* substituted a secular clergy of great authors for that of the Christian church. Matthiessen established Emerson's preeminence within the American canon when he described Emerson as the founder of a literary tradition comprising authors—the others were Whitman, Thoreau, Melville, and Hawthorne—responsible for the masterworks of American literature.

In adding Melville and Hawthorne to fill out his five-author paradigm, Matthiessen proposed that they be understood as counterweights to Whitman and Thoreau, who represented themselves as Emerson's disciples. He interpreted Melville's and Hawthorne's romances as investigations of moral ambiguity that served to chasten Emerson's optimism. According to Matthiessen, *Moby-Dick* brought contradictory versions of Emerson and American romanticism into apocalyptic confrontation: Captain Ahab demonstrates what happened when an Emersonian romantic aspired to effect a political transformation; Ishmael discloses the ineffectual results of an Emersonian effort to mount an opposition. Matthiessen found characters in Hawthorne's romances who are likewise critical of Emerson's character because they were, like Emerson, unable to enter into a sympathetic relationship with anyone who was not an extension of their will.

More important, with Emerson's romantic lineage as his warrant, Matthiessen forged an enduring alliance between liberalism in politics and romanticism in the arts and literature. He interpreted the doctrine of self-reliance as corroborating the core liberal beliefs in self-determination and the possessive individual. *American Renaissance* provided this alliance with a history and a coda. As the literary embodiment of ideals such as the free imagination, moral integrity, tactful judgment, and artistic innovation, the Matthiessen canon legitimated the ethos of liberal individualism.

Matthiessen, however, utterly ignored the generation of American and European romantics preceding Emerson. Matthiessen's ignoring the early strain of American romanticism stemmed from his desire to safeguard America's literary tradition from the incursions of revolutionary politics, and he found in Emerson's essays outstanding strategies of depoliticization. He advocated an interpretation of Emerson and American romanticism as a renaissance of imaginative energies rather than political activism, and he invoked the ghost of Shakespeare to produce an image of American romanticism as the recommencement of a period of British literary history notable for its imaginative excess and unregulated artistic invention. Rather than interpreting liberal democracy as a form of government, Matthiessen portrayed it as a way of life that requires protection against the totalitarian threats posed by Nazism and Stalinist Marxism. Emerson's works were well suited to Matthiessen's purposes because they allowed for an idealized description of the American literary tradition placed in opposition to the totalitarian ideologies emerging across Europe. When Matthiessen interpreted the liberal vision represented in Emerson's essays as continuous with Shakespeare's, he also renovated the core liberal values Emerson was made to represent. With the publication of *American Renaissance*, Matthiessen sought to glorify the nation-state by representing its literary heritage as comparable with England's during the Renaissance.

American Renaissance staged the rebirth of these liberal masterworks within the consecrated "renaissance" time a nation claims to renew when it takes its place in the world. With the subtitle *Art and Expression in the Age of Emerson and Whitman*, Matthiessen removed the masterworks American romantics from the contentious political context in which they were written and repositioned them so that, like a magic mirror, they reflected only the idealized images readers of *American Renaissance* found desirable.

AFTER EMERSON AND ROMANTICISM

In the aftermath of World War II, critics on every part of the political spectrum did homage to Emerson. The finest critics of that generation—Harold Bloom, Richard Poirier, and Stanley Cavell—brought their projects into prominence by finding the critical lexicon with which to come to terms with Emerson. Critics who came to maturity after the Cold War ended, however, have criticized Emerson's writings as endorsements of racial divisions and gendered hierarchies.

After he resigned from the ministry, Emerson claimed that he composed his work from within a place outside the social order, but recent critics have cited the following passage from the essay "Self-Reliance" as evidence that Emerson gained access to his sanctum by way of exclusions that reflected entrenched social prejudices:

> If an angry bigot assumes the bountiful cause of Abolition and comes to me with his last news from Barbadoes, why should I not say to him, "Go love thy infant, love thy woodchopper, be good-natured and modest. Have that grace, and never tarnish your hard uncharitable ambition with this incredible tenderness for black folk a thousand miles off. Thy love afar is spite at home." Rough and graceless would be such a greeting; but Truth is handsomer than the affectation of love. Your goodness must have some edge to it else it is none. The doctrine of hatred must be preached as the counteraction of the doctrine of love, when that pules and whines. I shun father and mother and wife and brother. When my genius calls me, I would write in the lintels of the door-post, "Whim." I hope it is better than whim at last, but we cannot spend the day in explanation.
>
> (*Bode and Cowler*, 1981, p. 142)

This passage is organized around an emotional contradiction. Emerson asserts that he wishes to be liberated from the affective alliances that undergird the abolitionist movement so that he can reinvest those emotions within his family. But the images of the woodchopper and the infant recall scenes of the slave's forcible separation and the violence of the auction block that they are supposed to supplant. The transition from family man to creative genius with which the passage ends turns on a complex figure that correlates the slave experience with residual metaphors from the Passover ceremony Emerson had discontinued: an allusion to the blood with which the Israelites marked their doorposts to ward of the Angel of Death.

In his journal, Emerson named this figure in whose name he rejected precedents as well as imitators the "anti-slave." The anti-slave resembled the slave in that he occupied a null site in the social order. Emerson's anti-slave was unlike any actually existing slave, however, in that he was released to his genius at this site. Emerson believed that when he exercised the powers of the anti-slave, he produced works that constituted an exception to the order of things. The African-American philosopher Cornel West has recently criticized the means whereby Emerson obtained access to the anti-slave as a reenactment of the terms of a racially exclusionary model of American nationalism that insisted on a racial difference between individuals who were capable of obtaining access to their genius and those who could not.

Feminist scholars have pointed to Emerson's assertion that the call of his genius required his dissociation from all domestic ties as evidence of his endorsement of the gendered basis for the division of intellectual labor. According to these critics, Emerson's separation of the site he entered when he exercised his genius from his wife, Lidian Emerson's domestic space reproduced a division of the gendered realms regulating woman's place within the social order.

When Emerson named the inspiration for his creativity "whim," he expressed his fear that commitment to the cause of abolitionism (or of women's rights) would require that he conform to the very social institutions from which he wished to remain independent. However, contemporary Americanist scholars understand literature to be inextricably linked with the more encompassing social processes Emerson repudiated. These revisionist scholars, unlike their predecessors, do not interpret Emerson as either an exemplar of American romanticism or as an exception to its rules. They instead interpret both Emerson's work and American romanticism in general as an evasion of the unfinished work of the American Revolution.

Rather than proposing alternative readings of the authors who are already categorized within Emerson's period of American romanticism, or advocating the addition of authors who give voice to neglected communities, contemporary Americanists characterize the period concept "Emerson and American romanticism" itself as a continuation of Anglo-American imperialism by literary means. Rob Wilson recapitulates this view of the Emerson archive when he cites the following passage from "Self-Reliance" as evidence of Emerson's adherence to U.S. imperial designs: "Vast spaces of nature, the Atlantic Ocean, the South Sea—long intervals of time, years, centuries—are of no account." "The reader must refuse full absorption," Wilson cautions, into "the Emersonian language of sublime transcendence by means of which Atlantic and Pacific spaces and peoples are mastered into ciphers and history into a diary of national (and private) self-empowerment."

Contemporary Americanist literary scholars believe that Emerson and the tradition of American romanticism founded in his name constituted an evasion of revolutionary social imperatives. These scholars have designated Emerson's "imperial self" as the nexus through which American romanticism was linked with the western expansion of an Anglo-American empire. In proposing Emerson's essays bear some responsibility for the historical injustices facilitated by the proponents of the European Enlightenment, however, these contemporary critics have made Emerson the representative of universal processes of human development from which he took pains to dissociate his project.

AFTERWORD

Emerson's representation of the American Revolution as an event internal to the individual consciousness was designed to obstruct its association with practices, whether progressive or reactionary, within the social sphere. Because Emerson refused to legitimate the structures of power that predominated at the time of his writing, it is difficult to understand how criticism of Emerson can be invoked to legitimate the overthrow of present-day social and political arrangements. The historical categorization "Emerson and American romanticism" has persistently failed to reduce the anomalies intrinsic to Emerson's figures of thought to a regulated sequence; so has the present-day resistance to that archive.

[See also Emerson, Ralph Waldo and Transcendentalism.]

FURTHER READING

Bloom, Harold. *The Anxiety of Influence: A Theory of Poetry*. New York and Oxford, 1973. Rethinks Anglo-American literary history in terms of a later poet's struggle to become emancipated from the literary influence of a precursor poet. The unique place Emerson occupies in Bloom's psychohistory sheds light on the difficulties Emerson posed for his contemporaries as well as his literary descendants.

Bloom, Harold. *Agon: Towards a Theory of Revisionism*. New York and Oxford, 1982. Spells out agonistic ordeals inherent in the production of Emerson's memorable essays as well as the literary tradition founded on those struggles.

Bode, Carl, and Malcolm Cowley, eds. *The Portable Emerson*. New York, 1981.

Cavell, Stanley. *Philosophical Passages: Wittgenstein, Emerson, Austin, Derrida*. Oxford, 1991. See the chapter "Emerson's Constitutional Amending" for a fine analysis of the complex relationship between Emerson's thinking and the slavery question.

Chai, Leon. *The Romantic Foundations of the American Renaissance*. Ithaca, N.Y., 1987. Provides a fine historical framework for a comparativist understanding of the historical relations between European and American romanticisms.

Foerster, Norman. *The Reinterpretation of American Literature*. New York, 1929, rev. ed. 1959. This book played a foundational role in the formation of American literature as an academic field.

Hobsbawm, Eric, and Terence Ranger, eds. *The Invention of Tradition*. New York, 1983. Essays explain the part romanticism played in engendering a cultural tradition that American literature was assigned the task of transmitting.

Matthiessen, F. O. *American Renaissance: Art and Expression in the Age of Emerson and Whitman*. New York and Oxford, 1941. The foundational critical work responsible for the articulation of the American literary canon as well as the framework through which it was to be interpreted.

Pease, Donald E. *Visionary Compacts: American Renaissance Writings in Cultural Context*. Madison, Wis., 1987. Places Emerson's essays within the context of the debates over slavery, expansionism, and secession.

Poirier, Richard. *The Renewal of Literature*. New York, 1987. Focuses on aspects of Emerson's writings that contradict attempts to assimilate Emerson's essays to the dimensions of cultural debates.

Shumway, David R. "Emerson and the Shape of American Literature." In *Disciplining English: Alternative Histories, Critical Perspectives*, edited by David R. Shumway and Craig Dionne. Albany, N.Y., 2002. A useful discussion of the role Emerson played in the formation of the field of American literature.

Wald, Priscilla. *Constituting Americans: Cultural Anxiety and Narrative Form*. Durham, N.C., 1995. Deftly links the Emerson project with anxieties over race and gender.

West, Cornel. *The American Evasion of Philosophy*. Madison, Wis., 1989. Interprets the optimism in Emerson's essays as grounded in his refusal to bear historical witness to the national tragedy of slavery.

Wilson, Rob. "Imagining 'Asia-Pacific' Today: Forgetting Colonialism in the Magical Free Markets of the American Pacific." In *Learning Places, The Afterlives of Area Studies*, edited by Masao Miyoshi and Harry Harootunian. Durham, N.C., 2002. Brings a range of revisionist readings of Emerson into a kind of summation.

HENRY ROTH

by Lani Wolf

Henry Roth, one of the twentieth century's most important Jewish authors, is known primarily for his first novel and masterpiece, *Call It Sleep* (1934), the story of a young Jewish boy named David Schearl growing up in a New York ghetto in the years before World War I. Sixty years would pass before the publication of his next major work, the first volume of *Mercy of a Rude Stream*, intended to be a series of six novels portraying the artistic, sexual, spiritual, and emotional development from childhood to old age of the protagonist, Ira Stigman. Both *Call It Sleep* and *Mercy of a Rude Stream* portray the immigrant experience, specifically that of the eastern European Jew, as an attempt to escape the trauma of one's social and familial environments. Both are also intensely psychological novels,

Henry Roth. (*Courtesy of Gale Research Company*)

exploring the development of an extremely perceptive and sensitive protagonist seeking enlightenment and personal redemption. Perhaps most importantly, both are great acts of memory and confession, not only for the protagonists but for the author himself.

BIOGRAPHY

Born on 8 February 1906 in Galicia, Austria-Hungary, now the Ukraine, Roth immigrated to the United States with his mother, Leah, when he was two years old. His father, Herman, had already arrived in New York City in 1907 and had found work and a home in the Brownsville section of Brooklyn. Shortly thereafter, however, Herman became disillusioned with his life in the "Golden Land," as the characters in *Call It Sleep* initially envision it. Like so many eastern European Jews, Roth's parents found the move difficult, exchanging the security of a pastoral village for the tumult of a modern city, the language of which

they did not speak. Adding to Herman's discontent was his estrangement from his wife, for his son's birth date and paternity were in question. This issue of paternity drives the principle conflict of *Call It Sleep*, the troubled relationship between Albert Schearl and his son, David, the sensitive young protagonist.

In 1910 the family, with their newborn daughter Rose, moved to New York's Lower East Side, a "virtual Jewish mini-state," as Roth later noted. The four years they spent in the bustling tenement neighborhood profoundly affected the young Roth, who absorbed sights, sounds, and experiences that would later emerge with great power in his writing. In 1914 the family moved to Harlem, then an Irish and Italian neighborhood, a difficult transition for Roth, for the close-knit Jewish community provided him with a sense of safety and security lacking in his home. As Roth later explained, the abrupt physical shift impeded not only the development of his personal identity but also his Jewish identity, for it took Roth from Hebrew school just before the critical stage of learning, the translation phase, in which he would learn the meaning behind Jewish words and scripture. His parents, in turn, did not reinforce Judaism at home. As a result, Roth strove to assimilate into the gentile Irish neighborhood of Harlem, declaring his atheism at age fourteen. Additional personal problems manifested themselves in his poor performance in school, his rapid weight gain, and his estrangement from his peers. A positive outcome of his introversion, however, was his developing interest in reading, particularly myths and fairy tales, which would later influence his writing.

In 1924 Roth enrolled in the City College of New York, intending to become a biology teacher or a zoologist. Instead, however, he met the literature professor and poet Eda Lou Walton, who would support him financially and emotionally until he finished his degree in 1928. The two lived together in her Greenwich Village apartment, where Roth became exposed to the fashionable New York community of literary intellectuals, for example, Hart Crane and Margaret Mead, an experience Roth relates in *Mercy of a Rude Stream*. In 1930 Roth accompanied Eda to Peterborough, an artists' colony, and began writing *Call It Sleep*. Aside from a creative college essay titled "Impressions of a Plumber," this was Roth's first attempt at fiction, extraordinary in that his entire artistic development took place in its evolution from straight autobiography to a highly structured, consciously shaped work of art.

In 1933 Roth joined the Communist Party, partially to assuage his guilt over his privileged lifestyle with Eda during the Great Depression and partly to regain a sense of community after his four years of comparative isolation while writing *Call It Sleep*. Despite positive critical reviews regarding its realism, vision, use of language, characterization, and plot, party members severely criticized the novel for not foregrounding the proletarian struggle. One reviewer declared, "It is a pity that so many young writers drawn from the proletariat can make no better use of their working class experience than as material for introspective and febrile novels." Shaken by such criticism, Roth abandoned his impulse to continue David's story into adolescence and adulthood and began work on a novel about a midwestern communist worker. Shortly after Scribners accepted the first section of the novel, publishing part of it as "If We Had Bacon" in a book called *Signatures: Work in Progress*, Roth stopped work on the novel, entering a profound writer's block that lasted nearly fifty years.

Eda and Roth continued living together until 1938, when he met his future wife Muriel Parker, a composer, at Yaddo, the artists' colony at Saratoga Springs, New York. In 1939 they married, and Roth began a series of odd jobs, for example, as a precision metal grinder during World War II, a high school math tutor, and later an orderly in a mental institution in Augusta, Maine, where he and Muriel had moved with their two sons. During the 1940s and 1950s he continued to publish short stories in such esteemed magazines as *The New Yorker* but found writing stories tiresome and uninspiring compared to his work on *Call It Sleep*. He was engaged in a waterfowl farming business in rural Maine when *Call It Sleep* was rediscovered in 1956. That year, the *American Scholar* published a special feature called "The Most Neglected Books of the Past 25 Years"; *Call It Sleep*

was the only book mentioned more than once. The critic Leslie Fiedler hailed it as a "neglected masterpiece" and "the best single book written by a Jew about Jewishness in America," commenting, "For sheer virtuosity, *Call It Sleep* is hard to best. . . . No one has reproduced so sensitively the terror of family life in the imagination of a child caught between two cultures." Alfred Kazin compared Roth in sensibility to Wordsworth and in self-conscious honesty to Dreiser. The novel was reissued in paperback and at once rose to the top of the best-seller lists, selling over one million copies; in addition, it was the first paperback ever to receive a front-page review in *The New York Times Book Review*. Reluctantly Roth gave up his literary anonymity, accepting a $2,500 grant from the National Institute of Arts and Letters in 1965 and the D. H. Lawrence Fellowship in 1968 at the University of New Mexico at Albuquerque.

By the 1970s Roth had relinquished his communist beliefs, instead taking a keen interest in the politics of the Arab-Israeli War, reawakening his faith in Judaism. While in Albuquerque, he began drafts of his second great literary achievement, *Mercy of a Rude Stream*, the story of a Jewish boy named Ira Stigman caught between his Jewish immigrant community and the fashionable community of New York artists, intellectuals, and writers he had entered as an aspiring novelist. It was not until after the death of Roth's beloved wife Muriel in 1990 that he published the first of the books, *A Star Shines over Mount Morris Park* (1994). Impelled by grief and anguish, he wrote as though in a fury, unburdening his mind and heart before his own death. The second installment, *A Diving Rock on the Hudson*, came out shortly before his death on 13 October 1995 at the age of eighty-nine, and the third, *From Bondage*, was published posthumously in 1996, a finalist in fiction for the National Book Critics Circle Award.

CALL IT SLEEP

Call It Sleep is the story of two years in the life of a six-year-old Jewish immigrant boy named David Schearl living—as Roth had himself—with his troubled family in the tenements of Brownsville and the Lower East Side. From a perspective that is simultaneously vulgar and ethereal, the novel relates David's experiences on the streets with neighborhood friends and anti-Semites, in Hebrew school, and in the home, where he is shielded by a loving, overprotective mother and tormented by his depressed, paranoid father. Frustrated with his menial job as a milk-truck driver, Albert Schearl is set in bold contrast to his sensitive and perceptive son, who, though very young, seeks spiritual enlightenment, living largely in his mind. Albert becomes convinced that David is the son of his wife's former lover, a gentile church organist in Austria, precipitating a profound identity crisis within David and Albert's own obsession with cuckoldry. These tensions lead to a menacing, nearly violent relationship between father and son; indeed, the title *Call It Sleep* refers to David's disturbed restlessness and mental anguish at the hands of his father. In one scene of the novel, after a terrible fight between David and Albert, David lies down next to his mother in bed, closes his eyes—and, "one might as well call it sleep."

As Roth himself has acknowledged, James Joyce's *Ulysses* greatly influenced *Call It Sleep*. Both novels are highly autobiographical and concerned with the lives of the people in the their immediate communities; as Roth explained, "What I gained [from reading *Ulysses*] was this awed realization that you didn't have to go anywhere at all except around the corner to flesh out a literary work of art." In addition, both Roth and Joyce are preoccupied with the father-son relationship. Both capture the chaotic daily life of the modern city, evoking its sights, sounds, and smells with a seemingly tangible reality. Both directly reveal their narrators' minds through stream of consciousness, or the interior monologue. Both structure their novels around recurring symbols and weave myth and archetype into their narratives. Both tell their stories in a foreshortened span of time, Joyce in one day, Roth in a few years, suggesting that past and future exist simultaneously within the present and that in essence, the present moment reveals a lifetime. Finally, both are preoccupied with linguistic considerations. Roth weaves a montage of language through his narrative: the interior language of David's mind, the Italian and Irish dialects of the streets, the Yiddish of the home, the immigrants' broken English, and Hebrew, "a strange and secret tongue." Roth uses this mixture of language to help establish character and atmosphere in the novel, but more importantly to explore the psychological effects of these various languages on David's mind. Yiddish, for example, is presented clearly and cleanly as correct English, while the immigrants' broken English is full of mispronounced words and misspellings, so that we must read it as though it were a foreign language. For example, David's mother Genya speaks a poetic, emotionally rich, and fluid Yiddish—"This is the way of the years, my son"—while her English comes out as "Herr-Mister. Ve-er-ve-go?" The reason for this striking presentation of Yiddish and English is verisimilitude; Roth wishes to re-create the immigrants' experience with language in the reader's mind. Another example occurs during the climatic scene of the novel, in which David tries to, in effect, crucify himself by touching a metal milk ladle to an electrified trolley line. The often crude vernacular of the immigrants on the streets is juxtaposed against the poetic interior language of David's consciousness, as one traumatic image after the next flashes through his mind. In a greater sense, however, the novel's emphasis on language points to David Schearl's search for his own voice.

As Bonnie Lyons (1976) suggests, the artistic differences between Roth and Joyce, however, are perhaps more significant than the similarities. Roth takes as his subject the revelation of character told in traditional narrative, unlike Joyce, who is primarily concerned with innovative novelistic technique. In a similar sense, Roth's structural symbols grow organically out of the text rather than being consciously imposed upon it. Finally, *Call It Sleep* lacks the intellectual difficulty of *Ulysses*, which is primarily a cerebral novel; as a result, the reader engages with greater intensity in David's psychic experience.

David's psychological development is primarily Freudian and Oedipal in nature. Roth's four structural symbols, the cellar, the picture, coal, and the rail, grow out of the workings of David's complex mind. The cellar is the locus of terror, bodily corruption, and impure sexuality. The picture of a field of cornflowers represents his mother Genya's nostalgia for her native rural Austria, alluding also to her love affair with a church organist, whom Albert fears is David's real father. Connected to the cornfield picture is Albert's set of bull horns, suggesting the peaceful, rural world he had left, and also his obsession with cuckoldry. Coal represents the uncleanliness and blackness of the cellar on the one hand, and on the other, David's spiritual purification through his association with the prophet Isaiah. Like Isaiah, who was empowered to speak God's voice when an angel touched his lips with a burning coal, David is a child mystic, visited by visions. Finally, as Lyons so finely explicates, the symbol of the trolley rail unifies the cellar, picture, and coal symbols in the climatic scene of the novel, which can be interpreted in Freudian terms. David plunges a metal milk ladle, signifying his father the milk-truck driver, into the electric portion of a trolley rail, nearly electrocuting himself. Signifying the sexual act, David's violent action is in direct response to his questionable paternity, leading to his father's rejection and his resultant identity crisis. Images of the cellar, associated with impure sexuality, and of the picture, representing illicit sexuality, flash through his mind. The result of his heightened state of awareness is a vision of God's burning coal, which allows him to transcend his symbolic state of death and be reborn into life. Thus, in this climatic scene, David undergoes the powerful process of archetypal initiation: torture, ritual death, and resurrection. Portrayal of David's developing consciousness through archetypal models is in part what makes the novel so powerful, engaging the reader's own subconscious.

MERCY OF A RUDE STREAM

Compared by critics to James Joyce's *Portrait of the Artist as a Young Man*, *Mercy of a Rude Stream* portrays the life of a boy named Ira Stigman engaged in profound emotional, spiritual, sexual, and artistic development from childhood through old age. The title comes from a speech by Cardinal Wolsey in Shakespeare's *Henry VIII*, suggesting that Roth viewed mankind as a "rude stream," a metaphor for the flaws and frailties of our mortal lives. Although Roth finished only three of the projected six novels, the series as a whole was intended to portray Ira's lifelong attempts to escape the stigma of his poverty, his sexual transgressions—"hideousities," as he calls his incestuous affairs with his younger sister and female cousin—and his parochialism. Individually the novels focus on different stages of his life.

Set in New York City in the years preceding World War I, *A Star Shines over Mount Morris Park* explores the struggle of the eight-year-old Ira struggling not only with the onset of adolescence and a disturbing sexual awakening but also with feelings of alienation from himself, his family, and the community, when his family moves from the all-Jewish Lower East Side to the non-Jewish Harlem. Like *Call It Sleep*, the novel is concerned with the effects of such dislocation on the young protagonist's emotional, sexual, and religious development.

Set in New York City in the Roaring Twenties, *A Diving Rock on the Hudson* begins with Ira's freshman year at the City College of New York. With the support of Edith Welles, Eda Lou Walton's fictional counterpart, Ira begins writing his first novel. Like Henry Roth himself, Ira is caught between his immigrant past and the "goyish" literary world of Greenwich Village. On a deeper level, however, the novel examines the dichotomy between his exciting outer life in the fashionable, literary world of Greenwich Village and his troubled inner life, as he seeks redemption from his plaguing guilt over his life's transgression, the unmentionable sin of incest with his younger sister.

From Bondage is narrated from the perspective of Ira as an old man looking back over his life. Many critics have recognized a Tolstoyian aspect to this work, as Ira confronts his imminent passing, drawing sustenance from the eroticized stories of his youth. The title, *From Bondage*, is a complex one, alluding to Ira's lifelong struggle to escape the real or perceived bondages of his immigrant past, his struggle with language and artistic expression, his alienation from self, family, and community, and the crushing guilt of his sexual sin. As Ira says of James Joyce: "It was language, language that could magically transmogrify the baseness of his days and ways into precious literature. . . . It could free him from this depraved exile, from this immutable bondage." This impulse toward escape, toward self-purification and redemption, describes not only Ira Stigman and David Schearl but also Henry Roth himself.

[*See also* Jewish-American Fiction.]

WORKS

Call It Sleep (1934)
"Broker" (1939)
"Petey and Yotsee and Mario" (1956)
"Somebody Always Grabs the Purple" (1966)
Nature's First Green (1979)
Mercy of a Rude Stream: A Star Shines over Mount Morris Park (1994)
Mercy of a Rude Stream: A Diving Rock on the Hudson (1995)
Mercy of a Rude Stream: From Bondage (1996)
Mercy of a Rude Stream: Requiem for Harlem (1998)

FURTHER READING

Allen, Walter. "Two Neglected American Novelists." *London Magazine* (May 1962): 79.

Books and Writers. "Henry Roth." http://www.kirjasto. sci.fi/henryr.htm.

Cohen, David. "Our Century: Henry Roth." *Nando Media*, 2000. http://archive.nandotimes.com/.Fiedler, Leslie A. "Henry Roth's Neglected Masterpiece." *Commentary* (August 1960): 106.

Fiedler, Leslie A., and Alfred Kazin. "The Most Undeservedly Neglected Books of the Past Twenty-five Years." *American Scholar* 25 (1956).

Lyons, Bonnie. *Henry Roth: The Man and His Work*. New York, 1976.

Ribelow, Harold U. "*The History of Henry Roth and* Call It Sleep." In his *Call It Sleep*. Paterson, N.J., 1960.

Sampson, Michelle R. "*Papers of Henry Roth.*" Center for Jewish History. December 2001. http://www.chj.org/academic/findingaids/AJHS/nhprc/HenryRothb.html.

"Special Issue on Henry Roth." *Studies in American Jewish Literature* 5 (1979).

Whittamore, Katherine. "Sneak Peeks, Fiction: *From Bondage.*" *Salon Daily Clicks*. http://www.salon1999.com/sneaks/sneakpeeks.html.

Wirth-Nesher, Hana, ed. *New Essays on* Call It Sleep. Cambridge, 1996.

PHILIP ROTH

by William H. Pritchard

Philip Roth's literary career is extraordinary in a number of ways other than its continued production of surprising, vital, imaginative works. It began when his first book, *Goodbye, Columbus*, a novella and five stories, won the National Book Award for 1959; it reached a peak of notoriety ten years later when *Portnoy's Complaint* became not only a best-seller but also a portent of the decay of American youth. (Students now came to college, declared Vice President Spiro T. Agnew, with pot and *Portnoy* secreted in their suitcases.) The career's most recent stage, beginning in 1993, shows a writer in his seventh decade who brought out no less than six novels, all of them distinctive, three of them possible examples of masterwork. At his seventieth birthday in March 2003, he stood as a writer who has exhibited astonishing staying power, but also one who has deepened, extended, and invariably transformed himself.

It is not easy to name the qualities that most distinguish Roth's work as a novelist. He has from first to latest shown a strong intelligence, fearsomely articulate in its ability to formulate positions, then argue with them by way of moving on to new ones just as temporary as the one abandoned. Everyone testifies to, even if they disagree about its ultimate value, his comic wit, often darkly sardonic but always incorrigibly playful. He has said that "Sheer Playfulness and Deadly Seriousness are my closest friends," and it may be said of him (as Robert Frost liked to say about himself) that he is never more serious than when joking. Roth's brand of serious play has been notably engaged in exploring, often in increasingly transgressive ways, the erotic life of American men and women in heterosexual relations that are usually combative, to say the least. One must speak also of what to some

Philip Roth.
(© Bettmann/Corbis)

readers may seem nebulous: the auditory satisfactions of Roth's narrative voices, whose lucidity and rhythmic movement are unsurpassed. Finally, and extending this remark about movement to the career as a whole, one notes with pleasure the way in which any book of his has succeeded its predecessor in a manner always surprising, yet somehow, upon thinking about it, inevitable. To describe the dynamic of that succession over the course of forty-four years is the burden of this account.

EARLY LIFE AND EDUCATION

Roth was born 19 March 1933, the second son of Herman and Bess Finkel Roth; his older brother, Alexander, would become a commercial artist. His father was assistant district manager in the Essex, New Jersey, office of Metropolitan Life Insurance; his mother, as we might assume from Roth's characterization of her in his autobiographical *The Facts* (1988), was a devoted housewife (the Yiddish word is *balabusta*). The Roths lived in the Weequahic section of Newark, a predominantly Jewish enclave celebrated in the first chapter of *The Facts*, "Safe at Home." Such safety and rooted affection for family and friends marked Roth's adolescence and young manhood, especially affection for his male compatriots and their shared conversations about life. In *The Facts* the mother of one of his school friends remarks, many years later, that she had never again seen anything like "the feeling there was among you boys"—to which Roth adds, "I told her, altogether truthfully, that I haven't either." A financial setback made it impossible for Herman Roth to assume the cost of Philip's education at an elite college, so in 1950 he enrolled in the Newark branch of Rutgers University; then, his father's fortunes having improved, in 1951 at Bucknell College in Lewisburg, Pennsylvania.

There he led an active literary and journalistic life (described well in the "Joe College" chapter of *The Facts*), graduated *magna cum laude* and Phi Beta Kappa, and, in 1954, published his first story in *The Chicago Review*. After taking an M.A. at the University of Chicago (1955), Roth enlisted in the army but was discharged a year later with a back injury. He returned briefly to Chicago as a Ph.D. candidate before deciding to forsake academic distinction and pursue his career as a writer. Accordingly, he published further stories in such magazines as *The Paris Review*, *Commentary*, and *The New Yorker*, while turning out a number of entertaining commentaries on television for *The New Republic*. Some of his stories received awards and were gathered together in *Goodbye, Columbus*, whose success more or less coincided with the beginning of a disastrous marriage to Margaret Martinson Williams, a divorced mother of two. Roth published his first novel, *Letting Go*, in 1962; moved to New York City; separated from his wife; taught at Princeton and the University of Pennsylvania; and spent five years in psychoanalysis. His second novel, *When She Was Good* (1967), emerged at the end of those difficult years, and his estranged wife was killed in an automobile accident the following year. These are a few events in the landscape of "early Roth," in which the young writer established himself as someone to be taken seriously.

EARLY FICTIONS: *GOODBYE, COLUMBUS* AND *LETTING GO*

Decades after it was first published, *Goodbye, Columbus* was reissued by the Modern Library, and Roth provided a short introduction describing the kind of literary creation he had been engaged in back then. The young man who had left the provincial enclosures of Jewish family life in northern New Jersey for a world of "intellectual consequence" in literature and criticism, was not content merely to reject and mock the life from which he had been liberated. His art in the stories was rather to "reimagine as a species of folk fiction" stories "that somehow stretched over the bones of the folktale a skin of satiric social comedy—what not that long before had been the undifferentiated everydayness of Jewish life along the route of Newark's Number 14 Clinton Place bus." So "the desire to repudiate and the desire to cling" were both given voice in Roth's art, an art similar to—though he does not make the comparison—Joyce's in his early book of stories, *Dubliners*. But there was nothing comparable in the critical reception of *Dubliners* to the plaudits that greeted *Goodbye, Columbus*. Novelists and critics

of established weight—Saul Bellow, Irving Howe, and Alfred Kazin—saluted and admired the way Roth had portrayed with exactitude the postwar Jewish-American upper middle class as observed in Newark and environs; a slightly younger critic, Leslie Fiedler, himself a son of Newark, testified that Roth had brought back to him his own childhood in that city. These critics, all of them Jewish, were dealing with Roth not merely as an individual talent but as a significant voice in Jewish-American fiction.

The 1950s had already produced some landmarks of such fiction, notably Bellow's *The Adventures of Augie March*—a most important book for Roth—a number of stories by Bernard Malamud and J. D. Salinger, and work by other now less well-known Jewish writers. What he had done in part was to make visible the materialistic success of "assimilated" Jews now living at some distance from the situation and mentality of their parents and grandparents, and feeling as much or more their identities as Americans than as Jews. Roth himself tells us that in adolescence he was a good deal more interested in sports and girls than in learning Hebrew or observing religious holidays. But the stories take on much of their energy from the critical eye cast on these assimilated young men and women: the triumphant philistinism of Brenda Patimkin and her family (in the story "Goodbye, Columbus") provokes something besides admiration in Neil Klugman, who falls in love with Brenda; and in "Eli, the Fanatic" the ease and safety of Jewish life in a Newark suburb is challenged by a black-garbed misfit out of the European *shtetl* past who eventually drives the story's protagonist, Eli Peck, into despair and madness.

In its leisurely 136 pages, *Goodbye, Columbus* combines satirical portraits of the upwardly mobile Patimkins, who have attained the suburban affluence of Short Hills (plenty of fresh fruit in the refrigerator, athletic equipment all over the house) and who serve both as magnet and as target for the narrator, who lives with his aunt and uncle and goes forth from his daily job at the Newark Public Library to visit and humorously anatomize the Patimkins. Roth's depiction is skillful, but tends toward the cartooning of these fairly easy marks. His more interesting and exploratory writing occurs in moments of lyric enchantment, as Neil drives out of Newark into another, suburban world, "past long lawns which seemed to be twirling water on themselves, and past houses where no one sat on stoops, where lights were on but no windows open. It was, in fact, as though the hundred and eighty feet that the suburbs rose in altitude above Newark brought one closer to heaven."

Or there is attractive Newark-directed observation of "the Lackawanna commuter trains...the sunny green cars, old and clean, with windows that open all the way." There are brief looks at the Newark Museum, and the department stores and theater marquees of Neil's boyhood memories—a vanishing Newark that, along with what replaced it, would be the subject of much of Roth's best writing in his later novels. Here it is touched on affectionately though lightly.

The "species of folk fiction" Roth identifies in these early stories is seen most clearly in "The Conversion of the Jews," when a stubborn little boy confronts his rabbi from the school's rooftop, and in "Eli, the Fanatic" with its tall-tale allegorical pitting of the individual against the law. But the best piece of writing in *Goodbye, Columbus* is the story that takes place in an army camp in Missouri, rather than Newark and its suburbs, and that works within a lucidly specified, authoritatively voiced realistic mode. Once again the situation is an oppositional one, with the voice of liberal reason and decency embodied in Nathan Marx, a Jewish army sergeant confronting a wheedling and manipulative private named Sheldon Grossbart, who is out to gain special treatment for himself and two of his Jewish mates. In its tough humor and moral intelligence, "Defender of the Faith" makes with grace and principle a case for what being a responsible human conscience entails. Roth would never write anything like it again, and indeed after *Goodbye, Columbus* he scarcely wrote any stories. "Defender of the Faith," which provoked criticism of Roth by certain Jewish groups, is a perfectly executed example of balanced "adult" literary performance of the sort he would soon forsake in his pursuit of a different kind of art.

Roth's first—it would also be his longest—novel appeared three years later, in 1962. Set mainly in Chicago, *Letting Go* is a leisurely paced, mainly unhumorous book about the fortunes of two young Jewish men beginning their adult careers as university English teachers. One of them, Gabe Wallach, an instructor at the University of Chicago, enters into a relationship with a divorced mother of two that eventually turns out badly (one of her children is killed in an accident, an event that ends the relationship with Gabe). The other, Paul Herz, has a wife, Libby, whom Gabe is strongly drawn to, and a marriage that is a litany of small disasters. Of the three epigraphs Roth chose to give more moral weight to a very moral book, one from Thomas Mann has it that "morality itself...forbids us to be true to the guileless unrealism of our youth"; another contains lines from Wallace Stevens's

"Esthétique du Mal" beginning "It may be that one life is a punishment / For another, as the son's life for the father's." So the novel's title seems to recommend, as moral realism, a necessary detachment from youthful illusions—about fathers, about other people. In speaking of the book four years later, Roth said that neither Gabe nor Paul "has understanding of what might be called the courage of detachment," and that the novel, by introducing them to suffering, forced them to discover "that some things are unresolvable."

Reviews of *Letting Go* were mixed (unlike those of *Goodbye, Columbus*), and in the most intelligent of them Stanley Edgar Hyman deftly balanced the novel's weaknesses with its strengths. Hyman rightly pointed out that its construction was faulty, that the two narratives into which it breaks are complementary only in a superficial way—that in fact the book is a series of vignettes, "dirty diapers and high thoughts among the instructors at a midwest university." But Hyman also pointed to impressive virtues in *Letting Go*, saying that Roth had the "finest eye for the details of American life since Sinclair Lewis," and that his ear was as good as his eye. He concluded that Roth would be a fine novelist if he were prepared to learn from his mistakes.

Letting Go is also the first of many Roth novels that makes the writing of literary predecessors a critical part of its literary action. Because of its relatively restrained pitch, by contrast with later, louder efforts, it is sometimes called Roth's Henry James novel. But *Letting Go* is unlike James in that absent from it are both the patient building up of a situation and James's urbane, humorous manner with the reader—much on display in *The Portrait of a Lady*, the James novel Gabe lends Libby Herz early in *Letting Go*. The novel is by contrast earnest, even dogged in worrying its material, and has little of the superb ease Roth would soon master in his narrative address to the reader.

WORKING UP TO *PORTNOY*: 1962–1969

The years following the publication of *Letting Go* were ones in which Roth experienced turbulence, both domestic and professional. In retrospect, and with Stanley Hyman's phrase in mind, one could say that he was learning from his mistakes, though doubtless it didn't look so fortifying at the time to the man making them. Legally separated from his wife (she refused to divorce him), living in New York, teaching, and undergoing psychoanalysis, he continued to come under attack from various Jewish individuals and groups for his insufficiently "positive" portrayals of Jewish characters. The attacks culminated in an unpleasant evening at Yeshiva University in New York (there is an account of it in *The Facts*) where hostile questions were directed at him from the audience. (Example: "Mr. Roth, would you write the same stories you've written if you were living in Nazi Germany?") Roth devoted considerable energy to answering these charges in a 1963 essay, "Writing About Jews" (collected in *Reading Myself and Others*, 1975); more important, this experience would serve as material to be explored more than once in the fiction to come, notably in *My Life as a Man* (1974) and *The Ghost Writer* (1979).

Meanwhile, his writing career issued in what Roth later called a series of "abortive forays" into what would become his second and third novels, *When She Was Good* and *Portnoy's Complaint*. Of interest is the fact that stylistically the two projects were conducted on entirely different lines: the "Lucy" project (the fiercely determined heroine of *When She Was Good* is named Lucy Nelson) employed a tense, hard-driving, impersonal narrative that realized itself mainly through the anxious consciousness of Lucy and her hapless husband, Roy; the *Portnoy* project, by contrast, was a freewheeling, first-person narrative about the embattled son of a Newark Jewish family. But the projects were different not merely stylistically, since the Lucy novel was set in a Midwest small town populated by not a single Jew (it would be Roth's only novel without Jewish characters), while the *Portnoy* one returned to the territory he had begun to explore in *Goodbye, Columbus*, but now with a fuller sense of neighborhood and milieu. If the presiding novelistic recipe for *When She Was Good* was Flaubert-like detachment combined with the "American" realism of Theodore Dreiser or Sinclair Lewis, *Portnoy* is an exercise in creative improvisation whose essence was vocal excess—the sort of extravagance Roth enjoyed in the comic performances of Chicago's Second City Theater (it opened in 1959), or that the comedian Lenny Bruce was outrageously practicing in the 1960s.

Despite these differences between the two projects, whose very disparity probably energized Roth as he worked on them, there are identifiable similarities, certainly to the novelist's retrospective eye. Both the protagonists, he said, embody "a grown child's fury against long-standing authorities believed...to have misused their power"; and in their respective feverish attempts to track down the sources of their grievances by locating them within the family, Lucy Nelson and Alexander Portnoy are truly soul mates. But more important than this connection is the fact that Roth's comments are typical of his recurrent, seriously undertaken effort to rationalize, to make sense

out of his own literary progress from book to book: his effort is to say how he got from there to there by bringing out interesting linkages and thematic preoccupations. In the imaginative intelligence with which he conducts this effort—as creative as it is "critical"—he may be compared among his contemporaries with Norman Mailer and John Updike, each of whom has been willing and eager, in interviews and essays, to criticize (and publicize) his own work by suggesting ways in which it should be understood.

The most relentless and unforgiving of Roth's novels, *When She Was Good* (the nursery rhyme concludes with "And when she was bad she was horrid"), pursues—almost literally—the young woman Lucy as she rejects her inadequate parents, especially her alcoholic father, and enters, pregnant, into a loveless marriage with the equally inadequate Roy Bassart that ends in her freezing to death. The mind of Roy, who is back from postwar army service in the Aleutians, sounds like this on important issues: "Look, marriage isn't something you just throw out of the window like an old shoe.... The more he thought about it the more he realized that marriage was probably the most serious thing you did in your whole life. After all, the family was the backbone of society." These are the "received ideas"—folk wisdom in its most cliched form—that Flaubert and the Joyce of *Dubliners* featured in their narratives, and that Roth employs by way of expressing the banality of thought, American Midwestern style, circa 1948. Lucy is equally self-justifying, though in a more monomaniacal fashion: "Had he not proved to her that his soul was an abyss, not just of selfishness, of mindlessness, but of heartless cruelty too?" These rhetorical performances—tirades, often, when Lucy is involved—make up most of the novel's action. In one sense they indicate Roth's narrative detachment from his characters; yet there is nothing objective or disinterested in his portrayal of those characters, since the novel's overall tone is overwhelmingly negative, Roth's eye and ear are both finely evident in *When She Was Good*, and to imagine a place and its inhabitants so remote from Jewish Newark was a feat in itself. But ultimately the novel will be seen as a curiosity: a road taken on one occasion, not to be followed afterward.

On the other hand, *Portnoy's Complaint*, Roth's attempt, as he put it later, "to raise obscenity to the level of a subject," exhibits for the first time the theatrical mode that would reappear in later novels like *My Life as a Man*, *Zuckerman Unbound* (1981), and, above all, *Sabbath's Theater* (1995). Cast in the form of Alexander Portnoy's confessions to his analyst, Dr. Spielvogel (who will appear again in *My Life as a Man*), the book is an extended comic improvisation on one man's trials with his Jewish family upbringing, his pursuit of non-Jewish "shikses," and above all his preoccupation with masturbation: "I am the Raskolnikov of jerking off," Portnoy declares early in the book, "the sticky evidence is everywhere." Alex's comparison of himself to Dostoyevsky's anguished hero in *Crime and Punishment* is a good example of the outrageous and funny replacing of a young Russian man's fantasies before and after he commits murder, with Portnoy's benign though fevered translation of them into tasteless travesties of serious matters: "LET'S PUT THE ID BACK IN YID" is one of his slogans. In response to "The Christmas Song," sung by the black artist Nat "King" Cole and featuring "Chestnuts roasting on an open fire, Jack Frost nipping at your nose," Alex exclaims "An open fire, in my house? No, no, theirs are the Noses whereof he speaks. Not his flat black one or my long bumpy one, but those tiny bridgeless wonders whose nostrils point northward automatically at birth. And stay that way for life!" Unlike Dostoyevsky's relatively uniform presentation of his anguished hero, Roth aspires to and succeeds in endowing Portnoy's first-person voice with—in Roth's words—"the turns, vibration, intonations, and cadences, the spontaneity and ease, of spoken language."

Although the novel was warmly received—Alfred Kazin called Roth "as marvelous a mimic and fantasist as has been produced by the most verbal group in human history"—it also occasioned not merely the aforementioned vice-presidential disapproval (pot and *Portnoy*) but also, three years after it appeared, the most devastating attack on his work Roth would ever receive—Irving Howe's "Philip Roth Reconsidered," which appeared in *Commentary* (December 1972), the Jewish magazine where Roth had published more than once. Howe remarked that "the cruelest thing you could do to *Portnoy's Complaint* is to read it twice," and went on to accuse Roth of vulgarity, of cheapening and reducing his characters into unrecognizable comic-strip shapes, and of being unable to render and explore "life" and human beings the way great novelists (such as Dostoyevsky) had done. *Portnoy* was no more than a series of "skits" performed by a stand-up comedian hungry for audience applause; the fact that it received so much applause meant to Howe that it was meretricious, an example of (he used the word twice, scornfully) "swinging" American debased culture in 1969.

One may agree with Howe that the novel is a series of related comic skits, but then insist that they are often very funny and inventive, and that there are other ways of writing interesting fiction than the "third-dimensional" exploration of character in a life-reverencing way. In fact, *Portnoy* has more than one moment of nostalgic, lyric elevation, as when Alex evokes baseball memories of playing center field, or of ice-skating on the lake in Irvington Park: "In winter, when the polio germs are hibernating and I can bank upon surviving outside of an iron lung until the end of the school year." The book goes on for too long, the "kvetching" becomes repetitive and oppressive. But no matter: with *Portnoy's Complaint* Roth did something original and exhilarating that helped free him into writing more substantial, humanly complicated books.

PUSHING THE ENVELOPE: ROTH IN THE 1970s

The humanly complicated novel Roth struggled to write after *Portnoy* eventually emerged in 1974 as *My Life as a Man*, a book that is centrally about the collapse of a disastrous marriage and its psychological and psychiatric consequences for the novelist-protagonist, Peter Tarnapol. In a chapter from *The Facts*, ironically titled "Girl of My Dreams," Roth recounts the story of his marriage to the woman he calls "Josephine Jensen," and says about *My Life as a Man* that not only the two stories (under the rubric "Useful Fictions") supposed to be written by Peter Tarnapol about a young man named Nathan Zuckerman, but the novel as a whole, was meant to show that he had "survived the consequences of my devastating case of moral simpletonism," namely, his deferential commitment to this "wretched" (Roth's word for her) woman. In an interview with the novelist Joyce Carol Oates, Roth called *My Life as a Man* a book he'd been "writing, abandoning, and returning to" ever since he finished *Portnoy*, and that while it was "simmering away on the 'moral' back burner," he brought out three novels of a very different character. Two of them, *Our Gang* (1971) and *The Breast* (1972), were short; the third, *The Great American Novel* (1973), feels in reading even longer than its almost four hundred packed pages. These "playful" novels may have owed some of that quality to the relief he felt in escaping, for a time, from the "serious" *My Life as a Man*. And since "Sheer Playfulness and Deadly Seriousness" were his closest friends, the three playful novels have, in intention at least, a serious component.

501

Still, these books are diversions, however sporadically engaging, in Roth's overall body of work. *Our Gang* (parenthetically subtitled *Starring Tricky and His Friends*) consists of six short chapters—sketches or skits would be more appropriate—in the life of President Trick E. Dixon, whose real-life counterpart (Richard M. Nixon) was then America's chief of state. As is the case with some of his other novels, especially those written around this time, Roth spoke interestingly and at length about *Our Gang*, placing it in a tradition of American political satire—and, going further back, to Swift and Defoe—but also pointing out that political satire thrives on the local moment, and therefore doesn't last. In 1971 Roth was disgusted by Nixon's behavior, especially by his response to the conviction of Lieutenant William Calley for his role in a massacre during the Vietnam War and to the war in Vietnam generally. But he was also fascinated by Nixon as a user of words, and the focus of *Our Gang* is on the debased political language the president so masterfully (for a while) exploited. The book's air of "buffoonery" (Roth's word), in which Nixon's anti-abortion concern for "the rights of the unborn" is combined with the killings in Vietnam, can still provoke dark laughter. "Tricky" is finally assassinated and stuffed into a plastic bag in the fetal position, an example of the active cultivation of bad taste achieved in *Our Gang*.

Irving Howe's nasty crack about how the cruelest thing one could do to *Portnoy's Complaint* was reread it, might more reasonably be made about both *The Breast* and *The Great American Novel*. The former features a new Roth protagonist, David Kepesh, who will appear twice more in later novels. He awakes one day to find himself metamorphosed into an enormous breast. The debt to Kafka's *The Metamorphosis*, as well as to Gogol's "The Nose," is patent: indeed Kepesh, himself a professor of literature, cites both predecessors in telling his story. Like those predecessors, Roth's strategy in his novella was to treat the potentially grotesque situation in an evenhanded tone, as Kepesh struggles to make some sort of sense out of his absurd plight. His situation may also be compared to that of earlier Roth protagonists who found themselves coming unmoored from the continuities of daily life. In an interview published the same year as the novella, Roth claimed that Kepesh was his first "heroic" character, since the situation in which he found himself is so extreme and intractable. Yet it seems doubtful that a reader can sympathize adequately with such heroism; the erotic details—as when Kepesh's lover, Claire Ovington,

manipulates his nipple so as to produce pleasurable relief—threaten to become simply ludicrous.

As for *The Great American Novel*, it is pure comic inventiveness, a mythical farce with baseball as its material. The fantasy is spun out by an imaginary sportswriter, one "Word" Smith (Red Smith was a famous American sportswriter), whose unstoppable verbal gymnastics, as he narrates the fortunes of a broken-down ball team in something called the Patriot League, know no limits. Here we have not only the unmooring of a character from a recognizable society, but also the unmooring of a novel from its traditional moral and representational energies into a world of pure play. It has the extravagance of burlesque, of a high-octane verbal performance—something Roth had to do once and not again.

When the troublesome *My Life as a Man* finally appeared in 1974, many reviewers used the word "solipsistic" to describe its overall claustrophobic atmosphere. The English novelist Martin Amis put it wittily when he pointed out that it "begins with two autobiographical short stories, presented as the autobiographical work of an autobiographical novelist, about a young autobiographical writer. The rest of the book is a first-person account of the autobiographical novelist's attempt to write a new autobiographical novel." Amis was noting the similarity between Nathan Zuckerman, the hero of two stories by Peter Tarnapol; Tarnapol, the writer-hero of Philip Roth's *My Life as a Man*; and Roth the novelist, the details of whose family and marital life bore (we may say) similarities to his creations. Although Roth said that the book was about the surprises one discovers in becoming a man, such dislocation is not to be settled or even come to terms with by clever narrative manipulation. More to the point, in suggesting the book's angry power, is the sustained narrative intensity with which these surprises are registered like body blows. By comparison, the anguish of *Portnoy's Complaint* feels lighthearted, constructed to elicit laughter.

Unlike *Portnoy*, the book was reviewed harshly and sold poorly, and a paperback edition of it soon went out of print. Its dogged, reiterative telling of the disastrous marriage between Zuckerman or Tarnapol, and Lydia Ketterer or Maureen Johnson; its extended treatment of Tarnapol's pre- and postmarital erotic adventures; its presentations of Tarnapol's sessions with Dr. Spielvogel, whose version of Tarnapol the novelist eventually rejects—all these story-oriented concerns, however skillfully they register, may obscure Roth's real contribution to American fiction: the novel's questioning of heterosexual relations as seen from the tormented male's point of view. One of the sections from Tarnapol's "My True Story," titled "Marriage À La Mode," contains extremely searching writing and thinking about midcentury sexual reality: the young man's felt obligation, in the 1950s, to become "mature," to form a permanent relationship by marrying a woman whether he wanted to or not, to have children, are subjected to an original analysis that is scarcely found in the fiction of Roth's American contemporaries, though some of it is there in the earlier writings of Mailer and in the novels and stories Updike began to produce in the 1960s. But Roth's voice, as projected through Tarnapol, manages to strike us as direct, sincere, and extremely intelligent in its efforts to determine how much the protagonist's difficult "life as a man" is reflective of larger patterns of male experience in the culture.

A similar "referential" interest marks *The Professor of Desire* (1977), in which we survey the (mainly erotic) life of David Kepesh before he found himself turned into an enormous breast. Much of the novel was by then familiar Roth territory: Kepesh's sexual discoveries with two Swedish young women; his painfully messed-up marriage to a Gentile woman; his psychoanalytic attempts to revive the now-depressed and sexually impotent "professor of desire" who is striving, not very successfully, to write a book about romantic disillusionment in the stories of Anton Chekhov. But, like *My Life as a Man*, the book's freshness manifests itself in a dimension other than that of plot or character, as from time to time Kepesh talks to his students, himself, and, most pertinently, to readers of the novel, about matters of life and art, reflected on by a man who is a devoted lifetime reader and teacher. Sitting on a bench in Prague's Old Town Square, Kepesh begins to compose an opening classroom lecture to his students, modeled on Kafka's story "Report to an Academy." (Kafka plays a large part in Kepesh's—and Roth's—imaginative life.) Why should his students cherish the classes and discussions that will make up their course in nineteenth- and twentieth-century fictions about eros and civilization?

> Because once you have left here people are rarely, if ever, going to talk to you or listen to you the way you talk and listen to one another and to me in this bright and barren little room. Nor is it likely that you will easily find opportunities elsewhere to speak without embarrassment about what has mattered most to men as attuned to life's struggles as were Tolstoy, Mann, and Flaubert.

As with the thoughtful pages in *My Life as a Man* about sexual relations between men and women in the American 1950s, Kepesh's reflections on the reading and teaching of literature—of Kafka, Chekhov, and the other greats—are of a sort rarely to be found within the pages of a novel, and are an indication of the boldness and seriousness of Roth's mind making something fresh out of "the novel."

ZUCKERMAN BOUND AND UNBOUND: ROTH IN THE 1980s

Between 1979 and 1983, Roth produced three novels that arguably constituted his most satisfying achievement to date. The grinding discontents and self-recriminations that, in their different shades of humor and seriousness, permeated *Portnoy's Complaint*, *My Life as a Man*, and *The Professor of Desire*, metamorphose, through the person of Nathan Zuckerman, into something more graceful, more comic in its poise. This is not to deny that Zuckerman in *The Ghost Writer* is full of romantic yearning toward the novelist's life or that, in *Zuckerman Unbound* and *The Anatomy Lesson* (1983), he suffers a severe comeuppance for having his dream translated into wild success and sheer misery: the author of a best-seller, the scandalous *Carnovsky*, is consequently dogged by the tribulations, physical and mental, of fame. Yet rather than striking us as depressing—as moments in the earlier novels come close to doing—Zuckerman's trials are exhilarating to a reader excited and charmed by Roth's narrative variety and changes of pace. Zuckerman will go on to figure importantly in *The Counterlife* (1986), then mainly as a sounding board for the obsessed heroes of Roth's novels in the 1990s. But he is most himself in the trilogy of books that in 1985 Roth collected under the apt title of *Zuckerman Bound*.

The first of these (*The Ghost Writer*) sets an attractively muted tone at its very beginning when the young, aspiring novelist Nathan Zuckerman visits a revered one, E. L. Lonoff, in his isolated farmhouse in the Berkshires:

> It was the last daylight hour of a December afternoon more than twenty years ago—I was about twenty-three, writing and publishing my first short stories—and like many a *Bildungsroman* hero before me, already contemplating my own massive *Bildungsroman*—when I arrived at his hideaway to meet the great man.

This ironic musing about the young man who already sees himself as the Teutonically solemn author-hero of a bildungsroman couldn't have been made by Zuckerman at age twenty-three; at forty-three (Roth was forty-seven when *The Ghost Writer* was published), and chastened by the consequences of his own literary success, he has learned irony. *The Ghost Writer* portrays Nathan's enchantment with the admirably monastic seclusion in which his mentor Lonoff lives in the company of a devoted wife and helpmate, Hope; he also meets and is attracted in a rather different way to a young woman named Amy Bellette, a guest at the Lonoffs', who works for the writer as a kind of secretary. A snowstorm results in Nathan's spending the night at the Lonoff house, where he is witness to a disruption between the novelist and his wife, who is fed up with serving a writer whose only mistress is Art, and also galled by the presence of the devoted, young, and beautiful Amy. The ensuing pages (only 178 in total) take on the air of a fable, when Zuckerman discovers (or fantasizes) that Amy is "really" Anne Frank, alive, somehow, in western New England. Overall, it is the understated, flexible humor of the narrative voice that makes *The Ghost Writer* unique in Roth's work and a point of relative stability after the feverish comedy of the works that preceded it.

Zuckerman Unbound reintroduces us to a Nathan who has become the "notorious" author of a novel that sounds very much like *Portnoy's Complaint*. Now, attempting to live in the quiet seclusion of a New York apartment, he is beset by various fans, kibitzers, and cranks, all devoted to setting him straight about life—his love life, his sartorial habits, how he should invest his money. The most persistent of these "fans" is Alvin Pepler, a fellow native of Newark, blessed with a photographic memory for every detail of popular culture. Pepler, once known as "the Jewish Marine," had reached the finals of one of the since-discredited, rigged television quiz shows, but was forced to take a dive and lose to a WASP contestant. Pepler dogs Zuckerman's steps, mainly as an engaging nuisance (he can with ease reel off the top ten tunes of 1950) until he turns against the novelist in a nastily ingenious way.

In its first three parts the novel is a fast-moving, wisecracking extravagance—Roth at the top of his form. Then in the final section the tone changes and deepens, as Zuckerman's father suffers a stroke and dies in Florida with the novelist at his bedside. After the funeral, flying back north with his brother Henry, he is accused by Henry of having broken his father's heart with the family revelations in *Carnovsky*. This charge, in conjunction with a visit to his old Newark neighborhood, now changed, changed utterly, is sufficient to unbind Zuckerman—not in the Aeschylean or Shelleyan positive sense of freedom and liberation, but in the painfully fraught sense of coming loose from all

human connections: "You are no longer any man's son, you are no longer some good woman's husband, you are no longer your brother's brother, and you don't come from anywhere anymore, either." This is Zuckerman's assessment of where he is at the end of the book. But Roth's manipulation of him is a thing of beauty: as John Updike put it in his brief review of the novel, Roth has become an "exquisitist," moving "among his by now highly polished themes with ever more expertness and care."

The Anatomy Lesson, last of the trilogy, is darker, more manic in its orbit. It contains an affecting scene involving the death of Zuckerman's mother, but mainly is a litany of the writer's suffering: from the incapacitating back trouble Nathan suffers during 1973, the year of Watergate; to the spectacle of Nixon trying to slither out of scandal; to the resentful rage Zuckerman feels at a dismissive article written about him by one Milton Appel (a clear stand-in for the critic Irving Howe). The book gathers torrential energy as Zuckerman decides to throw up the literary game and apply to medical school at the University of Chicago. His comeuppance, focused on a critical part of his anatomy, comes at the end of the book with an injury to his mouth—an organ that has been moving in nonstop activity, especially during the flight to Chicago when he impersonates a pornographer named Milton Appel, producer of a magazine titled *Lickety-Split*. The novel ends inconclusively, with Zuckerman a patient (rather than a doctor) in the hospital, "as though he still believed that he could unchain himself from a future as a man apart and escape the corpus that was his."

FURTHER VARIETIES OF IMPERSONATION

In the most revealing of the many interviews Roth has given over his career, the critic and biographer Hermione Lee asked him what happened when he "turned into" Nathan Zuckerman; Roth answered, "Nathan Zuckerman is an act. It's all the art of impersonation, isn't it? That's the fundamental novelistic gift." The novelist's art, he told Lee, "consists of being present and absent; he is most himself by simultaneously being someone else." Rather than abandon one's biography, "you distort it, caricature it, parody it, you torture and subvert it. You exploit it—all to give the biography that dimension that will excite your verbal life." These formulations of Roth were arrived at after twenty-five years of steady fictional work; they speak with salience to the practice of that work up to and centrally including the Zuckerman trilogy, but they have important reference as well to five books of varying character that he produced after the trilogy.

These books, to be treated here in the most cursory way, consist of three novels—*The Counterlife, Deception* (1990), and *Operation Shylock* (1993)—and two memoirs, one about himself (*The Facts*), the other about his father's illness and death (*Patrimony*, 1991). Each of them—even *Patrimony*, which would seem to eschew it—makes use of the art of personification in fresh, sometimes disturbing ways in order to, as Roth put it in the interview, give biography "that dimension that will excite your verbal life." They may be thought of as forays in several directions, each with its special, peculiar voice that cleared the decks for the "American" novels he would produce in the 1990s.

After *The Anatomy Lesson* was published, more than one reviewer expressed the hope that Roth had finally laid Zuckerman to rest and would turn to new material. It was not to be, however, since *Zuckerman Bound* added to the trilogy a longish epilogue, "The Prague Orgy" (a further adventure of Zuckerman's); then in 1986 came *The Counterlife*, in which once more Nathan plays a central role. This novel lays claim to being Roth's most complicated fictional performance, one that could sustain pages of commentary. Its five parts successively overturn one another; for example, in part one Zuckerman's younger brother Henry, a practicing dentist and father of three who has suffered the loss of erotic potency (he's on drugs after a heart attack), decides to have a difficult operation that will enable him to flee to Europe and set up a new love life with his mistress. Henry dies as a result of the operation, but in the next part is resurrected, a passionate member of an Israeli kibbutz who has abandoned his family for spiritual, ideological reasons. Nathan visits him at the kibbutz, tries to persuade him to come back home, but to no avail. But no—it turns out later on that it is Zuckerman himself who had the operation and died, while Henry, furious at his brother's novelistic indiscretions, goes through his effects and removes an incriminating part of a manuscript in which he, Henry, figures prominently. At the end of the novel "Nathan" is "alive," as a character in a novel written by Zuckerman, about to become a father even as his English wife, Maria Freshfield, threatens to leave him because of his violent response to what he perceives as English anti-Semitism. A clumsy attempt at paraphrase, like the one just made, may at least suggest the book's trickiness, its indulgence in many impersonations; but it can't confirm what is also the case—the thoroughly engaging fictional life created page by page.

The "personificating" strategy enters Roth's next book—his "novelist's autobiography" *The Facts*—by framing five chapters that straightforwardly narrate such events as early life in Newark, college days at Bucknell, a bad marriage to "Josephine Jensen," with an exchange of letters between "Roth" and his character Zuckerman. Should he publish the book? he asks at its beginning, and Zuckerman's lengthy reply in conclusion is no, since you've prettified and taken the exciting life out of your life by trying to be direct and sincere, rather than complicated and ambiguous, as you are in your fiction. Soon afterward, in *Deception*, Roth deceives us by writing a novel wholly in conversation taking place between a novelist named Philip and various female characters, one of whom may be his current lover if—so he explains to the woman he's living with—he hadn't been making it all up, creating literature rather than living life. In *Deception* the reader becomes an audiophiliac, the sex very much aural. Then in *Operation Shylock*, the novelist Philip Roth meets a bona fide impersonator who is passing himself off in Jerusalem as an impostor named "Philip Roth" with a utopian scheme for promoting a diaspora in which Jews leave Israel to resettle in the Europe whence they originally came. *Operation Shylock* is the novelist's most intransigent refusal to play it straight: subtitled *A Confession*, it ends with a note to the reader saying "This confession is false."

Finally, *Patrimony*, which won the National Book Award and is without doubt the most moving piece of writing Roth has produced, seems in its vivid and sympathetic rendering of a son's attempt to deal with his father's decline into death, to be, as it is subtitled, *A True Story*. Yet a story, however "true," is still a story, told by a narrator; and without impugning or discounting the strength of filial love and devotion chronicled in *Patrimony*, we can note that the literary effort—here a markedly successful one—was to create, to impersonate in words, the inexpressible feelings of pain and loss that the son had felt in life. In other words, it is no simple matter to tell a true story.

ROTH IN THE 1990s: A CREATIVE OUTPOURING

Roth's achievement as a major novelist is to be found in four substantial books he published between 1995 and 2000, from *Sabbath's Theater* to *The Human Stain* (2000). Although Nathan Zuckerman appears in all these novels with the exception of *Sabbath*, he is no longer the center of focus, but rather a listener to, and sometime writer of, the stories of others. After the elaborate games with character and narration played in *The Counterlife, Deception*, and *Operation Shylock*, the mode of presentation is realistic—like the early Roth, except now with the weight of a lifetime's practice behind it. Some biographical facts, mostly gathered from Roth's own books, are pertinent as backdrop. In 1976 he entered into a long relationship with the English actress Claire Bloom, living half the year in London, the other half in Roth's Connecticut farmhouse. In 1987 they moved to the United States to live there year round; in that same year, recuperating from bone surgery, Roth had a horrendous experience with the drug Halcion (recounted in *Operation Shylock*). Two years later his father died; just before that, Roth underwent quintuple heart bypass surgery. He and Bloom married in 1990; three years later they separated, the separation attendant upon severe depression on Roth's part (as described in Bloom's memoir *Out of the Doll's House*) and mutual recrimination. Recovered from his depression, no longer married to anyone or anything except his art, Roth began the production of those novels on which, it seems clear, his reputation will significantly rest.

SABBATH'S THEATER. More than any other book of Roth's, this is the one that divides readers, however much they may admire his other work. "The unknown about any excess is how excessive it's been," thinks the novel's protagonist, the aging, arthritis-ridden former puppeteer Mickey Sabbath, who in the 1950s ran something called The Indecent Theater on and off the streets of New York City. In this novel Roth set out to portray excess, predominantly sexual excess, by engaging with the unknown. As the critic James Wood put it, Sabbath is a "monk of fornication," dedicated to spiritual unhealth, to a breaking of every sexual taboo. Especially after his Croatian lover, Drenka Balich, with whom he has done everything, dies of cancer, Sabbath becomes the wild, old wicked man of the late W. B. Yeats poem, seeking out and hearing the voices of the dead by whom he is haunted: Drenka; his brother Morty, killed by the Japanese in World War II; his mother, whose response to Morty's death was herself to join the living dead; his first wife, Nikki, who disappeared decades previously but whom Sabbath is convinced he has murdered—and others. The death of a one-time New York friend who backed Sabbath's theatrical enterprise stimulates him to leave his present wife (a recovering alcoholic whom Sabbath berates for her AA vocabulary). In a dreamlike frenzy he drives to New York to his friend's funeral, impersonates King Lear on the subway, removes the panties from the drawer of his host's daughter (he carries them in his pocket to the funeral), and delivers a paean to suicide and to the politically incorrect,

as opposed to the "laudable ideologies" he despises. (He has already lost his job as a teacher at a New England college for indulging in phone sex with a student who taped and released it to administrative ears.)

The book's great sequence, the most sustained piece of eloquent writing Roth ever produced, consists of pages describing Sabbath's visit to the New Jersey shore town of Bradley Beach, in which he grew up, where he buys a grave for himself and communes with the spirit of the dead Morty. Sabbath encounters a vegetable peddler and cousin of the family, a very old man named Fish, who taught Sabbath and his brother to swim. Fish lives alone in his bungalow, cooks a lamb chop for his solitary lunch, doesn't remember Sabbath but reminisces about the day the Atlantic was so rough, it picked up the whole boardwalk and deposited it on Ocean Avenue. In a corner of Fish's room Sabbath discovers an American flag and a carton labeled "Morty's Flag and Things." Leaving Fish, who has gone off to have his lunch, he removes the carton and, parked on the beach at Ocean Avenue, reviews its contents. Among the many words contending in Sabbath's head are some lines from a Yeats poem, "Meru," as well as Fish's adjective "remarkable," used to describe the days long gone by. Suddenly things come together in a moment of powerful feeling and writing:

> The boardwalk was gone. Good-bye boardwalk. The ocean had finally carried it away. The Atlantic is a powerful ocean. Death is a terrible thing. . . . Remarkable. Yes, that's the word for it. It was all remarkable. Good-bye, remarkable. Egypt and Greece good-bye, and good-bye Rome.

The accumulated force of these sentences, scarcely sentences, coming after the previous hundred or so pages is indeed remarkable, like nothing else in Roth's work.

THE AMERICAN TRILOGY. *Sabbath's Theater* won the National Book Award, and in his acceptance speech Roth quoted Herman Melville's remark, after he had finished *Moby-Dick*, that he had written a "wicked" book and felt spotless as a lamb. Buoyed by the accolade given him for his riskiest venture, he turned his pen to three novels, in each of which the career of a doomed protagonist is played out against the social and political realities of American life in the twentieth century's second half. All Roth's fiction, in its scene and characters, had of course been "about" America. But *American Pastoral* (1997), *I Married a Communist* (1998), and *The Human Stain* are dense with the specifics of historical periods: the years of Vietnam protest and Watergate; the post–World War II anticommunist crusade, especially in the world of radio; the racial and sexual conflicts of recent decades. Serving as a thread to connect the novels is the muted presence of Nathan Zuckerman, now beyond the excitements of sex (his prostate has been removed) and living like a monk in a house near Athena College in the Berkshires, site of his visit decades earlier to the novelist Lonoff. Nathan now lives only to read and write, but in each book is drawn into the lives of individual men whose struggle with circumstances he sees as heroic, perhaps tragic. Nathan (with the help of Roth) serves as their writer, the artist who makes their lives into remarkable stories. In these books the presence of William Faulkner is felt more than once through a voice's persistent, never quite satisfactory attempt to put together sentences and paragraphs strong enough to suggest the torturous career under analysis (we think of Joe Christmas in *Light in August* or Thomas Sutpen in *Absalom, Absalom!*). Along with this rhetorical pressure goes a holding back of the antic humor that was Roth's trademark in so many books; indeed, these three "American" novels are the least humorous works he produced, though they are not without their quotient of grim wit.

American Pastoral, first of the three books, won the Pulitzer Prize and received plaudits from reviewers who had been put off two years previously by the obscenity of *Sabbath's Theater*. Divided into three sections—"Paradise Remembered," "The Fall," and "Paradise Lost"—it embodies those Miltonic categories in the life of Seymour Irving Levov, known to all as "Swede," a fantastic high school athlete who marries a Gentile woman, manages (with his father, Lou) a glove factory in Newark, and builds a handsome house in the country; then, with the defection of his daughter Merry (she blows up the local post office to protest the Vietnam War, killing a bystander), the Newark riots, and the generally culture-changing shock of the Vietnam years, he falls into a recognition of the world as unparadisial. In the opening section of the book, Zuckerman, who graduated from the same high school a few years after Swede, attends his high school reunion in Newark and finds out from Swede's brother Jerry that the hero has died of prostate cancer. Overcome by memories of the "paradise" of his high school days in the years just after World War II, Zuckerman begins—in a fantasy that grows increasingly rich and full as it develops—to tell Swede Levov's story.

The novel is full of finely rendered moments like Zuckerman's high school reunion, the dance floor filled with couples moving to Johnny Mercer's "Dream," a romantic hit of 1946. In meticulous detail we are taken through the glove factory managed by Swede's father as the son painstakingly explains the process by which a glove is manufactured. The most painful, indeed repellent, chapter in the book shows Swede meeting his lost daughter, who has now become a Jain (an extreme religious sect), in a hideous room in a decayed corner of Newark. The book's final third, set in 1973 with Watergate on everyone's mind and tongue, consists of a dinner party at the Levovs', the sequence of which—as Swede finds himself beleaguered in every way—is both pathetic and farcical. No novel Roth has written compares with *American Pastoral* in its inclusive, authoritative command of various modes of presentation, from denunciatory to elegiac to heroic. Along with *Sabbath's Theater*, it is Roth's masterwork.

I Married a Communist, which followed hard on the heels of *American Pastoral*, looks to have been written at white heat and with some fury. In 1996, Claire Bloom, obviously stung by the breakup and divorce initiated by Roth, published her memoir, a section of which concerned the events from the summer of 1993 that led to the end of their relationship. The woman who "married a Communist" is a Jewish actress named Eve Frame, whose daughter from an earlier marriage is a source of contention between Eve and her husband, Ira Ringold. The similarities between Eve Frame and Claire Bloom gave reviewers the hint that the imaginative creation here was not wholly disinterested; these circumstances, especially coming after the huge success of *American Pastoral*, couldn't have helped the new book's reception.

It is a novel top-heavy with feverish monologue, often for pages on end, as Zuckerman listens to his old high school teacher, Murray Ringold, try to make sense out of his brother Ira's rise and fall, from day laborer off the streets of Newark's Third Ward, to his mingling with the New York City cultural elite as the husband of a successful movie star (he himself appears in patriotic left-leaning radio plays), to his exposure by Eve in her tell-all confessional as a monster of corruption, political and otherwise. Ira's story is what fuels the novel, and in telling it, Roth and his narrators tell also of a moment in postwar America, poised on the brink of the Cold War and the war in Korea, with its attendant domestic anticommunist furor. It is still the age of radio, and in the book's most moving moment, Zuckerman, alone late at night on the deck of his house, remembers listening as an adolescent, with his brother, to their bedroom radio, a Philco Jr., "when I was a kid ambitious to change the world by having all my untested convictions masquerading as stories, broadcast nationwide." He concludes a paragraph dense with metaphoric speculation by asking, "Is it not at least a *semi*divine phenomenon to be hurled into the innermost wrongness of a human existence by virtue of nothing more than sitting in the dark, listening to what is said?" This is a novel that could have been written only by someone who was at an impressionable age when the magic of radio was entering its last days, and when the grand vision of America as savior of the world (land of the free, home of the brave) was about to be replaced by more painful and contested visions.

In 2001, Roth published two short works: *The Dying Animal*, a novella in which David Kepesh returns to the action as professor and lover, and *Shop Talk*, a collection of interviews with writers such as Primo Levi, Ivan Klima, and Milan Kundera, and an interesting critical essay on Saul Bellow's fiction. But the place to end this journey through the land of Roth is with *The Human Stain*, last of the "American history" trilogy. It is the most complicated and in some ways most improbable of the three novels, as in it Zuckerman befriends Coleman Silk, a professor of classics, a former dean, who retired in disgrace from Athena College after having fallen afoul of (as Sabbath called them) the "laudable ideologies." A remark Silk makes about two students absent from his class whom he hasn't yet met ("Are they spooks?") is taken as a racist slur, and Silk is harried into disgrace: his wife is stricken and dies; he retreats into recriminations and despair. Silk seeks out Zuckerman to write his story, then instead writes it himself and decides it won't do. With the aid of Viagra, he rediscovers sex as embodied in the form of a much younger divorced woman, Faunia Farley, whose husband, a disturbed Vietnam veteran named Les, hounds Coleman and Faunia and eventually kills them. But not before, with the listening aid of Zuckerman, Silk has revealed the amazing truth of his secret life—that rather than being a Jew, he grew up in a light-skinned "Negro" family in Newark, became a prizefighter known as "Silky Silk," and went on to pass as white, denying his familial and racial heritage.

Roth's attempts to give the book contemporary reference by placing Silk's humiliation against the Bill Clinton-Monica Lewinsky scandal of the summer of 1998 is of a piece with the novel's overall ambitiousness (it has an epigraph from *Oedipus Rex* about tragic purification). His toughest critic, James Wood, found the attempt to fuse Coleman Silk's unjust persecution by the denizens of political correctness at Athena College in the 1990s with

his lifelong effort to escape the "human stain" of racial marking, not only contrived but rigged in such a way as to protect its hero, sentimentalizing him by praising his victimhood. (Wood made a similar case about the treatment of Ira Ringold in *I Married a Communist*.) Yet the novel is continuously vivid and alive page by page, containing more various and distinct styles of presentation than are found in the relatively monovoiced novel that preceded it. Coleman Silk's growing up in New Jersey is one more example of Roth's mastery of that terrain, while the more satiric energies directed at thought police in the American academy who are dedicated to purging "unacceptable" attitudes form an apt focus for the novelist's animus. And the scene that ends the novel, in which Zuckerman confronts Les Farley—the man he believes is responsible for the deaths of Faunia and Coleman—ice fishing on a pristine lake in the Berkshires, is as riveting as anything in the Roth corpus.

Early in *American Pastoral*, after Zuckerman has singularly failed to understand Swede Levov at their dinner in New York City, he muses to himself about the general unknowability of human beings:

> The fact remains that getting people right is not what living is all about anyway. It's getting them wrong that is living, getting them wrong and wrong and then, on careful reconsideration, getting them wrong again. That's how we know we're alive: we're wrong.

As we listen and respond to the novelist's characters getting things wrong and wrong again, from *Goodbye, Columbus* to *The Human Stain*, we are reading right into the life of Philip Roth's fiction.

[*See also* Jewish-American Fiction.]

WORKS

Goodbye, Columbus (1959)
Letting Go (1962)
When She Was Good (1967)
Portnoy's Complaint (1969)
Our Gang (1971)
The Breast (1972)
The Great American Novel (1973)
My Life as a Man (1974)
Reading Myself and Others (1975)
The Professor of Desire (1977)
The Ghost Writer (1979)
Zuckerman Unbound (1981)
The Anatomy Lesson (1983)
Zuckerman Bound (1985)
The Counterlife (1986)

The Facts (1988)
Deception (1990)
Patrimony: A True Story (1991)
Operation Shylock: A Confession (1993)
Sabbath's Theater (1995)
American Pastoral (1997)
I Married a Communist (1998)
The Human Stain (2000)
The Dying Animal (2001)
Shop Talk (2001)

FURTHER READING

Baumgarten, Murray, and Barbara Gottfried. *Understanding Philip Roth*. Columbia, S.C., 1990. Survey of career up through *The Facts*.

Bloom, Harold, ed. *Philip Roth*. New York, 1986. Collection of essays on Roth.

Halio, Jay. *Philip Roth Revisited*. New York, 1992. Survey of the career up through *Patrimony*.

Lee, Hermione. *Philip Roth*. New York, 1982. Useful criticism of Roth's earlier books.

Rodgers, Bernard F., Jr. *Philip Roth: A Bibliography*. 2d ed. Metuchen, N.J., 1984.

Searles, George J., ed. *Conversations with Philip Roth*. Jackson, Miss., 1992. Generous selection of Roth being interviewed, full of interesting items.

Wood, James. "The Monk of Fornication: Philip Roth's Nihilism." In Wood's *The Broken Estate*. New York, 1999. Excellent criticism of *Sabbath's Theater*.

MURIEL RUKEYSER

by Jan Heller Levi

Muriel Rukeyser's category-defying work has yet to be fully acknowledged and integrated in the canon of twentieth-century American literature. For a continually growing audience, however, she is essential reading, and contemporary poets have hailed her influence. Adrienne Rich says that she found in Rukeyser "the poet I most needed in the struggle to make my poems and live my life." Galway Kinnell commented that Rukeyser was the one who discovered "the language of crisis" for the twentieth century. Anne Sexton referred to Rukeyser as "Muriel, mother of everyone."

Muriel Rukeyser. (*Courtesy of the Library of Congress*)

CHILDHOOD

Muriel Rukeyser was born in New York City on 15 December 1913. On her birth certificate, her father's occupation is listed simply as "cement." In fact, as president of Colonial Sand & Stone Company, Lawrence B. Rukeyser was fast becoming a significant player in New York's building boom. Colonial Sand & Stone was literally pouring the city into shape with its products. Later in her life, Rukeyser would write, in the section "Cement" from her poem "Searching/Not Searching": "They are setting the forms, / pouring the new buildings. / Our days pour down. / I am pouring my poems."

As his business continued to prosper into the 1920s, and with the arrival of a second daughter, Frances, in 1921, Rukeyser moved his family to Manhattan's Upper West Side. A summer residence on Long Island, box seats at the symphony, and a chauffeur-driven Pierce-Arrow attended the Rukeyser family's rise in the world. Muriel and her sister were looked after by a procession of nannies and governesses, and attended New York's private Ethical Culture Fieldston School. Muriel's mother, Myra Lyons Rukeyser, envisioned for her daughter a comfortable marriage to a successful doctor; while he was out on house calls, Myra imagined, Muriel could pursue writing poems as a hobby.

From an early age, however, Muriel Rukeyser evinced more than a hobbyist's interest in poetry. She was an excellent student, a voracious reader, and a dedicated young writer, already experimenting with demanding forms in her early teens. She was also, to the consternation of her parents, beginning to demonstrate a greater empathy with the workers who were building her city, rather than with the men, like her father, who employed them.

VASSAR, SCOTTSBORO, *THEORY OF FLIGHT*

Rukeyser entered Vassar College (where her classmates included writers Eleanor Clarke, Mary McCarthy, and the poet Elizabeth Bishop) in 1930, at the age of sixteen. In 1932 she took a leave of absence from Vassar and never returned. The faltering of her father's business played a role in her withdrawal, but Rukeyser was also eager to try her own wings, literally and figuratively, in the world. Fascinated by the young industry of aviation, she desperately wanted to learn to fly. Her parents, horrified by the thought, refused to grant permission for their daughter, still a minor, to enroll in pilot training. Rukeyser had to settle for taking only the courses for ground-crew workers at Roosevelt Aviation School in Long Island. With the same passion she felt for flight, she threw herself into the exciting literary and political life of New York's Greenwich Village, taking courses at the Rand School of Social Science and writing for the *Daily Worker*, the *Bookman*, and the *Student Review*, the newspaper of the radical National Student League.

By 1933 the plight of the Scottsboro Boys, nine young African Americans falsely accused and convicted of raping two white women, had become a leftist cause célèbre. Rukeyser talked the editor of the *Student Review* into letting her cover the upcoming retrial of the defendants.

She borrowed her father's Pierce-Arrow and headed for Alabama with some friends. Once there, they spent more time in the local jail than in the courtroom, when the Decatur sheriff detained the group overnight, ostensibly for distributing insurrectionary material (announcements for a National Negro Student Conference to be held later that year).

Scottsboro, strikers, and strivings for flight intertwine in Rukeyser's first book of poems, *Theory of Flight*. Awarded the prestigious Yale Series of Younger Poets prize, the collection was published in 1935, just two weeks shy of the author's twenty-first birthday. "Breathe-in experience, breathe-out poetry"—the opening lines of the collection—announced the arrival of a fervent, idealistic new voice in American poetry. Despite its occasional stumblings and overly dense passages, the multisectioned, multilayered, multivoiced *Theory of Fight*—its title drawn from Rukeyser's instruction manual at Roosevelt Aviation School—stands as an impressive, audacious experiment, merging high modernist linguistic energy with the radical social critique of the politically engaged poet. Rukeyser's shorter lyrics—poems of family, love offered and rejected, and of the difficulties implicit in any attempt at authentic intimacy, such as "Poem out of Childhood," "Sand Quarry with Human Figures," and the often-reprinted "Effort at Speech between Two People," show a young poet of intense, disconcerting authority.

GAULEY BRIDGE AND SPAIN

In the spring of 1936, with her photographer friend Nancy Naumberg, Rukeyser drove south again, but this time west as well, to Gauley Bridge, West Virginia. Here, as *Time* magazine reported, miners employed by Union Carbide and Carbon Corporation were "dropping like flies" from the lung disease silicosis. There was overwhelming evidence that Union Carbide had failed to warn its workers about—or protect them from—the health hazards of their work. The harrowing fruit of Rukeyser's journey to Gauley Bridge was her long multisectioned poem "Book of the Dead" (collected in her 1938 volume *U.S. 1*). Drawing on personal interviews, on transcripts of trials and congressional testimony, and on her own observations, and even incorporating into the poem an exact reproduction of Union Carbide's profit-and-loss statistics from the New York Stock Exchange listings, Rukeyser fashioned a chilling documentary of corporate greed and human suffering, a poem that, in accessing all kinds of "data," anticipates in many ways the communicative strategies of hypertext.

In 1936 Rukeyser also traveled to Spain to report on the People's Olympiad in Barcelona, the antifascist alternative to the regularly scheduled Olympic Games in Berlin. Rukeyser arrived by train in Spain just as the first days of fighting erupted in what was to become the Spanish civil war. She had a brief love affair with a young German athlete named Otto Boch, whom she had met on the Barcelona-bound train. Boch remained in Spain to join the Republican forces, while Rukeyser returned to New York. Boch subsequently lost his life in battle there, and references to him and his sacrifice appeared in her work throughout her life.

By early 1943 (still not yet thirty) Rukeyser had already published three full-length volumes of poetry, as well as a biography of the scientist Willard Gibbs. She had been awarded numerous prizes; she was regularly published in the outstanding literary journals of her day; in the *Saturday Review*, the prominent poet and anthologizer Louis Untermeyer called her "the most inventive and challenging poet of [her] generation." Rukeyser's place in American letters seemed assured.

PERSONAL HERESIES

By late 1943 early strains of what was to develop into the Red Scare campaign led by Senator Joseph McCarthy were beginning to show. The House Un-American Activities Committee, then headed by Congressman Martin Dies of Texas, was launching investigations into those whom they identified as "premature anti-fascists." Rukeyser was among scores of artists and writers, under pressure from this committee, who resigned their government positions (she had been working in the poster division of the Office of War Information).

Rukeyser left New York at the beginning of 1944 and spent much of the next seven years in the San Francisco area, lecturing at the California Labor School and working on her poetry and plays, with occasional extended trips east. In 1945, in California, she married the painter Glyn Collins; the marriage was annulled after six weeks. In 1946 she was at last able to fly solo in Carmel, California. A year later, Rukeyser became a mother. Her son was born in September 1947; Rukeyser never publicly revealed who the father of her child was. Yet she fully embraced maternity, and her "Nine Poems" dedicated to the unborn child (published in *The Green Wave*, 1948), and "Night Feeding" (published in her *Selected Poems*, 1951) show her claiming motherhood as a subject appropriate for serious literature.

Throughout the 1950s and early 1960s, while raising her young son (she returned with her child to New York in 1951) and teaching at Sarah Lawrence College, Rukeyser continued to write prolifically—poems, stories, children's books, film treatments, radio scripts, plays—but she was able to publish only a small part of her substantial output. During this time, a new school of critical theory was gaining authority. The New Criticism defined the poem as a world in itself, a self-contained organization of words and sounds, of formal negotiations of irony and ambiguity. To look *into* the poem, or to use the poem to look into the world in which it was written, the New Critics said, was to fall prey to the "personal heresy." (The term is the critic Cleanth Brooks's.) In some respects, Rukeyser's 1949 *The Life of Poetry* was her anti–New Criticism manifesto. With the New Criticism's continued hegemony, her work, replete with what could be described as personal heresy, went from being denigrated to dismissed. She was called sloppy, vague, self-indulgent. Her social concerns were considered passé, or, in the era of McCarthyism, "un-American." It took her more than half a dozen years, in this climate, to find a publisher for *One Life* (1957), her mythopoetic biography of 1940 presidential candidate Wendell Willkie, a book that Rukeyser called "a story and a song." Moreover, in 1964, at the age of fifty, Rukeyser suffered a debilitating stroke that robbed her of her powers of speech.

"THE WORLD SPLIT OPEN": 1968 AND BEYOND

By 1968, Rukeyser had battled herself back to health. A novelistic memoir, *The Orgy*, completed before her stroke, had been published in 1965. The publication of her first collection of poems after her illness, *The Speed of Darkness* (1968), coincided with the emergence of the second wave of the women's movement. The language of these poems, urgent, distilled, direct rather than dense, struck a chord in a new generation of women poets. They found in Rukeyser, and in her daring, self-interrogating poems, the neglected pioneer they had been seeking in their own efforts at speech.

"What would happen if one woman told the truth about her life? / The world would split open," and "No more masks!," lines from Rukeyser's poems "Kathe Kollwitz" and "The Poem as Mask," respectively, yielded the titles of two of the earliest and most influential feminist poetry anthologies published in the 1970s (*The World Split Open* and *No More Masks!*). In the last twelve years of her life, Rukeyser was an active antiwar protestor, traveling to

Hanoi, Vietnam, with the poet Denise Levertov and the activist Jane Hart. She published her speculative biography of the English mathematician Thomas Hariot; helped found the Teachers & Writers Collaborative in New York City; served as president of PEN American Center, and produced two more collections of poetry, *Breaking Open* (1973) and *The Gates* (1976). She dedicated her energies to numerous organizations committed to the struggle for social justice. In 1977 she was the recipient of both the Copernicus Award from the Academy of American Poets and the Shelley Memorial Award for lifetime achievement from the Poetry Society of America. She was scheduled to deliver an address to the Gay and Lesbian Caucus at the Modern Language Association's 1978 conference, where it was anticipated that she would publicly acknowledge her bisexuality and the sustaining influence that her love for women had had on her life, but she was too ill to attend the event. A series of smaller but damaging strokes, coupled with complications from diabetes, had seriously compromised her health. On 12 February 1980, soon after the publication of her 588-page *Collected Poems*, Rukeyser died in New York City at the age of sixty-six.

AN EVOLVING ASSESSMENT

Soon after Rukeyser's death, much of her work fell out of print, until the publication of *Out of Silence: Selected Poems* (1992), a volume of Rukeyser's poetry edited by Kate Daniels, and *A Muriel Rukeyser Reader* (1994), edited by Jan Heller Levi. These were followed by the Paris Press reissues of *The Life of Poetry* (1996) and *The Orgy* (1997). At the turn of the twenty-first century, Rukeyser's pioneering achievement, frequently sidelined in the past, is beginning to be more fully acknowledged. As expansive as Whitman, as subversive as Dickinson, she carried on and enlarged the American tradition of interrogating authority through a radical poetics of inclusiveness. As she herself once remarked, in what can serve as an incisive characterization of her contribution, "It is not that I bring things together, it is that I will not let things be torn apart."

[*See also* Long Poem, The.]

WORKS

POETRY

Theory of Flight (1935)
U.S. 1 (1938)
A Turning Wind (1939)
Beast in View (1944)
The Green Wave (1948)

Selected Poems (1951)
One Life (1957)
Body of Waking (1958)
Waterlily Fire: Poems, 1935–1962 (1962)
The Speed of Darkness (1968)
Breaking Open (1973)
The Gates (1976)
The Collected Poems of Muriel Rukeyser (1979)
Out of Silence: Selected Poems (1992)
A Muriel Rukeyser Reader (1994)

PROSE

Willard Gibbs (1942)
The Life of Poetry (1949; reissued 1996)

The Orgy (1965; reissued 1997)
The Traces of Thomas Hariot (1971)

FURTHER READING

Herzog, Anne F., and Janet E. Kaufman, eds. *How Shall We Tell Each Other of the Poet?: The Life and Writing of Muriel Rukeyser*. New York, 1999. The only book-length collection of critical essays about, and tributes (including reminiscences and poems) to Rukeyser. A valuable resource. Includes work by forty writers and scholars.

Kertesz, Louise. *The Poetic Vision of Muriel Rukeyser*. Baton Rouge, La., and London, 1980. A thoughtful critical study of Rukeyser's career and contributions.

J. D. SALINGER

by Brian Henry

J. D. Salinger's biography is in many ways a nonbiography, for the writer's fiercely defended privacy has thwarted nearly all biographical efforts since the 1950s. Thus, the information available about Salinger's life is largely that which was available in the 1950s and 1960s, before he withdrew from public life and stopped publishing. Although he published into the 1960s, Salinger began to resist his status as a public figure in the early 1950s; he has never agreed to a conventional interview, has forbidden his publisher from putting his photograph on his books—his photograph appears only on the first two editions of his first book—and has denied permission to reprint his work in anthologies. It seems both unfortunate and admirable that one of America's most beloved and enduring writers would decide to disappear from view,

leaving only his earlier works behind. (Although he has not published anything since 1965, Salinger reportedly continues to write for pleasure.)

Yet this reclusiveness has generated even more interest in Salinger, and therefore has not gone unchallenged by various reporters and writers. Salinger was the subject of a failed interview in *Life* magazine in 1961 ("The Search for the Mysterious J. D. Salinger: The Recluse in the Rye"). In 1980, Betty Eppes, a young woman from Louisiana, managed to meet Salinger for a brief conversation and published her account of their meeting in the *Baton Rouge Advocate*. (A longer version later appeared in the *Paris Review*.) Others have attempted with less success to learn why Salinger no longer publishes or makes public appearances. The most concerted effort to write Salinger's life,

J. D. Salinger. (© *Ted Russell/Corbis Sygma*)

Ian Hamilton's book-length biography, never appeared because Salinger sued Hamilton's publisher, Random House, in 1986 to prohibit the reprinting of personal correspondence, thus blocking the book from publication. Hamilton then wrote *In Search of J. D. Salinger* (1988), an examination of the biographical process and his experience writing Salinger's biography. To date, only one biography of Salinger—Paul Alexander's *Salinger: A Biography* (1999)—has been published; it relies considerably upon Hamilton's research but does not use any material to which Salinger holds the copyright. Despite Alexander's book, still very little is known about Salinger's life, an unusual situation for such a popular writer.

LIFE AND CAREER

Jerome David (J. D.) Salinger was born on 1 January 1919 to a Jewish father, Sol Salinger, and a Scots-Irish Christian mother, Marie Jillich Salinger. He had one sibling, a sister named Doris who was eight years older. After attending public schools in New York City, he enrolled in the private McBurney School in Manhattan in 1932 and failed out. He then attended the Valley Forge Military Academy in Pennsylvania from 1934 to 1936 and received his diploma. After briefly working in the pork business—his father's trade—in Poland, he returned to the United States, studying for a short time at New York University and Ursinus College in 1937 and 1938, respectively. In 1939 he took a course in short-story writing at Columbia University with Whit Burnett, the editor of *Story* magazine. Burnett encouraged Salinger's talent, and in 1940 he accepted Salinger's "The Young Folks" for *Story*, which was Salinger's first publication. This represented the beginning of Salinger's professional writing life, and he subsequently published short stories in magazines such as *Collier's*, *Esquire*, *The Saturday Evening Post*, and *The New Yorker*.

In 1942, Salinger was drafted into the U.S. Army, in which he attained the rank of staff sergeant and worked in counterintelligence. Salinger landed on Utah Beach in Normandy and fought in the Battle of the Bulge. While in the army he continued publishing short stories, and his publication rate accelerated after the war with stories in *Harper's*, *Mademoiselle*, *Cosmopolitan*, and *Good Housekeeping* as well as in *The New Yorker*, which became the primary outlet for Salinger's short fiction from the mid-1940s onward. His first marriage, to a European doctor, was short-lived, and he returned to New York City in 1946 after being honorably discharged from the army. Salinger lived with his parents in the city and worked

on *The Catcher in the Rye* (1951). In 1948 he moved to Westport, Connecticut, and five years later to Cornish, New Hampshire.

On 16 July 1951 his first and only novel, *The Catcher in the Rye*, appeared to widespread acclaim. In 1953 he published *Nine Stories* and met a young, English-born woman, Claire Douglas, whom he married in February 1955. They had two children: Margaret, born in December 1955, and Matthew, born in February 1960. After a difficult marriage, Salinger and his wife divorced in 1967. He became romantically involved with the writer Joyce Maynard and the television actress Elaine Joyce, among other women, and later married Colleen O'Neill, a woman decades younger than he. In 2000 his daughter Margaret published a memoir, *Dream Catcher*, that focuses mainly on her childhood and adolescence. It provides occasional glimpses of her father, whom she describes as charming and humorous but difficult and inaccessible; but by focusing on its author, Margaret's book fails to divulge much meaningful information about Salinger's life apart from hers.

Salinger's first two books attracted copious attention from critics and scholars while building a devoted following among general readers. *Franny and Zooey*, which consists of two stories that originally appeared in *The New Yorker* in 1955 and 1957, was published in 1961 and remained at the top of best-seller lists for ten months, thus achieving commercial success more rapidly than did The Catcher in the Rye. Salinger's work was the subject of a 1957 symposium in *The Nation*, and the first book-length critical work on Salinger's fiction, Frederick L. Gwynn and Joseph L. Blotner's *The Fiction of J. D. Salinger*, appeared in 1958. Salinger's last published book, *Raise High the Roof Beam, Carpenters and Seymour—An Introduction*, appeared in 1963. Both pieces were first published in *The New Yorker*, in 1955 and 1959, respectively. In 1965, Salinger published the epistolary novella "Hapworth 16, 1924" in *The New Yorker*, his first work in a magazine since 1959; almost uniformly dismissed by critics, at the beginning of the twenty-first century it remains his last publication.

THE CATCHER IN THE RYE

The Catcher in the Rye was a reasonable, but not resounding, commercial and critical success. A Book-of-the-Month Club selection, the novel was reviewed widely, if sometimes diffidently, in such influential newspapers and magazines as *The New York Times*, *Saturday Review of Literature*, *The Nation*, and *The New Republic*. While the reviews ranged from pure enthusiasm to moral denunciation, most critics offered approval. These initial critical responses to the novel did not foretell the emergence of *The Catcher in the Rye* as a minor classic and one of the most popular novels of the twentieth century. Since its appearance, the novel has sold more than 60 million copies worldwide. Alternately condemned and canonized, *The Catcher in the Rye* was published as a Modern Library edition in 1958, yet at the same time was being banned by schools and libraries around the country. As Joel Salzberg notes in his introduction to *Critical Essays on Salinger's* The Catcher in the Rye (1990), Salinger's novel "has enjoyed a readership that has transcended the boundaries of age, education, and culture, a phenomenon unparalleled in the history of modern and contemporary literature." Thus, the novel became an ideal vehicle for critics to explore postwar American culture along with its literature.

Early critics remarked on the novel's contemporaneity, social commentary, satire, balance of humor and despair, and portrayal of postwar adolescence. The generation of young readers (high school and university students) who admired the novel when it was first published established a future generation of critics and scholars essential to the book's ongoing critical reputation and canonization as an American classic. The first essay to place the novel in the tradition of great literature, "J. D. Salinger: Some Crazy Cliff" (1956), by Arthur Heiserman and James E. Miller Jr., examined *The Catcher in the Rye* in light of the epic tradition and generated intense scholarly interest. Gwynn and Blotner's *The Fiction of J. D. Salinger* was the first book-length study of Salinger's fiction and one of the most important. Critics approached the book from numerous angles, leading George Steiner, in a 1959 article in *The Nation* called "The Salinger Industry," to criticize both Salinger's modest literary achievements and the opportunistic critics writing about him. Nevertheless, Salinger criticism continued to appear regularly until the 1970s. Donald P. Costello introduced linguistic considerations of the novel, and Carl F. Strauch brought a strong formalist reading to it in his influential essay "Kings in the Back Row: Meaning through Structure—A Reading of Salinger's *The Catcher in the Rye*" (1961). Subsequent criticism approached the novel through Marxist, Freudian, psychoanalytic, and Buddhist lenses, revealing how many ways one can read *The Catcher in the Rye*. By 1980, critical writing on the novel was influenced primarily by pedagogical imperatives

or French literary theory, especially deconstruction and Lacanian psycholinguistics.

On a Saturday just before Christmas vacation, the novel's protagonist, sixteen-year-old Holden Caulfield, has failed out of Pencey Prep, a private boarding school in Pennsylvania. He spends most of the evening in his room, engaging in banter with other boys and eventually instigating a fistfight, which he loses, with his roommate, Stradlater, because the promiscuous Stradlater has been on a date with the object of Holden's (largely platonic) affection, Jane Gallagher. Holden gathers some of his belongings, sells his typewriter to another student, and, depressed and defiant, takes a train to Manhattan with the plan to spend a few days in the city before his parents learn of his expulsion. He thus sets into motion a journey that pits him against the falseness of the adult world and reveals him as one of the most memorable characters in twentieth-century American fiction.

After arriving in the city, Holden rents a cheap hotel room and starts drinking. He later tries to ingratiate himself with three older, intoxicated women who leave him with the bill. He hires and then refuses the services of a young prostitute, whose pimp coerces more money out of him and physically attacks him. On Sunday, Holden goes on a failure of a date, and after wandering the city he returns to his parents' apartment while they are out and talks to his sister, Phoebe. After a disillusioning experience with one of his former teachers, Holden spends the night in Grand Central Station. The next morning he goes to his sister's school to tell her he is running away but decides instead to return home with her. Throughout the weekend, Holden, feeling increasingly alienated, tries to reconnect with old friends, all of whom disappoint him. By the end of the novel, the reader learns that Holden is in a mental institution in California relating the events of that weekend to a doctor.

Repeatedly described by critics as a postwar Huckleberry Finn because of his age, informal way of speaking, and adolescent cynicism, Holden reacts violently against what he perceives as false, or "phony"—especially hypocrisy, snobbery, conceit, empty formality and convention, class privilege, and pretension—in the upper-middle-class culture in which he has been raised. Conversely, he embraces what he perceives as beautiful, particularly innocence, and thus is far more fond of children than of adults. His attraction to innocence emerges from his own loss of innocence and fall into adulthood. Many critics, including Ihab Hassan, Jonathan Baumbach, Joseph L. Blotner, and Frederick L. Gwynn, consider

Holden a quixotic, even saintly character—one destined to inspiring failure. Other critics, such as Peter J. Seng, consider Holden more tragic than saintly. Helen Weinberg has linked Holden to Franz Kafka's work, deeming him a modern hero pitted against society in search of truth but unable to find it. Several critics, including Warren French and A. Robert Lee, have written about Holden as a young artist, or an artist in the making, thus drawing a parallel between him and the Irish writer James Joyce's Stephen Dedalus, the protagonist of *A Portrait of the Artist as a Young Man* (1916). Some early critics equated Holden with his creator, reading Holden as a teenage version of the author, a position that Salinger did not discourage in interviews in the early 1950s.

Holden considers himself "crazy" and a "madman" and uses those words repeatedly to describe himself. Although he has failed out of school, Holden is unusually intelligent and sensitive. He still mourns the death of his younger brother, Allie, by leukemia, and he adores his younger sister, Phoebe. His perception of the world is sophisticated, but his ability to articulate his thoughts and feelings remains that of an adolescent, characterized largely by slang, obscenities, and clichés. He also indulges in numerous digressions that, while sometimes distracting, illuminate him as a character. Holden repeatedly sees through pretense, but must resort to words like "phony" to deflate what he sees. ("Phony," or some version of the word, appears in the novel more than forty times.) Despite its charm and specific quirks, his language is inadequate to his vision, a failure that makes Holden a sympathetic, but not pitiable, figure. Holden's strongest subject in school was English, and he reads literature—Thomas Hardy, F. Scott Fitzgerald, Ring Lardner, Isak Dinesen—and admires his brother, D.B., who is a writer. Holden's rejection of standard English in his speech stems partly from the fact that the educated language addressed to him—mainly by his teachers—is used only to convey platitudes and empty advice. Holden rejects not only these messages, but their means (proper English).

The novel, then, pits Holden against the corruption of the adult world, a corruption that appears in teachers, former friends, would-be girlfriends, and the doorman-pimp and prostitute at Holden's hotel. The only adults who do not disappoint Holden are two nuns, whose poverty nevertheless depresses him. Children are the only people with whom Holden feels a connection, but because he is on the cusp of adulthood, he cannot move freely in the world of children. Although many critics consider Holden cynical, it is remarkable that a teenager in his situation cares enough about the world to protest what he perceives as injustices. Continually confronted by falsehood, Holden seeks the truth, only to be disappointed by everyone he meets. Even his beloved former teacher, Mr. Antolini, fails him when Holden goes to his apartment for advice. Although Antolini has plenty of advice for the young man, he also makes what Holden perceives as a sexual advance at him (Antolini's intentions remain ambiguous), thus shattering Holden's confidence in the last authority figure whom he respects. For Holden, childhood remains the only place where innocence, and therefore truth, can exist, and much of his pain in the novel derives from his recognition of the disappearance of his own childhood.

This desire to remain childishly innocent even in adulthood appears most powerfully in the scene that gives the book its title. When Phoebe challenges Holden with the assertion that he does not like anything, he has difficulty answering her, and when he does, he says, "I like Allie.... And I like doing what I'm doing right now. Sitting here with you, and talking." But Phoebe points out that Allie is dead, and she asks Holden what he would like to be. Holden tells her he imagines "all these little kids playing some game in this big field of rye" near "some crazy cliff," and he is there to protect the children by stopping them from going over the cliff. "I'd just be the catcher in the rye," he says, reflecting his desire to protect innocence by protecting children. This concern for innocence explains why Holden is so upset by Stradlater going on a date with Jane Gallagher, why he declines sex with a young prostitute, why he worries about his mother's emotional state if he were to die, and why he stays with Phoebe rather than run away at the end of the novel. Despite Holden's feelings of alienation throughout *The Catcher in the Rye*, the ending emerges as affirmative, since Holden is moved to feel "so damn happy all of a sudden" by the simplest of pleasures—Phoebe riding a horse on a carousel in Central Park—and to recognize the centrality of love to human life. *The Catcher in the Rye*, then, emerges not only as a critique of postwar American culture but also as an affirmation of the beauty and necessity of innocence.

THE SHORT FICTION

Salinger's other three published books—*Nine Stories* (1953), *Franny and Zooey* (1961), and *Raise High the Roof Beam, Carpenters and Seymour—An Introduction* (1963)—are collections of short fiction. Although Salinger had published over twenty stories in national magazines by the time he assembled his first volume of short fiction, he considered only nine of those stories worthy of preserving in book form. (Seven of these stories originally appeared in *The New Yorker* and one appeared in *Harper's*.) The difference between *Nine Stories* and the next two books is profound and surprising, despite the later work's partial origin in the earlier work. *Nine Stories* presents nine relatively conventional, discrete, yet loosely related short stories, but *Franny and Zooey* and *Raise High the Roof Beam, Carpenters and Seymour—An Introduction* demonstrate determined stylistic innovation and focus exclusively on Salinger's most enduring obsession—the children of the Glass family. Because Salinger's last published work centers on the Glass children, the Glass stories retain an essential place in his oeuvre even though their aesthetic achievement does not always match their ambition.

NINE STORIES. The critical reception of *Nine Stories* was more consistently positive than that of *The Catcher in the Rye*. As with all of Salinger's books, *Nine Stories* was widely reviewed, most notably by Eudora Welty in *The New York Times Book Review*. All of the pieces in *Nine Stories* are concerned with the loss of innocence and the force of corruption. The adult world becomes the site of corruption in these stories, and childhood becomes a temporary stay against corruption. Even the innocence of childhood, however, cannot protect all children from the behavior of adults, as "Down at the Dinghy" demonstrates. Four-year-old Lionel Tannenbaum, daughter of Boo Boo (née Glass) Tannenbaum, has run away from home to the dinghy near the house because he has overheard the family maid call his father "a big—sloppy—kike." Although he does not understand the word and actually mistakes it for "kite," the hatred in the maid's voice is sufficient to terrify the boy. The specific situation is resolved when Lionel's mother manages to coax him out of the boat, but the general situation—anti-Semitism and the young boy's despair when confronted by the ugliness of the adult world—remains unresolved.

The intersection of childhood and adulthood in "Uncle Wiggily in Connecticut" deeply affects its protagonist. Two former college roommates, Eloise Wengler and Mary Jane, are drinking excessively at Eloise's house and talking about their college days during World War II. Mary Jane had married a man in the air force and divorced him after three months, never to marry again; Eloise had been expelled from college after being discovered in an elevator with a soldier, Walter Glass, who later was killed in an accident in Japan after the war. In their conversation,

Eloise reveals herself as bitter and insensitive but also nostalgic, especially for Walter, whom she still loves. Eloise is unhappy in her marriage—she does not respect her husband—and with her daughter, Ramona, who resembles her father. Ramona also has vision problems and lives primarily in her own imagination, therefore existing separately from Eloise's world. The crisis in the story occurs after Mary Jane loses consciousness and Eloise, having acted cruelly toward her daughter, her husband, and her maid, recognizes herself as the horrible person she has become when she sees her former self in her daughter. By indulging in nostalgic remembrance with Mary Jane, she has illuminated the contrast between her married life and her youth, between the miserable person she is and the hopeful person she was. Eloise then awakes Mary Jane to ask if she had not been "a nice girl" during her first year of college. The implication—that she no longer is "nice"—is clear, and the self-knowledge she attains in the story makes her a pitiable figure rather than a merely reprehensible one.

Salinger's most celebrated story, "For Esmé—With Love and Squalor," concerns the mental and emotional rehabilitation of Sergeant X, stationed in Bavaria after the Allied victory in World War II. Even though he has survived the war, he has not emerged "with all his faculties intact." While reading a book by the infamous Nazi Joseph Goebbels, *Die Zeit ohne Beispiel* (The Time without Example, 1941), he finds an inscription, written in German by a middle-aged Nazi woman whom he recently has arrested, that reads, "Dear God, life is hell." Because of the context, she clearly means Goebbels, and therefore Hitler, when she writes to "God." Beneath this inscription, X appends his own statement, borrowed from the Russian writer Fyodor Dostoyevsky's novel, *The Brothers Karamazov* (1879–1880): "Fathers and teachers, I ponder, 'What is hell?' I maintain that it is the suffering of being unable to love." Because Goebbels and the Nazis prohibited the possibility of love by refusing to recognize humanity, X's inscription can be read as a reaction against Nazism as well as an affirmation of human love. This affirmation becomes crucial to him because he is surrounded by superficial emotions—his wife, brother, and mother-in-law at home, his fellow soldiers in Bavaria—and the love he needs emerges later in the story when he meets an aristocratic thirteen-year-old English girl, Esmé, at a café. When she meets X, Esmé asks him to write a story about "squalor" for her. During their conversation, she reveals herself as both intelligent and sensitive, and her humane gesture thirty-eight days later—she sends X her deceased father's watch with a friendly letter—rescues X from the drudgeries of military life and from the despair into which he has sunk.

"A Perfect Day for Bananafish" also portrays a veteran of World War II, Seymour Glass, having difficulty coping with everyday existence, but the outcome of his crisis is less redemptive than Sergeant X's. A psychiatrist has told Seymour's father-in-law that "there's a chance—a very *great* chance . . . that Seymour may completely lose control of himself." Seymour's difficulties are compounded by his relationship with his shallow wife, Muriel, whom he calls "Miss Spiritual Tramp of 1948." Seymour and Muriel have gone to Florida for a vacation, and while Muriel talks to her mother on the telephone about him, Seymour is at the beach, where a young girl, Sybil Carpenter, engages his attention and delights him with her imagination. Seymour tells her a story about bananafish, which go into holes to eat bananas and often eat so many that they cannot leave the hole and eventually die. Seymour takes Sybil into the ocean on a float, and she claims to see a bananafish with six bananas in its mouth. Seemingly ecstatic, Seymour kisses the arch of her foot and quickly returns her to the beach. He goes back to his hotel room and shoots himself in the temple while his wife sleeps on the bed next to his. The abruptness of his suicide makes the story shocking and effective, but its brevity does not allow Salinger to imbue Seymour with much depth. In his next two books, *Franny and Zooey* and *Raise High the Roof Beam, Carpenters and Seymour—An Introduction*, Salinger develops Seymour as the spiritual and emotional center of the Glass family.

THE GLASS STORIES. Although three of the Glass children (Seymour, Walter, and Boo Boo) appear in three of the stories ("A Perfect Day for Bananafish," "Uncle Wiggily in Connecticut," and "Down at the Dinghy") in *Nine Stories*, Salinger does not treat them at length until "Franny" and "Zooey," which focus on the two youngest Glass children, both very gifted and tormented. All the Glass children have performed on the radio quiz show "It's a Wise Child," and they are "descended from an astonishingly long and motley double-file of professional entertainers." Their parents, Les Glass and Bessie Gallagher, were Irish-Jewish vaudevillians who performed together as Gallagher & Glass. Yet most of the Glass children are also intensely spiritual, and therefore combine the glittery surface of American culture and the depth of religion and philosophy. The oldest child, Seymour, was the spiritual teacher for Buddy, Franny, and Zooey, all of whom know a tremendous amount about Eastern religion and Western

philosophy because of him. The incredibly intelligent Seymour entered Columbia University at age fifteen and became a professor and poet before being drafted. Buddy has become a published writer, Zooey a television actor, and Franny a college student and emerging actress. The other Glass children—Boo Boo and the twins, Waker and Walter—are left largely undeveloped in Salinger's published work.

In "Franny," Franny is in the midst of a spiritual crisis that has led to a nervous breakdown, and in "Zooey" her brother Zooey tries to compel her back to a normal state. Franny's crisis has ruined her date with her boyfriend, Lane Coutell, a smug college student whose pretension Franny deflates at every opportunity, even as she apologizes for her behavior. Uncompromising in her abhorrence of ego wherever it appears, Franny is reminiscent of Holden Caulfield but is altogether more articulate. Despite her eloquence, she incessantly repeats "Lord Jesus Christ, have mercy on me" to herself in the hope that the repetition of the words will deliver her to a higher spiritual state. At the end of the story, she loses consciousness in the restaurant and awakes, still murmuring her prayer.

"Zooey," which is described by its narrator, Buddy, as "a sort of prose home movie" rather than a short story, is more formally ambitious and challenging than "Franny." The piece's unconventional structure, method of narration, and lack of economy were criticized at the time of publication; however, these elements mark "Zooey" as an early move by Salinger into the territory of postmodernism. The first half of "Zooey" occurs in the bathroom, during a conversation between the bathing Zooey and his mother, who sits on the toilet seat talking to her son. The comedy of this situation and their conversation contrasts with the piece's other, more profound and more emotional dialogue, between Franny—supine on the couch—and Zooey—alternately standing and lying on the floor. After failing to help Franny, Zooey goes into Seymour's room, where he uses the telephone—still working and listed under Seymour's name—to call Franny, pretending to be Buddy. Franny recognizes his ruse and Zooey, possibly inspired by being in Seymour's room, finally succeeds in communicating to Franny a way out of her impasse when he recalls Seymour's admonition, when they were performing on the radio show, to shine his shoes for "the Fat Lady," whom Zooey imagines as a pathetic figure in desperate need. Similarly, Seymour had told Franny to be funny for the Fat Lady. When Zooey tells Franny that everyone is the Fat Lady and that the Fat Lady is Jesus Christ, Franny feels able to connect the surfaces of her life with its spirituality, thus resolving her crisis.

"Raise High the Roof Beam, Carpenters" depicts Seymour's wedding day through Buddy's perspective. Seymour does not appear at his wedding, thus ruining the ceremony. Buddy, who has taken the train to New York City from his army base in Georgia, inexplicably finds himself on his way to the bride's parents' apartment in a limousine with the furious matron of honor, her husband, an aunt of the bride, and a great uncle of the bride. During the ride, the matron of honor harangues Seymour, referring to him as both a "latent homosexual" and "a really schizoid personality" and criticizing his reason for wanting to postpone the marriage. (He told the bride he was too happy.) When the limousine is stopped by a parade, the group leaves the car to find air conditioning and a telephone so the matron of honor can tell the bride why they have not arrived yet. Because Buddy and Seymour's apartment is nearby, Buddy offers to take them there, where he finds Seymour's diary. Reading it in the bathroom, Buddy finds Seymour's statement, "I'm a kind of paranoiac in reverse. I suspect people of plotting to make me happy." After the matron of honor uses the telephone, she informs the group that Seymour and Muriel have eloped, thus solving the problem of the nonmarriage. Of course, since Salinger's readers know that Seymour later commits suicide, his earthly happiness is necessarily temporary.

In "Seymour—An Introduction," the narrator, Buddy, is now forty years old and a writer-in-residence at a women's college in upstate New York. Buddy's aim in writing the piece is to introduce the reader to Seymour, but he admits that his "asides run rampant" and advises the "readers who seriously require only the most restrained, most classical, and possibly deftest methods of having their attention drawn" to "leave now." This self-consciousness manifests itself in direct addresses to the reader, self-admonitions, comments on the text as it is being composed, and frequent digressions, which cover such topics as Chinese and Japanese poetry, Seymour's own poetry, and large families. Although Buddy acknowledges that his digressions threaten "to turn this whole composition into a fool's soliloquy," this style, combined with Salinger's fondness for the footnote, the quotation, and such flourishes as a "bouquet of very early-blooming parentheses: ((((())))," make the story a proto-postmodernist work. Buddy justifies his unwieldy narrative structure by asserting that Seymour's complexity "lends itself to no legitimate sort of narrative

compactness." And he claims that his own "extremely pressing personal needs" in introducing Seymour forbid him the short story form, which "eats up fat little undetached writers" like himself. Rather, "Seymour" is written in "semi-diary form" and ends only when Buddy senses that his "time is *up.*" "Seymour" ultimately emerges less as an "introduction" than as hagiography, the portrayal of the life of a saint figure. However, Seymour's sainthood has been compromised by his suicide, a mortal sin, and Buddy's determination to make a saint out of Seymour becomes an enigmatic, perhaps futile act. Salinger's subsequent refusal to publish has kept Seymour an enigma.

[*See also* Short Story in America, The.]

SELECTED WORKS

The Catcher in the Rye (1951)
Nine Stories (1953)
Franny and Zooey (1961)
Raise High the Roof Beam, Carpenters and Seymour—An Introduction (1963)

FURTHER READING

Alexander, Paul. *Salinger: A Biography.* Los Angeles, 1999. The fullest biography of Salinger.

Alsen, Eberhard. *Salinger's Glass Stories as a Composite Novel.* Troy, N.Y., 1983. A persuasive reading of the Glass stories as a novel rather than as discrete works of short fiction.

French, Warren. *J. D. Salinger, Revisited.* Boston, 1988. French's second book on Salinger and a reassessment of his initial evaluations of Salinger's career. Especially useful is French's consideration of *Nine Stories* as a short-story cycle.

Grunwald, Henry Anatole, ed. *Salinger: A Critical and Personal Portrait.* New York, 1962. A diverse collection of critical essays with a biographical portrait, all of which is accompanied by Grunwald's incisive and spirited commentary.

Gwynn, Frederick L., and Joseph L. Blotner. *The Fiction of J. D. Salinger.* Pittsburgh, Pa., 1958. An influential monograph on Salinger's fiction, establishing the mainstream critical view of Salinger at the time.

Hamilton, Ian. *In Search of J. D. Salinger.* New York, 1988. A book not about Salinger, but about Hamilton's efforts to publish a biography of Salinger, which failed because of a lawsuit by Salinger.

Salinger, Margaret. *Dream Catcher: A Memoir.* New York, 2000. A poorly written, solipsistic memoir by Salinger's daughter that focuses on Salinger only as her father. Illuminating only for its personal view of Salinger.

Salzberg, Joel, ed. *Critical Essays on Salinger's* The Catcher in the Rye. Boston, 1990. A chronologically arranged collection of essential essays on the novel.

Strauch, Carl F. "Kings in the Back Row: Meaning through Structure—A Reading of Salinger's *The Catcher in the Rye*." Wisconsin Studies in Contemporary Literature (1961): 9–30.

Sublette, Jack R. *J. D. Salinger: An Annotated Bibliography, 1938–1981.* New York, 1984. The most comprehensive and useful bibliography of Salinger's work published to date. More than fourteen hundred entries list the various editions of Salinger's published writings, some letters, and unpublished writings as well as major works on Salinger, including biographies, critical books, book chapters, scholarly essays, book reviews, theses and dissertations, foreign criticism, and other material relevant to Salinger and his writing.

Wenke, John. *J. D. Salinger: A Study of the Short Fiction.* Boston, 1991. A multifaceted book on Salinger's short fiction, including not only essays on the short fiction but also "biographical reflections" on Salinger by Joseph Wenke and brief excerpts from other critics' writings.

See also the article on *The Catcher in the Rye*, immediately following.

J. D. SALINGER'S
THE CATCHER IN THE RYE

by Ted Weesner Jr.

Holden Caulfield, in the first chapter of *The Catcher in the Rye* (1951), tells the reader, "I felt like I was sort of disappearing." Indeed, throughout this cult classic novel, Holden faces a darkening existential crisis, with oblivion often threatening. And yet J. D. Salinger's best-known literary construction—and the novel he roams—have hardly disappeared. In the rarest of literary feats, Holden may be more alive today than he was upon birth in 1951.

AN ENDURING CLASSIC

Such unusual endurance springs from several places. Foremost, the novel is a masterfully composed work of art. Despite a colloquial tone—animated by Holden's idiosyncratic voice—it is a rare scene, paragraph, even word that feels extraneous. Because of this, and because the novel so poignantly captures the bewilderment of adolescence, *Catcher* has remained a staple of high school English classes. It has even been suggested that teachers assign the novel in an ongoing cycle of nostalgia, students and future English teachers wanting in turn to pass along a piece of their own memory. This literary daisy chain has not been difficult to sustain, as the novel's sensibility and pitch-perfect humor remain current.

Meanwhile, Salinger's withdrawal into the woods of New Hampshire, perhaps as much as anything, has endowed the novel with mystique. In fact, Holden anticipates his creator's future precisely when he floats his own escape fantasy: "[I'll] build me a little cabin somewhere with the dough I made and live there for the rest of my life," he says, "right near the woods." Certainly, Salinger's disappearance—the embodiment of Holden's philosophy—has managed to fuel the sense that Salinger is, in fact, Holden. Here is a character not only with sustained literary lifeblood; he actually exists! Or so one cannot help think.

The novel falls into four parts: Holden's last day at Pencey Prep is followed by his journey through the night in Manhattan, which is followed by his wandering throughout the next day and night. This picaresque journey ends with his first real human connection, a renewed bonding with his beloved sister, Phoebe. Having hit bottom, healing for Holden finally begins.

SCHOOL'S OUT

The reader bonds quickly with Holden, which is to say that Salinger wastes no words bringing him to life. In the first sentence his voice and vision, his attitude and operating philosophy, are in place. Speaking to the reader, Holden warns that he will not talk about his past—"all that David Copperfield kind of crap"—rather, he wants to tell us about "this madman stuff that happened to me around last Christmas." With that we are in his head and the dramatic terms of the novel are set.

The action opens with Holden standing on a hilltop overlooking Pencey Prep, the school from which he has just been expelled. Though it may appear he takes lightly his latest scholastic disaster—his ongoing biting commentary suggesting a hilltop view at any elevation—there are signs he is in deeper psychic trouble. If he has the mind of a highly perceptive adult, his emotional life is that of a disconnected, lonely, confused sixteen-year-old boy. He's "trying to feel some kind of good-by," a good-bye he has missed in the past and a hint of the searing grief he has avoided.

Human encounters at Pencey Prep provide little solace. First there is a visit to his history teacher, Spenser, who barely listens to him, making the extended scene wickedly funny and displaying the balance Salinger so often strikes between humorous attitude and a gulf of hidden feeling. When Spenser calls his parents "grand," Holden thinks, "There's a word I really hate. It's a phony," the word "phony" being perhaps the one most associated with the novel and an example of the falseness Holden sees in most adults. To calm himself as Spenser drones on, Holden pictures the ducks in Central Park, one of several iconic symbols that point to the purer, more immediate experience of a child.

Interactions with his dorm mates are no more sustaining; Holden's inanimate hunting hat provides the closest thing to comfort. Unlike Ackley, his annoying neighbor,

Holden's roommate, Stradlater, is probing the darker territory of adulthood, "snowing" women, having sex. That he is pursuing Jane, a girl Holden likes, terrifies him. This tension between the innocence of childhood and the compromised allures of adulthood does not cease.

While Stradlater is on his date with Jane, Holden occupies himself by writing a composition about his dead brother Allie's baseball glove. Here is a glimpse of the white-hot source of Holden's despair. After Allie died, Holden slept in the garage and "broke all the goddamn windows with my fist, just for the hell of it." Writing about the glove gives him satisfaction, a rare Caulfield sensation indeed. When Stradlater returns and implies he fooled around with Jane, Holden goes crazy. In effect, he forces Stradlater to beat him, as Ackley offers no safe haven. At this point Holden feels "so lonesome" that he thinks "I almost wished I were dead." Now, after midnight, he decides to "get the hell out of Pencey" and find a cheap hotel in New York for a few days until he must face his parents. Leaving the dorm, Holden yells, *"Sleep tight, ya morons!"*

IN THE DARK

After Holden's train ride into the city—he chats with a classmate's mother, embroidering a hilarious story about him—Holden makes his way to the "very crumby" Edmont Hotel. His hunger to connect flows through these next seven chapters, whether with a cabby, a waiter, a girl. Peeping out his hotel window, he spots a man "in a very tight black evening dress" and a couple squirting liquid at each other, exacerbating his loneliness. About sex he says, "I don't *like* the idea," yet he is drawn to contact, mind in regular battle with hungry body.

Before continuing into the night, Holden recalls his kid sister, Phoebe, the most important character in his life and the sharpest contrast to the sordidness around him. Described in a gorgeous density of detail—she is sweetly innocent, funny, smart—Phoebe will surface significantly toward the end. From this sweetness, Holden springs into darkness, first in the Lavender Room where he bumps up against several women. Outside of the relationship with Phoebe, his interactions with women are troubled and complex: "you fall half in love with them, and then you never know *where* the hell you are." When he recollects a time with Jane—"kissing her all over"—his memory gravitates to the more innocuous pleasure of holding hands.

At the next nightclub, Holden continues an aesthetic critique that is threaded through the novel, this time focusing on Ernie, the pianist, who knows he is good, too good, approaching "something holy." Read carefully, *Catcher* can be seen as Salinger's own guide to artistic creation. His critique does not end with art; Holden lets loose on "all those Ivy League bastards [who] look alike" and a phony former girlfriend of his brother's.

Holden's self-loathing spikes as he glimpses phoniness in himself. After extending a fake good-bye, he thinks "If you want to stay alive, you have to say that stuff." When he considers himself a "very yellow guy," Holden again contemplates suicide, an impulse he seems not able to avoid. The hotel elevator operator, Maurice, arranges for a prostitute to come to Holden's room, and not surprisingly—depression closing in, the dark possibility of sex before him—"sexy was about the *last* thing I was feeling." Instead, he feels sympathy for the girl, just as he feels unspoken sympathy for many he does not like, the unspokenness generating reader sympathy. The prostitute tries to wangle extra money out of him, gets upset, and leaves. In this terribly lonely moment, Holden turns to the solace of remembering Allie, then to prayer. Neither works. Body, mind, now spirit present a relief he cannot grasp. After Maurice returns to shake him down—Holden again asking for violence—he is ready to jump out the window. Yet his own quirkiness, Holden being Holden, saves him. He does not want "a bunch of stupid rubbernecks looking at me when I was all gory."

NOBODY ANYWHERE

Although the night is over, it seems to continue for Holden. In the next six chapters he confronts obstacles often suggesting an implicit Salinger critique. After arranging to meet Sally Hayes, a girl he knows, Holden deposits his bags at Grand Central and runs into two nuns. Here, Salinger turns his sights on the consumerist, conformist ways of the bourgeois. Holden relishes these women who wear steel glasses, eat sparsely, and practice genuine charity, a sharp contrast to Sally's mother, who would help only "if everybody kissed her ass for her when they made a contribution." Again the author's attention turns to aesthetics, first when Holden hunts for an old record for Phoebe, then when he considers actors and the movies. The underlying idea in these critiques of artistic presentation is that the creator spoils the performance if he knows he is good, partly the artist's fault, but also an adoring audience's.

The title of the novel surfaces when Holden spots a family, in particular a boy, walking on the sidewalk. This is a vintage Salinger moment in its capture of pure kidness—contentedly self-enclosed, in the moment—the boy "making out like he was walking a very straight line, the way kids do, and the whole time . . . singing and humming." The lyric he is singing "for the hell of it" includes the novel's title, making Holden feel "not so depressed any more." This theme is maintained when Holden roams the Museum of Natural History looking for Phoebe. The permanent exhibits display what he hankers for: "that everything stayed right where it was. Nobody'd move. . . . Nobody'd be different." It is hard not to think of Allie.

Holden throws himself at Sally, mind again at battle with body. As he puts it, "I'm crazy, I didn't even *like* her much." When they run into an old Ivy League friend of hers, his jealousy nears the Stradlater moment. The stream of loathing continues. When Holden finally reveals his true despair—"I'm in bad shape," he says, "I'm in *lousy* shape"—he proposes an escape fantasy, stunning in that it mirrors Salinger's later actions. They should drive north, he says, and "live somewhere with a brook." To this Sally rings the thudding note of conformity—"You can't just *do* something like that." The reader can feel Holden's heartbeat.

After a diatribe against war, surely informed by Salinger's own experience and perhaps by his alleged nervous breakdown, Holden meets an old classmate at a bar. Luce is an Ivy League intellectual, the type Holden cannot stand, and yet his level of ill ease is so heightened he will take advice from anyone. Of course Luce does not provide it, exhibiting only a lack of morals and compassion. Regardless, Holden grasps for connection. Further drunk, weeping, he heads to Central Park to "see what the hell the ducks were doing." As before, his siblings come to the rescue, first a recollection of Allie, then Phoebe, whom Holden decides he must see "in case I died and all." In what feels like the first heartening action of the novel, Holden starts home.

CATCHING PHOEBE

Only in the last quarter of the book does Salinger devote all of three chapters to a single scene. The space is warranted, however, when one considers the scene's importance. Following so much distress, Phoebe may be keeping Holden alive. Once he has sneaked into their apartment, he watches her sleep. On display is the unmediated beauty of childhood, with Holden's attitude dampening possible sentimentality. As Holden communes with the objects around her, Phoebe wakes, excited to see him.

Despite his evasions it is clear to Phoebe that Holden has been kicked out of school, and she repeats "Daddy'll

kill you!" When he tries to further divert her, she levels a wrenching indictment, one Holden cannot answer. "You don't like *any*thing that's happening," she says. After suggesting more excuses—some warranted—he tells her he wants to be "the catcher in the rye." The impossible allure of childhood resurfaces, Holden strangely picturing himself with thousands of little kids near a cliff and "if . . . they don't look where they're going I have to come out from somewhere and *catch* them." Phoebe (and the reader) are left wordless.

When they hear their parents return, a worried Phoebe lends Holden money. He gives her his prized hunting hat and makes his way to his old teacher's, Antolini. Though Salinger often disparages teachers, Antolini appears an exception. Yet when he delivers a lecture, Antolini is as unaware as Spenser, telling Holden he is "riding for some kind of terrible, terrible fall." Antolini does suggest a possible remedy that echoes Holden's earlier, satisfying experience writing about Allie's glove, namely that other "confused and frightened" persons have "happily . . . kept records of their troubles." This explicit call to make something of his suffering—to create!—may be Holden's way out. Things take an unexpected turn, however, when he wakes to find Antolini stroking his forehead. Holden interprets this as "perverty," though later he is unsure.

After sleeping in Grand Central, Holden, depressed as ever, says that "something very spooky started happening." Walking up Fifth Avenue, he once more becomes convinced he is disappearing. Again Holden invokes his brother. "Allie, please don't let me disappear," he pleads. With the same escape fantasy resurfacing, Holden decides he must leave the city and resolves to see Phoebe again.

Holden is deteriorating: sweating, about to vomit, almost fainting, suffering diarrhea. He spots the words "fuck you" on several school walls as he leaves Phoebe a note, and he wants to rub them out so she will not see. When Phoebe finally appears she is a devastating sight, wearing his hunting hat, dragging a suitcase. She wants to go with him! Holden is outraged, as Phoebe is in turn.

In the final scene Holden takes her to ride the carousel in Central Park. She wants him to ride too, but at last he is recognizing the faultline of adulthood he has crossed. It is here that Salinger delivers his hardest-earned piece of wisdom: if kids "want to grab for the gold ring, you have to let them do it, and not say anything. If they fall off, they fall off, but it's bad if you say anything to them." Holden is learning the same difficult truth. He cannot be a catcher in the rye. Phoebe returns the hunting hat to his head, like a piece of armor. Watching her on the carousel,

Holden says, "I felt so damn happy all of sudden, the way old Phoebe kept going around and around. I was damn near bawling, I felt so happy." Readers feel a similar relief. When he tells us, "God, I wish you could've been there," in his act of retelling, we have.

In a last short chapter, the action returns to Holden convalescing on the West Coast. He is ambivalent about telling this story, though lodged within one of his disclaimers Holden says, "About all I know is, I sort of *miss* everybody I told about." In the end Salinger suggests that at the heart of remembrance and creation there is sympathy and love.

FURTHER READING

Bloom, Harold, ed. *J. D. Salinger: Modern Critical Views.* New York, 1987.

French, Warren. *J. D. Salinger, Revisited.* Boston, 1988. A thorough overview of Salinger's life and work.

Grunwald, Henry Anatole. *Salinger: A Critical and Personal Portrait.* New York, 1962. The first collection of articles to appear, capturing the first decade of critical response following the novel's publication.

Hamilton, Ian. *In Search of J. D. Salinger.* New York, 1988. For two years, a restraining order initiated by Salinger held up publication of this intriguing, less-than-comprehensive biography.

Kotzen, Kip, and Thomas Beller, eds. *With Love and Squalor: 14 Writers Respond to the Work of J. D. Salinger.* New York, 2001. A slate of contemporary writers provide personal, quirky credence to Salinger's enduring influence.

Kubica, Chris, and Will Hochman, eds. *Letters to J. D. Salinger.* Madison, Wis., 2002. Writers, both renowned and anonymous, write unrequitedly to the man himself.

Lundquist, James. *J. D. Salinger.* New York, 1979. A proficient overview of the principal criticism up to the late 1970s.

Maynard, Joyce. *At Home in the World: A Memoir.* New York, 1998. Salinger's live-in lover for a year presents a largely unflattering portrait of the writer in seclusion and a completely unflattering portrait of herself.

Menand, Louis. "Holden at Fifty." *The New Yorker,* 1 October 2001, 82–87. A lively glimpse of how Holden has managed to age with grace.

Pinsker, Sanford. *The Catcher in the Rye: Innocence under Pressure.* New York, 1993. A sharply observed close reading, including historical background and critical reception.

Salinger, Margaret A. *Dream Catcher.* New York, 2000. A small-spirited, artless memoir by Salinger's daughter.

Salzberg, Joel, ed. *Critical Essays on Salinger's* The Catcher in the Rye. Boston, 1990.

Salzman, Jack, ed. *New Essays on* The Catcher in the Rye. Cambridge, U.K., 1991.

Steed, J. P., ed. The Catcher in the Rye: *New Essays.* New York, 2002.

Steinle, Pamela Hunt. *In Cold Fear:* The Catcher in the Rye, *Censorship Controversies, and Postwar American Character.* Columbus, Ohio, 2000.

Sublette, Jack R. *J. D. Salinger: An Annotated Bibliography: 1938–1981.* New York, 1984. A valuable compilation of all materials relating to the author up to 1982.

See also the article on J. D. Salinger, immediately preceding.

CARL SANDBURG

by Robert M. Dowling

Carl Sandburg was a poet, political activist, journalist, biographer, historian, traveling troubadour, honorary Ph.D. many times over, and two-time winner of the Pulitzer Prize. He published eleven books of poetry over a sixty-year period, and though he also published songbooks, children's books, compilations of his journalism, a six-volume biography of Abraham Lincoln, and a lengthy novel, he continues to be remembered best as the United States' great "Poet of the People." His finest collections of poetry include *Chicago Poems* (1916); *Cornhuskers* (1918); *Smoke and Steel* (1920); *Slabs of the Sunburnt West* (1922); *Good Morning, America* (1928); *The People, Yes* (1936); his Pulitzer Prize–winning *Complete Poems* (1950), which contains previously unpublished work; and his final performance, *Honey and Salt* (1963). Sandburg's great passion for American history ultimately inspired his monumental biography of Abraham Lincoln, which appeared in two installments: the two-volume *Abraham Lincoln: The Prairie Years* (1926) and the four-volume *Abraham Lincoln: The War Years* (1939), which won him a second Pulitzer Prize. His only novel, *Remembrance Rock* (1948), is a sweeping glance at America's past, covering the period from the Puritans' landing at Plymouth Bay to World War II and the dawn of the atomic age.

Sandburg was born into a Swedish immigrant family in Galesburg, Illinois, the site of the famous Lincoln-Douglas debates, on 6 January 1878. Neither of his parents received a formal education. His father, August Johnson (who later changed his name to the less common Sandburg to avoid confusion at work) was a railroad hand who never learned how to write, though he could read enough Swedish to study the Bible in that language. Carl's mother, Clara Anderson Sandburg, was a chambermaid in a small-town hotel. Sandburg enjoyed his midwestern childhood and

Carl Sandburg. (*Used by permission of the Trustees of the Carl Sandburg Family Trust. Courtesy of the Library of Congress*)

discovered reading and his love of language early. But with six brothers and sisters his parents could not support on their own, he went to work full time at the age of thirteen. The uneven tempo of his adult life began then; rather than finding stability in one job and learning it well, he dabbled in various trades, including carpentry, plumbing, painting, and retail. A year after Carl quit school, his two youngest brothers died of diphtheria on the same day. Thanks to his father, Carl was well-acquainted with the Midwest railroad system, and in 1897 he toured the countryside in the popular style of the hobo, traveling free from town to town and taking on short-term employment to sustain himself. In this way he immersed himself in the American landscape and vernacular for months—no experience could have provided him in so short a time with such a deep reservoir of images, expressions, and perspectives that could be tapped for material and inspiration for years to come. This adventurous period is best told by Sandburg himself in *Always the Young Strangers* (1953), an autobiography recounting his youth as a traveling hobo, a man of all trades, and a volunteer soldier.

On 15 February 1898, the U.S. battleship *Maine* was sunk in Cuba's Havana harbor. The American press blamed the Spanish, and goaded the United States into war. Sandburg was convinced, like most Americans, that the Spanish had to be expelled from the region, so he promptly signed up for service in the Sixth Infantry Regiment of Illinois Volunteers. Although he never saw battle, the experience broadened his purview further: he was first stationed in Virginia, then transported with his regiment to Guantánamo Bay, Cuba, and then to Guánica, Puerto Rico, because of a yellow fever epidemic in Cuba. Following his Caribbean escapades, Sandburg decided to pursue an undergraduate degree. Though he never spent a day in high school, Sandburg was a war veteran and therefore eligible to apply directly to college. After failing the U.S. Military Academy (West Point) entrance exams (in both mathematics and, ironically enough, English grammar), he was admitted to Galesburg's Lombard College. He spent four productive years there, writing for the literary magazine, playing basketball and baseball, acting in a musical, and working on the yearbook staff, though he mysteriously disenrolled before graduation in the spring semester of his senior year, May 1902, and never received a degree. While at Lombard, he formed a relationship with Professor Philip Green Wright, who acted both as mentor and advocate for the young Carl, then calling himself Charles. Wright had established a socialist poetry group known as the Poor Writer's Club in Galesburg along with a small press in his basement, Asgard Press. After a few months meandering through mid-Atlantic states (at one point, he was caught sneaking into a boxcar and spent ten days in a Pittsburgh jail), Sandburg returned home, unemployed and restive. He and Wright had corresponded during Sandburg's adventures in the East, and over the next few years, Wright published Sandburg's first four books of poetry under the Asgard imprint: *In Reckless Ecstasy* (1904), *Incidentals* (1907), *The Plaint of a Rose* (1908), and *Joseffy* (1910). In a letter to Wright (22 June 1903), Sandburg singled out four poets who most strongly influenced *In Reckless Ecstasy*—Walt Whitman, William Shakespeare, Joaquin Miller, and Rudyard Kipling—a group who together might easily be attributable to the excessively romantic verse found in these early books. (Sandburg later abandoned the idea of reprinting them, as he viewed them in maturity as "many odd pieces...not worth later print.") During this same period, however, he kept his eye on the one American writer who may be, along with Whitman (the poet to whom he is most often compared), his greatest influence—the "coal-heaver, the gold-hunter, the tramp, the war correspondent"—Jack London. "Keep your eyes on him, Professor," he wrote Wright on 8 December 1904, "he bids fair to outclass anything in all America's literary output." Along with Wright, London fueled Sandburg's passion for socialist reform, and the two eventually became friends and collaborated on writings for the *International Socialist Review* under various pseudonyms.

In that same letter, Sandburg informed his mentor that he had been invited to a dance party at the University of Chicago, where he hoped to meet "the ideal woman." Presciently admitting that "if only I could meet [her], I believe I could pull myself together and set the world by

the ears," Sandburg foresaw the grand alliance between him and his wife of fifty-nine years, Lilian Paula Steichen. Carl (then still going by Charles) met Lilian in 1908 at the headquarters of the Milwaukee Socialist Party; he was working as a recruiter and Lilian as a translator. Lilian was a graduate of the University of Chicago, where she was admitted to the prestigious Phi Beta Kappa society on the basis of her outstanding academic performance there. Her brother Edward, who became one of Sandburg's greatest friends and influences, was a distinguished photographer. After graduation, she became a teacher and an active socialist. They married that same year and remained together until Sandburg's death in 1967.

POET OF THE PEOPLE

Over the next decade, Sandburg campaigned for the Socialist Party candidate Eugene V. Debs in his 1908 bid for the presidency, lectured on Walt Whitman, wrote for the *Milwaukee News*, *Sentinel*, and *Journal*, and later contributed to liberal presses like the *Milwaukee Leader*, the *Chicago Daily World*, and more mainstream papers like the *Chicago Daily News*, where he was as a staff writer until 1926. More concerned with the everyday lives of working and immigrant classes than politics, Sandburg admired the achievements of the famous and effective "muckrakers" of the Progressive Era—notably, Lincoln Steffens, Ida Tarbell, and Upton Sinclair. But all the while, he viewed himself in artistic rather than political terms, with Lilian encouraging him to continue writing poetry and, significantly, to revert back to the more multinational name Carl. In 1914, he published what was to become his greatest, most highly acclaimed piece of writing—"Chicago" in Harriet Monroe's innovative journal *Poetry: A Magazine of Verse*. Two years later, his book *Chicago Poems* was published by Henry Holt and Company. (Alfred Harcourt, a novice editor there, had placed his job on the line to get the book under contract.) Sandburg's involvement with the editors of *Poetry* and his first great book *Chicago Poems* gave him a place in Chicago's literary renaissance, which included writers like Edgar Lee Masters, Sherwood Anderson, Floyd Dell, and Theodore Dreiser, all of whom were raised in the rural Midwest, pursued careers in journalism, harbored a strong connection to the regionalist school of American literary realism, and shared a suspicion of industrial capitalism and its effects on the new urban environment.

Sandburg struggled at first to find, as all authors do, a unique literary voice. Writing to Professor Wright on 22 June 1903, he grumbled, "tho I like them [his first poems] in a way, I feel they lack something." Years later, immediately following the release of *Chicago Poems*, Amy Lowell insinuated that Sandburg's problem was his inability to achieve the transcendent state of a great poet. Half as a criticism, half as a compliment, she wrote that "he can never get free of the actual, can never rise entirely above his world on the wings of a certain hope." In the collection's most vital poem, "Chicago," Sandburg does indeed fail to transcend the world he is describing. His subjects remain rooted in the quotidian, the coarse, the "unpoetic" material of an immigrant's son. But like Whitman before him, Sandburg's poetry was more than anything a celebration of American promise, though the perspective was radically narrowed. Personifying the city of Chicago as the archetype of the American workingman, Sandburg glorifies the inglorious:

> Hog Butcher for the World,
> Tool Maker, Stacker of Wheat,
> Player with Railroads and the Nation's Freight Handler;
> Stormy, husky, brawling,
> City of Big Shoulders

Walt Whitman's influence is clear, most easily attributable to "Mannahatta," in which Whitman closes with the lines, "City of hurried and sparkling waters! city of spires and masts! / City nested in bays! my city!" But if Whitman's New York is a benign space in which openness and hospitality are the rule, with millions of voices converging on the city and emanating outward refreshed and vitalized, Sandburg's Chicago is personified as a "tall bold slugger," "Fierce as a dog," "cunning as a savage," "Laughing as an ignorant fighter laughs," "Laughing the stormy, husky, brawling laughter of Youth, half- / naked, sweating." Sandburg insists that Chicago is a city under attack—considered "wicked," "crooked," and "brutal" by outsiders. These outsiders are correct, he informs us, but "I give them back a sneer and say to them":

> Come and show me another city with lifted head singing so proud to be alive and course and strong and cunning.
> Flinging magnetic curses amid the toil of piling job on job, here
> is a tall bold slugger set vivid against the little soft cities . . .

Sandburg's voice here echoes the stark defiance of the self-righteous workingman, a voice that often alienated the United States' genteel literary elite (no doubt deliberately), while at the same time elevating the standard and content of populist culture.

His next book, *Cornhuskers*, continued to explore the theme of populism, but this time at the source of populist American thought—the rural Midwest. The final section, "Shenandoah," looks across the Atlantic and weaves the midwestern experience he wrought out in the opening sections into the horrors of a foreign war. The rambling digressions of the first few sections address the social texture of the midwestern prairies and the people who inhabit them—members of the Salvation Army, inmates at Joliet penitentiary, workers on the Union Pacific railroad, and the "Slav miners, Italians, Scots, Cornishmen, Yanks" who fought in early American wars. As many Civil War veterans were still alive to stir the imaginations of the next generation that dreamed of war, Sandburg was able to realistically depict the effects of war stories on innocent youth. In the poem "House," for instance, two Swedish boys take in the battle yarns of their Uncle Joe, a Civil War veteran, until their heads are filled with "a big blur of guns, men, and hills," and one blurts out at the dinner table, "I wish we had a war now and I could be a soldier." Of course, in 1918 the United States had just entered World War I, and the Swedish boys get their wish. In the final poem of the volume, "The Four Brothers," Sandburg looks on powerlessly as young midwestern men parade off to Europe:

> Cowpunchers, cornhuskers, shopmen, ready in khaki;
> Ballplayers, lumberjacks, ironworkers, ready in khaki;
> A million, ten million, singing, "I am ready."
> This the sun looks on between seaboards,
> In the land of Lincoln, in the land of Grant and Lee.

The Socialist Party line in 1918 was peace. But once the United States entered the war, Sandburg eschewed his political colleagues and defended Woodrow Wilson's decision to enter the war, perhaps defending the "cornhuskers" who were losing their lives in Europe. During his efforts to acquire a visa to Stockholm as a war correspondent, he even went so far as to say in one letter, "I can even see how it might be reasonable, a reduction of hazardous contingencies, for certain authorities to rule that no man of ex-socialist connections and with known Bolshevist friends, should be permitted at this time to go to Stockholm" (12 September 1918).

Sandburg spent three busy months abroad, from October to December 1919, as a Newspaper Enterprise Association war correspondent, and sent back numerous secondhand accounts of the war. Back in New York, he was caught smuggling $10,000 and a mass of revolutionary literature intended for Santeri Nuortava, a Finnish Information Bureau agent in the United States who was a socialist fighting the Prussian-run provisional government in Finland. Sandburg was nearly tried in court for violating the Trading with the Enemy Act, but was exonerated by signing a statement that permitted the government to retain his contraband without protest, though he had earlier claimed in a letter to Sam Hughes that "75 percent has already been printed in publications in the United States and is now in public libraries and has been on sale nationwide at newsstands" (17 January 1919). Sandburg spent the next spring and summer covering the building racial tensions in Chicago that ultimately led to the Chicago race riots of July 1919. Alfred Harcourt collected these columns into a book, *The Chicago Race Riots* (1919).

In his next book of poetry, *Smoke and Steel* (1920), Sandburg drags out a conceit, or extended metaphor, over many poems that at first appear disjointed. *Smoke and Steel* is not a work of socialist realism as the title might imply. Rather, Sandburg interconnects nature and the American people, which Whitman did, by comparing men and animals to manmade machines, which Whitman did not. In it, smoke is blood, birds are chisels, steel laughs, sandpipers walk on wire legs, and skyscrapers love:

> One by one lights of a skyscraper fling their checkering cross
>   work on the velvet gown of night.
> I believe the skyscraper loves night as a woman and brings
>   her playthings she asks for, brings her a velvet gown,
> And loves the white of her shoulders hidden under the dark
>   feel of it all.
> The masonry of steel looks to the night for somebody
>   it loves,
> He is a little dizzy and almost dances...waiting...dark...

In *Smoke and Steel* Sandburg is experimenting, almost showing off, with a range of poetic forms, including Whitmanesque cataloguing, poetic prose, imagism, and haiku. Both the prodigious length of the volume and the irregular rhythm of the poetic variations make it one of his least accessible books.

AMERICAN ICON

Sandburg was now a prominent staff writer for the *Chicago Daily News* (he was known in the press rooms as "John Guts" for his tenacious style of reportage), an award-winning poet (including Poetry Society of America Awards in 1919 and 1921), and a father of three daughters, Margaret, Janet, and Helga, for whom he composed *Rootabaga Stories* in 1922 and *Rootabaga Pigeons* in 1923, each containing nonsensical fantasy tales reminiscent of Edward Lear. He lectured across the country, read his poetry at readings, and performed American folk songs

on guitar, many of which were collected in his book of folk songs, *The American Songbag* (1927). If *Smoke and Steel* is a difficult text for its length and variation, his fourth book of poetry, *Slabs of the Sunburnt West*, is a brief, referential text that will delight historically minded readers and admirers of naturalistic writers like Jack London and Theodore Dreiser. Much of it is a commentary on architecture, geography, war, the American frontier, and even celebrities like Charlie Chaplin and Robert Frost. Chicago is again Sandburg's subject in the opening poem, "The Windy City." But unlike "Chicago," the city is no longer an aggressive brute, poised to challenge the rest of the nation; this time, it invites the passersby to forgive its idiosyncrasies—its music, its noise, its pollution, and its immigrant population—and rather than attempt reform, accept the Chicago aesthetic and move on:

> Forgive us if the jazz timebeats
> Of these clumsy mass shadows
> Moan in saxophone undertones,
> And the footsteps of the jungle,
> The fang cry, the rip claw hiss,
> The sneak-up and the still watch,
> The slant of the slit eyes waiting—
> If these bother respectable people
> with the right crimp in their napkins
> reading breakfast menu cards—
> forgive us—let it pass—let it be.

The presence of jazz, the incantatory rhythm, and the rebelliousness toward respectability ("forgive us" has both contrite and ironic connotations) demonstrate to what extent Sandburg was a forerunner of the later Beat Generation poets of the 1950s and 1960s.

But while Sandburg continued to develop his craft, he had also been collecting material for a juvenile biography on Abraham Lincoln. After some months of writing, however, it became clear to both Sandburg and Harcourt that his work on the sixteenth president was more appropriate for a broader adult audience. In 1926, after two years of revising the original manuscript, Sandburg's *Abraham Lincoln: The Prairie Years* appeared—it was an enormous best-seller, but of dubious historical merit.

Covering most of Lincoln's life, from his Kentucky childhood to the explosive months leading up to the Civil War, *The Prairie Years* received popular acclaim, as it buttressed the Lincoln mythology and only challenged the audience's expectations stylistically; professional historians, on the other hand, either lambasted Sandburg's tendency to apply "poetic license" to the life of a major historical figure or they dismissed it entirely. Much of the material Sandburg used for this early biography was drawn from Ida Tarbell's two-volume *Life of Abraham Lincoln* (1900), which was based mainly on interviews by people who knew Lincoln as a young man rather than traditional scholarly sources. In a letter to Tarbell, Sandburg even hinted that he was more interested in "the Lincoln legend" Tarbell had helped construct than the Lincoln reality (9 February 1926).

Harvard University asked Sandburg to deliver the Phi Beta Kappa poem in June of 1928. The poem, entitled "Good Morning, America," alone took three years to write and became the title poem of his next collection. *Good Morning, America* opens with a list of thirty-eight definitions for "poetry," each starting, "Poetry is…" which together illuminate Sandburg's artistry. The book was a critical success, and the combination of *The American Songbag*, *Abraham Lincoln: The Prairie Years*, and *Good Morning, America* ensured Carl Sandburg's place as the lyrical voice of folksy America. And with the publication of *The People, Yes*, an ambitious epic poem containing 107 sections that revisit all of his subject matter up to that point—skyscrapers, the countryside, Lincoln's legacy, and the marching tempo of the American civilization—Sandburg became a true American icon. *The People, Yes* was a welcome flash of optimism in the midst of the Great Depression, giving a voice to those who felt most helpless. With it, we can fully understand that Sandburg's appeal did not lie in his ability to erect universal truths for humanity, but rather to record the many voices that converge to form the American mosaic.

The sequel to *Abraham Lincoln: The Prairie Years*, *Abraham Lincoln: The War Years*, appeared in 1939. This time, rather than producing another lyrical ode to the war president, Sandburg based his biography on a mass of primary source material which (though devoid of citations) overwhelmed both historians and the general public alike with its meticulous, hulking comprehensiveness. *The War Years* was a monumental four-volume study, based on factual data concerning the Lincoln presidency, the Civil War, and the political processes of mid-nineteenth-century American politics. Top historians, including James G. Randall, Milo M. Quaife, and Charles Beard, commended the poet-historian's grand effort. In the end, Sandburg's sequel won the 1940 Pulitzer Prize.

CRITICAL RECEPTION

Typical of Sandburg's critical reception as a whole, two of the most prominent American literature scholars of the twentieth century—Alfred Kazin and Edmund Wilson—were at odds in their interpretations of the complete, six-volume Lincoln biography. On the one hand, Kazin, in his groundbreaking analysis of the American modern period *On Native Grounds* (1942), distinguished Sandburg's work by claiming that its prodigious length adds texture to its overarching theme—Lincoln as "the greatest of all American works of art." After having read all six volumes, Kazin writes of the experience that:

> Out of the recovery of a period in time, a period restored day by day, month after month, layer on layer, a mound heap of human stories, Lincoln arose before the reader like a massive shadow of the racked civilization he had held together, a stupendous aggregation of all those American traits that were to find so ambiguous and moving an expression in him.

Edmund Wilson, on the other hand, in his equally distinguished study, *Patriotic Gore* (1962), found Sandburg's biographies imperfect tomes that peppered the reader with "romantic and sentimental rubbish." He grants that "Carl Sandburg is not obnoxious when he is strumming his homely guitar and singing American ballads or in his chunks of Middle Western rhapsody that combine the density of a Chicago block with the dryness of a Kansas drought; but," he continues, "Lincoln took him out of his depth, and the result was a long sprawling book that eventually had Lincoln sprawling."

Sandburg received his second Pulitzer Prize in 1951 for *Complete Poems*, which is a collection of his post-Asgard poetry with an additional section of new poems. He begins its preface by quoting prominent figures from high and low culture—Picasso and Babe Ruth, William Butler Yeats and Will Rogers, John Steinbeck and Ty Cobb—and all have the same, frustrating message: "The inexplicable is all around us. So is the incomprehensible. So is the unintelligible." His contemporary William Carlos Williams wrote a review of *Complete Poems* in *Poetry*, forty-five years after Sandburg made his debut in that magazine with "Chicago," attacking Sandburg for his inability to offer readers anything explicable, comprehensible, or intelligible in his verse:

> He had no answers, he didn't seek any. Without any attempt at the solace which the limitations of art…might bring, the formlessness of his literary figures was the very formlessness of the materials with which he worked. That was his truth.… That form he could accept but at a terrible cost: failure deliberately invited, a gradual inevitable slackening

off to ultimate defeat.... "Chicago," his first brilliantly successful poem, should have been his last.

Sandburg's popular and critical reception has been consistently inconsistent, and remains so to this day. His name appears in the oddest, most unliterary conversations (often with the oddest, most unliterary people) while almost never showing up on a graduate school syllabus, or even in a literature textbook. There are two main reasons for this scholastic disregard for Sandburg's poetry: first, he is not a technical poet, and second, his poetry rarely demands literary "unpacking," the explication and analysis that is the roux of literary criticism. In fact, much of his work has been graciously unpacked for us, as in the case of his imagist poem "Green Fishes": "Green fishes on a red-lacquered tray / are worn bringing a sea of beer / from draught faucets to bar tables / from bartenders to customers / they are losing their green fins." There exists little here beyond the physical image: the aesthetic of the bar, the abused tray, the consumption of beer.

The New Critics of the mid-twentieth century could not appreciate poetry like Sandburg's; it was too formless, too whimsical for scholars who preferred the more "cerebral, dense, and intricately allusive" verse of his contemporaries Ezra Pound and T. S. Eliot (Allen, 1972, p. 591). Sandburg confronts this issue head-on in his preface to *Complete Poems*:

> There is a formal poetry perfect only in form, "all dressed up and nowhere to go." The number of syllables, the designated and required stresses of accent, the rhymes if wanted—they come off with the skill of a solved crossword puzzle. Yet its animation and connotation are less than that of a "dead mackerel in the moonshine," the latter even as an extinct form reporting that once it was a living fish aswim in bright waters.

Rather than conform to the preferences of the 1940s and 1950s literary elite (the formalist school known as New Criticism went virtually unchallenged in academia during the period), Sandburg foresaw a brand of criticism that never fully emerged as a school of thought until the 1970s and 1980s—reader-response. There is no need to explain the approach here, as along with formalism, he defines reader-response in his preface as well:

> There stands the work of the man, the woman, who wrought it. We go to it, read it, look at it, perhaps go back to it many a time and it is for each of us what we make of it. The creator can say it means this or that—or it means for you whatever you take it to mean. He can say it happened, it came into

being and it now exists apart from him and nothing can be done about it.... *No two persons register precisely the same to a work of art.* (italics added)

Unlike his contemporary Robert Frost, he would never win a Nobel Prize, though Ernest Hemingway, the 1954 Nobel laureate, felt Sandburg was more deserving of it than he. In response to this, Sandburg told *The New York Times* staffer Harvey Breit that "some thirty years from now when the Breit boys are sitting around, one boy will say, 'Did Carl Sandburg ever win the Nobel Prize?' and one Breit boy will say, 'Ernest Hemingway gave it to him in 1954.'" In his final collection, *Honey and Salt*, Sandburg abandoned most of his signature traits—working-class rebelliousness, referential cataloging, American voices recorded in singular outbursts. Now in his eighties, he embraced the universality of what conventional critics have chosen as "great" writers. Throwing aside ethnic, racial, and class-based categories that in the past had broadened and limited his readers' perspectives, the last stanza of the last poem "Timesweep," says this:

> There is only one child in the world
> and the child's name is All Children.
> There is only one maker in the world
> and his children cover the earth
> and they are named All God's Children.

Sandburg answered Amy Lowell's 1917 call in his old age and transcended his world "on the wings of a certain hope." The last years of his life were spent at Connemara, a sizable farm in Flat Rock, North Carolina, with Lilian, his three daughters, and two grandchildren. By the time of his death on 22 July 1967, he had made radio broadcasts, recorded albums, played concerts, appeared on television, consulted in Hollywood, was interviewed by magazines, and utilized every publicity medium imaginable to achieve iconic stature in the United States and abroad. The popular icon's responsibility is to demonstrate that dreams are realizable, and if Carl Sandburg, the immigrant's son, the hobo, the college dropout, the war veteran, the beleaguered poet, the socialist, the self-promoter, achieved nothing else, he proved to common Americans that by embracing their democratic homeland, they are capable of being everything at once.

[*See also* Chicago Renaissance *and* Long Poem, The.]

SELECTED WORKS
POETRY

In Reckless Ecstasy (1904)
Incidentals (1907)

The Plaint of a Rose (1908)
Joseffy: An Appreciation (1910)
Chicago Poems (1916)
Cornhuskers (1918)
Smoke and Steel (1920)
Slabs of the Sunburnt West (1922)
Good Morning, America (1928)
The People, Yes (1936)
Poems of the Midwest (1946)
Complete Poems (1950)
Harvest Poems, 1910–1960 (1960)
Honey and Salt (1963)

NONFICTION

The Chicago Race Riots (1919)
Abraham Lincoln: The Prairie Years (1926)
The American Songbag (1927)
Steichen the Photographer (1929)
Mary Lincoln: Wife and Widow (1932)
Abraham Lincoln: The War Years (1939)
Storm over the Land (1942)
Home Front Memo (1943)
A Lincoln Preface (1952)
Always the Young Strangers (1953)
Abraham Lincoln: The Prairie Years and the War Years
  (1954)
The Sandburg Range (1957)
Breathing Tokens (1978)
Ever the Winds of Chance (1983)

FICTION

Remembrance Rock (1948)

FOR CHILDREN

Rootabaga Stories (1922)
Rootabaga Pigeons (1923)
Early Moon (1930)
Potato Face (1930)
Prairie-Town Boy (1955)
Wind Song (1960)
The Wedding Procession of the Rag Doll and the Broom
  Handle and Who Was in It (1967)

FURTHER READING

Allen, Gay Wilson. *Carl Sandburg*. Pamphlets on American Writers, Number 101. Minneapolis, Minn., 1972. Allen's work is particularly valuable for its literary analysis. He presents Sandburg's work more in the context of literary history than cultural or social history.

Golden, Harry. *Carl Sandburg*. Urbana, Ill., 1961. An anecdotal biography written in near-collaboration with Sandburg himself. Golden and Sandburg were good friends, and the book contains no scholarly apparatus—citations, bibliography, etc.

Lowell, Amy. *Tendencies in Modern American Poetry*. New York, 1917. No thorough analysis of Sandburg's life and works can avoid this book. Lowell's poetry study is the first major statement on Sandburg's career. On the merit of his *Chicago Poems* alone, Sandburg was one of six contemporary poets included in her study; the others are: Edwin Arlington Robinson, Robert Frost, Edgar Lee Masters, H.D., and John Gould Fletcher.

Meltzer, Milton. *Carl Sandburg: A Biography*. Brookfield, Conn., 1999. A more recent Sandburg biography. A finely written glance at Sandburg's career, focusing more on his writing than his personal life.

Mitgang, Herbert, ed. *The Letters of Carl Sandburg*. New York, 1968. Useful collection of Sandburg's correspondence.

Niven, Penelope. *Carl Sandburg: A Biography*. New York, 1991. The most comprehensive Sandburg biography to date; it is a massive, impressively researched compendium of Sandburg knowledge. She spent fourteen years organizing Sandburg's papers at Connemara, and collected them at the University of Illinois library for public access. No earlier Sandburg biographer brought to bear (or could have before her archival work was completed in 1983) as much primary source material as Niven.

Salwak, Dale. *Carl Sandburg: A Reference Guide*. Boston, 1988. Chronological collection of reviews and scholarly articles from 1904 to 1985 pertaining to Sandburg's work. As the critical reception of Sandburg is one of this most intriguing aspects of his career, this is an important book.

Sandburg, Margaret. *The Poet and the Dream Girl: The Love Letters of Lilian Steichen and Carl Sandburg*. Urbana, Ill., 1987. Collection of premarital letters between Lilian and Carl (then Charles).

Williams, William Carlos. "Carl Sandburg's 'Complete Poems.'" *Selected Essays of William Carlos Williams*. New York, 1954. The modern poet William Carlos Williams was perhaps Sandburg's most critical peer.

Yannella, Philip R. *The Other Carl Sandburg*. Jackson, Miss., 1996. A concentrated study focusing on Sandburg's early socialist journalism in Milwaukee, as well as his work for the *International Socialist Review*.

DELMORE SCHWARTZ

by Frederick Ethan Fischer

Delmore Schwartz was the poet of nighttime New York, who at age twenty-five published *In Dreams Begin Responsibilities* (1938), a collection of poems, a verse drama, and the title story, to much acclaim—"more than has come to any other American poet of his generation since Auden," wrote F. O. Matthiessen. A poet of consciousness, of intellect, and of city speech, Schwartz joins what he calls "the priceless particulars"—potatoes, subway grates, "The Beautiful American Word, Sure"—with ideas and abstractions, Time, History, Guilt. Into his poems enter Socrates, Freud, Marx, Orpheus, or Abraham, as a chorus that comments on the poet's origins.

Born to affluent Jewish parents on 8 December 1913 in Brooklyn, New York, Schwartz was precocious, voraciously

Delmore Schwartz, 1961.
(*Photograph by Rollie McKenna*)

reading philosophers, novelists, and poets, and expounding them brilliantly. He had always been fascinated with his immigrant ancestors, childhood, and change; autobiographical themes drive his poetry and fiction. Destined for divorce, his parents traumatized him, while the Depression defeated his hopes of inheriting wealth. Schwartz attended the University of Wisconsin for a year, impressing faculty and peers. His college letters reveal a devotion to literature and a thorough grasp of its traditions; already poetry was his vocation. In a letter to a childhood friend, Schwartz announced the credo to which he adhered all his life: "I shall devote myself to vision alone." He graduated from New York University, then studied philosophy at Harvard. Returning to New York, Schwartz finished the book *In Dreams Begin Responsibilities*, which won him celebrity and a letter from T. S. Eliot. Mark Van Doren proclaimed the verse "as good as any poetry has been for a long while, say at least a literary generation." Schwartz would never surpass the critical success of this first book.

FAME FROM EARLY SORROW

The book's title story envisions a silent movie that seems to star the narrator's own father and mother during a day of their courtship in 1909. From the darkened theater's audience, the Delmore-like narrator watches numbly, then in grief and horror as his young parents (after an afternoon at Coney Island) proceed to a proposal of marriage. He stands and protests aloud: "Don't do it. It's not too late to change your minds, both of you. Nothing good will come of it, only remorse, hatred, scandal, and two children whose characters are monstrous." Soon he is ejected from the theater. As Schwartz wrote in a letter to his fiancée, "memory is all we get from existence." His journey of self-discovery creates an art of memory recasting his life as fiction or verse. The poems of *In Dreams Begin Responsibility* balance polished irony and distance with naked confession: "I will forget the speech my mother made / In a restaurant, trapping my father there / At dinner with his whore" (from "Prothalamion"). Long before Sylvia Plath's work and well before his friend Robert Lowell wrote *Life Studies* (which includes a poem "To Delmore Schwartz"), Schwartz wrote confessional poetry, something raw and new.

Blessed and cursed with early fame, fearing it would not last, Schwartz became a teacher and editor. Thereafter he became central to the literary scene; he was a man of letters—poet, storyteller, playwright, translator, critic, wit, and professor to his generation (many of whom lived in Greenwich Village, hub of bohemian, radical thought). Schwartz saw his own life as a flawed epic reflecting the experience of American artists before, during, and after World War II. With his intellectual and lyric gifts, Delmore Schwartz was crafting work that dazzled greats such as Wallace Stevens, Ezra Pound, and Vladimir Nabokov. Yet later his friend, poet John Berryman, would call him "the most underrated poet in America."

Schwartz made a haphazard living teaching English at Harvard and other colleges. He worked also as poetry editor for the influential *Partisan Review*, as poetry and film critic for *The New Republic*, and as contributing editor to other periodicals. He had married Gertrude Buckman, who later worked for his publisher New Directions. Increasingly depressed or wildly elated, Schwartz toiled long for literature and generously promoted other writers. His work as critic remains impressive for its sympathy, discernment, and erudition. Such essays as "The Vocation of the Poet in the Modern World" (1951), and a wealth of reviews (he hailed Wallace Stevens as "sovereign of the mind and of light, master of reality") reveal Schwartz's belief that artists, though tragically alienated, are society's spiritual resources.

MODERNISM OLD AND NEW

Schwartz was a late apostle of modernism, the reigning artistic movement since World War I. Although no longer new, modernism influenced him deeply as he employed Eliot's idiom or that of other forbears. "In the Naked Bed, in Plato's Cave" shows how Schwartz blends echoes of great voices with his own: "In the naked bed, in Plato's cave, / Reflected headlights slowly slid the wall, / Carpenters hammered under the shaded window, / Wind troubled the window curtains all night long..." The modernist movement favored allusion, dream symbols, multiple voices, and ironic ambiguity, among other techniques. Schwartz responds (in "O Love, Sweet Animal"): "O love, dark animal, / With your strangeness go / Like any freak or clown: / Appease the child in her" (resembling Yeats and Edmund Waller). High modernism had brought a renaissance by the 1920s but may have dimmed stars like Hart Crane (whom Schwartz echoes in "Far Rockaway"). By 1940, Schwartz could be seen as the child of "a creed outworn," composing difficult poems appreciated by other learned poets. Nevertheless he sounds depths within himself, the youth who now proclaims, "The poet is a shepherd of being." Later adding motifs from vaudeville, film, or television, he would preview the postmodern era.

Schwartz sounds more of his own notes in the playful yet serious poem "The Kingdom of Poetry" ("For poetry is the sunlight of consciousness..."), or in "Vivaldi" as varied lines dance their homage. With his anthology pieces, "The Heavy Bear Who Goes with Me," "In the Naked Bed in Plato's Cave," and "Seurat's Sunday

Afternoon along the Seine," Schwartz lays his claim as heir to the moderns as he steps beyond them to a new music. "The Heavy Bear Who Goes with Me" weds clumsiness to grace, symbolizing the animal-spirit dilemma of humankind; the poem ends as the spirit bemoans a bearlike body "Dragging me with him in his mouthing care, / Amid the hundred million of his kind, / The scrimmage of appetite everywhere."

CHILDHOOD, LOVE, AND ALIENATION

Thematic in Schwartz is "the wound of consciousness," ruled by nightly fear or daily anger "exact as a machine." He remains a writer of human, often humorous, contradictions. Schwartz himself carried *Finnegans Wake* to baseball games. According to Saul Bellow, Schwartz joked that "history is a nightmare during which he was trying to get a good night's rest." In the later poems, despite sleeplessness, allusions to "love" abound. Laughter is present. This is displayed in the poem " 'I Am Cherry Alive,' the Little Girl Sang" (published posthumously as a children's book), or "Love and Marilyn Monroe" ("She is honest in her delight in womanhood and manhood"). Superb titles appear: "THE MIND IS AN ANCIENT AND FAMOUS CAPITAL" or "A Dog Named Ego, the Snowflakes as Kisses." A second book of poetry is entitled *Vaudeville for a Princess* (1950); his next two books of stories are *The World Is a Wedding* (1948) and *Successful Love* (1961).

His works seek hope in a world grown absurd or blind to art (Irving Howe calls him a "comedian of alienation"). Schwartz's stories depict families evolving from the Depression era through the post-war period. Although Schwartz downplays Jewish themes, they fuel much of his work; he is influenced by Franz Kafka's seemingly secular though gnostic fables (God being so distant that he seems absent). Schwartz stories indebted to Kafka include "The Statues," "Screeno," and "The Track Meet," wherein dream worlds grow real. Kafka imagines a man who becomes a huge beetle, but Schwartz crafts more homely metamorphoses. While not didactic, stories in *The World Is a Wedding* (whose title states Talmudic mystery) teach how past terrors haunt the present.

Other stories depict Schwartz-like sons straining to break free of a past fraught with old-world ritual. Schwartz portrays himself as typical (though with an absurd name: Hershey Green, Shenandoah Fish). Toward the end of "The Child Is the Meaning of This Life," Jasper, a Delmore-like character, asks himself: "What was the freedom to which the adult human being rose in the morning, if each act was held back or inspired by the overpowering ghost of a little child?"

TEACHING THE UNTAUGHT, SPEAKING THE UNSPOKEN

In classrooms Schwartz could be unpredictable, but students (such as the musician Lou Reed) remembered him with the devotion of friends ("the most magical human being I've known" says William Barrett). Schwartz had a comic, oracular air that mesmerized friends; Bellow dubbed him the "Mozart of conversation." (Schwartz somewhat resembles Samuel Johnson, the canonical English writer and conversationalist.) Schwartz's lilting letters preserve something of what people felt in his presence.

Thoroughly American, Delmore Schwartz, like his first hero Hart Crane, felt compelled to be "great" (equal to a bard perhaps, not a mere "second violinist"); such ambition called for an epic work to rival *The Waste Land* by Eliot or *The Bridge* by Crane. Schwartz feels that "America has to be discovered again and again by everyone in America, for America is always new and always full of the unknown and undiscovered" ("An American Fairy Tale"). But the America that barely remembered Walt Whitman's *Song of Myself* in *Leaves of Grass* was no more ready to love a long, autobiographical poem by Schwartz: *Genesis: Book One* (1943). In his essay "The Vocation of the Poet in the Modern World" (1951), the poet-critic recognizes the odds against popularity or greatness.

Schwartz continued to teach, publish, and edit with distinction until his death. The controversial later work departs from the style of his early successes. His verse play *Shenandoah* (1941) treated the family drama of his infancy; two years later, his narrative poem *Genesis: Book One* met with mixed reviews. Disappointed, the poet went on writing poems infused with tragicomic vision; however, slowly using softer tones he came to a transcendent music. Despite some poverty, various grants, prizes, and appointments came to him in time. Still his dark jests chill us, as when he speaks of man's confinement "to the coffin of his character." Childless, Schwartz was divorced and in 1949 married novelist Elizabeth Pollet (who later published his journals). Suffering spells of madness, he fought despair and paranoia with his art; he could sing of "The Deceptive Present, the Phoenix Year."

LATER WORKS

Mornings play a special role. His later poems resound with salutes to dawn. Schwartz's essential book *Summer Knowledge: New and Selected Poems (1938–1958)*, winner of the coveted Bollingen Prize in 1960, offers titles such as "The First Morning of the Second World," "A Little Morning Music," and "Gold Morning, Sweet Prince"; later the first part of *Last and Lost Poems of Delmore Schwartz* (1979) announces "DARKNESS BEFORE DELIGHT" (a telling pun). Robert Phillips sees him "celebrating the joys and vigors, enervations and languishments of the world's weathers." Thus in 1962 Schwartz could write, "Verse is pouring out of my fingers." In late translations (from Valéry lines like: "Time itself sparkles, to dream and to know are one") and in such poems as "The Studies of Narcissus," mornings open to him with new horizons: "Strong in hope once more, ever in eagerness. . . ." He borrows Van Doren's line, "Eternity is now."

Readers discern the change from the lean complexities of Schwartz's early poems to the cadenced, mystical rhapsody of his later work. Some critics disparage the latter as showing his diminished powers. Yet the poet's new singing voice represents an artistic evolution. Contrast "The Ballad of the Children of the Czar" with "O Child, Do Not Fear the Dark and Sleep's Dark Possession." The lines grew longer as Schwartz forsook Yeatsian tension for Whitmanesque song, an open road.

In 1966, Delmore Schwartz died of a heart attack alone in a New York City hotel, but he left behind a substantial body of work (much of it still unpublished). Early and late he strives for spiritual renewal even as he enters dark nights of the soul. In a review, Schwartz reaffirms his own stance: "But no matter how great the darkness, one cannot live by darkness" (*New Republic*, 1953). With a kind of innocence, he strove to live by light seen through art's kaleidoscope. One of his favorite poems, "Starlight Like Intuition Pierced the Twelve," concludes *Summer Knowledge* as follows: "And we shall never be as once we were, / This life will never be what once it was!"

[*See also* Bellow, Saul; Berryman, John; *and* Confessional Poetry.]

WORKS

In Dreams Begin Responsibilities (1938)
A Season in Hell (1939)
Shenandoah (1941)
Genesis: Book One (1943)
The World Is a Wedding (1948)
Vaudeville for a Princess and Other Poems (1950)
Summer Knowledge: New and Selected Poems, 1938–1958 (1959)

Successful Love and Other Stories (1961)
Selected Essays of Delmore Schwartz (1970; edited by Donald Dike and David Zucker)
In Dreams Begin Responsibilities and Other Stories (1978)
"I Am Cherry Alive," the Little Girl Sang (1979)
Last and Lost Poems of Delmore Schwartz (1979; edited by Robert Phillips)
Letters of Delmore Schwartz (1984; edited by Robert Phillips)
The Ego Is Always at the Wheel: Bagatelles (1986)
Portrait of Delmore: Journal and Notes of Delmore Schwartz (1986; edited by Elizabeth Pollet)
The Heights of Joy: Stories and Poems (2003)

FURTHER READING

Atlas, James. *Delmore Schwartz: The Life of an American Poet.* New York, 1977. An intelligent, lively biography that includes some critical interpretation of the work.

Bellow, Saul. *Humboldt's Gift.* New York, 1975. This brilliant novel by Schwartz's friend gives a comic (yet rather cruel) portrait of Delmore as Von Humboldt Fleisher.

Berryman, John. *The Dream Songs.* New York, 1969. See the series of poems numbered 146–160 in which a fellow poet reacts to the news of Schwartz's death.

Broyard, Anatole. *Kafka Was the Rage: A Greenwich Village Memoir.* New York, 1993. As a young man in Greenwich Village, Broyard knew Schwartz and in chapters 14 and 16 creates a vivid portrait of him.

Phillips, Robert. *Last and Lost Poems of Delmore Schwartz.* New York, 1989. This (and other posthumous Schwartz volumes) features an excellent introduction by Phillips who knew Schwartz and is also his literary executor.

Simpson, Eileen. *Poets in Their Youth: A Memoir.* New York, 1982. Laced throughout this loving memoir are scenes from her husband John Berryman's friendship with Schwartz as well as with other prominent, doomed poets of the mid-century.

Wetzsteon, Ross. *Republic of Dreams: Greenwich Village, the American Bohemia, 1910–1960.* New York, 2002. The brief biographical portrait "Alien in Residence" (chapter 14) places Delmore Schwartz in the setting of a half century's artistic ferment in New York City.

SCIENCE FICTION

by Vincent Standley

In a taxonomy of literature, science fiction would be found under the classification genre writing, as would its cousins the western, mystery, and romance. Genre writing implies mass production, mass appeal, and mass consumption. It implies formulaic, commercial, for-hire writing, employing a recognizable and repeatable set of writing practices and conventions that merely reinforce the status quo. The implications are severe but for the most part true. If you catalog the science fiction novels published in one year, some 200–300 new titles, only a handful will seem compromised by the genre writing label, and these will be given special attention as "quality" or "literary" science fiction, or they will be ignored. A growing number of books generally considered literary fiction employ elements of science fiction and are in effect shared by both communities. Kurt Vonnegut Jr. published his first stories in science fiction genre magazines. His work is called science fiction by the science fiction community despite vocal objections by the author. Thomas Pynchon, John Crowley, and, more recently, George Saunders have all been a part of the same tug-of-war.

From the point of view of science fiction writers and readers—its fans—the genre issue hardly matters. The range of motifs—utopias and anti-utopias, lost worlds, alien cultures, space travel, time travel, galactic empires, war, artificial life, postapocalyptic societies, biological experimentation, parallel worlds, ecological disasters, and so on—are numerous but fairly static. Writers and readers have accepted the basic premise of a fictional future history that was sketched out during the 1940s and 1950s in magazines like *Amazing Stories, Astounding, Magazine of Fantasy and Science Fiction*, and *Galaxy*. The future history is a set of conventions that writers can and generally do rely on as backdrops for their stories and that avid readers recognize and even expect.

However, the future history is also quite limber. That is, writers and readers alike expect new spins on the old rules, including the rejection and subversion of those rules, as long as the choice to do so is made by an informed agent. Implied here is a self-consciousness

Isaac Asimov. (*Courtesy of the Library of Congress*)

intrinsic to the genre. Following or breaking the rules is okay as long as the writer and reader know what the rules are. The conventions that externally define a genre are internally a contract between writer and reader. The contract creates several very practical advantages. The first is that future history is stable: each new story need not reinvent the whole universe. The author instead enriches or reenvisions what is already known or accepted. The originality of a story is found in the variations on a theme rather than in the introduction of new themes. Second, reading science fiction requires the command of a fairly unambiguous but mutable set of conventions (a requirement that is also one of the genre's strongest appeals), and the affirmation and/or disappointment of the reader's expectations becomes a very real rhetorical concern of the author. The interplay among writer, reader, and a set of genre conventions creates opportunities for a kind of irony not possible in literary fiction, at least not in literary realism, which expects conventions to be invisible. Finally, the contract between writer and reader creates a distinction between those inside and those outside of science fiction culture. Its conventions may keep science fiction bound within the confines of genre writing, but they also preserve and foster the continuity and community of science fiction fandom.

Until the 1960s few women wrote science fiction, and most of those who did wrote in a male idiom. Until the 1980s, the only prominent African-American science fiction writer was Samuel R. Delany—again with only a few possible exceptions. The insularity of science fiction culture minimizes the influence from other genres—except, perhaps, popular science writing. Consequently change is periodic, creating a stability that makes it perfect for the marketplace. Science fiction fandom emerged modestly out of fan clubs formed in the 1920s, when writers were paid a half penny per word, writing for pulp magazines that might fold after twenty or thirty issues. Kids today can identify with science fiction culture with the same fervor and conviction as their predecessors. Their defense of its rules and conventions gives them a shared knowledge, unique to real fans, while ensuring the repeatability and salability of product. This is an exhausted irony but one that may still have some poignancy, if only because it did not start out that way.

PULPS

Science fiction is clearly a fiction of speculation and wonder and as such belongs to vast body of writing that arguably can be traced back to *The Odyssey* and the Old Testament. Many examples from the Renaissance—like early utopian writing by Thomas More and Francis Bacon or the wilder astronomical tracts by Johannes Kepler, in which science decodes the music of the spheres—are preoccupied with imagining future societies and the true nature of the cosmos, motifs present to some degree in almost all science fiction. The union of science and rational thought in the pursuit of a greater good was a mainstay of the Enlightenment, one which has been equally integral to science fiction. Cautionary tales questioning the claim that science and reason are truly unified, that such a union is even possible, preoccupied science fiction in the years following World War II, after the bomb. Mary Wollstonecraft Shelley's *Frankenstein; or, The Modern Prometheus* (1818)—the prototypical science fiction story—is similarly preoccupied: the human endeavor to

transform nature is rewarded with a godlike creation that collapses in the face of a still unknowable nature.

Ultimately, though, science fiction is a product of the Industrial Revolution: science, reason, capital, labor, and the beyond-your-wildest-dreams consequences of their union. And the world became confusing because it was transforming and because the changes were wonderful and terrible at the same time. In France, Jules Verne (1828–1905) wrote adventures that hinged on scientific advance. The stories are about travel and discovery in hot air balloons, submarines, and steamships. The prose dwells on the little details of how each vessel works and may be as tedious as it was prophetic. In England, H. G. Wells (1866–1946), conversely, wrote a kind of speculative fiction more concerned with the welfare of the masses than with science. Between Verne and Wells can be found two sides of the genre that are still at odds with one another. "Hard" science fiction optimistically explores science, scientific probability, and progress. Humanistic science fiction explores societal want; sometimes pessimistic, it critiques for the greater good.

American science fiction began in the serial pulps of the 1920s and 1930s and remained a short-story form until mass-market paperbacks appeared in the 1950s. From the turn of the century into the 1920s, pulp magazines like *Argosy*, *All-Story*, and *Cavalier* were not genre specific and published a wide range of adventure and entertainment fiction, including gothic horror and science fiction.

In 1908, Hugo Gernsback (1884–1967) began publishing magazines like *Modern Electronics* and *Science and Invention* that combined quasi-scientific articles with "scientific fiction" stories. The new story form had no name yet and was called variously "scientifiction," "different stories," "scientific romance," and so on. Gernsback coined the term "science fiction" in 1929, but it is for publishing *Amazing Stories* between 1926 and 1929 that he is known as "The Father of Science Fiction."

Gernsback recognized that Edgar Allan Poe, Jules Verne, and H. G. Wells were important antecedents to the form and reprinted a number of stories by each author. He also recognized that the American writer Edgar Rice Burroughs (1875–1950), who had been publishing serialized novels in pulp magazines since 1912, was evidently in the same vein. Burroughs's first novel, *A Princess of Mars*, transports the Victorian romance to the planet Mars. Later, the center of the Earth (*Pellucidar*), the African jungle (*Tarzan*), and Venus (*Lost on Venus*) became locales for similar adventures. Burroughs successfully took the "lost race" story popularized by the English adventure writer H. Rider Haggard and expanded its horizon to include alien and alternative human races. And like Haggard, Burroughs catered to the audience that loved his stories, producing many books in long series. The Tarzan books, for instance, include twenty-four novels. He inspired many imitators, like Otis Adelbert Kline, who used the landscapes of Venus and Mars already charted by Burroughs.

Gernsback ran *Amazing Stories* for three years, editing only thirty-seven issues, but in that time he created the first science fiction audience and brought together a group of young writers who laid out the early ground rules of the genre, rules that have been built on, played against, and rejected outright ever since. Gernsback wrote and published science fiction that emphasized technological innovation, suggesting that what first appeared in fiction would become the landscape of the future. Under Gernsback's editorship *Amazing Stories* published work by the seminal American writers Bob Olsen, Jack Williamson, David H. Keller, Stanton Coblentz, and Philip Francis Nowlan, whose character Buck Rogers became a popular film and comic-strip hero. Perhaps the most memorable and influential writer in Gernsback's stable was E. E. "Doc" Smith, whose *Skylark* (1928) and *Lensman* (1937–1947) series left Burroughs's Mars and Venus far behind, pushing farther into space with gigantic spaceships capable of interstellar travel. The books are fast-paced and full of scientific invention and grand heroic themes.

By the 1940s, the positivist formula of *Amazing Stories* had fused with Burroughs's high adventure to produce the space opera in fiction, film, and comic books. Over the next decade, two camps emerged beneath the pulp umbrella: one started by Gernsback and *Amazing Stories;* the other by John Campbell and *Astounding.*

GOLDEN YEARS

During the late 1930s and through the 1940s, *Astounding,* under the editorship of John Campbell (1910–1971), abandoned much that had been set forth by *Amazing Stories,* ushering in what many have called the Golden Age of American science fiction. As editor and mentor Campbell demanded story over science and schmaltz. He encouraged writers to move away from the space-opera formula and the clichéd depiction of good versus evil.

Campbell was just twenty-seven years old when he began editing *Astounding* and would remain in that position for thirty-four years. He was already distinguished as a writer—*Amazing Stories* published his first story in 1930 alongside those of E. E. "Doc" Smith and Jack

Williamson—and brought to *Astounding* many of his instincts and beliefs about the genre.

The landscape remained space and the time was still the future. Spaceships and aliens still dominated. What had changed was the disposition toward these elements. Campbell introduced a humanistic eye to technology and its implications, and American science fiction became more concerned with morality and the relationship of the individual to society than it had been previously. The naive romance celebrating human progress and conquest of the stars was no longer convincing. Readers and writers demanded more. In no way was this an abandonment of the science in science fiction or even an abandonment of the faith in science and technology—that would come later. Rather, Campbell and *Astounding*'s writers strove for less commercialization, which demanded that writers take their subjects more seriously. The era of Buck Rogers was over.

The writers publishing in *Astounding* at this time—Isaac Asimov, Fritz Leiber, Theodore Sturgeon, Robert Heinlein, Lester del Rey, A. E. Van Vogt—had all grown up with the pulps; they were in fact the first generation to have lived through more than a decade of science fiction. Asimov and Del Rey both published their first stories as teenage fans. Their debt to the first generation as well as their desire to introduce more complexity into the genre is evident in their writing.

Asimov's story "Foundation" (1942), first published in *Astounding* and later published as a book with the same title, exemplifies many of the changes occurring within the genre during the early 1940s. In it, the Galactic Empire is beginning to decline, which means 25 million inhabited planets are on the brink of chaos after twelve thousand years of order. "Phychohistory," an exact science in which future mass behavior can be predicted and by extension controlled, indicates the probable collapse of the empire, unless a precise series of events are adhered to over the following several hundred years.

The scope of a future history added depth to what was possible in science fiction and set the scene for other writers to add to and develop their own histories of the sentient universe. Discussion between Campbell and his writers produced the prototypical universe from which stories of the next decade would be situated. While still adhering to a fairly conservative idea of what the characteristics of the future would be—empires, aliens, advancing technology, wars, and conquest—the stories became richer and more compelling than anything possible in the previous decade. In the few years between 1939 and the end of World War

II, many long-standing conventions of science fiction were established.

Robert Heinlein (1907–1988) developed a timeline of future history that outlined the social and technological changes to come. Many of his stories published in *Astounding* during this period remained true to the history and could be organized as a series of expanded historical moments. The stories, then, were interrelated and played off one another; more important, they gave the future history the depth of narrative. In 1941, Campbell even published a chart based on Heinlein's projection.

During this same time Asimov conceived of his three laws of robotics, which have such elegant simplicity they appeal to writers and scientists alike: "1) A robot may not injure a human being, or, through inaction, allow a human being to come to harm; 2) a robot must obey the orders given it by human beings except where such orders conflict with the First Law; and 3) a robot must protect its own existence as long as such protection does not conflict with the First or Second Law."

Another powerful component of the period during Campbell's early tenure at *Astounding* was the collaboration that occurred not just between Campbell and his writers but between writers and readers. Fandom had been slowly growing since the 1920s in the form of letters to the editor, fan clubs, and fanzines; eventually it came to include more organized and influential events like science fiction conventions (the first one was held in 1937) and awards (the Hugos, named after Hugo Gernsback, were first held in the early 1950s).

AFTER THE BOMB

The bombing of Hiroshima and Nagasaki marked the final blow against the naive idealization of technology, which had persisted even in *Astounding* during the post-Gernsback days. It was replaced by the nightmare consequences of technology. Nuclear annihilation, arms races, and radiation poisoning became some of the dominant themes in science fiction during the 1950s and remained so until the status quo was derailed by the British New Wave in the mid-1960s.

Before World War II there were more than sixteen science fiction magazines in publication. Most had disappeared by the end of the war. In the postwar years, however, there was another publishing boom, and in 1955 more than thirty-five science fiction and fantasy magazines were publishing in the United States. *Amazing* and *Astounding* were still going strong.

The two most influential new magazines were the *Magazine of Fantasy and Science Fiction* and *Galaxy*.

The *Magazine of Fantasy and Science Fiction* sought to elevate the writing, appealing to a more educated audience, privileging character and story in a way that had no precedent within the genre. Under the editorship of H. L. Gold—who had been publishing stories in *Astounding* since 1934—*Galaxy* expanded the "science" in "science fiction" to include psychology, sociology, and history. Physics and chemistry were, for the first time, no longer the raison d'être of science fiction. The human sciences made science fiction more porous to social issues and heightened its ability to critique and question as much as entertain—characteristics not seen since H. G. Wells's *The Time Machine* and *The War of the Worlds* in the late nineteenth century.

So far, American science fiction had been published almost exclusively in magazines, which meant it had been primarily a short-story form. In the 1950s science fiction anthologies began appearing, and a few hardback novels were published as well. In 1952, Ian and Betty Ballantine began publishing Ballantine Books, and for the first time science fiction appeared in trade paperback form. The modern science fiction novel was born. Novellas and serial stories first published in magazines were expanded and cobbled together to create novels. Asimov's *Foundation*, originally a series of interrelated stories published in *Astounding* during the 1940s, appeared as the first novel of the *Foundation* trilogy in 1951. Other examples of seminal novels that first appeared as stories or novellas are Theodore Sturgeon's *More Than Human*, James Blish's *A Case of Conscience*, Heinlein's *The Puppet Masters*, and Alfred Bester's *The Stars My Destination*. As a consequence magazines once again suffered, and by the mid-1960s most that had published through the 1950s were no longer in print. *Amazing, Astounding* (which became *Analog* in 1960), *Magazine of Fantasy and Science Fiction*, and *Galaxy* all survived.

The audience for science fiction had grown since the 1940s, which, coupled with the sudden availability of cheap paperbacks, created the publishing boom in the 1950s. The writers publishing in the *Magazine of Fantasy and Science Fiction* and *Galaxy*—Philip K. Dick, Theodore Sturgeon, Fredrick Pohl, Damon Knight, and Clifford Simak—began writing novels that would later became an unshakable part of the canon. However, the popularity and proliferation by paperback demanded that writers produce conformist, salable fiction in large quantities. The think-tank environment of Campbell's early years at *Astounding* was replaced by a hungry marketplace.

THE NEW WAVE

"New Wave" was originally coined by French journalists in 1959 to name the explosion of work by a group of young French filmmakers. The phrase was adopted by the science fiction community in the mid-1960s to describe a shift toward experimentation and a move away from the more commercial writing that had come to dominate the industry in England and America. The culture of conformism began looking conspicuous in light of the larger cultural changes occurring throughout the world, and a handful of mostly younger writers saw devices in literary fiction that might revitalize the genre. Calling this moment in science fiction history the New Wave is both understandable and misleading. Yes, it was a transformative moment inside an insular community of writers, editors, critics, and fans but one that only feebly echoed the thrust of literary modernism, which had begun well before the first issue of *Amazing Stories* hit the newsstands in 1926.

The New Wave began in 1965 when the British writer Michael Moorcock took over editorship of *New Worlds*, the British equivalent of *Astounding*. While postwar science fiction was preoccupied with the implications of nuclear war and had made a dramatic shift away from the overly simplistic depictions of technological advance and imperialistic and galactic expansion, the emphasis was nonetheless still problem-solving in the physical world. As the editor of *New Worlds*, Moorcock created a venue for writers who felt the standard motifs were exhausted. Along with Moorcock, the British writers J. G. Ballard and Brian Aldiss and the Americans Thomas M. Disch, Samuel R. Delany, and Roger Zelazny developed styles reflecting more interiority and formal experimentation.

The trend was quickly picked up in America, and in 1967 Harlan Ellison's anthology *Dangerous Visions* was published. The title was both a sensational description of content and a forceful declaration to writers and publishers that the industry had become complacent. Included in the anthology were many British writers associated with *New Worlds*. Notable among the Americans were Robert Silverberg, Philip José Farmer, Philip K. Dick, Carol Emshwiller, Fritz Leiber, Ursula Le Guin, and Kurt Vonnegut Jr. The anthology was nominated for numerous Hugo and Nebula awards, and Ellison received a Hugo as its editor.

Many of the American contributors had been publishing since the 1950s. Some, like Silverberg, had worked in a more conventional idiom and only now ventured into new territory. Others, like Dick and Emshwiller,

were simply gaining a wider reception of their already challenging work. Silverberg published his first story, "Gorgon Planet," in *Nebula Science Fiction* (1954) when he was nineteen years old and subsequently produced an enormous quantity of commercial writing through the remainder of the decade. During the early 1960s he stopped writing science fiction and turned to more lucrative nonfiction genres. His return to science fiction coincided with the industry's revolt against the formulaic writing that had been his bread and butter. This, coupled with the influence of early modernist experimentation on his own writing, allowed him to explore themes of alienation in a popular science fiction idiom. The novel *Thorns* (1967) and the stories "Passengers" (1968) and "Sundance" (1969) placed him at the forefront of the new literary science fiction.

Philip K. Dick, while never giving up the too hastily written pulp style, had been creating original and challenging fiction since his first publications in the early 1950s. His work epitomizes, perhaps better than that of any other science fiction writer, the kind of contradiction that is always possible in genre writing. Stylistically Dick is virtually never interesting and can be very often deplorable. And yet many of his novels, in particular *The Man in the High Castle* (1962), *The Three Stigmata of Palmer Eldritch* (1965), and *Ubik* (1969), are ambitious and successful in their depiction of paranoia and the anxiety surrounding confrontation with experience that can't be understood. The imaginative scope of his novels and the frameworks within which his protagonists are trapped render a shadowy world of imagination that is frightening and seductive.

The new voices and the new themes divided many writers, and the distinction between "hard" and humanist science fiction was never greater. The New Wave writers were calling William Burroughs their savior looking for influences outside of their genre. Less sympathetic voices like James Blish, Lester del Rey, and Donald Wollheim accused the New Wave of being nothing more than a rehash of European experimentalism from the 1920s and 1930s. They decried its pessimism and emphasis on style over believable depictions of speculative science. While it is true that the New Wave writers had not discovered anything new, writing works that were in large part derivative of modernist literature, they did introduce devices, like stream of consciousness and nonlinear narrative, that were new to the genre.

During the 1970s most science fiction returned to its old ways of telling the future. The New Wave did set a precedent, however, introducing higher writing standards and an ethos of social responsibility. A handful of older writers, including Robert Silverberg, Frederick Pohl, Damon Knight, Walter Miller, and Robert Sheckley, continued in a similar vein, producing quality, purposeful novels and short stories.

More women writers gained prominence during the 1970s, which to some degree the New Wave may have facilitated by calling conventions into question. It was, however, primarily the result of larger cultural changes—changes that science fiction had once again been unaware of because of its insularity and entrenched assumptions about who wrote science fiction. Anne McCaffrey, Kate Wilheim, Marion Zimmer Bradley, and Ursula Le Guin had all been writing during the 1960s, but it was not until the 1970s that they gained recognition commensurate with their work. Joanna Russ, a writer whose work has survived both inside and outside the genre, was writing fiction and criticism during the 1960s, and her first novel, *The Female Man*, was published in 1975. Decidedly utopian, feminist, comic, experimental science fiction, the novel indicates how much the genre can contain without collapsing under its own weight and makes one wonder why there isn't more science fiction as dynamic and challenging.

CYBERPUNK AND OTHER FUTURES

Cyberpunk, or "the Movement" as it is sometimes called, was a self-conscious attempt by a small group of mostly younger writers to revitalize the genre. Their point of departure was a critique of the industry similar to that of the New Wave writers, only this time the target *was* the New Wave and neo–New Wave writers (or, in general, the whole humanist subgenre of science fiction). The main complaint was the abandonment of the technology motif. In many ways cyberpunk is more a continuation or rejuvenation of the iconoclasm introduced by the New Wave, in the same way that the punk rock and 1960s countercultures are analogous. Particular to the cyberpunk writers, however, was an extremely unified vision of the future.

William Gibson and his first novel, *Neuromancer,* play a central role in casting the new future. It is the twenty-first century, and multinational corporations are more powerful than governments. Money, power, and information flow through cyberspace. Cyberspace is a consensual hallucination from which special operators can enter and steal or manipulate the content, which is controlled by the corporations. Cyberspace is one of the

novel's landscapes. The other is the urban landscape of the twenty-first century, which is like Tokyo under the influence of Reaganomics to the nth degree. Everything is high-tech, but there is an urban erosion, a noir grittiness, in which the characters operate.

The world of the novel overshadows the plot—a modest heist story—and, as with all compelling science fiction, the world is a wonderful hybrid, not a singular creation. *Neuromancer* was published in 1984, two years after the release of Ridley Scott's *Blade Runner*, Hollywood's revamp of Philip K. Dick's *Do Androids Dream of Electric Sheep? Neuromancer*'s unnamed America is a less glitzy, more street-smart version of *Blade Runner*'s Los Angeles. *Neuromancer* may not be derivative of *Blade Runner*, since both employ fairly simple and intuitive extrapolations of America during the 1980s: Reaganomics, Silicon Valley, and punk rock are present in each like the White Rabbit in *Alice's Adventures in Wonderland*.

While Gibson never pronounced cyberpunk "revolutionary" as Moorcock and Ellison had said of New Wave, another writer did. Bruce Sterling even earned himself the nickname "the Chairman" for his outspoken cheerleading about cyberpunk's role in science fiction history. During the 1980s he wrote cyberpunk manifestos in his fanzine *Cheap Truth* as well as influential stories and novels like "Swarm" (1982) and *Schismatrix* (1985). Other cyberpunk writers include Gardner Dozois, Rudy Rucker, and Greg Bear.

Technology is an ever-present element in cyberpunk, yet its role is never straightforward, often being a tool of both oppression and liberation, suggesting that technology itself is not moral but its implementation is. Politically cyberpunk is humanist, albeit a somewhat revised humanism, offering a more sophisticated answer to the question about technology's role in the genre. New Wave had moved the focus from outerspace to "innerspace," as J. G. Ballard has said, leaving technology out of the equation. Meanwhile, the "hard" science fiction writers held fast to their optimism about technological and scientific advancement that had been the status quo New Wave. Interestingly, while Gibson and Sterling were hammering out the new future of the twenty-first century—replete with the high-tech double-edged swords of cyberspace, prosthetic body parts, drugs, and all-powerful corporations—the consummate "hard" science fiction writers Larry Niven and Jerry Pournelle were lobbying President Reagan as outspoken advocates for the Star Wars missile defense system.

While most of the science fiction published in this country is written by Anglo-American men, including cyberpunk, the increasing racial and gender diversity within the genre suggests the old school insularity may be diminishing. As stated earlier, until the 1980s the only prominent African-American science fiction writer was Samuel R. Delany; it's hard to imagine a more conspicuous absence in a genre that is ostensibly concerned with socially relevant speculation about the future. There have been signs of change, however. Octavia Butler has come to prominence since the 1980s, publishing ten novels since 1977. Her stories "Speech Sounds" (1983) and "Bloodchild" (1984) won the Hugo and the Nebula awards respectively. Many of her novels are linked by a common future history about a superhuman species tied into a psychic web called the Pattern. The "mutes" lack psychic powers and are ruled by the Patternists. Her protagonists are usually strong black women, and while remaining easily within the science fiction idiom she creates complex explorations of gender, power, and master/slave relationships.

New epochs in science fiction are often marked by an anthology of work that challenges the old guard. In 1967 *Dangerous Visions* was published, ushering in the New Wave. In 1975 *Woman of Wonder*, edited by Pamela Sargent, announced the serious presence of women writing science fiction. And in 1986 Bruce Sterling edited *Mirrorshades: The Cyberpunk Anthology*. In 2000 a new anthology appeared, entitled *Dark Matter: A Century of Speculative Fiction from the African Diaspora*. Edited by Sheree Thomas, *Dark Matter* was the first anthology of black speculative fiction, including twenty-five stories, three novel excerpts, and five critical essays, spanning the period from 1887 to the end of the last century. (After *Dangerous Visions* was published in 1967, Harlan Ellison rejected the term "science fiction" to describe his own work, adopting instead the phrase "speculative fiction," a slightly looser term that includes horror and supernatural fiction.) *Dark Matter* is a surprising confluence of work that demands that the genre make some serious adjustments. Many of the themes are familiar science fiction fare—UFOs, robots, alien abduction, genetic mutation, space travel—while others, like Adam and Eve, astral travel, and an African civil war ring true but require a deeper set of conventions than the genre normally offers. Delany and Butler contribute an essay and a story each, along with newer work by other established writers like Amira Baraka, Ishmael Reed, and Walter

Mosley (known for his work in another genre: hard-boiled detective fiction). Writers working more strictly within the science fiction field include Nalo Hopkinson, Tananarive Due, Jewelle Gomez, and Steven Barnes, who has been publishing since the early 1980s.

Science fiction's future histories have a built-in shelf life because the future that was predicted becomes the present and writers have to start all over again. Starting over usually coincides with other cultural shifts that give urgency to change, and every ten years seems to bring a watershed moment. The test will be whether science fiction can articulate a future that recognizes the new present.

[*See also* Popular Fiction *and* Vonnegut, Kurt.]

FURTHER READING

Aldiss, Brian. *Trillion Year Spree: The History of Science Fiction*. New York, 1986. The authoritative history of science fiction by a science fiction author. The interpretative component of the book is full of generalizations and hasty conclusions. The historical component is quite detailed and firsthand.

Bloom, Harold, ed. *Classic Science Fiction Writers*. New York, 1995. A great resource for researching nineteenth- and early-twentieth-century science fiction authors; includes biographical essays and bibliographies.

Clareson, Thomas. *Some Kind of Paradise*. Westport, Conn., 1986. An informed and scholarly but readable discussion about early science fiction and the impact the two world wars had on the genre.

Clareson, Thomas D. *Understanding Contemporary American Science Fiction*. Columbia, S.C., 1990. A detailed chronology of science fiction writing from 1930 to 1970. The author has written many other books about the genre as well.

Gunn, James, ed. *The New Encyclopedia of Science Fiction*. New York, 1988. A wonderful compendium of essays about specific aspects of the genre by science fiction critics and writers. The book is an excellent starting point for research.

James, Edward. *Science Fiction in the Twentieth Century*. New York, 1994. A history of American science fiction writing.

Robinson, Frank. *Science Fiction of the 20th Century: An Illustrated History*. New York, 1998. Useful for exploring the early pulp magazines. The book is amply illustrated with original magazine covers.

Sterling, Bruce, ed. *Mirrorshades: The Cyberpunk Anthology*. New York, 1986.

Thomas, Sheree R., ed. *Dark Matter: A Century of Speculative Fiction from the African Diaspora*. New York, 2000.

Wingrove, David. *The Science Fiction Source Book*. New York, 1984. A concise resource for information about authors, books, and magazines. There is no revised second edition, so the book is not helpful for anything published after the early 1980s.

Wukel, Dieter, and Bruce Cassidy. *The Illustrated History of Science Fiction*. New York, 1989. A very well-written and compelling look at many aspects of the genre with an emphasis on European and literary science fiction. American science fiction is discussed mainly as an influence (usually a bad one) on European and eastern European science fiction.

SENTIMENTAL LITERATURE

Mary Louise Kete

To survey the history of sentimental literature in America is to gain insight into some of the most critical moments in American culture. As Thomas Paine's influential essay of 1776 explained, it is on the grounds of "common sense" that the colonial Englishman would be able to "generously enlarge his views beyond the present day" and so imagine and ultimately fight for independence. And the existence of common sense, Paine and his audience understood, was proved by the recognition that all people respond to the loss of their children in the same way. Sentimentality—featuring broken homes restored, dying children revived, and lost lovers found through the power of shared emotions—is a way to remind readers that at root we are all lost children, no matter how vast may seem the differences made apparent by logic and circumstance. Sentimentality expresses the utopian impulse to abolish boundaries and expand community upon which the ideological force of American identity depends. In other words, it is a term for a discursive mode, not a genre nor a historical period, that is used to construct a shared or common sensibility that hides the traces of its invention under the cloak of tradition.

The language of sentiment (what Walt Whitman called the "dialect of commonsense") may no longer direct Americans toward revolutionary political action; however, it certainly continues to inform American narrative, oratorical, and visual discourses in contemporary films, political speeches, and both popular and monumental visual arts. The continued (even if problematic) power of sentiment in America is due to its important role in both defining what it would mean to be an American and establishing the process by which one could become an American during the years between the Revolutionary War and the close of the Civil War.

WHAT IS SENTIMENTAL ABOUT SENTIMENTAL LITERATURE?

Sentimentalism is not confined to written works, and the discussion that follows could deal with visual, electronic, and aural as well as literary sentimentality. Even in the period focused on here, the mode of sentiment was dominant in nonliterary representations such as painting and sculpture, and even in landscape design. This definition adds sentimentality to the limited set of major expressive modes that includes irony, tragedy, romance, realism, and comedy.

Sentimentality is the set of symbolic gestures used to shape common sense through the simultaneous deployment of both conservative and generative impulses. These gestures operate on three axes (topic, diction, and rhetoric) to facilitate and even to enforce a collaborative effort against loss by engaging the subject and the object of sentiment in a constitutive economy of donative presentation and re-presentation. The three signal topics of sentimentality are lost homes, lost families, and broken bonds. The mere representation of these topics, however, does not in itself call for the adjective "sentimental." The sentimental mode also depends on the use of a distinctive vocabulary and rhetoric to present these topics. The defining vocabulary is a highly embellished, "literary" lexicon appropriated from recognized sources and mortared together with the diction of vernacular language.

Neither the presence of these topics nor the use of this language, however, demands the term "sentimental" unless a particular rhetorical trope, the apostrophe, is also present. Apostrophe, whether a direct address to an abstraction or one to an absent person, dramatizes the existence of multiple registers of imagined reality. Apostrophic address, in combination with certain topics and language, is the defining symbolic gesture of sentimentality because it is the vehicle through which the viewer or reader is encouraged to participate in the violation of these apparent planes of representation in order to reconstruct newer ones.

Despite what critics now recognize as the pervasiveness of sentimentality in American culture, the adjective "sentimental" has had dual valences—celebratory and pejorative—since it entered the lexicon in the eighteenth century. By 1776, Paine did not have to explain how it was that morality derives from those human faculties that allow us to share a common sensibility (sympathy) with one another. This idea had already become a critical commonplace supported in different ways by the ideas of Continental philosophers such as Jean-Jacques Rousseau and Emmanuel Kant and of British thinkers as various as Lord Shaftesbury, Adam Smith, and Francis Hutcheson. Whether in the register of fiction or in the register of political philosophy, Britons throughout the empire were increasingly exposed to a persuasive moral and aesthetic appeal to a shared common sensibility that was characterized by a feeling of loss. Thus, the novelist Samuel Richardson asked his reader to enter into sympathy with the parents of his heroine, Pamela, as Pamela asked her parents to enter into sympathy with her, and the philosopher Adam Smith asked his reader to believe in the recursive power of personal empathy to control the atavistic tendencies of the marketplace.

The problem that the sentimental mode addresses—how to create and perpetuate community once the traditional bounds of blood and geography have been loosened—was posed by Adam Smith in the *Theory of Moral Sentiments* (1759) as a problem of epistemology (How can we know?) concretized as a problem of communication (How can we share knowledge?). Since our own senses "will never carry us beyond our own person," we have to rely on something else. That something else, Smith explained, is imagination. Imagination allows us to communicate outside ourselves through a curious process of "representing to us what would be our own [case], if we were in the case" of another, even while we understand that it is the "impressions of our own senses only, not those of his, our imaginations copy" (p. 9). Smith, writing in the first flush of a truly mass culture brought about by the proliferation of cheap printed matter, was able to theorize the distinguishing paradox of sentimentalism: somehow, through the copying of our own impressions, we can generate new sensations that will in turn change the very nature of the feeling self. The imaginative reproduction of feeling allowed for an economy that in turn permitted the growth of this sentimental capital. "Right feeling," rather than appeal to an extrinsic source such as the Bible, became the standard measure of authentic moral judgment, and therefore of moral action.

However, the idea that feelings could be communicated only through representation raised the possibility and problem of counterfeiting, which has continued to color theoretical responses to the power of sentiment. Karen Haltunnen, for example, has traced the anxiety caused by the need of nineteenth-century Americans to distinguish authentic from sham sentiment. This anxiety, Haltunnen argues, is further evidence of the degree to which emotional force was valued. Especially within the American context, then, the term "sentimentalism" has generally been used to dismiss representations that seem to evoke an unwarranted emotional response. Walt Whitman, though celebrating the power of emotional imagination to allow him to experience and speak for the "Maternal as well as the paternal, a child as well as a man," was careful to describe himself as "no sentimentalist."

As scholarly attention to American literary history increased during the twentieth century and attempts were made to sort the literary heritage of the previous century, the question was posed as to whether the sensational designs of sentimentality (to use Jane Tompkins's [1985] term) were warranted, and when and by whom they might be legitimately employed. James Baldwin, in his seminal essay of 1949, "Everybody's Protest Novel," persuasively argued that there is no warrant, aesthetic or moral, for the literary mode that dominated the previous century. For Baldwin, Harriet Beecher Stowe's voyeuristic depiction of the pathos of slavery served only to reify racism and so was not warranted on a moral basis. Baldwin pointed out that the antirationality of sentimental identification, of common sense, is the basis for mob action, and that neither the reactionary power of mobs nor that of sentiment can be controlled. Like F. O. Matthiessen before him in the revolutionary study *The American Renaissance* (1941), Baldwin considered that the unambiguously political power of sentimentality conflicted fatally with any aesthetic claims that might be made for it. In fact, as Herbert Ross Brown's 1940s study, *The Sentimental Novel in America 1789–1860*, typifies, it was difficult for twentieth-century artists and cultural critics not to see "sentiment" and "aesthetics" as mutually exclusive terms.

Two developments in academic criticism of the late twentieth century fueled a revision of the term and the literature to which it refers. One was the historical recovery of the literary works produced by nineteenth-century women and black Americans. This ongoing project, though a conventional form of literary scholarship, is inspired by contemporary political needs to counter claims of the insignificance of women and blacks to the cultural history of America. The other development was a shift in formalist criticism toward a poststructuralist methodology that makes qualitative criteria (mass or elite, masculine or feminine, progressive or conservative, and so forth) part of the object of study. The very number of recovered works by "dis-remembered" nineteenth-century authors that could be described as "sentimental" testified to a poetics that was escaping current critical appreciation. To use Jane Tompkins's term, many of these works clearly had "sensational designs" upon their readers, with dead babies, whipped slaves, and empty hearths depicted in what seemed to be an awkwardly overwrought manner. But whereas an earlier generation of critics stopped at this realization and therefore felt justified in looking away ("dis-remembering") from the many traces of a literary culture in which women and blacks fully participated, a newer generation struggled to "re-remember" how to understand this large body of work. The critical questions then became "What are the codes governing sentimentality, and how do they function in particular contexts?" In other words, critics have begun to attempt to articulate the ways in which sentimental literature fulfilled some criteria of beauty (the question of aesthetics), and the ways in which it served some criteria of purpose (the question of poetics).

SENTIMENT IN EARLY AMERICA

Over the course of the eighteenth century, those trying hardest to reproduce the British self under colonial conditions created a kind of subjectivity whose "newness" and distinctiveness preceded the military and political creation of the new nation, the United States of America. J. Hector St. John de Crèvecoeur's *Letters from an American Farmer* (1782) exemplifies the eighteenth-century attempt to trace the sentimental process by which one "becomes an American." Only by "leaving behind him all his ancient prejudices and manners," explains Crèvecoeur's American Farmer, can a person enter into the free and mutual embrace that constitutes American identity. This identity, Crèvecoeur wrote, depends not on political or geographical boundaries that can be determined by logic and analysis of factors outside the self, but on the nature of one's feelings. In fact, the American Farmer ends his narrative by explaining the necessity of removing himself and his family beyond the borders of the new United States in order to preserve the conditions necessary to maintaining his feelings of "Americanness." In *Letters from an American Farmer*, as in Thomas Paine's various responses to the American crisis, sentimentality is a way of freeing the self so that it can enter into the liberal relationships on which the new society can be built.

In the years of the early republic, both authors and the subjects they addressed reflected the transatlantic nature of American identity, which depended on sentimentality

to help liberate American from British culture. Only later would writers turn the power of sentiment toward the problem of defining or limiting the nature of American culture. This was as true for writers of fiction and poetry as for essayists like Paine and Crèvecoeur. *Charlotte: A Tale of Truth* (1791) by Susanna Haswell Rowson (ca. 1762–1824) is a good example of what a novelist popular in America at that time would call the "power of sentiment." Born in England, Rowson spent time as a child on both sides of the Atlantic before choosing to become a paragon and proselytizer of American identity. *Charlotte* was written and first published in England but found its best audience in America, where, as the literary historian Cathy Davidson has traced, it attracted readers from all social classes, regions, and religions. Thematically, the story dramatizes a contest between sham and true feeling that makes a shambles of numerous homes over several generations. The recognition of common feeling repeatedly establishes voluntary communities in the form of families that must continually struggle against the tyrannical threat of the indulgence of selfish feelings.

Set during the years of the Revolutionary War, the main story concerns a young girl, Charlotte, who responds to the unsolicited affection of a thoughtless British officer, Montraville, by abandoning her own family to follow him to America. There, Charlotte is herself abandoned, but not before giving birth to an illegitimate daughter. This daughter, like the new nation she is born in, will have to establish an identity within a network of voluntary relationships because the story of her mother has shown how unreliable legal and blood relationships can be. Although it is not a typical eighteenth-century epistolary novel, in *Charlotte* the circulation of letters plays an important role in the plot as well as in the discourse. Through letters, the characters are able to address other characters despite geographical distance, and the narrator is able to redirect the reader's attention by shifting both the object and subject of focus. The language in the letters, no matter which character is supposed to have authored them, differs dramatically from the normative language of the narration and is distinctive to each fictional author. As extended apostrophes, these letters force the reader to exercise imaginative flexibility. The circulation and the obstruction of affections through letters drive the plot: Montraville seduces Charlotte through a letter that the young girl knows she should not have accepted; Montraville prevents the delivery of letters from Charlotte to her parents; the cad Belcour prevents Charlotte's letters to Montraville from being delivered; a letter of dismissal from Montraville breaks Charlotte's heart; and finally, the successful delivery of a letter to her parents allows for a deathbed reconciliation.

Rowson's novel typifies the sentimental novels that were read in the America of the early Republic. The signature sensationalism of sentimental literature in America is seen in Rowson's focus on the plight of unwed women, or rather, on the difference between legitimate and illegitimate affective associations. Her narrator explicitly asks her readers to "reflect how many errors we are ourselves subject to" before condemning "those unhappy women who fall victims to guilt and folly." But it also asks her readers to discriminate between kinds of feelings, because some reinforce community (imagined as a family formed on mutual, voluntary affections) while some are antithetical to it.

Rowson herself chose America as a place to become what she felt she had always been. She celebrated its potential in a number of popular plays, such as *The Female Patriot* and *The Columbian Daughter*. The feelings that are claimed to be most natural and most common—love of parents and love of children—are the ones that are most revolutionary and therefore to be fostered in the new nation. The feelings that are produced through the force of tradition or money or physical strength can only betray. In the early years of the new century, Rowson participated in the institutionalization of what had been revolutionary expressions by establishing a school for girls, devoted to preparing women to succeed as the kind of republican mother that her poor Charlotte Temple was so fatefully unsuited to become.

THE SENTIMENTAL EDUCATION OF AMERICA

If sentiment was used by early authors to liberate a self so that it could enter into some new, yet-to-be-defined American utopia, authors of the next few generations used sentiment to imagine what the details of this new community would be. Would the term "American" refer to women? To blacks? To Catholic immigrants? If anyone could be American who felt "American," then could it be that no one was American? Many authors of this period used sentimental poetry to try to answer these questions by defining and limiting the exact nature of America. Two of these, Lydia Howard Huntley Sigourney and

Lydia Huntley Sigourney by Charles Kennedy Burt. (© *Stapleton Collection/Corbis*)

Henry Wadsworth Longfellow, represent a varied group of poets who wielded much cultural power throughout the nineteenth century, only to be almost forgotten for much of the twentieth.

In early-nineteenth-century America, verse existed in a cultural space in which it was both widely revered and widely practiced. Narrative and lyric verse were privileged literary genres that differed significantly from both sanctioned and nonsanctioned prose forms. The conspicuous lack of institutional approval for novels such as Rowson's might have contributed to the attraction for them felt by the young and working people, who were apparently the initial purchasers of the numerous cheap editions. Verse aroused neither the suspicion that the novel did nor the solemn respect owed to sermons or prose histories, but it was nevertheless enthusiastically bought, sold, and shared. As Lawrence Levine (1988) has argued, the clear distinction between "high" or elite and "low" or popular arts is a phenomenon that arose in the late nineteenth century. Poetry was no exception: held in respect, but something anyone could practice. Thus, it provides us with unique insight into the "habitus" (cultural context and practices) of nineteenth-century America than do other more specialized, more professional literary practices.

The shift in taste that had occurred over the course of the eighteenth century in Britain—away from the neo-Augustan dictates of Pope and Dryden and toward an embrace of spontaneity and inspiration—had registered rather late in America. Even at the turn of the nineteenth century, major American poets such as the Connecticut wit Joel Barlow, Vermont's Royal Tyler, or Boston's Mercy Warren continued to deploy neo-Augustan forms and criteria of taste. It was not until the close of the War of 1812 that American poets begin to articulate what later literary historians would call a "romantic sensibility" in response to the cultural revolution across the ocean. The poetry columns of newspapers and the much-shared copies of British and domestic magazines began featuring Felicia Hemans, William Wordsworth, and Lord Byron as well as Hannah More, Thomas Gray, and Edward Young. Joining the stream of secular literary influences was that of religious verse, featuring the emotionally effusive hymns of Isaac Watts and John Wesley. Just as the canons of secular taste were being revised to sanction inspiration and spontaneity over intellectualism and wit, hymnals were being revised to embrace a newly gentled Jesus whose much-emphasized tears persuade rather than command conversion.

The publication in 1817 of William Cullen Bryant's poem "Thanatopsis" is often cited as the moment when British and European romantic poetry was appropriated for America, but in 1815 Lydia Sigourney had published *Moral Pieces in Prose and Verse*. This collection sold well and, like "Thanatopsis," brought together the themes of death, nature, and the individual. But where "Thanatopsis" did so to emphasize the sublimation of a self for whom no community can, by definition, exist, Sigourney combined these elements to establish the imaginary prerequisites of a *social* self. A peculiarity of American literary history, in contrast to European and British literary histories, has been the convention of subtracting the sentimental from discussions of American romanticism, but American readers of 1845 would not have hesitated to describe their two favorite poets, Longfellow and Sigourney, as sentimental.

Like John Greenleaf Whittier and Fanny Osgood (and Bryant himself in poems other than "Thanatopsis"), Sigourney and Longfellow sought to create a poetic idiom that was uniquely American without forgetting its connections with European culture. In an early poem, "Unspoken Language," Sigourney provided an excellent articulation of the theory of sentimental discourse through which this creation of American uniqueness would be accomplished. "Language," she began, "is slow, the mastery of wants / Doth teach it to the infant, drop by drop." "Years of studious toil / Unfold its classic labyrinths to the boy" who would "acquire / The speech of many lands." But this course is incomplete, according to Sigourney, if it does not recognize the prior and superior claims of the "unspoken language" of love, which is "Simple and sure, that asks no discipline / Of weary years." This "language of the soul" is learned in an instant of mutual identification between beholder and beheld. Sigourney established the mother and child as the epitome of this superior form of communication, for the "mother speaks as well / To the unfolding spirit of her babe." This nonverbal and extra-rational communication surpasses all others because, Sigourney hoped, it wears the "signet ring of truth." Sigourney and Longfellow are typical of pre–Civil War American poets for whom the unspoken language of the soul has a grammar and lexicon that can be reproduced, though only approximately, through words. In this way, as Longfellow wrote in "Dedication" (which opens his popular collection *From the Seaside to the Fireside*, 1849), "kind messages" can "pass from land to land." Through the mode of sentimentality, Longfellow replicated the process by which "the heart's deep history" and the "pressure of hand" may be shared across distances of time and space. "Dedication" suggests that he understood that the exchange of sentiments offered a way to bridge alienation, to collaborate with another in "endeavor[s] for the self same ends / With the same hopes, and fears and aspirations." Whether one looks at Longfellow's allegory "The Building of the Ship" or Sigourney's anthem "Our Country," the mode of sentiment functions to call into being an American who would be willing and able to participate in society, not flee from it.

This project was shared by novelists of the first half of the nineteenth century who, in the years following Rowson's death, developed a novel increasingly distinct from the its British counterpart. The novel, like poetry, was turned to the problem of how to make the American self "more perfect"; and the solution to this problem was, more often than not, through sentiment. The paradigmatic fictional character for this exploration remained, as for Rowson and her contemporaries, the young girl who is actually or effectively orphaned and so left to create herself. America's second "best-seller," Susan Warner's novel *The Wide, Wide World* (1840), exemplifies this as it establishes conventions that remain typical of much sentimental fiction even today. One of the most important contributions Warner made in this book was the degree to which she was able to invoke the sensational qualities of the everyday trials that beset an ordinary girl within a domestic setting. Where Rowson's book features scenes of abduction and seduction under extraordinary conditions of wartime, Warner's illustrates the moral drama inherent in learning to shop and to keep house. Warner, in her own gendered way, was responding to Emerson's appeal in "the American Scholar" to "embrace the common... explore and sit at the feet of the familiar, the low"; her skillful deployment of sentimentality helped her readers share the sorrow, confusion, and anger felt by the child Ellen Montgomery. Like Charlotte Temple, whose parents are unable to help her despite their own wishes, Warner's protagonist has parents and aunts and uncles who are at best unable to help, and at worst a positive hindrance. *The Wide, Wide World*, as is typical of the sentimental novel, posits as normative the failure of relationships that are not based on voluntary mutual consent. Instead, the plot consists of Ellen's learning how to exercise emotional discretion in choosing from whom to learn and with whom to enter into affectionate relationships. The object of Ellen's education is not Emersonian self-reliance but the reform of the self so as to be able to enter into and sustain voluntary relationships. The most important relationship for Ellen to choose and sustain is with God, who asks not for submission but for permission to participate in a collaborative project of improvement.

Many popular novels of the first half of the nineteenth century explore the possible variations of the pattern established by Warner. Denied the vote, the boardroom, and the pulpit, women authors in particular embraced the genre of the sentimental novel and tale. In this genre, authors were able to explore the political and philosophical problems that the project of America posed for women. While many sentimental novels by white authors concentrated on self-reform, others attempted to use sentiment directly to reform the self of the nation. Elizabeth Oakes-Smith (1806–1893) was one of many who tackled the endemic threat of alcoholism in temperance tales. Lydia Maria Child, Catherine Sedgewick, and E.D.E.N Southworth are only a few of the authors who marshaled sentiment on behalf of social reform in the years before the Civil War. However, the most important antebellum novel to deploy sentiment was Harriet Beecher Stowe's *Uncle Tom's Cabin; or, Life among the Lowly* (1852). Stylistically innovative, Stowe raised sentiment to its apogee in the service of an abolitionist agenda.

The main armature of Stowe's plot is shaped by the power of memory circulating through an economy of sentiment to bind characters, reader, and author together in a collaboration against legal and social mores that calls for nothing less than a reconfiguration of common sense. One concise example appears in the subplot concerning the escape of Eliza and her baby, Harry. Arriving at the house of a U.S. senator who has voted for the Fugitive Slave Act, the runaways pose an untenable challenge to the rational logic of the law. In response to the pietà-like vision of Eliza and the child she is trying to protect, Senator and Mrs. Bird present Eliza with the clothes of one of their own, recently dead children, which they had been preserving as keepsakes. The relics of the dead white child (the "things—of—of—poor little Henry's") are put into the service of the living black child's life and family. Giving, within the sentimental world, is one of the best ways of keeping: in this exchange, the memory of the dead child is enhanced and even allowed to act upon

the world. The process of exchange in this scene occurs under the rubric of mourning and hence is ostensibly a conservative, conserving gesture, yet it generates two subversive possibilities. On the one hand, as the title of Stowe's chapter suggests, it transforms the senator from an instrument of the state to "but a man" who will act on emotional evidence rather than on legal precedent. Mrs. Bird, Mr. Bird, and Eliza Harris share the common subject position as parents of children (one dead, one living) for whom they will do anything. On the other hand, this exchange is just the first gesture in the collaborative creation of a free black family. The revolutionary potential of this possibility has been explained to the reader by Eliza's husband, George, who understands the role played by the disruption of family and by natal alienation in the system of slavery. Stowe's book makes plain the connection between the right to maintain voluntarily a circle of family and friends and the ability to aspire to the status of possessive individualism predicated by liberal ideology.

The main thrust of Stowe's novel, as critics such as Philip Fisher (1987) and Gillian Brown (1990) remind us, was to persuade her white readers to recognize blacks as humans who shared the common sensibility and therefore the common inalienable rights to life, liberty, and the pursuit of happiness predicated by the Declaration of Independence. In other words, Stowe attempted to use sentiment on behalf of a group to which she did not belong and with which she could identify only through sympathy. But *Uncle Tom's Cabin* was also one of the fullest articulations of a feminine, if not feminist critique, of mid-nineteenth-century American society. In this sense, it is also a good example of how sentiment could be used on one's own behalf. If the scene discussed above illustrates the success of women in wielding moral suasion within a family bound by shared love and shared memories, numerous other scenes throughout the novel display its failure. "Moral suasion" was the name nineteenth-century reformers used to describe what they considered the most ethical political force. Though men could and frequently did try to exert it, moral suasion was only one of many political forces available to them. White men had the right to vote, as well as economic and physical power, as legitimate ways to express their political will. Moral suasion was the sanctioned way, and the only legitimate way, for white women to assert their political will in a world that could be imagined as composed of two separate but mutually dependent spheres: the feminine, domestic sphere of family and morality, and the masculine sphere of political and economic competition. Stowe's critique was directed not at extending the right of women to vote but at reforming America so that what she held as women's innate moral superiority could prevail.

Her numerous descriptions of the nightmarishly disordered kitchens at the center of slave-holding households symbolize the moral dislocation of all women under the conditions of slavery. Stowe's book as a whole describes the ultimate threat posed to the nation by a system that at best obstructed women from exerting their moral insights, and at worst corrupted the natural moral proclivities of women and prevented them from developing. But she also offered a powerful antidote to this dystopian vision in her fantasia on the kitchen of the Quaker Rachel Halliday, where the fathers are "anti-patriarchal" and "there was such an atmosphere of mutual confidence and good fellowship everywhere." This kitchen, unlike all others in the book, is a place where correct moral decisions are made by the mothers and carried out by the fathers, as the doctrine of separate spheres dictates. In this kitchen, families are reunited, not torn apart.

By the time Stowe was working on *Uncle Tom's Cabin*, she was able to draw on a large body of attempts by African Americans to exercise moral suasion on their own behalf in the form of slave narratives. These memoirs, as John Edgar Wideman suggests, might more accurately be called "freedom narratives" because they tell the story of the resistance of individuals to the ontological status of slavery. This resistance forms the substance of the plots of both major slave narratives, such as the *Narrative of the Life of Frederick Douglass, an American Slave, Written by Himself*, and the minor works that circulated both within and outside abolitionist circles. Douglass's *Narrative* begins with tally of negatives: he lacks "accurate knowledge of my age," his father's name, and even his "mother, to know her as such." This conventional starting point for the slave narrative emphasizes the importance of constitutive relationships to the American self as it testifies to the systematic process of natal alienation perpetuated by the slave-holding establishment. But it also testifies to the degree to which the sentimental arc from lost child to good parent structures the way in which black slaves plotted to gain freedom. In other words, the slave narrative shows how sentimentality enabled former slaves to make their experience transparent to themselves and to their readers. Douglass thus becomes not an alien being of dubious humanity but a familiar character whose feelings and actions are the same as all "right feeling" Americans.

Douglass for most part confined himself to the nonfiction genres of the memoir and speech, but African-American authors also used sentimentality within fiction to claim a place within mainstream American culture. African-American women such as Harriet Wilson and Harriet Jacobs may have turned to the sentimental novel because, it has been suggested, it allows for a greater degree of distance between the author and the narrator. In addition, where the slave narrative appeals to sympathy through the subjectivity of the lost child, the nineteenth-century African-American novel centers on the subject of the mother who is threatened with the loss of her child. Harriet Wilson's *Our Nig* (1859), occasioned by the author's need to take care of her child, depicts the way that racism systematically undermines the status of parent. The heroine is abandoned by her white mother, whose personal racism is so deep that it prevents her from loving either of the black men who rescue her from abject poverty. "Lonely Mag Smith," as Wilson calls the mother, suffers so deeply from racism that she calls her own children "black devils" and is able casually to walk away from Frado, the child whose attempts to resist becoming the deracinated possession connoted by the epithet "Our Nig" form the body of the text. The novel ends with the author averring that Frado, unlike her mother, is the opposite of lonely because she is enmeshed in a system of gift-giving through which she is connected to others whose most important identifying characteristic is not skin color but shared voluntary association. The author offers the story of Frado to her readers in an attempt to extend the economy of sentiment enough to allow her to redeem her child from the poorhouse. With her readers' help, the author hopes to counter the recurrent image of racist anti-mother who walks away from her child with an image of a woman for whom not race but relationship is the important category.

SENTIMENTAL SKEPTICISM

Although *Our Nig* ends by expressing the author's trust in the efficacy of sentiment, extratextual evidence suggests that Wilson's trust was unwarranted. Her book, literary historians such Henry Louis Gates tell us, failed to circulate enough in the contemporary literary marketplace to generate the money she needed to counteract the lifetime effect of poverty on her son's health. The child died, Wilson disappeared from the historical record, and the book was buried for almost one hundred years. Harriet Jacobs's 1861 *Incidents in the Life of a Slave Girl* also demonstrates the degree to which the conventions of the sentimental mode allowed black women authors simultaneously to claim middle-class values and to appeal for sympathy because of the degree to which racialized slavery prevented them from acting on these values. More self-consciously literary than Harriet Wilson, Jacobs signaled her reliance on the conventions of the mainstream (white) sentimentalism throughout the novel, but most tellingly at the conclusion, when the narrator breaks the fictional frame of reference to confront the sentimental expectations she has encouraged in her audience: "Reader, my story ends with freedom; not in the usual way, with marriage." Though sentiment may have allowed her to tell the story of how she physically freed herself and her children, some other mode would be necessary to imagine how she would obtain the property that would allow her to realize the "dream of my life," "a home of my own." Written on the brink of war, Jacobs's book demonstrates a growing awareness among American authors of the limits of sentimentality to achieve its end without violence. As Hazel Carby (1987) and Claudia Tate (1983) have convincingly argued, black women writers of the Reconstruction and post-Reconstruction eras (such as Frances Harper and Pauline Hopkins) deployed an increasingly sophisticated sentimentality as they tried to make a place for black Americans in the middle class. This is seen even in the work of black male writers of that era, such as Paul Dunbar, Charles Chesnutt, and W. E. B. Du Bois, who did not shrink from the knowing deployment of sympathy as well as reason.

In the same year that *Incidents in the Life of a Slave Girl* was published, Abraham Lincoln concluded his "First Inaugural Address to the Union" with a conspicuous shift in rhetoric. The body of the speech had laid out a measured argument against secession that derived from a logical reading of the Constitution and sought to assuage the anxieties of the slave-holding states. "Loth to close," Lincoln supplemented these rational appeals to the authority of the Constitution with an emotional appeal to the bonds of affection:

> Though passion may have strained, it must not break the bonds of our affection. The mystic chords of memory, stretching from every battlefield, and patriot grave, to every living heart and hearthstone, all over this brave land, will yet swell the chorus of the Union, when touched, as surely they will be, by the better angels of our nature.

The hope expressed by this language, a hope shared by many, betrays itself. The tropes and figures of sentimentality had already framed both the war and its foreseeable resolutions. As Lincoln himself had argued in 1858, "a house divided against itself cannot stand." Both sides fought on the ground of common sense to preserve an America that did not presently exist, nor had it ever. The resolution of the conflict between federalism and states' rights would necessitate a reinvention of a single story of inheritance by which the U.S. Constitution would generate one national tradition, not two. Within less than a generation after the war, Lincoln's language—the language of sentiment—would become the hallmark of institutionalized corruption that attempted to shield self-serving opportunism under the cover of altruism. The language of Lincoln was seen to be indistinguishable from the language of Dilworthy, the "Golden-tongued Statesman" of Mark Twain and Charles Warner's scathing political novel, *The Gilded Age*. In addition, the sentimental extension of the boundaries of inclusion around people of color and women threatened the racial and class privileges of white Americans.

Within the mainstream publishing market, the mode of sentiment came to be seen as appropriate only for children's literature. Writers for the adult white market increasingly abandoned sentimental topics, language, and rhetoric for what has come to be known as "realism." This disdain came as a reaction to the relatively successful efforts by disenfranchised groups, such as blacks and white women, to deploy sentiment in their own efforts to claim the status of "real" Americans.

CONCLUSION

At the beginning of what literary historians call the American Renaissance, Harriet Beecher Stowe asked her free white readers "how fast" they would run if it were their child who was threatened with being sold "down the river," then urged her readers actively to resist the Fugitive Slave Law. Reminding her readers of the power of their attachment for their own children, Stowe tried to force them to recognize the common humanity of black American slaves, even if this recognition might disturb their faith in their country. At the conclusion of the Civil War, fought to preserve the Union from the threats posed by a conflict between the common senses of what it meant to be an American, President Lincoln invoked the power of sentiment to "bind up the nation's wounds." Although the "better angels of our nature" called upon in the "First Inaugural Address" had not been able to prevent war from breaking out, at the close of the war Lincoln still hoped that "the mystic chords of memory" would somehow help to achieve the reconstruction of a national home for "him who shall have borne the battle and for his widow and his orphan."

In the years since, the project of reconstruction has not yet been completed, even though—or perhaps because of—a continued reliance on the strategies of sentimentality. The reception of Lincoln's "Second Inaugural Address" marks a shift in Americans' faith in the power of sentiment to effect unambiguously positive moral change. Postwar nineteenth-century black Americans such as Frances Harper attempted to use sentimentality to move themselves from the cultural margin to the secure middle-class center of American identity. But sentimentality, simultaneously marshaled by the white supremacists, limited this attempt by licensing brutal legal and vigilante negations of the claims of black Americans to common Americanness.

Ernest Hemingway expressed the bitterness of the twentieth-century modernists' relation to sentiment in his character Frederick Henry's embarrassment and disappointment in having seen in his experience of World War I "nothing sacred, and things that were glorious had no glory and the sacrifices were like the stockyards at Chicago if nothing was done with the meat." The force with which the American modernist writers disavowed the poetics and aesthetics of sentiment, however, testify to its persistent power in American popular culture. This power was particularly evident in the new electronic media of film, radio, and later television. Electronic media would bring into the family living room presidential candidate Richard Nixon's sentimental story of his children's affection for a campaign gift, the dog Checkers. It would also bring the Reverend Martin Luther King Jr.'s invocation of a dream of children joining hands and climbing to a new American future where people would be judged by their character and not by the color of their skin.

In the last third of the twentieth century, a shift away from the dominant values of modernism would be marked by a new embrace of the power to dissolve apparently preexisting boundaries through the formal strategies of sentimentalism, which take advantage of rather than oppose the tessellating power of emotional representation. Tony Kushner, for example, in his theatrical success of the 1990s, *Angels in America: A Gay Fantasia on National Themes*, used the formal strategies of sentimentality to engage his audience in an examination of the relationship between the failure of sympathy and the failure of community. Kushner, like Lincoln before him, invoked the better angels of our nature, knowing that these angels depend on the willingness of Americans to want a story that ends in freedom.

[*See also* American Autobiography: Slave Narratives; Baldwin, James; Chesnutt, Charles; Crèvecoeur, J. Hector St. John de; Douglass, Frederick; Du Bois, W. E. B.; Dunbar, Paul; Fireside Poets, The; Longfellow, Henry Wadsworth; Poetess in American Literature, The *and* Stowe, Harriet Beecher.]

FURTHER READING

Baldwin, James. "Everybody's Protest Novel." *Partisan Review* 16 (June 1949): 578–85. A still-important challenge to the American sentimental tradition.

Barnes, Elizabeth. *States of Sympathy: Seduction and Democracy in the American Novel*. New York, 1997. A model example of literary and political criticism.

Baym, Nina. *Woman's Fiction: A Guide to Novels by and about Women in America, 1820–1870*. Ithaca, N.Y., 1978. As an initiator of the feminist revision of American literary history, lays the groundwork for the reevaluation of the sentimental form.

Baym, Nina. "Reinventing Lydia Sigourney." *American Literature* 62 (1990): 385–404. An excellent analysis of the change in critical assessment of an author, following the reconfiguration of the field of American literary history that occurred between the 1970s and the 1990s.

Brown, Gillian. *Domestic Individualism: Imagining the Self in Nineteenth-Century America*. Berkeley, Calif., 1990. Pathbreaking reassessment of the underpinnings of American individualism.

Brown, Herbert Ross. *The Sentimental Novel in America, 1789–1860*. Durham, N.C., 1940. A still-fruitful survey of the genre.

Carby, Hazel. *Reconstructing Womanhood: The Emergence of the Afro-American Woman Novelist*. Oxford, 1987. A solid study of the deployment of sentiment by African-American women writers.

Clark, Suzanne. *Sentimental Modernism: Women Writers and the Revolution of the Word*. Bloomington, Ind., 1991. An important revaluation of modernism and the women's writing.

Dobson, Joanne. "Reclaiming Sentimental Literature." *American Literature* 69.2 (June 1997). A critical survey of the state of the field as of the mid-1990s.

Fisher, Philip. *Hard Facts: Setting and Form in the American Novel*. New York, 1987. One of the pathbreaking revisions of the American novel tradition to emerge in the mid-1980s in response to the new attention to the popular and sentimental traditions.

Haltunnen, Karen. *Confidence Men and Painted Women: A Study of Middle-class Culture in America, 1830–1870.* New Haven, Conn., 1982. A crucial study of the crisis of authenticity at the center of American efforts of self-definition.

Kete, Mary Louise. *Sentimental Collaborations: Mourning and Middle-class Identity in Nineteenth-century America.* Durham, N.C., 2000.

Levine, Lawrence W. *Highbrow / Lowbrow: The Emergence of Cultural Hierarchy in America.* Cambridge, Mass., 1988. An important study of the shifting parameters of taste and value during the nineteenth century.

Samuels, Shirley, ed. *The Culture of Sentiment: Race, Gender, and Sentimentality in Nineteenth-century America.* New York, 1992. A seminal book of some of the best essays exploring sentimentality in America.

Tate, Claudia. *Black Women Writers at Work.* New York, 1983.

Tompkins, Jane. *Sensational Designs: The Cultural Work of American Fiction, 1790–1860.* New York, 1985. One of the pathbreaking revisions of the American novel tradition to emerge in the mid-1980s that occurs in response to the new attention to the popular and sentimental traditions.

For Reference

Not to be taken from this room